FREEDOM OF THE PRESS

By **RALPH E. McCOY**

FREEDOM OF THE PRESS

An Annotated Bibliography

With a Foreword by Robert B. Downs

SOUTHERN ILLINOIS UNIVERSITY PRESS

Carbondale and Edwardsville

FEFFER & SIMONS, INC.

London and Amsterdam

PUBLISHED, 1968, BY SOUTHERN ILLINOIS UNIVERSITY PRESS
LIBRARY OF CONGRESS CATALOG CARD NO. 67-10032

PRODUCED BY CHANTICLEER PRESS, INC., NEW YORK
PRINTED IN AUSTRIA BY BRÜDER ROSENBAUM, VIENNA
DESIGNED BY ANDOR BRAUN

To Melba

Foreword by ROBERT B. DOWNS

IT IS HIGHLY SIGNIFICANT that when the Bill of Rights was added to the U.S. Constitution in December 1791, after being ratified by the required three fourths of the states, the First Amendment specifically stated, "Congress shall make no law . . . abridging the freedom of speech or of the press."

One hundred and fifty years later, when America was on the verge of war with the Axis powers, Franklin D.Roosevelt enunciated the Four Freedoms: "In the future days, which we seek to make secure, we look forward to a world founded upon four essential human freedoms. The first is freedom of speech and expression everywhere in the world."

Reaffirmation from another distinguished source came on December 14, 1946, when the UN General Assembly resolved, "Freedom of information is a fundamental human right, and the touchstone of all the freedoms to which the United Nations is consecrated."

Eloquent statements of faith in free expression have come from various spokesmen. Illustrative are the views of a great American jurist and a distinguished American historian, Louis D. Brandeis and Bruce Catton. Justice Brandeis, in *Whitney v. California*, emphasized that "Those who won our independence believed that . . . the deliberative forces should prevail over the arbitrary. They valued liberty both as an end and as a means . . . They believed that freedom to think as you will and to speak as you think are means indispensable to the discovery and spread of political truth; that without free speech and assembly discussion would be futile; . . . that the greatest menace to freedom is an inert people; that public discussion is a political duty; and that this should be a fundamental principle of the American government."

The same basic truth was restated by Bruce Catton: "The greatest of all American traditions is the simple tradition of freedom. From our earliest days as a people, this tradition has provided us with a faith to live by. It has shaped what Americans have done and what they have dreamed. If any one word tells what America really is, it is the one word—freedom . . . The secret of the American tradition is freedom—freedom unabridged and unadulterated, freedom that applies to everybody in the land at all times and places, freedom for those with whom we disagree as well as for those with whom we do agree."

Viewed in historical retrospect, censorship and all varieties of thought suppression are ancient phenomena, exhibiting the same characteristics in every era. One age may be predominantly concerned with religious heresy, another with political orthodoxy, and the next with obscenity and morality. No longer is it customary to burn authors at the stake—as happened, for example, to Michael Servetus and William Tyndale—though under totalitarian regimes they may be imprisoned or exiled, and in democracies deprived of their livelihoods.

Little is heard these days about religious heresy. There is intense concern, however, with obscenity and with unorthodox political opinions.

Legal precedents and practices relating to censorship in America, in common with other aspects of Anglo-American law, have British foundations. The antecedents of English censorship are ancient. Rigid restrictions on the press, in fact, were an important feature of ecclesiastical and state policy from the time of the invention of printing.

Henry VIII in the sixteenth century placed the entire press under a licensing system. Before anyone could publish he must submit his intended work to the government for approval. This licensing system prevailed in England until 1695. Throughout the Tudor and Stuart periods the primary function of the violently-hated Court of the Star Chamber was the censorship of books. Prior to the outbreak of the Civil War in 1642, several flagrant cases had aroused popular resentment against the censors. Offenders were sentenced to long terms in prison, were heavily fined, had their ears cut off and their noses slit, and were branded on the cheeks, pilloried, and otherwise subjected to cruel and inhuman punishments.

In the struggle between King Charles I and the Long Parliament, the detested Star Chamber was finally abolished by parliamentary action in 1641. With its passing, the great poet John Milton anticipated the lifting of arbitrary restrictions on a free press. Parliament, composed overwhelmingly of English Presbyterians, was alarmed, however, by the flood of "scandalous, seditious, and libellous" publications that began to appear as soon as the censorship was lifted. Accordingly, in 1643, the Parliament passed a new censorship act, modeled upon the old Star Chamber rules, but with the distinction that the censors were to be appointed by Parliament. Unlicensed printing was forbidden, and the Stationers' Company (the organized printers and publishers of the country) and the officers of Parliament were authorized to search out and destroy unlicensed presses, confiscate unlicensed books, and arrest all printers and authors who issued uncensored books.

It was at this point that Milton stepped into the censorship fight with a purposely unregistered and unlicensed pamphlet entitled *Areopagitica*, "for the liberty of unlicenc'd printing," the most celebrated of all his prose works, abounding in eloquent declarations on the transcendent importance of books and in compelling arguments supporting an unfettered press.

Milton's vigorous denunciation of censorship and licensing apparently had no perceptible impact on his own time. The Presbyterians were in an intolerant mood. Parliament was deaf to all suggestions for reform, and press control continued without moderation for the next fifty years. It was not until the accession of William and Mary to the throne in 1689 that a new spirit of tolerance allowed the press licensing act to die.

The first reported case on judicial censorship of obscene literature involved the poetry of a gay young rake, Sir Charles Sedley, early in the eighteenth century. A short time later, Edmund Curll's piratical and flourishing trade in obscene literature was legally estopped. In the same century, John Wilkes' prosecution for publishing his *Essay on Woman* gave that allegedly obscene poem great notoriety.

These isolated incidents were followed during the first quarter of the nineteenth century by a rash of cases implicating figures of considerably greater literary stature, notably Robert Southey's *Wat Tyler*, Lord Byron's *Cain* and *Don Juan*, and Shelley's *Queen Mab*.

England's laws dealing with obscenity are little more than a century old. In 1857 Lord Chief Justice Campbell drafted and steered through the British Parliament the statute of 20 and 21 Victoria. Its author described the measure as "intended to apply exclusively to works written for the single purpose of corrupting the morals of youth, and of a nature calculated to shock the common feelings of decency in any well regulated mind."

About a decade after its enactment, the Campbell statute received a classical interpretation at the hands of Chief Justice Cockburn in the case of *Regina v. Hicklin* (1868). The case involved a pamphlet entitled *The Confessional Unmasked Showing the Depravity of the Romish Priesthood; the Iniquity of the Confessional, and the Questions Put to Females in the Confession*, an anti-Catholic publication being distributed by a member of a Protestant union. In connection with the case Justice Cockburn formulated his famous rule for judging obscenity: "I think the test of obscenity is this, whether the tendency of the matter charged as obscenity is to deprave and corrupt those whose minds are open to such immoral influences, and into whose hands a publication of this sort may fall."

As David Fellman pointed out, "The objection to this test, of course, is that it fixes a standard for the community's reading matter geared to the feeblest mentality or most suggestible psyche in the community." Nevertheless, the Cockburn dictum has since served as a guiding principle for a majority of English and American judges. Only within recent years has there been any tendency to break away from its limitations.

Turning from British precedents, a review of "the rise and fall of prudery" or the relation of obscenity to morality in the United States is revealing. The changes in American standards of literary decency over the past three hundred years have been astonishing. We have moved so far from Puritan restrictions that most of the inhibitions of our grandparents seem grotesque. A little more than one hundred years ago, Robert Browning's *Man and Woman* was widely denounced as immoral; shortly afterward, Walt Whitman was accused of writing obscene poetry and discharged from the Interior Department for his *Leaves of Grass*; eighty years ago, Mark Twain's *Huckleberry Finn* was termed unfit reading for "pure minded lads and lasses;" and Hawthorne's *Scarlet Letter* was condemned for "perpetrating bad morals" and described as a "brokerage of lust." About the same time, a standard work on etiquette recommended that books by male and female authors not be placed on library shelves together, except for married couples.

For almost a century after the Revolution, the United States managed to get along without any censorship laws, though that did not prevent the suppression of unpopular literature during the colonial and early Federal period. The full flower of literary repression bloomed with the Comstock era in 1873, under the inspiration of a young man by the name of Anthony Comstock, who had emerged from the backwoods of Connecticut to lead a crusade against what he considered indecent literature. Under a special act of the New York State Legislature, Comstock organized the New York Society for the Suppression of Vice. The law gave the Society a monopoly in the field and its agents the rights of search, seizure, and arrest—rights which had previously belonged exclusively to the police authorities.

The idea spread quickly, and within a few years there were founded the Western Society for the Suppression of Vice, with headquarters in Cincinnati, and the New England Watch and Ward Society in Boston. The history of the latter organization has been ably chronicled by the author of the present work, Ralph E. McCoy, in his *Banned in Boston*.

Also in 1873, the moral forces obtained the passage of a federal statute entitled the "Comstock Law," providing penalties for the mailing of allegedly obscene publications. Comstock became a special post-office agent and instituted a series of famous prosecutions. For years the battle raged between what George Bernard Shaw called "Comstockery" and its opponents, as Comstock and his Society banned or attempted to ban innumerable works of art, science, literature, and drama. In its first seventy-three years of existence, the New York Society confiscated some 397,000 books and brought about the arrest of 5,567 defendants.

Then the tide began to turn. Censorship was discredited by ridicule, by the growth of liberal thought, and changing literary tastes. The transition from reticence to realism in our literature came slowly, but was speeded up considerably by World War I and such works as *All Quiet on the Western Front* and *What Price Glory?* Even so, few who were involved in the controversies over Dreiser's *Sister Carrie* and Cabell's *Jurgen* early in the present century would have imagined that in the nineteen sixties uninhibited books like Miller's *Tropic of Cancer*, Cleland's *Fanny Hill*, and Baldwin's *Another Country* would be circulated in the United States with minimal legal interference.

Legal precedents in the field of obscenity have a long history—for the most part a depressing one. Reviewing them over the past century and a half, one is left with an over-all impression of a labyrinth of judicial confusion, quibbling, hairsplitting, widely contradictory views, struggles with definitions, and general futility. The over-all murkiness is dispelled only occasionally by the enlightened, civilized views of such jurists as Augustus and Learned Hand, John M. Woolsey, William O. Douglas, Curtis Bok, and Jerome Frank.

One of the landmarks in the legal annals of censorship is the 1933 case of James Joyce's *Ulysses*, a storm center on both sides of the Atlantic for a number of years. Judge John M. Woolsey delivered the opinion of the federal court. Such a book, he stated, "must be tested by the Court's opinion as to its effect on a person with average sex instincts . . . who plays, in this branch of legal inquiry, the same role of hypothetical reagent as does the 'reasonable man' in the law of torts . . . It is only with the normal person that the law is concerned."

The same point was underlined by Walter Gellhorn, lawyer and political scientist, and a leading writer on intellectual freedom. "The stable and well adjusted members of the community," he said, "must make many sacrifices because there are unstable and disturbed members as well. But freedom of communication and freedom to read ought not to be among the sacrifices when the gain is so dubious and the deprivation so plain."

Another famous case is dated 1948. The Philadelphia police had raided fifty-four bookstores and seized without warrants about 2,000 allegedly obscene books, including works by William Faulkner, Erskine Caldwell, and James T. Farrell. In his opinion, the presiding judge, Curtis Bok, stated in part: "It will be asked whether one would care to have one's young daughter read these books. I suppose that by the time she is old enough to wish to read them she will have learned the biologic facts of life and the words that go with them. . . . Our daughters must live in the world and decide what sort of women they are to be, and we should be willing to prefer their deliberate and informed choice of decency rather than an innocence that continues to spring from ignorance."

Judge Bok's conclusion is most pertinent. Would-be censors almost invariably rest their cases on the protection of children and young people. The testimony of medical, psychiatric, and sociological authorities rebuts their contentions. Two research criminologists, Eleanor and Sheldon Glueck, intensively examined a thousand delinquent boys from the Boston area. The most significant factors contributing to delinquency, they found, were culture conflict, unwholesome family environment, educational deficiencies, socially undesirable use of leisure time (for example, gambling, drinking, drug addiction, and sex misbehavior), and psychological defects. There was no evidence that erotic or other types of reading matter were contributing elements in delinquency. In the same vein, George W. Smyth, one of the nation's outstanding children's court judges, listed for a New York state legislative commission 878 factors that had troubled children brought before him. Reading was not on the list, but *difficulty* in reading was. This point has been confirmed by other workers in the field of antisocial juvenile behavior. Far from discovering that delinquency grows out of reading, the clinicians report that it is more likely to grow out of inability to read. It is the

consensus, in short, that delinquent children read much less than do the law-abiding.

But granting that it is undesirable to expose immature minds to hard-core pornography and obscenity, normal adult readers hardly require such tender coddling. The definitive word on the subject was stated by a U.S. Supreme Court decision in 1957. Invalidating a Michigan statute designed mainly to protect young people, the court ruled: "The State of Michigan insists that, by thus quarantining the general reading public against books not too rugged for grown men and women in order to shield juvenile innocence, it is exercising its power to protect the general welfare. Surely this is to burn the house to roast the pig. The incidence of this enactment is to reduce the adult population of Michigan to reading only what is fit for children."

In the same year, an eminent English judge, Justice Stable, was asking a jury: "Are we to take our literary standards as being the level of something that is suitable for a fourteen-year-old girl? Or do we go even further back than that, and are we to be reduced to the sort of books that one reads as a child in the nursery? The answer to that is: of course not. A mass of literature, great literature, from many angles is wholly unsuitable for reading by adolescents, but that does not mean that the publisher is guilty of a criminal offense for making those works available to the general public."

The U.S. Supreme Court continues to have able and eloquent champions of the liberal point of view. Justice Douglas, for example, maintains that "if a board of censors can tell the American people what it is in their best interests to see or to read or to hear, then thought is regimented, authority substituted for liberty, and the great purpose of the First Amendment to keep uncontrolled the freedom of expression is defeated." His colleague Justice Harlan concurs: "The federal government," he declares, "has no business, whether under the postal or commerce power, to bar the sale of books because they might lead to any kind of 'thoughts.'"

Private pressure groups probably are more numerous, more vocal, and more active in the censorship field than in any other area. Innumerable veterans organizations, religious bodies, White Citizens Councils, superpatriotic societies, Congressional committees and similar groups appear to be working incessantly to place restrictions on what the American people may be allowed to read, see, or hear. They are voices calling for conformity, for unanimity of opinion, for eliminating all ideas with which they happen to disagree. Operating extralegally, such groups use, as their chief method, pressure on news dealers, drugstores, and booksellers, to force them to remove from their stocks every item on blacklists prepared by headquarters organizations. The books so listed have not been banned from the mails, and in an overwhelming majority of cases no legal charges have ever been brought against them.

The private pressure groups, following vigilante methods, deliberately ignore the fact that there are established legal channels for proceeding against books that are thought to be improper. The statute books contain adequate federal, state, and municipal laws to deal with real pornography. Furthermore, once started on their crusades for reform the "do-gooders" are constantly seeking new worlds to conquer. From cheap magazines and lurid-covered paperback books, they proceed to books of genuine literary merit, to serious motion pictures, and to the stage, radio, and television, determined, as Judge Bok phrased it, "to give others the courage of their convictions."

A well-known educator, Willard E. Goslin, has made fitting commentary on the activities of private pressure groups.

> No particular special interest group makes up the people. The people are not the Chamber of Commerce, or the labor unions, or the league for constitutional governments, or the Methodists, or the Parent Teacher Association, or the Catholics, or the Liberty Belles, or the American Legion, or the Protestants, or the Sons of the Golden West, or the Jews, or the American Association of University Women, or the Presbyterians, or the Rotarians, or the farmers, or the college graduates, or the whites, or the poor, or the Negroes, or the teachers, or the bankers, or the Democrats, or the commentators, or any other segmented or special interest group in America. The people, as we use the term, are that broad base of citizens representative of the diversity and strength of this nation.

Also full of common sense and broad toleration is a series of rules proposed by Father John Courtney Murray, for the guidance of minority groups, including the statement that "in a pluralist society no minority group has the right to impose its own religious or moral views on other groups, through the use of the methods of force, coercion, or violence."

Directly related to the activities of pressure groups is the problem of censorship in the schools. No institutions in our society are more vulnerable to pressures from every direction than are the public schools. It is perhaps surprising that the schools—close to the grass-roots level, their affairs always in the center of public attention, and dependent for support upon tax funds—retain any large degree of freedom. Economic, nationalistic, political, and religious groups, intent upon shaping the educational system to fit their particular ideologies, have sought to dictate to the schools what may or may not be taught. Also, legislatures in a number of states, sensitive to lobbies and other forms of organized pressure, have enacted statutes highly arbitrary and restrictive in nature to control textbook selection and curricula.

There would doubtless be universal agreement on the principle that textbooks used in U.S. schools should be American and should never be permitted to become vehicles for the propagation of obnoxious doctrines. The task of selection, however, is obviously not one to be delegated to self-appointed experts, with axes to grind. Instead, trust must be placed in the integrity, good faith, and plain common sense of the school boards and teachers of the country. As an investigating committee of the U.S. House of Representatives stated in its report: "If these educators are so utterly naive and untrained as to need help from a lobbying organization in selecting proper classroom materials, then our educational system has decayed beyond all help, a proposition we cannot accept."

A brief review of another major area for censorship activity—sedition and subversion—should be inserted here to round out a discussion of freedom of the mind. Throughout American history, so-called radical economic, political, and social ideas have been subject to attack. As long ago as 1689,

William Bradford, Pennsylvania's first printer, was arrested and prosecuted for printing the colony's charter for distribution among the people. The following year, an attempt to start a newspaper in the British colonies was suppressed after the first issue. Another celebrated case involved the second newspaper established in New York and its publisher, John Peter Zenger. The paper, the *New York Weekly Journal*, was strongly antagonistic to the government, and in 1734 Zenger was arrested and charged with libel. His defense was in the hands of able lawyers, who succeeded in having the case tried before a jury instead of a judge. Zenger was acquitted, thereby establishing the basis for a free press in New York.

Potentially, one of the most menacing attacks on freedom of political thought and expression was the infamous Alien and Sedition Acts, forced through Congress in 1798 by the Federalists, who were fearful of the threat of foreign ideas and of their subversive tendencies. The statutes made it a criminal offense for "brawlers against government" to voice opinions considered dangerous or revolutionary. Thomas Jefferson's unyielding opposition to the repressive legislation was overwhelmingly endorsed by the electorate, who sent Jefferson to the White House and the Federalists into political oblivion.

Postwar states-of-mind and political pressures were responsible for numerous unsavory episodes following after World War I and II. A notorious example was the so-called Palmer raids on liberal and radical political groups considered subversive by A. Mitchell Palmer, U.S. Attorney General in Wilson's cabinet.

Most disruptive to national unity of any such events in American history were the activities of Senator Joseph R. McCarthy in the early nineteen-fifties. In a long-drawn-out series of sensational statements and committee hearings, McCarthy claimed that the federal government was thoroughly infiltrated by Communist agents. One of his prime targets was the U.S. information libraries abroad. Here was an excellent system of 194 centers in sixty-one countries, standing high in prestige and influence, among the most effective ambassadors any country could have, with 30,000,000 visitors passing through their doors each year. Within a few months, violent attacks by McCarthy and investigations by his agents had demoralized the library staffs, seriously damaged the libraries' reputation for objectivity, reduced congressional appropriations, and spread the impression around the world that freedom of speech and of the press no longer existed in the United States. Fortunately for the nation, the Senate condemned McCarthy in 1954 for abusing other senators and his political influence declined thereafter. It is doubtful, however, whether even yet the information libraries have fully recovered from the scourge of "McCarthyism."

Such phenomena as McCarthyism, the Subversive Activities Control Act, passed over President Truman's veto in 1950, and the pressures in recent years for conformity and for restricting civil liberties have doubtless resulted from the sense of insecurity which the American people have felt since the end of the Second World War. As country after country was overrun by communism, the tempo of the Cold War stepped up, and the world subjected to a relentless barrage of Communist propaganda, Americans naturally reacted with strong counter-measures. Investigating committees of Congress and state legislatures invaded college and university campuses and examined teachers for their patriotism. A rash of loyalty oaths was devised for university professors, public school teachers, government workers, and others. Blacklists were drawn up of teachers, journalists, actors, and many others accused of being Communists, or of having joined organizations into which Communists had infiltrated, or who may simply have refused to testify as to their political beliefs. For such reasons, voices of dissent were stilled, the unorthodox was equated with treason, the free exchange of ideas diminished, and the nation became increasingly wedded to the status quo.

The extent of publishing coming within the scope of the present work on *Freedom of the Press* is astonishing. It is a tribute to the publishers' recognition of the fundamental bearing of these themes on the great American heritage. Likewise, it is gratifying to find that so many first-rate writers are preoccupied with essential rights and freedoms, especially when such concepts are under attack and misunderstood.

The availability of reading materials of all kinds to Americans and to the rest of the world is greater than ever before in history. In the United States alone, 30,050 book titles in a total considerably in excess of one billion copies were issued and sold in 1966. Four billion copies of magazines, exclusive of comic books, are sold annually, and about sixty million copies of newspapers appear every day. A preponderance of this vast quantity of printed matter is distributed without incident or interference. Most Americans believe that every adult should have freedom of choice to read whatever he wants to read whenever he wants to read, except for treason, fraud, and pornography. Viewed objectively, we remain a free people in the field of reading, but it is a freedom that cannot be taken for granted, casually and indifferently. Instead, its protection requires "eternal vigilance."

No one of our freedoms is an island, standing separate and alone, but is interdependent on others. As aptly phrased by J. R. Wiggins, editor of the *Washington Post*,

> A complex of many rights must co-exist unimpaired if the printed word is to be the effective agent of enlightenment. Men must have the right to discover the truth. They must have the right to print it without the prior restraint or pre-censorship of government. They must have access to printed materials. They must be able to print without fear of cruel or unusual punishment for publication alleged to be wrongful. They must have the right to put printed material into the hands of readers without obstruction by government, under cover of law, or obstruction by citizens acting in defiance of the law. Wherever these rights are threatened, the power of the printed word is incapable of performing its mission to mankind.

Taking the long view, the condemned books of one age are often the classics of later eras, because society's mores are constantly changing. In few instances since printing was invented has censorship resulted in the permanent loss or suppression of a literary work. Almost invariably copies survive and are subsequently revived under more hospitable conditions. To paraphrase Shakespeare's Mark Antony, the good that censors attempt to destroy lives after them; the evil is oft interred with their bones.

Freedom of the Press is destined to provide further strength and support for the great human rights of free press, free speech, and free expression.

Preface by RALPH E. McCOY

THIS IS AN ANNOTATED BIBLIOGRAPHY of some 8,000 books, pamphlets, journal articles, films, and other material relating to freedom of the press in English-speaking countries, from the beginning of printing to the present. "Press" is used generically to include all media of mass communications: books, pamphlets, periodicals, newspapers, motion pictures, phonograph records, radio, television, and, to a limited extent, stage plays. Subjects include heresy, sedition, blasphemy, obscenity, personal libel, and both positive and negative expressions on freedom of the press.

In format the entries range from a seventeenth-century pamphlet reporting a sedition trial to a Congressional hearing on pornography, to a tape recording of a radio discussion on modern libel laws. Entries are arranged alphabetically by personal or corporate author or by title where author is unknown. A comprehensive subject index identifies topics, concepts, countries, individuals, court decisions, and titles of censored works. Geographically, the bibliography includes the United States and Great Britain, as well as Ireland, Canada, India, Australia, and other present and former Commonwealth countries. Works relating to the *Index* of the Catholic Church have been included only when they appeared in the English language and were related to English or American practices.

In quality of expression the entries range from John Milton's eloquent defense of a free press, *Areopagitica*, to the irrational proposals of a vigilante group. In point of view, expressions cover a broad spectrum—from the views of a young London barrister who wrote in 1712 that all controversial ideas should be suppressed since they only lead to trouble, to the twentieth-century libertarians who would give absolute freedom to the printed and spoken word. In between are represented varying shades of restraint or freedom.

Generally excluded from the bibliography are the texts of laws, official reports of modern trials, newspaper or news-magazine articles, brief references to freedom of the press that appear as part of general works, and works on the broader topic of civil liberties. The subject of propaganda, unless it also relates to the converse area of censorship, has been excluded, since this field has been covered in the bibliographies of Harold D. Lasswell and associates. Banned books are not included per se, but references to them in annotations are brought out in the index. Within the above limits the bibliography is as complete as time and availability of sources have permitted.

The annotations are intended to be descriptive rather than critical and, within the stated scope of the bibliography, there has been little attempt at selectivity, except to exclude those accounts that were too brief (generally under two pages) or trivial. Occasionally, when a large number of articles reported the same news event, a few representative articles were selected. The length of annotation does not necessarily indicate the importance of the work, but rather the amount of explanation needed to delineate the subject. For example, an extensive quotation may be included from a brief article or pamphlet if, in the estimation of the compiler, it expresses a unique or interesting concept. Background information about events or people frequently has been supplied. I have indulged in an occasional fancy by including a curious or humorous item only slightly related to the topic, e.g. "bibliophagia," or the destruction of a book by eating it.

Interest in the subject of freedom of the press grew out of my doctoral dissertation, *Banned in Boston; The Development of Literary Censorship in Massachusetts*, at the University of Illinois (1956), suggested by Dean Robert B. Downs of the Graduate School of Library Science, himself a leading writer on freedom of the press. Dean Downs kindly agreed to write the foreword to this book.

This bibliography represents the labor of more than a decade, with intensive work being done during the past four years. Because of the lengthy production time required for the volume, an addendum, its entries identified in the Index by a degree symbol, provides for works issued or discovered after the body of the bibliography had been numbered.

Using more than a score of libraries either in person or by mail, most of the items in the bibliography were actually examined, if not read in their entirety. In addition to the author's personal collection and the Library of Southern Illinois University, the following major libraries were consulted: University of Illinois, Library of Congress, New York Public Library, Boston Public Library, University of Wisconsin, Harvard University, New York University Law Library, Northwestern University Law Library, Washington University Law Library, the Institute for Sex Research at Indiana University, the library of the American Civil Liberties Union, New York, the British Museum, and Trinity College, Dublin. Many other libraries supplied occasional unique items by interlibrary loan. The Free Public Library at New Beford, Mass., supplied by interlibrary loan reports of a number of American libel trials from their William L. Sanger collection. Among the special collections that provided rich sources of materials were the Ewing Baskett collection on freedom of the press at the University of Illinois (Mr. Baskett's widow permitted the compiler to use the collection while it was still in the hands of the family), the New York Public Library's collection, as noted in Carl L. Cannon's bibliographies, and the Theodore A. Schroeder collection at the Wisconsin Historical Society. It is a pleasure to express my appreciation to colleagues in these libraries for their resourceful and patient assistance.

The compiler is indebted to earlier bibliographies in this field, although incomplete and, in a number of cases, out-of-date. The most notable bibliographic effort was that of the great libertarian, Theodore A. Schroeder, in his *Free Speech Bibliography* (H. W. Wilson Co., 1922). Also useful, particularly for the literature of World War I, was Kimball Young and Raymond D. Lawrence, *Bibliography on Censorship and Propaganda* (University of Oregon, 1928); William F. Swindler, *A Bibliography of Law on Journalism* (Columbia University Press, 1947); Carl L. Cannon, *Journalism: A Bibliography* (New York Public Library, 1924); Warren C. Price, *The Literature of Journalism* (University of Minnesota Press, 1959); and Helen F. Conover, *Freedom of Information; A Selective Report on Recent Writing* (Library of Congress, 1949 and 1952). The *Catalogue of the McAlpin Collection of British History and Theology* at Union Theological Seminary and the study of *Burned Books* by its librarian emeritus, Charles Ripley Gillett (Columbia University Press, 1932), were useful for identifying seventeenth-century British works. Many clues to early works relating to the formation of the First Amendment

and the period of the Sedition Act of 1798 were gathered from Leonard P. Levy, *Legacy of Suppression* (Belknap Press of Harvard University Press, 1960). A valuable means of keeping in touch with recent publishing on freedom of the press, which has seemed to mushroom in the past decade, has been the *FOI Digest* (Freedom of Information Center, University of Missouri) and the *Newsletter on Intellectual Freedom* (American Library Association).

I am indebted to many librarians, faculty members, and booksellers who, knowing my interest in the subject, brought to my attention items that I might have overlooked. Alan Cohn, Ralph W. Bushee, and Hensley Woodbridge from the library staff of Southern Illinois University were especially alert for new references; Carl D. Cottingham previewed audio-visual material; and a number of graduate students in my seminar on freedom of the press uncovered items of interest. Much of the tedious work of preparing the manuscript for publication was done by my secretary, Mrs. Henrietta Miller; Mrs. Beatrice Moore of Southern Illinois University Press performed the herculean task of editing. Finally, my wife, Melba E. McCoy, helped with almost every phase of the project from preliminary searching to final proofreading.

A grant from Southern Illinois University's Cooperative Research in Communications helped to defray the cost of typing the manuscript.

Despite the time and effort that have gone into this work there are bound to be errors and omissions, hopefully not too many or too serious. While I am unwilling to commit myself to another decade of keeping this work up-to-date, I would be grateful to readers for any notes of errors or serious omissions.

Carbondale, Illinois
April 1967

Contents

FREEDOM OF THE PRESS

A

Abbott, Clarence M. "How They 'Censor' the Films at the National Board of Censorship." *Motion Picture Magazine*, 12 (10): 109–12, September 1917.　　　　**A1**
How the National Board in New York operates as an industry-wide voluntary censor of films. Accompanying cartoons by McNeel lampoon the censor, but the editor notes they are not aimed at the National Board but at the menace of *official* censors.

Abbott, Lawrence F. "The Roosevelt Libel Suit." *Outlook*, 104:325–29, 14 June 1913.　　　　**A2**
A libel suit brought by Theodore Roosevelt against George A. Newett in Marquette, Mich. Newett had published a vicious personal attack on Roosevelt. Token damages were awarded to the former President when the defense conceded the falseness of the publication.

Abbott, Leonard D. "Historical Side of the Birth Control Movement." *Mother Earth*, 11:451–56, April 1916.　　　　**A3**
Deals with the legal suppression of information on birth control in the United States and Europe and with the defiance of the restrictive laws.

――――. "Reflections on Emma Goldman's Trial." *Mother Earth*, 11:504–7, May 1916.　　　　**A4**
Trial and conviction of the anarchist leader, Emma Goldman, for disseminating birth control information.

――――. "Sanger Case." *Mother Earth*, 9:379–80, February 1915. 10:451–52, March 1915.　　　　**A5**
William Sanger was arrested in New York for giving birth control information to an agent provocateur.

"About a Book Named *Tropic*: Boston Courtroom Scene." *Evergreen Review*, 28: 81–84, January–February 1963.　　**A6**
The scene takes place in a courtroom in Boston as part of a drama entitled "Edward J. McCormack, Jr., Attorney General v. A Book

Named *Tropic of Cancer*." The cast: Ephraim London, attorney for the defense; Judge J. Goldberg; and Professor Harry T. Moore, witness for the defense. This excerpt from the court transcript is preceded by a poem by Anselm Hollo entitled "A Warrant Is Out for the Arrest of Henry Miller."

Abrams, Ray H. "The *Jeffersonian*, Copperhead Newspaper; a Case of Attempt at Suppression." *Bill of Rights Review*, 2: 284–89, Summer 1942.　　　　**A7**
In August 1861 a mob destroyed the offices of the *Jeffersonian*, a copperhead paper published in West Chester, Pa. Four days later the editor was arrested and brought to trial, charged with aiding and abetting the insurrection. The court exonerated him and ordered the restoration of his property. Editor John Hodgson sued the U.S. marshal for trespassing and won the case. The decision of the court represented a dispassionate appraisal of the freedom of the press during a period when wartime hysteria prevailed.

Abse, D. W. "Psychodynamic Aspects of the Problem of Definition of Obscenity." *Law and Contemporary Problems*, 20:572–86, Autumn 1955.　　　　**A8**
A psychiatrist considers the pathological conditions in which obscenity often figures; he explores the realm of the ugly "of which obscenity is a sub-species"; and suggests that the problem resolves itself into "setting a standard which both protects generally against noxious effect upon public taste without pandering to the pathological hypersensitive and does not threaten frustration of the artist in society." The author discusses *Lady Chatterley's Lover*, saying that its fine craftsmanship and sincerity are in contrast with pornography "that simply encourages people to luxuriate in morbid, regressive, sexual-sadistic fantasy."

"Absurdity of the Obscenity Laws." *Physical Culture*, 17:85–88, January 1907.　　　　**A9**
The editor of *Physical Culture* was arrested on charges of obscenity because of the scantily dressed muscle men appearing on the pages of the magazine.

"Access to Official Information—A Neglected Constitutional Right." *Indiana Law Journal*, 27:209–30, Winter 1950. **A10**
The author cites numerous examples of withholding public information, which he believes is a serious threat to democratic principles of government. Public officials should be imbued with a sense of responsibility to communicate their actions to the people. He calls for judicial recognition of the basic right to information.

Achorn, Robert C. "The Censors Have a Law." *American Editor*, 2(3):50–52, October 1958.　　　　**A11**
A critical look at the recently created Obscene Literature Advisory Commission of Massachusetts. When a publication seems to the Commission to violate the state's obscenity laws, the Attorney General is so advised.

Achwal, Madhao B. "The Literary Aspect of Obscenity." *Quest* (Bombay), 26:19–25, July–September 1960.　　　　**A12**
"The criteria of literary work, in so far as it is an expression, cannot be ethical or social, they can only be aesthetic." But a work of literature is also a "social fact" when it becomes an agent in communicating and involves the experience of the reader. The total impact of a literary work depends upon both the nature of the work and the individual reading it.

Ackerly, Will W. "Constitutional Freedom of Speech and of the Press." *Case and Comment*, 22:457–60, November 1915.　　　　**A13**
The right of freedom of speech and the press as guaranteed by the First Amendment is not to "unbridled license" but is subject to certain "necessary and reasonable restrictions." A review of judicial decisions.

Ackermann, Carl W. "Freezing the Press; Freedom of Speech but Not Freedom to Speak." *Vital Speeches*, 9:50–52, 1 November 1942.　　　　**A14**
The dean of the Graduate School of Journalism, Columbia University, charges that the United States government since the beginning of World War II has restricted and limited

freedom of the press so that "today the press is frozen by law, by censorship, by directives, by decrees and by executive action. In all governmental affairs the press is free only to report what is officially released. Editors and publishers are free to comment and to criticize. They are not free to investigate the war effort or to crusade and to report their findings."

————. "How Free Is the American Press?" *Vital Speeches*, 7:541–43, 15 June 1941. (Reprinted in Summers, *Wartime Censorship*, pp. 234–39.) **A15**
While the government in time of war has the power through legislation to control the press, there should be close cooperation between government and press to avoid a rigid official censorship.

————. "Keeping American News Lines Open." In *Problems of Journalism; Proceedings of the American Society of Newspaper Editors*. Washington, D.C., ASNE, 1941, pp. 135–41. **A16**
The author urges the ASNE to take an active role in working for a free and responsible press.

————. "The Prelude to War." *Annals of the American Academy of Political and Social Science*, 192:38–41, July 1937. **A17**
The surest safeguard against war is "to protect the freedom of the newspapers, the press associations and the radio from every attempt to manage or to control them by any group in government, in politics, in labor, in industry, or in public affairs."

————. "Relation of News to Global Peace; Freedom of International Communication." *Vital Speeches*, 9:247–50, 1 February 1943. **A18**
In an address at Haverford College, Dean Ackerman urges freedom of the press in the postwar world. Control over news is a certain prelude to war.

————. "Shall We Control the Press and Radio?" *Vital Speeches*, 4:382–84, 1 April 1938. **A19**
Comments on the German demand for press peace pacts with foreign governments, which would provide official control of the printed and spoken words of their respective citizens. Such a pact would be a violation of the United States Constitution. Included is the text of Dean Ackerman's letter on this subject addressed to Otto Dietrich, Reich press chief.

"The Act of Censorship." *Commonweal*, 68:139–40, 9 May 1958. **A20**
An editorial which defends the right to censor but is critical of Catholics who may be "moved by zeal rather than prudence" in their action.

"Action for Freedom of Information." *U.N. Bulletin*, 7:241–45, 1 September 1949. **A21**
"Ranging from study on corrective measures against war propaganda to procedures for dealing with communications, the Economic and Social Council made important recommendations in 16 resolutions on freedom of information and of the press." The resolutions grew out of the UN Conference on Freedom of Information at Geneva in 1948 and the third session of the Subcommission on Freedom of Information and of the Press.

Ad Hoc Committee [on *The Nation*]. *An Appeal to Reason and Conscience*. New York, The Committee, 1948. Broadside. **A22**
A statement of opposition and protest to the ban on *The Nation* in public high schools by the New York City Board of Education. The statement was endorsed by 34 organizations and 72 individuals, including leading lawyers, educators, government officials, editors, and scholars.

Adair, James. *Discussion of the Law of Libels as at Present Received, in which Its Authenticity is Examined with Identical Observations on the Legal Effect of Precedent and Authority*. London, Printed for T. Cadell, 1785. 97 p. **A23**
This moderate Whig lawyer joined Erskine in the defense of William Stone on trial for treason in 1796. Adair was also counsel for the defense in the Junius trials. He maintained that only works that were actually injurious to the public or created a breach of the peace should be considered libelous. A fear of the French Revolution, however, brought Adair into the prosecution against Horne Tooke and Thomas Hardy.

Adam, Kenneth. "Freemen of the Press?" *Fortnightly*, 144 (n.s.):34–41, July 1938. **A24**
Although public officials profess to admire and uphold freedom of the press, they often administer restrictions that are particularly troublesome to working journalists. The article discusses such factors as the British Official Secrets Act, the Judicial Proceedings Act of 1926, and British laws against libel and contempt of court.

Adams, Elbridge L. "Right of Privacy and Its Relation to the Law of Libel." *American Law Review*, 39:57–58, January–February 1905. **A25**

Adams, Franklin P. "Freedom of the Press." *New Republic*, 94:15, 9 February 1938. **A26**
A brief tale of a reporter who was fired for refusal to write an editorial that his boss wanted.

Adams, J. Donald. "Freedom of the Press." *Tomorrow* (New York), (4):20–23, December 1944. **A27**
The author considers the Newspaper Guild movement a dangerous threat to press freedom.

Adams, John. "Ostracised Frankness in America." *Bookman* (London), 64:224–25, August 1923. **A28**
The best evidence of freedom of the press in America is the free circulation of Upton Sinclair's *Brass Check*, a work violently critical of the press. Because of Sinclair's free use of actual names the work would have resulted in a libel suit if published in Britain.

Adams, Samuel H. "Appollyon v. Pollyana." *New Republic*, 30(sup):2–3, 12 April 1922. **A29**
A brief satirical essay on the League for Promotion of Purity.

[Adcock, A. St. John]. "Books That Have Been Banned." *Bookman* (London), 74:26–28, April 1928. **A30**
"You cannot suppress an evil by driving it underground; it usually flourishes longer there than it would have done if you had left it to look paltry and wilt in the common cleanness of the sunlight." Among the stupid misjudgments of the censor was the banning of the literary works of Theodore Dreiser.

Addison, Alexander. *Analysis of the Report of the Committee of the Virginia Assembly, on the Proceedings of Sundry of the Other States in Answer to Their Resolutions*. Philadelphia, Z. Poulson, Jr., 1800. 54 p. **A31**
A defense of the Alien and Sedition Acts of 1798 and a criticism of the Virginia Resolutions by a political judge who was later (1803) impeached and removed from the bench on charges of slander in court.

————. *Liberty of Speech and of the Press. A Charge to the Grand Juries of the County Courts of the Fifth Circuit of the State of Pennsylvania*. Albany, Loring Andrews, [1798]. 16 p. **A32**
A defense of the doctrine of seditious libel under the Alien and Sedition Acts of 1798.

[Addison, Joseph]. *The Thoughts of a Tory Author, Concerning the Press: With the Opinion of the Ancients and Moderns, about Freedom of Speech and Writing And an Historical Account of the Usage it has met with from Both Parties in England*. London, Printed for A. Baldwin, 1712. 33 p. **A33**
In a vein of "easy irony" the author defends the right of citizens to criticize their government, provided the expression is kept under

reasonable restraints of the common law. The work is ascribed by T. Holt White to Joseph Addison, who made similar arguments at about the same time in *The Spectator*. In No. 451 of that journal, Addison condemns pernicious libels against public officials, but blames the reader and distributor of libels as much as their author. The scurrility of the British press has given Britain the reputation among foreigners as "a nation of monsters." While condemning libelous works, Addison opposes any law against anonymity. To require that all publications be signed by their authors would effectively suppress all printed scandal but would also destroy learning as well—"it would root up the corn and the tares together."

An Address of the Minority in the Virginia Legislature to the People of That State; Containing a Vindication of the Constitutionality of the Alien and Sedition Laws. [n.p., 1799?]. 16 p.　**A 34**
On 21 December 1798, the majority in the Virginia House of Delegates had passed resolutions prepared by James Madison, condemning the Alien and Sedition Acts and defending the freedom of the press.

An Address to the People of Virginia, Respecting the Alien & Sedition Laws. By a Citizen of This State. Richmond, Va., Augustine Davis, 1798. 63 p.　**A 35**
The work has been attributed to Thomas Evans of Virginia.

Adler, Julius O. "The Free Press versus the Slave Press." *Vital Speeches*, 20:14–16, 15 October 1953.　**A 36**
To rule intelligently the people must know the facts. "Democracy will survive as a system of government only where the individual citizen has access to all information that is necessary for sound judgment and decision."

Adler, Mortimer J. *Art and Prudence.* New York, Longmans, Green, 1937. 686 p.
　A 37
Numerous references in the volume to censorship of art forms. Adler agrees with Milton that no form of literature can ever be by itself the essential cause of either vice or virtue. "Literature can only provide the matter, as does the rest of life, upon which the powers of the human soul must work for good or evil. Literature and kindred arts, therefore, perform an indispensable service of public education which is hindered, for the most part without any demonstrable profit, by censorship and control."

"Administrative Censorship of Motion Pictures." *Iowa Law Review*, 47:162–68, Fall 1961.　**A 38**
Deals with the case of *Times Film Corp. v. City of Chicago*, 81 Sup. Ct. 391 (1961), and related cases involving film licensing.

The Adult; A Journal for the Free Discussion of Tabooed Topics. London, Legitimation League, 1897–99. Monthly.　**A 39**
The first editor was George Bedborough. When he was arrested in 1898 for the sale of Havelock Ellis' *Studies in the Psychology of Sex*, Henry Seymour assumed the editorship. The short-lived journal crusaded for sexual freedom—the sexual emancipation of women, birth control, and sex education for the masses. It carried articles by such writers as Edwin C. Walker, Orford Northcotte, Tennessee Claflin (Lady Cook), William Platt, Lucy Stewart, and Lillian Harman. It reported news of attacks against the distribution of sex literature in England and the United States, including the case of Abner J. Pope and Moses Harman and, finally, the Bedborough case. Reports on the latter filled most of the second volume. The journal came to an ill-fated end when its founder, George Bedborough, deserted the cause of sex education and by pleading guilty of obscenity charges embarrassed the Free Press Defence Committee that supported him.

Advertising Federation of America. *Facts You Should Know about Anti-Advertising Propaganda in School Textbooks.* New York, The Federation, 1940. 10 p.　**A 40**
An attack on school textbooks, particularly those of Harold O. Rugg, which were allegedly damaging to the advertising industry. The pamphlet asks the reader to investigate the textbooks in his community to determine their sympathy or lack of sympathy with free enterprise.

"Advertising Groups Pursuing Professor Rugg's Books." *Publishers' Weekly*, 138: 1322–23, 28 September 1940.　**A 41**
An account of the attack launched by the Advertising Federation of America on textbooks written by Harold O. Rugg, because discussions of advertising in them allegedly reflected ideas of the Consumers Union and the U.S. Bureau of Standards. The American Legion joined in the attack.

"Aediles Were Busy This Summer." *Wilson Library Bulletin*, 38:21–22, September 1963.　**A 42**
Summary of recent events in censorship, including action against *Fanny Hill* (New York), *Tropic of Cancer* (California), *Dictionary of American Slang* (California), and *The Last Temptation of Christ* (California and New York).

L'Affaire Lolita; Défense de l'Ecrivain. Paris, Olympia Press, 1957. 105 p.　**A 43**
Although mainly an account of the difficulties encountered in France with the publication of Vladimir Nabokov's *Lolita*, there is a section on international censorship and references to the admission of *Lolita* through American Customs.

"Again the Literary Censor." *Nation*, 111: 343, 25 September 1920.　**A 44**

Discusses the New York vice society's action against James B. Cabell's *Jurgen*. While pitiably sincere, the vice societies are stupid and unable to distinguish between good literature and nasty books.

Agar, Herbert. "The British Press: Less and Less News Is Considered Fit to Print." *Column Review*, 8(1):1–4, March 1939.
　A 45
A discussion of self-censorship exercised by the British press through their Publishers' Association.

———. "If Freedom of the Press is to Endure." *Quill*, 26(10):3, 14, October 1938.
　A 46
Newspapers must bear a certain burden and must live up to certain responsibilities if freedom of the press is to endure.

Agler, Raymond B. "'Problem' Books Revisited." *Library Journal*, 89:2019–30, 15 May 1964. Reply by R. S. Bravard, 89:2470+, 15 June 1964.　**A 47**
A survey in depth of the small public library's book selection practices in controversial areas. Fifty-six libraries in four suburban Philadelphia counties responded to questionnaires relating to the handling of 20 fiction and 24 nonfiction titles. The study revealed that "no small segment of these librarians yielded to the pressures of anticipated trouble. Others relied on word-of-mouth criticism in forming their decision not to buy."

Agnew, L. R. C. "Celtic Twilight: The Irish Censorship of Publications Act, 1946." *Kansas Business Review*, 15(3):5–7, March 1962.　**A 48**
The author describes his recent experiences in Ireland, observing the suppression of literature in accordance with the *Register of Prohibited Publications*, an index which contains the names of many important works of modern literature.

Agronsky, Martin. "Armor-Plated Thought Control." *New Republic*, 120: 10–11, 9 May 1949.　**A 49**
Criticism of the first general order of the Public Information Office of the newly organized Department of Defense, which "applies military censorship to hundreds of thousands of members of the National Military Establishment" in time of peace.

Ahrens, Maurice. "Freedom to Learn: Censorship and Learning Materials." *Social Education*, 17:165–70, April 1953.
　A 50
Deals with the use of controversial materials in the teaching of the social studies. The author recommends as a desirable practice the involvement of representative groups of citizens in

the selection of controversial material and the keeping of the community informed regarding this method of teaching students about controversial issues.

Albig, William. *Modern Public Opinion.* New York, McGraw-Hill, 1956. 518 p. **A 51**

A new work, incorporating some of the material in the author's earlier text, *Public Opinion.* Chapters 12 and 13 deal with censorship. Of special interest is a chart (p. 244), Levels of Censorship in the United States. The author concludes that censorship is "based upon folk beliefs rather than upon data provided by social science."

————. *Public Opinion.* New York, McGraw-Hill, 1939. 486 p. **A 52**

Chapters 14 and 15 of this textbook discuss the various pressure groups (governmental, religious, social, and economic) which exert influence and control upon the formation and spread of ideas.

Alden, Edmund K. "Benjamin Franklin Bache." In *Dictionary of American Biography,* vol. 1, pp. 462–63. **A 53**

A brief biography of the grandson of Benjamin Franklin (1769–98), who, as editor of the Jeffersonian paper, the *Aurora,* was arrested under the Sedition Act of 1798.

Aldington, Richard. *Balls and Another Book for Suppression.* London, L. Lahr, 1930. 13 p. (Blue Moon Booklets, no. 7.) **A 54**

Following a humorous essay on "the Purity of our Public and Private life with balls," is a satirical essay on "Another Book for Suppression by Our Moral Expert in Literature." The imaginary expert reviews Shakespeare's *Songs,* which he finds disgusting and filthy-minded. "Whether he be in the pay of Moscow I know not, but who can doubt that a Communist wrote [the poem]." He calls on Scotland Yard to take "stern action in this flagrant case."

————. "Freedom of the Press." In his *Artifex; Sketches and Ideas.* London, Chatto & Windus, 1935, pp. 96–112. **A 55**

"The English law of libel was apparently designed for the discouragement of fiction, and the plaintiff always wins unless he happens to be an author." The opinion of the policeman is preferred over that of the literary expert in English courts of law. Not since the prosecution of Havelock Ellis have the courts prosecuted a scientist for obscenity. It is always the artist who is forbidden to write about sex. Aldington finds censorship a form of sadism, with the censor gaining satisfaction in destruction. The more popular the art form and the more widely read or attended, the greater are the chances of censorship. While acts of physical love may be censored as obscene, the most gruesome murder scenes are per-

mitted. However, "the existence of a censorship of books seems a very trivial matter" in an era where the real grief is the absence of passionately creative artists.

Aldred, Guy A. *Dogmas Discarded; Revised, Extended, and, in Parts, Abridged from an Autobiographical Fragment Published in 1908; Author's 1909 Trial for Sedition Affixed.* London, Bakunin Press, 1913. 31 p. **A 56**

Aldred was sentenced to a year's imprisonment for writing and publishing "certain scandalous and seditious libel" in the *Indian Sociologist* for August 1909, a journal of the Indian nationalist movement. Aldred's views on Indian independence and his expressions of philosophical anarchism were the basis of the prosecution. Aldred conducted his own defense.

————. "Introductory Account of Guy Aldred's Trial for Sedition." In his *Representation and the State.* London, Bakunin Press, 1910. 23 p. (Pamphlets for the Proletarian, no. 10, pp. 3–9.) **A 57**

Another account of the author's 1909 trial for sedition.

————. *Rex v. Aldred; London Trial, 1909, Indian Sedition: Glasgow Sedition Trial, 1921.* Glasgow, Strickland Press, 1948. 64 p. **A 58**

An account of the various sedition trials in which Aldred figured.

————. "Richard and the Georges." *Spur,* 2(9):73–75, February 1916. **A 59**

A comparison of the work of Richard Carlile with that of George J. Holyoake and George W. Foote, all associated in a crusade for freedom of thought and press. The author, editor of this workers' paper, attempts to discredit Holyoake and Foote in an effort to praise Carlile.

————. *Richard Carlile Agitator; His Life and Times.* 3 d ed. Glasgow, Strickland Press, 1941. 160 p. ("The Word" Library, 2 d ser., no. 3.) **A 60**

A sympathetic biography of the nineteenth-century British champion of freedom of the press by a kindred agitator of the twentieth century. Aldred, according to W. H. Wickwar, pictured the oft-imprisoned Carlile as a "demigod among demons." A brief account (39 p.) of Carlile, by the same author, was published in 1912 by the Bakunin Press, Glasgow.

Aldrich, Louise D. *Censorship of Television.* Washington, D.C., National Association of Radio and Television Broadcasters, 1951. 4 p. **A 61**

Alexander, Henry. "Obscenity and the Law." *Queen's Quarterly,* 60:161–69, Summer 1953. **A 62**

Literary censorship in Canada. "Our current crusade against pornographic books is here discussed in terms of existing methods of control and the wider implications—and dangers—of censorship."

[Alexander, James]. ["Freedom of Speech."] Four untitled essays in the *Pennsylvania Gazette,* numbers 466–69, 17 November to 8 December 1737, signed "X." (Reprinted in the Katz edition of the Zenger trial, 1963; also in Levy, *Freedom of the Press from Zenger to Jefferson,* pp. 61–74.) **A 63**

The original lawyer in the John Peter Zenger case (New York, 1735) supports Andrew Hamilton's arguments in defense of Zenger, answering the critical remarks of "Anglo-Americanus" which appeared in the *Barbados Gazette* of July 1737. Alexander draws upon history and common law in a spirited defense of freedom of speech and of the press, which he terms a "principal pillar in a free government." His arguments, however, fail to answer the basic issues raised by the critic, Anglo-Americanus. "To suppress enquiries into administration is good policy in an arbitrary government: But a free constitution and freedom of speech have such a reciprocal dependence on each other that they cannot subsist without consisting together." Duane attributes the essays to Benjamin Franklin, and Sparkes, on this basis, includes them in his collected works of Franklin. Larabee and Bell in *The Papers of Benjamin Franklin* (vol. 2, p. 184) find no internal or external evidence that Franklin was the author. Alexander was also the editor of the first edition of the report of the Zenger trial, listed in this bibliography under Zenger.

Alfange, Dean, Jr. "Balancing of Interests in Free Speech Cases: In Defense of an Abused Doctrine." *Law in Transition Quarterly,* 2:35–63, Winter 1965. **A 64**

After a review and analysis of the doctrine of "balancing of interests," which the author notes has not been popular among defenders of civil liberties, he concludes that judges are the last line of defense for protection of free speech and that faith in the judiciary should be demonstrated by "refusal to bind the courts through absolute rules under the first amendment, so that they may be free to decide cases in this area, as in all others, by balancing social considerations, and protecting all valid interests, not merely speech, to the greatest degree possible."

Alfred, *Brother.* "Francis Collins, First Catholic Journalist in Upper Canada." *Canadian Catholic Historical Association Report, 1938–39,* pp. 51–66. **A 65**

"Collins founded and edited the *Canadian Freeman* (1825–34) and his attacks on the Family Compact led to his imprisonment for libel."

Alfred, Vincent C. "Indecent Literature and the Law." *Catholic Mind*, 51:355–59, June 1953. (Reprinted from *Catholic Action*, April 1953) **A 66**
Some improvement in state and federal statutes will help in the control of obscene literature, but a real clean-up calls for organized public demand for better enforcement of existing laws.

Algie, R. M. *Journalists and the Law Relating to Defamation.* Aukland, N.Z., University of New Zealand School of Journalism, 1935. 24 p. (University of New Zealand Journalism Bulletin no. 2) **A 67**
English libel laws are applied to New Zealand.

Allain, Alex P. "The Trustee and Censorship." In Virgina G. Young, *The Library Trustee, a Practical Handbook.* New York, Bowker, 1964, pp. 113–15. **A 68**

Allbutt, Henry A. *Artificial Checks to Population; Is the Popular Teaching of Them Infamous? A History of Medical Persecutions.* London, George Standring, 1909. 35 p. **A 69**
An account of prosecutions for distributing birth control information.

[————]. *Trial of Henry A. Allbutt, by the General Medical Council of Great Britain and Ireland, at 299, Oxford Street, London, on November 23rd, 24th, and 25th, 1887, for the Publication of "The Wife's Handbook" at So Low a Price; with Press Criticisms on the Same Letter from Mr. Joseph Latchmore, of Leeds, to Sir Henry W. Acland.* Stanningley, Eng., J. W. Birdsall, 1887. 31 p. **A 70**
For having published this popular manual on birth control "at so low a price," Dr. Allbutt was judged by the Royal College of Physicians of Edingburgh and the General Medical Council of Great Britain as guilty of "infamous conduct" and his name was removed from their medical register.

Allen, Carleton K. "Movies and Morals." *Quarterly Review*, 245:313–30, July 1925. **A 71**
A history of control of the movies in England, beginning with the Act of 1909, which required local licensing for all public exhibitions of inflammable films. The author considers the work of the unofficial British Board of Film Censors and the 1917 Commission of Inquiry on the movies set up by the National Council of Public Morals. He reviews some of the specific areas of immorality in movie themes, noting from the evidence of a study on delinquency by Professor Cyril Burt, that the danger from films is not so much in imitative action of crime portrayed, as in the lowering of the general moral tone of the juvenile viewer.

Allen, Florence E. "Fair Trial and Free Press: No Fundamental Clash Between the Two." *American Bar Association Journal*, 41:897–900, October 1955. **A 72**
Judge Allen believes that the apparent conflict between the First Amendment, guaranteeing a free press, and the Fifth Amendment, guaranteeing due process of law and a fair trial, can be solved by the lawyers themselves, if they will enforce their own Canons of Professional Ethics.

Allen, Frank H. *Government Influence on News in the United States during the World War.* Urbana, Ill., University of Illinois, 1934. 263 p. (Unpublished Ph. D. dissertation) **A 73**
Contents: Control of News before April 1917, Rejection of Censorship Legislation, Formation of the Committee on Public Information (voluntary censorship), Dissemination of News by the Committee on Public Information, Military Censorship, Censorship and Publicity Activities of the Federal Departments and Bureaus, Legislation against Disloyalty (Espionage Act, Trading with the Enemy Act, including operation of postal censorship, action on foreign language newspapers), and Final Phases of Wartime Influence on News (including government restrictions on distribution of news of the peace conference).

Allen, Frederick L. *Frederick Baylies Allen: A Memoir.* Cambridge, Mass., Privately printed at Riverside Press, 1929. 102 p. **A 74**
An affectionate biography of one of the founders of the New England Watch and Ward Society, by his son, the late editor of *Harper's Magazine.*

Allen, George V. "U.S. Information Program." *Vital Speeches*, 14:702–4, 1 September 1948. **A 75**
The Assistant Secretary of State for Public Affairs states that the underlying theme of the overseas information program must be truth.

Allen, Harold B. "Mass Pressure on Radio and Journalism." *English Journal*, 38:447–53, October 1949. **A 76**
The author warns teachers of the communications arts to be aware of pressure groups and propaganda and of their effect upon mass communications. He discusses some of these effects on the press and radio.

Allen, Leslie H. *Bryan and Darrow at Dayton.* New York, Lee, 1925. 218 p. **A 77**
A reporter's account of the celebrated "evolution trial" of John T. Scopes. One of the books under attack was George W. Hunter's *Civic Biology.*

Allied Expeditionary Forces. Supreme Headquarters. *A History of Field Press*

Censorship in SHAEF, World War II. Paramus, N.J., 201st Field Press Censorship Organization, [1946?]. 123 p. **A 78**

Allin, C. D. "Belligerent Interference with Mails." *Minnesota Law Review*, 1:293–313, April 1917. **A 79**
Deals largely with the controversy between the United States and the Allied Powers (England and France) in World War I over the inviolability of the mails. The seizure and censorship of the mails, the author notes, is part of the larger question as to whether belligerents have the right under international law to bring a neutral ship into a home port for seizure. He concludes that the position of the United States is needlessly legalistic and obstructive. Up to the time of the Hague Convention there was no principle of international law prohibiting the search or even confiscation of the mail carried by sea in time of war.

Allis, Frederick S., Jr. "Boston and the Alien and Sedition Laws." *Proceedings, Bostonian Society*, 1951, pp. 25–51. **A 80**
The second section of the Sedition Act "interferes with freedom of speech in such a way as to raise serious questions as to the act's constitutionality, though it was never tested in the federal courts." The reaction of Federalist Massachusetts and Virginia resolutions against the Sedition Act showed "little sympathy for this Republican nonsense" and favored strict enforcement. There was only one case in Massachusetts; the state was hard put to find a Republican victim. This was David Brown, sentenced to 18 months in prison for erecting a liberty pole in Dedham, the home of arch-Federalist Fisher Ames. The offensive inscription was as follows: "No Stamp Act, no Sedition, no Alien Bills, no Land Tax: downfall to the Tyrants of America; peace and retirement to the President, long live the Vice-President and the minority; may moral virtue be the basis of civil government." Thomas Adams, editor of the *Independent Chronicle* of Boston was arrested for seditious libel under Massachusetts law rather than under the Federal Sedition Act. When he was too ill to stand trial his brother, Abijah, who had written the story, was tried and given a 30-day sentence. James Sullivan, the attorney general, used Blackstone's limited view of freedom of the press or freedom from prior restraint. Justice Dana refused to allow the defense to present a contrary point of view on the law. During the trial he delivered a lecture on the "monstrous position" of the Kentucky and Virginia resolution, but refused to permit Adams to print these remarks in his paper.

[Allison, Van K.] *Supreme Judicial Court for the Commonwealth; Suffolk County, March Sitting, 1917. Brief for the Defendant.* [Boston? 1917]. 26 p. **A 81**

Van K. Allison was convicted by the Supreme Judicial Court of Massachusetts (*Commonwealth v. Allison*) for distributing birth control information that was alleged to be obscene. Comment on the case appears in *Critic and Guide*, September 1916

Allison, William H. "Abner Kneeland." In *Dictionary of American Biography*, vol. 10, pp. 457–58. **A 82**
Kneeland is best known as the defendant in the famous blasphemy case in Boston, 1834.

Allsop, Kenneth. "I Am a Pornographer." *Spectator*, 205:594–95, 21 October 1960. **A 83**
An interview with Maurice Girodias of Olympia Press, Paris, whose "dirty books" get banned about a year after publication. "I accept the title of pornographer with joy and pride," comments Girodias. "I enjoy annoying people I dislike deeply—the bourgeois class which is in power everywhere, in France, Britain and America. I think it is very healthy to shock them."

———. *A Question of Obscenity*. London, Scorpion Press, 1960. 15 p. (Bound with *A Question of Obscenity* by Robert Pitman) **A 84**
While detesting "the cheapjack rib-nudger" that has flooded the book market with a "slightly more liberal law and a more sophisticated and tolerant taste" (Obscene Publications Act of 1959), Allsop opposes an increase in censorship. Censorship is absurd, inefficient, and without "justifiable function in a society which claims to be an adult and civilized democracy." To get rid of these weeds is "not to pass the job on to an efficiency expert who may grub up everything, but to develop taste and standards exacting enough to ensure that the weeds wither from lack of attention."

Almon, John. *The History of the Late Minority in Parliament during the Years 1762, 1763, 1764, and 1765*. London, Printed for John Almon, 1766. 332 p. **A 85**
Includes an account of the struggle over John Wilkes's publishing and the use of the general warrant for libel charges against authors, printers, and booksellers. Wilkes's copy of this work in the British Museum contains his own lengthy manuscript notes relating to the Wilkes Affair.

———. *Memoirs of John Almon, Bookseller, of Piccadilly*. London, John Almon, 1790. 262 p. **A 86**
Almon is perhaps best known as a friend and confident of John Wilkes. He participated as author, editor, or publisher in a series of tracts on libels and general warrants, appearing as an outgrowth of the Wilkes's trial. In 1770 Almon was arrested and fined for selling a copy of the *London Museum* containing a reprint of Junius' letters to the King.

[———]. *The Trial of John Almon, Bookseller . . . for Selling Junius's Letter to the K——. Before the Right Hon. William Lord Mansfield, and a Special Jury of the County of Middlesex, in the Court of King's-Bench, Westminster-Hall, on Saturday, the Second Day of June, 1770 . . .* London, Printed for J. Miller, 1770. 65 p. (Also in Howell, *State Trials*, vol. 20, pp. 803 ff.) **A 87**
Almon was a Piccadilly bookseller who offended the government by publishing the "Father of Candor" letters, by statements in his *Political Register*, and by publication of an account of the Zenger trial. He was ultimately tried and convicted for the sale of the Junius letters. A number of his pamphlets and those of his opponents were reprinted in *A Collection of Scarce and Interesting Tracts*, London, 1788. Rea, in *The English Press in Politics*, gives a full account of Almon's earlier trial for *A Letter Concerning Libels*.

Alpert, Leo M. "Judicial Censorship of Obscene Literature." *Harvard Law Review*, 52:40–76, November 1938. (Reprinted in Downs, *The First Freedom*, pp. 52–67) **A 88**
A history of the obscenity laws of Great Britain and the United States from the mid-seventeenth century to the twentieth century. Although the study is 25 years old, Downs terms it "the most adequate summary of legal developments" in the field of obscenity censorship. It supports the contention "that there is no evidence establishing the need for censorship; that on the whole the evidence points the other way. Strongly rooted feelings, however, lying deep within the present social organization, cannot be swept away." The author asks that "the approach to the problem be confined within the borders of the nature and function of literature with due regard to the pertinent psychological and sociological aspects of the effect of literature."

———. "Naughty, Naughty! Judicial Censorship of Obscene Literature." *Colophon*, 3(n.s.):47–54, 1939. (Reprinted in Downs, *The First Freedom*, pp. 4–8, and in Targ, *Carrousel for Bibliophiles*, pp. 208–9) **A 89**
The author examines the historical phases of censorship over three centuries, chiefly from the legal point of view, with references to the attitude of the British and American courts toward obscenity.

Altgeld, John P. "Anonymous Journalism and Its Effects." In his *Live Questions*. Chicago, Donohue & Henneberry, 1890, pp. 90–103. (Reprinted from *Belford's Magazine*, October 1889) **A 90**
The man who later became the controversial liberal governor of Illinois regrets the anonymity of newspapers of the day. Great editors in the past, he notes, did not hide behind

their papers, but stood erect "before all Israel and the sun." The effect of anonymity in journalism is to relieve the writer of personal responsibility and contribute to an irresponsible press. The public is entitled to know who is speaking. Freedom of the press would not be impaired, but rather enhanced by the requirement of a signature on everything appearing in a newspaper. Such a requirement would make for less bias, and would guarantee greater accuracy and fair play for the readers.

[Alverson, Luther]. *A Movie Censorship Decision*. Columbia, Mo., Freedom of Information Center, School of Journalism, University of Missouri, 1961. 7 p. (Publication no. 64) **A 91**
Text of the decision by Judge Luther Alverson of the Superior Court, Atlanta Judicial Circuit, holding as unconstitutional Atlanta's movie censorship ordinance. The case *Lobert Pictures Corp. v. City of Atlanta* involved the movie *Never on Sunday* and was decided for the plaintiff. The text is introduced by editorial commentary on state and municipal movie censorship.

Amdur, Leon H. *Copyright Law and Practice*. New York, Clark Boardman, 1936. 1332 p. **A 92**
A law textbook, particularly useful for its coverage of radio copyright.

Amen, Maurice. "Church Legislation on Obscenity." *Catholic Lawyer*, 10:109–28, Spring 1964. **A 93**
The author deals with the historical development of Church opposition to obscenity under two headings: The Patristic Condemnation of Obscene Literature and the Ecclesiastical Prohibition of Obscene Literature. Under the latter he considers action prior to the Council of Trent, the work of the Council of Trent, the events from the Council until Leo XIII, further prohibition by American bishops and the Leonene Reform of the prohibition of obscene literature. He concludes: "Only where there is some conformity of political legislation to the legislation of the Church, which determines the natural law in this matter, will there be that blending of truth and circumstances, of theory and practice, that is unimpeachable."

———. "The Church versus Obscene Literature." *Catholic Lawyer*, 11:21–32, 46–47, Winter 1965. **A 94**
"By enumerating some of the effects of obscenity, perhaps we can achieve some insights into the reasons behind the ecclesiastical legislation against obscene literature."

American Association of School Libraries. "Book Selection in Defense of Liberty in Schools in a Democracy." *ALA Bulletin*, 47:484, November 1953. **A 95**
A report by a school librarians discussion group at the Whittier Conference on Intellectual Freedom, Los Angeles, 20–21 June 1953. The statement rejects censorship of subject or

author, urges that all sides of controversial subjects be represented in school library materials, recommends that book lists be used as aids in book selection but not as final authority, and that responsibility for selection be retained within the school.

————. *Policies and Procedures for Selection of School Library Materials.* Chicago, AASL, 1961. 5p. (Reprinted in *Illinois Libraries*, May 1966) **A96**
This statement, adopted by the AASL, 3 February 1961, includes the School Library Bill of Rights and three examples of policy statements that treat the problem of censorship.

————. *School Library Bill of Rights.* Chicago, AALS, 1955. 1p. mimeo. **A97**
This statement, endorsed by the Council of the American Library Association, July 1955, reaffirms the Library Bill of Rights, applying its principles to the school library.

American Bar Association. "Statement on the Freedom to Read." *ALA Bulletin*, 47:486, November 1953. (Reprinted in Downs, *The First Freedom*, pp. 341–42, and in *Illinois Libraries*, May 1966) **A98**
Resolution adopted, House of Delegates, American Bar Association, 25 August 1953: "Resolved that the freedom to read is a corollary of the constitutional guarantee of the freedom of the press and American lawyers should oppose efforts to restrict it." The statement reviews recent efforts to remove books from government libraries abroad and the variety of attacks on libraries at home. "The smoke of burning books, like the smell of midnight oil in the rewriting of history by Nazi or Soviet historians to make it more palatable to their regimes, offends American nostrils. The place to stop is before the process begins. American lawyers have sufficient confidence in the common sense of our people and the stability of our institutions to urge that we can and should keep them free . . . A learned profession like ours is particularly aware that books contain the core of the great traditions of our history and civilization. No one should be allowed to tamper with them without sharp reaction from the Bar."

[American Book Company]. *Amercian Book Company Vindicated; The "Gates Pamphlet" a Libel. Jury Trial in Minneapolis at the March Term of the United States Circuit Court. Verdict against the Publisher of the Pamphlet and Large Damages Awarded.* (n.p.), 1897. 14p. **A99**
The "Gates pamphlet" charged bribery.

"American Book in British Courts; Sherwood Anderson's *Many Marriages*." *Literary Digest*, 79:30, 24 November 1923. **A100**

American Book Publishers Council. *Books and Our Constitutional Guarantees.* New York, The Council, 1953. 5p. mimeo. **A101**

————. *Censorship Bulletin.* New York, The Council. Published periodically since December 1955. Varying titles and frequency. **A102**
This publication of the trade association of book publishers reports from time to time on incidents of book censorship, actions or proposed actions by federal, state and local authorities, and by private groups that "tend to abridge the freedom to import, publish, distribute and circulate books through commercial and literary channels, or to deny access to information."

————. *Recent Censorship Developments.* New York, The Council, 1953. 6p. mimeo. **A103**

————. *Recent Pressures on Books.* New York, The Council, 1953. 12p. mimeo. **A104**

American Broadcasting Company. *Program and Advertising Policies.* New York, ABC, 1962. 68p. mimeo. **A105**
Contains standards of propriety for broadcasts of news and public affairs, programs involving religion, politics and controversial issues, contests, and programs intended for children.

"American by Decree." *New Republic*, 22:262–63, 28 April 1920. **A106**
Criticism of a proposal that only native-born American citizens be allowed to draw out foreign language books from public libraries, and of an Oregon law prohibiting the publication of foreign language newspapers and periodicals without an accompanying English translation.

The American [Catholic] Hierarchy. "Censorship." In *Catholic Mind*, 56:180–86, March–April 1958. **A107**
"Because freedom of the press is a basic right to be respected and safeguarded, it must be understood and defended not as license but as true rational freedom. The uncritical claims for liberty, so often made in our day, actually place that liberty in jeopardy." Annual statement of the American Hierarchy, 17 November 1957.

"American Censorship in France." *Review of Reviews*, 57:205–6, February 1918. **A108**
Censorship of American news of World War I by military authorities in France.

American Civil Liberties Union. *Academic Freedom and Civil Liberties of Students in Colleges and Universities.* New York, ACLU, 1961. 15p. **A109**
Includes statements on student publications, radio and television broadcasts, and distribution of pamphlets.

————. *Annual Report.* New York, ACLU. Published annually since 1920. **A110**
Each report reviews the significant civil liberties activities in the nation for the preceeding 12 months. The title and contents of the report have varied over the years. The 1943 annual report, *Freedom in Wartime*, for example, contrasts the freedom of public information in World War II and the lack of freedom in World War I; the 1963 report bears the title *To Secure—To Use—These Rights.* The 1964 report is titled *Defending the Bill of Rights: The Stakes Grow Higher.* This report, under the general heading, Freedom of Belief, Expression and Association, summarizes censorship of communications in general (books, magazines, motion pictures, radio, television, and newspapers), and discusses academic freedom, religion, general freedom of speech and association, and freedom of labor. The archives of the ACLU in the New York Public Library and Princeton University Library include scrapbooks, correspondence, and records relating to cases in which the Union has participated since its organization in 1917.

————. *Bills in Congress for Freedom of the Air.* New York, ACLU, 1936. 16p. **A111**
Bills provide for (1) equal facilities for both sides of controversial issues, (2) periods of unrestricted discussion of public issues, (3) complete, open station records on requests for time, (4) protection of stations from civil and criminal court actions, and (5) creation of a broadcasting commission.

————. *Bills in Congress for Freedom of the Air.* New York, ACLU, 1938. 12p. **A112**
Bills carry the same provisions as those in 1936, except for the omission of the broadcasting commission.

————. *The Case of Reed Harris, Student Editor at Columbia University. His Expulsion for Criticism of College Affairs, and Subsequent Reinstatement.* New York, ACLU, 1932. 16p. mimeo. **A113**
Harris was editor-in-chief of the *Columbia Daily Spectator.* His editorials had attacked college football, ROTC, anti-Semitism, the Republican Party, the secret society "Nacoms," and ultimately, the preparation and serving of food in the University's John Jay Hall. The last criticism led to his expulsion.

————. *Censorship of Comic Books.* New York, ACLU, 1955. 16p.　　**A114**
The statement opposes censorship of comic books as a violation of the First Amendment.

————. *Civil Liberties.* New York, ACLU. Published periodically since 1931; at present, monthly except July and August.
　　A115
Source of current events on press freedom and censorship in the United States. Includes reports on cases in which the ACLU is a party.

————. *Combatting Undemocratic Pressures on Schools and Libraries: A Guide for Local Communities.* New York, ACLU, 1964. 14p. (Reprinted in *Illinois Libraries*, May 1966)　　**A116**
"The purpose of this pamphlet is to prepare men and women in our cities and towns for such attacks [demands for immediate and drastic changes in our school curriculums and library policies] so that by careful, cool, and skillful organization—always using the democratic process, always permitting these outsiders and other pressure groups a proper hearing—these charges can be turned aside without impairing the basic soundness of our schools and libraries, or shaking the morale of the community. By doing so, the basic right of all citizens to criticize their public institutions, honestly and dispassionately, will be preserved."

————. *Jehovah's Witnesses and the War.* New York, ACLU, 1943. 36p.　　**A117**
Includes references to the freedom to distribute literature and the right to play records.

————. *Obscenity and Censorship. Two Statements of the Amercian Civil Liberties Union.* New York, ACLU, 1963. 8p.
　　A118
(1) Text of the public statement issued 28 May 1962, based on the Board of Directors action of 16 April 1962. (2) Text of the press release of 14 Febraury 1963, summarizing the amicus curiae brief filed with the U.S. Supreme Court by the ACLU and Ohio CLU.

————. *The Persecution of the Jehovah's Witnesses: The Record of violence against a religious organization unparalleled in America since the attacks on the Mormons.* New York, ACLU, 1941. 24p.　　**A119**

————. *Policy Statement on Pressure-Group Censorship.* New York, ACLU, 1952. 6p. mimeo. (Excerpts in Daniels, *The Censorship of Books*, pp. 58–59)　　**A120**

————. *The Post Office Ban on "Revolutionary Age"* . . . New York, ACLU, 1931. 7p.　　**A121**
In July 1930 the U.S. Post Office Department banned from second class mail *Revolutionary Age*, the weekly organ of a faction of the Communist Party. Action was taken under the Espionage Act of World War I, invoked for the first time in ten years. Judge John M. Woolsey of the U.S. District Court in New York upheld the ban, maintaining that the work advocated violent rather than constitutional measures for modifying the government. Arthur Garfield Hays argued for the defense that the language, while revolutionary in nature, did not suggest immediate forcible action. In this pamphlet the ACLU urges the repeal of the wartime law which permits the Post Office to serve as censor of political matter.

————. *Private Group Censorship and the NODL. A Statement by the American Civil Liberties Union.* New York, ACLU, 1958. 12p.　　**A122**
". . . a number of private groups, particularly church-related organizations, have prepared blacklists, threatened and imposed general boycotts, and awarded unofficial certificates of compliance. The most active of these groups is the National Office for Decent Literature."

————. *A Proposal to Promote Public Discussion over the Radio.* New York, ACLU, 1934. 8p. mimeo.　　**A123**

————. *The Prosecution of Mary Ware Dennett for "Obscenity."* New York, ACLU, 1929. 8p.　　**A124**
"After distributing her pamphlet 'The Sex Side of Life' for 10 years, Mrs Dennett was brought to trial by Post Office officials and convicted in the Federal Court at Brooklyn for sending 'obscene matter'—her pamphlet—through the mails. She was sentenced to pay a $300 fine or serve 300 days in jail." The Mary Ware Dennett Defense Committee, composed of leaders in educational, religious, and medical work, was organized by the American Civil Liberties Union to appeal the case and the defendant was represented by Morris Ernst and associates. The decision of the Federal Court was eventually reversed by the Circuit Court of Appeals, Judge Augustus N. Hand, writing the opinion.

————. *Radio Censorship. Report Submitted to the American Civil Liberties Union by a Special Committee Advocating a Thoroughgoing Inquiry by the Federal Government.* New York, ACLU, 1934. 9p. mimeo.
　　A125
A special committee, appointed by the ACLU to study restrictive practices in radio broadcasting, recommends a federal investigation.

————. *Religious Liberty in the United States Today: A Survey of the Restraint on Religious Freedom.* New York, ACLU, 1939. 48p.　　**A126**

————. *Repeal the Special Police Powers of the New York Vice Society.* New York, ACLU, 1931. 8p.　　**A127**

————. *Scandal and Defamation! The Right of Newspapers to Defame. Unique Minnesota Law empowers judges to suppress papers by injunction. First such use of judicial power in American history. Chicago Tribune takes the case to the U.S. Supreme Court, where it awaits decision.* New York, ACLU, 1931. 8p.　　**A128**

————. *Statement on Censorship Activities by Private Organizations and the National Organization for Decent Literature.* New York, ACLU, 1958. 12p. (Reprinted in Downs, *The First Freedom*, pp. 134–38 and Gardiner, *Catholic Viewpoint on Censorship*, pp. 173–78)　　**A129**
Appendix includes list of NODL banned books.

————. *The "Vanguard" Problem at Brooklyn College. Memorandum and Opinion of the Academic Freedom Committee of the American Civil Liberties Union.* New York, The Committee, 1951. 17p, 11p. mimeo.
　　A130
Report of an investigation of the revocation of the charter of *Vanguard*, the student newspaper at Brooklyn College, for alleged violation of a rule on "double editorials."

————. *War-time Prosecutions and Mob Violence Involving the rights of free speech, free press and peaceful assemblage. (From April 1, 1917, to March 1, 1919)* . . . New York, National Civil Liberties Bureau, 1919. 56p.　　**A131**
Includes reports on 56 espionage cases under World War I statutes involving freedom of the press or the distribution of literature. "This list of cases is compiled from the correspondence and press clippings of the National Civil Liberties Bureau. It is by no means a complete record." The Bureau later became the American Civil Liberties Union.

————. *War-time Restraints; Texts of federal laws and regulations affecting utterances, communication, enemy aliens, labor, etc.* New York, ACLU, 1942. 32p.　　**A132**

————. *What Freedom for American College Students? A Survey of the Practices Affecting Student Activities and Expressions.* New York, ACLU, 1941. 48p.　　**A133**
Student publications are discussed on pages 35–38.

————. *What Shocked the Censors.* New York, ACLU, 1933. 100 p. **A134**

A catalog of cuts made by movie censors of the state of New York.

————. *What's Obscene?* New York, ACLU, [1944?]. 8 p. **A135**

Relates to Post Office censorship of *Esquire, Sunshine and Health,* and Dr Popenoe's book, *Preparing for Marriage.*

American Committee for Democracy and Intellectual Freedom. *The Text Books of Harold Rugg: an Analysis* by George H. Sabine, Arthur N. Holcombe, Arthur W. MacMahon, Carl Wittke, and Robert S. Lynd. New York, The Committee, 1942. 28 p. **A136**

Statement by a group of social scientists on a series of high school texts under attack.

American Federation of Labor. *Buck's Stove and Range Company Injunction Suit and Contempt Proceedings. A Compilation of Reports of the Eexecutive Council and President Gompers to the Toronto Convention of the American Federation of Labor, November 8–20, 1909, together with the Report of the Committee on President's Report, Report of the Committee on Boycotts, and Vice-President Mitchell's Address, Etc.* Washington, D.C., AFL, 1910. 37 p. **A137**

Relates to a case of contempt of court for violating an injunction in an industrial dispute. The AFL had placed the Buck's Stove and Range Company on its "We Don't Patronize List," after which the company secured an injunction in the District of Columbia Court of Appeals against any action interfering with the company's product, including any publication. When the *American Federationist* carried a story about the case, President Gompers and two other AFL officials were found in contempt of court and given jail sentences. The case was in the courts until 1914 when it was settled under the Statues of Limitations.

[————]. *Organized Labor Says No.* New York, National Civil Liberties Bureau, 1919. 4 p. **A138**

Free speech and press resolutions adopted by the conventions of the American Federation of Labor and the National Woman's Trade Union League, June 1919.

American Forum of the Air. *Free Speech and Censorship in Wartime.* Washington, D.C., Ransdell, 1942. 11 p. (vol. 4, no. 10) **A139**

Participants: James L. Fly, Byron Price, Roy E. Larsen, Dwight Marvin, and Raymond G. Swing.

————. *What Are Your Children Reading?* Washington, D.C., Ransdell, 1953. 10 p. (vol. 16, no. 1) **A140**

Participants: Katharine St George, Morris Ernst, Charles Fahy, and Clarence Hall.

American Legion. Department of Michigan. *Evaluation of Instructional Materials; Statement Adopted at the Convention, Grand Rapids, Mich., August 19–22, 1948.* Detroit, The Legion, 1948. 5 p. mimeo. **A141**

In the midst of the widespread attacks on subversion in public school textbooks made by some members of the American Legion and other patriotic groups, a special committee of the Michigan Department of the American Legion issued this dispassionate and objective statement on evaluating textbooks. It was later adopted by the National Convention.

American Library Association. "How Libraries and Schools Can Resist Censorship." *Library Journal,* 87:908, 937, 1 March 1962. (Reprinted in *Illinois Libraries,* May 1966) **A142**

A statement approved by the Council of the Association, January 1962. Lists six principles that every library should establish to place the institution in a firm position with respect to censorship pressures, and six items of advice if an attack does come.

————. *Labeling; a Report of the ALA Committee on Intellectual Freedom.* Chicago, ALA, 1951. 4 p. (Reprinted from the *ALA Bulletin,* July–August 1951; also appears in the *ALA Bulletin,* November 1953) **A143**

This statement, adopted by the ALA Council, 13 July 1951, rejects the proposal sometimes made that controversial works in a library be so labeled. Labeling, the report states, is a censor's tool and violates the Library Bill of Rights.

————. "Library Bill of Rights." *ALA Bulletin,* 42:285, July–August 1948. (Reprinted in the *ALA Bulletin,* November 1953; in Downs, *The First Freedom,* p. 336; and as a separate broadside by the ALA) **A144**

Briefly speaking, this statement provides that no book be excluded from a library because of the race, nationality, or political or religious views of the writer; that books "should not be proscribed or removed from library shelves because of partisan or doctrinal disapproval"; that libraries should resist the pressures of censors; that libraries should enlist the support of allied organizations in resisting abridgment of free access to ideas; and that they should not deny the use of library facilities because of race, religion, national origin, or political views. By action of the ALA Council, 3 February 1951, the Library Bill of Rights was interpreted to apply to all materials and media of communication used or collected by libraries.

The statement was amended, 1 February 1961, to include this paragraph: "The rights of an individual to the use of a library should not be denied or abridged because of his race, religion, national origins, or political views." An earlier Library Bill of Rights, based on the Des Moines Public Library statement, was adopted by the ALA Council in 1939. A proposed revision of the Bill of Rights is presented in the 1 March 1967 issue of *Library Journal* (pp. 984–85).

————. "Overseas Library Statement." *ALA Bulletin,* 47:487, November 1953. (Reprinted in Downs, *The First Freedom,* pp. 339–40) **A145**

In June 1953 the Council of the American Library Association approved this statement defending the freedom of American overseas libraries, which were then under attack by a Congressional Committee and being subjected to the "confused and fearful response of the State Department."

————. Intellectual Freedom Committee. "Book Selection Principles." *ALA Bulletin,* 45:346–50, 5 November 1951. **A146**

The Committee examined the book selection policy of the Detroit Public Library, recommending a rewording of the section which deals with the distinction made in book selection between the main library and the branches. Librarian Ralph A. Ulveling replies to the Committee in the March 1952 issue of the *ALA Bulletin,* defending the Library's statement.

————. *Freedom of Book Selection; Proceedings of the Second Conference on Intellectual Freedom, Whittier, California, June 20–21, 1953 . . .* Edited by Fredric J. Mosher. Chicago, ALA, 1954. 132 p. **A147**

Contents: Introduction by Paul Bixler. I. *Areas of Controversy.* Science and Pseudo-Science by Louis N. Ridenour, Morality and Obscenity by Eric Larrabee, and Politics and Subversion by Harold D. Lasswell. II. *The Responsibility of Choice.* The Administrator's Problem by Virgil M. Rogers, The Publisher's Responsibility by Douglas M. Black, The Responsibility of the Literary Critic: Some Indirections for Selecting Good Books by Paul Jordan-Smith, The Librarian's Responsibility: Not Censorship, But Selection by Lester E. Asheim. The Appendix contains the statement on Freedom to Read adopted by the American Library Association and the American Book Publishers' Council, and President Eisenhower's Letter on Intellectual Freedom. The article by Lasswell is reprinted in Downs, *The First Freedom,* pp. 235–42. The conference was sponsored by the Committee on Intellectual Freedom, the Book Acquisitions Committee, and the Board on Acquisition of Library Materials of the American Library Association.

————. *Freedom of Communications; Proceedings of the First Conference on Intellectual Freedom, New York City, June 28–29, 1952 . . .* Edited by William Dix and Paul Bixler. Chicago, ALA, 1954. 143 p. **A148**
Contents: Introduction by Paul Bixler. I. *The Library and Free Communications* (William Dix, chairman). Free Communications—An American Heritage by Julian Boyd, The Significance of Free Communications Today by Alan Barth, and The Library's Responsibility in Free Communications by E. W. McDiarmid. II. *The Present Problems of Book Selection* (Milton E. Lord, chairman). The Large Research Library by Verner W. Clapp, The Large Public Library by Ralph Munn, The Small Public Library by Jerome Cushman, and The Problem—A British View by Robert L. Collison. III. *Pressures—Where From and How* (David K. Berninghausen, chairman). Pressure Groups and Intellectual Freedom by Harwood L. Childs, and A Statewide Experience (California) by John E. Smith. IV. *Our Common Stake in Free Communications* (Luther Evans, chairman). Book Publishing by Donald S. Klopfer, The Press by Lester Markel, and Broadcasting by Merle Miller. Conference Summary by Alan Barth. Appendix A, Library Bill of Rights; Appendix B, Labeling Statement; Appendix C, Selected Bibliography on Intellectual Freedom.

————. *Freedom of Inquiry. Supporting the Library Bill of Rights; Proceedings of the* [*Third*] *Conference on Intellectual Freedom, January 23–24, 1965, Washington, D.C. Sponsored by the American Library Association Intellectual Freedom Committee.* Chicago, ALA, 1965. 70 p. (Digested in Freedom of Information Center Publication, no. 149) **A149**
Contents: More Than Lip Service by Martha Boaz, Censorship and Obscenity by Dan Lacy, Can Reading Affect Delinquency? by William C. Kvaraceus, Censorship and the Public Schools by Lee A. Burress, Jr., Freedom to Read and Racial Problems by Charles Morgan, Jr., Freedom to Read and Religious Problems by Theodore Gill, Freedom to Read and the Political Problem by Wesley McCune, and Defending the Freedom to Read in the Courts by Edward de Grazia. A section on censorship as seen by other groups includes statements from the National Education Association, National Council of Teachers of English, American Studies Association, American Library Trustees Association, New Jersey Committee for the Right to Read, Freedom of Information Center, and National Book Committee.

————. *Newsletter on Intellectual Freedom.* Published periodically since 1952. Beginning with vol. 9, nos. 1–2, June 1960, the *Newsletter*, then a quarterly, was published for the American Library Association by the Freedom of Information Center, School of Journalism, University of Missouri. Beginning with vol. 11, no. 1, October 1962, the *Newsletter* became a bimonthly publication, issued by the Intellectual Freedom Committee, American Library Association, under the editorship of LeRoy C. Merritt. (A 14-year cumulative index, prepared by students of the School of Librarianship, University of California (Berkeley), is available in two parts: Part I, 1952–62; Part II, 1963–65) **A150**
Issues report news and opinions on the defense or abridgment of intellectual freedom, with special attention given to libraries and the mass media. New books and journal articles on intellectual freedom are listed.

————. *Reports.* Annually in *ALA Bulletin* since 1940. **A151**
In May 1940, the Council of the American Library Association created a standing Committee on Intellectual Freedom to Safeguard the Rights of Library Users to Freedom of Inquiry. The Committee was intended "to throw the force and influence of the ALA behind any individual librarian or any library board confronted with any demands for censorship of books or other material upon a library's shelves." The first brief report of the Committee under the chairmanship of Forrest B. Spaulding, appeared in the *ALA Bulletin*, August 1940.

American Library Association. Library Administrative Division. *Access to Public Libraries. A Research Project.* Prepared for the Library Administrative Division, American Library Association by International Research Associates, Inc. Chicago, ALA, 1963. 160 p. **A152**
"This is a study undertaken for the American Library Association. It is designed to examine the scope and extent of limited access to public libraries throughout the United States, with particular reference to the problem of racial segregation in Southern libraries. . . . The position of the American Library Association in this area has been recently emphasized by a revision of its Bill of Rights which proclaims that 'The rights of an individual to the use of a library should not be denied or abridged because of his race, religion, national origins, or political views.'"

American Library Association. Office of Library Film Advisor. "Special Edition on Censorship of Film Collections." *ALA Film Newsletter*, 15 September 1950. 4 p. mimeo. **A153**
Deals largely with the case of film censorship in the Peoria Public Library, "the first clear-cut instance of pressure upon public libraries to remove certain 16 mm films from public library film collections."

American Library Association and American Book Publishers Council. *Freedom to Read Statement.* Chicago, American Library Association, 1953. 8 p. (Prepared by the Westchester Conference of the ALA and the ABPC, 2 and 3 May 1953. Subsequently endorsed by the American Booksellers Association, the Book Manufacturers' Institute, and the National Education Association. Reprinted in the *ALA Bulletin*, November 1953, *Wilson Library Bulletin*, September 1953, Daniels, *The Censorship Books*, pp. 149–54, and in Downs, *The First Freedom*, pp. 337–39. Reprinted with comments in the *Saturday Review*, 11 July 1953, *Library Journal*, 6 July 1953, and *Time*, 6 July 1953 **A154**
Following a vigorous preamble against censorship, the statement lists six propositions, which are summarized as follows: publishers have an obligation to provide wide diversity of views without the necessity of endorsing views; a book should be judged as a book, not by the affiliations of the author; extralegal efforts to suppress reading matter should be rejected; labeling should be rejected; and both librarians and publishers should contest encroachment upon the freedom to read.

American Lutheran Church. Board for Christian Social Action. *The Church Looks at Immorality in Print and on the Screen.* Columbus, Ohio, The Board, [1959?]. 14 p. **A155**

American Municipal Association. *Regulation of Handbill Distribution: Legal Problems Involved.* Chicago, The Association, 1940. 20 p. (Report no. 136) **A156**
Examples of municipal ordinances and decisions are given as a guide to city officials.

American Newspaper Publishers' Association. *Bulletin.* New York, The Association, 1895–1926? Irregular. **A157**
A number of issues during the early years of the century were devoted to publishing the decisions of significant newspaper libel cases, in a subseries, headed "B" Special. Examples: *Frank N. Morse v. Times-Republican* (Iowa), 1904; *Kate Corr v. Sun Printing and Publishing Co.* (New York), 1904.

American Railway Literary Union. *"Knowledge and Virtue." The American Railway Literary Union; Its Origin, History and Constitution; for the United States and British American Provinces, March, 1865.* [Rochester, N.Y.]. Published for the Union, 1865. 15 p. **A158**
The Union was organized in 1857 by Jonathan Sturges of New York at the suggestion of a director of the Illinois Central Railroad "to

secure, with as little disturbance as possible of the business talent, capital, and engagements now existing, a healthful improvement in the Literature upon thoroughfares." A constitution was adopted in 1864. The organization, working closely with the Y.M.C.A., was a forerunner of the vice society, but its emphasis from the very beginning was on the positive side—providing good literature on trains and in stations.

American Railway Literary Union and Pure Literature Bureau. *Information and Suggestions Regarding Pernicious Literature. A Guide to All Who Would Aid in Its Suppression.* Philadelphia, 1882. (General Circular no. 5) **A159**
Advice to newsdealers, booksellers, and libraries on how to avoid pernicious literature.

American Recreation League. *The Menace of Motion Picture Censorship.* Washington, D.C., The League, n.d. 20p. **A160**
"How you can help to defeat the movement to shackle free speech and save the motion picture industry."

American Secular Union and Freethought Federation. *Answers by the American Secular Union and Freethought Federation in Reply to the Protests against Our Literature, which was Prepared for Circulation to Show the Folly and Illegality of Bible Reading in the Public Schools . . .* Chicago, American Secular Union, [1903]. 24p. **A161**
The answers were prepared by E. C. Reichwald.

American Society of Newspaper Editors. *Bulletin.* Wilmington, Del., 1941–date. Monthly. **A162**
Frequently contains reports and commentary on events related to freedom of the press.

————. "Canons of Journalism." In various issues of ASNE *Proceedings* of annual conventions; also in Schramm, *Mass Communications.* Urbana, Ill., University of Illinois Press, 1949, pp. 236–38. **A163**
Statement of the responsibility of a free press to society. I. Responsibility. II. Freedom of the Press. III. Independence. IV. Sincerity, Truthfulness, Accuracy. V. Impartiality. VI. Fair Play. VII. Decency. The Canons of Journalism were adopted by the Society in 1922 as a means of codifying sound practice and just aspirations of American journalism.

————. "A Declaration of Principles by the American Society of Newspaper Editors. Adopted July 12, 1957 in San Francisco." In *Problems of Journalism; Proceedings of the American Society of Newspaper Editors, 1958.* Washington, D.C., ASNE, 1958, p. 230. **A164**

The American people have an inherent "right to know." To exercise this right they must be able to gather information and to publish and distribute it without prior restraint or censorship and without fear of punishment not in accord with due process. The members of the Association are concerned, both as citizens and as agents of citizens, with threats to the "right to know." The Association has authorized its officers and directors to resist encroachment upon these liberties.

————. *Problems of Journalism; Proceedings of the Annual Meeting.* Washington, D.C., ASNE, 1923–date (except 1945). **A165**
Each annual proceedings discusses some aspect of freedom of information. For example, reports of the Committee on Legislation and Freedom of the Press prepared by R. J. Dunlap and Grove Patterson appear in the 1929 and 1930 volumes; a report of a Special Committee on Libel by Stuart H. Perry appears in the 1935 volume; a report of the Committee on World Freedom of Information by Erwin D. Canham appears in the 1948 volume; reports from the same Committee by Basil Walters appear in the 1949 and 1951 volumes; reports by James S. Pope and Carroll Binder appear in the 1951 volume. The 1951 volume also includes a summary of a report of the wartime Censorship Study Committee prepared by Jack H. Lockhart; and a summary of recent legal developments in The People's Right to Know by Harold L. Cross. A useful summary of the work and publications of the ASNE that relate to freedom of the press is given in U.S. Library of Congress, *Freedom of Information; a Selective Report on Recent Writings,* 1949.

————. "Report of the Committee on World Freedom of Information." *Editor and Publisher,* 78:5+, 16 June 1945 **A166**
The Committee proposes that the following provisions be included in the peace treaties following World War II: (1) not to censor news at the source, (2) not to use the press as an instrument of national policy, and (3) to permit a free flow of news in and out of signatory countries. The Committee consisted of Carl Ackerman, Wilbur Forrest, and Ralph McGill, chairman.

————. "Report on the Wechsler Case." *Nieman Reports,* 7(4):25–29, October 1953. **A167**
A committee was appointed by the president of the ASNE, at the request of James A. Wechsler, editor of the New York *Post,* to study and comment on the hearings before the U.S. Senate Subcommittee on Investigations of the Committee on Government, held 24 April and 5 May 1953. The case involved Senator McCarthy's questioning of Wechsler about books he had written and the editorial policies of the *Post.* The committee of newspaper men could not agree on whether or not the hearings constituted a threat to freedom of the press. In a separate statement, four members of the committee, J. R. Wiggins, Herbert Brucker, William M. Tugman, and Eugene S. Pulliam, Jr., concluded that freedom of the press was seriously endangered by the hearing. "Newspapers put to the necessity of explaining to government agencies, legislative or executive,

their news and editorial policies, under oath, would exist in such permanent jeopardy that their freedom to report fully and comment freely inevitably would be impaired. . . . The people suffer some diminution of their rights to know fully and comment freely upon their own government whenever a single newspaper, however worthy or unworthy, is subjected by one Senator, however worthy or unworthy, to inconvenience, expense, humiliation, ridicule, abuse, condemnation and reproach, under the auspices of governmental power . . . In our opinion, therefore, whatever inconvenience results, whatever controversy ensues, we [newspapermen] are compelled by every command of duty to brand this and every threat to freedom of the press, from whatever source, as a peril to American freedom."

American Textbook Publishers Institute. *American Way of Publishing: Your Safeguard against Subversion in Textbooks.* New York, The Institute, 1953. 8p. **A168**
Written in the form of a letter from a member of the Institute to a school superintendent. The publisher discusses how textbooks are prepared, how they can be improved, and how local school administrators can meet criticisms and attacks directed against textbooks.

————. *Attack on Textbooks.* New York, The Institute, 1951. 2p. **A169**

"The American Theatre and the Censors." *Life,* 2:17–21, 31 May 1937. **A170**
An account of the campaign by actors, playwrights, and theatergoers to defeat the theater licensing bill in New York; photographs of scenes from stage plays banned in New York, including *Mrs. Warren's Profession* (1905), *The Captive* (1927), and Mae West's *Sex* (1927).

Americanism Protective League, New York. *Smash Censorship! Report Grand Mass Meeting, Madison Square Garden, Jan. 14, 1924.* New York, The League, 1924. 22p. **A171**
The League was formed in opposition to the proposed New York Clean Books Bill and other censorship measures. Some 5,000 persons attended the mass meeting, addressed by Bernarr Macfadden, Herman Bernstein, Louis Joseph Vance, and U.S. Senator Magnus Johnson. Their speeches, and brief messages in opposition to censorship from Dr. Frank Crane, Senator William E. Borah, and Judge Ben B. Lindsey, are included. Dr. Crane calls for law instead of censorship. "Censorship implies that people shall be prevented from doing wrong. Law implies that every citizen shall be free to do wrong, but shall be held responsible for the wrong he does."

America's Town Meeting of the Air. *Do We Have a Free Press?* New York, Town Hall, 1939. 38p. (Bulletin vol. 4, no. 10) **A172**

Secretary of Interior Harold Ickes accuses the American press of being under the control of and dependent upon advertisers, more concerned with their pocketbook than with the public welfare. Frank E. Gannett, newspaper chain owner, defends the press and charges the Roosevelt administration with a systematic campaign against press freedom. Also included are newspaper editorials taking issue with Mr. Ickes' criticism.

————. *Is the American Press Really Free?* New York, Town Hall, 1946. 24 p. (Bulletin vol. 12, no. 25. Reprinted in Baird, *Representative American Speeches: 1946–47*, pp. 159–76) **A173**

Participants: George V. Denny, Jr., Erwin Canham, Morris Ernst, Michael Straight, and John R. McCrary, Jr. Attorney Ernst deplores the lack of press freedom in many cities where the newspaper and radio are under single control and where chains are forcing out small independent papers. He recommends a sliding scale for postal subsidies, revision of the tax laws, and divorcing control of newsprint and radio stations from newspaper owners. Erwin D. Canham of the *Christian Science Monitor* denies that diversity of ownership guarantees freedom of the press.

————. *Is There Too Much Censorship of War News?* New York, Town Hall, 1944. 23 p. (Bulletin vol. 9, no. 46) **A174**

War correspondent Henry J. Taylor believes that, while the Office of Censorship is doing a good job, censorship is sometimes being used to cover up military and political mistakes. Clifton M. Utley, Chicago newspaperman, believes that, while censorship is sometimes an annoyance, it is generally necessary to protect our military operations.

————. *Propaganda and Censorship in Wartime.* New York, Town Hall, 1941. 24 p. (Bulletin vol. 7, no. 9) **A175**

Participants: Roger Baldwin, Morris Ernst, Eugene Lyons, and John R. McCrary, Jr.

————. "Should Libraries Restrict the Use of Subversive Publications?" *ALA Bulletin*, 34:P5–P14, August 1940. **A176**

A "Town Meeting" program, conducted by George V. Denny at the fourth general session of the American Library Association Conference, 1940. Speakers were Gilbert Bettman and Arthur Garfield Hays. They were questioned by Carl H. Milam, Secretary, American Library Association.

————. *Should Minority Groups Exercise Censorship Over Books and Films?* New York, Town Hall, 1949. 22 p. (Bulletin vol. 15, no. 2) **A177**

The discussion revolved around objections to the movie, *Oliver Twist*, with opposite points of view taken by two prominent Jewish lawyers, Henry Epstein and Morris Ernst. Epstein argued that minority groups had a right to persuade others to reject false ideas about them even to the extent of using censorship. Ernst argued that no group, minority or majority, had a right to practice censorship, even to guarantee fairness to themselves. Freedom of ideas transcended the right of such security. Robert J. O'Donnell was the other member of the affirmative; John Mason Brown joined Ernst in representing the negative.

————. *What Is Freedom of the Press?* New York, Town Hall, 1936. 29 p. (Bulletin vol. 1, no. 20) **A178**

Three newspaper men, Heywood Broun, Will Irwin, and Julian S. Mason give their views on how the right of a free press is being exercised in the United States. Broun stresses the need for "integrity" of newspaper reporting as more significant than mere freedom to print or not to print. Mason sees Mr. Broun's movement to unionize newspaper writers (American Newspaper Guild) as a threat to a free press.

————. *What Should be the Function of Our Overseas Libraries?* New York, Town Hall, 1953. 16 p. (Bulletin vol. 19, no. 11) **A179**

United States overseas libraries became the center of controversy when Senator McCarthy's investigating committee charged that 30,000 volumes were written by Communists or fellow travellers, and the Department of State ordered their removal. Congressman Charles J. Kersten and Dan Lacy, managing director of the American Book Publishers Council, discuss the purpose of these libraries and the kinds of books that should be included.

Ames, Hector. "Censoring the Film Kiss." *Motion Picture Magazine*, 12(1):111–12, 166, December 1916. **A180**

A humorous reporting of the unofficial "kissing rules" announced by the Kansas state board which handles appeals of motion picture companies from decisions of the state movie censor. The report recommends a sliding scale on the length of movie kisses, depending on such factors as age and circumstances. "Soul kiss, dispute. Brewster [Attorney General] favors a limit of fifty-seven feet [a foot per second]; Sessions [representing the Governor] says not more than twenty-three feet. Botkin [Secretary of State] not voting."

Ames, Winthrop. "Censorship of the Stage: A Counter Proposal." *Review of Reviews*, 75:399–402, April 1927. **A181**

The chairman of the Committee of Nine Producers, Actors, and Authors outlines the proposal made by the Committee as an alternative to political or state censorship of the stage, such as that proposed in the bill pending in the New York legislature that would put the New York stage under control of the Regents of the University. The alternative proposal would have plays suspected of impropriety judged by a jury of seven members, drawn by lot from a panel of 300 representing "wise contemporary public opinion."

Amis, Kingsley. "The 'Cheesecake' Periodicals." *Author*, 66:28–30, Winter 1955. **A182**

Analysis of British magazines that consist of "representation, usually photographic, of scantily-clad young ladies in provocative poses." While the contents are often vulgar and trivial, there are "no reasons for regarding cheesecake as in itself wrong, dangerous or important."

Amory, Cleveland. "Speaking Out: Paperback Pornography." *Saturday Evening Post*, 236(13):10–12, 6 April 1963. **A183**

"It is high time that thinking persons stopped shouting 'censorship' in the pathetically few cases when a book is declared, by some duly constituted court, to be, in the court's considered judgment, obscene . . . Even one such action and clear court recognition of obscenity as obscenity would go a long way toward discouraging the large amount of paperback pornography which uses fear of censorship as its mask. What is needed on the obscene scene is, in short, less double-talk about censorship and more court action on obscenity."

Anderson, Archibald W. "*The Nation* Case." *Progressive Education*, 25:151–57, March 1949. (Reprinted in Downs, *The First Freedom*, pp. 353–59) **A184**

A history of the New York City Board of Education ban of *The Nation* from New York high schools. The author, a professor of education at the University of Illinois, quotes extensively from the various documents, pro and con, submitted in this widely publicized case.

Anderson, Frank M. "Contemporary View of the Virginia and Kentucky Resolutions." *American Historical Review*, 5:45–63, October 1899; 5:225–52, July 1900. **A185**

Contemporary newspaper commentary on the resolutions denouncing the Alien and Sedition Acts. The Virginia Resolution was the work of James Madison, the Kentucky Resolution the work of Thomas Jefferson.

————. "The Enforcement of the Alien and Sedition Laws." *Annual Report of the American Historical Association, 1912.* Washington, D.C., The Association, 1914, pp. 113–26. **A186**

A study of the enforcement of the Alien and Sedition Acts made from an examination of newspapers of the period, the Pickering and Jefferson papers, the archives of the State Department, and other contemporary records.

Anderson, John. *Military Censorship in World War I; Its Use and Abuse,* in *New Zealand.* Wellington, N.Z., Victoria University, 1952. 296p. (Unpublished Master's thesis) **A187**

Anderson, Paul Y. "Mainly about Publishers." *Nation,* 138:559–60, 16 May 1934. **A188**

The writer criticizes the report on freedom of the press adopted by the American Society of Newspaper Editors as a work of hypocrisy and smugness. The danger to freedom is not from Franklin D. Roosevelt and Hugh Johnson but "arises from the fact that so many of the men who have been intrusted with—or have acquired—the privilege of exercising that freedom have used it to grasp special privileges and profits for themselves." The "freedom of the press" clause has no place in the NRA code, which is concerned with business practices, not content of newspapers.

Anderson, Robert L. "Free Speech and Obscenity; A Search for Constitutional Procedures and Standards." *UCLA Law Review,* 12:532–60, January 1965. **A189**

"This comment directs itself to what appears to be a parallel development in the obscenity field to Kingsley and Roth. In two decisions handed down on the same day in 1964—*A Quantity of Copies of Books v. Kansas* and *Jacobellis v. Ohio*—the Supreme Court once again attempted to clarify the nonexisting law concerning the constitutional requirements for discovering and disposing of obscene materials, and the constitutionally imposed standards for determining what materials are obscene." The author concludes that the majority of the Court "intends to protect those forms of expression of a serious nature, maintaining a great deal of toleration for the manner of representation. In addition, it apparently will not proscribe materials having any artistic quality.... The Court will seemingly protect material which attempts to portray ideas, facts, concepts or interests that, though repugnant to the majority, nonetheless insures access to and expression of unorthodox views."

[Anderton, William]. *An Account of the Conversation, Behaviour and Execution of William Anderton, Printer.* [London, 1693]. **A190**

Anderton was charged with high treason and tried for printing two books which "tended to incite rebellion." He was found guilty and hanged on 16 June 1693. Siebert, in his *Freedom of the Press in England,* notes that Anderton and Twyn were the only printers to be executed for high treason in England during the later Stuart period.

[———]. "Mr. Anderton's Plea at the Old Bailey." In Sawbridge, *A Collection of Scarce and Valuable Papers.* London, 1712, vol. 1, pp. 228–32. **A191**

[———]. "Trial at Old Bailey for High Treason in Publishing Treasonable Libels, London, 1693." In Howell, *State Trials,* vol. 12, pp. 1245 ff. **A192**

Includes account taken from the British Sessional Papers and from reports published by Anderton's friends.

Andrew, M. G. "'A Free and Responsible Press': the Findings of an American Study of the Press and How They Apply to Canada." *Food for Thought,* 8:5–11, February 1948. **A193**

A discussion of the report of the Commission on Freedom of the Press.

Andrews, Alexander. *The History of British Journalism from the Foundation of the Newspaper Press in England to the Repeal of the Stamp Act in 1855, with Sketches of Press Celebrities.* London, Richard Bentley, 1859. 2 vols. **A194**

A comprehensive record, arranged topically, including biographical sketches of leading journalists. Vol. 1 carries through the eighteenth century and vol. 2 to 1855. There are accounts of some 75 British press trials and an extensive discussion of the American Colonial press.

Andrews, *Sir* Linton. "Cramping the Press." *Fortnightly* (London), 163 (n.s.): 391–97, June 1948. **A195**

The chairman of the Joint Editorial Committee of the Newspaper Society and the Guild of British Newspaper Editors charges that restrictions on newsprint limit seriously the free expression of opinion on public affairs. Reduced space forces editors to omit or compress news and to put different news in different editions.

Andrews, William. "Punishing Authors and Burning Books." In *Old Time Punishments.* London, Simpkin, Marshall, Hamilton & Kent, 1890, pp. 90–103. **A196**

Anello, Douglas A. *The Regulatory Role in Broadcasting.* Washington, D.C., National Association of Broadcasters, 1964. 21p. **A197**

The general counsel of the NAB, in an address before the Iowa Broadcasters Association, states that the "fairness doctrine" inhibits rather than encourages free discussion.

Angell, James R. "Radio as a Safeguard of Freedom in a Democracy." *Proceedings,* National Education Association, 1941. Washington, D.C., NEA, 1941, pp. 170–73. **A198**

Angell, *Sir* Norman. "Freedom of Discussion in War Time." *Annals of the American Academy of Political and Social Science,* 78:194–204, July 1918. **A199**

Censorship experience in World War I written from the British point of view.

[———]. "Raiding the Enemy's Diplomacy." *New Republic,* 11:324–27, 21 July 1917. **A200**

Censorship of the liberal press, while permitting free circulation of conservative and reactionary newspapers, has played into the hands of the German and Austrian militarists.

Anglo-Americanus, *pseud. Remarks on Zenger's Tryal, Taken out of the Barbados Gazette's. For the Benefit of the Students in Law, and others in North America.* [New York, Bradford, 1737]. 36 leaves. (Reprinted with bibliographic notes in Katz's edition of the Zenger trial, 1963, pp. 152 ff.) **A201**

A pamphlet critical of the legal arguments of the defense in the John Peter Zenger trial. Consists of two letters which originally appeared in the *Barbados Gazette* of 20 and 29 July 1737. The first letter (reprinted in the Katz edition) was signed "Anglo-Americanus." Evans' *American Bibliography* attributes the letter to Jonathan Blenman, King's Attorney of Barbados. The second letter, less persuasive and not reprinted in Katz, was signed "Indus-Britanicus." The first letter was answered by James Alexander in Franklin's *Pennsylvania Gazette.*

[———]. *Remarks on the Trial of John-Peter Zenger, Printer of the New York Weekly Journal, Who was Lately Try'd and Acquitted for Printing and Publishing Two Libels against the Government of that Province.* London, Printed for J. Roberts, 1738. 27p. **A202**

A London edition of the letters by "Anglo-Americanus" and "Indus-Britanicus," originally appearing in the *Barbados Gazette.*

Angoff, Charles. *Handbook of Libel; a Practical Guide for Editors and Authors.* New York, Duell, Sloan and Pearce, 1946. 410p. (Rev. ed. New York, Barnes, 1966. 454p.) **A203**

Beginning with an essay on the principles of libel, there follows a compilation of libel laws of all states and 17 significant decisions of the high courts, with an analysis of each.

Annual Register; A Review of Public Events at Home and Abroad. London, 1761–date. Annual. (Various publishers; since 1890, Longmans) **A204**

Includes in its Chronicle of Events section reports of trials, legislation, investigations, and incidents relating to freedom of the press in the United Kingdom and the British Commonwealth. Texts of state papers and excerpts of speeches relating to press freedom are sometimes included in the Public Documents section.

"Another Furor Over Books." *Ohio State University Monthly*, 55(4):8–12, December 1963. **A 205**

A report on two controversies being waged over books in Columbus, Ohio: (1) An attack on "objectionable, blasphemous, filthy, communistic and anti-white" books being used in a Columbus high school was made by anti-Communist study groups in the city. A delegation asked the school board to ban such works as *Catcher in the Rye*, *1984*, *To Kill a Mockingbird*, and *Brave New World* and to appoint a citizens committee to censor books used in the schools. The Superintendent of Schools and the School Board expressed confidence in the ability of their teachers and librarians to choose reading material for the school system. (2) The Columbus police vice squad "ruled" as obscene James Baldwin's *Another Country*, *Tropic of Cancer*, and *Tropic of Capricorn*, and told book dealers they would be arrested for selling these books. The article reprints protests of these censorship actions which appeared in the Ohio State University student daily, the *Lantern*.

Another Letter to Mr. Almon in Matter of Libel. London, John Almon, 1770. 184 p. (Reprinted in *A Collection of Scarce and Interesting Tracts*, 1787–88, vol. 4, pp. 5–113) **A 206**

An anonymous author, professing to be a retired lawyer, discusses in this pamphlet various points of law in the Woodfall libel case and in the decision of Lord Mansfield. While he was pleased with the prosecution of those who circulated the Junius letters he considered the libel law a "great canker-worm of the state." Attributed to the author of the "Candor" letter.

"Another Menace to the Press." *Nation*, 104:205–6, 22 February 1917. **A 207**

Editorial criticizing the censorship bill which the General Staff has produced and which it hopes to rush through Congress when war is declared.

"Another Repeal; Joyce's *Ulysses* Is Legal at Last." *Nation*, 137:693, 20 December 1933. **A 208**

A report on the Woolsey-Hand decisions clearing the often-banned *Ulysses*.

Ansari, Khalid. *Freedom of the Press in India*. Stanford, Calif., Stanford University, 1962. 116 p. (Unpublished Master's thesis) **A 209**

Anthony, Louise. "Censorship in the School Library." *ILA Record*, 7:94–96, April 1954. **A 210**

The honest desire of parents to protect their children from evil ideas, the honest desire of civic, patriotic, and religious groups to promote their own ideologies, as well as the questionable motives of those who seek to corrupt the schools, present problems for school librarians who are attempting to provide materials that will contribute to the preparation for intelligent citizenship. The author refers to her experience with a campaign against the Magruder textbook on *American Government*.

Anthony, Rose, *Sister*. *The Jeremy Collier Stage-Controversy (1698–1726)*. Milwaukee, Wis., Marquette University Press, 1935. 343 p. (Reprinted in 1966 by Benjamin Bloom, Bronx, N.Y.) **A 211**

"Anthony Comstock—An Heroic Suppressor or an Unconscious Protector of Vice?" *Current Opinion*, 56:288–89, April 1914. **A 212**

A review of Turnbull's sympathetic biography of Comstock, together with quotations less favorable to the vice crusader.

"Anthony Comstock Overruled." *Publishers' Weekly*, 45:942–43, 30 June 1894. **A 213**

News of the decision of Judge O'Brien of the New York Supreme Court clearing *Arabian Nights*, *Tom Jones*, *The Decameron*, and other classics in the receivership case of Worthington & Co. Anthony Comstock and the New York Society for the Suppression of Vice had charged that the books were morally unfit for sale.

Antieau, Chester J. "The Federalism of Freedom." *Kentucky Law Journal*, 42:404–22, 1953–54. **A 214**

Should there be any power in the states to abridge freedom of communications that concerns matters either of national legislation or national significance? Have courts recognized the impropriety of state negation of expression on matters of national concern? Is there a need for local interference with such communications?

———. "Judicial Delimitation of the First Amendment Freedoms." *Marquette Law Review*, 34:57–89, Fall 1950. **A 215**

The author considers the tests and principles utilized by the American judiciary in defining the conditions under which the First Amendment freedoms may be abridged. He cites two objective tests—Blackstone's limitation of freedom to that guaranteeing absence of prior restraint, and the "commercial criterion," employed in the case of movie films, crime, and sex magazines, works primarily for commercial rather than educational benefit. Among the subjective tests are: exclusion of abusive and licentious use, denial of rights of expression to those who would deny freedom to others, the "bad tendency" test, and the insistence on social significance. Another

criterion is the distinction between acts and speech or opinion, exemplified by the "clear and present danger" dictum of Justice Holmes. Finally, there is the recognition that other societal interests must be safeguarded and that freedom of expression of one must not interfere with freedom of another.

"Antiseptic of the Press." *Spectator*, 102:451–52, 20 March 1909. **A 216**

An answer to Hilaire Belloc's criticism of the law of libel, appearing in the *English Review* for March 1909. "The law of libel is the antiseptic of journalism . . . [it] is an admirable censor, whose work is automatic and unremitting. It operates not only as the protector of the public, but as the guardian of the press itself."

Antrim, Stanley E. "Obscene Publications and the Constitution—Censorship v. Freedom of the Press." *Washburn Law Journal*, 4:114–27, Winter 1964. **A 217**

Commentary on the case, *A Quantity of Copies of Books v. Kansas*, 84 S.Ct. 1723 (1964), and related cases. The Court quotes Irvin S. Cobb as saying: "If the depth of the dirt exceeds the breadth of the wit, then in my opinion the book is obscene."

Appleton's Annual Cyclopaedia and Register of Important Events . . . New York, Appleton, 1861–1902. Annual. **A 218**

The "Freedom of the Press" section in the various annual volumes is a source of information on contemporary events. Of special interest are volumes 1 through 4, carrying information on suppression of newspapers during the Civil War.

"Application of Censorship and Military Regulations to Advertising Copy." *Industrial Marketing*, 27(3):13–16+, March 1942. **A 219**

Policies of War and Navy Departments and Army Air Corps regarding reference in advertising to military activities, and procedure for securing permission to take photos.

Arber, Edward, *ed. English Reprints. John Milton. Areopagitica . . . Preceded by Illustrative Documents*. London, A. Murray, 1868. 80 p. **A 220**

Includes the Star-Chamber Decree concerning Printers (1637); Licensing Order of the House of Commons, 29 January 1642; Order of the House of Commons, 9 March 1643; Order of the Lords and Commons, 14 June 1643; and Milton's *Areopagitica*, reprinted verbatim from the first edition, 1644.

———. *An Introductory Sketch to the Martin Marprelate Controversy. 1588–1590 . . .* London, The Editor, 1879. 200 p. (English Scholar's Library no. 8) **A 221**

The Marprelate tracts were anonymously published in 1588 and 1589 by a group of Puritans in defiance of Elizabethan printing regulations. The press was moved from place to place, but eventually was discovered and destroyed by government agents.

"Arbitrary Ruling; Ban against *The Nation*." *Nation*, 168:627–28, 4 June 1949. **A222**

A report on the ban of *The Nation* from the New York City public schools.

Archer, Leonard B., Jr. "Intellectual Freedom Is the Issue." *Wisconsin Library Bulletin*, 60:161–86, May–June 1964. **A223**

An editorial in the special issue on intellectual freedom, which includes the Library Bill of Rights, the School Library Bill of Rights, and the Wisconsin Library Association statement on Intellectual Freedom in Libraries. A selected list of books, pamphlets, and periodicals, compiled by the editor and intended to provide librarians with background information in defense (or offense) against censorship, appears on pp. 181–86.

———. "It Is Later Than You Think: An Action Program Against Censorship." *Library Journal*, 88:3552–54, 1 October 1963. **A224**

The author calls for the creation of action committees of librarians to combat censorship, replacing the "weak and apathetic Intellectual Freedom Committees" that are largely discussion groups. He outlines the organizational structure and procedure for "an action program and a clobbering technique," to take rigorous action when a librarian or library is threatened.

Archer, William. "Censorship of the Stage." In his *About the Theatre; Essays and Studies*. London, Unwin, 1886, pp. 101–71 **A225**

———. "English Censorship." *New Review*, 6:566–76, May 1892. **A226**

A case for the abolition or radical reform of the institution of stage censorship in Britain. In principle the present censorship conflicts with the spirit of British institutions by placing unlimited power over the property and reputations of fellow citizens in the hands of one man. In practice, it fails to protect the stage from ribald buffoonery, while at the same time is repressive to the development of dramatic art. Archer recommends the substitution of stage control by reasonable public opinion and, in the case of nonliterary presentations, through the power of the police to proceed against violation of public decency.

Archibald, Samuel J. *Memo on Information Problems*. Columbia, Mo., Freedom of Information Center, School of Journalism, University of Missouri, 1961. 6 p. (Publication no. 56) **A227**

The staff director of the Special Subcommittee on Government Information, House of Repre-

sentatives Committee on Government Operations, outlines some of the public information problems in the federal government left over from the Eisenhower administration and new ones which have developed during the Kennedy administration.

———. *Secrecy from Peanuts to Pentagon*. Columbia, Mo., Freedom of Information Center, School of Journalism, University of Missouri, 1959. 3 p. (Publication no. 20) **A228**

Excerpts from a talk, giving examples of the withholding and suppression of public information by agencies of the federal government.

Arden, Caroline. *An Analysis of the Reports by Leading News Media of the New York Society for the Suppression of Vice, 1916–1947, Regarding the Suppression of Ten Specific Books*. Tallahassee, Florida State University, 1961. 117 p. (Unpublished Master's thesis) **A229**

The ten suppressed novels: *The Genius* by Theodore Dreiser, *Mademoiselle de Maupin* by Theophile Gautier, *Jurgen* by James B. Cabell, *Casanova's Homecoming* by Arthur Schnitzler, *Aphrodite* by Pierre Louys, *God's Little Acre* by Erskine Caldwell, *November* by Gustave Flaubert, *A World I Never Made* by James T. Farrell, *Memoirs of Hecate County* by Edmund Wilson, and *End as a Man* by Calder Willingham. The appendix includes the text of the Act of Incorporation of the Society (1873), and the New York State Penal Code.

Ardrey, Robert. "Hollywood's Fall into Virtue." *Reporter*, 16:13–17, 21 February 1957. **A230**

Includes a discussion of the Motion Picture Production Code and its part in the trend toward conformity. The author recounts his personal experiences while making the movie *Madame Bovary*.

"Are We to Have a Reptile Press?" *North American Review*, 209:9–12, January 1919. **A231**

Criticism of President Wilson for not meeting the press, but giving it instead the "creelings" from the Committee on Public Information. The article criticizes the Administration for taking control of the transoceanic cables when the war was practically over and for sending George Creel to Paris to "cover" or "censor" the news of the peace conference. The press policy of President Wilson, the article charges, is paternalistic and socialistic.

"*Areopagitica;* an Analysis and Criticism." *Retrospective Review*, 9 (pt. 1, art. 1):3–19, 1 February 1824. **A232**

This anonymous review of Milton's great work on freedom of the press presents the essay in its historical setting.

Areopagitica: an Essay on the Liberty of the Press. Dedicated to the Rt. Hon. Charles James Fox, the Friend of Truth and Liberty. London, Printed for J. Deighton, 1791. 68 p. **A233**

A criticism of the existing law of libel as laid down by Blackstone and reflected in English court decisions. "To say that the press is free when punishment of publication is certain is to place a trap for virtue, honor, and good conduct. The author is indeed in a much worse condition than he was in the times before mentioned, [i.e. under the licensing system] for he might then be secure by procuring a license. . . . The case of trial for a breach of the peace by the publication of truth, is surely a mockery of common sense and common justice." The work of this anonymous author, using the title of Milton's earlier tract, is dedicated to the author of the libel reform act that was made law by Parliament the following year.

Armitage, Gilbert. *Banned in England; an Examination of the Law Relating to Obscene Publications*. London, Wishart, 1932. 45 p. (Here and Now Pamphlets, no. 7) **A234**

A well-documented criticism of the British law of obscene libel.

Armour, Richard. "How to Burn a Book." *California Librarian*, 15:97–98, December 1953. **A235**

The author of *It All Started with Columbus* writes this witty article on book burning—"a charming old custom hallowed by antiquity. It has been practiced for centuries by fascists, communists, atheists, school children, rival authors, and tired librarians. Some scholars believe that the first instance of book burning occured in the Middle Ages, when a monk was trying to illuminate a manuscript."

Armstrong, O. K. "The Fight against the Smut Peddlers." *Reader's Digest*, 87:177–84, September 1965. **A236**

"The balance of power is shifting toward the decent-minded public, but the drive will fail unless a carefully mapped program is followed in every community." The author offers a three-point program: (1) Police and prosecutors must study obscenity laws and know the proper procedures to enforce them. (2) Try all obscenity cases in a criminal court, before a jury. (3) The public must strengthen and use every legal means to fight obscenity.

———. "Must Our Movies Be Obscene?" *Reader's Digest*, 87:154–56, November 1965. **A237**

"Immorality, infidelity, prostitution, rape—such are the subjects currently highlighted on movie marquees across the nation. Here's what you can do to help fight an alarming trend."

———. "Treason in the Textbooks." *American Legion Magazine*, 29:8–9+, September 1940. **A 238**
"The 'Frontier Thinkers' are trying to tell our youth that the American way of life has failed." A detailed attack on a number of textbooks, especially those by Harold O. Rugg, with objectionable books listed under the heading: Are These Books in Your Schools?

———. "You Can Help Fight Obscenity." *Christian Herald*, 83:14, 50, July 1960. **A 239**
An account of the organization of the Churchmen's Commission for Decent Publications, a Protestant counterpart of the Catholic National Office for Decent Literature.

Armstrong, Walter P. "Nothing But Good of the Dead?" *American Bar Association Journal*, 18:229–32, April 1932. **A 240**
The publication of critical biographies of Gladstone, George Sand, and Sam Huston, raise questions as to the rights and liabilities of biographers. The author refers to statutes of the various states involving the right of action for libel or slander of dead persons.

"Army Censorship." *Time*, 43:46+, 10 April 1944. **A 241**
Military censorship during World War II.

"Army's Index." *Literary Digest*, 58:31, 21 September 1918. **A 242**
Books forbidden to soldiers by the U.S. Army include works by J. W. Burgess, Frank Harris, F. C. Howe, and George S. Viereck.

[Arnall, William]. *The Case of Opposition Stated, between the Craftsman and the People . . .* London, J. Roberts, 1731. 64p. **A 243**
To the supporters of Walpole it seemed that the *Craftsman* in its bitter attacks upon the government claimed "an unbounded license to abuse all persons, and all things; to blast the fair reputation of any man; and to asperse the best councils of any ministry, without being made accountable for any means, right or wrong, which they think fit to make use of, and without justice, or equity of their proceedings." The *Craftsman* had been established in 1726 in the hope of driving Walpole from office.

Arndt, Murray. "Censorship and Perspective." *Catholic World*, 186:93–99, November 1957. **A 244**
Although the author defends the censorship policy of the Catholic Church, he believes that the negative actions have been overstressed and that more attention should be given to the education of Catholic youth and development of the Catholic press.

Arnebergh, Roger. "Pornography and 'Community Standards.'" *Dicta*, 37: 231–36, July–August 1960. **A 245**
The salacious expression, unlike the noxious ideology which could enrich the soil from which new ideas germinate, has no social value. It should be treated like any goods, wares, and merchandise deemed repugnant to the public welfare.

Arnold, A. J. "Film Censor Should Be Pitied, Not Blamed." *Saturday Night*, 61: 12–13, 13 April 1946. **A 246**
A description of the dual control system of movie censorship in Canada—self-censorship by the industry and pre-exhibition government censorship by provincial boards. Manitoba and Alberta boards use the film grading system. Reference is made to a Quebec court decision upholding provincial film censorship. A further court test is needed to determine the constitutionality of censorship.

[Arnold, Thurman]. "Decision in the Post-Office v. *Esquire* Case." *Saturday Review of Literature*, 28(24):16–18, 16 June 1945. **A 247**
The decision against the Postmaster General in his attempt to bar the magazine *Esquire* from the second-class mails is termed by the writer "the most important American legal opinion involving freedom from censorship and suppression since the famous 'Ulysses' decision."

Arnoult, L. A. "Problems of Prohibited Books: an Exploratory Discussion." *Catholic Theological Studies of America, Proceedings*, 15:137–43, 1960. **A 248**
Deals with the *Index of Forbidden Books* of the Catholic Church.

Aronowitz, Alfred G. "The Play that Rocked Europe." *Saturday Evening Post*, 237(8):38–39, 42–43, 29 February 1964. **A 249**
The Deputy, a Broadway play by Rolf Hochhuth, touched off a storm of criticism and demands for censorship because it accused the late Pope Pius XII of guilt by silence in the Nazi murder of 6,000,000 Jews.

[Aronson, A. Matthew]. "Constitutional Law—Obscenity—Scienter." *Brooklyn Law Review*, 26:289–92, April 1960. **A 250**
This article relates to the case of *Smith v. California*, 361 U.S. 147 (1959) in which the U.S. Supreme Court reversed the ruling of a lower court against a bookseller for unlawful possession of obscene books. The Court held that a statute that imposes absolute criminal liability upon a bookseller for mere possession of obscene literature violates the due process clause of the Fourteenth Amendment.

"Art for Dirt's Sake." *John Bull*, 46:8, 20 July 1929. **A 251**
An attack on D. H. Lawrence whose paintings had recently been seized by London police.

The article is in the form of a burlesque trial in which Judge John Bull rules that "any further filth from Florence shall be immediately consigned to the nearest public incinerator."

Arthur, William R., and Ralph L. Crosman. *The Law of Newspapers.* 2d ed. New York, McGraw-Hill, 1940. 615p. **A 252**
A standard American text. The appendix contains text of state and federal laws relating to freedom of the press.

Asbury, Herbert. "The Day Mencken Broke the Law." *American Mercury*, 73: 62–69, October 1951. **A 253**
On 5 April 1926, H. L. Mencken sold a copy of his *American Mercury* to the Rev. J. Frank Chase of the New England Watch and Ward Society and was promptly arrested by the Boston police. This account of the 25-year-old event is told by the author of the offending "Hatrack" article

Asgill, John. *Argument to Prove that Death is Not Obligatory on Christians; by the Celebrated John Asgill, esq., M. P., with Introductory Essay, Memoirs, Notes and Ministerial Testimony by the Rev. Tresham D. Gregg.* New York, Ennis Brothers, 1875. 135p. **A 254**
This is a reprint of the work for which the author was expelled from the English and Irish Parliaments. Also reprinted are resolutions of the English and Irish Parliaments ordering the burning of the book, and other documents relating to the trial.

[———]. *An Essay for the Press.* London, Printed for A. Baldwin, 1712. 8p. **A 255**
A libertarian politician and mystic, Asgill argues for freedom of the press as a "natural right of mankind." He objects to licensing and taxation as means of restraining the press and proposes that anonymity be outlawed, although his own essay was published anonymously.

———. *Mr. Asgill's Defence upon His Expulsion from the House of Commons of Great Britain in 1707. With an Introduction, and a Postscript . . .* London, A. Baldwin, 1712. 87p. (A summary of the trial appears in Schroeder, *Constitutional Free Speech . . .*, pp. 318–22) **A 256**
In 1703 Asgill was expelled from the Irish Parliament and in 1707 from the Parliament of Great Britain for publishing a heretical book arguing that man may be translated into eternal life without passing through death. The book was ordered burned by the common hangman and Asgill was given the nickname of "Translated."

[Ashbee, Henry S.]. *Bibliography of Prohibited Books . . .* By Pisanus Fraxi. New Hyde Park, Jack Brussel, University Books, 1952. 3 vols. **A 257**

A reprint of the three volumes on erotica first issued in 1877, 1879, and 1885, under the pseudonym of Pisanus Fraxi: *Index Librorum Prohibitorum, Centuria Librorum Absconditorum,* and *Catena Librorum Tacendorum* (A258–60). Introduction by G. Legman.

[——]. *Catena Librorum Tacendorum: Being Notes Bio-Biblio-Icono-graphical and Critical on Curious and Uncommon Books.* By Pisanus Fraxi, pseudonym for Henry Spencer Ashbee. London, Privately printed, 1885. 593 p. (Vol. 3 of series)   **A 258**
This volume and the following two represent a single scholarly bibliography of erotica. They are included here because of the introductory essays on obscenity in each volume and for the detailed accounts of certain works that have had a history of suppression or have become *causes celebre*, e.g., John Wilkes's *Essay on Woman, The Confessional Unmasked* (Hicklin case), John Cleland's *Memoirs of a Woman of Pleasure,* and *The Awful Disclosures of Maria Monk.* While not approving of the works he describes, the author, writing in the 1880's, sees obscenity as less harmful than crime stories. "I am of opinion that more youths have become criminals through reading of deeds real or fictitious, of murders, pirates, highwaymen, forgers, burglars, etc., than have ever developed into libertines from the perusal of obscene novels."

[——]. *Centuria Librorum Absconditorum: Being Notes Bio-Biblio-Icono-graphical and Critical on Curious and Uncommon Books.* By Pisanus Fraxi, pseudonym for Henry Spencer Ashbee. London, Privately printed, 1879. 593 p. (Vol. 2.of series)   **A 259**

[——]. *Index Librorum Prohibitorum: Being Notes Bio-Biblio-Icono-graphical and Critical on Curious and Uncommon Books.* By Pisanus Fraxi, pseudonym for Henry Spencer Ashbee. London, Privately printed, 1877. 542 p. (Vol. 1 of series)   **A 260**

Asheim, Lester E. "Layman vs. Librarian." *Library Journal*, 80:253–58, 1 February 1955.   **A 261**
"A case history in mutual education develops as a layman and a librarian view controversial material in a library." The dean of the Graduate Library School, University of Chicago, and a lawyer who read Dean Asheim's article Not Censorship But Selection, engage in an exchange of ideas relating specifically to the library's handling of books about communism. The layman, while recognizing the importance of allowing freedom for diverse opinion, believed that "librarians owe a duty . . . not to allow their libraries to become an outlet for the spread of false propaganda designed to weaken and destroy our 'way of life' nor to become an outlet for the spread of the false, the malicious, the sub-standard on any subject."

——. "Library Book Selection in a Democracy." *Michigan Librarian*, 19:7–12, December 1953.   **A 262**
Beginning with references to censorship in overseas information libraries, the author defines the proper function of a library, and discusses the difference between censorship and selection.

——. "Not Censorship But Selection." In *Freedom of Book Selection; Proceedings of the Second Conference on Intellectual Freedom.* Chicago, American Library Association, 1954, pp. 90–99. (Reprinted in *Wilson Library Bulletin,* 28:63–68, September 1953; Daniels, *The Censorship of Books,* pp. 186–90; and Marshall, *Books, Libraries, Librarians,* pp. 347–56)   **A 263**
"The major characteristic which makes for the all-important difference seems to me to be this: that the selector's approach is positive, while that of the censor is negative . . . Selection, then, begins with a presumption in favor of liberty of thought; censorship, with a presumption in favor of thought control."

——. "Problems of Censorship in Book Selection." *Bay State Librarian,* 52:5–9, 13 January 1962. (Reprinted in *Wilson Library Bulletin,* 59(1A):80–82, January 1963)   **A 264**
A paper presented at the Institute on Adult Book Selection in Public Libraries, Simmons College, 14 September 1961, by the dean of the Graduate Library School, University of Chicago.

Ashhurst, Henry F. "Freedom of the Press." *Congressional Record,* 55:2004–11, 9 May 1917. (Reprinted in *Congressional Record,* 79:7789–92, 20 May 1935)   **A 265**
Speech opposing censorship, delivered in the U.S. Senate during World War I.

Ashley, Paul P. *Essentials of Libel. A Handbook for Journalists.* Seattle, University of Washington Press, 1948. 71 p.   **A 266**
"This handbook offers the long-needed compressed, yet complete and practical presentation of the law of libel."

——. *Say It Safely; Legal Limits in Publishing, Radio, and Television.* Seattle, University of Washington Press, 1966. 169 p.   **A 267**
Relates to libel, slander, contempt of court, and the right of privacy.

Aspinall, Arthur. "The Circulation of Newspapers in the Early Nineteenth Century." *Review of English Studies,* 22: 29–43, January 1946.   **A 268**

An account of the wide readership of the radical newspapers of the period by the working class, despite the stamp tax, because of their availability in the coffee-houses and public-houses. At one time the temperance party urged repeal of the stamp tax to keep the workingmen out of the pubs.

——. *Politics and the Press, c. 1780–1850.* London, Home and Van Thal, 1949. 511 p.   **A 269**
Based on archival and manuscript sources this work shows how the British newspaper press managed to emancipate itself from the control of the politicians during the first half of the nineteenth century. Chapter 2, Freedom of the Press, deals with publishers and booksellers who risked arrest and punishment by challenging the strict interpretation of the libel laws.

Aspland, Lindsey M. *Law of Blasphemy: Being a Candid Examination of the Views of Mr. Justice Stephen . . . with an Appendix Containing an Essay on Religious Offenses Indicated at Common Law, by the Late Edgar Taylor and the Speech of Lord Mansfield in the House of Lords in 1767 in the Case of the Sheriffs of London.* London, Stevens and Haynes, 1884. 48 p.   **A 270**

Associated Press. *The Dangers of Libel: A Summary for Newsmen by the Associated Press.* New York, The AP, 1964. 24 p.   **A 271**
"This booklet on libel is 'must' reading for every Associated Press staff member. It is based upon practical and legal experience and has been approved by Associated Press counsel." Includes advice on libel and the right of privacy, and procedures for handling "kills" and "correctives."

——. *Member Editorials on the Monopoly Complaint Filed by Government Against the Associated Press on August 28, 1942.* New York, The AP, 1942. 2 vols.   **A 272**
A collection of editorials supporting the Associated Press in its refusal to sell its services to the *Chicago Sun.* The federal government brought an antitrust suit against the AP in the U.S. District Court to force the news service to accommodate any paper willing to pay the cost. The government's case was upheld.

"The Associated Press." *Outlook,* 107: 631–32, 18 June 1914.   **A 273**
The editor believes that while the Associated Press performs a public service of great moment it also possesses powers for evil as well as good. The need is becoming more acute for "regulating these powers in the interest of public welfare."

Association of National Advertisers. *Self-Regulation in Advertising.* New York, The Association, 1960. 68 p.　　**A 274**
Report of a special meeting of the Association held 2 February 1960 to review procedures and plans for self-regulation of advertising. Includes talks by Paul B. West, Donald S. Frost, and Gilbert H. Weil from the advertising industry, and Earl W. Kintner, chairman of the FTC. In discussions of what the various media are doing to regulate advertising, Robert Kintner (NBC), James T. Aubrey, Jr. (CBS), and Donald H. McGannon (National Association of Broadcasters) represent the broadcasting industry; Gibson McCabe (Magazine Advertising Bureau) represents the magazine industry; John D. Thees (Newspaper Advertising Executives) represents newspaper advertising; and Robert M. Ganger (American Association of Advertising Agencies) represents the agencies.

Association of the Bar of the City of New York. "Report on Book Burning." *Record of the Association of the Bar of the City of New York*, 10:143–47, March 1955.　**A 275**
This report of the Committee on the Bill of Rights deals with the attempt of private groups to censor community reading. It recommends that the Association condemn "the attempts of any individuals or group, private or public, to interfere in any manner with the publication, circulation, or reading of any published matter, other than by means of regular applicable statutory procedures and standards."

———. "Selected Materials on Political Broadcasting." *Record of the Association of the Bar of the City of New York*, 18:47–51, January 1963.　　**A 276**
Bibliography includes references on Section 315 (equal time for political broadcasting) and liability of broadcasters for defamatory statements made by candidates.

"The Assumers." *Times Literary Supplement*, 3224:1031, 12 December 1963.　**A 277**
Editorial on certain "predetermined attitudes, based on unquestioned assumptions" which Englishmen fall into when talking about obscenity. In the debate in the House of Commons the previous week on the importation of obscene publications from abroad and the seizure of 1,360,000 copies, assumptions were that reading matter of this sort is harmful, and that there is a level of literature where the authorities can reasonably be allowed a free hand. These and similar assumptions need to be questioned.

Atkin, Kenward L. "Federal Regulation of Broadcast Advertising." *Journal of Broadcasting*, 3:326–40, Fall 1959.　**A 278**

Atkinson, *Sir* Edward H. T. *Obscene Literature in Law and Practice.* London, Christophers, 1937. 32 p.　　**A 279**
A lecture on the English law of obscene libel, delivered at King's College, London, by the director of public prosecutions.

Atkinson, Wilmer. *A Bogy Unveiled; Argument against the Adoption by Congress of H. R. Bill 6071, Known as the Loud Bill.* [Philadelphia, The Author], n.d. 48 p.　　**A 280**
Atkinson, the founder and long-time publisher of the *Farm Journal*, was active in many crusades of his day including woman suffrage, quack medicines, and rural free delivery. His concern with freedom of the press was limited to freedom from post-office control over his business methods as publisher.

———. *Earnest Appeal to Members of the 61st Congress (Codifying, Revising and Amending the Postal Laws) to Safeguard the Liberty of the Press, and to Let the Papers Circulate without Government Supervision, Espionage or Interference.* Philadelphia, The Author, 1910. 8 p.　　**A 281**
Editor Atkinson opposes a bill to increase the discretionary power of the Postmaster General over the periodical press.

———. *An Inquiry into the True Meaning and Intent of the Postal Laws Relating to the Public Press.* Philadelphia, The Author, 1908. 16 p.　　**A 282**
"A denial of the second-class rate throws the publication into the third class, which signifies that it must cease to be published. The Post Office Department claims the right to determine to which class the publication belongs; it claims the right, therefore, to kill any publication."

———. *The Old Battle Renewed for Freedom of the Press.* Philadelphia, The Author, 1907. 55 p.　　**A 283**
Atkinson protests against the Post Office for its arbitrary exclusion of periodicals from second-class mailing privileges. His concern seems to be chiefly from the viewpoint of freedom for the use of the printing press as a tool of trade and, in fact, he endorses restrictions on the press as a vehicle of thought.

"Attack on Books in Libraries." *Wilson Library Bulletin*, 27:807–12, June 1953.　　**A 284**
Notes and excerpts from a preliminary session of the Library Public Relations Council dealing with intellectual freedom. Moderator Edward L. Bernays opened the meeting by suggesting a three-point program of action for librarians: community survey, community action, and community publicity. John Mackenzie Cory of the New York Public Library stressed the futility and dangers of censorship, and presented an outline of types of censorship, special problems, and deterrents to censorship (produced in the summary). Helen A. Ridgway, former ALA public libraries specialist, described her experience with the censor. Roger H. McDonough, director of the New Jersey State Library was the final member of the panel.

Auerbach, Joseph S. "Authorship and Liberty." *North American Review*, 207: 902–17, July 1918. (Also in Auerbach, *Essays and Miscellanies*, New York, Harper, 1922, vol. 2, pp. 130–65)　　**A 285**
Argument for the defense before the Appellate Division of the New York Supreme Court in the case of *The Genius* by Theodore Dreiser. The book was suppressed at the instigation of the New York Society for the Suppression of Vice. In 1923 *The Genius* was published in New York in defiance of the ban.

Aurthur, Robert A. "TV: The 21" Bore." *Nation*, 201:227–31, September 1965.　　**A 286**
Television programming will not improve until the monopolistic control of the networks is broken.

Australia. Broadcasting Control Board. *Television Programme Standards. Determined by the Board in Pursuance of the Broadcasting and Television Act, 1942–1956.* Canberra, A. J. Arthur, Govt. Print. Off., 1956. 29 p.　　**A 287**

Australia. Department of Customs and Excise. *Decisions Relating to Publications Submitted to Central Office for Review in Terms of the Customs (Prohibited Imports) Regulations.* Canberra, Govt. Print. Off., 1962. (Various lists, issued irregularly)　　**A 288**

[Australia. Ministry for Trade and Culture]. "Movie Censorship in Australia." *Light*, 172:38–44, September–October 1926.　　**A 289**
A summary of the report of the Australian censor for 1925.

Australia. Royal Commission on Moving Picture Industry. *Report of the Royal Commission on the Moving Picture Industry in Australia.* Canberra, H. J. Green, Govt. Printer, [1928]. 31 p.　　**A 290**
The Board, under the chairmanship of Walter M. Marks, recommends the establishment of a permanent Board of Film Censors. The report was summarized in *The Light*, January–February 1929.

Australia. Royal Commission on Television." Control of Political Broadcasting in English Speaking Countries." *Journal of Broadcasting*, 2:123–36, Spring 1958. **A 291**

Excerpted from the Report of the Royal Commission. Relates to broadcasting of political and controversial issues in Great Britain, Canada, Australia, and briefly, the United States.

———. *Report* . . . Canberra, A. J. Arthur, Govt. Print. Off., 1954. 131p. **A 292**

"Australia and the *Labour Monthly*." *Labour Monthly* (London), 10:215–16, April 1928. **A 293**

Relates to the barring of the *Labour Monthly* from Australia and India by actions of the Commonwealth Minister of Customs under the Customs Act. Thirty-six books and eight periodicals are reported to have been banned under this Act.

"[Australia] Civil Censorship." In *Australian Encyclopaedia*. East Lansing, Mich., Michigan State University Press, 1958, vol. 2, pp. 316–19. **A 294**

"Australia: The Censorship of Books." *Round Table*, 25:614–17, June 1935. **A 295**

Authors League of America. *Freedom to Write. A Declaration by the Authors League of America presented at the National Assembly of Authors and Dramatists at New York on May 8, 1957*. New York, The League, 1957. 4p. (Also in Downs, *The First Freedom*, pp. 252–53) **A 296**

While recognizing that public welfare requires certain safeguards against unrestrained obscenity, direct incitement to crime, and defamation of character, there has been a dangerous drift in the United States toward censorship, a drift coming mainly from a few religious and patriotic organizations. Self-appointed censors take it upon themselves to deny the public access to certain writings. The League holds that any individual or group has the right to disapprove of a writing or a writer and to state publicly that disapproval, but it denies the right of any individual or group to set limits on the freedom to write, publish, and distribute writings. This must be left to legislatures and courts, subject to the basic guarantees of the Constitution. The League calls on the press, the universities, the clergy and "all thinking patriots" to join in the battle against authoritarian censorship.

Axford, H. William. "The Crucial Battle for the Minds of Men." *Library Journal*, 90:2499–2503, 1 June 1965. **A 297**

The article reviews the basic book selection policy of U.S. Information Agency libraries abroad and its change during the McCarthy era from "one reflecting fundamental American belief in intellectual freedom to one of rigid censorship, reflecting the widespread paranoia affecting American society in the early 1950's." While the McCarthy episode has passed there is still a lingering danger. Axford questions the present book selection policy of USIA, including reliance on the book review service of a commercial agency.

Axon, William E. A. "Milton and the Liberty of the Press." In *Milton Memorial Lectures, 1908*. London, Royal Society of Literature of the United Kingdom, 1909, pp. 39–58. **A 298**

———. *Plea for Free Speech: an Address at the Inaugural Meeting of the Manchester Eclectic Society, June 11th, 1872*. London, Trübner, [1872]. 16p. **A 299**

Ayres, Donald L. "Censorship of Literature as a Curriculum Problem." *Journal*

of Secondary Education, 37:61–63, January 1962. **A 300**

"The most effective steps to protect the school's objectives are to satisfy the parent, in this case its supporters. This does *not* mean to censor and withdraw every work of fiction by a questioned author from the library shelves as all too often has been the case. Rather, it means convincing the parents the school merits their confidence in educating their children along socially accepted lines." Confidence can be gained by: (1) an effective system of school-parent communications and (2) establishment of textbook committees of professionally qualified teachers.

———. "What Can the Teacher Do?" *NEA Journal*, 52:24, May 1963. **A 301**

"If books are selected which are suitable to the curriculum and to the students concerned the possibility of encountering censorship is minimized." (Part of an 11-page feature on textbook censorship.)

Azikiwe, Nnamdi. *Suppression of the Press in British West Africa*. Onitska, Nigeria, African Book Co, [1946?]. 15p. **A 302**

Azkoul, Karim and Carroll Binder. "How Free Shall the Press Be?" *UN World*, 5(8):22–24, August 1951. **A 303**

The case of restriction of press freedom by government to prevent abuse is presented by Dr. Azkoul, Lebanon representative on the UN Subcommittee on Freedom of Information. This view is defended on the ground that such control is necessary in those nations where the media are insufficiently developed. The representative of the United States, Mr. Binder, espouses the principle of absolute freedom of the press on the ground that any attempt to give government the authority to suppress possible abuses would automatically subject the media to unlimited control.

B

B., J. *The Poets Knavery Discouered, in all their lying pamphlets: Wittily and very ingeniously composed, laying open the names of every lying lybel that was printed last yeare, and the authors who made them. . . . Written by J. B.* London, Printed for T. H., [1642]. **B1**
A witty pamphlet describing how writers of the time, when sources of news dried up, proceeded to manufacture news for their readers. They were not brought to account because the government was busy with more pressing matters. The British Museum catalog attributes the work to James Boyd.

"The B. A. at Work: the Censor." *Living Age*, 256:55–57, 4 January 1908. (Reprinted from *Punch*) **B2**
A humorous, imaginary, conversation about censorship, that might appropriately take place between a young debutante and her dinner partner.

Bach, Harry. "Censorship of Library Books and Textbooks in American Schools, 1953–1963." *Journal of Secondary Education*, 40:3–15, January 1965. **B3**
A general review of the efforts by individuals and groups to suppress evil by preventing the dissemination of evil ideas and "error" in the schools, and the measures that librarians under attack can take to resist both. "If pressure groups are allowed to determine the content of books, teaching in American schools will degenerate into indoctrination. The antidote to authoritarianism is not some form of American authoritarianism; the answer is free inquiry."

[Bache, Benjamin Franklin]. *Truth Will Out! The Foul Charges of the Tories against the Editor of the Aurora Repelled by Positive Proof and Plain Truth, and His Base Culminators Put to Shame . . .* Philadelphia, 1798. 12p. **B4**
The editor of the anti-Federalist Philadelphia *Aurora* was one of the chief targets of the Sedition Law of 1798. In this pamphlet he accuses the Adams administration of studied attempts to curb the press. Mrs. Adams urged action against Bache, writing that unless Bache's press and other Republican newspapers were suppressed civil war might be expected. William Cobbett, then in America, and later to stand trial for libel both in America and England, urged suppression of the *Aurora* and that Bache be treated as "a Traitor, a Jew, a Jacobin, or a Dog." Bache was arrested in June 1798, three weeks before the Sedition Act was signed, for libeling the President, but died before trial.

Back, Howard K. *Rights of Access of Radio to the News*. Columbus, Ohio State University, 1951. 117p. (Unpublished Master's thesis) **B5**
"The thesis will attempt to investigate those areas in which the radio newsman does not have, by law, the same access to news as do other newsmen. It will look into those areas in which the radio newsman's right to gather material has not been clearly defined, and those areas of radio and television which have special access problems not facing other media."

Bacon, Corrine. "What Makes a Novel Immoral?" *New York Libraries*, 2:4–12, October 1909. (Based on articles in the *Springfield Republican* appearing in 1903. Reprinted in *Wisconsin Library Bulletin*, December 1909; *Library World*, November 1910; and in a separate pamphlet by H. W. Wilson Co., 1914) **B6**
An immoral novel is one that "leaves us worse than it found us." This is accomplished by (1) appealing to our lower nature, (2) confusing right and wrong, and (3) being untrue to life (pure fantasy excluded), i.e. based on impossible psychology, distortion and half-truths, morbidness, and containing false information. The author illustrates her points with numerous examples from literature. "The book that degrades our intellect, vulgarizes our emotions, kills our faith in our kind, is an immoral book; the book which stimulates thought, quickens our sense of humor, gives us a deeper insight into men and women and a finer sympathy with them, is a moral book, let its subject-matter have as wide a range as life itself." The author was on the staff of the New York State Library.

Bacon, Francis, *Viscount St. Albans*. "Of Sedition and Troubles." In his *Essays or Counsels Civill and Morell* (first published, 1597–1625). In *Selected Writings of Francis Bacon*, edited by Hugh G. Dick, New York, Modern Library, 1955, pp. 38–44. **B7**
Bacon notes that when libels and licentious discourses against the state are frequent and open it is a sign of trouble. We do not remedy the trouble by silencing the complaints—"the going about to stop them doth but make a wonder long-lived"—but by removing the cause of the complaint.

Bagdikian, Ben H. "Behold the Grass-roots Press, Alas!" *Harper's*, 229:102–7, December 1964. **B8**
"The myth of the small-town editor as the great opinion maker is fading; often he is no more than a print-shop proprietor looking for a piece of 'editorial' mat to fill the space between ads. Thus, for a modest fee, or even for free, it is possible to get a 'message' on the editorial pages of many small-town papers." Quoted from *FOI Digest*.

———. "Death in Silence." *Columbia Journalism Review*, 3(1):35–37, Spring 1964. **B9**
The 1964 decision of the U.S. Supreme Court in the *New York Times* libel case, freeing the printed word from massive legal retaliation by affronted public officials, prompts this discussion of the implications of the decision and the practice of the press in drawing a cloak of silence on libel cases concerning itself. While holding as a sacred principle that a newspaper does not suppress news just because it may make someone unhappy, "yet when the someone is a newspaper and the news is a significant libel suit, a majority of papers give themselves protection that they do not extend to other news-makers. . . . What's needed is the normal standard of news in the reporting of public events, now suspended for newspaper libel cases."

———. "The Gentle Suppression." *Columbia Journalism Review*, 4(1):16–19, Spring 1965. **B10**

A news quarantine by Washington papers in reporting activities of American Nazis, the author argues, is not in the public interest.

———. "The News Managers." *Saturday Evening Post*, 236(15):17–19, 20 April 1963.
B11
"Congress and reporters fear vital facts are hidden, and wonder if they can believe the government . . . Each week the Pentagon's censors classify enough documents to form a pile higher than the Empire State Building... The fact that government, which has to live with danger, with error and embarrassment, will disagree with the press on what should be secret is only natural, but it is the strength of democracy that this is a continuing battle and that over the years the battle has settled the issue better than any rigid rule."

———. "Press Agent—But Still President." *Columbia Journalism Review*, 4(2):10–13, Summer 1965.
B12
President Lyndon Johnson is both originator and editor of the news. Heavy pressures are brought to bear on White House correspondents not to print anything critical of the President.

———. "Press Independence and the Cuban Crisis." *Columbia Journalism Review*, I(4):5–11, Winter 1963.
B13
"In the wake of the international crisis of last fall, an old issue arose cast in new dimensions: What are the obligations of journalism and government in a national emergency?" The press by high performance and conditioning the public to expect competent and significant news can protect freedom of information and can exert counterpressure in time of crisis against government efforts to establish tight controls.

———. "What Happened to the Girl Scouts?" *Atlantic*, 195:63–64, May 1955.
B14
An account of the attack on the 1953 edition of the Girl Scout handbook for its "international friendship" theme.

Bagg, William E., III. *A Survey of Reasons for Proposed Legislation Limiting Liability for Defamation by Radio and Television in Massachusetts.* Boston, Boston University, 1953. 139p. (Unpublished Master's thesis)
B15

Baginski, Max. "Anthony B. Comstock's Adventures." *Mother Earth*, I:27–29, September 1906.
B16
The article ridicules Comstock and his sex censorship.

[Bailey, Samuel]. *Essays on the Formation and Publication of Opinions, and on Other Subjects.* Philadelphia, R. W. Pomeroy, 1831. 240p. (First edition published in London, 1821)
B17
An intellectual's appeal for freedom of the press as an influential factor in the "natural progress of knowledge" and in "a judicious and gradual adaptation of their institutions to the inevitable changes of opinion." Bailey believed that no power could arrest the "silent march of thought" made possible by a free press. This work went through three editions in ten years and was considered by well-informed radicals of the 1820's as a major contribution to the moral sciences. The essays were praised by James Mill in the *Westminster Review* for July 1826 and by Thomas Cooper in the preface of his *Treatise on the Law of Libel and the Liberty of the Press* (1830).

———. *Essays on the Pursuit of Truth, and on the Progress of Knowledge, and the Fundamental Principle of All Evidence and Expectation.* 2d ed. London, Longman, *et al*, 1844. 278p. (First published in 1829)
B18
Sequel to Bailey's *Essays on the Formation and Publication of Opinion*, 1821.

Bailey, William S. *Prosecution of William S. Bailey for Publishing the "Free South."* [Newport, Ky., 1845?]. 2p.
B19
This Newport, Ky., publisher expressed anti-slavery sentiments in his paper. His shop was attacked by a mob.

Bainbridge, John. "Danger's Ahead in the Public Schools." *McCall's*, 80:56+, October 1952.
B20
Deals with attacks on the public schools—the efforts to censor textbooks, to ban speakers, to standardize the curriculum, to eliminate teaching about communism and the United Nations, to discredit teaching methods, and to change the pattern of teaching from one that educates to one that indoctrinates.

Baker, Ernest A., *et al.* "The Poisonous Literature Scare." *Library Association Record*, 12:1–8, 15 January 1910.
B21
Editor Baker invites members of the Library Association to respond to Canon Rawnsley's charge that objectionable books are making their way into the public libraries of England. The discussion, entered into by C. W. Sutton, Lawrence Inkster, W. H. K. Wright, Alfred Lancaster, and A. O. Jennings considers the censorship activities of the Circulating Libraries Association in relation to the book selection policies of public libraries.

Baker, George. "*Lolita*: Literature or Pornography." *Saturday Review*, 40(25):18, 22 June 1957.
B22
With the U.S. Customs declaring it unobjectionable, *Lolita* becomes a book that must be smuggled out of France but can be legally imported into the United States. A French publication noted that "France has shown herself to be more intolerant and more puritanical than an English-speaking country."

[Baker, George M.]. *The Freedom of the Press; a Farce.* Boston, Walter H. Baker, 1865. 21p. (Also in *The Amateur Drama*, 1893, pp. 162–83)
B23
Trials and tribulations of the editor of *The Bird of Freedom*. The would-be editor closes with the line: "I'm convinced, that, while the press is a mighty engine, it needs a great deal of care and attention; and, of all freedom, that which is most comfortable and easy for its possessors is not the freedom of the press."

Baker, Nancy. *Criticisms of Broadcast News.* Columbia, Mo., Freedom of Information Center, School of Journalism, University of Missouri, 1963. 4p. (Publication no. 111)
B24
A compilation of criticisms leveled against radio and television newscasts, by government officials, the public, and the broadcasting industry.

———. *New York Newspaper Strike.* Columbia, Mo., Freedom of Information Center, School of Journalism, University of Missouri, 1963. 8p. (Publication no. 104)
B25
An analysis of the New York newspaper strike which lasted from 8 December to 31 March 1963.

———. *Reporters' Privilege Worldwide.* Columbia, Mo., Freedom of Information Center, School of Journalism, University of Missouri, 1964. 7p. (Publication no. 116)
B26
A survey of professional secrecy and shield laws in the United States and abroad and the arguments for and against the claims of privileged relations between the reporter and his news source.

Baker, Sir Richard. *Theatrum Redivivum; or, The Theatre Vindicated by Sir Richard Baker [!]; in Answer to Mr. Pryn's Histrio-Mastix: wherein His Groundless Assertions against Stage-plays Are Discovered, His Misstaken Allegations of the Fathers Manifested, as Also What He Calls His Reasons, to Be Nothing but His Passions . . .* London, Printed by T. R. for F. Eglesfield, 1662. 141p.
B27

Baker, Sidney J. "The Hoax of Censorship." *International Journal of Sexology*, 2(2):111–14, November 1948.
B28

Bakewell, Paul. "*The Menace* and the Post Office." *Catholic Mind*, 13(2):25–44, 22 January 1915.
B29

An open letter to W. H. Lanpir, Solicitor of the Post Office Department, from a St Louis lawyer who claims it is the legal duty of the Postmaster General to suppress a publication that is "dirty, vile, and filthy." He refers to the anti-Catholic journal, *The Menace*, published in Aurora, Mo., by B. O. Flower. The same issue of *Catholic Mind* contains the text of an earlier letter from Bakewell on the same subject (pp. 45–51), an article entitled Your Money and the Mail, noting that Catholics through their taxes were helping to subsidize the mailing of *The Menace* (pp. 51–53); and a list of Anti-Catholic Periodicals (pp. 55–56).

Balderston, John L. "The Freedom of the Pen: A Conversation with George Moore." *Fortnightly Review*, 102(n.s.): 539–51, October 1917.   **B 30**
An American correspondent reports his conversations with George Moore, using extensive quotes. Moore rejects the "Anglo-Saxon fallacy" that morality depends upon literature. He also exposes the inconsistency of reformers in attacking current literature for its immorality while neglecting the classics. Moore's report of the same conversation is presented in his book, *Avowals*.

Baldus, David C. "Pennsylvania's Proposed Film Censorship Law—House Bill 1098." *Duquesne University Law Review*, 4:429–40, Spring 1966.   **B 31**
"A few simple amendments to Pennsylvania's Comic Book Act will produce a less radical and far more effective system than the one recommended by House Bill 1098."

[Baldwin, Charles N.]. *Report of the Trial of Charles N. Baldwin for a Libel in Publishing, in the Republican Chronicle, Certain Charges of Fraud and Swindling, in the Management of Lotteries in the State of New-York. Containing, the Publications in Relation to This Interesting Subject—The Evidence—The Speeches of the Counsel on Both Sides, and the Charge of His Hon. C. D. Colden, Mayor of the City of New-York, to the Jury. The Trial Commenced on Tuesday the 10th of November, and Lasted Until Friday Morning 2 O'clock, when the Jury Returned a Verdict of "Not guilty . . ."* New York, 1818. 124p.
                    B 32

Baldwin, Hanson. "Managed News: Our Peacetime Censorship." *Atlantic*, 211: 53–59, April 1963.   **B 33**
A criticism of the news management policy of the Kennedy administration, which Baldwin charges with increased centralization and restriction of government news and with using such devices as dispensing "exclusive" stories to favored papers, arranging for high-

level "leaks," using FBI agents to trace unplanned "leaks," and, during the Cuban crisis, the use of news blackout and deliberate falsehood.

Baldwin, Judith M. *Access Laws*. Columbia, Mo., Freedom of Information Center, School of Journalism, University of Missouri, 1962. 7p., 11p., 11p., 8p. (Publication nos. 86–89)   **B 34**
Thirty-four states have laws permitting the public and the press to inspect the records of public bodies and public officials and 28 states have laws stating that meetings of governmental bodies must be open to the public and the press. The author reports on this legislation in 4 monographs: Development (no. 86), Comparison (no. 87), Interpretations (no. 88), and Defeats (no. 89).

Baldwin, Roger N. "The Truth Shall Make You Free." *Survey Graphic*, 35: 498–500, December 1946.   **B 35**
The director of the American Civil Liberties Union discusses the forces for international freedom in communications that can be counted upon to combat such obstacles as tariffs and taxes on motion pictures, censorship of films and printed material, copyright complications, discriminatory cable rates, and government control of radio which prevails virtually everywhere outside of the United States.

Ball, Horace G. *Law of Copyright and Literary Property*. Albany, N.Y., Bender, 1944. 976p.   **B 36**

Ball, Joseph A. "Fair Trial." *California State Bar Journal*, 32:212–25, May–June 1957.   **B 37**
A review of the conflict between a fair trial and a free press, with special reference to California. The author urges the State Bar of California "to declare a rule of conduct which will prohibit trial by newspaper, radio, or television."

Ball, W. Macmahon, *ed. Press, Radio and World Affairs; Australia's Outlook*. Melbourne, Melbourne University Press, 1938. 146p.   **B 38**
A series of essays on sources of public opinion in Australia on world affairs. The author criticizes the censorship of radio broadcasting by the government and recommends changes in the law.

Ball, W. Valentine. *The Law of Libel as Affecting Newspapers and Journalists*. London, Stevens, 1912. 165p.   **B 39**
A series of lectures on the law of libel presented at the British Institute of Journalists. Topics: What Constitutes a Libel, Construction of Libels, Privilege, Reports of Parliamentary Debates, and Criminal Law of Libel.

————, and Patrick Browne. *The Law of Libel and Slander*. 2d ed. London, Stevens, 1936. 229p.   **B 40**
Summary of modern English libel law relating to newspapers.

Ball, William. *A Briefe Treatise Concerning The Regulating Of Printing, Humbly presented to the Parliament of England*. London, 1651. 16p. (Reprinted in Clyde, *The Struggle for the Freedom of the Press*, pp. 298–313)   **B 41**
An appeal to Parliament to regulate printing, presented in behalf of Mathew Barker, who sought a monopoly in printing the Bible.

Ball, William B. "Legal Aspects of Obscene Literature." *Guild of Catholic Psychologists Bulletin*, 8:79–87, April 1961.
                    B 42
Consideration of the mounting indignation over smutty and violence-inciting material and efforts to stem such publications by private action groups and, on the other hand, the equally indignant protests of those who object to censorship. The author examines in detail and with scepticism the idea that no relationship exists between obscenity and overt sexual misbehavior. He charges that a small body of "anti-restriction" literature is being given undue emphasis.

Ball, William W. *The Freedom of the Press in South Carolina and Its Limitations*. Columbia, S.C., [1916?]. 15p. (Originally published by the *News and Courier* of Charleston, S.C., 28 June 1913)   **B 43**

Ballinger, Kenneth. *Florida Law of the Press—Newspaper, Radio, Television*. Tallahassee, Fla., Capital Printers, 1954. 101p.
                    B 44

Balter, Harry G. "Freedom of Speech and Press Prevail in Clash with Court's Contempt Power." *California State Bar Journal*, 17:8–13, January 1942.   **B 45**
By a 5 to 4 decision, the U.S. Supreme Court in the "Bridges" and the *Times* cases, "dramatically reaffirms broadest principles of freedom of speech and freedom of press in the very teeth of war emergency."

————. "Some Observations Concerning the Federal Obscenity Statute." *Southern California Law Review*, 8:267–87, June 1935.
                    B 46
Deals with federal regulation of the use of the mails for transmittal of books, papers, letters, pictures, or other written matter which has been declared by federal statutes to be non-mailable.

The Bang. New York, 1907–17. Weekly. Edited by Alexander Harvey.   **B 47**
The entire eight-page issue of this radical paper was frequently devoted to questions relating to freedom of speech or the press. For example, the industrial dispute at Paterson, N. J. (11 October 1915); John S. Sumner and the New York vice society (28 February 1916); ridicule of judicial tests of obscenity (6 March 1916); and postal censorship against Socialists (16 July 1917).

"Bang! You're Dead or You're Dead, Bang!" *Broadcasting*, 61(6):62–74, 7 August 1961.   **B 48**
Account of a symposium on freedom and responsibility in broadcasting, held at Northwestern University.

Banks, William. "The Press Censorship." *Canadian Magazine*, 46:152–55, December 1915.   **B 49**
Press censorship in Canada during World War I.

"Banned, Branded, Burned: Partial List of Writers and Artists Whose Works Have Been Banned, Branded, or Burned in the Recent Period by Federal, State and Local Officials in the United States." *Masses and Mainstream*, 6:10–13, August 1953.   **B 50**
Following the list, the journal reprints the "Freedom to Read" statement formulated by the American Library Association and the American Book Publishers Council.

Banning, Margaret C. "Filth on the Newsstand." *Reader's Digest*, 61:115–19, October 1952.   **B 51**
"The volume of public protest at the sexy and debasing magazines grows. Can publishers and distributors police themselves or must we have an unwanted and possibly undiscriminating censorship?"

———. "The Restricted Shelf: Censorship's Last Stand." *Saturday Review*, 19:3–4+, 29 October 1938. Reply by G. F. Bowerman, *Saturday Review*, 19:9, 12 November 1938. (Reprinted in Downs, *The First Freedom*, pp. 320–23)   **B 52**
A novelist and essayist condemns the practice in some public libraries of having a "restricted shelf," largely for books on sex. "If the restricted shelf cannot be abandoned, and fear of aldermen will take care of that for a while, the shelf should be made useful. It should not be a patchwork of prejudice but a shelf containing books for which some prerequisite of reading is necessary." Librarian Bowerman comments favorably on Mrs Banning's article, noting that books are often placed on restricted shelves not so much to protect the reader but to prevent the books from being stolen.

———. "The Side of the Angels." *ALA Bulletin*, 47:391–92+, October 1953.   **B 53**
Mrs. Banning defends her testimony before the House of Representatives Committee investigating pornography. She describes her study of the "girlie" magazines on the newsstands and reiterates the opinion that they are an affront to decency, and should be subject to vigorous police enforcement under the obscenity laws. She calls for adequate control within the magazine publishing industry. The only really effective method of defeating pornography, however, is the development of a sense of discrimination and a sense of value in the home, in the school, and through support of libraries.

"The Banning of Books in Boston." *Publishers' Weekly*, 111:1254–55, 19 March 1927.   **B 54**
Booksellers are protecting themselves from threatened prosecution by withdrawing many books from sale. Books recently withdrawn include *The Rebel Bird* (Diana Patrick), *The Hard-Boiled Virgin* (Frances Newman), *Marriage Bed* (Ernest Pascal), and *The Beadle* (Pauline Smith). References are made to censorship activities of the Boston Booksellers' Committee.

"Banning the Sale of Literature, 1814 and 1944." *Wilson Library Bulletin*, 19:213, November 1944.   **B 55**
Printed side-by-side are (1) a statement by Thomas Jefferson, made 19 April 1814, expressing mortification that efforts have been made to suppress a book by M. de Bécourt and affirming the right of every man to read what he pleases, and (2) a resolution adopted by the Massachusetts Library Association, 12 May 1944, deploring police censorship in Boston and reminding the public that "in the long run the best and most effective suppression of objectionable books results from voluntary action by individuals in refusing to buy or countenance them."

Barber, Owen G. "Competition, Free Speech, and the FCC Network Regulations." *George Washington Law Review*, 12:34–53, November 1943.   **B 56**

[Barber, William E.]. "Censorship." In *Encyclopaedia Britannica*, 13th ed., 1926, vol. 1 of sup., pp. 559–60.   **B 57**
British censorship during World War I.

Barco, George J. "'The Free Press' and 'A Fair Trial.'" *Pennsylvania Bar Association Quarterly*, 31:63–77, October 1959.   **B 58**
A general discussion of the controversy over Canon 35 of the American Bar Association and the implications of the various positions taken by the bar and the press.

Bard, Isaiah S. *Section 315 of the Communications Act of 1934 and the Presidential Election of 1952.* New York, New York University, 1956. 292p. (Ph.D. dissertation, University Microfilms, no. 21, 692)   **B 59**

Barker, Ambrose G. *Henry Hetherington (1792–1849).* London, Issued for the Secular Society by the Pioneer Press, [1938]. 62p   **B 60**
Hetherington played a leading role in the struggle for an untaxed newspaper press in England during the 1830's, issuing his *Poor Man's Guardian* in defiance of the tax law.

[Barker, Jacob]. *Suspension of the National Advocate.* New Orleans, Estafette du Sud Printing Office, 1863. 12p. (English and French texts)   **B 61**
The publication of the *National Advocate* "was suspended by Major General Butler's Special Order No. 513, from a mistaken view taken of the opinions I had advanced, in relation to foreign intervention. This being satisfactorily explained, the publication was allowed to be resumed after a single day's suspension." The correspondence between Editor Jacob Barker and Major General Butler ensues.

Barker, Lucius, and Twiler W. Barker, Jr. *Freedoms, Courts, Politics: Studies in Civil Liberties.* New York, Prentice-Hall, 1965. 320p.   **B 62**
Includes discussions of civil liberties problems in the following areas: religion and the public schools, freedom of speech and assembly, obscenity and freedom of expression (*Alberts v. California*), communism, race relations, and right of counsel. "In addition to the role of judges, legislators, and administrators, the book also describes (1) how civil liberty problems arise, (2) the role of organized interest groups, (3) the impact of community attitudes and public opinion, and (4) what happens after a court decision is made, especially reactions to the decision and attempts to comply with, circumvent, or overcome it."

Barkley, John. *Report of the Trial of John Barkley, (one of the shop-men of Richard Carlile,) prosecuted by the Constitutional Association for publishing a Seditious and Blasphemous Libel . . .* London, Printed by R. and A. Taylor and published by Effingham Wilson, 1822. 20p. (A second edition the same year includes the proceedings in the House of Commons on the petition of the defendant)   **B 63**
Barkley, one of the volunteer clerks who operated Carlile's bookshop when the latter was in prison, was brought before Common Sergeant Newman Knowlys, found guilty, and sentenced to six months in prison.

Barkocy, Michael A. "Censorship against *Time* and *Life* International Editions." *Journalism Quarterly*, 40:517–24, Autumn 1963. **B 64**
"During the past 23 years *Time* or *Life* has been censored abroad 857 times. The author analyzes the types of censoring, by countries, and the reasons for the actions, using the files of Time-Life International."

Barksdale, N. P. "Why and How Censor?" *Wilson Library Bulletin*, 15:380–81, 1 January 1941. **B 65**
The librarian should "worry less about the printed page and think more about developing an open, critical attitude in the reader."

Barlow, Samuel L. M. "The Censor of Art." *North American Review*, 213:346–50, March 1921. **B 66**
The trial of James Branch Cabell's *Jurgen* in New York, at the instigation of the New York Society for the Suppression of Vice, forms the basis of the author's discussion. Bringing *Jurgen* to trial violates the constitutional right of the author to be tried by a jury of his peers. While America is faced with local Comstock laws affecting literature, Great Britain is faced with stage censorship by central authorities. The author quotes Arnold Bennett as saying of stage censorship: "The existence of the censorship makes it impossible for me to even think of writing plays on the same plane of realism and thoroughness as my novels." And H. G. Wells: "The censorship, with its wanton powers of suppression, has ever been *one* of the reasons why I haven't ventured into play-writing." The author believes that the people can be trusted to support good literature and drama and to reject the indecent without aid of censor.

Barnard, Thomas. *Observations on the Proceeding of the Friends of the Liberty of the Press, &c. Dec. 22, 1792. And an Answer to Mr. Erskine's Speech, of January 19, 1793.* London, J. Evans, 1793. 39p. **B 67**
On 22 December 1792 a group of gentlemen assembled at Free Mason's Tavern as the Friends of the Freedom of the Press. They passed nine resolutions with respect to a free press and heard an address by Thomas Erskine, who had recently defended Thomas Paine for the publication of his *Rights of Man*. The author of this pamphlet criticizes the assemblage and expresses support of the constitutional societies in much the same vein as his contemporary, John Bowles.

[Barnes, Edward]. "Newspapers—and the Stamp Question." *British Quarterly Review*, 15:135–62, February 1852. **B 68**
Commentary on the report of the House of Commons Select Committee on Newspaper Stamps (1851), listing the various objections to a stamp tax—difficulties in defining a "newspaper," evasions, limitation of the circulation of papers, discrimination against the poor, and the major objection that "news" is not a fit subject for taxation.

Barnes, Harry Elmer. *The Struggle Against the Historical Blackout.* Cooperstown, N.Y., Privately printed, 1950. 87p. **B 69**
The author charges that efforts were made to suppress facts about our entry into World War II.

———, and Oreen M. Ruedi. *The American Way of Life.* 2d ed. New York, Prentice-Hall, 1950. 931p. **B 70**
A chapter on censorship includes: nature and development, types, obscenity and libel laws, political censorship, and restrictions in radio and the movies.

Barns, Margarita. *The Indian Press; A History of Public Opinion in India.* London, Allen & Unwin, 1940. 491p. **B 71**

Barnstein, Harold. *British Press Council.* Columbia, Mo., Freedom of Information Center, School of Journalism, University of Missouri, 1963. 6p. (Publication no. 96) **B 72**
An appraisal of the work of the British Press Council, established in 1953 as an outgrowth of a recommendation of the first Royal Commission on the Press in Britain. References are made to the two Royal Commissions on the Press (the report of the second appeared in 1962), the Pilkington report on British broadcasting, and the report of the Hutchins Commission in the United States. "The British Press Council and proposed councils in other countries are beset by many of the same difficulties: controversy over composition; lack of influence over the press if the council cannot level sanctions, and cries of 'censorship' if it can and does; and the threat to freedom of the press through enlargement of the council with possible government involvement."

———. *Broadcast Self-Regulation.* Columbia, Mo., Freedom of Information Center, School of Journalism, University of Missouri, 1962. 13p. (Publication no. 91) **B 73**
A survey of noncode members of the National Association of Broadcasters (stations that chose not to subscribe to the NAB Code) and a discussion of the broadcast industry's self-regulatory efforts.

Barnum, Phineas T. *Liberty of the Press. The Nation's Bulwark. Oration on the Freedom of the Press. On the Liberation of P. T. Barnum, Editor of the Herald of Freedom, from Imprisonment, for an Alleged Libel.* New Haven, Conn., 1832. **B 74**
Three times in 3 years young Barnum was prosecuted for libel for his frank and caustic accusations against citizens of Bethel and Danbury, Conn. In the first trial the jury did not agree; in the second he was fined; in the third he was given a sentence of 60 days in Danbury jail for describing Seth Seelye, a local deacon, as a "canting hypocrite" and accusing him of exacting "usurious interest" from an orphan boy. In his autobiography Barnum describes the incident and the celebration following his release from prison.

Barr, Stringfellow. "Censorship in a Dialectical Republic." In John Cogley, *Religion in America.* New York, World, 1958, pp. 208–22. **B 75**
Censorship is the most crucial case of conflict between church and state in a free society. It is only justified as a means of preventing monopoly of the dialectical process and not as a means of preventing "the preaching of false doctrine." The author agrees with Plato that censorship is proper in the guardianship of minors, but that there is no excuse for protecting grown men and women. He criticizes religious pressure groups that attempt to silence opinion by manipulation of power rather than by persuasion. We ought to hold the aesthetic dialectic (literature and art) as well as the political dialectic free from the censor.

Barrett, C. R. B. "Napoleon I and the British Press." *Royal United Service Institution Journal* (London), 61:814–19, November 1916. **B 76**
A study to determine the extent to which careless publication of naval and military intelligence in the British press was beneficial to Napoleon. The emperor restricted the press of France but took advantage of a free press in England.

Barrett, Cyril. "Censorship." *Studies; An Irish Quarterly Review*, 53:149–58, Summer 1964. **B 77**
The author considers the conflict between art and morality in appraising works of art and literature and questions the logic in exempting them from censorship. "It is possible to censor a work (and so satisfy the moralists) while at the same time admitting that it is a work of art and even, as far as the artist is concerned, morally irreproachable. On the other hand, it is possible to allow for the circulation of work among certain sections of the public however reprehensible the artist's intentions . . . Thus the moral merits and demerits will be decided on moral grounds, and the artistic merits and defects on artistic grounds." He rejects the idea that art and immorality are any more incompatible than art and morality.

Barrett, Edward L. *The Tenney Committee; Legislative Investigation of Subversive Activities in California.* Ithaca, N.Y., Cornell University Press, 1951. 400p. **B 78**
Numerous references to attacks on books, magazines, and school texts that were considered subversive.

————, Paul W. Bruton, and John Honnold. *Constitutional Law; Cases and Materials*. Brooklyn, Foundation Press, 1959. 1225 p.   **B 79**
Chapter 10 deals with freedom of expression—control of subversive speech; defamatory, obscene communications and problems of censorship. In the area of sedition, the Schenck case is included; in the area of scandal and obscenity the following cases are included: *Near v. Minnesota (Saturday Press), Joseph Burstyn, Inc. v. Wilson (The Miracle, film); Roth v. United States, Alberts v. California,* and *Kingsley Books, Inc v. Brown.* Also included is the case of *Beauharnais v. Illinois,* involving group libel.

Barrett, Edward W., and John O. Pastore. "Is Speech on Television Really Free?" *TV Guide*, 11:22–25, 18 April 1964.   **B 80**
Views on the "fairness doctrine."

Barrett, Wilton A. "The National Board of Review of Motion Pictures; How It Works." *Journal of Educational Sociology*, 10:177–88, November 1936.   **B 81**
The executive secretary of the Board describes the work of this volunteer citizen group, organized to review films in New York City before they are released for general exhibition to the public.

————. "The Work of the National Board of Review." *Annals of the American Academy of Political and Social Science*, 128:175–86, November 1926.   **B 82**
A summary of the work of this voluntary film reviewing agency.

"Barriers to Free Flow of Information; Summary of Discussions at Third Session of Sub-commission on Freedom of Information and the Press." *U.N. Bulletin*, 7:22–25, 1 July 1949.   **B 83**

Barrington, Margaret. "The Censorship in Eire." *Commonweal*, 46:429–32, 15 August 1947. (Reprinted in Downs, *The First Freedom*, pp. 398–402)   **B 84**
This Irish writer, wife of novelist Liam O'Flaherty, reviews the current Irish censorship and includes a partial listing of authors who are banned.

Barron, Jerome A. "The Constitutional Status of Freedom of Speech and Press in Canada: The History of a Quiet Revolution." *Northwestern University Law Review*, 58:73–106, March–April 1963.   **B 85**
The author describes the "rise of a judicially-created theory of implied constitutional protection" for political freedoms, including the freedom of the press. Such a development parallels the American constitutional pattern

and illustrates the generative power of the American Bill of Rights. In recent years "the Jehovah's Witnesses have been responsible for a line of decisions by the Supreme Court which have partially constructed an implied Bill of Rights for Canada."

Barrus, Clara. *Whitman and Burroughs, Comrades*. Boston, Houghton Mifflin, 1931. 392 p.   **B 86**
Chapter 13, The Suppression of *Leaves of Grass*, deals with the action by Boston authorities in suppressing the 1882 edition of that work.

Barry, John. *Erotic Censorship*. Springfield, Mass., Victory Publishing Co., 1958. 23 p.   **B 87**
An impassioned personal plea to join the fight against censorship.

Barry, Richard. "Freedom of the Press?" *North American Review*, 208:702–9, November 1918.   **B 88**
The author urges the press to exercise its rights to freedom of opinion, despite the threat of post-office censorship.

Barry, William. "The Censorship of Fiction." *Dublin Review*, 144:111–31, January 1909.   **B 89**
The author condemns the immoral literature that is "spreading like a pestilence over the land." While the Home Office should keep a firm control on vile literature, plays, and photographs, the law alone cannot solve the problem and a censor is unlikely to flourish. Parents and teachers should unite in a purity crusade against moral anarchy. "No efforts can be too speedy or too strenuous to prevent [Pagan democracy's] chief instrument of propaganda, romantic fiction, from poisoning the source of a better life by its atheism and ethical desease."

Barth, Alan. "Freedom and the Press." *Progressive*, 26(6):29–33, June 1962.   **B 90**
"A press which serves faithfully and fearlessly as a censor of the government is a source of great national strength." Adopted from his paper, The Press as Censor of Government, delivered as the first Nieman Chair Lecture, College of Journalism, Marquette University.

————. "Freedom from Contempt." *Nieman Reports*, 3(2):11–16, April 1949.   **B 91**
The U.S. Supreme Court of the 1940's redefined freedom of the press along libertarian principles through three decisions: *Bridges v. California, Pennekamp v. Florida,* and *Craig v. Harney.* The decisions "grant to newspapers a virtual immunity from discipline by judges through summary contempt proceedings, at least so far as out-of-court editorial comment is concerned."

————. *The Government and the Press; Sixth Annual Memorial Lecture, Sponsored by the Twin Cities Local, American Newspaper Guild, CIO, and School of Journalism, Uni-

versity of Minnesota, Minneapolis, December 5, 1952.* [Minneapolis, 1953]. 14 p. (Annual Memorial Lecture no. 6)   **B 92**

————. "Position of the Press in a Free Society." *Annals of the American Academy of Political and Social Science*, 250:82–88, March 1947.   **B 93**
The author discusses the basic American doctrine of a free press in relation to economic limitations and the services it actually performs.

————. *The Price of Liberty*. New York, Viking, 1961. 212 p.   **B 94**
Hazards to freedom of speech and the press, arising from Congressional investigations.

————. "The Significance of Free Communication Today." In *Freedom of Communication; Proceedings of the First Conference on Intellectual Freedom . . .* Chicago, American Library Association, 1954, pp. 19–24.   **B 95**

Barth, Roger V. "Pennsylvania—A Cinematic Gomorrah?" *Buffalo Law Review*, 11:389–96, Winter 1962.   **B 96**
A discussion of the situation in Pennsylvania where a series of judicial decisions "have done much to preclude any formal control over the quality of movie films which may be exhibited. Pennsylvania is here examined because of a recent decision of its Supreme Court, *William Goldman Theatres, Inc. v. Dana,* and because its present situation reflects the increased reliance which must now be placed on informal means of control in this important area."

Barthelemy, J. *Respectfully Submitted to the State Convention of A.D. 1846, by a Victim of the Mal-administration of Criminal Justice in New York; Flagrant Subversion of the Liberty of the Press.* New York, Printed by Michael Z. O'Connor, 1846. 24 p.   **B 97**

Bartholomew, Paul C. "Movie Censorship and the Supreme Court." *Michigan State Bar Journal*, 40(8):10–16, August 1961.   **B 98**
A review of the court's interpretation of movie censorship from the 1915 Mutual Film Corp. case through the Times Film Corp. case of 1961.

Bartholomew, Robert O. *Report of Censorship of Motion Pictures and of Investigation of Motion Picture Theaters of Cleveland, 1913.* Cleveland, Council of City of Cleveland, 1913. 32 p.   **B 99**

The Cleveland censor of motion pictures, at the request of Mayor Newton D. Baker, made a study of censorship of films, and an inspection of movie theaters. He recommends that all films circulating in the city be censored. State censorship is preferable, but if a pending state bill does not pass Cleveland should establish its own censorship board.

Bartlett, James. "Press Censorship." *Fortnightly*, 158(n.s.):253–59, October 1945. **B 100**

A brief history of censorship of British foreign correspondents. Wartime censorship was first experienced at the end of the Crimean War when Whitehall lost its tolerance for free reporting. In the 1920's newspapermen abroad began to find themselves hampered when reporting nonmilitary affairs because of restrictions in countries in which they were posted.

———. "World Free Press." *Fortnightly*, 157(n.s.):296–302, May 1945. **B 101**

A British journalist sees in government controls the greatest threat to a free press in the postwar years.

Bartley, Robert T. *Regulation of Programs—How Far? How Good?* Washington D.C., U.S. Federal Communications Commission, 1961. 19 p. **B 102**

Address before the Florida Association of Broadcasters.

Bascom, John. "Public Press and Personal Right." *Education*, 4:604–11, July 1884. **B 103**

The great extension in the freedom of the press "has tended to remove the slightest protection which the law had previously provided for personal rights." There are few prosecutions for libel and even fewer successful ones. Liberty is given to the press with the supposition that it will be conscientiously used. "If the supposition is not true, the weightiest plea for liberty is taken away."

Bassett, Robert C. "Freedom of the Press." *Marquette Law Review*, 25:28–33, December 1940. **B 104**

The fundamental purpose of the First and Fourteenth Amendments with respect to freedom of the press is "not to guarantee to publishers the right to print, but to guarantee the American people the right to read what is printed, to learn the facts concerning public affairs, to weigh conflicting opinions, and to form their own judgments, unhampered by the dictates of any one branch of government." A general discussion of the concept of press freedom in America.

Bastwick, John. *The Confession of the faithfull Witnesse of Christ . . .* London, 1641. 8 p. **B 105**

The author's own account of his life and martyrdom. Dr. Bastwick was a physician and Puritan theologian who was brought to trial, along with Henry Burton and William Prynne, before the Star Chamber for his *Apologeticus* (1636) and *Leteny* (1637). He accused the court of having decided the case "a long time in advance of the trial," and the clerk of the court with mispronouncing the Latin in the objectionable works.

[———]. "Trial of John Bastwick, M.D., Henry Burton, Clerk, and William Prynne, Esq., for Seditious Libels, 1637." In Borrow, *Celebrated Trials*, vol. 1, pp. 467–68. **B 106**

Dr. Bastwick, along with Burton and Prynne, were tried and convicted by the Star Chamber for their heretical writings. The three were fined, pilloried, shorn of their ears, and given life imprisonment. In 1640 they were released as heroes by the Long Parliament.

Bate, Henry. "The Right of Privacy: Right or Wrong?" *Journalist's World*, 3:6–8, September 1963. **B 107**

Efforts by the Press Council in Great Britain, in the absence of judicial decisions, to uphold the right of privacy.

Bates, Ernest S. "Comstock Stalks." *Scribner's Magazine*, 87:355–66, April 1930. **B 108**

"The ghost of a ginger-whiskered censor of the 1870's inspires the Federal Customs Service and the police censors of Boston today. Anthony Comstock dead is a more powerful enemy of freedom and liberal thought than he was when alive. Mr. Bates in a telling article attacks the principles of censorship." The real aim of censorship is suppression of thought, not of vice, and the war is primarily against ideas, not indecent language. "One motive underlies all the attacks—fear of sex enlightenment."

———. *This Land of Liberty.* New York, Harper, 1930. 383 p. **B 109**

A description of the many attacks made on liberty in the United States, including the use of private constabularies, illegal searches and seizures, the espionage law, the activities of the Post Office Department during World War I, and the Palmer raids after the war. There is also a description of propaganda and pressure groups and "major minority" tyranny.

[Bates, Henry M.]. "Freedom of Press and Use of the Mails." *Michigan Law Review*, 29:728–31, May 1921. **B 110**

A critical review of decisions of the U.S. Supreme Court on the "tendency" test as a limit of freedom in the area of sedition. The discussion centers around the case of *U.S. ex rel. Milwaukee Social Democrat v. Burleson* (255 U.S. 407). During World War I the *Milwaukee Leader* was denied second-class mailing privileges for its denunciation of the draft law.

Bates, Miner S. *Religious Liberty: an Inquiry.* New York, International Missionary Council, 1945. 604 p. **B 111**

This study, prepared under the auspices of the Foreign Missions Conference of North America and the Federal Council of Churches of Christ in America, has numerous references to suppression of heretical publications throughout the world.

Bath, Gomer. "The Libraries Buy Propaganda." *Freeman*, 2:535–37, 19 May 1952. **B 112**

"How public libraries are buying and circulating 'one-world' and pro-Soviet propaganda films is shown by the controversy in Peoria, Illinois." Bath, a columnist for a Peoria newspaper, was one of those who attacked the Peoria Public Library's film-buying program leading to the library's experiment with labeling of controversial films.

"Battle Against Censorship." *Theatre Arts*, 31:13–14, April 1947. **B 113**

A brief editorial supporting the bill before the New York City Council which provided that "a license shall not be refused nor shall a licensee be punished for showing a picture or giving a performance where there has not been a prior conviction."

"Battle over Birth Control." *Current Opinion*, 59:339–40, November 1915. **B 114**

The William Sanger case before New York Municipal Court Judge McInerney who, in pronouncing sentence, stated that proposals for birth control were "a crime not only against the laws of man but against the laws of God." Judge William N. Gatens of Portland, Oregon, dismissed a similar case against two others who had distributed Mrs. Sanger's pamphlets, with a statement defending sex education.

"Battling the Wolves." *Christian Century*, 48:470–71, 8 April 1931; 48:892–93, 8 July 1931. **B 115**

"If the wolves of the literary underworld are not held at bay, the destruction of social and moral standards that will ensue is something not to be lightly contemplated." A defense of the Rev. Philip Yarrow, superintendent of the Illinois Vigilance Association, who was convicted of malicious prosecution by a Chicago jury and made liable for $5,000 damages. Yarrow had earlier brought suit against a Chicago bookseller for selling obscene literature. The bookseller was acquitted and sued the minister for malicious prosecution.

Bauer, Harry C. "Censorship or Fair Trial." *Library News Bulletin* (Washington State Library), 15:87–91, May–June 1947. **B 116**

"The committee [appointed by the Mayor of Seattle] therefore believes that books or other printed material dealing with the subject of sex—aside from out-and-out pornographia—

should, like controversial or substandard writing on other subjects, be challenged not in a negative but in a positive fashion by subjecting it to the competition of unquestionably healthy work, and that the task of both our institutions and our public spirited citizens is to do everything in their power to stimulate the recognition of good literature."

—————. "The Censorship Rides at Anchor." *Pacific Northwest Library Association Quarterly*, 25:82–90, January 1962. **B117**
A discussion of the work of the two most active bodies in the field of censorship—the National Office for Decent Literature, a Catholic organization that opposes the distribution of salacious literature and endorses legal suppression of obscene matter, and the American Civil Liberties Union that takes the opposite view that all censorship is wrong, and opposes the NODL lists. The efforts of the two bodies seem to balance each other.

—————. "The Dream and Reality." *Antiquarian Bookman*, 30:919, 3–10 September 1962. **B118**
"If I were King, there would be no censorship in my kingdom," the author writes of his dream world. But, facing reality, he finds that the plethora of printing today acts against an interest in reading. "Publications are so plentiful, they are impenetrable . . . Nowadays, the surest way of keeping a secret is to publish it. Paradoxically, to censor is to broadcast, and to publish is to repress."

—————. "The Minority Pace." *Library Journal*, 89:3923–25, 15 October 1964. **B119**
"Minorities should be wooed and catered to by the one institution deliberately designed, established, and maintained for them—the library . . . A good library is one that serves a sufficient number of individuals or minorities of one to justify its existence, and not so many individuals as to overwhelm service capabilities."

—————. "Seattle Takes Action on Salacious Literature." *Library Journal*, 72:712–13, 1 May 1947. **B120**
A committee, appointed by the Mayor to consider the spread of salacious literature, agreed upon a plan "to emphasize the good, play down and expose the bad, but not to resort to censorship which would be futile even if attempted."

Baum, Terry L. "On Obscene Matter: California's New Law." *Journal of the State Bar of California*, 36:625–35, July–August 1961. **B121**
The deputy legislative counsel of California discusses the new California law on obscene matter and its implication to the various media.

Baxter, A. B. "Censorship and Sex." *Maclean's Magazine*, 70:6, 47–48, 3 August 1957. **B122**
Censorship of obscenity in Great Britain.

Baxter, Richard. *Life of the Rev. Richard Baxter* . . . London, The Religious Tract Society, [186—?]. 160p. **B123**
Includes account of his trial for seditious libel.

[—————]. "Proceedings against Richard Baxter, clerk, for a seditious Libel, at Guildhall, before Lord Chief Justice Jeffreys, 1685." In Howell, *State Trials*, vol. 11, pp. 493–502 and in *Modern Reports*, vol. 3, pp. 68–69. (Also reported in Schroeder, *Constitutional Free Speech* . . . , pp. 302–4) **B124**
This English minister was brought to trial in 1685 for his book, *A Paraphrase upon the New Testament*, critical of orthodox Christianity and of the bishops of the established church. The court presided over by the notorious Jeffreys, found Baxter guilty of sedition. Baxter was unable or unwilling to pay his fine of £500 and so spent two years in prison. In 1688 Baxter's book, *Holy Commonwealth or Political Aphorisms Opening the True Principles of Government*, was burned at Oxford.

Bayle, Pierre. *An Explanation Concerning Obscenities.* (Appeared originally in the 2d ed. of Bayle's *Dictionnaire Historique et Critique*; English edition, edited by M. Des Maizeaux, London, D. Midwinter, 1738, vol. 5, pp. 837–58; published separately (1879) in Bruxelles as *Sur les obscénités*; reprinted in Schroeder, *Free Press Anthology*, pp. 114–48) **B125**
This French rationalist was cited by the consistory of the Church for alleged obscenities in his famous dictionary (1697). He was required to make alterations in the second edition. In his explanation concerning obscenities (Eclaircissement sur les Obscénités) Bayle anticipates most of the present-day objections to frankness in sex expression. Henry S. Ashbee considers this essay "one of the most just, liberal, and forcible strictures ever written" on the subject of obscenity. In volume 10, page 330, of the English edition, Bayle also discusses defamatory libel, noting that "those who are pleased with reading defamatory libels, so far as to approve the authors and dispensers of them, are as guilty as if they had composed them."

Bayley, *Sir* John. *Speech in Passing sentence on Richard Carlile, in the Court of King's Bench, Nov. 16, 1819, for Publishing The Age of Reason and for Reprinting Palmer's Principles of Nature.* London, [1819]. 12p. **B126**

A Beacon Set on Fire. London, 1652. 16p. (Includes an *Index Expurgatorius* of "popish" books) **B127**
A group of Presbyterian stationers and printers, known as the "Beacon Firers," protested the publication of popish and sectarian books. They suggested a strict licensing system administered by "godly men," with the fines for violations awarded to the informer. The Levellers answered this appeal with *Beacons Quenched*.

Beacons Quenched. London, Printed by Henry Hills, 1652. **B128**
The Levellers charged the stationers with wanting to suppress the press in the interest of Presbyterianism. The stationers answered with a pamphlet entitled: *The Beacon Flameing* . . . The stationers issued *A Second Beacon Fired by Scintilla.* For the Levellers' answer to *A Second Beacon* see John Goodwin's *Fresh Discovery* . . . William M. Clyde gives a detailed account of the "Beacon Firers" in his *Struggle for the Freedom of the Press*, pp. 225 ff.

Beale, Howard K. "Freedom for the School Teacher." *Annals of the American Academy of Political and Social Science*, 200:119–43, November 1938. **B129**
Includes a section on censorship of textbooks and a review of the subjects which most frequently cause trouble—religion, science, history, politics, patriotism, peace and war, social and economic questions, and radicalism.

Beard, Charles A. "Count Karolyi and America." *Nation*, 120:347–48, 1 April 1925. **B130**
Address given at an American Civil Liberties Union meeting honoring Count Michael Karolyi. The State Department, at the request of the rulers of Hungary, had refused Count Karolyi permission to speak or write, but modified the directive to permit him to speak, but not on politics. Mr. Beard's address is a protest against the decision as an insult to the intelligence of the American people.

—————. "Freedom of Speech and Press." In his *The Republic*, New York, Viking, 1944, pp. 149–63. **B131**
The author discusses with his imaginary friends, Doctor and Mrs. Smyth, the meaning of the First Amendment and its interpretation by the courts. Particular attention is given to the operation of the laws against sedition and espionage and to court decisions relating thereto.

—————. "Great American Tradition." *Nation*, 123:7–8, 7 July 1926. (Reprinted in Beman, *Censorship of Speech and the Press*, pp. 28–34) **B132**
Historian Beard traces the development of the idea of freedom of the press from the time of

Jefferson to the sedition legislation of World War I. He urges that during peacetime we consider the implications of wartime sedition. He quotes Justice Hughes as wondering whether, in view of the severity of peacetime sedition laws, "this republic could survive another great war."

————. "In defense of Civil Liberties." *Current History*, 44:66–68, April 1936. **B 133**

Includes comments on the U.S. Supreme Court decision declaring void the Louisiana statute imposing a tax on newspaper revenues.

————. "On the Advantages of Censorship and Espionage." *New Republic*, 27: 350–51, 24 August 1921. **B 134**

Commenting on the Lusk "subversive activities" bills before the New York legislature, Beard recalls the experience of the French in the mid-eighteenth century, when an edict against criticism of the government only stimulated such writing. The tyranny "revealed the system from which it sprang and multiplied its enemies." Secondly, it sharpened the wits of writers in their efforts to evade the law and thus improved French literature. Thirdly, it produced more writing than would have otherwise occurred, and fourthly, it made the forbidden more attractive. He quotes a wit who wrote in 1767: "It is necessary now for a publisher to beg a magistrate to burn a book in order to make it sell."

Beattie, A. M., and Frank A. Underhill. "Sense and Censorship: On Behalf of Peyton Place." *Canadian Library Association Bulletin*, 15:9–16, July 1958. **B 135**

Text of the testimony of a professor of English and a former professor of history in behalf of *Peyton Place* at a hearing before the Canadian Tariff Board. The Board handed down a majority ruling which permitted the entry of the book into Canada. The statements give "a distinction between obscenity and realism in literature and an interpretation of modern fiction."

Beatty, Joseph M., Jr. "An Essay in Critical Biography—Charles Churchill." *PMLA*, 35:226–46, 1920. **B 136**

Biography of the profligate but fearless coauthor, with John Wilkes, of the suppressed *North Briton*.

Beaty, John O. "Censorship, Gangs, and the Tyranny of Minorities." In *Image of Life*. New York, Nelson, 1940, pp. 131–53. **B 137**

Freedom of the press in the United States is threatened by publishers themselves in their glorification of vice and in their deliberate deceptions. The author recommends self-censorship, citing as a good example the British press censorship in the Simpson-

Edward VII affair and American Catholic pressures against bad films. The latter efforts, he believes, should be extended to print. The world is tired of obscenities imposed on the majority by the minority.

Beck, James M. *Constitutionality of the New Federal Law Regulating Journalism*. New York, 1912. 17 p. **B 138**

The law requires publicity as to owners of periodical publications.

————. *Jefferson and the Liberty of the Press*. n.p., 1931. 13 p. mimeo. **B 139**

Address given 20 October 1931 by a Pennsylvania Representative at the dedication of a room at Jefferson's Monticello to the liberty of the press.

Beck, John B., *et al. Report of the Trial on an Indictment for Libel in "The American Lancet," Containing the Whole Evidence, Speeches etc. Accusers in Behalf of the State, Drs. J. B. Beck, E. G. Ludlow and Others against J. G. Vought, Wm. Anderson and Samuel Osborn*. New York, 1831. 48 p. **B 140**

Becker, Callie. "Censorship Workshop at A.S.U." *Arizona Librarian*, 21:7–8, Winter 1964. **B 141**

Report on a workshop in Censorship and Controversial Books held by the Department of Library Science at Arizona State University, Summer 1964.

Becker, Carl L. *Freedom and Responsibility in the American Way of Life*. New York, Vintage Books, 1958. 135 p. (First published, 1945) **B 142**

Chapter 2, Freedom of Speech and Press. If freedom of speech and the press are to be maintained "the people must have sufficient intelligence and honesty to maintain them with a minimum of legal compulsion."

Becker, William, and John H. Colburn. *Pre-Verdict Publicity Dialogue*. Columbia, Mo., Freedom of Information Center, School of Journalism, University of Missouri, 1964. 6 p. (Publication no. 124) **B 143**

Points of view of the bar and the news media in the matter of fair trial and fair news coverage, presented at the University of Missouri's Joint Conference on News Coverage of Crime and the Courts.

Beckerly, J. G. "Government Control of Technical Data." *Confluence*, 5:147–57, July 1956. **B 144**

"The secrets we keep are determined by small groups of men, often unidentified to the general public." The author calls for an overall government policy and review by a competent body acting in the public interest.

"Becoming Intolerable." *Crucible*, 3:1, 8, February 1920. **B 145**

Reprint of a statement from the Seattle *Union Record* that the *New Republic* and *Survey* are excluded from the high school library.

Bedborough, George. "Comstock Rex." *Adult*, 2:63–65, April 1898. **B 146**

The editor reports on the American suppression of publications of D. M. Bennett (*Truth Seeker*) and Dr. Kime, editor of the *Iowa Medical Journal. The Firebrand*, Emil Ruedebusch's *Our New Humanity*, and Oswald Dawson's *Outcome of Legitimation* are also reported on.

[————]. "Police and the Press; Scotland Yard Censorship." *Review of Reviews*, 18:162, 15 August 1898. **B 147**

Bedborough was arrested for selling Havelock Ellis' *Studies in the Psychology of Sex*.

[————]. "Trial of George Bedborough; Verbatim Report." *Adult*, 2:333–38, December 1898. **B 148**

Bedborough was brought to trial on obscenity charges for selling Ellis' *Studies in the Psychology of Sex; The Adult*, of which he was editor; and Oswald Dawson's *Outcome of Legitimation*. Much to the embarrassment of the Free Press Defence Committee, formed in his behalf, Bedborough pleaded, guilty. Schroeder, in his *Free Speech Bibliography*, states that Bedborough was both fearful of the competency and honesty of his lawyer and wanted to protect one of his financial backers who "had a skeleton in his closet." Reports on the Bedborough trial consumed most of the second volume of *The Adult*. In the December 1898 issue (p. 331) Bedborough writes an apology to his friends and supporters for letting them down. The article is entitled, George Bedborough: Coward.

Bedford, Arthur. *Evil and Danger of Stageplays: Shewing their Natural Tendency to Destroy Religion, and Introduce a General Corruption of Manners, in Almost Two Thousand Instances, Taken from the Plays of the Last Two Years . . .* Bristol, Eng., Bonny, 1706. 227 p. **B 149**

The author, a vicar in Bristol, was an associate of Jeremy Collier in a crusade against the stage which he charged was a promoter of vice and a blasphemer of religion.

————. *Serious Remonstrance in Behalf of the Christian Religion, against the Horrid Blasphemies and Impieties Which Are Still Used in the English Play-houses*. London, Hammond, 1719. 383 p. **B 150**

Bedinger, Margery. "Censorship of Books by the Library." *Libraries*, 36:390–95, November 1931. **B 151**

The author is concerned with "books of literature or fiction that have been kept away from the public on the pleas of the danger they carried to the morals of the young." It is her contention that "instead of keeping information away from youth, it is rather our duty to let them have all we can give them, provided it is true knowledge sincerely expressed." Emotion and sentiment instead of logic and scientific investigation have too often determined decisions.

Beecher, Edward. *Narrative of Riots at Alton: in Connection with the Death of Rev. Elijah P. Lovejoy.* Alton, Ill., George Holtman, 1838. 159p. (Reprinted with an introduction by Robert Merideth. New York, Dutton, 1965. 98p. Dutton Paperback) **B152**
A contemporary account of the "premeditated murder" of Lovejoy, written by his friend the president of Illinois College. Rev. Beecher describes Lovejoy as "the first martyr in America to the great principles of the freedom of speech and of the press." Lovejoy was an abolitionist editor who lost four printing presses and finally his life at the hands of a mob. Beecher notes in the introduction that the original manuscript sent from Jacksonville, Illinois, to New York never arrived and "must either have been lost or otherwise disposed of." The introduction to the 1965 edition is entitled "Edward Beecher's *Narrative* and Conservative Abolitionism."

Beford, Sybille. "The Last Trial of *Lady Chatterley*." *Esquire*, 55(4):132–55, April 1961. **B153**
A novelist's detailed report of the trial, *Crown v. Penguin Books, Ltd.*, before Mr. Justice Byrne and a jury at the Central Criminal Court, London, 20 October–2 November 1960, in which D. H. Lawrence's *Lady Chatterley's Lover*, is found to be not obscene under Britain's Obscene Publications Act of 1959. The book was for the first time in Great Britain judged as a whole, with its literary merit permitted as a justification, and with expert evidence allowed.

Beichman, Arnold. "The Unmanageable Issue behind 'Managed News'!" *Columbia University Forum*, 6(2):4–10, Spring 1963. **B154**
"A press fretful about 'managed news' might remember that it cannot be both critic and confidant of government when survival of the nation, or the earth itself, is in peril." The real issue is: "Does democracy today charge us to place in the hands of a civilian Chief Executive the power to issue ultimatums, to respond to hostile actions or not to respond, to do nothing, when whatever he alone decides may become, as never before, irrevocable for eternity?"

Beinart, B. "Postal Censorship." *South African Law Journal*, 67:350–71, November 1950. **B155**

A review and criticism of South African postal regulations permitting clandestine censorship, probably never intended by the Legislature.

Bell, Clair H. "What the Censor Saw." *University Chronicle* (University of California), 21:347–68, 1919. **B156**
Censorship in the United States during World War I.

Bell, Clive. *On British Freedom.* London, Chatto and Windus, 1923. 86p. **B157**
A caustic and sometimes witty attack on present-day restriction of British freedoms including sex expression in literature.

Bell, Edward P. *The British Censorship. An Examination of This Institution, and of the General Position of American Correspondents in London, from the Point of View of One of Their Number . . .* London, Unwin, [1916]. 21p. **B158**
Criticism of British military censorship given in an address before the American Luncheon Club, London, 19 November 1915. "The Censorship is discharging its function improperly and has become a grave menace to the successful prosecution of the war." The charges are answered by "Libra" in the March 1916 issue of *English Review.*

———. "Foes of Press Freedom." *Quill*, 28(9):13, 16, September 1940. **B159**
Government and wealth may be foes of press freedom, but the deadliest foe is the self-applied censorship.

Bell, Howard H. "The Relativity of Freedom." *Journal of Broadcasting*, 5:199–204, Summer 1961. **B160**
"Mr. Bell holds that freedom of speech guarantees should apply to the communication of ideas, regardless of the technology of the medium; and that flourishing economic competition should dispel fears resulting from technological monopoly." He believes that "while it is technologically essential that the allocation of spectrum space be controlled, the program output must be left to the free interplay of the market-place."

[Bell, Robert]. *A Few more Words, on the Freedom of the Press, Addressed by the Printer, to the Friends of Liberty in America.* Philadelphia, Robert Bell, 1776. 4p. (Appended to Josiah Tucker, *The True Interest of Britain, set forth in regard to the Colonies . . .* published by Robert Bell) **B161**
"If new modes of Government, are either in reality, or in appearance, approaching towards the inhabitants of America; it is more peculiarly necessary on these extraordinary occasions, that the liberty of the press should be freely exerted: For, if in these changes, we do not fully retain all our present happy privileges, but weakly suffer any restrictions or curtailings of liberty to advance upon us with new

establishments, it will afterwards be next to impossible, to regain the desirable possession."

Bell, W. S. *Liberty and Morality; a Speech by W. S. Bell at the New York Free Thinkers Convention at Watkins, August 26, 1882.* Boston, W. S. Bell, 1882. 36p. **B162**
References to censorship of literature dealing with sex education, pp. 16–19.

Bellamy, Paul. *Challenge of War to Freedom of the Press.* New York, Department of Journalism, New York University, 1943. 19p. **B163**

———. "Why Print Crime News?" In *Attorney General's Conference on Crime. Proceedings, 1934.* Washington, D.C., Govt. Print. Off., 1936, pp. 86–97. **B164**
"I regard the publication of crime news as one of the primary obligations of a newspaper, arising out of its mission to improve society. I believe that we shall not make a better society on the hush-hush method." The author was then editor of the Cleveland *Plain Dealer*.

Bellanger, Claude. *Press Clandestine, 1940–1944.* Paris, Armand Colin, 1961. 264p. **B165**
The story of the underground newspapers in Europe during World War II.

Belle, Minnie. *Public Library Practices in the Exclusion and Restriction of Printed Materials.* New York, School of Library Service, Columbia University, 1941. 95p. (Unpublished Master's thesis) **B166**

Belloc, Hilaire. *The Free Press.* London, Allen & Unwin, 1918. 102p. **B167**
A group of essays attacking "the evils of the modern capitalist press" and in defense of "its correction by the formation of small independent organs." Originally published serially in *The New Age.*

———. "Modern Life; the Source of Information." *English Review*, 1:799–808, March 1909. **B168**
"The whole mass of public information upon which Englishmen depend for the nourishment of public opinion, has long been, and is now everywhere admitted to be tarnished at the source." Belloc detects a conspiracy of secrecy that can only be combatted by public opinion which develops an attitude that "mistrusts secrecy above all things, and would actively punish, in some social way, every alias, and every anonymity." Belloc demonstrates how he would name names; the editors, however, mindful of British libel laws and also to reinforce Belloc's thesis, have deleted the names by black slugs of type.

Bellowings of a Wild-Bull. [London, 1680].
3 p.   **B 169**
A pamphlet attacking Chief Justice William
Scroggs for his attempts to suppress the Whig
press. Scroggs is depicted as a wild bull who
roared that whoever invented the heretical
art of printing should be "frying in hell."

Bellows, Henry A. "Is Radio Censored?"
Harper's, 171:697–709, November 1935.
(Excerpted in Summers, *Radio Censorship*,
pp. 102–3)   **B 170**
"It is censored by the Federal Communications
Commission, despite the law, through interference with program quality and content,
made possible by the threat of refusal to
renew licenses; it is censored by the broadcasters themselves because, owing to the
limitation of facilities, they cannot do otherwise." There is no censorship in the sense of
denial of the air to critics of the administration.

[Belmont, August]. *A History of the Libel
Suit of Clarence H. Venner against August
Belmont. How a plaintiff who had been called
a practical blackmailer discontinued his suit for
libel when confronted with an order for his
examination as to the truth of the charges.*
[New York, 1913?] 155 p.   **B 171**
Venner had distributed circulars attacking
the management of the Interborough Rapid
Transit Company and assailing the validity
of a bond issue. Both suits were dismissed by
Judge Hough in the U.S. District Court
because "complainant has shown no right to
maintain these actions."

Beltran, Pedro G. "Freedom of the Press
in a Republic." In *The Enduring American
Press.* Hartford, Conn., *Hartford Courant*
and Connecticut Mutual Life, 1964,
pp. 7–10.   **B 172**
The publisher of *La Prensa* of Lima, Peru, and
president of the Inter American Press Association discusses the struggle for press freedom in Latin America, in which he has played
a part. The occasion of the talk is the 200th
anniversary of the *Hartford Courant.*

Beman, Lemar T., *comp. Selected Articles on
Censorship of Speech and the Press.* New York,
Wilson, 1930. 507 p. (Wilson Handbooks,
series 3, vol. 5)   **B 173**
A compilation of articles dealing with various
aspects of censorship, pro and con, arranged
so that the material might be useful to
debaters. Part I deals with general background
and history; Part II deals with free speech,
particularly as it relates to propaganda for the
overthrow of the United States Government;
Part III considers the Minnesota Nuisance
Law that had just been upheld by the Minnesota Supreme Court; and Part IV considers the
proposition that the federal government create
a Board of Review for all books of fiction, with
power to deny copyright to obscene works
and exclude them from the mails.

————. *Selected Articles on Censorship of the
Theater and Motion Pictures.* New York,
Wilson, 1931. 385 p. (Wilson Handbooks,
series 3, vol. 6)   **B 174**
A collection of articles, pro and con, compiled
to assist debaters.

[Benbow, William]. *The Trial of William
Benbow, for publishing certain Libels (alledged
to be licentious), in "The Rambler's Magazine," and a Translation of a French Romance,
entitled "The Amours of the Chevalier Fau-
blas;" with a full report of the eloquent and
successful Speech of the Celebrated Irish
Barrister, C. Phillips, Esq. against the Society
for the Suppression of Vice.* London, Printed
for Wilson and Smith, 1822. 21 p. (Also
in Macdonell, *Report of State Trials*, vol. 6,
pp. 228 ff.)   **B 175**
Benbow, a Strand bookseller and publisher,
was prosecuted for the sale of a French novel,
but was found not guilty when it was proved
that an English translation had been available
in English circulating libraries for more than
30 years. This was the first time in its 19 years
that the vice society failed to get a conviction
in a case of obscene libel. Benbow is said to
have pirated Byron's *Cain* and to have published
anything anyone was likely to object to.

Bendiner, Robert, "The FCC—Who Will
Regulate the Regulators?" *Reporter*, 17:
26–30, 19 September 1957.   **B 176**
A criticism of the FCC, an agency administered
by men who are reluctant to regulate—"A
regulatory system of regulation by anti-
regulators." Reference is made to the investigation of FCC by the House Subcommittee
on Legislative Oversight.

Benenson, Peter. *A Free Press.* London,
Fabian Society, 1961. 36 p. (Fabian Research Series, 223)   **B 177**
A discussion of freedom of the press in relation
to the individual, the state, the newspaper
owners, the journalists, and the advertisers.

————. "The Law's Pressures on the
British Press." *IPI Report* (International
Press Institute), 11:1–2, Janaury 1963.
                                           B 178
A British lawyer comments, generally in
agreement, on the charges made by Cecil
Harmsworth King in a report of the General
Council of the Press, that the British press
operates under oppressive legal censorship.

Benét, Stephen Vincent. *They Burned the
Books.* New York, Farrar and Rinehart,
1942. 25 p. (Reprinted in *Wilson Library
Bulletin*, May 1945, and in Benét, *We
Stand United*)   **B 179**
A radio play, written at the request of the
American Writers' War Board to remind the
world of the declaration of war against mankind that took place 10 May 1933. On this date
the Nazis made a bonfire of 25,000 books in
which men had set down their belief in
themselves.

[Benjafield, John, *plaintiff*]. *Statement of
Facts, together with the Trial of the Printer
and Proprietor of the "County Chronicle" for
a libel, 22nd December 1812.* Bury Saint
Edmunds, Eng., [1813].   **B 180**
Benjafield, former publisher of the paper,
brought suit against the present publisher
J. Wheble, for accusing him of accepting a
government annuity for suppressing information. Benjafield lost the suit.

Benjamin, Harry. "Sex Censorship in
Medicine." *Sex and Censorship*, 2:4–16,
Spring 1958.   **B 181**

Benjamin, Hazel C. "Lobbying for Birth
Control." *Public Opinion Quarterly*, 2:
48–60, January 1938.   **B 182**
A description of techniques used by the
National Committee on Federal Legislation
for Birth Control during the years leading
up to the decision of the Second Circuit Court
of Appeals in the case of *U.S. v. One Package . . . ,*
dismissing a federal libel suit against contraceptive materials.

Benn, *Sir* Ernest J. P. *The BBC Monopoly.*
London, Individualist Bookshop, 1941.
23 p. (Post-war Questions, no. 6)   **B 183**
A British publisher criticizes the British
Broadcasting Corporation as a government
monopoly that tends to standardize opinion.
While crediting the BBC with doing a good
job in an impossible task, he recommends
legislation to insure effective competition in
the radio broadcasting industry.

Bennett, Arnold. "Censorship by the
Libraries." In his *Books and Persons . . .*
London, Chatto & Windus, 1917, pp.
167–77; 181–94.   **B 184**
A collection of satirical comments originally
appearing in *The New Age* during the hubbub
caused by British circulating libraries setting
up a censorship committee to screen current
novels. Comments on the committee's passing
of Elinor Glyn's novel, *His Hour*, also elicit a
satirical essay (pp. 271–77). The suppression
of passages in certain editions of Oscar Wilde's
De Profundis is discussed on pp. 217–21.

————. ["On Censorship"]. *Authors'
League Bulletin*, 15(1):18, April 1927.
                                           B 185
"I regard censorship as a great nuisance to a
respectable dramatist, but as a smaller nuisance
than the absence of censorship." Some controls
over drama are necessary and the present
British system works fairly well.

———. "The Public and the Censor." *Harper's Weekly*, 59:508–10, 28 November 1914. **B186**

Bennett offers suggestions for ways to comprehend the principles on which the wartime censorship works so that the British public may be able to judge facts accurately concerning the war and not "live in a world of illusions."

Bennett, De Robigné M. *Anthony Comstock; His Career of Cruelty and Crime. A Chapter from "The Champions of the Church"* by D. M. Bennett. New York, Liberal and Scientific Publishing House, 1878, pp. 1009–1119. **B187**

"Those who in the name of morality and the Christian religion have been persecuted and annoyed." Bennett cites 26 cases prosecuted by Comstock: Charles Mackey, James Sullivan, Leander Fox & Sons, Mrs. Woodhull and Miss Claflin, George Francis Train, John A. Lant, Mr. Simpson, Hunter & Co., David Massey, Dr. John Botts, Mr. Kendell, Mr. Weil, Dr. William Morrison, Charles Conroy, Dr. E. B. Foote, Dr. E. C. Abbey, John Manning, A. Prosch, Charles F. Blandin, Louis Wengenrath, Edgar W. Jones, E. H. Heywood, D. M. Bennett, Frank Rivers, Edward W. Baxter, and Madam Restell. The cases range from the criminal abortionist and pornographer to the respectable bookseller and the sex educator.

———. *Eighth and Last Letter from Ludlow Street Jail, Where Obscenity Is.* New York, D. M. Bennett, 1879. 79 p. (Truth Seeker Tracts, no. 162) **B188**

———. *From Behind the Bars; a Series of Letters Written in Prison, by D. M. Bennett ... Imprisoned Ostensibly for Depositing Prohibited Matter in the Mail, but Really for Entertaining and Speaking His Honest Convictions.* New York, Liberal and Scientific Publishing House, 1879. 565 p. **B189**

A collection of letters, most of which were published in Bennett's paper, *Truth Seeker.*

———. *Letters from the Albany Penitentiary. By the Editor of the Truth Seeker, While Serving Out an Unjust Sentence.* New York, D. M. Bennett, 1880. Various paging. (Four of the letters are Truth Seeker Tracts, nos. 165–68) **B190**

———. *An Open Letter to Samuel Colgate Touching the Conduct of Anthony Comstock and the New York Society for the Suppression of Vice.* New York, D. M. Bennett, 1879. 93 p. **B191**

For more than 20 years Colgate, a soap manufacturer, was president of the New York Society for the Suppression of Vice.

———. *Trial of D. M. Bennett in the United States Circuit Court, Judge Charles L. Benedict, Presiding, New York, March 18, 19, 20 and 21, 1879, upon the Charge of Depositing Prohibited Matter in the Mail ...* New York, Truth Seeker Office, 1879. 189 p. **B192**

Bennett was the iconoclastic editor of the *Truth Seeker*, a weekly paper devoted to free thought and a crusade against the vice societies. Anthony Comstock considered Bennett the embodiment of all that was vile and blasphemous. In 1878 Bennett, then aged 60, was arrested for selling a copy of Ezra Heywood's *Cupid's Yokes*, a birth control pamphlet. He was convicted of mailing obscene matter and sentenced to 13 months at hard labor. His case became a cause célèbre for liberals and Bennett achieved the martyrdom he seemed to be seeking. Broken in health, Bennett died within a year and a half of his release.

Bennett, Edward H. *An Investigation of Censorship in the Libraries of Massachusetts.* Boston, School of Library Science, Simmons College, 1953. 43 p. (Unpublished Master's thesis) **B193**

[Bennett, George C.]. *The Strong-Bennett Libel Suit. Senator Demas Strong v. George C. Bennett. Proprietor Brooklyn Daily Times. Damages Claimed, $10,000, as Found by the Jury, Six Cents ...* Brooklyn, 1866. 151 p. **B194**

The charge against Bennett was for accusations of bribery which appeared in his Brooklyn paper.

Bennett, James O. *Deceiving the Whole World. American Newspaper Men Arrested in London for Telling the Truth about Germany—A Personal Letter.* Chicago, The Chicago Tribune, 1914. 4 p. (Reprinted from the *Chicago Tribune*, 6 October 1914) **B195**

Bennett, a *Chicago Tribune* correspondent, was later criticized by George Creel, chairman of the wartime Committee on Public Information, for sending pro-German cables from Stockholm.

Benson, Allan L. "Press Not Free to Give True Information to the People." *Pearson's Magazine*, 28(6):97–106, December 1912. **B196**

"The Federal Constitution guarantees free speech and a free press but we have neither. We have free speech just so long as it pleases city councils—and no further. We have free speech so long as we say nothing that displeases the men who run our towns—that's all. Our press is free of oppressive laws, but it is a long way from being free of advertisers. No newspaper prints much that would hurt a big advertiser ... —Editors." The article accuses

the press of protecting wealthy businessmen, of not telling the truth about political candidates, failure to inform the public of a lack of fire safety in department stores, accepting political subsidies (small town papers), suppressing facts about socialists and radicals. "Every line of politics they read in their newspapers should be read with suspicion. If it does not contain outright lies it probably at least suppresses the truth."

Bensusan, S. L. "Ghouls and Garbage in Literature." *Contemporary Review*, 188:336–39, November 1955. **B197**

An attack on the writers who besmirch the reputations of deceased famous persons and the publishers who publish such "garbage."

Bent, Silas. *Ballyhoo: The Voice of the Press.* New York, Boni, Liveright, 1927. 398 p. **B198**

A debunking account of the pressures that influence American journalism. Chapters 14 and 15 relate to the press and state.

———. *Newspaper Crusaders; a Neglected Story.* New York, Whittlesey House, 1939. 313 p. **B199**

Includes chapters on Colonial newspaper editors who fought for freedom, editors who were persecuted under the Alien and Sedition Acts, and editors who were martyrs in the fight against slavery.

Bentham, Jeremy. *The Elements of the Art of Packing, as applied to Special Juries, particularly in Cases of Libel Law.* London, Effingham Wilson, 1821. 269 p. (Also in his *Works*, Edinburgh, William Tait, 1843, vol. 5, pp. 65–186) **B200**

Bentham attacked the system of keeping a corps of special jurors who were paid by and took their orders from the agents of the Crown. The jury packing was an issue in the libel trials of John Horne Tooke and T. J. Wooler. When Bentham's work was first published in 1821, a note in the edition indicated that the work had been printed many years earlier (1809) but "circumstances prevented its being at that time exposed to sale." If the causes of the suppression were brought to view, the note states, "those causes would afford a striking illustration of the baneful principles and practices [this work] is employed in unveiling."

———. "Liberty and Licentiousness of the Press." In his *Book of Fallacies.* London, John Hunt, 1824. (Also in his *Works*, Edinburgh, William Tait, 1843, vol. 2, pp. 451–53, "Sham Distinctions") **B201**

Bentham attacks the "sham popular distinction" between "liberty" and "license." Licentiousness of the press, he points out, is charged when suppression is to the advantage of the government. Liberty of the press is the right of any expression that does not inconvenience those in power.

————. *On the Liberty of the Press, and Public Discussion.* London, Printed for William Hone, 1821. 38p. (Also in his *Works*, Edinburgh, William Tait, 1843, vol. 2, pp. 275–97) **B 202**

This philosopher, jurist, and political theorist took an active part in the struggle for a free press during the last decade of his life, defending both Carlile and Cobbett, though he disagreed with many of the ideas of the former and personally disliked the latter. The present work is written in the form of a series of letters to the Spanish people in opposition to a proposed censorship law. The letters were not delivered in time to prevent the objectionable law from passage, but the pamphlet was widely distributed in England. In his *Fragment on Government*, Bentham took issue with Blackstone's limited concept of a free press. He believed a man should be free to "make known his complaints and remonstrances to the whole community" and that the people should "practice every mode of opposition short of actual revolt, before the executive power can be legally justified in disturbing them."

————. *Truth v. Ashhurst; or, Law As It Is, Contrasted with What It Is Said to Be.* London, Richard Carlile, 1823. 16p. (Written in December 1792; first published in 1823. Also in his *Works*, Edinburgh, William Tait, 1843, vol. 5, pp. 231–37) **B 203**

Bentham in this first work on freedom of the press, attacked the English common law of libel as being judge-made and dangerously undefinable. He comments on the practice of excluding truth as a defense in libel cases: "I fear this paper is a sad libel—there is so much truth in it." Bentham wrote this essay in 1792 in answer to a charge delivered to a grand jury by Sir William Ashhurst, Judge of King's Bench, and printed by the Constitutional Association of that time, but Bentham's essay was not printed until 1823.

Bentley, Eric. "Release the *Evergreen Review!*" *Village Voice*, 9(33):5, 4 June 1964. **B 204**

A Grove Press advertisement reprinting an editorial in which the theater critic urges the police to release the 20,000 copies of *Evergreen Review* seized at the bindery in Nassau County on orders of the District Attorney for alleged obscenity.

Benton, Josiah H., Jr. *A Notable Libel Case. The Criminal Prosecution of Theodore Lyman, Jr. by Daniel Webster in the Supreme Judicial Court of Massachusetts, November Term, 1828.* Boston, Goodspeed, 1904. 117p. **B 205**

Lyman was a wealthy Bostonian who supported Jackson in the election of 1828. An article by Lyman in the *Jackson Republican* (29 October 1828) so infuriated Webster that he sued Lyman for criminal libel, alleging that Lyman had accused him and other Federalists of wishing to break up the Union and reannex New England to England. The jury could not agree and the case was dismissed.

Benton, Paul. "If This Be Heresy——" *Quill*, 19(1):9, January 1931. **B 206**

Individuals have rights just as newspapers have rights; there are two sides to freedom.

Benton, William L. "Freedom of Information: the Role of the State Department." *Department of State Bulletin*, 16:352–67, 23 February 1947. **B 207**

The Assistant Secretary of State reviews the campaign for a free world press being waged through the United Nations.

————, and Paul Porter. "Freedom of the Press—World Wide." *Department of State Bulletin*, 14:156–62, 3 February 1946. **B 208**

The role of the United Nations in establishment of world freedom of information. Economic factors form a major barrier in the international transmission of news.

Berg, Louis. "How End the Panic in Radio-TV? The Demagogic Half-Truth v. the Liberal Half-Lie." *Commentary*, 14:315–25, October 1952. **B 209**

A proposal on how to clear innocent performers, unjustly accused by *Red Channels* of Communist associations.

Berger, Marcel, and Paul Allard. *Les Secrets de la censure pendant la guerre.* Paris, Éditions des Portiques, 1932. 383p. **B 210**

Exposé of allied military censorship in Paris during World War I, written by former censors.

Bergman, Robert E. "Should We Censor Political Broadcasts or Risk Liability for Defamation." *South Dakota Law Review*, 4:173–80, Spring 1959. **B 211**

Deals with the dilemma created by the *Port Huron* decision of the Federal Communications Commission, 12 F.C.C. 1069 (1948).

Bergson, Philip. "State Censorship of Television." *Federal Bar Journal*, 10:151–61, April 1949. **B 212**

"Censorship of television film programs by state authorities represents a radical departure from the concept of uniform regulation and imposes a heavy economic burden that will fatally retard the development of the infant industry."

Berkman, Alexander. "*Blast* Raided." *Mother Earth*, 11:726–27, January 1917. **B 213**

The Blast was an anarchist periodical edited by Berkman, which came under government surveillance for its antimilitary expression during World War I.

————, and Emma Goldman. *Anarchism on Trial; Speeches . . . before United States District Court in the City of New York, July.* [New York, 1917]. 87p. (Reprinted from *Mother Earth*, July 1917) **B 214**

The authors were convicted under the wartime espionage act for issuing pamphlets urging disobedience to the draft.

Berkowitz, Leonard. "The Effects of Observing Violence." *Scientific American*, 210(2):35–41, February 1964. **B 215**

"Experiments suggest that aggression depicted in television and motion picture dramas, or observed in activity, can arouse certain members of the audience to violent action." The findings have a direct bearing on discussions of the harm or lack of harm to the immature viewer observing violence. The author concludes that "effective catharsis [offered as a defense of violence in TV] occurs only when an angered person perceives that his frustrater has been aggressively injured. From this I argue that filmed violence is potentially dangerous. The motion picture aggressivism has increased the chance that an angry person, and possibly other people as well, will attack someone else."

Berkson, Seymour. "Facing the Foreign Censor." *Journalism Quarterly*, 13:7–16, March 1936. **B 216**

Efforts by European dictators to restrain American correspondents.

————. "Freedom of the Press and American Foreign Policy." In Quincy Wright, ed., *Foreign Policy for the United States.* Chicago, University of Chicago Press, 1947, pp. 339–48. **B 217**

"Only if such universal freedom of information becomes an accepted and established fact in our global life shall we be truly on the road to mutual understanding and real world peace." The author appeals for greater attention to world freedom of communication as a dynamic weapon against international hatreds and misunderstanding.

Berman, Manuel K. "Regulation of Radio Broadcasting." *Boston University Law Review*, 13:60–73, January 1933. (Reprinted in Buehler, *American v. British System of Radio Control*, pp. 202–19) **B 218**

A review of the development of regulatory legislation, including the Radio Act of 1927 which is discussed in detail. The author recommends extending the powers of the Federal Radio Commission.

Bernays, Edward L. "Needed: A Grand Strategy." *Saturday Review of Literature*, 25(10):10, 7 March 1942. **B 219**
Editorial in a special issue devoted to censorship and propaganda. The issue also includes Bernay's review of Mock's *Censorship, 1917*.

Bernberg, Benedict. "Freedom to Read." *Times Literary Supplement*, 3194:357, 17 May 1963. **B 220**
A letter to the editor discussing the powers of British customs, post office, and police to confiscate allegedly obscene matter, particularly as these powers are affected by the passage of the Obscene Publications Act of 1959.

Berndt, Frank. "Anti-Obscenity Legislation." *Western Reserve Law Review*, 12: 425–30, March 1961. **B 221**
Notes on *Commonwealth v. Blumenstein*, 396 Pa. 417, 153 A. 2d 227 (1959).

———. "A Free Press and a Fair Trial: England v. the United States." *Western Reserve Law Review*, 13:147–61, December 1961. **B 222**
A comparative study of the handling of the dilemma created by the conflicts of two democratic principles.

Berninghausen, David K. "Book Banning and Witch-Hunts." *ALA Bulletin*, 42: 204–7, May 1948. **B 223**
"All librarians must become acutely aware of the trend toward suppression of opinion. They must protest against all attempts at censorship and all legislation or acts of government agents that could threaten intellectual freedom." The author describes censorship attempts by various groups and efforts by librarians to combat them.

———. "The Case of *The Nation*." *American Scholar*, 19:44–55, Winter 1949–50. **B 224**
"The issue involved in *The Nation's* ban ⸢from the New York City schools⸣ is not the study of religious beliefs, nor is it tolerance versus intolerance . . . The issue is freedom of inquiry, freedom to examine alternative points of view before coming to a conclusion." Letters in the *American Scholar* for Spring 1950 (pp. 234–36) support and defend the charges made against the New York City Board of Education.

———. "Climate of Intellectual Freedom in America Today." *Michigan Librarian*, 28:5–11, March 1962. **B 225**

———. "Film Censorship." *ALA Bulletin*, 44:447–48, December 1950. **B 226**
An account of the restrictions placed on certain films at the Peoria (Ill.) Public Library after objections to them from the American Legion. The episode led the Council of the American Library Association to declare that the Library Bill of Rights shall apply to films and all media of communications used or collected by libraries.

———. "Free American Library." *Bulletin, New Hampshire Public Libraries*, 47:73–76, September 1951. **B 227**
In a talk before the New Hampshire Library Association, the author advises librarians to stress the importance of the Library Bill of Rights, to enlist the aid of respected citizens, and to adopt a positive program of book selection.

———. "Frontiers of Freedom." *Library Journal*, 76:1071–73, July 1951. **B 228**
Suggestions on how librarians can meet attacks of pressure groups, including the use of the Library Bill of Rights.

———. "History of the ALA Intellectual Freedom Committee." *Wilson Library Bulletin*, 27:813–17, June 1953. **B 229**
Talk given at the American Library History Round Table, Chicago, February 1953.

———. "Los Angeles County Has Censorship Board." *Library Journal*, 73:1545–46+, 1 November 1948. **B 230**
"Los Angeles County supervisors decided on September 28 to create a board of censors to examine all books in the county library. Each five supervisors will appoint one censor to control books purchased and circulated . . . In other cities attempts at censorship have been made by individuals or groups, but here is the first open creation of an *official* board of censors, appointed by county supervisors."

———. "On Keeping Our Reading Free." *Educational Leadership*, 6:104–8, November 1948. (Reprinted in *Educational Digest*, January 1949) **B 231**
"The seeker after knowledge is entitled to access to alternate views and the right to learn in an unbiased atmosphere . . . and the well-ordered school library offers this balanced set-up for freedom of thought and expression."

———. "Publicity Wins Intellectual Freedom." *ALA Bulletin*, 43:73–75, February 1949. **B 232**
The chairman of the ALA Committee on Intellectual Freedom describes recent incidents where censorship efforts collapsed when such activities were brought to the attention of scholars, educators, parents, publishers, and authors.

———. "The Right To Read." *Nation*, 175:30–31, 12 July 1952. **B 233**
A summary of the position of the American Library Association determined in its Committee on Intellectual Freedom meeting on the subject of the dissemination of information, 28 and 29 June. Quotations from members of the committee.

———, and Richard W. Faunce. "An Exploratory Study of Juvenile Delinquency and the Reading of Sensational Books." *Journal of Experimental Education*, 33:161–68, Winter 1964. **B 234**
The authors test the working hypothesis that there is no relationship between juvenile delinquency and the reading of "sensational books," matching 39 institutionalized juvenile delinquent boys with 39 nondelinquents. The study showed that delinquent boys were no more apt to have read sensational books than the nondelinquents, although they were more prone to have read adult books with erotic content. No inference of a causal relationship between delinquency and the reading of sensational books was made.

Berns, Walter F. *The Case of the Censored Librarian: Censorship of Obscenity*. Chicago, American Foundation for Continuing Education, 1959. 30p. (Case Stories in American Politics, no. 8) **B 235**
A fictional but plausible account of a public library board faced with charges, brought by a local society of Minute Women, of having obscene books on the library shelves. The issue, intended to stimulate adult group discussions, is presented objectively, without a conclusion.

———. *Freedom, Virtue and the First Amendment*. Baton Rouge, La., Louisiana State University Press, 1957. 264p. **B 236**
A review of what the author regards as widespread dissatisfaction with the U.S. Supreme Court decisions in First Amendment cases made in the 1950's. Includes a table of cases.

Bernstein, Charles. "Cameras in the Courtroom." *Quill*, 48(12):12–14+, December 1960. **B 237**
A review of Canon 35 of the American Bar Association, from its inception following the Lindbergh-Hauptmann trial to the present.

Bernstein, Harry. "Free Minds in the Americas." In Ángel del Río, ed., *Responsible Freedom in the Americas*. New York, Doubleday, 1955, pp. 224–38. **B 238**
On the "free circulation and exchange of ideas" between North and South America since 1700.

Berry, Dean L. "Validity of Motion Picture Licensing Statute." *Michigan Law Review*, 58:134–37, November 1959. **B 239**
Discussion of the U.S. Supreme Court ruling in *Kingsley International Pictures Corp. v. Regents of the University of the State of New York*, 360 U.S. 684 (1959). The distributor of the motion

picture, *Lady Chatterley's Lover*, had applied to the Motion Picture Division of the New York State Education Department for a license and became involved in decisions which eventually reached the Supreme Court. The Court ruled that the licensing statute was an unconstitutional restraint on free speech, since it denied a license to a film simply because it advocated certain ideas.

[Berry, Ira]. *The Liberty of the Press Vindicated and Truth Triumphant! State versus Ira Berry for an Alleged Libel on Cyrus Weston* . . . [Augusta, Maine? 1832?]. 20 p. **B 240**

"Victim of the desperation and folly of the federal party."

Berry, John L., and W. M. Goodrich. "Political Defamation—Radio's Dilemma." *University of Florida Law Review*, 1:343–59, Fall 1948. **B 241**
The radio broadcaster is faced with a conflict in opinions of the courts and the FCC as to whether he is liable for defamatory material presented by political candidates, who are given time in accordance with FCC directives. The authors recommend that Congress clarify the ambiguity of the Communications Act.

Berry, John N., III. "Demand for Dissent?" *Library Journal*, 89:3912–17, 15 October 1964. **B 242**
The article reports on a survey of public library coverage of "the fringes of political and social thoughts," responses from 100 public libraries on their holdings of periodicals on a "roster of dissent." The author found librarians generally willing to cooperate with the analysis. "In many libraries the attempt to provide material presenting all points of view is an emphatic success. More often, however, it is eroded by the reliance on selection criteria of doubtful validity—demand and available indexing—or it is left to chance . . . We are left with the feeling that public libraries in the United States continue, very cautiously, to cling to the middle of the road."

——. "'I Fear for the Ladies.'" *Bay State Librarian*, 53(2):9–10, 12 April 1963. **B 243**
Account of a hearing before a Committee of the Massachusetts legislature to consider a bill to abolish the state's Obscene Literature Control Commission. The Civil Liberties Union of Massachusetts and the Massachusetts Library Association supported the bill. "The censors irrelevantly used mother, God, and country, in old fashioned fourth of July style to overwhelm a committee of legislators, of politicians." The bill was reported unfavorably.

Bertram, G. B. "Young Girl." *New Zealand Librarian*, 14:244–46, September 1951. **B 244**

A public librarian comments on the traditional concern of patrons who wish to protect the young girl from the immorality of modern fiction. He notes that library books are sometimes burned by an irate patron (but only after they have been read through) "in an attempt to shift the conviction of sin in reading on to the source of supply or the corrupt writer."

Besant, Annie. *An Autobiography*. London, Unwin, 1893. 368 p. **B 245**
In 1877 this English theosophist and social reformer published, with Charles Bradlaugh, a birth control pamphlet entitled *Fruits of Philosophy*, a work written by the American physician, Charles Knowlton, and first published in 1832. They were tried on charges of immorality (*Regina v. Charles Bradlaugh and Annie Besant*) but were acquitted. "We are unanimously of opinion that the book in question is calculated to deprave public morals, but at the same time we entirely exonerate the defendants from any corrupt motives in publishing it." The trial attracted widespread attention in England and over 200,000 copies of the Knowlton booklet are said to have been sold within a few weeks.

——. *Is the Bible Indictable?* London, [Freethought Publishing Co., 1877?]. Pamphlet. **B 246**
During the obscenity trial for publishing Charles Knowlton's birth control pamphlet, Mrs. Besant published a series of articles in the *National Reformer* entitled, Does Not the Bible Come Within the Ruling of the Lord Chief Justice as to Obscene Literature? These were later condensed and issued as a separate pamphlet under the title *Is the Bible Indictable?* The pamphlet quotes some 150 Bible passages which, under existing English law, would likely be considered obscene.

Bess, Donovan. "Miller's *Tropic* on Trial." *Evergreen Review*, 6:12–37, March–April 1962. **B 247**
At the time of writing this article, at least 50 criminal cases had been brought to trial in the United States for the sale of Henry Miller's *Tropic of Cancer*. This is the dramatic account of the 9-day trial in San Rafael, Calif., in which Mark Schorer and other literary figures testified for the defense. The jury found the defendant not guilty.

[Best, Paul]. *To Certaine Noble and Honourable Persons of the House of Commons assembled in Parliament. The Petition of Paul Best, Prisoner in the Gate-house in Westminster*. London, 1646. **B 248**
In 1644 Best, an educated gentleman and student of theology, submitted his manuscript on the doctrine of the Trinity to a minister friend "for his Judgment and advice only." The "friend" turned the manuscript over to the authorities; Best was ordered by the House of Commons to be hanged for his offense. There was some dispute over the legality of the form of punishment for such an offense and, instead, he served three years in prison.

Beth, Loren P. "The Legion and the Library." *New Republic*, 127:11–13, 14 July 1952. (Reprinted in Daniels, *The Censorship of Books*, pp. 169–72) **B 249**
The attack on the film program of the Peoria (Ill.) Public Library by the Americanism Committee of American Legion Post No. 2, which precipitated a heated dispute over censorship. The films objected to as containing Communist propaganda were: *Brotherhood of Man*, *Boundary Lines*, and *Peoples of the USSR*. An explanatory reply to Beth's article by Hazel C. Wolf, member of the Peoria Public Library Board, appears in *New Republic* for 11 August 1952.

——. "Toward a Model Movie Censorship Law." *Massachusetts Review*, 2:770–74, Summer 1961. **B 250**
The author opposes a system of prior censorship of the movies on the grounds that it assumes guilt before there is reason to suppose that a crime has been committed; it does not allow a trial or even an administrative hearing, and, contrary to practices in a criminal trial, the defendant must prove his innocence, often at great cost. Beth suggests that the real reason for treating the movies differently than other media is that they have a greater mass appeal and are more likely to corrupt the ordinary person. He calls for replacing prior censorship with court action after the fact.

Bettelheim, Bruno, *ed*. "Sex and Violence in Books, Magazines and Television: How Much Can—and Should—Parents Censor?" *Redbook*, 123:60, 132–49, May 1964. **B 251**

Betten, Francis S. *The Roman Index of Forbidden Books Briefly Explained for Catholic Booklovers and Students . . . With a Summary of the Index*. St. Louis, Herder, 1909. 69 p. (Also in Fordham University's *Catholic Mind* series, nos. 23 and 24, 1907; 2d ed., Loyola University Press, 1932) **B 252**

Bettman, Alfred, and Swinburne Hale. *Do We Need More Sedition Laws? Testimony of Alfred Bettman and Swinburne Hale, Late Captain Military Intelligence Division, General Staff, U.S.A., before the House of Representatives*. New York, American Civil Liberties Union, 1920. 22 p. **B 253**
Testimony before the Committee on Rules, U.S. House of Representatives.

Betz, I. H. "Dr. Thomas Cooper." *Humanitarian Review*, 10:56–61, July 1911. **B 254**
Biographical sketch of Cooper, including his conviction under the Sedition Act of 1798 and his resignation as professor of chemistry at South Carolina College, in 1834, because of liberal religious views.

Beytagh, Francis X., Jr. "Right of News Media Personnel to Refuse to Disclose Confidential Sources of Information." *Michigan Law Review*, 61:184–91, November 1962. **B 255**
Appeal of Alan L. Goodfader, 367 P. 2d 472 (Hawaii, 1961).

[Biddle, John]. *The Spirit of Persecution Again broken loose, By An Attempt to put in Execution against Mr. John Biddle Master of Arts, an abrogated Ordinance of the Lords and Commons for punishing Blasphemies and Heresies. Together with, A full Narrative of The Whole Proceedings upon that Ordinance against the said Mr. John Biddle and William Kiffen Pastor of a baptised Congregation in the City of London.* London, For Richard Moone, 1655. 23 p. **B 256**
Biddle, a theologian and "father of Unitarianism," was imprisoned on several occasions for publishing blasphemous doctrines and his books were ordered to be burned. This pamphlet, probably published by his friend Richard Moone, accuses the "Beacon Firing" Presbyterians with responsibility for the persecution of Biddle. (The case against the Rev. John Biddle is summarized in Schroeder, *Constitutional Free Speech*, pp. 265–69.)

Bierstadt, Edward H. "Mon Ami Moore." *Bookman*, 56:719–22, February 1923. **B 257**
History of the *Jurgen* case, with quotations from the court's decision.

———, Barrett H. Clark, and Sidney Howard. *Jurgen and the Censor. Report of the Emergency Committee Organized to Protest against the Suppression of James Branch Cabell's "Jurgen."* New York, Privately printed for the Committee, 1920. 77 p. (Edition limited to 458 copies) **B 258**
Contents: Preface by James B. Cabell, Letter from John S. Sumner of the New York Society for the Suppression of Vice, Report of the Emergency Committee, Morals, Not Art or Literature by Edward H. Bierstadt (title borrowed from Anthony Comstock), List of Signers of the Protest, Letters to the Emergency Committee (from prominent authors), Letters to the Publisher, and Echoes from the Press.

Bignell, M. A. *Report of the Meeting of the Inhabitants of Calcutta Held 5th January, 1835, to Take into Consideration the Propriety of Petitioning the Governor-General in Council or the Legislative Council of India to Repeal the Press Regulation Passed in 1823 . . .* Calcutta, 1835. **B 259**

[Bijur, Nathan]. "A Decision for Liberty." *Birth Control Review*, 1(14):2, 8, June 1917. **B 260**

The opinion of Justice Bijur of Superior Court of New York in the case of Message Photoplay Co., producers of the film, *Birth Control*, v. George H. Bell, commissioner of licenses, New York, granting an injunction against the commissioner. "The libertarians of America will read with hope the views of freedom expressed therein."

Biklé, Henry W. "The Jurisdiction of the United States over Seditious Libel." *American Law Register*, 50:1–26, January 1902. **B 261**
"The power of the United States . . . results from its power to maintain its own integrity and establish its own efficiency. Seditious libels . . . are such as threaten to impair that integrity and destroy that efficiency. Over such libels, therefore, the jurisdiction of the United States must be held to exist in order that the true balance between liberty and licentiousness of the press may be maintained within the jurisdiction of the nation, as well as within that of the state."

Bilgrey, Felix J. "Some Questions Concerning Movie Censorship and the First Amendment." *Record of the Association of the Bar of the City of New York*, 18:32–46, January 1963. **B 262**
In discussing the issues of movie censorship the author raises these broader questions: Should society restrain freedom of expression in *any* manner? Should we admit the existence of other interests so overriding that they can justify the displacement of speech? He predicts that legislatures, sensitive to the pressures for regulatory schemes, may enact measures which will ultimately be struck down by the courts.

———, and Ira Levenson. "Censorship of Motion Pictures—Recent Judicial Decisions and Legislative Action." *New York Law Forum*, 1:347–52, September 1955. **B 263**

Bill of Rights of the United States. 16 mm. b/w and color movie, 20 min. Chicago, Encyclopaedia Britannica Films. **B 264**
The story of the struggle for human freedom culminating in the American Bill of Rights, including development of the freedom of the press.

"A Bill to Secure the Liberty of the Press." *Dublin Review*, 7:518–40, November 1839. **B 265**
A history of the English law of libel, prompted by an attempt at codification of the law by the Maltese Commissioners. The author criticizes the extreme harshness of existing British libel law and notes the efforts of the Commissioners to remedy the arbitrary exercise of power in applying the law to the Island of Malta.

Binder, Carroll. "The Dangers of Secrecy." *Nieman Reports*, 9(3):32–34, July 1955. **B 266**

Large doses of government secrecy, like large doses of patent medicines, may destroy the body we are trying to save.

———. "Failure of a Mission; Not Freedom but Restriction is Aim of Majority of UN Subcommission on Information." *Nieman Reports*, 6(4):12–15, October 1952. **B 267**
"Mr. Binder wrote this report of the UN Subcommission on Freedom of Information . . . as he finished his term on the commission and returned to his editorship of the *Minneapolis Tribune*."

———. "A Plea for Adequacy of News Distribution and Free Flow of Information." *U.S. Department of State Bulletin*, 26:508–12, 31 March 1952. **B 268**
In a statement before the UN Subcommission on Freedom of Information, the United States representative presents the American views on the free flow of information. There are three major weaknesses in world news coverage: lack of objectivity, lack of adequate coverage in underdeveloped countries, and restrictions on movement of correspondents and censorship of what they write.

———. "Shadow of Global Censorship." *Saturday Review of Literature*, 34(12):8–9, 33–35, 24 March 1951. **B 269**
A report on the deliverations in the United Nations over a preamble for a Convention on Freedom of Information, presented by one of the United States representatives. He reports on the determined effort of some delegates to restrict freedom of information in the name of the United Nations.

———. "U.S. Urges Noncompromise on Principles of Freedom of Information." *U.S. Department of State Bulletin*, 24:194–97, 29 January 1951. (Also in *Vital Speeches*, 1 March 1951) **B 270**
The United States representative on the United Nations Committee to Draft Convention of Freedom of Information sets forth the American objections to Article 2, limitations to press freedom. The American position was for complete freedom for correspondents and newspapers.

———, and Raul Noriega. "Freedom of Information." *Rotarian*, 79:6–7, October 1951. **B 271**
An American and a Mexican delegate to the UN committee, writing a convention on freedom of information, present their views on the subject. "The right to seek, receive, and impart information without government or any other control is one of the most precious of all freedoms. Without such freedom of information no other freedom can be secure."

Bingham, Major, William Bingham, and Patrick Lavelle. *Report of the Trial of an Action for Libel . . . wherein the Rev. J. P. Lyons, Parish Priest of Kilmore . . . was Plaintiff, and Major Bingham, William Bingham, Esq. and Patrick Lavelle, were Defendants . . . Taken down by Walter Glascock.* Dublin, Printed for George Folds, 1834. 102 p. **B 272**
The defendants were brought to trial for a letter in the *Mayo Constitution* that was allegedly abusive to the parish priest. The trial exposed the unsavory conditions of the time, the quarrel between Catholics and Protestants, the oppressive taxation of state and church, and brought forth a series of cross-charges that were humorous at times. The jury could not agree on a verdict and the case was dismissed.

[Bingley, William]. *The Extraordinary Case of William Bingley, Bookseller, Who, on the 11th of June, 1768, was Committed to Newgate upon a Writ of Attachment of Contempt.* London, William Bingley, 1770. 121 p., 15 p. **B 273**
Proceedings against the vendor of No. 50 and No. 51 of John Wilkes's paper, *North Briton,* including an account of his arrest, his commitment to prison for supposed contempt, "where he has ever since remained, without trial, conviction, or sentence."

[———]. *A Sketch of English Liberty! Illustrated by Precedents for Proceeding in Attachment and by Interrogatories in the Court of King's Bench, in a Matter of Libel; Being the Case of a Free Citizen (William Bingley) who was . . . Imprisoned for a Supposed Libel, Without Trial, etc.* London, William Bingley, 1793. **B 274**
Bingley was a printer who was brought before Lord Mansfield, in 1768, on charges of seditious libel for having published a letter from John Wilkes reflecting on the administration of courts of justice in general and Mansfield's in particular. Instead of a jury trial the Justice substituted "interrogatories" and when Bingley refused to submit to questioning, sentenced him to jail for contempt of court. Bingley, backed by friends and contributions, steadfastly refused to submit, spending three years in prison before Judge Mansfield was finally persuaded, on threat of a Parliamentary investigation, to release him. Bingley continued to edit *North Briton* from his jail cell. The Bingley episode in relation to the larger political scene is described in Rea, *The English Press in Politics, 1760–1774.*

Birch, J. E. V. "Librarian's Daughter." *New Statesman,* 48:184, 14 August 1954. Discussion, 48:210, 21 August 1954; 48:234, 28 August 1954. **B 275**

The borough librarian of Taunton, Eng., discusses the handling of complaints from readers who object to literary works in the library, complaints usually prefaced by the question: "Would you be happy if you knew your daughter was reading stuff like this?"

Birchall, Frederick T. "Getting at the Facts Despite the Censor." *New York Times Magazine,* 15 October 1939, pp. 3 ff. **B 276**
Difficulties of American correspondents in getting news past European censorship.

Bird, F. B. K. "Freedom on the Air." *Canadian Welfare,* 27:2–3, February 1952. **B 277**
The author defends the four principles of free speech adopted by the Canadian Broadcasting Corp., against critics who do not approve of broadcasts of controversial issues.

Birkenhead, Frederick E. S. "William Cobbett's Libel Trial." In his *Famous Trials of History.* New York, Boardman, 1929. vol. 2, pp. 253–62. **B 278**
Cobbett's trial before Lord Ellenborough, 15 June 1810.

Birkhead, L. M. *Missouri University Sex Questionnaire and Its Significance.* Girard, Kans., Haldeman-Julius, 1929. 63 p. (Little Blue Book, no. 1498) **B 279**
Story of the ban of a questionnaire on student sex practices and opinions, issued by a research agency of the University of Missouri. The affair caused a furor throughout the state and several faculty members were fired. A copy of the questionnaire is included.

[Birney, James G.]. *Narrative of the Late Riotous Proceedings Against the Liberty of the Press, in Cincinnati. With Remarks and Historical Notices, Relating to Emancipation. Addressed to the People of Ohio, by the Executive Committee of the Ohio Anti-Slavery Society.* Cincinnati, Ohio Anti-Slavery Society, 1836. 48 p. **B 280**
Relates to public sentiment in Cincinnati against abolitionists and the destruction of the presses of A. Pugh, printer of the *Philanthropist,* the Ohio Anti-Slavery Society organ.

Birney, William. *James G. Birney and His Times.* New York, Appleton, 1890. 443 p. **B 281**
Birney was a leader in the fight to overthrow the power of the slavery interests in suppressing freedom of press, speech, and right of trial by jury.

Birrell, Augustine. *Seven Lectures on the Law and History of Copyright in Books.* New York, Cassell, 1899. 228 p. **B 282**

Origin of copyright in England, the relation of the Stationers' Company to copyright, the battle of the English booksellers for perpetual copyright, legislative enactments since Queen Anne, and the copyright situation in England at the turn of the century.

Birth Control Review. New York, 1917–33; new series 1933–40. Monthly. Edited by Margaret Sanger. **B 283**
This journal, in taking a positive position in behalf of freedom of birth control information, frequently met with opposition from postal authorities. It was suspended from July through November 1917; again in August 1918 it was banned because of a review of Marie Stopes's *Married Love.* The journal was mailable in Canada but not mailable in the United States.

Bixler, Paul H. "Censorship and Selection: The Librarian as a Trustee of the Public's Right to Know." In University of Illinois Library School, *The Nature and Development of the Library Collection,* Champaign, Ill., Illini Union Book Store, 1957, pp. 117–33. (Allerton Park Institute, no. 3) **B 284**

———. "Don't Split Collections." *Library Journal,* 76:2064–65, 15 December 1951. (Reprinted in Daniels, *The Censorship of Books,* pp. 175–77). **B 285**
We do not win the war against communism "by imitating the censoring, repressive tactics of the enemy" or by "putting the words of Lenin, Marx, Stalin, and William Foster out of sight in a locked case, or simply by talking to ourselves about democracy." This is in answer to a proposal by Detroit Librarian Ralph Ulveling (*Library Journal,* August 1951) to segregate the public library collection.

———. "Footnote on Propaganda." *Progressive Librarians' Council Bulletin,* 2:3–4, February 1941. **B 286**
The author recommends two basic tests to apply to propaganda: "(1) Is the source or part of the source hidden? (2) Is the propaganda fundamentally 'dishonest'?" If the answer is "yes" the propaganda should not be added to the library.

———. "Introduction." In *Freedom of Book Selection; Proceedings of the Second Conference on Intellectual Freedom . . .* Chicago, American Library Association, 1954, pp. 1–9. **B 287**

———. "Introduction." In *Freedom of Communication; Proceedings of the First Conference on Intellectual Freedom . . .* Chicago, American Library Association, 1954, pp. 1–8. **B 288**

Bjorseth, Lillian. *Turbulence in the Privacy Field*. Columbia, Mo., Freedom of Information Center, School of Journalism, University of Missouri, 1964. 7 p. (Publication no. 133)   **B 289**
"In this paper is explained the lack of statutes in this area and the further unrest caused by the entrance of electronic eavesdropping."

Black, Creed C. "On the Way: Standby Censorship." *Bulletin of the American Society of Newspaper Editors*, 466:1, 4, 1 July 1963.   **B 290**

Black, Douglas M. "The Responsibility of Choice: The Publisher's Responsibility." In *Freedom of Book Selection; Proceedings of the Second Conference on Intellectual Freedom* . . . Chicago, American Library Association, 1954, pp. 67–74. (An adaptation appears in the *Antioch Review*, December 1953)   **B 291**
A publisher discusses the publisher's obligation to issue controversial books, illustrating his views from his own publishing experience with Velikovsky's *Worlds in Collision*, Edmund Wilson's *The Memoirs of Hecate County*, and the impending publication of Lord Jowett's book on the Hiss trial.

Black, Edwin, and Harry P. Kerr. *American Issues: A Sourcebook for Speech Topics*. New York, Harcourt, Brace & World, 1961. 243 p.   **B 292**
Section 5 deals with censorship. Following an introduction, there are reprints of speeches and articles by Leslie G. Moeller and Clark Mollenhoff (freedom of access to information), Fred B. Millett (The Vigilantes), John Fischer and John C. Murray (pros and cons on the National Organization for Decent Literature). Questions that follow (pp. 198–200) relate largely to forensic points.

Black, Forrest R. "Debs v. the United States—a Judicial Milepost on the Road to Absolutism." *University of Pennsylvania Law Review*, 81:160–75, December 1932.   **B 293**
The author contrasts the liberal decision of the U.S. Supreme Court in the Schenck case ("high-water mark" of liberalism in freedom of speech) with the departure from these liberal views (one week later) in the Debs case in order to "get its man." Neither decision went so far as to accept Jefferson's idea as expressed in the *Acts of Toleration*: "It is time enough for the rightful purpose of civil government for its officers to interfere when principles break into overt acts against peace and order." The author discusses the Debs case in the framework of the evolution of freedom of the press and speech in Anglo-American law.

Black, H. Campbell. "Libel of the Dead." *American Law Review*, 23:578–87, July 1889.   **B 294**
Libel of the dead "is still indictable at the common law in England and it is recognized as a specific offense, by statute in some American states and is indictable in the others unless the common-law rule has been expressly abridged."

Black, Henry T. "Radical Periodicals; Their Place in the Library." Mena, Okla., Commonwealth College, 1937. 12 p. mimeo.   **B 295**
Four pages of text introduce a selected list of left-wing periodicals. "Radical periodicals cannot be ₍logically₎ barred from the library merely because they contain propaganda . . . since 'conservative' and 'reactionary' journals abound in all libraries, if the library itself is to escape being an agency of propaganda, it must provide a more balanced diet." The fact that they are not indexed is not a valid excuse.

Black, Hugo L. "The Bill of Rights." *New York University Law Review*, 35:865–81, April 1960.   **B 296**
In the first annual James Madison lectures, Justice Black discusses the extent to which the Bill of Rights limits the federal government. No superior public interest justifies the abridgment of the Bill of Rights. The First Amendment itself and the interpretation of it by James Madison, who introduced it in Congress, is unequivocal. "If the Constitution withdraws from Government all power over subject matter in an area, such as religion, speech, press, assembly, and petition, there is nothing over which authority may be exerted." Justice Black considers the First Amendment "the heart of the Bill of Rights. The Framers balanced its freedom in religion, speech, press, assembly and petition against the needs of a powerful central government, and decided that in those freedoms lies this nation's only true security. They were not afraid for men to be free."

[———]. "Justice Black and First Amendment 'Absolutes': A Public Interview." *New York University Law Review*, 37:549–62, June 1962.   **B 297**
In an interview by Professor Edmond Cahn of New York University School of Law, Supreme Court Justice Black declares that when the First Amendment states that "Congress shall make no law respecting . . . abridging the freedom of speech, or of the press," it means *no law*. The intent of the First Amendment was extended to apply to the states by the Fourteenth Amendment. Upon questioning, Justice Black stated he would apply the prohibition to laws relating to personal as well as seditious libel. The latter, he said, consists of prosecuting people who are on the wrong side politically. When asked if he would exclude obscenity in the coverage by the First Amendment he replied that "my view is, without deviation, without exception, without any ifs, buts, or whereases, that freedom of speech

means that you shall not do something to people either for the views they have or the views they express or the words they speak or write." He further stated that he does not subscribe to the "clear and present danger" rule.

The Black Dwarf, A London Weekly Publication. London. Edited by Thomas J. Wooler. Vol. 1, no. 1, 29 January 1817 to vol. 12, December 1824.   **B 298**
A periodical devoted to radical reform, dedicated to the Prince Regent "hoping that he will wake to a full knowledge of Himself, his Ministers, and his People, before it is too late." It was frequently critical of royal and parliamentary acts that abridged freedom of expression. Volume 1 (1817) contains numerous articles dealing with freedom of the press: (1) Southey, the poet laureate of England is criticized for taking legal measures to suppress his own youthful work, *Wat Tyler* (no. 9). (2) William Cobbett is accused of "running away" to America in the face of a threat to his liberty (no. 11). (3) The arrest and trial for libel of Editor Wooler, on an "ex officio information," for an article on the right of petition is reported in issues nos. 15, 17, 19, 20, and 23. (4) A series of letters to the editor by "Fabricus," dealing with the law of libel (nos. 23 through 28). (5) Death of the Trial by Jury in Cases of Alleged Libel, an attack on packing of juries by the Office of Master of Crown (no. 45). (6) Progress of Persecution: Approaching Trial of the Editor, including a discussion of the prevailing doctrine that "truth is a libel" and that "the greater the truth, the greater the libel" (no. 47). (7) Mr. Hone's Acquittals (nos. 48 and 49). A list of nineteenth-century English unstamped and radical papers is given in the *Cambridge Bibliography of English Literature*, vol. 3, pp. 815–18.

"Black Out." *Times Literary Supplement*, 3193:341, 10 May 1963.   **B 299**
Comments on the South African Sabotage Act (1962) which prohibits reporting of any remarks made by a list of about 100 citizens, and the Publications and Entertainments Act.

Blackburn, Anna F. "Recent Decisions on the Extensive and Intensive Aspects of the Guarantee of Free Speech and Free Press." *Ohio State Law Journal*, 5:89–98, December 1938.   **B 300**
A summary of state and municipal court decisions.

Blackmur, R. P. *Dirty Hands or the True-Born Censor*. Cambridge (Eng.), Minority Press, 1930. 15 p. (Minority Pamphlet no. 5; reprinted in *Censorship*, quarterly report of the Congress for Cultural Freedom, London, Spring 1965)   **B 301**

A British literary critic interviews an American customs censor, whose definition of a classic is "a dirty book somebody is trying to get by me."

"Blackout Journalism." *Columbia Journalism Review*, 2(2):5–12, Spring 1963. **B 302**

This issue of the journal is devoted to presenting basic data for understanding the New York newspaper strike. It includes a staff report on the extent of the interim news devices, the tenor of the national debate over the strike, and the immediately perceptible effect on the established papers. The issue carries a report on strike negotiations written by A. H. Raskin (pp. 14–27) and an article entitled A Public Policy on a Newspaper Strike by Clayton Knowles and Richard P. Hunt (pp. 28–33). An editorial discusses the implication of the strike on First Amendment freedoms.

Blackstone, *Sir* William. "Libels; Liberty of the Press." In *Blackstone's Commentaries on the Laws of England (1765–1769)*. Edited by St. George Tucker. Philadelphia, Birch and Small, 1803. Book IV, chap. 11, par. 13, pp. 149–53. (A modern edition of Blackstone was edited by Bernard C. Gavit and published in Washington, D.C., by Washington Law Book Co., 1941. 1040 p.) **B 303**

Blackstone's concept of freedom of the press, followed religiously by many eighteenth-century English jurists and by some Americans in the early days of the Republic, was narrowly proscribed. "The liberty of the press," he stated, "is indeed essential to the nature of a free state; but this consists in laying no *previous* restraints upon publications, and not in freedom from censure for criminal matters when published . . . if he publishes what is improper, mischievous, or illegal, he must take the consequences of his own temerity." Utterances, both spoken and written, true or false, which defamed the government, were criminally libelous. The editor of this edition, the eminent Virginia jurist St George Tucker, gives his own more liberal interpretation in Appendix to vol. 1, pt. 2, Note G, pp. 1–30.

Blackwell, Leslie, and Brian R. Bamford. *Newspaper Law of South Africa.* Capetown, Juta & Co., 1963. 112 p. **B 304**

Includes such restrictions on the freedom of publication as registration and licensing of newspapers, restrictions on court reporting, and laws relating to defamation, indecency and obscenity, sedition, and race relations.

[Blackwood, William]. *Report of the Trial by Jury, Professor John Leslie against William Blackwood, for Libel in "Blackwood's Edinburgh Magazine." Reported by William Bennet. July 22, 1822.* Edinburgh, Printed for W. and C. Tait, 1822. 161 p. **B 305**

A professor of physics at the University of Edinburgh was awarded damages for libel in an article that accused him of claiming for his own other men's discoveries.

Blades, William. *The Enemies of Books.* London, Trübner, 1880. 110 p. (Revised edition published by Elliot Stock in 1902 in the Book-Lover's Library) **B 306**

A whimsical essay which includes chapters on destruction of books by fire, water, dust and neglect, ignorance and bigotry, bookbinders, collectors, servants, and children. The edition examined, ironically, is printed on such poor paper that a mere turning of the page is enough to crumble it.

Blagden, Cyprian. *The Stationers' Company; A History, 1403–1959.* London, Allen & Unwin, 1960. 321 p. **B 307**

A general account of the history of the agency that played a major role in controlling the production and distribution of books and printing in England during the sixteenth and seventeenth centuries. References are made to the Company's role in the licensing of printing, the granting of the right of search and seizure of unauthorized printing, the carrying out of various decrees of the government to control printing, and the role of the Company in copyright.

Blair, Ross M. *Pennsylvania's "Right to Know" Laws.* Columbia, Mo., Freedom of Information Center, School of Journalism, University of Missouri, 1960. 1 p. (Publication no. 39) **B 308**

Discussion of the Open Meeting Law and the Open Record Law, passed by the Pennsylvania legislature in 1957.

[Blair, Sam C.]. *A Judge Favors TV Cameras.* Columbia, Mo., Freedom of Information Center, School of Journalism, University of Missouri, 1958. 5 p. (Publication no. 2) **B 309**

An account of the first television coverage of a murder trial in Missouri, approved by Circuit Judge Sam C. Blair. Includes text of an interview with Judge Blair by KOMU-TV News-Director Phil Berk, in which TV coverage of the trial is discussed.

Blakely, Robert J. "Threats to Books." *ALA Bulletin*, 46:291–92+, October 1952. **B 310**

"Books must be regarded as a symbol of the process of free communication." The author examines the enemies of free communications, then lists four ways in which the library can offer leadership in the field of liberal adult education—ways to combat ignorance, anti-intellectualism, and similar enemies of free communication.

Blakeman, Charles E. *Thoughts on Books to Read and Books to Burn. A Compilation in Three Parts, Containing Evidence that Pure Minds and Useful People are Not the Product of the Cheap Trashy Novel.* [Hermon?], Calif., 1906. 152 p. **B 311**

Blanchard, Florence B., *comp. Censorship of Motion Pictures.* [Chicago?], General Federation of Women's Clubs, 1919. 24 p. **B 312**

The Federation prefers state movie censorship boards to the National Board of Review, an agent of the industry. The compiler, chairman of the Federation's Motion Picture Committee, quotes from movie trade journals to "show the real views of the industry when they talk among themselves." The pamphlet includes a model state censorship bill, lobbying instructions, and advice in setting up a motion picture study program to promote censorship.

Blank, Blanche D. *Municipal Regulatory Licensing; a Study of Sixteen American Cities.* New York, Columbia University, 1952. 293 p. (Ph. D. dissertation, University Microfilms no. 3681) **B 313**

The study concludes with a review of two special licensing problems: censorship and public relations, the former an "unnecessary evil."

Blank, Joseph P. "The Ordeal of John Henry Faulk." *Look*, 27:80–96a, 7 May 1963. **B 314**

A blacklisted TV performer wins $3,500,000 libel damages against the publishers of *Aware* and vindication of his reputation in a 6-year court battle. Bulletin 16 of *Aware*, the publication of a private organization "to combat the Communist conspiracy in entertainment communications," had blacklisted Faulk. This led to his dismissal from CBS and kept him from getting any work in the communication industry. Louis Nizer was the attorney for Faulk. The editors of *Look* comment: "The guilt for John Henry Faulk's ordeal is shared by all—magazines, newspapers, radio and television, advertising agencies and just plain citizens."

Blanshard, Paul. *American Freedom and Catholic Power.* Boston, Beacon, 1950. 350 p; 2d ed., rev. and enl., 1958. 402 p. **B 315**

This controversial study of the American Catholic hierarchy as a pressure group includes a chapter on censorship and boycott relating to books, magazines, radio, and the motion picture. In the Personal Prologue: The Duty to Speak, appearing in the revised edition, the author writes of the efforts to suppress and discredit the first edition of his book, including a *New York Times* ban on advertisements of the book (later lifted) on grounds that the chapter on birth control was "particularly objectionable since it involved highly controversial matter of a religious nature." The Calendar of Significant Events, 1947–1957, in the revised edition, lists various efforts by the Church at censorship of books and movies.

———. "The Catholic Church as Censor." *Nation*, 166:459–64, 1 May 1948; 166:499–502, 8 May 1948. **B 316**
The first article deals with Catholic censorship of books and magazines, the second article with Catholic motion picture censorship. Blanshard concludes: "No one questions the *right* of the hierarchy to influence its people in matters of art and literature . . . But the censorship operations of the hierarchy have gone far beyond religion and decency. They have extended into the world of politics, medicine, and historical research, and have impaired the integrity of the media of information which serve non-Catholics as well as Catholics. Most serious of all, the hierarchy has stifled judgment among its own people by refusing them permission to read both sides of important controversies on matters of social policy."

———. *Communism, Democracy and Catholic Power*. Boston, Beacon, 1951. 340p. **B 317**
A comparative study of systems of thought control as exercised by the Vatican and the Kremlin, and the relation of each to the American tradition of intellectual freedom.

———. *The Irish and Catholic Power; an American Interpretation*. Boston, Beacon, 1953. 375p. **B 318**
A study of Ireland as "The No. 1 exhibit of Roman Catholic power in the English-speaking world." Numerous references to censorship of books, movies, and birth control information.

———. *The Right to Read; the Battle against Censorship*. Boston, Beacon, 1955. 339p. **B 319**
A survey of censorship as it is practiced in the United States today in the realms of politics, religion, race, sex, education, and crime. Includes essential historical and legal background.

———. "Roman Catholic Censorship: Movies." *Nation*, 166:499–502, 8 May 1948. **B 320**
While supporting the Legion of Decency's opposition to pornography, Blanshard charges the organization with being "far more concerned with Catholic dogma and with Catholic social philosophy than with decency."

"Blasphemy." *Correspondent*, 2:204–6, 21 April 1827. **B 321**
The writer advocates free expression of religious ideas and opposes legal protection from criticism for any specific body of religious thought. The Bible itself, he maintains, is filled with blasphemies.

"Blasphemy." *Westminster and Foreign Quarterly Review*, 120(n.s.):1–25, July 1883. **B 322**
A review of six recent publications relating to blasphemy law: James Stephens, *A History of the Criminal Law of England* (1883), four reports of the blasphemy trials of G. W. Foote, and a report of the trial of George Bradlaugh. The editor concludes that "these prosecutions are opposed both to the spirit and the interests of Christianity itself" and are contrary to the laws of England.

"Blasphemy and Blasphemous Libels." *Canada Law Journal*, 19:183–88, 15 May 1883. **B 323**
A discussion of the British law of blasphemous libel as revealed by the case against Charles Bradlaugh for publication of the *Freethinker*. Judge Coleridge points out that if attacks on the Christian religion are to be punished criminally because the Christian religion is part of the law of the country, it would be reasonable to punish criminally attacks upon the monarchy, primogeniture, or marriage laws—all part of the fundamental law.

"The Blasphemy Controversy." *Spectator*, 56:348–49, 17 March 1883. **B 324**
In order to be fair, we should punish the writer who ridicules Christianity only to the extent that we would be willing to punish one who ridicules a non-Christian religion.

Blasphemy Laws; What They Are and Why They Should Be Abolished. London, Committee for the Repeal of the Blasphemy Laws, 1912. 4p. **B 325**

"The Blasphemy Sentence." *Spectator*, 56:313–14, 10 March 1883. **B 326**
Defense of George W. Foote (*Queen v. Foote, Ramsay, et al.*), in his conviction for blasphemy in distributing the Christmas number of the *Freethinker*. The author, while defending the blasphemy laws, objects to the severity of punishment (one year in prison). He also questions the inequity of punishing only for vulgar atheistic expression while allowing refined expression of the same ideas to go free.

Blau, Lois. "The Novel in the High School Library; Censorship or Selection." *Wisconsin Library Bulletin*, 60:178–80, May–June 1964. **B 327**

Bleackley, Horace W. *Life of John Wilkes*. London, Lane, 1917. 464p. **B 328**
A vindication of Wilkes, whose fame, the author argues, has been "influenced more adversely by political prejudice" than that of most public men. Wilkes is best known today as a symbol for the fight for freedom of the press in eighteenth-century England. R. W. Postgate, in his biography, *That Devil Wilkes*, rates this work as "incomparably the best" among numerous Wilkes biographies.

Bledsoe, Thomas, "Hierarchy over Hollywood." *Protestant*, 7:8–18, June–July 1946. **B 329**
"If Roman Catholic domination of censorship continues, the film screens of most of the world will be flooded with pictures such as *Going My Way*, *The Song of Bernadette*, and *The Bells of St. Mary's*, which glorify priests and the Roman Catholic Church. But even the faintest suggestion of the church's role in support of fascism in Italy and Spain and other countries, or its alignment with the rich and reactionary, as in Mexico, against the people will be entirely suppressed. Also, in the past, when any criticism of organized religion or its representatives is made, Protestants or Jews will bear the brunt of the dubious or villainous roles."

Bleyer, Willard G. "Freedom of the Press and the New Deal." *Journalism Quarterly*, 11:22–35, March 1934. **B 330**

———. *Main Currents in the History of American Journalism*. Boston, Houghton Mifflin, 1927. 464p. **B 331**
Includes an account of the historical development of freedom of the press and censorship in the United States.

Blied, Benjamin J. "The 'Prisoner of State' and Its Author." *Historical Bulletin*, 27:81–83, May 1949. **B 332**
The story of Dennis A. Mahony, editor of the *Dubuque Herald*, and his imprisonment in Washington, D.C., for alleged disloyalty, 1862.

"Blind Guides." *Freeman*, 7:172, 2 May 1923. **B 333**
An editorial in opposition to the New York censorship bill sponsored by the Clean Books League and critical of the National Association of Book Publishers for not taking a stand against the bill.

Bliven, Bruce. "The Future of Free Speech." In *Problems of Journalism; Proceedings of the American Society of Newspaper Editors, 1934*. Washington, D.C., ASNE, 1934, pp. 124–31. (Summarized in *Quill*, June 1936) **B 334**
The editor of the *New Republic* describes three types of self censorship: censorship to please the readers, censorship for reasons of economic profit, and censorship to keep out of trouble. The current economic crisis threatens freedom of the press.

———, and E. H. Harris. "Should the Government Operate Radio Broadcasting?" *Public Utility Fortnightly*, 14:747–51, 6 December 1934. **B 335**
Summary of a debate before the Fourth Annual Assembly of the National Advisory Council on Radio in Education, Chicago, 9 October 1934. Bliven was editor of the *New Republic*; E. H. Harris was chairman of the radio committee of the American Newspaper Publishers' Association.

Blodgett, Virginia J. "Censorship and the Teacher of English." *Hoosier School Libraries*, 2:16–18, April 1963. **B 336**

"Blood and Rage." *Newsweek*, 27:100–102, 24 June 1946. **B 337**

A Greenwich Village bookseller was the first to defy attempts to censor Albert C. Hick's biography of Trujillo, *Blood in the Streets*.

Bloom, Edward A. "Johnson on a Free Press; a Study in Liberty and Subordination." *ELH*, 16:251–71, December 1949. **B 338**

A study of Samuel Johnson's philosophy of a free press and the basic problem of human liberty upon which it was founded. "At times Johnson appears to be conservative in the matter of a free press to a point little short of reaction. Yet at other times he is almost radical in denouncing violations of liberty. The answer involves no inconsistency by Johnson. Actually he was quite positive in his deference to reasonable authority but as firmly adverse to any acts which, according to his own lights, constituted oppression by that authority."

———. "Neoclassic 'Paper Wars' for a Free Press." *Modern Language Review*, 56:481–96, October 1961. **B 339**

A study of the period in England between the expiration of the licensing act in 1694 and the passage of the Fox Libel Act of 1792, a period that "witnessed an unprecedented outpouring of fugitive publications—mainly broadsides and pamphlets—devoted to the subject of a free press."

Bloom, Sigmund L. "Newspaper Advertising—an Interference with a Fair Trial by Jury?" *University of Pittsburgh Law Review*, 22:601–9, March 1961. **B 340**

Notes on cases involving newspaper advertising which bear on an issue currently before the courts, including the recent case of the *Washington Observer*, Washington, Pa.

Bloomenthal, Lawrence R. "No Pictures Allowed." *American Photography*, 33:492–96, July 1939. **B 341**

The right to take pictures of unwilling subjects is still a source of controversy. The author discusses a decision by the Maryland Supreme Court relating to photographing and publishing the pictures of defendants in a criminal trial.

Bloss, Meredith. "For Action." *ALA Bulletin*, 47:463–64, November 1953. **B 342**

An itemized program for positive action by librarians in helping to preserve the freedom to read.

[Blount, Charles]. *A Just Vindication of Learning, and of the Liberty of the Press: or, an Humble Address to the High Court of Parliament In behalf of the Liberty of the Press, by Philopatris.* London, 1679. 24 p. (Reprinted in *Harleian Miscellany*, vol. 8, pp. 290–300) **B 343**

Blount, a deist and radical Whig, writing under the pseudonym of *Philopatris*, argues against the continuation of the English licensing act which is about to expire. He recommends liberty of the press as the best cure for ignorance, giving nine arguments against licensing: (1) censorship is the evil creation of the Inquisition, (2) censorship is an affront to learning, (3) it is prejudicial to the book and the author, (4) it vilifies the whole nation, (5) it is a reflection on the church and clergy, (6) it is a dangerous practice for any government, (7) it injures the licensers, (8) we can hardly blame the Mohammedans for their ignorance when we practice the same restrictions, and (9) "licensing and persecution of conscience are two sisters that ever go hand in hand." Sensabaugh, in his *That Grand Whig, Milton* (pp. 58–61) by parallel text, the striking similarity of idea and phrasing to Milton's *Areopagitica*. In 1693 *A Just Vindication of Learning* was ordered to be burnt by the common hangman. Similar action was taken against Blount's *Anima Mundi* (1673) and his *Life of Apollonius Tyaneus* (1680). The latter cast doubt on Christian miracles.

[———]. *Reasons Humbly offered for the Liberty of Unlicens'd Printing. To which is Subjoin'd, The Just and True Character of Edmund Bohun, The Licenser of the Press. In a Letter from a Gentleman in the Country, to a Member of Parliament.* London, 1693. 32 p. (Signed "J.M.") **B 344**

An attack on the English press licensing system in general and Edmund Bohun, the Surveyor of the Imprimery (censor), in particular. The pamphlet, designed to influence the discontinuance of the licensing act which had been revived in 1685, is based largely upon Milton's *Areopagitica*, as was Blount's earlier pamphlet, *A Just Vindication of Learning* (1679). Sensabaugh, in *That Grand Whig, Milton* shows the similarity between *Areopagitica* and *Reasons Humbly offered* by use of parallel texts (pp. 155–62). T. Holt White, in his 1819 edition of *Areopagitica*, terms Blount's pamphlet as "sort of an abridgement of Milton's work," noting that the initials are presumably for John Milton, fellow Whig. While Blount copied from Milton, Locke, in turn, is believed to have been influenced by Blount in drafting the House of Commons document favoring the discontinuance of licensing. Hilgers, in his *Der Index der verbotenen Bücher*, gives Blount as much credit for ending licensing as Milton and Locke combined. Blount was responsible for getting Bohun dismissed from his job as censor by means of a trick. He presented for licensing a work, *King William and Queen Mary Conquerors*, which Bohun, failing to recognize as satire, had approved. *Reasons Huuubly offered* is reprinted in Blackburne's *Remarks on Johnson's Life of Milton* (1780) and in a volume of tracts edited by Francis Maseres in 1809.

Blount, *Sir* Thomas P. *Censura Celebriorum Authorum: sive, Tractatus in quo varia virorum doctorum de clarissimis cujusque seculi scriptoribus judicia traduntur . . .* London, Richard Chiswel, 1690. 746 p. **B 345**

"It is a bibliographical dictionary of a peculiar kind, and may be described as a record of the opinions of the greatest writers of all ages on one another" (DNB). This work deals more with literary criticism than with freedom of the press, but it is the source of much information on censorship of particular works.

Blow, George. "Press Comment on Pending Trials." *Virginia Law Review*, 38:1057–74, December 1952. **B 346**

"The Blue Pencil." *New Statesman* (London), 6:57–59, 23 October 1915. (Reprinted in *Living Age*, 18 December 1915) **B 347**

A lampooning of Britain's wartime press censorship. "If the Press Censorship does not grow more effective, it at least grows more amusing." The author cites examples of blue penciling of Kipling and Browning. "The censorship is justified in throwing as much dust in the eyes of the Germans as it can; it is not justified in stuffing as much cottonwool as it can in the ears of the English . . . The censor must not work in the spirit of a priest overlooking the choice of books in a village free library, but in the spirit of an admiral preventing the leakage of supplies into the hands of the enemy."

"Blue Pencils: 'Strong' Drama Wins over Censorship in New York and Omaha." *Literary Digest*, 123(22):7, 29 May 1937. **B 348**

New York's Governor Lehman vetoes a theater licensing bill; Methodist Bishop Oxnam defends *Idiot's Delight* in Omaha.

Blumenfeld, F. Yorick. *Regulation of Television.* Washington, D.C., Editorial Research Reports, 1959. (*Editorial Research Reports*, 2:953–70, 1959) **B 349**

Inquiries into network programming and existing controls over broadcasting in the United States and Great Britain. New proposals for regulating television are considered: imposition of programming standards by the FCC, network policing, magazine concept of programs, advisory groups, and reform from within.

Blumenthal, Walter H. "American Broadside Whipt." *American Notes & Queries*, 3:67–68, January 1965. **B 350**

An extraordinary case of the whipping of an offending broadside, Edward Cole's *A Letter to A Gentleman in New York*, by the "common Whipper" in Milford, Conn., 21 November 1755. The work tended "to beget Ill Will."

Blunden, Edmund C. *Leigh Hunt's "Examiner" Examined* . . . New York, Harper, 1928. 263 p. (Reprinted by Archon Books, Hamden, Conn., 1967)   **B 351**

In 1812 John and Leigh Hunt, editors of the London *Examiner*, were found guilty of libel on the Prince Regent and given prison sentences of two years. In 1821 John was again imprisoned for political libel. The book discusses the trials and gives general consideration of the law of libel and political liberalism.

["Blushing Post Office and the Fine Arts."] *Metropolitan Magazine*, 39:6, March 1914.   **B 352**

An editorial discussing the temporary suspension of the magazine by the New York postmaster for reproducing Paul Manship's *Wood Nymph's Dance* and *Playfulness*.

B'nai B'rith. Anti-Defamation League. *The Broadcaster's Code. More or Less Free Speech?* Chicago, The League, [1939?]. 8 p. (Fireside Discussion pamphlet, no. 27)   **B 353**

"The Fireside Discussion Group of the Anti-Defamation League presents for open discussion the very controversial issue of the Code recently adopted by the National Association of Broadcasters. This pamphlet . . . is prepared for educational purposes only. There is no intent to influence one side or the other in this controversy."

Boas, Magda van E. "'Naked' and 'Nude' in Art." *Sexology*, 28:388–91, January 1962.   **B 354**

Boaz, Martha T. "ALA's Intellectual Freedom Committee." *Wilson Library Bulletin*, 39:651, April 1965.   **B 355**

The chairman describes the Committee's areas of responsibility—watching for proposed or actual restrictions on authors, books, booksellers, or libraries; seeking ways to give assistance to those involved in abridgment of the Library Bill of Rights; enlisting the support of other groups; seeking support for a legal aid program; and initiating research on the effects of reading.

———. "Censoring Censorship." *Michigan Librarian*, 17(3):16–17, October 1951.   **B 356**

"In light of the First Amendment to the Constitution, we believe that it is not only desirable, but essential to curb censorship and to promote freedom of speech in order to maintain a free world."

———. "What to do Before the Censor Comes—and After." *Newsletter on Intellectual Freedom.* (American Library Association), 14(5):59–60, September 1965.   **B 357**

These 20 suggestions to librarians who may become involved in censorship cases represent practices and policies which have been tried and found useful in several communities.

"*Bobbsey Twins*, the *Swimming Hole*, and Censorship in South Carolina." *Southeastern Librarian*, 6:87–89, Summer 1956.   **B 358**

Bodas, Mahader R. *Freedom of the Press in India; Its Origin and Progress.* Poona, "Shri Manik Prabhu" Press, 1898. 33 p.   **B 359**

The author is High Court Pleader in Bombay.

Bode, Carl. "Columbia's Carnal Bed." *American Quarterly*, 15:52–64, Spring 1963.   **B 360**

The author explores the serious and frivolous (generally rare) literature dealing with sex in nineteenth-century America, some of which met with censorship. Among the serious sex works are those of Robert Dale Owen (*Moral Physiology*), Charles Knowlton (*Fruits of Philosophy*), Nicholas F. Cooke (*Satan in Society*), and David G. Croly (*The Truth About Love*). Bode also gives examples of early American pornography.

Bodwell, Charles S. "Enforcement of the Obscenity Laws." *Light*, 192:5–7, January–February 1930.   **B 361**

A report in this journal of the World Purity Federation, from the secretary of the New England Watch and Ward Society.

Bogart, G. Henri. "One Bane of Prudery." *Medicine Times*, 31:341–46, February 1912.   **B 362**

Censorship of works on sex education and birth control.

Bohun, Edmund. *The Diary and Autobiography of Edmund Bohun, Esq., with an Introductory Memoir, Notes, and Illustrations, by S. Wilton Rix.* Beccles, Eng., Privately printed by Read Crisp, 1853. 148 p. (Edition limited to 150 copies)   **B 363**

Bohun was appointed licenser of the press under William and Mary, a position which he found painful and difficult. He held it only five months and was dismissed when he approved Blount's work, *King William and Queen Mary Conquerors*. Bohun subsequently moved to America where he became chief justice of South Carolina. In his autobiography, Bohun reports in detail on his experience before the House of Commons leading to his dismissal, and on other aspects of his brief career as licenser. The editor provides extensive notes on the licensing system.

Bok, Bart J., Francis Friedman, and Victor Weisskopf. "Security Regulations

in the Field of Nuclear Research." *Bulletin of the Atomic Scientists*, 3:321–34+, November 1947. (Reprinted in Summers, *Federal Information Controls in Peacetime*, pp. 65–71)   **B 364**

Three physicists evalute security regulations with respect to the release of scientific and technical data developed by the U.S. Atomic Energy Commission and the effect of these restrictions on research.

Bok, Curtis. "Censorship and the Arts." In *Civil Liberties under Attack*. Philadelphia, University of Pennsylvania Press, 1951, pp. 107–28.   **B 365**

An essay by the Philadelphia judge whose decision in the case of *Commonwealth v. Gordon*, 1948, has been cited as an example of a mature and sophisticated approach to sex expression in modern literature.

———. "Censorship through the Open Market Rather than the Police Station." *Publishers' Weekly*, 157:1885–87, 29 April 1950. (Also separately published by the Philadelphia Book Clinic, 1950. 13 p.)   **B 366**

An address by a Philadelphia judge at the Fifth Annual Philadelphia Book Show at Franklin Institute. "I believe in the censorship of the open market rather than the police station. No publisher who prints a lot of smut because a ban has been lifted will make much money: actually, it is the ban that keeps the price up—when the market is open the demand seals itself off and the pickings are scarce."

———. *Commonwealth v. Gordon, et al. The Opinion of Judge Bok.* New York, Printed for Blanche and Alfred Knopf by Grabhorn Press, 1949. 57 p.   **B 367**

A famous decision on obscenity which freed the five Philadelphia booksellers arrested in a police raid and brought to trial, 3 January 1947, on charges of violating the Pennsylvania obscenity statutes.

———. "If We Are to Act Like Free Men . . ." *Saturday Review*, 37(7):9–10, 56–57, 13 February 1954.   **B 368**

In an address at the National Book Award ceremony, the Philadelphia judge who received acclaim in the literary world for his decision in the obscenity case, *Commonwealth v. Gordon*, speaks of some of the philosophical aspects of law and the First Amendment, noting that abridgment of the right of free speech takes on different shapes, on different occasions, at different times. In recent months the efforts to regulate sound-trucks caused a great outcry, while the ten-day strike which silenced New York newspapers was generally accepted. The present tolerant mood of the courts toward free expression could change if, for example, crime comics could be linked positively with delinquency. The force of custom is more effective than the force of law in applying sanctions on publishing and reading.

[————]. "Judge Bok Clears the Nine Novels Involved in Pennsylvania Trial." *Publishers' Weekly*, 155:1512–13, 2 April 1949. **B 369**
Summary of the 53-page opinion in *Commonwealth v. Gordon*, a case involving definition of obscenity in literature. Novels included are by James Farrell, William Faulkner, and Erskine Caldwell.

————. "This Duty of Freedom." *Saturday Review*, 36:27–28, 11 July 1953.(Reprinted in Daniels, *The Censorship of Books*, pp. 36–39; Downs, *The First Freedom*, pp. 457–60) **B 370**
An eloquent plea for freedom of speech and the press: "Above the bare legal right to speak or to read is the courage to use these rights well: to speak clearly, bravely, and accurately, and to read with understanding. On the other side is the right to maintain a lighted silence, and this right must still be fought for."

Boles, Donald E. *The Bible, Religion, and the Public Schools.* 3d ed. Ames, Ia., Iowa State University Press, 1965. 408 p. **B 371**
From one point of view the exclusion of the Bible from the classroom is an effort to separate church and state; from another point of view it represents censorship. This work gives the historical background on the issue and discusses state constitutions, laws, court cases, and attitudes of pressure groups. A list of important court cases and a bibliography are included.

Bolitho, William. "Eyes and Ears of Democracy." *Survey*, 57:731–33, 1 March 1927 **B 372**
"The modern news press can be killed so easily—but never used." The author draws from experiences in Great Britain during the General Strike, in Italy under dictatorship, and in Europe under wartime control, showing that the press becomes the first victim of a despot.

Bollan, William. *The Freedom of Speech and Writing upon Public Affairs Considered, with an Historical View of the Roman Imperial Laws against Libels . . . the Bringing of the Rock into the Tower . . . The Different Treatment of Libels There . . . with Observations on the Proper Use of the Liberty of the Press . . .* London, Baker, 1766. 160 p. (A 49-page abridgment was published in

London in 1772 under the title *Essay on the Right of Every Man in a Free State to Speak and Write Freely . . .* Excerpts and commentary appear in Levy, *Freedom of the Press from Zenger to Jefferson*, pp. 83–94) **B 373**
A legal history of suppression of free speech and press, from ancient times to mid-eighteenth century. The author is best known as Massachusetts' colonial agent in London. He criticizes the tyranny of the Star Chamber, the persecutions of the Levellers, and the existing practice of substituting trial by judge for trial by jury. While accepting the general principles of seditious libel, Bollan argues for reforms in procedures—the right of the accused to plead truth as a defense, and the right of juries to judge falsity and malice. The former was recognized in America in the decision of the Zenger trial; the latter was recognized in England by the Fox Libel Act of 1792. Levy (p. 83) calls Bollan's work, "surely the eighteenth century's most learned work in English on the liberty of the press."

Bolte, Charles G. "Security Through Book Burning." *Annals of the American Academy of Political and Social Science*, 300:87–93, July 1955. (Reprinted in Downs, *The First Freedom*, pp. 242–47) **B 374**
A witty and sententious article with numerous quotes from those who approve and those who disapprove of book burning. Lenin is quoted as favoring censorship, a fact "offered free of charge to those who still want proof that any American who favors book burning is guilty of Communism by association." "For us," Bolte writes, "there can be no security through book burning; only the rigid crust of conformity."

[Bonaparte, Charles J.]. *Transmission through the Mails of Anarchist Publications . . .* Washington, D.C., Govt. Print. Off., 1908. 11 p. (Senate Document no. 426, 60th Cong., 1st sess.) **B 375**
The statement of the Attorney General advising President Theodore Roosevelt that "in my opinion, the Postmaster-General will be justified in excluding from the mails any issue of any periodical, otherwise entitled to the privileges of second-class mail matter, which shall contain any article constituting a seditious libel and counseling such crimes as murder, arson, riot, and treason." In transmitting the letter, Roosevelt expresses his intention to act on this advice. "When compared with the suppression of anarchy [Roosevelt writes] every other question sinks into insignificance. The anarchist is the enemy of humanity, the enemy of all mankind, and his is a deeper degree of criminality than any other. No immigrant is allowed to come to our shores if he is an anarchist; and no paper published here or abroad should be permitted circulation in this country if it propagates anarchist opinions." Relates to the suppression of *La Questione Sociale* of Paterson, N. J.

Bond, Edward. "Censor in Mind." *Censorship*, 4:9–14, Autumn 1965. **B 376**
The author of the play *Saved* describes his experience with censorship by the Lord Chamberlain. One of the banned scenes is reproduced. "If dramatists were given the new freedom that has finally been given . . . to novelists, there might be a powerful renaissance in the English theatre, a striking assertion of the cultural and moral ability—at a time when it is being said we have to rediscover a national identity."

Bond, Elizabeth M. "Censorship and Your Library." *Minnesota Libraries*, 17:208–10, September 1953. (Reprinted in *Illinois Libraries*, May 1966) **B 377**
The head of the Reference Department, Minneapolis Public Library, examines the Library Bill of Rights, point by point, explaining what it means, what the implications are, what pressures have been brought to bear by groups, and how such pressures can be met.

Bond, Richmond P., and Katherine K. Weed. *Studies of British Newspapers and Periodicals from Their Beginning to 1800.* Chapel Hill, University of North Carolina Press, 1946. 233 p. **B 378**
A source of bibliographical information on the struggles of early British newspapers.

Bonnard, G. A. "Two Remarks on the Text of Milton's *Areopagitica*." *Review of English Studies*, 4:434–38, 1928. **B 379**
Commentary on the accuracy of the various texts. The author believes T. Holt White's text to be more accurate than those edited by John W. Hales and Edward Arbor.

Bonner, Hypatia (Bradlaugh). *Charles Bradlaugh, a Record of His Life and Work, by His Daughter, Hypatia Bradlaugh Bonner. With an Account of His Parliamentary Struggle, Politics and Teachings, by John M. Robertson.* London, Unwin, 1894. 2 vols. **B 380**
Bradlaugh was a British social reformer and advocate of freethought. In 1868 he was brought to trial under the Stamp Act for publication of the *National Reformer*, and acquitted. Collett, in his *History of the Taxes on Knowledge*, calls the defense of Mr. Bradlaugh "the most valuable personal contribution ever made to the liberty of the press." Bradlaugh was associated with Annie Besant in the publishing of Charles Knowlton's *Fruits of Philosophy*, for which they were both brought to trial.

————. *Penalties upon Opinion; or Some Records of the Laws of Heresy and Blasphemy . . .* London, Watts, 1912. 113 p. **B 381**

A résumé of the efforts in England, from the twelfth century to the early twentieth, to challenge the restrictions of church and state against heresy and blasphemy. Includes references to significant state trials and acts of Parliament.

Bonwick, James. *Early Struggles of the Australian Press.* London, Gordon & Gotch, 1890. 82 p. **B 382**
References to early newspaper libel trials, personal confrontations, and difficulties with government officials. Arrangement is by province and then by name of newspaper.

"Booby Trap." *Time,* 59(10):73–75, 10 March 1952. **B 383**
An account of the problems faced by the American delegation to the UN Conference on Freedom of Information, a project which Delegate Carroll Bender announced had "boomeranged."

"Book Ban Attempted in California; Ministers and Priests of Arcadia." *Christian Century,* 79:1576, 26 December 1962. **B 384**
An editorial concerning the Arcadia, Calif., council of churches' request to the city council to order the public library board to ban Nikos Kazantzakis' *The Last Temptation of Christ.* The editor defends the right of people to read and decide for themselves whether or not the book is worthy.

Book Banning. 14 min., b/w movie. New York, Columbia Broadcasting System. (*See It Now* television program) **B 385**
The story of the woman who conducted a crusade to ban certain works from San Francisco high schools.

"Book Burning: Where U.S. Officials Stand." *U.S. News & World Report,* 34:37–40, 42, 45–46, 26 June 1953. **B 386**
Text of President Eisenhower's "Don't Join the Book Burners" statement at Dartmouth, 14 June 1953; testimony of James Conant, U.S. High Commissioner for Germany, made under questioning by Senator McCarthy at hearing, 15 June 1953, to the effect that Communist books should not be on the shelves of U.S. information libraries overseas, and McCarthy's retort: "They were not removed till we exposed them." Report of an interview on the same day with Secretary of State Dulles dealing with his Department's policies on "book burning." Text of interview with President Eisenhower two days later, explaining what he meant by his earlier reference to "book burners."

"Book Censorship Condemned as Un-American and Undesirable." *Current Opinion,* 73:517–18, October 1922. **B 387**
Discussion of proposals for voluntary censorship in America made by John Sumner of the New York vice society. There are quotations from Mr. Sumner and from such opponents of the proposal as George Creel, Booth Tarkington, and Heywood Broun.

"Book Censorship in Ireland." *Literary Digest,* 100:23, 2 February 1929. **B 388**
George Russell, in the London *Spectator,* gives the background and some of the provisions of the censorship bill pending in Ireland. "The Irish Free State through the publicity given to its censorship bill, and because of other activities by its moralists, has become, with Tennessee, a butt for the wits of the world."

"Book Censorship in Ireland." *Saturday Review* (London), 146:262–63, 1 September 1928. **B 389**

"Book Censorship in New Zealand." *Bookseller,* 3017:1756–59, 19 October 1963. **B 390**
An account of the Indecent Publications Act of 1963, which aroused a storm of controversy within the government and the book trade. Under the Act a tribunal of five appointed members "would appear to have the power to ban any book considered by it to be undesirable and to confiscate stocks."

"Book Censorship in the Air." *New Zealand Libraries,* 13:118–19, June 1950. **B 391**
Press comment on proposals to modify New Zealand's Customs censorship.

"Book Censorship in the Commonwealth." *Author,* 71:91–93, Autumn 1960. **B 392**
The article considers obscenity law and administration in Britain, New Zealand (the new Indecent Publications Act), South Africa, and Canada. "At present . . . it seems that the Commonwealth, in its attitude to writers and readers, is considerably less liberal than we are at least trying to be in this country, and less venturesome than America, which has struggled harder than most countries toward an adult standard of literacy."

"Book Censorship Is Reaching Epidemic Proportions." *Publishers' Weekly,* 163:1058–60, 28 February 1953. **B 393**
A review of recent efforts by local censorship groups to ban books and magazines through extralegal means as an outgrowth of the hearings of the Gathings Committee. References are made to efforts to enact drastic legislation against obscenity. The 30 May 1953 issue reports further censorship efforts in many localities.

"Book Selection or Censorship; Summary of a Panel Discussion Which Took Place at the APLA Conference, May 20, 1960." *APLA Bulletin* (Atlantic Provinces Library Association), 25:17–22, Fall 1960. **B 394**

The Bookseller. London, J. Whitaker & Sons, 1858–date. Weekly. **B 395**
This organ of the British book trade carries notes and news about book censorship problems at home and abroad.

"Boom or Boycott." *Spectator,* III:238–39, 16 August 1913. **B 396**
Relates to the action of the British Circulating Libraries Association's rejection of Hall Caine's *The Woman Thou Gavest Me,* and Caine's attack on the policies of the Association.

Boone, Ilsley. *Evolutionary Psychology . . . Also, some information by and about Theodore Schroeder.* Stamford, Conn., The Next Century Fund, 1949. 62 p. **B 397**
Biographical and testimonial data on a leading proponent of freedom of speech and the press.

———. *On the Non-Obscenity of Nudist Pictures.* [Mays Landing, N.J., American Sunbathing Association, 1942]. 4 p. (Reprinted from *Sunshine & Health,* October 1942) **B 398**
The executive secretary of the American Sunbathing Association presents the nudist point of view, citing court decisions, with particular reference to the official journal of the Association, *Sunshine & Health.* He concludes that "such pictures as are illustrative of bona fide nudist publications, whether books or periodicals, cannot fall within scope of the statutes directed against lewd, lascivious, obscene and indecent pictures." He argues that to deny the organization the right to set forth its teachings by use of nude figures would be to deprive it freedom of the press guaranteed by the Constitution. The obscenity law was not intended to be used as a weapon by which a minority social view might be suppressed. An article on censorship and the nudist press by Donald Johnson, appears in the 1961 *Eden Annual.*

Booth, George F. "The Freedom of the Press." In Worcester Fire Society, *One Hundred and Fiftieth Anniversary of the Worcester Fire Society.* Worcester, Mass., The Society, 1943, pp. 16–33. **B 399**
The publisher of the Worcester *Telegram and Gazette* reviews the struggle for a free press in America that took place during the lifetime of the Society. "The freedom of the press is not primarily for the protection of newspapers and other publications; it is for the protection of the rights of the whole people. With the right of free speech, a free press is the greatest protection against tyranny . . . that we, as a people, possess . . . A free press is the organ through which democracy breathes."

Booth, Wayne C. "Censorship and the Values of Fiction." *English Journal,* 53:155–64, March 1964. **B 400**

A professor of English advises high school English teachers to keep a "freedom portfolio" of arguments to combat censorship. He submits a statement entitled What to Do with a Literary Work before Deciding to Censor It, which he recommends giving to a parent who wants to censor *Catcher in the Rye*. He argues that a good censor will refuse to draw conclusions on any element of a book taken out of context, but will read the complete work and, in fact, study it as in a classroom situation A good censor should judge the true value o a book as a whole, not by the expressed value or behavior of a single character, which may be repudiated by the author's implied criticism. After analyzing *Catcher in the Rye* he concludes that it is a moral and important work; by contrast *Peyton Place*, aside from the sexual offenses, is immoral and shoddy and deserving of contempt.

Borah, William E. *Andrew Hamilton. Remarks of Hon. William E. Borah of Idaho in the Senate of the United States, Monday, January 15 . . . 1934. Inscription on Tablet to Commemorate the Distinguished Public Service of Andrew Hamilton; also Address of Harry Weinberger, Chairman of Tablet Committee* . . . Washington, D.C., 1934. 7p. **B 401**

Hamilton was the defense attorney in the celebrated John Peter Zenger libel case.

————. "Censorship Heavier Than Russian Muzzle: Senator Borah Characterized the Espionage Bill; Senator Cummins in Voicing his Opposition, Criticises President Wilson." *New York Times Magazine*, 29 April 1917, p. 2–3. **B 402**

————. "Free Speech for Free Americans." *Christian Century*, 52(18):570, 1 March 1935. **B 403**

"The great problem of representative government, as I see it, is not alone that of coping with those who openly advocate the destruction of representative government, but rather how to deal with the forces—economical and political—which grow restless and sometimes defiant under the restraint of law." It is a libel on the American people to assume that so considerable a number are susceptible to infection by foreign "isms" that they need to be watched, protected, and controlled. Loyalty means "loyalty of the government to the people just as much as it means loyalty of the people to the government." Extracts from an address before the American Society of Newspaper Editors.

Boroson, Warren. "'Introduction' to 'Some Thoughts on the Science of Onanism' by Mark Twain." *Fact*, 9(2): 19–21, March–April 1964. **B 404**

"Suppressed since 1879, a minor masterpiece by America's greatest humorist is here published for the first time . . . In the entire history of bawdy literature, perhaps no work has been the subject of such high-handed suppression and such shamefaced secrecy."

Borrow, George. *Celebrated Trials and Remarkable Cases of Criminal Jurisprudence from the Earliest Records to the Year 1825*. London, Knight and Lacy, 1825. 6 vols. **B 405**

Includes a number of sedition and censorship trials, listed elsewhere in this bibliography under the name of the defendant.

Borthwick, John. *Observations upon the Modes of Prosecuting for Libel, According to the Laws of England*. London, Ridgway 1830. 44p. **B 406**

————. *Treatise on the Law of Libel and Slander, as Applied in Scotland, with Appendix of 48 Unreported Cases*. Edinburgh, W. & C. Tait, 1826. 491p. **B 407**

Bose, Sudhindra. "Book Censorship in America." *Modern Review* (Calcutta), 55: 286–88, March 1934. **B 408**

Criticism of the United States Customs laws restricting obscene and radical works.

Boston. Advisory Committee on Sex Publications. *Constitution*. Boston, The Committee, 1921. 3p. mimeo. **B 409**

Boston booksellers, seeking expert advice on sex hygiene books that were "flooding the country" after World War I, organized an Advisory Committee on Sex Publications. It consisted of three physicians, two representatives of the Watch and Ward Society, and two booksellers. The purpose of the Committee was "to act as a voluntary board to assist publishers, booksellers, and any organization or group of citizens interested in the public welfare, and to this end pass upon the suitability for publication and distribution of popular sex publications." The Committee decided whether the books were suitable for (1) general distribution, (2) medical and legal professions only, or (3) unsuitable. Publishers were encouraged to submit manuscripts of sex hygiene books to the Committee for its opinion before publication.

"Boston Discusses Its Censorship Problem." *Publishers' Weekly*, 111:2118–19, 28 May 1927. **B 410**

A news report on a public meeting in Boston called by the Woman's City Club, to find a solution to the mass censorship wave in that city. Rev. Raymond Calkins spoke for the Watch and Ward Society; Hiller C. Wellman, librarian of Springfield, pleaded for tolerance and for frankness in modern literature and urged revision of the obscenity laws; Publisher

Alfred Harcourt suggested that Boston had gotten itself into a ridiculous situation in censorship as a result of "too much machinery."

"The Boston Trial of *Naked Lunch*." *Evergreen Review*, 9(36):40–49, 87–88, June 1965. **B 411**

Excerpts from the testimony of Norman Mailer and Allen Ginsberg in behalf of William S. Burroughs' *Naked Lunch*, the defendant, in Boston's Superior Court. There is also a statement from Edward de Grazia, defense attorney for the book and its publisher, Grove Press.

"Boston's Book Censorship." *Literary Digest*, 93:31–32, 2 April 1927. **B 412**

Press comments on the banning by Boston police of nine current novels including *The Plastic Age* by Percy Marks and *As It Was* by Helen Thomas.

Bostwick, Andrew L. "Censorship of Moving Picture Films." *National Municipal Review*, 2:332–33, April 1913. **B 413**

Bostwick, Arthur E. "The Librarian as a Censor." *Library Journal*, 33:257–64, July 1908. (Also in his *Library Essays*, New York, Wilson, 1920, pp. 121–39) **B 414**

Discussion of the censorship activities of the librarian who selects books for the general public. Bostwick recommends three bases for such book selection—"the Good, the True, and the Beautiful." The librarian should inquire of a questionable book whether it is objectionable "because of falsity, of evil morality or of impropriety." The author was librarian of the St. Louis Public Library.

Boswell, Peyton. "Cultural Censorship." *Art Digest*, 16:3, 15 April 1942. **B 415**

Brief comments on the banning of *Life* magazine in Boston for reprinting six nude pictures then on public exhibition at the Dallas Art Museum.

————. "Protection against Maturity." *Art Digest*, 12:3–4, 1 October 1937. **B 416**

Comments on the conviction of a New York art supplies firm for selling *The Body Beautiful*, a volume of nude photographs published for artists and art students. The book was seized by a police officer on complaints from unnamed citizens.

Bothwell, *Mrs*. Austin. "The Problem of Controlling the Reading of Undesirable Periodical Literature; Brief Presented to Saskatchewan Library Advisory Council." *Ontario Library Review*, 31:125–36, May 1947. **B 417**

The librarian of the Province summarizes arguments for and against certain classes of periodical literature (salacious and pornographic, low grade crime, love and westerns, confession magazines, movie magazines, and comic books) and presents various suggestions for controlling their circulation. Among the possible methods of control are: legal (Criminal Code, postal regulations, Customs Act, embargo, and grading of publications as "adult" and "juvenile"), the counterattack with good reading, influencing the content of undesirable publications, intelligent use of comics, and immunization of children against undesirable literature.

Bottiger, R. Ted. "Washington Comic Book Statute." *Washington Law Review*, 34:160–67, Summer 1959. **B 418**
Notes on *Adams v. Hinkle*, 51 Wn. 2d 763, 322 P. 2d 844 (1958), in which the Washington State Supreme Court declared void the 1955 state "Comic Book Act," which attempted to give the State supervisor of children and youth services regulatory control over the publication and distribution of comic books to be sold in that state.

Boudin, Louis B. "Freedom of Thought and Religious Liberty under the Constitution." *Lawyers Guild Review*, 4(3): 9–24, June–July 1944. **B 419**
Includes a discussion of Jehovah's Witnesses cases before the U.S. Supreme Court (the *Lovell* and *Opelika* cases). The Supreme Court rulings with respect to the power of the State to require conformity are summarized: "The State has no authority whatsoever in the domain of thought. Freedom of thought is absolute. In the domain of conduct the State has a right to protect itself against imminent serious danger."

———. "'Seditious Doctrines' and the 'Clear and Present Danger' Rule." *Virginia Law Review*, 38:143–86, February 1952; 38:315–56, April 1952. **B 420**

Bourke, Vernon J. "Censorship in American Culture." In Catholic Library Association. *Proceedings*, 33rd Conference, Louisville, 1957, pp. 72–77. **B 421**

———. "Moral Problems Related to Censoring the Media of Mass Communication." *Marquette Law Review*, 40:57–73, Summer 1956. **B 422**
"Censoring is only called for when people fail to exercise due restraint over their personal inclinations to endanger the good order of their community in various types of communications. Censoring, then, is the mark of some degree of moral failure in a society. Those who resent and criticize it are partly right. But the thing to do is not passively to suffer the evils which censoring is designed to avoid but actively to work for standards of public conviction which would remove the very reasons for censoring."

Bourne, H. R. Fox. *English Newspapers: Chapters in the History of Journalism.* London, Chatto and Windus, 1887. 2 vols. **B 423**
A general history of English journalism from 1621 to 1887. Includes detailed accounts of the Wilkes and Junius affairs and the seditious libel cases both before and after the Fox Libel Act of 1792.

———. *The Life of Locke.* London, H. S. King, 1876. 2 vols. **B 424**
When the English licensing act was up for renewal in 1694, Locke drew up a section by section criticism of it which his friend, Edward Clarke, presented to a joint committee of Parliament appointed to study the measure. Unlike the eloquence of Milton in *Areopagitica*, Locke's statement took a more practical approach, stressing the inconvenience of the act rather than the pernicious principle on which it was based. It is believed that Locke's statement helped influence the decision of the committee to disapprove renewal. An extract of Locke's statement appears in volume 2, pp. 311–16.

Bourquin, Jacques. *La Liberté de la Presse.* Paris, Presses Universitaires de France, 1950. 621 p. **B 425**
Includes a general discussion of freedom of the press; an historical survey of press freedom in France, the United States, Great Britain, and Switzerland since the seventeenth century; and techniques of control. The author was active in the UNESCO conference on press freedom.

Boutwell, William D. "What's Happening in Education [Book-banning]" *PTA Magazine*, 56:15–16, April 1962. **B 426**
"We have been going through one of those book-banning fevers that strike when you least expect them. This time it is 'The Scarlet Letter' by Hawthorne. A few parents say it is salacious and should be banned by the high school library."

"Bow Street and After." *Bookseller*, 3035: 1074–76, 22 February 1964; 3036: 1156–59, 29 February 1964. **B 427**
The first article reports on a document signed by 20 members of Parliament protesting action taken against *Fanny Hill* by a Bow Street magistrate. "This decision was given after two minutes reflection . . . was contrary to all the evidence given by expert and reputable witnesses." The book, the statement said, is healthier in tone than many books which are not subject to censorship by police. The second article reports on the Publishers' Association statement deploring the methods used by the director of public prosecutions in proceeding against *Fanny Hill*.

Bowden, Witt. "Freedom for Wage Earners." *Annals of the American Academy of Political and Social Science*, 200:185–209, November 1938. **B 428**

One of the basic freedoms of the worker is the right of free inquiry and discussion. The author discusses these freedoms as they have been sustained or denied by law, executive action, and court decision.

[Bowdler, Thomas]. *Liberty; Civil and Religious. By a Friend to Both.* London, Printed for J. Hatchard, 1815. 73 p. **B 429**
Religious liberty is "the being able to profess a true faith, and to practice a right mode of worship." Civil liberty is not liberty to think and do what one will; this is license. Rather, it is to be "able to do what he ought to will."

Bowen, John. "Gamesmanship with *Fanny Hill*." *New York Times Book Review*, 15 March 1964, p. 4. **B 430**

Bowen, Louise de Koven. *Five and Ten Cent Theatres; Two Investigations by the Juvenile Protective Association of Chicago, 1909 and 1911.* Chicago, The Association [1911?]. 10 p. **B 431**

Bowen, Marjorie, *pseud. Peter Porcupine; a Study of William Cobbett, 1762–1835.* London, Longmans Green, 1935. 312 p. **B 432**
A somewhat simplified story of the life and adventures of William Cobbett, farmer, linguist, fiery pamphleteer, and rebel, including references to his many trials for libel both in England and the United States.

Bower, George S., *ed. A Code of the Law of Actionable Defamation.* 2d ed. London, Butterworth, 1923. 469 p. **B 433**

Bowerman, George F. "Censorship and the Public Library." *Libraries*, 35:127–35, April 1930; 35:182–86, May 1930. (Reprinted in his *Censorship and the Public Library, with Other Papers.* New York, Wilson, 1931) **B 434**
The librarian of the Washington, D.C., Public Library discusses the problems faced by public librarians in selection of books, including the activities of pressure groups. He favors the locked case device for some books, limiting them to the use of serious students. He would put in the case books on such subjects as sex psychology (Havelock Ellis) and certain medical works dealing with sex.

Bowker, Richard R. *Copyright; Its History and Its Law; Being a Summary of the Principles and Practice of Copyright with Special Reference to the American Code of 1909 and the British Act of 1911.* Boston, Houghton Mifflin, 1912. 709 p. **B 435**

A comprehensive treatise on copyright, tracing the legal history back to classic times and including American and British law up to 1912. The work is divided into six parts which suggests its broad scope: Literature and general copyright; dramatic, musical, and artistic copyright; copyright protection and procedure; international and foreign copyright; business relations and literature. The appendix gives in detail the copyright provisions of American, British, and International and Pan-American Union conventions.

Bowles, John. *Considerations on the Respective Rights of Judge and Jury, particularly upon Trials for Libel*. 2d ed. London, 1791. 56 p.

B 436

Bowles, a barrister of the Inner Temple, held the view espoused by Lord Mansfield, that the jury in libel trials should consider only the fact of publication. Whether or not the matter published was libelous should be left to the wisdom of the judge.

————. *A Letter to the Right Hon. Charles James Fox, occasioned by his Motion in the House of Commons respecting Libels: and suggesting the Alarming Consequences likely to ensue, if the Bill now before the Legislature upon that Subject should pass into a Law*. London, Printed for Whieldon and Butterworth, 1792. 34 p.

B 437

One of several letters written on this subject in support of Lord Mansfield's limitations on juries in libel trials and opposing the liberalizing measure proposed by Fox. The Fox Libel Act was passed the same year.

[————]. *Letters of the Ghost of Alfred, addressed to the Hon. Thomas Erskine, and the Hon. Charles James Fox, on the occasion of the State Trials at the close of the year 1794, and the beginning of the year 1795*. London, Printed for J. Wright, 1798. 126 p. **B 438**

The letters were originally published in the *True Briton* to protest the acquittal of Hardy, Tooke, and Thelwall in the sedition trials of 1794. Erskine had been defense counsel in the trials and Fox had been responsible for the revision of the libel law which put the power of decision in the hands of the jury rather than the judge. The letters oppose liberalizing the libel act and favor strengthening laws that would protect the country against the dangerous influence of the French Revolution.

[————]. *A Protest Against T. Paine's "Rights of Man": Addressed to the Members of a Book Society, in Consequence of the Vote of their Committee for Including the above Work in a List of New Publications Resolved to Be Purchased for the Use of the Society. . . .* London, Printed for T. Longman, etc., 1792. 37 p. **B 439**

The anonymous author states that the majority voted for Paine's mischievous book through a mistaken zeal for freedom of discussion.

————. *A Second Letter to the Right Honourable Charles James Fox, upon the Matter of Libel: suggesting The dangerous Tendency of the Bill now before the Legislature upon the above Subject, both with Respect to the Constitution itself and the Whole System of English Law*. London, Printed for Whieldon and Butterworth, 1792. 58 p.

B 440

Bowles also issued an 8-page appendix to the second letter, *Brief Deductions from First Principles Applying to the Matter of Libel*, in which he lists 32 legal principles with respect to libels.

————. *A Short Answer to the Declaration of the Persons calling themselves The Friends of the Liberty of the Press*. London, J. Downes, 1793. 24 p. **B 441**

Bowles was a member of the Association for Preserving Liberty and Property Against Republicans and Levellers. In this pamphlet he defends the constitutional associations and their attempts to enforce the laws against seditious publications. "Those who serve the licentious excess to which the Freedom of the Press is still daily carried, will be of opinion that it stands in no great need of the proffered protection of this new-formed phalanx of defenders."

Bowman, Ben C. "Censorship in University and Research Libraries." *ILA Record* (Illinois Library Association), 7: 96–99, April 1954. **B 442**

Encroachments on the selection of books for academic and research libraries have not been a widespread problem. In the matter of book selection in a scholarly library, the author notes that "whatever interferes with the freedom of the process of questioning and investigating is censorship, and whoever would impose it is a censor."

Bowron, Albert. "*Tropic* in Canada." *Library Journal*, 87:184, 15 January 1962.

B 443

The effects in Canada of the debanning of the works of Henry Miller by the U.S. Department of Justice. Royal Canadian Mounted Police used a blanket search warrant to repossess copies of Miller's work in Vancouver. The Toronto Public Library was requested to return copies to the local Collector of Customs.

Bowyer, William. "John Wilkes." In his *Literary Anecdotes of the Eighteenth Century*. London, Printed for the Author, 1815. vol. 9, pp. 453–80. **B 444**

Boyce, W. D. "Genesis of the Censorship Proposition." *Advertising News*, 25: 30–32, 26 May 1917. **B 445**

A review of prosecutions under the Alien and Sedition Acts in light of proposals for censorship in World War I. From an address given during Journalism Week at the University of Missouri.

Boyd, Ernest A. "Adult or Infantile Censorship?" *Dial*, 70:381–85, April 1921.

B 446

If we are to have censorship it should be by legally constituted authorities and not by professional "smuthounds." Boyd cites the French trial of Flaubert for writing *Madame Bovary* as preferable to the American attack on *Jurgen*.

————. "Puritan: Modern Style." In his *Portraits: Real and Imaginary*. New York, Doran, 1924, pp. 106–17. **B 447**

One of the imaginary portraits deals with a modern-day Puritan who is "conspiring against freedom of thought, freedom of art and personal liberty."

[————, and John S. Sumner]. *Debate. Subject: Resolved, That limitations upon the contents of books and magazines as defined in proposed legislation would be detrimental to the advancement of American literature. Ernest Boyd, Affirmative, versus John S. Sumner, Negative. Introduction by Clifford Smyth, Foreword by John Farrar*. New York, League for Public Discussion, 1924. 77 p.

B 448

Boyd was an Irish literary critic and essayist, at one time a member of the editorial staff of the New York *Evening Post*. Sumner was Secretary of the New York Society for the Suppression of Vice.

Boyd, Francis. "A Free Press." *Spectator*, 209:385–86, 21 September 1962. **B 449**

Comments on the report of the Royal Commission of the Press concerning the number of newspapers ceasing publication and "the extent to which a few proprietors dominate the actual supply of news and opinion through the daily and Sunday press." The author is in favor of the public knowing who controls which papers. "For, if economic forces must be allowed, the best hope of retaining a press which is not only free but varied is to produce papers which are demanded because they are judged to be good by the best tests the public can apply."

Boyd, Julian P. "Free Communication— An American Heritage." In *Freedom of Communication; Proceedings of the First Conference on Intellectual Freedom . . .* Chicago, American Library Association, 1954, pp. 10–18. **B 450**

————. "Subversive of What?" *Atlantic Monthly*, 182:19–23, August 1948. (Reprinted in Downs, *The First Freedom*, pp. 224–30) **B 451**

The former librarian of Princeton and editor of Thomas Jefferson's papers considers some lessons learned from Jefferson as to the nature of subversion and loyalty. Boyd describes Jefferson's defense of the bookseller, Nicholas Dufief, arrested in Philadelphia for the sale of Regnault de Bécourt's *Sur la Création du Monde*. Every man in the United States has the right to buy and read what he pleases, Jefferson maintained. "To preserve the freedom of the human mind and freedom of the press every spirit should be ready to devote itself to martyrdom; for as long as we may think as we will and speak as we think, the conditions of man will proceed in improvement."

Boyd, Maurice R. *The Effect of Censorship Attempts by Private Pressure Groups on Public Libraries, 1945–57.* Kent, Ohio, Kent State University, 1958. 69p. (Unpublished Master's thesis)   **B 452**

Boyenton, William H. "Origins of Advertising Censorship in the New York Newspapers." *Journalism Quarterly*, 19: 137–49, June 1942.   **B 453**
Based on a Master's thesis, *Development of Advertising Censorship by New York City Newspapers.* New Brunswick, N.J., Rutgers University, 1940. 104p.

Boyer, Paul S. "Boston Book Censorship in the Twenties." *American Quarterly*, 15:3–24, Spring 1936.   **B 454**
"Boston was particularly susceptible to censorship in the twenties and the Watch and Ward Society provided the institutional apparatus through which censorship was exercised." The author describes the events in which the Society, the booksellers, the Catholic press, and the police combined to give Boston its reputation as the censorship capital of the United States. He refers especially to the cases against the *American Mercury*, Dreiser's *An American Tragedy*, and Lawrence's *Lady Chatterley's Lover* (the Dunster House Bookshop case), and analyzes the factors that combined to make possible such a climate.

Boylan, William A. "Legal and Illegal Limitations on Television Programming." *Federal Communications Bar Journal*, 11: 137–49, Autumn 1950.   **B 455**

Boyle, Donzella C. "The Textbook Problem." *D.A.R. Magazine*, December 1960. (Reprinted as a separate pamphlet by the National Defense Committee, D.A.R.; also in *Warped Manuscripts; A Report on "Slanted Textbooks".* Fullerton, Calif., Educational Information, 1962, pp. 1–4)   **B 456**
Mrs. Boyle charges that a socialist program of thought control is taking place in America through a powerful educational monopoly that dictates the contents of textbooks. This is done through swinging "enough big city and state adoptions to control the content of

textbooks for everybody." The available school textbooks are unsympathetic with Americanism and the free enterprise system. She urges school boards to demand a different kind of textbook. "Confidentially, I think the textbook publishers would like to be free, too, and they would welcome the opportunity to bid for your business." An address before the Minnesota Association of Public Schools.

Boyle, Hugh C. "The Legion of Decency—a Permanent Campaign." *Ecclesiastical Review*, 91:367–70, October 1934.   **B 457**
The Bishop of Pittsburgh is heartened by the success of the Legion of Decency's campaign against immoral movies and calls for continuing support of the crusade.

Boyle, Humphrey. *Report of the Trial of Humphrey Boyle. Indicted at the Instance of the Constitutional Association, as "a man with name unknown," for Publishing[!] an Alleged Blasphemous and Seditious Libel, as One of the Shopmen of Mr. Carlile; Which Took Place before Mr. Common Sergeant Denman, and a Common Jury, at the Old Bailey Sessions House, on the 27th of May, 1822. With a Narrative of the Proceedings against the Defendant before Trial. To Which is Attached, the Trial of Joseph Rhodes, under the Name of Wm. Holmes, as forced upon him, for Publishing a Copy of the Same Pamphlet.* London, Printed by R. Carlile and Published at the Koran Society's Office, 1822. 32p. (Also in Macdonell, *Report of State Trials*, vol. 6, pp. 42 ff., 103, 189; vol. 8, p. 155)   **B 458**
Boyle, one of Mr. Carlile's voluntary shopmen, was tried for blasphemous libel, found guilty, and sentenced to 18 months in prison. At the trial Boyle insisted in reading "obscene" passages from the Bible. Mr. Rhodes, another shopman, refused to give his name so was prosecuted under the name of Holmes. He was found guilty and given a 2-year sentence. John Barkley, a 17-year-old printer was sentenced to six months with hard labor.

Boyle, Robert. "Literature and Pornography." *Catholic World*, 193:295–302, August 1961.   **B 459**
Society must stamp out pornography but it must also protect literature. Neither the church nor state is competent to judge literature; this is the task of a trained literary critic.

———. "Teaching 'Dirty' Books in College." *America*, 100:337–39, 13 December 1958.   **B 460**
An author-priest defends the teaching of such works as Graham Greene's *The End of the Affair* and James Joyce's *Ulysses* to college students "on the assumption that contemplation of the perfectly expressed visions of

contemporary as well as classical artists is essential to the full development of our students."

Boyle, T. O'R. "We Are All Censors." *Commonweal*, 21:226–28, 21 December 1934.   **B 461**
The author discusses arguments against the Legion of Decency presented in *The Nation*, *Today*, and *Liberty*, and defends the Legion against its critics.

Bracken, Brendan. "Wartime Censorship; How England Keeps Its Freedom of the Press." *Life*, 12:71–74, 16 March 1942.   **B 462**
The head of Britain's Ministry of Information describes how wartime censorship works, "how in practice we reconcile the conflicting demands of freedom and of security."

Braden, Thomas W. "Today's Threat to Librarians." *Bulletin, School Library Association of California*, 33:17–18, May 1962.   **B 463**

———. "The Trouble with Censorship." *San Francisco Magazine*, 5:42–43, 45, July 1963. (Reprinted in *California Librarian*, October 1963)   **B 464**

[Bradlaugh, Charles]. *Champion of Liberty: Charles Bradlaugh.* New York, Freethought Press, 1933. 346p. (Issued for the Centenary Committee)   **B 465**
Includes a section on Bradlaugh and the Liberty of the Press, by Sir J. A. Hammerton, pp. 299–308.

[———]. *The Laws Relating to Blasphemy and Heresy; an Address to Freethinkers.* London, Freethought Publishing Co., 1878.   **B 466**

[———, and Annie Besant]. "Publishers' Preface." In Charles Knowlton, *Fruits of Philosophy; a Treatise on the Population Question.* London, Freethought Publishing Co. [1876?], pp. 2–3. (Issued in numerous editions in England and the United States)   **B 467**
Mr. Bradlaugh and Mrs. Besant relate the 40-year English publishing history of Dr. Knowlton's birth control tract, leading to the arrest of the English publisher Charles Watt. When Watt pleaded guilty of an obscenity charge and the work did not come before the court, Bradlaugh and Besant republished it as a test case.

[———]. *The Queen v. Charles Bradlaugh and Annie Besant* . . . London, Freethought Publishing Co., 1877. 324 p. **B 468**
The defendants were indicted for having published an obscene libel, Dr. Charles Knowlton's pamphlet, *Fruits of Philosophy*. They were acquitted when the jury found the book obscene but the defendants without any corrupt motive in publishing it. "It was for the sake of free discussion that we published the assailed pamphlet when its former seller yielded to the pressure put upon him by the police; it was not so much in defence of this pamphlet, as to make the way possible for others dealing with the same topic, that we risked the penalty which has fallen upon us." The defendants, in the introduction, note that Lord Campbell himself, under whose act they were being tried, "limited its object to the seizure of the foul literature of passion and sensuality."

Bradley, J. R. A. "The Case of *The Well of Loneliness*." *New Adelphi*, 2:350–52, June 1929. **B 469**
The English obscenity law makes the discussion of homosexuality have about as much chance of a fair hearing as the mouse had in *Alice in Wonderland*.

Bradley, Lawrence J., and Joseph A. Marino. "Freedom of Speech—Obscenity, 1958–1960." *Notre Dame Lawyer*, 35: 537–46, August 1960. **B 470**
The authors examine recent legal developments, including whether obscenity is protected under the First Amendment, the problem of prior restraint, what measures may be taken to protect youth, and who shall decide what is and what is not obscene. They believe that a program of limited censorship is in order to protect certain impressionable segments of the population, especially children.

Bradshaw, Michael. "Slanting the News." *Atlantic Monthly*, 174:79–82, August 1944. **B 471**
Freedom of the press is in danger from the menace of local news slanting. If the people can trust the press they will come to its defense.

Brady, Robert A. "Monopoly and the First Freedom; Censorship over the Media of Communications." *Hollywood Quarterly*, 2:225–41, April 1947. **B 472**
An economist criticizes Morris Ernst's indictment of big business control of the mass media in his book, *The First Freedom*. With the increase of monopoly in the modern world, the traditional formulae for "competition" are no longer practical. Brady argues for acceptance of man's production and control by organized democratic action.

———. "The Problem of Monopoly in Motion Pictures." *Annals of the American Academy of Political and Social Science*, 254:125–36, November 1947. (Reprinted in Schramm, *Mass Communications*, pp. 168–85) **B 473**
An analysis of the complex monopoly in the motion picture industry by which five major companies control production, distribution, and exhibition. Includes a detailed summary of the important court decree against Paramount Pictures (1946) which placed a number of restraints on the film industry.

Brailsford, H. N. *The Levellers and the English Revolution. By H. N. Brailsford. Edited and prepared for publication by Christopher Hill.* Stanford, Calif., Stanford University Press, 1961. 715 p. **B 474**
References throughout to the Levellers' efforts in behalf of freedom of the press, including the cases of Lilbourne, Walwyn, Overton, and Bastwick.

Brailsford, Mabel R. *A Quaker from Cromwell's Army: James Nayler.* New York, Macmillan, 1927. 200 p. **B 475**
Nayler was a Quaker whose books and pamphlets were considered blasphemous by the English Parliament. His books were burned and he was subjected to cruel punishment. Proceedings of the House of Commons against Nayler for blasphemy in 1656 are reported in Howell, *State Trials*, vol. 5, p. 801 ff.

Brandt, Joseph A. "Freedom of Communication within the Nation." *Educational Record*, 29:392–99, October 1948. **B 476**
In an address before the American Council on Education, Brandt reviews the report of the Commission on Freedom of the Press and suggests steps to be taken to carry out some of its recommendations.

Brandwen, Maxwell. "Battle of the First Amendment: a Study in Judicial Interpretation." *North Carolina Law Review*, 40:273–96, February 1962. **B 477**
The author, a member of the New York Bar, argues that if the consequences of abuse of freedom of speech and press under the First Amendment "are too alarming to society, then the alternative is constitutional amendment, not judicial or congressional whittling down. If the first amendment is outmoded and no longer conforms to modern insights, tastes and mores, and if the needs of society must be liberated from the thraldom of the words of the framers of the first amendment, then let the constitutional method of amendment be observed . . . Meanwhile, let the first amendment be immune from encroachment."

Brantley, Rabun L. "A Southern Paper and the Civil War." *Journalism Bulletin*, 2(2):23–28, June 1925. **B 478**
The trials of one southern paper, the Macon *Telegraph*—difficulties in getting paper and news, threats of conscription of its editors, and the cutting of telegraph lines by federal troops.

Bratt, Eyvind. "Government and the Press: a Comparative Analysis." *Journalism Quarterly*, 21:185–99, September 1944. **B 479**
A Swedish consular officer discusses the ideologies influencing the relationship between the press and government. He considers the liberal, totalitarian, and socialist concepts of press freedom and the operation of these doctrines in the United States, Britain, Sweden, and the Soviet Union.

Braumueller, Gerd. *Der Weg zur Pressefreiheit; die Entwicklung des Presserechtes in den Vereinigten Staaten.* Bonn, L. Röhrscheid, 1953. 104 p. **B 480**
A general treatise on the development of press freedom in the United States.

Braun, Theodore A. "Obscenity in the Bookstore." *United Church Herald*, 7:31, 1 February 1964. **B 481**

Bray, J. J. "Censorship." *Australian Library Journal*, 13:60–70, June 1964. **B 482**
Following a general review of the English heritage of freedom of the press, the author discusses the present legal position with respect to censorship in Australia—federal restrictions placed on book importations and obscenity prosecutions in South Australia at common law or under the Police Offences Act. Australians are denied the right to read books by distinguished writers which circulate in other parts of the English-speaking world. The author does not see much hope for success in recasting the complex system of federal and state laws, but suggests that constant pressures be applied to exert a liberalization in the administration of the law.

Bray, Robert J., Jr. "Censorship—Motion Picture—Licensing Statute Is Not an Unconstitutional Prior Restraint." *Villanova Law Review*, 6:567–71, Summer 1961. **B 483**
Regarding *Times Film Corp. v. City of Chicago*, 365 U.S. 43 (1961).

Brechner, Joseph L. "A Statement on the 'Fairness Doctrine.'" *Journal of Broadcasting*, 9(2):103–12, Spring 1965. **B 484**
A broadcaster argues that the FCC should cease to impose the test of "fairness" on broadcast editorializing.

Breckinridge, Harry. "Persecution of Margaret Sanger." *Mother Earth*, 9: 296–97, November 1914. **B 485**

The author, writing in this American anarchist periodical, ascribes opposition to birth control to capitalist greed.

Breen, Walter. "Censorship; the Real Issue." *Panic Button*, 14:20–29, Summer 1963.　　　**B 486**
The three common, oversimplified positions about censorship—the conservative who is interested in preserving the status quo, the moderate whose concern is solely for protection of the welfare of the child, and the liberal who believes all censorship is bad—present a danger. The conservative does not realize that historically censorship has been ineffective in preventing change; the moderate does not realize that there is no evidence that children are harmed by radical political or sexual expression; the liberal fails to realize that freedom of the press in itself is not sufficient so long as the press is under the control of big business and advertisers, and that the opinions of ordinary citizens do not always get into print. To protect against propaganda the author recommends the teaching of a healthy scepticism; to protect against violence and sadism, he recommends orienting society toward sexual freedom and away from its substitute—violence.

Breger, Dave, ed. *But That's Unprintable! About the Taboos in Magazine and Newspaper Comic Cartoons.* New York, Bantam, 1955. 149p.　　　**B 487**
A collection of 135 "unprintable" cartoons, never published because they violate certain journalistic taboos. The drawings are accompanied by Breger's general discussion of these taboos—what causes them and who enforces them.

Brégy, Katherine. "Literature of Libel." *Catholic World*, 116:444–53, January 1923.　　　**B 488**
The author attacks the "literature of libel" which maligns and debunks moral standards, religious faith, and basic institutions.

Breit, Harvey, and Alan U. Schwartz. "A Right to License the Licentious?" *Saturday Review*, 48(8):34–35, 2 February 1960.　　　**B 489**
A critique of the book, *Pornography and the Law*, by Eberhard and Phyllis Kronhausen, and their attempts to draw a distinction between erotic realism in literature and "hard-core" pornography.

Breitenfeld, Frederick, Jr. "Reason and the Absolute." *Journal of Broadcasting*, 5:191–98, Summer 1961.　　　**B 490**
"Mr. Breitenfeld's central point is that guarantees of the First Amendment have little relation to current criticisms and actions being directed against broadcasters who possess a technical monopoly (although with economic competition) of a priceless national resource." The author compares the power of broadcasting as a force to nuclear energy, and suggests they should be viewed similarly.

Brend, William A. *Sacrifice to Attis; a Study of Sex and Civilization.* London, Heinemann, 1936. 350p.　　　**B 491**
Numerous references to social control of obscenity and the doctrine of obscene libel.

Brennan, Jerome T. "City May Constitutionally Require that a Movie Be Submitted for Censorship before Public Showing." *Illinois Bar Journal*, 50:248–51, November 1961.　　　**B 492**
Regarding *Times Film Corp. v. City of Chicago*, 365 U.S. 43 (1961).

Brennan, William J., Jr. "Law, Liberty and Librarians." *Library Journal*, 88:2417–20, 15 June 1963.　　　**B 493**
"A Supreme Court Justice calls for greater cooperation between schools and libraries, and outlines the library's role as 'the guardian of freedom to read.' . . . It is not hard to understand, then, how easily the freedom to read might be placed in jeopardy were it not for the determination of the great public libraries to keep alive the full spectrum of our literature even where booksellers and others either cannot or care not, or dare not do so." The article is drawn from a speech given at a dinner celebrating the 75th anniversary of the Newark Public Library, 1 May 1963.

Brenner, D. J. *Covering Local Government.* Columbia, Mo., Freedom of Information Center, School of Journalism, University of Missouri, 1963. 9p. (Publication no. 106)　　　**B 494**
The responsibilities and problems faced by the reporter and the editorial writer in fair coverage of local government and politics.

Brentford, William Joynson-Hicks, Viscount. "Censorship of Books." *Nineteenth Century*, 106:207–11, August 1929.　　**B 495**
The British Home Secretary denies there is censorship of books in England in the sense of the censorship of plays and films, but affirms the responsibility of the Government for the moral welfare of the community. He defends his policy of reading manuscripts and books submitted to him by the publisher or the general public and advising whether the publication is actionable under the Obscene Publications Act of 1857, and especially with respect to his adverse decision on *Well of Loneliness*.

———. *Do We Need a Censor?* London, Faber, 1929. 24p. (Criterion Miscellany, no. 6)　　　**B 496**
Sir William states the case for British censorship of obscenity in books, plays, and movies, defending his own record against charges of "establishing a dictatorship in the realm of literature and morals." It was during his administration that action was taken against *Ulysses* and *Well of Loneliness*.

Brenton, Cranston. "Motion Pictures and Local Responsibility." *American City*, 16:125–31, February 1917.　　　**B 497**
The article is in support of the National Board of Review of Motion Pictures which is "unqualifiedly opposed in principle to all forms of legalized pre-publicity censorship as being unnecessary, un-democratic, un-American and unjust." Citizens are urged to co-operate with the National Board by informing that agency what pictures are objectionable in the local community.

Brenton, Myron. *The Privacy Invaders.* New York, Coward-McCann, 1964. 240p.　　　**B 498**
The author charges that public lives have become public property by invasion of the mass media. He lays blame on the social scientists, the schools and universities, and the direct-mail advertisers.

Brett, William H. "Improper Books." *Library Journal*, 20:36–37, December 1895.　　　**B 499**
In selecting books for libraries, there are three categories: those the librarian selects, those which he simply omits, and those he absolutely excludes. It is in the question of morals and conduct that he has the right of exclusion. Comments of the librarian of the Cleveland Public Library in one of a series of papers on undesirable books in public libraries given at the Denver Conference of Librarians.

Brettman, John. "Freedom of the Press: Power to Revoke the Second-Class Mail Privilege." *California Law Review*, 34:431–35, June 1946.　　　**B 500**
A consideration of the *Esquire* case in which the U.S. Supreme Court held that the Post Office has no power to consider the "worth" of a publication in approving its application for second-class mail privilege.

Breuer, *Mrs.* M. H. "Notes for an Article on Censorship." *Progressive Librarians' Council Bulletin*, 2:6–7, December 1940.　　　**B 501**
The books most often rejected by libraries are those advocating progressive thought and social change. The rejection is done quietly, often with the excuse of a limited budget. The author asks whether librarians will have the courage to buy pacifist books during wartime.

Brewer, George D. "*The Fighting Editor*" or, "*Warren and the Appeal.*" *A Word Picture of the Appeal to Reason Office. Biography of Fred D. Warren.* . . . 2d ed. Girard, Kan., The Author, 1910. 211p.　　　**B 502**

Biography of the editor of *Appeal to Reason*, the Socialist paper, and a history of events leading up to his sentence of 6 months in prison and a fine of $1,500. The offense was the mailing of 25,000 circulars, with an envelope message containing "threatening and scurrilous language." The book includes Warren's speeches before the Federal Court at Fort Scott, Kan., and the Appellate Court at St. Paul, Minn. There is also a chapter on the refusal of Canadian Customs to accept *Appeal to Reason* (1906).

Brewer, Weldon. "Should the School Newspaper Have a Censor?" *School Activities*, 21:251–52+, April 1950.
B 503

"The school newspaper, to be an effective, democratic voice of the students, must be freed from faculty domination." No sponsor should permit personal, abusive attack in the newspaper; by using methods outlined in the article, the sponsor would rarely have to censor anything. When censorship is necessary students do it themselves.

Brewerton, William W. "Words Adjudged to Be Slanderous." *Case and Comment*, 22:478–80, November 1915. **B 504**
A review of pertinent court decisions.

Brewin, F. A. "Civil Liberties in Canada during Wartime." *Bill of Rights Review*, 1:112–27, Winter 1941. **B 505**
Censorship in Canada during World War I was achieved more by voluntary cooperation than by coercive action of government censors, although sweeping powers were given the government.

Brewster, Kingman, Jr. "Allied Freedom: Press and Academic." In *The Enduring American Press*. Hartford, Conn., The *Hartford Courant* and Connecticut Mutual Life, 1964, pp. 4–6. **B 506**
Talk given by the president of Yale University on the occasion of the 200th anniversary of the *Hartford Courant*.

[Brewster, Thomas]. "Trial for Publishing a Book Called *Speeches and Prayers of Some of the Late King's Judges*, and other Seditious Works, 1663." In Howell, *State Trials*, vol. 6, p. 513. **B 507**

Bridgeman, George F. L. *The Pressman and the Law*. London, Pitman, 1928. 105 p.
B 508

A practical handbook for newspapermen including sections on libel, contempt, copyright, and restrictions on publication.

Brier, Warren J. "Political Censorship in the *Oregon Spectator*." *Pacific Historical Review*, 31:235–40, August 1962. **B 509**
The first English-language newspaper in the far western states, the *Oregon Spectator* of Oregon City, established in 1846, for a year managed to maintain a strict ban on political discussion, despite the strong political convictions of the pioneers.

Briffault, Robert, *et al*. "'Obscene' Literature." *English Review*, 62:504–6, April 1936. **B 510**
Twelve prominent scientists and writers, including Robert Briffault, J. B. S. Haldane, and Julian Huxley, sign this letter to the editor protesting the recent suppression of a work of science as an "obscene libel." It was published by a reputable firm on advice of well-known doctors and scientists. The publisher had been fined as a common pornographer.

Briggs, Asa. *The History of Broadcasting in the United Kingdom*. London, Oxford, 1961, 1965. 2 vols. **B 511**
Vol. I, The Birth of Broadcasting; vol. II, The Golden Age of Wireless; vol. III (not yet published) will deal with broadcasting during World War I. References throughout the two volumes to problems of broadcasting control and censorship.

Brill, Henry. "Will We Gag Italian Films?" *Nation*, 175:132–33, 16 August 1952.
B 512

Account of a campaign by the American Catholic Legion to impose an indirect censorship on Italian-made films. Two priests, sent to Italy, point out to a producer before the film is made that certain things are unacceptable to Americans.

Brindze, Ruth. *Not to Be Broadcast; the Truth about the Radio*. New York, Vanguard, 1937. 310 p. **B 513**
The author charges that America has surrendered freedom of the airwaves to private monopoly; that the party in power exerts political controls and interference; and that the Federal Radio Commission exerts a direct and positive censorship (Star Chamber proceedings) over broadcasting. She discusses the taboos and prohibitions imposed on controversial topics and criticizes propaganda of the "Ford-Cameron sermons." She recommends that limitations be placed on radio stations' authority to censor; that a portion of the new ultra-high frequencies be set aside for nonprofit public use, with possible financing from tax on commercial stations.

Bristol, Roger P. "It Takes Courage to Stock Taboos." *Library Journal*, 74: 261–63, 15 February 1949. **B 514**
A survey of public libraries in the Boston area to determine the handling of two controversial books—Kinsey's *Sexual Behavior in the Human Male* and Mailer's *The Naked and the Dead*—reveal a great divergence in practice. For the most part, the survey indicates, librarians have been exercising courage in making available controversial works.

"The British House of Commons and Obscene Publications." *New Zealand Libraries*, 17:241–44, November–December 1955. **B 515**
The author describes recent treatment of obscenity in the British Parliament, in light of recent amendments to the New Zealand Indecent Publications Act.

"British Library Association Council Approved Statement on Censorship." *Library Journal*, 88:2658, July 1963.
B 516

Statement also appears in *Liaison*, May 1963; *ALA Bulletin*, July 1963; and in *ALA Intellectual Freedom Newsletter*, July 1963.

"The British Press: Its Growth, Liberty, and Power." *North British Review*, 30: 367–402, May 1859. **B 517**
An essay based on a review of several volumes, including Andrews, *History of British Journalism* (1859); John Stuart Mill, *On Liberty* (1859); and Macaulay, *History of England from the Accession of James the Second* (1857). The reviewer is particularly critical of the pseudoliberalism of Mill. "Coming to the perusal of it [*On Liberty*] fresh from the grand thoughts of such advocates of freedom of opinion as Milton, Burke, Fox, Mackintosh, and Robert Hall . . . our ardour received a shock."

Britton, Beverly. "Censored Uncensored." *Nieman Reports*, 7(2):33–34, April 1953.
B 518

Account of the courtmartial and dismissal from service of Lt. Colonel Melvin B. Voorhees, former censor with the Eighth Army in Korea, charged with failure to submit the manuscript of his book, *Korean Tales*, for review, and for refusal to withdraw it from publication when ordered to do so.

Broadcasting. Washington, D.C., Broadcasting Publications, 1931–date. Weekly.
B 519

A trade magazine of the radio-television industry, often containing both news and editorial comment on activities of the industry and government agencies that relate to freedom of broadcasting.

"Broadcasting Bunk." *Hygeia*, 8:418–19, May 1930. **B 520**
An editorial concerning the radio broadcasting by Brinkley promoting his goat-gland grafting, and a man named Baker who is advertising cancer cures, the latter over Station KTNT, Muscatine, Iowa. "If the Federal Radio Commission wants to merit public confidence it must find some way to curb this type of broadcasting."

Broadhurst, Thomas. "The Middle Ground." *Authors' League Bulletin*, 15(1): 15–16, April 1927. **B 521**
A defense of the proposal for drama censorship in New York by a Committee of Nine.

Brock, Henry I. *Meddlers, Uplifting Moral Uplifters*. New York, Ives Washburn, 1930. 307 p. **B 522**
Chapter V, The Volunteer Fireman, deals with the activities of vice societies and the censorship pressures of the Catholic church and other religious bodies.

Brockett, Paul. *Scientific Publications from Germany*. [National Research Council, Washington, D.C., 1917?]. (Reprinted from the *Proceedings*, National Academy of Sciences, vol. 3, pp. 717–21, December 1917) **B 523**
Relates to shipments of books from Germany detained by British authorities during World War I.

Broderick, Dorothy. "Freedom for Whom to Read What?" *Iowa Library Quarterly*, 19:115–19, January 1963. **B 524**

———. "I May, I Might, I Must." *Library Journal*, 88:507–10, 1 February 1963. **B 525**
"Some philosophical observations on book selection policies and practices and the freedom to read. One of three papers relating to selection of controversial materials given at a staff meeting of librarians working with young adults at the Free Library of Philadelphia."

Broeker, Galen. "Jared Sparks, Robert Peel and the State Paper Office." *American Quarterly*, 13:140–52, Summer 1961. **B 526**
Account of the assault on the rules of the State Paper Office by Jared Sparks in the 1820's when he was combing the archives of the United States, England, and France for information on the American Revolution. His success in gaining access to British state papers "established a noteworthy precedent to be cited by those who believed that the search for historical truth should not be hampered by the nationality of the historian or official attitudes toward his subject."

Broker, Warren W. *A Study of the Meaning of "Freedom of the Press" as Interpreted by the United States Supreme Court*. Milwaukee, Marquette University, 1940. 143 p. (Unpublished Master's thesis) **B 527**

Bromberg, Benjamin. "Five Tests for Obscenity." *Chicago Bar Record*, 41: 416–22, May 1960. **B 528**

The assistant state's attorney of Cook County, Ill., devised five tests for obscenity which enabled him to win every obscenity case he prosecuted: the signature test (who wrote the book?), the channels of distribution test, the price test, the reputation test, and the advertising methods test. In addition, he added the ultimate test—pornographic intent.

Bromberg, Frederick G. *Correspondence of Frederick G. Bromberg with Central Law Journal, St. Louis, Mo., on Freedom of Speech in Time of War and Eighteenth Amendment to the Constitution of the United States 1919 and 1920, and Correspondence with Virginia Law Review*. Mobile, Ala., 1920. 13 p. **B 529**

Bromley, Dorothy D. "Free Press v. Fair Trial." *Harper's Magazine*, 202: 90–96, March 1951. **B 530**
A staff writer on the *Herald Tribune*, discusses the conflict between the First Amendment, which guarantees freedom of the press, and the Fifth Amendment, which assures every citizen a fair trial. Many newspapers interfere with trials (e.g., the Hess case and the Hauptmann case) without giving the defendant the benefit of the doubt until he is proven guilty. The author suggests reforms in newspaper coverage of trials.

Bronson, Edward H. "Self-Regulation by Stations." *Journal of Broadcasting*, 1:119–28, Spring 1957. **B 531**
The author was director of Television Code Affairs, National Association of Radio and Television Broadcasters.

Brook, Peter. "A Flaming Issue." *Censorship*, 4:2, Autumn 1965. **B 532**
A poetic essay beginning: "How can we understand the burning issue of censorship in a country [England] where censorship is mild." The essay concludes that censorship in England begins with autocensorship, which reflects a way of life.

Brooks, Alexander D. *Civil Rights and Liberties in the United States. An Annotated Bibliography . . . with a Selected List of Fiction and Audio-Visual Materials Collected by Dr. Albert A. Alexander and Virginia H. Ellison*. New York, Civil Liberties Educational Foundation, 1962. 151 p. **B 533**
Includes a section on free expression in mass communications, pp. 37–42, and lists a number of films dealing with freedom of the press.

Brooks, George. "Freedom of the Press and Collective Bargaining." *American Federationist*, 44:282–93, March 1937. **B 534**

"This is a summary of some of the instances during the past three years in which the newspaper publishers have raised the cry that the free press was in danger . . . the cry has been raised indiscriminately as a blind behind which the publishers have sought (and largely obtained) an immunity from ordinary governmental regulation."

Brooks, Sydney. "Lord Northcliffe and the War." *North American Review*, 202: 185–96, August 1915. **B 535**
Relates largely to the publication in Lord Northcliffe's *Daily News* of an attack on Lord Kitchener for allegedly supplying shrapnel instead of the needed shells, causing the deaths of thousands of British soldiers. The public reaction was largely against the newspaper because of the personal nature of the attack. The author considers the journalistic ethics in the case.

———. "The Press in War Time." *North American Review*, 200:858–69, December 1914. **B 536**
"Part of the art of war in a democratic State must be to keep the democracy intelligently interested." The author criticizes the "urbane fatuity" of the censors in the British Press Bureau for preventing sympathetic reporting of the war by the foreign press. Happily, he finds the situation improving.

———. "The Press in War-time: the Muzzling of the War Correspondent Raises the Larger Question of the Relation of the Press to Modern Organized Society." *Harper's Weekly*, 56:21, 27 December 1912. **B 537**

Broom, John L. "The Sins of Puritans." *Assistant Librarian*, 49:189–90, December 1956. **B 538**
The author opposes existing British laws against obscene literature on the grounds that (1) a person should be allowed to read what he pleases, (2) there is lack of agreement on what is obscene, (3) censorship brings all people down to the lowest common denominator, and (4) censorship illogically claims that it is always the other person who needs to be protected from an offending publication.

Brophy, Brigid. "The British Museum and Solitary Vice." *London Magazine*, 2(n.s.):55–58, March 1963. **B 539**
According to the author, the practice of the British Museum in keeping certain books in locked cases is an act of censorship.

———. "An Open Letter to the Director of Public Prosecutions." *Books*, 9(11): 11–12, August 1964. **B 540**

Advice from a novelist and critic who believes the public prosecutor's legal training does not qualify him for that portion of his job which requires him to decide what is obscene. "You are . . . being asked to administer not a law but a primitive superstition . . . Usually, incitement is a crime only if what people are incited to—breaching the peace, for instance—is a crime. From the obscenity of a book no crime follows, and not even the demonstrable corruption of a single person. The crime is the *being* 'obscene': being taboo."

Brougham and Vaux, Henry Peter Brougham, *1st Baron. Speech (at the Durham Assizes, August 6, 1822) . . . in the Case of the King v. Williams for a Libel on the Clergy; etc.* London, 1822. 18 p.　**B 541**

──────. *Taxes on Knowledge. Stamps on Newspapers* . . . London, Printed by J. R. and C. Childs, 1834. 8 p.　**B 542**
Extracts of evidence presented by Baron Brougham and Vaux, Lord High Chancellor of England, before the Select Committee of the House of Commons, on libel law. He points out the evil to society from the stamp duty on newspapers, the impolicy of the government in continuing the tax, and its interference with the spread of useful knowledge.

Broun, Heywood. "After Its Fashion." *Nation*, 141:47–48, 10 July 1935.　**B 543**
"If labor wants to get a press which is fair to labor it will first have to organize its own newspapers. Our present press is free to do as it pleases, and it pleases to be always on the side which carries the heaviest butter."

[──────]. "American Censorship in France." *Review of Reviews*, 57:205–6, February 1918.　**B 544**
Excerpts from an article by Broun in the New York *Tribune* asserting that American wartime censorship is the strictest in the world and urging the appointment of a civilian censor, independent of military control, except for army news.

──────. "Censoring the Censor." *Bookman*, 53:193–96, May 1921. (Reprinted in Downs, *The First Freedom*, pp. 273–75; also in MacLean and Holmes, *Men and Books*, pp. 301–5)　**B 545**
An attack on John Summer and the New York vice society for its censorship of *Jurgen*. Broun advocates abolishing official censorship. The playgoing and reading public, he believes, will act as its own censor.

──────. "Heywood Broun Comes to the Rescue of Immoral Books." *Current Opinion*, 67:315–16, December 1919.　**B 546**

The New York *Tribune* literary critic comments on the suppression of *Madeleine* in New York at the instigation of the vice society, and the disapproval of Maugham's *Moon and Sixpence* by certain New York librarians. "The business of public libraries is not to promote morality, but to promote reading . . . Anybody who restricts his reading to moral books will miss much delightful literature." Broun cites an allegory of Lucifer and the Angels to illustrate his point.

──────. "It Seems to Heywood Broun." *Nation*, 125:144–45, 26 October 1927. (Reprinted in Downs, *The First Freedom*, pp. 404–6)　**B 547**
Broun comments on the sensitivity of the Irish in New York which prompts the commissioner of licenses to censor movies and stage plays that might offend that nationality.

──────. "Piece that Got Me Fired." In *Collected Edition of Heywood Broun*, New York, Harcourt, Brace, 1941, pp. 220–23.　**B 548**
Broun deplores the lack of a liberal press in New York. He contends that New York newspaper editors live in mortal terror of the power of the Catholic Church and that they generally lack the courage to stand up to racial, religious, and national groups. He dubs the Irish as the "cry-babies of the Western world. Even the mildest quip will set them off into resolutions and protests."

──────. "Where Does Censorship Start?" *Colliers*, 67:14–15+, 14 May 1921.　**B 549**
A discussion of the Pennsylvania State Board of Censors of Motion Pictures and its many deletions and prohibitions. "No matter what the law," writes Broun, "the real basis of censorship is the public itself."

──────, and Margaret Leach. *Anthony Comstock, Roundsman of the Lord.* New York, Boni, 1927. 285 p.　**B 550**
A colorful biography of the controversial founder of the New York Society for the Suppression of Vice and sponsor of the federal and state obscenity laws that bear his name. Comstock was a deeply religious man whose 40-year crusade was directed against frank expression of sex in works of literature as well as against pornography.

Brown, Alec. "Good Censor." *Dublin Magazine*, 4(2):21–30, April 1929.　**B 551**
While disapproving of "bad censorship," i.e. the banning of books by the police, the author defends "good censorship" as needed to protect society. "The good censor . . . is first and foremost the constructive censor. His first qualification would be, not a knowledge of the intricacies of the law . . . but a knowledge as wide as humanly possible of the making of human society." The censor should be selected by responsible writers to represent their corporate conscience. Such self-censorship makes police censorship unnecessary.

Brown, Burdette B. *Legalized Limitation of Press News.* [New York, 1936]. 9 p.　**B 552**

Brown, Charles T. "A Legal Discussion of the Obscenity Laws." *Physical Culture*, 15:395–97, April 1906.　**B 553**
References to the case of Moses Harman (portrait). Opposition to the application of the "into whose hands" rule in obscenity cases as class legislation. While permitting physicians to write on topics of sex in medical journals for the benefit of other physicians, they may not discuss sex matters in papers intended for the common man.

Brown, *Mrs.* Clifford. "Censorship in School Libraries; a Statement of Belief." *Michigan Librarian*, 21(3):30–34, October 1955.　**B 554**
"If a book has real literary merit, if it offers the student enough in story and in writing quality, most will not be affected, except momentarily, by a few questionable scenes." The school librarian must be clear-minded and honest in examining books and in estimating their value and effect in relation to students.

Brown, F. Clement. "The Catholic Question in Canada. I. A Struggle for Freedom." *Arena*, 17:742–47, April 1897.　**B 555**
Discusses action brought by the Catholic hierarchy to suppress *L'Electeur*, the leading liberal paper of Quebec.

Brown, George R. "Lynching of Public Opinion." *North American Review*, 209:795–802, June 1919.　**B 556**
A denunciation of the Wilson administration for the arrogant handling of war news, for the use of press agents, and for stifling public opinion. He contrasts the situation with the greater freedom under the Taft and Roosevelt administrations.

Brown, Henry B. "The Liberty of the Press." *American Law Review*, 34:321–41, May–June 1900.　**B 557**
A justice of the U.S. Supreme Court criticizes the cruelty with which the press, in ill-directed zeal, often assaults the character and invades the privacy of innocent persons, and indulges in excessive sensationalism. Libel trials are not often resorted to because of the expense and attendant evils. He rejects censorship as a solution and opposes the California law against anonymity. He calls upon newspapers themselves to practice restraint, upon the public to refuse to buy, and upon business to refuse to advertise in papers that are irresponsible.

Brown, Henry H. "The Old Scots Law of Blasphemy." *Juridical Review*, 30:56–68, 1918.　**B 558**

Blasphemy was a high crime (a capital offense at common law and by statute) under old Scots law. Lawyers were not troubled by the doubts attendant to English cases in such trials as that of Edward Moxon for his publication of *Queen Mab*. "They had no doubts that such prosecutions were not only expedient but necessary in public interest, and they had a clear view of what constituted the crime."

Brown, Ivor. "*Parnell* and the Lord Chamberlain." *New Statesman and Nation*, 11(n.s.):666–67, 2 May 1936. **B 559**
A protest of the veto by the Lord Chamberlain of Elsie T. Schauffer's play, *Parnell*. The author suggests that the Lord Chamberlain publish the rules of his office for the guide of playwrights.

Brown, James W. "Life and Times of John Peter Zenger." *Editor and Publisher*, 86:11+, 14 March 1953; 86:14+, 21 March 1953; 86:12+, 28 March 1953; 86:12+, 4 April 1953; and 86:12+, 11 April 1953. **B 560**
On the occasion of the erection of a permanent memorial to John Peter Zenger and a Free Press in the Sub-Treasury Building in New York City, the president of the Zenger Memorial Fund, Inc., presents this article on Zenger, in five installments.

———. "The Zenger Memorial Is Now a National Shrine." *Quill*, 41(6):8–9, June 1953. **B 561**
"The federal government takes over the exhibit depicting the career of the printer who defied a royal governor to win America's first battle for a free press."

Brown, John. *Thoughts on Civil Liberty, on Licentiousness, and Faction.* Dublin, Printed for A. Leathley, J. Exshaw, W. Watson, and S. Watson, 1765. 192 p. **B 562**

Brown, John Mason. "Topsy-Turvy; *Uncle Tom's Cabin* Barred in Bridgeport and New Haven." *Saturday Review*, 28:24–25, 6 October 1945. **B 563**

———. "Wishful Banning." *Saturday Review of Literature*, 32(11):24–26, 12 March 1949. (Reprinted in Downs, *The First Freedom*, pp. 155–58) **B 564**
In his Seeing Things column, the literary critic comments favorably upon the point of view of John Haynes Holmes's article (26 February) criticizing censorship by racial and religious minorities. "We get nowhere by banning books just because they contain characters which do not flatter us. We get nowhere by pretending that there are not heroes and villains of all creeds and colors. Minorities should not be allowed to enjoy "literary immunity."

Brown, Karline. "The Public Be Banned!" *ALA Bulletin*, 38:443–48, November 1944. **B 565**
After citing numerous historical examples of censorship of the press the author finds that "history bears articulate testimony against censorship and the sagacity of the censor."

Brown, Louise F. "On the Burning of Books." In *Vassar Mediaeval Studies*, ed. Christabel F. Fiske. New Haven, Yale University Press, 1923, pp. 249–71. **B 566**
An account of the burning of books in mediaeval Europe to suppress heresy, taken largely from treatises written in the seventeenth and eighteenth centuries. "The first great book bonfire of the fifteenth century was that in the courtyard of the arch-episcopal palace of Prague, in 1410, where more than two hundred of the works of Wycliffe . . . were given to flames. Two years later the Synod of Pisa condemned Wycliffe's works, and they were burned at Oxford." By the end of the fifteenth century, with the spread of printing, church and state authorities recognized that bonfires as a means of destruction of books could not be made big enough, and so they turned to a new technique. The censor replaced the common hangman except for symbolic burning. The author concludes: "What contributions to thought has the world lost that it might have had from those men who, having cast the precious firstfruits of their labors upon the fire, turned sadly to safer pursuits, and from others who, watching the conflagration, refrained from putting on paper thought that might be destined only to kindle other bonfires."

Brown, Peter C. "Executive Papers—the President and the Congress." *Congressional Record*, 94:A–4896–98, 4 August 1948. **B 567**
An analysis of the constitutional rights of the executive and legislative branches of the federal government, presented in an address before the New York State Bar Association, 1 July 1948.

Brown, R. Jardine. "Freedom of the Ether." *BBC Quarterly*, 1:58–61, July 1946. **B 568**

Brown, Ray W. "Freedom of the Press: Injunctions: Obscene Literature." *Cornell Law Quarterly*, 42:256–61, Winter 1957. **B 569**
In the case of *Kingsley Books, Inc. v. Brown* (1957), the New York Supreme Court found the booklets obscene and upheld the New York statute. The reviewer supports the decision, believing that, in a conflict of morality and free press where no social or literary merit is present, the former should be protected. There is no clear rule, however, for drawing the line. The booklets in question were entitled *Nights of Horror*. The statute was later upheld by the U.S. Supreme Court.

Brown, Robert (Bob). *Gems; A Censored Anthology.* [*By*] *Bob Brown*. Cagnes-sur-Mer, France, Roving Eye Press, 1931. 109 p. **B 570**
A devastating and witty attack on censors and censorship, consisting of an essay on pornography—those who produce it, those who sell it (book-leggers), and those who buy it secretly (but object to others reading it). The major portion of the work is intended to support the author's contentions that obscenity is in the mind of the reader and that censorship only serves to emphasize the banned. To illustrate this he quotes widely from famous works of poetry by Shakespeare, Wordsworth, Browning, Tennyson, Longfellow and others, blocking out certain innocuous key words, leaving the meaning to the imagination of the reader. Gershon Legman calls this book by the expatriate American, "the greatest spoof ever published at the expense of censorship."

Brown, Robert U. "ASNE Reports Progress on Free Press Pledges; Report of ASNE Committee on World Freedom of Information." *Editor and Publisher*, 78(25):5, 64, 66, 68, 16 June 1945. **B 571**
The members of the Committee on World Freedom of Information of the American Society of Newspaper Editors were Wilbur Forrest of the New York *Herald-Tribune*, chairman; Ralph McGill of the *Atlanta Constitution*, and Dean Carl W. Ackerman of the Columbia University Graduate School of Journalism.

———. "Editors Exhorted to Fight 'Arrogant Suppression.'" *Editor and Publisher*, 84(18):17, 112, 114+, 28 April 1951. **B 572**
A report on the work of the Freedom of Information Committee of the American Society of Newspaper Editors in "uncovering numerous instances of news suppression and restriction of access to public records all over the country."

Brown, Robert W. "Is Press Freedom Infringed by License Tax? One Judge Decides It Is." *Nieman Reports*, 6(2):18–19, April 1952. **B 573**
The editor of the Columbus (Ga.) *Ledger* discusses the business license tax being levied on newspapers in a number of cities and the ruling of Superior Court Judge R. Bruce Findley in Riverside, Calif., that the Corona, Calif., ordinance was unconstitutional.

Brown, Rome G. "Some Points on the Law of the Press." *Central Law Journal*, 95:59–71, 28 July 1922. **B 574**
Résumé of laws restricting newspapers during wartime, the use of the injunction against newspapers, the regulation of mailing privi-

leges, the law of libel, and contempt of court. The author recommends additional laws to give courts greater power to restrict "trial by newspaper."

Brown, S. J. M. "Note on Censorship of Literature." In his *Libraries and Literature from a Catholic Standpoint*, Dublin, Browne & Nolan, 1937, pp. 293–304. **B 575**
Arguments in favor of government censorship, especially with reference to sex literature.

Brown, Spencer. "Dilemma of Liberal Censorship." *Education Digest*, 30:4–6, September 1964. **B 576**
The author writes of liberals who may be tempted to accept censorship rather than offend some ethnic, cultural, or religious minority. He cites pressures from Negroes to exclude *Little Black Sambo* from libraries; pressures from Jewish groups to censor *Oliver Twist* and *The Merchant of Venice*. Even the Bible as a work of literature is suspect for fear of charges of sectarianism.

Brown, Steven R. *United States Information Agency.* Columbia, Mo., Freedom of Information Center, School of Journalism, University of Missouri, 1962. 11 p. (Publication no. 70) **B 577**
A history of this agency, created in 1953 to carry news of America to the people of other countries. Includes a brief account of the agency's predecessors, the Office of War Information, the Interim International Information Service, the Office of International Information, and the U.S. Information Service. References are made to the attacks on the overseas information program during the McCarthy era.

Brown, Stuart G. "Politics and Mr. Crosskey's Constitution, II. The Constitution in the Debates on the Alien and Sedition Acts." *Syracuse Law Review*, 7:27–37, Fall 1955. **B 578**
The author challenges the interpretation of the political issues in the debate over the Alien and Sedition Acts of 1798 contained in William W. Crosskey's *Politics and the Constitution in the History of the United States.* The Federalists, Brown contends, turned to the Sedition Act as the most effective means of stifling Republican opposition. They preferred federal to state action to get around Republican governors.

[Brown, William Montgomery]. *In the Matter of the Presentment of Bishop William Montgomery Brown. Appeal from the Court for the Trial of a Bishop. Transcript of the Records. Charles L. Dibble, Church Advocate, John H. Smart, of Counsel. Joseph W. Sharts,*

Counsel for Accused, Edward Bushnell, of Counsel. [Cleveland, Gates Publishing Co., 1924]. 251 p. **B 579**
Bishop Brown was tried in the church court for the trial of a bishop, 27–31 May 1924, on charges of holding and teaching in his book, *Communism and Christianism*, doctrine contrary to that held by the Protestant Episcopal Church in the United States. In October 1925, a vote of 95 to 11 by the General Convocation of the Church, held in New Orleans, deposed him from the office of bishop. Another report of the trial, published in Galion, Ohio, by the bishop's friends, *The Man of Galion before the Sanhedrin*, contains A Critical Review of the Heresy Trial, by Theodore A. Schroeder. Edward Bushnell, one of the bishop's legal counsels prepared an account, *The Narrow Bed; a Bird's Eye View of the Trial*, published by Bradford-Brown Educational Co., Galion.

[———]. *My Heresy; The Autobiography of an Idea.* New York, John Day, 1926. 273 p. **B 580**
Bishop Brown's own account of his conversion to the naturalism of Darwin and Marx and of his trial and removal from the position of bishop of the Protestant Episcopal Church for publication of his views. Following the trial he continued to publish his doctrines in "*Bad Bishop Brown's*" *Quarterly Lectures*, issued by Bradford-Brown, Galion, Ohio.

Browne, Edward E. "Free Speech and Free Press." *Congressional Record*, 55(Appendix):257–58, 31 May 1917. **B 581**
The Congressman from Wisconsin spoke in the House against proposed wartime restrictions upon freedom of speech and the press. Existing laws, he maintained, were adequate to permit the President to use his powers to protect information on troops and military movements. "It is well settled that war does not suspend the provisions of the Constitution. In times of war freedom of the press is of more importance than in times of peace."

———. "Free Speech Kin to Freedom of Worship." *La Follette's Magazine*, 12:27, February 1920. **B 582**
Congressman Browne lauds free speech while justifying existing abridgments of it.

Browne, George L. *Narratives of State Trials in the Nineteenth Century . . . 1801–1830.* London, Sampson, Low, 1882. 2 vols. **B 583**
Includes English trials of Jean G. Peltier, James Perry, William Cobbett, and Leigh Hunt.

Brownell, Herbert, Jr. "Fair Trial with a Free Press; the Public's Right to News and the Individual's Right to Justice." *Vital Speeches*, 21:793–96, 15 October 1954. **B 584**
A speech by the Attorney General of the United States.

———. "Freedom and Responsibility of the Press in a Free Country." *Fordham Law Review*, 24:178–86, Summer 1955. **B 585**
A speech delivered before the Federal Bar Association.

———. "Press Photographers and the Courtroom—Canon Thirty-Five and Freedom of the Press." *Nebraska Law Review*, 35:1–12, November 1955. **B 586**
A speech delivered before the annual convention of the National Press Photographers Association.

Brownrigg, *Sir* Douglas E. R. *Indiscretions of the Naval Censor.* New York, Doran, 1920. 315 p. **B 587**
The autobiographical narrative of a retired admiral of the Royal Navy who was chief censor of radio-telegraphy during World War I.

Brubacher, John S. "Loyalty to Freedom: Scrutinizing School Textbooks." *School and Society*, 70:792–93, 10 December 1949. **B 588**
In a University of Illinois commencement address a Yale professor criticizes censorship of textbooks, exaction of loyalty oaths, and infringement of academic freedom as contrary to the American tradition of freedom to which all citizens should be dedicated.

[Bruce, Archibald]. *Reflections on Freedom of Writing; and the Impropriety of Attempting to Suppress It by Penal Laws. Occasioned by A Late Proclamation against Seditious Publications, and the measures consequent upon it; Viewed Chiefly in the aspect they bear to Religious Liberty, and Ecclesiastical Reform. By a North British Protestant.* Edinburgh, W. Berry, 1794. 168 p. **B 589**
A scholarly theologian of great piety and a lively imagination, Bruce urged tolerance in religion and politics. He considers the proclamation an error effected by faulty counsel of ministers. While not a member of the Friends to the Liberty of the Press, he praises the society and publishes an "Ode" to its members, written by Mr. Armstrong.

Brucker, Herbert. "A Crack in Canon 35." *Saturday Review*, 47(28):48–49, 10 July 1965. **B 590**
Although the U.S. Supreme Court ruled that television had prejudiced the Texas trial of Billie Sol Estes, the decision was 5 to 4, with an opening for further consideration.

———. "The Free Trial v. the Free Press." *Texas Bar Journal*, 20:438–44, August 1957. **B 591**
The premise on which total prohibition of the taking of photographs in the courtroom rests (American Bar Association's Canon 35)

is false. It is no longer necessarily true that taking photographs in a courtroom detracts from the dignity of the court. To say that the taking of photographs is an invasion of privacy is a rationalization inasmuch as witnesses, lawyers, and judge are already in the public glare. Brucker pleads for adequate newspaper coverage of trials. Publication of trial and pretrial information, he argues, does not necessarily prejudice justice.

———. *Freedom of Information.* New York, Macmillan, 1949. 307 p. **B 592**
In order to survive and flourish, democracy requires an environment of free public information. Citizens must have reliable information about the world in which they live in order to make wise decisions. The author develops the thesis that newspapers, radio, and other mass media must serve as the fourth branch of government and must be protected and encouraged so that they can withstand pressures from within and without. The press should be free both from government and from business monopoly.

———. "The Government Copyright Racket." *Saturday Review,* 45(32):36–37, 11 August 1962. **B 593**
Criticism of the growing practice of government officials to copyright their reports for private revenue.

———. "Let's Abolish Canon 35." *Saturday Review,* 45:63–64+, 8 December 1962. **B 594**
An appeal to permit coverage of trials by news photographers and television, now prohibited by Canon 35 of the American Bar Association and widely supported by the judiciary. Brucker believes photography need not imperil a fair trial if the physical layout is properly controlled.

———. *Men in the Dark.* Tucson, University of Arizona Press, 1960. 12 p. (The John Peter Zenger Award for Freedom of the Press, no. 6) **B 595**
The 1959 award went to Herbert Brucker, editor of the *Hartford Courant,* for his "tireless efforts as an advocate of freedom of information." In addition to his record as a newspaper man, Mr. Brucker is recognized for his work as chairman of the Freedom of Information Committee of the American Society of Newspaper Editors and for his classic work on the concept of *Freedom of Information.* The theme of Mr. Brucker's talk is that "men in the dark cannot be free."

———. "Official Controls versus Self-Regulation of Communications Media." In *Lectures in Communications Media, Legal and Policy Problems, Delivered at University of Michigan Law School, June 16–June 18, 1954.* Ann Arbor, University of Michigan Law School, 1954, pp. 99–108. **B 596**

Editor Brucker discusses the history and alternatives of government control, advocating that "free, private ownership must do the job through self-regulation."

———. "Storing up Trouble." *Saturday Review,* 34:22–23, 26 May 1951. **B 597**
An editorial commenting on the conflicting Soviet and Anglo-Saxon concepts of freedom of the press and the difficulty in convincing the people of the world to accept the Anglo-Saxon doctrine.

Brunini, John G. "The Endangered Press." *Commonweal,* 24:609–11, 23 October 1936. **B 598**
The greatest threat to a free press is in the action of publishers and editorial writers who deliberately embody their viewpoints and philosophy in news reports, who suppress news more vital than much that is included, and who play up certain news out of proportion to its value.

Brustein, Robert. "Artists and Bureaucrats." *New Republic,* 149:36–38, 2 November 1963. **B 599**
A general complaint against government interference with the communications arts—vice squad action against the stage performance of Lenny Bruce, FCC "stall" in renewing the broadcast license of Pacifica Foundation, the closing of New York's Living Theater by the Internal Revenue Service, and the interruption of the author's favorite TV program for a documentary favorable to the Kennedy administration.

Bryan, Carter R. "Economic Intervention: Prelude to Press Control." *Journalism Quarterly,* 38:67–75, Winter 1961. **B 600**
"Freedom of the press can be affected by economic limitations, both private and governmental, including interventions made to aid the press. In this survey of world press systems, the uses of economic interventions and controls by non-democratic regimes are particularly examined."

———. "Security and the News in Liberal Countries." *Journalism Quarterly,* 38:485–96, Autumn 1961. **B 601**
National security restrictions on news in Great Britain and Commonwealth countries, Europe, and the United States.

[Bryan, Frederick Van Pelt]. "Grove Press v. Postmaster of City of New York." *Evergreen Review,* 3(9):37–68, Summer 1959. (Also in McCormick, *Versions of Censorship,* pp. 232–50) **B 602**
Text of the decision of Justice Bryan rescinding the Post-Office ban on *Lady Chatterley's Lover* in the case of *Grove Press v. R. K. Christenberry,* U.S. District Court, Southern District of New York, 1959.

Bryant, Ashbrook P. "Responsibility for Broadcast Matter." *Journal of Broadcasting,* 5:3–16, Winter 1960–61. **B 603**
The author was chief counsel for the FCC study of radio and television network broadcasting.

Bryant, E. T. "Book Selection and Censorship." *Librarian,* 44:65–76, April 1955. **B 604**
The author recommends that if a complaint against a book is justified on moral grounds, yet the book has literary merit and sincerity, it should be withdrawn from open shelves but retained in reserve stock. The article reports on the response to questionnaires circulated to 80 British libraries on the handling of 12 controversial books.

Bryant, Louise. "A New Adventure in Arcadia." *Mother Earth,* 10:235–41, September 1915. **B 605**
An account of the arrest, conviction, appeal, and discharge of Emma Goldman and Ben Reitman, at Portland, Oregon, for distributing birth control information.

Brychta, Ivan. "The Ohio Film Censorship Law." *Ohio State Law Journal,* 13:350–411, Summer 1952. **B 606**
Notes on film censorship in Ohio and its interpretation by the state courts, 1913–52.

Bryson, Lyman. "Freedom of Information." In UNESCO's *Freedom and Culture,* New York, Columbia University Press, 1951, pp. 119–56. **B 607**
The Universal Declaration of Human Rights, adopted by the UN General Assembly in 1948, acknowledges the universal right to information. We fall short in realizing this freedom, however, because of economic and political factors. In the first instance, "a large portion of the peoples of the world are still too poor in material resources to make more than meagre use of the machinery for spreading information," and in the second instance, "governments of the world are divided on the meaning of the [word] 'freedom,' and follow different policies in controlling the dissemination of facts."

———. *Time for Reason about Radio; from a Series of Broadcasts on CBS.* New York, Stewart, 1948. 127 p. **B 608**
Includes two discussions: (1) Lyman Bryson, CBS consultant on public affairs, and Charles A. Siepmann, former consultant to the Federal Communications Commission, discuss the FCC role in licensing and the "public interest." (2) Robert D. Leigh discusses Freedom and Responsibilities of American Broadcasting, emphasizing that the air belongs to the public, not to the radio industry.

Buchanan, J. W. "Books and Bookmen." *Library Review*, 100:247–50, Winter 1951. **B 609**

An essay on censorship prompted by recent press reports of Scottish booksellers being prosecuted. While recognizing that some books are "vicious or shoddy or unreal" and have no place in a library that is supported by public funds, "serious books, exceptionally frank in language or theme," cannot be justifiably withheld.

Buchanan, N. B. "Some Thoughts on Censorship." *Library World*, 37:208–9, March 1935. **B 610**

"We see and hear things in everyday life, which are . . . far worse than any which get into print . . . We cannot very well censor life, so why bother unduly about the books . . . Censorship is so often a form of mental coddling which lowers one's powers of resistance against evil, that it is difficult to appreciate the mentality of anyone who will argue in its favor." Books on sex fall into two classes: the obviously prurient, and the serious work of science or literature which deals frankly with sexual subjects.

Buchanan, Robert W. *On Descending into Hell: A Letter Addressed to the Right Hon. Henry Matthews, Q. C. Home Secretary, Concerning the Proposed Suppression of Literature.* London, Ridgway, 1889. 38 p. (Excerpts in *Physical Culture*, October 1907 and in Schroeder, *Free Press Anthology*, pp. 162–67) **B 611**

Buchanan, long a critic of the "fleshly school" of literature, unexpectedly came to the defense of Henry Vizetelly when that elderly Briton was imprisoned for publishing novels by Emile Zola. He urges the Home Secretary to intercede in Vizetelly's behalf. Zola's works, Buchanan states, while unsavory in their examination of "social sewage," should not be regarded as criminal. "It is one thing to dislike the obtrusion of things unsavory and abominable, and quite another to regard any allusion to them as positively criminal." The common people who can read and can afford to buy books are "robust and healthy-minded enough, familiar with the world enough to discriminate for themselves . . . The milliner, will frisk without the aid of Zola, and the young clerk will follow the milliner, even within the protective shadow of a Young Men's Christian Association. Wholesale corruption never yet came from corrupt literature which is the effect, not the cause, of social libertinage . . . The man who says that a book has power to pollute his soul ranks his soul below a book. I rank mine infinitely higher."

Buck, Philo M., Jr. "Milton on Liberty." *University Studies of the University of Nebraska*, 25:1–41, January 1925. **B 612**

Buckingham, Joseph T. *Trial: Commonwealth v. J. T. Buckingham, on an Indictment for a Libel, before the Municipal Court of the City of Boston, December term, 1822.* Boston, Office of the New England Galaxy, 1822. 60 p. **B 613**

Trial for an alleged libel against John N. Maffitt in the *New England Galaxy*. Buckingham, the publisher, was a ferociously outspoken editor, much after the style of William Cobbett, who engaged in numerous battles of words which sometimes involved him in libel suits. His journal was open to the free expression of opinion. The plaintiff charged plagiarism, falsehood, and licentiousness.

Buckle, Henry T. "Need of Increased Liberty of Discussion." In his *Miscellaneous and Posthumous Works*. London, Longmans, 1872. vol. 1, pp. 51–62. (Part of a longer essay entitled, Mill on Liberty, appearing in *Fraser's Magazine*, May 1859) **B 614**

An appeal for liberty of discussion and publication. Minority opinion should have free reign. "We can never be sure that the opinion of the majority is true. Nearly every opinion held by the majority was once confined to the minority. Every established religion was once a heresy." Furthermore, if truth is to triumph it needs to engage in conflict with error. "All hail therefore to those who, by attacking a truth, prevent that truth from slumbering . . . Of all evils, torpor is the most deadly." Buckle criticizes the blasphemy case, in 1857, against Thomas Pooley, who was given 21 months' imprisonment. "It should be clearly understood that every man has an absolute and irrefragable right to treat any doctrine as he thinks proper; either to argue against it, or to ridicule it. If his arguments are wrong, he can be refuted; if his ridicule is foolish, he can be out-ridiculed. To this there can be no exception. It matters not what the tenet may be, nor how dear it is to our feelings. Like all other opinions, it must take its chance; it must be roughly used; it must stand every test; it must be thoroughly discussed and sifted."

Buckley, J. M. "The Suppression of Vice." *North American Review*, 135:495–501, November 1882. **B 615**

The Rev. Mr. Buckley defends the New York vice society and its special agent, Anthony Comstock. The enforcement of the obscenity laws "cannot safely be left to public sentiment" because of the indelicate subject matter. The Society has adopted the most efficient methods of combating obscenity, has managed its affairs with prudence, and is one of the most important reformatory movements of modern times.

Buckley, Michael J. "State Censorship of Movies." *Catholic World*, 180:24–27, October 1954. **B 616**

A Jesuit priest argues for state censorship of movies. He criticizes the opinion of U.S. Supreme Court Justice Douglas concurred in by Justice Black—that "every writer, actor, or producer, no matter what medium of expression he may use, should be freed form the censor."

Buckley, William F., Jr., and Arthur M. Schlesinger, Jr. "The Issue of Free Speech on Television." *TV Guide*, 11:15–19, 25 April 1964. **B 617**

Two views on the "fairness doctrine" in broadcasting. Mr. Buckley: "I would favor passage of a law . . ." Professor Schlesinger: "The ideal should always be more debate . . ."

Buehler, E. C., *comp. American v. British System of Radio Control*. New York, Wilson, 1933. 361 p. (The Reference Shelf, vol. 8, no. 10) **B 618**

A collection of articles assembled to represent pros and cons on the debate topic. Resolved: That the United States should adopt the essential features of the British system of radio control and operation.

Buick, William G. "Statement of Principles and Policies on the Freedom to Read." *Australian Library Journal*, 12:105–7, June 1963. **B 619**

Bullard, F. Lauriston. "Boston's Book Ban Likely to Live Long." *New Yrok Times*, 28 April 1929, sec. 3, pp. 1, 7. **B 620**

An account of the trial and conviction of Theodore Dreiser's *An American Tragedy* in the Massachusetts courts. Bullard describes the hysteria in Boston over obscene books and the fear of the booksellers who no longer have the assurance of the former gentleman's agreement in which the booksellers policed book sales. In the present situation the police, the district attorney, the Watch and Ward Society are all in the act. "It is possible for anyone to have a book suppressed in Boston merely by advancing the idea."

Bundy, June. "Censorship Eases on Aired Lyrics as Acceptance Grows." *Billboard*, 71:2+, 19 January 1959. **B 621**

Bunzel, Peter. "Shocking Candor on the Screen; a Dilemma for the Family." *Life*, 52(8):88–102. **B 622**

The author predicts that the trend toward more frank portrayal of such themes as lesbianism, incest, and homosexuality, may lead to further pressures for censorship.

Buranelli, Vincent. "Peter Zenger's Editor." *American Quarterly*, 7:174–81, Summer 1955. **B 623**

The story of James Alexander, editor of the account of the John Peter Zenger trial, and Alexander's influence on the New York *Weekly Journal* and the Zenger trial.

———, ed. *The Trial of Peter Zenger*. New York, New York University Press, 1957. 152 p. **B 624**

A modern edition of the celebrated Zenger trial, consisting of a popularly written account of the trial and biographical information on Zenger and his lawyers, James Alexander and Andrew Hamilton. There is also a chapter on the significance of the trial. H. V. Kaltenborn has written the foreword.

Burch, Angelus T. "Free Press and Fair Trial." *Journal of the Bar Association of the State of Kansas*, 23:352–62, May 1955. **B 625**

A defense of the right of the press to report criminal proceedings. "If we seem to 'usurp' the investigating functions of the police and of the prosecutor's aides once in a while it is merely because they are not doing the job themselves." An address by the associate editor of the *Chicago Daily News* at a meeting of the Bar Association of the State of Kansas.

———. "News Media and the Law." *Chicago Bar Record*, 43:297–304, March 1962. **B 626**

In an address before the Chicago Bar Association, Editor Burch considers such topics as: whether juveniles should be shielded by anonymity, the difficulties of the press in keeping up with the vast amount of court and executive activities of the big city, newspaper libel, and contempt and Canon 20.

———. "'Trial by Newspaper' Is Often Exercise of a Public Duty to Yell 'Stop Thief!'" *Quill*, 52(10):7–9, 15–16, October 1954. **B 627**

"The real foe to justice is not newspaper coverage of a trial but indifference and political corruption."

"The Burden of Books." *Saturday Review* (London), 102:541–42, 3 November 1906. **B 628**

The writer approves of the whimsical suggestion of Lord Rosebery that there be a balance between intellectual imports and exports and that a commission be appointed to eliminate all unnecessary books. "The human spirit would be relieved from an oppressive incubus and there would be a startling burst of originality." In the same vein he suggests that "a University should really be an institution to restrict to its most useful minimum both reading and writing. If an ardent young man has access to a large library he will read too much that is useless either because it lacks quality or because it is obsolete and lacking in authority."

[Burdett, *Sir* Francis]. "Trial of Sir Francis Burdett, Baronet, before Mr. Justice Best and a special jury at the Spring Assizes at Leicester, on March 23, 1820, on an information for publishing a seditious libel, 1820." In Macdonell, *Reports of State Trials*, vol. 1, new series, London, 1888, pp. 1–170. **B 629**

The case involved the publication of an address to the electors of Westminster which the defendant represented in Parliament and which the government maintained was an incitement to rebellion. Sir Francis was found guilty and sentenced to three months in prison and fined £2,000.

[Burgess, Herbert R.] *Alice's Adventures in Censorland*. Boston, The Author, 1930. 4 p. **B 630**

Burgh, James. "Of the Liberty of Speech and Writing on Political Subjects." In his *Political Disquisitions* . . . Philadelphia, Robert Bell and William Woodhouse, 1775. vol. 3, pp. 246–66. **B 631**

The author objects to the unnatural attempts "to lay a restraint" on those who would criticize the conduct of men who undertake to conduct the public's business. Our public officials are not infallible; history shows that in order to preserve liberty we need to have a watchful eye on our public servants. "Punishing libels public or private is foolish, because it does not answer the end, and because the the end is a bad one, if it could be answered." The writer reviews the history of criminal libel in English common law.

Burgman, Charles F. *Case of Helen Wilmans*. [Philadelphia, The Author, 1904?]. 8 p. **B 632**

The case involves the Post-Office suppression of literature relating to the religious and mental cure of illness.

Burke, Edmund. "Speech on a Motion . . . for Leave to Bring in a Bill for Explaining the Powers of Juries in Prosecutions for Libels." In his *Works*, Boston, Little, Brown, 1839. vol. 5, pp. 414–26. **B 633**

Burke supported a bill in Parliament for giving juries the power to try every part of matter referred to them in libel indictments. "If the intent and tendency [of a libel] be left to the judge, as legal conclusions growing from the fact, you may depend upon it you can have no public discussion of a public measure; which is a point, which even those who are most offended with the licentiousness of the press (and it is very exorbitant, very provoking) will hardly contend for."

Burke, Edward L. "The Right of Privacy and Television." *Notre Dame Lawyer*, 28:389–98, Spring 1953. **B 634**

Notes on cases involving the violation of privacy, 1948–52.

Burke, John A. V. "The Church, the Cinema, and Censorship." *Sight and Sound*, 17(66):85–86, Summer 1948. **B 635**

Written by Father Burke in his capacity as a member of the Office Catholique International du Cinema.

Burke, Redmond A. "The *Index* and Its Implications for College and University Libraries." In Catholic Library Association, *Proceedings, 33rd Conference*. Louisville, 1957, pp. 78–84. **B 636**

———. "Student Reading in Catholic Colleges." *Catholic Library World*, 35:141–46, November 1963; 35:219–21, December 1963; 35:222–23, December 1963. **B 637**

Father Burke discusses types of books in the college library and justifications for book control by the Catholic Church. He describes general classes of restricted literature (Canon 1399) and immoral literature. In part two he considers the treatment of restricted literature in the college library. A final section consists of Better Known Authors and Books Listed in the *Index of Forbidden Books*.

———. *What Is the Index?* Milwaukee, Bruce, 1952. 129 p. **B 638**

"The present work attempts to supply . . . a factual description of the modern system of the Church's book legislation with an exposition of its rationale, as expounded by authoritative canon lawyers . . . This present work is written from the point of view of culture at large and in language that should be understood by the average layman, Catholic and non-Catholic." The appendix contains: Censorship of Special Classes of Books, Various Forbidden Authors and Titles, and The Great Books Program. Father Burke is director of libraries, DePaul University, and the book is based on a doctoral dissertation at the University of Chicago, 1948.

Burke, Richard K. "Contempt by Publication." *Arkansas Law Review*, 1:162–66, Winter 1946–47. **B 639**

Includes the "clear and present danger" test adopted as the rule in the Arkansas courts.

[Burleson, Albert S.]. "Postmaster General Explains to Editors Purpose and Operation of New Law." *Editor and Publisher*, 50:5, 16 October 1917. **B 640**

A discussion of government policies for dealing with disloyal and seditious publications during World War I.

Burlingame, Roger. "Freedom and the Lone Wolf." *Harper's Magazine*, 169:82–90, June 1934. **B 641**

"Freedom of speech or of the press we do, according to a current fiction, still maintain. Else how could our friend write what he wrote to the *Herald-Tribune* or view with alarm the tendency of dictatorship to censor and suppress? The speculation I am about to enter on is this: Suppose our president became in fact a dictator; suppose he forbade all criticism of himself, his administration, his party, or his political thought; suppose, for instance, a censorship as strict as that of Italy or even that of Germany. Suppose that at the same time he removed all of the censorship now imposed by industry and business. Should we then be more or less free in speech and writing than we are now?" The author considers the extent to which industry and trade dominate our freedoms.

Burn, John S. "Books Burned by the Common Hangman." *Notes and Queries*, 8(ser. 1):346–48, 8 October 1953. **B 642**
Relates to the suppression of Dr. James Drake's *Anglo-Scotia* in 1703.

"Burn the Books!" *Saturday Review of Literature*, 4:273, 5 November 1927. **B 643**
An essay on book burning inspired by Chicago Mayor Thompson's attack on pro-British books. Books are burned not as a convenient way of suppressing knowledge, but rather, using fire as a symbol. Opinion must not only be suppressed, according to the book burners, but must be suppressed by violence.

Burnett, Leo. "The Challenge of Economic Pressures on Freedom of the Press." *Nieman Reports*, 12(4):16–19, October 1958. **B 644**
Advertising pressures to influence editorial policies of the press are infrequent and not generally effective.

Burnett, R. G., and E. D. Martell. *The Devil's Camera; Menace of a Film Ridden World*. London, Epworth Press, 1932. 130p. **B 645**

Burnham, Philip. "The Outstretched Fist." *Commonweal*, 49:364–65, January, 1949. **B 646**
The author denies any question of press freedom is involved in the ban of *The Nation* from New York City schools. However, he considers the publication "a positive enemy of Christianity and the Catholic Church."

Burr, George L. "Anent Bonfires." *Cornell Era*, 39:205–9, February 1907. **B 647**
Professor Burr, class of '81, recounts the old custom of the Cornell students who at the end of the freshman year tossed their "all too learned" textbooks into a huge campus bonfire. Burr compares this college prank with the more earnest book burning in the early European universities where students, led by their professors, burned heretical books before they could contaminate readers. He describes Martin Luther's bonfires at Wittenberg. The young, Burr declares, are both the fiercest persecutors and the boldest heretics.

Burress, Lee A., Jr. "Censorship and the Public Schools." In *Freedom of Inquiry; Supporting the Library Bill of Rights; Proceedings of the Conference on Intellectual Freedom, January 23–24, 1965, Washington, D. C.* Chicago, American Library Association, 1965, pp. 20–28. (Also in *ALA Bulletin*, June 1965) **B 648**
The author notes an increase in censorship pressures in schools, caused, in part, by a greater awareness by teachers of controversial works and a broadening of reading assignments which include these works. He draws upon the recent study of censorship in Wisconsin schools for his comments. He refers to the possible use of professional sanctions against school systems where intellectual freedom is violated. Many school librarians and English teachers labor under the present distorted method of teaching literature, based upon a canon of what is good and bad, which may result in what Northrop Frye terms an aesthetic form of censorship.

———. *How Censorship Affects the School.* ⌐Oshkosh, Wis.⌐. Wisconsin Council of Teachers of English, 1963. 23 p. (*Special Bulletin* no. 8) (Also reported in *Wisconsin English Journal*, October 1963, and summarized in *Top of the News*, May 1964, and in *Education Digest*, January 1964) **B 649**
In a survey of censorship pressures in Wisconsin public schools (questionnaires returned by some 600 administrators and teachers) a fifth of all returns reported various kinds of censorship episodes. "Approximately one-third of all the returns contained evidence of one sort or another supporting the major conclusion that a substantial proportion of the teachers in Wisconsin feel the continuing presence of censorship pressures, and have experienced, or expect to experience, an overt expression of that pressure." The author recommends further cooperation among professional groups in resisting censorship, a written policy on book selection, and greater publicity for open schools and the right to read, with possible sanctions against those systems that do not permit freedom of book selection. Includes A Sample School Board Policy Statement and Books Objected to in Wisconsin, 1961–63.

———. "Is the *Areopagitica* Out of Date?" *Illinois Libraries*, 47:458–69, May 1965. **B 650**
In an address before the Southern Wisconsin Education Association, an English professor considers the various arguments against censorship made by John Milton in 1643 in light of present-day pressures for censorship, particularly in the public schools. The real issue is the student's right to read or right *not* to read. But "the right *not* to read does not mean the right to keep others from reading." Commenting on the two reactions of teachers to pressure—resistance or acquiescence—he states: "I think the American public wishes the schools to remain free of any pressure group, to be representative of the whole society, to enable all ideas to be expressed and to maintain intellectual freedom. Where teachers have publicly sought support, it has been forthcoming. Where they kept silent, they tended to lose their professional freedom, and their students lose the opportunity to get acquainted with the best literature of our time."

Burroughs, William. "Censorship." *Transatlantic Review*, 11:5–10, Winter 1962. **B 651**
In his introduction the author questions "the right of government to decide what people will think, what thought material or word or image will be presented to their minds." If all censorship were removed, he doubts if there would be any serious effect. The main body of his article is an experiment with the "fold in method" of writing, making a composite text by placing a page of text folded down the middle on another page of text so that a composite text is then read across half one text and half the other. By way of example he takes two texts he read at the Writers' Conference and folds them into newspaper reports of the conference. The subject matter is largely that of censorship and the effect is unusual.

Burrows Charles W. "Postal Rates and Literature." *Yale Review*, 14:343–60, February 1906. **B 652**
A criticism of the postal laws of 1874 and 1885 which give special rates to second-class matter. The privilege is being abused by inferior publications that are filled with advertising. Superior magazines are handicapped rather than aided by the working of this law.

⌐Burton, Henry⌐. *Narration of the Life of Mr. Henry Burton* . . . London, 1643. 51p. (Also in Howell, *State Trials*, vol. 3, pp. 714 ff. and in Schroeder, *Constitutional Free Speech*, pp. 212–24) **B 653**
Burton was an English Puritan minister who, along with William Prynne and John Bastwick, was persecuted for writing "libellous books against the hierarchy." On several occasions he was brought before the Star Chamber at the instigation of Bishop Laud for his criticism of popish practices of the prelates. His books and papers were seized, his testimony refused, and in 1637 he was committed to "prisoner of the fleet," where he remained until released by Parliament in 1640.

Bury, John B. "Freedom of Speech and the Censorship." *R. P. A. Annual, 1919*, London, Rationalist Press Association, 1919, pp.16–19. **B 654**
A certain limited censorship of opinion is necessary in wartime.

———. *A History of Freedom of Thought*. New York, Holt, 1913. 256p. (Home University Library of Modern Knowledge, no. 69) **B 655**

A professor of history at Cambridge has written this concise but scholarly work, tracing the freedom of thought from the freedom of Greece, through the persecution of the medieval church and state, to the rise of religious toleration and rationalism.

Bush, W. S. "Federal Censorship is Wholly Bad." *Moving Picture World*, 28:1853–54, 10 June 1916.   **B 656**

Busher, Leonard. *Religions Peace : Or A Plea for Liberty of Conscience. Long since presented to King James, and the High Court of Parliament then sitting, by Leonard Busher Citizen of London, and Printed in the Yeare 1614. Wherein is contained certain Reasons against Persecution for Religion; Also a designe for a peaceable reconciling of those that differ in opinion . . .* London, Printed for John Sweeting, 1646. 38 p. (Reprinted in Edward B. Underhill, *Tracts of Liberty of Conscience and Persecution*, pp. 1–81)   **B 657**
"It be lawful for every person or persons, yea, Jews and papists, to write, dispute, confer and reason, print or publish any matter touching religion, either for or against whomsoever; always provided they allege no fathers for proof of any point of religion, but only the holy scriptures . . . By which means, both few errors and few books will be written and printed, seeing all false ministers, and most people, have little or nothing else, besides the fathers, to build their religion and doctrine upon."

Bushnell, Robert J. "Banned in Boston." *North American Review*, 229:518–25, May 1930.   **B 658**
District Attorney Bushnell describes his prosecution of *Lady Chatterley's Lover* in Boston (*Commonwealth v. James A. Delacey*). While he conducted a vigorous case against the bookseller, Delacey, with ultimate success in the Supreme Judicial Court of Massachusetts, Bushnell did so with distaste because of the entrapment methods employed by the Watch and Ward Society. His blasts against the Society during the trial and the supplemental brief he filed criticizing the Society's tactics led to widespread public criticism of the vice society and a movement to amend the Massachusetts censorship law.

Busser, Ralph C. "Free Press and Fair Trial." *Temple Law Quarterly*, 27:178–93, Fall 1953.   **B 659**
Notes on court decisions relating to the publication of information that might prejudice the impartiality of trials, 1935–53.

Butcher, Maryvonne. "Films and Freedom." *Commonweal*, 69:65–70, 17 October 1958.   **B 660**
The fine artistry in many films emanating from countries under authoritarian control (U.S.S.R., Czechoslovakia, Poland, and Spain) suggests to the author, an English film critic, that box office pressures in the democracies "are more harmful to artistic creation than are the restrictions of ideological controls."

Butler, D. M. *The Law of Newspaper Libel.* Lincoln, Nebr., Legal News Printing Co., 1899. 44 p.   **B 661**
A practical handbook for newspaper editors giving specific examples of "libelous language" and "language not libelous."

Butler, William J. "The Right of Free Listening." *Catholic World*, 168:200–204, December 1948.   **B 662**
Criticism of the decisions of the U.S. Supreme Court favorable to Jehovah's Witnesses which allowed them to use loud-speakers and phonograph records on the streets.

Butterfield, Elizabeth. "Is a Public Library Its Brother's Keeper?" *Wilson Library Bulletin*, 17:835–36, June 1943.   **B 663**
The author rejects the principle that every book be considered in the light of its appropriateness for a 16-year-old. She examines the factor of "good taste," which is really a matter of community values. "The public library should be its brother's inspiration and help, but not its brother's keeper."

Button, Wilfred A. *Principles of the Law of Libel and Slander.* 2d ed. London, Sweet and Maxwell, 1946. 255 p.   **B 664**
"Mr. Button's object has been to state as shortly and clearly as possible the main principles of the law of defamation as they have been established by authoritative decisions of our ₍English₎ Courts of Justice,

and to support his précis of these principles by extracts from the reported judgments of eminent Judges . . . and by reference to decisions in leading cases."

Byington, Steven T. "On the Interference with the Environment: VI. The Question of Obscenity." *Egoist*, 1:15–16+, 1 January 1914; 2:34–35, 15 January 1914.   **B 665**
Since it is impossible for the law to satisfactorily define obscenity, "a man of ordinary prudence settles the question by regarding as probably legally obscene everything that opinions might differ on . . . to the considerable injury to the public." The writer attempts to reach a point of peaceful agreement between two divergent groups—those who find the nude body aesthetically acceptable and those who find it obscene.

Byrom, H. J. "Edmund Spenser's First Printer, Hugh Singleton." *Library*, 14 (4th ser.):121–56, September 1933.   **B 666**
Biography of a Puritan printer during the days of Elizabeth I. Part 2 of the article deals with Singleton's trial for secretly printing *The Discourie of a Gaping Gulf*, criticizing Queen Elizabeth's proposed marriage to a Catholic. The author, John Stubbe, and the printer, Singleton, were condemned to lose their right hands. Stubbe's hand was chopped off, but for some unaccountable reason the sentence on Singleton was never carried out.

The Bystander (London). "Special Censor Number." 61:217–60, 29 January 1919. (Excerpted in *Literary Digest*, 15 March 1919)   **B 667**
"For four and a half years ₍the censor₎ has been fair game for the lovers of this gentle pastime ₍leg-pulling₎, but never until now have we dared to indulge our inevitable propensities." Includes brief satirical articles, spoofs, jokes, and cartoons under the headings: The Censor's Blind Eye, That Queer "Censation," A Brain-Wave in the Censor's Office ₍analysis of the x's at the end of a love letter₎, As the Artist Might Have Drawn It—As the Censors Would Certainly Prefer It ₍e.g., "an issue of rum" v. "tea in the trenches"₎, and Censor Among the Poets.

C

[Cabell, James B.]. *The Judging of Jurgen.* Chicago, Bookfellows, 1920. 13 p. (Reprinted from the *New York Tribune*) **C1**

The publishers of James Branch Cabell's *Jurgen* were brought to trial in the New York courts on an obscenity charge at the instigation of the New York Society for the Suppression of Vice. The case was dismissed in 1922 by a judge who recognized that the erotic symbols in the novel could be understood only by the sophisticated reader.

———. *Taboo; A Legend Retold from the Dirghic of Saevius Nicanor, with Prolegomena, Notes, and a Preliminary Memoir.* New York, McBride, 1921. 40 p. (Limited to 920 numbered copies) **C2**

The work purports to retell the legend of an early civilization in which all references in literary works to eating were considered indecent and subjected the work to banning. Cabell dedicates his satire with an introduction to John S. Sumner, agent of the New York vice society whose aid (action against *Jurgen*) "obtained for me overnight the hearing I had vainly sought for a long while."

Cairns, Huntington. "Freedom of Expression in Literature." *Annals of the American Academy of Political and Social Science,* 200:76–94, November 1938. **C3**

The literary advisor to the U.S. Customs discusses the legal and extralegal control of literature and pictorial art, giving evidence of the thinking which led to censorship laws and court decisions. He points out the danger of intellectual distortion through censorship. "No matter how explicit its consideration, art never conflicts with the interests of national morality and is altogether beyond its provence." The article lists books acquitted by New York courts from 1920 to 1938.

Cairns, Robert B., James C. N. Paul, and Julius Wishner. "Sex Censorship: the Assumptions of Anti-Obscenity Laws and the Empirical Evidence." *Minnesota Law Review,* 46:1009–41, May 1962. **C4**

"In the following article, a lawyer and two behavioral scientists explore the consequences of exposure to obscenity. Their main purpose is to summarize the empirically demonstrated effects of psychosexual stimuli. In doing so, the authors examine and analyse the behavioral science investigations in this area. The article points out that the effects of sexual stimuli have rarely been studied in adequately controlled experimental investigations. This situation, of course, makes definite conclusions impossible. The authors, however, do evaluate that which is available and these evaluations will provide the reader with further insights into the problem at hand."

Caldwell, Edward C. "Censorship of Radio Programs." *Journal of Radio,* 1:441–76, October 1931. **C5**

A résumé of the historical development of free speech and the laws now governing that right, followed by an application of the law to radio broadcasting. The author points out the apparent conflict existing between freedom of speech via radio and the duty of the government to ensure best use of very limited facilities. If one yields to the other, it should be the latter that should give way.

Caldwell, Erskine. *God's Little Acre.* New York, Viking, 1933. 303 p. **C6**

The appendix to the fifth printing gives a seven-page account of the prosecution of the book in New York Municipal Court and Magistrate Benjamin Greenspan's decision freeing the book, considered a milestone in the fight against censorship. He ruled that the book must be considered in its entirety, that it was honest and sincere in its intent, that it had no tendency to incite its readers to behave like its characters, and that coarse and vulgar language was essential to the people portrayed. "The Court," he said, "may not require the author to put refined language in the mouths of primitive people."

———. "My Twenty-Five Years of Censorship." *Esquire,* 50(4):176–78, October 1958. **C7**

The author of *God's Little Acre* describes various efforts to suppress this work—the suit in New York against Viking Press (1933) brought by the New York vice society, in Massachusetts where the Supreme Judicial Court (1949) banned the book, and in Philadelphia where *God's Little Acre* was among a group of books freed by a decision of Judge Curtis Bok. Caldwell also discusses action against his *Tobacco Road* and *Tragic Ground.*

———. "Protest against Columbia University's Ban on *Tobacco Road* and *God's Little Acre.*" *New Republic,* 79:184–85, 27 June 1934. **C8**

Caldwell, Henry C. "Trial by Judge and Jury." *American Federationist,* 17:385–89, May 1910. **C9**

Deals with contempt of court cases and censorship by injunction in labor disputes.

Caldwell, J. B. "Statement." *Christian Life,* 2:19–22, November 1890. **C10**

The author was arrested on an obscenity charge for advocating "coition for offspring only" and for publishing a defense of Moses Harman, birth control advocate, in an issue of *Christian Life.*

Caldwell, Louis G. *American Press and International Communications.* New York, American Newspaper Publishers' Association, 1945. 58 p. **C11**

The author opposes merger of American communications companies, which, he believes, would bring greater government control of information.

———. "Censorship is Censorship—Regardless." *Broadcasting,* 30(13):25, 69, 1 April 1946. **C12**

The former general counsel of the Federal Radio Commission charges that the FCC's report in *Public Service Responsibility of Broadcast Licensees* is based on the fiction that the slogan "public interest, convenience or necessity" embraces government regulation of broadcast programs.

———. "Freedom of Speech and Radio Broadcasting." In *Annals of the American Academy of Political and Social Science,*

177:179–207, January 1935. (Excerpts in Summers, *Radio Censorship*, pp. 77–80) **C 13**
"My principal thesis is that, on the basis of legal and factual data now before us, broadcasting enjoys a liberty of expression far more circumscribed than that of the press, and that whereas the press has won a very substantial immunity, broadcasting has no immunity in time of war, and in time of peace it must be content in the main with lip service to the principle instead of the principle itself. The scope of freedom of speech by radio should be no whit less than the scope of freedom of the press, not only for the sake of the broadcaster and his listening public, but as well for the sake of the publisher and his reading public. Theirs is a common cause, liberty of expression, and a defeat suffered by either will eventually expose the other to a flank attack."

————. "Legal Restrictions on Broadcasting Programs." *Air Law Review*, 9:229–49, July 1938. (Excerpts in Summers, *Radio Censorship*, pp. 62–77) **C 14**
Address before the Second International Congress on Comparative Law, The Hague, 4 August 1937.

Calhoun, Harold G., Dorothy Calhoun, *et al. Let Freedom Ring!* Washington, D.C., U.S. Office of Education, 1937. 379 p. (Bulletin 1937, no. 32) **C 15**
Contains the scripts of 13 national broadcasts of the radio series, *Let Freedom Ring*, presented in the spring of 1937 over Columbia Broadcasting System. Script 4 deals with freedom of the press and introduces the Martin Marprelate tracts, William Prynne, Milton's *Areopagitica*, the trial of John Peter Zenger, the Alien and Sedition Acts, and the Minnesota gag law. Music production notes are included.

Calhoun, John C. "Minority Report of Senator Calhoun on Suppressing Anti-Slavery Agitation." In M. M. Miller, *ed., Great American Debates*. New York, Current Literature Publishing Co., 1913. vol. 4, pp. 125–28. **C 16**
President Jackson, in his message to Congress in 1835, had recommended legislation to prevent the Post Office from accepting anti-slavery publications and Calhoun was made chairman of a special committee of three Southerners and two Northerners to draft such legislation. The committee brought in a bill subjecting a postmaster to penalties for accepting such matter. A minority of the committee submitted this controversial report, drafted by Calhoun, opposing the bill, favoring instead, action by the states. The bill was finally rejected by a vote of 29 to 19. Daniel Webster spoke against it because its vagueness threatened press freedom. On page 161, a cartoon is reproduced with the caption "Joshua [Calhoun] Commanding the Sun [The Press] to Stand Still."

California. Assembly. Judiciary Committee. *Report of the Subcommittee on Porno-*

graphic Literature. Sacramento, Calif., The Assembly, 1959. 45 p. (Assembly Interim Committee Reports, 1957–59, vol. 20, no. 9) **C 17**

California. University. School of Librarianship. *The Climate of Book Selection; Social Influences in School and Public Libraries. Papers Presented at a Symposium Held at the University of California, July 10–12, 1958.* Edited by J. Periam Danton. Berkeley, Calif., The School, 1959. 98 p. **C 18**
Papers by a group of social scientists, emphasizing the ideological atmosphere in which books are selected and retained. Includes: The Atmosphere of Censorship by Harold D. Lasswell and Book Selection and Retention in California Public and School Libraries by Marjorie Fiske, author of a full-length study on book censorship in California libraries.

Callahan, Daniel. "The Ivy Curtain; Censorship of Campus Publications." *Critic*, 22(4):9–14, February–March 1964. **C 19**
Catholic college publications "suffer all the handicaps of the non-Catholic products, and, for good measure, a few others besides." The most notable handicap is the omnipresent reality of prior censorship. The present brand of college student is unwilling to accept this administrative paternalism. He is discovering "progressive" Catholicism. The author, associate editor of *Commonweal*, recounts the censorship cases at Catholic University (*Tower*), Notre Dame (*Scholastic*), and Chicago's Loyola (*Loyola Times*). The only advantage of censorship is that it safeguards the university; there is no educational value to the student.

Callahan, North. "Jefferson's Contribution to America's Free Press." *Quill*, 48(3):8, 20–21, March 1960. **C 20**
A professor of history at New York University reviews Jefferson's statements and activities with respect to the press.

Callanan, James A. S. *A History of Literary Censorship in England*. Boston, Boston University, 1941. 632 p. (Unpublished Ph. D. dissertation) **C 21**
The author traces the origin of censorship from ancient Rome and the *Index Romanorum*, to special edicts of English sovereigns and to the appointment of a Master of Revels for drama; censorship of the Church of Rome up to the time of the Reformation when the Church of England and the Star Court Chamber took over; the Star Chamber until abolished in 1641 and the subsequent development of censorship by parliamentary statute until licensing ended in 1694. After interpreting the laws against slander, libel, and blasphemy, and Lord Campbell's Act in 1857 against obscenity, he presents a chronological survey of book censorship from earliest times down to the present day. One section of the survey deals with censorship of plays from the

appointment of the Master of Revels in 1545 until the present day action of the Lord Chamberlain. Another section deals with wartime censorship, showing the close kinship between censorship and propaganda. A final section deals with the development of radio and film censorship in England. Appendices include: List of Masters of Revels and Examiners of Plays, Copy of Oath Taken by Examiner of Plays, Copy of License Issued by Lord Chamberlain for a Stage Play, Number of Plays Licensed and Refused, 1852–1912, and samples of war cartoons on the topic of censorship.

[Callender, James T.]. "Proceedings in the High Court of Justiciary against James T. Callender, Walter Berry, and James Robertson for Publishing a Seditious Pamphlet, 1793." In Howell, *State Trials*, vol. 23, pp. 79 ff. **C 22**
Callender and his associates were indicted in Edinburgh in 1792 for the publication of the *Political Progress of Great Britain*. To escape trial for sedition, Callender fled to the United States, where within a decade he was convicted under the Sedition Act.

[————]. "Trial for Seditious Libel, Richmond, Va., 1800. (*U.S. v. Callender*)." In Wharton, *State Trials*, pp. 688–90; also in *American State Trials*, vol. 10. pp. 813–76. **C 23**
Callender, a disreputable literary hack, was brought to trial for publication of a libel against President Adams in a pamphlet entitled, *The Prospect before Us*. The case involved the question of whether the jury had the right to consider the constitutionality of the law, in this case the Sedition Act. Judge Chase believed it did not. Callender was found guilty of seditious libel and sentenced to nine months' imprisonment. The trial became a debate between the Federalist judge and the Republican defense attorneys, three of Virginia's most distinguished lawyers, Philip N. Nicholas, George Hay, and William Wirt. Throughout the trial freedom of the press was an issue. A full account of the Callender case appears in James M. Smith, *Freedom's Fetters*, pp. 334–58.

Callwell, *Sir* Charles E. "Press Censorship." *Nineteenth Century*, 85:1132–45, June 1919. (Abstracted in *American Review of Reviews*, August 1919) **C 24**
Considers the necessity of a competent press censorship in time of war.

A Calm Inquiry into the Evidences of the Christian Revelation and Reflections suggested by the Late Trials of Carlile and Others, for Blasphemy, &c. London, John Glanville, 1819. 31 p. **C 25**
"Carlile's defence was all a falsehood. No man of common sense could believe him to have

had any point in view beyond the guilty profit of his publications . . . They who do not honour the King, must be made to respect his authority. They who do not fear God, must be prevented from balspheming his Holy Word." The author ("A Layman") calls on all Britons to defend the honor of God and country against attacks of the anarchist and atheist as represented by Carlile.

Calverton, Victor F. *Sex Expression in Literature*. Introduction by Harry E. Barnes. New York, Boni, 1926. 337 p. (Chapter on "Contemporary Sex Release in Literature" is reprinted in McDermott, *Sex Problem in Modern Society*, pp. 351–79) **C 26**

Sex expression is presented here in relation to its social origin and social control. The denial of things sexual and the condemnation of sex episode and diction by the bourgeoisie (Puritans) is the outgrowth of the social economy. "It is but a defense mechanism unconsciously designed to protect the private-property concept upon which it has thrived."

————, and S. D. Schmalhausen, *eds. Sex in Civilization*. New York, Macaulay, 1929. 709 p. **C 27**
Includes essays on Sex Censorship and Democracy by Waldo Frank, Sex and the Law by Huntington Cairns, Sex in Education by Harry E. Barnes, and Sex and the Novel by Robert M. Lovett.

Cameron, Angus. "The Freedom to Publish." *Masses and Mainstream*, 8(1): 43–47, January 1955. **C 28**
Deals with the application of the First Amendment to the books (largely Communist) issued by International Publishers, directed by Alexander Trachtenberg, and the belief of "a handful of witch-hunters" that the publications are "dangerous to the safety of our country."

Campbell, Alexander. "A Censorship of the Censor." *English Review*, 22:58–63, January 1916. **C 29**
Wartime censorship "is discharging its functions improperly and has become a grave menace to the successful prosecution of the war . . . An exclusive military censorship we must have, but nothing more."

Campbell, I. D. "Indecent Publications Amendment Act 1954: A Commentary." *New Zealand Law Journal*, 30:293–94, September 1954. **C 30**

Campbell, Laurence R. "Freedom of Information Study in Florida Shows Progress and Problems." *Quill*, 45(6):11–12, 36, June 1957. **C 31**

In a survey conducted by Florida State University School of Journalism, the local press and radio and television newsmen report on problems involved in covering government meetings and obtaining access to public records.

Campbell, Lily B. "The Suppressed Edition of *A Mirror for Magistrates*." *Huntington Library Bulletin*, 5–6:1–16, November 1934. **C 32**
A revision of the history of the *Mirror* "in order that it may be viewed as work of political and historical significance." The article discusses "the data at hand concerning the origin of the *Mirror*, the date of the original issue, and the reason for its suppression."

Campbell, Theophila (Carlile). *The Battle of the Press, as told in the Story of the Life of Richard Carlile, by his Daughter . . .* London, A. and H. B. Bonner, 1899. 319 p. **C 33**

The story of Carlile's trial for publication of Thomas Paine's *Age of Reason* and his role in the Manchester riots of 1819. For his radical writings and efforts to secure the freedom of the press this English publisher and journalist spent more than nine years in prison. The author is Carlile's youngest daughter. Although she hardly remembered her father, she knew a number of his friends and had access to some of his correspondence.

Campbell, Walter B. "Censorship of Literature in Queensland." *University of Queensland Law Journal*, 3:244–57, December 1958. **C 34**
A critique of the administration of the Objectionable Literature Act of 1954.

[Campion, William, *et al.*]. *The Reports of the Trials of William Campion, Thomas Jefferies, Richard Hassell, John Clarke, William Haley, William Cochrane, and others, for the sale of Anti-Christian Publications in the Shop of Richard Carlile, 84, Fleet Street, London. Tried at the Old Bailey Sessions, for June, 1824, before Newman Knowlys, the Recorder, and Common Juries*. London, R. Carlile, 1824. 136 p. **C 35**
When Richard Carlile went to prison for the sale of blasphemous or seditious works, various volunteers kept shop for him and, in turn, went to prison for the sale of works of Thomas Paine and other "blasphemous" writers. Campion was sentenced to three years, Hassell to two years, and Jefferies to two months (Jefferies pleaded guilty) for sale of *Age of Reason*. Clarke, Haley, and Perry were given three years and Cochrane six months for sale of an issue of *The Republican*.

"Can It Happen in Massachusets?" *Massachusetts Library Association Bulletin*, 42:1–3, January 1952. **C 36**

A Massachusetts public librarian, writing anonymously, describes a "frightening" disagreement on the library board which prevented the adoption of the Library Bill of Rights.

"Can the Ban Be Justified? Banning *The Nation* from New York City High Schools." *Nation*, 167:569–71+, 20 November 1948. **C 37**

Canada. Censorship Coordinating Committee. *Handbook: Press and Radio Broadcasting Censorship*. Ottawa, Patenaude, 1940. 23 p. **C 38**

Canada. Royal Commission on Broadcasting. *Report*. Ottawa, Queen's Printer, 1957. 518 p. **C 39**
In this general study of the Canadian broadcasting system, sponsored by the Fowler Commission, chapter 4 relates to the regulation of broadcasting. No fundamental change is suggested in arrangements for control; in general, the system has worked well. The report supports the continuation of "a single system in which both public and private stations are all integral parts and which is regulated and controlled by a single board [there had been agitation for a separate board for private broadcasters] representing the public interest and responsibility to Parliament." A brief history of Canadian broadcasting is given as an appendix. Reference is made to the Aird Commission (Sir John Aird) of 1928–29 which recommended the present system of national control and established the principle of public interest. The report of that Commission led to the Canadian Radio Broadcasting Act. The Royal Commission on National Development in the Arts, Letters, and Sciences, 1949–51, under the chairmanship of Vincent Massey, recommended continued public control of broadcasting in Canada.

[*Le Canada-Revue*]. *La Grande Cause Ecclesiastique. Le Canada-Review v. Mgr. E. C. Fabre. Procédure, Preuve, Pièces du Dossier, Plaidoyers des Avocats, Reproduction des Textes Originaux et des Notes Sténographiques Officielles*. Montreal, John Lovell, 1894. 342 p. **C 40**
A celebrated suit against the Archbishop of Montreal for interference with the publication of *Le Canada Revue*.

"Canada's Ban on Certain American Publications." *Literary Digest*, 88:17–18, 27 March 1926. **C 41**
Liberty was banned by the Canadian Customs "because of the publication of a series of articles said to reflect on the character of the late King Edward VII and the Prince of Wales." The New York *Daily Mirror* was banned following the allegation in the Canadian Parliament that it was "immoral."

Canadian Bar Association. Saskatchewan Sub-Committee on Civil Liberties. "Report on Censorship and Obscenity." *Saskatchewan Bar Review*, 25:80–87, September 1960. **C 42**

"The opinion is expressed that laws which seek to regiment public taste have no place in a democratic society, since such laws generally play into the hands of pedants and tyrants." A review of censorship powers of the Department of National Revenue, censorship under the criminal code of Canada, and provincial censorship legislation.

Canadian Library Association. Committee on Intellectual Freedom. "This Freedom." *Canadian Libraries*, 19:329–30, March 1963. **C 43**

The statement on intellectual freedom and censorship adopted by the Council of the Canadian Library Association: "The libraries and those responsible for libraries must stand as leaders for intellectual freedom and must resist social influences tending to restrict the legitimate right to provide Canadians with worthwhile books."

"Canadian Secrecy." *Time*, 34(21):49–50, 20 November 1939. **C 44**

Wartime censorship in Canada under the sweeping regulations of the Minister of National Defense is more rigorous than in Great Britain itself.

Canby, Henry S. "Something about Fig Leaves." *Saturday Review of Literature*, 4:249–50, 29 October 1927. **C 45**

A review of James Branch Cabell's, *Something About Eve*, including remarks on Cabell's experience with censorship.

———. "*Strange Fruit.*" *Saturday Review of Literature*, 17(14):14, 1 April 1944. **C 46**

Editorial on the banning in Boston of Lillian Smith's novel because of the use of a four-letter word. He calls for an end to the bootlegging of four-letter words. "Any word in the great English language is a good one, if honestly and properly used." In a letter to the editor in the 22 April issue, Arthur Garfield Hays points out that there is no legal prohibition on the use of four-letter words.

Candid Considerations on Libels. In Which is Represented: I. Their Influence upon the Human Mind. II. The Necessity of Refuting Them. III. The Inexpediency of the Law against Them. IV. The Insufficiency of Obtaining Redress Thereby, and the Consequent Propriety of Appealing to the Publick. With Some Observations of the Liberty of the Press. By a Friend to Harmony. Boston, Printed by E. Freeman and L. Andrews, [1789]. 22p. **C 47**

Candor, *pseud. A Letter from Candor to the Public Advertiser: Containing a Series of Constitutional Remarks on Some Late Interesting Trials, and Other Points, of the Most Essential Consequence to Civil Liberty* . . . 2d ed. London, Printed for J. Almon, 1764. 54p. (Also in *A Collection of Scarce and Interesting Tracts*, London, Almon, 1773, vol. 1, pp. 1–40) **C 48**

Following the verdict against John Wilkes for publication of a seditious libel in the printing of no. 45 of the *North Briton*, an anonymous Gray's Inn lawyer, writing as "Candor," expressed his approval of the verdict and of Lord Mansfield's interpretation of the common law of seditious libel. Freedom of the press, said Candor, was simply freedom from prior restraint and did not imply freedom from prosecution after the event. Truth itself was no defense in a libel case and the judge, not the jury, should determine whether the work was libelous. The libel law, Candor maintained, served as "an excellent device for keeping the scribbling race from meddling with political questions . . . The advantage of inoffensive speech or writing, and absolute submission to the government is so great, that I am sure every man ought to rejoice in such wholesome regulations." There is every reason to believe that the Candor pamphlet was actually a satire on Lord Mansfield, the judgment of the court, the House of Commons, and the conservative stand on seditious libel. This was the first in a series of pamphlets between Candor and his opponents (principally one writing under the pseudonym, "Father of Candor") and proponents, which focused attention on the administration of British libel laws. The identity of Candor has been ascribed to John Dunning, Lord Camden (Charles Pratt), Lord Ashburton, Sir Philip Francis, and to the publisher, John Almon.

Canham, Erwin D. *The Content of Our Information.* Columbia, Mo., Freedom of Information Center, School of Journalism, University of Missouri, 1958. 4p. (Publication no. 8) **C 49**

An address by the editor of the *Christian Science Monitor* on the occasion of the First-Day-Issue ceremony for the commemorative stamp honoring journalism and the freedom of the press.

———. "General Assembly Adopts Draft Convention on International Transmission of News and Right of Correction; Statement by E. D. Canham, and Text of Convention and Resolutions Adopted." *U.S. Department of State Bulletin*, 20:678–85, 29 May 1949. **C 50**

Canham was alternate United States delegate to the UN General Assembly.

———. "How a Free Press Can Help Freedom Survive." *Quill*, 40(6):5, 12–14, June 1952. **C 51**

Editor Canham believes that the newspaper, like other agencies of a free society, faces a crisis of confidence in liberty.

———. "International Freedom of Information." *Law and Contemporary Problems*, 14:584–98, October 1949. **C 52**

An American delegate on the UNESCO Sub-Commission on Freedom of Information discusses the task before the Fourth General Assembly of the United Nations in considering the second Draft Convention on Freedom of Information.

———. "Press as a Safeguard of Freedom in a Democracy." In *Proceedings*, National Education Association, Washington, D.C., 1941, pp. 176–79. **C 53**

———. "Report of Committee on World Freedom of Information." *Problems of Journalism; Proceedings of the American Society of Newspaper Editors, 1948.* Washington, D.C., ASNE, 1948, pp. 150–57. **C 54**

The report recommends (1) preservation of freedom of the press at home as "still our first task," (2) issuing visas into the United States for any bonafide news correspondents unless there is a real security risk, (3) co-operation in an attempt to organize an International Federation of Associations of Editors, and (4) study of the proposals of the International Institute of the Press.

———. "The Responsibility of Freedom of the Press." *Problems of Journalism; Proceedings of the American Society of Newspaper Editors, 1944.* Washington, D.C., ASNE, 1944, pp. 108–15. **C 55**

"Freedom of the press is never going to be impaired in the United States for very long unless American newspapers and newspaper men let it happen here. We are the basic masters of our destiny. Upon what we do depends what happens to us."

———. "The Right to Know." *Christian Science Monitor*, 16 July 1949, p. 6. **C 56**

Victory in battle for men's souls is seen through maintenance of freedom and democracy. From remarks at a Yale University luncheon on the occasion of the author's receiving an honorary doctorate.

Canning, Rita M. *A Study of Elijah Parish Lovejoy's Views on Freedom of the Press.* Carbondale, Ill., Southern Illinois University, 1957. 144p. (Unpublished Master's thesis) **C 57**

Cannon, Carl L., *comp. Journalism: A Bibliography.* New York, New York Public Library, 1924. 360 p. (Also in *New York Public Library Bulletin*, vol. 27, nos. 2–8, February–August 1923; reprinted by Gale Research Co., Detroit, 1967)　**C 58**

A comprehensive bibliography on American and British journalism for the nineteenth and early twentieth centuries, based on the extensive collection of the New York Public Library. Sections containing books and articles relating to freedom of the press are as follows: jurisprudence (includes numerous censorship and libel trials), liberty of the press, and military censorship. Most of the entries from these sections of Cannon's list have been included in this bibliography, except for personal libel cases not involving the issue of freedom of the press.

———. "Who Shall Decide What We Can't Read?" *Library Journal*, 54:1024–26, 15 December 1929.　**C 59**

The Book Buying Committee of the American Library Association opposes the provision in the tariff bill before Congress which provides that clerks of the U.S. Customs shall decide whether any book, pamphlet, or other writing imported into the United States is obscene or seditious.

Cannon, Garland H. "Freedom of the Press and Sir William Jones." *Journalism Quarterly*, 33:179–88, Spring 1956.　**C 60**

An account of the eighteenth-century British linguist who was brought to trial charged with seditious libel for his pamphlet, *Principles of Government.*

Cannon, Lucius H., *comp. Motion Pictures: Laws, Ordinances and Regulations on Censorship, Minors and Other Related Subjects.* St. Louis, Municipal Reference Library, 1920. 68 p.　**C 61**

Cannon, Ralph A. *An Analysis of Sex Exploitation on the Newsstands; A Sickness in Society.* Washington, D.C., Methodist Board of Temperance, 1958. 32 p.　**C 62**

———. "Pornography, Sex and the Church." *Christian Century*, 80:576–79, 1 May 1963.　**C 63**

"Behind the fact that peddlers of pornography find ready markets is the even more disturbing fact that our culture suffers from a fundamental confusion concerning the nature of human sexuality . . . Since the Supreme Court has stated that contemporary community standards are the basis for judging obscenity, we should get busy reshaping these standards." The Church should also take a more active part in sex education, should minister compas-sionately to those with sexual problems, should seek a more genuinely artistic presentation of sex, and should join forces with community organizations for decent literature, "but not before examining the assumptions and procedures of such organizations."

Cantril, Hadley, *ed.* "Liberty of the Press." In *Public Opinion, 1935–1946.* Princeton, N.J., Princeton University Press, 1951, pp. 416–18.　**C 64**

Includes summaries of 30 public opinion polls on liberty of the press.

"Canutes and the Press." *Times Literary Supplement*, 1296:873–74, 2 December 1926.　**C 65**

A brief history of the conflict between the press and the regulation of printed books: the round fought by the Catholic church, beginning with the Bull Inter Multipices (1501); the round fought in England beginning in 1408 with Arundel, the Archbishop of Canterbury; the round fought in France; the fifth and unfinished round begun immediately after Waterloo, which was to have a large part in the struggle for freedom in the epochs of revolutions not yet ended. "The ordered freedom of the Press will become the measure of complete nationhood."

Capouya, Emile. "Varieties of Love." *Nation*, 197:457–59, 28 December 1963.　**C 66**

"If evil communications do, in fact, corrupt good manners, the young have more to fear from the books that are freely available to them than from those the postmaster has been impounding since Mrs. Grundy first took the job . . . The case against censorship is always that the best books are the most controversial and therefore the first to be suppressed . . . What is most patently cheap and corrupting in our literature does not in the ordinary course attract the censor's attention." Capouya discusses three categories of erotica: love as a religious experience, love as a cosmic joke, and love as the banal decoration on the canvas of life.

Capp, Al. "Al Capp Views the Networks." *Nieman Reports*, 6(2):11, April 1952.　**C 67**

The cartoonist finds freedom in the American press but an "immovable, frightening Iron Curtain in American radio and TV." In Russia you must think as the Kremlin thinks; on the American air you must think as the sponsor thinks. A note to the article states: "This provocative statement by Al Capp was heard on March 12 by a Boston audience of several hundred. But the broadcasting and reporting facilities assigned to the meeting failed in their function."

Carden, Philip M. "The Supreme Court and Obscenity." *Vanderbilt Law Review*, 11:585–98, March 1958.　**C 68**

The net result of 7 obscene publication cases before the U.S. Supreme Court in the 12 months through January 1958 appears to be "that the controlling constitutional issue in obscenity cases hereafter will be the proper application of the definition of obscenity laid down by the five-man majority in Roth." The author examines in detail both majority and minority opinions in the Roth-Alberts cases.

Cardim, Elmano. *Freedom of Thought and Freedom of the Press in a World of Democracy.* Rio de Janeiro, Journal of Commerce, 1943. 33 p.　**C 69**

A lecture delivered 15 September 1943 before the Brazilian Academy of Letters, one of a series organized by the P.E.N. Club of Brazil with a view to studying the problems of organization of the postwar democratic world. The scope of the address is world-wide.

"The Cardinal's Crusade." *Commonweal*, 19:449–50, 23 February 1934.　**C 70**

An editorial supporting the action taken by Cardinal Hayes in "proclaiming a crusade for Christian decency in regard to reading, as part of the general program of the Catholic hierarchy of the United States to promote the Catholic press."

Cardwell, Richard W. *Keeping the Press Free.* Columbia, Mo., Freedom of Information Center, School of Journalism, University of Missouri, 1963. 8 p. (Publication no. 103)　**C 71**

The author, general counsel for the Hoosier State Press Association, reviews the legal rights of the press as expressed in the Constitution and by the courts. In addition to freedom from prior restraint and from undue prosecution after publication, the right of access to public information must be guaranteed. The tendency of the courts has been toward acceptance of the balancing theory. "What this means is that the current method of deciding First Amendment questions is by setting a statute or regulation or competing interest and the reasons for it on one side of the scale, and the protected right and the substantiality and probable effects on its restriction on the other and see which falls the fastest. The heaviest one wins." The newspaper is often in an unfavorable position with the legislature, in part because of its role as critic and public conscience. The general public has not always supported the press in its opposition to threats to the First Amendment because it has not always identified the newspaper's right of free expression with its own right as a citizen. He urges newspaper publishers to understand more fully their rights, to help the public to understand their mutual interests, and to help legislative representatives recognize issues and problems.

Care, Henry, *comp. English Liberties, or the Free-born Subject's Inheritance . . .* 4th ed. London, Printed by E. McNutt and K. Gosling for A. Bettesworth and J. Hooke, 1719. 356 p. Revised by William

Nelson. (First American edition, Boston, James Franklin, 1721. 288 p.) **C 72**

Includes a section, "That Juries are Judges of Law in Some Respects, as well as of Fact." This refers to the controversy as to whether the jury or the judge should determine whether a work was libelous, an issue in Care's trial of 1680.

[————]. *Triall of Henry Carr, Gent., at London, 2nd of July, 1680; upon Information... Charging Him to Be the Author of a Certain False, Scandalous and Malitious Book Intituled The Weekly Pacquet of Advice from Rome; or, The History of Popery . . .* London, R. Taylor, 1681. 26 p. (Reprinted in Howell, *State Trials*, vol. 7, pp. 1111 ff., and in Schroeder, *Constitutional Free Speech*, pp. 298–99) **C 73**

Care (or Carr) was arrested for attacks on the Pope that appeared in his periodical, *The Weekly Pacquet of Advice from Rome*. Chief Justice Scroggs declared it illegal to publish any news whatever without permission and ruled that the jury was to determine only the fact of publication; the judge would determine whether or not the matter was libelous. The jury found Care guilty.

[Carlile, Jane]. *Report of the Trial of Mrs. Carlile, on the Attorney-General's Ex-officio Information for the Protection of Tyrants; with the Information and Defence at Large before Mr. Justice Abbott and a Special Jury at the Guildhall.* London, J. Carlile, 1821. 24 p. (Reprinted in Macdonell, *Reports of State Trials*, 1(n. s.):1365 ff.) **C 74**

When her husband, Richard Carlile, went to jail for publishing Paine's *Age of Reason*, Mrs. Carlile took over the shop and continued to sell the offending work. She was arrested for the sale of a report of her husband's trial which included quotations from Paine's work. Charges, brought at the instigation of the vice society, were dropped when she agreed to sell no more copies. But within a week she was again arrested for sale of Sherwin's *Life of Paine*. She was found guilty of blasphemous libel and eventually joined her husband at Dorchester Prison. Richard's sister, Mary-Anne, took over the shop until she also went to prison.

[————]. *The Trials, with the Defences at Large of Mrs. J. Carlile, M. A. Carlile, W. Holmes . . . and T. R. Perry . . . who were Prosecuted for Selling the Publications of R. Carlile . . .* London, J. Carlile, 1825. 32 p. **C 75**

The trials of Richard Carlile's wife, Jane, his sister Mary-Anne, and two shopmen, Holmes and Perry. While neither wife nor sister supported the radical ideas of Carlile, they came to his defense out of indignation at the injustice of his loss of freedom.

[Carlile, Mary-Anne]. *Bridge-Street Banditti, versus The Press. Report of the Trial of Mary-Anne Carlile, for publishing a New-Year's Address to the Reformers of Great Britain; written by Richard Carlile; at the Instance of the Constitutional Association. Before Mr. Justice Best, and a Special Jury, at the Court of King's Bench, Guildhall, London, July 24, 1821. With the Noble and Effectual Speech of Mr. Cooper in defence, at Large.* London, R. Carlile, 1821. 53 p. **C 76**

The sister of Richard Carlile was brought to trial at the instigation of the Constitutional Association ("Bridge-Street Gang") for the sale of her brother's pamphlets. The Association consisted of a group of Tories dedicated to protect the Crown and government against seditious libel, a counterpart of the Society for the Suppression of Vice, which operated against blasphemy and obscenity. Miss Carlile was acquitted largely through the spirited defense of a young liberal lawyer, Henry Cooper. This pamphlet is dedicated to Cooper, who died shortly after the trial.

[————]. *Suppressed Defence. The Defence of Mary-Anne Carlile, to the Vice Society's Indictment, against the Appendix to the Theological Works of Thomas Paine; which Defence Was Suppressed by Mr. Justice Best, Almost at its Commencement; and, on the Propriety of Which Suppression, the Public, as the Highest Tribunal, is now appealed to and called upon to Judge between the Defendant, Her Prosecutors, and Her Judge. With a Report of the Proceedings before the Defence was Suppressed.* London, Printed and published by R. Carlile, 1821. 46 p. **C 77**

Miss Carlile was tried and convicted for selling a blasphemous libel, a part of a vice society campaign against the Carlile print shop. Later the same day she was acquitted of a charge of seditious libel.

[————]. *Trial of Mary-Ann Carlile for a Blasphemous Libel Before Mr. Justice Best and a Special Jury in the Court of King's Bench, Guildhall, on July 24, 1821. Motion for New Trial (Before Abbott, C. J. and Bayley, Holroyd, and Best, J. J) on November 12, 1821.* London, [1821]. 10 p. (Reprinted in Macdonell, *Reports of State Trials*, 1(n. s.):1033–51) **C 78**

[Carlile, Richard]. *Carlile and Paine's Age of Reason. British Forum . . . June 25th, 1819. Question, Ought the Conduct of Mr. Carlile in Continuing to Publish Paine's Age of Reason . . . to be Censured? . . .* London, 1819. Single sheet folded. **C 79**

James Mill's speech on the occasion is entered under the speaker's name.

[————]. *Constitutional Remarks Addressed to the People of Great Britain on the Subject of the Late Trial of R. Carlile for Republishing Paine's Age of Reason.* By a Member of Gray's Inn. London, 1819. 72 p. **C 80**

[————]. *A Dialogue on the Approaching Trial of Mr. Carlile, for Publishing the Age of Reason, with the trial Anticipated . . .* London, T. J. Wooler, 1819. 16 p. (From Wooler's *British Gazette*, 18 April 1819) **C 81**

[————]. *Jail Jottings (1820–1825); with an Introductory Account of Carlile's Mock Trial for Blasphemy and His Speech from the Dock.* Edited and Compiled by Guy A. Aldred. London, Bakunin Press, 1913. 48 p. **C 82**

Commentary written by Carlile while serving a jail sentence for publication of Paine's *Age of Reason*.

[————]. *Jail Journal. Prison Thoughts and Other Writings.* Edited and Selected by Guy A. Aldred. Glasgow, Strickland Press, 1942. 91 p. ("The Word" Library, 2d ser., no. 6) **C 83**

[————]. *"The King against Richard Carlile, 1831."* In Macdonell, *Reports of State Trials*, 2(n.s.):459–93. **C 84**

Carlile was brought to trial on 10 January 1831 before the Recorder of London for publishing seditious and revolutionary sentiments in his unstamped paper, *The Prompter*. He delivered a five and one-half hours' speech in his own behalf. After two verdicts of guilty for publishing *only*, which the Recorder refused to accept, the jury at last found Carlile guilty and he was fined and sentenced to two years in jail. He served this sentence plus an additional eight months in lieu of payment of the fine. Later the same year Cobbett was freed by a jury for the same offense.

[————]. *A Letter to Sir Samuel Shepherd Knt. His Majesty's Attorney-General, upon the subject of his prosecutions of Richard Carlile, for publishing Paine's Age of Reason.* London, R. Carlile, 1819. 28 p. **C 85**

While in jail awaiting trial for publishing Paine's *Age of Reason* Carlile wrote this open letter to the Attorney-General, anticipating the arguments of the prosecution, and answering each. The letter is signed "Philalethes."

[————]. *A Letter to the Society for the Suppression of Vice, on their Malignant Efforts to Prevent a Free Enquiry after Truth and Reason.* London, Carlile, 1819. 13 p. **C 86**

Carlile wrote this open letter while in jail awaiting trial on charge of blasphemy for publication of Paine's *Age of Reason*. He challenged the Society, which was responsible for his arrest, to prepare a refutation of Paine's arguments which he would publish and sell in an effort to present "a fair exposition of both our views."

[————]. *A List of the Jurors Nominated to Try the Two Informations by the Attorney-General, and Three Indictments by the Society for the Suppression of Vice against Mr. Carlile, for Publishing Paine's Age of Reason, Sherwin's Register and Palmer's Principles of Nature, in the Deist, a Work Now Publishing in Weekly Numbers.* London, Printed and Published for Mr. Carlile, 1819. 8 p. **C 87**

————. *A New Year's Address to the Reformers of Great Britain.* London, Printed by M. A. Carlile, [1821]. 16 p. **C 88**
The first of six pamphlets written by Carlile while serving his blasphemy sentence in Dorchester Goal. In the last, dated 20 December 1821, he reports satisfaction that the first four "have been considered worthy of indictment" (Mrs. Susannah Wright was sentenced to prison for their sale) and the fifth "has staggered the enemy in perceiving the strength it exhibits on my part." The sixth pamphlet contains the correspondence between Carlile and his friends, and Carlile's account of his quarrels with William Benbow and Thomas Wooler, also prosecuted for libel.

[————]. *The Report of the Proceedings of the Court of King's Bench, in the Guildhall, London, on the 12th, 13th, 14th, and 15th Days of October; Being the Mock Trials of Richard Carlile, for Alledged Blasphemous Libels, in Publishing Thomas Paine's Theological Works and Elihu Palmer's Principles of Nature; Before Lord Chief Justice Abbott, and Special Juries.* London, Printed and published by R. Carlile, 1822. 203 p. (Issued in numerous editions; reprinted in Borrow, *Celebrated Trials*, vol. 6, pp. 297–301) **C 89**
Carlile went to jail for six years; his wife was given a two-year sentence, and his sister a similar penalty. Carlile called for volunteers to continue publication of *Age of Reason* in his shop. Over the years, according to Gimbel in *Thomas Paine's Fight for Freedom*, "more than one hundred fifty persons responded, who collectively served more than 200 years' imprisonment in this battle for the freedom of the press . . . His heroic efforts finally won the battle, and the *Age of Reason* has ever since been in print." In 1818 Carlile challenged the government censors with the publication of Paine's *Age of Reason*, a work twice before condemned by the courts. To assure arrest, he advertised the publication widely. At the

instigation of the Society for the Suppression of Vice, Carlile was arrested and brought to trial. He faced three charges for selling Paine's work, a fourth charge for selling a copy of the *Deist* containing Elihu Palmer's *Principles of Nature*, and the fifth charge for the sale of *Sherwin's Register*. After long delays Carlile was tried for blasphemy and found guilty both for publishing *Age of Reason* and, in a second trial, for *Principles of Nature*. The sedition charge for publishing *Sherwin's Register* was dropped. Wickwar, in his comprehensive account of the Carlile case, stated that blasphemy was at the time considered more offensive to the average man than sedition, and offenders more likely to be convicted. Carlile insisted upon conducting his own defense and did so without much skill. He was found guilty and sentenced to three years in prison and given a heavy fine. Unable to pay his fine, Carlile spent a total of some six years in jail. The Carlile trial was one of the most talked-about events of the year, and the publication of it and *Age of Reason* was widespread. More serious to Carlile than the fine imposed was the seizure of his book stock by the sheriff. Following Carlile's imprisonment his wife Jane and his sister Mary-Anne continued to operate the shop and sell the offending publication. For this they were also arrested and served two years in prison. Between 1821–22, six volunteer shopmen were given sentences of from six months to two years each (Susanna Wright, George Beer, John Barkley, Humphrey Boyle, Joseph Rhodes, and William Holmes). Later James Watson and William Tunbridge served sentences. In 1824 nine more shopmen went to jail: Thomas Jefferies, William Haley, William Campion, Richard Hassell, Michael O'Connor, William Cochrane, John Clarke, John Christopher, and Thomas Riley Perry. The government limited its prosecution to the sellers of the offending works whom they considered as publishers, and did not take action against the authors. Carlile was never brought to trial for anything he wrote.

[————]. *Vice versus Reason. A Copy of the Bill of Indictment, found at the Old Bailey Sessions, January 16, 1819, against Richard Carlile, for Publishing Paine's Age of Reason . . .* London, R. Carlile, 1819. 13 p. **C 90**
Text of the indictment drawn up at the instigation of the Society for the Suppression of Vice, together with the defendant's comments on the act of the "distinguished boobies."

[———— *et al.*]. *The Trials with the Defences at Large of Mrs. Jane Carlile, Mary-Anne Carlile, William Holmes, John Barkley, Humphrey Boyle, Joseph Rhodes, Mrs. Wright, William Tunbridge, James Watson, William Campion, Thomas Jefferies, Richard Hassell, William Haley, John Clarke, William Cochrane, and Thomas Riley Perry, being the Persons who were Prosecuted for selling the publication of Richard Carlile in various Shops.* London, R. Carlile, 1825. Various paging. **C 91**

Under this title page are collected the various separate reports of trials, some of which are entered in this bibliography as separate publications.

Carlson, Oliver. "A Slanted Guide to Library Selections." *Freeman*, 2:239–42, 14 January 1952. (Reprinted in Daniels, *The Censorship of Books*, pp. 160–69) **C 92**
The author charges Helen Haines with a pro-Soviet bias in the revised edition of her *Living with Books*, a standard guide to library book selection. Elinor S. Earle replies in the *ALA Bulletin*, April 1952.

Carlson, W. H. "Preparers of the Mind and Heart." *Library Journal*, 61:182–85, 1 March 1936. **C 93**
To withstand the vicious international propaganda war "librarians are going to have to be specialists in falsehood and distortion of the truth in print." If such propaganda becomes a real threat to the existing order, librarians are justified in opposing it in their professional capacity. Librarians "may, paradoxically, have to be militant in their opposition to a social order which threatens their freedom."

Carlton, Henry F. *Right to Print the Truth.* Edited by Claire T. Zyve. New York, Bureau of Publications, Teachers College, Columbia University, 1932. 32 p. **C 94**
A radio play dealing with John Peter Zenger, part of a series, "Dramatic Hours in Colonial History."

Carlyle, Edward I. *William Cobbett; a Study of His Life As Shown in His Writings.* London, Constable, 1904. 318 p. **C 95**
G. D. H. Cole describes this biography of a man involved throughout his life in issues of press freedom, as "painstaking and competent, but dull."

Carmer, Carl L. *For the Rights of Men.* New York, Hinds, Hayden & Eldredge, 1947. 64 p. **C 96**
Popular dramatizations of "heroes who risked their lives and fortunes in the struggle for civil liberties." Includes Andrew Hamilton, John Peter Zenger, Matthew Lyon, Thomas Paine, William Lloyd Garrison, and Elijah Lovejoy.

Carnes, Paul N., and F. J. Cavalier. "Censorship." *Library Journal*, 80:1445–51, 15 June 1955. **C 97**
Paul N. Carnes, Unitarian minister, expresses the opinion that the moral censor is less interested in morality than in moralizing. If he were really concerned with morality he would not stop with the law, but would promote good reading habits in children and better relationship between children and their parents. Mr. Cavalier, a municipal judge,

considering the legal aspects of censorship, reviews the law enforcement problems connected with book censorship, with special reference to Ohio. The task of law enforcement is to control purveyors of trash who disregard all bounds of decency, but to permit writers "the just and full expression of their genius." While legal action against an offending work is difficult it is the only legitimate way to proceed. Talks given at a conference of the Ohio Library Association.

Carney, William P. "Fighting the Censor." *Scribner's*, 101:33–38, June 1937. **C98**
An account of censorship abroad, by a veteran foreign correspondent of the *New York Times*. "World censorship of news is in a bull market in 1937. On practically all fronts, the dispatches which keep American readers in contact with world affairs are being snipped, slashed, or held up until valueless ... War-born in 1914, censorship in open or undercover form now covers all of European and Asian countries, with the exception of the British Empire, Holland, Switzerland, and Scandanavia." An accompanying map shows the approximate conditions of censorship prevailing throughout the world.

Carnovsky, Leon. "Can the Public Library Defend the Right to Freedom of Inquiry?" *ALA Bulletin*, 38:255–57, July 1944. **C99**
A proposal by the Intellectual Freedom Committee of the American Library Association of a program to make the Library Bill of Rights more effective. Libraries affected by suppression should report the details to the Committee, which will, in turn, give wide publicity to the case.

———. "The Obligations and Responsibilities of the Librarian Concerning Censorship." *Library Quarterly*, 20:21–32, January 1950. (Reprinted in Downs, *The First Freedom*, pp. 312–20; in Marshall, *Books, Libraries, Librarians*, pp. 324–42, and in *Illinois Libraries*, May 1966; excerpted in *ALA Bulletin*, November 1953) **C100**
A classic statement about censorship and the librarian, by the editor of *Library Quarterly*. He distinguishes between book selection and censorship, and, after reviewing the historical development of the concept of a free press as defined by the American courts, he considers how librarians might intelligently meet various censorship situations. The fear of objection may lead a librarian to avoid purchase of controversial books. In assuring a minority the right of expression, the librarian must not permit them to dictate the reading matter of others. "Censorship is an evil thing. In accepting it, in compromising, in 'playing it safe,' the librarian is false to the highest obligations of his profession. In resisting it, he retains his self-respect, he takes his stand with the great champions of free speech, and he reaffirms his fundamental faith in the dignity of man."

Carpenter, Edward. *My Days and Dreams, Being Autobiographical Notes*. London, Allen & Unwin, 1916. 340 p. **C101**
Includes a discussion of efforts to restrict and censor the author's frank expressions in matters of sex.

Carpenter, William. *Political Letters and Pamphlets, Published for the Avowed Purpose of Trying with the Government the Question of Law—Whether All Publications Containing News or Intelligence, However Limited in Quantity or Irregularly Issued, Are Liable to the Imposition of the Stamp Duty of Fourpence, &c.; with a Full Report of the Editor's Trial and Conviction, in the Court of Exchequer, at Westminister*. London, William Carpenter, 1830–31. (Thirty-three letters, each with a different title and separate paging, prefaced by an account of William Carpenter's Trial, 14 May 1831) **C102**
Carpenter, in protest against the Stamp Act, issued this series of letters. He claimed it was not a newspaper under the definition of the Stamp Act because (1) it was not regularly issued, (2) it did not bear a single title, and (3) there was no numerical designation of the parts. The Crown argued that if it contained news it was a newspaper. The jury found Carpenter guilty and he was required to pay £120 and back taxes.

Carr, Frank. "The English Law of Defamation." *Law Quarterly Review*, 18:255–73, July 1902; 18:388–99, October 1902. **C103**
An historical and interpretive work based on the author's doctoral dissertation at Cambridge University. Special references are made to the distinction between libel and slander.

[Carr, *Sir* John, *plaintiff*]. *Liberty of the Press, Sir John Carr against Hood and Sharpe, Report of the above Case Tried at Guild Hall before Lord Ellenborough, the 25th of July, 1808, to which Are Added Several Letters on the Subject written by Earl Mountmorris, Sir Richard Phillips, and the Author of "My Pocket Book."* London, Wilson, 1808. 39 p. **C104**
Edward Dubois had written a satire on Sir John's "Tour in Ireland," entitled "The Stranger in Ireland in 1805, by a Knight Errant," for which the publishers were prosecuted for libel. They were found not guilty.

Carrigan, Mike. "North Dakota's Fight for Open Court Records." *Quill*, 49(5): 15–16, 19, May 1961. **C105**
The article relates to a North Dakota Supreme Court ruling on the 1957 public records act that newsmen had no right to inspect records of the county courts.

[Carrington, Charles]. *Forbidden Books: Notes and Gossip in Tabooed Literature. By an Old Bibliophile*. Paris, For the Author and His Friends, 1902. 227 p. (375 copies printed) **C106**
The publisher and probably the author of this work was the notorious English pornographer who conducted a flourishing publishing business in erotica and pornography in Paris, beginning about 1893. His sales were largely to English buyers. For a time English Customs prohibited "any books published by Carrington." His activities were the source of considerable annoyance to authorities both in France and England and his name figured prominently in the 1907 Parliamentary hearings on lotteries and indecent advertisements. The author gives a synopsis of three books: John Cleland's *Fanny Hill*, Anatole France's *Thais*, and the anonymous *My Secret Life*.

Carrington, Walter, "Laws to Suppress Anarchy and Sedition." *Virginia Law Register*, 5(n.s.):606–9, December 1919. **C107**
The author favors a resolution adopted by the Missouri Bar Association urging Congress and state legislatures to pass legislation to suppress anarchy and sedition.

Carroll, Paul. "Big Table: The Way It Was." *Choice*, 2:156–58, 1962. **C108**
A former editor of the *Chicago Review* writes of the suppression of the Winter 1959 issue of that little magazine by the University of Chicago and the subsequent launching of *Big Table*, later suppressed by the Post Office.

Carroll, Thomas F. "Freedom of Speech and of the Press During the Civil War. *Virginia Law Review*, 9:516–51, April 1923. **C109**
Includes sections on control of reporters, telegraphic censorship, exclusion from the mails, arrest of editors, suppression of papers, and use of martial law.

———. "Freedom of Speech and of the Press in War Time: The Espionage Act." *Michigan Law Review*, 17:621–65, June 1919. **C110**
A study of the Espionage Act of 1917 and its interpretations by the courts: (1) the freedom of the press is limited by the protective right of the community; (2) the right of circulation is collateral with the right of publication; (3) the censorship provision of the Act was rejected by Congress out of respect for the traditional opposition of the press and the people to any form of censorship; (4) the doctrine of administrative discretion has been strengthened; (5) the future of the Espionage Act to suppress bolshevism is in doubt.

————. "Freedom of Speech and the Press in the Federalist Period: The Sedition Act." *Michigan Law Review*, 18:615–51, May 1920. **C111**
While no authority over the press was given to Congress by the Constitution, Congress might exercise needful control by virtue of the necessary and proper clause. The First Amendment does not provide a positive denial to Congress of any power over the press. Freedom of the press seems to imply freedom to publish such sentiments as do not interfere with the government exercise of its constitutional functions. The Sedition Act as it was enforced was little, if any, less severe than the common law of libels. It was the last act of its kind passed by the Congress.

Carson, Doris M. "The Price of Liberty; a Statement Prepared by the Intellectual Freedom Committee, Kansas Library Association." *Wilson Library Bulletin*, 36:392–93, January 1962. **C112**
Advice to librarians on how to meet censorship pressures and maintain intellectual freedom.

Carter, Boake. "Foreword." In his *I Talk as I Like*, New York, Dodge, 1937, pp. xi–xiii. (Excerpted in Summers, *Radio Censorship*, pp. 132–34) **C113**
The entire book deals with "the headaches with which I have battled in the last eight years, promoted solely from intolerance of Mr. Average Man" who, when he did not approve of the radio commentator's views, showered commercial sponsors with "the intolerance of threats to destroy their business." He calls on radio listeners, in the interest of freedom of reporting, to refrain from such actions and on advertisers and radio stations to disregard such demands for censorship. The book is dedicated to Philco Radio and Television Corp., which withstood such pressures. An article, What's Happened to Boake Carter? appeared in *Radio Guide*, 29 April 1939, and was reprinted in Summers, *Radio Censorship*, pp. 255–58.

Carter, John S. "Injunction of Newspaper's Publication as Nuisance." *Cornell Law Quarterly*, 17:126–31, December 1931. **C114**
A discussion of the case of *Near v. Minnesota*, in which the U.S. Supreme Court held unconstitutional the so-called Minnesota "gag law" that declared that a newspaper regularly engaged in publication of malicious and scandalous material could be enjoined as a nuisance.

Carter, Robert L. "Two Thousand Years of Censorship." *Library Journal*, 79:1003–5, 14 June 1954. **C115**
Report on an exhibit of banned books, 200 B.C. to A.D. 1953, at the Enoch Pratt Free Library, Baltimore.

Carter, Roy E., Jr. "Newspaper 'Gatekeepers' and the Sources of News." *Public Opinion Quarterly*, 22:133–44, Summer 1958. **C116**
Consideration of research possibilities in the relationship between the newspaper "gatekeepers" (the desk editors who decide what is to be published) and the news sources.

————. "Radio Editorializing Aboard the New Mayflower." *Journalism Quarterly*, 28:49–53, Fall 1951. **C117**

Cartwright, Frances D., *ed. The Life and Correspondence of Major Cartwright. Edited by His Niece.* London, Henry Colburn, 1826. 2 vols. **C118**
Major John Cartwright, who devoted a lifetime to liberal reforms, played an important part in the campaign against the British tax on newspapers. He supported the defendants in many of the libel trials of the period and refers to them in his letters—Thelwall, Wooler, Hardy, Muir, Holt, and Tooke. Daniel Holt had been convicted in 1793 for publishing *An Address to Tradesmen . . .*, written in 1782 by Cartwright. The biography contains a lengthy account of the prosecution of John Horne Tooke and Cartwright's testimony in his behalf.

Cartwright, John. *English Constitution Produced and Illustrated.* London, Printed by Richard Taylor and sold by T. Cleary, 1823. 446p. (Excerpts from sections on freedom of discussion are included in Schroeder, *Methods of Constitutional Construction*, pp. 85–106) **C119**
Major Cartwright, although a monarchist and opposed to the republican propaganda of Thomas Paine, was a staunch believer in freedom of opinion and was one of the founders of the Friends to the Liberty of the Press and the Society for Constitutional Information. His book, favorably reviewed by Thomas Jefferson, contains many references to freedom of speech and of the press.

Cary, Joyce. "Censorship Plot." *Spectator*, 194:275–76, 11 March 1955; discussion, 194:320, 18 March 1955; 194:390, 1 April 1955. **C120**
An attack on the proposed British Censorship Bill aimed at the horror comics. "The horror comics, in themselves are thoroughly bad; but censorship is worse." Cary sees the bill as an opening wedge for censorship on a wider front. J. C. C. Armitage, in a letter to the editor in the 1 April issue, believes Mr. Cary fails to distinguish between horror comics for children and erotic literature for adults. It is only the former that are to be banned and rightly so.

Cary, William J. "Espionage Bill: Shall the Declaration of Independence and the Bill of Rights Be Deleted by a Censor?" *Congressional Record*, 55:1949–52, 5 May 1917. **C121**

The Case against the Saturday Review of Literature . . . Chicago, *Poetry*, 1949. 71p. **C122**
While not strictly an issue on the freedom of the press, the spirited controversy over the awarding of the 1948 Bollinger Prize in Poetry to Ezra Pound, under indictment for treason, raised a number of related points, notably whether a man's literary work can be legitimately judged apart from his public life, and what should be the relationship of art and the state. Opposition to the award, made by the Fellows in American Letters of the Library of Congress, centered in the pages of the *Saturday Review of Literature* (two articles by poet Robert Hillyer and several editorials); the defense of the award (or opposition to the *Saturday Review's* attack) was summed up in this pamphlet with statements by the Committee of the Fellows, including Allen Tate, Malcolm Cowley, Archibald MacLeish, and others. Some of these articles appeared previously in *New Republic*, *Hudson Review*, and *Poetry*.

"The Case Against Trial by Newspaper: Analysis and Proposal." *Northwestern University Law Review*, 57:217–54, May–June 1962. **C123**
An examination and evaluation of methods employed in the past in "an effort to reach some workable solution to the problem of how to assure a fair trial by an impartial jury to every criminal defendent, while not unconstitutionally limiting freedom of the press." Includes a model statute as an attempt to eliminate many of the abuses of unrestrained crime reporting.

"The Case for Censorship." *Living Age*, 346:172–73, April 1934. **C124**
An editorial observing that "the ideal of personal liberty has waned with prosperity," and quoting author Jean Schlumberger as questioning whether the right of the artist to express his ideas without restraint "is as essential to civilization as we have come to believe."

"A Case for News Suppression." *Columbia Journalism Review*, 2(3):11–12, Fall 1963. **C125**
An anonymous southern business man applauds local management of the news in the interest of achieving equitable race relations and civil order. Editorial comment follows.

"The Case of Canon 35—As Debated on WSB Radio, Atlanta." *Quill*, 50(12): 12–15, 24, December 1962. **C126**
The program, Court of Public Inquiry, discussed the American Bar Association stand against photography, broadcasting, or television coverage of court proceedings. The text of the broadcast is given.

"Case of *Hagar Revelly*." *Green Bag*, 26: 115–19, March 1914.　　　　**C 127**
Hagar Revelly was found obscene by a New York court but Judge Hand questioned the Cockburn rule on obscenity, a product of Victorian England, as not reflecting "the understanding and morality of the present time."

"The Case of John Hadlow." *New Statesman and Nation*, 38:603–4, 26 November 1949; discussion, 38:635, 647, 3 December 1949.　　　　**C 128**
The case, subject of a discussion in Parliament, involves the right of an editor to protect the confidence and anonymity of his writers, a right which the author defends.

"The Case of *The Well of Loneliness*." *New Adelphi*, 2:199–209, March–May 1929.　　　　**C 129**
The editor of the *New Adelphi* discusses the case of Radclyffe Hall's book which was condemned to be burnt as "obscene" by a Bow Street magistrate. The case should never have been brought to court, which is not qualified to pass judgment. "All that was needed was common sense and courage in the Home Secretary." A footnote states that the case could not be reported in the last issue of *New Adelphi* without contempt of court because an appeal, since denied, was pending.

[Casey, Paul C.]. "The Casey Judgement." *Tamarack Review*, 21:58–70, Autumn 1961.　　　　**C 130**
The text of the decision against *Lady Chatterley's Lover* given by Mr. Justice Casey in the Province of Quebec.

Casey, Ralph D. "Professional Freedom and Responsibility in the Press." In Wilbur Schramm, *Communications in Modern Society*, Urbana, Ill., University of Illinois Press, 1948, pp. 205–18.　　　　**C 131**

Cashman, Gerald, and Marlowe Frake. "Canon 35 as Voiced by the Illinois Judiciary." *Journal of Broadcasting*, 2: 295–310, Fall 1958.　　　　**C 132**
A questionnaire survey of 66 Illinois judges indicated "almost unanimous regard of photo-radio-TV coverage as psychologically and physically distracting in the courtroom."

Casner, Margaret S. *The Prosecutions of Newspapers under the Espionage Acts of 1917 and 1918*. Urbana, Ill., University of Illinois, 1929. 42 p. (Unpublished Master's thesis)　　　　**C 133**

Castagna, Edwin. "The Climate of Intellectual Freedom—Why Is It Always So Bad in California." *ALA Bulletin*, 59: 27–33, January 1965.　　　　**C 134**

The author considers the phenomenon of a state that once offered hospitality to the controversial ideas of Jack London, Lincoln Steffens, Upton Sinclair, Cary McWilliams, Hiram Johnson, John Steinbeck and Dr. Townsend, but since the days of Senator McCarthy has become a national center for censorship and suppression. Despite the "stinking smogs of anti-intellectualism" many California librarians have stood up against attacks on intellectual freedom, setting courageous examples to librarians across the nation.

———. "Courage and Cowardice: The Influence of Pressure Groups on Library Collections." *Library Journal*, 88:501–6, 1 February 1963.　　　　**C 135**
The director of Enoch Pratt Free Library, Baltimore, describes the characteristic approaches and behaviors of censors of library books, gives examples of censorship attempts, and relates some of the accomplishments of librarians in the struggle for intellectual freedom.

Castberg, Frede. *Freedom of Speech in the West; a Comparative Study of Public Law in France, the United States, and Germany*. London, Allen & Unwin, 1960. 475 p.　　　　**C 136**
Part 2 considers constitutional provisions on freedom of expression in the United States—an historical survey, laws, Supreme Court decisions, and administrative ruling. Similar sections deal with Germany and France. A final section attempts to compare the ideological and practical expression of free speech in the three countries. Compiled largely from secondary sources. The author is former Rector, University of Oslo.

Castiglione, Emily P. *Recent Trends in the Judicial Handling of Obscenity in Literature*. Columbia, Mo., University of Missouri, 1948. 87 p. (Unpublished Master's thesis)　　　　**C 137**
Largely a discussion of court decisions on modern fiction in New York and Boston during the 1930's and 1940's. Consideration is given to the changed scene in Boston with the decisions on *Strange Fruit* and *Forever Amber*.

Cathcart, Arthur M. "Constitutional Freedom of Speech and of the Press." *American Bar Association Journal*, 21: 595–600, September 1935. (Reprinted in Johnsen, *Freedom of Speech*, pp. 86–96)　　　　**C 138**
"Guarantees of free speech and free press control government action only. Prohibition of these rights clearly assumes a pre-existing freedom which is far less extensive than is generally supposed. Its sources are the English Common Law and the great principle of popular liberty for which the American Revolution was professedly fought." Address before the Commonwealth Club of California, 29 March 1935, by a professor of law at Stanford University.

[Catholic Church in the United States. Bishops]. *Censorship; Statement of the Bishops of the United States*. Washington, D.C., National Catholic Welfare Conference, 1957. 3 p. (Reprinted in Gardiner, *Catholic Viewpoint on Censorship*, pp. 185–92)　　　　**C 139**
"Through the National Legion of Decency and the National Office for Decent Literature, we Catholics give public expression to our opinion on this subject. Through these agencies we voice our concern over conditions which, tolerated, merit expression of public indignation. But we assert that our activities as carried out by these organizations cannot justly be termed an attempt to exercise censorship." The statement was signed in the name of the Bishops of the United States by members of the Administrative Board, National Catholic Welfare Conference. Comments on the statement appear in *Commonweal*, 6 December 1957.

[———]. "Films: Freedom and Responsibility: Statement." *Catholic Mind*, 59: 563–66, December 1961.　　　　**C 140**
A statement on film censorship by the Catholic Bishops of the United States who had established the Legion of Decency in 1933 and the National Office for Decent Literature in 1938.

[Catholic Church in the United States. Episcopal Committee for Motion Pictures, Radio and Television]. *Advisory-Film Classification, a Contemporary Obligation of Society*. Huntington, Ind., Our Sunday Visitor, n.d. 23 p. (Bound with John E. Fitzgerald, *Film Classification, the Bishops Speak Again*)　　　　**C 141**
The statement was issued by the Committee on 7 December 1962.

[Catholic Church in the United States. Newark Archdiocese. Office of Communications and Entertainment]. *Organization and Procedures. Decent Literature and Decent Motion Pictures, Archdiocese of Newark*. Newark, n.d. 15 p. mimeo.　　　　**C 142**

Catlin, George E. G. "Freedom of Speech and Television." *Contemporary Review*, 184:337–43, December 1953.　　　　**C 143**
A discussion of freedom of speech in relation to the monopoly of the British Broadcasting Corp. "The question is: who settles what is moral service and what is vice? Should we choose to accept the democratic philosophy, then I submit that it follows that the public must have a right to experiment in what is right, even if wrong; to be crude and clumsy; to learn by its errors; to grow."

———. "This Giant Air Monopoly." *Fortnightly Review*, 135(n.s.):577–85, May 1934.　　　　**C 144**

The English people who have prided themselves on freedom of the press have allowed a censor, appointed by a government monopoly, to determine news and opinion on radio. The author calls for a challenge to the B.B.C. system and its standardization of ideas.

Catt, Carrie Chapman. "Open Letter to D.A.R." *Woman Citizen*, 12(n.s.):10–12, 41–42, July 1927. **C 145**
The author criticizes the Daughters of the American Revolution for the use of libel as a campaign method in the organization's pamphlets which charge innocent women with Communist sympathies and associations. In particular, Mrs. Catt refers to vilification of members of the Women's League for Peace and Freedom, of which Jane Addams is president.

Causton, Bernard, and G. Gordon Young. *Keeping It Dark, or the Censor's Handbook.* London, Mandrake Press, 1930. 83 p. Foreword by Rebecca West. **C 146**
Deals with literary, dramatic, and film censorship in Great Britain.

Cavanagh, John R. "The Comics War." *Journal of Criminal Law and Criminology,* 40:28–35, May–June 1949. **C 147**
The author concludes that no one has conclusively demonstrated that comics are harmful and that no normal child under 12 is likely to be harmed by them. Certain types of comics may be harmful to adolescents. He argues that campaigns to eliminate comics are useless and serve only to release the aggressive feeling of the crusaders; that parents are the best judges of what their children should read.

Caygill, Harry W. "Press Censorship in Wartime." *Artillery Journal*, 78:262–68, 358–63, 1935; *Infantry Journal*, 42:344–50, July–August 1935; 42:441–46, September–October 1935. **C 148**
Based on an unpublished Master's thesis, Columbia University, 1932, entitled *Press Censorship in the American Expeditionary Forces.*

Cecil, *Lord* Robert. *Why Mail Censorship Is Vital to Britain; an Interview with the Rt. Hon. Lord Robert Cecil as Published with a Preface by Arthur S. Draper of the New York Tribune. Together with a Brief Memorandum on the American Note Dealing with the Censorship of Mails, by the Rt. Hon. Sir Maurice De Bunsen . . .* London, Truscott, 1916. 10 p. **C 149**
Deals with British military censorship in World War I.

Celler, Emanuel. "The Book and Censor." *ALA Bulletin*, 47:479–80, November 1953. **C 150**
Extension of remarks made by the New York Congressman, reprinted from the *Congressional Record*, 14 April 1953. Representative Celler dissented from the majority report of the House Select Committee on Current Pornographic Materials, 82d Congress.

———. "A Study of the Concentration of Ownership and the Decline of Competition in News Media." *Brooklyn Barrister*, 14:82–88, January 1963. **C 151**
Abstracts from an address by Congressman Celler before the Overseas Press Club.

Cellier, Elizabeth. *Malice Defeated: Or a Brief Relation of the Accusation and Deliverance of Elizabeth Cellier, Wherein her Proceedings both before and during her Confinement, are Particularly Related, and the Mystery of the Meal-Tub fully discovered. Together with an Abstract of her Arraignment and Tryal, Written by her self, for the satisfaction of all Lovers of undisguized Truth.* London, Printed for Elizabeth Cellier, 1680. 44 p. **C 152**
A famous London midwife was accused of involvement in a plot to kidnap the king, and incriminating documents were found in a meal tub in the Cellier kitchen. She was found not guilty, whereupon she wrote an exposé of her trial called *Malice Defeated . . .* This work offended authorities and brought about her trial and conviction for scandalous libel. She was fined, pilloried, and her books burned at the pillory.

———. *The Tryal and Sentence of Elizabeth Cellier; for Writing, Printing, and Publishing, a Scandalous Libel Called Malice Defeated, &c. at the Sessions in the Old Bailey, Held Saturday the 11th and Monday the 13th of Sept. 1680. Whereunto Is Added Several Depositions, Made before the Right Honorable, the Lord Mayor.* London, T. Collins, 1680. 39 p. (Reprinted in Howell, *State Trials*, vol. 7, pp. 1183 ff.) **C 153**

"Celluloid Censorship." *Time*, 27(22):40–42, 1 June 1936. **C 154**
British censorship of the *March of Time* movie.

"The Censor and the Screen." *State Government*, 7:183–86, September 1934. **C 155**
The work of State boards of review is considered in the light of the recent movement for motion picture censorship.

"The Censor as Britain's Deadly Peril." *Literary Digest*, 50:1238–40, 22 May 1915. **C 156**
A book, *Britain's Deadly Peril* by William Le Queux, which criticized England's war effort and complained of its policies on censorship, was itself the victim of the censor.

"Censor over Ads." *Business Week*, 667:48–51, 24 January 1942. **C 157**
A discussion of Army and Navy censorship of advertising in World War II, operating under the broad policy of the Interdepartmental Committee on War Information.

"Censored Faun." *Current Opinion*, 60:176, March 1916. **C 158**
A reproduction of the censored picture.

"Censored: *From Here to Eternity;* Photographs." *Look*, 17:41–43, 25 August 1953. **C 159**
Suppression of the "on the beach scene" from the movie, *From Here to Eternity.*

Censored Mother Goose Rhymes. New York, Mother Goose, 1926. 32 p. **C 160**
A collection of Mother Goose rhymes with certain key words provocatively blacked out. "Dedicated to the Censors who have taught us how to read naughty meanings into harmless words."

"Censored Songs: Why You Hear New Words with the Old Tunes." *U.S. News*, 43:102–3, 9 August 1957. **C 161**

"Censoring Art." *Bazaar* (London), 121:9, 13 July 1929. **C 162**
The anonymous writer approves the seizure by the London police of D. H. Lawrence's paintings and the seizure by U.S. Customs of a book of drawings by Epstein.

"Censoring Poverty Pictures." *Public*, 11:171–72, February 1908. **C 163**
Brief editorial criticism of Chicago police for confiscating lantern slides showing wide contrasts of poverty and wealth in the United States.

"Censoring the Movies." *Public*, 17:579–90, 19 June 1914. **C 164**
While approving censorship of lewdness and violence in films, there is a danger that censorship might also be employed for political purposes.

"Censors and the Library." *Saturday Review of Literature*, 38(27):10–13, 36, 2 July 1955. **C 165**
Lois Purdin reports on Brooksville, Fla., "where a lady with a foreign-sounding name was accused of attempting to stock the library there with 'filthy Communist propaganda'";

Robert S. Ricksecker reports on Galion, Ohio, "where the father of a young high-school girl objected to the fact that his daughter found Richard Wright's 'filthy' novel 'Native Son' on the shelves of her school library"; Tomme C. Call reports from San Antonio, Texas, where a housewife had compiled a REaD READING list, used as a basis for an attack on the school and public libraries; John D. Paulus reports on Mt. Lebanon, Pa., where the small community was split into several contending groups over library censorship; Lawrence J. Kipp reports on Boston, where an attempt to censor books in the Public Library was rejected by the board of trustees.

"Censors and Their Enemies." *Literary Digest*, 93(10):29, 4 June 1927. **C166**
Because of various forms of literary censorship becoming widespread in this country writers "begin to view with alarm the encroachments of constituted authority on the free expression of their literary divinings." The New York *Herald Tribune* reports the meeting of "two-score authors, poets, and writers" to organize a "Committee for the Suppression of Irresponsible Censorship to combat the insistent activities of the descendents of Anthony Comstock." The organization was prompted by the passage of the theater "padlock" bill in New York and police action against many modern novels.

"The Censors Raise a Howl." *Life*, 25:57–8+, 25 October 1948. **C167**
"All over the world moviemakers find themselves in sudden trouble with church, state and plain citizen." The article is illustrated with scenes from current movies banned in one country or another for political, racial, or religious reasons.

"Censors' Stag Party." *Economist*, 187:690, 24 May 1958. **C168**
A brief satire on the decision of the town councillors of Brighton to exclude women from their Watch Committee because of the embarrassment of seeing films that might have to be banned.

"Censorship." *Literary Review*, 4:385, 22 December 1923. **C169**
If censorship is to be performed it should be by the courts, not by an arbitrary censor who is not competent to judge.

Censorship. London, The Congress for Cultural Freedom, 1964–1966. Quarterly. Editor: M. Mindlin; advisory editors: Daniel Bell (U.S.A.), Armand Gaspard (Switzerland), Anthony Hartley and Richard Hoggart (Great Britain), and Ignazio Silone (Italy). **C170**
Contents: Issue 1, Autumn 1964, opens with an essay, The Guardians and the New Populism by Richard Hoggart, and carries reports on censorship in Australia, France, East Germany, West Germany, Ireland, Italy, Poland, the Soviet Union, Yugoslavia, South Africa, and

the United States (Alan Reitman). Issue 2, Spring 1965, deals largely with film censorship in various countries including England and United States. Issue 3, Summer 1965, includes articles on the Mihajlov affair, censorship in Indonesia, Rhodesia, France, as well as articles by Maurice Girodias (Confessions of a Book-legger's Son), Donald Thomas, and B. S. Johnson. Issue 4, Autumn 1965, features stage censorship in England and reports briefly on censorship in Portugal, Ghana, Malaysia, and Australia. Articles dealing with United States and Great Britain are listed separately in this bibliography under the name of the author.

"Censorship." *Nation*, 116:508, 2 May 1923. **C171**
A discussion of the current censorship epidemic which is not confined to attacks on impure literature but is also aimed at ideas. "Among the most absurd of these attacks are the attempts to revise history, according to some nationalistic or economic bias, to supplant one alleged prejudice with another."

"Censorship." *Survey*, 46:231–32, 21 May 1921. **C172**
On the occasion of the passage of a New York movie censorship bill, the author discusses movie censorship in other states.

"Censorship." *Transactions of the California Commonwealth Club*, San Francisco, 1921, pp. 181–221. **C173**
Concerns motion picture censorship.

Censorship: A Question of Judgment. 16 mm. color film, 5½ minutes. Chicago, International Film Bureau, 1964. **C174**

"Censorship Abroad." *Nation*, 99:513–14, 20 October 1914. **C175**
Censorship of war news prevents American readers from learning the truth about the enemy.

"The Censorship Again." *Truth Seeker*, 43:100–101, 12 February 1916. **C176**
Suppression of *The Masses* from the New York elevated and subway newsstands because of objections to a poem, "The Ballad of Joseph," a satire on the Virgin Birth.

"The Censorship and Its Effects." *Quarterly Review*, 225:148–63, January 1916. **C177**
Commentary on wartime censorship in Great Britain. While criticizing the unnecessary suppression of news, the author believes that some failures of reporting result from it being "nobody's business to publish them." He rejects the idea that England should indulge in spreading false news to delude the enemy. "Our press will never lend itself readily to Government control; but if it cannot be adapted to cripple the enemy's strength, let us see that neither by sins of omission or commission it cripples our own."

"Censorship and Obscenity: a Panel Discussion." *Dickinson Law Review*, 66:421–44, Summer 1962. **C178**
An edited transcript of a panel discussion, cosponsored by the Greater Philadelphia Branch of the American Civil Liberties Union and the Public Affairs Committee of the Philadelphia Ethical Society. Panelists are Arlen Specter, assistant district attorney of Philadelphia; William B. Ball, general counsel, Pennsylvania Catholic Welfare Committee; Dr. Philip Q. Roche, psychiatrist; and Julian E. Goldberg, general counsel ACLU of Greater Philadelphia. "The panelists were asked to address their opening remarks to three questions: What is the duty of government with respect to the preservation of accepted standards of sexual morality? To what extent is control over printed words and pictures necessary in order to fulfill this duty? What form should such control take, and where does the responsibility rest for setting the standards and for deciding what offends standards?"

"Censorship and Open Diplomacy Discussion." *Proceedings*, Academy of Political Science in the City of New York, 7:369–74, July 1917. **C179**
Participants: Paul U. Kellogg, Philip Marshall Brown, Dixon Merritt, Edward T. Devine, and Maurice Léon. Presented at the National Conference on Foreign Relations of the United States.

"Censorship and Prohibition." *Christian Century*, 40:901–3, 19 January 1923. **C180**
The author considers common problems in control of alcoholic beverages and corrupting books and plays. In the interest of the young, if we are to prevent the fountains of literature and drama to be poisoned, a national censorship is the only solution.

"Censorship and Suppression." *Nation*, 104:424–25, 2 April 1917. **C181**
Objection to the barring of certain foreign journals during World War I.

"Censorship and the Espionage Act." *New Republic*, 11:316, 21 July 1917. **C182**
The Act gives the Post Office too much censorship authority.

"Censorship and the Freedom to Read." *Publishers' Weekly*, 187:85–87, 18 January 1965. **C183**
Review of court decisions and censorship activities during 1964. The major court battles of the year were won by supporters of the freedom to read, though local courts and citizen vigilantes continued to harry certain books for reasons of obscenity or politics. The most important censorship case of the year was the Jacobellis case, involving the movie, *The Lovers*.

"Censorship and the Freedom to Read; 1963 in Review." *Publishers' Weekly*, 185:88–89, 20 January 1964.   **C184**
"Proponents of the freedom to read won a few rounds and lost a few in 1963." A review of court decisions and other actions affecting censorship and the various books which came under attack in 1963.

"Censorship and the Peace Conference." *New Republic*, 17:61–63, 16 November 1918.   **C185**
Criticism of the Wilson government for extending wartime censorship to Peace Conference negotiations. "Crusaders for freedom are themselves" applying "the very methods and principles against which they fight."

Censorship and Trade. London, Eyre and Spottiswoode, 1916. 24 p.   **C186**
Refutation of a suspicion in the United States that Great Britain, during World War I, used information obtained from censorship of mails to gain advantage over neutral trade.

"Censorship as Finally Enacted." *Survey*, 38:245–46, 9 June 1917.   **C187**
Relates to the defeat in the U.S. House of Representatives of a more stringent wartime censorship clause in the espionage bill.

"Censorship as Self-Control." *New Republic*, 50:5–7, 23 February 1927.   **C188**
The article approves of the police closing three undesirable plays. The blatant sex plays in the American theater during the present season have offended the public to such an extent that some kind of administrative censorship is unavoidable. The article describes the self-censorship jury set up by the Committee of Nine to be administered by the Actors Equity Association.

"Censorship Beaten in New York Court." *Publishers' Weekly*, 102:801–4, 16 September 1922.   **C189**
New York Magistrate George W. Simpson freed three books—Schnitzler's *Casanova's Homecoming*, Lawrence's *Women in Love*, and the anonymous *A Young Girl's Diary*—of obscenity charges brought by the New York Society for the Suppression of Vice against publisher Thomas Seltzer. Text of the decision and comments by Mr. Seltzer.

"Censorship by Judicial Construction." *New Republic*, 26:123–25, 30 March 1921.   **C190**
A criticism of the censorship action by the Postmaster General, with special reference to the case of the *Milwaukee Leader*.

"The Censorship Column." *Library Journal*, 88:2556–58, July 1963.   **C191**
A résumé of recent censorship news including favorable action on *Tropic of Cancer* (Wisconsin Supreme Court), dismissal of a suit which attempted to ban four books from a Virginia county library, and the court decision (U.S. District Court in Philadelphia) against the magazine *Eros*.

"Censorship Fantasia." *Time*, 39:64, 8 June 1942. (Reprinted in Summers, *Wartime Censorship*, pp. 190–92)   **C192**
A criticism of Army censorship of Washington correspondents reporting on a tour of war plants.

"Censorship Fight over Movie Morals." *Life*, 5:50–55, 18 July 1938.   **C193**
A group of pictures illustrating scenes cut from American movies by the Hays Office, by state and municipal censorship boards, and by foreign censors. Special attention is given to Catholic boycott action against the Spanish Civil War film, *Blockade*.

"Censorship for the Mass Audience: A Protection or a Threat?" In *Platform*. Published by Newsweek Club and Educational Bureau, September 1953, pp. 1–23. (Reprinted in Daniels, *The Censorship of Books*, pp. 18–22)   **C194**

"Censorship from the Inside." *Bookman*, 57:374–75, May 1923.   **C195**
A brief editorial, reprinted from the New York *World*, dealing with censoring by the city of Minneapolis of the list of magazines suitable for juvenile prisoners. *Saturday Evening Post*, *Red Book*, and *Ladies Home Journal* were removed by the City Council because each in some way offended one of the members.

"Censorship Ground Rules." *Time*, 39(4):56–58, 26 January 1942.   **C196**
A discussion of the wartime censorship code and its reception by the American press.

"Censorship Grows Bold." *Time*, 39(14):51–53, 6 April 1942.   **C197**
Deals with the British controversy over wartime censorship and government threats against the *Mirror* for its criticism of the war effort.

"Censorship in Boston." *Commonweal*, 12:656, 29 October 1930.   **C198**
Reference to the suppression of Thomas Á Kempis' *Imitation of Christ* in the Massachusetts Bay Colony, 1669.

[Censorship in Canada]. *Mother Earth*, 5:275–77, November 1910.   **C199**
Editorial comment on the exclusion of radical literature and the deportation to Russia of Savva Federenko.

"Censorship in Washington." *Democratic Digest*, 3:28–35, November 1955.   **C200**
Government cover-ups begin "with censorship of information, then hush-hush treatment of small mistakes and ineffeciencies. From there, it is only a matter of time and degree for some grave blunder or failure to be hidden from sight in the ordinary course of business." A criticism of government censorship under the Eisenhower administration.

"Censorship—Informal Prior Restraint through Lists of 'Objectionable' Books and Threats to Recommend Prosecution." *Iowa Law Review*, 49:161–69, Fall 1963.   **C201**
Bantam Books, Inc. v. Sullivan, 372 U.S. 58 (1963), relating to action of the Rhode Island Commission to Encourage Morality in Youth.

"Censorship Issues: an Appraisal of Obscenity and Censorship." *Information Service*, National Council of Churches, 39:1–8, 24 December 1960.   **C202**

"Censorship Issues and Legal Cases." *Publishers' Weekly*, 181:68–71, 15 January 1962.   **C203**
A review of censorship cases and court decisions during 1961.

"The Censorship: Its History and Purposes." *Common Sense* (London), 3:54, 28 July 1917; 3:68, 4 August 1917; 3:83, 11 August 1917; 3:116, 25 August 1917; 3:134, 1 September 1917; 3:183, 22 September 1917; 3:198, 29 September 1917; 3:230, 13 October 1917; 3:344, 22 December 1917.   **C204**
In nine installments the author reports on censorship in Great Britain during World War I—early laws and regulations, the operation of censorship under the three Defence of the Realm Acts, the work of the British Press Bureau, the widespread criticism of this agency, and efforts to modify the agency's powers and directives.

"Censorship—Morality Commission's Action in Compiling Lists of 'Obscene' Paperback Books and Threatening to Recommend Prosecution of Distributors Held Not to Infringe Constitutional Guarantee of Free Speech." *University of Pennsylvania Law Review*, 110:1162–65, June 1962.   **C205**
Review of the case *Bantam Books, Inc. v. Sullivan*, 176 A. 2d 393 (R.I. 1961), with the conclusion: "By requiring a strict cause-and-effect relationship between censorship and financial injury, the present case permits a state to do by indirection what it may not do directly; the very effectiveness of the methods employed leads to the conclusion that the absence of appropriate safeguards rendered the Commission's actions inimical to the first and fourteenth amendments."

"The Censorship Muddle." *Nation,* 104: 648–49, 31 May 1917. **C 206**
Editorial criticism of the Committee on Public Information rules for the guidance of newspapers. Along with the rules, the Committee lists subjects which it considers "dangerous" and "of service to the enemy" and therefore not to be discussed in the press.

"Censorship of Motion Pictures." *Yale Law Journal,* 49:87–113, November 1939. **C 207**
"It is the contention of this comment that legal censorship by previous restraint is an impediment to full development of the cinema, and that the maturity of the industry now renders this form of control unnecessary." A documented study of motion picture censorship, a confused pattern of voluntary and compulsory restrictions, exercised at all levels. The author recommends that motion pictures be brought under the protection of the First Amendment.

"Censorship of Moving Picture Films As an Interference with the Freedom of the Press." *Virginia Law Review,* 2: 216–18, December 1914. **C 208**
Regarding *Mutual Film Co. v. Industrial Commission of Ohio.*

"Censorship of Newspapers." *Museum of Foreign Literature and Sciences,* (Philadelphia), 16:94–95, January 1830. **C 209**
Brief comments on censorship of newspapers in Madras, India, and reports on the printing of the 20 March 1829 issue of the *Modern Courier* with white spaces to represent censored portions.

"Censorship of Obscene Literature by Informal Governmental Action." *University of Chicago Law Review,* 22:216–33, Autumn 1954. **C 210**
The author considers the less formal action taken by government to avoid giving undue publicity to an obscene work and "to avoid the practical difficulties on one hand and the constitutional difficulties of prior restraint on the other." He discusses the problems raised when local police attempt to prevent distribution of objectionable literature by informal methods. Numerous examples of local police action are cited.

"A Censorship of Opinion." *Literary Digest,* 54:1767–68, 9 June 1917. **C 211**
Newspaper comments on George Creel's recently published *Regulations for the Periodical Press of the United States during the War.*

"Censorship of Plays." *Quarterly Review,* 213:352–76, October 1910. **C 212**
Extensive comment on the report from the Joint Committee of the House of Lords and the Commons on the Stage Plays (Censorship) of 1909 and the 1907 protest of British authors against stage censorship by the Lord Chamber-

lain. The author agrees with the report of the Select Committee, that "more facts, a more complete basis for calculation, are necessary before it can be decided whether or not it would be safe to give it [drama] complete freedom." He examines the various alternative proposals for replacing the nearly two hundred years of "thraldom of drama."

"Censorship of Telegrams Transmitted by Cable and Wireless." *American Journal of International Law,* 9:270–313, July 1915. **C 213**
Treats of the interference with official correspondence between the United States and belligerent powers.

"The Censorship of the Drama." *Spectator,* 135:189–90, 1 August 1925. **C 214**
A committee of churchmen, not satisfied with present drama censorship of the Lord Chamberlain, will demand that censorship be taken out of his hands and given to the London County Council. The writer, supporting the "aristocratic principle," favors retaining the Lord Chamberlain as censor but agrees with the 1909 Joint Committee recommendation that the theater manager be given an option—either submit for prior review or take the risk of a forced closing.

"The Censorship of the Drama; Mr. G. B. Shaw, Sir J. Forbes-Robertson, Miss Rose Macaulay, Mr. Basil Dean, Mr. Noel Coward & others State Their Views." *Spectator,* 135:261–62, 15 August 1925. **C 215**
A sampling of answers to the question as to whether stricter censorship is needed for the stage. There was no concensus, but a majority wanted to abolish censorship entirely. Those who did want to retain it preferred the Lord Chamberlain as censor to the London County Council.

"Censorship of the Mind." *Spectator,* 141:258–59, 1 September 1928. **C 216**
Concerns censorship of *Well of Loneliness.* The author believes the censor acted wisely in asking the publisher (Cape) to withdraw the book, and the publisher is to be congratulated for complying.

"Censorship of the Press." *Nation,* 105: 361–62, 4 October 1917. **C 217**
An editorial ciricizing an amendment to the Trading with the Enemy Act, which makes it unlawful to transport any foreign language material made unlawful by the Espionage Act. This denies a publisher, whose case may be pending in court for a violation of the Espionage Act, the right to distribute his material in any way whatever before it is decided judicially that he has violated any law.

["Censorship of the Stage"]. *Blackwood's Magazine,* 186:852–56, December 1909. **C 218**

The article approves retention of stage censorship by the Lord Chamberlain as recommended in the report of the Parliamentary Committee, but disagrees with the recommendation that it should be legal "to perform an unlicensed play whether it has been submitted or not," but at the risk of prosecution. Such a "double system" is an unhappy compromise—retention of censorship to please the managers who want security, and setting it aside to please the playwrights who want freedom.

"Censorship, of Which the Less the Better . . ." *Fortune,* 23:88, 153–61, June 1941. (Reprinted in Summers, *Wartime Censorship,* pp. 19–28) **C 219**
The article concerns the problems of wartime censorship and includes a statement of censorship policy which *Fortune* believes to be in the best interests of the nation. It concludes that "the deepest duty of a democratic press in wartime is to remain aggressively free, critical, and informative."

"Censorship on the Campus; Report." *Bulletin of the Atomic Scientists,* 18:46–48, November 1962. **C 220**
A report of the New York County Lawyers' Association Committee on Civil Rights cites numerous cases of refusal of campus administrators to allow speakers who had been scheduled. "The standard which should be applied in both public and private institutions is this: any written idea or discussion or speaker should be permitted full exposure on the campus, so long as the basic purpose of the exposure is not to violate the law. Anything short of this, we think, is inimical to a free society."

"Censorship or Not." *Literary Digest,* 77:27–29+, 23 June 1923. **C 221**
A number of leaders in literature, drama, and religion were asked to jot down their views on the subject of ensorship, whether there should be more, less, or none at all. The article quotes from replies by Irving S. Cobb, H. L. Mencken, George Ade, Sherwood Anderson, Owen Johnson, George Barr McCutcheon, F. Scott Fitzgerald, Brander Matthews, Bliss Perry, Henry S. Canby, James Harvey Robinson, and Heywood Broun. Clergy represented include Thomas Nicholson, William Burt, William F. Anderson, S. Parkes Cadman, William Houston, William I. Haven, and Bob Jones.

"Censorship—Private Brand." *Business Week,* 1160:130–31, 24 November 1951. **C 222**
"New TV code and movie incidents spotlight rise in censorship by private groups. Telecasters would set up sweeping standards to cover almost all aspects of programming . . . The rise of private control—censorship by the entertainment industry itself and by racial, political, and religious groups . . . By taking matters into their own hands, the telecasters hope to quiet both the public and Congress."

"Censorship Rules Affect Industry." *Modern Industry*, 3:80–81, 15 April 1942. (Reprinted in Summers, *Wartime Censorship*, pp. 142–44) **C 223**
A discussion of the difficulties that industry faces in getting statistics and other information needed in the course of doing business because of wartime censorship.

"The Censorship Scandal." *English Review*, 10:725–27, March 1912. (Signed "S.O.") **C 224**
Attack on the office of stage censorship for its ban of two plays—Israel Zangwill's *The Next Religion* and Eden Phillpotts' *The Secret Woman*. While allowing inanities in drama, the office of the Lord Chamberlain vetoes serious plays. The author calls for the organization of an actor's union to defend their lawful right of expression and to press for censorship reform in Parliament.

Censorship Scoreboard. Chicago. Censorship Scoreboard, Inc. Published monthly in 1959–63. **C 225**
"Round-up of information about the fight against censorship and bigotry."

Censorship: Should Books be Banned? 1 hour teletape. Bloomington, Ind., National Educational Television and Radio Center, University of Indiana (distributor). Produced by WNDT, New York, 1963. (Court of Reason no. 3) **C 226**
Morris L. Ernst, attorney, Anne Fremantle, novelist, Robert B. McKay, law professor, and Eric Larrabee, managing editor of *Horizon*, give variant views on the banning of books. The Court member is Robert K. Merton, Columbia University professor.

"Censorship under Three Flags." *Living Age*, 355:310–21, December 1938. **C 227**
The first section is concerned with control of opinion in England by government interference, with particular reference to pressures brought to bear during "Crisis Week." The remainder of the article deals with censorship in Japan and Italy.

Censura contra las Artes y el Pensamiento. Paris, Patrocinado por el Congreso por la Libertad de la Cultura, 1964–1966. Quarterly. (Also a French edition, *Censure contre les Arts et la Pensée*). Editors: J. Bloch-Michel, Ignacio Iglesias. **C 228**
Issue 1, July–September 1964, carries articles on Argentina, Australia, Brazil, Columbia, France, Hungary, Ireland, Poland, Portugal, and the U.S.S.R. Issue 2, October–December 1964, reprints an article on pornography and censorship by Sidney Hook (*New York Times Book Review*, 4 December 1964), and reports on censorship in Argentina, Czechoslovakia, Indonesia, Italy, Mexico, Spain, and Yugoslavia. Issue 3, January–March 1965, carries articles on Africa, Argentina, Australia, England, Switzerland, and Turkey. Issue 4, April–June 1965, carries articles on East Germany, South Africa, China, Spain, India, Mexico, U.S.S.R., Uruguay, and Yugoslavia.

"La Censure en Irlande." *Journal des débats*, 35(2):841, 23 November 1928. **C 229**
A report of Irish attacks on modern fiction.

Center for the Study of Democratic Institutions. *Broadcasting and Government Regulation in a Free Society.* New York, The Fund for the Republic, 1959. 39 p. (Occasional Paper) **C 230**
A transcript of two panel discussions dealing with the administration of regulatory responsibilities of the Federal Communications Commission. The panel considers such questions as: How much regulation should there be? How is the public interest defined? How is it maintained? What is the balance between freedom and responsibility in a privately-owned, federally-regulated broadcasting system? Participants are: Clifford J. Durr, James L. Fly, Eric F. Goldman, Robert M. Hutchins, Frank K. Kelly, Robert W. Horton, and Joseph P. Lyford (first panel); Rosel H. Hyde, Benedict P. Cottone, Raymond F. Kohn, Newton N. Minow, Herbert Alexander, Charles Clift, Eric F. Goldman, Frank K. Kelly, and Robert W. Horton (second panel).

———. *The First Amendment: Government of the Mind.* Santa Barbara, Calif., The Center, 1964. Tape Recordings, nos. 85–88. **C 231**
Four discussions, each approximately one hour long, led by Joseph Tussman, University of California philosophy professor, who proposes that since government already assumes responsibility for protecting the physical health of citizens through such measures as the food and drug laws, that it also assume responsibility for protecting the moral and intellectual development of the mind. Most of the participants, including Professor Alexander Meiklejohn, dissent.

———. *The First Amendment: Libel and Slander.* Santa Barbara, Calif., The Center, 1964. Tape recording, no. 89. **C 232**
Harry Kalven, Jr., leads a discussion which "examines the legal reasoning that determines when the law may compromise the principle of free speech in order to protect the individual from injury, and when the law 'privileges' free speech, despite personal injury, in order not to infringe upon the right to speak."

Cerf, Bennett. "The Case of Ezra Pound." *Saturday Review of Literature*, 29(6):26–27, 9 February 1946; 29(11):32–36, 49–53, 16 March 1946. **C 233**
An exchange of letters between Bennett Cerf and Lewis Gannett over the moral issues of omitting 12 poems by Ezra Pound from *An Anthology of Famous English and American Poetry*, an action taken by publisher Cerf over the objections of the editor. A wide variety of opinion on the controversy is seen in letters to the Trade Winds column appearing in the 16 March issue, including letters from Norman Rosten, Clyde Brion Davis, Harry L. Hopkins, Robert Hillyer, and Francis Hackett. Cerf concluded that future editions of the anthology would contain Pound's poems "because we concede that it may be wrong to confuse Pound the poet and Pound the man."

———. ["Post-Office Censorship of *Esquire*"]. *Saturday Review of Literature*, 27(6):20–21, 5 February 1944. **C 234**
In his Trade Winds column Cerf describes the "nonsensical farandoles" in the action of Postmaster General Frank Walker's banning of *Esquire* from the mails.

Cestre, Charles. *John Thelwall, a Pioneer of Democracy and Social Reform in England during the French Revolution.* London, Sonnenshein, 1906. 204 p. **C 235**
In 1820 a group of London citizens formed a Constitutional Association for Opposing the Progress of Disloyal and Seditious Principles. Its purpose was to see that those who disseminated seditious literature, including criticism of men in public affairs, were brought to trial. One of the first victims of the Association was John Thelwall, publisher of the weekly *Champion* and friend of Horne Tooke. Thelwall was arrested along with a number of other printers and charged with seditious libel. After long delays he was acquitted and the Association came in for considerable public criticism for its persecutions. Thelwall had earlier (1794) survived, along with Tooke, Hardy, and others, the treason trials of the "English Jacobins."

Chafee, Zechariah, Jr. *The Blessings of Liberty.* Philadelphia, Lippincott, 1956. 350 p. **C 236**
A book of reminiscences from a retired member of the Harvard Law School faculty and a foremost champion of civil liberties. Chapter 3 consists of a 40-year survey of freedom of speech and press, beginning with the events of World War I. In Chapter 4, Chafee answers the question, "Does freedom of speech really tend to produce truth?" In Chapter 11, he discusses his work with the United Nations in advocating world-wide freedom of speech and press.

———. *Censorship in Boston . . . as Told by Prof. Zechariah Chafee . . .* Boston, Civil Liberties Committee of Massachusetts, 1930. 24 p. **C 237**
Discussion of the recent epidemic of book banning in Boston, the result of the combined efforts of the Watch and Ward Society, the District Attorney, and compliant booksellers. Books are being withdrawn largely on threat or fear of threat. Theater censorship is less active against serious works, but not burlesque. Threat of revocation of theater license is the means of control.

———. "Censorship of Plays and Books." *Bill of Rights Review*, 1:16–23, Summer 1940. **C238**

Where and how is a line to be drawn between decency and indecency in literature? Who shall draw the line? Should it be drawn before or after the act? What are the consequences of an unfavorable decision on the persons concerned? Chafee believes the decision should be made by citizens through qualified juries. The practical problem is how to lessen the risk of the producer and publisher who want to know the legal status before going ahead with a work.

———. "A Contemporary State Trial— the United States v. Jacob Abrams, *et al.*" *Harvard Law Review*, 33:747–74, April 1920. **C239**

An analysis and criticism of the famous sedition case of World War I in which Abrams and four other pamphleteers were given extended prison sentences, a decision confirmed by the U.S. Supreme Court. Justice Holmes, in his dissenting decision, said: "In this case sentences of twenty years imprisonment have been imposed for the publishing of two leaflets that I believe the defendants had as much right to publish as the Government has to publish the Constitution of the United States now vainly invoked by them." For this article Professor Chafee was widely criticized; a Harvard University committee, appointed to investigate the matter, vindicated him. Comments on the investigation appear in *Harvard Law Review*, November 1921.

———. "Danger of Repression." *Bulletin*, League of Free Nations Association, 1:2–3, 5 March 1920. **C240**

Professor Chafee pleads for more freedom of speech.

———. "Ezra Hervey Heywood." In *Dictionary of American Biography*, vol. 8; pp. 609–10. **C241**

A biographical sketch of the Massachusetts crusader for free expression in the matter of sex education who spent many months in jail as the result of the counter-crusade of Anthony Comstock.

———. *Free Speech in the United States.* Cambridge, Mass., Harvard University Press, 1942. 634 p. (A revision of his *Freedom of Speech*, published in 1920) **C242**

A basic reference book on the subject, written by a leading advocate of civil liberties who was a longtime member of the faculty of Harvard Law School. Professor Chafee traces the history of freedom of speech and the press from the prosecutions of World War I to the events on the eve of World War II, giving full documentation of cases. There are also sections on the history of the sedition law, and methods of controlling discussion in peacetime. The appendix contains a list of federal and state laws affecting freedom of speech and the press.

———. "Freedom of Speech." *New Republic*, 17:66–69, 16 November 1918. **C243**

An attack on political prosecutions under the wartime Espionage Act as a violation of the First Amendment and a break with the great tradition of freedom in English and American law.

———. *Freedom of Speech.* New York, Harcourt, Brace, 1920. 431 p. **C244**

Although partly superseded by the author's later study, *Free Speech in the United States*, this work is still valuable as a documented account of free speech prosecutions during World War I, written during and immediately after the events.

———. *Freedom of Speech and Press.* New York, Carrie Chapman Catt Memorial Fund, 1955. 59 p. (Freedom Agenda Pamphlet no. 11) **C245**

"This pamphlet is one of a series prepared under the auspices of the Freedom Agenda Committee for the assistance of local Freedom Agenda Projects in their study of individual liberty. It is intended to present the reader with an accurate picture of the long struggle for freedom of expression from the ancient world to our own time, in such a manner as to make clear the profound advantages of free speech and a free press for our American system of individual liberty."

———. "Freedom of Speech and States Rights." *New Republic*, 25:259–62, 26 January 1921. **C246**

Eleven states and territories considered the severe federal Espionage Act of World War I an insufficient protection against seditious pamphlets and oratory and supplemented it by more drastic local legislation. Chafee deals largely with the Montana and Minnesota Sedition Acts, which imposed a maximum of 20 years on violators.

———. "Freedom of Speech as I See It Today." *Journalism Quarterly*, 18:158–63, June 1941. **C247**

In a paper read on the Boston University Founders' Day program, Chafee declared that it is not enough to insure that a speaker will not be interfered with, but we must provide a means by which free discussion can be carried on. Action against extremists may serve as a threat to others; it may serve to drive ideas underground. Open controversy should be an accepted part of life in a community.

———. "Freedom of Speech in War Time." *Harvard Law Review*, 32:932–73, June 1919. (Reprinted in Association of American Law Schools, *Selected Essays on Constitutional Law*. Chicago, 1938, vol. 2, pp. 1024–59, and as Senate Document 95, 66th Congress, 1st Session; also in

Dunster House Papers, no. 1, Dunster House Bookshop, Cambridge, Mass.) **C248**

"Never in the history of our country, since the Alien and Sedition Laws of 1798, has the meaning of free speech been the subject of sharp controversy as today." Portions of the article were incorporated in the first chapter of Chafee's *Freedom of Speech*.

———. *Government and Mass Communications. A Report from the Commission on Freedom of the Press.* Chicago, University of Chicago Press, 1947. 2 vols. **C249**

Chafee deals with government efforts to supress discussion through libel laws, control of obscenity in the mails and in the customs service, laws against treason, sedition, and contempt of court. He discusses the affirmative activities of government in encouraging dissemination of news and ideas. Unlike Morris Ernst (*The First Freedom*) he recommends "watchful waiting" in matters of legal restraint and enforcing of antitrust laws, believing that a more satisfactory solution to bad journalism lies in development of discriminate readers.

———. "The Great Liberty: Freedom of Speech and Press." In Kelly, Alfred H., ed., *Foundations of Freedom in the American Constitution.* New York, Harper, 1958, pp. 52–87. **C250**

———. *The Inquiring Mind.* New York, Harcourt, Brace, 1928. 276 p. **C251**

Collection of essays on liberty and free speech. Includes a review of important court decisions and a chapter on the Bimba blasphemy case.

———. "Investigations of Radicalism and Laws against Subversion." In *Civil Liberties under Attack*, Philadelphia, University of Pennsylvania Press, 1951, pp. 46–84. **C252**

———. "Legal Problems of Freedom of Information in the United Nations." *Law and Contemporary Problems*, 14:545–83, October 1949. **C253**

An American delegate on the UNESCO Sub-Commission on Freedom of Information explains the relation to the American Constitution of the article on freedom of expression in the UN Covenant of Human Rights.

———. "Milwaukee Leader Case." *Nation*, 112:428–29, 23 March 1921. **C254**

Criticism of the unrestricted power of postal censorship and the lack of judicial qualifications of postal censors as revealed by this wartime espionage case.

———. "An Outsider Looks at the Press." *Nieman Reports*, 7(1):5–7, January 1953. **C 255**

There are two startling paradoxes about the American press: It is the only large, wealthy, and powerful business in the country subject to very little legal accountability; newspapers are both educational agencies and money-making enterprises. Chafee considers three topics raised by the Commission on Freedom of the Press: the truthful and intelligent reporting of the news, the proposal of a system of correction and retraction of errors to replace the present unsatisfactory libel suits, and the lack of adequate press competition in many cities. He believes the press is in greater danger than it has been since Jeffersonian newspapers were suppressed by the Sedition Act of 1798.

———. "Possible New Remedies for Errors in the Press." *Harvard Law Review*, 60:1–43, November 1946. **C 256**

The article comprises two sections of the author's book, *Government and Mass Communications*. It discusses the wisdom of a possible criminal statute punishing inaccuracies, and the feasibility of compulsory correction of errors in the press. The chief cure for falsehoods in the press should be sought outside the realm of law, in the responsible standards of a community's press.

———. "The Press Under Pressure." *Nieman Reports*, 1(2):19–21, April 1948. **C 257**

Freedom *from* something is not enough. It should also be freedom *for* something. Chafee discusses the criticisms of the American press made by two groups—the Commission on Freedom of the Press and the foreign representatives of the UN—and the lessons that can be learned from both.

———. "Sedition." In *Encyclopaedia of the Social Sciences*, vol. 13, pp. 636–39. **C 258**

———. "Tariff Bill's Prohibition of Revolutionary Literature." *School and Society*, 30:407–8, 21 September 1929. **C 259**

Statement from Professor Chafee in opposition to the amendment to the 1843 customs law prohibiting importation of obscene literature. "This law is a kindergarten measure which assumes that the American people are so stupid and untrustworthy that it is unsafe to let them read anything about revolutions because they would immediately be converted." The editor observes that such a law in Great Britain would prevent the importation of the Declaration of Independence.

———. *Thirty-five Years with Freedom of Speech*. New York, Roger N. Baldwin Civil Liberties Foundation, 1952. 40p.

(Presented as a lecture at Columbia University, 12 March 1952) **C 260**

Chafee reviews the 35-year span of his career as law professor and as observer, participant, and reporter in freedom of speech cases. He deals with the criminal syndicalist period (1917–20), the period of growth (1920–30), the period of achievement (1930–45), and the renewed struggle and subtle suppression since 1945. Talking and writing about freedom of speech and press, he concludes, helps to preserve it.

Chalker, Thomas P. "'Book Burning' in Alabama." *Christian Century*, 69:1169, 8 October 1952. **C 261**

A letter to the editor tells of attempts to ban a high school history text, *The Challenge of Democracy* by Blaich and Baumgartner, from the Birmingham schools because it contained a passage objected to as un-American by the real estate board.

Challman, Jean C. "Adults Si, Children No." *Library Journal*, 89:807–9, 15 February 1964. **C 262**

The confessions and conclusions of a librarian who is against censorship but in favor of control. She pleads for "a kind of national facing up to the problem" of dealing with various age groups in a public library, and "a serious consideration of the differences between children—even those bibliophilic drunks of children all libraries know—and adults." She suggests that librarians and book publishers explore the British film category scheme as it might be applied to children's books.

Chalmeley, R. F. "Bad Books." *Library*, 5(2d ser.):225–38, July 1904. **C 263**

A whimsical essay on the changing tastes in reading and the compilation of a list of bad books. A list of the "hundred worst books," the author suggests, could almost be compiled from the same catalog as those of the "hundred best books."

Chamberlain, Edward W. "In the Midst of Wolves." *Arena*, 10:835–37, November 1894. **C 264**

Deals with obscenity cases against Moses Harman and Lois Waisbrooker.

[———]. *United States v. Heywood. Why the Defendant Should Be Released. Mr. Chamberlain's Letter to Mr. Harrison*. New York, National Defense Association, [1891?]. 21p. **C 265**

A New York lawyer and one of the defense counsels in the Ezra H. Heywood case, urges President Benjamin Harrison to pardon Heywood, who was given a two-year sentence on an obscenity charge. The pamphlet includes the text of Judge Carpenter's charge to the jury, and an abstract of the petition for pardon submitted by Heywood's friends.

Chamberlain, William H. "Censorships I Have Known." *Christian Science Monitor Magazine*, 30 September 1939, p. 6. **C 266**

A veteran foreign correspondent describes his experience with foreign press censorship.

Chambers, *Sir* Edmund K. *Notes on the History of the Revels Office under the Tudors*. London, Bullen, 1906. 80p. **C 267**

The Revels Office was the licensing agency for the stage in Elizabethan England.

Chandhuri, J. "Law of Sedition in India." *Juridical Review*, 10:385–94, 1898. **C 268**

Following a brief history of the press policy of the British government in India from the time of the East India Company to the date of publication, the author considers the recent amendment to the law of libel. It is "one of those periodic attempts on the part of the Government to put public opinion under executive control, on the same old apprehensions of political danger if discussion be freely allowed." A promised second installment to the article failed to appear.

Chandler, Peleg W., *ed. American Criminal Trials*. Boston, Little and Brown, 1841. 2 vols. **C 269**

Volume 1 includes the trial of Thomas Maule for a slanderous and blasphemous publication (Salem, 1696), and the trial of John Peter Zenger for two libels on the government (New York, 1735).

Chandos, John, *ed. "To Deprave and Corrupt . . ." Original Studies in the Nature and Definition of "Obscenity."* New York, Association Press, 1962. 207p. **C 270**

Ten original studies dealing with the problem of obscenity from the literary, legal, sociological, and moral points of view: John Chandos, My Brother's Keeper; William B. Lockhart and Robert C. McClure, Why Obscene?; Lord Birkett, The Changing Law; Norman St. John-Stevas, The Church and Censorship; Ernest Van den Haag, Quia Ineptum; Maurice Girodias, More Heat than Light; Walter Allen, The Writer and the Frontiers of Tolerance; Claire and W. M. S. Russell, The Natural History of Censorship; and John Chandos, Unicorns at Play. "The contributors have been chosen, not for the opinions they may have been believed to hold, but for their experience of one aspect or another of the cause and effect of censorship." Chandos, the editor, has written widely on literary and social history. Professors Lockhart and McClure of the University of Minnesota Law School collaborated in a comprehensive study of literature and the law of obscenity in the United States; Lord Birkett steered the Obscene Publications Bill (1959) through the House of Lords in Great Britain; St. John-Stevas was legal advisor for the Committee which drafted the bills and is author of *Obscenity and the Law*; Professor Van den Haag is a New York psychoanalyst; the Russells are behavioral scientists; Maurice Girodias is managing director of the Olympia

Press of Paris which has issued English editions of many works liable for seizure in England and the United States (he advocates total abolition of censorship); and Walter Allen is formerly literary editor of the *New Statesman* and a member of the A. P. Herbert Committee that drafted the Obscene Publications Bill.

Chandra, Ram. "Press Censorship in India." *Mother Earth*, 12:89–92, May 1917. **C 271**

The suppression of 400 periodicals for sedition under wartime censorship.

Chapman, Leland L. "The Power of the Federal Radio Commission to Regulate or Censor Radio Broadcasts." *George Washington Law Review*, 1:380–85, March 1933. **C 272**
An analysis of court decisions (Dr. Brinkley and Rev. Shuler cases) involving license renewal and "free speech that is in the public interest."

Chapmann, H. S. "Mr. Spring Rice and the Tax on Knowledge, with a postscript on the French King and the Press." In Roebuck, John A., *ed. The Evils of a House of Lords* . . . London, T. Falconer, 1836. **C 273**

———. "State of the Newspaper Stamp Question." In Roebuck, John A., *ed. The King's Speech* . . . London, Charles Ely, [1835?]. **C 274**

"Charles H. Keating Jr., National Co-chairman of Citizens for Decent Literature." In *The Smut Hunters*. Los Angeles, All America Distributors Corp., 1964. 4 p. **C 275**
Some insight into the man and supplemental information on the Visalia, Calif., obscenity trial in which Keating testified for the prosecution.

Charnley, Mitchell V. "Should Courtroom Proceedings Be Broadcast?" *Federal Communications Bar Journal*, 11:64–72, Summer 1950. **C 276**

Charter, William H. *Censorship of Motion Pictures*. Washington, D.C., Editorial Research Reports, 1950. (*Editorial Research Reports*, 1:257–74, 1950) **C 277**
Public concern over morals of the movies, private pressures and public censorship (self-regulation, Legion of Decency, state and municipal boards), free speech v. censorship of films.

Charters, Zelda S. "The *Call* Raid: a Study in Mob Psychology." *New York Call*, 12 May 1919, pp. 2, 7. **C 278**

An account of the May Day mobbing of the publication office of the New York *Call*.

Chase, Harry W. "Academic Freedom and Freedom of the Press." *Vital Speeches*, 7:286–87, 15 February 1941. **C 279**
The chancellor of New York University, addressing the American College Publicity Association, states that the ultimate test of a free press is the use made of liberty. The freedom to criticize is not enough; we must have also the freedom to be constructive. We are passing out of a period of negativism into a period of affirmation.

Chase, J. Frank. "Cleaning Up the Magazines." *Light*, 28:5–11, May–June 1925. **C 280**

Chase describes the cooperation in Boston between the police and the Watch and Ward Society, carried on through the Massachusetts Magazine Committee. He cites, as an example, the case of *Snappy Stories* and the conviction of the circulation manager by a Massachusetts court. The article includes a melodramatic address by District Attorney Thomas C. O'Brien.

———. "The New Puritanism." *Harvard Advocate*, 112:9–16, May 1926. **C 281**
An address by the secretary of the New England Watch and Ward Society before the Student Liberal Club of Harvard. Chase describes the work of the Society in enforcing the law against indecent literature as "the American System of Censorship." He decries the influence upon the U.S. Post Office Department of liberal decisions by Tammany judges in obscenity cases. He praises the work of certain Harvard professors who applied their brains "to the public service of reading and deciding as experts what is obscene in certain modern novels." He also praises the "high-minded" booksellers and their association for appointing a Booksellers' Committee. "When a bad book appears, if it is convictable, the Booksellers' Committee itself notifies the trade throughout the State, and quietly it is immediately withdrawn. If it is sold thereafter, the law is applied by law enforcement agencies. Many books have thus been suppressed."

———. "Next Step in Fight against Morbid Magazines." *Light*, 28:11–15, September–October 1925. **C 282**
Chase proposed that the U.S. Bureau of Standards establish a Department of Literary Standards, staffed by psychologists and sociologists who would measure the amount of smut in a given work of literature. Chase also developed an "obscenity cycle" theory similar to a "panic of economy" that ought to be controlled by government action.

———. "Preventive Criticism and Endocrinic Literature." *Light*, 27:34–38, May–June 1924. **C 283**
In an address before the Massachusetts Librarians' Club, the secretary of the Watch and Ward Society describes the operation of

the "gentlemen's agreement" among Boston booksellers which prevents objectionable books from being sold. "If a bookseller disagrees with his committees he is at liberty to sell and take the risks which are swift and stern. Such a man might have fine courage, but we could not think much of his judgment." Chase also condemns the libidinous sex hygiene books and speaks of the work of the Boston Advisory Committee on Sex Publications. He prefers the term "criticism" (from the Greek) to "censorship" (from the Latin) because of the unfavorable connotation of the latter. He coins the term "endocrinic literature" for those books that stir the "animal lusts."

———. "Report of Department of Contributory Vices." *Light*, 17:50–55, March–April 1914. **C 284**
Chase describes the unwholesome "problem novels" and works treating with sex that are flooding the country.

[Chase, Samuel]. *Report of The Trial of Hon. Samuel Chase, an Associate Justice of the Supreme Court of the United States, Impeached by the House of Representatives for High Crimes and Misdemeanors, before the Senate of the United States*. Baltimore, 1805. (Also in *Annals of Congress*, 8th Cong., 2d sess., 1804–5, pp. 80–675+) **C 285**
Justice Chase's impeachment grew out of his conduct of the Callender sedition trials (he had also presided at the trial of Thomas Cooper), in which he was alleged to have shown partiality against the Jeffersonians. Chase was acquitted by the Senate.

Chase, Stuart. *Democracy Under Pressure*. New York, Twentieth Century Fund, 1945. 142 p. **C 286**
A study of the effects of pressure groups on the making of government policy and the carrying out of executive directives. In modern society the activity and influence of pressure groups tend to cancel each other and are not the evil that they once were. Free discussion of issues through the media of mass communication is the most effective antidote to pressures in a democracy.

Chase, William S. *The Case for the Federal Supervision of Motion Pictures*. Washington, D.C., International Reform Federation, 1927. 36 p. **C 287**
Canon Chase was president of the New York Civic League.

———. *Catechism on Motion Pictures in Interstate Commerce: Shall This Interstate Business, Dangerous to Morals and to Politics, Be Nationally Controlled, a Trust Prevented, a Demoralized Business Be Reorganized, and*

---

an Attack upon Free Government Be Thwarted?
3d ed. Albany, N. Y., New York Civic
League, 1922. 159p.   **C 288**
Canon Chase answered in the affirmative.

————. "The Motion Picture Situation."
Light, 165:17–27, July–August 1925.
                                        C 289
A review of industry efforts to control the
immorality of the movies, the various city
censorship boards, and legislation before
Congress. The author urges passage of the
Upshaw bill (H.R. 6821) presently before
Congress, which would place motion pictures
under federal control.

[————, and John S. Sumner]. "The
Arguments for Stage Censorship." *Review
of Reviews*, 75:403–4, April 1927.   **C 290**
Canon Chase, representing the New York
Civic League, calls for stage censorship by
state law, with administrative enforcement
officers from whose decisions appeals may be
made to the courts. John S. Sumner, representing the New York Society for Suppression of
Vice, supports the measure pending in the
New York legislature to place the stage under
the same control as exists in the state for
motion pictures.

"Chatter Checked." *Newsweek*, 21:92–94,
22 February 1943.   **C 291**
The blue-penciling of portions of the news
script of Walter Winchell and Drew Pearson
by the Blue Network.

Chauncy, Charles. *The only Compulsion
proper to be made Use of in the Affairs of
Conscience and Religion. A Sermon . . .* Boston,
J. Draper and J. Edwards, 1739. 26p.
                                        C 292
A liberal Boston minister pleads for liberty of
expression in matters of religion; but licentiousness is not to be tolerated. "And as it is
no Argument, that men ought not to eat or
drink, because they may be intemperate, so
neither is it an Argument, that they mayn't
have the Use of Liberty, because they be
licentious. The Abuse of any thing is no
argument against its Use."

Checkley, John. *The Speech of Mr. John
Checkley, upon His Tryal at Boston in New-
England for Publishing The Short and Easy
Method with the Deists: To Which Is Added,
A Discourse Concerning Episcopacy; In De-
fence of Christianity, and the Church of
England against the Deists and Dissenters.
To Which is Added the Jury's Verdict; His
Plea in Arrest of Judgment and the Sentence
of the Court.* 2d ed. London, J. Applebee,
1738. 40p. (Reprinted in Slafter, *John
Checkley*, vol. 2, pp. 1–37)   **C 293**

In 1724 John Checkley, an advocate of Episcopacy, came to Boston with a stock of his book,
A Short and Easy Method with Deists, which he
had been forbidden to print in Massachusetts
5 years before. The Council ordered the attorney general to prosecute the author. Checkley
was brought to trial, convicted, and fined
£50. An appeal to Superior Court resulted in
a second conviction. The trial is of interest
because the jury brought in a special verdict
to the effect that if the book was libelous
Checkley was guilty; if it was not libelous,
he was not guilty. This followed the English
practice of leaving up to the judge the question
of the criminality of the alleged libel. Checkley's lawyer, John Read, made an eloquent plea
for acquittal based on the duty of the jury
to decide whether or not the work was libelous,
a principle not recognized in English law until
the passage of the Fox Libel Act of 1792.

[Cheetham, James]. *A Narrative of the
Suppression by Col. Burr, of the History of the
Administration of John Adams . . . Written
by John Wood . . .* 2d ed. New York,
Denniston and Cheetham, 1802. 72p.
                                        C 294
Cheetham, who identifies himself only as
"A Citizen of New York," reveals the story
back of the suppression of John Wood's history
of the Adams administration. Aaron Burr and
his friends threatened the publishers with a
libel suit, according to Cheetham, and asked
Wood to arrange for the suppression of the
entire edition. After a long controversy the
publishers surrendered the 1,250 copies to
Van Ness, an agent of Burr, on receipt of
$1,000. Wood wrote his own explanation of
the censorship episode in *A Correct Statement . . .*

[————]. *Speech of Counsellor Sampson, on
the Trial of James Cheetham, for Libelling
Madame Bonneville, in his Life of Thomas
Paine; with a Short Sketch of the Trial.* New
York, Charles Holt, 1810. 27p.   **C 295**
Cheetham had implied that Paine had a son
by Madame Bonneville whom he had seduced.
For this statement Cheetham was convicted
of libel and fined $150. The speech is reprinted
from issues of the *Columbian*.

[————]. *The Trial of the Hon. Maturin
Livingston, against James Cheetham, for a
Libel . . . on the Twenty-Eighth of Nov.,
1807. Before the Hon. Judge Spencer.* New
York, S. Gould, 1807. 63p.   **C 296**
Cheetham was accused of libeling Livingston
by charging in the *Republican Watch Tower*,
14 September 1805, that the latter cheated at
cards. The defendant was found guilty and
fined $1,000.

Chenery, William. *Freedom of the Press.*
New York, Harcourt, Brace, 1955. 256p.
                                        C 297
An account of the concept of freedom in the
Western world, with emphasis on the great
turning points in the struggle for a free press.
The author is a veteran journalist who draws
upon a half century of personal experience.

Chennell, Frank E. "Few Words on the
Censor in the Library." *Library World*,
2:316–18, June 1900.   **C 298**
The author rejects the notion held by some
librarians and expressed by Sir Anthony
Absolute that "a circulating library in a town
is an evergreen tree of diabolical knowledge,"
and that, in censoring, the librarian is doing
a little judicious pruning.

Chervin, Harriet T. "Birth Control
Propaganda in Oregon." *Mother Earth*,
11:641–43, October 1916.   **C 299**
An account of the conviction of Carl Rave for
obscenity in selling birth control information.

Cheshire, Herbert, and Maxine Cheshire.
"The Menace in Your Letterbox." *Ameri-
can Mercury*, 87:137–42, August 1958.
                                        C 300
"Mail order filth may destroy your child."
The article is concerned with pornography
being mailed to children and teenagers.

Cheslau, Irving G. *John Peter Zenger and
"The New-York Weekly Journal"; A Historical Study.* New York, [Zenger Memorial
Fund, 1952?]. 32p.   **C 301**
An account of John Peter Zenger, his newspaper, and the historic trial of 1735, "in which
the defense made an eloquent plea for freedom
of the press and anticipated the modern laws
of libel by three-quarters of a century." The
Zenger case, Cheslau notes, although a milestone in American freedom, did not establish
a legal precedent and "did not sweep out
the rigors of the common law" of libel.

Chesterfield, Philip Dormer Stanhope,
4th Earl. *The E—— of C——f——d's
Speech in the H[ou]se of L[or]ds against the
bill for licensing all dramatic performances.
To which are prefixed, Some loose Thoughts
that were found in a closet of a Gentleman
lately deceased.* Dublin, 1749. 10p. (Also
in *A New Miscellany for the Year 1737*,
pp. 17–21, and in the appendix to Fowell
and Palmer, *Censorship in England*)   **C 302**
Lord Chesterfield vigorously championed the
freedom of the stage in opposition to the
Theatres Act of 1737 in a speech in the House
of Lords, but to little avail.

Chesterton, G. K. "About the Censor."
In his *As I Was Saying; a Book of Essays.*
New York, Dodd, Mead, 1936, pp. 31–36.
                                        C 303
"There were some who seemed to hold that
any artistic experiment, however anarchical or
abnormal, or manifestly and even medically
insane, had a mysterious right of its own to
override any social custom or convenience,
any common-sense or ordinary civic dignity...
Even the worst play must take precedence of
the best law . . . Anyhow, the theory of the

thing seemed to be that supreme spiritual authority in this world belongs to art . . . I was never able to accept this highly modern and credulous conception; because I am unable to imagine any human being accepting any authority that he has not originally reached by reason."

———. "On a Censorship of Literature." In his *Come to Think of It . . .* New York, Dodd, Mead, 1931, pp. 27–32.   **C 304**
A witty argument against censorship, revealing the muddled thinking that lies behind it. Three totally distinct things are often confused in censorship involving sexual decorum: antisocial sex theories, descriptive writing likely to excite sex appetites, and use of objectionable terms. Society must first agree upon a morality before it can have a censor of morals. We ought to be making a fuss about real life and let fiction take care of itself. Many who demand censorship "are really demanding that we should tolerate in life what we will not tolerate in literature."

———. "Prohibition and the Press." In his *Fancies Versus Fads*, 3d ed., London, Methuen, 1927, pp. 80–85.   **C 305**
A criticism of American Prohibition, applying John Milton's arguments for liberty of the press (*Areopagitica*) to liberty in drinking. True freedom gives to man the "ownership of his own body and his own bodily activities" whether it is in speaking, writing, or drinking beer. There is as much risk involved in the freedom to print as in the freedom to drink.

[Cheynell, Francis]. *Chillingworthi Novissima. Or the Sicknesse, Heresy, Death and Burial of William Chillingworth (in his own phrase) Clerk of Oxford . . . and a short Oration at the Buriall of his Hereticall Book.* London, 1644.   **C 306**
A unique form of censorship is proposed by this Calvinist minister—the burial of the offending works of the rationalist theologian, William Chillingworth. Pastor Cheynell had previously refused to bury the author.

Cheyney, Edward P. "Freedom and Restraint: A Short History." *Annals of the American Academy of Political and Social Science*, 200:1–12, November 1938. (Reprinted in Schramm, *Mass Communications*, pp. 121–37)   **C 307**
The author traces freedom of speech and of the press in America, from the adoption of the Bill of Rights (1791) to present-day subversive activity probes. Such episodes as the Sedition Act, the oppression of abolitionists, and the "criminal syndicalism" trials represent exceptions in a country which has been remarkably free of government threat to personal liberty. "Popular passion" has always been the greatest threat to civil liberties. Cheyney also served as editor of this entire issue of *The Annals*, which was devoted to "Freedom of Inquiry and Expression." He sums up the series of studies in Observations and Generalizations, pp. 275–91. "Freedom of expression is not

merely a personal privilege, nor is it only a defense against tyranny of government or of any other possessors of power; it is a condition of progress."

Chicago. Commission upon Moving Picture Censorship. *Report.* Chicago, The Commission, 1920. 184 p.   **C 308**
The Commission was appointed by the Committee on Judiciary of the Chicago City Council to study and recommend revision of the city's ordinance on censorship of motion pictures. Its 20 members included a judge, Methodist and Episcopal ministers, a Catholic priest, and representatives of the Holy Name Society and the Knights of Columbus. Conclusions: (1) There is no legal or constitutional restriction on prior censorship of movies. (2) Censorship should be removed from the police department. (3) A Department of Motion Pictures should be created to have exclusive authority over licensing of movies. (4) The Department should approve motion picture advertising and should stamp its approval on each reel of film and each advertisement approved. (5) The "pink permit" section of the present ordinance ("adults only" films) should be repealed. "No picture should be exhibited," the report concluded, "that could not be shown before the father and mother in company with their children." Text of the proposed ordinance is included.

Chicago. Municipal Reference Library. *Censorship of Motion Picture Films in Cities in the United States Other than Chicago.* Chicago, The Library, 1918. 18 p. mimeo.   **C 309**
The report favors municipal censorship of movies.

Chicago. Police Department. "Obscene Literature." *Training Bulletin*, 3(47, 48), 19 November, 26 November 1962. 3 p.   **C 310**
Definitions of obscenity as indicated in recent court decisions, and procedures to be followed by the police when handling suspected obscene publications.

"Chicago Booksellers Join to Fight Censorship." *Publishers' Weekly*, 186:83+, 6 July 1964.   **C 311**
Editorial on the establishment of the Greater Chicago Booksellers' Association for the purpose of organizing opposition to city censorship.

Chicago Civil Liberties Committee. *Pursuit of Freedom; a History of Civil Liberty in Illinois, 1787–1942 . . .* Chicago, The Chicago Civil Liberties Committee and the Illinois Civil Liberties Committee, 1942. 221 p.   **C 312**
Chapter 3 deals with freedom of the press in Illinois; Chapter 4 with censorship. The editorial committee, Edgar Bernhard, Ira Latimer, and Harvey O'Connor, prepared the report.

"Chicago Movie Censorship." *Literary Digest*, 48:702–3, 28 March 1914.   **C 313**
Pros and cons in the press regarding the new board of movie censorship. The *Advocate* is quoted as criticizing the Chicago newspapers for their opposition to the censorship and for their failure to measure up to "their responsibility in the emergency of morals brought about by the picture-theaters."

[*Chicago Tribune*]. *What American Editors Said about the Ten Million Dollar Libel Suit. Editorial Comment in American Press on the Lawsuit Brought in the Name of the City of Chicago against the Chicago Tribune.* Chicago, *Chicago Tribune*, 1921. 154 p.   **C 314**
The city of Chicago had brought a $10,000,000 libel suit against the *Chicago Tribune* for alleged damages to the city's credit inflicted by the *Tribune's* exposures of municipal corruption. The Illinois Supreme Court ruled in favor of the *Tribune*, declaring that "the people have the right to discuss their government without fear of being called to account in the courts for their expression of opinion."

"Chicago Vice Committee Report Excluded from the Mail." *Nation*, 93:308–9, 5 October 1911.   **C 315**
A famous case of Post-Office censorship is the exclusion from the mails of *The Social Evil in Chicago*, a report prepared by the official Vice Commission of Chicago for distribution to clergymen, editors, and social workers.

Chidley, Samuel. *The Dissembling Scot Set forth in his Coulours Or a Vindication of Lieu. Col. John Lilburn and others, From those Aspersions cast upon them by David Brown in his idle pamphlet . . .* London, 1652.   **C 316**
Chidley, although an impassioned Leveller and a disciple of the exiled Lilburne, did not agree with his brethren on freedom of the press. The license systems, he argued, should be rigorously enforced, at least against such pamphleteers as David Brown. Brown had informed on Lilburne and testified against him at the sedition trial.

[Chidley, William J.]. "Chivied Chidley; His Immurement as Insane; He Describes His Callan Park Experiences; Cries of Souls in Grievous Agony." *Truth; the People's Paper*, 21 September 1913.   **C 317**
Chidley, an Australian minister, had written and published a book, *The Answer* (Melbourne, Australian Author's Agency, 1911. 79 p.), in which he offered a strange theory on sexual intercourse, discussed in religious context. The work was judged obscene and ordered burnt. Chidley was arrested, committed to an asylum and later sent to jail. His case was discussed in the Australian Parliament. Numer-

ous accounts of the episode appear in the Melbourne and Sydney papers over the period from 1911 through 1914 and are listed in Schroeder, *Free Speech Bibliography*.

[Child, David L.]. *Trial of the Case of the Commonwealth versus David Lee Child, for Publishing in the Massachusetts Journal a Libel on the Honorable John Keyes, before the Supreme Judicial Court, Holden at Cambridge, in the County of Middlesex. October term, 1828. Reported by John W. Whitman.* Boston, Dutton and Wentworth, 1829. 119p. **C 318**

Child, Richard W. "The Critic and the Law." *Atlantic Monthly*, 97:620–29, May 1906. **C 319**
"From a legal point of view, then, we as critics are all held to a high standard of fairness. We must not comment on any but matters of public interest. We must be honest and sincere, but we may express any view, no matter how prejudiced or exaggerated it may be, so long as it does not exceed the limits to which a reasonably fair man would go."

Childs, Harwood L. "Pressure Groups and Intellectual Freedom." In *Freedom of Communication; Proceedings of the First Conference on Intellectual Freedom . . .* Chicago, American Library Association, 1954, pp. 73–88. **C 320**

Childs, Marquis. "'Managing' News: An Old Practice With New Twists." St. Louis *Post-Dispatch*, 31 March 1963, Editorial Section, p. 1. **C 321**
"In this reporter's nearly 30 years in Washington, there has never been a day that the news has not been managed . . . When, as has happened since the war, news management is linked to 'national security' and the growing practice of stamping almost any document secret or top secret, there is reason for grave concern."

——. "What Signs Threaten Free Press?" *Nieman Reports*, 5(3):7–10, July 1951. **C 322**
An address by the syndicated Washington columnist on receiving the University of Missouri School of Journalism award. He lists present dangers to freedom of the press and describes the action needed to preserve "the right of independent opinion for a newspaper, for an editor, and for the individual in our society who elects to stand alone."

[Christesen, C. B.]. "Censorship and Cant." *Meanjin Quarterly; a Review of Arts and Letters in Australia*, 23:223–24, 1964. **C 323**
An editorial criticizing censorship practices of Australian Customs in prohibiting such works as *Lady Chatterley's Lover*, *Lolita*, and *Another Country*.

"Christian Civilisation in War and Peace." *Mother Earth*, 7:253–54, October 1912. **C 324**
The article includes the cartoon for which Ludovico Caminita was arrested for alleged provocation of war with Italy.

Christiansen, Paul. "Prior Censorship and Movies." *Rocky Mountain Law Review*, 33:421–24, April 1961. **C 325**
Notes on *Times Film Corp. v. City of Chicago*, 365 U.S. 43 (1961).

Christie, J. R. "Liability of Publishers of Newspapers for Advertisement Containing False Statement Not ex facie Libelous, but Containing an Imputation on Character When Read by Person Acquainted with Circumstances Unknown to Publishers." *Juridical Review*, 22:254–60, October 1910. **C 326**

Christinger, Raymond. *Le Développement de la Presse et son Influence sur la Responsabilité Internationale de l'Etat*. Lausanne, Switz., Roth and Cie, 1944. 155p. **C 327**
A survey of the national press systems in operation at the beginning of World War II—free, state-directed, and state-controlled. Discusses principles of international responsibility of the press in time of peace and war.

Christman, Henry. "'Nobly Save or Meanly Lose.'" *Survey Graphic*, 35:436–40, December 1946. **C 328**
In an introduction to a special issue of *Survey Graphic* devoted to communications, the editor calls on America to take the leadership in providing people of the postwar world with information and understanding. But freedom begins at home and we must "re-evaluate boldly our own record at home" with respect to the right to know. The title is a Lincoln quotation.

Christophilus, *pseud*. *Vindiciae Britannicae: Christianity interested in the Dismissal of Ministers. A Vindication of the People from the Charge of Blasphemy, and a Defence of the Freedom of the Press. In Six Letters, Addressed to W. Wilberforce, Esq. M.P., and the Religious Public.* 2d ed. London, 1821. (*The Pamphleteer*, London, 1822, vol. 19, no. 37, pp. 161–99; 369–429) **C 329**
A general discussion of blasphemy and sedition.

Churchill, Randolph S. *What I Said about the Press*. London, Weidenfeld and Nicolson, 1957. 112p. **C 330**
A transcript of the author's successful libel case against Odhams Press and Harry Ainsworth, together with the speeches and articles which gave rise to the case.

Ciardi, John. "Across the River and Into New Jersey." *Saturday Review*, 44(18):35, 6 May 1961. **C 331**
Concerns the demand by a Catholic War Veterans group in New Jersey for the suppression of a Rutgers University literary magazine.

——. "Banned in Boston." *Saturday Review*, 48(10):14, 6 March 1965. **C 332**
Observations on the Boston trial of William Burroughs' *Naked Lunch* and obscenity trials in general.

——. "The Book Banners." *Saturday Review*, 45(25):39, 23 June 1962. **C 333**
The publisher may clear a book through the courts in one jurisdiction only to be prosecuted in another city. Because of recent court decisions he will eventually win if he fights long enough and can afford the legal fees.

——. "The Book Banners Again (and Again and Again)." *Saturday Review*, 48(35):21, 28 August 1965. **C 334**
Comments on the decision of Judge Eugene A. Hudson in the Boston trial of William Burroughs' *Naked Lunch*, finding the book obscene. While the verdict "is the best effort of an able and learned judge," Ciardi concludes that "the law itself is incapable of doing honor to itself in such trials," and that a judge is incompetent to serve as "a capable agent of literary criticism."

——. "Book Banning and Juvenile Delinquency." *Saturday Review*, 46(31):16, 10 August 1963. **C 335**
Ciardi doubts that any child becomes a juvenile delinquent because of what he reads—how can it ever be the consequence of anything but parental delinquency? While admitting the stimulation of sexy literature on the adolescent, "nothing suggests sex more movingly than a girl to a boy and a boy to a girl" and there is always an ample supply of both.

——. "The Book Burners and Sweet Sixteen." *Saturday Review*, 42(26):22, 30, 27 June 1959. **C 336**
Editorial comment on the edict from University of Chicago's Chancellor Kimpton against the publication in the *Chicago Review* of anything that would "offend a sixteen-year-old girl" and the Post-Office action against *Big Table*, a magazine privately published by student editors who had resigned over the restrictions. Two of the works featured were: Jack Kerouac's Old Angel Midnight and William S. Burroughs' Ten Episodes from *Naked Lunch*.

——. "Last Exit to Nowhere." *Saturday Review*, 48(14):12, 3 April 1965. **C 337**

"Someday, and soon I hope, the Supreme Court will hear a book-banning case and issue a ruling that not only clears the book but enunciates legal principles so firmly that the everlastingly reiterated harassment of books by the lower courts will be brought to a halt." Ciardi rejects the two charges usually brought against a book—that it contributes to juvenile delinquency and that it offends community standards. There is no demonstrable connection between juvenile delinquency and any reading habit; a book has no way of intruding upon the community and it offends an individual only when he seeks it out.

―――――. "A Public Answer." *Saturday Review*, 45(31):11, 4 August 1962. **C 338**
An answer to letters received after his defense of Henry Miller's *Tropic of Cancer*, charging that he would have a different attitude if his children could read the book. Ciardi reveals his attitude as a parent and his belief in children reading at any age what they want to read, so long as they discuss it with their parents.

―――――. "Student Publications and the Tufts Plan (or Alma Mater, Yours in Pride)." *Saturday Review*, 48(37):20–22, 11 September 1965. **C 339**
Discussion and text of the Tufts College statement on university policy toward student publications. The University will not act as a censor; it leaves the right to publish with the editors and faculty advisors, subject to no revision by the University.

―――――. "*Tropic of Cancer*." *Saturday Review*, 45(26):13, 30 June 1962. **C 340**
"*Tropic of Cancer* must be defended, but not as 'a great book.' It must be defended as the work of a serious artist enlarged by talent and passionately engaged in giving form (and thereby meaning) to his view of life."

―――――. "What Is Pornography?" *Saturday Review*, 46(28):20, 13 July 1963. **C 341**
To the question "Is *Fanny Hill* pronography?" Ciardi answers: "It certainly is: it was written as such, it has had a clandestine history in which all scholars have held it to be such, and such it is today and will be to the dark end of time's last bookshelf."

Cibber, Colley. "C――y C――'s Letter to *The Craftsman*. To Caleb D'Anvers, Esq." In *A New Miscellany for the Year 1737*. London, 1737, pp. 22–29. **C 342**
This letter from the actor, playwright, and poet laureate of England deals with the licensing of stage plays.

"Circulating Libraries Association and Banned Books." *Library Association Record*, 18:383, 15 September 1916. **C 343**
Invitation to librarians to become librarian associates of the Association, which recently established a Committee to "classify" books on the basis of their morality.

["Circulating Libraries Association Censorship of Books"]. *Library Association Record*, 12:28–29, 15 January 1910. **C 344**
Text of letter announcing the censorship policy of the Circulating Libraries Association.

A Citizen of Georgia. *Remarks on Slavery, Occasioned by Attempts to Circulate Improper Publications in the Southern States*. Augusta, Ga., 1835. **C 345**
The writer argues that suppression of abolitionist literature is desirable because, if slaves could read, it would "tend to make them restless and discontented" and hence lead to their ruin.

Citizens for Decent Literature. *Criminal Obscenity Convictions in Which United States Supreme Court Has Denied Review—1957–65*. Cincinnati, The CDL, 1965. 8p. **C 346**
From Roth-Alberts to Wenzler-Imlay.

―――――. *Fight Newsstand Filth. The Law Is Your Weapon*. Cincinnati, The CDL, 1960. 31p. **C 347**
"A question and answer booklet that describes the aims and the methods used by Citizens for Decent Literature to wipe out the evil, billion dollar, printed filth racket." An interview with Charles Keating, Jr., founder of the CDL, conducted by Douglas J. Roche. "The CDL doesn't set itself up as a judge and tell people they can't read this or that. The CDL wants the courts to judge if certain publications are obscene."

―――――. *National Decency Reporter; National News Letter of Citizens for Decent Literature*. Cincinnati, The CDL, 1963–date. Approximately monthly. **C 348**
Reports news of local, state, and national CDL groups, court cases, and legislation, and gives advice to members on methods of fighting the spread of pornographic books and magazines in local communities.

―――――. *Printed Poison. A Community Problem*. Cincinnati, The CDL, 1960. 32p. **C 349**
"The sordid story of the muck merchants, their efforts to sell printed filth to the youngsters of America . . . The author provides a forceful reminder that it is even more necessary to protect our children's minds than it is their bodies."

―――――. *Procedures Handbook for Establishing a Citizens for Decent Literature Group in Your Town*. Cincinnati, The CDL, n.d. 12p. **C 350**

―――――. *Vanguard; Young Adults News Letter*. Cincinnati, The CDL, 1963–date. Monthly. **C 351**

Civil Liberties Committee of Massachusetts. *Censorship in Boston* . . . Boston, The Committee, 1938. 14p. (The material for the pamphlet was collected by Constantine Aristides) **C 352**
No motion picture censorship board exists in Boston but there are severe restrictions on Sunday showings. The law of 1936 assures stage plays one uncensored production before the City License Commission makes recommendation of cuts; a hearing is also provided for. The Watch and Ward Society has withdrawn from book censorship but the booksellers use their own system which has deprived Boston citizens of works of literature available in other cities. A Censorship Committee of the Police Department acts arbitrarily against offending magazines.

―――――. *Censorship in Time of Crisis. A Symposium* . . . Boston, The Committee, 1941. 34p. **C 353**
Includes: Is Regulation Necessary by Bruno Lasker, Censuring the Censor (the Massachusetts scene) by Zechariah Chafee, Jr., and Publication by Handbill (a Worcester, Mass., case) by Sidney Grant and Samuel Angoff.

"Civil Liberties in Great Britain and Canada during War." *Havard Law Review*, 55:1006–18, April 1942. **C 354**
A comparison of censorship and internment policies of England and Canada during the early years of World War II. England liberalized its policies after the first few months of war; Canada maintained strict enforcement. In both countries, however, consent of central authorities was required before proceedings under the regulations could take place.

Claghorne, Kate H. "Alien and Sedition Bills Up-to-Date." *Survey*, 42:590–92, 19 July 1919. **C 355**
An account of bills pending before the Congress.

Clancy, William P. "The Catholic As Censor." *Commonweal*, 68:142–44, 9 May 1958. **C 356**
The author defends some censorship as necessary for "the common good." Such organizations as the Legion of Decency and the National Office for Decent Literature play a necessary role. Catholic censors should confine their efforts to obvious obscenity and not seek to control even indirectly the artistic and intellectual freedom of adults.

―――――. "The Catholic as Philistine." *Commonweal*, 53:567–69, 16 March 1951. **C 357**
An English professor at Notre Dame University criticizes the crusade of Catholics against *The Miracle* and other works they consider blasphemous. He calls upon Catholic educators to press for a more mature attitude toward freedom of expression.

————. "Freedom of the Screen." *Commonweal*, 59:500–502, 19 February 1954. **C 358**

The author agrees with U.S. Supreme Court decisions reversing the ban on *The Miracle*, *La Ronde* and *M*. He feels that there should not be prior film censorship by state or city authorities, and that the setting of moral standards should be the province of religious authorities. An answer to this article, written by Martin H. Work, appears in the issue for 12 March 1954.

Clapp, Verner W. "Book Selection in the Large Research Library." In *Freedom of Communication; Proceedings of the First Conference on Intellectual Freedom . . .* Chicago, American Library Association, 1954, pp. 38–43. **C 359**

Clark, Allen C. "William Duane." In *Records of the Columbia Historical Society*. Washington, D.C., The Society, 1906, vol. 9, pp. 14–62. **C 360**

Duane, who succeeded Bache as editor of the *Aurora*, was brought to trial under the Sedition Act, in 1800. The author observes that Duane's articles were written with "venom, vehemence, violence, vituperation, and vilification" in an age of public passions. A bibliography of Duane's writings is attached. The paper was read before the Society, 13 February 1905.

Clark, Barrett H. *The Blush of Shame; a Few Considerations on Verbal Obscenity in the Theater*. New York, Privately published, 1932. 16 p. **C 361**

Despite a greater freedom of expression in the theater than ever before, there is still a self-imposed code of producers to avoid certain words that have become common in printed literature. The line between decent and indecent language, however, is becoming thinner and thinner.

————. *Oedipus or Pollyanna, with a Note on Dramatic Censorship*. Seattle, University of Washington Book Store, 1927. 37 p. (University of Washington Cahpbooks, no. 4) **C 362**

Clark, Charles D. L. "Obscenity, the Law and Lady Chatterley— I. and II." *Criminal Law Review*, 1961:156–63, March 1961; 1961: 224–34, April 1961. **C 363**

I. A. review of obscene libel in England from the first recorded case, *R. v. Read* (1708), to the test case under the 1959 Obscene Publications Act. II. A review of the case of *R. v. Penguin Books, Ltd.* and a discussion of the 1959 Obscene Publications Act under which the case was tried.

Clark, Christopher J. "Motion Picture Censorship—Artistic Merit of Film as Whole Not Sufficient to Redeem Obscene Parts." *Villanova Law Review*, 9:671–75, Summer 1964. **C 364**

Regarding *Trans-Lux Distrib. Corp. v. Regents*, 14 N.Y. 2d 88, 248 N.Y. S. 2d 857 (1964).

Clark, Eleanor G. *Ralegh and Marlowe; A Study in Elizabethan Fustian*. New York, Fordham University Press, 1941. 488 p. **C 365**

Throughout this study in Elizabethan and Jacobean fustian, with particular reference to the Marlowe-Ralegh relationship, the author considers the work of the stage censor and the licensing system.

Clark, Grenville. "The Limits of Freedom of Expression." *United States Law Review*, 73:392–404, June 1939. **C 366**

"My theme is an inquiry into the principles upon which expression may be justifiably suppressed or punished, without violation of the essential spirit of English-American liberty under which we live."

Clark, Mary E. *Peter Porcupine in America. The Career of William Cobbett, 1792–1800 . . .* [Gettysburg, Pa., Printed by Times and News Publishing Co.] 1939. 193 p. (Ph. D. dissertation, University of Pennsylvania, 1937) **C 367**

Chapter 5. The Quarrel with the Bradfords and Pamphlet Warfare. Chapter 8. Liberty of the Press—First Libel Suit, 1797. Chapter 10. Departure from Philadelphia and the Rush Trial, 1799 (libel of Dr. Benjamin Rush for which Cobbett was fined $5,000).

Clark, William L. "Lockhart's Last Journey." *Rail Splitter*, 3:4, December 1918. **C 368**

An account of Lockhart's conviction on obscenity charges. According to the author it was because of Lockhart's opposition to Catholicism.

————. *Reminiscences of a Reformer's Life; or, Twenty-five Years on the Skirmish Line against Political Romanism*. [Milan, Ill., The Author] 1913. 229 p. **C 369**

Includes an account of mobbings for anti-Catholic lectures; also his arrest on an obscenity charge for sale of his book, *Hell at Midnight in Springfield* [Ill.].

————. *The Story of My Battle with the Scarlet Beast*. [Milan, Ill., The Rail Splitter Press, 1932]. 441 p. **C 370**

The author describes his lifelong and often violent crusade against the Catholic Church and the alleged vices of its clergy. The latter part of the book is largely a reporting of the various efforts to suppress Clark's paper, *The Rail Splitter*, and other anti-Catholic literature, and his 1911 arrest and trial in Peoria, Ill., for an alleged obscene book—*Hell at Midnight in Springfield*—an exposé of vice and corruption in Springfield, Ill. Theodore A. Schroeder and the Free Speech League gave Clark legal aid. Clark also reports on the prosecution of B. O. Flower's anti-Catholic paper, *The Menace*. The fourth edition of *Hell at Midnight* (1914) gives an account of the Peoria trial.

Clarke, Austin. "Banned Books." *New Statesman*, 45:606+, 23 May 1953. **C 371**

Comments on modern Irish censorship. Irish authors who write in English can have their works published in England or America; but the position of the new Gaelic literature is precarious. Its writers depend upon government or the Gaelic Book Club publication. There is little chance of publication for those who write with the candor of Liam O'Flaherty.

Clarke, G. E. "Propaganda." *Library World*, 42:62–63, October 1939. **C 372**

Librarians have a responsibility for discarding unsound books of yesteryear. In the eyes of the public, the fact that they are on the shelves confers upon them an endorsement.

Clarke, George T. "Improper Books." *Library Journal*, 20:33–35, Denver Conference of Librarians, 1895. **C 373**

Books selected "should either be capable of adding to the general store of knowledge, of exercising some beneficial influence upon the mind, or of providing wholesome amusement or recreation." This excludes many works being currently published. Comments of the librarian of the San Francisco Public Library in one of a series of papers on undesirable books in public libraries.

[Clarke, John *et al.*]. "The Trial of John Clarke, Robert Knell, and Joseph Carter, Printers of *Mist's Weekly Journal*, 1729." In Howell, *State Trials*, vol. 17, pp. 666–68. **C 374**

For printing in the issue of 24 August 1729 a letter signed "Amos Dudge," reflecting unfavorably on the late King George II, Clarke and Knell were given six months at hard labor and twice pilloried; Carter and Richard Nutt, apprentices, were given one month at hard labor and required to walk about London with paper hats describing their offense. Nathaniel Mist, publisher, had previously (1721) been imprisoned at the order of the House of Commons for criticism of the government.

Clarkson, Lawrence. *Truth Released from Prison to Its Former Libertie; or, A True Discovery Who Are the Troublers of Israel, the Disturbers of England's Peace . . .* London, 1646. **C 375**

Clarkson (or Claxton) was an Anabaptist who published an "impious and blasphemous" tract, *The Single Eye, All Light No Darkness, or Light and Darkness One*, for which he was condemned by the House of Commons and banished from the country. Action was taken upon a report from a House Committee for Suppressing Licentious and Impious Practices. An official broadside (27 September 1650) decreed that the book be seized and burnt by the common hangman and anyone possessing a copy deliver it to the nearest Justice of the Peace. Wing reports only a single known copy survives in the Thomason collection.

Clay, Cassius M. *Appeal of Cassius M. Clay to Kentucky and the World.* Boston, J. M. Macomber and E. L. Pratt, 1845. 35 p.   **C 376**
Clay published unpopular antislavery sentiments in his Lexington, Ky., newspaper, *The True American.* A vigilante committee demanded that the paper cease publication. When Clay refused, the members, unopposed by city officials, boxed up the press and shipped it at Clay's direction, to Cincinnati. The pamphlet deals with the suppression of the paper.

————. *The Life of Cassius Marcellus Clay... Written and compiled by Himself* . . . Cincinnati, J. F. Brennan, 1886. 600 p.   **C 377**
Includes references to the suppression of his newspaper, *The True American,* because of its abolitionist stand.

Clayton, Bertram. "The Cinema and Its Censor." *Fortnightly Review,* 109(n.s.): 222–28, February 1921.   **C 378**
A criticism of the president of the British Board of Film Censors for his efforts to be "reasonable and conciliatory" toward the film interests. The film industry, the author charges, is turning more and more to "bookstall trash." The sole virtue of the silent drama is that it *is* silent and the accompanying music is the better part of the performance.

Clayton, Charles C. *Fifty Years for Freedom: The Story of Sigma Delta Chi's Service to American Journalism, 1909–1959.* Carbondale, Ill., Southern Illinois University Press, 1959. 244 p.   **C 379**
This professional journalism society has been concerned with keeping open the channels of information and assuring the journalist's freedom to report the news. Its rituals, its awards, and the work of its Committee on the Advancement of Freedom of Information reflect interest in freedom of the press. A number of its annual conventions have featured themes relating to press freedom and the Society's historical sites program has included markers for Anthony Haswell, Elijah P. Lovejoy, and John Peter Zenger.

Clean Books League, New York. *Criminal Obscenity Rampant: a Simple Remedy for a Loathsome Disease.* New York, The League, [192—?]. 36 p.   **C 380**
The pamphlet calls for amendment to the New York obscenity laws to make it impossible for the courts to follow the decision of

People v. Brainard and Harper & Brothers (New York Appellate Division), which in 1920 killed the effectiveness of the 1909 New York obscenity law. The legislation was supported by Judge John Ford and the New York Society for the Suppression of Vice, and by such writers as Hendrik W. Van Loon, Edwin Markham, and Hamlin Garland.

"The Clean Books League; the Views of its Defenders and Critics." *Publishers' Weekly,* 103:940–41, 17 March 1923.   **C 381**
Justice John Ford of the New York Supreme Court established the League to serve as a committee of readers to advise the public what books to avoid. The New York press was almost unanimously opposed to the League, but many religious and civic groups favored it. Chief City Magistrate McAdoo is quoted at length in pointing out the difficulties of attempting to introduce literary reforms by law and police methods.

"Clean Hands." *Saturday Review of Literature,* 6:227, 237, 12 October 1929.   **C 382**
An editorial attributes the excesses of censorship, in part, to the provocation of sensationalism and indecency exhibited in recent stage plays. Opponents of censorship "must come into court with clean hands."

"Clear and Present Danger Re-examined." *Columbia Law Review,* 51:98–108 January 1951.   **C 383**
A reconsideration of the dictum of Justice Holmes in applying a legal test for sedition.

Cleaton, Irene, and Allen Cleaton. *Books & Battles; American Literature, 1920–1930.* Boston, Houghton Mifflin, 1937. 282 p.   **C 384**
The revolt against Puritanism and Victorianism in literature that led to battles among the critics and in the courts. Chapter 3, Censorship: From Limbs to Legs, deals with activities of the vice societies. Other efforts at censorship are discussed briefly throughout the book.

Clemens, Samuel L. "License of the Press." In *Mark Twain's Speeches.* New York, Gabriel Wells, 1923, pp. 46–52.   **C 385**
"There are laws to protect the freedom of the press's speech, but none that are worth anything to protect the people from the press . . . I have a sort of general idea that there is too much liberty of the press in this country, and that through the absence of all wholesome restraint the newspaper has become in a large degree a national curse, and will probably damn the Republic yet." From a talk before the Monday Evening Club of Hartford in 1873. Mark Twain's caustic criticism reflects the corrupt state of the press in the period following the Civil War.

[Clement, William I.]. *Report of the Action, Wright v. Clement, for Certain Libels Published in Cobbett's Political Register, Tried in*

the Court of King's Bench at Westminster, on Friday, the 10th of December, 1819, before Lord Chief Justice Abbott, and a Special Jury. London, Printed by T. C. Hansard for J. Wright, 1819. 55 p.   **C 386**
John Wright, formerly associated with William Cobbett in the publishing of the Parliamentary Debates, sued Clement, a London bookseller, for the sale of issues of *Cobbett's Weekly Register,* which Wright charged contained two libels on him. Cobbett was then in America and could not be brought to trial so action was taken against the distributor of the paper. The verdict was for the defendant on the first libel; and, on the second, for the plaintiff, with a fine of £500.

Clements, Robert J. "Forbidden Books and Christian Reunion." *Columbia University Forum,* 6:26–31, Summer 1963.   **C 387**
The author, a student of the Renaissance, considers the *Index Librorum Prohibitorum* as an institution that has kept alive the divisive spirit of the Reformation. It is no longer relevant to an age concerned with uniting Christianity and, on the eve of its 400th birthday, should be the next book proscribed.

Clements, Traverse. "Censoring the Talkies." *New Republic,* 59:64–66, 5 June 1929.   **C 388**
The addition of sound to motion pictures has increased the worries of censors in 8 states and some 30 cities where there are movie censorship laws. The article reviews some of the recent actions of movie censors and decisions of the courts. The chairman of the Pennsylvania Board of Censors stated that the President of the United States has no right to deliver a speech in that state through the medium of talking movies without the Board's approval.

Cleveland, Arthur. "Defamation in the Local and Ecclesiastical Courts." *Law Magazine and Review,* 40:271–81, May 1915.   **C 389**

Cleveland Chamber of Commerce. *Shall the Movies Be Censored?* Cleveland, The Chamber, 1922. 22 p. (Reprinted in Rutland, *State Censorship of Motion Pictures,* pp. 133–46)   **C 390**
A review by the Municipal Committee of the case for censorship, with recommendations for a federal (not state or local) board of review. A minority report from the Committee opposed all forms of film censorship.

Cleyre, Voltairine de. "Our Police Censorship." *Mother Earth,* 4:297–300, November 1909.   **C 391**

A speech at a protest-meeting over suppression of the anarchist writings of Emma Goldman.

Cliff, Norman. "Free Press in India." *New Statesman*, 45:512–14, 2 May 1953. **C 392**

Commentary on the summoning of the *Times* of India editor before the Bombay Legislative Assembly for his criticism of Prohibition.

Clift, David H. "Enduring Rights." *Wilson Library Bulletin*, 28(10):851–54+, June 1954. (Reprinted in Downs, *The First Freedom*, pp. 331–36) **C 393**

The executive director of the American Library Association, in an address at the opening of the New Haven (Conn.) State Teachers College Library, 21 February 1954, speaks of the increased efforts of private and public groups to challenge man's right to knowledge. "So many of our apprehensions are directed against an ideology. The expression of a dissident idea becomes then a thing feared, in itself, and there is a tendency to react against it as against a hostile deed . . . The solution is not by the suppression of dissident ideas but by the very widest exposure accompanied by thoughtful anaysis. And for this to become wholly true, libraries have a clear and unalterable responsibility."

Clissold, Stephen. "Radio in the Crisis." *Fortnightly*, 139(n.s.):338–44, March 1936. **C 394**

A discussion of the control of radio by the British government to influence opinion on the Italian war in Ethiopia. The author believes that the duty of B.B.C. should be to give informative and impartial news and to counteract "the hysteria of the popular press."

Close Up. London, Poal, vol. 1–10, 1927–33. **C 395**

This publication contains numerous articles on film censorship including The English Censorship by R. Herring, It Rests with Local Authorities by L. B. Duckworth, Acts under the Acts by R. Bond (April 1930); Films and the Law by I. M. Banner Mendus (September 1930); and The Cinema and the Censors by H. G. Weinberg (October 1930).

Clough, Frank C. "Operations of the Press Division of the Office of Censorship." *Journalism Quarterly*, 20:220–24, September 1943. **C 396**

A report from the former managing editor of the *Emporia Gazette*, a member of the staff of the Office of Censorship.

[Clowes, *Sir* William Laird]. *Bibliotheca Arcana seu Catalogus Librorum Penetralium, being Brief notices of books that have been secretly printed, prohibited by law, seized, anathematized, burnt or Bowdlerized. By Speculator Morum.* London, George Redway, 1885. 141 p., 25 p. **C 397**

The preface, which reviews the history of censorship of erotica, is attributed to the Rev. John B. McClellan, the compilation of the annotated bibliography has been sometimes attributed to Sir William Laird Clowes and to Henry S. Ashbee. It is believed that less than 100 copies were issued. There are 630 erotic works, with brief descriptions of their content and, in some instances, the occasion of their suppression. A 25-page preface discusses erotica and the efforts at bibliographic control, particularly by French bibliographers Gay, Peignot, and Delepierre.

Clulow, T. I. M. "Public Libraries and Propagandist Literature." *Library Assistant*, 28:163–67, July 1935. **C 398**

"The librarian is obligated as a matter of professional ethics to provide free access to literature representing all shades of opinion, propagandist or not."

Clyde, William M. *The Struggle for the Freedom of the Press from Caxton to Cromwell.* London, Oxford University Press, 1934. 360 p. (St. Andrews University Publications, no. 37) **C 399**

A study of the freedom of the press in Great Britain from the first printing (1476) through the period of the Protectorate (1658). It includes the beginning of licensing, the action of the Star Chamber, the protests of Milton and others against licensing, the revolt of the licensers, the suppression of newsbooks, and the action of the Levellers in behalf of a free press. This work is followed, chronologically, by Hanson's *Government and the Press, 1695–1763* and Rea's *The English Press in Politics, 1760–1774.* Siebert's *Freedom of the Press in England, 1476–1776,* covers the combined period as does Gillett's *Burned Books.* The latter emphasizes the works rather than the events. These four works are continued, chronologically, by Wickwar's *Struggle for Freedom of the Press, 1819–1832,* and Aspinall's *Politics and Press, 1780–1850.*

Coase, R. H. *British Broadcasting; a Study in Monopoly.* Cambridge, Harvard University Press, 1950. 206 p. (Published for the London School of Economics and Political Science) **C 400**

An historical study of the monopolistic organization of broadcasting in Great Britain—how the monopoly came into existence, its effect on the development of competitive services, and views held pro and con on the subject of the monopoly.

Coatman, John. "The B.B.C., Government and Politics." *Public Opinion Quarterly*, 15:287–98, Summer 1951. **C 401**

"Mr. Coatman describes the development of broadcasting policy in Great Britain, particularly as regards controversial and political issues, and concludes that the role of the Government in the shaping of this policy has been and must be dominant."

Cobb, Frank I. "Press and Public Opinion." *New Republic*, 22:144–47, 31 December 1919. **C 402**

An editorial writer on the New York *World* opposes censorship as a method of combating foreign ideologies.

———. *Public Opinion.* Washington, D.C., Govt. Print. Off., 1920. 12 p. (S. doc. 175, 66th Cong., 2d sess.; also in *LaFollette's Magazine*, January 1920) **C 403**

In an address before the Women's City Club of New York on 11 December 1919, Cobb urges the repeal of wartime restrictions on the free play of public opinion. "I am not afraid of bolshevism in the open, where the American people can examine it and weight it and consider it . . . There is no surer way to give those doctrines a foothold than to proscribe them." Newspapers must fight the rising tide of Prussianism in the form of censorship and government propaganda.

[Cobbett, William]. *The Democratic Judge: or the Equal Liberty of the Press, As Exhibited, Explained, and Exposed, In the Prosecution of William Cobbett, For a pretended Libel against The King of Spain and his Ambassador, before Thomas McKean, Chief Justice of the State of Pennsylvania. By Peter Porcupine.* Philadelphia, 1798. 102 p. (Appears also in vol. 7 of *Porcupine's Works,* 1801) **C 404**

A savage attack on Chief Justice McKean, a powerful Democrat, whom Cobbett called a "wife-beater," "drunkard," "judicial murderer," etc. Commenting on Judge McKean's statement that the liberty of the press is "a phrase much used but little understood," Cobbett remarks: "Had the judge called the liberty of the press a thing much talked about, much boasted of, and *very little enjoyed,* I would most readily have subscribed to his assertion; for, of all the countries under the Sun, where unlicensed presses are tolerated, I am bold to declare and the contents of this pamphlet will establish the truth of my declaration, that none ever enjoyed less *real* liberty of the press than America has for some years past." Abridgment of the freedom of the press has come from "popular prejudice, by the influence of the party, the fear of mobish violence, or of government tyranny."

[———]. *A Full and Accurate Report of the Trial of William Cobbett, Esq. (Before Lord Tenterden and a Special Jury), on Thursday, July 7, 1831, in the Court of King's Bench, Guildhall.* London, W. Strange, 1831. 45 p. (Also in Macdonell, *Reports of State Trials,* n.s., vol. 2, pp. 789–904) **C 405**

Cobbett had been sympathetic with the revolt of the agricultural laborers in his *Political Register* of 11 December 1830, and it was for these sentiments that he was brought to trial. Cobbett, then aged 68, delivered an eloquent defense in his own behalf. The jury, despite a plea from the judge, failed to reach a verdict and Cobbett was released. Richard Carlile, who had been more outspoken in behalf of the same revolt, was sentenced to two years. This report of the Cobbett defense was distributed throughout England.

[————]. *A Report of an Action for a Libel, Brought by Dr. Benjamin Rush, against William Cobbett, in the Supreme Court of Pennsylvania, December term, 1799, for Certain Defamatory Publications in a Newspaper Entitled Porcupine's Gazette, of which the Said William Cobbett Was Editor.* Philadelphia, Printed by W. W. Woodward, 1800. 70 p.　　　　**C 406**
Cobbett made an abusive attack on the Philadelphia physician, Benjamin Rush, for the medical advice the doctor had given in the yellow fever epidemic of 1793. After a long delay in bringing the case to trial, the Court awarded Dr. Rush a verdict of $5,000. To meet this Cobbett was forced to sell his Philadelphia property.

[————]. "Trial for a Libel Published in *Cobbett's Weekly Political Register.*" In Borrow, *Celebrated Trials*, vol. 6, pp. 56–68. (Also in Birkenhead, *Famous Trials*, vol. 2, pp. 253–62)　　　**C 407**
In 1810 Cobbett was brought to trial before the unsympathetic Lord Ellenborough, accused of sedition for articles appearing in his *Political Register*. He insisted in pleading his own case, which he did very poorly because of his lack of legal training, and was convicted. There was a long delay in sentencing during which it is believed Cobbett tried to negotiate with the government, even to the point of giving up his *Register*. This fell through and he was sentenced to two years in Newgate Prison. He continued to edit his *Register* from prison, but his financial situation forced him to sell his *Debates, Parliamentary History*, and *State Trials* to his printer, Hansard, who continued them.

[————]. "Trial for Libels upon Lord Hardwicke and Other High Officers of Ireland, 1804." In Howell, *State Trials*, vol. 29, pp. 1 ff.　　　**C 408**
Cobbett was fined for publishing criticism of the administration of Ireland in his *Political Register*.

————. *Trial of Republicanism; or, A Series of Political Papers, Proving the Injurious and Debasing Consequences of Republican Government and Written Constitutions; with an Introductory Address to the Hon. Thomas Erskine, Esq.* London, Cobbett and Morgan, 1801. 63 p.　　　　**C 409**
Various references to freedom of the press in America.

[————]. "Trial of William Cobbett for Libel, Philadelphia, 1797." In *American State Trials*, vol. 6, pp. 675–86, and Wharton, *State Trials*, pp. 322–32.　**C 410**
This English journalist, in exile in the United States, directed abusive criticism against the King of Spain in his *Porcupine Gazette*. At the request of the Spanish Minister he was brought to trial before Chief Justice McKean of the Pennsylvania Supreme Court. McKean, after a statement on the law of libel as it was directed against irresponsible and scurrilous personal invective, assumed the role of prosecutor, and in so doing is believed to have libeled the prisoner. The Grand Jury refused to return an indictment.

Cobbett's Weekly Political Register. London. Vols. 1–89, 1802–35. Title varies. Suspended April–June 1817, June–July 1819.
　　　　C 411
This political journal, edited by the violent and sarcastic William Cobbett, carried articles that led to his various arrests for libel. It also reported on the prosecution of libel cases in the English courts, his own and others. During Cobbett's imprisonment for libel (1810–12) he continued to edit the *Register*, which carried his letters from Newgate Prison, some of which discussed the issues of seditious libel and freedom of the press. The supplement to vol. 8 of *Niles Political Register*, 26 August 1815, reproduces several of Cobbett's letters relating to freedom of the press.

Cockburn, Henry C. *An Examination of the Trials for Sedition Which Have Hitherto Occurred in Scotland.* Edinburgh, David Douglas, 1888. 2 vols.　　　**C 412**
A critical study of legal aspects of the infamous sedition trials that took place in Scotland, principally in 1793 and 1794, growing out of the hysteria that swept the country with the events of the French Revolution. The author was a prominent British jurist, but not to be confused with Lord Chief Justice Alexander Cockburn who formulated the famous test for obscenity. This work includes commentary on the cases of William Callender, Walter Berry, James Robertson, Thomas Muir, Thomas F. Palmer, Joseph Gerrald, and others.

Cocks, O. G. "Applying Standards to Films; Voluntary Censorship in England." *Survey*, 32:337–38, 27 June 1914.　　**C 413**

Codding, George A., Jr. *Broadcasting without Barriers.* Paris, United Nations Educational, Scientific and Cultural Organization, 1959. 167 p.　　　**C 414**
"The task undertaken in this study is threefold: to determine the extent to which broadcasting has been made available to the world's peoples; to define the obstacles—political, economic and technical—which impede its full and proper use as a medium of communication; and to examine possible ways and means of extending its benefits more widely." A section on freedom to listen deals with problems concerning the right of persons to listen to broadcasting from another country, the type of program which should or should not be broadcast to the people of another country, and the right of a country to stop, by jamming, programs from other countries.

Coggeshall, Reginald. "Was There Censorship at the Paris Peace Conference?" *Journalism Quarterly*, 16:125–35, June 1939.
　　　　C 415

Coghlan, Ralph. "Contempt Citations against Newspapers." In *Problems of Journalism; Proceedings of the American Society of Newspaper Editors, 1940.* Washington, D.C., ASNE, 1940, pp. 158–67.
　　　　C 416
Based largely on the writer's experience on the St. Louis *Post-Dispatch*.

Cogley, John. "How Much Discussion, How Free?" *Commonweal*, 66:182, 17 May 1957.　　　**C 417**
The Columbia Broadcasting System would not broadcast the talk prepared for the Church of the Air by Father Thurston Davis because it touched on the controversial areas of birth control, censorship, and parochial schools.

————. *Report on Blacklisting.* New York, Meridian, 1956. 2 vols.　　**C 418**
Study of blacklisting in the movies (vol. 1) and television (vol. 2). Sponsored by The Fund for the Republic.

————. "The Rutgers Affair." *Commonweal*, 53:329–30, 5 January 1951.　**C 419**
The publication of a short story in Rutgers University *Antho*, which was essentially the case history of an abortion, brought mass pressures and charges of blasphemy from the Knights of Columbus and the Catholic War Veterans. The author quotes the passage labeled as blasphemous which had been lifted from context and misread to be so labeled. He says "the man or group who takes on the obligations of the censor, more especially who assumes the burden of defending God, the Church and religion in general, should be eminently thoughtful, responsible and sure. This is not the kind of cause that is served by bluster, mere vehemence, prejudice or hasty judgment."

Cohen, Chapman. "L[ondon] C[ounty] C[ouncil] and Freedom of Propaganda." *Freethinker*, 39:379–80, 3 August 1919.
　　　　C 420

The article deals with prohibiting the sale of free-thought and Socialist papers in London public parks.

Cohen, Gerda L. "Obscenity at London Airport." *Twentieh Century*, 163:256–59, March 1958.   **C 421**

A personal experience with the British Customs which confiscated a book the author had been reading. Investigation revealed it was on a list open to the public. The conflict between the Customs and the Olympia Press, Paris, is also revealed in an interview with the director of the press.

Cohen, Steven I. "Wisconsin Provides Civil Action against a Book." *Wisconsin Law Review*, 1960:309–24, March 1960.   **C 422**

A discussion of the recent Wisconsin obscenity act and the Massachusetts statute on which it was based. "The Massachusetts statute has been in effect since 1945 and the Massachusetts court has never doubted its constitutionality."

Cohn, Marcus. "Religion and the FCC." *Reporter*, 32(1):32–34, 14 January 1965.   **C 423**

While the U.S. Supreme court has been gradually strengthening Jefferson's concept of the separation between church and state, the FCC has been doing the opposite by labeling religious broadcasts as being in the public interest.

Cohn, Morris E. "The Censorship of Radical Materials by the Post Office." *St. Louis Law Review*, 17:95–119, February 1932.   **C 424**

Congressional action to deny the use of the mails by refusal to grant a second-class mailing permit is held to be a violation of the First Amendment.

Cokinos, George. "The School Librarian, Censor of Books." *Maryland Libraries*, 29: 13–14, 25, Fall 1962.   **C 425**

"The salvation lies in our recruitment of individuals who are flexible, who can adapt to varied situations, who are well read in all fields or at least have varied interests aside from books." The author discusses the special problems faced by school librarians who operate as part of regulated and controlled systems and are often caught in the conflict between teachers who recommend controversial material and students who feel everything should be available to them and, on the other hand, school administrators who are more restrained in their views and sensitive to outside pressures.

Colburn, John C. *The Press and an Informed Electorate.* Tucson, Ariz., University of Arizona Press, 1963. 12 p. (The John Peter Zenger Award for Freedom of the Press, no. 9)   **C 426**

An address by the 1962 recipient of the award, the managing editor of the Richmond (Va.) *Times Dispatch,* "representative of what is best in today's journalism and in its fight for the people's right to know."

Colden, Cadwallader. *History of William Cosby's Administration as Governor of the Province of New York, and of Lieutenant-Governor George Clarke's Administration through 1737.* Albany, New York Historical Society, 1935, pp. 326–39. (Collections, 68)   **C 427**

Contains a lengthy contemporary account of the John Peter Zenger trial, drawn largely from the *Brief Narrative,* believed to have been written by Andrew Hamilton.

Cole, G. D. H. *The Life of William Cobbett...* London, Collins, 1927. 455 p.   **C 428**

This biography of one of England's most formidable pamphleteers, political journalists, and social reformers, was written by an English economist and social hostorian. During a long life of intensive and violent political controversy, Cobbett was often involved in attempts by government authorities to suppress his writings, in England as well as in America where he spent a self-imposed exile. Cobbett's attack on the reputation of the Spanish king in the *Porcupine Gazette* led to his arrest in Philadelphia (1797); two years later he was convicted in Philadelphia for libeling Dr. Benjamin Rush. In 1804, having returned to England, Cobbett was fined by authorities for libeling the Irish administration; in 1810 he was sentenced to two years in a London prison for seditious articles in his famous *Political Register;* and in 1831 he pled his own case successfully in another sedition trial. Cobbett started his career in critical and often abusive journalism as a Tory, but later turned radical. A full account of his prolific publishing is recorded in a biobibliography by L. P. Pearl.

———. *Richard Carlile, 1790–1843.* London, Gollancz, 1943. 37 p. (Fabian Society Bibliographical Series, no. 13)   **C 429**

A brief but comprehensive sketch of the English radical who devoted the greater part of his short life to a crusade for a free press.

Cole, Marley. *Jehovah's Witnesses; the New World Society.* New York, Vantage, [1955]. 229 p.   **C 430**

Chapter 7, Defending and Legally Establishing the Good News, deals with the Jehovah's Witnesses' battle for freedom of speech, press, and worship through the courts of the United States, Canada, and in 22 other countires. The Appendix contains summaries of the decisions, including 46 cases in the U.S. Supreme Court.

Colegrove, Albert M. "Attitudes toward Crime News." *National Probation and Parole Journal,* 4:313–19, October 1958.   **C 431**

[Coleman, Edward]. *The Trial of Edward Coleman, gent. for Conspiring the death of the King etc.* London, Printed for R. Pawlet, 1678. (Also in Howell, *State Trials,* vol. 1, p. 7)   **C 432**

A Catholic news writer, executed for treason, was one of the first victims of Titus Oates's testimony in the "popish plot."

Coleman, Peter. *Obscenity, Blasphemy, Sedition: Censorship in Australia.* Brisbane, Jacaranda Press, 1962. 196 p.   **C 433**

The history of literary censorship in Australia from the first Obscenity Acts of the 1880's to the present day when the crusade against government censorship is almost over. "The *dramatis personae* are church groups, women's groups, moralists, booksellers, publishers, freethinkers, revolutionaries, journalists, pornographers, sex-reformers, muck-rakers, religious bigots, race cranks, politicians, lawyers, judges, magistrates, customs officers, postal officials and policemen." A serious study written in a light ironical style.

Coleman, William. *A Faithful Report of the Trial of the Cause of Philip I. Arcularius, and William Coleman, gent. etc. being an Action for a Libel, Held at the Sittings before His Honor Judge Livingston, on the Third of January, 1807 . . . Taken by Mr. Sampson . . .* New York, Bernard Dornin, 1807. 62 p.   **C 434**

A suit for an alleged libel published in the *New York Evening Post.* Coleman, who was a militant Federalist editor and friend of Hamilton, made frequent and scurrilous attacks on the Republicans in his paper.

Coleridge, John Duke Coleridge, *1st baron. Law of Blasphemous Libel: the Summing up in the Case of Regina v. Foote and Others; Revised and with a Preface by the Lord Chief Justice of England.* London, Stevens, 1883. 32 p.   **C 435**

George W. Foote, editor of the *Freethinker,* was sentenced to one year in prison for blasphemous libel, in a case heard by Judge Coleridge. Foote published his own three-hour defense in a pamphlet, *Defence of Free Speech,* in which he praised the fairness of Lord Coleridge's handling of the trial.

Coleridge, Samuel T. "Duty of the Communication of Truth . . ." In his *The Friend; a Series of Essays . . .* London, Edward Moxon, 1863, pp. 30–103. (First published as a collected edition in 1818)   **C 436**

Essays 5 through 13 deal with the duty to communicate the truth, and the conditions under which it may be safely communicated. Includes relationship between an individual and his conscience, between the publisher and the state, the law of libel, despotism and insecurity without a free press, and the "only solution of the difficulties of the law of libel compatible with a free press: toleration and tolerance."

A Collection of Scarce and Interesting Tracts. London, John Almon, 1788. 6 vols.

C 437

Printer Almon has brought together numerous contemporary political tracts, including those for and against prosecutions for seditious libel, general warrants, and seizure of papers. This collection includes Lord Somers' treatise on grand juries, the accounts of the libel trials of Zenger and Owen, and the Candor and Father of Candor letters which previously had been published separately. Over a period of years Almon issued various editions of collected tracts, bearing different titles and with varying contents.

A Collection of Scarce and Interesting Tracts Written by Persons of Eminence; upon the Most Important, Political and Commercial Subjects, during the Years 1763 . . . [to] 1770 . . . London, Printed for J. Debrett, 1787–88. 4 vols.

C 438

Volume 1 includes Charles Townshend, *A Defence of the Minority in the House of Commons, on the Question Relating to General Warrants;* Charles Lloyd, *A Defence of the Majority . . .,* and *A Letter concerning Libels, Warrants, the Seizure of Papers.* Volume 3 includes George Grenville, *Speech . . . on the Motion for Expelling Mr. Wilkes, Mr. Wilke's Letter to Mr. Grenville in Answer to his Speech,* and *A Letter on the Public Conduct of Mr. Wilkes.* Volume 4 includes *Another Letter to Mr. Almon, In Matter of Libel, Substance of the Pleadings of the Crown Lawyer and of Mr. Woodfall's Counsel* [trial of Henry S. Woodfall, 3 July 1770], *Postscript and A Second Postscript to a Late Pamphlet, entitled, a Letter to Mr. Almon, in Matter of Libel,* and Philelutherus Anglicanus, *A Summary of the Law of Libel.*

Collection of the Most Interesting Letters on the Government, Liberty, and Constitution of England, Which Have Appeared in the Public Papers, from the Time that Lord Bute Was Appointed First Lord of the Treasury, to the Death of the Earl of Egremont . . . London, [Almon?], n.d. 3 vols.

C 439

"In these volumes are contained all the authentic papers relative to the *North Briton* and the case of Mr. Wilkes; examined with the originals."

Colledge, Stephen. *The Arraignment, Tryal and Condemnation of Stephen Colledge for High-Treason, in Conspiring the Death of the King, the Levying of War, and the Subversion*

of the Government. Before the Right Honourable Sr. Francis North, Lord Chief Justice of the Court of Common Pleas, and other Commissioners of Oyer and Terminer . . . the 17th and 18th of August 1681. London, Printed for Thomas Basset and John Fish, 1681. 102 p. (Also in Howell, *State Trials,* vol. 8, pp. 549–746)

C 440

Colledge (or College) was a fanatical antipapist, whose coarse verse and "scandalous" pamphlets contributed to his arrest and trial for sedition. He was also accused of threatening the king and of riding armed to Oxford where Parliament was in session. Colledge was found guilty, executed, drawn, and quartered.

Collet, Collet Dobson. *History of the Taxes on Knowledge: Their Origin and Repeal.* Introduction by George Jacob Holyoake. London, Unwin, 1899. 2 vols. (Reprinted in 1933 in the *Thinker's Library,* no. 33)

C 441

In 1712 the first newspaper tax was enacted in England, which provided the government with a device that replaced the licensing system as a potential means of censorship. This is the story of the 157-year crusade to abolish these "taxes on knowledge," which ended with the repeal of the last such tax in 1869. The author was himself active in the movement.

Collier, Arthur. "Two Purity Societies." *Adult,* 2:207–9, August 1898.

C 442

The author praises the work of the National Vigilance Association and its executive, W. A. Coote, for the society's attack on sex ignorance. He criticizes the National Association for the Abolition of State Regulation of Vice, as an agency based on childish ignorance of the nature of prostitution and sexual tyranny.

Collier, Jeremy. *A Defence of the Short View of the Profaneness and Immorality of the English Stage, etc.; Being a Reply to Mr.* [William] *Congreve's Amendments, etc., and to the Vindication of the Author of the Relapse,* [Sir J. Vanbrugh]. London, Keble, Sare & Hindmarsh, 1699. 139 p.

C 443

Congreve and Vanbrugh answered Collier's attack (*A Short View,* etc.) on them and their plays. Collier followed with this work and a *Second Defense . . .,* the latter in answer to James Drake's *The Ancient and Modern Stages Surveyed.*

———. *A Short View of the Immorality and Profaneness of the English Stage, together with the Sense of Antiquity upon this Argument.* London, Keble, Sare & Strahan, 1698. 288 p.

C 444

This devastating criticism of the English theater had an important influence on the establishment of a permanent system of stage censorship in Great Britain. Collier, a nonjuring clergyman with a literary bent, attacked dramatists and their plays by name, citing

incidents of vulgarity. King William was sympathetic with Collier's efforts at reform and used his actual words in admonishing the Master of Revels to take a firmer hand in the licensing of plays.

Collier, John. "Anthony Comstock— Liberal." *Survey,* 35:127–30, 6 November 1915.

C 445

A favorable appraisal of the work of the vice crusader, written on the occasion of Comstock's death.

———. "Censorship; and the National Board," *Survey,* 35:9–14+, 2 October 1915.

C 446

A discussion of the National Board of Censorship of Motion Pictures, the conditions leading to its creation and an analysis of its work. The author concludes: "Censorship is impracticable and dangerous because the means involved are too crude for the ends sought; are indeed largely unrelated to the ends sought; and because the indirect damage of censorship infinitely exceeds the direct good which may be accomplished."

———. "Censorship in Action." *Survey,* 34:423–27, 7 August 1915.

C 447

The author, cofounder in 1909 of the National Board of Censorship of Motion Pictures (a voluntary agency), traces the growth of film censorship in the United States from the first city censorship board (Chicago, 1907) and the first state censorship board (Pennsylvania, 1909) to the recent (1915) Supreme Court decision upholding motion picture censorship. He favors voluntary censorship and is sharply critical of much of the legal censorship of city and state boards which he finds unenlightened, irresponsible, pathetic, and harmful to the serious development of the movie art.

———. "Film Shows and Lawmakers." *Survey,* 29:643–44, 8 February 1913.

C 448

A protest concerning the delay by the New York Board of Aldermen in enacting the ordinance framed by the Mayor's Committee on Moving Pictures.

———. "The Learned Judges and the Films." *Survey,* 34:513–16, 4 September 1915.

C 449

A criticism of the U.S. Supreme Court ruling that precensorship of films is legal. The Court had the option of deciding whether the framers of the Constitution intended to secure the freedom of political, economic, and religious discussions in whatever form, or merely sought to protect newspapers, books, and public utterances. In choosing the limiting second option the court "ignored the voluminous evidence . . . that the motion picture theater had already become . . . an important form of press, of publication and of speech directed toward religious, economic and political subjects." The author, an advocate of voluntary censorship of films, fears for the future in the extension of legal censorship.

———. "'Movies' and the Law." *Survey*, 27:1628–29, 20 January 1912. **C 450**
A member of the Committee on Moving Pictures appointed by New York Mayor Gaynor reports on the main points of interest in the proposed ordinance which was framed by the Committee and presented to the New York Board of Aldermen.

Collins, Anthony. *Discourse of Free-thinking, Occasion'd by the Use and Growth of a Sect Call'd Free-thinkers.* London, 1713. 140p. **C 451**
An argument for the necessity and expediency of rational thinking and intellectual freedom, especially on subjects of religion. His work, which set forth the position of the deists, was widely criticized by theologians and satirized by Jonathan Swift. It was placed on the Roman *Index* in 1715.

[———]. *A Discourse of the Grounds and Reasons of the Christian Religion . . . To which is prefix'd an Apology for free debate and liberty of writing . . .* London, 1724. 62p., 285p. **C 452**
This disciple of John Locke maintained that all belief must be based on free inquiry. In a preface to the *Discourse*, Collins defends the liberty of writing of the man (William Whiston) whose essay on the Old and New Testaments he is criticizing in the text. Collins argues that every man has a "natural right" to think and judge for himself, to freely profess and publish his opinions and attempt to convince others of their truth. An attempt to suppress opinions that are different from one's own only sheds doubt on the opinions of the suppressor. Clergymen especially should have full liberty to inquire after truth and teach what they believe. "Men have no reason to apprehend an ill consequence to truth from free debate; but on the contrary to apprehend ill consequence from free debate disallow'd." True debate will lessen the number of controversies, contribute to knowledge and the arts, and lead to a solid and lasting peace. Thomas Cooper, in his *Treatise on the Law of Libel and the Liberty of the Press*, 1830, acknowledges the influence of Collins.

Collins, Blanche. "Ordeal at Long Beach." *Library Journal*, 90:2486–90+, 1 June 1965. **C 453**
The librarian of the Long Beach, Calif., Public Library reports on the long fight of that library against censorship pressures of the radical right. First, there was the campaign to remove Kazantzakis' *The Last Temptation of Christ* from the shelves. More recently charges were made by the Education Society of Long Beach, resulting in a five-hour public hearing

before the City Council, that the library was excluding "books and periodicals which present points of view which may be described as pro-American and anti-Communist." The library staff cooperated with its critics by patiently checking long lists of books and providing other information requested. The Long Beach episodes, the author points out, are part of "a pattern in this war on public libraries which goes back several years and extends throughout our country. We have had access to the John Birch Society *Bulletin* and find in it material which ties in with all of this . . . I have realized that we must fight the issue on a broad scale and not get caught fighting the little fight on the little branch of the tree." She writes with appreciation for the support of the city manager, the library staff, the local newspaper, and many community leaders.

Collins, J. P. "Cult of the Hyena." *Nineteenth Century*, 123:535–49, May 1938. **C 454**
A barbed criticism of the popular press, likened to the hyena for its subbestial behavior, its interest in carrion and garbage, and its intrusion into the private lives of the people. The press faces public clamor for restrictions unless it changes its way.

[Collins, John]. "Trial of John Collins before Littledale, J., and a common jury, at the Warwick Summer Assizes, on August 5, 1839, for publishing a seditious libel." In Macdonell, *Reports of State Trials*, vol. 4, pp. 1149–76. **C 455**

Collins, LeRoy. *Remarks by LeRoy Collins, President, National Association of Broadcasters to Conference on Freedom and Responsibility in Broadcasting, at Northwestern University School of Law, Chicago, Ill., August 3, 1961.* Washington, D.C., The National Association of Broadcasters, 1961. 6p. **C 456**

Collins, Robert H. "Books Defaced with Stickers of Minutemen." *St. Louis Post-Dispatch*, 27 September 1964. p. 10A. **C 457**
Stickers bearing the words "A Gun Did Not Kill Kennedy—A Communist Did" and the identification "Minutemen, Norborne, Mo.," were pasted on the title pages of numerous books in a St. Louis bookstore, concentrated largely on books about the late President. Several months earlier books in the Washington University library were similarly defaced with anti-Communist slogans.

Collins, Seward. "Chronicle and Comment; Censorship." *Bookman*, 70:648–56, February 1930. **C 458**
Collins takes issue with William Allan Neilson and Edward Weeks over their recent articles in the *Atlantic Monthly* opposing censorship.

Censorship, he argues, is needed to prevent corruption of the reader. He favors enforcing censorship laws through the cooperative efforts of two groups—the prosecuting agency and a judicial agency such as the Watch and Ward Society, made up of churchmen and educators.

Collison, R. L. W. "The [Book Selection] Problem—A British View." In *Freedom of Communication; Proceedings of the First Conference on Intellectual Freedom . . .* Chicago, American Library Association, 1954, pp. 55–62. **C 459**

———. "Books Are Not for Burning." *Assistant Librarian*, 49:35–37, March 1956. **C 460**
A review of the second edition of Anne Lyon Haight's *Banned Books* and Rubinstein and Farley's catalog of a University of Kansas exhibit on censorship. In the December 1956 issue of *Assistant Librarian* the author comments on certain criticisms of Mrs. Haight's work (references to East Germany), observing that censorship may take subtle as well as overt form.

———. "The Fight for Freedom." *Library Assistant*, 45:3, 35–38, March 1952; 45:133–34, November 1952. **C 461**
A discussion of the activities of the American Library Association's Committee on Intellectual Freedom and the conference held in June 1952 to discuss attacks on library book selection policies by individuals and pressure groups.

———. "What Is Censorship?" *Assistant Librarian*, 49:191–93, December 1956. **C 462**

Colorado. Legislative Council. *Comic Books: Related Matters and Problems; Report to the General Assembly.* Denver, The Council, 1956. (Research Publication no. 19) **C 463**

Colson, John. "Municipal Administration and the Freedom to Read." *Wisconsin Library Bulletin*, 60:175–78, May–June 1964. **C 464**

[Colton, Calvin]. *Abolition a Sedition. By a Northern Man.* Philadelphia, G. W. Donahue, 1839. 187p. **C 465**
Antiabolitionist sentiment as applied to press regulations.

Columbus, *pseud. Letter to a Member of Congress; Respecting the Alien and Sedition Laws . . .* [n.p. 1799]. 48p. **C 466**

Combe, Abram. *An Address to the Conductors of the Periodical Press, upon the Causes of Religious and Political Disputes, with Remarks on the Local and General Definition of Certain Words and Terms which have been often the Subject of Controversy.* Edinburgh, Printed by James Auchie, 1823. 48 p.   **C 467**

The writer claims that much of the distress in the world is caused by ignorance, and that the periodical press has a responsibility to give full and accurate information on all sides of a controversy, that truth may be perceived. Much of the pamphlet is devoted to a study of different meanings given to terms used in controversial literature of the time, and the writer uses a work of William Cobbett for this study of the semantics of politics.

Combe, George. *Suppressed Documents; or, An Appeal to the Public against the Conductors of the Scottish Guardian.* Glasgow, J. McLeod, 1836. 14 p.   **C 468**

Come, Arnold B. "The Christian and Censorship: Some General Principles." *Issue*, 1(1):9–11, Winter 1963.   **C 469**

A theology professor opposes civil censorship as contrary to Christian doctrine, which exaults freedom of the human spirit. Resistance to evil thought should be the responsibility of the church, the home, and the school, rather than the law and government. Abuses to freedom of the press should be met largely through appeal to conscience and public opinion. "The abuses of the freedom of thought and expression are finally controlled and adequately dealt with only by that thought and expression that opposes error with truth." Dr. Come was witness for the defense in the Marin County *Tropic of Cancer* trial.

Comfort, Alex. "Social Aspects of Censorship & Pornography." *Now*, 8:11–14, May–June 1947.   **C 470**

In a power society censorship has operated against three main threats to itself—criticism of power, criticism of religion, and open discussion of sexual matters—"the last in part because rulers have always had a hardly-conscious conviction that sexual freedom was in some way related to political liberty, and in part because of the need to appear as the upholders of a morality increasingly based upon fear . . . Censorship by power against sedition and heresy is easy to understand, but the censorship of genuine pornography is illogical—pornography tends to stabilize an ill-adapted society, rather as prostitution does . . . The most serious feature of the history of pornography is its progressive deviation away from mere sexual ribaldry toward more and more abnormal outlets." Present-day pornography has ceased to be bawdy and has become brutal and scabrous.

"Comic Books and Children: a Radio Script." *Illinois Libraries*, 37:43–46, February 1955; 37:98–102, March 1955.   **C 471**

A critique of Frederic Wertham's book, *Seduction of the Innocent*, an indictment of horror comics, conducted by a panel of teachers and librarians.

["'Comics' and 'Obscene Publications'"]. *Bookseller*, 2551:1646–50, 13 November 1954.   **C 472**

Calls for reform of the obscenity law in England which puts legitimate publishers "under the shadow of Old Bailey." It is hypocritical to condemn books as unfit for children that are not intended to be read by children and at the same time claim that horror comics written for children are not "technically" obscene.

"The Comics: Do They Or Don't They?" *Juvenile Delinquency Digest*, 1(2):1–4, March 1955.   **C 473**

Comics Magazine Association of America. *Facts About Code-Approved Comic Magazines.* New York, The Association, 1963. 32 p. (The Code is reprinted in McNickle, *Policing the Comics*)   **C 474**

"Included is a description of how the Code Authority operates, a brief background of the comics magazine industry and of the C.M.A.A., an analysis of the content of Code-approved comics, their educational as well as entertainment values, documentary material on the efficacy and public approval of the self-regulation program, and the complete text of the Code."

Commager, Henry S. "The Blasphemy of Abner Kneeland." *New England Quarterly*, 8:29–44, March 1935.   **C 475**

Kneeland was the freethinking editor of *Investigator*, who had defied Boston authorities in 1833 by publishing the second edition of Dr. Charles Knowlton's birth control book, *Fruits of Philosophy*. In the following year he was brought to trial on a blasphemy charge for irreverently ridiculing the doctrine of prayer and the miracles, and denying the divinity of Christ. The case dragged through the courts for 4 years and inspired numerous sermons, articles, and pamphlets. Kneeland was found guilty in a Boston court and sentenced to 60 days. Despite a petition signed by some of the most illustrious names in Boston, the Supreme Judicial Court of Massachusetts upheld the sentence, thus upholding the constitutionality of the blasphemy statute. Commager writes of the effect of the Kneeland trials: "Society was rocked to its foundation, the pillars of morality and religion tottered, and the commonwealth seemed doomed, but in the end the forces of light triumphed over the powers of darkness, immorality was rebuked, and blasphemy silenced."

———. "A Fighting Printer—and a Free Press." *New York Times Magazine*, 19 April 1953, pp. 13, 63–67.   **C 476**

The story of John Peter Zenger and the role he played in establishing America's freedom of the press. Written on the occasion of the opening of the Zenger Memorial Room in

New York City's Federal Hall, on the site of old City Hall where Zenger was imprisoned, tried, and acquitted.

———. *Freedom, Loyalty, Dissent.* New York, Oxford University Press, 1954. 155 p.   **C 477**

"The great danger that threatens us is neither heterodox thought nor orthodox thought, but the absence of thought." In his essay on Free Enterprise in Ideas, Commager presents a vigorous case for freedom of speech and press. This essay is reprinted in Downs, *The First Freedom*, pp. 230–35.

———. "Jefferson and the Book-Burners." *American Heritage*, 9(5):65–68, August 1958.   **C 478**

"When he offered Congress his library, his foes charged that it was full of books which 'never ought to be read' and probably ought to be burned." An account of the action of Congress, with quotes from various sources, in approving the payment to Jefferson of $23,900 for his library of about 6,000 volumes. Quotations from *Niles Register*, 1814–15, vol. 7, Supp., pp. 63–65.

———. "The Problem of Dissent." *Saturday Review*, 47(51):21–23, 81, 18 December 1965.   **C 479**

Commager defends the right of criticism of American government policies on Vietnam, citing precedent in American history. If government officials "can silence criticism by the argument that such criticism might be misunderstood somewhere, then there is an end to all criticism, and perhaps an end to our kind of political system. . . . We do not need to fear ideas, but the censorship of ideas. We do not need to fear criticism, but the silencing of criticism. We do not need to fear excitement or agitation in the academic community, but timidity and apathy."

———. "The Right of Dissent." *Current History*, 29:197–203, October 1955. **C 480**

The editors of *Current History* had referred to the "almost tragic conflict between the need for security and the democratic idea of liberty and justice." Commager disagrees with this viewpoint and feels that security and freedom are interdependent as are freedom and democracy.

"A Commentary." *Criterion*, 8:185–88, December 1928.   **C 481**

A comparison of censorship in Ireland and Boston.

"Comments on the New York Textbook Censorship." *New Yorker*, 25:19, 9 October 1949.   **C 482**

Satirical comments on a New York Board of Education pamphlet setting up 23 criteria for selecting textbooks and library books for use in the public schools. Three criteria, selected for special barbs, are the requirement that materials selected must be "free from subject matter that tends to irreverence for things held sacred," that materials must present both sides of a controversial issue with fairness, and must be free of objectionable slang expressions. "Irreverence for things held sacred has started many a writer on his way, and will again . . . the Board should strive for a well-balanced library, not a well-balanced book."

The Commission on Freedom of the Press. *A Free and Responsible Press; a General Report on Mass Communications: Newspapers, Radio, Motion Pictures, Magazines, and Books.* Chicago, University of Chicago Press, 1947. 138 p. **C 483**
A general summary of the findings of the Commission, composed of a group of scholars, headed by Robert M. Hutchins. The study of mass communications "deals with the responsibilities of the owners and managers of the press to their conscience and the common good for the formation of public opinion." The Commission found that although the mass media had increased in importance and influence, the number of persons who were able to express their ideas through it had decreased. The Bill of Rights protects the press and other media from government but not from the private interests which control it. The Commission recommends ways in which the press itself, the government, and the public can bring about a more responsible press. It proposes that the government publicize its works and aims when the private media fail to do so; it recommends that the press accept the responsibility of being a common carrier of information and ideas; and that the public be encouraged to augment the commercial press with its own nonprofit press. The Commission recommends that antitrust laws be used sparingly. The following special studies were issued by the Commission: Hocking, *Freedom of the Press: A Framework of Principle;* Chafee, *Government and Mass Communications;* Inglis, *Freedom of the Movies;* White and Leigh, *Peoples Speaking to People,* and White, *The American Radio.* The Library of Congress bibliography, *Freedom of Information,* devotes a section, pp. 75–83, to the report and its critics.

[————]. "Press Reactions to Freedom of the Press Report." *Nieman Reports,* 1(3): 14–20, July 1947. **C 484**
Excerpts from press comments, pro and con.

Committee on Evaluation of Comic Books. *An Evaluated List of Comic Books.* Cincinnati, The Committee, 1951. 4 p. **C 485**
"The Committee . . . with its 75 trained reviewers has evaluated the 423 comic books available. These books are placed in the categories of No Objection, Some Objection, Objectionable, and Very Objectionable. Those in the first two are deemed suitable for use by children and young people." The list also contains Criteria for Evaluating Comic Books, as to (1) cultural area, (2) moral area, and (3) morbid emotionality.

"Communist Propaganda Ban Complicates Postal Bill." *Congressional Quarterly (Weekly Report),* 20:503–5, 30 March 1962. **C 486**
Background and discussion of the debate in Congress over the proposal to direct the Post Office to screen Communist propaganda.

Comstock, Anthony. "The Children of Our Nation and Their Foes." *Light,* 99:17–19, September–October 1914. **C 487**
A brief account of the author's work in the fight against obscene books and pictures.

————. "Combatting the Moral Cancer Planters." *Light,* 53:58–63, January 1907. **C 488**
The secretary of the New York Society for Suppression of Vice reports on censorship of obscene literature in an article written for delivery to the National Purity Conference in Chicago. Comstock was unable to attend.

————. *A Defense of Detective Methods. An Open Letter to Judge Jenkins of Milwaukee, Wis.* New York, 1892. 16 p. (Reprinted from *The Christian at Work*) **C 489**
A defense against public criticism of the entrapment methods used by agents of the New York vice society.

————. "Demoralizing Literature." In *Papers, Addresses . . . First National Purity Congress . . . 1895.* New York, American Purity Alliance, 1896, pp. 418–22. **C 490**
The systematic corruption of youth through demoralizing literature is the first cause of delinquency. (Photograph of Comstock on p. 419.)

————. *Frauds Exposed, or How the People Are Deceived and Robbed, and Youth Corrupted. Being a Full Exposure of various Schemes operated through the Mails and unearthed by the Author in a Seven Years' Service as a Special Agent of the Post Office Department and Secretary and Chief Agent of the New York Society for the Suppression of Vice.* New York, J. Howard Brown, 1880. 576 p. **C 491**
While the work deals largely with the campaign against using the mails for lotteries, bogus schemes, and patent medicines, there are also chapters on Fight Against Obscene Literature, Obscene Publications, Infidelity Wedded to Obscenity, a detailed account of the D. M. Bennett trial, and Comstock's fight with the liberals of the National Defense Association.

————. *Morals, Not Art or Literature v. Laws and Brief.* New York, New York Society for the Suppression of Vice, 1914. 68 p. **C 492**
Contents: Art Indictable If It Tends to Corrupt Morals, Freedom of the Press, Lewd Defined, Test of Obscenity, and Standard Works Indictable.

————. *Morals versus Art.* New York, J. S. Ogilvie, 1888. 39 p. (*The People's Library* vol. 12, no. 406) **C 493**
Having recently attacked the "obscene classics" of Balzac and Boccaccio, Comstock turned to works of pictorial art. In 1887 he made a raid on the New York art gallery of Herman Knoedler, seizing 117 prints of French masterpieces. In this pamphlet Comstock attempts to state his case that art is not above morals; that where the two conflict, morals must prevail. He charges that the youth of the country is endangered by importation of "lewd French art—a foreign foe."

————. *Obscene Publications and Immoral Articles of Mail.* New York, J. S. Ogilvie, 1888. **C 494**

————. "The Suppression of Vice." *North American Review,* 135:484–89, November 1882. **C 495**
Comstock describes the circumstancs surrounding the founding of the New York Society for the Suppression of Vice in 1873. The purpose of the Society is to see that the federal and state laws against obscenity are enforced. Evidence of violation is frequently discovered through advertisements. He describes the Society's methods of trapping the vendor of obscene matter and enumerates some of the successes of the Society in destroying offensive material and securing the arrest and conviction of offenders. In the same issue J. M. Buckley defends the society (pp. 495–501) and O. B. Frothingham states his opposition to vice societies (pp. 489–95).

————. *Traps for the Young.* New York, Funk and Wagnalls, 1883. 253 p. (Reprinted in 1967 by Belknap Press, with introduction by Robert Bremner) **C 496**
The founder of the New York Society for the Suppression of Vice has written this book to expose "the mighty forces for evil that are to-day exerting a controlling influence over the young" in the form of pernicious literature. He specifically warns against the modern novel, the daily and weekly paper with its news of crime and sex, the half-dime novel and story paper, pornography by mail, free-love literature, artistic and classical traps "catering to the animal in man," and infidel and liberal tracts, which "in some respects are worse" than the criminal and obscene. He discusses his fight with liberal groups over the "Comstock" postal laws.

―――. "Vampire Literature." *North American Review*, 153:160–71, August 1891. **C 497**
Comstock reports on his crusade against immoral literature.

―――. "The Work of the New York Society for the Suppression of Vice, and Its Bearings on the Morals of the Young." *Pedagogical Seminary*, 16:403–20, September 1920. **C 498**

―――, *et al.* "Comstock in Cold Type: His Address before the Brooklyn Philosophical Association." *Truth Seeker*, 29(52): 822–24, 27 December 1902. **C 499**
Comstock discusses the controversial Craddock case (Miss Ida Craddock was an eccentric crusader for sex education, who committed suicide rather than face a prison sentence for obscenity). He is followed by opposition speakers E. C. Walker, Henry Rawley, Moncure D. Conway, and Hugh A. Pentecost.

"Comstock as a Psychologist." *Truth Seeker*, 34:179, 23 March 1907. **C 500**
A critical view of the vice crusader.

Conder, George W. *Free Press versus Free Speech: being a reply to strictures in the British Banner of May 17th, in a letter to the editor.* London, William Freeman, 1854. 27p. **C 501**
A Congregational minister from Leeds takes the editor of the Church paper, *British Banner*, to task for, among other things, his interpretation of liberty of the press in the discussion of Church matters. The editor, in a lengthy piece on the liberty of the press, had accused Condor of threatening freedom of the press. The issue of press freedom is not clearly drawn.

Conference on Thought Control in the United States. *Thought Control in U.S.A. Complete Proceedings of the Conference on Thought Control.* Hollywood, Calif., Arts, Sciences & Professional Council, Progressive Citizens of America, 1947. 432p. Edited by Harold J. Salemson. **C 502**
A conference of West Coast scientists, educators, lawyers, doctors, writers, actors, artists, musicians, and other professional people to consider the extent of thought control in their respective fields and report findings to the Conference as a whole. "The conclusions of the reports were of overwhelming unanimity that there is an alarming trend to control the cultural life of the American people in accordance with reactionary conceptions of our national interest." Among the contributions relating specifically to freedom of the press are the following: Toward a Free Press by Charles J. Katz; Thought Control in American Advertising by Joe Weston; Radio in a Free Culture by Reuben Ship; FCC and Freedom of the Air by Milton S. Tyre; The Threat to Freedom (radio) by Sam Moore; The Writer as the Conscience of the People (re: Zola) by Albert Maltz; Medical Care and Thought Control by Medical Division, HASPC; With Whom Is the Alliance Allied? (Motion Picture Alliance for the Preservation of American Ideals) by Carey McWilliams; You Can't Do That (motion pictures) by Adrian Scott; and the Screen Writer and Censorship by Richard Collins.

"Confidentiality of News Sources under the First Amendment." *Stanford Law Review*, 11:541–46, May 1959. **C 503**
Deals with the case of *Garland v. Torre*, 358 U.S. 910 (1958), in which the U.S. Supreme Court reversed the contempt charge against a newspaper correspondent for refusing to name a news source.

"Confused Standards of Literary Censorship." *Literary Digest*, 53:1033–34, 21 October 1916. **C 504**
Criticism of the suppression of Theodore Dreiser's *The Genius* by the New York Society for the Suppression of Vice.

Congressional Digest. [Special Censorship Issue]. 9:33–57, Februrary 1930. **C 505**
A panel discussion, Is Official Censorship of Books Desirable, concerns the issue before Congress as to whether objectionable foreign books should be prohibited by the U.S. Customs. Favoring censorship are Senators Reed Smoot, Frederick H. Gillett, Guy D. Goff, Park Trammell, J. Thomas Heflin, Editor G. W. Ochs-Oakes, Judge John Ford, former Supreme Court Justice Joseph Story, and author Hendrick W. van Loon. Opposing censorship are Senators Bronson Cutting, Millard E. Tydings, Robert M. LaFollette, Jr., and Burton K. Wheeler, Professor Zechariah Chafee, Jr., Alfred Bettman, and William A. Neilson. Articles on censorship in the issue include Freedom of Communication in America by Leon Whipple, Censorship in Early European History by George H. Putnam, and The U.S. Customs Service and Its Censorship of Foreign Publications by Seymour Lowman. There is also a summary of state laws regulating obscene literature. The March 1957 issue of *Censorship Bulletin*, American Book Publishers Council, reprinted a verse by Ogden Nash entitled "Invocation," poking fun at Senator Reed Smoot's proposals to put a tariff ban on improper books. The verse had originally appeared in an issue of the *New Yorker* during the 1930 hearings.

[Congreve, William]. *Amendments of Mr. Collier's False and Imperfect Citations, &c From the Old Batchelour, Double Dealer, Love for Love, Mourning Bride, By the Author of those Plays.* London, Printed for J. Tonson, 1698. 109p. **C 506**
An answer to Jeremy Collier's attacks on the London stage.

Conn, Marshall J. "Constitutional Censorship of Motion Pictures—An Iconoclastic View." *University of Pittsburgh Law Review*, 17:637–59, Summer 1956. **C 507**
The Constitution seems to take sides with "free thinkers," although not on the side of immorality. That problem seems to be left to the jurisdiction of the parent, the teacher, the social worker, or clergyman. "The social order may demand morality, and it is free to attempt to reach its goal so long as it honors the demands of the first and fourteenth amendments."

Connally, Peter R. "Censorship." *Christus Rex*, 13:151–70, July 1959. **C 508**
A discussion of censorship in general, Irish censorship in particular.

Conrad, Joseph. "Censor of Plays." In his *Notes on Life and Letters*. London, Dent, 1921, pp. 76–80. (Appeared originally in the *Daily Mail*, 12 October 1907) **C 509**
An appeal against stage censorship in England as an affront not only to the self-respect of the artist but also to the public. Conrad describes his own contact with the licensing system, which came as a shock. A man who is courageous enough to occupy the post of Censor of Plays in the twentieth century "must be either an extreme megalomaniac or an utterly unconscious being. . . . Is it not time to knock the improper object (censorship) off its shelf?"

―――. *Letters from Conrad, 1895 to 1924. Edited with Introduction and Notes by Edward Garnett.* London, Nonesuch Press, [1928]. 335p. **C 510**
Several letters to Edward Garnett deal with censorship of *The Breaking Point* and reveal Conrad's opposition to censorship: "The institution should be attacked on moral grounds as a cowardly expedient."

"Considerations in Determining the Limitations on State Power to Regulate Motion Picture Content." *Indiana Law Journal*, 30:462–76, Summer 1955. **C 511**

Considerations on the Legality of General Warrants, and the Propriety of a Parliamentary Regulation of the same, [with] *a postscript on a pamphlet concerning Juries, Libels, etc.* 2d ed. London, W. Nicoll, 1765. 50p. **C 512**
Answered in Father of Candor's *A Letter Concerning Libels.*

Constant de Rebecque, Henri B. *On the Liberty of the Press; or An Enquiry How Far Government May Safely Allow the Publication of Political Pamphlets, Essays,*

and Periodical Works. Translated from the French exclusively for the *Pamphleteer.* [London], 1815. 33 p. (*Pamphleteer*, vol. 6, no. 11, pp. 205–38)　　　　**C513**
The author is a disenchanted Bonapartist who became a prominent pamphleteer for civil liberties and government reforms. This pamphlet, widely circulated in France and England, urges France to follow the more liberal policy of England toward freedom of the press.

The Constitution and Censorship. 30 min., b/w movie. New York, Center for Mass Communication, Columbia University. (Decision: The Constitution in Action Series)　　　　**C514**
The issue of "prior restraint" is presented in the case of *Burstyn v. Wilson,* dealing with the ban of *The Miracle* by the New York State film censorship board and in the case of *Cantwell v. Connecticut,* involving a Jehovah's Witnesses minister, arrested for going from door-to-door playing a phonograph record which attacks religious doctrines. The film is documentary in character.

"Constitutional Association." *Edinburgh Review,* 37:110–21, June 1822.　　**C515**
An address to the Earl of Liverpool on the degraded state of the government press and its supporters. The author observes that a period of excessive suppression of the press had been followed by a period of government indifference. Recent censorship cases indicate a revival of severity. The Constitutional Association was established to enforce the law against seditious libel.

[Constitutional Association for Opposing the Progress of Disloyal and Seditious Principles]. "Address, 17 April 1821." In Mence, *Law of Libel,* vol. 1, pp. 186 ff.　　　　**C516**
The Constitutional Association was formed in 1820 by English Tories who wanted a counterpart of the vice society to suppress disloyal and seditious publications. The suppression of licentiousness of the press, the address argued, would, in effect, secure the true liberty of the press, by suppressing the false. A work is criminal, if it makes any private person look ridiculous, and especially if that person is entrusted with the administration of public affairs. The Association, called the "Bridge-Street Gang," survived for only a short time and was generally discredited when prosecutions sponsored by its agents were rejected by the courts. The final discrediting came in the prosecution of a poor book-vendor, David Ridgeway, described in Wickwar's *Struggle for the Freedom of the Press.*

———. *Documents Relating to Libels.* London, Ellerton & Henderson, 1821. 16 p.　　　　**C517**

Constitutional Freedom in Peril. The Jehovah[’s] Witnesses' Case. Winnipeg, Winnipeg Free Press, 1954, 23 p. (Winnipeg Free Press Pamphlet no. 48)　　**C518**
Relates to the decision of the Supreme Court of Canada (6 October 1953) in favor of Jehovah's Witnesses' freedom to distribute printed matter on the streets. The decision was widely hailed as a victory for constitutional rights, but in reality, it "was a defeat for these and other constitutional rights . . . Thus while the Witnesses won, the real constitutional issue of jurisdiction was decided in favor of the provinces [Quebec] and against the Federal Parliament."

"A Constitutional Shock: Disclosure of Anonymous Authorship." *South African Law Times,* 2:204–5, October 1933. **C519**
Deals with a case in Southern Rhodesia in which an editor was jailed for refusing to reveal to the police the name of the writer of an allegedly libelous letter appearing in his paper.

"Constitutional Status of Antileaflet Ordinances." *Monthly Labor Review,* 48: 881–85, April 1939.　　　　**C520**
References to the case of *Lovell v. City of Giffin,* 303 U.S. 444, in which the U.S. Supreme Court held the ordinance against Jehovah's Witnesses to be unconstitutional.

"The Consumer and Federal Regulation of Advertising." *Harvard Law Review,* 53:828–42, March 1940.　　**C521**
Several indictments leveled against advertising copy have led the public to demand some regulation of advertising. The author reviews the regulatory activities of the Post Office Department, the Federal Alcohol Administration, the Federal Food and Drug Administration, and the Federal Trade Commission. The mere prevention of outright falsehood is not the ultimate solution, but the creation of practicable standards on a wide scale is both paternalistic and difficult to administer. A possible solution is the creation of a centralized federal agency dedicated to consumer welfare and education.

"Control of the Press." *Economist* (London), 151:85–86, 20 July 1946.　　**C522**
Personalism, not monopoly, is the chief threat to freedom of the press in Great Britain. The practice of certain publishers in using their newspapers "merely as giant megaphones for their own whims and prejudices" is a menace to a free press. Raising the standards of education and popular taste, however, will be more effective in achieving reform than the enactment of dangerous legal restraints on the press.

"Controlling Press and Radio Influence on Trials." *Harvard Law Review,* 63: 840–53, March 1950.　　**C523**
The article considers three questions: Is the news reporting practice one which can be

seriously harmful? If so, what is the likelihood that it will be? What is the social cost of preventing the harm, and would the particular methods used be constitutional? Possible remedies are voluntary action by press and radio to restrain crime reporting, a change of venue, a new trial, contempt of court, and prevention of disclosure to the press.

"Controversial Books." *Kansas Library Bulletin,* 32:28–30, June 1963.　　**C524**
A group of librarians discuss practical methods for the selection of controversial books in areas of politics, religion, and sex, and steps to take in the wake of demands for censorship.

Controversy, Freedom of Speech, and Majority Rule. 30 min. b/w movie. San Francisco, Alfred T. Palmer Productions. (The Great Idea Series)　　　　**C525**

[Converse, Sherman]. *Report of the Case of Joshua Stow vs. Sherman Converse, for a Libel; containing a History of Two Trials before the Superior Court, and some account of the proceedings before the Supreme Court of Errors.* New Haven, Conn., S. Converse, 1822. 183 p.　　　　**C526**
Stow, a leading political figure, sued Converse for libel for accusing him of being an infidel (in Converse's newspaper, the *Connecticut Journal* of 16 March 1819.) The award was to the plaintiff. The trial is significant because it involves questions of introduction of evidence as to truth or falsehood and also of the practice of returning a jury to a second and third consideration of their verdicts.

"Conviction of Heresy." *Truth Seeker,* 33: 756–57, 1 December 1906.　　**C527**
An editorial on the expulsion of the Reverend Algernon S. Crapsey from the Episcopal Church because of his beliefs concerning the physical being and the life of Christ, as expressed in his book, *Religion and Politics.* In 1924 Crapsey published his autobiography, *The Last of the Heretics.*

Conway, Moncure D. *Blasphemous Libels* ... London, E. W. Allen, [1883]. pp. 277–88. (Lessons for the Day, no. 24)　　**C528**

———. *Liberty and Morality; A Discourse Given at South Place Chapel, Finsbury.* London, Freethought Publishing Co., 1878. 15 p. (Reprinted in Truth Seeker Tracts, no. 153)　　　**C529**
A liberal minister criticizes British efforts at suppression of obscenity and disagrees with the prosecution of Mrs. Besant, Mr. Bradlaugh, and Mr. Truelove. The vice societies have departed from their original purpose of suppressing vice to attack unorthodox expression and honest sex education. "They who menace man's freedom of thought and speech are tampering with something more powerful than gunpowder."

———. *The Life of Thomas Paine: With a History of His Literary, Political, and Religious Career in America, France, and England.* London, Putnam, 1892. 2 vols. **C530**

A defense of Paine by a British author, editor, and liberal minister. Includes a sketch of Paine by William Cobbett. Throughout the biography there are references to the suppression of Paine's unorthodox works on politics and religion.

Cook, Benning P. "The Right to Censure: A Lockian View." *Issue,* 1(1):19–22, Winter 1963. **C531**

According to the author, a graduate student in philosophy at the University of California, John Locke asserts that men have given up their natural right of self-protection in order to be regulated by law of the community. The right of personal religion and morality are retained rights, however, and never surrendered. "The allegiance of any man is first owed to God, his Creator; and then to the community in which he dwells. Therefore he is obliged to resist the community to death, where the community is believed to have violated the laws and commandments of God."

Cook, Bruce. "*Candy* Comes to Chicago." *Nation,* 199:125–26, 14 September 1964 **C532**

The banning of the sale of *Candy* in Chicago and the organization of booksellers in that city for mutual defense against strict police censorship.

Cook, *Sir* Edward T. *The Press Censorship, Interview Given by Sir Edward T. Cook to the Associated Press.* London, Burrup, Mathieson, and Sprague, 1916. 12p. **C533**

An account of wartime censorship by the chief British censor, World War I.

———. *The Press in War-Time. With Some Account of the Official Press Bureau; An Essay.* London, Macmillan, 1920. 200p. (Spanish translation published in Buenos Aires in 1923 by L. Bernard) **C534**

Reminiscences of Britain's chief censor in World War I. He describes methods used and the difficulties as well as fallacies of censorship.

Cook, G. Bradford. "Motion Picture Censorship." *Nebraska Law Review,* 40: 491–502, April 1961. **C535**

An historical review of the development of modern screen censorship through the second *Times Film Corp.* case, 365 U.S. 43 (1961). The author believes that court decisions, in permitting previewing of *any* film, permit previewing of *all* films. Such a procedure could be time-consuming and costly. "The

benefit of censorship laws to society is doubtful, and the harm to a free society is obvious."

Cook, Harold M. "Freedom of Speech and Press vs. National Security." *Alabama Lawyer,* 3:78–89, January 1942. **C536**

An analysis of major cases under the wartime Espionage Act of 1917 including *Schenck v. U.S., Frohwerk v. U.S.* (articles in a German language newspaper), *Debs v. U.S., Abrams v. U.S.* (pamphlets opposing the American Expeditionary Force to Russia), *Schaefer v. U.S.* (editorial in a German language newspaper), and *Gitlow v. N.Y.* (publication of a revolutionary manifesto). The Gitlow case came under the New York criminal anarchy law. The author draws the conclusion that "the collective right of organized society must take precedence over individual liberty where the same are in irreconcilable conflict."

Cooke, George W. *Treatise on the Law of Defamation.* London, O. Richards, 1844. 512p. **C537**

Includes the changes in English libel law resulting from the Lord Campbell Act of 1843, which recognized truth as evidence.

₁Cooley, John G.₁ *Report of the Trial of John G. Cooley, Editor of "The Reporter," a Temperance Paper, for an Alleged Libel upon K. H. Van Rensalaer, Keeper of a Fashionable Grop Shop . . . Before the Superior Court at Norwich, 1847 . . .* Norwich, Conn., John G. Cooley, 1847. 80p. **C538**

The case was dismissed when the jury could not agree.

Cooley, Thomas M. *Constitutional Limitations Which Rest upon the Legislative Power of the States of the American Union.* 8th ed. Boston, Little, Brown, 1927, 2 vols. **C539**

Chapter 12, Liberty of Speech and of the Press, reviews legal decisions of state and federal courts dealing with such issues as libel upon the government, publication of privileged communications, privilege of publishers of news, publication of legal proceedings, the jury as the judge in libel cases, and the doctrine of "good motives and justifiable ends."

Coons, John E., *ed. Freedom and Responsibility in Broadcasting.* Evanston, Ill., Northwestern University Press, 1961. 252p. **C540**

Speeches by Newton N. Minow, Le Roy Collins, Louis L. Jaffe, and Roscoe Barrow, and discussion by participants at a conference on broadcasting held at Northwestern University. Includes a history of the FCC.

Cooper, Courtney R. "This Trash Must Go!" *Forum,* 103:61–64, February 1940. **C541**

The author urges action be taken against the "torrent of smutty magazines" flooding the newsstands. He gives examples of local community efforts in controlling obscene magazines, particularly the work of the Permanent Committee on Public Decency, Buffalo, N.Y.

Cooper, Geoffrey. *Caesar's Mistress: the BBC on Trial.* London, Venture Publications, 1948. 113p. **C542**

A critical inquiry into charges of bribery, corruption, and inefficiency in the operation of the British Broadcasting Corporation, made by a Member of Parliament. The B.B.C. Advisory Council, he believes, should be a representative body reflecting both producer and consumer interests.

₁Cooper, James F.₁ *Cooper versus Horace Greeley and Thomas McElrath: a Brief Statement of the Pleadings and Argument in the Case, with Running Commentaries on the Law.* New York, 1843. 16p. **C543**

Between 1837 and 1845 the novelist James Fenimore Cooper waged a war against the American press, bringing a total of 14 private libel suits and 2 criminal libel suits against newspapermen, including Horace Greeley of the New York *Tribune.* "The entire nation breaths an atmosphere of falsehoods," Cooper charged in *The American Democrat* (1838). "The country cannot much longer exist in safety under the malign influence that now overshadows it. . . . ₁The press₁ as a whole owes its existence to the schemes of interested political adventurers."

Cooper, Kent. *Anna Zenger; Mother of Freedom.* New York, Farrar, Straus, 1946. 345p. **C544**

"This novelized biography of Anna Zenger ₁wife of John Peter Zenger₁ has been written in this form to give co-ordinating details for the actual incidents that I believe were the genesis of freedom in this land." A number of documents in the Zenger case are reproduced at the back of the volume.

———. *Barriers Down; the Story of the News Agency Epoch.* New York, Farrar and Rinnehart, 1942. 324p. **C545**

Cooper relates the longtime efforts of the Associated Press, of which he was head, to extend its coverage of world news and to break the monopoly of foreign news held by the British agency, Reuters.

———. "Free News: First Step in Peace." *Free World,* 8:225–29, September 1944. **C546**

With this article, Mr. Cooper begins a campaign for international agreements on world press freedom. Free exchange of news and information among peoples of the world, he asserts, will remove causes for war.

———. "A Free Press in a Free World; A Check upon Government Propaganda." *Vital Speeches*, 11:209–11, 15 January 1945. **C 547**

A speech in behalf of a world-wide free press and freedom of international news exchange as the most powerful forces for world peace.

———. "Freedom of Information; Call for Unhampered Flow of World News." *Life*, 17:55–58+, 13 November 1944. **C 548**

The former head of Associated Press is generally credited with having started the crusade for world press freedom as a method of preventing war, a campaign undertaken by the American Society of Newspaper Editors.

———. "Government, the Press, and World News Freedom." *United Nations World*, 1:20–21, September 1947 **C 549**

The author stresses the need for world freedom of news coverage and especially for full reporting of U.N. activities.

———. *The Right to Know; An Exposition of the Evils of News Suppression and Propaganda.* New York Farrar, Straus, and Cudahy, 1956. 335p. **C 550**

The former head of Associated Press reviews the history of government control of the press, exposing the tragic results of the use of censorship and propaganda as a device of public policy. Many of the examples are taken from the author's own wide experience. Cooper urges that government withdraw from news gathering and news dispensing activities. Included is a detailed account of the case of Edward Kennedy, AP newsman, who defied government censorship of news concerning the end of World War II.

———. "To Prevent War, No News Blackout." *New York Times Magazine*, 11 March 1945, pp. 33, 35. **C 551**

We must spread truth and make it a shield to guard world peace. America should hold out in the peace settlement for two things that make a world-wide community of interest possible: a world-wide free press and a communications system adapted to serve the press everywhere.

Cooper, Morton. "*Fanny Hill* vs. The Constitution." *Pageant*, 19:14–20, June 1964. **C 552**

Cooper, Sanford L. "Censorship." In *Newsmen's Holiday.* Cambridge, Mass., Harvard University Press, 1942, pp. 112–26. **C 553**

The cable editor of the *Pittsburgh Press* discusses current wartime censorship—that imposed by the military and that imposed by the Office of Censorship in Washington. While censorship thus far is mild, the author reports the fears of some that it may become more severe, that it may become positive, using information (true or false) as a propaganda tool, and that censorship may be extended beyond essential war news to silence all criticism of government. We can keep censorship in its proper place by using freedom of the press with common-sense restraint.

Cooper, Thomas. *An Account of the Trial of Thomas Cooper, of Northumberland; on a Charge of Libel against the President of the United States. . . . With a Preface, Notes, and Appendix.* Philadelphia, Printed by John Bioren for the Author, 1800. 64p. (Reprinted in *American State Trials*, vol. 10, pp. 774–812, and in Wharton, *State Trials*, pp. 659–81) **C 554**

Cooper was an English radical who had moved to the United States in 1794, during the conservative reaction to the French Revolution that swept England. He took up residence in Northumberland, Pa., near his friend Joseph Priestley. Cooper was trained as a lawyer, owned a textile mill, attained some renown as a chemist, and from 1820 to 1833 was president of South Carolina College. He was also an articulate anti-Federalist and wrote various articles against the Alien and Sedition Acts. In 1800 he was arrested and brought to trial in the Circuit Court of the United States under the Sedition Act of 1798 for libeling President Adams. Cooper conducted his own defense, arguing with great conviction and logic that his writings were both true and made with honest intent; that the denial of peaceful persuasion during a presidential campaign was to defeat democracy. Judge Samuel Chase, departing from impartiality, argued for the prosecution and Cooper was found guilty. He served six months in prison where he continued to criticize the President and the Federalists, assuming the role of political martyr.

———. *Defence of Dr. Cooper, before the Trustees of South Carolina College, Columbia.* Boston, Printed at the Times & Gazette Office, 1833. 64p. **C 555**

Cooper was forced to resign from his presidency of South Carolina College in 1833 and from his professorship the following year because of liberal religious views expressed verbally and in publications. He had earlier been forced from the faculty of the University of Virginia because of attacks by clergy. John Adams called Cooper "a learned, ingenious, scientific, and talented madcap."

———. *Political Essays, Originally Inserted in the Northumberland Gazette, with Additions.* Northumberland, Pa., Andrew Kennedy, 1799. 64p. **C 556**

Includes extracts from a speech by Thomas Erskine on the English doctrine of libel and comments on the Alien and Sedition Acts.

———. "The Right of Free Discussion." In his *Lectures on the Elements of Political Economy.* 2d ed. Columbia, S.C., 1829. 17p. (Also published as an appendix to *Treatise on the Law of Libel*, and as a separate pamphlet published in London by J. Watson, 1840. 22p.) **C 557**

———. *A Treatise on the Law of Libel and the Liberty of the Press; Showing the Origin, Use, and Abuse of the Law of Libel . . .* New York, G. F. Hopkins, 1830. 184p. **C 558**

The author, president of Columbia College in South Carolina, had 30 years earlier been the defendant in a sedition trial. His doctrines on a free press, he writes, grew out of the earlier statements of Milton (*Areopagitica*, 1644), Anthony Collins (1724), his own earlier tract (1787), Robert Hall (1821), Samuel Bailey (1821), and Thomas Herttell (1828). His legal researches led him to protest against the common law doctrine of libel and blasphemy. Appendix I deals with heresy and blasphemy.

Cooper, Thompson. "William Carter." In *Dictionary of National Biography*, vol. 3, pp. 1116–17. (Also referred to in the *Catholic Encyclopedia*, vol. 15, p. 630) **C 559**

Carter operated a secret Catholic press which was discovered by the authorities in 1579. In 1582 he was arrested for publishing a *Treatise of Schism*, in which a cryptic passage was interpreted as urging the assassination of Queen Elizabeth. For this he was found guilty, hanged, boweled, and quartered. Siebert states that Carter was the only person put to death for his publishing activities during the Tudor period.

Cooper, William C. *A Sketch of the Life of . . . Henry Cooper . . . of the Norfolk Circuit; as also of his Father (Charles Cooper). (Report of the Trial of M. A. Carlile, for Publishing a New Year's Address to Reformers of Great Britain . . .)* London, W. & H. S. Warr, 1856. 139p. **C 560**

Henry Cooper was a young liberal lawyer, an intimate friend and intended biographer of Thomas Erskine. Shortly after a brilliant and successful defense of Mary-Anne Carlile on trial for seditious libel in 1821, Cooper died. This sketch was written by his brother. Cooper's speech at the Mary-Anne Carlile trial is reprinted as an appendix.

Coote, William A., *ed. Pernicious Literature; Debate in the House of Commons; Trial and Conviction [of Henry Vizetelly] for Sale of Zola's Novels.* London, National Vigilance Association [1889]. 32p. **C 561**

Coote was head of the National Vigilance Association that brought Vizetelly to trial.

———. *A Romance of Philanthrophy; being a record of some of the principal incidents connected with the exceptionally successful thirty years' work of the National Vigilance Association.* London, The Association, 1916. 235 p. **C 562**
Chapter 3 deals with the Association's attack on indecent literature and exhibitions, since its founding by W. T. Stead in 1885. Chapter 4 is on the origin of the Censorship Committee of the Bill Posters' Protective Association, which cooperated with the Vigilance Association in eliminating objectionable placards and posters. Chapter 5 describes the Association's action against the Rabelais Gallery of Pictures and the clandestine selling of obscene prints. Chapter 6 contains a discussion of the prosecution of the publisher of *The Yoke* and the censorship of the unpublished works of Sir Richard Burton. Lady Burton, who died in 1896, had appointed Mr. Coote as one of her literary trustees. He was to supervise publication of her husband's work so that not a single immodest, coarse, or indecent word would appear in print. Also included in the book are reports of the various international purity conferences in which the Association participated.

Copinger, Walter A. *Copinger and Skone James on the Law of Copyright . . .* 8th ed. Edited by F. E. Skone James. London, Sweet & Maxwell, 1948. 664 p. **C 563**
Leading English work on copyright, first published in 1870.

[Corbet, William]. *Reports of the Trial, F. E. Jones v. William Corbet, Proprietor of the Hibernian Telegraph.* Dublin, 1810. **C 564**
Corbet was ordered before the House of Lords to answer for a libel on Lord Aldborough that appeared in the *Hibernian Telegraph.* Corbet was reprimanded for publishing an account of the proceedings of Parliament.

[Corbett, James A.]. "Trouble at Cochise." *Arizona Librarian,* 22(3):7–10, 40–43, Summer 1965. **C 565**
An open letter to the Governing Board of Cochise College, Douglas, Ariz., from the librarian whose contract was not renewed after a controversy over the library's book selection policy. Corbett defends the freedom of the college library against extralegal censorship. The college newspaper was suspended, an art exhibit censored, and the student literary magazine, *El Librito,* condemned by the college administration. A sequel, reporting on the Arizona Civil Liberties Union investigation of the situation, is given in the Fall 1965 issue of *Arizona Librarian.*

[Corbo, John]. "Subjecting the Sale of Books to Prior Administrative Restraints with Extra-Legal Sanctions." *New York Law Forum,* 9:385–90, August 1963. **C 566**

Bantam Books, Inc. v. Sullivan, 372 U.S. 58 (1963), relating to censorship activites of the Rhode Island Commission to Encourage Morality in Youth.

Corey, Herbert. "Radio Is Censored." *Public Utilities Fortnightly,* 23:588–96, 11 May 1939. **C 567**
Radio newscasters lack the freedom of newspaper reporters because of broadcast licensing regulations.

———. "Radio's Growing Pains—The FCC and Control in Public Interest." *Nation's Business,* 27:17–19, 62–64, February 1939. **C 568**

"Correspondence in Regard to the Censorship of Scientific Journals." *Science,* 96:216–21, 4 September 1942. **C 569**
An exchange of letters between J. McKeen Cattell, editor of *Science,* and Colonel W. Preston Corderman, chief postal censor, relating to the demand of the censor that certain items dealing with recent medical discoveries be deleted from copies of *Science* mailed overseas on the ground that the information might promote health or limit disease among the people of the countries with which we are at war. Cattell charges that such action is a betrayal of the ethics of the medical profession and contrary to the spirit of a democracy at war. He notes that in World War I the Surgeon General ruled that "we should not consider for a moment holding back a life-saving discovery on the ground that the enemy could also make use of it."

Corry, J. A. "Free Trade in Ideas." *Queen's Quarterly,* 56(1):1–14, Spring 1949. **C 570**
The author considers the controversy over allowing free inquiry and expression to "those who will not acknowledge a reciprocal obligation to defend them for others." He finds that "it is always a question of balancing the dangers of unrestricted expression against those which flow from suppression. At the present time, the hazards on both sides are greatly intensified because we live in an unsettled and dangerous world." He calls for frequent reassessment of risks and dangers.

Corwin, Edward S. "Bowing Out 'Clear and Present Danger.'" *Notre Dame Lawyer,* 27:325–59, Spring 1952. **C 571**

———. "Constitutional Law in 1919–1920. The Constitutional Decisions of the Supreme Court of the United States in the October Term, 1919 . . . Freedom of Speech and the Press." *American Political Science Review,* 14:655–58, November 1920. **C 572**
A summary of court decisions relating to enforcement of the Espionage Act of 1917.

———. "Freedom of Speech and Press under the First Amendment: A Résumé." *Yale Law Journal,* 30:48–55, 1920. (Also in Maggs, *et al.,* eds., *Selected Essays on Constitutional Law.* Chicago, Foundation Press, 1938. vol. 2, pp. 1060–68) **C 573**
A comparison of the Sedition Act of 1798 with the Espionage Act of 1917 and a consideration of the latter in the light of history and the intention of the Constitution. "The cause of freedom of speech and press is largely in the custody of legislative majorities and of juries, which, so far as there is evidence to show, is just where the framers of the constitution intended it to be."

Cory, John M. "Libraries and Censorship." *ILA Record,* 3:1–4, September 1949. **C 574**
A summary of the recent incidents of book and magazine censorship in America and what librarians are doing to withstand local pressures and to adhere to the Library Bill of Rights. As alternatives to censorship, Cory recommends the "counter-attack" with good literature and the "immunization" technique which involves providing a normal healthy environment.

Coryell, John R. "Comstockery." *Mother Earth,* 1:30–40, March 1906. (Excerpts in Schroeder, *Free Press Anthology,* pp. 178–80) **C 575**
The writer of the Nick Carter detective stories attacks Comstock and the vice societies. Includes an account of the suppression of Hans Markart's *Triumph of Charles V.*

———. "Indecency on the Stage." *Mother Earth,* 4:24–28, March 1909. **C 576**
A satire on sex censorship.

[Costa, Joseph]. *Canon 35: Matter Closed?* Columbia, Mo., Freedom of Information Center, School of Journalism, University of Missouri, 1963. 16 p. (Publication no. 97) **C 577**
A report on the American Bar Association vote in the convention on 5 February 1963, to continue, with minor changes, its prohibition against photographs and broadcasting in the courtroom. The report includes the arguments of Joseph Costa, of the National Association of Press Photographers, to the American Bar Association, and the transcript of the proceedings leading to the decision.

———. "Does Press Freedom Include Photography?" *Nieman Reports,* 6(4):3–7, October 1952. **C 578**
The case against the barring, restricting, or interfering with cameramen, whose picture record is an essential part of the news.

———. *The Public's Image of the Press.* Columbia, Mo., Freedom of Information Center, School of Journalism, University of Missouri, 1959. 4 p. (Publication no. 17)

C 579

The author discusses the lack of public confidence in the news media ("Therein lies the 'clear and present danger' to freedom of the press.") and what the media can do to regain it.

Costello, M. Joseph. "Ecclesiastical Traditions and Controversial Books." *Catholic Educational Review*, 61:176–88, March 1963.

C 580

Reviews the tradition and codes of the Catholic Church in dealing with Catholic literary criticism and its application in Catholic schools. Defends the Church's point of view against the claims in recent years of Catholic critics and educators on advantages to be gained in reading "controversial" literature.

Couch, W. T. "The Sainted Book Burners: Because of Undercover Censorship by Liberals, the Freedom to Read that Is Piously Championed by the American Library Association May Well Become the Freedom to Read Propaganda." *Freeman*, 5:423–26, April 1955.

C 581

Coughlin, William J. *Conquered Press; the MacArthur Era in Japanese Journalism.* Palo Alto, Calif., Pacific Books, 1952. 165 p.

C 582

A history of the handling of the Japanese press and American correspondents by the Supreme Command for the Allied Powers during the occupation of Japan after World War II. Chapter 4 deals specifically with censorship.

[Coulson, Frederick R.]. "Corrupting the Morals of Her Majesty's Subjects." *University Magazine*, 10:443–47, July 1898.

C 583

An account of the Bedborough Case, involving publication of Havelock Ellis' *Studies in the Psychology of Sex.* The article is signed with the pseudonym, Democritus.

———. *Darwin on Trial at the Old Bailey. By Democritus.* London, The University Press, [1900?]. 39 p. (Bound with George Astor Singer, *Judicial Scandals and Errors*, pp. 41–86 and Appendix, "The English Press and the Prosecution," pp. 87–107)

C 584

A mock trial before an imaginary London court for the prosecution of a bookseller charged with obscene libel for the sale of a book entitled *Sexual Selection and Human Marriage.* The burlesque is based on the Bedborough trial for the sale of Havelock Ellis' *Studies in the Psychology of Sex*, 1898.

Coulson, H. J. W. "Laws Relating to Blasphemy." *Law Magazine and Law Review*, 9:158–78, February 1884. **C 585**

The prosecution of Mr. Bradlaugh and Messrs. Ramsey and Foote for blasphemous libel, and the severe sentences passed by Justice North on the two latter persons at their first trial, prompts the author to review the law and court decisions on blasphemy. He notes that the cases are old and the principles on which they were decided are "repugnant to modern ideas." He concludes, by quoting Henry T. Buckle, that "every man has an absolute and irrefragable right to treat any doctrine as he thinks proper; either to argue against it, or to ridicule it."

Coulton, G. G. *The Death Penalty for Heresy from 1184 to 1921 A. D.* London, Simpkin, Marshall, Hamilton, Kent, 1924. 88 p. (*Medieval Studies*, 2d ser., no. 18)

C 586

The author, a member of the faculty of St. John's College, Cambridge, traces the foundation of the idea of exterminating heretics, expressed in Canon law of the Catholic Church and carried out by popes and temporal rulers.

———. "New Roman *Index.*" *Nineteenth Century*, 107:378–90, March 1930. **C 587**

A caustic criticism of the Roman Catholic *Index Librorum Prohibitorum.*

Council for Democracy. *Censorship.* New York, The Council, 1942. 46 p. (Democracy in Action, no. 10) **C 588**

A popular presentation of censorship problems in America, particularly with respect to wartime restrictions. Readers are advised to use native intelligence in interpreting news during the period of wartime censorship and to be on guard for any trend toward unreasonable and drastic censorship.

"Council Urges Title V Repeal," *Publishers' Weekly*, 146:571–73, 19 August 1944. **C 589**

Recommendations of the Council on Books in Wartime for repeal of Title V of the Soldiers Vote Act which bans the distribution of political books to service personnel. Includes the text of Senator Theodore F. Green's new bill to rescind the objectionable censorship provisions of Title V.

"Council's Appeal to Safeguard Rights of Correspondents." *U.N. Bulletin*, 11:264–65, 15 September 1951. **C 590**

The Economic and Social Council of the U.N. voiced its "extreme concern" at governmental action that systematically excludes bona fide correspondents, imposes arbitrary personal restraints, and punishes them solely because of their attempts to perform their news-gathering and news-transmitting duties.

Counterattack. *Red Channels. The Report of Communist Influence in Radio and Television.* New York, Counterattack, 1950. 213 p.

C 591

Alphabetical lists of prominent radio and television personalities and their alleged affiliations with "organizations espousing Communist causes." The same publisher issues a periodic newsletter entitled *Counterattack* which follows a similar line. Elizabeth Dilling's *The Red Network, A Who's Who and Handbook of Radicalism for Patriots* (1934) was a forerunner of *Red Channels.* The Dilling book however, was not limited to the communications industry and was international in scope. Merle Miller reports on blacklisting in radio and television in his *The Judges and the Judged.*

"Court Order Prohibiting Photographing of Spectators on Streets and Sidewalks Surrounding Courthouse, Held Not to Be Abuse of Discretion of Court." *DePaul Law Review*, 10:151–56, Autumn–Winter 1960. **C 592**

Atlanta Newspapers, Inc. v. Grimes, 216 Ga. 74, 114 S. E. 2d 421 (1960).

Courtney, James C. "Absurdities of the Law of Slander and Libel." *American Law Review*, 36:552–64, July 1902. **C 593**

Courtney, Paul. "The *Southern Parish* Case." *Commonweal*, 55:191–93, 30 November 1951. Reply by F. J. Baechle, 55:594–95, 21 March 1952. **C 594**

The story of the suppression of Father Joseph H. Fichter's *Southern Parish: The Dynamics of a City Church*, by a church reviewing committee. The book was a sociological study scheduled for publication in four volumes by the University of Chicago Press. Only one volume was published.

Cousins, Norman. "Censoritis." *Saturday Review of Literature*, 27(27):12, 1 July 1944.

C 595

An editoral comment on the rejection by the Council on Books in Wartime, of Catherine Drinker Bowen's *Yankee from Olympus* and Charles A. Beard's *The Republic* for Army and Navy use because they allegedly violate the Soldiers' Vote Act. In the 15 July issue Senator Robert Taft denies that the Act was ever intended to ban such books. In the 29 July issue Editor Cousins reports on a meeting between Senator Taft and Army officials, arranged by *Saturday Review*, to iron out difficulties in Title V of the Soldiers Vote Act.

———. "Free Press and Free Enterprise." *Saturday Review of Literature*, 34(22): 20–21, 2 June 1951. **C 596**

A censorship controversy in India between the government and the press.

———. "Group Libel." *Saturday Review of Literature*, 30(5):20, 1 February 1947. **C 597**

The editor proposes a libel law to enable groups to protect themselves against untruthful and harmful speech or print. He asked for comments and received many. The general tide ran against the proposal. Some of the letters are printed in the 15 March issue. Among those generally favorable to the proposal were Bernard M. Baruch, Senator Arthur H. Vandenberg, and Justice Bernard L. Shientag. Among those opposed were Judge Learned Hand, Senator Elbert D. Thomas, and Representative Frank A. Mathews, Jr.

———. "The N.Y. Post Office and the SRL." *Saturday Review of Literature*, 27(21): 14–15, 20 May 1944. **C 598**

In answer to a letter from the New York postmaster stating that any issue of the *Saturday Review* containing advertising of *Strange Fruit* would be unmailable, the editor notifies the postmaster of his intent to defy the ruling: "We not only protest your order; we refuse to follow it without due process of law." A response from the Post Office Department (it decided not to press the case) and letters to the editor in the matter appear in the issues for 3 June and 17 June.

———. "Open the Books!" *Saturday Review*, 36(28):30–31, 11 July 1953. (Reprinted in Daniels, *The Censorship of Books*, pp. 116–19) **C 599**

An editorial criticizing the American government suppression of controversial books in U.S. Information Libraries abroad. "We have the astonishing spectacle of the American Government placing a ban on books that are controversial as being synonymous with subversion." Through "our own hideous ineptness we have done damage to ourselves far beyond anything done against us by the Soviet propaganda machine."

———. "What We Don't Know Can Kill Us." *Saturday Review*, 44(2):24, 14 January 1961. **C 600**

Criticism of the lack of adequate news coverage of world events as indicated in the Laos conflict.

[Covington, Hayden C.]. *Defending and Legally Establishing the Good News*. Brooklyn, N.Y., Watchtower Bible and Tract Society, 1950. 96 p. **C 601**

The legal counsel for Jehovah's Witnesses has prepared these guides to advise members on their rights in preaching and distributing religious literature and to advise lawyers and city officials of the constitutional guarantees of freedom of speech, press, and worship. The pamphlet cites numerous court cases, many of which involved the Witnesses.

[———]. *Freedom of Worship*. Brooklyn, N.Y., Watchtower Bible and Tract Society, [1943]. 64 p. **C 602**

Cowen, D. V. *Freedom of Thought and Its Expression in South Africa*. Cape Town, National Union of South African Students, [1960?]. 30 p. **C 603**

An address on censorship and freedom of the press delivered by a professor of law, University of Cape Town. The occasion is the opposition to the Publications and Entertainment Bill which establishes "machinery for total control of thought by government" in South Africa.

Cowley, Malcolm. "Artists, Conscience, and Censors." *Saturday Review*, 45:8–10+, 7 July 1962. **C 604**

There is a moral code of authors to turn out an honest work of literature. But art can be good or bad in its public effects and "censorship is one of the means by which society defends itself against enemies, external and internal, and by which it tries . . . to prevent social change." Cowley speaks of some of the dilemmas over censorship: welfare of the adult v. the child, freedom of presentation in the movies and television v. the press, and the right of expression in literary work v. expression in crude and tawdry form. Certain principles, however, are generally agreed upon: no prior censorship, no secret or private censorship, and action against the work and not the author. The battle between free expression and restraint is never ended. All we can hope for is "that the battle be conducted according to rules."

———. "Gammon for Dinner." *Interim*, 14:21–24, 1954. **C 605**

The writer describes the unsuccessful campaign against him as a visiting professor at the University of Washington, Seattle, first on the basis of his political associations and later on charges that his poetry was immoral.

———. "There Have to Be Censors." *New Republic*, 94:364–65, 27 April 1938. **C 606**

The author finds arguments for and against political censorship of works of art both substantially unassailable. "The censors are right in attacking books and pictures which they regard as immoral or subversive. The artists are right in counterattacking the censor and in fighting not only to save but to widen their own freedom of expression. There is no final decision to be reached, but there is a temporary stability to be achieved as the result of struggle."

Cowley, W. H. "All God's Chillun Got Wings." *School and Society*, 66:145–50, 30 August 1947. **C 607**

An appeal for greater freedom of communication in all the media and an improvement in the quality of what gets communicated. Special references to censorship on radio.

Cowper, B. H. "Books Burnt." *Notes and Queries*, 11 (ser. 1):77–78, 3 February 1855; 99–100, 10 February 1855; 120–21, 17 February 1855; 161–62, 3 March 1855; 1(ser. 2):397–98, 17 May 1856; 498–99, 21 June 1856. **C 608**

A collection of notes taken in the course of the author's readings pertaining to the destruction of books by fire, either by accident or design. The comments are arranged in approximate chronological order, with printed sources cited in many instances. There is no restriction as to time or country. The series attracted other readers to contribute notes on book-burning and these appear in issues of *Notes and Queries* for several years. They may be located through the index to Series 1 and 2.

Cox, C. B., *et al.* "Pornography and Obscenity." *Critical Quarterly*, 3:99–122, Summer 1961. **C 609**

A symposium generated by the recent trial of *Lady Chatterley's Lover*. Following quotations on obscenity from D. H. Lawrence, these editorial topics are presented: The Teaching of Literature by C. B. Cox, The English Censorship Laws by Norman St. John-Stevas, Literature and Morality by Donald Davie, A Christian View by Martin Jarrett-Kerr, and Four Letter Words by C. S. Lewis.

Cox, Harvey G., Jr. "Obscenity and Protestant Ethics." *Christian Century*, 76: 415–17, 8 April 1959. **C 610**

Cox, Kenneth A. "The Federal Communications Commission's 'Fairness Doctrine' with Respect to Broadcasting Matter Dealing with Controversial Issues." *Brief* (Phi Delta Phi), 60:16–24, Fall 1964. **C 611**

Coyle, Edward L. "Limiting the Freedom of Speech by Suppressing the Advocacy of Direct Action." *University of Cincinnati Law Review*, 4:211–16, March 1930. **C 612**

Crafts, Wilbur F. "Hard Fight on Federal Censorship on Motion Pictures." *Light*, 98:21–23, July–August 1914. **C 613**

Discussion of the bill before Congress to establish a Motion Picture Commission as part of the U.S. Bureau of Education. The agency would provide censorship prior to copyright and shipment in interstate commerce. Rev. Crafts recommends complete and prompt establishment of federal censorship.

Craftsman. London. Nos. 1–44 (1726–27); continued as *The Country Journal; or, The Craftsman*. Nos. 45–1159 (1727–50).

Edited by the imaginary Caleb D'Anvers, Bencher of Gray's-Inn. Semiweekly. **C 614**

The *Craftsman* was a newspaper, started in 1726 by Lord Bolingbroke formerly Queen Anne's Secretary of State, and the two Pulteneys (Daniel and William) as a political organ to attack the Walpole administration. During the first four years of publication eight issues were deemed offensive to the government and led to prosecution of the publishers. In 1729 the publisher, Richard Francklin, was tried but found not guilty; in 1731 he was again tried and sentenced to a year in prison; in 1737 the new publisher, Henry Haines, was also given a year's sentence. During the course of the various trials the pages of the *Craftsman* were filled with discussions of the freedom of the press. In the issue for 3 September 1737 the editor writes: "The great benefit of the Liberty of the Press, consists in the freedom of discussing matters of religion and government, all disputable points, with a proper regard to decency and good manners, tho' even they ought to give place in case of extremity, to the publick good."

"The *Craftsman* and Its Contributors." *Bookworm*, 2:13–17, 1890. **C 615**

An account of the origin and publication of the *Craftsman* (1726/27) and an identification of some of its contributors.

The Craftsman's Doctrine and Practice of the Liberty of the Press, Explained to the meanest Capacity. London, J. Roberts, 1732. 61 p. **C 616**

Bolingbroke helped to found the *Craftsman* for the purpose of denouncing the action of the Walpole administration in prosecuting Tory opinion as seditious libel. This anonymous Whig pamphlet comes to the defense of Walpole and exposes the hypocrisy of Bolingbroke who, the author shows, suppressed the opinions of those out of power when he was Secretary of State under Queen Anne.

Craies, W. F. "Censorship of Stage Plays." *Journal of the Society of Comparative Legislation*, 8:196–202, 1907. **C 617**

"The outcry lately raised on the disallowance [by the Lord Chamberlain] of a play named *Waste*, written by Mr. Granville Barker, affords occasion to consider the history and law with reference to the licensing and control of representations of plays and similar productions on a public stage." The article describes the method by which objectionable plays are banned.

Craig, Alec. *Above All Liberties.* London, Allen & Unwin, 1942. 205 p. **C 618**

Discussion of the effects on literature, art, science, and society of the British laws against literary obscenity. This sequel to *The Banned Books of England* contains special chapters on the United States, France, and censorship of the works of Havelock Ellis.

———. "B.M. Catalogue." *Times Literary Supplement*, 2870:129, 1 March 1957. **C 619**

References to the omission of the "Private Case" books from the British Museum catalogue.

———. *The Banned Books of England and Other Countries.* London, Allen and Unwin, 1962. 243 p. (Published in the United States by World Publishing Co., under the title *Suppressed Books; A History of the Conception of Literary Obscenity*, with a foreword by Morris L. Ernst) **C 620**

"The subject of this book is the conception of literary obscenity as found in law and practice and its cultural and social effects. My primary concern is the restraint which the conception exercises on serious literature and consequently on intellectual freedom and artistic creation. In surveying this subject I have devoted the greatest space to England because that is the country which first developed a law of libel to fill the vacuum created by the abolition of direct censorship by church or State authorities." The author includes much of the past history from his earlier books (*Banned Books of England* and *Above All Liberties*), but extends his remarks to recent developments and includes America, France, and other countries "where freedom of the Press has traditionally been held in esteem." Special attention is given to the cases of Sir Charles Sedley, Edmund Curll, and John Wilkes, the Lord Campbell Act and the Cockburn definition of obscenity, the Bradlaugh and Besant trial, Havelock Ellis, British Customs, the Joint Select Committee on Lotteries and Indecent Advertisements, D. H. Lawrence and James Joyce, Count Potocki of Montalk, and the Obscene Publications Act, 1959. There is a chapter on Comstockery, the *Ulysses* and other landmark cases, and *Lady Chatterley's Lover*. A final chapter deals with pornography.

———. *The Banned Books of England; with a Foreword by E. M. Forster.* London, Allen & Unwin, 1937. 207 p. **C 621**

An explanation of the workings of the British law of obscene libel, with suggestions for reform. In chapter 4 the author draws a comparison between English and American practices. In the appendix are lists of eminent persons who have opposed censorship, citation of important obscenity cases, and titles of certain reputable books that have been banned.

———. "Censorship of Sexual Literature." In The *Encyclopedia of Sexual Behavior*, edited by Albert Ellis and A. Abarbanel. New York, Hawthorn Books, 1961, vol. 1, pp. 235–46. **C 622**

———. "The Law of Dirty Books." *University Libertarian*, 6:5–6, Spring 1958. **C 623**

———. "Recent Developments in the Law of Obscene Libel." In A. P. Pillay and Albert Ellis, *Sex, Society and the Individual*, Bombay, 1953. **C 624**

The article continues the account (introduced in *Above All Liberties*) of British laws against literary obscenity, and includes reference to the case of Eustace Chesser's *Love Without Fear*.

———. *Sex and Revolution.* London, Allen & Unwin, 1934. 144 p. **C 625**

The law of obscene libel is dealt with as a factor in the current controversy over sexual ethics.

———. "Wider Censorship." *New Statesman and Nation*, 14:516–17, 9 October 1937. **C 626**

The writer condemns the practice of excluding books from public libraries in England because reactionary local public opinion considers the books immoral.

[Crandall, Reuben]. *The Trial of Reuben Crandall, M.D., charged with Publishing and Circulating Seditious and Incendiary Papers, &c. in the District of Columbia, with the intent of Exciting Servile Insurrection . . . By a Member of the Bar.* Washington, D.C., Printed for the Proprietors, 1836. 48 p. **C 627**

A notice in the pamphlet states: "The Trial of Crandall presents the first case of a man charged with endeavoring to excite insurrection among slaves and the free colored population that was ever brought before a judicial tribunal." Dr. Crandall was charged with promulgating false doctrines that the black man had equal rights with the white; with casting reflections on the chivalry of the south; and with intent to cause unrest among Negroes. Dr. Crandall had written publications urging immediate emancipation of slaves. The jury found him not guilty.

[———]. *The Trial of Reuben Crandall, M.D., charged with publishing Seditious Libels, by circulating the publications of the American Anti-Slavery Society. Before the Circuit Court for the District of Columbia, held at Washington, in April, 1836, Occupying the Court the Period of Ten Days.* New York, H. R. Piercy, 1836. 62 p. (Bailey Pamphlets, v. 39, no. 5) **C 628**

A New York edition of the same pamphlet.

Crane, Jonathan M., and James F. Morton, Jr. "Moses Harman." *Mother Earth*, 5:10–15, March 1910. **C 629**

A brief biography and appreciation of a Kansas crusader for sex education, imprisoned on obscenity charges.

Crane, Verner W. "Benjamin Franklin and the Stamp Act." *Publications of the*

Colonial Society of Massachusetts; Transactions 1933–37, 32:56–77, 1937. **C 630**
An account intended to clarify Franklin's seeming equivocal conduct relative to the stamp act. The author reviews Franklin's attempt to dissuade Grenville from adopting the scheme, his philosophical acceptance of the measure when enacted, and his eventual impassioned plea for the removal of the tax in a hearing before the House of Commons.

Cranfield, G. A. *The Development of the Provincial Newspaper (1700–1760)*. Oxford, Clarendon, 1962. 287 p. **C 631**
Chapter 7 deals with Prosecution and the Press. "The growing importance of the provincial press [eighteenth century] was faithfully reflected in the number of prosecutions it suffered as the century progressed."

Crawford, Carolyn. "Controversial Literature in the Public School Libraries." *Hawaii Library Association Journal*, 20:17–18, Fall 1963. **C 632**

Crawford, Charles T. "Movie Censorship." *Kansas Law Review*, 4:584–89, May 1956. **C 633**
Notes on the present status of state and municipal motion picture censorship following the Supreme Court's reversal of the Kansas State Board of Review's ban of the motion picture, *The Moon Is Blue*.

Crawford, W. Rex. "Freedom in the Arts." *Annals of the American Academy of Political and Social Science*, 200:95–101, November 1938. **C 634**
"In part, the conflict over freedom of expression [in the arts] centers around what the artist is trying to express and the limitless possibilities that his utterance, verbal or otherwise, may be construed as an attack on the sacred, the cherished, the vested interest."

Creel, George. "American Newspaper; What It Is and What It Isn't." *Everybody's Magazine*, 40(4):40–44, 92, April 1919. **C 635**
Discussion of the work of voluntary press censorship in World War I. The author praises the American press for its wartime activities and calls for certain postwar reforms in the public interest.

[———]. "Authors Discuss Censorship." *Publishers' Weekly*, 102:1930, 25 November 1922. **C 636**
The chairman of the Committee on Censorship of the Authors League of America defends the voluntary jury system for the New York stage against criticism from the League. He describes how the Committee has stemmed "a tide of beadleism" which had threatened to bring literature under official supervision.

———. *How we Advertised; the First Telling of the Amazing Story of the Com-* mittee on Public Information that Carried the Gospel of Americanism to Every Corner of the Globe. New York, Harper, 1920. 466 p. **C 637**
American censorship and propaganda efforts told by the chief American censor in World War I.

———. "The Plight of the Last Censor." *Collier's*, 107:13+, 24 May 1941. (Reprinted in Summers, *Wartime Censorship*, pp. 69–75) **C 638**
"America's first official censor hopes that he will be the last one." He points out why voluntary censorship will not work in this war any better than it did in the last one. He suggests putting radio and cables under guard but leaving the press free.

———. "Public Opinion in War Time." *Annals of the American Academy of Political and Social Science*, 78:185–94, July 1918. **C 639**

———. *Rebel at Large: Recollections of Fifty Crowded Years*. New York, Putnam, 1947. 384 p. **C 640**
Autobiography of the head of the World War I Committee on Public Information; includes a chapter on wartime censorship.

———. "The Truth Shall Make You Free." *Collier's*, 108(18): 17, 27–29, 1 November 1941 **C 641**
Creel gives public advice on wartime control of information to President Franklin D. Roosevelt, based on the policy of President Woodrow Wilson.

———. "Wanted: Opposition." *American Mercury*, 54:666–71, June 1942. **C 642**
The man who served as chief American censor in World War I defends freedom of expression in wartime as essential to a democracy.

"Crime Comics and the Constitution." *Stanford Law Review*, 7:237–60, March 1955. **C 643**
The author concludes that the U.S. Supreme Court might uphold legislation restricting sale of crime comics of there is a serious enough threat to the morals of the community. But more objective investigations of the comic book problem are needed before legislatures should take action. "Do they pose so great a problem that another inroad on fundamental freedoms is warranted?"

"Criminal Libel and Freedom of the Press." *Outlook*, 94:275, 5 February 1910. **C 644**
Relates to the Panama libel case.

"Criminal Obscenity Statute Held Unconstitutional for Lack of Scienter."

Ohio State Law Journal, 23:355–60, 1962. **C 645**
In the case of the *City of Cincinnati v. Marshall*, 172 Ohio Stat. 280 (1961), the Supreme Court of Ohio reversed a lower court decision, declaring unconstitutional a Cincinnati city ordinance making the possession or sale of obscene writings or pictures a misdemeanor. The ordinance was "fatally defective due to its omission of the element of *scienter*, or knowledge, in defining the offense." The Ohio ruling followed the U.S. Supreme Court decision in *Smith v. California*, involving a similar Los Angeles ordinance.

Croft, Taylor. *The Cloven Hoof: A Study of Contemporary London Vices*. London, D. Archer, 1930. 176 p. **C 646**
Contains a chapter on Pornography and Obscene Displays.

Croope, J. *Conscience-Oppression; or A Complaint of wrong done to the Peoples Rights, etc.* London, 1657. 56 p. **C 647**
One of the Liberty of Conscience party during the Protectorate counsels for freedom for Dissenters to publish their opinions without persecution. Quoted in Clyde, *The Struggle for the Freedom of the Press*, p. 288.

Crosby, John. "Censorship on the Air." In his *Out of the Blue, a Book about Radio and Television*. New York, Simon and Schuster, 1952, pp. 271–81. **C 648**
Deals largely with the N.B.C. network censorship of Fred Allen, "possibly the most censored man in radio."

———. "Movies Are Too Dirty." *Saturday Evening Post*, 235(40):8, 11, 10 November 1962. **C 649**
Most "adult" pictures produced today aren't fit for grownups, let alone children, according to this movie critic. He objects violently to the degenerate, childishly prurient, and repellent treatment of sex by the movies and suggests that we solve the problem by classification of films as in Great Britain and by indignant complaints. Censorship is not the answer—it always fails "because the wrong things get censored for the wrong reasons by the wrong people." *Walk on the Wild Side*, a "rampantly sexual, really dirty movie" got the seal of the Legion of Decency because the prostitute was redeemed, while *Never on Sunday*, a "far more wholesome movie" was condemned by the Legion because the prostitute seemed to enjoy her work.

Crosby, William D. "Basis of Liability in Radio Defamation." *Boston University Law Review*, 29:90–97, April 1949. **C 650**

Crosman, Ralph L. "Freedom of the Press in 1931." *Journalism Quarterly*,

9:149–69, June 1932.　　**C 651**
A survey of censorship events of that year.

————. "Legal and Journalistic Significance of the Trial of John Peter Zenger." *Rocky Mountain Law Review*, 10:258–68, January 1938.　　**C 652**

Cross, Farrell. "Creeping Censorship in Our Libraries." *Coronet*, 50:40–45, May 1961.　　**C 653**
Cites instances where "self-righteous book burners" such as Governor Ross Barnett of Mississippi and San Antonio's "Minute Women" have censored American libraries.

Cross, Harold L. "Current Libel Trends." *Nieman Reports*, 5(1):7–11, January 1951.　　**C 654**

A discussion of libel in its flexible and varying forms by "one of America's great specialists in libel," former professor of journalism, Columbia University.

————. *The Executive Privilege to Withhold.* Columbia, Mo., Freedom of Information Center, School of Journalism, University of Missouri, 1958. 4p. (Publication no. 9, reprinted from the *ASNE Bulletin*, August 1958)　　**C 655**
The counsel for the American Society of Newspaper Editors writes of his doubts of the existence of executive privilege to withhold information from Congress and the people.

————. "The People's Right to Know: Its Nature and Needs." In *Lectures on Communications Media, Legal and Policy Problems, Delivered at University of Michigan Law School, June 16–June 18, 1954.* Ann Arbor, University of Michigan Law School, 1954, pp. 46–60.　　**C 656**
The author of a book of the same title discusses further the right of access to public records and proceedings. The right of the people "to examine public records and to attend public proceedings is the foundation without which the structure of freedom of speech, free press, and public trial cannot be built."

————. *The People's Right to Know. Legal Access to Public Records and Proceedings.* New York, Columbia University, 1953. 405p. (Cumulative Supplement no. 1, 1953, 36p.; no. 2, 1959, 114p.)　　**C 657**
An analysis of state and federal statutes, court decisions, opinions of attorneys general, and official regulations that determine rights of public and press access to public records and proceedings. Following a general discussion on the right of inspection, there are chapters on inspection of state and municipal nonjudicial records, inspection of state judicial records, access to judicial proceedings, access to state and municipal legislative and administrative proceedings, and federal nonjudicial records and proceedings. Appendixes include, newspapers as parties litigant in applications for compulsory inspection, state statutes which define the term "public records," state statutes which create, define, or state a general right of inspection of public records, and status of records for purposes other than inspection. This is a comprehensive reference work prepared by an authority on newspaper law for the Freedom of Information Committee of the American Society of Newspaper Editors.

————. "The People's Right to Know; Legal Developments in 1957–1958." In *Problems of Journalism; Proceedings of the Annual Meeting, American Society of Newspaper Editors, 1958.* Washington, D.C. ASNE, 1958, pp. 231–47.　　**C 658**
Events are summarized under the headings: The Federal Scene, In the States, and Legislation.

————. *The Right to Know.* Columbia, Mo., Freedom of Information Center, School of Journalism, University of Missouri, 1960. 6p. (Publication no. 26)　　**C 659**
An assessment of recent gains and losses in the public's "right to know."

————. "Some Twilight Zones in Newspaper Libel." *Cornell Law Quarterly*, 1:238–56, May 1916.　　**C 660**
It is becoming "increasingly difficult for the courts and journalists to steer a safe course between the Scylla of undue restraint and the Charybdis of abuse." The author discusses the Code of Civil Procedure with respect to libel action, noting some of the problems presented, and suggesting principles which should determine the decisions.

————. "Where Stands the Battle Line on Press Freedom?" *Nieman Reports*, 8(4):40–47, October 1954.　　**C 661**
A review of the historic right of freedom of the press and the modern conditions affecting this constitutional guarantee. The author finds expanded freedom in the matter of contempt of court, but elsewhere freedoms are abridged in various indirect ways.

Crosthwait, Charles. "Censorship and the School Library." *Wilson Library Bulletin*, 39:670–72, April 1965.　　**C 662**
Reviews the historic pressures against controversial works in school libraries. Some of the present targets of the censor are the teaching of such subjects as the United Nations, the New Deal, communism, race relations, and religion and morals. He suggests ways to meet such controversies.

[Croswell, Harry]. *The Speeches at full length of Mr. Van Ness, Mr. Caines, the Attorney-General [Ambrose Spencer] Mr. Harrison, and General Hamilton, in the Great Cause of the People, against Harry Croswell, on an Indictment for a Libel on Thomas Jefferson, President of the United States.* New York, Printed by G.&R.Waite, 1804. 78p. (Also in *American State Trials*, vol. 16, pp. 40–77. A summary of Hamilton's argument and commentary appears in Levy, *Freedom of the Press from Zenger to Jefferson*, pp. 377–99)　　**C 663**
Croswell, editor of the Federalist publication, *The Wasp*, of Hudson, N.Y., was charged with seditious libel at the instigation of Jefferson's friend, Governor George Clinton of New York. Croswell had accused Jefferson in his paper of paying James T. Callender to denounce Washington and Adams. A Democratic judge cited the opinion of Lord Mansfield in the case of the Dean of St. Asaph's, that truth was not a defense in seditious libel and that the judge, not the jury, decided whether or not the statement was libelous. On appeal, Alexander Hamilton represented Croswell, declaring that freedom of the press "consists in the right to publish, with impunity, truth, with good motive, for justifiable ends, though reflecting on government, magistracy, or individuals." The prosecution again insisted on the narrow definitions of Blackstone and Mansfield. Croswell was eventually acquitted by an evenly divided court. Thus we have the anomaly of the Jefferson administration adopting tactics of suppression against its critics that it had denounced under the previous administration of John Adams. In the following year the New York legislature passed a bill permitting truth as a defense and allowing a jury to decide whether or not the work was libelous.

Crotty, Robert T. *The Irish Press.* Columbia, Mo., Freedom of Information Center, School of Journalism, University of Missouri, 1962. 4p. (Publication no. 80)　　**C 664**
A survey of self-censorship in the Irish press.

Crouse, Jay. "'Off-the-Record' Is Form of Censorship." *Quill*, 48(7):16, 20, July 1960.　　**C 665**
"Off-the-record" conferences are subterfuges which stifle the voice of the press and deprive the people of its right to know.

Crow, Peter. *Access to News: Gray Areas.* Columbia, Mo., Freedom of Information Center, School of Journalism, University of Missouri, 1965. 4p. (Publication no. 148)　　**C 666**
"There are many incidents involving access to information in which the interests of the public and the interests of the individual citizens are almost equally balanced."

Crowell, Chester T. "My Daughter, Oh My Daughter." *New Republic*, 38:281–83, 7 May 1924.   **C 667**
A humorous account of a managing editor faced with the protests of a father concerned with the effect of news stories on his twelve-year-old daughter.

Crowell, Robert L. "'A Little Bit of Censoring.'" *Wilson Library Bulletin*, 39:652–57, April 1965.   **C 668**
The president and chairman of the board of the Thomas Y. Crowell Company describes the attacks on his company's *Dictionary of American Slang* in California where "in the minds of some voters, this book had now become associated with the deterioration of the English language, sexual perversion, liberalism, Communism, the alleged softening of the boys in Korea, and urban renewal." The title of the article is taken from a statement by California's State Superintendent of Public Instruction, Max Rafferty, who stated that "we ought to do a little bit of censoring" and advised the removal of the *Dictionary of American Slang* from California school libraries. Thomas W. Braden, president of the State Board of Education introduced a resolution against statewide banning of books from the public schools, which was unanimously approved by the Board. Crowell refers to a five-page statement from Professor S. I. Hayakawa on behalf of the *Dictionary*, to the effect that knowledge of evil does not incite evil, least of all dictionary words and definitions. About three out of four newspaper stories and editorials opposed the censorship. The company decided not to take legal action on the grounds of either libel or copyright violation (various groups had extracted and reproduced in pamphlets the most offensive entries and large quantities of these pamphlets were distributed, some among high school students), but to await the verdict of community opinion. "I wonder if perhaps it wasn't better that way. The people decided what the courts did not. The book was vindicated, and the attackers were discredited."

Crowell, William B. "Libel of Public Officials." *Bench and Bar*, 5(n.s.):104–15, July 1913.   **C 669**

Crowley, Ellen. "Who Do You Think You Are!" *Wyoming Library Roundup*, 5:[3–8], July 1950.   **C 670**
Librarians should be neither guardians of books nor censors of what the public reads.

Crowther, Bosley. *Movies and Censorship*. New York, Public Affairs Committee, 1962. 28p. (Public Affairs Pamphlet no. 332)   **C 671**
The motion picture critic of the *New York Times* reviews the history of censorship of movies and recent court decisions relating thereto. He discusses the various methods used to restrict obscene movies—the industry code, film classification (compulsory or advisory), and the British system. He lists some of the available independent film rating services.

———. "The Strange Case of *The Miracle*." *Atlantic Monthly*, 187:35–39, April 1951. Discussion, 188:15–16, July 1951.   **C 672**
"To what extent shall books, plays, and films be restricted in this country by what one or another religious group believes to be sacrilegious? The question has been posed directly by the recent efforts of Catholic authorities in New York City to cause the withdrawal of an Italian film and to achieve a boycott of the theatre which, under a court injunction, persisted in showing it." A record of events by which the Italian film, *The Miracle*, was hamstrung and harassed in New York; a demonstration "of the vehemence of a campaign waged by powerful elements of the Catholic church to restrain the subject matter of films shown in this country."

Crowther, Jonathan. *An Apology for the Liberty of the Press among the Methodists; Being an Examination of the Claim to restrain the Preachers from publishing; and an Investigation of the Subject of Hawking Booksellers*. 2d ed. Halifax, P. K. Holden, 1810. 8p.   **C 673**
A Methodist minister protests the prohibition upon the Methodist clergy from publishing works outside the official publishing agency of the Church and selling them via hawkers rather than through the Methodist bookrooms. He believes such restraints deny the "unalienable rights of men and true Christian Liberty." The loss of profits by the book-rooms are too small to be considered. He defends sale of religious books by hawkers or peddlers as a means of reaching families who do not patronize bookshops.

Crum, Mark. "Facing up to Controversy." *Michigan Librarian*, 28:11–12, March 1962.   **C 674**
Advice from the librarian of the Kalamazoo Public Library on what to do before a censorship issue arises, when an issue is raised, and when confronted with a genuinely fanatical person.

"Crusade against Boccaccio and Rabelais." *Publishers' Weekly*, 64:1397–98, 5 December 1903; 64:1491, 19 December 1903.   **C 675**
The campaign of Boston's Watch and Ward Society against four booksellers for selling the *Decameron* and the works of Rabelais. In the second article a Boston municipal judge is reported as declaring Boccaccio and Rabelais "impure" and imposing fines on the booksellers.

"Crusade against Unclean Books." *Literary Digest*, 76:30, 31 March 1923.   **C 676**
Discusses the work of New York's Clean Books League.

"Crusade for Truth." *Fortune*, 31:146–49, 185–91, April 1945.   **C 677**

Reviews the work of Kent Cooper in organizing a world tour of the American Society of Newspaper Editors to enlist international support for agreement on freedom of information. The *Fortune* editors conclude that Cooper was promoting both an ideal and freedom of cable rates and wireless transmission for the Associated Press of which he was director. He was also fighting for the right of free competition among news agencies.

Cummings, Arthur J. *The Press and a Changing Civilization*. London, Lane, 1936. 139p. (Twentieth Century Library)   **C 678**
There are chapters on The Early Struggle of the Press, Press in Wartime (World War I), and The Menace of Freedom (from Nazi and Soviet taint of state control).

Cummings, J. Joseph. "Television and the Right of Privacy." *Marquette Law Review*, 35:157–66, Fall 1952.   **C 679**

Cunningham, Glenn. "Operation Yorkville, a Major Force in the Battle against Obscene Literature." *Congressional Record*, A3704–6, 10 June 1963.   **C 680**

[Curll, Edmund]. "Trial for Publishing an Obscene Libel, 1727." In Howell, *State Trials*, vol. 17, pp. 154ff.   **C 681**
Curll, a London publisher, was brought to trial in Court of King's Bench for selling a pamphlet, *Venus in the Cloister, or, The Nun in her Smock*. The Court rejected an earlier decision by Judge Holt, in the case of *Rex v. Read*, that works tending to corrupt public morals ought to be tried in spiritual not temporal courts. The majority of justices found Curll guilty of obscene libel. Lord Fortescue dissented, calling the work bawdy, but not libelous, and performing the useful function of exposing corrupt priests. In 1720 Curll was brought before the House of Commons for announcing publication of the works of the Duke of Buckingham; in 1722 his edition of Pope's *Correspondence* was seized until the House could determine that it contained no letters from a Peer. At the time, Parliament considered it unlawful for the press to even mention the names of its members.

Curran, John P. ["Speech at the Trial of Doctor Drennan"]. In *Speeches of the Right Honourable John Philpot Curran . . . edited by Thomas Davis*. London, Bohn, 1847. pp. 220–33.   **C 682**
Dr. Drennan was indicted for having written and published a seditious libel, a proclamation addressed to United Irishmen. He was defended by Curran and acquitted by the jury. Archibald H. Rowan who signed the proclamation as secretary, and John Robb, the printer for the *Northern Star* in which the

address was published, were tried separately and found guilty. Curran's speeches at the Rowan trial are on pp. 161–211; his speech at the trial of the proprietors of the *Northern Star* are on pp. 233–39.

———. ["Speech at the Trial of Hamilton Rowan"]. In *Speeches of the Right Honourable John Philpot Curran . . . edited by Thomas Davis*. London, Bohn, 1847, pp. 161–211. (Text also appears in separate reports of the Rowan trial)   **C 683**
Curran defended Rowan in a libel trial for publication of an address to the Dublin United Irishmen.

———. ["Speech at the Trial of Peter Finnerty"]. In *Speeches of the Right Honourable John Philpot Curran . . . edited by Thomas Davis*. London, Bohn, 1847. pp. 330–62.   **C 684**

The publisher of the *Dublin Press*, a propagandist organ of the United Irishmen, was tried and convicted of libel for publishing a criticism of the trial and execution of William Orr, which he termed "murder." For his criticism of the trial Finnerty received a two-year sentence.

Curry, William L. *Comstockery; a Study in the Rise and Decline of a Watchdog Censorship; with Attention Particularly to the Reports of the New York Society for the Suppression of Vice, to Magazine Articles and to News Items and Editorials in the New York Times, Supplementing Other Standard Studies on Comstock and Censorship*. New York, Teachers College, Columbia University, 1957. 273 p. (Ph. D. dissertation, University Microfilms, no. 21,779)   **C 685**

Curtis, Bernard A. "The Morality of Catholic Censorship." *Christian Century*, 82:772–75, 16 June 1965.   **C 686**
"No one man nor even ten men should dare to judge and reject a book which explores Catholic dogma."

Curtis, George T. *Treatise on the Law of Copyright*. London, Sweet & Maxwell, 1847. 450 p.   **C 687**
An early study of English and American copyright.

Curtis, Thomas B. *Political Information Curbs*. Columbia, Mo., Freedom of Information Center, School of Journalism, University of Missouri, 1961. 3 p. (Publication no. 50)   **C 688**
In testimony before the Special House

Committee to Investigate Campaign Expenditures, Representative Curtis considers the role of the news media, the rising power of pressure groups, and the decline of power and responsibility of the parties. One of the greatest problems is the practice of the news media in giving "free" publicity to a favored candidate and denying proper publicity to an unfavored one.

Cusack, Mary A. *Editorializing in Broadcasting*. Detroit, Wayne State University, 1960. 273 p. (Ph. D. dissertation, University Microfilms, no. 60–2319)   **C 689**

———. "The Emergence of Political Editorializing in Broadcasting." *Journal of Broadcasting*, 8:53–62, Winter 1963–64.   **C 690**
The historical development of political editorializing as a concern of the American broadcasting industry.

Cushing, Marshall H. *Story of Our Post Office: The Greatest Government Department in All Its Phases*. Boston, Thayer, 1893. 1034 p.   **C 691**
Sex censorship of the mails is discussed on pp. 609–24; antilottery censorship, pp. 535, 540–41, 546; frauds, pp. 503, 567–78.

Cushman, Jerome. "Book Selection in the Small Public Library." In *Freedom of Communication; Proceedings of the First Conference on Intellectual Freedom . . .* Chicago, American Library Association, 1954. pp. 50–54.   **C 692**

———. "The Hidden Persuaders in Book Selection." *Library Journal*, 90:3553–58, 15 September 1965.   **C 693**
"Subtle pressures by the community, the library board, and the book selection staff itself are among the hidden persuaders in book selection."

———, et al. "Book Rejection: Is It Censorship?" *Library Journal*, 87:2298–2304+, 15 June 1962.   **C 694**
The editors ask the question: How does a librarian reject a book, particularly a controversial book, without incurring charges of censorship? Views of those librarians responding include Jerome Cushman, Edwin Castagna, Stuart C. Sherman, Ray Smith, Zada Taylor, John F. Anderson, Donald V. Black, and Robert B. Downs.

Cushman, Robert E. *Civil Liberties in the United States; a Guide to Current Problems and Experience*. Ithaca, N.Y., Cornell University Press, 1956. 248 p. (Cornell Studies in Civil Liberty)   **C 695**
Chapter 1 deals with freedom of speech, press, assembly, and petition. It includes government

protection of public morals and decency, protection of private interests against libel and slander, protection against speeches and publications alleged to be nuisances, and postal censorship.

———. "'Clear and Present Danger' in Free Speech Cases: a Study in Judicial Semantics." In Milton R. Konvitz and Arthur E. Murphy, eds., *Essays in Political Theory Presented to George H. Sabine*, Ithaca, N.Y., Cornell University Press, 1958, pp. 311–24.   **C 696**

———. *Keep Our Press Free!* New York, Public Affairs Committee, 1946. 32 p. (Public Affairs Pamphlet no. 123)   **C 697**
A popularly presented history of freedom of the press—wartime and peacetime sedition, obscene literature, Supreme Court test cases, and economic restraints. The author is an authority on constitutional law.

———. "National Police Power under the Postal Clause of the Constitution." *Minnesota Law Review*, 4:402–40, May 1920.   **C 698**
The purpose of the article is "to trace the various lines along which this national police power has developed under the postal clause of the constitution, to examine the conflicting views regarding the constitutional propriety of that development, and to determine, if possible, what are the true limits of the police power as derived." Problems are treated under four principal topics: (1) Police regulations which Congress has enacted to protect the safety and efficiency of the postal system. (2) Police regulations enacted to prevent the postal system from being used for purposes which are injurious to the public welfare. (Fraud order legislation and the obscene literature acts fall into this group.) (3) Those regulations which deny the right to use the mails for the purpose of violating or evading the laws of the states. (4) The proposals that conformity to general police regulations be made the price of the enjoyment of postal privileges.

———. "Some Constitutional Problems of Civil Liberty." *Boston University Law Review*, 23:335–78, June 1943.   **C 699**
The first part discusses freedom of the press, noting three groups that must play a part in preserving this freedom: the legislature, the government official, and the ordinary citizen.

Cusseres, Benjamin de. "Case of Prudery Against Literature; Attack on Gautier's Novel Brings to Mind Many Historic Examples of Law's Moral Censorship of Books." *New York Times*, section 7, p. 3, 23 May 1920.   **C 700**
Historical discussion of sex censorship, prompted by the court awarding damages

against the New York vice society for malicious prosecution of a book clerk (*Raymond D. Halsey v. John E. Sumner*) in the sale of Gautier's *Mademoiselle de Maupin*.

"Customs Censorship." *Publishers' Weekly*, 117:984–85, 22 February 1930. **C 701**

Discussion of the forthcoming debates over the censorship clause in the Tariff Bill before the U.S. Senate, and opposition to the clause by the New York Library Association.

Cuthell, John. "Trial for Publishing a Seditious Libel, a Pamphlet Written by Gilbert Wakefield, 1799." In Howell, *State Trials*, vol. 27, pp. 642 ff.; also in Erskine, *Speeches*, vol. 5, pp. 213–46. **C 702**

Bookseller Cuthell was tried and convicted of selling Rev. Gilbert Wakefield's pamphlet attacking the Pitt administration. In his defense Thomas Erskine maintained that Cuthell had no knowledge of the content of the work and therefore no criminal intent. Lord Kenyon ignored this distinction, declaring the work libelous, and then invited the jurors to make up their own minds. The jury found Cuthell guilty. Lord Kenyon stated the issue of libel in these simple terms: "A man may publish any thing which twelve of his countrymen think is not blameable, but that he ought to be punished if he publishes that which is blameable."

Cutler, Charles R. "The Post Office Department and the Administrative Procedure Act." *Northwestern University Law Review*, 47:72–80, March–April 1952. **C 703**

Notes on Post-Office "control over the morals and manners of the mails" in relation to due process, 1946–51.

Cutler, S. Olney. "The Clear and Present Danger Test—Schenck to Dennis." *George-*

town *Law Journal*, 40:304–20, January 1952. **C 704**

Covers the period from the Schenck case, 249 U.S. 47 (1919) through the Dennis case, 341 U.S. 494 (1951).

Cutting, Bronson, Reed Smoot, *et al.* ["The Customs Censorship"]. *Congressional Record*, 71:4433–39, 10 October 1929; 71:4445–72, 11 October 1929; 72:5414–33, 17 March 1930; 72:5487–5522, 18 March 1930. (Extracts of the speeches in Beman, *Censorship of Speech and the Press*, pp. 431–66) **C 705**

Lengthy discussions on an amendment to the tariff act, offered by Senator Bronson Cutting, to exempt literature from the operation of the U.S. Customs censor. Senator Reed Smoot was the chief opponent. The amendment failed, but a modified amendment passed.

D

"D——!" *Librarian*, 3:281–83, March 1913.　**D1**

The banning of *Tom Jones* by the Library Committee of Doncaster, prompts this witty essay on banning books because of objectionable words.

Dahl, Francis W., and Charles W. Moton. "Dahl's Boston." *Atlantic Monthly*, 178(5): 55–60, November 1946.　**D2**

The cartoonist whose caricatures of Watch and Ward censors appeared frequently in the *Boston Herald*, describes the "noncensorship technique of suppressing books" used by the Watch and Ward, the Boston booksellers, and the police.

Daily Worker (London). *The Case of the Daily Worker. By the Members of the Former Editorial Board: J. B. S. Haldane (Chairman); Sean O'Casey; Councillor J. Owen; R. Page Arnot.* London, Editorial Board, *Daily Worker*, [1941?]. 20p.　**D3**

A protest against the suppression of the London *Daily Worker* during World War II, under a wartime regulation permitting the British Home Secretary to prohibit the issue of a newspaper that systematically publishes "matter calculated to foment opposition to the prosecution of the war to a successful issue."

[Dakin, Edwin F.]. *The Blight that Failed*. New York, Blue Ribbon Books, [1930?] 16p.　**D4**

"Being an account of how Mr. Edwin Franden Dakin's outstanding biography, 'Mrs. Eddy: The Biography of a Virginal Mind,' came to be published; of the efforts made by officials of the Christian Science Church to obtain access to the MS. in order to censor it; of the methods adopted to induce booksellers and libraries not to stock or circulate the book, and of the failure of this concerted effort to put a blight on the liberties of free speech, free thought, and a free press."

[——]. "Foreword." In his *Mrs. Eddy; The Biography of a Virginal Mind*. New York, Blue Ribbon Books, [1930], pp. vii–x.　**D5**

The author's foreword refers to the suppression of the Georgine Milmine biography of Mrs. Eddy, the plates having been bought by a friend of Mrs. Eddy and destroyed. The publisher's preface of the present book describes the unsuccessful efforts of an "organized Minority" to suppress the Dakin volume. Dakin's bibliography cites other works on the Christian Science "index expurgatorius." G. P. Putnam withdrew the fourth volume of the *Cambridge History of American Literature* in 1921 when the Christian Science Committee on Publication objected to Professor Woodbridge Riley's article on *Science and Health* (he had referred to Mrs. Eddy as "the thrice-married female Trismegistus"). An article by the Rev. Lyman P. Powell was substituted. Powell also wrote a replacement article for Professor Riley's *The Book of Mormon*, objected to by members of that sect (*New York Times*, 19 April 1921; 4 September 1921).

Dalcourt, Gerald J. "The *Index* [of Prohibited Books]: Past, Present, Future." *Catholic Library World*, 32:45–50, October 1960.　**D6**

A revision of the Catholic *Index* is expected, bringing it more in line with present-day thinking.

——. "Pornography, the Law, and the Kronhausens." *Catholic Library World*, 32:343–47, March 1961.　**D7**

A critique of *Pornography and the Law* by Phyllis and Eberhard Kronhausen. The author questions many of the assumptions and conclusions in this study. "It should be obvious that the arguments of the Kronhausens against censorship are completely unacceptable for a Christian. Nor are they very persuasive from a philosophical and scientific point of view . . . The analysis of hard-core pornography is the only major section of the Kronhausen book which is durable."

[Dale, Alan]. "Censors Are Bleaching Plays Abroad." *Current Opinion*, 77:328–37, September 1924.　**D8**

A Hearst drama reporter, after a tour of theatrical performances abroad, notes that London was more puritanical and Paris more prudish than New York was in the heydey of Comstockery.

——. "Dramatic Censors and Some New Plays." *Cosmopolitan Magazine*, 47: 74–80, June 1909.　**D9**

"Our moral censors are so busy denouncing the evils of the stage that they never find time to advise us to see the fine and inspiring products."

Dalrymple, Ian. "The Film Censorship." *Spectator*, 155:895–96, 29 November 1935.　**D10**

An appeal for lighter censorship and a more tolerant attitude toward the motion picture on the part of public officials. The reaction of the public can be depended upon to preserve the public morality.

Daly, J. Bowles. *The Dawn of Radicalism*. London, Sonnenschein, 1892. 252p. (First published in 1886 under the title *Radical Pioneers of the Eighteenth Century*.)　**D11**

Largely the story of John Horne Tooke and John Wilkes and their efforts in behalf of the freedom of the press in Great Britain during the latter years of the eighteenth century. Includes a discussion of the prosecution of Woodfall for the Junius letters, the sedition trials of Paine, Muir, Palmer, Hardy, and other victims of the hysteria that swept England during the French Revolution.

Daly, John Charles. "Ensuring Fair Trials and a Free Press: A Task for the Press and the Bar Alike." *American Bar Association Journal*, 50:1037–42, November 1964.　**D12**

This television personality and reporter states that reforms are needed in reporting the news about sensational criminal cases, and he blames both the news media and the Bar for the unsatisfactory handling of publicity about trials like those of Jack Ruby and the Sinatra kidnappers. His proposed remedy is similar to that recommended by the Warren Commission in its report on the Kennedy assassination.

——. *News—Broadcasting's First Responsibility*. Washington, D.C., National Association of Broadcasting, 1957. 16p.　**D13**

The vice-president of the American Broadcasting Company speaks against Canon 35 of the American Bar Association's Judicial Ethics which forbids broadcasting of courtroom proceedings or taking of photographs during court sessions.

Dameron, Charles E., III. "Obscenity Statute—Proof of Scienter." *North Carolina Law Review*, 38:634–38, June 1960. **D 14**

Notes on four cases: *Smith v. California*, 361 U.S. 147 (1959); a West Virginia case, a New York case, and a Wisconsin case.

Dana, John Cotton. "Public Libraries as Censors." *Bookman*, 49:147–52, April 1919. **D 15**

"Skill in the art of exclusion" is demanded of every librarian who must live within a limited book budget. The line between books included and books excluded shifts in accordance with the character of the community, stock on hand, funds, and anticipated demand. The librarian's personal tastes and views should not be injected. The author, librarian of the Newark Free Public Library, relates some of his experiences with patrons who challenged his decisions in book selection. He describes library censorship as a "benign necessity."

Danahey, J. D., and D. A. Ruen. "Freedom of Speech and Press, Extension of Personal Rights under Fourteenth Amendment." *University of Detroit Law Journal*, 3:80–85, January 1940. **D 16**

Dang, Charlotte L. "How to Answer Would-Be Censors." *Hawaii Library Association Journal*, 22:14–16, Fall 1964. **D 17**

Dangerfield, George. "Invisible Censorship." *North American Review*, 244:334–48, Winter 1937–38. **D 18**

A discussion of British self-censorship, the result of predatory libel laws, monopoly newspaper ownership, and "a willingness on the part of the public to blind itself to unpleasant facts." He contrasts the British self-restraint on publication in the realms of politics (the Simpson Affair) and sex (James Hanley's *Boy*) with the greater freedom in America.

"A Dangerous Bill." *Outlook*, 109:549–50, 10 March 1915. **D 19**

Opposition to a measure in Congress to extend the bill which excludes obscene publications from the mails so that it will also exclude scurrilous and libelous matter. Such an extension, which he believes was prompted by the Catholic Church, would constitute censorship of the press.

"Dangerous Thoughts: Zone of Silence." *Nation*, 170:525, 27 May 1950; 171:39, 8 July 1950. **D 20**

"The Observer" notes numerous instances of censorship and blacklisting in radio and television, which force the media into a "zone of silence," the name being taken from an area of shipwreck and disaster near Vancouver Island.

"Dangers to Press Freedom." *Fortune*, 35:2–5, April 1947. **D 21**

A review of the general report of the Commission on Freedom of the Press.

Daniels, Jonathan. "Book-Burners and Their Motives." *Nation*, 153:375, 18 October 1941. **D 22**

Condemnation of "people out to destroy the freedom of books," in particular, the Georgia Board of Education which banned, along with a dozen or so other books, *A Man Named Grant* by Helen Todd.

———. "The Naval Censor." *Nation*, 152:130, 1 February 1941. **D 23**

A letter marked "confidential" from Secretary of Navy Knox concerning regulation of the press prompts this discussion of the dissemination of military information. "Both the army and the people would be safer from the consequences of military mistakes if there were a clearer understanding all down the line in Washington about just what constitutes legitimate information and a more efficient system of getting it through the press to the people."

———. *They Will Be Heard; America's Crusading Newspaper Editors.* New York, McGraw-Hill, 1965. 336p. **D 24**

Includes chapters on John Peter Zenger, Elijah P. Lovejoy, William Duane and other editors who were victims of the Sedition Act, the editors who defied the stamp act, and the pioneer San Francisco editor, James King of William.

Daniels, Josephus. "Jefferson's Contribution to a Free Press." In *The Writings of Thomas Jefferson.* Memorial Edition. Washington, D.C., Thomas Jefferson Memorial Association, 1907, vol. 18, pp. i–xlvii. **D 25**

"Mr. Jefferson's contribution to the free press was not bounded by geographical lines or limited by any period of time. It was for all countries and all ages. In his life, whether laboring in the land of his birth to obtain, safeguard and make permanent the freedom of the press, or seeking to aid the people of France, groping through the darkness with only the dim gleam of a censored press, to secure the 'liberty of speaking and writing which guard all other liberties,' he was always animated by faith in the capacity of man to control his own affairs, and by this oath of 'eternal hostility against every form of tyranny over the human mind.'"

Daniels, Walter M., *ed. The Censorship of Books.* New York, Wilson, 1954. 202p.

(The Reference Shelf, vol. 26, no. 5.) **D 26**

A compilation of readings and introductory notes arranged under the following topics: Nature of the Problem, Moral Censorship, Political Censorship, United States Libraries Abroad, Textbooks, and Censors and the Librarian. Most of the articles reprinted are contemporary, and, taken together, form a substantial picture of the pros and cons of censorship.

Danna, Sammy R. *Broadcast Editorializing.* Columbia, Mo., Freedom of Information Center, School of Journalism, University of Missouri, 1965. 7p. (Publication no. 141) **D 27**

The author traces the development of editorializing through the FCC "fairness doctrine." He presents the FCC hearings beginning with the Mayflower case and gives arguments for and against editorializing. He uses surveys to show the number of stations that air their opinions.

Da Ponte, Durant. "Some Evasions of Censorship in *Following the Equator*." *American Literature*, 29:92–95, March 1957. **D 28**

An examination of certain passages in *Following the Equator* as examples of a "possible attempt on Mark Twain's part if not to defy, at least to circumvent the influence of the oppressive morality of his times."

Darling, Edward. *How We Fought For Our Schools.* New York, Norton, 1954. 255p. **D 29**

A documentary novel built around the tactics of national pressure groups in attacking school textbooks.

Darrow, Clarence, and Harriet Vittum. "Censorship of 'Movies': Clarence Darrow and Harriet Vittum Debate New Ordinance." *City Club Bulletin* (Chicago), 11:187–88, 3 June 1918. **D 30**

Relates to Chicago's movie censorship ordinance.

Date with Liberty. 20 min., b/w movie. New York, Anti-Defamation League of B'nai B'rith. **D 31**

Based on William O. Douglas' *Almanac of Liberty.* One of the five sequences deals with a martyr to freedom of the press, Elijah P. Lovejoy.

Daughters of the American Revolution, National Society. National Defense Committee. *Textbook Study, 1958–1959.* Washington, D.C., DAR, 1960. 20p. **D 32**

Criticism of the nation's school textbooks, largely on ideological grounds, with a listing of satisfactory and unsatisfactory titles. Suggestions are given as to how members can influence local school officials to get satisfactory books back into the school system. "You will be challenging the entrenched 'liberal' position. You will find there is no one so intolerant or vindictive as the 'liberal' who is quick to deny freedom of speech if it includes criticism of the propaganda in textbooks."

Davenport, Walter. "The Dirt Disher." *Collier's*, 81:26+, 24 March 1928. **D 33**
An account of Richard Kyle Fox and the *Police Gazette*. "He had watched his original stake of $2 multiply to $2,000,000 through the business of peddling scandal and racy chitchat."

———. "You Can't Say That." *Collier's*, 107(7)19, 62–65, 15 February 1941. **D 34**
Prediction of wartime censorship and a sketch of Lowell Mellett, "who will very likely be the American censor should the United States slip into this war. Sometime ago Mr. Roosevelt assigned Mr. Mellett to work up a plan." The job actually went to Byron Price.

Davidson, Clifford. "St. Cloud—How the Flames Spread." *New Republic*, 128(26): 13–14, 29 June 1953. **D 35**
Influenced by a group of Catholic clergy, St. Cloud, Minn., passed a city ordinance banning salacious comic books. A board of review took action against works of James T. Farrell, Richard Wright, and Somerset Maugham. A fight against the censorship, centered in the faculty and student body of the St. Cloud Teachers College, led to the board of review being suspended by the city council.

Davidson, Donald. "Decorum in the Novel." *Modern Age*, 9:34–48, Winter 1964–65. **D 36**
The author expresses concern "when novelists lose all conception of prose fiction as high art and are willing in the name of freedom, to practice novel-writing as a low art," abandoning common restraints in subject matter and language and crossing the border into the realm of obscenity. "Censorship, then, would be the deplorable fate toward which the liberationists are hustling us."

Davidson, Philip. *Propaganda on the American Revolution, 1763–83*. Chapel Hill, N.C., University of North Carolina Press, 1941. 460 p. **D 37**
While largely a study of propaganda emanating from both Whigs and Tories, several sections of the volume discuss efforts to counteract wartime propaganda. Chapter 9 describes efforts of the Sons of Liberty to suppress pro-

British pamphlets and newspapers through boycott, censorship, burnings, and intimidation of the printers.

Davie, Emily. "*Profile* and the Congressional Censors." *Saturday Review*, 38:11+, 5 November 1955. (Reprinted in Downs, *The First Freedom*, pp. 247–50) **D 38**
The author discusses the Congressional attack on her book, *Profile of America: an Autobiography of the U.S.A.*, and the refusal of Congress to provide funds for distribution of copies requested for U.S. Information Libraries abroad. Although the work carried a foreword by Charles A. Lindbergh and was widely praised in the United States and abroad, certain Congressmen objected to the pictures of a little red school house, a dust storm, and a quotation from Thoreau.

Davies, J. Eric. "Is There Sense in Censorship?" *Student Librarian*, 4:3–5, July 1964. **D 39**

Davis, Elmer. "The Comstock Load." *Saturday Review of Literature*, 3:689–91, 2 April 1927. **D 40**
A lengthy review with commentary on Broun and Leech's *Anthony Comstock: Roundsman of the Lord*.

———. "News and the Whole Truth." In his *But We Were Born Free*, Indianapolis, Bobbs-Merrill, 1954, pp. 147–77. **D 41**
A criticism of news coverage by the American press which, he says, often falls short of telling the whole truth. "Too much of our news is one-dimensional, when truth has three dimensions (or maybe more)."

———. "Security and the News." *Public Administration Review*, 12(2):85–88, Spring 1952. **D 42**
A discussion of the implications of the President's order concerning security of information and classification of government documents.

———, and Byron Price. *War Information and Censorship*. Washington, D.C., American Council on Public Affairs, 1943. 79 p. **D 43**
Davis, head of the Office of War Information in World War II, describes the work of that agency in the distribution and control of war information. Price, head of the Office of Censorship, explains the system of voluntary cooperation of the press and radio under the codes of wartime practices.

Davis, Ewin L. "Regulation of Radio Advertising." *Annals of the American Academy of Political and Social Science*, 177:154–58, January 1935. **D 44**
The chairman of the Federal Trade Commission describes the work of his agency in

protecting legitimate business and the public from false and misleading advertising. The job is carried out with the support of advertisers, press, and broadcasters.

Davis, Forrest. "How to Burn a Book." *National Review*, 2:9–11, 27 June 1956. **D 45**
The author describes attempts to suppress publication of the U.S. Senate subcommittee document, *The Communist Party of the United States*.

Davis, Jerome. *Liberty, Censorship and the Fish Committee*. New York, American Civil Liberties Union, 1931. 6 p. mimeo. **D 46**
A speech by Professor Davis of Yale over Station WEAF discusses the proposal of the Fish Committee (Congressional Committee to Investigate Communist Activities, headed by Hamilton Fish, Jr.) to outlaw free speech for Communists.

Davis, Norris G. *Freedom of the Press in Texas: A Comparative Study of State Legal Control of Mass News Media*. Minneapolis, Minn., University of Minnesota, 1954. 575 p. (Ph. D. dissertation, University Microfilms, no. 8450) **D 47**
The study analyzes the legal restraints on freedom of the press in Texas and compares the Texas law with that of New York.

———. *The Press and the Law in Texas*. Austin, University of Texas Press, 1956. 244 p. **D 48**
Includes chapters on Freedom of the Press in Texas, Civil Libel, Criminal Libel, and Access to Public Records.

———. "Print That Picture at Your Peril!" *Quill*, 30(11):3–4, November 1942. **D 49**
Deals with the publication of newspaper photographs as an invasion of privacy.

Davis, Peter. "Thinking Man's Radio." *Fact*, 1(2):23–29, March–April 1964. **D 50**
The story of the controversial Pacifica Foundation broadcasting chain (New York, Berkeley, and Los Angeles), its provocative programs, its struggle to survive without advertising support, and the long controversy with the FCC over renewal of a broadcasting license.

Davis, Philip R. *Obscene Literature and the Constitution*. Chicago, [Boswell Club?], 1944. 14 p. **D 51**
In an address to the Boswell Club, 28 February 1944, a Chicago lawyer concludes that the final legal test of obscenity is whether the work is literature as distinct from pornography; all doubts should be resolved in favor of the work—book, play, art, or movie.

Davis, Richard Harding. "War Correspondent: Change from Independence to Close Surveillance." *Collier's Weekly*, 48: 21–22, 30, 7 October 1911. **D 52**
The position of the war correspondent has changed in the course of a decade from one of a welcome free-lance reporter with complete independence to that of a prisoner and a suspected spy. This veteran war correspondent calls for greater acceptance of correspondents by the military as a legitimate and necessary part of military campaigns.

Davis, Thurston N. "A Time for Silence or a Time to Speak?" *America*, 96:670–72, 16 March 1957. **D 53**
Father Davis discusses the denial of clearance of an address over the C.B.S. "Church of the Air" because of its controversial nature.

Davison, Thomas. *The Trial of Thomas Davison, for publishing a Blasphemous Libel in the Deist's Magazine, in the Court of King's Bench, Guildhall London, on Monday, October 23d, 1820. With a prefatory letter to Mr. Justice Best . . .* London, Printed for the editor, by R. Helder, 1820. 58p. **D 54**
The trial of Davison in 1820 for sale of pamphlets published by Richard Carlile is noteworthy because Justice Best fined the defendant for objectionable remarks made in his own defense, an action widely denounced in the press. This account also contains a letter from Erasmus Perkins criticizing Justice Best for the "extraordinary interference with the Defendant in the progress of his defence." The trial had been brought about at the instance of the Society for the Suppression of Vice. Davison was given a two-year prison sentence.

Davson, *Sir* Geoffrey L. S. *Elinor Glyn: A Biography* by Anthony Glyn [pseud.]. Garden City, N. Y., Doubleday, 1955. 348p. **D 55**
The grandson of Elinor Glyn devotes a portion of the biography of his grandmother to the Boston censorship of her voluptuous novel, *Three Weeks*, a best seller almost from the time of its publication in 1907. A movie burlesque of the novel, *Pimple's Three Weeks (without the option)* brought forth a libel suit filed by Mrs. Glyn (*Glyn v. Western Feature Film Co.*) in which the judge found for the defendants. "It is enough for me to say that to a book of such a cruelly destructive tendency no protection will be extended by a court of equity. It rests to others to determine whether such a work ought not to be altogether suppressed."

Dawbarn, Charles. "Abuse of the English Press." *English Review*, 21:490–96, December 1915. **D 56**
The author condemns the docility of the British press and notes the difficulty in wartime of telling the truth without fear or favor. The public often condemns the press as muckraking when it merely tells the truth. The press is "hopelessly browbeaten and battered by a snobbery that deserves the guillotine." The ungenerous public does not deserve the press it is getting.

Dawes, Manasseh (Matthew). *The Deformity of the Doctrine of Libels, and Informations Ex Officio, With a View of the Case of the Dean of St. Asaph, and an Enquiry into the Rights of Jurymen; in a Letter to the Hon. T. Erskine.* London, J. Stockdale, 1785. 40p. **D 57**

———. *England's Alarm! On the Prevailing Doctrine of Libels, as Laid Down by the Earl of Mansfield, in a Letter to his Lordship by a Country Gentleman [with] the Dialogue between a Gentleman and a Farmer by Sir William James, with Remarks thereon and the case of the Dean of St. Asaph.* London, 1785. 56p. **D 58**
Dawes was a lawyer of the Inner Temple whose liberal views on freedom of the press corresponded to those of Thomas Erskine and clashed with those of Chief Justice Mansfield. He was one of the first English writers to advocate the overt acts test in political libel—that an expression was not actionable unless it advocated the commission of a crime. This was in direct opposition to the prevailing bad-tendency test.

[Dawson, Francis W.]. *The Great Libel Case. Report of the Criminal Prosecution of the News and Courier, for Libelling Sheriff and Ex-congressman C. C. Bowen. The State v. F. W. Dawson.* Charleston, S. C., [The News and Courier], 1875. 96p. **D 59**

Dawson, Gladys, and Oswald Dawson. *Free Press Fiasco; Balance Sheet and Counter Manifesto.* Leeds, A. S. Fryer, 1898. 28p. **D 60**
Concerns the controversy which arose from George Bedborough's plea of guilty in the trial for selling Havelock Ellis' *Studies in the Psychology of Sex.*

Dawson, Mitchell. "Censorship on the Air." *American Mercury*, 31:257–68, March 1934. (Reprinted in Summers, *Radio Censorship*, pp. 172–78) **D 61**
Reviews cases of radio censorship by the Federal Radio Commission under the phrase: "No person within the jurisdiction of the United States shall utter any obscene, indecent or profane language by means of radio communication." Recommends a more constructive social policy on the part of the licensing authority.

———. "Paul Pry and Privacy." *Atlantic Monthly*, 150:385–94, October 1932. **D 62**

Contemporary Paul Prys are the tabloid reporters, radio gossips, Sunday supplement writers, cameramen, wire-tapping Prohibition agents, blackmailing shysters, and back-fence biographers. The author protests the exploitation of the public appetite for sensational news, but opposes any government control of the press. Instead there should be a reasonable restraint, voluntarily imposed, which would protect "the indiscriminate betrayal and destruction of private lives and sensibilities."

Dawson, Oswald. "Millard and Thompson Cases." *Adult*, 2:84–87, April 1898. **D 63**
The acquittal of *Book for Women* and the judicial condemnation of the use of lantern slides of nude women in a lecture "for ladies only."

———. *Personal Rights and Sexual Wrongs.* London, William Reeves, 1897. 62p. **D 64**
In defense of Moses Harman of Valley Falls, Kan., and his crusade for the emancipation of women through sex education.

Dawson, Samuel A. *Freedom of the Press: A Study of the Legal Doctrine of "Qualified Privilege."* Foreword by Henry W. Sackett. New York, Columbia University Press, 1924. 120p. **D 65**
Deals with the legal aspects of libel and the rights of newspapers in reporting the actions of legislatures, courts, and government officials. "The heart of the doctrine of qualified privilege is the right of the people of a free nation to have published for their information what their rulers—their public officials—are doing . . . This is a brief account of the efforts of the public press to achieve this right in England and America."

Dawson, Thomas. *The Law of the Press.* 2nd ed. London, Staples Press, 1947. 222p. **D 66**
A summary of English newspaper law, including the law of libel, qualified privilege, fair comment, seditious, blasphemous and obscene libel, and copyright.

Deacon, William A. *Sh—h—h . . . Here Comes the Censor! An Address to the Ontario Library Association, March 26, 1940.* Montreal, Macmillan, 1940. 16p. **D 67**

"The Dead Hand Again." *Times Literary Supplement*, 3257:665, 30 July 1964. (Reprinted in *Censorship*, Autumn 1964) **D 68**
Mostly about censorship in South Africa.

Deakin, Terence J. "B. M. and B. N." *Times Literary Supplement*, 3191:295, 26 April 1963. **D 69**

References to the handling of erotica by the British Museum and the Bibliothèque Nationale.

————, comp. *Catalogi Librorum Eroticorum. A Critical Bibliography of Erotic Bibliographies and Book Catalogues.* London, Cecil and Amelia Woolf, 1965. 28 p. (400 copies) **D 70**

Dean, Joseph. *Hatred, Ridicule or Contempt: A Book of Libel Cases.* London, Constable, 1953. 271 p. **D 71**
An analysis of 40 British libel cases from 1824 to 1946, some momentous, others absurd. Each case was chosen to embody some aspect of the libel law.

Dearmer, Percy, *ed. Religious Pamphlets . . .* London, Paul, Trench, Trüber, 1898. 380 p. **D 72**
Documents and commentary tracts include the Marprelate libels, the anti-Marprelate libels, and the trials of William Prynne, John Bastwick, Richard Baxter, and Daniel DeFoe.

de Bekker, L. J. "America and Rabelais." *Spectator,* 129:363–64, 16 September 1922. **D 73**
A letter to the editor tells of censorship of such classics as the works of Boccaccio, Rabelais, and *The Arabian Nights.*

Dedmond, Francis B. "Poe's Libel Suit Against T[homas] D[unn] English. *Boston Public Library Quarterly,* 5:31–37, January 1953. **D 74**
Poe was awarded $225 damages against the publishers of the New York *Evening Mirror* for alleged libelous remarks made by English in a quarrel in print between the two writers.

Defence of the Drama, Containing Mansel's Free Thoughts, Extracts from the Most Celebrated Writers, and a Discourse on the Lawfulness & Unlawfulness of Plays; by the Celebrated Father Caffaro . . . New York, G. Champley, 1826. 294 p. **D 75**

"Defenders of Books and Public Schools Analyze Recent Attacks." *Publishers' Weekly,* 160:1381–83, 29 September 1951. **D 76**
A summary of recent articles and pamphlets by professional educators answering attacks on school textbooks.

Defoe, Daniel. *The Best of Defoe's Review: An Anthology.* Compiled and edited by William L. Payne. New York, Columbia University Press, 1951. 289 p. **D 77**
The section on The Press: License and Liberty, pp. 71–103, contains these excerpts: Of Truth, and Freedom of the Press (1712); A Proposed Tax Examined (1711); and Of Taxing the Press (1712).

————. *An Essay on the Regulation of the Press.* Introduction by John Robert Moore. Oxford, Published by Blackwell for the Luttrell Society, 1948. 29 p. (Luttrell Reprint no. 7) First published in 1704. **D 78**
Defoe presents cogent arguments against prior licensing, showing that the system lends itself to arbitrary action by the party in power and encourages bribery. While recognizing the need to curb "licentious extravagence" of the press, he finds licensing as a cure is like cutting off the leg to cure the gout in a man's toe. Instead he proposes a law which will state precisely what is illegal to publish "so that all men will know when they transgress," and so that judges will not impose their personal opinions as to what is licentious. Defoe agrees with John Locke that the author's and publisher's names should appear on the publication so that there will be someone to answer for the work. Written in 1704 while Defoe was serving a prison sentence for his *The Shortest Way With Dissenters.*

[————]. *A Hymn to the Pillory.* London, 1703. 15 p. (Reprinted in James T. Boulton's edition of *Daniel Defoe,* pp. 100–109 and in Isadore Abramowitz, *The Great Prisoners . . . The First Anthology of Literature Written in Prison,* pp. 289–303) **D 79**
While Defoe stood in the pillory for his offense in writing *The Shortest Way With Dissenters,* this pamphlet from his pen was sold on the streets of London. In it Defoe said he considered it no dishonor to stand where earlier defenders of a free press—Prynne, Burton, and Bastwick—had stood.

[————]. *A Letter to a Member of Parliament, shewing the Necessity of Regulating the Press . . with a Particular Answer to the Objections that have of Late been Advanced against it.* Oxford, G. West and H. Clements, 1699. 67 p. **D 80**
Wing attributes this to Defoe.

[————]. *A Vindication of the Press; or, an Essay on the Usefulness of Writing, on Criticism, and the Qualification of Authors . . .* London, T. Walker, 1718. 36 p. (Reprinted with an introduction by Otho Clinton Williams. Los Angeles, William Clark Memorial Library, University of California, 1951. 36 p.) (Augustan Reprint Society. Publication no. 29) **D 81**
This pamphlet, attributed to Defoe, does not seem to be written for any special occasion, but as a general apology for a free press and as a defense of accepting pay for political writing from both parties. Defoe served both Whigs and Tories. At one time, he was hired by the Whigs to take a job with a Tory paper for the purpose of sabotage. Only two copies of this rare pamphlet are known—one is at the Bodleian, the other at the New York Public Library.

de Grazia, Edward. "Defending the Freedom to Read in the Courts." *ALA Bulletin,* 59:507–15, June 1965. **D 82**
A defender of numerous books and magazines in the courts advises librarians on ways to implement the Library Bill of Rights. "It is my opinion that under present law no book selected by a librarian for his shelves can constitutionally be found obscene. Why? Because any such book must have at least some slight redeeming social importance." Two areas of caution must be observed—the placement of the work in the collection and practices where minors are concerned. There is need, nevertheless, for librarians to have able legal counsel available to them. De Grazia bases his view on the *Roth* decision of the U.S. Supreme Court, which has come to be viewed as the law of the land in matters of obscenity. A publication is obscene if its *dominant* appeal is to the *prurient interests* of the *average person* applying *contemporary standards.* This decision embodies many earlier court rulings on obscenity, but not the concept expressed by Judge Jerome Frank (*Roth v. Goldman,* 1948) that arousal of erotic feeling is not socially harmful, or Judge Curtis Bok's point of view that a book is obscene only if it can be demonstrated as the cause of a crime or intent to commit a crime. De Grazia calls attention to the case of *Smith v. California* (1959) in which the Supreme Court ruled that proof of "guilty knowledge" on the part of a bookseller was essential in a conviction of obscenity and that the obscenity laws should not be enforced in such a way as to require a bookseller to screen and censor books.

————. "Equal Defamation for All: Section 315 of the Federal Communications Act." *George Washington Law Review,* 20:706–25, June 1952. **D 83**

————. "Obscenity and the Mail: a Study in Administrative Restraint." *Law and Contemporary Problems,* 20:608–20, Autumn 1955. **D 84**
"The United States Post Office Department enjoys the dubious distinction of being the only governmental agency, federal or state, fully empowered to censor obscene literature and art . . . It is with the powers and procedures, standards, and rationales employed by the postal authorities in their exercise of this far-reaching power that this paper is concerned."

————. "Sex and the Stuffy Librarian." *Library Journal,* 90:2483–85, 1 June 1965. **D 85**

Unless librarians "first entrench the intellectual freedom principle underlying the Library Bill of Rights securely in their own shops—for every battle won in the courtroom by virtue of legal measures developed and provided through conferences and defense funds, 20 other censorship battles will be privately lost in the librarians' own chambers—the Library Bill of Rights will be deflated." He calls upon librarians to show their faith in the principle of intellectual freedom by making available avant-garde controversial works. The author served as general counsel for Grove Press in various censorship cases.

De la Bedoyere, Michael. "Censorship: More or Less?" *Criterion*, 13:252–69, January 1934.   **D 86**
The author considers the question of censorship of films in Great Britain. "Our ideal scheme of film censorship would therefore include the State, the Churches, the Universities and the trade itself." He considers that B.B.C., operating as a State corporation, provides a means of functioning in the best public interest, understanding liberty and authority.

Deland, Paul S. "Battling Crime Comics to Protect Youth." *Federal Probation*, 19(3):26–30, September 1955.   **D 87**
The associate editor of the *Christian Science Monitor* summarizes legal action and community drives taken throughout the nation "to stem the flood of horror comics that now run to some 90 millions published weekly, doing a business estimated at $350,000,000 a year."

Delany, Hubert T., and Seymour D. Altmark. "Radio Censorship." *National Lawyers Guild Quarterly*, 1:401–8, December 1938.   **D 88**
"The problem presented by the American system of broadcasting is, essentially, not one of illegal censorship, but of encouraging and, if needs be, compelling the use of radio facilities in the public interest." The article considers whether radio can, "through regulation, serve the democratic function of a market place for free and uncensored discussion and thought," and what form such regulation must take.

De Laune, Thomas. *De Laune's Pleas for the Non-Conformists . . . With a Narrative of the Remarkable Tryal and Sufferings underwent for Writing, Printing and Publishing hereof . . . Printed Twenty-Years ago; But being seiz'd by the Messenger of the Press, was afterwards Burnt by the Common-Hang-Man: And is now Re-printed from the Author's Original Copy; and Published by a Protestant Dissenter, who was the Author's Fellow Prisoner at the Time of his Death, for the Cause of Non-Conformity.* London, 1704. 46 p.   **D 89**

———. *A Narrative of the Tryal and Sufferings of Thomas De Laune for Writing, Printing and Publishing a late Book, called A Plea for the Non-Conformists with some modest Reflections thereon. Directed to Doctor Calamy; in Obedience to whose Call, that Work was Undertaken . . .* London, Printed for the author, 1683. 66 p.   **D 90**

———. *A Plea for the Non-Conformists. In three Parts. I. The True State of their Case . . . II. [Image of the Beast] III. [A Narrative of the Sufferings of Thomas de Laune, For Writing, Printing and Publishing a late Book, call'd, A Plea for the Non-Conformists: With some modest Reflections thereon . . .] Printed from the original Copy, and corrected from many Faults escaped in former Impressions.* London, Printed for Joseph Marshall, 1733. 135 p. (Preface signed "D.F." i.e., Daniel Defoe, discusses the persecution of De Laune. A summary of the case appears in Schroeder, *Constitutional Free Speech*, pp. 300–302)   **D 91**
De Laune was a Baptist layman and school teacher. In 1683 he wrote *A Plea for the Non-Conformists*, a classic, well-reasoned, argument in answer to a sermon in behalf of uniformity delivered of Dr. Benjamin Calamy. De Laune argued that Dissenters should be treated as "weak brethren," so long as they did not disturb the peace and are "not ruined by penalties for not swallowing what is imposed." For this work De Laune was arrested and brought to trial. He was convicted, fined, and his books were burned. Being unable to pay the fine, he spent the rest of his life (18 months) in Newgate prison. His wife and two children joined him in prison and all three died of the foul conditions. The *Narrative of the Sufferings Underwent*, included in this reprinting, was written in jail. De Laune's punishment was one of the most cruel and vindictive in English history. De Laune also wrote (1684) *Two Letters to Benjamin Calamy . . . on His Imprisonment.*

[Delavan, Edward C.]. *Report of the Trial of the Cause of John Taylor vs. Edward C. Delavan, Prosecuted for an alleged Libel and Mr. Delavan's Correspondence with the Executive Committee of the Albany City Temperance Society, etc.* Albany, N.Y., Hoffman, White & Visscher, 1840. 48 p.   **D 92**
A brewer's suit against Delavan for an alleged libel in the *Evening Journal*, 12 February 1835. The jury found for the defendant.

Delepierre, Joseph Octave. *Des Livres Condamnés au Feu en Angleterre.* Paris, Philobiblon Society, n.d.   **D 93**
Cited in Henry S. Ashbee (Pisanus Fraxi), *Catena Librorum Tacendorum*, pp. 500–507,

who lists the publications and persons condemned, according to Delepierre's paper.

Dell, Floyd. "Morality and the Movies." *New Review*, 3:190–91, August 1915.   **D 94**
Art and literature, writes Dell in this brief satire, have historically encouraged wickedness, but not so the new art of the movies. The movies began without freedom and therefore were pure from the beginning. In movies, unlike books, "good people are good and bad people are bad and anybody can tell the difference . . . Unfortunately, the movies are dependent to a great extent on those tainted arts, fiction and drama, for their natural materials." But the movies manage to emasculate the original work in such a way as to remove the danger and also most of the quality. He cites Ibsen's *Ghosts* and Prévost's *Manon Lescaut* as examples of works sterilized, emasculated, and made completely innocuous for the public.

———. "Story of the Trial." *Liberator*, 1:2–18, June 1918.   **D 95**
Trial of the editors of the *Masses* for opposition to the draft in World War I. Includes Max Eastman's speech in his own defense.

Demaus, Robert. *William Tyndale. A Biography, A Contribution to the Early History of the English Bible.* New edition, revised by Richard Lovett. London, The Religious Tract Society, 1886. 468 p.   **D 96**
Unable to get his English translation of the New Testament printed in England because of opposition from Cardinal Wolsey, Tyndale went to Germany, where the work was printed. When copies were smuggled into England, the Cardinal ordered Tyndale seized. He was ultimately arrested in Antwerp, tried, and condemned to death. He was strangled at the stake and his body burned. Tyndale's New Testament became the first printed book to be burned in England.

De Mille, William C. "Bigoted and Bettered Pictures." *Scribner's Magazine*, 76:231–36, September 1924.   **D 97**
Discusses the effects of censorship on motion pictures and the shackling caused by narrow-minded, arbitrary rules. If the people want the art of the motion picture to grow, they must make their own decisions as to what they want to see on the screen, and cease to delegate their power of acceptance or rejection to a small group of political appointees.

Dempsey, David. "Teaching Librarians to Fight Back." *Saturday Review*, 48(9):20–21, 40, 27 February 1965.   **D 98**
A review of the ALA Intellectual Freedom Conference held in Washington, D.C., together with the author's own observations.

"In numberless communities throughout the country, that timid creature of our folkways—the local librarian—has become the storm center of controversy." He cites examples of courageous action by librarians and reviews the suggestions made by the speakers for "fighting back" when censorship strikes.

Denison, Merrill. "Freedom, Radio, and the F.C.C." *Harper's Magazine*, 178: 629–40, May 1939.　　　**D 99**
The author discusses steps that brought the FCC into being, its duties under the Radio Communications Act of 1927, its ambiguous powers under "the public convenience, interest, and necessity" clause, the pressures it is subjected to, and the dangers inherent in its powers, such as "the exercise of the Commission's judicial function which is called into play whenever a station's program activities are reviewed in connection with the renewal of a license." When Congress again examines radio law in the light of actual experience, "the goal to be sought for is not the maximum but the minimum of arbitrary legislation."

Dennett, Mary Ware. *Birth Control Laws; Shall We Keep Them, Change Them, or Abolish Them.* New York, Hitchock, 1926. 309 p.　　　**D 100**
An encyclopedic compilation of birth control laws, including comments on their history, proposed changes, and the opposition to changes.

————. "*Married Love* and Censorship." *Nation*, 132:579–80, 27 May 1931.　**D 101**
The author of *The Sex Side of Life* discusses the freeing of Dr. Marie Stopes's *Married Love* by Judge John M. Woolsey after a 13-year ban by Customs.

[————]. "What Mrs. Dennett Wrote." *New Republic*, 58:329–32, 8 May 1929.
　　　D 102
The editors reprint a major portion of the pamphlet, *The Sex Side of Life*, for which Mrs. Dennett was found guilty of sending obscene matter through the mails. They carefully omit the passages on which she was found guilty to avoid loss of their mailing privilege, but assure their readers that the omitted passages are "dignified, straightforward, and entirely in the tone of those we print."

————. *Who's Obscene?* New York, Vanguard, 1930. 281 p.　　　**D 103**
An account of the trial of Mrs. Dennett, April 1929, before a U.S. District Court in New York, for the distribution through the mails of the defendant's pamphlet, *The Sex Side of Life*. She was declared guilty, but on appeal to the U.S. Circuit Court of Appeals the decision of the lower court was reversed.

Mrs. Dennett also discusses other cases of Post Office suppression.

[Denny, Charles, *et al.*]. *A Report of the Trials of Charles Denny and Patrick Byrne—and of Samuel Himson and George French, for Publishing an Alleged Libel upon Elisha Bloomer, a Hatter . . . With Introductory Remarks, by John Lomas . . .* New York, 1834. 16 p.　　　**D 104**

Dent, R. K. "Introduction to Discussion on Blacking Out of Sporting News in Libraries." *Library*, 6:127–29, 1894.
　　　D 105

[Denton, William]. *An Apology for the Liberty of the Press.* [London, 1681]. 9 p.
　　　D 106
The author attributes padlocking of the press to the influence of the Catholic church. He objects to the practices of the Church in requiring an imprimatur, a practice which "stifles books in the womb" and is injurious to the truth. It is a trick of the priests to keep the laity ignorant, even of the Scriptures for which are substituted doctrinal works of the Fathers. Denton was an anti-Catholic physician who joined Blount and other Whigs in their campaign against the renewal of the Licensing Act. He takes Milton's ideas on the origin of licensing and, with slight rewording, presents them as his own. Sensabaugh, in *That Grand Whig, Milton* (pp. 62–65), shows by parallel text how Denton crudely but effectively adapted Milton's *Areopagitica.*

De Palma, Samuel. *Freedom of the Press; an International Issue.* Washington, D.C., U.S. State Department, 1949. 24 p. (Publication 3687; reprinted from 14 November 1949 issue of *Department of State Bulletin*)　**D 107**
The UN debate on the Convention on International Transmission of the News and the Right of Correction, reported by the technical secretary to the United States delegation to the UN Conference on Freedom of Information.

De Pereda, Prudencio. "Red Straits." *Nation*, 172:492–93, 26 May 1951.　**D 108**
"A Report on the Subversive Activities of Certain Contributors to Radio Not Covered by 'Red Channels.'" A satire listing names, activities, and associates of such "subversives" as Beethoven, Mark Twain, Shelley, Jefferson, and Voltaire.

Depew, Chauncey M. *The Liberty of the Press. Address before New York State Press Association at Madison Square Theatre, New York, June 19, 1883.* New York, 1883. 20 p.
　　　D 109
"The one man to whom the Press is more indebted than all others is that marvelous genius, who with rarest indifference to personal fame, buried his personality in

devotion to his principles, and wrote under the name of Junius. . . . The most important effect of its liberty and growth upon the Press itself, has been to elevate journalism from a trade to one of the liberal professions."

De Selincourt, Oliver. *Art and Morality.* London, Methuen, 1935. 284 p.　**D 110**
A philosophical discussion of the conflict and compatibility of art and morality, with indirect implication to the freedom and suppression of creative literature. "Human experience is a whole which cannot, without danger to truth, be divided up into parts or elements wholly unrelated to one another."

De Silver, Albert. "Freedom of Speech." *Arbitrator*, 3:1–6, January 1921.　**D 111**
An historical and legal defense of free speech.

Des Moines Public Library. Board of Trustees. "The Library's Bill of Rights." *ALA Bulletin*, 33:51, December 1939.
　　　D 112
A statement of policy adopted by the Board of Trustees of the Des Moines Public Library, 21 November 1938, which served as the basis for a similar statement by the American Library Association.

Desmond, Charles S. "Censoring the Movies." *Notre Dame Lawyer*, 29:27–36, Fall 1953.　　　**D 113**
The author defends the constitutional and moral right of the government, in the interest of public order and decency, to censor films. It should "stop the evil at its source, and need not wait and punish after the harm has been done."

————. "Legal Problems Involved in Censoring the Media of Mass Communications." *Marquette Law Review*, 40:38–56, Summer 1956.　　　**D 114**
"My thesis . . . is that there is nothing in American law, constitutional, statutory or conventional, to prevent precensorship for obscenity, and that such precensorship, applied reasonably and justly and without impingement on the public right to be informed and without destruction of real literary values, is not offensive to the historic American tradition of freedom of publication."

Desmond, Robert W. "Of a Free and Responsible Press." *Journalism Quarterly*, 24:188–92, June 1947.　　　**D 115**
An editorial criticism of the report of the Hutchins Commission on Freedom of the Press, by the president of the American Association of Schools and Departments of Journalism.

————. *The Press and World Affairs.* New York, Appleton-Century, 1937. 421 p.　　　**D 116**
In a general survey of the collection and

distribution of news throughout the world, this American journalist discusses the obstacles of censorship which the foreign correspondent encounters in the years just before World War II. The final chapter, Autocrats of the Press, deals with influences and restrictions faced by the free press of democratic nations.

Desrochers, Edmond. "A Catholic Librarian Looks at Intellectual Freedom in the Canadian Setting." *Canadian Library*, 19:123–25, November 1962.　　**D117**

———. "Catholic Viewpoint on Censorship." *Catholic Library Association Bulletin*, 15:147–49, 9 January 1959.　　**D118**

[Destruction of Charlotte Towle's Book by the Federal Security Administrator]. *Social Service Review*, 25:248–49, June 1951.
　　D119
A manual for social workers, entitled *Common Human Needs*, prepared by Charlotte Towle of the University of Chicago faculty, was ordered destroyed by the Federal Security Administrator after the president of the American Medical Association charged that it was "viciously un-American" and that it advocated state socialism.

Detroit Public Library. *Radio Control: A List of References on the Subject, Resolved, That All Radio Broadcasting in the United States Should Be Conducted in Stations Owned and Controlled by the Federal Government.* Detroit, Civics Division, Detroit Public Library, 1933. 11 p. mimeo.　　**D120**

Deutsch, Eberhard P. "Federal Equity Jurisdiction in cases Involving the Freedom of the Press." *Virginia Law Review*, 25:507–27, March 1939.　　**D121**

———. "Freedom of the Press and of the Mails." *Michigan Law Review*, 36:703–51, March 1938.　　**D122**
An historical summary of postal powers in relation to censorship of the mails.

Deutsch, Monroe E. "Freedom of the Press." In his *The Letter and the Spirit . . .*, Berkeley, University of California Press, 1943, pp. 39–55.　　**D123**

Devane, Richard S. "The Committee on Printed Matter." *Irish Ecclesiastical Record*, 28:357–77, October 1926; 28:449–66, November 1926; 28:583–95, December 1926. (Reprinted in a separate publication, *Evil Literature: Some Suggestions, with a foreword by the Rt. Hon. Sir E. Cecil*, Dublin, Browne and Nolan, 1927)　　**D124**

The three articles by Father Devane deal with the work of the Irish government's Committee on Evil Literature. In the first article he discusses three basic problems: (1) combating the evils of imported British publications, (2) an inadequate obscenity law, and (3) the "stupid writing" and "loose-thinking" in defending as "freedom of the press" what is really "license of the press." The article includes a list of publications rejected by Canadian Customs. The second article proposes legislation and the creation of a blacklist, and argues against the proposal of moral suasion as an effective weapon against indecent literature. In the third article the author sums up his own recommendations for legislation: (1) a new definition of "indecency," (2) establishment of a blacklist, (3) creation of a state censor in the Ministry of Justice, (4) ban of all birth control information, (5) registration of imported journals other than scientific, (6) licensing of news vendors, and (7) licensing of booksellers.

Devoe, Alan. "Any Sex Today?" *American Mercury*, 41:175–78, June 1937.　　**D125**
Deals with the racket of selling publications advertised as forbidden erotica, but which are, in reality, entirely innocuous.

DeVoto, Bernard. "The Decision in the *Strange Fruit* Case: The Obscenity Statute in Massachusetts." *New England Quarterly*, 19:147–83, June 1946.　　**D126**
A critique of the court decision, written by a strong opponent of Massachusetts censorship and a principal in the case. Faced with the threat of police censorship, Boston booksellers withdrew *Strange Fruit* from sale. The Civil Liberties Union thereupon decided to make a test case of the Massachusetts obscenity statute and arranged for a copy to be sold in Cambridge to DeVoto. The bookseller, Abraham Isenstadt, was convicted and the decision affirmed by the Supreme Judicial Court. The test was made with the thought that *Strange Fruit* was of such high literary quality and social significance that it could not be reasonably considered obscene. Judge Stone of the District Court, however, considered it "appealing to pornographic minds," and criticized the defendants for using the courts for a test case. There was widespread criticism of the decision, both in Boston and throughout the country. A group from the Bar Association of Boston denounced the criticism of the court as "unconstitutional." DeVoto calls this response of the lawyers "a state of mind which at best is craven and cringing and at worst must be regarded as dangerous to the liberties of the Commonwealth."

———. "The Easy Chair: Boston Censorship." *Harper's Magazine*, 188:525–28, May 1944.　　**D127**
The recent banning of *Strange Fruit* prompts DeVoto to attack the cultural leadership of Boston in which Catholic and Protestant "bigots" are joined by a third group, "the well-born, the rich, the cultivated, the heirs

of the old ruling class" who will not accept social responsibility or exercise leadership.

———. "The Easy Chair: Four Letter Words." *Harper's Magazine*, 197:98–101, December 1948.　　**D128**
Deals with the breaking down of the taboo against use of many "four letter words" formerly considered obscene.

———. "The Easy Chair: Liberal Decisions in Massachusetts." *Harper's Magazine*, 199:62–65, July 1949.　　**D129**
Discuss three recent liberal decisions on books in the Massachusetts courts: Justice Donahue finding *Forever Amber* not obscene and Justice Fairhust finding *God's Little Acre* and *Serenade* not obscene. He also praises the "landmark" decision of Judge Curtis Bok in Philadelphia in finding nine novels not obscene.

———. "The Easy Chair: Sex and the Coed." *Harper's Magazine*, 195:156–59, August 1947. (Reprinted in Downs, *The First Freedom*, pp. 201–5)　　**D130**
DeVoto reveals the removal of his article, "Sex and the Coed," from the May 1926 issue of *American Mercury*. The April issue containing the famous "Hatrack" story was before the courts under an obscenity charge and Mencken and his lawyers did not wish to prejudice their case. DeVoto summarizes his hilarious article on sex education in a typical university of the mid-twenties.

———. "The Easy Chair: Soldier Voting Bill." *Harper's Magazine*, 189:330–33, September 1944.　　**D131**
A satirical essay attacking the restrictions on distribution of political literature to members of the armed services and particularly the part played by Senator Taft in the enactment of the bill. The restrictions, DeVoto finds, are more asinine than sinister.

———. "The Easy Chair: The Case of the Censorious Congressman." *Harper's Magazine*, 206:42–45, April 1953. (Reprinted in Downs, *The First Freedom*, pp. 205–9)　　**D132**
An attack on the Gathings Committee on Pornographic Materials of the U.S. House of Representatives. "Such ignorance and prejudice as the Committee shows are routine in obscenity crusades, but also there is something new." This is the belief of the Committee "that the freedom guaranteed by the First Amendment ought to be abridged and . . . that Congress has power to act."

———. "The Easy Chair: The *Forever Amber* Case." *Harper's Magazine*, 194:408–11, May 1947.　　**D133**

The columnist reports a sudden improvement in the censorship situation in Massachusetts with the decision of Judge Frank J. Donahue of the Superior Court in *Commonwealth v. "Forever Amber."* Judge Donahue freed the book of obscenity charges.

―――. "The Easy Chair: The *Strange Fruit* Case." *Harper's Magazine,* 189: 148–51, July 1944.   **D 134**
Following a brief account of the author's involvement in the test case of the Massachusetts obscenity law by the purchase of a copy of *Strange Fruit,* he launches into a discussion of the right to purchase and possess erotic literature. "The right to own and read pornography appears to me unquestionable . . . The ordinary adult should be secure in his right to read in his own home any kind of book he may desire to read—and to buy it free of imputation and penalty." He agrees to one limitation—that the surreptitious sale of pornography to adolescents be forbidden.

―――. "The Easy Chair: The *Strange Fruit* Case." *Harper's Magazine,* 190: 225–28, February 1945.   **D 135**
"As Lillian Smith's *Strange Fruit* has progressed through the courts of Massachusetts, it has become clear that the defense of literary freedom has got to be shifted to firmer and bolder grounds than those from which liberals have so far argued . . . Meanwhile I feel obliged as an American correspondent resident in Massachusetts to keep you informed about the local censorship . . . I must be careful, however, to say 'suppression,' not 'censorship,' for the official position is that Massachusetts has no censorship."

―――. "The Frustrated Censor." *Harper's Magazine,* 175:109–12, 7 June 1937.   **D 136**
"[Censorship] tries to improve society instead of policing it. It tries to infuse with morality an area that society considers non-moral. It fails to distinguish between fiction and reality. It mistakes a verbalism for a psychological and ethical principle. And it is perpetually out of touch with society as it is, and so finds itself stopped by social energies which it perpetually misunderstands." The only solution to the problem of censorship is to do away with it entirely.

―――. "Literary Censorship in Cambridge." *Harvard Graduates' Magazine,* 38: 30–42, September 1930.   **D 137**
The case of James A. Delacey, proprietor of the Dunster House Book Store in Cambridge, arrested and convicted of selling *Lady Chatterley's Lover* to an agent provocateur of the Watch and Ward Society. DeVoto was one of the leaders in Delacey's defense.

De Wagstaffe, William. "The Creel Press Cabinet; an Insight into the Censorship." *Forum,* 58:447–60, October 1917.   **D 138**
A discussion of the Creel Committee, its policy and its work in censorship during World War I.

Dewees, Curtis. "On the Suppression of Homosexual Literature." *Mattachine Review,* 4(8):14–16, August 1958; 4(9):7–12, September 1958.   **D 139**

Dewey, John. "Conscription of Thought." *New Republic,* 12:128–30, 1 September 1917.   **D 140**
Concern with "the historically demonstrated inefficacy of the conscription of mind as a means of promoting social solidarity and the gratuitous stupidity of measures that defeat their own ends." Wartime censorship of unorthodox political ideas may ultimately harm the attacker more than the attacked.

―――. "Freedom of Thought and Work." *New Republic,* 22:316–17, 5 May 1920.   **D 141**
"Because liberty is essentially mental, a matter of thought, and because thought is free only as it can manifest itself in act, every struggle for liberty has to be reinacted on a different plane. The old struggle for liberty of speech, assemblage and publication was significant because it was part of a struggle for liberty of worship, and security of property . . . Freedom of speech and of the franchise is now significant because it is part of the struggle for freedom of mind in industry, freedom to participate in its planning and conduct."

―――. "New Paternalism; Molding of Public Opinion." *New Republic,* 17:216–17, 21 December 1918.   **D 142**
Public opinion is being molded by the press through a combination of paternalism and censorship. Dewey is concerned with the mental attitude brought on by submission to war censorship.

DeWolf, Richard C. "Copyright and Morals." *Authors' League Bulletin,* 4(6): 3–4, September 1916.   **D 143**
"In the United States we have no cases reported in which copyright has been denied or opposed on the ground of the libellous, seditious or blasphemous character of the matter involved, but we have several cases in which immorality, in the narrower sense of the term, has been held a reason for refusing to protect the work which showed it."

Dialogue between a Country Farmer and a Juryman on the Subject of Libels. London, 1770. 30 p.   **D 144**

Dialogue between a Methodist Preacher and a Reformer. Newcastle, Eng., John Marshall, 1819. 8 p.   **D 145**

A Methodist minister is quoted as decrying the seditious libels in the "twopenny trash." The reformer responds: "Is there no Sixpenny Trash? . . . And if books become dangerous when they are cheap, how are we to defend our Cheap Religious Tract Societies? Now, if Cobbett, Wooler, Sherwin, and other popular writers of Political Tracts, promulgate false doctrines, the Press is open, refute them. If they publish misstatements, overwhelm them by the production of irresistible facts . . . Defeat them upon their own ground. But do not run in an affected fright to a Police Officer." Many of the Methodist clergy who had supported radical reform, he notes, now fear the action of the extremists.

Dialogue on the Approaching Trial of Mr. Carlile for publishing the Age of Reason . . . From Wooler's British Gazette, Sunday, Arpil 18, 1819. London, Wooler, 1819. 16 p.   **D 146**
An imaginary conversation, written in a satirical vein.

Dicey, Albert V. *Introduction to the Study of the Law of the Constitution.* Introduction by E. C. S. Wade. 10th ed. London, St. Martin's, 1959. 535 p.   **D 147**
Chapter 6, The Right to Freedom of Discussion, contains an analysis of the evolution of freedom of the press in England from the Star Chamber to the date of publication.

―――. *Lectures on the Relation between Law and Public Opinion in England during the Nineteenth Century.* London, Macmillan, 1914. 506 p.   **D 148**
An attempt to draw a relationship between a century of English legislation and successive currents of opinion. References to freedom and restriction of opinion are made throughout. The lectures, delivered at Harvard Law School over a period of years, represent reflection and interpretation rather than a compilation of facts.

Dickerson, Oliver M. "British Control of American Newspapers on the Eve of the American Revolution." *New England Quarterly,* 24:453–68, December 1951.   **D 149**

Dickinson, Edwin D. "The Defamation of Foreign Governments." *American Journal of International Law,* 22:840–44, October 1928   **D 150**
Deals with the case of Hearst newspapers publishing documents which were claimed to have been abstracted from the secret archives of Mexico. The incident occurred at a time when the United States and Mexico were involved in difficult negotiations.

Dickinson, Robert L. "The Birth Control Movement." *Medical Journal and Recorder,* 125(10):654, 18 May 1927.   **D 151**

Dickinson, Thomas H. "The Theory and Practice of the Censorship." *Drama*, 18:248–61, May 1915.　　　**D 152**
An impartial review of the development of stage censorship in the United States.

Dickinson, William B., Jr. *Libel Suits and Press Freedom.* Washington, D.C., Editorial Research Reports, 1963. (*Editorial Research Reports*, 2:885–902, 1963)　　**D 153**
A review of the growing magnitude of libel awards including the Alabama case against the *New York Times*, the Butts action against the *Saturday Evening Post*, the case of *Reynolds v. Pegler*, and the John Henry Faulk case against *Aware, Inc.*, followed by a summary of the basic elements of the law of libel and the relation to First Amendment freedoms.

————. *Peacetime Censorship.* Washington, D.C., Editorial Research Reports, 1961. (*Editorial Research Reports*, 1:461–78, 1961)　　**D 154**
Deals with current issues relating to government security v. free access to information, a review of experience with censorship in World Wars I and II, and modes of news control in foreign countries.

————. *Privileged Communications.* Washington, D.C., Editorial Research Reports, 1959. (*Editorial Research Reports*, 2:895–910, 1959)　　**D 155**
Deals with the protection of news sources in the courts, the position of the press in Congress, and recognized confidential communications (husband-wife, lawyer-client, physician-patient, confidences to priest or pastor). Includes a discussion of the Marie Torre case.

Dietrich, John H. *The Conspiracy of Silence About Sex.* Minneapolis, The First Unitarian Society, [1931?]. (The Humanist Pulpit Series, vol. 13, no. 8)　　**D 156**

————. *The Vexing Problem of Censorship.* Minneapolis, The First Unitarian Society, [1931?]. (The Humanist Pulpit Series, vol. 13, no. 3)　　**D 157**

Digest of the Law Concerning Libels; Containing All the Resolutions in the Books on the Subject, and Many Manuscript Cases, the Whole Illustrated with Occasional Observations; by a Gentleman of the Inner Temple. London, Owen, 1765.　　**D 158**

Digges, Isaac W. "Radio Broadcast and Libel." *Printers' Ink*, 169(6):73–77, 8 November 1934.　　**D 159**
Some important decisions that can guide advertisers in matters of libel, pending a U.S. Supreme Court ruling.

Dill, Glenn. "Fairness Doctrine for the Press." *North Dakota Law Review*, 40:317–28, July 1964.　　**D 160**
"The real answer to the problem of centralized communication is to maintain the minority viewpoint; the most practicable means being a governmental broadcasting system. It is in the area of spot news reporting which broadcasting has largely pre-empted from the press, that minority groups are likely to encounter the limited-access medium, the area where the government is then obligated to give aid. And it is because of the limited-access aspect that a 'fairness doctrine' is the least expeditious. . . . Many stations and newspapers, each with an individual viewpoint, will more adequately present minority views than few stations and newspapers each presenting many viewpoints."

Dillard, James H. "History and Free Speech." *Public*, 22:236–37, 8 March 1919.　　**D 161**
General arguments for unlimited freedom of speech and press, with special mention of post-office censorship of abolition literature.

Dilliard, Irving. "Censorship and the Freedom to Read." *Illinois Libraries*, 47:449–55, May 1965.　　**D 162**
It is the "basic mission of the public library to stand firm against those who set themselves up as censors or attempt in some other way to control the thinking of the community through what it reads." The author, who received the Intellectual Freedom Award of the Illinois Library Association in 1964, suggests titles of books on freedom that should be in every public library and brought to the attention of the public.

————. "The Development of a Free Press in Germany, 1945–46: an Aspect of American Military Government." In *Edmund J. James Lectures on Government*, 5th series. Urbana, Ill., University of Illinois Press, 1951, pp. 35–66.　　**D 163**

————. "How America's First Press Martyr Gave His Life for Freedom." *Quill*, 40 (10):8–9, 15–16, October 1952.　　**D 164**
The editor of the editorial page of the St. Louis *Post-Dispatch* presents, in the form of a contemporary dispatch, the story of Elijah P. Lovejoy's fight for freedom of the press. The occasion is the dedication of a Sigma Delta Chi historical marker in Alton, Ill., to the memory of the martyred editor.

————. "The Press and the Bill of Rights." *Nieman Reports*, 8(1):13–18, January 1954. (Excerpted in the *Nation*, 12 December 1953)　　**D 165**
In the second annual Lovejoy Lecture at Colby College, 5 November 1953, the St. Louis

editor criticizes the American press for maintaining a double standard, tending "to have one standard when it measures the performance of officials and public figures, and another standard when it comes to measuring its own performance . . . The press holds other institutions up to searching scrutiny but is unwilling to have the same scrutiny applied to itself." Most of the press of today is indifferent to infringements of civil rights and is not fighting for the principles and causes that the Bill of Rights embodies.

Dillon, John. *The Censorship and the War. Remarkable Speech . . .* London, National Council for Civil Liberties, 1917. 14p. (From the *Official Reports*, vol. 90, no. 8)　　**D 166**
A member of Parliament objects to the Government's policy of secrecy in the conduct of World War I.

Dillon, Merton L. *Elijah P. Lovejoy, Abolitionist Editor.* Urbana, Ill., University of Illinois Press, 1961. 190p.　　**D 167**
A study of Elijah Lovejoy's life and thought, set within the larger framework of the American abolitionist movement.

Dillon, William T. "Censorship in Education." *Catholic Lawyer*, 3:322–29, Autumn 1957.　　**D 168**
Monsignor Dillon's thesis is that education is made effective largely through discipline, criticism, and censorship. While decrying legal censorship, he favors educational censorship which he generally defines as criticism.

Dilworth, Nelson. *Responsibility for Selection of School Books.* Washington, D.C., National Defense Committee, National Society of the Daughters of the American Revolution, 1957. 6p. (Also issued by Education Information, Inc., Amarillo, Tex.)　　**D 169**
An address by California State Senator Dilworth before the Commonwealth Club of San Francisco. "Is it censorship if, in selecting books for our school children's desks and libraries, that our school board members insist on books that 'impress on the minds of the pupils the principles of morality'? If that be censorship let's have more of it. Is it censorship for board members to insist on the selection of books that teach patriotism?" The speaker notes that removal of a book once selected is a difficult one. The emphasis should be on proper selection, and a record should be kept of who recommended the selection of every book.

Dimmock, Thomas. *Lovejoy. An Address Delivered by Thomas Dimmock, at the Church*

of the Unity, St. Louis, March 14, 1888 . . . St. Louis, 1888. 28 p.   **D170**
This account of the life and martyrdom of Elijah P. Lovejoy is by a St. Louis newspaper-man, who, as a young man in Alton shortly after the riots, became interested in the Lovejoy affair. He interviewed witnesses, examined documents, and in 1864 was instrumental in marking Lovejoy's grave.

"Discussing the Social Evil." *Nation*, 93:308–9, 5 October 1911.   **D171**
Editorial criticism of the action of the post office in excluding from the mails the report of the Chicago Vice Commission.

Disher, M. Willson. "The Throne Is the Censor." *Theatre World*, 27:56, February 1937.   **D172**
Stage censorship in England is incorporated in no written law. The throne is the censor, with the Lord Chamberlain exercising powers upon which no limits have been set, delivering judgment according to his own opinion rather than by recorded law.

Disraeli, Isaac. *The Calamities of Authors.* New York, Widdleton, 1875. 2 vols.   **D173**
Vol. 1 contains an essay on Dangers Incurred by Giving the Result of Literary Inquiry (pp. 294–305), largely an account of the persecution of Dr. Cowell for his work, *The Interpreter*. Vol. 2 has a chapter on Martin Marprelate (pp. 357–92).

———. *Curiosities of Literature* . . . New York, Armstrong, n. d. 4 vols. in 3. (Volumes of this work were first published over a period of years, from 1791 to 1834)   **D174**
Sections relating to freedom of the press: Vol. 1, Persecuted Learned (pp. 78–80), Imprisonment of Learned (pp. 87–89), Destruction of Books (pp. 101–12); Vol. 2, The Bible Prohibited and Improved (pp. 175–80), Licensers of the Press (pp. 399–414); Vol. 3, Condemned Poets (pp. 37–43), Of Suppressors and Delapidators of Manuscripts (pp. 200–212), and Expression of Suppressed Opinion (pp. 29–44).

"Distinction between Selection and Censorship." *Wilson Library Bulletin*, 36:598+, April 1962.   **D175**
A brief note reporting the case of a Savannah, Ga., resident who charged the public librarian with censorship for not labeling as "subversive" Foreign Policy Association literature; a Spartanburg, S.C., resident who accused the public librarian of censorship for not buying Edgar Rice Burroughs' *Tarzan* books.

"Distribution of Leaflets and Handbills—Municipal Regulation— Public Order."

Canadian Bar Review, 19:49–50, January 1941.   **D176**
The author is concerned with the tendency "to exalt order at the cost of liberty" and with the absence of the protection of legislation permitting distribution of controversial literature.

Ditchfield, Peter H. *Books Fatal to Their Authors.* London, E. Stock, 1895. 244 p. (Book-lover's Library)   **D177**
A series of essays, based on the author's wide reading and research, dealing with writers who lost their lives because of their unorthodox ideas. Topics include Theology; Fanatics and Freethinkers; Astrology, Alchemy and Magic; Science and Philosophy; History; Politics and Statesmanship; Satire; Poetry; Drama and Romance; Booksellers and Publishers; Some Literary Martyrs. A lecture by the author, Literature Martyrdoms, including much of the material from the book, was published by the Royal Society of Literature of the United Kingdom in *Essays by Divers Hands*, 2nd ser., vol. 2, pp. 35–69.

Ditzion, Sidney. "Censorship and Exclusion." In his *Arsenals of a Democratic Culture.* Chicago, American Library Association, 1947, pp. 183–87.   **D178**
The author traces the efforts by city fathers, pressure groups, and librarians, to censor or exclude works from libraries.

———. *Marriage, Morals, and Sex in America. A History of Ideas.* New York, Bookman, 1953. 440 p.   **D179**
America's sexual behavior from colonial times to the Kinsey Report. There are sections on the birth control movement and the struggle for freedom of sex education, Comstock laws, and references to such figures as Thomas Cooper, Mary Ware Dennett, Ezra Heywood, Abner Kneeland, Margaret Sanger, and Theodore A. Schroeder.

———. "Problems of Propaganda Magazines." *Wilson Bulletin*, 11:21–24, September 1936.   **D180**
Advice on selection of magazines of a controversial nature that will represent minority points of view without allowing such groups to use the library for propaganda purposes.

Dix, William. "Intellectual Freedom." *Library Trends*, 3:299–307, January 1955.   **D181**
The librarian of Princeton University summarizes the work of the American Library Association "in formulating the concept of the intellectually free library, in promoting discussion and understanding of this concept among librarians, library trustees, and the public, and in responding to the recurring threats to intellectual freedom in an era marked by strong currents of anti-intellectualism."

———. "The Public Library and the Citizen's Right to Find Out." *Public*

Libraries, 7:1–2, 14–15, February 1953.   **D182**

Dixon, Eric. "Obscene Publications." *Penrose Annual*, 54:73–77, 1960.   **D183**
"The [British] Obscene Publications Act 1959, which makes a number of important improvements, is very much to be welcomed by the printing industry." The author discusses past problems and events leading up to the enactment of the Act.

Dixon, F. J. *Dixon's Address to the Jury. In Defence of the Freedom of Speech . . . and Judge Galt's Charge to the Jury. In Rex v. Dixon.* Winnipeg, The Defence Committee, 1920. 126 p.   **D184**
Dixon was charged with publishing seditious libels in connection with a general strike.

Dixon, R. *Billy Hughes and Censorship.* [Sydney], Legal Rights (for Victory) Committee, 1942. 4 p.   **D185**
Relates to the Communist Party of Australia.

Dixon, Thomas. "Censorship." *Publishers' Weekly*, 105:1698–1701, 24 May 1924.   **D186**
"As an author, I am bitterly and uncompromisingly opposed to pre-publication or pre-viewing censorship, either of pictures or books . . . not only is censorship undemocratic and in violation of the fundamental principles upon which this Republic rests, but the establishment of a censorship will never accomplish the purpose for which it is established." Dixon calls upon book publishers to stand up and fight for their books. He comments on his own efforts to combat film censorship in Ohio, Virginia, and New York.

D'Joinville, Luigi A. "Necessity of Birth Control Propaganda." *Mother Earth*, 12:53–55, April 1917.   **D187**
A defense of the freedom to provide information on birth control.

"Do You Want Radio Censorship?" *Look*, 3:6–11, 14 February 1939.   **D188**
A pictorial account of recent censorship cases and the campaign for government censorship of radio that is confronting Congress.

Doan, Edward N. *The Basis and Operation of Wartime Censorship in the United States.* Madison, Wisc., University of Wisconsin, 1944. 363 p. (Unpublished Ph. D. dissertation)   **D189**
The author concludes that "despite the misgivings of a great many people, the operation of the Office of Censorship with respect to the voluntary code of censorship over news was successful to the point that it had the respect and goodwill of all practicing newspapermen and broadcasters." But, he also notes, from the point of view of both the

disseminators of news and the general public, "the basic thinking of the armed forces with respect to 'policy' censorship needs overhauling" in the interest of an informed public in a democracy at war.

————. "Organization and Operation of the Office of Censorship." *Journalism Quarterly*, 21:200–216, September 1944. **D190**
Government censorship in the United States during World War II; a summary of findings in the author's doctoral study.

Doctrine of Libels discussed and examined; a treatise showing from the best authorities, what shall be deemed Defamatory Writings, and how far the same are punishable by our laws. London, 1728. 136p. **D191**

Doerfer, John C., and Oren Harris. *Questions of Responsibility.* Columbia, Mo., Freedom of Information Center, School of Journalism, University of Missouri, 1960. 8p. (Publication no. 29) **D192**
Debate between the former chairman of the Federal Communications Commission (Doerfer) and Representative Harris, chairman of the Legislative Oversight Committee, in the matter of government responsibility for radio and television programming.

Doering, Edward A. *Federal Control of Broadcasting versus Freedom of the Air.* Washington, D.C., Georgetown University, 1939. 56p. (Unpublished S. J. D. dissertation) **D193**
Discusses the licensing of radio broadcasting, based on a study of cases before the Federal Communications Commission. In place of the existing system for periodic renewal of licenses, which he believes creates insecurity, Doering recommends permanent "authorities" be granted to those who prove their operation is in the public interest.

Dolan, Edward. *The Tree of Liberty and Palladium of the Press; the Advocate and Preservative of the People's Rights.* 2nd ed. Detroit, Martin Geiger, 1847. 56p. **D194**

Dolan, John P. *Radio Censorship; a Social Problem.* St. Louis, St. Louis University, 1940. 80p. (Unpublished Master's thesis) **D195**

Dolan, Marguerite. "Books to Beat the Band." *Cosmopolitan*, 156:32, May 1964. **D196**

[Dolby, Thomas]. ["Trial, 1821"]. In *Hansard's Parliamentary Debates*, 5:1114ff., 6 June 1821. **D197**

Dolby, long a proponent of reform in his *Parliamentary Register*, was arrested at the insistence of the Constitutional Association for an alleged libel in his paper, *Pasquin.* A few days later he was again arrested for selling *A Political Dictionary.* His original bail was forfeited and second bail required. There was a general outcry in the press opposing such tactics being used against a tradesman, and a petition of redress was submitted to Parliament. At the trial it developed that the jury was selected by the sheriff who was a member of the prosecuting Association. Dolby was eventually convicted but was not sentenced when he agreed to give up bookselling.

Dollen, Charles. "Censorship and Thought Control." *Catholic Library World*, 36:158–59, November 1964. **D198**
The *Index* of the Catholic Church as now constituted is ineffectual and the confusion it raises calls for a solution from the Fathers of Vatican II. "If the *Index* consisted of *Monita* [calling attention to error] rather than prohibitions, it would be a useful guide to the Catholic scholar and a real help in his work."

————. "Freedom All Over the Place." *Library Journal*, 86:764–65, 15 February 1961. **D199**
"When does liberty become license? When the advocates of freedom become bigots themselves, that's when." The library director of the University of San Diego presents a case for censorship. Librarians should put their know-how at the service of parents in the drive for decency in literature. Written in response to Lloyd W. Griffith's review of Downs's *The First Freedom*, in *Library Journal*, 15 December 1960.

Dolye, H. G. "Censorship of Student Publications." *School and Society*, 28:78–80, 21 July 1928. **D200**

Doms, Keith. "The Challenge and the Small Public Library." *ALA Bulletin*, 47:465–66, November 1953. **D201**
A six-point program for action by the small public library "at the grass roots level" to preserve the freedom to read.

Don R. Mellett Memorial Fund. *Lectures.* New York, School of Journalism, New York University. Annual since 1931. **D202**
The lectureship was founded "to perpetuate in the free press of America the spirit of Don Mellett, who was assassinated July 16, 1926, by enemies made in his crusade against vice, corruption, and lawlessness permitted by the city government of Canton, Ohio." Each year, at a designated place in the United States, a lecture is delivered by a person selected by the committee. Among the lectures dealing specifically with freedom of the press were: The Right of Free Hearing; the Freedom of the Reader by Carl C. Magee (New York University *Bulletin*, vol. 33, no. 29, 1933); Freedom of News by Ray Roberts (*Bulletin*, vol. 34, no. 31, 1934); The Challenge

of War to Freedom of the Press by Paul Bellamy (New York University, unnumbered bulletin, 1943); The Only Solid Basis for All Our Rights by Mark Ethridge (New York University, unnumbered bulletin, 1944); The Free and Responsible Press by George E. Sokolsky (New York University, unnumbered bulletin, 1947).

Donahue, Charles. "Art and Censorship." *Commonweal*, 66:84–85, 26 April 1957. **D203**

Donleavy, J. P. "What They Did in Dublin; an Account of the Closing of *The Ginger Man* in Dublin." In his *The Ginger Man.* New York, Random House, 1961, pp. 1–41. **D204**

Donnelly, Gerald B. "The Motion Picture and the Legion of Decency." In *Public Opinion in a Democracy.* Proceedings of the Institute of Human Relations. Issued as a special supplement to the January 1938 issue of *Public Opinion Quarterly*, pp. 42–44. **D205**
The Legion was organized to persuade the film industry to adopt a code of self-regulation. "The Legion resorted to the organization of public opinion and public pressure to induce the industry to establish and obey its own censors."

Donnelly, Richard C. "Defamation by Radio—A Reconsideration." *Iowa Law Review*, 34:12–40, November 1948. **D206**
The author proposes that defamatory statements made over the radio be classified as libel and not slander, that the radio station be held liable for defamation in programs not presenting adverse views on questions and persons of public interest, that the station not be held liable for utterances of candidates for public office. He endorses the White Bill which would relieve the radio station from liability for defamation.

————. "Government and Freedom of the Press." *Illinois Law Review*, 45:31–56, March–April 1950. **D207**
The author notes these shortcomings in freedom of the press: (1) exclusion of movies in a definition of "press," (2) failure to subject the postal power to the guarantees under the First Amendment, (3) hesitancy to use the principle of disclosure legislation to attack clandestine anti-democratic propaganda, and (4) reluctance of the courts to employ the "clear and present danger" test in obscenity cases.

————. "History of Defamation." *Wisconsin Law Review*, 1949:99–126, January 1949. **D208**

A history of the development of the concept of defamation in Anglo-American law, including the twin interests to protect the honor and reputation of the individual and the interest in the public peace and security. The advent of modern commercial media calls for the overhauling of the law of defamation.

————. "The Law of Defamation: Proposals for Reform." *Minnesota Law Review*, 33:609–33, May 1949. **D 209**

————. "Right of Reply—An Alternative to an Action for Libel." *Virginia Law Review*, 34:867–900, November 1948. **D 210**

Notes on radio law and court decisions, 1929–48.

Donogh, Walter R. *The History and Law of Sedition and Cognate Offenses, Penal and Preventive, with a Summary of Press Legislation in India and an Excerpt of Acts in Force Relating to the Press, the Stage, and Public Meetings.* 3d ed. Calcutta, Thacher, Spink, 1917; London, W. Tacker, 1917. 285 p. **D 211**

Includes a discussion of notable Indian sedition laws.

Donoghue, Denis. "Eight Propositions on Censorship." In International Writers' Conference, *The Novel Today (Programme & Notes).* Edinburgh, Edinburgh International Festival, 1962, pp. 51–53. **D 212**

The author is a lecturer in English at University College, Dublin. "The greatest danger facing a writer from the direction of censorship," he concludes, "is not that he will be silenced, but that by meeting force with force he will undermine his own imagination." The fourth day of the Conference dealt with censorship.

Doob, Leonard W. *Public Opinion and Propaganda.* New York, Holt, 1948. 424 p. (2d ed., Hamden, Conn., Archon Books, 1966. 612 p.) **D 213**

A general work on propaganda but with numerous references to pressure groups as censors, e.g., the New York Society for the Suppression of Vice, pp. 206–12.

Doren, Electra C. "Action upon Bad Books." *Library Journal*, 28:167–69, April 1903. **D 214**

Tells of the formation of a committee representing 23 organizations in Dayton, Ohio, to encourage and raise money for wider use of public school libraries in cooperation with public library neighborhood projects. A subcommittee of 9 was named to suppress bad books and to recommend prosecution of vile literature and sensational plays.

Dorman, P. H. *Content Analysis Study of Articles Dealing with Censoring Activities in the United States, 1950–1957.* Atlanta, School of Library Service, Atlanta University, 1959. 39 p. (Unpublished Master's thesis) **D 215**

"Dorothy the Librarian." *Life*, 46:47, 16 February 1959. **D 216**

Brief editorial criticizing as "tiresome and spurious" the advice of the Florida state librarian, urging libraries to withdraw such books as *Uncle Wiggly*, *Tom Swift*, *Tarzan*, and the *Wizard of Oz*, because they are "poorly written, untrue to life, sensational, foolishly sentimental, and consequently unwholesome for the children in your community."

Dorrance, Dick, and Jo Ranson. "You Cant' Sing That!" *American Mercury*, 48:324–26, November 1939. **D 217**

"More frequently than the listener realizes, the lyrics of songs to which he dances at home have been amended or completely rewritten before given the right of the airwaves."

Dorsen, Norman. "Libel and the Free Press." *Nation*, 198:93–95, 27 January 1964. **D 218**

Discussion of the *New York Times* libel case, in which the Alabama Supreme Court awarded to the plaintiff. The decision was ultimately reversed by the U.S. Supreme Court.

Dorward, Theo E. *The Development of the Civil Libel Law in Texas as It Concerns Newspapers.* Austin, Tex., University of Texas, 1940. 118 p. (Unpublished Master's thesis) **D 219**

Doty, Elias. *Doty's Commentaries on the Moot Courts of Iowa.* [Cedar Rapids, Iowa, The Author, 1903?]. 155 p. **D 220**

Concerns the case of Elias Doty, charged with keeping for sale and with selling obscene pictures.

[Dougherty, Daniel]. "License of the Press." *Weekly Law Bulletin*, 19:333–38, 21 May 1888. **D 221**

Excerpts from an address before the State Bar Association of New York.

Dougherty, Kathryn. "Motion Pictures on Trial. Do You Want Censorship?" *Photoplay*, 46:32–33, 96, October 1934. **D 222**

Douglas, James S. "Early Press Censorship." *Antiaircraft Journal*, 94(3):25–26, May–June 1951. **D 223**

On the effort of General Ambrose E. Burnside, commanding the Department of the Ohio in the Civil War, to suppress the *Chicago Times*, 1863.

Douglas, William O. *An Almanac of Liberty.* New York, Doubleday, 1954. 409 p. **D 224**

A collection of brief essays and sketches on aspects of American freedom, including the following topics pertaining to freedom of the press: Alien and Sedition Laws, Trial of Zenger, Law of Obscenity, The Book *Ulysses*, Jefferson on Censorship, Trial of Thomas Paine, Stamp Act, Elijah P. Lovejoy, Governor Shute and Censorship, Distribution of Religious Literature, Licensing of the Press, Book Burning, Milton on Freedom of the Press, Books Banned by the State Department, Trial of Richard Carlile, Censorship of the American Stage, Censorship of the English Stage, and the Library Bill of Rights. A motion picture based on this work is distributed by the Anti-Defamation League of B'nai B'rith, New York.

————. "The Black Silence of Fear." *New York Times Magazine*, 13 January 1952, pp. 7, 37–38. **D 225**

Deals with the growing intolerance in America to unorthodox opinion. "The times demand a renaissance in freedom of thought and freedom of expression, a renaissance that will end the orthodoxy that threatens to devitalize us."

————. *Freedom of the Mind.* New York, American Library Association in Cooperation with the Public Affairs Committee, 1962. 44 p. (Reading for an Age of Change Series, no. 3) **D 226**

An Associate Justice of the U.S. Supreme Court explains in popular language why freedom of the mind is a necessary principle in a democratic society and a major concern today. "Why and how the basic constitutional rights of freedom of thought, press, speech, and assembly have been threatened or actually curtailed. How freedom of information develops more responsible citizens." Reviewed in ALA *Newsletter on Intellectual Freedom*, January 1963, pp. 1–2.

————. "The Public Trial and the Free Press." *Nieman Reports*, 14(3):3–7, July 1960. (Also in *Rocky Mountain Law Review*, 33:1–10, December 1960) **D 227**

"Since defendants' rights are the interests protected by the public trial, the end is best served by banning all photography, broadcasting, and televising. The camel should be kept out of the tent, lest he take it over completely." The annual John E. Coen Lecture, delivered by Justice Douglas at the University of Colorado Law School, 10 May 1960.

————. *The Right of the People.* New York, Doubleday, 1958. 238 p. (North Lectures delivered at Franklin and Marshall College, 1957; reprinted by Pyramid Books) **D 228**

Lecture I deals with freedom of expression, including the philosophy of the First Amendment, the conflict between free expression and other community values, and censorship and prior restraint. Justice Douglas concludes that the only protection against tyranny of the few or tyranny of the mob is "more freedom of expression rather than less."

Dover, Simon Thomas Brewster, and Nathan Brooks. "Trial, 1663." In Howell, *State Trials*, vol. 6, pp. 539th ff.   **D 229**
For publishing seditious pamphlets the three men were sentenced to be fined, pilloried, and held in prison during the king's pleasure. The king's chief censor, Roger L'Estrange, testified against the defendants. The judge commented that, except for the compassion of the king, the three should have been put to death for treason.

Dow, Lorenzo. *The Stranger in Charleston! or, The Trial and Confession of Lorenzo Dow, Addressed to the United States in General, and South Carolina in Particular.* 3d ed. Wheeling, Va., Printed by R. I. Curtis, 1826. 94 p. (First edition published in Boston, 1821)   **D 230**
Libel on the Rev. William Hammett, in Charleston, in the State Court of Sessions, 17 May 1821.

Dow, Orrin B. "*The Last Temptation* and The First Freedom." *NCLA Odds and Bookends*, 43:9–11, Fall 1963.   **D 231**
A public library board (Farmingdale, N.Y.) by unanimous vote defended the library's purchase of copies of Kazantzakis' *Last Temptation of Christ* against charges of blasphemy. Opposition to the board's action, particularly from the Independent Active Citizens of Farmingdale, was believed to have been responsible for the defeat at the polls of the library's budget. This article includes text of a leaflet used in the campaign—"Protesting Defamation of Christ (in your local library)" and urging a "no" vote on the library's budget. A reactivated Friends of the Library, following the election, waged a vigorous campaign on behalf of the library and when the budget was resubmitted to voters it passed.

Dowden, Wilfred S., and T. N. Marsh, eds. *The Heritage of Freedom; Essays on the Rights of Free Men.* New York, Harper, 1962. 283 p.   **D 232**
Includes Benjamin Franklin's An Apology for Printers, from the *Pennsylvania Gazette*, 10 June 1731 (pp. 76–82); J. S. Mill's On Liberty of Thought and Discussions (pp. 5–33); Elmer Davis' Men and the Whole Truth, from his *But We Were Born Free* (pp. 57–75); Milton's *Areopagitica* (pp. 83–111); Alexis de Tocqueville's Liberty of the Press in the United States (pp. 112–18); Zechariah Chafee Jr.'s Freedom of Speech and Press, from his *A Freedom Agenda* (pp. 140–56); and John Locke's A Letter Concerning Toleration, 1689 (pp. 231–53).

Dowell, Eldridge. "Criminal Syndicalism Legislation, 1935–1939." *Public Opinion Quarterly*, 4:299–304, June 1940.   **D 233**
Efforts by several states to alter the statutes covering criminal syndicalism.

———. *A History of Criminal Syndicalism Legislation in the United States.* Baltimore, Johns Hopkins University, 1939. 176 p. (Studies in Historical and Political Science, series 57, no. 1)   **D 234**

Dowling, Margaret. "Sir John Hayward's Trouble over His *Life of Henry IV*." *Library*, 11(4th ser.):212–24, 1931.   **D 235**
Hayward was tried for treason in 1600 because his book was found objectionable to Queen Elizabeth. The Bishop of London ordered it to be burnt. Hayward was sentenced to imprisonment and would have lost his life but for the support of Sir Francis Bacon.

Downfall of Temporizing Poets, unlicenst Printers, upstart Booksellers, Trotting Mercuries, and bawling Hawkers. Being a very pleasant Dialogue between Lightfoot the Mercury, and Suck-bottle the Hawker, Rednose the Poet being Moderator between them; the corruptions of all which by their conference is plainly described. London, J. Barker, 1614. 5 p.   **D 236**
A ribald description of the unrestrained and irresponsible trade of printing and bookselling that existed in seventeenth-century England, with frequent issues of scandalous and untruthful works.

Downs, Robert B. "Apologist for Censorship." *Library Journal*, 86:2042, 44, 1 June 1961.   **D 237**
A criticism of James J. Kilpatrick's *Smut Peddlers.* Kilpatrick begins his researches in obscenity, writes Downs, with a reasonably unbiased viewpoint but "emerges embracing and condoning the NODL, the Citizens for Decent Literature, Americans for Moral Decency, and similar extra-legal private pressure groups, and advocating stringent repressive legislation." Testimony of medical, psychiatric, and sociological authorities, Downs points out, does not support the contention that pornography is a significant factor in contributing to juvenile delinquency.

———. "Book Banning v. the Right to Read." *Kansas Business Review*, 15(3):2–4, March 1962. (Also in *College Store Journal*, 29:100–104, August–September 1962)   **D 238**
Banning a book automatically creates a universal desire to read it and frequently makes a bestseller out of a mediocre work that would otherwise be overlooked. Censorship, furthermore, is futile since ideas cannot be killed by destroying the book that contains them.

———. "The Book Burners Cannot Win." In *Robert S. Allen Reports,* newspaper column distributed by Hall Syndicate, 14 September 1953. (Reprinted in Downs, *The First Freedom,* pp. 310–12)   **D 239**
During the controversy over censorship in U.S. Information Libraries overseas, the retiring president of the American Library Association discusses the issues from the point of view of librarians. Would-be censors never learn two basic facts about censorship: (1) censorship creates a desire for the banned book, and (2) ideas cannot be killed by suppression.

———. "Censorship." In the *American Library Annual and Book Trade Almanac,* 1959. New York, Bowker, 1958, pp. 91–92.   **D 240**
A summary of the year's events involving libraries and the work of the ALA Committee on Intellectual Freedom.

———. "Communist Propaganda." *Library Journal*, 87:2506–7, July 1962.   **D 241**
A statement prepared for the American Council on Education for use in testimony in opposition to the "Cunningham Amendment" to the Postal Revision Act of 1962. The amendment provides that no international mail determined by the Attorney General to be Communist propaganda may be handled by the U.S. Post Office and that no Communist propaganda mailed within the United States may be sent under any postal rate established by the Act. Downs comments on the effect this legislation, if passed, would have on library resources and research activities.

———. *The First Freedom; Liberty and Justice in the World of Books and Reading.* Chicago, American Library Association, 1960. 469 p.   **D 242**
An anthology of 88 notable writings of the past 50 years by American and British authors on the censorship of books. The first two chapters place the problem of censorship in its historical setting and present the broad issues. The remaining chapters deal with famous legal decisions, pressure groups, obscenity, political subversion, the attitude of writers and librarians, censorship in the public schools, censorship in Ireland and under dictatorships. The final chapter deals with prospects for the future. Downs has written introductions to each chapter and each selection. The collection brings together in one volume many important but elusive works in the development of freedom of the press.

———. "Liberty and Justice in Books." *ALA Bulletin*, 51:407–10, June 1957.   **D 243**

The first American Library Association Liberty and Justice Book Awards presented 25 April 1957 in New York furnished "another demonstration of its long-time concern with American tradition of freedom." An account of the awards and the winners, and a list of the distinguished panel of judges.

———. "Trustees and Intellectual Freedom." *Illinois Libraries*, 45:256–59, May 1963. **D 244**

Doyle, Donald D. "If You Believe in Freedom." *California Librarian*, 18:43–44, 59–60, January 1957. **D 245**

The chairman of the Education Committee of the California Legislature, describes for the Intellectual Freedom Committee of the California Library Association the legislative history of Senate Bill 1671. This bill, which failed of passage, provided that every school board in the state adopt regulations for selection and review of all material in school libraries and that their regulations should prohibit "books or other materials which teach, advocate, sponsor, or otherwise tend to propagate ideas or principles contrary to or at variance with" the state education code which provides for teaching principles of morality, truth, justice, and patriotism.

Doyle, James. *A Special Report of the Trial of the Rev. Vladimir Petcherine (one of the Redemptorist Fathers) in the Court House, Green-Street, Dublin, December 1855, on an indictment charging him with burning the Protestant Bible, at Kingston.* Dublin, James Duffy, 1856. **D 246**

A Catholic priest was brought to trial for allegedly burning two copies of the Protestant Bible along with two wheelbarrow loads of books considered "pestilential." He was acquitted. A lengthy article in defense of Father Petcherine, who, the author believed, was being persecuted for his religious zeal while infidel literature was allowed to flourish, appears in the *Dublin Review*, March 1856, under the title, Bible Blasphemy.

Doyle, James A. "Free Speech and Fair Trials." *Nebraska Law Review*, 22:1–16, March 1943. **D 247**

Discussion of the effect of U.S. Supreme Court decisions upon constitutional doctrine respecting the absoluteness of freedom of the press in relation to reporting of court trials.

Drakard, John. "Trial for a Seditious Libel, 1811." In Howell, *State Trials*, vol. 31, pp. 495 ff. **D 248**

Drakard was brought to trial for publishing in his *Stamford News* an article criticizing corporal punishment in the Army. He was convicted and given 18 months' imprisonment.

Draper, John, W. *History of the Conflict between Religion and Science.* New York, Appleton, 1896. 367 p. (First published in 1876) **D 249**

The historic struggle between the doctrines of the Catholic Church and the discoveries of science. Numerous references to censorship and suppression of thought. The work itself was placed on the Catholic *Index*.

———. *Thoughts on the Future Civil Policy of America.* New York, Harper, 1865. 325 p. **D 250**

Chapter 3 deals with the political force of ideas. Censorship of literature and art are discussed on pp. 284 ff.

Dreiser, Theodore. "Life, Art and America." *Seven Arts*, 2:363–89, February 1917. **D 251**

The author comments on America's moral and social drift as it relates to mental freedom. He is "constantly astonished by the thousands of men, exceedingly capable in some mechanical or narrow technical sense, whose world or philosophic vision is that of a child." The tendency today is to even narrower and more puritanic standards than in the past. "Personally, my quarrel is with America's quarrel with original thought." Dreiser protests the activities of reformers, such as Comstock, and their followers, and regards such interference with serious art and serious minds as an outrage.

———. "The Meddlesome Decade: How Censorship Is Making Our Civilization Ridiculous." *Theatre Guild Magazine*, 6(8):11–13, 61–62, May 1929. **D 252**

"Today we are faced with one of the most fanatical and dangerous forms of censorship that ever existed, because the effect of all such activity is to reduce all human intelligence to one level—and that level about that of a low grade (not even a high-grade) moron!" Dreiser speaks of "'Bands' and 'clubs' and 'societies' and 'daughters' of this or 'sons' of that or 'mothers' of the other thing—the sole purpose of which is the protection and guidance of public manners and morals." He gives numerous examples from newspaper articles, city ordinances, bills in the legislatures, and court decisions, which attest to the hysteria in America in the decade following World War I. "Censorship by threat, without protection of law," has become the established system in America.

Drinker, Eugene. "Ordinance Prohibiting Anonymous Handbills." *Wayne Law Review*, 6:420–25, Summer 1960. **D 253**

Regarding *Talley v. California*, 362 U.S. 60 (1960), *Lovell v. Griffin*, 303 U.S. 444 (1937), and related cases.

Drinker, Henry S. *Some Observations on the Four Freedoms of the First Amendment: Freedom of Speech, Freedom of the Press, Freedom of Assembly and Petition, Freedom of Religion.* Boston, Boston University Press, 1957. 69 p. (The Gasper G. Bacon Lectures on the Constitution of the United States) **D 254**

General considerations which prompted the adoption of the First Amendment and the court decisions that have interpreted it. Drinker recommends as a test, the determination as to whether a person in a particular case has been deprived of a substantial right of one of the basic freedoms.

Drinnon, Richard. *Rebel in Paradise; A Biography of Emma Goldman.* Chicago, University of Chicago Press, 1961, 349 p. **D 255**

A biography of the American anarchist who, for more than 50 years, was an "archetype rebel," challenging the social, political, and intellectual convictions of the American people. She was frequently involved in issues of freedom of speech and the press, either in her own behalf or in defense of others. She figured prominently in the birth control movement, she challenged Comstock and the vice societies, and took part in wartime espionage cases. Her journal, *Mother Earth*, often reported attacks on press freedom.

Driver, Tom F. "Shylock on Television." *Christianity and Crisis*, 22:126–27, 23 July 1962. **D 256**

Editorial comment on the objection of the New York Board of Rabbis to the television presentation of Shakespeare's *Merchant of Venice*. He calls their stand ill-advised. "We do not understand why it is not obvious, especially to a group long subjected to 'minority' discrimination, that the surest way to excite hostility is to restrain freedom of speech."

Drone, Eaton S. *A Treatise on the Law of Property in Intellectual Productions in Great Britain and the United States . . .* Boston, Little, Brown, 1879. 774 p. **D 257**

An early American study of copyright theory and practice; still useful for historical reference.

Drummond, Isabel. *The Sex Paradox.* New York, Putnam, 1953. 369 p. **D 258**

This study of the legal aspects of sexual delinquency includes a chapter on Obscenity and Defamation, in which the author discusses the historical development of obscenity and efforts to control it, and the application of defamation laws in the realm of sex expression.

Drummond, J. Roscoe. "Open Letter about 'Book Burning.'" *Nieman Reports*, 7(3):38, July 1953. (Reprinted from *Christian Science Monitor*, 16 June 1953) **D 259**

The letter relates to the suppression of books in U.S. overseas libraries. Other newspaper articles and editorials on the topic are also reprinted in this issue of *Nieman Reports*.

———. "Public Duty of a Free Press." In *Public Opinion in a Democracy*. Proceedings of the Institute of Human Relations. Issued as a special supplement to the January 1938 issue of *Public Opinion Quarterly*, pp. 59–62. **D 260**
The editor of the *Christian Science Monitor*, which prints no crime news, recommends that newspapers "make 1 per cent of crime news look like 1 per cent and not 50 per cent," thus recognizing the social importance of the news. A free press "is not guaranteed merely for either the convenience or the commerce of newspapers but to protect free speech and free institutions, to preserve the free processes of democratic government." The major danger to a free press is from within and lies with publishers and editors who do not use their freedom to good purpose.

Dryer, Sherman H. *Radio in Wartime*. New York, Greenberg, 1942, 384 p. **D 261**
Criticism of the failure of radio to realize its full potential in meeting wartime challenges. Following the author's views, differences of opinion are provided by the comments of seven distinguished critics.

[Duane, William]. *Biographical Memoir of William J. Duane*. Philadelphia, Claxton, Remsen & Haffelfinger, 1868. 28 p. **D 262**
Duane succeeded Bache as editor of the Republican *Aurora* and continued the paper's invective against the Adams administration. He was brought to trial on a charge of seditious libel. The case was dropped when Duane insisted on producing an Adams letter in his defense. In March 1800 a committee of the U.S. Senate, after a bitter controversy over the freedom of the press, found Duane guilty of seditious utterances in his reporting of proceedings of the Senate and ordered him to appear before that body to defend his conduct. Duane employed Alexander J. Dallas and Thomas Cooper as his counsels, but they refused to represent him before the Senate. "I will not degrade myself by submitting to appear before the Senate with their gag in my mouth," wrote Cooper. Duane failed to appear before the Senate and his arrest was ordered. He went into hiding until Congress had adjourned. He was later indicted by a federal grand jury under the Sedition law, but the proceedings were dropped with the advent of the Jefferson administration. A full account of "William Duane, the *Aurora*, and the Alien and Sedition Laws" is given in Smith, *Freedom's Fetters*, pp. 277–306. Senator Jonathan Dayton's "Report on Libels on the Senate," dealing with the *Aurora* case, appears in the *Journal of the Senate*, 6th Congr., 1st sess., pp. 170–74, 194–95.

[———, *et. al.*]. "Trial of Duane, Reynolds, Moore and Cuming, for Seditious Riot. In the Court of Oyer and Terminer for the County of Philadelphia, 1799." In Wharton, *State Trials*, pp. 345–91. **D 263**

The trial has no direct relation to freedom of the press, but pertains to a charge of stirring up a seditious riot outside a Catholic church in attempting to get signatures on a petition to repeal the Alien Act. While Duane played only a minor role in the affair, as editor of the Republican paper he was considered by the prosecution to be the most important figure in the case. The jury acquitted the defendants, and the Federalists lost the first skirmish in their campaign to suppress the Republican editor.

Dubois, Jules. *Freedom Is My Beat*. Indianapolis, Bobbs-Merrill, 1959, 295 p. **D 264**
A correspondent for the *Chicago Tribune* writes of his 30 years experience in seeking to preserve and extend press freedom throughout Latin America. In 1951 Dubois was named chairman of the Freedom of the Press Committee of the Inter American Press Association.

Duckett, Kenneth W., and Francis Russell. "The Harding Papers: How Some Were Burned . . . and Some Were Saved." *American Heritage*, 16(2):24–31, 102–10, February 1965. **D 265**
"Controversy, the inevitable result of secrecy and suppression, still swirls about the life and Presidency of Warren Gamaliel Harding, who came to the White House in 1921 in the bright sunlight of landslide victory and left it in death, shadowed by scandal, less than three years later . . . Tampering with his papers—even the outright burning of many of them—began almost with Harding's funeral; the censorship has continued over the decades since. That story is told . . . by the curator of manuscripts at the Ohio Historical Society, Kenneth W. Duckett . . . Francis Russell gives his account of the recently publicized Harding-Phillips love letters; he found them in Marion, Ohio, and tried to place them in the custody of the Ohio Historical Society, with explosive results into which this magazine has been drawn."—The Editors.

Dudley, Dorothy. *Forgotten Frontiers; Dreiser and the Land of the Free*. New York, Smith and Haas, 1932. 484 p. **D 266**
Numerous references to the suppression of Theodore Dreiser's novels.

Dudley, Edward P. "Danger to Libraries." *Assistant Librarian*, 49:202–3, December 1956. **D 267**
The threat of pressure groups producing an intolerance of that which does not conform. This is a greater danger to libraries than overt political and government action.

"Due Process for Whom—Newspaper or Defendant?" *Stanford Law Review*, 4: 101–11, December 1951. **D 268**
The primary concern should be to secure a fair trial. If newspapers adhere to ethical standards in reporting, the problem would be minimized. Where newspapers are unfair, a change of venue may be necessary.

Duesenberg, Richard W. "Crime Comic Books: Government Control and Their Impact on Juvenile Conduct." *Mercer Law Review*, 7:331–51, Spring 1956. **D 269**
While society demands measures to preserve and protect the health and welfare of youth, the interest of freedom of the press militates against the regulation of comic books. For this reason and because of the lack of evidence with respect to the effect of the reading of comic books on juvenile behavior, anticomic book legislation should not be upheld. The author recommends a countermovement of private organizations to produce results.

Duess, Harriet G. "Between the Devil of Censorship and the Deep Sea of Propaganda." *Matrix*, 20(3):7, February–March 1935. **D 270**
Problems of a foreign correspondent.

[Duffin, Patrick W., and Thomas Lloyd]. *The Trial of P. W. Duffin, a Late Captain of the Fourth Company in the Volunteer Regiment of Irish Brigade, Dublin. And Thomas Lloyd, a Citizen of the United States of America, for a Supposed Libel. To which is annexed, a Letter to Thomas Pinckney, the American Minister; wherein Thomas Lloyd claims the Interference of the United States of America, to obtain him a Satisfaction for the Unparalleled Tortures, and cruel Oppressions which he has experienced under the British Government . . .* 2d ed. London, Printed for D. J. Eaton, 1793. 46 p. **D 271**
Duffin and Lloyd were charged in 1792 with posting libelous and seditious notices on the chapel of Fleet prison: "This house to let . . . on or before the 1st day of January, 1793, being the commencement of the first year of liberty in Great Britain!!" Their actions reflected the support in England of the French Revolution. Lloyd was given three years in Newgate prison and pilloried; Duffin was sentenced to two years in prison at New Compter.

Dugan, Frank H. "An Illinois Martyrdom." Illinois State Historical Society, *Papers in Illinois History and Transactions for the Year 1938*, pp. 111–57. **D 272**
The story of Elijah P. Lovejoy and his death in defense of a free press in Alton, Ill., in 1837. The author gives special attention to the part which the Puritan minority played in the events leading to the Alton riots. He has relied largely on contemporary letters and newspaper accounts. The article is based on a Master's thesis at Northwestern University.

Dugan, John T. "License of Liberty: Art, Censorship, and American Freedom."

Journal of Aesthetics, 12:366–72, March 1954.   **D 273**

Under the First Amendment art should be entitled to the same freedom from censorship prior to exposure, as a newspaper. Censorship of the arts is an insult both to the intelligence and the moral strength of American citizens.

————. "Right to Dissent: Fear or Freedom for the American Dramatist?" In *Theatre Annual, 1955.* New York, The Theatre Library Association, 1955, pp. 7–15.   **D 274**

"We must have the courage born of faith in the aesthetic, political, and moral rightness of our freedom to produce and enjoy drama which reflects truth and beauty as we see it, whether this vision is contrary to the transient mores of the times or not." The dramatist should have the same freedom of expression as artists working in other media. Not censorship, but fear of it, has prevented many great ideas from being expressed in the theater.

Dulles, Avery. *The Legion of Decency.* Washington, D.C., America Press, 1956. 31 p.   **D 275**

A pamphlet explaining the purpose and method of operation of the Legion and answering objections to its program.

Dunbar, Mathilda. "*Dictionary of American Slang* Controversy." *Manitoba Library Association Bulletin*, 12:14–17, Winter 1964–65.   **D 276**

Duncan, W. G. K. "A Librarian's First Loyalty." *Australian Library Journal*, 10:163–74, October 1961; also in *ALA Bulletin*, 56:509–19, June 1962.   **D 277**

The librarian's vocation is "to promote and foster the free flow of information and ideas throughout his community; . . . no matter what a librarian thinks and feels as a private person, he should feel obliged, *qua* librarian, to resist the pressures in his community towards censorship."

Duniway, Clyde A. *The Development of Freedom of the Press in Massachusetts.* Cambridge, Mass., Harvard University Press, 1906. 202 p. (Harvard Historical Studies, vol. 12)   **D 278**

A study of the evolution of press freedom in the colonies, and particularly in Massachusetts. The author begins with a survey of English restrictions on printing and the development of English common law. He discusses the institution of royal control over the colonial press, the struggle of Massachusetts editors and publishers against executive and legislative restrictions and the stamp act, the development of constitutional guarantees, persecution under the Sedition Act, and, finally, the passage in 1827 of a just and reasonable libel law. A well-documented and basic source of information on censorship in the American colonies.

Dunker, George F., Jr. "Constitutional Law: State Commission's Extralegal Censorship." *California Law Review*, 51:620–26, August 1963.   **D 279**

Bantam Books, Inc. v. Sullivan, 372 U.S. 58 (1963), relating to action of the Rhode Island Commission to Encourage Morality in Youth.

Dunkerley, Madeline. "Censorship in Public Libraries." *Australian Library Journal*, 7(2):22–23, April 1958.   **D 280**

A report of the chief librarian of Burwood, New South Wales, to the City Council in answer to charges made by a citizen that immoral novels were in the public library. Miss Dunkerley describes the library's book selection policy, noting that it was not the business either of the librarian or the City Council to impose standards of morality on the adult members of the community through censorship of books. If a book is banned by court authority it is not placed on the library shelves. "Otherwise my choice of adult fiction and literary works is not influenced by moral, religious or political considerations, nor do I think it should be." The library recognizes the right of citizens to be repelled by certain books and to express their repulsion to others "but not the right to force their standards on others by demanding the suppression of what they dislike." The Council commended Miss Dunkerley for her handling of the situation and recommended that a copy of her statement be sent to the complainant.

Dunkley, *Mrs.* G. S. "Selection Policies Defended to Allay Fears of Censors." *Library Journal*, 80:2881–83, 15 December 1955.   **D 281**

Dunlap, Andrew. *A Speech delivered before the Municipal Court of the City of Boston, in Defence of Abner Kneeland, on an Indictment for Blasphemy. January Term, 1834. By Andrew Dunlap.* Boston, Printed for the Publisher, 1834. 132 p.   **D 282**

An eloquent address in behalf of Abner Kneeland, delivered by his attorney who, while dissenting from the doctrine of the defendant, claimed for him "the same legal right to the enjoyment, and the maintenance of his opinions, by his voice and his pen, which we claim for ourselves, as our political birthright, guaranteed by our glorious Revolution; and proclaimed in our immortal Bill of Rights." Dunlap based his defense on two grounds—the offense charged was not within the Statute and the Statute was a violation of the letter and spirit of the Constitution. When the judge inquired of Kneeland's religious beliefs, Dunlap responded: "That is an affair between him and God, not between him and your Honor. He does not consider that he is bound to make a confession of faith here." Dunlap concluded his defense: "If the defendant shall fall in this prosecution, a nobler victim will fall with him, for the blow which is aimed at the prisoner at the bar, is a fatal blow to the Constitution of his country."

Dunlap, Leslie W. "Censorship." In *American Library Annual for 1957–1958.* New York, Bowker, 1958, pp. 134–36.   **D 283**

A summary of the year's events involving censorship in libraries.

Dupee, F. W. "*Lolita* in America." *Encounter*, 12:30–35, February 1959.   **D 284**

Account of the publishing history of Nabokov's *Lolita* and its reception in America.

Durham, Frank M. "Mencken as Missionary." *American Literature*, 29:478–83, January 1958.   **D 285**

Mencken's protest at the attempt to suppress Theodore Dreiser's, *The Genius.*

Durham, M. E. "A Very Free Press." *New Statesman and Nation*, 1:352–53, 2 May 1931.   **D 286**

The author describes his experience under a completely free press in Albania after the Young Turk revolution of 1908, which was so abused by scurrilous personal attacks that it led of action in Defence of the Realm and the expulsion of the editor. 'Too much Freedom,' the author concludes, "is not really good for anyone."

"Durham, 1964. The A.A.L. and Censorship." *Assistant Librarian*, 57:113–17, July 1964.   **D 287**

In a conference of the Association of Assistant Librarians held at Durham, T. S. Broadhurst of Liverpool University Library discussed why books are censored and what legal measures can be applied; Bill Smith, editor of *Books and Bookmen*, spoke about censorship of films, stage, and television, as well as books; T. E. Callander, chief librarian of Croydon, spoke from the point of view of the practicing librarian.

Durr, Clifford J. "Freedom of Speech for Whom." *Public Opinion Quarterly*, 8:391–406, Fall 1944.   **D 288**

The author, a member of the Federal Communications Commission, expresses dissatisfaction with the restrictions placed on content of radio programs by the networks, who in turn are influenced by the advertisers.

Dutt, R. Palme, and R. Page Arnot. "Press Freedom." *Labour Monthly*, 30:113–19, April 1948.   **D 289**

The reply made by the editors of this Marxist intellectual journal to the questionnaire of the Royal Commission on the Press. The statement reviews the struggle for freedom of the press in Great Britain. True press freedom requires the social ownership of the press, in place of the present monopoly-capitalist ownership.

"The Duty of a Newspaper." *Spectator*, 115:649, 13 November 1915. **D 290**
Wartime censorship on reporting of Parliamentary debate.

Duvillard, E. "The Censorship of Films for the Young." *International Review of Educational Cinematography*, 3:136–42, February 1931. (Translated from the French) **D 291**
"M. Duvillard asserts that film censorship has missed its aim and that the chief reason of its inefficiency lies in the fact that it attempts to replace the authority and mind of the father of the family, and to impose, as representing the majority's will, views that do not correspond to general opinion." He objects to creating a special censorship of films for children; this is the responsibility of the parents.

Dwight, Timothy. *Essay on the Stage; in Which the Arguments in Its Behalf, and Those Against It, Are Considered; and Its Morality, Character and Effects Illustrated.* Middletown, Conn., 1824. 166p. **D 292**

Dyer, George. *Address to the People of Great Britain, on the Doctrine of Libels, and*

the *Office of Juror*. London, The Author, 1799. 120p. **D 293**

Dyke, Stewart. *USIA: The Murrow Years.* Columbia, Mo., Freedom of Information Center, School of Journalism, University of Missouri, 1964. 6p. (Publication no. 127) **D 294**
"Murrow did more to redefine, reshape and upgrade the role of the United States Information Agency than anyone else in the ten-year history of the agency."

E

E., D. "The Candor Pamphlets." *Notes and Queries*, 5(2d ser.):121–23, 13 February 1858; 5(2d ser.):141, 20 February 1858; 5(2d ser.):161–63, 27 February 1858. **E1**
A careful analysis of the Candor pamphlets of the 1760's "in which great constitutional battles were fought and by which they were won." The pamphlets laid down the principle that, in questions of libel, juries are judges of law as well as facts. The author of this article shows by external and internal evidence that the authors of the Candor letter (satire) and the Father of Candor letters (logic) were one and the same. He also believes Candor was "Philelutherus Anglicanus" who wrote *A Summary of The Law of Libel*. He favors Lord Camden as author of the Candor pamphlets, but is inclined to the opinion that the author of the Candor pamphlets and the Junius letters were not the same.

"E & P Panel Suggests Studies for Press Self-Improvement." *Editor and Publisher*, 82:5–7, 40–41, 45–48, 50, 26 March 1949. **E2**
A panel of six newspaper men and four educators, including Professors Hocking and Niebuhr of the Commission on Freedom of the Press, discuss a program for appraisal of problems and performance of American newspapers. The group was formed as an outgrowth of newspaper criticisms of the report of the Commission.

Eager, Alan R. "Who Killed Cock Robin?" *Assistant Librarian*, 49:196–98, December 1956. **E3**
In this whimsical essay, an Irishman discovers hidden and sinister meaning in *My First Book of Nursery Rhymes* and decides to place it out of reach of his little daughter.

Eagleton, Clyde. "Interference with American Mails." *American Journal of International Law*, 34:315–20, April 1940. **E4**
A discussion of the rights of a neutral against interference with the mail by belligerents in time of war, written in the light of a recent American protest to the British Foreign Office.

Eakin, M. L. *Censorship in Public High School Libraries*. New York, School of Library Service, Columbia University, 1948. 102 p. (Unpublished Master's thesis) **E5**
"What persons attempt to exercise censorship over the purchase and use of public secondary school library materials and to what extent do they succeed? For what reasons have books been censored and which of these factors have operated most frequently in restricting purchases or use of materials? By what methods do librarians restrict the purchase or use of doubtful materials? What titles have been censored in high school libraries, how often, and for what reason?"

Easley, Ralph M. "What Is Obscenity in Literature?" *Light*, 190:17–24, September–October 1929. **E6**
An open letter of appreciation to the 12 jurymen who convicted Mrs. Mary Ware Dennett for her book, *The Sex Side of Life*. Easley, one of the founders of the National Civic Federation, objects to Mrs. Dennett's work as unsavory and improper sex education. He protests against her role as martyr.

Eastman, Max. "Is the Truth Obscene?" *Masses*, 6(46):5–6, March 1915. (Reprinted by the Free Speech League) **E7**
An attack on the practice of U.S. postal authorities in suppressing birth control information. Eastman describes his interview with William Sanger who had just been arrested for giving a copy of his wife's birth control pamphlet to an agent provocateur of the New York vice society. Eastman urges the public to come to Sanger's support.

———. *Max Eastman's Address to the Jury in the Second Masses Trial, in Defense of the Socialist Position and the Right of Free Speech*. New York, Liberator Publishing Co., [1918]. 46 p. (Liberator Pamphlets no. 1) **E8**
A defense of the Socialist position and the right of free speech in the espionage trial against the publishers of the *Masses*. Eastman was editor from 1914 until it was suspended by the Post Office Department in 1917. It is

"the underlying intention of our publication... to publish a free, vigorous, satirical, humorous and somewhat reckless magazine, with poetry and picture and argument addressed to the people from the socialist point of view." He defends the right of editors "who are opposed to the war on political grounds, but who want to conform to the regulations and don't want to impede the military operations of the government." He accuses Postmaster General Burleson of bungling in the handling of postal affairs under the Espionage Act.

———. "The Post Office Censorship." *Masses*, 9:24, September 1917. **E9**
An account of the suppression of the *Masses* by the Post Office Department during World War I.

———, and Morris Hillquit. "Speeches of Max Eastman and Morris Hillquit at the *Masses* Dinner, May 9, [1918]." *Liberator*, 1:19–23, June 1918. **E10**
Eastman became editor of the *Liberator* when his paper, *Masses*, was suspended under the wartime Espionage Act. Hillquit was a leader of American Socialists.

Eastman, Newton L. A. *Open Door to Hell; a Brief Account of the Trial of Bishop Eastman; Every Article for Which He Was Indicted Is Herein Printed*. Milan, Ill., Truth and Light Publishing House, [1908?]. 34 p. **E11**
Between 1905 and 1908 Eastman, Bishop of the Gospel Workers of America, was indicted five times in New York and federal courts for libel and obscenity for anti-Catholic articles appearing in his *Gospel Worker*. He was eventually acquitted on all charges.

Eaton, Clement. "Censorship of the Southern Mails." *American Historical Review*, 48:266–80, January 1943. **E12**
Experience of the South during three decades of antebellum censorship of incoming mail from Northern states. "The Southern record demonstrates the difficulty of suppressing pernicious and dangerous propaganda without at the same time destroying the literature of reform, of protest, and of sanative criticism."

————. "A Dangerous Pamphlet in the Old South." *Journal of Southern History*, 2:323–34, August 1936. **E13**
"During the late autumn of 1829 a dangerous incendiary pamphlet was found circulating among the blacks at Savannah, Georgia." The pamphlet, *Walker's Appeal in Four Articles Together with a Preamble to the Colored Citizens of the World, But in Particular and Very Expressly to those of the United States of America*, was written by a free Negro whose father was a slave. It frightened two states into enacting laws prohibiting the circulation of incendiary publications and forbidding the teaching of reading and writing to slaves.

————. "The Freedom of the Press in the Upper South." *Mississippi Valley Historical Review*, 18:479–99, March 1932. **E14**
A record of the fight for freedom of the press in the Old South "waged in the borderland between the fire-eating cotton kingdom and the free North." Freedom was "enjoyed only in the fringes of the Old South, and for brief interims, in Kentucky." On grounds of protecting the public safety, freedom of the press was denied to even the mildest opponents of slavery.

————. *Freedom of Thought in the Old South*. Durham, N.C., Duke University Press, 1940. 343 p. (Rev. ed., New York, Harper Torchbooks, 1964. 418 p.) **E15**
A study of intellectual freedom (or lack of it) in the antebellum South, including accounts of the suppression of the newspaper press over the slavery issue, and opposition to heterodoxy in religion. Reports of numerous trials. "This study of the cultural history of the South between 1790 and 1860, in which freedom of thought and speech is the central theme, is offered as a case history in the record of human liberty and intolerance."

Eaton, Daniel I. *The Proceedings, on the Trial of Daniel Isaac Eaton, upon an Indictment for selling a supposed libel, "The second part of the Rights of Man, combining principle and practice." By Thomas Paine. At Justice Hall, in the Old Bailey. Before the Recorder of London. On Monday, the third Day June, 1793*. London, Printed and published by Daniel I. Eaton and sold by James Ridgway, [1793]. 50 p. (Also in Howell, *State Trials*, vol. 22, pp. 753 ff.; vol. 31, pp. 927 ff.) **E16**
Eaton, a London publisher and bookseller, was indicted in 1793 for selling Paine's *Rights of Man* and, later the same year, Paine's *Letter Addressed to the Addressers*. He was acquitted in both cases. In 1812 Eaton was tried before Lord Ellenborough for publishing Paine's *Age of Reason*, was found guilty of a blasphemous libel and sentenced to be pilloried and to spend 18 months in prison. In Newgate he wrote a pamphlet exposing the extortion and abuses in the prison. In

his final challenge to the censor, Eaton published a translation of *Ecce Homo* for which he was indicted but never brought to trial because of his advanced age.

————. *The Trial of Daniel Isaac Eaton, before Lloyd Lord Kenyon, and a Special Jury, in the Court of King's Bench, Guildhall, London, July the Tenth, 1793; for Selling a Supposed Libel, A Letter Addressed to the Addressers, by Thomas Paine*. London, [1793]. 65 p. **E17**

————. *The Trial of Daniel Isaac Eaton, for Publishing a Supposed Libel, Intitled Politics for the People; or Hog's Wash: at Justice Hall in the Old Bailey, February Twenty-fourth, 1794*. London, Published for Daniel Eaton, 1794. 62 p. (Also in Howell, *State Trials*, vol. 23, pp. 1013 ff.) **E18**
Having been freed the year before from charges of sedition in the publication of Paine's *Rights of Man*, Eaton was again brought to trial in 1794 for this objectionable pamphlet, a story in which the king appeared as a gamecock. Eaton was again acquitted. In 1796 he was twice brought to trial—first for the publication of Pigot's *Political Dictionary* and second for *Duties of Citizenship*. To escape punishment he fled to America where he remained more than 3 years. On his return he found his property seized and his books burned and he was confined to prison for 15 months. In 1793 he published a satirical pamphlet, *The Pernicious Effects of the Art of Printing upon Society*.

————. *The Trial of Mr. Daniel Isaac Eaton, for Publishing the Third & Last Part of Paine's Age of Reason . . .* London, 1812. 80 p. **E19**
Eaton was convicted of blasphemy and sentenced to 18 months in prison. On hearing of this conviction, the young poet Shelley wrote a spirited letter of protest to the presiding judge, Lord Ellenborough. Wickwar notes that "It was easier to convict Eaton of blasphemous libel in 1812 than it had been to convict him of seditious libel in 1793–4."

Eaton, Walter P. *Free Speech*. Boston, American Unitarian Association, 1935. 20 p. (*Tracts*, series II, no. 342) **E20**
A drama critic considers the right of free speech as it applies to the preacher, the dramatist, the author, the radio performer, and the agitator.

Eaton, William D. "Press Censorship Calmly Considered." *Paladin* (St. Louis), 1:1 (1918). **E21**

Eddy, J. P. "Obscene Publications: Society of Authors' Draft Bill." *Criminal Law Review*, 1955:218–26, April 1955. **E22**

An examination of the bill to amend the British law on obscene publications, a proposal made by a Committee of the Society of Authors, first presided over by Sir Alan Herbert and subsequently by Sir Gerald Barry.

Edelman, Murray. *The Licensing of Radio Services in the United States, 1927 to 1947; a Study in Administrative Formation of Policy*. Urbana, Ill., University of Illinois Press, 1950. 229 p. (Illinois Studies in Social Sciences, vol. 31, no. 4) **E23**
Deals with the manner of development of rules and decisions which govern the licensing of broadcasting. A chapter on Conduct of Applicants and Licensees includes discussion of policies relating to program content and balance, and broadcasts on controversial public issues.

Edelstein, Alex S. "Not a Blunt Instrument, But a Sword." Columbia, Mo., Freedom of Information Center, School of Journalism, University of Missouri, 1958. 6 p. (Publication no. 11) **E24**
An abstract of the section on freedom of information from the author's doctoral dissertation, *The Marshall Plan Information in Western Europe as an Instrument of United States Foreign Policy, 1948–1952*.

Edgcomb, Ernest I. "Freedom of the Press." In *Problems of Journalism; Proceedings of the American Society of Newspaper Editors, 1930*. Washington, D.C., 1930, pp. 92–102. **E25**

Edge, John D. "A Report of the Trial of John Jones versus Thomas Sheehan, for Libel, Tried in the Court of Common Pleas on Monday, 2nd December, 1839." In *An Epitome of the Case of Irish Corporations . . .* Dublin, George Faulkner, 1839. 76 p. **E26**

Edgerton, Alice. "Lost Art of Censorship." *Freeman*, 2:369–70, 29 December 1920. **E27**
A satire on the suppression of heretics.

Edinborough, Arnold. "Arnold Edinborough Opposes Hard Core Pornography Along with Censorship." *Saturday Night*, 79:12–14, May 1964. **E28**

————. "Pornography and Public Taste." *Saturday Night*, 74:7–9, 42, 1 August 1959. **E29**
After analyzing sex and crime magazines on the Canadian newsstands, the author concludes

that those featuring crime and violence come nearer to meeting the Lord Cockburn definition of obscenity than those trading on the bare bosom. "There is a certain amount of questionable, immoral literature on our book stands. But the small amount of obscenity, there, should not be allowed to stampede the authorities into wholesale book banning."

————. "Sex and Violence in the Bookstalls." *Canadian Author and Bookman*, 36(1):10–14, Spring 1960. **E 30**
The editor of *Saturday Night* proposes a positive program of good reading as an antidote to widespread dissemination of obscene literature in Canada.

Editor and Publisher. New York, Editor and Publisher Co., 1901–date. Weekly. **E 31**
Freedom of the press is frequently discussed in both news and editorial columns of this trade publication of the newspaper press. News coverage is both domestic and foreign. An annual survey of Legal Decisions and Rulings Affecting Newspapers appears in the January issue. During World War II the column Shop Talk at Thirty carried frequent reports on wartime restrictions on the press. Curtis D. MacDougall, in his *The Press and Its Problems*, indexes the recent reports appearing in *Editor and Publisher* on such topics as: federal government restrictions on the "right to know" during the Truman, Eisenhower, and Kennedy administrations (pp. 310–14); the Moss Committee activities on government news secrecy (pp. 315–16); protection of news sources (pp. 348–49); to print or not to print (pp. 376–77); government news management during the Cuban and U–2 affairs (pp. 379–81); gag laws (pp. 416–17); and trial by newspaper (pp. 417–19).

"Editor Leech Goes to Jail for 'Contempt of Court.'" *Literary Digest*, 62:50–52, 30 August 1919. **E 32**
Edward T. Leech, editor of the *Memphis Press*, was sentenced to ten days in jail for alleged contempt of court, which grew out of an editorial criticizing, in general terms, the quality of judicial service rendered in Memphis. This article quotes some of his reflections written in jail, and a lengthy comment from the editor of the *Chattanooga News* on the freedom of the press, which concludes: "A free press is as important to the people as the right to vote."

["Editorial on Irish Censorship"]. In *An Leabharlann, Journal of the Library Association of Ireland*, 14:3–4, March 1956. (Quoted in Downs, *The First Freedom*, p. 380) **E 33**
The Irish librarian, faced with arbitrary and rigid censorship under the Censorship of Publications Act of 1946, has three alternatives: He can buy according to his own judgment,

hoping his selections will not be banned; he can buy on approval, holding the books for possible return; or he can limit his purchase of fiction to nothing but light romance, cowboy stories, and a few mysteries.

"Editor's Notebook." *Film Quarterly*, 13(3):2–3, Spring 1960. **E 34**
A massive film censorship movement may be in the offing, according to the trade papers. The situation "reveals a typical lack of both nerve and intelligence on the part of the film industry" in combating censorship. The industry "has no principle in these matters except where commerce dictates: if there is enough money in it censorship will be fought."

Editors of *Life*. "Hell Breaks Loose in Paradise." *Teachers College Record*, 65:651–53, May 1964. (Reprinted from *Life*, 26 April 1963) **E 35**
A social studies teacher in Paradise, Calif., who encouraged her students to read widely divergent points of view on controversial issues, is accused of being a Communist and her job is threatened in an episode that ripped the town into factions. A student was enlisted to spy on the teacher by means of a tape recorder concealed in a book.

[Edmondson, Robert E.]. *The Rape of the Press; American Free Speech Subversion Unmasked. Democracy Propaganda Fraud "Exploded."* Bend, Ore., 1954. 39p. **E 36**
The pamphlet charges that advertisers, organized labor, press associations, and Communist elements are subverting America's free press. He calls for legal separation of advertising from editorial policies in the press, with the "treason penalty" as "punishment for violation because of the enormity of the crime."

Edmunds, James. *Orrin B. Judd vs. James Edmunds. Action for Libel: Tried before Hon. Charles P. Daly and a Jury, at New York, Nov. 1859. Closing Address to the Jury, for the Plaintiff, by John Graham, esq., and Charge of His Honor Judge Daly; together with the Letter of Rev. Archibald Maclay, D.D. on His Resignation as President of the American Bible Union.* New York, Ervin H. Tripp, 1860. 112p. **E 37**
Dr. Judd was awarded $2,000 in damages for Edmunds' alleged libelous review of Judd's *Review of the American Bible Society* that appeared in the Louisville *Journal*.

Education Information, Inc. *The Interlocking Relationship of the NEA–ALA; "Censorship" and the "Dictionary of American Slang." A Report on Monopoly and Pressure Patterns in the Field of Education.* Amarillo, Tex., Education Information, Inc., 1964. 12p. (Education Report, ser. 8, no. 10) **E 38**

The report charges librarians, under the guise of the "freedom to read," with defending the presence of objectionable books in libraries (obscene and subversive) and at the same time "blacklisting" books of conservative persuasion. It suggests a conspiracy among such agencies as the American Library Association, the National Education Association, Foreign Policy Association, American Book Publishers' Council, the Fund for Adult Education, and UNESCO. The episode of the campaign against the *Dictionary of American Slang* in California schools is discussed at length.

————. *A Second Report on Slanted Textbooks; The Texas Textbook Investigation.* Fullerton, Calif., Education Information, Inc., 1962. 26p. (Education Report, vol. 8, no. 4) **E 39**
The report examines the investigation being conducted by a special Texas House of Representatives Textbook Study Committee. The Committee was appointed because of widespread dissatisfaction over selection of school textbooks by the State Textbook Committee, and as the result of a drive spearheaded by Texans for America. Included is the testimony against certain textbooks, given at a hearing of the investigating committee and a background article on Pressure Patterns and Slanted Textbooks.

Educational Reviewer. Chicago, Published for the Committee on Education, Conference of American Small Business Organizations, 1949–53. Quarterly. Lucille C. Crain, editor. **E 40**
A quarterly review of educational materials to combat collectivist doctrines in the public schools. The issue for 15 January 1953, for example, carried an article, Choose Honest, Unbiased Textbooks, calling for the Indiana State Textbook Commission to do a more careful job of screening school textbooks to eliminate biased economic doctrines. The issue for 29 October 1949 included an attack on the Magruder textbook on American government.

Edwards, P. L. "Free Speech and Free Press in Relation to the Police Power of the State." *Central Law Journal*, 58:383–86, 13 May 1904. **E 41**
A defense of the right of state legislatures and the Congress to restrain immoral publications "based on the police power of the state to protect society from attacks on its safety, and to prevent moral degradation."

Eek, Hilding. *Freedom of Information as a Project of International Legislation; a Study of International Law in Making.* Uppsala, Lundequistska Bokhandeln, 1953. 176p. (Uppsala Universitets Ärsskrift, 1953:6) **E 42**
Appendix 3 is the text of the Convention on the International Transmission of News and the Right of Correction. Appendix 5 is The

Draft Convention on Freedom of Information (various texts). Appendix 6 is a Statement of the Rights, Obligations and Practices to Be Included in the Concept of Freedom of Information.

Efron, Edith. "Can TV Drama Survive?" *TV Guide*, 13(39):8–12, 25 September 1965. **E43**
Six TV writers agree that television drama is dying because of the NAB code, network censorship, pressure groups, Congressional hearings on sex and violence in TV drama, and ratings.

————. "Television: America's Timid Giant." *TV Guide*, 11:4–11, 18 May 1963. **E44**

————. "Why Speech on Television Is Not Really Free." *TV Guide*, 11:4–9, 11 April 1964. **E45**
A critique on the "fairness doctrine."

Egan, Beresford, and P. R. Stephensen. *Policeman of the Lord; a Political Satire . . .* London, Issued in the Public Interest by the Sophistocles Press, [1929?]. 30p. **E46**
A lampooning of Sir William Joynson-Hicks, the British Home Secretary and official censor, who is quoted as stating: "It may possibly be that in the near future I shall have to deal with immoral and disgusting books." The authors comment, "A Socrates as Home Secretary would hesitate to define morality in terms of Police action. Not so a Jix [a term for Joynson-Hicks used by his critics]. In the mind of this essentially simple character, the problems of morality, which have exercised the profoundest philosophical minds of all ages, are solved and even acted upon without the hesitation which would be natural to a more tutored intellect." "I am attacked [Sir William is quoted] by those people who put freedom of thought and speech and writing before everything else in the world." "Precisely, Sir William" [conclude the authors]. Cartoons accompanying the text bear the following captions: An Astral Body; Twinkle, Twinkle, Little Jix; Hands Off; Visit to a Night Club; Leave the Well Alone; A Visit to the Attic; Street Offences; and We Will Not Have Purgatory. The pamphlet closes with a five-page poem lampooning the censor and, finally, a mock imprimatur.

Eggleston, Wilfred. "Press Censorship." *Canadian Journal of Economics and Political Science*, 7:313–23, August 1941. **E47**
A definition of censorship and its objectives, and an outline of the machinery existing in Canada for its application. An article on press censorship by Eggleston also appears in *Encyclopedia Canadiana*, vol. 2, pp. 298–99.

Ehlers, Henry, and Gordon C. Lee, eds. *Crucial Issues in Education.* Rev. ed. New York, Holt, 1959. 342p. **E48**

Part I deals with Freedom in Education, and Chapter 1 with Censorship by Whom? The case for responsible control is presented by excerpts from works of Walter Lippmann, I. B. Berkson, and the Rev. Francis J. Connell. The case against censorship is presented by excerpts from the work of Thorwald Esbensen, Julian Pleasants, Archibald MacLeish, and *The New Yorker.* There follow questions and readings for further study.

Ehling, William P. *Contempt by Publication and Freedom of the Press; an Historical Analysis of the Theories and Practices of the Judicial Contempt Power.* Syracuse, N.Y., Syracuse University, 1954. 1312p. (Ph. D. dissertation, University Microfilms, no. 10,070) **E49**

Ehrlich, J. W., ed. *Howl of the Censor.* Edited with introduction by J. W. Ehrlich. San Francisco, Nourse Publishing Co., 1961. 144p. **E50**
The actual court proceedings, *People of the State of California v. Lawrence Ferlinghetti,* in the prosecution of the booklet, *Howl and Other Poems* by Allen Ginsberg, on an obscenity charge. After lengthy testimony of literary critics, Judge Clayton W. Horn, in a classic summary of modern obscenity law, found the book not obscene. Ehrlich, counsel for the defense, is a noted trial lawyer and author of a number of legal works. The book includes extracts from *Howl.*

Eichelberger, Rosa K. "Freedom to Be Well-Informed." *Senior Scholastic,* 51(7): 22–23, 27 October 1947. **E51**
A popular, illustrated account of freedom of the press from Zenger to William Allen White.

Eisenhower, Dwight D. ["Don't Join the Book Burners"]. Address delivered at Dartmouth College Commencement, Hanover, N. H., 14 June 1953. In *Vital Speeches of the Day,* 19:570–71, 1 July 1953. (Also in Daniels, *The Censorship of Books,* pp. 101–3) **E52**
"Don't join the book burners. Don't think you are going to conceal faults by concealing evidence that they ever existed. Don't be afraid to go in your library and read every book as long as any document does not offend our own ideas of decency. That should be the only censorship."

————. "Letter [on Intellectual Freedom] to Robert B. Downs, President of the American Library Association, 24 June 1953." In *ALA Bulletin,* November 1953, p. 484; *Wilson Library Bulletin,* September 1953, pp. 59–60; Daniels, *The Censorship of Books,* pp. 154–55; and Downs, *The First Freedom,* pp. 340–41. **E53**
Letter from President Eisenhower during the

controversy over censorship of U.S. Information Libraries abroad, read to the American Library Association conference in Los Angeles, 26 June 1953. "The libraries of America are and must ever remain the home of free inquiring minds."

Eldon, John Scott. *Speech of the Lord Chancellor [1st Earl Eldon] and Judgment of the House of Lords . . . 1802, in the Appeal of John Morthland, Advocate, and John Johnstone, Printer in Edinburgh, against John Cadell.* Edinburgh, J. Johnstone, 1802. 16p. **E54**
Eldon was a reactionary Tory, opposed to both Catholic emancipation and liberal reform. He had earlier prosecuted John Horne Tooke and other sympathizers with the French Revolution.

Eldredge, Lawrence H. *Development of Freedom of the Press in Colonial America; Address before the Society of Colonial Wars in the Commonwealth of Pennsylvania, March 14, 1940.* Philadelphia, Printed by order of the Society, 1940. 23p. (Historical Publications of the Society of Colonial Wars in the Commonwealth of Pennsylvania, vol. 5, no. 4) **E55**

Elias, Erwin A. "Obscenity: The Law, a Dissenting Voice." *Kentucky Law Journal,* 51:611–64, Summer 1963. **E56**
"Although emphatically opposed to capricious censorship . . . there is no inclination to embrace what appears to be the prevailing view of most commentators and the Supreme Court that whatever is in fact published is entitled to near absolute protection." While preferring a middle ground between the extreme of complete censorship and complete absence of restraint, if a choice must be made, "the writer is inclined more and more toward favoring regulation and even censorship with respect to publications dealing with sex . . . These views do not carry into the area of political speech where the considerations involved weigh heavily on the side of free expression." Free society cannot exist without frank political discussion but it can get along without degrading portrayal of sex relations.

Eliasberg, W. G. "Art: Immoral or Immortal?" *Journal of Criminal Law, Criminology and Political Science,* 45:274–78, April 1954. **E57**
A New York psychiatrist uses the "pornographic criterion" to judge the immorality in art. "The true work of art, by its artistic quality, is moral in as much as it lifts the mind of the onlooker or the reader into the sphere of his own problems and urges him to find a solution within the framework of the civilization in which he lives."

Eliel, Richard H. "Freedom of Speech During and Since the Civil War." *American Political Science Review*, 18: 712–36, November 1924. **E 58**
"It is to the two great crises of American history, the Civil War and the World War that we must look for the best example of the theory and practice of free speech." War forces a re-examination of the guarantees under the Constitution. The author considers the theory of expedient suspension of free speech practiced during the Civil War; Blackstone's theory of prior restraint and its modification by Cooley; the theory of liberty v. license; and the liberal interpretation of the use-abuse theory expressed by Holmes, Brandeis, Hand, Pound, and Chafee. The doctrine of the liberals is that "argument should be met with argument, for if force is used who can be sure that it will be used on the right side? If force is used truth loses its superior survival values."

Elkin, Frederick. "Censorship and Pressure Groups." *Phylon Quarterly*, 21:71–80, Spring 1960. **E 59**
Underlying demands for censorship are three basic assumptions: (1) Messages of the mass media express norms, values, and ideas; (2) messages have an impact on the audience; and (3) the impact threatens the existence of the society or a subgroup. Not all ideas which attack accepted norms are considered threatening—it depends upon such factors as the size of the menace, the context, the public symbols of the characters involved, and the security of the group threatened. Pressure groups perceive those ideas to be threatening that either relate to the public interest or the welfare of their own group. The author gives numerous examples of censorship efforts by pressure groups within the framework of his classification.

"Ellen Glasgow on Censorship and Sinclair Lewis." *ALA Bulletin*, 56:618, July 1962. **E 60**

[Elliot, James B.?]. "Jefferson's Friend Cooper; an English Freethinker and Philosopher Who Followed Paine in Adopting America as a Home. By Historicus." *Truth Seeker*, 37:342, 28 May 1910. **E 61**
A brief account of Thomas Cooper's removal as professor at South Carolina College and his conviction under the Sedition law.

Elliott, Desmond. "Books That Shocked." *Books and Bookmen*. A series beginning April 1959. **E 62**
(1) *The Well of Loneliness*, 4(7):7, April 1959; (2) Elinor Glyn and Sin, 4(8):18, May 1959; (3) Most Banned Author (D. H. Lawrence), 4(9):18, June 1959; (4) Fight for Romance; Fifty-Year War with Society of Dr. Marie Stopes (birth control), 4(11):12, August 1959; (5) Regina v. Warburg, 4(12):15, September 1959; (6) Really, Mr. Sinclair (Upton Sinclair), 5(1):17, October 1959; (7) Scandal over Studs (trial over James Farrell's *Studs Lonigan*), 5(2):23, November 1959; (8) The Passing of Little Nell (censorship not involved); (9) Field Day for the Righteous (*Sleeveless Errand* by Norah C. James), 5(4):17, January 1960; (10) Genius or Rubbish? (Elliot condemns the literary pundits and suggests we are missing nothing by banning Miller's *Tropic of Cancer*), 5(5):17, February 1960; (11) The Ego of Henry Miller, 5(6):10, March 1960; (12) Disciple of the Devil; the Eroticism of Aleister Crowley, 5(7):20, April 1960; (13) The Book That Shocked Paris; Strange Story of *Madame Bovary*, 5(9):11, 46, June 1960; (14) Mark Twain's Dilemma, 5(10):13–14, June 1960; (15) The Book That Caused a War (*Uncle Tom's Cabin*), 5(12):16, 20, September 1960; (16) The Bodley Head Bombarded (the arrest of Oscar Wilde caused not only a mob at his publisher's door, but also, ironically, the sacking of an editor [Beardsley] who had consistently refused Wilde's work), 6(1):15, October 1960; (17) The Mighty Marie (Cordelli; censorship not involved). Articles 18, 19, and 20 in the series are listed under Godfrey Harrison.

Elliott, George. *The Newspaper Libel and Registration Act, 1881. With a Statement of the Law of Libel as Affecting Proprietors, Publishers, and Editors of Newspapers.* London, Stevens & Haynes, 1884. 130 p. **E 63**

Elliott, George P. "Against Pornography." *Harper's Magazine*, 230:51–60, March 1965. **E 64**
The author approaches a consideration of pornography from what he admits are two not very compatible points of view—"a liberal suspicion of censorship and a conservative dislike of pronography"—seeking some sort of compromise. Psychologically the trouble with pornography is that it intrudes upon the rights of others. It is only when it becomes public that it deserves attention from the state. To purveyors of pornography he would say: "Bother your neighbors, especially children, and you will be punished; leave others untroubled by your vice and you will be viewed with disapproval by the law but left alone." Elliott suggests three valid arguments against censorship of pornography: the impossibility of law offering a clear and sure guide, the scientific uncertainty of the affect of pornography on the user, and the harm of increasing the power of state and police. Less persuasive are the arguments that decent citizens can stop pornography, that pornography may have a value in releasing sexual tensions, that censorship attaches unfortunate prurience to reading of literary works, and that an obvious solution is to abolish all sex taboos. "Decent people had better learn now," he advises, "to censor moderately, or the licentiousness released by liberal zealots may arouse their brothers the puritan zealots to censorship by fire." He offers as a civilized method of censorship the use of a censorship board consisting of three general categories of citizens—the lawyer, the humanist, and the social worker-psychologist-clergyman, with right of appeal to the courts. Finally, he deals with the use of pornography by such writers as Jean Genet and Henry Miller as a weapon of nihilistic destruction.

Ellis, Albert. "Adventures with Sex Censorship." *Independent*, 62:4, January 1957. **E 65**

———. *The Folklore of Sex.* New York, Boni, 1951. 313 p. **E 66**
To determine the American attitude toward sex, Ellis examines the popular press, magazines, books, radio, TV, and the stage and presents his findings in an entertaining style. Chapter 22 deals with Sex Control and Censorship.

Ellis, Elmo. "'The Right to be Heard': Free Men and Free Thought in a Changing World." *Southeastern Librarian*, 14:89–96, Summer 1964. **E 67**

Ellis, Havelock. *A Note on the Bedborough Trial.* London, University Press, 1898. 23 p. (Reprinted by Douglas C. McMurtrie, New York, 1925. 26 p.) **E 68**
The author's account of his work, *Sexual Inversion*, and the trial of George Bedborough for sale of a copy. Appendix A contains letters to Mr. Ellis; Appendix B contains excerpts from book reviews. A review of this pamphlet appeared in *The Adult*, December 1898.

———. "Obscenity and the Censor." *Saturday Review* (London), 146:642–43, 17 November 1928. (Reprinted in Downs, *The First Freedom*, pp. 168–70) **E 69**
Ellis, an authority on the psychology of sexual behavior, uses his review of Ernst and Seagle's *To the Pure* as an occasion to express his own views on censorship.

———. "The Revolution of Obscenity." In his *More Essays of Love and Virtue.* New York, Doubleday, Doran, 1931, pp. 99–136. (Also published separately by Hours Press, Paris, 1931. 40 p. Limited to 200 signed copies) **E 70**
This essay has been called by Huntington Cairns "perhaps the most adequate study of the nature of obscenity we possess." Ellis likens the fear of obscenity that possessed the Victorian age to that of the earlier fear of witchcraft. He believes that sex education rather than law is the answer to obscenity. He criticizes D. H. Lawrence's essay on obscenity as confused and "muddle-headed."

———. "Studies in Sex: a History." *American Mercury*, 37:14–21, January 1936. **E 71**

A history of the publication of Ellis' *Studies in the Psychology of Sex*, the difficulties encountered in publishing the first two volumes in England, and the trial involved in the sale of the first volume.

———. *Studies in the Psychology of Sex.* New York, Random House, 1936. 2 vols.
E 72

Ellis, a British psychologist, was one of the earliest writers to adopt a scientific approach to the treatment of problems of sexual behavior. The first volume of his *Studies in the Psychology of Sex*, despite its wide acceptance by the scholarly world, was termed "filthy and obscene" by Sir Charles Hall, judge in the famous Bedborough case. The foreword to this edition, written by Ellis, describes the strange publishing history of the work, including the trial of George Bedborough for the sale of a copy. Bedborough, much to the chagrin of his backers, made a deal with the prosecution, and the obscenity issue was not settled. The Postscript to part 3 of volume 2, Sex in Relation to Society, also deals with the attack on this work.

———, *et al.* "The 'Censorship' of Books." *Nineteenth Century*, 105:433–50, April 1929.
E 73

A symposium, with the following contributors: I. Lord Darling, who writes against proposals for an official government censor, but accepts the need for action against obscenity under the rule of Lord Chief Justice Cockburn. II. Havelock Ellis, who opposes censorship, making 6 points—(1) it is impossible to define obscenity, (2) banning creates an artificial demand for the product banned, (3) our censors are too tangled in their own taboos about sex, (4) it is a mistake to identify censorship with the Puritans, since they had no horror of plain speech or even plain action, (5) the Bible and all great literature have obscene elements, and (6) for wholesomely born and bred persons obscenity is no problem. III. Stephen Foot, a schoolmaster, who maintains that indecent books do an immense amount of harm to all boys between the ages of 14 and 19. IV. E. M. Forster, who objects to the application of the Campbell Act, intended to suppress pornography, to works of literary merit. While agreeing that people should not be corrupted by blasphemy he sees no reason why they should not be shocked or that the law should be called in to avenge a man's private opinions. Nonpornographic works on homosexuality, which is a fact of life, ought not be suppressed. V. Virginia Woolf, who believes that the police magistrate's power to suppress obscene books should be limited to those whose intent is to corrupt and not to those whose indecency is incidental to another purpose—scientific, social, or aesthetic. VI. Carrol Romer, editor, who gives a résumé of the obscenity law and the manner in which it came about.

Ellison, Bill. *Free Speech and Sedition Since 1946.* Columbia, Mo., Freedom of Information Center, School of Journalism, University of Missouri, 1961. 6 p. (Publication no. 60)
E 74

A review of the decisions of the Vinson Court (1946–53) and the Warren Court (1953–date).

Ellsworth, Ralph E. "Comments on Censorship." *Stechert-Hafner Book News*, 4:17, October 1949.
E 75

A university librarian complains of the "general indifference [of librarians] to the widespread and apparently increasing practice of censorship." Librarians fail to realize that they must protest each act of censorship as it occurs, that censorship is going to show itself through all media, not just through the book, and that "the tyrant always does his foul work under guise of legality."

———. "Is Intellectual Freedom in Libraries Being Challenged?" *ALA Bulletin*, 42:57–58, February 1948.
E 76

A guest editorial calls for librarians to consider anticipatory actions against future assaults on libraries, in order to protect intellectual freedom. Currently the major assaults are in other areas than libraries, and the basic question at present for librarians to face is "whether or not, individually or collectively, they wish to exert their influence in defense of freedom outside of the libraries where freedom is being assaulted."

"*Elmer Gantry* Banned in Boston." *Publishers' Weekly*, 111:1569–71, 16 April 1927.
E 77

Account of the withdrawal of Sinclair Lewis' book from Boston bookstores on threat of prosecution by the District Attorney.

Elsten, Harold L. "Mass Communication and American Democracy." In Waples, *Print, Radio, and Film in a Democracy.* Chicago, University of Chicago Press, 1942, pp. 3–13.
E 78

The author examines the implications of "free competition" in the communications industry and the extent to which it serves the public interest in a democracy.

Elston, Laura. "Censorship. The What and Why of Movie Censorship." *Canadian Magazine*, 79:6, 48–50, May 1933.
E 79

"Canadians accept a viewpoint on morals that varies with each province. It is imposed [by government officials] at a substantial cost that they only occasionally stop to consider." The author questions whether Canadians need a more rigid censorship than Britain or the United States. She does not question the need for censorship of films, but rather the cumbersome administrative structure.

Elton, Oliver. *C. E. Montague, a Memoir.* London, Chatto and Windus, 1929. 335 p.
E 80

Chapter 6 is on Press Censorship.

Elvin, Rene. "Film Censorship: Its Evolution and Practice in Britain and

America." *Persuasion*, 20:48–55, Autumn 1950.
E 81

A comparison of film censorship in the United States and Great Britain. "In some respects, the British censorship practice is more liberal than the American. Thus, it shows itself more tolerant of profanity in language and even of certain sexual license, though here it discriminates against serious discussions of sex problems while showing lenience to 'glamorous' or humorous treatment of sex." The British film censor is more "pusillanimous" in treating religious and political subjects than his American counterpart. The censors have contributed toward the elimination of much vulgarity and pornography in the making of innocuous mass entertainment. The censors, however, cannot be held responsible for the industry's tendency to aim at the broad, uncultured masses.

Elwall, Edward. *The Triumph of Truth; Being an Account of the Trial of Mr. E. Elwall before Judge Denton, for Publishing a Book in Defence of the Unity of God; at Stafford Assizes; in the year 1726 . . .* [Birmingham Eng.], Printed and sold by M. Swinney, 1788. 12 p. (Summarized in Schroeder, *Constitutional Free Speech*, pp. 334–37)
E 82

Elwall, a Sabbatarian, was brought to trial on a blasphemy charge for his tract, *A True Testimony for God*, which defended the Unitarian doctrine. After he had presented a lengthy argument in behalf of his ideas, and prominent citizens had testified to his honesty, the judge dismissed the case. Schroeder concludes that charges were not pressed because "unitarian blasphemy was politically harmless." The first edition of the account of the trial was probably issued in 1726. Editions continued to be published for almost a century. Joseph Priestley has written the preface to a number of editions.

———. *The Triumph of Truth; Being an Account of the Trial of Mr. E. Elwall, for Heresy and Blasphemy, at Stafford Assizes, before Judge Denton. To which are added, Extracts from William Penn's Sandy Foundation Shaken . . .* 2d ed. London, Printed for J. Johnson, [1788?]. 24 p. **E 83**

In the preface to this edition the editor explains why William Penn's work is relevant to the Elwall heresy trial. He accuses Penn of "unworthy prevarication" in matters of Unitarian doctrine in order to get out of prison, where he was sent in 1668 for his *Sandy Foundation Shaken*. If he had taken a stronger stand in behalf of this work, it "would have been infinitely more to his honour than being the founder of Pennsylvania."

Ely, Catherine B. "Life in the Raw." *North American Review*, 226:566–69, November 1928.
E 84

The author charges that it is chiefly women, taking advantage of their increased freedom, who support with pocketbook and gossip the current purveyors of "literary carrion."

Embree, Raymond. "What to Do Until the Censor Comes." *Ohio Library Association Bulletin*, 34:24–26, July 1964.

E 85

The author suggests that librarians keep a written record of reasons for purchasing a title; that they be sure that their trustees have full knowledge of and are in agreement with the library's buying policies; that librarians, by cultivating good relations with the press and civic organizations, be prepared in advance for censorship pressures.

Emerson, Thomas I. "The Doctrine of Prior Restraint." *Law and Contemporary Problems*, 20:648–71, Autumn 1955.

E 86

"The concept of prior restraint, roughly speaking, deals with official restrictions imposed upon speech or other forms of expression in advance of actual publication" as distinguished from punishment imposed after the communication has been made. The author, professor of law at Yale University, treats of the development of this concept in American law. Only two exceptions to the rule against prior restraint are indicated: military operations in time of war and "traffic" controls where communication facilities are limited. Exceptions beyond these limited categories "are dangerous and tend to nullify the doctrine."

———. "An Essay on Freedom of Political Expression Today." *Lawyers Guild Review*, 11(1):1–17, Winter 1951.

E 87

The author discusses the theory of freedom of expression in America and traces its history through the encroachments on freedom of political expression by the Sedition Act, the Espionage Act, and the more recent Smith and McCarran Acts. He reviews both the actions of the Congress and the decisions of the federal courts. He considers such devices as the McCarran Act, the Federal Loyalty Program, and the use of the administrative rather than the judicial process to determine guilt or innocence, as dangerously undermining the whole legal structure protecting freedom of political action.

———. "Freedom of Association and Freedom of Expression." *Yale Law Review*, 74:1–35, November 1964.

E 88

This article has attempted to explore some of the doctrines on freedom of association as they relate to the field of freedom of expression, particularly "issues presented when the government seeks to impose restrictions on an organization or its members for the purpose of reconciling interests in freedom of expression with other social interests."

———. "Toward a General Theory of the First Amendment." *Yale Law Journal*, 72:877–956, April 1963. (Issued in book form by Random House, 1966. 245 p.)

E 89

"In the first part of this article we have attempted to set forth the various factors upon which any non-verbal interpretation of the first amendment must rest." Two major conclusions emerge. "One is that the essence of a system of freedom of expression lies in the distinction between expression and action . . . The other conclusion is that conditions in a modern democratic society demand that a deliberate affirmative, and even aggressive effort be made to support the system of free expression." In the second part of the article the author attempts "to formulate a basic theory and specific legal doctrines which would take into account the underlying factors . . . The endeavor has been to demonstrate that a comprehensive and consistent theory of the first amendment, providing a rational basis for explaining apparent exceptions and remedying deficiencies in existing doctrine, is possible."

———, and David Haber, *eds. Political and Civil Rights in the United States*. 2d ed. Buffalo, Dennis, 1958. 2 vols. (United States Case Book Series)

E 90

Chapter 4 includes historical background of political expression in the United States—the First Amendment, the Sedition Act, and wartime restrictions. Chapter 5 deals with cases on obscenity, group libel, individual libel, and slander. Chapter 6 covers control of the specific mass media—newspapers, radio, and motion pictures.

Emery, Edwin, and Henry L. Smith. *The Press and America, An Interpretive History of Journalism.* 2d ed. Englewood Cliffs, N.J., Prentice-Hall, 1962. 801 p.

E 91

A general history of the press and more recent media of mass communication, presented as part of America's economic, political, and social life. Numerous references throughout to censorship.

Emery, Walter B. *Broadcasting and Government: Responsibilities and Regulations.* East Lansing, Mich., Michigan State University Press, 1961. 482 p.

E 92

The book explains the role of the FCC and other government agencies in the control of wire and radio communication, particularly broadcasting, and presents the important policies and regulations that govern these media. Part 1 covers the basic technical and economic factors of regulation; part 2, the powers and functions of the FCC and other regulatory agencies; part 3 deals with technical rules and regulations; part 4 deals with problems of getting a license and keeping it; part 5 includes requirements regarding programming and use of material; part 6 analyzes some of the current problems of broadcast regulation and suggests possible remedies.

———. "Government's Role in the American System of Broadcasting." *Television Quarterly*, 1:7–13, February 1962.

E 93

A survey of the government's relation to broadcasting and the powers and limitations of the FCC in encouraging more effective use of the airwaves.

———. "Legal Restrictions on Use of Program Materials." *Journal of Broadcasting*, 4:241–52, Winter 1959–60. **E 94**

Deals with the use of copyright materials, unfair competition, and the right of privacy.

Emlyn, Thomas. "A True Narrative . . . of the Proceedings of the Dissenting Ministers of Dublin against Mr. Thomas Emlyn; and of His Prosecution . . ." In Emlyn, *A Collection of Tracts . . . ,* London, 1719. **E 95**

England's first Unitarian minister was brought to trial at the urging of his fellow ministers of Dublin, on charges of publishing a blasphemous libel. The offending tract was *An Humble Inquiry into the Scripture Account of Jesus Christ.* Before a civil court composed largely of clergy, the defense was browbeaten and Emlyn was refused permission to speak in his own behalf. He was found guilty and sentenced to a year's imprisonment, given a heavy fine, and placed on life probation. Numerous editions of the account of the trial have been published.

Emmerich, Oliver. "Is Our Freedom Immortal?" *Nation's Business*, 28:15–16, 56–57, December 1940. **E 96**

The author contrasts the controlled press of totalitarian countries which he has visited, with the free press of America, and calls for vigilance in upholding the right of minority opinion, the first area that the dictator attacks.

"End of the Censor's Reign of Terror." *Literary Digest*, 60:30, 15 March 1919.

E 97

Extracts and illustrations from and commentary on the special 29 January issue of *The Bystander* (London), celebrating the end of wartime censorship in England.

"End to Censorship." *Public*, 21:1398–99, 16 November 1918. **E 98**

The author calls for an end to wartime censorship practices which "lose all their sanction now that the war is over." He pleads for return to the antebellum tolerance of dissenting opinion.

"Enemies of Society." *New Republic*, 58:318–20, 8 May 1929. **E 99**

The enemies of society are the "dirty-minded, snobbish and ignorant spy or censor" who takes action against such worthy works as Mary Ware Dennett's book on sex education. "They have done injury not only to a principle but to the children of the nation."

"The Enforcement of Laws against Obscenity in New York." *Columbia Law Review*, 28:950–57, November 1928. **E100**

"Nowhere, except in the closely related conflicts over free speech, do parties align themselves with such bitterness and such irreconcilable attitudes" as in the enforcement of laws against obscenity. The article examines the treatment by the legislature and courts of New York of the ethical and administrative problems raised by this phase of public opinion. "There is probably no field of the law in which administrative bodies are so perplexed in gauging public opinion as in the enforcement of the laws against obscenity."

"England Says Hush; Posters, Comic and Grim, Warn War Gossipers to Hold Tongues." *Life*, 8:47–48, 18 March 1940. **E101**

"England Suppresses an English Novel, *The Well of Loneliness*." *Living Age*, 335:447–48, February 1929. **E102**

"England's Blindfold Eyes." *Literary Digest*, 50:100–101, 16 January 1915. **E103**

Comments from London papers covering the censorship of war news and the fact that the English papers are forbidden to print news which has already been published in America and Germany.

"England's Censorship Mania." *Literary Digest*, 44:483–84, 9 March 1912. **E104**

Comments on the confusion that exists between the censorship of a stage play and freedom for the play in printed form. Reference to the recent deputation headed by John St. Loe Strachey, to impose censorship on pernicious books, and the opposition to the movement by numerous authors and publishers.

Englisch, Paul. *Memoiren eines Freudenmädchens (Fanny Hill) von John Cleland; Ein bibliographischer Versuch*. Stuttgart, J. Püttmann, 1929. 80p. (Abhandlungen zur Geschichte der Erotischen Literatur, 1) **E105**

A bibliographical study of the often suppressed piece of English literary pornography.

"The English and Their Censor." *Current Literature*, 52:695–96, June 1912. **E106**

An account of contemporary British stage censorship which, the author claims, tends to make British drama dull.

Epps, P. H. "Who Shall Write Unbiased Textbooks." *School and Society*, 74:345–56, 1 December 1951. **E107**

The author is distressed by the implications of an announcement that the Cotton Manufac-

turers Association of Georgia, finding only biased textbooks on industrial relations in Southern colleges, is preparing its own book.

Epstein, Samuel B. *Opinion in the Case of Franklyn S. Haiman, et al. v. Robert Morris, et al*. Chicago, 1962. 15p. **E108**

A reprint of Judge Epstein's opinion in Superior Court of Cook County, Ill., finding Henry Miller's *Tropic of Cancer* "not obscene as defined in the law, and that interference by the police in its free distribution and sale should be enjoined."

[———]. "Statement in Support of the Freedom to Read." *Evergreen Review*, 6(25) cover page+, July–August 1962. (Also issued in 4-page processed form by Grove Press, New York) **E109**

A brief statement signed by authors, publishers, and booksellers in support of Judge Epstein's defense of the freedom to read in his historic decision in the *Tropic of Cancer* case. The opinion enjoined the Chicago and suburban police from preventing sale of the book.

"Equity—Injunction—Injury to Trade or Business—Freedom of Speech—Threat of Prosecution." *Michigan Law Review*, 25:74–75, November 1926. **E110**

A review of the decision in *American Mercury, Inc. v. Chase, et al*. Judge Morton granted a temporary injunction against the New England Watch and Ward Society and sustained a $50,000 damage claim against the Society for threats of prosecution against H. L. Mencken's *The American Mercury*. This is the famous "Hatrack" case.

"Equity Jurisdiction—Freedom of the Press—Libel." *Marquette Law Review*, 17:132–38, February 1933. **E111**

A review of cases involving equity jurisdiction in newspaper libel, beginning with the "unfortunate dicta" of Lord Eldon in *Gee v. Pritchard* (1818) that equity will not enjoin publication of a libel because such publication is a crime and equity has no jurisdiction to prevent crimes. The author favors the use of equity to enjoin personal libels.

Erbe, Norman A., and Arlo F. Craig, Jr. "Freedom from Obscenity." *Cleveland-Marshall Law Review*, 10:123–35, January 1961. **E112**

"The purpose of this article is to discuss obscenity laws from a propitious point of view, pointing out the sound basis for their existence and enforcement, and examining some of the arguments made against them." He concludes that a more aggressive enforcement of the laws is needed "so that citizens can be assured of freedom from obscenity."

Ernst, Morris L. *The Best Is Yet*. New York, Harper, 1945. 291 p. **E113**

"It has been one of the profoundly satisfactory portions of my life as a lawyer to be called

upon to represent dozens of authors and publishers against censors, private or public." This leading advocate of a free press devotes two chapters in his autobiography to book censorship cases in which he participated, with notable success, including *Well of Loneliness*, *Ulysses*, and the birth control pamphlets of Mrs. Dennett. He also discusses his work with the American Civil Liberties Union, the American Newspaper Guild, and his defense of the right of privacy.

———. "Censorship by the Back Door; a Court Decision Threatens to Gag the Theatre." *Theatre Guild Magazine*, 6(7): 11–12, 60, April 1929. **E114**

Reference is to the Supreme Court of Pennsylvania upholding the State Board of Censorship in the Fox Film case. "If speech in a talking film drama can legally be subjected to censorship, is there anything illogical in censoring the same speech in the same drama just across the street?" Censorship of the stage is at the back door.

———. "A Danger in Big Libel Awards." St. Louis *Post-Dispatch*, 85(241):2C, 1 September 1963. **E115**

A civil liberties lawyer considers the trend toward awarding punitive damages in libel cases as a threat to the mass media. "We must promptly design a more precise definition of money punishment beyond the direct compensation of the injury done to the libeled in order to curb the carelessness of the mass media and still not imperil their very existence . . . The present explosion of punitive damages by guesswork may . . . make all organs of opinion timid and cowardly." Written in the wake of the news on the libel award against the *Saturday Evening Post*.

———. *The First Freedom*. New York, Macmillan, 1946. 316p. **E116**

The author discusses freedom, or lack of it, in the American press, radio, and movies, showing that, with few exceptions, government has observed the Bill of Rights and the courts have upheld it. The greatest threat today comes from the control of the mass media by private monopolies that need to be checked by public opinion, legislation, and enforcement of the antitrust laws. He gives a detailed account of historic court cases, including many in which he participated.

———. "Freedom to Read, See and Hear." *Harper's Magazine*, 191:51–53, July 1945. (Reprinted in Lorch, *Of Time and Truth*, pp. 333–37) **E117**

Freedom of speech and of the press means more than freedom for the speaker or writer, it means "freedom for the rest of us to read and to hear; and that includes, if it is to be effective, chances to get information and ideas from a number of sources." We must prevent a few powerful agencies from monopolizing the American public's access to news and ideas. Ernst suggests a number of methods for restoring the right of diversity.

———. "The Importance of Diversity." *Grassroots Editor*, 5(4):3–6, October 1964.　　**E118**

Excerpts from the Sigma Delta Chi lecture at the International Conference of Weekly Newspaper Editors, Southern Illinois University. Ernst deplores the reduction in number of newspapers, the control of the air waves by three men, and other trends which limit diversity of ideas in America. He calls for a national inquiry into the communications media, along the lines of the British press inquiries.

———. "Radio Censorship and the Listening Millions." *Nation*, 122:473–75, 28 April 1926.　　**E119**

Criticism of legislation before Congress which would regulate radio for private profit and stabilization of investment, without regard for protection of free speech. Ernst outlines amendments recommended by the American Civil Liberties Union which would prevent station censorship, prevent domination of radio by two or three large concerns, and insure the free expression of public opinion.

———. "Reflections on the *Ulysses* Trial and Censorship." *James Joyce Quarterly*, 3(2):3–11, Fall 1965.　　**E120**

Reminiscences of the James Joyce *Ulysses* trial of 1933, written in 1959 by the attorney who defended the book.

———. "Sex Wins in America." *Nation*, 135:122–24, 10 August 1932.　　**E121**

The article depicts the period from 1870 until 1920 during which campaigns were conducted against everything connected with sex. "Censorship spread over the land like a prairie fire." Before this period most taboos were against blasphemy, or were applied only to certain groups, such as literature appropriate for women. After 1920 the first real signs of a shift appeared in the legal attitudes toward sex in literature.

———. "The So-Called Market Place of Thought." *Bill of Rights Review*, 2:86–91, Winter 1942.　　**E122**

There are two major effective barriers to the realistic expansion of the idea of the market place of thought—the disclosure of the identity of our sources of knowledge, and the interference with the diversity of these sources.

———. *So Far So Good*. New York, Harper, 1948. 271p.　　**E123**

A sequel to *The Best Is Yet*, with further references to cases on freedom of the press.

———. "Some Aspects of Censorship." *Wilson Library Bulletin*, 39:668–69, April 1965.　　**E124**

In place of legal censorship and vigilante efforts, the tawdriness in the mass media, particularly the sadistic fare on television, should be corrected by cross-criticism. Since "corporations can't blush," protests against unwholesome and debilitating programs should be aimed personally at the heads of the networks—David Sarnoff, William S. Paley, or Leonard Goldenson.

———. "Who Shall Control the Air?" *Nation*, 122:443–44, 21 April 1926.　　**E125**

"For the first time in history the problem of free speech becomes an administrative problem, for the Government controls the licensing of stations and the distributing of wave lengths." Censorship is exercised by the selection of concerns that are permitted to go on the air and by action of the stations themselves.

———. "Why Not a First Freedom Treaty?" *Survey Graphic*, 35:445–48+, December 1946.　　**E126**

"With nations not totalitarian we are ready now to write First Freedom Treaties based on the reciprocal theory of the Hull Trade Treaties, but this time dealing exclusively with the commodities of the mind—books, magazines, newspapers, radio, movies, and so on." Specifically, Ernst calls for the abolition of postage rates and tariffs on books, magazines, and newspapers, a priority given to the free flow of currency used in the mass media, and for the United States to join the Berne International Copyright Convention.

Ernst, Morris L., and A. J. Katz. "Speech: Public and Private." *Columbia Law Review*, 53:620–31, May 1953.　　**E127**

"The speech with which we are concerned here is only that speech which has as its object an *illegal* end . . . the spread of thought by print, the air-waves, celluloid or the vocal cords." A distinction is made between public speech which "attempts to create a majority will," and secret or covert speech "which attempts to undermine it." The authors recommend protection of open public speech but not of secret speech, to which the "overt act" test should apply. Secret speech may drive out the more socially desirable free and open discussion.

Ernst, Morris L., and Alexander Lindey. "The Censor Marches On . . ." *Esquire*, 11:42, 174–77, June 1939; 12:49, 108–12, July 1939; 12:58–59, 142–45, August 1939; 12:76–77+, September 1939.　**E128**

A series of four articles "on the Puritan's progress, and setbacks, in the war on freedom in art." I. A review of some of the obscenity cases in the courts beginning with Gautier's *Mademoiselle de Maupin* (1916), the *Madeleine* case (1920), and some of the cases introduced by the New York and Boston vice societies. II. "So it was ruled that books be judged by their effect on normal people, not the immature, the subnormal or insecure." This article deals with U.S. Customs censorship, the *Ulysses* case, and the banning of James T. Farrell's *A World I Never Made*. III. "A list of the works that were banned during the last three thousand years reads like civilization's honor roll." IV. "Censorship proceeding from coercion is stupid, dangerous, and from the censor's own point of view, futile."

———. *The Censor Marches On; Recent Milestone in the Administration of the Obscenity Law in the United States*. New York, Doubleday, Doran, 1940. 346p.　　**E129**

A sequel to *To The Pure . . .*, with emphasis on censorship cases taking place between 1925 and 1940. The authors present a spirited protest against arbitrary action of government and private groups guarding sex expression in literature. Present laws against obscenity are adequate to take care of the public morals. Precensorship of movies comes in for special criticism. The Broadcasters' Code and Motion Picture Code are reproduced on pages 313–28. Substantially the same text as the articles that appeared in issues of *Esquire* during 1939.

———. *Hold Your Tongue! Adventures in Libel and Slander*. New York, Abelard, 1932. 357p.; London, Methuen, 1936. 312p.; Rev. ed. 1950. 304p. (English edition has introduction by A. P. Herbert)　　**E130**

A popular account of libel and slander, illustrated with historic cases involving the spoken and printed word and such prominent figures as Theodore Roosevelt, James McNeill Whistler, John Ruskin, James Fenimore Cooper, and Oscar Wilde. There is a detailed account of the libel case involving the New York *World*, the result of its Panama Canal Zone investigations that took place in the early 1900's.

———. "*Strange Fruit* and *Forever Amber*." *Author, Playwright and Composer*, 57:19–21, Winter 1946.　　**E131**

The *Strange Fruit* decision in Massachusetts is "an astonishing document." While exuding "reasonableness, liberality, and tolerance," the decision against the work came as an anticlimax. *Forever Amber* is yet to be tried under the new obscenity act. (*Forever Amber* was subsequently freed.)

Ernst, Morris L., and Pare Lorentz. *Censored: The Private Life of the Movies*. New York, Cape & Smith, 1930. 199p.　　**E132**

The foibles of motion picture censorship in the United States are revealed in this irreverent indictment of the political guardianship of public morals. Heywood Broun, in his introduction to the book, suggests that the authors could almost have proved their case by printing the pictures of the censors.

Ernst, Morris L., and Gwendolyn Pickett. *Birth Control in the Courts; a Résumé of Legal Decisions Clarifying and Interpreting Existing Statutes.* New York, Planned Parenthood Federation of America, 1942. 58 p. plus 19 p. mimeo.   **E133**

Ernst, Morris L., and Alan U. Schwartz. *Censorship; the Search for the Obscene.* With an introduction by Philip Scharper. New York, Macmillan, 1964. 288 p. (Milestones of Law Series)   **E134**
"This new volume treats with the Law of the Obscene—its origins in our culture, the forces that shaped it and are still shaping it, and above, all, the pivotal opinions—pro and con—rendered by judges high and low." Beginning with a survey of sexual folkways, the authors discuss some of the early legal cases in England and America (*Commonwealth of Pennsylvania v. Sharpless,* 1815, and *Commonwealth of Massachusetts v. Holmes,* 1821, the latter for *Fanny Hill*), early statutes here and abroad, the introduction of the Comstock laws, and various efforts of the courts to define "obscene" and to find a solution to the problem. In a chapter entitled Cowboys and Indians the authors discuss the "vigilantism" of private censorship groups. The work quotes widely from actual judicial opinions. An appendix entitled Lagniappe presents a modern obscenity case in its pristine state, with all the citations, footnotes, and other assorted gobbledygook left in for the amusement and instruction of the reader.

——. *Privacy: The Right to Be Let Alone.* New York, Macmillan, 1962. 238 p. (Milestones of Law Series)   **E135**
The legal dilemma of two basic American rights: the right of the individual to be let alone and the right of the public to be informed. The authors discuss a new legal concept and consider "whether existing law affords a principle which can properly be invoked to protect the privacy of the individual; and, if it does, what the nature and extent of such protection is."

Ernst, Morris L., and William Seagle. "The Subterranean Censorship." *Bookman,* 68:36–40, September 1928.   **E136**
How the English circulating libraries selling three-volume novels were able to maintain effective censorship for many years by banding together to refuse to place on their shelves any book which one of them considered immoral. There are also references to methods of subterranean censorship practiced by public libraries.

——. *To the Pure . . . A Study of Obscenity and the Censor.* New York, Viking, 1928. 336 p. (Chapter on "Sex Control" reprinted in McDermott, *Sex Problems in Modern Society,* pp. 389–404)   **E137**

A lively presentation of the case against literary censorship, giving historical background on freedom of expression in matters pertaining to sex. The lawyer-authors show the contradictions and absurdities, the follies of the crusaders, and the vagaries of the courts. The appendix contains excerpts from important court decisions, lists of books banned by various authorities, Annie Besant's list of offending Bible passages, and Henry Vizetelly's list of English classics which should logically be suppressed.

Erskine, John. "Censorship." *Century Magazine,* 113:629–30, March 1927.   **E138**
Erskine objects to any proposed censorship of the theater or of literature.

——. "Literary Discipline: Decency in Literature." *North American Review,* 216: 577–91, November 1922. (Also in his *The Literary Discipline,* Indianapolis, Bobbs-Merrill, 1923, pp. 3–43)   **E139**
The author finds censorship in the area of morals difficult to perform because of changing notions of decency and a lack of fixed definitions. "The role of the censor would take on some dignity if there ever were a censor who was a connoisseur, who was the patron of good poets and painters, who actually supported a clean stage." But such a person, he decides, would hardly devote his life to detecting indecency. "Human nature is wiser in the long run than any censor; in the long run the books of the highest decency hold their place in fame by crowding out the others. The public suppresses indecent books by reading decent ones." The censor, on the other hand, is so preoccupied with evil he fails to notice the good.

Erskine, Thomas Erskine, *Baron. The Celebrated Speech of the Hon. T. Erskine, in Support of the Liberty of the Press. Delivered at Guild hall, December 18, 1792 . . . to Which is Prefixed a Preface by a Scotch Member of Parliament.* Edinburgh, J. Buel, 1793. 68 p. (Reprinted in *Erskine's Works,* Ridgway edition, vol. 2, pp. 87–182)   **E140**
Erskine's speech before the Court of King's Bench in the trial of Thomas Paine (in absentia) for seditious libel in the publication of the second part of *Rights of Man.* The jury showed its contempt of Paine and his counsel by reaching a verdict without leaving the chamber, but the crowd outside gave Erskine a rousing cheer and bore him from the Guildhall on their shoulders.

——. *Christianity Vindicated in the Admirable Speech of the Hon. Tho. Erskine, in the Trial of T. Williams, for publishing Paine's "Age of Reason."* 24th June, 1797. From the Twelfth London Edition. Philadelphia, Printed by J. Carey for

G. Douglas, 1797. 24 p. (Reprinted in *Erskine's Works,* Ridgway edition, vol. 2, pp. 185–204)   **E141**
One of the many reprints of Erskine's anti-blasphemy speech, widely circulated in various countries by Paine's detractors.

——. *The Rights of Juries Vindicated. The Speeches of the Dean of St. Asaph's Counsel.* London, 1785. 81 p. (Reprinted in *Erskine's Works,* Ridgway edition, vol. 1, pp. 151–393)   **E142**
Erskine defended William Davies Shipley, Dean of St. Asaph, charged with libel for publishing a tract on representative government written by his brother-in-law, Sir William Jones. Justice Francis Buller ruled that the jury should decide only the fact of publication, leaving to the court the decision as to whether or not it was libelous. Erskine objected to this view, arguing for expanded rights of juries. His views were widely publicized in the campaign for the adoption of the Fox Libel Act of 1792.

——. *The Speech of the Hon. Thomas Erskine, at a Meeting of the Friends to* [sic] *the Liberty of the Press, at Free-Mason's Tavern, Dec. 22, 1792. With the Resolutions, etc. of that Patriotic Society.* London, Printed for James Ridgway, 1792. 16 p. (Reprinted in *Erskine's Works,* Ridgway edition, vol. 4, pp. 427–42)   **E143**
Erskine, who had just lost his case in defense of Thomas Paine for publication of *Rights of Man,* joined in the formation of this group made up of men who were concerned with preserving freedom of the press in the face of the hysteria over sedition. The organization hoped to counteract the vigilante tactics of the Association for Preservation of Liberty and Property against Republicans and Levellers and to protest against the persecution of the press by the antisedition campaign of the Pitt government. Erskine's talk was actually given at the second meeting, held 19 January 1793 at Crown and Anchor Tavern, and it was adopted as a Declaration on Freedom of the Press. At a third meeting, 9 March 1793, arrangements were made for fund raising and wide distribution of the Declaration. The proceedings of the Society and the declaration appear in many contemporary editions and in the various editions of Erskine's speeches.

——. *The Speeches of the Hon. Thomas Erskine, in the Court of King's Bench, June 28, 1797, before the Right Hon. Lloyd Lord Kenyon and a Special Jury, on the Trial: the King versus Thomas Williams, for Publishing the Age of Reason, Written by Thomas Paine; together with Mr. Stewart Kyd's Reply, and Lord Kenyon's Charge to the Jury.* London, Printed for J. Debrett,

1797. 24 p. (Also in Howell, *State Trials*, vol. 26, pp. 653 ff.; *Erskine's Speeches*, Ridgway edition, vol. 2, pp. 185–204)
E144

Thomas Erskine, who had earlier (1792) defended Thomas Paine in the sedition charge against his book, *Rights of Man*, appears here for the prosecution. He had accepted the assignment at the request of the Society Opposed to Vice and Immorality. Erskine acknowledges that he cannot grant the same freedom to attack the Christian religion that he grants to attack the authority of the state. He objects to *Age of Reason* because it treats the Christian faith "with the most shocking contempt." To attack the Christian religion in order to promote civil liberties he believes is false, for these liberties are founded on the Christian ethic. Williams, a poor bookseller, was found guilty and given three years in prison. Erskine returned his fee when the Society refused to recommend leniency. In consideration of the destitution of the Williams family, Erskine persuaded the judge to reduce the sentence to one year.

————. *The Speeches of the Hon. Thomas Erskine (now Lord Erskine), when at the Bar, on Subjects connected with the Liberty of the Press, and against Constructive Treasons. Collected by James Ridgway.* London, Printed for J. Ridgway, 1810. 4 vols. (A fifth volume was published in 1812.) (Reprinted in two volumes by Reeves and Turner, London, 1870)
E145

Erskine was a British jurist and trial lawyer who devoted his skills and eloquence during the 1790's to defense of the freedom of the press. This was during a period when mass hysteria swept England as a result of the French Revolution. Erskine defended Thomas Paine's *Rights of Man* against charges of sedition; he defended John Horne Tooke and Thomas Hardy, charged with high treason for their publishing activities. His defense of the Dean of St. Asaph led to the revision of the British libel laws. Erskine, believing in the natural right of man, opposed the traditional view of the libel laws as exemplified by the interpretation of Blackstone. Erskine's speeches are classics in the defense of the freedom of the press.

"Erskine on the Limits of Toleration." *Secular Thought*, 37:51–55, February 1911.
E146

Ervine, St. John G. *Francis Place, the Tailor of Charing Cross.* London, The Fabian Society, 1919. 27 p. (Fabian Tract no. 165)
E147

Place (1771–1854) was active in both the English birth control movement and the efforts to remove the tax from newspapers.

Esbensen, Thorwald. "How Far Have the Book Burners Gone?" *School Executive*, 76:69–71, May 1957. (Condensed in *Education Digest*, October 1957)
E148

The South Dakota Free Library Commission has issued a list of some 150 authors "not to be purchased, not to be circulated and not to be mended or repaired." It includes such unliterary old favorites as Tom Swift, Uncle Wiggily, The Bobbsey Twins, and the Oz books. The author relates numerous other restrictions placed on book selection in school libraries, including a South Carolina legislative ban on *The Swimming Hole* because of integrated swimming; the Galion, Ohio, school board order to store all novels until they could be screened for moral content; the case of Mrs. Ada White of the Indiana Textbook Committee, who attempted to ban *Robin Hood*; and the case of Mrs. Anne Smart of Larkspur, Calif., whose book burning crusade included the following authors: Carl Sandburg, Sherwood Anderson, John Hersey, Pearl Buck, Dorothy Canfield Fisher, and Eleanor Roosevelt.

Escott, T. H. S. *Masters of English Journalism; a Study of Personal Forces.* London, Unwin, 1911. 868 p.
E149

Includes reference to the work of the following journalists involved in issues on freedom of the press: John Almon, William Cobbett, Daniel Defoe, John and Leigh Hunt, Roger L'Estrange, John Wilkes, and Henry Woodfall.

Esquire. A Summary of the Essential Facts in the Case of Esquire v. Postmaster General, together with a Selection of Representative Press Comments. [New York, Esquire, 1944]. 47 p.
E150

The U.S. Supreme Court in 1946 ruled in behalf of *Esquire*, limiting the power of the Postmaster General to censor magazines by means of the withdrawal of second-class mailing privileges.

"The *Esquire* Case. A Novel Extension of the Postmaster General's Power of Classifying the Mail." *Yale Law Journal*, 53:733–57, September 1944.
E151

Esterquest, Ralph T. "Books Stand Trial in Oklahoma." *Progressive Librarians' Council Bulletin*, 3:5, December 1941.
E152

An account of the Oklahoma trials for criminal syndicalism of persons accused of owning subversive books.

Ethical Culture Society of Bergen County, N.J. ["Statement on Censorship"]. In *Library Journal*, 88:2218, 1 June 1963.
E153

The statement applies specifically to the freedom of reading by teenagers and was prepared by the group to combat pressures in Paterson and East Paterson to restrict their reading.

Ethridge, Mark F. "The Government and Radio." *Annals of the American Academy of Political and Social Science*, 213:109–15, January 1941.
E154

A newspaperman and former president of the National Association of Broadcasters examines some of the basic differences between the Federal Communications Commission and the broadcasters as to the extent to which government regulation of radio broadcasting should go.

————. "Of Whom Shall I Be Afraid?" *Nieman Reports*, 7(3):3–6, July 1953. **E155**

In a Kentucky State College commencement address, 2 June 1953, the publisher of the Louisville *Courier-Journal* decries the fear of subversion that pervades America and threatens our historic freedom of speech and press. America's strength lies in this freedom and those who, in their hysterical drive for security, abridge this freedom are creating real subversion by their acts.

Evans, B. Ifor. "The Lessons of the *Areopagitica*." *Contemporary Review*, 166:342–46, December 1944.
E156

A tribute to Milton's *Areopagitica* on the 300th anniversary of its publication, together with a study of Milton's plea for unlicensed printing as applied to modern conditions. "If England is to be mentally alive in a free and vigorous atmosphere after the war the press must be released from the tyranny of power without responsibility and radio from the dull compromises which have resulted from State monopoly."

Evans, Bergen. "The Storm over *Lady Chatterley's Lover*." *Coronet*, 47:144–50, December 1959.
E157

[Evans, E. W., and John Lyle King]. *Speeches of E. W. Evans and John Lyle King, Counsel for the plaintiff in the Wilkinson-Tribune Libel Suit. Circuit Court of Cook County* [Ill.] *December term, 1868. George Buckley, Reporter.* Chicago, Round and James, Printers, 1869. 92 p. (Bound with *The Chicago Tribune as A Libeler of Men, A Defamer of Women, and A Menacer of Courts and Juries*, by A. C. Ellithorpe. 15 p.)
E158

Mrs. Frances M. Wilkinson, a Civil War widow, brought suit against the *Tribune* for libel because of an article suggesting she had been intimate with her married landlord. The *Tribune* was found guilty and assessed damages of $7,500. The case is of interest because of the issue of freedom of the press that appeared in the speeches of counsels for plaintiff and defense and in the judge's introduction to the jury. On 1 January 1869 the *Tribune* carried an article on the trial, headed A Malicious Verdict. It said, in part, "It is in behalf of the freedom of the press—in behalf of the freedom of every other paper in the country, and in behalf of the liberty of the people themselves—that we arraign this verdict as an embodiment of an ignorance whose stolidity is only equalled by its personal malignity."

Evans, Luther H. "The Challenge of Censorship." In Louis Shores, *Challenges to Librarianship.* Tallahassee, Fla., Florida State University Press, 1953, pp. 39–54. (Florida State University Studies no. 12) **E159**

Evans, then Librarian of Congress, discusses the fear and suspicion that prompts censorship. Many would-be defenders of the Bill of Rights have used specious arguments to justify abridgments of these very rights. Political censors are "cowards unwilling to live the American dream."

———. "The Problem of Censorship in Public Libraries." *Library of Congress Information Bulletin,* 11(23):1–2, appendix I, 2 June 1952. **E160**

[Evans, Thomas A.]. *Nelson's Sword v. Lord Denman's Law; or, What Is Libel? Being Illustrations of the Summing-up of the Judge, the Shrewdness of Counsel, the Triumph of the Times, and Sagacity of the Eminent Solicitor of that Impartial Journal,* as Displayed in the Recent Trial of Evans v. Lawson for Libel . . . London, T. A. Evans, 1848. 45 p. **E161**

Evans, Thomas W. "New Freedom of Speech in Politics." *New York Law Forum,* 10:333–49, September 1964. **E162**

"The purpose of this article is to review the historical development of absolute privilege and to examine the consequences which the recent extension in this state will have on the pleading and proof of defamation actions. An attempt will also be made to define the effect which the changed status of the law is likely to have on the conduct of a political campaign and political criticism." Regarding *Sullivan v. New York Times.*

"Everybody's Business." *Aurora,* 1:42, 22 August 1834. **E163**

A brief editorial on freedom of the press. "The free press is everybody's business—its freedom is established in the great compact of July 4, 1776. Its freedom is essential to a free state—and that freedom comprehends the right of individual judgment upon all subjects which are within the reach of the human mind."

"Examining the Examiner." *Nation,* 89: 147, 12 August 1909. **E164**

Review of the testimony of George A. Redford, examiner of plays in England, given before the Joint Committee of Lords and Commons on the Censorship.

"Excitement in the South." *Niles Register,* 38:87–88, 27 March 1830. **E165**

Mayor Harrison Gray Otis of Boston sends a letter of apology to the mayor of Savannah, Ga., expressing his "deep abhorrence" and his legal inability to restrain a "free black man" of Boston from sending inflamatory pamphlets (urging slave revolts) into that state. Also quoted is a bill before the Georgia General Assembly prohibiting printing, writing, or circulating any publication advising slave rebellion, and prohibiting the teaching of slaves to read or write. The bill passed the House but was rejected by the Senate.

"Expanding Postal Powers." *Columbia Law Review,* 38:474–92, March 1938. **E166**

An inquiry into the content and limitations of the power of Congress in the regulation of the mails. The article discusses the legal history of the postal system, the power of Congress to encourage or discourage use of the mails, the limitations on postal power imposed by the Bill of Rights, and the power of the states with respect to the mails.

F

Faber, Geoffrey C. "On Censorship: Notes on a Proposed Literary Censorship." In his *A Publisher Speaking*. London, Faber & Faber, 1934, pp. 145–50. **F1**
The veteran British publisher marshals arguments against current proposals to establish a censorship department in the government. Any literary censorship, if it is to be effective, must include newspapers as well as books and magazines, for nine-tenths of the "immoral and disgusting" works emanate from this source. To screen effectively all works of the publishing industry would require a government organization of such a grand scale that it would collapse of its own weight. Censorship, even if it were thoughtfully administered, would thwart literary efforts, would hamper the spread of new ideas, and would be followed by a general decline in reading.

Fabricus, *pseud*. "Law of Libel." *Black Dwarf*, 1:366–68, 383–84, 398–400, 412–15, 427–30, 441–45, June and July 1817. **F2**
A series of six letters to the editor containing observations on the libel laws. In the first letter Fabricus recommends that to adjust the balance between liberty and libel in the interest of the public the judge should state the issues clearly and leave the verdict to the jury. In the second letter he considers the extent to which an author should be able to discuss public affairs and public officials without fear of libel. In subsequent letters Fabricus affirms three rights of the press: (1) to publish every legislative act or measure; (2) to report on the conduct of public officials; (3) to comment the propriety of an act or measure.

Fabry, Elizabeth. "To Hold in Trust: the Trustees' Responsibilities for Intellectual Freedom." *Wisconsin Library Bulletin*, 60:173–75, May–June 1964. **F3**

Facey, Paul W. *The Legion of Decency: A Sociological Analysis of the Emergencies and Development of a Social Pressure Group*. New York, Fordham University, 1945. 206 p. (Unpublished Ph. D. dissertation) **F4**
Father Facey, a Jesuit priest, was one of the Catholic leaders in the movement to establish the Legion of Decency, a national organization dedicated to elevating the moral standards of the cinema in the United States. His dissertation is based on both published and unpublished documents of the Legion.

"Facing the Tide of Obscenity." *Christianity Today*, 9:729–31, 9 April 1965. **F5**

"Facts of Life." *Time*, 31(16):57–58, 18 April 1938. **F6**
The banning of *Life* magazine for 11 April 1938, which contained a series of pictures entitled The Birth of a Baby.

Fagan, Edward T. "Obscenity Controls and Minors—The Case for a Separate Standard." *Catholic Lawyer*, 10:270–84, Autumn 1964. **F7**
"The aim of this article . . . is twofold. First, it shall delineate the separate classification, in law, of minors as a prospective audience for obscenity. This distinction has been uniformly recognized and accepted throughout the evolution of obscenity law and continues to exist to the present time . . . Secondly, it will endeavor to provide suggestions and *caveats* for the formulation of this separate standard to draftsmen who may presently be working on remedial obscenity legislation. It will also explore possible collateral aids to implement the enforcement of such a separate standard once statutorily defined."

Fagan, John E. "Liberty of the Press." *American Catholic Quarterly Review*, 48:68–71, January 1923. **F8**
The author deplores the misuse of freedom by large segments of the press.

"Fair Trial and Free Press: Opinion by the Supreme Court of Puerto Rico." *American Bar Association Journal*, 43:1108–10, December 1957. **F9**
In a decision reversing a murder conviction, the Supreme Court of Puerto Rico discusses at some length the issue of "trial by newspaper."

"Fairfax (Va.) County Library Storm Shifts from Film to Book Protests." *Library Journal*, 88:2462, 15 June 1963. **F10**
A suit has been filed by lawyer Paul Peachey seeking removal of four books from the public library: *Without Magnolias* by Bucklin Moon, *A Month Soon Goes* by Storm Jameson, *Color Blind* by Margaret Halsey, and *The Big Sky* by A. B. Guthrie. A further account appears in *Library Journal*, July 1963, and in *ALA Intellectual Freedom Newsletter*, July 1963.

Fairlie, Henry. "The Useless Press." *Spectator*, 210:346–47, 22 March 1963. **F11**
Criticism of Sir William Haley of *The Times* and his interpretation of freedom of the press. "Freedom (or, rather, the spirit of freedom) is declining in this country, and will continue to decline, largely as a result of democracy . . . But it is also declining because of the growth over the last century of the pernicious idea that people (and, therefore, institutions) are to be judged and rewarded according to their usefulness to the community. I know no one who more sedulously spreads this idea than the editor of *The Times* in his moral addresses to the nation." The author claims the right to life, liberty, and the pursuit of happiness whether he is useful or not.

Fairman, Milton. "Bookseller Victorious in Chicago Reformer's Campaign." *Publishers' Weekly*, 117:566–68, 1 February 1930. **F12**
A Chicago municipal court freed a bookseller of charges of selling an obscene book, *A Night in a Moorish Harem*. The defense had pleaded entrapment by a vice society agent since the book was not in stock but was ordered for and at the request of the agent. Evidence also showed that the society intended to share in the anticipated fine as an informer. The freed bookseller expressed the intention of filing suit for damages against the agent, the Rev. Philip Yarrow. A subsequent issue of *Publishers' Weekly* (4 July 1931) reports on the arrest and jailing of Mr. Yarrow for failure to pay damages assessed by the court.

———. "Censorship in Chicago." *Publishers' Weekly*, 117:213–14, 11 January 1930. **F13**
An account of the alleged use of entrapment methods by the superintendent of the Illinois Vigilance Association, the Rev. Philip Yarrow, to effect the arrest of Chicago booksellers for

the sale of obscene books. Books were allegedly seized by police without a search warrant.

———. "Clean Books in Chicago." *Publishers' Weekly*, 110:327–28, 31 July 1926. **F14**
Plan for an advisory board of critics to guide Chicago's district attorney in prosecution of booksellers charged with selling obscene books.

———. "Superintendent McAndrew and Chicago Textbooks on Trial." *Publishers' Weekly*, 112:1627–29, 29 October 1927. **F15**
An account of the trial before the school board of the suspended superintendent of Chicago schools, charged with recommending textbooks that were pro-British, that would cause children to regard the Declaration of Independence as old-fashioned, and that omitted names of American heroes. At one of the hearings a former judge accused the American Library Association of circulating pro-British propaganda through its "Reading with a Purpose" series. A former Illinois congressman, John J. Gorman, reported on an investigation he made for Chicago's Mayor Thompson showing that school textbooks such as those by Muzzey and Schlesinger were part of a pro-British plot. The author treats the affair as "a comedy in the most gorgeous manner."

A Faithful History of the Late Discussions in Bengal, on the Power of Transportation without Trial, assumed as a Right by the Supreme Government of India. To be exercised on any Englishman who may honestly avail himself of the Freedom of the Press, as by Law Established. With copies of the Official Correspondence between W. B. Bayley, Esq., Chief Secretary to Government, and Mr. Buckingham, the late Editor of the Calcutta Journal. Calcutta, 1823. 28 p. **F16**
The introduction indicates it is an exchange of correspondence "printed exclusively for the Private information of the Editor's Friends—but neither Published nor Sold." The editor complains, not of libel cases brought to trial, but of "forcible banishment from the country, without conviction or trial" as punishment for alleged offenses in the press.

Falardeau, Ernest R. "The *Index* and Vatican II." *Catholic Library World*, 36:155–57, November 1964. **F17**
"The last 50 years have brought in such tremendous changes within and without the Church that the *Index of Forbidden Books* and its corresponding legislation seems not only out of date and out of tune, but impractical and impracticable as well." Father Falardeau mentions various solutions, in keeping with the spirit of Vatican II, that have been proposed.

Fankhauser, Eduard. *Nudism, Obscenity and the Law.* Chicago, Althea, 1951. 72 p. **F18**

Translated from the German by Alois S. Knapp, who has also written the foreword.

Faris, Barry. "Curses on the Censor!" *Quill*, 28(4):7–8, April 1940. **F19**
The difficulties that foreign correspondents assigned to war zones have with military censorship.

Farley, John. "Censorship Isn't That Simple." *Library Journal*, 87:3107–11, 15 September 1962. **F20**
"What is most needed, and what professional library literature has not been providing, are rational, unemotional bases for a dialogue on censorship in the schools." He defines six bases: definition, philosophical basis for freedom, where to set the limit on freedom, voluntary censorship by school librarians, effect of reading, and question of authority for selection and rejection. LeRoy C. Merritt takes issue with the author in the matter of voluntary censorship in school libraries (*ALA Newsletter on Intellectual Freedom*, December 1962) and defends his own point of view.

Farmer, Arthur E. "Pressure Group Censorship—and How to Fight It." *ALA Bulletin*, 42:356–62, September 1948. **F21**
A New York lawyer whose practice is largely concerned with literary property, discusses the "bases upon which the law presumes to exercise censorship"—obscenity, contraception, criminal libel, sedition, and incitement to riot—citing pertinent court decisions.

Farrell, James T. "The Author as Plaintiff: Testimony in a Censorship Case." In his *Reflections at Fifty and Other Essays.* New York, Vanguard, 1954, pp. 188–223. (Also in Downs, *The First Freedom*, pp. 286–301) **F22**
In 1948 three novels by Farrell were banned by the Philadelphia police. In an injunction proceedings brought against the police by the publisher, Farrell defends his works and expresses his intention "to present life as it is, in so far as I can see it."

———. "Canada Bans Another Book." *Canadian Forum*, 26:176–78, November 1946. **F23**
When Farrell's novel, *Bernard Clare*, was banned by Canadian Customs the author protested to Prime Minister Mackenzie King. This article discusses Canadian censorship and the attitude of Canadian officials toward freedom of expression.

———. "Censorship in Prison." *New Masses*, 11:22, 1 May 1934. **F24**
Letter to the editor in the Correspondence section.

[———]. *The Dominion of Canada vs. "Bernard Clare," a Novel by James T. Farrell.* New York, Vanguard, 1947. 8 p. **F25**

———. "Is the Press Really Free?" [etc.]. *Call*, 14:4, 14 May 1947; 14:6, 21 May 1947; 14:4, 6, 28 May 1947; 14:6, 11 June 1947; 14:4, 18 June 1947; 14:4 25 June 1947; 14:6, 9 July 1947. **F26**
A series of articles analyzing the reports of the Commission on the Freedom of the Press.

———. "*Lonigan*, Lonergan, and New York's Finest." *Nation*, 158:338, 18 March 1944. **F27**
Concerning the New York Police Department investigation of Farrell's *Studs Lonigan*.

———. "Moral Censorship and the Ten Commandments." In his *Literature and Morality*, New York, Vanguard, [1947], pp. 90–100. (Also in *Humanist* [Salt Lake City], 6(3):105–13, Autumn–Winter 1946–47) **F28**
Farrell rejects as psychologically unsound the moral censorship of works of art as embodied in the Production Code of the motion picture industry. "Art cannot be made into an instrument for making human beings keep the Ten Commandments . . . A good man, so-called, will remain good in the face of stimuli to evil. Otherwise he is not a good man." If a young man is sexually suppressed he does not need an obscene work of art or literature in order to indulge in sexual fantasies. Moral censors would do well to devote their time to cleaning up slums instead of cleaning up art which reflects the conditions of the slums. The essay was written in 1938.

Farrer, James A. *Books Condemned to Be Burnt.* New York, A. C. Armstrong, 1892. 206 p. (The Book-Lover's Library) **F29**
A history of the English practice of suppressing books by having them burned by the common hangman, beginning with Tyndale's English translation of the New Testament, the first book so treated (1546), and ending with *The Present Crisis* (1775), the last book to be condemned to the public fire in England.

Father of Candor, *pseud. An Enquiry into the Doctrine lately propagated, concerning Libels, Warrants, and the Seizure of Papers . . . In a Letter to Mr. Almon from the Father of Candor.* London, Printed for J. Almon, 1764. 135 p. **F30**
A reply to the conservative doctrine on seditious libel, expressed by Candor, came from this anonymous writer who called himself "Father of Candor." The exchange grew out of the trial of John Wilkes, convicted for a libel published in no. 45 of the *North Briton*. This important libertarian work has sometimes been attributed to the writer of the Junius letters, to Publisher John Almon, or to the anonymous author of the "Candor" tracts.

Father of Candor defended the right of the press to criticize a bad administration of government and attributed the present unwise doctrine of seditious libel and the mode of prosecution to the historic influence of the Star Chamber. The English jury, not the judge, should decide the question of libel, and truth should be an absolute defense. Referring to the Wilkes case, he stated: "The writing of anything quietly in one's study, and publishing it by the press, can certainly be no actual breach of the peace. Therefore, a member who is only charged with this, cannot thereby forfeit his Privilege." He repudiated the bad-tendency test for libel and espoused the test of overt acts. This work appeared in numerous editions and with various postscripts, including a collected edition (7th ed.) entitled *A Letter Concerning Libels, Warrants . . .,* 1765. In 1858, an author signing as "D. E.," writes in *Notes and Queries:* "There can be no doubt that 'Candor' and 'The Father of Candor' were *alter et idem.*" Candor was vivacious, entertaining, and satirical, while Father of Candor was meant to express the same ideas in serious, argumentative, and legal form. "The satire of the one is but a form of the logic of the other." Rea, in his *The English Press in Politics,* gives credence to the speculation that John Dunning wrote the Father of Candor letters with the aid of Lord Camden.

————. *A Letter Concerning Libels, Warrants, the Seizure of Papers, and Sureties for the Peace or Behavior; with a View to some late Proceedings, and the Defence of Them by the Majority.* London, J. Almon, 1765. (Reprinted in *A Collection of Scarce and Interesting Tracts . . .,* vol. 1, pp. 93–274) **F 31**

A revision of an earlier pamphlet entitled, *An Enquiry into the Doctrine lately propagated, concerning Libels, Warrants, and the Seizure of Papers . . .* John Almon, the publisher, was brought to trial for issuing this pamphlet.

————. *A Postscript to the Letter, on Libels, Warrants, & in Answer to a Postscript in the Defence of the Majority, and Another Pamphlet, Entitled, Considerations on the Legality of General Warrants.* London, Printed for J. Almon, 1765. 9 p. (Reprinted, along with a "Second Postscript" in Almon, *A Collection of Scarce and Interesting Tracts . . .,* vol. 4, pp. 126–96) **F 32**

Further comments on the doctrine expressed by Candor and by Charles Lloyd in his pamphlet, *Defence of the Majority in the House of Commons, on the Question relating to General Warrants . . .* By 1765, writes Robert R. Rea, "this pamphlet exchange [in the war over the use of general warrants in libel cases] had reached the point at which postscripts to postscripts in answer to pamphlets in reply to other pamphlets were commonplace."

"Fatherhood of the Unstamped." *Tait's Edinburgh Magazine,* 1(n.s.):733–34, December 1834. **F 33**

The story of William Carpenter who, after passage of the Stamp Act, first published a series of unstamped papers in an irregular series of *Political Letters.* Carpenter was tried before Lord Chief Justice Baron in the Court of Exchequer where he conducted his own defense. He was found guilty and sentenced to six months in prison.

Faught, Albert S. "Three Freedoms in the Eighteenth Century and the Effect of Paper Shot." *University of Pennsylvania Law Review,* 94:312–21, April 1946. **F 34**

A discussion of four historic trials relating to freedom of speech and the press: William Penn (1670); the case of the Seven Bishops (1688); John Peter Zenger (1735); and the Dean of St. Asaph (1784).

[Faulder, Robert]. "Proceedings on the Trial of Robert Faulder, Bookseller (one of Forty against whom Actions were brought for selling the *Baviad*), for Publishing a Libel on John Williams, Alias Anthony Pasquin, Esq. . . ." In William Gifford, *The Baviad, and Maeviad.* 6th ed. London, Printed for J. Wright by W. Bulmer, 1800, pp. 135–88. **F 35**

In 1797 John Williams brought charges against Faulder for sale of *The Baviad,* which he declared contained a "false, scandalous, defamatory, and malicious libel" on him as an author. *The Baviad* was a lengthy satirical poem on the "wretched taste" of the Cruscan school of writers and was particularly harsh on one, Anthony Pasquin, whom Faulder identified as John Williams. Pasquin's poetry, Gifford charged, was "at once licentious and dull beyond example." Williams was represented in court by Thomas Erskine. The bookseller was acquitted and the 40 other actions against booksellers were dropped. Gifford's introduction to this edition also refers to the trial. He notes that Williams himself was a common libeler, fattened "on the filthy dregs of slander and obscenity . . . who lived by violating the law."

Faulk, Alfred T. *Does Advertising Harm or Benefit Consumers?* New York, Bureau of Research and Education, Advertising Federation of America, 1939. 10 p. **F 36**

A critical review of the chapter in Professor Harold O. Rugg's high school textbook, *An Introduction to Problems of American Culture,* which had attacked advertising. "When parents send their children to school, they have a right to expect unbiased education and truthful teaching. It is the responsibility of school authorities to see that they get it. Harold Rugg's textbook does not fill the bill."

Faulk, John H. *Fear on Trial.* New York, Simon and Schuster, 1964. 398 p. **F 37**

"The story of his six-year battle to clear his name, culminating in the dramatic, history-making trial that exposed the true nature of the [radio and television] blacklisters and helped break their grip on American life." While much of the broadcasting industry exhibited timidity in challenging the vigilante activities of the self-appointed censors of the entertainment industry, Faulk, with his lawyer, Louis Nizer, instituted a libel suit against AWARE, Inc., and its associates, and won an unprecedented $3,500,000 in damages. The Appellate Division of the New York State Supreme Court later reduced the award as being excessive and unrealistic, and Faulk settled with the estate of Lawrence A. Johnson, one of the defendants, for $175,000.

Faulkner, Alex. "How Tough is American Censorship?" *Harper's Magazine,* 186: 502–9, April 1943. **F 38**

Experiences of a British correspondent under American wartime censorship. He makes "a plea for a more liberal administration of the censorship of press messages leaving the United States, being convinced that in this matter America has nothing more, and nothing less, than her reputation for freedom of speech to defend." American censorship is not political, in the sense that it is employed for the political advantage of the party in power, but is based on the tendency to "soft-pedal controversial subjects."

Faulkner, Joseph W. "Chicago Booksellers and Censorship." *Illinois Libraries,* 47: 470–78, May 1965. **F 39**

The president of the Booksellers' Association of Greater Chicago describes the "dangerous censorship situation" in that city. Chicago booksellers have banded together to protect themselves against the injustice of law enforcement as it now exists. "With the help of the public, we may be able to put the prosecution of books on the more legal basis enjoyed by other cities."

Fawcett, James W. "Free Press: How to Maintain It; Read before the Woman's Peace Party of New York City, August 7, 1917." *Dawn,* 1:2–3, 1 September 1917. **F 40**

Faÿ, Bernard. "Benjamin Franklin Bache, a Democratic Leader of the Eighteenth Century." *Proceedings,* American Antiquarian Society, 40(n.s.):277–304, 1931. **F 41**

A vindication of the young Philadelphia journalist, favorite grandson of Benjamin Franklin, who dared to criticize the administrations of Presidents Washington and Adams in his paper, *Aurora.* For this he was vilified by the Federalist press, charged under the Sedition Act, and ambushed and brutally beaten. Despite the yellow fever that raged in Philadelphia in 1798, Bache continued to publish the *Aurora* until he contracted the disease and died at the age of 29.

————. *The Two Franklins: Fathers of American Democracy.* Boston, Little, Brown, 1933. 397 p. **F 42**

The story of Benjamin Franklin and his grandson, Benjamin Franklin Bache. The latter was the young Philadelphia publisher, charged under the Sedition Act for libel on George Washington in his paper, *Aurora.* Faÿ describes Bache, as "the most outspoken, the most reckless, the most generous, and the most neglected leader in the second revolution" that broke the power of the Federalists.

FCC. v. "Overcommercialization." Columbia, Mo., Freedom of Information Center, School of Journalism, University of Missouri, 1964. 7 p. (Publication no. 115) **F 43**

A summary of points of view of broadcasters, advertisers, the public, and the Federal Communications Commission on the issue of overcommercialization, i.e., the amount of time devoted to advertising in relation to program time on the air, and the propriety of applying government limitations and controls.

FCC's "Blue Book" (1946). Columbia, Mo., Freedom of Information Center, School of Journalism, University of Missouri, 1962. 16 p. (Publication no. 90) **F 44**

A digest of the Federal Communications Commission's report, *Public Service Responsibility of Broadcast Licensees* (1946), known in the industry as the "Blue Book." The report criticized the industry's interpretation of public service and affirmed the authority and duty of the Commission "to give full consideration to program service." A campaign by the broadcasting industry against possible government interference in programming led to the setting aside of the report. In the late 1950's when public attention was focused on broadcasting abuses and deceptions and there was a demand for tighter program controls, the Blue Book again came to public attention.

"The FCC's Concept of Freedom of the Press." *Virginia Law Review,* 36:496–519, May 1950. **F 45**

Fearing, Franklin. "A Word of Caution for the Intelligent Consumer of Motion Pictures." *Quarterly of Film, Radio and Television,* 6:129–42, Winter 1951. **F 46**

A discussion of problems involving children and motion pictures, censorship, and the effect of films on people's attitudes and opinions.

Fearnside, W. Ward. "Thoughts about the Integrity of a Library." *Wilson Library Bulletin,* 30:239–43, November 1955. **F 47**

A University of California professor who saw the vacant newspaper hooks in the Bonn University Library during the Nazi regime, pleads for freedom for libraries to present wide points of view on any topic worthy of the

attention of the public. He considers and refutes the arguments sometimes given for library censorship: (1) A taxpayer's money should not be spent for library materials whose contents interest only a small minority. (2) Libraries should install labels to warn the unwary of Communist propaganda. (3) Communist or other objectionable material should be placed on special shelves or in locked cases. (4) Reading Communist literature is ideologically seductive. He observes that research requires freedom to examine heretical as well as approved ideas, and, finally, that "toleration of political expression of the most extreme sort is more effective than suppression in a society whose institutions are strong enough to stand comparison with others."

Fearon, John. "Movies and Morals." *America,* 91:277–79, 5 June 1954. **F 48**

Father Fearon, parish priest at St. Dominic's, Los Angeles, discusses the motion picture production code.

Feasey, Eveline I. "The Licensing of *The Mirror for Magistrates.*" *Library,* 3: (ser. 4):177–93, December 1922. **F 49**

According to the author, the suppression of the 1554 edition and the difficulty in obtaining a license for the 1559 edition was caused by the political significance of three poems: "Humfrey Duke of Glocester," "Elinour Cobham," and "Duke of Somerset."

Featherer, Esther J. *Advertising Ethics.* Columbia, Mo., Freedom of Information Center, School of Journalism, University of Missouri, 1964. 6 p. (Publication no. 126) **F 50**

"The following monograph reviews the history of advertising regulation and what codes of ethics say about advertising."

————. *Electronic Access to Public Meetings.* Columbia, Mo., Freedom of Information Center, School of Journalism, University of Missouri, 1963. 8 p. (Publication no. 114) **F 51**

The right or privilege of broadcasters and photographers to cover meetings of administrative and legislative bodies, unlike the right to cover the courts, has not been as vigorously pursued by the journalism profession. The author examines the extent of this denial of coverage at all levels of government and sets forth the major arguments in the controversy.

————. *The Leak: Bane and Blessing.* Columbia, Mo., Freedom of Information Center, School of Journalism, University of Missouri, 1964. 4 p. (Publication no. 132) **F 52**

An examination of recent news leaks, including the Oswald diary, the Bobby Baker case, the Pentagon and PFX contract, and Adlai Stevenson and the Cuban crisis, with an appraisal of the advantage and disadvantage

of this source of information. The author notes the lack of a code of ethics covering such news.

————. *The Moss Committee, 1955—.* Columbia, Mo., Freedom of Information Center, School of Journalism, University of Missouri, 1963. 14 p. (Publication no. 110) **F 53**

To assess the work of the House Committee on Government Information (Moss Subcommittee), the author brings together material on how and where the Subcommittee operates, giving examples and criticism of its work.

————. *Overcoverage and the Pool System.* Columbia, Mo., Freedom of Information Center, School of Journalism, University of Missouri, 1964. 7 p. (Publication no. 128) **F 54**

Overcoverage of special events has been justified as an exercise of freedom of the press, but it has also been criticized as hindering fair and objective reporting. One solution is pool reporting, where representatives of the media are chosen to cover the event and then to brief other newsmen.

————. *Pressures on the Libraries.* Columbia, Mo., Freedom of Information Center, School of Journalism, University of Missouri, 1964. 8 p. (Publication no. 134) **F 55**

A survey of pressures exerted on public librarians to censor books, with numerous examples indicating the geography and kind of duress, and the recourses open to librarians and friends of libraries in meeting the pressures. The author concludes: "The censors' verbosity and potential power must be met by the librarian's reliance on budget, conscience, accepted criteria of library function and service, established and good relations with the community, intelligent and responsible citizens, guidelines and book reviews in professional journals and the ALA's standards of practice."

————. *The Toils of Pay Television.* Columbia, Mo., Freedom of Information Center, School of Journalism, University of Missouri, 1965. 6 p. (Publication no. 136) **F 56**

California voters recently outlawed pay television as a threat to free television. The author reviews the action against pay TV in California and the experience elsewhere, where it has been more successful.

Featherstonhaugh, Duane. "You Can't Take That!" *American Photography,* 36: 8–10, July 1942. **F 57**

A press photographer discusses wartime restrictions established by the Office of Censorship ("surprisingly few") governing press and amateur photographers.

Feder, Edward L. *Comic Book Regulation.* Berkeley, Calif., Bureau of Public Administration, University of California, 1955. 59 p. (1955 Legislative Problems, no. 2) **F 58**

A concise review prepared for the California legislature. Includes efforts at regulation by various government agencies as well as by the comic book industry.

"Federal Censorship—Revised Standard for Obscenity." *Fordham Law Review,* 31:570–77, February 1963. **F 59**

Notes on the case of *Manual Enterprises, Inc. v. Day,* 370 U.S. 478, 488 (1962). The Post Office charged and the lower court affirmed that nude male figures portrayed in the publication tended to arouse prurient interest in the average homosexual. The U.S. Supreme Court reversed the ruling, holding that the materials were not so patently offensive as to violate "the national standard of decency."

"Federal Communications Commission." *Fortune,* 17:60–62+, May 1938. **F 60**

The article is concerned with radio as a social and governmental problem and with the Federal Communications Commission—what it is empowered to do, what it ought to be empowered to do, and the men who are its members.

Federal Council of the Churches of Christ in America. Department of Research and Education. *The Public Relations of the Motion Picture Industry.* New York, The Council, 1931. 155 p. **F 61**

A statement of the scope and activities of the Council with respect to motion pictures, including the relations with the Hays Office.

"Federal Program Scrutiny Considered." *Broadcasting,* 14:17, 1 January 1938. **F 62**

Sharper scrutiny of programs by the FCC may be a result of the "Mae West—N.B.C." incident. Heavy complaints were received following the "Adam and Eve" skit in which Mae West appeared with Charlie McCarthy, the Edgar Bergen dummy. N.B.C. had approved the script but had not anticipated the inflection given to the words by Miss West.

Federal Records Law Debate. Columbia, Mo., Freedom of Information Center, School of Journalism, University of Missouri, 1964. 4 p. (Publication no. 117) **F 63**

Consideration of debate on legislation affecting the right of Congress to request and receive information from the executive branch. A brief history of criticism and support of 5 U.S.C. 1002, with special attention to the Long bill (S. 1666) and the debate it provoked.

"Federal Sedition Bills: Speech Restrictions in Theory and Practice." *Columbia Law Review,* 35:917–27, June 1935. **F 64**

A documented review of various repressive measures recently introduced in Congress. The continuance of economic distress "finds an increasing tendency on the part of governing bodies to meet the incident unrest with repressive measures."

Federation of American Scientists. Committee on Secrecy and Clearance. "How Far Should Military Censorship Extend?" *Bulletin of the Atomic Scientists,* 4:163–65, June 1948. (Reprinted in Summers, *Federal Information Controls in Peacetime,* pp. 133–39) **F 65**

Feinberg, Wilfred. "Recent Developments in the Law of Privacy." *Columbia Law Review,* 48:713–31, July 1948. **F 66**

A discussion of recent cases involving the common law right of privacy, a number of which involve invasion of privacy by news media. The author finds the doctrine well established, at least nine states having given recognition to the doctrine for the first time during the previous decade.

Feinsilber, Myron. "Censorship and Libraries." *Illinois Libraries,* 47:456–57, May 1965. **F 67**

Reprinting of a news account of recent censorship attempts on public libraries.

Feipel, Louis N. "Questionable Books in Public Libraries." *Library Journal,* 47:857–61, 15 October 1922; 47:907–11, 1 November 1922. **F 68**

Results of a questionnaire sent to libraries, indicating their treatment of controversial books. Most respondents oppose censorship.

Fellman, David. *The Censorship of Books.* Madison, Wis., University of Wisconsin Press, 1957. 35 p. **F 69**

A brief but cogent review of the history of book censorship, delivered by a political scientist in an address at the annual meeting of the Association of American University Presses, Lincoln, Neb., May 1957. "Freedom to discuss is built upon apprehensions concerning the use of power by those who have in their hands that enormous leviathan, the state machinery. It is rooted in a profound skepticism about the nature of human nature, and therefore exposes the men of power to ceaseless criticism and political opposition. Our system denies the legitimacy of either permanent or absolute power and rejects the assumptions concerning human infallibility which lie at the base of a closed society."

Censorship represents the efforts of authority to suppress this challenge.

———. *The Limits of Freedom.* New Brunswick, N.J., Rutgers University Press, 1959. 144 p. (Brown and Haley Lectures, no. 7) **F 70**

Lecture 1. Religious Freedom—More or Less. Lecture 2. The Right to Communicate. Lecture 3. The Right to Talk Politics.

———. "The Supreme Court as Protector of Civil Rights: Freedom of Expression." *Annals of the American Academy of Political and Social Science,* 275:61–74, May 1951. **F 71**

The author, professor of political science at the University of Wisconsin, discusses U.S. Supreme Court decisions affecting freedom of speech.

Fellows, Harold E. "Freedom of Expression on the Air." *Annals of the American Academy of Political and Social Science,* 300:13–19, July 1955. **F 72**

The author is chairman of the Board and president of the National Association of Radio and Television Broadcasters.

[Fenner, Arthur]. *Report of the Case of John Dorrance against Arthur Fenner, Tried at the December Term of the Court of Common Pleas, in the County of Providence, A.D. 1801. To Which Are Added, the Proceedings in the Case of Arthur Fenner vs. John Dorrance . . .* Providence, Wheeler, 1802. 116 p. **F 73**

Fenton, Frances. *The Influence of Newspaper Presentations upon the Growth of Crime and other Anti-social Activity; a Dissertation Submitted to the Faculty of the Graduate School of Arts and Literature in Candidacy for the Degree of Doctor of Philosophy.* Chicago, University of Chicago, 1911. 96 p. **F 74**

In this study of the causal connection between the newspaper and crime the investigator finds that newspapers influence people "directly, both unconsciously and consciously, to commit anti-social acts. It also has a more indirect anti-scocial influence on public opinion during criminal trials through its accounts of these trials and through its partisan selection of evidence, and, finally, it aids in building up anti-social standards, and thus in preparing the way for anti-social acts." The author recommends that suggestive antisocial matter be excluded from newspapers; that inclusion or suppression of news not be based on commercial influences but upon the advantageous social results; that new and adequately enforced laws be passed "defining strictly the power of newspapers to deal with news, laws analogous to those already in operation in regard to the use of the mails, billboards, etc."

Ferguson, Charles K. "The Los Angeles *Times* Contempt Case." *Public Opinion Quarterly*, 4:297–99, June 1940. **F 75**
The case before the U.S. Supreme Court raises the issue whether or not "freedom of the press" is subordinate to "independence of the judiciary." The case originated with the Los Angeles Bar Association objection to five editorials commenting on local court cases in the process of trial and two additional editorials commenting on the Bar Association objections.

Ferguson, Fred S. "Honor-Bound Censorship Is Greatest Menace." *Editor and Publisher*, 56:4, 24 November 1923. **F 76**
The author was a correspondent at the Versailles Peace Conference which followed World War I.

Ferguson, George V. *Freedom and the News.* Toronto, Canadian Institute of International Affairs, 1948. 18 p. (*Behind the Headlines*, vol. 8, no. 6) **F 77**
The Canadian representative at the UN Conference on Freedom of Information discusses the foundation of a free press and the basic barriers to free flow of information. He believes that private ownership of the mass media, operating without government controls, shows a "steadily growing sense of responsibility" in presenting full and free information.

———. "Freedom of the Press." In *Press and Party in Canada: Issues of Freedom.* Toronto, Ryerson, 1955, pp. 1–23. (Seventh Series of Lectures under the Chancellor Dunning Trust, delivered at Queen's University, Kingston, Ontario, 1955) **F 78**
The author is editor of the Montreal *Star*. Among other matters he considers the charges that advertisers and a capitalist monopoly influence the news. He endorses the recommendation of the Hutchins Commission on the Freedom of the Press, especially that section calling for an independent appraisal agency. He favors the development of a greater sense of responsibility on the part of the press without the use of government controls.

———. "Have We Got, Can We Keep, Freedom of the Press?" *Saturday Night*, 63:6–7, 3 April 1948. **F 79**
The Canadian heritage of freedom of the press.

———. *Information: Keystone of Freedom. A Lecture delivered at the University under the auspices of the Canadian Club of Vancouver. Thursday, January 13th, 1949.* Vancouver, University of British Columbia, 1949. 13 p. **F 80**
The author deals largely with the World Conference on Freedom of Information.

Ferguson, Homer. "The Iron Curtain at Home." *Congressional Record*, 94:10272–77,

7 August 1948. (Reprinted in Summers, *Federal Information Controls in Peacetime*, pp. 146–57) **F 81**
A criticism of the growing practice on the part of public officials to conduct their affairs in secret and to withhold information from the press, the public, and the Congress. Remarks of the Senator from Michigan before the U.S. Senate.

Ferguson, Otis. "The Legion of Decency Rides Again." *New Republic*, 105:861, 22 December 1941. **F 82**
A criticism of the Catholic Legion of Decency which "has proved itself an enemy of the specious truth, and actual abettor of petty filth."

Ferlinghetti, Lawrence. "Horn on *HOWL*." *Evergreen Review*, 1(4):145–58, 1957. **F 83**
Account of the confiscation of *HOWL and Other Poems* and the trial of its publishers for issuing and selling obscene writings. Includes statements made in behalf of *HOWL* as literary writing and excerpts from the 39-page opinion of Judge Clayton Horn in finding the publishers not guilty.

Fernald, John. "Is Censorship in the Theatre Out of Date?" *Listener*, 59:318, 20 Feburary 1958. **F 84**
"While we may have been right to tolerate the censorship up to now, it really is up to us to find something better, from now on, if we do not want to look too foolish in the eyes of the world."

Fernandez, Perfecto V. "Freedom of the Press in the Philippines." *Philippine Law Journal*, 33:473–95, September 1958. **F 85**
Contents: historical introduction, protection and scope, limitations on freedom of the press (public order, public morals), restrictions in connection with reputation and the right of privacy, and restrictions in connection with inherent powers of public bodies.

Ferran, Angel. "The Censorship and the Censors." *International Review of Educational Cinematography*, 6:529–33, August 1934. **F 86**
The film censor is inclined to attribute much of present-day immorality to the "pernicious influence of the cinema." He makes no distinction between films intended for adults and those for children, "cutting down everything with the same knife." The censor begins his work as an enemy of the cinema, but gradually comes to enjoy the films he forbids others to see. In attempting to protect the public he unwittingly poisons himself. It is the censor who may need protection from an absorption of evil.

Fessler, Aaron L., *comp.* "Selective Bibliography of Literary Censorship in the

United States." *Bulletin of Bibliography*, 20:188–91, May 1952. **F 87**

Festival Theatre Review. Cambridge, Eng., Cambridge Festival Theatre, 1926–35. Weekly. Title varies. **F 88**
The following issues carry articles on stage censorship in England: 9 March, 6 May, and 6 June 1927 (*Don Juan*); 24 October 1927 (*Salomé*); 21 January 1928 (*Etain and Bella*); 23 February and 27 May 1928, 18 April, 25 April, and 9 May 1931 (*Roar China*); 24 October and 7 November 1931 (*Eater of Dreams*); and 14 November 1931 (*Salomé*).

[Fetzer, Herman]. *Alice in Justice Land.* By Jake Falstaff [pseud.]. New York, American Civil Liberties Union, 1935. 11 p. (Reprinted from "Pippins and Cheese," a column appearing in the *New York World*, during the summer of 1929) **F 89**
In this parody of *Alice in Wonderland*, the White Knight explains to Alice a too-common practice in American justice: "It's much easier to convict a man of something he didn't do than it is to prove that what he really was doing was a crime. So if a man is guilty of passing tracts, we charge him with littering the streets . . . If he is a freethinker, we charge him with bootlegging. If he writes a book which doesn't agree with our economic notions, we have him arrested on a charge of obscenity."

Fetzer, John E. "The Television Code of the National Association of Radio and Television Broadcasters." In *Lectures in Communications Media, Legal and Policy Problems Delivered at University of Michigan Law School, June 16–June 18, 1954.* Ann Arbor, University of Michigan Law School, 1954, pp. 147–61. **F 90**
The author is chairman of the Television Code Review Board, National Association of Radio and Television Broadcasters.

Feuer, Lewis S. "Pornopolitics and the University." *New Leader*, 48:14–19, 12 April 1965. **F 91**
An appraisal of the use of a new genre, which the author terms "pornopolitics," i.e. the use of pornography as an instrument of student activists in the University of California (Berkeley) free speech movement.

Fey, Harold E. "Censorship and Cultural Rebellion." *Library Journal*, 90:2473–78, 1 June 1965. **F 92**
The former editor of *Christian Century* writes of the wave of anti-intellectualism in the United States, whose adherents rely upon censorship and thought control in the interest

of their reactionary creed. Libraries are particularly exposed to their manipulations. Censorship "is always based on the assumption that there is or should be a concensus, a basis of national agreement, or what constitutes national orthodoxy . . . National unity is desirable and necessary, but it is achieved and must be achieved on a voluntary basis by the consent of the governed . . . Americans who fear the exercise of freedom of thought, who seek to restrain that exercise by censorship or other forms of cultural vigilantism, may do so from patriotic motives, but the only result, where their efforts are successful, is to weaken our nation and to discredit democracy as a genuine alternative to Marxism."

————. *A Free, Responsible Religious Press.* Columbia, Mo., Freedom of Information Center, School of Journalism, University of Missouri, 1958. 4 p. (Publication no. 5)
F 93
The editor of *Christian Century* discusses the role of the liberal journal of Christian thought that "seeks the truth believing that discovery of truth in any field is discovery of God." He treats of the contribution of John Milton who believed that freedom of expression was necessary to the proper service of God. Among other aims, the liberal religious press is concerned with maintaining freedom of thought within the Churches.

Ficke, Arthur D. *The Problem of Censorship; a Paper Read Before the Contemporary Club, Davenport, Iowa, March 20, 1922.* Davenport, The Contemporary Club, 1922. 18 p.
F 94

Ficklen, Imogen S. *Three Landmarks in the Anglo-American Struggle for Freedom of Speech.* Chapel Hill, University of North Carolina, 1960. 86 p. (Unpublished Master's thesis)
F 95
The three landmark writings on freedom of expression are: Milton's *Areopagitica*, Jefferson's *Kentucky Resolutions*, and Mill's *On Liberty*. The study analyzes the events that prompted these statements and their impact on contemporary and later thought.

"Fiction in Public Libraries." *Review of Reviews*, 15:604, May 1897.
F 96
Newspaper discussion occasioned by the removal of certain popular works of fiction from the shelves of the Carnegie Free Library at Alleghany, Pa.

Fiedler, Leslie A. "The Literati of the Four Letter Word." *Playboy*, 8(6):85, 126–38, June 1961.
F 97
A contentious critic castigates the treatment of sex in the contemporary novel. "Sex has come to seem to us the essential subject for our time, not only because . . . it represents

the last survival of Nature for the city dweller, but also because it is what a hundred years of literature left out, what almost all of American literature, for instance, ignored completely until our century had begun. And in the century of official silence, the language for speaking of the physical aspects of love decayed, fell apart into brutal vulgarities and polite obscenities." The author writes of the attempts of D. H. Lawrence and others to break out from the bonds of conventional silence.

Field, David Dudley. *The Lawyer and His Clients. The Rights and Duties of Lawyers; the Rights and Duties of the Press; the Opinions of the Public Correspondence of Messrs. David Dudley and Dudley Field, of the New York Bar with Mr. Samuel Bowles, of the Springfield Republican.* Springfield, Mass., Republican Office 1871. 20 p.
F 98
Correspondence between the two Fields and Samuel Bowles reveals divergent points of view in the defense of newspaper clients accused of criminal libel.

————. "The Newspaper Press and the Law of Libel." *International Review*, 3:479–91, July 1876. (Reprinted in his *Speeches*, New York, Appleton, 1884, vol. 1, pp. 547–61)
F 99
The author deplores the irresponsibility of journalism in this country and the difficulty of obtaining judgment against slander under the present laws of libel. He suggests changes in the law which might bring under control the abuses in the press against public and private individuals.

Field, Marshall. *Freedom Is More than a Word.* Chicago, University of Chicago Press, 1945, 190 p.
F 100
The Chicago publisher states his views on freedom of expression. He believes that the consolidation tendency that results in single ownership of the newspaper press is dangerous to democracy. One chapter deals with his own experience with *PM, Chicago Sun*, and the AP wire exclusion case.

Fifoot, Cecil H. S. *Lord Mansfield.* Oxford, Clarendon, 1936. 262 p.
F 101
A sympathetic treatment of the legal contributions of Chief Justice Mansfield, whose limited concept of the role of the jury in libel trials was evident in the eighteenth-century trials of Woodfall, Almon, and others.

"The Fight against Poisonous Literature." *Current Literature*, 52:468–71, April 1912.
F 102
A review of the campaign in England against "demoralizing" and "poisonous" literature. Quotes from Canon Rawnsley in *Hibbert Journal* and J. St. Loe Strachey in the *Spectator*, favoring censorship; from George Moore in the *Irish Times*, against literary censorship.

"A Fight for Freedom of the Press." *Literary Digest*, 90:9, 14 August 1926.
F 103
Press reaction in the case of George R. Dale, editor of the Muncie, Ind., *Post-Democrat*, who was cited for contempt of court and sentenced to jail for an editorial criticizing the court and grand jury.

"Fight to Lift the Ban on *The Nation*." *Nation*, 167:299–301, 11 September 1948.
F 104
Concerns the banning of *The Nation* from the New York City public schools.

"The Film Censorship." *Justice of the Peace*, 90:545–47, 2 October 1926; 96:131–32, 27 Feburary 1932; 97:179–80, 25 March 1933; 98:551–53, 25 August 1934; 116:342–43, 31 May 1952.
F 105
A favorable account of the work of the British Board of Film Censors, an unofficial body but with official support through a system of licensing of public exhibitions. "As the law stands, the whole structure of censorship is built on the inflammability of films, but if a really non-inflammable film be ever invented and came into general vogue, there is no doubt the law would immediately be extended so that it too could be censored." The 1932 report notes that while the Board performs a voluntary censorship, it is likely that local licensing authorities would disapprove any film not regarded by the Board as acceptable. The 1933 report discusses the activity of the newly organized Film Consultative Committee. The 1952 report observes that, unlike the American system, the British Board has no written code, but treats each picture, incident, and dialogue on its merits.

"Film Censorship against the Background of the First and Fourteenth Amendments." *New York Law Forum*, 7:424–37, November 1961.
F 106
A review of motion picture censorship and opinions of the courts relating thereto. "Free individuals rebel against a state of affairs wherein another has the power to determine what motion picture is or is not correct for them to see; besides an unacceptable standard today may be the accepted standard of tomorrow. The scales of justice must weigh every situation to determine whether legislation is in effect imposing unconstitutional restraints upon the individual or whether there exists a harm to the public welfare of sufficient proportion to justify regulation."

"Film Censorship: an Administrative Analysis." *Columbia Law Review*, 39:1383–1405, December 1939.
F 107
A survey of the various methods used in controlling the content of films in the United States, with an evaluation of their efficacy and desirability. "Only in the case of obscenity is there any justification for censorship. If it is to be continued, the censor should be made responsive to prevalent public concepts of

morality. A possible solution would be to have the censors elected by the people at periodic intervals . . . Complete absence of control might occasionally allow the presentation of a film better left unknown. Yet it is far more desirable that this should occur than that art and free expression be trampled under our present system of censorship."

"Film Censorship and the Admission of Children to Cinemas." *Municipal Review*, 8:116–20, April 1947. **F108**
Minutes of a London conference of municipal agencies convened to discuss charges as to the harmful effects of "A" category films on children who are attending such adult movies in increasing numbers.

Filmer, Edward. *Defence of Plays; or, The Stage Vindicated from Several Passages in Mr. Collier's Short View, etc. . . .* London, 1707. 167 p. **F109**
The author defends the English stage against the criticism of Jermey Collier (1697). "Had those strait-laced partisans of Collier's, with Mr. Collier's charitable assistance, once gained their point against plays, we should find them nibbling at most of our other diversions, and giving our ladies as frightful an idea perhaps of Hyde Park or the Mall as Mr. Collier has already done of the play-house."

"Films and Birth and Censorship." *Survey*, 34:4–5, 3 April 1915. **F110**
Conflicting points of view on censorship arise in two New York cases: the approval of the movie, *Birth of a Nation*, by the National Board of Censorship of Motion Pictures in a divided vote, and the publication of Margaret Sanger's birth control pamphlet, *Family Limitation*. The latter was attacked by the New York vice society and defended by The Free Speech League.

"Findings of Fact and Order for Decree." *Bay State Librarian*, 52:11–13, Winter 1962. **F111**
An account of the decree of the Superior Court, Commonwealth of Massachusetts, against *Tropic of Cancer*. The Supreme Judicial Court's reversal of the decision is reported in the October 1962 issue.

Fine, Benjamin. "The Truth about Schoolbook Censorship." *Parents' Magazine*, 27:46+, December 1952. (Reprinted in Daniels, *Censorship of Books*, pp. 121–24 and Downs, *The First Freedom*, pp. 349–52) **F112**
The education editor of the *New York Times* recounts incidents of censorship of school and college textbooks that have taken place throughout the nation in recent years, both at the hands of public and private groups.

"A Fine Play Banned: *Young Woodley.*" *New Statesman*, 30:593–94, 18 February 1928. **F113**

The disapproval of John van Druten's play by the Lord Chamberlain is considered the most serious blunder of the drama censor in 50 years. The play was banned, the author believes, more because of its criticism of the public schools than because of its treatment of sex.

[Finerty, Peter]. *Trial of Mr. Peter Finerty, Late Printer of The Press, for a Libel against His Excellency Earl Camden, Lord Lieutenant of Ireland, in a Letter Signed Marcus in that Paper.* Dublin, 1798. 62 p. (Also in Howell, *State Trials*, vol. 26, pp. 901 ff., and Thomas MacNevin, *Leading State Trials in Ireland*, pp. 402–598) **F114**
The publisher of the Dublin *Press* was found guilty of a seditious libel, pilloried, and given two-years' imprisonment for criticizing the trial of William Orr, Court of King's Bench.

Finlason, W. F. "Catch v. Shaen; the Right of Free Discussion." *Law Journal*, 6:8–11, 2 January 1871. (Also in *Law Times*, 17 December 1870) **F115**
The author of a letter to the editor appeals for protection in the right of free discussion in the case of Mr. Shaen, who was brought to trial for libel in issuing three pamphlets critical of an investigation of conditions in a public workhouse.

Finlay, Thomas. *Defence, prepared for delivery, by Thomas Finlay, charged before the High Court of Justiciary, City of Edinburgh, 24th July, 1843, with Vending Blasphemy, and Printed by Order of "The Scottish Anti-Persecution Union."* Edinburgh, W. & H. Robinson, 1843. 32 p. **F116**
This is the address that the elderly Edinburgh bookseller intended to use at his trial for sale of "blasphemous" and "infidel" works. His son-in-law, Henry Robinson, and Charles Southwell, arrested with Finlay, were given 12- and 15-month sentences respectively, but, because of an incorrectly drawn indictment, Finlay was not brought to trial in July. In November 1843 he was rearrested for sale of a book "containing a denial of the truth and authority of the Holy Scriptures" and was tried the following month. He delivered his own defense somewhat along the lines of this intended speech, which was published in advance to raise funds for his defense. Finlay was found guilty and sentenced to 60 days in prison. The intended defense is a spirited attack against the laws of blasphemy. The Anti-Persecution Union, with Holyoake as secretary, was organized to defend those indicted under the blasphemy laws. It issued a weekly *Gazette*. An account of the various Scottish blasphemy trials also appears in issues of Holyoake's *Oracle of Reason*.

Finletter, Thomas K. "Intellectual Freedom and the National Defense; Address Delivered at the California Library Association Meeting in San Jose, October 26,

1955." *California Librarian*, 17:83–89, April 1956. **F117**
The speaker was formerly Secretary of the Air Force.

Finley, John H. "Free Press from Plato to Peter Zenger." *Vital Speeches*, 4:122–23, 1 December 1937. **F118**
A brief account of Zenger's contribution to a free press and its significance today.

[Finnegan, Richard J.]. *The Copy of a Free Press Is Not in Commerce . . .* Chicago, 1943. 105 p. **F119**
The editor of the Chicago *Times* prepared this "memorandum of events in the story of American freedom of expression and conscience, showing that newspaper 'copy' before publication is immune from any authority of government, including the power of Congress to regulate commerce." Brief filed 6 July 1943 on behalf of the Chicago *Times* in the District Court of the United States for the Southern District of New York in the case of *U.S. v. The Associated Press, et al.*

First, Joseph M. "Freedom of the Press." *Pennsylvania Bar Association Quarterly*, 30:200–207, March 1959. **F120**
Address by the editor of the *Quarterly* before the Ventnor Foundation, 1 February 1959 at Atlantic City, as part of a program for German-Austrian medical interns. The speech presents the American concept of a free press, with special references to Philadelphia and the medical profession.

———. "Freedom of the Press in Wartime." *Pennsylvania Bar Association Quarterly*, 14:225–31, April 1943. **F121**
The author calls upon the legal profession to watch each censorship move made by the government and to allow no controls not immediately connected with winning the war.

"First Amendment Requires Qualified Privilege to Publish Defamatory Misstatements about Public Officials." *University of Pennsylvania Law Review*, 113:284–90, December 1964. **F122**
Concerning the case of *New York Times Co. v. Sullivan*, 376 U.S. 254 (1964).

Fischer, Henry G., ed. *Pike & Fischer Radio Regulation*. Washington, D.C., Pike & Fischer, 1948. Loose-leaf volume. **F123**
A compilation of significant statutes, Congressional reports, FCC rules, and court decisions.

Fischer, John. "The Harm Good People Do." *Harper's Magazine*, 213:15–20, October 1956. (Reprinted in Downs, *The

First Freedom, pp. 138–41, in Gardiner, *Catholic Viewpoint on Censorship*, pp. 157–63, and in Black and Kerr, *American Issues*, pp. 184–90) **F124**

The editor of *Harper's* in his Easy Chair column, directs his attack largely against the work of the NODL, which he says is "not aimed at Catholics alone, and . . . is not attempting to *persuade* readers to follow its views. It is *compelling* readers, of all faiths, to bow to its dislikes, to denying them a free choice in what they buy."

Fisher, Boyd. "The Regulation of Motion Picture Theaters." *American City*, 7: 520–22, December 1912. **F125**

"Provisions for the Physical, Moral and Intellectual Control of a Form of Popular Entertainment Possessing Great Educational Values." Deals with the provisions of an ordinance then pending in New York City, which was later (1913) passed and put into effect.

Fisher, Harry M. *Freedom of the Press; Opinion of Hon. Harry M. Fisher . . . in the Ten Million Dollar Libel Suit brought by Corporation Counsel Samuel A. Ellelson in the name of the City of Chicago against The Chicago Tribune. With an Introduction and Summary of the History of the Struggle for Free Press during Three Centuries since the Invention of Printing*. Chicago, The Chicago Tribune, 1921. 37 p. **F126**

Judge Fisher of the Circuit Court of Cook County, Ill., sustained the demurrer of the *Tribune* that the libel charge against that newspaper was a violation of the free press provisions in the Constitutions of the United States and of Illinois.

Fisher, Joseph R. "Chapter in the Law of Libel." *Law Quarterly Review*, 10: 158–63, April 1894. **F127**

The practice of making a clean distinction between written and spoken scandal, with the former (libel) being the greater offense, is recognized only in English law. The distinction is a comparatively recent development.

————, and James A. Strahan. *The Law of the Press: a Digest of the Law Affecting Newspapers in England, India, and the Colonies. With a Chapter on Foreign Press Codes*. London, W. Clowes, 1891. 297 p. **F128**

Fisher, Paul. *FOI in the U.S., 1960*. Columbia, Mo., Freedom of Information Center, School of Journalism, University of Missouri, 1961. 4 p. (Publication no. 46) **F129**

A brief résumé of the climate for freedom of information in the United States during 1960.

————. *Making Communications Be Good*. Columbia, Mo., Freedom of Information Center, School of Journalism, University of Missouri, 1963. 4 p. (Publication no. 107) **F130**

The executive secretary of the Freedom of Information Center, in an address before the Mississippi Press Association, discusses the present tendency for the government, in the interest of the public welfare, to force the communications media to conform to certain norms of social repsonsibility. Such a trend is not only a direct threat to a free press but, indirectly, encourages timidity and caution. "You cannot be hurt, the communicator reasons, if you say nothing." Fisher calls for newspapers to serve as a prime mover in calling attention to this drift toward government control and to restate the First Amendment in its boldest scope.

Fisher, Vardis. "Parable for Librarians on Why Ignorance Is Bliss." *Pacific Northwest Library Association Quarterly*, 4:7–9, October 1939. **F131**

A humorous and satirical talk dealing with the practices of librarians in restricting controversial books. "The only dangerous thing in this world is the thing we can understand." When a book is quaint and old-fashioned and no longer understood, it is safe to put on open shelves.

Fisk, Theophilus. *The Nation's Bulwark. An Oration, on the Freedom of the Press, delivered at the Court House in Danbury, Con. Wednesday Dec. 5, 1832. On the liberation of P. T. Barnum, Esq. Editor of the Herald of Freedom, from Imprisonment, for an alledged libel. To which is appended an account of the proceedings on that occasion, together with a Letter addressed to him [by Fisk] while in prison*. New Haven, Examiner and Watch Tower of Freedom, [1832]. 16 p. **F132**

Fisk, a former Universalist clergyman of Charleston, S.C., and then editor of the New Haven *Examiner*, delivered the address on the liberation of P. T. Barnum, editor of the *Herald of Freedom*, from imprisonment. Barnum had spent 60 days in jail on a libel conviction. There follows a newspaper account of the celebration in Danbury.

————. *An Oration on the Freedom of the Press; to Which is appended the doings of a Public Meeting held in Charleston, July 28th 1837*. Charleston, S.C., Office of The Examiner, 1837. 48 p. (Bound with Fisk's *Oration on Banking, Education, &c*) **F133**

In addition to publication of Fisk's address on freedom of the press at the Barnum celebration, Danbury, Conn., 1832, there is the text of his speech on banking and education, delivered at the Queen-Street Theatre in Charleston, July 4th 1837, which ended in riot, and an account of a public meeting held in that city on 28 July by "friends of freedom of Speech and of the Press," in protest of the physical and journalistic attacks on the Rev. Mr. Fisk for his talk on baking reform. The speakers at the meeting and editorials in the Charleston *Examiner* charged the leaders of the anti-Republican banking institutions of the city with organizing mob violence at the meeting.

Fiske, Marjorie. *Book Selection and Censorship*. Berkeley, Calif., University of California Press, 1959. 158 p. **F134**

Fear of controversy among school and public librarians in California, as a result of censorship pressures, is revealed in this study conducted by a social psychologist and financed by the Fund for the Republic. Miss Fiske investigated the extent to which restrictions in book selection were imposed on librarians from without and the extent imposed by librarians themselves. Some of the findings are also presented in *The Climate of Book Selection*, pp. 66–76, California University, School of Librarianship. The work is reviewed by Marie Jahoda in *Public Opinion Quarterly*, Spring 1961.

Fitch, Robert E. "Four-Letter Words to the Wise." *Commonweal*, 76:78–80, 20 April 1962. **F135**

The dean of the Pacific School of Religion discusses the issues in the jury trial of a California bookseller, arrested for selling Henry Miller's *Tropic of Cancer*. Freedom of the press is not an issue here, he states, but rather "the fetishes and clichés of two social classes," the uplifters who insist that the book is degrading to public morals and the eggheads and liberals who proclaim that the book is "an assertion of the sanctity of the individual, a legitimate protest against the mechanized uniformity of our society, and a genuine work of literary art." Both positions are false, he maintains, but the article is concerned with the falsity of the latter.

[Fitzgerald, Thomas J.] "Interview with Msgr. Fitzgerald of the National Office for Decent Literature." *Publishers' Weekly*, 171:12–15, 20 May 1957. **F136**

————. "The Menance of Indecent Literature." *Ave Maria*, 84(12):8–9, 28–30, 22 September 1956. **F137**

The executive secretary of the National Office for Decent Literature discusses the Church's campaign against the placement of indecent literature in the hands of children.

————. "NODL States Its Case." *America*, 97:280–82, 1 June 1957. (Reprinted in Gardiner, *Catholic Viewpoint on Censorship*, pp. 179–84) **F138**

Monsignor Fitzgerald has written this article to clarify the position of the National Office for Decent Literature and to state its policies. He presents the code by which objectionable literature is evaluated.

Fitz-Gerald, W. G. "Dramatic Censorship in England.' *Harper's Weekly*, 51:947, 5 January 1907. **F139**

"Never since the evil days when Walpole established the Dramatic Censorship in England . . . has the British Lord Chamberlain and his Examiner of Plays been placed in so embarrassing a position as that which recently resulted from the sudden ban on 'The Mikado.'"

[Fitz-Harris, Edward]. *The Arraignment and Plea of Edw. Fitz-Harris, Esq.; with all the Arguments in Law, and Proceedings of the Court of Kings-Bench, Thereupon, in Easter Term, 1681*. London, Printed for Fr. Tyton, and Tho. Basset, 1681. 66 p. **F140**

Fitz-Harris was tried for high treason and executed for publishing a pamphlet, *The True Englishman speaking plain English in a Letter from a Friend to a Friend*. In the pamphlet he accused King Charles II of conspiring with the Pope and the French to introduce Popery and arbitrary government. It is believed he might have intended to plant the pamphlet in the house of a Whig member of Parliament, then pretend to discover it and earn for himself the reward of an informer, but was betrayed by an accomplice.

[————]. *The Tryal and Condemnation of Edw. Fitz-Harris, esq.: for High-Treason, at the Barr of the Court of King's Bench, at Westminster . . . the 9th of June . . . 1681 . . .* London, 1681. 103 p. **F141**

Fixx, James F. "Library Goes to Market." *Saturday Review*, 45(14):14–15, 7 April 1962. **F142**
A discussion of the way in which public libraries go about selecting their books. "Although all libraries, from the very best to the very worst, have their share of failings and misjudgments, each of them tries, sometimes clumsily, sometimes with a skill approximating art, to provide its public with a reliable and useful collection of books. In this task they are ordinarily guided by formal statements of policy that have been thoughtfully worked out to explain to themselves, to their readers, and to the potential book-banners why they choose the books they do."

————. "When Extremists Attack the Press." *Saturday Review*, 48(7):72–73, 13 February 1965. **F143**
An account of the attempt by right wing extremist groups to silence by personal harassment Bill Sanders, liberal cartoonist of the Kansas City *Star*. Sanders' editor, Richard B. Fowler, also subject to pressures, backed his cartoonist.

Fladeland, Betty. *James Gillespie Birney: Slaveholder and Abolitionist*. Ithaca, N.Y., Cornell University Press, 1955. 323 p. **F144**
The biography of the Southern abolitionist editor and crusader whose fight for civil liberty "helped to maintain freedom of speech and

press in a time when censorship and gag laws were threatening the North as well as the South." Various references to the suppression of "incendiary" publications of the abolitionists.

Flaherty, Francis. "Censorship in Canada." *Quill*, 28(3):10–11, March 1940. **F145**
A member of the Press Gallery in the Canadian House of Commons, describes how Canada's newspapers have been affected by wartime censorship.

————. *Freedom of the Press in Canada*. Ottawa, Buchanan's Bulletin Reg'd, 1957. 16 p. **F146**
A series of articles appearing in the Canadian press during 1955, for which the author received the Bowater Award for distinguished journalism.

————. "Press Censorship." *Canadian Spokesman*, 1:13–16, January 1941. **F147**
A discussion of censorship as practiced in Canada.

Flechuck, Anna J. *The Index of Forbidden Books of the Roman Catholic Church, Described and Explained*. Cleveland, School of Library Science, Western Reserve University, 1951. 47 p. (Unpublished Master's thesis) **F148**
The author discusses the history and religious significance of the *Index* from the Catholic viewpoint, the method of proscribing a book, and the influence of the *Index* on a Catholic librarian in a public library.

Fleishman, Stanley. "Legal Control of Sex Literature." *California Librarian*, 21:107–12, April 1960. **F149**
A review of recent court decisions concerning definition and control of sex expression.

————. "Obscenity and Post Office Censorship." *Law in Transition*, 22:222–30, Winter 1963. **F150**
Review of the U.S. Supreme Court decision in *Manual Enterprises, Inc. v. Day*, 370 U.S. 478 (1962), in which the Court voided the Post-Office order that declared the magazines of this publisher obscene and unmailable.

————. "Sex, Censorship, Literature and Freedom." *Rogue*, 7:16–18+, November 1962. **F151**

————. "Times Film Corporation v. City of Chicago: Obscenity and Prior Restraint." *Law in Transition*, 21:235–43, Winter 1962. **F152**

————. "Witchcraft and Obscenity: Twin Superstitions." *Wilson Library Bulletin* 39:640–44, April 1965. **F153**

Borrowing the title from Theodore A. Schroeder, pioneer critic of the obscenity laws, a Los Angeles attorney explores the similarities of witch-hunting and obscenity-hunting, both outgrowths of misguided religious fervor. He reviews recent American court decisions which indicate a movement toward a more libertarian view of sex expression. He gives special attention to the Roth and Alberts cases, the *Tropic of Cancer* case, and the decision on the film *The Lovers* (*Jacobellis v. Ohio*). He quotes from a decision of New York Justice Shapiro, defending the right of so-called "trashy" books, which, while they do not appeal to educated people, have a social importance of their own, and an equal right to protection under the First Amendment: "What I have tried to suggest is that obscenity is not a crime. At most, it is sex speech which some find in poor taste, and others may find sinful. But neither sin nor taste are matters with which the law has any proper concern. Those are personal matters best left to the individual to resolve for himself."

Fleming, Peter. "Blood Out of Stone." *Spectator*, 200:619, 16 May 1958. **F154**
Criticism of the unwarranted restrictions placed by Whitehall on the use of documents of World War II.

Fleming, W. S. "The Menace of the Movie." *Light*, 145:20–25, May–June 1922. **F155**
Address of the manager of the National Reform Association, given before the National Purity Congress, Chicago.

Fletcher, Alan. "Obscene Books and the Law." *Author*, 64:37–38, Winter 1953. **F156**
Analysis of current British obscenity law.

Fletcher, W. I. "The 'Infernos' in Public Libraries." *Critic*, 12:275, 30 November 1889. **F157**
A letter to the editor refers to an article in the *North American Review* charging that books in libraries kept in the "inferno" are used for evil purposes. The writer assures the author that in his experience as an assistant in the Boston Athenaeum, he had only once given out an "inferno" book, and then to a reputable gentleman to be used in the library. But when the chief, Dr. Poole (now of the Newberry Library), came in, he took the book from the man and locked it up again.

Flexner, Stuart. "The Man Who Corrupted California." *Esquire*, 61(3):82–83, 151–55, March 1964. **F158**
The coeditor of the *Dictionary of American Slang* reports on the furor his book created in California, beginning with its withdrawal from the library by a high school student in Sacramento. "Censorship disputes grew so hot that the book was banned in some places,

marked for burning in others . . . There were demonstrations in the California capital, and Democrats and Republicans, liberals and ultraconservatives went forth to battle. The uproar could even affect the outcome of California's next gubernatorial election." The action against the reference book was stimulated, in part, by the denunciation of the work by Maxwell Rafferty, California Superintendent of Public Instruction, who urged the book be removed from school library shelves. Thousands of copies of mimeographed lists of the extracted "dirty" words were circulated by such groups as the Christian Citizens for Moral Action.

Flick, Hugh M. "Control and Regulation of Motion Pictures." In *Lectures in Communications Media, Legal and Policy Problems Delivered at University of Michigan Law School, June 16–June 18, 1954.* Ann Arbor, Mich., University of Michigan Law School, 1954, pp. 109–26. **F159**
The author is director of the Motion Picture Division, New York State Education Department.

Flicker, Theodore J. "Censored." *Plays and Players*, 9:23, September 1962. **F160**
The director of the London production, *The Premise*, presents a selection of the sketches that were banned from the play by the Lord Chamberlain because they poked fun at President Kennedy and his family. The scenes were retained in the New York and Washington production and President Kennedy is said to have approved.

Flower, Benjamin. *The Proceedings of the House of Lords in the Case of Benjamin Flower, Printer of the Cambridge Intelligencer, for a Supposed Libel on the Bishop of Llandaff; With Prefatory Remarks, and Animadversions on the Writings of the Bishop of Llandaff, the Rev. R. Ramsden . . ., and the Rev. Robert Hall . . . To which are Added, the Argument in the Court of King's Bench on a Motion for an Habeas Corpus, and . . . Remarks on the Judgment of that Court, by Henry Clifford . . .* Cambridge, The Author, 1800. (Also in Howell, *State Trials*, vol. 27, pp. 986 ff.) **F161**
Proceedings on Flower's commitment by the House of Lords for libel and breach of privilege for an article in his paper, *Cambridge Intelligencer.* He was convicted and sentenced to six months in prison, despite a spirited defense by his lawyer, Henry Clifford.

Flower, Benjamin O. "Conservatism and Sensualism an Unhallowed Alliance." *Arena*, 3:126–28, December 1890. **F162**
A melodramatic editorial defending Tolstoy's *Kreutzer Sonata* and regarding the attempt to suppress the work as "another striking illustration of conservatism protecting vice by assailing all who seek to purify life in the only way in which society can ever be purged of immorality."

————. "Free Press Lives—*Menace* Acquitted." *Menace*, 248:1, 4, 22 January 1916. **F163**
Discussion of the Federal Court trial in Joplin, Mo., of the publishers of *The Menace*, for alleged "obscene" criticism of the Catholic Church. A synopsis of the four-day trial, in which the defendants won, is given on page 4. Speeches of the defense attorneys, John L. McNatt and J. I. Sheppard, are given in the 12 February issue of *The Menace.* Articles throughout the pages of *The Menace* charge the Catholic hierarchy with efforts to silence criticism by use of the postal laws against obscenity and the wartime Espionage Act. Thomas E. Watson, in the 6 January 1916 issue of his weekly *Jeffersonian* (Atlanta) took up the defense of *The Menace*, with a lengthy criticism of the censorship practices of the Church of Rome.

[————]. "The Freedom of the Press as Viewed by Mr. Roosevelt and by Jefferson and Tocqueville." *Arena*, 41:218–19, February 1909. **F164**
By way of contrast to the antagonistic attitude of President Theodore Roosevelt to the press, the editor cites various statements of Thomas Jefferson in behalf of a free press (letters to Lafayette, Judge Tyler, Edward Carrington, and Charles Lancey), and a quotation from Tocqueville's *Democracy in America.*

————. "The Postmaster-General and the Censorship of Morals." *Arena*, 2:540–52, October 1890. **F165**
Condemnation of action by the Postmaster General in refusing to transmit Tolstoy's *Kreutzer Sonata* through the mails because of alleged obscenity. He sees this action as a dangerous precedent "toward the establishment of a despotic censorship of the press" and explores the results of such censorship. He refers to the efforts of Anthony Comstock to convict four persons for selling *Kreutzer Sonata.*

————. *Sound Morality versus Morbid Pruriency.* New York, Free Speech League, 1906. 7 p. **F166**
Published with Theodore A. Schroeder's *Our Vanishing Liberty of the Press.*

————, comp. *Story of the Menace Trial. A Brief Sketch of this Historic Case, with Reports of the Masterly Addresses by Hon. J. L. McNatt and Hon. J. I. Sheppard.* Aurora, Mo., United States Publishing Co., 1916. 61 p. **F167**
Flower was a Boston social reformer and liberal editor (*American Spectator, The Arena, The Menace*) who, in later life, was obsessed with the idea that the Roman Catholic hierarchy was a menace to American democracy. His journal, *The Menace*, published in Aurora, Mo., was devoted to an anti-Catholic crusade. Flower was president of the Free Press Defense League and the National League for Medical Freedom. He was a descendent of the English liberal, Benjamin Flower, 1755–1829. The editors of *The Menace* were charged with sending obscene matter through the mails (Federal Court, Joplin, Mo., 1916). Part of the indictment was for quotations from Jeremiah J. Crowley's book. Crowley, a former Catholic priest, appeared for the defense. The editors were acquitted.

Flower, Benjamin O., *et al. In Defense of Free Speech. Five Essays from The Arena (Trenton, N.J.) and Written by B. O. Flower, Rev. Eliot White, Louis F. Post, and Theodore Schroeder.* New York, Free Speech League, 1908. 24 p. **F168**
Contents: The Sinister Assault on the Breastworks of Free Government (Flower); The Lawless Suppression of Free Speech in New York (Schroeder); Denial of Free Speech in Massachusetts (White); Free Speech and Good Order (Post); and the Growing Despotism of Our Judiciary (Schroeder). The essays deal largely with the suppression of anarchist propaganda and partly with contempt of court as a means of censorship.

Flues, A. Gilmore. "Public Library Censorship?—No!" *Wilson Library Bulletin*, 23:56–57, September 1948. **F169**
The president of the Friends of the Toledo Public Library made this anticensorship talk at a Toledo Town Meeting. "We still gamble on the average American—that given access to all sides of a question, and being allowed to pursue without hindrance the answer to that question, he will come reasonably close to the conception that our forefathers had of him." Printed with Mr. Flues' talk is a newspaper editorial which appeared two days later criticizing the other speaker, George D. Hawkins, executive secretary of the Toledo Small Business Association, for his stand favoring censorship. The editorial gives strong support of freedom for the Toledo Public Library.

Fly, James L. "Freedom of Speech and Press." In Edward L. Bernays, *Safeguarding Civil Liberties Today.* Ithaca, N.Y., Cornell University Press, 1945, pp. 61–75. **F170**
The former chairman of the FCC argues that freedom of the press is dangerously controlled by monopolies of newspaper and broadcasting chains, press associations, syndicates, and the major Hollywood studios. The interest of a free press is best served by diversity.

————. "Freedom to Hear: Radio." *Survey Graphic*, 35:474–76, 514, December 1946. **F171**
The author considers the barriers against easy access to radio, both on the domestic scene and internationally.

————. "Regulation of Broadcasting in the Public Interest." *Annals of the*

American Academy of Political and Social Science, 213:102–8, January 1941. **F172**

The chairman of the Federal Communications Commission discusses problems in safeguarding the public interest by regulation of radio broadcasting. "My own view is that a free market in ideas over the air can be attained without special interest stations and without the creation of a multitude of 'propaganda' stations . . . a licensee must serve the public at large, not any special interests; and the public interest can be served only if the licensee permits the presentation of all the facts and all points of view."

Flynn, James R. *The United States Government's Theory of Free Speech on the Air.* Chicago, University of Chicago, 1955. 143 p. (Unpublished Master's thesis) **F173**

Fode, Bennet. "Canadian Film Censorship." *Tamarack Review*, 21:71–77, Autumn 1961. **F174**

Censorship of Canadian entertainment "is now applied only to the cinema, whereas the other mass media of visual entertainment—the theatre, television, Telefusion—have never been subjected to this form of official narrow mindedness. All ten provinces have statutes requiring motion pictures to be censored prior to their exhibition to the public."

Fogarty, Frank P. *Canon 35 and the Broadcast Media.* Columbia, Mo., Freedom of Information Center, School of Journalism, University of Missouri, 1961. 6 p. (Publication no. 61) **F175**

The vice-president of Meredith Broadcasting Company believes that lawyers should take a fresh look at Canon 35 in the light of today's conditions. "If you will admit cameras and microphones to the courtrooms you will not jeopardize the rights of your clients; on the contrary you will actually insure them."

———. *A Time for Fundamentals.* Columbia, Mo., Freedom of Information Center, School of Journalism, University of Missouri, 1960. 4 p. (Publication no. 28) **F176**

The author examines two fundamentals: (1) the concept of "public interest, convenience, and necessity" as applied by the FCC to broadcasting, and (2) the concept that self-regulation can and does succeed in American society.

FOI Digest. Columbia, Mo., Freedom of Information Center, School of Journalism, University of Missouri, 1959–date. Bimonthly. **F177**

A publication devoted to news of freedom of information, or the lack of it, in all media of communications throughout the United States. Each issue includes brief notes on current articles and books.

Foil, Frank F. "Constitutional Law—Censorship of Motion Picture Films." *Louisiana Law Review*, 21:807–12, June 1961. **F178**

Concerning the case of *Times Film Corp. v. Chicago*, 365 U.S. 43 (1961).

Foley, Francis C. "Constitutional Law—Freedom of Speech and the Press." *Boston University Law Review*, 12:261–63, April 1932. **F179**

Relates to the case, *Near v. Minnesota*, 283 U.S. 697. Liberty of speech and the press, the court holds, is within the liberty safeguarded by the due process clause of the Fourteenth Amendment from invasion by state action.

Folkard, Henry C. "Injunction to Restrain Libels." *Law Magazine and Review*, 22(4th ser.):63–73, November 1896. **F180**

A review of the English law of libel in view of recent discussions on the use of the injunction to prevent publication of alleged libel, which has "the effect of striking a serious blow at the liberty of the press."

———. *The Law of Slander and Libel, Founded upon the Treatise of the Late Thomas Starkie . . . including the Procedure, Pleading, and Evidence, Civil and Criminal, with Forms and Precedents: Also Contempts of Court, Criminal Informations, &c. &c., and an Appendix of Statutes.* 7th ed. London, W. Clowes, 1908. 711 p. **F181**

Includes numerous citations to English cases of seditious and blasphemous libel. Folkard was editor of the last (1869) edition of Starkie's treatise on the law of libel, but subsequently Folkard's own work replaced that of Starkie's.

[Folkard, Henry T.]. "Obliteration of Racing News." *Library Association Record*, 9:24–29, 1907. **F182**

A survey of practices among 138 English libraries indicates that 27 obliterate betting news, 49 have decided against it, and 62 have not considered the question.

Folsom, Robert, *et al.* "How Free Is College Journalism?" *New Republic*, 134:11–14, 2 April 1956. **F183**

"The story told here of suppression of opinion at Florida State University prompted the *New Republic* to query student editors of publications in seven other state universities in the South [Texas, Maryland, Georgia, Virginia, Oklahoma A & M, North Carolina, and Mississippi] who were asked how much independence and freedom of editorial comment they are allowed." Texas, Maryland, and Georgia indicate censorship; the others reported having free rein.

Fondren, Lee. *Advertising—1980.* Columbia, Mo., Freedom of Information

Center, School of Journalism, University of Missouri, 1961. 6 p. (Publication no. 62) **F184**

A fantasy on the total destruction of advertising in America and its effect on society—an attack on government control of advertising.

"Fooling the Americans Again." *Nation*, 115:680, 20 December 1922. **F185**

Because of censorship abroad, particularly in the Balkans, the American people are getting biased accounts of foreign affairs.

Foot, Dingle, *et al.* "The Freedom of Our Press." *Listener*, 20:1337–38, 1370–71, 22 December 1938. (Also in *Vital Speeches*, 1 February 1939) **F186**

Discussion by Dingle Foot, M.P., Nicholas Macaskie, K.C., and Sir Stanley Reed, M.P., with Lord Meston as chairman. Lord Meston concludes: "It isn't boasting to say that, all in all, our British Press is the best in the world; the more reason, Mr. Macaskie would say, for preserving its virtue. The more reason, Mr. Foot would say, for refusing to curb its freedom and its discretion; certainly the more reason, we should all admit, for as little as possible of the dictation which is making a mockery of the Press in some great countries today."

Foote, Edward Bliss. *Confidential Pamphlet for the Married; Words in Pearl for Married People Only.* New York, The Author, 1875. 32 p. **F187**

The pamphlet contains the text of a suppressed work bearing the same title. In place of the offending section on "reliable preventives," the text and criticism of the statutes prohibiting birth control information is given.

———. *A Fable of the Spider and the Bees . . .* [New York, National Defense Association, 1881]. 61 p. **F188**

In this fable, which appeared originally in *Foote's Health Monthly*, the spider is permitted by the bees who rule the insect community to spin a web to keep undesirable insects out of the garden. The web serves this purpose but it also traps butterflies, useful in pollination. The bees pay no heed to the complaints of the insect community because they are powerful enough to fly through the web. An analogy is drawn to the suppression of literature on sex education, free thought, and radical social ideas by the web of the Comstock society. Three cases are cited: The suppression of Dr. Foote's pamphlet, *Words in Pearl for Married People Only*, and his fine of $3,500 for sending the work through the mail; the blasphemy trial of D. M. Bennett of the *Truth Seeker*; and the trial of Ezra Heywood for his *Cupid's Yokes*. The book quotes press criticism of the New York Society for the Suppression of Vice.

————. *In the Matter of the Repeal or Modification of a Certain Postal Law.* [*Address by Dr. E. B. Foote to the Committees on Revision of Laws in Senate and House of Representatives*]. New York, E. B. Foote. 7 p. **F189**

An attack on postal censorship and its use to exclude legitimate works on health and sex education

————. "Plea for Liberty to Apply Sexology v. Sexual Chaos." *Dr. Foote's Health Monthly*, 19:2–11, February 1894. **F190**

An appeal for freedom of information on sex and sex hygiene.

————. *Step Backward; in Reviewing Inconsiderate Legislation, Concerning Articles and Things for the Prevention of Conception.* New York, Issued by the Author [Murray Hill Publishing Co.], 1875. 16 p. **F191**

Opposition to legislation that prevents distribution of birth control information.

Foote, Edward Bond. *Comstock Versus Craddock.* [New York? 1902?]. 4 p. **F192**

An attack on Anthony Comstock for his persecution of Ida Craddock for "obscenity." This self-styled "purity lecturer" was convicted and served a three-month jail sentence for her pamphlet, *The Wedding Night.* Following a second conviction she committed suicide. "I am taking my life," she wrote, "because a judge, at the instigation of Anthony Comstock, has declared me guilty of a crime which I did not commit—the circulation of obscene literature."

————. *In the Matter of the Repeal or Modification of a Certain Postal Law.* New York, The Author, n.d., 7 p. **F193**

Address of Dr. Foote to the Committees in the Senate and House of Representatives on revision of the Comstock law.

————. "Plea for Necessity of a Free Medical Press." *Eclectic Review*, 8:171–74, July 1905. **F194**

An appeal for freedom of expression in matters of sex hygiene in the nation's medical journals. Dr. Edward Bond Foote is the son of Dr. Edward Bliss Foote. Both were New York physicians.

Foote, George W. *Blasphemy No Crime . . .* London, H. A. Kemp, 1882. 24 p. **F195**

Published during the author's prosecution for blasphemous libel for publishing the *Freethinker.* Foote reviews the history of the prosecution during which a law that had lain dormant for a quarter of a century was revived.

He gives a brief history of the blasphemy law in England and earlier prosecutions under it; he defends blasphemy as "simply scepticism expressed in plain language and sold at the people's price."

————. *Defence of Free Speech. Being a Three Hours' Address to the Jury in the Court of Queen's Bench before Lord Coleridge on April 24, 1883 . . .* New edition with introduction and footnotes. London, Progressive Publishing Co., 1889. 45 p. (Reprinted in 1932 by Pioneer Press, London, with introduction by H. Cutner) **F196**

George W. Foote, editor of the *Freethinker*, who was brought to trial for blasphemy, reviews the history of freethinking and comments on his earlier trial before Judge North, which he felt was unfairly conducted. In his address to the jury Foote discusses in eloquent language the legal concept of religious freedom in England and pleads to the jury to "check that spirit of bigotry and fanaticism which is fully aroused . . . proclaim that henceforth the press shall be absolutely free, unless it libel men's characters or contain incitements to crime, and that all offences against belief and taste shall be left to the great jury of public opinion." The jury was in disagreement, but the case was heard again four days later and Foote was found guilty and given a year's sentence. Foote praised the fairness of Judge Coleridge.

————. *Hall of Science Libel Case, with a Full and True Account of "The Leeds Orgies,"* Edited, with Introduction, by G. W. Foote. London, R. Forder, [1895?]. 58 p. **F197**

A Christian Evidence lecturer, Walton Powell, charged in a speech (later published in the *Anti-Infidel* and as a pamphlet) that the Hall of Science where the National Secular Society held its meetings was used for a class in which boys were taught unnatural vices. The Society took civil action against the publisher of the pamphlet and won the verdict. The trial was unique in that the council for the plaintiff made an appeal for freedom of the press, showing that false and malicious charges represented a threat to freedom.

————. *Mr. Bradlaugh's Trial and the Freethought Party.* London, Charles Watts, [1899]. 16 p. **F198**

"The prosecution of Mr. Bradlaugh and Mrs. Besant for publishing [Charles] Knowlton's *Fruits of Philosophy* was, as the Lord Chief Justice told the Solicitor-General, a mischievous mistake. It gave wide circulation to an obscure pamphlet which many think indecent and which even its defenders admit to be comparatively unimportant . . . At the normal rate of sale it would have taken two centuries to circulate as many copies as the prosecution has spread amongst the people during the last two months . . . The prosecution was, too, a mischievous mistake in another respect; it was an unnecessary interference with the liberty of the Press. Nobody was compelled to

purchase the *Fruits of Philosophy*, it was not liable to fall into juvenile hands, nor was it extensively advertised." Foote criticizes Mr. Bradlaugh and Mrs. Besant who started the affair, but allowed others (Mr. Truelove, the bookseller) to take the brunt of the persecution. Bradlaugh and Besant were more interested, he charges, in notoriety than in furthering the cause of the Freethought Party. The Knowlton pamphlet, in the estimation of Foote, was an obsolete work of quackery.

————. *Prisoner for Blasphemy.* London, Progressive Publishing Co., 1886. 180 p. **F199**

After two trials, the editor of the British agnostic journal, *Freethinker*, was convicted of blasphemy for the Christmas issue (1882) and served a year in prison. Two months after sentencing by Lord North, Foote was tried for another blasphemous libel. This is reported in his *Defence of Free Speech.* In the present book Foote gives an account of his three trials and life in prison. He discusses the history of blasphemy laws and cases in England, noting that the last case preceding his was in 1857. "It is more than possible that I shall be the last prisoner for blasphemy in England." On his release, Foote acquired his own printing plant so that the production of the *Freethinker* and other "blasphemous" literature might be done under his own roof.

[————, W. J. Ramsey, and H. A. Kemp]. *Verbatim Report of the Two Trials of G. W. Foote, W. J. Ramsey, and H. A. Kemp, for Blasphemous Libel in the Christmas Number of the "Freethinker." Held at the Old Bailey on Thursday March 1st, and on Monday, March 5th, 1883, Before Mr. Justice North and Two Common Juries.* London, Progressive Publishing Co., 1883. 112 p. (Another edition was published by Edward B. Aveling) **F200**

Foote, the editor of *Freethinker*, was sentenced to 12 months; Ramsey, the proprietor, to 9 months; and Kemp, the printer, to 3 months. In the sentencing the judge recognized the relative responsibility of the three men for the libel. The spectators in the court reacted so violently to the verdict that the judge cleared the court before passing sentence. Notes on the trials appear in *Central Law Journal*, 13 July 1883.

Foote's Health Monthly. New York, 1876–96? **F201**

Under the editorship of Dr. Edward Bliss Foote and his son, Dr. Edward Bond Foote, New York physicians, this journal became the organ for medical freedom, sex hygiene, sexual emancipation of women, and birth control. The Footes were both active in free-thought circles and in the fight against censorship, and their journal reflects these interests. The senior Foote opposed the Comstock law in New York in 1872; two years later Anthony Comstock retaliated by having Dr. Foote arrested for distributing birth control pamphlets. Both father and son were active in the

National Defense Association, organized to oppose the Comstock laws.

"For a Sensible Censorship." *Nation*, 104:518–19, 3 May 1917.　　**F 202**
Wartime censorship should not include the suppression of criticism of acts of public officials.

"'For Adults Only': The Constitutionality of Government Film Censorship by Age Classification." *Yale Law Journal*, 69:141–52, November 1959.　　**F 203**
American constitutional issues in adopting the British system of film classification. Notes on *Paramount Film Distribution Corp. v. City of Chicago*, 172F Supp. 69, the first court test of age classification in the United States.

Forbes, Archibald. "War Correspondents and the Authorities." *Nineteenth Century*, 7:185–96, January 1880.　　**F 204**
An historical and critical review of government censorship of news in wartime.

Forbes, M. Z. "Obscene Publications." *Australian Law Journal*, 20:92–99, July 1946.　　**F 205**
Consideration of the more important provisions of the New South Wales Act (1901) as interpreted by judicial decisions and the effect of the Obscene and Indecent Publications (Amendment) Act, 1946. The occasion for the review was the prosecution of Angus & Robertson for publication of Lawson Glassop's *We Were the Rats.*

Forbush, William B. "Barnyard Literature." *Christian Century*, 40:1615–16, 13 December 1923.　　**F 206**
A complaint against the disgusting fiction coming from the "new school of unrestraint." He advises readers and critics to ignore this "barnyard literature."

Ford, Douglas M. "The Growth of the Freedom of the Press." *English Historical Review*, 4:1–12, January 1889.　　**F 207**
The history of freedom of the press in England from the repeal of the licensing act in 1695. Mostly concerned with the history of newspaper publishing, the achievement of the right to publish full and fair reports of parliamentary debates, and the newspapers' struggle against strict libel laws.

Ford, Frederick W. *Broadcasting Political and Controversial Issues.* Washington, D.C., U.S. Federal Communications Commission, 1962. 9 p.　　**F 208**
A FCC commissioner, in an address before the Ohio Broadcasters' Association, points out the difficulties in applying the "fairness doctrine" and urges that the FCC be given "the authority to make rules, regulations and interpretations on the use of broadcast facilities for political campaigns, and for affording a reasonable opportunity for the discussion of conflicting views on issues of public importance."

———. "The Fairness Doctrine." *Journal of Broadcasting*, 8:1–16, Winter 1963–64. (Also issued in pamphlet form by the U.S. Federal Communications Commission, 1963. 13 p.)　　**F 209**
Commissioner Ford discusses the history and application of the "fairness doctrine" in broadcasting, maintaining that it does not result in regulation and censorship, and does not contribute to the revocation of broadcast licenses.

———. "The Meaning of the 'Public Interest, Convenience or Necessity.'" *Journal of Broadcasting*, 5:205–18, Summer 1961.　　**F 210**
An analysis of the legislative and judicial history of the "public interest" standard in broadcasting and a defense of the FCC report on programming policy.

Ford, Guy S. "Censorship." *Encyclopedia Britannica*, 12th ed., 1922. vol. 30, pp. 591–96.　　**F 211**
Special emphasis on wartime censorship in Great Britain and the United States.

Ford, James L. "Plea for the Free Theater." *Munsey's Magazine*, 28:148–52, October 1902.　　**F 212**

Ford, John. *Criminal Obscenity, a Plea for Its Suppression.* New York, Revell, 1926. 143 p.　　**F 213**
A New York judge, shocked by finding his daughter reading D. H. Lawrence's *Women in Love*, carried on a vigorous crusade against obscenity as expressed in the modern novel. He was active in the organization of the Clean Books League and urged the passage of the "clean books" bill in the New York legislature. Judge Ford favors upholding and strengthening existing obscenity laws, and interpreting them according to Lord Cockburn's definition of obscenity. The appendix contains: The Law of England, *King v. Curl, Queen v. Hecklin, U.S. v. Harman, People v. Muller, Commonwealth of Massachusetts v. Buckley*, and American Laws and Statutes against Obscenity.

———. "Judicial Repeal of Legislative Action." *St. John's Law Review*, 3:216–24, May 1929.　　**F 214**
Judge Ford is alarmed over the narrowing judicial interpretation of obscenity legislation.

Ford, John A. "We will Gamble on the American." *Library Journal*, 74:917–19, 15 June 1949. (Reprinted in Downs, *The First Freedom*, pp. 329–31)　　**F 215**
A member of the Los Angeles County Board of Supervisors expresses his faith in the average

American citizen to arrive at he truth when faced with controversial points of view represented by books in the public library.

Ford, Paul L., *ed. Journals of Hugh Gaines, Printer.* New York, Dodd, Mead, 1902. 2 vols.　　**F 216**
Censorship in the American colonies is discussed on pages 56–62.

Ford, Worthington C. "Benjamin Harris, Printer and Bookseller." *Massachusetts Historical Society Proceedings*, 57:34–68, 1923.　　**F 217**
Harris was publisher of the first newspaper printed in the American colonies, *Publick Occurrances, both Foreign and Domestick*, and suppressed by authorities after the first issue (1690).

———, *ed. Thomas Jefferson and James Thomson Callender, 1798–1802.* Brooklyn, Historical Printing Club, 1897. 45 p.　　**F 218**
"Of all the foreigners who were connected with journalism in the United States at the beginning of the century, James Thomson Callender was easily first in the worst qualities of mind and character." Jefferson befriended the man, only to have him turn on him as he had on other public figures "as ready to libel him as any member of the Federalist Party." A collection of letters between Jefferson and "this scandalmonger and partisan scribbler." Ford also published a general account on "Jefferson and the Newspapers" in *Records of the Columbia Historical Society*, vol. 8, pp. 78–111.

"Foreign Policy and a Free Press." *Nation and Athenaeum*, 33:108–9, 28 April 1923.　　**F 219**
Because of false information on foreign affairs the nation is faced with a serious menace to freedom. "We hope the Labor Party . . . will devote its whole mind and resources to devising ways and means of surmounting this obstacle."

Forer, Lois G. "A Free Press and a Fair Trial." *American Bar Association Journal*, 39:800–803, 843–49, September 1953.　　**F 220**
The 1953 winner of the Ross Prize Essay. The author suggests that "comment and report by all media of mass communication be unrestricted except during the limited period commencing with the empanelling of the jury and ceasing with the rendering of the verdict. During this time, no information which has not been introduced into evidence should be disseminated." A voluntary code could accomplish this. An appendix lists and classifies cases involving contempt by publication since 1928.

"The Forgotten Village: The Board of Regents of the State of New York; in the Matter of Appeal from the Action of the Director of the Motion Picture Division in Refusing to License a Motion Picture Entitled the *Forgotten Village*; Petition for Review." *Twice-a-Year*, 8–9: 321–42, 1942. **F 221**

The *Forgotten Village* was a motion picture, with actual native scenes depicting Mexican life, written by Steinbeck, directed by Herbert Kline, and produced in Mexico. The motion picture censors in New York objected to the showing of a native woman nursing her baby and a woman in labor as "indecent." The legal counsel for the film company defended the movie for its artistic and social integrity. After two appeals the Board reversed its decision and granted a license. The article includes text of documents in the case as well as commentary.

Forman, Harry B[uxton]. *The Vicissitudes of Shelley's Queen Mab. A Chapter in the History of Reform.* London, Printed for private circulation [by Richard Clay], 1887. 23 p. (Twenty-five copies printed) **F 222**

"This book, which [Shelley] never even published, but merely printed for private distribution and circulated sparingly, appears and re-appears in his life… and he was as powerless to check its vitality as his wife's imaginary *Frankenstein* was to unmake the monster he had made." Shelley composed his iconoclastic *Queen Mab* when still in his teens and, failing to find a publisher, he had it printed about 1813 (approximately 250 copies). In 1816 the poem was used as evidence against Shelley in his trial to get custody of his two children. The work was charged with being anti-religious, anti-King, and antimarriage. In 1821 William Clark issued a piratical edition in London. Shelley, then in Italy, was amused but embarrassed. "Because I wish to protest against all the bad poetry in it, [Shelley wrote] I have given orders to say that it is done against my desire, and have directed my attorney to apply to Chancery for an injunction, which he will not get." The Society for the Suppression of Vice stepped in, however, and secured the arrest and conviction of Clark for the sale of the poem. Some of the unbound stock fell into hands of Richard Carlile, who used it in his pirated edition. Hetherington and Watson later put out a better edition. Various booksellers over the years were prosecuted for the sale of *Queen Mab*. When Mrs. Shelley's collected edition of her husband's work was published by Mr. Moxon, W. J. Linton arranged for a test case against the publisher. "There should not be one law for the 'low bookseller of the Strand' and another for the aristocratic booksellers of Dover Street." Moxon was prosecuted for blasphemous and seditious libel and, despite the eloquent plea of his attorney, Talfourd, was heavily fined. Shelley had brushes with the censors early in life. He was expelled from Oxford for writing a pamphlet denying the existence of God; he attacked Lord Ellenborough because of the sentence he passed on Daniel I. Eaton for publishing the third part of Paine's *Age of Reason;* and he defended Richard Carlile, arrested on a similar charge.

Forster, E. M. "Liberty in England." In Forster's *Abinger Harvest*, London, Arnold, 1936, pp. 63–70. (Reprinted from *London Mercury*, August 1935) **F 223**

Paper read at the International Congress of Authors held in Paris, 1935. Includes remarks on the wartime Sedition Act and recent British cases of obscene libel.

[————]. "Mr. D. H. Lawrence and Lord Brentford." *Nation and Athenaeum* (London), 46:508–9, 11 January 1930. **F 224**

A critique of Lawrence's *Pornography and Obscenity* and Lord Brentford's *Do We Need a Censor?* The two have in common emotional uncertainty; each would censor "genuine pornography"; each detests indecency, but would define it differently. "Lord Brentford wants to suppress everything except marriage, and Mr. Lawrence to suppress nothing except suppression . . . the one sounds the trumpet of duty, the other the trumpet of passion . . . in the valley between them lie the inert forces of the general public." Signed "E.M.F."

[————]. "The New Censorship." *Nation and Athenaeum*, 43:696, 1 September 1928; 43:726, 8 September 1928. **F 225**

An unsigned letter from Forster in the 1 September issue and a letter signed jointly by Forster and Virginia Woolf in the 8 September issue deal with the suppression of Radclyffe Hall's *The Well of Loneliness*.

[————]. "The Tercentenary of the *Areopagitica*." In his *Two Cheers for Democracy*. London, Arnold, 1951, pp. 62–66. **F 226**

Forsythe, Richard H., and Carl Hamilton. "Freedom and the Student Press." *News of Iowa State*, 17(6):6, July–August 1965. **F 227**

Two faculty members of Iowa State University express different points of view on the extent of freedom that should be permitted a student newspaper. Forsythe argues for some editorial guidance from faculty because the monopoly makes the campus paper different from the commercial newspaper; Hamilton argues for freedom, even at the cost of controversy. "The alternatives to freedom are infinitely worse."

Forsythe, Robert. "Who Speaks for Us?" *New Theatre*, 3(8):6–9, August 1936. **F 228**

Censorship in the theater.

Fort, Charles. "The Law of Libel as Applied to Newspapers." *Law Times*, 68:28, 8 November 1879; 68:48–49, 15 November 1879. **F 229**

In a paper delivered before a meeting of the Incorporated Law Society, U.K., Fort traces the growth of the law of libel as it applies to newspapers and considers what changes are called for.

Fortunoff, Daniel G. "Liability of Radio Corporations for Defamatory Statements Uttered on the Air." *Air Law Review*, 12:316–33, July 1941. **F 230**

Forum on Newspaper Censorship as Presented during National Newspaper Week. October 1–8, 1955. Gainesville, Fla., School of Journalism and Communications, University of Florida, 1955. 24 p. **F 231**

Foster, George, Jr. "The 1931 Personal Liberties Cases." *New York University Law Quarterly Review*, 9:64–81, September 1931. **F 232**

Background and analysis of two cases involving the right of free speech and the press—*Stromberg v. California* (283 U.S. 359), concerning the so-called "red flag" law, and *Near v. Minnesota* (283 U.S. 697), involving the newspaper "gag" act. The latter involved a statute that permitted the suppression of a newspaper as a public nuisance.

Foster, Henry H., Jr. "'Comstock Load'; Obscenity and the Law." *Journal of Criminal Law*, 48:245–58, September–October 1957. **F 233**

Anthony Comstock's crusade against vice is being revived today by a number of well-organized pressure groups. This article examines "the history of the concept of 'obscenity,' its meaning, the different tests which have been applied in obscenity cases, and some of the psychological and constitutional questions inherent in the problem."

Foster, J. Donald. "Another Side to Censorship." *Christianity Today*, 6:22–23, 2 February 1962. **F 234**

The author, an instructor in sociology and editor of the quarterly, *Religious and Theological Abstracts*, defends censorship of obscenity.

Foster, J. Herbert. "Necessities of Censorship and of Free Inquiry." *Sexual Life*, no. 35, February 1909. **F 235**

The motive of the author and the character of the readers should be the basis of judgment against a work charged as obscene.

Foster, James E. "Censorship as a Medium of Propaganda." *Society and Social Research*, 22:57–66, September–October 1937. **F 236**

An analysis of censorship as a negative form of propaganda. While propaganda attempts to control the conduct of a group by directing stimuli that reach it, censorship sets up barriers between the stimuli and the group. "Censorship at its best can do nothing more than protect an attitude from competing propaganda, and in any complex civilization even the most firmly rooted attitude needs something more than mere protection if it is to survive."

Foster, Roger. "Trial by Newspaper." *North American Review*, 144:524–27, May 1887.   **F 237**
In light of unfair news coverage of the trial of New York aldermen for bribery, the author suggests that some of the controls of the press which the courts inherited from England and long since abrogated, need to be restored. He calls for the press to "stand off" in news coverage until a verdict has been rendered.

"Foster Lyrics, Southern Fried Style." *Variety*, 207:1+, 31 July 1957; 207:47+, 28 August 1957.   **F 238**
Congressmen and music teachers object to radio and television network and textbook censorship of *Sewanee River*, *Ole Black Joe*, and *My Old Kentucky Home* to meet Negro criticism.

"*The Fourth Estate*." *North British Review*, 13:159–88, May 1950.   **F 239**
A review of F. K. Hunt's *The Fourth Estate*, with specific attention to his discussion of freedom of the press, and some new information and interpretation.

Fowell, Frank, and Frank Palmer. *Censorship in England*. London, Frank Palmer, 1913. 390p.   **F 240**
A history of British stage censorship from the fifteenth century to about 1913. A documentary rather than critical presentation, with special attention given to the celebrated Masters of Revels, Examiners or Licensers of Plays, and the changes in the legal control of dramatic productions. Chapter 10 devotes considerable space to the report of the 1909 Select Committee and the widespread criticism of dramatic censorship. The appendix contains, a table of plays licensed and refused, 1852–1912; text of play licenses issued by the Lord Chamberlain; Lord Chesterfield's speech in the House of Lords protesting the 1737 stage censorship bill; text of the 1737 Theatre Act; and the 1912 petition to the king against the Lord Chamberlain's censorship of plays, signed by some 60 British dramatists.

Fowell, Myron W. *A Suggested Approach to the Problem of Obscene Literature for Local Church Social Action Committees.* Boston, Massachusetts Council of Churches, 1959. 4p. mimeo. (Also in *Bay State Librarian*, Summer 1959)   **F 241**

Fowle, Daniel. *An appendix to the late Total eclipse of liberty. Being some thoughts on the end and design of civil government; also the inherent power of the people asserted and maintained; that it is not given up to their representatives* . . . Boston, [D. Fowle], 1756. 24p. (Reprinted in *Magazine of History with Notes and Queries*, 40(2):35–55; extra number 158, 1930)   **F 242**
Fowle, a Boston printer, spent six days in prison in 1754 for offending the Massachusetts House of Representatives by his humorous satire, *Monster of Monsters*. He described his persecution in this pamphlet. In 1755 Fowle sued the Commonwealth of Massachusetts for £1,000 for false arrest, but lost the case. He moved to New Hampshire, but continued to press for recompense. In 1766, 12 years after the prison sentence, the persistent printer was awarded £20 by the Commonwealth of Massachusetts "on account of his sufferings."

———. *A Total Eclipse of Liberty, Being a True and Faithful Account of the Arraignment, and Examination of Daniel Fowle before the Honorable House of Representatives of the Province of the Massachusetts-Bay in New-England, Octob. 24th 1754, Barely on Suspicion of His Being Concern'd in Printing and Publishing a Pamphlet Intitled, The Monster of Monsters. Also His Imprisonment and Sufferings . . . Written by Himself* . . . Boston, Printed in the Year 1755. 32p. (Reprinted in *Magazine of History with Notes and Queries*, 40(2):5–34; extra number 158, 1930)   **F 243**

Fowler, Albert. "Can Literature Corrupt?" *Modern Age*, 3:125–33, Spring 1959.   **F 244**
A discussion of the conflict over moral censorship between the American Civil Liberties Union and the National Office for Decent Literature. "The Civil Liberties Union is right," the author asserts, "in arguing that the method of compelling the removal of publications from neighborhood racks is ill suited to a problem of this magnitude, not so much because it violates the right of the individual to buy and sell as he chooses as because it does almost nothing to change the state of public taste and responsibility for the values of modern literature." This emphasis on the things that should not be done, however, "tends to minimize the importance of the problem itself and to discourage sincere efforts to deal with it." The author criticizes the ACLU for failure to explore with the NODL a positive approach to the problem.

Fox, Harold G. *The Canadian Law of Copyright.* Toronto, University of Toronto Press, 1944. 770p.   **F 245**

Fox, Jay. "The Nude and the Prudes." *Mother Earth*, 7:28–29, March 1912.

(Reprinted from *Agitator*, 1 July 1911; also published in broadside form by the Free Speech League)   **F 246**
The author was given two months in jail for publishing this article, which the court said tended to create disrespect for law. The case is commented on in "Two Months in the Tank," *Agitator*, 15 February 1912.

Fox, *Sir* John C. *The History of Contempt of Court.* Oxford, Eng., Clarendon, 1927. 252p.   **F 247**
A classic work on the development of the concept of contempt of court. The author maintains that the modern judicial doctrine that courts have an "inherent" power to punish contempt by publication is founded on a false view of the scope of summary judicial power at common law.

Fox, R. M. "Censorship in Ireland." *Nation*, 128:570–71, 8 May 1929.   **F 248**
An article from Dublin describing the current censorship situation in Ireland. A new Censorship Bill has just passed the Dail. It is based on findings of the Committee on Evil Literature. The writer comments on the findings of that Committee and on the activities of other supporters of censorship, concluding that the struggle "in essence is the same as that between the fundamentalists and the modernists . . . The only way to insure that people will not read the wrong books is to keep them ignorant."

———. "Censorship in the Irish Free State." *Nation*, 133:49–50, 8 July 1931.   **F 249**
Books in Ireland are subjected to two censorships, official action by the Censorship Board and unofficial action by public opinion. "Certain authors, certain publishers are unofficially 'discouraged.'"

Foxon, David F. "John Cleland and the Publication of *Memoirs of a Woman of Pleasure*." *Book Collector*, 12:476–87, Winter 1963.   **F 250**
An account of the author and the circumstances surrounding the publication of the oft-banned *Fanny Hill*.

———. "Libertine Literature in England, 1660–1745." *Book Collector*, 12:21–36, Spring 1963; 12:159–77, Summer 1963; 12:294–307, Autumn 1963. (Also issued as a separate publication, London, *Book Collector*, 1964. 63p.)   **F 251**
The first part deals with the earliest references to erotic literature in England and the legal proceedings against it. In 1660 John Garfield was imprisoned for writing *The Wandering Whore*; in 1668 in his diary Samuel Pepys records buying a "mighty lewd book . . .

L'eschalle des filles" and after reading it, burning it "that it might not be among my books to shame." In 1688 there were convictions for the sale of the English edition of the same book, *The School of Venus*, and in 1708 was the famous decision, *Rex v. Read*, in which the publisher of *The Fifteen Plagues of a Maidenhead* was freed on the grounds that obscenity was a matter to be dealt with by the ecclesiastical rather than civil courts. In 1728, in a reversal of the Read opinion, Edmund Curll was found guilty of obscenity for publishing *Venus in the Cloyster*. The second and third parts of Foxon's article deal in detail with six erotic works, including *The School of Venus* and *Venus in the Cloyster*. The author makes general observations on the aesthetic and moral problems that pornography raises. He concludes that erotic fantasies have their functions, if properly used, in providing "a temporary escape from the stresses and deprivations of real life . . . but the personality which clings to a fantasy view of the world is clearly sick."

Fraenkel, Osmond K. "For Free Speech." *Menorah Journal*, 24:97–101, April–June 1936. **F 252**
The author objects to laws such as one in New Jersey, prompted by anti-Semitism in Germany, which punishes as a misdemeanor any publication that "incites, counsels, promotes, or advocates hatred, violence or hostility" against any person in the state by reason of race, color, religion, or manner of worship. Such laws run counter to American guarantees of free speech. "Reason will not flourish where men are punished for their ideas and the expression of them—not even when the ideas are hateful ones." He calls on Jews to disassociate themselves from anti-Nazi laws and join the movement for freedom of speech.

————. "The Lynch Bill—A Different View." *Lawyers Guild Review*, 4:12–15, March–April 1944. **F 253**
The author considers a bill prohibiting false and defamatory racial and religious matter from the mails as a violation of the First Amendment. "Repression of the expression of opinions will never save democracy; eventually it will undermine it. Only truth beats falsehood. Repression breeds martyrs, neurotics and criminals, and fosters the dictator." An article in support of the Lynch Bill appeared in the January–February issue.

————. "One Hundred and Fifty Years of the Bill of Rights." *Minnesota Law Review*, 23:719–75, May 1939. **F 254**
On pages 751–62, the author discusses the changing legal concepts of freedom of the press and speech, largely in the area of political expression.

————. *Our Civil Liberties.* New York, Viking, 1944. 277p. **F 255**
Chapter 7, Freedom of Speech and of the Press, summarizes legal aspects of libel, obscenity,

blasphemy, sedition, race libel, and distribution of literature.

————. *The Supreme Court and Civil Liberties; How the Court Has Protected the Bill of Rights.* 9th ed. Dobbs Ferry, N.Y., Published for the American Civil Liberties Union by Oceana Publications, 1963. 189p. **F 256**
A classic study of the Bill of Rights by a leading constitutional lawyer and general counsel for the ACLU. The chapter on Freedom of Expression summarizes court decisions under the following headings: restrictions on the states, censorship and permits, postoffice restrictions, punishment based on "clear and present danger," punishment for content (seditious matter, disorderly conduct, obscenity, defamation, contempt of court), punishment depending on the manner of expression, indirect restrictions (newspapers, "guilt by association," government employees, unions and employers, registration and reports), and the right to be silent. Leading cases are listed in the appendix. Introduction by Joseph O'Meara, dean, Notre Dame Law School.

France, Joseph I. "Bourbonism against Free Speech; History Will Repeat with Same Disastrous Consequences the Results of the Alien and Sedition Laws, Opposed by Washington, Hamilton and Jefferson." *La Follette's Magazine*, 12:26–27, February 1920. **F 257**
"Reprinted [from the *Congressional Record*] because of the unanswerable argument advanced by him for the toilers whose viewpoint on this legislation he so characteristically presented."

France. Ministry of Foreign Affairs. *Conférence Internationale relative à la Répression de la circulation des publications obscènes.* Paris, Imprimerie Nationale, 1910. 148p. **F 258**
A complete record of the transactions of this conference, instigated by the antiobscenity crusade of French Senator Bérenger and resulting in the International Agreement for the Suppression of Obscene Publications, signed at Paris, 4 May 1910. An early effort to distinguish frank literary expression from pornography.

Frank, Dorothy. "I Was Called Subversive." *Collier's*, 131:68–73, 28 March 1953. **F 259**
A Los Angeles housewife describes her experience as education chairman of a women's committee to promote the study of UNESCO in the city s schools. The article describes the nightmare of bigotry and hate which attended the efforts of certain individuals and groups to keep a discussion of UNESCO out of the schools.

Frank, Glenn. "Critical Function in Democracy." *Vital Speeches*, 1:550–52, 20 May 1935. **F 260**

The president of the University of Wisconsin believes that the press and the universities face "the common problem of preserving unhampered the prophylactic process of corrective criticism in the midst of pressures from the world around for an uncritical surrender to the will, if not indeed to the whim of excessively centralized power."

————. "Is Free Speech Dangerous?" *Century Magazine*, 100:355–60, July 1920. **F 261**
A defense of free speech in the form of 14 principles in which the author believes in relation to freedom of thought and expression in a democracy.

[Frank, Jerome]. *A Man's Reach: The Philosophy of Judge Jerome Frank.* Edited by Barbara Frank Kristein. New York, Macmillan, 1965. 450p. **F 262**
The chapter Censorship: The First Amendment, includes an abstract of Judge Frank's opinion in the U.S. District Court in the case of *Samuel Roth v. Albert Goldman* in which he analyzes the obscenity statutes. Reviewed in *ALA Newsletter on Intellectual Freedom*, May 1965.

[————]. "On Censorship and the Constitution." *Publishers' Weekly*, 155:1156–57, 5 March 1949. **F 263**
Quotations from the opinion of Judge Frank of the U.S. District Court of Southern District of New York, in the case of *Samuel Roth v. Albert Goldman.* He finds the book obscene, but hopes that the U.S. Supreme Court "will review our decision, thus dissipating the fogs which surround this subject."

Frank, Joseph. *The Beginnings of the English Newspaper, 1620–1660.* Cambridge, Harvard University Press, 1961. 384p. **F 264**
This comprehensive and well-documented history of the first 40 years of the English newspaper includes many references to control and censorship of the press by the Crown and by Parliament. Early editors faced not only the vicissitudes of business, including government subsidies to their competitors, but were under pressure from licensing authorities, were sometimes subject to searches and seizures, and occasionally served jail sentences. The seeds of both good and bad journalism, the author observes, were planted during this early period of political and social upheaval, civil war, and intellectual ferment.

————. *The Levellers; a History of the Writings of Three Seventeenth-Century Social Democrats: John Lilburne, Richard Overton, William Walwyn.* Cambridge, Harvard University Press, 1955. 345p. **F 265**
An analysis of the intellectual contributions of the Levellers as seen in their publications. Written from primary sources, including an examination of some 500 contemporary pam-

phlets. The author finds that many of the freedoms the western world enjoys today, including freedom of the press, were born in the struggle of these seventeenth-century reformers. In addition to extensive consideration of Lilburne, Overton, and Walwyn, there are also references to the writings of Bastwick, Burton, and Prynne who also figured in the fight for freedom of the press.

Frank, S. B. "Headaches of a Movie Censor." *Saturday Evening Post*, 220: 20–21+, 27 September 1947.　**F 266**

Frank, Waldo. "Our Censors." *New Republic*, 55:12–15, 23 May 1928.　**F 267**
"A force that restrains in rhythm with organic growth is a control; a force that restrains against that rhythm is a censor . . . Censorship is the one way of ordering a world that does not create its own organic order."

Franke, Lewis. "Censorship of Obscenity in Literature—Prior Restraints." *American University Law Review*, 12:211–16, June 1963.　**F 268**
In the case of *Bantam Books, Inc., et al. v. Sullivan*, 372 U.S. 58, the U.S. Supreme Court declared invalid the action of a Rhode Island Commission to Encourage Morality in Youth which set up an informal system of censorship, employing "extralegal means without an immediate judicial determination on the obscenity of certain publications."

Frankenstein, R. *A Victim of Comstockism, being the History of the Persecution of George E. Wilson, by the Agent of the Western Society for the Suppression of Vice . . .* Compiled from the original records by R. Frankenstein. Chicago, George E. Wilson, 1894. 100p. (Wilson Library, no. 16, vol. 2, 10 July 1894)　**F 269**
An Indiana bookseller was fined for mailing Boccaccio's *Decameron*, pronounced obscene by the Post Office inspector.

Frankfurter, Felix. "Press Censorship by Judicial Construction." In *Law and Politics; Occasional Papers of Felix Frankfurter, 1913–1938.* Edited by Archibald MacLeish and E. F. Prichard, Jr. New York, Harcourt, Brace, 1939, pp. 129–34.　**F 270**
The selection, appearing originally as an unsigned editorial in the *New Republic*, 10 March 1921, deals with the U.S. Supreme Court decision in the Milwaukee *Leader* case, which "immediately affects only a despised Socialist sheet, but which involves nothing less than the control of the press."

Franklin, Benjamin. *An Apology for Printers.* New York, Book Craftsmen Associates, 1955. 16p. (Also in *A*

Benjamin Franklin Reader, edited by Nathan G. Goodman, New York, Crowell, 1945, pp. 252–58; and in Levy, *Freedom of the Press from Zenger to Jefferson*, pp. 3–10)　**F 271**
Franklin's eloquent statement on the value of a free press to a free people, originally published in the *Pennsylvania Gazette*, 10 June 1731, is reprinted on the 250th anniversary of Franklin's birth. It is unreasonable, Franklin argues, to imagine that printers approve of everything they print or that printers ought not to print anything of which they do not approve. If this were the case there would be nothing to read but what happened to agree with the opinion of printers. Also, if printers determined not to print anything that might offend someone, there would be very little printed.

[———]. "On Freedom of the Press; an Account of the Supremest Court of Judicature in Pennsylvania, viz., the Court of Press." *Federal Gazette*, 12 September 1789. (Reprinted in *A Benjamin Franklin Reader*, edited by Nathan G. Goodman, New York, Crowell, 1945, pp. 261–65)　**F 272**
A satire on the press abuse in attacking the reputation of a man without giving him the opportunity of defense—a practice later known as "trial by newspaper." "If by the liberty of the press were understood merely the liberty of discussing the propriety of public measures and public opinions, let us have as much of it as you please. But if it means the liberty of affronting, culminating, and defaming one another, I, for my part, own myself willing to part with my share of it when our legislators shall please so to alter the law, and shall cheerfully consent to exchange my liberty of abusing others for the privilege of not being abused myself." Franklin recommends as a legal check to these abuses of the liberty of the press that a citizen be permitted "the liberty of the cudgel." If an impudent writer attacks your reputation "you may go to him openly and break his head."

[Franklin, Charles L.]. [*Fred A. Burnham, President Mutual Reserve Fund Life Association v. Charles L. Franklin, editor of "The Interview."* New York? 1901.] 18p.　**F 273**
Criminal libel charges were brought by Burnham against the editor of *The Interview*, a paper which had been devoting a major portion of space to denouncing the Mutual Reserve Fund Life Association. The pamphlet consists of a reprinting of contemporary news articles about the case.

Franklin, Richard (Francklin). *Trial at Westminster for Publishing a Seditious Libel in the Craftsman, 1731.* (In Howell, *State Trials*, vol. 17, pp. 625ff., and in Abel Boyer, *Political State of Great Britain*)　**F 274**

Franklin was found guilty and given a year in prison for an article appearing in *The Craftsman*, which criticized the treaty between France, Spain, and England. Lord Chief Justice Raymond instructed the jury to find the defendant guilty if (1) Franklin was the publisher and (2) if the article referred to the king and his ministers. The jury was denied the right to decide whether or not the offense was libelous. In his *Government and the Press*, Hanson refers to a slightly different account of the trial by Richard Hollings in a British Museum MS (Add. MS. 36115).

Franklin, Robert D. "A Game of Chicken." *Library Journal*, 89:3918–19, 15 October 1964.　**F 275**
"Some librarians are afraid to apply book selection standards. Instead, pressured by cries of 'freedom,' they play . . . A Game of Chicken." While agreeing with "*some* aspects of the new freedoms from taboo and the disarming by the courts of would-be censors," the author believes that librarians still have a responsibility for evaluation, guidance, and selection of reading material.

Frantz, Laurent B. "The First Amendment in the Balance." *Yale Law Journal*, 71:1424–50, July 1962.　**F 276**
"The first amendment provides that 'Congress shall make no law . . . abridging the freedom of speech . . .' In determining whether this provision has been violated should a court 'balance' the 'competing interests' involved in the particular case?" The author concludes that "the 'balancing' test does not permit the first amendment to perform its function as a constitutional limitation . . . Not only does 'balancing' first amendment fail to protect freedom of speech, but it becomes a mechanism for rationalizing and validating the kinds of governmental action intended to be prohibited."

Fraser, Hugh. *Principles and Practices of the Law of Libel and Slander.* 7th ed. Edited by Gerald Osborne Slade and Neville Faulks. London, Butterworth, 1937. 371p.　**F 277**
Standard treatise on both civil and criminal libel, first published in 1889, and continuing the efforts of Starkie and Folkard.

———. "The Privileges of the Press in Relation to the Law of Libel." *Law Quarterly Review*, 7:158–73, April 1891.　**F 278**
Discussion of special defenses open to a defendant under British statutory law in an action of libel contained in a newspaper or other periodical publication. Special attention is given to reporting of Parliamentary proceedings, court proceedings, and other public meetings.

Fraser, R. B. "Free Speech and Thin Skins." *Maclean's Magazine*, 66:5, 74, 15 March 1953. **F 279**
Radio censorship in Canada.

———. "Our Hush-Hush Censorship: How Books Are Banned." *Maclean's Magazine*, 62:24–25, 44, 15 December 1949. **F 280**
Canadian censorship.

"Frederick Palmer Explains 'Mysteries' of the American Censorship in France." *Editor and Publisher*, 50:5–6, 27, 16 February 1918. **F 281**
Military censorship in World War I.

Fredericks, Pierce G. "Censored." *Park East*, 12(5):10–11, April 1951. **F 282**
"About Huntington Cairns, T-Man extraordinary, who sifts art from pornography for the U.S. Customs."

"Free Air or Hot Air? FCC Ruling on Editorializing and Free Speech." *Commonweal*, 50:334–36, 15 July 1949. **F 283**

"Free Press and Fair Trial." *Quill*, 52(2):8–14, February 1964. **F 284**
A symposium on limits to pretrial newspaper coverage, in light of the ban on electronic coverage of the Jack Ruby trial in Texas.

[Free Press Association, New York]. "Constitution of the Free Press Association." *Correspondent*, 1:63–64, 17 February 1827. **F 285**
This Association was founded 29 January 1827 in New York to give support to a press which, without fear of political party, private interest, or public opinion, would report the truth in all realms of knowledge. The preamble charges that books in libraries contribute to darkness rather than provide illumination; the work of journalists reflects the influence of party and private interests rather than public good.

Free Press Defence Committee, London. *The Bedborough Case*. London, The Committee, 1898. 7 p. (Also in *Adult*, August 1898) **F 286**
The Committee was formed to support the defense of Mr. Bedborough in the sale of Havelock Ellis' book, *Sexual Inversion*. Henry Seymour was honorary secretary. The Committee raised funds and held meetings, which the press ignored. Bedborough subsequently pleaded guilty and the Committee withdraw its support. An eight-page general and financial report was also issued bearing the title *Bedborough Case—Balance Sheet*.

Free Press Persecution; or, The Steel Trust Alarmed; Information Charging "Seditious and Criminal Libel" against the Alleged Committee in Charge of the Free Press. New Castle, Pa., Free Press Publishing Co. [1910]. 31 p. **F 287**
A seditious libel case against McCarthy, Flannigan, and others in an industrial dispute.

"Free Speech Anarchist." *Secular Thought*, 23:310–13, September 1907. **F 288**
Criticism of Theodore A. Schroeder's advocacy of freedom for sex discussion.

"Free Speech and Its Enemies." *Case and Comment*, 22:471–75, November 1915. **F 289**
Favorable commentary on the work of the Free Speech League and its efforts in behalf of Moses Harman, indicted on an obscenity charge.

"Free Speech and Movies." *Commonweal*, 73:495–96, 10 February 1961. **F 290**
Editorial comment on the decision of the U.S. Supreme Court in *Times Film Corp. v. Chicago*, objecting to prior restraint. "With Justice Warren and the other dissenters, we fear that the power to withhold a license from a film—or a book or anything else—without the necessity to show cause or even give a reason, is not in the best interests of a healthy democracy."

Free Speech League. *Free Speech: Self-Evident Truths about It, by Many Authors*. New York, The League, 1916. 20 p. **F 291**
This small pamphlet reprints excerpts on freedom of speech and the press from such prominent men as Lincoln Steffens, Felix Adler, Robert Louis Stevenson, Wendell Phillips, William Lloyd Garrison, T. B. Macaulay, Sir Oliver Lodge, Herbert Spencer, Sir Leslie Stephen, Rev. Robert Hall, and Leonard Abbott.

"Free Speech Suppressed." *Independent*, 70:807–8, 13 April 1911. **F 292**
Reference to the forced resignation of Professor Banks from the University of Florida for his article, "A Semi-Centennial View of Secession."

"Free Speech v. Fair Trial in English and American Law of Contempt by Publication." *University of Chicago Law Review*, 17:540–53, Spring 1950. **F 293**

"Free State Censorship." *New Statesman*, 31:632–33, 1 September 1928. **F 294**
With a sense of irony the ministers of the Irish Free State issued a text of the Censorship of Publications Bill on the same day that Yeats and Shaw were honored with literary awards at the Tailteann Games. The ecclesiastical authorities are the principal backers of the

censorship bill and their main object is to prevent advice on artificial birth control.

Freedman, Edward. "*Equal Time*"—Then and Now. Columbia, Mo., Freedom of Information Center, School of Journalism, University of Missouri, 1960. 8 p. (Publication no. 23) **F 295**
An effort has been made to present an objective view of the attitude of both industry and government toward "equal time" legislation.

Freedman, Norman J. "Fair Trial—Freedom of the Press." *Osgoode Hall Law Journal*, 3:52–75, April 1964. **F 296**
The article considers the American and Canadian views in an attempt to resolve "this inevitable conflict" between the bar and the press. Legislation should be enacted to the effect that "after an accused has been arrested the press may only publish the bare facts of arrest and charge, along with any procedural abuses which they may discover . . . At trial, the press should be able to accurately report the trial but without comment on the merits till after the verdict."

Freedman, Warren. "News Media Coverage of Criminal Cases and the Right to a Fair Trial." *Nebraska Law Review*, 40:391–412, April 1961. **F 297**
The author concludes, after a review of the conflict between the concepts of a fair trial and freedom of the press, that the courts must resolve the conflict "in such a way as to satisfy a maximum of human wants with a minimum of sacrifice of others."

"Freedom in Radio." *Education by Radio*, 9:32–40, December 1939. **F 298**
A history of the development of freedom for American broadcasting, beginning with David Sarnoff's speech before the First National Conference on Educational Broadcasting, continuing with the adoption of the industry code of self-regulation in 1939, and concluding with the controversy over the question: Is radio so different from other media of communications that it needs to be treated differently?

Freedom of Communication. 30 min., b/w movie. Bloomington, Ind., National Educational Television and Radio Center, University of Indiana. (Essentials of Freedom Series) **F 299**

"Freedom of Communications." *Public Opinion Quarterly*, 10:85–92, Spring 1946. **F 300**
"In the following extracts from a panel discussion held under the auspices of the American Association for the United Nations and the Commission to Study the Organization of Peace, leading spokesmen of the newspaper and radio industries express the conventional concept of their limited obligation: 'When you report the facts and report full

information honestly, you have done your job in either press or radio.'" Discussion, under the chairmanship of David Sarnoff, chairman of the board of N.B.C., included the following panel members: A. A. Schechter (M.B.S.), Francis J. Starzel (AP), Lyman Bryson (C.B.S.), Harry Flory (UP), and Robert Saudek (A.B.C.).

"Freedom of Expression in a Commercial Context." *Harvard Law Review*, 78: 1191–1211, April 1965.   **F 301**
"This Note first examines the protection afforded political expression by a business enterprise or union, and then turns to the first amendment limitations on regulation of advertising, private economic elections, and picketing."

"Freedom of Film and Press." *Christian Century*, 55:136–37, 2 February 1938.
                                                    F 302
Discusses the ban of *March of Time* by the Chicago Motion Picture Board under the control of the police commissioner, noting the dangers of police censorship of news.

"Freedom of Information." *Free World*, 8:164–69, August 1944; 8:219–29, September 1944; 8:433–36, November 1944.
                                                    F 303
A series of articles urging international guarantees for freedom of the press, published on the occasion of the forthcoming UN conference on freedom of information. Includes articles by Kent Cooper, president of the Associated Press (he urges a free press as a means of removing the causes of war); James L. Fly, chairman of the Federal Communications Commission; Under-Secretary of State Sumner Wells; Christopher Chancellor, manager of Reuter's news agency; and Hugh Baille, president of the United Press.

"Freedom of Information: A New Program of Study and Work." *U.N. Bulletin*, 13:457–65, 15 November 1952.   **F 304**
A summary of the work of the Third Committee (Social, Humanitarian, and Cultural) of the UN General Assembly, considering the draft convention on freedom of information, including the attitudes of the various delegates toward aspects of freedom, censorship, codes of ethics, war propaganda, and false news.

Freedom of Information Center Publications. Columbia, Mo., Freedom of Information Center, School of Journalism, University of Missouri, 1958–date. Irregular.   **F 305**
Each publication deals with a separate topic related to freedom of information. Publication no. 00 (November 1958) contains a brief chronology of the Freedom of Information idea taken from the files of Hugh Boyd, publisher, *Home News*, New Brunswick, N.J., a member of the National Editorial Association's Freedom of Information Committee, 1952–53. The account closes with a resolution of the Association to establish a Freedom of Information Center at the University of Missouri "for the purpose of advancing the right of the people to know and be informed through all means of communications, printed,

oral, and visual." Nancy Baker describes the work of the Center in the *ALA Bulletin*, June 1965. Publications of the Center are listed in this bibliography under individual authors.

Freedom of Information Conference. University of Missouri. School of Journalism. *Speeches, First Annual Freedom of Information Conference . . . , December 11–12, 1958.* Columbia, Mo., Freedom of Information Center, School of Journalism, University of Missouri, 1959. 57p. **F 306**
Contents: Freedom of Information: A Ten-Year-Old Prodigy by James S. Pope; What You Don't Know Won't Hurt You by Samuel J. Archibald; The Great American Jury by Murray Snyder; Books and Censorship by Dan Lacy; Do Access Laws Serve the Public Interest? by Coleman A. Harwell; Access in the Age of Electronic Journalism by Howard Bell; New Horizon for Press Photography If . . . by Joseph Costa; A Look Ahead by J. Russell Wiggins.

———. *Speeches, Second Annual Freedom of Information Conference . . ., November 5–6, 1959.* Columbia, Mo., Freedom of Information Center, School of Journalism, University of Missouri, 1960. 42p.
                                                    F 307
Contents: Censorship by Terror by Jules Dubois; The American School Textbook and the Freedom to Know by W. MacLean Johnson; Ohio's Open Doors by Charles A. Mosher; The Right to Advertise by C. James Proud; Broadcasting: A Panorama of Challenges by Vincent T. Wasilewski; Which Way the Press of Uncommitted Countries? by Boleslaw Wierzbianski; Harold L. Cross: Arch Foe of Secrecy by James S. Pope.

———. *Speeches, Third Annual Freedom of Information Conference . . ., November 17–18, 1960.* Columbia, Mo., Freedom of Information Center, School of Journalism, University of Missouri, 1961. 48p.
                                                    F 308
Contents: Secrecy in Federal Government by V. M. Newton, Jr.; Oh, Touch Not the Press by O. R. Stackbein; Privacy Intrudes on Public Education by Robert Finkelstein; The Hennings Committee and Freedom of Information: 1955 to 1960 by Charles H. Slayman, Jr.; Exegesis of the Danish Study Circle by Vincent Naeser; Toward Closer Cooperation Between the Journalists of the Western Hemisphere by Nicholas Pentcheff; Now, After the Election by Kenneth G. Crawford; The Philosophy of the Right to Know by Herbert Brucker.

———. *Speeches, Fourth Annual Freedom of Information Conference . . ., November 2–3, 1961.* Columbia, Mo., Freedom of Information Center, School of Journalism, University of Missouri, 1962. 64p. (Sponsored by the School of Journalism and School of Law)   **F 309**

Contents: Criminal Procedure by Frank J. Remington; Contempt by Publication and the First Amendment by John W. Oliver; The Right to Privacy by Leon Green; Access to Judicial Records by Albert M. Spradling; Executive Privilege and Discovery against the Government by Harry Blanton; The Bill of Rights—Its Relationship to a Criminal Trial by William H. Becker.

———. *Speeches, Fifth Annual Freedom of Information Conference . . ., November 15, 16, 19, 1962.* Columbia, Mo., Freedom of Information Center, School of Journalism, University of Missouri, 1963. 30p.   **F 310**
Contents: Between Old Europe and New America by Lewis Galantiere (Free Europe Committee); Gathering News in Latin America by Henry W. Goethals; . . . Twenty-three Years in the State Department by Lincoln White; High-Level Handouts and the Responsibility of a Free Press by Clark R. Mollenhoff; Vietnam: Underdeveloped Freedom to Know by Nguyen Thai.

———. *Speeches, Sixth Annual Freedom of Information Conference . . ., November 7–8, 1963.* Columbia, Mo., Freedom of Information Center, School of Journalism, University of Missouri, 1964. 41p.
                                                    F 311
Contents: Censors and Their Tactics by Jack Nelson; Freedom from Filth by Joseph L. Badaracco (Citizens for Decent Literature); Where the Real Power Lies (textbook selection) by Campbell Hughes; Do Teachers Encroach on the Students' Right to Read? by Mrs. Enid M. Olson; How Good Can Better Books Be? by Robert C. McNamara, Jr. (textbook publisher); The First Manner of Freedom (student reading) by Harold B. Allen.

———. *Speeches, Seventh Annual Freedom of Information Conference . . ., November 16–17, 1964.* Columbia, Mo., Freedom of Information Center, School of Journalism, University of Missouri, 1965. 32p. (Sponsored by the Motion Picture Association of America and the Freedom of Information Center)   **F 312**
Contents: The Harold L. Cross Memorial Lecture by Michael V. DiSalle; Freedom and American Films Overseas by Gordon Stulberg; The Film Industry and Self-Regulation by Geoffrey Shurlock; The Artist and Film Freedom by Tippi Hedren; The Screen Writer and Freedom by Michael Blankfort; The Legal Aspects of Freedom and Film by Barbara Scott.

"Freedom of Speech and Group Libel Statutes." *Bill of Rights Review*, 1:221–25, Spring 1941.   **F 313**

Group libel laws such as the New Jersey law which prohibits false racial propaganda, jeopardize freedom of legitimate expression of opinion. "It might be preferable to bear the mad harangues of bigots rather than to extend the criminal law so that it might in the future become an instrument of oppression."

"Freedom of Speech and of the Press; Guaranteed by the Constitution of the United States and of the Several states." *Niles Register*, 49:236–37, 5 December 1835. (Reprinted from the *Richmond Compiter*) **F 314**
An extract from the Constitution of the United States and the several states showing that "no law can constitutionally be passed for the purpose of restraining the fanatics of the north in their crusade against our rights."

"Freedom of Speech and of the Press—Prerequisite for Damage Awards to Public Officials Resulting from Defamatory Falsehoods Concerning Their Official Conduct." *Iowa Law Review*, 50:170–76, Fall 1964. **F 315**
Concerning *New York Times Co. v. Sullivan*, 84 Sup. Ct. 710 (1964).

"Freedom of Speech and Press—Federal Statute Authorizes Post Office to Detain Communist Political Propaganda unless Addressee Requests Delivery." *Harvard Law Review*, 77:1165–70, April 1964. **F 316**
A review of the statute which authorizes detention of mail, other than sealed letters, which originates in a foreign country and is found to be Communist political propaganda. The author considers the act a violation of the First Amendment.

The Freedom of Speech and Writing upon Public Affairs Considered; with an Historical View of the Roman Imperial Laws against libels . . . With Observations on the Proper Use of the Liberty of the Press, and Its Abuses, Particularly of Late with Respect to the Colonies; and a Brief State of their Origin and Political Nature, Collected from Various Acts of Princes and Parliaments. London, S. Barker, 1766. 160 p. **F 317**
English libel laws, the author believes, were in a measure drawn from the unfavorable Roman imperial laws. He traces the persecution for free expression from Roman times to eighteenth-century England, describing the work of the Star Chamber, the action against Prynne, Leighton, and Lilburne, and the recent press restrictions on the Colonies.

"Freedom of Speech, Press, and Assemblage." *Canadian Congress Journal*, 17:9, March 1938. **F 318**

Editorial on freedom of the press in Canada, with reference to the Alberta law "to ensure the publication of accurate news and information."

"Freedom of Speech—Prior Restraint on Motion Picture Exhibition." *Vanderbilt Law Review*, 14:1525–32, October 1961. **F 319**
Review of *Times Film Corp. v. City of Chicago*, 365 U.S. 43 (1961). "Considering the dangers to free speech inherent in pre-censorship, it is suggested that the state has failed to bear the heavy burden of proof which would warrant prior restraint in an area designated by the Supreme Court as a 'significant medium for the communication of ideas.'"

"Freedom of Speech: Whose Concern?" *New Republic*, 18:102–4, 22 February 1919. **F 320**
Freedom of speech would be supported by conservatives as well as liberals if they understood the long-range implications.

"Freedom of the Air." *Nation*, 119:90–91, 23 July 1924. **F 321**
Three short articles: Uncensored and Uncontrolled by David Sarnoff; Radio Control by Grover A. Whalen; and Radio—the Fulcrum by Hudson Maxim. Sarnoff states that "the danger to freedom of speech by radio is not the danger that any one interest will ever be able to monopolize the air. The real danger is in censorship, in over-regulation." Whalen believes that radio broadcasting should be free in every respect from control by private corporation, that any control should be by the government. "Broadcasting should be as free as the air through which the sound waves are impelled, except for such government control as may be necessary and advisable." Maxim confesses to being puzzled concerning the control of radio. "I distrust the wisdom of allowing radio broadcasting to be controlled by any private monopoly, but I also distrust the wisdom and the ability and the justice of federal control of radio."

"Freedom of the Films." *Spectator*, 154:109–10, January 1935. Reply by Ronald Kidd, *Spectator*, 154:209, 8 February 1935. **F 322**
Discusses the deputation for more adequate control of motion pictures made to the Prime Minister by a group headed by the Archbishop of Canterbury. The deputation favors a broad inquiry. Ronald Kidd of the National Council for Civil Liberties asks why censorship should be extended to noninflammable films when the original justification for censorship was on grounds of public safety from fire.

"Freedom of the Press?" *Grassroots Editor*, 5(1):20, January 1964. (Translated from German text editorial, *Belleviller Zeitung*, Belleville, Ill., 5 September 1861) **F 323**
The editor complains of the suppression of several Northern newspapers and the revocation of mailing privileges of others accused

of supporting the Southern rebellion. Such administrative action is illegal and unconstitutional; charges of treason should be handled by the courts.

"Freedom of the Press." *Literary Magazine and American Register*, 5:243–46, April 1806. **F 324**
Comments on the folly and futility of censorship, with reference largely to the Catholic *Index*. A bookseller's plot to burn Erasmus' *Colloquies* in order to increase the sale (it sold 24,000 copies) is also mentioned. "The worst abuse of the press is more tolerable than would be such a violation of liberty." The author advises leaving the culminators of falsehoods to their own fate.

"Freedom of the Press." *New Statesman*, 27:4–5, 17 April 1926. **F 325**
Answer to critics who charge that an English newspaper has no right to criticize the internal affairs of another country. Reference is made to criticism of the Fascist regime in Italy.

"Freedom of the Press." *New Statesman*, 27:116–17, 15 May 1926. **F 326**
The writer considers as indefensible the General Council of the Trade Union Congress' refusal to set tpye in an attempt to suppress a newspaper with which they disagree.

"Freedom of the Press?" *North American Review*, 208:702–9, November 1918. **F 327**
Republished under title "Muzzling the Press," in *La Follette's Magazine*, December 1918. Describes some aspects of war censorship.

"Freedom of the Press." *Survey*, 24:365–68, 4 June 1910. **F 328**
The founding of the *Boston Common*, a weekly newspaper published by a cooperative company, occasioned this supporting editorial which noted the widespread distortion, misinterpretation, and suppression of news in much of the daily press. "Until the ideal and perfectly free daily is founded, we shall have to read more than one newspaper and check up the gaps in their news by a combination of weeklies and monthlies none of which has space for all the facts about everything."

Freedom of the Press. 51 frame, b/w filmstrip. New York, Office of Educational Activities, New York Times Co. **F 329**

Freedom of the Press. 16 mm., b/w movie, 17 min. New York, United World Films. Produced by the U.S. Information Agency. **F 330**
A historical review of freedom of the press in America, from the famous Zenger trial to modern times.

Freedom of the Press. 5-inch phonotape, 30 min. Boulder, Colo., National Tape Repository, University of Colorado. (Jeffersonian Heritage Series) **F 331**

Thomas Jefferson (played by actor Claude Rains) discusses the development of freedom of the press in the United States.

Freedom of the Press and Biblical Christianity Re-considered: by a Bible Christian. Lodiana, 1859. 23 p.　**F 332**
Listed in Schroeder's *Free Speech Bibliography.* Copy not located.

"Freedom of the Press—Nuisance—Power of State to Enjoin Publication of Newspaper as Public Nuisance." *Minnesota Law Review*, 14:787–98, June 1930.　**F 333**
Notes on the case of *State ex rel. Olson v. Guilford* (1928) in which the Supreme Court of Minnesota held that a statute declaring a newspaper regularly engaged in publishing malicious and scandalous material to constitute a nuisance and enjoinable as such was not an abridgment of freedom of the press. The decision was ultimately reversed by the U.S. Supreme Court.

"Freedom of the Press to Publish Reports of Current Judicial Proceedings." *Yale Law Journal*, 45:360–63, December 1935.　**F 334**

"Freedom of the Press: Topics of the Day." *Dalhousie Review*, 17:510–13 January 1938.　**F 335**
Discussion of the Quebec padlock law and Aberhart's attempt to limit freedom of the press in Alberta.

"Freedom of the Press Vindicated." *Harper's Magazine*, 57:293–98, July 1878.
　F 336
A dramatic report of the Zenger trial.

"Freedom to Read." *Times Literary Supplement*, 3196:389, 31 May 1963.
　F 337
The article attempts to answer questions posed by a reader: Who lists the books British customs officials are instructed to confiscate from British citizens returning from abroad? By what legal authority? Who lists the books Post Office officials are entitled to confiscate?

Freedom to Read. 16 mm., b/w movie, 14 min. New York, Center for Mass Communication, Columbia University Press, 1954.　**F 338**
A librarian upholds the right of the public library to provide books on all aspects of controversial issues against censorship pressures in the community. The film was produced to stimulate civic and classroom debate during Columbia University's bicentennial celebration.

[Freeland, Edward B.]. "The Freedom of the Press." *Continental Monthly*, 4: 361–67, October 1863.　**F 339**

"The government has seen fit at various times, through its authorities, civil and military, to suppress the circulation and even the publishing of journals, which, in its judgment, give aid and comfort to the enemy." The author approves of wartime censorship if it is not despotic. He calls for restraint in public criticism in time of crisis. "The *political* liberty which [the political leaders] possess of free thought and free speech, has imposed upon them the *moral* duty of using this wisely for the welfare of humanity." References are made to a convention of editors, headed by Horace Greeley, to consider the government's policy on press censorship.

Freeman, A. C. "Enjoining the Publication of Libels." *Central Law Journal*, 4:171–73, 23 February 1877.　**F 340**
A general review of the legal history of enjoining the publication of libel in Great Britain and the United States. The author deplores the presence of small publications in both countries that carry on a business of blackmail, and pleads for laws and decisions to put them out of business. He disagrees with the court rulings that equity has no jurisdiction to restrain the publication of a libel, even though its publication threatens to prove ruinous to reputation and property of the person libeled.

Freeman, Alden, *comp. Fight for Free Speech. A Supplement to "Law-Breaking by the Police." Including a Legal Opinion by Theodore Schroeder, Attorney for the Free Speech League.* East Orange, N.J., The Author, 1909. 36 p.　**F 341**
Freeman was a Mayflower descendent who became aroused over police treatment in suppressing anarchist Emma Goldman's speech in East Orange, N.J. He compiled this collection of addresses, news stories, quotations, and editorials for use by workers in a campaign for free speech.

———. *The Suppression of Free Speech in New York and New Jersey. Being a True Account of an Eye Witness of Law-Breaking by the Police Department of New York City . . . May 23, 1909. By the City Authorities of East Orange . . . June 8, 1909 . . . Together with the Full Text of the Suppressed Lecture by Emma Goldman and the Address of Leonard Abbott and Alden Freeman at the Thomas Paine Centenary . . .* East Orange, N.J., The Author, 1909. 28 p.　**F 342**

Freeman, Marilla W. "Censorship in the Large Public Library." *Library Journal*, 53:221–24, 1 March 1928.　**F 343**
It is the duty of the public librarian to furnish important material on every side of a question engaging public attention, including thought in fictional form. Includes statement on how large public libraries, particularly the Cleveland Public Library, handle controversial books.

Freethinker's Convention. *Proceedings and Addresses at the Freethinker's Convention Held at Watkins, N.Y. August 22d, 23d, 24th, and 25th, '78.* New York, D. M. Bennett, 1878. 398 p.　**F 344**
Much of the convention discussion concerned freedom of speech; a resolution was adopted calling for repeal of the obscenity laws. During the convention D. M. Bennett, W. S. Bell, and Josephine S. Tilton were arrested for selling Ezra Heywood's *Cupid's Yokes.*

Frend, William. *An Account of the Proceedings in the University of Cambridge, against William Frend . . . for Publishing a Pamphlet, Intitled Peace and Union &c Containing the Proceedings in Jesus College, the Trial in the Vice Chanceller's Court, and in the Court of Delegates.* Cambridge, Eng., Published by the Defendant; Printed by B. Flower, 1793. 262 p. (Also in Howell, *State Trials*, vol. 22, pp. 523 ff.)　**F 345**
Frend, a fellow of Jesus College, Cambridge, published a pamphlet entitled *Peace and Union recommended to the Associated Bodies of Republicans and Anti-Republicans*, which college authorities found objectionable and seditious. After a lengthy trial in the Court of Vice-Chancellor, Frend was "banished" from the University. Appeals to the Court of Delegates and the Court of King's Bench were unsuccessful.

Freston, Edwin. "Prior Restraint of Motion Pictures." *Southern California Law Review*, 34:362–66, Spring 1961.　**F 346**
Notes on the case, *Times Film Corporation v. City of Chicago*, 1961.

Freund, Ernst. "Freedom of Speech and Press." *New Republic*, 25:344–46, 16 February 1921.　**F 347**
Criticism of the juridical status of free speech, inspired by Zechariah Chafee's book on the subject.

———. *The Police Power, Public Policy and Constitutional Rights.* Chicago, Callaghan, 1904. 819 p.　**F 348**
A discussion of the inherent power of the government to protect the general welfare, including control of advertising and obscene publications.

Friedenthal, Jack H., and Richard J. Medalie. "The Impact of Federal Regulation on Political Broadcasting: Section 315 of the Communications Act." *Harvard Law Review*, 72:445–93, January 1959.
　F 349

"The authors re-examine the statutory requirement that equal opportunities to broadcast be given to candidates for public office. They analyze the problems involved in determining what constitutes equal opportunities, to whom and when they must be afforded, and the difficulties that state defamation law creates. Judicial and agency interpretations of section 315 [equal time provision] are criticized and various statutory changes suggested."

Friedman, Joel. "Music on Networks Gets Scissors; Sex Is Not Here to Stay." *Billboard*, 68:1+, 9 June 1956. **F 350**
"The broadcast industry has evolved a system of self-regulated censorship of music which appears to be an intelligent approach to a generally sensitive subject." With the influx of rock and roll, network censors are keeping a cautious ear for material that might corrupt the young.

Friedman, Jon L. "A New Approach to Obscenity." *University of Pittsburgh Law Review*, 19:166–73, Fall 1957. **F 351**
"It is the purpose of this note to examine and analyze the previous tests [of obscenity] and attempt to predict whether or not the present test [model Penal Code as used in *Roth v. United States*] will be an improvement over its predecessors." The author finds that the present test has eliminated most of the weaknesses in earlier tests and has greater flexibility and adaptability to the varying customs of society.

[Friedman, Samuel]. "Constitutional Law—Motion Picture Censorship." *Brooklyn Law Review*, 26:112–17, December 1959. **F 352**
Notes on the decision of the U.S. Supreme Court in the case of the refusal of a license to the movie, *Lady Chatterley's Lover*, by the Motion Picture Division of the New York Educational Department. The Court held that censorship may not constitutionally be imposed upon a motion picture, solely because acts of sexual immorality are therein presented as acceptable or desirable behavoir. (*Kingsley Corp. v. Regents*, 360 U.S. 684).

Friedrich, Carl J. "The FCC 'Monopoly' Report; a Critical Appraisal." *Public Opinion Quarterly*, 4:526–32, September 1940. **F 353**
A critique of the report of the FCC investigations of chain broadcasting, by the director of Harvard's Radiobroadcasting Research Project.

————, and Jeannette Sayre Smith. *An Analysis of the Radiobroadcasting Activities of the Federal Agencies.* Cambridge, Mass., Littauer Center, Harvard University, 1940. 118 p. (Radiobroadcasting Research Project. Studies in the Control of Radio, no. 3) **F 354**
A selection of excerpts from testimony before government agencies, private conversations, and comments from industry sources, involving social aspects of broadcasting control.

————. *Controlling Broadcasting in Wartime: a Tentative Public Policy.* Cambridge, Mass., Littauer Center, Harvard University, 1940. 34 p. (Radiobroadcasting Research Project. Studies in the Control of Radio, no. 2) **F 355**
The report recommends leaving the control of wartime radio in the hands of private owners, subject to necessary military censorship. It also recommends a federal agency be established to control government broadcasts.

————. *The Development of the Control of Advertising on the Air.* Cambridge, Mass., Littauer Center, Harvard University, 1940. 39 p. (Radiobroadcasting Research Project. Studies in the Control of Radio, no. 1) **F 356**
The history of control of radio advertising from 1922, when the first national conference on broadcasting endorsed advertising as a source of income for radio, to 1939 when the National Association of Broadcasters adopted the code for good taste in advertising and placed the responsibility for censorship on the local station or network.

Friedrich, Carl J., and Evelyn Sternberg. "Congress and the Control of Radio Broadcasting." *American Political Science Review*, 37:797–818, October 1943; 37:1014–26, December 1943. **F 357**
"In general, the record is one of confused efforts to 'regulate' a very young industry in response to a multitude of complaints and pressures, but with no real understanding of the situation." The authors recommend that a regular committee of Congress devote its entire time to communication problems. Conclusions of a Harvard research study on radio broadcasting.

————. *Congress and the Control of Radiobroadcasting.* Cambridge, Mass., Littauer Center, Harvard University, 1944. 35 p. (Radiobroadcasting Research Project. Studies in the Control of Radio, no. 5) **F 358**
Discusses Congress as a law-making agency (Radio Act and Federal Communications Act), its relations with the FCC, including monopoly control, public service responsibilities, and censorship. Various references are made to Congressional investigations of the broadcast industry.

A Friend to Harmony, *pseud. Candid Consideration on Libels . . . With Some Observations on the Liberty of the Press.* Boston, Freeman & Andrews, 1789. 22 p. **F 359**

Friends to the Liberty of the Press. *Proceedings of the Friends to [sic] the Liberty of the Press on December, the 22d, 1792 and January 19th, and March 9th, 1793.* London, Printed by order of the Committee, 1793. 22 p. **F 360**
On the eve of the trial of Thomas Paine's *Rights of Man* (1792), a retired colonel formed the Association for Preservation of Liberty and Property against Republicans and Levellers. This right wing group was intended to combat the efforts of the various English reform societies that had been organized to correspond with French revolutionists. The aim of the Association was to bring seditious activities to the attention of authorities and to see to it that such activities were prosecuted. On 22 December, a few days after Thomas Erskine's valiant but unsuccessful defense of Thomas Paine's *Rights of Man*, a group, not sympathetic with the radical activities of the French revolutionists but concerned with freedom of the press in England, met in Mason's Tavern. The meeting, chaired by Gerard Noel Edwards, passed a resolution affirming the historic English right of a free press and free discussion of public issues. It also protested against the current sedition prosecutions and the vigilante activities of certain societies that have "held out general terrors against the circulation of writings, which, without describing them, they term Seditious." The resolution paid tribute to the contribution of Thomas Erskine in behalf of freedom of the press in recent trials. At the second meeting, 19 January, Erskine himself delivered an eloquent address in defense of a free press, which was subsequently adopted as the Declaration of the Friends to the Liberty of the Press and was signed by more than 500 persons. At the third meeting on 9 March, with R. B. Sheridan as chairman, the group decided to distribute 10,000 copies of the Declaration and to serve as a clearing house for information on cases of persecution for circulation of seditious papers.

————. *The Resolutions of the First Meeting of the Friends to [sic] the Liberty of the Press, December 19th, 1792. Also the Declaration of the Second Meeting, January 22nd, 1793, Written by the Hon. Thomas Erskine; to Which Is Added A Letter to Mr. Reeves, Chairman of The Association for Preserving Liberty and Property; by Thomas Law . . .* London, Printed for J. Ridgway, 1793. 27 p. (Reprinted with introduction in *Erskine's Speeches*, vol. 4, pp. 411–46) **F 361**
Thomas Law, a member of the Association for Preserving Liberty and Property, objects to the Association's undemocratic methods in combating alledged sedition. It was the questionable activities of this group that led to the formation of the Friends to the Liberty of the Press. The dates of the Friends' meetings

given in this pamphlet vary slightly from the official printing (above), which is probably correct.

Froeschle, Ferd. "Freedom of Information Becomes Law After Legislators Hear Case Stated." *Quill*, 45(10):17–18, October 1957. **F 362**
The press in North Dakota sponsors a new law guaranteeing freedom of access to public records.

Frohlick, Louis D., and Charles Schwartz. *The Law of Motion Pictures including the Law of the Theatre* . . . New York, Baker and Voorhis, 1918. 943 p. **F 363**
An early casebook on motion picture law, now largely of historic interest. Sections 115–16 deal with Regulation Amounting to Prohibition, and Prohibition—Immorality; section 119 deals with Censorship. The work summarizes the law and gives a digest of cases.

"Front Page Revolution." *Time*, 26(10):51–52, 2 September 1935. **F 364**
A news account of the antisedition bill passed by the Alabama legislature and repealed during the same session after the editor of the Dothan *Eagle* suggested that citizens arm themselves with shillalahs and "whale Hell out of members of the Alabama Legislature" for their action.

Frost, B. John. "Some Thoughts on Censorship and Youth." *Library Journal*, 70:792–93, 15 September 1945. **F 365**
The solution to the problem of book selection is to apply to a book the question, "Is it of such nature that it tends to weaken or destroy our Christian concepts of morality?" The author, librarian of St. Charles Boys' Home, Milwaukee, believes that "character [is] so malleable that a man can be depraved through reading a book." Leaders of the Church are justified in protecting the faith and morals of their faith, as is done in the Catholic Church by the *Index of Forbidden Books*.

Frost, S. E., Jr. *Is American Radio Democratic?* Chicago, University of Chicago Press, 1937. 234 p. **F 366**
A study of the American system of radio regulation, control, and operation as related to the democratic way of life, with emphasis on its educational aspects. Chapter 2 deals with federal regulation of aural broadcasting in the United States. The author finds that the present American system makes possible much that can be judged democratic, but its commercial foundation makes impossible a fairly reasonable advance in this direction. "Private profit, censorship for commercial ends, a dictatorial selection of program material, among other things make inevitable the subordination of public welfare to private or corporate gain and a resultant warping of the individual both in thinking and in action." Recommendations are made for revisions in the regulatory laws to lessen the station owner's power of dictatorial censorship and

to open radio to a broader discussion of public issues. Based on the author's doctoral dissertation.

[Frothingham, David]. "Trial of David Frothingham, for a Libel on General Hamilton, 1799." (In Wharton, *State Trials of the United States*, pp. 649–51) **F 367**
Frothingham was fined and sentenced to four years in prison for publication of a libel against Alexander Hamilton in his newspaper, *Argus*.

Frothingham, Octavius B. "The Suppression of Vice." *North American Review*, 135:489–95, November 1882. **F 368**
A noted Unitarian minister of Boston states his opposition to censorship activities of vice societies. (1) Vice societies are belligerants, not judicial bodies, yet they pretend to perform judicial tasks; (2) they are sectarians who wish to impose their notions of blasphemy, infidelity, and obscenity on others; (3) their methods of attack have kept many infamous books alive that would have otherwise died; and (4) the sources of corruption will be dried up only so fast as common enlightenment proceeds. Anthony Comstock and J. M. Buckley comment on the subject in the same issue.

Fry, John. *The Accuser sham'd; or A Pair of Bellows to blow off that Dust cast upon John Fry, a Member of Parliament . . . By the Accused J. J.* London, John Harris, 1648. (Case summarized in Schroeder, *Constitutional Free Speech*, pp. 272–75) **F 369**
Fry was accused in Parliament of publishing two books, *The Clergy in their Colors* and *The Bellows*, which were attacks against "Doctrine and assertions of the true Religion." The books were ordered burnt and Fry "disabled to sit as a Member of this House" of Parliament.

Frye, Northrop. "Dr. Kinsey and the Dream Censor." *Canadian Forum*, 28:85–86, July 1948. **F 370**
The author uses the threat of censorship of the Kinsey report in Canada to attack censorship in general. "Censorship and democracy don't mix, and there is no argument in favor of censorship that does not assume an anti-democratic social tendency." It is the adult book, the work of the serious author, not the adolescent, titillating work, that has to fight to be read.

Fryer, Peter. *Mrs. Grundy; Studies in English Prudery.* New York, London House and Maxwell, 1964. 368 p. **F 371**
A study of English prudery (interference, organized or unorganized, in other people's pleasures) as it is found in various fields since the Middle Ages. Part 1 deals with the taboos and consequent euphemisms used to express parts of the body, sexual activity, excretion, and certain articles of clothing. The section includes a frank account of the "four-letter

words," their derivation, and their substitutes, including the ban of certain combinations of initials in motor vehicle registration plates. An article based on portions of the book appears in *Horizon*, Spring 1964.

"Full Text of the Cleveland Newspaper Contempt Case. Court of Appeals for Cuyahoga County." *Ohio Law Bulletin and Reporter*, 31:394–412, 24 March 1930. **F 372**

Fuller, Edmund. "Books, Beds and Bromides." *Saturday Review of Literature*, 32(2):6–7, 33, 8 January 1949. **F 373**
The author discusses frankness of sex expression in modern literature, arguing that it should be used sparingly and only when artistically necessary. He disapproves of both censorship and the lack of restraint in modern fiction.

———. "The Post-*Chatterley* Deluge." *Critic*, 20(6):9–13, June–July 1962. **F 374**
This literary critic believes that the freeing of such literary works as *Lady Chatterley's Lover* and *Tropic of Cancer*, has broken the dam of restraint so that a "free invitation is offered to any Tom, Dick and Harry to write with absolute license without the tests of proving themselves which made Joyce, Lawrence, and Miller the men they are, for better or worse. The whole concept of *avant garde* vanishes if no price must be paid for a bold departure from a previous convention." Fuller believes that those who write, edit, and publish must make themselves "the responsible referees of our literary freedom."

Fuller, John. "Cibber, *The Rehearsal at Goatham*, and the Suppression of *Polly*." *Review of English Studies*, 13(n.s.):125–34, May 1962. **F 375**
Presents some hitherto unnoticed material relating to the contemporary belief that Colley Cibber had a hand in the suppression of *Polly*.

Fuller. W. A. "Books in the Dock." *Spectator*, 156:873–74, 15 May 1936. **F 376**
Discussion of a proposal under consideration by the British Publishers' Association and the Authors' Society to set up a new central court, the Obscene Books Commissioner, to settle all disputed issues of obscenity in publications.

Fuller, Walter D. "Freedom for What?" *Vital Speeches*, 7:467–71, 15 May 1941. **F 377**
The president of the National Association of Manufacturers, addressing the National Editorial Association, urges the preservation of a free press as the guardian of American democracy.

[Fuller, William]. *Tryal of W. Fuller, upon an Information for Being an Imposter, and of Ill Name and Reputation; Falsely . . . and Seditiously Contriving . . . to Delude and Deceive, and Discords between Said Late King [William] and his Peers, and the Noblemen of this Kingdom, to Excite and Stir up, by Publishing Two Scandalous Libels, the One Called The Original Letters from the Late King; the Other Called, Twenty-six Depositions of Persons of Quality and Worth . . .* London, I. Cleave, 1702. 13 p. (Also in Howell, *State Trials*, vol. 14, pp. 517 ff.) **F 378**

The House of Lords directed Fuller's imprisonment and trial as a "cheat and imposter." He was found guilty of having published spurious letters from the late King William.

Fulton, E. D. "How Canada Has Dealt with the Comic Book Situation Through Legislation." *Religious Education*, 49: 416–18, November 1954. **F 379**

———. "Problem of the Publication and Distribution of Obscene and Salacious Literature." *Canadian Library Association Bulletin*, 15:111–13, November 1958. **F 380**

Fulton, William. "Social Sciences and the Self-Appointed Censors." *Audio-Visual Instruction*, 9:714, December 1964. **F 381**

Editorial on the growth and power of "well-financed radical dissident groups dedicated to the self-appointed job of censuring and 'book burning' activities." Reference to the John Birch Society and related groups and their activities through the PTA's, the Chambers of Commerce, and other community groups.

Funnye, Doris V. *Book Censorship in America, 1945–1955.* [New York, New York University], 1957. 89 p. (Unpublished Master's thesis) **F 382**

Furnas, J. C. "Moral War in Hollywood." *Fortnightly*, 137(n.s.):73–84, January 1935. **F 383**

A humorous tribute to Will Hays' skill in placating the reformers and at the same time allowing movie producers free rein.

Furneaux, Philip. *Letters to the Honourable Mr. Justice Blackstone, concerning His Exposition of the Act of Toleration, and Some Positions relative to Religious Liberty, in his Celebrated Commentaries on the Laws of England. 2d ed. With Additions, and an Appendix, containing Authentic Copies of the Argument of the late Honourable Mr. Justice Foster in the Court of Judges Delegates, and of the Speech of the Right Honourable Lord Mansfield in the House of Lords, in the Cause between the City of London and the Dissenters.* London, T. Cadell, 1771. 284 p. **F 384**

The Reverend Philip Furneaux was a critic of Blackstone's limited concept of toleration and, according to Theodore A. Schroeder, was responsible for inducing Blackstone to modify his views somewhat. Furneaux believed that a line should be drawn between mere religious principles and those overt acts which might affect the public peace. Only in the latter should civil law take jurisdiction. Punishing a man for the tendency of his principles is punishing him before he is guilty, for fear he should be guilty. The Virginia religious liberty statute is said to be derived largely from Furneaux's work.

"Futility of Censorship." *Nation*, 116: 508, 2 May 1923. (Reprinted in Beman, *Censorship of Speech and the Press*, pp. 466–70) **F 385**

"Behind the efforts to tighten the laws affecting the publication and sale of 'unclean' and otherwise dangerous books are two motives, more or less blurred. One is the honest impulse to protect society, especially the young and the weak from sinful ideas. The other is a perversion or exaggeration of the tendency, which we all have in some degree, to impose our ideas on the other fellow." The article was prompted by Justice John Ford's sponsorship of the "clean-books bill" before the New York Assembly.

G

G., N. "Newspapers in Contempt of Court." *Solicitors' Journal*, 104:135–36, 19 February 1960. **G1**
Relates to the *Scottish Daily Mail* case.

Gabriel, Gilbert W. "Behind the Asbestos Curtain." *Nation*, 174:625–28, 28 June 1952. **G2**
The article is concerned with effects of anti-subversive hysteria on the theater, and on actors, authors, and producers of plays. The author has served for several years as chairman of the Anti-Censorship Committee of the Authors League of America.

Gadgil, Gangadhar. "Report on the Seminar on 'Obscenity in Literature.'" *Quest*, 26:84–85, July–September 1960. **G3**
The seminar was organized under the joint auspices of the I.C.C.F. and the P.E.N. Participants included Smt. Bhagwat, A. R. Wadia, C. C. Shah, Jyotindra Dave, and Madhao Achwal, whose paper is published on pages 19–25 of this issue.

Gaines, Ervin J. "Birchers Denied Access to Brockton Library." *Bay State Librarian*, 53:11–12, April 1953. **G4**

———. "CDL on the Local Scene." *ALA Bulletin*, 59:17–18, January 1965. **G5**
Criticism of the "newly enlarged influence of the Citizens for Decent Literature, which seems to have established a kind of canned doctrine for use in local brouhahas over 'dirty books.'"

———. "Chicago—New Censorship Capital." *ALA Bulletin*, 58:983–84, December 1964. **G6**
A report on recent efforts at censorship of books and magazines in Chicago with evidence that the "current agony" has official sanction and that back of it is the effort of Citizens for Decent Literature and the National Office for Decent Literature. Includes comments by Joseph Faulkner, head of the Chicago Booksellers' committee.

———. "Church, State, and Freedom to Read." *ALA Bulletin*, 59:785–86, October 1965. **G7**
A discussion of charges of censorship against the librarian of the Belleville, Ill., Public Library for rejecting the periodical *Church and State*, which he stated was disqualified under the Library Bill of Rights because it was not "sound factual authority."

———. "The Dangers of Censorship." *ALA Bulletin*, 58:595–96, July–August 1964. **G8**
An answer to the charge of Father Leo F. Petit (p. 590 of the issue) that Gaines, in his column, "brings an absolutist, dogmatic mentality" to the issue of freedom to publish and freedom to read, which is a simple solution but hardly realistic.

———. "Freedom to Read in New Hampshire." *ALA Bulletin*, 57:1009–10, December 1963. **G9**
A recent survey of holdings of New Hampshire libraries indicates many libraries have not purchased titles of such representative modern authors as Mailer, Baldwin, Steinbeck, and Faulkner. The avoidance of many "controversial" novels may be attributed to economic handicaps of small libraries, a conservative intellectual climate, and antiquated obscenity laws.

———. "Legal Defenses for Public Librarians." *ALA Bulletin*, 59:343–44, May 1965. **G10**

———. "The Passionate Pursuit of Pornography." *ALA Bulletin*, 59:99–100, February 1965. **G11**
"The passionate pursuit of pornography keeps opening up in new cities, resembling very much the annual hunting season which features men shooting anything that moves—sometimes even their friends."

———. "The Purpose of Censorship." *ALA Bulletin*, 58:87–89, February 1964. **G12**
The author explores the diametrically opposed positions on censorship held by Father Terrence J. Murphy (*Censorship: Government and Obscenity*) and Alec Craig (*Suppressed Books*). The former holds the classic position in favor of censorship, the latter, a libertarian point of view. Gaines refers to an unresolved thought falling between the two positions, "the imposition of unsolicited materials through flagrant display . . . dubious use of the mails," citing André Gide and Joyce Cary's comments on such invasion of privacy.

———. "Silence, Too, Is a Form of Censorship." *ALA Bulletin*, 58:17–18, January 1964. **G13**
Censorship is seen as a means of preserving the *status quo* by choking off threatening information at the source. The blackout of news represents a conspiracy of silence no less dangerous than suppressing a work after it has been published.

———. "Stubborn Resistance Is Not Enough." *ALA Bulletin*, 57:817–18, October 1963. **G14**
Sheer stubborn resistance to the incursion of censorship, necessary as it is, does not suffice. The library profession should shift the debate to higher ground; should support research to establish the effects of literature on human behavior.

———. "A Substitution and a Suggestion." *ALA Bulletin*, 57:711–12, September 1963. **G15**
The author explores the problem of the librarian and obscenity laws in light of recent court decisions, concluding that despite a more enlightened approach (e.g. Massachusetts recent rulings) "librarians are not free and clear of the danger of arrest, and that it would be wise to find out where they do stand."

———. "Summer Storms in Minnesota." *ALA Bulletin*, 59:693–94, September 1965. **G16**
Recent pressures for and against censorship in Minnesota.

———. "Sunshine on the Vigilant." *ALA Bulletin*, 58:675–76, September 1964. **G17**

The bright sunshine of freedom of the press is seen in the trend toward greater freedom in decisions of the U.S. Supreme Court. Contrasting shadows are seen in the favorable action on a bill in the House of Representatives giving postal authorities powers to interfere with mailing privileges of "immoral" publications. The author criticizes librarians for not taking a more vigorous part in opposing such legislation at local and state levels.

————. "Time for a Defense Fund." *ALA Bulletin*, 58:345–47, May 1964.

G 18

Recommendation that a fund be established to help librarians who are faced with a fight for the freedom to read.

————. "Words and Deeds Are Not Identical." *ALA Bulletin*, 59:605–6, July–August 1965. **G 19**

The U.S. Supreme Court decision to overthrow the Connecticut birth control law has free speech implications. "The significance of laws which attempt to suppress an activity or a behavior pattern by recourse to censorship of information about that activity ought to be the constant concern of librarians."

Gallichan, Walter M. *The Poison of Prudery; an Historical Survey.* Boston, Stratford, 1929. 235 p. **G 20**

In his chapter on Pornography and Prudery the author describes the common mental attitude toward our amative nature as "an unwholesome mixture of Lewdness, Shame, and Prudery," which he believes encourages pornography, "an intellectual and moral poison which spreads like cancer and suicide, with the march of civilization." The disease is not cured by censorship; this only heightens the demand. "Wholesome inquiry is the true remedy for prurience and mere lasciviousness. To educate the mind is to refine it." In the chapter on The Banning of Books he notes that, in attempting to suppress the obscene, the vice societies have often taken action against legitimate studies of sex ethics and sex psychology, the very works which will help to reduce false shame and prudery.

Gallup, Donald. "Some Notes on Ezra Pound and Censorship." *Yale Literary Magazine*, 126(5):37–41, December 1958.

G 21

"At various times in his career, Ezra Pound has run afoul of the censor, particularly in England, where public sensitivity in matters of indecorum and, especially libel, has been refined to a somewhat greater degree than in the United States." The article deals largely with suppression and censorship of Pound's work by his publishers and printers.

Gallup, George. "Set Owners Found against Censorship." *Broadcasting*, 14(4): 40, 15 February 1938. **G 22**

The Gallup poll found that 59 per cent of set owners believe government censorship of programs is harmful; 41 per cent believe it would do good. Only 14 per cent said they had heard a program in the past year that they considered vulgar.

Galphin, Bruce, *ed.* "The News Management Issue As Washington Sees It." *Nieman Reports*, [17?](1):3–15, March 1963. **G 23**

Opinions on news management expressed by Washington correspondents Alan Barth, Douglas Cater, Richard Dudman, Julius Duscha, Robert H. Fleming, Richard L. Harwood, David J. Kraslow, John J. Lindsay, Murrey Marder, John L. Steele, Robert C. Toth, and Donald L. Zylstra.

[Galsworthy, John]. *A Justification of the Censorship of Plays, together with a Demand for the Extension of the Principle of that Office to Other Branches of the Public Service.* London, Heinemann, 1909. 32 p. (The essay also appears under the title, "About Censorship" in Galsworthy, *The Inn of Tranquility; Studies and Essays.* New York, Scribner's, 1913, pp. 236–53, and is reprinted in Downs, *The First Freedom*, pp. 265–70) **G 24**

A satirical essay directed against British censorship of plays by the Lord Chamberlain. Galsworthy, with tongue-in-cheek, suggests that such a beneficial institution should be extended to literature in general and to the realms of art, science, religion, and politics.

Galt, Thomas F. *Peter Zenger, Fighter for Freedom.* New York, Crowell, 1951. 242 p. **G 25**

Fictionized biography of the New York editor and his trial for seditious libel in 1735.

Gannett, Frank E., and T. Swann Harding. "Freedom of Speech—Should It Be Curbed?" *Rotarian*, 18–19+, June 1939. **G 26**

A debate between Frank E. Gannett, publisher, and T. Swann Harding, publicist. Gannett believes that the individual should be his own censor, held accountable in court under the libel laws, but that there should be no prior restraint. Harding believes that anything antisocial should be suppressed. "What we really want when we discuss censorship, is not its complete abolition, but its control in line with the most scientifically informed intelligence of the time."

Gannon, Patrick J. "Art, Morality and Censorship." *Studies* (Ireland) 31:409–19, December 1942. **G 27**

Art owes its origin to religion, but has too frequently turned on its foster mother. Art, no less than religion, should mirror the essential, the ideal, and the eternal, but not moral ugliness. Pathological subject matter as seen in modern plays, novels, and films is not a legitimate subject for art, even though it may be true to life. Popularity of such works is due to man's morbid curiosity about sex since the Fall. The literati trade on this weakness. Immorality in publications is one of the major causes of "the rake's progress." Legislative action, regrettably, is necessary to control books, films, and plays. Father Gannon quotes an Irish censor as saying of American films: "Ireland is not so much in danger of Anglicisation as Los Angelesisation." He defends the Irish Free State censorship policies against such critics as G. B. Shaw and Sir John Keane, "the mouthpiece of the literati" in the Irish Senate. Even Milton comes in for criticism for his *Areopagitica*, the work of an apologist for divorce. The censors have "the common people of Ireland on their side, and it is in the interest of the common people of Ireland that they exercise the unpleasant and unrequited functions of censorship."

————. "Literature and Censorship." *Irish Monthly*, 65:434–47, 1937. **G 28**

A defense of Irish censorship which, the author maintains, is intended to operate only against pornography. "The censorship set up by law in The Free State is very restricted in scope and reasonable in its purpose, though, like every piece of legislation, it calls for prudence in its application." If this is Puritanism, "then call the Church Puritan."

Gannon, R. D. "Censorship and High School Libraries." *Wilson Library Bulletin*, 35:46–47, September 1960. **G 29**

Ganzel, Dewey. "Patent Wrongs and Patent Theatres: Drama and the Law in the Early Nineteenth Century." *PMLA*, 76:384–96, September 1961.

G 30

Edward Bulwer (later Bulwer-Lytton) sponsored legal reform of the British theater in the 1830's, initiated by the Select Committee on Dramatic Literature of which he was chairman. Dramatists were given copyright protection and the monopoly was broken. Despite continuing dramatic censorship, which the author describes, the theater managed to flourish.

Gaquin, Thomas E. "The Law Is Not Enough." *Bay State Librarian*, 53(2):8, 12–15, April 1963. **G 31**

The auhtor, a Boston businessman, is concerned with the vicious influence on young people of the onrushing tide of obscene books and magazines. Legal efforts in all 50 states have met with failure because of the "shrinking definition of what is considered obscene in the eyes of the courts." He describes the decent literature campaign of the Holy Name Society, "an extra-legal method to complement what the law is attempting to do." He denies that these efforts are an interference with freedom under the First Amendment, but rather a limitation on license. The campaign is in accordance with the Roth decision of the U.S. Supreme Court which indicated that contemporary community standards shall determine the acceptability of printed matter. The parish, in this instance, is the community.

Gardiner, Harold C. *Catholic Viewpoint on Censorship*. Garden City, N.Y., Hanover House, 1958. 192 p. (The Catholic Viewpoint Series) **G 32**
A Jesuit priest, literary editor of *America*, presents the Catholic position on censorship, both in its theory and practical application. He examines the two main Catholic groups involved in the censorship controversy, the National Legion of Decency (movies) and the National Office for Decent Literature, and considers the charges leveled against them by the American Civil Liberties Union and the American Book Publishers Council. "This is an admirable book particularly for anti-Catholic bigots," writes Morris Ernst in the *Saturday Review of Literature* for 19 April 1958, "and for men of goodwill it is an invitation to sober thought even in that area of the problem not dealt with—literature about birth control, family planning, and the race between population and food."

———. "The Imprimatur." *Library Journal*, 88:60–62, 1 January 1963. **G 33**
A discussion of the purposes and mechanics of prepublication censorship by the Catholic Church.

———. *In All Conscience; Reflections on Books and Culture*. New York, Hanover House, 1959. 288 p. **G 34**
Chapter 3, Censorship, Movies, TV, reprints selections of Father Gardiner's articles appearing in the magazine *America*.

———. "Moral Principles towards a Definition of the Obscene." *Law and Contemporary Problems*, 20:560–71, Autumn 1955. **G 35**
Canon Law of the Catholic Church forbids the reading of obscene works, but does not define obscenity. In the interpretation of Canon Law the emphasis has been "on the *tendency* of the book, of the work of art, to exude some sort of allure that panders to the passions of sex." Obscenity "has a restricted meaning, which the whole tone and practice of moral theology and Canon Law refrains from extending to works, which, however much to be discouraged on other grounds, cannot be called objectively obscene." Whether a work "falls within that carefully staked-out definition is a matter of prudential judgment . . . In the dearth of such certainty, the probability that the work falls within the definition is enough to have the force of law."

———. "One Way to Tackle Obscenity." *America*, 106:849, 31 March 1962. Comment by Rodman C. Herman. 107:91+, 28 April 1962. **G 36**
The author suggests control of the distribution of obscenity, such as making it illegal to sell "girlie" magazines or paperbacks that exploit sex to persons under 18. The comment is a letter from the president of the Catholic Lawyers Guild, Essex County, N.J., referring to the Guild's efforts to control "tie-in" sales, giving storekeepers the right to accept only those publications they want.

———. *Tenets for Readers and Reviewers*. Washington, D.C., America Press, 1944. 24 p. **G 37**
The literary editor of *America* states principles for judging "the soundness and decency of moral values of a work of literature." The reviewer should consider the merit of the book apart from the author; he should consider the effect of the whole book; sin, if portrayed, should be recognized for what it is and should never be described "as to become a temptation to a normally discriminating reader."

———, et al. "The *Index of Forbidden Books*: A Symposium." *Critic*, 20:54–59, April–May 1962. **G 38**

Gardiner, Samuel R., ed. *Documents Relating to the Proceedings against William Prynne, in 1634 and 1637. With a Biographical Fragment by the Late John Bruce*. Westminster, Eng., Printed for the Camden Society, 1877. 121 p. (Camden Society Publications, n.s. 18) **G 39**

———. *Speech of Sir Robert Heath, Attorney-General, in the Case of Alexander Leighton, in the Star Chamber, June 4, 1630. Edited with a Preface by the late John Bruce . . . By Samuel Rawson Gardiner . . . .* London, Printed for the Camden Society, 1875. 22 p. plus 10 p. (Camden Miscellany, vol. 7, no. 2; part of the Society's Publications, new series 14) **G 40**
Dr. Leighton was brought to trial, convicted, imprisoned, and tortured for a "most scandalous, libellous, and seditious book," entitled *An Appeale to the Parliament or Sion's Plea against the Prelacye*.

Gardner, Mary A. *Inter American Press Association. Its Fight for Freedom of the Press, 1926–1960*. Austin, Tex., Published for the Institute of Latin American Studies by University of Texas Press, [1967]. 217 p. (Latin American Monographs, no. 6) **G 41**
A nonprofit voluntary membership association of more than 550 Western Hemisphere publications and individuals pledged, among other things, to guard freedom of the press. The organization grew out of the first Pan American Congress of Journalists, held in Washington, D.C. in 1926. Since 1950 it has alternated annual meetings between the United States and Latin America. The Association took an active role in the battle in behalf of the suppressed *La Prensa*. The freedom of the press,

the author notes, is a cause to which members rally, without respect to national barriers.

Garfield, James A. "Necessity of the Freedom of the Press." In *Works of James A. Garfield*, Boston, Osgood, 1882–83, vol. 2, pp. 575–85. (Reprinted in Beman, *Censorship of Speech and the Press*, pp. 329–35) **G 42**
Address delivered before the Ohio Editorial Association, Cleveland, 11 July 1878.

Garnett, Edward. *The Breaking Point, a Censured Play. With Preface and a Letter to the Censor*. London, Duckworth, 1907. 116 p. **G 43**
The Breaking Point was rejected by the British stage censor because it dealt with the problems of an unmarried mother. In the preface to this edition Garnett defends the play and lambasts the censor and the British censorship system that permits "flashy lewdness" while rejecting the serious drama of Ibsen, Maeterlinck, and Brieux. In an appendix he suggests the formation of a Society for the Defence of Intellectual Drama. The letter to the censor, George Alexander Redford, although signed by Garnett, was actually written by William Archer.

———. "The Censorship of Public Opinion." *Fortnightly Review*, 86(n.s.): 137–48, July 1909. **G 44**
A paper read before the Playgoers' Club. "The main issue is that no official or bodies of officials shall dictate the dramatist what he ought to say or how he shall say it, but that public opinion shall do its own censuring." Using examples from censored plays, he shows why he believes that censorship of plays is contrary both to the interests of the stage and the public.

Garrett, George P. "Free Speech and the Espionage Act." *Journal of the American Institute of Criminal Law and Criminology*, 10:71–75, May 1919. **G 45**
The author examines the Espionage Act in terms of the Constitutional guarantee of the freedom of speech.

———. "Free Trade in Ideas." *Journal of the American Institute of Criminal Law and Criminology*, 11:181–90, August 1920. **G 46**
A comparison of present-day (1920) radical critics of the government with those of the period of the Sedition Act of 1798. The author defends free exchange of ideas and full discussion and criticism directed to governmental affairs.

Garrett, Jo L. *The Leveller Movement and the Liberal Theory of the Press*. Urbana,

Ill., University of Illinois, 1959. 92 p. (Unpublished Master's thesis) **G 47**

Garrison, William L. *A Brief Sketch of the Trial of William Lloyd Garrison, for an Alleged Libel on Francis Todd, of Newburyport, Mass.* Boston, Printed by Garrison and Knapp, 1834. 24 p. (Bailey Pamphlets, vol. 39, no. 7) **G 48**
Garrison was tried for publising an article charging Todd, a shipowner, with engaging in the slave trade.

———. "'The Rights of God'—Free Discussion—Freedom of the Press." *Liberator*, 16:18, 30 January 1846. **G 49**
Garrison defends the policy of his abolitionist paper in allowing free expression of unorthodox ideas, including ideas of which he, himself, disapproves. "The fact, that men are more or less ignorant—that they misapprehend the truth, and conflict in their views of it—demonstrates the absolute need of freedom of conscience and speech . . . as also the absurdity and cruelty of putting reason under ban, or of affixing pains and penalties to heretical opinion."

Garwood, W. St. John. "Free Speech and the Public Library." *Library Journal*, 77:1128–33, July 1952. **G 50**
A plea for freedom of ideas by an associate justice of the Texas Supreme Court.

Gary, Hampson. "Regulation of Radio in the U.S." *Annals of the American Academy of Political and Social Science*, 177:15–21, January 1935. **G 51**
The chairman of the Broadcast Division of the Federal Communications Commission traces the development of regulation of broadcasting in the United States from the earliest days through the passage of the Communications Act of 1934.

Gascoigne, Bamber. "Protection Racket." *Spectator*, 206:214, 17 February 1961. **G 52**
Publication of a letter from the Office of the Lord Chamberlain to the Garrick Theatre requiring explicit deletions in the scenes and dialogue of *Fings Ain't Wot They Used T' Be*. The letter and the whole function of dramatic censorship are ludicrous, the author charges. "To prove this, try and write that letter to the Garrick *without* making it seem ridiculous."

"Gathings Committee Reports on 'Pornographic' Books." *Publishers' Weekly*, 163: 125–27, 10 January 1953. **G 53**
A summary of the final reports of the House of Representatives Select Committee on Current Pornographic Materials, which followed a lengthy study of publications, largely paperbacks, and hearings at which various proponents and opponents of censorship appeared. While opposing censorship, the report recommended powers be given to the Postmaster General to impound mail, pending court action, addressed to anyone selling "obscene" matter by mail and exempting the Post Office Department from holding hearings prior to impounding such mail. The report also calls for action by the publishing industry against "borderline" publications. A minority report takes "vigorous exception to the general approach to the complex nature of the subject under investigation," indicating that the committee has not recognized the distinction between what is patently obscene and what is free thought and creative expression. The minority report charges that "highly arbitrary and unfair" accusations are made against the paperback book industry which is "deserving of better treatment than wholesale condemnation."

Gatley, Clement C. *Libel and Slander in a Civil Action, with Precedents and Pleadings.* 5th ed. Edited by Richard O'Sullivan and Roland G. Brown. London, Sweet & Maxwell, 1964. 820 p. **G 54**

Gatzka, Charles A. *Detroit Newspaper Strike.* Columbia, Mo., Freedom of Information Center, School of Journalism, University of Missouri, 1965. 4 p. (Publication no. 143) **G 55**
The author examines the events leading up to the 134-day strike of two Detroit newspapers, the effect on the newspapers' employees and advertising, and the efforts that were made to bridge the news gap.

Gavin, Clark. *Foul, False and Infamous; Famous Libel and Slander Cases of History.* New York, Abelard, 1950. 237 p. (Published in paperback under the title, *Famous Libel and Slander Cases of History*, by Crowell-Collier, New York, 1962. 188 p.) **G 56**
Contents: For Socrates, the Hemlock Cup . . . ; John Peter Zenger's America; A Friend of Mr. Jefferson's (Thomas Cooper); For Where There Are Irish . . . (Sir William Wilde); . . . But Is It Art? (James McNeill Whistler); Heritage of the Wager (Sir William Gordon-Cumming); and There's One Born Every Minute (*Collier's v. Grape Nuts and Postum*).

Gayler, J. L. "Librarian and the Law of Defamation." *Library World*, 39: 273–78, November 1950. **G 57**
Is the librarian who allows a book containing a defamatory statement to go into circulation liable to the person to whom that defamation statement relates? If the librarian is so liable are there any special rules in English law which may mitigate that liability?

Gaynor, William J. "Libel in England and America." *Century Magazine*, 82: 824–31, October 1911. **G 58**
The mayor of New York believes that "freedom of speech and of the press means freedom to speak and write the truth, not falsehood or abuse." He draws a comparison of the libel laws and definition of libel between the United States and England, showing the differences in interpretation and judgments by the courts.

Gedye, G. E. R. "What a Book Famine Means." *Publishers' Weekly*, 135:1754–55, 13 May 1939. (Reprinted in Downs, *The First Freedom*, pp. 408–10) **G 59**
A London newspaper correspondent describes what happened to the bookstores of Europe when the Nazis and Fascists came into power.

[Gee, Edward]. *Letter to the Superiors (whether Bishops or Priests), which Approve or License the Popish Books in England, Particularly to those of the Jesuit Order, Concerning Lewis Sabran, a Jesuit.* London, W. Rogers, 1688. 14 p. **G 60**

Geere, Frank. "The Press in Time of War." *Journal of the Military Service Institution of the United States*, 56:9–23, January 1915. **G 61**
The author recommends that a press "censorate" be organized prior to the beginning of hostilities, to avoid the unnecessary confusion of wartime.

Geis, Gilbert. "Basic Issue in Canon 35 Is Right of Defendant to Impartial Trial." *Quill*, 45(5):9–10, 20, May 1957. **G 62**
A survey of lawyers, judges, and criminologists, reveals deep-seated suspicion of motives of newspapers in insisting on camera coverage of trials.

———. "Preliminary Hearings and the Press." *UCLA Law Review*, 8:397–414, 1960–61. **G 63**
"This article considers the conflict between the policies of a fair trial and a free press as encountered in preliminary hearings in England and the United States . . . The author concludes that the Parliamentary Committee recommendations (resulting from the 1957 trial of Dr. Adams) strikes the best balance yet found between the policies in question."

Gellhorn, Walter. "Restraints on Book Reading." In his *Individual Freedom and Governmental Restraints.* Baton Rouge, Louisiana State University Press, 1956, pp. 49–104. (Edward Douglass White Lectures on Citizenship; reprinted in Downs, *The First Freedom*, pp. 20–41) **G 64**
A presentation of the basic concepts underlying censorship and opposition to censorship,

developed as an outgrowth of discussions by a three-man study group, appointed by the National Book Committee to inquire into the theory of censorship (Richard McKeon, Robert K. Merton, and Walter Gellhorn). "The advocates of censorship," writes Gellhorn, "regard it as a means by which to prevent debasement of the individual values, the cultural standards, and the common security of democracy. Its opponents regard it, by contrast, as a danger to the freedom which fosters these virtues and standards, and without which democracy cannot survive." Gellhorn examines the present-day concern with obscenity and the difficulties of definition. He explores the controversy over the impact of reading on conduct, questioning whether there is enough evidence to support the charges of Dr. Frederick Wertham and others. Gellhorn surveys the mechanics of restraint—the censorship board (stage plays and movies), the volunteer organization (NODL), and police action (Detroit). He points out that the government as a consumer offers a potential source of censorship since about half the hard cover books in America are sold to libraries, to the armed forces, or as textbooks to schools. He discusses the efforts of the Post Office Department and Customs Bureau to exclude foreign propaganda and to regulate the distribution of matter considered seditious or obscene. Artificial stifling of criticism, he believes, is more dangerous to democracy than the free reign of un-American doctrine. He concludes with an appeal to go back to the common-sense or common-law approach to offensive ideas: that "no person should be deemed free to obtrude upon another an unwilling exposure to offensiveness." Individuals, and to some extent communities, he believes, must have freedom of choice. "None should be compelled to read or listen to what he abhors . . . None should be precluded from writing or reading as his own rather than another's taste may determine." Encouragement of good books and reading rather than censorship of the bad should be the American goal.

——. *Security, Loyalty and Science.* Ithaca, N.Y., Cornell University Press, 1950. 300 p. **G 65**
A study of "the impact upon our civil liberties of current governmental programs designed to ensure internal security and to expose and control disloyalty or subversive conduct." Chapters 1 through 3 deal with the American government system for keeping secrets and with the balance of security versus dissemination of essential information. The study is critical of unnecessary restrictions of scientific data in the interest of security. "Secrecy is antithetical to the spirit of science."

——. "Security, Secrecy, and the Advancement of Science." In *Civil Liberties Under Attack.* Philadelphia, University of Pennsylvania Press, 1951, pp. 85–106.
G 66

Genest, John. *Some Account of the English Stage, From the Restoration in 1660 to 1830.*

Bath, Eng., Printed by H. E. Carrington, 1832. 10 vols. (Available on Microcard)
G 67
Discusses the licensing of the stage and gives numerous accounts of attacks on the stage and players and the suppression of stage productions, beginning with William Prynne's *Histrio-Mastix* (1633). The work is considered both thorough and accurate.

Gentleman's Magazine. London, 1731–1907. Monthly. **G 68**
The issues of 1737–38 frequently contain articles dealing with freedom of the press and the libel laws of England, including a number of articles by Caleb D'Anvers, reprinted from *The Craftsman.* A few examples are: Of The Arts of Printing, and Liberty of the Press, March 1737; The Liberty of the Press, January 1738 (reprint of article on the Zenger trial from *The Craftsman,* 21 January 1738); The Importance of the Liberty of the Press, January 1738 (reprinted from *Common Sense,* 7 January 1738); and Whether There Is Now Any Liberty of the Press, April 1738 (reprinted from *The Craftsman,* 29 April 1738).

Gentz, Friedrich von. "Reflections on the Liberty of the Press in Great Britain. Translated from the German of the Celebrated F. von Gentz." *Pamphleteer* (London), 15:455–96, 1819. (Also printed as a separate pamphlet) **G 69**
This friend and advisor to the Austrian prince, Metternich, considers the contemporary English press as existing in "a state of absolute anarchy." Unless more strict press controls are instituted, this absolutist writer warns, the English press might as well be abandoned to its own devices. Specifically, English press law is unclear, leaving decision to the arbitrary action of the court. Nevertheless, he considers how the English system might be used as a model for other states by recognizing the difficulties and dangers where the state is "not favored by local circumstances." Reviewed in *The Monthly Review or Literary Journal,* 88:(ser. 2):270–85, March 1819.

George, J. W. "Lucky Strike Campaign Starts Fight over Radio Censorship." *Advertising and Selling,* 12:22, 65, 26 December 1928. **G 70**
The cigarette company's campaign, aimed at substituting smoking for the eating of sweets, brought forth complaints to government authorities from the candy and restaurant industries and raised questions with respect to control of radio advertising in the public interest.

George, John. *A Treatise on the Offence of Libel; with a Disquisition on the Right, Benefits, and Proper Boundaries of Political Discussion.* London, Taylor and Hessey, 1812. 361 p. **G 71**

George, Walter L. "Sincerity: The Publisher and the Policeman." In his *Literary*

Chapters. Boston, Little, Brown, 1918, pp. 111–35. **G 72**
The circulating libraries of England that have rejected so many works of literary importance reflect, rather than create, the Puritan climate of the time. The author places the real blame for censorship on the publishers for their timidity and the police for taking action against works of merit and frankness. "We cannot be sincere because the police dare not allow it."

Georgia Literature Commission. *A Report . . . to the Governor, the General Assembly, and the People of Georgia.* Atlanta, State of Georgia, 1955. 60 p. **G 73**
The Committee was formed by the legislature in 1953, according to Governor Talmadge, "for the purpose of ridding our newsstands of lewd and obscene literature which are deleterious to the morals and good order of our communities and state. It is a study agency, has no powers of censorship, nor authority to punish offenders." The report is signed by the chairman of the Committee, James Pickett Wesberry. After the abolition of the Rhode Island Commission to Encourage Morality in Youth, according to *Publishers' Weekly,* 8 June 1964, Georgia remained the only state with a morality commission.

Gerald, J. Edward. *The British Press under Government Controls.* Minneapolis, University of Minnesota Press, 1956. 235 p. **G 74**
A professor of journalism analyzes the effect of government economic controls (supply of newsprint and labor) on the British press, controls that began as security measures at the onset of World War II and continued into the postwar decades. He evaluates the control legislation both as to its impact on the press as a social institution and its probable use in the future to influence newspaper content. He also discusses the work of the Royal Commission on the Press.

——. *The Press and the Constitution, 1931–1947.* Minneapolis, University of Minnesota Press, 1948. 173 p. **G 75**
Development of the concept of freedom of the press in the United States on the basis of constitutional law during the period beginning with the Minnesota gag-law case in 1931 (*Near v. Minnesota*) and ending with the Taft-Hartley Act in 1947. The author includes in his discussion the antitrust laws, newspaper taxes, wage and hour legislation, censorship, picketing, licensing, and the contempt of court power.

——. *The Social Responsibility of the Press.* Minneapolis, University of Minnesota Press, 1963. 214 p. **G 76**
The author considers the theory of diversity

in communications in a democracy, a concept growing out of English law and embodied in the American Bill of Rights. He traces a parallel development of business enterprise in which entrepreneurs arrive at their own theories of publishing and broadcasting. He explores problems arising from this conflict in interest and considers the various criticism of the mass media. "When the claims are balanced and a course of future action sought, it should be remembered that the freedom given to business and the press is solely for accomplishing the ideals of the open society and the community's concern for man as man." The final chapter deals with professional organization. "Professional spirit is a powerful defense against the acceptance of imbalanced government, against technological captivity, against coercion and disruption of political communication, because it attracts and trains persons able to cope with tasks of such magnitude."

―――. "Study of Press Freedom Teaches American Heritage." *Journalism Quarterly*, 26:68–71, March 1949. **G 77**

Gerber, Albert B. "A Suggested Solution to the Riddle of Obscenity." *University of Pennsylvania Law Review*, 112:834–56, April 1964. **G 78**
The author suggests "concepts which might eliminate the untenable posture that the law has adopted with respect to criminal obscenity." He reviews the historical background leading to the present confusion. "Every problem of obscenity must be tested under the criterion of balancing the claim that the material is obscene against the harm to the area of conduct protected by the first amendment." The courts "must recognize that they are rendering a decision in a dynamic field."

Gerbner, George. "Mental Illness on Television: a Study of Censorship." *Journal of Broadcasting*, 3:293–303, Fall 1959. **G 79**
The article illustrates some aspects of the dynamics of network censorship in one area of national concern: the treatment of mental illness and the mental health professions on television.

―――, and Percy H. Tannenbaum. "Regulation of Mental Illness Content in Motion Pictures and Television." *Gazette; International Journal for Mass Communications Studies*, 6:365–85, 1961. **G 80**

A report of "some studies and observations probing into the effects of motion pictures and broadcast censorship upon the communication of ideas and images of mental illness."

"German and English Censorship." *Living Age*, 332:270–71, 1 February 1927. **G 81**
Comments on the censorship law (Schmutz und Schund) recently passed in Germany which provides for a board of censors in every federal state to review books, and the recent English censorship law aimed at checking "scandalous and salacious reports of divorce proceedings" in newspapers.

Gerrard, John. "Irish Censorship—or Fighting for Cleaner Cinema." *Sight and Sound*, 18(70):81–82, Summer 1949. **G 82**
James Montgomery, first holder of the office of Irish [movie] Censor (1923), "took the Ten Commandments as his code and swung into a full-blooded battle against the low standards prevailing at the time. Of the 1,307 features submitted to him in 1924, he rejected 104 and administered severe cuts to 166." He was urged by Catholic newspapers to be even more strict. In 1941 Montgomery was succeeded by Dr. Richard Hayes who applied "the simple moral code and the principles on which civilization and family life are built." No political censorship is applied, but Dr. Hayes noted that "anything advocating Communism or presenting it in an unduly favourable light gets the knife!"

[Gerry, Elbridge]. [*Message of Governor Elbridge Gerry on Newspaper Libels*]. Boston, 1812. 12 p. **G 83**
Governor Gerry requests the Massachusetts legislature to pass a law clarifying the offense of libel, now subject to the uncertainty of the common law. The courts, he said, have ruled that truth can be given as a defense in the case of an offense against an elected official but not a judge or an appointed official. Judges, he said, should not be exempt. He cites a report (attached) from the Attorney and Solicitor General of the Commonwealth itemizing 253 libels appearing in Boston papers in the past 9 months.

Gertz, Elmer. *Censored: Books and Their Right to Live*. Lawrence, Kan., University of Kansas Library, 1965. 19 p. (12th Annual Public Lecture on Books and Bibliography) **G 84**
Observations of a Chicago lawyer based on a lifetime fight against censorship. Includes references to Frank Harris' *My Life and Loves* (Gertz wrote the first serious study of Harris) and Henry Miller's *Tropic of Cancer*, which he defended successfully in Chicago. He tends to agree with Justice Black in rejecting all forms of censorship. There are bad books, but they should be rejected by the reader, not by the police or even the courts, which cannot agree on what should be banned. Furthermore, there is no real evidence to show the effect of bad books on the reader.

―――. "The End of All Censorship." *Nation*, 201:7–10, 5 July 1965. (Reprinted in St. Louis *Post-Dispatch*, 8 July 1965) **G 85**
Lawyer Gertz, long a student of the obscenity laws, describes the evolution of his own thinking about obscenity, beginning with the point of view of legally proscribing works that represent "utterly worthless obscenity" to his present belief "that adults should be permitted to read anything, literally anything." He compares the U.S. Supreme Court's efforts at balancing freedom of the press and local pressures and passions against obscenity with its earlier efforts to balance civil rights and racial prejudice by the doctrine of separate-but-equal facilities. It is time that the Supreme Court says that the adult is free to chose not only its rulers but its reading matter. "There must be an end to all censorship of books for adults."

―――. *A Handful of Clients*. Chicago, Follett, 1965. 379 p. **G 86**
In chapters 6 and 7 Gertz describes the Chicago ban on Henry Miller's *Tropic of Cancer* and the court case which resulted in the freeing of the book by Judge Epstein. Gertz was the lawyer for the publishers, Grove Press.

―――. "Illinois Battle over *Tropic of Cancer*." *Chicago Bar Record*, 46:161–72, January 1965. **G 87**
A lawyer's account of the *Tropic of Cancer* case in the Illinois courts, with extensive quotations from opinions of the courts, not otherwise in print. In March 1962 Judge Samuel B. Epstein of the Supreme Court of Cook County had declared the book not obscene. He said, in part, "Let the parents control the reading matter of their children; let the tastes of the readers determine what they may or may not read; let each reader be his own censor; but let not the government or the courts dictate the reading matter of a free people." Superintendent Wilson of the Chicago police appealed the case to the Appellate Court of Illinois, which referred the case to the Illinois Supreme Court on constitutional grounds. On 18 June 1964 that court unanimously reversed Judge Epstein's decision, declaring the book obscene and not entitled to constitutional protection. Four days later the U.S. Supreme Court, in a Florida case, *Grove Press v. Gorstein*, ruled the book not obscene. On 7 July, the Illinois Supreme Court withdrew its earlier decision and ordered the judgment of the Superior Court of Cook County affirmed and the book cleared.

―――. "Test case: *Tropic of Cancer*." *Focus Midwest*, 1(2):12–14, July 1962. **G 88**
The Chicago attorney who represented Grove Press and Henry Miller in the Chicago courts, discusses the implications of the case. The test of a free people, he maintains, is the freedom to read.

―――. "The *Tropic of Cancer* Litigation in Illinois." *Kentucky Law Journal*, 51:591–610, Summer 1963. **G 89**
Another account of the case against the Grove

Press edition of Henry Miller's work before the Superior Court of Cook County, Illinois, told by the defense attorney. Gertz outlines the evidence for the defense adduced at the trial, using the language of the statutes: "(1) The character of the audience for which the material was designed. . . . (2) What the predominent appeal of the material would be for ordinary adults or a special audience. . . . (3) The artistic, literary, scientific, educational or other merits of the material. . . . (4) The degree . . . of public acceptance. . . . (5) Appeal to the prurient interest, or [absence] thereof, in advertising or other promotion of material. . . . (6) Purpose of the author. . . ."

Gessler, Charles A. "Comic Book Ordinance Unconstitutional." *Southern California Law Review*, 35:325–31, Spring 1960.　　**G 90**
Relates to *Katzev v. County of Los Angeles* (1959) in which the California Supreme Court declared unconstitutional the Los Angeles County Ordinance prohibiting the sale of crime comic books to children.

Gibb, Mildred A. *John Lilburne, the Leveller; A Christian Democrat*. London, Drummond, 1947. 359 p.　　**G 91**
The first full-length biography of the impassioned leader of the English Levellers during the Puritan Revolution, based on examination of Lilburne's own writings, contemporary manuscripts, records, and pamphlets. For his published criticisms of the established Church and parliament Lilburne was tried and convicted by the Star Chamber in 1638. Two years later he was released by Cromwell but in 1646 was again imprisoned for his pamphlets calling for democratic reform in the constitution and parliament. The oft-imprisoned Lilburne described himself as "an honest, true-bred, free-born Englishman, that never in his life loved a tyrant nor feared an oppressor." This work includes illustrations of Lilburne, Dr. Bastwick, William Laud, and William Prynne, all of whom figured in the seventeeth-century fight for press freedom.

Gibbon, Monk. "In Defense of Censorship." *Bell* (Dublin), 9:313–22, January 1945.　　**G 92**
The author warmly defends the principle, if not the practice, of literary censorship. Every nation has the right to defend its young from harmful reading "for what youth thinks matters at least as much as what it eats, perhaps more." Writers have a profound influence, for good or bad, on current mentality, if not morality. The Catholic Church and Soviet Russia both understand that realistically "certain authors and certain books are better left unread." The author comments in some detail on what he believes is good literature and what is bad. Answers to Gibbon from G. B. Shaw, Sean O'Casey, and others appear in the February 1945 issue.

Gibson, Morgan. "A Warning from Milwaukee: The *Tropic* Trial." *Michi-*

gan's *Literary Quarterly*, 3(1):41–44, Winter 1962–63.　　**G 93**
An account of the Milwaukee trial of *Tropic of Cancer* related by a witness for the defense. Circuit Court Judge Ronald A. Drechsler declared the book obscene. In the same issue (pp. 48–49) the editor, Robert Bassil, discusses episodes of censorship of student magazines and newspapers.

Gilbert, Robert W. "Union Publications and the Unlawful Purpose Doctrine." *Labor Law Journal*, 5:175–82, March 1954.　　**G 94**

Gildersleeve, Virginia C. *Government Regulation of the Elizabethan Drama*. New York, Columbia University Press, 1908. 259 p. (Columbia University Studies in English, 2d ser., vol. 4, no. 1; reprinted by Burt Franklin, New York, 1961)
　　G 95
An account of the laws and regulations, national and local, which affected drama during this important period of its history, including the standing of players and playhouses in the eyes of the law. Chapter 3 deals with the Nature of Censorship.

Gilfond, Duff. "Arbiters of Obscenity in the Post Office Department." *New Republic*, 59:119–21, 19 June 1929.　　**G 96**

———. "Customs Men Keep Us Pure." *New Republic*, 59:176–77, 3 July 1929.
　　G 97

Gill, John. *Tide Without Turning: Elijah P. Lovejoy and Freedom of the Press*. Boston, Beacon, 1958. 256 p.　　**G 98**
The story of the Lovejoy martyrdom, based on original papers and dramatically told. Lovejoy was a young abolitionist editor of Alton, Ill., who was shot to death by a mob in 1837 while attempting to defend his press from destruction. The mob leaders were acquitted in what is considered one of the most flagrant miscarriages of justice in the nation's history.

Gill, Theodore. "The Freedom to Read and Religious Problems." *ALA Bulletin*, 59:477–83, June 1965.　　**G 99**
The president of San Francisco Theological Seminary asks that librarians not blame religion for all the problems raised in its name. The political zealot and the sex-obsessed, who, in the name of religion, demand that churches, schools, and libraries conform to their own beliefs are not the emissaries of the church. "They are part of a problem we share with you." Dr. Gill speaks of the reawakening taking place in both Catholic and Protestant theology in confronting public issues, including freedom to read. Protestants thought is shifting from a "content Christianity" to a

"context Christianity," which says that "the meaning of any act or any word is determined not by traditions about their use but by the context in which they occur this time." This is not only good theology but enlightened self-interest for "we simply know that the abridgers of anyone's thinking could abridge ours."

Gilleland, LaRue. *Obscenity—"Anybody's Guess."* Columbia, Mo., Freedom of Information Center, School of Journalism, University of Missouri, 1961. 4 p. (Publication no. 53)　　**G 100**
The author considers the controversy over whether or not the reading of an obscene book is likely to result in the commission of an antisocial act.

Gillett, Charles R. *Burned Books; Neglected Chapters in British History and Literature*. New York, Columbia University Press, 1932. 2 vols. (Reprinted by Kennikat Press, Port Washington, N.Y., 1960)
　　G 101
A well-documented study of book censorship in Great Britain, developed chronologically around specific books that were condemned to the flames. Beginning with pre-Reformation manuscripts, the study covers the burnings under Elizabeth and the Stuarts (including Archbishop Laud's persecutions), the destruction of the secret tracts of the English Civil War, the persecution of works of the Levellers and Socinians, books burned under Charles II and James II, books burned under William III (including Irenic books), and a brief survey of burnings in the eighteenth and nineteenth centuries. "Most of the books to be mentioned were the product of a purpose which had in view the reformation or the overthrow of a system that was regarded as false, vicious, or unjust. Some of these systems were political, some of them were ecclesiastical, and those who lighted the fires were politicians or clerics who foresaw the threatened destruction of that which they held sacred, or that on which they fattened." Only a negligible number of works were burned on the basis of immorality. After the Restoration, burning as a means of suppressing books gradually went out of fashion. "The burning of a book," the author observes, "gave advertising which resulted frequently in a wider dissemination of the offending views than might otherwise have been obtained." About 100 of the burned books referred to are represented in the McAlpin Collection in the library of the Union Theological Seminary.

Gillmore, Donald M. *Free Press and Fair Trial*. Washington, D.C., Public Affairs Press, 1966. 254 p.　　**G 102**
A documented account of the conflict between press and bar over the right of the press and the public to full coverage of court news and the right of the accused to a fair trial. Attention is given to state, federal, and Supreme Court

decisions, and to the Jack Ruby, Billie Sol Estes, and other celebrated trials involving conflict of interests. Recommendations of the Warren Report and press-bar codes of ethics are included.

————. "Free Press and Fair Trial in English Law." *Washington and Lee Law Review*, 22:17–42, Spring 1965. **G 103**
In England Parliament and the courts have "already given priority to fair trial, and, through the consistent and vigorous use of the contempt power, have greatly restricted press comment on judicial proceedings."

————. "Free Press v. Fair Trial: A Continuing Dialogue." *North Dakota Law Review*, 41:156–76, January 1963. **G 104**
A professor of journalism considers the contribution of recent communications research, suggesting further study in the nature of experiments, interviews, content analysis, and participant observations.

————. "Free Press versus Fair Trial: A New Era?" *Journalism Quarterly*, 41: 27–37, Winter 1964. **G 105**
Legislation rather than contempt of court might be the answer to pretrial publicity if self-regulation is unsuccessful.

————. "Freedom in Press Systems and the Religious Variables." *Journalism Quarterly*, 39:15–26, Winter 1962. **G 106**
"Although there appears to be a relationship between Christianity and political democracy, of which freedom of expression is a part, concomitant variables also need to be considered. An examination of the world's great religions suggests that few of them, when considered in isolation, are incompatible with press freedom."

————. *"Trial by Newspaper"*: The Constitutional Conflict between Free Press and Fair Trial in English and American Laws. Minneapolis, University of Minnesota, 1961. 386 p. (Ph. D. dissertation, University Microfilms, no. 62–1781) **G 107**

Gillmore, Frank. "The Theatre Stands under the Shadows of a Padlock." *American Federationist*, 35:316–20, March 1928. **G 108**
The secretary of Actors' Equity denounces the Wales Padlock bill, amending the New York Penal Code, providing that any theater which has housed a play convicted of immorality by the state courts might have its license revoked for a period of one year. "The theatre may need an occasional cleaning up, but a padlock is a poor instrument for such work."

Gillotti, Chris F. "Book Censorship in Massachusetts: The Search for a Test for Obscenity." *Boston University Law Review*, 42:476–91, Fall 1962. **G 109**
A review of the legal concept of obscenity in Massachusetts from Colonial days to the present, including such noteworthy cases as *Commonwealth v. Holmes* (1821), *Commonwealth v. McCance* (1894), *Lady Chatterley's Lover* (1930), *An American Tragedy* (1930), *Strange Fruit* (1945), and the most recent case, *Tropic of Cancer* (1962). While Massachusetts decisions are now liberalized and the old stigma of "banned in Boston" has disappeared, the Commonwealth still does not have a legal definition of "obscenity" and, in view of the narrow majority in decisions of the Supreme Judicial Court, "the author who has something to say, and intends to say it at any cost still runs the risk of judicial censure."

Gimbel, Richard. "Thomas Paine Fights for Freedom in Three Worlds, the New, the Old, the Next. Catalogue of an Exhibition Commemorating The One Hundred Fiftieth Anniversary of His Death. Yale University Library, October 1959." *Proceedings, American Antiquarian Society*, 70(n.s.):397–492, 19 October 1960. **G 110**
A bibliographical record of one of the world's most often-suppressed writers. The annotations give evidence of action in America and England against Paine's *Rights of Man* and *Age of Reason*. The exhibition is from the Paine collection of Richard Gimbel. Item 117 in the catalog is a contemporary manuscript of *Age of Reason*. After the work had been declared blasphemous, Gimbel notes, printed copies of the work were so scarce that manuscript copies were circulated.

Gimlette, Thomas. "Books Burnt." *Notes and Queries*, 12(ser. 1):31, 14 July 1855. **G 111**
Reference to the burning in Ireland (1715) of *A Long History of a Short Session of a Certain Parliament in a Certain Kingdom.*

Ginger, Ray. *Six Days or Forever? Tennessee v. John Thomas Scopes.* Boston, Beacon, 1958. 258 p. (Reprinted as Signet Book by New American Library, 1960) **G 112**
A dramatic and humane account of the famous Tennessee "monkey trial" over the teaching of the theory of evolution in the public schools. This 1925 case involved the use of a high school textbook, George Hunter's *Civic Biology.* Chapter 10 of Ginger's work refers to other cases of textbook censorship. Scrapbooks of clippings relating to the Scopes trial are on file in Princeton University Library.

Ginsburgh, Abraham R. *War Correspondents in the American Expeditionary Forces.* Columbia, Mo., University of Missouri, 1931. 197 p. (Unpublished Master's thesis) **G 113**

Ginzburg, Ralph. "*Eros* on Trial." *Fact*, 2(3):1–64, May–June 1965. **G 114**
The entire issue is devoted to an account of the Post Office action against *Eros*, a magazine "devoted to the joys of love and sex," and two other works published by Ginzburg, and the ensuing trial in the U.S. District Court for the Eastern District of Pennsylvania. Ginzburg was sentenced to 5 years in prison and $42,000 in fines. The U.S. Court of Appeals affirmed conviction. At the time of writing the case is before the U.S. Supreme Court. (On 21 March 1966 the U.S. Supreme Court in a 5 to 4 decision affirmed the conviction of Ginzburg.) Included in the article is defense testimony of art professor Horst W. Janson, literary critic Dwight Macdonald, psychiatrist Dr. Peter G. Bennett, and the Rev. George Von Hilsheimer III, and the direct examination by the defense of the prosecution's witness, psychiatrist Dr. Frignito. This issue of *Fact* also includes A Portfolio of the Most Beautiful Art from *Eros*. Three *amici curiae* briefs were filed with the Supreme Court—the ACLU, the Authors League of America, and one signed by 111 leaders in art, science, theology, education, law, and entertainment. Ginzburg notes that, "despite the fact that this brief carried the most impressive sponsorship of any brief ever filed in the entire history of the United States Supreme Court, not one single word concerning the brief . . . appeared anywhere in the American press. The big newspaper story published about free speech during the week of the brief's filing had to do with a poet who was unable to get his poems published in Russia."

————. *An Unhurried View of Erotica.* New York, Helmsman, 1958. 128 p. Introduction by Theodor Reik; preface by George J. Nathan. **G 115**
A collection of excerpts and fragments from the erotic and scatological writings that have moved under the surface of English literature from the first traces in the Anglo-Saxon *Exeter Book* up to the pornographic works of our time. These samples are brought together into an interpretive and explanatory context to provide an informative and often witty account. Dr. Reik comments on the psychological and sociological implications of erotica. A bibliography of 100 titles is given on pages 117–25.

Girodias, Maurice. "Advance Through Obscenity." *Times Literary Supplement*, 6 August 1964, pp. 708–9. **G 116**
Commentary on the author's establishment of the Olympia Press in Paris to "push the white-hot brand of pornography down the censor's throat." Girodias believes that literary censorship in England and America will have disappeared in five or ten years.

[————]. "The Arrest of Maurice Girodias; Literary Censorship in France." *City Lights Journal*, 2:7–13, 1964. **G 117**

An account of the conviction of the publisher of the Olympia Press, Paris, on obscenity charges for publication of six English-language books. Includes text of letter of protest to Minister of Cultural Affairs André Malraux from a group of French writers, also references to an earlier letter of protest of bans on Olympia Press books (1959) from prominent British and American writers.

————. "Confessions of a Booklegger's Son." *Censorship*, 3:2–16, Summer 1965.
G 118

The founder of the Olympia Press in Paris (his father, Jack Kahane, had founded the Obelisk Press), which published English editions of such works as Nabokov's *Lolita*, Genet's *Our Lady of the Flowers*, and works of Henry Miller, as well as a host of "dirty books" for the English and American trade, tells the story of his publishing career. From 1956 onward, French censorship descended upon Girodias, and the result of numerous trials was "eighty years' personal ban from all publishing activities, from four to six years unsuspended prison sentences, and some £29,000 in fines." While England and America have moved to a new level of moral and artistic freedom, "the very concept is being denied, denigrated, and officially ostracised in France."

————. "Pornography Is My Business." *Books and Bookmen*, 7(11):31–34, August 1962.
G 119

"To deprave and corrupt is my business. It is my business to publish those forbidden books, those outrageous obscenities." The author is head of the Olympia Press, Paris, and the article is a chapter from the book *To Deprave and Corrupt* . . .

Gladstone, J. M. "Censorship." *Library Assistant*, 37:2–8, March–April 1944.
G 120

A brief sketch of British censorship from the sixteenth century to the present.

Glasgow, Ellen. *Five Letters from Ellen Glasgow concerning Censorship and Other Matters of Interest to a Library Board Member. With an Introductory Note by Louis D. Rubin, Jr.* Richmond, Friends of the Richmond Public Library, 1962. 10 p.
G 121

When there was public furor over Sinclair Lewis' *Elmer Gantry*, the librarian of the Richmond Public Library solicited the views of the distinguished library board member, Ellen Glasgow. She wrote on 14 March 1927: "I am unequivocally opposed to such censorship in a public library."

[Glasgow, J. Wesley]. *In the Supreme Court of the United States; October Term, 1911. No. 1123. [J. Wesley Glasgow, Appellant v. Wm. H. Moyer, Warden, Appellee.] Brief for Appellant.* Columbian Printing Co., 1911. 21 p.
G 122

The U.S. Supreme Court affirmed Glasgow's conviction of obscenity for his book, *Personal Beauty and Sexual Science.* (*Glasgow v. Moyer*, 225 U.S. 420)

Glenesk, William B. ["The Reverend William B. Glenesk exhibits a copy of *Fanny Hill* from the pulpit of the Spencer Memorial Presbyterian Church, Brooklyn, N.Y., on March 3, 1964."] *Wilson Library Bulletin*, 39:664–65, April 1965.
G 123

A photograph taken in the church sanctuary of the minister who delivered a sermon protesting the court ban of *Fanny Hill* and displayed copies of the book and a dozen other works once banned.

Glenn, Garrard. "Censorship at Common Law and under Modern Dispensation." *University of Pennsylvania Law Review*, 82:114–28, December 1933.
G 124

A review of the long history of efforts made in England and America to use censorship as a matter of state policy, to control expression and bring about conformity in the realm of religion, politics, and morals. The author observes that there has always been a frame of control around us, but in recent years it has been somewhat loosened. "We had better continue in a wholesome state of watchfulness, for who knows what may break through again?"

Glick, Alvin M. "Group Libel and Criminal Libel." *Buffalo Law Review*, 1:259–67, Spring 1952.
G 125

[Godden, Gertrude M.]. *The Stage Censor, an Historical Sketch: 1544–1907 . . . With 16 Illustrations from photographs of rare prints, and contemporary portraits by Marie Léon. By G.M.G.* London, Sampson Low, Marston, 1908. 128 p.
G 126

The author traces the development of stage censorship from the Tudor period, when the Master of Revels, the Privy Council, and the Star Chamber dealt harshly with dramatists and actors, to modern censorship under the Lord Chamberlain dating back to 1737. Includes discussion of the laxness of Stage Censor Thomas Killigrew during the Restoration, the attacks on the immorality of the stage by Jeremy Collier, and censorship of the plays of Dryden, Gay, Thomson, Garnett, and Maeterlinck, to name a few. There are portraits of Lord Chancellor Rich, sixteenth-century examiner of plays; Philip Massinger, author of a play personally expurgated by Charles I; James Shirley (1594–1666), author of a play expurgated by the Master of Revels; Sir William D'Avenant (1605–68), stage licenser; Thomas Killigrew (1611–82), Master of Revels; John Dryden, John Gay, James Thomson, and Theodore Hook, author of an expurgated farce; Mary Russell Mitford (1789–1855), author of two banned plays; Edward Garnett, whose play, *The Breaking*

Point, was prohibited; and Granville-Barker, author of *Waste*, prohibited in 1907. The dramatic author of 1907 finds himself under an authority derived with little change from the Tudor kings, "still unaltered and uncontrolled, 'the one irresponsible and secret tribunal in the land.'" The appendix contains a letter addressed to the Prime Minister opposing censorship of plays in England, signed by 71 prominent authors and playwrights.

Goette, John. "I've Learned Something New About Censors!" *Quill*, 27(1):10–11, January 1939.
G 127

How and why American newsmen can tell the truth about the Sino-Japanese war.

Golden, Aubrey. "Aubrey Golden Opposes Saddling the Courts with the Thankless Job of Censorship." *Saturday Night*, 79:14–15, May 1964.
G 128

Golden, Harry. "Protest for Eleven Books." In his *Only in America*, Cleveland, World, 1958, pp. 289–92.
G 129

An essay on book burning in which Golden recalls the great works of past generations that were destroyed.

Golden, John. "Our Decadent Drama." *Authors' League Bulletin*, 15(1):9–11, April 1927.
G 130

"If we don't clean up our house from the inside, there will be forced on us a thing that strangles art, expression, and all progress in the theatre—censorship."

"Golden Bowl and Silver Porringer." *New Statesman*, 67:212–14, 7 February 1964.
G 131

A discussion of the sexual revolution of the present century and the fact that the "cause of literature is now often thought to be closely associated with the cause of sexual emancipation." The case of *Fanny Hill*, to be decided before a magistrate, is the basis for the editorial, which concludes: "The indignant, the high-minded, the private grievers, are not the only ones who may lay claim to literary merit. The celebration of the body's pleasures may also be an act of the spirit. Even when it is not, though it may not be literature, it is hardly a crime."

Goldenson, Leonard H. *Responsible Broadcasting: The Freedom to Inform, the Duty to Protect.* New York, American Broadcasting Company, 1964. 8 p.
G 132

An address by the president, American Broadcasting Co., upon receipt of the 1963 Gold Medal Award from the Poor Richard Club, Franklin Institute, Philadelphia, 17 January 1964. While recognizing that we must "strike a balance between the need to inform the American people against the need to protect an individual's right," the writer urges re-examination of rules and attitudes toward electronic coverage of trials, hearings, and other public events covered by the newspaper press. It is now technically possible to cover such events without massive equipment and without interference with the conduct of the trial.

Goldfarb, Ronald. "Ensuring Fair Trials." *New Republic*, 150(9):11–14, 29 February 1964.   **G 133**
The lawyer as well as the newspaper should avoid pretrial publicity.

———. "Public Information, Criminal Trials and the Cause Celebre." *New York University Law Review*, 36:810–38, April 1961.   **G 134**
"One of the most vexing contemporary legal problems is that posed by the effect of the reporting of the facts of a crime by the communications media upon the right of a criminal accused to a fair trial. When the right to a fair trial and freedom of the press conflict, there is little agreement on how to handle the situation." The author raises the various problems and complexities in the conflict and reports remedies that have been offered. "Unfortunately the solution seems to be slipping further from our grasp."

"*Goldfarb* Case Fought by Anti-Censorship Forces." *Publishers' Weekly*, 187:105–6, 18 January 1965.   **G 135**
Reviews the case of the temporary injunction by the New York Supreme Court against the distribution or showing of the film, *John Goldfarb, Please Come Home*, with quotations from Justice Greenberg's opinion. The article quotes from briefs filed in the Appellate Division in behalf of the defendant by the American Book Publishers Council and the American Civil Liberties Union.

Goldhill, Walter A. "Censorship of Political Broadcasts." *Yale Law Journal*, 58:787–95, April 1949.   **G 136**
The history of political broadcasting leading to the *Port Huron* decision of the Federal Communications Commission. Radio stations were required by the Communications Act of 1934 to grant equal time to qualified political speakers, without censorship. Some state laws, on the other hand, held stations liable for defamatory statements made in political broadcasts. The *Port Huron* decision stated that state laws must be suspended in favor of the federal law guaranteeing freedom of expression in the particular circumstances.

Goldman, Albert. "One Law for the Lion & Ox." *Censorship*, 2:2–6, Spring 1965.   **G 137**
The Lenny Bruce conviction in New York for

giving an "obscene" performance "dramatically demonstrated the inadequacy of the current legal code to deal with the complex and conflict-laden issues of the sexual content of modern art and entertainment." Goldman concludes that "censorship rests on conditions of social homogeneity and respect for authority that are waining in a country like the United States. Blake's proverb, 'one law for the lion & ox is oppression,' has for us a meaning that becomes more poignant every day."

[Goldman, Emma]. [Conviction of Van K. Allison]. *Mother Earth*, 11:562–63, August 1916.   **G 138**
The editor of *The Flame* was given three years in prison for distributing birth control information.

[———]. "Despite Jehovah and the Police." *Mother Earth*, 11:730–33, January 1917.   **G 139**
Deals with the arrest of Ben Reitman in Cleveland for distributing birth control information.

[———]. "Emma Goldman before the Bar." *Mother Earth*, 9:496–507, May 1916. (Also in the *Masses*, June 1916)   **G 140**
Argument presented at the trial of Emma Goldman for disseminating birth control information. (*State of New York v. Emma Goldman.*)

———. "My Arrest and Preliminary Hearing." *Mother Earth*, 11:426–30, March 1916.   **G 141**
The author's account of her arrest for distributing birth control information.

[———]. ["Poor Dear Anthony Has Passed Away"]. *Mother Earth*, 10:260–61, October 1915.   **G 142**
An editorial on the death of Anthony Comstock, commending his work for having made plain that "sexual pleasure is rendered doubly enticing by a dash of indecency."

[———]. ["Suppression of *Rabochaya Rech*"]. *Mother Earth*, 11:663, November 1916.   **G 143**
An editorial on the suppression of the *Worker's Voice* by the Post Office Department.

[———]. ["Suppression of *Volné Listy*."] *Mother Earth*, 11:532–33, July 1916.   **G 144**
An editorial on the Post Office suppression of this Bohemian anarchist paper. The publisher was required to submit an English translation of the 15 June issue.

[———]. "Trial and Conviction of Emma Goldman and Alexander Berkman." *Mother Earth*, 12:129–63, July 1917.   **G 145**

Relates to the conviction of two American anarchist leaders under the wartime Espionage Act. Reprinted in book form with the addresses of Harold A. Content, assistant U.S. Attorney, and the defendants to the jury.

Goldstein, Elmer J. "Constitutionality of Legislation Limiting Freedom of Speech and Press." *University of Cincinnati Law Review*, 9:265–72, May 1935.   **G 146**

Goldwater, A. L. "Abstract of Dr. A. L. Goldwater's Speech." *Mother Earth*, 11:460–63, April 1916.   **G 147**
Speech delivered before a mass meeting held at Carnegie Hall, New York City, 1 March 1916, to protest the arrest of Emma Goldman and others for distributing birth control information.

———. "The Need for Free Discussion of Birth Control Methods." *Birth Control Review*, 1(2):5, March 1917.   **G 148**

Goldwater, John L. *Americana in Four Colors; A Decade of Self Regulation by the Comics Magazine Industry.* New York, Comics Magazine Association of America, 1964. 63 p.   **G 149**
The president of Comics Magazine Association of America reports on the ten-year experience with the Comic Code Authority, which he states "has proved to be one of the most constructive achievements in publishing history." The codes for both editorial matter and advertising are included in the pamphlet.

Golin, Milt. "Bottling the Facts at the Factory." *Quill*, 52(2):24–25, February 1964.   **G 150**
A criticism of the practices of the Food and Drug Administration in premanagement of science news.

Gompers, Samuel. "As Others View Justice Wright's Decision." *American Federationist*, 16:216–22, March 1909.   **G 151**
Editorial on the contempt of court decision against Gompers, Mitchell and Morrison, quoting press comments in support of the defendants.

———. "Buck's Stove and Range Company Injunction Modified." *American Federationist*, 16:336–45, April 1909.   **G 152**
The decision in the appeal of the AFL against the injunction imposed by Justice Gould in the Buck's Stove case. The decision "eliminates the prohibition of free press and free speech as to printing or discussing *anything* in relation to the Buck's Stove and Range Company or discussion of the injunction itself." The text of the decision is given on pp. 313–35.

————. "Constitutional Liberty Imperilled." *American Federationist*, 16: 222–25, March 1909. **G153**
Gompers considers the broad implication of Justice Wright's decision against officers of the AFL as it pertains to a free press.

————. "Court of Appeals Decision; Justice Wright's Abuse of Judicial Discretion." *American Federationist*, 20: 449–60, June 1913. **G154**
In a second contempt of court case involving officers of the AFL, Justice Wright reaffirmed his earlier sentences; the Appeals Court upheld Wright, but reduced the sentences. Chief Justice Shepard dissented both in the injunction and the contempt case, holding, with Blackstone, that "every freeman has an undoubted right to lay what matter he pleases before the public." Any abuse of the right should be punished under laws made for the purpose. Gompers presents his own commentary as well as those of others on Judge Wright's actions.

[————]. *Dissenting Opinion of Mr. Justice Shepard of the Court of Appeals of the District of Columbia, in the Contempt Case of Gompers, Mitchell and Morrison v. Buck's Stove and Range Co. Trial by Judge and Jury by Hon. Henry Clay Caldwell . . .* [Washington, D.C.], American Federation of Labor, 1910. 16p. **G155**
Convinced that the court was without authority to order Gompers, *et al.*, to refrain from publication on the case, Judge Shepard believed that the contempt decree should be reversed.

————. "Free Press and Free Speech Invaded by Injunction Against the A. F. of L." *American Federationist*, 15:98–105, February 1908. **G156**
An editorial denouncing as an invasion of the liberty of the press and the right of free speech the injunction issued 18 December 1907 by Justice Gould of the Supreme Court of the District of Columbia, enjoining the AFL and its officers from any reference whatsoever to the Buck's Stove and Range Company's relations to organized labor, either by printed, written, or spoken word.

————. "Free Speech and the Injunction Order." *Annals of the American Academy of Political and Social Science*, 36:255–64, September 1910. **G157**
President Gompers of the American Federation of Labor reviews the two court charges against the Federation (injunction and contempt) in the Buck's Stove and Range Company case. Both charges, he argues, are a violation of the constitutional right of free press and free speech. It is the duty of the people to protest a court decision that violates not only the Constitution but the inherent rights of man. He notes a tremendous popular

indignation against the attempt of the court to abolish the right of free speech and press.

————. "Guilty of Contempt, Says Justice Wright." *American Federationist.* 19:601–11, August 1912. **G158**
Justice Wright of the Supreme District Court of the District of Columbia, following the U.S. Supreme Court reversal of the decision against the officers of the AFL, once again imposes sentences on Gompers and Mitchell for contempt. Gompers quotes Judge James B. McGuire as stating that Judge Wright's decision "is the most far-reaching step yet to undermine and destroy the freedom of speech and of the press guaranteed by the Federal Constitution. Primarily it is intended to curb the governing power of organized labor, if not to destroy the labor movement. . . . If finally upheld, it must ultimately lead to the general censorship of speech and the press: If a court may, by injunction or otherwise, determine in advance what subjects may or may not be discussed, or what may or may not be said in a labor paper, why may it not in like manner abridge the freedom of all other publications."

————. "Injunction Contempt Proceedings." *American Federationist*, 15:852–58, October 1908. **G159**
An editorial denying that officers of the AFL have disobeyed the spirit of a court injunction forbidding them from discussing the Buck's Stove and Range Company's labor relations. They insist upon the constitutional right to report to their members through their journal events in the case. "We have repeatedly and emphatically declared that it is not our purpose to violate the order of the court, but we can not consent to surrender the constitutional right of editorial expression upon any subject. If a test is to be made in our case, we shall not flinch from its consequences."

————. "Justice Wright's Decision and Sentence in the Gompers, Mitchell and Morrison Case; the Appeal and Judge Parker's Magnificent Argument." *American Federationist*, 16:438–56, May 1909. **G160**
Comment on and quotations from the address by the defense attorney for the AFL in the Buck's Stove case.

————. "Justice Wright's Denial of Free Speech and Free Press." *American Federationist*, 16:130–32, February 1909. (Issued also as a separate 32-page pamphlet) **G161**
The entire issue deals with Justice Wright's decision in the Buck's Stove case, sentencing Samuel Gompers, John Mitchell, and Frank Morrison to prison for one year, nine months, and six months respectively for contempt of court, or, as Gompers put it "for exercising their constitutional rights of free speech and freedom of the press." The court proceedings

and decision are given on pp. 102–24; replies of the defendants as to why sentence should not be imposed, pp. 129, 151; editorial comments, pp. 132–48; call for funds, pp. 149–50; letters of protest, pp. 152–67.

————. "No Jail for Gompers, Mitchell and Morrison—Yet." *American Federationist*, 18:458–61, June 1911. **G162**
Comment on the reversal by the U.S. Supreme Court of the sentences imposed by the District of Columbia courts against officers of the AFL in the Buck's Stove case, but leaving open right of lower courts to punish "by a proper proceeding, contempt, if any, committed against it."

————. "Sedition Bill Is Blow to Liberty . . ." *International Molders Journal*, 56:97–99, February 1920. **G163**
The president of the American Federation of Labor opposes a peacetime sedition law because it would continue a censorship of the American press not needed, and, in fact, harmful in time of peace.

Goodell, A. C., Jr. "Remarks on the Censorship of the Press in Massachusetts." *Proceedings, Massachusetts Historical Society*, 8(ser. 2):271–73, 1892–94. **G164**
A brief survey of censorship in the colonial period.

Goodhart, Arthur L. "Freedom of Speech and Freedom of the Press." *Washington University Law Quarterly*, 1964:248–69, June 1964. **G165**
The author believes we may avoid total uncontrolled publication or, on the other hand, the imposing of censorship of the press under another name "if we construe the First Amendment as meaning that no *unreasonable* limitation or hindrance shall be placed on publication."

————. "Newspapers and Contempt of Court in English Law." *Harvard Law Review*, 48:885–910, April 1935. **G166**
A review of the English law relating to press coverage of trials indicates that the law of constructive contempt of court meets with general approval. It has been successful in preventing prejudice of the trial by "newspaper convictions or acquittals." Since the trial itself is public and fully reported, only the sensational forms of gossip are eliminated.

[Goodkind, Gilbert E.]. "Goodkind, for A.B.A., Answers Hearst Drive." *Publishers' Weekly*, 150:810–11, 24 August 1946. **G167**
The executive secretary of the American Booksellers' Association issues a statement in answer to the nationwide campaign against alleged indecent literature launched by Hearst papers.

Goodman, Christopher. *How Superior Powers Oght to be Obeyd. Reproduced from the Edition of 1558 with a Bibliographical Note by Charles H. McIlwain.* New York, Published for the Facsimile Text Society by Columbia University Press, 1931. 234 p.   **G 168**
This work is a chief source for later theories of political disobedience. A proclamation issued by Philip and Mary decreed death for anyone found in possession of the book. In 1683, 125 years after publication, it was burned at Oxford University as a "treasonable" work.

Goodman, Jules E. "A Censor or Censorship." *Authors' League Bulletin*, 15(1): 13–14, April 1927.   **G 169**
The author approves the proposed censorship of plays by a Committee of Nine as necessary to stave off less sympathetic censorship.

Goodman, Paul. "Censorship and Mass Media." *Yale Political*, 3(1):23, 40, Autumn 1963.   **G 170**
"At present, other factors of censorship are small potatoes in comparison with the aggrandizement and centralized control of mass-media; broadcasting, newspapers, national magazines, merging publishing houses with giant presses, advertising agencies. . . . They dictate for the public the limits of acceptable knowledge, feeling, and conversation with regard to what is news, what is decent as a standard of living, what is realistic as political policy, what is the norm of artistic expression, etc."

———. "Dr. Reich's Banned Books." In his *Utopian Essays and Practical Proposals.* New York, Random House, 1962, pp. 138–44. (Appeared originally in *Kultur*, 1960)   **G 171**
The author objects to the banning of Dr. Reich's book, *The Function of the Orgasm; The Cancer Biopathy*, etc., by the Food and Drug Administration. That government agency objected to "statements pertaining to the existence of orgone energy." Goodman notes: "It is the hallmark of genius to pay attention to such dark and *suppressed* areas, and to find connections among entities that tend to be neglected." He accuses the *New Republic* of commissioning and then banning as scandalous a review of *The Sexual Revolution* and *The Mass-Psychology of Fascism*.

———. "Pornography, Art and Censorship." *Commentary*, 31:203–12, March 1961; reply with rejoinder, 32:156–61, August 1961. (Reprinted in his *Utopian Essays and Practical Proposals*, pp. 51–69)   **G 172**

Censorship as "part of a general repressive anti-sexuality, causes the evil, creates the need for sadistic pornography sold at a criminal profit." Goodman predicts that censorship by police, administrators, and lower courts will continue to fail and will continue to create the evil it attempts to destroy. The author calls for a more principled high-level policy on obscenity that takes our mores into consideration.

Goodman, Robert W. "The Constitutional Guarantee of Freedom of the Press—Does It Cover the Right to Gather News?" *Journal of Public Law*, 8:596–601, 1959.   **G 173**
Garland v. Torre, 259 F 2d 545 (C.A. 2d, 1958).

[Goodman, Walter]. "How to Deal with Obscene Books." *Redbook*, 110(1):45, November 1957. (Reprinted in Downs, *The First Freedom*, p. 161)   **G 174**

Goodrich, Herbert F. "Does the Constitution Protect Free Speech?" *Michigan Law Review*, 19:487–501, March 1921.   **G 175**
A review of judicial decisions under war censorship, from the viewpoint of a liberal.

Goodwin, John. *A Fresh Discovery Of The High-Presbyterian Spirit. Or The Quenching of the second Beacon fired. Declaring I. The Un-Christian Dealings of the Authors of a Pamphlet, Entituled, A Second Beacon Fired, &c. In presenting unto the Lord Protector and Parlament, a falsified passage out of one of Mr John Goodwins Books, as containing, either Blasphemie, or Error, or both. II. The Evil of their Petition for subjecting the Libertie of the Press to the Arbitrariness and will of a few men. III. The Christian Equity, that satisfaction be given to the Person so notoriously and publickly wronged. Together with the Responsatory Epistle of the said Beacon Firers, to the said Mr. Goodwin, fraught with further revilings, falsifications, scurrilous language, &c. insteed of a Christian acknowledgment of their errour. Upon which Epistle some Animadversions are made.* . . . London, Printed for the Author, and are to be sold by H. Cripps, and L. Ll., [1655]. 84p. (Reprinted in part in Clyde, *Struggle for the Freedom of the Press*, pp. 328–35)   **G 176**
An answer to pamphlets by the "Beacon Firers." "The setting of Watchmen with authority at the door of the press to keep errors and heresies out of the world is as weak a project and design, as it would be to set a company of armed men about a house to keep

darkness out of it in the night season." This work is considered a landmark in expression on freedom of the press, although written in less elevated language than Milton's *Areopagitica*.

Goodwin, Maud W. "The Zenger Trial." In her *Dutch and English on the Hudson: A Chronicle of Colonial New York.* New Haven, Yale University Press, 1919, pp. 193–205. (Chronicles of America Series, 7)   **G 177**

Goodwine, John A. "Problems Respecting the Censorship of Books." *Jurist*, 10: 152–83, April 1950.   **G 178**
Paper read at the regional meeting of the Canon Law Society of America, May 1949. Deals largely with prior-censorship by the Catholic Church.

Gordiner, Nadine. "Censored, Banned, Gagged." *Encounter*, 20:59–63, June 1963.
                                          G 179
A South African novelist complains of the tight censorship controls imposed by the South African government on both locally published and imported works. Many of the suppressions are on political grounds, because they undermine the traditional race policy of the Republic. Censorship is imposed by a Publications Control Board in the Ministry of Interior and encompasses books, periodicals, plays, and films. Newspapers are exempt because the newspaper proprietors association accepted a self-censorship code. For fear of censorship booksellers are wary of books on contemporary affairs by South African authors, so book sales are consequently restricted.

Gordon, Edward. "Freedom to Teach and to Learn." *PTA Magazine*, 58:4–7, October 1963.   **G 180**
Censors, as individuals or national groups, object to many different things with the result that many schools are afraid to present any ideas that are controversial. Crises over books should be brought out into the open. The article includes a form, prepared by the National Council of Teachers of English, to be filled out by a person objecting to a book, and to be submitted to a committee of teachers and administrators for consideration.

Gordon, Rosalie M. "Why You Can't Find Conservative Books in Public Libraries." *Human Events*, 18:591–94, 8 September 1961.   **G 181**
Accusation against the "liberal" review journals for their bias which affects the selection of books for public libraries. "A publicly-supported library has no right to depend entirely on these 'liberal' media in the purchase of books." The author urges conservatives to demand adequate provision of conservative works but not to try to ban or eliminate leftward-leaning books.

Gorer, Geoffrey. "The Uses of Pornography." *London Magazine*, 1(5):38–49, August 1961. (Also in Hewitt, *Does Pornography Matter?* pp. 27–40) **G182**
"To the best of my knowledge, there is no record of a society which has used literacy for profane and imaginative purposes and which has not produced books dealing with sexual topics." There are two contradictory fears which prompt censorship of pornography: first, that the reader will be excited into executing in real life the activities he has been seeing or reading about, and, secondly, that he will find sufficient stimulation in the fantasy so that he will not react sexually. The author believes that the latter is the more realistic response. He recommends some restriction, but not total prohibition, as a matter of public policy.

The Gorgon. London. 23 May 1818 —24 April 1819. Weekly. **G183**
A penny half-sheet paper which espoused the causes of reform and philosophical radicalism, and attacked the aristocracy, Whig journalists, and the Society for Suppression of Vice. It frequently carried articles on freedom of the press. Edited by John Wade.

[Gorton, Samuel]. *Simplicities Defence against Seven-Headed Policy. Or Innocency Vindicated, being unjustly Accused, and sorely Censured, by that Seven-headed Church-Government United in New-England: or That Servant so Imperious in his Masters Absence Revived, and now thus re-acting in Nevv-England. . . .* London, Printed by J. Macock, 1646. 111p. (In Peter Force, *Tracts*, vol. 4, no. 6, 116p.; also in Rhode Island Historical Society, *Collections*, Providence, 1835. vol. 2) **G184**
Among the documents that Gorton quotes as evidence of the intolerance of the Church-Government of the Massachusetts colony, is the verbatim account of his own trial for blasphemy. He was ordered to be confined "to Charlstowne, there to be set on worke, and to wear such bolts or irons, as may hinder his escape, and so to continue during the pleasure of the Court," and if, in the meantime, he "either by speech or writing, publish, declare, or maintaine any of the blasphemous or abominable heresies" such as contained in the two books used as evidence, he would be tried, and, upon conviction, executed. Gorton's bolts were eventually filed off and he was banished from the colony and, subsequently, returned to England where this exposé was published.

Goss, C. W. F. "Nasty Literature." *Library Association Record*, 14:517–18, 15 October 1912. **G185**
Editorial recommending a middle course between unbound freedom and "grandmotherly legislation" which might suppress works of literary merit.

Gossage, Howard. "The Fictitious Freedom of the Press." *Ramparts*, 4(4):31–36, August 1965. **G186**
"In this century we have seen effective control of the press shift from the public, for whom it presumably exists, to the advertiser, who merely uses it to sell his wares to the public. It has shifted so much that the life or death of a publication no longer depends on whether its readers like it, but on whether advertisers like it." The author is an advertising man.

Gosse, *Sir* Edmund W. "Censorship of Books." *English Review*, 4:616–26, March 1910. (Reprinted in *Living Age*, 16 April 1910; excerpted in Downs, *The First Freedom*, pp. 1–2, and in Beman, *Censorship of Speech and the Press*, pp. 476–81) **G187**
Discussion of the current hubbub over the censorship activities of the English circulating libraries. The Circulating Libraries Association, formed to protect the British book trade from criticism, established a policy of refusing to "circulate or sell any book considered objectionable by any three members of the Association." It required publishers to submit books to the Association prior to publication. According to Gosse, the Association failed to consider the wishes of the author, and George Moore, whose books were not approved, set out to buck the system. As background to the present situation Gosse traces the history of censorship which he terms a Papal invention dating back to the fourth century.

Gott, J. W. "Gott in Jail for Libeling Christianity." *Crucible* [Seattle, Wash.], no. 38, 22 December 1917. **G188**
The author tells of his conviction and that of J. J. Riley for blasphemy.

[————]. "Special." *Freethinker* (London), 41:105, 13 February 1921; 41:169, 13 March 1921. **G189**
The articles state the attitude of the [British] National Secular Society to the arrests of J. W. Gott on charges of blasphemy and obscenity. The first arrest was for distribution of an antireligious pamphlet, *Rib Ticklers*; the second arrest was for a pamphlet, *How to Prevent Conception.*

Gottesman, A. Edward. "Letter from London." *Record of the Association of the Bar of the City of New York*, 18:371–76, June 1963. **G190**
Relates to criticism on the floor of the House of Commons of the protection of "lobby journalists," while at the same time other journalists (Vassall investigations) were convicted for refusing to reveal news sources. "The lobby privilege, sanctified by long usage, but not by law, allows a member of the House, or a Minister, to give the press inside hints on future developments or present problems while requiring the newsmen not to reveal the source of their information. . . . It is the counterpart of the 'leak' well-known

to the American press, but less formally recognized in the web of United States press institutions."

Goucher College, Baltimore. Julia Rogers Library. "Books and Freedom." In *The College Library in a Changing World.* Baltimore, Goucher College, 1953, pp. 48–68. **G191**
A panel discussion on the freedom to read. Felix Morley speaks of the development of the critical faculty; Alan Barth speaks against "the barbarian invaders who now threaten to take away" the independence of American universities; Amy Winslow discusses freedom of access to books and information, drawing parallels between the dangerous trend in this country and methods now employed behind the Iron Curtain and giving special attention to labeling and blacklisting; Lloyd A. Brown discusses the printed book as a commodity "far more explosive than dynamite."

Goudeau, John M. "Intellectual Freedom." *Aspects of Librarianship*, 7:1–12, Summer 1955. **G192**
Brief account of the American Library Association's Library Bill of Rights and recent attempts at library censorship.

Gould, Kenneth M. "The Scarsdale Story." *Humanist*, 12:145–59, July–August 1952. **G193**
A report of "the clash of issues between the forces of liberty and those of obscurantism in our public schools" in the attempt to ban school textbooks in Scarsdale, N.Y. The Board of Education held to the "principles of educational freedom and responsibility . . . that books and speeches should be judged on the merit of their content and the educational use that is made of them."

"Government Clarifies Policy of Book and Library Program." *Publishers' Weekly*, 164:184–87, 18 July 1953. **G194**
A statement from the U.S. State Department (Robert L. Johnson) clarifying government policy on overseas library service which had earlier, under pressure of criticism by Senator Joseph R. McCarthy, led to confusion and book banning.

"Government Exclusion of Foreign Political Propaganda." *Harvard Law Review*, 68:1393–1409, June 1955. **G195**
"Faced with a flood of propaganda materials sent from abroad criticizing the United States or defending the policies of nations hostile to it, the Customs Bureau and the Post Office Department are undertaking a broad program of exclusion which appears to have rather doubtful statutory authority."

[Grady, Thomas]. *An Authentic Report of the Interesting Trial for a Libel, contained in the Celebrated Poem, called "The Nosegay," wherein George Evans Bruce, Esq. was Plaintiff, and Thomas Grady, Esq., Defendant . . . At Summer Assizes, 1816. Containing the Speeches of Messrs. Goold, O'Connell, Burton, and Pennefeather . . .* Limerick, Ire., Printed by A. J. Watson, for the Editor, [1816?]. 76 p. **G 196**

The plaintiff asked for £20,000 damage for a passage in Mr. Grady's long narrative poem, *The Nosegay*, that accused Bruce of no less than 40 offenses, from swindling to treason. The attorney for the plaintiff declared the poem a work of undoubted genius, but at the same time the most malignant ever before issued from the human mind, and as never before applied to the human character. The judge, in his charge to the jury, declared the work to be libelous beyond doubt, the only question was to what extent the plaintiff's reputation was damaged. The jury found for the plaintiff with a verdict of £500 damages. The editor of this report of the trial, in a preface, charges the editor of the *Southern Reporter* of Cork with suppressing the publication of the trial, hinting of bribery.

Graham, Arthur F. "Film Censorship Upheld." *Ohio State Law Journal,* 20: 161–64, Winter 1959. **G 197**

Notes on the case, *Kingsley International Pictures Corp. v. Regents of University of State of New York,* 358 U.S. 897 (1958).

Granahan, Kathryn. "When Pornography Aims at Your Home." *Christian Herald,* 83:12, 72–74, July 1960. **G 198**

The chairman of the House of Representatives Subcommittee on Postal Operations discusses her bill, designed to help to restore "clean mail" service by giving postmasters authority to detain mail destined for suspected pornographers.

Grannis, C. B. "The Right to Read and the Responsibility to Teach." *Publishers' Weekly,* 182:35, 19 November 1962.
G 199

Grant, Arnold. "Censorship and Sex." *Sexology,* 3:238–39, December 1935.
G 200

Grant, James. *The Newspaper Press: Its Origin, Progress, and Present Position.* London, Tinsley, 1871. 2 vols. **G 201**

A comprehensive history of the press of England, with numerous anecdotes on publishing and excerpts from interesting or unusual papers. There are references throughout to efforts at restraint of the press, with special treatment of the sixteenth-century licensing and Roger L'Estrange, *The Craftsman,* restric-

tions on Parliamentary reporting, the John Wilkes case, letters of Junius, the trial of John Horne Tooke, and the fight against "taxes on knowledge."

[Grant, M. R.]. *Americanism vs. Roman Catholicism.* Meridan, Miss., Truth Publishing Co., 1920. 173 p. **G 202**

Chapter 10 quotes Catholic clergy on the divine authority of the Church to establish a censorship.

Grant, Sidney S., and S. E. Angoff. "Censorship in Boston." *Boston University Law Review,* 10:36–60, January 1930; 10:147–94, April 1930. **G 203**

Part 1. Review of recent censorship that has brought ridicule and scorn to a city and state that were once centers of intellectual freedom. Specifically, the authors discuss the work of the Watch and Ward Society, the *American Mercury* case, the ban of Eugene O'Neill's *Strange Interlude,* and the police raids of 1929. The article concludes with a general account of the development of the concept of obscenity in common law. Part 2. Development of court decisions on obscenity in Massachusetts: *Commonwealth v. Holmes* (1821), *Commonwealth v. Buckley* (Elinor Glyn's *Three Weeks*), and the Dunster House case over *Lady Chatterley's Lover.* The authors contrast the severe interpretation of obscenity statutes in Massachusetts with the more liberal interpretation of similar laws by New York courts. They also comment on Massachusetts restrictions on birth control information. The authors recommend the appointment of a government board of censorship to judge offending books, thus protecting the bookseller from police censorship.

———. "Recent Developments in Censorship." *Boston University Law Review,* 10:488–509, November 1930. **G 204**

The authors discuss the recent liberal decision of the New York court in the obscenity case of *U.S. v. Dennett* in contrast with the Massachusetts restrictions on works dealing with sex education. They review the recent Massachusetts cases of *Commonwealth v. DeLacey* (*Lady Chatterley's Lover*), and *Commonwealth v. Friede* (*An American Tragedy*). They report on the passage of a new and liberalized censorship law in Massachusetts which would judge the book rather than the bookseller. The law was sponsored by a Massachusetts Citizens Committee for the Revision of the Book Law, headed by Edward A. Weeks of *Atlantic Monthly.*

Graphia, Anthony J. "The Louisiana Obscenity Statute and Freedom of Speech and Press." *Louisiana Law Review,* 23: 604–9, April 1963. **G 205**

Grasty, Charles H. "Reasonable Restrictions upon Freedom of the Press." *Papers and Proceedings, Ninth Annual Meeting, American Sociological Society,* 9: 117–22, 1914. **G 206**

A discussion of Henry Schofield's paper on freedom of the press (pp. 67–116) with respect to newspapers. "The relation of the newspaper to its chief source of revenue, and how this strictly private business relation can be maintained without doing violence to the restraints and control of public opinion, is the largest single problem of journalism." Comments on this discussion are to be found on pp. 117–22.

Graves, John T. "The Value of a Free Press." *Proceedings, Academy of Political Science in the City of New York,* 7:365–68, July 1917. **G 207**

Address delivered at the National Conference on Foreign Relations of the United States by a representative of Hearst Publications.

Graves, William B., *ed. Readings in Public Opinion; Its Formation and Control . . .* New York, Appleton, 1928. 1281 p.
G 208

Chapter 31, on Censorship and Public Opinion, includes the following readings: (1) Newell D. Hollis, Censorship in a Democracy, (2) Brenda Ueland, Censoring the Movies (from *Liberty,* 20 March 1926), (3) Text of a State Censorship Law, (4) Some City Ordinances for Regulating the Moving Pictures, (5) Governor Samuel R. McKelvie's Veto Message of Nebraska Motion Picture Censorship Bill, 1921, (6) The Philadelphia Board of Theater Control, (7) Resolution Opposing Legal Censorship of Moving Pictures, Adopted January 16, 1925 by National Better Films Conference, and (8) Mrs. A. Starr Best, The Drama League of America.

Great Britain. Cinematograph Films Council. *Tendencies to Monopoly in the Cinematograph Film Industry.* London, H.M. Stat. Off., 1944. 41 p. **G 209**

A study of the threat of monopoly domination of the British film industry both by American and British producers. The Council recommends legislation to prevent further expansion of film combines.

Great Britain. Commissioners on Criminal Law. *Sixth Report of Her Majesty's Commissioners on Criminal Law. Dated the 3rd Day of 1841. Presented to both Houses of Parliament by command of Her Majesty.* London, H.M. Stat. Off., 1841. **G 210**

Libel was one of the three offenses considered in this report. This is quoted extensively in *Law Magazine,* August 1841.

Great Britain. Committee on the Law of Defamation. *Report.* London, H.M. Stat. Off., 1948. 52 p. (Cmd. paper 7536)
G 211

The Porter Committee was appointed to consider British libel laws, long criticized for their severity. Evidence was presented by representatives of book publishers, newspapers, and broadcasting. Charges were made that the laws were too complicated and costly to enforce, that they were unpredictable, tended to stifle discussion on matters of public interest, and often favored the "gold-digging" plaintiff. The Committee recommended broadening of the defenses of justification and fair comment.

Great Britain. Council of State. *Sedition scourg'd, Or a View of that Rascally & Venemous Paper, entitled a Charge of high-treason exhibited against Oliver Cromwell, Esq: for several treasons by him committed.* London, By Hen. Hills, for Rich. Baddeley, 1653. **G 212**

This pamphlet is a reply to John Lilburne's charges against Cromwell. The author blames the government for not suppressing the pamphleteers.

Great Britain. Court of Star Chamber. *A Decree of Starre-Chamber, Concerning Printing, Made the eleuenth day of July last past. 1637.* London, Robert Barker, 1637. 32 p. (Reprinted by the Grolier Club, New York, 1884. 93 p.; summarized in Clyde, *Struggle for the Freedom of the Press*, pp. 295–97) **G 213**

This decree declares it unlawful, without special authorization, to make, buy, or keep types or presses, or to practice the trade of a printer, publisher, or bookseller. It states that all books must be licensed by the Company of Stationers; it forbids the importation of English books printed overseas; and requires "vpon paine of imprisonment" to reserve one copy for the library at Oxford. It was expected that the fear of punishment combined with the hope of getting government printing favors would keep the printers in line. The decree, humanely omits references to punishment more severe than public whipping (a month before the enactment of the decree Prynne's ears had been chopped off), but the English public was in no mood for even this repression. Four years later the Court of Star Chamber was abolished and by the end of the century all prior restraints on printing came to an end.

———. *Reports of Cases in the Courts of Star Chamber and High Commission.* Edited by Samuel Rawson Gardiner. [Westminster, Eng.] Printed for the Camden Society, 1886. 328 p. (Camden Society, Publications, new series, vol. 39) **G 214**

Part I includes Star Chamber Reports (1631–32) of *John Smith v. Crakew and Wright* for printing and selling a libel against the plaintiff; *Micha Smith and others v. Marten and others* for a scandalous libel. Part II includes High Commission Reports (1631–32) of Dr. Slater for adding a scandalous table to the Psalms, Bookseller Sparke for misprinting the Bible, Richard Blagrave for keeping Geneva Bibles, Mr. Barker, printer, for misprinting the Bible, Bookseller Whittacres for printing scandal against Queen Elizabeth, and Henry Goskin for printing a blasphemous ballad.

Great Britain. Foreign Office. *Correspondence between His Majesty's Government in the United Kingdom and the Government of the United States regarding the Censorship of Mails, December 1939–January 1940.*... London, H.M. Stat. Off., 1940. 7 p. (United States, no. 1, 1940; Cmd. paper 6156) **G 215**

Printed in part in United States *Department of State Bulletin*, 6 January 1940.

———. *Correspondence with the Swedish Minister on the Subject of the Detention by the Swedish Government of the British Transit Mail to Russia as a Reprisal for the Search of Parcels Mail by His Majesty's Government.* London, Harrison and Sons, 1916. 26 p. (Misc. no. 28, 1916; Cmd. paper 8322) **G 216**

———. *Correspondence with the United States Ambassador Respecting the Treatment of Mails in Neutral Vessels.*... London, Harrison and Sons, 1916. 3 p. (Misc. no. 5, 1916; Cmd. paper 8173) **G 217**

A note from the United States government regarding the examination of parcels and letter mails appears as Misc. no. 20, 1916, Cmd. paper 8261, in continuation of Misc. no. 9, Cmd. paper 8223.

———. *The Mails as a German War Weapon; Memorandum on the Censorship of Mails Carried by Neutral Ships.* London, Eyre & Spottiswoode, 1916. 24 p. **G 218**

British postal censorship in World War I.

———. *Memorandum Addressed by the French and British Governments to the United States Government Regarding the Examination of Parcels and Letter Mails.* London, Harrison and Sons, 1917. 10 p. (Misc. no. 2, 1917; Cmd. paper 8438; in continuation of Misc. no. 23, 1916; Cmd. paper 8294) **G 219**

———. *Memorandum Presented by His Majesty's Government and the French Government to Neutral Governments Regarding the Examination of Parcels and Letter Mails*... London, Harrison and Sons, 1916. 7 p. (Misc. no. 9, 1916; Cmd. paper 8223) **G 220**

Great Britain. General Council of the Press. *The Press and The People: The Annual Report of the General Council of the Press.* London, The Council, 1954–date. (Since 1962, known as The Press Council) **G 221**

The Council was established by the Royal Commission on the Press to safeguard the freedom of the press and to combat abuses of that freedom. The Council makes annual reports of press performances and suggests ways of improvement. Specific complaints against the press investigated by the Council are summarized or reported in appendices. The 1964 report, for example, reports on the following cases adjudicated during the year: intrusion into grief, late telephone calls by reporters, deliberate misleading reports, refusal to publish a letter to the editor, identifying a minor brought before Juvenile Court, a satirical editorial taken seriously, the refusal to accept certain minority group advertisements, and what constitutes clear retraction of errors in print. Beginning with the eighth annual report (1961) signed articles appear as follows: Some Legal Aspects of Press Freedom by Lord Birkett (1961); Subtle Censorship Is Shackling Britain's Press by Cecil H. King (1962); Curbs on the Rights of Disclosure by Lord Shawcross (1963).

Great Britain. General Staff. *Censorship Orders and Regulations for Troops in the Field.* [n.p., 1917]. 14 p. **G 222**

Printed in France during World War I.

Great Britain. Home Department. *Correspondence Respecting the International Conferences on Obscene Literature and the "White Slave Traffic," Held in Paris, April and May, 1910*... London, H.M. Stat. Off., 1912. 45 p. (Cmd. paper 6547) **G 223**

Great Britain. Parliament. *An Act against Unlicensed and Scandalous Books and Pamphlets, And for better Regulating of Printing.* London, Printed by John Field for Edward Husband, 1649. 17 p. (Reproduced in Firth and Rait, *Acts and Ordinances of the Interregnum*, vol. 2, p. 245; extracted in Clyde, *Struggle for the Freedom of the Press*, pp. 187–88) **G 224**

———. *An Act For Reviving of a former Act, Entituled, An Act against Vnlicensed and Scandalous Books and Pamphlets, and for better Regulating of Printing.*... London, Printed by John Field, Printer to the Parliament of England, 1652. (*Collection of Acts of Parliament, 1648–54*, vol. 3, pp. 1923–28; reproduced in Clyde, *Struggle for the Freedom of the Press*, pp. 314–18) **G 225**

The Act is dated 7 January 1653.

———. *Correspondence Respecting the Suppression of the "Bosphore Egyptien."* London,

H.M. Stat. Off., 1885. 42 p. (Sessional Papers, 1884–85, vol. 89)   **G 226**

British authorities in Egypt suppressed a French paper, *Bosphore Egyptien*, that had been critical of the British, thus precipitating a controversy with the French and Egyptian governments. After a lengthy exchange of diplomatic messages, the British government agreed that the press be reinstated.

————. *The History of Two Acts, entitled, "An Act for the Safety and Preservation of His Majesty's Person and Government against Treasonable and Seditious Practices and Attempts, and an Act for the more effective preventing Seditious Meetings and Assemblies," including the Proceedings of the British Parliament and of the Various Popular Meetings, Societies and Clubs, throughout the Kingdom . . .* London, 1796. 800 p. plus.   **G 227**

Contains hundreds of petitions, manifestoes, declarations, and resolutions of various societies and groups, both pro and con with respect to these acts, under which many of the eighteenth-century trials for seditious libel were undertaken.

————. *Ordinance of the Lords and Commons Assembled in Parliament Against Unlicensed and Scandalous Pamphlets, And For better Regulating of Printing. . . .* London, Printed for Edward Husband, Printer to the Honorable House of Commons, 30 September 1647. 8 p.   **G 228**

————. *Ordinance of the Lords and Commons Assembled in Parliament for the Utter Suppression and Abolishing of All Stageplays and Interludes . . .* Imprinted at London for J. Wright, 1647. 5 p. (Reprinted, London, 1869)   **G 229**

Great Britain. Parliament. Broadcasting Committee. *Memoranda Submitted to the Committee.* London, H.M. Stat. Off., 1951. 583 p. (Report 8117, 1950–51, vol. 9)   **G 230**

Testimony submitted by the B.B.C., other government agencies, advisory bodies, unions, performers, producers, educators, and representatives of religious and minority groups. A summary of the evidence presented by the National Council for Civil Liberties is given on pp. 313–14. The NCCL report criticizes the B.B.C.'s tendencies "to abrogate to itself the right, in normal times, to censor the expression of views by outside speakers invited to the microphone." The Council also referred to information that "certain well-known public figures are blacklisted."

All censorship policies should be made public and "all future cases of censorship and blacklisting should be listed and made available to all members of Parliament and all members of Advisory Committees."

————. *Report of the Broadcasting Committee, 1949.* London, H.M. Stat. Off., 1951. 327 p. (Report 8116, 1950–51, vol. 9)   **G 231**

The Committee was appointed by the Lord President of the Council and the Postmaster General jointly "to consider the constitution, control, finance and other general aspects of the sound and television broadcasting services of the United Kingdom . . . and to advise on the conditions under which these services and wire broadcasting should be conducted." The Committee was under the chairmanship of Lord Beveridge. The main report summarizes British broadcasting practices and raises the various issues of controversy, including program content, religious broadcasting, political broadcasting, and degree of government control and licensing. In addition to recommendations as to constitution and powers of broadcasting authority, the Commission suggested a number of policies to govern broadcasting of programs dealing with religion, political parties, and controversial issues: "The allocation of opportunities for ventilation of controversial views, should not be guided either by simple calculation of the numbers who already hold such views, or by fear of giving offense to particular groups of listeners." The majority approved the continuation of broadcast control under a single corporation; a minority report by Selwyn Lloyd disagreed with the continuation of a public monopoly. A separate statement by six committee members states the case against sponsored broadcasting and commercial advertising (pp. 213–26). Members Joseph Reeves and Dr. Stephen Taylor present an expanded statement on civil liberties in broadcasting (pp. 233–37).

Great Britain. Parliament. Committee on Broadcasting, 1960. *Memoranda Submitted to the Committee. . . . (Appendix E).* London, H.M. Stat. Off., 1962. 1268 p. (Report 1819 and 1819–1, 1961–62, vols. 9 and 10)   **G 232**

Memoranda from the B.B.C. and the Independent Television Authority includes such topics related to freedom of broadcasting as religious broadcasting, control of advertising, and control of program. There are statements from performers, associations, and organizations representing minority religious and political groups.

————. *Memorandum on the Report of the Committee on Broadcasting, 1960.* London, H.M. Stat. Off., 1962. 12 p. (Report 1770, 1961–62, vol. 31)   **G 233**

A summary of recommendations of the Committee and proposals for Government action based upon the Report of the Committee (Cmd. 1753).

————. *Report of the Committee on Broadcasting, 1960.* London, H.M. Stat. Off., 1962. 342 p. (Report 1753, 1961–62, vol. 9)   **G 234**

The Committee, headed by Sir Henry Pilkington, was appointed by the Postmaster General to consider the future of broadcasting services in the United Kingdom. The report recommends no basic changes in arrangements for the discharge of the government's ultimate responsibility for the social consequences of broadcasting. The Committee rejected proposals for censorship and also proposals for a Broadcasting Consumers' Council; it approved of continuing the veto power of the Postmaster General on particular programs or classes of programs. It recommended that the B.B.C. remain the main instrument of broadcasting in the United Kingdom. On political broadcasting it stated: "We re-affirm the recommendation of the Ullswater Committee that 'The BBC must, of course, continue to be the judge of the amount of political broadcasting which the programme will stand.'" The Corporation must never be under an express obligation to make time available. The Committee recommends strict control of the amount and nature of commercial advertising; it recommends continued prohibitions on paid religious and political advertising and the extending of prohibitions to subliminal advertising.

Great Britain. Parliament. House of Commons. Committee for Suppressing Licentious and Impious Practices under Pretence of Religion, Liberty, etc. *The Confession of Lawrence Clarkson, touching the Making and Publishing of the Impious and Blasphemous Book, Called the Single Eye, and also Mr. Rainborow's Carriages. . . .* London, 1650. Broadside.   **G 235**

This resolution sentences Clarkson to the house of correction for a month, thereafter to be banished from the country. All copies of his book are to be seized and burnt by the common hangman.

Great Britain. Parliament. House of Commons. Committee of Secrecy. *Report . . .* London, John Stockdale, 1799. 111 p. (Another edition was issued by J. Plymsell at the Anti-Jacobin Press. 90 p.)   **G 236**

Largely concerned with the activities of the Society of United Irishmen. Includes reports on suppressing seditious publications and on the action taken against members of the London Corresponding Society—Hardy, Tooke, Thelwall, and others.

Great Britain. Parliament. House of Commons. Secret Committee on Seditious Societies. *Report from the Committee of Secrecy. 1st, 2d and Supplement to 2d Report with Appendix.* London, 1794. 3 vols. in 1.   **G 237**

Concerning the Society for Constitutional Information, London; London Corresponding Society.

Great Britain. Parliament. House of Commons. Select Committee on the Law of Libel. *Report from the Select Committee on the Law of Libel: with Proceedings of the Committee.* London, 1880. 6 p. (Report 284, 1880, vol. 2) **G 238**

———. *Report . . . together with the Proceedings of the Committee, Minutes of Evidence, and Appendix.* London, Ordered by the House of Commons to be Printed, 1879. 108 p. (Report 343, 1879, vol. 4) **G 239**

The Committee was appointed "to inquire into the Law in relation to Libel in newspapers and journals, and as to the mode of proving the Publication of such Libels, and the means of rendering the Proprietors and Publishers of Newspapers and Journals responsible Civilly and Criminally for Libels contained therein." After extensive testimony the Committee recommended an extension of privilege to newspaper reporting of public meetings, if reported fairly and accurately, without malice, and to the public benefit. The Committee also recommended that no criminal prosecution be commenced against a newspaper for libel without the fiat of the Attorney General being first obtained.

[Great Britain. Parliament. House of Commons. Select Committee on the Obscene Publications Bill]. *Memoranda of Evidence Submitted to the Select Committee . . . by the Progressive League, Alec Craig, the Society of Labour Lawyers.* London, Progressive League, 1958. **G 240**

This testimony before the Committee did not appear in the published *Minutes of Evidence*, but was privately published.

———. *Minutes of Evidence. . . .* London, H.M. Stat. Off., 1958. 154 p. (Report 122, 1957–58, vol. 6) **G 241**

The following witnesses testified on the proposed bill: Sir Frank Newsam, Undersecretary of State; J. K. Jones, legal adviser, and S. H. E. Burley of the Home Office; Sir Theobald Mathew, director of public prosecutions; M. G. Wittome, W. J. Sellers, and B. Rose of Customs; Sir John Nott-Bower, T. MacD. Baker, and Inspector D. McLeod of the Metropolitan police; Sir Alan Herbert, Norman St. John Stevas, and C. R. Hewitt from the Society of Authors; Sir Geoffrey Faber, R. H. Code Holland, and F. J. Warburg from the Publishers Association; and A. C. West and Sir Charles Martin from the Association of Chiefs of Police.

———. *Report from the Select Committee . . . together with the Proceedings of the Com-*

mittee, Minutes of Evidence and Appendices. London, H.M. Stat. Off., 1958. 96 p. plus 28 p. (Report 123–1, 1957–58, vol. 6; reprinted in U.S. House of Representatives. 86th Cong., 2d sess., Committee on Post Office and Civil Service. *Hearing before the Subcommittee on Postal Operations,* 27 May 1960, pp. 51–60) **G 242**

The Committee was appointed to consider whether it was desirable to amend and consolidate the law relating to obscene publications. "We have considered it inadvisable to depart substantially from the definition laid down in *R. v. Hicklin*. The test laid down by Cockburn, C.J. in that case has been subjected to considerable judicial interpretation which has removed some, though not all, of its uncertainties. . . . Our recommendations on amendment of the law are therefore divided into two parts, the first designed to bring greater certainty to the law of obscene publications . . . , and the second to strengthen the powers for suppressing the pornographic trade." The Committee recommended the following changes in the obscenity law: (1) The class of persons liable to be depraved and corrupted should be defined in accordance with the decision in *R. v. Secker*. (2) The effect of the work as a whole should be considered. (3) The defense of literary merit should be afforded. (4) The author should have the right to be heard in court. (5) A defense should be afforded the bookseller. (6) Consent of the director of public prosecutors should be required to initiate obscenity proceedings. (7) The 1857 Act should be amended to omit proof of sale and to permit power of seizure and the search of stalls and vehicles. Testimony included that of authors T. S. Eliot and E. M. Forster, a memorandum submitted by the Public Morality Council, a complaint from the British Federation of Master Printers as to the ambiguity of the obscenity law with respect to the liability of the printer, and a letter from Mr. R. H. Code Holland answering the question, How many books failed to be published because the printers refused to print them: "None that ought to be published."

Great Britain. Parliament. House of Commons. Select Committee on Theatres and Places of Entertainment. *Report . . . together with the Proceedings of the Committee, Minutes of Evidence, Appendix, and Index.* London, H.M. Stat. Off., 1892. 592 p. (Report 240, 1892, vol. 8) **G 243**

The Committee was appointed "to inquire into the operation of Acts of Parliament relating to the Licensing and Regulation of Theatres and Places of Public Entertainment, and to consider and report any alterations in the law which may appear desirable." Testimony was taken both in favor of the Lord Chamberlain continuing as stage censor and as opposed to the system. Drama critic William Archer objected to the present system of censorship of plays on the ground of its failure to eliminate the indecent at the same time it suppressed the serious dramatic work, e. g. Shelley's *The Cenci*. The public, he argued, is the only reliable judge of the worth of a play. Any

indecency on the stage should be a matter of police action. The Committee concluded that the censorship of plays has worked satisfactorily and that it should be continued and extended to performances in music halls and other places of public entertainment, echoing the recommendation of a similar investigating committee made in 1866.

Great Britain. Parliament. House of Commons. Select Committee on Theatrical Licenses and Regulations. *Report . . . together with the Proceedings of the Committee, Minutes of Evidence and Appendix.* London, Ordered by House of Commons to be Printed, 1866. 333 p.; index 66 p. (Report 373, 1866, vol. 11) **G 244**

The evidence given before the Select Committee of 1866 constitutes one of the most important documents on British stage censorship. The witnesses included the Lord Chamberlain, Spencer Cecil Brabazon Ponsonby, who reported on the stage censorship activities of his office (very few plays were refused license—only 19 in 13 years) and urged continuation of censorship to prevent immorality in the theater; the then censor, William Bodham Donne, who described his method of operating; novelist Charles Reade who found the present censorship satisfactory if accompanied by the right of appeal; author Shirley Brookes, who described the censorship of his dramatization of *Coningsby*, and would abolish censorship, leaving the judgment to the audience; John B. Buckstone, proprietor of the Haymarket Theatre who believed stage censorship did not interfere with freedom of authorship; and John Hallinghead, author and signer of the petition of the Dramatic Authors' Society, who objected to the present censorship as both unnecessary and ineffective. The Committee concluded that censorship of drama under the Lord Chamberlain had worked satisfactorily and that it should be continued and extended to music halls and other places of entertainment.

Great Britain. Parliament. House of Lords. Select Committee Appointed to Consider the Law of Defamation and Libel. *Report . . . with the Minutes of Evidence Taken before the Committee, and an Index.* London, H.M. Stat. Off., 1843. 192 p. (Report 513, 1843, vol. 5) **G 245**

The investigation resulted in the Lord Campbell's Libel Act, which permitted the defendant in a case of criminal libel to plead the truth of the matter charged, if published for public benefit. The Act was drawn up by Thomas Starkie, author of *Treatise on the Law of Slander and Libel* and modeled on the Benthamite code of Louisiana.

———. Parliament. Joint Select Committee on Lotteries and Indecent Ad-

vertisements. *Report; Together with the Proceedings of the Committee, Minutes of Evidence, and Appendices. Ordered by the House of Commons, to Be Printed, 29th July, 1908.* London, Printed for H.M. Stat. Off., by Vacher & Sons, 1908. 120 p. (Cmd. paper 275)   **G 246**
Contains evidence of the lucrative trade in pornography, including the activities of "Roland de Villiers" and Charles Carrington. The report recommends a revamping of the obscenity laws into a single comprehensive act aimed at pornographic matter, but excluding works of artistic or literary merit. The recommendations were not acted upon.

[Great Britain. Parliament. Joint Select Committee on Stage Plays (Censorship)]. *Censorship and Licensing (Joint Select Committee). Verbatim Report of the Proceedings and Full Text of the Recommendations, with an Appendix Containing Further Statements by Mr. G Bernard Shaw, Mr. Henry Arthur Jones, Mr. Charles Frohman &c., and Articles from "The Stage."* London, The Stage, 1910. 228 p.   **G 247**

————. *Report . . . on the Stage Plays (Censorship); together with the Proceedings of the Committee, Minutes of Evidence, and Appendices . . .* London, H.M. Stat. Off., 1909. 413 p (House of Lords Reports and Papers, no. 21; Cmd. paper 303, vol. 3)   **G 248**
The Select Committee was appointed "to inquire into the censorship of stage plays as constituted by the Theatres Act of 1843, and into the operations of the Act of Parliament relating to the licensing and regulation of theatres and places of public entertainment, and to report any alterations of the law or practice which may appear desirable." The Committee examined 49 witnesses, including the Comptroller of the Lord Chamberlain's Department, the Examiner of Plays, members of the clergy, drama critics, actors, and theater managers. Among the opponents of the present stage censorship were William Archer, critic; Granville-Barker, actor, author, and manager, who testified that the censorship retarded the advancement of English drama and made uncertain the profession of authors; and playwright J. M. Barrie, who favored abolishing the national censor, but retaining the licensing of theaters and leaving the action against immoral plays to local authorities; G. K. Chesterton, who preferred to trust 12 ordinary men as censors, but not one; Hall Caine, who stated that present censorship implies that the theater is merely a place of amusement and that serious drama is suspect; John Galsworthy, Laurence Housman, George B. Shaw, Israel Zangwill, and Professor Gilbert Murray. Despite contrary evidence of the

literary greats the Committee concluded that (1) the law which covers indecency, blasphemy, and libel in print was inadequate to cover the theater and, therefore, that special laws were needed; (2) producers should have access, prior to production, to a public authority impowered to license plays; (3) license authority should not have power of veto on a play; (4) public authority should have the power by a summary process to suspend the performance of an unlicensed play that appears to be improper, in which case the producer is libel to penalty; (5) the propriety of the future performance of an unlicensed play should be courts of law in cases where indecency is alleged, and in other cases, a mixed committee of the Privy Council. St. John Ervine, in his biography of Shaw states: "Such a galaxy of mind and wit had never appeared in a Blue Book before, nor has it been seen since."

[Great Britain. Postal Censorship Bureau]. *The London Censorship, 1914–1919, by Members of the Staff, Past and Present.* [London, Printed by Harrison & Sons for Private Circulation, 1919.] 69 p.   **G 249**
Anecdotes of censorship during World War I.

————. Royal Commission on the Press, 1947–1949. *Memoranda of Evidence Submitted . . .* London, H.M. Stat. Off., 1947–48. 262 p. in 5 vols.   **G 250**
Contents: (1) Charges made by the National Union of Journalists of a financial monopoly in the newspaper industry. The NUJ recommends legislation to prevent monopolies, reform in libel law, fixed ratio of advertising versus editorial space, and an industry self-regulatory body. (2) The Institute of Journalists believes monopoly control exerts little influence over free expression in the press. It is more concerned with restrictive union practices of the NUJ, control of official news, and restrictions on supplies of newsprint. The IJ recommends a self-regulatory code. (3) Replies to a questionnaire dealing with various proposals for reform, received from 95 publishers of newspapers and periodicals. (4) Replies to questionnaire sent to newspaper editors and publishers association. Both groups found that the chief obstacle to freedom of the press was newsprint restrictions, and that self-regulatory measures were preferable to government controls. (5) Reply of Advertising Association to questionnaire, denying that advertising interests influence editorial policy.

————. *Minutes of Evidence . . . 19 June 1947—10 June 1948.* London, H.M. Stat. Off., 1947–48. 38 separate reports, totalling more than 1,000 pages.   **G 251**
The Commission heard evidence from a variety of witnesses. The first memorandum presents a full statement of the case against newspaper monopoly presented by representatives of the National Union of Journalists. They were followed by other journalists, editors, publishers, and representatives of the advertising associations. Points of discussion included charges of Communists infiltration

in the NUJ, the low standards of the popular press, sensational intrusion of privacy, training of journalists, and newsprint restrictions.

————. *Report.* London, H.M. Stat. Off., 1949. 363 p. (Cmd. paper 7700)   **G 252**
Final report of a Commission, created at the recommendation of the Government and the National Union of Journalists to study freedom of the press in Great Britain. The first part of the report relates to the organization of the press—ownership and control, policy formation, news agencies, and the growth of chains. The second part deals with performance of the press—how standards are set and carried out, and factors of external influence. Final chapters make recommendations. The report supports free enterprise against state control and vindicates the press, in general, against charges of monopoly and corruption. It recommends that reform and supervision should come from within the profession rather than from government control. The Commission recommends the establishment of a General Council of the Press, to be made up of members of the profession, to safeguard press freedom and to encourage higher journalistic standards. The Council was subsequently created. Like the American Commission on Freedom of the Press, whose report appeared just as this Commission was named, the Royal Commission consisted entirely of impartial experts with no representatives of the press. A full description of the documents of the Commission and comments about its findings are presented in U. S. Library of Congress, *Freedom of Information*, pp. 103 ff.

Great Britain. Royal Commission on the Press, 1961–1962. *Documentary Evidence.* London, H.M. Stat. Off., 1962. 5 vols. (Cmd. papers 1812–4 through 9)   **G 253**
Vol. 1, National Newspaper Undertakings; vol. 2, Provincial Daily and Sunday Newspapers, etc.; vol. 3, Weekly Newspapers, Magazine and Periodical Undertakings; vol. 4, Associations and Trade Unions; vol. 5, Advertising Agents and Associations, etc.; vol. 6, Miscellaneous (including associations, societies, and unions).

————. *Minutes of Oral Evidence.* London, H.M. Stat. Off., 1962. 3 vols. (Cmd. papers 1812, 1812–1 and 2)   **G 254**
Vol. 1, Individuals, Associations, etc., Newspaper and Periodical Proprietors; vol. 2, Trade Unions and Associations, etc., vol. 3, Miscellaneous.

————. *Report.* London, H.M. Stat. Off., 1962. 239 p. (Cmd. paper 1811)   **G 255**
This second Royal Commission on the Press was appointed "to examine the economic and financial factors affecting the production and sale of newspapers, magazines and other periodicals in the United Kingdom, including (a) manufacturing, printing, distribution and other costs; (b) efficiency of production; and

(c) advertising and other revenue, including any revenue derived from interests in television; to consider whether these factors tend to diminish diversity of ownership and control or the number or variety of such publications, having regard to the public interest, of the accurate presentation of news and the free expression of opinion." The Commission was under the chairmanship of Hartley William, Baron Shawcross. Among the recommendations were that newspaper interests in television be terminated, that no Government press subsidy be granted, that newspapers be required to disclose ownership and control, reporting such information to a reconstituted Council of the Press, that such a Council "act as a tribunal to hear complaints from editors and journalists of undue influence by advertisers or advertising agents and of pressure by their superiors to distort the truth or otherwise engage in unprofessional conduct." Further amalgamations of newspapers should be submitted to a Press Amalgamations Court for consent.

Great Britain. Special Commission to Inquire into Charges and Allegations against Certain Members of Parliament and Others. *Parnellism and Crime. The Special Commission . . . Reprinted from the Times.* London, G. E. Wright, 1880–90. 35 vols. **G 256**
The Commission was appointed to inquire into charges made by the defendants, John Walter, the registered proprietor, and G. E. Wright, the printer and publisher of the *Times* newspaper, in the course of proceedings in action entitled *O'Donnell v. Walter and Another.* Charles S. Parnell, the Irish nationalist, and others brought charges against the London *Times* for defamation, in printing, among other things, statements that Parnell had approved the Phoenix Park assassinations. The article was based on alleged letters from Parnell, sold to the *Times* by one Richard Pigott. Under cross-examination of Sir Charles Russell, Pigott admitted forging the letters. Parnell was exonerated of the *Times* charges by the special commission of judges. The report of the judges appears in vol. 35.

Great Britain. War Office. Army. *Memorandum on the Censorship . . .* London, H.M. Stat. Off., 1915. 5 p. (Cmd. paper 7679) **G 257**
Official policy on censorship of the press, the mail, and cables in Great Britain during World War I.

———. *Memorandum on the Official Press Bureau.* London, H.M. Stat. Off., 1915. 3 p. (Cmd. paper 7680) **G 258**
British censorship plans, World War I, presented by John T. Graves.

Grebstein, Sheldon N. *Monkey Trial: The State of Tennessee vs. John Thomas Scopes.* New York, Houghton Mifflin, 1960. 221 p. **G 259**

A casebook of the famous evolution trial in which lawyers William Jennings Bryan and Clarence Darrow were pitted against each other. The case involved the use of a high school textbook, George Hunter's *Civic Biology.* The present work includes large sections from the transcript of the trial, newspaper accounts, the court decision, and other documents.

———. "Sex, Censorship, and Morality in the Modern Novel." *Kentucky Library Association Bulletin,* 25:16–25, January 1961. **G 260**

[Greeley, Horace]. *The Littlejohn Libel Suit. The Case of DeWitt C. Littlejohn against Horace Greeley, Tried at the Oswego Term of the Supreme Court of the State of New York, at Pulaski, Sept. 10–13, 1861 . . . Containing the Rulings of Judge [William J.] Bacon, the Arguments, and Points of Messrs. D. H. Marsh, I. T. Williams, John H. Porter, Chas. S. Sedgewick, and Henry T. Foster. Phonographically Reported by James L. Crosby.* New York, The Tribune Association, 1861. 56 p. **G 261**
Relates to a charge of libel against the editor of the New York *Tribune* for articles appearing in that paper. The jury disagreed—nine were for the defendant, two for nominal damages, and one for heavy damages—so the case was dismissed.

Green, Beriah. *The Martyr. A Discourse, in Commemoration of the Martyrdom of the Rev. Elijah P. Lovejoy, delivered in Broadway Tabernacle, New York; and in the Bleecker Street Church, Utica.* New York, American Anti-Slavery Society, 1838. 18 p. **G 262**
A eulogy on Lovejoy as a Christian martyr and an assault on the institution of slavery. Only incidentally touches on freedom of the press.

Green, Bernard. "Federalism and the Administration of Criminal Justice: The Treatment of Obscenity in the United States, Canada and Australia." *Kentucky Law Journal,* 51:667–702, Summer 1963. **G 263**
"It is the purpose of this article to examine how each of three countries—the United States, Canada, and Australia—has tried to solve these obscenity problems in the context of their particular circumstances." The author examines the three countries under three major categories: the federal structure, the testing of obscenity as formulated by the legislatures and interpreted by the courts, and the obscenity laws in operation.

———. "Obscenity, Censorship and Juvenile Delinquency." *University of Toronto Law Journal,* 14:229–52, 1962. **G 264**

"There is widespread belief that a causal relationship exists between an allegedly increased dissemination of obscene material and the increase of juvenile delinquency ratio. It is the purpose of this paper to examine the evidence for this belief with a view to deciding whether present methods of controlling the content of communication are justified or adequate." The author finds "no scientific studies showing that exposure to obscenity is a causal factor in juvenile delinquency. . . . The view that seems to be supported best by the evidence is that obscenity is unlikely to harm any but the disturbed juvenile, and that, even in this case, the effect is probably slight." Nevertheless, because of widespread popular belief of the harmfulness of obscenity to children and the inability of parents to cope with the problem, some state intervention seems necessary. "A system of age classification would seem to offer the best hope." Such a system would not restrict the free flow of adult material to adult readers or viewers, but would protect juveniles. Books and magazines could be imprinted with a special sign prohibiting sale to anyone under a specified age; adult radio and television shows could be scheduled for late evening hours. A proposed censorship board should be staffed by child psychologists, psychiatrists, educators, communications experts, and teachers of English drawn from universities. Due process must be preserved; counsel must have the right to submit evidence and make arguments; and the decision must be open to the public. Such a system of classification-censorship, which will protect juveniles, should obviate the need for extralegal censorship.

Green, Edward. "How Can the Public Mind Be Safeguarded: The Problem of Library Censorship." *Municipal Journal,* 44:1823–24, 11 October 1935. **G 265**

Green, Francis V. "Uses and Misuses of Censorship; Modern War Function Has Developed until Many of its Rules Serve Only to Annoy People at Home Without Concealing News from the Enemy." *New York Times Magazine,* 28 April 1918, pp. 4–5. **G 266**

Green, Reginald H. "Freedom, Responsibility and the Student Press." *Masthead,* 10(2):14–16, Spring 1958. **G 267**
A National Student Association officer states that student newspapers should not be under the control of the university administration, that faculty advice is welcome but not faculty control. "We contend that freedom of the collegiate press is theoretically desirable and practically obtainable."

Greenaway, Emerson. "An Informed Public." *Library Journal,* 77:1123–27, July 1952. **G 268**

The librarian of Enoch Pratt Free Library, Baltimore, describes how that library, through its "statement of objectives" in book selection, seeks to provide freedom for ideas. He discusses the danger of censorship and how public libraries can combat it.

Greene, William V. "Your Catholic Conscience: Is That Book on the *Index?*" *Our Lady of Perpetual Help Magazine*, 3:317–19, July 1940.   **G 269**

Greenfield, Meg. "How We Got Protected from Communist Propaganda." *Reporter*, 27:22–25, 25 October 1962.

G 270

An account of the passage of the Cunningham amendment to the federal bill increasing postal rates (1962), whereby unsealed mail that comes into the country from abroad and is designated Communist propaganda will be held and the addressee notified that such mail will be delivered only on request. There is a "white list" of legitimate recipients exempted from the restrictions.

Greenslade, D. R. W. "The Press Council of Great Britain as Seen by a Working Journalist." *Grassroots Editor*, 6(2):5–9, April 1965.   **G 271**

The editor of the Mansfield *Chronicle Advertiser* concludes that "from the point of view of journalistic ethics the Press Council is doing a useful job in providing a yardstick for behavior and possibly a deterrent from excess."

Greenslet, Ferris. "Are All Things Pure?" *Saturday Review of Literature*, 5:333–34, 10 November 1928.   **G 272**

A review of Ernst and Seagle's *To the Pure . . .*, with Mr. Greenslet's own ideas on obscenity laws, particularly in Massachusetts. The book, he believes, is better calculated to provide ammunition and entertainment to the proponents of complete freedom than to convince the objectors. He concludes his remarks with the observation that in the millennium "not the shocking volume but the shocked reader may be haled into court."

[Greenspan, Lou, *ed.*]. "The Journal Looks at Film Censorship around the World." *Journal of the Screen Producers Guild*, 11(6):1–42, December 1963.   **G 273**

A brief history of film censorship in the United States is presented by Geoffrey Shurlock, administrator of the Production Code; Britain's independent censorship is described by John Trevelyan, secretary of the British Board of Film Censors; Canadian film censorship is described by Hye Bossin; Australia's "liberal censorship" by Colin J. Campbell, chief Commonwealth film censor. The case for and against film censorship in the United States is presented by Kenneth MacGowan. There

are also brief articles on movie censorship in Argentina, France, Germany, Japan, Sweden, Mexico, Brazil, Belgium, and Spain.

[———]. "The Journal Looks at Film Classification." *Journal of the Screen Producers Guild*, 7(9):1–27, September 1961.

G 274

A cross section of opinion on the question: Should the American film industry adopt a rating system similar to that used in Great Britain. Eric Johnston looks at both sides of the classification system in his article, Classification—a Noise or an Echo? Father Harold C. Gardiner writes favorably of classification; John Trevelyan, secretary of the British Board of Film Censors, describes the British system; Albert M. Pickus, president of the Theater Owners of America, presents the views of the exhibitor; Msgr. Thomas F. Little, of the Legion of Decency, favors classification; film critic Richard L. Coe believes "the complete categorizing of films would defeat what we boast of as freedom"; Charles Schnee, president of the Writers' Guild of America, favors having the industry try classification; and S. Franklin Mack, of the National Council of Churches, favors advisory classification from the industry to help the people make their own selections.

[———]. "The Journal Looks at the Production Code . . . Should It Be Abolished?" *Journal of the Screen Producers Guild*, 7(1):1–38, March 1965.

G 275

"Has the Code actually outlived its usefulness and should it, perhaps, be put to rest? Or, is it doing its best to 'hold the line' and should it be encouraged to go on?" The following writers discuss the issue: Walter M. Mirisch, producer; Bishop Gerald Kennedy, of the Methodist Church; John Houseman, producer; Richard L. Coe, critic; Michael Blankfort, writer; Geoffrey Shurlock, administrator of the Code; Max E. Youngstein, producer; William H. Mooring, Catholic film critic; Sumner M. Redstone, theater operator; Charles A. Alicoate, publisher of *Film Daily*; and George Cukor, producer.

Greenway, Cornelius. "In the Name of Religion." *Library Journal*, 77:1342–43, 1 September 1952.   **G 276**

Excerpts from an address by the pastor of All Souls Universalist Church, Brooklyn, to the Religious Round Table of the American Library Association. Dr. Greenway stated that many distinguished propagandists "sin against our public libraries. These self-styled and self-appointed censors are sorely tempted to look down upon and harshly condemn those with whom they differ in politics, religion, or race. It is the duty of the librarian and his staff to keep free the circulation of ideas. . . . It is the public's duty to defend the librarians and their staffs from all the attacks by the various pressure groups."

Greg, *Sir* Walter W. *Licensers for the Press, &c to 1640; a Biographical Index*

Based Mainly on Arber's Transcript of the Register of the Company of Stationers. Oxford, Eng., Oxford Bibliographical Society, 1962. 109p. (Publications, new series, vol. 10)   **G 277**

———. *Some Aspects and Problems of London Publishing Between 1550 and 1650.* London, Oxford University Press, 1956. 131p. (Lyell Lectures, Oxford, Trinity Term, 1955)   **G 278**

Based on records of the Company of Stationers, these six lectures relate to the printing monopoly it held in England. Lecture 3 deals with the licensing of the press. Lecture 6 deals with the question of whether copies of a play were sometimes entered in the Stationers' Register, not with the intention of publication, but rather in order to prevent publication.

Gregg, Pauline. *Free-Born John; a Biography of John Lilburne*. London, Harrap, 1961. 424p.   **G 279**

A full-length biography of the colorful leader of the seventeenth-century Levellers. For his fight for freedom of the press Lilburne was whipped and pilloried by the Star Chamber, imprisoned by the Long Parliament, banished, and twice put on trial for his life. This scholarly biography is based on the prolific tracts of Lilburne himself and on other contemporary documents.

Gregorius, Adam S. "Literary Volsteadism." *Saturday Review of Literature*, 5:1180, 13 July 1929.   **G 280**

In a letter to the editor the writer notes that whatever the original intent of the Tariff Act of 1922 with respect to obscenity, its present effect is to give complete protection to American publishers by keeping out foreign production of books readily obtainable in America.

Gregory, Francis. *A Modest Plea for the Due Regulation of the Press, In Answer to several Reasons lately Printed against it.* London, R. Sare, 1698. 46p.   **G 281**

Written as an answer to Mathew Tindal's *A Letter to a Member of Parliament . . .*, in which Tindal opposed government licensing of the press. Gregory, the Rector of Hambleton, argues that "since this unlimited Liberty of the Press would certainly be . . . an in-let to Schisms, Heresies, and a great variety of Opinions and Practices in matters of Religion; the allowance of it can never consist with that Command of God . . ." Two years earlier, in his *A Divine Antidote against a Devilish Poyson*, Gregory recommended burning for John Smith's *A Designed End to the Socinian Controversy* (1693), which he described as "so abominably foul, that nothing can purge it, save only that which consumes it."

Gregory, Goldwin. "Canada Mollycoddled by Press, Radio." *Saturday Night*, 57:6–7, 20 September 1941.   **G 282**

The Canadian press and radio have not been presenting a full and accurate picture of world conditions. The fault is not with the Press Censor, who is reasonable, but with the publishers of the daily papers. "The offenses range from outright distortion or faking of news; through the deliberate withholding of news; through the expression editorially of opinions based on deliberately falsified news items; through the use of headlines which misleadingly color the news; right down to the comparatively trivial, but nonetheless inexcusable offense of reporting matters of political import with a bias to correspond to the party allegience of the particular newspaper."

Gregory, Horace. "The Return of Lady C." *Nation*, 188:501–2, 30 May 1959. **G 283**

In his novel Lawrence "advanced two warnings to his readers: the dangers of sexual and intellectual sterility; a growing lack of actual communication between human beings." Only the unexpurgated edition "deserves the promise of immortality." Censorship makes the book uneasily suggestive and intellectually dishonest.

Gregory, Robert. "Postal Censorship. Why the Postoffice Has No Time for Your Mail." *One*, 9(8):5–18, August 1961. **G 284**

In 1957 the U.S. Supreme Court, *One, Inc. v. Olesen*, reversed a lower-court ban on the mailing rights of this publication which calls itself, "The Homosexual Magazine."

Gregory, Ruth, *comp.* "Readings on Book Selection and Intellectual Freedom, 1954–1961." *ALA Bulletin*, 56:145–49, February 1962. "A Selected List, 1962–67." *ALA Bulletin*, 62:64–69, January 1968. **G 285**

An annotated list that includes a section on Sensitive Areas and Controversies.

Greig, George. *Facts Connected with the Stopping of the South African Commercial Advertiser. A Facsimile Reproduction of the Original Handbill and Its First Postscript together with a Transcript of the Subsequent Postscript.* Cape Town, Africane Connoisseurs, 1963. 29 p. **G 286**

[Grenville, George]. *Speech of the Right Honourable Gentleman on the Motion for Expelling Mr. Wilkes, Friday, February 3, 1769.* London, J. Almon, 1769. 54 p. (Reprinted in *A Collection of Scarce and Interesting Tracts . . .*, vol. 3, pp. 3–40) **G 287**

Relates to the case of John Wilkes, expelled from Parliament for his *North Briton* and *Essay on Woman*. Grenville joined with Burke in arguing against expulsion on the grounds of futility in rejecting a member who would only be returned in the next election.

Gressle, Lloyd E. "The Pastor and Censorship." *Pastoral Psychology*, 12:39–48, January 1962. **G 288**

"When the clergyman moves into the area of censorship he runs the danger of playing God and dictating to others on the basis of his own level of taste; the Church cannot meet the problem of obscenity unless it sheds its pose of self-righteous respectability and meets it with keen insight based on all the scientific factors available."

Grey, James G., *comp. Freedom of Thought and Speech in New Zealand, a Serious Menace to Liberty; the Story of the Boers, Things Worth Knowing.* Wellington, Wright & Grenside, 1900. 80 p. **G 289**

Griffin, John H. "Current Trends in Censorship." *Southwest Review*, 47:193–200, Summer 1962. **G 290**

A summary of recent episodes in censorship in the United States with special attention given to the Texas scene. The author describes in some detail the recent attack on history textbooks by a group calling itself "Texans for America." J. Evetts Haley, speaking for this organization declared: "The stressing of both sides of a controversy only confuses the young and encourages them to make snap judgments based on insignificant evidence. Until they are old enough to understand both sides of a question, they should be taught only the American side." Griffin is the author of *The Devil Rides Outside*, under attack in Detroit but freed in a U.S. Supreme Court ruling, *Butler v. Michigan.*

———. "Prude and the Lewd—Wherein the Bigger Peril?" *Nation*, 181:382–84, 5 November 1955. (Reprinted in Downs, *The First Freedom*, pp. 148–51) **G 291**

The author attacks local censorship groups which perform extralegal pressures to attain their ends. "No one would deny the right of any sectarian group to discourage its members from reading books which are offensive to it, but such a prerogative becomes vicious when it is used to deprive others who are not members of that particular group, from access to the work to which they have a perfect right, according to the legal standards of the United States. . . . Censorship, by depriving the community of the right of access to serious works because it cannot distinguish pornography from realism, thereby commits mankind to a cultural and ethical hara-kiri."

Griffin, William J. "Notes on the Early Control of the Stage." *Modern Language Notes*, 58(1):50–54, January 1943. **G 292**

———. *Tudor Control of Press and Stage.* Iowa City, State University of Iowa Press, 1939. 198 p. **G 293**

In the first chapter the author outlines the development of press control in Tudor England under the Stationers' Company and

stage control under the Revels Office. Chapter two includes a calendar of evidence which bears on the subject of press and stage control. Incidents are arranged in chronological order, beginning with the appointment of Peter Actors, in 1485, as Stationer to the King, through the death of Elizabeth in 1603. In that year plays were prohibited for five days before and two weeks after Elizabeth's death. The study is not a history of regulations but the chronological organization of materials from which such a history could be written.

Griffith, David W. *The Rise and Fall of Free Speech in America.* Los Angeles, The Author, 1916. 42 p. **G 294**

Criticism of the widespread censorship of movies that hampers free expression and the serious development of the cinema art. A collection of editorials, speeches, and satirical cartoons.

Griffith, Emlyn I. "Mayflower Rule —Gone but Not Forgotten." *Cornell Law Quarterly*, 35:574–91, Spring 1950. **G 295**

Court decisions relating to editorializing on the air, 1941–49.

Griffith, Hubert F. *Red Sunday; a Play in Three Acts . . . With a Preface on the Censorship.* London, Cayme Press, 1929. 90 p. (First published in 1912) **G 296**

The preface (pp. vii–xxiv), "contributed by an eminent authority," is in the form of a letter to the author, purportedly from a native of the South Pacific Island, Ping-Pang-Bong. The writer discusses the reasons for the ban of *Red Sunday* by the Lord Chamberlain—because it deals with the Russian Revolution, too recent an event to be shown on the English stage, and because it portrays the late Czar Nicholas II, a relative of the ruling house of England. The author follows with a general history and criticism of English stage censorship. "The free play of thought that has always been one of the glories of your island, and that has perhaps been the best of all your gifts to the world, should be as unrestricted in your theatre as in your literature."

Griswold, Erwin N. "When Newsmen Become Newsmakers." *Saturday Review*, 47(43):21–23, 24 October 1964. **G 297**

"The Warren Report [investigating the Kennedy assassination] makes clear that the press did more than cover a story in Dallas a year ago. Here the dean of the Harvard Law School argues the case for a measure of restraint."

Griswold, Whitney. "A Little Learning." *Atlantic Monthly*, 190:49–53, November 1952. (Stearns Lecture given at Phillips Academy, Spring 1952) **G 298**

In a criticism of shortcomings in American education, the President of Yale University describes the strange state of mind that reasons "if a little learning is a dangerous thing, a lot of learning is a much more dangerous thing." At one point he discusses the banning of books. "Books won't stay banned. They won't burn. Ideas won't go to jail. In the long run of history, the censor and the inquisitor have always lost. The only sure weapon against bad ideas is better ideas."

Gronouski, John A. "Control Without Censorship." *Yale Political*, 3(1):12, 29–30, Autumn 1963.   **G 299**
"In this, his first official policy statement in the field of obscenity control, the Postmaster General defends our present laws as an effective weapon against pornography yet asserts that the role played by the Post Office is not that of a censor."

[Grosman, Alan M.]. "Obscenity—Censorship of Obscene Literature—Constitutional Law." *New York Law Forum*, 9:371–84, August 1963.   **G 300**
Grove Press lost the New York battle in its nationwide campaign for unrestricted distribution of Henry Miller's *Tropic of Cancer* in a split decision by the New York Court of Appeals, July 1963.

"*The Group:* Australian Uproar." *Bookseller*, 3042:1594–95, 11 April 1964.
                                                G 301
"The uncertainty about the workings of the obscenity law in this country that followed the Bow Street condemnation of *Fanny Hill* is as nothing compared with that which has followed the Victoria State action against *The Group* in Australia."

"Group Libel Laws: Abortive Efforts to Combat Hate Propaganda." *Yale Law Journal*, 61:252–64, February 1952.
                                                G 302

Grove Press. *A Digest of Press Opinion: The U.S. Post Office vs. Lady Chatterley's Lover.* New York, Grove Press, [1959]. 8 p.   **G 303**

"Growing Demand for the Suppression of the German-American Press." *Current Opinion*, 63:151–52, September 1917.
                                                G 304

"The Growth of the Law of Libel." *Law Magazine and Review*, 3(n.s.):679–91, August 1874.   **G 305**
Deals with the period before the abolition of the Star Chamber in England.

Gruber, F. C. "Radio and Television and Ethical Standards." *Annals of the American Academy of Political and Social Science*, 280:116–24, March 1952.   **G 306**
The author considers the need for a positive policy in governing the public interest in radio and television broadcasting. Programming for children, he maintains, is "one of the weakest spots in radio-television."

Gruening, Ernest H. *The Public Pays; a Study of Power Propaganda.* New York, Vanguard, 1931. 273 p.   **G 307**
"An abstract of the last three years' investigation by the Federal Trade Commission of the propaganda of the public utilities, especially those dealing in power and light." Two chapters relate to freedom of the press: Rewriting the Textbook: The Index Electricus Expurgatorius, and Pressure and the Press.

Guernsey, Roscellus S. "When a Libel Is Not a Libel." *Yale Law Review*, 20:36–43, November 1910.   **G 308**
A libel is *malicious* "if no justification or excuse therefore is shown." It is *justifiable* "when the matter charged as libelous is true, and was published with good motives and for justifiable ends." It is *excused* when 'honestly made in the belief of its truth and upon reasonable grounds for this belief, and consists of fair comments upon the conduct of a person."

Guest, Edgar A. "Mrs. Malone and the Censor." In his *Collected Verse*, Chicago, Reilly, Lee, 1934, pp. 289–90.   **G 309**
A humorous poem involving a censored letter from a soldier: "I'm chokin' wid news I'd like to relate, / But it's little a soldier's permitted t' state."

Guha, Dhirendra N. *Law of Defamation and Malicious Prosecution.* 5th ed. Calcutta, Eastern Law House, 1964. 410p.   **G 310**

Guider, John W. "Liability for Defamation in Political Broadcasts." *Journal of Radio Law*, 2:708–13, October 1932.   **G 311**
Discussion of the Nebraska Supreme Court case of *Sorenson v. Wood and KFAB Broadcasting Co.* (1932), the first case on defamation by radio to come before an appellate court in the United States.

Guinzburg, Harold K. "Free Press, Free Enterprise, and Diversity." In *Books and the Mass Market*, Urbana, Ill., University of Illinois Press, 1953, pp. 1–19. (Fourth Annual Windsor Lectures in Librarianship)   **G 312**
The president of Viking Press "shows that the three concepts are interdependent, and that there must be constant vigilance to protect them against the pressures of censorship, monopoly control, and high production costs."

Gunston, David. "Film Censor in Britain." *Contemporary Review*, 191:342–46, June 1957.   **G 313**
Censorship of such a powerful mass medium as the film is, regrettably, necessary, but the censor can raise the level of public appreciation by approving "courageous and experimental films."

Gunther, John. "Funneling the European News." *Harper's Magazine*, 160:635–47, April 1930.   **G 314**
"The news from perhaps six hundred million people reaches the United States funneled through the agency of perhaps three hundred men ... American journalists, living abroad ... Who gets this news? What are its sources? And how is it controlled?"

Guthrie, A. B., Jr. "The *Peter Rabbit* Library?" *Nieman Reports*, 12:17–18, April 1958. (Reprinted in Downs, *The First Freedom*, pp. 285–86)   **G 315**
When a missionary complained that Guthrie's novel, *Big Sky*, contained lustful passages, the Grand Jury of Whitley County, Ky., questioned whether the book should be in the local Corbin Public Library. At the request of the Kentucky State Library Extension Division, Mr. Guthrie prepared this statement. He feared that if works containing references to "lust" were to be banned from the library, the Bible, and works of Shakespeare, Voltaire, Dreiser, Hemingway, Steinbeck, and many others would have to go—leaving only *The Tale of Peter Rabbit.*

Gwynne, H. A. "The Press in War." *Royal United Service Institution Journal* (London), 57:1616–31, December 1913.
                                                G 316
The editor of the *Morning Post* suggests the establishment of a committee of ten journalists to determine what could reasonably be released to the press in wartime. The proposal was made on the eve of World War I. A lively discussion follows the talk.

H

H., W. E. "Proposed Reduction of the Stamp Duty on Newspapers." *London and Westminster Review*, 25:264–70, April 1836. **H1**

Haas, Warren J. *English Book Censorship.* Rochester, N.Y., University of Rochester Press for the Association of College and Research Libraries, 1955. 80p. (2 cards) (ACRL Microcards, no. 49) **H2**
A general survey prepared as a bachelor's thesis in library science at the University of Wisconsin.

Hachten, William A. "The Press as Reporter and Critic of Government." *Journalism Quarterly*, 40:12–18, Winter 1963. **H3**
"Pointing out how the press itself can utilize the machinery of government to bring about the continuing adjustments necessary to maintain its freedom and vigor, a Wisconsin scholar urges further studies so that the political theory of the government and the press may be restated in more realistic terms."

Hackett, Francis. "The Invisible Censor." *New Republic*, 21:11–13, 3 December 1919. **H4**
The invisible censor is the reader "who feels that social facts must be manicured and pedicured before they are fit to be seen." Each of us becomes an invisible censor in opposing certain ideas whether they are on suffrage, sex, or politics. The author's comments are an outgrowth of his favorable review of Strachey's *Eminent Victorian*.

———. "A Muzzle Made in Ireland." *Dublin Magazine*, 11 (n.s.):8–17, October 1936. (Reprinted in Downs, *The First Freedom*, pp. 393–98) **H5**
The Irish-American biographer and novelist discusses Irish censorship law under which his own novel, *The Green Lion*, was banned. "The Censorship law is repugnant to every instinct of a free man, ignorant in its conception, ridiculous in its methods, odious in its fruits, bringing the name of self-governing

Irishmen into contempt wherever the freedom of literature is understood, and revealing the muddle and immaturity of our statecraft." He challenges the Irish people to get rid of this self-imposed law.

Hackett, Paul. *Obscenity Trial.* New York, New American Library, 1964. 144p. (A Signet Book) **H6**
A novel developed around an obscenity trial involving the sale of a book surveying human sexual behavior. The arguments for prosecution and defense bring out the various issues on the suppression of freedom of sex expression.

Hackwood, Frederick W. *William Hone, His Life and Times.* London, Unwin, 1912. 373p. **H7**
A biography of the English political satirist and pamphleteer who, in 1817, was arrested under an "ex-officio information" and tried for blasphemous libel for his three political parodies. The parodies were modeled on the Catechism, the Litany, and the Apostle's Creed. Hone was acquitted in each of three separate trials. The real basis of prosecution was Hone's attacks on the ministries of Lords Sidmouth and Castlereagh in his *Reformists' Register*.

Hadfield, John. "Book Censorship in Britain at War." *Publishers' Weekly*, 139:2362–64, 14 June 1941. **H8**
The editor for Dent outlines the book censorship situation as it has existed in England since the start of the war. Censorship of materials intended for use outside Great Britain is compulsory and largely automatic; censorship of material intended for publication within Great Britain is on a voluntary basis.

Haefner, John H. "The Battle of the Books." *National Education Association Journal*, 42:227–28, April 1953. **H9**
The author charts a general course of action which schools may take to weather textbook attacks.

Hager, J. W. "Civil Libel and Slander in Oklahoma." *Tulsa Law Journal*, 2:1–31, January 1965. **H10**

"In this article I hope to give the reader a survey and sometimes critical analysis of the law of libel and slander in Oklahoma as such law is reflected in the Constitution, the statutes, and the cases. . . . For a long time there were comparatively few actions brought for defamation, but it would appear from newspaper reports . . . that within the past few years there has been a great increase in the number of defamation cases filed both in Oklahoma and in the other states, and a corresponding increase in the amount of damage sought by the plaintiffs."

Hagerty, Sheward. "Censorship." *Show Business Illustrated*, 1(7):30–35, 44, 72–74, 28 November 1961. **H11**
An examination of movie censorship in some detail as practiced by the Production Code and by city boards, as movies delve into more provocative themes. Despite sporadic outbursts, the author finds that formal censorship in local communities is on the wane, the courts have given movies greater freedom, and the Production Code is decidedly more liberal.

Hahesy, J. E. "Declaratory Relief in Obscenity Proceedings." *California Librarian*, 25, 177–80, July 1964. **H12**
A consideration of the declaratory relief section of the California Code of Civil Procedure by which books believed to be obscene may be brought before the Superior Court for a judgment, before there has been any breach of an obligation by any party. The case under discussion is *Zeitlin v. Arnebergh* and the book involved is Henry Miller's *Tropic of Cancer*. The California Supreme Court held that this was a proper case for declaratory judgment. "The use of the relief process, instead of criminal procedure, in the field of censorship will be a salutary change from the standpoint of the public, the bookseller, and the librarian."

Haig, Robert L. *The Gazetteer, 1735–1797. A Study in the Eighteenth-Century English Newspaper.* Carbondale, Ill., Southern Illinois University Press, 1960. 335p. **H13**
"The [London] *Gazetteer* was distinguished by being one of the first papers chosen for prosecution by the House of Commons, and its printer being one of the first to resist."

The *Gazetteer* was one of the papers that came to the defense of "Wilkes and Liberty" and faced indictment for publishing the famous Junius letter. The paper was also prosecuted for a libel on the Russian ambassador.

Haight, Anne L. *Banned Books: Informal Notes on Some Books Banned for Various Reasons at Various Times and in Various Places.* 2d ed. rev. and enl. New York, Bowker, 1955. 172 p.   **H 14**
A chronological list of books banned from 387 B.C. to 1954, showing, by means of commentary, the trend in censorship throughout the years and the change in thought and taste. Included are books condemned because of heresy, treason, or obscenity; some have withstood the condemnation of their times to become classics of today. The appendix contains statements on Nazi book-burning, Senator McCarthy's attacks on the United States overseas libraries, censorship in public libraries, the action against comic books, and textbook censorship. Excerpts from notable statements on freedom of the press, court decisions, and customs and postal regulations are included. A bibliographic check list is given on pages 158–62.

Haight, George I. "Freedom of Speech and of the Press—Now." *Bill of Rights Review*, 1:278–85, Summer 1941.   **H 15**
An appeal for straight thinking and calm appraisal to avoid hysteria that might lead to unwise abridgment of a free press in wartime.

Haiman, Franklyn S. *Freedom of Speech: Issues and Cases.* New York, Random, 1965. 207 p.   **H 16**
A selection of statements on freedom of speech extracted from court decisions and the writings of scholars and public officials. Each document is placed in perspective, and its philosophical, legal, and psychological implications are considered. Attention has been concentrated on three broad areas which include most of the major American cases of the twentieth century—speech that inflames an audience and creates a danger of disorder; speech that is viewed as a threat to national survival; and speech that is regarded as corrupting to public morality. The work is intended as a text for the study of the problems of freedom of speech.

Haimbaugh, George D., Jr. "Film Censorship Since Roth-Alberts." *Kentucky Law Journal*, 51:656–66, Summer 1963.   **H 17**
The author discusses the cases of *Roth v. U.S.* and *Alberts v. California*—in which the Supreme Court held that obscenity is not constitutionally protected—and the film censorship cases that followed. *Roth-Alberts* provided a prurient interest test; *Times Film Corp. I* (1957) helped to restrict the legal meaning of obscenity to "hard-core" pornography; *Kings-*

ley Pictures (*Lady Chatterley's Lover*) in 1959 held that a movie depicting immorality cannot be required by state law to show that such conduct does not pay; and *Times Film Corp. II* (*Don Juan*) in 1961 "held that a statute providing for prior restraint is not invalid per se, and may have hinted that obscenity could be an exception to the general rule against prior restraints."

———. "Free Press Versus Fair Trial: The Contribution of Mr. Justice Frankfurter." *University of Pittsburgh Law Review*, 26:491–520, March 1965.   **H 18**
"Resolution of conflict between competing constitutional provisions is nowhere more crucial than in contempt of publication and trial by newspaper cases. The conflict in these areas, however, is clearly defined by the differing views of Mr. Justice Frankfurter and the majority of the United States Supreme Court. Professor Haimbaugh, in this article, presents a critical exposition of Mr. Justice Frankfurter's opinions as they relate to the constitutional conflict by contrasting them with those of the majority of the Court."

Haines, Fred. "City of Angels vs. *Scorpio Rising.*" *Nation*, 199:123–25, 14 September 1964.   **H 19**
An art theater manager in Hollywood was found guilty on an obscenity charge for showing the movie, *Scorpio Rising*.

Haines, Helen E. "Balancing the Books: Reason Enthroned." *Library Journal*, 73: 149–54, 1 February 1948.   **H 20**
An appeal to librarians to resist attempts by pressure groups to suppress everything they consider subversive, but to balance their collections with books that will develop a better understanding of world cooperation, tolerance, etc.

———. "Committee on Intellectual Freedom." *California Library Association Bulletin*, 2:117–18, December 1940.   **H 21**
A review of the charges made by O. K. Armstrong in the *American Legion Magazine* (September 1940) that American schools were harboring subversive literature. Armstrong's blacklist includes books of Harold O. Rugg and Charles and Mary Beard. The Committee advises librarians to become familiar with the background and progress of the American Legion attack.

Haines, Henry. *Treachery, Baseness, and Cruelty Display'd to the Full; in the Hardships and Sufferings of Mr. Henry Haines, Late Printer of the Country Journal, or, Craftsman, . . .* London, 1740. 32 p.   **H 22**
Haines became printer of *The Craftsman* in 1731, after Richard Franklin's imprisonment. Six years later he was arrested for an article likening George II to Shakespeare's King John; he was fined and given a year in prison. Haines is bitter, not only because of the sentence, but because his employers failed to pay his fine,

and since he was unable to raise the money he faced perpetual imprisonment.

Haldeman-Julius, Emanuel. "The Downfall of a Smut Hound." *Debunker*, 12(4): 24–26, September 1930.   **H 23**
An amusing story of how an agent provocateur for a vice society was himself trapped by a Pittsburgh bookseller. The author of the article is the publisher of the Little Blue Books, frequently the subject of public controversy.

———. "*Why I Do Not Believe in Censorship.* Girard, Kan., Haldeman-Julius, 1930. 32 p. (Little Blue Book no. 1549)   **H 24**
"The real animus of censorship lies in a dislike for art that, whether imaginatively or realistically, runs counter to notions of respectability which the censors personally regard as sacrosanct and which they pretend have the just force of great social necessities . . . Censorship is foolish and the censors personally illustrate its foolishness to the last degree."

Hale, William G. "Freedom of Speech and of the Press—Resolution of the Missouri Bar Association." *Illinois Law Bulletin*, 2:440–52, February 1920.   **H 25**
In spite of the general merit of the resolution proposing a peacetime sedition act, the author sees danger unless its application is confined to cases where the criminal intent is clear and the likelihood of causing lawless acts is imminent.

———. "Freedom of Speech and the Press." *Quill*, 11:3–4, 10 May 1923.   **H 26**
The dean, University of Oregon School of Law, reviews the historical development of freedom of the press in England and the United States, criticizing the existing restrictions on political expression which began with wartime censorship but continued after the war. He criticizes state legislation against anarchy and radicalism which suppresses a free press.

———. *The Law of the Press.* 3d ed. St. Paul, West, 1948. 691 p.   **H 27**
Standard casebook containing statutes, cases, and a general discussion of legal issues. Covers areas of constitutional guarantees, libel, contempt, and invasion of privacy.

Halewyck de Heusch, Michel. *Le Régime Légal de la Presse en Angleterre . . .* Louvain, C. Peeters, 1899. 142 p. (Bibliothèque de l'Ecole des Sciences Politiques et Sociales de Louvain, 14)   **H 28**
Traces the legal concept of freedom of the press from the seventeenth through the nineteenth centuries, with special attention to the English law of libel.

[Hall, A. Oakey]. *The People of the State of New York vs. John A. Dix, and Five*

Others. Outlines of Argument of District Attorney Hall, for Prosecution. New York, Baker & Godwin, 1864. 10 p. **H 29**
Arguments of the prosecution in the case of the State of New York against Major-General John A. Dix and others for ordering and carrying out the order for troops to seize and occupy the premises of the *New York World* and *Journal of Commerce* as a wartime measure. Hall cites legal precedence in support of freedom of the press in time of crisis and argues for the preservation of "these great safeguards of civil freedom, the habeas corpus, the right of trial by jury, and the right of personal liberty, unless deprived thereof for crime by due process of law."

Hall, Clarence W. "The Book They Couldn't Ban." *Christian Herald,* 73(7): 17–18, 60–63, July 1950. **H 30**
Account of the unsuccessful effort to ban Paul Blanshard's *American Freedom and Catholic Power.*

———. "Poison in Print and How to Get Rid of It." *Reader's Digest,* 84:94–98, May 1964. **H 31**
The story of Citizens for Decent Literature (CDL), founded in Cincinnati by Charles H. Keating, and its spread to other cities. Keating defends local action against dealers rather than national action against publishers, which, he maintains, ends up in the crowded dockets of the federal courts.

Hall, G. Stanley. *Life and Confessions of a Psychologist.* New York, Appleton, 1923. 623 p. **H 32**
This pioneer psychologist and first president of Clark University, accepted the presidency of the New England Watch and Ward Society in 1909 in order to change the Society's emphasis from censorship to a campaign for sex education. The Society did not choose to follow his leadership and he served only one term. In his autobiography, Hall reveals with great candor his almost morbid interest in the social evils of the day, especially during his association with the Society. In his work in behalf of sex education he was closely associated with Theodore A. Schroeder, an arch enemy of the vice societies.

Hall, James P. "Free Speech in War Time." *Columbia Law Review,* 21:526–37, June 1921. **H 33**
The author defends the Espionage Acts as war measures, not likely to be retained in time of peace.

Hall, John M. "Preserving Liberty of the Press by the Defense of Privilege in Libel Actions." *California Law Review,* 26: 226–39, January 1938. **H 34**
"The defense of privilege in the law of libel is founded on the theory that in certain situations the individual's right to protection of his reputation must yield to the rights of others. It recognizes that there are times when the 'public benefit from . . . publicity' is paramount to individual immunity." This doctrine of qualified privilege is a mainstay to the freedom of the newspaper press.

Hall, Martin. "Revolt against Reason; Basis of Book-Burning." *Nation,* 178: 30–32, 9 January 1954. **H 35**
The author compares book burning and banning in America with similar activities under the Nazis in Germany twenty years earlier.

Hall, Robert. *An Apology for the Freedom of the Press, and for General Liberty: to Which are Prefixed Remarks on Bishop Horsley's Sermon, Preached on the 30th of January Last.* London, Printed for G. G. J. and J. Robinson, 1793. 103 p. (Reprinted with related documents in *The Works of Robert Hall,* edited by Olinthus Gregory, London, Bohn, 1845. vol. 3, pp. 61–202) **H 36**
This eloquent statement, delivered by a prominent Baptist minister, is a landmark in the development of the idea of press freedom. Hall protested vigorously against the sedition trials of Muir, Palmer, and others, and the blasphemy prosecutions of Hone and Carlile, declaring that all men should have absolute liberty to discuss "every subject which can fall within the compass of the human mind." He opposed the vigilante societies that were being formed in England in the hysteria over the French Revolution. Societies, he said, are unable to make the subtle distinctions between liberty of the press and licentiousness. They transform great people into a race of spies and informers. "The law hath amply provided against *overt acts* of sedition and disorder, and to suppress mere opinion by any other method than reason and argument, is the height of tyranny." Hall was denounced by fellow clergymen as a radical whose opinions were contrary to the Scriptures. But he maintained his stand and reopened the controversy in 1821 by a republication of his original pamphlet. The collected work listed here contains the original statement, selected editorial charges, and Hall's replies.

Hall, Walter P. *British Radicalism, 1791–1797.* New York, Columbia University Press, 1912. 262 p. (Studies in History, Economics and Public Law, vol. 49, no. 1) **H 37**
A study of the radical reform movement that swept England and Scotland during the period of the French Revolution and was ultimately crushed by the suppressive measures of the Pitt government. Efforts at suppressing radical thought and the "seditious" pamphleteering brought prosecution against John Horne Tooke, the whimsical representative of old-time radicalism, William Cobbett, the Tory warrior, Daniel I. Eaton, Major Cartwright, John Thelwall, William Frend, and Thomas Spence. Two landmark cases in the history of freedom of the press are discussed—the sedition trials of Thomas Muir in Scotland

and Thomas Paine in England. In the latter Erskine made his illustrious defense of freedom of the press.

Hall, William E. *An Analysis of Post-World War II Efforts to Expand Press Freedom Internationally.* Iowa City, State University of Iowa, 1954. 397 p. (Ph. D. dissertation, University Microfilms, no. 10,213) **H 38**

Haller, Frederick. "New Phase of the Contempt Cult." *New Review,* 2:388–90, July 1914. **H 39**
Deals with the Samuel Gompers case and free speech injunctions in industrial disputes.

Haller, William. "'For the Liberty of Unlicenc'd Printing.'" *American Scholar,* 14(3):326–33, Summer 1945. **H 40**
Comments on Milton's reasons for writing *Areopagitica,* based on an address given by Professor Haller at Columbia University on the 300th anniversary of the publication of this classic on freedom of the press.

———. *Liberty and Reformation in the Puritan Revolution.* New York, Columbia University Press, 1955. 410 p. **H 41**
An account of English Puritanism based on the reading of the tracts, sermons, and other literature of the period. This scholarly work covers the pamphleteering in behalf of unlicensed printing that took place during the Puritan Revolution, with references to Milton's *Areopagitica,* and to the persecution of William Prynne, Henry Burton, Richard Overton, John Lilburne, and others of the Leveller party.

———. "Two Early Allusions to Milton's *Areopagitica.*" *Huntington Library Quarterly,* 12:207–12 (1949). **H 42**

———, ed. *Tracts on Liberty in the Puritan Revolution, 1638–1647.* New York, Columbia University Press, 1934. 3 vols. (Records of Civilization; Sources and Studies, no. 18) **H 43**
A critical survey of the Puritan Revolution literature, works that are important as revealing the beginning of democracy and freedom of the press. The commentary appears in volume 2; the facsimile text of 19 tracts, relating to the doctrine of liberty, are reproduced in volumes 2 and 3. These include tracts of John Lilburne, William Walwyn, and Richard Overton, all persecuted for their writings.

———, and Godfrey Davies, eds. *The Leveller Tracts, 1647–1653.* New York, Columbia University Press in Cooperation with Henry E. Huntington Library and Art Gallery, 1944. 481 p. **H 44**

The reprinted tracts, with extensive introductory notes giving bibliographical data as well as background information on the occasion for their original publication. Sixteen tracts are reproduced including, A Declaration or, Representation; A Declaration of Some Proceedings; The Bloody Project; The Humble Petition; England's New Chains Discovered; A Manifestation; An Agreement of the Free People of England; Walwyn's Just Defence; The Legall Fundementall Liberties of the People of England (excerpts); and The Just Defence of John Lilburn.

Hallgren, Mauritz A. *Landscape of Freedom; the Story of American Liberty and Bigotry.* New York, Howell, Soskin, 1941. 444 p. **H 45**

A popular history of efforts to suppress liberty in America, from the Zenger trial and religious persecution in colonial days to attacks on sex expression in literature during the 1920's and 30's. There are references to the Bache sedition trial and others under the Alien and Sedition Acts, the suppression of anarchist thought and atheism, birth control, the Comstock laws, and recent censorship of movies and stage plays.

Halliday, E. M. "Man Who Cleaned up Shakespeare." *Horizon* 5(1):68–71, September 1962. **H 46**

"While Dr. Bowdler is long dead, his spirit of expurgating the Bard lives on in our schools—though at the corner drugstore pupils can get the real thing, and Henry Miller too."

Halligan, John T. "An Attempt at Censorship." *Library Journal*, 88:4002–3, 15 October 1963. **H 47**

How one high school (Carlsbad, Calif.) faced up to a campaign against *The Dictionary of American Slang*. The matter reached the State Board of Education, which, in opposition to the State Superintendent of Public Instruction, voted unanimously to return the "stolen" book to the library shelves.

Hallis, Frederick. *The Law and Obscenity.* London, Harmsworth, 1932. 40 p. **H 48**

A brief survey of English laws and court decisions on obscene literature. The author argues that the law of obscene libel is bad jurisprudence.

Halpenny, Marie. "Books on Trial in Texas." *Library Journal*, 78:1179–82, July 1953. (Reprinted in Daniels, *The Censorship of Books*, pp. 98–101) **H 49**

A report by the chairman of the San Antonio Committee to Fight Censorship. Concerns the attacks on the San Antonio Public Library for

having "REaD READING," and a bill in the Texas legislature to censor textbooks.

Hamburg, Morris. "Case of the Subversive Text." *School Executive*, 77(8):59–61, April 1958. (No. 1 in a series of case studies) **H 50**

This hypothetical case involves the charge by a parent that her sixth-grade daughter is being exposed to Communist propaganda through a social studies textbook.

Hamel, Frank. "English Books in the Indexes *Librorum Prohibitorum et Expurgandorum.*" *Library*, 1:(3d ser.)351–83, October 1910. **H 51**

A general survey of the "curious medley" of English books placed on one or more of the many Catholic indices, and the reasons and circumstance of the listing. Comparatively few English works appeared on the *Index* before mid-seventeenth century. Over the centuries the indices have included works of such writers as Hobbes, Thomas Browne, Robert Boyle, John Selden, Addison, Steele, Defoe, Richardson, Sterne, Swift, Locke, Newton, Hume, and Bentham. Strangely missing from lists are Darwin, Huxley, and Tyndall. Because of frequent inaccuracies, Hamel cautions against reliance upon contemporary newspaper accounts of books placed on the *Index*.

[Hamilton, Alexander]. "Liberty of the Press." In *The Federalist*, no. 84 ("Why the Constitution Needs No Bill of Rights"). New York, 1788. Lodge edition, pp. 537–38. (Also in Charles A. Beard, *The Enduring Federalist*, pp. 364–65) **H 52**

In one of the last of the famous *Federalist* papers, Hamilton, writing under the pseudonym "Publius," argues that a bill of rights to the Constitution is unnecessary: "For why declare that things shall not be done which there is no power to do? Why, for instance, should it be said that the liberty of the press shall not be restrained, when no power is given by which restrictions can be imposed?" The security of a free press, "whatever fine declarations may be inserted in any constitution respecting it, must altogether depend on public opinion, and on the general spirit of the people and of the government."

Hamilton, Archibald. *Report of the Trial by Jury of the Action of Damages for a Libel in the Beacon Newspaper.* Edinburgh, J. Robertson, 1822. 154 p. **H 53**

Hamilton, Clayton. "Movie, Censor and the Public." *Literary Review, New York Evening Post*, 30 December 1922. (Reprinted in Rutland, *State Censorship of Motion Pictures*, pp. 123–33) **H 54**

Objections to Ellis P. Oberholtzer's proposals for film censorship.

Hamilton, Jack. "Hollywood Bypasses the Production Code." *Look*, 23:80–84, 29 September 1959. **H 55**

Today there is a more liberal interpretation of the motion picture production code which governs treatment of morality. "Hollywood coexists with a code that is flexible while stubborn, logical while confusing."

Hamilton, John J. *Plea for the Business Freedom of the American Press; an Address Delivered before the Congressional Postal Commission at New York, October 2, 1906; by John J. Hamilton of the Iowa Homestead. Speaking as Member of the Postal Commission of the National Agricultural Press League.* Des Moines, Homestead Co. [1906]. 22 p. **H 56**

Hamilton, Robert C. "Censorship of Obscene Literature by Informal Governmental Action." *University of Chicago Law Review*, 22:216–33, Autumn 1954. **H 57**

Hamman, Mary. "Do You Want Your Movies Censored?" *Good Housekeeping*, 110:13, 93, April 1940. **H 58**

Hammargren, Russell J. "I'm Tired of the Word 'Censor.'" *Quill*, 25(1):5, 18, January 1937. **H 59**

A journalism professor believes there is far too little censorship of campus publications.

Hammitt, Frances E. "The Burning of Books." *Library Quarterly*, 15:300–312, October 1945. **H 60**

An account of the practice of book burning—its background, sponsorship, efforts at total eradication of books, and the effects.

Hammond, Arthur. "Obscenity in Montreal." *Canadian Forum*, 40:74–75, July 1960. **H 61**

Police confiscation of *Lady Chatterley's Lover*.

Hampden, *pseud. A Letter to the President of the United States, touching the Prosecutions, under his patronage, before the Circuit Court in the District of Connecticut . . . By Hampden.* New Haven, Conn., Oliver Steele, 1808. 28 p. **H 62**

This anonymous Federalist writer takes President Jefferson to task for permitting Republican prosecutions in Connecticut which violate freedom of press and speech. He describes the libel proceedings taken against eleven Connecticut magistrates, clergymen, and printers who were critical in speech or publication of the Jefferson administration. Those indicted included Judge Tapping Reeve of the Connecticut Supreme Court, Thomas Collier, publisher of the *Monitor*, and Hudson and Goodwin, editors of the Federalist *Connecticut Courant* of Hartford. All except one of the indictments (Hudson and Goodwin) were defeated or voluntarily abandoned by the public prosecutor. The Hudson and Goodwin case was appealed to the U.S. Supreme Court, which handed down a decision (1812) that the federal courts did not have jurisdiction over the common law of seditious libel.

Hampton, Benjamin B. *A History of the Movies.* New York, Covici-Friede, 1931. 456 p. plus plates.　**H 63**
Chapter 13 relates to the Hollywood scandals and censorship which gave rise to the film production code.

Hance, Myrtle G. *A Report on Our San Antonio Public Libraries, Communist Front Authors and Their Books Therein.* San Antonio, Tex., 1953. 15 p. mimeo. (Quoted in Daniels, *The Censorship of Books,* pp. 96–97)　**H 64**
A San Antonio housewife checked the public library for books by Communist-front authors. She recommends all such books be stamped in red and that a citizens' committee keep the library board informed on pro-Communist books for future stamping.

Handover, P. M. *Printing in London from 1476 to Modern Times. . . .* London, Allen & Unwin, 1960. 224 p.　**H 65**
Includes discussion of the Star Chamber decrees on printing, the licensing system, the struggle for power in the Stationers' Company, and the crusade against "taxes on knowledge."

Haney, Robert W. *Comstockery in America; Patterns of Censorship and Control.* Boston, Beacon, 1960. 199 p.　**H 66**
A review of censorship and control of sex expression in the United States as it affects the printed word, the movies, radio, and television. The author cites important court cases and describes the efforts of unofficial pressure groups that operate today.

Hanighen, Frank C. "Propaganda on the Air; the International Problem of Radio Censorship." *Current History,* 44:45–51, June 1936.　**H 67**
Broadcasts from London, Rome, or Geneva may be pure propaganda instead of "authoritative news." The listener will have to be "alert in appraising the value and significance of the various broadcasts by identifying the stations and station announcements with the political color of the views they propagate."

Hankin, Edward. *Letter to the Right Honourable the Earl of Liverpool—on the Licentiousness of the Press, as Destructive of the Monarchy and the Public Morals . . .*

London. Printed for White, Cochrane, 1814. 96 p.　**H 68**

[Hansard, John]. "Action of Libel by John Joseph Hansard . . . Tried before Lord Denman, C. J., and a special jury at Westminster, on February 7, 1837." In Macdonell, *Reports of State Trials,* vol. 4, pp. 723–964.　**H 69**
In a series of legal actions extending over several years, the publisher Stockdale attempted unsuccessfully to bring fellow publisher Hansard to terms on a libel charge. The Hansard firm had printed, by order of the House of Commons, a Report of the Inspector of Prisons in which there was reference to some obscene books alleged to have been printed by Stockdale. The defense entered a plea of privilege, which the House of Commons supported to the extent of imprisoning the sheriff who attempted to collect the fine. In 1840 a law was passed protecting printers of official parliamentary reports.

———. *Judgment in Error in the Case of Stockdale v. Hansard, by the Court of Common Sense.* London, Longman, Orme, Brown, 1840. 190 p.　**H 70**

Hansen, Harry. "Dilemma of Modern Writing." *Survey Graphic,* 37:30–31, January 1948.　**H 71**
The dilemma is "how to preserve intellectual freedom and at the same time cultivate a sense of literary responsibility."

———, *et al.* "The Censorship Forum." *Publishers' Weekly,* 117:2734–37, 31 May 1930.　**H 72**
With book critic Harry Hansen as chairman, four prominent persons debate censorship: Morris L. Ernst, lawyer ("I believe that the laws on the question of obscenity are an insult to the American population."); Mary Ware Dennett, whose sex education pamphlet was suppressed; John S. Sumner, secretary of the New York Society for the Suppression of Vice, who denies that police action against obscenity is censorship; and H. V. Kaltenborn, radio analyst, who accuses the vice societies of failure to distinguish between "dominant pornography and incidental realism" in their effort to control public taste. Photograph of Mrs. Dennett on p. 2735.

Hansen, Victor R. "Broadcasting and the Antitrust Laws." *Law and Contemporary Problems,* 22:572–83, Autumn 1957.　**H 73**

Hanser, Richard. "Shakespeare, Sex . . . and Dr. Bowdler." *Saturday Review,* 38: (17)7–8, 23 April 1955. (Reprinted in Downs, *The First Freedom,* pp. 15–18)　**H 74**
An account of the work of the English editor, Thomas Bowdler, who took it upon himself

to prepare expurgated versions of Shakespeare, omitting those words and expressions that were "unfit to be read aloud by a gentleman in the company of ladies" and to suppress anything that could "raise a blush on the cheek of modest innocence." Bowdler's name became a byword for prudish expurgation of literary works.

Hanson, Elisha. "American Newspaper Publishers' Association." *Public Opinion Quarterly,* 2:121–26, January 1938.　**H 75**
The counsel for the ANPA defends the Association against charges made by Virginius Dabney, editor of the Richmond *Times-Dispatch.* Dabney said (April 1937 issue of *POQ*) that publishers indulge in self-laudation, use "freedom of the press" as a shibboleth to press selfish interests, and band together to oppose progressive legislation which might affect their profit. Hanson, in answer to the second charge, recited a long list of cases in which ANPA defended freedom of the press.

———. "Freedom of the Press and Judicial Contempt." In *Lectures in Communications Media, Legal and Policy Problems, Delivered at University of Michigan Law School, June 16–June 18, 1954.* Ann Arbor, University of Michigan Law School, 1954, pp. 63–78.　**H 76**
A history of the use of the contempt power of the courts to restrict public information.

———. "Freedom of the Press, Is It Threatened in the United Nations." *American Bar Association Journal,* 37: 417–20, June 1951.　**H 77**
Opposition to the United Nations Freedom of Information Convention as controverting the Bill of Rights of the United States Constitution.

———. "The Guaranty of a Free Press." *Vital Speeches,* 6:433–35, 1 May 1940.
H 78
The general counsel of the American Newspaper Publishers' Association discusses the relationship of the constitutional guaranty of a free press to the interests of the advertiser and the consumer in the United States. Address before the Advertising Club of New York.

———. "Liberty's Debt to the Press." *Vital Speeches,* 4:752–56, 1 October 1938.
H 79
The author contrasts the American theory of press freedom, "the great bulwark of all liberty," with that of the authoritarian theory as exemplified in Nazi Germany. He is critical not only of German controls but of efforts by the Roosevelt administration to control the press through various economic recovery and labor laws. He calls on the nation's press to maintain its vigilance.

————. "Life, Liberty and Property." *Vital Speeches*, 4:254–56, 1 February 1938. **H 80**

The author calls for Americans to take heed of the loss of press freedom in European dictatorships and "to battle those in authority who attempt to restrain it in the exercise of its functions of gathering and disseminating information." He criticizes the propaganda barrage of government agencies and their restrictions on free access to officials and records.

————. "The Supreme Court on Freedom of the Press and Contempt by Publication." *Cornell Law Quarterly*, 27:165–89, February 1942. **H 81**

"The majority opinion gives unstinted support to a free press as a right of the people throughout the land."

————. "The Two Bulwarks of Liberty. A Free Press and an Independent Judiciary." *American Bar Association Journal*, 41:217–20+, March 1955. **H 82**

In an address at the University of Michigan Law School, Hanson cites many cases where publicity by newspapers was virtually the only means of securing justice. Those who would seek to censor the press in the performance of its function of "reporting on judicial proceedings have seized upon the epithet 'trial by newspaper' as the shibboleth in their campaign."

Hanson, Laurence. *Government and the Press, 1695–1763.* London, Oxford University Press, 1936. 149 p. **H 83**

An account of the relationship between the government and the press in England, from the expiration of the Licensing Act (1695) to the publication of no. 45 of *North Briton* by John Wilkes (1763). Largely limited to regulation of the newspaper press and to matters of politics, excluding prosecutions for obscenity and blasphemy. There are numerous references to trials for seditious libel.

Hapgood, Hutchins. *A Cold Enthusiast.* Hillacre, Riverside, Conn., Privately printed, 1913. 10 p. **H 84**

An appreciation of Theodore A. Schroeder, secretary of the Free Speech League and lifelong crusader for freedom of expression in the realm of sex.

————. "Fire and Revolution." New York, Free Speech League, 1912. 16 p. **H 85**

The author argues for the expediency of permitting most violent opinions.

Hapgood, Norman. "How Fighting Governments Suppress Opinion." *Harper's Weekly*, 61:76–78, 24 July 1915. **H 86**

How the countries of Europe dealt with the organization of opinion stemming from events leading to World War I. In Germany the government controlled opinion; England, among all the powers at war, permitted the greatest freedom. "If we [Americans] go to war, infinite tact will be required, but nevertheless a firm censorship will also be required. The advantages of free speech must not be forgotten, but neither must newspaper owners conduct the war."

Hard, William. "Mr. Burleson, Espionagent." *New Republic*, 19:42–45, 10 May 1919; 19:76–78, 17 May 1919. **H 87**

A critical account of the Postmaster General's actions in banning books and newspapers from the mails during the period immediately following World War I.

————. "Perhaps the Turning of the Tide." *New Republic*, 21:313–16, 11 February 1920. **H 88**

Opposition to a sedition bill before a Congressional committee.

[Hardy, Thomas]. *The Genuine Trial of Thomas Hardy, for High Treason, at the Sessions House in the Old Bailey, from October 28 to November 5, 1794 . . . By Manoak Sibly, shorthand writer to the City of London.* 2d ed. London, Printed for J. S. Jordan, 1795. 2 vols. **H 89**

————. *Memoir of Thomas Hardy, Founder of, and Secretary to the London Corresponding Society . . . for Promoting Parliamentary Reform, 1742, until his Arrest on a False Charge of High Treason, 12 May 1794. Written by Himself.* London, 1832. 127 p. **H 90**

[————]. *State Trials for High Treason. Containing the Trial of Thomas Hardy to Which is Prefixed Lord Chief Justice Eyre's Charge to the Grand Jury . . . Taken in Short-Hand by a Student in the Temple.* Edinburgh, J. Robertson, 1794. 268 p. (Also in Howell, *State Trials*, vol. 24, pp. 199 ff.) **H 91**

[————]. *The Trial of Thomas Hardy for High Treason, at the Session House in the Old Bailey, on Tuesday the Twenty-eighth . . . [to] Friday the Thirty-first of October; and on Saturday the First . . . [to] Wednesday the Fifth of November, 1794 . . . Taken in Short-hand by Joseph Gurney.* London, Sold by Martha Gurney, 1794–95. 4 vols. (Also in *The Speeches of the Hon. Thomas Erskine*, vol. 3, pp. 53–503) **H 92**

Hardy, the secretary of the London Corresponding Society, was charged with high treason for circulating pro-Jacobin propaganda in England. Among the offending publications was Hardy's *The Patriot*, which included discussions of the writings of Thomas Paine. Hardy was arrested along with eight others, including the eminent John Horne Tooke whom the Pitt government especially wished to silence. Thomas Erskine defended Hardy, arguing that reform rather than revolution was the aim of Hardy and the Society. Defense witnesses included Richard B. Sheridan and Philip Francis, the latter the reputed author of the Junius letters. Shocked by the barbarous sentences at the recent Scottish treason trials and aroused by strong public sentiment in behalf of the defendents, the jury brought a verdict of not guilty. Tooke and John Thelwall, in trials that followed, were likewise acquitted; the charges against the others were dropped.

Hargreaves, William. *Is the Anonymous System a Security for the Purity and Independence of the Press? A Question for the Times Newspaper.* London, William Ridgway, 1864. 32 p. ("Revelations from Printing-House Square") **H 93**

The author condemns the practice in England, as exemplified by *The Times*, of concealing the name of the writer in order to preserve his independence and integrity. The reader has a right to know whose opinions he is reading. It is an aspersion on the writer and the public to suggest that anonymity protects the writer from the duelist's pistol or from the "corruptions of the Government." The anonymous system of journalism is a threat to the freedom of the press.

Harlan, William K. "Book-Burning Birchers." *California Crossroads*, 5:13–15, October 1963. **H 94**

An account of the vigorous but unsuccessful efforts of a citizens committee led by a John Birch Society organizer, to ban the *Dictionary of American Slang* from the Tulare County, Calif., library. The author is an English teacher at the College of the Sequoias.

Harley, J. H. "Ourselves and Our Censors." *Polish Review*, 2:109–15, June 1918. **H 95**

The article concerns the detention of the *Polish Review* by the British Army Council during World War I. The action was taken without warning and for no stated reason, except: "Instructions have been given to detain all copies of the *Polish Review* found in course of transmission from the United Kingdom." The editor believes that mention of possible Bolshevik activities in Poland may have prompted the ban. The banned issue contained a letter to the editor from President Wilson.

Harley, John E. "Some Case Studies of Official National Censorship of Motion Pictures." *World Affairs Interpreter*, 21:428–33, January 1951. **H 96**

New Zealand film censorship.

————. *World-wide Influences of the Cinema; a Study of Official Censorship and the International Cultural Aspects of Motion Pictures.* Los Angeles, University of Southern California Press, 1940. 320p. (Cinematography series no. 2) **H 97**

The work cites examples of censorship around the world, including the operation of the British Board of Film Censors.

Harlin, Melvin N. *An Examination of the Freedom of the Press Concept.* Lawrence, Kan., University of Kansas, 1937. 69p. (Unpublished Master's thesis) **H 98**

Harlow, Alvin F. "Martyr for a Free Press." *American Heritage,* 6(6):42–47, October 1955. **H 99**

An account of the printer, Matthew Lyon, 1750–1822, who was tried and imprisoned under the Sedition Act in 1798.

Harman, Moses. *The Kansas Fight for Free Press. The Four Indicted Articles.* Valley Falls, Kan., Lucifer Publishing Co., 1889. 11p. **H 100**

Relates to the indictment of Moses Harman for disseminating "obscene" literature through the mails. This consisted of four articles contained in issues of Harman's *Lucifer, the Light Bearer,* a newspaper which advocated sexual emancipation of women. Harman was found guilty on this and subsequent charges and for the next ten years he either served in jail or was under bond.

[————]. *The Persecution and Appreciation. Brief Account of the Trials and Imprisonment of Moses Harman Because of His Advocacy of Freedom of Women from Sexual Enslavement and the Right of Children to be Born Well. Together With an Account of the Public Reception Given to Him on His Release from Prison.* [Chicago, Lucifer Publishing Co., 1907.] 58p. **H 101**

The editor of *Lucifer, the Light Bearer,* a journal devoted to freedom of the press in matters of sex education and the sexual emancipation of women, was imprisoned for ten months under the Comstock laws for circulating "obscene" literature through the mail. This pamphlet records the celebration on New Year's day, 1907, given to Mr. Harman on his release from prison. Included are addresses by the Rev. William H. MacPherson, Methodist minister; Parker H. Sercombe, editor; Lucinda B. Chandler, crusader for social hygiene; and Gertrude Breslau Hunt. Mr. Harman's own account of his crusade is given in an article entitled, Lucifer and the Obscenity Laws.

————. *Whither Are We Drifting?* [Chicago, Lucifer Publishing Co.? n.d.]. 4p. **H 102**

Deals with conditions in the U.S. House of Representatives, 3 March 1873, when the postal censorship bill was passed.

[————, *et al.*] *Free Press: Arguments in Support of Demurrer to the Indictment of M. Harman, E. C. Walker, and Geo. Harman, under the Comstock Law, by C. C. Clemens and David Overmeyer. Also Judge Foster's Decision Overruling the Demurrer.* Valley Falls, Kan., Lucifer Publishing Co., 1889. 43p. **H 103**

The pamphlet contains the written brief and oral arguments presented to Judge Foster and the decision of the judge overruling the demurrer. The defense constitutes arguments against the Comstock obscenity laws.

Harned, Thomas B. "Whitman and His Boston Publishers." *Conservator,* 5:150–53, December 1895; 6:163–66, January 1896. **H 104**

An account of the suppression of the Boston edition of *Leaves of Grass,* told by one of Whitman's literary executors. The book was withdrawn by the publisher, James R. Osgood, after pressures were exerted by the district attorney, who in turn had been under pressure from the New England Watch and Ward Society.

Harnett, Bertram, and John V. Thornton. "The Truth Hurts: A Critique of a Defense of Defamation." *Virginia Law Review,* 35:425–44, May 1949. **H 105**

Notes on the legal aspects of speaking or publishing true but damaging facts, with special attention to the law of privacy.

[Harper, Edward]. *The Harper and Maine Slander Case. Commonwealth versus Harper. Trial for an Alleged Slander against Sebeus C. Maine, in the Superior Court, Criminal Session, December 29, 1862.* [Boston, 1863]. 68p. **H 106**

Relates to the distribution of a handbill attacking Sebeus C. Maine, nominated for justice of the police court, Boston, as being a "lying and licentious scoundrel." The case was one of the first to be tried under the amended libel law of Massachusetts (1855) which permitted truth as a sufficient justification, unless malicious intent is proved. The jury found Harper guilty on two counts, not guilty on a third.

Harpster, James E. "Obscene Literature." *Marquette Law Review,* 34:301–9, Spring 1951. **H 107**

"It would seem most reasonable for the legislatures to confer upon the courts the authority to enjoin all obscene literature, which literature could be defined with detailed exactness. Such a listing should contain, *inter alia,* magazines devoted wholly or in part to the pictorial presentation of nude

and seminude females . . . , nudist publications; comic books emphasizing sex or crime; publications which identify lust with love or which relate in detail either licit or illicit sexual intimacies; publications carrying suggestive cartoons; books and magazines presenting immorality in an attractive light; and magazines carrying advertising for such immoral literature. The list of course could and should be expanded . . . To prove the necessity for such a statute, one needs only to go down to his corner drugstore and watch what children read."

Harris, Albert W., Jr. "Movie Censorship and the Supreme Court: What Next?" *California Law Review,* 42:122–38, Spring 1954. **H 108**

How the states have responded to the U.S. Supreme Court decision, *Joseph Burstyn Inc. v. Wilson,* in which the Court ruled that motion pictures were entitled to the protection of the First Amendment. The author speculates on the implication of this decision in relation to the future of movie censorship.

[Harris, Benjamin]. *A Short but Just Account of the Tryal of Benjamin Harris, Upon an Information Brought against him For Printing and Vending a late Seditious Book called An Appeal from the Country to the City, for the Preservation of His Magesties Person, Liberty, Property, and the Protestant Religion.* [London, Benjamin Harris], 1679. 8p. (Also in Howell, *State Trials,* vol. 7, pp. 926ff.) **H 109**

The book, *An Appeal from the Country to the City,* had been written anonymously by Charles Blount and published by Harris. The latter was brought to trial in 1679 for publishing a seditious libel. Chief Justice Scroggs declared: "You can hardly read a more bad, and pernicious book, to put us all into a Flame." Scroggs ruled that under the Regulation of Printing Acts it was illegal to publish anything about the government without permission. Harris was not permitted to speak in his own defense and the jury was not permitted to read the book. Harris was found guilty, and, in default of a fine, was sent to prison. Upon his discharge he published *Triumphs of Justice over Unjust Judges,* which he dedicated to Justice Scroggs, and continued his attacks on the papists in his newsbook, *Domestic Intelligence.* He was able to escape punishment inasmuch as the Printing Act had accidentally been allowed to expire in 1679. In 1686 Harris moved to Boston where he opened a print shop and on 25 September 1690 published *Publick Occurrences Both Foreign and Domestick,* the first newspaper printed in America, which was banned after its first issue.

————. *To the Honorable House of Commons Assembled in Parliament. The Case, and Humble Petition, of Benjamin Harris Book-*

seller, lately come from New-England. [London, 1695?]. Broadside. **H110**
Harris, a London publisher who had spent time in jail for printing seditious works, had just returned from a nine-year stay in America. His petition asks for clearance of the earlier censorship cases against him so that he might support himself and his family.

Harris, E. H. "Shall the Government Own, Operate, and Control Radio Broadcasting?" *Proceedings*, National Advisory Council on Radio in Education. Chicago, University of Chicago Press, 1934, pp. 90–96. (Reprinted in Johnsen, *Freedom of Speech*, pp. 271–75) **H111**

Harris, Frank. "Mr. Sumner under the Microscope." *Pearson's Magazine*, 38(2): 79–80, August 1917. **H112**
Deals with John Sumner's management of the finances of the New York vice society and his conduct as censor. "In the last two years in New York Mr. Sumner has done more harm than any other man or society in the city."

———. "Mortal Disease—the Censorship." *Pearson's Magazine*, 38:367–68, February 1918. **H113**

———. *My Life and Loves*. Edited, with an introduction by John F. Gallagher. New York, Grove, 1963. 5 vols. in 1 (1070p.). **H114**
In his foreword to this often-suppressed autobiography, Harris writes of the history of opposition to sex expression in English and American literature and of his determination to rebel "against this old maid's canon of deportment" by writing freely of his sex life, an ingredient omitted in most biographies. His ultra frankness in describing his numerous amours (one writer calls it his "sexual gymnastics") resulted in the work being widely banned. Opposition to *My Life and Loves* in England and Germany, Harris notes, was as much based on his unflattering portrayal of the English nobility as on alleged obscenity. References to the long record of censorship of his work as well as comments on obscenity censorship in general in the United States, England, Germany, and France, appear in the general introduction, in prefaces to volumes 2, 3, and 5, and in chapter 14 of volume 4, Prosecution of *My Life*.

———. "Sumner and His Satellites." *Pearson's Magazine*, 38:362–63, February 1918. **H115**
This article refers to some of John Sumner's activities as New York sex censor and questions his financial management of the Society.

———. "Sumner and His Vice." *Pearson's Magazine*, 38(3):130, September 1917. **H116**
A vitriolic personal attack on Sumner, the "chief inquisitioner."

———. "Sumner and Indecency." *Pearson's Magazine*, 37:556–58, June 1917. **H117**
Sumner and his assistants had seized the May issue of *Pearson's Magazine* because of Harris' article on the vices of the New York Night Court. The case had not yet come up for trial. Harris comments bitterly on an earlier brush with the vice society when it attempted to suppress his book, *Oscar Wilde*. He also refers to the prosecution of Bruno for publishing Kreymborg's *Edna, Girl of the Street*.

Harris, George W. *Contempt of Court as It Affects Newspapers*. Evanston, Ill., Northwestern University, 1931. 73 p. (Unpublished Master's thesis) **H118**

Harris, Henry W. *The Daily Press*. Cambridge, Eng., University Press, 1943. 146 p. **H119**
An analysis of the contemporary British press by the editor of the *Spectator*. Harris believes that commercialization, monopoly, fear of libel in exposing abuse, and government pressures, have made some, but not serious, inroads on press freedom. He recommends reform of libel and contempt of court laws. Self-imposed professional restraints are to be preferred to more government control.

Harris, K. A. "Censorship in Kansas: A Dilemma." *Your Government; Bulletin of the Governmental Research Center* (University of Kansas), 19(4):1–3, 15 December 1963. **H120**
Kansas is one of 4 states maintaining film censorship boards, despite court decisions questioning the legality of such boards. The author of the article discusses the changed standards of movie censorship as influenced by public opinion and the courts. He estimates that over a period of 40 years the board consistently altered some 10 to 20 per cent of the movies it reviewed.

Harris, Sydney J. "You Get Soiled in Hunt for Dust." In his *Last Things First*. Boston, Houghton Mifflin, 1961, pp. 188–89. **H121**

Harrison, Austin. "Gott Strofe All Intellect." *English Review*, 24:470–73, May 1917. **H122**
Criticism of the British government ban on *The Nation*.

———. "The Lion in Blinkers." *English Review*, 19:204–15, January 1915. **H123**

Accusation that Britain, fighting a war under voluntary conscription which depends upon support of public opinion, is governed by a despotic press censorship. "A democracy which does not trust itself, that is to say, its Press, is a poor thing."

———. "Literature and the Policeman." *English Review*, 38:358–65, March 1924. (Reprinted in Downs, *The First Freedom*, pp. 46–49) **H124**
An appeal to leave literature and art to the judgment of the critic and artist and not to the policeman. Literary offenses must be tried, if at all, before a special jury of literary people. The strict moral code in literary expression makes it "almost impossible to write truthfully about things in England."

[———]. "The New Censorship." *English Review*, 7:530–40, February 1911. **H125**
We have a mania for pretending we are not grown up. Fiction intended for adult readers is banned by the censor on grounds that it might be harmful to children. While we allow the newspaper press free rein in reporting sex and crime, we object to the same realism in fiction. Banning of Neil Lyons' *Cottage Pie* is an example. The present practices of the British lending libraries in making all words safe for children is "really a declaration of our mothers' bankruptcy." Harrison calls on the feminists to direct their energy against the vigilance societies. "Does the public know that literature is in the hands of the informers?"

———. "Off with the Blinkers." *English Review*, 21:317–23, October 1915. **H126**
The editor calls upon the new coalition government to free the press to tell the truth about the conduct of the war. "Only the Press can arouse the people to see the war as it is and take the proud step essential to victory." The Press should demand that government take off the blinkers.

———. "Under the Collar." *English Review*, 13:477–85, February 1913. **H127**
An editorial critical of the part English circulating libraries have played in censoring books and intimidating authors and publishers. Harrison recommends that authors take the initiative in fighting for a free press.

Harrison, Earl G. "Television and Censorship." *Pennsylvania Bar Association Quarterly*, 21:128–35, January 1950. **H128**
Reference to the first test of the power of the state to impose censorship on television broadcasting, *Allen B. DuMont Laboratories, Inc. et al. v. Carroll et al.* (1949). The case involves regulations of the Pennsylvania Board of Censors.

Harrison, G. B. "Books and Readers, 1599–1603." *Library*, 14(4th ser.):1–33, June 1933. **H129**
Discusses such controversial publications as John Hayward's *The First Part of the Life and*

Reign of Henry the Fourth, the suppression of nine other books, and the ban on English histories.

Harrison, Godfrey. "Burned by the Hangman." *Books and Bookmen*, 8(5):17, February 1961. (Books that Shocked, no. 18)　　　　**H130**
"Some aspects of seventeenth-century persecution when authors were liable to lose their ears." (Earlier articles in the series were written by Desmond Elliott.)

———. "The Royal Mistress." *Books and Bookmen*, 8(7):17, 20, April 1961. (Books that Shocked, no. 20)　　　　**H131**
Account of the burning of a biography of Madame de Pompadour in London at the request of the French king and carried out with the help of his agent, Beaumarchais, himself a censored author.

Hart, Fred B. "Power of Government over Speech and Press." *Yale Law Journal*, 29:410–28, January 1920.　　**H132**
The author defends the constitutionality of the 1917 Espionage Act, on the basis of the right of government to punish persons advocating disobedience of the law.

Hart, William H., *comp. Index Expurgatorius Anglicanus: or a Descriptive Catalogue of the Principal Books Printed or Published in England, which have been suppressed or burnt by the Common Hangman, or censured, or for which the authors, printers, or publishers have been prosecuted.* London, Smith, 1872–78. Parts 1–5 (290p.). (Reprint announced by Burt Franklin, New York)　　**H133**
An early effort at a comprehensive bibliography of banned British books, issued in 5 paperbacked sections during 1872–78. The first 4 sections, examined in the New York Public Library, contained 260 entries, all fully annotated. The first book recorded as being banned was *A Supplicacyon for the Beggers*, compiled by Simon Fyshe and published in 1524. It offended Cardinal Wolsey, who had it suppressed. The second and third offending books were William Tyndale's translation of the New Testament and his *Parable of the Wicked Mammon*. These 3 works and several others were proscribed by a proclamation of 1530. Hart's list includes the many banned works of the Puritan Revolution and the last entry (Part 4) is for Henry Carr's *English Liberties, or the Freeborn Subject's Inheritance*, 1682.

Hartley, Jack. "Censorship and the School Librarian." *Arizona Librarian*, 18(3):9–10, Summer 1961.　　**H134**
"The teacher-librarian is on the firing line in any problem involving censorship. This is exactly where he should be . . . he must always look to his first line of defense—a knowledge of his books."

[Hartman, L. O.]. "Polluting the Springs: A Discussion of Censorship from Another Point of View." *Publishers' Weekly*, 102:1785–86, 11 November 1922.　　**H135**
The editor of the Methodist Church's *Zion's Herald* condemns the trend toward immorality in literature, but believes the most effective censorship is informed public opinion and an exposure of the "literary charlatans who have prostituted their abilities for the sake of the almighty dollar or a cheap popularity." He calls upon the publishing industry to put its house in order to avoid the pressure for literary censorship.

Hartnett, B., and J. V. Thornton. "Truth Hurts—A Critique of a Defense to Defamation." *Virginia Law Review*, 35:425–45, May 1949.　　**H136**

Hartz, F. R. "Obscenity, Censorship, and Youth." *Clearing House*, 36:99–101, October 1961.　　**H137**
Young people are not generally attracted to the book that has excellent literary qualities but is undesirable for adolescent reading. These books are generally of a "heavy nature." If such a book is chosen, to take it away only whets the curiosity and calls undue attention to the work. "It all comes down to the fact that you can't keep children in cotton wool. They come up against life in hundreds of ways and in many guises often worse than what they read in books. There is greater danger in a false picture of life than in the admission of certain true but disagreeable facts."

Harum, Albert E. "Remolding of Common Law Defamation." *American Bar Association Journal*, 49:149–54, February 1963.　　**H138**
Discussion of the common-law distinction between libel and slander, and commentary on the law of defamation in relation to radio and television.

[Harvey, Daniel W., and John Chapman]. "Trial of Daniel Whittle Harvey and John Chapman, for a libel on George 4, before Abbott, C.J. and a special jury at Guildhall, on October 30, 1823." In Macdonell, *Report of State Trials*, vol. 2, pp. 1–67.　　**H139**
The defendants had published in their newspaper a statement "from authority" that King George IV was insane. The defense counsel admitted the statement was false, but pleaded it was not made with malicious intent. Judge Abbott ruled the effect presumed to have been intended was the effect which the publication was calculated to produce. The defendants were convicted.

Harvey, Holman. "Help Stamp Out This Vile Traffic." *Reader's Digest*, 74:69–73, March 1959.　　**H140**

"Obscene photographs and lewd movies 'for private showing' aimed at school children, circulate by the millions and constitute a dangerous threat to the morals of our youth." The author urges citizens to notify the post office when pornography arrives in the mail; to launch a drive against the sale of pornography in school areas; to help to put teeth in the state and local laws against pornography; and to make certain that children receive a sound and sensible sex education.

Haskins, Doug. "The Many Faces of Censorship." *Canadian Forum*, 33:57–58, June 1953.　　**H141**
Comments on a British Columbia court decision against *Tobacco Road*.

[Haswell, Anthony]. "Trial for a Seditious Libel, Windsor, Vt., 1800." In Wharton, *State Trials*, pp. 684–87, and in *American State Trials*, vol. 6, pp. 695–99.　**H142**
The publisher of the *Vermont Gazette* was fined and imprisoned for two months for publishing critical articles reflecting on the prosecution of Matthew Lyon under the Sedition Act of 1798. James Morton Smith gives a full account of the Haswell case in his *Freedom's Fetters*.

Hatch, Azel F., *comp. Statutes and Constitutional Provisions of the States and Territories of the United States and the Statutes of England, on Libel and Slander, with Suggestions of Amendments.* Compiled under the auspices of, and published by the American Newspaper Publishers Association. Brooklyn, Press of Eagle Book Printing Department, [1895]. 162p.　　**H143**

Hatch, Robert L. "*Latuko*—The Naked and the Censor." *Reporter*, 7:36–38, 8 July 1952.　　**H144**
A review of the anthropological documentary film, *Latuko*, which was shown elsewhere in the country but banned in New York because of the code which prohibits nakedness. The film was made by the Museum of Natural History.

[Hatchard, John]. *Report of the Trial of the King v. J. Hatchard, for a Libel on . . . Sir James Leith . . . Feb. 20, 1817, together with Mr. Justice Bayley's Address in Pronouncing the Sentence of the Court.* London, Whitmore & Fenn, 1817. 134p.　**H145**

Hatt, Frank. "Right to Read and the Long Revolution." *Library Association Record*, 65:11–16, January 1963.　**H146**

Now that "as a nation we have more or less won literacy" and the right of access to books is recognized, librarians should be more concerned with guidance in reading and in the choice of what to read.

Hawes, William. "Television Censorship: Myth or Menace?" *Television Quarterly*, 4(3):63–73, Summer 1965.　　**H 147**
"From this historical review of the various restrictions on TV drama, one might conclude that regardless of whether programming changes because of television executives, sponsors, critics, or the public—*it does change.* The careful regulations predicted for television 20 years ago are now obsolete. TV drama may soon enjoy all the freedom of novels, theater and films."

Hawthorne, Julian. *In Behalf of Personal Liberty.* New York, Twentieth Century, 1891. 8 p. (Twentieth Century Library, no. 34)　　**H 148**
An open-letter of protest against the imprisonment of Ezra Heywood of Princeton, Mass., for circulating sex-education pamphlets through the mails. While "not eager to associate with Mr. Heywood's theories" and questioning the propriety of "open discussion of matters physiological and obstetrical," Hawthorne defends both the honesty of Heywood's motives and his right to free expression. "It would be better to have the country flooded with genuinely vicious and obscene literature, than to establish the precedent of imprisoning men for publishing their honest opinions." There follows a letter from Moses Harman of Topeka, Kan., relating his arrest on similar charges.

[Hay, George]. *An Essay on the Liberty of the Press; Respectfully Inscribed to the Republican Printers Throughout the United States. By Hortensius.* Philadelphia, Printed at the Aurora Office, 1799. 51 p. (Excerpted in Levy, *Freedom of the Press from Zenger to Jefferson*, pp. 186–97)　　**H 149**
A member of the Virginia House of Delegates, U.S. attorney in the Jefferson administration, and the prosecutor in the Burr conspiracy trial, Hay is one of the earliest and most eloquent exponents of the libertarian philosophy on the freedom of the press. No person should be punished for his opinions, regardless of the truth or falsity, and regardless of the intent. It was the purpose of the First Amendment that all men be free to criticize and condemn the government and its officers. He rejected the Blackstonian doctrine of freedom of the press being limited to freedom from prior restraint. Hay believed that "a man may say every thing which his passions suggest; he may employ all his time, and all his talents, if he is wicked enough to do so, in speaking against the government matters that are false, scandalous, and malicious" without being subject to prosecution. From this absolute freedom he would exempt only libels on private reputations. This essay deals largely with an attack on the Sedition Act, followed by Hay's radical views on freedom of expression. "My object is to demonstrate to the people, and to you, that the constitution of the United States, has been violated . . . If, Sir, these arguments shall excite in your mind, a doubt concerning the power of Congress, to define and punish libels, my purpose will be accomplished." Leonard Levy, in his *Legacy of Suppression*, gives a full account of the importance of Hay's opinion in the formulation of the Jefferson-Madison doctrine of a free press.

————. *An Essay on the Liberty of the Press, Shewing, That the Requisition of Security for Good Behavior from Libellers, is Perfectly Compatible with the Constitution and Laws of Virginia.* Richmond, 1803. 48 p.　　**H 150**
A later edition of Hay's essay, bearing his name as author.

Hayes, John C. "Survey of a Decade of Discussions on the Law of Obscenity." *Catholic Lawyer*, 8:93–109, Spring 1962.　　**H 151**
Beginning with the case of *Burstyn v. Wilson*, 343 U.S. 495 (1952), involving the New York film licensing statute, the author traces a decade of movement away from strict legal controls on obscenity. "Between the legally punishable and the morally evil there is a great gap. To accept as morally inoffensive all that is legally unpunishable would be to lower greatly our standards." The author sees the need for private agencies to evaluate the communications products, to publicize these evaluations, and, as parents and citizens, to seek legal means for action.

Haygood, William C. "Enclaves of America Overseas." *Saturday Review of Literature*, 36(28):29, 33, 11 July 1953.　　**H 152**
An account of attempts to discredit and undermine the U.S. Information Service libraries abroad through censorship of books.

Hayne, Isaac W., *comp. The Mercury's Course, and the Right of Free Discussion.* Charleston, S.C., Walker, Evans and Co., 1857. 45 p.　　**H 153**
A compilation of extracts from Charleston newspapers, relating to freedom of the press in the election for representatives in the state legislature held 25–26 August 1857.

Haynes, E. S. P. *The Case for Liberty.* London, Richards, 1919. 128 p.　　**H 154**
Chapter 3, Freedom of Discussion, extends remarks made in the author's earlier book, *Decline of Liberty in England*, showing that during World War I there was both the loss of faith in the citizen and loss of a sense of internal and external security, leading to "a curious inversion of the whole problem of free discussion."

————. *The Decline of Liberty in England.* London, Richards, 1916. 238 p.　　**H 155**
Chapter 5, Freedom of Discussion, considers the areas of religion, morals, and politics. Liberty of discussion is secured by four conditions—faith in the rationality and intelligence of citizens, a strong sense of internal and external security, a conviction that in certain cases it is impossible to suppress discussion of a subject, and an acceptance of the fact that the state must be the final arbiter for the sake of law and order.

————. *Religious Persecution: A Study in Political Psychology.* London, Duckworth, 1904. 208 p.　　**H 156**
Numerous references to incidents of suppression of published works on the grounds of heresy or blasphemy.

————, [Edward Carpenter, and Havelock Ellis]. "Taboos of the British Museum Library." *English Review*, 16:123–34, December 1913.　　**H 157**
Books in the British Museum that are "subversive of throne, of religion, and of propriety" are omitted from the general catalog and recorded separately.

Hays, Arthur G. "Censors and Gag Laws." *Library Journal*, 60:792, 15 October 1935.　　**H 158**
"We censor . . . in order that people should not be perverted to what we regard as views which may tend to upset our social or economic system or our moral view." The effect of gag laws and censorship has a broad significance and bars progress to an extent that cannot be measured. Librarians should "support to the fullest extent the untrammeled freedom of the human mind."

————. "Censorship." In Fred J. Ringel, ed., *America as Americans See It.* New York, 1932, pp. 267–71.　　**H 159**

————. "Civil Liberties in War Time." *Bill of Rights Review*, 2:170–82, Spring 1942.　　**H 160**
References to various actions taken against "objectionable" publications, including the paper, *Social Justice*.

————. *Let Freedom Ring.* New York, Boni and Liveright, 1928. 341 p.　　**H 161**
"This book narrates some half dozen cases on freedom of education, speech and assemblage, press, residence, stage and opinion, with which the writer happened to be connected. They all occurred between the years 1922 and 1927 and have one common characteristic, fear." Includes the famous "Hatrack" case, in which Hays was counsel for H. L. Mencken, editor of the *American Mercury*.

Hays, Will H. *The Memoirs of Will H. Hays.* Garden City, N.Y., Doubleday, 1955. 600 p.　　**H 162**

Part 4 of Hays's autobiography deals with his career as administrator of the Motion Picture Production Code Administration, an agency of the film industry for the regulation of the moral content of movies. The agency has come to be known as the "Hays Office."

———. "Motion Pictures and Their Censors." *Review of Reviews*, 75:393–98, April 1927. **H163**
Discussion of the background of motion picture censorship as practiced by state and municipal boards. The motion picture industry is opposed to political censorship "as un-American, unnecessary and ineffective." Self-regulation of the industry is being attempted through the Motion Picture Distributors and Producers of America, as a means of improving pictures and avoiding political censorship.

"The Hays Office." *Fortune*, 18:68–72, pp. 139–44, December 1938. **H164**
An account of the growth of power in the "Hays Office," self-censorship agency for American movies, from its establishment to the present. In cutting "cuss words, navels, attractive adultry, and irrelevant drunks . . . it has saved the screen for entertainment by warding off political censorship."

[Hayter, Thomas]. *An Essay on the Liberty of the Press. Chiefly as it respects A Personal Slander.* London, Published for J. Raymond, 1775. 47p. **H165**
The Bishop of London defends the right of a free press as an outgrowth of the natural and constitutional right of free speech. The latter he traces, mistakenly, to the Magna Carta. He considers (1) how far the liberty of the press is connected with the liberty of the subject, (2) whether the complaints of the abuse of the press be well-grounded, and (3) whether the peace and security, which any individual may derive from a new restraint of the press, will compensate for the mischiefs which may result from such restraint. Personal slander he considered a "subordinate evil," and punishment should be confined to damages. Even criticism of men in public life should not be a public offense. A free press is useful to reveal the designs of evil men so that they can be detected and restrained. While decrying the abuses that freedom of the press permits, he maintains that the advantages of freedom outweigh the disadvantages. The statement, along with that of his contemporary, the Reverend Robert Hall, represents one of the most liberal of the times.

Hayward, Max. "*Zhivago's* Suppression—A New Theory." *Library Journal*, 84:1562–63, 15 May 1959. **H166**
The cotranslator of *Dr. Zhivago* theorizes about the reasons it is not being published in Russia. His belief is that the original decision not to publish it was to a large extent based on personal animosities rather than political reasons.

Hazeltine, Charles, *ed. Narcissus Scrap Book: Containing an Account of the Seizure of a Nude Statuette by the City Marshal of New Bedford, the Trial of the Owner, His Suit Against the Marshal, and Comments of the Press, with Trial in the Superior Court.* New Bedford, Mass., E. Anthony, 1873. 60p. **H167**

Headlam, Cecil. *An Argument Against the Abolition of the Daily Press.* Oxford, Eng., Blackwell, 1904. 16p. **H168**
A satire, ostensibly in favor of keeping the press, despite public clamor to abolish it. The author supports freedom of the press despite the fact that press coverage is often trivial and personal, always incorrect and misleading, encourages betting, enables us to enjoy sports without fatigue, may involve us in war, discourages good literature, etc.

———. "Censorship of the Press." *Quarterly Review*, 234:132–46, July 1920. **H169**
Censorship in England by the Press Bureau during and immediately following World War I.

Heaford, William. "Restoration of Ferrer's Books." *Freethinker* (London), 32:250–51, 21 April 1912. **H170**
Deals with the unsuccessful effort to have the books of Francisco Ferrer destroyed, after the author had been shot by official order.

Heaney, Donald. "Obscene Literature Statutes." *Wisconsin Law Review*, 1955:492–98, May 1955. **H171**
The article (1) lists the factors which the courts have seemed to weigh in applying obscenity statutes, (2) considers the alternatives open to the Wisconsin Legislative Council [under direction to present recommendations to the 1955 Legislature], and (3) suggests the results of adopting any one alternative.

Heaps, W. A. "Textbook Controversies and the School Librarian." *Wilson Library Bulletin*, 16:42–43, September 1941. **H172**
The possibility of extending the current censorship of textbooks to censorship of school libraries suggests that librarians should be alert to attacks. They should "acquaint themselves with the nature of current criticism, the methods used in various localities in treating such attacks, and the tenets of academic freedom as reflected in printed materials."

[Hearst, William Randolph]. *William Randolph Hearst's Views on NRA and Freedom of the Press.* [New York, 1934?]. 36p. **H173**
Editorials reprinted from the New York *American* and other Hearst papers dealing largely with the rights of the press under the NRA codes. The editorial of 18 October

1933 supports Secretary of Labor Frances Perkins in her rebuke of a labor conciliator who threatened a local editor with prosecution for printing articles in alleged violation of the NRA.

Heartman, Charles F. *Charles F. Heartman Presents John Peter Zenger, and His Fight for the Freedom of the American Press, together with a Genuine Specimen of the New York Weekly Journal Printed by John Peter Zenger.* Highland Park, N.J., Printed for Harry B. Weiss, 1934. 60p. **H174**
A privately printed collector's item, issued on the occasion of the 200th anniversary of Zenger's trial. Each of the 99 printed copies presumably has an insert of an original issue of Zenger's paper. The text includes a review of the trial, facsimile pages of Lawyer John Chamber's brief, and Cadwallader Colden's manuscript account of the Zenger troubles.

———. *The Necessity of Prohibiting the German Press. From a Different Point of View.* [New York, The Author, 1918?]. 6p. **H175**
The author, later known for his bibliographical work and as a dealer in Americana, "dropped a bombshell" in German-American circles by urging that the American government suppress the German-American papers because of their pro-German sentiments and their opposition to the war. Heartman, a young newspaperman, had left Germany some years earlier because of his opposition to the Kaiser.

Heath, Gary E. "On Immoral Books." *Literary Review*, 3:637, 21 April 1923. **H176**
A letter to the editor charges the vice societies with going after works of literary value, such as *Many Marriages*, while ignoring such insincere and foolish works as *The Sheik*. "If the public is sincere in wanting to do away with the cheap, trashy, obscene books, as it claims to be, why does it continue to read them by the thousands?"

Heath, S. Burton. "Press is Freedom's Skirmish Line." *Nation's Business*, 35:44, 46, 68–71, February 1947. **H177**
A Pulitzer award winner explains why censorship at any level can curb freedom by taking away "the right to read."

Heath, William H. "They, Too, Build Major Barriers Against Freedom of Information." *Bulletin*, American Society of Newspaper Editors, 387:10–11, May 1956. **H178**
The attitudes of parents, teachers, and students are often hostile to freedom of the press. As evidence, the author cites a questionnaire submitted to high school students in Haverhill, Mass., by the Chamber of Commerce.

A typical answer referred to the "reactionary press which tends to tear down civic pride by printing the sorry details of each city council meeting." Similar evidence is contained in an article, Teen-Age Thinking on Press Freedom, in the April 1956 issue.

Hechinger, Fred M., *et al*. "The Textbook in America: A Symposium." *Saturday Review of Literature*, 36(16):14–23+, 19 April 1952.   **H179**
An analysis of the American school textbook problem by a publisher, two critics, an author, a parent, a school superintendent, and a college professor. Frequent references are made to attacks by pressure groups against particular textbooks.

Hecht, Ben, and Maxwell Bodenheim. *Cutie, a Warm Mamma*. Chicago, Privately printed by the Hechtshaw Press, 1924. 69 p. (Limited to 200 copies) (Reprinted by Boar's Head Books, New York, 1952, with a preface by Bodenheim)   **H180**
Two literary rebels of the 20's poke fun at the censor in a risqué volume describing the naughty adventures of Rudolph Pupich, censor and "smut hound." This work first appeared under the signature of Ben Hecht in the Chicago *Literary Times*.

Hedley, T. H. "Consumer's Guide to Henry Miller." *Hawaii Library Association Journal*, 18:14–17, Spring 1962.   **H181**

Heffron, Edward J. "Free Air or Hot Air?" *Commonweal*, 50:334–36, 15 July 1949.   **H182**
Comments on the FCC ruling on editorializing over radio and the reconsideration of the so-called Mayflower decision that required balanced presentation of all responsible viewpoints.

———. "Radio and Free Speech." *Commonweal*, 29:489–91, 24 February 1939.   **H183**
Government control of radio is essential to the public welfare.

———. "Should Radio Be as Free as the Press?" *Commonweal*, 47:466–69, 20 February 1948.   **H184**
The author objects to giving radio the same right to editorialize as held by newspapers. Since radio is under government control through licensing, minorities **might** not have their viewpoints broadcast.

[Hefner, Hugh M.]. *The Playboy Philosophy I*. [Chicago, *Playboy Magazine*, 1963]. 47 p.   **H185**

The editor-publisher of *Playboy* discusses the magazine's guiding principles and editorial credo in a series of seven installments that appeared originally in the magazine from December 1962 through June 1963. Much of the discussion deals with the magazine's treatment of sex. The third editorial in the series considers the sexual revolution that has taken place in the United States as reflected in literature and the movies, with particular reference to censorship activities of the NODL and the Post Office Department. The fifth editorial deals with religious curbs on freedom of sex expression; the sixth and seventh editorials discuss obscenity and the law, the latter quoting at some length from an interview with Justice Hugo Black, conducted by Professor Edmond Cahn of the New York University School of Law. Hefner writes in the seventh editorial: "The anti-sexual in our society so fail to understand the true sexual nature of man that they try to suppress what is unsuppressible. In so doing, they hurt society in three distinct ways: 1. The censor curtails freedom . . . 2. The censor attempts to control our thoughts . . . 3. The censor impairs our mental health and well-being." *Playboy*'s crusade for a censor-free society is not promoted by self-interest, Hefner writes, since the magazine "has never attempted to push to the outer boundaries of what was censorable," but because of a belief that citizens "will be happier in an America in which all men are allowed to exercise full freedom of speech, of press, of religion, and of association." An answer to the "*Playboy* philosophy" by J. Claude Evans, chaplain of Southern Methodist University, appears in *Catholic World*, October 1964.

[———]. *The Playboy Philosophy II*. [Chicago, *Playboy Magazine*, 1963]. 52 p.   **H186**
Installments eight through twelve continue the statements by *Playboy*'s editor relating to freedom of sex expression. Editorial eight considers various points of view of sex freedom as expressed by such writers as Dr. Kinsey and Mrs. Margaret C. Banning. The ninth and tenth editorials trace the history of sexual expression from early Christendom through the Victorian era and the relationship of historic concepts to present-day sex prohibitions and taboos. Editorial eleven and twelve deal largely with censorship of obscenity in Chicago, including the recent action taken against the author himself. The influence of the hierarchy of the Catholic Church and the controversy over the distribution of birth control information by the Illinois Public Aid Commission are also included.

Heidenheimer, Arnold J. "Techniques of Intimidation." *New Republic*, 125:14–15, 29 October 1951.   **H187**
A review of methods used to intimidate persons who hold unorthodox views, including attacks against high school and college textbooks and college newspapers.

Heiskell, John N. *The Newspaper: Keeper of the Community Conscience*. Tucson, Ariz., University of Arizona Press, [1965]. 12 p.

(The John Peter Zenger Award for Freedom of the Press, 1964)   **H188**
The author, recipient of the award, is editor of the *Arkansas Gazette*.

"Helen and Galahad Under Fire." *Literary Digest*, 92:26–27, 8 January 1927.   **H189**
John Erskine's *Private Life of Helen of Troy* and *Sir Galahad* are denounced in the press as "moral filth."

Helffrich, Stockton. "Broadcast Censorship: Past, Present, Future." *Television Quarterly*, 1(4):62–68, November 1962.   **H190**
The manager of the New York Code Office of the National Association of Broadcasters discusses some of the misconceptions concerning broadcast censorship. "The chief occasions on which censorship is truly needed are those where integrity in the attainment of a reasonable objective is missing." Healthy development in broadcasting censorship includes: "an increasing freedom for maturity in program fare; an increasing rejection of any lingering poppycock in broadcast advertising claims."

Hellrung, Gregory L. "Obscenity—Evidence—Contemporary Community Standards—Prurient." *Catholic University Law Review*, 12:53–55, January 1963.   **H191**
Review of the Maryland case, *Yudkin v. State*, dealing with *Tropic of Cancer*, and related cases involving contemporary community standards concerning obscenity.

[Helwys, Thomas]. *Persecution for Religion Judg'd and Condemn'd . . .* London, 1615; reprinted 1662. (Reprinted in Edward B. Underhill, *Tracts of Liberty of Conscience and Persecution*, pp. 85–180)   **H192**

Hemenway, Henry B. "Report of the Committee on Publishing Details of Suicides in the Public Press." *Bulletin*, American Academy of Medicine, 12:253–63, October 1911.   **H193**
The Committee considers the reporting of a crime as an incentive to commission of one.

Hempel, William J., and Patrick M. Wall. "Extralegal Censorship of Literature." *New York University Law Review*, 33:989–1026, November 1958.   **H194**
An analysis of the use of extralegal methods to suppress works of literature, with an account of campaigns by such private groups as the National Office of Decent Literature, the American Legion, the General Federation of Women's Clubs, the Daughters of the American Revolution, and the Parent Teachers Association. References are made to official pressures in such cities as Detroit, Port Huron, Mich., and New York City. There is also a section

on control of literature in the Armed Forces. The authors consider legal remedies against nonstatutory censorship by private groups and public officials, including malicious prosecution, defamation, and action against secondary boycott. Existing law is adequate to protect the public from extralegal censorship by public officials, but not from private groups, especially when they employ the boycott. Laws should be enacted which provide that coercive interferences with publication or distribution of published material are unlawful and that injunctions and actions in equity may be brought under the statute. Private groups would be protected in their freedom of expression concerning any printed matter, but would be encouraged to espress their opposition under the obscenity or other applicable statutes. Appendix I: Publications Disapproved for Youth by the National Office for Decent Literature, October 1955; Appendix II: Communities in which Reading Material Available to the Public Has Been or Is Determined to Some Extent by Public Officials; Appendix III: Partial List of Pocket Books Banned by the Police in Detroit, Michigan, 1950 to 1955.

Hempstead, Walter E., Jr. "Licensing of the Press under the N.I.R.A." *Oregon Law Review*, 13:359–64, June 1934. **H 195**
The author concludes that the licensing of the press contemplated under the N. I. R. A., even if exercised, would be no unconstitutional thwarting of political expression. If other business may be licensed, publishing activities may be likewise restricted.

Henderson, Gerard. "What is Left of Free Speech." *New Republic*, 21:50–52, 17 December 1919. **H 196**
Criticises the opinion of the U.S. Supreme Court in the Abrams case, where friends of Soviet Russia were sentenced to 20 years in jail for opposing American intervention.

Henderson, James M. "James Fraser, 1645–1731." *Aberdeen University Review*, 25:138–46, 1938. **H 197**
A biographical sketch of the licenser of printing who succeeded Roger L'Estrange.

Henderson, John. "Censorship in Montana." *Wilson Bulletin*, 10:480–81, 1 March 1936. **H 198**
Comments on the exclusion from state university libraries of Vardis Fisher's *Passions Spin the Plot*, by action of the Montana State Board of Higher Education.

Henderson, William G. *Concise Summary of the Law of Libel as it Affects the Press.* Rutherford, N.J., Chemical Bank, 1915. 120 p. **H 199**

Henkin, Louis. "Morals and the Constitution: The Sin of Obscenity." *Columbia Law Review*, 63:391–414, March 1963. **H 200**

"I believe, despite common assumptions and occasional rationalizations, that obscenity laws are not principally motivated by any conviction that obscene materials inspire sexual offenses. Obscenity laws, rather, are based on traditional notions, rooted in this country's religious antecedents, of governmental responsibility for communal and individual 'decency' and 'morality.'"

Hennelly, Edmund P. *Advertising's Most Important Challenge.* Columbia, Mo., Freedom of Information Center, School of Journalism, University of Missouri, 1959. 4 p. (Publication no. 18) **H 201**
The author discusses the threat to the freedom of advertising in various legislative proposals. "Every bill in Congress which affects the freedom from unreasonable restraint of business affects your freedom—even if the bill has no remote connection with freedom of the press. Economic freedom and political freedom are inseparable."

Hennings, Thomas C. "Constitutional Law: The People's Right to Know." *American Bar Association Journal*, 45:667, July 1959. **H 202**

———. "A Legislative Measure to Augment the Free Flow of Public Information." *American University Law Review*, 8:19–27, January 1959. (Reprinted in U.S. Senate hearings, 86th Cong., 1st sess., Committee on the Judiciary, *Freedom of Information and Secrecy in Government*, 1959) **H 203**
Senator Hennings discusses the work of the House of Representatives' subcommittee of the Committee on Government Operations, devoted to various aspects of government secrecy, and the bill proposed to "clarify and protect the right of the public to information."

———. "Secrecy—Threat to Freedom." *Progressive Magazine*, 23:21–24, April 1959. (Reprinted in U.S. Senate hearings, 86th Cong., 1st sess., Committee on the Judiciary, *Freedom of Information and Secrecy in Government*, 1959) **H 204**
Senator Hennings demonstrates the practices and techniques used to restrict information about government activities. He suggests a program to combat undue secrecy in government.

Henriques, Fernando. "The Perils of Pornography." *Twentieth Century*, 172:157–70, Summer 1962. **H 205**
A lecturer in social anthropology at University of Leeds looks at the trade in "hard-core" pornography on both sides of the Atlantic and assesses its influence. He finds that the rise in juvenile delinquency in America is the result of complex social factors, hardly affected by trade in pornography, which is

more likely to encourage private fantasies than overt action. Pornography is not a serious danger to the community; more dangerous is the apparatus of censorship. For those who insist on the destructive character of pornography, the only way to eliminate it is "to remove the forest of taboo which luxuriates around sexual activity. The open acceptance of sex as a natural function destroys the necessity for the obscene."

Henry, E. William. "The FCC and Freedom of the Frequencies: A Federal View." *Yale Political*, 3(1):20, 35–36, Autumn 1963. **H 206**
The chairman of the FCC believes his agency must constantly be under scrutiny. Since it assigns frequencies to broadcasters, it must insure that they serve the public interest. By insisting upon a broad choice of programs the FCC is widening freedom of speech. A broadcaster's view is presented by Donald McGannon in an accompanying article.

Hentoff, Nat. "Trial by Newspaper; A Free Press Versus the Right of the Defendant." *Commonweal*, 82:110–13, 16 April 1965. **H 207**

Hepple, Alexander. *Censorship and Press Control in South Africa.* Johannesburg, The Author, 1960. 78 p. **H 208**
A review of present censorship laws and the actions of pressure groups, particularly those intent on keeping literature white. The author fears further government controls in carrying out the Report of the Cronje Commission (Commission of Enquiry in Regard to Undesirable Publications).

Herd, Harold. *Seven Editors.* London, Allen and Unwin, 1955. 126 p. **H 209**
One of the seven biographical sketches is about William Hone, bookseller, who was tried for blasphemy in publishing parodies of the Creed and the Litany.

Herrick, Robert. "What Is Dirt?" *Bookman*, 70:258–62, November 1929. **H 210**
A discussion of recent censorship activities, with special reference to deletions made by the American publisher in *All Quiet on the Western Front* and the banning of the magazine carrying Hemingway's *Farewell to Arms*. "Better to allow free pronography than to leave to any censor or board of censors the choice of what we can read and think! Less harm to public morals would be done with complete license than from the sort of censoring we suffer from at present—haphazard, ignorant, vacillating."

Herring, Clyde L. "Is Radio Censorship Necessary." In Summers, *Radio Censorship*, pp. 221–26. **H 211**

The U.S. Senator from Iowa writes in behalf of a National Council for Radio, Press, and Moving Pictures to provide voluntary industry regulation of media-content to avoid undesirable government censorship.

Herring, E. Pendleton. "Politics and Radio Regulation." *Harvard Business Review*, 13 : 167–78, January 1935. **H 212**
Consideration of the question before the Federal Communications Commission as to "whether or not commercial broadcasters shall continue to dominate the air to the virtual exclusion of other interests." The author reviews the experiences of the Federal Radio Commission and government regulation of radio, and proposes possible solutions to the problem of control of the air.

Herring, James M. "Public Interest, Convenience or Necessity in Radio Broadcasting." *Harvard Business Review*, 10 : 280–91, April 1932. (Reprinted in Buehler, *American vs. British System of Radio Control*, pp. 90–110) **H 213**

———, and Gerald C. Gross. *Telecommunications: Economics and Regulation.* New York, McGraw-Hill, 1936. 544 p. **H 214**
Includes regulations on national and international cables and radio transmission.

Hershey, Amos S. "So-called Inviolability of the Mails." *American Journal of International Law*, 10 : 580–84, July 1916. **H 215**
"Recent correspondence between Allied and United States Governments has called renewed attention to the so-called inviolability of postal correspondence on the high seas during maritime warfare." A review of the international conventions and practices.

Herttell, Thomas. *The Demurrer; or, Proofs or Error in the Decision of the Supreme Court of State of New York Requiring Faith in Particular Religious Doctrine as a Legal Qualification of Witnesses* . . . New York, E. Conrad, 1828. 158 p. **H 216**
A friend of Dr. Thomas Cooper, Herttell presents a strongly-worded legal argument of the right of the American citizen to form his own opinions in matters of religious faith and to state them without prejudice to his civil rights. The right of a free press is incidental to the statement, but Cooper cited it in his own treatise on the liberty of the press as a landmark on free discussion.

[Hervey, John, *Baron* Hervey of Ick'worth]. *Further Observations on the Writings of the Craftsman.* London, Printed for J. Roberts, 1730. 28 p. **H 217**
In his *Observations . . .*, *Sequel . . .*, and *Further Observations . . .*, Lord Hervey accuses Bolingbroke of using *The Craftsman* not as a champion of a free press but to blacken the Walpole administration. He objects to Bolingbroke's use of historical parallels to avoid libel, accusing him of expounding "as unfairly, and as ignorantly [upon English history], as his Holiness ever did on the Scriptures." He also comments on the offense of Robert Nixon, imprisoned for ridiculing acts of Parliament, calling him "a nonjuring parson half mad." These pamphlets, published anonymously, have also been attributed to Sir William Yonge.

[———]. *Letter to Mr. D'Anvers concerning the liberty of the press.* London, Printed for J. Roberts, 1729. 24 p. **H 218**
An answer to Caleb D'Anvers of *The Craftsman*, written to vindicate the liberty of the press from some abuses that were agreeable to D'Anvers. Attributed to Lord Hervey or one of his Whig associates.

[———]. *Observations on the Writings of the Craftsman.* London, Printed for J. Roberts, 1730. 31 p. **H 219**

[———]. *Sedition and Defamation Display'd: In a Letter to the Author of the Craftsman. . . .* London, J. Roberts, 1731. 48 p. **H 220**

[———]. *Sequel of a Pamphlet intitled Observations on the Writings of the Craftsman . . .* London, Printed for J. Roberts, 1730. 29 p. **H 221**

Hervey, John G., and Joseph J. Kelley, Jr. "Some Constitutional Aspects of Statutory Regulation of Libels on Government." *Temple University Law Quarterly*, 15 : 453–92, July 1941. **H 222**
On the eve of war the authors consider the history and development of seditious libel, through English common law in the formation of the First Amendment, during the War of 1812, the Civil War, and World War I (a lengthy discussion). They also discuss the syndicalist trials of the 1920's and the freedom of speech issues in labor relations during the 1930's. They conclude that there is no blanket rule to measure validity of statutes controlling libel of government; each case must be determined on its merit and upon the climate of opinion. Final approval or disapproval of actions taken by both the legislature and the court rests with the people.

Hester, Mary, *Sister*. "The High School Librarian and the Controversial Novel." *Catholic Library World*, 36 : 161–66, November 1964. **H 223**
The author gives advice to school librarians on book selection, admonishing them to accept the responsibility of keeping harmful matter from the immature while at the same time avoiding capricious condemnation. She notes Cardinal Newman's comment that it is impossible to write about a sinful humanity without reference to sin. The real obligation of the Catholic librarian is to stress the natural law of the Church by which each individual is bound to avoid reading matter that would be harmful to his faith and morals. "Let us take all prudent precautions to safeguard the inexperienced in this matter of reading, but let us also respect our student sufficiently to insist that . . . he is the responsible guardian of his own soul."

[Hetherington, Henry]. *A Full Report of the Trial of Henry Hetherington, on an Indictment for Blasphemy, before Lord Denman and a Special Jury, at the Court of Queen's Bench, Westminster, on Tuesday, December 8, 1840; for Selling Haslam's Letters to the Clergy of all Denominations: With the Whole of the Authorities Cited in the Defence, at Full Length.* London, H. Hetherington, 1840. 32 p. (Reprinted in Macdonell, *Report of State Trials*, vol. 3, pp. 563–99) **H 224**
Hetherington, a newspaper editor who had played a leading part in the struggle for an untaxed press in the 1830's, was tried and convicted of blasphemy for selling Charles Junius Haslam's series of pamphlets criticizing the Bible as "abominable trash." Hetherington conducted his own defense, replying to the charge of Haslam's use of "objectionable" language, that on that basis the Bible itself must be prohibited. He had before him a list of such passages which he refrained from reading. Hetherington also objected to the singling out of certain passages while ignoring the general nature of the work. Includes an open letter to Lord Denman criticizing the conduct of the trial, signed "Publicola."

Hettinger, Herman S., and William A. Porter. "Radio Regulation: a Case Study in Basic Policy Conflicts." *Annals of the American Academy of Political and Social Science*, 221 : 122–37, May 1942. **H 225**
An examination of the basic economic, social, and technical aspects of radio broadcasting as well as the "public interest" principle. The authors trace the development of regulatory legislation and the important decisions of the Federal Communications Commission which have set the pattern of the American system of regulation.

Hewett, Barnard, *et al.* "Censorship." *Theatre Arts Monthly*, 21 : 243–46, March 1937. **H 226**
To test the actual opposition to freedom of the theater, the journal recorded the experience of directors in various parts of the country: a teacher of drama at the University of Arizona; a director of the Division of Drama, University of Washington, Seattle; a director of a little theater in Minnesota; and an anonymous author from a southern university.

[Hewitt, Cecil R.]. "After *Lady Chatterley*." *New Statesman*, 60:730–33, 12 November 1960.   **H 227**

The author, writing under the pseudonym, C. H. Rolph, discusses the acquittal of *Lady Chatterley* (Penguin Books) in England under the new Obscene Publications Act and projects the implications for the future.

[———]. "Banning Books." *New Statesman*, 40:452–53, 18 November 1950. Reply by Norman Haire, 40:545, 2 December 1950.   **H 228**

The author (C. H. Rolph, *pseud.*) writes of his own early experience in translating objectionable French papers so that the British court might take action against their sale. He criticizes the uneven prosecution for obscenity in America and England. It is unwise to expect the judge to be a literary critic; it is chaotic to enforce the obscenity law in some districts and not in others; it is unfair for England to have an official *Index Librorum Expurgatorius* for government use. He recommends that the courts accept the judgment of the professional council of reputable publishers. Mr. Haire, president of the Sex Education Society, in a letter to the editor, adds the further suggestion that if authorities were to make the banning of a book in one part of the country automatically extend to other parts, the prospect of financial loss to publishers would induce them to defend the unfortunate bookseller, which they have not always been willing to do.

[———]. "Books in the Dock." *Author*, 74:14–17, Spring 1964.   **H 229**

Status of obscenity prosecutions in Great Britain under the Obscene Publications Act, 1959, and the reforms that are still needed.

[———]. "The *Chatterley* Legacy." *Author*, 71:5–6, Spring 1961.   **H 230**

A review of recent press and public opinion following the freeing of *Lady Chatterley*, in the case of *Regina v. Penguin Books*.

[———]. "Common Law Censorship." *New Statesman*, 65:418, 420, 22 March 1963.   **H 231**

The author discusses the possible use of the common law for "conspiracy to publish" in England to avoid acquittal of obscene works, following the freeing of *Lady Chatterley* under the Obscene Publications Act of 1959.

[———]. "'Conspiracy' and Censorship." *Author*, 72:15, Autumn 1962.   **H 232**

The use of conspiracy indictments in obscenity cases instead of the Obscene Publications Act, places the matter, once again, under common law, which the Act was intended to prevent.

[———]. "*Lady Chatterley's* Triumph." *New Statesman*, 60:682, 5 November 1960.   **H 233**

The trial and acquittal of *Lady Chatterley* (Penguin Books). "The defence triumphantly

proved that an author with a conscience can deal with sex honestly and seriously—and still be published."

[———]. "Obscene Publications." *Author*, 68:94–96, Summer 1958.   **H 234**

Comments on the report of the Select Committee on Obscene Publications.

[———]. "Obscene Publications Bill." *Solicitors' Journal*, 103:317–18, 24 April 1959.   **H 235**

Report on the status of the bill in the House of Commons.

[———]. "Obscenity and Common Law." *Author*, 71:10–13, Autumn 1961.   **H 236**

[———]. "Sense and Censorship." *Author*, 66:59–61, Spring 1956.   **H 237**

A review of current publications on sex censorship.

[———, ed.]. *Does Pornography Matter?* Edited by C. H. Rolph, [*pseud.*]. London, Routledge & Kegan Paul, 1961. 112 p.   **H 238**

A collection of essays bringing many points of view to the broad problem considered in the title: Lord Birkett as a lawyer, Sir Herbert Read from his interest in aesthetics, Goeffrey Gorer as a sociologist, Dr. Donald Soper and Dr. Dom D. Rutledge from differing religious viewpoints, and Dr. Robert Gosling as a practicing psychoanalyst. C. R. Hewitt, a British editor, draws upon his legal, literary, and publishing experience to present his views in a summary chapter.

[———, ed.]. *The Trial of Lady Chatterley: Regina v. Penguin Books Limited.* Edited by C. H. Rolph, [*pseud.*]. Baltimore, Penguin Books, 1961. 250 p. (A Penguin Special 192)   **H 239**

Lady Chatterley's Lover was the first novel prosecuted under the British Obscene Publications Act of 1959. This Act was intended to do away with the common law on obscene libel and to liberalize prosecutions so that works of literature and science would not be proscribed. The new law required the court to consider the book as a whole; it permitted booksellers a defense of "innocent dissemination"; it permitted publishers and authors to defend their books against destruction; and it protected private libraries from police raids. It also permitted expert testimony, and 35 experts—authors, editors, critics, theologians—testified at the *Lady Chatterley* trial. The verdict was "not guilty." The editor of this account had been secretary of the "Herbert Committee," responsible for bringing about reforms in the censorship law. This account is taken from the transcript of the trial.

[Heywood, Ezra H.]. *The Evolutionists: Being a Condensed Report of the Principles,*

Purposes and Methods of the Union Reform League as revealed in its three Conventions held in Princeton, Mass., during the Summers of 1879, 1880, 1881. Princeton, Mass. Cooperative Publishing Co., 1882. 16 p.   **H 240**

The League was organized in Princeton, Mass., in 1879, to promote the repeal of legislative restrictions on natural rights and to encourage diffusion of knowledge and cooperative action in all progressive movements. A resolution was adopted at the first convention (1879) in behalf of D. M. Bennett, imprisoned for circulating a physiological pamphlet on marriage; a resolution at the second convention (1880) called for the abolition of Comstock laws and compulsory Bible reading in the public schools; another resolution, offered by Stephen Pearl Andrews (president), called for an effort to redeem so-called vulgar sex words by washing them clean and putting them to good use in society. "That since there is no obscenity in Nature, no obscenity in Science, and no obscenity in Art, there seems no place left for obscenity, but in the defilement of our own imaginations; and that, therefore when our thoughts and imaginations are freshened to the naturalness of nature, used to the clean-cut precision of science, and to the gracious sweetness of Artistic beauty, obscenity will cease to exist among us." The account is written by Ezra H. Heywood, secretary.

[———]. *Free Speech: Report of Ezra H. Heywood's Defense before the United States Court in Boston, April 10, 11 and 12, 1883; together with Judge Nelson's Charge to the Jury, Notes of Anthony Comstock's Career of Cruelty and Crime; Tragic and Comic Incidents in the Malicious, Savage Persecution, Suffered by Moral Scientists Devoted to Social Evolution, and Other Interesting Matter.* Princeton, Mass., Cooperative Publishing Co., [1883?]. 55 p.   **H 241**

Heywood was arrested by Comstock for the second time, in 1882. The charge was sending obscene matter through the mails, namely: Heywood's pamphlet, *Cupid's Yokes*, quotations from two Walt Whitman poems in the August 1882 issue of Heywood's magazine, *The Word*, and advertisements for a contraceptive device that Heywood waggishly called "the Comstock Syringe." Judge Nelson rejected the first two charges, leaving only the advertisement, but the jury refused to convict.

[———]. *Proceedings of the Indignation Meeting held in Faneuil Hall, Thursday Evening, August 1, 1878, to Protest against the Injury Done to the Freedom of the Press by the Conviction and Imprisonment of Ezra H. Heywood . . .* Boston, Benjamin R. Tucker, 1878. 68 p.   **H 242**

Heywood, a respected citizen of Princeton,

Mass., was a socialist freethinker and advocate of a single standard of sexual morality. His pamphlet, *Cupid's Yokes*, was a serious, though somewhat crude, treatise on love and marriage. Comstock considered it "too foul for description" and arrested Heywood. He was convicted of sending obscene matter through the mails and sentenced to two years at hard labor. The mass meeting, presided over by Elizur Wright, petitioned President Hayes to remove Comstock from his position as postal inspector and to release Heywood from jail. President Hayes, on advice of his Attorney General, released Heywood after he had spent six months in jail. The publisher and secretary for the meeting was Benjamin R. Tucker, a friend of Walt Whitman, who later became famous as a philosophical anarchist. The pamphlet includes testimonial letters from Alfred E. Giles, Theron C. Leland, Parker Pillsbury, A. J. Grover, and D. M. Bennett. Elizur Wright's speech in behalf of Heywood is published in the 15 August 1878 issue of *The Index*, organ of the National Liberal League.

[————]. *United States v. Heywood; Why the Defendant Should Be Released; Mr. Chamberlain's Letter to President Benjamin Harrison.* New York, National Defense Association, 1891. 21p. **H 243**
Documents relating to the conviction of Heywood on an obscenity charge for his pamphlet, *Cupid's Yokes*, including Judge George M. Carpenter's charge to the jury, a letter from the defense counsel, Edward W. Chamberlain of New York, to President Benjamin Harrison, reviewing the case and asking in the interest of justice for the pardon of Heywood, and an abstract of the petition of pardon from his friends, including those from his home town. Petitions were also sent from Canada, England, and Scotland.

Hibbard, Darrell O. "The Moving Picture—The Good and the Bad of It." *Outlook*, 101:598–99, 13 July 1912. **H 244**
Calls for nationwide supervision of public exhibitions of moving pictures under the Department of Education or Child Welfare, to safeguard children. The National Board of Censors is inadequate as a means of control since only those films which are submitted by their makers reach the Board.

[Hickeringill, Edmund]. *The Late Famous Tryal of Mr. Hickeringill, Rector of All-Saints, in Colchester; and Author of the Naked-Truth, the Second Part . . .* London, F. Smith, 1681. 14p. **H 245**
Hickeringill was brought to trial for blasphemy for, among other charges, the publication of his book, *The Naked-Truth*, which criticized the jurisdiction and ritual of the Church of England. In the introduction of a subsequent book, *The Ceremony-Monger*, Hickeringill refers to his banishment from house and family because of his writing, and discusses the nature of libel: "Nothing can be a libel but

what is false; and then it may be false, and yet no Libel, if it do not tend to Discord; and consequently be malicious or seditious."

[————]. *A Speech Without-Doors: Or some Modest Inquiries Humbly Proposed to the Right Honourable the Convention of Estates, Assembled at Westminster, Jan. 22, 1688/9 Concerning . . . Restraint of the Press.* London, George Larkin, 1689. 36p. **H 246**
One of the five brief essays in this work concerns restraint of the press. The author, rector of All Saints Church, Colchester, and himself a victim of restraint of the press, observed that "no Books vend so nimbly as those that are sold (by Stealth as it were) and want Imprimaturs." While acknowledging the need for the Catholic Church to maintain an *Index*, the Church of England should not be the only "door-keeper" to the press. He recommends a law against anonymity.

Hicks, Frederick C. "Legal Liability of Libraries in Time of War." *Papers and Proceedings*, American Library Institute, 1918, pp. 43–49. **H 247**
A law librarian discusses the legal liability of librarians and trustees under the Trading with the Enemy Act (1917) and the Espionage Act (1917), the latter of which seems to involve questions of both compulsory and voluntary censorship of libraries. A discussion follows in which A. E. Bostwick expresses strong support for the responsibility of libraries to preserve enemy propaganda for historic purposes. He also objects strenuously to suppression of works in the German language, since the language has nothing to do with the present attitude of the German government. If we do not make this distinction we will alienate many loyal Americans of German ancestry.

Hicks, Granville. "How Red Was the Red Decade?" *Harper's Magazine*, 207:53–61, July 1953. (Reprinted in Daniels, *The Censorship of Books*, pp. 89–96) **H 248**
Hicks, well-known student of social and intellectual history and an avowed Communist from 1935 to 1939, gives an estimate of the influence of communism during those years. "Communism scarcely made a dent on any of the mass media—the popular magazines, the movies, the radio." The notion that communism dominated American culture in the thirties is false.

————. "In the Mind of the Reader." *Saturday Review*, 45(35):11, 1 September 1962. **H 249**
A discussion of the once-forbidden four-letter words. The emergence of the words in accepted literature is a victory over censorship. To disapprove of censorship, however, is not to approve of the works censored, some of which are trash. But censorship does not get at the real evil; it is an evil in itself.

————. "Introduction." In *Banned*, New York, Berkley, 1961, pp. vii–xii. (Also as an "Afterwords" in *Banned #2*, New York, Berkley, 1962, pp. 247–54) **H 250**
Comments on censorship are used as an introduction to this anthology of excerpts from books that have been banned. While recognizing that "the relationship between art and morality is not . . . a simple one," and that some literature is undoubtedly sexually stimulating, Hicks believes that we should insist on the right to read any serious author, no matter what he writes about, no matter what language he uses. It is better to have some pornography slip by in a broad interpretation of "serious" rather than be "denied the opportunity to read work of merit."

————. "*Lolita* and Her Problems." *Saturday Review*, 41(33):12, 38, 16 August 1958. **H 251**
The reviewer believes that the future will exonerate *Lolita* from the charges of pornography as completely as we of today have exonerated *Ulysses*.

Hickson, Oswald S., and P. F. Carter-Ruck. *The Law of Libel and Slander.* London, Faber, 1953. 290p. **H 252**

Hier, Frederick P., Jr. "When Boston Censored Walt Whitman." *New York Times*, 19 June 1927, sec. 4, pp. 7, 10. **H 253**
How the Watch and Ward Society of Boston stopped the publication of the Osgood edition of *Leaves of Grass*.

Higgins, Alexander P. "Treatment of Mails in Time of War." In *British Year Book of International Law, 1928.* London, Oxford University Press, 1928, pp. 31–41. **H 254**
Traces the development of international understandings (or lack of them) for protecting neutrals from interference by belligerants, from the Second Hague Peace Conference (1907) through the Eleventh Hague Convention. Includes a discussion of the situation in World War I in which postal correspondence by sea was not guaranteed by the belligerents.

Higgins, E. M. "Censorship in Australia: The Ban on Working Class Literature." *Labour Monthly* (London), 11:57–58, January 1929. **H 255**

High, Stanley. "Not-So-Free Air." *Saturday Evening Post*, 211(33):8–9, 73–74, 76–77, 11 February 1939. **H 256**
A discussion of some of the controls exercised over radio programs by government agencies. The radio in the United States is "jittery because of the growing and substantiated fear that the Administration's appetite is too expansive." The author suggests that radio

take to the air in its own behalf to build up public support of a free radio.

———. "Press Fights on Two Fronts." *Reader's Digest*, 41:126–30, December 1942.   **H 257**
A charge against Washington bureaucrats for practicing political censorship, not necessary for the war effort. He absolves the "ably managed office of Chief Censor Byron Price." Only the alertness of the press has prevented creeping paralysis of information.

Highet, Gilbert. "I Wuz Robbed; Fearless Reporter Battles Censors." *Nation*, 155: 581–82, 28 November 1942.   **H 258**
Written in the form of a diary by an American reporter, the account bitterly denounces British censorship for prohibiting his broadcasts concerning the war in North Africa and his criticism of the British conduct of the war.

Highmore, Anthony. *Reflections on the Distinction Usually Adopted in Criminal Prosecutions for Libel; and on the Method, Lately Introduced, of Pronouncing Verdicts in Consequence of Such Distinction.* London, 1791. 192 p.   **H 259**

Hildebrand, Joel H. "How Not to Control Atomic Energy." *ALA Bulletin*, 41:273–81, 1 September 1947. (Reprinted in Summers, *Federal Information Controls in Peacetime*, pp. 84–86)   **H 260**
Scientists need not only laboratory facilities but also freedom to consult with each other. They need "free enterprise" and their own "free press" in order to be effective in their work.

Hildesheimer, Esriel E. "Censorship." In *Universal Jewish Encyclopedia*. New York, The Encyclopedia, 1941. Vol. 3, pp. 80–83.
                                              H 261
History of the censorship of Hebrew works by Christian ecclesiastical and civil authorities.

Hill, Alexander. "Responsibility for Public Taste." *Library*, 7(n.s.):257–63, 1906.   **H 262**
The author charges the public library with responsibility for keeping out bad books as they would keep out bad men. The library "book-tasters" should "reject such books as are poisonous to the moral nature."

Hill, Derek. "The Habit of Censorship: 'We're Paid to Have Dirty Minds.'" *Encounter*, 15:52–62, July 1960. Reply by John Trevelyan, 15:61–64, September 1960.   **H 263**
A review of a half century of film censorship under the British Board of Film Censors. The author formulates principles which seem to

have prompted the action of the Board in cutting or banning films, although no written code has been issued. Examples of films cut or banned are given. The reply is by the secretary of the Board, pointing out what he considers inaccurate or false in the article, and defending the work of the Board.

Hill, Frederick T. *Decisive Battles of the Law; Narrative Studies of Eight Legal Contests Affecting the History of the United States between the Years 1800 and 1886.* New York, Harper, 1906. 267 p.   **H 264**
Contains a full account of the trial of James T. Callender in 1800 for seditious libel under the Sedition Act of 1798.

Hill, Lister. "Freedom and Responsibility in Publishing." In Alfred Stefferud, *ed.*, *Wonderful World of Books*, New York, Houghton Mifflin, 1952, pp. 212–14.
                                              H 265
The Alabama senator discusses the educational responsibility of the newspaper and book publishing industries. "Freedom carries its own responsibility, perhaps a heavier one than if freedom were absent."

Hill, Marjorie B. "Censorship in Perspective." *Wilson Library Bulletin*, 19: 319–20, January 1945.   **H 266**
A brief view of censorship over the years. "If we agree that censorship is undemocratic in its assumption that the average man cannot think for himself, that it fails to achieve its purpose, and is attended by bigotry, intolerance, and spiritual self-righteousness, then let us bring about greater liberality in our laws and in our minds in order to free literature from the shackles of the censor."

Hilliard, Samuel. *A Narrative of the Prosecution of Mr. Sare and His Servant, for Selling the "Rights of the Christian Church" in Answer to What Relates to the Prosecution in the Second Part of Defence of the Said Book.* London, 1709.   **H 267**
Richard Sare, a London bookseller, and his apprentice, Mr. Williams, were brought to trial along with the author of this account, for selling Matthew Tindal's *Rights of the Christian Church Asserted*. The work was critical of the Church of England and the influence of its "Romish" priests.

Hillyer, Robert. "Treason's Strange Fruit." *Saturday Review of Literature*, 32(24):9–11, 28, 11 June 1949.   **H 268**
An attack on the award of the 1949 Bollinger Prize for poetry to Ezra Pound, who was then awaiting trial under charge of treason. In his article poet Hillyer, supported by a statement from the editors, calls the award a "permanent disgrace." The criticism of the award is continued in the issue for 18 June 1949. In that issue (page 7) the editors state that while maintaining that "political considerations should not interfere with the evaluation of art,

the principle did not obtain in the case of the award to Ezra Pound . . . both because of the political coloration of the book itself and because it seemed to us that the award was being utilized to take the curse off Pound's political activities against the United States during the War."

Hiltner, Seward. "Four Letter Words." *Pastoral Psychology*, 13:7–9+, October 1962.   **H 269**
"As signs, they seem to be more offensive to some persons than the actions they signify." If such taboo words could become domesticated "a book would be judged on whether the action to which it alluded was proper (or prurient) in print, and not on whether the language in which the allusion was made was proper or not."

Hilton, O. A. "Freedom of the Press in Wartime, 1917–19." *Southwestern Social Science Quarterly*, 28:346–61, March 1948.
                                              H 270
A study of legislative and judicial encroachment of free speech during World War I through the enforcement of war statutes relating to newspapers and periodicals. An earlier article by the author, Public Opinion and Civil Liberties in Wartime, 1917–1919, appeared in the December 1947 issue.

Himes, C. F. *Life and Times of Judge Thomas Cooper.* Carlyle, Pa., Dickinson School of Law, 1918. 70 p.   **H 271**
Contains brief reference to Cooper's trial for sedition and a lengthy account of his trial for teaching heresy to the students of Columbia [S.C.] College. According to Theodore A. Schroeder, the author feared to discuss Cooper's conviction under the 1798 Sedition law, because of the Espionage Act of World War I then in force.

Himes, Norman E. "Charles Knowlton." In *Dictionary of American Biography*, vol. 10, pp. 471–72.   **H 272**
A biographical sketch of the early American physician whose book on birth control, *Fruits of Philosophy*, was attacked by censors in America and England.

———. "History of Birth Control." In *Encyclopaedia of Sexual Knowledge*. New York, Dingwall-Rock, 1936, pp. 46–57.
                                              H 273
Includes references to the various efforts to prevent the dissemination of information about birth control.

———. *The Truth about Birth Control, with a Bibliography of Birth Control Literature.* New York, Day, 1931. 28 p. (John Day Pamphlets, no. 4)   **H 274**

Hine, Al. "Chief Defect of Current Film-Censor Groups Is That They Don't Represent Movie-Goers." *Holiday*, 2: 134–36, August 1947. **H 275**
The author considers various groups that exert censorship influence on movies for political, religious, or other reasons. If there is to be censorship at all, it should be by the movie-goers themselves; otherwise we might try the idea of no censorship at all.

Hints to Radical Reformers, and Materials for True. London, Printed for J. Hatchard, 1817. 164 p. **H 276**
Includes a section on theatrical licentiousness and corruption of the press, pp. 89–107. "Immoral publications must be deterred by all the rigour of existing law. And, where they evade its force, and seem to satisfy its forms, their price must be raised beyond the reach of poorer purchasers." The anonymous author suggests a tax on books whose sole purpose is "food for idle appetite or vain amusement."

Hints to the Jurors on the Liberty of the Press. Dublin, 1813. **H 277**
Pamphlet listed in Brian Inglis, *Freedom of the Press in Ireland.* Copy not located.

Hintz, C. W. E. "Which Propaganda?" *College and Research Libraries*, 1:170–75, March 1940. **H 278**
The propaganda of the present and future "will be far more subtle and insidious than heretofore" and more effective unless steps are taken to counteract it. The usual library policy of presenting all sides of a subject so long as it is in good taste, style, and method of presentation, will not be adequate in dealing with modern propaganda. He calls for co-operative efforts in reaching a solution to the problem.

Hirsch, William R. "Liability of a Radio Station for Defamatory Utterances." *Washington University Law Review*, 1950: 95–108, Winter 1950. **H 279**

Historical Highlights of Birth Control . . . London, International Planned Parenthood Federation, [1955?], 18 p. **H 280**
A chronological history of efforts in behalf of birth control and the prosecution of those distributing literature relating thereto.

"The History Censorship in Chicago." *Library Journal*, 52:1026, 1 November 1927. **H 281**
Article about the controversy in Chicago resulting from the efforts of Mayor William Hale Thompson to prove Superintendent of Schools William McAndrew guilty of disseminating pro-British propaganda in the public schools. A member of the board of the Chicago Public Library threatened to remove and burn pro-British books from that Library, but was prevented by an injunction from destroying taxpayers' property.

Hitchcock, Curtice. "Boston and *Strange Fruit*." *Publishers' Weekly*, 145:1447–48, 8 April 1944. **H 282**
The publisher of *Strange Fruit*, in a letter to the editor, criticizes bookseller Richard Fuller and the Boston book trade for outrunning the police in their eagerness to ban a book.

Hoar, Roger S. "Freedom of Speech and Its Limitations." *American Mercury*, 10: 202–4, February 1927. **H 283**
Deals with the "two fundamental, but opposed rights: the right of freedom of speech, and the right to be let alone."

Hobbes, Thomas. *An Historical Narration Concerning Heresie, And the Punishment thereof.* London, 1680. 18 p. (Also in *Somers Tracts*, vol. 7, pp. 373–81) **H 284**
Hobbes defends his publication, *Leviathan*, the object of the passage of a bill in the House of Commons (1666) to punish theism.

Hobbs, Perry. "Dirty Hands; a Federal Customs Officer Looks at Art." *New Republic*, 62:188–90, 2 April 1930. **H 285**
A book dealer interviews the customs censor at an eastern port, who claimed to have read more dirty books than any man in New England. The censor admitted "getting a kick" out of the stuff but took seriously his job of keeping such books out of the hands of innocent youths. He was especially hard on the classics which he defined as "a dirty book someone is trying to get by me."

Hobhouse, *Sir* Benjamin. *Treatise on Heresy, as Cognizable by the Spiritual Courts. And an Examination of the Statute 9th and 10th of William III. c. 32, Entitled, an Act for the More Effective Suppression of Blasphemy and Profaneness. By a Barrister at Law.* [London?]. 1792. 146 p. **H 286**

Hobson, John A. "Liberty of Unlicensed Printing." *Nation and Athenaeum* (London), 44:831–32, 16 March 1929. **H 287**
A change in the habit of speech and thought has taken place in recent years; there has been an "abandonment of the sentimental prudery which sought thrills of secret pleasure from revelations of the 'shocking,' in favour of a more open and honest attitude toward . . . 'the facts of life.' Education and public opinion have a higher prophylactic value than legal force."

Hockenberry, Scott H. "Pennsylvania's Courtroom Ban on Camera Equipment." *Pennsylvania Bar Association Quarterly*, 36: 76–83, October 1964. **H 288**
According to a Pennsylvania survey there is more diversity of opinion on the part of Pennsylvania newspaper editors concerning the merit of courtroom photography than there is within the legal profession in upholding the ban on camera equipment. "Since the legal profession has the power to enforce its rulings, courtroom photography will not become a standard press activity in Pennsylvania."

Hocking, William E. *Freedom of the Press; a Framework of Principle. A Report from the Commission on Freedom of the Press.* Chicago, University of Chicago Press, 1947. 243 p. **H 289**
A philosophical discussion of the basis for press freedom, developed by the author, a member of the Commission. Footnotes indicate comments of other members of the Commission. The thesis is that freedom of the press is a means to an end and not an end in itself.

———. *Freedom of the Press in America.* Leiden, Universitaire Pers Leiden, 1947. 24 p. **H 290**
Inaugural address delivered on his entrance into office as guest professor at the University of Leyden.

Hodges, Elizabeth D. "What Can the Library Committee Do?" *NEA Journal*, 52:25–26, May 1963. **H 291**
"A school library with a defensible book collection, a united faculty, a well-informed supporting public, and a plan of action in case of attack should be able to offer a formidable front to any assult upon freedom to read."

Hodges, William T., and C. Lawrence Stagg. "Broadcasting and Television Trials Versus Free Press." *University of Florida Law Review*, 11:87–98, Spring 1958. **H 292**
A summary of the issues, with special attention to practices in Florida and references to a modification of Canon 35 in Colorado.

Hoffman, Carl. "A Psychiatric View of Obscene Literature." *Guild of Catholic Psychiatrists Bulletin*, 8:3–13, January 1961. (Reprinted by Citizens for Decent Literature, Cincinnati, 1961. 6 p. mimeo.) **H 293**
While recognizing the complex matter of delinquency, Dr. Hoffman cites his own studies and those of a number of other psychologists that support the dangers that arise from the reading, hearing, and seeing of obscene material and pornography. He disagrees with the conclusions of Drs. Phyllis and Eberhard Kronhausen as to the effect of pornography.

Hoffmann, Frank A., *et al.* "Panel on Folk Literature and the Obscene." *Journal* of *American Folklore*, 75:189–259, July–September 1962. **H 294**

Most of the issue is devoted to problems of gathering, classifying, and publishing obscene folklore. The introduction is by Frank A. Hoffmann; definition and problems are presented by Herbert Halpert; the work of field-collecting erotica as part of general folklore collecting is discussed by Horace P. Beck; misconceptions in erotic folklore is discussed by Gershon Legman. Several articles relate to identifying and classifying the genres. Restrictions on publication of erotic folklore are referred to throughout.

Hogan, Robert. "O'Casey and the Archbishop." *New Republic*, 138:29–30, 19 May 1958. **H 295**

A review of the years of censorship, suppression, and vilification of the Irish theater. The issue was brought once again to public attention through the action of the impending Dublin International Theatre Festival which decided to drop the production of McClelland's *Bloomsday* and caused O'Casey to withdraw his play, *The Drums of Father Ned*, because of demands for alterations.

Hoggart, Richard. "The Guardians and the New Populism." *Censorship*, 1:2–4, Autumn 1964. **H 296**

In matters of freedom of expression in the arts Britain may be going from Vestigial Guardianship (consisting of senior clergy, leader writers, presidents of national volunteer bodies, headmasters) to a New Populism, a superficial grassroots movement that claims to "speak for the body of ordinary decent people" in threatening the freedom of expression, "bypassing the alternatives a literate democracy is supposed to offer."

Hohman, Agnes C. *An Analysis of the Literature on the Outstanding Issues and Opinions on Censorship, 1940–50.* Washington, D.C., Catholic University of America, 1952. 182 p. (Unpublished Master's thesis) **H 297**

Special attention is given to episodes during the decade covered, including the cases of *Esquire* and *The Nation*, and objections to paperback books.

Holcroft, Thomas. *Narrative of the Facts, relating to a Prosecution for High Treason; including the Address to the Jury, Which the Court Refused to Hear; with Letters . . . and the Defence the Author Had Prepared, If He Had Been Brought to Trial.* 2d ed. London, Printed for H. D. Symonds, 1795. 215 p. **H 298**

Holcroft was charged with high treason along with Thomas Hardy, John Horne Tooke, and John Thelwall.

Holdsworth, *Sir* William S. "Defamation in the Sixteenth and Seventeenth Cen-

turies." *Law Quarterly Review*, 40:302–15, September 1924; 40:397–412, October 1924; 41:13–31, January 1925. **H 299**

"The wrong of defamation is sometimes a crime pure and simple, sometimes a tort pure and simple, and sometimes it can be treated either as a crime or a tort at the option of the injured person." The author traces the origin of modern law of defamation in the court decisions of the sixteenth and seventeenth centuries—civil libel growing from the common law belief that damages were recoverable for defamation; the criminal law concept growing from the philosophy of the Star Chamber. The legal differences between libel and slander are explained. The author recommends that the rules of libel be applied to all kinds of defamation.

———. "Press Control and Copyright in the 16th and 17th Centuries." *Yale Law Journal*, 29:841–58, June 1920. **H 300**

The Tudors and Stuarts employed three methods of controlling the press: punishment as criminal offenses for those works considered treasonable, seditious, and heretical; grant of powers of control over printing to the Stationers' Company; and the issuance of comprehensive Royal ordinances. The paper deals with the second two measures by which unlicensed printing was suppressed and copyright was originated. The differences between the controls exercised by the Stationers' Company and the Crown are at the root of two different theories on the origin of copyright.

———. "The Right of Liberty of Discussion." In his *A History of English Law.* London, Methuen, [1938]. vol. 10, pp. 672–96. **H 301**

Includes a discussion of the conflict in point of view between Thomas Erskine and Lord Mansfield and the libel cases that took place in England during the last decades of the eighteenth century and which led to the Fox Libel Act of 1792.

Holland, Denys C. "Freedom of the Press in the Commonwealth." *Current Legal Problems*, 9:184–207, 1956. **H 302**

The author surveys the status of freedom of the press in the British Commonwealth, concluding that "freedom of the press as we know it in Great Britain does not exist in many dependent territories. . . . The Executive should not possess the arbitrary powers of controlling the press, independent of judicial control, which they enjoy in so many of our dependent territories at present."

Hollander, John. "The Old Last Act: Some Observations on *Fanny Hill*." *Encounter*, 21(4):69–77, October 1963. **H 303**

Comments on the confusions between the two "genres" of the novel and the pornographic work, which have multiplied during the past half century. Analysis of the background, style, and content of *Fanny Hill*.

Holliday, Yvonne. "Expurgatoria." *Library Review*, 51:126–30, August 1939. **H 304**

The author's theme is that "censorship should be left to the people," since librarians and patrons can seldom agree upon what is fit for circulation. She cites numerous examples of library censorship observed during her career.

Hollingshead, John. *Theatrical Licenses. Reprinted from "The Daily Telegraph" and "Times".* London, Chatto and Windus, 1875. 24 p. **H 305**

Hollis, Christopher. "State Censorship." *Commonweal*, 62:49–51, 15 April 1955. (Excerpts from an article in the London *Tablet*, 12 February 1955) **H 306**

Deals with the difficulty of defining the obscene book and the position of the State in condemning the corrupt book. The author believes that the "powers of censorship of the secular State should be most severely limited."

Holloway, George. "Controversy on Film." *Library Journal*, 88:513–15, 1 February 1963. **H 307**

The experience of the Free Library of Philadelphia with the controversial film, *Operation Abolition*. Lists special criteria to consider in film selection. One of three papers relating to selection of controversial materials given at a staff meeting of librarians working with young adults at the Free Library of Philadelphia.

Holman, Frank E. "The Convention on Freedom of Information: Threat to Freedom of Speech in America." *American Bar Association Journal*, 37:567–70, August 1951. **H 308**

A former president of the American Bar Association opposes the acceptance by the United States of the UN Convention as being in conflict with the Bill of Rights of the United States Constitution and as opening the way to dictatorship.

Holmes, D. T. "Another Feature of Doubtful Literature." *Library World*, 13:236–37, February 1911. **H 309**

The author shows, in an extract (The Principle of Opposition) from his book, *A Scot in France and Switzerland*, that the reader doesn't necessarily respond in the direction of the author's intention, but rather to the contrary. Literature of crime, passion, and squalor does not necessarily encourage emulation. Likewise, moral literature (often boring) may have little effect.

Holmes, John Haynes. "Sensitivity as Censor." *Saturday Review*, 32(9):9–10, 23, 26 February 1949. Discussion: 32:23–24,

19 March 1949; 32:23–24, 26 March 1949. (Reprinted in Downs, *The First Freedom*, pp. 152–55) **H 310**

A New York clergyman and board chairman of the American Civil Liberties Union decries "the informal yet drastic censorship" in the current attempts by organized minority groups to suppress books, movies, and radio programs that are offensive to their interests. Holmes refers especially to the case of the movie version of *Oliver Twist* (objection to the portrayal of the Jew, Fagin), the movie, *Birth of a Nation* (objections from Negroes), and *The Nation* magazine (objections from Catholics). He denies that minority groups have the right of literary immunity. The true libertarian believes that all men shall have the right to express and publish their ideas, however disagreeable or even dangerous they appear to be. Censorship means assumption of personal infallibility; the imposition of this judgment upon the entire community by group pressure, law, or force; and the arrogance of a minority using its power to persecute the majority. Instead of outlawing serious literary and dramatic works, let the minority protest through the pulpit, platform, and press; let them confront error with truth. "So long as men are free thus to bear witness against defamation, they need not be afraid." This article and a supporting one by John Mason Brown (12 March) was followed by an avalanche of letters, pro and con, including letters from Margaret Halsey (19 March, 7 May) who defended the right of Jews and Negroes to literary immunity; Arnold Forster of the Anti-Defamation League of B'nai B'rith (26 March) who believes Holmes has confused censorship with censuring, which is the right of majority or minority to protest; and Elmer Davis and Elmer Rice (16 April) who come to Mr. Holmes's defense. The three-month debate was followed by a Town Meeting of the Air broadcast and concluded by an editorial by Norman Cousins in the issue of 28 May in which he affirmed the right of the author to produce, the right of the offended to protest, and, finally, the right of a counterprotest condemning minority action. "The only time a controversy such as this becomes dangerous is when government intervention is sought or invoked."

————, comp. *Freedom of Speech and of the Press.* New York, National Civil Liberties Bureau, 1918. 30 p. **H 311**

A collection of quotations on freedom of expression, including selections from Jefferson, Garrison, Thoreau, Milton, Locke, Bentham, Hall, Mill, Erskine, Godwin, and Galsworthy. Selections are intended to assist pacifists in protesting against war censorship.

Holmes, Marjorie. "A Mother Speaks up for Censorship." *Today's Health*, 40:50–51+, January 1962. **H 312**

"Movies glorifying prostitution, books that smile on adultery, even songs about infidelity—this is what we've tolerated until smut has finally taken over. What's the next step—the acceptance by society of complete sexual freedom, with all its consequences?" The author, as a writer and as a parent, begs for some controls over the mass media, particularly over the movies where sex, used as a money-maker, is flouted regardless of consequences to the young.

Holmes, Mary. "Censorship and Civil Rights." *Social Order*, 7:242–49, June 1957. **H 313**

A prize-winning essay by a student at Maryville College presents the point of view of the Catholic Church in drawing a line between freedom and restraint. The author considers the arguments, pro and con, over "the role of the government as censor and over the censorship efforts of minority groups."

Holmes, Oliver W. *The Dissenting Opinions of Mr. Justice Holmes; arranged by Alfred Lief . . .* New York, Vanguard, 1929. 314 p. **H 314**

Free Press in Wartime, pp. 41–43; Free Speech Not Free, pp. 231–35; Eugene V. Debs Case, pp. 242–47.

————. "Schenck v. United States: Opinion of Oliver Wendell Holmes for the Supreme Court, 1919." In S. G. Brown, ed., *We Hold These Truths.* New York, Harper, 1941, pp. 300–362. **H 315**

Decision upholding the constitutionality of the Espionage Act. Contains the famous "clear and present danger" dictum relating to freedom of speech under the First Amendment. This decision along with Holmes's dissenting opinion in *Abrams v. United States* in which the clear and present danger doctrine is advanced further, are reprinted in Haiman, *Freedom of Speech*, pp. 52–56.

[Holmes, William V.]. *Report of the Trial of William Vamplew Holmes, (One of Mr. Carlile's Shopmen,) on a charge of Sedition and Blasphemy, before the Common Serjeant and a London jury, at the Sessions House, Old Bailey, March 1st, 1822 . . .* London, R. Carlile, 1824. 24 p. **H 316**

Holmes, one of the men who volunteered to tend the bookshop while Richard Carlile was in jail, was himself found guilty of sale of a seditious work. He served a two-year sentence and upon his release opened his own bookshop and continued to sell the offending works.

Holorenshaw, Henry. *Levellers and the English Revolution.* London, Gollancz, 1939. 96 p. (The New People's Library, vol. 21) **H 317**

A Marxian interpretation of the Leveller movement in Cromwell's England, a movement which first awakened the spirit of English freedom of the press.

Holt, Daniel. *A Vindication of the Conduct and Principles of the Printer of the Newark Herald: an Appeal to the Justice of the People of England, on the Result of the Two Recent and Extraordinary Prosecutions for Libels.* Newark, Eng., Holt, 1794. (Also in Howell, *State Trials*, vol. 22, pp. 1189 ff) **H 318**

Holt was brought to trial before Lord Kenyon for the publication of two pamphlets urging parliamentary reform. Despite the able defense of Thomas Erskine, Holt was fined and given four years' imprisonment. One of the offending pamphlets was sanctioned and probably written by the Duke of Richmond and Mr. Pitt.

Holt, Francis L. *Law of Libel.* Edited by Anthony Bleecker. New York, Stephen Gould, 1818. 328 p. (First edition published in London, Butterworth, 1812) **H 319**

An American edition of one of the major digests of the English law of libel. Holt gives a résumé and apology for existing English libel laws on which early American cases were based; Bleecker added a selection of American cases.

Holt, Guy, ed. *Jurgen and the Law; a Statement with Exhibits, Including the Court's Opinion, and the Brief of the Defendants on Motion to Direct an Acquittal.* New York, McBride, 1923. 78 p. **H 320**

"People of the state of New York against Guy Holt, Robert M. McBride & Company, and Robert M. McBride for having in possession with intent to sell, a book called *Jurgen*, by James Branch Cabell, in violation of section 1141 of the Penal Law, concerning obscene prints and articles. In the Court of General Sessions for the County of New York."

Holtzoff, Alexander. "The Relation between the Right to a Fair Trial and the Right of the Press." *Syracuse Law Review*, 1:369–79, Spring 1950. **H 321**

Notes concerning court cases, 1918–49.

Holyoake, George J. *The History of the Last Trial by Jury for Atheism in England: a Fragment of Autobiography . . .* London, James Watson, 1851. 100 p. **H 322**

Holyoake, who served as editor of the *Oracle of Reason* while its original editor, Charles Southwell, served a prison sentence for blasphemy, was himself convicted for blasphemy at Cheltenham in 1842 and served six months in the Gloucester jail. This is the story of the Holyoake trial. The publisher, James Watson, was also a veteran in the cause of the liberty of the unlicensed press.

————. *The Life and Character of Richard Carlile.* London, Austin & Co., [1849?]. 40 p. **H 323**

A sympathetic biography of the nineteenth-century English martyr, written by a friend and associate in the struggle for press freedom.

Wickwar calls this biography of Carlile "the first, the best, and the shortest." In 1817 Carlile began his fight against censorship by hawking Wooler's *Black Dwarf* on the streets of London and by publishing Southey's *Wat Tyler*, when the poet laureate was trying to suppress this early work. In 1818 Carlile reprinted Paine's political works and William Hone's parodies, serving 18 weeks in prison for the latter. By the end of 1819, 6 indictments were pending against him and he began a prison sentence which was to total some 6 years. His wife and younger sister took over the shop and were jailed. Under pressure from the Constitutional Association, numerous convictions were secured against Carlile's friends who took over the shop. They served from 6 months to 2 years. Eventually a vending device was rigged up at the shop whereby the purchaser could select a book on a clock dial, pay his money, and receive the book without seeing the vendor. The shop prospered because of the prosecution rather than in spite of it. By 1829, when all the convicted had been released from prison, the freedom to publish was virtually assured in Great Britain.

————. *Sixty Years of an Agitator's Life.* 3d ed. London, Unwin, 1893. 2 vols.

H 324

The autobiography of an English social reformer, Chartist, and freethinker. Holyoake spent 6 months in jail on a blasphemy charge and played a major role in the fight for an untaxed press. When the last warrant was issued against him for flouting the newspaper tax, the total penalties amounted to some $3,000,000.

————. *The Spirit of Bonner in the Disciples of Jesus; of the Cruelty and Intolerance of Christianity, Displayed in the Prosecution, for Blasphemy, of Charles Southwell, Editor of the Oracle of Reason.* London, [185?]. 16p.

H 325

————. *The Suppressed Lecture at Cheltenham.* London, Frederick Farrah, 1864. 8p. (Utilitarian Tracts; from *The Reasoner*, no. 827)

H 326

In 1841 when Holyoake gave a free-thought lecture in Cheltenham he was arrested and sentenced to 6 months' imprisonment; in 1864 he again attempted to lecture in that city but the authorities turned off the lights. He prints here for circulation in Cheltenham a digest of his intended remarks to the effect that freedom of expression had greatly improved during the 23-year interval, that "it is impossible to inflict punishment for opinion any more in England."

————. *The Trial of George Jacob Holyoake, on an Indictment for Blasphemy, before Mr. Justice Erskine and a Common Jury, at Gloucester, August the 15th, 1842. From Notes Specially Taken by Mr. Hunt . . .* London, Printed and published for the "Anti-

Persecution Union," by Thomas Paterson, 1842. 68p.

H 327

Holyoake was the second editor of *The Oracle of Reason* to be tried for blasphemy. He was sentenced to six months in prison. The trial proceedings include an address before the Anti-Persecution Union, formed to assist in the defense of those persecuted for free publication of opinion. Paterson, publisher of the account of the trial, subsequently followed Holyoake to prison as the third editor of the *Oracle*.

[————], ed. *The Life and Character of Henry Hetherington.* London, J. Watson, 1849. 16p.

H 328

Prepared as a memorial by a Committee of the Directors of the Literary and Scientific Institution under the editorship of Mr. Holyoake. Includes an abridgment of the life of Hetherington from Thomas Cooper's *Éloge*, Hetherington's last will and testimony, the funeral oration by Mr. Holyoake, and tributes from James Watson and W. J. Linton.

Homans, T. S. "Comstockery and Sex Morality." *Altruria*, 2:12–13, March 1911.

H 329

An attack on censorship of sex education.

[Hone, William]. *Don John, or "Don Juan" Unmasked . . . Being a Key to the Mystery Attending that Publication*, 3d ed. London, Hone, 1819.

H 330

Byron arranged for the private publication of *Don Juan* despite the opposition of the "cursed puritanical committee." When no action was taken against it William Hone, who had two years before been brought to trial for his parodies, protested. This pamphlet is an ironical appeal for impartial prosecution. He accuses the publisher, John Murray, of having government protection which permitted him to defy the vice society while less fortunate publishers would face prosecution. He challenged the censors by conveniently quoting from the parody on the Ten Commandments (Canto I, Stanzas 105, 106).

[————]. *Don Juan, Canto the Third.* London, Hone, 1819. 58p.

H 331

A parody on Byron's *Don Juan*, dealing with a radical "news-retailer" who was arrested for seditious libel. The two genuine cantos by Byron were also published by Hone without the poet's permission. Byron and his authorized publisher attempted to get an injunction to prevent breach of copyright (*Byron v. Dugdale*, 9 August 1823) but Hone's agent argued that the book was obscene and therefore not worthy of government protection. The judge refused the injunction. John Hunt wrote in the *Examiner* that even an immoral book deserved protection by the court and that a jury not a judge should decide whether a work was obscene, and if it were judged obscene the criminal laws should be invoked.

[————]. *Man in the Moon* [*a Speech from the Throne to the Senate of Lunataria. In*

the Moon.]. London, Hone, 1820. 16p.

H 332

Parody on a speech of the Prince Regent urging vigilance against the "dissemination of the doctrines of treason and impiety." The work was impiously illustrated by George Cruikshank, showing the Holy Alliance dancing around the burning figure of Liberty seated on a printing press. It was dedicated to George Canning. Although more libelous than many other works prosecuted it was never charged, probably because of the levity the reading of the verse might create in the courtroom.

[————]. *The Political House that Jack Built.* London, Hone, 1819. 24p.

H 333

This is Hone's most famous satire, illustrated by Cruikshank, in which he attempts to show the power of pen over sword. He strikes out at the despised ex-officio informations against printers. Of the printing press he writes: "This is The Thing, that, in spite of new Acts, And attempts to restrain it, by Soldiers or Tax, Will *poison* the Vermin, That plunder the Wealth, That lay in the House, That Jack Built." Despite an invitation to prosecution for libel, no action was taken against Hone for this satire.

[————]. *The Political Showman—at home! Exhibiting his cabinet of curiosities and Creatures—All Alive!* London, Hone, 1821. 32p. (24 illustrations)

H 334

The Political Showman consisted of a hand press with human legs, and an inkpot and quills for a hat. The illustrations (by Cruikshank) and dialogue (by Hone) combine to celebrate the triumph of the people and the press over government suppression. Among the creatures shown are a crocodile, a locust, a scorpion, black rats, a bloodhound, and a vampire—all representing contemporary political figures and situations.

[————]. *A Slap at Slop and the Bridge-Street Gang.* London, Hone, 1822. 56p.

H 335

A satire on the Constitutional Association that had sponsored so many prosecutions against the pamphlet press. "Doctor Slop" represents John Stoddart, editor of *The New Times* and a leader in the Constitutional Association.

[————]. *The Three Trials of William Hone, for Publishing Three Parodies; viz. The Late John Wilkes's Catechism, The Political Litany, and The Sinecurist's Creed; on Three Ex-officio Informations, at Guildhall, London, during Three Successive Days, December 18, 19, & 20, 1817; before Three Special Juries, and Mr. Justice Abbott, on the First Day, and Lord Chief Justice Ellenborough, on the Last Two Days, December*

19th and 20th. London, Hone, 1818. 48 p. 45 p., 44 p. (Each trial has a separate title page and separate paging. Varying editions of the separate trials have been bound together. An 1876 edition contains introduction and notes by the publisher, William Tegg) **H 336**
The 3 trials dealt with charges of blasphemy for the publication of political parodies. (1) John Wilkes's Catechism, a parody on the Apostle's Creed, the Lord's Prayer, and the Ten Commandments, (2) The Political Litany, a parody on the Litany in the Book of Common Prayer, and (3) The Sinecurist's Creed, a parody on the Athanasian Creed. Hone provided his own defense and was acquitted in all 3 trials. It is said that nearly 100,000 copies of the parodies in numerous editions were sold, largely stimulated by the trials.

[———]. *Trial by Jury and Liberty of the Press. The Proceedings at the Public Meeting, December 29, 1817 at the City of London Tavern, for the Purpose of Enabling William Hone to Surmount the Difficulties in which He Has Been Placed by Being Selected by the Ministers of the Crown as the Object of Their Persecution . . . With the Resolutions and the Speeches . . .* Fifth ed. London, Hone, 1818. 27 p. (Sometimes bound with the *Three Trials of William Hone;* reprinted by Freethought Publishing Co., London, 1880) **H 337**
A defiant meeting of friends of Hone (Hone was not present) celebrating his victory and the victory of a free press. The speakers emphasized that the charge of blasphemy was used in lieu of the real offense, which was political. Speakers included Robert Waithman, Sir Francis Burdett, Alderman Thorp, Mr. Perry, Mr. P. Walker, Lord Cochrane, Charles Pearson, Mr. Sturch, and Thomas Wooler, who had undergone a similar prosecution earlier that year. Appended is a list of subscribers to the benefit of William Hone.

Honigman, John J. "A Cultural Theory of Obscenity." *Journal of Criminal Psychopathology,* 5:715–33, April 1944. **H 338**

Hood, B. G. "Dirt Seekers and Mind Moulders: Further Thoughts on Censorship." *New Zealand Librarian,* 12:30–34, March 1949. **H 339**
The author cites three barriers imposed by censorship: government action, particularly through Customs (unjust rulings should be protested often and tenaciously both by individuals and through the New Zealand Library Association); a too-narrow book selection policy of librarians; and pressure from individuals and groups to withdraw a book from the shelves.

Hook, Sidney. "Pornography and the Censor." *New York Times Book Review,* 69(15):1, 38–39, 12 April 1964. **H 340**
Recommends literary criticism and more strict standards of literary merit rather than censorship as a means of combating cheap and vulgar writing.

Hoover, Donald D. "For a Freer Press." *Quill,* 18(3):7, 15, March 1930. **H 341**
A hoosier newspaperman moves to change Indiana's procedures in contempt of court cases.

Hoover, Herbert C. "Free Speech and Free Press." In his *Addresses upon the American Road, 1933–1938.* New York, Scribner's 1938, pp. 276–80. **H 342**
Lovejoy lecture, Colby College, 8 November 1937.

[———]. "Radio Gets a Policeman." *American Heritage,* 6:73–76, August 1955. **H 343**
As one in a group of interviews with Americans who were involved in the early history of radio, former President Hoover recounts his experience in setting up federal radio controls when he was Secretary of Commerce. He speaks wistfully of a suggestion he made in the 1920's that commercials be limited to brief statements by the sponsors at the beginning and end of a program rather than interrupting the program with long and "hideous repetition." But the idea, he noted, received little attention. Hoover also speaks of the prevalence of defamation on radio and the difficulty of ordinary people to answer such charges. "If our libel and slander laws were restored on the British basis, we would have less such rotten statements poured out over radio."

Hopkins, John B. "Liberty and Libel." *Gentleman's Magazine,* 233:185–95, August 1872. **H 344**
The author finds the present (1872) British law of libel "needlessly oppressive to the press . . . We should insist upon the utmost liberty of criticism which is compatible with respect for the right of the individual to have his reputation protected by law."

———. "The Liberty of the Press." *Tinsleys' Magazine,* 40:120–35, February 1887. **H 345**
"The British juror, by his undue sympathy for the plaintiff in a libel action against a newspaper, inflicts an injury on the Press." Such action is an "infringement of the just and wholesome liberty of the Press." Judges treat newspapers as if there were a presumption in the law that the newspaper is probably in the wrong. The author complains of the ruling of the Lord Chief Justice that "facts affecting private character" should not be broadcast through the press, a restriction which would prevent coverage of most criminal trials. The author also objects to proposals that coverage of public meetings be limited to reporting prepared speeches.

Hopkins, Mary A. "Birth Control and Public Morals. An Interview with Anthony Comstock." *Harper's Weekly,* 60:489–90, 22 May 1915. **H 346**
Comstock, long-time secretary of the New York vice society, defends the existing laws banning obscene literature, contraceptives, and pornography. Article contains photograph of Comstock.

Hoppe, Harry R. "John Wolfe, Printer and Publisher, 1579–1601." *Library,* 14 (4th ser.):241–88, December 1933. **H 347**
Wolfe, a London printer in the days of Elizabeth I failing to obtain a printing monopoly from the government proceeded to print what he pleased in defiance of authority. He was imprisoned for a time and his presses were seized. In later life he turned "respectable" and used his talents in behalf of the government to track down other rebel printers.

Hoppin, Frederick S. "Wanted—a Cato!" *Forum,* 78:3–6, July 1927. **H 348**
A satire on censorship, suggesting we apply national prohibition to "art, literature, and music" so that these cultural areas, like prohibition of liquor, "could also be made subjects of vital and argumentative importance in every American family."

Horchler, Richard. "Literature and Morality." *Commonweal,* 69:559–61, 27 February 1959. **H 349**
The moralist who criticizes literature must be competent to judge it within the aesthetic context which gives it meaning.

Horiguchi, Robert Y. *Observations on Censorship of Daily Newspapers in the United States from 1920 to 1930.* Columbia, Mo., University of Missouri, 1932. 123 p. (Unpublished Master's thesis) **H 350**

Horn, K. A. R. "The Censorship of Indecent Publications in New Zealand." *New Zealand Libraries,* 12:25–29, March 1949. **H 351**
A review of obscenity censorship in New Zealand, applied under the Customs Act of 1913 and the Indecent Publications Act of 1910.

Horne, Alistair. "It Pays to be Libeled in London." *National Review,* 7:205–8, 212, 18 July 1959. **H 352**
"Under Britain's tax structure, one thing which still pays off is a successful libel case, as E. Waugh, R. Churchill and A. Bevin have found." A British journalist summarizes the libel situation in England.

Horsley, W. F. "The Prior Restraint of Speech and Press—a Critique of the Doctrine." *Alabama Law Review,* 15: 456–60, Spring 1963. **H 353**

"The danger of superficially analyzing prior restraint and subsequent punishment is that courts tend to examine the *means* rather than the *ends* of speech control methods. What is prior restraint in form may be subsequent punishment in fact, and the converse is equally true. In the future more emphasis might well be placed upon operational effect than outward appearance."

Hoskins, John A. "Delinquency, Comic Books and the Law." *Ohio State Law Journal*, 18:512–37, Autumn 1957. **H 354**
A review of efforts nationally and in the state of Ohio to curb obscene and crime comics. The author cites three basic proposals that have been introduced by various governments: the censorship board (common abroad but objected to in the United States); prohibition of sale of sex and crime comics to minors (Ohio's statute is of this type); and court action against a particular publication. The author recommends enactments that will protect the child while maintaining the maximum freedom of reading for the adult.

Hoskins, Percy. "The Press and the Administration of Justice." *Federal Probation*, 22(2):31–35, June 1958. **H 355**
A British newspaperman reviews practices with respect to "fair trial and a free press."

Hossom, Kenneth. *Freedom of Speech and Public Opinion*. Princeton, N.J., Princeton University, 1952. 255 p. (Ph. D. dissertation, University Microfilms, no. 2977) **H 356**

Hostetter, Joseph C. "Freedom of the Press." In *Problems of Journalism; Proceedings of the American Society of Newspaper Editors*, Washington, D.C., 1930, pp. 86–92; 1932, pp. 41–58. **H 357**
Advice on the legal aspects of journalism, court trials, and libel.

"Hot Cakes." *New Statesman*, 28:201–2, 27 November 1926. **H 358**
The Whispering Gallery is selling like hot cakes in the United States as a result of its suppression in England. The author of this article deplores the subjection of eminent men to malicious gossip.

Hotchkis, Preston. "Quest for Truth through Freedom of Information." *U.S. State Department Bulletin*, 30:682–86, 3 May 1954. **H 359**
A statement made by the U.S. Representative on the Economic and Social Council, United Nations, to the Council, 9 and 13 April 1954. He speaks of proposals made in three areas: government restrictions; economic and technical barriers; and professional standards, rights, and responsibilities. He closes with a protest against "the physical snatching away and imprisoning of journalists" by Chinese Communists.

Hottman, Henry. *Some Problems of Federal Regulation of Radio Broadcasting*. Boulder, Colo., University of Colorado, 1947. 336 p. (Unpublished Ph. D. dissertation) **H 360**

Hough, Graham. "The Moral Censor." In his *The Dream and the Task; Literature and Morals in the Culture of Today*. New York, Norton, 1964, pp. 28–41. **H 361**
The work of imaginative literature is a thing in itself, worth having for its own sake, and "its value as a social or moral force outside itself is only incidental." The author advocates an "all-embracing literacy acceptance." The greater the appreciation of literature, the wider and more comprehensive it will become. Two "vermin" that need to be kept down are the anticulture or hatred of art and letters, and the set of ideas that narrows the range of literary curiosity and appreciation.

Hough, Richard L. "The Jehovah's Witness Cases in Retrospect." *Western Political Quarterly*, 6:78–92, March 1953. **H 362**
Views on cases involving freedom of speech, 1938–46.

Hoult, Thomas F. "Comic Books and Juvenile Delinquency." *Sociology and Social Research*, 33:279–84, March–April 1949. **H 363**
A study "aimed at discovering if there is actually, as the layman so often assumes, any relationship between juvenile delinquency and the reading of comic books." A study was made of 235 boys and girls arrested for delinquency and a matched group of nondelinquent children. Both groups read about the same number of "harmless" comics, but the delinquent read many more "questionable" or "harmful" comics.

House, Frederick B. *The Application of the Law of Disorderly Conduct to Illegal Public Speaking and the Distribution of Improper Printed Matter*. New York, City Magistrate, 1917. 16 p. **H 364**
"Intended as a partial aid to the city magistrates and the police authorities in dealing with the present condition in the city of New York." Any matter breaching the peace, the pamphlet notes, is illegal, and can be dealt with under existing laws.

"House Group Closes Hearings on Pornographic Books." *Publishers' Weekly*, 162:2318–21, 2329, 13 December 1952. **H 365**
Summary and editorial comments on the "Gathings Committee" hearings, including testimony by publishers, booksellers, authors, lawyers, religious leaders, and government officials.

Housman, Laurence. "The Censorship of Literature." *Week-end Review*, 26:393–94, March 1932. **H 366**

While expressing no concern in protecting the reader who wants to be debauched, Housman believes that the young and immature who have been sheltered by "fussy inhibitions" about sexual matters, need to be protected from the "moral" shock of frank expression. Such protection lies almost entirely with parents and teachers; any legal restrictions imposed on current literature should not apply to the reading of adults. He quotes the Archbishop of Canterbury as saying: "I would rather have all the risks which come from free discussion of sex than the great risks we run by a conspiracy of silence." The two great problems of today are war and sex.

———. "A King's Proctor for Plays." *Fortnightly Review*, 94:852–56, 1910. **H 367**
Housman proposes that "instead of the Censor, with his present power of veto before production, there should be an Examiner of Plays, whose functions would be somewhat similar to those of a King's Proctor, and whose duty it would be to consider plays from a strictly legal standpoint." If the Proctor believed the play would be liable to prosecution as an offense against the common law he would so warn the theater manager.

———. "My Thirty Years' Fight with the Censor." *Living Age*, 353:264–65, November 1937. (Reprinted from the *Evening Standard*, London). **H 368**
The author tells of his experiences with the censor, with particular reference to his plays, *Bethlehem*, *Pains and Penalties*, and *Victoria Regina*.

———. *Pains and Penalties; an Historical Tragedy, in Four Acts. With a Preface on the Censorship*. London, Sidgwick & Jackson, 1911. 89 p. **H 369**

"How Came 'Comstockery.'" *Literary Digest*, 93:32–33, 2 April 1927. **H 370**
"Play censorship in this country got a thrill over Shaw's *Mrs. Warren's Profession*, but the net result seems to have been the addition of a new word to the language—'Comstockery.'"

"How Free is the Air?" *Nation*, 143:5–6, 4 July 1936. (Reprinted in Summers, *Radio Censorship*, pp. 92–95) **H 371**
Editorial criticizing the FCC ruling forbidding rebroadcast of foreign programs without the written consent of the Commission.

"How Much Freedom for the Student Editor?" *Quill*, 51(9):8–12, September 1963. **H 372**
College presidents, student publications' advisors, former college editors, and others having a close relationship to the student press give their views.

"How Much Management of the News?" *Newsweek*, 61(14):59–63, 8 April 1963. **H 373**

The article cites three groups that are responsible for charging the Kennedy administration with managing the news: some Republicans who have found in news management a political issue; the "outs," reporters who enjoyed an inside track in previous administrations; and the professional "freedom writers." It quotes the Washington *Evening Star* as saying: "If the press devoted the energy to covering the news that it devotes to bellyaching about freedom of information, the public would be much better off." It attributes to President Kennedy the belief that reporters, by their own admission, have more access to news than ever before, and that they can be managed only if they want to be managed. Good reporters will not be victimized. It takes two to manage the news.

"How Nations at War Search the Mails." *Popular Science*, 136:90–92, May 1940. **H 374**

"How News Is 'Managed' by Officials in Washington." *U.S. News and World Report*, 54(15):38–42, 15 April 1963. **H 375**

Criticism of news management by the Kennedy administration during the Cuban invasion.

"How the Press May be Russianized." *La Follette's Magazine*, 1:3–4, 20 March 1909. **H 376**

Deals with the Panama Canal libel case.

[Howard, Granby S., *plaintiff*]. *Report of the Trial of the Libel Suit of Dr. G. S. Howard, of Carleton Place, Ont., against the "Montreal Star"* . . . [Montreal], 1898. 136 p. **H 377**

Howard, R. H. "Some of the Lessons of the War." *Ladies Repository*, 22:171–76, March 1862. **H 378**

The Civil War, with all its horrors, will bring certain benefits including freedom of speech and opinion and the defeat of professional dogmatism. The suppression of free discussion of the iniquities of slavery, this minister writes, was a factor in causing the war. We should use our newly-found freedom of expression for God's purposes. Churches must carry religion and morality into political life and never again be silent in the face of evil.

Howard, Sidney. "Theatre Censorship." *Authors' League Bulletin*, 14(12):18–19, March 1927. **H 379**

"The censorship which now threatens the American theatre outstrips in severity any that the English speaking stage has known since the days of Cromwell."

Howarth, Edmund. "Birth Control Prosecution." *Liberator*, 1:2, [1920]. **H 380**

Account of the trial of Edmund Howarth for circulating an "obscene" pamphlet, *Large or Small Families*, by George H. Suasey. Howarth was found guilty on an obscenity charge in Durham, England.

Howe, Frederic C. "What To Do With the Motion-Picture Show; Shall It Be Censored?" *Outlook*, 107:412–16, 20 June 1914. **H 381**

The chairman of the National Board of Censorship of Motion Pictures discusses the question of motion picture censorship, followed by a review of the work of the Board which was organized in 1909 by the People's Institute of New York. The article includes a listing of the standards of judgment announced by the Board.

Howe, P. P. *Malthus and the Publishing Trade*. New York, Kennerley, 1913. 29 p. **H 382**

A satire on the overpopulated world of books, the flood of ordinary books that is driving out the good books. Howe recommends the application of Malthusian principles, that no more books be born than the public can support. "Moral restraint" on the part of publisher and author is advised to prevent indiscriminate conception.

Howe, Quincy. "Policing the Commentator: A News Analysis." *Atlantic Monthly*, 172:46–49, November 1943. **H 383**

Recommends that (1) sponsorship of "straight" news broadcasts should be permitted, (2) slanted commentary should not be labeled as news, and (3) networks should maintain news analysts who are free to present objective interpretation of the news.

Howell, Rex G. "Fairness . . . Fact or Fable?" *Journal of Broadcasting*, 3:321–30, Fall 1964. **H 384**

To keep fairness from becoming a farce rather than a force for good, it must be kept a two-way street encouraging free discussion rather than silencing opposition.

Howell, T. B., and T. J. Howell, *eds. A Complete Collection of State Trials and Proceedings for High Treason and Other Crimes and Misdemeanors, from the Earliest Period to the Year 1783 . . . and Continued from the Year 1783 to the Present Time*. London, Hansard, 1816–28. 34 vols. **H 385**

This collection includes summaries and proceedings of most of the important British trials relating to freedom of the press from the sixteenth century to 1820. A *General Index* to the trials, edited by David Jardin (London, Longman, Rees, 1828), gives a brief abstract of each trial. The early volumes of the *State Trials* were published by William Cobbett.

Trials contained in the Howell collection are listed in the present bibliography under the name of the defendant.

Howey, Walter, *ed. Fighting Editors*. Philadelphia, McKay, [1948?] 163 p. **H 386**

A collection of stories originally appearing in the *American Weekly*, dealing with adventures of brave editors and reporters in crusades for truth in reporting. In addition to the famous case of John Peter Zenger, there are the lesser known cases of Carl Magee who exploded the Teapot Dome scandal; John D. Pennekamp of the *Miami Herald*, whose right of criticism of the Florida courts was upheld by the U.S. Supreme Court; the newspapermen who exposed the Georgia Klan; Editor Hazel Brannon of Lexington, Miss., whose contempt of court was reversed by the Mississippi Supreme Court; and James King of William, who sacrificed his life in exposing the graft and crime during the gold-rush days in San Francisco. Most of the articles were written by Paul Gallico and William Engle.

Hoyt, Palmer. "Last Chance; Mutual Unrestricted Freedom of News." *Vital Speeches*, 12:60–62, 1 November 1945. **H 387**

The publisher of the Portland *Oregonian* calls for world-wide freedom of the press as the last chance in an atomic civilization. "A civilization that is not informed cannot be free and a world that is not free cannot endure."

———. "Let's Face the Facts; No Matter How Bitter!" *Quill*, 30(4):3–4, April 1942. **H 388**

Hoyt charges that the American people are not getting the facts about the war as promptly as they should and that when they do get them the news is not always properly presented.

———. "News Suppressed Today Becomes News Distorted Tomorrow." *Quill*, 32(2):3–4, March–April 1944. **H 389**

A discussion of news handling, manipulation, suppression, and distortion in wartime, together with an appeal for newspaper support of the Office of War Information.

———, Basil L. Walters, and James S. Pope. *The John Peter Zenger Award, 1954–1955–1956. Addresses by Palmer Hoyt, Basil L. Walters and John S. Pope*. Tucson, Ariz., University of Arizona Press, 1957. 48 p. **H 390**

The John Peter Zenger Award was inaugurated by the University of Arizona through its Department of Journalism in 1954 to acknowledge "leadership in the endless battle to protect the freedom of the press and the people's right to know." The first three awards, whose addresses are presented here, went to Palmer Hoyt, editor and publisher of the *Denver Post* (1954); Basil L. Walters, executive editor, *Chicago Daily News* (1955);

and James S. Pope, executive editor, *Louisville Courier-Journal* (1956). Excerpts of the Palmer talk are also given in *Nieman Reports*, January 1955.

[Hubbard, H. P.]. *The Law of Libel; Important for Those Who Get into Hot Water.* New Haven, H. P. Hubbard, 1887. 8 p. (Bound with *How to Write an Adv't.*) **H 391**
"The law in all its points, briefly discussed in plain terms, that he who runs may read and live to heed some other day." The H. P. Hubbard Co. was an advertising agency.

Hubbard, James M. "Are Public Libraries Public Blessings?" *North American Review*, 149:339–46, September 1889. **H 392**
The public library, originally organized to counteract novel-reading by children, now freely circulates novels to children. The author would prefer that no novels be lent to children, but if this cannot be achieved, state laws should make it a criminal offense to lend an immoral book to a child. Public libraries should be required to submit to the Board of Education each year a list of all immoral books purchased, the cost, and number of times consulted.

———. *The Public Library and School Children; an Appeal to the Parents, Clergymen, and Teachers of Boston.* Boston, The Author, 1881. 23 p. **H 393**

———. *The Public Library and the Children; a Second Appeal.* Boston, The Author, 1883. 12 p. **H 394**
Hubbard, a former cataloger with the Boston Public Library, carried on a one-man crusade against the immoral influence of fiction in that library. He lists and describes such fiction in great detail, demanding that such works be removed from the shelves and that all novels be kept out of the hands of children. The Boston newspapers supported his crusade but the library trustees rejected his demands with a sharply worded declaration of independence from would-be censors.

Huber, M. J. "Help Clean up the Mails!" *Liguorian*, 47:7–9, July 1959. **H 395**
This publication of the Redemptionist Fathers speaks against the complacency about filth in the mails that is being brazenly sent to teenagers and even younger children.

Hudon, Edward G. *Freedom of Speech and Press in America. Foreword by Justice William O. Douglas; Introduction by Morris L. Ernst.* Washington, D.C., Public Affairs Press, 1963. 224 p. **H 396**
This well-documented study, the work of a lawyer-librarian, "delves into the British law of speech and press as it existed in England and Colonial America prior to the Revolution, and also into the theories of law and sovereignty

which permitted this English and Colonial law to follow the course that it did." The author considers at length the threat to freedom by the Alien and Sedition law of 1798 and traces the major Supreme Court decisions relating to freedom of speech, press, and the movies. He gives particular attention to the development of the concept of "clear and present danger" and to the applications of the "natural law" principles to intellectual freedom.

———. "Speech, Press and the Supreme Court." *National Publisher*, 43(9):22–23, 38, September 1963. **H 397**
A summary of important cases during the 1962–63 term of the U.S. Supreme Court.

Hudson, George E. "Censorship vs. Freedom." *Library Journal*, 87:1955–58, 15 May 1962. **H 398**
Analysis of the author's survey, "Problem of Censorship in the Public Secondary School Libraries of Nassau County, New York," a study to determine whether or not the kind of censorship which results in proscription and rejection of certain titles is common practice. He found that 82 per cent of the librarians are committed to censorship, their motive being good public relations; 13 per cent are convinced that censorship should not be practiced by school librarians and that complete freedom of selection is imperative.

Hudson, J. K. *The Legal and Political History of the Suits Brought by Hon. Cassius Gaius Foster, Judge of the U.S. District Court of Kansas, against Maj. J. K. Hudson, Editor Daily Capital, of Topeka, Kansas. Giving the Origin, Facts, Letters, Charges, Indictments, Editorials, and Decisions of the Cases of 1890 and 1895.* Topeka, Kan., 1895. 94 p. **H 399**
Libel case relates to prohibition of alcoholic beverages in Kansas.

Hughes, Charles E. "Near v. Minnesota: Opinion of Charles E. Hughes for the Supreme Court." In S. G. Brown, *ed.*, *We Hold These Truths*, New York, Harper, 1941, pp. 303–17. **H 400**
A classic decision invalidating the Minnesota "gag-law" which enabled the state to prosecute an offending newspaper as a public nuisance.

Hughes, Edward. "English Stamp Duties, 1664–1764." *English Historical Review*, 56:234–64, April 1941. **H 401**
An investigation of "the antecedents of the famous Stamp Act which was fraught with such consequences for the American colonies."

Hughes, Frank L. *Prejudice and the Press, a Restatement of the Principles of Freedom of the Press with Specific Reference to the*

Hutchins-Luce Commission. New York, Devin-Adair, 1950. 642 p. **H 402**
A devastating attack on the findings of the Commission on Freedom of the Press, written by a staff member of the *Chicago Tribune*. The study purports to present "first, a complete and valid restatement of American political philosophy and the principles of American liberty; second, a critical examination of the 'Commission on Freedom of the Press' and its private brand of philosophy, including the sources of the latter; third, a critical examination of the kind of 'liberalism' the 'commission' is attempting to introduce as our way of life in the United States today; and, fourth, a presentation of the facts about the press and about freedom of the press in America." In presenting his case, Hughes goes into the personal, professional, and business backgrounds of each Commission member.

Hughes, Rupert. "Viewing with Alarm." *Bookman*, 49:263–67, May 1919. **H 403**
The moving picture is "no more dangerous to childhood than the printed page, the trusted nurse, the neighborhood companion, or the opportunities of solitude."

Hull, Julius H. "Judicial Review of Orders by the Postmaster General Revoking Second Class Mailing Privileges." *Georgetown Law Journal*, 34:77–78, November 1945. **H 404**
"The duty imposed on publishers to contribute to the public good did not confer on the Postmaster General the power to censor if his standards were not met . . . The duty to classify does not confer the power to censor."

Hullfish, H. Gordon. "Indirect Censorship." *Educational Leadership*, 14:511, May 1957 (Reprinted in *Education Digest*, October 1957) **H 405**
The author objects to the suggestion that free propaganda and promotional material furnished to teachers should be consigned to the wastebasket. Free material should be admitted or rejected on the same terms as other material in a classroom—whether or not it contributes to the educative function. "We shall not serve education well by black-listing (and to withhold is to blacklist by default) writings we do not approve, especially when these writings have been widely publicized."

Hullinger, Edwin W. "Free Speech for Talkies?" *North American Review*, 227:737–43, June 1929. **H 406**
"How the lately quiescent problem of State film censorship has been revived in acute form since the silver screen found its synchronized tongue." Comments on the "intramural" censorship of the industry, set up to ward off the state censor. The author asks: Why should the movies and talkies be subjected

to a supervision that magazines, playwrights, and comic strip artists escape?

Hulme, Harold. "The Winning of Freedom of Speech by the House of Commons." *American Historical Review*, 61:825–53, July 1956. **H 407**
An essay whose purpose is "to trace in detail the course of the quarrel between the Commons and King James I and to show precisely how and when freedom of speech was won by the members of the lower House."

"An Humble Inquiry." *Nation*, 107:362, 5 October 1918. **H 408**
Editorial criticizing the Post Office ban of two issues of the *Truth Seeker* for referring to the YMCA as a commercial organization. The action was taken under the Espionage Act which the courts had interpreted as covering the work of voluntary religious and humanitarian organizations engaged in war work.

Hume, David. "Of the Liberty of the Press." In his *Philosophical Works*, Boston, Little, Brown, 1854, vol. 3, pp. 6–10; also in his *Essays, Moral, Political and Literary*, edited by T. H. Green and T. H. Grose, London, Longmans, 1907. vol. 1, pp. 94–98. (Originally published in 1742)
H 409
Hume cites the unique freedom of the press enjoyed by the English, which he believes is derived from the mixed form of government—monarchial and republican—with republican dominating. This situation creates a mutual watchfulness and jealousy which promotes freedom. Reading, he states, is a rational way for considering controversial ideas in public affairs. Liberty of the press, even if abused, "can scarce ever excite popular tumults in rebellion." Hume believes that sedition and libel laws "are at present as strong as they possibly can be made." To go beyond this would be a violation of English liberty.

Humphreys, Robert. "How Your News is Censored." *Saturday Evening Post*, 215 (13):16–17, 113–14, 26 September 1942. **H 410**
How the wartime Office of Censorship works.

Hunnings, Neville M. ["Film Censorship]: Great Britain." *Censorship*, 2:8–11, Spring 1965. **H 411**
"Film censorship in Britain is a peculiar amalgam of historical accident and a lurching attempt to resolve all the conflicting interests and pressures. The powers of the local authorities to license cinemas was given them to stop fire risk, while their power to supervise the content of the films shown in them is a legacy from the law governing music halls."

Under the Cinematograph Act of 1952 all commercial film is subject to censorship under power held by the county councils which have in effect "delegated the task of viewing and classifying to a private body which is appointed by the film industry but is formally responsible only to itself."

———. ["Film Censorship]: India." *Censorship*, 2:23–25, Spring 1965. **H 412**
While the conduct of film censorship in India raises little complaint from the trade, it is "one of the strictest in the world, both in the wide ranging numbers and the particular criteria followed by the individual censor." If film censorship were challenged by the courts it is likely that they would adopt the attitude that so long as there were adequate procedural safeguards against abuse and the right of appeal, the principle of censorship would be upheld as a reasonable restriction on free expression.

Hunscot, Joseph. *The Humble Petition and Information of Joseph Hunscot, Stationer, to both the Hon. Houses of Parliament Now Assembled, against Divers Scandalous Libels . . .* [London, 1646]. **H 413**

Hunt, Frederick K. *The Fourth Estate; Contributions toward a History of Newspapers, and of the Liberty of the Press.* London, David Bogue, 1850. 2 vols. **H 414**
One of the earliest general histories of the English newspaper press. Volume one ends with 1800; volume two covers from 1800 to 1850. The author succeeded Dickens as editor of the *Daily News* and took an active part in the fight against the newspaper tax. The detailed provisions of the tax are given in this work. Chapter 3 deals with the early struggles of the press, including the origin of censorship and licensing and the Star Chamber persecutions of Leighton and Prynne. Chapter 4 discusses the press during the Commonwealth and the Restoration, including Milton's plea for unlicensed printing, the trial and fate of Twyn, and Roger L'Estrange as censor. Chapter 5 includes the trial of Tutchin, the stamp act, and the case of John Wilkes. Chapter 6 covers the period of 1788 to 1800 and includes the numerous prosecutions for libel including that of Thomas Paine. Chapter 7 includes a discussion of the trials of Peltier, Hunt, Cobbett, Carlile, and the repeal of the taxes on knowledge. Chapter 11 includes a discussion of the early restrictions on reporting of parliamentary debates.

Hunt, Joel A. "French Texts and American Editors." *French Review*, 28:241–45, January 1955. **H 415**
Many American editors of French texts "do not hesitate to expurgate and, in some cases, even to rewrite phrases or passages which they judge offensive."

[Hunt, John]. *Report of the Trial of the King v. John Hunt, for a libel on the House of Commons, in the Examiner; Tried in the King's Bench, February 21st, 1821. The Defence Verbatim, with a Preface, being an Answer to the Attorney-General's Reply. By Henry L. Hunt the Son of the Defendant.* London, Printed for William Hone, 1821. 40p. (Also in Macdonell. *Report of State Trials*, vol. 1, p. 1367) **H 416**
Hunt, the proprietor of the *Examiner* was charged on an "information" with libeling the members of the House of Commons in an article which he wrote and published in his paper. Commenting on the attitude of the House toward the king's marital affairs, Hunt accused its members of being "venal borough-mongers, grasping placemen, greedy adventurers . . . in short, containing a far greater portion of public criminals than public guardians." Hunt defended himself by citing incidents of corruption and misconduct of members, some evidence gathered from the records of the Parliament itself. He was found guilty and imprisoned for one year. This was John Hunt's fifth arrest for attacking a public abuse; and the second prison sentence. He was at liberty only a short while before being convicted for a third offense.

[———]. "Trial of John Hunt for publishing a seditious libel, on January 15, 1824, before Abbott, C. J., and a special jury." In Macdonell, *Report of State Trials*, vol. 2, pp. 69–103. **H 417**
Hunt was brought to trial for publishing a "defamatory libel" concerning the late king (Byron's *Vision of Judgment*). This was the first indictment during this period for publishing a poem and the last inspired by the Constitutional Association, then on its last legs. Byron, who relished the controversy, died a few months after the prosecution. Hunt was found guilty, but unlike earlier offenses for which he served prison sentences, he was merely fined.

[———, and Leigh Hunt]. *The King vs. John and Leigh Hunt. A Report of the Trial "The King vs. John and Leigh Hunt," for a Libel on the Prince Regent: before Lord Ellenborough and a Special Jury, at the Sittings in the Court of King's Bench, Westminster, on Wednesday, December 9, 1812 . . .* London, Mr. Jones, 1812. 25p. **H 418**
The Hunt brothers, editors of the *Examiner*, had been acquitted in 1811 of the charge of seditious libel for criticizing military flogging. In December 1812 they were found guilty of libel on the Prince Regent and sentenced by Lord Ellenborough to two years in different prisons. The offending article had referred to the Prince as "an Adonis of fifty," a libertine, and a man who had just closed half a century without one single claim on the gratitude of his country or the respect of posterity. Brougham appeared for the defendants. The Hunt trial is also reported in the no. 6 issue of Wooler's *The Republican*.

[———]. *The Prince of Wales v. the Examiner. A Full Length Report of the Trial of*

John and Leigh Hunt, Proprietors of the Examiner . . . Decided by Lord Ellenborough, and a Special Jury, in the King's Bench, Westminster, on Wednesday, the 9th of December, 1812. To Which Are Added Observations on the Trial, by the Editor of the Examiner . . . London, [1813?]. 63 p. **H 419**

Hunt, Leigh. The Autobiography of Leigh Hunt. Edited by J. E. Morpurgo. London, Cressett Press, 1948. 512 p. **H 420**
In 1813 Leigh Hunt and his brother, John, were sentenced to two years' imprisonment for libel against the Prince Regent in articles in the Examiner. The episode is described in chapters 13 and 14.

Hunter, [Robert, plaintiff]. Great Libel Case. [Dr. Hunter v. Pall Mall Gazette.] Being a Verbatim Report of the Medical Evidence Given by Dr. Williams [and others] etc. Showing Their Opinions on the Nature, Causes and Cure of Consumption, with Explanatory Remarks by Dr. Hunter, the Plaintiff. London, C. Mitchell, 1867. 404 p. **H 421**

Hunter, William A. Blasphemy Laws: Should They Be Abolished? Plymouth, Eng., Association for the Repeal of the Blasphemy Laws, 1884. 23 p. **H 422**
A draft of a law repealing the blasphemy laws of England is given on the last page.

——. Past and Present of the Heresy Laws. London, Freethought Publishing Co., 1878. 23 p. **H 423**
The author was professor of jurisprudence, University College, London, and had been counsel for Edward Truelove in his trial for blasphemy.

Huntington, Henry S. "The Philadelphia Book Seizures." Nation, 167:205-7, 21 August 1948. **H 424**
An account of the wholesale book seizures in Philadelphia of some 2,000 copies of 18 different titles (including Raintree Country, Studs Lonigan, and Never Love a Stranger) seized without warrant by the police under a provision of the Pennsylvania law allowing police to take possession of obscene literature on sight.

Huntington, Trumbull. "Censorship: A Bookseller's View." Publishers' Weekly, 185:57-58, 2 March 1964. **H 425**

Hurd, John C. The Law of Freedom and Bondage in the United States. Boston, Little, Brown, 1858–62. 2 vols. **H 426**
Includes references to acts passed to prevent distribution of abolitionist propaganda.

Hurlbut, E. P. Liberty of Printing: an Address at Second Annual Congress of the National Liberal League at Syracuse, Oct. 26, 1878. 22 p. (Truth Seeker Tract no. 150) **H 427**
Judge Hurlbut of Albany, N.Y., speaks in favor of federal legislation excluding obscenity from the mails. He defends the right of the federal government to enact obscenity laws and argues for the need of such laws to prevent licentiousness of the press. He offers a draft obscenity statute with a clause that would exclude from censorship serious works and treatise even though "if carried into practise, would have a bad influence on society." T. B. Wakeman's reply is given in the same tract.

Hurleigh, R. F. Should the News Be Censored? Evanston, Ill., Northwestern University on the Air: The Reviewing Stand, 1945. 12 p. **H 428**

Hurley, Richard J. "Talking Shop: [Book Selection in Senior High Schools]." Catholic Library World, 35:467-68, March 1964. **H 429**
The supervisor of school libraries, Fairfax, Va., objects to assigned reading of such books as Steinbeck's Grapes of Wrath, and Dreiser's American Tragedy. He suggests that librarians buy such "controversial" books if they are requested by classroom teachers but that the books not be added to the library. Eric Moon replies to the article in the Library Journal, 15 May 1964.

Hurley, Timothy. A Commentary on the Present Index Legislation. With a Preface by the Most Rev. Dr. Claney . . . New York, Benziger Brothers, 1908. 252 p. **H 430**
Relates to the Index Librorum Prohibitorum of the Catholic Church.

Hurt, Walter. "Comstockism Is Indicated; Infamous Law, Framed Solely to Serve the Ends of Injustice, Now Being Used by the Romish Oppressor to Destroy the Menace and Imprison Its Staff—Comstock's Alliance with Catholicism Is Demonstrated Beyond All Doubt." Menace, 233:1, 9 October 1915. **H 431**
An account of the arrest of Benjamin O. Flower, editor of The Menace, for his attacks on the Catholic Church, and of the author's arrest in 1899 under the obscenity law.

——. "Despotism." Assayer, 2:9, June 1899. **H 432**
Hurt was arrested for alleged "obscenity" in his periodical, Gattling Gun. He charged that the real reason was that he had printed "some inside facts about certain shady epochs in the career of Senator Hanna and his political friends."

——. "Great Conspiracy." To-morrow, 2:68–72, September 1906. **H 433**
A criticism of postal censorship of publications advocating sexual and labor reforms.

——. "Moses Harman, an Analysis and an Appreciation." To-morrow, 2:26–28, April 1906. **H 434**
Harman, editor of Lucifer, the Light Bearer, was frequently arrested and harrassed for articles advocating sex reform.

Hutchins, Robert M. "Hutchins Chastises Editorial Writers; Offer to Hutchins." Editor and Publisher, 81:6, 38, 27 November 1948. **H 435**
Text of an address by the chairman of the Commission on Freedom of the Press criticizing the critics of the Commission's report. The Editor and Publisher offers to contribute to the cost of an impartial body to review the performance of the press. Such a panel was appointed and its first meeting is reported in the 26 April 1949 issue of the journal.

Hutchins, Shelby V. "Obscenity Law Imposing Strict Liability Declared Unconstitutional." Ohio State Law Journal, 22:242–44, Spring 1960. **H 436**
Smith v. California, 361 U.S. 147 (1959).

Hutchinson, Henry S. "The Bookseller's Responsibility for the Book he Sells." Publishers' Weekly, 103:1620–26, 26 May 1923. **H 437**
A New Bedford, Mass., bookman, addressing the convention of the American Booksellers' Association, declared it is the responsibility of the bookseller to guard his customers by refusing to sell immoral and neurotic books. Arthur Proctor, a Detroit bookseller, replies: "I say that the duty, the responsibility of the bookseller toward his customer, toward the general public, is not just to sell books . . . that have a sweet ending, but . . . to get them the books [they want] in spite of the censorship . . . of such men as Mr. John Sumner." A heated discussion follows in which obscenity is associated by some with Bolshevism. Despite protests from Frederick G. Melcher, the convention voted to expunge Mr. Proctor's remarks from the record. R. F. Fuller of Boston described how that city keeps unfit books from sale with the help of the Watch and Ward Society.

Hutchinson, Paul. "Is the Air Already Monopolized?: Freedom of the Air." Christian Century, 47:441–44, 1 April 1931. **H 438**
An account of the difficulties exponents of unorthodox ideas have in getting time on the air. In an article in the 8 April issue, Hutchinson charges that broadcasting policy is reaching

the point where nothing can go on the air "except by the grace of the business interests."

Hutnyan, Joseph D. "New Jersey Newsmen Win Important Victory for Freedom of the Press." *Quill*, 45(12):10, 21–22, December 1956.   **H 439**
The New Jersey State Senate abandoned closed sessions after vigorous opposition by the press.

[Hutton, Tom, et al.]. [*The "Suppressed" Report.*] Fullerton, Calif., Education Information, 1961. 16p.   **H 440**
A reprinting (together with notes on its suppression) of a study entitled The Supreme Court as an Instrument of Global Conquest, by Col. Tom Hutton, SPX Research Associates for the Subcommittee to Investigate the Internal Security Acts and Other Internal Security Laws, 85th Cong., 2d sess., re: S2646. "The U.S. Printing Office was required to bury this Report in a voluminous document making the cost of additional copies prohibitive."

Huxley, Aldous. "Censorship." *Fortnightly Review*, 128(n.s.):415–16, September 1930. (Reprinted in Downs, *The First Freedom*, pp. 272–73)   **H 441**
In this review of Causton and Young's *Keeping It Dark, or the Censors Handbook*, Huxley presents his own appeal for a sensible attitude toward censorship. "The remedy against pornography is in the hands of everyone who chooses to use it. If you do not like a book, all you have to do is not to read it. Let every man be his own censor."

————. "Censorship and Spoken Literature." In his *Tomorrow and Tomorrow and Tomorrow and Other Essays*. New York, Harper, 1956, pp. 115–27. (Also in *Esquire*, October 1955)   **H 442**
In democratic countries there is no political censorship, except in regard to military secrets, but there is unintentional economic censorship caused by the steady rise in cost of producing books, plays, and films. "The great silencer" to every channel of intellectual and artistic expression is money. Subsidies offer only a partial solution. Huxley suggests a revival of spoken literature since phonograph records may be cheaper to make than books and, more important, they will reach the nonreader. Furthermore, reading aloud the literature of wisdom will counteract the popular philosophy of life formulated by writers of advertising copy.

————. "Lord Campbell and Mr. Charles." *New Statesman and Nation*, 10:673–74, 9 November 1935.   **H 443**
The Lord Campbell Act of 1857, dealing with obscene publications, has been stretched so as to punish many offenses which its author never intended it to punish. The latest example is the case of *The Sexual Impulse* by Edward Charles, judged obscene for six objectionable passages, three of which were taken from books against which no objections had ever been raised.

————. *Vulgarity in Literature.* London, Chatto and Windus, 1930. 39p. (Extracted in Downs, *The First Freedom*, pp. 210–13)   **H 444**
"Vulgarity is a lowness that proclaims itself," writes Huxley. "There is a vulgarity in the sphere of morals, a vulgarity of emotions and intellect, a vulgarity even of the spirit." Huxley comments on the changing fashions in vulgarity that have led to the erratic action of the censor. Expressions and themes that are taboo in one generation may be acceptable in the next. Emotions and episodes insincerely or crudely expressed are vulgar; the same emotions and episodes expressed with sincerity and artistry may become great literature.

Hyde, H. Montgomery. *A History of Pornography. With an Introduction by Morris Ernst.* New York, Farrar, Straus and Giroux, 1964. 246p.   **H 445**
"The historical survey of the subject which has been undertaken in the following pages is designed to cover both kinds of pornography [i.e., artistic and crude] although that which possesses an element in varying degrees of literary or artistic merit necessarily has the principal place. It will also involve some consideration of the measures which different societies at different periods in history have employed to deal with it, by means of administrative action through the operation of an official or unofficial censorship, and legal action through the courts. Finally, we shall take a brief look at contemporary conditions mainly at English-speaking countries, which, while ostensibly aiming at suppressing pornography, are constantly creating and stimulating the demand for it through various media of mass communication and promoting a fruitful climate in which it can flourish." The author is an English lawyer and criminologist. The *Fanny Hill* case, prosecuted in England under the Obscene Publications Act of 1959, is discussed in detail as an appendix. (Reviewed in ALA *Newsletter on Intellectual Freedom*, May 1965.)

————. "Siobhan and the BBC." *Spectator*, 202:658–60, 8 May 1959.   **H 446**
The canceling of Edward R. Murrow's television show, "Small World," in Northern Ireland because of objection to an interview with actress Siobhan McKenna, speaking from Dublin.

————, ed. *Privacy and the Press; the Daily Mirror Press Photographer Libel Action. Lea v. Justice of the Peace, Ltd. and R. J. Acford, Ltd.* London, Butterworth, 1947. 250p.   **H 447**
This case involved the alleged invasion of privacy by the taking of photographs of a wedding, against the wishes of the bridegroom.

Hyman, Stanley E. "In Defense of Pornography." *New Leader*, 46:13–15, 2 September 1963.   **H 448**
The author comments on two recent publications, *Fanny Hill*, the eighteenth-century work which he terms a "good example of pornography," and *The Housewife's Handbook on Selective Promiscuity*, "a good example of obscenity." Both books, he believes, are suppressible under the law, but neither should be banned. The law should be changed to permit the publication of any work even those works "without the slightest redeeming social importance" and with no literary merit.

Hynd, Alan. "Comstock: Crusade against Sin." *American Mercury*, 69:184–91, August 1949.   **H 449**
An American novelist tells the story of Anthony Comstock and the New York vice society.

I

Ickes, Harold L. *America's House of Lords; an Inquiry into Freedom of the Press.* New York, Harcourt, Brace, 1939. 214 p. **I1**
The Secretary of the Interior in the Franklin D. Roosevelt administration criticizes the nation's press for its failure to live up to the ethical rules of the American Society of Newspaper Editors. He decries the practice of certain editors who "keep raising the smokescreen of 'Freedom of the Press,' which often amounts to nothing but *their freedom to suppress.*" The real danger to press freedom, Ickes maintains, is from the "selfish and sinister" interest within the industry itself and not from government interference.

————, ed. *Freedom of the Press Today; a Clinical Examination by 28 Specialists. Assembled, with an Introduction by Harold L. Ickes.* New York, Vanguard, 1941. 308 p. **I2**
"Here is an attempt to discover whether, and how, American newspapers perform the obligation imposed upon them when a democratic people wrote into their fundamental law a guarantee of freedom of the press." Do pressure groups—economic, religious, etc.—affect freedom of the press? What role, if any, does advertising play? Is the press merely a business enterprise? Is there a conflict between trying to run a business and serving the public? Leading figures from the newspaper world contribute varying points of view to these and other questions relating to a free press. Contributors are Herbert Agar, Bruce Bliven, Manchester Boddy, Irving Brant, Arthur Capper, William L. Chenery, Raymond Clapper, Kenneth G. Crawford, Richard J. Finnegan, George H. Gallup, J. B. S. Hardman, Ralph Ingersoll, Edward Keating, Freda Kirchwey, Frank Knox, Harold D. Lasswell, Max Lerner, Archibald MacLeish, Vernon McKenzie, Franz B. Noyes, Nelson P. Poynter, Arthur Robb, Louis Stark, J. David Stern, Tom Wallace, William Allen White, A. F. Whitney, and Richard L. Wilson.

I'd Rather Have a Paper Doll. 30 min. color movie. Cincinnati, Citizens for Decent Literature. **I3**
"The story of a marriage, and how it is jeopardized and finally destroyed by the influence of obscene magazines on the young

husband. A penetrating look at the results of pornography on family life and society."

"Idaho Case." *Outlook*, 103:151–54, 25 January 1913. **I4**
A summary of the case against the editors of a daily newspaper who were fined and jailed for contempt of court.

Ikuta, Masateru. "Freedom of Speech and Public Welfare." *Nieman Reports*, 12(4): 1–6, December 1958. **I5**
Self-control of the press is the only satisfactory solution to the dilemma of press freedom versus public welfare.

Iliffe, J. A. "The Australian 'Obscene Publications' Legislation of 1953–55." *Sydney Law Review*, 2:134–39, January 1956. **I6**
A summary of the main points of the obscenity legislation.

————. "Objectionable Literature." *Sydney Law Review*, 2:374–79, January 1957. **I7**
Deals with the case, *Transport Publishing Co., Ltd., et al. v. Literature Board of Review*, the first case to test the new legislation which created a Board of Review in Queensland.

Illinois Legislative Council. *Restrictions upon Comic Books.* Springfield, Ill., The Council, 1956. 29 p. (Bulletin 2–585) **I8**
Contents: Comic Books and Juvenile Delinquency, Constitutional Issues, Existing Restrictions on Comic Books, Possible Solutions to the Constitutional Problem, State Legislation Aimed at Objectionable Comic Books, Statutory Descriptions of Objectionable Comic Books, Statutory Citations to "Comic Book" Laws.

Illo, John. "The Misreading of Milton." *Columbia University Forum*, 8(2):38–42, Summer 1965. **I9**
"The restriction of a conditional, not absolute, freedom of expression for the elect is the main proposition of the *Areopagitica* . . . The majority perhaps of English intellectuals,

surely of European intellectuals . . . are excluded from Milton's tolerance, and the speech for the liberty of unlicensed printing denies the only toleration that means anything, the toleration of radical dissent." The pamphlet, the author charges, has been misread by three centuries of intellectuals. It was not liberal or libertarian even in its time, but a "militant and exclusivist revolutionary pamphlet," a device for maintaining Protestant harmony.

"Imitations." *Living Age*, 291:494–97, 25 November 1916. **I10**
The influence of the "cinematograph" on the youth who see the pictures and tend to imitate what they see is discussed in this editorial from *The New Statesman*. Censorship is not the answer to the complaint that the motion picture is upsetting the morals of the young. Censorships of movies or of books are "defenders not of morals but of conventions." They are "almost always as unintelligent as they are useless."

The Importance of the Liberty of the Press: Shewing How greatly it Affects all Degrees of Men, as well with respect to Religion, as Private Property and National Liberty. Being Six Papers, publish'd in the Old England, began November 28, 1747; and now reprinted. London, M. Cooper, 1748. 36 p. **I11**

"Impropriety in Plays and Revues; a Warning by the Lord Chamberlain." *Justice of the Peace*, 79:236, 15 May 1915. **I12**

"Impurity, Vulgarity, Obscenity." *Woodhull & Claflin's Weekly*, 23 October 1875. **I13**
Vulgarity and obscenity is not of the body but is in the mind of those who make complaints about it. An editorial in this New York libertarian paper, edited and published by the controversial sisters, Victoria C. Woodhull and Tennessee Claflin.

"In Defense of Liberty, Macfadden's

Arrest." *Physical Culture*, 17:301–2, April 1917. **114**

An account of the arrest of Bernarr Macfadden, publisher of *Physical Culture*, for alleged obscenities in this journal.

"In the Interpreter's House." *American Magazine*, 76:92–93+, August 1913. **115**

Review of a study of motion pictures recently conducted in Cleveland. The editor of *American Magazine* disapproves of censorship except that which is self-imposed by the motion picture exhibitors. The best guarantee of good shows is public opinion in their behalf.

Inbau, Fred E., *ed. Free Press—Fair Trial. A Report of the Proceedings of a Conference on Prejudicial News Reporting in Criminal Cases.* Evanston, Ill., Northwestern University School of Law and Medill School of Journalism, 1954. 202 p. **116**

"Indecency in the Public Press." *Law Times*, 52:171, 6 January 1872. **117**

Calls for the extension of Lord Campbell's Act to cover reporting of scandalous affairs in the daily press.

"Indecent Publications Tribunal: The First Decision." *New Zealand Libraries*, 27:62–63, April 1964. **118**

The Indecent Publications Tribunal, following a public hearing, decided that James Baldwin's novel, *Another Country*, was not indecent and refused to place restrictions on its free circulation.

"Independence for Editors." *New Republic*, 16:61–63, 17 August 1918. **119**

The purchase of the New York *Evening Post* by Thomas W. Lamont prompts this discussion of the effect of ownership on control of editorial policy. The author suggests how a newspaper owner can guarantee a free editorial policy and still retain financial control.

"Independence of the American Press." *Army and Navy Chronicle*, 11:72, 30 July 1840. **120**

An editorial declaring that American newspapers cannot exist as free institutions; they must espouse a cause or support a political party if they are to be financially successful.

"The *Index* Crosses the Atlantic." *Independent*, 65:724–26, 24 September 1908. **121**

Commentary on the announcement by the Catholic Church, emanating from Rome, which condemned articles in the *New York Review*. Rome is now attempting to ban

"modernist heresy" in America as it has done in Europe.

"Indirect Censorship of Radio Programs." *Yale Law Journal*, 40:967–73, April 1931. **122**

Although the Federal Communications Commission may have no power to scrutinize and reject programs prior to their release, "the power to revoke or refuse the renewal of a license is in many cases so effective a means of 'censorship' as to make unconvincing any legalistic distinction between 'previous restraint' and a refusal to renew a license because of the character of past programs."

"Information et propagande." *Renaissances* (Paris), 20:3–55, April 1946. **123**

A group of articles dealing with conflicting ideas over freedom of information in the UN. One of the papers, Un Explosif Dangereux: la Liberté de la Press by Géraud Jouve, concerns the ideological conflict between the USSR and the United States. The prewar capitalist liberal ideal of press freedom, the writer believes, will not satisfy the postwar generation in Europe. The press that came out of the resistance tends to reject the right of anyone who has the funds to found and exploit a journal.

Ingersoll, Ralph, *et al.* "*Time;* the Weekly Fiction Magazine." *Fact*, 1:3–23, January–February 1964. **124**

"At *Fact's* invitation, celebrities from all walks of life tell of their bitter experiences with *Time's* distortions, omissions, and lies." Comments from Ralph Ingersoll, Irving Shaw, Mary McCarthy, Dwight Macdonald, Sloan Wilson, Igor Stravinsky, James Gould Cozzens, Tallulah Bankhead, P. G. Woodhouse, Bertrand Russell, John Osborne, Taylor Caldwell, Vincent Price, Burgess Meredith, Senator John McClellan, and others.

Ingersoll, Robert G. *Liberty in Literature, Testimonial to Walt Whitman . . . An Address Delivered in Philadelphia, Oct. 21, 1890 . . .* New York, Truth Seeker, 1890. 77 p. **125**

[———]. *Trial of C. B. Reynolds for Blasphemy at Morristown, N.J., May 19th and 20th, 1887. Defense by Robert G. Ingersoll.* New York, C. P. Farrell, 1899. 84 p. (The Agnostic Library, vol. 1, no. 5) **126**

Reynolds, a free-thought lecturer, was accosted by a mob during a New Jersey lecture tour. In a subsequent engagement in Morristown, N.J., he circulated a satirical pamphlet describing the attack against him. He was brought to trial, convicted, and fined for issuing a blasphemous work. Ingersoll served as defense attorney.

Ingle, Lorne. "Control of the Press." *Alberta Law Quarterly*, 3:127–30, April 1939. **127**

A discussion of Alberta's 1937 press act which would have given the government power of complete control over the press, had it not been declared *ultra vires* by the Supreme Court of Canada. The "gag" act was aimed at suppressing Communist doctrine.

Inglis, Brian. "Freedom of the Press." *Spectator*, 194:725–26, 10 June 1955. Reply by R. A. Paget-Cooke, *Spectator*, 194:769, 17 June 1955. **128**

Three threats to freedom of the press are: advertising, the State, and labor troubles. Inglis complains of official press officers and PRO's.

———. *The Freedom of the Press in Ireland, 1784–1841.* London, Faber, [1950?]. 256 p. (Studies in Irish History, vol. 6) **129**

The work traces the course of relations between press and state in Ireland from 1784, when statutory limitations were first enacted, until the end of the tranquil Whig administration in 1841, when the threat of rebellion brought press and state into conflict. It is based on research in contemporary newspapers and periodicals as well as state papers and manuscripts.

———. "Smuggled Culture." *Spectator*, 189:726, 28 November 1952. (Reprinted in Downs, *The First Freedom*, pp. 402–4) **130**

The author discusses the work of the Irish Censorship of Publications Board which has brought ridicule from the literary world. He sees no real demand for the abolition of censorship in Ireland, unless the government, sensitive to ridicule, feels that it has had enough.

Inglis, Ruth A. *Freedom of the Movies; a Report on Self-Regulation from the Commission on Freedom of the Press.* Chicago, University of Chicago Press, 1947. 241 p. **131**

This special report from the Commission on Freedom of the Press analyzes the system of self-regulation by means of which the motion picture industry avoids outside censorship. It discusses the nature of the pressures on the movie industry from within and without and how they have been met by the Production Code. The author recommends the use of antitrust action, the application of "freedom of the press" principles to the movies, and the establishment of a National Advisory Board (public) to propose change in the motion picture code.

———. "Freedom to See and Hear: Movies." *Survey Graphic*, 35:477–81, 506–7, December 1946. **132**

The author considers the barriers both within the movie industry and outside that prevent a realization of the screen's greatest potential. Films both of fact and fiction can make for increased understanding and tolerance between peoples.

——. "Need for Voluntary Self-Regulation." *Annals of the American Academy of Political and Social Science*, 254:153–59, November 1947. **133**

A member of the research staff of the Commission on Freedom of the Press discusses the history, problems, and possible future of what she calls "private monopoly censorship" of the movies.

Inglis, William. "Morals and Moving Pictures." *Harper's Weekly*, 54:12–13, 30 July 1910. **134**

"The interesting work of the newly established Board of Censors which passes upon the films intended for exhibition in the 7,500 moving picture houses where five million Americans seek their chief theatrical diversion."

Ingram, Brian R. "New Light on Lear." *Assistant Librarian*, 49:204–6, December 1956. **135**

In this whimsical article the author discovers in the "seemingly meaningless and innocuous limerick" of Edward Lear, evidence of Communist and other radical doctrine, which he illustrates with quotations.

"Intellectual Hospitality." *Truth Seeker*, 38:281, 6 May 1911. **136**

The author maintains that liberty includes the right to use scurrilous language. The article was prompted by the Mockus blasphemy trial.

"Intent and Motive as Bearing on Obscene Publications." *Solicitors' Journal*, 21:666–67, 30 June 1877. **137**

An editorial opposing the requirement of "wicked intent" as a factor in obscenity convictions. The editor favors the ruling in the case of *Queen v. Hicklin*.

Inter American Press Association. Committee on Freedom of the Press. *Report of the Committee on Freedom of the Press*. San Juan, Puerto Rico, The Association, 1962. various paging. mimeo. **138**

This first report of the Committee, prepared for consideration by the Board of Directors of the Association, contains an introduction summarizing press freedom or lack of it in the various states of North and South America. Following are reports on each of the countries, including a 20-page report on the suppression of the press in Cuba, prepared by the National Association of Newsmen in Exile; a 7-page report on the Dominican Republic, which has finally achieved press freedom, and a report on radio censorship in Puerto Rico. This voluntary organization of western newspaper publishers and editors grew out of the First Pan-American Congress of Journalists, meeting in Washington, D.C., 1926. The organization, which alternates its meetings between Latin American states and the United States, has frequently turned its attentions to press freedom, notably in the battle for *La Prensa* of Buenos Aires.

——. *Report of the Committee on Freedom of the Press*. Mexico City, The Association, 1964. 28 p. mimeo. (Report to the XX General Assembly, October 1964. Doc. 18) **139**

Following a general survey of the freedom or lack of freedom in the press of the Americas from the period 21 November 1963 to 21 October 1964, detailed reports are made of the state of the press in each of the American nations. The reports indicate there is no freedom of the press in Bolivia, Honduras, Cuba, Haiti, and Paraguay. During the year freedom of the press was resumed in Guatemala. A lengthy section on the United States indicates there is freedom of the press, but notes certain threats that exist, including the threat of the International Typographical Union to control the printing facets of computer operation.

——. *Report of the Committee on Freedom of the Press*. San Diego, Calif., The Association, 1965. 34 p. mimeo. (Report to the XXI General Assembly, October 1965. Doc. 16E) **140**

As with earlier reports, brief statements describe the freedom or lack of freedom in Latin American countries, Canada, and the United States. There are lengthy statements on Argentina (freedom) and the Dominican Republic (lack of freedom).

Interchurch World Movement of North America. *Public Opinion and the Steel Strike; Supplementary Reports of the Investigators to the Commission of Inquiry . . .* New York, Harcourt, Brace, 1921. 346 p. **141**

This report deals with the treatment of the Pittsburgh steel strike of 1919–20 by the various media of communications. Chapter II by M. K. Wisehart of the New York *Evening Sun* deals with the role of the Pittsburgh newspapers in covering the strike. The Commission of distinguished Protestant churchmen found that the papers accepted advertising relating to the strike without regard to its truth, represented strikers as radicals, were silent on the grievances of workers and on denials of free speech and assembly, published misleading statistics, published only the employers' point of view on violence, and suppressed "news whose tendency would have been to inspire a fair-minded examination of repressive conditions in the Pittsburgh district." The Commission was headed by Bishop Francis J. McConnell of the Methodist Church.

International Juridical Association. *Ordinance Restricting Leaflet Distribution; an Analysis of the Ordinances and Court Decisions*. New York, American Civil Liberties Union, 1937. 12 p. (Reprinted from the Association's *Bulletin*, June 1937) **142**

International Neo-Malthusian Bureau of Correspondence and Defence. *Memorandum concerning the prosecution of Mrs. Mar-*

garet H. Sanger of New York, U.S.A., for her advocacy of Birth Control and her issue of a Pamphlet entitled "Family Limitation" describing various methods of restricting families. [London? 1915?]. 8 p. **143**

International Press Institute. *Government Pressures on the Press*. Zurich, The Institute, 1956. 130 p. (IPI Survey, no. 4) **144**

A survey of pressures on the press, based on law and on such economic and political factors as subsidies and bribes, newsprint distribution, advertising, and trade unions. Fifty-three countries, including United States and Great Britain, are covered. Countries of authoritarian ideologies are excluded.

——. *I.P.I. Report*, Zurich, The Institute, May 1952–date. Monthly. **145**

Bulletin of the Institute contains world news regarding freedom and responsibility of the press.

——. *Improvement of Information*. Zurich, The Institute, 1952. 32 p. (IPI Survey, no. 1) **146**

A basic objective of the International Press Institute, an agency recommended by UNESCO and supported with grants from Ford and Rockefeller Foundations, is a broadening and strengthening of the flow of news among all peoples. A questionnaire completed by editors from 41 countries where the press is relatively free from government control reveals 3 major problems: (1) barriers to the flow of news erected by totalitarian countries, (2) shortage of newsprint and its prohibitive price, and (3) the heavy toll of cable charges which are beyond the scope of newspapers in many countries of the world.

——. *Press Councils and Press Codes*. 4th ed. Zurich, The Institute, 1966. 134 p. **147**

The first part of the study examines the working of press councils and courts of honor in 18 countries, including United Kingdom, United States, Canada, India, and South Africa. The second part gives the texts of 3 international codes of ethics—UN Draft International Code of Ethics, Declaration of Principles on the Conduct of Journalists of the International Federation of Journalists, and Code of Journalistic Press Association. Text of 17 internal codes are given including Australia, Canada, India, South Africa, United Kingdom, and United States.

——. *Professional Secrecy and the Journalist*. Zurich, The Institute, 1962. 242 p. (IPI Survey, no. 6) **148**

"In undertaking this study of professional secrecy, the International Press Institute has turned for detailed reports to authorities within representative countries. On the basis of their own special familiarity with the indigenous conditions and circumstances, they have in each case provided information bearing upon the journalist's right, or lack of right, to protect his sources." Reports from 20 countries (including Canada, United Kingdom, and United States) include summaries of the law, court decisions, custom, and ethical codes. Part two consists of views of the profession on the subject of professional secrecy, as determined by response to a questionnaire.

International Writers' Conference. Edinburgh International Festival. [*Proceedings . . . Thursday 23rd August, 1962*]. Edinburgh, The Conference, 1962. 27 p. mimeo. (Bound with proceedings for 20, 21, 22, 24 August. Separate paging; common title page) **149**
This session of the five-day conference, under the chairmanship of Mary McCarthy, was devoted to an informal discussion of censorship. Participants included Dutch writer Jacques den Haan and German publisher Hans Robart (he considered censorship of Henry Miller's *Tropic of Cancer*), William Burroughs, Norman Mailer (he played the devil's advocate), Stephen Spender, Colin MacInnes, Maurice Girodius, Van Het Reve (he discussed pornography), Henry Miller, Lawrence Durrell, Erich Fried, Muriel Spark (a Roman Catholic writer who recommended abolishing the *Index*), Rebecca West, Alexander Reid, Marian Frieman (she discussed South African censorship), and an unidentified man from the audience who introduced himself as a "professional ex-pornographer." At an earlier session (Wednesday, 22 August) Alan Paton, who was prevented from attending by the withdrawal of his passport, sent a message on censorship in South Africa.

Inter-University Case Program. *The Regional Director and the Press.* Washington, D.C., The ICP, 1952. 4 p. (ICP Case Series, no. 5). (Also in Harold Stein, *Public Administration and Policy Development*, New York, Harcourt, Brace, 1952, pp. 741–45) **150**
"This case deals with alleged partiality on the part of the National Labor Relations Board Regional Director for the 9th Region, a partiality that in the view of the Committee's investigator had led the Regional Director to suppress or tamper with the free flow of news at its source."

"Invalidity of Ordinance Imposing Absolute Criminal Liability on Bookseller Possessing Obscene Material." *New York University Law Review*, 35:1086–91, May 1960. **151**
Case notes on *Smith v. California*, 361 U.S. 147 (1959).

Ireland. Department of Justice. *Censorship of Films Act, 1923–5. Statement of Receipts and Expenditures from 1st December, 1923, to 21st March, 1930.* Dublin. Stationery Office, 1930. **152**

———. Department of Justice.Committee on Evil Literature. *Report.* Dublin, Stationery Office, 1927. 20 p. (Reports 34) **153**

Ireland (Eire). Department of Justice. Censorship of Publications Board. *Register of Prohibited Publications.* Dublin, Stationery Office, 1931?–date. Revised periodically, usually annually. Title varies. **154**
Published by the Censorship of Publications Board in accordance with directions of the Minister for Justice, pursuant to the Censorship of Publications Acts of 1929 and 1946. The 1961 edition (431 pages) is in two sections: (1) alphabetical list of prohibited books, and (2) alphabetical list of prohibited periodicals. Among the authors with books banned are Ernest Hemingway, John Dos Passos, William Faulkner, William Saroyan, C. P. Snow, Robert Penn Warren, Sinclair Lewis, Aldous Huxley, Arthur Koestler, H. G. Wells, Dylan Thomas, Emile Zola, and Morris Ernst. The catalog of the Irish Stationery Office lists various forms available for complaints against books and periodicals under the Censorship of Publications Act, and for use in appeals by author or publisher.

———. *Report of the Censorship of Publications Board and of the Censorship of Publications Appeal Board.* Dublin, Stationery Office, 1946–date. Annual. **155**

"The Irish Press Prosecution." *Solicitors' Journal*, 12:223–24, 10 January 1868. **156**
The prosecution of the editor of *The Irishman* for seditious libel prompts this general discussion of British libel laws.

"An Irish War on Immoral Prints." *Literary Digest*, 44:430, 2 March 1912. **157**
"'Vigilance committees' in Limerick, Cork, Dublin, and elsewhere in Ireland are carrying on a vigorous crusade against 'immoral literature,' generally in the shape of certain objectionable English periodicals."

Irvis, K. Leroy. "Influencing of Jurors by Publication." *University of Pittsburgh Law Review*, 15:640–43, Summer 1954. **158**
Notes on the case, *Hoffman v. Perrucci*, 117 F. Supp. 38 E.D. Pa. (1953), relates to the publication of four newspaper advertisements.

Irwin, James W. "Radio Should Fight for Greater Freedom." *Broadcast*, 24(26):28, June 1943. **159**
A public relations counselor calls for a concentrated industry campaign to guard the independence of broadcasting.

Irwin, Leonard B. "Group Pressure and Censorship." *Social Studies*, 40:178–79, April 1949. **160**
"The inevitable effect of these attempts at private censorship will be not only to endanger the right of free speech for everyone, but to bring upon these minorities the very kind of attitude they are seeking to avoid."

"Is Any Book Legally Obscene Anymore?" *Life*, 55:8, 27 September 1963. **161**

"Is Censorship Fair to Teens?" *Ingenue*, 5(4):72–74, April 1963. **162**
The article "distinguishes between censorship in its broadest sense, as practiced in Russia, and that which many small groups try to impose because of their own self interest, both of which it condemns as alien to the American idea of freedom of the press."

"Is Censorship Useless as a Weapon Against Literary Obscenity?" *Current Comment*, 56:298–99, April 1914. **163**
Pros and cons from the American press. Lucian Cary of the Chicago *Evening Post* is quoted as writing: "The evils of censorship are certain even though its benefits doubtful. . . . There is only one way to discover the truth about an idea. That way is to set it free to fight for its life with other ideas. One idea can destroy another; nothing else can. But a dangerous idea is doubly dangerous for being suppressed. There have been superstitions which have persisted for ages simply because they have never been permitted to come out into the open and be destroyed."

"Is Criminal Libel Freedom of the Press?" *Outlook*, 91:415–16, 27 February 1909. **164**
An editorial concerning indictments against the New York *World* and the Indianapolis *News* for publishing libelous allegations against Theodore Roosevelt, William H. Taft, Charles P. Taft, Douglas Robinson, William Nelson Cromwell, Elihu Root, and J. Pierpont Morgan in statements about the purchase of the Panama Canal rights. The editorial is critical of newspapers for slandering honest men on "framed-up" charges under the pretense of freedom of the press.

"Is Government Control of Wireless Intended?" *Scientific American*, 117:116, 3 February 1917. **165**
Navy-sponsored legislation for government ownership and control of radio communications is opposed in this editorial.

Is Limitation of the Family Immoral? Judgment on Annie Besant's "Law of Population." Delivered in the Supreme Court of New South Wales by Mr. Justice Windeyer. London, Freethought Publishing Co., 1889. 26 p. **166**

"Is the Censor Coming?" *New Republic,* 49:344–45, 16 February 1927.   **167**

Comments on pressures for censorship arising from the sordid coverage of the Peaches and Daddy Browning case and the "homosexual comedy-drama," *The Drag.* The author calls for the theater to provide its own internal control and for the press to assume public responsibility. Censorship, imposed from without, is thoroughly undesirable.

"Is the Censorship of Books Justified?" *Library Assistant,* 7:152–53, May 1910.   **168**

A debate held during a meeting of the Yorkshire Branch of the Library Assistants Association, in which N. Treliving (Leeds) took the affirmative and A. J. Hawkes (Leeds) the negative.

Isaacs, Norman. "Free Press and Fair Trial." *Frontier,* 16(11):8–10, September 1965.   **169**

The controversy over free press v. free trial often is the result of careless police reporting that is unfair to the defendant. Thoughtful reporting might eliminate the problem.

Ishill, Joseph, *et al. Theodore Schroeder, an Evolutionary Psychologist . . . An Extract from "A New Concept of Liberty" Including Three Unpublished Letters by Harold L. Ickes, Forest Frazier, and Dr. Ben L. Reitman.* Berkeley Heights, N.J., Oriole Press, 1964. 19p.   **170**

Eulogies in behalf of the pioneer leader in freedom of expression, including an article, A Maverick Psychologist by Maynard Shipley, reprinted from *The New Humanist,* March–April 1933. Ishill's biography of Schroeder first appeared in *A New Concept of Liberty,* published by The Oriole Press in 1940.

Issue: Censorship. Berkeley, Calif. The Coordinating Council of the United Campus Christian Fellowship, vol. 1, no. 1, Winter 1963.   **171**

The first issue of this "journal of opinion" devoted to the discussion of controversial issues "arising from our commitment and life within the Christian community," is given over to censorship. It contains the following essays: The American As Moral Censor by William L. O'Neill; The Christian and Censorship: Some General Principles by Arnold B. Come; Aspects of Southern Censorship by John E. Rinehart, Jr., and Tom L. Beauchamp, III; Indirect Censorship—Does It Mean Anything? by Raymond W. McNamee, Jr.; and The Right to Censor: A Lockian View by Benning P. Cook.

"It Happened in Pasadena." *California Librarian,* 14:89–90, December 1952.   **172**

A statement by Paul G. Hoffman before the Los Angeles Board of Education in behalf of providing UNESCO materials in the Los Angeles schools; resolutions of the Board of Education on the matter, and a resolution of the California Library Association opposing censorship or elimination of books and materials on subjects relating to UNESCO from class-rooms and libraries.

"It's a Bad, Bad Book." *New Republic,* 34:34–35, 7 March 1923.   **173**

A criticism of the practice of censors in considering passages out of context.

Iversen, William. *The Pious Pornographers.* New York, Morrow, 1963. 214p.   **174**

The title of this book of irreverent essays is taken from the first essay which exposes the obsession of women's magazines in America with sexual themes—"how to muss up the marriage bed and keep one's mate aroused." Another essay, Sex, State and the Sin-Snoopers, treats of the suppression of sex expression in Soviet Russia. "As a result of more than forty

years of censorship and state control of every aspect of art, literature and information, it is literally impossible for the average Russian to be sexually stimulated by anything he reads, sees, or hears within the confines of his official culture." Both Americans and Russians exhibit "a similar prudish desire to suppress sexuality by a masochistic denial of the flesh."

Ives, Sumner. "Five Hundred Years of Censorship." *Forum* (University of Houston), 4(4):16–19, Spring–Summer 1964.   **175**

"The areas in which censorship have been imposed have been, in order, religion, government, and artistic expression. The continuing question has been what constituted danger in each area. The trend has been toward a more and more liberal interpretation of this question. The means has largely been shifted from public law to private pressure. And, so far as one can tell, no attempts at censorship have permanently prevented the dissemination of knowledge or of that which has artistic merit."

Iyengar, K. R. Srinivasa. "Literature and Pornography." In his *The Adventure of Criticism.* Bombay, Asia Publishing House, 1962, pp. 662–67. (Essay first appeared in *Bhavan's Journal,* 1959)   **176**

"Literature *can* present sex or vice or perversion, and yet remain literature, so long as these are imaginatively seized and fully consumed in the whole design. . . . Literature that boldly and purposefully describes those aspects of human experience over which polite society feels compelled to throw a blanket of silence is a kind of strong meat which may conceivably injure weak or diseased stomachs, but these risks of indigestion are the necessary concomitants of all good things."

J

Jack, Guy. *Captain Guy Jack's Iconoclast Being an Exposure of Hypocritical Christians and Corrupt Jews of Murder, Arson, Robbery, Perjury, Forgery and Bribery of Officials and Private Citizens in Kemper and Adjacent Counties in Mississippi, whose Efforts Have Been to Defeat Justice—all Graphically Disclosed by the Author Who Figured Personally in the furious Fires of Human Greed for Filthy Lucre, and Felt the Scathing Flames of Hellish Persecution Dealt Out by Men Claiming to Be His Friends and Fellow Sympathizers. 3d ed. The First Having Been Burned in an Effort to Destroy Testimony Which Would Have Disgraced the Author's Enemies.* ₒScooba, Miss., 1919₁. For the Author. 107p. **J1**
Theodore A. Schroeder called this work "probably the most extraordinary collection of libels ever published in the same space, giving names, dates and details." Some 60 murders are charged against wealthy Mississippi citizens, as well as many other crimes not included on the title page. The publisher was charged with criminal libel and after a spectacular and sometimes hilarious trial he was acquitted.

Jack, Homer A. *Blue Pencil Over Chicago. The Fine Art of Censorship.* Chicago, Chicago Division, American Civil Liberties Union, 1949. 20p. **J2**
This pamphlet was adapted from a sermon by the minister of the Unitarian Church of Evanston. It deals with Chicago censorship of stage and motion picture performances. The occasion was the refusal to allow the performance of Sartre's play, *The Respectful Prostitute*, to be performed in Chicago. Dr. Jack discusses methods of stage censorship elsewhere (the Boston system, the Quincy plan) and national movie censorship.

Jackson, Gardner. "My Brother's Peeper." *Nation*, 130:64–65, 15 January 1930. **J3**
The author describes current activities of the New England Watch and Ward Society, particularly the trial of James A. DeLacey, manager of Dunster House Bookshop, for selling copies of D. H. Lawrence's *Lady Chatterley's Lover.* He also reports on activities in opposition to the Society, including a drive conducted by the Boston *Herald.* In the 12 February 1930 issue of *The Nation* the president of the Watch and Ward, the Reverend Raymond Calkins, defends the Society from the charges of its critics.

Jackson, Holbrook. *The Fear of Books.* New York, Scribner's, 1932. 199p. **J4**
"It is to the glory of books that ignorance and fanaticism are their enemies and that their history is disfigured with calamities, persecution and neglect." In a series of witty essays filled with literary illusions, the author advances examples from the broad scope of history of books that have been feared and often banned or destroyed. In his chapter on The Consequences of Fig Leaves, the author notes that moralists who delight in suppressing sex expression in literature "give it undeserved prominence and thus defeat their supposed ends by making it a greater danger than it is." Repression has stimulated a commerce in pornography, but the only books the Customs catch are works of genius. He devotes chapters to the "traditional sport" of pursuing aphrodisiacs and to the widespread taste for forbidden books (The Locked Cupboard). In a final chapter Jackson discusses remedies, both serious and humorous, for destroying books, including the application of birth control to the publishing industry—"all bookmen of goodwill should resist the temptation to encourage indiscriminate bookbreeding that can end only by turning a bookshop into a slum." The work is an extension of Jackson's *The Anatomy of Bibliomania.*

Jackson, Joseph H. "On Banning Books." *Nieman Reports*, 7(4):51, October 1953. **J5**
In his column, Between the Lines, in the San Francisco *Chronicle*, Jackson charges that private censoring groups fail to trust the people and the courts to recognize and properly dispose of "dirt" and communism. He comments favorably on the Westchester declaration of the American Library Association and the American Book Publishers' Council.

Jackson, Mabel. "Censorship and Problem- Area Books." *Hawaii Library Association Journal*, 20:11–13, Fall 1963. **J6**

Jackson, Thomas A. "Essays in Censorship." *Labour Monthly* (London), 11: 233–39, April 1929. **J7**
Before World War I Britain had an enviable reputation for freedom. A tightening of censorship that began with the war has been continued and broadened in the postwar decade to cope with class movements. The serious treatment of sex and not its bawdiness has led to recent action by the Home Secretary. Any "fundamental critique of social relations . . . cannot fail, in an age of literacy and libraries, to shatter all those optimisms upon which a disintegrating social system always relies."

———. *Trials of British Freedom, Being Some Studies in the History of the Fight for Democratic Freedom in Britain.* London, Lawrence & Wishart, 1945. 192p. **J8**
Contents: On British Freedom; "Wilkes and Liberty!"; Thomas Paine and the Rights of Man; The Scottish Jacobins and the British Convention of 1793; The English Jacobins; Castlereagh and Sidmouth's Spies; Peterloo and Henry Hunt; Richard Carlile and his Shopmen; The Tolpuddle Martyrs; Chartism—the First Crisis; Chartism—the Second Crisis; Chartism—the Third Crisis; The Freethinkers (Bradlaugh's Battle); The Socialists and the Riots of 1886–7; The Communists (the Twelve of 1925); Epilogue—Treason, Sedition, Blasphemy.

Jacobs, Harvey C. "Freedom to Know." *Vital Speeches*, 22:590–93, 15 July 1956. **J9**
The assistant editor of *The Rotarian* discusses the American heritage of a free press in an address at Warren Central High School, Indianapolis, citing numerous examples and anecdotes.

Jaffe, Carolyn. "The Press and the Oppressed—A Study of Prejudicial News Reporting in Criminal Cases." *Journal of Criminal Law, Criminology, and Police*

Science, 56:1–17, March 1965; 56:158–73, June 1965. **J10**

In part 1 the author examines the standards of impartiality which a jury must meet, the kinds of "prejudicial publicity" which can render a trial unfair, and the methods used to prevent conviction of defendants by juries rendered partial by publicity. In part 2 she examines possible solutions and the importance of formulating and making known to the press, bar, and police, the kinds of material likely to deprive a defendant of fair trial. The author proposes a remedial statute. Results of a poll of lawyers, police officials, and newsmen are given in the appendix to part 2.

Jager, Harry A. *Let Freedom Ring! Manual Adopting to Use in Classroom and Assembly, and in Local Broadcasting Station, Radio Series Let Freedom Ring . . .* Washington, D.C., U.S. Office of Education, 1937. 83 p. (Bulletin 33) **J11**

Jahoda, Marie, *et al. The Impact of Literature: A Psychological Discussion of Some Assumptions in the Censorship Debate.* Prepared for the American Book Publishers Council by Research Center for Human Ralations, New York University, 1954. 64 p. Photocopy of typescript. **J12**
Dr. Jahoda and her staff attempted to discover what research was available on the question as to "whether so-called 'obscene' reading matter has a detrimental effect on young people in the sense of inducing socially or individually harmful habits and actions." The result is largely an analysis of psychological aspects relating to (1) the causes of juvenile delinquency and (2) the nature of the process by which literature affects the mind of the reader. The study found that in the first case "there is no evidence available in the vast literature on juvenile delinquency which would justify the assumption that reading matter has a major motivating force in it." On the second point, they found that "it is virtually impossible to isolate the impact of one of these media [newspapers, television, movies, printed fiction] on a population that is exposed to all of them." Further research is needed to provide positive evidence on the impact of literature.

James, C. L. *An Appeal to the Women of America in Behalf of Liberty and Justice to and for the Prosecuted and Persecuted Defenders of the Wives and Mothers of Our Land.* Topeka, Kan., Moses Harman, 1891. 12 p. **J13**
An appeal for public support in behalf of Moses Harman, prosecuted on obscenity charges under the Comstock law for sending sex education information through the mails. The author attacks the law as it is applied to the suppression of sex education and sex hygiene.

James, Robert R. "Fifty-Year Rule." *Spectator*, 213:233–34, 21 August 1964. **J14**
An examination of some of the problems involved in official restrictions covering inspection of British public records and the assault on these restrictions by those opposing the 50-year rule imposed upon historians by the Public Records Act of 1958.

Jamieson, John. "Censorship and the Soldier." *Public Opinion Quarterly*, 11:367–84, Fall 1947. **J15**
"For the first time the full story is told of wartime censorship in Army libraries. Most of the censorship of soldiers' reading materials in World War II resulted from the War Department's efforts to enforce Title V of the Soldier Voting Law . . . However well-intended the legislation may have been, its sweeping powers and obscure language produced violent, chaotic, even ludicrous results . . . Finally, a vigorous press campaign, touched off by a release of the civilian Council on Books in Wartime, led to a sensible modification of an unworkable censorship law."

———. "Censorship and the Soldier Voting Law." In his *Books for the Army; the Army Library Service in the Second World War.* New York, Columbia University Press, 1950, pp. 212–29. **J16**
Except for the enforcement of the Soldier Voting Law, there was almost no army-wide censorship for moral or political reasons and very little imposed at the post level. Title V of the Soldier Voting Law prohibited the distribution of "political propaganda" to the armed forces. A strict interpretation by the Adjutant General resulted in the suppression of many significant books and magazines. After much criticism in the press, the law was amended to remove the unreasonable restrictions.

Janes, Lewis G. *Samuell Gorton: a Forgotten Founder of Our Liberties; First Settler of Warwick, R.I.* Providence, R.I., Preston and Rounds, 1896. 141 p. **J17**
Gorton, who came to America in 1637, was banished from both Boston and Plymouth for his heresies. In 1642, after a turbulent stay in Providence, R.I., he bought Indian lands and founded Shawomet, Mass. Here again he was jailed for his unorthodox religious views. He returned to England and reported on his persecutions in *Simplicities Defence against Seven-Headed Policy* (1646).

Janes, Robert W. *The Legion of Decency and the Motion Picture Industry.* Chicago, University of Chicago, 1939. 75 p. (Unpublished Master's thesis) **J18**

Jansen, William. *Should Religious Beliefs Be Studied and Criticized in an American Public High School?* New York, Board of

Superintendents of the New York City Schools, 1948. (Excerpted in *The Nation*, 20 November 1948) **J19**
A defense of the New York City Board of Education in banning *The Nation* from public high schools, written by the Superintendent of Schools. This pamphlet answers *An Appeal to Reason and Conscience*, a statement opposing the ban, signed by 107 persons and representing 34 organizations. *The Nation* excerpts are accompanied by replies from some of those who signed the *Appeal.*

Jansky, Maurice. "Analysis of the Standards of Public Interest, Convenience and Necessity as Defined by the Federal Communications Commission." *George Washington Law Review*, 6:21–45, November 1937. **J20**

Jarett, Lawrence. "Circulation as an Essential Element of a Free Press." *St. John's Law Review*, 13:81–93, November 1938. **J21**
A review of court decisions involving distribution of printed matter by mail and by hand, particularly the Grosjean and Lovell cases. "Liberty of circulation is as essential as liberty of publishing."

[Jarves, James J.]. *Report of the Case of Peter Allen Brinsmade . . . versus James Jackson Jarves, editor of the Polynesian, for Alleged Libelous Publications, decided upon grounds of law by Hon. Lorrin Andrews . . .* Honolulu, Charles E. Hitchcock, 1846. 104 p. **J22**

Jast, L. Stanley. "Library Politics." *Library Review*, 40:364–69, Winter 1936. **J23**
The librarian "cannot be indifferent to the Bolshevik discovery of the value of the public library as an organ of simple propaganda for the economic, social, and religious or anti-religious ideas of the government in power." Librarians should take care not to allow such propaganda to threaten the freedom of the shelves.

———. "Public Libraries and Doubtful Books." *Library Association Record*, 16:77–78, 14 February 1914. **J24**
The Secretary of the Library Association, in an address before the National Council of Public Morals, defends public library practices in book selection. "A public library authority does not reject books; it selects, a rather different thing." Jast emphasizes the responsibility of the public librarian in reflecting the attitude of his community. He refers to an open letter from Hall Caine to the Library Association, noting the essential difference

between the purposes of the Circulating Libraries Association, which had banned his latest novel, and the Library Association, the former being a commercial organization with a profit motive, the latter representing the public interest.

Javits, Jacob K. "So All the People May See and Hear." *TV Guide*, 11(19):6–9, 11 May 1963.　　　　　　**J 25**
The New York Senator urges television coverage of some sessions of the U.S. Senate.

Jay, William. "Freedom of Speech and Press." In his *Miscellaneous Writings on Slavery*. Boston, Jewett, 1853, pp. 530–37.　　　　　　**J 26**

Jefferson, Thomas. ["Censorship of Books"]. In Saul K. Padover, ed., *The Complete Jefferson*. New York, Duell, Sloan & Pearce, [1943], p. 889.　　**J 27**
In a letter to Dufief, 19 April 1814, Jefferson protests the ban on De Becourt's *Sur la Création du Monde, un Système d'Organisation Primitive*. He is "mortified" that the sale of a book is a subject of criminal inquiry and can be carried before a civil magistrate. "Are we to have a censor whose imprimatur shall say what books may be sold, and what we may buy . . . Whose foot is to be the measure to which ours are all to be cut or stretched . . . If M. de Becourt's book be false in its facts, disprove them; if false in its reasoning, refute it. But, for God's sake, let us freely hear both sides, if we choose." It is a book "not likely to be much read if let alone, but, if prosecuted, it will be generally read. Every man in the United States will think it a duty to buy a copy, in vindication of his right to buy, and to read what he pleases."

[Jefferson, Thomas]. *The Kentucky Resolutions, 1798*. (Reprinted in Saul K. Padover, ed., *The Complete Jefferson*, New York, Duell, Sloan & Pearce, [1943], pp. 128–34)　　　　　**J 28**
These resolutions, a protest against the Alien and Sedition Acts, were adopted by the Kentucky legislature on 10 November 1798. Jefferson kept his authorship of them a secret. The third resolution states in part "that no power over the freedom of religion, freedom of speech, or freedom of the press being delegated to the United States by the Constitution, nor prohibited by it to the States, all lawful powers respecting the same did of right remain, and were reserved to the States or the people: that thus was manifested their determination to retain to themselves the right of judging how far the licentiousness of speech and of the press may be abridged without lessening their useful freedom, and how far those abuses which cannot be separated from their use should be tolerated, rather than the use be destroyed." The Sedition Act "which does abridge the freedom of the press, is not law, but is altogether void, and of no force."

———. ["Second Inaugural Address, Washington, D.C., 4 March 1805"]. In Saul K. Padover, ed., *The Complete Jefferson*. New York, Duell, Sloan & Pearce, [1943], pp. 410–15.　　　　　　**J 29**
Jefferson speaks against the licentiousness of the press in attacking his administration. "These abuses of an institution so important to freedom and science, are deeply to be regretted, inasmuch as they tend to lessen its usefulness, and to sap its safety; they might, indeed have been corrected by the wholesome punishments reserved and provided by the laws of the several States against falsehood and defamation; but public duties more urgent press on the time of public servants, and the offenders have therefore been left to find their punishment in the public indignation."

Jefferson and Our Times: The Experiment of a Free Press. 33 1/3 r.p.m. recording. Prepared by the Fund for Adult Education, Experimental Discussion Project. (Program no. 5)　　　　　　**J 30**
Part of a series of ten programs, prepared for use in discussion groups in conjunction with Dumas Malone's book, *Jefferson and Our Times*. This episode deals with Jefferson, in retirement, recounting his experience with a free press during his terms as President, and the events which threatened his experiment.

Jeffries, James H., III. "Municipal Ordinance Restricting Distribution of Handbills." *Kentucky Law Journal*, 49:423–28, Spring 1961.　　　　　　**J 31**
People v. Talley, 172 Cal. App. 797:332 P. 2 d 447 (1958).

[Jehovah's Witnesses]. *Jehovah's Witnesses in the Divine Purpose*. Brooklyn, N.Y., Watchtower Bible and Tract Society of New York and International Bible Student Association, 1959. 311 p.　　　**J 32**
This history of Jehovah's Witnesses contains frequent references to efforts made to censor publications of this religious sect, beginning with the wartime sedition charges in Canada in February 1918.

[Jenkins, Benjamin G.]. [*William Inman v. Benjamin G. Jenkins, defendant.*] *The Loss of the "City of Boston." A Action for Libel Tried at the Liverpool Assizes . . .* Liverpool, Lee and Nightingale, 1870. 85 p.　　**J 33**
Jenkins was convicted of libel for a letter in *The Times* accusing the owners of the steamship line of overloading the ship. The ship was never heard from after it left Halifax. Jenkins was found guilty and fined £250. Considerable criticism of the verdict appeared in the press.

Jenkins, Clive. *Power Behind the Screen; Ownership, Control and Motivation in British Commercial Television*. London, Macgibbon & Kee, 1961. 288 p.　　　　　**J 34**

Jenkins, Daniel. "Evil Communications: the Responsibility of Controllers." *Frontier*, 4:131–37, Summer 1961. (A chapter from the author's book, *Equality and Excellence: A Christian Commitment on Britain's Life*. London, Published for the Christian Frontiers Council by SCM Press, 1961)　　　　　　**J 35**
Criticism of the mass media and their disrespect for the public they are serving. "Those who trade upon the weaknesses of society in the realms of the mind and spirit should not be regarded as its successful leaders, but as members of its shoddy underworld." The author calls not for legal controls, but for a greater public sensitivity and awareness of the behavior of controllers of the mass media.

Jenkins, Iredell. "The Laissez-faire Theory of Artistic Censorship." *Journal of the History of Ideas*, 5:71–90, January 1944.　　　　　　**J 36**
A critical analysis of the theory of noninterference in the field of artistic endeavor, the laissez-faire theory. The author attempts to define the theory and identify its position in the light of the new role that we expect art to play, that of a part of life for every one, instead of a luxury for a few as in earlier times.

———. "Legal Basis of Literary Censorship." *Virginia Law Review*, 31:83–118, December 1944.　　　　　　**J 37**
Trends in literary censorship during the past 30 years and a plea for freedom of artistic expression. Special references are made to the *Strange Fruit* and *Esquire* cases.

[Jenkins, J. C.]. *Decision of Judge J. C. Jenkins of the Court of First Instance for the Judicial District of Manila. Part IV, in the Action for Damages Brought by Dean C. Worcester against the Owners, Directors, Writers, Editors and Administrators of the Newspaper Known as "El Renacimiento y Muling Pagsilang."* [Manila, Press of Methodist Publishing House, 1910?]. 23 p.　　　　　　**J 38**

Jenkins, Roy. "Obscenity, Censorship, and the Law; the Story of a Bill." *Encounter*, 13:62–66, October 1959.　**J 39**
An account of the five-year struggle for the passage of the 1959 British Obscene Publications Act which allows the law of censorship in literature "to advance beyond the points at which Lord Campbell, in his Act of 1857, and Chief Justice Cockburn, in his Hicklin judgment of 1868, had previously established it."

———. "Reforming the Censorship." *Spectator*, 198:372–73, 22 March 1957.　　　　　　**J 40**
A member of Parliament discusses the Obscene Publications Bill presently before that body.

Jenks, George M. "J'Accuse!" *Newsletter on Intellectual Freedom*, 13:13–14, March 1964. (Reprinted from *The Australian Library Journal*, December 1963) **J 41**
The author charges that librarians in Australia have been "conspicuous by their absence as opponents of censorship."

Jennison, Peter S. "Censorship: Strategy for Defense." *Publishers' Weekly*, 185: 58–61, 2 March 1964. **J 42**
Advice to booksellers on how to meet attacks by the censors. Jennison advises librarians and booksellers to "make common cause, and whenever possible, in a mutual defense treaty, identify and mobilize their allies in anticipation of attack." The first line of defense, he advises, is the bookseller himself, "his prudence, responsibility and courage."

———. "The Censorship War on Low-Priced Books." *Chicago Sunday Tribune, Magazine of Books*, 27 January 1963, p. 2. **J 43**

The popularity, availability, and price of the paperback that makes them so attractive and successful also subjects them to the censor, while the clothbound edition "seldom draws the lightning of censorship."

———. *Freedom to Read*. New York, Public Affairs Committee, 1963. 20 p. (Public Affairs Pamphlet no. 344) **J 44**
A summary of present efforts in America to restrict freedom to read and what is being done to counteract these threats. Includes discussion of attacks on textbooks, libraries and the censors, the fear of obscenity, and vigilante action.

———. "Sense and Censorship." *Ohio Library Association Bulletin*, 33:3–6, 26–28, January 1963. **J 45**

———. "Today's Challenge to the Book World." *Library Journal*, 82:2319–25, 1 October 1957. **J 46**
Includes a commentary on the dangers of "anticipatory" censorship.

Jensen, Jay W. "Toward a Solution of the Problem of Freedom of the Press." *Journalism Quarterly*, 27:399–408, Fall 1950. **J 47**
"After illustrating how the traditional Anglo-American concept of a free press has been undermined by the Romantic Revolt and the Darwin-Einstein revolution, the author suggests a starting point for the reconstruction of its principles with a contemporary framework." Freedom of the press should be more than the absence of restraint and it should encompass all media.

Jensen, William P. *Newspaper Libel in Iowa.* Lawrence, Kan., University of Kansas,

1940. 92 p. (Unpublished Master's thesis) **J 48**
An analysis of the laws and court decisions pertaining to libel in the state of Iowa, with emphasis upon court decisions involving newspapers. The author finds that Iowa courts have dealt liberally with newspapers involved in libel offenses—truth alone is allowed as a defense in civil suits, a great deal of leniency is given to newspaper comment on public officials and candidates, and considerable latitude is permitted in the coverage of trials.

Jephson, Henry L. *The Platform: Its Rise and Progress.* New York, Macmillan, 1892. 2 vols. **J 49**
The term "Platform" refers to the public discussion of political issues in England, an institution, the author maintains, ranking in importance with four others—Crown, Lords, Commons, and the Press. This work traces the history of the Platform and public debate of political questions from the middle of the eighteenth century to the end of the nineteenth. Although largely a history of the struggle for free speech, the events parallel those for a free press, beginning with the agitation for John Wilkes, and following with the development of the doctrine of seditious libel, the practices of ex-officio information, the reform brought about by the Fox Libel Act, the prosecutions of seditious writing and speaking (Seditious Meetings Act of 1795) during the period of the French Revolution, the revival of restrictive legislation in 1817 and in 1820, the Roman Catholic emancipation agitation, and the rising power of Press and Platform during the period of reform.

Jessen, Lowell. *A Newsman Sees FOI Blind Spots.* Columbia, Mo., Freedom of Information Center, School of Journalism, University of Missouri, 1958. 3 p. (Publication no. 3) **J 50**
A California newspaperman discusses that State's laws permitting secret meetings of state boards and committees, and the successful efforts to remove such clauses. He also discusses the efforts in Washington to combat secrecy. Other blind spots in freedom of the press are the use of news handouts, and the failure of the schools to teach the lessons of American freedom.

Jèze, Gaston P. A. *Le Régime juridique de la presse en Angleterre pendant la guerre.* 2d ed. Paris, Giard and Brière, 1915. 185 p. (Reprinted from issues of *Revue du Droit Public et de la Science Politique*, 1915–16) **J 51**

British press controls during World War I.

Johansen, Alan H. "Right of Privacy— When Is It Invaded by Publication of News Items and Photographs?" *Oregon Law Review*, 35:42–50, December 1955. **J 52**
Notes on cases coming before the American courts, 1890–1955.

John Peter Zenger Award Lectures, University of Arizona. *Annual Lectures.* 1954–date. Tucson, University of Arizona, 1957–date. (The first three lectures are published in one volume; subsequent lectures are published separately) **J 53**
Each annual lecture deals with an aspect of freedom of the press, e. g., the 1958 lecture by John E. Moss on What You Don't Know *Will* Hurt You; the 1959 lecture by Herbert Brucker on Men In the Dark; the 1960 lecture by Virgil M. Newton, Jr. on The Press and Bureaucracy; the 1961 lecture by Clark R. Mollenhoff on Deadly Dilemma: Defense and Democracy; the 1962 lecture by John C. Colburn on The Press and an Informed Electorate; the 1963 lecture by James B. Reston on The Press in a World of Change; and the 1964 lecture by John Netherland Heiskell on The Newspaper: Keeper of the Community Conscience.

"John Wilkes and the Liberty of the Press." *Law Magazine*, 22(4th ser.): 213–16, August 1897. **J 54**
An account of the presentation made in 1772 by the City of London of a silver cup to John Wilkes to celebrate his defense of the liberty of the press. The article is accompanied by an illustration and description of the cup, the design, depicting the death of Caesar, having been suggested by Wilkes himself.

Johnsen, Julia E., *comp. Freedom of Speech.* New York, Wilson, 1936. 317 p. (The Reference Shelf, vol. 10, no. 8) **J 55**
Includes three articles on censorship of radio: Louis G. Caldwell, Censorship of Radio from *Annals of the American Academy of Political and Social Science*, January 1935; E. H. Harris, Shall the Government Own, Operate and Control Radio Broadcasting? from *Proceedings of the National Advisory Council on Radio in Education*, 1934; and H. V. Kaltenborn, Radio Must Continue Free, from *Printers' Ink*, February 1935.

———. *Selected Articles on Birth Control.* New York, Wilson, 1925. 369 p. (Handbook Series) **J 56**
References deal with pros and cons of the debate topic, Resolved: That the dissemination of knowledge and means of contraception should be made legal. Includes a reprinting of chapter 9 from Annie Besant's autobiography dealing with the Bradlaugh-Besant trial over publication of Charles Knowlton's early birth control pamphlet.

Johnson, Alvin W., and Frank H. Yost. *Separation of Church and State in the United States.* Minneapolis, University of Minnesota Press, 1948. 279 p. **J 57**
Chapter 3, Bible Reading in the Public Schools; chapter 14, Litigation Relating to Bible Reading in the Public Schools; chapter 18, Religion and Freedom of the Press.

Johnson, B. S. "Pi Printers." *Censorship*, 3:43–45, Summer 1965. **J 58**
The censorship practiced by printers in refusing to set a manuscript in type. He cites the case of James Joyce's *Dubliners* and his own novel, *Albert Angelo*. Of all those engaged in the book trade, the printer takes the least risk financially.

Johnson, Burges. "More Murmurings of a Common Scold." *Harper's Magazine*, 143:391–94, August 1921. **J 59**
"The greatest danger that lies in the recognition of the rights of censorship is that thoughtless people will grow to believe that any such real right exists." Education is the best protection against any "emanations of diseased minds."

Johnson, C. D. "The Legal Status of the Librarian." *Library Journal*, 81:1847–52, 1 September 1956. **J 60**
Deals with the legal rights of librarians who face attempts by groups and associations to suppress information. "What are your rights and what can you do as a legal and practical matter to protect yourself and protect the right to free access to all proper types of information?"

Johnson, Caleb. "Franklin on Liberty." *American Press*, 52(12):5, September 1934. **J 61**
The author reprints, with evidence of its authenticity, a little-known letter from Benjamin Franklin expressing his ideas on freedom of speech. In the eighth letter in the "Silence Dogwood" series, published in no. 49 of the *New England Courant*, July 1722, Franklin says in part: "Without Freedom of Thought, there can be no such Thing as Wisdom; and no such Thing as publick Liberty, without Freedom of Speech; which is the Right of every Man, as far as by it, he does not hurt or control the Right of another: And this is the only Check it ought to suffer, and the only Bounds it ought to Know."

Johnson, Claudius O. "Status of Freedom of Expression under the Smith Act." *Western Political Quarterly*, 11:469–80, September 1958. **J 62**
While a decision of the Supreme Court in the Yates case, 345 U.S. 340 (1957), reversed 33 convictions, the wartime Alien Registration Act of 1940 (Smith Act) is still a threat to unorthodox expression. There is legal uncertainty as to whether the written or spoken word advocating overthrow of government by force contains an actual incitement to action to that end.

Johnson, Donald. "Wilson, Burleson, and Censorship in the First World War."
Journal of Southern History, 28:46–58, February 1962. **J 63**
An account of Post Office censorship during World War I, directed by Postmaster General Albert S. Burleson, which went far beyond the wartime needs and suppressed Socialist and liberal newspapers and pamphlets.

Johnson, Dorothy E. "What Price Censorship?" *Minnesota Libraries*, 17:211–12, September 1953. **J 64**
Censorship is a doubtful method of either reducing the amount of crime or protecting the social order and the "American Way."

Johnson, Edwin H. *What Constitutes Libel in Missouri*. Columbia, Mo., University of Missouri, 1938. 110p. (Unpublished Master's thesis) **J 65**

Johnson, Eugene I., and L. E. Salisbury. "Thought Control in America? Censorship in the News; Cartelized Information." *Far Eastern Survey*, 15:151–54, 22 May 1946. **J 66**
Johnson, former chief censor in the Chinese Theater in World War II, discusses problems of getting Asian news at the source and warns readers to be aware of the editorial policy of the newspaper or magazine carrying the news. The second article charges newspaper and magazine editors rather than reporters with censoring and coloring news from Asia.

Johnson, F. L. "Obscene Publications, Pictures, and Articles—Whether or Not a Phonograph Record, Containing Obscene, Lewd, and Lascivious Words, Songs, or Other Matter is an Article or Instrument of Indecent or Immoral Use or Purpose Within the Prohibition of Obscenity Statutes." *Chicago-Kent Law Review*, 28:163–70, March 1950. **J 67**
Many states, because of narrow statutory language, are ill-equipped to punish persons for production and sale of obscene phonograph records; other states with broader statutes and proper legal interpretations can punish such offenses.

Johnson, Franklin. "How Britain's Blacklists and Censorship Affect American Traders." *Export Trade & Shipper*, 43(4): 3–5, 3 March 1941. **J 68**
The publisher of *American Exporter*, who made up the first U.S. blacklist of enemy firms in World War I, discusses British controls in World War II. He discounts stories of British use of wartime censorship to capture American business. He believes American business can expect greater controls but can learn to live with them.

Johnson, Gerald W. "American Freedom and the Press." In Allen Maxwell, *ed.*,
The Present Danger; Four Essays on American Freedom. Dallas, Southern Methodist University Press, 1953, pp. 19–41. **J 69**
A review of the historic development of a free press in America and its importance in the preservation of democracy. "But no freedom exists without a corresponding responsibility. Because I am free to read anything, it becomes my duty to read the truth; and by the same token, it becomes the duty of the newspapers to print it."

———. "The Devil Is Dead and What a Loss." *American Scholar*, 16:395–403, Autumn 1947. **J 70**
A satirical inquiry as to why censorship should exist in a country that is economically and politically more secure than ever before. The spirit of Puritanism, he finds, "has never been wholly eradicated from the American mind, and it is characteristic of Puritanism that while it may get along comfortably enough without God . . . it has always found the Devil indispensable." Now that Hitler is dead we have created a papier-mâché devil in censorship. "We need one that can be worked on by the F.B.I., the Ku Klux Klan, the American Legion . . ."

———. "The Freedom of the Newspaper Press." *Annals of the American Academy of Political and Social Science*, 200:60–75, November 1938. **J 71**
The editor of the Baltimore *Sun* discusses the constitutional freedom of the press as it is amended and interpreted by court decisions, limitations and controls of advertising, community taboos, the right of privacy, regulation of trade practices (NRA), labor relations (closed shop), and pressures of interest groups. Public apathy is the chief threat to press freedom in America.

———. "Newspapers on Guard." *Atlantic Monthly*, 169:156–61, February 1942. **J 72**
"The American press is facing not merely the usual prohibitions that always go into force with the outbreak of hostilities, but positive duties unlike those laid upon it in any previous war."

———. *Peril and Promise: an Inquiry into Freedom of the Press*. New York, Harper, 1958. 110p. (Excerpts in Downs, *The First Freedom*, pp. 88–111) **J 73**
One of America's most distinguished journalists presents a literate and philosophical analysis of press freedom. "A free press is the creature, not the creator of freedom," Johnson asserts. The influence of enlightened readership as well as the courageous efforts of responsible leadership are needed to preserve press freedom. Monopoly and mediocrity are the twin threats that may well invite government controls.

———. "Unfortunate Necessity." *Century Magazine*, 112:41–47, May 1926. **J 74**
A résumé of the history of freedom of the press

in the United States. If the press is not only to be free but to inspire public confidence it must practice better journalism and eliminate yellow sensationalism.

Johnson, Hubert A. "The Trustee's Role." *ALA Bulletin*, 57:631–33, July–August 1963. **J 75**
A trustee of the Free Library, Wallingford, Pa., calls for strong support of the Library Bill of Rights on the part of public library trustees. Where a compromise on the Library Bill of Rights has been necessary you will generally find weak trustees. "It can be weakness in failing to support a good librarian, or it can be weakness in abiding a librarian who is running scared."

Johnson, Humphrey. "Some Reflections Suggested by Canon 1399." *Downside Review*, 74:215–27, Summer 1956. **J 76**
Canon law of the Catholic Church dealing with forbidden literature.

Johnson, James D. "We Censors Are Frustrated Humans." *Saturday Evening Post*, 218(12):34, 22 September 1945.
J 77
A Post Office censor discusses his problems.

[Johnson, Samuel (c. 1686)]. *An Account of the Proceedings against Samuel Johnson: Who was Tryed at the Kings-Bench-Bar, Westminster, For High Misdemeanour: And found Guilty of Writing and Publishing Two Seditious and Scandalous Libels against the Government, on Monday the 21th. of June. 1686.* London, Printed for A.M., 1686. broadside (Also reported in Howell, *State Trials*, vol. 11, p. 1339 ff.) **J 78**
For publishing anti-Catholic pamphlets Johnson, a clergyman, was brought to trial, found guilty, and sentenced to be whipped by the common hangman "from Newgate to Tyburn." The ordeal consisted of 317 lashes. In order to avoid the scandal to a clergyman, an *ad hoc* Ecclesiastical Commission degraded Johnson. In 1689 Parliament declared the trial procedure, including the Ecclesiastical Commission, illegal and the punishment cruel; Johnson was awarded a pension by the king.

[Johnson, Samuel (1709–84)]. *A Compleat Vindication of the Licensers of the Stage, from the malicious and scandalous Aspersions of Mr. Brooke, Author of Gustavus Vasa, With a Proposal for making the Office of Licenser more Extensive and Effective. By an Impartial Hand.* London, 1739. (Also in his *Works*, edited by Arthur Murphy, New York, Harper, 1873, vol. 2, pp. 539–44) **J 79**
The first action of the Lord Chamberlain under the 1737 Stage Licensing Act was to

ban Henry Brooke's *Gustavus Vasa* on political grounds ("there was a good deal of liberty in it"), whereupon the sale of the book flourished. Dr. Johnson's satirical pamphlet was directed against the Walpole administration in general and the Stage Licensing Act in particular. "Let the poets remember, when they appear before the licenser, or his deputy, that they stand at the tribunal from which there is no appeal permitted, and where nothing will so well become them as reverance and submission." In conclusion, he suggests that a more sure and silent way to control the spread of ideas without a direct attempt on freedom of the press would be to make it a felony to teach children to read without a license from the Lord Chamberlain.

Johnson, Thomas H. "Jonathan Edwards and the 'Young Folk's Bible.'" *New England Quarterly*, 5:37–54, January 1932.
J 80
An account of an investigation in Northampton in 1744 of the widespread but secret reading of a certain volume on midwifery for pornographic purposes, under the guise of sex education for young people.

Johnson, Thomas M. *Without Censor; New Light on Our Greatest World War Battles.* Indianapolis, Bobbs-Merrill, 1928. 411 p. **J 81**
"The war-time version of the war was so often not the true version. The War God slew the maiden Truth to make way for the twin Furies, Censorship and Propaganda. The first lowered before exact and often ugly reality a screen whereon the second threw attractive pictures." In telling the "true story" of American participation in World War I, this New York *Sun* correspondent with the AEF, describes the ways in which censorship operated to prevent news from France from getting to the American press. A chapter, The Propaganda Front, describes the mechanism of censorship and includes a photograph of the Paris Bourse, "where the blue pencil flourished."

Johnston, Eric. *Agreement—Not Compulsion.* Washington, D.C., Motion Picture Association of America, 1946. 11 p. **J 82**
The president of the Motion Picture Association of America defends the industry's program of self-regulation of movies.

———. *The Freedom to Choose.* Columbia, Mo., Freedom of Information Center, School of Journalism, University of Missouri, 1960. 4 p. (Publication no. 30) **J 83**
In an address before a conference of the Child Study Association, Johnston urges a crusade for freedom of choice instead of censorship. The freedom to accept or reject, to approve or disapprove of movies, radio and television programs, books, or newspapers belongs to the people. Parents have a responsibility to help their children exercise good judgment in selecting their entertainment.

———. "Report from Europe." *Screen Writer*, 4(4):4–6, 17–18, October 1948.
J 84
The president of the Motion Picture Association defends American movies from its critics; he calls for freedom from restrictions on American movies shown abroad.

Jones, Alexander F. "Urges Press Seek Access to Federal Records as Legal Right, Not Favor." *Quill*, 40(1):7, 16, January 1952. **J 85**
The president of the American Society of Newspaper Editors urges legislation to compel government officials to allow newspapers access to official records.

———, et al. "How Does Freedom of Information Affect You?" *Reviewing Stand*, Northwestern University, Evanston, Ill., 1951. 11 p. (Vol. 17, no. 6) **J 86**
Participants: Alexander F. Jones, president, American Society of Newspaper Editors; Kenneth E. Olson, dean, Medill School of Journalism, Northwestern University; and Tom Wallace, president, Inter American Press Association. James H. McBurny, dean, School of Speech, Northwestern University, was moderator.

———, George B. DeLuca, and Louis Waldman. "Fair Trial—Free Press: A Panel Discussion." *New York State Bar Bulletin*, 26:202–25, July 1954. **J 87**
An editor (A. F. Jones), a district attorney (G. B. DeLuca), and the chairman of the Committee on Civil Rights of the New York State Bar Association (Louis Waldman) discuss Canon 20 of the American Bar Association's Canons of Professional Ethics.

Jones, C. H. M. "Censor and Ship News." *National Marine*, 13:33–38, June 1919.
J 88
An account of naval censorship in World War I.

Jones, Caroline L. "Censorship in Rural Libraries." *Wilson Bulletin*, 2:307–11, November 1924. **J 89**
The public libraries in small towns need to resist requests to stock the cheaply-written oversentimental fiction that is flooding the market. While the author recommends a liberal policy in purchasing modern fiction of quality, some extreme works need to be kept off the open shelves and made available only on request. Cheaply written children's work, especially those in series, should be avoided even though children like them. She cites statements of juvenile court officials to the effect that "cheap stories" are a major cause of delinquency.

Jones, Henry A. "After the Censorship Committee." In his *Foundations of a*

National Drama . . . London, Chapman & Hall, [1913], pp. 337-58.　　**J 90**

A review of censorship of drama in Great Britain since the sittings of the Censorship Committee in the fall of 1909 and up to the fall of 1912. The author repeats his recommendation for an Inspector-General to replace the present Examiner of Plays in the Office of the Lord Chamberlain.

————. "The Censorship Muddle and a Way Out of It." In his *Foundations of a National Drama* . . . London, Chapman & Hall, [1913], pp. 282-336. (Also separately published by Chiswick Press, 1909. 58 p.)
　　J 91

A letter addressed to Herbert Samuel, chairman of the committee to examine the working of the censorship of plays in the United Kingdom (September 1909). Jones recommends the appointment of an Inspector-General, responsible to the Government, but concerned with "indecency" and not "morality." The playgoers themselves should be the judge of the latter.

————. "The Licensing Chaos in Theatres and Music Halls." In his *The Foundations of a National Drama* . . . London, Chapman & Hall, [1913], pp. 269-81.　　**J 92**

A lecture delivered to the National Sunday League, 27 February 1910. "I ask you not to rest until every theatre and music hall in the kingdom has letters patent from you as playgoers to give and perform whatever entertainment the manager may choose, and the audiences may wish to see; the only restriction being that such entertainment shall not be indecent, or dangerous, or harmful to the general public."

Jones, Howard Mumford, *ed. Primer of Intellectual Freedom.* Cambridge, Mass., Harvard University Press, 1949. 191 p.
　　J 93

A collection of significant pronouncements in behalf of freedom of inquiry and expression. Includes John Stuart Mill's *On the Liberty of Thought and Discussion* (1859), Milton's *A Speech for the Liberty of Unlicensed Printing* (1644), Oliver Wendell Holmes's *Dissenting Opinions,* and Zechariah Chafee's *Freedom of Speech in the Constitution.*

————. "Reflection in a Library." *Saturday Review,* 43:34+, 9 April 1960.　　**J 94**

The author explores the position that "the public library is the greatest force for censorship in the country after the postmaster and the police sergeant. . . . A librarian's purchasing power is limited by his budget, the advice he gets from his staff and from professional journals, the policies or prejudices of his governing board, the taste of his clientele, his notion of the needs of the community, the educational policy of the local school board (of which he is never a member), religious pressures, and the reading ability of his clientele."

Jones, John. *De Libellis Famosis; or the Law of Libels.* London, S. Rousseau, 1812. 73 p.　　**J 95**

Jones, John G., *et al. Substance of the Speeches of John Gale Jones delivered at the British Forum, March 11, 18, & 22, 1819, on the . . . Question: "Ought the Prosecutions Instigated against Mr. Carlile . . . for Publication of Paine's Age of Reason, to be Approved . . . or Censured?"* London, 1819. (Appeared in various editions)　　**J 96**

While Richard Carlile awaited trial for publication of Paine's *Age of Reason,* the British Forum at Westminster debated for three weeks whether the prosecution should be "approved as necessary to prevent the further increase of infidelity, and vindicate the doctrines of Christianity?—or censured as an officious and ill-timed interference on a subject not cognizable before any human tribunal, and an infringement upon the Freedom of Opinion that ought to be exercised upon all topics essential to the welfare and happiness of mankind?" When Carlile continued to publish and sell *Age of Reason* in defiance of the authorities, the Forum again debated whether Carlile should be "censured as a serious aggravation of his offense" or approved as a "bold and manly perseverance in the cause of reason and truth?" James Mill was among the speakers in the second debate.

Jones, Matt B. *Thomas Maule, the Salem Quaker, and Free Speech in Massachusetts Bay. With Bibliographical Notes.* Salem, Mass., Essex Institute, 1936. 42 p. (Reprinted from *Essex Institute Historical Collections,* January 1936)　　**J 97**

Maule was the first person in the Massachusetts province to be prosecuted for the crime of libel. The importation from New York of his Quaker pamphlet, *Truth held forth and Maintained,* led to Maule's being brought before the Council and eventually the courts. While copies of his work were ordered to be burnt, by adroit reference to the current reaction to the miscarriage of justice in the witchcraft prosecutions, Maule was able to win an acquittal. During the course of his testimony, Maule shocked the court by attempting to prove that the Bible was fallible, having as many errors in it as were in his own work.

Jones, Pierre, *et al.* "Blueprint from Minnesota; the Rise and Fall of the Bill on Obscene Literature in the 1953 Minnesota Legislature." *Library Journal,* 78: 955-57, 1 June 1953.　　**J 98**

Jones, Robert W. *Journalism in the United States.* New York, Dutton, 1947. 728 p.
　　J 99

A general work on the history of American journalism, especially useful for its extensive quotations and emphasis on recent newspaper history. Chapter 44 deals with censorship in World War I and II and the operation of the Espionage Act.

————. *The Law of Journalism, Including Matters Relating to the Freedom of the Press, Libel, Contempt of Court, Property Rights in News, and Regulation of Advertising.* Brooklyn, Metropolitan Law Books, 1940. 395 p.　　**J 100**

A standard textbook including text of law and court cases. Includes a chapter on blasphemous publications.

Jones, Walter E. *Legal Problems Involved in Governmental Regulation of Radio Broadcasting.* Boulder, Colo., University of Colorado, 1939. 91 p. (Unpublished Master's thesis)　　**J 101**

Jordan, Henry D. "The British Press Inquiry." *Public Opinion Quarterly,* 11: 558-66, Winter 1947-48.　　**J 102**

A consideration of the forthcoming Royal Commission on the Press, appointed to study monopoly conditions in the British newspaper industry. The author denies that the inquiry is "the first step in a socialist attack on the freedom of the press," and believes that the only opposition will come from the extreme right.

Jordan, Wilbur K. *The Development of Religious Toleration in England.* Cambridge, Mass., Harvard University Press, 1932-40. 4 vols.　　**J 103**

This scholarly work traces the development of religious toleration from the beginning of the English Reformation to the Restoration of the Stuarts. The conflicts over freedom of the press in the realm of religion are treated throughout the work, from the persecution of William Tyndale for heresy to the action against the Levellers.

Jordan-Smith, Paul. "The Responsibility of the Literary Critic: Some Indirections for Selecting Good Books." In *Freedom of Book Selection; Procedings of the Second Conference on Intellectual Freedom.* . . . Chicago, American Library Association, 1954, pp. 75-89.　　**J 104**

Jorgensen, Emil O. *The Betrayal of Our Public Schools.* . . . Chicago, Education Protective Association of America, 1930. 31 p.　　**J 105**

The secretary of the Association addresses "an open letter to the officers of the National Education Association protesting against their action in ruling out of the schools the propaganda of the radical, liberal and reform organizations while admitting into the schools the propaganda of the 'power trust' and other special interests."

Jose, Victor. "Press Freedom Begins at Home." *Quill*, 40(9):11, 16, September 1952.   **J106**
"If small-town newspapermen can make the principle of 'official records are public records' a reality in their communities, no restrictions in Washington will stop them."

Josephson, Matthew. "The Battle of the Books." *Nation*, 174:619–24, 28 June 1952.   **J107**
Description and analysis of the mass hysteria concerning communism and the attacks by superpatriots on textbooks and book publishing, and the "intense activity in peddling the propaganda of prejudice, fear and hate." The author concludes that writers and publishers, on the whole, have not made an issue of freedom of thought versus censorship and have been meek during this crisis. Resistance has come from school principals and teachers and, particularly, members of the American Library Association.

Journalism Quarterly. Minneapolis, Association for Education in Journalism, School of Journalism, University of Minnesota, 1924-date. Quarterly.   **J108**
A journal devoted to research in journalism and mass communications, frequently containing articles on freedom of the press.

Jovanovich, William. *Now, Barabbas*. New York, Harper and Row, 1964. 228 p.   **J109**
This commentary on book publishing by a New York publisher contains a number of references to book censorship including an account of the Yugoslav interference with the American publication of the work of Milovan Djilas.

Joyce, James. "A Curious History." *Egoist*, 1:26–27, 15 January 1914.   **J110**
A letter from Ezra Pound which includes two letters from James Joyce, relating to difficulties in publication of *Dubliners* in England and Ireland. The New York publisher, B. W. Huebsch, issued the letters, written by Joyce from Trieste, in a promotional broadside, 5 May 1917.

———. [*Letter to Bennett Cerf re Publication of Ulysses*] In Modern Library edition of *Ulysses*. New York, Random House, 1934, pp. xv–xvii.   **J111**
In answer to a request from Bennett Cerf of Random House, who expressed his determination to fight for the legalization of *Ulysses* in the United States, Joyce wrote of "the history of its publication in Europe and the complications which followed it in America." This edition of *Ulysses* also includes Judge John M. Woolsey's decision lifting the ban on *Ulysses*

(1933) and a foreword by the defense council, Morris L. Ernst.

[———]. *Ulysses*. London, John Lane, 1936. 768 p.   **J112**
Appendix A contains the injunction of Joyce against Samuel Roth in the pirated edition of *Ulysses* and the international protest of authors against this unauthorized and mutilated edition. Appendix B contains a letter from Joyce to Bennett Cerf, publisher of the first American edition; the decision of Judge John M. Woolsey of the U.S. District Court, who ruled that *Ulysses* was not obscene within the meaning of the federal statutes; the decision of Judge Augustus N. Hand of the Circuit Court of Appeals, affirming the decision of the lower court; and the foreword to the Random House edition by Morris L. Ernst, counsel for the defense. The Woolsey and Hand decisions, which did much to liberate the Customs censorship in the United States are also reproduced in Downs, *The First Freedom*, pp. 83–89. Judge Curtis Bok of the Court of Quarter Sessions, Philadelphia, refers to these decisions in his own decision, *Commonwealth v. Gordon.*

Joyce, Jeremiah. *Account of Mr. Joyce's Arrest for "Treasonable Practices"; His Examination before His Majesty's Most Honourable Privy Council; His Commitment to the Tower, and Subsequent Treatment; together with Remarks on the Speeches of Mr. Windham, etc.* 2d ed. London, Printed for the Author, 1795. 30 p.   **J113**
Joyce was one of the English Jacobins, arrested and imprisoned for high treason for speaking and publishing activity in behalf of the London Corresponding Society and for alleged sympathy with the French Revolution. When Thomas Hardy, John Horne Tooke, and John Thelwall were freed by the juries in consecutive trials, the government dropped the charges against Joyce and the others.

Judge, Mark H. "Should Not the Publishing of False News Be by Law a Misdemeanor?" *Westminster Review*, 166:617–18, December 1906.   **J114**
The author believes that the offending newspaper should be punished, the first offense by a withdrawal of mailing privileges and special press telegraph rates, the second offense by stronger measures.

"Judge as a Literary Critic." *Catholic World*, 116:392–99, December 1922.   **J115**
Editorial criticizing the New York court ruling that dismissed the obscenity charges against *Satyricon*. It criticizes the demoralizing influence of the literati in defeating efforts at censorship. "A genuine Catholic needs no other censor than a Catholic conscience. But what about non-Catholic America?"

"Judge Woolsey on *Ulysses*; with Editorial Comment." *Saturday Review*, 10:352, 356, 16 December 1933.   **J116**

An account of Judge John M. Woolsey's classic decision in freeing James Joyce's *Ulysses*.

"Judges of Obscenity." *New Republic*, 145:7, 27 November 1961.   **J117**
Editorial relating to the charges brought by the police of Provincetown, Mass., against William V. Ward for publishing a story, "Tralala," in the *Provincetown Review*. The editor questions the qualifications of police and politicians to draw a line between art and pornography.

"Judgment by Television." *Columbia Journalism Review*, 3(1):45–47, Spring 1964.   **J118**
A review of steps taken toward clarifying and resolving the debate on free press and television versus fair trial, in the wake of the murder of Lee Harvey Oswald.

"Judicial Regulation of Birth Control under Obscenity Laws." *Yale Law Review*, 50:682–89, February 1941.   **J119**
Commonwealth (Mass.) v. Corbett, 29 NE (2d) 151.

Junius, *pseud. The Letters of Junius, Edited with an Introduction by C. W. Everett. . . .* London, Faber & Gwyer, 1927. 410 p. (An exact reprint of the Henry Sampson Woodfall edition of 1772. The first American edition appeared in Philadelphia in 1791)   **J120**
A series of letters appeared in Henry Woodfall's *Public Advertiser* in 1769 under the pseudonym Junius. Letter no. 35 in the issue of 19 December was openly critical of the king and his policies. The letter was reprinted in various other papers during the next few days and created a considerable stir. Five printers and one bookseller, John Almon, were charged with seditious libel. Almon was tried first, found guilty and fined. Lord Chief Justice Mansfield had charged the jury to consider only two issues: (1) whether Almon had published the paper, and (2) whether the information it contained was as described. It was for the judge, he said, to decide whether the matter was libelous. Woodfall, the original publisher, was tried next, but the jury failed to agree. Two printers were found "not guilty" and the others were apparently not brought to trial. The identity of Junius was never revealed, but speculation as to his identity embraced many prominent statesmen and writers of the time. Everett lists 44 persons to whom authorship has been attributed. The Junius prosecutions caused considerable public criticism, but it was not until 1792 that the Fox Libel Act liberalized the rights of juries in libel cases. Junius' letters contain references to libel prosecutions of Wilkes, Almon, and Woodfall, as well as Junius' views on the use of the general warrant and the right of juries in libel cases. Junius disagreed with Lord Mansfield's restrictions on the power of juries.

Junker, Howard. "Smut Hunters: The New Jurisprudery." *Nation*, 201:358–60, 15 November 1965. **J121**

A criticism of the activities of the Citizens for Decent Literature.

Jupp, Alan, and Anthony H. Newton. *Resolved: Advertising Is a Menace*. Columbia, Mo., Freedom of Information Center, School of Journalism, University of Missouri, 1961. 5 p. (Publication no. 58) **J122**

Excerpts from a debate at the University of Missouri, featuring two Oxford College students—Jupp taking the affirmative, Newton the negative.

The Juryman's Touchstone: or, A Full Refutation of Lord Mansfield's Lawless Opinion in Crown Libels, Addressed to All the Jurors of England. By the Censor General. London, T. Evans, 1771. 95 p. **J123**

The author cites laws and general grounds refuting Lord Mansfield's opinion in the Woodfall case. He argues that English juries in libel cases are competent to judge both the fact of publication and also the law.

Just, Ward S. "The Day the News Managers Quit." *Reporter*, 28:36–37, 9 May 1963. **J124**

An imaginary account of what would happen if Washington officials left news coverage entirely to the reporters.

"Justice Hugo Black on the 1st Amendment." *Editor & Publisher*, 95(24):15+, 16 June 1962. **J125**

U.S. Supreme Court Justice Hugo Black believes that the First Amendment should be interpreted literally and absolutely when it says "Congress shall make no law . . ."

Justice of the Peace, Ltd. *Obscene Publications; Being a series of articles reprinted from the "Justice of the Peace and Local Government Review."* London, Justice of the Peace, [1954?]. 21 p. **J126**

A review of some of the legal aspects of censorship in Great Britain with suggestions for alteration in existing laws.

Justitia, *pseud*. "Survival of the Inquisition." *Adult*, 2:329–30, December 1898. **J127**

The anonymous author defends Havelock Ellis' *Studies in the Psychology of Sex* in the obscenity case against George Bedborough for selling it.

K

Kacedan, Basil W. "The Right of Privacy." *Boston University Law Review*, 12:353–95, June 1932; 12:600–647, November 1932. **K1**

A history of the legal concept of the right of privacy, including unwarranted publication of letters and personal photographs. The right of privacy, early recognized as a fiction in protection of property, was given outright recognition in 1905. The author gives three remedies for violation of the right of privacy: action in tort for damages, relief by injunction, and criminal liability by statute. He opposes further legislation, favoring instead action under common law.

Kadin, Theodore. "Administrative Censorship: a Study of the Mails, Motion Pictures and Radio Broadcasting." *Boston University Law Review*, 19:533–85, November 1939. **K2**

An extensive survey of administrative censorship in the United States as indicated by cases brought before the courts. Administrative censorship is exercised in motion pictures by a "straightforward examination in advance; in radio broadcasting through a licensing system, an unacknowledged scrutiny of past conduct; in the mails, a combination of both licensing and prior review . . . Even if censorship is necessary, then the methods employed in the three fields have not been intelligently applied." Censorship of any of the media should be applied only if there is a clear social danger. Then society must ask: Will it cope with the supposed social danger? Will it destroy esthetic ends? Will it create any undesirable results?

Kahane, Jack. *Memoirs of a Booklegger.* London, M. Joseph, 1939. 287p. **K3**

Includes a history of the Obelisk Press of Paris and its experience with the censors.

Kahn, Dorothy. "Abe Goff, Our Chief Censor." *Reporter*, 12:27, 19 May 1955. **K4**

An interview with Abe Goff, solicitor of the Post Office and the federal government's chief censor. "He is also, it appears, a general arbiter of American intelligence and literacy." The legal basis for banning foreign publications

(examples are given) is a letter written by the Attorney General in 1940 stating his opinion that the Foreign Agents Registration Act of 1938 could be used as a basis for excluding mail from abroad if the sender had not registered as a foreign agent.

Kahn, E. J., Jr. "The Wayward Press." *New Yorker*, 26:109–24, 15 April 1950. **K5**

Deals with newspaper coverage of the libel case instituted by Larry Adler and Paul Draper, musician and dancer respectively, against Mrs. John T. McCullough.

"Kahn, Morgan, and *Salome.*" *Saturday Review*, 47(22):60, 30 May 1964. **K6**

Previously unpublished letter from Otto H. Kahn to Richard Strauss (29 May 1908) charging J. P. Morgan as the one responsible for banning Strauss's *Salome* from the New York Metropolitan Opera after a single performance in 1907.

Kallen, Horace M. "Blasphemy." In *Encyclopaedia of the Social Sciences.* New York, Macmillan, 1930–35. vol. 2, pp. 586–88. **K7**

A history of the concept of blasphemy as an offense subject to prosecution by civil authorities.

———. "Censorship, or the Ethos of Procrustes." *Gazette des Beaux-Arts*, 28 (ser. 6):23–24+, July 1945. **K8**

A chapter in a lengthy article entitled Freedom and the Artist. Other chapters are: The Experience of Freedom; Freedom and Society; The Economy of Free Thought; Criteria of Freedom; Freedom of the Artist; Technique, Tradition, and Freedom; Ethos and the Freedom of Art; The Freedom of the Artist Depends on Free Communication; and Free Art and Free Society Are Interdependent. "That this identification of private expression with public meanings which we call ethos must be spontaneous and uncoerced is just as true for authoritarian as for free societies. The endeavor to impose identity, to make conformation coercive is, however, institutional and seems as inveterate as art itself. We call it censorship. It consists in procrustean

prescriptions of what shall be expressed and how it shall not be expressed. It is dictatorship over the content and methods of the arts, and it is effective dictatorship in the degree that the censors have power to control the media of communication. . . . The liberty of the artist is the avatar of all the liberties of man. It subdues all discipline. It diversifies all doctrine . . . Where the artists keep free, no other sort or condition of man long remains bond."

———. "Fear, Freedom, and Massachusetts." *American Mercury*, 18:281–92, November 1929. **K9**

Philosophical insight into political freedom, with a review of the conflict in Massachusetts, particularly Boston, between the native post-Puritan and the Catholic descendents of Irish immigrants, resulting in a "paranoiac condition."

———. *Indecency and the Seven Arts.* New York, Liveright, 1930. 246p. **K10**

A series of essays and lectures dealing with literary criticism and censorship, of which the first two are particularly pertinent to freedom of the press: Indecency and the Seven Arts; and The Censor, the Psychologist, and the Motion Picture.

———. "Protean Censorship." *Freeman*, 3:370–72, 29 June 1921. **K11**

Deals with the suppression of James B. Cabell's *Jurgen.*

———, ed. *Freedom in the Modern World.* New York, Coward-McCann, 1928. 304p. **K12**

A series of lectures given at the New School for Social Research, including How a Catholic Looks at Freedom by Rev. J. A. Ryan, The Protestant View of Freedom by F. J. Foakes-Jackson, Liberty and the Law by Zechariah Chafee, Jr., Freedom of Speech, Conscience and the Press by S. Bent, and Freedom in the Fine Arts by R. M. Lovett.

Kallgren, Edward E. "Group Libel." *California Law Review*, 41:290–99, Summer 1953. **K13**

Notes on cases of group libel in the American courts, 1890–1952.

Kalven, Harry, Jr. "Metaphysics of the Law of Obscenity." In *The Supreme Court Review, 1960*. Chicago, University of Chicago Press, 1961, pp. 1–45.　**K 14**
The purpose of the article is to examine some of the recent decisions of the U.S. Supreme Court relating to obscenity to see how it has resolved the perplexities inherent in the problem and what issues remain. Constitutional problems are of two kinds: the first revolves around the ambiguity of the meaning of the term "obscene"; the second relates to the interpretation of the clear-and-present-danger test. Obscenity legislation has considered four possible dangers, "(1) the incitement to anti-social sexual conduct; (2) psychological excitement resulting from sexual imagery; (3) the arousing of feelings of disgust and revulsion; and (4) the advocacy of improper sexual values." The author analyzes five cases, *Butler v. Michigan*, 352 U.S. 380 (1957); the two cases decided together, *People v. Alberts* and *United States v. Roth*, 354 U.S. 476 (1956); *Kingsley Pictures Corp. v. Regents*, 360 U.S. 684 (1959); and *Smith v. California*, 361 U.S. 147 (1959). The author concludes with three observations on the difficulties of the task. First, the topic of obscenity is fraught with "all the anxieties and hypocrisies of society's attitude toward sex." Second, the matter comes "close to major doctrine about free speech and free press." Third, decisions are made in an institutional context that necessarily raises many issues relating to the function and role of the court. In a footnote the author suggests four possible judicial roles in obscenity cases: urbane resignation, irreverent amusement, uncompromising concern for free speech, and "the role of the responsible man of affairs who feels that there are limits to what the public will tolerate."

———. "The *New York Times* Case: A Note on 'The Central Meaning of the First Amendment.'" In *Supreme Court Review, 1964*. Chicago, University of Chicago Press, 1964, pp. 191–221.　**K 15**
Relates to the U.S. Supreme Court decision in *New York Times Co. v. Sullivan*, in which the Court unanimously held that a libel judgment rendered under Alabama law was violative of First Amendment principles. "In brief compass, my thesis is that the Court, compelled by the political realities of the case to decide it in favor of the *Times*, yet equally compelled to seek high ground in justifying its results, wrote an opinion that may prove to be the best and most important it has ever produced in the realm of freedom of speech." The author concludes that the decision offers the Court an "invitation to follow a dialectic progression from public official to government policy to public policy to matters in the public domain . . . If the Court accepts the invitation, it will slowly work out for itself the theory of free speech that Alexander Meiklejohn has been offering us for some fifteen years now."

———. "Obscenity and the Law." *Library Quarterly*, 27:201–8, July 1957.　**K 16**
A review of two works on the legal aspects of obscenity: the book *Obscenity and the Law* by Norman St. John-Stevas and the personalized essay by Judge Jerome Frank, issued as an appendix to his opinion in *United States v. Roth*.

Kansas. State Board of Review (Moving Pictures). *Publications*. Topeka, The Board, 1917+.　**K 17**
In 1913 Kansas adopted a state censorship law, creating a Moving Picture Censorship Appeal Commission. The law was declared constitutional by the U.S. Supreme Court in 1915. This agency was replaced in 1917 by the Kansas State Board of Review, which has continued to disapprove films that are "cruel, obscene, indecent or immoral, or such as tend to debase or corrupt morals." Publications of the Board have included *A Complete List of Motion Picture Films Presented to the Kansas State Board of Review for Censorship* (1917–41; numbered reports irregularly issued, later ones annually); monthly mimeographed reports (1942–52); *Biennial Reports* to the Governor, beginning in 1920.

Kansas. University. The Library. *An Exhibition of books which have survived Fire, the Sword and the Censors*. Lawrence, Kan., The University Library, 1955. 28 p.　**K 18**
A list of 150 banned books with informative annotations describing the cause and occasion for banning, compiled by Joseph Rubinstein and Earl Farley. A traveling exhibit of 33 of the books was made available to other libraries.

Kansas Library Association. Intellectual Freedom Committee. "Price of Liberty." *Wilson Library Bulletin*, 36:392–93, January 1962.　**K 19**
A statement on the defense of the freedom to read, with practical suggestions to Kansas librarians on how to meet would-be censors.

Kaplan, Abraham. "Obscenity as an Esthetic Category." *Law and Contemporary Problems*, 20:544–59, Autumn 1955.　**K 20**
The author, in his discussion of the philosophy of art, considers the questions: "Can a work of art be obscene and still be esthetic in status and function? What part, if any, does the obscene play in the esthetic experience? What characteristics of the art object mark its occurrence?" He identifies several species of the obscene: *conventional obscenity*, the quality of a work which attacks accepted standards of sexual behavior (Zola, Ibsen, Shaw); *Dionysian obscenity*, consisting of excessive sexualism, expressing an exuberant delight in sexual pleasures (Aristophanes, Boccaccio, Rabelais), and *the obscene of the perverse*, a calculated indecency or sex for the sake of dirt (Huysmans, de Sade).

Kassner, Minna F. "Radio Censorship." *Air Law Review*, 8:99–111, April 1937.

(Excerpted in Summers, *Radio Censorship*, pp. 183–90)　**K 21**
An examination of both official censorship, practiced by the Federal Communications Commission, and so-called "editorial selection," practiced by commercial broadcasters and generally known as "private censorship." The author recommends changes in the Radio Act and the passage of bills sponsored by the American Civil Liberties Union requiring stations to give greater attention to the "public interest."

———, and Lucien Zackaroff. *Radio Is Censored! A Study of Cases Prepared to Show the Need of Federal Legislation for Freedom of the Air*. New York, American Civil Liberties Union, 1936. 56 p.　**K 22**
In support of federal legislation for greater freedom of the air, the authors present 25 typical cases of local station censorship. The pamphlet is prefaced by a description of how radio censorship works in such areas as politics, minorities, labor, special interests, race, birth control, and humor. Legislation supported by the ACLU would require stations to set aside daily a regular period of choice time for discussion of economic, social, and political issues; to present at least one opposing view on a controversial issue. The legislation would free the station, not the speaker, from legal liability; would require stations to keep a record of requests for time—those granted and those denied.

Kasson, Constantine D. "Constitutional Law—Due Process—Freedom of Expression—Moving Picture Censorship." *Michigan Law Review*, 52:599–602, February 1954.　**K 23**
Consideration of the film censorship case, *Burstyn v. Wilson*, and related cases that have come before the U.S. Supreme Court.

Katz, Daniel. "Psychological Barriers to Communication." *Annals of the American Academy of Political and Social Science*, 250:17–25, March 1947.　**K 24**
"Physical barriers to communications are rapidly disappearing, but the psychological obstacles remain. These psychological difficulties are in part a function of the very nature of language; in part they are due to the emotional character and mental limitations of human beings." Specifically, the author mentions (1) the failure to refer language to experience and reality, (2) the inability to transcend personal experience in intergroup communication, (3) stereotypes, and (4) the confusion of percept and concept.

Kauffmann, Reginald W. "The News Embargo." *North American Review*, 208:831–41, December 1918.　**K 25**
A scathing criticism of American military censorship in World War I, by an American overseas correspondent. He recommends that censorship boards be composed of educated civilians under a civilian head answerable not

to any detective (Army Secret Service), general, or to any member of the Cabinet, but to Congress. While giving the Army the credit that it is due and keeping secret military information from the enemy, censorship should give the American public legitimate news of its fighting men.

Kauffmann, Stanley. "God's Belittled Acre." *New Republic*, 138:21, 30 June 1958. **K 26**

Objections to censorship of the movie version of Erskine Caldwell's book, although the author himself is quoted as having no disagreement with the production.

————. "*Lady Chatterley* at Last." *New Republic*, 140:13–16, 25 May 1959. **K 27**
The challenge to the obscenity laws by the publication for the first time in America of the unexpurgated edition of D. H. Lawrence's *Lady Chatterley's Lover* by Grove Press. The obscenity laws in America have been geared to the level of the weakest members of society. "Is it not madness," Kauffmann writes, "to abolish freedom because some would abuse it?" The greatest support of the censor comes from the "liberal" who believes in freedom only for serious literature, but would ban trash. "Suppose there are people who want to read trash? What about their civil liberties?" He criticizes the defenders of *Lady Chatterley* who deny that the work is sexually stimulating, suggesting that, if it were, the work could not be defended.

————. *The Philanderer*. 2d ed. London, Secker & Warburg, 1954. 300 p. **K 28**
This edition of Kauffmann's novel contains a summing up of the decision of Justice Stable in the British court (Central Criminal Court, 2 July 1954). The Court recommended that the 1868 Cockburn test of obscenity be interpreted in the light of modern standards. The publishers were found not guilty.

Kaufman, Paul. "A 'Revoluntionary' Edition of the *Areopagitica*." *AmericaneNotes & Queries*, 2:116–18, April 1964. **K 29**
Notes on a forgotten edition of Milton's *Areopagetica*, published by James Losh in 1791. This was three years after Mirabeau (1788) published his French *Sur la liberté de la Presse*, based on Milton's work.

Kauper, Paul G. "Censorship: Protecting the Public Morals." In his *Civil Liberties and the Constitution*. Ann Arbor, University of Michigan Press, 1962, pp. 52–89. **K 30**

An essay by an American legal scholar.

Kavados, Thomas, Jr., and John R. Martzell. "Free Speech—City Ordinance Requiring Motion Pictures to Be Censored Prior to Public Exhibition Not Invalid as Violation of First Amendment." *Notre Dame Lawyer*, 36:406–10, May 1961. **K 31**

Times Film Corp. v. City of Chicago, 81 S. Ct. 391 (1961).

Kayser, Jacques. *Mort d'une Liberté-Techniques et Politique de l'Information*. Paris, Librarie Plan, 1955. 338 p. **K 32**
A monograph on freedom of the press with special reference to the United States and the Soviet Union.

Kazan, Elia. "Pressure Problem. Director Discusses Cuts Compelled in *A Streetcar Named Desire*." *New York Times*, 21 October 1951, sect. 2, p. 5. **K 33**

[Keach, Benjamin]. "The Trial of Mr. Benjamin Keach, at the Assizes at Aylsbury, in Buckinghamshire, for a Libel, 1665." In Howell, *State Trials*, vol. 6, pp. 702–10, and in *A Collection of the Most Remarkable and Interesting Trials* ... London, R. Snagg, 1775. vol. 1, pp. 211–17. (Also reported in Schroeder, *Constitutional Free Speech*, pp. 282–85) **K 34**
Keach, a minister of the Armenian Baptists, was arrested and tried in 1664 for expressing doctrines on infant baptism and other matters contrary to the Church of England in his *The Child's Instructor; or, A New and Easy Primmer*. Keach was fined, sentenced to a fortnight in prison, pilloried, and his book was burned before his eyes.

Kearney, Patrick. "Taboos of the Vice Agents." *Freeman*, 1:542–43, 18 August 1920. **K 35**
The author criticizes various acts of sex censorship by the vice societies, including the suppression of Freud's *Leonardo da Vinci*.

Keating, Charles H., Jr. *Typical CDL Talk*. [Cincinnati, Committee for Decent Literature, n. d.] 9 p. **K 36**
Information on the pornography traffic in the United States, its dangers, and the way in which a Citizens for Decent Literature group can take action against the traffic. Intended for use in local campaigns against pornography.

Keating, Joseph. "Civil Censorship: Theory and Practice." *Month* (London), 159:239–49, March 1932. **K 37**
A defense of film censorship and a criticism of the inadequate and clumsy supervision exerted by the British Board of Film Censors. It is the duty of the community to guide the moral character of its people. "For civilization is not properly measured by the development of the arts, or of the comforts and amenities of life, although these things accompany its growth, but by the taming of the beast in man, the restoration of reason to its throne, the development of his power to recognize truth, to love good, to appreciate beauty." The State (Britain) no longer has a clear and definite moral standard of its own, having

gotten rid of it along with the Catholic faith in the Protestant Reformation. The author praises the strong hand of Mussolini in removing filth from Italy. He praises Ireland's censorship of films and books. England should emulate this censorship, but Protestants are not likely to support it.

Keeler, Charles C. "Taxes upon Advertising Media." *Villanova Law Review*, 4:442–45, Spring 1959. **K 38**
Notes on the case, *Baltimore v. A. S. Abell*, in which the Maryland courts (1958) declared unconstitutional a Baltimore city tax upon purchasers and sellers of certain advertising.

Keen, Harold. "Wave of Censorship ... or Persecution?" *San Diego*, 17:72, 98, June 1965. **K 39**

"Keeping Out German Newspapers." *Nation*, 106:670–71, 8 June 1918. **K 40**
Editorial criticism of the policy whereby German newspapers are handled through the British government, which will not allow any to come to the United States except those destined for the federal government.

Keeton, G. W. "The Tercentenary of the *Areopagitica*." *Contemporary Review*, 166:280–86, November 1944. **K 41**
"The problems with which [Milton] grappled so courageously three centuries ago are to-day living issues for each one of us, for personal freedom and freedom of thought are rights which must be vindicated afresh in each successive century."

Kefauver, Estes. "Obscene and Pornographic Literature." *Federal Probation*, 24(4):3–12, December 1960. **K 42**
Senator Kefauver reviews a Senate subcommittee's investigations of the pornography racket in the United States. He calls for greater research by the behavioral scientists in "the effect of visual and auditory stimuli on overt behavior." This information is needed in solving the problems of obscenity.

Kegler, Stanley B., and Stephen Dunning. "A Minority Report on Censorship." *English Journal*, 51:667–68, December 1962. **K 43**
The authors examine cases of book censorship of the previous year, concluding that many cases of school censorship might have been avoided if teachers had worked constantly to bring together "the right books for the right child at the right time."

[Keith, George, *et al.*]. *New England's Spirit of Persecution Transmitted to Pennsilvania, and the Pretended Quaker found Persecuting the True Christian-Quaker, In* the *Tryal of Peter Boss, George Keith, Thomas Budd and William Bradford At the Sessions held at Philadelphia the Nineth, Tenth and Twelfth Days of December, 1692 . . . Giving an Account of the most Arbitrary Procedure of that Court.* [New York], printed by William Bradford, 1693. 38 p.　**K 44**

A theological quarrel among the Quakers resulted in the arrest and imprisonment of several Quakers and their printer, William Bradford, for publishing an account of unorthodox religious views. The charge was "sedition," but the jury failed to agree and the case was dismissed. Bradford's press was seized by the court and he had difficulty in getting it returned. The principle that the jury should decide the law as well as the fact of publication was established by this Philadelphia trial for seditious libel. In the *First Year of Printing in New York*, 1928, Eames writes: "This seems to be the joint production of George Keith and Thomas Budd, including Bradford's own account of the trial."

Keller, Joseph E. *Federal Control of Defamation by Radio.* Washington, D.C., Georgetown University, 1935. 109 p. (Unpublished J. D. dissertation)　**K 45**

Kellerman, Dana F. *Censorship of the Northern Press during the Civil War.* Urbana, Ill., University of Illinois, 1960. 130 p. (Unpublished Master's thesis)　**K 46**

Kelley, D. O. "Librarians and Proposed Legislation Relating to Obscenity." *New Mexico Library Bulletin*, 28:2–4, January 1959.　**K 47**

Kellock, Harold. *Freedom of Communications.* Washington, D.C., Editorial Research Reports, 1944. (*Editorial Research Reports*, 1(12):1–14, 1944)　**K 48**

A discussion of the proposal of the Federal Communications Commission for merger of American companies that provide overseas radio and cable service and the effect of such a merger on freedom of the press.

Kelly, Frank K. *Citizens' Commission Proposed.* Columbia, Mo., Freedom of Information Center, School of Journalism, University of Missouri, 1960. 4 p. (Publication no. 34)　**K 49**

In a talk before the Freedom of Information [Study] Group of Southern California, the vice-president of the Fund for the Republic endorses a National Citizens Advisory Board for Radio and Television.

———. *Communication in a Free Society.* Columbia, Mo., Freedom of Information

Center, School of Journalism, University of Missouri, 1961. 6 p. (Publication no. 57)　**K 50**

The author discusses the status of American mass communication, endorsing William Benton's proposal for a national Citizens Advisory Board for Radio and Television.

———. "The Press on Censorship." *Nieman Reports*, 8(2):33–34, April 1954.　**K 51**

A consultant, American Book Publishers Council, reports on news coverage and editorial comment on its review of censorship in the United States.

Kelly, Gerald, and John C. Ford. "The Legion of Decency." *Theological Studies*, 18:387–433, September 1957.　**K 52**

"The main purpose is . . . to give more information about the Legion than is usually available to theologians, so that some of the more practical of the moral problems can be reasonably discussed, if not perfectly solved."

Kelly, John. "Criminal Libel and Free Speech." *Kansas Law Review*, 6:295–333, March 1958.　**K 53**

"This article will outline briefly the history of criminal libel in England and the United States, concentrating on the modifications of the early law engendered by the American Revolution and the subsequent Constitutional declarations of freedom of speech and press. Then something of the present theory and practice will be discussed, and, in conclusion, the history and theory treated will be applied to an analysis of the decision in *Beauharnais v. Illinois*, the most recent and significant Supreme Court decision regarding criminal libel."

Kelly, Richard J. *The Law of Newspaper Libel. With Special Reference to the State of the Law as Defined by the Law of Libel Amendment Act of 1888.* London, Clowes, 1889. 258 p.　**K 54**

———. "Liberty of the Press in America, Germany and France." *Irish Law Times*, 30:432–34, 26 September 1896.　**K 55**

A history and comparison of the state of press freedom in the three countries, read before the Institute of Journalists, Belfast.

Kem, James P. "Senator Asks Showdown on Federal Information." *Quill*, 40(2):11, February 1952.　**K 56**

Not only the press, but Congress, is hampered by censorship in the guise of national security. A Missouri senator criticizes President Truman's order restricting release of government information.

Kemler, Edgar. *The Irreverant Mr. Mencken.* Boston, Little, Brown, 1950. 317 p.　**K 57**

A biography of one of America's most militant

foes of censorship, particularly in the realm of sex. Chapter 6 deals with Mencken's part in the defense of Dreiser; chapter 9 discusses The Battle of the Books that took place in America during the 1920's; and chapter 13 covers the famous "Hatrack" case in which Mencken sold a copy of his *American Mercury* on the Boston Common in defiance of the Watch and Ward Society.

Kempton, Murray. "Impurities in Yorkville: With Pornography One Thing Leads to Another." *New Republic*, 148: 13–15, 16 March 1963.　**K 58**

A campaign against pornography in Manhattan's East Side, led by Father Morton Hill of St. Ignatius Loyola Catholic Church.

Kennan, George. "The Associated Press: A Defense." *Outlook*, 107:240, 249–50, 30 May 1914.　**K 59**

A defense of the practices of the Associated Press, particularly of its rules "not to contradict any statement for which the Associated Press itself was not responsible," and not to give competing organizations the news of their own localities. A criticism of the AP by Gregory Mason appears in the same issue.

Kennan, George F. "No Concessions . . ." *ALA Bulletin*, 47:470, November 1953.　**K 60**

"In my opinion, NO concessions ought to be made to the prevailing hysteria, and a library should carry in a normal way, and with no distinctions other than those indicated by normal functional considerations, any material of communist origin which fits naturally with the library's purpose and the general nature of its holdings." From a letter written by the former ambassador to Russia to William S. Dix, chairman, ALA Intellectual Freedom Committee.

Kennan, Richard B. "Freedom of Selection for School Libraries—The Lesser Risk." *ALA Bulletin*, 47:461–62, November 1953.　**K 61**

The author is secretary of the National Commission for the Defense of Democracy through Education. He deplores the atmosphere of fear and suspicion that has been responsible in some instances for the "drying up of the well springs." He cites and quotes from these important statements on freedom: The Public School and the American Heritage, endorsed by ten education organizations; the NEA resolution on freedom of thought and expression; and the Scarsdale, N.Y., statement in support of the freedom to read.

———, *et al.* "Censorship as Seen by Other Groups." *ALA Bulletin*, 59:523–30, June 1965. (ALA Conference on Intellectual Freedom, 23–24 January 1965)　**K 62**

Statements by Richard B. Kennan, NEA's Commission on Professional Rights and Responsibilities; Enid M. Olson, National Council of Teachers of English; Robert

F. Lucid, American Studies Association; Charles E. Reid, American Library Trustees Association; Harold F. Flanders, New Jersey Committee for the Right to Read; Nancy Baker, Freedom of Information Center, University of Missouri; and Peter Jennison, National Book Committee.

Kennedy, Crammond. *The Liberty of the Press; Its Uses and Abuses. An Essay.* Washington, D.C., 1887. 23 p. (Reprinted from the *Christian Union*) **K 63**
A prize-winning essay, first published in 1876, giving a brief history of the development of freedom of the press in England and the United States. The abuses of the present day are: inaccurate and unauthenticated news-gathering, publishing of gossip rather than facts, coloring and distorting of news, public defamation of character, and journalistic blackmail. The press is shorn of its real power by the abuse of liberty.

Kennedy, Edward. "I'd Do It Again." *Atlantic Monthly*, 182:36–41, August 1948. **K 64**
An answer by the former chief of the Paris Bureau of the Associated Press to critics who claimed he violated SHAEF's release agreement when he filed the first bulletin to reach American readers with news of Germany's capitulation, May 1945. His account gives details of the signing of the Peace at Reims and his reasons for breaking the 24-hour "hold" on the release of the news.

Kennedy, Gerald. ["Censorship"] *Together*, 7(10):58–59, October 1963. **K 65**
In his column, Browsing in Fiction, a bishop of the Methodist Church criticizes the efforts of self-appointed groups of citizens to put pressure upon librarians and booksellers to ban books. The occasion for the article is the demands in California for the ban of the *Dictionary of American Slang* on grounds of obscenity. There is a censorship mentality which "usually springs from an unhealthy attitude toward life and indicates an abnormal interest in anything that has to do with sex." Children go through a period of seeking out sex words in such books as Shakespeare and the Bible, but most of them outgrow it. While recognizing the right of individuals to object to any particular book, Bishop Kennedy believes that censorship should be left to the courts. Words can be dangerous weapons and they can corrupt as well as redeem, but "you must . . . commit yourself either to the general principle of liberty or of censorship, and there is no such thing as a little censorship."

Kennedy, J. S. "Attitude Toward the *Index*." *Catholic Mind*, 52:623–25, October 1954. **K 66**
Relates to the *Index of Forbidden Books* of the Catholic Church.

Kennedy, John F. [Statement on Freedom to Read]. In "The Candidates and the Arts." *Saturday Review*, 43(44):43–44, 29 October 1960. **K 67**
In answer to a request of the two candidates for President to comment on government support of the arts, Mr. Kennedy stated in part: "American libraries should be open to all—except the censor. We must know all the facts and hear all the alternatives and listen to all the criticisms. Let us welcome controversial books and controversial authors. For the Bill of Rights is the guardian of our security as well as our liberty."

Kennedy, Ludovic. "Letters to Master Thompson." *Spectator*, 212:35–56, 10 January 1964. **K 68**
The author recounts his unsuccessful efforts to get access to the transcript of the trial of Stephen Ward, for use in writing a book on the trial. Who are the judges, he asks, to decide what books shall or shall not be encouraged.

Kennedy, M. D. "This Freedom of the Press; The Great Illusion." *Nineteenth Century*, 122:166–78, August 1937. **K 69**
The article deals with "the craze for sensationalism in reporting foreign news and the way it affects the foreign news correspondents . . . Under cover of 'freedom of the press' there is a great deal of high-handed action on the part of editors and managers which is the reverse of true freedom."

Kennedy, Renwick C. "Alabama Book-Toasters." *Christian Century*, 71:428–29, 7 April 1954. (Reprinted in Downs, *The First Freedom*, pp. 375–77) **K 70**
A Presbyterian minister writes of the Alabama "poison label" law which required that every book used in schools and colleges of the state be labeled as to whether or not its author is an advocate of communism or socialism. He recounts the amusing and ridiculous situations that the law presented for publishers, librarians, and school administrators. The *Montgomery Advertiser* dubbed supporters of the bill "one degree removed from a book-burner—which, we suppose, is a book-toaster."

Kennedy, Robert E. "How Much Freedom for Student Editors?" *Masthead*, 9(4):9–12, Fall 1957. **K 71**
An editor of the Chicago *Sun-Times* maintains that while it is healthy for student editors to battle out issues of freedom of expression with college officials, "they have no more 'right' to insist on their views prevailing over that of the 'publisher' than have those of us who earn our living in journalism."

Kennedy, Robert P. "Right to Privacy in the Name, Reputation and Personality of a Deceased Relative." *Notre Dame Lawyer*, 40:324–29, April 1965. **K 72**
The author finds that no strong case has been made in court decisions for or against the recognition of this relational right. "Recognition of this relational right would protect

against crass invasions of privacy which are becoming frequent in these days when radio, television, motion pictures, newspapers and magazines intrude into our lives."

Kennedy, William S. *The Fight of a Book for the World* . . . West Yarmouth, Mass., Stonecraft Press, 1926. 304 p. **K 73**
An account of the reception of Walt Whitman's *Leaves of Grass*, including the suppression of the Osgood edition in Boston. Further references to the suppression are contained in Kennedy's *Reminiscences of Walt Whitman*.

———. "Suppressing a Poet." *Conservator*, 5:169–71, January 1895. **K 74**
An account of the suppression of Walt Whitman's *Leaves of Grass* in Boston and the writer's experience in ferreting out the instigator of the action, the New England Society for the Suppression of Vice.

Kenner, Hurnard I. *The Fight for Truth in Advertising; a Story of What Business Has Done and Is Doing to Establish and Maintain Accuracy and Fair Play in Advertising and Selling for the Public's Protection.* New York, Round Table Press, 1936. 298 p. (Sponsored by the Advertising Federation of America) **K 75**

Kenney, Louis A. "Censorship." *Illinois Libraries*, 41:327–36, May 1959. **K 76**
The first part of the article identifies the groups who are exerting censorship pressures on American libraries. The second part deals with examples of modern censorship carried to an extreme in Nazi Germany.

———. "Censorship." *Ontario Library Review*, 43:222–24, August 1959. **K 77**

Kenny, James. "Correspondents in Eire Couldn't Say 'Boo.'" *Saturday Night*, 60:11, 16 June 1945. **K 78**
"Many strange things were suppressed by the war censorship in Eire. News that Ginger Rogers had become engaged to an American marine was taboo for Eirann newspapers. Correspondents couldn't write about a German parachutist who was at large in the country even though his photograph was displayed prominently outside every civic guard station."

Kent, C. B. R. *The English Radicals; an Historical Sketch.* London Longmans, 1899. 451 p. **K 79**
This history of the radical movement in England, from 1761 through the Chartist period, includes accounts of the thinking and activities of many crusaders for freedom of the press. Included in the early period (1761–89) are John Wilkes and his *North Briton*,

John Horne Tooke, and Major Cartwright. Included in the second period (1789–1831) that reflected the French Revolution are Thomas Paine, Thomas Hardy and others in the state sedition trials; John Thelwall, Richard Carlile, William Cobbett, Thomas Wooler and his *Black Dwarf*, John and Leigh Hunt and their *Examiner*, Jeremy Bentham, Francis Place, and James Mill. The last three were active in the fight against "taxes on knowledge."

Kent, Frank R. "Filth on Main Street." *Independent*, 114:686–89, 20 June 1925. (Reprinted in Beman, *Selected Articles on Censorship*, pp. 425–31) **K 80**
On a recent tour of the United States the author became concerned about the stream of "pornographic periodicals and dirty fiction magazines" which has been flooding the newsstands. He is concerned with the social implications of pornography, but believes that censorship is not the answer since such efforts are "nearly always futile, often worse."

——— "Lurid Literature in the United States." *Spectator*, 135:9–10, 4 July 1925. **K 81**
An American journalist writes that the abundance of lurid sex magazines on the American newsstands takes "the lead in luridness" away from France. He refers to such pulps as *Hot Dog*, *Red Pepper*, and *Whiz Bang*.

Kent, James. *Commentaries on American Law*. 14th ed. Edited by John M. Gould. Boston, Little, Brown, 1896. 2 vols. (First published in four volumes, 1826–30) **K 82**
Lecture 24, section 2 (vol. 2) deals with the rights of persons with respect to slander and libels. Numerous cases are cited, beginning with the colonial courts, as evidence of the development of the law of libel in the United States. Kent was a noted justice of the New York Supreme Court and his *Commentaries* were as influential in America as those of Blackstone in England.

Kenyon, George T. *The Life of Lloyd, First Lord Kenyon, Lord Chief Justice of England*. London, Longmans Green 1873. 403 p. **K 83**
A sympathetic biography of the justice who, in the last decade of the eighteenth century, sat in judgment at the sedition trials of Cuthill, Stockdale, Williams, and others. His strict, legalistic interpretation was later tempered by enactment of the Fox Libel Law.

Kerby, Phil. "How Free Is The Free Press?" *Nieman Reports*, 6(4):21–23, October 1952. **K 84**

An exposé of the biased and irresponsible coverage of news by large segments of the press—freedom without responsibility.

Kerr, Charles. "Shall We Have a Free Press?" *Outlook*, 121:18–19, 1 January 1919. **K 85**
The author is concerned with the right of the press to discuss public questions and to lead in solving questions of reconstruction following the war. He reviews the history of the John Peter Zenger case, with a quotation from the speech of Andrew Hamilton.

Kerr, Dora F. "Conversion of Mrs. Grundy." *Adult*, 2:96–101, May 1898. **K 86**
A lecture before the Legitimation League opposing sex-censorship.

Kerr, James M. "Criminal Libel, Libeling a Class." *Central Law Journal*, 86:334–38, 10 May 1918. **K 87**
Recommends use of criminal libel laws to throttle the "vicious elements which are threatening the government and civilization itself," including anarchists, Bolsheviki, Socialists, and the IWW.

———. "*World* Libel." *Central Law Journal*, 68:253–54, 2 April 1909. **K 88**
Correspondence on the prosecution of certain publishers by the federal government in the Panama Canal case.

Kerr, Walter. *Criticism and Censorship*. Milwaukee, Bruce, 1954. 86 p. (Gabriel Richard Lecture, cosponsored by the National Catholic Educational Association and Trinity College, Washington. D.C.) **K 89**
The drama critic of the New York *Herald Tribune* discusses the age-old conflict between "the critic who is passionately devoted to the arts and the censor who is worried about the possible indiscretions of the arts," a conflict yet unresolved. Favorably reviewed by Charles Donahue in *Commonweal*, 26 April 1957.

Kerwin, Jerome G. *The Control of Radio*. Chicago, University of Chicago Press, 1934. 27 p. **K 90**
A brief review of the early history of radio including the Radio Act of 1927, with comparisons between control in the United States and other countries.

Ketch, John. *The Speech of John Ketch, Esq., at the Burning of a Late Scandalous and Malicious Preface . . .* London, 1712. Broadside. **K 91**
Ketch was chief executioner under James II. He presided over the destruction of books as well as persons.

Keup, Erwin J. "Obscenity Not Within the Area of Constitutionally Protected Speech or Press." *Marquette Law Review*, 41:320–28, Winter 1957–58. **K 92**
Notes on the U.S. Supreme Court decision in *Roth v. United States* and earlier obscenity cases.

Keyhoe, Donald E. "U.S. Air Force Censorship of the UFO Sightings." *True*, 332:38–41, 84–86, January 1965. **K 93**
A retired Marine Corps major charges the Air Force with suppression of information on unidentified flying objects ("flying saucers"). A comprehensive *Report on Unidentified Flying Objects* by Edward J. Ruppelt, former head of the Air Force Project Blue Book, published by Doubleday in 1956, reviews the considerable literature on the subject of the UFO.

Kidd, Ronald. "Censorship of Films." *New Statesman and Nation*, 9:170–71, 9 February 1935. **K 94**
The author finds that British film-licensing agents have exceeded their authority by performing censorship under the Cinematograph Act of 1909 which was intended as a fire safety protection against inflammable films.

———. *Fight for a Free Press*. London, National Council for Civil Liberties, 1942. 20 p. (Historic Struggles for Liberty, no. 1) **K 95**
A popularly written history of the development of a free press—the licensing act, "taxes on knowledge," reporting the proceedings of Parliament, the British state trials during the period of the French Revolution, the cases of William Cobbett, John Wilkes, Richard Carlile, and wartime controls.

Kidgell, John. *A Genuine and Succinct Narrative of A Scandalous, obscene, and exceedingly profane Libel, entitled, An Essay on Woman, as also, of Other Poetical Pieces, containing The most atrocious Blasphemies. Submitted to the Candor of the Public . . .* London, Printed for James Robson and J. Wilkie, [1763]. 16 p. (Reprinted in Wilkes, *Essay on Woman*. London, 1871, pp. 201–8; also reported in *Gentleman's Magazine*, November 1763) **K 96**
Kidgell, a dissolute clergyman and chaplain to the Earl of March and Ruglen, managed to get hold of a copy of John Wilkes's obscene parody, *An Essay on Woman*, never intended for publication. Feigning shock at Wilkes's poem, he reveals it to the public in this pamphlet, describing the blasphemies in detail but taking care to avoid the actual words. Kidgell took the offensive poem to the Earl, who assured his chaplain that proper measures would be taken "for the Discovery and Punishment of so avowed an Enemy of Society." Each copy of this folio pamphlet is personally inscribed by the author, "To The violated Laws, The abused Liberty, and the Insulted Religion of our Country." The Rev. Mr. Kidgell figured in the Wilkes trial.

Kiley, Roger J. "Let Me Alone!" *Books on Trial*, 15:57–58, 97–100, October 1956.
K 97
An Illinois Appellate Court judge discusses the right of privacy and its violation in modern times by personal exposé in books and magazines.

———. "Obscenity in Literature." *Critic*, 16(2):11–12, 57–58, October 1957. **K 98**
A brief history of the "three hundred year war" carried on between those representing extreme views in matters of obscenity—the literati and the censors.

———. "That's Libel! But Is It?" *Critic*, 17(4):15–16, 86–88, February-March 1959. **K 99**
A judge discusses the many complexities of the modern law of libel as interpreted by court decisions.

Kilgore, Bernard. "Press Freedom of a Sort Is Not Enough." *Quill*, 50(1):12–13, January 1962. **K 100**
The president of the *Wall Street Journal*, on receipt of the tenth annual Lovejoy Award at Colby College, states that freedom of the press is simply a right to own a printing press and to use it to comment on public affairs. It has nothing to do with quality of news, ethics of journalism, the right of the people as a whole, nor the business regulations and taxes applied to the publishing business. He opposes stretching the concept of freedom of press to radio and television industries that, for technical reasons, must operate under government license.

Kilmer, Joyce. "War Censorship Modeled on That of the Church; Archbishop Bonzano, Apostolic Delegate Here, Says That Nations of Europe Got their Idea of Censorship from *Index Expurgatorius*." *New York Times Magazine*, 2 September 1916, p. 13–14. **K 101**

Kilpatrick, James J. *Smut Peddlers*. New York, Doubleday, 1960. 323 p. **K 102**
A documented study of today's obscenity racket and the operation of the law of obscenity censorship. The author, editor of the Richmond *News Leader*, attempts to find a middle group between the need to suppress harmful pornography on the one hand and the need to protect freedom of legitimate sex expression on the other. Table of cases, pp. 295–306. Exchange of comments on the book between the author and R. B. Downs appear in *Library Journal*, 1 June 1961 and August 1961. The book is reviewed by Godfrey Harrison in the March 1961 issue of *Books and Bookmen*.

Kilpatrick, James J., and Robert B. Downs. "Censorship Debate." *Library Journal*, 86:2580–82, August 1961. **K 103**

In a letter to the editor Kilpatrick charges Downs, dean of library administration, University of Illinois, with resorting to "every contemptible trick of the polemicist" in the unfavorable review of his book, *Smut Peddlers* (*Library Journal*, 1 June 1961). Downs responds by accusing Kilpatrick of "suffering from a split personality on the question of censorship . . . Conscientiously attempting to weigh all the pros and cons of censorship he falls between two stools and fails to present a convincing case for either side." Accompanying the "debate" is an illustration of the Post Office Department's smutmobile," displaying books by Margaret Mead and D. H. Lawrence along with "girlie" and "true romance" magazines.

[Kimball, Edmund]. *Reflections upon the Law of Libel, in a letter addressed to "A Member of the Suffolk Bar."* By a Citizen. Boston, Wells and Lilly, 1823. 55 p. **K 104**
Written in defense of Judge Josiah Quincy's decision in *Commonwealth v. Buckingham* and in reply to H. G. Otis' *Letter to Hon. Josiah Quincy . . . on the Law of Libel . . .* Kimball explores British common law on libel and reviews major British and American cases. "The question is not whether the licentiousness of the press be an evil, but whether this evil is of equal magnitude with that which would ensue from a tyrannical restraint." An arbitrary, corrupt, or weak government, Kimball argues, cannot long resist criticism from the press. A good government will not fear it. The author does not agree with contemporary critics who charge that libels have muitiplied with increased press freedom. The fear of a critical press keeps many officials honest who might not be honest from principle.

Kimball, Reginald S. "Stamping Out the Weeds of Literature." *Educational Review*, 73:112–16, February 1927. **K 105**
While deploring the rise of "gutter literature" in this country, the author feels that promotion of good literature is a better answer than attempts at suppression of the bad.

Kinchen, Robert P. "Everyone Knows His Name—Now!" *Top of the News*, 20:289–91, May 1964. **K 106**
A discussion of the books of James Baldwin and their place in the young-adult literary world. Professional librarians should know Baldwin well, recommend his books in appropriate circumstances, and inform young readers of some of his literary limitations. "But to deny Baldwin on the basis of controversy is to deny education."

King, Cecil H. "Subtle Censorship Is Shackling Britain's Press." In Great Britain. General Council of the Press. *The Press and The People*. London, 1962, pp. 11–15. **K 107**
A British publisher declares that the British press "is so hedged about by legal restrictions and penalities that it can no longer be called

free." We only have freedom when what we say is ineffective or unheeded. The British press is censored "by the arbitrary operation of a series of loosely drawn laws which make it hazardous in the extreme for newspapers to comment or even report on a number of issues of vital public importance." He refers to the restrictions imposed by the law of contempt of court, the Official Secrets Acts, the law against libel, and the law of parliamentary privilege.

King, Frank N., Jr. "Right to Inspect Public Records." *Kentucky Law Journal*, 49:597–600, Summer 1961. **K 108**
Relates to the denial of a petition by the *Courier Journal* and the Louisville Times Co. for the right to inspect shorthand notes of a statement made by a murder defendant in the privacy of the judge's chambers.

King, John. *A Decade in the History of Newspaper Libel. A Paper read at the Annual Meeting of the Canadian Press Association held at Ottawa, March 6th–7th, 1892. . . .* Woodstock, Ont., Sentinel-Review, 1892. 50 p. **K 109**
Many changes in the law of libel have been the result of changes in public sentiment over the years, without legislative action. Other changes, especially in Canada and its Provinces, have been due to direct intervention of the legislatures, Dominion or Provincial. These last have been brought about by the press association. The decade covered is that immediately following the Newspaper Libel Act of 1882 in Ontario.

———. *The Law of Criminal Libel. A Treatise on Libel as a Criminal Offense . . . at Common Law and under the Canadian Criminal Code*. Toronto, Carswell, 1912. 400 p. **K 110**

———. *The Law of Defamation in Canada. A Treatise on the Statutes of the Canadian Provinces Concerning Slander and Libel . . .* Toronto, Carswell, 1907. 896 p. **K 111**

———. "The Newspaper Press and the Law of Libel." *Canadian Monthly*, 8:394–405, November 1875. **K 112**
A general review of the English and Canadian libel laws including the 1874 law of the Dominion of Canada which had recently been enacted.

King, Joseph A. *Birchers Try to Burn a Dictionary*. Visalia, Calif., The Author, 1963. 10 p. mimeo. **K 113**
After California's Superintendent of Public Instruction urged the removal of the *Dictionary of American Slang* from school library shelves

because it contained certain four-letter words, a group of Tulare County citizens, with the aid of a John Birch Society organizer, formed a committee to remove the book from the county library. At a heated public hearing on the matter the librarian, the author of this article (an instructor at the local college), and several others defended the book against obscenity charges made by committee members, the John Birch organizer, local ministers, etc. The Board of Supervisors gave the librarian a unanimous vote of confidence. King describes the accusations and personal threats made against him by members of the committee. "I had a kind of Hate directed at me that I have never experienced before."

———"Books and Banners: A Case History." *Saturday Review*, 46(45):28–29, 66, 9 November 1963. **K114**

An English instructor at the College of Sequoias describes a rightist effort in Tulare County, Calif., to ban the *Dictionary of American Slang*.

King, Judson. *Freedom of Thought and the Censorship*. Washington, D.C., National Popular Government League, 1930. 5 p. mimeo. (Bulletin no. 132) **K115**

Favorable review of Senator Bronson Cutting's speech against the amendment to Section 305 of the Tariff Act. Quotes from his speech with references to the U.S. Customs ban on Aristophanes and legitimate medical and scientific works.

———. *Shall the Censorship Be Made Absolute?* Washington, D.C., National Popular Government League, 1929. 4 p. mimeo. (Bulletin no. 128) **K116**

Opposition to a proposed amendment to the tariff law to prohibit seditious literature. Includes letter from Zechariah Chafee who calls the amendment "an effective censorship over (all) foreign literature" which gives the Customs Office the duty of deciding what our universities and libraries shall import. "The Law is a kindergarten measure." Reference is made to Customs Office action against *Candide*.

King, Stoddard. "The Writer and the Asterisk." In his *What the Queen Said and Further Facetious Fragments*. New York, Doran, 1926, pp. 21–22. **K117**

"A writer owned an Asterisk,
And kept it in his den,
Where he wrote tales (which had large
sales)
Of frail and erring men;
And always, when he reached the point
Where carping censors lurk,
He called upon the Asterisk
To do his dirty work."

Kingdom, Frank. "Literature and Sex." In *The Encyclopedia of Sexual Behavior*,

edited by Albert Ellis and A. Abarbanel. New York, Hawthorn Books, 1961. vol. 2, pp. 631–40. **K118**

Kingston, Gertrude. "How Came We to Be Censored by the State." *Nineteenth Century*, 64:1003–49, December 1908; 65:504–20, March 1909. **K119**

An historical review of stage censorship in England. The author calls the English theater the Cinderella of the arts. "No State-ridden art will ever flourish, whether the stage be dictated by a sovereign emancipated from the thraldom of the Puritan, or by a State given back to the tyranny of the proletariat." If the stage takes too much liberty and ridicules the sacred, the public can show its displeasure by staying away. The dramatic author is "oppressed by a narrow tyranny of time-honoured prejudices" and "finds himself merely in a position of a nursery-governess amusing a kindergarten pupil. Not Shakespeare nor Goethe nor Cervantes could have turned their lays or sung their songs under such conditions as these."

Kinsley, Philip H. *Liberty and the Press; a History of the Chicago Tribune's Fight to Preserve a Free Press for the American People*. Chicago, The Chicago Tribune, 1944. 99 p. **K120**

A *Tribune* reporter recounts his newspaper's record in defending the freedom of the press in such cases as the Henry Ford libel suit (1919), the libel suit of the City of Chicago (1920), the Minnesota gag law case (1928), prosecutions under the New Deal, and the Associated Press membership case (1943).

Kintner, Earl W. "1961—Armageddon for Advertising?" *Printers' Ink*, 275(11):21–26, 16 June 1961. **K121**

A former FTC chairman "documents the case for self-regulation of advertising and against more federal power."

Kipp, Lawrence J. "Boston—The Library Did Not Burn." *New Republic*, 128(26):15–16, 29 June 1953. **K122**

The Boston *Post* accused the Boston Public Library of having Communist publications. "We believe," an editorial stated, "that pro-Soviet literature should be suppressed in our public libraries." The librarian, backed by a majority of the library board, rejected the censorship role of the library. Strong support of the library came from three other Boston papers, the *Herald*, the *Christian Science Monitor*, and the *Pilot*, a Catholic diocesan paper.

———. "Report from Boston." *Library Journal*, 77:1843–46+, 1 November 1952. **K123**

An account of an attack spearheaded by the Boston *Post* against the public library for buying and having literature of a pro-Communist nature in the library. City and library officials who agreed with the *Post* brought

charges before the library trustees and City Council. Trustees, by a vote of 3 to 2, adopted two resolutions—the first to the effect that all points of view concerning the problems and issues of our times shall be available to the public, and the second to the effect that the director shall effect arrangement of any Communist propaganda material to prevent abuse or misuse. An editorial entitled Strong in the Faith, commending the action of the trustees appears in *Library Journal* for 15 November 1952.

Kirby, Ethyn W. *William Prynne*. Cambridge, Mass., Harvard University Press, 1931. 228 p. **K124**

Prynne was one of the most prolific and zealous of the Puritan pamphleteers of the seventeenth century, best known for his willingness to suffer torture and imprisonment for the right to express himself in print. For his criticism of the English stage in *Histrio-Mastix* (1633), a work interpreted as casting aspersions on the king and queen, Prynne was imprisoned and shorn of his ears.

Kirby, Sidney. "Question of Censorship." *Library World*, 14:257–59, March 1912. **K125**

The public librarian needs the shield of a selection committee behind which he may find safe shelter in matters of book selection and censorship.

Kirchwey, George W. *A Survey of the Workings of the Criminal Syndicalism Law of California*. Los Angeles, California Committee, American Civil Liberties Union, 1926. 47 p. **K126**

Kirgo, George. "The Name is *Chatterley*— and I'm no Lady; How to Write a Banned Best Seller." In his *How to Write Ten Different Best Sellers Now—in Your Spare Time* . . . New York, Simon and Schuster, 1960, pp. 144–155. **K127**

An hilarious account of how to write a book that will be banned by the Postmaster General and hence become a best seller.

Kirk, Russell. "Censorship." In *Collier's Encyclopedia*. New York, P. F. Collier, 1960. vol. 4, pp. 518–21. **K128**

The article traces the history of censorship from Roman days to the present, with emphasis on censorship of church and state. "In the twentieth century, the recrudescence of state censorship appears to coincide with the ominous extension of private censorship, or the suppression of opinion by conscious or unconscious conspiracy of silence among persons substantially in control of publishing and publicizing." A coterie in one or two cities controls opinion in accordance with the current fad or ideology of their "charmed circle of cognoscenti," which is often in sharp variance with views of the majority. The author notes that no society has long existed without some form of censorship and that persons who advocate that nothing be censored "may come to find themselves saddled with a state censorship more inflexible than anything they ever dreamt of."

――――. "War against Good Books." *National Review*, 14:407, 21 May 1963. **K129**
Account of efforts in high schools throughout America to remove such books as *Scarlet Letter*, *Huckleberry Finn*, *Bell for Adano*, *War and Peace*, and *Brave New World*, and replace them with inane literature.

Kirkendall, Lester A. "Obscenity and the U.S. Supreme Court." *Sexology*, 32:242–45, November 1965. **K130**
The difficulty of arriving at a standard definition of pornography.

――――, and Richard D. Railton. "The Law and Dissemination of Sex Information." In Ralph Slovenko, *Sexual Behavior and The Law*. Springfield, Ill., Thomas, 1965, pp. 807–28. **K131**

Kirkpatrick, Evron M. *National Regulation of False and Misleading Advertising*. New Haven, Conn., Yale University, 1939. (Unpublished Ph. D. dissertation) **K132**

Kirkpatrick, William S. "Showing German Editors a Free Press at Work." *Journalism Quarterly*, 26:29–36, March 1949. **K133**
Comments on a seminar for German editors and publishers, given at the School of Journalism, Columbia University.

Kirkus, Virginia. "Books and Your Thinking." *Louisiana Library Association Bulletin*, 14:68–73, Summer 1951. **K134**
A discussion of controversial books as reviewed by the author's commercial reviewing service and others. She discusses criticisms of reviews and reviewers, the refusal to buy, the refusal to review in the press, and attacks upon libraries and bookstores for stocking certain books.

Kirsch, Robert R. "California Blue Pencil Brigade." In *The Smut Hunters*. Los Angeles, All America Distributors Corp., 1964. 4p. (Originally published in the *Los Angeles Times*, 22 November 1964) **K135**

"Prominent book reviewer reports his experience at Visalia, California trial, actions of Charles H. Keating, Jr., [Citizens for Decent Literature] and warns that the act of separating obscenity from constitutionally protected expression may be purchased at too great a price—especially where censorship groups demonstrate contempt for the laws which guarantee that freedom."

――――. "Custodians, Eunuchs, and Lovers." *Wilson Library Bulletin*, 39:647–50, April 1965. **K136**
"By the very nature of the public library and the democratic system, which sponsors it," writes the literary editor of the *Los Angeles Times*, "the library finds itself, now more than ever, in the center of ferment, quarrel, and argument . . . It is not the responsibility of librarians to avoid controversy, but rather to deal with it in ways compatible with professional standards, training, and a firm commitment to the freedom to read." The author traces the historic role of the public librarian, first as "gentle custodian" of a harmless collection of books; then, as the potency of books was recognized, as a "gentle eunuch," unharmed by the dangerous contents of books; and, finally, as a book-lover and passionate defender of reading "confronted by a literate and sophisticated group of individuals who are products of our schools and who cannot be shrugged off." The librarian needs to communicate the love of books and the love of freedom to the largest possible segment of the community, to help to educate the community to a cultural understanding of books, and, since freedom is indivisible, to defend intellectual freedom wherever it is under assault.

――――. "Obscenity—U.S. Style." *ALA Bulletin*, 58:269–72, April 1964. (Reprinted from the *Los Angeles Times*, 12 January 1964) **K137**
An account of the prosecution in Grand Rapids, Mich., of 8 paperback books, one of which was declared obscene (*Sex Life of a Cop*). The defendants were given a total of 15 years in prison (3 consecutive 5-year terms) and fined $69,000. An account of the amazing background of the case involving book raids in Fresno and Burbank, Calif., and a decision of the California Supreme Court in which the author testified for the defense. The U.S. Supreme Court reversed the conviction. Stanley Fleishman discusses the case in an introduction to the 1967 edition of the book.

Kitchin, George. *Sir Roger L'Estrange. A Contribution to the History of the Press in the Seventeenth Century*. London, Kegan Paul, 1913. 440p. **K138**
During the English Restoration L'Estrange served as the powerful and often ruthless Surveyor of the Press (1663–80), acting as official publisher for the government, sole licenser of printing, and censor. He was responsible for the searches, arrests, and prosecution of numerous printers and publishers, taking over many of the duties of the Stationers' Company. The printer John Twyn was hanged, drawn, and quartered in 1664 under the persecution of L'Estrange.

Kittredge, Daniel W. *All the World Loves a Quarrel; an Introduction to One by D. W. Kittredge*. Cincinnati, Marwick, 1911. 92p. **K139**
The quarrel between St. Loe Strachey, the editor of the London *Spectator*, and Austin Harrison, the editor of the *English Review*,

sometimes called "The Great Adult Review." The *Spectator* attacked the *English Review* for its objectionable articles, one of which was by Frank Harris recommending freer sexual morals—"a little excess in youth in the gratification of natural desire [said Harris] is less harmfull than the abstinence generally recommended in England." A distinguished group of 50 literary figures including Hardy, Shaw, Bennett, Wells, Galsworthy, Walpole, Yeats, and Lawrence, some of whom admitted being shocked by Harris' sentiments, came to the defense of the *English Review* in a signed statement, reprinted on pp. 89–90. "Its suppression can be justified only by arguments which would justify the suppression of every organ of advanced or reactionary thought in Europe, and could easily be pushed for party or sectarian purpose to the destruction of the liberty of the press . . . We feel bound to protest against the attempt to annul the compact of tolerance upon which the maintenance of the highest literature and the best journalism depends for its very existence."

[Klafter, Samuel]. "Education Law—Censorship of Motion Pictures—N.Y. Licensing Statute—Indecency." *Albany Law Review*, 22:186–91, January 1958. **K140**
A discussion of the legal status of moving picture licensing that arose out of the case of *Excelsior Pictures Corp. v. Regents of the State of New York* and the motion picture, *Garden of Eden*.

Klapper, Joseph T. *The Effects of Mass Communication*. Glencoe, Ill., Free Press, 1960. 302p. **K141**
Part 2 deals with the effects of specific types of media material—crime and violence, escapist media, adult TV fare—on child audiences and the conclusions which bear on the need for social controls.

Klee, Bruce B. "Woolcott v. Shubert: Dramatic Criticism on Trial." *Educational Theatre Journal*, 13:264–68, December 1961. **K142**
An account of the dispute and legal contest in 1915 between the *New York Times* drama critic, Alexander Woolcott, and the Shubert brothers, theatrical producers. The stand taken by Woolcott and the *Times* "helped to establish independent criticism as a norm from which it has become increasingly less desirable or necessary to deviate."

Klieneberger, H. R. "Librarianship and Humanism." *Library World*, 56:119–24, February 1955. **K143**
If the librarian is to select books that will lead to a broad cultural background some form of censorship is necessary. The public library can improve the cultural level of its readers and save funds for more worthy use by rejecting cheap fiction.

Klopfer, Donald S. "Our Common Stake in Free Communication: Book Publishing." In *Freedom of Communication; Proceedings of the First Conference on Intellectual Freedom . . .* Chicago, American Library Association, 1954, pp. 102–7. **K144**

Klotz, Johann C. *De Libris Auctoribus Suis Fatalibus Liber Singularis.* Leipzig, Langenheim, 1768. 205 p. **K145**

An early account of censored, prohibited, and burned books, including references to such English figures as John Toland, George Buchanan, John Selden, Edmund Richards, and Thomas Woolston.

Klotzer, Charles L. "Censorship or Editing?" *Focus/Midwest,* 1(5):10–14, October 1962. **K146**

A column entitled Freedom Forum is censored because a State Chamber of Commerce official thinks "it might hurt some of our friends." The young reporter resigned rather than submit to the blue-penciling of his column by the general manager of the Missouri Press Association. The column reported on plans for holding a Freedom Forum at the Missouri Military Academy under the auspices of "the aberrant National Education Program of Searcy, Ark." The author raises the question whether the column was "censored" to accommodate rightist pressures or only "edited."

[Kneeland, Abner]. *An Appeal to Common Sense and the Constitution, in behalf of the Unlimited Freedom of Public Discussion: Occasioned by the late trial of Rev. Abner Kneeland, for Blasphemy.* Boston, 1834. 14 p. **K147**

"Is it consistent with common sense, or the principles of our republican constitution, to repress the expressions of opinion, however false or absurd those opinions may be, or to shackle the liberty of discussion, however that liberty may be perverted to the support of false doctrines?" While most would agree that fair argument and sober discussion should be unshackled, many object to permitting ridicule of sacred truths. "If we deprive an opponent of the privilege of ridicule, we strip him of one of the sharpest weapons of controversy . . . Ridicule is one of the means essential to a free discussion of any topic." The author denounces the confusion in thinking that associates two such dissimilar offenses as blasphemy and obscenity into a compound crime. As to the Massachusetts Bill of Rights, when it says "that no man shall be molested for his religious sentiments, he certainly must be allowed not only to choose his creed among such as may offer, but likewise to reject the whole." The anonymous author hopes the Kneeland case will result in the repeal of the blasphemy laws which are antiquated and unconstitutional.

————. *An Introduction to the Defence of*

Abner Kneeland, charged with Blasphemy; before the Municipal Court, in Boston, Mass., at the January Term, in 1834. Boston, Printed for the Publisher, 1834. 43 p. **K148**

While awaiting trial Kneeland wrote this defense in which he objects to the lifting of passages from their context in order to sustain a charge of blasphemy. The offending passage which questioned the virility of Jesus, was a reference from Voltaire, appearing in an essay by Ben Krapac of Mobile, Ala. Kneeland had republished three of Krapac's essays (originally appearing in the New York *Free Inquirer*) in his own *Boston Investigator*, he stated, without reading them in their entirety. He admits to an offense against good taste. He reprints the three essays in this pamphlet written prior to the first trial, with explanatory footnotes, using Greek to conceal the objectionable word. Kneeland was convicted in Municipal Court and the case appealed to the Massachusetts Supreme Court. The speech of the defense attorney, Andrew Dunlap, was issued separately and is entered in this bibliography under his name.

[————]. *Report of the Arguments of the Attorney of the Commonwealth, at the Trials of Abner Kneeland, for Blasphemy, in the Municipal and Supreme Courts, in Boston, January and May, 1834.* Boston, Printed by Beals, Homer, 1834. 93 p. (Collected and published at the request of some Christians of various denominations) **K149**

"Some friends of religion and law thought it might be useful to the cause of truth, to obtain the views and arguments of the prosecuting officer as expressed at the trials, and place them before the public with accuracy and authenticity." This compilation, issued by those opposed to Kneeland, appeared following the first trial before the Massachusetts Supreme Court in which the jury could not agree. Quotations from the arguments of the Attorney of the Commonwealth are reproduced in McCormick, *Versions of Censorship,* pp. 167–70, under the heading, Corruption of the Poor and Unlearned by Certain Opinions. The gist of the argument was that the press is free to express opinions provided they do not offend the beliefs of others; that the crime of blasphemy is aggravated when it is conveyed in a newspaper "easily circulated, soon read, and finding its way to the poor and unlearned, to those who have not learning nor leisure enough to consider and refute its falsehoods." The Courts should act as "moral Boards of Health" to denounce and restrain blasphemy and obscenity.

[————]. *A Review of the Prosecution against Abner Kneeland, for Blasphemy. By a Cosmopolite.* Boston, 1835. 32 p. **K150**

A spirited defense of Kneeland and an appeal for the preservation of a free press, an issue involved in the Kneeland trial. "We enter the investigation . . . to rescue that important instrument [the Constitution of Massachusetts], which our fathers left for an inheritance,

from the ruthless grasp of blind fanaticism, prowling ignorance, canting hypocrisy and judicial usurpation." The author quotes from the testimony and charge of the judges in the several trials and pays tribute to the dissenting juror, Mr. Greene, and the defense attorney, Mr. Dunlap.

————. *Review of the Trial, Conviction and Final Imprisonment in the Common Jail of the County of Suffolk, of A. K., for the Alleged Crime of Blasphemy; Written by Himself.* Boston, George A. Chapman, 1838. 132 p. **K151**

This account was written by Kneeland while serving his 60-day jail sentence.

[————]. *Sketches of Arguments of Attorney of the Commonwealth, at Trials for Blasphemy, Municipal and Supreme Court.* Boston, 1834. 32 p. **K152**

————. *Speech of Abner Kneeland, Delivered before the Full Bench of Judges of the Supreme Court, in His Own Defence, for the Alleged Crime of Blasphemy. Law term, March 8, 1836.* Boston, J. Q. Adams, 1836. 44 p. **K153**

Following Kneeland's conviction by the Massachusetts Supreme Court in November 1835, the case was appealed to a full bench of the judges, with Chief Justice Lemuel Shaw, presiding. Kneeland's attorney at earlier trials, Andrew Dunlap, having died, the defendant pleaded his own case. The earlier decision was upheld, with Chief Justice Shaw holding that the blasphemy law was constitutional and that the defendant had violated it. Mr. Justice Marcus Morton dissented, arguing that a work must not only be blasphemous but must have malicious intent to be liable and there was no evidence of the latter. Kneeland prefaces the report with a brief review of the November 1835 trial in which he had been found guilty; this includes a statement on the freedom to discuss religion taken from the opinion of Judge Jay of New York and delivered before the Grand Jury of West Chester County.

[————]. *Speech of Abner Kneeland, Delivered before the Supreme Court of the City of Boston, in His Own Defence, on an Indictment for Blasphemy. November Term, 1834.* Boston, J. Q. Adams, 1834. 32 p. **K154**

This was Kneeland's third trial for blasphemy and the second before the Massachusetts Supreme Court. This trial, as in the case of the earlier one, ended in disagreement by the jury. S. D. Parker was the prosecutor; Andrew Dunlap, the defense attorney.

[————]. "The Trial of Abner Kneeland for Blasphemy, Boston, 1835." In *American State Trials,* vol. 13, pp. 450–75. **K155**

A summary and analysis of the Kneeland blasphemy case by Henry S. Commager appears in the March 1935 issue of *New England Quarterly*.

Knepper, Max. "Don't Chain the Movies!" *Forum*, 108:265–69, November 1947. **K156**
The answer to undesirable movies lies in audience control rather than production interference. The author charges that the more vocal censorship enthusiasts are using the juvenile delinquency charge as a means to an end—"to mould public thought in line with their own dogmas."

———. "Is Hollywood Growing Up?" *Forum*, 105:880–85, June 1946; 106: 21–27, July 1946. **K157**
A survey of the movie industry published in two parts. The first article deals mainly with the movies as a commercial enterprise, the second with the cultural status of motion pictures, including a discussion of censorship and the operation of the Production Code Administration. "There is sound argument for the premise that censorship—if the evil must be supported—should be at the exhibiting rather than producing end."

Knight, Arthur. "Who's to Classify?" *Saturday Review*, 49(9):42, 62, 26 February 1966. **K158**
Awards recently made to adult movies by both Catholic (National Catholic Office for Motion Pictures) and Protestant (Broadcast and Film Commission of the Federal Council of Churches) groups suggest that the movie industry should make an attempt to unite such enlightened leadership in formulating an effective classification system. Such a system would be preferable to the censorship by police and pressure groups now taking place with the liberalization of legal controls.

Knight, John S. "Censorship as Viewed from London." In *Problems of Journalism; Proceedings of the American Society of Newspaper Editors, 1944*. Washington, D.C., ASNE, 1944, pp. 94–103. **K159**
The working of wartime censorship in England as observed by the head of an American newspaper chain.

———. "World Freedom of Information." *Vital Speeches*, 12:472–77, 15 May 1946. **K160**
The president of the American Society of Newspaper Publishers opposes any plan for creation of a permanent international communications agency, as only encouraging censorship. Newspaper press associations should be independent of government.

Knight, Mary. "Secret War of Censors v. Spies." *Reader's Digest*, 48:79–83, March 1946. (Condensed from the *Washington Post*, 3 February 1946) **K161**
How American censorship checkmated scores of dangerous Japanese and German agents during World War II, is told by wartime censor.

Kniskern, Maynard. "Are Basic Communist Works a Menace in Public Libraries—and If So, to Whom?" *Idaho Librarian*, 5(4):29–31, October 1953. (Reprinted from *ALA Newsletter on Intellectual Freedom*, January 1953) **K162**
"Communists are never made in libraries; they are made in slums, gutters, dark alleyways, and dingy meeting halls . . . Now such individuals are almost never confirmed in their course by reading books; and anyhow, if they ever do get around to pursuing 'basic' communist works it is only after the damage has been done. Normally, however, such people read only crudely-written pamphlets produced specifically for them—stuff that is far too low-grade to be accorded a place in any library."

Knowles, Dorothy. *The Censor, the Drama and the Film, 1900–1934*. London, Allen and Unwin, 1934. 294 p. **K163**
After a brief history of drama censorship in England, the author considers the growing case against the censor that came to a head in 1909 with the banning of Shaw's *The Shewing up of Blanco Posnet* and the appointment of the Select Committee of Parliament. The author discusses the continuation of censorship following the investigation and during the decade after World War I. Part 2 of the volume deals with censorship of films in Great Britain, beginning with the Cinematograph Act of 1909 and the work of the Board of Film Censors, "a body appointed by the trade in self-defence against the public." Sex rather than excessive violence was the concern of the censor in the various films studied by the author. In a preface, Hubert Griffith reminisces on some of the plays that the censor deprived him of seeing during his 12 years as a drama critic. Contains a comprehensive bibliography on British censorship of drama and films.

Knowles, Freeman T. *Our Press Censorship: The Case of Freeman Knowles of the Lantern*. Deadwood, S. D., The Author, 1908. 16 p. **K164**
Knowles was convicted and fined $500 in federal court for sending "lewd, obscene and lascivious matter through the mail." The charge was based on an article in Knowles's paper, the *Lantern*, 30 May 1907, which dealt with the case of an unnamed local girl who died from an abortion. Knowles attacked society for contributing to the shame of unmarried motherhood. Eugene V. Debs, in a letter to Knowles suggests the real reason for the prosecution was Knowles's socialist views and his criticism of President Theodore Roosevelt. Knowles served a jail sentence rather than pay the fine. Comments on the editor's conviction appear in the 28 May and 8 July 1908 issues of *Lanterr*.

Knowlton, Charles. *Fruits of Philosophy or the Private Companion of Adult People.*

Edited with an Introductory Notice by Norman E. Himes . . . with Medical Emendations by Robert Latou Dickinson . . . Mount Vernon, N.Y., Peter Pauper, 1937. 107 p. (Edition limited to 450 copies) **K165**
"This little book, first published anonymously in New York in 1832, by an obscure, western Massachusetts physician, has done much to revolutionize the sexual habits of the English speaking world . . . It has intrinsic merit as well as historical importance. The *Fruits of Philosophy* is the most important treatise on birth control technique for seventeen centuries." In the introduction Professor Himes discusses the significance of the work and traces efforts at suppressing it in the United States and Great Britain. Knowlton bears the historical distinction of being the first man in birth control history to go to jail for his opinions. No sooner was Knowlton released from the Cambridge, Mass., jail in 1833, than Abner Kneeland, editor of the Boston *Investigator*, defied Boston authorities by issuing an edition of the Knowlton work, with an appendix that had been written by Knowlton during his incarceration. More than 40 years later (1877–78) Charles Bradlaugh and Annie Besant were brought to trial in England for republishing the work.

———. *Two Remarkable Lectures Delivered in Boston, by Dr. C. Knowlton, on the Day of His Leaving the Jail at East Cambridge, March 31, 1833, Where He Had Been Imprisoned, for Publishing a Book*. Boston, A. Kneeland, 1833. **K166**
Knowlton's pamphlet on birth control, *Fruits of Philosophy; or the Private Companion of Young Married People*, was a temperate and serious discussion by a respected physician, first published in New York in 1832 and reprinted the following year in Boston by Abner Kneeland. Although Massachusetts did not yet have a law banning contraceptive information (the first act was in 1847) there was strong sentiment against publicizing such information as being offensive to common decency. Knowlton was fined in Taunton, Mass., for the sale of the New York edition; in Cambridge he was sentenced to three months at hard labor; he was arrested again in Greenfield, Mass.

"Knox's Censorship." *Time*, 37(25):41–42, 23 June 1941; 37(11):45–46, 15 September 1941. **K167**
Navy censorship rules as interpreted by Secretary of the Navy Frank Knox and criticism of them by the press.

Knudson, Marie. "Sense of Censorship." *Minnesota Libraries*, 17:213–15, September 1953. (Reprinted in *Illinois Libraries*, May 1966) **K168**
The author examines the kinds of pressures on librarians to buy or not to buy books—the

man who knows the truth and anything which does not agree with his ideas of the truth is objectionable; the do-gooder; the liberal and the conservative who insist on their books being represented; the gift bringer; and the persons who demand a closed shelf. "If a book is worthy of being in the library, it is worthy of standing in its rightful place on the shelf."

Knudson, Theodore S. "Apparent Conflict between Free Press and Free Trial Comes in Focus Again." *Hennepin Lawyer*, 23:67–72, February 1955. **K169**
Special references to the case of Donald Lyng in Minneapolis and the Jelke case in New York. Judge Knudson recommends strengthening Canon 20 of the American Bar Association.

Knutson, Andie L. "The Commission Versus the Press." *Public Opinion Quarterly*, 12:130–35, Spring 1948. **K170**
A social psychologist reviews the report of the Commission on Freedom of the Press, taking issue with some of the unfavorable press reviews of the report.

Koch, Adrienne, and Harry Ammon. "The Virginia and Kentucky Resolutions: An Episode in Jefferson's and Madison's Defense of Civil Liberties." *William and Mary Quarterly*, 5(3rd ser.):145–76, April 1948. **K171**
The authors analyze the historic manifestos drawn by Jefferson and Madison which advanced the theory of States' Rights as a practical and spirited means of protecting the civil rights of individuals. The resolutions were in answer to the passage by Congress in 1798 of the Alien and Sedition Acts, which represented to Jefferson a negation of one of the principles he held most sacred: "To preserve the freedom of the human mind then and the freedom of the press [he wrote to William Green Munford, 18 June 1799] every spirit should be ready to devote itself to martyrdom; for as long as we may think as we will, and speak as we think the condition of man will proceed in improvement."

Koch, Theodore W. "British Censorship and Enemy Publications." *Library Journal*, 42:697–705, September 1917. **K172**
The work of the British censors in World War I whose aim was to examine and send on as rapidly as possible everything that did not contain information of value to the enemy.

———. *War Libraries and Allied Studies.* New York, Stechert, 1918. 287p. **K173**
Includes references to British censorship and treatment of enemy publications.

Koenig, Harry C. "Forbidden Books in a High School Library." *Catholic Library World*, 17:109–11+, January 1946. **K174**

———. "What Is an Imprimatur?" *Library Journal*, 75:1358–61, 1 September 1950. **K175**
The librarian of St. Mary of the Lake Seminary explains the purpose of the imprimatur (it may be printed) found in the books written by Catholic authors which concern faith or morals. "The purpose of censorship in the Catholic Church is not to keep people ignorant but to preserve them from error."

Koenigil, Mark. *Movies in Society (Sex, Crime and Censorship).* New York, Robert Speller, 1962. 214p. **K176**
A member of the Brazilian Motion Picture Congressional Commission presents a rambling account of the foreign film industry and the effect of films on the morals of the viewers, particularly children and adolescents. His own point of view, expressed briefly in the epilogue, is that some form of censorship is necessary to protect the people against the depravity of greedy producers who thrive on the exploitation of human weaknesses. He recommends the establishment by UNESCO of "an international censorship advisory council to help member nations control, on an enlightened basis, the public exhibition of obscenity, depravity and other antisocial manifestations." Appendix III deals with *Censorship of Motion Pictures in the U. S. A.*

Koether, George. *Free Market and Free Press.* Columbia, Mo., Freedom of Information Center, School of Journalism, University of Missouri, 1960. 5p. (Publication no. 31) **K177**
A steel company public relations man considers freedom of the press in the sense of freedom of the ownership and use of property.

Konecky, Eugene. *The American Communications Conspiracy in Standard Broadcasting, Frequency Modulation, Television, Facsimile, Shortwave, Newspaper.* New York, Peoples Radio Foundation, 1948. 168p. **K178**
A leftist exposition of monopolistic controls of American radio and television. The author claims the FCC has been made the tool of big business.

Konkle, Burton A. *The Life of Andrew Hamilton, 1676–1741.* "The Day-Star of the American Revolution." Philadelphia, National Publishing Co., 1941. 168p. **K179**
Chapters 11 through 14 deal with the part played by this eminent American lawyer in the defense of John Peter Zenger and his *New York Weekly Journal* in 1735. For his service to the cause of freedom of the press Gouverneur Morris called Hamilton "the day-star of the American Revolution." There is a frontispiece of Hamilton and (opposite page 70) a reproduction of an oil painting of Hamilton during the Zenger trial.

Konvitz, Milton R. *Fundamental Liberties of a Free People: Religion, Speech, Press, Assembly.* Ithaca, N.Y., Cornell University Press, 1957. 420p. (Cornell Studies in Civil Liberty) **K180**
A study of the concepts of freedom of religion, speech, press, and assembly, with extensive documentation of court cases. The doctrine of "clear and present danger" is treated in some detail. Chapter 18 deals with obscene literature and chapter 21 with taxes on knowledge. The appendix contains a table of cases.

———, ed. *Bill of Rights Reader: Leading Constitutional Cases.* 3d ed., Ithaca, N.Y., Cornell University Press, 1965. 941p. (Cornell Studies in Civil Liberty) **K181**
Leading constitutional cases on the Bill of Rights are presented in actual text, together with introductory and background information. Emphasis is on recent decisions on such topics as Bible reading and Bible distribution in the schools, police power and freedom of speech and the press, previous restraints on censorship, the "clear and present danger" doctrine, indecent and obscene literature, movie censorship, and contempt by publication.

———. *First Amendment Freedoms; Selected Cases on Freedom of Religion, Speech, Press, Assembly.* Ithaca, N.Y., Cornell University Press, 1963. 926p. **K182**
This comprehensive case book on freedoms guaranteed by the First Amendment devotes four of its six chapters to cases relating to freedom of speech and press. Chapter 3 includes the subject of group libel (*Beauharnais v. Illinois*), previous restraints or censorship (*Near v. Minnesota, Lovell v. Griffin, Niemotko v. Maryland, Kunz v. New York,* and *Rockwell v. Morris*), taxes on knowledge (*Grosjean v. American Press Co.*), and freedom of anonymous publications (*Talley v. California*). Chapter 4 deals with cases on the "clear and present danger" doctrine and the Communist conspiracy. Chapter 5 deals with cases on loyalty and security. Chapter 6 deals with cases on censorship and contempt by publication: (1) Indecent and obscene literature, a) Post-Office control (*Hannegan v. Esquire, Inc., Grove Press v. Christenberry, Manual Enterprises v. Day*), b) Customs control (*U. S. v. One Book Called "Ulysses"*), c) Police control (*Commonwealth v. Gordon, Roth v. U.S., Alberts v. California, Kingsley Books, Inc. v. Brown, Butler v. Michigan, Smith v. California, Bantam Books v. Sullivan,* and *Attorney General v. The Book Named "Tropic of Cancer"*). (2) Movie censorship (*Burstyn, Inc. v. Wilson, Kingsley International Pictures Corp. v. Regents of University of State of New York,* and *Times Film Corp. v. Chicago*). (3) Contempt by publication (*Bridges v. California*). (4) Censorship on advice as to use of contraceptives (*Poe v. Ullman*). This work is an expansion of the First Amendment portion of Konvitz' earlier book, *Bill of Rights Reader.*

Koop, Theodore F. "Equality of Access for Radio in Covering Washington News."

Journalism Quarterly, 34:338–40, Summer 1957. **K183**

———. *Weapon of Silence*. Chicago, University of Chicago Press, 1946. 304 p. **K184**

A study of civilian censorship of the press and radio in the United States during World War II, told by the assistant director of the Office of Censorship. Three chapters deal with wartime censorship in the Civil War and World War I, and compare these with the voluntary system of World War II.

Kordus, Claude. "Censorship of Textbooks." *Marquette Law Review*, 39:268–74, Winter 1955–56. **K185**

"The purpose of this comment is to evaluate the legal issues presented to the textbook committees of American public schools when reading materials intended to be used in public school libraries contain attacks on religious groups." The author concludes that the local school board must not be hindered in the effort to keep the public schools free of the "strife of sects." While approving the fair-minded evaluation of tenets of faith, the author believes that Paul Blanshard's articles in *The Nation* "go far beyond any impartial evaluation of the principles of Catholicism" and he approves the banning of the magazine in the Newark schools.

Kostelantz, Richard, *et al.* "Pornography." *Twentieth Century*, 174:4–29, Summer 1965. **K186**

A group of articles by Richard Kostelantz, Father Corbishley, Dan Snee, John Calder, David Stafford-Clark, Michael Rubinstein, and Maurice Girodias. Henry Miller had been asked to contribute but wrote, "I have written myself out on that subject, I fear, couldn't possibly do another." Kostelantz suggests that pornography might be classified in five rough categories: vulgar, clichéd, sentimentalized, realistic, and imaginative; he gives examples of each. Father Corbishley believes that pornography, while most harmful to the adolescent, may also harm the adult who has not developed a well-balanced view of sex. The suppression of the traffic will be achieved only by a public opinion that will not tolerate it. Dan Snee writes satirically of Henry Miller's pursuit of freedom by writing of sex, and of the growing trade of serious pornography. John Calder notes that children have no interest in pornography, adolescents have little need for artificial stimulation, but the chief readers are the middle-aged. He examines the "pornographic method," which he believes should be tolerated if used to benefit society, exposed where it is not. David Stafford-Clark reports on the press criticism of his ultrafrank talk on the sexual aspects of marriage, delivered at a conference of the Scottish Marriage Guidance Council. Michael Rubinstein concludes that "campaigns for the suppression of 'suggestive' literature are promoted, pursued and publicized by the corrupt." Maurice Girodias, founder of The Olympia Press, writes of his own publishing experience.

Kotschnig, Walter M. "U.S. Proposes New Convention for Freedom of Information." *U.S. Department of State Bulletin*, 25:504–9, 24 September 1951. **K187**

Proposals of the United States Deputy Representative on the UNESCO Sub-Commission on Freedom of Information, which had reached an impasse over international freedom for correspondents and newspapers.

Koudelis, George. "Fair Trial v. Freedom of the Press in Criminal Cases." *Temple Law Quarterly*, 35:412–32, Summer 1962. **K188**

The author concludes that "reinstating the power to punish constructive contempts would be the most effective and feasible way to approach the problem . . . The original common-law power should be revived with the United States Supreme Court as final arbiter."

[Kough, Jack, *et al.*]. "Dealing with Censorship Pressures." *Publishers' Weekly*, 181(24):29–31, 11 June 1962. **K189**

Summary of a panel discussion on censorship pressures given at the annual meeting of the American Textbook Publishers Institute. Participants included Robert C. McNamara, Jr. (chairman), John Spaulding, Jack Kough, and W. MacLean Johnson. Mr. Kough defined four groups of censors—the organized negative, the excited but lonesome negative, the misinformed constructive, and the very informed constructive.

Kraft, Joseph. "Politics of the Washington Press Corps." *Harper's*, 230:99–105, June 1965. **K190**

If there is a threat to a free press, it lies "in the intellectual poverty of the press itself" that accepts the government-managed news and deals with the favored sources.

"*Kreutzer Sonata*." *American Law Review*, 25:102–4, January–February 1891. **K191**

"The attempt of the post-office department to exclude one of Tolstoi's celebrated books, called *Kreutzer Sonata* from the mails, resulted in the very object which it was intended to prevent, in giving enormous circulation to the book."

Kreymborg, Alfred. *Edna: The Girl of the Street. Including George Bernard Shaw's Advice to the New York Society for the Suppression of Vice Regarding Edna and the Complete Story of the Arrest and Subsequent Trial of Guido Bruno*. New York, 1919. 27 p. **K192**

The text of Kreymborg's short story, together with documents relating to the publication of the work by Guido Bruno and his arrest and trial in New York on an obscenity charge. Frank Harris appeared in Bruno's behalf.

Krieghbaum, Hillier. "The Office of War Information and Government News

Policy." *Journalism Quarterly*, 19:241–50, September 1942. **K193**

The official control of news in the United States during World War II.

Kris, Ernst. "Mass Communication under Totalitarian Government." In Douglas Waples, *Print, Radio and Film in a Democracy*. Chicago, University of Chicago Press, 1949, pp. 14–38. **K194**

Discusses control of information during wartime—the experience under British and German governments in both world wars. After each war, the public is left with a distrust of mass communications which has to be overcome. The author suggests the formation of a new élite, consisting of specialists dealing with news, who would establish a body of professional ethics as a means of controlling the mass media to "prevent the death of public confidence in the news."

Krock, Arthur. "A Free Press in War Time." In Thomas H. Johnson, *ed.*, *Men of Tomorrow*. New York, Putnam's, 1942, pp. 209–25. **K195**

The head of the Washington bureau of the *New York Times* describes censorship conditions prevailing in the United States in World War II, following a brief history of censorship in earlier wars. He objects to the use of "voluntary" to a censorship which is really "compulsory." Krock recommends putting "the military and nonmilitary news control under a small committee, with a civilian in the chair, which would lay down sensible, elastic rules so that you would get much timely news of events." Such an agency, the Office of War Information, was subsequently formed under the direction of Elmer Davis.

———. "The Press and Government." *Annals of the American Academy of Political and Social Science*, 180:162–67, July 1935. **K196**

The article is about the conflict between the press and the restrictions sometimes attempted by government officials. "In repayment of liberties without parallel, the American newspaper and its makers must seek and deserve the friendship of the public alone, to whom the Government belongs."

———. "Press v. Government—a Warning." *Public Opinion Quarterly*, 1:45–49, April 1937. **K197**

The Central Information Bureau, proposed by the Brownlow-Gulick-Merriam committee on government reorganization, would be a menace to the legitimate flow of news to the public.

———. "Public Information and National Security: A Journalist's View." *Yale*

Political, 3(1):19, 35, Autumn 1963.
K 198

"Mr. Krock decries the inadequate and slanted information the people are receiving about the activities of their government. While censorship may be justified in times of a national emergency such as war, such justification does not apply to merely critical situations such as the Cold War." A government view is presented in an accompanying article by Arthur Sylvester.

Kronhausen, Eberhard, and Phyllis Kronhausen. *Pornography and the Law; the Psychology of Erotic Realism and "Hard Core" Pornography.* New York, Ballantine Books, 1959. 317 p. Foreword by J. W. Ehrlich; Introduction by Dr. Theodor Reik. Revised edition, 1964. 416 p. **K 199**

According to the authors, both psychologists, there is no reliable evidence that pornography is a major cause of juvenile delinquency. Some psychologists, they state, believe that erotic emotion is actively purged and sublimated by this means. The authors attempt to delineate between "erotic realism" and "hard core pornography," giving examples of both categories from classic and modern writings. They discuss such books as Frank Harris' *My Life and Loves,* Henry Miller's *Tropic of Cancer,* D. H. Lawrence's *Lady Chatterley's Lover,* and (in the revised edition) the case of *Fanny Hill.* Part II of the book deals with obscenity and the law, with comments on the Supreme Court definition of obscenity and the concept of "contemporary community standards." The revised edition contains a section on Erotica of Tomorrow, and a postscript indicating that in the five years since the first edition there has been no further evidence of positive correlation between reading erotic material and overt antisocial acts. In a pro and con review of the work (*Saturday Review,* 20 February 1960), Harvey Breit believes the authors have found "a viable, even dramatic distinction" between pornography and erotica. Alan U. Schwartz, in the same source, believes the Kronhausens have largely failed of their aim through a misunderstanding of the basic legal problems involved.

———. "Psychology of Pornography." In *The Encyclopedia of Sexual Behavior,* edited by Albert Ellis and A. Abarbanel. New York, Hawthorn Books, 1961. vol. 2, pp. 848–59. **K 200**

Kronick, David A. "Unadmitted Rule of Why Censor." *Wilson Library Bulletin,* 16:467–69, February 1940. **K 201**

"The librarian practices censorship whether he wishes to or not, as a result of the limitations of his book fund. It is a censorship of omission rather than commission; a censorship implied in the necessity of selecting from the thousands of titles which pour from the presses of the commercial publishers every year . . . It is a problem that is closely involved in many aspects of library policy; the criteria of book selection, the freedom of access to the literature of sex education, the practice of library publicity (lack of publicity and difficulty of access may amount to censorship), the question of the library's attitude toward obscenity in literature, and many others."

Krug, Mark M. "'Safe' Textbooks and Citizenship Education." *School Review,* 68:463–80, Winter 1960. **K 202**

An analysis of charges being made that in the interest of balance and objectivity school textbook writers have taken out any ideas to which anybody might possibly object. He calls for a "responsible reappraisal of the policy of omitting or glossing over controversial issues, of avoiding a clear-cut commitment to the fundamental democratic rights and to the obligation to work for the betterment of our democratic society."

Krutch, Joseph Wood. *Comedy and Conscience After the Restoration.* New York, Columbia University Press, 1924. 300 p. **K 203**

In chapters entitled The Onslaught on the Stage, the author deals with attacks made on Restoration drama, which centered around Jeremy Collier's *A Short View of the Immorality and Profaneness of the English Stage* (1688).

———. "Freedom for Radio and Television; the Risks Involved." *Commentary,* 10:434–38, November 1950. **K 204**

A favorable review with commentary on Siepmann's *Radio, Television, and Society.*

———. "The Indecency of Censorship." *Nation,* 124:162–63, 16 February 1927. **K 205**

"It is impossible to set any legal standard of decency, for the simple reason that decency is purely a matter of changing convention." But to this literary critic the final and conclusive argument against censorship "is the character of the censor himself, since there never was one who was not utterly ridiculous."

Kugelmass, J. Alvin. "Smut on Our Newsstands." *Christian Herald,* 75:21–22+, May 1952. (Reprinted in Daniel, *The Censorship of Books,* pp. 51–55) **K 206**

Advice to citizens on how to go about cleaning up the newsstands. Laws are available to get the job done, but fear of the "censorship bugaboo" has made officials hesitant to act.

Kuh, Frederick. "The British Press in Wartime." *New Republic,* 104:522–24, 21 April 1941. **K 207**

Many believed Britain would adopt Fascist techniques in controlling the press in wartime, but, in fact, the government under both Chamberlain and Churchill "has allowed the press a latitude in criticism which is a constant and refreshing surprise."

Kuh, Richard H. "Obscenity: Prosecution Problems and Legislative Suggestions." *Catholic Lawyer,* 10:285–300, Autumn 1964. **K 208**

The author discusses the recent experience in New York County with enforcement of the obscenity law (films, books and magazines, sales to minors, high-priced erotica, the movies, and live performers). He reviews the judicial trend on obscenity and recommends a legislative program, the keystone of which is "keeping objectionable items from being foisted upon children." Such legislation should limit its protective cloak to those under 16; should limit its interdiction to those "outsiders" who sell to children; and should be extremely explicit in what is barred.

Kuhl, Ernest. "The Stationers' Company and Censorship (1599–1601)." *Library,* 9(4th ser.):388–94, March 1929. **K 209**

From official records the author presents evidence "that the Church during the political crisis took active part in the condemnation of [the Earl of] Essex, and in suppressing Essex propaganda of a non-dramatic nature. It was this ecclesiastical body, in turn, that held accountable (at least during those fifteen months) the company of Stationers."

Kuhn, Bowie K. "Right of a Newsman to Refrain from Divulging Sources of His Information." *University of Virginia Law Review,* 36:61–83, February 1950. **K 210**

An extensive discussion of statutes and court cases relating to protection of newsmen from divulging sources of information. So-called "confidence laws" exist in 12 states. The author believes these laws are undesirable on broad public grounds and the tendency to give special privilege to occupational groups is unhealthy. Each case should be considered on its own merits. "Privilege to refrain from answering proper questions cannot be extended too far before the administration of justice becomes seriously impaired."

Kuhn, Irene C. "Who Are the Censors?" *Catholic Digest,* 19(1):86–89, November 1954. **K 211**

The real censors are the Communists who try to prevent books opposing their ideas from being published and, if published, from being reviewed. Books unfavorable to communism are "smothered under the counters of bookstores by disciplined communists put there for that purpose, or by misguided, susceptible clerks."

———. "Why You Buy Books that Sell Communism." *American Legion Magazine,* 50:18–19+, January 1951. (Reprinted in Daniels, *The Censorship of Books,* pp. 82–88) **K 212**

The author alleges Communist infiltration of the book trade and left-wing domination of book reviewers for the *New York Times* and the *New York Herald Tribune*. She cites names of reviewers and titles of books.

———. "Your Child Is Their Target." *American Legion Magazine*, 52(6):18–19, 54–60, June 1952.   **K 213**
"How a small but well organized minority is attempting to manipulate our public schools to condition our children for what they call 'a new social order.'" The author attacks "progressive" educators John Dewey, William H. Kilpatrick, John L. Childs, George S. Counts, and Harold O. Rugg. She claims that honest citizens who are indignant at this development are being charged with a "plot" against the public schools.

Kuhn, Lesley, comp. *Theodore Schroeder: The Sage of Cos Cob; The Definitive Bibliography of His Published Works . . . Compiled and Annotated by Lesley Kuhn, With Comments by Roland Baughman . . . Ethel Clyde, Harry Golden, H. L. Mencken, Havelock Ellis, and Others.* New York, Psychological Library, 1964. 46p.   **K 214**
Includes an inventory of Schroeder's works in leading American libraries. Schroeder is probably the most prolific of all modern writers on the subject of freedom of the press, especially on those aspects relating to blasphemy and obscenity.

———, et al. *Theodore Schroeder's Last Will.* New York, Psychological Library, 1958. 40p.   **K 215**
Tribute to a leading advocate of the freedom of the press, Theodore A. Schroeder (1864–1953), by Alison Reppy, Ethel Clyde, and Lesley Kuhn. The volume contains an account of Schroeder's will, leaving his estate to Mrs. Clyde and Mr. Kuhn for the purpose of collecting, arranging, and publishing his writings, and the decision of the Connecticut Supreme Court holding the trust invalid and awarding the estate to cousins. Judge O'Sullivan stated that "the law will not declare a trust valid when the object of the trust, as the finding discloses, is to distribute articles which reek of the sewer." A lower court judge had found that

Schroeder's works "extol anti-social ideas" and were offensive to religious beliefs of Mormons and Catholics. Schroeder had opposed polygamy and favored birth control.

Kunitz, Stanley J. "Anti-American Way." *Wilson Library Bulletin*, 15:258–59, November 1940.   **K 216**
In his column, The Roving Eye, Kunitz is concerned with the intellectual climate of America when a state library trustee objects to too many "anti-American" books in our libraries; the Librarian of Congress "indicts our post-war writers, including himself, for telling the truth, the awful truth, about the war they lived through"; President Butler of Columbia University "warns his faculty, in extraordinary assembly, that professors and students not in sympathy with his pro-war stand should resign"; the chairman of the New York State Economic Council organizes a movement to ban the social science textbooks of Professor Harold O. Rugg.

Kunstler, William M. "Andrew Hamilton." In his *The Case for Courage*. New York, Morrow, 1962, pp. 17–45.   **K 217**
An account of the courage of the New York lawyer in defending John Peter Zenger, an impoverished printer accused of criminal libel. A century after his death, Hamilton's interpretations of the law of criminal libel have been accepted by the English-speaking world.

Kupferman, Theodore R., and Philip J. O'Brien, Jr. "Motion Picture Censorship: the Memphis Blues." *Cornell Law Quarterly*, 36:273–300, Winter 1951.   **K 218**
"The purpose of this article is to examine the bases of the Mutual Film decision in light of subsequent law and of fuller appreciation of the role of the motion picture and the censor to the community, and to determine how the issue may again be raised in order to give due weight to the intellectual menopause." This was the case of *Mutual Film Corp. v. Industrial Commission* in 1915, in which an Ohio statute providing for a board of censors of motion pictures was held by the U.S. Supreme Court to be constitutional. Much of the discussion

relates to the Memphis censorship of the movie, *Curley*, and the decisions of the courts.

Kutner, Luis. "Unfair Comment: A Warning to News Media." *University of Miami Law Review*, 17:51–74, Fall 1962.   **K 219**
"This article . . . proposes to delineate the steps to be taken in the light of existing case law to insure the defendant's right to a fair trial when unfavorable publicity may have reached and clouded the impartial judgment of the jurors."

Kvaraceus, William C. "Can Reading Affect Delinquency?" *ALA Bulletin*, 59: 516–22, June 1965.   **K 220**
The author explores some of the factors that relate to the fear, implicit in censorship, that reading of books will corrupt behavior. He considers these factors in terms of five focal principles: the wide gulf between knowing and doing, the highly individualistic reaction to literary works, the book as a source of hard-to-get information on sex, the principle of therapy, and the principle of guidance. "Reading must be viewed more as a symptom than a cause of adjustment or maladjustment. Reading tends to enforce what is already present and what has already been learned or experienced, frequently as far back as the early childhood years . . . Reading a specific book will seldom cause a 'normal' or 'average' child to go out and commit a similar act."

Kyle-Keith, Richard. *The High Price of Pornography.* Washington, D.C., Public Affairs, 1961. 230p.   **K 221**
A survey of the manufacture and dissemination of pornography in all forms of the mass media, presented as a serious social problem in the United States. Mr. Kyle-Keith cites evidence of the close connection between pornography and crimes of violence. He concludes: (1) Society must alter the sex directed tendencies in the mass media to avoid creating a need which cannot be satisfied under currently accepted mores. (2) Unless voluntary standards are applied by the media, public opinion will force a more rigid control.

L

La Barre, Weston. "Obscenity: an Anthropological Appraisal." *Law and Contemporary Problems*, 20:533–43, Autumn 1955. **L1**
"This discussion has attempted to show, through comparative examples, the anthropological relativity of obscenity, whether in words, artistic representations, nudity of various parts of the body, or publicly prohibited acts." This article is part of a series on Obscenity and the Arts.

"Labelling, Another Form of Thought Control." *New Zealand Libraries*, 15:17–18, January–February 1952. **L2**

Lacy, Dan M. [*Censorship and Freedom*]. *Address at Session on Censorship and Freedom, 1960 Biennial Conference of American Civil Liberties Union.* [New York, ACLU, 1960]. 30 p. mimeo. **L3**
The managing director of the American Book Publishers Council covers the broad field of the government and freedom of communications, including censorship in the realm of subversive literature and obscenity (discussion of *Roth v. U.S.*), freedom and secrecy of government information, the government's role as buyer and purveyor of books, and the relationship of government to the communications system in the United States through policies of the FCC, antitrust laws, postal rates, and copyright.

——. "Censorship and Obscenity." *ALA Bulletin*, 59:471–76, June 1965. **L4**
Unlike seditious and heretical work, objected to because they may lead to an illegal or undesirable action, blasphemy and obscenity are considered as offenses in themselves. The intensity of objection to verbal and pictorial reference to sex arises from the fact that "in no other area of human life does society attempt to exercise a control so rigorous over an appetite so imperative." Such intensity is paralleled only in reaction against communism or racial integration—"the other two foci of censorship." Lacy charges librarians with responsibility not only for defending their own rights to acquire and circulate material but to provide community leadership in opposing censorship.

——. *Freedom and Books*. Address to the Georgia Library Association, 24 October 1953. New York, American Book Publishers Council, 1953. 12 p. mimeo. (Reprinted in *Nieman Reports*, January 1954; excerpts in Daniels, *Censorship of Books*, pp. 155–59) **L5**
The importance in a democracy of the freedom to write and read. Advice to librarians for withstanding the pressure of censorship.

——. "Freedom and Books." *Southeastern Librarian*, 4:14–26, Spring 1954. **L6**
A review of recent efforts in the United States to ban books that describe sexual experience in detail. Censorship takes three forms: state or municipal commissions, police lists, and unofficial committees. In attempting to combat pornography without resort to court action, these groups are likely to interfere with legitimate books. Personal views and prejudices of the individuals or groups may become the standards employed. Publishers object to a code of self-regulation because the real pornographers would not join and because the code, in itself, would be an act of censorship. Librarians are under pressure from unofficial groups to exclude books that are obscene, that deal favorably with the United Nations, or whose authors are suspected of left-wing association. They are also criticized for not having books with the point of view of the complainants.

——. *Freedom and Communications*. Urbana, University of Illinois Press, 1961. 63 p. (7th annual Windsor Lectures) (2d ed., 1965. 108 p.) **L7**
The author looks at the whole system of communications—books, newspapers, magazines, radio, television, films, schools, and libraries—noting the great technical changes and the growing demands placed upon the agencies of communications. He also notes serious weaknesses in the communications system, such as the failure to achieve wide enough distribution of knowledge and the tendency for uniformity and oversimplification. He calls for a reassessment of public policy in the area in which the communications industry operates.

——. "Freedom of the Press." *Religion in Life*, 30:7–16, Winter 1960–61. **L8**
Christian concern with freedom of the press must include opposition to extralegal censorship, encouragement of the press to give a fair voice to minority views, concern with legislation affecting broadcasting, support of the schools as a free forum of wide-ranging views, and support of school and public libraries. The Church should resist well-intentioned but hysterical efforts to set up committees outside the law to attack textbooks, purge newsstands, ban books from libraries, or exert pressures on newspapers.

——. "Obscenity and Censorship." *Christian Century*, 77:540–43, 4 May 1960. **L9**
The author examines the charge that dissemination of pornographic materials in the United States has reached dangerous proportions. He discusses four categories of sex literature: hard-core pornography, borderline "girlie" magazines, frank fiction, and scientific sexual works. He finds little evidence that the relative importance of hard-core pornography has grown greatly or that there is any cause for hysteria. Few psychologists see sex literature as a major cause of juvenile delinquency; such literature reflects rather than influences moral standards.

——. *On Obscenity and Censorship*. Columbia, Mo., Freedom of Information Center, School of Journalism, University of Missouri, 1960. 10 p. (Publication no. 38) **L10**
An address at the 1960 biennial conference of the American Civil Liberties Union. Lacy considers the problem of the government as censor—the moderate censorship of Customs, the "almost furtively administered" Foreign Agents Registration Act as it pertains to mailing of political propaganda, and the Post Office Department's action against obscene publications. He recommends that the ACLU, in light of the Roth decision, concern itself with defending only those publications having some slight "redeeming social importance." He notes the growing trend toward secrecy in government affairs and in the control of information derived from government-sponsored scientific research. Another area of government control is in the selection

of textbooks for schools. Since the only feasible way for tens of millions of Americans to get books is through public libraries, there must be freedom of library book selection. He sees a reduction in threats to libraries. Finally, he considers the government's role in influencing the economic circumstances in which the media of communications operate.

————. "A Self-Policing Code for Book Publishing?" *Publishers' Weekly*, 177: 48–50, 8 February 1960. (Also issued as a separate pamphlet by the American Book Publishers Council) **L11**
Testimony before the U.S. House of Representatives Subcommittee on Postal Operations in opposition to a publishing industry code or reviewing authority which he believes would be "a grave, indeed an intolerable, mistake . . . Any 'code' that forecloses discussion of specified themes or situations, or predetermines the attitudes to be taken toward them, or defines in advance the language that may be used in describing them, or otherwise prescribes for an author what parts of life he may deal with and in what ways he may deal with them—though it will not outwit the evil-minded—will by that much limit the freedom of the writer of integrity . . . I hope . . . that the day will never come in this country when books are not free to challenge and attack, to shock and offend, to call established institutions and traditional thinking into question, to confront complacency with impudence and to test with the weapons of ridicule and satire."

————. "Should the Book Publishing Industry Set up a Self-Policing Program?" *American Scholar*, 29:407–8+, Summer 1960. **L12**
The author is opposed to a code for book publishing.

————, and George P. Thomson. "Censorship." In *Encyclopaedia Britannica*, 1959. vol. 5, pp. 117–21. **L13**
Historical development of censorship in the United States and Great Britain, including actions by customs and postal authorities and censorship of motion pictures, radio, and television. Special attention is given to wartime restrictions.

Lacy, George. *Liberty and Law: Being an Attempt at the Refutation of the Individualism of Mr. Herbert Spencer and the Political Economists; an Exposition of Natural Rights, and of the Principles of Justice, and of Socialism and a Demonstration of the Worthlessness of the Supposed Dogmas of Orthodox Political Economy.* London, Sonnenschein, Lowrey, 1880. 377 p. **L14**
Chapter 10 deals with Liberty of the Press and Freedom of Speech. The author opposes unabridged freedom of expression.

Ladas, Stephen P. *The International Protection of Literary and Artistic Property.*

New York, Macmillan, 1938. 2 vols. (Harvard Studies in International Law, no. 3) **L15**
Vol. 1, International Copyright and Inter-American Copyright. Vol. 2, Copyright in the United States of America and Summary of Copyright Law in Various Countries.

Lader, Lawrence. *The Margaret Sanger Story and the Fight for Birth Control.* New York, Doubleday, 1955. 352 p. **L16**
"In 1912, when she launched her crusade for birth control, to print a pamphlet on the subject or to open a birth control clinic was a serious crime." Mrs. Sanger battled the police and the vice societies and frequently went to prison in defiance of the Comstock law, which classified all information on contraception as pornography.

"*Lady Chatterley:* Judged by Her Peers." *Economist*, 197:1215–16, 17 December 1960. **L17**
Editorial on the debate in the House of Lords on a motion to ban for all time not only *Lady Chatterley* but all the writings of D. H. Lawrence or any other writer of books of a similar nature.

"*Lady Chatterley:* Turn Up for the Book." *Economist*, 197:536, 5 November 1960. **L18**
Editorial on the trial of *Lady Chatterley's Lover* under the Obscene Publications Act and the acquittal of the publisher, Penguin Books.

"*Lady Chatterley's Lover:* Printers' Censorship?" *Economist*, 195:518, 7 May 1960. **L19**
An unexpurgated Penguin edition was postponed because printers declined to set it in type, presumably through fear of legal action.

La Follette, Robert M. "People Demand a Free Press." *La Follette's Magazine*, 12:161, November 1920. **L20**
In a front page editorial La Follette charges that education is of little avail so long as the "sources of current news are poisoned and editorial comment controlled by sordid and mercenary influences . . . It is doubtful if the American people can ever emancipate themselves from the merciless exploitation of the colossal monopoly which controls markets and prices, until they shall establish a free and independent press."

Laidler, Harry W. *Boycotts and the Labor Struggle; Economic and Legal Aspects . . . with an Introduction by Henry R. Seeger.* London, Lane, 1914. 488 p. **L21**
Includes a discussion of press control in labor conflicts and "conspiracy" charges as a means of suppressing boycott propaganda. The author affirms that boycott notices are protected as a part of freedom of the press.

Lake, Albert C. "Pursuing a Policy." *Library Journal*, 90:2491–94, 1 June 1965. **L22**
In advocating a written policy in public library book selection, the author states, "I am not only concerned with its effectiveness in improving the quality of library collections but also in its use as a defense against outside pressures." Despite the official position of the profession on intellectual freedom as expressed in the Library Bill of Rights and the articulate position of the library press, there is a lack of unanimity among librarians on the relative importance of intellectual freedom as a library problem. He calls for "rational debate in the library profession with the widest possible participation, not necessarily to achieve a consensus but rather to bring about a greater understanding of the issues involved."

Lamar, William H. "The Government's Attitude toward the Press." *Forum*, 59:129–40, February 1918. **L23**
The solicitor of the Post Office Department interprets that agency's ruling with respect to the Trading with the Enemy and Espionage Acts.

Lamb, Edward. *No Lamb for Slaughter.* New York, Harcourt, Brace & World, 1963. 248 p. **L24**
An American financier describes (chapters 10 through 13) his four-year ordeal in clearing himself of false charges of being a Communist. The charges were levied against him by the Federal Communications Commission and sustained by a parade of hired witnesses when he attempted to renew his radio and television licenses. When Lamb was cleared by the Commission in 1957, *TV Digest* wrote: "It is clear now that the Lamb case was conceived by an inept and fumbling Commission which bowed to pressures of the times when communist hysteria was at its peak." Former Attorney-General Howard McGrath served as defense attorney; Senator Estes Kefauver wrote the foreword to the book.

————. *Trial by Battle: The Case History of a Washington Witch Hunt.* Santa Barbara, Calif., Center for the Study of Democratic Institutions, 1964. 24 p. (Occasional Paper on the Free Society) **L25**
A revised version of the section of Lamb's autobiography, *No Lamb for Slaughter*, dealing with the melodramatic trial in which Lamb was forced to defend himself against charges of being a Communist in order to renew his radio and television licenses. In an introduction, Harry S. Ashmore, of the *Arkansas Gazette*, notes that "many of the hired character assassins employed by the federal government in the trial went off the federal payroll only to find similar employment with official agencies of the Southern states." The Lamb case is the lineal antecedent of the 1964

favorable ruling on the Pacifica Foundation broadcasting licenses, the text of which is given as an appendix. The ruling stated in part: "We recognize that as shown by the complaints here that provocative programming as here involved may offend some listeners. But this does not mean that those offended have the right, through the Commission's licensing power, to rule such programming off the airwaves . . . No such drastic curtailment can be countenanced under the Constitution, the Communications Act, or the Commission's policy, which has consistently sought to insure the maintenance of radio and television as a medium of freedom of speech and freedom of expression for the people of the Nation as a whole."

[Lambert, John]. *The Case of Libel, the King v. John Lambert and Others, Printer and Proprietors of the Morning Chronicle: With the Arguments of Counsel, and Decision of the Court* . . . London, Printed for J. Debrett, 1794. 68 p. (Also in Borrow, *Celebrated Trials*, vol. 6, pp. 69–85 and Erskine, *Speeches*, vol. 2, pp. 371–453) **L 26**
Lambert, the printer, and James Perry, the editor, were tried before Lord Kenyon for a libel against the king. Thomas Erskine delivered a notable speech for the defense and Perry spoke in his own behalf. The jury delivered a verdict of "guilty of publishing, but with no malicious intent." When Lord Kenyon refused to accept this as a verdict the jury found the defendants "not guilty." A New York edition, including the trial of William Cobbett, was published by D. C. & P. Burkloe in 1810.

Lambert, Richard S. *The Cobbett of the West. A Study of Thomas Latimer and the Struggle between Pulpit and Press at Exeter.* London, Nicholson and Watson, 1939. 254 p. **L 27**
The story of Thomas Latimer, editor of the *Western Times*, Exeter, England. A lifelong champion of liberal causes and freedom of the press, he was prosecuted for libel on several occasions, once by the militant Bishop of Exeter. In this case, which involved the right of the press to criticize the pulpit, Latimer was acquitted after a distinguished defense by Alexander Cockburn. The verdict was widely acclaimed by the English press.

Lamm, Richard. "Constitutionality of Local Ordinance Prohibiting Distribution and Sale of 'Crime Comic' Books. *Katzev v. County of Los Angeles* (Cal. 1959)." *California Law Review*, 48:145–51, March 1960. **L 28**

Lamont, Corliss. *Freedom Is as Freedom Does; Civil Liberties Today.* New York, Horizon, 1956. 340 p. **L 29**

In a chapter, entitled The Drive Against Cultural Freedom, Lamont summarizes the attacks made by government and private groups during the last decade to curb expression in art, literature, science, and religion. He refers to attacks on such movies as *Pinky*, *The Birth of a Nation*, *The Moon Is Blue*, *Oliver Twist*, and *The Miracle*, the blacklisting of radio and television performers, and the controversy in Detroit over the art work of Diego Rivera. He also refers to the book-burning in State Department overseas libraries during the McCarthy era and the various Post-Office actions against "subversive" publications.

Lamont, William A. *Marginal Prynne, 1600–1669.* London, Routledge and Paul, 1963. 250 p. (Studies in Political History) **L 30**
A new study of the public life of this prolific Puritan pamphleteer, who suffered torture and imprisonment for defying the authorities in his writings. Based largely on a study of Prynne's pamphlets and the vast amount of literature that surrounds them.

Lamoreux, Stephen, *comp.*, *The Right of Privacy—A Bibliography: 1890–1961.* Pullman, Wash., Washington State University Press, 1963. 54 p. mimeo. **L 31**
An annotated listing of books, pamphlets, and articles covering various phases of the right of privacy, prefaced by an essay on the subject. Includes numerous brief or specialized articles not listed in this bibliography.

Lander, Byron G. "Stillness in Lincoln, Illinois." *Focus/Midwest*, 2:10–11, May 1963. **L 32**
"College officials [Lincoln College] sided and abetted the local news media in suppression of the news so that they could quietly dismiss an instructor whose views differed from those of donors of the college."

Landis, James M. "Freedom of Speech and of the Press." *Encyclopaedia of the Social Sciences.* New York, Macmillan, 1931. vol. 6, pp. 455–59. **L 33**

Landis, Simon M. *A Full Account of the Trial of Simon M. Landis, M.D., for Uttering and Publishing a Book Entitled "Secrets of Generation." Phonographically Reported by C. R. Morgan, M.D.* Philadelphia, The First Progressive Christian Church, 1870. 76 p. **L 34**
The case of *Commonwealth v. Landis*, Philadelphia, 1870. Dr. Landis, a minister and physician, was charged with having published a sex education book that was "lewd, filthy, and corrupt." Despite able counsel, a verdict against the defendant was assured when Judge William S. Pierce refused to allow fellow physicians to offer testimony of the medical truth or value of the book. A new trial was refused and the maximum sentence imposed—$500 fine and one year in prison.

Landon, Perceval. "War Correspondents and the Censorship." *Nineteenth Century*, 52:327–37, August 1902. **L 35**
"The present article will attempt to indicate some of the conditions under which correspondents work on active service, and a rough scheme for securing the ends of both the censor and the censored will be suggested, though it is the opinion of the writer that the true course is rather to exercise care in the appointment of censors and in the original formation of the corps of correspondents than to hamper the latter with irritating restrictions afterwards."

Landor, Ronald A. "The Fallacy of 'Balance' in Public Library Book Selection." *Library Journal*, 91:629–32, 1 February 1966. **L 36**
"A sane community is one that seeks to identify its real problems and to discuss them rationally. The public library is more likely to be helpful in this quest if its materials are selected according to criteria of excellence and not by a balancing act." Irresponsible, badly written political writings have no more place on the shelves of the public library than does hard-core pornography.

Landry, Robert J. "Radio and Government." *Public Opinion Quarterly*, 2:557–69, October 1938. **L 37**
"In conclusion, we find that commercial broadcasting criticizes the FCC for being too harsh. Pressure groups to the contrary declare it is not strict enough."

Lane, Tamar. *What's Wrong with the Movies?* Los Angeles, Waverly, 1923. 254 p. **L 38**
Contains a chapter on movie censorship.

Lang, Andrew. "The Evolution of Literary Decency." *Book Lover*, 2(5):1–5, Autumn 1900. **L 39**
The author attributes the rise in prudishness in English fiction, which had once been robust and bawdy, to the rise in the readership of the middle class, particularly of women, and to the moral revolution of the Wesleyan movement.

Lang, Fritz. "Freedom of the Screen." *Theatre Arts*, 31:52–55, December 1947. **L 40**
A Hollywood film producer with experience under the Nazis is critical of all censorship, but censorship of the movies in particular. "The way of real security and progress lies neither in the blind acceptance nor in the indiscriminate rejection of new ideas; they must be scrutinized, tested, and, if found of value, adopted. The censor would deny us the right to examine what is new." Censorship never cured a social evil. It is sheer hypocrisy to suppose that those who serve as censors are wiser or more mature than those whom they strive to protect. Children, evidence shows, absorb from pictures what they have already learned from their environment.

While recognizing that some self-censorship of the movie industry may be necessary, it should be flexible and sensitive to changes in public understanding and taste.

Lang, George. "Free Press and Religious Freedom." *Vital Speeches*, 5:693–99, 1 September 1939. **L 41**
"A free press is at one with the Christian religion in affirming the dignity and worth of the plain man. It is also obvious that a free press is at one with those who affirm the service of reason to promote human welfare."

Langford, John A. *Prison Books and Their Authors*. London, W. Tegg, 1861. 357p. **L 42**
Contents: Boethus, Earl of Surrey, Cervantes, Walter Raleigh, Robert Southwell, George Withers, Lovelace, Bunyan, Dr. Dodd, James Montgomery, Leigh Hunt, and Thomas Cooper.

Lanning, R. J. "German Periodicals and Canadian Censorship; An Interim Report." *Pacific Northwest Library Association Quarterly*, 4:47–48, January 1940. **L 43**
Discusses Canadian censorship of German periodicals during World War II under the Trading with the Enemy Act.

"Lantern Bearers; Censorship and the National Board." *Survey*, 35:9–14, 2 October 1915. **L 44**
Censorship of the movies in the early days of the industry.

La Palombara, Joseph. "Is the Press Too Free?" *Pacific Spectator*, 7:51–60, Winter 1953. **L 45**
American newspapers are operating in twentieth-century society with a nineteenth-century concept of press freedom. The newspaper publisher often considers his paper as private property, immune from private or government interference. The author recommends vigorous application of the antitrust laws to newspapers, a legal compulsion to publish a reply or to correct erroneous statements, the creation of trusteeship newspapers such as the London *Times*, and, as a last resort, the establishment of municipally owned newspapers for those cities with a newspaper monopoly.

Lapica, Ray. "The FCC: Protector or Censor?" *Southern California Law Review*, 38:634–66, Summer 1965. **L 46**
"The FM program-splitting rule seems to be a questionable extension of FCC control, for it seeks to accomplish through government regulation what economic pressure will gradually solve."

Laprade, William T. "The Freedom of the Press: an Outworn Shibboleth?" *South Atlantic Quarterly*, 35:212–19, April 1936. **L 47**

The author reconsiders the question of freedom of the press in light of the change in the character of the daily newspaper from that familiar to the controversialists of the seventeenth and eighteenth centuries and the framers of the Constitution to the modern daily newspaper and its publisher who has become a merchandising capitalist. "The monopolistic character of the enterprise of gathering and dispensing news and current comment and its profound influence of the material thus dispensed in shaping mass emotions certainly raise the question whether a publisher chiefly interested in earning profit is the most suitable trustee of this undertaking?"

Lardner, John. "Let 'em Eat Newspapers." *Newsweek*, 45:92, 14 March 1955; 45:95, 21 March 1955. **L 48**
An exposé of widespread police censorship in Detroit and the work of Inspector Herbert W. Case. Action was taken against works of Hemingway, Farrell, Dos Passos, Salinger, Havelock Ellis, and Hans Christian Anderson. The obscenity list, known as the "Detroit Line," is compiled each month by Inspector Case.

Larned, J. N. "Improper Books." *Library Journal*, 20:35, Denver Conference of Librarians, 1895. **L 49**
"It is important that every possible effort should be made, in the management of a public library, to avoid the appearance of an assumption of arbitrary censorship over the literature supplied to its readers." The attitude of the library toward questionable books is one that "will cast responsibility for the possession and use of them, as far as may be, on the public for whom the library is maintained." Comments of the superintendent of the Buffalo Public Library in one of a series of papers on undesirable books in public libraries.

Larrabee, Eric. "The Cultural Context of Sex Censorship." *Law and Contemporary Problems*, 20:672–88, Autumn 1955. (Reprinted in Downs, *The First Freedom*, pp. 193–201) **L 50**
Based in part on the author's paper on Morality and Obscenity in the American Library Association's *Freedom of Book Selection*. Larrabee observes "the universal human inability to draw a sharp line between lust and love."

———. "Morality and Obscenity." In *Freedom of Book Selection; Proceedings of the Second Conference on Intellectual Freedom . . .* Chicago, American Library Association, 1954, pp. 23–41. **L 51**

———. "Pornography Is Not Enough." In his *The Self-Conscious Society*. New York, Doubleday, 1960, pp. 99–118. (Also in *Harper's Magazine*, November 1960) **L 52**
A review of the struggle between the literati and the Philistines over censorship of sex

expression. "The true obscenities of American life," according to Larrabee, "lie in our vicious consumption of human suffering, in virtually every form and medium. By comparison, the literature of sexual love would seem vastly to be preferred. The only real question is whether pornography is enough, whether literature alone can do the trick, and whether the tentative liberties now allotted to a handful of authors will undo the damage of over a century of censorship before another puritan cycle begins." This chapter originated in a speech published in the American Library Association's *Freedom of Book Selection*, 1954.

Larsen, Samuel J. "The Stroke of the Blue Pencil." *Catholic Digest*, 20(11):72–75, September 1956. (Condensed from the *Home Messenger*, August 1955) **L 53**
While most objections to censorship come from those who wish to produce something really censorable, some objections are well taken. The censor has sometimes blundered and banned a work of art, e.g., Shaw's *Mrs. Warren's Profession*. The most damaging thing that can be said of censors is that they ignore artistic expression. "About 75% of the films rated as 'morally unobjectionable,' might also be listed as 'morally inane.'"

Larson, Cedric. "The British Ministry of Information." *Public Opinion Quarterly*, 5:412–31, Fall 1941. **L 54**
An account of the early and often hectic years of the agency established in Great Britain to counteract Nazi propaganda efforts.

———. "Censorship of Army News During the World War, 1917–1918." *Journalism Quarterly*, 17:313–23, December 1940. **L 55**

———, and James R. Mock. "The Lost Files of the Creel Committee of 1917–19." *Public Opinion Quarterly*, 3:5–29, January 1939. **L 56**
In the course of writing a book on the Committee on Public Information (Creel Committee) in World War I, the authors discovered in the basement of a War Department building a Committee file that had lain forgotten and untouched for 20 years. The article is based on information revealed by the documents. Some documents are reproduced in print or facsimile.

Larson, Lorentz. "Censur och lagstiftning mot mindelvärdig litteratur." *Skolbiblioteket*, 3:70–73, 1957. **L 57**
A review of legislation against objectionable comics and "inferior literature" in Great Britain, Germany, Austria, and France.

Lasch, Robert. "For a Free Press." *Atlantic Monthly*, 174:39–44, July 1944.

(Reprinted in S. S. Morgan, *Opinions and Attitudes in the Twentieth Century*, pp. 472–83) **L 58**
An editorial writer on the Chicago *Sun* has written this prize-winning essay on freedom of the press in which he charges irresponsible editorial control as a major obstacle to a free press.

———. "A Real Threat to Freedom." *Nieman Reports*, 1(3):7–8, July 1947. **L 59**
If the Associated Press decision handed down by the U.S. Supreme Court is undone by House Resolution 110, protection from press monopoly is removed.

Lasker, Albert D. "Freedom of Advertising and a Free Press." *Vital Speeches*, 1:27–32, 8 October 1934. **L 60**
"No more vicious calumny has ever been put forth than the suspicion that the press in any major or important way can be influenced editorially by the advertising patrons." A free press is possible in America because of its advertisers. "End free advertising and you will largely end a free press such as we have known." Address of the chairman of the board of Lord & Taylor before a Conference on Retail Distribution.

Lasker, Edward. "Censorship of Motion Pictures Pursuant to Recent Supreme Court Decisions." *UCLA Law Review*, 1:582–92, June 1954. **L 61**

Laski, Harold J. "Civil Liberties in Great Britain in Wartime." *Bill of Rights Review*, 2:243–51, Summer 1942. **L 62**
Includes a discussion of the powers and operation of the British Home Secretary, under Regulation 2D, to suppress objectionable publications.

———. *Freedom of the Press in Wartime.* London, National Council for Civil Liberties, 1941. 16 p. **L 63**
The intellectual leader of the left wing of Britain's Labour Party criticizes the action of the Ministry of Information in the wartime suppression of the *Daily Worker* and the *Week*. Laski prefers that the government issue a warning and require the editor to offer proof that his intentions were not subversive.

———. . . . *Laski v. Newark Advertiser Co., Ltd. & Parlby, before Lord Goddard, Lord Chief Justice of England and a Special Jury.* London, Daily Express, [1947]. 398 p. **L 64**
The well-known political scientist and leader in the Labour Party brought action against the newspaper for a statement quoting Laski as declaring that if the policy of the Labour Party should not be put into effect by con-stitutional means, he advocated "revolution by violence." The jury found that the news-paper report was fair and accurate and judg-ment was given for the defendants.

———. "Sedition: The Case of the *Daily Worker*." *New Statesman and Nation*, 2:743, 12 December 1931. **L 65**
The recent convictions of the printers and journalists connected with the *Daily Worker* for incitement of the armed forces of the Crown to mutiny prompts the author to a criticism of the Seditious Libels Act. He recommends the interpretation of the sedition laws given by American Justice Holmes in the Abrams case.

Laski, Marghanita. "Obscene Literature." *New Statesman*, 47:634, 15 May 1954. Discussion, 47:664, 22 May 1954; 47:700, 29 May 1954; 47:733, 5 June 1954; 48:44, 10 July 1954. **L 66**
In a letter to the editor the writer challenges some of the thinking about corruption by literature. For example, she points out, 5,000,000 copies of a particularly corrupting series have been sold. At 2 readers per copy, "this means that one-fifth of the population is already corrupt." No corrupted young person has ever been offered in evidence. Miss Laski is answered by several correspond-ents, including S. D. Francis in the 29 May 1954 issue.

Lasswell, Harold D. "Atmosphere of Censorship." In California. University. School of Librarianship. *Climate of Book Selection.* Berkeley, The School, 1959, pp. 41–49. **L 67**

———. "Censorship." In *Encyclopaedia of the Social Sciences.* New York, Macmillan, 1931. vol. 30, pp. 290–94. **L 68**
A discussion of the concept of censorship from the earliest times to the present day, with selected examples.

———. "Politics and Subversion." In *Freedom of Book Selection; Proceedings of the Second Conference on Intellectual Free-dom.* . . . Chicago, American Library Association, 1954, pp. 42–55. **L 69**
"The continuing study of national security problems calls for self-knowledge, knowledge of the Soviets, knowledge of the peoples in between."

———. "Propaganda and Mass In-security." *Psychiatry*, 13:283–99, August 1950. (Reprinted in Stanton and Perry, *Personality and Political Crisis*) **L 70**
A discussion of interrelations among propa-ganda, mass insecurity, censorship, totali-tarianism, individual freedom, and national security.

———, Ralph D. Casey, and Bruce L. Smith. *Propaganda and Promotional Activities: An Annotated Bibliography.* Min-neapolis, University of Minnesota Press, 1935. 450 p. **L 71**
This volume, together with a continuation of the work by Smith, Lasswell, and Casey, *Propaganda, Communication, and Public Opinion*, represents a comprehensive bibliographic coverage of propaganda literature. A section on censorship is given on pp. 382–401.

Lathrop, Charles N. *The Motion Picture Problem.* New York, Federal Council of Churches of Christ in America, Com-mission on Church and Social Service, 1922. 51 p. (Excerpts on Control of the Motion Pictures in Rutland, *State Censor-ship of Motion Pictures*, pp. 146–62) **L 72**
An objective discussion of various proposals for improvement of the moral quality of movies: the "thirteen points" for regulating standards of films, set up by the National Board of Review; arguments pro and con on state regulatory boards and provisions of the five laws in operation (Maryland, Ohio, Pennsylvania, Kansas, and New York); and proposals for federal licensing of producers to do business through interstate commerce. The author is inclined to favor some form of general business licensing, rather than censorship boards, which would place respon-sibility upon the industry rather than the government.

Laud, William. *The History of the Troubles and Tryal of the Most Reverend Father in God, and Blessed Martyr, William Laud, Lord Archbishop of Canterbury. Wrote by Himself, during his Imprisonment in the Tower.* . . . London, Printed for Ri Chis-well, 1695. 616 p. **L 73**
Under the Long Parliament, Archibishop Laud was brought to trial on charges of high treason for his conduct of the licensing of books. The enemies he had made among the Puritans (especially William Prynne) by his Star Chamber proceedings now returned to perse-cute him with a vengeance. Laud was found guilty of more serious charges and was hanged. His chaplain and licenser was required to make public recantation from the pulpit of the errors of his judgment on printing.

———. *A Speech Delivered in the Starr Chamber, on Wednesday, The XIVth of June, MDCXXXVII. At The Censvre, of John Bastwick, Henry Burton, & William Prinn; Concerning pretended Innovations In the Church.* London, Richard Badger, 1637. 77 p. **L 74**
The Archbishop of Canterbury, an arch enemy of the freedom of the press, especially when it involved the Puritans, delivered this speech praising the king and members of the Star Chamber and vilifying the defen-dants and their theology. Prynne and the

others were shorn of their ears and sentenced to life imprisonment. The king ordered the printing and distribution of Laud's speech but it was generally received with bitterness.

Laugesen, Richard W. "Freedom of Speech and Press—Anonymous Communication." *Dicta*, 37:384–88, November–December 1960. **L75**
Notes on the anonymous handbill case, *Tally v. California*, 1960.

[*Laughing Horse*]. "Symposium of Criticism, Comment, and Opinion on the Subject of Censorship." *Laughing Horse* (Taos, New Mexico), no. 17, February 1930. 32 p. (Willard Johnson, editor) **L76**

In response to Editor Johnson's request for comments on Senator Bronson Cutting's fight in the U.S. Senate against Customs censorship, a group of prominent literary and public figures express their opinions. Brief but cogent and often witty comments from Carl Sandburg, Maxwell E. Perkins, Edward C. Aswell, Will Irwin, John Dewey, Arthur D. Ficke, Sherwood Anderson, B. W. Huebsch, William Allen White, Witter Bynner, Margaret Larkin (she accuses the publishers of encouraging censorship), Ellery Sedgwick, Alfred A. Knopf, Mabel Dodge Luhan, W. W. Norton, Upton Sinclair, Mary Austin, E. B. W. (assistant editor, *The New Yorker*), Camilo Padilla, John Metcalfe, John Collier, Haniel Long, Lincoln Steffens, Evelyn D. Scott (reports on interview with John Sumner), Harriert Monroe, Henry G. Leach, Cyril Kay-Scott, Josie Turner, and Logan Clendening. Ironically, an insert notes, a cartoon by Will Shuster, intended for the publication, was suppressed by the man who was entrusted to send the cartoon to the engravers.

Launer, Seymour. "News-Gathering Agencies and Freedom of the Press." *St. John's Law Review*, 19:128–34, April 1945. **L77**
Discusses the issues raised in the case, *U.S. v. Associated Press*, 52 F. Supp. 362 (1943), then awaiting a U.S. Supreme Court decision. The supporters of the Associated Press maintain that mandatory requirements with respect to changes in the Association's bylaws are an infringement on the right of a free press; the Government position is that, under cover of a Constitutional right, the Association is attempting to monopolize the free flow of information.

Laurencelle, Ulric G. "Censorship and Obscenity." *Canadian Bar Journal*, 4: 223–32, June 1961. **L78**
A discussion of the "Saskatchewan paper," a report of the Saskatchewan subcommittee on civil liberties dealing with censorship and obscenity which was presented to the Canadian Bar Association at its annual meeting in September 1960. The report stated that "the utmost freedom possible should be accorded the general adult public in its choice of literary

materials, films, and other exhibitions, and that each group should have the right to establish its norms and standards, so long as none attempts to force these norms and standards upon others, and so long as they are not positively and clearly harmful to classes such as children who require special care and protection." The committee favored positive measures to promote good reading rather than negative controls, which are largely ineffective.

Lauter, Vita, and Joseph H. Friend. "Radio and the Censors." *Forum*, 86: 359–65, December 1931. (Reprinted in Summers, *Radio Censorship*, pp. 154–68) **L79**

"Radio censorship, practiced by all commercial broadcasters, is governed throughout by the caprice of the broadcaster, who is limited only by the provisions of the Federal Radio Act of 1927." The author mentions instances of censorship to show how controversial issues, both large and small, are aired, or not aired, in a censored way. He is unsure whether government control would in any way ameliorate the present situation, but thinks perhaps it might clear away some of the inconsistency now prevalent in censorship.

Lavine, Harold, and James Wechsler. *War Propaganda and the United States*. New Haven, Yale University Press, 1940. 363 p. **L80**
A contemporary study of World War II propaganda published for the Institute for Propaganda Analysis. Numerous references to the related topic of censorship.

Law, William. *Absolute Unlawfulness of the Stage-entertainment Fully Demonstrated*. London, W. & J. Innys, 1726. 50 p. **L81**

"The Law and *Fanny Hill*." *Bookseller*, 3038:1326–28, 14 March 1964. **L82**
Discussion in the House of Commons of prosecutions of *Fanny Hill* under the Obscene Publications Act, 1959, and the confusion existing in the prosecution and sale of the work in England and the United States.

"The Law and the Obscene." *Economist*, 182:985, 23 March 1957. **L83**
Editorial concerned with the "outdated muddle" of the present law of obscenity in England under which magistrates have to order the destruction of the good along with the bad.

"The Law of Blasphemy." *London Magazine*, 19(n.s.):360–62, November 1827. **L84**
A satirical criticism of Lord Tenterden for his decision in the case of the Reverend Robert Taylor, convicted of blasphemy. The author criticizes the use of the meaningless phrase—"for Christianity is part and parcel of the law of the land." It is no more part and parcel of

the law of the land than it is part and parcel of Lord Tenterden's wig. It is solely a belief in the truth, subject to critical inquiry.

"Law of Contempt; Liberty of the Press Defined by Idaho Supreme Court." *Lawyer and Banker*, 6:73–81, April 1913. **L85**

"The Law of Libel." *Western Law Journal*, 2(n.s.):499–503, August 1850. (Reprinted from the *New York Tribune*) **L86**

"The Law of Libel and Its Results." *Law Journal*, 13:611–15, 5 October 1878. **L87**
A criticism of the law of libel as it is now interpreted and administered. The author suggests it is in the public interest to leave to the jury the decision whether or not the information complained of is in the public interest and whether its publication can be considered malicious. He cites the case of heavy loss at sea because of the pernicious practice of sending out unseaworthy ships, a practice not properly criticized in the press because of an earlier, unfavorable decision in a libel case against a press that had criticized the practice.

"Law of Libel and Liberty of the Press." *Westminster Review*, 3:285–321, April 1825. **L88**
An essay based on reviews of two current books: Francis Place, *On the Law of Libel; With Strictures on the Self-Styled Constitutional Association* (London, John Hunt, 1823. 73 p.) and Richard Mence, *The Law of Libel* (London, Maxwell, 1824. 595 p.). The review, published anonymously but attributed to John Stuart Mill, seeks to prove that "the law of England is as unfavorable to the liberty of the press, as that of the most despotic government which ever existed." Whatever liberty exists is not because of but in spite of the law.

["Law of Libel; Review of a Treatise on the 'Law of Libel and the Liberty of the Press' . . . by Thomas Cooper; and of *The People v. Croswell*"] *Southern Quarterly Review*, 12:236–68, July 1847. **L89**

The Law of Libels . . . London, Printed and sold by M. Thrush, 1765. 304 p. **L90**
Contents: Trial of the *North Briton*; Defence of the Liberty of the Press; The Most Considerable Cases in the Law Books Relating to Libels, Precedents of Remarkable Sentences for Libeling; Trial of the Seven Bishops; History of the British Constitution; Trial of John Peter Zenger; Rights of the Lords and Commons to Suppress as Enemies; Ministers of Arbitrary Power; and the Magna Charta.

"The Law of Obscene Literature." *Albany Law Journal*, 16:220–23, 29 September 1877. **L91**

An account of the Bradlaugh-Besant trial in London for publication of the birth control pamphlet, *Fruits of Philosophy*.

"The Law of Obscenity." *Social Service Review*, 11:108–9, March 1937. **L92**

Two court cases are discussed—one dealing with birth control articles, other the with the 1937 decision of a New York magistrate in dismissing a complaint against James T. Farrell's *A World I Never Made*.

"The Law of Obscenity: New Significance of the Receiving Group." *Indiana Law Journal*, 34:426–41, Spring 1959. **L93**

By confining the test of prurient effect on the receiving group, it is possible to allow scientific organizations to pursue research under existing obscenity laws. Notes involve the Institute for Sex Research at Indiana University in the case of *U.S. v. 31 Photographs* (1957).

"The Law of Sedition in India: A Study." *Bombay Law Journal*, 8:5–23, June 1930; 8:82–84, July 1930. **L94**

A brief history of sedition law in India, beginning with the 1837 penal code and including prosecutions for sedition during 1924–29. The author notes the disparity between the severity of punishment in India and in England. The second article compares Indian and South African sedition law.

"The Law Relating to Blasphemy." *Law Journal*, 64:182–83, 17 September 1927. **L95**

A review of British statutory and case law on a subject which "has caused our judges to differ amongst themselves more intensely than they have ever done upon any other." Special attention is given to the case, *Bowman v. The Secular Society* (1917).

"Law Relating to Blasphemy." *Law Magazine*, 8(3d ser.):247–80, 1860. **L96**

Lawrence, D. H. *A Propos of Lady Chatterley's Lover; being an essay extended from "My Skirmish with Jolly Roger."* London, Mandrake Press, 1930. 63 p. **L97**

Lawrence's own account of the suppression and pirating of his book. He discusses his use of taboo words that shocked the readers and led to censorship both in England and America, and the purpose behind the sex frankness of the book. "I want men and women to be able to think sex, fully, completely, honestly, and cleanly." He concludes with a discussion of the historic attitude of the Church toward sex expression.

———. "Introduction to These Paintings." In his *Paintings of D. H. Lawrence*. London, Mandrake Press, [1929]. 33 p. unnumbered. **L98**

In this criticism of contemporary English painting and praise of modern French painting, Lawrence considers the English fear of sex, beginning in the Renaissance, a major reason why England has produced so few painters. Fear of syphilis, particularly, gave a fearful blow to English sexual life, and in turn affected artistic expression. English painters have delighted and excelled in landscape paintings but have avoid the human figure. In the introduction to his *Pansies* (London, Secker, 1931, pp. 5–6), Lawrence refers to the Scotland Yard seizure of the MS and the need to omit certain poems in order for the book to be published.

———. *Pornography and Obscenity*. New York, Knopf, 1930. 40 p. (First published in *This Quarter* [Paris], July–September 1929; in London published by Faber and Faber [1936] as the first essay in Lawrence's *Pornography and So On*, pp. 11–53; reprinted in Lawrence, *Sex Literature and Censorship*, edited by Harry T. Moore, pp. 64–81, and in Downs, *The First Freedom*, pp. 171–80) **L99**

"What is pornography to one man," writes Lawrence, "is laughter of genius to another." Lawrence defends the role of the arts in openly stimulating sex feelings. Pornography, on the other hand, is the "dirty little secret," insulting and degrading to sex, and indefensible. He denounces word prudery as a mob habit.

———. *Sex, Literature, and Censorship*. Edited by Harry T. Moore. New York, Viking, 1959. 128 p. (Compass Books, C58) **L100**

Includes an introduction, D. H. Lawrence and the "Censor-Morons" by Harry T. Moore and the following essays by Lawrence relating to freedom of sex expression: Introduction to *Pansies* (unexpurgated edition, dealing with taboo words); State of Funk (the Englishman's fear of sex expression); *Pornography and Obscenity* (an attack on the "dirty little secret"); and *A Propos of Lady Chatterley's Lover*. The book includes the full text of Judge Bryan's decision in the U.S. District Court (1959) restraining the New York postmaster from excluding from the mails the Grove Press edition of *Lady Chatterley's Lover*. The English edition of *Sex, Literature, and Censorship* (Heineman, 1955) contains an essay by H. F. Rubinstein, The Law Versus D. H. Lawrence.

[———, and Henry Miller]. *Pornography and Obscenity; Handbook for Censors. Two Essays by D. H. Lawrence and Henry Miller.* Foreword by Russell F. Knutson. Introduction by Maurice Parmelee. Preface by Florenz Arslen-Masratoff. Michigan City, Ind., Fridtjof-Karla, 1958. 54 p. **L101**

Pornography and Obscenity by D. H. Lawrence was originally published by Alfred Knopf in New York in 1930; *Obscenity and the Law of Reflection* by Henry Miller is reprinted from *Remember to Remember*, New York, New Directions, 1947.

Lawrence, David. "International Freedom of the Press Essential to a Durable Peace." *Annals of the American Academy of Political and Social Science*, 72:139–41, July 1917. **L102**

———. "The Vanishing First Amendment." In American Society of Newspaper Editors, *Proceedings of the Annual Meeting, 1944*. Washington, D.C., ASNE, 1944, pp. 80–94. **L103**

"I do not believe that the First Amendment of the Constitution of the United States is today an adequate protection for the freedom of the press in America. Judicial interpretation has nullified the original purpose. I believe there must be an additional amendment to safeguard the freedom of the press." Lawrence objects to the application to newspapers of the constitutional power to regulate commerce. He complains particularly of the abuses of labor and postal authority.

Lawrence, Edmund, *pseud.* "Radio and the Richards Case." *Harper's Magazine*, 205:82–87, July 1952. **L104**

An anonymous southern California newsman discusses the four-year case of G. A. Richards before the FCC. Richards had been charged with misuse of his three powerful stations to attack his racial, political, and personal antagonists. With Richards' death, FCC was released from having to make a clear-cut decision on the misuse of radio facilities.

Lawrence, Eugene. "The Freedom of the Press in New York in 1733–35; An Epoch in American Journalism." *National Magazine*, 18:113–27, July-August 1893. **L105**

Account of the John Peter Zenger trial.

———. "New York and the 'Liberty of the Press.'" *Harper's Weekly*, 38:703, 28 July 1894. **L106**

Account of the John Peter Zenger trial.

Lawrence, James. *Dramatic Emancipation; on Strictures on the State of the Theatres, and the Consequent Degeneration of the Drama; on the Partiality and Injustice of the London Managers; on many Theatrical Regulations on the Continent, for the Security of the Literary and Dramatic Property; particularly deserving the attention of the Subscribers for a Third Theatre.* London, 1813. (The *Pamphleteer*, vol. 2, no. 4) **L107**

"The Laws against Blasphemy. Mr. Sergeant Talfourd's Defence of Moxon." *Law Magazine*, 26:139–52, August 1841.
L108
The publisher Edward Moxon was found guilty of blasphemous libel in publishing the works of Shelley.

Lawson, John D., *ed. American State Trials . . .* St. Louis, Thomas Law Book Co., 1914. 18 vols. **L109**
Summarizes historic American trials, including a number of sedition trials involving freedom of the press. These are referred to in the present bibliography under the name of the defendant.

Lawson, W. P. "Do You Believe in Censors?" *Harper's Weekly*, 60:86–88, 23 January 1915. **L110**
Article opposes legal censorship of the movies and defends the type of voluntary censorship represented by the National Board of Censorship.

———. "How the Censor Works." *Harper's Weekly*, 60:39–40, 9 January 1915. **L111**
Account of the forming of the National Board of Censorship by the People's Institute of New York in cooperation with the motion picture manufacturers, and explains the procedure of the Board in passing upon films.

———. "Standards of Censorship." *Harper's Weekly*, 60:63–65, 16 January 1915. (This article and others in the series were reprinted by the National Board of Censorship, *Movies: Their Importance and Supervision*, 1917. 20 p.) **L112**
Statement of the basic policy of the National Board of Censorship in its review of motion pictures. Movie censors are "chosen for their sincerity, their breadth of sympathy, and the diversity of their training and experience."

Layard, George S. *Suppressed Plates, Wood Engravings, &c. Together With Other Curiosities Germane Thereto; Being an Account of Certain Matters Peculiarly Alluring to the Collector.* London, Adam and Charles Black, 1907. 254 p. **L113**
An account of book illustrations that have been suppressed, usually by the publishers or artists, because of error, disapproval, or fear of libel, but not because of indecency.

Layton, *Sir* Walter T. *Newsprint, a Problem for Democracy.* London, O'Donoghue, 1946. 20 p. **L114**
The chairman of the rationing committee of Britain's wartime Newsprint Supply Co. describes the wartime rationing of newsprint. He argues for more and larger papers as a means for free expression. Government restric-

tions on newsprint supply were relaxed in January 1949. A review of the wartime restriction on newsprint supplies and its consequences is given in a 42-page report, *Newsprint, 1939–1949.*

Lazarsfeld, Paul F., and Harry Field. *The People Look at Radio; Report on a Survey Conducted by the National Opinion Research Center, University of Denver.* Chapel Hill, N.C., University of North Carolina Press, 1946. 158 p. **L115**
Résumé of a national opinion survey, sponsored by the National Association of Broadcasters, to determine the public's opinion of radio programs and commercials. Freedom of speech is discussed (pp. 73–79) as a triangle of citizen, government, and industry.

Leach, John. *Considerations on the Matter of Libel; Suggested by Mr. Fox's Notice in Parliament, of an Intended Motion on That Subject.* 2d ed. with additions. London, J. Johnson, [1790?]. 29 p. **L116**

League of Nations. Advisory Commission for the Protection and Welfare of Children and Young People. *The Cinema.* Geneva, The League, 1928. 34 p. (League of Nations Publications, IV. Social. 1928. IV. 21) **L117**
Replies to a 1927 questionnaire from the Child Welfare Committee record conditions for admission of minors to motion picture shows in 34 countries. Included is the text of official regulations for the control of films exhibited to minors.

League of Nations. Advisory Committee on Social Questions. *Circulation and Traffic in Obscene Publications. Summary of Annual Reports . . .* Geneva, The League, 1926–46. Various paging. (League of Nations Publications, IV. Social. 1926. IV. I through IV. Social. 1946. IV. 2) **L118**
Reports from the various governments for the years 1926 through 1944–45.

League of Nations. Conference of Press Experts. *Final Report.* Geneva, The League, 1927. 32 p. (League of Nations Publications, General. 1927. 15) **L119**
Resolutions on improving international telecommunications, facilitating the distribution of newspapers between countries, limiting censorship in peacetime, and providing international freedom for journalists.

———. *Report on Laws on Protection of Press Information.* Geneva, The League, 1927. 28 p. (League of Nations Publications, General. 1927. 5) **L120**
Texts of laws on protection of the press in 18 countries including Australia, New Zealand, and the Union of South Africa.

League of Nations. International Conference for the Suppression of the Circulation of and Traffic in Obscene Publications. *Final Act.* Geneva, The League, 1923. 4 p. **L121**
The Convention, signed at Geneva, 12 September 1923, appears in League of Nations Treaty Series, 27(658):215, 1924 and in *The American Journal of International Law*, 20:178–89, 1926.

———. *Records of the International Conference . . . Held at Geneva from August 31st to September 12th, 1923.* Geneva, The League, [1924]. 129 p. **L122**

League of Nations. Traffic in Women and Children Committee. *Obscene Publications. Replies from the Governments to the Committee's Questionnaire.* Geneva, The League, 1931. 39 p. (League of Nations Publications, IV. Social. 1931. IV. 3) **L123**
A copy of the questionnaire and additional replies are recorded in a 14-page supplement, IV. Social. 1931. IV. 9.

Lear, John. "You Can't Say That on the Air." *Saturday Evening Post*, 220(2): 22–23+, 12 July 1947. **L124**
A humorous account of the humorless foibles of radio censorship and particularly the throttling of the comics. The network censor exercises more control over radio than do advertisers or the government.

Leary, Thomas B., and J. Roger Noall. "Entertainment: Public Pressures and the Law; Official and Unofficial Control of the Content and Distribution of Motion Pictures and Magazines." *Harvard Law Review*, 71:326–67, December 1957. **L125**
"The authors interviewed members of censorship boards, law enforcement officers, private attorneys, executives in the business of producing and distributing motion pictures and magazines, theater owners and retail dealers, clergymen, and representatives of private organizations concerned with the regulation of motion pictures and magazines." The discussion considers three means of control: by prior restraint, by subsequent sanctions, and by unofficial action (self-regulation, action of private groups). The authors found that all forms of regulation are imposed to a surprising extent by extralegal, even informal means. Such action is often not brought to the attention of the public. Except in isolated pockets there is very little suppression of genuine artistic expression. All forms of censorship "rest upon the premise that the public as a whole must be protected from its own tastes in entertainment." In a

democratic society, those who justify this premise should be required to assume the burden of proof that censorship is necessary.

Leatherwood, Dowling. *The "Freedom of the Press" in Florida*. Atlanta, Ga., Department of Journalism, Emory University, 1938. 12 p.　　　**L126**
Florida laws and court decisions relating to newspaper libel.

Lechtreck, Roy. "Chafee on Law and Freedom of Speech." *Catholic Lawyer*, 11:41–46, Winter 1965.　　　**L127**
Chafee believes that the greatest value of freedom of speech is not to the minority who want to speak, but to the majority who do not want to listen.

Lederman, Lorna F. "New York Statute Censoring 'Sexual Immorality' in Motion Picture Film Held Unconstitutional." *Temple Law Quarterly*, 33:242–46, Winter 1959.　　　**L128**
The case of *Kingsley International Pictures Corp. v. Regents of the University of the State of New York*, 360 U.S. 684 (1959).

Lee, Alfred M. "Can the Individual Protect Himself against Propaganda Not in His Interest?" *Social Forces*, 29:56–61, October 1950.　　　**L129**
"The extent to which a person can so protect himself depends—within the limits of available knowledge and competence—upon the extent to which he has benefited from a liberal arts education." The author comments on the difficulty of access to propaganda and propaganda analysis.

———. "Freedom of the Press: Services of a Catch Phrase." In *Studies in the Science of Society*, edited by George P. Murdock. New Haven, Yale University Press, 1937, pp. 355–75.　　　**L130**
A survey of the use of the term "freedom of the press" from the late eighteenth century to the present day.

———. "Violations of Press Freedom in America." *Journalism Quarterly*, 15:19–27, March 1938.　　　**L131**
A review of the nonlegal forces at work in America to control the mass media.

Lee, Carolyn T. *Contemporary Catholic Attitudes toward Censorship for Catholics*. Minneapolis, University of Minnesota, 1958. 93 p. (Unpublished Master's thesis)　　　**L132**

Lee, Edward T. *The Freedom of the Press. Address Delivered to the Graduating Class of the John Marshall Law School*. Chicago, The School, 26 June 1929. 14 p. (Reprinted in *Commercial Law League Journal*, October 1929)　　　**L133**
The dean of the law school attacks the modern newspaper, a "monstrous city gargoyle," whose business interests have dominated its policies to the detriment of the people it is intended to serve. He criticizes its evil and corrupting influence, its invasion of private homes and businesses in the guise of freedom of the press, and its threat to legislators and the courts. He discusses the newspaper as "a business affected with a public interest," citing two court decisions (*Munn v. the People*, and *Inter Ocean v. Associated Press*) which "contain the germ of the solution of . . . how the press may be made the servant instead of being, as now, the tyrant of the public." If newspapers are to be treated as mere articles of trade, without regard to the public interest, then the law should exhibit no special tenderness toward them.

Lee, Frederick G. *Immodesty in Art: An Expostulation and Suggestion; a Letter to Sir Frederick Leighton*. 4th ed. London, G. Redway, 1887. 23 p.　　　**L134**
Favors censorship of sex expression in art.

Lee, James M. "Censorship of the Press." *Bellman*, 25:325–26, 21 September 1918.　　　**L135**
A comparison of wartime censorship in Great Britain and the United States. American censorship at the front must meet regulations of both France and the United States. The author calls for some uniformity in the requirements of the two censorship codes, for the benefit of American correspondents.

Lee, Joseph. "The Dunster House Case." *North American Review*, 230:381–82, August 1930.　　　**L136**
The vice-president of the Watch and Ward Society defends the methods used by the Society in entrapment of the proprietor of Cambridge's Dunster House Book Store for the sale of *Lady Chatterley's Lover*. The article is in answer to one by District Attorney Robert J. Bushnell in the May issue. Bushnell, while prosecuting the case with vigor, charged the Society with illegal methods of entrapment.

Lee, Mary. "Seek to Clear up Boston's Book Ban." *New York Times*, 22 January 1928, sec. 3, pp. 1, 6.　　　**L137**
This reporter visited Boston in January 1928, going from bookseller to police, to district attorney, to the Watch and Ward to get to the bottom of the mass book-banning, only to learn of an "imaginary censor" operating in a panic of fear.

Lee, R. W. "The Law of Blasphemy." *Michigan Law Review*, 16:149–57, January 1918.　　　**L138**
Occasioned by the decision, *Bowman v. The Secular Society, Ltd.* (1917) the dean of the Faculty of Law, McGill University, reviews the British law of blasphemy. He finds that the Bowman decision was unsuccessful in restating the law of blasphemy. Is there no alternative but to punish blasphemy as it tends to breach the peace?

Lee, Robert E. A. "Censorship: A Case History." *Christian Century*, 74:163–65, 6 February 1957.　　　**L139**
An officer of Lutheran Church Productions, which made the film *Martin Luther*, discusses efforts to ban the film. He cites, as a by-product of the controversy, "the encouragement to claim and defend freedom to think and speak and choose according to one's conscience."

Leeds, Josiah W. *Common Weal vs. the News-Stand*. [Philadelphia, 1894]. 16 p. (Reproduced from the *Christian Statesman*, 13 January 1894)　　　**L140**
Appeal to newsdealers and booksellers to exclude from sale dime novels and such "trash." Noting train robberies are on the increase, the author suggests that "express companies refuse to act as carriers of train robbery and like literature, and let them and all the affiliated railroad interests write in asking from Congress a bill excluding the debasing and brutalizing stuff from the mails."

———. "The Relation of the Press and the Stage to Purity." In National Purity Congress. *Papers, Addresses . . . First National Purity Congress . . . 1895*. New York, American Purity Alliance, 1896, pp. 320–26.　　　**L141**
Criticism of the press for publishing theater news and reviews, and for advertising the immoral stage.

Lees, Gladys L. "Censorship as It Affects the School Library." In A. H. Lancour, *ed.*, *School Library Supervisor*. Chicago, American Library Association, 1956, pp. 39–51.　　　**L142**

Lefebvre, Florent. *The French-Canadian Press and the War*. Translated and edited by J. A. Biggar and J. R. Baldwin. Toronto, Ryerson, 1940. 40 p. (Contemporary Affairs no. 2)　　　**L143**

"Legal History of the Problems Posed by the Publication of 'Obscene' Literature Traced—Protection of First and Fourteenth Amendments and Standards of Obscenity Discussed." *New York Law Forum*, 6:313–20, July 1960.　　　**L144**

"Legal Presumptions [of Recklessness in Use of Fictitious Name of Author and

Publisher Ignorant of Fact That Plaintiff Bore Same Name]." *Canada Law Journal*, 46:319–23, 16 May 1910.　　**L145**

"Legal Techniques for Protecting Free Discussion in Wartime." *Yale Law Journal*, 51:798–819, March 1942.　　**L146**

Legality of Governmental Copyrighting Challenged by Leading Editors and Scholars. [Washington, D.C., M. B. Schnapper, *et al.*, 1962]. 1 p. Broadside.　　**L147**
Twenty-three editors, librarians, journalism professors, and civil liberties leaders condemn the practice of copyrighting government publications as contrary to the guarantees of the First Amendment and to the specific provisions of copyright law. "Anyone who has the right to copyright has the legal right to restrict and censor." The petitioners urge the executive and legislative branches of the federal government to "take appropriate corrective action." The petition is an outgrowth of the agitation of M. B. Schnapper of Public Affairs Press.

Le Gallienne, Richard. "Limited Editions." In his *Prose Fancies*. New York, Putnam, 1894, pp. 119–25.　　**L148**
Le Gallienne, in this whimsical essay, views publishers of limited editions as malthusians who restrict careless procreation. No book should be brought into the world, he believes, which is not sure of love and lodging on some comfortable shelf.

[Legate, Bartholomew]. "Anglicans and Dissenters under James I; a Text without Note or Comment [relating to Bartholomew Legat, who was Burned for Heresy at Smithfield, in 1612]." *British Review*, 5:208–12, 1914.　　**L149**

[———, and Edward Wightman]. "Cases against Bartholomew Legate and Edward Wightman for Heresy, 1612." In Howell, *State Trials*, vol. 3, pp. 727–42.　　**L150**
Legate and Wightman were burned to death in 1612 for their heretical and blasphemous opinions on Church doctrine. Legate was the last person to be burned in London, Wightman the last to die in England for religious beliefs and writings. Case abstracted in Schroeder's *Constitutional Free Speech*, pp. 181–85.

Leggett, Robert D. "Motion Picture Censorship." *University of Cincinnati Law Review*, 23:259–63, Spring 1954.　　**L151**
Notes on *Superior Films, Inc. v. Department of Education of the State of Ohio* and *Commercial Pictures Corp. v. Regents of the University of the State of New York*, 74 Sup. Ct. 286 (1954).

Leggett, William. *Collection of the Political Writings of William Leggett, Selected and Arranged, with a Preface by Theodore Sedgwick, Jr.* New York, Taylor & Dodd, 1840. 2 vols.　　**L152**
Volume two, pp. 7–27, contains letters and editorials on postal and other suppressions of abolitionist literature.

"Legislative Measures in India for Restraining the Freedom of the Press." *Jurist; or, Quarterly Journal of Jurisprudence and Legislation*, 1:74, 1827.　　**L153**
An essay on the history of censorship in India.

Léglise, Paul. "Censorship: A Double-Edged Weapon." *UNESCO Courier*, 16(4): 28–32, April 1963.　　**L154**
Consideration of industry efforts to control production of films to prevent governments from applying censorship. How such systems work in the United States, Great Britain, Germany, and a number of Latin American countries. Special reference to protection of youth, including positive efforts made by the International Centre of Films for Children in Brussels, under the sponsorship of UNESCO.

Legman, Gershon. *The Horn Book; Studies in Erotic Folklore and Bibliography.* New Hyde Park, N.Y., University Books, 1964. 565 p.　　**L155**
A group of bibliographical articles "sampling and describing at length some of the more typical but elusive masterpieces of erotic literature in various languages." Contents: The Bibliography of Prohibited Books (Pisanus Fraxi), The Horn Book and Other Bibliographical Problems, Great Collectors of Erotica, The Rediscovery of Burns' *Merry Muses of Caledonia*, and a series of articles on erotic folklore including the bawdy song, the limerick, and erotic humor. References are made throughout to incidents of censorship including action of the U.S. Customs and the Post Office.

———. *Love and Death, a Study in Censorship.* New York, Breaking Point, 1949. 95 p. (2d ed. New York, Hacker Art Books, 1963)　　**L156**
Legman discusses literary sadism which he believes is intensified by censorship of sex expression. "His motif," writes Eric Larrabee, "is the shameful anomaly of American mores which make love, which is legal in fact, illegal on paper, while murder, which is illegal in fact, is not only legal on paper but the basis of the greatest publishing successes of all time." The substitution of sadism for prohibited sex in the entertainment arts will lead to the "most sinister abnormalization of the whole psychic structure of future generations."

Lehman, Milton. "Who Censors Our Movies?" *Look*, 18:86–92, 16 April 1954.　　**L157**
"The U.S. Supreme Court and Hollywood itself re-examine old taboos, good as well as bad, as the chaotic question of film censorship

receives nationwide attention." Discusses types of censors movies must satisfy: (1) legal censors in some 50 cities and 7 states, (2) pressure groups, and (3) the industry's own Production Code.

Lehmann, Leo H. "The Catholic Church in Politics." *New Republic*, 97:34–36, 16 November 1938; 97:64–66, 23 November 1938; 97:94–96, 30 November 1938; 97:122–25, 7 December 1938.　　**L158**
The first article in the series deals with The Church and Freedom of Speech; the second and third with Censorship by the Church; the fourth with Church and Social Legislation (including birth control information); and the final article with The Church and Some Social Issues.

Lehrer, Tom. "Smut." In *That Was the Year That Was, TW3 Songs & Other Songs of the Year.* New York, Reprise Records, 1965. Side one, 3:15. (Reprise Records R–6179)　　**L159**
A humorous and irreverent song in behalf of pornography and opposed to censors and censorship.

Leigh, Robert D. "Intellectual Freedom." *ALA Bulletin*, 42:363–69, 1 September 1948.　　**L160**
Discusses the ways in which librarians can, as a group, meet the pressures of censorship. Address at American Library Association convention, 15 June 1948.

———. "Problems of Freedom." In Lyman Bryson, *Communication of Ideas.* New York, Harper, 1949, pp. 197–208.　　**L161**
An analysis of the factors involved in creating a free and responsible press. Based on the author's experience as director of the Commission on Freedom of the Press.

[Leighton, Alexander]. *An Epitome or Brief Discovery from the Beginning to the End of the Great Troubles that Dr. Leighton Suffered in His Body, Estates, and Family, Wherein Is Laid Down the Cause of Those Sufferings, Namely, that Book Called Sion's Plea Against Prelacie.* London, 1646.　　**L162**
The trials of Dr. Leighton are reported in Schroeder, *Constitutional Free Speech*, pp. 194–207.

[———]. "Proceedings in Star-Chamber against Him for Publishing An Appeal to the Parliament, or Sion's Plea against

Prelacie, 1630." In Howell, *State Trials*, vol. 3, pp. 383ff., and Rushworth, *Historical Collections . . .*, part 2, pp. 55–58. **L163**

For his pamphlet criticizing the English clergy as "anti-Christian and satanical," Dr. Leighton, a physician and divine, was tried before the Star Chamber Court and found guilty without being permitted to appear in person or to speak in his own behalf. He was degraded from the ministry, pilloried, whipped, one ear was cut off, his nose split, his face branded, and he was imprisoned at the king's pleasure. He was eventually released by the Long Parliament and honored for his martyrdom.

[————]. *Whereas Alexander Leighton, a Scottish-man borne . . . Printing and publishing a very Libellous and Scandalous Booke . . . escaped out of the Prison of the Fleete . . . he hath a yellowish Beard, a high Forehead, betweene forty and fifty yeeres of age. Dated this eleuenth of Nouember. 1630.* [London, 1630]. Broadside. (STC 8967) **L164**

Leipold, L. E. "Parent Fears about Books Pupils Read in Class and Library." *Clearing House*, 30:36–37, September 1955. **L165**

Leiter, Bernard K. "How Harrell Beat the Censor." *Grassroots Editor*, 6(3):14–15, 32, July 1965. **L166**

During the Civil War the editor of the Cairo, Ill., *Gazette* beat the military censor who demanded submission of all copy in advance of publication, by inundating him with "massive rolls of matter" that he had no intention of publishing.

Lemon, Courtney. *Free Speech in the United States.* New York, Free Speech League, [1917]. 11p. (Reprinted from *Pearson's Magazine*, December 1916) **L167**

So far as free speech in the United States is concerned "our only advantage is the possession of a rhetorical tradition of freedom to which appeal can be made in the fight to establish those rights which the average American citizen fondly imagines himself to possess, but which do not in fact exist." Free speech in the United States is curtailed by (1) acts of state legislatures, (2) court usurpations, (3) police outrages, (4) postal legislation and rulings, and (5) vice societies.

L'Engle, Madeleine. "The Mystery of the First Law of Thermodynamics." *Library Journal*, 89:4851–54, 15 December 1964. **L168**

Many of the books which fill our bookstores and library shelves "are afraid of the mysteri-

ous, leave nothing to our imagination, and try to break the first law of thermodynamics" (energy and heat are mutually convertible, but if you get heat you lose energy and vice versa). In the "climate of mystery, passion can flourish far more strongly than in the clinical glare of the laboratory." The reader searching for pornography is "not unlike dope addicts looking for a cheap jag . . . something for nothing." The author believes that librarians, through person to person communication and concern "can help to control the influx of trading stamp sex, not through censorship or in manipulation. . . . It is in the meeting of human beings that we find our answer to censorship; it is the meeting of persons that provides an influence that is free and vital and that speaks far more loudly and truthfully than pressure groups trying to impose their own opinions and imperatives."

Lenin, V. S. "On the Freedom of the Press." *Labour Monthly*, 7:35–37, January 1925. (First published in 1917) **L169**

"The capitalists . . . define 'freedom of the Press' as the suppression of the censor and the power for every party to publish newspapers as they please. In reality that is not freedom of the Press, but freedom for the rich, for the bourgeoisie, to deceive the oppressed and exploited masses of the people." State monopoly of newspaper advertising is the only solution.

LeQueux, William T. *Britain's Deadly Peril. Are We Told the Truth?* London, S. Paul, 1915. 176p. **L170**

The peril of wartime government censorship.

Lerner, Max. "On Lynching a Book." In his *Public Journal.* New York, Viking, 1945, pp. 131–34. (Reprinted in Downs, *The First Freedom*, pp. 209–10) **L171**

Deals with the Massachusetts *Strange Fruit* case in which Bernard DeVoto precipitated a test case in Cambridge, Mass. The bookseller's conviction for selling a copy to DeVoto was upheld by the Massachusetts Supreme Judicial Court, thus affirming that state's rigid censorship laws. This article is followed by Cartels in Ideas, pp. 134–37.

Lesher, Dean. "What do the Espionage and Sedition Acts Forbid?" *Journal of the State Bar of California*, 17:204–13, July–August 1942. **L172**

A California newspaper publisher reviews the historical background of legislation and court decisions relating to wartime sedition. He believes that limitations on a free press should be strictly construed even in time of war. He notes a calmer, sounder approach to the problems in World War II than in World War I.

"The Lesion of Decency." *Ramparts*, 4:3–4, September 1965. **L173**

An editorial criticism of the Legion of Decency, suggesting the following minimum requirements be accepted by this Catholic agency:

(1) that the issue is clear-cut, (2) that the approach to the issue is tenable within their house, and (3) that they make no false claims with respect to precisely whom they represent.

Leslie, Shane. "The Suppression of a Book." *Bookman*, 66:181–84, October 1927. **L174**

A satirical description of the author's feelings when his novel, *The Contab*, was tried in London for obscenity. The novel, an account of the author's life at Cambridge, included the "hopeless confusion in religious and sexual questions" the English undergraduate feels.

"Lesson for Liberals." *Nation*, 175:121–22, 16 August 1952. **L175**

Editorial concerning the dismissal of James A. Wechsler, editor of the New York *Post*, from the television program "Starring the Editors," because the *Journal American* had exposed his membership in the Young Communist League in his college days. Wechsler's 15-year record of anticommunism was disregarded. The writer believes the *Post's* anti-McCarthyism crusade precipitated the attack.

L'Estrange, Roger. *Considerations and Proposals in Order to the Regulation of the Press; together with Diverse Instances of Treasonous and Seditious Pamphlets, Proving the Necessity Thereof.* London, Printed by A. C., 1663. 33p. **L176**

"Roger L'Estrange has won a notoriety for his harsh proceedings as 'Surveyor of the Imprimery and Printing Presses,' an office to which he was appointed shortly after the appearance of this pamphlet. It is stated therein that the number of presses at the time, amounting to sixty, is unnecessary and dangerous; only twenty ought to be licensed. Much more stringent rules were proposed for the regulation of printers than had previously been in force; among them one to the effect 'that no printing-house be permitted with a back door to it.' The surveyor of the press was to have the right to search at any time, and printers guilty of publishing objectionable books were to be punished with 'death, mutilation, imprisonment, corporal peyns (torture)', as well as minor penalties; such as the pillory, whipping, branding, &c." (Bigmore and Wyman. *A Bibliography of Printing*, vol. 1, p. 434.) L'Estrange was appointed surveyor of the press by Charles II in 1663 and exercised dictatorial powers over the English press for almost 20 years.

————. *A Memento. Treating, of the Rise, Progress, and Remedies of Seditious: with some Historical Reflections upon the Series of Our late Troubles.* 2d ed. London, Reprinted for Joanna Brome, 1682. 138p. (First printed 1642) **L177**

Seditions arise from seven interests—the Church, the Bench, the Court, the Camp, the City, the Country, and the Body Representative. L'Estrange discusses the nature of each and methods of prevention. Largely a classification of heresies.

[————]. *A Modest Plea both for the Caveat and the Author of It.* London, 1661. **L178**
L'Estrange protests the prevalence of seditious opinion in the press and urges action against offending printers. This brochure led to L'Estrange being appointed in 1663 to exercise the controls on printing that he recommended. There are references to action taken against the Baptist publisher, Livewell Chapman, and others in the publication of *The Phoenix of the Solemn League and Covenant.* This is also referred to in L'Estrange's *Truth and Loyalty Vindicated* (1662).

————. *Notes upon Stephen College. Grounded Principally upon his own Declarations and Confessions. And Freely submitted to Publique Censure.* 2d ed. London, Printed for Joanna Brome, 1681. 48 p. **L179**
In defense of the sentence on College.

————. *A Seasonable Memorial in Some Historical Notes upon the Liberties of the Presse and Pulpit; with the Effects of Popular Petitions, Tumults, Associations, Impostures, and Disaffected Common Councils.* London, Printed for H. Brome, 1680. 37 p. **L180**
A defense of the abridgment of freedom of the press and speech by the official English censor. Unlicensed printing (the Licensing Act had been allowed to expire) could lead to the collapse of established religion and the constituted authority of the State. L'Estrange considered the revealing of corruption in government as the first step in a dangerous evolution that ends in treason against Church and State.

————. *Toleration Discuss'd; in two Dialogues; I. Betwixt a Conformist, and a Non-Conformist; Laying open the Impiety, and Danger of a General Liberty. II. Betwixt a Presbyterian, and an Independent; Concluding, upon an Impartial Examination of their Respective Practices, and Opinions, in Favor of the Independents.* 3d ed. London, Printed for H. Brome, 1681. 164 p. **L181**

————. *A Word Concerning Libels and Libellers* . . . London, Printed for Joanna Brome, 1681. 13 p. **L182**
L'Estrange reviews the precedent in the libel cases against Richard Baldwin, Richard Janeway, John Starkey, Langley Curtis, and Henry Care, noting the points of law involved in each.

Lethbridge, *Sir* Roper. "Government Relations with the Press: an Indian Precedent." *Nineteenth Century*, 83:403–11, February 1918. **L183**
The author describes the creation of the Press Commissionership in India by Lord Lytton in 1877, and suggests that such a position would serve Britain in wartime.

Letourneau, Jean. "Freedom of Information." *Vital Speeches*, 14:538–40, 15 June 1948. **L184**
The chief of the French delegation to the United Nations Conference on Freedom of Information presents the French conception of worldwide freedom of the press.

A Letter of Consolation to Dr. Shebbeare. [London, 1758?]. 44 p. **L185**
John Shebbeare was an English physician and political writer whose *Sixth Letter to the People of England* in 1758 caused his arrest and trial for seditious libel. Dr. Shebbeare had attributed the calamities of England to the House of Hanover. He was convicted and sentenced by Judge Mansfield, who ruled that satires on dead kings were punishable by three years in prison. The anonymous writer of this pamphlet believes the doctor should rejoice at the mildness of his fate; for much less serious libels under the Stuarts, whom Shebbeare praises, he might have lost his head. The writer reviews the numerous convictions for seditious libel prior to the accession of the Hanovers. Shebbeare had served an earlier sentence for writing a novel, *The Marriage Act,* that had been critical of Parliament.

"A Letter to a Censor." *Survey*, 54:107–8, 15 April 1925. **L186**
An "open-letter" to the censor whom he addresses: "Unhappy man: People do not make sex. Sex makes people. . . . I hope you won't try to censor sex out of life." Is there some way, he asks, of doing away with the nasty commercial pornography without giving the censor the power to destroy new ideas and useful discussions of sex? If we err, it should always be on the side of liberty.

A Letter to a Great Man; Concerning the Liberty of the Press. London, J. Wilford, 1729. 14 p. **L187**
The "great man" is Sir Robert Walpole. The author cautions the government against striking out against critics by restraining the press. "The Fall of this one particular Instance of Liberty, will soon be followed by the Fall of Others." Even if the government "should hang or starve all the Printers in England, I shall find means to convey it [ideas] to future ages."

A Letter to a Member of Parliament, Shewing the Necessity of Regulating the Press: . . . With A Particular Answer to the Objections that of late have been Advanced against it. Oxford, George West and Henry Clements, 1699. 71 p. **L188**
Written anonymously in answer to Mathew Tindal's *A Letter to a Member of Parliament, Shewing that a Restraint On the Press Is inconsistent with the Protestant Religion.* The author argues that it is the duty of the magistrate to control the press in order to protect the church from attacks, and recommends the reenactment of a licensing law.

A Letter to Sir Charles Forbes, Bart., M.P. on the Suppression of Public Discussion in

India and the Banishment, without Trial, of Two British Editors from that Country by the Acting Governor-General, Mr. Adam. By a Proprietor of India-Stock. London, 1824. 48 p. (*Pamphleteer*, vol. 24, no. 47) **L189**

Letter to the Archibishop of Canterbury concerning Persecution for Religion and Freedom of Debate. London, J. Peel, 1732. 56 p. **L190**
Persecutions in any degree are contrary to the Gospel; debate about religion is "not only consistent with Christianity, but recommended in the New Testament, as previously necessary before we can arrive at a certainty of Truth."

A Letter to the Right Honourable the Earls of Egremont and Halifax, His Majesty's Principal Secretaries of State, on the Seizure of Papers. London, J. Williams, 1763. 31 p. **L191**
Relates to the John Wilkes case.

Letters on the Subject of the Proper Liberty of the Press. By An Englishman. First Published in the Paper of the World. London, Reprinted for P. Byrne, etc., 1790. 58 p **L192**
A sharply worded criticism of the judgment of Lord Mansfield in libel cases, stated in a series of nine letters, dedicated to the "Jurors of Dublin who defended Freedom of the Press." Lord Mansfield's intention, wrote the author, "was simply to maintain power, and to act *as a Soldier for the Crown*; and in doing this, he became lost in a labyrinth of absurdity." The maxim he left was that truth is a libel. "In the wide, and dark, and troubled Ocean of what is now demonstrated to be Libel, nothing can be said in private, nothing can be written of living or even dead persons, but what may be liable to this objection. If History be not impeached, if Epitaphs be not prosecuted, and Religious Discourses be not arraigned at the Bar, it is carelessness that passes them over—for as the law now stands—Every Human thing, that is not Panegyric, is indictable."

Letters to the Marquis of Hastings, on the Indian Press; with an Appeal to Reason and the British Parliament, on the Liberty of the Press in General; by a Friend to Good Government. London, J. M. Richardson, 1824. 120 p. **L193**
Argues forcefully for a free press as the best protection against sedition, and applies the argument to British India.

"Levels of Freedom." *Times Literary Supplement*, 3198:445, 14 June 1963. **L194**

Mostly about French and German censorship, but also about South Africa, and is intended to show a comparison with England.

Levenson, Joseph. "Censorship of the Movies." *Forum*, 69:1404–14, April 1923. (Reprinted in Rutland, *State Censorship of Motion Pictures*, pp. 81–92)   **L195**
Supports regulatory legislation of movies "as an absolutely necessary part of the government of civilized countries." The great power of the cinema in moulding thought, particularly among young people, makes censorship necessary. The author refutes the various arguments advanced in opposition to movie censorship, noting that nowhere has movie regulatory legislation, once enacted, been repealed.

Levien, Sonya. "New York's Motion Picture Law." *American City*, 9:319–21, October 1913.   **L196**
The educational secretary of the National Board of Review of Motion Pictures describes what she considers a model motion picture ordinance: the New York law for regulating movie theaters, passed in 1913. While the law has to do mostly with fire control and other physical facilities, it also gives discretionary power to the License Bureau to preserve the moral tone of the performance.

Levin, Arthur. "Censorship Now?—No!" *Scribner's Commentator*, 10:85–89, September 1941.   **L197**
The author fears a licensed press during wartime. He reviews censorship laws enacted during the last war and new controls of public opinion added since; he calls upon newspapers and the public to maintain vigilance to prevent any further infringement on free speech and free press and to oppose any attempt to exercise those powers already granted the administration.

Levin, Bernard. "Lady's Not for Burning." *Spectator*, 205:677–78, 4 November 1960.   **L198**
An account of the *Lady Chatterley's Lover* trial in England, the first case to be brought against a serious work under the Obscene Publications Act of 1958.

———. "Very Dirty Books." *Spectator*, 205:270–71, 19 August 1960.   **L199**
In anticipation of action against Penguin Books for publication of *Lady Chatterley's Lover*, the author suggests the American court decisions in the *Ulysses* case might be cited as "noble judicial dicta."

———. "Why All the Fuss?" *Spectator*, 202:32–33, 9 January 1959.   **L200**
About publishing *Lolita* in England. "No intelligent person . . . can any longer seriously believe in the corrupting power of a book like *Lolita*. Can it seriously be maintained that if it were published numbers of middle-aged men would take to seducing twelve-year-old girls? And, if not . . . why all the fuss?"

Levin, Harry. "The Unbanning of the Books." *Atlantic Monthly*, 217(2):77–81, February 1966.   **L201**
"As the courts free more and more books from the contraband shelf, there is not much left in literature that can consistently be banned, says Harvard professor and literary critic Harry Levin. Here he assesses what the new candor in literature could mean to the critic and to the reader."

Levin, Harvey J. *Broadcast Regulation and Joint Ownership of Media.* New York, New York University Press, 1960. 208 p.   **L202**
Discussion of the public policy and economic questions raised by joint ownership of radio, television, and newspapers.

———. *Cross-Channel Ownership of Mass Media; a Study in Social Evaluation.* New York, Columbia University, 1953. 289 p. (Ph. D. dissertation, University Microfilms, no. 5197)   **L203**

———. "Organization and Control of Communications Satellites." *University of Pennsylvania Law Review*, 113:315–57, January 1965.   **L204**
The article gives a description of the new type of legal entity under the Communications Satellite Act of 1962 (the creation of the Communications Satellite Corp., Com Sat) to operate a global system of communications satellites. He considers why the new type of joint government-private enterprise venture was chosen, the nature of the rejected alternatives, and the potential dangers to Com Sat's fulfillment of its sponsors' expectation. "To avoid serious impairment of international confidence in American leadership in space communication, therefore, foreclosed or inequitable access by any class of users or suppliers must be prevented."

———. "Social Welfare Aspect of FCC Broadcast Licensing Standards." *American Journal of Economics and Sociology*, 12:39–55, October 1953.   **L205**

Levin, Meyer. "The Candid Cameraman: Hollywood Producers Submit to Foreign Dictators, Incidentally Giving America War-minded Films." *Esquire*, 6(5):125, 211–12, November 1936. (Condensed in *Reader's Digest*, December 1936)   **L206**
American war movies destined for foreign markets (40 per cent of output) must glorify war or else risk censorship. Americans, therefore, are served prowar pictures because they are more profitable for Hollywood producers.

Levinthal, Louis E. "Reminiscences of 'A Cause Celebre,'" *Pennsylvania Bar Association Quarterly*, 37:39–45, October 1965.   **L207**
A Philadelphia judge recalls one of his most interesting cases, an appeal from the State Board of Censors to ban the documentary film of the Spanish civil war, *Spain in Flames*. The decision of the Court of Common Pleas (Levinthal, Bok, and Flood) reviewed the decision, ruling that the film was in the nature of a newsreel and exempt from censorship.

Levy, A. B. "Taboo or Not Taboo." *Realist*, 1:15–16, April 1959.   **L208**

Levy, Bernard S. "Obscenity—A Perusal and a Proposal." *Temple Law Quarterly*, 32:322–31, Spring 1959.   **L209**
A general discussion of the Federal and Pennsylvania statutes relating to obscenity. The author attempts a definition of pictorial obscenity.

Levy, H. Philip. "Wilkes and Liberty." *Spectator*, 195:298, 2 September 1955.   **L210**
"The reasons given for the banning of reports of Parliamentary debates in the 18th century were much the same as the reasons given for the fourteen-day-rule—and other restrictions on broadcasting today." (Preserve Parliamentary dignity, protect members from pressure, and prevent premature comment.) Wilkes was responsible for demolishing the ban on Parliamentary reporting in the eighteenth century and Parliament subsequently gave up the attempt to muzzle the press.

Levy, Leonard W. "Did the Zenger Case Really Matter?" *William and Mary Quarterly*, 17(3d ser.):35–50, January 1960.   **L211**
The verdict for Zenger was more the result of the magnificent forensics of a great lawyer, Andrew Hamilton, than a milestone in the change of common law on seditious libel. "The Zenger case at best gave the press the freedom to print the 'truth' but only if the truth were directed away from the assembly. . . . No cause was more honored by rhetorical denunciation and dishonored in practice than that of freedom of expression during the revolutionary period, from the 1760's through the War of Independence."

———. *Jefferson & Civil Liberties; the Darker Side.* Cambridge, Mass., The Belknap Press of Harvard University Press, 1963. 225 p.   **L212**
The author's thesis is that Thomas Jefferson, long revered as the apostle of American liberty, "did not directly apply to practical political problems a libertarian creed to which he adhered consistently." Levy found "a strong pattern of unlibertarian, even antilibertarian thought throughout Jefferson's long career."

Chapter 3 deals with problems of a free press. While Jefferson was deeply devoted to freedom of religious, scientific, and philosophical expression, he was less tolerant of political dissent. While supporting freedom of the press in the abstract, Jefferson distrusted the press and, following the ideas of Blackstone, approved prosecution for falsity. His opposition to prosecutions under the Sedition Act, seldom vigorous, was based on the opinion that prosecution of the abuses in the press should be left to the states. He remained silent when state authorities acted against the Philadelphia editor, Joseph Dennie, and New York editor, Harry Croswell, and was long silent when his Connecticut party leaders took libel action against critics of Jefferson and his administration. By the time Jefferson left the presidency, he was so convinced of the licentiousness of the press "that he professed to believe that it was doing more harm than would result from its prosecution." Levy recounts Jefferson's efforts at censorship at the University of Virginia and his endorsement of Baxter's edition of the works of David Hume, which the editor had altered silently "to make it what truth and candor say it should be."

———. *Legacy of Suppression: Freedom of Speech and Press in Early American History.* Cambridge, Mass., The Belknap Press of Harvard University Press, 1960. 353 p. (A revised edition with a new preface was issued in 1963 by Harper Torchbooks)　**L213**

A "revisionist" interpretation of the origins of the freedom of speech and the press clause in the First Amendment, showing that "the generation which adopted the Constitution and the Bill of Rights did not believe in a broad scope of freedom of expression, particularly in the realm of politics." In this documented study Professor Levy traces the development of the ideas of freedom of expression from the days of Milton and Locke in seventeenth-century England to the emergence of an American libertarian theory. The latter began to emerge when the Jeffersonians were forced to defend themselves against the Sedition Act of 1798. In the preface to the Torchbook edition, Levy writes: "I am still convinced that the First Amendment was not intended to supersede the common law of seditious libel, that the legislatures rather than the courts were the chief suppressive agencies, that the theory of freedom of speech in political matters was quite narrow until 1798, that English libertarian theory was in the vanguard of the American, that the Bill of Rights was in large measure a lucky political accident, and that the First Amendment was more an expression of federalism than of libertarianism." The Levy thesis attracted considerable attention from reviewers, who argued the case pro and con. Reviews by James Morton Smith in *William and Mary Quarterly*, January 1963, Merrill Jensen, *Harvard Law Review*, December 1961, John J. Cound, *New York Law Review*, January 1961, and Harold L. Nelson, *Journalism Quarterly*, Winter 1961, are included.

———. "Liberty and the First Amendment: 1790–1800." *American Historical Review*, 68:22–37, October 1962.　**L214**

The author develops the thesis that there was "a sudden break-through in American libertarian thought on freedom of speech and press" in 1798 which repudiated the Blackstonian concept that freedom of the press meant merely freedom from prior restraint. This new libertarianism, which originated as an "expedience of self-defense on the part of a beseiged political minority . . . established virtually all at once and in nearly perfect form a theory justifying the rights of individual expression and of opposition parties."

———. "Satan's Last Apostle in Massachusetts." *American Quarterly*, 5:16–30, April 1953.　**L215**

The story of Abner Kneeland, the last man to be jailed in Massachusetts for the crime of blasphemy. The antireligious views he expressed in his newspaper, *Boston Investigator*, got him into trouble with the authorities. In the decision, *Commonwealth v. Kneeland*, 37 Mass. Reports 206 ff. (1838), the judge warned of the consequences if Kneeland's doctrines became widespread among the poor—they might become dissatisfied with their lot. On release from prison Kneeland emigrated with members of his First Society of Free Inquirers, to form a utopian society in frontier Iowa.

———, ed. *Freedom of the Press from Zenger to Jefferson.* Indianapolis, Bobbs-Merrill, 1966. 409 p. (American Heritage Series)　**L216**

"This anthology is valuable on two levels. On the one it is the first compendium of the classic American statements on freedom of the press from Andrew Hamilton's defense in the Zenger case (1735) to Alexander Hamilton's defense in the Croswell case (1804), including the full texts of oft-quoted opinions of Benjamin Franklin, James Madison, and Thomas Jefferson. On the second level, Professor Levy offers a documentary defense of his provocative thesis [see his *Legacy of Suppression*]. Thus here are assembled a representative selection of the only substantial writings that enable us to weigh the intent of the drafters of the first amendment—James Wilson, Richard Henry Lee, William Cushing, and John Adams. Here occupying a major section of the collection are the statements of 'The New Libertarianism' of 1799–1800 which hitherto have been available only in rare book depositories: the tracts of George Hay and John Thomson, Madison's *Virginia Reports*, Albert Gallatin's speech in Congress, and generous excerpts from Tunis Wortman's *A Treatise Concerning Political Inquiry* . . . Finally, here are some two dozen lengthy selections from the letters and state papers of Thomas Jefferson that will enable readers to draw their own conclusions as to whether Professor Levy's negative verdict in *Jefferson and Civil Liberties* . . . is warranted."— Alfred Young in the Foreword.

Lewis, Alfred H. "That Idaho Contempt Case." *Hearst's Magazine*, 24:224–34, August 1913.　**L217**

Criticism of the Idaho Supreme Court for

conviction of three editors for publishing President Roosevelt's criticism of the judiciary of the state.

Lewis, Anthony. "Cameras in Court—A growing Debate." *New York Times Magazine*, 2 October 1960, p. 224.　**L218**

———. "The Case of 'Trial' by Press." *New York Times Magazine*, 18 October 1964, pp. 31 ff.　**L219**

Criticizes excessive pretrial publicity and urges the press to find ways of preventing abuses instead of complaining about threats to the freedom of the press.

———. "Law and the Censor." *New York Times*, 112:12, 20 February 1963.　**L220**

Deals with the U.S. Supreme Court's 8 to 1 decision holding unconstitutional certain activities of the Rhode Island Commission to Encourage Morality in Youth. The activities concerned the Commission's efforts to remove objectionable publications from the newsstands.

———. "The Most Recent Troubles of *Tropic*: A Chapter in Censorship." *New York Times Book Review*, 67(3):4–5, 16, 18, 21 January 1962.　**L221**

A report on the nationwide controversy over the Grove Press publication of Henry Miller's *Tropic of Cancer*, which went "further in vulgarity of subject matter and candor of treatment than many Americans are now prepared to accept."

———. "Sex . . . and the Supreme Court." *Esquire*, 59(6):82–83, 141–43, June 1963.　**L222**

"Applying steady pressure, nine calm men are dragging the censor, kicking and screaming, into the twentieth century . . . Gradually, without much notice but with developing momentum [the Supreme Court] has cut back the censor's power over literature and the arts generally." The article reviews the decisions of the court in matters of obscenity in the last decade. "The swift change in legal standards during the last decade has left us all with one burden—the volume of pretentious trash that fills the bookshelves." Now that crude sex expressions are no longer forbidden they may pass out of fashion. The choice of reading good or bad literature, within the expanding limits of the courts, is now up to the reader—"as the Constitution intended it should be."

Lewis, C. S. "Four-Letter Words." *Critical Quarterly*, 3(2):118–22, Summer 1961.　**L223**

———. "Prudery and Philology." *Spectator*, 194:63, 21 January 1955.　**L224**

The author considers this literary problem: Why have societies in general been willing to accept a drawing of a naked human body, while objecting to an equally detailed description of the same object in words? What is the cause of this seemingly arbitrary discrimination?

Lewis, Denslow. "Practical Prophylaxis." *Medical Record*, 72:594–600, 12 October 1907. **L225**
An account of various acts of sex censorship, all of which the author opposes.

Lewis, Edward G. "Lese Majesty." *Woman's National Weekly*, 14:2, 19 August 1911. **L226**
Shows how criticism of the postal officials in periodicals is punished by departmental action.

[Lewis, Freeman, *et al.*]. "Freedom to Read." *Publishers' Weekly*, 181(21):26–28, 21 May 1962. **L227**
Summary of a panel discussion at the annual meeting of the American Book Publishers Council. Participants: Freeman Lewis (chairman), Richard Corbin, and Richard Morgan.

Lewis, Shippen. "Action for Libel Where Defendant Has Used a Fictitious Name." *University of Pennsylvania Law Review*, 58:166–69, December 1909. **L228**
A British case in which a fictitious name used in a newspaper fiction coincided with that of a real person and led to a libel suit. There are three categories of intent: (1) The author intends the statements about the plaintiff, but does not intend them to be libelous; (2) he intends to make an innocent statement, but through a mistake it is libelous; and (3) defendant has no idea of any reference to the plaintiff, which is the present case.

[Lewis, Sinclair]. "Fearless Press Is Why *It Can't Happen Here*." *American Press*, 54(2):3, December 1935. **L229**
In an interview with Percy B. Scott, Lewis states that he chose a country newspaper publisher as the central figure in his novel *It Can't Happen Here* because such publishers are today "the best line of defense we have or will have for some time to come to prevent the establishment of a dictatorship."

Lewis, Thomas P. "Freedom of Speech and Motion Pictures—the *Miracle* Decision." *Kentucky Law Journal*, 41:257–64, January 1953. **L230**
"In *Burstyn v. Wilson*, the Supreme Court of the United States for the first time was presented squarely with the question: Are motion pictures within the ambit of protection which the First Amendment, through the Fourteenth Amendment, secures to any form of speech or the press? The question was answered in the affirmative and a 37-year-old anomaly in Constitutional Law—based on an application of a state constitution—was thereby abandoned." The case was based on *The Miracle*, banned by the Board of Regents of New York.

Lewis, Walker. "The Right to Complain: The Trial of John Peter Zenger." *American Bar Association Journal*, 46:27–30, 108–11, January 1960. **L231**
A Washington lawyer retells the trial for seditious libel of John Peter Zenger (1735), setting forth in some detail the arguments of the defense counsel, Andrew Hamilton.

Lewis, William D. "English Cases on the Restraint of Libel by Injunction." *American Law Register*, 51:322–40, June 1903. **L232**

———. "The Law of Blasphemous Libel." *Solicitors' Journal*, 4:45–49, 26 November 1859. (Also in *Papers*, Juridical Society, 2:250–82, 1858–63) **L233**
Paper read at a meeting of the Juridical Society, 21 November 1859; discussed at a subsequent meeting of the Society and the discussion reported in the issue for 10 December 1859.

Lewis, Wyndham. *The Writer and the Absolute*. London, Methuen, 1952. 202 p. **L234**
"It is dangerous to live, but to write is much more so." Lewis discusses the freedom or lack of freedom of the creative writer, who he believes should have "freedom to speculate, to criticize, to create, on the same terms as those enjoyed by the men of science." The man of letters should have the same freedom to deal with "history-in-the-making" as the historian has freedom to deal with past events. Lewis discusses the unorthodox social and political views of prominent British authors and their reception. He fears that political events today lead "one to believe that the individual may not be allowed for very much longer to express himself in writing."

"Liabilities of Editors." *Law Times*, 48:142, 25 December 1869. **L235**
The case of Dr. Shorthouse, convicted for a libel in the *Sporting Times*. The Court held that the editor is responsible for everything that appears in his paper.

"Liability for Libels." *Law Journal*, 12:728–30, 15 December 1877. **L236**
Regarding *Milissich v. Lloyds*, which involves the right of publication of fair reports of trials and discussion of affairs of public interest, and *Queen v. Holbrook*, which holds that a newspaper proprietor who had no knowledge of the publication of a libel in his paper is not held responsible. Also reported in *Solicitors' Journal*, 8 December 1877, and in *Irish Law Journal*, 16 February 1878.

"Libel and the Freedom of the Press." *Quarterly Review*, 117:519–39, April 1865. **L237**
The author reviews four publications, including two dealing with the topic of freedom of the press—Thomas Starkie's *Treatise on the Law of Libel and Slander*, 3d ed., and *A Bill to Amend the Law of Libel*, introduced by Sir Colman O'Loghlen and others. The author objects to the Bill in part because of a clause which relieves the publisher of a newspaper from libel in reporting a public speech containing libelous matter, provided the defendant has been given the right of response.

Libel Cases; Benjamin F. Butler vs. The Publisher and Editor of the Lowell Courier. n. p., n. d. 15 p. **L238**
Trial held at the Court of Common Pleas, Cambridge, Mass., 1852.

"Libel: Liability of the Printer." *Law Journal*, 6:225, 7 April 1871. **L239**
Messers. Spottiswoode & Co. were convicted of libel for merely printing a journal that they did not own or edit.

"Libel on a Government; Authority and Precedent in Libel Cases." *Law Journal*, 44:42, 23 January 1909. **L240**
Comments on the libel suit by the United States government against the New York World.

"Libels on Deceased Persons." *Law Times*, 59:257–58, 7 August 1875. **L241**
A review of the law which enables relatives of deceased persons to protect the dead from libelous assertions.

"Libels on Professional Men." *Solicitors' Journal*, 9:518–19, 22 April 1865. **L242**
The law of libel furnishes doctors, lawyers, engineers, and other professional men greater protection than it affords statesmen and men of letters who have chosen to place themselves in the public eye.

"Libels Which Are No Libels." *Irish Law Times*, 15:204–5, 16 April 1881. (Reprinted from *Justice of the Peace*) **L243**
Too many thin-skinned people are bringing libel charges before justices, where no case really exists.

Liber, B. "Dr. Liber and Post Office." *New Republic*, 20:61, 13 August 1919. **L244**
Tells of the suppression of Liber's book on sexual life on the pretense of its being obscene, but with private confession that it is too radical in its economic explanation of disease and prostitution.

"Liberalism and the Censor." *New Republic*, 34:148–49, 4 April 1923. **L245**

Censorship is usually the tool of the Tory who doesn't object to vice and war portrayed in print or on the stage but believes they ought to be kept in their place. The Liberal knows that a better world is possible and strives to eliminate the evils by breaking down the barriers to understanding.

Liberty Defense Union; Purpose; to Organize Popular Support in Behalf of Persons Prosecuted for the Exercise of their Constitutional Right of Free Speech and Free Press. New York City, [1918].   **L246**

"Liberty of Criticism, and the Law of Libel." *Fraser's Magazine*, 68:35–45, July 1863.   **L247**
A review of the English law of libel in light of the awarding of damages to Dr. Campbell against the *Saturday Review* (*Campbell v. Spottiswoode*). The author believes the decision did not limit the law of libel in protecting the right of free discussion.

The Liberty of the Press. London, Printed for W. Nicoll, [176–?]. 58 p.   **L248**
Written soon after the Wilkes *North Briton* affair. While defending freedom of the press, the author objects to the scurrility and abuses. "Let us endeavor to enlarge its [the Press's] Power of doing good. . . . But since it is confessedly capable of producing much Mischief, let it be restrained by that power of Law, which marks the Boundaries of the Prerogatives, and in all other Instances, the Rights of the People." The unknown author calls on Parliament to do its duty.

"Liberty of the Press." *Edinburgh Review*, 18:98–123, May 1811.   **L249**
A free press in England is restricted by the law of libel which punishes "all those who dare to speak ill of the ministers." It is, in effect, "liberty to speak ill of all those who are the minister's enemies." The article is prompted by Emanuel Ralph's book *La Liberté de la Presse.* Attributed to James Mill by his biographer, Alexander Bain.

———. *Niles Register*, 33:359–60, 26 January 1828. (Reprinted from the *Charleston City Gazette*)   **L250**
Deals with a debate in the South Carolina Senate over a bill requiring editors to reveal the source of their news. The bill failed to pass.

———. *Scottish Review*, 38(n.s.):1–5, Spring 1915.   **L251**
Press censorship cannot be excused or defended save on grounds of urgent public necessity and hardly then. The author objects to wartime censorship; he complains of the suppression of certain Irish journals on grounds of being subsidized by German interests. The real reason, he charges, is that their ideas are objectionable to English Liberals. Scotland, thus far, is free of censorship.

"Liberty of the Press and Its Abuses." *Edinburgh Review*, 27:102–44, September 1816.   **L252**
A discussion of the libel law of England and its restriction on the liberty of the press. The article is prompted by the publication of the second edition of Holt's *Law of Libel.*

[Liberty of the Press; Sedition Law of 1798]. *Southern Review*, 3:450–67, May 1829.   **L253**
A review with commentary on the resolution submitted in the U.S. House of Representatives, declaring unconstitutional the Sedition Act of 1798 and providing for a restoration of fines levied against those convicted under the Act. The author argues for the resolution, pointing out that it was not enough to let the act expire, that "effective securities ought to be obtained against any effort, in future, to make what are generally called political libels, punishable by the authority of the United States, and consequently cognizable in the Federal Courts."

Libra, *pseud.* "The Press Censorship." *English Review*, 22:261–72, March 1916.   **L254**
A defense of Britain's wartime Press Bureau against its many critics, particularly Alexander Campbell, whose criticisms appeared in the *English Review*, January 1916, and Edward P. Bell, American correspondent.

"Librarians and Censorship." *Bookseller*, 3044:1712, 25 April 1964.   **L255**
General principles of censorship, the present state of the law, the librarians' position, and practical ways of dealing with sexy books and unpopular subjects were discussed in the 1964 Weekend School of the Association of Assistant Librarians, Durham, 10–12 April.

["Librarians' Responsibility in the Treatment of Bad Literature"]. *Library Journal*, 33:347–48, September 1908.   **L256**
Editorial discussing what libraries should do about the "unfortunate deluge of bad books" now being published, especially in the form of fiction. Not to select or buy is one answer, another is to lock away those already on the shelves. Librarians should bring public sentiment against such books to bear on publishers.

"Libraries Everywhere Involved in *Tropic of Cancer* Fight." *Library Journal*, 87:65–68, 1 January 1962.   **L257**

"Library Board's Policy on Censorship." *Australian Library Journal*, 13:59, June 1964.   **L258**
Policy adopted by the Library Board of New South Wales.

"Library Censorship of Current Fiction: Some Principles to be Observed." *New York Libraries*, 9:208–9, February 1925.   **L259**

A book is not to be accepted because it is innocuous, nor rejected because it is written from a point of view alien to the librarian; it is not to be rejected because a few people call it bad or because it is not suitable for all ages and grades of intelligence.

Library Employes Union of Greater New York. "Public Libraries and Censorship." *Library Journal*, 49:885–86, 15 October 1924.   **L260**
Summary of charges in a report to the Executive Board of the American Federation o Labor to the effect that Carnegie libraries are not controlled by the municipalities in which they exist but by a board of trustees appointed, generally, by the foundations themselves; that there is coming into being a system under which only books approved in a certain manner may be placed on foundation library shelves; and that an unjust certification o librarians is coming into practice.

Library Journal. New York, R. R. Bowker, 1876–date. Semimonthly (September–June), monthly (July–August).   **L261**
A major source of articles and news relating to freedom of the press and freedom to read, as applied to libraries.

"The Licentiousness of the Press." *Brownson's Quarterly Review*, 3(n. s.):517–43, October 1849.   **L262**
The writer defends the restraints on the radical press in England, citing a speech on the law of the press by Count de Montalembert, given in the French Assembly, 21 July 1849. The Count discounts the influence of the press in England and the United States because it "disdains logic and renders reason superfluous." The European press, he argues, should be subjected to greater restraint because it exerts greater influence for good or evil and because "mental culture there is of a superior order."

Lichtman, Richard. "Sex Censorship in a Free Society." *University of Kansas City Review*, 28:55–64, October 1961.   **L263**
"The fact that our culture is saturated with sexually provocative material and suffering from forms of maladjustment such as increasingly juvenile and violent crimes leads a certain element of the population to link the two and to demand elimination of the first as a significant requirement for the elimination of the second." The author criticizes censorship of sexual expression for three reasons: (1) it is a flat contradiction of the First Amendment, (2) there is no evidence that adult sex crimes are the result of contact with erotic material, and (3) nobody can agree on what is pornographic. He comments on the difficulty of keeping the power of a censor in check and the likelihood of anyone who accepts the job being unaware of the aesthetic values in literature. There is no easy solution, but it is not in suppression.

Lichtman, W. T. *Certain Restrictions in the Acquisition and Use of Books in Undergraduate Liberal Arts College Libraries.* New York, School of Library Service, Columbia University, 1939. 95 p. (Unpublished Master's thesis) **L264**

Lidschin, Rose. "Censorship and the American Heritage, or 'You Can't Read that!'" *Public Libraries*, 5:3, 56–60, June 1951. **L265**
The author emphasizes the responsibility of the librarian to provide material on all sides of a controversy and, by wide community contacts, to build up support of the library as a positive agent in the dissemination of knowledge.

Lieberman, Irving. "Reflections of an American Librarian: Intellectual Freedom and Libraries." *Librarian*, 42:25–26, February 1953. **L266**
Reviews the efforts in the United States to uphold the Library Bill of Rights and cites some of the attempts at censorship—attacks on the UNESCO pamphlet used in the Los Angeles schools and the newspaper crusade against Communist literature in the Boston Public Library.

Lieberman, J. Ben. *Changing Concepts of Freedom of the Press.* Stanford, Calif., Stanford University, 1952. 332 p. (Ph. D. dissertation in Political Science) **L267**
The purpose of the study is (1) "to delineate the various major concepts which have been labeled 'freedom of the press,'" (2) "to study contemporary opinion and actions for implicit new concepts, and relate them to the main body of concepts," and (3) to offer a thesis as to a serviceable general concept under conditions now developing. "Under the emerging conception," the writer finds, "Freedom of the Press is the right to serve, without government interference, the more fundamental right of Freedom of Information, the latter being the right of the people to assure themselves of the fullest supply of information possible."

————. "Restating the Concept of Freedom of the Press." *Journalism Quarterly*, 30:131–38, Spring 1953. **L268**
"The only answer to those who insist on confusing responsibilities with freedom of the press is to go back to first principles. . . . Freedom of the press still rests, therefore, on the faith that public policy is better served by absolutely uncontrolled expression on political matters than by any method of control, no matter how benignly devised."

————. "Should the School Press Be Free?" *California Journal of Secondary Education*, 24:340–46, October 1949. (Reprinted in *Education Digest*, January 1950) **L269**
The principles involved in constitutional freedom of the press should be applied to school newspapers. Under the present system too often the only example of the press that the students really know—the student paper—operates on an entirely different basis. The article is concerned with developing editors and writers who will defend freedom of the press, and with ways a free student press may help to accomplish this objective.

Lieberman, Marvin S. "Obscenity Is Not Within the Area of Constitutionally Protected Speech and Press." *University of Illinois Law Forum*, 1957:499–505, Fall 1957. **L270**
Roth v. United States, 354 U.S. 476 (1957).

Liebling, A. J. "The End of Free Lunch." In his *The Press.* New York, Ballantine, 1964, pp. 3–12. **L271**
In this foreword to the author's collection of witty and caustic commentary on the state of the press, he describes the American press as being in a monopolistic situation where "the paper can cut out news as the saloons cut out free lunch." In another section, No News, he discusses the practice of "the expert, who writes what he construes to be the meaning of what he hasn't seen." He illustrates this by the American press coverage of Stalin's death and the events that followed.

The Light. Published by the World's Purity Federation, LaCrosse, Wis., bimonthly, 1897–1937. **L272**
The Light was known as "the magazine that broke the age-old conspiracy of silence on problems of life and sex." It was the organ of the World's Purity Federation and was edited by B. S. Steadwell of LaCrosse, Wis., beginning in 1897 until his death in 1937. It brought together, through the Federation, curious fellow travelers, who could agree on only one thing—the need for sex hygiene, although not on the kind of literature that promoted the cause. The Federation at one time included Anthony Comstock and J. Frank Chase from the vice societies, the WCTU's Frances Willard, the columnist Dorothy Dix, and the libertarian lawyer and enemy of censorship, Theodore A. Schroeder. J. Frank Chase was editor of the magazine's Department of Contributory Vices. A picture of Steadwell appears on the cover of the November–December 1926 issue.

Lilburne, John. *A Christian Mans Triall or a Trve Relation of the first apprehension and severall examinations of Iohn Lilburne, with his Censure in Star-Chamber, and the manner of his cruel whipping through the Streets: whereunto is annexed his Speech in the Pillory, and their gagging of him: also the severe Order of the Lords made the same day for fettering his hands and feet in yrons, and for keeping his friends and monies from him . . .* London, 1638. 39 p. (Second edition by William Larnar in 1641; in various other editions during Lilburne's lifetime) **L273**
Writing from prison, Lilburne, the leading crusader for the freedom of the press during the Puritan Revolution, describes his arrest, arraignment, and trial. He was accused of printing seditious tracts (Bastwick's *Letany* and other antiprelatical works), brought before the Star Chamber, convicted, and sentenced to solitary confinement. He was set free by the Long Parliament and continued his career as radical pamphleteer. Joseph Frank in *The Levellers*, describes the style of this pamphlet as "hasty, emotional, undisciplined." Much of it is legalistic and relates to Lilburne's refusal to answer questions at the trial.

[————]. *A Conference with the Souldiers.* London, 1653. **L274**
An anonymously published defense of Lilburne in his trial for libel against Cromwell.

————. *A Copie of a Letter, Written by John Lilburne Leut. Collonell to Mr. William Prinne Esq. . . .* London, 1645. 7 p. (Facsimile reprint in Haller, *Tracts on Liberty in the Puritan Revolution*, vol. 3, pp. 181–87) **L275**
Lilburne demands freedom of the press as a right of every freeborn English subject. He accuses Prynne and the Presbyterians of intolerance to the ideas of others because of fear of their own cause. Prynne, who had himself suffered under the Star Chamber for his writings, was influential in having Lilburne imprisoned in Newgate for this attack.

[————]. *Englands Birth-Right Justified Against all Arbitrary Usurpation, whether Regall or Parliamentary, or under what Vizor soever . . .* London, Larner's Press, 1645. 49 p. (Facsimile reprint in Haller, *Tracts on Liberty in the Puritan Revolution*, vol. 3, pp. 258–307) **L276**
In this tract, written for the common man, Lilburne turns to the Magna Charta as the supreme charter of popular liberty, including liberty of conscience, freedom of the press, and economic justice. He opposes the monopoly in religion granted the clergy and the printing monopoly granted the Stationers' Company.

————. *Free-Mans Freedome Vindicated.* London, 1646. 12 p. **L277**
Written from Newgate prison, this pamphlet is an account of Lilburne's defiance of the House of Lords when he was being questioned about an offending pamphlet. The frontispiece of *Free-Mans Freedome* is a portrait of Lilburne with prison bars across his face and a caption: "The Liberty of The Freeborne English-man, Conferred on him by the house of lords." The House of Lords ordered the pamphlet burned by the common hangman.

[———]. *A Jury-man's Judgement upon the Case of Lieut. Col. John Lilburn: Proving, by Well-grounded Arguments, both to His Own and Every Jury-man's Conscience, that They May Not, Cannot, Ought Not Finde Him Guilty upon the Act of Parliament Made for His Banishment, and to Be a Felon for Returning to England* . . . [n. p., 1653?]. 15 p. **L278**

———. *The Legall Fundamentall Liberties of the People of England, Reviewed, Asserted, and Vindicated* . . . London, "Printed in the grand yeer of hypocriticall and abominable dissimulation," 1649. 75 p. **L279**
Written by Lilburne when he was imprisoned in the Tower of London.

———. *Malice detected, In Printing certain Informations And Examinations Concerning Lieut. Col. John Lilburn. The morning of his Tryal: And Which were not at all brought into his Indictment.* London, 1653. **L280**
Lilburne, having been brought to trial for a libel against Cromwell, wrote this pamphlet in his own defense, *A Charge of High-Treason exhibited against Oliver Cromwel.* This was another episode in Lilburne's long fight against all forms of tyranny—first against the bishops, then against the Presbyterians, and finally against Cromwell, whom he had once served, and Parliament. Lilburne cherished his role as martyr, folk hero, and champion of the rights of the common Englishman. He was the rallying figure for the Levellers and the many years he spent in prison he used to dramatize the cause of freedom. The Council of State characterized him as the greatest libeler of his time. He can also be considered the greatest champion of freedom of the press.

———. *The Picture of the Councel of State, held forth to the Free People of England by Lieut. Col: John Lilburn, Mr. Thomas Prince, and Mr. Richard Overton, now prisoners in the Tower of London* . . . London 1649. 54 p. **L281**
A narrative of the arrest and examination, consisting of a signed statement of each prisoner. Walwyn gives his account in *The Fountain of Slander Discovered.* Frank, in his book, *The Levellers* (p. 196), writes: "Each of the four dramatic accounts is essentially similar, yet each reveals certain differences in the personalities, though not in the social ideals, of these Leveller leaders."

———. "Proceedings in the Star-Chamber against Him and John Wharton for Publishing Seditious Books, 1637." In Howell, *State Trials*, vol. 3, pp. 1315 ff; in Borrow, *Celebrated Trials*, vol. 1, pp. 469–82; and in Rushworth, *Historical Collections*, pt. 2, pp. 463–69. **L282**

An account of Lilburne's trial in Star Chamber for publication of Bastwick's *Letany* and other tracts, the first of Lilburne's many persecutions.

[———]. *The Triall, of Lieut. Collonell John Lilburne, By an extraordinary or special Commission, of Oyear and Terminer at the Guild-Hall of London, the 24, 25, 26. October 1649. Being as exactly pen'd and taken in short hand, as it was possible to be done in such a croud and noyes, and transcribed with an indifferent and even hand, both in reference to the Court, and the Prisoner; that so matter of Fact, as it was there declared, might truly come to publick view.* . . . *Published by Theodorus Varax.* . . . London, Printed by Hen. Hils, [1649]. 168 p. **L283**

Lilienthal, David E. "The American Press in War Time." *Quill*, 30(10):3–4, 14, October 1942. **L284**
Observations on the role of a free press in a democracy during war, voiced by the chairman of the Tennessee Valley Authority.

———. "The People, the Atom, and the Press." In Summers, *Federal Information Controls in Peacetime*, pp. 61–64. **L285**
The chairman of the U.S. Atomic Energy Commission, in an address before the New York State Publishers' Association, 19 January 1948, describes the responsibility of the Commission both with regards to national security and to keeping the public informed. A well-informed public is essential in the formulation of public policy.

Lilly, W. S. "The Ethics of Journalism." *Forum*, 7:503–512, July 1889. **L286**
In democracies, the newspaper press undertakes to guide the people to an understanding of matters of state. Liberty of the press is essentially ethical—"liberty to state facts, liberty to argue upon them, liberty to denounce abuses, liberty to advocate reforms." The press of continental Europe falls far short of this goal.

"Limits of Libel." *Law Times*, 47:421–22, 16 October 1869. **L287**
An analysis of recent libel cases suggests to the author that we have gone far enough in allowing for the plaintiff.

Linck, Anna A. *Freedom of the Press in the United States in World Wars I and II.* Columbus, Ohio State University, 1947. 172 p. (Unpublished Master's thesis) **L288**

Lincoln, Abraham. [Letter to Erastus Corning and Others]. In his *Collected Works.* New Brunswick, N.J., Rutgers University Press, 1953. vol. 6, pp. 260–69. **L289**

In a letter dated 12 June 1863, Lincoln defends the wartime restrictions on freedom of the press and the suspension of habeas corpus. He denies the danger "that the American people will, by means of military arrests during the rebellion, lose the right of public discussion, the liberty of speech and the press, the law of evidence, trial by jury, and Habeas corpus, throughout the indefinite peaceful future" anymore than "a man could contract so strong an appetite for emetics during temporary illness, as to persist in feeding upon them through the remainder of a healthful life." On a number of occasions Lincoln disapproved of the action of military commanders against newspapermen. On 1 October 1863 he wrote to General Schofield (pp. 492–93), "Under your recent order, which I have approved, you will only arrest individuals, and suppress assemblies, or newspapers, when they may be working palpable injury to the Military in your charge; and, in no other case will you interfere with the expression of opinion in any form, or allow it to be interfered with violently by others."

Lincoln, William S. *Alton Trials: of Winthrop S. Gilman who was indicted with Enoch Long [et al.] for the Crime of Riot Committed on the night of the 7th of November 1837, while engaged in defending a Printing Press from an attack made on it at that time, by An Armed Mob. Written out from notes of the trial, taken at the time, By a member of the Bar of the Alton Municipal Court. Also, the trial of John Solomon [et al.] for a Riot Committed in Alton [the same night] in unlawfully and forcibly entering the Warehouse of Godfrey, Gilman & Co., and breaking up and destroying a Printing Press* . . . New York, John F. Trow, 1838. 158 p. **L290**
The only record of the trials growing out of the Alton riots and the murder of Elijah P. Lovejoy, presented without comment. Widely circulated as an antislavery pamphlet.

Lindey, Alexander. *Entertainment; Publishing and the Arts; Agreements and the Law.* . . . New York, Boardman, 1963. 1248 p. **L291**
This compendium of practical information on the law of the communications field includes references to such topics as freedom of expression, censorship, invasion of privacy, libel, and copyright. The reference work is arranged by medium: books, magazines, newspapers, plays, motion pictures, television and radio, music, art work, phonograph recordings, and photographs.

———. "The *Forever Amber* Trial." *Author, Playwright and Composer*, 57:68–70, Summer 1947. **L292**
A 50-year taboo has been broken in Massachusetts with the freeing of *Forever Amber*

in a civil jurisdiction. "The case has shown that censorship proceedings cannot and must not be tried as run-of-the-mill criminal affairs."

———. "Thank the Censor!" *Publishers' Weekly*, 125:1508–10, 21 April 1934. **L 293**

A New York lawyer thanks the censor for rendering a social service by bringing significant books to the attention of the public and by forcing the courts to uphold freedom of the press. References to the work of the New York Society for the Suppression of Vice and Judge Woolsey's decision in the *Ulysses* case.

Lindley, Ernest K. "Basic Pattern for News Censor's Shears." *Newsweek*, 18:22, 29 December 1941. **L 294**

Comments on plans for wartime censorship. News of the appointment of Byron Price as wartime censor is reported on pp. 50–51.

———. "Freedom of Information." *Newsweek*, 24:47, 11 December 1944. **L 295**

A favorable review of the stand on worldwide freedom of information taken by the American Society of Newspaper Editors. News report on page 88.

———. "Report on Growing Pains of Censorship." *Newsweek*, 19:29, 16 February 1942. **L 296**

Conflict between the Office of Censorship and the Army over information on war production.

Lindsay, John V. "Censorship Feeds on Complacency." *Library Journal*, 89:3909–12, 15 October 1964. **L 297**

"No doubt one reason why private censorship groups have proliferated in recent years is that they have not been checked by countervailing efforts by other private groups. . . . It is important for the future of the reading public that persons representing all sides of the question make themselves known, heard, and effective." The author was then Republican Congressman from New York's 17th District, later mayor of New York City.

———. "Intellectual Freedom and the Federal Government." *Publishers' Weekly*, 183:18–22, 27 May 1963. **L 298**

In an address before the American Book Publishers Council, Representative Lindsay analyzes recent attacks on the First Amendment, including stringent curbs proposed on freedom of speech and the press. He calls upon citizens to shield the First Amendment as the "greatest legal protection of our liberties."

Linenthal, Eleanor T. *Freedom of Speech and the Power of Courts and Congress to Punish for Contempt*. Ithaca, N.Y., Cornell University, 1952. 333 p. (Ph. D. dissertation, University Microfilms, no. 19,157) **L 299**

The contemporary conflict between the tradition of free speech and the doctrine that courts and Congress may punish for contempt, derives, in a large measure, from changed patterns of legal, political, and constitutional thought with respect to the functions of government, the scope of individual liberties, and the nature of the judicial process.

Linfield, Seymour L. *Laws relating to Birth Control in the United States and Its Territories*. New York, Birth Control Clinical Research Bureau, 1938. 61 p. (Foreword by Margaret Sanger; introduction by Morris L. Ernst) **L 300**

A compilation of federal and state statutes prohibiting or controlling the dissemination of information on birth control. The statutes, Ernst points out, stem from the Comstock Act of 1873 when "literature discussing birth control could be characterized as 'obscene.'" "The reading of the birth control laws of the nation which this pamphlet makes possible (writes Ernst) is the most effective argument for their repeal which could be advanced."

Linington, Elizabeth. *The Long Watch*. New York, Viking, 1956. 377 p. **L 301**

A novel of Revolutionary War days in which the central theme is the struggle of a New York newspaper to survive the British occupation.

Linton, W. J. *James Watson: A Memoir of the Days of the Fight for a Free Press in England, and of the Agitation for the People's Charter*. Manchester, A. Heywood, [1880?] 93 p. **L 302**

Watson, an English publisher, was associated with W. J. Linton, Henry Hetherington, and George J. Holyoake, in the fight against the stamp tax. Watson's earliest service in behalf of freedom of the press was in 1823 in the sale of Palmer's *Principles of Nature*, for which Carlile and Tunbridge had already been imprisoned. Watson sold the book as a volunteer salesman for Carlile. The work, dealing with evolution, was deemed blasphemous and Watson was given a year in prison. Watson pleaded his own case, arguing that the volume was "maliciously bought [by a police officer who came into the shop] but not maliciously sold by me," and that the jury would be committing perjury by finding him guilty. In 1833 he was imprisoned for six months for selling Hetherington's *Poor Man's Guardian* and in 1834 for another six months for selling Hetherington's unstamped paper, *Conservative*. It is said that he took his prison sentences philosophically, using the time to catch up on his reading. Watson's print shop was for many years headquarters for radicals and Chartists.

Lippmann, Walter. "Free Speech and Free Press as Factors in International Affairs." *Bulletin*, League of Free Nations Association, 1:1–2, March 1920. **L 303**

———. "Liberty and the News." *Atlantic Monthly*, 124:779–87, December 1919. **L 304**

"The task of liberty, therefore falls under three heads: protection of the sources of the news, organization of the news so as to make it comprehensible, and education of human response . . . We shall advance when we have learned humility; when we have learned to seek truth, to reveal it and publish it; when we care more for that than for the privilege of arguing about ideas in a fog of uncertainty."

———. *Liberty and the News*. New York, Harcourt, Brace, 1920. 104 p. **L 305**

In two of the three essays which comprise this volume, What Modern Liberty Means and Liberty and the News, both originally published in the *Atlantic Monthly*, Lippmann describes the liberty of the press as "the name we give to measures by which we protect and increase the variety of the information on which we act." There is no absolute freedom of the press. Milton, Mill, and Russell all imposed qualifications on liberty. During wartime we impose restrictions; and various factors restrict and modify our daily news reporting. It is more critical, Lippmann believes, to protect the stream of news that reaches the public than it is to protect opinion based on the facts. Lippmann cites restrictions and limitations in recent news coverage of World War I and the Peace Conference. Reviewed in *Current Opinion*, March 1920.

———. "The Nature of the Battle over Censorship." In his *Men of Destiny*, New York, Macmillan, 1927, pp. 93–106. **L 306**

Lippmann examines the nature of liberty and the reasons for efforts to suppress certain ideas. The censor has traditionally not so much feared ideas as "the circulation of the idea among the classes which in his judgment are not to be trusted with the idea." Censorship "is actually applied in proportion to the vividness, the directness, and the intelligibility of the medium which circulates the subversive idea." Suppression is generally practiced by those who consider themselves guardians of the state, the church, the family, and property and who feel that the unattached and impressionable might be seduced by unorthodox ideas.

———. "The Press." *Vital Speeches*, 1:362–63, 11 March 1935. **L 307**

Freedom of the press depends on something more than legal guarantees under the Constitution; it must be achieved by the action of newspaper men.

———. *Public Opinion*. New York, Macmillan, 1922. 427 p. (Reprinted in Macmillan Paperback edition, 1960) **L 308**

The first serious attempt made to study the underlying principles of censorship, propaganda, publicity, electioneering, news, and intelligence work, particularly as it relates to the life of a democracy. Chapter 2 deals with Censorship and Privacy and relates largely to wartime experiences as do other portions of the volume. Still considered a classic study.

————, and Charles Merz. "A Test of the News." *New Republic*, 23:sup. 1–42, 4 August 1920. **L309**
An examination of news reports in the *New York Times* on the coverage of a world event, the Russian Revolution, to determine the adequacy and objectivity of coverage and the extent of bias. The authors find too great a reliance on official sources; the use of untrustworthy correspondents; and the policy of the editors at times influencing the news columns.

"Literary Censorship." *Dial*, 48:135–37, 1 March 1910. **L310**
An editorial condemning the power of English circulating libraries to censor books. The American public library system, supported by taxation, and with each library free to make its own selection, is much better.

"Literary Censorship." *Yale Literary Magazine*, 8:156–65, February 1843. (Signed: L.U.C.) **L311**
A criticism of literary reviews. While "criticism founded on truth and justice is necessary for the health of our literature," too much of criticism is "microscopic" rather than "telescopic."

"Literary Censorship and the Novels of the Winter." *Current Opinion*, 55:353, 377+, November 1913. **L312**
A report on Anthony Comstock's arrest of Mitchell Kennerley for publication of *Hagar Revelly* by D.C. Goodman, and, in England, the refusal of the Circulating Libraries Association to list Hall Caine's *The Woman Thou Gavest Me*, W. B. Maxwell's *Devil Garden*, and Gilbert Cannan's *Round the Corners*.

"Literary Censorship in South Africa." *South African Libraries*, 23(3):77, January 1956. **L313**
A statement on censorship, approved by the Council of the South African Library Association.

Literary Liberty Considered; in a Letter to Henry Sampson Woodfall. London, Printed for J. Johnson, 1774. 32 p. **L314**
The imprisoning of London publishers has become so fashionable that a newcomer must pass through jail on his way to popularity. The author complains of the licentiousness and rebelliousness of the press, believing that the public has suffered more from the abuse of the press than from its restraint. "Of late years two opposite monsters have presided at the helm of political affairs: their names, *Libel* and *Panegyric*. . . . From these parents have sprung falsehood, scurrility and adulation." The writer professes a great respect for proper freedom of the press but "an utter foe

to intellectual licentiousness. . . . In a right cause I should find as much gratification in being a champion of a Printer as of a Prime Minister; and should labour with equal zeal to rescue from infamy Mr. Woodfall or his Sovereign."

"Literature and Morals in England." *Nation*, 94:205–6, 29 February 1912. **L315**
While one group of Britons, led by John St. Loe Strachey, editor of the *Spectator*, is urging censorship of literature similar to dramatic censorship, another group is protesting the censorship of the stage.

Littell, Philip. "Books and Things." *New Republic*, 32:20, 30 April 1922. **L316**
Critical comments on the work and dour personality of John Sumner, successor to Anthony Comstock, as head of the New York vice society.

[Little, Joseph J.]. *Statement of Facts Regarding the Indictment for Criminal Libel, Found by the Grand Jury against Nicholas Murray Butler, Professor of Philosophy in Columbia University, and Others, upon the Complaint of Joseph J. Little, President of the Board of Education of the City of New York.* [New York, 1899]. 24 p. **L317**
Relates to charges brought by Commissioner Little against Butler, editor, and Henry Holt & Co., publishers of the *Educational Review*, for an allegedly libelous editorial in the February 1899 issue of that journal. In the article Little was described as a "fine old educational mastodon" supported by Tammany and by "two other representative antediluvians." This is Little's formal statement, issued to "correct understanding of the case through the imperfect statements that have appeared in the daily press."

Litsky, Leo. *Censorship of Motion Pictures: A History of Motion Picture Censorship and an Analysis of its Most Important Aspects.* New York, New York University, 1947. 380 p. (Unpublished Ph. D. thesis; abstracted in School of Education, *Abstracts of Theses, 1947–48*, pp. 45–50) **L318**
The study describes and analyzes the early development of censorship of motion pictures, including the National Board of Review, the industry's answer to censorship (self-regulation), censorship by local, state, and federal agencies, censorship activities of such pressure groups as the Legion of Decency, and the Protestant Motion Picture Council. The author recommends that "some methods be adopted for making the Production Code and the Advertising Code more representative of the people"; the abolition of "legal censorship" by government boards, possibly by means of a test case carried to the U.S. Supreme Court, which would accord to films the right to freedom of expression. He also recommends that responsibility for Customs censorship "be

more tightly fixed and a simple system of appeal be instituted . . . Pressure groups serve a very useful purpose in informing the industry of the desires of its member," so long as one group does not exercise a monopoly. He points out the need for pressure groups to promote film quality and to emphasize the social and educational potential of the films.

The Livery-man; or, Plain Thoughts on Publick Affairs. In which The present Situation of Things, some late Writings concerning the Liberty of the Press, the General Disposition of the People, the Insults offered to the City of London, and the true Nature and infallible Characteristicks of Publick Spirit, in Contradistinction to that of a Faction, are consider'd and explain'd. Addressed to the Lovers of Truth and Liberty . . . London, Printed for James Smith, 1790. 64 p. **L319**

"Nature teaches us to complain when we are aggrieved; and therefore there can be nothing more unnatural than to take away the Power of Complaining." Historically, it was the illegal freedom of the press which brought many of the blessings now enjoyed by the English people through the overthrow of tyrannical government. Libels are an evil and libelers deserve punishment, but too often the outcry is directed against the press instead of the libeler. The author objects to setting up a system of licensing the press comparable to that governing the stage. "Power is an intoxicating thing, and therefore all Concessions in its favor are dangerous. . . . It is like giving ground to the Sea, or opening a Gate to a mad Bull; we may escape afterwards, but if we do, it is more than we deserve, and we can never recover our Reputation."

Livingston, Robert. "Censorship—The Test of Obscenity as a Standard for the Censorship of Literature." *Boston University Law Review*, 34:208–12, April 1954. **L320**
Deals with the case, *New American Library of World Literature v. Allen*, involving a Youngstown, Ohio, ordinance prohibiting the sale and distribution of obscene books. The chief of police had informed the local distributor of paperback books that failure to remove books on a submitted list would result in arrest. The Federal District Court held that while the ordinance was constitutional, the plaintiff had been deprived of a property right without due process of law. The article discusses the various tests for obscenity and the conflicts arising between the divergent interests—guardian of public morals and guardian of the right of creative, realistic, and original works of literature.

[Lloyd, Charles]. "A Defence of the Majority in the House of Commons, on

the Question Relating to General Warrants. In Answer to the *Defence of the Minority.*" In *A Collection of Scarce and Interesting Tracts . . .* London, J. Debrett, 1787–88, vol. I, pp. 73–92. **L 321**
An answer to Charles Townshend's *A Defence of the Minority . . .*, written in 1764 by the secretary to George Grenville, First Lord of the Treasury. The majority had defeated Whig efforts to outlaw the use of the general warrant for seizing authors, printers, and booksellers. Discussed in Rea, *The English Press in Politics*, chapter 7.

Loble, Lester H. "Juvenile Crime and Law in Montana." *Washington Newspaper*, 50(1):6+, October 1964. **L 322**
Calls for publicity rather than secrecy on juvenile offenses as a method of curbing juvenile violence and crime.

"Local 'Blackouts' on Public Affairs Television." *Columbia Journalism Review*, I(1):40–47, Spring 1962. **L 323**
A survey of the extent of turn-down by local television stations of public service programs offered by the networks. A second look at the situation, showing much the same results, appears in the Spring 1966 issue.

Locke, John. *Essay Concerning Toleration.* In *Works of John Locke*, 11th ed., London, 1812, vol. 6; also in Bourne, *Life of John Locke*, and in various collections of Locke's essays. **L 324**
Locke's essay and his *Letters on Toleration* (1685) were notable pleas for liberty of thought, particularly in religion. Locke believed in allowing the utmost freedom of opinion in religious matters, with the state interfering only when, under cloak of religion, the ideas espoused were political or social views at variance with the best interest of the community. Religious liberty consisted in limiting the power of the magistrates to matters clearly necessary to the preservation of the peace. His was a more restricted doctrine on freedom of opinion than Milton's in *Areopagitica*. No specific reference is made to the press, but it was Locke who drew up the case against continuance of licensing of the press, which brought an end to the Licensing Act.

————. ["Observations on the Licensing Act"]. In Lord King, *The Life of John Locke, with Extracts from His Correspondence, Journals, and Common-Place Books.* London, Henry Colburn. 1829, pp. 201–8. (Also in Bourne, *Life of John Locke*, vol. 2, pp. 312–15) **L 325**
Locke made notes on each paragraph of the offensive Act for the licensing of printing, probably in 1694 when the Act was up for renewal. Lord King prints the 17 paragraphs

from the Act together with Locke's critical but concise arguments against each. Unlike Milton's philosophical eloquence in *Areopagitica*, Locke's paper was a straightforward, businesslike appeal to common sense, addressed to the officials of the Government and pointing out the practical inconvenience of the Act. The submission of this memorandum by a friend (Edward Clarke) to a Parliamentary committee on 18 April 1694, is credited with turning the tide to allow the Act to expire.

Lockhart, Andrew F. "Interesting Account of [Free Press Defense] League's Activities . . . Persecuted Editor of *Chain Lightning* Sentenced to Federal Prison." *Menace*, 320:1, 9 June 1917. **L 326**
A. F. Lockhart, editor of *Chain Lightning*, was sentenced to federal prison for alleged obscenity in anti-Catholic articles.

————. "Lockhart Case." *Rail Splitter*, 3:1–2, March 1918. **L 327**
In his magazine, *Chain Lightning*, Lockhart attacked "political romanism," which he maintained supplied the real motive for his arrest and conviction on an obscenity charge.

Lockhart, William B., and Robert C. McClure. "Censorship of Obscenity: The Developing Constitutional Standards." *Minnesota Law Review*, 45:5–121, November 1960. **L 328**
"The authors discuss the constitutional criteria controlling recent decisions of the United States Supreme Court in the area of obscenity censorship and demonstrate that substantial protection has been given to published material dealing with sex. In considering the development of a test to identify censorable obscenity, they examine the nature of pornography and conclude that it provides a useful guide. They find that 'hard-core pornography' is the foundation for the 'constant' concept of obscenity currently applied by the Court; and they advocate a 'variable' concept which would make the validity of censorship depend upon the particular material's primary audience and upon the nature of the appeal to that audience. The authors also discuss: (1) the requirement that material be judged as a whole on the basis of its dominant theme, (2) the weight to be given 'redeeming social importance,' (3) the protection of 'immoral' ideas and the 'end of ideological obscenity,' (4) the requirement of scienter, (5) the meaning and application of 'contemporary community standards,' and (6) the need for independent judicial review of obscenity findings."

————. "Literature, the Law of Obscenity, and the Constitution." *Minnesota Law Review*, 38:295–395, March 1954. **L 329**
The entire issue is devoted to a well-documented study of the law of obscenity in the United States as interpreted by the courts. The account begins with the U.S. Supreme Court ruling to uphold the conviction of

Doubleday in the case of the *Memoirs of Hecate County.* A review of censorship today includes action against paperback books and an extended treatment of the National Organization for Decent Literature. The authors discuss the various concepts of obscenity and trace court decisions from the Lord Cockburn dicta in *Queen v. Hicklin* to the Woolsey-Hand decisions on *Ulysses.* They consider the effect of reading on thoughts, actions, community moral standards, and the probable audience. One section deals with works of educational and scientific value that have been charged as obscene—sex education and birth control literature. They discuss the extent to which the constitutional guarantees cover sex expression and the application of Mr. Justice Holmes's "clear and present danger" phrase to sex expression. The authors consider the use of secret lists as the greatest threat to free expression in the realm of sex.

————. "Obscenity in the Courts." *Law and Contemporary Problems*, 20:587–607, Autumn 1955. **L 330**
This article largely recapitulates portions of an earlier study, Literature, the Law of Obscenity, and the Constitution, that appeared in the *Minnesota Law Review*, March 1954.

Lodge, *Sir* Oliver. "The Responsibility of Authors." *Fortnightly Review*, 87(n. s.): 257–67, February 1910. **L 331**
In a talk given before the Authors' Club, 20 December 1909, Sir Oliver shows by example how "contemporary criticism may be mistaken, and that a hasty censorship may commit much injustice," especially when it tries to restrict circulation of an idea. Freedom is essential to literature and the other arts.

Loevinger, Lee. "Broadcasting and Religious Liberty." *Journal of Broadcasting*, 9(1):3–23, Winter 1964–65. **L 332**
The author calls for a reappraisal of FCC practices and doctrines on supervision of religious programming in light of recent Supreme Court decisions.

————. "The Role of Law in Broadcasting." *Journal of Broadcasting*, 8:113–26, Spring 1964. **L 333**
The FCC Commissioner believes that regulations should be limited to listing forbidden acts rather than attempting to list what the station or industry must do.

[Lofft, Capell]. *An Essay on the Law of Libels; with an Appendix Containing Authorities; Subjoined, Remarks on the Case in Ireland of Attachment and the Letter of T. Erskine, on the Subject.* London, 1785. 110p. **L 334**
Lofft, an English rationalist and follower of the doctrine of Thomas Erskine, insists on the right of the jury rather than the judge to decide whether a work is libelous. He defends the right of the people to censure public men and measures, as necessary to a free government. His ideas come close to denying the entire concept of seditious libel.

Lofton, John. "Justice and the Press; Communication Inside and Outside the Courtroom." *St. Louis University Law Journal*, 6:449–88, Fall 1961.　**L335**
The article offers an "analysis of the interaction of the public press and the courts. It is hoped that this analysis will be of help in determining under what circumstances and in what ways the individual right to due process should take precedence over the collective public right to know, and, conversely, where free news reporting may be allowed without unduly jeopardizing the individual's right to an impartial trial."

————. "The Press Manages the News." *Progressive*, 27(7):16–20, June 1963.　**L336**
A criticism of the employment of news by editors "as a weapon of the cold war rather than a source of enlightenment about world events."

"*Lolita* in the Dock." *New Zealand Libraries*, 23:180–83, August 1960.　**L337**

[London, Ephraim]. "There Must Be Freedom to Expound All Ideas: An Interview with Ephraim London Conducted by Mary Batten." *Film Comment*, 1(4):2–19, 1963. (Reprinted, University of Missouri, Freedom of Information Center, Publication no. 121)　**L338**
Verbatim report of an interview with a lawyer who has fought many cases of film censorship, including *The Bicycle Thief* and *The Miracle* case (1952) in which the U.S. Supreme Court held that the motion picture was protected under the First Amendment. London rejects the idea that the film requires special regulation because of its great impact. "The more effective the medium, the greater the freedom it should have." Films are subject to greater censorship than stage plays because they are a more popular and less expensive form of entertainment. He discusses the work of various state and local film censorship boards, including Providence, R.I., where police censorship is in force. He comments especially on the Kansas board's action against *The Sky Above, The Mud Below*, because of scenes of a few naked aborigines. He defends the rights of organizations such as the Legion of Decency to recommend and condemn films although he disagrees with their judgment and opposes government action to enforce their recommendations. Every policy and philosophy no matter how distasteful or evil it may be should be allowed to be shown on film; the same medium can and should be utilized to counteract hate and evil. London does not favor the British system of classifying films for children; while he feels it is not a violation of the Constitution, it is not effective. Librarians, he states, "more than any other group, have insisted on the freedom to read." Complete freedom of the films, as with all media, is the answer to censorship.

London. County Council. *Censorship of Cinematograph Films. Special Committee on Procedure for Licensing Places of Public Entertainment. Report to the Clerk of the Council.* London, County Council, 1929. 8 p.　**L339**

————. Public Morality Council. *Annual Reports.* London, The Council, 1901–date?　**L340**
The Council superseded the National Vigilance Association in 1899, which, in 1885, had succeeded the Society for the Suppression of Vice. The Council was for a time called the London Council for the Promotion of Public Morality. From 1954 onwards, issues of the report are entitled *Public Morals*.

————. Public Morals Conference. *The Nation's Morals; Being the Proceedings of the Public Morals Conference Held in London on the 14th and 15th July, 1910 . . . With a Preface by the Rt. Hon. Alfred Emmott . . .* London, Published for the National Social Purity Crusade by Cassell and Co., [1910?]. 263 p.　**L341**
Section 3 deals with Books, Newspapers, Theatres. Three topics are discussed: (1) How may the organization of publishers, news agents, circulating libraries, journalists, and authors check the production and circulation of noxious reports and publications? (2) Should the law be strengthened, having due regard to the liberty of the press and for the suppression of noxious publications? Among the contributors to this section are John St. Loe Strachey, editor of *The Spectator*, Canon H. D. Rawnsley, and Anthony Comstock. (3) The relation of the theatre to public morals.

————. Stationers' Company. *A Transcript of the Registers of the Company of Stationers of London . . . 1554–1640 . . .* Edited by Edward Arber. London, Privately printed, 1875–94, 5 vols.　**L342**
Source of information on the rules and regulations of the Company of Stationers, the licensing or refusal to license printing, and the controversies over the licensing system.

The London Printer, His Lamentation; or, the Press Oppressed, Or Overpressed. London, 1660. 8 p. (Also in *Harleian Miscellany*, vol. 7, pp. 104–11)　**L343**
A brief history of printing in England, including its regulation by the Crown up to 1640. The lament is against the monopoly granted to certain printers by the Crown, in which printing is prostituted for every vile purpose, both in Church and State. He accuses printers Christopher Barker, John Bell, Thomas Newcomb, John Field, and Henry Hills of inflaming the people against the king.

[Long, Howard R.]. "Case Studies in Stewardship." *Grassroots Editor*, 5(1):2–5, January 1964. (Digested in St. Louis *Post-Dispatch*, 8 March 1964)　**L344**

An account of three editors of small-town papers (Midlothian, Tex., Morrilton, Ark., and Holmes County, Miss.) who have been awarded the Elijah Parish Lovejoy Award for Courage in Journalism by the Department of Journalism, Southern Illinois University. Despite financial losses, boycotts, and threats of violence they continued to fight for freedom of the press.

Long, Joseph R. "The Freedom of the Press." *Virginia Law Review*, 5:233–46, January 1918.　**L345**
A general summary of the struggle for a free press in the United States and Great Britain.

Longacre, Charles S. *Freedom, Civil and Religious; the American Conception of Liberty for Press, Pulpit, and Public, as Guaranteed in the Federal Constitution. Issued by the Religious Liberty Association, Washington, D.C.* Washington, D.C., Review and Herald Publishing Association, 1920. 128 p.　**L346**
A Seventh-day Adventist work.

[Loomis, Horatio N.]. *Report of the Trial. [The people v. Dr. Horatio N. Loomis, for Libel.] Tried at the Erie County Oyer and Terminer, June, 24, 1850; Justice Mullett Presiding.* Buffalo, N.Y., Press of Jewett, Thomas & Co., 1850. 50 p.　**L347**
Trial relates to the practice of midwifery.

López, Salvador P. "Freedom of Information." *Vital Speeches*, 20:411–13, 15 April 1954.　**L348**
The Filipino delegate to the United Nations, chosen to prepare a report which would assist the UN in its effort to facilitate the free flow of news throughout the world, discusses the proposals in his report. He pays tribute to the English language as "kindling wood" for freedom.

————. *Freedom of Information, 1953.* New York, UNESCO, 1953. 64 p.　**L349**
A report to UNESCO on contemporary problems and developments in freedom of communications, with evidence of surviving authoritative controls, and recommendations for practical action.

Lorch, Fred W., W. P. Jones, and Keith Huntress, eds. *Of Time and Truth.* New York, Dryden, 1946. 590 p.　**L350**
A section on Freedom of Expression includes the following: Morris Ernst, Freedom to Read, See, and Hear; Plato, Censorship in *The Republic*; John Milton, *Areopagitica*; a selection from Thomas Hobbes' *Leviathan*, asserting the right of the sovereign to censor; expressions of Thomas Jefferson on the role of a

free press in a democracy; Walt Whitman's "Shut not Your doors to me proud libraries..." from his *Leaves of Grass*; Mark Twain's speech on freedom of the press; and a selection from Marshall Field's *Freedom Is More Than a Word*.

Lord, Daniel A. *The Motion Pictures Betray America*. St. Louis, The Queen's Work, 1934. 48 p.   **L351**
"I accuse the Motion Picture Industry of the United States of the most terrible betrayal of public trust in the history of our country. I charge them with putting the profits of the box office ahead of all considerations of decency, respect for law, or love of a nation's health and happiness." Despite the 1930 Production Code, Father Lord believes the movies continue to be objectionable, with a few men fighting to enforce the Code and others trying to evade it. He calls upon Catholics to follow the lead of the Bishops by boycotting objectionable pictures.

"Lord Campbell's Bill." *Law Magazine and Law Review*, 3(3d ser.):283–86, 1857.   **L352**

A criticism of Lord Campbell's obscenity bill as being "well-meant" to attack a real evil, but an "ill-devised measure" that would give the informer, the magistrate, and the policeman power over literature. Article attributed to Lord Brougham.

"Lord Chamberlain: The Regulator." *Economist*, 204:682, 25 August 1962.   **L353**
Editorial expressing the hope that the new Lord Chamberlain will reduce his theatrical censorship activities to the minimum. "It is easier to be a straightforward censor of morals (which the Lord Chamberlain is not) than a judge of public taste."

Lorensen, W. D. "The Journalist and His Confidential Source: Should a Testimonial Privilege Be Allowed." *Nebraska Law Review*, 35:562–80, May 1956.   **L354**

"Los Angeles Bumps Bump Dancer Out of Show." *Art Digest*, 16:12, 1 March 1942.   **L355**
When the California Watercolor Society's 21st annual exhibition was moved from San Francisco to Los Angeles, the charge of censorship was raised by a Hollywood newspaper because one of the pictures was not hung but kept in the back room.

Los Angeles *Daily Journal*. *Report on Pornography*. Los Angeles, *Daily Journal*, 1958. 24 p.   **L356**
A comprehensive survey of obscene literature, cartoons, photographs, and films in southern California.

Los Angeles *Times*. *Freedom of the Press Affirmed*. Los Angeles, The *Times*, 1941. 19 p.   **L357**
"What the contempt of court victory of the Los Angeles *Times* in the United States Supreme Court means to the American public and to American newspapers."

Loth, David. *The Erotic In Literature. A historical survey of pornography as delightful as it is indiscreet*. New York, Messner, 1961. 256 p.   **L358**
A survey of pornography from the Golden Age of Greece down to present-day underground traffic in salacity. The author believes there is great confusion as to what constitutes a forbidden obscenity, who should declare it so, from whom it should be kept, and how the prohibition should be enforced. In the final chapter he considers the various proposals for meeting the present-day problem of pornography.

Louaillier, Alfred R. *Government Regulation of Radio Programming*. Lawrence, University of Kansas, 1955. 143 p. (Unpublished Master's thesis)   **L359**

Loucks, Philip G. "Section 315." *Federal Communications Bar Journal*, 18:33–36, 1963.   **L360**
This paper, the result of a study of the Communications Act of 1934 conducted by the Federal Communications Bar Association, recommends the repeal of Section 315 which provides for equal time for political candidates.

Louisiana Legislative Council. *The Regulation of Obscenity, Indecency, and Salacious Literature in the United States*. Baton Rouge, La., The Council, 1959. 72 p. mimeo.   **L361**

Lounsbury, Thomas R. "A Puritan Censor of the Stage." *Yale Review*, 12:790–810, July 1923.   **L362**
An account of William Prynne's criticism of the stage in his work *Histrio-Mastix* (1633), for which he was arrested, convicted, and imprisoned.

Louthan, Shirley. *The McCarthy Sub-Committee and the American Overseas Libraries*. Cleveland, Western Reserve University, School of Library Science, 1958. 59 p. (Unpublished Masters' thesis)   **L363**

Lovat-Fraser, James A. *Erskine*. Cambridge, Eng., Cambridge University Press, 1932. 155 p.   **L364**
An appraisal of the career and character of the eloquent defender of freedom of the press in the sedition and libel trials of late eighteenth-century England.

Lovejoy, Joseph C., and Owen Lovejoy. *Memoir of the Rev. Elijah P. Lovejoy; Who Was Murdered in Defence of the Liberty of the Press, at Alton, Illinois, Nov. 7, 1837. With an Introduction by John Quincy Adams*. New York, John S. Taylor, 1838. 382 p.   **L365**
The story of Lovejoy, written by two of his brothers immediately after Elijah's death, is the major source of material on his life and the Alton riot. The work consists of editorials, news stories, testimonials, and family letters, joined together with brief comment. Lovejoy was murdered when he attempted to protect his printing press from a proslavery mob.

Lovell, James. *Copy of a Letter . . . to the President of the United States, Supposed by the Writer to be Fitted, Specially, for the Eye and Courage of the "Young Federal Republicans of Boston" and also to be Calculated, Generally, to Promote the Comfort of All Grey-Headed as well as Green-Headed "Free Citizens," Everywhere*. Boston, A. Newell, [1805]. 8 p.   **L366**
Liberty of the press is "a broad sword of Defense," but, in the hands of the licentious, an equally broad instrument of offense. The cause of false use is the "nonsensical trinitarian partition of Man into thought, *word*, and action," instead of a simple division of thought and action. Speaking and writing, according to the author, is action "as truly as sneezing, coughing, even spitting; and Words, directed slyly to the Ears and Eyes of a free citizen of proper sensibilities, may be as offensive as any of those other actions directed plumply into his face."

Lovett, William. *Life and Struggles of William Lovett in His Pursuit of Bread, Knowledge, and Freedom, with Some Short Account of the Different Associations He Belonged to and of the Opinions He Entertained. With an Introduction by R. H. Tawney*. New York, Knopf, 1920. 2 vols. (Reprinted from the first edition of 1876)   **L367**
Lovett was a nineteenth-century English radical and a colleague of Hetherington, Place, and Watson in the attack on taxes on knowledge. In 1839 Lovett and a colleague were tried for publishing a "seditious libel" (a Chartist resolution) and sentenced to a year in prison.

[————]. *Trial for Seditious Libel, Assizes at Warwick*. London, 1839. 19 p. (Also in Macdonell, *Report of State Trials*, vol. 4, pp. 1177–88)   **L368**

Lowenstein, Ralph L. *Assault on the Press, 1964*. Columbia, Mo., Freedom of Information Center, School of Journalism, University of Missouri, 1965. 8 p. (Publication no. 145)   **L369**

An examination to determine the nature, reasons, and results of the numerous attacks made on the press during 1964.

——. *Obscenity and the Supreme Court.* Columbia, Mo., Freedom of Information Center, School of Journalism, University of Missouri, 1966. 6p. (Publication no. 154)
L370
A review of the history of obscenity rulings of the federal courts and an examination of the issues in obscenity cases now before the Supreme Court.

Lowenthal, David. "Macaulay and the Freedom of the Press." *American Political Science Review*, 57:661–64, September 1963.
L371
Review and commentary on Macaulay's ideas of freedom of the press as expressed in his *History of England.* The author concludes that "Macaulay's liberalism was and is inconsistent and inadequate. He did not allow his principles and perceptions to converge."

Lowry, Edward G. "The Reform in the Movies." *World's Work*, 50:329–33, July 1925.
L372
In praise of the film industry's efforts at self-improvement and self-censorship.

Lubasz, H. M. "Public Opinion Comes of Age: Reform of the Libel Law in the Eighteenth Century." *History Today*, 8: 453–61, July 1958.
L373
Account of the struggle in the eighteenth century for freedom of the press which, in the context of this essay, was "the freedom to express political opinion publicly and in writing." In legal form it "was a contest over the respective powers of judge and jury in trials for political libel." Cases are considered which led to the Fox Libel Act of 1792.

Lucas, Edward. "Mr. Mill upon Liberty of the Press." In Henry E. Manning, *Essays on Religion and Literature* . . . London, Henry S. King, 1874, pp. 142–73. **L374**
Lucas refutes the thesis of Mill's *Essay on Liberty* that there is a "natural right to deny the existence of God, or to call in question the commonly received doctrines of morality." Man's inherent right of liberty is only to speak or write the truth, not to believe and promulgate falsehood. Since God has revealed Himself and His will to man, to refute this revelation is to express false opinion. To suppress such opinion will rob mankind of nothing.

Lucey, Cornelius. "The Freedom of the Press." *Irish Ecclesiastical Record*, 50(ser. 5): 584–99, December 1937. **L375**
Freedom of the press is guaranteed in the new Irish constitution. Father Lucey supports the statement that blasphemy is punishable by law (he wishes it would also include "anti-religious" publications) but believes the libel laws are too severe in prohibiting criticism of public men. Legal freedom of the press is "only half the real freedom of the Press;" the press must be free of business pressures and must express varying points of view.

Luchsinger, John A. "A Blueprint for Censorship of Obscene Material: Standards for Procedural Due Process." *Villanova Law Review*, 11:125–38, Fall 1965.
L376
"Prior restraint by an administrative or law enforcement agency is not permitted. Censorship boards or commissions may be set up, if standards of education and competency of its members are designed to guard against arbitrary decisions. Decisions by such commissions may not be used to threaten a publisher, distributor, or vendor. It is submitted that decisions by such commissions should be used only to aid law enforcement agents in obtaining possibly objective material."

Lucidus, *pseud.* "Peoples' Press." *Canadian Forum*, 18:77–79, June 1938. **L377**
"We want to make the Canadian press directly dependent on the support of its readers instead of the support of its wealthy owners and advertisers. We want to make it possible for any faction or school of thought, no matter how poor its adherents may be, to have access to some organ which will present its views." Recommends a provincial press commission.

Lucifer, The Light-Bearer. Published at Valley Falls, Kan.; Topeka, Kan.; Chicago. Edited by Moses Harman and (for a time) E. C. Walker. 1883–1907. Weekly.
L378
"A journal of Investigation and Reform Devoted to the Emancipation of Women from Sex Slavery; An Untrammeled Peace." The issues of this paper frequently attack the Comstock laws and postal censors, and defend persons under prosecution for obscenity or blasphemy. Articles appearing in the paper and separately published tracts dealing with birth control resulted in Harman's spending some ten years either in jail or under bond on obscenity charges.

Ludwig, Frederick J. "Journalism and Justice in Criminal Law." *St. John's Law Review*, 28:197–219, May 1954. **L379**
A professor of law reviews the struggle between press and the courts over the conduct of judicial proceedings—an issue involving two historic constitutional rights. He finds no instantaneous solution, but rather the "patient application of highly specific remedies on a case by case, trial and error basis."

Lundberg, Ferdinand. "Crusade for a Free Press Cartel." *Common Sense*, 14: 34–37, May 1945. **L380**
"Newspaper publishers are calling for a free press over the world . . . Their motives however are not unselfish. . . . They want to take over the extensive, government-built news transmission facilities. . . . They want government aid in entering new press markets. . . . The only visible enemies in the world of free distribution of information are totalitarian governments, the big private newspaper cartels, and secret alliances between any type of government and private press cartels."

Lundevall, Karl-Erik, *et al. Förbjudna Böcker och Nordisk Debatt om Tryckfrihet och Sedlighet.* Stockholm, Wahlstrom & Widstrand, 1958. 324p. **L381**
Includes chapters on censorship of the works of Darwin (Åke Gustafsson), Joyce's *Ulysses* (Gunnar Brandell), Lawrence's *Lady Chatterley's Lover* (Olof Lagercrantz), in addition to chapters relating to censorship in the Scandinavian countries.

Lundy, Inez G. "Legislative Delegation of Authority to Administrative Agency—Constitutional Law—Freedom of the Press." *Temple Law Quarterly*, 35:334–37, Spring 1962. **L382**
The California District Court held unconstitutional the California Business and Professional Code which prohibited the exhibition or distribution of printed matter on certain subjects except through designated state agencies.

Lunn, A. Jean E. "Bibliography of the History of the Canadian Press." *Canadian Historical Review*, 22:416–33, December 1941. **L383**
Includes references to freedom of the press.

Luraschi, Luigi. "Censorship at Home and Abroad." *Annals of the American Academy of Political and Social Science*, 254:147–152, November 1947. **L384**
The director of censorship for Paramount Pictures discusses the film industry's self-censorship under the Production Code and the regulations of states, cities, and foreign governments. He also discusses the various themes that are offensive to audiences in various countries and which must be avoided or deleted for film export.

Luscher, Thomas. "Freedom of Speech and Press as a Limitation on the Contempt Power." *Marquette Law Review*, 40:313–24, Winter 1956–57. **L385**
Notes on *Bridges v. California* (1941) in which the U.S. Supreme Court held that [to quote from the author of the article] "the power of state courts to impose criminal punishment for contempt on individuals who, by public comment, attempt to exert influence over judicial proceedings, was subject to the freedoms of speech and press guaranteed by the First Amendment."

Lusk, Louis B. "The Present Status of the 'Clear and Present Danger' Test—A Brief

History and Some Observations." *Kentucky Law Journal*, 45:576–606, Spring 1957. **L 386**

The "clear and present danger" test was an attempt on the part of the U.S. Supreme Court to answer the question: How much freedom and how much restraint? The article reviews the history of that doctrine and appraises its present status.

Lutnick, S. M. "Who Should Choose the Books?" *Library Journal*, 87:1951–54, 15 May 1962; also in *School Library Journal*, 8:19–22, May 1962. **L 387**

"School librarians who shudder at the word 'controversial' must not be entrusted with the crucial task of selecting the books our youngsters will read. The question, then, is . . . 'Who Should Choose the Books?'" The author, a history professor, claims that school librarians are being forced to give ground in the matter of controversial books, yielding to pressure of superintendent or principal, who in turn yields to outside pressure groups. He feels that the classroom teacher should have final authority to recommend specific titles for the school library.

[Lyman, Theodore, Jr.]. *Report of a Trial in the Supreme Judicial Court, Holden at Boston, Dec. 16th and 17th, 1828, of Theodore Lyman, Jr., for an Alleged Libel on Daniel Webster, a Senator of the United States, Published in the Jackson Republican, Comprising All the Documents and Testimony Given in the Cause, and Full Notes of Arguments of Counsel, and the Charge of the Court . . .* Boston, Putnam and Hunt, 1828. 76 p. **L 388**

The style of the indictment against Lyman is of special interest, being based upon the law of *scandalum magnatum*, or slander of great men. The offense originated with the English Star Chamber but was never recognized in the common law of the United States. The case is also reported in Benton, *A Notable Libel Case.*

Lynch, Frederick. "Censorship and Art." *Christian Century*, 44:297–98, 10 March 1927. **L 389**

A discussion of the increasing indecency of the New York stage and the difficulties in efforts at a clean-up. Unless the managers and producers initiate sweeping reform, censorship is inevitable. A recent play-jury was unsuccessful. The writer suggests the appointment of a state censor "who shall have oversight of public morals in general—the theatre, the revues, the moving pictures, the books, and magazines."

Lynch, James J. "The Right to Read—and Not to Read." *Modern Age*, 9:18–33, Winter 1964–65. **L 390**

A summary of the various concepts of freedom to read, including the development of legal doctrine, as expressed by recent writers. Special attention is given to the attacks on censorship in the schools by the National Council of Teachers of English. Alongside the "right to read" is an even more fundamental right—"the right not to read." An individual has the right to impose a censorship on himself.

Lynch, John J. "Forbidden Reading." *Books on Trial*, 15:297–98, 344–50, March 1957. **L 391**

Father Lynch discusses books prohibited by the Catholic Church and the bases for the restrictions.

Lynd, Robert. "The Bounds of Decency." *Atlantic Monthly*, 139:748–59, June 1927. **L 392**

A glance through literature brings the author to the conclusion that "everybody is shocked by somebody or something . . . the sense of decency is . . . an eternal and universal part of human nature." The author feels that a decorum of one sort or another is essential. He observes that today it is not the comic writers but the writers who never make a joke who transgress the bounds of decency.

Lyne, Fritz. "Defamation as Applied to a Group or Class." *Texas Law Review*, 21:819–22, June 1943. **L 393**

Regarding *Knupffer v. London Express Newspaper, Ltd.*, 167 L.T.D. 376 (1942). Defamation of a group will not afford an individual member cause for libel action unless the group is so small as to identify members completely, or when words purport to refer to a class but, in fact, refer to one or more individuals who are identifiable.

[Lyon, Matthew]. "Trial for Seditious Libel, Vergennes, Vt., 1798." In Wharton, *State Trials*, pp. 333–44; also in *American State Trials*, vol. 6, pp. 687–94. **L 394**

Congressman Lyon was the first to be prosecuted under the Sedition Act, accused of publishing an antiadministration letter in his Vermont paper, *The Scourge of Aristocracy*. A rabid Republican member of Congress, Lyon conducted his own defense, was convicted, fined $1,000 and sentenced to 4 months in jail. He was re-elected to Congress while serving his prison term. In 1840 Lyon's heirs were refunded the $1,000 fine (U.S. Senate Doc. 106, 16th Cong., 1st sess.). A full account of the case is given in Smith, *Freedom's Fetters*, chapter 11.

Lyons, Eugene. "The *Esquire* Affair." *American Mercury*, 58:317–18, March 1944. **L 395**

Editorial criticism of Postmaster-General Walker's action in revoking second-class mailing privileges of *Esquire*. "As long as one man remains the judge of any paper's or magazine's right to share in a general privilege, freedom of the press is an empty phrase."

Lyons, Louis M. "A Free and Responsible Press." *Nieman Reports*, 1(2):1–3, April 1947. **L 396**

Review of the report of the Commission on Freedom of the Press.

————. "Liebling, Libel, and the Press." *Atlantic Monthly*, 213(5):43–48, May 1964. **L 397**

A review of recent criticism of the press (including that of A. J. Liebling) and an appraisal of the Alabama libel case against the *New York Times*, involving reporting and advertising on the racism that has afflicted the state. The U.S. Supreme Court held for the newspaper, affirming that criticism in good faith is entitled to protection. The opinion stated that "the constitutional guarantees require, we think, a Federal rule that prohibits a public official from recovering damages for a defamatory falsehood relating to his official conduct unless he proves that the statement was made with 'actual malice.'"

————. "The Press and Its Critics." *Atlantic Monthly*, 180:115–16, July 1947. **L 398**

The lack of coverage by newspapers of the report of the Commission on Freedom of the Press illustrates the need for the internal criticism of the press that the Commission recommended.

————. "What's Fit to Print?" *New Republic*, 144:17–19, 5 June 1961. **L 399**

Comments on newspapermen's reactions to President Kennedy's request, following the Cuban missile crisis, for more restraint by the press in covering news involving national security, and specifically, his proposal that the newspapers themselves appoint a journalist of some stature to serve as a voluntary clearing house for security matters. The author discusses the problem of how much restraint to exercise in reporting manifest activities of the CIA.

————, Clark Mollenhoff, and Edwin A. Lahey. *Secrecy in Government*. Columbia, Mo., Freedom of Information Center, School of Journalism, University of Missouri, 1959. 7 p. (Publication no. 13) **L 400**

Transcription of a television program.

————, Theodore White, and John K. Fairbank. *The News from China*. Columbia, Mo., Freedom of Information Center, School of Journalism, University of Missouri, 1959. 7 p. (Publication no. 12) **L 401**

Transcript of a television panel in which two newspapermen and a professor of China-studies criticize State Department policy that prevents Americans from getting adequate news from Communist China.

[Lytton, Edward R. B.]. "Liberty of the Press; an Old Fable." *Fortnightly Review*, 24:178–88, August 1875. **L 402**

A "modern" poem based on the Prometheus legend.

M

M., D. L. "Plea for Cinderella." *Nation and Athenaeum* (London), 31:602–4, 29 July 1922. **M1**
Discussion of the refusal of the Lord Chamberlain to grant a license to the play, *The Queen's Minister*, because it might be offensive to living people. "It is apparently held that the theatre is either so vile that it needs a special guard to be set over it, or so trivial and contemptible that the liberating process which has almost wholly freed literature and the other arts from the regime of State surveillance and repression, may well stop short at the drama."

M., R. B. "Censorship in 1615." *Devon and Cornwall Notes and Queries*, 15:181–82, October 1928. **M2**
A brief note on the action of the government of James I against William Martin's *Historie and Lives of the Kings of England*. Martin was summoned before the authorities, but released when he repented of certain passages objected to by the king.

Maas, Peter. "Merchants of Obscenity." *Saturday Evening Post*, 235:26–27, 13 October 1962. **M3**

McAnany, P. D. "Motion Picture Censorship and Constitutional Freedom." *Kentucky Law Journal*, 50:427–58, Summer 1962. **M4**
"In January 1961 the Supreme Court decided its ninth case dealing with the censorship of motion pictures. For the first time since 1915 [Mutual Film Corp. case] the decision ran in favor of the censor." Father McAnany reviews the history of court decisions on the movies, including the famous Burstyn case (1952), Kingsley International Pictures Corp. (1959), and the *Times Film Corp. v. City of Chicago* (1961), noting the changing patterns of thought. The Court "has shown a continuing interest in protecting the right of films to be communicated to the public at large as long as they do not infringe the counter right of the state to protect the community against the corrupting effects of obscene or pornographic movies."

"MacArthur and Censorship." *Harper's Magazine*, 188:537, May 1944. **M5**

An editorial on Army censorship of an article about MacArthur intended for *Harper's Magazine*. The article was banned by Army authorities to whom it was submitted for clearance, "on grounds of military security." The editor charges the real reason was that the article contained, along with praise, considerable criticism of the General. The Army ruled that the article "undermines the confidence of this country, Australia, and particularly the troops in that theatre, in their commander and his strategics and tactical plans."

Macaulay, Thomas B. [On the Suggested Suppression of the Works of Wycherley, Congreve, &c.]. In his *Critical and Historical Essays*. London, 1843. vol. 3, p. 256. **M6**
"The whole liberal education of our countrymen is conducted on the principle that no book which is valuable, either by reason of excellence of its style or by reason of the light which it throws on the history, polity and manners of nations, should be withheld from the student on account of its impurity. . . . We are therefore by no means disposed to condemn this publication [the plays of Wycherley, Congreve, Vanbrugh, and Farquhar] though we certainly cannot recommend the handsome volume before us as an appropriate Christmas present for young ladies."

McCabe, George P. *Forces Molding and Muddling the Movies . . . A Paper on Censorship of Motion Pictures in the United States with Suggestions for Sane Regulatory Laws.* Washington, D.C., n.p., 1926. 47 p. **M7**
This booklet is an impartial study of the activities of various city and state censorship boards.

McCabe, Joseph. *The History and Meaning of the Catholic Index of Forbidden Books.* Girard, Kan., Haldeman-Julius, 1931. 107 p. **M8**

———. *Life and Letters of George Jacob Holyoake.* London, Watts, 1908. 2 vols. **M9**

A sympathetic biography of the English social reformer and Chartist. Chapter 4 deals with his trial and imprisonment on blasphemy charges; chapter 12 with his part in the fight against "taxes on knowledge"; and chapter 19 with his relationship to the obscenity trial of Annie Besant and Charles Bradlaugh. Richard Carlile, the lifelong crusader for a free press, also appears throughout the work.

McCabe, Robert K. "No News Is Bad News." *Nieman Reports*, 15(3):24–27, July 1961. **M10**
Criticism of the government policy that keeps American reporters out of Communist China.

McCarroll, Tolbert H. "Freedom of Speech and Press—Censorship of Films." *Oregon Law Review*, 34:250–56, June 1955. **M11**
A review of recent cases dealing with prior restraint on film exhibition.

MacCarthy, Desmond. "Censorship of Plays." *New Quarterly Review*, 2:599–614, 1909. **M12**
Commentary on the recommendations of the Joint Select Committee of the Lords and Commons upon the Censorship of Plays. "The Committee may find that in attempting to give freedom to the drama of ideas, by sanctioning the performances of unlicensed plays, they have by the creation of this new tribunal for controlling them, made it almost impossible for a manager, who wishes to produce an unlicensed play to get a theatre in which to perform it." The alternative to prior censorship, offered by the Committee, was to face a closing of the theatre, if, after the performance, the play was found to be objectionable.

———. "Literary Taboos." *Life and Letters*, 1:329–41, October 1928. **M13**
Discussion of the ban on the *Well of Loneliness* and the taboo against certain sex discussions that has led to the suppression of such plays as Shaw's *Mrs. Warren's Profession*, Ibsen's *Ghosts*, Brieux's *Damaged Goods*, and Havelock Ellis' book, *Psychology of Sex*. "History shows that only those communities have flourished in which men were allowed to pool their experience and comment freely on life, and

that the suppression of freedom is a graver risk to civilization than the circulation of any particular book to morality." On pages 327–35, the author reviews English obscenity law in light of recent action against *Well of Loneliness* and *Sleeveless Errand.*

McCarthy, John. "New Needs for the Legion of Decency." *Catholic Digest,* 18(7):1–6, May 1954. **M 14**
Relaxed standards of the film industry, violations of the Code, and recent Supreme Court rulings call for greater vigilance by the Legion of Decency. The author describes how the organization works in discouraging films it believes are bad.

McCarthy, Joseph R. *Confusing Freedom of the Press with Prostitution of the Press. Speeches in the Senate of the United States, December 15, 19, 1950 and January 5, 1951.* Washington, D.C., U.S. Govt. Print. Off., 1951. 32 p. **M 15**

———. "Sen. McCarthy Questions Pres. Conant on 'Book Burning.'" *Nieman Reports,* 7(3):35–37, July 1953. (Reprinted from the Boston *Globe,* 16 June 1953) **M 16**
Questions and answers in Senator McCarthy's examination of Harvard President James B. Conant before the U.S. Senate Appropriations Committee, relating to U.S. information libraries abroad.

McCarthy, Mary T. "The Menace to Free Journalism in America." *Nieman Reports,* 7(4):46–48, October 1953. (Reprinted from *The Listener,* 14 May 1953) **M 17**
The greatest menace to free journalism is not Senator McCarthy but "the conceptualized picture of the reader that governs our present-day journalism like some unseen autocrat. The reader, in this view, is a person stupider than the editor, whom the editor both fears and patronizes."

———. "No News, or What Killed the Dog." In her *On the Contrary.* New York, Farrar, Straus and Cudahy, 1961, pp. 32–42. **M 18**
Freedom to circulate works of art and literature is more or less intact in the United States. The paradox is that, while ideas circulate, the individuals who espouse them, believe in them, or practice them are persecuted, banned, or jailed, or exiled from the country. Article based on a speech given at the conference of the American Committee for Cultural Freedom, March 1952.

McCarthy, Michael J. F. *Jesuits and the British Press.* Edinburgh, Oliphant, Anderson & Ferrier, 1910. 71 p. **M 19**

A Protestant views the unofficial censorship and control of the press by Catholics.

McCausland, Elizabeth. "*The Blue Menace.*" Springfield, Mass., The *Springfield Republican,* 1928. 28 p. **M 20**
A series of articles reprinted from the *Springfield Republican,* 19–27 March 1928, discussing the drive against liberalism, the curtailment of free speech in Massachusetts and elsewhere by means of blacklists, attacks on liberal colleges and churches, and the "DAR protest."

Macchiaroli, Michael A. "Recovery for Libel of Public Official Requires Proof of Actual Malice." *Villanova Law Review,* 9:534–39, Spring 1964. **M 21**
Regarding *New York Times Co. v. Sullivan,* 84 S. Ct. 710 (1964).

McClellan, Sidney. *Censorship of Radio Broadcasts . . .* Washington, D.C., Georgetown University, 1938. 80 p. (Unpublished S.J.D. dissertation) **M 22**
"This dissertation will concern itself primarily . . . with the restrictions, restraints, or censorship of radio broadcasts imposed by the Communications Act of 1934 as administered by the Federal Communications Commission and the allied problem of defamation by radio. The law applicable to the cinema and press will be discussed only by way of analogy and comparison with the laws applicable to radio broadcasting."

McClure, Alexander K. *Bench, Bar and Press. Argument of Alexander K. McClure before Supreme Court, for Plaintiffs in Error. In Matter of the Rules Disbarring Andrew J. Steinman and William U. Hensel, Attorneys.* [Philadephia? 1880?]. 30 p. **M 23**
The attorneys, who were also editors of a newspaper, published in their paper an article, charging a judge with prostituting the machinery of justice in a certain case to serve party purpose. Thereupon the court disbarred them for misbehavior in office, although they were not professionally associated with the case under discussion. McClure, editor of the Philadelphia *Times,* speaks eloquently against the arbitrary judgment of the court and its threat both to the freedom of the press and the right of the legal profession. Judge Sharwood, speaking for the Pennsylvania Supreme Court, ruled (95 Penn St. 220) that the action of Judge Patterson in the lower court was a violation of the state's 1874 Bill of Rights.

McClure, Robert C. "Obscenity and the Law." *ALA Bulletin,* 56:806–10, October 1962. **M 24**
A century of confusion as to what is obscene, which began with the English case of *Regina v. Hicklin,* may soon be resolved when one of the *Tropic of Cancer* cases comes before the U.S. Supreme Court. Professor McClure believes the court will rule that this book does not meet the constitutional standards for obscenity

and that, henceforth, only hard-core pornography can be constitutionally censored. He reviews recent legal cases that seem to lead to this interpretation.

Maccoby, Simon. *English Radicalism, 1762–1785. The Origins.* London, Allen & Unwin, 1955. 535 p. **M 25**
A history of the years in which modern English radicalism was born, containing references to the work of the radical press, the various trials for seditious libel, in which the juries sometimes refused to convict, the John Wilkes affair, the Junius letters, and the activities of the Society for Constitutional Information.

———. *English Radicalism, 1786–1832; From Paine to Cobbett.* London, Allen & Unwin, 1955. 559 p. **M 26**
This study covers the period of English history that witnessed the great state trials for seditious and blasphemous libel, the prosecution of Paine (1792–93), Hone (1817), Hardy (1794), Carlile (1817), Eaton (1793), Tooke (1794), Cobbett (1831), Spence (1801), Hunt (1821), Thelwall (1794), and Williams (1822).

McConn, Max. "Authors' Bureau of Censorship." *Nation,* 113:40–41, 13 July 1921. **M 27**
An amusing satire on censors and censorship.

McCormack, Thelma H. "Canada's Royal Commission on Broadcasting." *Public Opinion Quarterly,* 23:92–100, Spring 1959. **M 28**
A review of the report of the Fowler Commission that examined television and radio broadcasting in Canada. "Once again Canadian broadcasting, with its unique combination of private and public ownership, was given a vote of confidence." Among the recommendations of the report was the establishment of a new regulatory agency, the Board of Broadcast Governors, with C.B.C. as an interested party only.

McCormick, John, and Mairi MacInnes, eds. *Versions of Censorship; an Anthology.* Garden City, N.Y., Doubleday, 1962. 374 p. (Anchor book) **M 29**
The editors have brought together an unusual collection of opinions relating to censorship, some famous, some obscure, but all contributing to the historical development of the idea. The first section, Censorship and Belief, begins with Milton's *Areopagitica* and continues with statements on the Roman Catholic *Index,* the condemnation of Galileo, and a selection from Spinoza. The second section, Censorship and Ideas, deals with the development of secular concepts of freedom. It includes selections from Hobbes' *Leviathan,* Julian Huxley's *Soviet Genetics,* Claud Cockburn's *Discord of Trumpets,* Tocqueville's *Democracy in America,* Abner Kneeland's *Trial for Blasphemy,* Chafee's *Free Speech in the United States,* and the Congressional testimony of Patrick M. Malin

of the American Civil Liberties Union, entitled Smut, Corruption, and the Law. The third section, Censorship and Imagination, deals with the realm of art, literature, and the theater, and includes Henry Miller's testimony in the *Sexus* case, Judge Bryan's opinion on *Lady Chatterley's Lover* in the Grove Press case, George Orwell's The Prevention of Literature, Rousseau's case for censorship of the theater, and Lord Chesterfield and Bernard Shaw's arguments against theater censorship. A final section, Self-Censorship, contains Dream-Censorship by Freud and The Legend of the Grand Inquisition from Dostoyevsky's *The Brothers Karamazov*. Appropriate commentary by the editors brings a unity to the various selections and to the entire compilation.

McCormick, Robert R. *Assaults upon the Constitution; a Series of Addresses Broadcast over WGN and the Mutual Broadcasting System, September 26–December 26, 1953.* [Chicago, *Chicago Tribune*, 1954]. 53 p.
M 30

———. *The Case for the Freedom of the Press; An Address by Robert R. McCormick . . . before the New York State Chamber of Commerce. New York City, November 16, 1933.* Chicago, *Chicago Tribune*, 1933. 28 p.
M 31
The publisher of the *Chicago Tribune* gives a brief history of the development of a free press in England and the United States, followed by more detailed references to the then current restrictions placed on the press by the NRA codes.

———. *The Fight for the Freedom of the Press; an Address by Robert R. McCormick before the New York Advertising Club, New York, N.Y., April 25, 1935.* [Chicago, *Chicago Tribune*, 1935]. 19 p.
M 32

———. *The Freedom of the Press. A History and an Argument Compiled from Speeches on this Subject Delivered over a Period of Fifteen Years.* New York, Appleton-Century, 1936. 116 p.
M 33
The publisher of the *Chicago Tribune* gives a brief summary of the history of the freedom of the press from the Middle Ages to the New Deal, stressing the current problems that face the newspaper publisher. He refers especially to the famous *Tribune* libel case, the Minnesota gag laws, and government action under the NRA codes.

———. *The Freedom of the Press; an Address by Col. Robert R. McCormick . . . before the Inland Daily Press Association, Chicago, Oct, 18, 1933.* [Chicago, *Chicago Tribune*, 1933]. 23 p.
M 34

———. *The Freedom of the Press Still Furnishes that Check upon Government Which No Constitution Has Ever Been Able to Provide.* Chicago, *Chicago Tribune*, 1934. 36 p.
M 35
A pamphlet directed against the newspaper codes under the NRA.

McCoy, Bruce R. "Freedom of the Press in Democratic and Totalitarian States." In Robert B. Heilman, *ed., Aspects of Democracy.* Baton Rouge, Louisiana State University Press, 1941, pp. 90–96.
M 36
A brief look at the press restrictions in Japan, Russia, Italy, and Germany by way of contrast with the freedoms in England and America.

McCoy, Ralph E. "The ABC's of Illinois Censorship, 1965." *Illinois Libraries,* 48: 372–77, May 1966.
M 37
A review of three Illinois cities—Alton, Belleville, and Chicago—that made the headlines in 1965 because of book censorship. The first two involved cases of public library censorship. Chicago dealt with a protest over James Baldwin's *Another Country* as required reading at Wright Junior College and the conviction of bookseller Paul Romaine for sale of *Fanny Hill.* Also mentioned is the removal of paintings by George G. Kokines from an exhibit in the Chicago Public Library. This entire issue of *Illinois Libraries* features Intellectual Freedom.

———. *Banned in Boston: The Development of Literary Censorship in Massachusetts.* Urbana, Ill., University of Illinois, 1956. 345 p. (Ph. D. dissertation, University Microfilms, no. 18,173)
M 38
The New England Watch and Ward Society was formed in Boston in 1878 as part of the Comstock crusade against obscenity. It received widespread support from the Boston Brahmins, who were unwilling to concede the same freedom in sex expression that they supported in the realms of politics and religion. In an attempt to enforce a rigid concept of sexual purity in literature, the Society, in 1882, with official sanctions, suppressed the Boston edition of Whitman's *Leaves of Grass.* The Society reached the height of its power in 1909 when the state's Supreme Judicial Court upheld the ban on Eleanor Glyn's *Three Weeks.* Following this decision Massachusetts booksellers, unwilling to risk further arrests, joined forces with the Society in a "gentlemen's agreement" which kept much of modern fiction from bookstores of the Commonwealth. This arrangement was brought to an end in 1926 when H. L. Mencken defied the Society's edict by selling an issue of *American Mercury* on the Boston Common and was cleared by a municipal judge. In the confusion that followed, the Boston police, with strong Catholic support, launched a wholesale attack on modern novels. Liberalization of Massachusetts obscenity laws in 1930 and 1945, the awakening of the Boston press, and the activities of an emerging civil liberties movement supported by lawyers, librarians, and book publishers, helped to erase the long-standing stigma on Boston as the censorship capital of America.

———. "Intellectual Freedom." *Illinois Library Association Record,* 10(2):30–32, October 1956.
M 39
A review of some of the problems faced by librarians in attempting to follow the Library Bill of Rights and suggestions on how to deal with the problems.

———. "Public Library Censorship." *Illinois Library Association Record,* 7:89–93, April 1954.
M 40
A review of recent attacks on public libraries, and some of the censorship threats that libraries and booksellers have faced in past generations in areas of religion, politics, and sex. Censorship practiced by librarians as well as pressures from outside are discussed. Among the questions raised are: Does the refusal of the library to accept propaganda literature from deviant religious, social, and economic groups constitute censorship? Do minority groups have a right to practice censorship in order to guarantee fairness to themselves? How far can a pressure group go in its objection to publications before it is a menace to freedom? The author offers advice to librarians and library boards in resisting demands for censorship.

McCracken, George W. "World Security and Freedom of Information." *Queens Quarterly,* 52(1):91–99, Spring 1945.
M 41
An appeal for world freedom of information made on the eve of the San Francisco Conference. He quotes the Canadian Prime Minister in support: "I believe that freedom of exchange of international news is essential for informal opinion of international affairs, without which there can be no peace. I hope that the necessary limitations of wartime censorship will be lifted as soon as the reasons for the existence have disappeared, and trust that in the post-war world no government will be permitted to insulate its people from the current of thought outside their national boundaries."

McCrea, Tully. "Publishing of Juvenile's Name Serves No Useful Purpose." *Washington Newspaper,* 51(3):4–6, December 1965.
M 42
The author is a regional director of the National Council on Crime and Delinquency.

MacCulloch, Campbell. "How Free Is Speech?" *Motion Picture Classic,* 32(1): 24–25, 90, September 1920.
M 43
A brief history of movie censorship which "really began in 1908 in New York City when Mayor George B. McClellan issued an order closing every one of the five hundred picture houses in the city on December 24 of that year, on the ground that they were unclean and immoral. Three days later a court order reopened them. Then a volunteer organization,

the People's Institute, offered to examine all films intended for exhibition, and approve or disapprove them." In six states—Kansas, Maryland, New York, Ohio, Pennsylvania, and Virginia—the people have their movies "carefully denatured for them." The New York censor "allows baby shirts" but disapproves of political slams; the Pennsylvania censor frowns on any mention of "the Expected Event."

McCullough, John M. "Free Press and Fair Trial." *Pennsylvania Bar Association Quarterly*, 25:237–44, April 1954.　**M 44**

McCune, Wesley. "The Freedom to Read and the Political Problem." *ALA Bulletin*, 59:500–506, June 1965. (ALA Conference on Intellectual Freedom, 23–24 January 1965)　**M 45**
The director of Group Research, Inc., who has made studies of groups seeking to affect public issues, comes to the conclusion that the right wing of American politics and economics is growing stronger in every measurable way—membership, leadership, public relations, political activity, financial support, and publishing. While in favor of having right- and left-wing literature on library shelves in balance, he notes that "a larger bill of fare is being offered by the right-wing" and it will be pressed upon libraries with enthusiasm, if not outright fanaticism. He offers a guide to identifying the "literature" of the right-wing so that librarians will not be inundated by it.

McDermott, John F., ed. *The Sex Problem in Modern Society*. New York, Modern Library, 1931. 404 p.　**M 46**
A section on Sex in Literature contains the following articles: Contemporary Sex Release in Literature by V. F. Calverton, Hermaphrodites by Robert Herrick, and Sex Control by Morris L. Ernst and William Seagle. The Calverton article appeared originally in *Sex Expression in Literature*; the Herrick article in the *Bookman*, July 1929; the Ernst and Seagle article in their *To The Pure*.

McDermott, John F., and Kendall B. Taft. *Sex in the Arts; a Symposium*. New York, Harper, 1932. 328 p.　**M 47**
A discussion of sex expression in various forms of Communications: poetry (Henry Morton Robinson), fiction (John Cooper Powys), drama (Elmer Rice), biography (Ernest Boyd), motion pictures (Struthers Burt), journalism (Henry F. Pringle), and advertising (Silas Bent). Morris L. Ernst has a chapter on Sex and Censorship.

McDiarmid, E. W. "The Library's Responsibility in Free Communication." In *Freedom of Communication; Proceedings of the First Conference on Intellectual Freedom* . . . Chicago, American Library Association, 1954, pp. 25–33.　**M 48**

MacDonagh, Michael. "Can We Rely on Our War News?" *Fortnightly Review*, 63(n.s.):612–25, April 1898.　**M 49**
The author evaluates difficulties encountered by British journalists in obtaining war news, and the attitudes of the War Office toward correspondents in the field. The war correspondent is now an established figure in journalism and the public will not tolerate too much hampering of him in the field of action.

Macdonald, Dwight. "Censorship Without Control?" *Yale Political*, 3(1):13, 30, Autumn 1963.　**M 50**
"Opposing all forms of censorship with the exception of military information during a war, Dwight Macdonald examines the problems in determining what should be censored and who should do the censoring." If we must have censors, they should not be cops or postmen, but should be writers, artists, scholars, or other intellectuals. "The only trouble is few such individuals would want the job. I wouldn't."

MacDonald, Eugene M. *Colonel Robert Ingersoll As He Is; a Complete Refutation of His Clerical Enemies' Malicious Slanders*. New York, The Truth Seeker, 1896. 100 p.　**M 51**
Among other refutations, the author deals through letters and documents with Ingersoll's defense of freedom of expression in matters of religion and free thought but his opposition to obscenity.

Macdonald, George E. *Fifty Years of Freethought; being the Story of the Truth Seeker, with the Natural History of its Third Editor*. New York, The Truth Seeker, 1929–31. 2 vols.　**M 52**
The Truth Seeker, founded by D. M. Bennett in 1875 to offset censorship efforts of Anthony Comstock's vice society, carried reports of many censorship cases during its years of publication. This history of the journal refers to the Bennett case, the Reynolds and Mockus blasphemy trials, the persecution of Ida Craddock, and the Scopes evolution trial. There are photographs of such freedom of the press leaders as Charles Bradlaugh, Elizur Wright, Benjamin Tucker, Dr. E. B. Foote, Jr., Dr. E. B. Foote, Sr., and Theodore A. Schroeder.

————. *Letter to Solicitor Lamar*. New York, 1918. Broadside.　**M 53**
Reprinted from *The Nation*, 5 October 1918, along with an editorial from *The Truth Seeker*. Both deal with suppression of *The Truth Seeker* by the solicitor of the Post Office Department. "Another number of *The Truth Seeker* (Sept. 28, 1918) has been found nonmailable. . . . I renew my request that *The Truth Seeker* be removed from the list of 'suspects.'"

McDonald, John. "Will Hays' New Rival: Government Review." *Nation*, 156:484–86, 3 April 1943.　**M 54**
Criticism of a proposal of the Office of War Information to review movies prior to release. The author urges that the movies be given the same freedom from government censorship as that enjoyed by the newspaper press.

McDonald, Joseph A., and Ira L. Grimshaw. *Radio Defamation*. New York, National Broadcasting Co., 1937. 29 p.　**M 55**

MacDonald, W. A. "How Censored Are We?" *Canadian Business*, 32:60, 66, November 1959.　**M 56**
In practice censorship is left to the discretion of customs officials and to local police boards. The present tightening of Canada's censorship legislation is at variance with Britain's opposing trend. The author opens the door on Canada's censorship code with its many peculiarities and problems.

MacDonald, William. "The Press and the Censorship in England and France." *Nation*, 105:287–89, 13 September 1917.　**M 57**
"No reputable correspondent needs a censorship, no official ought to be shielded by it, no secret diplomatic intrigue ought to be fostered by it. Least of all should it find tolerance in a war which, like the present one, is being fought by democracies for the safeguarding of democracy."

Macdonell, *Sir* John. "Blasphemy and the Common Law." *Fortnightly Review*, 39:776–89, June 1883.　**M 58**

————, and J. E. P. Wallis, ed. *Report of State Trials*. New Series, 1820–58. London, 1888–98. 8 vols. (Published under the Direction of the State Trials Committee)　**M 59**
Includes trials of the following involving freedom of the press: Sir Francis Burdett, Mary Ann and Richard Carlile, John Chapman, William Cobbett, John Collins, Daniel W. Harvey, Henry Hetherington, John Hunt, William Lovett, Edward Moxon, Daniel O'Connell, John Stockdale, Samuel Waddington, and John A. Williams.

MacDougall, Curtis D. "College Editors Should Be Free." *Masthead*, 10(2):20–22, Spring 1958.　**M 60**
A professor of journalism takes issue with Robert E. Kennedy of the Chicago *Sun-Times* (Fall 1957 issue of *Masthead*) on the role and rights of a college newspaper. A college paper should not be regarded "as merely an arm of a college's public relations department," but should have the right of independent views. MacDougall favors the 1947 resolution

of the American Association of Schools and Departments of Journalism which "opposed censorship of undergraduate publications in any form whatever, *de jure* or *de facto*."

———. *The Press and Its Problems*. Dubuque, Ia., Brown, 1964, 532p.   **M 61**
A major portion of the problems dealt with in this journalism textbook relates to freedom of the press. Chapter 2, The Press and Democracy: What is the freedom of the press guaranteed by the first amendment of the Constitution? To what extent can government legislate regarding newspapers without violating the constitutional provision? What should be the attitude of the press toward the other so-called civil liberties? Chapter 6, The "Controlled" Press: What is the extent and nature of capitalistic-owner influence upon editorial policy? How and to what extent do advertisers influence editorial policy? What are the methods and importance of pressure groups other than advertisers? Chapter 8, The Newspaper and the Law: What are the limits to the newspaper's right to gather information about public affairs? To comment on the news? What is libel and how can the newspaper avoid committing it? Chapter 9, The Individual and the News: What is the legal and ethical relationship between a newspaper and a news source? What right should a newspaper concede to the individual to control news relating to himself? To control the use of pictures of himself? Chapter 10, To Print or Not to Print: Is the press ever justified in suppressing news at the request or in the interest of private individuals or groups of individuals? Business? Government? Numerous specific cases are cited in answering the questions. Each chapter has an extensive bibliography.

[MacDougall, Peter]. "Open Meeting Statutes: The Press Fights for the 'Right to Know.'" *Harvard Law Review*, 75: 1199–1221, April 1962. (Also in *Public Management*, February 1963)   **M 62**
A discussion of the open meeting principle, the extent of legislative enactment, and the results. "Ensuring the people access to the greatest possible amount of information about government activities is an unimpeachably sound concept and, as a basic tenent of democratic government, merits legislative recognition. If the limits and operation of the open meeting principle are defined with the greatest possible precision, many difficulties will be resolved, and both press and officials will have a more workable standard for conduct." Includes text of a proposed open meeting statute.

McElroy, Robert M. "And He Answered the Red Stranger." *Arbitrator*, 2:7–9, August 1919.   **M 63**
The author answers Norman Thomas and A. De Silver, denying that war censorship created political prisoners and opposing amnesty for such prisoners

McElroy, William E. "A Menace to America's Children." *Illinois Libraries*, 42: 186–91, March 1960.   **M 64**

The postmaster of Springfield, Ill., discusses the use of the mails "for the wholesale promotion and conduct of mail order business in obscene and pornographic materials." He describes what the Post Office is doing to banish smut from the mails, and what citizens can do to help combat the racket.

McEvoy, Andrew T., Jr., and Thomas R. Newman. "Free Press; Fair Trial—Rights in Collision." *New York University Law Review*, 34:1278–98, November 1959.   **M 65**
"The only way to give real meaning to the guarantee of an impartial jury trial is to restore to the courts the power to control constructive contempts."

McEvoy, J. P. "Back of Me Hand to You." *Saturday Evening Post*, 211(26):8–9, 46–48, December 1938.   **M 66**
The story of Joseph Breen, the man who administers the Film Production Code which dictates what the movies can and can't do.

Macfadden, Bernarr. "Comstock, King of the Prudes." *Physical Culture*, 14: 561–63, December 1905.   **M 67**
Publisher Macfadden was arrested for "obscene" pictures in two issues of *Physical Culture*. In one the cover design by Carl Victor was offensive. The instigator of the arrest was Anthony Comstock of the New York vice society, whose "distorted conception of the human body," Macfadden charged, "is that of sheer prudery, which is the curse of the present day." He suggests that readers who are devoted to the physical culture idea write Comstock of their objections to the arrest.

[———]. *The Macfadden Prosecution: A Curious Story of Wrong and Oppression under the Postal Laws*. [Battle Creek, Mich., 1908]. 16p.   **M 68**
The publisher of *Physical Culture* magazine was brought to trial in the federal courts on charges of mailing obscene matter. The objection was to a serial story, Growing to Manhood in Civilized? Society, an appeal for enlightened sex education. Macfadden was found guilty and sentenced to a fine of $2,000 and 2 years in prison, but because of a technicality, the sentence was never carried out. Issues of *Physical Culture* from December 1907 through March 1908 carry news and editorials on the case. A summary of the case appears in *Physical Culture*, February 1910, pp. 130–36.

[———]. "Press Muzzled by Patent Medicine Companies." *Physical Culture*, 15:24–27, January 1906.   **M 69**

Macfarlane, John. "Pamphlets and the Pamphlet Duty of 1712." *Library*, 1(n.s.): 298–304, 1 June 1900.   **M 70**
Quotes from broadsides of the period with respect to the Pamphlet Act, designed not

only for revenue but to check "false and scandalous Libels."

———. "The Paper Duties of 1696–1713; Their Effect on the Printing and Allied Trades." *Library*, 1(n.s.):31–44, 1 December 1899.   **M 71**
Contemporary accounts of the effects of duties on imported papers and also those made in England and the high import duty on books.

McFee, William. "Censoring a Classic." *New Republic*, 38:315–16, 14 May 1924.   **M 72**
Criticism of the emasculation of Dana's *Two Years Before the Mast* in an edition for school children. "We can assure parents and pedagogues that there is nothing in the book as Dana wrote it to give offense to any modern child who can spare the time from the movies to look it over."

McGannon, Donald. "The FCC and Freedom of the Frequencies." *Yale Political*, 3(1):21, 36, 39, Autumn 1963.   **M 73**
The president of Westinghouse Broadcasting Company sees the need for federal regulations, while he also points out that broadcasters must respond to the taste of the audience. He shows concern at the lack of definitive standards involved in the revocation of a broadcast license. A federal view is presented by FCC Chairman Henry in an accompanying article.

[M'Gavin, William]. *Report of a Trial in the Jury Court, Edinburgh on the 25th June, 1821, for an Alleged Libel: In the Case of A. Scott, versus William M'Gavin and Others*. Glasgow, University Press, 1821. 140p.   **M 74**
M'Gavin was a lay minister who had written a series of tracts, entitled *The Protestant*, critical of the Catholic Church. He was charged with libel by a Catholic priest, Andrew Scott, for statements he made relative to the building of a Catholic chapel in Glasgow. M'Gavin was found guilty and fined £100.

McGee, Gale W. *The Fairness Doctrine—A Challenge for Responsibility in Broadcasting*. Washington, D.C., U.S. Senate, 1964. 4p.   **M 75**
In an address before the Academy of Television Arts and Sciences, Senator McGee emphasizes that fairness means more than a mere offering of equal time. "What is required is a direct effort to find a taker for the use of that time."

McGhee, Paul A., *et al.* "Points of View in Book Publishing: I. Book Censorship."

Publishers' Weekly, 153:316–17, 24 January 1948. **M 76**

Summary of a discussion on censorship at the first session of a New York University course on publishing. The participants were: Morris Ernst (lawyer), the Reverend Samuel L. Hamilton (theology professor), Ben W. Huebsch (publisher), John S. Sumner (vice society head), and Ken McCormick (book editor).

McGill, Ralph. "There is Time Yet." *Atlantic Monthly*, 174:61–65, September 1944. **M 77**

The editor of the *Atlanta Constitution*, who saw freedom lost in Austria when the Germans moved in, says freedom exists in this country only so long as it exists in the enlightened minds of the people. Newspapers must help the people keep alive the feeling for freedom; they must merit the confidence of the people by good journalism.

MacGregor, Ford H. "Official Censorship Legislation." *Annals of the American Academy of Political and Social Science*, 128: 163–74, November 1928. **M 78**

A history of movie censorship legislation by the federal, state, and municipal governments in the United States and a brief account of government control of films in England and Commonwealth nations. "Compared with the unprecedented development of the moving picture industry and the magnitude of the interests involved, official censorship legislation has made little progress in the United States during the past twenty-five years."

McGuigan, James L. "Crime Reporting: the British and American Approaches." *American Bar Association Journal*, 50: 442–45, May 1964. **M 79**

"Against the background of the American press's reporting of the assassination of President Kennedy, the author contrasts the approaches in Great Britain and the United States to the regulation of crime reporting that prejudices fair trials of accused persons. While our specific constitutional guarantees of free speech and press must be preserved, he concludes, we might consider borrowing something from the British system of control through the exercise of constructive contempt powers."

McGuire, Dave. "Another View on Comic Book Control." *American City*, 64:101, January 1949. **M 80**

Summary of a 59-page report on municipal regulation on comic books presented by the author to the mayor and Commission Council of the City of New Orleans. McGuire recommends control through recognition of better comic books and improvement or elimination of the worst.

McGuire, W. D., Jr. "Censoring Motion Pictures." *New Republic*, 2:262–63, 10 April 1915. **M 81**

————. "Freedom of the Screen Versus Censorship." *Survey*, 44:181–83, 1 May 1920. **M 82**

The executive secretary of the National Board of Review of Motion Pictures supports the prevailing "Boston Plan," operating as part of the National Board of Review, rather than a system of state movie censorship, as proposed in Massachusetts (*Survey*, 17 April). Only 4 states have state movie censors; the system has been repudiated in 28 states.

MacInnes, Colin. "On Censorship." In International Writers' Conference, *The Novel Today*. Edinburgh, Edinburgh International Festival 1962, pp. 55–56. **M 83**

"While plays and films are subject to overt control in our country, censorship of the printed word is indirect." In books he considers censorship of the printers (typographers) and libraries; in radio the policy (B.B.C.) of removing all controversy from the discussion of controversial topics; in television the policy of attempting "to give maximum reality to a maximum audience." The fourth day of the Conference dealt with censorship.

McIntyre, Dina G. "Constitutional Law —Censorship—Not All Prior Restraint on Exhibiting Motion Pictures Is Unconstitutional." *University of Pittsburgh Law Review*, 23:229–33, October 1961. **M 84**

Regarding *Times Film Corp. v. Chicago*, 365 U.S. 43 (1961).

McIntyre, William R. *Control of Obscenity*. Washington, D.C., Editorial Research Reports, 1959. (*Editorial Research Reports*, 2:555–72, 1959) **M 85**

Considers new controversies over postal censorship (rising tide of pornographic, lewd, and borderline materials), law and court decisions on obscenity (state, federal), and current application of obscenity tests.

McKavitt, Matthew A. "Ideas and the Spirit of Censorship." *Library World*, 47:158–61, May 1945. **M 86**

A critique of the article, A Few Thoughts on Libraries and the Spirit of Censorship (*Library Journal*, 1 November 1944), in which the reviewer raises numerous questions as to who shall pass judgment on the morality of books and on what bases.

Mackay, Charles R. *Life of Charles Bradlaugh, M. P.* London, D. J. Gunn, 1888. 468 p. **M 87**

Biography of the nineteenth-century English champion of freedom of the press, particularly in the area of religion. According to Peter Fryer (*Private Case—Public Scandal*) this work, which contains a section of the trial of Bradlaugh for obscene libel, was itself withdrawn from general circulation at the British Museum in 1892 because Bradlaugh's family considered it libelous.

Mackay, R. S. "Hicklin Rule and Judicial Censorship." *Canadian Bar Review*, 36: 1–24, March 1958. **M 88**

An examination of the decision in the Canadian obscenity case, *R. v. American News Co., Ltd.*, (1957), which the author considers important for two reasons: it is the most comprehensive and thorough judgment of a Canadian court on the question of obscenity under the present law, and it demonstrates that it is imperative to change the law. "It would be a shame if, in 1968, we had to celebrate the hundredth anniversary of the *Hicklin* rule."

————. "Judicial Censorship—Recent Developments in the Law of Obscenity." *Canadian Bar Review*, 32:1010–18, November 1954. **M 89**

Discusses the British case of *R. v. Martin Secker & Warburg, Ltd.* (1954) and *Conway v. The King* (1944) which did for Canadian law what the *Ulysses* case did for the United States in re-evaluating the Hicklin rule on obscenity. These decisions brought a new "anti-authoritarian" point of view, with emphasis on liberty and the protection of legitimate literature.

McKean, Addison G. "Indictment for Publishing Obscene Matter." *Central Law Journal*, 21:488–89, 4 December 1885. **M 90**

Text of the decision and notes in the case of *Commonwealth v. Wright* before the Supreme Judicial Court of Massachusetts. The accused was charged with distributing a business card with an inscription so obscene that it could not with decency be described in the records of the court. The indictment was quashed because it did not set forth the offense in a manner required by law.

McKelvie, Samuel R. *Veto of Motion Picture Censorship Bill*. New York, National Board of Review of Motion Pictures, 1921. 4 p. mimeo. **M 91**

Veto message of the Nebraska governor.

McKelway, B. M. "Freedom of the Press— From What?" *Quill*, 51(1):20–22, January 1963. **M 92**

Management of news during the Cuban crisis is the most recent incident in the history of conflict between government and press.

McKenna, Daniel J. "John Peter Zenger." *Commonweal*, 22:399–401, 23 August 1935. **M 93**

An account of "the first great American criminal trial" and background of events leading up to the trial. It had a decisive effect "in formulating the traditional American policy of free speech."

MacKenzie, A. J. *Propaganda Boom*. London, The Right Book Club, 1938. 368p.
M 94
A discussion of the growing importance of propaganda as a national weapon and as a Fourth Defence Service in time of war. The major portion of the book is devoted to the employment of propaganda by the Communist, Nazi, and Fascist governments. Chapter 12 deals with the censor as an "invaluable ally of the propagandist," with reference to press, film, and radio censorship in the democracies that have been "thrown back on the defensive."

Mackenzie, Peter. *Life of Thomas Muir, esq., Advocate . . . Who Was Tried for Sedition . . . With a Full Report of His Trial*. Glasgow, W. R. M'Phun, 1831. 60p.
M 95

McKeon, Richard P., R. K. Merton, and Walter Gellhorn. *The Freedom to Read: Perspective and Program*. New York, Published for the National Book Committee by R. R. Bowker, 1957. 110p. **M 96**
An inquiry into the theory of censorship and the freedom to read, from the viewpoints of philosophy, sociology, and law, conducted by a commission engaged by the National Book Committee under a grant from the Fund for the Republic. The three scholars concluded that the problems of censorship occur in the context of larger problems of internal development and values in individuals and in society. "The freedom to read can be advanced ultimately only by raising the level of reading tastes, and so changing the demand they generate, and by encouraging the work of creative artists and thinkers in contemporary society." The authors recommend a three-part program to advance freedom to read: "I. a comprehensive statement of the grounds and implications of censorship, to provide grounds for the formation of public policy; II. empirical investigation to test the assumptions commonly made concerning the effects of books, to study the formation of reading taste, and to investigate the consequences of decisions to control or not to control; III. action to protect the freedom to read and to correct the abuses and misapplications of censorship."

McKeown, E. J. "Censoring the Moving Picture." *Common Cause*, 4:8–16, July 1913.
M 97
The author describes how movies, in the interest of catering to the lowest and basest human interest, began to degenerate and thus bring about a public clamor for controls. Censorship began when New York's Mayor McClellan closed all of that city's movie houses. Out of a subsequent investigation conducted by John Collier of People's Institute, the idea of a national board of movie censors originated. This was an industry-sponsored, voluntary agency offering a seal of approval on films that passed the reviewers.

McKerrow, R. B. "The Supposed Calling-in of Drayton's *Harmony of the Church*, 1591." *Library* 1(3d ser.):348–50, October 1910.
M 98
This book was suppressed, according to a statement in the Roxburghe Club edition of Drayton's poem. Actually, it was a Puritan work of a somewhat similar title that was suppressed.

McKillop, Alan D. "Thomson and the Licensers of the Stage." *Philological Quarterly*, 37:448–53, October 1958. **M 99**
The experience of the poet, James Thomson, with the stage censor under the Licensing Act of 1737. According to the article, Thomson wrote the unacknowledged preface to the 1738 republication of Milton's *Areopagitica*.

Mackin, Tom. "Taboo on TV." *Pageant*, 18:62–69, November 1962.
M 100

McKinney, John F. "Poetry and Pornography." *Spirit; a Magazine of Poetry*, 32:16–18, March 1965.
M 101
The poem is never art when the means distort the end. The use of pornography as a means of conveying realism insults the reader's sensitivity and only indicates the paucity of the poet's imagination.

McLaughlin, James F. *Matthew Lyon, the Hampden of Congress, A Biography . . .* New York, Wynkoop, Hallenbeck, Crawford Co., 1900. 531p.
M 102
A eulogistic biography of the Vermont soldier and Republican leader who served four months in jail under the Sedition Act for a letter critical of the Adams administration that appeared in the *Vermont Journal*. There was suspicion of jury packing.

Maclean, Charles. *The Affairs of Asia considered in their effects on the Liberties of Britain, in a Series of Letters, addressed to the Marquis Wellesley, Late Governor-General of India; including A correspondence with the Government of Bengal under that Nobleman and a Narrative of Transactions involving the Annihilation of the personal Freedom of the Subject, and the Extinction of the Liberty of the Press in India: With the Marquis's Edict for the Regulation of the Press*. 2d ed. London, C. Maclean, 1806. 172p.
M 103

MacLeish, Archibald. *Brief Amicus Curiae Submitted by Archibald MacLeish on behalf of a Number of Individuals and Organizations Who Have Protested the Action of the Board of Superintendents in This Case*. [New York, 1948]. 21p. mimeo. (Reprinted in *Nation*, 16 October 1948)
M 104

An *ad hoc* committee of 34 organizations and 72 individuals was organized to protest the banning of *The Nation* from New York high schools on the recommendation of the Board of Superintendents of New York City Schools, sustained by the Board of Education. The brief by MacLeish urges the Commissioner to reaffirm the right of freedom of inquiry in the libraries of New York City Schools and "instruct the Board of Superintendents that lists of library materials issued by them shall be regarded as advisory and not exclusive."

———. *A Free Man's Books; an Address Delivered at the Annual Banquet of the American Booksellers Association; together with a Letter by Franklin D. Roosevelt*. Mt. Vernon, N.Y., Peter Pauper Press, [1942?]. 17p. (Edition limited to 310 copies for the Typophiles) **M 105**
"We all know that books burn—yet we have the greater knowledge that books cannot be killed by fire."—Roosevelt, 6 May 1942. Books are "the strongest and the most enduring weapon in our fight to make the world a world in which the free can live in freedom."—Archibald MacLeish. He challenged the book trade to become more than mere vendors of a commercial product.

———. [Letter to Barney Rosset]. In D. H. Lawrence, *Lady Chatterley's Lover*. New York, Grove Press, 1959, pp. v–vii.
M 106
Relates to the censorship history of Lawrence's book. A brief bibliographical note by Mark Schorer appears on pp. 367–68.

———. "Loyalty and Freedom." *American Scholar*, 22:393–98, Autumn 1953. **M 107**
The Constitution was founded upon the belief of our ancestors that "loyalty to the liberty of every man to believe what he chooses would outlast loyalty to any formulation of belief whatever." MacLeish observes that the present generation seems to have suffered a "loss of faith in freedom" to a conviction that we must conform in opinion and beliefs or the Communists will take over. David Riesman, in the Winter 1953–54 issue of *American Scholar*, replies to MacLeish. Riesman believes that there is sufficient "faith in freedom" in America and that we ought not be too concerned over the recent attacks being made on liberty. MacLeish's remarks are based on an address given at Haverford College, Riesman's remarks on an address given at Mills College.

———. "A Tower Which Will Not Yield." *ALA Bulletin*, 50:649–54, November 1956. **M 108**
Former librarian of Congress, Pulitzer Prize-winner in poetry, and Harvard professor, in an address at the dedication of Carleton College Library, urges librarians "to despise

objectivity when objectivity means neutrality and neutrality when neutrality interferes with the performance of their duties as librarians. . . . As long as the fight to subvert freedom continues, libraries must be strong points of defense."

————, William S. Paley, and Edward R. Murrow. *In Honor of a Man and an Ideal: Three Talks on Freedom.* New York, Columbia Broadcasting System, 1941. 35 p. **M 109**
The occasion was a dinner in honor of Mr. Murrow, chief of the European staff of C.B.S. The three talks relate to freedom of expression in wartime. Mr. Murrow's talk refers to British censorship.

McMahon, Charles A. "Inviting Motion Picture Censorship." *Child Welfare Magazine*, 19:23–25, September 1924. **M 110**
"A new evil threatens in the field of motion pictures. It is the evil of the filmed sex novel." The author advises parents to keep their children from attending such exhibitions, to stay away from the film themselves, and to organize community sentiment to protest to film producers and exhibitors. Censorship via the box office is the most effective way. If this cannot be achieved, government censorship may be the only remedy.

McMahon, Joseph H. "The Battle for Decency." *Commonweal*, 20:441–43, 7 September 1934. **M 111**
Father McMahon expounds some of the principles underlying the Legion of Decency, including instructions issued in 1927 to all the bishops of the Church from the Congregation of the Holy Office stating principles of guidance with regard to literature. Such principles are equally applicable to the screen.

McMahon, Robert S. *Federal Regulation of the Radio and Television Broadcast Industry in the United States, 1927–1959, with Special Reference to the Establishment and Operation of Workable Administrative Standards.* Columbus, Ohio State University, 1959. 357 p. (Unpublished Ph. D. dissertation) **M 112**
The major purposes of this study are "to determine whether or not it was the intent of the Congress that the Commission expand its broad 'public interest' mandate into firm and dependable policies; and to determine whether in fact the FCC has expanded its broad mandate into 'firm and dependable' policies; and to determine whether failure by the FCC to establish firm and dependable policies can be attributed to a lack of sufficient 'guidance' from Congress; and if such a need for clarification can be demonstrated, the author will as a final measure, suggest certain specific areas where this further guidance will

be most appropriate." The author gathered much of his data as an investigator for the Subcommittee on Legislative Oversight.

McMahon, Sandra. "A Review of Censorship." *Iowa Publisher*, 32(9):8–11, September 1960. **M 113**
Review of group controls and pressures on obscene literature and the prevailing attitude of the courts.

McManus, Martin J. *Federal Legislation Regulating Radio.* Los Angeles, University of Southern California, 1946. 55 p. (Unpublished Master's thesis) **M 114**

McManus, Patrick J. "What Constitutes Obscene Literature?" *Physical Culture*, 19:125–26, February 1908. **M 115**
"When any part of the human body is described or illustrated for the sake of art, or medicine, or scientific research, or for any other legitimate purpose, such as, for example, the improvement of the part itself, obscene literature is *not* produced by the description." Under present court interpretation the Bible could be considered obscene because it speaks frankly of sex.

McMaster, John B. "A Free Press in the Middle Colonies." *Princeton Review*, 61: 78–90, January 1886. **M 116**
An account of William Bradford, "the first man in America to stand up boldly for unlicensed printing." Quaker authorities in Philadelphia suppressed Bradford's publication of the *Almanac* of Daniel Leeds in 1687 and later refused him permission to print an English translation of the Bible. Bradford, after twice being brought before the governor, three times censored by the meeting, once placed under heavy bonds, and once thrown in jail by the Quaker government, moved to New York (1693) where he established a press. Six years elapsed before Pennsylvania had another printer; the new press was placed under the censorship of a committee.

McMillan, George M. "Administrative Law—Post Office—Second-class Mail Privileges—Power of Postmaster General." *George Washington Law Review*, 14:518–21, April 1946. **M 117**
A discussion of the issues in the case of *Hannegan v. Esquire* in which the U.S. Supreme Court ruled that the withholding of second-class mailing privileges must not be used to interfere with freedom of the press.

McMillin, John E. "New Voices in a Democracy." *Television Quarterly*, 3(3): 27–52, Summer 1964. **M 118**
The author was commissioned by the Television Information Office to make this study of the history, current status, and problems posed by television editorializing. "The problem of controlling or regulating TV's

new editorial voices [almost 200] can never be settled satisfactorily by trying to define, in precise, bureaucratic terms, how each editorial should be handled 'in the public interest.' The real challenge lies in finding ways to encourage, develop and enlarge, within the framework of American ideals, TV's already healthy editorializing movement."

McMullan, John. "Freedom of the Press in Reporting Crime News." *Add I*, 1(4):28–32, Summer 1962. **M 119**
Summary of a symposium on free press versus fair trial, held at Northwestern University. The author, a participant, believes the conflict could be solved in part by willingness of newsmen to impose voluntary restraints on their urge to editorialize.

McMurrin, Sterling M. "Academic Freedom in the Schools." *Teachers College Record*, 65:658–63, May 1964. **M 120**
A former U.S. Commissioner of Education reflects on academic freedom in the public schools. "Censorship in the schools that denies intellectual freedom to teachers robs the student of that same freedom. And the freedom to learn is clearly no less precious than the freedom to teach."

McNae, L. C. J., *ed. Essential Law for Journalists.* 2d ed. London, Staples, 1963. 322 p. **M 121**
A compilation of information on British press law, including chapters pertaining to restrictions on publications, contempt and privilege, defamation, slander and injurious falsehood, criminal libel, the Official Secrets Act, and illegal advertisements.

McNamara, Robert C., Jr. "What Can the Publisher Do?" *NEA Journal*, 52: 27–28, May 1963. **M 122**
Considering the content of public school textbooks, the author observes that "rights of public and parents, professional rights of teachers, and the student's right to read must be reconciled. . . . This will not come from simple proposals to secure more freedom of choice for some by denying the rights of others." (Part of an 11-page feature on textbook censorship.)

McNamara, Samuel G. "Recent Developments Concerning Constitutional Limitations on State Defamation Laws." *Vanderbilt Law Review*, 18:1429–55, June 1965. **M 123**
"The primary purpose of this discussion is to point out the practical effect which the decisions [*New York Times Co. v. Sullivan* (1964) and *Garrison v. Louisiana* (1964)] will have on state law, both statutory and decisional. This note is concerned primarily with those aspects of the law of defamation dealing specifically with the conditional or qualified privilege to criticize the official acts and qualifications of public officials and candidates."

McNamee, Raymond W., Jr. "'Indirect Censorship'—Does It Mean Anything?" *Issue*, 1(1):15–19, Winter 1963. **M124**
In a Socialist state the individual may have the right to express unpopular ideas, but not the means of distributing them in a state monopoly of the mass media. The capitalist system, with its dispersed centers of wealth, not beholden to the state, provides a source of distribution of unorthodox thought. These centers, while they may be described as "indirect censorship," may, from another point of view, provide greater liberty. Indirect censorship is "really custom and convention ordering human activities. This ordering, far from inhibiting freedom, enhances it, by making the punishments for dissent much more mild than would be the case should law pre-empt custom. . . . The less law governs and the more custom controls our acts in lieu of law the better." The author is a research chemist, formerly active in the Berkeley Student Chapter of the Intercollegiate Society of Individualists.

McNeal, Archie L. "Censorship." In *American Library and Book Trade Annual, 1961*. New York, Bowker, 1960, pp. 157–59. **M125**
A summary of the year's events involving libraries and the work of the American Library Association Committee on Intellectual Freedom.

———. "Censorship." In *Annual of Library and Book Trade Information, 1962*. New York, Bowker, 1962, pp. 127–28. **M126**

———. "Censorship." In *Annual of Library and Book Trade Information, 1963*. New York, Bowker, 1963, pp. 144–45. **M127**

———. "Defending the Right to Read." *The Rub-Off*, 15:2–7, November–December 1964. **M128**

———. "Fear of Books." *Alabama Librarian*, 11:62–64, July 1960. **M129**
To combat pressures for censorship, the author recommends that librarians be informed on the issues, that library boards adopt well-defined book selection policies, that state library associations have strong intellectual freedom committees, and that library schools give greater attention to problems of censorship.

———. "Intellectual Freedom and Censorship." *Teachers College Record*, 66:574–78, April 1965. **M130**
The author sketches a program and indicates useful materials for combating censorship in the schools. He stresses preventive policies and extensive community involvement.

———. "Intellectual Freedom and the State Library Association." *Pennsylvania*

Library Association Bulletin, 18:5–6, 1963. **M131**

MacNeil, Neil. *Without Fear or Favor*. New York, Harcourt, Brace, 1940. 414p. **M132**
The story of the *New York Times*. The chapter on Libel, Ethics, Principles discusses freedom v. license and stresses the importance of good taste and accuracy. The chapter on Freedom of the Press warns against a class press as a threat to freedom of objective news coverage.

MacNevin, Thomas. *Leading State Trials in Ireland from the Year 1794 to 1803 . . .* Dublin, James Duffy, 1844. 598p. **M133**
Contains accounts of the trials of Peter Finerty and Archibald H. Rowan.

McNickle, Roma K. *Policing the Comics*. Washington D.C., Editorial Research Reports, 1952. (*Editorial Research Reports*, 1:223–38, 1952) **M134**
Contents: Public concern over impact of the comics, rise of the comic in American newspapers, methods of controlling objectionable comics, and serious uses of comic strip techniques. Includes code of comic magazine publishers.

MacQueary, Howard. "Moral and Immoral Literature." *Arena*, 8:447–54, September 1893. **M135**
A work is not immoral simply because it discusses ugly sins; but "when it lacks a spark of talent or a lofty purpose it is both degrading to the mind and depraving to the heart . . . The remedy is not denunciation, but displacement of bad by good literature . . . Prohibition has always increased a desire for the forbidden fruit . . . In ignorance alone is danger; in knowledge alone is safety."

McWilliams, Carey. *A Frank Appraisal of the Press*. Columbia, Mo., Freedom of Information Center, School of Journalism, University of Missouri, 1961. 7p. (Publication no. 54) **M136**
The editor of *The Nation* cites seven weaknesses of the American press: the handling of big city politics, political bias, labor-business bias, susceptibility to demagogic manipulation, overexposure of trivia, subservience to official policy, and narrow range of opinion.

Macy, Ethelrid S. "The Top Bookshelf." *American Home*, 38:128–30, October 1947. **M137**
The author deals with the attraction of forbidden books to children. He believes that "children, from the time they begin reading to themselves, should have free run in the library."

Maddaloni, Arnold. *Schroeder—The Public Excuser; a Biographical Outline to which*

Are Added Some Published Opinions Concerning His Personal Traits. Stamford, Conn., The Author, 1936. 12p. **M138**
Biographical data and photograph of Theodore A. Schroeder, a leading proponent of freedom of speech and the press.

Madden, Henry M. "The Intellectual Freedom Front." *California Libraries*, 20:161–62, July 1959. **M139**
A report of the work of the Intellectual Freedom Committee of California.

———. "Mr. and Mrs. Grundy in the Library and in Court." *Library Journal*, 89:4857–62, 15 December 1964. **M140**
A summary of a preconference meeting on intellectual freedom, California Library Association. "In essence, the pre-conference dealt directly with two aspects of Grundyism—first, a philosophical and legal survey of the present state of freedom of the press and, second, a series of case studies in attempted censorship, reported by librarians and trustees who had been in the fight." The philosophical and legal considerations were presented by book critic Robert Kirsch in Custodian, Eunuch, or Lover; by Professor Paul Ferguson in Pornography or Censorship—Which is Worse? and by Attorney Stanley Fleishman in Obscene Literature and Constitutional Law. Case histories were presented by Mrs. Cay Mortenson, trustee of Arcadia Public Library; Virginia Ross, chairman of California Library Association's Intellectual Freedom Committee; Ursula Meyer, county librarian of Butte County; and Mrs. Hilda Collins, county librarian of Tulare County. The Arcadia case dealt with *The Last Temptation of Christ*; Virginia Ross reported on her appearance before the State Legislature in opposition to antiobscenity bills; Ursula Meyer reported on her experience in the field of political extremism; Mrs. Collins presented the case of the *Dictionary of American Slang* "in which the John Birch Society flexed its muscles, Dr. Max Rafferty cheered from the side lines."

———. "On the Firing Line in a Bad Climate." *ALA Bulletin*, 59:33–34, January 1965. **M141**
At a general session of the California Library Association Conference on 6 November 1964, Henry Madden, editor of *California Librarian*, reported on a preconference on Intellectual Freedom held earlier in the week. This excerpt from his report summarizes a panel of case histories.

Madden, Richard R. *The History of the Irish Periodical Literature, from the End of the 17th to the Middle of the 19th Century. Its Origin, Progress, and Results; with Notices of Remarkable Persons Connected with the Press in Ireland during the Past Two Centuries.*

London, J. C. Newby, 1867. 2 vols. **M 142**

References throughout to licensing of newspapers, application of the law of libel, and prosecution of editors and printers.

Madison, James. [Letter to N. P. Trist, 23 April 1828]. In *Letters and Other Writings of James Madison*. New York, Worthington, 1884. vol. 3, pp. 629–31. **M 143**

Madison refers to Jefferson's letter to Mr. Norvell complaining of the licentious character of the press. The solution, Madison believes, is in having rival papers, but this is not always possible at a given time or place. He asks, half-seriously: "Could it be so arranged that every newspaper, when printed on one side, should be handed over to the press of an adversary, to be printed on the other, thus presenting to every reader both sides of every question, truth would always have a fair chance." Elsewhere he questions whether a reader would turn the paper to the side opposed to that he embraced.

———. "Public Opinion and Press." *Complete Madison; His Basic Writings*, edited by Saul K. Padover. New York, Harper, 1953. **M 144**

Selections include: The Nature of Public Opinion (*National Gazette*, 19 December 1791); Freedom of the Press (address to the General Assembly of Virginia, 23 January 1799); Abuses of the Press (letter to N. P. Trist, 23 April 1828); and Freedom of Opinion (address to the General Assembly of Virginia, 23 January 1799).

Maeterlinck, Maurice. "On the Prosecution of *The Adult*." *Adult*, 2:202, August 1898. **M 145**

Letter approving of "Fellis," by William Pratt, published in *The Adult*, February 1898, and declared "obscene" in the prosecution of George Bedborough.

Magee, John. *The Trial of John Magee, for Printing and Publishing a Slanderous and Defamatory Libel, against Richard Daly, Esq. held before the Right Honorable Lord Viscount Clonmel, by a Special Jury of the City of Dublin . . . June 28, 1790*. Dublin, P. Byrne, 1790. 68 p. **M 146**

Magee, publisher of the *Dublin Evening Post*, was one of the most persistent, though sometimes erratic, champions of a free press in Ireland from the 1780's to 1814. His first imprisonment was in 1785 when he was given a month in jail for criticizing court procedure in his own libel trial. Then, as in subsequent trials, he appeared before Baron Earlsfort (later to become Lord Clonmel) who enjoyed meting out stiff punishment to troublesome

journalists, and Magee was his major protagonist. Most of Magee's trials came as a result of his crusades against government corruption and incompetency. In this case, however, Magee was charged with libeling John Daly, manager of the Theatre Royal of Dublin, affecting the theater's patronage. The offending verse was undoubtedly scurrilous, but a sympathetic jury awarded the plaintiff only 200 of the £8,000 damages asked. The odious *fiat* was used in this case as in a number of others against Magee. It was a legal device that enabled a judge to hold a man in jail indefinitely by assessing heavy bail.

Magee, John, Jr. *Trial of John Magee, Proprietor of the Dublin Evening Post, for a Libel on the Duke of Richmond . . .* Dublin, J. Magee, 1813. 171 p. **M 147**

The new proprietor of the *Dublin Evening Post*, son of the irascible John Magee, published articles charging the administration of the Duke of Richmond with corruption. Magee, who was championing the Catholic cause, was brought to trial before an all-Protestant jury, found guilty and sentenced to two years in prison. The Kilkenny Catholic Committee passed resolutions condemning the government's treatment of Magee, which Magee published in his paper. For this offense Magee received an additional six months. As a further persecution of the Peel government, stamps for the mailing of Magee's newspapers were withheld, requiring Magee to transfer ownership of the paper to his brother James.

Magruder, Jane N. *Development of the Concept of Public Interest as It Applies to Radio and Television Programming*. Columbus, Ohio State University, 1959. 335 p. (Unpublished Ph. D. dissertation) **M 148**

Mahony, Dennis A. *The Prisoner of State*. New York, Carleton, 1863. 414 p. **M 149**

The autobiography of the editor of the Dubuque *Herald*, who was arrested ("kidnapping" he calls it) and imprisoned for three months in 1862 for writing editorials critical of the "usurpation of power by the President" in time of war.

"Mail Snooping." *New Republic*, 153:6–7, 21 August 1965. **M 150**

"The Post Office, alert to violations of obscenity laws, now routinely visits employers of persons suspected of receiving 'obscene' mail."

Maisel, Albert Q. "The New Battle Over Birth Control." *Reader's Digest*, 82: 54–59, February 1963. **M 151**

An account of the debate being waged in Illinois over proposals of the Illinois Public Aid Commission to issue birth control information and supplies to indigent families.

———. "The Smut Peddler Is After Your Child." *Woman's Home Companion*, 78: 24–25+, November 1951. **M 152**

[Makemie, Francis]. *A Narrative Of a New and Unusual American Imprisonment Of Two Presbyterian Ministers: And Prosecution of Mr. Francis Makemie One of Them for Preaching one Sermon at the City of New York. By a Learner of Law and a Lover of Liberty*. Printed for the Publisher, 1707. 56 p. (Also in Peter Force, *ed. Tracts and Other Papers*, 1847, vol. 4, no. 4) **M 153**

Francis Makemie and John Hampton, Presbyterian ministers, were arrested for preaching without a license, to the disturbance of the established Church. Makemie published his sermon and was brought to trial for seditious libel. The defense argued that the Act of Tolerance of 1689 applied to the Colonies and protected them. The New York jury found Makemie "not guilty," scoring a victory for religious tolerance in speech and press.

Makowski, Kenneth W. "Obscenity Statute Declared Unconstitutional Due to Vagueness." *Temple Law Quarterly*, 33: 359–65, Spring 1960. **M 154**

Relates to the case, *Commonwealth v. Blumenstein*, 396 Pa. 417 (1959), involving the closing of a drive-in theater for showing a film that allegedly violated the Pennsylvania Penal Code.

Makris, John N. *The Silent Investigators: The Great Untold Story of the United States Postal Inspection Service*. New York, Dutton, 1959. 319 p. **M 155**

Includes accounts of action against use of the mails for extortion, to advertize fraudulent or harmful medicine, for blackmail, and to distribute pornography. The last is presented in chapter 19, Merchants of Filth. Much of the chapter is devoted to investigations of the Gathings Committee and the 30-year efforts against pornographer Samuel Roth, sentenced in 1956 to 5 years in prison. The conviction was upheld by the U.S. Supreme Court in a decision upholding the constitutionality of the obscenity statute.

Maley, Michael. *Catholic-Committee Persecution. Reports of Two Trials for Libel in which Mr. M. M. and George Bryan, Esq., were Plaintiffs;—Edward J. B. Fitzsimons, Esq., Barrister-in-law and His Father, John Bourke Fitzsimons, Esq., Defendant*. Dublin, Espy & Cross, 1813. 36 p. **M 156**

Maley, a journalist, sued the editor of a government paper, *Hibernian Journal*, for libel, but the judge dismissed the case, ruling that an editor could not be held responsible. A Major Bryan of the Catholic Board had sued the *Journal's* two proprietors for libel, but an unsympathetic judge and jury awarded Bryan only £5.

Malin, Patrick M. "Smut, Corruption, and the Law." In McCormick, *Versions of Censorship*, pp. 203–17. **M 157**

Testimony of the executive director of the American Civil Liberties Union before Senate Subcommittees on Juvenile Delinquency and Constitutional Amendments, January 1960. One constitutional amendment opposed by the ACLU would allow each state to decide questions of decency and morality on the basis of its own public policy, a second amendment would declare obscene material outside the bounds of protection under the First Amendment.

Malkin, Sol. M. "Censorship Confusion." *Antiquarian Bookman*, 20:282–84, 29 July 1957. **M158**
In February 1957 the U.S. Supreme Court unanimously reversed a lower court ruling convicting a Detroit bookseller of obscenity for selling Griffin's *The Devil Rides Outside*. In June of the same year, in a series of three split decisions on alleged "obscene" books, the Court upheld the validity of one federal and two state "obscenity" statutes. The author believes the Court instead of clarifying the issue has "yielded to expediency and has compounded the many more 'test cases' certain to arise."

———, *et al.* "Special Book Censorship Issue." *Antiquarian Bookman*, 22:1875–92, December 1958. **M159**
A compilation of some of the most pertinent material on censorship events of the year: court decisions, actions of the Post Office Department and other U.S. agencies, state and city censorship, literary censorship, and action against books, magazines, motion pictures, newspapers, radio and television. Includes advice to booksellers and librarians on what to do when the attack comes.

Malone, Dumas. "The First Years of Thomas Cooper in America, 1784–1801." *South Atlantic Quarterly*, 22:139–56, April 1923. **M160**
Includes an account of Cooper's arrest and trial under the Sedition Act of 1798, for libeling President Adams.

———. *The Public Life of Thomas Cooper, 1783–1839.* New Haven, Yale University Press, 1926. 432 p. (Yale Historical Publications, Miscellany 16) **M161**
The standard biography of one of the earliest American defenders of freedom of the press. Cooper, a British-born American scientist and educator was convicted under the Sedition Act and imprisoned for his political writing. His *Treatise on the Law of Libel and the Liberty of the Press*, first published in 1830, is one of the earliest attempts to formulate a libertarian doctrine on freedom of the press.

Manchester, William R. *Disturber of the Peace; the Life of H. L. Mencken. With an introduction by Gerald W. Johnson.* New York, Harper, 1951. 336 p. (Published in England under the title, *The Sage of Baltimore*) **M162**

A full-length biography of the Baltimore journalist whose aversion to hypocrisy and prudery brought him into the van of the attack on literary censorship of the 20's. Of special interest are the chapters on the Scopes evolution trial and the famous "Hatrack" case. In the latter Mencken personally challenged the power of the Boston censors by selling a copy of his April 1926 *American Mercury* on the Boston Common to J. Frank Chase of the Watch and Ward Society. The issue contained an article entitled "Hatrack," offensive to the Society. In a surprise decision by a Boston municipal court judge, Mencken and the *American Mercury* were cleared of the obscenity charge.

Mandeville, Bernard. *The Fable of the Bees or, Private Vices, Publick Benefits.* With a Commentary Critical, Historical and Explanatory by F. B. Kaye. Oxford, Eng., Clarendon Press, 1924. 2 vols. **M163**
The *Fable*, published during the first quarter of the eighteenth century, was widely denounced as heretical and twice presented to the Grand Jury as a public nuisance. In France it was buried by the common hangman. In his defense Mandeville denies any blasphemy, profaneness, or immorality, offering to recant and even burn his own book if evidence to the contrary can be found. The editor's notes and commentary contain evidence of the censorship. A Vindication of the Book, from the Aspersions Contain'd in a Presentment of the Grand Jury of Middlesex, and An Abusive Letter to Lord C. (first published in 1724) is contained in pages 381–412 of volume one.

Mandeville, Ernest W. "Gutter Literature." *New Republic*, 45:350–52, 17 February 1926. (Reprinted in Beman, *Censorship of Speech and the Press*, pp. 275–81) **M164**
An attack on the sex story and confession magazines of the 20's, but with no recommendations for censorship.

Mangravite, Peppino. "Freedom of Expression; Excerpts." *American Artist*, 11:47, September 1947. **M165**
Today the real danger for the artist in regard to freedom of expression "lies in the fact that cultural and political patterns are forcing the personality of the artist to become subservient to their doctrines . . . Freedom of expression can be maintained by the artist only if he has the strength to remain an independent identity." Excerpts from an address before the American Federation of Arts, May 1947.

[Manners and Miller, Buchan and Others against the King's Printers]. "Judgment of the Court of Sessions, on May 12, 1826, as to the Royal prerogative in regard to printing Bibles . . ." In Macdonell, *Report of State Trials*, vol. 2, pp. 215–43. **M166**

Mannes, Marya. "Hidden Censorship in the United States." *Listener*, 801–2, 15 May 1958. **M167**
A discussion of the serious restrictions placed by advertisers and pressure groups on the content of American television programs. The danger zones are race, religion, politics, and sex. The result is often superficial and evasive treatment of a theme. The author finds the Republicans more sensitive to satire and criticism of their administration, but "since sputnik, the voice of dissent is steadily growing in volume." When the people wake up to their deprivation, the hidden censors will be out of jobs and shackled writers will be free to communicate.

———. "The Public Right to Prurience." New York *Herald Tribune Book Week*, 2(14):2, 13 December 1964. **M168**
The publishing world is "encouraging a nation of Peeping Toms, avid for sexual intimacies which they themselves apparently fail to achieve." Pornography is purveyed under cover of sociology, satire, and art. "The public has the double enjoyment of being sexually excited and morally instructed." The author rejects censorship as a solution but calls for the revival of standards of taste in writing and publishing.

Manning, Robert J. "Foreign Policy and the People's Right to Know." *Department of State Bulletin*, 50:868–77, 1 June 1964. **M169**
In an address before the Massachusetts Bar—Press Symposium, the Assistant Secretary of State for Public Affairs explores the complex ethical as well as practical issues faced by the government in meeting the dual responsibility of informing the public and protecting national security. Specifically, he discusses several "deceptively easy distinctions" that are often introduced into arguments, yet offer unsatisfactory solutions: (1) the distinction between fact and policy, between things you can count and decisions about those things; (2) the distinction between a code of conduct in time of war and in time of peace; (3) the view that it is the government's job to keep secrets and the job of the press to try to pry them loose and print them. He calls for a greater understanding within government, particularly in the diplomatic profession, of the requirement of public knowledge and a greater awareness of the working of government on the part of journalists, based on direct experience in government. The public must also promote its own interest by "rejecting the bogus and ridiculing the oversimplicities."

Manson, T. W. "Freedom of Thought and Expression." In Ernest F. Jacob, *What We Defend: Essays in Freedom by Members of the University of Manchester.* London, Oxford University Press, 1942, pp. 33–45. **M170**

"We defend these three rights: 1. Freedom of access to the facts. 2. Freedom to think about them including freedom to think aloud with other people, that is to discuss, without the dead hand of an official and orthodox interpretation paralyzing the discussion, and without spies listening in to the debate. For freedom of exchange of thought is an essential and integral part of freedom of thought itself. 3. Freedom of expression, i.e. freedom to publish the results of inquiry, reflection and discussion." He considers the limitations of these freedoms of expression within the framework of a democratic state in normal times and in time of war.

The Manual of Liberty: or, Testimonies in Behalf of the Rights of Mankind; Selected from the Best Authorities, in Prose and Verse, and Methodically Arranged. London, Printed for H. D. Symonds, 1795. 406 p. **M 171**
Includes quotations relating to freedom of the press, from John Milton, Lord Chesterfield, David Hume, and others.

Manvell, Roger. "The Cinema and the State: England." *Hollywood Quarterly*, 2:289–93, April 1947. **M 172**
An advocate of organized social pressures (film societies) as a means of improving the quality of the British movies discusses Labour Party proposals for partial nationalization of the British film industry.

Maple, William L. "Be Careful What You Write." *Quill*, 19(2):3, 5 March 1931. **M 173**
The director of the School of Journalism, Washington and Lee University, writes of the legal pitfalls to newspapers in the area of libel.

Marbut, Frederick B. "Newspaper Libel in Pennsylvania." *Dickinson Law Review*, 59:232–38, March 1955. **M 174**
A review of recent court decisions involving newspaper libel.

Marcellus, *pseud. Essays on the Liberty of the Press. By Marcellus. Originally Published in the Virginia Argus, in December, 1803.* Richmond, Printed by S. Pleasants, Jr., 1804. 19 p. **M 175**
The author, commenting on measures then before the Virginia Assembly, urges the rejection of the British common law of libels, as expounded by Blackstone, in favor of the American Bill of Rights and the "celebrated report of the Virginia legislature in the session of 1799." While recognizing the right of an individual citizen for redress of a personal libel, he calls for a jury trial rather than decision by a magistrate.

March, John. *Actions for Slaunder, or A Methodicall Collection under certain Grounds and Heads, of what words are actionable in the Law, and what not? . . .* London, Printed by F. L. for M. Walbank and R. Best, 1647. 241 p. **M 176**
"A Treatise of very great use and consequence to all men, especially in these times, wherein actions for Slaunder are more common, and do much more abound then in times past: And when the malice of men so much increases, well may their tongues want a Directory. To which is added, Awards or Arbitrements, methodised under severall Grounds and Heads . . . wherein is principally shewed, what Arbitrements are good in Law, and what not . . . By Jo. March of Grayes-Inne, Barister." This work, published three years after Milton's *Areopagitica*, is probably the first English work on libel and slander.

Marcus, Steven. "Mr. Acton of Queen Anne Street, or, The Wisdom of Our Ancestors." *Partisan Review*, 31:201–30, Spring 1964. **M 177**
"The following essay is the first chapter of a study whose subject is writings about sex and sexuality in mid-nineteenth century England. The largest part of that body of literature consists of writings of a pornographic character, and it is toward an examination of such works that this essay moves."

———. "Pisanus Fraxi, Pornographer Royal." *Partisan Review*, 32:13–32, 99–113, Winter 1965. **M 178**
An account of the life and scholarship of the English bibliographer, Henry Spencer Ashbee (1834–1900) who compiled the first bibliography in the English language devoted to writings of a pornographic or sexual character. His bibliographical trilogy "is not only the first work of its kind in English; it is undoubtedly the most important in any language." References also to English pornographer John Camden Hotten.

Marcus, William E. "Censorship from the Viewpoint of a Trustee." *Wisconsin Library Bulletin*, 27:152–53, June 1931. **M 179**
Reference to the frequent rejection of the factually unchallenged *Strange Death of President Harding* and the acceptance of a debunking biography of George Washington by Rupert Hughes, and the bases for judgment of each.

[Marcus Graham Freedom of the Press Committee]. *Freedom of Thought Arraigned. Four Year Persecution of "Man!" . . .* [Los Angeles, The Committee, 1939]. 20 p. **M 180**
A protest of the "19-year persecution of Marcus Graham" and the San Francisco anarchist publication, *Man*. The pamphlet invites support of the Marcus Graham Freedom of the Press Committee, consisting of prominent authors and scholars. Among them are Sherwood Anderson, Witter Bynner, George S. Counts, John Dewey, Vardis Fisher, Louis Untermeyer, and Ruth Suckow.

Marcuse, Ludwig. *Obscene; The History of an Indignation.* London, MacGibbon & Key, 1965. 327 p. **M 181**
This study of obscenity by a German professor (first published in 1962 by Paul List Verlag) centers around leading obscenity trials: Friedrich Schlegel's *Lucinde* (Jena, 1799), Gustave Flaubert's *Madame Bovary* (Paris, 1857), Arthur Schnitzler's *Round Dance* (Berlin, 1920), D. H. Lawrence's *Lady Chatterley* (London, 1960), and Henry Miller's *Tropic of Cancer* (Los Angeles, 1962). A chapter is also devoted to the crusade of Anthony Comstock and the New York Society for the Suppression of Vice. Marcuse describes Comstock as "a cross between Barnum and McCarthy." A final chapter entitled Seven Theses to Disarm Indignation gives the gist of the author's views on obscenity.

Margolis, Richard J. "The Well-Tempered Textbook." *Teachers College Record*, 66: 664–70, May 1965. **M 182**

Margolis, William J. "Censorship Is Their Kind of Hate." *Miscellaneous Man*, 13:1–3, Autumn 1957. **M 183**
Relates to the confiscation of *Miscellaneous Man*, no. 10, by the San Francisco Customs authorities.

Marion, George. *The "Free Press" Portrait of a Monopoly.* New York, New Century, 1946. 48 p. **M 184**
A Marxian-oriented attack on news coverage by the "capitalist" press, particularly in the coverage of foreign news by the Associated Press. The author charges that the press is controlled by a capitalist class which gags the expression of labor and liberal thought. Curbing the reactionary block would improve the press, but only a program that takes socialism as its ultimate goal can seriously approach the problem of press freedom.

———. *Stop the Press! Being Volume 1 of The Next Hundred Years.* New York, Fairplay, 1953. 224 p. **M 185**
An attack on the American press which Howard Fast, who writes the introduction, charges is a corrupt monopoly "ruthlessly directed against the welfare of the people." Published by the author after he was unable to place the work with an established publisher. Marion considers the capitalist press of America "the most powerful, concentrated—and dangerous—monopoly, this world has ever known." His thesis that freedom of the press in America is a myth is also dealt with in a 1946 pamphlet, *The "Free Press": Portrait of a Monopoly.*

Marion, Kitty. "Selling the *Birth Control Review*." In the *Papers* of the Sixth Annual International Neo-Malthusian and Birth Control Conference. New York, The American Birth Control League, 1926, pp. 175–78. **M 186**

The author writes of the opposition and support given her when she volunteered to help Margaret Sanger distribute the *Birth Control Review*.

Marion, Séraphin. "Liberté de la Presse (au Canada Français depuis 1808)" *Culture*, 3:183–92, June 1942. **M 187**
The history of freedom of the press in French Canada since 1808.

Mark, Norman. "The Anonymous Smut Hunters." *Nation*, 201:5–7, 5 July 1965. **M 188**
An analysis and criticism of the operation of the Citizens for Decent Literature, a nationwide organization to combat obscenity.

Marke, Julius J., ed. *A Catalogue of the Law Collection at New York University with Selected Annotations*. New York, The Law Center of New York University, 1953. 1372 p. **M 189**
Includes the following pertinent sections: civil rights, libel and slander, and trials (libel and slander, and state). The collection of historic English and American trials is extensive.

Markel, Lester. "Our Common Stake in Free Communication: The Press." In *Freedom of Communication; Proceedings of the First Conference on Intellectual Freedom . . .* Chicago, American Library Association, 1954, pp. 108–15. **M 190**

Markland, Ben C. *Editorializing Practices of American Radio Stations: a Study of the Mayflower Decision and Its Revocation*. Evanston, Ill., Northwestern University, 1951. 101 p. (Unpublished Master's thesis) **M 191**

Marks, Sidney. "What Is Obscene Literature Today." *United States Law Review*, 73:217–23, April 1939. **M 192**
The author explores the legal confusion in the attempts over the years to find a definition for "obscenity."

Markun, Leo. *Mrs. Grundy, a History of Four Centuries of Morals Intended to Illuminate Present Problems in Great Britain and the United States*. New York, Appleton, 1930. 665 p. **M 193**
References throughout to action taken for moral reasons against books and the theater and to squeamishness in reading tastes.

Marquette University. *Problems of Communication in a Pluralistic Society. Papers Delivered at a Conference on Communications . . .*

[Milwaukee], Marquette University Press, 1956. 166 p. **M 194**
Includes: Legal Implications of, and Barriers to the Right to Know by Leon R. Yankwich; The Right to Know Government Business from the Viewpoint of the Government Official by William P. Rogers; The Role of the Press in Safeguarding the People's Right to Know Government Business by J. R. Wiggins; Moral Problems Related to Censoring the Media of Mass Communications by Vernon Bourke; and Legal Problems Involved in Censoring the Media of Mass Communications by Charles S. Desmond.

Marsh, Michael. *Controls over Advertising*. Washington, D.C., Editorial Research Reports, 1951. (*Editorial Research Reports*, 2:611–26, 1951) **M 195**
Deals with advertising in a national emergency, the growth and criticism of advertising, government regulation of advertising, and controls in the advertising of liquor.

[Marshall, John]. *Address of the Minority in the Virginia Legislature to the People of that State; containing a vindication of the constitutionality of the Alien and Sedition laws*. [Richmond?]. 1799. 16 p. **M 196**
When the Virginia legislature passed resolutions against the Alien and Sedition Laws, Federalist John Marshall wrote this minority report. While supporting the constitutionality of the laws, Marshall considered them useless and unwise.

[————]. *The Letters of Curtius to General J. Marshall, Late Envoy to France. Likewise the Alien and Sedition Laws; together with Part of the Constitution of the United States. From the Virginia Argus*. Washington, Pa., Printed by John Israel, 1799. 35 p. **M 197**
John Marshall's opinion on the Alien and Sedition Acts are revealed in this exchange of letters with "Curtius."

Marshall, Max S. "Sense and Censorship." *College and University*, 40:11–14, Fall 1964. **M 198**
A California professor says "censorship is a daily, almost an hourly, occurrence. We are surrounded by it and do some censoring of our own. Not censorship itself, but its rules are at stake."

Marshall, S. L. A. "Curious Is the Course of the Censors." *Quill*, 30(5):3–4, 12, May 1942. **M 199**
The author, a newspaperman, military critic, and historian, writes of the problems of military censorship. The publication of all "safe" military news in wartime, even if it is bad news, serves a direct military end because it builds civilian morale.

Martel, John S. "Fair Trial v. Free Press in Criminal Trials." *California Law Review*, 47:366–73, May 1959. **M 200**

After an examination of the factual situations of these two consitutionally protected rights and after reviewing court decisions, the author concludes that both Canon 35 and 20 of the American Bar Association should be adopted as rules of court, enforceable by contempt proceedings. "Our system of justice demands that in an area fraught with doubts, such doubts be resolved in favor of the accused as long as they persist."

Martin, Albert B. *The Federal Communications Commission and the Regulation of Broadcasting*. Pittsburgh, University of Pittsburgh, 1938. 107 p. (Unpublished Master's thesis) **M 201**

Martin, Everett D. *Liberty*. New York, Norton, 1930. 307 p. **M 202**
A philosophical study of the concept of liberty down through the ages; an understanding of the great classical statements of Milton, Locke, and Mill and the conflicts among the various traditions of liberty we have inherited from the past. While not limited to consideration of press freedom, the ideas expressed lie at the base of the various concepts of a free press. The implications of Milton's *Areopagitica* are discussed on pp. 203 ff.

Martin, Frederick R. "A Plea for an Uncensored Press." *Proceedings*, Academy of Political Science in the City of New York, 7:360–64, July 1917. **M 203**
Address of the assistant manager of the Associated Press before the National Conference on Foreign Relations of United States.

Martin, Harold. "The Manila Censorship." *Forum*, 31:462–71, June 1901. **M 204**
Military censorship in the Philippines under American Army jurisdiction which banned any reproach or criticism of the army or news of any army failures in attempts at political dealings with the Philippines.

Martin, Harold C. "Books and Boys." *Horn Book*, 35:355–67, October 1959. **M 205**
A professor discusses the barriers that librarians sometime erect between readers and books.

Martin, J. C. "A Free Press." *Criminal Law Quarterly*, 1:21–24, 1958–59. **M 206**
General commentary on freedom of the press in Great Britain and Canada.

Martin, Kingsley. "Censorship during the Crisis." *Political Quarterly*, 10:128–34, January 1939. **M 207**
Alleged distortion of news by the British government during the crisis of September 1938.

————. *Fascism, Democracy and the Press.* London, *New Statesman and Nation,* 1938. 32 p. (*New Statesman* pamphlet)   **M 208**
Brief statement on the issues involved in the controversy over the British Official Secrets Act.

————. "The Freedom of the Press." *Political Quarterly,* 9:373–88, July 1938.
    M 209
In the abortive conversations between England and Germany in the winter of 1937, Germany is said to have demanded the suppression of anti-Nazi articles and cartoons in the British press. Had the British government wished to comply there are four legal weapons at their disposal, under the legal doctrine of Blackstone which still holds good: the laws to defend public morals, the law of contempt of court, the law of libel, and the laws against espionage and dispensing of official secrets. Most of these laws could not be counted upon as useful for the purpose, but "most of the daily Press, if properly handled, could be brought into line without special legislation." While many of the journalists, in private life, express more or less Leftist opinions, they work for a conservative press and must conform in order to earn a living. Those who are concerned with maintaining freedom of the press should turn their attention to the question of organization and professional independence of journalists.

————. "The Press in Britain, Is It Subject to Censorship? *New Republic,* 98:183–85, 22 March 1939.   **M 210**
Criticism of the lack of political independence of the press because "a few great commercial trusts own the vast bulk of the press." Further restrictions are placed on the press by the potent laws of libel, the laws against sedition, and the Official Secrets Acts. The author fears the survival of liberties in another war since already there is evidence that government measures of suppression have been imposed.

————. *The Press the Public Wants.* London, Hogarth Press, 1947. 143 p.   **M 211**
Inspired by the Royal Commission inquiry on a free press, the Socialist editor of the *New Statesman and Nation* advocates that newspapers, as public concerns, be run by responsible and independent groups, much along the lines of the *Times* and the *Manchester Guardian,* rather than as commercial monopolies. He believes that a critical public, demanding truth in the news and fairness in editorial comment, will eventually support such a public service, with a minimum of government control.

Martin, Laura K. "What Are We Afraid Of? Some Notes on Censorship." *ALA Bulletin,* 42:599–600, December 1948.
    M 212
"School library organizations should follow the lead of state and national library associations in setting up machinery for the discussion of censorship problems as they arise . . . The major function of the machinery suggested should be to anticipate actions of censorship, to call to the attention of administrators the fact that there is established policy in this field, and to insist on the careful examination, by librarians, of materials whose value has been questioned."

Martin, Olga J. *Hollywood's Movie Commandments, a Handbook for Motion Picture Writers and Reviewers.* New York, Wilson, 1937. 301 p.   **M 213**
The former secretary to the director of the Production Code Administration analyzes the Code from the standpoint of the theme of the story and the regulations that determine its its moral acceptability. Chapters 1 through 10 deal with the decency campaign which led to the Code; subsequent chapters are concerned with factors of crime, sex, and other objectionable matters. The Code of 1930 and its amendments are given in the appendices.

Martin, Philip. "Footnote to Censorship." *Wilson Library Bulletin,* 15:222–23, November 1940.   **M 214**
An imaginary but credible eposide of the banning of *Grapes of Wrath* by the Board of Trustees of "Doan County." There is implied criticism of the American Library Association for not taking an active hand in support of the librarian and those members of the library board who objected to the banning.

Martin, Robert P. "The MacArthur Censorship." *Nieman Reports,* 2:3–4, April 1948.   **M 215**
Arbitrary restrictions deny to the United States press its best base for coverage in Asia.

Marvin, James S. "Legal Censorship of Obscene Literature." *Syracuse Law Review,* 12:58–68, Fall 1960.   **M 216**
"The purpose of this note is to examine the obscenity statutes of the United States and of New York State, and the cases which have arisen thereunder . . . The scope of this article is limited to a discussion of those cases which have involved works of literature."

Marvin, Oliver W. "Freedom of Photography." *American Photography,* 35:42–45, January 1941.   **M 217**
The rights of freedom of the press and free speech include the right to freely take pictures. "Like all other rights guaranteed by law, the rights of freedom of the press and freedom of speech are not limitless and unbounded. They do not confer the privilege or license of abuse or misuse of language or pictures with immunity."

————. "Legal Aspects of Photography." *American Photography,* 39:22–25, January 1945; 39:18–21, Feburary 1945; 39:12–14, March 1945; 39:20–23, April 1945; 39:20–23, May 1945.   **M 218**
The series includes discussion of the right of privacy, libel, and copyright.

"Mary Baker Eddy." *Saturday Review of Literature,* 6:581–82, 21 December 1929.
    M 219
An account of extralegal methods used by the Christian Science Committee to suppress Dakin's book on Mary Baker Eddy. Reports of the nationwide boycott of stores selling the book are given in *Publishers' Weekly,* 5 October 1929 and 14 December 1929.

"The Mary Ware Dennett Case." *Journal of Social Hygiene,* 16:220–29, April 1930.
    M 220
Concerns the post-office censorship of Mrs. Dennett's pamphlet, *The Sex Side of Life.*

Mary Ware Dennett Defense Committee. *Sex Education or Obscenity? The Mary Ware Dennett Case.* New York, The Committee, [1929]. 8 p.   **M 221**
John Dewey was chairman of the Committee.

Maryland. State Board of Motion Picture Censors. *Annual Reports.* Baltimore, The Board, 1916/17–date?   **M 222**
The Board was created in 1916 by the State Legislature. Its duties include the examination of all motion picture films or views to be exhibited or used in the State, with the exception of news reels which were exempted in 1955. The reports for 1957–58 and 1958–59 contain general discussions on state censorship of motion pictures as well as application of court rulings to the Maryland Board.

Maryland Library Association. "Supplement to Freedom of Inquiry Statement As It Relates to *Tropic of Cancer.*" *ALA Bulletin,* 56:207, March 1962; also in *Maryland Libraries,* 28:14+, Summer 1962.
    M 223

[Maseres, Francis]. *An Enquiry Into the Extent of the Power of Juries, on Trials of Indictments or Informations, for Publishing Seditious, or other Criminal Writings, or Libels. Extracted from a Miscellaneous Collection of Papers that were Published in 1776, Intitled, Additional Papers Concerning the Province of Quebec.* Dublin, D. Lynch, 1792. 48 p.   **M 224**
A severe critic of the English seditious libel trials of the late eighteenth century, Maseres, in the year 1776, argued for the "overt acts test," which held that a work should not be considered seditious unless it "actually occasioned the disturbance which it seemed to be intended to create." This was a forerunner of the "clear and present" dictum of Mr. Justice Holmes.

Mason, Gregory. "American War Correspondents at the Front." *Bookman*, 40:63–67, September 1914. **M 225**
Includes censorship regulations under which correspondents operated at the beginning of World War I.

————. "The Associated Press: A Criticism." *Outlook*, 107:237–40, 30 May 1914. **M 226**

A history of the Associated Press and a review of its present power and practices. The author says that "criticism and suspicion of this great news-gathering agency will continue as long as it holds to its present form of an exclusive private club and as long as the form of its organization tends to prevent its members from buying and selling news elsewhere." A defense of the AP is given by George Kennan in the same issue. The two articles are introduced by the following editorial comment: "The *Outlook* has already referred editorially to the suit brought by the New York *Sun* against the Associated Press, in which are involved charges of the monopolization of news and of alleged unfair or oppressive action toward other news associations and individual newspapers. This legal controversy, and also the action taken by the Associated Press against the editors of *The Masses* for alleged libelous publication, have brought before the reading public large questions of news control and distribution. The two articles which follow discuss these questions from different standpoints."

Mass Meeting of Protest against the Suppression of Truth about the Philippines. Faneuil Hall, March 19 . . . Testimony of some of the witnesses who were refused a hearing before the Senate Committee. Boston, 1903. 60 p. **M 227**

Speeches and resolutions protesting the U.S. Government suppression of information on the conditions and government of the Philippine Islands and refusal of the Senate Committee of Affairs in the Philippines to hear testimony critical of American occupation of the Islands. The meeting was chaired by Col. Thomas Wentworth Higginson.

Massachusetts. House of Representatives. *The Defence of Young and Minns, Printers to the State, before the Committee, of the House of Representatives. With an Appendix, containing the Debate.* Boston. Gilbert & Dean, 1805. 68 p. **M 228**

————. Legislative Research Bureau. *Report Relative to Government Censorship of Obscene Material.* Boston, The Bureau, 1960. 18 p. **M 229**

————. State Commission to Investigate and Study the Relation between Juvenile Delinquency and the Distribution and

Sale of Publications Portraying Crime, Obscenity and Horror. *Report, July 1956.* Boston, Wright & Potter, 1956. 27 p. (House document 3205) **M 230**

Massachusetts Advisory Committee on Juvenile Reading. *Statement.* Boston, The Committee, 12 March 1952. 3 p. mimeo. **M 231**

At the suggestion of Boston bookseller, Richard F. Fuller, the Massachusetts Attorney General established this advisory committee to consider comic books, paperbacks, magazines, and books. The committee consisted of 32 members, representatives of schools, libraries, churches, PTA's, women's clubs, and patriotic societies. On the basis of the committee's recommendations, the Attorney-General warns firms offering objectionable reading matter.

"Massachusetts Board of Education Lifts Ban on *The Nation.*" *Nation*, 167:385, 9 October 1948. **M 232**

"Massachusetts Censorship Legislation, and Text of Massachusetts Act on Obscenity." *Library Journal*, 54:69, 15 January 1929. **M 233**
A committee of the Massachusetts Library Club in conference with booksellers and publishers, prepared a bill for introduction in the Massachusetts legislature amending the present obscenity law.

Massachusetts Library Association. "Statement of the Intellectual Freedom Committee of the M. L. A." *Bay State Librarian*, 52:10, January 1962. **M 234**
Statement on freedom to read, given before the Obscene Literature Control Commission, considering whether Henry Miller's *Tropic of Cancer* is obscene. Presented by Ervin J. Gaines, chairman.

————. "Suggested Changes in the Statute Relating to Obscene Books." *Massachusetts Library Association Bulletin*, 35:11–12, January 1945. **M 235**

Masters, Edgar Lee. "Censorship." *Authors' League Bulletin*, 15(1):11–13, April 1927. **M 236**
"No one can object to censorship by an audience, to the killing of a play because the people will not have it . . . There is no higher appeal than public taste. . . . Works of art can safely be entrusted to the laws of aesthetics and these alone."

Matchett, William T. "Boston Is Afraid of Books." *Saturday Review of Literature*, 26:6–7+, 15 July 1944. **M 237**
A general summary of Boston's long history of literary censorship, dating back to the suppression of Whitman's *Leaves of Grass*. The

writer believes that Boston "has yet to grow up in its approach to literary censorship."

Mathews, George. *An Account of the Trial of the Rev. T. Emlyn, 1703, Queen's Bench, Dublin, for a Publication against the Doctrine of the Trinity. With a Sketch of his Associates . . .* Dublin, 1839. 80 p. **M 238**
Thomas Emlyn, a Unitarian minister, was found guilty of blasphemy in the publication of his tract *An Humble Inquiry into the Scriptural Account of Jesus Christ*, and sentenced to a year in prison.

Mathias, James F., Jr. *The Court of Star Chamber, 1603–1627.* New Haven, Yale University Press, 1939. (Unpublished Ph. D. dissertation) **M 239**

Matthews, Brander. "Books That Are Barred." *Munsey's Magazine*, 50:493–97, December 1913. **M 240**
Matthews, the conservative literary critic who frequently came to the defense of the Watch and Ward Society, here criticizes the Society for taking action against Eleanor Glyn's *Three Weeks*, which he calls "a cheap tale of superficial cleverness" which would have sunk "swiftly beneath the waters of oblivion" without the need for censorship. The most effective method for the suppression of indecent literature is through enlightened public opinion.

Matthews, John. "Trials for High Treason in Printing a Libel Asserting the Title of the Pretender to the Crown, 1719." In Howell, *State Trials*, vol. 15, pp. 132 ff. **M 241**

Matthews, an 18-year-old printer, had published a pamphlet, *Vox Populi, Vox Dei*, asserting that the Pretender had a legitimate title to the crown. According to a 1707 statute such printed words constituted treason and Matthews was hanged. Frederick Siebert cites this as "the only conviction [in England] for treason for publishing seditious material in the eighteenth century."

Matthews, Miriam. "California Library Association and California Librarians Join Censorship Fight." *Library Journal*, 72:1172–73, 1 September 1947. **M 242**
The chairman of the Intellectual Freedom Committee of the California Library Association describes the protests made by librarians to the attacks on Marguerite Stewart's *Land of the Soviets* and the *Building America* textbook series, and the Committee's opposition to a censorship bill in the state legislature.

Matthews, Sidney T. "Control of the Baltimore Press During the Civil War."

Maryland Historical Magazine, 36:150–70, June 1941. **M 243**

Mattison, Walter J. "Restraints on Freedom of the Press." *Marquette Law Review*, 13:1–8, December 1928. **M 244**
Freedom of the press is not an absolute right and the term is a relative one. In no jurisdictions have newspapers, under guise of freedom, been given the right to invade the constitutional guarantees that are given to the general public, including the right of a fair trial.

Matz, Elsa. "Film Censorship." *International Review of Educational Cinematography*, 3:1113–22, December 1931. **M 245**
Deals largely with Germany and the Continent, but includes a section on proposals for an International Code.

Maude, Aylmer. *Marie Stopes: Her Work and Play*. New York, Putnam, 1933. 299 p. **M 246**

A biography of a British leader in the movement for sex education and information on birth control.

Maude, William C. "The Law of Blasphemy." *Month*, 131:320–28, April 1918. **M 247**
Points raised by the case of *Bowman and Others v. Secular Society, Ltd.* (1917).

Maverick, Maury. "San Antonio—More Fire Fighters than Fire." *New Republic*, 128(2):12–13, 29 June 1953. **M 248**
An account of a book burning campaign conducted by San Antonio "Minute Women" who would include works by Einstein, Thomas Mann, Dorothy Canfield Fisher, Dorothy Parker, and Louis Adamic, and the widespread denunciation of the censors by civic leaders. Maverick headed an opposition group, known as the American Activities Committee.

Maverick, Maury, Jr. "The Texas Brand in the Library." *Nation*, 176:525, 20 June 1953. **M 249**
Speech delivered before the Texas legislature in the course of debate on a bill to "brand" certain books in the public libraries of Texas. He enumerates various books, including the Bible, which would be removed from libraries if the unconstitutional law being considered were enacted. On page 515 of the same issue is an account of the "Minute Women" of San Antonio and their efforts at book branding, written by Maury Maverick, Sr.

Maw, T. E. "Immoral Fiction." *Library Association Record*, 2:453–54, August 1900. **M 250**

Letter to the editor urging librarians to reject immoral fiction even at the risk of being thought "straitlaced."

Maxse, Leopold J., *ed*. "Gleanings from the Unofficial Press Bureau." *National Review*, 65:276–86, 1915. **M 251**
British censorship in World War I.

Maxwell, Manuel. "Federal Radio Commission—Supervision—Censorship." *American Law Review*, 2:269–72, April 1931. **M 252**
Relates to the powers of the FCC to regulate radio broadcasts by use of its licensing powers. Examines the case of Dr. Brinkley's station KFKB.

Maxwell, Neal A. "Is Freedom of the Press Compatible With National Security?" In *Great Issues Concerning Freedom*, edited by Waldemer P. Read. [Salt Lake City], University of Utah Press, 1962, pp. 41–60. **M 253**

The author reviews the history of government restrictions on the press in time of national emergency and makes a strong plea against unnecessary withholding of official news and in favor of an aggressively free press. "Total national security . . . cannot exist without a free press . . . which can help to call the cultural cadence, which prods us when we become lethargic as individuals, and which warns us of dangers when our sentinels sleep or are strangely silent. Information is our political plasma, our lifeblood." Comments by Hays Gorey and William B. Smart, both newspapermen, follow.

May, Frederick. "Concupiscence of the Oppressor: Some Notes on the Absurdity of the Book Censorship." *Australian Library Journal*, 13:73–84, June 1964. **M 254**

The author believes that to deprive men of their rights to read what they will when they will is brutish and degrading, and to prove his point he cites from numerous works of literature. Censorship in Australia, he charges, is both unenlightened and capricious. "If nothing was banned, terror, superstition and spurious authority would vanish in a cloud of revelatory boredom—for your man in the street has (quite properly), little desire to do the exacting work called for with a serious piece of writing . . . Man must be freed from terror and superstition exploited by authority; man must be free to respond with all of himself to a work of art; he must accept the full responsibility of his own judgment. Never can he be free if information and evidence are denied him."

May, H. R. D. "Immorality of the Modern Burglar Story and Burglar Play." *Nineteenth Century*, 77:432–44, 15 February 1915. (Also in *Living Age*, 285:90–98, 10 April 1915) **M 255**

"It is the plain duty of the moral public to say that they will no longer lend the cloak of their approbation to vulgar thieves masquerading as heroes."

May, *Sir* Thomas E. "The Press, and Liberty of Opinion." In his *Constitutional History of England Since the Accession of George the Third*. Edited and continued to 1911 by Francis Holland. New York, Longmans Green, 1912. vol. 2, chapters 9 and 10, pp. 1–123. **M 256**
Content: Chapter 9. The press under censorship and afterwards; its contacts with government early in the reign of George III; Wilkes and Junius; the right of juries; Mr. Fox's Libel Act; progress of free discussion, 1760–1792; reaction caused by the French Revolution; and repressive policy, 1792–1799. Chapter 10. Repressive policy of the regency; measures of 1817; trials of Watson and others, 1817; trials of Hone, 1817; the "Six Acts"; the Constitutional Society, 1821; Duke of Wellington's prosecutions of the press, 1830; Cobbett's trial, 1831; taxes on knowledge. Chapter 11. Liberty of the Subject deals briefly with the general warrant aspects in John Wilkes's arrest.

Mayberry, Richard S. "Obscenity in New York: Law, Fact, or Both?" *Buffalo Law Review*, 11:369–84, April 1963. **M 257**

Review of recent New York obscenity cases, including *Bunis v. Conway*, 17 A.D. 2d 207, 234 N.Y.S. 2d 435 (1962), relating to *Tropic of Cancer*. The author concludes that "the best manner of discovering the 'definition of obscenity' in each case is to go to its source, the average adult." A jury, not a judge should decide.

Mayer, Arthur L. "How Much Can the Movies Say?" *Saturday Review*, 45(44): 18–20+, 3 November 1962. **M 258**
A leader in the movie industry considers recent developments in movie censorship in the United States, including decisions of the courts. Censorship boards and the industry production code are becoming more lenient, but the system is inflexible. A picture is either accepted or rejected without regard to the audience. Mayer favors some kind of audience rating system, a solution rejected by the Motion Picture Producers Association. He believes the solution will ultimately come, not from the industry or the state, but from the local theater owner, the community, and individual viewers.

———. "A Movie Exhibitor Looks at Censorship." *Reporter*, 10:35–40, 2 March 1954. **M 259**
"Our movies have survived the depredations of censor boards, government agencies, and self-regulation, but their future is dark indeed if the test of their suitability for public showing has become their political or economic orthodoxy and blameless private lives of those who make them. There is little hope for good films

dealing with the realities of modern life if such attacks are not resisted, resisted both by those who make films and by those who look at them."

———. "A Movie Man's Faith." *Library Journal*, 78:1056–57, June 1953.   **M 260**
The author is concerned with the "fear of Communist infiltration that now agitates the entire American entertainment industry." Every art and medium of communication must unite against "the dark powers of intolerance."

———. "Sense and Censorship." *Esquire*, 34(4):98, 167–68, October 1950.   **M 261**
Views on censorship by a former U.S. military government movie censor in Germany.

Mayer, J. P. "Children and the Cinema: Discusses the Ineffectual Film Censorship Provisions in Britain and Proposes an Experiment in Municipal Cinemas." *Socialist Commentary*, 17:63–64, March 1953.   **M 262**

Mayer, Milton. "How to Read the *Chicago Tribune*." *Harper's Magazine*, 198:24–35, April 1949. (Reprinted in W. H. Stone, and R. Hoopes, *eds.*, *Form and Thought in Prose*, pp. 91–112)   **M 263**
A devastating critique of an article by Frank Hughes, news reporter for the *Tribune*, which appeared in the 14 November issue under the headline: "Name Angels of Moves to Curb Press." In his article Hughes had attacked the report of the Commission on Freedom of the Press and the "angels" who financed it.

Mayerberg, S. S. "Summum Bonum of Library Service." *ALA Bulletin*, 32:815–17, 15 October 1938.   **M 264**
Abridgment of a talk given by a Kansas City rabbi at the American Library Association Conference. While not advocating the exclusion of propaganda, he suggests librarians submit controversial books to experts for their evaluation and then mark them with such notation as: "The facts in this book are reliable, but we do not endorse the conclusion of the author," or, "This work, or article, is contrary to truth, it is obviously propaganda. As its antidote, we recommend such and such a volume."

"The Mayflower Doctrine Scuttled." *Yale Law Journal*, 59:759–70, March 1950.   **M 265**
On editorializing by radio stations and industrial licensees over their own facilities, 1941–49.

Mayo, Louis H. "Comments Concerning the First Amendment and the People's Right to Know." In *Lectures on Communications Media, Legal and Policy Problems Delivered at University of Michigan Law School, June 16–June 18, 1954*. Ann Arbor, University of Michigan Law School, 1954, pp. 3–45.   **M 266**
Examination of the doctrine of "the people's right to know" and the provision of full information on the judicial, executive, and legislative processes.

"Mayor Walker as a Movie Censor." *Literary Digest*, 98:11, 28 July 1928.   **M 267**
Criticism of the arbitrary action of New York's Mayor James Walker.

Meacham, Denver W., II. "Privilege of Newsmen to Conceal Source of Information." *Oklahoma Law Review*, 15:453–56, November 1962.   **M 268**
The author observes that the U.S. Supreme Court "has never expressly decided whether compelling a reporter to disclose his confidential news source constitutes an infringement of the freedom of the press guaranteed by the first amendment." He believes that where the question asked of the reporter is definitely relevant to the plaintiff's claim, "his freedom of the press must yield to the administration of justice even if it results in the reporter losing some of his sources of information."

Mead, Margaret. "Sex and Censorship in Contemporary Society." In *New World Writing*, 3rd Mentor Selection. New York, New American Library, 1953, pp. 7–24.   **M 269**
An anthropologist discusses the various forms of censorship that ancient and modern societies have exerted in matters of sex expression. She draws a distinction between pornography, the secret vice that is condemned in every modern society, and the bawdy, the ribald, and the vulgar that are the safety valve of most social systems.

Meager, Ruby. "The Sublime and the Obscene." *British Journal of Aesthetics*, 4:214–27, July 1964.   **M 270**
"Whereas the sublime promises to bundle an eternity of significant reflection into a moment of illumination, the obscene promises to suppress our perennial distracting concern with objective truth and the last effects of thoughts and behavior on personal relations, self-respect and human dignity, liberating us for pure irresponsible enjoyment of the fantasies and sensations of the moment." Obscenity has become a serious aesthetic danger. It is "an aesthetic disvalue in literature."

Mecklin, John M. "Freedom of Speech for Clergymen." *Annals of the American Academy of Political and Social Science*, 200:165–84, November 1938.   **M 271**
While the clergyman is protected legally under the First Amendment, he is limited practically and sociologically in his expression by the doctrines and discipline of his sect. The author discusses the degrees of liberty permitted, referring to such issues as theological liberalism, middle-class ideology, slavery, the Ku Klux Klan, the social gospel, science, evolution, and personal piety.

Meek, Thomas. *An Essay on the Liberty of the Press: in Which the National and Prudential Limits of the Noble Invention of Printing are Properly Defined . . .* South Shields, Eng., Printed for the Author by W. Hallgarth, 1799. 50p.   **M 272**

Mehrotra, Baikunth N. *The Law of Defamation and Malicious Prosecutions, Civil and Criminal*. Allahabad, India, Law Publishers, 1963. 229p.   **M 273**

Meiklejohn, Alexander. "The First Amendment and the Evils that Congress Has a Right to Prevent." *Indiana Law Journal*, 26:477–93, Summer 1951.   **M 274**
Notes on the doctrine of "clear and present danger," 1919–50.

———. "The First Amendment Is an Absolute." In *The Supreme Court Review*, Chicago, University of Chicago Press, 1961, pp. 455–66.   **M 275**
In an effort to seek a clarification of the meaning of the First Amendment, the former president of Amherst College presents the absolutist views of Justice Hugo Black and the more limited interpretation of Justice Harlan, as well as his own views.

———. *Free Speech and Its Relation to Self-government*. New York, Harper, 1948. 107p.   **M 276**
A series of lectures considering recent interpretations of the First Amendment to the Constitution. Special attention is given to Justice Holmes's doctrine of a "clear and present danger," which the author finds inadequate. He believes that in discussion of public issues, which he distinguishes from private issues, there is greater danger in suppression than in widespread discussion. He concurs with Justice Brandeis' opinion so long as there is physical freedom for the exchange of ideas; the presence of danger is no excuse for censorship. Zechariah Chafee, Jr. reviews the Meiklejohn book in the *Harvard Law Review*, January 1949.

Meissner, Gerhard. *Die Liberale Pressefreiheit Englands im Lichte Englischer Kritik*. Frankfurt, Moritz Diesterweg, 1939. 198p. (Zeitung und Zeit, Schriftenreihe des Instituts für Zeitungswissenschaft an der Universität Berlin. n.F., Reihe A, Bd. 13)   **M 277**

This study of English press freedom consists of four parts: (1) historical development; (2) restraint of the press from such internal influences as the publishers and editors and from such external influences as the advertisers, the readers, government and law; (3) abuse of press freedom through sensationalism, personal libel, and biased treatment of foreign politics and especially the relationship between England and Germany; and (4) the English conception of freedom of the press. The study claims objectivity because it makes use of British sources, but it actually reflects throughout the bias of Nazi Germany. A section deals with the influence of Jews on the British press. The author concludes that there is greater freedom of the press in Germany under the Nazi government than in England where the press is under capitalist domination.

Melcher, Frederic G. "The Banning of Books in Boston." *Publishers' Weekly* 111:1254–55, 19 March 1927. (Reprinted in *Authors' League Bulletin*, April 1927) **M 278**
A description of the "Boston book massacre" in which the police and district attorney took wholesale action against many works of modern fiction in the bookstores. The booksellers are protecting themselves from threatened prosecution by withdrawing many books from sale.

————. "Freedom to Read: Books." *Survey Graphic*, 35:457–61, 502, December 1946. **M 279**
The editor of *Publishers' Weekly* "feels the pulse of new, vaster audiences—and gauges this challenge to writers, scholars, and publishers." He finds little direct censorship of books and no evidence that the publishing business is in the control of too few hands. Nor does he believe that publishers interject their own beliefs unduly into their product. Paper shortage and the problems of book distribution are limiting factors in freedom to read books. He calls upon publishers to "take with full seriousness the responsibilities that rest squarely on them to augment the percentage of books of more than trifling value."

Melchionne, Theresa M. "One Step Further." *Police Management Review*, 2(2):8–13, October 1964. **M 280**
Statement by deputy commissioner of the Youth Program, New York Police Department, before the New York State Joint Committee on Pornographic Materials.

Melgund, Gilbert John (Elliot-Murray-Kynynmound), *Viscount*. "Newspaper Correspondents in the Field." *Nineteenth Century*, 7:434–43, March 1880. **M 281**
"I am convinced, from personal observation

in different campaigns, that every word in the new press regulations is necessary."

"The Menace of Irresponsible Journalism." *Arena*, 38:170–80, August 1907. **M 282**
"Recent examples of the prostitution of the press in the interests of the industrial society." Special reference to the Boston press and to the New York *World*'s attacks on Mary Baker Eddy.

Menace Publishing Company, *et al. In the District Court of the United States; Western District of Missouri, Southwestern Division. no. 253* [*United States, Plaintiff, v. The Menace Publishing Company, a Corporation, Wilber F. Phelps, Bruce M. Phelps, Theodore C. Walker and Marvin Brown, Defendants*]. *Brief of Defendants on Motion to Quash and on Demurrer.* Kansas City, Mo., Smith-Grieves, [1913]. 200 p. **M 283**
The defendants were indicted for issues of the *Menace* and for a book by Father Crowley, *The Pope, Chief of White Slavers, High Priest of Intrigue*, all alleged to be obscene. The court overruled the demurrer, but the jury found the matter not obscene and acquitted all defendants.

Mence, Richard. *Law of Libel.* London, A. Maxwell, 1824. 595 p. **M 284**
A general defense of intellectual liberty and a criticism of existing laws of libel. An essay based on this book, entitled Law of Libel and Liberty of the Press and attributed to John Stuart Mill, appears in the *Westminster Review*, April 1825.

————. "Law of Libel—State of the Press." *Quarterly Review*, 35:566–609, 1827. **M 285**
A review of Starkie's *The Law of Slander, Libel, Scandalum Magnatum, and False Rumours* and Holt's *The Law of Libel*.

Mencher, Melvin. "Press Freedom for the Campus Newspaper." *Quill*, 49(8):11–17, August 1961. **M 286**
A professor of journalism discusses the merits of a completely free versus a limitedly free college press, preferring the former, despite the possible embarrassment from time to time that will come to the university in the exercise of this freedom.

Mencken, H. L. *A Book of Prefaces.* New York, Knopf, 1917. 288 p. **M 287**
Mencken, the "Sage of Baltimore," was one of the most outspoken critics of censorship in all its forms. He exposed the absurdities of censorship in his writing, he defended his author friends against the attack of the censor, and he himself faced the Boston censor in the famous "Hatrack" case. The essay on Theodore Dreiser contains many references to Dreiser's conflict with the censor. The

essay on Puritanism as a Literary Force, is an attack on the new spirit of Puritanism spreading over America and restricting sex expression in art and literature. The activities of Comstock societies come in for special invective.

————. *The Hatrack Case, 1926–1927 The American Mercury vs. the New England Watch and Ward Society, the Postmaster General of the United States et al. by H. L. Mencken, with Newspaper Reports and Other Documents.* Baltimore, 1937. 8 vols. (In Enoch Pratt Free Library, Baltimore) **M 288**
In these eight unpublished scrapbooks Mencken has preserved hundreds of documents relating to the famous "Hatrack" case—correspondence, newspaper clippings, telegrams, photographs, and his own lengthy Prefatory Note in vol. 1, summarizing the case. After Mencken had been freed by a Boston judge for the sale of the April 1926 issue of the *American Mercury*, he faced a Post Office ban of the issue in New York, prompted by the Watch and Ward Society. An injunction against the Society for its interference with the freedom of the press brought an end to the case. A list of newspaper and journal references to the "Hatrack" case is given in Betty Adler and Jane Wilhelm, *ed., H.L.M., the Mencken Bibliography*, p. 388.

————. *James Branch Cabell.* New York, McBride, 1927. 32 p. **M 289**
This little pamphlet is in praise of Cabell and his works, particularly *Jurgen*, and an attack on the "patriotic" and "pornographic" Comstocks that are attempting to suppress this book.

————. *Prejudices: Fifth Series.* London, Jonathan Cape, 1926. 307 p. **M 290**
Two brief essays in this collection, Birth Control and Comstockery, relate to censorship. In the latter essay Mencken suggests that the support of sex education and birth control literature by some members of the vice societies might spell the doom for "Comstockery," which was based on the doctrine that "virtue and ignorance were identical." The Comstockery essay is reprinted in Downs, *The First Freedom*.

————. *To The Friends of the American Mercury. A Statement by the Editor.* [New York?], 1926. 7 p. **M 291**
Mencken's own account of the "Hatrack" case, including the text of Boston Judge Parmenter's opinion dismissing the charge against Mencken and the *American Mercury*. The offending article in the April issue, entitled Hatrack, was written by Herbert Asbury and related to a prostitute in a small Missouri town. The pamphlet is dated 16 April 1926.

Mendelson, Wallace. "Clear and Present Danger—Another Decade." *Texas Law Review*, 39:449–56, April 1961. **M 292**

Supplements earlier history of this dictum in *Columbia Law Review*, March 1952.

————. "Clear and Present Danger—from Schenck to Dennis." *Columbia Law Review*, 52:313–33, March 1952. **M 293**
Covers court decisions from the first use of the dictum in the Schenck case, 249 U.S. 47, through the Dennis case, 341 U.S. 494.

————. "The Clear and Present Danger Test—a Reply to Mr. Meiklejohn." *Vanderbilt Law Review*, 5:792–95, June 1952. **M 294**
Commentary on views of Alexander Meiklejohn (*Indiana Law Journal*, Summer 1951) on the First Amendment.

————. "The Degradation of the Clear and Present Danger Rule." *Journal of Politics*, 15:349–55, August 1953. **M 295**
Notes on cases from 1919 to 1952.

————. "First Amendment and the Judicial Process: a Reply to Mr. Frantz." *Vanderbilt Law Review*, 17:479–85, March 1964. **M 296**
"The author combines a debate with Mr. Laurent Frantz on the meaning of the first amendment and the 'balancing of interests' in free speech cases. He suggests that every judicial decision involves a balancing approach, and concludes that it is desirable that this balancing be clearly articulated."

————. "On the Meaning of the First Amendment: Absolutes in the Balance." *California Law Review*, 50:821–28, December 1962. **M 297**
"I suggest that the language of the first amendment is highly ambiguous, and this ambiguity is at best compounded by history." A criticism of the point of view expressed by Laurent Frantz in *Yale Law Journal*, July 1962.

Menon, K. B. *Press Laws of India*. Bombay, Indian Civil Liberties Union, 1937. 52 p. **M 298**

[Meredith, *Sir* William]. *A Reply to the Defense of the Majority*. London, John Almon, 1764. 48 p. **M 299**
In support of Charles Townshend's defense of the minority (Whig) position in the matter of general warrants and opposed to the government's statement as issued by Charles Lloyd. The Whig minority wished to abolish the use of the general warrant against authors, printers, and booksellers and Meredith introduced a motion to this effect. In this pamphlet he states: "It is unhappily blended with the Nature of Liberty, to degenerate often into Licentiousness; but, 'tis so impossible to draw the line between them, that if you resort to more than legal power to

suppress the One, you will soon Destroy the Other."

Merey, P. E. *Analysis of the Books Removed from the United States Information Service Libraries*. Philadelphia, School of Library Science, Drexel Institute of Technology, 1954. 53 p. (Unpublished Master's thesis) **M 300**

Meriwether, James B. "The Dashes in Hemingway's *A Farewell to Arms*." *The Papers of the Bibliographical Society of America*, 58:449–57, Fourth Quarter 1964. **M 301**
An examination of M. Coindreau's copy of the first American edition of *A Farewell to Arms* into which Hemingway had penciled the obscenities expurgated by the publishers.

Merriam, *Mrs.* Charles E. "Motion Pictures—Past, Present and Future." *Light*, 180:17–27, January-February 1928. **M 302**
Address of the former president of the Film Council of America before the International Purity Conference, La Crosse, Wis., 1927. Suggested regulatory measures follow the address.

Merriam, Clinton L. *Obscene Literature; Speech of Hon. Clinton L. Merriam, of New York, in the House of Representatives, March 1, 1873, on the Bill (S. no. 1572) for the Suppression of Trade in and Circulation of Obscene Literature and Articles of Immoral Use*. Watertown, N.Y., Ingalls, Brockway & Skinner, 1873. 8 p. **M 303**

Merrill, Samuel. *Newspaper Libel: A Handbook for the Press*. Boston, Ticknor, 1888. 304 p. **M 304**
An early handbook on libel, compiled for newspaper offices by a member of the staff of the Boston *Globe*. Includes a brief introduction to the history of libel, civil and criminal action, libels as contempt of court, language that is libelous, privileged communications, and political libels.

Merritt, LeRoy C. "Censorship Afoot." *California Librarian*, 19:177–78, July 1958. **M 305**
A review of the recent work of the Intellectual Freedom Committee, California Library Association.

————. "Intellectual Freedom." In *Bowker Annual of Library and Book Trade Information, 1964*. New York, Bowker, 1964, pp. 125–28. **M 306**
A résumé of intellectual freedom and censorship activity during the fifteen months ending 30 September 1963, drawn from the American Library Association's *Newsletter on Intellectual Freedom*.

————. "Intellectual Freedom." In *Bowker Annual of Library and Book Trade Information, 1965*. New York, Bowker, 1965, pp. 170–74. **M 307**
A summary of events of the past year relating to censorship and freedom of the press, including important court decisions (*Tropic of Cancer* and *Fanny Hill*), and the activities of such pressure groups as the National Organization for Decent Literature and Citizens for Decent Literature.

————. "Intellectual Freedom." In *The Bowker Annual of Library and Book Trade Information, 1966*. New York, Bowker, 1966, pp. 185–87. **M 308**
A summary of the events of the past year, including legislation, court decisions, and censorship incidents involving books, films, and libraries. There are references to the Supreme Court action against the Post Office practice of intercepting mail it deemed to be foreign Communist propaganda and the Court's ruling the film censorship statutes of Maryland and New York unconstitutional. A similar report by Merritt appears in the 1967 annual volume.

————. "Keeping Up With Censorship." *California Librarian*, 20:57–59, January 1959. **M 309**

————. "Notes of Merritt." *Library Journal*, 86:4158–60, 1 December 1961. **M 310**
In his regular column Merritt reprints the policy statement of the Intellectual Freedom Committee of the California Library Association and the Book Selection Policies Committee of the School Library Association of California.

————. "The Right to Read." *California Teachers Association Journal*, 61:18–20, 44–48, January 1965. **M 311**
Discussion of censorship and the forms it assumes and the opposition to it in the defense of the right to read. Text of the Library Bill of Rights and the Statement of Purpose recently adopted by the New Jersey Committee for the Right to Read are included.

Merryweather, F. Somner. *Bibliomania in the Middle Ages*. New York, Meyer, 1900. 322 p. **M 312**
The introductory chapter refers to destruction of books and manuscripts of the monasteries during the Middle Ages, during the British Civil War and the French Revolution. There are scattered references to book destruction throughout the volume.

Merson, Martin. *The Private Diary of a Public Servant*. New York, Macmillan, 1955. 171 p. **M 313**

A personal account of the book burning practiced by government overseas libraries in 1953, stimulated by the antisubversive crusade of Senator Joseph R. McCarthy.

Metzger, Charles R. "Pressure Groups and the Motion Picture Industry." *Annals of the American Academy of Political and Social Science*, 254:110–15, November 1947. **M 314**
No other business is watched so closely and subjected to so many negative suggestions from religious, professional, trade, and racial groups. In addition to these external pressures, the industry itself exerts pressures on producers in an effort not to offend potential customers.

Meurant, Louis H. *Sixty Years Ago*. 2d ed. Cape Town, Africane Connoisseurs, 1963. 116p. **M 315**
"Reminiscence of the struggle for freedom of the press in South Africa, and the establishment of the first newspaper in the Eastern Province." Originally published in Cape Town by S. Solomon, 1885.

Meyer, A. G. *Modesty and the Printed Word*. Milwaukee, Wisconsin Committee, National Organization for Decent Literature, [196—?]. 6p. **M 316**
The Archbishop of Milwaukee reports on indecency in print and its relation to the law of the Catholic Church and the responsibility of Christian leaders.

Meyer, Bernard S. "Free Press v. Fair Trial: The Judge's View." *North Dakota Law Review*, 41:14–23, November 1964. **M 317**
A justice of the Supreme Court of the State of New York proposes to ameliorate the difficulty with a statute restricting the time of publication of information relevant to a pending case. This article is preceded by Frank Stanton's, which gives the broadcaster's view.

Meyer, Bernard S., *et al*. "Symposium: Fair Trial—Free Press." *Criminal Law Bulletin*, 2(3):3–37, April 1966. **M 318**
Other participants: Herbert Brucker, editor, Hartford *Courant*; Frank G. Raichle, American College of Trial Lawyers, and Harris B. Steinberg, moderator.

Meyer, Sylvan. "We Call It Privilege, They Call It Smear." *Nieman Reports*, 19(4):9–14, December 1965. **M 319**
A plea for more thorough newspaper coverage of libel cases. "In straightforward coverage of libel cases and their results, the reader sees the broad rules applied to the specific instance.

Over the long haul this is bound to be constructive. For the public's sake we should print more stories of libel trials and educate the people to their stake in the press and to what libel entails."

Meyerfeld, Max. "Censor and Other Tales." *Nineteenth Century*, 69:460–70, March 1911. **M 320**
A German drama critic believes that the British merit their stage censor because of the public indifference to good drama. Even if the censor were abolished there would be no guarantee of good plays or public appreciation of them. He calls for education of the public, and the creation of a national theater "released from any moral muzzle."

Michael, George. *Handout*. New York, Putnam, 1935. 242p. **M 321**
The author charges that the federal government seeks to control the nation's press through a well-organized plan of employing newspapermen as press agents and by exercising favoritism in the release of news. An exposé of the New Deal propaganda organization.

Michael, Kenneth E. "Freedom of the Press under Our Constitution." *West Virginia Law Quarterly*, 33:29–63, December 1926. **M 322**
A brief historical survey of the development of freedom of the press and a determination of the statutes of freedom of the press under federal and West Virginia constitutions.

Middleton, Janet. "Literary Censorship in Australia—with a Commentary on the L.A.A.'s Action." *Student Librarian*, 5:25–28, 1965. **M 323**

Middleton, John. *Citizens for Decent Literature*. Columbia, Mo., Freedom of Information Center, School of Journalism, University of Missouri, 1960. 5p. (Publication no. 37) **M 324**
An account of a new national organization engaged in "the fight against newsstand filth" using duly constituted legal measures instead of lists of banned books, boycotts, and demands for more legislation.

[Midgely, Robin]. "*Victor*—Or The Chamberlain Takes Over." *Plays and Players*, 11(12):10, September 1964. **M 325**
Frank Cox interviews the director of the controversial play, *Victor, or the Children Take Over*, which ran into censorship difficulties in London during rehearsal.

Mightier Than the Sword. 20 min., b/w movie. New York, Prepared by a Committee of the National Council for Social Studies to Cooperate with Teaching

Film Custodians, 1964. (Accompanied by study guide) **M 326**
One in a series of four films on the tradition of American journalism, adapted from the "Cavalcade of America" television series. This film is intended to present the basic concept of freedom of the press and to provide a background for study of the First Amendment. It is a dramatization of the libel case of John Peter Zenger. The other films in the series are: *One Nation Indivisible* (Horace Greeley as a moulder of public opinion); *The Tiger's Tail* (Thomas Nast, cartoonist, and Boss Tweed); and *Six Hours to Deadline: A Free and Responsible Press* (analysis of social and ethical problems of journalism).

Mikva, Abner J. "Chicago: Citadel of Censorship." *Focus/Midwest*, 2:10, 16–17, March–April 1963. **M 327**
"Chicago, for all its alleged cosmopolitanism and for all its actual bawdiness, has been a citadel of censorship." Two cases involving the Police Department's Censor Board of Motion Pictures have gone before the U.S. Supreme Court. In the case involving *Game of Love*, the ban was reversed; in *Don Juan*, the court upheld precensorship of movies by a 5 to 4 decision. Stage plays banned have included Sartre's *Respectful Prostitute*, *Tobacco Road*, and *The Children's Hour*.

Milam, Aubrey, *et al*. "Pressure Groups and the Library: Symposium." *Southeastern Librarian*, 7:50–56, Summer 1957. **M 328**
The participants include Aubrey Milam, trustee of the Atlanta Public Library; M. E. Sterne, trustee of the Birmingham Public Library; and J. Maynard Magruder, member of the Virginia State Library Board. Mr. Sterne refers to the proposed labeling bill in Alabama; Mr. Magruder considers the legal history of the freedom to read.

Milam, Carl H. "Library and Today's Problems." *ALA Bulletin*, 33:721–22, December 1939. **M 329**
The author, executive secretary of the American Library Association, writes of the importance of a courageous stand on the part of libraries in the matter of censorship, recalling his experience with the "black out" of a free press during World War I.

Mildmay, Paulet St. John. "*Don't Sit on the Safety Valve*"; or Reconstruction and the Press Bureau, Being a Protest against the Institution of "Government-by-Concealment" in England under the Guise of "Democracy." London, Kibble, [1918?]. 16p. **M 330**
A criticism of British censorship in World War I.

Miles, Dudley D. "The Constitutionality of Anti-Birth Control Legislation." *Wyoming Law Journal*, 7:138–42, Spring 1954. **M 331**
Notes on cases, 1938–43.

Miles, [Nelson A.?]. "Criticism in War." *English Review*, 23:538–43, December 1916.　　　　　　　　　**M 332**
Military reporting and criticism, the author complains, is largely left to nonmilitary amateurs, not always well-informed, while those who know the facts are prevented by military censorship from informing the public.

Miles, Vincent M. "A Letter from the Solicitor of the Post Office Department." *Saturday Review of Literature*, 27:17–18, 3 June 1944.　　　　　　　　　**M 333**
The letter reveals the procedures employed by the Post Office Department in censoring the mail.

Miles, William E. *Damn It . . . A Book of Bluenoses and Self-Made Censors . . .* Evanston, Ill., Regency Books, 1963. 156p.　　　　　　　　　**M 334**
A popular account of efforts at censorship in the United States and Great Britain. Includes chapters on the use of profanity, nude illustrations, the comics, objectionable songs, the movies, radio and television, Anthony Comstock and the vice societies, censorship of literary works, textbook censorship, censorship by religious groups, wartime censorship, libel, and pornography.

Mill, Herbert V. *Rev. W. Sharman and the Blasphemy Laws.* Colne, Eng., R. Hyde, [1883]. 8p.　　　　　　　　　**M 335**
Account of the resignation of the Rev. Mr. Sharman, Unitarian Minister at Plymouth, in consequence of his support of Messrs. Foote, Ramsay, and Kemp, charged with blasphemy.

Mill, James. *Essays on Government, Jurisprudence, Liberty of the Press, and Law of Nations. Written for the Supplement to the Encyclopaedia Britannica, [5th ed., 1821] and Printed by Permission of the Proprietors of the Encyclopaedia. . . . Not for Sale.* London, Printed for J. Innes, [1825?]. Each essay separately paged; Liberty of the Press, 34p. (The Liberty of the Press essay has appeared in various reprints including Philip Wheelwright's *Jeremy Bentham . . . , James Mill . . . ,* pp. 253–80; and Theodore Schroeder's *Methods of Constitutional Construction.* Extracts from the essay were issued in a separate pamphlet by the Free Speech League in 1913 (36p.), with an introduction by Theodore Schroeder)
　　　　　　　　　M 336
Mill was one of the leading "scientific radicals" of his day; he was a friend and disciple of Jeremy Bentham and father of John Stuart Mill. He frequently wrote for the radical papers on the subject of a free press, criticizing government prosecution of publishers. In this article Mill argues that the press has a

responsibility to make the people dissatisfied with poor government to such an extent that the ruling group cannot ignore the popular will. He advocates the freedom to resist government and the freedom to censor the conduct of its officials. Undeserved praise, he argues, is as mischievous as undeserved blame. Limitations on freedom lead to its destruction. "No opinion ought to be impeded more than another, by any thing but the adduction of evidence on the opposite side."

———. *The Speech Delivered at the British Forum . . . on the . . . Following Question: "Ought the conduct of Mr. Carlile, the Bookseller, in continuing to Publish Paine's Age of Reason . . . to be censured as a serious aggravation of his offense, and an obstinate defiance of the established religion of his country; or approved, as a striking instance of the rectitude of his intentions, and of his bold and manly perseverance in the cause of reason and truth?* London, R. Carlile, 1819. 14p.
　　　　　　　　　M 337
The conclusion was that "Mr. Carlile was justified in continuing the sale of his books until a jury should forbid him to do so."

[Mill, John Stuart]. [*J. S. Mill on Blasphemy*]. *Report of an Article Contributed to the "Westminster Review" for July, 1824, occasioned by the Prosecution of Richard Carlile.* London, Progressive Publishing Co., 1883. 30p.　　　　　**M 338**
Unsigned article attributed to Mill by his father's biographer, Alexander Bain. The article reviewed Rev. W. B. Whitehead's *Prosecutions of Infidel Blasphemers briefly Vindicated* and *On the Recent Prosecutions of Persons Vending Books against Christianity,* the latter dealing with the prosecution of Richard Carlile.

———. *On Liberty.* London, J. W. Parker, 1859. 207p. (Available in various modern editions including Gateway Edition, Chicago, Regnery, 1955. 171p. With Introduction by Russell Kirk)　**M 339**
In this classic of libertarian thought Mill states his belief in the dignity of the human intellect. He considers freedom of discussion indispensable to the working of a democracy through representative government. In the chapter on liberty of thought and discussion Mill argues that to silence contrary opinion assumes infallibility of both the person and the age in which he lives. Opinions that are mostly false may contain a portion of truth and opinions mostly true may be partially false. The whole truth becomes known only through a collision of opinion. Even the whole truth is best kept alive by frequent restatement. Milton had spoken of truth as always triumphing over falsehood. Mill says that unfortunately this is not true. Commenting on the present status of a free press in England, Mill notes that we still persecute those whose ideas are offensive, though not so violently, and cites the cases of Holyoake and Truelove,

and in a footnote refers to the "ill-judged" interference with public discussion under the Government Press Prosecutions of 1858, dealing with the doctrine of tyrannicide.

———. *Prefaces to Liberty: Selected Writings of John Stuart Mill.* Edited by Bernard Wishy. Boston, Beacon, 1959. 367p.
　　　　　　　　　M 340
Includes three letters on free discussion published in 1823 in the *Morning Chronicle* as part of the Benthamites campaign on behalf of the persecuted Richard Carlile. The letters are signed "Wickliff" and "assume that freer formation of public opinion will serve truth and that public opinion will be predominantly benign in its effect." Another letter protests the barring of reporters from court. Also included are Mill's reviews of books by Francis Place and Richard Mence on the law of libel, appearing in *Westminster Review,* April 1825, in which Mill asserts that popular rule and free discussion serve truth. Free discussion "is equal in value to good government, because without it good government cannot exist." There is an article from the *Spectator* of 19 August 1848 condemning French restrictions on the press. Finally, the collection includes Mill's famous essay, *On Liberty.*

Millard, Oscar E. *Underground News; the Complete Story of the Secret Newspaper that Made War History.* New York, McBride, 1938. 287p.　　　　　　　**M 341**
The story of *Libre Belgique,* the clandestine newspaper published during German occupation of Belgium in World War I.

Millay, Richard P. "The Power of the Executive to Withhold Information from Congressional Investigating Committees." *Georgetown Law Journal,* 43:643–60, June 1955.　　　　　　　　**M 342**
A history of the development of the legal concept, 1787–1954.

Miller, Donald F. "Is Censorship Necessary in Your Life?" *Liguorian,* 49:1–7, May 1961.　　　　　　　　　**M 343**
Comments of a Redemptorist priest.

———. *Should Your Reading be Censored?* Liguori, Mo., Redemptorist Fathers, 1954. 24p. (Reprinted from the *Liguorian* 42:65–70, Feburary 1954)　　　**M 344**

Miller, Edward G., Jr. "Freedom and Responsibility." *U.S. Department of State Bulletin,* 23:617–19, 626, 16 October 1950.
　　　　　　　　　M 345
An address before the Sixth Inter-American Press Conference in New York, reviewing the American concept of freedom of the press.

"We citizens of the United States believe that the press has one fundamental and over-riding moral duty . . . to seek the truth, and to report all available facts as objectively as possible."

Miller, Edwin H. "Censorship." In his *The Professional Writer in Elizabethan England*. Cambridge, Mass., Harvard University Press, 1959, pp. 171–202.

M 346

Miller, Henry. "*Defense of the Freedom to Read,*" *A Letter to the Supreme Court of Norway in Connection with the Ban on "Sexus" ("The Rosy Crucifixion")*. Oslo, J. W. Cappelens, 1959. 27 p. (Also in *Two Cities*, 15 July 1959; *Evergreen Review*, Summer 1959; McCormick, *Versions of Censorship*, pp. 223–30; and in Lawrence Durrell, *The Best of Miller*, New York, 1959)

M 347

The author of *Sexus*, on request of the Oslo Town Court, defends his book. In 1957 *Sexus* was confiscated by the Attorney General of Norway as "obscene writing" and in 1958 two booksellers were found guilty of selling the book. The case was appealed to the Norwegian Supreme Court which found the defendents not guilty, but upheld the ban on the book.

———. "I Defy You." *Playboy*, 9(1):102, January 1962.

M 348

The author of *Tropic of Cancer* defies the censor, specifically the Massachusetts Obscene Literature Control Commission, which had acted against Miller's work. He cites four arguments against the censorship: (1) There is no valid definition of obscenity. (2) "No man, no group, no court of law has the right to tell us what we may or may not read." (3) There is no proof that reading a so-called obscene book ever demoralized a reader. (4) By attempting to protect youth we restrict the freedom of the adult. We are "burning down the house to roast the pig."

———. *Obscenity and the Law of Reflection*. Yonkers, N.Y., Hunt Turner, 1945. 24 p. (750 copies) (Reprinted in Miller's *Remember to Remember*. New York, New Directions, 1947, and in the Summer 1963 issue of *Kentucky Law Journal*, pp. 577–90)

M 349

The only effect which censorship has had upon his book, *Tropic of Cancer*, writes Miller, is to drive it underground and give it the best kind of publicity—word of mouth recommendation. "The book is a living proof that censorship defeats itself. It also proves once again that the only ones who may be said to be protected are the censors themselves, and this only because of a law of nature known to all who over-indulge."

———. "Obscenity in Literature." In *New Directions in Prose and Poetry: 16*. New York, New Directions, 1957, pp. 232–46.

M 350

This often-banned author argues for freedom of expression of man's universal human passions. "It is my honest conviction that fear and dread which the obscene inspires, particularly in modern times, sprang from the language employed rather than the thought." People are shocked to see in print sex words that they have known since childhood. He quotes Montaigne as writing: "It is amusing that the words which are least known, least written, and most hushed up, should be the best known and most generally understood." "Deceit and hypocrisy," writes Miller, "have a way of provoking honest men to explosive language, to shocking language." But, "ideas are in the air . . . and the artist does but make use of them." The real evil by which we are being destroyed is not obscenity but the making and planning of war. As a preliminary to his essay Miller discusses the censorship of his own books both in France and the United States.

[Miller, John]. *The Evidence, (As Taken down in Court) in the Trial wherein the Rt. Hon. John, Earl of Sandwich, was Plaintiff, and J. Miller, Defendant, before William, Lord Mansfield, and a Special Jury, In the Court of King's Bench, July 8, 1773*. London, Printed for George Kearsley, 1774. 48 p.

M 351

Miller was found guilty of libel for publishing a letter in the *London Evening Post* accusing the earl of the sale of a Navy job. The defendant was assessed £2,000 damages.

[———]. "Trial in London for Re-printing Junius's Letter to the King, 1770." Howell, *State Trials*, vol. 20, pp. 869 ff.

M 352

Miller had published Junius letter no. 35 in his *London Evening Post* and also in his monthly *London Museum*. The letter, originally appearing in Woodfall's *Public Advertiser*, had attacked the king for alleged evils in his administration and had warned him that a crown "acquired by one revolution . . . may be lost by another." Miller was brought to trial as were several other printers and booksellers. He was ably defended by Mr. Serjeant John Glynn, who had been attorney for Wilkes, and found not guilty.

Miller, John C. *Crisis in Freedom: the Alien and Sedition Acts*. Boston, Little, Brown, 1951. 253 p.

M 353

An account of two years of American history (1798–1800) when freedom of speech and the press was seriously abridged by the Alien and Sedition Acts. In a period of hysteria brought on by the French Revolution, the Federalists enacted these laws to protect their administration from criticism by the Jeffersonian Republicans. The work includes accounts of sedition trials against Benjamin Bache, Thomas Cooper, James T. Callender, Matthew Lyon, and others.

Miller, Justin. "The Broadcasters' Stand: A Question of Fair Trial and Free Information." *Journal of Broadcasting*, 1: 3–19, Winter 1956–57.

M 354

This discussion of Canon 35 of the American Bar Association, dealing with broadcasting and televising of court proceedings, is digested from the September 1956 *American Bar Association Journal*.

Miller, Merle. "Freedom to Read: Magazines." *Survey Graphic*, 35:462–67, December 1946.

M 355

"Over all it can be said that a dozen to fifteen magazines today control the mass circulation field."

———. *The Judges and the Judged*. Garden City, N.Y., Doubleday, 1952. 220 p. Foreword by Robert E. Sherwood.

M 356

A report on blacklisting in radio and television prepared for the American Civil Liberties Union. The investigation was occasioned by pressures exerted on the radio and television industries and the relating advertising agencies by the book, *Red Channels*, and the weekly newsletter, *Counterattack*, which listed persons in the entertainment world who had alleged Communist affiliations.

———. "Our Common Stake in Free Communication: Broadcasting." In *Freedom of Communication; Proceedings of the First Conference on Intellectual Freedom . . .* Chicago, American Library Association, 1954, pp. 116–23.

M 357

———. "The Real Danger." *Saturday Review of Literature*, 31(50):20–21, 11 December 1948.

M 358

The author cites numerous cases of pressures on librarians to suppress books, particularly in Los Angeles County. The real danger is in the pressures exerted against librarians suspected of having liberal thoughts and in the complacency of writers to threats of censorship.

———. "Trouble on Madison Avenue, N.Y." *Nation*, 174:631–36, 28 June 1952.

M 359

The president of the Authors Guild of America criticizes the radio-television industry for knuckling under to the "three wartime appointees of the Federal Bureau of Investigation" who published the 213-page *Red Channels*, the most powerful among a number of blacklists used by the industry.

Miller, Nellie B. "Fighting Filth on Main Street." *Independent*, 115:411–12+, 10 October 1925.

M 360

The chairman of the literature committee of the General Federation of Women's Clubs describes some of the attempts made by her organization to halt the flow of pornographic publications. The article is a follow-up of Frank R. Kent's article, Filth on Main Street.

Miller, Neville. "Legal Aspects of the Chain Broadcasting Regulations." *Air Law Review*, 12:293–98, July 1941.
M 361

———. *Let's Keep Radio Free.* Washington, D.C., National Association of Broadcasters, 1942. 51p.
M 362
Testimony of the president of NAB before a House committee considering an amendment to the Federal Communications Act of 1934.

———. "Radio's Code of Self-Regulation." *Public Opinion Quarterly*, 3:683–88, October 1939.
M 363

———. "Reappraisal of the Federal Communications Commission's Policies Regarding Issuance of Broadcast Licenses." In *Lectures in Communications Media, Legal and Policy Problems Delivered at University of Michigan Law School. June 16–June 18, 1954.* Ann Arbor, University of Michigan Law School, 1954, pp. 206–18.
M 364
The author is chairman of the Committee on Communications, American Bar Association.

———. "Self-regulation in American Radio." *Annals of the American Academy of Political and Social Science*, 213:93–96, January 1941.
M 365
Miller cites the operation of the code of broadcasters as an "outstanding example of American industrial democracy. Through it, industry volunteers to do for itself what some would have done through legislative enactment." The code "is concerned with the development and the strengthening of wholesome and fair considerations which should govern the broadcast licensee as he determines the selection or rejection of speakers and subjects for broadcast."

———, and Paul Hutchinson. "Can U.S. Radio Regulate Itself?" *Rotarian*, 57:18–19+, July 1940.
M 366
"Yes!" says Neville Miller, president, National Association of Broadcasters. "Not only *can* radio in the United States regulate itself—it *must*—in its own and the public's interest. What is more, it has already shown that it can keep its own vast house and yard in order, by adopting and *adhering* to the voluntary but exacting code of its own trade association, the National Association of Broadcasters." "No!" says Paul Hutchinson, managing editor, *Christian Century*. He believes there is no such thing as self-regulation in the broadcasting industry. In order to correct the weaknesses in our present system, he would like to see "the establishment of competition in the form of at least

two alternative systems, one supported by the Government and one endowed by public-spirited foundations."

Miller, Paul V. "Censorship in Japan." *Commonweal*, 46:35–38, 25 April 1947.
M 367
Criticism of the censorship policy of the American occupation authorities in Japan as too strict, placing the Japanese theater, dance halls, radio, and the mails under close surveillance. Needless antagonisms are being aroused by unwise policies.

Miller, Robert C. "News Censorship in Korea." *Nieman Reports*, 6(3):3–6, July 1952.
M 368
"Our critics are right. We are not giving them the true facts about Korea, we haven't been for the past sixteen months and there will be little improvement in the war coverage unless radical changes are made in the military censorship policy."

Miller, Susan. *City Council Executive Sessions.* Columbia, Mo., Freedom of Information Center, School of Journalism, University of Missouri, 1964. 4p. (Publication no. 118)
M 369
Report on the use of "executive sessions" as a device to keep council proceedings from the public.

Miller, Vernon K. "Defamation in Newspaper Cases." *Loyola Law Review*, 4:25–49, June 1947.
M 370

Millett, Fred B. "The Vigilantes." *Bulletin*, American Association of University Professors, 40:47–60, Spring 1954. (Reprinted in Edwin Black and Harry P. Kerr, *American Issues*, New York, Harcourt, Brace & World, 1961, pp. 178–84)
M 371
Lists some contemporary examples of censorship in television, motion pictures, and literature, and gives evidence why he believes "(1) censorship in the field of literature and the other arts is usually stupid, and always unintelligent, (2) the censorship of literature is invariably self-defeating, (3) the censorship of literature is undemocratic."

Milner, Lucille B. "Freedom of Speech in Wartime." *New Republic*, 103:713–15, 25 November 1940.
M 372
Historical review of constitutional rights in World War I.

———, and Groff Conklin. "Wartime Censorship in the United States." *Harper's Magazine*, 180:187–95, January 1940. (Reprinted in Summers, *Wartime Censorship*, pp. 76–85)
M 373
A review of censorship experience during

World War I, with predictions "that censorship in a coming war will be more complete, more drastic, and even less concerned with the constitutional rights of freedom of speech and press than was that of the last war." The predictions proved to be wrong.

Milner, Michael. *Sex on Celluloid.* New York, Macfadden-Bartell, 1964. 224p.
M 374
A veteran of the movie industry writes a detailed account of the treatment of sex in the movies—the pornographic film racket, the experimental and impressionistic films, the "nudies," and the feature films from Hollywood and abroad. He covers in detail the subject of sex as substance and content in the different movie forms, considering the story and the performer (nudity, premarital and extramarital sex, prostitution, perversion, incest, abortion, rape, and obscene language). Chapter 4 deals with regulating sex on the screen—self-regulation, unorganized public regulation, organized public regulation (including the Legion of Decency and the Film Estimate Board of National Organizations), and official regulation. A brief description is given of movie censorship abroad—England, Italy, Ireland, West Germany, France, Canada, Mexico, Australia, Africa, and Pakistan. The appendix includes the text of the Film Production Code and a table of standards of public regulation of movies in certain American cities.

Miloradovitch, G. A. "Boston Shocks Moscow." *Bookman*, 72:266–69, November 1930.
M 375
The author as a child in Moscow had a New England governess who objected to their reading Oscar Wilde's *Lady Windermere's Fan* and substituted *Little Women.* His mother was shocked by one of the passages in the latter work and insisted that the governess return to reading Oscar Wilde.

Milton, George F. "Can Minds Be Closed by Statute?" *World's Work*, 50:323–28, July 1925.
M 376
An article on the background of Tennessee's evolution trial.

———. "Freedom of the Press." In American Society of Newspaper Editors, *Proceedings of the Annual Meeting, 1937.* Washington, D.C., ASNE, 1937, pp. 59–68.
M 377
The editor of the Chattanooga *News* discusses the antipress gag bill before the Tennessee General Assembly.

Milton, John. *Areopagitica; A Speech of Mr. John Milton For the Liberty of Unlicenc'd Printing, To the Parliament of England . . .* London, 1644. 40p. Later editions include: James Thomson (1780),

T. H. White (1819), John W. Hales (1866), Edward Arber (1868), R. C. Jebb (1872), Henry Morley (1886), James R. Lowell (Grolier Club, 1890), H. B. Cotterill (1904), Eragny Press (1904), Doves Press (1907), and William Haller (1927). A facsimile edition was published in London by Noel Douglas, 1927. Early editions are listed in T. H. White's edition (London, R. Hunter, 1819) which also reprints prefaces to earlier editions. Of those editions still in print Cottrell's (Macmillan, St. Martin's Press) has been recommended for the general reader.

M 378

The most perfect literary expression on freedom of the press and the most widely quoted work on the subject. Milton wrote *Areopagitica* as a classic unspoken oration in protest of Parliament's re-establishment of press censorship. It appeared without the name of the printer, in defiance of the Parliamentary order of 14 June 1643. Milton defends freedom of the press as essential to the life and progress of the nation. There should be no prior licensing and no punishment after publication save on legally proved charges of libel or blasphemy. He views censorship as an unholy product of the Inquisition and introduces almost all of the arguments against censorship employed, generally less eloquently, by later writers: Censorship is a barrier to learning. No man can be sure he has discovered the truth until he has examined all points of view and is free to make his own choice. A strong nation requires unity, not artificially imposed from above, but the result of a blend of individual differences. Without freedom of expression there can be no progress. No man is wise enough to serve as censor. Truth will defeat falsehood when the two are left free. No one is infallible. Censorship is an insult to the mind of the free Englishman. Milton's arguments stopped short of a complete libertarian view, for he would exempt two categories of thought: popish ideas and impious works that are offenses against faith or manners. Despite the popularity of the work today, Milton's pamphlet attracted little attention at the time of publication except in learned circles. It was less effective than the tracts of contemporary but less erudite writers such as Lilburne and Blount. Charles Blount quoted *Areopagitica* in his *A Just Vindication . . .* (1679) and *Reasons Humbly Offered . . .* (1693) and the work was paraphrased by Mirabeau in his tract, *Sur la Liberté de la Presse*, 1788. *Areopagitica* was reprinted for the first time in 1738 to protest the licensing of the stage.

————. *Areopagitica: A Speech to the Parliament of England for the Liberty of Unlicensed Printing, by John Milton; with Prefatory Remarks, Copious Notes, and Excursive Illustrations, by T. Holt White, Esq.*

To which is subjoined A Tract Sur la Liberté de la Presse, imité de l'Anglois de Milton par Le Comte de Mirabeau. London, Printed for R. Hunter . . . , 1819. 311 p. **M 379**

In addition to the 1644 text, there are prefatory remarks by White, a preface by James Thomson, observations on the invention of printing, a reprinting of the preface to the 1772 edition, a list of editions of *Areopagitica*, commendatory testimonials, a "glossarial index," and the Mirabeau adaptation of 1788.

Mims, Sam. "No One Has Burned Any Books." *American Mercury*, 78:17–22, April 1954. **M 380**

Attack on teachers and others concerned with "book burning," and a defense of the Congressional committee and its raids of the shelves of U.S. Information Centers abroad.

Minattur, Joseph. *Freedom of the Press in India. Constitutional Provisions and their Application.* The Hague, Martinus Nijhoff, 1961. 136 p. **M 381**

"This study is intended to present to the reader the main provisions of law affecting freedom of the press in India. It is especially concerned with examining how far freedom of the press obtains in free India."

Miner, Worthington. "The Terrible Toll of Taboos." *Television*, 18:42–47, March 1961. **M 382**

The effect of taboos and censorship on television. "When all searching into politics, religion, and sex are removed—when every 'damn' and 'hell' is gone—when every Italian is no longer a 'wop' and every Negro is no longer a 'nigger'—when every gangster is renamed Adams or Bartlett, and every dentist is an incipient Schweitzer, when, indeed, every advertiser and account executive smiles—what is left? . . . Synthetic hogwash and violence!"

Minow, Newton N. *Equal Time; The Private Broadcaster and the Public Interest.* Edited by Lawrence Laurent. New York, Atheneum, 1964. 316 p. **M 383**

A collection of speeches and writings by the chairman of the Federal Communications Commission under the Kennedy administration. Beginning with Mr. Minow's celebrated "vast wasteland" speech in 1961 which triggered a national dialogue over the proper role of television in American society, the speeches include comments on the effects of editorializing; a proposal that would give the broadcaster not the advertiser the final word on program content; and an outlining of the various evils in the industry that have been damaging to the public interest. In an introductory essay Mr. Minow suggests methods of improvement in political broadcasting which will extend equal opportunity to the worthwhile but poor candidate.

————, and Lawrence Laurent. "Is There No Way Out of This Madness." *TV Guide*, 13(5):4–9, 30 January 1965. **M 384**

The authors call for new legislation that will give broadcasters the same kind of freedom now enjoyed by the newspaper press.

Mintz, Joseph D. "Liabilities of the Extra-Legal Censor." *Buffalo Law Review*, 5:328–33, Spring 1956. **M 385**

An examination of the liability of censorship groups which attempt to suppress literature through means other than the courts or mere persuasion by the exercise of free speech. The author considers the areas of property or trade damage, injunction, and declaratory judgment.

"The *Miracle* Decision." *Commonweal*, 56:235–36, 13 June 1952. **M 386**

"By refusing to allow the wise distinctions between civil and religious power to be obscured, by speaking boldly for freedom of ideas on the screen, and questioning local prior censorship of this medium, the Supreme Court has rendered an historic service to the cause of both civil and religious liberty."

"*Miracle* on 58th Street." *Harper's Magazine*, 202:106–8, April 1951. **M 387**

A review of the controversy over the film, *The Miracle*, the most recent censorship being the withdrawal of approval for public showing by the New York State Education Department. Censorship of the film, the author believes, has reached the point of absurdity.

Mirams, Gordon. "Drop That Gun!" *Quarterly of Film, Radio and Television*, 6:1–19, Fall 1951. **M 388**

Interim results of a comprehensive survey of motion picture content on which the author (chief government censor and registrar of films in New Zealand) worked. He compares violence in American films with that in foreign films.

[Mist, Nathaniel]. *A Collection of Miscellany Letters Selected out of Mist's Weekly Journal.* London, 1722. 2 vols. **M 389**

The preface discusses Mist's frequent persecution for publication of objectionable pieces in his *Weekly Journal*. His first arrest was in 1717 for printing libels against the government. In 1721 he was summoned before the House of Commons for printing "a false, malicious, scandalous, infamous and traitorous libel." When he refused to answer questions put to him, including requests for names of his contributors, he was committed to Newgate prison. In 1728 no less than 22 persons were arrested for publication of the *Journal* of 24 August. They included authors, publishers, printers, and even some members of their households—maids and children. Daniel Defoe, a friend and contributor to the *Weekly Journal*, helped Mist assemble this collection of letters while the latter was in prison.

"Mr. Foote and the Blasphemy Laws." *Spectator*, 56:1121–22, 1 September 1883. **M 390**

The writer takes the position that Christianity

should not be protected by civil law but its professors should be protected from insulting parodies on their beliefs as a matter of maintaining the public peace. He refers to the blasphemy trials of George W. Foote.

"Mr. Hall Caine Banned." *English Review*, 15:310, September 1913.   **M 391**
A discussion of the censorship of *The Woman Thou Gavest Me*.

"Mr. Roosevelt's Libel Suit." *Current Opinion*, 55:5–6, July 1913.   **M 392**
Newspaper comment on Theodore Roosevelt's libel suit against George A. Newett, proprietor of *Iron Ore*.

"Mr. Roosevelt's Vindication." *Literary Digest*, 46:1321–22, 14 June 1913.   **M 393**
Newspaper comments on the winning of the slander case by Theodore Roosevelt against Mr. Newett, who had accused him of being drunk. Includes the retraction read by Mr. Newett.

"Mr. Wells and the *Daily Mail*." *New Statesman*, 18:250–51, 13 December 1917.
                                                              M 394
An account of the London *Daily Mail*'s censorship of dispatches from its New York correspondent, H. G. Wells, because of his criticism of France.

Mitchell, John J., *et al. Five Bases for "Executive Privilege."* Columbia, Mo., Freedom of Information Center, School of Journalism, University of Missouri, 1958. 6 p. (Publication no. 10)   **M 395**
The five bases cited by the executive branch of government in withholding information from Congress and the public are: three statutes, an executive order, and a Presidential letter. They are reprinted here with comments by John J. Mitchell, Clark R. Mollenhoff, and Harold L. Cross.

Mitford, Jessica. "The Disease that Dr. Kildare Couldn't Cure." *McCall's*, 92(12):102–3+, September 1965.   **M 396**
An account of the National Broadcasting Company's ban of a two-part television show ("Dr. Kildare" and "Mr. Novak") dealing with venereal diseases. The question arose as to whether this was fit and appropriate as entertainment. The program had been recommended by the National Education Association, and the U.S. Surgeon General's Office, and was to have been filmed by MGM to help combat the alarming increase in the VD rate among high school students. Despite appeals from leaders in the field of education, religion, and public health, the network refused to permit the program.

Mitgang, Herbert. *Freedom to See: The Khrushchev Broadcast and Its Meaning to Television.* New York, Fund for the Republic, 1958. 17 p.   **M 397**

On 2 June 1957, the Columbia Broadcasting System telecast an interview with Nikita Khrushchev. The network thought it was performing a public service, but a good many people, including President Eisenhower, did not appear to agree. At the request of the Fund for the Republic, Herbert Mitgang of the *New York Times* was commissioned to study and report on the incident. Mitgang concluded that the interview raised the fundamental question "Does American television in its role as a news gatherer and broadcaster, have the same freedom as the American newspaper?" He argues that television should have the same rights as the press under the First Amendment.

Mitra, S. M. "The Press in India, 1780–1908." *Nineteenth Century*, 64:186–206, August 1908.   **M 398**
"The relations between the Government and the Press have developed . . . since 1780 from a system of arbitrary, not to say despotic, treatment, through periods of Press censorship, restriction, liberty, temporary restraint renewed freedom, a Vernacular Press Act for four years, legislation (twice) by amendments of the ordinary law against sedition." In 1908 a new press Act was passed, armed not against sedition but against incitement to murder, revolt, and secret diabolical schemes. It remains to be seen whether the new act is sufficient to maintain peace and order.

Mitter, Vishnu. *Law of Defamation and Malicious Prosecution, Civil and Criminal.* 4th ed. Allahabad, India, Law Book Co., 1965. 316 p.   **M 399**

[Mobley, Carlton]. *A Liberal Contempt Decision.* Columbia, Mo., Freedom of Information Center, School of Journalism, University of Missouri, 1961. 3 p. (Publication no. 47)   **M 400**
Text of the decision of the Georgia Supreme Court in reversing a contempt charge against the Atlanta *Journal* and the Atlanta *Constitution* (*Atlanta Newspapers, Inc. v. The State of Georgia*). Publication of the arrest record of a defendant in a criminal trial was found legal inasmuch as the account appeared after the jury had been impaneled and the trial was underway.

Mock, James R. *Censorship, 1917.* Princeton, N.J., Princeton University Press, 1941. 250 p.   **M 401**
An historical study of censorship during World War I, showing the extent to which the First Amendment was set aside by government action, and the extent to which wartime repressive measures were carried over into an era of peace for the sake of stifling political, economic, and social reform. Edward L. Bernays reviews the book in the 7 March 1942 issue of *Saturday Review of Literature*.

———, and Cedric Larson. "Activities of the Mexico Section of the Creel Committee, 1917–1918." *Journalism Quar-*

terly, 16:136–50, June 1939.   **M 402**
A study of one aspect of government censorship during World War I, the result of a year's research in the National Archives.

———. *Words that Won the War; the Story of the Committee on Public Information, 1917–1919.* Princeton, N.J., Princeton University Press, 1939. 372 p.   **M 403**
A study of government censorship in the United States during World War I, as seen in the work of the so-called Creel Committee. The study was prepared at the eve of World War II, as an attempt to demonstrate that "the advance of censorship power can be silent and almost unnoticed as wave follows wave of patriotic hysteria." The work is based largely on the records of the Committee that are in the National Archives.

Mock, James R., *et al.* "The Limits of Censorship: a Symposium." *Public Opinion Quarterly*, 6:3–26, Spring 1942.   **M 404**
Mock discusses the limits of censorship in a democracy, using for a base his study of World War I censorship. He recommends wartime censorship only by the government and at the source. These views are commented on by George Creel, official censor in World War I, Neville Miller, president of the National Association of Broadcasters, Professor Zechariah Chafee, Jr. of Harvard University, Professor Ralph D. Casey of University of Minnesota, and Arthur Krock of the *New York Times*.

[Mockus, Michael X.]. "At Waterbury, Conn., U.S.A., Rev. Michael Mockus, Unitarian Minister Has Been Prosecuted for Blasphemy." *Freethinker*, 4:37, 28 February 1917.   **M 405**

[———]. "Case of Michael Mockus for Blasphemy." *Outlook*, 115:111, 17 January 1917.   **M 406**
Mockus was a Unitarian minister of Detroit who was found guilty on blasphemy charges in Waterbury, Conn. The text of oral arguments at the retrial are given in Schroeder, *Constitutional Free Speech Defined and Defended in an Unfinished Argument in a Case of Blasphemy*.

Modder, Montagu F. "The Censorship of Literature." *Peabody Journal of Education*, 7:281–84, March 1930.   **M 407**
"Since it is the function of literature to *present life as a whole*, it should be the endeavor of the teacher and student to study not only the 'obscene' but also the beautiful." While it is necessary to include the seamy side of life in literature, constant emphasis on the sordid is unhealthy.

"Modern Ideals and the Liberty of the Press." *Dublin Review*, 81:191–222, July 1877.   **M 408**

A philosophical discussion of the difference in meaning of a free press as seen by "liberals" and Catholics. Where there is a "true synthesis" of belief in a society, Catholic doctrine, according to the author, states that liberty of expression is not allowable; it is an evil and a snare. The law should interfere for the sake of protecting the true synthesis.

A Modest Proposal for the Prohibition of Speech, Humbly Offered to the Consideration of Parliament. Dublin, Printed for Peter Wilson, 1743. 16 p.   **M 409**
The anonymous author argues that a prohibition of speech would save all from saying foolish things or giving offense to wise men obliged to hear, would silence defamation and scandal, would abolish shocking oaths and curses, would save innocent young creatures from infamy and ruin resulting from beguiling tongues, would save public revenues used to silence critics of the administration, and would require people to show their intent by actions rather than words.

Moeller, Leslie G. "How Free Is The Press?" *Vital Speeches*, 23:750–54, 1 October 1957. (Also in Black and Kerr, *American Issues*, New York, Harcourt, Brace, 1961, pp. 163–68)   **M 410**
The director of a Journalism school discusses the proper and judicious use of freedom. "Right of access" is the greatest problem area today in the realm of freedom of the press. There are three groups involved: the "Policy Definers" or "Policy Controllers" (mostly in government), the "Active Defenders" (from the press, law, education, and the ACLU), and the "Usually Passive Beneficiaries." These average citizens, according to various polls which the author cites, are too often indifferent to the issue of freedom of the press. He suggests ways in which the media can bring about an improvement in the climate of freedom.

[Moens, Herman M. B.]. "Injustice to a Holland Scholar by the Department of Justice." *Medico-Legal Journal*, 37:77–80, September 1920.   **M 411**
An account of the prosecution of Professor Moens, his conviction, appeal, and final acquittal on a charge of obscenity in photographic studies of nudes showing race mixture, intended for an anthropological study. The fear-psychology of the war, according to Theodore A. Schroeder, induced groundless suspicious that Moens was a German spy.

[———]. "Three Black Bands." *Medical Review of Reviews*, 25:719–23, December 1920.   **M 412**
Reference to his own prosecution for having in his possession a series of anthropological photographs of nudes, and an account of the support he received from scientists and artists.

The September issue of the *Medical Review* reproduced some of the pictures with black bands across the genitalia.

Mohr, J. W. *Report on a Study of Obscene and Indecent Literature.* [Toronto?], The Author, 1958. 102 p. mimeo.   **M 413**
A report prepared for the Committee on Obscenity and Indecent Literature of the Attorney General's Department, Province of Ontario, Canada.

Moley, Raymond. *The Hays Office.* Indianapolis, Bobbs-Merrill, 1945. 266 p.   **M 414**
A eulogistic account of the Motion Picture Producers and Distributors of America under the direction of Will Hays and the efforts of this organization to promote self-regulation in the movie industry. Part II, Evaluation of Self-Regulation, deals largely with the operation of the Production Code.

———. "Strange Roads to Freedom." *Newsweek*, 14:64, 20 November 1939.   **M 415**
The author objects to the kind of free press proposed by Harold Ickes and Max Lerner, who charge a sinister monopoly of the channels and sources of opinion. What these men want, Moley writes, is not a completely free press or radio, but "merely control over the instruments of public education."

Molina G, M. I. *La Libertad de Prensa en los Estados Unidos de Norte América, La Prensa en el Mundo Socialista.* Caracas, Venezuela, [Editorial Cantaclaro]. 1961. 47 p.   **M 416**

Mollenhoff, Clark R. "The Answer to Secrecy." *Nieman Reports*, 8(1):3–7, January 1954.   **M 417**
"Follow through—that is the newspaper answer to secrecy in government." A talk presented before the Iowa Radio Press Association at the State University of Iowa, September 1953.

———. "Congressional Inquiry on Government Secrecy Aids the Press' Cause." *Quill*, 45(8):15–16, 20, August 1956.   **M 418**
What the Moss Committee of the U.S. House of Representatives has done to ease executive news barriers.

———. *Deadly Dilemma: Defense and Democracy.* Tucson, University of Arizona Press, 1962. 12 p. (The John Peter Zenger Award for Freedom of the Press, number 7)   **M 419**
The 1961 recipient of the award was Pulitzer Prize-winning Washington correspondent of the Cowles Publications. His lecture explores the problems of national security versus the rights and responsibilities of a free press.

———. "Is the Press Alert to a Dangerous Precedent on Executive Secrecy?" *Quill*, 43(12):9–10, 37–38, December 1955.   **M 420**
A criticism of the current use of the Eisenhower-Wilson letter, issued during the Army-McCarthy hearings, to keep certain executive matters confidential.

———. "Managing the News." *Nieman Reports*, 16(4):3–6, December 1962.   **M 421**
The Harold L. Cross Memorial Lecture to the National Editorial Association in St. Louis, 16 November 1962.

———. "News 'Weaponry' and McNamara's Military Muzzle." *Quill*, 50(12): 8–9, December 1962.   **M 422**
A criticism of the control of information by the Defense Department during the Cuban missile crisis. Arthur Sylvester, Assistant Secretary of Defense, answers the criticism: "No distortion, no deception, no manipulation of news."

———. "Secrecy in Washington." *Atlantic Monthly*, 204:54–59, July 1959.   **M 423**
The author examines the "executive privilege" doctrine as proclaimed by the Eisenhower administration and the withholding of information from Congress and the press by the federal, executive, and independent agencies under this doctrine. The basic question is: "Can the President or his department heads arbitrarily override a specific law of the Congress which requires the production of records of 'financial transactions and methods of business' in all agencies?"

———. "Shield of Secrecy." *Nieman Reports*, 14(1):20–25, January 1960. (Reprinted in Black and Kerr, *American Issues*, New York, Harcourt, Brace 1961, pp. 168–78)   **M 424**
In the 8th annual Lovejoy Lecture, Colby College, December 1959, Mollenhoff discusses the use of executive privilege to withhold information from the Congress and the public. He describes the use of official news handouts, unavailable officials, favoritism, and the misuse of security classification as forming the shield of secrecy.

———. *Washington Cover-Up.* New York, Doubleday, 1962. 239 p. (Reprinted in Popular Library, 206 p.)   **M 425**
How increasing cover-up in the executive branch of the federal government has prevented Congress, the press, and the people from learning about incompetency, laxity, bungling, and even fraud. Although a practice that is as old as government, beginning with the Truman administration the executive branch has become increasingly highhanded in withholding information that might be critical of the party in power. Under the Eisenhower administration the practice of "executive

privilege" became a constitutional right to withhold government records. While President Kennedy has spoken against secrecy in government, the practice of "news management" continues.

[Molz, Kathleen]. "More Than Lip Service." *Wilson Library Bulletin*, 39: 537–40, March 1965.　**M 426**
A summary of the proceedings of the conference sponsored by the American Library Association's Intellectual Freedom Committee, 23–24 January, Washington, D.C., with the theme, More than Lip Service: Backstopping the Library Bill of Rights. The reviewer compares the general scope and nature of this conference with the one sponsored by the Committee in 1952, noting an increase in number and magnitude of censorship incidents over the past decade, the group nature of the censor, and the "inverse" censorship pressure to add books, particularly of the right persuasion.

Monaghan, Frank. "Benjamin Harris, Printer, Bookseller, and the First American Journalist." *Colophon*, 1932. Pt. xii, 8 unnumbered pages.　**M 427**
Account of the publishing career of Benjamin Harris, convicted in England in 1680 for publishing a newsbook without a license. Ten years later he published the first American newspaper, which was suppressed after the first issue. Includes checklist of Harris' American printing.

———. *Heritage of Freedom; the History & Significance of the Basic Documents of American Liberty*. [*Presenting and Explaining the Documents on the Freedom Train*]. Princeton, N.J., Princeton University Press, 1947. 150 p. (Published in cooperation with the American Heritage Foundation)　**M 428**
Includes three items relating to John Peter Zenger; a copy of Benjamin Franklin's defense of the freedom of the press; a copy of John Wilkes's no. 45 issue of *North Briton*; an account of Elijah Lovejoy's martyrdom; a first edition of George Hay's essay (1799); a first edition of Milton's *Areopagitica*; a polygraph copy of Jefferson's letter to Thomas Seymour declaring that an honest press is "Equally the Friend of Science and Civil Liberty"; and Jefferson's letterpress copy of a letter to Edward Carrington with the famous quotation, "Were it left to me to decide whether we should have a government without newspapers, or newspapers without a government I should not hesitate to prefer the latter."

Mondschein, Morris. "Constitutional Law: Motion Picture Censorship." *Cornell Law Quarterly*, 44:411–19, Spring 1959.　**M 429**
Regarding *Kingsley International Pictures Corp. v. Regents of the University of New York* (1958), in a case involving the film, *Lady Chatterley's Lover*.

Monroe, Bill. "The Electronic Press: How Free?" *Quill*, 49(11):13, 15, November 1961.　**M 430**
Increased government regulation of broadcasting in the area of entertainment, as proposed, may have serious effect upon the atmosphere of news-gathering and reporting. Broadcast journalism "has more to offer the American people in freedom than the government regulators have to offer them by methods of official persuasion."

Monroe, James O. *Freedom of Speech in Illinois in 1935. An Address in the Illinois State Senate on May 18, 1935, on a Bill to Repeal the Seditious Utterance Act*. Collinsville, Ill., The Author, 1935. 40 p.　**M 431**
Senator Monroe, a Collinsville newspaper publisher, urges the repeal of Illinois's criminal syndicalism law, passed in 1919.

Monroe, Margaret E. "The Sleeping Dog vs. the Stolen Horse." *Wisconsin Library Bulletin*, 60:170–72, May–June 1964.　**M 432**
Deals with the general public and its understanding of the principles of intellectual freedom. "The sleeping dog must be awakened so that he can meet the thief at the barn door."

Montagu, Ivor G. *The Political Censorship of Films*. London, Gollancz, 1929. 44 p.　**M 433**
In this pamphlet on the conditions for exhibiting films, a member of Parliament discusses the equivocal position on film censorship which involves Acts of Parliament, and action of Scotland Yard and local authorities. "Unofficial" suppression of films is more stringent than official banning and prevents the public showing of many serious educational works that are deemed "controversial."

Montague, Charles E. *Disenchantment*. London, Chatto and Windus, 1928. 228 p.　**M 434**
Information on military censorship in World War I by a British journalist who served as a military censor.

———. "Would Truth or Lies Cost More?" *Nineteenth Century*, 90:27–34, July 1921.　**M 435**
The author explores the proposal that in the next war "we might do well to draw a wide, opaque veil of false news over the whole face of our country," noting cynically that "one morality has to be practiced in peace and another in war."

Montague, Gilbert H. "Censorship of Motion Pictures before the Supreme Court." *Survey*, 34:82–83, 24 April 1915.　**M 436**
"Mr. Montague here puts the case of those who believe that so far as censorship of 'movie'

films is needed at all, it should be official. Their hands have been strengthened by three decisions of the Supreme Court which he quotes." In February 1915 the Supreme Court in three unanimous decisions sustained the Ohio and Kansas statutes creating official censorship of motion pictures before exhibition. (236 U.S. 230, 247, 248.)

Montague, Henry B. "Pornography." In International Association of Chiefs of Police, *Police Yearbook*. St. Louis, 1963, pp. 35–38.　**M 437**

Montague, Peter. "Controversial Books." *Catholic Library World*, 36:166–68, November 1964.　**M 438**
Brother Montague observes that books are not so much good or bad in themselves but as they affect particular readers. We get out of a book what we bring to it. "The real problem is not banning controversial books, but finding a way of allowing them to be read by the more mature students, and yet not giving them to the younger or less mature student."

[Montague, Richard]. "Proceedings in Parliament against Richard Montague for Publishing a Factious and Seditious Book, 1625." In Howell, *State Trials*, vol. 2, pp. 1257 ff.　**M 439**
Chaplain Montague's pamphlet, *An Appeal to Caesar*, was considered an offense to the Archbishop of Canterbury and an encouragement to Popery. The House of Commons recommended punishment, but in the concern with more important trials, no action was taken.

Montcalm, Henry, *pseud*. "How Free Is Canada's Air?" *Nation*, 174:253, 15 March 1952.　**M 440**
An anonymous Canadian journalist deals with recent attacks on the Canadian Broadcasting Corporation for so-called antireligious broadcasts and the question whether freedom of speech is possible on the air. The row began over six lectures by the British physicist, Fred Hoyle.

Montgomery, James. "The Menace of Hollywood." *Studies* (Ireland) 31:420–28, December 1942.　**M 441**
The man who was Ireland's film censor from 1923 to 1940 discusses the cinema as "an ever increasing danger to the manners and morals of our people." He is particularly concerned with the harmful effect on children, despite the inconclusive result of studies of effect. While Ireland's Censorship of Films Act of 1923 (it installed a "sin-filter") provided for issuing limited certificates for "adults only" films, the provision was not used for fear it would advertise films to adolescents. Instead, all films were drastically cut down to render them harmless

to children. The cinema production industry, especially in America, has fallen into evil hands and its product is shameful. The author refers to the good work of the Production Code and the Legion of Decency. But this has not been enough to stop the production of rubbish. When the Legion tried to restrain eroticism, sadism took its place. He calls for an Irish Film Company to provide a renaissance of true cinema art.

Montgomery, Reid H. *Publication Laws of South Carolina.* Columbia, S.C., School of Journalism, University of South Carolina, [1964]. 38 p. **M 442**

Montvéran, Tournachon de. *De la Législation anglaise sur le Libelle, la Presse et les Journaux. . . .* Paris, Alexis Eymery, 1817. 120 p. **M 443**

Mood, Robert G. "Let 'em Read Trash." *Elementary English*, 34:444–50, November 1957. (Condensed in *Education Digest*, February 1958) **M 444**
The author discusses recent tendencies to exercise censorship over children's books. He examines the dangers inherent in censorship as contrasted with the "worse dangers" claimed by certain groups if children are permitted to read objectionable books.

Moody, Howard. "Toward a New Definition of Obscenity." *Christianity and Crisis*, 24:284–88, 25 January 1965. **M 445**
"Should we not as Christians raise a new standard of 'obscenity' not obsessed with sex and vulgar language, but defined rather as that material which has as its dominant theme and purpose the debasement and depreciation of human beings—their worth and their dignity."

————. "Which of These Pictures Is Obscene?" *Pageant*, 21:112–18, September 1965. **M 446**

Moon, Eric. "The Benefit of the Doubt." *Wilson Library Bulletin*, 39:663–67, 704, April 1965. **M 447**
The editor of *Library Journal* discusses three kinds of censorship: (1) that emanating from legal or governmental sources, (2) that stemming from action of individuals or groups "who wish either to limit the access of others to materials with which they do not agree, or to enforce their own opinions and materials to the forefront at the expense of others," and (3) self-censorship and censorship by librarians, "perhaps the worst kind." Writing largely of the third category, Moon observes that too often library "book selection is one of fear and timidity, of deliberate avoidance of those books which dare to challenge the

accepted or which hint of the possibility of repercussions." While librarians may risk popularity by honest book selection, they will gain respect. Even where there is a book selection policy, it is often expressed in such generalities to be useful only as a crutch. Moon questions the practice of librarians catering to majority interests to the neglect of minorities. He also questions the double standard in which the librarian is more circumspect and rigorous in selection of books addressed to a serious or controversial theme than those that are "trite and mediocre and harmless." In all cases where responsible opinions differ, Moon concludes, "it is the book which should be given the benefit of every possible doubt."

————. "Coalinga to Philadelphia." *Library Journal*, 40:2980–81, July 1965. **M 448**
In light of the decision of the Coalinga, Calif., District Library to classify controversial books (controversial and restricted, controversial but open shelf, open shelf), Editor Moon considers the restrictive policies of libraries (including Philadelphia Free Library) and the position of the American Library Association's statement on "labeling."

————. "Defensive about 'The Defenders.'" *Library Journal*, 88:2210, 1 June 1963. Discussion 88:2580, July 1963. **M 449**
Editor Moon criticizes an editorial in the *ALA Bulletin* that protested the 30 March teleplay, "The Defenders," as damaging to the librarians' image. The editorial, Moon charges, "makes no attempt to discuss whether the program succeeded or failed in its central purpose or whether the 'total' effect of the program was for good or ill." A professional association should not react this way to a single portrayal of a character. In the July 1963 issue Sidney L. Jackson defends the *ALA Bulletin* editorial.

————. "In Place of Panacea." *NCLA Odds and Books Ends*, 43:3–8, Fall 1963. **M 450**
A talk on censorship given before the Nassau County Library Association by the editor of *Library Journal*. Since we can't apply consistent standards in book selection in both categories, "it would be better to reverse the double standard . . . that is, apply more rigorous judgment to the trite and mediocre and harmless than to the book which deals with a challenging idea or subject."

————. "Integration and Censorship, Two Thorny Issues at ALA's Midwinter Conference." *Library Journal*, 87:904–8+, 1 March 1962. **M 451**

[————]. "More Than Lip Service; A Report on a Special Two-Day Conference Sponsored by ALA's Committee on Intellectual Freedom." *Library Journal*, 90:1067–72, 1 March 1965. **M 452**

A report on a conference "to discuss infringement of intellectual freedom and censorship problems in libraries and to discuss ways and means of implementing the Library Bill of Rights," and, specifically, "to work out steps librarians may take when confronted with censorship problems." Papers appear in the *ALA Bulletin*, June 1965, and as a separate publication of the proceedings of the conference under the title *Freedom of Inquiry*. Each paper is listed under the author in this bibliography. A summary of the conference also appears in the *Antiquarian Bookman*, 8 February 1965.

————. "New York Letter: Courage and Cowardice." *Library World*, 63:293–96, May 1962. **M 453**
A review of recent American censorship. While regretting incidents of library censorship, "one can feel nothing but pride for the record of the profession as a body, at least as represented by the American Library Association." He reviews the ALA's long record on intellectual freedom.

[————]. "'Problem' Fiction." *Library Journal*, 87:484–96, 1 February 1962. **M 454**
"How many libraries provide home for unorthodox ladies like *Lolita* or *Lady Chatterley*? Is the *Tropic of Cancer* too hot to handle? Will you find *The Carpetbaggers* or the sex-surveyors of *The Chapman Report* on the open shelves, under the counter, or in the stacks? A recent *Library Journal* survey, which queried public libraries on their book selection in the area of contemporary controversial fiction, provides some of the answers."

Moore, Charles C. *Behind the Bars; 31498.* Lexington, Ky., Blue Grass Printing Co., 1899. 303 p. **M 455**
Moore was the editor of the free-thought magazine, *Blue Grass Blade*, who served numerous terms in prison for his outspoken attacks on the Bible and theology. This autobiography was written while in prison for blasphemous articles appearing in his paper. In 1900, in the case of *United States v. Moore*, the District Court D., Kentucky, ruled that a publication to be prohibited from the mails must be "lewd and lascivious" as well as "obscene" and that it could not be banned because it offends the religious sentiments of the majority of the people by attacking the doctrine of the immaculate conception of Christ, even though worded in coarse or obscene language. The publication must have a tendency to induce sexual immorality.

Moore, Donald P. "Chicago Censorship Ordinance Held Enforceable." *University of Illinois Law Forum*, 1954:678–84, Winter 1954 **M 456**
American Civil Liberties Union v. Chicago, 3 Ill. 2d 334, 121 N.E. 2d 585 (1954). A test case involving showing of the film, *The Miracle*. The Illinois Supreme Court upheld the Chicago ordinance, observing that the U.S. Supreme Court, in holding unconstitutional the New

York film board banning of *The Miracle* (*Burstyn v. Wilson*), reserved judgment on the validity of "a clearly drawn statute designed and applied to prevent the showing of obscene films."

Moore, Everett T. "Amazing What Turns up in a Library." *ALA Bulletin*, 56:395–96, May 1962. (Reprinted in Moore, *Issues of Freedom in American Libraries*, pp. 58–59) **M 457**

A view of Miss Cloud, the librarian in John Hersey's *The Child Buyer*, who, when questioned by Senator Skypack whether she had "dished up" any sex books to the boy, answered: "I dish up whatever a young mind wants and needs, sir."

————. "Bartlesville, and After." *ALA Bulletin*, 54:815–17, November 1960. (Reprinted in Moore, *Issues of Freedom in American Libraries*, pp. 12–13) **M 458**

A recounting of the persecution of the librarian of the Bartlesville Free Public Library, dismissed in 1950 for having in the library such journals as *The Nation* and *New Republic*.

————. "*Catcher* and *Mice*." *ALA Bulletin*, 55:227–30, March 1961. (Reprinted in Moore, *Issues of Freedom in American Libraries*, pp. 67–68, and in Marvin Laser and Norman Fruman, ed., *Studies in J. D. Salinger*, pp. 130–34) **M 459**

Opposition to having J. D. Salinger's *The Catcher in the Rye* and John Steinbeck's *Of Mice and Men* in school libraries.

————. "Censorship; and Threats of Censorship." *California Librarian*, 16:226–28+, July 1955. **M 460**

————. "Censorship in the Name of Better Relations." *ALA Bulletin*, 55:617–18, July–August 1961. (Reprinted in Moore, *Issues of Freedom in American Libraries*, pp. 69–70) **M 461**

Censorship of books because they are offensive to the National Association for the Advancement of Colored People.

————. "A City in Torment over Kazantzakis." *ALA Bulletin*, 57:305–6, April 1963. (Reprinted, with author's note, in Moore, *Issues of Freedom in American Libraries*, pp. 62–63) **M 462**

Attacks on libraries in southern California for having on their shelves *The Last Temptation of Christ* by Nikos Kazantzakis.

————. "D. H. Lawrence and the 'Censor-Morons.'" *ALA Bulletin*, 54:731–32, October 1960. (Reprinted in Moore, *Issues of Freedom in American Libraries*, pp. 60–61) **M 463**

An up-to-date summary of the difficulties encountered in the publication of *Lady Chatterley's Lover*.

————. "A Dangerous Way of Life." *Illinois Libraries*, 46:165–74, March 1964. **M 464**

In an address before the Illinois Library Association, the author discusses the anti-intellectualism in America that has resulted in fear and suspicion of ideas, of books that convey them, and of librarians that select the books. He recounts some of the attacks against books and the efforts of American librarianship to withstand the attacks. "We are committed to a way of life, therefore, that is dangerous." But there are "other priceless elements that make our way of life well worth the hazards involved . . . We have been given the happy and solemn task of seeing to it that every man shall have a chance to read without fear of the meddling censor and the obstructive hater of books and ideas."

————. "For Reference Only." *ALA Bulletin*, 55:19–20, January 1961. (Reprinted in Moore, *Issues of Freedom in American Libraries*, pp. 19–20) **M 465**

Controversy in Santa Barbara, Calif., over whether the magazine, *New World Review*, should remain on the open shelves of the public library. The case was resolved by treating the book as a reference work, for use only when requested.

————. "Friends and 'True Friends' in New York." *ALA Bulletin*, 57:387–88, May 1963. (Reprinted in Moore, *Issues of Freedom in American Libraries*, pp. 30–31 **M 466**

"Seldom, if ever, has so direct an attack on the Library Bill of Rights been recorded, as the one made by the 'True Friends of the Library' of New City, New York (a few miles north of New York City) in the midst of the turmoil in that town over book selection policies of the Free Library."

————. "The *Huckleberry Finn* Matter: Some Facts Overlooked." *ALA Bulletin*, 56:629–30, July–August 1962. (Reprinted in Moore, *Issues of Freedom in American Libraries*, pp. 71–72) **M 467**

A correction of a *New York Times* story that *Huckleberry Finn* had been dropped from the approved textbook list of the New York City schools. It was only the "adapted" and expurgated edition that was dropped and, the author notes, the school authorities are to be congratulated.

————. "The Innocent Librarians." *ALA Bulletin*, 55:861–62, November 1961. (Reprinted in Moore, *Issues of Freedom in American Libraries*, pp. 37–38) **M 468**

Comments on Rosalie M. Gordon's accusations that librarians show a decided left-wing bias in their book selection and are being "used" by the liberal review media.

————. *Issues of Freedom in American Libraries*. Chicago, American Library Association, 1964. 80 p. **M 469**

"All of the pieces in this books were first published in the 'Intellectual Freedom' department of the *ALA Bulletin*, the official journal of the American Library Association. They are now reissued in this form to provide a record and an interpretation of a number of problems concerning freedom which were faced by librarians in the United States mainly during the period 1960–63, and, in a few instances, in earlier years." The articles are grouped under the following headings which suggest their scope: The Nature of the Problem, Charges of Subversion, On Defining Obscenity, Concerning Our Children, and Who May Use the Library?

————. "Justice Douglas on 'Freedom of the Mind.'" *ALA Bulletin*, 56:985–86, December 1962. (Reprinted in Moore, *Issues of Freedom in American Libraries*, pp. 21–23) **M 470**

A review of Justice William O. Douglas' pamphlet, published for the American Library Association.

————. "L. A.'s *Tropic* Decision and the Geography of Community Standards." *ALA Bulletin*, 56:301–3, April 1962. (Reprinted in Moore, *Issues of Freedom in American Libraries*, pp. 50–52) **M 471**

An account of the spirited testimony for both prosecution and defense in the case of the *Tropic of Cancer*, convicted in the Los Angeles Municipal Court. Moore comments on the crazy-quilt pattern of southern California bookstores and libraries stocking or not stocking the book.

————. "Learning Without Fear." *PNLA Quarterly*, 28:6–14, October 1963. **M 472**

A look at the "wave of fear that has overwhelmed so many people in this country and has made them wary of almost all kinds of reading—particularly of reading by others." Similar to the author's article in *Illinois Libraries*, March 1964.

————. "Librarians and the 'Decency Committees.'" *ALA Bulletin*, 54:571–73, July–August 1960. (Reprinted in Moore, *Issues of Freedom in American Libraries*, pp. 41–42) **M 473**

The campaign to curb distribution of "smut literature" by various decency groups is a potential threat to libraries because in many cases such groups have gone on to demand restriction of book selection in libraries.

————. "A Library Burns in the Los Angeles Riot." *ALA Bulletin*, 59:983–86, December 1965. **M 474**

An account of the burning of the Willowbrook branch of the Los Angeles County Public Library during the race riot of August 1965.

————. "Massachusetts Provides First Major *Tropic* Decision." *ALA Bulletin*, 56:785–86, October 1962. (Reprinted, with author's note, in Moore, *Issues of Freedom in American Libraries*, pp. 55–57) **M 475**

The Supreme Judicial Court of Massachusetts ruled that the book was entitled to the protection of the First Amendment, and that it could not be held obscene in the constitutional sense.

————. "The Nature of Our Problem: There Have Been Some Changes." *ALA Bulletin*, 57:488–92, June 1963. (Reprinted in Moore, *Issues of Freedom in American Libraries*, pp. 7–9) **M 476**

How the library profession came to change its emphasis from defender against immorality and indecency in literature, to defender of readers against the censor himself.

————. "Objections to the Foreign Policy Association: A Familiar Pattern." *ALA Bulletin*, 55:684–86, September 1961. (Reprinted in Moore, *Issues of Freedom in American Libraries*, pp. 16–18) **M 477**

The American Legion's objection to holding of the Great Decisions programs, sponsored by the Foreign Policy Association, in the Miami Public Library, recalls earlier attacks on the Association in the 1930's.

————. "Open to All—Except the Censor." *California Librarian*, 25:153–60, 183–84, July 1964. **M 478**

A review of current efforts at censorship in California, viewed as a manifestation of the fear of intellectualism that exists throughout America.

————. "Raising Hell with the Legionnaires." *ALA Bulletin*, 57:222–26, March 1963. (Reprinted, with author's note, in Moore, *Issues of Freedom in American Libraries*, pp. 26–29) **M 479**

Account of attacks by the American Legion on the treasurer of the Ringwood (N.J.) Library Association for alleged Communist affiliations, and on a social science teacher in Paradise, Calif., for brainwashing students in a unit on American government. The teacher was accused, among other things, of requiring students "to read salacious literature" and with "teaching sex." The Board of Education voted their confidence in the teacher.

————. "A Rationale for Bookburners: A Further Word from Ray Bradbury."

ALA Bulletin, 55:403–4, May 1961. (Reprinted in Moore, *Issues of Freedom in American Libraries*, pp. 39–40) **M 480**

Comments on Ray Bradbury's novel, *Fahrenheit 451*, written during the panic and wholesale book burning of the McCarthy era, and Mr. Bradbury's comment on the continued validity of his attack on tyranny over the mind.

————. "Screening the Propaganda Once Again." *ALA Bulletin*, 57:17–19, January 1963. (Reprinted, with author's note, in Moore, *Issues of Freedom in American Libraries*, pp. 24–25) **M 481**

"Many librarians feel that the federal government turned back the clock last fall by writing a 'mail-screening' program into the statutes books for the first time." The screening was aimed at censorship of "communist political propaganda." Public, college, and university libraries are exempt from the screening.

————. "Still No Decision in Albany." *ALA Bulletin*, 57:111–16, February 1963. (Reprinted, with author's note, in Moore, *Issues of Freedom in American Libraries*, pp. 77–80) **M 482**

Relates to the campaign against racial segregation in the Carnegie Public Library, Albany, Ga.

————. "The 'Study-In' as Reported in Jackson, Mississippi." *ALA Bulletin*, 55:497–99, June 1961. (Reprinted, with author's note, in Moore, *Issues of Freedom in American Libraries*, pp. 75–76) **M 483**

The episode of Mississippi's first "study-in" at the city's main public library, which is for whites only.

————. "Sustaining the Atmosphere of Caution." *ALA Bulletin*, 55:100–104, February 1961. (Reprinted in Moore, *Issues of Freedom in American Libraries*, pp. 64–66) **M 484**

An account of the activities of the Daughters of the American Revolution and America's Future, Inc., in passing on the fitness of school and college textbooks.

————. "*Tropic* Controversy: Not Yet Concluded." *ALA Bulletin*, 56:492–94, June 1962. (Reprinted in Moore, *Issues of Freedom in American Libraries*, pp. 53–54) **M 485**

Ruling on the literary merit or lack of it in *Tropic of Cancer*, including Chicago Judge Samuel B. Epstein's ruling that the book was not obscene.

————. "*Tropic of Cancer* (Second Phase)." *ALA Bulletin*, 56:81–84, February 1962. (Reprinted in Moore, *Issues of Freedom in American Libraries*, pp. 47–49) **M 486**

Efforts to suppress the first American edition of Henry Miller's book.

————. "*Tropic of Cancer*; the First Three Months." *ALA Bulletin*, 55:779–80, October 1961. (Reprinted in Moore, *Issues of Freedom in American Libraries*, pp. 45–46) **M 487**

Legal action against Miller's book, published in the United States by Grove Press 27 years after its first publication in Paris.

————. "Vexation on the Right." *ALA Bulletin*, 54:433–34, June 1960. (Reprinted in Moore, *Issues of Freedom in American Libraries*, pp. 14–15) **M 488**

An account of complaints from conservatives that librarians are discriminating against their periodicals.

————. "What Harm Will Befall?" *ALA Bulletin*, 56:213, March 1962. (Reprinted with author's note on the *Fanny Hill* case in Moore, *Issues of Freedom in American Libraries*, pp. 43–44) **M 489**

A brief discussion of the difference of opinion on the effect of reading an obscene book, a discussion prompted by the reading of Paul and Schwartz, *Federal Censorship*.

————. "Why Do the Rightists Rage?" *ALA Bulletin*, 56:26–31, January 1962. (Reprinted in Moore, *Issues of Freedom in American Libraries*, pp. 32–36) **M 490**

Article tells of pressure brought by rightists on public librarians to change their policies of book selection in order to emphasize rightist literature. Includes a list of authors and some of their recent articles which are used by rightists to espouse their cause.

Moore, George. "Apologia pro Scriptis Meis." *Fortnightly Review*, 112(n.s.): 529–44, October 1922. **M 491**

Moore discusses his controversy with the firms of Mudie and Smith and their refusal to circulate his books because of the unconventional writing. "Conventions there must be . . . but man's instincts are always invading the moral law, and may loosen the conventions of prose narrative still further."

————. *Avowals*. New York, Boni & Liveright, 1926. 308 p. **M 492**

In chapter 3 Moore reports his conversations with the young American correspondent Balderson, which deal with literary censorship in England. Moore describes his experiences with the English lending libraries over his books *Esther Waters* and *A Mummer's Wife*, because of their requirement that sordid stories must have moral endings. In their conversation Balderson and Moore present a mock enactment of the trial of Henry Vizetelly for publishing the works of Zola, with Moore's sleeping black cat representing the judge. Balderson's account of the conversation appears in the *Fortnightly Review* for October 1917.

———. *Literature at Nurse or Circulating Morals.* London, Vizetelly, 1885. 22p.

M 493

Strictures upon the selection of books for circulation at Mudie's Library.

Moore, Harry T. *The Intelligent Heart; the Story of D. H. Lawrence.* New York, Farrar, Straus, and Young, 1954. 486p. (Also in Penguin edition, 1960; Grove Press edition, 1962)

M 494

In this biography of Lawrence there are many references to the banning and bowdlerizing of his work, with particular attention given to the publishing history of *Lady Chatterley's Lover* and Lawrence's views on obscenity.

Moore, John R. *Daniel Defoe; Citizen of the Modern World.* Chicago, University of Chicago Press, 1958. 409p.

M 495

A biography of one of England's most prolific satirists and political pamphleteers. For his *The Shortest Way With the Dissenters* (1703), a satire recommending death to dissenters, Defoe was pilloried, fined, and spent 18 months in prison. The pamphlet was burned by the common hangman. At Newgate prison Defoe continued his writing. He experienced numerous arrests and frequent imprisonment throughout his life, largely for his attacks on the Tories and the High Church.

———. "'Robin Hog' Stephens: Messenger of the Press." *Papers of the Bibliographical Society of America*, 50:381–87, 1956.

M 496

One of the most disliked of the government spies who reported to the authorities the existence of printing that was unlicensed or otherwise objectionable.

"A Moral Pestilence." *Nation*, 129:767–68, 25 December 1929.

M 497

While defending the political rights of Catholics in this country, this editorial is critical of doctrines of the Catholic Church which claim to the Church the right to prescribe in detail, through the *Index of Prohibited Books*, what may or may not be read. The editor calls upon liberal Catholics in this country to make known their sentiments in the hope of having some ultimate influence upon the official doctrines of the Church.

"Morality Commission's Action in Compiling Lists of 'Obscene' Paperback Books and Threatening to Recommend Prosecution of Distributors Held Not to Infringe Constitutional Guarantee of Free Speech." *University of Pennsylvania Law Review*, 110:1162–65, June 1962.

M 498

Relates to the Rhode Island Commission to Encourage Morality in Youth that had prepared a list of books it considered objectionable for sale to minors. *Bantam Books, Inc., v. Sullivan*, 176 A. 2d 393 (R. I. 1961). The decision was later reversed by the U.S. Supreme Court.

"The Morality Crisis." *Newsweek*, 65(16):98, 101–2, 19 April 1965.

M 499

The Motion Picture Production Association, faced with the influx of racy foreign films, the production of films by independents, and the apparent public acceptance of more sex and nudity in films, has announced the intention of a massive overhaul of its code provisions. Commentary on such frank and permissive productions as *Kiss Me, Stupid, The Pawnbroker*, and *The Amorous Adventures of Moll Flanders*.

Mordell, Albert, ed. *Notorious Literary Attacks.* New York, Boni & Liveright, 1926. 255p.

M 500

A collection of contemporary reviews of such works as *Jane Eyre, The Scarlet Letter, Leaves of Grass*, and the poetry of Swinburne, revealing the hostility to frank expression, particularly in the realm of sex.

"More Condemned Books." *Literary Digest*, 59:27, 12 October 1918.

M 501

Books on the "Index" of the U.S. Army during World War I.

"More of the Same: Massachusetts Supreme Court and Dreiser's *An American Tragedy*." *Outlook*, 155:214, 11 June 1930.

M 502

The highest court of Massachusetts upheld the state's obscenity law by finding Dreiser's work in violation.

Morecroft, J. H. "What about Libel by Radio?" *Radio Broadcast*, 9:118–19, June 1926.

M 503

Morel, E. D. *The Persecution of E. D. Morel. The Story of his Trial and Imprisonment.* Glasgow, [1917?]. 11p.

M 504

Morel was sentenced to six months in prison for sending a copy of his book, *Africa and the Peace of Europe*, to Romain Rolland, then residing in Switzerland, for which he was technically guilty of a felony in wartime. Introduction by Sir D. M. Stevenson.

[———]. *Rex v. E. D. Morel. Trial at Bow Street.* London, Published by the Union of Democratic Control, printed by the National Labour Press, [1917?]. 30p.

M 505

A verbatim report of the court proceedings at Bow Street, on 1 and 4 September 1917, before Mr. E. W. Garrett. A photograph of Morel appears on the cover.

Morgan, Charles. "Censorship of Books." *Review of Reviews* (London), 82:56–57,

November 1932; discussion, 83:87, January 1933; 83:84, February 1933.

M 506

The author of *The Fountain* disagrees with a proposal of the Morality Council of London that books in England be placed under a censorship similar to that of films. The public is already adequately protected from pornography and obscenity under existing laws. Any further censorship of books would endanger ideas in politics and religion as well as in the realm of love. Do not pass a general censorship in order to meet a particular case; do not restrict literature at its source in order to restrict your daughter's reading.

Morgan, Charles, Jr. "The Freedom to Read and Racial Problems." *ALA Bulletin*, 59:484–90, June 1965.

M 507

"From the Negro revolution has come a new literature and new expressions of old sensitivity. Public school curricula come under attack; books are viewed for their racelessness or for their dedication to southern ways; and sex and race combine to arouse the ire of the censors." The author, a Birmingham lawyer and director of the Southern regional office of the American Civil Liberties Union, describes the efforts at racial censorship in the South—"the white southerner frantically clinging to the last straws of his youth"—and efforts of The Movement in the North to "wipe clean the slate of literature" by censoring those works which the emancipated Negro finds offensive.

Morgan, Edward P. "Censorship." In his *Clearing the Air.* Washington, D.C., Robert B. Luce, 1963, pp. 155–62.

M 508

Includes two radio broadcast essays dealing with muzzling the military and one essay on academic freedom.

Morgan, James A. *The Law of Literature . . .* New York, James Cockcroft, 1875. 2 vols.

M 509

Volume one contains sections on the libel laws as they relate to literature—newspapers, periodicals, and books. The appendix contains text of American, English, French, and German copyright laws then in force.

Morgan, Murray. "Books They Don't Want You to Read." *Cosmopolitan*, 64:130–34, April 1950.

M 510

U.S. Customs censorship and the work of Huntington Cairns, chief literary advisor.

Morgan, Robert S. *Section 315 of the Communications Act of 1934: An Overview of the Development of Political Broadcast Regulation.* Boston, Boston University, 1960. 321p. (Unpublished Master's thesis)

M 511

Morgenthau, Hans J. "The Democratic Dilemma." *Yale Political*, 3(1):15, 27–28, Autumn 1963. **M 512**
"Can a democratic nation suppress antidemocratic ideologies and still maintain its democratic integrity? My answer is in the negative." The suppression of antidemocratic minorities as a legitimate act of democratic self-defense tends to degenerate into the illegitimate suppression of all dissent.

Morris, J. Conway. "Literary Censorship and the Law." *Quarterly Review*, 252:18–27, July 1929. **M 513**
Prompted by the reading of Ernst and Seagle's book, *To the Pure*, the author comments on sex censorship in England. He considers the historical development of the law and interpretation by the courts. He shows that the Obscene Publications Act of 1857 was not intended to deal with works of literary importance and that the Hicklin decision, now the basis for many actions, is difficult to reconcile with the basic act. Parliamentary action may be necessary.

Morris, James. "Reflections on the Chatterley Case." *New York Times Magazine*, 4 December 1960, p. 24. **M 514**

Morris, Jill. "The New Look In Nudes." *U.S. Camera*, 26(7):58–61, 72–77, July 1963. **M 515**
"America's growing sexual and social freedom provides new opportunities for nude photography . . . Nudity today is hardly a thing to be shocked at. Proof of this lies in the increasing degree in the last 10 years to which nudity has entered all of our communications media—movies, theater, magazines, advertising, and television."

Morris, Joe Alex. "How Your News is Censored." *Saturday Evening Post*, 213(27):18–19, 64–66, 4 January 1941. **M 516**
How the censors of Europe work to prevent foreign correspondents from telling all the facts. Efforts by American correspondents to evade the censor have been ingenious but not too successful. A comparison of wartime censorship techniques used by the British, Germans, and Russians.

Morris, Richard B. "Freedom of Expression: Its Past and Its Future." *New York History*, 31:115–35, April 1950. **M 517**
Incidents in the history of freedom of the press in America, beginning with the Zenger trial.

[Morris, Robert]. *A Letter to Sir Richard Aston, Knt., one of the judges of His Majesty's Court of King's Bench, Containing a reply to his scandalous abuse, and some Thoughts on the modern doctrine of Libels*. 2d ed. London, George Pearch, 1770. 68 p. **M 518**
An English lawyer and secretary of the Society for Supporters of the Bill of Rights criticizes Judge Mansfield for denying the jury's right to accept truth as a defense in a libel trial as "the most pernicious and abominable doctrine."

Morrow, Marco. "Is the Press Free?" *Quill*, 18(9):10–13, September 1930. **M 519**
Pros and cons on press freedom. The press has more freedom than it knows how to use and has the courage to use. The press is only as free as the public demands.

Morrow, William L. *Some Constitutional Aspects of the Communications Act of 1934*. Washington, D.C., Georgetown University, 1938. 91 p. (Ph. D. dissertation) **M 520**
Limited to consideration of emergency powers, including wartime controls.

Morse, Arthur D. "Who's Trying to Ruin Our Schools?" *McCall's*, 78:26–27+, September 1951. **M 521**
An account of the attack on the public schools, including social studies textbooks, made by Allen Zoll (National Council for American Education), Lucille Cardin Crain (*Educational Reviewer*), and others concerned with "subversion."

Morse, J. M. "*Forever Amber*; Defendant at Trial in Suffolk County Superior Court, Boston." *New Republic*, 116:39–40, 6 January 1947. **M 522**
The novel was ultimately cleared of obscenity charges by the Massachusetts Supreme Judicial Court.

Morse, Sidney. *The Siege of University City; the Dreyfus Case of America*. St. Louis, University City Publishing Co., 1912. 772 p. **M 523**
"The arbitrary discretion exercised by the Postmaster-General under existing postal laws hangs like a veritable sword of Damocles over the periodical publishers of the United States." A lengthy and spirited defense of Edward Gardner Lewis, St. Louis promoter-publisher, whose two periodicals, *Woman's Magazine* and *Woman's Farm Journal*, were denied second-class mailing privileges by the U.S. Post Office on grounds of the questionable business practices of the publisher. One chapter is devoted to a history of the second-class postage act of 1879 and its administration.

Morse, Wayne. "Censorship and the Public's Right to Know." *Yale Political*, 3(1):11, 26–27, Autumn 1963. **M 524**
"Freedom of the press, according to Senator Morse, implies an often ignored dependent freedom of access to information. Without such access, he contends that neither Congress nor the people can fulfill their responsibilities of legislating and voting."

Mortimer, John. "The Lord Chamberlain." *Censorship*, 4:3–8, Autumn 1965. **M 525**
"The censorship of plays in England [by the Lord Chamberlain] is performed in a manner that is so ludicrous and outdated that its abolition is only a matter of time."

Morton, James F., Jr. *Do You Want Free Speech?* Home, Wash., The Author, [1902?]. 16 p. **M 526**
The author, active in the Free Speech League, charges a "corrupt religio-political clique" with attempting to suppress all thought in America that they consider blasphemous, immoral, or seditious. He views Comstockism as a wedge to control all deviant points of view. "Comstock is the greatest enemy of purity in the United States, as Philip the Second of Spain was in reality the deadliest foe of Christianity, and as those who suppress the utterance of Anarchist opinions are the worst traitors to the government they profess to adore." In addition to attacks on "Comstockism" the author attacks the suppression of freedom by American imperialists in Cuba, Puerto Rico, and the Philippines, the persecution of anarchist expression, and the crushing of progressive papers in the interest of postal economy—the latter which he terms "Maddenism" after Edwin C. Madden, third assistant Postmaster General.

————. *The Rights of Periodicals. The Most Dangerous of Assassins is he who Strikes at the Liberty of the Press*. New York, The Author, 1905. 32 p. (Reprinted from the *Public*, 26 August 1905) **M 527**
The author charges Post Office bureaucracy with misuse of its powers to classify second-class matter, allegedly for economy reasons, but actually in the interest of suppressing "personal advertising."

————. "Origin and Working of the Comstock Law." *Birth Control Review*, 3:5–7, May 1919. **M 528**
Use of the Comstock law in suppression of birth control information.

————. "Our Foolish Obscenity Laws." *Case and Comment*, 23:23–27, June 1916. (Reprinted in *Publishers' Weekly*, 8 July 1916) **M 529**
The obscenity statutes place "the liberty of every citizen in the hands of a jury who have no criterion imposed on them beyond that of their own prejudices." He calls the obscenity laws outrageous and would do away with all of them, keeping instead a pornography law, "exactly and specifically defined so as to allow no room for quibbling . . . All beyond this is undemocratic, against the constitutional right of freedom of expression."

Mosby, Thomas S. "The Anglo-Saxon Crime." *Arena*, 36:373–75, October 1906. **M 530**

Opposes censorship by "contempt of court" proceedings.

Moskin, Morton. "Inadequacy of Present Tests as to What Constitutes Obscene Literature." *Cornell Law Quarterly*, 34:442–47, Spring 1949. **M 531**

Notes on *Doubleday v. New York*, 335 U.S. 848, involving Edmund Wilson's *Memoirs of Hecate County*. The courts have failed to hit upon a reasonably predictable test for obscenity.

Moss, John E. *Local Battlers Needed for FOI Rounds*. Columbia, Mo., Freedom of Information Center, School of Journalism, University of Missouri, 1958. 3 p. (Publication no. 4) **M 532**

Excerpts from a speech by the chairman of the House of Representatives Subcommittee on Government Information, discussing the campaign of California editors for the passage of public record bills. "The battle for freedom of information begins on the local level."

———. *What You Don't Know Will Hurt You*. Tucson, University of Arizona Press, 1959. 15 p. (The John Peter Zenger Award for Freedom of the Press, 1958) **M 533**

The 1958 award went to Congressman John E. Moss in recognition of his work as chairman of the Subcommittee on Government Information of the Government Operations Committee and his efforts to remove restrictions on government information.

Mother Earth. New York, 1906–18. Monthly. **M 534**

This anarchist journal was founded by Emma Goldman and for many years was edited by her. It frequently espoused the cause of freedom of the press and speech for radicals and in the area of sex expression and birth control. The July 1915 issue reports the trial and imprisonment of Emma Goldman and Alexander Berkman. The April 1916 issue was devoted to birth control, centered around the prosecution of Emma Goldman in New York for distribution of birth control leaflets. *Mother Earth* and many other radical journals that ran into difficulty with the censor are listed in Walter Goldwater, *Radical Periodicals in America, 1890–1950*, Yale University Press, 1964.

Motion Picture Association of America. *An Advertising Code for Motion Pictures and Regulations for Its Administration*. New York, The Association, 1950. 4 p. **M 535**

The Advertising Code was first adopted in 1930; amended in 1947 and in 1950. The purpose is "to apply to motion picture advertising, publicity and exploitation, within their range, the high principles which the Production Code applies to the content of motion pictures."

———. *Censorship Classification of Films in Britain*. New York, The Association, 1961. 4 p. mimeo. **M 536**

A report on the work of the British Board of Film Censors and its system of film classification that began in 1913. The Association considers the system unsatisfactory.

———. *The Free Screen; Statement of the Motion Picture Association of America before a Committee of the United States Congress*. Washington, D.C., The Association, 1960. 16 p. (U.S. House of Representatives. Committee on Post Office and Civil Service. Subcommittee on Postal Operations. Hearings, 2 February 1960) **M 537**

Four representatives of the Association testify before the Subcommittee that was making a study of obscene and pornographic materials, defending self-regulation of the movies under the Production and Advertising Codes.

———. *Memorandum: Motion Picture Classification*. New York, The Association, 1960. 13 p. mimeo. **M 538**

A collection of statements and quotations opposed to government classification of films as a form of censorship. The system of government classification used in Great Britain and many other countries has not taken root in the United States, the report asserts, because "classification in this country has been for long the devoted, jealous and democratic privilege of citizens … groups and publications as opposed to government agencies. This is right and proper for a heterogeneous society such as ours."

———. *The Motion Picture Production Code*. New York, The Association, 1956. 12 p. (Earlier editions are reproduced in the appendix of Moley's *Hays Office* and in Inglis' *Freedom of the Movies*) **M 539**

An industry-adopted moral code to regulate content of motion pictures, first adopted by the so-called "Hays Office" in 1930 and revised from time to time. The general principles state that no picture shall be produced which will lower the moral standards of those who see it; that correct standards of life, subject only to the requirements of drama and entertainment, shall be presented; and that law—divine, natural, or human—shall not be ridiculed. The Code deals with specific applications with respect to crime, brutality, sex, vulgarity, obscenity, blasphemy and profanity, costumes, religion, national feelings, and cruelty to animals.

———. *Self-Regulation in the Motion Picture Industry*. New York, The Association, 1938. 31 p. **M 540**

Report by Will H. Hays, president. Hays assumed active direction of the Motion Picture Producers and Distributors of America in 1922. At the request of the new "czar", Eric Johnston, the official name of the regulatory

organization was changed to the Motion Picture Association of America in 1945.

———. *A Wolf in Sheep's Clothing: Motion Picture Classification by State Censors*. New York, The Association, [1960?]. 4 p. **M 541**

A statement in opposition to film classification by any government agency.

"Motion Picture Censorship—A Constitutional Dilemma." *Maryland Law Review*, 14:284–98, Summer 1954. **M 542**

Notes on *Superior Films, Inc. v. Department of Education of the State of Ohio and Film Censorship Division* and *Commercial Pictures Corp. v. Regents of the University of State of New York*, 346 U.S. 587 (1954).

"Motion Picture Censorship: The Aftermath of Burstyn v. Wilson." *Northwestern University Law Review*, 49:390–99, July–August 1954. **M 543**

"In the United States the status of film censorship still remains unsettled after the two most recent Supreme Court decisions."

Motion Picture Theater Owners of America. *Case Against Censorship: A Brief Compendium of Facts, Figures and Arguments Showing the Follies and Failures of Censorship*. New York, MPTOA, 1921. 8 p. **M 544**

"Motion Pictures and the First Amendment." *Yale Law Journal*, 60:696–719, April 1951. **M 545**

A documented review of court decisions on movie censorship. The author believes that there will be a "temptation to use the present highly discretionary powers of administrative regulations" as movies attempt to present controversial subjects. The First Amendment protection will then become more important.

"Motion Pictures: Safety and Decency." *Outlook*, 103:103, 18 January 1913. **M 546**

Comments on an ordinance before the New York Board of Aldermen providing safeguards as to health conditions, fire risks, etc., in the operation of movies. An amendment provided that no licenses would be issued except to movies approved by censors appointed by the Board of Education. Mayor Gaynor vetoed the bill on the ground that no censorship should be established by law to control what may or may not be printed or published. The editor calls for a separation of the two issues—safety and censorship.

Mott, Frank L. *American Journalism; a History, 1690–1960*. 3d ed. New York, Macmillan, 1962. 901 p. **M 547**

There are frequent references in this work to episodes involving freedom of the press. Chapter 8, covering the period 1783 to 1801, describes the persecution of editors and publishers under the Sedition Act. In chapter 18, Attitudes Toward the Press, Mott discusses the attacks on the abolitionist press, including the murder of Lovejoy; in chapter 36, he gives an account of censorship during World War II. There are references throughout to cases of newspaper libel

————. *Jefferson and the Press*. Baton Rouge, Louisiana State University Press, 1943. 65 p. (Journalism Monographs no. 2)
M 548
Mott has examined Jefferson's philosophy of the press, particularly the controversy over the apparent contradictions in ideas appearing in letters to friends over a period of years. He finds no real inconsistency. Despite all that Jefferson suffered from a hostile press, he held to his basic principle of a free press. "Jefferson stands out as the foremost exponent in history of a free press in any system of popular government. No other man has stated that principle so well."

————. ed. *Journalism in Wartime*. Washington, D.C., American Council on Public Affairs, 1943. 216 p.
M 549
A collection of 32 articles dealing with problems of the press in World War II. Four articles deal with censorship: The American Way by Byron Price, director of the Office of Censorship; The Use and Abuse of Restraints by Palmer Hoyt, publisher of the *Portland Oregonian*; The Battle for News by Erwin D. Canham, managing editor of the *Christian Science Monitor*; and Dispatches Going Abroad by Raymond Clapper, columnist for the Scripps-Howard papers.

————, and Ralph D. Casey, eds. *Interpretations of Journalism: A Book of Readings*. New York, Crofts, 1937. 534 p.
M 550
The section on Freedom of the Press includes the following documents: John Milton's *Areopagitica*, Andrew Hamilton's *Address to the Jury in the Zenger Case*, Alexander Hamilton's and Melancton Smith's *Debate on a Constitutional Provision for Liberty of the Press*, Thomas Erskine's *Defense of Thomas Paine*, several Thomas Jefferson letters showing his theory of the unfettered press, an excerpt from James Madison's *The Danger of Tampering with Liberty of the Press*, Alexander Hamilton's *The Right to Criticize Public Men* (from the case of the *People v. Harry Croswell*), Alexis de Tocqueville's *Liberty of the Press in the United States* (from his *Democracy in America*), Clarence K. Streit's *The Problem of False News* (a report to the League of Nations), William Allen White's editorial *To an Anxious Friend*, and Charles Evans Hughes's *Decision in the Minnesota "Gag-Law" Case*. There is also a section on newspaper ethics.

"Movie Censorship." *Life*, 21:79–82, 84, 28 October 1946.
M 551
Illustrations of scenes banned from movies under the Motion Picture Production Code.

"Movie Censorship Standards under the First Amendment." *De Paul Law Review*, 9: 44–51, Autumn–Winter 1959.
M 552

"Movies and Censorship." In Carroll C. Arnold, *et al.*, *The Speaker's Source Book; an Anthology, Handbook, and Glossary*. Chicago, Scott, Foresman, 1961, pp. 121–28. (C.B.S. "Small World" Telecast, 10 April 1960)
M 553
Guests on Edward R. Murrow's discussion program, "Small World," were Monsignor John J. McClafferty of Catholic University of America and formerly secretary of the Legion of Decency; Deborah Kerr, actress; and Otto Preminger, producer-director, whose movie, *The Moon Is Blue*, was condemned by the Legion of Decency. The program, filmed and edited by Murrow and Fred W. Friendly, was a unique four-way transoceanic conversation, with participants located in Washington, D.C., Switzerland, Rome, and Hong Kong.

"The Movies on the Water Wagon." *Literary Digest*, 29:28–29, 7 August 1926.
M 554
"Anything making light of the Prohibition Law and of law in general is voluntarily to be excluded from the movies," a ruling adopted at a meeting of the Motion Picture Producers and Distributors of America. Most of the press commended the action.

"Moving Pictures and Child Welfare." *School and Society*, 7:55–57, 12 June 1918. (Reprinted from *The Child*, London)
M 555
A review of the report of the cinema commission appointed by the National Council of Public Morals (Great Britain) which recommended state censorship.

Mowrer, Paul S. "War and Journalism." In Pierce Butler, *ed.*, *Books and Libraries in Wartime*. Chicago, University of Chicago Press, 1945, pp. 67–87.
M 556
A veteran foreign correspondent discusses conflicts and compromises of war reporting and censorship. In general he approves of the conduct of the system of voluntary censorship on the home front, but is critical of the operation of military censorship in battle zones abroad. He makes two criticisms of the handling of war news by American newspapers—a tendency to minimize failure and exaggerate success, and a tendency to give disproportionate credit for war effort to our own troops.

[Moxon, Edward]. "Trial of Edward Moxon for publishing a blasphemous libel before Lord Denman, L.C.J., and a special jury in the Court of Queen's Bench at Westminster, June 23, 1841." In Macdonell, *Report of State Trials*, vol. 3, pp. 693–722.
M 557
A brief account of this case against Moxon

for publication of Shelley's *Queen Mab* is given in Harold G. Merriam, *Edward Moxon*, New York, Columbia University Press, 1939, pp. 101–3.

Mozley, E. N. "The Government, Religious Liberty, and the BBC." *Hibbert Journal*, 44:125–31, January 1946.
M 558
"A very sharp criticism of the B.B.C.'s policy of denying time for religious broadcasts by those (e.g., Unitarians and Friends) whose doctrines are not in the mainstream of the Christian tradition."

————. "Religious Liberty, and the B.B.C." *Hibbert Journal*, 40:38–48, October 1941.
M 559
Article protests the broadcasting on B.B.C. of religious programs limited to the interests of orthodox Christianity and confined to the Christian tradition.

Muddiman, Joseph G. "Benjamin Harris, the First American Journalist." *Notes & Queries*, 163:129–33, 147–50, 166–70, 273, (1932).
M 560
The publisher of the first newspaper in what is now the United States. The paper was suppressed after the first issue.

[————]. *A History of English Journalism to the Foundation of the Gazette, by J. B. Williams, pseud. . . .* London, Longmans, Green, 1908. 293 p.
M 561
"Much of the harsh criticism directed against them [seventeenth-century periodicals] by contemporaries was due to defective intelligence, the corrupt system of licensing, or the even more shameful official press. The liberty of the press was closely connected with liberty in religious matters, and it is noteworthy that in both, toleration appeared simultaneously. Freedom from the tutelage of an official licenser was not obtained until the year 1695, and before the attainment of that freedom this book ends (1665)."

Mueller, Gerhard O. W. "Problems Posed by Publicity to Crime and Criminal Proceedings." *University of Pennsylvania Law Review*, 110:1–26, November 1961.
M 562
The article attempts to present "the issues at stake and the American efforts to reduce the ferocity of conflict between the right to know, so important for intelligent popular government . . . and the right to be free from criminal depredations, which demands a certain amount of secret strategy against crime, an atmosphere of calm judicial determination . . . and possibly even restraint in providing the public with information about crime."

[Muggleton, Lodowick]. "A Modest Account of the Wicked Life of that grand Impostor, Lodowick Muggleton: . . .

1676." In *Harleian Miscellany*, vol. 1, pp. 610–12. **M 563**

[———]. *True Narrative of the Proceedings at the Sessions-House in the Old Bayley, at a Sessions There Held on Wednesday the 17th of January 1676/7. Giving a Full Account of the True Tryal and Sentence of Lodowick Muggleton for Blasphemous Words and Books*. London, 1676/7. Edition printed in London by T. Fever in 1808. 24p. **M 564**

In 1652 Muggleton and his cousin John Reeve, members of a band of religious fanatics who considered themselves vested with prophetic gifts and divine powers, published a work entitled *Transcendent Spiritual Treatise*. For this they were charged with blasphemy in denying the Trinity and were committed to prison for six months. Muggleton argued during his trial that a temporal court had no jurisdiction over a religious matter. In 1677 he was again brought to trial for a book, *Neck of the Quakers Broken*. He was convicted, fined, pilloried, and his books ordered burned over his head. He spent six months in jail in default of the fine. Schroeder, in his *Constitutional Free Speech*, summarizes the Muggleton case and cites further contemporary references both favorable and unfavorable to the accused.

Muir, Thomas. *An Account of the Trial of Thomas Muir, Younger, of Huntershill, before the High Court of Justiciary, at Edinburgh. On the 30th and 31st Days of August, 1793, for Seditious Practices . . .* Edinburgh, printed for William Creech, 1793. 135p. **M 565**

Muir, a supporter of the French Revolution and leader in British constitutional reform, was charged with circulating the works of Thomas Paine. An able lawyer, Muir conducted his own defense, but Lord Braxfield, presiding as Lord Chief Clerk, recommended conviction and the jury dutifully obliged. Muir was sentenced to fourteen years' transportation to Botany Bay. This miscarriage of justice became a *cause célèbre* on both sides of the Atlantic. The case of Muir and that of Thomas F. Palmer were brought before the House of Commons, but in vain. The events that followed were no less than melodramatic. American sympathizers outfitted a privateer which rescued Muir from Botany Bay, shortly after his arrival. The ship was wrecked on the coast of California and after a hectic voyage in a Spanish warship, a sea battle with the British in which he was wounded, Muir finally arrived in Paris where he was given a hero's welcome. Muir died in France in 1799, the result of his exhausting travels. In 1837 the Town Council of Edinburgh erected a monument to Muir and the other martyrs of the Scottish sedition trials—Muir, Gerrald, Palmer, Skirving, and Margarot.

[———]. "Trial in the High Court of Justiciary for Sedition, 1793." In Howell, *State Trials*, vol. 23, pp. 117ff.; in Borrow,

Celebrated Trials, vol. 5, pp. 205–12; in Cockburn, *Examination of Trials for Sedition in Scotland*, vol. 1, pp. 144–83. **M 566**

[———]. *The Trial of Thomas Muir, Younger, of Huntershill, . . . before the High Court of Justiciary, upon Friday and Saturday the 30th and 31st days of August, 1793. On a Charge of Sedition . . . with an Elegant Portrait of Mr. Muir. To Which is Annexed an Appendix; Containing all the Papers referred to in the course of the Trial . . .* Edinburgh, Printed for and sold by Alexander Scott. [1793?]. 71p. plus 16p. **M 567**

Proceeds from the sale of this edition of the trial were, at Mr. Muir's request, to be used for the relief of poor prisoners.

Muir, Willa. *Mrs. Grundy in Scotland.* London, Routledge, 1936. 187p. **M 568**

The effect of the imaginary Mrs. Grundy, who "suspected licentiousness in everything outside the home," on the code of propriety in Victorian Scotland.

Muldoon, J. J. "Press Participation in Criminal Trials." *Chicago-Kent Law Review*, 33:338–43, September 1955. **M 569**

A review of recent court decisions involving the proper conduct of criminal trials and the freedom of the press to cover such trials.

Mullaly, Charles J. "Does It Pay Editors to Insult Catholics?" *America*, 38:436–37, 11 February 1928. **M 570**

The author describes the activity of a Catholic action group, the Washington Truth Society, that conducted a campaign of boycott against newspapers that printed false information about Catholic nuns. The group worked on advertisers, news dealers, and on other newspapers.

Mulroy, Thomas R. "Obscenity, Pornography and Censorship." *American Bar Association Journal*, 49:869–75, September 1963. **M 571**

The author examines the U.S. Supreme Court's recent pronouncements on obscenity and points out that, even if the Court is moving toward a test that would bar only "hardcore" pornography, there is still no judicially approved definition of the term.

Mumby, Frank A. *Publishing and Bookselling; a History from the Earliest Times to the Present Day.* 4th ed. London, Cape, 1956. 442p. **M 572**

This general history of the book trade contains numerous references to press restrictions, from the suppression of the Tyndale New Testament to revision of the libel laws in 1952, and includes early licensing by church and government, the Marprelate tracts, the

action of the Star Chamber against printers, the crusade of the Levellers, and L'Estrange's harsh rule as censor during the Restoration.

Mumford, L. Quincy. "Report from Cleveland." *Library Journal*, 78:788–89, 1 May 1953. **M 573**

The librarian of the Cleveland Public Library opposes a broad censorship ordinance before the Cleveland City Council.

Mundt, Karl E. "Government Control of Sources of Information." *Annals of the American Academy of Political and Social Science*, 250:26–31, March 1947. **M 574**

A Congressman describes conditions of government thought-control in Europe and urges American people to guard against any, even slight, attempt in this country. He cites as the first departure of our rule of freedom the 1942 Supreme Court ruling which permits the FCC to consider the content of radio programs as a factor in determining whether to renew a station's license.

Munford, W. A. "Public Library and the Left." *Library Association Record*, 40:74–75, February 1938. **M 575**

It is the duty of the public librarian to have representative left wing publications in the library, even though it may not always be possible to balance them by comparable right wing publications.

———. "Selection or Censorship?" *Library World*, 36:207–9, March 1934. **M 576**

"Book selection means the choice of . . . the best books. In censorship some other criterion is superimposed . . . Amateur censors must receive no quarter."

Munn, Melvin. "Dirt Is Never Clean." *Life Line*, No. 67–M, 16 June 1965. (Published script of a Washington, D.C., radio program, sponsored by Life Line Foundation) **M 577**

"In the name of modern 'culture' every art form known to our people has been invaded, to some degree, by smut merchants who thrive on ignorance, curiosity, and intellectual snobbishness. . . . Despite recent rulings of courts, including the United States Supreme Court, that give protection and comfort to some of the worst offenders of American life, the general public wants this traffic stopped."

———. "Pornography & the Pornographer." *Life Line*, No. 35, 1 December 1965. (Published script of a Washington, D.C., radio program, sponsored by Life Line Foundation) **M 578**

Comments about *Playboy*, the UNESCO

translation of *The Life of An Amorous Woman*, the publishing activity of David Zentner, Ralph Ginzburg, and Maurice Girodius.

———. "Smut Fighters." *Life Line*, No. 18-D, 6 August 1965. (Published script of a Washington, D.C., radio program, sponsored by Life Line Foundation) **M 579**

Comments on the antiobscenity campaign of the General Federation of Women's Clubs; the Washington, D.C., Conference to Combat Obscenity; action against the movie, *Kiss Me, Stupid*, by students of Aquinas High School, Augusta, Ga.; organization of a speakers' bureau against indecent literature by the Knights of Columbus, Arlington, Va.; and other efforts to fight obscenity.

Munn, Ralph. "Book Selection in the Large Public Library." In *Freedom of Communication; Proceedings of the First Conference on Intellectual Freedom . . .* Chicago, American Library Association, 1954, pp. 44–49. **M 580**

———. "Segregation of Questionable Material." In American Library Association, *Freedom of Communications, Proceedings of the First Conference on Intellectual Freedom.* Chicago, 1954, pp. 44–49. (Reprinted in Daniels, *Censorship of Books*, pp. 177–82) **M 581**

The director of Pittsburgh's Carnegie Library identifies seven types of materials relating to Russia and communism: (1) official expositions of communism by Marx, Engels and others, (2) biographies, (3) histories, (4) factual explanations of the Soviet system of government, (5) official yearbooks and statistical documents, (6) popular books dealing with the current scene, and (7) undisguised propaganda, such as the *Daily Worker*. Munn would accept all forms and make them freely available except for those items in category six that are *disguised* Russian propaganda. He would reject these (except by way of examples of propaganda) on the ground that "a book shall be honest, that it shall be what it purports to be." A discussion of this point of view follows.

Munro, W. Carroll. "Cameras Don't Lie." *Current History*, 46:37–42, August 1937. **M 582**

Newsreels of the clash between police and strikers at the gates of the Republic Steel Corporation in South Chicago were suppressed by Paramount and testimony "essential to the case of labor" withheld. The newsreels were later released.

Munroe, Pat. "Government Secrecy." *Nieman Reports*, 10(2):6–8, April 1956. **M 583**

Congress, now intent upon investigating secrecy in the executive branch of government, should put its own house in order.

Murphy, C. B. "Sex, Censorship, and the Church." *Bell* (Dublin), 2:11–30, September 1941. **M 584**

The editor charges that Irish censorship goes far beyond what is required by the canons of the Church and is "an attempt of Victorianism to survive in Ireland after the English people, including the English Catholics, had very sensibly dropped it." Furthermore, "the average Irish mind has not, and perhaps never had, a properly balanced outlook upon sex. Either it runs away from sex or it runs after it."

Murphy, Charles F. "A Seal of Approval for Comic Books." *Federal Probation*, 19(2):19–20, June 1955. **M 585**

The author is administrator of the Code Authority, Comic Magazines Association of America, Inc.

Murphy, E. F. "Value of Pornography." *Wayne Law Review*, 14:255–80, Summer 1964. **M 586**

"It is time that the venue over obscenity was withdrawn from the courts and the concern shifted to those personal levels in routine life where it belongs. The censors, the legislators, the prosecutors, the police, the judges, and all the forces of repression have had their day since 1800; and it is time another approach was tried."

Murphy, E. J. "Blasphemy." *Canadian Criminal Cases*, 48:1–22, 1927. **M 587**

The Crown prosecutor in the blasphemy case of *Rex v. Sterry* reviews the English common law on blasphemy, the two earlier Canadian cases, *Rex v. Pelletier* (1900) and *Rex v. Kinler* (1925), as well as the current case of Ernest Sterry, publisher of the *Christian Enquirer*, Toronto. Sterry was convicted and sentenced to 60 days in jail; the Supreme Court of Ontario confirmed the conviction.

Murphy, Lawrence W. "Thomas Maule: The Neglected Quaker." *Journalism Quarterly*, 29:171–74, Spring 1952. **M 588**

Maule is a little-known but important figure in the fight for freedom of expression. The case is the first in the Salem area, so far as the writer has discovered, where a jury as a whole sided with the accused against the colonial authorities in a matter involving printing and authorship.

Murphy, T. J. "Massachusetts Advisory Committee on Juvenile Reading." *Massachusetts Library Association Bulletin*, 39:45–47, June 1949. **M 589**

Excerpts from the speech of the assistant Attorney General of Massachusetts on obscenity laws of the Commonwealth of Massachusetts, delivered before a meeting of the Massa-

chusetts Library Association. Includes text of the policy statement of the Committee.

Murphy, Terrence J. *Censorship: Government and Obscenity*. Baltimore, Helicon, 1963. 294 p. **M 590**

"After a clarifying discussion of the meaning of the term 'obscenity,' Father Murphy places the question of constitutional guaranteed freedom—and its limits—in its historical context within our democratic society. He describes the various Congressional attempts to deal with obscenity and analyzes all the important Court decisions, distinguishing the complicated problems that vary from medium to medium, from juvenile to adult." He criticizes the recent Supreme Court decisions which, while not nullifying the obscenity laws, greatly diminish public control of obscenity. The libertarian decisions of the Court represent the substantive values of a minority. Policy making is no longer in the hands of the officials chosen by the people.

———. "Legal Aspects of Book Censorship and Their Relationships to Academic Libraries." *College and Research Libraries*, 29:39–42, January 1963. **M 591**

Freedom is accorded a high, even preferred place, in American values. But it is not the only social value in our society. Book selection policies must consider the doctrine of "balancing the interest," which may be complex. The academic librarian has a responsibility to respect the right of the parent in the upbringing of his child. In church-related institutions the school may serve *in loco parentis*. A system of classifying books by age of reader might be appropriate. The library also has a responsibility to taxpayers or donors, which must be respected in determining library policies.

Murrah, A. P. *A Judge Looks at the Press*. Columbia, Mo., Freedom of Information Center, School of Journalism, University of Missouri, 1958. 3 p. (Publication no. 1) **M 592**

A federal judge discusses freedom of the press in coverage of court trials. He favors relaxing Canon 35 and Rule 53 only if modern equipment can cover trials without physical interference or distraction in any way.

Murray, Gilbert. "Obscenity in Literature." *Nation and Athenaeum* (London), 44:876, 23 March 1929. **M 593**

The author attacks the fashionable trend in writing which deals with "excretory, sudatory, and procreative systems" and the critics who defend such writing as representing courage. The serious literature of the past is generally free from obscenity. Obscenity destroys the higher imagination in literature, and those who indulge in reading, like a drunkard, soon lose a taste for all else. Murray's article brought forth a host of answers, presented in subsequent issues. Lytton Strachey (30 March) refuted the statement that all great literature is pure, giving as examples Catullus, Rabelais, and Swift. He also denied that obscenity has a power to destroy the higher imaginative values, referring readers to the third and fourth acts of *King Lear*. Philip Kerr supported Murray against his critics (6 April). In the same issue Murray answered Strachey to the effect that the critics apparently can recognize neither obscenity nor great literature. Darsie Yapp, reported from Paris that that city viewed the controversy much like London viewed the "monkey trial" in the United States. She defended bawdy books: "Dirty stories seem to me to be a tonic in some way." G. E. G. Catlin of Cornell University wrote (18 May): "It is supposed that repression will cure obscenity; there is much in experience to indicate that it is rather repression which is the cause of obscenity . . . One suspects that the source of obscenity, as of the obscene joke, lies in the furtive mind." The effect of obscenity, he writes, is likewise difficult to assess; it is a problem in medicine and psychology rather than law. He recommends that the energy spent in censorship be directed toward the study of moral psychology.

Murray, James. "The Role of Government." *Survey Graphic*, 35:449+, December 1946. **M 594**
Responsibilities of Congress in safeguarding the American right of free expression are described by the chairman of the Senate Committee on Education and Labor.

Murray, John C. "The Bad Arguments Intelligent Men Make." *America*, 96: 120–23, 3 November 1956. (Reprinted in Gardiner, *Catholic Viewpoint on Censorship*, pp. 164–72; also in Edwin Black and Harry P. Kerr, *American Issues*, Harcourt, Brace & World, 1961, pp. 190–97) **M 595**
The Jesuit editor of *Theological Studies* answers John Fischer's article (*Harper's*, October 1956) on censorship activities of the National Office for Decent Literature.

———. "Literature and Censorship." *Books on Trial*, 14:393–95+, June–July 1956; abridged article in *Commonweal*, 64:349–51, 6 July 1956 and in Downs, *The First Freedom*, pp. 215–22; also issued as a separate pamphlet by the Fund for the Republic. **M 596**
Father Murray, in an address on the seventeenth anniversary of the Thomas More Association, suggests four rules to govern divergent groups in their interrelated freedom of expression: (1) Each minority group has a right to censor for its own readers, if it so chooses. (2) No minority group has a right to demand that government shall impose a general censorship. (3) Any minority group has a right to work through persuasion and pacific argument for elevation of standards of public morality. (4) No minority group has a right to impose its own religious or moral values on other groups. "Our chief problem, of course, is not literary censorship but literary creation." James T. Farrell reviewed this lecture in *New Republic*, 12 November 1956, under the title A Jesuit on Censorship.

———. "Should There Be a Law?" In his *We Hold These Truths: Catholic Reflections on the American Proposition*. New York, Sheed & Ward, 1960, pp. 155–74. **M 597**
Censorship should be left to public authority and not practiced by amateurs. The greatest danger is in not reading good books.

Murray, June A. "Statutory Innovation in the Obscenity Field." *Buffalo Law Review*, 6:305–16, Spring 1957. **M 598**
An appraisal of a New York Statute (section 22 a of the Code of Criminal Procedure) which "provides for a civil injuncture proceeding which, in effect, tries the book for obscenity and if it is found guilty, the seller is compelled to surrender all his copies to the sheriff, who is directed to destroy them." The author believes that "if full effect is to be given to the freedom guaranteed by the First Amendment section 22(a) as well as section 1141 must be held to be unconstitutional."

Murray, Lindley, *comp*. Extracts from the *Writings of Divers Eminent Authors, of Different Religious Denominations; and at Various Periods of Time, Representing the Evils and Pernicious Effects of Stage Plays, and Other Amusements; with Some Additions*. Philadelphia, Benjamin & Jacob Johnson, 1799. 24 p. **M 599**

Murray, Robert K. *Red Scare: A Study in National Hysteria, 1919–1920*. Minneapolis, University of Minnesota Press, 1955. 337 p. **M 600**
A full-length analysis of the national hysteria that swept the United States immediately following World War I as a reaction to bolshevism and other radical movements. The fear of radicalism led to criminal syndicalist legislation and the seizure of radical literature. Included is the Schenck case involving the distribution of antienlistment literature, which brought forth the famous "clear and present danger" principle from Justice Holmes.

Murray, Samuel H. "The Extent of Government Immunity from Federal Rule 34." *Virginia Law Review*, 41: 507–22, May 1955. **M 601**
Notes on the privileged character of certain public records and the conditions under which a government may refuse "discovery." Covers court decisions, 1849–1954.

Murray, W. H. H. "An Endowed Press." *Arena*, 2:553–59, October 1890. **M 602**
A plea to free the press from the corrupting power of commercial interests which has led to license rather than liberty. Recommends endowments to create a free press.

Murray, William. "Books are Burning:

The Spreading Censorship." *Nation*, 176: 367–68, 2 May 1953. **M 603**
A survey of recent censorship activities, with special consideration to investigations by the Gathings Committee of Congress of "current pornographic materials."

Murrill, Judith. *Canon 35: A Summary*. Columbia, Mo., Freedom of Information Center, School of Journalism, University of Missouri, 1962. 7 p. (Publication no. 77) **M 604**
A summary of recent events relating to the American Bar Association Canon of Judicial Ethics which prevents photography, broadcasting, and telecasting in the courtroom. Includes an extensive bibliography.

———. *The Development of Access Legislation*. Columbia, Mo., University of Missouri, 1962. 184 p. (Unpublished Master's thesis) **M 605**

———. *Hutchins Commission*. Columbia, Mo., Freedom of Information Center, School of Journalism, University of Missouri, 1962. 15 p. (Publication no. 69) **M 606**
A digest of the major criticisms and recommendations of the media of communications made by the Commission on Freedom of the Press (Hutchins Commission), and some of the reactions they caused.

———. *Press Commission Suggestions*. Columbia, Mo., Freedom of Information Center, School of Journalism, University of Missouri, 1961. 4 p. (Publication no. 68) **M 607**
A review of the various proposals for establishing a press commission in the United States, including proposals of William Benton, Ernest K. Lindley, Harry Ashmore, Gordon Gray, Edward R. Murrow, Roland E. Wolseley, and others.

Murrow, Edward R. "TV and Fear of Controversy." *New Republic*, 139:11–13, 10 November 1958. **M 608**
In an address before the Association of Radio and Television News Directors, Murrow criticizes the timidity of the networks. While not advocating "a 27-inch wailing wall" he writes, "I would just like to see it [television] reflect, occasionally, the hard, unyielding realities of the world in which we live. I would like to see it done inside the existing framework, and I would like to see the doing of it redound to the credit of those who finance and program it."

"Murrow's TV Program Exposes Book Banning." *Library Journal*, 80:1245–46, 15 May 1955. **M 609**

Murry, J. Middleton. "An Immortal Pamphlet: The Charter of the Fourth Estate." *Aryan Path*, 33:483–88, November 1962. (First published in *Aryan Path*, November 1944) **M 610**

A tribute to John Milton's *Areopagitica*, on the 300th anniversary of that classic on freedom of the press.

Murthy, N. V. K. "Freedom of the Press and Fair Trial in the U.S.A." *Journalism Quarterly*, 36:307–13, Summer 1959. **M 611**

An Indian scholar, examining cases in the United States and Great Britain, believes that "the balance between the concepts of free press and free trial is an extremely delicate one, but it can be maintained if both press and the judiciary recognize their fundamental identity of purpose."

Mussey, Henry R. "The Christian Science Censor." *Nation*, 130:147–49, 5 February 1930; 130:175–78, 12 February 1930; 130:241–43, 26 February 1930; and 130:291–93, 12 March 1930. (Reprinted in Beman, *Censorship of Speech and the Press*, pp. 22–26) **M 612**

The first article in the series, The Machinery of Suppression, deals with the structure of the "smoothest-running publicity (and anti-publicity) machine operated in the United States during the twentieth century" and particularly with the work of the Church's Committee on Publication. The second article, Obnoxious Books, deals with efforts of the Committee to suppress unfavorable biographies of Mary Baker Eddy. The third article, Freedom of the Press, deals with activities of local Committees in monitoring local news and radio stories to seek "corrections" of articles unfavorable to the Church. The fourth article reviews efforts of the Church to suppress Dakin's biography of Mrs. Eddy, through a nationwide boycott of booksellers who did not yield to the request that the book be withdrawn from sale.

"Must We Go to Jail?" *North American Review*, 206:673–77, November 1917. **M 613**

The author considers the Espionage Act, insofar as it prohibits publication of any matter of a seditious nature, "wicked, vicious, tyrannous, and ought never to have been enacted." He suggests that Postmaster-General Burleson study the First Amendment and reflect on the fate of John Adams when he tampered with freedom of the press.

Muzzey, David S. "John Milton—an Apostle of Liberty." *Ethical Addresses*, 16:93–112, December 1908. **M 614**

[Myers, Allen O.] "Contempt." *Weekly Law Bulletin*, 19:302–15, 7 May 1888. **M 615**

The case against Allen O. Myers, convicted of contempt of court because his letter, appearing in the *Cincinnati Enquirer*, charged packing of the grand jury (*State of Ohio v. Allen O. Myers*). In the article the author reviews the law of contempt by newspapers.

Myers, Paul. "The Blue Hand of Censorship." *Theatre Time*, 1:62–64, Summer 1949. **M 616**

"Since 1948 there have been growing indications that considerable pressure is being brought to bear upon legislative bodies and—in turn—upon artistic expression." There is as much danger in threatened use of the blue pencil as in actual exercise. References are made to censors at work in such cities as Chicago, Philadelphia, and Washington, where there is an official censorship. Philadelphia is the city in which "the most recent abuse has taken place," the barring of Sartre's *The Respectful Prostitute*.

N

Nadelmann, Kurt H. "The Newspaper Privilege and Extortion by Abuse of Legal Processes." *Columbia Law Review*, 54: 59–74, March 1954. **N1**
Notes on abuses resulting from newspaper publication or comment on a case filed with a judicial officer but not yet tried.

Nafziger, Ralph O. *International News and the Press: an Annotated Bibliography*. New York, Wilson, 1940. 193 p. **N2**
Part I covers works on world press associations, including press censorship during the war. Part II covers the foreign press, geographically arranged.

———. "World War Correspondents and Censorship of the Belligerents." *Journalism Quarterly*, 14:226–43, September 1937. **N3**
The author reports on censorship of news during World War I as revealed by the files of professional and trade publications in the United States and Great Britain. Abstract of a chapter in his doctoral dissertation, *The American Press and Public Opinion during the World War, 1914 to 1917*.

"The Naked and the Obscene." *Economist*, 156:1126–27, 18 June 1949. **N4**
Review of "the existing mechanisms by which censorship is or can be imposed" in Great Britain and of the weaknesses of the present system. The editor recommends an amendment to the Libel Act of 1888 "that no prosecution for alleged obscene writings should be launched without the fiat of the Attorney General," to protect author and publisher from nuisance prosecution.

Natarajan, Swaminath. *A History of the Press in India*. New York, Asian Publishing House, 1962. 425 p. **N5**
A study of the growth of the press in India and the obstacles it encountered in a struggle for freedom.

Nathan, George Jean. "The Censor Psyche [etc.]" *American Mercury*, 11: 113–15, May 1927. (In his Clinical Notes column) **N6**
"The men who devote themselves to censorship are simply men who have not, with the aid of experience, wisdom, and honor, outgrown the childish desire for indiscriminate havoc. They are thus what may be designated as emotional morons . . ." In another note, Nathan attributes to censorship the encouragement of literary craftsmanship. "The author is put to it to defeat censorship with the devious complexities of the literary art, the subtle shadings, the fine circumlocutions, all the shrewd and masterly jugglings of the English language."

———. "Deceptio Visūs." *American Mercury*, 11:243–44, June 1927. **N7**
While admitting that censorship at some point might be justified (e.g., selling *Fanny Hill* to school children at a nickel a copy) his quarrel is with the censor, who is generally stupid. "It is they who are ruining the cause of censorship amongst even censorship's more rational proponents."

———. "If Holly Wood came to Dunsinane." *American Mercury*, 63:598–604, November 1946. **N8**
The author considers what the legitimate stage would be like if a code similar to that of the Motion Picture Producers and Distributors of America were in effect. He lists code regulations and specifications and, under each, examples of plays which could not be produced without alterations.

———. "In the Matter of the Lid." *American Mercury*, 17:242–43, June 1929. **N9**
"The one big unanswered question concerning censorship as we engage in it in this day and hour is this: Why is it that censorship, designed by its own admission to safeguard the young, the susceptible and the ignorant, four times out of five disports itself not in that quarter at all but exercises itself sedulously against institutions and works whose appeal is directly and almost entirely to unsusceptible and intelligent adults."

———. "Master Minds of Censorship. Some Reflections on the Inconsistency of the Guardians of Our National Soul." *Vanity Fair*, 26:57, 102, July 1926. **N10**
While New York burlesque, which caters almost exclusively to hardened audiences, is subject to frequent police raids, New York legitimate theater, far dirtier, but attended by a more genteel audience, is untouched by the censor. Nathan cites 67 episodes, in plays produced during the past season, of rape, seduction, incest, degeneracy, etc.—more than one-third of the plays showing. "Not a voice has been raised against any of them. And yet the moralists go down into a remote corner of the town, where men and women are tough as stale beefsteaks, and demand that the lid be clapped on the innocent spectacle of a fat girl shaking her middle."

———. "A Programme for Censorship." *American Mercury*, 13:369–71, March 1928. (Reprinted in Downs, *The First Freedom*, pp. 279–80) **N11**
Writing in the Clinical Notes column of *American Mercury* during the 20's Nathan frequently applied his witty and irreverent remarks against censorship and the censors. In this article Nathan recommends that since we cannot get rid of censorship altogether, we settle the argument between the "smutsters" and the "liberals" by altering the present obscenity statute so that the artist is condemned after the commission of the crime, not before it. Nathan would require proof that a person has been corrupted by a book. "Let us have the witness in the box and let him swear on the Bible to his ruin." In Clinical Notes for April 1926, Nathan notes the spread of the "doctrine that there is considerable humor in sex" as opposed to an earlier view that "sex is a grim, serious and ominous business."

[Nation, Carrie]. "Mrs. Nation Discharged; Well-Known Saloon Smasher Acquitted by Commissioner May." *Hatchet*, 2:11, 1 September 1906. **N12**
This militant prohibitionist was arrested and brought to trial before U.S. Commissioner A. W. May, charged with sending obscene matter through the United States mails. The offending publication was the 1 July issue of *The Hatchet*, mailed in Guthrie, Okla., containing an article on masturbation entitled

"Private Talk to Little Boys." The same issue chides President Theodore Roosevelt for not taking action against the "113 whore houses within six blocks of the White House." The case was dismissed, the Commissioner finding the article to be not obscene.

"*The Nation* and the Post Office." *Nation*, 107:236–37, 28 September 1918.   **N13**
Editorial criticizing the banning of the 14 September 1918 issue of *The Nation* by the Post Office Department because of an article critical of the government's labor policies. Mr. Burleson is no longer merely seeking to prevent sedition, but is aiming "to control public opinion."

"*Nation* Ban." *Nation*, 168:647–49, 11 June 1949.   **N14**
Ban of *The Nation* from the New York City public schools.

National Association of Book Publishers. "Publishers Outline Stand on Censorship." *Publishers' Weekly*, 104:1837, 8 December 1923.   **N15**
To meet the criticism that their stand on censorship was unknown, the publishers' association adopted this statement which proclaims that publishers stand back of their books and authors. The statement decries censorship efforts of private groups; it calls for admission of expert testimony at book trials, consideration of a book as a whole, and consideration of the intent and purpose of the author. It urges that books written for adults not be judged on the effect they might have on the immature.

National Association of Broadcasters. *Addresses at the 39th Annual Convention of the National Association of Broadcasters*. Washington, D.C., The Association, 1961. 39 p.   **N16**
Includes addresses by President John F. Kennedy, LeRoy Collins, president of the NAB, and Newton N. Minow, chairman of the FCC. Minow's talk was given wide publicity for his sharp criticism of the "vast wasteland" in television programs. While stating his opposition to government censorship he warned that the FCC would consider the station's contributions to the public interest at the time of license renewal. He called upon the industry to live up to the great potential of the medium.

————. *Broadcasting and the Bill of Rights* . . . Washington, D.C., The Association, 1947. 322 p.   **N17**
A collection of statements presented by representatives of the broadcasting industry before the Senate Committee on Interstate and Foreign Commerce (17–27 June 1947) opposing the White Bill (S. 1333) which would expand functions of the FCC to include program control. The spokesmen not only presented specific criticisms and recommendations on the proposed bill, but expressed convictions relating to the whole subject of federal regulation in the field of radio broadcasting. Text of the bill is included.

————. *Editorializing on the Air*. Washington, D.C., The Association, 1959. 40 p.   **N18**
Includes a report of the Committee on Editorializing and a resolution of the NAB, adopting the report and approving a policy favoring and encouraging editorializing by broadcasters. The FCC report on Editorializing by Broadcast Licensees of 2 June 1949 is printed in full. It authorizes identified editorializing, providing "the public has a reasonable opportunity to hear different opposing positions on the public issues of interest and importance in the community."

————. *N.A.B. Wartime Guide*. Washington, D.C., The Association, 1941. (Reprinted in Summers, *Wartime Control of Press and Radio*, pp. 283–86)   **N19**

————. *An Operational Guide for Broadcasting the News*. Washington, D.C., The Association, 1958. 28 p.   **N20**
A brief history of news broadcasting, policies on editorializing, a statement on the responsibility of broadcasters to keep the public informed, and a code of conduct in covering public meetings and court proceedings. Prepared by the Freedom of Information Committee.

————. *Radio Code of Good Practices*. Washington, D.C., The Association, 1962. 12 p.   **N21**
First adopted by the industry in 1937; revised from time to time. The Code deals with program standards and ethics relating to such matters as news, public issues, political broadcasts, religious programs, and children's programs. It also includes a section on advertising standards.

————. *Seal of Good Practice*. Washington, D.C., Television Code Authority of the National Association of Broadcasters, [1963?]. 11 p.   **N22**
A popular presentation of the purpose of the Television Code, how the Code functions, and what it means to the viewer.

————. *The Television Code*. 9th ed. Washington, D.C., The Association, 1964. 30 p.   **N23**
The Television Code of good practice was enacted in 1952 by the Television Board of the National Association of Broadcasters. The Code is administered by the Television Code Authority. Revisions of the Code have been made from time to time. The 14 chapters of the present Code are as follows: Advancement of Education and Culture, Responsibility toward Children, General Program Standards (covers obscenity, profanity, ridicule of race or religious faith, brutality, etc.), Community Responsibility, Treatment of News and Public Events, Controversial Public Issues, Political Telecasts, Religious Programs, General Advertising Standards, Presentation of Advertising, Advertising of Medical Products, Contests, Premiums and Offers, and Time Standards for Advertising.

National Board of Review Magazine. New York, National Board of Review of Motion Pictures, 1926–42. Monthly. Superseded by *New Movies*.   **N24**
The news organ of the National Board of Review of Motion Pictures, which published the judgment of the Board on movies and frequently carried commentary on movie control.

National Board of Review of Motion Pictures. *Boston (Mass.) Method of Motion Picture Regulation*. New York, The Board 1919. 8 p.   **N25**

————. *Brief by Mayor Gaynor in Opposition to Censorship of Motion Pictures*. New York, The Board, n. d. 8 p.   **N26**
New York's mayor opposed legislation for state control of motion pictures.

————. *Case Against Federal Censorship of Motion Pictures*. New York, The Board, 1916. 5 p.   **N27**

————. *Handbook on the Regulation of Motion Pictures; Including a Model Ordinance, Based on the Report of the Special Committee of the New York State Conference of Mayors and Other City Officials* . . . New York, The Board, 1921. 8 p.   **N28**

————. *The National Board of Review of Motion Pictures; Its Background, Growth and Present Status*. New York, The Board, n. d. 15 p.   **N29**

————. *Objection to State Censorship of Motion Pictures*. New York, The Board, 1921. 6 p.   **N30**

————. *Official Opinion on Censorship and an Ordinance for the Regulation of Motion Pictures*. New York, The Board, 1917. 5 p.   **N31**

————. *Policy and Standards of the National Board of Review of Motion Pictures*. New York, 1915. 23 p.   **N32**

———. *Question of Motion Picture Censorship*. New York, The Board, 1921. 16p.
N 33

———. *Report*. Annual, 1910/11—1919/20?
N 34

———. *Repudiation of Motion Picture Censorship in New York City; Report of the Committee on General Welfare of the Board of Aldermen, June 10, 1919*. New York, The Board, 1919. 6p.
N 35

———. *Standards of the National Board of Review of Motion Pictures Adopted by the National Association of the Motion Picture Industry, January 19, 1917*. New York, The Board, 1917. 15p.
N 36

———. *State Censorship of Motion Pictures*. New York, The Board, 1921. 6p. (Reprinted in Rutland, *State Censorship of Motion Pictures*, pp. 117–23)
N 37
Arguments against censorship include: It is an invasion of constitutional rights; the censors can't agree; there is no popular demand for censorship; movie censorship represents unjust discrimination against one medium; censor confuses good taste with morals; and censorship would reduce the movies to child's entertainment. An account is given of the work of the National Board of Review, founded in recognition of the screen's right to freedom.

———. "What the National Board of Review Stands For." *Motion Picture Magazine*, 14(8):43–44, September 1917.
N 38
A report on the activities of the organization that reviews "practically 99% of all photoplays exhibited in the United States."

National Broadcasting Company. *NBC Radio and Television Broadcast Standards*. New York, N.B.C., 1956. 43p.
N 39
Chapters on standards of program content, advertising content, and operating procedures. Program content includes such topics as controversial public issues, political campaigns, religion, sex, profanity and obscenity, defamation, race and nationality, and references to living persons.

National Catholic Welfare Conference. "The U.S. Bishops' Statement of 1957 on Censorship." In Gardiner, *Catholic Viewpoint on Censorship*, pp. 185–92.
N 40
This statement from the Conference's administrative board presents the position of the Catholic Church with respect to moral censorship. Along with freedom of expression in America is also the "duty to exercise it with a sense of responsibility." Freedom of

expression is not absolute; it has a moral dimension. "Obscenity cannot be permitted as a proper exercise of a basic human freedom." Legal restraints should be applied prudently and cautiously, leaving to the Church the responsibility for upholding standards of morality. The National Office for Decent Literature and the Legion of Decency (films) are twin organizations of the Church intended to oppose harmful and offensive materials on the stage and screen and in publications. They evaluate materials and seek to "enlist in a proper and lawful manner the cooperation of those who can curb the evil. . . . Neither agency exercises censorship in any true sense of the word."

"National Censorship of Motion Pictures." *Survey*, 26:469–70, 1 July 1911.
N 41
Brief review of the work of the National Board of Censorship of Motion Pictures.

National Conference on the Freedom of the Press. London. *Freedom of the Press. Conference held at The Central Hall, Westminster, June 7th 1941; Convened by the National Union of Journalists and the National Council for Civil Liberties*. London, The National Council and The Union [1941]. 12p., 6p., 4p.
N 42
Contains statements on press freedom from secretaries of the National Union of Journalists, National Federation of Building Trade Operatives, Paul Rotha, Frank Owen of the *Evening Standard*, and Sunder Kabadi of the *Bombay Chronicle*, among others. A resolution on freedom of the press was adopted. Bound with the report of the conference is a statement, Censorship of the Indian and Colonial Press, and Indirect Censorship, the latter dealing largely with the actions of the National Association of Wholesale Newsagents.

National Council for Civil Liberties. *Civil Liberties Defended. Case Book of the National Council* . . . London, The Council, 1941. 19p.
N 43
Includes references to freedom of the press in wartime Britain.

———. *Civil Liberty*. London, The Council. Published periodically since 1937. **N 44**
Source of information on current events in freedom of the press and censorship in Great Britain.

———. *The Press and the War*. London, The Council, [1941?]. 22p.
N 45
Criticism of government restrictions on the press in wartime. "If Britain is to remain free the Press, too, must remain free, and . . . restrictions upon the freedom of expression are a prelude to national disaster." Report prepared by John White for the Press Freedom Committee headed by Frank Owen of the *Evening Standard*.

———. *Press Freedom*. London, The Council, 1942. 21p.
N 46
The Council objected to the use by the British Home Secretary of Defence Regulation 2D to suppress the newspaper press; to the withdrawal of the subsidy to export *Picture Post* to the Middle East; to censorship of the press in Palestine; and to the extension of cable censorship by the Minister of Information. The Council requests the abolition of Defence Regulation 2D and the lifting of the ban on the *Daily Worker*. It also condemns individual reporting that gives a distorted picture of British war efforts.

———. *Your Freedom in Danger. Why Civil Liberty Today Is Essential in the Defence of the Nation*. London, The Council, [1943?]. 12p.
N 47

National Council for the Social Studies. "The Treatment of Controversial Issues in the Schools." *Social Education*, 15:232–36, May 1951.
N 48
A report by the Committee on Academic Freedom, adopted by the Board of Directors in 1950 and 1951. The statement defines the role of the teacher in the study of controversial issues and suggests criteria for evaluating teaching materials in these areas.

National Council of Jewish Women. "Censorship and Complacency in Education." *Council Platform*, 7:5, May 1963.
N 49
A discussion of the impact of censorship as opposed to concensus on American education.

———. *Censorship: Safeguard or Threat*. New York, The Council, 1956. 45p.
N 50
Prepared by Mrs. Betty Rosen and Miss Helen Raebeck and designed as a discussion guide in the Council's Freedom Campaign.

National Council of Public Morals (Great Britain). Cinema Commission of Inquiry. *The Cinema: Its Present Position and Future Possibilities. Being the Report of and Chief Evidence Taken by the Cinema Commission of Inquiry*. London, Williams and Norgate, 1917. 372p.
N 51
An unofficial committee of religious, scientific, and cultural leaders instituted this study of "the physical, social, educational, and moral influences of the cinema, with special references to young people" to investigate "complaints which have been made against cinematography exhibitions." Testimony includes statements from representatives of the movie industry, education, public welfare, ministers, police officers, YMCA, the Billposters Association, and the British Board of Film Censors. The report recommends continuance of present

censorship; that local authorities show only films "on the white list, issued by the trade"; and that the public refuse to enter a theater which does not restrict itself to films on the list. The report also recommends the exclusion of social, moral or religious propaganda films and the appointment of a national film advisory council. A questionnaire circulated indicated that 75 per cent found no objection to the films for children and observed no harmful effects. Only 35 per cent reported local censorship, mostly by the police. "If British producers will follow such high standards," the report concluded, "and free us from the nauseating stuff, much of which is imported from America, they will help to make the cinema a worthy asset in national life." A survey of movie censorship practices in other countries is given in the appendix.

The National Council of Teachers of English. *Censorship and Controversy; Report of the Committee on Censorship of Teaching Materials for Classroom and Library.* Chicago, The Council, 1953. 56 p.　　**N 52**

The report was prepared to help teachers meet the threats of censorship of textbook and library materials, restrictions on speakers, and denial of the right to consider controversial topics in the classroom. The report considers the problem as a joint responsibility of teachers, students, administrators, parents, and community leaders. It suggests procedures in meeting criticism, principles for selecting materials, and statements of other organizations relating to academic freedom, such as the National Education Association, National Council for the Social Studies, American Library Association, Association of American Colleges, National Congress of Parents and Teachers, American Textbook Publishers Institute, American Book Publishers Council, and American Legion.

――――. *Resolution on Censorship.* Champaign, Ill., The Council, 1960. 1 p. mimeo.　**N 53**

――――. *The Students' Right to Read.* Champaign, Ill., The Council, 1962. 21 p. (Reprinted in *Illinois Libraries*, May 1966; excerpted in *Education Digest*, May 1963)　　**N 54**

A guide to teachers and administrators on how to resist local campaigns that seek to prevent students from reading well-established authors. The Council senses growing community pressures to remove important books from classrooms and libraries. A program of action and a procedure by which a citizen may request the reconsideration of a book used in a school is included.

The National Council of the Churches of Christ in the United States of America. ["Censorship Issue"]. *Information Service*, 39(21-I):1–8, 24 December 1960.　**N 55**

The entire issue, prepared by the Council's Bureau of Research and Survey, deals with problems of censorship.

National Council on Freedom from Censorship. *Abolish Motion Picture Censorship in New York State. A Brief in Support of a Bill Now Pending in the New York State Legislature to Abolish the Board of Censors . . .* New York, The Council, 1933. 5 p. mimeo.　　**N 56**

――――. *The "Bad Book" Bill.* New York, The Council, 1933. 4 p. mimeo.　　**N 57**

Brief in support of a bill before the New York State Legislature to amend procedures in prosecuting obscene and indecent literature.

――――. *Censorship Covers up but Does Not Cure . . .* New York, The Council, 1941. 7 p.　　**N 58**

The Council was organized in 1932 by the American Civil Liberties Union. It undertook a nationwide campaign to oppose censorship in all forms, in all areas of communications. Its three-point program called for repeal of censorship laws; test cases in the court; and an information campaign. The Council considered the post office and customs as the offenders and obscenity as "their big card." Quincy Howe is listed as chairman of the Council, which includes prominent authors, editors, and educators.

――――. *Censorship of Motion Pictures.* New York, The Council, 1939. 12 p.　　**N 59**

――――. *Freedom from Censorship.* New York, The Council, 1946. 8 p.　　**N 60**

Brief paragraphs on the definition of obscenity, censorship by the post office and customs, censorship of books, radio, motion pictures, and the stage. Includes a statement on the platform and program of the Council.

――――. *Memorandum in Support of a Bill Abolishing the Censorship of Motion Pictures and Increasing the State's Revenue from Taxes on Films, New York State Legislature, 1934.* New York, The Council, 1934. 19 p.　　**N 61**

Arguments: Censorship of movies has not accomplished the intended purpose of protecting the public; the system entails public expenditures without public benefits; artificial standards are maintained; control should be left to the same measures as for press and education; only a jury should judge, not a professional censor; censorship is generally discredited over the country; and moral persuasion is superior to legal suppression.

――――. *"The Miracle" Decision.* New York, The Council, 1952. 6 p.　　**N 62**

"The Supreme Court, by unanimous vote, has just rendered two historic decisions on movie censorship. On May 26, it declared unconstitutional a New York State ban on the Italian film 'The Miracle'; and on June 2 it invalidated a municipal ordinance of Marshall, Texas, under which showings of the American film 'Pinky' had been prohibited."

――――. *An Outline History of the Post Office Censorship.* New York, The Council, 1932. 29 p. mimeo.　　**N 63**

Includes 12 brief case-histories and 20 examples of conflicting court decisions.

――――. *The Post Office Censor . . .* New York, The Council, 1932. 13 p.　　**N 64**

In support of a bill before Congress to abolish postal censorship and substitute jury trial for all seized matter. The pamphlet describes how postal censorship works and what actions have been taken against works involving sex education and birth control, politics, and religion.

――――. *Repeal the Theatre Padlock Law and Abolish Censorship by the Prosecutor's Office.* New York, The Council, 1933. 5 p. mimeo.　　**N 65**

A brief in support of a bill now pending in the New York State Legislature to amend a law which provides that a theater may be padlocked for one year if a theatrical production playing there is convicted of indecency or obscenity.

――――. *What Shocked the Censors!* New York, The Council, 1933. 98 p.　　**N 66**

"A complete record of cuts in motion picture films ordered by the New York State censors from January, 1932 to March, 1933." Foreword by Hatcher Hughes, chairman of the Council, and introduction by Professor Edward C. Lindeman.

National Defense Association. *Constitution.* New York, The Association, [1879?]. 4 p.　　**N 67**

The objectives of the Association were to investigate all questionable cases of prosecution under federal and state Comstock laws and to defend persons "unjustly assailed by the enemies of free speech and free press." Rev. A. L. Rawson was the first president and Dr. E. B. Foote the first secretary.

――――. *Words of Warning to Those Who Aid and Abet in the Suppression of Free Speech and Free Press.* New York, The Association, 1879. 61 p.　　**N 68**

The Association, formed in 1879 to aid victims of the Comstock laws, helped to secure a petition of 50,000 names to present to Congress urging repeal. Comstock's friends were more influential lobbyists, however, and prevented any changes in the law. An auxiliary of the National Defense Association was the Boston Defense Association, formed in January 1879 to help the victims of the New England vice society. Benjamin R. Tucker was one of its officers.

National Institute of Municipal Law Officers. "Obscene Literature and Comic Books: Workshop No. 3, Proceedings of the 1959 Annual Conference." *Municipal Law Review*, 23:498–544, 1959. **N 69**
Discussion centered around the U.S. Supreme Court case of *Roth v. United States* and the case involving *Lady Chatterley's Lover* (Kingsley International Pictures Corp.). Actions against obscene publications in New York, Chicago, Cincinnati, Greensboro, Los Angeles City and County were reported. Text of the Los Angeles County ordinance, held unconstitutional by the California Supreme Court (*Katzev v. County of Los Angeles*, 1959), is included.

National Legion of Decency. National Center for Film Study. [*Classification List*]. New York, The NLD, 1935?–date. Biweekly. **N 70**
Lists films by classification (A, B, C), according to moral standards established by this Catholic group. The organization publishes on alternate weeks a *Catholic Film Newsletter*, which includes lengthy annotations of recommended films. The two publications are prepared by the National Center for Film Study (a division of the Catholic Adult Education Center, Chicago) which is the educational affiliate of the National League of Decency. The classification system is described in Gardiner, *Catholic Viewpoint on Censorship*, pp. 94 ff.

National Liberal League. [*First Annual Congress*]. *Equal Rights in Religion. Report of the Centennial Congress of Liberals, and Organization of the National Liberal League, at Philadelphia on the Fourth of July, 1876.* Boston, The League, 1876. 190 p. **N 71**
The League was made up largely of New York and Boston intellectuals, including Elizur Wright, James Parton, O. B. Frothingham, and Francis E. Abbot as president. While the League was unanimously opposed to the Comstock laws, its membership was split over whether the laws should be modified or repealed. When repeal advocates took over, Abbot resigned and Wright became president. The final decision on the Comstock laws was postponed for a subsequent convention.

———. [*First Annual Congress*]. *Patriotic Addresses to the People of the United States, adopted at Philadelphia on the Fourth of July, 1876, by the National Liberal League . . .* Boston, The League, 1876. 23 p. **N 72**
Includes texts of resolutions passed at the first convention of the League, which emphasize separation of church and state. They call for the prohibition of Bible reading in the public schools and urge freedom of expression for all religious ideas, orthodox or heterodox.

———. [*Second Annual Congress*]. *Circular to the Auxiliary Leagues for 1878 and 1879, Containing Address of the President and Directors . . . Official Report of the Proceedings*

Had and Resolutions Passed at Syracuse, N.Y., October 26th and 27th, 1878 . . . New York, The League, 1879. 42 p. **N 73**
In his address to the second annual convention Elizur Wright comments on the difference of opinion of members over obscenity legislation, some wishing repeal, others modification, but all agreeing that the federal postal laws as administered had been "a most flagrant attack upon the freedom of the press." The resolution of the conflict over the obscenity laws was postponed for another year.

———. *Third Annual Congress Held at Cincinnati, Ohio, September 13 and 14, 1879.* New York, Liberal and Scientific Publishing House, 1879. 115 p. **N 74**
President Elizur Wright's address deals largely with freedom of the press including references to the persecution of Editor D. M. Bennett. The convention passed resolutions, proposed by Colonel Ingersoll, favoring freedom of the mails for all matters "irrespective of the religious, irreligious, political, and scientific views," but opposing dissemination of obscene matter through the mails, including the Bible, until it can be expunged of passages "that cannot be read without covering the cheek of modesty with the blush of shame." "Good morals and habits," the resolution stated, "can be better fostered by education, persuasion, industry, and healthy amusement, than by force and government interference." The League held a fourth meeting in Chicago in 1880 and it was at that meeting that Ingersoll resigned over the resolution for repeal of the Comstock law. The League was reorganized as the American Secular Union in 1885.

"National Library Week Brings Film Furor to Fairfax County." *Library Journal*, 88:2216–17, 1 June 1963. **N 75**
Fairfax County (Virginia) public libraries celebrated National Library Week by showing documentary films on brotherhood and international good will. American Legion Post 177 detected subversion and a censorship hassle developed.

National Office for Decent Literature. *The Drive for Decency in Print. Report of the Bishops' Committee Sponsoring the NODL.* Huntington, Ind., Our Sunday Visitor Press, 1939. 218 p. **N 76**
Includes a report of progress of the NODL against salacious literature, cooperation of law enforcement agencies, new state laws, support of related Catholic agencies, and A Guide for Judging Magazines According to the NODL Code.

———. *NODL Newsletter.* Chicago, NODL, 1956–date. Quarterly. **N 77**
In 1938 the Catholic bishops of the United States established a National Organization for Decent Literature (name changed to "Office" in 1955) "to set in motion the moral forces of

the country . . . against the lascivious type of literature which threatens moral, social and national life." The quarterly newsletter reports on activities and procedures in the crusade and lists comic books, magazines, and paperbacks it considers contrary to the NODL Code and objectionable for youths.

———. *What is NODL?* Chicago, NODL, n.d. 19 p. **N 78**
Includes a statement on how the lists of objectionable publications are prepared and how they are intended to be used in local communities.

National Purity Congress. *The National Purity Congress, Its Papers, Addresses, Portraits . . . Baltimore, October 14, 15 and 16, 1895. Edited by Aaron M. Powell . . .* New York, American Purity Alliance, 1896. 453 p. **N 79**
The first convention of the purity movement in the United States, a forerunner of modern social hygiene, brought together a curious association of men and women, normally antagonistic, but with a common concern in sexual purity. The one group, represented by Anthony Comstock, was mainly interested in suppression of sexually demoralizing literature; the other, which later included the free speech advocate Theodore A. Schroeder, sought freedom for sex education. The organization ultimately became the World's Purity Federation, with headquarters in LaCrosse, Wis., led by B. S. Steadwell. Its publication was *The Light*. Included here are papers by Anthony Comstock, Demoralizing Literature, and Josiah W. Leeds, The Relation of the Press and the Stage to Purity. A photograph of Comstock appears on page 419; a photograph of B. O. Flower, editor of the *Arena*, appears on page 305.

[National Union of Journalists and the National Council for Civil Liberties]. *Freedom of the Press and the Challenge of the Official Secrets Acts . . .* [London, NUJ and NCCL, 1938]. 30 p. **N 80**
Speeches made by Major G. Lloyd George, Dingle Foot, Compton Mackenzie, L. C. White, A. P. Herbert, Kingsley Martin, C. J. Bundock, and R. Willis at a conference called by the National Union of Journalists and the National Council for Civil Liberties. The purpose of the conference was to call attention to dangerous tendencies towards suppression of free opinion in Britain and particularly to the perils contained in the Official Secrets Acts.

National Vigilance Association for the Repression of Criminal Vice and Public Immorality. *Reports.* London, The Association, 1885–99. Annual. **N 81**
This Association superseded the Society for the Supression of Vice, and was itself succeeded

in 1899 by the Public Morality Council. Its work was comparable to that of the New York Society for the Suppression of Vice, serving to instigate proceedings against obscene literature. The Association was formed at the time of the "Maiden Tribute" (white slave) scandal and was headed for many years by William Alexander Coote. Its first major censorship effort was against Henry Vizetelly for publication of the novels of Zola.

The Nationalization of the Bill of Rights. Freedom of the Press. 30 min., b/w movie. New York, Encyclopaedia Britannica Films. (Structure and Functions of American Government Series) **N 82**

Professor Peter H. Odegard discusses the importance of freedom of the press in the formation of American democracy.

"The Nation-wide Battle over Movie Purification." *Literary Digest*, 69:32–33, 14 May 1921. **N 83**

Reports on the conflict over what reforms should take place in the motion picture industry—many state officials urging censorship boards, the industry opposing censorship, and the press taking sides, but mostly against censorship.

Neal, John S., Jr. "The Federal Communications Commission and Its Licensing Function in the Public Interest." *Temple Law Quarterly*, 21:135–39, October 1947. **N 84**

Nealy, W. A. *Motion Picture Censorship and Organized Labor.* New York, National Board of Review of Motion Pictures, [1920?]. (Reprinted in Rutland, *State Censorship of Motion Pictures*, pp. 106–13) **N 85**

The president of the Massachusetts Federation of Labor expresses the opposition of organized labor to film censorship, quoting a resolution to this effect from the 1916 convention report of the AFL and a report from the Executive Council. State censorship of films, he states, "is inimical to the free institutions of this country."

[Nearing, Scott]. *Free Speech and Press Go to Trial with Scott Nearing.* [New York, 1918?]. 8 p. **N 86**

Background of the Scott Nearing espionage case, with a brief account of Nearing's life and philosophy and an appeal for contributions for his defense.

————. *Scott Nearing's Address to the Jury. The Speech before the Jury when Charged with a Violation of the Espionage Act.* New York, The Rand School of Social Science, [1919?]. 30 p. **N 87**

[————]. *The Trial of Scott Nearing and the American Socialist Society. Presiding Judge—Julius M. Mayer; Attorneys:—for the Government, Earl B. Barnes; for the Defense, Seymour Stedman . . . S. John Block . . . Walter Nelles . . . [and] I. M. Sackin . . . United States District Court for the Southern District of New York, New York City, February 5th to 19th, 1919.* [New York, The Rand School of Social Science, 1919]. 249 p. **N 88**

Scott Nearing, a leader in radical thought in America and a teacher at the Rand School, was indicted under the Espionage Act of 1917 for having written *The Great Madness*, a pamphlet expressing his views of the relation of big business to the conduct of World War I. The work was charged with obstructing the draft. Nearing was acquitted but the same jury convicted the American Socialist Party for publishing the work.

Nebraska. University. School of Journalism. *Latin American Journalism.* [Lincoln, Nebr.], The School, 1954. 31 p. (Contribution to Bibliography in Journalism) **N 89**

Contains a number of references to books and journal articles on freedom of the press in Latin American countries. Arranged by countries.

Nedham, Marchamont. *The Great Accuser cast down; Or, A Publick Tryal of Mr. John Goodwin of Colemanstreet, London, At the Bar of Religion & Right Reason. It Being a full Answer to a certain Scandalous Book of his lately published, Entituled. The Triers Tried and Cast, &tc. Whereupon being found Guilty of High Scandal and Malediction both against the present Authority, and the Commissioners for Approbation and Ejection, He is here sentenced and brought forth to the deserved Execution of the Press.* London, Printed by Tho. Newcomb, for George Sawbridge, 1657. 137 p. **N 90**

A violent attack on Goodwin by a fellow journalist who hoped by it to gain favor with Cromwell.

"Need to Know; Meeting at Northwestern University." *Newsweek*, 38:57–58, 8 October 1951. **N 91**

Highlights of a conference on freedom of information attended by representatives of American press and radio.

Neep, Edward J. C. *Seditious Offenses. With an Introductory Note by Harold J. Laski.* London, Fabian Society, 1926. 30 p. (Fabian Tracts no. 220) **N 92**

Nehls, Edward, ed. *D. H. Lawrence: A Composite Biography . . .* Madison, University of Wisconsin Press, 1959. 3 vols. **N 93**

These volumes contain references throughout to censorship action taken against Lawrence's work—the ban on *Lady Chatterley's Lover*, the seizure of the *Pansies* manuscript (including debate in Parliament over the incident and the Obscene Publications Act), and seizure of Lawrence's paintings by London police. The events are often reported in correspondence between Lawrence and friends.

[Neilson, Samuel, et al.]. *A Faithful Report of the Second Trial of the Proprietors of the Northern Star for the Insertion of the Society of United Irishmen's Address to the Volunteers of Ireland on the 19th December, 1792. By a Barrister.* Belfast, 1795. 56 p. (A similar report of the first trial was published in 1794) **N 94**

The formation of the Society of United Irishmen in Belfast in 1791, urging Irish independence, served to increase government persecution of the opposition press. This was carried out through such measures as use of spies, bribery, military raids, and, ultimately, libel charges in the courts. The *Northern Star* became the United Irishmen's spokesman. Its 12 proprietors, including Samuel Neilson, who also served as editor, were arrested in December 1792 for publishing the Dublin United Irishmen's *Address to the Volunteers*. After an 18-month delay, a part of the harassment plan, they were brought to trial before Lord Clonmell, but for a different libel. The printer was sentenced; the proprietors freed. At a second trial (November 1794) for the original libel, the defense was assured a verdict of "not guilty" by showing that a loyal paper, the Belfast *News-letter*, had published the same *Address* a day before it appeared in the *Northern Star*. In May 1797 a military party entered the office of the *Northern Star* without a warrant and destroyed the printing plant.

Neilson, William A. "The Theory of Censorship." *Atlantic Monthly*, 145:13–16, January 1930. **N 95**

The president of Smith College explores "what principles are implied in the suppression of books and other forms of expression and whether these are in harmony with common sense and the ideas which lie at the basis of our social structure." Neilson closes with a quote from the critic, Sir Walter A. Raleigh, referring to the novels of Fielding: "Books are written to be read by those who can understand them; their possible effect on those who cannot is a matter of medical rather than literary interest."

Neilson, Winthrop, and Frances Neilson. *Verdict for the Doctor; The Case of Benjamin Rush.* New York, Hastings, 1958. 245 p. **N 96**

The celebrated Philadelphia libel case against William Cobbett, 1799. Cobbett had published a series of scurrilous articles in his *Porcupine's Gazette* attacking Dr. Rush for his methods of treating patients during the yellow fever epidemic in Philadelphia. Arguments in the trial were based on whether or not Cobbett's attacks were privileged under "freedom of the press." The case became a struggle between Federalist supporters of Cobbett and Republican supporters of Rush, although Rush had the support of both Adams and Jefferson. The jury ruled in behalf of Dr. Rush, fining Cobbett $5,000. Cobbett departed soon afterwards for England. Rush's lawyers were Joseph Hopkinson, William Lewis, Moses Levy, and Jared Ingersoll; Cobbett's lawyers were William Rawle, Edward Tilghman, and Robert Goodloe Harper.

Nekvasil, M. E. *Control of Public Diffusion of Knowledge and Ideas: Fascist, Communist, Liberal.* Chicago, University of Chicago, 1957. 65 p. (Unpublished Master's thesis) **N 97**

Nelles, Walter, ed. *Espionage Act Cases, with Certain Others on Related Points; New Law in Making As to Criminal Utterance in Wartime.* New York, National Civil Liberties Bureau, 1918. 92 p. **N 98**
Contains extracts from significant court decisions and statutes.

———, and Carol W. King. "Contempt by Publication in the United States." *Columbia Law Review*, 28:401–31, April 1928; 28:525–62, May 1928. (Reprinted by American Civil Liberties Union, 1928. 79 p.) **N 99**
A reconsideration of the doctrine that the courts have "inherent" power to punish summarily contempts by publication. The first part of the study deals with the development of the doctrine down to the passage of the Federal Contempt Statute in 1831. The second part deals with court decisions since that date. An appendix gives a table of statutory provisions by states.

Nelson, Harold L. "Home-Grown Suppression: Press Restraint in Colonial America." *Grassroots Editor*, 2:12–13+, October 1961. **N 100**
"The colonial press was more effectively throttled by home-grown entities than by the towers of aristocratic authority holding power under the king." The author cites the elected assemblies (after 1736) as "the fiercest oppressor of the press that existed in colonial times." After 1765 they were joined by patriot groups in suppressing printers.

———. *Libel in News of Congressional Investigating Committees.* Minneapolis, University of Minnesota Press, 1961. 174 p. **N 101**

"This study attempts to discover and describe activities of legislative investigating committees that may not furnish a basis for the immunity of the press from liability from libel in reporting such activities."

Nelson, Helen. "Watchdog of the British Press." *Saturday Review*, 47(32):42–43, 8 August 1964. **N 102**
A report on the work of the British Press Council, set up in 1953 at the suggestion of the First Royal Commission of the Press. Through the investigations of questionable practices, the Council developed a body of case law on newspaper ethics. There were numerous decisions defending theater and film critics from undue pressure from editors and advertisers, defending reporters from unethical demands of editors and unjust criticism from the public, and defending reporters who refused to disclose news sources. Reprimands were also issued by the Press Council to papers that had "sunk below the accepted levels of decency."

Nelson, Jack. "What Is the Problem?" *NEA Journal*, 52:19–21, May 1963. **N 103**
A survey of the nationwide attacks on school textbooks. "In nearly a third of our state legislatures, textbooks came under fire from the early part of 1958 until the end of 1962." (Part of a 11-page feature on textbook censorship.)

———, and Gene Roberts, Jr. *The Censors and the Schools.* Boston, Little, Brown, 1963. 208 p. **N 104**
A report on an investigation by two Nieman Fellows of the activities of pressure groups which attempt to influence the selection and content of public school textbooks. Included are the activities of the DAR, American Legion, America's Future, Inc., Texans for America, and the NAACP. Individuals taking a leading part in censorship efforts include Lucille Cardin Crain of the *Educational Reviewer*, E. Merrill Root, and J. Evetts Haley.

Nelson, S. C. *The Latest Literary Boycott: A Bookseller's Censorship.* London, 196 Strand, [1898?]. 8 p. **N 105**
Smith & Son of London refused to stock a novel entitled *God Is Love* by T. M. Ellis because they objected to the title for a work of fiction. The author complained both to the lending library and to the Society of Authors. This pamphlet urges that the book be ordered by mail.

Nerboso, Salvatore D. "McCarthy og de amerikanske informationsbiblioteker i udlandet." *Bogens Verden*, 36:167–68, May 1954. **N 106**
Senator McCarthy and the attack on American information libraries abroad.

———. "U.S. Libraries." *Library Journal*, 79:20–25, 1 January 1954. (Reprinted in

Daniels, *Censorship of Books*, pp. 107–11) **N 107**
An account of the furor over censorship of books in U.S. information libraries overseas.

Nethercot, Arthur H. "Birth Control and *The Fruits of Philosphy*." In his *The First Five Lives of Annie Besant*. Chicago, University of Chicago Press, 1960, pp. 107–30. **N 108**
Among her many activities, Mrs. Besant was the first prominent woman to fight openly for birth control. This chapter deals with the famous court case, *Queen v. Besant and Bradlaugh* (1878) for the sale of Charles Knowlton's book on birth control.

Netherlands. Department van Buitenlandsche Zaken. *Diplomatieke Bescheiden Betreffende de Inbeslagneming door de Britsche Autoriteiten van over Zee Vervoerde Brievenpost.* Gravenhage, Algemeene Landsdrukkerij, 1916. 5 p. **N 109**
Postal censorship in Great Britain during World War I.

Neville, Laurence E. "Free Speech and Broadcasting." *Broadcast*, 16(3):40, 1 February 1939. **N 110**
An editorial exploring various aspects of the confused state of mind with respect to freedom in broadcasting—the uncertainties in the application of administrative law by the FCC, the consideration by the broadcaster of his advertisers, and the difference between newspapers and broadcasting with respect to laws of libel and slander.

New Bedford, Mass. Free Public Library. *The William L. Sayer Collection of Books and Pamphlets Relating to Printing, Newspapers, and Freedom of the Press.* New Bedford, Mass., Free Public Library. Part 1, 1914 (38 p.). Part 2, 1920 (24 p.). **N 111**
A list of 161 titles (80 in part 1, 81 in part 2) including many reports of early trials relating to freedom of the press. Particularly strong in newspaper libel cases. The pertinent publications are listed in the present bibliography.

"A New Bill to Amend the Obscene Books Law." *Massachusetts Library Club Bulletin*, 19:8–9, March 1929. **N 112**
The text of the Shattuck bill, sponsored by the Massachusetts Library Club.

"New Censorship Bill; Massachusetts Citizens' Commitee for the Revision of the Book Law." *Publishers' Weekly*, 116:2820–21, 21 December 1929. **N 113**

Draft of a bill to amend the Massachusetts obscenity statutes to solve "the distressing situation which has brought the ridicule of the entire civilized world upon the city of Boston." Edward L. Weeks, editor of the *Atlantic Monthly*, was chairman of the Revisions Committee.

"New Constitutional Definition of Libel and Its Future." *Northwestern University Law Review*, 60:95–113, March–April 1965.　　　　　　　　　**N 114**
An analysis of the doctrine on libel enunciated by the U.S. Supreme Court in the *New York Times* case and the prospects for expansion of the doctrine.

New England Society for the Suppression of Vice. *Appeal for Support.* Boston, The Society, 1878. 4 p.　　　　**N 115**
The Executive Committee, headed by Professor Homer B. Sprague, appeals for financial support of the newly organized vice society of Boston, "to aid in purifying our literature and checking our immorality." The Appeal also invited parents and teachers to report any evidence of immoral publications.

New England Watch and Ward Society. *Dunster House Book Shop Case. A Statement by the Directors of The New England Watch and Ward Society.* Boston, 1930. 25 p.　　　　　　　　　　　　　**N 116**
The Watch and Ward Society secured the arrest of James A. Delacey, proprietor of the Dunster House Book Store in Cambridge, and his clerk, for the sale of *Lady Chatterley's Lover* to an agent provocateur of the Society. Both were fined and given short prison sentences. The method of entrapment greatly aroused the public and the Boston press against the Society. The case (*Commonwealth v. Delacey*) was appealed to the Supreme Judicial Court of Massachusetts, where the verdict of the lower courts was sustained, but the jail sentences remitted. This report was prepared by Thomas W. Proctor, attorney for the Society, to justify its part in the affair. "I have seen nothing in the activities of the agents of the Society in this case that was not in the public interest," Proctor concluded. The case had the effect of bringing about a change in the tactics of the Society and, indirectly, a modification of the Massachusetts obscenity law.

———. *Reports.* Boston, The Society. Annual, 1878–date. (From 1878 to 1891, the organization was known as the New England Society for the Suppression of Vice)　　　　　　　　　　　**N 117**
The Society was organized in 1878 as an outgrowth of the Comstock movement to suppress the traffic in pornography. Gradually the efforts of the Society's agents turned on legitimate works of literature, succeeding in 1882 in suppressing the publication of Whitman's *Leaves of Grass* and stopping the sale of various classics and best sellers. Its successful action against the popular novel *Three Weeks* (*Commonwealth v. Buckley*), in 1907 brought the Society to the peak of its power. During the 20's it received the cooperation of the Boston booksellers in a system of self-censorship which kept from the bookstores many of the frank novels of the post-World War I period. In 1925 H. L. Mencken successfully challenged the Society by selling a copy of his *American Mercury* on the Boston Common to Frank Chase, longtime agent of the Society, and in 1930 the Society was subjected to public ridicule in the entrapment of a Cambridge bookseller for the sale of *Lady Chatterley's Lover*. In the 1950's the Society turned from literary censorship to a program of education against corruption, graft, and juvenile delinquency. During most of its history the Society had the backing of prominent Boston leadership and had the support of the city officials, the courts, and the press.

New Jersey. Assembly. Committee to Study and Investigate Obscenity in Certain Publications. *Final Report. Pursuant to Assembly Concurrent Resolution No. 15, 1960.* [Trenton], The Assembly, 1962. 38 p.　　　　　　　　　　　　**N 118**

———. *Public Hearing Held Assembly Chamber, State House, Trenton, New Jersey, October 17, 1961.* [Trenton, 1961]. 93 p.　　　　　　　　　　　　　　　**N 119**

New Jersey Committee for The Right to Read. *The Readers' Right.* Caldwell, N.J., The Committee, 1964–date. Bimonthly.　　　　　　　　　　　**N 120**
A mimeographed newsletter issued to report on New Jersey events relating to censorship. The Committee "is organized to support local action groups with guidance and with information relating to censorship groups and their activities, while also maintaining a statewide educational and public relations program."

"New Jersey's Journalistic Perils." *Literary Digest*, 46:1366–67, 21 June 1913.　**N 121**
Excerpts from newspaper editorials defending editor Alexander Scott who had been convicted and imprisoned for "daring to impugn the Paterson police in his *Weekly Issue*."

New Orleans. Public Relations Section. *Report on Comic Books, to Mayor Morrison and the Common Council of City of New Orleans.* [New Orleans, 1948]. 49 p.　　　　　　　　　　　　　　　**N 122**
Report was prepared by Dave McGuire, city director of public relations.

"New Pennsylvania Libel Law." *Outlook*, 74:202–3, 23 May 1903.　　　**N 123**
The ban on caricatures of political figures in the press is an abridgment of freedom of the press. Relates to the case of Governor Pennypacker, sponsor of a more severe libel law.

"New Phases of the Government's War upon Disloyalty." *Current Opinion*, 63: 223–24, October 1917.　　　　　**N 124**
Deals with the suppression of radical papers and meetings during World War I. Lists some of the papers being suppressed and the groups forbidden to have meetings.

"The New Pornography." *Time*, 85(16): 28–29, 16 April 1965.　　　　　**N 125**
With the liberalizing court decisions on what is obscene, just about anything is now printable in the United States. The pornographer finds himself hard put to stay ahead of the avant-garde literary publishers. This essay treats of the "new immoralist" whose writings add up to "homosexual nihilism" (the Genet-Burroughs crowd). Their writings are not pornographic in the sense of arousing sexual excitement; they create a pornographic nausea and are an offense against hedonism. The article quotes a Methodist minister as saying: "A return to ribaldry would be a very good thing. People ought to laugh in bed, and at some of the current writing about bed."

A New Project for the Destruction of Printing and Bookselling; for the Benefit of the Learned World . . . London, Printed from the Dublin copy, and sold by J. Roberts, [1729].　　　　　　**N 126**
This eighteenth-century pamphlet is the subject of W. G. Clifford's book of essays, *Books in Bottles*, London, Bles, 1926. The gist of the pamphlet, presumably a piece of whimsey, is that since "sounds are nothing but Air put in Motion," ideas expressed in sound could be bottled for future use, enabling printed books to be destroyed. Ideas could be stored like wine and released with a corkscrew.

New Republic. "A Special *New Republic* Report on Book Burning." *New Republic*, 128(26):7–17, 29 June 1953.　　**N 127**
Contains a summary of Senator McCarthy's attack on the overseas library program of the U.S. State Department, excerpts from McCarthy's questioning of James C. Conant, U.S. High Commissioner for Germany, and articles on voluntary censorship in San Antonio by Maury Maverick; St. Cloud, Minn., by Clifford Davison; and Boston by Lawrence J. Kipp.

"New Varieties of Censorship." *Survey*, 43:222–24, 13 December 1919.　**N 128**
Relates to the suppression of the *Seattle Union Record* and the arrest of its editors on charges under the Espionage Act, and the arrest of the editor of the *Business Chronicle*, an extreme antiunion weekly in Seattle, both actions part of the aftermath of the Armistice Day killings at Centralia, Wash.

New York (State). Legislature. Joint Committee Investigating Seditious Activities. *Revolutionary Radicalism; Its History, Purpose and Tactics with an Exposition and Discussion of the Steps Being Taken and Required to Curb It . . .* Albany, The Committee, 1920. 4 vols. **N 129**
A chapter on Freedom of Speech (vol. 3) summarizes the federal and New York laws relating to espionage and criminal anarchy and cites cases tried under the acts. The Committee recommends no further legislation, believing that the New York anarchy law is adequate. The text of anarchy statutes is given for the following states and territories: Alaska, California, Indiana, Iowa, Kansas, Louisiana, Michigan, Minnesota, Nebraska, New Hampshire, New Jersey, New York, Ohio, Oregon, Pennsylvania, Rhode Island, South Dakota, and West Virginia. Volume 2 contains a section analyzing Communist propaganda in the United States, with quotations taken from newspapers and periodicals that are "either frankly revolutionary and seditious, or those which show an apologetic attitude toward all subversive movements." It is not suggested that the works should be suppressed. There is also a description (pp. 1979–89) of the activities of the American Civil Liberties Union and a reprinting of an ACLU pamphlet stating that organization's views on freedom of speech and the press.

———. Legislature. Joint Legislative Committee to Study the Publication and Dissemination of Offensive and Obscene Material. *Reports.* Albany, Williams Press, 1951–date. Annual except for 1953; before 1955 called Joint Legislative Committee to Study the Publication of Comics. The reports appear in the Legislative Documents series. **N 130**
The Committee was organized in 1949 to consider the effect of "comic books" on juvenile delinquency and to recommend appropriate legislative action. The Committee later expanded its concern to include all printed matter (including greeting cards), motion and still pictures, phonograph records, radio, and television. The Committee conducted hearings, received testimony, compiled exhibits of offending works, and, in its reports, summarizes the legislative and judicial events of the preceding year and recommends statutory changes. The 1958 report contains an article by Judge Charles S. Desmond on Free Speech and Obscenity; a report of the case of *People of State of New York v. Richmond County News*, relating to knowledge of a work being obscene; a report on The Scienter Requirement in Obscenity by R. Marshall Witten; the case of *Charles H. Tenney, Corp. Counsel City of New York v. Liberty News Distributors*; a Guide for Neighborhood Committees for Decent Literature; a report on the use of paperback books in the Buffalo Public Schools; statements of the Roman Catholic Episcopal Committee for Motion Pictures, Radio, and Television; and proposed federal legislation creating a commission on noxious and obscene matters and materials.

———. Legislature. Law Revision Committee. *Report and Study Relating to Problems Involved in Conferring upon Newspapermen a Privilege which Would Legally Protect them from Divulging Sources of Information Given to Them.* Albany, Williams Press, 1949. 146 p. (Legislative Document 1949, no. 65–A) **N 131**

———. Motion Picture Commission. *Annual Reports, 1921–26.* Albany, J. B. Lyon, 1922–27. 5 vols. (Continued by the Report of the Motion Picture Division, University of the State of New York) **N 132**
Reports include statistical record of objectionable sections of film eliminated and for what causes. Extracts from the 1922 report, consisting of arguments for State regulation of motion pictures, are published in Rutland, *State Censorship of Motion Pictures*, pp. 63–68.

"New York County Lawyers' Association Conference on Fair Trial-Free Press." *Bar Bulletin*, New York County Lawyers' Association, 11:7–51, May 1953. **N 133**
The entire issue is devoted to reporting on the conference, opened by Edwin M. Otterbourg, president of the Association. Participants include Simon H. Rifkind, F. A. Vallat (British practice), Arthur G. Hays, James A. Wechsler, Lloyd P. Stryker, Herbert B. Swope, Stuart N. Updike, and Sig Mickelson. A special committee was appointed to formulate a declaration of principles respecting the proper scope of public reporting on court proceedings.

New York Society for the Suppression of Vice. *Annual Reports.* New York, The Society, 1874–1948? From 1874 (vol. 1) to 1937 (vol. 64) the publication bore the title, *Annual Report*; beginning in 1938 (vol. 65) it was entitled *Year Book*. The name of the society was changed in 1947 to the Society to Maintain Public Decency. No record of reports found since 1948 (75th annual). **N 134**
The first of the American vice societies was incorporated 16 May 1873 under New York law with the object of "enforcement of the laws for the suppression of the trade in and circulation of obscene literature and illustrations, advertisements and articles of indecent and immoral use, as it is forbidden by the laws of the State of New York or of the United States." The act of corporation required the New York city police to "aid this corporation, its members or agents, in the enforcement of all laws . . . for the suppression of the acts and offenses specified in . . . this Act." The act also permitted the Society to retain one-half of the fines collected through action of the Society. The Society was organized through the efforts of Anthony Comstock and he was for many years its secretary and guiding hand.

———. *Periodical Letter.* New York, The Society, 1925–1934. Issued irregularly. 2- to 4-page printed letters. **N 135**
Letters addressed to members and friends of the Society, each copy personally signed by John S. Sumner, the Society's secretary. The letters generally reported on special cases and developments in the Society's campaigns against indecent literature.

———. *65th Milestone.* New York, The Society, 1938. 18 p. plus some unnumbered pages. **N 136**
A brief history of the Society followed by letters of congratulation and appreciation from President Franklin D. Roosevelt, District Attorney Thomas E. Dewey, and others.

New York State Conference of Mayors and Other City Officials. *Report on State Censorship of Moving Pictures.* Albany, The Conference, 1930. 10 p. (Reprinted in Rutland, *State Censorship of Motion Pictures*, pp. 95–106) **N 137**
The Committee appointed to investigate the regulation of motion pictures reported "unalterably opposed to any form of state censorship." Among the reasons given: the principle is un-American; it is a backward step in the progress of civilization; it is fundamentally wrong to enact morals by legislation; it would be unsatisfactory to administer; it is subject to political pressure; it would retard the development of motion pictures; it is class legislation; it usurps the function of parents. Legalized censorship of films "is no less dangerous than a censorship of the press or the stage, for it places a ban on ideas."

New York University. School of Law. *Annual Survey of American Law.* New York, The School, 1942–date. **N 138**
Each annual volume contains recent legislation and court cases relating to freedom of the press as a part of the section on civil rights. Since 1946 the section has been compiled by Ralph F. Bischoff.

"New Zealand Government Is Making Legislative Attempt to Ban Books Secretly." *Library Journal*, 88:3041, 1 September 1963 **N 139**

New Zealand Library Association. "Report of the Censorship Committee." *New Zealand Libraries*, 9:189–91, November 1946. **N 140**
This report, sent to the Prime Minister, asserts the position of the Association as "unalterably averse to the censorship of books on qualitative grounds." It recommends a tribunal which will restrict censorship to its necessary scope, give it the sanction of public opinion, and make it operate with little hardship to all concerned. Specifically, the

report recommends consideration of the pattern of the Australian Literary Censorship Board, but warns of the experience with such a board in Eire. The report calls for close cooperation with similar agencies in Britain and the United States.

"New Zealand Tribunal's First Judgment." *Bookseller*, 3041:1526–27, 4 April 1964.   **N 141**
"The New Zealand Tribunal appointed under the Indecent Publications Act, giving its first judgment, says that five members of the Tribunal had 'no hesitation' in deciding that the novel, *Another Country*, by James Baldwin, was not indecent within the meaning of the Act." Includes text of findings.

[Newbolt, William]. "The Trial of William Newbolt and Edward Buttler, Printers, for High Treason, in Composing and Imagining the Death of . . . King William and Queen Mary. Now first published from the Harleian MSS. in the British Museum, circ. 1692–95." In Howell, *State Trials*, vol. 15, pp. 1404–8.   **N 142**
The offending work was *The Late King James's Declaration*. Both men were found guilty but there is no record of the punishment.

Newell, Martin L. *The Law of Slander and Libel in Civil and Criminal Cases*. 4th ed. Chicago, Callaghan, 1924. 1109 p. First edition 1890.   **N 143**
Leading American treatise on slander and libel, including important British and American cases, indicating the historical development of the law.

Newell, Thomas M., and Albert Pickerell. "California's Retraction Statute: License to Libel?" *Journalism Quarterly*, 28:474–82, Fall 1951.   **N 144**

Newgate Monthly Magazine, or Calendar of Men, Things, and Opinions. London, Richard Carlile, 1824–26. Monthly.   **N 145**
While in Newgate prison for defying the authorities in the sale of Thomas Paine's works, Carlile edited this paper and his voluntary shopmen, Campion, Hassell, and Perry, printed and distributed it. The magazine contained essays on science, technology, and especially freedom of expression. The motto on the masthead was: "Error alone needs artificial support. Truth can stand by itself."

Newman, Bruce L. "Constitutional Law: The Problem with Obscenity." *Western Reserve Law Review*, 11:669–79, September 1960.   **N 146**

Newman, Edwin S., *ed. The Freedom Reader*. New York, Oceana, 1955. 256 p. (Docket Series vol. 2)   **N 147**
A collection of writings on civil liberties, including excerpts from court decisions and prominent opinion-moulders. Includes the "clear and present danger" formula of Justice Holmes (*Schenck v. U.S.*), Judge Woolsey's decision on obscenity in the *Ulysses* case, the *Hannegan v. Esquire* decision, the Supreme Court decision in *The Miracle* film censorship case (*Burstyn v. Wilson*), and the Supreme Court decision in the case of *Winters v. New York* which related to the publication of crime news. Also included is the American Civil Liberties Union statement on censorship of comic books and the Freedom to Read statement of the American Library Association and the American Book Publishers Council.

Newman, James R. "Control of Information Relating to Atomic Energy." *Yale Law Journal*, 56:769–802, May 1947. (Reprinted in Summers, *Federal Information Controls in Peacetime*, pp. 86–97)   **N 148**
We must recognize the dangers to the fundamental values of our democratic system "implicit in an uncritical policy of placing immediate security considerations before everything else." Based on material in the book, *The Control of Atomic Energy*, by Newman and Miller.

———, and Byron S. Miller. *The Control of Atomic Energy; a Study of the Social, Economic, and Political Implications*. New York, Whittlesey, 1948. 434 p.   **N 149**
Chapter 10 deals with control of information. Restriction on freedom of communications among the scientists is symptomatic of a broader assault on the freedom of ideas in the interest of national security. We must scrutinize all measures which purport to serve security purposes at the expense of individual liberty, and reject those that are not essential or well-designed to serve the intended purpose.

———. "Freedom of Science in America." *Atlantic Monthly*, 180:27–32, September 1947.   **N 150**
"Secrecy. There is a present danger that American research may be stifled. In technical skill and inventiveness the United States has been pre-eminent; but for basic research in fundamental science Americans have leaned heavily on the work of German, Italian, Scandinavian, English and other foreign scientists . . . Is our policy of atomic secrecy shutting our scientists off from the rest of the world and from one another?"

Newman, M. W. *The Smut Hunters*. Los Angeles, All American Distributors, 1964. 30 p. (Originally published as a series in the *Chicago Daily News*, starting 31 August 1964 and running through 10 September 1964)   **N 151**

A detailed account of recent book-banning in Chicago, conducted under the direction of municipal officials and with the prompting of the Citizens for Decent Literature. The scene has brought forth charges that "the harassing of reputable book dealers is worse in Chicago than in any other city in the country" and that Chicago is now the "Boston" of America. The article recites specific cases, including the action against *Candy* and *Tropic of Cancer* and gives names of those involved both in censorship and combating censorship.

Newman, Robert, and Robert Anderson. *Freedom in Company Communications*. Columbia, Mo., Freedom of Information Center, School of Journalism, University of Missouri, 1964. 8 p. (Publication no. 131)   **N 152**
A viewpoint on controversial Section 8(c) of the Taft-Hartley Act relating to the free flow of management-labor communications by Robert Newman, information specialist for General Electric, followed by a general explanation of the National Labor Relations Board's historic position in interpretation of this section of the act, presented by Robert Anderson, executive assistant to the general counsel of the NLRB.

"News v. Security: Excerpts from a Debate between the President [John F. Kennedy] and the Press." *Columbia Journalism Review*, 1:45–47, Fall 1961.   **N 153**
Quotations from President Kennedy and from newspaper editorials dealing with the issue of the press v. national security, a debate occasioned by the Cuban crisis.

Newsman, [pseud.]. "The Press in the Provinces." *Fortnightly*, 167:350–57, May 1947.   **N 154**
A survey of the condition and ownership of the provincial press of England, with a recommendation for a study of the ownership scheme of the *Manchester Guardian* (ownership by private trust), so that newspapers will become "a public service and not an instrument of private power or private profit."

The Newspaper Conscience. 14 min., 5-inch phonotape. Boulder, Colo., National Tape Repository, University of Colorado. (That You May Know Series)   **N 155**

"Newspaper Law." *Albany Law Journal*, 19:188–89, 8 March 1879; 19:208–9, 15 March 1879; 19:228–29, 22 March 1879; and 19:248–49, 29 March 1879.   **N 156**
A lawyer observes the abuses of editorial privilege and the practical application of the law of newspaper libel as it is being interpreted by the American courts in the 1870's.

Newspaper-Radio Committee. *Freedom of the Press—What It is, How It Was Obtained,*

How It Can Be Retained. New York, The Committee, 1942. 105 p. **N157**
The Committee was organized for the defense of newspaper ownership of radio stations in the FCC monopoly investigations of 1941. Six witnesses testified for the Committee, citing concepts of the freedom of the press.

"Newspaper Reporting as a Political Engine." *Eclectic Museum*, 3:423–24, November 1843. (Reprinted from *Spectator*) **N158**
Criticizes the practice of summoning newspaper reporters as witnesses in court. While they should not be exempt from testifying, the prosecution should know that "whenever a newspaper reporter is called as a witness, injury is done to that organ of general publicity which is one efficient safeguard of peace and good government."

"Newspaper Tax." *Edinburgh Review*, 61:96–99, April 1835. **N159**
Newspaper taxes amounting to 200 per cent are supported by the large newspapers, according to the author, because they tend to keep out competitors. The newspaper tax keeps information and knowledge away from the poor who are unable to pay for higher priced papers. The article was prompted by a Petition from the Inhabitants of the City of London against the Newspaper Stamps.

"Newspapers and Private Life; a Poll of the Press." *Outlook*, 104:329–30, 14 June 1913. **N160**
Quotations from newspaper editorials on the outcome of the Theodore Roosevelt libel case. The New York *Tribune* believes the verdict "will warn those who think that they can safely repeat in a public way the irresponsible stories which they hear about men of prominence."

"Newspapers and the Codes." *Christian Century*, 50:1361–62, 1 November 1933. **N161**
The newspapers' opposition to the proposed NRA code as a threat to freedom of the press is a false issue. Newspapers should be free as organs of opinion to support or criticize the government as they will. As manufacturing establishments they should not enjoy special exemptions.

"Newspapers in Defense of a Free Press." *Viewpoint* (West Coast News Co.), 1(2):1–4, 1960. **N162**
Reports opinions and action taken by the press against censorship threats to the various mass media.

"Newsstands: a National Disgrace." *Catholic Preview of Entertainment*, 6:24–28, September 1962. **N163**
An attack on the pornography being sold on American newsstands

Newsweek. Club and Educational Bureau. *Censorship for the Mass Audience: a Protection or a Threat?* New York, The Bureau, 1953. 23 p. (Platform Study Guide) **N164**

Newton, Virgil M. *An Editor Views Bureaucracy, Part I*. Columbia, Mo., Freedom of Information Center, School of Journalism, University of Missouri, 1959. 4 p. (Publication no. 14) **N165**
The managing editor of the *Tampa Tribune* and chairman of the Freedom of Information Committee of Sigma Delta Chi, discusses secrecy in government. "Over the last 25 years, an arrogant federal bureaucracy has clamped a tight vise of secrecy over all records of government at Washington."

———. *An Editor Views Bureaucracy, Part II*. Columbia, Mo., Freedom of Information Center, School of Journalism, University of Missouri, 1959. 4 p. (Publication no. 15) **N166**
A discussion of the *Tampa Tribune's* crusade for information about the affairs of Tampa and the State of Florida.

———. "A Growing Threat to Democracy: Secrecy in Government." *Quill*, 41(9):7, 14–17, September 1953. **N167**
A summary of six months of work by the Freedom of Information Committee of Sigma Delta Chi.

———. *Newsman's Free Press Brief*. Columbia, Mo., Freedom of Information Center, School of Journalism, University of Missouri, 1963. 8 p. (Publication no. 105) **N168**
Portion of the *amicus curiae* brief submitted by the chairman of Sigma Delta Chi's Freedom of Information Committee, in the mandamus suit of three Long Island newspapers to examine the records of the Long Island State Park Commission. After seven months, officials of the Commission bowed to the newspapers' demands. The brief includes historic, philosophical, and legal arguments for public access to records.

———. *The Press and Bureaucracy*. Tucson, University of Arizona Press, 1961. 8 p. (The John Peter Zenger Award for Freedom of the Press, number 7) **N169**
The 1960 recipient of the award was the managing editor of the *Tampa Tribune*, for eight years chairman of Sigma Delta Chi's Freedom of Information Committee and a vigorous crusader for freedom of the press.

Next Revolution; or, Woman's Emancipation from Sex Slavery. Valley Falls, Kan., Lucifer Publishing Co. [1890?]. 34 p. **N170**

Contains matter on the Moses Harman obscenity case and the arrest of J. B. Caldwell, editor of *Christian Life*, for supporting Harman's crusade for the sex emancipation of women.

Nicholas, George. *A Letter from George Nicholas, of Kentucky, to His Friend, in Virginia, Justifying Conduct of the Citizens of Kentucky, as to Some of the Late Measures of the General Government; and Correcting Certain False Statements, Which Have Been Made in the Different States, of the Views and Actions of the People of Kentucky*. Lexington, Ky., Printed by James Bradford, 1798. 42 p. Reprinted by James Carey, Philadelphia, 1799. 39 p. **N171**
A defense of the Kentucky Resolutions, which were critical of the Alien and Sedition laws. Nicholas was a leading anti-Federalist who had cooperated with James Madison in the struggle for religious freedom. Nicholas' letter is answered by an anonymous writer, *Observations on a Letter from George Nicholas . . .*

Nicholas, H. G. "Parliament and Press." *Nineteenth Century and After*, 143:249–55, May 1948. **N172**
An account of the differences between Parliament and the press in matters of disclosures by journalists.

Nichols, Lewis. ["Customs Censorship"]. In his "In and Out of Books" column, *New York Times Book Review*, 10 July 1960, p. 8. **N173**
The author reports on his visit with the U.S. Customs censor and on his interview with Huntington Cairnes of the National Gallery of Art, who serves as literary advisor to the Customs Office.

Nicholson, Margaret. *A Manual of Copyright Practice for Writers, Publishers, and Agents*. 2d ed. New York, Oxford University Press, 1956. 273 p. **N174**

Nicholson, Watson. *The Struggle for a Free Stage in London*. London, Constable, 1906. 475 p. (Reprinted in 1966 by Benjamin Bloom, Bronx, N.Y.) **N175**
"The subject of this volume is the story of the long struggle to free London of the theatrical monopoly, a struggle which began almost within the lifetime of the second Charles himself, and culminated in the parliamentary act of 1843." This was the Theatre Regulation Act which deprived the two patent theaters, Drury Lane and Covent Garden, of the monopoly they had possessed for nearly two centuries.

Nicoll, De Lancey. *Panama Libel Case. The United States, Plaintiff in Error v. Press*

Publishing Company. Writ of Error to the Circuit Court of the United States for the Southern District of New York Sued out by the Government to Review a Judgment Quashing an Indictment Charging the Publication . . . of Alleged Libels Printed in the New York World. Argument of De Lancey Nicoll, Esquire, of Counsel for the Defendant, before the Supreme Court, Washington, October 24, 1910. [New York, 1910]. 43 p.

N 176

Nieburg, Harold L. *Nuclear Secrecy and Foreign Policy.* Washington, D.C., Public Affairs, 1964. 255 p. **N 177**
This work attempts to put into a coherent whole the story of nuclear secrecy, its political, military, and diplomatic significance.

Nieman Reports. Cambridge, Mass., Society of Nieman Fellows, 1947–date. Monthly.

N 178

In addition to articles on freedom of the press, this periodical often carries news articles, editorials, and notes on the subject.

Nierman, F. K. "Propaganda and the College and University Library." *News Notes*, 17(2):19–21, July 1941. **N 179**
If the library collects propaganda pamphlets they should be filed separately. The University of Texas files such material geographically by country of origin. While taking a liberal view of accepting minority opinion, the author believes that in time of crisis it may be necessary to reject some propaganda.

Nightingale, G. M. "Vulgar Postcards." *Justice of the Peace*, 118:5–6, January 1954.

N 180

Advice to local law enforcement officers on the legal authority and procedure for taking action against allegedly obscene postcards. Court decisions are cited.

Nimmer, Melville B. "The Constitutionality of Official Censorship of Motion Pictures." *University of Chicago Law Review*, 25:625–57, Summer 1958. **N 181**
The article is concerned with official censorship by legally constituted authorities of state or local government, and the limitations imposed on them by the federal constitution. The study was conducted under a grant from the Fund for the Republic.

Nineteen Numbers of the Radical Reformer, and Working Man's Advocate: a Philadelphia Weekly Publication, Edited and Published by Thomas Brothers: to Which is appended;

A Letter to Mr. Daniel Webster . . . Philadelphia, Coates, Printer, 1836. 208 p.

N 182

Includes an account of William Cobbett's trial and Remarks of Benjamin Franklin on Toleration. Cited in Theodore Schroeder's *Free Speech Bibliography.*

"The 1964 Obscene Publications Bill Creates a New Offense." *Bookseller*, 3051: 2168–72, 13 June 1964; 3052:2226–30, 20 June 1964; 3054:12–16, 4 July 1964; 3055:62–63, 11 July 1964; 3058:970–74, 1 August 1964. **N 183**
The first article discusses the reasons for introduction in the House of Commons of amendments to the 1959 Act. The proponents believed the 1959 Act less effective than was intended in checking pornography with no literary merit. "The new Act created a new offence of having an obscene article of publication for gain." Mere possession with intent to sell would be actionable. The second article (20 June) carries an account of the debate in the House of Commons over right of trial by jury. The third article (4 July) continues the debate on the bill, with reference to the recent cases against *Fanny Hill.* The fourth article (11 July) reports the bill as passing third reading in the House. The fifth article (1 August) reports the passage of the bill by the Lords and the discussion by that body which included reference to the action against *Lady Chatterley* and *Fanny Hill* under the 1959 Act. The bill was sent back to the House of Commons without amendment.

Nissen, David R. "Freedom of Speech and Press Includes the Right to Distribute Handbills Anonymously." *University of Illinois Law Forum*, 1961(1):169–72, Spring 1961. **N 184**
Relates to the Talley case, 362 U.S. 60 (1960).

Nixon, Raymond B. "Factors Related to Freedom in National Press Systems." *Journalism Quarterly*, 37:13–28, Winter 1960. **N 185**
A comparison of press freedom in various countries as reported by the International Press Institute and UNESCO. "Utilizing new data and a new theory appearing in a recent book, the Editor of the *Quarterly* makes a cross-country comparison of four variables in 85 national press systems. The results indicate that socio-economic and cultural factors are closely related to the degree of freedom reported by IPI and IAPA surveys."

———. "Problem of Newspaper Monopoly." In Schramm, *Mass Communications*, Urbana, University of Illinois Press, 1949, pp. 158–67. **N 186**
The author takes issue with Morris Ernst's belief that the government should break up concentration of ownership of the press. He points out that such a monopoly is the result of economic factors, that monopoly does not

in itself insure "badness" nor independence insure "goodness." Many good papers are parts of chains. Nixon believes monopolies are here to stay, that there has been and will be adequate competition from other media.

———. "Propaganda and Censorship in America's Next War." *Journalism Quarterly*, 16:237–44, September 1939. **N 187**
A prediction of the laws and procedures likely to be put into effect to control attitudes and opinion in wartime.

[Nixon, Robert]. *The Tryal of Robert Nixon . . . for a High Crime and Misdemeanour: In Contriving, Writing, Printing, Publishing and Blowing Up in Westminster-Hall A False, Scandalous, Seditious Libel, on Five Acts of Parliament . . .* London, Printed for Ed. Cook, 1737. 10 p. **N 188**
Nixon was charged with issuing a pamphlet that criticized acts of Parliament. He was found guilty and sentenced to five years in prison, assessed a fine, and required to tour the courts bearing a hat that described his offense. Nixon refused to defend himself at the trial and prejudiced his case by literally exploding (using explosives that caused noise and fire) the offending pamphlet in Westminster Hall while the court was in session.

Nizer, Louis. *New Courts of Industry: Self-Regulation under the Motion Picture Code; Including an Analysis of the Code.* New York, Longacre Press, 1935. 344 p. **N 189**
The operation of the code for fair competition under the National Recovery Act, which has no relationship to the motion picture production code. The latter regulates the content of the film, the NRA code relates to economic control.

———. "Reputation: The Libel Case of Quentin Reynolds v. Westbrook Pegler." In his *My Life in Court.* New York, Doubleday, 1961, pp. 17–152. (Condensed in *Reader's Digest*, August 1962, pp. 90–95+) **N 190**
The story of the sensational libel suit brought by Quentin Reynolds, war correspondent and author, against newspaper columnist Westbrook Pegler. Nizer was attorney for the plaintiff. Pegler had made a venomous attack on Reynolds' war record, his morals, his sympathies with communism, and even his physical appearance. In the course of the trial, Pegler retracted many of his statements and others were disproved by witnesses. At one point in the trial, Nizer reported, "we counted 130 times that he said he made a mistake under oath." Pegler and his publishers were found guilty and a total of $175,000 punitive damages was assessed. Appeals to the U.S. Court of Appeals and the U.S. Supreme Court failed to reverse the decision. In his argument before the U.S. Court of Appeals, Nizer said: "Reckless attacks equivalent to character assassination have become too frequent an occurrence in personal column editorializing.

Newspapers are like cannon. They must not be shot carelessly and with abandon. This case afforded an opportunity to encourage the old tradition of checking facts, and to control reckless writers who build circulation by extremism and sensationalism." Nizer reports on the John Henry Faulk blacklisting case in *The Jury Returns*, New York, Doubleday, 1966, pp. 225–438.

————. "Right of Privacy: a Half Century's Developments." *Michigan Law Review*, 39:526–60, February 1941. **N191**
The right of privacy represents a struggle between the right of the individual and the right of society. "With gradual adjustment of the weight given to these forces, a balance will be achieved" between the two opposite ideals—complete privacy and complete public information.

"No Time for Comedy." *Time*, 39:60–62, 16 February 1942. **N192**
Inconsistencies of present-day censorship in the United States.

Noah, Mordecai M. *Report of the Trial of an Action on the Case, Brought by Sylvanus Miller, esq., Late Surrogate of the City and County of New-York, against Mordecai M. Noah, Esq., Editor of the National Advocate, for an Alleged Libel. Tried at the City-Hall, in the City of New-York, before the Circuit Court held in the First Judicial District in the State of the New-York, by his Honour Samuel R. Betts, Esq., on Friday, the 12th day of December, 1823. By L. H. Clarke.* New-York, Printed by J. W. Palmer, 1823. 72 p. **N193**

Nobbe, George. *The North Briton; a Study in Political Propaganda.* New York, Columbia University Press, 1939. 274 p. (Columbia University Studies in English and Comparative Literature, no. 140) **N194**
A study of the weekly paper of John Wilkes that in its short career of less than a year played an important role in freedom of the press in England and in establishing the responsibility of the ministers for the content of the royal speech. Wilkes and his associates "were exposed to every kind of fair and foul attack . . . His printers were threatened and intimidated when they could not be bribed. Twice he was involved in duels with government partisans." He was exiled and spent a period in jail. Nobbe has referred to original manuscript materials, and for quotations he used the 1763 edition of *The North Briton* which Wilkes printed on his private press.

Noble, John. "Notes on the Libel Suit of Knowles v. Douglass in the Superior Court of Judicature, 1748 and 1749." In *Publications of the Colonial Society of Massachusetts*, 3:213–40, March 1896. **N195**

The case of Commodore Charles Knowles and Dr. William Douglass.

"Noise in Public." *Times Literary Supplement*, 3328:1159, 9 December 1965. **N196**
An editorial objecting to a jury conviction in Blackburn, England, of the editor of a little magazine, *Poet-meat*. "It was a prosecution which once again showed the idiocy of our present laws with reference to obscene publications." See also *Dust*, Winter 1966.

Nokes, Gerald D. "The Future of the Blasphemy Laws." *Nineteenth Century*, 107:391–401, March 1930. **N197**
An analysis of the British law against blasphemy and recommendations for its modification or abolition.

————. *A History of the Crime of Blasphemy.* London, Sweet & Maxwell, 1928. 178 p. **N198**
A documented study of the development of the laws of blasphemy, both common and statutory, with particular reference to England. The appendix contains tables of prosecutions for blasphemy, from 1617 to 1922, giving the nature of the offense, name of the court, verdict, and sentence.

Nolan, Michael S. "Constitutional Law: Obscenity Censorship in Wisconsin." *Marquette Law Review*, 47:275–81, Fall 1963. **N199**
Relates to *McCauley v. Tropic of Cancer*, 20 Wis. 2d 134, 121 N.W. 2d 545 (1963).

["Nomination for Literary Heroine of the Month"]. In "Talk of the Town" column, *New Yorker*, 37(26):17, 12 August 1961. **N200**
Comments on the vigilante action of Miss Katherine McCardle of Glasgow, who, disapproving of a window display of copies of *Lady Chatterley's Lover*, painted the window black, and was jailed: "If books have the right to paint people black, people should have the right to paint books black . . . Censorship, whether in the form of banning, burning or blacking, pays books the high compliment of taking them seriously . . . More anti-intellectual than censorship is its apathetic absence. So paint on, Miss McC. You are on the wrong side, but of the right fence."

"Non-Criminal Obscenity Regulation and Freedom of Expression." *Washington University Law Quarterly*, 1962:474–514, December 1962. **N201**
Notes: Obscenity Debate, Circa 1962; Constitutional Setting; Form and the Effect of the Test; Criminal Enforcement Techniques; Prior Restraint; Search and Seizure; *Marcus v. Search Warrant*; Problem in Louisiana and California; Search and Seizure as a Prior Restraint; and Postal Department (Marcus standards).

Noordenbos, O. "Verboden Boeken."

Bibliotheekleven, 18:174–93, October 1933. **N202**
A brief survey of the history of censorship in various countries of Europe including English censorship from the time of the first secular index by Henry VIII in 1526 to the repeal of the licensing law in 1695.

Norden, Helen B. "The Crime of Censorship." *Vanity Fair*, 43:48, 50, September 1934. **N203**
An attack on movie censorship as "colossal stupidity . . . one of those unfortunate recurrences of mob epidemics which sometimes sweep our land, revealing us, by and large, as still pretty much in our mental infancy, and making us the laughing stock of the other nations." If "parents feel that their progeny really are too susceptible—they pick up things so quicky the little tykes!—let them keep them home from allegedly objectionable pictures." In order to protect children we should not inflict censorship on a nation of adults.

Noriega, Raul. "Draft Convention on Freedom of Information with Text." *U.N. Bulletin*, 10:210–13, 1 March 1951. **N204**
The author, chairman of the Committee on Freedom of Information, reports on the 27 meetings of the Assembly's Committee on the Draft Convention on Freedom of Information.

Norris, Hoke. "*Cancer* in Chicago." *Evergreen Review*, 6(25):40–66, July–August 1962. **N205**
The book review editor of the *Chicago Sun-Times* reports the trial of *Tropic of Cancer* before Judge Samuel B. Epstein in Cook County, Illinois, Superior Court. The case grew out of action taken by Chicago suburban police against the Henry Miller book. Judge Epstein found the book not to be pornographic, but coming under the protection of the First and Fourteenth Amendments. The book has both social and literary significance and its effect on children is irrelevant. "Let the parents control the reading matter of their children; let the tastes of the readers determine what they may or may not read; let not the government or the courts dictate the reading matter of a free people."

North, Anthony. "Extra! Extra! Has America a Free Press?" *New Outlook*, 163:13–17, April 1934. **N206**
The author comments on the various threats to a free press within the industry itself, including unionization of the printing trades, the Newspaper Guild, and the NRA, but believes the most serious threat is an economic one—action by the public in refusing to buy newspapers critical of the New Deal.

The North Briton. Nos. 1 to 45. London,

printed for G. Kearsley, 5 June 1762—23 April 1763 (folio). An additional number (46) was issued 12 November 1763, printed for J. Williams. The first collected edition was published in 2 vols. (small octavo) for J. Williams in 1763. Bingley's folio reprint, "Corrected and revised by a Friend to Civil and Religious Liberty," was issued in a 164-page folio volume by W. Bingley in 1769.   **N 207**

The periodical published by John Wilkes which led to his arrest and imprisonment. It was started with the purpose of opposing the government-licensed *Briton*, and many of its articles relate to government control of political discussion. It was the now-famous issue no. 45, published 23 April 1763, that brought government action against Wilkes. For reprinting no. 45 in his own house as part of the first collected edition, Wilkes was fined and imprisoned; J. Williams, the publisher, was fined, imprisoned, and pilloried. A full account of the bibliographical history of *The North Briton* is contained in *Notes and Queries*, 9:104–6 (7th ser.), 8 February 1890, signed J.T.Y. The account also refers to suppressed vol. 3, contents of which are described in *Notes and Queries*, 10 August 1889. Only a few copies of this third volume have survived.

[Norwood, Robert]. *A Brief Discourse Made by Capt. Robert Norwood on Wednesday last, the 28 of January, 1651. In the Upper-Bench-Court at Westminster: With some Arguments by him then given, in defence of himself, and prosecution of his Writ of Errour by him brought upon an Indictment found and adjudged against him upon an Act against Blasphemy, at the Sessions in the Old Bayly. . . .* London, 1652. 6p.   **N 208**

Norwood was brought to trial for blasphemy at the instigation of his pastor to whom he had given a paper to read outlining his religious beliefs. Norwood was excommunicated and given a six-month sentence. In the course of his defense, Norwood objects to the use of a joint indictment with one, M. Tany, and to the introduction of evidence based on the spoken word.

Nossaman, Walter A. "Free Speech in Wartime." *California State Bar Journal*, 17:109–15, May–June 1942.   **N 209**

"Notes on the Newspaper Stamp." *Fraser's Magazine*, 44:339–54, September 1851.   **N 210**

A discussion of the controversy over a stamp tax versus newspaper postage as it relates to freedom of the press. Commentary on the report of a House of Parliament Select Committee.

"The Novelist Rebels." *Nation*, 113:255–56, 7 September 1921.   **N 211**

An imaginary conversation between a novelist and his friend, in which the novelist analyzes the difficulty of examining the psychical grounds of human action in fiction in the presence of opposition through ignorance and fanaticism. He concludes, "We must destroy the censorship not because it forbids books but because it corrupts souls."

Nowell, Dix W. "Defamation of Public Officers and Candidates." *Columbia Law Review*, 49:875–903, November 1949.   **N 212**

The author suggests that much of the uncertainty of the law would be avoided "if all comments and statements about political officers and candidates would be conditionally privileged." This would provide needed encouragement to those who wish to speak out honestly, but would at the same time guarantee adequate protection to officers and candidates.

Noyes, Theodore W. *Newspaper Libels, The National Capital, and Notes of Travel.* Washington, D.C., B. S. Adams, 1894. 131p.   **N 213**

"The Nude in Art; The Nude in Education." *Outlook*, 83:871–72, 18 August 1906.   **N 214**

An editorial on Anthony Comstock's attempt to suppress a periodical published by the Art Students' League. Two press comments are quoted: Harvard Professor Charles H. Moore, who disposes of "certain superficial defenses interposed on behalf of the indiscriminate publication of the nude in art," and Charles Henry Smith, Professor of American History at Yale, who is critical of suppression of pictures and statues of the human body in education and calls for more familiarity with the appearance of the human body.

Nugent, J. C. "Speaking of Censorship." *Authors' League Bulletin*, 15(1):8–9, April 1927.   **N 215**

Playwright Nugent favors some censorship, preferably from within the profession, that "establishes quickly and firmly the legitimate limits of our legitimate profession."

Nullius Nominis, *pseud. An Apologie for the Six Book-Sellers, Subscribers of the Second Beacon Fired. Or A Vindication of them from the foul and unjust aspersions cast upon them by M. John Goodwin in a late Pamphlet Intituled A Fresh Discovery of the High Presbyterian Spirit . . .* London, Printed by S. G. for Matthew Keinton, 1655. 12p.   **N 216**

No. 49040. "Writing the Hard Way." *Saturday Review*, 48(37):34, 11 September 1965.   **N 217**

The prison censorship faced by inmates who attempt to get their manuscripts published. The author has been an inmate of various reformatories and prisons since 1950 and hopes to write professionally when he is released.

Nutting, Charles B. "Definitive Standards in Federal Obscenity Legislation." *Iowa Law Review*, 23:24–40, November 1937.   **N 218**

The author traces the development of federal legislation "designed to keep from the mails and other channels of interstate commerce those things which have been regarded as unfit for the public eye." He is critical of the present act because it places too much power in the hands of the Postmaster General in interpreting and controlling obscene matter. That official is, potentially, "a most powerful literary critic and censor of morals."

Nye, Russel B. *Fettered Freedom; Civil Liberties and the Slavery Controversy, 1830–1860.* East Lansing, Michigan State College Press, 1949. 273p. rev. ed., 1965. 353p.   **N 219**

In this study of the slavery controversy as it affected the civil liberties of the American people two chapters deal especially with the freedom of the press: Chapter 2, The Right of Petition and the Right to Use the Mails; Chapter 4, Abolitionism and Freedom of the Press. In the latter there is a discussion of the work of James G. Burney and Cassius Clay, and the martyrdom of Elijah P. Lovejoy.

————. "Freedom of the Press and the Antislavery Controversy." *Journalism Quarterly*, 22:1–11, March 1945.   **N 220**

A brief report of a study, made under a Rockefeller Foundation grant, and later published as a book under the title *Fettered Freedom.*

Nyholm, J. P. "American Way." *Wilson Library Bulletin*, 14:555–59, April 1940.   **N 221**

If American libraries are to operate as democratic institutions they must accept the literature of minority groups and the literature of sex, both imaginative and scientific. A reply by J. A. Work, Jr., appears in the November 1940 issue.

O

Oakes, George W. Ochs. "Unclean Books." *Light*, 153:28–32, July–August 1923. **O 1**
Address by the editor of *Current History* before the Federation of Women's Clubs, New York.

Oakes, John B. "The Paper Curtain of Washington." *Nieman Reports*, 12(4):3–5, October 1958. **O 2**
The federal government limits freedom of information by means of censorship at the source, management of news, and restrictions on reporters.

Oakes, Philip. ". . . Something Blue." *Spectator*, 205:432+, 23 September 1960. **O 3**
A description of the lurid and sadistic sex books and magazines in the British shops, openly available to minors, while *Lady Chatterley's Lover* is under wraps.

Oare, Lenn J. "What Is Liberty of the Press?" *Case and Comment*, 22:476–77, November 1915. **O 4**
"Freedom of the press means, in fact, the right to bring the government of the people before the public bar of justice." The guarantee of a free press, however, has never been construed as interfering with libel laws.

Oberholtzer, Ellis P. "Censor and the 'Movie Menace.'" *North American Review*, 212:641–47, November 1920. (Reprinted in Rutland, *State Censorship of Motion Pictures*, pp. 29–36) **O 5**
The secretary of the Pennsylvania Board of Motion Picture Censors urges censorship of movies.

———. *Morals of the Movies*. Philadelphia, Penn Publishing Co., 1922. 251 p. **O 6**
An American historian recounts his experiences in serving for six years as a member of the Pennsylvania State Board of Censors, which regulates and controls the issue and circulation of motion picture films in that state. Oberholtzer is concerned not only with the effect on Americans, especially children, of the low moral standards of many of the movies, but objects to the export of false values to the outside world. The appendix includes a proposed federal film censorship bill (1914), the Pennsylvania censorship law, a proposed Chicago ordinance (1921), the Portland, Ore., ordinance (1915), the law of Massachusetts, the proposed Missouri bill (1919), the law of Quebec, and Senator Myers' resolution for a federal investigation of the film industry.

———. "Moving Pictures: Obiter Dicta of a Censor." *Yale Review*, 9(n.s.):620–32, April 1920. **O 7**
The Pennsylvania censor presents a general denunciation of the movies and a denial of the right of freedom of speech for the movie producer whose products show he has "so low an estimate of his social responsibility." The author objects to industry control of movies as merely a device to forestall public action. He calls for state censorship of films.

———. "What Are the Movies Making of Our Children?" *World's Work*, 41:249–63, January 1921. (Reprinted in Rutland, *State Censorship of Motion Pictures*, pp. 36–47) **O 8**

Oboler, Eli M. "Congress as Censor." *Library Journal*, 77:1927–30, 15 November 1952. (Reprinted in Daniels, *Censorship of Books*, pp. 29–31) **O 9**
A review of censorship legislation introduced in the 82d Congress.

———. *The Freedom to Read: A Selected List*. [Pocatello, Idaho], Idaho State College Library, 1963. 28 p. mimeo. (Reading List no. 35) **O 10**

———. "Idaho Libraries and Intellectual Freedom." *Idaho Librarian*, 17:101–4, July 1965. **O 11**

———. "Idaho School Librarians and Salinger's *Catcher in the Rye*: A Candid Report." *Idaho Librarian*, 15:137–39, October 1963. **O 12**

O'Brian, John L. *Civil Liberty in War Time*. Paper Presented at the Forty-Second Annual Meeting of the New York State Bar Association Held in the City of New York on January 17 and 18, 1919. Washington, D.C., Govt. Print. Off., 1919. 22 p. (Senate document no. 434, 65th Cong., 3d sess.) **O 13**
The special assistant to the Attorney General for war work discusses the work of the Justice Department in enforcing the wartime sedition laws. Includes section on the prosecution of publications and speakers.

"Obscene Literature." *Albany Law Journal*, 12:37–38, 17 July 1875. **O 14**
An attack on two sex education books, Elizabeth Edson Evans' *The Abuse of Maternity*, and Dr. Dio Lewis' *Chastity, or Our Secret Sins*. The former is dangerous because it proposes that a woman "have the legal right to the control of her own person in sexual matters." The latter, which discusses sex hygiene, "ought to be suppressed by the public authorities." The ideas espoused in these works are the product of "long-haired men and short-haired women." In the 7 August issue a letter to the editor offers the bold suggestion that such books as the above should be given to our children to teach them the facts of life. The editor retorts that this would be fine if society were organized upon ideas that regulate horse-breeding.

"Obscene Literature and Pictures." *American Journal of Dermatology*, 15:442, August 1911. **O 15**
Brief editorial reporting on the suppression of the June issue because of an illustrated article by Dr. W. P. Carr on scrotal surgery. A review by Dr. Robert W. Shufeldt of Theodore Schroeder's *Obscene Literature and Constitutional Law* appears on pages 424–25 of the August issue.

"Obscene Publications." *Justice of the Peace*, 118:664–66, 23 October 1954; 118:680–82, 30 October 1954; 118:694–97, 6 November 1954; 118:709–11, 13 November 1954; 118:725–26, 20 November 1954; 118:812–18, 25 November 1954. **O16**

A discussion of the present state of obscenity in Great Britain and the application of the law by local officials and the courts. The author draws widely from history, law, and the opinions of literary critics, as well as from the practical experience of police and magistrates. He suggests Parliamentary reform in the Obscene Publications Act of 1857.

"Obscenity and the Post Office: Removal From the Mail under Section 1461." *University of Chicago Law Review*, 27:354–68, Winter 1960. **O17**

Congress has the power, within limits, to decide what matter will be carried in the mail. Section 1461 authorizes the removal of obscene matter, which is not protected under the First Amendment. Only the procedures for determining censorship may be successfully attacked. "What probably will survive is censorship of an ill-definable collection of matter by the federal letter-carrying agency under the watchful eye of federal courts."

"Obscenity—Comparison Evidence Inadmissible for Purpose of Establishing Community Standards under 'Hard-Core Pornography' Test." *Harvard Law Review*, 76:1498–1501, May 1963. **O18**

Notes on the case of *People v. Finkelstein*, 11 N.Y. 2d 300.

"Obscenity—Constitutional Obscenity: The Supreme Court's Interpretation." *DePaul Law Review*, 12:103–15, Autumn–Winter 1962. **O19**

"What concerns this writer is the Court's hesitance to recognize that an expression's distributive freedom is limited where its primary audience is incapable of mature judgment . . . It is obvious that the inquiring and immature mind of a child should be channeled and protected until it develops at least a youthful maturity."

"Obscenity—Construction and Constitutionality of Statutes Regulating Obscene Literature." *New York University Law Review*, 28:877–90, April 1953. **O20**

The purpose of this note is "to point out that obscenity statutes may cause more harm than good to society, and that there exists a need for a re-examination of the current law."

"Obscenity—Declaratory Judgments—Massachusetts Provides for Declaratory Action against Obscene Book with Jury Trial on the Issue of Obscenity." *Harvard Law Review*, 59:813–16, May 1946. **O21**

A new Massachusetts law puts the offending book, rather than the bookseller or publisher, on the stand. The article reviews the legal background of obscenity in Massachusetts.

"Obscenity—Evidence—Admission of Contemporary Critical Evaluation of Libeled Book." *Minnesota Law Review*, 35:326–30, February 1951. **O22**

Case notes on *U.S. v. Two Obscene Books*, 92 F. Supp. 934 (N.D. Cal. 1950). The case involves the importation of Henry Miller's *Tropic of Cancer* and *Tropic of Capricorn*.

"Obscenity in the Mails: Post Office Department Procedures and the First Amendment." *Northwestern University Law Review*, 58:664–84, November–December 1963. **O23**

"It is the purpose of this commentary to examine these ¡Post Office¡ procedures with the aim of determining what safeguards may be necessary at each stage—from removal of allegedly obscene matter from the mails through judicial review—in order to meet constitutional standards."

"Obscenity Law Anomalies." *Bookseller*, 3094:1744–46, 10 April 1965. **O24**

A member of Parliament complains of the unfairness of the administration of the Obscene Publications Act which allows a public library to stock books which booksellers had been prevented from selling and copies of which had been confiscated.

"Obscenity—Mailability of Magazines Which Appeal to Homosexuals." *Vanderbilt Law Review*, 16:251–57, December 1962. **O25**

Manual Enterprises, Inc. v. Day, 370 U.S. 478 (1962).

"Obscenity Test—A Legal Poser." *Newsweek*, 67(14):19–22, 4 April 1966. **O26**

"Perhaps nowhere was the uncertainty and unease over the limits of publishing and peddling pornography better illustrated than in the Supreme Court last week. In the course of upholding the obscenity conviction of publisher Ralph Ginzburg and overturning the ruling that the eighteenth-century novel *Fanny Hill* was obscene, members of the Court filed no fewer than ten separate opinions."

Observations on a Letter from George Nicholas, of Kentucky, to His Friend in Virginia; in Which, Some of the Errors, Misstatements, and False Conclusions in that Letter Are Corrected, and the Late Measures of the Government, Which Have Been Complained of in Kentucky, Are Justified; by an Inhabitant of the Northwestern Territory. Cincinnati, Printed by E. Freeman, 1799. 46p. **O27**

The writer upholds the Alien and Sedition laws, in disagreement with the recently-passed Kentucky Resolutions which had been defended in *A Letter from George Nicholas . . .*

The Observator Observ'd: or, Protestant Observations upon Anti-Protestant Pamphlets. ¡London¡, By T. C. for Edw. Dod, ¡1656¡. **O28**

A Whig pamphlet ridiculing the ex-licensor of printing, Roger L'Estrange.

Ockham, David, "Freedom of the Films." *Saturday Review* (London), 150:783, 13 December 1930. **O29**

Objections to self-censorship in the British movie industry. The author prefers an official film censorship comparable to that of the stage.

———. "The Mandarins of Wardour Street." *Saturday Review* (London), 149:516–17, 26 April 1930. **O30**

"The Film Censorship is responsible to nothing or nobody not even to the trade which created it." Special concern over the censor's entering the realm of politics.

O'Connell, Michael. "Censorship on Campus." *America*, 111:611–13, 14 November 1964. Discussion, 112:17–18, 2 January 1965. **O31**

A student's plea for granting responsible freedom to Catholic college editors.

O'Connor, Frank. "Frank O'Connor on Censorship." *Dubliner*, 2:39–44, March 1962. **O32**

"On Wednesday, February 14th, 1962, in Trinity College, Dublin, at a meeting of the College Historical Society, Mr. Frank O'Connor proposed the motion 'that Irish censorship is insulting to Irish intelligence.' The motion was opposed by the Hon. Mr. Justice Kevin Haugh. It was carried by forty votes to nine. We publish here the text of Mr. O'Connor's speech."

O'Connor, J. D. "Censorship of Motion Pictures." In *Union of Nova Scotia Municipal Proceedings*, 1922, pp. 59–65. **O33**

O'Connor, Ulick. "Censorship on the Irish Scene." *Chicago Tribune Books Today*, 2(31):9, 1 August 1945. **O34**

A brief account of Irish Customs censorship of John McGahern's *The Dark*. Now that the Censorship Board is operating on a more reasonable basis, the customs officials seem to have stepped up their censorship activity.

O'Connor, William D. "Another Recovered Chapter in the History of *Leaves of Grass*." *Conservator*, 7:99–102, September 1896. **O35**

Horace Traubel wrote in the introduction: "The letter that follows was addressed to the New York *Tribune*, under date of September 16th, 1882, and, so far as I can discover, was not there or elsewhere printed. I have come into possession of the manuscript through the generosity of the widow of its author." O'Connor's playful title to the piece was Tobey or Not Tobey? That Is the Question. It is an account of the efforts of Boston's postmaster, Mr. Tobey, to exclude from the mails excerpts from Whitman's *Leaves of Grass* contained in a weekly journal published by George Chainey.

――――. *The Good Gray Poet. A Vindication.* New York, Bunce & Huntington, 1866. 46p. (Reprinted in Richard M. Bucke, *Walt Whitman.* Philadelphia, McKay, 1883, pp. 99–130)   **O 36**
In June 1865 Walt Whitman was dismissed from his clerkship in the U.S. Department of Interior by Secretary Harlan because he had written *Leaves of Grass*, a work "full of indecent passages." Whitman's young Irish friend wrote this eloquent defense of the poet and his poetry, a devastating attack on Harlan's action and on censors in general. The essay is filled with allusions to efforts that have been made to suppress or expurgate great works of literature.

[――――]. "Mr. Comstock as Cato the Censor." In *Walt Whitman Review*, 5: 54–56, September 1959.   **O 37**
A hitherto unpublished letter from William D. O'Connor to the editor of the New York *Tribune* relating to the suppression of Whitman's *Leaves of Grass* by the Boston authorities in 1882. Includes a note by William White, editor of the *Walt Whitman Review*.

Odgers, William B. *Digest of the Law of Libel and Slander and of Actions on the Case for Words Causing Damage . . .* Edited by Robert Ritson. 6th ed. London, Stevens, 1929. 824p. (First published, 1881)   **O 38**
The 1881 edition, according to the editor, cited every case in England and Ireland for the previous 15 years, earlier cases more sparingly. Leading American and Canadian cases are also cited, with notation where the law differs. Subsequent editions add later English cases. Appendix B of the 1929 edition digests statutes relating to newspaper libel.

――――. "Law Relating to Heresy and Blasphemy." *Modern Review*, 4:586–608, 1883.   **O 39**

O'Donnell, T. J. "Military Censorship and the Freedom of the Press." *Virginia Law Review*, 5:178–89, December 1917.   **O 40**
An emotional plea for strict wartime censorship in the interest of national defense. "There are probably in this country a million traitors and alien enemies who have the disposition to destroy our military and naval forces and defeat us in this war." Their activities and publications should be banned. We should not even permit journals to be published in the enemy language.

Oertel, William J. *How Free Is Freedom?* Columbia, Mo., Freedom of Information Center, School of Journalism, University of Missouri, 1960. 4p. (Publication no. 40)   **O 41**
A discussion of the right to advertise, including laws proposed or enacted by various states to provide "free enterprise" in advertising.

Oestreicher, Jack C. "But the News Came Through!" *Quill*, 22(10):16–17, 36, October 1934.   **O 42**
Foreign correspondents have braved many dangers and the censor's wrath to report recent events.

――――. "Censorship." In *The World Is Their Beat.* New York, Duell, Sloan, and Pearce, 1945, pp. 128–41.   **O 43**
An American war correspondent discusses his experience and that of fellow correspondents with military censorship during World War II.

Oetting, Richard F. "The New Star Chamber—TV in the Courtroom." *Southern California Law Review*, 32:281–92, Spring 1959.   **O 44**
The author argues that the principles of Canon 35 are not necessary for the maintenance of the high tradition of judicial conduct. Granting the television industry the right to reveal the actual workings of the court will not corrupt the ideas. The right of television under the First Amendment and the interest of the public in a public trial "should be restricted only when it appears there is an actual conflict with equally important interests." He calls for modification or repeal of Canon 35.

Oexeman, Robert J. *Obscenity and the Law in Illinois.* Carbondale, Ill., Southern Illinois University, 1965. 138p. (Unpublished Master's thesis)   **O 45**
A study of the obscenity law (literature and motion pictures) in Illinois as it has been interpreted by decisions of the Illinois Supreme Court and in light of recent decisions of the U.S. Supreme Court.

"Of Censorship and Decency." *Christian Century*, 75:125, 29 January 1958. **O 46**
Editorial concerning the recently set up Churchmen's Commission for Decent Publications which "proposes to coordinate efforts to eliminate the sale and distribution of 'indecent and obscene' material and publicize the need for federal, state, and local laws to curb the spread of such material; to encourage high standards of publication . . . and to issue evaluation lists of publications."

O'Faolain, Sean. "Love Among the Irish." *Life*, 34:152–54, 16 March 1953. (Quoted in Downs, *The First Freedom*, p. 379)   **O 47**

An Irish novelist attributes the declining Irish birth rate to a fear of sex. The symbol of this fear is expressed in the arbitrary censoring as indecent and obscene of most works of modern fiction. The register of books banned by the Irish Censorship Board (150 pages) is so lengthy "that the motto of the Censorship Board could be, 'If it's good we've got it.'"

"Off with Her Head." *Nation*, 108:18, 14 January 1919.   **O 48**
The arrest of Theodora Pollock in Sacramento for having in her possession a copy of *Solidarity* and her own unpublished poem, "Peace."

"Official Correspondence Relating to the Censorship of Telegrams Transmitted by Cable and Wireless." *American Journal of International Law*, 9(Sup.):270–313, July 1915.   **O 49**

"Official Secrets Bill: Widespread Press Opposition." *U.S. News*, 12:21, 6 March 1942.   **O 50**
Most editors believe the bill goes far beyond the censorship powers needed for the war.

O'Flaherty, Liam. "Irish Censorship." In *American Spectator Year Book*, New York, Stokes, 1934, pp. 131–34.   **O 51**
Censorship in Ireland is the work of "the illiterate ruffians who control Irish life at present." The Irish people love art and beauty but it is kept from them by the priests. "The militant puritans in Ireland have, in my opinion, staged their last great parade. Before very long they'll be all hurled into the clean Atlantic, together with their censorship, their dung, their bawdy books, their bawdy houses and their black booze."

Ogden, Rollo. "A Defense of the Press." In *Proceedings*, American Political Science Association, December 1912. New York, The Association, 1913, pp. 194–200. (Reprinted in Beman, *Censorship of Speech and the Press*, pp. 342–50)   **O 52**
A New York newspaper editor states that a newspaper can be all-powerfull or impotent, depending upon the will of the people. "The community always holds the power of life or death over newspapers. No form of property is more precarious." The public should show active hostility toward newspapers that are vulgar and unreliable.

Ogilvie, R. A. "Keeper of the Keys." *Wilson Library Bulletin*, 14:640–41, May 1940.   **O 53**
The librarian has the duty, while providing information on all sides of controversial questions, to reject propaganda that is false and that is harmful to minority groups.

O'Higgins, Harvey J. "Freedom of Speech." *Century*, 95:302–3, December 1917. **O 54**
"In the freest of countries, in the most peaceful of times, freedom of speech and freedom of the press were never more than the limited freedom to say what you pleased and print what you pleased and take the consequences." He rejects as unwarranted the cries of many against wartime censorship—those who want not only to be free but to be immune from the consequences.

————. "Natural Censorship." *Outlook*, 149:6–7, 2 May 1928. **O 55**
There is a natural censorship, which is seen among primitive people as "fear of the omnipotent word." In a heterogeneous society, such as ours, the more puritanical citizens often find judges and juries not as shocked as they by some of the books and plays, brought before them. Hence, they ask for prosecution to be put in the hands of censors who represent the same point of view as the complaining members of the community. "The wise artist . . . will say: 'You may pass all the laws you please against moral turpitude in books and plays so long as you leave the enforcement of those laws to judges and juries. I don't expect to move any faster than the civilization in which I live. But don't set up a private Judge Lynch to censor one according to his personal sense of shock. That is a return to barbarism which the community may come to regret.'"

————, and Edward H. Reede. "Anthony Comstock and P. T. Barnum." In their *The American Mind in Action*. New York, Harper, 1924, pp. 132–54. **O 56**
The authors deal with two diverse products of the Puritan mind, Anthony Comstock and P. T. Barnum. Comstock's life long crusade against obscenity is taken largely from the sympathetic biography by Trumbull.

Ohio. Department of Education. Division of Film Censorship. *Ohio Censorship Law*. Columbus, Ohio, Banks-Baldwin, 1938. 7p. **O 57**
This pamphlet was edited by E. N. Dietrich. Ohio's censorship law was passed in 1913, became a storm-center of controversy soon afterwards and led to the Supreme Court decision in 1915 upholding state movie censorship. In 1921 the censorship functions were transferred from the Industrial Commission to the State Board of Education. State censorship was abolished by the Department of Education in 1952 after a decision of the U.S. Supreme Court (*Burstyn v. Wilson*) in effect declared the Ohio censorship law unconstitutional. The law, though no longer enforced, has not actually been repealed.

Ohio Anti-Slavery Society. *Narrative of the Late Riotous Proceedings against the Liberty of the Press, in Cincinnati. With Remarks and Historical Notices, Relating to Emancipation . . .* Cincinnati, The Society, 1836. 48p. **O 58**
Relates to public sentiment in Cincinnati against the abolitionists and the destruction of the presses of A. Pugh, printer of the *Philanthropist*, organ of the Ohio Anti-Slavery Society.

"Ohio Supreme Court Upholds Conviction under Statute Prohibiting 'Knowing Possession' of Obscene Literature." *DePaul Law Review*, 10:156–61, Autumn–Winter 1960. **O 59**
The case of *State of Ohio v. Mapp*, 170 Ohio St. 427, 166 N. E. (1960), in which a landlady was found guilty of "knowing possession" of obscene matter when she stored the belongings of a roomer. The reviewer believes that "knowing possession" should be coupled with some intent to sell or distribute.

"The O'Keefe Case and The Law of Libel." *Law Times*, 55:75, 31 May 1873. **O 60**
Relates to two alleged libels published by Cardinal Cullen, the questions turning upon the relationship between a Catholic priest and his superior and rights under civil law.

Oklahoma Library Association. Committee on Intellectual Freedom. "Censorship in Bartlesville." *Oklahoma Librarian*, 1:7, 17, Winter 1950–51. (Also in *ALA Bulletin*, March 1951, and *Nieman Reports*, July 1951) **O 61**
Report on censorship in Bartlesville, Okla., where the public librarian was discharged after 30 years of service because of her refusal to submit to censorship demands. "The action of the Citizens' Committee in Bartlesville, Okla., constitutes a violation of the Bartlesville Public Library's integrity and is a grave infraction of the freedom of inquiry, thought and expression. It is an act of intolerance."

O'Laughlin, John C. *Army and the Press; Address before the Army War College.* Washington, D.C., [1913]. 18p. **O 62**

————. *Relation of Press Correspondents to the Navy before and during War.* Washington, D.C., Naval War College Extension, 1913, 16p. **O 63**

Old Playgoer, *pseud.* "Miss Goldman's Trial." *Pearson's Magazine*, 38(3):132–43, September 1917. **O 64**
Dramatic account of the espionage trial of Emma Goldman and Alexander Berkman.

O'Leary, Jeremiah A. *Awake! Awake! The Constitution Attacked; a Letter on a "Free Press," . . . Occasioned by an Attempt* of the Post Office Department and the Administration to Suppress "Bull," a Satirical Monthly. New York, American Truth Society, 1917. 8p. **O 65**
O'Leary, an outspoken advocate of Irish independence, was indicted for treason and lost the mailing privileges for his publication, *Bull*, when it opposed wartime cooperation with the British. The letter is addressed to Congressman Daniel J. Riordan.

————. *My Political Trial and Experience. Including a Biographical Sketch of the Author by Major Michael A. Kelly . . . With Preface by Joseph W. Gavan.* New York, Jefferson Publishing Co., 1919. 546p. **O 66**

Olesen, Pete. "Censorship Reviewed." *Idaho Librarian*, 15(1):26–31, January 1963. **O 67**
A general review of the works of literature that have over the years been banned and the various forces that have operated for and against the freedom to read.

Oliva, Peter F. "The Dilemma of Censorship." *Educational Forum*, 25:499–502, May 1961. **O 68**
"The dilemma of censorship is that of reconciling freedom with restraint. Freedom in a democracy requires self-restraint." The author proposes the following steps in partial answer to the dilemma: (1) The product—film, book, or other art work should be clearly labeled when for adults only. (2) Film exhibitors should enforce ban on sale of children's tickets to adult films. (3) Previews of coming film attractions should be carefully made by the industry. (4) Parents should take a greater hand in screening literature read and films seen by their children.

Oliver, John W. "Contempt by Publication and the First Amendment." *Missouri Law Review*, 27:171–92, April 1962. **O 69**
The meaning of contempt of court and the development of the law in the United States. A major problem we face today "is the constitutional balance between the exercise of the freedom of the press and the right for one to have a fair trial free from outside pressure of trial by newspaper."

————. *Grand Jury: Out of the Cave.* Columbia, Mo., Freedom of Information Center, School of Journalism, University of Missouri, 1962. 11p. (Publication no. 78) **O 70**
A federal judge discusses the grand jury and its powers to report its proceedings.

Oliver, L. Stauffer. "A Famous Colonial Lawyer and the Zenger Trial." In *Historical Publications of the Society of*

Colonial Wars in the Commonwealth of Pennsylvania, 5(3):13–17, 1939. **O 71**
Biographical sketch of Andrew Hamilton, John Peter Zenger's lawyer.

Olson, Enid M. "What Do the Censors Fear?" *Teachers College Record*, 66:566–73, April 1965. **O 72**
The author makes a vigorous attack on the problem of academic freedom for the lower schools. He argues that the fabric of freedom is seamless and that censorship of our schools is dangerous, primarily because it easily becomes a habit of mind that jeopardizes the democratic community.

Olson, Paul R. *The Regulation of Radio Broadcasting in the United States.* Iowa City, State University of Iowa, 1931. 250 p. (Unpublished Ph. D. dissertation) **O 73**

The Olympia Press. *On the Old Theme of Literature & Censorship.* [Paris], The Olympia Press, 1958. 31 p. **O 74**
A discussion of the major points of evidence brought out in hearings on the British Obscene Publications Bill, 1958.

O'Meara, Carroll. "Not on the Air!" *Forum*, 103:301–8, June 1940. **O 75**
A discussion of the tight radio censorship, largely self-imposed, to avoid offense to certain minorities. The author believes that censorship has about reached its peak and that "some of the prudish barriers and narrow restrictions in drama and intelligent discussion will be gradually knocked down."

O'Meara, Joseph J. "Freedom Versus Authority." *Commonweal*, 63:516–18, 17 February 1956. **O 76**
"The contest between freedom and authority, even in a democracy, is an unequal contest, with the advantage on the side of authority, for authority has power . . . So freedom should have the benefit of every doubt . . . No man's rights are safe unless all men's rights are respected."

———, and Thomas L. Shaffer. "Obscenity and the Supreme Court: A Note on Jacobellis v. Ohio." *Notre Dame Lawyer*, 40:1–12, December 1964. **O 77**
Criticism of the U.S. Supreme Court's opinion that the Court itself must weigh and decide the issues in obscenity cases; that it must decide whether material is obscene and according to the standards of the community, that is, the whole country. The authors believe the Court should "recognize the jury as the authentic alter ego of the community, reflecting its morals and mores more truly than even the wisest of judges."

"An Ominous Sign of the Times." *Outlook*, 105:68–70, 13 September 1913. **O 78**

Vulgar works exploiting sex are tolerated while great works of frank and moral vigor such as *Anna Karenina* and *Scarlet Letter* are banned.

"On Proceedings for Blasphemous Libel." *Monthly Law Magazine*, 9:144–56, 1840. **O 79**

"On Protecting a Defendant Against the Creation of Prejudice." *American Law Review*, 30:597–601, July 1896. **O 80**
Concerns the right to produce a play based upon the facts of a criminal case pending its trial. *The Crime of the Century*, by Durrant, based on the San Francisco murders of Blanche Lamont and Minnie Williams, was stopped by the police at the end of the first act, and the actors arrested for contempt of court.

[*On the Law of Libel* and *The Law of Libel*] *Westminster Review*, 3:285–321, April 1825. **O 81**

Favorable reviews of Francis Place, *On the Law of Libel*, and Richard Mence, *The Law of Libel*, with further commentary by the reviewer. He concludes that if any freedom of discussion exists in England it is because it cannot be suppressed for fear of adverse public opinion.

On the Taxes on Knowledge. London, Robert Heward, 1821. 32 p. (Reprinted from *Westminster Review*, July 1831) **O 82**

One; The Homosexual Magazine. One & the U.S. Post Office . . . Los Angeles, One, Inc., 1957. 24 p. **O 83**
An account of the Los Angeles Post Office ban of the October 1954 issue of *One* on grounds of obscenity. The Federal District Court ruled the magazine nonmailable and the decision was upheld by the Ninth District Court of Appeals. The text of the latter is included. On 13 January 1958 the U.S. Supreme Court reversed the decision against *One* and took similar action on two nudist magazines.

"One Editor Missing." *Time*, 60(7):59–60, 18 August 1952. **O 84**
Account of the dropping of Editor James A. Wechsler from a TV discussion at the request of the advertiser because the New York editor had become a "controversial" figure.

One Nation Indivisible. 61 min. b/w movie. New York, McGraw-Hill. (Part I of Constitution Series) **O 85**
Includes a dramatization of the Alien and Sedition Acts.

O'Neill, James M. *Catholicism and American Freedom.* New York, Harper, 1952. 287 p. **O 86**
The book, by a Catholic layman, is a defense of American Catholics and an answer to

Paul Blanshard's *American Freedom and Catholic Power*. Chapter 8 deals with "Catholic 'Censorship.'"

———. "Nonsense about Censorship." *Catholic World*, 187:347–55, August 1958. **O 87**

The author "excoriates the nonsense about censorship found in recent books by Morris Ernst, Paul Blanshard, Kent Cooper, William Chenery and others." He considers the opinions of Justices Black and Douglas in the *La Ronde* and *M* cases of 1954 as "irresponsible utterance" on the moral issue. He also attacks Haight's *Banned Books* and McKeon, Merton, and Gellhorn's *Freedom to Read*.

———. "Semantics and Responsibility." *Catholic Library World*, 24:5–10, October 1952. **O 88**
The author's views on the relation of Catholics to censorship, with references to Paul Blanshard's books and the Supreme Court ruling on the film *The Miracle*. While defending the right of the Church to oppose and criticize a book or a film, he believes it is a mistake for Catholics to picket, boycott, or otherwise take action to prevent the work from being available to others.

———. "Sense about Censorship." *Catholic World*, 187:257–63, July 1958. **O 89**
Comments on Father Harold C. Gardiner's book, *Catholic Viewpoint on Censorship*, as "an especially reliable treatise on the aspects of censorship covered by Catholic doctrine and on the similarities between this body of doctrine and the basic concepts underlying the laws abridging freedom of speech and press in the United States under the federal and state constitutions."

O'Neill, William L. "The American as Moral Censor." *Issue*, 1(1):4–8, Winter 1963. **O 90**
The formal moral censorship of the Victorian era, represented by Anthony Comstock, began to fade in the 1920's, "when it became impossible to enforce the standards of a single group upon the nation." The emergence of new racial and ethnic groups brought to an end the period of formal censorship, to be succeeded by informal control exerted through moral, social, and economic pressures. The Catholic Church is the leading practitioner of such pressures and has been most successful in mobilizing informal vigilante groups to discourage booksellers from distributing books of which the Church disapproves. The author fears that with the tendency toward cultural uniformity in America we will again face threats of formal censorship. Article based on the author's doctoral dissertation at the University of California, Berkeley.

"Open Meeting Statutes: The Press Fights for the 'Right to Know.'" *Harvard*

Law Review, 75:1199–1221, April 1962. **O 91**

The article undertakes to "consider the arguments for and against open-meeting laws, to explore the statutory techniques adopted to accommodate conflicting considerations, to examine the reaction to these statutes of the press and of the officials to whom they apply, and to propose a model open-meeting statute adapted to resolving competing interests and considerations."

"Opinion on Obscene Books." *Journal of Social Hygiene*, 17:354–58, June 1931. **O 92**

Text of Judge Woolsey's opinion on Dr. Marie Stopes's book, *Married Love*.

"Opinions on the Clean Books Bill." *Publishers' Weekly*, 103:1328–30, 28 April 1923. **O 93**

Pros and cons on the proposed New York bill against immoral books. Includes quotations by Bliss Perry (pro) and New York newspaper editorials (con).

[Oppenheim, Jerry]. "Constitutional Law—Motion Picture Censorship—Pre-Exhibition Licensing." *Brooklyn Law Review*, 27:343–46, April 1961. **O 94**

The U.S. Supreme Court held, in the case of *Times Film Corporation v. City of Chicago* (1961), that a censorship statute requiring submission of a motion pictures prior to its exhibition is not, of itself, void. The dissent, through Chief Justice Warren, although recognizing that different media present different problems, refuses to include licensing or prior censorship as an "exceptional case."

Oppenheimer, Walter O., Jr. "Television and the Right of Privacy." *Journal of Broadcasting*, 1:194–201, Spring 1957. **O 95**

Based on the author's thesis at American University, 1956.

The Oracle of Reason: Or, Philosophy Vindicated. London, Various publishers, 1841–43. Weekly. (A bound edition of volume 1, 1841–42 issues, was published by Thomas Paterson in 1842; a bound edition of volume 2, 1843 issues, was published by William Chilton in 1843. Each volume containes an introduction and index) **O 96**

This journal was begun in November 1841 by Charles Southwell and George J. Holyoake as an organ of atheistic thought and as a challenge to those who would suppress the freedom of the press. First, Editor Southwell was arrested and imprisoned on blasphemy charges; then Editor Holyoake went to jail for the same offense and was succeeded by Thomas Paterson and by George Adams who were, in turn, imprisoned and succeeded by William Chilton. The journal ceased publication with no. 103, in December 1843. Its columns were filled not only with attacks on organized religion but reports on the trials of the editors and other incidents of suppression of a free press. Accounts of the organization and activities of the Anti-Persecution Union also appear in *The Oracle*. The Union was organized to promote the right of free discussion and to help those prosecuted for atheist expression. Maltus Q. Ryall was the Secretary.

"Ordinance Forbidding Dissemination of Crime Comic Books to Children Held Violative of Free Press Liberties Inherent in Fourteenth Amendment." *Univeristy of Pennsylvania Law Review*, 108:747–53, March 1960. **O 97**

Notes on the case, *Katzen v. County of Los Angeles*, 341 P. 2d 310 (Cal. 1959).

"Ordinance Prohibiting Distribution of Handbills Without Identification of Author Violates Fourteenth Amendment." *Vanderbilt Law Review*, 14:392–97, December 1960. **O 98**

Talley v. California, 362 U.S. 60 (1960).

"Ordinance Requiring that Source of All Handbills Be Identified Held Unconstitutional." *Columbia Law Review*, 60:1173–79, December 1960. **O 99**

The U.S. Supreme Court held, in the case of *Talley v. California*, 362 U.S. 60 (1960), that the broad Los Angeles ordinance prohibiting the distribution of any anonymous handbills in any place under any circumstances is void on its face as an unconstitutional interference with freedom of speech and press.

O'Reilly, W. Cresswell. "Film Censorship in Australia." *Light*, 168:14–15, January–February 1926. **O 100**

The author is Australia's chief film censor.

Orians, G. Harrison. "Censure of Fiction in American Romances and Magazines, 1789–1810." *PMLA*, 52:195–214, 1937. **O 101**

Deals largely with the widespread objection to novels and novel-reading. The author finds that (1) despite evidences of liberality, there was a considerable audience who considered novels as subversive to the highest moral principles, (2) the atmosphere of the period was a little frigid for the ambitious novelist, (3) novels were charged as being mawkish and melodramatic, (4) novels were read largely by females, and (5) as the novel became better established and addiction to novel-reading was noticeable, greater attention was given to its morality, ethics, and prudence, and the need to regulate any "over-indulgence."

Orme, Frank. "Morals on Your TV." *Nation*, 174:601–3, 21 June 1952. **O 102**

The editor of *TV Magazine* criticizes the television code as unrealistic and unenforceable. He recommends dropping "the subterfuge of the code, and to come up with fair and open effort" to improve the situation.

———. "The Television Code." *Quarterly of Film, Radio and Television*, 6:404–13, Summer 1952. **O 103**

The author is concerned primarily with such negative elements as censorship, improper controls, and programming that is possibly injurious to segments of the television audience.

O'Rourke, Dennis. "Freedom of the Press and Contempt of Court." *George Washington Law Review*, 7:234–42, December 1938. **O 104**

A history of the long-standing feud between the exponents of civil liberties and the power of the courts to inflict summary punishment for contempt.

Orvis, Caroline. "Censorship of Fiction in the Public Library." *South Dakota Library Bulletin*, 16:9–11, March 1930. **O 105**

Suggestions for limiting the circulation of "adult" books to the mature reader only.

Orwell, George. "The Prevention of Literature." *Atlantic Monthly*, 179:115–19, March 1947. (Reprinted in Downs, *The First Freedom*, pp. 411–17; in McCormick, *Versions of Censorship*, pp. 285–99; and in Orwell, *Shooting an Elephant and Other Essays*. New York, Harcourt, Brace, 1945, pp. 104–21) **O 106**

Comments by the English novelist and critic of totalitarianism on freedom of speech and the press: "Though other aspects of the matter are usually in the foreground, the controversy over freedom of speech and of the press is at bottom a controversy over the desirability, or otherwise, of telling lies. What is really at issue is the right to report contemporary events truthfully." Intellectual freedom is under attack on the one hand by apologists of totalitarianism and, on the other, by the drift toward monopoly and bureaucracy.

Osborn, Tom. "Censor by Jury?" *Plays and Players*, 11(12):9, September 1964. **O 107**

"Disagreement this month between the Lord Chamberlain and the Royal Shakespeare Company over Roger Victrac's *Victor* at the Aldwych again spotlights the weaknesses in the stage's antiquated form of censorship. Tom Osborn here puts the case for more democratic methods."

Osgood, Herbert L. "Controversies during the Administration of Cosby and Clarke, the Zenger Episode, 1730–1740." In *The American Colonies in the Eighteenth Century.* New York, Columbia University Press, 1924. vol. 2, pp. 443–82.　**O108**

An account of the Zenger case as an episode in the history of the New York colony.

Oshkosh Public Library. *The Freedom to Read: A Guide to Selection of Materials in the Media of Communication at the Oshkosh Public Library.* Oshkosh, Wis., The Public Library, 1963. 13 p.　**O109**

An example of a public library book selection policy statement, prefaced by the American Library Association's *Freedom to Read* statement, adopted by the Oshkosh Public Library Board. There follows an outline of the library's role in the community and the criteria used in the selection of various materials. "The library will not indicate, through the use of labels or other devices, particular philosophies outlined in a book. To do so is to establish in the reader's mind a judgment before the reader has had an opportunity to examine the book personally." Many library boards have adopted similar statements.

Osman, Alfred. "Are Photographers Pornographers?" *Photography*, 19:28–33, November 1964.　**O110**

Deals with the effect of the new Obscene Publications Act in Great Britain.

O'Sullivan, Richard. *A Guide to the Defamation Act, 1952.* London, Sweet & Maxwell, 1952. 50 p. (Current Law Guide no. 10)　**O111**

An analysis of the British law of libel, as radically changed by the 1952 Defamation Act.

[Otis, Harrison G.]. *Letter to Hon. Josiah Quincy, Judge of the Municipal Court, in the City of Boston, on the Law of Libel as Laid Down by Him in the Case of the Commonwealth v. Buckingham. By a Member of the Suffolk Bar.* Boston, Wells and Lilly, 1823. 62 p.　**O112**

———. *Mr. Otis's Speech in Congress, on the Sedition Law, With Remarks by the "Examiner"* [Benjamin Austin] *on This Important Subject.* Boston. [1789]. 35 p.　**O113**

"The above speech was delivered by Mr. Otis on the petition of Matthew Lyon (a member of Congress), who was prosecuted under the sedition law." Otis expressed the Federalist point of view that freedom of the press was limited to exemption from prior restraints. Austin was a violent anti-Federalist from Massachusetts.

Otterbourg, Edwin M. "Fair Trial and Free Press." *Journal of the American*

Judicature Society, 37:75–80, June 1953.　**O114**

A plea for lawyers and the press to resolve the apparent conflict between the constitutional guarantees of fair trial and of free press, to avoid solution by legislative fiat or by judicial decree. Text of proposed Code on Fair Trial and Free Press follows the article.

———. "Fair Trial and Free Press." *New York State Bar Bulletin*, 27:103–10, April 1955.　**O115**

The chairman of a Special Committee on Fair Trial and Free Press of the New York County Lawyers' Association presents his Committee's proposal of a reasonable court rule governing fair trial and a free press.

———. "Fair Trial and Free Press; A 'New Look' in 1954." In *Lectures on Communications Media, Legal and Policy Problems Delivered at University of Michigan Law School, June 16–June 18, 1954.* Ann Arbor, University of Michigan Law School, 1954, pp. 78–95.　**O116**

The author proposes a voluntary agreement among press, bench, and bar, rather than legislative action to insure fair coverage of trials. Includes the text of the proposed code submitted by the New York County Lawyers' Association Committee.

———. "Fair Trial and Free Press: a Subject Vital to the Existence of Democracy." *American Bar Association Journal*, 39:978–81, November 1953.　**O117**

The author cites abuses of professional ethics by lawyers and editors in "trial by newspapers." Includes a list of cases and a proposed code on fair trial and free press.

———. "The Right to Enforce Canon 20." *Bar Bulletin*, New York County Lawyers' Association, 13:197–99, March 1956.　**O118**

Responding to criticism of his Committee's attempts to amend American Bar Association Canon 20 (Paul Williams, pp. 196, 200–201) the author states that no "gag" on lawyers or the press is possible or intended by the proposed changes.

———, and Herbert Brucker. ["Fair Trial and a Free Press"]. *Connecticut Bar Journal*, 29:423–35, December 1955.　**O119**

An attorney's point of view was presented by Edwin M. Otterbourg, chairman of the New York County Lawyers' Association Committee on Fair Trial and Free Press that had proposed a new code of ethics. The point of view of a newspaperman was presented by Herbert Brucker, editor of the *Hartford Courant.* Presented at the 1955 annual meeting of the State Bar Association of Connecticut.

Ould, Herman, *ed. Freedom of Expression.*

A Symposium Based on the Conference Called by the London Centre of the International P.E.N. to Commemorate the Tercentenary of the Publication of Milton's Areopagitica: 22–26th August, 1944. London, Hutchinson International Authors, 1945. 184 p.　**O120**

Thirty-one distinguished men of science, letters, religion, and philosophy took part in what has been described as "probably the most impressive tribute that has ever been paid to the power and significance of a single book." E. M. Forster was president of the Conference. Among the contributions relating especially to freedom of the press are: Milton and the Modern Press by B. Ifor Evans; Liberty in Society by Salvador de Madariaga; a Materialist on Freedom and Values by J. B. S. Haldane; The Philosophical Basis of Toleration by Rev. W. R. Matthews; Leaven in the Loaf by Richard Church; Science, Culture and Freedom by John R. Baker; on Milton's *Areopagitica* by Herbert Read; Culture, Liberty and Science by George Catlin; The Conception of Literary Obscenity and the Freedom of Letters by Alec Craig; An Editor's View by Kingsley Martin; The Example of Milton by Mulk Raj Anand; An American's Tribute by Herbert Agar; and The *Areopagitica* of Milton after 300 Years by Harold J. Laski. P.E.N. is the International Association of Poets, Playwrights, Editors, Essayists, and Novelists.

———. *Writers in Freedom; A Symposium Based on the XVII International Congress of the P.E.N. Club Held in London in September 1941.* London, Hutchinson, 1942. 152 p.　**O121**

For 4 days in wartime London, professional writers from 35 countries discussed literature in relation to the wartime world and the world after the war and this volume is a record of their deliberations. "We all know," writes Ould in his introduction, "that the democratic way of life has to be defended all the time, in war and peace, by ceaseless vigilance, by free discussion, by keeping the ideal ever before us; and that is where the writer comes in . . . it is his business to see that the lines of communication are not cut. Books are the lines of communication between free men, and it is not merely out of caprice but for more sinister reasons that dictators burn, ban, and mutilate books. If it is important that men should come from all parts of the world to defend freedom on the battlefield, it is no less important that men should be recruited to defend it in the intellectual field."

"Our Censorship Committee." *Scribner's Magazine*, 51:762–63, June 1912.　**O122**

A tongue-in-cheek article about the columnist's duties as a member of the library censorship committee. The members read the shocking books so that they might forbid their children to read them. "Yet, in spite of all this, the youngsters seem to know them about as well as we do ourselves."

Oursler, Will. "Books on Trial." *Library Journal*, 78:173–78, 1 Feburary 1953. **O123**

A review of the "Report of the Select Committee on Current Pornographic Materials, House of Representatives, Eight-second Congress, Pursuant to H. Res. 596, a Resolution Creating a Select Committee to Conduct a Study and Investigation of Current Pornographic Materials."

Outland, Ethel R. *The "Effingham" Libels on Cooper.* Madison, Wis., University of Wisconsin Press, 1929. 272 p. (Studies in Language and Literature no. 28) **O124**

A documentary account of the famous libel suits brought against the American press by the novelist James Fenimore Cooper in the years 1837–45. Cooper won most of the suits in his bitter war against the nation's press, but the severity of the court rulings contributed to the movement for more moderate libel laws.

Overton, Grant. "On Morality and Decency in Fiction." *English Journal*, 18: 14–23, January 1929. **O125**

"We waste far too much time on decency and the details of current morality." We should instead judge the inner intention, the effect of the book on the spirit.

Overton, Nelson T. "The Virginia 'Right of Privacy' Statute." *Virginia Law Review*, 38:117–25, January 1952. **O126**

An examination of the State's privacy statutes and cases since 1902.

[Overton, Richard]. *The Araignement of Mr. Persecution . . . By Yongue Martin Mar-Preist . . .* London, Printed by Martin Claw Clergie, 1645. 46 p. (Reproduced in Haller, *Tracts on Liberty in the Puritan Revolution*, vol. 3, pp. 205–56) **O127**

With Lilburne and Walwyn, Overton was one of the three outstanding Leveller pamphleteers. Through his many tracts, which he printed on his own secret press, he gave vigorous and fiery support to the doctrines of the natural rights of man, religious toleration, popular government, and freedom of the press. *The Araignement of Mr. Persecution* was an allegorical account of persecution for political and religious nonconformity. In it he accuses the Presbyterians of wishing to displace the prelates as censors. The true authorship was not immediately discovered, but it stirred the Stationers' Company to action in suppressing the clandestine press.

———. *A Defiance against all Arbitrary Usurpations or Encroachments, either of the House of Lords, or any other, upon the Sovereignty of the Supreme House of Commons . . . or upon the Rights, Properties and Freedoms of the people in generall . . .* London, 1646. 26 p. **O128**

Written from Newgate prison where he was sent for his support of Lilburne and his refusal to answer questions about his pamphleteering put to him by the House of Lords. *A Defiance* gives an account of Overton's arrest and conviction. Frank, in his book, *The Levellers* (pp. 86–87), calls the pamphlet a work of art which "combines the broad humor of Dickens, the suspense of a good detective story, the indignation of Lilburne, and the insight of Walwyn."

[———]. *A Remonstrance of Many Thousand Citizens, and other Freeborn People of England, To their owne House of Commons. Occasioned through the Illegall and Barbarous Imprisonment of that Famous and Worthy Sufferer for his Countries Freedoms, Lieutenant Col. John Lilburne . . .* London, 1646. 20 p. (Reproduced in Haller, *Tracts on Liberty in the Puritan Revolution*, vol. 3, pp. 353–70) **O129**

This protest of the persecution of Lilburne, signed by "98,064 hands," urges Parliament to "let the imprisoned Presses at liberty, so that all mens understandings may be more conveniently informed." The tract was declared "scandalous," and a committee was appointed to discover its author and publisher. The pamphlet, published anonymously and without license or imprint, is generally attributed to Overton. Wolf states that Walwyn probably collaborated with Overton in the writing.

Owen, Ralph D. "Jehovah's Witnesses and Their Four Freedoms." *University of Detroit Law Journal*, 14:111–34, March 1951. **O130**

[Owen, William]. "Trial for Publishing a Seditious Libel, 1752." In Howell, *State Trials*, vol. 18, pp. 1203 ff. (Also issued with the Almon edition of John Peter Zenger trial, London, 1765, pp. 49–59) **O131**

Owen was brought to trial for publishing a pamphlet critical of the House of Commons, *The Case of the Hon. Alexander Murray . . .* Possibly influenced by the widely publicized Zenger case in New York, the jury failed to convict the defendant, despite the instructions of Lord Chief Justice Lee to ignore the intent of the offending publication.

Oxford University. *The Judgment and Decree of the University of Oxford, past in their Convocation, July 21, 1683, against certain pernicious books, and damnable doctrines, destructive to the sacred persons of princes, their State and Government, and all Human Society.* Oxford, 1683. 9 p. (Reprinted in Farrer, *Books Condemned to Be Burnt*, pp. 191–99) **O132**

Following the Rye House Plot to kill Charles II, Oxford University issued this decree for the public burning of certain pernicious books, including works by Milton, Goodwin, Baxter, Knox, and Hobbes.

Ozman, Howard A., Jr. "Better Dead than Well-Read?" *Phi Delta Kappan*, 43:222–23, February 1962. **O133**

"Texans for America" found 50 out of 100 history textbooks to be "un-American." "If there is anything that America needs, it is to be better read . . . When we censor the writings of great men we not only make it more difficult for the present generation to understand the world they live in but we also—because of the climate of conformity that censorship promotes—prevent future writers from expressing themselves freely."

P

P., J. *Mr. L'Estrange Refuted with His Own Arguments.* [London, 1681]. 35 p. **P 1**
A Whig attack on the former licenser of printing who was out of a job with the lapse of the Licensing Act.

Pack, Ernest. *The Trial and Imprisonment of J. W. Gott for Blasphemy.* Bradford, Eng., The Freethought Socialist League, [1912?]. 149 p. **P 2**
Following a review of the history of blasphemy prosecution in England and the United States, the author gives an account of the career and trial of John W. Gott in Leeds, England. Gott was arrested, convicted, and sentenced to four months in prison in 1911–12 for publishing a pamphlet entitled *Rib-Ticklers*, or *Questions for Parsons*, which poked fun at religious thought. The author of this report, Ernest Pack, was a fellow freethinker. Many prominent Englishmen, including members of Parliament and churchmen, petitioned the Home Secretary for Gott's release arguing that punishment for blasphemy was an unwarranted form of religious persecution.

Pack, Richard, and Mark Marain. *Censored! The Censors See Red! The Record of the Present Wave of Terrorism and Censorship in the American Theatre, by Richard Pack. For a Free Stage; the Program of the Committee Against Censorship by Mark Marain.* New York, National Committee Against Censorship of the Theatre Arts, 1935. 29 p. (Reprinted in *New Theatre*, May 1936) **P 3**
A crusade for a free theater in America, with special attention to conditions in Newark, Boston, and Philadelphia. The Committee included such prominent literary critics as Brooks Atkinson, John Mason Brown, and Joseph Wood Krutch.

Pages of Death. 16 mm. color movie, 30 min. Cincinnati, Citizens for Decent Literature, 1962. (Produced by Karl Holtsnider) **P 4**
A true story (with actors rather than documentation) of the rape and murder of a 12-year-old girl, the cause being attributed to the reading of obscene literature by the youthful killer. The offending publications, the film emphasizes, were available from the neighborhood drugstore. A 4-page brochure describes the film. "This film is suitable for showing to all age groups of eighth grade level and above."

Paine, Donald F. "Obscenity Legislation in Tennessee." *Tennessee Law Review*, 29: 562–72, Summer 1962. **P 5**
A survey of current obscenity legislation in Tennessee—the state statutes in relation to decisions of the U.S. Supreme Court, and the municipal ordinance on obscenity in four cities—Knoxville, Memphis, Chattanooga, and Nashville.

Paine, Paul M. "The Library Must Be Free." *New York Libraries*, 11:42–44, February 1928. **P 6**
Discussion of the pressures on public libraries to buy or not to buy certain books, and an appeal to the librarian to "maintain the cause of freedom in book selection."

[Paine, Thomas]. *The Genuine Trial of Thomas Paine, for a Libel Contained in the Second Part of Rights of Man; at Guildhall, London, Dec. 18, 1792, before Lord Kenyon and a Special Jury: together with the Speeches at Large of the Attorney-General and Mr. Erskine, and Authentic Copies of Mr. Paine's Letters to the Attorney-General and Others, on the Subject of the Prosecution. Taken in Short-hand by E. Hodgson.* London, Printed for J.S. Jordan, 1792. 109 p. (2d ed., corrected, 1793. 143 p.) **P 7**
Erskine accepted the brief for the defense despite the opposition of the Prince of Wales. Paine was found guilty by the jury without waiting for the summing up. Erskine was dismissed from his office of Attorney-General to the Prince of Wales.

———. *Letter Addressed to the Addressers, on the Late Proclamation* [*for suppressing seditious publications, etc.*]. London, H. D. Symonds and Thomas Rickman, 1792. 40 p. (Reprinted in *Complete Writings of Thomas Paine*, edited by Philip S. Foner, vol. 2, pp. 469–511) **P 8**
In this satirical eulogy on the British constitution Paine criticizes the government for prosecuting his *Rights of Man*, noting that it was only when cheap editions of his book were offered to the public that the government took action. This indicated that the officials feared the common man. The royal proclamation for suppressing seditious publications, Paine charged, is indictable as an effort to influence the verdict in a pending case. In one place he declares: "It is a dangerous attempt in any government to say to a Nation, *thou shalt not read.*" Gimbel states that both Symonds and Rickman, the printers, were prosecuted for the publication; Rickman escaped to Paris and Symonds served a two-year jail sentence. This pamphlet is sometimes referred to as the third part of Paine's *Rights of Man*.

———. *A Letter to the Hon. Thomas Erskine, on the Prosecution of Thomas Williams, for Publishing the Age of Reason, by Thomas Paine . . . With His Discourse at the Society of the Theophilanthropists.* Paris, Printed for the Author, 1797. 32 p. (Also published by Richard Carlile, London, 1826. 29 p.) **P 9**
Paine argued that a man's religion was a personal affair and that the government had no right to interfere. Paine published the letter in English in Paris where he was serving as a member of the French National Convention, and sent copies to England for circulation.

[———]. "On the Liberty of the Press." In *Two Letters, being a Correspondence between Andrew A. Dean . . . and Thomas Paine . . . also, Mr. Paine's Description of the Liberty of the Press.* New York, 1823, pp. 7–8. (Reproduced in *Complete Writings of Thomas Paine*, edited by Philip S. Foner, vol. 2, pp. 1010–11) **P 10**
Paine quotes Jefferson's remark of 1787 that "the licentiousness of the press produces the same effect as the restraint of the press was intended to do. The restraint was to prevent

things from being told, and the licentiousness of the press prevents things being believed, when they are told." Paine defines liberty of the press as meaning in America, as in England, freedom from prior restraint and "not at all to the matter printed, whether good or bad." The public at large or the jury must be the judges of the content.

[———]. "The Prosecution of *Rights of Man*." In *Complete Writings of Thomas Paine*, edited by Philip S. Foner, New York, Citadel, 1945. vol. 2, pp. 441–513.
P 11

Paine's replies to his accusers include a letter to the Attorney General, Sir Archibald Macdonald, letters to Mr. Secretary Dundas, letters to Onslow Cranley, a letter to the sheriff of the County of Sussex, and a *Letter Addressed to the Addressers on the Late Proclamation*, issued in pamphlet form in 1792.

[———]. *The Trial of Thomas Paine, for a Libel, Contained in the Second Part of Rights of Man, before Lord Kenyon, and a Special Jury, at Guildhall, December 18. With the Speeches of the Attorney General and Mr. Erskine, at Large*. London, Printed for C. and G. Kearsley, 1792. 45 p. (Also in Howell, *State Trials*, vol. 22, pp. 357 ff., and Erskine, *Speeches*, vol. 2, pp. 1–184)
P 12

Thomas Paine (1737–1809) was undoubtedly the most censored author of the eighteenth century, both for his radicalism in politics (*Rights of Man*) and religion (*Age of Reason*). To many persons in authority in both America and England, Paine's works represented the most undesirable influences of the French Revolution. When the second part of *Rights of Man* appeared in 1792 (it applied the principles of the French Revolution to Britain), Paine was arrested and brought to trial. Between the preliminary hearing in June and the formal trial scheduled for December, feeling against Paine ran so high that, at the insistance of his friends, Paine left for France. Paine was tried *in absentia* and, despite Thomas Erskine's eloquent defense, he was found guilty of seditious libel and declared an outlaw. His book became contraband. Erskine had argued that since Paine's intent was honorable reform, the work could not be considered seditious. On the eve of the trial a retired army officer organized an anti-Paine society called the Association for the Preservation of Liberty and Property Against Republicans and Levellers. Following the trial the government stepped up its drive against seditious literature and a number of publishers who were authorized to issue Paine's work were brought to trial.

———. *Two Letters to Lord Onslow, Lord Lieutenant of the County of Surry; and One to Mr. Henry Dundas, Secretary of State, on* the Subject of the Late Excellent Proclamation for Suppressing Seditious Publications. 3d ed. London, Printed for J. Ridgway, 1792. 36 p.
P 13

[———]. *The Whole Proceedings on the Trial of an Information Exhibited Ex Officio against Thomas Paine for a Libel upon the Revolution and Settlement of the Crown and Regal Government as by Law Established; and also upon the Bill of Rights, the Legislature, Government, Laws and Parliament of this Kingdom, and upon the King. Tried by a Special Jury in the Court of King's Bench, Guildhall, on Tuesday, the 18th of December, 1792, before the Right Honourable Lord Kenyon. Taken in Short-hand by Joseph Gurney*. London, Printed by Martha Gurney, 1793. 196 p.
P 14

Paine was tried *in absentia* since he was in France at the time, sitting as a member of the jury in the trial of Louis XVI.

Paley, William S. *First Paralyzing Blow at Freedom of the Air in the United States. A Statement by William S. Paley*. New York, Columbia Broadcasting System, 1941. 4 p.
P 15

"New regulations by Federal Communications Commission sound innocent—actually they would destroy existing broadcasting structure."

———. *The Freedom of Radio*. New York, Columbia Broadcasting System, [1944?]. 18 p.
P 16

Statement of the president of Columbia Broadcasting System before the Interstate Commerce Committee of the U.S. Senate at the hearing on S. 814, known as the White-Wheeler Bill, 9 November 1943.

———. *Radio and Its Critics*. New York, Columbia Broadcasting System, 1946. 32 p.
P 17

An analysis of the current criticism of radio. The cure must ultimately be found in the field of public opinion rather than in government control. Paley favors a new and detailed Code of Program Standards which will prohibit practices which detract from the good name of radio, and strict enforcement of the Code under the spotlight of publicity.

Palladium of Conscience; or, The Foundation of Religious Liberty Displayed, Asserted and Established, Agreeable to Its True and Genuine Principles, above the Reach of All Petty Tyrants Who Attempt to Lord it over the Human Mind; Containing Furneaux's Letters to Blackstone, Priestley's Remarks on Blackstone, Blackstone's Reply to Priestley, and Blackstone's Case of the Middlesex Election . . . Philadelphia, Robert Bell, 1773. 155 p.
P 18

Palmer, Charles. "Press Control in War Time." *Nation* (London), 17:677–78, 21 August 1915.
P 19

The editor of the *Globe* replies to articles by "Tiercel" appearing in earlier issues and urging strict wartime press controls. Palmer advises telling the whole truth to the country when it can be told without detriment to national interests. He denies the right of the British Press Bureau to suppress proper criticism of the government.

Palmer, Elihu. *Posthumous Pieces by Elihu Palmer, Being Three Chapters of an Unfinished Work Intended to Have Been Entitled "The Political World."* . . . London, R. Carlile, 1824. 30 p.
P 20

One piece (pp. 26–30) is on the liberty of the press. Five years earlier Carlile, the publisher of this pamphlet, had been convicted of blasphemy for publishing Palmer's *Principles of Nature*.

Palmer, Frederick. "Things You Don't Know about the War." *Colliers*, 55:5–6+, 17 April 1915.
P 21

Because of military secrecy newspapermen covering the front have great difficulty writing other than bits of minor news.

———. *With My Own Eyes: A Personal Story of the Battle Years*. Indianapolis, Bobbs-Merrill, 1933. 396 p.
P 22

Autobiography of the chief censor of news dispatches, American Expeditionary Forces, World War I.

Palmer, John L. *The Censor and the Theatres*. London, Unwin, 1912. 307 p.
P 23

"The larger half of the present essay is based upon the evidence given before the Joint Select Committee [Great Britain] of 1909. . . . After discussing the origin of censorship, and . . . the law as it stands to-day, I propose to group the evidence for and against the censor, to outline . . . the . . . remedies . . . and to sum up . . . in favor of the . . . remedy of abolition, and the single license for theatre and music-hall."

———. *The Future of the Theatre*. London, G. Bell, 1913. 196 p.
P 24

Palmer states that the British Theatres Act was intended to keep intellectual life out of the theater. He charges the Lord Chamberlain with isolating the theater from the intellectual and imaginative life of the time.

Palmer, Thomas F. "The Case of Thomas Fyshe Palmer, September 1793." In Cockburn, *Examination of Trials for Sedition in Scotland*, vol. 1, pp. 184–220. (Arguments of Mr. Haggart, defense counsel, in

Howell, *State Trials*, vol. 23, pp. 276 ff.)
P 25

————. *A Narrative of the Sufferings of T. F. Palmer and W. Skirving, During a Voyage to New South Wales, 1794, on Board the Surprise Transport.* 2d ed. Cambridge, Eng., Printed by Benjamin Flower, 1797. 80 p.
P 26
Palmer and William Skirving were among the Scottish Jacobins convicted of sedition in 1793–94 and sentenced to transportation to Botany Bay. Skirving died soon after arrival; Palmer died on the journey home after he had served his fourteen-year sentence. This account of the voyage to Botany Bay was written by Mr. Palmer, according to the foreword by Jeremiah Joyce, "to vindicate his own [Mr. Palmer's] and Skirving's character from the charge of conspiracy and mutiny, on board the Surprise Transport."

————. *The Trial of the Rev. Thomas Fyshe Palmer, before the Circuit Court of Justiciary, Held at Perth, on the 12th and 13th September 1793. On an Indictment for Seditious Practices. Taken in Court by Mr. Ramsey* … Edinburgh, W. Skirving, 1793. 195 p.
P 27
Palmer, a respected Unitarian minister of Dundee, Scotland, was sentenced to seven years' transportation for publishing a "seditious" pamphlet for the Dundee society, Friends of Liberty, and for encouraging the reading of Thomas Paine's works. The offending pamphlet was written by George Mealmaker who five years later was also sentenced to transportation. The pamphlet expressed some of the political sentiments of Thomas Paine and advocated universal suffrage.

Paltsits, Victor H. "New Light on *Publick Occurrences*, America's First Newspaper." *Proceedings*, American Antiquarian Society, 59(n. s.):77–88, 1949.
P 28
The first publication of a letter from Cotton Mather to his kinsman John Cotton, 17 October 1690, sheds new light on the suppression of America's first newspaper. Although disclaiming authorship of the paper, Mather endorses it as a "very Noble, useful, & Laudable Design."

Pangborn, Arden X. "Can Self-Regulation Preserve a Free Press and a Free Trial?" *Quill*, 52(3):7, 15–16, March 1954.
P 29
An Oregon editor reviews the history of contempt citations and suggests ways to resolve the ancient conflict between the First and Fifth Amendments through voluntary agreement.

"Papal Raids on St. Louis Book Stores; Prosecuting Attorneys Said by Rome to Be Leading the Motley Aggregation of 'Heresy' Hunters." *Menace*, 403:1, 8 January 1919.
P 30

Pardey, Hans. *Das Recht der englischen Presse, Grundlagen und Systematik.* Hamburg, Lütcke & Wulff, 1928. 77 p. (Hamburgische Universität. Abhandlungen und Mitteilungen aus dem Seminar für Öffentliches Recht, Heft 20)
P 31

Park, A. E. W. "Public Bodies (Admission to Meetings) Act, 1960." *Modern Law Review*, 25:204–9, March 1962.
P 32
The first part of the article describes the historical background of the bill, which was enacted by Parliament and came into force on 1 June 1961; the second part concerns the legal effect of the Act; the third part discusses questions raised by those clauses of the bill which did not become law.

Park, Robert E. *The Immigrant Press and Its Control.* New York, Harper, 1922. 488 p.
P 33
Part 4 deals with control of the press through advertising, manipulators, enemy propaganda, and alliance.

Parker, Dorothy. "Sex—Without the Asterisks." *Esquire*, 50(4):102–3, October 1958.
P 34
In her book review column the author makes this observation: "Certainly no one wants to complain about sex itself; but I think we all have a legitimate grievance in the fact that as it is shown in present-day novels, its practitioners are so unnecessarily articulate about it. There is no more cruel destroyer of excitement than painstaking detail." She looks back with nostalgia to the day of the asterisk.

[Parker, Henry?]. *To the High Court of Parliament: the Humble Remonstrance of the Company of Stationers [asking for "such a perfect regulation of the Presse, as may procure the publike good of the State, by the private prosperity of the Stationers Company"].* London, 1643. 8 p. (Reproduced in Clyde, *Struggle for the Freedom of the Press*, pp. 319–22)
P 35
The Stationers' Company demanded of Parliament the appointment of regular licensers with the authority to control the undisciplined press, which they charged with being "scandalous and enormious" and with having "been the fewell in some measure of this miserable Civill-Warre." Parliament agreed and forbade all unlicensed publications. Authorship of the pamphlet is attributed by George Thomason to Henry Parker.

Parmelee, Maurice. *Nudism in Modern Life. The New Gymnosophy.* 5th ed. May's Landing, N.J., Sunshine Book Co., 1952.

Introduction by Havelock Ellis. **P 36**
This edition contains the text of the decision of the U.S. Court of Appeals for the District of Columbia, relating to the charges of obscenity against the book for its illustrations. Copies of the book, being imported from England, had been seized by the Customs. The decision of a lower court finding the work obscene was reversed by the Court of Appeals, with Justice Vinson dissenting.

[Parnas, Raymond I.]. "Obscenity Regulation and Enforcement in St. Louis and St. Louis County." *Washington University Law Quarterly*, 1964(1):98–127, February 1964.
P 37
Includes information on the operation of the Decent Literature Commission of St. Louis County and the St. Louis chapter of Citizens for Decent Literature.

————. "Will the First Prevail?" *Focus/Midwest*, 3(10–11):21–22, 1965.
P 38
Action by St. Louis city and county authorities against obscene publications.

A Parody on the Tent-Scene, in Richard the Third. Principal Characters—Lord Castlebrag, Cashman, Brandreth, Turner, and Ludlam. From the Independent Whig. London, R. Carlile, 1818. 8 p.
P 39
The scene takes place the night before Hone's third trial. The parody is an attack on Lord Castlereigh and his "spies" who had participated in the various libel trials.

Parrish, Wayne W. "Pornography at Airports." *American Aviation*, 29:45, July 1965.
P 40

Parsons, Roy. "Indecent Publications and the New Act of 1963." *New Zealand Libraries*, 27:49–63, April 1964.
P 41

Parton, James. ["Letters to the Editor in Opposition to Comstock Laws"]. *Truth Seeker*, 5:617, 28 September 1878; 6:504, 9 August 1879; 7:664, 19 October 1880.
P 42
The noted biographer took an active part in the campaign against the Comstock laws, in support of D. M. Bennett and others prosecuted by the vice societies.

Partridge, Eric. *The First Three Years.* London, Scholartis Press, 1930. 54 p.
P 43
An account and bibliography of the Scholartis Press. Contains a review of the *Sleeveless Errand* case.

"Passed by Censor." *Time*, 55(25):74–76, 19 June 1950. **P 44**
Censorship problems faced by American press correspondents abroad.

"'Passed by the National Board of Censorship.'" *Review of Reviews*, 50:730–31, December 1914. **P 45**
Description of the National Board of Censorship, its authority, organization, and the standards it uses in judging pictures.

"The Passing of the Indecent." *Outlook*, 106:795–96, 11 April 1914. **P 46**
The editor sees an abatement of "the tide of indecency which has rolled over the country during recent years and left its traces in fiction, on the stage, in dress, in dancing, and in other less obvious ways."

"Passing Show." *Agitator*, 1:1, 15 April 1911. **P 47**
An account of a man fined $50 for distributing a political cartoon.

Patch, Buel W. *Access to Official Papers and Information.* Washington, D.C., Editorial Research Reports, 1953. (Editorial Research Reports, 1:417–33, 1953) **P 48**
Contents: The White House and Freedom of Information, Congress and Access to Executive Papers, Access of the Press to Government News.

———. *Protection of Official Secrets.* Washington, D.C., Editorial Research Reports, 1948. (*Editorial Research Reports*, 1(8):1–15, 1948) **P 49**
A description of security measures taken by the government to prevent leaks in military information, including a review of the security classification of official documents. The report also reviews the program of voluntary censorship of press and radio.

———. *World Press Freedom.* Washington, D.C., Editorial Research Reports, 1945. (*Editorial Research Reports*, 2(20):1–23, 1945) **P 50**
A summary of efforts by the American Society of Newspaper Editors and the press associations to establish an international free press. U.S. and Soviet views of a free press are contrasted.

Paterson, James. *The Liberty of the Press, Speech, and Public Worship. Being Commentaries on the Liberty of the Subject and the Laws of England.* London, Macmillan, 1880. 568 p. (Reprinted in London by Sweet and Maxwell, 1930) **P 51**
An important and authoritative commentary on English and American legal principles and practices relating to all aspects of freedom of expression. Includes such topics as licensing, the newspaper tax, blasphemy, obscene libel, sedition, libeling the sovereign, libeling the ministers, libeling the constitution, ex-officio informations, the right to publish parliamentary debates and court procedure, personal libel and slander, and censorship of plays. Well-documented as to statutes and court decisions.

[Paterson, Thomas]. *God versus Paterson. The Extraordinary Bow-Street Police Report . . . Trial of Thomas Paterson, Editor of the "Oracle of Reason," Taken on a warrant charged with exhibiting in view a profane paper in a thoroughfare, under the Police Act.* London, George Clarke [1843]. 92 p. **P 52**
"Bull-dog" Paterson took over editorship of the *Oracle of Reason* after its previous editors, Charles Southwell and G. J. Holyoake, were imprisoned for blasphemy. Paterson, in turn, was imprisoned for one month for blasphemy and William Chilton became editor.

[———, et al.]. *The Trial of Thomas Paterson, for Blasphemy before the High Court of Justiciary, Edinburgh, with . . . the Trials of Thomas Finlay and Miss Matilda Roalfe (for Blasphemy) in the Sheriffs' Court. With Notes and a Special Dissertation on Blasphemy Prosecutions in General, by the Secretary of the "Anti-Persecution Union."* London, Published for the Anti-Persecution Union by Henry Hetherington . . . and Matilda Roalfe (Edinburgh), 1844. 80 p. **P 53**
Shortly after Paterson was released from a London jail for "blasphemous" placards, he went to Edinburgh to defy the blasphemy laws there. He took possession of a bookshop and boldly announced by placard his intention to sell blasphemous and infidel works, including works of Palmer, Hume, Paine, Shelley, Carlile and others, waggishly offering "a liberal allowance to Sunday Schools." He was arrested and tried on 11 charges, "as many different acts of publication," found guilty, and sentenced to 15 months in prison. Shortly thereafter, Thomas Finlay, the elderly bookseller whose shop Paterson had used for his sales, was arrested for the sale of 2 infidel books. At his trial Finlay spoke in his own behalf, quoting from various authorities on freedom of the press and citing decisions in earlier trials. He argued that if Christians had the right to attack atheists, it was only fair that atheists be given the right of reply. He was found guilty and sentenced to 60 days in jail. Whereupon Matilda Roalfe came from London to Edinburgh and took over sales from the "Atheistical Depot," 105 Nicolson Street, issuing a manifesto listing persecuted works offered for sale. She was arrested at the instigation of the procurator fiscal and brought to trial, where she spoke in her own defense. She was found guilty and given a 60-day sentence. Following the imprisonment of Miss Roalfe, it was announced that "Mr. Baker of the United Order of Blasphemers, London, has arrived in Edinburgh, to take the superintendence of the Atheistic Depot." George J. Holyoake, who had himself served a jail sentence for editing *Oracle of Reason*, has written an introduction to the three trials (pp. 9–12) and A Dissertation on Blasphemous Prosecutions (pp. 3–8).

The Patriot; a Periodical Publication, Intended to Arrest the Progress of Seditious and Blasphemous Opinions, too Prevalent in the year 1819. Manchester, Eng., J. Aston, 28 August 1819—1 January 1820. 19 numbers. **P 54**
The editors complain that the stamp tax not only makes the spread of sedition more difficult by rendering it more expensive, but it also operates against the loyal press as well.

"Patriotism in Chicago." *Publishers' Weekly*, 112:1630–31, 29 October 1927. **P 55**
The Mayor of Chicago ordered a survey of the historical collection of the Chicago Public Library to find volumes tainted with British propaganda. Librarian Carl Roden objected to proposed book burning, suggesting as an alternative that offending books be locked up. The article also deals with the suit of Professor David S. Muzzey against a former Illinois Congressman, John J. Gorman, who claimed Muzzey's *History of the American People* was dictated from Buckingham Palace.

Patten, McClellan. "Radio Gets the Jitters." *American Magazine*, 127:42–43, March 1939. (Excerpted in Summers, *Radio Censorship*, pp. 261–65) **P 56**
A discussion of the strange taboos on radio resulting from pressures of minority groups. A new definition of the licensing and other powers of the FCC is needed. "On guard against government censorship, radio has clamped its own hand over its own mouth in a self-censorship as rigid as, if not more rigid than, anything the government could order." References are made to the antics of the censor against such comics as Fred Allen and Phil Baker, and the celebrated fan dancer, Sally Rand.

Patterson, Giles J. *Free Speech and a Free Press.* Boston, Little, Brown, 1939. 261 p. **P 57**
A concise history of legal concepts of freedom of political expression, including the Continental background, the struggle in England, and the evolution of freedom of the press in the United States under the First Amendment. The author, a lawyer, has written the work to give the general public an appreciation of the "legacy that our ancestors acquired by the colossal fight . . . waged against government's greed for power."

Patterson, Grove. "Social Responsibilities of the American Newspaper." *Vital Speeches*, 14:435–38, 1 May 1948. **P 58**

A Boston University Founders' Day speech by the editor of the *Toledo Blade*. "American newspapers are confronted by these three major responsibilities. First, to provide objective reporting and to furnish the people with unslanted facts. Second, to represent the whole people and not special interests, to assume the task of interpretation and leadership, and to deserve, by moral behavior, the freedom of the press. Third, to join in a constructive, specific and practical effort to raise their own standards."

[Patterson, Thomas]. "Liberty Imperilled through the Encroachments of the Judiciary." *Arena*, 35:189–94, February 1906.
P 59
Deals with the case of the U.S. Senator from Colorado, convicted by the Supreme Court of Colorado for "constructive contempt" and fined $1,000. Senator Patterson had published articles and cartoons in his paper, *Rocky Mountain News*, critical of the state's judiciary. The article includes the text of Senator Patterson's defense and one of the cartoons objected to by the Court.

[———]. "Nullification of the Ends of Free Government through Judicial Usurpations in the Interests of Corporate Wealth." *Arena*, 36:309–11, September 1906.
P 60
Further commentary on the contempt conviction of Senator Patterson.

Patterson, W. D. "The Censors and the Public." *Saturday Review*, 35:22–23, 6 September 1952. (Excerpted in Daniels, *The Censorship of Books*, pp. 66–67)
P 61
Consideration of the work of the Gathings Committee investigation of immoral literature. "The answer to censorship in a democracy is the progressive education of the public taste to reject the bad and demand the good, without recourse to official censors or to the extremism of many private pressure groups." To trust the people's judgment is the real test of a democracy.

Paul, Elliot. *Film Flam*. London, Muller, [1956]. 160 p.
P 62
An exposé of the Hollywood film industry by a writer who had spent the last 15 years in the film capital, written in a mood of benevolent satire. Includes chapters on Censorship, the Bugaboo, and The Hays Code. Paul reviews "the censorship pestilences which have followed one another in Hollywood, like ghosts of dead men in material leather shoes, marching on and on, again to haunt our hours of ease and rest." The Hays Code, he maintains, was written "by the late Rev. Daniel A. Lord, S.J., and the former editor of a tract called *Decency in Motion Pictures*, one Martin Quigley . . . I maintain that Art cannot be '*morally good*' or 'unclean'. It can be enchanting or lousy, or so-so, which probably is the worst."

———, and Luis Quintanilla. *With a*

Hays Nonny Nonny. New York, Random House, 1942. 188 p.
P 63
A burlesque of the taboos in the production of Hollywood movies as reflected in the handling of various Biblical stories. The Hays Office and its rulings come in for frequent spoofing in both text and illustrations. "The Marx brothers could not hope to be funnier than the Hays Code itself."

[Paul, James C. N.]. "Libel Actions by Political Organizations: Freedom to Smear vs. Freedom to Criticize." *University of Pennsylvania Law Review*, 98:865–84, May 1950.
P 64
Notes on cases covering the period 1925–49.

———. "The Post Office and Non-Mailability of Obscenity: An Historical Note." *U.C.L.A. Law Review*, 8:44–68, 1960–61.
P 65
The author "finds that the basic purpose of Congress was to provide criminal sanctions for the dissemination of obscenity via the mails, and concludes that there is a serious question whether an independent censorship program such as that assumed by the Post Office has been authorized by Congress."

———, and Murray L. Schwartz. *Federal Censorship; Obscenity in the Mail*. Glencoe, Ill., Free Press, 1961. 368 p.
P 66
Two legal experts explore the problems relating to censorship of the mails and customs in the United States, presenting their findings in nontechnical language. They trace the evolution of federal obscenity laws from the English common law to the Comstock laws and on down to the *Ulysses* case of 1930 that marked a change in the attitude of the federal courts. The last half of the volume deals with recent developments resulting from court decisions and administrative action. In a final section the authors discuss alternative proposals for treatment of objectionable materials. The appendix includes extensive case notes and excerpts from statutes and regulations.

———. "Obscenity in the Mails: a Comment on Some Problems of Federal Censorship." *University of Pennsylvania Law Review*, 106:214–53, December 1957.
P 67
A brief interim report on a broader study published in book form in 1961.

Paulu, Burton. *British Broadcasting: Radio and Television in the United Kingdom*. Minneapolis, University of Minnesota Press, 1956. 457 p.
P 68
This general description and appraisal of British broadcasting includes references to the legal control of the B.B.C. and the extent of its freedom in programming. There is discussion of the Fortnight Rule, regulating

discussion of Parliamentary debate, and the handling of controversial issues.

———, comp. *A Radio and Television Bibliography; Books and Magazine Articles on the Nontechnical Aspects of Broadcasting Published between January 1, 1949 and June 30, 1952*. Urbana, Ill., National Association of Educational Broadcasters, 1952. 129 p.
P 69

Payne, George H. *History of Journalism in the United States*. New York, Appleton, 1920. 453 p.
P 70
Mott considers this general history important because of its emphasis on the relations between government and press, especially its treatment of press freedom.

Payne, John C. "Certain Limitations upon the Rule that Publications Shall Not Be Subject to Prior Restraints." *University of South Carolina Selden Society Yearbook*, 2:2–18, January 1938.
P 71
The author notes prevailing exceptions in the United States to the Blackstonian rule that there shall be no prior censorship: mail censorship and withholding of second-class mailing privileges, publications involving strikes and labor conflict (Buck's Stove case), newspaper tax and nuisance laws, court injunctions on reporting of trials, wartime censorship of news, and the entire motion picture production.

Payne, Margaret. "Selection—or Censorship." *Books; Journal of the National Book League*, 356:209–13, November–December 1964.
P 72
A children's librarian urges librarians to buy the better quality children's books for these are the ones that are not generally available to children through other sources. To buy these exclusive of poor and indifferent books is not censorship.

Paz, Alberto G. "Eyes and Tongues of Our People." *Vital Speeches*, 18:73–74, 15 November 1951.
P 73
The editor of the suppressed Buenos Aires paper, *La Prensa*, discusses the importance of a free press in a speech accepting the Freedom House award, 7 October 1951.

Peairs, C. A., Jr. "Freedom of the Press." *Kentucky Law Journal*, 28:369–410, May 1940.
P 74
The author traces the freedom of the press "from the aspect of the constitutional guarantees supporting it, with a brief historical sketch of the growth of the doctrine." The freedom of minority opinion, he believes, may be threatened by popular pressures in a political or moral crisis.

Pearce, Lillian. "Book Selection and *Peyton Place.*" *Library Journal*, 83:712–13, 1 March 1958. **P 75**
Article concerns a letter written by Margaret Cole of Queens Borough Public Library in reply to a letter objectioning to the inclusion of *Peyton Place* in one of the branch libraries. The letter was written to clarify and explain the book selection policies of the library.

Pearl, M. L. *William Cobbett; a Bibliographical Account of His Life and Times.* London, Oxford University Press, 1953. 266p. **P 76**

Pearson, Edmund L. "The Evil That Books Do." *Public Libraries*, 16:188–91, May 1911. (Reprinted in *Illinois Libraries*, May 1966) **P 77**
In a witty essay on the good and bad effect of books, especially on children, the author concludes that the "evil influence of books is smaller than many of us suppose, and should cause less disquiet [to the librarian] than it does at present." While admitting that dime novels lack artistic merit and are not appropriate for libraries, they ought not to be excluded as immoral (they actually have a high moral standard) and that boys found reading them should not be treated as criminals. Finally, he quotes a prison chaplain as stating that "the place of pernicious literature in the list of formative agencies in the genesis of precocious criminalism is incidental."

Pearson, Lester B. *The Free Press; a Reflection of Democracy* . . . Williamsburg, Va., Colonial Williamsburg, [1958]. 16p. **P 78**
An address by Lester B. Pearson, a leader of the Liberal Party of Canada, on the occasion of the celebration of the Prelude to Independence, 15 May 1958.

Pearson, Richard M. "Can Textbooks Be Subversive?" *Phi Delta Kappan*, 33:248–50, January 1952. **P 79**
A textbook publisher examines his product. Careful planning, scrutiny, and editing ensures the most objective possible writing.

Pease, A. S. "Notes on Book-Burning." In H. M. Shepherd, *ed., Munerosa Studiosa.* Cambridge, Mass., Episcopal Theological School, 1946, pp. 145–60. **P 80**

Pease, Theodore C. *The Leveller Movement. A Study in the History and Political Theory of the English Great Civil War.* Washington, D.C., American Historical Association, 1916. 406p. (Reprinted by Peter Smith, Glouchester, Mass., 1965) **P 81**

A sympathetic history of this group of political radicals of the Commonwealth, led by John Lilburne. The Levellers fought for their ideas of religious toleration, the sanctity of the individual, and the right of the common man to speak his mind for the good of the nation. They contributed to the freedom of the press by their vigorous and fearless pamphleteering in the face of persecution and imprisonment.

Peattie, Donald C. "Freedom on Trial." *Reader's Digest*, 51:41–44, July 1947. **P 82**
Popular account of the censorship trial of John Peter Zenger.

Pedrick, William H. "Freedom of the Press and the Law of Libel: the Modern Revised Translation." *Cornell Law Quarterly*, 49:581–608, Summer 1964. **P 83**
An examination of the "task of balancing the societal interest in the free flow of information against the interest in securing responsibility in dissemination of information and in protecting individual reputation from unwarranted injury." Interpretation of decisions, particularly *New York Times Co. v. Sullivan*, 376 U.S. 254 (1964).

———. "Senator McCarthy and the Law of Libel: A Study of Two Campaign Speeches." *Northwestern University Law Review*, 48:134–84, May–June 1953. **P 84**

Peele, David A. *Lollipops or Dynamite— Shall We Censor the Comics?* Cleveland, Western Reserve University, 1951. 46p. (Unpublished Master's thesis) **P 85**

Peet, Creighton. "Our Lady Censors." *Outlook*, 153:645–47+, 25 December 1929. **P 86**
Discussion of the various censors affecting motion pictures and their production, including the work of organized clubwomen intent on protecting children. "Among all the subjects upon which the censor lavishes his handiwork, the movies suffer the most; not so much from the actual elimination of essentially trivial 'damns,' 'hells' and bedroom scenes by state and city boards, as from too much motherly care and too many stultifying prenatal cautions from the dozens of unofficial reviewing organizations."

Peltason, Jack. *Constitutional Liberty and Seditious Activity; Individual Liberty and Governmental Security.* New York, Carrie Chapman Catt Memorial Fund, 1954. 55p. (Freedom Agenda Pamphlet no. 12) **P 87**
The purpose of the pamphlet is "to give the reader a basic understanding of the history and theory of governmental policy in the control of seditious political activity. The pamphlet makes no attempt to resolve the

conflict between the American principle of freedom of opinion and the requirements of national security but instead merely sets forth the alternatives of policy."

[Peltier, Jean]. *The Trial of Jean Peltier, Esq. for a Libel against Napoleon Buonaparte . . . At the Court of King's-Bench . . . 21th of February, 1803. Taken in Short-Hand by Mr. Adams, and the Defence revised by Mr. Mackintosh.* London, Printed by Cox, Son, and Baylis for M. Peltier, 1803. 312p; 147p. **P 88**
The voluminous bilingual report of the trial of a French national residing in England, for his alleged attempts to incite Frenchmen, through his pamphleteering, to assassinate Napoleon. Lord Ellenborough, in his charge to the jury, said the works were written with the intent to vilify, and the verdict of guilty was not unexpected. The report concludes with an impassioned address by the author following the verdict. Peltier was never sentenced because of the outbreak of war with France. Mr. Mackintosh's defense of Peltier is reprinted in Howell's *State Trials*, vol. 28, pp. 529ff.

Pemberton, John de J., Jr. "Prurience or Redeeming Social Importance?" *Iowa Library Quarterly*, 19:109–12, January 1963. **P 89**

Pemberton, Thomas. *Letter to Lord Langdale on the Recent Proceedings in the House of Commons on the subject of Privilege.* London, Charles Hunter, 1837. 99p. **P 90**
Relates to the question whether Parliamentary papers sold by order of the House of Commons are a privileged publication though they contain false and scandalous matter reflecting upon individuals. The letter also discusses the broader question of whether or not Parliament has the right to assert its privileges over against the courts of law. The issue grew out of action against Hansard, the state printer, to recover damage for alleged libel contained in a government report.

[Pennell, William B., and Marc L. Swartzbaugh]. "Retroactivity and First Amendment Rights." *University of Pennsylvania Law Review*, 110:394–435, January 1962. **P 91**
An analysis of the issue of retroactive government action and the rights guaranteed by the First Amendment. "The Supreme Court has not expressly acknowledged that the first amendment prohibits retroactive governmental action."

Pennsylvania. State Board of Censors (Motion Pictures). *Acts and Rules.* Harrisburg, Pa., The Board, 1914, 1915, 1926, 1941?, 1951?. 5 issues. (Issued as *Rules and Standards*, 1926–51.) **P 92**

—————. *List of Subjects Condemned for the Year Ending June 30, 1916.* Harrisburg, Pa., The Board, 1916. 5 p.　**P 93**
Such a list, in addition to an annual report, was issued by the Board from time to time between 1916 and 1922 (10 issues).

—————. *Notice [concerning rule change].* Harrisburg, Pa., The Board, 1919. 4 p.
　P 94
Reproduces certificate and seal of approval.

—————. *Reports, 1914–1918.* Harrisburg, Pa., The Board. 1915–1919.　**P 95**
The first state censorship of films (State Board of Censors; later called the Board of Motion Picture Control) was created in Pennsylvania in 1911. Historian Ellis P. Oberholtzer was secretary of the Board for a number of years. In 1923 the Board was transferred to the Department of Public Instruction. It functioned until 1961 when the laws creating it were declared unconstitutional by a decision of the State Supreme Court (405 Pa. 83). The reports were issued semiannually and annually (5 issues) between 1914 and 1918.

Pennypacker, Samuel W. "Sensational Journalism and the Remedy." *North American Review*, 190:587–93, November 1909.　**P 96**
The former governor of Pennsylvania charges that the press by its sensationalism "has come to be the most conspicuous example of the very wrong to correct which its privileges were conferred—that is, the secret use of arbitrary power." Individuals and institutions are attacked and libeled and "nobody knows whose is the hand which strikes the blow or what the motive which inspires it." The author recommends that newspapers be prevented by injunction from publishing falsehood and scandal. "Such material has no part in the liberty of the press any more than sewage has place in the streams."

Penstone, Giles H. "Meaning of the Term Public Interest, Convenience, and Necessity under the Communications Act of 1934, as Applied to Licenses to Construct New Broadcast Stations." *George Washington Law Review*, 9:873–917, June 1941.　**P 97**

Pentcheff, Nicholas. *Trade Unions and the Press.* Columbia, Mo., Freedom of Information Center, School of Journalism, University of Missouri, 1961. 6 p. (Publication no. 65)　**P 98**
The treasurer of the Inter-American Federation of Working Newspapermen's Organization discusses the mutual interests of the free press and the free labor movement. "The most deadly enemies of free expression and free labor organizations have been and continue to be autocratic and totalitarian governments." He discusses the lack of press freedom and labor freedom in Communist and Nazi states. In a democracy threat to labor and a free press may come from party interests, financial interests, newspaper monopolies, the government bureaucrat, or the unscrupulous labor leader. "We must fight any interest that would have us distort the news for their selfish ends. . . . All enemies of democracy and the freedom of the press are our enemies."

Penton, Brian C. *Censored! Being a True Account of a Notable Fight for your Right to Read and Know, with some Comment upon the Plague of Censorship in General.* [Sydney, Australia, Shakespeare Head Press, 1947]. 108 p.　**P 99**
An account of the growing censorship in Australia that was "equalled on the moral side only by Eire's and on the political side came closer to the model of totalitarian censorship than any democratic or pseudo-democratic State in the World." The matter came to a head, according to the author, with the wartime suppression of a number of newspapers in Sydney, Melbourne, and Adelaide. The work is largely an account of the wartime censorship of the newspaper press in Australia.

Penty, George, and James Crown. "The Books Didn't Burn in Brooksville." *Nation*, 178:120, 13 February 1954.
　P 100
An account of the removal of controversial books from the Brooksville (Fla.) Public Library after pressures from "super-patriots" and the return of the books following President Eisenhower's address to the American Library Association opposing book burning.

"People Who Have Eaten Books." *Scientific American*, 94:267, 31 March 1906.　**P 101**
A brief history of bibliophagia, or the eating of books as a means of destroying them.

The People's Choice. Columbia, Mo., Freedom of Information, School of Journalism, University of Missouri, 1962. 4 p. (Publication no. 74)　**P 102**
Are the communications media giving the American public what it wants? Here is a collection of "recent odds-and-ends answers to the question."

PEP (Political and Economic Planning). Press Group. *Report on the British Press, a Survey of Its Current Operations and Problems with Special Reference to National Newspapers and Their Part in Public Affairs.* London, PEP, 1938. 333 p. (An adaptation of chapter 9, Legal Restrictions on the Press, is published in the *United States Law Review*, October 1938)　**P 103**
This comprehensive discussion of the state of the British press on the eve of World War II is the result of a three-year study made by a Keynesian-oriented group. The report includes comments on freedom of the press and monopoly

control. Among the recommendations are proposals for reform in libel and contempt laws and various alternatives by which press ownership might be shared by private enterprise and public groups so that freedom of editing and reporting might be preserved.

Periodical Distributors Association. "Distributors: Censorship Forum Presents Contrasting Views and Policies." *Publishers' Weekly*, 178:35–37, 17 October 1960.　**P 104**
"Basic differences of opinion on the subject of censorship were made apparent during a discussion of censorship held by three clergymen and the managing director of the American Book Publishers Council at the first general session of the Council for Periodical Distributors Association convention." The clergy were Msgr. Thomas J. Fitzgerald, Rev. Dan M. Potter, and Rev. William F. Rosenblum; Dan Lacy represented the American Book Publishers Council. John Butler, attorney for the Periodical Distributors Association, discusses a "model statute" on obscenity.

"Periphery of War." *Living Age*, 357:215–24, November 1939.　**P 105**
Four contributions on wartime censorship: (1) Triumph of Anastasie (French censorship); (2) Blackout of Humor by Lamar Middleton; (3) The Censors in Three Capitals by C.B.S. Broadcasters William L. Shirer (Berlin), Thomas B. Grandin (Paris), and Edward R. Murrow (London); (4) The Man Who Knows (a story about wartime rumors taken from the London *Times*).

Periscope, *pseud.* "Sedition and the Censor." *English Review*, 39:653–59, November 1924.　**P 106**
The writer praises the present government of the Irish Free State for allowing, for the most part, "seditious" and "republican" literature, press, and plays on the theory that if left alone such passion will "burn itself out."

Perkins, F. B. "Free Libraries and Unclean Books." *Library Journal*, 10:396–99, December 1885.　**P 107**
The librarian of the San Francisco Free Public Library states his arguments for refusing to buy or circulate what he considers "dirty books" even though there may be requests for them from adults.

Perlés, Alfred. *My Friend Henry Miller. An Intimate Biography.* New York, John Day, 1956. 255 p.　**P 108**
References throughout to action taken in England and the United States against Miller's books, *Tropic of Cancer* and *Tropic of Capricorn*. Excerpts are given from the case of *Besig v. United States*.

Perlman, David. "How Captain Hanrahan Made *Howl* a Best-Seller." *Reporter*, 17: 37–39, 12 December 1957. **P 109**

Account of the case in San Francisco, when Police Captain William Hanrahan brought Lawrence Ferlinghetti, proprietor of the City Lights Pocket Bookshop, and his clerk to trial for selling *Howl and Other Poems*, by Allen Ginsberg. Judge Horn's verdict was "not guilty." Part of his opinion is quoted.

Perlman, Nathan D., and Morris Ploscowe. "False, Defamatory Anti-Racial and Anti-Religious Propaganda and the Use of the Mails." *Lawyers Guild Review*, 4:13–23, January–February 1944. **P 110**

The authors defend the Lynch Bill which bars defamatory antiracial and antireligious matter from the mails. This point of view is opposed by O. K. Fraenkel in the March–April issue.

Perlman, William J., ed. *The Movies on Trial: The Views and Opinions of Outstanding Personalities anent Screen Entertainment Past and Present.* New York, Macmillan, 1936. 254p. **P 111**

Comments from a representative group of leaders—civic, religious, cultural—on the controversy over the American movies, growing out of charges made during the late 20's and 30's that the motion picture industry was exploiting indecency and that some form of controls were needed. Includes statements from William Allen White, the Reverend John J. Cantwell, Edward G. Robinson, Raymond J. Cannon (member of Congress who introduced the censorship bill in 1934), Judge Ben B. Lindsey, William Lyon Phelps, Upton Sinclair, the Reverend John Haynes Holmes, and Rabbi Sidney E. Goldstein.

Pernicone, Joseph M. "Church Prohibition of Books." *Catholic Lawyer*, 3:286–91, Autumn 1957. **P 112**

Bishop Pernicone describes the law of the Catholic Church as it relates to reading, publishing, and bookselling.

Perry, Bliss. *Pernicious Books . . .* 2d ed. Boston, New England Watch and Ward Society, 1927. 15p. (Also published in *The Light*, July–August 1923) **P 113**

Address given at the annual meeting of the Society, 22 April 1923. Perry, along with such authors and critics as Hamlin Garland, Irving Bacheller, Edwin Markham, Brander Matthews, and Paul Elmer Moore, supported the work of the vice societies and the Clean Books League and deplored pernicious contemporary literature. In this lecture Perry refers to George Moore as "a satyr in his seventieth year," and observes that "the chief mark left thus by Freudian psychology upon contemporary literature is a very dirty one." While opposing prior censorship, Perry approves of

taking an offensive book to court. The Watch and Ward, he states, is merely acting as proxy for busy citizens who want to see the law enforced against pernicious literature.

Perry, James. "Trial for Seditious Libel, 1793." In Howell, *State Trials*, vol. 22, pp. 953 ff., and in Erskine, *Speeches*, vol. 2, pp. 372–453. **P 114**

In the first libel trial after the passage of the Fox Libel Act, the jury found Perry and the two other defendants, John Lambert and James Gray, not guilty. The three had been charged with publishing in their *Morning Chronicle* an address of a society for political information. Thomas Erskine was defense attorney; James Perry spoke in his own behalf.

Perry, Stuart. *The Indecent Publications Tribunal: A Social Experiment.* Foreword by Sir Kenneth Gresson. Wellington, N.Z., Whitcombe and Toombs, 1965. 169p. **P 115**

The city librarian of Wellington, N.Z., who is also a member of New Zealand's Indecent Publications Tribunal, describes how this official censorship body has operated since its creation in 1964. The appendix gives the text of New Zealand censorship legislation dating back to 1892. Eric Moon, in reviewing the book in *Library Journal*, 15 March 1966, notes the reasonably liberal record of the Tribunal and that the experiment "has left New Zealand's censorship problems, if not solved, at least less messy and less injurious for the moment than some of ours have been in the U.S. in recent years."

Perry, Stuart H. "Trial by Newspaper." *United States Law Review*, 66:374–83, July 1932. **P 116**

A lawyer-newspaperman comments on problems created by sensational reports of criminal trials.

———. "Twin Evils Cast Disturbing Shadows Over Press and Judiciary." *Quill*, 21(3):3–4, 10, March 1933. **P 117**

The evils are the interference of the press with the administration of criminal justice and the traffic between officers of the law and the press whereby information is exchanged for publicity.

———, and Edward J. White. *Newspapers and the Courts.* Columbia, Mo., University of Missouri, 1928. 24p. (University of Missouri Bulletin, vol. 29, no. 28, Journalism Series no. 51) **P 118**

Address by S. H. Perry, The Press under Fire; address by E. J. White, The Press and the Judiciary.

Perversion for Profit. 16 mm. color movie, 30 min. Cincinnati, Citizens for Decent Literature. Narrated by George Putnam. **P 119**

The theme of the movie is that one of the main causes of juvenile delinquency, violence, and especially sex crimes, is obscene literature. A large portion of the film shows examples of pornographic literature (with patches introduced at appropriate spots) classified as to type of perversion—homosexuality, sadism, etc. The film also calls for precensorship of films. "The film is for showing to adult groups only."

Peter, Emmett, Jr. "Do Our Contempt of Court Laws Need Modernizing?" *Quill*, 49(4):15–16, 19, April 1961. **P 120**

The author suggests that "a fact-finding study could bring press-judicial conflict into focus and perhaps suggest ways of resolving some of the issues in dispute." A tightening and clarification of contempt laws, with reasonable restraints, is needed.

Peters, John. "Where the Sex Appeal Corrupts." *Light*, 29:27–31, May–June 1926. **P 121**

Discusses the danger of sex literature in the hands of adolescents and the need to control its distribution.

Peters, William. "What You Can't See on TV." *Redbook*, 109(3):28–29, 80–83, July 1957. **P 122**

"Is it 'good taste' or sheer cowardice that keeps valuable programs off your screen? Here are the facts on television's quiet but deadening censorship—and how you can help overcome it."

Peterson, Houston. *Havelock Ellis Philosopher of Love.* Boston, Houghton Mifflin, 1928. 432p. **P 123**

Chapters 11 and 12 contain an account of the attack on *Studies in the Psychology of Sex* and the Bedborough prosecution in England.

Peterson, Theodore. "The Fight of William Hone for British Press Freedom." *Journalism Quarterly*, 25:132–38, June 1948. **P 124**

A brief account of the prosecution for political libel of the pamphleteer and satirist who shocked and amused London in 1817.

———. "The Social Functions of the Press." In National Society for the Study of Education, *Mass Media and Education*, 53d Yearbook. Chicago, University of Chicago Press, 1954. pt. 2, pp. 30–53. **P 125**

To improve the social services of the press, account must be taken of the commercial basis of the press and reforms or remedies to improve the press must be based on the combined efforts of press, public, and government. The freedom of the press must be re-examined, considering it not only as the right of the individual to speak, but as the obligation of those who control the media to present a wide range of representative views.

Petrov, B. "Current Tendencies in Bourgeois Library Science." *ALA Newsletter on Intellectual Freedom*, 13:73, 82–84, November 1964. (From *Bibliotekar*, 7:55–58, July 1964. Translated by Rudolf Lednicky) **P126**
"In actuality the principle of 'freedom to read' in capitalist countries serves above all as a cover for the dissemination of politically reactionary literature which in one form or another promotes the propaganda of capitalist ideology. . . . 'Freedom to read' means that in the acquisition of library material, comics, detective stories, 'horror novels,' anti-communist libels, racist fabrications, open and half-concealed pornography, all of which is thrust upon the reader by deafening advertisements with the aid of press, radio and television, must be widely represented in the libraries' book collections." Reference is made to a report on Libraries of the U.S.A. and Censorship by B. P. Kanevskii, who observes that while American librarians sometimes show genuine courage in opposing censorship from ultrareactionary organizations, they themselves to a marked degree share anti-Communist prejudices. Soviet librarians openly acknowledge the party nature of their work and subordinate all their work to advancing Communist ideas among readers.

Pettijohn, C. C. "How the Motion Picture Governs Itself." *Annals of the American Academy of Political and Social Science*, 128:158–62, November 1928. **P127**
The general counsel for the Motion Picture Producers and Distributors of America describes and defends the self-censorship of movies by the industry, against the alternative of political censorship by state and municipal bodies.

———. *Self-Regulation versus Censorship.* New York, [Motion Picture Producers and Distributors of America?]. 1938. 11p. **P128**
Favors self-regulation of the movies under the Production Code.

P[etty], Sir W[illiam]. *The Advice of W. P. to Mr. Samuel Hartlib, For the Advancement of Some Particular Parts of Learning.* London, 1648. 34p. (Also in *The Harleian Miscellany*, vol. 6, pp. 141–57) **P129**
A British physician and statistician proposes to condense all books into "one book, or great work, though consisting of many volumes." One writer has called the proposal a threat to end bookselling for all time and to regiment books "in slavish squads, each volume numbered like a bound convict, its contents rationed to a comma." Books would be marketed by the yard. Sir William suggests

that all that is "nice, contentious, and merely fantastical" be in some measure suppressed, and "brought into disgrace and contempt with all men."

Pew, Marlen E. "So Long as Editorial Freedom Remains." *Quill*, 21(11):8–10, November 1933. **P130**
The editor of *Editor and Publisher* considers the importance of editorial criticism as a constructive influence on public affairs.

Pezet, Washington. "Common-Censorship." *Forum*, 73:742–46, May 1925. **P131**
The author, dealing largely with stage censorship, objects to the establishment of an "authoritative guardian of morals and manners."

Pfeffer, Leo. "Heresy, American Democracy and *The Miracle*." *Jewish Frontier*, 17:14–18, August 1951. **P132**
An account of the banning of the film, *The Miracle*, and implications of the action. "A case history of Catholic power in American democracy is presented by the dramatic short-lived career of the forty-minute Italian picture which opened at the Paris Theatre in New York City, on December 12, 1950, and was closed by order of the State Board of Regents on February 16, 1951." The action was taken, according to the author, at the instigation of Cardinal Spellman. "Shall American democracy continue the Jeffersonian tradition of freedom in religion, or shall we return to the Augustinian dogma of the duty of the State to extirpate heresy?"

———. *The Liberties of an American; the Supreme Court Speaks.* Boston, Beacon, 1956. 309 p. **P133**
In this general work on the decisions of the U.S. Supreme Court which interpret the Bill of Rights, three chapters deal with freedom of the press: Chapter 2, Liberty of Belief and Disbelief, which includes decisions relating to religious freedom; Chapter 3, Liberty of Speech and Silence, covering sedition, and the doctrine of "clear and present danger"; and Chapter 5, Liberty of Knowledge and Learning, which surveys the development of freedom of the press in England and America from the beginning of printing.

Pfeiffer, George E., and Edward L. Knoedler. *Police Court, First District [The People, etc., on the Complaint of Anthony Comstock vs. George E. Pfeiffer and Edward L. Knoedler].* New York, 1888. 17p. **P134**
Anthony Comstock raided the Knoedler art galleries in New York City on 17 November 1887, seizing 117 photographs of masterpieces of French art. He charged that the youth of the country was endangered by obscenity in the shape of "lewd French art—a foreign foe." The New York *Evening Telegram* reproduced some of the pictures in outline drawings. The court held that the pictures were not obscene.

Phelps, Edith M., *ed.* "British System of Radio Control." In *University Debaters' Annual, 1932–33.* New York, Wilson, 1933, pp. 97–133. **P135**
A debate between students of the University of North Carolina and George Washington University on the topic, Resolved: That the United States shall adopt the British system of radio control.

———. "British System of Radio Control and Operation." In *University Debaters' Annual, 1933–34.* New York, Wilson, 1934, pp. 12–52. **P136**
An international debate between students of Cambridge University and University of Iowa on the topic, Resolved: That the United States should adopt the essential features of [British] radio control and operation.

———. "Censorship." In *University Debaters' Annual, 1929–30.* New York, Wilson, 1930, pp. 287–326. **P137**
A debate between two student teams from Bates College on the topic, Resolved: That legal censorship be abolished.

———. . . . *Civil Liberty.* New York, Wilson, 1927. 194p. (The *Reference Shelf*, vol. 4, no. 9) **P138**
"This volume contains the essential material on the freedom of expression of opinion from the viewpoint of the arguments for and against restrictions upon it." It includes quotations relating to freedom of the press from the following: James Mill, Jeremy Bentham, John Milton, Robert Hall, and Zechariah Chafee. Quotations favoring censorship include those from James Kent and William Blackstone. Among the documents included are the Kentucky and Virginia Resolutions of 1798 and 1799, the Sedition Law of 1798, the California Criminal Syndicalist Act (1919), and the Tennessee Anti-Evolution Law (1925).

———. "Freedom of Speech." In *University Debaters' Annual, 1928–29.* New York, Wilson, 1929, pp. 231–79. **P139**
Resolved: That the principle of complete freedom of speech on political and economic questions is sound. The emphasis in this college debate topic is largely on oral speech rather than the printed word, but there is some material relating to post-World War I sedition. Western Reserve University and Oberlin College are the participants.

———. "Freedom of Speech in Time of National Emergency." In *University Debaters' Annual, 1941–42.* New York, Wilson, 1942, pp. 405–56. **P140**
Resolved: That the Federal Government should restrict freedom of speech and press during national emergencies. A symposium

participated in by students of Western Reserve University, College of Wooster, and Ohio Wesleyan University.

————. "Power of the Press." In *University Debaters' Annual, 1927–28.* New York, Wilson, 1928, pp. 189–238. **P141**
A debate between students of the University of Idaho and Marquette University on the topic, Resolved: That the power of the press has increased, is increasing and should be diminished.

————. "Regulation of the American Press." In *University Debaters' Annual, 1940–41.* New York, Wilson, 1941, pp. 281–344. **P142**
"Is the American press meeting its social responsibilities?" This is the topic of discussions in the form of a committee hearing between debaters from Colgate and Princeton Universities, held at Colgate University, 9 May 1941. A verbatim report of the hearing is presented here. The discussions take into consideration the charges of unfairness leveled against the press by the government (Ickes), labor leaders, editors who oppose the American Newspaper Publishers' Association, and public opinion polls. One of the proposals for reform is the creation of a Federal Press Commissioner. An 11-page bibliography covers the literature on freedom of the press that appeared during the years 1938–40.

————. "Suppression of Propaganda for the Overthrow of the United States Government." In *University Debaters' Annual, . . . 1919–20.* New York, Wilson, 1920, pp. 293–372. **P143**
Chapter 7 deals with the topic, Resolved: That Congress shall take all measures necessary to suppress propaganda having for its purpose the overthrow of the United States Government. Included are speeches delivered by the teams representing Yale University in debate with Harvard and Princeton. Chapter 8 deals with the topic, Resolved: That Congress should suppress all propaganda advocating the overthrow of the government of the United States by force and violence. It is a report of debate between University of Washington and Harvard.

Phelps, Edward B. "Neurotic Books and Newspapers as Factors in the Mortality of Suicide and Crime." *Bulletin,* American Academy of Medicine, 12:264–306, October 1911. **P144**

Phelps, William Lyon. "Are We Going to Have a Censorship of Printed Books?" *Scribner's,* 72:631, November 1922. (Excerpts in Beman, *Selected Articles on Censorship,* 391–92) **P145**

The blame for literary censorship lies with "those who destroy freedom by their selfish excesses."

Philathes, Tho., *pseud. New-England Pesecutors* [sic] *Mauld With Their Own Weapons Giving some Account of the bloody Laws Made at Boston against the Kings Subjects from their way of Worship. Together With a brief Account of the Imprisonment and Tryal of Thomas Maule of Salem, for Publishing a Book entituled, Truth held forth and Maintained. By Tho. Philathes.* [New York, W. Bradford, 1697]. 60 p. **P146**
In 1695 Thomas Maule, a Salem Quaker, was brought to trial for distribution of his religious tract, *Truth Held Forth & Maintained,* which he had arranged to have printed in New York. Because of the current reaction against the witchcraft prosecutions, Maule was acquitted. This was the first criminal trial in Massachusetts for a printed libel. This pamphlet, giving the account of the trial, was probably published for Maule.

Philbrick, Herbert A. "Should Communist Books Be Freely Available in Public Libraries?" *Massachusetts Library Association Bulletin,* 43:1–3, January 1953. **P147**
The FBI counterspy in the Communist Party and author of *I Led Three Lives,* defends the right of the American people to read Communist works and the right of libraries to stock controversial materials without labeling, in a speech presented during the attack on the Boston Public Library.

Phileleutherus Anglicanus, *pseud. A Summary of the Law of Libel: In Four Letters, Signed Phileleutherus Anglicanus, Addressed to, and printed in, The Public Advertiser, by H. S. Woodfall.* London, Printed for S. Bladon, 1771. 34 p. (Also in *A Collection of Scarce and Interesting Tracts,* vol. 4, pp. 197–221) **P148**
The four letters, possibly written by Woodfall, relate to the libel trials of Almon and Woodfall. Letter 1, An Englishman cannot be found guilty of any crime except by a jury. Letter 2, The usual order in criminal trials is to (1) establish that crime was committed, (2) establish the nature of the crime, and (3) establish who perpetrated it. Under Lord Mansfield the order was reversed. Letter 3, Criticism of the Court's judgment in the Woodfall case as legally unsound. Letter 4, The oppressive sentence in the Almon case was uncalled for.

Philip, A. J. "Blacking Out." *Library World,* 7:261–63, April 1905. **P149**
The public librarian at Gravesend, while defending the practice of "blacking out" betting news, not for moral reasons but to prevent the nuisance use of public library reading-rooms, treats as "an ingenious burlesque" the proposals before Watford Public Library to similarly obliterate references to divorce court and stock exchange news.

Phillips, Martha A. *The Legal Restrictions of the Press in Texas.* Austin, Tex., University of Texas, 1930. 119 p. (Unpublished Master's thesis) **P150**

Phillips, Wendell. *The Freedom Speech of Wendell Phillips. Faneuil Hall, December 8, 1837, with Descriptive Letters from Eye Witnesses.* Boston, Wendell Phillips Hall Association, 1870. 10 p. (Also in Bernard Smith, *The Democratic Spirit.* New York, Knopf, 1941, pp. 382–90, and in A. Craig Baird, *American Public Addresses.* New York, McGraw-Hill, 1956, pp. 138–44) **P151**
When the word of Elijah Lovejoy's murder was received in Boston late in 1837 a protest meeting was held in Faneuil Hall, chaired by the Rev. William E. Channing and attended by many distinguished citizens. Following resolutions in behalf of the martyrdom of Lovejoy, the Attorney General of Massachusetts, James T. Austin, spoke from the floor: Lovejoy "died as the fool dieth"; he deserved to be killed because he wrote and spoke against property rights. Young Wendell Phillips asked to be heard and from the platform made a memorable improptu speech in answer and in defense of free speech. This pamphlet reprints the speech, with statements of eye-witnesses, for the benefit of the Phillips Memorial Fund. Baird notes that the oration was taken in shorthand by B. F. Hallett and printed in the *Liberator.* An edited version appeared in Phillips', *Speeches, Lectures, and Letters.* Boston, J. Redpath, 1863.

[Philodemos], *pseud. An Enquiry whether the Act of Congress . . . Generally Called the Sedition Bill Is Unconstitutional or Not.* Richmond, Printed by S. Pleasants, 1798. 15 p. (Duane Pamphlets, vol. 53, no. 13) **P152**

Phocion, *pseud. Phocion in Reply to Cato, in Defence of the People of England, and in Vindication of the Public Press, with a few words in conclusion to the Earl of Liverpool. By a Barrister.* 2d ed. London, 1821. 17 p. (*The Pamphleteer,* 18(35):259–76) **P153**
Written in reply to two letters under the signature, "Cato", appearing in the *New Times,* 14 December 1820 and 12 January 1821. Cato had charged that the revolutionary press was the prime cause of the rebellious spirit of the day and that "it must be scathed by the lightnings of the law, it must be destroyed by the strong arm of power; if the existing laws be not sufficient, subsidiary laws must be created." Phocion denies both the charge and the remedy. The press did not cause, but only reflects the revolutionary spirit, as is its proper function.

Pichel, Irving. "Areas of Silence." *Hollywood Quarterly*, 3:51–55, Fall 1947. **P154**
"Drama deals with the strains to which human relationship are subject and the conflicts that result from them." Today we limit the use of a medium, the screen, in depicting "those sources of strain and conflict which have the greatest contemporary interest for us."

Pickerell, Albert G. "Secrecy and the Access to Administrative Records." *California Law Review*, 44:305–12, May 1956. **P155**

Pickering, Timothy. *To P. Johnston, of Prince Edward County, Virginia.* Trenton, Sept. 29, 1798. *A Letter Written in His Capacity of Secretary of State, in Regard to Insulting Addresses sent to the President of the United States Relating Principally to the Alien and Sedition Laws, and the Conduct of France toward the United States.* Trenton, 1798. Broadside. **P156**

Piel, Gerard. *Science, Censorship and the Public Interest; a Talk at Conference on Scientific Editorial Problems. American Association for the Advancement of Science.* [New York, Scientific American, 1956]. 11 p. (Reprinted in *Public Relations Journal*, July 1957) **P157**
"We have always opposed the tendency in our Executive Departments to make government a private affair. We know from experience how secrecy can shelter corruption and incompetence and promote incest and sterility in the making of policy. Now we have a new reason for opposing secrecy in the operation of government: it obstructs the progress of science." A summary of the testimony of the publisher of *Scientific American* before the Moss Committee of the U.S. House of Representatives.

Pierce, Bessie L. *Public Opinion and the Teaching of History in the United States.* New York, Knopf, 1926. 380 p. **P158**
Chapter 6, Attempts to Control Textbooks, deals with antebellum action by Southerners against textbooks that criticized the institution of slavery; efforts by Confederate and Union veterans' groups to secure favorable treatment for their repsective causes; and pressures brought by Catholic groups to revise and expurgate textbooks having passages they considered objectionable. Chapter 7, dealing with the period following World War I, reports on the attacks by the Hearst newspapers against allegedly pro-British history texts; reports on the agitation by Catholics and Irish, by patriotic and fraternal groups, and the two investigations of history textbooks conducted in New York City in the 1920's. The latter, conducted by David Hirshfield, Commissioner of Accounts, with the assistance of inexpert investigators, became an attack

on history books for their failure to instill patriotism. The chapter closes with comments on the attitudes of the press toward censorship efforts.

Pierce, William. *An Historical Introduction to the Marprelate Tracts; a Chapter in the Evolution of Religious and Civil Liberty in England.* London, Constable, 1908. 350 p. (Reprinted by Burt Franklin, New York, 1963) **P159**
The Marprelate tracts, issued 1588–89 from a secret press, stirred a major religious controversy in sixteenth-century England. These Puritan tracts, published under the assumed name of Martin Marprelate, attacked in witty and satirical language the episcopacy and defended the Presbyterian system of church government. The tracts were written and published in defiance of an edict of the Star Chamber, requiring prior licensing of religious publications. The press was moved from place to place, but eventually was discovered and destroyed by government agents. John Penry and John Udall, suspected of authorship, were brought to trial. Penry was executed and Udall died in prison of brutal treatment. Job Throckmorton, also suspected of being the author, denied this at the trial of Penry and escaped punishment. All three, Penry, Udall, and Throckmorton, wrote pamphlets declaring their innocence. Pierce exonerates Udall; believes that Penry and Throckmorton's complicity cannot be dismissed, but that the real author may be a "Great Unknown." The *Dictionary of National Biography* calls Penry the chief author of the tracts.

——. *John Penry, His Life, Times and Writings.* London, Hodder and Stoughton, 1923. 507 p. **P160**
Penry, a Welsh Puritan, spent 12 days in prison in 1587 for his work, *A Treatise on . . . the Aequity of an Humble Supplication,* which called the attention of Parliament to the ignorance and religious destitution of his fellow Welshmen. For his contribution to the writing and printing of the anticlerical Marprelate tracts, Penry was brought before the Court of High Commission, charged with intent to excite rebellion and insurrection. A major portion of this book deals with his association with the publishing of the tracts, his trial, and execution which took place 29 May 1593.

Pierson, Frank R. "The Censorship of Television." *New Republic*, 140:23–24, 23 March 1959; 140:21–23, 30 March 1959. **P161**
The confusion over censorship of television grows out of public indecision as to whether television is a news medium, an amusement, or an art. Television has yet to prove by some standard of freedom of its own that it deserves protection under the First Amendment. The author believes that Dr. Winick in his *Taste and the Censor in Television* fails to recognize the extent of control by the sponsor and the pressures from the government. In the second article the author attacks the television

industry code. "There is no freedom of expression under such a code no matter who administers it." The more subtle censorship is the discouragement of writers and producers. Nothing is gained by censorship "but a convenience of not having to make up one's own mind to switch off programs one doesn't like, the convenience of not having to discipline and watch over one's own children."

Pierson, Robert M. "'Objectionable' Literature: Some False Synonymies." *Library Journal*, 89:3920–23, 15 October 1964. **P162**
"Some of our troubles in the censorship area, our author argues, arise from failures in logic and communication." Among the false synonymies are: identifying *immoral* with *sexually immoral,* equating *high moral tone* with *poetic justice, immoral* with *dangerous,* and *dangerous to some* with *dangerous to all.* He also questions the assumption that books can do good but that they can do no evil. "They fail to realize that if we question the dangers of reading we must also question its benefits; one cannot rule out bad effects and admit good . . ., the 'books that changed men's minds' could have led to sin quite as much as to virtue."

Pierson, W. Theodore. "The Active Eyebrow—A Changing Style for Censorship." *Television Quarterly*, 1:14–21, February 1962. **P163**
Criticism of the FCC's efforts to change content of TV broadcasts. The writer argues for free competition as the best assurance of a balanced program. Substitution of government censorship for private censorship isn't the answer. He believes that TV, as it matures, will solve many of the problems of diversified programming without government intervention.

——. *Broadcast Responsibility and the FCC.* Columbia, Mo., Freedom of Information Center, School of Journalism, University of Missouri, 1962. 4 p. (Publication no. 75) **P164**
Criticism of the FCC efforts to use "every device at hand to effect changes in the content of broadcast communications," which will ultimately lead to "centralized dictation and control by government." The author discusses the problem of scarcity of facilities and selection of program. Free and open societies have resulted from the choice of free selectors.

——. "The Electronic Press: How Free?" *Quill*, 49(11):12, 14, November 1961. **P165**
The author is alarmed at the proposals, in the interest of improved programming, to turn over control of selection to a government agency. "A free and open society cannot exist if its mass communicators are centrally controlled."

[Pigott, Richard]. *Report of the Proceedings upon the Committal of Richard Pigott for Contempt of Court, by Certain Writings in the "Irishman" Newspaper Respecting the Trial of Robert Kelly . . . at Dublin Commission Court, November, 1871* . . . Dublin, Printed by Alexander Thom, 1874. 106 p.   **P166**
The editor of the *Irishman* was brought to trial, convicted, and given a four-month sentence, for an editorial that appeared during the trial of Robert Kelly, charged with the murder of a constable during the Fenian conspiracy. Pigott had accused the chief justice of "shameless bias," a witness of perjury, and had questioned "whether it is a moral crime at all to rid the earth of an informer."

Pilley, Charles. *Law for Journalists.* 2d ed. London, Isaac Pitman, 1932. 174 p.   **P167**
A practical handbook for newspapermen that includes sections on libel, contempt, and copyright.

Pillsbury, Parker. *"Cupid's Yokes" and the Holy Scriptures Contrasted in a Letter from Parker Pillsbury to Ezra H. Heywood.* Boston, Albert Kendrick, 1878. 14 p.   **P168**
Parker Pillsbury, a prominent freethinker, writes to Heywood who was in prison on an obscenity charge for sending his pamphlet, *Cupid's Yokes,* through the mails. Pillsbury examines the copy marked by the prosecuting attorney with the offending passages. He compares, passage by passage, what he considers the innocuous language of Heywood with comparable passages in the Bible, which he considers obscene.

The Pilot. Boston, 1835–date. Weekly. Official paper of the Boston diocese of the Roman Catholic Church.   **P169**
The paper made frequent attacks on modern literature during the 20's and 30's. In November 1929 it launched a "Catholic Literature Campaign" under the direction of the Rev. Francis Phelan. *The Pilot* indirectly stimulated Catholic support of the censorship action of the Boston police, including the ban of the book *Elmer Gantry* and the play *Strange Interlude.* An earlier editor of *The Pilot,* John Boyle O'Reilly, came to the defense of Walt Whitman in 1882–83, when Whitman's *Leaves of Grass* was under attack by the vice societies.

Pilpel, Harriet F. "But Can You Do That?" *Publishers' Weekly,* various issues since March 1955.   **P170**
Mrs. Pilpel, a member of the New York Bar, writes regularly for *Publishers' Weekly* under this heading, usually in the last issue of the month. Topics have included copyright, defamation and libel, censorship, and freedom of the press.

————. "'The Desperate Hours' and the Right of Privacy." *Publishers' Weekly,* 188(18):32–33, 1 November 1965. (But Can You Do That? series)   **P171**
Regarding *Hill v. Hayes and Time, Inc.* in which the New York Supreme Court ruled that an article in *Life* magazine violated the privacy of the Hill family. Also comments on *Walker v. Courier-Journal* in which a federal judge in Kentucky dismissed a libel complaint against former General Edwin A. Walker, ruling that the First Amendment was not limited to "public officials" but extended to other figures involved in matters of public concern.

————. "The *Esquire* Case: What It Did and Did Not Decide." *Twice a Year,* 14–15:486–94, Fall–Winter 1946–47.   **P172**
A member of the law firm that represented *Esquire* in the Post Office censorship case, points out that the court opinion in that case did not decide the basic question of constitutional law, whether "clothing a man [the Postmaster General] with a power by fiat to prevent distribution of the press is compatible with our democracy."

————. "Evolution of a Sensible Doctrine of Censorship." *Publishers' Weekly,* 180(13): 29–30, 25 September 1961. (But Can You Do That? series)   **P173**
The author cites hearings and legal decisions which show a trend toward a more rational approach to the problem of obscenity. Particular reference is made to the decision of the Supreme Court of New Jersey in a recent case involving indictments against a wholesaler of books, magazines, and newspapers.

————. "Firm Restrictions Placed on Pre-'Publication' Censorship." *Publishers' Weekly,* 180(13):30–31, 25 September 1961. (But Can You Do That? series)   **P174**
Comment on the case of *Zenith International Film Corp. v. City of Chicago,* involving the movie, *The Lovers.* The U.S. Court of Appeals reversed the ruling of a lower federal court which had supported the censorship action of the Chicago Film Review Board. The Appeals Court stated that the administrative procedures of the Film Review Board offered "the antithesis of a fair determination of the obscenity of the film in question." The case helps establish procedural protection, if censorship in advance of release is possible, as permitted by the U.S. Supreme Court in the case *Times Film Corp. v. City of Chicago.*

————. "The Libel Pendulum Continues to Swing." *Publishers' Weekly,* 189(13): 40–42, 28 March 1966. (But Can You Do That? series)   **P175**
Discussion of four recent freedom of the press cases: *Linn v. United Plant Guard Workers of America* (libel relating to labor dispute), *Henry v. Barrymore Theatre Corp.* (right of privacy involving portrayal in a play), *Bookcase, Inc. v. Broderick* (obscenity and the rights of children), and *Estate of Ernest Hemingway v. Random House, Inc.* (request for injunction against A. E. Hotchner's book, *Papa Hemingway*).

————. "Relief for Booksellers from Censorship Pressures." *Publishers' Weekly,* 183:36–37, 25 February 1963. (But Can You Do That? series)   **P176**
Discussion of various legal devices by which a bookseller can be relieved from threats of prosecution: the *in rem* laws, requiring that a book be judged obscene before a criminal prosecution can be pressed; and the use of a declaratory judgment procedure to determine in advance of sale whether or not a book is actionable.

————, and Nancy F. Wechsler. "The Law and *Lady Chatterley.*" In *New World Writing, 16.* Philadelphia, Lippincott, 1960, pp. 231–40.   **P177**
A review of the state of obscenity law in the United States in light of the 1959 decision of Judge Frederick van Pelt Bryan of the U.S. District Court for the Southern District of New York, freeing D. H. Lawrence's *Lady Chatterley's Lover.*

————, and Theodora S. Zavin. *Rights and Writers; a Handbook of Literary and Entertainment Law.* New York, Dutton, 1960. 384 p.   **P178**
Based on Mrs. Pilpel's column, But Can You Do That? appearing in *Publishers' Weekly,* March 1955—August 1959.

Pinchot, Ann. "How One Community Cleaned House." *Christian Herald,* 83: 13–14, 72–74, July 1960.   **P179**
An account of a crusade against obscene literature in West Springfield, Mass. The crusade was started in 1958 by a minister of the First Congregational Church to drive obscene books and magazines from the newsstands and to encourage good reading.

"Pinero v. Goodlake." *Solicitors' Journal,* 11:325–26, 9 February 1867.   **P180**
The case "marks the progress which has been made by newspapers during the last forty years in acquiring a resonable privilege for the publication of matter of general importance."

Piñón Tiana, Antonio. *The Freedom of the Press; A Critical Evaluation of the Totalitarian and Liberal Theories.* Manila, University of Santo Tomas Press, 1960. 572 p. (Also in *Unitas,* vol. 27–28, 1954–55)   **P181**
Following an extensive review of the concepts of freedom of the press, the writer argues

that the liberal theory confuses thought, which is spiritual, and expression, which is the outward manifestation. The press can only be free when it speaks the truth. Because it is a social expression, the press "must enter within the framework and jurisdiction of the public authority," which looks after the public good. The freedom of the press excludes, among other things, sedition, lies, and propaganda that "cause tension and sow distrust among nations," scandalmongering, libel, prejudices, and suspicions, "telling the truth in inauspicious circumstances" and "spreading harmful errors even though held sincerely and in good faith."

Pinsky, Abraham. "Freedom of Speech under Our Constitution." *West Virginia Law Quarterly*, 31:273–92, June 1925.
P182

An historical study of freedom of speech and of the press during times of crisis in war and peace. The writer favors a conservative approach. Freedom of speech and the press, as with "every other right enjoyed in human society, is subject to restraints which separate right from wrong."

Pitman, Robert. *A Question of Obscenity*. London, Scorpion Press, 1960. 21 p. (Bound with *A Question of Obscenity* by Kenneth Allsop)
P183

"The purpose of this essay is to argue against any repeal of the Jenkins Act [Obscene Publications Act, 1959]; to argue for more self-restraint by publishers; to demand a tougher moral attitude from the weightier critics and the literary weeklies. Under those conditions it may be that we shall find the road back from Sleazy Street at last." Pitman criticizes the "Lilac Establishment," a term he uses for the present-day intelligentsia who support obscenity in literature.

Pitt, William P. *The Law of Libel of West Virginia*. New York, Columbia University, 1930. 60 p. (Unpublished Master's thesis)
P184

Pius XI, *Pope. On Motion Pictures. Encyclical Letter of His Holiness, Pope Pius XI ("Vigilanti Cura")*. Washington, D.C., National Catholic Welfare Conference, 1936. 18 p.
P185
The Legion of Decency is praised for its "holy crusade against the abuses of motion pictures."

Pius XII, *Pope. Miranda Prorsus On Motion Pictures, Radio & Television. Encyclical Letter of His Holiness Pope Pius XII, September 8, 1957*. Washington, D.C., National Catholic Welfare Conference, [1957]. 40 p.
P186

A letter "concerning the grave dangers which can beset Christian faith and morals if the powerful inventions of motion pictures, radio and television are perverted by men to evil uses."

[Place, Francis]. *A Letter to a Minister of State, Respecting Taxes on Knowledge. 2d ed.—with a Postscript! and Appendices. Not for Sale*. London, J. Innes, printer, [1831]. 13 p.
P187

An outspoken attack on the newspaper stamp tax, used as a basis for presentations in Parliament.

[————]. *On the Law of Libel, with strictures on the self-styled Constitutional Association*. London, John Hunt, 1823. 76 p.
P188
Place attacks the concept of seditious libel held by the Constitutional Association, namely, that anything that made an official of the government look ridiculous was subject to criminal prosecution. The Constitutional Association was formed in London in 1820 for "opposing the Progress of Disloyal and Seditious Principles," and for strict enforcement of the law of libel. The *New Times* of 5 January 1821, in supporting the Constitutional Association, argued that present-day libels were more serious than those of earlier generations because now they were being read by the lower classes who are barely able "to distinguish between a cabbage and a potato." Place charges the Association, which he said never met or issued a proceedings, with being a money-making venture. The pamphlet contains a passionate account of the persecution of an innocent bookvendor, David Ridgeway, for selling Richard Carlile's *New Year's Address* . . . to an agent provocateur of the Association. This volume is a collection of anonymously published articles.

[————]. *Repeal of the Stamp Duty on Newspapers*. Edited by J. A. Roebuck. London, Charles Ely [1835?]. 16 p. **P189**
One of Place's many articles attacking the newspaper tax, this appears as part of Roebuck's series of unnumbered pamphlets, issued without payment of the tax. Place wrote articles against the "taxes on knowledge" for any paper that would take them.

[————]. *St. Paul and William Campion: a parallel between the cases of St. Paul the Apostle and William Campion*. London, Richard Carlile, 1824. 16 p. **P190**
Campion was one of Richard Carlile's volunteer shopmen arrested for selling works of Thomas Paine. He defended himself in a lengthy and impassioned criticism of Christianity and a defense of morality. For thus "glorying in his crime" he was given a three-year sentence. Place compares Campion's martyrdom with that of the Apostle Paul. Each was brave and stood firm for his beliefs and each attacked the superstitions of the day. The difference was that Paul was violating Jewish law; Campion was violating no law, only the opinion of the judges. Wickwar attributes this pamphlet to Francis Place; a copy is to be found in the Place Collection in the British Museum.

————. *The Taxes on Knowledge*, by Francis Place. The *"Morning Advertiser"* and Mr. Wakley, by J. A. Roebuck. Victims of the Unstamped Press, by H. S. Chapman. Edited by J. A. Roebuck. London, John Longley, [1835?]. 16 p. **P191**
Place, whose tailor shop was a meeting place for fellow radicals, took an active role in most of the reform movements of the day including the crusade against the English newspaper tax. He served as treasurer of the Association for the Repeal of the Taxes on Knowledge. These pamphlets in opposition to the tax were probably part of the series of unnumbered news pamphlets issued by J. A. Roebuck as a device to avoid the payment of the objectionable tax.

The Place of Radio. Winnipeg, Winnipeg Free Press, 1951. 8 p. (Winnipeg Free Press Pamphlet no. 39) **P192**
Editorial considering the Canadian radio as a form of "the press" as that term is used in defining freedom of the press. A general discussion of freedom of radio broadcasting in Canada.

"The Plague of Pornography." *Christian Herald*, 88:6–11, August 1965. **P193**

Plain Facts in Five Letters to a Friend on the Present State of Politics; in Which Are Included Thoughts and Observations on the Liberty of Speech . . . London, J. S. Jordan, 1798. 105 p. **P194**

Plante, William L., Jr. "Open Meeting Law in Massachusetts." *Quill*, 47(3):10, 15, March 1959. **P195**
Prompted by the press, the Massachusetts legislature passed an open meeting bill in 1958.

[Platform Slanderers and Newspaper Libellers; Discussion Based on the issues of the *Law Journal* and the *Jurist* for 1858]. *Dublin Review*, 45:413–28, December 1858. **P196**
The author attacks the English law of libel as "irrational, inconsistent, and fraught with injustice and iniquity," particularly the concept of "the greater the truth the greater the libel." He would transfer the risk of libel by public speeches from the reporting press to the offending speaker, making public speaking legally equivalent to printing and publishing.

Platt, William. "The *Chronicle* and the Unthinking." *Adult*, 2:325–27, December 1898. **P197**
Criticizes sex-censorship and the suppression of Havelock Ellis' *Studies in the Psychology of Sex* in the case of George Bedborough.

————. "Free Speech." *Adult*, 2:172–75, July 1898. **P 198**
Sexual tyranny leading to the suppression of sex education, is greater than religious and political tyranny because there are more practitioners. The author condemns man's inhumanity to woman by the attempts to keep her sexually pure and sexually ignorant.

————. "In Defence of Free Discussion." *Adult*, 2:292–93, November 1898. **P 199**
Criticizes the prosecution of George Bedborough for selling Havelock Ellis' *Studies in the Psychology of Sex*.

————. "Worship of Ignorance." *Adult*, 2:197–200, August 1898. **P 200**
An attack on the suppression of sex education.

"Play Safe but Be Suggestive; Hollywood's Movie Code." *New Republic*, 115:907–9, 30 December 1946. **P 201**
The author charges the administrators of the Hollywood movie code with hypocrisy, with approving "suggestive sexiness" and brutality while showing a prurient display of moral righteousness over frank expression of sexuality.

Playfair, W. E. ["Watch and Ward"]. Boston *Herald*, 3 September 1944, 4 September 1944, and 5 September 1944. **P 202**
A series of three articles on the past, present, and future of the New England Watch and Ward Society. The final article presents a proposal of Louis J. Croteau, executive secretary of the Society, for the creation of a board of review to examine books and other publications and to share the responsibility for censorship.

"Plays that Catholics Censor." *Literary Digest*, 53:1603–4, 16 December 1916. **P 203**
Relates to the Catholic Theater Movement and its "white list" of plays that are "free from objectionable and vulgar features." Quotes criticism of the group's judgment by Heywood Broun.

Plomer, Henry R. "The Protestant Press in the Reign of Queen Mary." *Library*, 1(3 d ser.):54–72, January 1910. **P 204**
The author, by careful examination of evidence, suspects that the secret printer of news critical of Queen Mary and the Catholic religion was Hugh Singleton who may have joined Humphrey Powell in exile in Dublin, once life in London became risky.

————. "Secret Printing During the Civil War." *Library*, 5(n.s.):374–403, October 1904. **P 205**
Study of the clandestine operations of the press and the book trade during the British Civil War and the Commonwealth, 1640–50, particularly those employed by Lilburne and Overton.

————. "Some Dealings of the Long Parliament with the Press." *Library*, 10(n.s.):90–97, January 1909. **P 206**
Pertains to the action of the Committee on Printing in dealing with authors and printers who incurred the wrath of the Presbyterian majority. Includes action against George [Gregory?] Dexter, Richard Herne, Francis Couler, Thomas Bates, and William Botler.

Plucknett, Theodore F. T. "Libel and Slander." *Encyclopaedia of the Social Sciences*. New York, Macmillan, 1931. vol. 9, pp. 430–35. **P 207**

[Plumer, William]. *Freedom's Defence; or A Candid Examination of Mr. Calhoun's Report on the Freedom of the Press, Made to the Senate of the United States, Feb. 4, 1836: By Cincinnatus [pseud.]*. Worchester, Mass., Dorr, Howland, 1836. 24 p. **P 208**
Calhoun had recommended postal censorship of abolitionist literature.

Plumptre, James. *The English Drama Purified: Being a Specimen of Select Plays, all the Passages that Have Appeared to the Editor to Be Objectionable in Point of Morality Are Omitted or Altered. With Prefaces and Notes*. Cambridge, F. Hudson, 1812. 3 vols. **P 209**
Plumptre was a Fellow of Clare-Hall, Cambridge. The general preface to the work explains his purpose and method of bowdlerizing the plays in the collection (pp. i-xxvii).

[Pocklington, John]. "Proceedings against Dr. John Pocklington, for Innovations into the Church of England, 1641." In Howell, *State Trials*, vol. 5, pp. 747–65. (Schroeder reproduces portions of the offending pamphlet in his *Constitutional Free Speech Denied*, pp. 230–52) **P 210**
In addition to such offenses as turning the communion table altarwise and using an altar cloth in his services, this English minister was charged with publishing two pamphlets advocating "Popish" practices in the Church of England. He was deprived of his preferments and his books were ordered burned by the common hangman. For the offense of prior licensing of the two pamphlets, the Rev. William Bray was required to preach a recantation sermon.

Pocklington, Peter D. "The Aftermath of *Lady Chatterley*." *Library World*, 67:219–22, March 1965. **P 211**
A new look at the handling of sex books in British public libraries in light of present liberal attitudes and the Obscene Publications Act of 1959. "I am quite convinced that we do more harm by trying to keep books with a sexual content away from adolescents than by allowing them free rein to read what they like."

Podell, Albert N. "Censorship on the Campus: the Case of the *Chicago Review*." *San Francisco Review*, 1(2):71–87, Spring 1959. **P 212**
The story of the suppression of the *Chicago Review* by the University of Chicago, told by a former member of the staff of that literary quarterly.

Podhoretz, Norman, and Brian O'Doherty. "The Present and Future of Pornography." *Show*, 4(6):54–55+, June 1964. **P 213**
Podhoretz discusses pornography in the bookstalls, including *Candy*. O'Doherty discusses pornography openly displayed under the label "art."

"The Poem That Caused a Campus Controversy." *Realist*, 7:17–18, April 1959. **P 214**
Reports an incident at Queens College, New York.

"Poetic Licenses; a Forecast." *Littell's Living Age*, 183:509–11, 23 November 1889. (Reprinted from *Punch*) **P 215**
A humorous one-act play founded on supposed censorship of songs.

Poffenberger, A. T. "Motion Pictures and Crime." *Scientific Monthly*, 12:336–39, April 1921. (Reprinted in Rutland, *State Censorship of Motion Pictures*, pp. 58–63) **P 216**
Recommends censorship of films to eliminate portrayal of crime that might be harmful to the child.

Poindexter, Miles. "Your Right to Speak Freely." *Forum*, 60:670–76, December 1918. **P 217**
"If the free operation of public opinion is essential in time of peace it is more essential in time of war because of the vital character of the issues involved." The author is a U.S. Senator from the state of Washington.

"Police against the Publisher." *New Statesman and Nation*, 48:380, 2 October 1954. **P 218**
Lack of judgment in an anti-obscenity campaign which doesn't distinguish between literary works and trash makes laughing stock of the Home Secretary and of the law.

"Police as Literary Censor." *Literary Digest*, 44:533–34, 16 March 1912.   **P 219**
A satire on the use of the police to enforce moral standards in literature.

"Police Censorship in Toronto." *Secular Thought*, 37:147–50, May 1911.   **P 220**
Deals with case of Albert Britnell, convicted of selling *Three Weeks* and *The Yoke*.

"Policy for the Library Association of Australia." *Australian Library Journal*, 13:55–57, June 1964.   **P 221**
An editorial urging the Library Association of Austrialia to adopt an official statement on the freedom to read.

Polier, Shad. "The *Times* 'Libel' Case." *Nieman Reports*, 17?(1):29–32, March 1963.   **P 222**
A civil liberties lawyer discusses the significance of the issues in the Alabama libel suit against the *New York Times*, brought before the U.S. Supreme Court. "The suit . . . presents squarely for the first time for decision by the United States Supreme Court the question of what limitations upon the law of libel are imposed by the First Amendment." Polier criticizes the nation's press and broadcasting industry for relative silence upon the issues.

Politella, Dario. *Patterns of Press Freedom in a Selected Group of Colleges and Universities in Indiana, 1964.* Syracuse, N.Y., Syracuse University, 1965. 440p. (Ph.D. dissertation, University Microfilms no. 65-7977)   **P 223**

"Political Censorship Threats Studied by Publishers." *Publishers' Weekly*, 159: 2527–28, 23 June 1951.   **P 224**
Report on trend toward political censorship of books made by the Anti-Censorship Committee of the American Book Publishers Council.

Political Prisoners Defense and Relief Committee. *Sentenced to Twenty Years Prison.* New York, The Committee, [1919]. 32p.   **P 225**
Case of Jacob Abrams, Samuel Lipman, Hyman Lachowsky, and Mollie Stimer, who were sentenced to twenty years for distributing a circular, the essence of which was, "Will you allow the Russian revolution to be crushed? The Russian revolution calls to the workers of the world for help."

Pollack, Jack H. "Newsstand Filth: A National Disgrace!" *Better Homes and Gardens*, 35:10–11+, September 1957.   **P 226**
An attack on obscene magazines that are flooding the newsstands. The author calls on citizens to protest to dealers; to work through

clubs, church groups, professional organizations to make their protests felt; to bring the matter to the attention of local law enforcement officials; and to watch what teenage children are reading.

Pollard, Graham. "The Company of Stationers before 1557." *Library*, 18(4th ser.):1–38, June 1937.   **P 227**
The economic structure of the early London book trade and the corporate organization in which it was reflected. Relates to censorship only indirectly.

———. "The Role of the Censorship." *Labour Monthly*, 11:433–38, July 1929.   **P 228**
A brief historical summary of censorship of Church and State which in every generation is called forth by decaying society. "As an old man must eschew the pleasures of the flesh, so the ageing bourgeoisie can have no place for unremunerative art." While there is an increasing philistinism in Britain, the U.S.S.R. promotes art. "The only hope for the future of art is the united front of the intellectuals and the proletariat against the dead hand of the philistine capitalist censorship."

Pollard, James E., and E. M. Martin, *eds. Ohio Newspapers and the Law.* Columbus, Ohio, Ohio State University Press, [1956]. 210p. (Journalism series, no. 16)   **P 229**

Pollard, Robert S. W. *Abolish the Blasphemy Laws.* London, Society for the Abolition of the Blasphemy Laws, [1957]. 15p.   **P 230**

———. "A Prosecution for Obscenity." *Journal of Sex Education*, 3:50–52, October–November 1950.   **P 231**
Case tried in Blackpool, England, 24 July 1950, involved several books on sex education, including the works of Havelock Ellis.

Pollitt, Daniel H. "Campus Censorship: Statute Barring Speakers from State Educational Institutions." *North Carolina Law Review*, 42:179–99, December 1963.   **P 232**
"The last place in a democracy to expect restrictions on the thinking process is in a university or college. Yet the censorship of ideas in such institutions is not rare. A brief exploration of these restrictions will put the North Carolina law in sharper focus and proper perspective." The article considers control of teachers, control of the curriculum, control of textbooks, and control of outside speakers.

Pollock, Channing. "Swinging the Censor." *Authors' League Bulletin*, 4(12):3–9, March 1917. (Reprinted from *Photoplay*, May 1916)   **P 233**

"A censor is the politicians' way of correcting Nature, which gave us five senses and only one conscience. . . . A motion picture censor is one of eighteen or twenty persons paid to tell an hundred million what they can see and enjoy. . . . We are a decent-minded majority, and it is as normal for us to demand clean entertainment as to demand clean collars. While this is true, we do not need censors, and, when it ceases to be true, censors will be merely futile fools trying to sweep back the sea."

Pollock, Jack, and Mack Lundstrom. *A Survey of Freedom of Access to News in Nebraska.* Lincoln, Nebr., School of Journalism, University of Nebraska, n.d. 17p. (Studies in Nebraska Journalism, no. 2)   **P 234**
"Forty-one newspapers across the state [Nebraska], or 69 percent of the respondents, listed 143 cases of current abridgement of freedom of information in 33 categories. Of the 59 papers that returned the questionnaire, 18 reported that they have no trouble with either closed meetings or closed access to news sources. . . . The largest number of respondents named county welfare and unemployment agencies as suppressors of news."

Pollock, John. "The Censorship." *Fortnightly Review*, 91(n.s.):880–94, May 1912.   **P 235**
A survey of British censorship past and present, with criticism of contemporary censorship practices.

Pontifex, W. S. "Suppressio Veri." *Socialist Review* (London), 14:145–50, May–June 1917.   **P 236**
The English press concealed news about the crimes and horrors of Tsarist Russia while presenting a full account of the war crimes of the Germans. The Russian Revolution came as a "bolt from the blue" to the British people, who had not been told of the corrupt Russian court and of the attempts to make a separate peace with Germany.

Pool, Ithiel de Sola. "Free Discussion and Public Taste." *Public Opinion Quarterly*, 24:19–23, Spring 1960.   **P 237**
Testimony at public hearings held by the FCC on 11 December 1959. Recommends FCC-sponsored research which will determine what reforms are needed to see that broadcaster monopoly is used for the public good.

Poole, Frederic. "The Philadelphia Stage Censorship." *Authors' League Bulletin*, 15(4–5):11–13, July–August 1927.   **P 238**
"We believe we have created a relationship between censorial authority, local managers, visiting producers, and the city administration and the public, that has enabled us to secure

tangible results without friction and with the commendation of the public at large in the city of Philadelphia." Comments on the Philadelphia Board of Theatre Control.

Pope, James S. "The Cult of Secrecy." *Nieman Reports*, 5(4):8–10, October 1951. **P 239**

The chairman of the Committee on Freedom of the Press of the American Society of Newspaper Editors discusses the control of government information in a Kappa Tau Alpha lecture at the University of Illinois.

————. "Freedom Is Indivisable." *Nieman Reports*, 7(1):30–34, January 1953. **P 240**
The executive editor of the Louisville *Times* and the *Courier-Journal* delivers the first Lovejoy Lecture at Colby College, 6 November 1952.

————. *No Sustained Colloquy.* Columbia, Mo., Freedom of Information Center, School of Journalism, University of Missouri, 1962. 3 p. (Publication no. 73) **P 241**

The author calls for a sustained colloquy between government and the press in preserving the coexistence of truth and security in a democracy. He suggests a number of informal, voluntary codes to be observed by government and the press.

————. "The Suppression of News." *Atlantic Monthly*, 188:50–54, July 1951. Discussion, 188:16–17, September 1951. (Reprinted in *Atlantic Essays*, pp. 395–405) **P 242**

"The free press guaranteed by our Constitution is encountering a new—and growing—obstacle: A flat refusal by many public officials to divulge what is going on in their conduct of office." The author examines ways in which federal, state, and local government suppress information.

————. "U.S. Press Is Free to Print the News but Too Often Is Not Free to Gather It." *Quill*, 39(7):9, 21–22, July 1951. **P 243**
How officials dam up the news that it is the people's business to know.

————. "We Have Just Begun to Fight for Press Freedom." *Quill*, 47(11):39–41, November 1959. **P 244**
A review of the recent achievements in freedom of information and some of the problems yet to be solved.

Popkin, Henry. "The Famous and Infamous Wares of Monsieur Girodias."
New York Times Book Review, 65(16):4, 17 April 1960. **P 245**
The Olympia Press of Paris, which has thrived on publication of pornography and banned books, expects to be forced out of business in five or ten years by the weakening of British and American censorship.

Pore, Harry R., Jr. "A Trustee Looks at the Freedom to Read." *Pennsylvania Library Association Bulletin*, 18:6–9, May 1963. **P 246**
A newspaper editor and public library trustee considers ways in which the library can meet the threats of censorship. "The basic weapons are what they have always been—courage, determination, a love of truth, and a respect for the opinion of others."

"Pornography and the Censor." *New Statesman*, 34:219–20, 23 November 1929. **P 247**
Reviews of D. H. Lawrence's *Pornography and the Law* and Viscount Brentford's *Do We Need a Censor?* "We cannot remember ever having seen the two sides of an important publishing controversy set forth with so much vigor and such unimpeachable integrity. . . . In our view Lawrence wins hands down." The censor would have been wiser to suppress the essay than to attempt to answer it.

"Pornography and the Young." *Times* (London), *Educational Supplement*, 2560: 1634, 12 June 1964. **P 248**
Quotes from opposing views on the effect of pornography on the young as stated during parliamentary debate on the Obscene Publications Bill.

"Pornography . . . The New Black Plague." *National Parent-Teacher*, 54(1): 20–22, September 1959. **P 249**

Porritt, Edward. "The Government and the Newspaper Press in England." *Political Science Quarterly*, 12:666–83, December 1897. **P 250**
"The purpose of this article is to trace the change which, during the last century, has come over the connection of the government with the newspaper press, so far as concerns the use of the press by the government and the attitude of the government towards newspapers, newspaper proprietors and journalists." The author sees no danger of political indoctrination.

Port, M. L. "Standards for Judging Obscenity—Who? What? Where?" *Chicago Bar Record*, 46:405–11, June 1965. **P 251**
A statement of the relationship of the various courts in considering obscenity cases and procedures under which the cases are handled. The author describes 12 steps that must take place before a defendant is found guilty by a jury of selling obscene material.

Porter, Garrett. "Thomas Cooper, Apostle of Freedom." *Scribner's Commentator*, 9: 99–103, April 1941. **P 252**
Abstract of a radio dramatization of Thomas Cooper's opposition to the Sedition Act, his testing of it in the courts, his trial and imprisonment. The script quotes from his words in defense of free expression of opinion and the right of dissent.

Porter, Gary. "A Contrast in Press Freedom." *Journal of the Student Press*, 2(1): 12–13, Autumn 1963. **P 253**
Comment on the remarks of Vlademir V. Vashendchenko, Washington bureau-chief of Tass, in a talk at the University of Illinois.

Porter, James N. "Libel Law Reform." *Macmillan's Magazine*, 47:437–42, April 1883. **P 254**
Relates to reforms proposed by the Select Committee of the House of Commons and enacted as the Newspaper Libel and Registration Act of 1881. Further changes are needed.

Porter, Robert B. "Library Problem." *Ontario Library Review*, 32:310–11, November 1948. **P 255**
Dozens of American fiction titles, by reason of their "rawness," never see the inside of Canadian public libraries despite their literary merit. "They cannot, for obvious reason, be purchased, for they may disgust and revolt many excellent readers of discriminating taste, and they may run counter to the upbringing and training of others." If some of the border-line novels "have to go to maintain goodwill, to keep confident patrons, then it is a good thing and wholly justified. No library is doing its job if it should defy this principle, for the public library is above all a public institution, and must cater to its owners."

Portnoy, Julius. "Creators, Censors, Censorship." *Teachers College Record*, 66: 579–87, April 1965. **P 256**
A professor of philosophy examines the "creator" and the "censor" as personality types, each contributing to the complex of attitudes which defines a democratic civilization. Each poses his distinctive threats, but of the two, the censor, is far more dangerous. "Some censorship is necessary, but when it becomes excessive itself by making unwarranted inroads into our lives, then it turns from a moderating influence into an evil." He suggests a federal bureau of aesthetics to advise the courts on censorship of the arts.

"A Possible Paterson." *Outlook*, 104: 318–21, 14 June 1913. **P 257**
During the Paterson, N.J., strike an editor was accused of subverting organized government. The editor of the *Outlook* comments: "Freedom of speech and of the press does not mean freedom to lie and to slander; but if, under the guise of such freedom, any editor claims the right to libel a public official, he should be accused, not of hostility to government, but of libel, and be made to justify his libel or to suffer the consequences."

Post, Langdon W. "Placing the Responsibility." *Publishers' Weekly*, 117:718–19, 8 February 1930.　**P 258**
A New York legislator proposes a change in the obscenity law to shift responsibility from bookseller to book publisher.

Post, Louis F. "American Postal Censorship." *Government*, 2:27–34, October 1907.　**P 259**
Opposes postal censorship of works on sex education.

———. "Growing Power of the Postal Censorship." *Public*, 8:778, 7 October 1905.　**P 260**
Deals with the E. G. Lewis case involving refusal of second-class mailing privileges.

———. "Legal Limitations upon the Use of Language." *Public*, 11:147–49, 15 May 1908.　**P 261**
The editor answers a letter from Theodore A. Schroeder criticizing Post for saying that some speech may be prohibited.

———. "Our Advancing Postal Censorship." *Public*, 8:290–91, 12 August 1905.　**P 262**
Deals with the Post Office ban on the periodical, *Lucifer, the Light Bearer*.

———. "Our Despotic Postal Censorship." *Public*, 8:815–20, 10 March 1906.　**P 263**
Further comment on the Post Office ban on *Lucifer*. This article, together with the preceding article and various other comments of Editor Louis F. Post, have been reprinted by Schroeder in his *Free Press Anthology*, pp. 149–62. They have also been issued in a 35-page pamphlet by the Public Publishing Co., Chicago, 1905.

"Post Cards and Policemen." *Justice of the Peace*, 118:213–14, 3 April 1954.　**P 264**
The author cautions local officials against too hasty and too zealous application of the law of obscenity. "The practical harm to young people, from the exhibiting of the great mass of vulgar post cards, is almost negligible." He cites the difficulty in determining whether an item is obscene because of the lack of any scientific criteria. Obscenity is not subject to the same kind of inspection and analysis as milk or sausage.

"Postal Sanctions: A Study of the Summary Use of Administrative Power." *Indiana Law Journal*, 31:257–70, Winter 1956.　**P 265**
"The present use of these powers [postal sanctions] by the Post Office Department is without judicial precedent or legislative authority. Clearly it is the duty of the courts to declare such usurpation of authority illegal."

References are made in the study to impounding unmailable matter and interim stoppage of incoming mail.

Postgate, Raymond W. *That Devil Wilkes*. New York, Vanguard, 1929. 275 p. (Rev. ed. issued by Dennis Dobson, London, 1956. 249 p.)　**P 266**
A biography of the British political leader who became the symbol in eighteenth-century England of opposition to government tyranny and suppression of a free press. Wilkes was four times expelled from Parliament, spent four years in exile, and many months in prison for his political expressions. Despite his early reputation as a rake, Wilkes devoted most of his life to public service, challenging the abuse of the general warrant, defending the right to criticize the government and the king, asserting the right to publicize the proceedings of Parliament, and paving the way for a reform of the libel law.

"Postmaster General Cannot Refuse to Deliver Mail Pertaining to Future Issues of Obscene Magazines." *Harvard Law Review*, 68:1458–60, June 1955.　**P 267**
The fact that one issue of a magazine is declared obscene by the courts does not give postal authorities blanket permission to refuse future issues of the magazine.

"Postmaster General's Order to His Postmasters." *Appeal to Reason*, no. 653, 4 July 1908.　**P 268**
A discussion of the use of sex censorship to exclude Socialist papers from the mails.

Potocki, *Count* Geoffrey W. Vaile (of Montalk). *Whited Sepulchres. Being an Account of My Trial and Imprisonment for a Parody of Verlaine and Some Other Verses*. London, Right Review, 1936. 48 p.　**P 269**
British-born Count Potocki, grandson of a Polish nobleman, was sentenced to six months in prison in 1932 for showing his five "obscene" poems to someone in an attempt to get them published. In this statement which he prepared following his conviction, Potocki explains his experimental use of taboo sex words. He attacks the British obscenity law, the conduct of his defense attorney, and the judge, and accuses the prosecution of printing and privately circulating his poems.

Potter, Horatio. *Intellectual Liberty; or, Truth to be Maintained by Reason, Not by Physical Power*. Albany, N.Y., Packard & Van Benthuysen, 1837. 16 p.　**P 270**
An essay on freedom of expression, inspired by the killing of Elijah P. Lovejoy, abolitionist editor.

Pound, Ezra. "Honor and the United States Senate." *Poetry*, 36:150–52, June 1930.　**P 271**

Praise of Senator Cutting for his support in exempting the classics from seizure by the U.S. Customs.

Pound, Roscoe. "Equitable Relief Against Defamation and Injuries to Personality." *Harvard Law Review*, 29:640–82, 1915–16.　**P 272**

———. "Government in Time of War." *Vital Speeches*, 7:375–76, 1 April 1941. (Reprinted in Summers, *Wartime Censorship*, pp. 60–64)　**P 273**

"Pound of Waltzing Mice." *Time*, 48(24):24–25, 9 December 1946.　**P 274**
Action against Edmund Wilson's *Memoirs of Hecate County* in a New York court. "Finding a yardstick for proving a serious book indecent is as difficult as weighing a pound of waltzing mice."

Powell, Arthur C. *Law Specially Affecting Printers, Publishers and Newspaper Proprietors; 2 d Issue, Comprising Several Additional Subjects, Including the Law of Libel Amendment Act*. London, Stevens, 1889. 255 p.　**P 275**

Powell, B. "Smith the Censor." *Free Review*, 5:337–51, January 1896.　**P 276**
Describes the unofficial censorship of British newsstands.

Powell, L. F., Jr. "Right to a Fair Trial." *American Bar Journal*, 51:534–38, June 1965.　**P 277**
The most serious conflict between press and Bar is in the field of pretrial publications which have the potential of prejudicing defendant's right to a fair and impartial trial. The author describes and analyzes problems to be considered in working out a solution.

Powell, L. W. *Resolution on Freedom of the Press by Senator L. W. Powell, 23 June 1864*. Washington, D.C., Govt. Print. Off., 1864. 1 p. (Senate Document 131, 38th Cong., 1st sess.)　**P 278**
The resolution condemns the military order which interfered with freedom of the press at Cincinnati, Ohio, and requests that the order be revoked.

———. *Resolution on Suppression of Newspapers by Senator L. W. Powell, 26 May 1864*. 1 p. (Senate Document 120, 38th Cong., 1st sess.)　**P 279**
The resolution stated that the conduct of the executive authority of the Government in

suppressing the publications of the *World* and *Journal of Commerce*, of New York City, was unwarranted in itself, dangerous to the cause of the Union, in violation of the Constitution, and subversive of the principles of civil authority.

Powell, Robert. "Britain Explains the Censor's Role." *Living Age*, 360:76–78, March 1941. **P 280**

An analysis of the criticism of British wartime censorship by American correspondents.

"Power of the State to Enjoin Publication of a Newspaper as a Public Nuisance." *Minnesota Law Review*, 14:787–98, June 1930. **P 281**

Relates to the Minnesota case, *Olson v. Guildford*, in which the Supreme Court of that state held that a statute declaring a newspaper regularly engaged in the publishing of malicious, scandalous, and defamatory material to constitute a nuisance and enjoinable as such was not an abridgment of freedom of the press. The author considers the meaning and limits of constitutional guarantees in light of this decision and concurs with the decision. The U.S. Supreme Court later declared the act unconstitutional (*Near v. Minnesota*).

Powers, Florence. "Must Fiction + Sex = Censorship?" *California Libraries*, 20: 224–26, 258, October 1959. **P 282**

The Long Beach Public Library policy, in dealing with potentially troublemaking books, includes a book selection policy, a thorough study by the staff, and, on at least one occasion, a public discussion.

Powers, Francis J. *Religious Liberty and the Police Power of the State; a Study of the Jurisprudential Concepts Underlying the Problem of Religious Freedom and Its Relationship to the Police Power in the United States with Special Reference to Recent Decisions of the United States Supreme Court on the Subject.* Washington, D.C., Catholic University of America Press, 1948. 184 p. **P 283**

"The primary purpose of this study is to appraise, in the light of scholastic principles, the jurisprudential concepts underlying the problem of the relationship between religious freedom, as constitutionally guaranteed and protected, and the police power of the state." "On the whole," the author finds, "the courts' pronouncements have harmonized favorably with the tenets of scholastic jurisprudence." The author gives considerable attention to the implications of decisions with respect to Jehovah's Witnesses.

[Poynder, John]. *Observations upon Sunday Newspapers; tending to show the Impiety of such a Violation of the Sabbath, the Religious and Political Evils Consequent upon the Practice, and the Necessity which exists for its Suppression. By a Layman.* London, n.p., 1820. **P 284**

Poynder was a lay theological writer who participated in various religious and social crusades in England and was author of a number of doctrinal works.

Pratt, Fletcher. "How the Censors Rigged the News." *Harper's Magazine*, 192: 97–105, February 1946. **P 285**

Critical of wartime censorship, this foreign correspondent places on the censors and press relations officers considerable blame for the inefficient reporting of the war. He sees a danger in continued government censorship. "The official censors have pretty well succeeded in putting over the legend that the war was won without a single mistake, by a command consisting exclusively of geniuses, who now have asked to be rewarded by being placed in the control of all scientific thought and utterance."

Pratt, Ralph E. "Obscenity: Obscene Publications, Pictures, and Articles: Prohibition of Importation." *Kansas Law Review*, 7:216–19, December 1958. **P 286**

Notes on the reversal of the decision under the Tariff Act of 1930 prohibiting the import of a collection of photographs intended for Dr. Kinsey's Institute for Sex Research, *U.S. v. 31 Photographs.*

Prentice, Archibald. *Historical Sketches and Personal Recollections of Manchester. Intended to Illustrate the Progress of Public Opinion from 1792 to 1832.* 2 d ed. London, C. Gilpin, 1851. 432 p. **P 287**

The publisher of the *Manchester Times* includes in his memoirs a discussion of many of the cases of prosecution of publishers during the hysteria that swept England during the French Revolution and under the Sidmouth and Castlereagh governments: William Cobbett, John and Leigh Hunt, John Edward Taylor, and Prentice's own trial for libel in 1831 in which he turned to Jeremy Bentham for advice. He also reports on a Manchester "society to put down levellers" formed in 1792 to systematically "bring to justice the authors, publishers, and distributors of all seditious and treasonable writings . . . The official name of the society was the Association for Preserving Constitutional Order, Liberty, and Property, against the Various Efforts of Levellers and Republicans."

"Press and Crime." *Bulletin*, American Academy of Medicine, 12:253–316, October 1911. **P 288**

Contains the report of a committee, appointed to consider the publishing of details of suicides in the public press and other related papers.

"The Press and Its Readers." *Christian Century*, 51:1616–17, 19 December 1934. **P 289**

Commenting on the newspapers' fear of the powers of the Federal Communications Commission, the editor believes it is the freedom of the reader that is threatened by the economic and political powers of the press.

"The Press and the Bar." *Law Times*, 5:85–86, 3 May 1845. **P 290**

Accusation against the *Times* for maliciously removing the name and remarks of Serjeant Talfourd from reports of law cases in which he appears.

"The Press and the Law of Libel." *Solicitors' Journal*, 2:657–58, 12 June 1858. **P 291**

The right of a newspaper to publish fair reports of court proceedings.

"The Press and the Law of Libel." *Irish Law Times*, 20:425–26, 4 September 1886. **P 292**

Editorial comment on the case, *Armstrong et al. v. Armit, et al.*, involving newspaper libel. The newspaper as a "watchdog of civilization" does not believe in keeping silent just because there is nothing to bark at; the law sometimes needs to let fly its bootjack to silence unnecessary howling.

The Press and the People; a Series of Television Programs produced by WGBH-TV, Boston, Mass., with a Grant from the Fund for the Republic. New York, The Fund, n.d., nos. 1–15. **P 293**

These programs, for which edited scripts are available, are moderated by Louis M. Lyons, Curator of Nieman Fellowships, Harvard University. The programs "are designed to bring television audiences informed discussion of the problems and performance of the American press in reporting the leading questions of the day." Many of the programs deal, at least indirectly, with freedom of the press. No. 1, The News from China; No. 4, Secrecy in Government; and Nos. 8 and 9, The Responsibilities of Television.

"The Press and the People—A Survey." *Fortune*, 20(2):64–65, 70–78, August 1939. **P 294**

A public opinion poll reveals that the majority consider radio news mor free of prejudice than newspapers; newspaper reporting fair and unprejudiced, except in matters of politics; and news unfavorable to the publishers' interest likely to be suppressed. The majority believe the American press is free "except as it inhibits itself or kowtows to men with financial or political influence." The majority also believe that the press should be limited only by public opinion and the editor's good taste, not by government controls.

The Press and the Public Service. By a Distinguished Writer. London, G. Routledge, 1857. 272 p. **P 295**

The book was written anonymously in defiance of current government distrust of anonymity (the Secretary of State had required persons in his department suspected of anonymous writing to prove they had not written a piece or be discharged). The author asks "whether publishers and editors can be indirectly forced to betray their clients and be thus virtually compelled to destroy the right of anonymous writing on which the liberty of the Press is chiefly founded?" Chapters deal with Liberty of the Press, Anonymous Writing, The Law of Honor, and Official Secrets and Persecutions, Recriminations, and Dismissal.

"The Press Censorship." *Economist* (London), 79:909–10, 21 November 1914. (Reprinted in *Living Age*, 9 January 1915)
P 296

"In time of war foreign newspapers can manufacture quite freely whatever opinion they wish to attribute to politicians or newspapers in this country." And this being so, the argument that controversy in the British Press may comfort and assist the enemy loses all value. If the British Press were muzzled, as is the German press, "the effect upon neutral opinion would be much more mischievous."

"Press Censorship! a Revival of Mediaeval Animosity to the Press, the Old Henderson Bill . . . the Liberty of Unlicensed Printing in Danger! Shall an Inquisition Be Established on American Soil?" *Advertiser's Guide*, May 1894, pp. 4–8. **P 297**
Contains interviews with congressmen and extracts from a report of a congressional committee on extending the power of the Postmaster General over the content of the mails, by extending the present censorship of publications on sex education.

"Press Censorship by Judicial Construction." *New Republic*, 26:123–25, 30 March 1921. **P 298**
The author criticizes the nation's press for its approval or indifference to the recent conviction of the *Milwaukee Leader*, for seditious libel "in a decision which immediately affects only a despised Socialist sheet, but which involves nothing less than the control of the press."

"The Press in War-Time." *Fortnightly Review*, 79(n.s.):528–36, March 1906. **P 299**
"Secrecy is the essence of successful warfare. Publicity is the essence of successful journalism. How is a common ground to be found?" A careful bill should be written in peacetime to lie dormant until needed.

"The Press: Its Fairness and Freedom." *Fortune*, 16(4):170, 173, October 1937. (*Fortune* Survey X) **P 300**
The survey asked: Do newspapers present news fairly? Do you think newspapers should be allowed to print anything they choose except libelous matter?

"Press Law." In *Encyclopaedia Britannica.* 11th ed., 1911. vol. 22, pp. 299–304. **P 301**
Comprehensive treatment of the laws concerning the restrictions of the press in various countries, with fullest accounts of current legislation in Great Britain and the British Dominions.

Press Restrain'd: A Poem Occasion'd by a Resolution of the House of Commons, to consider that Part of Her Majesty's Message to the House, which relates to the great License taken in Publishing false and scandalous Libels. London, John Morphew, 1712. 16p. **P 302**
A light-hearted lampooning of the radical pamphleteering of the day. The poet thinks we may now return to more delightful themes of love, but also volumes of greater size and weight.

"The Press under Post Office Censorship." *Current History*, 7:235–36, November 1917. **P 303**
Quotes clauses from the Trading with the Enemy Act and the Espionage Act which put press control during the war under the Postmaster General. This official has "the power to adjudge a publisher guilty in advance of trial by any judicial tribunal, and to destroy his business through a mere edict."

Pressley, Harold, Jr. "Expanding Civil Liberties in the Supreme Court." *Texas Law Review*, 22:230–35, February 1944. **P 304**
The U.S. Supreme Court has ruled in recent years that municipal ordinances that abridge freedom of speech and the press are unconstitutional.

Preston, William, Jr., *Aliens and Dissenters; Federal Suppression of Radicals, 1903–1933.* Cambridge, Mass., Harvard University Press, 1963. 352 p. **P 305**
Treats the "red-scare" of 1919–20, which resulted in the seizure of numerous radical pamphlets, as the outcome of passions, policies, and methods that had arisen some 30 years before World War I. The raids represented the traditional treatment accorded aliens and radicals and not the result of postwar fears.

"Previous Restraints upon Freedom of Speech." *Columbia Law Review*, 31: 1148–55, November 1931. **P 306**
The occasion for the comments is the U.S. Supreme Court decision in *Near v. Minnesota* in which the Court declared prior censorship unconstitutional. The author considers other acts of prior censorship that have been held constitutional, such as those connected with the mails, radio broadcasting, the Tariff Act, and local police regulations.

Price, Byron. "Censorship an Evil of War." *Vital Speeches*, 9:158–60, 15 December 1942. **P 307**
The director of the Office of Censorship in World War II discusses wartime news dissemination in a speech delivered at the *New York Times* Forum.

———. "Censorship and Free Speech." *Indiana Law Journal*, 18:17–22, October 1942. **P 308**
Price discusses the work of the Office of Censorship—to censor all communications entering or leaving the country and to withhold certain information of military value at home. The latter rests largely upon voluntary participation of the various agencies of dissemination, with the Government acting, by consent, as umpire.

———. "Censorship of the Press." In *Problems of Journalism; Proceedings of the American Society of Newspaper Editors, 1942.* Washington, D.C., ASNE, 1942, pp. 26–30. (Reprinted in Summers, *Wartime Censorship*, pp. 29–35) **P 309**
A description of the work of the U.S. Office of Censorship and some of the problems it faces and the techniques it uses. ASNE President Marvin commented in introducing Price: "Voluntary censorship is in safe hands."

———. "Freedom of Press, Radio, and Screen." *Annals of the American Academy of Political and Social Science*, 254:137–39, November 1947. **P 310**
Local censorship of the movies constitutes a threat to the American principle of freedom of the press.

———. "Governmental Censorship in War Time." *American Political Science Review*, 36:837–49, October 1942. **P 311**
Censorship in time of war is "justifiable only in so far as it aids prosecution of the war." The head of the United States censorship agency during World War II discusses his ideas on news control.

———. "Radio: a New Weapon." In Summers, *Wartime Censorship*, pp. 35–40. **P 312**
Discussion of the Code of Wartime Practices for American Broadcasters; an address delivered to the National Association of Broadcasters, 11 May 1942.

———. ["Remarks on the Occasion of the Award of ASNE Scroll to Price for Wartime Directorship of Office of Censorship"]. In *Problems of Journalism; Proceedings of the American Society of Newspaper*

Editors, 1946. Washington, D.C., ASNE, 1946, pp. 209–11. **P 313**

————. "What Can and What Cannot Be Printed in Wartime." *Congressional Digest*, 21:36–37, February 1942. **P 314**
A statement on the censorship code for newspapers and periodicals during the war. Price covers "specific information which newspapers and magazines are asked not to publish except when such information is made available officially by appropriate authority."

Price, Warren C. *The Literature of Journalism. An Annotated Bibliography.* Minneapolis, University of Minnesota Press, 1959. 489 p. **P 315**
A general descriptive bibliography of literature pertaining to journalism in the broadest sense, with special attention to historical and biographical books in the English language. Includes sections on Appraisals of the Press, Ethics of the Press, and Law of the Press.

————. "Reflections on the Trial of John Peter Zenger." *Journalism Quarterly*, 32:161–68, Spring 1955. **P 316**
"There is danger in making a too easy assumption that the 'symbol' of Zenger offers present-day protection against efforts to limit press freedom, and ignoring underlying causes and 1735 opposition to the trial verdict."

Priestley, J. B. "Real Clean-Up." In his *Thoughts in the Wilderness.* New York, Harper, 1957, pp. 60–65. **P 317**
Priestley recommends that the cleaners-up stop thinking about sex and take a look at the sadistic fiction. There is "so much sex in most people's heads that a writer would have to work very hard to put in any more." There is something wrong with persons who "prefer a sexual dream life, dubiously heightened by trashy novels, to the strenuous give-and-take of reality." Prosecuting a few writers will not help very much. Priestley calls upon publishers to refuse to publish "sadistic muck"; reviewers to condemn it; and booksellers to boycott it.

————. "Taking the Lid Off." *Twentieth Century*, 170:29–33, Spring 1962. **P 318**
"What I dislike is the idea that some people's private lives are sacred and other people's are there for show." The author believes that "either more lids should be removed" so that all private lives are open to the public, or that "all lids, outside criminal courts, should be respected and left untouched." He prefers the latter.

Priestley, Joseph. *An Appeal to the Serious and Candid Professors of Christianity on the Following subject . . . An Account of the Trial of Mr. Elwall for Heresy and Blasphemy at the Stafford Assizes.* London, J. Johnson, 1783. 72 p. **P 319**
Elwall espoused the Unitarian doctrine in his tract, *A True Testimony for God*, for which he was brought to trial. Priestley, a clergyman and chemist, was an early advocate of Unitarianism, first in England and later in the United States, where he emigrated to avoid persecution for his support of the French Revolution.

"The Prime Minister and the Press." *Nation* (London), 24:41–42, 12 October 1918. **P 320**
Editorial charging the government with presenting "a new set of perils to truth and freedom" by, for the first time, taking the press seriously in hand as an instrument of national psychology. Censorship, in the sense of suppression, is less serious than the positive propaganda efforts of the government.

Pringle, Henry F. "Comstock the Less." *American Mercury*, 10:56–63, January 1927. **P 321**
A member of the staff of the New York *World* writes about John S. Sumner, the tame successor to the fiery and colorful Comstock as head of the New York Society for the Suppression of Vice.

————, and Katherine Pringle. "Congress and the Plunging Neckline." *Saturday Evening Post*, 225:25+, 27 December 1952. **P 322**
Review of the congressional investigation of charges of immoral and offensive programs on radio and television.

Pringle, H. N. "The Protested Magazines." *Light*, 181:30–32, March–April 1928. **P 323**
An estimated 100 of the 1,300 magazines published in U.S. are objectionable. He describes their publishing history and action taken against them. He offers to send lists of protested magazines and books to reform societies on request.

The Printers' Case with Their Proposals for Regulating the Press. London, 1712. Single sheet folio. **P 324**
The London printers petitioned Parliament for a registration of presses to exclude printers who had not served an apprenticeship. They objected to the provision in the regulations that required the author's name to appear on a publication, believing that modesty of the writer might prevent publication and in other cases prejudice against a writer might interfere with acceptance of his ideas.

"Prior Restraint—Administrative Censorship of Motion Pictures." *Iowa Law Review*, 47:162–68, Fall 1961. **P 325**
Comment on the decision in *Times Film Corp. v. City of Chicago,* 365 U.S. 43 (1961). In view of the decision "an administrative agency or an individual acting within the authority given him by a statute or ordinance can suppress in advance the exhibition of any motion picture."

"Prior Restraint on Motion Picture Exhibition." *Vanderbilt Law Review*, 14:1525–32, October 1961. **P 326**
Times Film Corp. v. City of Chicago, 365 U.S. 43 (1961).

Pritt, D. N. "Freedom of Discussion and the Law of Libel." *Political Quarterly*, 6:173–89, 1935. **P 327**
Criticism of the law of libel in England, an example of overdeveloped case-law which "constitutes by reason of its complexity, uncertainty, and breadth of application, a grave obstacle to freedom of discussion." The author summarizes existing law, its historical development, and possible remedies.

"Privileged Criticism." *Law Times*, 53:310–11, 24 August 1872. **P 328**
The libel case of *Henwood v. Harrison.*

"Privileges of the Press in Relation to the Law of Libel." *Law Quarterly Review*, 7:158–73, 1891. **P 329**

Proffatt, John. "Law of Newspaper Libel." *North American Review*, 131:109–27, August 1880. **P 330**
Freedom of the press is no longer a blessing but operates a "dangerous and unrestrained license in the vituperation of private character, in the publication of much that is vile and demoralizing, and in the misrepresentation of public men and measures." The writer reviews the laws and court decisions on newspaper libel in the realm of (1) comment concerning public men, (2) reckless criticism of literature and art, and (3) reports of judicial proceedings.

Prompter. London. Nos. 1–53, 13 November 1830—12 November 1831? Edited by Richard Carlile. **P 331**
One of the many periodicals edited by Carlile which includes articles in behalf of a free press and his own trials. Other Carlile papers are, *The Deist* (1819–20); *The Republican* (1819–20; 1822–26); *The Moralist* (1823); *The Newgate Monthly Magazine* (1824–25), edited by Carlile's shopmen when he was in prison; and *The Lion* (1828–29). Carlile also wrote regularly for *The Gauntlet* (1832), published by Eliza Sharples, and *The Cosmopolite* (1832–33), edited by Alexander Somerville.

"Propaganda and Censorship." *Psychiatry*, 3:628–32, November 1940. **P 332**
The functions of propaganda and censorship in world unrest, considered from the point of view of psychotherapy.

"Prosecution for Obscenity." *Journal of Sex Education*, 3:152–62, February–March 1951. **P 333**

Report of a meeting of the Sex Education Society, London, 15 January 1951, at which Dr. Norman Haire discussed obscenity censorship from 1620 to date.

"Prosecution Scores Two Hits as Witnesses Deny Imputations in Guy Jack Criminal Libel Trial." *New Orleans Item*, 292:2, 3 April 1919. **P 334**
Trial for publishing Captain Guy Jack's *Iconoclast*.

Prosser, William L. "Interstate Publication." *Michigan Law Review*, 51:959–1000, May 1953. **P 335**
Notes on separate torts constituted in each state by nationwide "publication" of slander, libel, etc., by newspapers, radio, and television, 1849–1953.

————. "Libel per Quod." *Virginia Law Journal*, 46:839–55, June 1960. **P 336**
A distinction in law is made between two types of libel—"per se" where libel is apparent on the face of the publication, and "per quod," whose defamatory imputation is not apparent on the face and arises out of facts known to the reader. Prosser concludes that where the defamatory meaning can be made out only by resort to extrinsic facts, the libel, as a libel, is incomplete. Laurence H. Eldredge takes issue with this interpretation in The Spurious Rule of Libel per Quod (*Harvard Law Review*, February 1966) arguing that the prevailing view of the courts is that all libel claims are actionable without proof of special damages. Prosser defends his views in a second article, More Libel per Quod (*Harvard Law Review*, June 1966).

"Prudes in Council." *Saturday Review* (London), 142:605–6, 20 November 1926. **P 337**
The article repeats charges made in the 15 November *Daily News* that public librarians are "illiterate busybodies," exercising discrimination against many authors, and quoting a Croydon library official as saying "we keep watch on readers of a certain type of book." In the following issue (27 November) Croydon's head librarian, W. C. Berwick Sayers, declared the charges fantastic and without foundation. The editors apologized.

"Prurient Motion-Picture Advertising in Times of Increased Sex Crimes." *Journal of Social Therapy*, 1:146–47, April 1955. **P 338**

Prynne, William. *Histrio-Mastix. The Players Scourge, Or, Actors Tragaedia, Divided into Two Parts. . . . That popular Stage-plays (The very Pompes of the Divell which we renounce in Baptisme, if we beleeve the Fathers) are sinfull, heathenish, lewde, ungodly Spectacles, and most pernicious Corruptions; condemned in all ages, as intolerable*

Mischiefes to Churches, to Republickes, to the manners, mindes and soules of men. And that the Profession of Play-poets, of Stage players; together with the penning, acting, and frequenting of Stage-plays, are unlawfull, infamous and misbeseeming Christians. . . . London, Printed by E. A. and W. I. for Michael Sparke, 1633. 1046 p. **P 339**
A lengthy Puritan attack on stage plays in England culminated in William Prynne's *Histrio-Mastix* which summarized and amplified all previous attacks, as is indicated in the full title. "For publication of this book the author was sentenced to pay a fine of £5,000, lose both ears, one at Westminster and the other at Cheapside, to be deprived of his university degrees, to be excluded from Lincoln's Inn, and to be imprisoned for life. The book was condemned to be burned before his face by the hangman."—C. R. Gillett in *Catalogue of the McAlpin Collection*.

[————]. *A New Discovery Of The Prelates Tyranny, In their late prosecutions of Mr. William Pryn, an eminent Lawyer; Dr. John Bastwick, a learned Physitian; and Mr. Henry Burton, a reverent Divine. Wherein the separate, and joynt proceedings against them in the High-Commission, and Star-Chamber. . . .* London, Printed for M. S., 1641. 224 p. (Reprinted in *Harleian Miscellany* and forms the basis for the account in Howell, *State Trials*) **P 340**
This unsigned pamphlet was written by Prynne while serving his second sentence in prison, this time for his attacks on the prelates of the church. Along with Henry Burton and John Bastwick, he was fined, pilloried, shorn of his ears (or what was left of them after an earlier mutilation), and given life imprisonment. This illicitly printed pamphlet describes the trial and the suffering of the three prisoners. Prynne and the others were released as heroes by the Long Parliament in 1640. Contains portraits of Laude, Prynne, Bastwick, and Burton.

[————]. "Proceedings in the Court of Star Chamber against him for publishing a book entitled *Histrio-Mastix*, and against Michael Sparke for printing, and William Buckner for licensing the same, 1634." In Howell, *State Trials*, vol. 3, pp. 562 ff; Borrow, *Celebrated Trials*, vol. 1, pp. 405–26; and Rushworth, *Historical Collections*, pt. 2, pp. 220–41. **P 341**
Prynne was an English Puritan whose book, *Histrio-Mastix*, a criticism of the immorality of the stage, became the first book in England to be burned by the common hangman. For his alleged aspersions on the queen in that book, Prynne was imprisoned, pilloried, and shorn of his ears. The persecution of Prynne was directed by Archbishop Laude. Throughout his life Prynne continued to write controversial religious and political pamphlets, incurring the wrath of both sides—the

prelates and the Levellers. Like many of the Puritan writers in England and America, Prynne fought for his own freedom of expression but was not always willing to grant the same to others. In one of his pamphlets he appealed to Parliament to suppress anything written against Calvinistic doctrines.

[————, et al.]. *A Briefe Relation Of Certain speciall, and most materiall passages, and speeches in the Starre-Chamber, Occasioned And delivered, June the 14th, 1637, at the Censure of those three worthy Gentlemen, Dr. Bastwicke, Mr. Burton, and Mr. Prynne. . . .* London, 1638. 30 p. (Reprinted in the *Harleian Miscellany*, vol. 4, pp. 12–26) **P 342**

The Public. Vols. 1–22; April 1898–6 December 1919. Weekly. Edited by Louis F. Post and published during most of its life in Chicago. **P 343**
A journal of liberal thought which conducted frequent crusades for freedom of the press, dealing with Post Office censorship, restrictions on birth control information, and, shortly before its demise, with wartime censorship.

"Public Confidence and the Censor." *World's Work*, 34:243–44, July 1917. **P 344**
Objection to Creel as not having "sufficient of the public's confidence to give him a good chance to succeed in so difficult a position [i.e. wartime censor]."

"Public Librarian as Censor." *Library Association Record*, 16:83–85, 14 Feburary 1914. **P 345**
Summary of a spirited discussion on whether and to what extent the public librarian should perform the duty of censor, presented at a meeting of the Liverpool and District Association of Assistant Librarians. Participants were H. Tempest (Liverpool Athenaeum), R. Cochran (Wavertree), E. C. Wickens (Liverpool Reference), and S. A. Firth (Birkenhead).

"Public Opinion in Wartime." *New Republic*, 12:204–7, 22 September 1917. **P 346**
Accuses the conservative press of acquiescing in the most doubtful stretch of the espionage law to secure suppression of Socialist and radical publications.

The Publications Laws of the State of Colorado. Boulder, Colo., University Extension Division, University of Colorado, 1932. 277 p. **P 347**

Publicity and Juvenile Courts. Columbia, Mo., Freedom of Information Center, School of Journalism, University of Missouri, 1965. 6p. (Publication no. 140)   **P 348**

"This paper briefly summarizes provisions of the juvenile codes and coverage policies of news media. The bulk of the paper is concerned with the identification issue—to name or not to name, to make known to or keep secret from the public who the youthful offenders are—and the arguments that are made for and against such full disclosure. Finally there is a summary of what scientifically controlled studies have found out about the effects of communications on young people."

"Publishers Protest Leipzig Congress." *Publishers' Weekly*, 133:211–13, 15 January 1938; reply, 1606–8, 16 April 1938.   **P 349**

American book publishers, refusing to attend a meeting of the International Publishers' Congress to be held in Leipzig, sent a letter to the Congress secretary protesting against German censorship. Karl Baur, leader of the German publishers' organization, answers the letter.

"Publishers Speak Out Against Censorship." *Publishers' Weekly*, 148:1830–32, 20 October 1945.   **P 350**

Text of A Statement About Censorship, signed by 26 publishers, appearing in the Boston papers, protesting the decision of the Massachusetts Supreme Court in the *Strange Fruit* case.

Publishers' Weekly. New York, R. R. Bowker, 1872–date. Weekly.   **P 351**

This news journal of the book industry regularly carries news and editorial comments on issues and events relating to freedom of the press and censorship. It is a major source for news of censorship action taken against particular books by pressure groups, police officers, and the courts. It is also a source of information on state and federal legislation relating to freedom of the press.

[Pulteney, William]. *The Honest Jury, or, Caleb Triumphant.* London, 1729. folio broadside.   **P 352**

A ballad written by Pulteney, under the pseudonym of Caleb D'Anvers, to celebrate the verdict of the jury freeing Richard Francklin, publisher of *The Craftsman*, of libel charges.

Pumphrey, Byron. "Censorship of Radio Programs and Freedom of Speech—Beginning with the Case of KFKB Broadcasting Association v. Federal Radio Commission." *Kentucky Law Journal*, 22:634–41, May 1934.   **P 353**

Purcell, Gillis. "Wartime Censorship in Canada." *International Journal*, 2:250–61, Summer 1947.   **P 354**

"The analysis outlines the principles on which censorship in Canada [World War II] was based, its organization, and its operation. It traces the underlying factors in censorship and their relation to the operation of a fighting democracy."

Purcell, William L. "A Knock on the Door; Censorship Strikes a Librarian at Home." *Library Journal*, 88:526+, 1 February 1963.   **P 355**

A librarian writes of the seizure, by postal inspection at the time of mail delivery to his home, of a book, *Housewife's Handbook on Selective Promiscuity*, by Mrs. Ray Anthony, published by Documentary Books, New York. Purcell defends the book and his right to read it.

Purified Proverbs and Censored Quotations. New York, Amour Press, 1930. 32p.   **P 356**

This "fig-leaf edition" turns a few innocuous quotations into highly suggestive sentences by the deletion of occasional words. The booklet is waggishly dedicated to the memory of Anthony Comstock and a note offers to send the unexpurgated edition in a plain envelope to ministers, doctors, teachers, etc., who are 21 or over.

Purvis, Hoyt. "The Dean's Blue Pencil." *Motive*, 25:35–38, November 1964.   **P 357**

Administrative censorship of college newspapers and magazines.

Putnam, George H. *Books and their Makers during the Middle Ages* . . . New York, Putnam's, 1896. 2 vols.   **P 358**

Privileges and Censorship in Italy, pp. 343–406; Privileges and Regulations in Germany, pp. 407–36; Control and Censorship in France, pp. 347–63; Literary Property in England, pp. 464–599. The last section relates to the development of controls under the Stationers' Company.

———. "A Censor for Books?" *Review of Reviews*, 75:404–5, April 1927.   **P 359**

In response to the request of the editors for an expression of his opinion on censorship, the author submits a report of his contentions maintained at a hearing in Albany before the committee in charge of the Censorship Bill in the previous year. Experience has shown that no person has qualifications that make him worthy to act as censor, that is, no one is absolutely free from prejudice.

———. "Censorship." *Bookman*, 52:234–40, November 1920.   **P 360**

Putnam recognizes the contribution of the vice society in controlling obscenity, but believes it should not have final decision on books since it was not established by popular vote. Political literature presents the more

serious difficulty. Government "is entitled to make a presentment against literature the circulation of which the officials believe to be antagonistic to the maintenance of law and order, but that such presentment ought itself be passed upon by a commission representing the authority of one of the existing courts, or of a special court constituted for the purpose."

———. *The Censorship of the Church of Rome and Its Influence upon the Production and Distribution of Literature* . . . New York, Putnam's, 1907. 2 vols.   **P 361**

"A study of the history of the prohibitory and expurgatory indexes, together with some consideration of the effects of Protestant censorship and of censorship by the State." Putnam deals with early indexes issued by Henry VIII, before the time of the first papal *Index*, the "Index" of Thomas James, librarian of the Bodleian Library, 1627, and the translations of the Bible. He deals briefly with later suppression of religious works in England by the government and Protestant clergy.

———. "The Growth of the Censorship Idea." *Independent*, 110:334–35, 26 May 1923. (Reprinted in Beman, *Censorship of Speech and the Press*, pp. 22–28)   **P 362**

A brief review of the history of censorship from 400 B.C. to the 1920's. More mischief has been brought about through unwise censorship than through allowing books that might be pernicious. A commission representing the authority of a court should condemn a book before the Postmaster General has a right to exclude it from the mails.

———. "Literary Censorship." In *A Cyclopedia of Education*, edited by Paul Monroe. New York, Macmillan, 1914. vol. 4, pp. 32–41.   **P 363**

A history of censorship going back to the early Christian Church and the Roman Empire and coming down to the present time (1914) in England, Germany, and the United States.

Putnam, George P., ed. *Nonsensorship* . . . *Sundry Observations Concerning Inhibitions and Illegalities.* New York, Putnam's, 1922. 181p.   **P 364**

A group of "not-too-serious thinkers" set down their pet aversions to various forms of censorship and prohibition. Contributors include Heywood Broun, Ben Hecht, Frederick O'Brien, and Dorothy Parker. J. Frank Chase of the Watch and Ward Society wrote an unfavorable review of the book in *The Light*, January–February 1923, pp. 44–48.

———. *Wide Margins: a Publisher's Autobiography.* New York, Harcourt, Brace, 1942. 351p.   **P 365**

Contains numerous anecdotes relating to censorship in the book publishing world—*Married Love*, *Jurgen*, and the incident of Comstock's action against the painting, *September Morn*, which Putnam states was created by a press agent, Harry Reichenback.

Putnam, Samuel P. *400 Years of Freethought*. New York, Truth Seeker, 1894. 874 p.

P 366

This encyclopedia of the free-thought movement contains biographical material on many persons who participated in the crusade against blasphemous, or obscene libel. Includes sketches and portraits of Annie Besant, Charles Bradlaugh, E. B. Foote, Jr., and Sr., G. W. Foote, Ezra H. Heywood, G. J. Holyoake, Abner Kneeland, T. B. Wakeman, E. C. Walker, and Elizur Wright.

Putney, Bryant. *Censorship of Press and Radio*. Washington, D.C., Editorial Research Reports, 1939. (*Editorial Research Reports* 2(12):228–88, 1939)

P 367

A review of U.S. censorship during World War I and subsequent policies of voluntary censorship by the newspaper and radio industries. Survey of censorship in Europe after the outbreak of World War II.

Pyburn, George. *The Conspiracy against Free Speech and Free Press*. New York, Edwin C. Walker, 1902. 32 p.

P 368

This tiny (12 cm) pamphlet by an M. D. criticizes the lack of free speech and press in the hysteria following the assassination of President McKinley: the press criticism of remarks by Senator Wellington (Md.); efforts to remove the free speech clause from the Virginia bill of rights; seizure of anarchist publications; and the "tyranny" of the Post Office Department in refusing to carry publications containing alien doctrine.

Pyle, Fitzroy. "The Prohibited Issue of *A Mirror for Magistrates*." *Hermathena; a Series of Papers on Literature, Science, and Philosophy* (Dublin), 51:1–28, May 1938.

P 369

A chapter on the history of Marian printing. This collection of versified moralization of English history, probably published before June 1554 without authorization, was disapproved because it gave too much scope for tactless Protestant commentary and employed a technique that, it was feared, might be applied to the ruling dynasty.

Q

"Qualified Privilege to Report Legislative and Judicial Proceedings as a Guarantee of Freedom of the Press." *Virginia Law Review*, 36:767–80, October 1950. **Q1**
Historical notes, 1789–1950.

Qualter, T. H. "Politics and Broadcasting: Case Studies of Political Interference in National Broadcasting Systems." *Canadian Journal of Economics and Political Science*, 28:225–34, May 1962. **Q2**
Examples are from Great Britain and New Zealand.

Quarrington, W. "Detroit, Michigan, Minister's Stand. The Secular Press of Detroit Refused to Print This Discourse." *Menace*, 376:1, 13 July 1918. **Q3**
Sermon criticizing a Detroit ordinance prohibiting the sale of publications defamatory to religion. According to the author, the ordinance was designed to protect Catholicism.

Quennell, Peter. "Introduction" to *John Cleland's Memoirs of a Woman of Pleasure*. New York, Putnam's, 1963, pp. v–xiv. **Q4**
Since first published in the middle of the eighteenth century, John Cleland's erotic work, better known as *Fanny Hill*, has been both widely read and frequently suppressed. This introduction discusses the history and literary qualities of the publication. A note on the American History of the work (pp. xv–xxviii) includes reference to the case of Peter Holmes, *Commonwealth v. Holmes*, 17 Mass. 336 (1821), indicted for sale of *Memoirs of a Woman of Pleasure*. This is generally believed to be the first recorded American case of suppression of a literary work on grounds of obscenity. The note closes with a report of the freeing of the Putnam edition by the New York Supreme Court, with Justice Arthur Klein's opinion printed in full. A bibliographical record of *Fanny Hill*, taken largely from Pisanus Fraxi's *Catena Librorum Tacendorum*, is printed as an appendix.

"The Question of Literary Censorship; Symposium." *Independent*, 110:191–93, 17 March 1923. Discussion, 110:258, 14 April 1923. **Q5**
A group of articles attacking literary censorship, particularly critical of the efforts of Justice Ford and the Clean Books League. Theodore Dreiser, in Why Attack Books, accuses women of being "responsible for this censorship talk" and for not raising the intellectual level of the nation. H. W. Boynton, in Native Versus Alien Standards, states that public taste and tolerance shape literature along racial and natural lines and that nothing is to be gained by official censorship but publicity for the banned book. Horace B. Liveright, in The Absurdity of Censorship, states that only the highest type of intellectual is capable of judicious censorship and such a person will not accept the assignment. Various points of view are given in letters to the editor on page 258. The Liveright article is reprinted in Beman, *Censorship of Speech and the Press*, pp. 470–73.

Quiat, Marshall. "The Freedom of Pressure and the Explosive Canon 35." *Rocky Mountain Law Review*, 33:11–22, December 1960. **Q6**
Suggests a code of rules and regulations for editorial and news comment to be agreed upon by editors and publishers along the lines of that of the Denver area broadcasters. "If responsibility is assumed by editors of mass media, the problem loses importance."

Quigley, Martin. *Decency in Motion Pictures*. New York, Macmillan, 1937. 100 p. **Q7**
Quigley, a Catholic layman and publisher of a motion picture trade journal, was the originator of the motion picture production code (1930). In this volume he describes the basis for self-regulation of film content—to meet the public demand for morality without government censorship.

Quill. Chicago, Sigma Delta Chi, 1912– date. Monthly. **Q8**
This journal of the professional journalism society frequently publishes articles, editorials, and news items reflecting the Society's concern for freedom of the press. The Society also publishes an annual report of the Advancement of Freedom of Information Committee.

Quirk, James R. "The Wowsers Tackle the Movies." *American Mercury*, 11:349–56, July 1927. **Q9**
In a humorous vein the author describes the attempt to set up a Federal Motion Picture Commission, which failed. He cites ways in which different groups, states, and cities censor or attempt to censor motion pictures.

R

Rabi, Isidor I. *Science and Public Policy.*
Columbia, Mo., Freedom of Information
Center, School of Journalism, University
of Missouri, 1960. 3 p. (Publication no. 42)
R 1
A physicist argues that "to live at peace with
the atom we must find our way back to the
fundamental principles on which this republic
was founded. We must again become a nation
of free men informed by a free press."

Radcliffe, Cyril J., *Lord. Censors. The Rede
Lecture, 1961.* Cambridge, Eng., Cambridge
University Press, 1961. 32 p.   **R 2**
Philosophical observations on the nature of
censorship and censors; an examination of the
ideas of Milton's *Areopagitica* in light of the
more complex society of today and a new
pattern of authoritarianism. Lord Radcliffe
comments particularly on the implications of
the *Lady Chatterley's Lover* trial under the
1959 Jenkins Act. The trial "marked
dramatically a final turning away from the
older idea that words can be things dangerous
enough to merit punishment for the man who
has let them loose on society . . . and an
acceptance of the idea . . . that it is the evil
and intended purpose only that is the badge
of crime." Censorship of the future will be
not so much by law as by pressures for
standardization of average opinion. It is in the
power of inertia that there lies a modern and
effective censorship. John Sparrow, in his
Independent Essays, reviews Lord Radcliffe's
lecture, commenting favorably on the point
of view of censorship as "the old aedile
business of keeping the roads clean and the
air sweet."

———. *Freedom of Information: A Human
Right* . . . Glasgow, Jackson, Son &
Company, Publishers to the University,
1953. 30 p.   **R 3**
Lord Radcliffe's lecture on the Montague
Burton Foundation in the University of
Glasgow, delivered 6 March 1953.

Raddatz, Leslie. "Have You Been
Shocked, Outraged or Scandalized by
Television?" *TV Guide,* 11(45):16–19,
9 November 1963.   **R 4**

A description of the work of the television
network censors: Continuity Acceptance
(A.B.C.), Program Practices (C.B.S.), and
Broadcast Standards (N.B.C.).

———. "Smut in the Living Room."
TV Guide, 13(15):3–7, 10 April 1965. **R 5**
A tightening of the broadcast industry's code
of self-regulation may be needed if and when
the present trend in movie "smut" gets to
television.

Radin, Max. "The Library's Role in a
Democracy Today." *Wilson Library Bulletin,* 16:17–20, September 1941.   **R 6**
In attempting to serve as an educator the
librarian must not assume the role of the
censor. There should be free access to all
types of doctrines in a library and the librarian
must withstand the growing pressures from
various groups to reject unorthodox literature.
The author believes that there are few really
dangerous books and even these should be
available.

"Radio Censorship and the Federal
Communications Commission." *Columbia
Law Review,* 39:447–59, March 1939. **R 7**
It must be recognized that "there does not
exist in this country any such thing as
'freedom of the air.'" The individual licensees
of stations exercise a power of censorship under
the guise of "editorial selection." "If radio
facilities were unlimited, such censorship
would be of little importance, for everyone
would have an opportunity to be heard."
But limited channels led to the enactment in
1927 of a regulating act on the basis of
"public interest, convenience, or necessity."
The article discusses the development of
such regulations with reference to various
court decisions.

"Radio Editorials and the Mayflower
Doctrine." *Columbia Law Review,* 48:
785–93, July 1948.   **R 8**
"In 1941, by way of dictum in a license renewal
report, Mayflower Broadcasting Corp., 8 F.C.C.
333, 340 (1941), the Federal Communications
Commission announced as a rule of policy that
the radio broadcaster and his station should
be allowed neither to editorialize nor to take

a stand on any controversial matter." The
article discusses the legal justification for the
doctrine and its value as a policy.

Radoff, Maurice L. "Censorship among
the Learned." *American Mercury,* 28:
206–10, February 1933.   **R 9**
A professor of Romance languages writes this
humorous article based on charges that works
of Freud are to be found in the library of the
University of North Carolina, available to
anyone who wants to read them. He discusses
efforts at censoring texts used by students in
studying foreign literature.

Rafferty, Max, and Thomas Braden.
"Should Schoolmen Serve as Censors?"
Nation's Schools, 73:62–64, September 1964.
R 10
"That's what they're paid for, argues Max
Rafferty [superintendent of public instruction
for the state of California] who points out that,
in education, screening is really a form of
censorship." "If schoolmen must censor,
Thomas Braden [president of the California
State Board of Education] contends, their
censorship should not stop pupils from learning
how to use free choice."

Rainolds, John. *The Overthrow Of Stage-
Playes, By the way of controversie betwixt
D. Gager and D. Rainolds, wherein all the
reasons that can be made for them are notably
refuted; the objections answered, and the
case so cleared and resolved, as that the judgement of any man, that is not Froward and
perverse, may easilie bee satisfied. Wherein
Is Manifestly Proved, that it is not onely
unlawfull to be an Actor, but a beholder of
those vanities* . . . Oxford, Eng., Printed by
John Lichfield for E. Forrest & W. Webbe,
1629. 190 p.   **R 11**
Rainolds (or Reynolds) was a prominent
Puritan clergyman, one time president of
Corpus Christi College, Oxford.

Rairigh, W. N. *Judicial Opinion Concerning
Censorship of Library Materials, 1926–1950.*
Philadelphia, School of Library Science,

Drexel Institute of Technology, 1950.
59 p. (Unpublished Master's thesis) **R 12**

Raleigh, *Sir* Walter A. *The War and the Press; a Paper Read March 14th, 1918 to the Essay Society, Eton College.* Oxford, Eng., Clarendon Press, 1918. 19 p. **R 13**
The author is a literary critic, essayist, and official historian of the Royal Air Force in World War I.

Ralph, James. *The Case of Authors by Profession or Trade, Stated. With Regard to Booksellers, the Stage, and the Public, No Matter by Whom . . .* London, R. Griffiths, 1758. 68 p. **R 14**
This commentary on the political press of the day contains an account of Nicholas Amhurst, the author of an article in *The Craftsman* critical of George II. Amhurst was arrested along with the publisher, Henry Haines.

Ramsey, G. V., and M. Varley. "Censorship of the Kinsey Report." *Journal of Social Psychology*, 33:279–88, May 1951. **R 15**

Ramsey, W. J. *In Prison for Blasphemy . . .* London, R. Forder, [1883?]. 16 p. **R 16**
An account of the author's nine months in Holloway Gaol following a blasphemy conviction for publication of the *Freethinker*.

Rand School of Social Science, New York. *The Case of the Rand School. Manifesto by Civil Liberties Bureau. Seeking to Silence Truth. Letter of Samuel Untermeyer. Story of the Rand School by Algernon Lee. From Editorial Comments . . .* New York, Rand School of Social Science, 1919. 16 p. **R 17**
The Rand School of Social Science was a Socialist and labor college maintained by the American Socialist Society. In addition to its instruction, it maintained a large public library and readingroom, a bookstore, and conducted a large mail-order business in Socialist publications. The School, along with a number of its faculty, came under attack during the 1920's, the result of the Lusk and the Criminal Anarchy Acts. Proceedings against the School were dropped with the repeal of the Lusk laws. Zechariah Chafee, Jr., argued that a school for adults should be given the same legal protection as newspapers and books.

Randall, James G. "The Newspaper Problem in Its Bearing upon Military Secrecy during the Civil War." *American Historical Review*, 23:303–23, January 1918. **R 18**
"Acting under no effective governmental restraint, the newspapers of the North, though in many ways deserving of admiration, undoubtedly did the national cause serious injury by continually revealing military information, undermining confidence in the management of public affairs, and giving undue publicity to the virtues of ambitious generals and the sensational features of the war . . . Voluntary restraint or popular pressure had far greater effect in keeping improper material out of newspapers than official repression."

Randall, R. G. "Film Censorship." *Nation and Athenaeum* (London), 47: 9–11, 5 April 1930. **R 19**
Concerns political censorship of the Russian films, *Mother, Ten Days That Shook the World, The Fall of St. Petersburg*, and *The General Line*, by the London County Council. The author calls for an advisory body such as counsels the Lord Chamberlain on stage censorship, that would consider the film as a serious medium of expression.

———. "Youth and Censorship." *Nation and Athenaeum* (London), 45:701–3, 31 August 1929. **R 20**
Discusses the attitude of modern youth toward obscenity, using Julian Hall's two categories—the sceptics and the conspirators. The modern youth believes that the laws against blasphemy, obscenity, and treason "upholster a respect for superstition that he regards as quite out of date." He demands the right to express himself rationally about royalty, frauds, obscenity, holiness, and perfectibility.

Ransom, Charles F. "Intellectual Trust v. Suppression." *Library Journal*, 75: 262, 15 February 1950. **R 21**
A Des Moines editor comments on the controversial books a library should buy. "You always have to compromise somewhat between 'the best' and 'the most in demand'—between what the community needs, what it wants, and what it will stand for. But any attitude which goes all out to avoid controversy is a betrayal of intellectual trust, and self-defeating at that."

Ransom, Harry. *The First Copyright Statute: An Essay on an Act for the Encouragement of Learning, 1710.* Austin, Tex., University of Texas Press, 1956. 145 p. **R 22**
An account of the first copyright law enacted by the English Parliament and the major influences on literary property in England from the establishment of Caxton's press in 1476 to the year 1710.

[Rapier, John L.]. *Freedom of the Press; in the Supreme Court of the United States, ex parte in the Matter of John L. Rapier, upon a Petition for Writs of Habeas Corpus and Certiorari, against the Constitutionality of the Recent Act of Congress Generally Known as the Anti-lottery Law.* n.p., n.d. 48 p. **R 23**
Deals with postal prohibition of lottery information.

Raskin, A. H. "What's Wrong With American Newspapers?" *New York Times Magazine*, 11 June 1967, pp. 28–29, 77–84. **R 24**
"The real long-range menace to America's daily papers, in my judgment, lies in the unshatterable smugness of their publishers and editors, myself included."

———. "Who Needs Newspapers?" *Reporter*, 33(7):33–35, 21 October 1965. **R 25**
Criticism of the apathy on all sides toward ending the 1965 New York newspaper strike.

Ratcliff, Nora. "Censorship." In her *Rude Mechanicals. A Short View of Village Drama.* London, Nelson, 1938, pp. 119–30. **R 26**
"The censorship of the Lord Chamberlain's reader is kindness, benevolence, encouragement itself, compared with the rigorous though unofficial tyranny which is exerted locally, on the village group's choice of play. The censorship is usually a tripartite one of Church, gentry, and public opinion."

[Ratcliffe, Ebenezer]. *Two Letters Addressed to the Right Rev. Prelates Who a Second Time Rejected the Dissenters' Bill.* London, J. Johnson, 1773. 123 p. **R 27**
A follower of Philip Furneaux, the Reverend Ratcliffe considered that the mere expression of an idea was not actionable unless such an utterance actually "produced criminal overt acts, evidently injurious to society." He considered the risk of seditious opinion as "no great price to pay for truth and the privilege of expressing our sentiments without control."

Rawnsley, H. D. "Pernicious Literature." *Hibbert Journal*, 10:462–68, January 1912. **R 28**
A British clergyman protests the prevalence of obscene literature and suggests means for combating it. He urges distributors and newspapers to aid in banning it.

Ray, Roy R. "Truth: A Defense to Libel." *Minnesota Law Review*, 16:43–69, December 1931. **R 29**
The author discusses the inception of this defense in English law and its growth in English and American jurisprudence. He examines the basis of the rule making truth a complete defense, showing that the rule "has obstructed the fullest usefulness of the law of libel." The rule, if in a statute, "should be amended as to make it only prima facie a defense, i.e., where there are good motives and justifiable ends."

Raymond, Allen. *The Denial to the American Press of Access to Information to the Federal Government.* New York, American Civil Liberties Union, 1955. 65 p. **R 30**

————. *The People's Right to Know.* New York, American Civil Liberties Union, 1955. 48 p. **R 31**
Raymond, a veteran newspaper man, was commissioned by the ACLU to investigate charges that government agencies were suppressing news at its source and thus narrowing "the market-place of opinion." His report shows evidence of the validity of some of the charges.

————. "Press Freedom v. Army Regulations." *Reporter,* 8:17–20, 24 June 1952. **R 32**
Analysis of the code of regulations governing the accreditation of war correspondents to United States military commands.

[Rayner, John]. *A Digest of the Law Concerning Libels: Containing All the Resolutions in the Books on the Subject and Many Manuscript Cases, with Observations. By a Gentleman of the Inner-Temple.* Dublin, W. Hallhead, 1778. 139 p. **R 33**
The author has gathered together cases relating to definition, seizure, printing, publishing, bookselling, printing of parliamentary proceedings, informations and indictments, evidence, and punishments. The occasion for the volume was the current wave of sedition trials. Cases are presented without editorial comment. "This book it should seem might serve as an argument for the Liberty of the Press, since it shows the little Necessity there is of any further Restraint upon it, by demonstrating, that every one who prints any thing with a mischevous Intent, does so at his peril."

[————]. *An Inquiry into the Doctrine Lately Propagated, Concerning Attachments of Contempt, the Alteration of Records, and the Court of Star-Chamber. Upon the Principles of Law, and the Constitution, Particularly as They Relate to Prosecutions for Libels . . .* London, Printed for J. Williams, 1769. 98 p. **R 34**
Published during a period when the English laws of libel were being challenged in the courts. In 1792 the Fox Libel Act adopted the more liberal views espoused by Thomas Erskine.

Rayner, William. "The Unstamped Press." *Notes and Queries,* 10 (4th ser.):367–68, 9 November 1872. **R 35**
Notes on the history of "unstamped newspapers" of Great Britain, with a list of most of them.

Rea, Robert R. *The English Press in*

Politics. Lincoln, Neb., University of Nebraska Press, 1963. 272 p. **R 36**
A study of the political press of England during the eighteenth century—the controversial newspapers, pamphlets, and broadsides which provoked government officials, and their authors, printers, and publishers who suffered arrest and sometimes imprisonment for exercising their freedom. Considerable attention is given to the use of general warrants to suppress seditious libel, to the controversy over reporting the acts of parliament, to the Junius affair, and to the prosecution of such figures as John Wilkes, John Almon, and H. S. Woodfall. Sixteen contemporary illustrations include "Wilkes and Liberty," Hogarth's famous leering Wilkes, and the "Burning of *North Briton* No. 45."

————. "John Almon: Bookseller to John Wilkes." *Indiana Quarterly for Bookmen,* 4:20–28, January 1948. **R 37**
An account of publishing agreements and disagreements between two men who figured in the fight for freedom of the press in eighteenth-century England.

————. "Mason, Walpole, and That Rogue Almon." *Huntington Library Quarterly,* 23:187–93, February 1960. **R 38**
"In the case of Mason's satires and their publisher, John Almon, Walpole presents the misleading picture of a hapless author betrayed by a rascally bookseller for a few pieces of silver. Re-examination of the evidence and the witnesses exculpates the publisher from most of Walpole's charges and throws new light upon his relations with Mason."

Read, Allen W. "Noah Webster as a Euphemist." *Dialect Notes,* 6:385–91, 1934. **R 39**
The spirit of euphemism reached its height during the 1830's when the King James version of the Bible was criticized as containing "language too foul to be uttered in decent society." Webster brought out a version of the Bible in 1833 which, in addition to removing obsolete words and expressions, he deleted or replaced those words which "cannot be uttered in families without disturbing devotion." He was concerned with frank references to parts of the body (*teats* were replaced by *breasts*), secretion and excretion (*piss* was removed entirely), and sex acts (*whore* was replaced by *harlot*).

Read, Herbert E. *Freedom, Is It a Crime? The Strange Case of the Three Anarchists Jailed at the Old Bailey, April 1945; Two Speeches by Herbert Read.* Foreword by E. Silverman. London, Freedom Press Defence Committee, 1945. 14 p. (Reprinted in *Twice-A-Year,* Fall–Winter, 1946–47) **R 40**
"This crime is conspiracy to cause disaffection by certain articles which appeared in *War Commentary.* The Jury found them guilty." The three anarchists were sentenced to nine

months in prison. The pamphlet criticizes the police raid of the offices of Freedom Press and the homes of the accused anarchists for antiwar pamphlets. It calls for the restoration of peacetime freedom of speech and of the press. A Freedom Defence Committee was formed, headed by Herbert Read and including such prominent British writers as Housman, Orwell, and Priestley.

Reade, Charles. "The Prurient Prude." In *Readiana; Comments on Current Events . . .* London, Chatto & Windus, 1896, pp. 296–301. **R 41**
The prurient prude, Reade wrote in 1866, "itches to attract attention by a parade of modesty . . . or even by rashly accusing others of immodesty." Reade attacks critics of his novel, *Griffith Gaunt, or Jealousy,* for bringing a foul mind to the reading of a sincere work of literature. He threatens libel action against the American journal, *The Round Table.* In the chapter "Second-Hand Libel" (*Readiana,* pp. 302–3) he threatens to sue publishers of the *Globe* and *London Review* for quoting an American review that stated the work is "indecent and immoral."

Reardon, William R. *Banned in Boston: A Study of Theatrical Censorship in Boston from 1630 to 1950.* Palo Alto, Calif., Stanford University, 1953. 253 p. (Ph.D. dissertation, University Microfilms, no. 5386) **R 42**
A contemporized record and evaluation of theatrical censorship in Boston to which has been appended a total appraisal of Boston censorship. The first three chapters deal with legislative prohibition on the theater in Massachusetts during the seventeenth, eighteenth, and nineteenth centuries as preliminary to the major portion of the dissertation on the period from 1890 to 1950. Special attention has been given to the influence of the Watch and Ward Society and of the clergy of the Catholic Church. A tabulation of the performances censored is found on pages 231–38.

————. "The Tradition Behind Bostonian Censorship." *Educational Theatre Journal,* 7:97–101, May 1955. **R 43**
Account of the imposition of total theatrical censorship upon Boston for a period of over 160 years—by whom it was imposed and for what reasons.

Recap. A Digest of Recent Trends in Academic Freedom in California Public Schools. Los Angeles, vol. 1, no. 1, Fall 1962. Issued periodically. **R 44**
"*Recap* grew out of a concern by a group of parents, teachers, administrators, and school board members over increasing attempts to limit texts, tests, and other materials used in schools to those promoting a special viewpoint.

Our chief purpose is to give sources of materials related to these irresponsible attacks."

"Recent Development in the Law of Motion Picture Censorship." *St. John's Law Review*, 31:93–103, December 1956. **R 45**

A review of recent court decisions suggests that limited censorship is still constitutional and a narrow though indefinite area is still open to prior restraint.

"Recent Limitations on Free Speech and Free Press." *Yale Law Journal*, 48:54–80, November 1938. **R 46**

Notes on the *Los Angeles Times* case, the right of the press to comment on "pending cases," and specific cases relating to freedom under the Wagner Act.

["Recent Prosecutions for Blasphemy"]. *Christian Examiner*, 16:90–95, March 1834. **R 47**

A report on "recent" blasphemy cases in the United States, as part of a review of the Knowles biography of Roger Williams. The reviewer believes that "by the highest judicial authorities in various parts of the United States blasphemy has been adjudged as an offense against the laws of the commonwealth." He cites cases in New York and Pennsylvania. While the law does not protect particular sects, it protects offenses against religion and God. It is based, at least in part, on the power of the state to prevent corruption of morals and disturbance of the peace.

"Record of Congressional Debate on Censorship of Immoral Books." In M. S. MacLean, and Elizabeth K. Holmes, *Men and Books*. New York, Long and Smith, 1932, pp. 347–59. (Reprinted from the *Congressional Record*, vol. 72, no. 79) **R 48**

A portion of the U.S. Senate debate between Senators Cutting and Smoot over the proposed Customs ban on obscene literature. Deals largely with the presence of Rabelais and other French classics in American libraries.

"Recruiting and the Censorship." *Quarterly Review*, 233:130–58, January 1915. **R 49**

The author criticizes wartime controls of public information exerted by the Press Bureau, the Admiralty, and the War Office, as having "worked in a way inimical to recruiting." The witholding of information and the delay in transmission of news have caused grave annoyance in the United States, which fact he believes is humiliating to the British and does harm to their reputation for fair play.

"Red Hysteria." *New Republic*, 21:249–52, 28 January 1920. **R 50**

Discredits the hysteria on which war censorship was largely based and Bolshevik hysteria of the postwar period on which further legislation is demanded. Includes statement from Judge George W. Anderson.

Redman, Ben Ray. "Is Censorship Possible?" *Scribner's Magazine*, 87:515–17, May 1930. (Reprinted in Downs, *The First Freedom*, pp. 213–15) **R 51**

"Although religious and political censorship can be moderately effective, and military censorship exceedingly effective, sex-censorship has never had and never will have a chance of accomplishing a fraction of its intention." Such censorship seeks "to control an uncontrollable force by the futile expedient of eliminating external stimuli that are infinitely replaceable. Obscenity does not reside in the stimulating object, but in the determined-to-be-stimulated subject; the sin, if sin there be, is not outside us, it is within."

———. "Obscenity and Censorship." *Scribner's Magazine*, 95:341–34, May 1934. **R 52**

The author believes that the legal definition of obscenity, enunciated by Judge Woolsey in the *Ulysses* case, "bears no relation to the facts of life and the realities of literature." The legal concept of obscenity needs to be transformed through a change in the thought behind the law. Regardless of the fluctuations of manners and revisions of laws, censorship is generally incapable of suppressing either good or evil in the printed word.

———. "Pictures and Censorship." *Saturday Review of Literature*, 19:3–4, 13–14, 31 December 1938. **R 53**

A critique of the activities of the Hays Office. This agency, the creation of the motion picture industry, stands between the producers and the state, city, and local censor boards and between the studios and the innumerable pressure groups interested in influencing the American screen.

Redwood, Hugh. "News in War Time." *Contemporary Review*, 106:651–57, November 1914. **R 54**

Review of difficulties encountered by British newspapers in obtaining and publishing war news. Criticism of the government Press Bureau, which was created primarily as a channel for official war news, but which instead constituted itself the chief censoring authority and relegated news distribution to second place.

Reece, B. Carroll. "How the *Encyclopaedia Britannica* Was Gobbled Up." *Congressional Record*, 102(11):14927–31, 26 July 1959. (Extension of remarks in the House of Representatives) **R 55**

The Representative from Tennessee attacks the *Encyclopaedia Britannica*, acquired by the University of Chicago under Chancellor Robert M. Hutchins. This respected reference book, the Congressman charges, through a "well-conceived strategy," has used its power to influence public opinion in behalf of "Socialists of all hues," materialistic, and anticonservative and utopian thought. He calls upon Congress to take a look at economic power to mould public opinion that rests in the hands of tax-exempt foundations and institutions.

Reed, Arthur W. "The Regulation of the Book Trade before the Proclamation of 1538." *Transactions*, Bibliographical Society (London), 15:155–86, 1917–19. **R 56**

An analysis of five early records (1524–28) regulating the London book trade, showing the working of the diocesan and ecclesiastical control which preceded that by the king and Privy Council. The five cases were: 1. Bishop Tunstall's first monition to the booksellers (1524). 2. The case of the Vicar-General against Wynkyn de Worde, printer (1525). 3. The case of the Vicar-General against Thomas Bartlett (1525–26). 4. Bishop Tunstall's second monition to the booksellers (1526). 5. The case of the Vicar-General against Robert Wyer, printer (1527).

Reed, Clifton. "Radio Censors Labor." *Nation*, 141:357, 25 September 1935. (Reprinted in Summers, *Radio Censorship*, pp. 181–83) **R 57**

Deals with charges by the American Civil Liberties Union against Crosley Radio Corporation, owners of radio station WLW, Cincinnati, for practicing "unjustified and anti-labor censorship." Quotes a memorandum by the station prohibiting references to strikes in news reports.

Reed, James A. "The Liberty of the Press." In *Problems of Journalism; Proceedings of the American Society of Newspaper Editors, 1927*. Washington, D.C., ASNE, 1927, pp. 28–39. **R 58**

The author is U.S. Senator from Missouri.

Reed, John. "About the Second *Masses* Trial." *Liberator*, 1:36–38, December 1918. **R 59**

The second sedition trial against *The Masses*, in contrast with the first, was conducted in a less emotional atmosphere. The judge was fair-minded throughout, defending the right to criticize the government so long as it did not interfere with recruiting or cause mutiny. A disagreement of the jury was a victory for the defendant, The Masses Publishing Co. Max Eastman and Art Young were among the witnesses for the defense. Reed believes that political offenses are dealt with more harshly in the United States than anywhere in the world.

———. "On Intervention in Russia." *Liberator*, 1:14–17, November 1918. **R 60**

Deals with suppression of information as to Russian conditions by our war censorship.

Reed, John J. "Permission to Read Forbidden Books." *Theological Studies*, 19:586–95, December 1958.　**R 61**
Father Reed discusses some of the problems in granting permission to Catholics to read books that are on the *Index*.

———. "Problems of Prohibited Books: an Exploratory Discussion." *Catholic Theological Studies of America, Proceedings*, 15:45–53, 1960.　**R 62**

Reed, Ralph. "Crime and the Press." *Lancet-Clinic*, 106:460–62, 4 November 1911.　**R 63**
Reply to an argument for freedom, *Bulletin of the American Academy of Medicine*, October 1911. Report of the committee on publishing the details of suicides in the public press.

Reed, Roy. "How to Lynch a Newspaper." *Atlantic*, 214(5):59–63, November 1964.　**R 64**
The story of Eugene Henry Wirges, an Arkansas small-town newspaper editor who tried to fight the local political machine under the Faubus regime, but was finally put out of business by a community's use of the libel law.

Reed, William. "Background of World Freedom of Information." *Editor and Publisher*, 80(16):13+, 12 April 1947; 80(17):18+, 19 April 1947; 80(18):108+, 26 April 1947.　**R 65**
Three articles trace progress toward the ideal of a free flow of information throughout the world: 50 Years of Resolutions Form Stage for UN Talks; Freedom v. Responsibility—a Perennial Press Issue; U.S. at One Extreme in Responsibility Issue. The last article indicates the difference of opinion on methods of achieving freedom of world news coverage held by the American press, the State Department, and the Hutchins Commission.

Reeder, Frank G. "Prohibitions on the Publication or Distribution of Anonymous Campaign Literature." *Michigan Law Review*, 60:506–9, February 1962.　**R 66**
Regarding *U.S. v. Scott*, 195 F. Supp. 440 (1961) and *Talley v. California*, 362 U.S. 60 (1960).

Reedy, William M. "The Censorship of Literature." *Bruno's Weekly*, 3:1118, 30 September 1916.　**R 67**
A protest against the efforts by the "successor of Anthony Comstock" to suppress Dreiser's *The Genius*. "Literary censorship is an intolerable institution. It cramps imagination and cripples invention. It has a paralytic influence upon thought. And it does not help morals in the least. Indeed, it puts a premium upon the meanest nastiness that circulates clandestinely. The best disinfectant of base art is freedom."

Bruno's Weekly was edited by Guido Bruno in his Washington Square garret, New York.

———. *The Myth of a Free Press; an Address Delivered before the Missouri Press Association at Excelsior Springs, Mo., May 28, 1908 . . .* St. Louis, The Mirror, 1908. 31 p.　**R 68**
The editor of *Reedy's Mirror* deals with the economic controls of the press and the influence of the advertisers.

[Reeves, John]. "Trial at the Suggestion of the House of Commons for a Libel upon the English Constitution, 1796." In Howell, *State Trials*, vol. 26, pp. 529 ff.　**R 69**
Reeves, a Tory journalist, alarmed by the spread of reformist pamphlets and newspapers, was instrumental in forming (1792) the Association for Preserving Liberty and Property against Levellers and Republicans, with its main purpose the suppression of seditious literature. A few years later Reeves himself was a victim of suppression, and the Whigs who had opposed press restraints, were the oppressors. Sheridan, backed by Pitt, demanded in Parliament that Reeves's pamphlet which had been critical of both Houses, be burnt by the common hangman and that the author be prosecuted. Reeves was brought to trial. The jury found the pamphlet "improper," but Reeves "not guilty."

Reformists' Register and Weekly Commentary. London, 1 February 1816—25 October 1817. Weekly. Edited by William Hone.　**R 70**
This short-lived periodical (two-penny sheet) was devoted to radical reform and defense of the freedom of expression. Its editor was brought to trial for libel.

Regan, John J. "The Supreme Court, Obscenity and Censorship." *Catholic World*, 200:142–48, December 1964.　**R 71**

Regnery, Henry. "Bias in Book Reviewing and Book Selection." *ALA Bulletin*, 60:57–62, January 1966.　**R 72**
This conservative publisher was asked to investigate the charges sometimes made that libraries tend to purchase liberal books and pass over conservative ones, following advice from biased book reviewing media. Regnery concludes: "I think that bias is indicated reflecting a liberal point of view in reviewing, but the conservative position, all things considered, is given a fair chance. The liberals enjoy a strong and commanding position in the communication of ideas, but a conservative who has something to say can still get a hearing."

"'Regulating' the Press." *Nation*, 100:348–49, 1 April 1915.　**R 73**

Editorial advising the American press to set its house in order to head off regulatory legislation.

"Regulation of Comic Books." *Harvard Law Review*, 68:489–506, January 1955.　**R 74**
"An effective system of self-limitation by the comic book industry would appear to be the best way to eliminate crime, horror, and sex in comic books. . . . If legal regulation is necessary, state laws prohibiting tie-in sales of comic books would be an unobjectionable means of reducing the circulation of such comic books. If it is found desirable to enact a statute prohibiting the sale of comic books, a post-publication statute limited to the sale of comic books to children would be the type least subject to constitutional objections."

"The Regulation of Films." *Nation*, 100:486–87, 6 May 1915.　**R 75**
Editorial commenting on the film, *Birth of a Nation*, and the widespread indignation and race hatred it aroused. Approves an official film censor, responsible to the mayor, as "the best way out."

"Regulation of Wireless Telegraphy." *Scientific American*, 106:282, 30 March 1912.　**R 76**
Discussion of a bill introduced in the Congress to regulate radio-communications.

Reichler, Oxie. "Those Homemade Iron Curtains." *Nieman Reports*, 5(3):19–21, July 1951.　**R 77**
The iron curtains are the restrictions imposed by state, county, and municipal agencies against access to public records and proceedings.

———. "You Can't Print That." *National Municipal Review*, 47:58–61, February 1958.　**R 78**
The editor of the Yonkers *Herald Statesman* believes the public's business should be conducted "in a goldfish bowl." He condemns censorship in city hall.

Reid, Hugh. "What's the Matter with the Post Office." *Public*, 22:1041–43, 27 September 1919.　**R 79**
An historical account of the growth of Post Office censorship in the United States down to the present restrictive practices under Postmaster General Burleson. The author attacks the theory of unmailability which is extended from year to year. "We shall never have a free press in America until we wipe out the whole system of handling judicial questions by purely administrative procedure."

Reid, John C. *Broadcast Defamation.* Columbia, Mo., Freedom of Information Center,

School of Journalism, University of Missouri, 1963. 8 p. (Publication no. 108)
R 80

Reifin, Melvin H. "The Constitutionality of Obscenity Laws: U.S. and Ohio." *University of Cincinnati Law Review*, 31: 285–96, Summer 1962. **R 81**

Reiner, Donald F. "Motion Picture Censorship Re-examined." *Albany Law Review*, 23:152–68, January 1959. **R 82**
An examination of recent decisions of the courts, beginning in 1952 with the *Joseph Burstyn v. Wilson* case in which the U.S. Supreme Court reversed its field and decided that the First and Fourteenth Amendments do clearly require the states to apply protection to motion pictures. The author explores the idea of the abolition of all film censorship.

Reitman, Alan. "The Battle Continues on Subtler Levels." *Censorship*, 1:30–36, Autumn 1964. **R 83**
In this survey of the censorship scene in the United States, the author notes that "traditional forms of censorship, governmental bans or prosecutions, are not today's major pressure points." New and complex methods being substituted include "harassment by private groups, extra-legal coercion (some direct and some subtle) and classification of material for specialized audiences."

Reitman, Benjamin L. "Cleveland Myth." *Mother Earth*, 11:761–65, February 1917. **R 84**
Story of the trial and conviction of Reitman for giving birth control information.

Reitzel, William. "William Cobbett and Philadelphia Journalism: 1794–1800." *Pennsylvania Magazine of History and Biography*, 59:223–44, 1935. **R 85**
Includes an account of Cobbett's *Porcupine's Gazette* and the libel against Dr. Benjamin Rush.

"Religious Bigotry and Persecution in the United States." *Secular Thought*, 24: 169–70, 14 April 1900. **R 86**
References to the exclusion of free-thought papers from Canada.

Religious Liberty Association. *Freedom, Civil and Religious; the American Conception of Liberty for Press, Pulpit and Public, as Guaranteed in the Federal Constitution.* Washington, D.C. Review and Herald Publishing Association, 1920. 128 p.
R 87

"Religious Prosecutions and Free Discussion." In *Free Thinkers' Information for the People.* 1:165–71, 1842. **R 88**
The author attacks Christians for their intolerance. They "boast a long array of martyrs" who have flouted the orthodoxy of their time; but now that they are in power they crush those who differ with them. Truth can only be determined by free discussion; falsehood requires coercion.

Remmers, D. H. "Recent Legislative Trends in Defamation by Radio." *Harvard Law Review*, 64:727–58, March 1951. **R 89**
The study deals with the advisability of legislation relieving a radio station from liability for defamations broadcast by it in instances in which the speaker was not a member of the staff and where the station could not, by exercise of due care, have prevented the utterance. "The solution of the proposed federal legislation and the Port Huron case, denying the right of censorship but exempting from liability for defamation, provides a fair and workable solution."

Remmo, C. G. "Freedom of the Press." *Notre Dame Lawyer*, 20:314–21, March 1945. **R 90**
A brief review of the restrictions placed on freedom of the press in the area of obscenity and wartime sedition. Even these restrictions need to be guarded zealously.

[Remson, Evelyn S.] "Constitutional Law—Criminal Contempt—News Photographs." *Brooklyn Law Review*, 23:304–6, April 1957. **R 91**
A case involving the infrared photographing of a convicted murderer enroute to the courtroom for sentencing raises questions in the interpretation of the American Bar Association Canon 35.

"Repeal of the Blasphemy Laws." *Spectator*, 59:476–77, 10 April 1886. **R 92**
Criticism of Courtney Kenny's bill in Parliament "to abolish Prosecutions against Laymen for the Expression of Opinions on matters of Religion." Any such bill should also contain protection of the individual whose religious beliefs are insulted by scurrilous speech or writing.

The Report on Radio. Winnipeg, Winnipeg Free Press, 1951. 28 p. (Winnipeg Free Press Pamphlet, no. 36) **R 93**
Editorial comments on the Massey Commission report on radio and television in Canada. The report considered broadcasting as a state monopoly operated and controlled in the pulic interest. Private broadcasting should be part of the national system, subject to control of the public corporation, the C. B. C.

Reppler, Agnes. "Good News and Bad." *Commonweal*, 3:16–17, 11 November 1925.
R 94

This American author disagrees with the policy of the *Christian Science Monitor* "to avoid reporting crimes, disasters, epidemics, deaths or trifling gossip." The world the *Monitor* describes is not the world we live in. Crime and disaster should be reported because they exist.

Representation of the Impiety and Immorality of the English Stage; with Reasons for Putting a Stop Thereto; and Some Questions Addrest to Those Who Frequent the Play-house. 3 d ed. London, 1704. 12 p. **R 95**

The Republican. London, 1817–26. Weekly.
R 96
The Republican was started in 1817 by W. T. Sherwin, with Richard Carlile as distributor. Its name was changed after a few issues to *Sherwin's Political Register*, and continued under that name until 27 August 1819 when Carlile took it over and renamed it *The Republican.* Except for the year 1821, when the paper was dropped, it continued until 1826, edited by Richard Carlile and, when he was in jail, by his wife, his sister, or his shopmen. *The Republican* carried accounts of the various sedition trials, including those of the Carliles, the Carlile shopmen, and Henry and Leigh Hunt.

"The Requirement of Scienter in Obscenity Statutes." *De Paul Law Review*, 9: 250–54, Spring–Summer 1960. **R 97**

Resnick, Edward H. "Prior Restraint— the Constitutional Question." *Boston University Law Review*, 42:357–72, Summer 1962. **R 98**
A discussion of "recent developments relating to the doctrine of prior restraints and the historical development of the doctrine, including a discussion of the area of communication to which it has been applied. There will be no consideration of censorship in radio or television, which come within the aegis of the Federal Communications Commission, or of the large number of cases which has been decided under the censorship statutes applicable to the Post Office Department." Areas of application include newspapers and books, speech in public places, distribution of literature, and motion pictures. Special attention is given to the case of *Times Film Corp. v. Chicago*, 365 U.S. 43 (1961), which "removed the last vestige of absoluteness from the prior restraint doctrine."

Reston, James B. "Secrecy and the Reporter." *Atlantic*, 185:39–42, April 1950. **R 99**
Diplomatic correspondent of the *New York Times* says too much national policy is fully formed in these days before press and the public are let in on the facts. Calls for earlier action, and more of it, by the reporters.

———, and Murray Kempton. "The Right to Know v. the Right to Strike."

New Republic, 148(13):15–18, 30 March 1963. **R 100**
The text of Reston's column on the New York newspaper strike, censored from the 12 January 1963 *New York Times* western edition and wire service, with Kempton's comments on Reston's stand.

"The Restraint of Libellous Publications." *Law Times*, 53:112–13, 15 June 1872. **R 101**
The case of *A'Beckett v. Mortimer*.

"Restrictions on the Freedom of the Press." *Harvard Law Review*, 16:55–56, November 1902. **R 102**
Comments on cases involving free speech as guaranteed by the Constitution conflicting with the misdemeanor of endangering the public peace. Various decisions "show that these provisions—found in so many of our constitutions—mean only that a man may freely speak and write what he chooses, so long as he does not thereby disturb private rights, the public peace, or attempt to subvert the government."

Revell, Peter. "Censorship Facts." *Ontario Library Review*, 46:95–96, May 1962. **R 103**
The chairman of the Ontario Library Association's Intellectual Freedom Committee discusses Canadian censorship under the Customs Tariff Act, the Criminal Code, and the powers of the Postmaster General.

———. "Propaganda and Pornography." *Library Journal*, 88:3552, 3585, 1 October 1963. **R 104**
In light of the publication of John Cleland's *Fanny Hill*, written as intentional pornography, the author calls for a re-examination of the whole question of obscenity, pornography, and what used to be called hard-core pornography. He suggests research along the line of that done by the Institute for Propaganda Analysis, 1937–41.

"Revision of the Book Law." *Massachusetts Library Club Bulletin*, 20:5–6, January 1930. **R 105**
Endorsement by the Massachusetts Library Club of the proposed revision of the obscene book law, as drafted by a committee under the chairmanship of Edward A. Weeks, Jr.

"Revocation of Mailing Privilege Violation of Espionage Act." *Virginia Law Register*, 3(n.s.):537–41, November 1917. **R 106**
The U.S. District Court for the Southern District of Georgia upholds the constitutionality of the Espionage Act in the case of *Jefferson Publishing Co. v. West*. The case involved the revocation of second-class mailing privileges of *The Jeffersonian* for its opposition to wartime conscription.

"The Revolt against the Revolting." *Literary Digest*. 92:31–32, 19 February 1927. **R 107**
"The public is becoming aroused, we are told, against the filth and lewdness being paraded on the stage and screen and in books, magazines and the 'yellow press,' and several newspapers have met the issue presented by an evil-smelling trial by adopting voluntary censorship. In Washington, and Albany, New York, bills have been introduced to bring the daily parade of vice to an end through legal means."

Rex, Frederick, *comp. Motion Picture Censors' and Reviewers' Manual: A Handbook for the Instruction and Use of State and City Board of Censors of Motion Pictures, Producers and Distributors, Citizen Motion Picture Councils, Better Films Committees, Women's Clubs and Parent-Teacher Organizations*. Hubbard Woods, Ill., The Author, 1934. 34 p. **R 108**

[Reynolds, Charles B.]. "Trial for Blasphemy, Morristown, N.J., 1887." In *American State Trials*, vol. 18, pp. 795–857. **R 109**
Reynolds was found guilty and fined for publication of a pamphlet. Robert Ingersoll was the defense counsel, a fact which attracted attention throughout the country. This was the first blasphemy case to be tried in the New Jersey courts.

Reynolds, James B. "Reasonable Restrictions upon Freedom of Speech." *Papers and Proceedings, Ninth Annual Meeting, American Sociological Society*, 9:46–59, 1914. **R 110**
The legal counsel of the American Public Hygiene Association discusses cases involving restriction of free speech in relation to public morals and social well-being.

Reynolds, John W. *Wisconsin's "Anti-Secrecy Law."* Columbia, Mo., Freedom of Information Center, School of Journalism, University of Missouri, 1960. 3 p. (Publication no. 24) **R 111**
Wisconsin's Attorney General discusses the right to know and Wisconsin's new "open meetings" law.

Rhode Island. House of Representatives. Commission to Study the Sale and Distribution of "Comic" Books, Etc., in Rhode Island. *Report*. Providence. Ordered printed by the House of Representatives, 1956, 16 p. **R 112**
The report assesses the responsibility of publishers, distributers and citizens (parents) in meeting the problem of salacious "comic" books. The Commission recommends a permanent agency be established to educate the public and to canvass the state for violation of present obscenity laws. It calls for the exclusion of objectionable "comics" on state property. The Rhode Island Commission to Encourage Morality in Youth, established as a result of these recommendations was abolished by the Legislature in 1964 following a ruling of the U.S. Supreme Court, that the Commission was engaged in extrajudicial and unconstitutional censorship.

Rhodon, *pseud*. "The *North Briton* and the Journeymen Printers." *Notes & Queries*, 166:137, 24 February 1934. **R 113**
Brief account of the arrest of the 14 journeymen printers, 1763.

———. "Wilkes and the *North Briton*." *Notes & Queries*, 161:165–66, 5 September 1931. **R 114**
Further bibliographic details and differences noted over J.T.Y.'s notes on *North Briton*, 41 years earlier.

Rhyne, Charles S. *Comic Books—Municipal Control of Sale and Distribution—a Preliminary Study*. Washington, D.C. National Institute of Municipal Law Officers, 1948. 16 p. (Report no. 124) **R 115**

Riback, Harold L. *The Development of Obscenity Administration in Relation to the American Press*. New York, New York University, 1949. 81 p. (Unpublished Master's thesis) **R 116**

Rice, Elmer L. "Censorship." In his *The Living Theatre*. New York, Harper, 1959, pp. 276–86. **R 117**
A brief review of stage censorship throughout the world with special attention to the United States where there "has never been a theatrical censorship, nor any sort of play-licensing system, either nationally, or, as far as I know, in any of the states." He discusses scattered examples of municipal censorship but notes that in New York, the only important play-producing center, the stage has on the whole, "been happily free from censorship . . . Thus, while threats to the freedom of the stage are ever present, and occasionally successful, the American theatre as a whole is an unrestricted institution and nowhere in the world is the communication of drama less impeded by censorship than in the United States."

———. "Entertainment in the Age of McCarthy." *New Republic*, 128:14–17, 13 April 1953. **R 118**
"No objective observer can have failed to note, in the past 20 years, an accelerating deterioration in our standards of freedom, particularly freedom of expression of opinion."

The author discusses extralegal police action against books and stage plays, the *Miracle* case, and current blacklisting in radio and TV.

————. "New Fashions in Censorship." *Survey*, 88:112–15, March 1952. "Reply with Rejoinder." *Survey*, 88:148, April 1952. (Reprinted in Downs, *The First Freedom*, pp. 141–46)   **R 119**
With the decline of official censorship as a result of liberal court decisions, a more devious and more effective form of unofficial censorship by pressure group has developed. The author, a Pulitzer Prize-winning playwright, attacks the militant minority groups that threaten freedom of speech and press by applying pressure on the mass media. Two conditions are necessary for free speech: diversity of ownership and control of the media of communications and a modification of the tactics of minority pressure groups.

————. "No Quarter to Censorship." *Authors' League Bulletin*, 15(1):17, April 1927.   **R 120**
"The distinction between voluntary and involuntary censorship is purely illusory. Censorship is censorship and in accepting it in principle or in fact the public surrenders itself into the hands of the Comstockians."

————. *The Supreme Freedom*. Whitestone, N.Y., The Graphics Group, 1949. 32 p. (Graphics Group Book 11. Illustrated by Kelly Oechsli. Reprinted in The Institute for Religious and Social Studies, *Great Expressions of Human Rights*, pp. 105–25)   **R 121**
A popular summary of freedom of expression or the lack of it in present-day America, prepared for the Institute for Religious and Social Studies by the chairman of the National Council on Freedom from Censorship. The "supreme freedom" is the freedom to think, talk, and write with independence and without threat.

[————]. "The U.S.O. and *Races of Mankind.*" *Saturday Review of Literature*, 27(29):13, 15 July 1944.   **R 122**
An account of the suppression by the U.S.O. of the pamphlet, *Races of Mankind*, by Ruth Benedict and Gene Weltfish. Chester I. Barnard, president of the U.S.O., had defended the suppression. The article includes Mr. Rice's denunciation of Mr. Barnard's defense.

Rice, George P., Jr. "Freedom of Speech under Law." *Vital Speeches*, 21:1527–29, 1 October 1955.   **R 123**
The educational director, National Foundation for Education in American Citizenship, in an address before the Sigma Delta Kappa honorary legal fraternity, Indianapolis, Ind., urges members to be well-informed in the basic concepts of freedom of speech and in the important rulings of the Supreme Court in this area.

Rice, Warner G. "A Note on *Areopagitica.*" *Journal of English and German Philology*, 40:474–81, 1941.   **R 124**
A reconsideration of Milton's classic work on freedom of the press. The author notes that the essay received little attention during Milton's lifetime and for a century after his death. Its reputation rose in the eighteenth century with the triumph of Whig liberalism. The author considers the limitations Milton placed on freedom of the press; Milton "the humanistic—aristocrat," opposed prior licensing but would agree with "judicious censorship" after the event.

Richards, Robert K. "Freedom of Air at Stake." *Broadcasting*, 30(11):15, 101–2, 18 March 1946.   **R 125**
Criticism of the FCC's report on *Public Service Responsibility of Broadcast Licensees*, which the author considers "the Commission's latest and most overt bid for control of America's free radio."

Richardson, Elliot L. "Freedom of Expression and the Function of the Courts." *Harvard Law Review*, 65:1–54, November 1951.   **R 126**
"It has been the purpose of this paper, by defining the issues in free speech cases, to indicate which of them are wholly committed to the courts, especially the Supreme Court of the United States, and which belong primarily to legislatures and to the states . . . The great battles for free expression will be won, if they are won, not in the courts but in committee rooms and protest meetings, by editorials and letters to Congress, and through the courage of citizens everywhere."

Richardson, Ernest C. "The Question of Censorship in Libraries." *Library Journal*, 43:152–54, March 1918.   **R 127**
"The problem of library censorship is not a simple one, and it involves the whole question of free discussion." The author, in his presidential address before the American Library Association, introduces the problem and recommends it as a field for special research.

Richardson, J. Hall. "Should Divorce Cases Be Reported?" *Fortnightly Review*, 117(n.s.):813–20, June 1925.   **R 128**
The article is occasioned by a bill before Parliament which would impose restrictions on the publication of reports of judicial proceedings relating to the dissolution of marriage.

Richardson, Samuel. *The Necessity of Toleration In matters of Religion. Or, Certain Questions propounded to the Synod, tending to prove that Corporal punishments ought not to be inflicted upon such as hold Errors in Religion, and that in matters of Religion, men ought not to be compelled, but have liberty and freedom . . .* London, 1647. 22 p. (Reprinted in Edward B. Underhill, *Tracts of Liberty of Conscience and Persecution*, pp. 235–85)   **R 129**

[Richmond, Alexander B., *plaintiff*]. *Trial for Libel, in the Court of Exchequer, Guildhall, London . . . Alexander B. Richmond, Plaintiff; versus Simpkin & Marshall, and Others, defs.* London, Muir, Gowans, 1834. 64 p.   **R 130**
The suit was against Simpkin and Marshall, London booksellers and agents for *Tait's Edinburgh Magazine*, for publishing a series of alleged libels against the plaintiff arising from a review of a work called *The Exposure of the Spy System*, wherein the plaintiff was designated a government spy. As evidence in the "spy trial" developed against the plaintiff he elected to be "non-suited" and the case was dropped.

[Riddell, George Allardice, *baron*]. "Censorship." *Encyclopaedia Britannica*, 13th ed., 1926. vol. 1 of supp., pp. 560–62.   **R 131**
British press censorship in World War I.

Riddell, William R. "Libel on the Assembly: A Pre-Revolutionary Episode." *Pennsylvania Magazine of History and Biography*, 52:176–92; 249–79; 342–60, 1928.   **R 132**
Deals largely with the case of William Moore, brought before the Bar of the Pennsylvania Assembly on charges of misconduct as justice of the peace and also for writing and publishing his *Address to the Governor*, which the House had resolved to be a libel against the Constitution and the Assembly. Riddell denied the right of the House to try for such libel, but was convicted, sent to jail, and denied the right of habeas corpus. Also charged and convicted was Professor William Smith, provost of the College and Academy of Philadelphia. He was convicted for abetting Moore and publishing the *Address* in his German-language newspaper. The author discusses the legal issues involved in libel and contempt of a colonial legislature.

Ridenour, Louis N. "Military Security and the Atomic Bomb." *Fortune*, 32:170–71+ November 1945. (Reprinted in Summers, *Federal Information Controls in Peacetime*, pp. 73–84)   **R 133**
A physics professor believes that the net effect of blanket efforts to keep the atomic bomb "secret," now that the war is over, can only be harmful to the United States by retarding scientific progress in nuclear physics. He suggests the removal of all security barriers to the publication of basic scientific information in nuclear physics.

————. "Science and Pseudo-science." In *Freedom of Book Selection; Proceedings of* the Second Conference on Intellectual Freedom . . . Chicago, American Library Association, 1954, pp. 12–22. **R 134**

Ridgeway, James. "Snooping through the Mails." *New Republic*, 152(12):11–13, 20 March 1965. **R 135**
Relates to the Post Office practice of maintaining lists of persons receivings Communist propaganda.

Ridgeway, William. *A Report of the Trial of Hugh Fitzpatrick for Libel*. Dublin, 1813. 105 p. **R 136**
Fitzpatrick was a Dublin bookseller who issued a book on penal laws written by Denis Scully. It was objected to by the authorities and Fitzpatrick, rather than reveal the name of the author, went to jail. Inglis states that this was the only important trial against a book during that period in Irish history.

———. *A Report of the Trial of Peter Finerty*. Dublin, 1798. 113 p. **R 137**
Finerty, listed as printer and proprietor of the *Dublin Press*, though not yet of legal age, was arrested for that paper's attack on the government and criticism of the trial and execution of William Orr. Finerty was found guilty and sentenced to two years in prison.

Ridings, Donald J. *Access to Information in Missouri*. Columbia, Mo., Freedom of Information Center, School of Journalism, University of Missouri, 1959. 4 p. (Publication no. 19) **R 138**
A survey of access to news in Missouri towns and cities, conducted through a questionnaire answered by 100 newspaper publishers.

———. *Concepts of Contempt*. Columbia, Mo., Freedom of Information Center, School of Journalism, University of Missouri, 1961. 10 p. (Publication no. 48) **R 139**
Abstract of a Master's thesis in journalism, University of Missouri. The author concludes: "Although they are often deserving of the punishment they receive, the crux of the matter seems to be that newspapers do not have the chance to prove themselves. When citing newspapers for contempt, judges claim they are protecting the due process of law. Where is due process for the newspaper?"

———. *Survey Assesses World FOI*. Columbia, Mo., Freedom of Information Center, School of Journalism, University of Missouri, 1959. 9 p. (Publication no. 21) **R 140**
Survey of the status of freedom of information in 35 countries as reported by correspondents. Includes Canada, Ireland, South Africa, Hong Kong, and the Philippines.

[Ridpath, George]. *The Stage Condemn'd, and The Encouragement given to the Immoralities and Profaneness of the Theatre by the English Schools, Universities and Pulpits, Censur'd . . . The Arguments of all the Authors that have Writ in Defence of the Stage against Mr. Collier, Consider'd . . . Together with The Censure of the English Stage and of several Antient and Modern Divines of the Church of England upon the Stage . . .* London, Printed for John Salusbury, 1698. 216 p. **R 141**
A defense of Jeremy Collier's *Short View of the Immorality and Profaneness of the English Stage*.

Riegel, Oscar W. *Mobilizing for Chaos; the Story of the New Propaganda*. New Haven, Yale University Press, 1934. 231 p. **R 142**
The role of nationalism in the exploitation of the world's newspapers and radio communication. How propaganda and censorship have been used to achieve the political aims of totalitarian and quasi-totalitarian states.

Rielly, Thomas L. *Censorship and the Post Office*. Chicago, University of Chicago, 1958. 106 p. (Unpublished Master's thesis) **R 143**

Riesel, Victor, and O. John Rogge. "Must Reporters Tell All." *Controversy*, 1(4):8+, August 1959. **R 144**
Reporter Riesel believes disclosure of news sources would weaken "the effectiveness of one of the principal tools a newsman uses in keeping the public informed." Lawyer Rogge argues that where an individual's liberty, reputation, or property is at stake, the anonymity of the informer should not be protected.

Riesman, David. "Democracy and Defamation: Control of Group Libel." *Columbia Law Review*, 42:727–80, May 1942. **R 145**
An exhaustive study of the law of group libel as it pertains to political offenses in America and a comparison with the law in Europe and Latin America.

———. "Democracy and Defamation: Fair Game and Fair Comment." *Columbia Law Review*, 42:1085–1123, September 1942; 42:1282–1318, November 1942. **R 146**
In these articles Riesman continues his discussion of political defamation as it is applied against individuals, concluding with recommendations for reform.

Rifkind, Simon H. "When the Press Collides with Justice." *Journal of the American Judicature Society*, 34:46–52, August 1950. (Reprinted in *Quill*, March 1951) **R 147**

To solve the conflict between a free trial and a free press the author recommends a clear statement be prepared as to the objectives of fair reporting and the restraints the press is expected to observe. He further suggests a watchdog committee of the bar to review individual cases.

———. "When the Press Hampers Justice." *American Mercury*, 71:14–24, July 1950. **R 148**
A judge discusses the controversy between court and press over "trial by newspaper," a conflict between two great constitutional principles. He suggests ways in which the bar and bench might obtain better newspaper cooperation in maintaining justice.

Riggs, Arthur S. "The Free American Press and Its Function in a Free World." *Catholic World*, 160:106–14, November 1944. **R 149**
"Men, not things, are the measure of a successful and constructive press. Government has no part in it: nor Capital, nor Labor, nor Church, each as such. Only men, free men, fearless men, above all honest men, can make free and keep free a great national press."

———. "Of Value to the Enemy." *Public Opinion Quarterly*, 6:367-77, Fall 1942. **R 150**
A member of the staff of the Cable and Radio Censorship Division of the Office of Censorship, considers the use of censorship as a weapon in war.

"The Right of Free Discussion." *American Biblical Repository*, 9:368–421, April 1937. **R 151**
The discussion is based on three major works: John Milton's *Areopagitica*, Jeremy Taylor's *The Liberty of Prophesying*, and Robert Hall's *An Apology for the Freedom of the Press*, works which the writer considers eloquent expressions of the right of free discussion, the foundation of all other rights in the land. "We deem it the duty of every man to lift up his voice . . . in defense of these great principles of republican liberty and of the Protestant religion." The author warns against the use of the arbitrary power of censorship by ecclesiastical authorities to enforce the doctrines of the church. Condemnation of books is being used today in lieu of committing their authors to the flame; it is unworthy of men in a land of freedom, it is an insult to a thinking age, and it is as ineffective as it is unworthy.

"Right of Newspapers Arbitrarily to Discriminate in Accepting Advertising." *United States Law Review*, 68:4–8, January 1934. **R 152**
References to an Iowa Supreme Court decision, *Shuck v. Carroll Daily Herald*, 247 N.W. 813 (1931), which decided that a newspaper was

a private enterprise and its publishers had a right to accept or reject advertising.

"The Right to a Good Name." *Outlook*, 90:891–92, 26 December 1908.   **R 153**
Editorial commending the action of John D. Rockefeller, Jr., in bringing criminal proceedings against Hearst's *American*, for libel. While not prejudging the case, the editor believes that a libelous newspaper editor and publisher should be imprisoned because the "liberty of the press does not mean liberty maliciously to vilify any private citizen or public official who happens to have aroused the hostility of the newspaper."

"Right to Restrain the Right of Free Speech or a Free Press When Necessary to Make Effective the Terms of an Injunction Restraining a Boycott." *Central Law Journal*, 68:207–8, 19 March 1909.
     R 154
Brief comment on the famous Buck's Stove contempt of court case involving Samuel Gompers and the American Federation of Labor.

Riley, Frank. "The Curious Case of Connor Evarts: Obscenity?" *Los Angeles Magazine*, 8:35–37, 56–61, September 1964.   **R 155**

Rinehart, John E., Jr., and Tom L. Beauchamp III. "Aspects of Southern Censorship." *Issue*, 1(1):11–15, Winter 1963.
     R 156
"We shall attempt to show that censorship in the South is deeply influenced and fostered by the pietistic and moralistic attitudes which prevail in the southern region." The authors, graduate students at Southern Methodist University, cite numerous examples of censorship in the South, beginning with recent episodes in Dallas, Tex. "If obscenity and indecency do exist in the arts, they should be countered through competent criticism and not with banishment. Open dialogue . . . promotes freedom in the community rather than stifling it. Book burnings and censorship committees have no place in a free society."

Ringler, William. "The First Phase of the Elizabethan Attack on the Stage, 1558–1579." *Huntington Library Quarterly*, 5(4):391–418, July 1942.   **R 157**

Riordan, Mary E. *Literary Censorship in Ireland, 1929–1961.* Chicago, University of Chicago, 1964. 165 p. (Unpublished Master's thesis)
     R 158

Ripley, Joseph M. "Policies and Practices Concerning Broadcasts of Controversial Issues." *Journal of Broadcasting*, 9(1):25–32, Winter 1964–65.   **R 159**
While broadcasting policies generally provide for fair treatment of "both sides of an issue," in practice too few stations allow adequate time for programming of controversial issues.

———. *The Practices and Policies Regarding Broadcasts of Opinions about Controversial Issues by Radio and Television Stations in the United States.* Columbus, Ohio State University, 1961. 279 p. (Ph. D. dissertation, University Microfilms, no. 62–805)
     R 160
A report of two studies of broadcasting stations and their handling of controversial public issues. A great many stations failed to meet their obligation to devote time to public affairs.

Rittenhouse, David C. "Obscenity and Social Statics." *William and Mary Law Review*, 1:303–24, 1958.   **R 161**
"The purpose of this paper is to illustrate some of the changes which have taken place in obscenity as an idea and the struggle which has taken place in an effort to formulate a stabilized concept which may be applied with some assurance of fairness by man with his limited understanding." The author concludes that the test for obscenity has passed through two periods of development— the period of the Hicklin Rule and the *Ulysses* Rule, and is now entering a third period arising from the Roth case, marked by the "Prurient Interest Test."

Rivard, Adjutor. "De la Liberté de la Presse." In the Royal Society of Canada. *Proceedings and Transactions*, 17(1):33–104, May 1923.   **R 162**
Following a general discussion of the history of press freedom in England and France, the author considers the press law of the province of Quebec, including such aspects as libel, privacy, reporting of public meetings, comment on public officials, and the right of reply. Bibliography of French and English legal works on pp. 102–3.

Rivkin, Allen. "The Hollywood Letter." *Free World*, 11:50–51, June 1946.   **R 163**
The difficulties in administering the Film Production Code because of complaints from movie-goers in matters of morality. He believes a small minority might bring enough pressure to effect government controls.

Roalfe, Matilda. *Law Breaking Justified . . .* Edinburgh, Matilda Roalfe & Co., 1844. 16 p.   **R 164**
The author argues that "to resist bad laws, is no less a duty than to respect good ones." The "bad law" the author broke and for which she went to jail was the law against blasphemy. She was convicted of selling heterodox works. "The law which forbids the publication of heterodoxy shall never be obeyed by me. I will publish irreligious opinions, be the consequences to myself what they may."

Robb, Arthur. "Shop Talk at Thirty; Florida Censorship." *Editor & Publisher*, 73:36, 7 March 1942.   **R 165**
The case of voluntary suppression of news stories of a ship sinking off the Florida coast during World War II, a fact widely known and talked about by residents of Palm Beach. One of a number of censorship issues dealt with in the editor's column during World War II.

Robbins, Alexander H. "The Action of the Government Against the New York *World* as a Revival of the Offence of *Scandalum Magnatum*." *Central Law Journal*, 68:135–36, 19 February 1909.   **R 166**
Relates to federal government charges of criminal libel because of allegations made against government officials with respect to the purchase of the French interests in the Panama Canal. "The rule of the civil law is recognized today as the rule of a higher civilization than that out of which grew the doctrine of *scandalum magnatum*."

———. "Obscenity; What Constitutes an Indecent Publication." *Central Law Journal*, 65:64–69, 26 July 1907.   **R 167**
The case of *People v. Eastman* before the Court of Appeals of New York, 21 May 1907. The defendant, N. L. A. Eastman, was charged with obscenity for an anti-Catholic attack on the confessional box in his newspaper, *The Gospel Worker*. The Court of Appeals upheld the lower court decision freeing Eastman. While agreeing that the work was "improper, intemperate, unjustifiable, and highly reprehensible," it was not "indecent" as the word is employed in the penal code. A portion of the text of the offending article is reprinted, along with the text of the decision and a minority opinion.

Roberts, Clifford J. "Freedom of the Press and Fair Judicial Administration." *Texas Law Review*, 21:309–14, January 1943.   **R 168**
A discussion of the contempt of court case against the *Times-Mirror* of Los Angeles for publication of five editorials. The conviction involved an extension of the "due process" clause to include the regulation of the court's power to punish summarily. *Times-Mirror Co. v. Superior Court of the State of California*, 314 U.S. 252 (1941).

Roberts, Gene, Jr. *The Censors and the Schools.* Washington, D.C., National Education Association, Commission on Professional Rights and Responsibilities, 1963. 7 p. mimeo.   **R 169**
In an address before the NEA convention, Detroit, 4 July 1963, the coauthor (with Jack Nelson) of the study, *The Censors and the Schools*, reports on some of the activities of textbook censors in the United States during the past

five years. "Textbook censorship is far from dead. It is better organized, better financed than in any period in our history."

[Roberts, William]. *The Whole Proceedings on the Trial of an Action brought by Thomas Walker, Merchant, against William Roberts, Barrister at Law, for a Libel. Tried by a Special Jury at the Assizes at Lancaster, March 28, 1791 . . . Taken in shorthand by Joseph Gurney.* Manchester, Eng., Printed by Charles Wheeler, 1791. 208 p. **R 170**
For the issuing of handbills of an abusive nature against Walker, in the course of a personal feud, Roberts was convicted and fined £100.

Robertson, C. Grant, *ed. Select Statutes, Cases and Documents to Illustrate English Constitutional History, 1660–1832.* London, Methuen, 1904. 452 p. **R 171**
Includes the 1662 Licensing Act and reports on the censorship trials of Benjamin Harris, John Tutchin, and John Wilkes

Robins, Lee N. *Birth Control in Massachusetts; the Analysis of an Issue through an Intensive Survey of Opinion.* Cambridge, Mass., Radcliffe College, 1951. 242 p. (Unpublished Ph. D. dissertation) **R 172**

Robinson, Arthur R. *Freedom of Speech and of the Press; Speech in the Senate of the United States, January 18, 1934.* Washington, D.C., 1934. 4 p. (Reprinted from *Congressional Record*, 78(7): 862–65) **R 173**
The Senator from Indiana advises that the national emergency faced by the United States not be used as an excuse to restrict the freedom of speech and press. He offers a resolution (S. Res. 146) to investigate restrictions on freedom of speech placed by the Federal Radio Commission.

[Robinson, Henry]. *Liberty of Conscience. or the Sole means to obtaine Peace and Truth . . .* [London, 1643]. 62 p. (Reprinted in Haller, *Tracts on Liberty in the Puritan Revolution*, vol. 3, pp. 107–78) **R 174**
Robinson, a merchant-philosopher, issued his ideas on freedom of the press on 24 March 1644, eight months before Milton's more famous *Areopagitica.* He recommended freedom of speech and press as a logical extension of the laissez-faire economic doctrine. "No man can have a natural monopoly of truth." Religious opinion should be "fought out upon eaven ground, on equall termes, neither side must expect to have greater liberty of speech, writing, Printing . . . then the other." The pamphlet was published anonymously and without license or publisher's imprint.

Robinson, Howard. *Bayle the Sceptic.* New York, Columbia University Press, 1931. 334 p. **R 175**

Pierre Bayle, eighteenth-century sceptic, had frequent clashes with church authorities, especially over his *Historical and Critical Dictionary*, which was cited for its "obscenities."

Robinson, James H. "The Threatened Eclipse of Free Speech." *Atlantic Monthly*, 120:811–18, December 1917. **R 176**
Concerns restraints imposed upon free speech during war, what these are, why they develop, and the groups that create them. The restraints are transient, however, and conditions are favorable in the state of the world for the rapid extension of an unprecedented degree of toleration.

Robinson, Thomas P. *Radio Networks and the Federal Government.* New York, Columbia University Press, 1943. 278 p. **R 177**
A comprehensive study of the history of radio broadcasting in the United States and its regulation by government agencies. Chapter 7 deals with Radio Censorship and Free Speech.

Robinson, Victor, *ed. Encyclopaedia Sexualis.* New York, Dingwall-Rock, 1936. 819 p. **R 178**
Contains the following articles pertaining to freedom of expression in matters of sex: Annie Besant; History of Birth Control; Charles Bradlaugh; Catholic Church and Sex Problems; Censorship of Sex Instruction Books; Anthony Comstock; Havelock Ellis; Sex Problems in Icelandic Literature; Literature and Love (lengthy treatment by Samuel P. Putnam); Legal Aspects of Obscenity (Theodore A. Schroeder); and the World League for Sexual Reform.

———. *Pioneers of Birth Control in England and America.* New York, Voluntary Parenthood League, 1919. 107 p. **R 179**
A brief history of the birth control movement in conflict with efforts to suppress it, beginning with Malthus' *Essay on the Principles of Population* and the work of Francis Place, the father of the movement. References are made to publishing activities of Richard Carlile and Robert Dale Owen, the trial of Annie Besant and Charles Bradlaugh for the sale of Charles Knowlton's *Fruits of Philosophy*, Dr. Alice Drysdale and the Malthusian League, the trial of Edward Truelove, the trials of Moses Harman and Ezra Heywood, Drs. E. B. Foote, Jr. and Sr., of the Free Speech League, Mrs. Mary Ware Dennett, and Mrs. Margaret Sanger.

[Robinson, William J.]. "Forbidden Book." *Medical Critic and Guide*, 22:202–4, June 1919. **R 180**
Without naming the book, it reports on the suppression by postal authorities of Marie C. Stopes's *Married Love.*

———. "Most Atrocious Law; Extracts from Address Made at Carnegie Hall Meeting, March 1, 1916." *Mother Earth*, 11:457–60, April 1916. **R 181**

Protest by Dr. Robinson over arrest of Emma Goldman and others for distributing birth control information.

———. "An Open Letter to Anthony Comstock." *Critic and Guide*, 16:225–26, July 1913. **R 182**
Deals with postal censorship of information on birth control.

Robson, Norman. "The Official Secrets Act and the British Press." *Journalism Quarterly*, 15:253–58, September 1938. **R 183**
Comments on current British governmental activities to curb the press.

Robson, William A. "British Films are Pure." *Nation*, 131:547–48, 19 November 1930. **R 184**
Analyzes the 1929 report of the British Board of Film Censors as to rejected films and reasons for rejection. "It is obvious that the films will never develop into a true art so long as they are subjected to the cramping influence of the censor as it exists at present; for no art can flourish while it is pinioned to an elaborate code of social hypocrisy and unreal convention."

Rochat, Carl R. *Analysis of the Freedom of the Press Clauses in the American Constitutions.* Urbana, Ill., University of Illinois, 1948. 308 p. (Unpublished Master's thesis) **R 185**
Freedom of the press clauses in present and past state constitutions are analyzed as to wording and intent. The appendix contains the complete text of clauses and some debate relating to their passage.

Roche, John P. "Security and the Press." *Current History*, 29:229–35, October 1955. **R 186**
The author sets forth what he feels to be the functions of a free press in a democratic society and the proper scope and purpose of a security program, with some suggestions for relating the security program to the press. He feels it unwise and unnecessary "to establish any large-scale program of press supervision."

Rockwell, Dorothy. "Radio Censors Itself." *Nation*, 149:217–19, 26 August 1939. **R 187**
A discussion of the new self-regulatory code ratified by most radio station owners and managers at the suggestion and under the auspices of the National Association of Broadcasters. The code means "that the 400 strongest stations have so arranged matters that on the one hand the FCC can't complain that the industry is unable to police itself, and on the other the government,

like everyone else, must find a way to hurdle these rules if it wants more than its allotted time or to ban its opponents from the air."

Rodale, Robert. "Our Personal Fight for Freedom of the Press." *Prevention; the Magazine for Better Health*, 17(2):43–45, February 1965. **R 188**
The publisher of *Prevention* and of various books on health describes his fight against efforts of the Federal Trade Commission "to limit the advertising of ideas in health books only to those concepts which meet the approval of their medical advisors." Specifically, the FTC objected to advertising of a 946-page encyclopedia, *The Health Finder*, and two pamphlets. The publisher claims that the traditional right to freedom of the press embraces advertising of the ideas in books and that "a hostile government could stamp out almost any type of publication it was opposed to merely by acting against the advertising or distribution of that publication." Quoted is the minority opinion of one Commissioner who voted to dismiss the FTC complaints as "an unwarranted intrusion of the Commission into an area from which it is excluded by the Constitution and the statute."

Rodell, Fred. "TV or No TV in Court?" *New York Times Magazine*, 12 April 1964, pp. 16 +. **R 189**

Roden, Carl B. "The Library as a Censor of Books." *Illinois Libraries*, 4:167–70, October 1922. **R 190**
The librarian of the Chicago Public Library describes that library's policy on "objectionable books." Novels by reputable authors, published by respectable publishers, and that are considered of literary merit are selected without regard to their ethical content. Books of ill-fame, though of literary value, are secluded and are available only to the mature reader. The same treatment is given to books on sex hygiene.

Roderick, Colin. "Censorship in Australia." *New Zealand Libraries*, 22:8–10, January–February 1959. **R 191**
A summary of measures against obscene literature passed by the various states since 1953. Recommends federal jurisdiction.

Rodgers, E. C. "Tennessee Courts and the Freedom of the Press." *Public*, 22: 877–78, 16 August 1919. **R 192**
Imprisonment of Edward T. Leech, editor of the *Memphis Press*, on contempt of court for an editorial criticizing political and judicial corruption.

Roe, Gilbert E. "Free Speech and Free Press; . . . Discusses Need, in Time of War, of Obtaining Collective Judgment of the People on the Conduct of the War." *La Follette's Magazine*, 9:8–10, August 1917. **R 193**

Roe, Wellington. "Connecticut's Index Expurgatorius: The Catholic Boycott of Bookshops and Newstands Purveying *The Grapes of Wrath*, the *New Republic*, *Life* and all other 'Subversive' Literature." *New Masses*, 34:8–10, 13 Feburary 1940. **R 194**

Roebuck, John A. *Life and Letters of John A. Roebuck* . . . Edited by Robert Eadon Leader. London, Edward Arnold, 1897. 392 p. **R 195**
Roebuck was one of the leaders during the 1830's in opposing the English "tax on knowledge." He served as editor of a series of 36 *Pamphlets for the People* aimed at repeal of the stamp tax.

———, ed. *Pamphlets for the People*. London, Charles Ely, John Longley, 1835–36. 2 vols. (Nos. 1–36) **R 196**
Roebuck was a member of Parliament who was active in the fight to repeal the stamp duty on newspapers. Like William Carpenter's efforts a few years earlier, Roebuck circumvented payment of a newspaper tax on a series of weekly pamphlets he issued, by omitting dates and numbers that would identify them as a serial publication. The first pamphlet in the series, "On the Means of Conveying Information to the People," was published 11 June 1835; the final pamphlet in February 1836. A total of 36 was published. Various writers (H. S. Chapman, Francis Place, Thomas Falconer) contributed articles and various publishers were employed, the pamphlets supported various radical proposals and frequently attacked "taxes on knowledge" with Roebuck always serving as editor. Some of the individual articles, 16 to 20 pages in length, were apparently also issued separately by various publishers. Following are some of the titles dealing with the newspaper tax: On the Means of Conveying Information to the People, The Stamped Press of London and Its Morality, Persecution of the Unstamped Press, all by John A. Roebuck; Repeal of the Stamp Duties on Newspapers, and Taxes on Knowledge, by Francis Place; Crusade against the Unstamped, Victims of the Unstamped, The Newspaper Stamp Return, Conduct of the Authorities, Toward an Unstamped Press, and The Great Unstamped Acknowledged to be Invincible, by H. S. Chapman.

[———]. *A Short Account of the Political Martyrs of Scotland, Sufferers in the Cause of Parliamentary Reform, viz.: Thomas Muir, Thomas Fyshe Palmer, William Skirving, Joseph Gerrald and Maurice Margarot* . . . London, H. Hetherington, [1837]. 6 p.

(Extracted from Hetherington's *London Dispatch*) **R 197**
On 20 February 1837, a group of gentlemen assembled at the Crown and Anchor Tavern, London, to commemorate the anniversary of the "First Martyrs of Political Liberty in Scotland" during the "reign of terror" of 1793–94. This pamphlet was prepared for the occasion to give a summary of the lives and sacrifices of the five men. Muir and Palmer had both been sentenced to transportation for circulating seditious literature. The pamphlet was probably prepared by John A. Roebuck, but much of it was from the pen of William Tait, magazine editor and treasurer of a campaign to raise funds for a monument to the martyrs. The monument was erected in 1844 at Calton Hill, Scotland.

Roeburt, John. *The Wicked and the Banned*. New York, Macfadden Books, 1963. 159 p. **R 198**
A popularly written summary of censorship in America, covering books, motion pictures, television, and the theater, with emphasis on recent cases. Numerous references to specific incidents of film and television censorship, the self-regulation of the movies and the networks, and consideration of such censorship cases as *Ulysses*, *Tropic of Cancer*, *Lady Chatterley*, *Lolita*, and the trial of William V. Ward of the *Provincetown Review*.

Rogers, Bruce. "In Alaska." *Liberator*, 1:45–46, February 1919. **R 199**
An account of the author's conviction for publishing the statement: "To be an American patriot be willing to die in defense of the trade supremacy of the British Empire and her subjugation of India and Ireland."

Rogers, Cameron. "A Bookseller's Censorship." *World's Work*, 50:218–20, June 1925. **R 200**
Praise for the Boston system by which the booksellers quietly provide their own censorship. The system, according to Rogers, staves off the Watch and Ward, prevents police raids, protects the public, gives no unwelcome publicity to bad books, and brings fewer cases before the courts. When a book is brought to court the judge only need to ask the opinion of the Boston Bookseller's Committee and that is that.

Rogers, Edward S. "Copyright and Morals." *Michigan Law Review*, 18:390–404, March 1920. **R 201**
An immoral work is one which will not "promote the progress of science and useful arts" and, therefore, is not entitled to copyright protection. The author discusses some of the problems that the court faces in determining what is or is not immoral. In this area, the author remarks, one finds "some of the finest gems of judicial literature." He discusses cases and decisions under the headings of (1) works that offend public order, and (2) works that offend public decency.

Rogers, Harold D. "Canon 35: Cameras, Courts and Confusion." *Kentucky Law Journal*, 51:737–61, Summer 1963. **R 202**
With the reaffirmation by the American Bar Association in 1963 of Canon 35, which provides that press photography and radio or television broadcasts shall not be permitted in the courtroom, the writer reviews the problem as seen by the media, the legal profession, and the courts.

Rogers, Helen C. "Scripture and the Devil." *Library Journal*, 75:1782–87, 15 October 1950. **R 203**
"Censorship in its devious forms offers a challenge to the librarian."

Rogers, James L. *A Study of Prospective High School Teachers' Attitudes toward Daily Newspapers and Freedom of Information.* Columbia, Mo., University of Missouri, 1955. 173 p. (Ph. D. dissertation, University Microfilms, no. 10,129; summarized in *Journalism Quarterly*, Spring 1955) **R 204**
The author finds that "only half of a representative group of prospective high school teachers have attitudes favorable to newspapers, and their attitudes toward freedom of information show even less understanding and stability."

Rogers, Lindsay. "The Extension of Federal Control through the Regulation of the Mails." *Harvard Law Review*, 27:27–44, November 1913. **R 205**
The author criticizes as an indirect encroachment upon press freedom the newspaper publicity law, recently upheld by the U.S. Supreme Court. The law requires publication of officers, owners, stockholders, etc., of all publications entered as second-class mailing matter. It also requires the labeling of all advertisements that consist of editorial or reading matter.

———. "Federal Interference with Freedom of the Press." *Yale Law Journal*, 23:559–79, May 1914. **R 206**
"The decisions of the Supreme Court which have been quoted lead to no conclusion other than that any attempt on the part of Congress to place a previous restraint upon the press, or even to deny it postal facilities, for no discernible reason, would receive a judicial veto. The exclusion of obscene matter, lottery tickets, and other writings inimical to the public morals, has clearly been within the power of Congress, and legislation forbidding seditious and anarchistic publications or banning them from the mails, would be constitutional."

———. "Freedom of the Press in the United States." *Contemporary Review*, 114:177–83, August 1918. (Reprinted in *Living Age*, 28 September 1918) **R 207**

"In the United States the [wartime] restrictions thus far imposed do not abridge the constitutional guaranty, nor do they give much cause for objection to those who argue that discussion of the war should be allowed great latitude. The danger lies in the enforcement of the regulations through the post office and the possible denial of mail privileges without a judicial review."

———. *The Postal Power of Congress; a Study in Constitutional Expansion.* Baltimore, Johns Hopkins Press, 1916. 189 p. (Johns Hopkins University Studies in Historical and Political Science, series 34, no. 2) **R 208**
Chapter 4 on Limitations on the Postal Powers deals with constitutional restrictions against unreasonable searches and seizures and against infringing the freedom of the press; chapter 5 deals with the Power of the States to Interfere with the Mails; and chapter 6 deals with The Extension of Federal Control through Exclusion from the Mails. A scholarly work with numerous citations to court decisions.

Rogers, Virgil M. "Don't Let Censors Take You Unaware." *Library Journal*, 80:2879–81, 15 December 1955. **R 209**
A schoolman's advice to school and children's librarians on aims and objectives and proper handling of controversial materials and effective lines of communications with children, parents, and teachers.

———. "The Responsibility of Choice: The Administrator's Problem." In *Freedom of Book Selection; Proceedings of the Second Conference on Intellectual Freedom. . . .* Chicago, American Library Association, 1954, pp. 58–66. **R 210**

———. "Textbooks under Fire." *Atlantic*, 195:42–48, February 1955. **R 211**
The dean of the School of Education, Syracuse University, after more than 30 years of service in public schools, evaluates the attacks on textbooks thought to be "subversive." He shows that today the task of educators has become that of "educating our children for the making of choices which to be intelligent have to be based upon carefully wrought definitions." Good textbooks help in the task of educating the young to make intelligent choices.

———. "Toward Intellectual Freedom." *ALA Bulletin*, 51:243–47, April 1957. **R 212**
An educator praises the Library Bill of Rights and other documents that defend intellectual freedom.

Rogers, William P. "The Right to Know Government Business, from the Viewpoint of the Government Official." *Marquette Law Review*, 40:83–91, Summer 1956. **R 213**

At the time of writing the author was Deputy Attorney-General of the United States.

Rogge, B. A. "Complexity in Hades." *Teachers College Record*, 65:654–57, May 1964. **R 214**
The dean of Wabash College comments on issues and implications in the case of the social studies teacher in Paradise, Calif., threatened with loss of her job for exposing students to a variety of points of view on public issues.

Rogge, O. John. "Congress Shall Make No Law . . ." *Michigan Law Review*, 56:331–74, January 1958; 56:579–618, February 1958. **R 215**
Recent cases before the U.S. Supreme Court "call for a re-examination of the circumstances leading to the adoption of the federal bill of rights, the framers' intent in drafting the First Amendment, its subsequent construction, particularly the development and application of Justice Holmes' clear and present danger test, which he enunciated in *Schenck v. United States*, and the respective areas of federal and state power."

———. *The First and the Fifth. With Some Excursions Into Others.* New York, Nelson, 1960. 358 p. (Brief treatment in *New York Law Review*, May 1959) **R 216**
A discussion of two American rights which secure to the individual freedom from the state's intrusion—freedom of utterance, guaranteed by the First Amendment and freedom of silence, protected by the Fifth Amendment. A chapter is devoted to Justice Holmes's clear and present danger test; and a chapter to sedition and obscenity. Well-documented with citation to court decisions. The author was formerly Assistant Attorney General of the United States.

Rogin, Lawrence. "Postoffice Censorship Again." *Nation*, 132:379–80, 8 April 1931. **R 217**
The author criticizes the action of the Post Office in refusing second-class mailing privileges to such Communist periodicals as, *Revolutionary Age, Young Worker,* and *Young Pioneer.* "Political censorship of any sort in a democracy is an anomaly. To vest the power of such censorship in an official whose decisions, for all practical purposes, are final, is to introduce autocracy in an extreme form."

Romberg, Martin. *Der Lügenfeldzug gegen Deutschland.* Schwerin i. Mecklb., F. Bahn, 1915. 22 p. **R 218**
British censorship in World War I.

[Romeo, Francesco]. *Letters, to the Marquis of Hastings, on The Indian Press; with an Appeal to Reason and the British Parliament, on the Liberty of the Press in General. By a Friend to Good Government.* London, J. M. Richardson, 1824. 120p.　　**R 219**

Twenty-one letters cite arguments for a free press: the best protection against revolution; conversely suppression encourages revolt; the best protector against foreign intrigue; possible abuses and lack of sufficient education of natives are not sufficient reasons for proscribing the press; English libel laws offer sufficient protection and obviate prior censorship; a free press in India would secure the government from contempt and enable Indians to express their grievances; a free press is compatible with views of British Parliament; censorship of the Indian press is injurious to interests of the East India Company; censorship in India gives an advantage to the rivals of England.

[Romilly, *Sir Samuel*]. *A Fragment on the Constitutional Power and Duty of Juries upon Trials for Libels.* London, 1785. 16p.　　**R 220**

Expresses the libertarian point of view of Thomas Erskine.

"Romish Plot against Heretic Press Uncovered; No Less Than Nineteen Roman Catholic Editors in Various Parts of the Country Helped to Spring the Trap on Unwary Heretics in Detroit." *Menace*, 376:1, 13 July 1918.　　**R 221**

Part of an anti-Catholic crusade of the editor, B. O. Flower.

Roney, Joseph A. "NAB Code and Father Coughlin." *Commonweal*, 31:114–16, 24 November 1939.　　**R 222**

Defends the NAB Code against charges that it was written to exclude Father Coughlin from the air. The section prohibiting the airing of controversial issues on sponsored commercial programs (in favor of free time in the public interest) grew out of criticism of talks by W. J. Cameron of Ford Motors. Radio frequencies, unlike newspapers, the author maintains, are public property and subject to control in the interest of the public.

Rooney, E. M. "Morality and the Selection of Books for the High School Library." *Catholic Library World*, 28:394–400, May 1957.　　**R 223**

Roosevelt, Franklin D. ["A Letter to the American Society of Newspaper Editors on Free Speech and a Free Press. April 16, 1941"]. In his *Public Papers and Addresses, 1941 Volume.* New York, Macmillan, 1950, pp. 120–21.　　**R 224**

"Free speech and a free press are still in the possession of the people of the United States."

———.["On Newspapers and Editors—A Letter of Congratulations to the St. Louis *Post-Dispatch*. November 2, 1938."] In his *Public Papers and Addresses, 1938 Volume.* New York, Macmillan, 1941, pp. 577–83.　　**R 225**

In this tribute to the *Post-Dispatch* and its editors, President Roosevelt observes: "I have always been firmly persuaded that our newspapers cannot be edited in the interests of the general public from the counting room." And later, that "freedom of news" rather than "freedom of the press" should be the chief concern.

———. [The President Issues a Statement and Establishes the Office of Censorship. Executive Order No. 8985, December 19, 1941.] In his *Public Papers and Addresses, 1941 Volume.* New York, Macmillan, 1950, pp. 574–79.　　**R 226**

"All Americans abhor censorship, just as they abhor war. But the experience of this and of all other Nations has demonstrated that some degree of censorship is essential in wartime, and we are at war." The Executive Order and related documents follow.

Roosevelt, Theodore. "A Disagreeable Duty." *Outlook*, 104:316–18, 14 June 1913.　　**R 227**

Statement by the former President giving his reasons for bringing the libel suit against George A. Newett at Marquette, Mich., and expressing gratitude to those testifying in his behalf.

———. "Lincoln and Free Speech." In his *Works.* New York, Scribner's, 1926. vol. 19, pp. 289–300. (From *The Great Adventure*, 1918)　　**R 228**

Comments on the wartime activities of the Wilson administration in light of the policies of the Lincoln administration during the Civil War.

[———, *plaintiff*]. *Roosevelt v. [George A.] Newett. A Transcript of the Testimony taken and Depositions read at Marquette, Mich.* n. p., Privately printed, [W. Emlen Roosevelt], 1914. 362p.　　**R 229**

Libel action against the publisher of *Ishpemeng Iron Ore* for $10,000 for a statement made during the Presidential campaign that Theodore Roosevelt was frequently drunk. The defendant conceded the mistake in fact and claimed lack of malice. Roosevelt asked that no damages be assessed; the judge directed a verdict of guilty with nominal damages of 6 cents. The judge gives an extended charge to the court, differentiating between the right of a newspaper to discuss freely the fitness of a person for public office, including opinions and inferences from honest belief, and the use against a candidate of "words which are both defamatory and untrue."

"Roosevelt and the Slanderers." *Review of Reviews*, 48:16–18, July 1913.　　**R 230**

A series of editorials concerning the attempt to besmirch the personal reputation of Theodore Roosevelt, the libel suit against the Michigan editor printing the charges, the trial and testimony for Roosevelt, and the complete vindication of the former President.

"Roosevelt's Law of Libel." *Nation*, 90:104–5, 3 February 1910.　　**R 231**

Editorial commenting on the attempt by President Theodore Roosevelt to revive the doctrine that the government of the United States can be libeled. A government suit was brought against the New York *World* and the Indianapolis *News*, but Federal Judge Hough decided "that the President's law was unsound, and that the principle which he sought to establish had in it 'consequences of a very serious character.'"

Root, David. *Liberty of Speech and of the Press. A Thanksgiving Sermon Delivered November 26, 1835 to the Congregational Church & Society in Dover, N. H.* Dover, N. H., Printed at the Inquirer Office, 1835. 16p.　　**R 232**

A Congregational minister traces to the scriptures the doctrine of free speech and press as expressed in the federal constitution and the constitutions of the several states. It is a right granted by the Creator which no human authority can lawfully deny. "We ought to obey God rather than man" (Acts V:29). Rev. Root eloquently denounces the mob violence that was then preventing free discussion of the evils of slavery.

Root, E. Merrill. *Brainwashing in the High School.* New York, Devin-Adair, 1958. 277p. (Issued in a paperback edition by the Church League of America, 1962)　　**R 233**

The author analyzes 11 American history textbooks used in high schools, charging a bias in favor of "liberal" historians and collectivist apologists and an avoidance of references to revisionist historians and radical conservatives. The effect, the author charges, is to indoctrinate high school students with subversive ideas and to keep from them a proper appreciation of patriotic nationalism, the private ownership of property, and the idealogy of economic individualism. He urges a thorough housecleaning of the tainted sources and that parents and teachers demand new textbooks.

———. "The Proposed Program of Our Academic Hucksters." *American Legion Magazine*, 53(6):18–19, 56–58, December 1952.　　**R 234**

"How left-wing super-salesmen operating under the slogan of 'academic freedom' exploit youth's desire to fight for the underdog and build a better world." An attack on the alleged collectivism in American schools.

Root, Robert. "The Freedom and Responsibility of the Press." *American Editor*, 2(4):5–15, 56–59, January 1958. **R 235**
To "temper the excesses of the irresponsible press and to facilitate the efforts of the responsible press," the author considers the formation of a press commission along the lines of the British Royal Commission. He also explores cooperative ownership of newspapers, the creation of tax-supported state and local papers, and a press sponsored by a university or foundation.

Roote, Betty. *FCC Network and Programing*. Columbia, Mo., Freedom of Information Center, School of Journalism, University of Missouri, 1965. 6 p. (Publication no. 147) **R 236**
This paper traces the background of FCC involvement in network programming and examines the current controversy over proposals that the FCC limit network ownership of prime-time shows.

———. *Federal Records Law Debate*, II. Columbia, Mo., Freedom of Information Center, School of Journalism, University of Missouri, 1966. 4 p. (Publication no. 157) **R 237**
This paper follows the progress of S. 1666 and subsequent public records bills during 1964 and 1965. This continues a history of legislation that was presented in Center Publication no. 117, entered under the title, *Federal Records Law Debate*.

———. *State Regulation of Obscenity*. Columbia, Mo., Freedom of Information Center, School of Journalism, University of Missouri, 1966. 3 p. (Publication no. 155) **R 238**
"Virtually every Supreme Court decision on obscenity forces a change in obscenity laws and enforcement on the state and local levels. The condition of the 'war on obscenity'—as it affects print media—on the state and municipal levels is reviewed in this paper."

Rorty, James. "The Attack on Our Libraries." *Commentary*, 19:541–49, June 1955. (Reprinted in Downs, *The First Freedom*, pp. 303–10) **R 239**
"Sketches the ordeal of the libraries: the nature and direction of the attacks, and the way that many communities—though, alas, far from all—were able to fight off the incursions." Includes censorship cases that took place in the 1950's in the Bartlesville (Okla.) Public Library, the Boston Public Library, Galion (Ohio) public school, Mt. Lebanon (Pa.) Public Library, and the San Antonio Public Library. The San Antonio Minute Women conducted a crusade against alleged Communist books which later spread to San Francisco and other communities.

———. "The Embattled Textbook Publishers." *Jewish Frontier*, 23(6):18–22, June 1956. **R 240**
Attempts by individuals and organizations to censor public school textbooks. "During the postwar decade the public schools have been almost continuously under fire from the right, and in these attacks, the attempts of conservative and patriotic pressure groups to make 'progressive education' synonymous with subversion have been frequently coupled with the political censorship of school textbooks." While the campaigns of Allen A. Zoll and other "sadists of freedom" (term coined by Luther Evans) have been ineffectual and there have been few firings and no burnings, the campaigns and pressures have contributed to appeasement and timidity. Zoll's National Council for American Education and Mrs. Crain's organization, sponsored by the Conference of Small Business Organizations, provided much of the ammunition.

———. "The Harassed Pocket-Book Publishers." *Antioch Review*, 15:411–27, Winter 1955–56. **R 241**
Account of private and public censorship drives on the production and distribution of paperback books, with special attention to censorship activities by the National Office for Decent Literature.

———. "It Ain't No Sin!" *Nation*, 139:124–27, 1 August 1934. **R 242**
Discussion of current movie censorship, with particular reference to the Legion of Decency, the Motion Picture Research Council, and their activities. The author feels that movie magnates have a "thoroughly deserved headache." In making poor films and films exploiting sex and social and moral values, instead of honest films dealing with honest values, the industry has created a situation ripe for censorship.

———. "The Libraries in a Time of Tension." *Commentary*, 20:30–37, July 1955. **R 243**
The author considers the demands made upon libraries in time of international tension, particularly the demand of many patriotic societies for a more rigid control and identification of library books on anything to do with the Communist problem.

———. *Order On the Air!* New York, John Day, 1934. 32 p. (John Day pamphlets no. 44) (Excerpted in Summers, *Radio Censorship*, pp. 43–50) **R 244**
The author "analyzes radio's sins of commission and omission, and describes the several kinds of conflicting censorships by which radio is shackled and minority pressure groups are kept off the air. He calls for order—or at least orderly conflict—on the air and joins with the American Civil Liberties Union in urging as a basis for legislation, an investigation and recommendations by a non-political commission appointed by the President." The ACLU report, *Radio Censorship*, embodies some of the material presented by Rorty.

[Rose, Alfred, comp.]. *Registrum Librorum Eroticorum. Vel (sub hac specie) Dubiorum: Opus Bibliographicum et Praecipue Bibliothecariis Destinatum . . .* Compiled by Rolf S. Reade (*pseud.*) London, Privately Printed, 1936. 2 vols. (Original edition limited to 200 copies; reprinted by Jack Brussel, New York, 1965) **R 245**
While this work is an alphabetical list of erotica rather than of books that have been banned, the preface (pp. vii–xi) relates the list to the censorship of the works included.

Rose, Cornelia B. *National Policy for Radio Broadcasting; a Report of a Committee of the National Economic and Social Planning Association*. New York, Harper, 1940. 289 p. **R 246**
The report recommends that the government define the relationship of member stations with the network system and formulate positive standards and objectives for assuring the public interest. Content control, however, should be left to the broadcasters.

Rose, John. "The Unstamped Press, 1815–1836." *English Historical Review*, 12:711–26, October 1897. **R 247**
A study of the illegal newspapers and periodical pamphlets published in England during the years 1815–1836. These "unstamped" papers reveal the struggle of the press for freedom as well as the many reform movements of the period that were supported by the radical press.

Rose, Kenneth. "The Growth of Freedom in the Reporting of Parliamentary Debates." *Gazette; International Journal of the Science of the Press*, 2:223–32, 1957. **R 248**
A review of the battle in the history of journalism for freedom to report the proceedings in Parliament which began in the seventeenth century and is not yet completely won. "The right to publish Parliamentary reports remains a privilege which at any moment in theory, if not in practice, may be withdrawn from the Press."

Rose, Oscar, ed. *Radio Broadcasting and Television: An Annotated Bibliography*. New York, Wilson, 1947. 120 p. **R 249**
Contains a section on Systems and Legislation, Censorship, and Related Media.

Rosenberg, Albert. "A New Move for the Censorship of Owen Swiney's *The Quacks*." *Notes & Queries*, 5 (n.s.):393–96, September 1958. **R 250**
The real reason why this 1705 farce was censored and the opening performance postponed was the attacks the play made on the

Kit-Cat Club and Jacob Tonson. "There is good reason to believe that some offensive passages were removed from the play before it was allowed to be performed."

Rosenberg, James N. *Censorship in the United States. An Address before the Association of the Bar of the City of New York on March 15th, 1928.* New York, Court Press, 1928. 28 p. (Reprinted in *Law Notes*, June and July 1928)　　**R 251**
A review of recent developments in censorship of stage, movies, and books in the United States, with some reference to historical background. Rosenberg believes that "the narrow limits which the courts have laid on themselves to set aside acts of police power or of quasi-judicial or administrative boards almost nullify the practical value of such a review." He decries the increased pressures and support for censorship that have swept the nation and the feeble attempts of leaders to stand up against this dangerous and powerful adversary.

————. *Group Defamation and Freedom of Speech.* New York, National Conference of Jews and Christians, 1937. 12 p.　**R 252**
How shall this country meet the menace of group defamation? By speech or suppression? The author rejects the use of suppression and gag laws. Liberals should not leave the arena to the demagogues, but should actively fight for the truth. The greatest menace of free speech is inertia. "Let there be more, not less, of speech." An address delivered at the Williamstown Institute of Human Relations, Williams College, 1 September 1937.

————. "Padlocking the Talkies." *Nation*, 127:601–2, 5 December 1928.　**R 253**
The censor's power to muzzle the silent movie has been established by statute and court decision. Pennsylvania has already asserted the power to throttle speech in the talking movie. What has become of our constitutional safeguard of freedom of speech?

Rosenberg, Marvin. "The 'Refinement' of *Othello* in the Eighteenth Century British Theatre." *Studies in Philology*, 51: 75–94, January 1954.　**R 254**
"*Othello* more than any of the other major Shakespearean tragedies builds on thoughts and words and incidents involving the sexual act. In the eighteenth century, British culture became increasingly sensitive to public allusions to sex. The theatres, patronized now largely by middle class audiences, began to eliminate from the play language and action that was erotic, 'indelicate,' or in 'bad taste.' Thus began a pattern of social censorship that culminated in the late Victorian period, when nearly every reference in the play to physical love, however indirect, was driven from the stage, and only the barest hints remained of the playwright's carefully integrated pro-jection of sexual imagery motivating Othello's jealousy."

————. "Reputation Oft Lost Without Deserving." *Shakespeare Quarterly*, 9:499–506, Autumn 1958.　**R 255**
Bowdler, who refined Shakespeare's plays "to protect the purity of British womanhood from contamination by indecent language," kept the basic structure of the play untouched, but changed only offending words and lines.

Rosenburg, Bernard. "Censorship of Books." *Truth Seeker*, 44:615–16, 29 September 1917.　**R 256**

Rosenfield, John. "Vigilantes Riding." *Southwest Review*, 41:vi, 198–203, Spring 1956.　**R 257**
A historical sketch of vigilantism in America and its recent application to the arts in the form of censorship and boycott of movies and art exhibits on the basis of immorality and subversion.

Rosenthal, Elias. *Theodore Dreiser's "Genius" Banned.* n. p., 1917. 8 p.　**R 258**
Suppression of *The Genius* in New York in 1916 by threat of prosecution under the obscenity laws. The New York vice society objected to the work because certain female delinquents did not suffer ill consequences from their sin.

Rosenthal, Eric. *Apology Refused.* London, Bailey & Swinfen, 1958. 187 p.　**R 259**
Report of a South African libel case.

Rosenthal, Irving. "Editorial: The Complete Contents of the Suppressed Winter 1959 *Chicago Review*." *Big Table*, 1:3–6, Spring 1959.　**R 260**

Ross, Albert. "What Is Immoral in Literature?" *Arena*, 3:438–45, March 1891. (Reprinted in *Freethought*, 21 March 1891)　**R 261**
We do not care so much that vice exists as that it is well-dressed. The nude in literature is on trial. It is almost as sinful to write about sexual sin as to commit it. The professional conservators of morality in print who experience difficulties in drawing the line between the moral and immoral "have never hit upon the excellent plan of letting everybody make the decision for himself."

Ross, Edward A. "Freedom of Communication and the Struggle for Right." In his *Social Trends*, New York, Century, 1922, pp. 195–213. (Extracted in *Survey*, 9 January 1915)　**R 262**
The president of the American Sociological Society denounces the shocking denial of freedom of communications to organized labor and others who are appealing for the redress of social wrongs. "The tactics for controlling subversive ideas is not the application of the gag but the redress of real grievances." For organized society to allow the weapon of a free press to be wrenched from the hands of the laboring class in their struggle against oppression constitutes "connivance in one of the greatest iniquities that could be committed."

————. "The Suppression of Important News." *Atlantic Monthly*, 105:303–11, March 1910. (Also as a chapter in his *Changing America*, New York, Century, 1912)　**R 263**
A sociologist discusses the owner-advertiser censorship that he believes is the "damning count against the daily newspaper" in America. He proposes the creation of endowed newspapers that will have freedom to publish news that might be suppressed by commercial papers.

Ross, Irwin. "Trial by Newspaper." *Atlantic Monthly*, 216(3):63–68, September, 1965.　**R 264**
A former newspaperman considers the serious flaw in American justice whereby an accused is tried, convicted, and damned by newspapers before he has had his day in court. He considers various proposals, including the British system, for providing a fair trial and yet permitting reasonable press coverage. "The only approach that has a chance to work is one that would stop the flow of prejudiced material at its source: the police department and the prosecutor's office." The defense counsel should be under the same restraints.

Ross, Sherwood. "Violence on the Air." *Progressive*, 25(11):28–31, November 1961.　**R 265**
Industry's self-regulation of broadcasting has not succeeded in freeing the air of violence. Calls for government establishment and enforcement of program standards.

Ross, Virginia. "The Growing Menace." *California Librarian*, 21:37–38, 73, January 1960.　**R 266**
The librarian of the San Mateo County Free Library believes that "the present California law is adequate to deal with the problem [of obscenity]" and that violations "should be handled through proper legal channels, not by volunteer citizen action." She questions two premises in the matter of concern over "girlie" magazines—(1) that youths are the major purchasers, and (2) that reading these magazines is a causative factor in delinquency.

Rosten, Leo. "Is Fear Destroying Our Freedom?" *Look*, 18:21–25, 7 September 1954.　**R 267**
A record of cases growing out of hysteria over communism which threatens the freedom of ideas.

Rostenberg, Leona. *Literary, Political, Scientific, Religious & Legal Publishing,*

Printing & Bookselling in England, 1551–1700 : Twelve Studies. New York, Burt Franklin, 1965. 2 vols. (Portions of the work appeared earlier in *The Papers of the Bibliographical Society of America*) **R 268**

A study of 12 members of the Stationers' Company, publishers, printers, and booksellers in seventeenth-century England. "This book embraces a study of their publications, their careers, the milieu in which they lived and worked, their influence upon the period and the period's influence upon them. Often suffering personal indignity, persecution and financial ruin, they nevertheless pursued the specific cause they espoused and abetted." Among these are: Nathaniel Butter, whose newsbooks were "supprest and inhibited" by the Star Chamber and who, in 1643, was held prisoner in the Fleet for his seditious works; William Dugard, schoolmaster and printer, imprisoned during the Commonwealth; the Puritan publisher Michael Sparke, who suffered at the pillory along with William Prynne; Livewell Chapman, publisher to the Fifth Monarchy (a radical religious society), who was imprisoned during the Restoration; Nathaniel Thompson, Tory-Catholic publisher, whose "popish" books brought him more than 6 jail sentences; the licenser of printing, Roger L'Estrange and his "messenger" Robert Stephens ("Robin Hog"); and Richard and Anne Baldwin, Whig pamphleteers and champions of English press freedom. Facsimiles of title pages reproduced include the following associated with press freedom: William Prynne's suppressed *Histrio-Mastix* (p. 177); *An Account of the Proceedings against Nat. Thompson, Mr. Farwell, & Mr. Paine* (p. 337); Roger L'Estrange's *Considerations and Proposals in Order to the Regulation of the Press* (p. 344); and Elizabeth Cellier's *Malice Defeated* (p. 357).

Roth, Edwin. "Britain's Libel Laws Keep Profumo Case Under Cover." *Editor and Publisher*, 96(24):11, 68, 15 June 1963. **R 269**

"A story of immense political significance, which could overthrow the government . . . was not printed in Britain for almost half of a year [until War Minister John Profumo had resigned] during which almost every newspaperman in Fleet Street knew it." The reason was the British libel law under which "even an absolute truth can be legally libelous if it exposes anyone to hatred, ridicule or contempt."

Roth, H. O. "America Shows the Way; Dealing with the Political Censor." *New Zealand Libraries*, 12:35–39, March 1949. **R 270**

A report on the wave of political censorship in America—censorship action of such groups as the House Un-American Activities Committee, the American Legion, and the DAR. References also to efforts of the American Library Association to counteract censorship.

Roth, Samuel. "Advertisement." In the *Education of a French Model; Kiki's Memoirs*,

New York, Boars Head, 1950, pp. 5–8. **R 271**

In his preface to these memoirs, Roth discusses his own experience with the censor—Anthony Comstock and the Post Office Department. Roth was later involved in an obscenity case before the U.S. Supreme Court, which upheld his conviction.

Rothenberg, Ignaz. *The Newspaper: a Study in the Workings of the Daily Press and Its Laws*. London, Staples, 1946. 351 p. **R 272**

A comparative study of newspaper laws in various countries. The introduction deals with liberty of the press; other sections deal with anonymity, libel and the right of reply, blasphemy and obscenity, reporting of court and parliamentary proceedings, and legal restrictions on advertising.

———. "The Peeping Camera." *Nieman Reports*, 14(4):31–33, October 1960. **R 273**

An attorney describes incidents of reckless violation of privacy by news photographers.

———. "The Right of Reply to Libels in the Press." *Journal of Comparative Legislation and International Law*, 23(3d ser.): 38–59, 1941. **R 274**

The press laws of most countries give the right of an immediate reply to be published in the paper. "Among the countries without special regulations concerning a right of reply Great Britain and the U.S.A. are the most outstanding."

Rothman, Bernard, and Norman Harris. "Control of the Movies by Criminal Law." *Commercial Law Journal*, 61:360–63, December 1956. **R 275**

The article suggests two bases which can be used for controlling movies without violation of the freedom of the medium as defined by the U.S. Supreme Court. One statute would protect the unwary from offense by requiring some form of notice of the nature of the movie; the other involves the right of a person to direct the education of his children, requiring the parents' consent before permitting them to see immoral movies.

Rothrock, Mary V. "Censorship of Fiction in the Public Library." *Library Journal*, 48:454–56, 15 May 1923. **R 276**

An appeal for open-mindeness in selection of fiction dealing with controversial subjects.

Rothschild, John. "Brass Checks and Michigan." *New Republic*, 34:43–45, 7 March 1923. **R 277**

Implications of the censorship of the *Michigan Daily* by the Board of Control of Student Publication at University of Michigan.

Rotnem, V. W., and F. G. Folsom, Jr. "Recent Restrictions upon Religious

Liberty." *American Political Science Review*, 36:1053–68, December 1942. **R 278**

Includes reference to municipal ordinances against circulation of literature by Jehovah's Witnesses.

Roughead, William. "An Advocate of Reform; or, Sedition and Botany Bay." *Juridical Review*, 50:231–56, 1938. **R 279**

An account of the trial, conviction, and transportation to Botany Bay of Thomas Muir, advocate of reform and freedom of the press in Scotland during the period of the French Revolution. Accompanying portrait of Muir (etching) by John Kay.

Rourke, Francis E. "Administrative Secrecy: A Congressional Dilemma." *American Political Science Review*, 54:684–94, September 1960. **R 280**

Study of administrative secrecy and the cross-pressures complicating "the task of finding a balance between secrecy and publicity in administrative operations . . . At the root of the congressional dilemma over administrative secrecy is the fundamental difficulty of reconciling the divergent claims of publicity and privacy in the operations of democratic government."

———. *Secrecy and Publicity*. Baltimore, Johns Hopkins Press, 1961. 236 p. (Excerpted in *Saturday Review*, 13 May 1961) **R 281**

Secrecy in government (the suppression of information critical of government officials and policies and the restrictions on access to public records) is examined alongside a parallel issue of expanding government public relations activities and the use of mass persuasion. Both secrecy and publicity are considered in terms of their simultaneous impact upon national security and individual freedom.

———. "Secrecy in American Bureaucracy." *Political Science Quarterly*, 72: 540–64, December 1957. **R 282**

American political tradition holds that administrative secrecy should be "held within the narrowest limits consistent with the safety of such state secrets as must of absolute necessity be concealed from unfriendly foreign eyes." The author considers the role of secrecy, beginning with Max Weber's classic analysis of secrecy as an inherent characteristic of administrative institutions. He examines the American tradition of publicity, the recent growth of pressures for administrative secrecy, the legal basis for executive secrecy, and decisions of the courts relating to the withholding of information by government agencies.

Routledge, James. *Chapters in the History of Popular Progress, Chiefly in Relation to the Freedom of the Press and Trial by Jury.*

1660–1820. With an Application to Later Years. London, Macmillan, 1876. 631 p. **R 283**

A sympathetic account of the struggle for freedom of the press in England, with emphasis on the contributions made by eighteenth- and early nineteenth-century liberals and radicals, such men as Thomas Erskine, John Wilkes, Thomas Wooler, William Hone, Richard Carlile, John Horne Tooke, Junius, William Cobbett, and the Scottish and English Jacobins. Gives a detailed treatment of the prosecution of William Hone.

Rovere, Richard H. "Letter from Washington." *New Yorker*, 39:163–69, 30 March 1963. **R 284**

Comments on news management in Washington, an old practice, not limited to the executive branch but extending to Congress.

Row, C. A. "Mr. Foote and the Blasphemy Laws." *Spectator*, 56:1121–22, 1 September 1883. **R 285**

Deals with the conviction of George W. Foote. Canon Row states, "I do not contend that Christianity should be protected by the civil power, but I urge that it is unendurable that its numerous professors in this country should be insulted by parodies of Him whom they consider to be the Holy One of God . . . being publicly exhibited in the streets; and that the civil power is bound to prevent it, in its capacity of conservator of the peace."

[Rowan, Archibald H.]. *A Full Report of the Trial at Bar, in the Court of King's Bench, in which the Right Hon. Arthur Wolfe, His Majesty's Attorney General, prosecuted, and A. H. Rowan, Esq. was defendant. On an Information filed ex officio against the Defendant, for having published A Seditious Libel. January 29, 1794.* Dublin, W. McKenzie, 1794. 116 p. **R 286**

[————]. *Report of the Trial of Archibald Hamilton Rowan, Esq. on an Information filed, ex officio, by The Attorney General for the Distribution of a Libel; with the Subsequent Proceedings thereon, containing the Arguments of Council, the Opinion of the Court, and Mr. Rowan's Address to the Court, at Full.* Dublin, Printed for Archibald H. Rowan and sold by P. Byrne, 1794. 152 p. (Also in MacNevin, *Leading State Trials in Ireland*, pp. 482–598) **R 287**

Rowan was brought to trial for seditious libel along with Dr. Drennan and the proprietors of the Belfast *Northern Star*, for publication of the *Address to the Volunteers* by the Dublin United Irishmen. Dr. Drennan had written the address, Rowan had signed it as secretary,

and the *Northern Star* had published it 5 December 1792.

Rowell, Chester H. "The Freedom of the Press." *Annals of the American Academy of Political and Social Science*, 185:182–89, May 1936. **R 288**

The editor of the *San Francisco Chronicle* describes indirect restrictions on press freedom by subscribers, advertisers, and business practices.

Rowell, John A. "Black Rabbits, Red Herrings, and *Lorna Doone*." *Pennsylvania Library Association Bulletin*, 18:9–12, May 1963. **R 289**

How to meet the pressures for censorship in the school library.

Rowse, Arthur E. "The Great Smokescreen." *Fact*, 1(2):3–9, March–April 1964. **R 290**

"An editor of the Washington *Post* tells how fear of reprisal of tobacco advertisers kept newspapers from publicizing the link between smoking and cancer for 25 years."

Roy, P. G. "L'Emprisonnement d'Etienne Parent en 1838–39." *Bulletin des Recherches Historiques*, 43:216–17, July 1937. **R 291**

Account of the imprisonment of Etienne Parent and Jean-Baptiste Fréchette, publishers of *Canadien*.

Rubenstein, Bernard J. "Obscenity." *Brooklyn Law Review*, 24:49–69, December 1957. **R 292**

"It is about time our courts realize judicial breadth of vision is needed to help stop the moral corrosion that is eating away at our national greatness." The author accuses the judiciary with giving obscenity and subversive matters "more than fair trials" and the U.S. Supreme Court with giving them "undue preference on review and in lengthy treatment."

Rude, George. *Wilkes and Liberty. A Social Study of 1763 to 1774.* Oxford, Clarendon, 1962. 240 p. (Oxford Paperbacks, no. 91) **R 293**

Rugg, Harold O. "A Study in Censorship Good Concepts and Bad Words." *Social Education*, 5:176–81, March 1941. (Reprinted in Downs, *The First Freedom*, pp. 344–49) **R 294**

The author of widely used social science textbooks that have frequently been attacked as "un-American," discusses concepts about America that can be mentioned in school textbooks with impunity and those that bring wide-spread protest from "the patrioteers." Rugg names those who are spearheading the the attack on school textbooks.

————. *That Men May Understand; an American in the Long Armistice.* New York, Doubleday, Doran, 1941. 355 p. **R 295**

An American educator and author of numerous textbooks for secondary schools, discusses the banning and burning of his books on social science. The Englewood school case is discussed in Chapter 2.

Rundell, Hugh A. *The American Radio and Freedom of Speech.* Madison, University of Wisconsin, 1947. 57 p. (Unpublished Master's thesis) **R 296**

Ruppenthal, J. C. "Criminal Statutes on Birth Control." *Journal of the American Institute of Criminal Law and Criminology*, 10:48–61, May 1919. **R 297**

A digest of state and national laws against the dissemination of information on birth control.

Rush, Richard H. *The Regulation of Network Broadcasting.* Cambridge, Mass., Harvard University, 1950. 367 p. (Unpublished Ph. D. dissertation) **R 298**

Rushworth, John, ed. *Historical Collections of Private Passages of State, Weighty Matters in Law, Remarkable Proceedings . . . Beginning the Sixteenth Year of King James, Anno. 1618 and Ending . . . 1648. Digested in Order of Time . . .* London, R. Boulter, 1680–1701. 8 vols. **R 299**

Contains trial proceedings and reports to Parliament on a number of cases involving freedom of the press (1618–1648), including those of Alexander Leighton, William Prynne, and John Lilburne. An *Order for the Regulation of Printing*, dated 14 June 1643, appears in part 3, vol. 2, pp. 335–36.

Russell, Bertrand. "The Recrudescence of Puritanism." In his *Skeptical Essays*, New York, Norton, 1928, pp. 124–31. **R 300**

In this attack on the modern puritan influence in England and America, Russell cites the laws against obscene publications, which suppress much that is desirable along with the base, and the laws against birth control, whereby it is illegal to give information to a wage-earner but legal to give it to an educated person. "The harm done by the enforced ignorance . . . [is] regarded by our Puritan lawgivers as smaller evils than the hypothetical pleasure of a few foolish boys."

[————]. *Rex v. Bertrand Russell, Report of the Proceedings before the Lord Mayor at the Mansion House Justice Room, 5 June 1916.* London, No-conscription Fellowship, 1916. 23 p. **R 301**

Lord Russell had been charged with violation of wartime conscription laws for his leaflet in defense of Ernest F. Everett, given 2 years at hard labor for refusing military service. Russell was fined £100 and costs. This is a publication of Lord Russell's defense.

———. "The Taboo on Sex Knowledge." In his *Marriage and Morals*. New York, Liveright, 1929. (Reprinted as *Bantam Classic*, 1959, pp. 63–79) **R 302**
A British philosopher and social critic attacks the prevailing taboo, backed by law in England and America, that declares bluntly that children and young people must not know the facts of life. He refers to the prosecutions of Margaret Sanger, Mary Ware Dennett, and Havelock Ellis. "Ignorance in sexual matters is extraordinarily harmful to the individual, and therefore no system whose perpetration demands such ignorance can be desirable."

———. "Virtue and the Censor." *Encounter*, 3:8–11, July 1954. **R 303**
"Censorship of literature, which has existed in some form in all modern civilized countries, has two main purposes: one is to prevent people from thinking about politics, and the other is to prevent them thinking about sex." The article is concerned with the latter situation in England and the legal weapons in the hands of "prurient elderly bigots," who attempt to deter the young from thinking or knowing about sex.

[Russell, *Sir* Edward]. *A Report of the Trial of Sir Edward Russell at the Liverpool Assizes for Criminal Libel in the "Liverpool Post and Mercury," together with the Proceedings on the Application for a Rule before the Divisional Court*. Liverpool, Daily Post and Mercury, 1905. 251 p. **R 304**
The trial of Sir Edward Russell, editor, and Alexander G. Jeans, publisher of the Liverpool paper, charged with criminal libel for criticizing the administration of beer-hall licensing by the licensing judges. The history and legal precedent in newspaper libel comes in for discussion throughout the trial. The jury found the defendants not guilty.

Russell, George W. (AE) "The Censorship in Ireland." *Nation & Athenaeum* (London), 44:435–36, 22 December 1928. (Reprinted in Downs, *The First Freedom*, pp. 391–93) **R 305**
AE, along with William Butler Yeats, a leader in the Irish literary renaissance, was an outspoken critic of Irish censorship. He wrote this brief attack during the debates over the Censorship Bill. AE notes the Freudian preoccupation in Ireland with sexual sins, "almost the only ones seriously regarded by our moralists." Sex in Ireland has come to have an obscene significance and the objectionable bill defines indecent literature as anything "calculated to excite sexual passion," a definition which "would suppress in Ireland half the literature of the world which deals with passionate love between men and women."

Russell, Herbert. "News Censorship in War." *Fighting Forces*, 2:181–92, June 1925. **R 306**
A British correspondent in World War I maintains that "much in the censorship of news in wartime is supererogatory, futile, and therefore, ineffective."

[Russell, Joseph]. *Trial of Joseph Russell, for a Political Libel, being Mr. Hone's Parody on the Litany*. Birmingham, Eng., 1819. 48 p. **R 307**
A Birmingham bookseller was convicted in the sale of William Hone's parody, a publication which a London jury laughed at and refused to find libelous.

Russell, W. M. S. "The Two Censors." *Listener*, 67:416–18, 8 March 1962 **R 308**
The dividing line between what is permitted and what suppressed "never seems to be in the same place. It wobbles . . . Each society, like each individual, draws the dividing line between its own beliefs and behavior and any others, rational or not. But the pattern of society changes, and the line shifts with it."

Rutherfurd, Livingston. *John Peter Zenger, His Press, His Trial and a Bibliography of Zenger Imprints . . . Also a Reprint of the First Edition of the Trial*. New York, Dodd, Mead, 1904. 275 p. (Edition limited to 360 copies; reprinted in 1941 by Peter Smith) **R 309**
This is the standard biography of the newspaper publisher who figured in the most celebrated case of freedom of the press in American history. The Rutherfurd work includes a bibliography of the issues of the Zenger press, 1725–51, and a list of the issues of Zenger's *New York Weekly Journal* that are available in libraries. There is also a bibliography of the Zenger trial, beginning with the *Brief Narrative of the Case . . .*, issued in 1736 and probably written by James Alexander, to Chandler's *American Criminal Trials*, 1841, an abridgment of the 1736 edition.

Rutland, James R., *comp. State Censorship of Motion Pictures*. New York, Wilson, 1923. 177 p. (*Reference Shelf*, vol. 2, no. 1) **R 310**
A compilation of articles and statements, pro and con, on censorship of the movies, compiled at the close of the first significant decade of the movie industry. Among the articles favoring some form of censorship are: Censor and the "Movie Menace," and What Are the Movies Making of Our Children? by Ellis P. Oberholtzer, secretary of the Pennsylvania Board of Motion Picture Censors, and Reasons for Regulation, an extract from the annual report of the New York State Moving Picture Commission. Opposing censorship is the report of the investigating committee of the New York State Conference of Mayors, a statement from the National Board of Review of Motion Pictures, and from the Massachusetts Federation of Labor. A bibliography on state censorship of motion pictures is given on pages 16 to 28.

Rutland, Robert A. *The Birth of the Bill of Rights, 1776–1791*. Chapel Hill, N.C., Published for the Institute of Early American History and Culture by the University of North Carolina Press, 1955. 243 p. (Also in Collier paperback edition) **R 311**
A study of the process by which the Bill of Rights became the first ten amendments of the federal Constitution. The account traces the background in English common law, in American colonial history, and in the written codes of the various states.

Ryan, John A. "Freedom of Speech in Wartime." *Catholic World*, 106:577–88, February 1918. **R 312**

Ryan, John K. "Are the Comics Moral?" *Forum*, 95:301–4, May 1936. **R 313**
The author gives examples of "sadism, bestial and degenerate scenes and characters" found in comic strips which he feels have bad effects upon immature minds. "The prevention and correction of such effects are a task for an aroused public conscience."

Ryckman, Charles S. "Why We Banned Fight Ballyhoo." *Quill*, 18(2):9, 16, December 1930. **R 314**
The elimination of fight news in the Fremont, Neb., *Tribune*, as news unfit to print.

S

S., E. "A Forgotten Journalist." *Athenaeum*, 3734:626, 20 May 1899. **S1**
William Bingley, printer of John Wilkes's *North Briton*, was brought to trial for seditious libel. His "known career begins with a bookseller's shop opposite Durham Yard in the Strand. Here he continued the *North Briton* after Wilkes had relinquished it." For unguarded words (in no. 50) he was committed to Newgate and remained in prison about two years.

Sabadosh, Audrey. "Teenagers View Censorship." *Top of the News*, 22:278–80, April 1966. **S2**
A report on a questionnaire about reading distributed to English classes in Brecksville (Ohio) High School, indicating a wide variety of views for and against censorship.

Sabsay, David. "The Challenge of the 'Fisk Report.'" *California Libraries*, 20:222–23, 256, October 1959. **S3**
A critique of the study on book selection and censorship in California libraries made by Marjorie Fisk. The author suggests ways in which the library profession can improve the situation.

[Sacheverell, Henry]. *The Tryal of Dr. Henry Sacheverell, before the House of Peers, for High Crimes and Misdemeanors; upon an Impeachment by the Knights, Citizens and Burgesses in Parliament Assembled, in the Name of Themselves, and of all the Commons of Great Britain* . . . London, Published by order of the House of Peers by Jacob Tonson, 1710. 335p. (Also in Howell, *State Trials*, vol. 15, pp. 1ff., and in Borrow, *Celebrated Trials*, vol. 3, pp. 293–321) **S4**
This eminent English minister was impeached by Parliament for criticism of the Whigs in two printed sermons. He was sentenced not to preach for three years and his sermons were ordered burned by the common hangman.

Sachs, Ed. "I Want *Candy*." *Focus/Midwest*, 3(2):11–13, 23–24, 1964. **S5**
The author, learning that the current novel, *Candy*, was not being sold in Chicago, set out to investigate Chicago police censorship. After interviews with police and city officials (including a man in the police department who has spent most of the past three years reading dirty magazines), the publisher, and numerous Chicago book dealers, the author finds that Chicago may be "the most severe city in the United States" in restricting magazines and books—a "New Boston."

Saerchinger, César. "Radio, Censorship and Neutrality." *Foreign Affairs*, 18:337–49, January 1940. **S6**
"We do not want radio, now that it has become such a powerful medium of publicity, to be controlled or bureaucratically censored from 'above.' On the other hand, we do not wish to see it exploited by unseen forces beyond our control."

"Safe-guarding Our Minds." *Nation*, 107:795, 28 December 1918. **S7**
Criticism of Post Office censorship of books, including reading matter for soldiers, as "a disgrace to the American intelligence."

Sagarin, Edward. *The Anatomy of Dirty Words*. New York, Lyle Stuart, 1962. 220p. Introduction by Allen Walker Read. **S8**
The author believes that modern man exhibits an unwholesome and antibiological attitude toward the physical functions of the body by his use of taboo or "dirty" words as expressions of abusive negative qualities. The current relaxation of restriction on the use of taboo sex terms does not solve the basic social problem. The increased frequency of use of these words reinforces and intensifies as well as reflects the unwholesome attitudes.

St. George, Maximilian, and Lawrence Dennis. *A Trial on Trial; the Great Sedition Trial of 1944*. n.p., National Civil Rights Committee, 1945. 503p. **S9**
Two of the defense attorneys in the mass sedition trial of 1944 write a criticism of the government prosecution and "the use of criminal law and criminal procedures as an instrument of political policy and as a tool of political propaganda." The defendants, because of written and spoken words, were accused of contributing to a Nazi world-movement.

[Saint-John, Henry, *Viscount* Bolingbroke]. *The Doctrine of Innuendo's Discuss'd; or, the Liberty of the Press maintain'd: being some thoughts upon the present treatment of the printer and publishers of the Craftsman*. London, Printed for the author, 1731. 26p. **S10**
This anonymous pamphlet, probably written by either Bolingbroke or William Pultney, defended the right of men to state their thoughts in print "on state matters as well as others," and objected to the government practice of charging "sedition" for the slightest innuendo. This forced the writers of *The Craftsman* to develop an ingenious method of avoiding offense and libel by drawing upon facts and parallels of history to attack the present administration. Lord Hervey had challenged the integrity of such methods in his *Observations on the Writings of The Craftsman*.

[———]. *Final Answer to the Remarks on the Craftsman's Vindication, and to All the Libels, which Have Come, or May Come from the Same Quarter against the Person, Last Mentioned in the Craftsman of the 22d of May*. London, R. Francklin, 1731. 32p. (Also appears in Lord Bolingbroke's *Works*. Philadelphia, Cary and Hart, 1841. vol. 1, pp. 456–73) **S11**
Lord Bolingbroke, one of the anonymous sponsors of the publication, *The Craftsman*, defends the editorial policy of the paper against its critics and makes general comments on the law of libels. His answer is directed especially against a pamphlet entitled *Remarks on The Craftman's Vindication*. The publisher of *The Craftsman*, Richard Francklin, was freed of libel charges in 1729.

[———]. *A Proper Reply to a late Scurrilous Libel; intitled, Sedition and Defamation display'd. In a Letter to the Author. By Caleb D'Anvers, of Gray's-Inn* . . . London, R. Francklin, 1731. 36p. **S12**

The imaginary editor of *The Craftsman* defends that paper against libel charges leveled by the spokesmen of the Walpole administration in their pamphlets, *Sedition and Defamation Display'd . . .*, *Observations on the Writings of the Craftsman, Sequel . . .*, and *Further Observations . . .* Authorship is attributed to Lord Bolingbroke or William Pultney.

St. John-Stevas, Norman. "Art, Morality and Censorship." *Ramparts*, 2:40–48, May 1963. **S13**
The political editor of the *Economist* argues for freedom of expression in matters of sexual morality and behavior. This is "the only sphere, apart from blasphemy and sedition, where freedom of expression is materially restricted in western liberal societies. The need for such freedom is greater than ever today, when literature and especially the novel is so closely concerned with psychological problems and a naturalistic or realistic presentation of life." While creative writers need to be free of legal restraints in order to create literature, they also have an obligation to exercise self-discipline. He cites three "interior restraints": the exercise of prudence, the recognition of moral values of a universal character, and the imposition of the discipline imposed by the work of art itself.

———. "The Author Wins His Battle." *Catholic World*, 195:34–42, April 1962. **S14**
In a continuation of an earlier article, the author traces obscenity law from the Victorian period to the recent furor over *Lady Chatterley's Lover*. Authors have won their fight for protection now that British law and American courts have arrived at substantially the same test for obscenity. We must now battle "hard-core pornography."

———. "Author's Struggles with the Law." *Catholic World*, 194:345–50, March 1962. **S15**
In an address before the First Amendment Forum, the writer shows that the obscenity law first was restricted to the control of pornography, but eventually began to mishandle literature. He traces the early development of English obscenity law from the appearance of *Venus in the Cloister* (1727) to the enactment of the law against obscene libel (1857).

———. *Birth Control and Public Policy. A Report to the Center for the Study of Democratic Institutions.* Santa Barbara, Calif., The Center, 1960. 84 p. **S16**

———. "Censorship and Law." *Commonweal*, 70:146–48, 8 May 1959. **S17**
"With the passage of the Obscene Publications Bill, English law will closely approximate that of the United States." A discussion of the present state of obscenity law in the United States and England. Primary responsibility for a moral literature, the author points out, rests not upon the law but upon the standards of integrity of authors.

———. "The Censorship of Plays." *Writer*, 67:54–57, Spring 1957. **S18**
A brief history of British stage censorship under the Lord Chamberlain; how it has survived and how it operates at the present time.

———. "Intent and the Law." *New Statesman*, 48:428–29, 9 October 1954. **S19**
The development of the obscenity law in England and current proposals for handling the infection of the crime comic, largely imported from America.

———. "Obscenity and the Law." *Criminal Law Review*, 1954:817–33, November 1954. **S20**
A general history of obscenity under English common and statutory law, followed by an analysis of some of the important questions on which the law is uncertain—intention of author or publisher, defenses that are permissible, tests of the character of the book, and evidence that is admissible. The author comments favorably on the abandonment of the Hicklin formula in the American decision on Joyce's *Ulysses*.

———. "Obscenity and the Law Reform." *Spectator*, 194:119–20, 4 February 1955. **S21**
Consideration of the proposal by the Herbert Committee for reform of the British Obscene Publications Act.

———. *Obscenity and the Law. With an Introduction by Sir Alan P. Herbert.* London, Secker & Warburg, 1956. 289 p. **S22**
A study that approaches the problem of obscenity from both the legal and literary points of view. The author, who is both a writer and lawyer, traces the development of obscenity law from the days of the ecclesiastical courts and Star Chamber to the latest decision of the British courts. While largely devoted to the British scene, a chapter is devoted to Irish censorship and censorship in the United States—the *Ulysses* case, *God's Little Acre*, the NODL, the Gathings Committee, and attacks on comic books. Appendices include a draft bill for the reform of the British obscenity law, comparative law of the Commonwealth and foreign countries, and a list of reported cases in England and the United States. A lengthy review of the book by Harry Kalven, Jr., appears in the July 1957 issue of *Library Quarterly*.

———. "Obscenity, Literature and the Law." *Dublin Review*, 230(471): 41–56, Summer 1956. (Reprinted in Downs, *The First Freedom*, pp. 67–75) **S23**
An English lawyer and author examines the existing British obscenity laws which he states still reflect the thinking of Chief Justice Cockburn as laid down in the Hicklin case in 1868. He discusses the provisions of the reform bill drafted by the Herbert Committee

which abolishes the old common law offense of obscene libel. The bill was subsequently enacted.

———. "Obscenity, Literature and the Law." *Catholic Lawyer*, 3:301–11, Autumn 1957. **S24**
The author is concerned with "how far the state should intervene to protect members of society from corruption by the dissemination of obscene literature." He considers the changing standards of obscenity in England from the Hicklin case down to proposed changes in the British law in which an effort is made to distinguish pornography from serious works that may, by contemporary standards, be considered shocking or obscene.

———. "Printers' Censorship." *Spectator*, 195:792–94, 9 December 1957. **S25**
"Printers all over the country have employed extra readers to hunt through manuscripts, especially novels, and to mark passages which some old lady or police might consider obscene. Until such passages have been deleted they refuse to print the book." A reform in the obscenity law, giving security to the printer, is needed to prevent growth of this insidious censorship.

St. Louis *Post-Dispatch. Symposium on Freedom of the Press.* St. Louis, *Post-Dispatch*, 1939. 76 p. (Reprints from the *Post-Dispatch* from 13 to 25 December 1938) **S26**
Brief statements from 120 representative Americans on the freedom of the press, including an introductory letter from Franklin D. Roosevelt.

Sait, Edward McChesney. *Clerical Control of Quebec.* New York, Truth Seeker, n.d. 158 p. **S27**
Contents: Theocratic Quebec, Educational System, Clerical Censorship of Press and Theatre, and Undue Influence in Elections.

Salant, Richard S. *The 1960 Campaign and Television.* Columbia, Mo., Freedom of Information Center, School of Journalism, University of Missouri, 1961. 9 p. (Publication no. 66). **S28**
The president of C.B.S. News, in an address before the 1961 annual meeting of the American Political Science Association, discusses the great television debate between John F. Kennedy and Richard M. Nixon—its origin, its implications, and its significance.

———. "Television's Access to News." *ASNE Bulletin*, 461:5–6, 1 February 1963. **S29**
Defends the right of the people to televised coverage of Congress and the Supreme Court.

[Salmon, Lucy M.]. "Censorship." *Encyclopaedia Britannica*, 13th ed., 1926. vol. I of supp., pp. 562–63.　**S 30**
General statement on United States wartime censorship (World War I) based on the author's personal clipping collection on censorship and propaganda, now in Vassar College Library.

————. *The Newspaper and Authority*. New York, Oxford University Press, 1923. 505 p.　**S 31**
The author attempts to discover "how far the restrictions placed on the newspaper press by external authority have limited its serviceableness for the historian in his attempt to reconstruct the past." Chapters include Theory of Censorship, Preventive Censorship (wartime), Punitive Censorship, Regulation of the Press, Taxes on Knowledge, Clandestine Press, and Libel. The study embraces United States, Great Britain, France, Germany, and, to a lesser extent, a number of other countries. A companion volume to the author's *The Newspaper and the Historian*.

————. *The Newspaper and the Historian*. New York, Oxford University Press, 1923. 566 p.　**S 32**
The purpose of the volume is to discover the advantages and limitations of the newspaper press to the historian in reconstructing the past. Several sections relate to press control and freedom. Chapter 3, Guarantees of Probability, considers guarantees of freedom and accuracy imposed by law and self-imposed; Chapter 7, The Official Reporter, considers restrictions in parliamentary reporting and the withholding of public information by government agencies; Chapter 9, The War Correspondent, considers military censorship; and Chapter 16, The Authoritativeness of the Press, explores the suppression of news by the government and by the press itself. A companion volume to the author's *The Newspaper and Authority*.

Salmon, Thomas. *A New Abridgement and Critical Review of the State Trials . . .* London, Printed for J. R. and J. Hazard, *et. al.*, 1738. 922 p.　**S 33**
Includes brief accounts of the following trials relating to press freedom: William Anderton, John Bastwick, Nathan Brooks, Henry Care, Elizabeth Cellier, Stephen College, William Fuller, Benjamin Harris, John Lilburne, William Prynne, Henry Sacheverell, John Tutchin, John Twyn, and John Wharton.

Salter, Katharine H. *An Open Letter to Charles Taft, President of the Federal Council of the Churches of Christ in America*. Oberlin, Ohio, The Author, 1947. 41 p.　**S 34**
The purpose of the pamphlet, according to the author, is to bring to the attention of the American public some basis facts concerning church-backed antidiscrimination legislation

and the difficulties that have been placed in the way of those fighting the measure "to use the 18th century bill of rights—freedom of speech, press, assembly . . . and religion, in a normal fashion, to state their side of the case."

"The Salvation of Mediocrity." *Independent*, 118:326–27, 26 March 1927.　**S 35**
Criticizes the action of the Boston police in demanding that nine novels be withdrawn from booksellers' shelves as "silly and unwise." Censorship "never protects and it usually does little more than draw attention to what would otherwise have gone relatively unknown."

Samuel, Herbert L. "Liberty of Speech and of the Press." *New Statesman*, 9: 223–25, 9 June 1917.　**S 36**
Wartime censorship in Britain has exceeded that necessary for military reasons. The writer would take the responsibility for political censorship out of the hands of the military, who are "rather prone to see only the direct advantage of repression without the harm of restricting freedom." Reference is made to the suppression of the overseas circulation of *The Nation*.

Samuels, Alec. "Obscenity and the Law: the Balance between Freedom to Publish and Public Decency." *Law Society's Gazette*, 61:729–37, November 1964.　**S 37**
"How can we suppress pornography (literally the writing of prostitutes) and at the same time protect literature?" The author considers the problem in light of recent court decisions under the British Obscene Publications Act of 1959.

[Sancroft, William, *Archbishop of Canterbury, et al.*]. *The Proceedings and Tryal in the Case of . . . William Lord Archbishop of Canterbury, and . . . William Lord Bishop of St. Asaph . . .* London, Printed for Thomas Basset and Thomas Fox, 1689. 140 p. (Also in Howell, *State Trials*, v. 12, pp. 183 ff.)　**S 38**
The case is commonly known as the "trial of the seven bishops" who were accused of "publishing, and causing to be publish'd, a seditious libel." The questions of both publication and libel were left to the decision of the jury who found the defendants "not guilty." The precedent established by this case in allowing the jury to judge whether the work was libelous, was not followed in later cases until established in law by the Fox Libel Act of 1792. Laurence Hanson states that "the verdict of 'not guilty' immensely furthered the Revolution." The Bishops of Ely, Chichester, Bath and Wells, Peterborough, and Bristol were the others standing trial.

Sanders, Robert E. *The Great Debate*. Columbia, Mo., Freedom of Information Center, School of Journalism, University of Missouri, 1961. 28 p. (Publication no. 67)　**S 39**

An analysis of the television debates between John F. Kennedy and Richard M. Nixon during the 1960 presidential election campaign, together with comments from informed observers.

Sandwell, B. K. "Censorship." In *Encyclopedia Americana*. New York, Encyclopedia Americana, 1955. vol. 6, pp. 193a–f.　**S 40**

————. "Freedom of Speech by Radio." *Saturday Night*, 67:4–7, 17 November 1951.　**S 41**
The author favors retaining present restrictions on broadcasting of opinions over Canadian radio. He bases his point of view on the technical nature of radio, which permits a limited number of channels and because of radio's unique position in a household.

————. "Guard the Juvenile Mind." *Canadian Home Journal*, 38:3, 43, August 1941.　**S 42**

————. "Mr. Duplessis Moves In; TV Censorship in Quebec." *Saturday Night*, 68:7, 15 November 1952.　**S 43**
The Province of Quebec claims the right to censor its telecasts. The author doubts that the central Dominion authorities have the right to control content, but only the physical facilities of broadcasting.

————. "Radio Free Speech: The Pitches Are Limited." *Saturday Night*, 67:4–5, 19 January 1952.　**S 44**
The author draws a distinction between limiting the expression of ideas on radio and in books and newspapers. Since channels of communications are limited, every citizen cannot have an absolute right to speech over radio. "Somebody has to determine who shall speak over the radio and who shall not." Other media are available to citizens.

San Francisco, California. *Power of City and County to Enact Ordinances Regulating Traffic in Obscene Literature*. San Francisco, The City, 1960. 14 p. mimeo.　**S 45**

Sanger, Margaret. *An Autobiography*. New York, Norton, 1938. 504 p.　**S 46**
An American leader in the fight for birth control describes her experiences which include numerous threats to freedom of speech and press: The Post Office banning of her book, *What Every Girl Should Know*, and the first issue of *Woman Rebel* (March 1914); her flight to Canada to avoid prosecution under the Comstock law; the difficulties in getting her *Family Limitations* pamphlet published in New York and the various arrests for its distribution. She also relates her efforts in the 1930's to amend the Comstock law to permit distribution of information on contraceptives. The campaign was conducted by the National

Committee on Federal Legislation for Birth Control. Several chapters deal with her work with British Neo-Malthusians.

———. *Birth Control Through the Ages. A Chronological History of the Birth Control Movement from Ancient to Modern Times.* New York, Planned Parenthood Federation of America, 1940. 15 p. **S 47**
Numerous references to suppression of publications and trials and imprisonment of authors and publishers.

———. *Case for Birth Control; a Supplementary Brief and Statement of Facts, Prepared by Margaret Sanger to Aid the Court in Its Consideration of the Statute Designed to Prevent the Dissemination of Information for Preventing Conception.* New York, The Author, 1917. 251 p. **S 48**
This was prepared as part of Mrs. Sanger's defense before the New York courts, on a charge of circulating information for prevention of conception.

[———]. *A Catalogue of the Margaret Sanger Papers, 1914–1939 in The Library of Congress. Gift and Deposit by Mrs. Sanger, 1942.* [New York, 1943]. 202 p. Typescript. (Prepared by Florence Rose, personal secretary to Mrs. Sanger) **S 49**
A comprehensive listing of correspondence, manuscripts, legal documents, photographs, clippings, and publications dealing with the career of Margaret Sanger and the birth control movement in America and abroad. There are introductory and explanatory remarks relating to the various associated organizations. Includes files on court cases involving suppression of information on birth control and the opposition of the Catholic Church.

———. "Letter from Margaret Sanger." *Mother Earth*, 10:75–78, April 1915. **S 50**
Account of the Post Office suppression of *Woman Rebel* for March, May, July, August, September, and October 1914, and the arrest of Mrs. Sanger, its editor, on a charge of obscenity.

———. *My Fight for Birth Control.* New York, Farrar & Rinehart, 1931. 360 p. **S 51**
The American leader of the birth control movement recounts her lifelong crusade, including frequent brushes with the authorities for distribution of birth control literature.

———. "Shall We Break This Law?" *Birth Control Review*, 1(1):4, February 1917. **S 52**
"If she must break the law to establish her right to voluntary motherhood, then the law shall be broken." The same issue carries an

article by Havelock Ellis on Birth Control in Relation to Morality.

———. *The Suppressed "Obscene" Articles.* [New York? 1914?] 16 p. **S 53**
Deals with the New York Post Office suppression of issues of the *Woman Rebel* for March 1914. Contains the text of the objectionable articles: The Prevention of Conception, Open Discussion, and The Birth Control League.

[———]. *Supreme Court, Appellate Division—Second Department.* [*People of the State of New York ex rel Margaret Sanger, Ethel Byrne and Fannie Mindell*] *Appellant's Brief in Support of Motion for Stay of Proceedings.* New York, Hecla Press, n.d. 56 p. **S 54**
Margaret Sanger, Ethel Byrne, and Fannie Mindell were convicted for giving birth control information.

———. "The War Against Birth Control." *American Mercury*, 2:231–36, June 1924. **S 55**
Margaret Sanger, through her experience of ten years of suppression and persecution, touches "upon certain aspects of the psychology of these thought-suppressors—aspects perhaps unfamiliar to many who have never incurred their enmity."

———, et al. [*"Birth Control"*]. *Nation*, 134:89, 102–14, 27 January 1932. **S 56**
A group of advocates, including Robert S. Allen, Henry Pratt Fairchild, William Allen Pusey, John Dewey, and Morris L. Ernst, discuss various aspects of birth control, including the record of suppression of birth control information.

[Sanger, William]. *The Trial of William Sanger, September 10th, 1915, With an Introduction by James Waldo Fawcett.* New York, 1917. 15 p. **S 57**
The story of the arrest, trial, and conviction of William Sanger for giving a copy of his wife's pamphlet on birth control, *Family Limitations*, to an agent provocateur of the vice society. Unwilling to pay the fine imposed by the Court, Sanger spent 30 days in the city prison. The story is made up of excerpts from the *New York Call* and *New York Times*.

Sankey-Jones, Nancy E. *Theodore Schroeder on Free Speech; a Bibliography.* New York, Free Speech League, 1919. 24 p. **S 58**
A bibliography of the published writings of this prominent crusader for freedom of speech and press. Covers the years 1896–1919.

Santayana, George. "Censor and the Poet," In *Soliloquies in England.* New York, Scribner's, 1922, pp. 155–59. **S 59**
Santayana's "censor" is "an important official of the inner man" whose function is to

"forbid the utterance . . . of unparliamentary sentiments, and to suppress all reports not in the interest of our moral dignity." If erotica could be passed by the censor and treated judiciously "it would enrich the arts and at the same time disinfect the mind." Europeans, unlike Orientals, cannot seem to treat natural things naturally. Under the circumstances "public art and the inner life have to flow separately, the one remains conventional, the other clouded and incoherent." Poets under such conditions would not only offend the public but would do an injustice to their theme. It is well, therefore, that the censor, "by imposing silence, keeps them from attempting the impossible."

Sapp, Phyllis W. "It Happened to One Book." *Christian Century*, 75:432–33, 9 April 1958. **S 60**
Account of deletions from a Southern Baptist study book about home mission work with Negroes, to avoid offending Southerners. Despite the revisions, the book was withdrawn from Baptist bookstores for a time. "Some people feared study of the book would provide discussion."

Sargeant, Howland. "Voice of the Free World." *U.S. Department of State Bulletin*, 22:330–34, 27 February 1950. **S 61**
Excerpts from a speech about the "Voice of America" breaking the censorship of the Iron Curtain countries.

Sargent, Noel. "Press Censorship." *Central Law Journal*, 85:60–68, 27 July 1917. **S 62**
In light of proposed wartime censorship, the author attempts to answer the question: Under the Constitution how far can Congress go in passing laws regulatory of the press? He believes that only military news should be prevented from free distribution, but that this should be released when the action is over and it can no longer harm the war effort. Military commanders should not be permitted indefinite suppression of news.

Sarnoff, David. "In Favor of Self-Regulation." In Summers, *Radio Censorship*, pp. 230–32. **S 63**
From a statement on network broadcasting before the FCC made by the president of the Radio Corporation of America, 14 December 1938. Printed in pamphlet form by RCA under the title, *To the Stockholders.*

Sarnoff, Robert W. *Through the Regulatory Looking Glass—Darkly.* New York, National Broadcasting Co., 1965. 17 p. **S 64**
In an address to the N.B.C. Television Affiliates meeting, the chairman of the Board of N.B.C. attacked the old enemies of government regulation—equal time restrictions, "the official meddling fostered by the

so-called 'fairness doctrine,'" prohibition of television access to legislative and judicial proceedings—and the more recent inroads into programming and business practices. "The Commission was not given the mission of reforming broadcasting to serve the interests of the few rather than the many." If FCC undertakes to tinker with the basic mechanisms of television it will create more problems than solutions.

Saroyan, William. "A Cold Day." In his *The Daring Young Man on the Flying Trapeze.* New York, Random House, 1934, pp. 153–63. (Reprinted in Downs, *The First Freedom*, pp. 281–84) **S 65**
Saroyan considers burning old books—even to keep warm—as blasphemous, in this brief sketch which is possibly autobiographical.

Saunders, Stephan L. "Catholics, Censorship and Classification." *Catholic Preview of Entertainment*, 5:26–28, October 1961. **S 66**

Classification by exhibitors cannot possibly satisfy all groups. But Catholics have the Legion of Decency which classifies movies on the basis of established moral standards. Catholics are advised to form local film councils in cooperation with the Legion of Decency and to follow their advice. The best control is exercised by the movie patron at the box office.

Saunders, W. C. "Tom Watson Marked." *Down Homer*, 6:1–7, July 1912. **S 67**
Account of Watson's arrest for "obscene" criticism of Catholicism.

[Savage, George, *et al.*]. "Mr. Hearst and Sex; Report of a Citizens Committee, Seattle." *Saturday Review*, 30:16–17, 32, 12 July 1947. **S 68**
During the fall of 1946 the Hearst paper, the Seattle *Post-Intelligence* launched a crusade against salacious literature. Seattle's Mayor Devin appointed a citizens committee, headed by Professor George Savage of the University of Washington, to consider the issues. Other members were: J. B. Harrison, Mrs. A. M. Walrath, Rev. Allan Lorimer, Harry C. Bauer, and John Richards. After months of deliberation the committee gave birth to a "sane and stimulating statement" printed here.

Savage, William S. "Abolitionist Literature in the Mails, 1835–1836." *Journal of Negro History*, 13:150–84, April 1928. **S 69**

An account of the efforts of Southerners to keep abolitionist literature out of the mails. Includes the controversy faced by the Postmaster General, President Jackson, and the Congress, which resulted in a Post-Office policy which took the decision on what was to be sent through the mails out of the hands of local postmasters.

————. *The Controversy over the Distribution of Abolition Literature, 1830–1860.* Washington, D.C., The Association for the Study of Negro Life and History, 1938. 141 p. **S 70**
The controversy began in the 1830's with efforts of the abolitionist societies to distribute their newspapers in the South. This account discusses the dispute over freedom of the mails as it related to antislavery literature, a dispute that was waged for three decades in the state legislatures, the Congress, the office of the President, and finally in the courts.

"Save America from Ruin." *Missionary Review*, 47:10–12, January 1924. **S 71**
An attack on the vast quantity of pernicious literature that the author believes is flooding America.

Saveth, Edward N. "What to Do About Dangerous Textbooks." *Commentary*, 13: 99–106, February 1952. **S 72**
A discussion of attacks made on textbooks both from the left and the right: "Qualified criticism, not pressure tactics, is the appropriate means of making one's views felt insofar as the writing and revision of textbooks are concerned."

Saville, William B. *The Press and the House of Lords, 1696–1780.* Urbana, Ill., University of Illinois, 1947. 146 p. (Unpublished Master's thesis) **S 73**
Includes prosecution for libels on members and for printing reports of Parliament, with special attention given to the John Wilkes case.

Sawilowsky, Yale S. *Censorship and the Librarian.* University, Miss., University of Mississippi, 1964. 60 p. (Unpublished Master's essay) **S 74**

Sawyer, Geoffrey. *A Guide to Australian Law for Journalists, Authors, Printers, and Publishers.* Melbourne, Melbourne University Press, 1949. 96 p. **S 75**
Includes laws on copyright, defamation, court coverage, obscenity, blasphemy, sedition, and control of advertising.

Say, H. B. "Censorship and Security." U.S. Naval Institute *Proceedings*, 79: 134–41, February 1953. **S 76**
Discussion of censorship principles and practices in World War II and in the period of the cold war, with special reference to the armed forces.

Sayers, Dorothy L. "How Free is the Press?" In *Unpopular Opinions.* London, Gollancz, 1946, pp. 127–33. **S 77**

This essay, written in 1941, is a caustic criticism of the British press, free in a technical and legal sense, but "shackled to its own set of overlords" and exercising "a powerful bondage upon its readers and on the public in general." The press "exists not so much to express opinion as to manufacture it." Specifically, the writer complains of the sensational headlines, the false emphasis, the suppression of context, the garbling, the inaccurate reporting or reversing of facts, the random and gratuitous invention, the deliberate miracle-mongering, and the flat suppression. The reader is helpless to oppose the vested interests. The press, not the reader, possesses the freedom.

Sayers, Frances Clarke. "If the Trumpet Be Not Sounded." *Wilson Library Bulletin*, 39:659–62, 684, April 1965. **S 78**
"Librarianship is only now emerging from uncertainty into an awareness of its obligation to profess a strong belief in intellectual freedom and to substantiate that profession with action, when it is necessary." Looking across the years at the changing concepts of librarianship—as teacher, censor, and umpire—Mrs. Sayers sees an emerging role as "inciter, arouser, as trumpeter and champion." She describes the persecution of ideas and of librarians that took place during and immediately following World War I, and the greater maturity of judgment in the library profession that enabled librarians to withstand the hysteria of McCarthyism and the obsession with communism that followed World War II. She describes her own experience in being faced with the persecution techniques of the censor when she was superintendent of work with children in the New York Public Library. "No other profession is as well equipped for the confrontation with the future as is our profession. . . . As people who hold to the redemptive power of books, we have books behind us, and we know them well enough to have acquired an historical perspective of the vagaries of men's minds. . . . We are vital because we function at the center of the passion and action of our time. . . . We will be the explorers, the discoverers and the sounders of trumpets."

Sayers, W. C. Berwick. "Banning of Books in Libraries." *Library Review*, 1:184–87, Spring 1928. **S 79**
While deploring the moral bankruptcy of modern novelists, Sayers advises public librarians to remember the interests of the patrons and to keep out personal bias. "My own view of [the rules of selection] is simply this: no novel written in recent years has sufficient quality to be a source of trouble between a public and its people. Buy it, if the reviewers praise it enough; circulate it freely until someone objects; and in that event withdraw it from the open shelf, but leave it in the catalogue. The person who wants it will ask for it, and if that person is of mature years, may be allowed, without question, to have it."

Scanlon, Arthur J. "The Cardinal Hays Literature Committee." *Catholic Action*, 15:7–8, 10, February 1933. **S 80**

The secretary of the Committee considers the work of the organization in the promotion of good literature and discouragement of bad. Advice to the reader includes preparation of a "white list" of approved plays. The Committee also offers advice to publishers, authors, and the general public.

Scanlon, Helen L., *comp. Freedom of Communication in Wartime. Select List of References on Censorship in Time of War.* Washington, D.C., The Library, Carnegie Endowment for International Peace, 1942. 11 p. mimeo. (Select Bibliographies, no. 12) **S 81**

Scarboro, J. A. "Free Press on Trial in America." In William L. Clark, *Hell at Midnight in Springfield, Illinois.* 4th ed. Milan, Ill., The Author, 1914, pp. 122–45. **S 82**

The editor of *The Liberator*, Magnolia, Ark., reports on the prosecution of publishers "who print the truth about Romanism, for sending obscene matter through the mails." He describes the cases of William Lloyd Clark in the Peoria, Ill., trial for publishing *Hell at Midnight . . .*, *The Appeal to Reason* case, Girard, Kan., the case of Thomas E. Watson of Georgia, and *The Menace* of Aurora, Mo. Other commentary on the Clark trial is given on pp. 146–88.

Schafer, Joseph. "Popular Censorship of History Texts." *Wisconsin Magazine of History*, 6:450–61, June 1923. **S 83**

Editorial comments on a unique Wisconsin law forbidding adoption of a textbook in Wisconsin public schools "which falsifies the facts regarding the War of Independence or the War of 1812 or which defames our nation's founders or misrepresents the ideals and causes for which they struggled and sacrificed, or which contains propaganda favorable to any foreign government."

Schall, James V. "Censorship in the Church." *Commonweal*, 83:601–3, 25 February 1966. **S 84**

Scharper, Philip J. *You Can't Ban Those Books and Films!* New York, Information Features, n.d. 8 p. (Reprint from monthly publication of the Paulist Fathers) **S 85**

Questions on the work of the Catholic Church's National Office for Decent Literature, answered by a Catholic editor.

Schary, Dore. "Censorship and Stereotypes." *Saturday Review of Literature*, 32(18):9–10, 30 April 1949. **S 86**

A film producer takes exception to the views of John Haynes Holmes and John Mason Brown (26 February and 12 March) who criticize censorship activities by sensitive minority groups. The use of uncomplimentary stereotypes of racial groups is propaganda for bigotry, and minority groups have a right to defend themselves against such abuse. Such efforts ought not be condemned by an unsympathetic demand for freedom of expression.

Schattenfield, Thomas S. "Judicial Independence and Freedom of the Press." *Western Reserve Law Review*, 6:175–82, Winter 1955. **S 87**

Notes on cases, 1831–1954.

Schenk, Gretchen K., *ed.* "Meeting the Censorship Problem." *Wilson Library Bulletin*, 36:484, February 1962. **S 88**

Brief reference to the use of a "Request for Review of Library Materials" used at Santa Fe (River) Regional Library, Fla., which gives the reading public a chance to be critical of books in the library.

Scher, Jacob. "Access to Information: Recent Legal Problems." *Journalism Quarterly*, 37(1):41–52, Winter 1960. **S 89**

———. *5 U.S.C. 1002 Change Discussed.* Columbia, Mo., Freedom of Information Center, School of Journalism, University of Missouri, 1960. 4 p. (Publication no. 45) **S 90**

The chief counsel of the House Subcommittee on Government Information comments on the Committee's proposal to change the public information section of the Administrative Procedure Act.

———. *On Executive Privilege.* Columbia, Mo., Freedom of Information Center, School of Journalism, University of Missouri, 1960. 9 p. (Publication no. 43) **S 91**

This paper is based upon a longer study prepared by the writer for the House Subcommittee on Government Information.

———. "Some Comments on the Law of Obscenity." *Northwestern University Tri-Quarterly*, 2(3):3–10, Spring 1960. **S 92**

Schick, Franz. "Propaganda and the Library." *California Library Association Bulletin*, 3:61–63, December 1941. **S 93**

The librarian had always been advised to play the role of a neutral, seeing to it that all points of view in a controversy were represented in the collection. The present world crisis, however, requires that librarians no longer be impartial, that subversive propaganda be rejected and that a self-imposed censorship be instituted.

Schlesinger, Arthur M. "Colonial Newspapers and the Stamp Act." *New England Quarterly*, 8:63–83, March 1935. **S 94**

"Since the first widespread employment of newspaper propaganda in America coincided with the adoption of the Stamp Act, a consideration of the circumstances and results may serve as a sort of knot-hole through which to view the first stages of a developing journalistic warfare which eventually led to revolution and independence." The article describes the widespread defiance of the stamp tax by the colonial newspapers that viewed the tax as a threat to the freedom of the press. Schlesinger's book, *Prelude to Independence: The Newspaper War on Britain, 1764–76* (New York, Knopf, 1958) records British overseas policy on freedom of the press.

Schloff, Kay D. "Prior Censorship of a Motion Picture by a State is Not a Violation of Free Speech and Press." *University of Detroit Law Journal*, 38:483–89, April 1961. **S 95**

Times Film Corp. v. Chicago, 365 U.S. 43 (1961).

Schlytter, Leslie E. "Jural Esthetics and Jural Ethics." *Saturday Review of Literature*, 29(6):23–24, 9 February 1946. **S 96**

In a letter to the editor the author discusses the principle that scientifically valid jural esthetics must be controlled by jural ethics. He refers to efforts to define obscenity.

Schmeiser, D. A. *Civil Liberties in Canada.* Oxford, Eng., Oxford University Press, 1964. 302 p. **S 97**

Chapter 5 deals with the communicative freedoms, a discussion of legislative jurisdiction (the role of Parliament versus legislatures), criminal sanctions as applied to blasphemy, defamatory libel, sedition (with special reference to Communist expression), contempt of court, and obscenity. Obscenity law is "the most muddled law in Canada today."

Schmidt, Godfrey P. "A Justification of Statutes Barring Pornography from the Mail." *Fordham Law Review*, 26:70–97, Spring 1957. **S 98**

Schmidt, Harold R., and William K. Unverzagt. "Defamation in Pennsylvania." *University of Pittsburgh Law Review*, 2:1–16, October 1935. **S 99**

Schmitt, Gladys. "Censorship and the Immature." *Library Journal*, 75:652–55, 15 April 1950. **S 100**

We have been careful to exercise our function of guidance in the area of the obscene, but have not exercised it in the area of the neurotic, nor examined the social, political and ethical concepts in the works of literature we give our youth.

Schmulowitz, Nat. "Thou Shalt Not Read the *Rights of Man*." *United States Law Review*, 73:271–86, May 1939. **S101**
An account of the criminal prosecution against Thomas Paine, at the end of the eighteenth century, for his book, *Rights of Man*.

Schnapper, M. B. *Constraint by Copyright; a Report on "Official" and "Private" Practices*. Washington, D.C., Public Affairs, 1960. 154 p. **S102**
"The purpose of this report is to call the attention of the American people to a problem vitally affecting the interests of every citizen: extensive copyrighting of official material by public officials who flagrantly disregard or deftly by-pass laws barring such activities." The private copyrighting of government documents, the author maintains, is contrary to the free press guarantees in the Bill of Rights as well as a specific prohibition of the Copyright Act. He cites specifically the case of Admiral Rickover's speeches and the decision of the U.S. Court of Appeals.

Schneiderhahn, Edward V. P. *Motion Pictures: Influence, Benefits, Evils, Censorship*. St. Louis, St. Louis University, 1917. 68 p. **S103**

Schofield, Henry. "Freedom of the Press in the United States." *Papers and Proceedings, Ninth Annual Meeting, American Sociological Society*, 9:67–116, 1914. (Also in his *Essays on Constitutional Law and Equity*. Boston, Northeastern University Law School, 1921, vol. 2, pp. 510–71) **S104**
This study by a professor of law at Northwestern University has been referred to as a classic statement on the historical development and meaning of the liberty of the press in the United States. Schofield traces American press freedom from the English common law through the First Amendment to the United States Constitution and its subsequent interpretation by the courts. He believes that the Constitution does not provide complete immunity from legislative regulation of the liberty of the press. He considers it desirable for state and federal legislation to be enacted that will give "better protection by the courts of personal reputation and property from defamatory falsehood." "Constitutional liberty of the press in the United States is nothing more nor less than a fine popular attempt to employ the law and its machinery to realize the great saying: 'And ye shall know the truth, and the truth shall make you free.'" Comments on this paper are to be found on pages 123–32 of *Papers and Proceedings*.

"School Boards, Schoolbooks and the Freedom to Learn." *Yale Law Journal*, 59:928–54, 1950. **S105**
A well-documented analysis of the legal issues in public school censorship. The author considers in some detail the banning of *The Nation* in the New York City schools because of articles offending Catholics, and the "encore," i.e. the demand to ban works of Dickens and Shakespeare that were offensive to Jews. The author finds justification in neither law nor theory. "Administratively, its inherent evil is an incapacity to draw the line. Once a book-banning precedent is established, future exclusions are made simpler. . . . Alternatively, a positive approach to the challenges of intolerance and hostile ideology appears necessary. . . . Perhaps school boards might better devote their energies towards establishing merit of school programs wherein basic controversial issues would be openly studied and discussed."

"School Teachers as Film Censors." *World's Work*, 48:248–49, July 1924. **S106**
A report on recommendations made by the Better Film Committee of the National Council of Mothers and Parent-Teacher Associations, to the effect that parents and teachers should take joint action to discourage children from attending unsuitable movies. Two suggestions for teachers: request students to list good movies attended, and pour on the homework while a poor movie is in town. Mrs. Charles E. Merriam was chairman of the Committee.

Schramm, Wilber. *Responsibility in Mass Communications*. New York, Harper, 1957. 391 p. (Prepared under the direction of a study group authorized by the Federal Council of Churches) **S107**
The first part of the book deals with the changing nature of the mass media. The second part traces the main currents of change in the public philosophy of mass communications, including The Four Concepts of Mass Communications which were discussed more fully in Siebert, *et al.*, *Four Theories of the Press*. The third part considers some of the ethical problems confronted by the media—freedom, the right to know, truth and fairness, and popular art. The final section considers the social responsibility of government, the media, and the public in the control and regulation of the mass media.

———, ed. *Communications in Modern Society; Fifteen Studies of the Mass Media* . . . Urbana, Ill., University of Illinois Press, 1948. 252 p. **S108**
Frederick S. Siebert in Communications and Government, presents the fourfold relationship of government to communications (restricting, regulating, facilitating, and participating) and favors a government-sponsored information service to supplement commercial sources. Raymond B. Nixon in Implications of the Decreasing Numbers of Competitive Newspapers takes issue with the charges made by Morris Ernst that monopolies are destroying freedom of the press. Ralph D. Casey in Professional Freedom and Responsibility in the Press, and Robert J. Blakely in The Responsibilities of an Editor, write of the dedication of the profession to a "sacred trust."

———, ed. *Mass Communications; a Book of Readings* . . . Urbana, Ill., University of Illinois Press, 1949. 552 p. **S109**
One section of this anthology relates to Control and Support of Mass Communications. Schramm writes in the introduction: "The problems of who should control communications and how media should be supported, how free they should be and what should be the nature of their social responsibility, have always existed. They have come into the forefront of our thinking since communications have begun to be *mass* communications, and therefore potent political weapons and exceedingly expensive institutions."

Schriftgiesser, Karl. "The Boston Stage Censor: John Michael Casey." *Authors' League Bulletin*, 15(3):7–11, June 1927. **S110**
Since 1904 Mr. Casey has been enforcing the "dictates of propriety and refinement" on the Boston stage under what has come to be known as the Boston Plan. Casey operates as city censor in the licensing division of the mayor's office. "My sole object as 'censor'", Casey states, "is to protect the man whose money is invested in the show or the theater, and the general theatrical public whose one desire is to see clean, wholesome plays."

———. "Boston Stays Pure." *New Republic*, 58:327–29, 8 May 1929. **S111**
A denunciation of the verdict in Suffolk Superior Court in Boston against publisher Donald S. Friede for the sale of Theodore Dreiser's *The American Tragedy*. Until the Massachusetts obscenity law is changed or the courts set aside the verdict, "all modern literature in Massachusetts hovers in fear under the tyrannical figure of the law!"

———. "How Little Rollo Came to Rule the Mind of Boston; History of the Censorship of Plays and Books That Attracts the Attention of the Country." *Boston Transcript*, 21 September 1929, Magazine Section, pp. 1–2. **S112**
An exposé of Boston's police censorship of drama, written during the controversy over banning of Eugene O'Neill's *Strange Interlude*. Includes an account of the appointment by Mayor Patrick A. Collins, in 1904, of Boston's first official drama censor, John Michael Casey. Casey qualified for the job by having served as a drummer in Boston burlesque for twenty years. The author quotes Casey's views on stage morality: "I believe that nothing should be placed upon the stage of any theater anywhere to which you could not take your mother, sweetheart, wife, or sister." Casey attends first night performances and reports any improprieties to a three-man committee consisting of the mayor, the chief justice of the Municipal Court, and the police commissioner, who take the necessary action.

Schroeder, Theodore A. "Abstract of Theodore Schroeder's Speech at Birth Control Meeting, Carnegie Hall, New York City, March 1, 1916." *Mother Earth*, 11:463–67, April 1916. **S 113**

Schroeder (1864–1953), attorney for the Free Speech League and legal counsellor to the Medico-Legal Society of New York, devoted a lifetime to a crusade for freedom of speech and the press, particularly in the area of sex expression. His libertarian views were the subject of considerable controversy, which extended even after his death to a ruling on his will by the Connecticut courts. He has probably written more on the subject of free speech and obscenity than any other writer, his articles appearing in legal, medical, psychological, and radical journals such as the article in *Mother Earth*. On this occasion Schroeder defends the anarchist, Emma Goldman, arrested for circulating birth control literature. He discusses the mental attitude of judges and legislators toward the subject.

————. "Absurdity of the 'Obscenity' Laws." *Physical Culture*, 17:85–88, January 1907. **S 114**

"They are absolutely opposed to elementary common sense and the first principles of modern law." The laws are so absurd, he declared, that even the Bible has been judged obscene (Clay Centre, Kansas, 1895). Abridged from an address, Liberty of Speech and Press Essential to Purity Propaganda, delivered at the National Purity Conference, Chicago, 10 October 1906.

————. "Argument on Blasphemy; the Former Attitude of the English Courts and Recent Changed Constructions." *Truth Seeker*, 43:822–24, 23 December 1916. **S 115**

————. *Blasphemy and Free Speech, being Sample Portions of an Argument which a Connecticut Judge Refused to Read. Printed to Promote the Repeal of the Blasphemy Laws.* New York, Free Speech League, 1918. 53 p. **S 116**

Chapter 1, Statement on the Mockus Case; Chapter 18, Review of Blasphemy Prosecutions; Chapter 21, Roger Williams, James Madison and Thomas Jefferson; Chapter 22, Christianity and the Law.

[————]. "Brief for Free Speech; the Blasphemy Argument Brings up the History of Toleration in New York; the Animus of Justice Kent in the Ruggles Case—his Clerical Antecedents; Overruling of Justice Kent by Judge Parker in the case of Charles C. Moore." *Truth Seeker*, 44:70–71, 3 February 1917; 44:86, 10 February 1917; 44:102–3, 17 February 1917. **S 117**

————. "Censoring Free Speech Advocates." *Call Magazine*, 1:34, 16 November 1919. **S 118**

How a U.S. educational department asked for and then rejected a gift of free-speech literature. Rejected titles are listed.

————. "Censorship of Sex Literature." *Medical Council*, 14:91–98, March 1909. (Reprinted in Schroeder, *"Obscene" Literature and Constitutional Law*, pp. 42–73) **S 119**

————. *A Challenge to Sex Censors.* New York, Privately printed, 1938. 159 p. **S 120**

A development of the thesis that legally and psychologically the words *witchcraft* and *obscenity* "represent only different rationalizations for the same superstition . . . The witches and wizards of old are now the producers of sexy books, pictures, and plays."

————. "Concerning the Meaning of 'Freedom of the Press.'" *Central Law Journal*, 68:227–34, March 1909. (Reprinted in *"Obscene" Literature and Constitutional Law*, pp. 142–53) **S 121**

————. "The Constitution and Obscenity Postal Regulations." *Albany Law Journal*, 26:334–39, November 1907. (Also issued in revised form by Free Speech League under the title, *Unconstitutionality of All Laws Against "Obscene" Literature.* 16 p.) **S 122**

————. *Constitutional Free Speech Defined and Defended in an Unfinished Argument in a Case of Blasphemy.* New York, Free Speech League, 1919. 456 p. **S 123**

The occasion for the book is the argument by Mr. Schroeder, attorney for the Free Speech League, on behalf of the defendent, Michael X. Mockus, a free-thought lecturer, charged with blasphemy in the state of Connecticut. Through both historical and legal argument, Schroeder presents the thesis that blasphemy cannot be a crime under the First Amendment. Beginning with the opinions of Blackstone, which he considers undemocratic, he discusses various English and American decisions and cases relating to blasphemy including that of Abner Kneeland. He draws upon numerous historical documents—reports of trials, speeches, philosophical treatises, and political tracts—both in American and British history to illustrate the evaluation of thinking with respect to freedom of religious thought. He quotes at length from many important but often obscure sources, so that the work becomes "a small encyclopedia of source-material on the question." Included are references to the thinking of Jeremy Bentham, Tunis Wortman, St. George Tucker, Roger Williams, Robert Hall, and Charles Blount.

He summarizes the proceedings of the freedom of the press trials of Alexander Leighton, William Prynne, Henry Burton, John Pockington, Paul Best, John Archer, John Biddle, John Fry, Benjamin Keach, Lodowick Muggleton, Henry Care, Thomas DeLaune, Richard Baxter, John Asgill, Matthew Tindal, Edward Elwall, Bernard Mandeville, Thomas Woolston, Jacob Ilive, Peter Annett, Daniel I. Eaton, George Houston, and James Adair.

————. "Constructive Obscenity, an Unconstitutional Crime." *Physical Culture*, 17:363–64, May 1907. **S 124**

This article was stimulated by the arrest of Bernarr Macfadden, publisher of *Physical Culture*, on obscenity charges. All the safeguards of liberty under due process of law to prevent punishment for constructive crimes "are being violated under the pretext of the 'virtuous' suppression of 'obscene' literature. Obscenity is never the quality of a book or a picture, but always and ever only the quality of the viewing mind." The article also appeared in *Blue Grass Blade* (Louisville, Ky.), 17 March 1907, under the title, Test Case on Obscenity.

————. *The Criminal Anarchy Law and Suppressing the Advocacy of Crime; A Lecture.* New York, Mother Earth Publishing Co., 1907. 16 p. (First appeared in the January 1907 issue of *Mother Earth*; reprinted in Schroeder, *Free Speech for Radicals*, pp. 23–36) **S 125**

————. "Erskine on the Limits of Toleration." *Secular Thought* (Toronto), 37:51–55, February 1911. (Reprinted in Schroeder, *Free Speech for Radicals*, pp. 45–53) **S 126**

Schroeder concludes, after a careful examination of Thomas Erskine's speeches in defense of freedom of the press, that this eighteenth-century English lawyer "was a true believer in a real unabridged liberty of utterance, where no man could be punished so long as the mere verbal portrayal of his ideas is the only factor involved."

————. "Etiology and Development of Our Censorship of Sex-Literature." *Pacific Medical Journal*, 53:213–22, April 1910; 53:279–94, May 1910. (Reprinted in Schroeder, *"Obscene" Literature and Constitutional Law*, pp. 42–73) **S 127**

————. "Evolution of Comstockery." *Altruria*, 2(3):13–17, March 1907. **S 128**

————. "Free Speech and the War." *New Review*, 3:158–61, March 1915. **S 129**

———. *Free Speech Bibliography, Including Every Discovered Attitude toward the Problem, Covering Every Method of Transmitting Ideas and of Abridging Their Promulgation upon Every Subject Matter.* New York, Wilson, 1922. 247 p. **S130**
Contents: Before 1800, General Discussions, Alien and Sedition Laws, Economic Motive, Personal Motive, Religious Motive, Sedition, Sex Motive, and War Motive. A list of suppressed publications is given on pp. 227–39. The Schroeder bibliography includes many topics not covered by the present bibliography—general freedom of thought and opinion, religious freedom, freedom of association, public speech, church and state relations, and religion in the schools. There are also many references to legal briefs and newspaper stories, omitted in the present bibliography.

———. *The Free Speech Case of Jay Fox.* New York, Free Speech League, 1912. 12 p. **S131**
An appeal on behalf of Jay Fox, who was convicted in the State of Washington for violating a state law prohibiting any publication encouraging disrespect for law. The offending article appeared in the *Agitator* of Home, Wash., and was entitled, The Nude and the Prudes, a defense of the rights of a group of nudists. This pamphlet argues that the state law invoked in the Fox case "clearly penalizes every attempt to get a law amended or repealed, for manifestly one cannot make an argument for a repeal or an amendment of a statute without tending to create disrespect for that particular law."

———. *Free Speech for Radicals.* Enlarged edition. Riverside, Conn., Hillacre Bookhouse, 1916. 206 p. (Published for the Free Speech League) **S132**
Ten republished essays on liberty of speech and press, principally from the *Arena* and *Mother Earth*, 1906 to 1915: Our Vanishing Liberty of the Press, Lawless Suppression of Free Speech in New York, On Suppressing the Advocacy of Crime, The Meaning of Unabridged Freedom of Speech, Erskine on the Limits of Toleration, Liberal Opponents and Conservative Friends of Unabridged Free Speech, Our Progressive Despotism, Methods of Constitutional Construction, History of the San Diego Free Speech Fight, and Free Speech and the War. The appendix contains an excerpt from the Final Report of the U.S. Commission on Industrial Relations.

———. *Freedom of the Press and "Obscene" Literature; Three Essays . . .* New York, The Free Speech League, 1906. 71 p. **S133**
Contents: More Liberty of Press Essential to Moral Progress (address to National Purity Federation, Chicago, 1906). What Is Criminally Obscene? A Study of the Absurd Judicial Cases (*Proceedings* of the XV Congrès International de Médecine, Lisbon, 1906). Liberty of Discussion Defended with Special Application to Sex Discussion (*Liberal Review*, August and September 1906).

———. "Government by Spies." *Twentieth Century*, 3:140–44, November 1910. **S134**
Schroeder complains of the vast army of government employees who are checking on the activities of the American people, including what mail they send and receive.

———. "Historical Interpretation of 'Freedom of Speech and of the Press.'" *Central Law Journal*, 70:184–89, 10 March 1910; 70:201–11, 28 March 1910; 70:223–28, 25 March 1910. **S135**
Part 1 covers early English theories of libel and the enactment of the Fox Libel Act of 1792. Part 2 discusses the Star Chamber treatment of sedition, the defense of a free press by Milton, Montesquieu, Robert Hall, and Thomas Jefferson. Part 3 discusses the fight against the taxes on knowledge in England during the early decades of the nineteenth century.

———. "In Defense of Liberty: Macfadden's Arrest." *Physical Culture*, 17:301–2, April 1907. **S136**
Bernarr Macfadden, editor of *Physical Culture*, was arrested and afterward convicted for alleged obscenity in a story published in *Physical Culture* entitled, Growing to Manhood in Civilized Society, written by John R. Coryell.

———. "Intellectual Liberty and Literary Style." *Open Court*, 34:275–78, May 1920. (Reprinted in the *Crucible*, 18 July 1920) **S137**
Freedom of speech and press should not be limited to those with literary facility: "If constitutional free speech is recognized as a 'human right,' then every human must have an 'equal' right to express his own ideas, in his own way, with his own vocabulary, in the service of his own temperment." This includes the right to use scurrilous language. The framers of the Bill of Rights did not intend a "stylists' aristocracy." The article was prompted by the Mockus blasphemy case.

———. "Judicial Destruction of Freedom of the Press." *Albany Law Journal*, 70:323–26, November 1908. (Reprinted in his *"Obscene" Literature and Constitutional Law*, pp. 154–62) **S138**
Freedom of the press is a proposition almost everyone professes to believe yet everyone can be relied upon to endorse some abridgment of it. "The courts have promptly and almost uniformly amended the constitutional guarantees of freedom of speech and press by dogmatically writing into them new exceptions and limitations."

———. "Judicial 'Tests of Obscenity' Applied by Theodore Schroeder." *Alienist and Neurologist*, 31:497–501, November 1910. (A revised version in *"Obscene" Literature and Constitutional Law*, pp. 240–57) **S139**
The author criticizes the judiciary for attempting to make judgments in an area of abnormal and sexual psychology in which they do not have adequate scientific knowledge. They fail to recognize that "obscenity is the contribution of the reading mind."

———. *Law of Blasphemy: The Modern View Exhibited in Model Instructions to a Jury.* New York, Free Speech League, 1919. 18 p. (Reprinted from *Truth Seeker*, 31 August and 7 September 1918) **S140**
While one American court has held that laws against blasphemy are not unconstitutional (*People v. Ruggles*, 8 John 290; 5 Am. Dec. 335) the author believes that a judge might appropriately show that our guarantees of liberty compel a change in the judicial interpretation of blasphemy, a fact to be brought out in the instructions to the jury. The author, therefore, presents suggestions for such a statement. The issues of the *Truth Seeker* carrying these articles were banned by the Post Office Department under the wartime espionage law.

———. "The Lawless Suppression of Freedom of Speech in New York." *Arena*, 39:694–99, June 1908. **S141**
Deals with action by the New York police against the anarchist, Emma Goldman, including threats against those who sold her periodical, *Mother Earth*.

———. "Legal 'Obscenity' and Sexual Psychology." *Alienist and Neurologist*, 29:1–35, August 1908. **S142**
The editor of the *Medico-Legal Journal* refused to publish this article without editing it. Accordingly, it was withdrawn and published in full in the St. Louis journal, *Alienist and Neurologist*, August 1908.

———. *Liberal Opponents and Conservative Friends of Unabridged Free Speech. Being Notes of a Lecture Delivered March 13, 1910, before the Brooklyn Philosophical Association. . . .* New York, Mother Earth Publishing Association, 1910. 16 p. (Also published in *Mother Earth*, May 1910, and in Schroeder, *Free Speech for Radicals*) **S143**
Schroeder replies to critics who take issue with his views that obscenity exists only in the minds of the reader and that any restrictions on expression in this realm as in others is a violation of freedom of the press. He points out that his opponents are strange bedfellows—radical and free-thought leaders such as Robert Ingersoll, Edwin C. Walker, and the editors of the *Truth Seeker*, *Secular Thought*, and *The Public* are in agreement with Anthony

Comstock and the vice societies. On the other hand, support for his libertarian views has come from such political conservatives as Havelock Ellis, Sir Oliver Lodge, and Sir Leslie Stephen. There are three major groups agitating for free speech and press: (1) Socialists, (2) advocates of sex freedom, including the author, and (3) Emma Goldman in behalf of anarchism. Ingersoll's attitude on the obscenity laws is quoted from his book, *As He Is*.

————. *Liberty of Speech and Press Essential to Purity Propaganda. An Address Prepared for the National Purity Conference, and to be Delivered October 10th, 1906, Lincoln Center, Chicago.* [New York, Free Speech League, 1906]. 50p. (Reprinted in *The Light*, January 1907, and in Schroeder, *Freedom of the Press and "Obscene" Literature*, 1906) **S144**
Schroeder urges legal freedom for sex education as the most important step in the purity movement. He recommends abolishing present tests for obscenity and the repeal of all existing laws on obscenity as applied to adults. As for children, Congress should place control of their mail in the hands of their parents. Sex instruction should be offered in the schools in an effort to get rid of the morbid curiosity about sex education books. Anthony Comstock was unable to attend the Conference but a paper by him was read. William A. Coote of the London vice society attended.

————. "A Lobby for Liberty." New York, Free Speech League, 1910. 8p. (Reprinted from *Editorial Review*, March 1910) **S145**
A plea for a lobby to further the case for liberty of the press and speech and to urge repeal of oppressive legislation. Such a lobby is not now in existence because there is no market value represented.

————. "May It Please The Court." *Medico-Legal Journal*, 48:22–25, January–February 1931; 48:60–63, March–April 1931; 48:89–95, May–June 1931. **S146**
In a mock obscenity trial, Schroeder as defense attorney claims that obscenity has no more objective existence than witches and that the court is tempermentally and psychologically incapable of understanding scientific evidence with respect to obscenity. The entire concept of obscenity is a "mass delusion."

[————]. *May It Please the Court, by Amicus Curiae* [pseud.]. *One Experienced with "Obscenity" Now Portrays the Difficulties that Beset the Accused and His Attorney . . .* Mays Landing, N.J., Sunshine Book Company, 1945. 35p. **S147**
In behalf of the nudist press.

————. *Meaning of Free Speech (for Pacifists).* New York, Free Speech League, 1917. 16p. **S148**

Statement made at a free speech meeting held in Madison Square Garden, New York, 1 August 1917, to protest against the arbitrary suppression of 18 radical and pacifist periodicals. No one should be disadvantaged by the state for a psychological offense, and for the mere use of words the state has no rightful jurisdiction to punish except for material injury or overt act. Constitutional free speech includes protection against privately inflicted injury as well as official interference.

————. "The Meaning of Unabridged 'Freedom of Speech.'" In Alden Freeman, *The Fight for Free Speech*, pp. 21–24, and *Central Law Journal* (St. Louis), 26 March 1909. **S149**

————. *Methods of Constitutional Construction. The Synthetic Method Illustrated on the Free Speech Clause of the Federal Constitution . . . With Three Supplements Bearing on the Rights of Revolutionists by James Mill, J. L. De Lolme and John Cartwright.* New York, Free Speech League [1914]. 106p. **S150**
Includes the text of James Mill's *On Liberty of the Press*, J. L. De Lolme's *Right of Resistance* (De Lolme was a French lawyer who admired the British constitution and, according to Schroeder, was the author of the Junius letters), and John Cartwright, a British major who was dismissed from the army for sympathies with the American and French Revolutions. Cartwright was active in the government reform movement of the early 1800's and helped to form the Association for Constitutional Information.

————. *Much Needed Defense for Liberty of Conscience, Speech and Press, with Special Application to Sex Discussion.* New York, Free Speech League, 1906. 23p. (Reprinted from the *Liberal Review*, August and September 1906) **S151**
Persecution of opinion "seems to be an eternal inheritance of humans." It can be traced down through the ages in areas of religious bigotry, and more recently, sex bigotry. "Moral concepts are a matter of geography and evolution. The morality of one country or age is viewed as the moral poison of another country or age." The laws for the suppression of "obscene" literature as administered today deny adults access to part of the necessary facts about their sex nature, and therefore, are a violation of the inalienable right of every individual to acquaintance with the process of nature. "If you are a true liberal you will be ever ready to defend the right of every other man to disagree with you upon every conceivable subject."

————. *A New Concept of Liberty from an Evolutionary Psychologist.* Berkeley Heights, N. J., Oriole Press, 1940. 153p. (Edition limited to 200 copies) **S152**

Eight selections from Schroeder's writings, including his An Indictment of Puritan Censorship and Our Vanishing Liberty of the Press. Contains a brief biography of Schroeder by Joseph Ishill, proprietor of the Oriole Press.

————. *"Obscene" Literature and Constitutional Law; A Forensic Defense of Freedom of the Press.* New York, Privately printed for forensic uses, 1911. 439p. **S153**
This is an encyclopedic work on obscenity laws and court decisions, representing Schroeder's crusade against existing legal attitudes toward obscenity which he believes place pernicious restrictions on the freedom of the press. Much of the book is composed of articles by Schroeder appearing in various legal, medical, or public affairs journals during the early 1900's. It is Schroeder's contention that all laws against obscene literature are unconstitutional.

————. "'Obscene' Literature at Common Law." *Albany Law Journal*, 69: 146–49, May 1907. **S154**
A brief review of the English and American precedence showing that no "obscene libel" was recognized under common law.

————. "On the Implied Power to Exclude 'Obscene' Ideas from the Mail." *Central Law Journal*, 65:177–83, 6 September 1907. (Reprinted in his *"Obscene" Literature and Constitutional Law*, pp. 29–41) **S155**
"Postal laws against 'obscene' literature conflict with constitutional restraints upon Congressional powers" and should be repealed.

————. "Opposition to Freedom of the Press." *American Journal of Eugenics*, 1:1–6, July 1907. (Reprinted in *Secular Thought*, Toronto, August 1907) **S156**
Deals with criticism of those supporting sex censorship.

————. "Our Censorship of Literature." *Tomorrow*, 4:42–44, November 1908. **S157**
Discusses the suppression of *Mrs. Warren's Profession* by the New York vice society.

————. *Our Prudish Censorship Unveiled.* New York, Free Speech League, 1915. 16p. (Reprinted from *Forum*, 1915; published also in *Pacific Medical Journal*, June 1915) **S158**
Schroeder discusses freedom of sex knowledge including sex hygiene, physiology, and the psychology of sex. He protests against any form of censorship on any subject as constitut-

ing a violation of the Constitution. "Always the cure for the sorrows of misinformation and half knowledge is more information."

————. *Our Vanishing Liberty of the Press.* New York, Free Speech League, 1907. 7 p. (Bound with B. O. Flower's *Sound Morality, Versus Morbid Pruriency.* The Schroeder article is reprinted from the December 1906 *Arena*; it also appears in Schroeder, *Free Speech for Radicals,* pp. 1–10) **S159**

"By gradual encroachments and precedents we are rapidly approaching the stage in which we will enjoy any liberties only by permission."

————. "Prosecution for 'Obscenity'; Case of the Polish People's Publishing Co." *Truth Seeker,* 38:226, April 1911. **S160**

The cause of the arrest was the publication of a cartoon offensive to Catholics.

————. *Protest of the Free Speech League against the Passage of Senate Bill No. 1790, Assembly Bill No. 650, New York Legislature, 1911, which Proposes to Penalize Certain Medical Advertising and Intelligence.* New York, Free Speech League, 1911. 12 p. **S161**

The bill relates to advertising treatment for venereal diseases. Whatever may be legally done, Schroeder argues, may be legally advertised.

————. "Psychic Lasciviousness and Purity Legislation." *Medical Critic and Guide,* 7:109–11, October 1907. **S162**

————. *Psychologic Study of Judicial Opinion.* New York, Privately printed for the Friends of Free Speech, 1918. 45 p. (Reprinted from the *California Law Review,* January 1918) **S163**

————. "Psychologic Study of Modesty." *Medical Council* (Philadelphia), 14:18–22, January 1909. (Reprinted in Schroeder, *"Obscene" Literature and Constitutional Law,* pp. 315–25) **S164**

————. "Right of Free Speech; a Peppery Correspondence [with the editor of the *Outlook*]." *Truth Seeker,* 36:34–35, 16 January 1909. **S165**

————. "Rights of Moses Harman under the Constitution; How They Were Denied." *American Journal of Eugenics,* 3:13–15, April 1910. **S166**

Harman was several times convicted of "obscenity" for advocating sex reforms.

————. *Sex and Censorship: The Eternal Conflict.* New York, 1927. 13 p. (Reprinted from the *Medical Journal and Record,* 16 November 1927) **S167**

"Obscenity exists exclusively in the viewing or reading mind, and never is a quality of the thing read or viewed."

————. "Testimony of Mr. Theodore Schroeder." In U.S. Senate. Commission on Industrial Relations. *Industrial Relations; Final Report and Testimony....* Washington, D.C., Govt. Print. Off., 1916, pp. 10840–52, 10866–96 (Doc. 415, 66th Cong., 1st sess.) **S168**

The attorney for the Free Speech League gives testimony before the Commission on violations of freedom of speech and the press in labor disputes. In a prepared statement Schroeder cites examples of government efforts to suppress the speech and publications of radicals. Included examples are: the speech of Fred Warren, editor of *Appeal to Reason,* before the U.S. Circuit Court of Appeals in Minneapolis, where he was tried on charges of sending scurrilous matter through the mail on an outside wrapper; the criminal libel charges against *The Masses;* and the use of the obscenity laws against Freeman Knowles, South Dakota Socialist editor, and the Denver Socialist paper, *Up the Divide.* Schroeder incorporates the text of the article on prostitution from the June 1911 issue of the Denver paper which was suppressed by the Post Office Department. He also cites the suppression, on grounds of obscenity, of the New York *Daily Call,* the Oklahoma *Social Democrat,* and Mrs. Margaret Sanger's *Woman Rebel.* He reports on the trial for seditious libel of Ludobico Comminita, editor of a radical paper at Paterson, N.J., and of the publishers of the *Free Press* of New Castle, Pa. Schroeder includes the text of the offending article, The Nude and the Prude, for which Jay Fox, editor of the anarchist-syndicalist paper, *Agitator,* of Home, Wash., was given a jail sentence for creating disrespect for the law.

[————]. "Theodore Schroeder; an Unconventional and Non-Professional Educator." *Lawyer and Banker,* 8:64–66, February 1915. **S169**

A biographical sketch of one of the leading advocates of freedom in sex expression. Portrait at front of issue.

[————]. *Theodore Schroeder's Last Will.* New York, Psychological Library, 1953. 40 p. **S170**

A decision of the Supreme Court of the State of Connecticut upheld a lower court decision breaking the will of one of America's leading fighters for freedom of press and speech. Schroeder had left his estate to be expended in the collection, arrangement, and publication of his writings. The Court found the writings of no social value and offensive to religion. Judge O'Sullivan found that "the object of the trust . . . is to distribute articles which reek of the sewer." The pamphlet is edited and compiled by Leslie Kuhn, with an Introduction by Alison Reppy, dean of the New York Law School, and an Appreciation by Ethel Clyde.

————. "Twin of Witchcraft. Such Is Blasphemy. Born of the Same Book, the Same Age, the Same Ignorance." *Truth Seeker,* 43:801–3, 16 December 1916. **S171**

————. "Varieties of Criteria of Guilt in Obscenity Cases." *Central Law Journal,* 71:150–56, 2 September 1910. (Reprinted in Schroeder, *"Obscene" Literature and Constitutional Law,* pp. 326–42) **S172**

————. "Varieties of Official Modesty." *Albany Law Journal,* 70:226–31, August 1908. (First published in *American Journal of Eugenics,* December 1907; reprinted in Schroeder, *"Obscene" Literature and Constitutional Law,* pp. 302–15) **S173**

"The purpose of this essay is to exhibit a portion of the official and juridical evidence to prove that 'obscenity,' as used in the statutes by which we now destroy the freedom of the press as to sex discussion, has no exact or definable meaning."

————. *What About You?* Selected, edited, and with an Introduction by Ethel Clyde. New York, Psychological Library, 1951. 60 p. **S174**

Includes selections of Schroeder's writings on sex education, obscenity, freedom of speech and freedom for silence.

————. "What Is Criminally 'Obscene'?" *Albany Law Journal,* 68:211–17, July 1906. (Reprinted from the *Proceedings,* XV Congrès International de Médecine, Lisbon, April 1906, Section XVI) **S175**

The author objects to the legal assumption that the term "obscene" permits of "exact general definition or tests, such as are capable of universal application, producing absolute uniformity of result, no matter by whom the definition or test is applied." Today every medical book that treats of sex is free only by tolerance, not by right. It is a futile struggle for the courts to attempt a definition of "obscenity."

————. "Where Speech is Not Free." *Call Magazine,* 2:8–9, 5 September 1920; 2:6–7, 12 September 1920; 2:6–7, 19 September 1920. **S176**

A summary of the laws of the states and the

United States which in any way abridged freedom of speech before the enactment of war censorship.

———. *Where Speech Is Not Free—In the USA. An Appeal to the Record.* Mays Landing, N.J., Open Road Press, 1944. 50p. **S177**
Schroeder has gathered together evidence of the lack of free speech in the United States in the realms of labor, sex, birth control, socialism, and free thought.

———. "Why Do Purists Object to Sex-Discussion?" *American Journal of Eugenics*, 1:118–23, September 1907. **S178**
An attack on various schools of moral sentimentalists about sex—Comstockians, Mormon polygamists, "spiritual lovers," and lascivious ascetics. "Erotophobia" or "erotomania" should both be rejected on scientific evidence; sex censorship is attacking the result rather than the cause of a problem. "The desire for pornographic literature is but the evidence that healthy and natural curiosity has grown morbid through the purist's success in suppressing the proper information."

———. *Why: "Obscene" Literature and Constitutional Law, a Forensic Defense of Freedom of the Press . . . ; Is Not Sold to You.* New York, Privately printed for forensic uses, 1911. 8p. **S179**
A prospectus for and defense of the author's book on obscenity, which, if sold, might violate the obscenity laws.

———. "Why the 'Obscenity' Laws Should Be Annulled." *Physical Culture*, 18:169–70, September 1907. **S180**
The author gives eight reasons for repealing the postal laws on obscenity: (1) Congress has no implied power to make such regulations under the Constitution. (2) Our Constitution precludes the punishment of mere psychological crimes. (3) The laws are void under the First Amendment. (4) The statute furnishes no standard or test by which to differentiate that which is obscene from that which is not. (5) The statute, because of its uncertainty, presents no clear guide to citizens to enable them to keep from violating the law, and is therefore a violation of due process of law. (6) Every conviction is secured under an *ex post facto* law and, therefore, unconstitutional. (7) "When the law is uncertain there is no law." (8) Congress has delegated to courts not only the power to judge whether an act has been committed, but whether or not it constitutes a crime.

———. *Witchcraft and Obscenity; Twin Superstitions.* New York, Free Speech League, 1912. 16p. (Portions appear in the *Free Press Anthology*, "Obscene" Literature and Constitutional Law, in *Lucifer, the Light*

Bearer, 6 June 1907, and in *Physical Culture*, June 1907) **S181**
Obscenity, like witches, exists only in the mind. Schroeder criticizes those opponents of the censorship of obscenity who accept censorship in principle, but oppose its application in a particular work. "As for me, I am not content to protest merely against the abuse of arbitrary power; I want that power itself destroyed. . . . I demand that a searching and fearless inquiry be made as to the objective characteristics of obscenity as well as witches." Schroeder quotes from a letter he received from Havelock Ellis: "It seems to me that there can be no doubt whatever regarding the soundness of your view of 'obscenity' as residing exclusively, not in the thing contemplated, but in the mind of the contemplating person."

———, comp. *Free Press Anthology.* New York, Free Speech League and the Truth Seeker, 1909. 267p. **S182**
Contents: Milton's *Areopagitica*, Peter Bayle's *An Explanation Concerning Obscenities*, historic defenses of free press made by John Locke, Robert Hall, Thomas Erskine, Tunis Wortman, Jeremy Bentham, Thomas Cooper, G. J. Holyoake and others; more recent statements relating to obscenity censorship by Louis F. Post, Robert Buchanan, B. O. Flower, Theodore A. Schroeder, and Edwin C. Walker; references to the obscenity cases against Moses Harman and D. M. Bennett. The appendix contains brief accounts of censorship cases against sex-literature: Dr. William W. Sanger's *History of Prostitution*, Mortimer A. Warren's *Almost Fourteen*, Clark's *Marriage Guide*, Havelock Ellis' *Studies in the Psychology of Sex*, Dr. C. W. Malchow's *The Sexual Life*, and Mrs. Ida C. Craddock's *The Wedding Night*. A bibliography of magazine articles by Schroeder on freedom of speech and press appears on pp. 264–67.

———, ed. *Edward Bond Foote. Biographical Notes and Appreciatives.* New York, Free Speech League, 1913. 85p. **S183**
Appreciation of Dr. Foote as a friend of freedom of speech and the press and founder of the Free Speech League.

———, ed. *List of References on Birth-Control.* New York, Wilson, 1918. 52p. **S184**
A list of books, pamphlets, and articles in English, Dutch, French, German, Italian, Spanish and other languages in support of birth control.

———, and John S. Sumner. "Should the Movies be Censored? Surely, Says Vice-Suppressing Chief. Why? Asks Free Speech Advocate." *New York World*, Editorial Section: 1, 3 April 1921. **S185**

Schultz, John. "Border Crossing." *Evergreen Review*, 30:99–112, May–June 1963. **S186**

A description of the grueling search for "treasonable" and "obscene" materials by U.S. Customs officials when the author crossed from Mexico to the United States at Laredo, Texas. Even standard works published and sold in the United States were suspect. The author's manuscript was seized and only returned by Customs after protest from the American Civil Liberties Union.

Schumach, Murray. *The Face on the Cutting Room Floor; The Story of Movie and Television Censorship.* New York, Morrow, 1964. 305p. **S187**
After considering Hollywood's current controversy over nudity on the screen, the author describes the events of the 1920's and 30's that led to the self-censorship of movies under the Production Code. In the second part, Quality and Control, he discusses particular movies that were the object of controversy—*The Outlaw, The Moon is Blue, The Man With the Golden Arm, Streetcar Named Desire, From Here to Eternity,* and *Double Indemnity.* Part 3 deals with Pressures and Politics, the activities of the Legion of Decency, pressures from such minority groups as the NAACP, Jewish organizations, and the quiet pressures of government agencies. In Part 4, Aftermath of Cowardice, the author discusses the blacklist of Hollywood actors, writers, and producers for their espousal of liberal or left wing causes, and the answer to the blacklist—"Hollywood Underground." Part 5, Boudoirs and Blood, treats in detail Hollywood's handling of themes of sex and violence. Part 6, Trial and Error, discusses the action of the courts in such movie censorship cases as *The Miracle (Burstyn v. Wilson), Lady Chatterley's Lover (Kingsley International Pictures v. Regents), Garden of Eden (Excelsior Pictures Corp. v. Regents),* and *Don Juan (Times Film Corp. v. City of Chicago).* Part 7 deals with television censorship, and Part 8, What Next?, considers future solutions to the movie censorship dilemma, including classification of movies. The Appendix contains: Curious Examples of Foreign Censorship, How Some Foreign Countries Classify Films, and the text of the Motion Picture Production Code.

Schuyler, Livingston R. *The Liberty of the Press in the American Colonies before the Revolutionary War. With Particular Reference to Conditions in the Royal Colony of New York.* New York, Thomas Whittaker, 1905. 86p. (Published also in *Magazine of History*, May–June, July, November and December 1905) **S188**
A study based largely on an examination of the records of the New York General Assembly and O'Callaghan's *Documents Relative to the Colonial History of New York.* Includes an account of the Zenger case. Chapter 1 deals with the press in England before the nineteenth century; chapter 2, the press in Massachusetts; chapter 3, the press in Pennsylvania; chapter 4, the press in New York; and chapter 5, conclusions and bibliography.

Schuyler, Philip. "2 Civil Liberties Champions Clash on Press Freedom." *Editor and Publisher*, 77(50):7+, 9 December 1944. **S 189**

Arthur Garfield Hays is confident the press is and will remain free provided the government does not pass new restraining laws; Morris L. Ernst sees a grave threat in the "growing economic domination of the pipelines of mass communication."

Schwab, Jeffrey A. "Statute Prohibiting Obscene Materials in the Mails." *Brooklyn Law Review*, 29:325–28, April 1963. **S 190**

A review of recent court decisions, including the case of *Manuel Enterprises, Inc., et al. v. Day*, 370 U.S. 478 (1962).

Schwartz, Bernard, *ed. Protection of Public Morals through Censorship*. New York, New York University School of Law, 1953. 88 p. (Social Meaning of Legal Concepts, no. 5) **S 191**

Contents: A Lawyer Looks at Censorship by James M. Landis; The View of an Artist by Elmer Rice; The Ethical Aspects of Censorship by Horace M. Kallen; and Some Effects of Censorship upon Society by Goodwin B. Watson. (Excerpts from the Watson paper appear in Daniels, *The Censorship of Books*, pp. 39–45.)

Schwartz, Elias. "Sir George Buc's Authority as Licenser for the Press." *Shakespeare Quarterly*, 12:467–68, Autumn 1961. **S 192**

Quotes relevant parts of a letter from George Chapman to Sir George Buc upbraiding him for refusing Chapman a license to print Byron plays, the refusal evidently coming after the protest by the French Ambassador to the performance of these plays early in 1608.

Schwartz, Louis B. "Criminal Obscenity Law; Portents from Recent Supreme Court Decisions and Proposals of the American Law Institute in the Model Penal Code." *Pennsylvania Bar Association Quarterly*, 29:8–17, October 1957. **S 193**

Deals with the tentative section on obscenity in the Model Penal Code (Section 207.10).

Schwartz, Murray L. "The Mail Must Not Go Through—Propaganda and Pornography." *UCLA Law Review*, 11:805–58, July 1964. **S 194**

———, and James C. N. Paul. "Foreign Communist Propaganda in the Mails: A Report on Some Problems of Federal Censorship." *University of Pennsylvania Law Review*, 107:621–66, March 1959. **S 195**

The authors "report on these activities, examine the legal bases for the operation and weigh a number of legislative alternatives against the constitutional guarantee of free expression." Part of a study financed by the Fund for the Republic. A full-length book by the authors on censorship of the mail is entered under James C. N. Paul.

"Science Hush-Hushed." *Time*, 39:90, 11 May 1942. (Excerpt in Summers, *Wartime Censorship*, pp. 144–45) **S 196**

The affect that wartime secrecy has on the reduction of scientific reporting at the meetings of national science societies.

Scileppi, John F. "Obscenity and the Law." *New York Law Forum*, 10:297–306, September 1964. **S 197**

"The prevailing judicial attitude which has unwisely enlarged our historical concepts of freedom of the press has resulted in a violation of society's right to maintain and protect its moral fiber. Justice therefore requires the restoration of that balance which is essential to the preservation of conflicting constitutional rights."

Scofield, Cora L. *A Study of the Court of Star Chamber, Largely Based on Manuscripts in the British Museum and the Public Record Office*. Chicago, University of Chicago Press, 1900. 82 p. **S 198**

A study of the origin, composition, and action of the court, including its operation in the suppression of printing. Gives methods of procedure in trials.

Scoler, Jerome A. "Statutes Prohibiting Dissemination of Birth Control Knowledge." *Boston University Law Review*, 23:115–18, January 1943. **S 199**

In the case of *Tileston v. Ullman*, 26 A (2d) 582 (Conn.) the court decided that the Connecticut statute against dissemination of birth control information does not violate either the Constitution of Connecticut or that of the United States.

"Scope of Blasphemy Laws." *Truth Seeker*, 43:838–39, 30 December 1916. **S 200**

The case of Michael X. Mockus, under indictment in Connecticut for blasphemy, prompts this historical review and criticism of the blasphemy laws of England and the United States. Theodore A. Schroeder was the attorney for Mockus in the appeal before the District Court.

"Scope of Statutes Censoring Obscene Literature." *Illinois Law Review*, 40:417–21, January–February 1946. **S 201**

The Massachusetts decision on *Strange Fruit*

prompts the editor to review the interpretation of obscenity statutes by the courts. "At least one court has gone so far as to grant literature immunity from obscenity censorship provided obscene parts do not overbalance artistic or educational merits." This forces the court to determine what is artistic and educational and "this sort of determination is not a proper one for the court to make."

"The Scope of the PLAIFC: a Symposium." *Pennsylvania Library Association Bulletin*, 18:9–12, May 1963. **S 202**

Comments by members of the executive board of the newly-created Intellectual Freedom Committee of the Pennsylvania Library Association with respect to the scope of the Committee.

Scott, F. R. "Freedom of Speech in Canada." In Canadian Political Science Association, *Papers and Proceedings*. Ottawa, The Association, 1933, pp. 169–89. **S 203**

Consideration of freedom of speech and, to a lesser degree, of the press in Canada in light of the economic crisis of the 1930's. The author reports on the restrictions placed on works dealing with economic and social radicalism.

Scott, George R. *"Into Whose Hands,"* an Examination of Obscene Libel in Its Legal, Sociological and Literary Aspects. London, Swan, 1945. 236 p. (Reprinted by Waron Press, Brooklyn, 1961) **S 204**

Deals with the origin and development of laws and court decisions relating to obscenity in England and the United States. The author describes the trials and tribulations of authors, publishers, and booksellers who have been subjected to the pressures of censorship. He suggests alteration in existing English laws dealing with obscenity. The title of the book is derived from the classic test of obscenity stated by Lord Chief Justice Cockburn in 1868: "I think the test of obscenity is this, whether the tendency of the matter charged as obscenity is to deprave and corrupt those whose minds are open to such immoral influences and *into whose hands* a publication of this sort may fall."

———. "The Law Relating to Obscenity and Its Dangerous Implications." *Journal of Sex Education*, 3:148–52, February–March 1951. **S 205**

Scott, Leroy. "Hays Organization Co-operates with Authors' League." *The Authors' League Bulletin*, 15(9):6–7, January 1928. **S 206**

Agreement between a Motion Picture Committee of the League and the Hays office on the basis and procedure for banning plays and fiction by the latter, to give authors and their work adequate protection from arbitrary and capricious action.

Scott, Paul W. "War Censorship." *Wilson Library Bulletin*, 14:291, 295, December 1939.   **S 207**
A comparison of Canadian censorship of 1939 with United States regulations in World War I. Canadian censorship regulations of World War II provide for the suppression of "any adverse or unfavorable statement, report or opinion likely to prejudice the defence of Canada or the efficient prosecution of the war."

Scott, W. J. "The *Lolita* Case." *Landfall*, 58:134–38, June 1961.   **S 208**
Deals with the prosecution of the book, *Lolita*, under the New Zealand Indecent Publications Act. In the decision the literary and artistic merits of the book were subordinated to the tendency of the work to corrupt and deprave.

Scott-James, R. A. "The Firm Censorship." *Saturday Review* (London), 151: 8–9, 3 January 1931.   **S 209**
If official censorship is to be retained for the theater and extended to the cinema as has been proposed, it should be reformed. It should reflect public opinion, and the defendent should have the right to plead his case before a tribunal. The censor should be the servant of the people, not the master.

———. "Should Reviewers Be Censors?" *Spectator*, 150:280–281, 3 March 1933.
                                                S 210
Defends the right and duty of reviewers to say that a bad book is bad.

"Scouring the Smut From the Newsstand." *Literary Digest*, 92:31–32, 12 February 1927.   **S 211**

"Screening Public School Textbooks in Indiana." *Nation*, 173:511, 15 December 1951.   **S 212**

[Scripps-Howard Newspapers]. *Synopsis of the Law of Libel and the Right of Privacy.* New York, Scripps-Howard, 1963. 29 p.
                                                S 213
This handbook "is published for the purpose of alerting newspaper editors, reporters, desk men and others in the newspaper field of the dangers arising from the use of libelous words, statements, expressions and pictures, and from the invasion of a person's privacy."

Scroggs, *Sir* William. *The Lord Chief Justice Scroggs, His Speech in the Kings-Bench, the First Day of This Present Michaelmas Term, 1679. Occasion'd by the Many Libellous Pamphlets Which Are Publisht against Law, to the Scandal of the Government, and Publick Justice* . . . London, R. Pawlet, 1679. 8 p. (Also in Howell, *State Trials*, vol. 7, pp. 701 ff.)   **S 214**

Scroggs was a Restoration judge who presided with a heavy hand over a number of sedition cases, attempting to regulate printing through the court. He maintained, in his speech, the right of the court in the interest of public safety to "take care to prevent and punish the mischiefs of the Press." If the press were not contained, the country would be at the mercy of the libels of the Papists, the factious, and the mercenaries. According to Scroggs it was illegal under the Regulation of Printing Acts to publish anything whatever about the government. Scroggs was later impeached for his arbitrary acts in connection with sedition trials.

Scrutineer, *pseud.* "Secret Blacklist; Untold Story of the USIA." *Nation*, 179:376–79, 30 October 1954.   **S 215**
The Washington correspondent of a New York newspaper reports anonymously on the compilation and use of a whitelist and a blacklist of writers, artists, and composers, by the U.S. Information Agency overseas. The blacklist contains some 7,000 names of (1) avowed Communists, (2) invokers of the Fifth Amendment, (3) persons convicted of crimes involving national security, and an unpublicized fourth category—"additional data" cases, where there is derogatory information about the person in the files.

Seabury, William M. *Motion Picture Problems; the Cinema and the League of Nations.* New York, Avondale Press, 1929. 426 p.   **S 216**
Section 6 deals with The Broken Reeds, Censorship and the Industry. "The nations should agree upon a few fundamental specifications of pictures," Seabury states, "the showing of which should be prohibited internationally by such agreement and nationally by appropriate executive or legislative enactment. . . . Inspection, instead of censorship, applied at the source of production, by inspectors designated by the League of Nations, in behalf of all of the nations request ing such action, would achieve highly desirable results."

———. *The Public and the Motion Picture Industry.* New York, Macmillan, 1926. 340 p.   **S 217**
Seabury was former general counsel to the National Association of the Motion Picture Industry. He discusses block booking and circuit booking as restraints of trade, Treasury Department censorship, copyright restrictions, restrictions on attendance by children, and Sunday closing. Chapter 11 deals with The Futility of Censorship. "While there should be no state or other censorship of pictures before their exhibition and hence no censorship commission with its attending expense and utterly futile activity, there should nevertheless be legislative authority to prevent the exhibition of pictures which it is obvious to everyone but those engaged in the industry should not be exhibited even though they may not be actually obscene."

Seagle, William. *Cato; or The Future of*

Censorship. London, Paul, Trench, Trübner, 1930. 96 p.   **S 218**
A classic analysis of censorship of sex expression in literature. "The great crime is now neither blasphemous nor seditious libel, but 'obscene libel.'" Art rather than religion or politics is under attack today. Censorship is only practical when ideas are likely to affect the masses. The "penny pamphlet" is more dangerous to authority than the "three guinea book," but a work in a foreign language is considered safe. The writer distinguishes between two kinds of obscenity: that which represents "excessive sexualism and contravenes the sense of shame, and that which has less sexual exhibitionism but tends to bring accepted morality into contempt. It is the latter, the sexual radicalism, that is subject to the more severe censorship. The newspaper, Seagle notes, has won comparative freedom of expression through years of struggle. The book and especially the stage play have less freedom. Seagle traces the development of sex censorship in England and America and looks into the future. Ultimately, he predicts a psychological censorship in which "perfection of the mind of man will be the ruling passion of the government of society."

———. "Paradox of American Censorship." In S. D. Schmalhausen, ed., *Behold America.* New York, Farrar and Rinehart, 1931, pp. 343–59.   **S 219**
The reason for the compatibility of democracy and censorship is plutocracy. America has traditionally demanded freedom from prior restraint, but not from subsequent punitive censorship. While Americans have objected to government interference with their freedom, they have allowed self-censorship and censorship by private societies. In the minds of some, obscenity became an offense of the same order as murder and arson, and unorthodox sex ideas were akin to radical social and economic doctrines. "The censorship of the Machine Age dominates in all countries where capitalism and industrialization flourish. But it has been carried to its greatest lengths naturally in America." The author sees in the monopolies of the capitalist system the greatest threats to freedom of expression.

———. "The Technique of Suppression." *American Mercury*, 7:35–42, January 1926.
                                                S 220
Deals with three types of statutes by which various states have eroded the freedoms guaranteed in the Bill of Rights. These statutes are known popularly as Red Flag, Criminal Syndicalism, and Criminal Anarchy or Sedition Laws.

[Sealy, George, and Joseph Hodson]. *An Address to the Public, relative to a late Trial at Salisbury Assizes, in March 1774, on a curious Information, The King, at the Suit of Wm. Buckler, Esq. (A Justice of the Peace for Wilts) against the Printers of the*

Salisbury Journal ₁Sealy *and* Hodson₎. *Together with a Copy of the said Information, and the Argument of Council, before the Court of King's Bench at Westminster.* London, 1774. 45 p.　**S 221**
The printers were found guilty of publishing a libel on Justice of the Peace William Buckler in the form of an anonymous public apology. The decision was rendered by Lord Mansfield, who denied that freedom of the press was an issue. Included is a letter from William Temple of Trowbridge, inviting those who wished to protest the decision in the name of freedom of the press to meet at his house.

"A Season of Censorship Discussion." *Publishers' Weekly*, 111:1566–69, 16 April 1927.　**S 222**
Editorial on the recent wave of censorship in New York and Boston.

A Second Letter to Sir Charles Forbes . . . on the Suppression of Public Discussion in India, and the Banishment, without Trial, of Two British Editors from that Country by the Acting Governor-General, Mr. Adam. By a Proprietor of India-stock. London, Printed for J. M. Richardson, 1824. 70 p. (*East India Pamphlets*, vol. 2, no. 8; also in *The Pamphleteer*, 1825, vol. 25, pp. 33–60)　**S 223**

A Second Letter to the Right Honourable The Earl T——E. In Which The Proceedings relative to J——N W——S, from March 28th to June 18th are Mutually considered; the Person clearly pointed out who was the Cause of the present Distractions: and A Curious Anecdote, With regard to Lord M——D's Family, Never published before . . . London, A. Henderson, n.d. 44 p.　**S 224**
Deals unsympathetically with John Wilkes and favorably with Lord Mansfield, who presided at Wilkes's libel trial.

"Seditious Libels." *Law Times*, 48:431–32, 2 April 1870.　**S 225**
A summary of the sedition law as it stands today, with recommendations now before the Government to extend the law in the interest of suppressing the Irish national press.

Seelman, Ernest P. *Law of Libel and Slander in the State of New York.* . . . Albany, Williams Press, 1933. 742 p. Supplement 1941. 180 p.　**S 226**
Swindler describes this work as the "most comprehensive study yet made of libel law within the boundaries of one state's laws and court cases."

Segal, Paul M. "Recent Trends in Censorship of Radio Broadcast Programs." *Rocky Mountain Law Review*, 20:366–80, June 1948.　**S 227**
Notes on court decisions, 1931–47.

Segal, Roland. "South Africa: The End of Free Speech." *Writer*, 10–11, Winter 1962.　**S 228**
A South African writer in exile describes the new apparatus of censorship established under the Nationalist Government.

Seitz, Don C. "Newspapers and the War." *American Review of Reviews*, 50:465–68, October 1914.　**S 229**
Effects of English and German censorship on American newspapers at beginning of World War I.

Seldes, George. "Abettors of Tyranny; New Critics of the Press." *Nation*, 180: 138–40, 12 February 1955.　**S 230**
Concern with "the most dangerous activity of the McCarthyite movement"—the attempt to destroy an opposition by using a red smear to arouse popular opinion against it.

——. *Can These Things Be.* New York, Brewer, Warren & Putnam, 1931. 433 p.　**S 231**
A sequel to *You Can't Print That!* An exposé of propaganda and censorship that the author claims exists in the coverage of foreign news by the American press. His attacks are aimed at the influence of fascism, the official foreign press, and the Catholic Church.

——. *The Catholic Crisis.* New York, Messner, 1939. 357 p.　**S 232**
A candid discussion of pressures brought to bear by the Catholic Church against the American press, movies, and book publishers. Considerable attention is given to the Legion of Decency and to the efforts of the Church to influence American public opinion in behalf of the Fascists in Spain.

——. *Freedom of the Press.* Indianapolis, Bobbs-Merrill, 1935. 380 p.　**S 233**
The author describes what he considers the corrupting influences of big business on the press—the utilities, oil, and drug companies. He shows how, over the years, news has been suppressed or perverted to suit vested interests. He describes the fight of the independent press against "invisible government" and pressure groups.

——. *Lords of the Press.* New York, Messner, 1938. 408 p.　**S 234**
A violent attack on the American Newspaper Publishers' Association and certain individual publishers who, he claims, have used the pretext of protecting freedom of the press to protect vested interests.

——. *Los Amos de la Prensa, Prólogo, notas y Epílogo de Gregorio Selser.* Buenos Aires, Editorial Triangulo, 1959. 479 p. (Colección "Historia Viva")　**S 235**

——. "New War on the Press; 'Reform' from the Right." *Nation*, 180:113–16, 5 February 1955.　**S 236**
"For the first time in American history the press, which Jefferson described as playing a greater role in a democracy than government itself, is under sustained attack from the right—the reactionary or potentially fascist element in the United States." Account of McCarthyism and its efforts to discredit and destroy democratic elements in the press.

——. "The Poisoned Springs of World News." *Harper's Magazine*, 169:719–31, November 1934.　**S 237**
Seldes is concerned with the control and manipulation of news from those countries with dictatorships. He calls for the press of the free world to fight for the news and for the newspapers to stand behind their correspondents against the censorship of dictators.

——. *You Can't Print That! The Truth Behind the News, 1918–1928.* New York, Payson & Clarke, 1929. 465 p.　**S 238**
A newspaper correspondent recounts his experience with censorship and propaganda during and immediately after World War I. The first part deals with United States and British censorship of news during the war; the remainder of the book deals largely with postwar censorship in Italy, Russia, Arabia, and Mexico.

Seldes, Gilbert. *The Great Audience.* New York, Viking, 1950. 299 p.　**S 239**
In a section on the movies the author discusses the Production Code as it operates primarily against sex, and the pressure groups that bear on the movie industry. The Code "sets out to uphold the sanctity of the institution of marriage and ends by undermining the moral foundation upon which marriage stands." Seldes considers the public-interest responsibility of radio and television and proposes a revolution of the popular arts in terms of physics rather than aesthetics, in terms of social significance rather than private pleasures.

——. "Law, Pressure, and Public Opinion." *Hollywood Quarterly*, 1:422–26, July 1946.　**S 240**
The author offers "an incomplete thesis: that social controls which operate effectively on such older forms as books and newspapers are not sufficiently developed to give us standards in radio and the movies. This, in turn, means that we are developing controls of the popular arts by trial and error; and that both laws and pressures may be useful, as they certainly may be vicious."

——. "Pressures and Pictures." *Nation*, 172:104–6, 3 February 1951; 172:132–34, 10 February 1951.　**S 241**

The order given by the New York City commissioner of licenses for the Paris Theater to end its presentation of the film *The Miracle* began "a case more complex than most in the history of civil liberties." The Board of Regents is expected to decide whether the picture may continue. "If they decide against the picture, the issue will be taken to the courts and the interested public will discover that *movies are not protected by the First Amendment*. If the decision is to continue the picture, a powerful organized drive will be undertaken to alter the New York State law in order to subject the Board of Regents to minority pressure." The articles discuss the forms and limits imposed by pressures and the particular danger for movies since they are not legally considered as part of the press or organs of public opinion.

————. *The Public Arts*. New York, Simon and Schuster, 1956. 303 p. **S 242**
In this critical analysis of the movies, radio, and television, Seldes considers, among many facets of broadcasting, the three major problems relating to apsects of freedom—the right to broadcast, the right to editorialize, and immunity from censorship. He also devotes a chapter to Edward R. Murrow's challenge to Senator McCarthy and the concept of "equal time" that was involved.

————. "A Short Angry View of Film Censorship." *Theatre Arts*, 35:56–57, August 1951. **S 243**
A picture of film censorship—by the Johnston office under the Code and before the picture is made; by State boards of review before the film has been shown; and by police power after a film is exhibited. The "dwindling privilege of free expression in the films corresponds to the dwindling exercise of free expression in schools, in politics, in newspapers, in broadcasts."

"Self-Censorship of the Stage." *Literary Digest*, 90(1):25, 3 July 1926. **S 244**
Comments on the voluntary play-juries established to review New York stage productions for possible deletion or termination.

Selwyn, James. "The Town That Battled over Sex Education." *Redbook*, 110(1); 54–55, 106–8, November 1957. **S 245**
Citizens of Argenta, Ill., were alarmed over the flood of pornography. When the Superintendent of Schools proposed a sex education program as a solution, a controversy was touched off, with an organization known as Parents Unlimited leading the opposition to the use of certain movies, books, and talks. In a town vote, sex education won by 386 to 103.

Selz, Jay, and Howard K. Smith. "The Nervous Networks." *Progressive*, 27(9): 20–23, September 1963. **S 246**
News-analyst Smith reveals, in an interview, the pressures applied against television newsmen.

Semar, John. "The Censor and *The Mask*." *Mask*, 2:49–52, October 1909. **S 247**
An essay by the editor, in defense of the censor of drama, calling for more rather than less censorship to prevent London from being flooded by vulgarity. "The theatre is not the property of the mob and is not a place for exhibitions, animal or human."

Semeta, Ramutis R. "Journalist's Testimonial Privilege." *Cleveland-Marshall Law Review*, 9:311–22, May 1960. **S 248**
In examining the contention that newsmen have statutory privilege to refuse to reveal the source of their news, the author finds the journalist's cause for such a grant inadequate. Such decisions should be left to judicial tribunals.

Semmler, Clement. "James Joyce in Australia." In his *Uncanny Man*. Sydney, Angus and Robertson, 1963, pp. 13–30. **S 249**
An account of the censorship of Joyce's books in Australia.

"Senate Debates 'Censorship.'" *Publishers' Weekly*, 117:1668–69, 22 March 1930. **S 250**
Debate between Senators Reed Smoot on one side and Bronson Cutting and Burton K. Wheeler on the other, over the obscene and seditious book clause in the tariff bill. Smoot defended Customs censorship; Cutting and Wheeler argued against legislation that reflected fear of foreign literature.

Senator Hennings and FOI. Columbia, Mo., Freedom of Information Center, School of Journalism, University of Missouri, 1960. 3 p. (Publication no. 41) **S 251**
A résumé of Senator Hennings' efforts to increase the flow of information from government to the people.

Sensabaugh, George F. *That Grand Whig, Milton*, Stanford, Calif., Stanford University Press, 1952. 213 p. (Stanford University Publications, University Series, Language and Literature, volume 11) **S 252**
A study showing the impact of Milton's political thoughts in the latter part of the seventeenth century when the Whigs were in power. The author shows how the ideas in Milton's great work on the freedom of the press, *Areopagitica*, which probably created very little stir during the Puritan Revolution, were revived in the works of Charles Blount and William Denton to attack the licensing act. He demonstrates by use of parallel text how Blount and Denton borrowed heavily from Milton both for ideas and actual phrasing in their pamphlets. He also discusses at some length Blount's pamphlet, *Reasons Humbly Offered . . .*, which attacked the licenser, Edmund Bohun.

"Sense and Censorship." *Literary Digest*, 54:1318–19, 5 May 1917. **S 253**
Comments by newspapers and Congressmen on the censorship clause in the wartime espionage law.

Sercombe, Parker H. "Free Speech? Not Yet—Not Yet!" *Physical Culture*, 18:48, July 1907. **S 254**
Excerpts from an address made in Chicago at a reception for Moses Harman, released from prison after serving a sentence for obscenity. Includes comments on the mobbing of the editor of *Voice of the Negro*.

Serviss, Trevor K. "Freedom to Learn: Censorship in Learning Materials." *Social Education*, 17:65–70, February 1953. **S 255**
A textbook editor discusses the attacks on school textbooks. Sincere, constructive criticism of textbooks is welcomed by publishers, but much of it comes from "self-appointed, dogmatic guardians of a way of life in which we must live according to the prescription of the few." He reports on the *New York Times* study of textbook censorship, and discusses at some length the care and safeguards that are observed in the preparation of school textbooks.

Sethre, Robert A. "Freedom of Information Scores on the Campus." *Quill*, 43(5):13–14, May 1955. **S 256**
"Steady prodding by the *University of Washington Daily* opens the door to Board of Control sessions."

Sevareid, Eric. "Censors in the Saddle." *Nation*, 160:415–17, 14 April 1945. **S 257**
"Among the miserable legacies this war will leave in many parts of the world is a system of censorship which has become such an intricate, cunning mechanism, such a deeply ingrained habit of the official mind that free journalists are now confronted with the most exhausting obstacle course the profession has known in decades."

Seven Arts. London, Hansom Books, 1956–date. Monthly. **S 258**
A composite of the monthly periodicals *Books and Bookmen*, *Films and Filming*, *Dance and Dancers*, *Music and Musicians*, *Plays and Players*, and *Records and Recordings*, which sometimes carry news and comment on freedom of expression related to the various media.

Severson, Thor. "The Last Outpost of Feudal Journalism: Copper Controls the Press of Montana." *Nieman Reports*, 6(4): 39–42, October 1952. **S 259**
"This is from the first of six articles in the *Denver Post* on the influence of the Anaconda

Copper Mining Company on the public in Montana through its chain of newspapers."

Seward, William H. "Law of Libel and Slander." *Western Law Journal*, 2:465–72, July 1845. **S 260**
Extracts from a speech by William H. Seward in the case of *Cooper v. Greeley and McElrath*, before the Supreme Court of the State of New York. Seward calls for a review of the law of libel which puts an undue restraint on free expression by the public press. He states that the American courts have "extended still wider the broad and dangerous definitions of libel, which in an unfortunate age were adopted in England, and have rendered it impossible to justify any libel, however true."

Sex and Censorship. Vol. 1, no. 1, 1958. San Francisco, Mid-Tower Publishing Co. Wallace de Ortega Maxey, editor. A total of three issues published during 1958–59. **S 261**
A sensational exposé of censorship, presented for popular appeal. The first issue contains an article by Henry Miller, The Censor Censored; an article by James Kepner, Jr., *One* Magazine Cleared; and articles on the court decision on Allen Ginsberg's *Howl*.

"Sex and Censorship in Literature and the Arts." *Playboy*, 8(7):27–28+, July 1961. **S 262**
A panel discussion by Judge Thurman Arnold; Dr. Albert Ellis, psychologist; Ralph Ginzburg, author; Maurice Girodias, publisher; Norman Mailer, author; Otto Preminger, movie director; and Barney Rosset, publisher. The aim of the discussion is to shed some light on the writer—and those in allied arts—confronted with the conflict between his work, as it relates to sex, and the forces of censorship.

Seymour, Charles. "How Free Can Speech Be in Time of War?" *New York Times Magazine*, 12 April 1942, pp. 13, 32. **S 263**
When war rages there is a conflict between freedom of speech and national security. The president of Yale University believes that we can continue to have both.

Seymour, Gideon. "American Society of Newspaper Editors Report on Atomic Information Problems." *Bulletin of the Atomic Scientists*, 4:211–12, July 1948. (Reprinted in Summers, *Federal Information Controls in Peacetime*, pp. 116–21) **S 264**

Seymour, Henry. "Literary 'Hall-mark' of the Old Bailey." *Adult*, 2:323–25, December 1898. **S 265**

A critique of the Bedborough trial and criticism of the "contemptible part played by George Bedborough," whom Seymour and *The Adult* had supported, and the unfair remarks made by the judge. The case involved Havelock Ellis' *Studies in the Psychology of Sex*.

———. "Our Conventional Virtue." *Adult*, 2:289–91, November 1898. **S 266**
Inspired by opposition to the prosecution of George Bedborough for selling Havelock Ellis' *Studies in the Psychology of Sex*.

———. "To the Breech, Freeman!" *Adult*, 2:157–60, July 1898. **S 267**
An account of the arrest of George Bedborough for the sale of Ellis' *Studies in the Psychology of Sex*. Includes a statement of the Free Press Defence Committee, formed in Bedborough's behalf and headed by Seymour, who succeeded Bedborough as editor of *The Adult*.

Seymour, Whitney N. "Authority of the FCC Over Broadcast Content." *Journal of Broadcasting*, 4:18–26, Winter 1959–60. **S 268**
Testimony of the special counsel of the National Association of Broadcasters before the FCC.

Sforza, Carlo. "A Basic Condition of International Reconstruction: Freedom of Opinion and Press." *American Political Science Review*, 37:838–50, October 1943. **S 269**
Freedom of information is a basic factor in the prevention of international misunderstandings which lead to war. It has the power to preserve other freedoms.

Shaffer, Helen B. *Bad Influences on Youth.* Washington, D.C., Editorial Research Reports, 1955. (*Editorial Research Reports*, 2:499–518, 1955) **S 270**
Includes a discussion on the influence of pornography, crime and horror comics, movies, and television, voluntary censorship of movies and television; and difficulties in enforcement of the Comic Book Code.

———. *Censorship of Movies and TV.* Washington, D.C., Editorial Research Reports, 1961. (*Editorial Research Reports*, 1:265–82, 1961) **S 271**
A summary of the current status of censorship under these topics: Movie Tribulations and the Courts, Censorship—Official and Non-Official, and Dilemma Posed by Conflicting Demands (protection of child v. freedom of adult).

———. *Status of Birth Control.* Washington, D.C., Editorial Research Reports, 1958. (*Editorial Research Reports*, 2:775–92, 1958) **S 272**
Controversy over birth control therapy, a summary of American and foreign birth-

control laws, and obstacles to acceptance of birth control, including the position of the Catholic Church.

"Shall There Be a Book Censorship?" *Literary Digest*, 74:31–32, 26 August 1922. **S 273**
John Sumner of the New York Society for the Suppression of Vice proposes a system of voluntary censorship. Article includes comments from the press.

Shaman, Dianna L. "Margaret Sanger: Mother of Birth Control." *Coronet*, 4(3): 66–73, March 1966. **S 274**

[Shanks v. American News Co.]. *Albany Law Journal*, 23:401, 421, May 1881. **S 275**
Editorial comment on the libel case in which Shanks, a lawyer, won a $2,500 libel suit against the newspaper *Truth*.

"The Shape of Things." *Nation*, 173:201–2, 15 September 1951. **S 276**
Two editorials, the first concerning the withdrawing of *Reader's Digest* from the 113 Catholic schools of the diocese of Green Bay, Wis., for publication of an article: Margaret Sanger: Mother of Planned Parenthood. The second editorial concerns the efforts of the Sons of the American Revolution to put into effect their resolution calling on public libraries and schools to label Communist literature with a stamp or sticker.

Shapiro, Martin. *Freedom of Speech: The Supreme Court and Judicial Review.* Englewood Cliffs, N.J., Prentice-Hall, 1966. 182 p. **S 277**
In the first chapter the author considers the conflict between the "judicially modest," who want to keep the Supreme Court free from political process and the "judicially activist" who represent in the area of First Amendment freedoms those whose methods and idealogies have no other defenders. In chapter two the author discusses the "clear-and-present-danger" rule, widely used for activist judicial protection of freedom of speech. In chapter three he discusses an alternative doctrine—"balancing of interests," which he considers "little more than a tactical device adopted by the modest to avoid the activist implication of the danger rule." The final chapter discusses the preferred position doctrine for freedom of speech and how the clear-and-present-danger rule can implement this preference.

Shaplen, Robert. "Scarsdale's Battle of the Books. How one Community Dealt with 'Subversive Literature.'" *Commentary*, 10:530–40, December 1950. (Reprinted in Downs, *The First Freedom*, pp. 359–70; also in C. W. Scott and C. M. Hill, *eds.*, *Public Education under Criticism*, pp. 322–26) **S 278**

What happened when a group of zealots in Scarsdale, N.Y., tried to purge the school libraries of the works of Howard Fast, an acknowledged Communist, and other authors known or alleged to have Communist leanings. The story tells of two years of attack from the ultra-right Committee of Ten. School officials met the issues patiently and intelligently and the attack was defeated.

Sharp, Eugene W. *The Censorship and Press Laws of Sixty Countries*. Columbia, Mo., University of Missouri, 1937. 50 p. (*University of Missouri Bulletin*, vol. 37, no. 24, Journalism Series, no. 77) **S 279**
Part IV deals with legislation then current on censorship, suppression, and control of the press.

———. "Cracking the Manila Censorship in 1899 and 1900." *Journalism Quarterly*, 20:280–85, December 1943. **S 280**
"Study of a little-known censorship episode that occurred during the Philippine insurrection of 1899."

Shattuck, C. H. "E. L. Bulwer and Victorian Censorship." *Quarterly Journal of Speech*, 34:65–72, February 1948. **S 281**
How the plays of Bulwer were shaped by moral and political pressures from the stage censor. "He could not dig deep into problems of human passion, he could not cut wide swaths across social ills; for all questions of ability aside—those regions were closed to him."

Shaw, Archibald B. *Censorship of Materials and Program*. Washington, D.C., National Education Association, Commission on Professional Rights and Responsibilities, 1963. 6 p. mimeo. **S 282**
The associate secretary, American Association of School Administrators, in a talk before an NEA convention, describes some of the pressures to alter or exclude materials and programs in the schools. Among areas under attack are the United Nations and sex educations.

———. "What Can the Superintendent Do?" *NEA Journal*, 52:22–23, May 1963. **S 283**
Deals with textbook censorship. "The wise superintendent doesn't wait until the flames of controversy have been fanned into a book-burning conflagration, just as he doesn't wait for the school to burn down before turning in the fire alarm. The sagacious superintendent prepares three levels of defense—good structure, good routines, and good emergency drill." (Part of an 11-page feature on textbook censorship.)

Shaw, Elton R. *What Shall We Do with the "Comstock" Law and the Post Office Censorship Power?* Washington, D.C., National Committee for Revision of the Comstock Law, [1938]. 44 p. (Also a Chapter in Shaw's book, *The Body Taboo*.) **S 284**
The occasion for the pamphlet was the obscenity charges against Mrs. Mary Ware Dennett. The author, executive secretary of the National Committee for Revision of the Comstock Law, reviews the long history of government action against alleged obscenity. He cites arguments against the obscenity laws by authors, lawyers, and others. He quotes from the September 1937 issue of *Sunshine & Health*, Editor Ilsley Boone's account of the seizure of the July 1937 issue of that nudist magazine.

Shaw, Fred. "A Call to Arms." *ALA Bulletin*, 56:1001–4, December 1962. **S 285**
Words of advice to librarians on censorship. Some old ideas on the subject expressed in colorful language: "I feel that witch-hunters are more dangerous than witches." "One of the predictable results of the recent *Tropic* trial in Dade County was that many teenagers who were hardly mature enough for the Hardy boys were trying to read Henry Miller." "A probation officer of my acquaintance says he knows many delinquents who are in trouble because they can't read, but not one who is because he can." "What we have to worry about is the insidious pressure to remove books from the shelves, the telephone calls to administrators, and antagonism from the Mrs. Grundys who are willing to admit that they haven't read the books they object to." It is sex that usually gives the trouble. He quotes a minister friend who argues that we ban the wrong books. The most obscene books are the sickening novels that picture the world as it is not.

Shaw, George Bernard. *The Author's Apology from Mrs. Warren's Profession. By Bernard Shaw. With an Introduction by John Corbin, The Tyranny of Police and Press*. New York, Brentano's, 1905. 66 p. **S 286**
Shaw's defense of his play, *Mrs. Warren's Profession*, first appeared in England in 1902 when the play was produced there after an eight-year ban. The essay is reproduced on the occasion of the censorship of Arnold Daly's American production by New York Police Commissioner McAdoo. John Corbin's introduction was reprinted in part from the *New York Sun*.

———. "Censorship of the Drama." *Spectator*, 135:405–6, 12 September 1925. **S 287**
Shaw denies the report (*Spectator*, 15 August) that he favors retention of censorship by the Lord Chamberlain. "The one person on earth who should have nothing to do with a largely satirical and discourteous art which raises fierce controversy on subjects on which the Court is constitutionally obliged to be neutral, is the Lord Chamberlain." Shaw would limit action to prosecution of the manager for obscenity, blasphemy, or sedition.

———. "The Censorship of the Stage

in England." *North American Review*, 169:251–62, August 1899. (Also in *Shaw on Theatre*, edited by E. J. West. New York, Hill and Wang, 1958, pp. 66–80) **S 288**
Criticism of stage censorship in England where "no play may be publicly performed until a certificate has been procured from the Lord Chamberlain that it 'does not in its general tendency, contain anything immoral or otherwise improper for the stage.'" Shaw believes that "nothing short of abolishing the monarchy" could get rid of the censorship system in England. He warns Americans who may attempt to set up stage censorship to "remember how the censorship works in England, and DON'T."

———. *The Doctor's Dilemma, Getting Married, and The Shewing-up of Blanco Posnet*. New York, Brentano's, 1911. 443 p. **S 289**
In the Preface to *The Shewing-Up of Blanco Posnet* (pp. 323–42). Shaw recounts the case of the suppression of this work by the Lord Chamberlain. In a Rejected Statement (pp. 345–80). Shaw pleads for abolition of the licensing system, before a Joint Select Committee of the Parliament. His plea is rejected by the Committee. In Preface Resumed (pp. 385–405). Shaw resumes his attack on the censorship activities of the Lord Chamberlain. The Rejected Statement appears in Downs, *The First Freedom*, pp. 254–65; excerpts from the Preface appear in McCormick, *Versions of Censorship*, pp. 334–44.

———. "Preface." In *Three Plays by Brieux, Member of the French Academy. With Preface by Bernard Shaw. English Versions by Mrs. Bernard Shaw, St. John Hankin and John Pollock*. 2d ed. New York, Brentano's, 1911, pp. vii–liv. **S 290**
In the preface, Shaw discusses the censorship of Brieux's plays in France and England. In France, censorship was broken; in England, where a censor of plays is part of the king's retinue, it is more difficult to abolish. The prohibition of Brieux plays in England in 1909 led to the appointment of a Select Committee of Parliament to investigate censorship. The English system, Shaw states, suppresses plays such as those by Brieux "dealing seriously with social problems whilst allowing frivolous or even pornographic plays to pass unchallenged." He discusses English stage taboos and explains "why the unmentionables must be mentioned on the stage."

———. "Prosecution of Mr. Bedborough." *Adult*, 2:230–31, September 1898. **S 291**
"The prosecution of Mr. Bedborough for selling Havelock Ellis' book [*Studies in the Psychology of Sex*] is a masterpiece of police stupidity."

———. "[Review of] H. Belloc's *The*

Free Press." Nation (London), 22:599–602, 9 February 1918. **S 292**

"I found out early in my career that a Conservative paper may steal a horse when a Radical paper dare not look over a hedge, and that the rich, though very determined that the poor shall read nothing unconventional, are equally determined not to be preached at themselves. In short, I found that only for the classes would I be allowed, and indeed tacitly required, to write on revolutionary assumptions. I filled their columns with sedition; and they filled my pockets (not very deep ones then) with money. In the press as in other departments the greatest freedom may be found where there is least talk about it."

————. *"Saint Joan* Banned: Film Censorship in the United States." In *Shaw on Theatre,* edited by E. J. West. New York, Hill and Wang, 1958, pp. 243–52. (Originally appeared in *London Mercury,* October 1936) **S 293**

Shaw discusses the request of the Hays Office to modify his play for an American movie production in order to meet obligations of the Catholic Action group. The absurd modifications requested, Shaw notes, "represent not the wisdom of the Catholic Church, but the desperation of a minor official's attempt to reduce that wisdom to an office routine." Censors are popular with theater managers because they afford police protection. They interfere with serious work without preventing real pornography. "I must continue to insist on the evil they do, on the good that they fail to do, and on the better ways of achieving their purpose that are readily available."

————. *Shaw on Censorship; Being an Extract from the Minutes of Evidence Before the Joint Select Committee of the House of Lords and the House of Commons on the Stage Plays (Censorship), 1909.* London, Shaw Society, 1955. 19 p. (Shavian Tract, no. 3) **S 294**

————. *Statement of the Evidence in Chief of George Bernard Shaw before the Joint-Committee on Stage Plays (Censorship and Theatre Licensing).* London, Printed privately, confidentially, 1909. (Also appears in the Brentano edition of *The Shewing-Up of Blanco Posnet,* pp. 345–80; and in Downs, *The First Freedom,* pp. 254–65) **S 295**

Shaw was one of a number of prominent authors and dramatists called before the Joint Select Committee of the Parliament in 1909 to consider Britain's stage censorship. The investigation grew out of the furor caused when Shaw's play, *The Shewing-Up of Blanco Posnet,* was rejected by the Lord Chamberlain as blasphemous. Shaw's testimony in opposition to censorship was rejected by the Committee and omitted from their printed report, but this privately circulated version became a collector's item. In the Preface to his banned play, *The Shewing-up of Blance Posnet,* Shaw recounts the events of the investigation. In The Rejected Statement Shaw argues not only against the existing censorship by the Lord Chamberlain which he considers imbecilic and mischievous, but against censorship by more enlightened critics, or by a panel of arbitrators. He pleads for the same freedom of expression for stage plays as for newspapers and pamphlets— that is, no prior restraint. He recommends that censorship be abolished, and that licensing of theaters be transferred to local authorities with specific legal protection given to theater managers against unreasonable restraints.

————, Gilbert Murray, *et al. The Censorship of Plays in the Office of the Lord Chamberlain: The Case for Abolition.* Letchworth, Printed at the Arden Press, 1908. 44 p. **S 296**

Articles by Shaw, Murray, and others suggesting various lines of reform. Includes a brief history of stage censorship in England and a list of plays recently approved or censored. In a section on censorship in practice, Shaw notes that one of the worst features of the existing arrangement is the practice of the examiner of plays to take no cognizance of the author as such and his refusal to communicate directly with any author concerning the work which he has condemned in the secrecy of St. James's Palace. The system operates largely against the serious drama. "The creator of a statute of the early years of the last century says that our prophets shall not use the theatre as a forum." In an article reprinted from *The Nation,* Shaw criticizes both the system and the present censor, Mr. Redford. The first and most intolerable rule of the censor is that "dramatic art is too unclean a thing to be allowed to be religious. It may be lewd, and it may be silly; but it must not dare touch anything sacred." There are three great taboos on the question of sex—you must never mention abortion, incest, or venereal disease. The play may wallow in vice, but must never show the serious consequence. The banning of Shaw's own play, *Mrs. Warren's Profession,* and Ibsen's *Ghosts* are examples of the taboo on these serious sex themes. Shaw rejects the solution of employing a tribunal of eminent men of letters as censors. "The sensible course is obvious. Abolish the censorship of plays altogether, root and branch." If necessary license theaters, managers, and even dramatists but let the play "be born and take its chance with the consciences of men just as it came from the conscience of the author."

————, Sean O'Casey, *et al.* "Censorship: Comments by Readers." [i.e., G. B. Shaw, Sean O'Casey, T. C. Kingsmill Moore, and James Hogan]. *The Bell* (Dublin), 9:395–409, February 1945. **S 297**

Comments on Monk Gibbon's defense of censorship, appearing in the January 1945 issue. The editor, Sean O'Faolain, observes, "We now have, here, a Literary Censorship, a Film Censorship, the Censorship of the secret reports of the Librarians' Association, and the private censorship which any citizen irrespective of class, education, age, or sanity may exercise over any book in a public library merely by objecting to it." Shaw (pp. 395–401) notes that all governments suppress, persecute and punish offenders under the headings of blasphemy, sedition, and libel "to maintain conformity of conduct and doctrine." Civilization has traditionally obstructed and penalized change, yet "without change there can be no development." People who do not believe as everyone else does "must suffer persecution until their numbers grow sufficiently to intimidate their persecutors." A licensing system would work perfectly "if the licensing authorities and the censors were wise and benevolent . . . were omnipotent and ubiquitous gods with unlimited time to spare." There is mischief in assuming that "the authorities should be members of the profession they are appointed to restrain and regulate, much as if judges should be burglars and murderers. . . . The censorship is damned, not by the rare masterpieces it suppresses but by the heaps of pernicious trash its license prevents the police from prosecuting." Shaw suggests that "the remedy is to abolish the censorship and trust to the licensing from year to year by the local authorities of all places of public entertainment." O'Casey (pp. 401–67) disputes Gibbon's claims of the importance and influence of books. Food is more important to children than thought; children get more of their ideas from their parents than from the printed word; Hitler was more influential than any writers of books. The problem is not so much what people have missed by censorship (reading people have always read what was banned) but how long Ireland is going to stand "this pompous, ignorant, impertinent and silly practice." Authors must always fight the enemies of free thought whether they be official censors or such unofficial guardians as the Watch and Ward Society or The National Office for Decent Literature. Moore (pp. 407–8) believes every man not only has the right to form and hold his own views but "this, in turn, involves the right of access to known facts and to the opinion of others." Professor Hogan believes that "the further you get away from activity with social implications the less censorship there should be. . . . Censorship of literature should be at the very minimum by comparison with the censorship which the community enforces against various forms of political opinion."

Shaw, Ralph R. *Literary Property in the United States.* Washington, D.C., Scarecrow Press, 1950. 277 p. **S 298**

The purposes of the book are to clarify the objectives and scope of copyright and of common-law rights, to describe the present state of common and statutory law covering literary property as it affects scholarship, to identify literary property rights which do not appear to be recognized by our laws and court decisions, and to indicate areas for restudy.

Shaw, Robert. "Forms of Censorship." *Hollywood Quarterly,* 1:199–210, January 1946. **S 299**

"It is the purpose of this article to examine as objectively as possible some recent trends toward radio censorship and restriction."

Shayon, Robert L. "Editorials on the Air." *Saturday Review*, 43(46):113–14, 12 November 1960. **S 300**
Many stations abstain from editorializing for fear of inviting regulation by the FCC.

———. "Looking at the Birchers." *Saturday Review*, 48(33):41, 14 August 1965. **S 301**
Report of a 90 minute program featuring the John Birch Society, presented over National Educational Television, in which founder Robert Welch told the commentator: "There aren't two sides to every question. This is one of those smart-sounding phrases that have been introduced largely by liberals to promote certain ideas."

———. "Mr. Percy's Torch for Television." *Saturday Review*, 43(41):61–62, 8 October 1960. **S 302**
Tribute to an advertiser, Charles H. Percy of Bell & Howell, who sponsored a controversial television program (C.B.S. Reports) despite a threat of boycott of his product.

———. "The Public May Be Heard." *Saturday Review*, 48(26):44, 26 June 1965. **S 303**
Deals with efforts before the FCC, of the Office of Communication of the United Church of Christ in behalf of the public interest in broadcasting, indicating that public interest groups can play a part in the granting and renewal of broadcast licenses.

———. "The Show that Wasn't There." *Saturday Review*, 47(33):27, 15 August 1964. **S 304**
Account of the censorship of a play on WMSB, Michigan State University's television station. The drama dealt with race relations.

———. "The Uphill Fight of Pay-TV." *Saturday Review*, 48(7):55–57, 24 April 1965. **S 305**

Shearman, Montague, and O. T. Raynor. *The Press Laws of Foreign Countries*. London, H. M. Stationery Office, 1926. 328 p. **S 306**
Text of press laws of leading countries (in English and French) with an appendix on the press laws of India. Now out of date and of historical interest only.

Sheavyn, Phoebe. "Writers and Official Censors under Elizabeth and James I." *Library*, 8:134–63, April 1907. (Reprinted in her *The Literary Profession in the Elizabethan Age*. Manchester, Eng., Manchester University Press, 1909, pp. 39–63) **S 307**
The representatives of authority in Elizabethan England so far as literature was concerned were four: The Privy Council and Court of Star Chamber, the Court of High Commission, the Stationers' Company, and the City Corporation. The author describes the work of each.

Shedd, Kendrick P. *The Right of Free Speech; Address Delivered in Shubert Theatre, Rochester, N.Y., Sunday, February 26, 1911*. Rochester, N.Y., The Labor Lyceum, 1911. 23 p. **S 308**
Address given on the occasion of a protest against the Rochester mayor's prohibition on the use of public buildings to a speaker who had discussed world-wide socialism in a public school building.

Shee, *Sir* Martin A. *Alasco: a Tragedy in Five Acts . . . Excluded from the Stage, by the Authority of the Lord Chamberlain*. London, Sherwood, Jones, 1824. 169 p. **S 309**

Sheehan, Harold. "Reporter vs. the Law On News Source Protection." *Quill*, 48(12):15–16, 22 December 1960. **S 310**

Sheerin, John B. "The American Priest and Freedom of the Press." *Catholic World*, 185:1–4, April 1957. **S 311**
The U.S. Supreme Court's decision to void a Michigan statute against obscene literature and other recent decisions of that Court point out "the fact that the court is not so much concerned with juvenile innocence as it is about freedom of the press. This means more liberty for our Catholic children and more and more responsibility for the priests that shepherd their souls."

———. "Art, Movies and the Censor." *Catholic World*, 178:403–5, March 1954. **S 312**
Critical comment on the ruling of the U.S. Supreme Court that the censors of New York and Ohio had acted beyond the scope of their authority in refusing to license two movies for public showing. New York had banned *La Ronde* as "immoral" and Ohio had rejected *M* as "inviting to crime."

———. "Censorship in Contemporary Society." *Catholic Lawyer*, 3:292–300, Autumn 1957. **S 313**
The editor of the *Catholic World* believes that censorship is necessary to conserve essential values of the American way of life. Freedom is not the highest value; it exists for the preservation of purity, truth, and justice.

———. "Free Speech and Obscenity Censorship." *Catholic World*, 194:132–36, December 1961. **S 314**

A summary of discussions at the *Catholic World's* seminar on Freedom of Speech and Obscenity Censorship. The discussion revealed that censorship is a complex and deep-rooted problem, that further clinical studies are needed; that censorship laws designed to protect the young have a better chance of Supreme Court approval than do laws to protect adults.

———. "Sex and Censorship." *Catholic World*, 177:241–45 July 1953. **S 315**
"By censorship and other legal safeguards, children must be protected against constant sexual stimulation and annoyance." The author notes the similarity of views of the Catholic Church toward censorship and those of Margaret Mead as stated in her article, Sex and Censorship in Contemporary Society, in *New World Writing*, May 1953.

Sheldon, John P. *Statement of the Trial of John P. Sheldon, Editor of the Detroit Gazette . . . on an Attachment for Contempt*. n.p., [1828]. 40 p. **S 316**

Shell, Dan H. "First Amendment Rights and Restrictions." *Mississippi Law Journal*, 36:41–53. December 1964. **S 317**
"This paper seeks to deal primarily with freedoms of speech and press, and more specifically with the dangers to the society when these rights are unconditionally protected. . . . Particular attention will be directed to the attitude of the U.S. Supreme Court toward the freedoms as they are applied to the activities of Communist Party sympathizers."

Shelley, Percy Bysshe. "Letter to Leigh Hunt on the Trial of Richard Carlile for Publishing Paine's *Age of Reason*." In *The Prose Works of Percy Bysshe Shelley*, edited by Harry B. Forman. London, Reeves and Turner, 1880. vol. 4, pp. 291–300. **S 318**
Shelley expresses his indignation over the trial. He argues that Carlile has a right to be tried by his peers, persons of a similar social status and of like philosophical views who will not bring prejudice to the decision.

———. "A Letter to Lord Ellenborough, Occasioned by the Sentence he Passed on Mr. D. I. Eaton, as Publisher of the Third Part of Paine's *Age of Reason*." In *The Prose Works of Percy Bysshe Shelley*, edited by Harry B. Forman. London, Reeves and Turner, 1880. vol. 1, pp. 401–24. (Reprinted in a 16-page pamphlet, *Shelley on Blasphemy*, by the Progressive Publishing Co., London, 1883) **S 319**
"But I raise my solitary voice, to express my disapprobation, so far as it goes, of the cruel

and unjust sentence you passed upon Mr. Eaton." In March 1812 Lord Ellenborough sentenced the London bookseller to 18 months in prison and to stand in the pillory once a month.

Shepard, A. G. "Freedom of Speech in Industrial Disputes." *Case and Comment*, 22:466–70, November 1915.   **S 320**

Shepherd, Robert E., Jr. "The Law of Obscenity in Virginia." *Washington and Lee Law Review*, 17:322–28, Fall 1960.   **S 321**

Shepherd, William G. "The Forty-two Centimeter Blue Pencil." *Everybody's Magazine*, 36:470–82, April 1917.   **S 322**
An American war correspondent who has fought censorship comments: "I don't exactly sympathize with the censor. But I have seen enough of war to know that the side which dropped censorship would be immediately defeated on land and sea."

Sheppard, W. *Action upon the Case for Slander*. 2d ed. London, 1674. 287 p.   **S 323**
"A methodical collection of thousands of cases of what words are actionable, and what not, and of a conspiracy, and a libel." The first edition appeared in 1662, two years after the advent of the Stuart Restoration.

Shera, Jesse H. "*A Book for Burning*". *Wilson Library Bulletin*, 37:790, May 1963.   **S 324**
Comment on the TV play, *A Book for Burning*, in "The Defenders" series. While the librarian in the play was presented as a prudish old maid who defends censorship, "the stereotype of the librarian is not to be improved by protest but by educating librarians who will give the lie to the image we abhor." He hopes that the ALA will not protest the treatment but will "keep its corporate mouth shut."

———. "Officer, Arrest That Book!" *Wilson Library Bulletin*, 36:488, February 1962.   **S 325**
"Against humor and comedy the censor is defenseless, because he fears that which he cannot understand and cannot manage. Humor can save the book in the future as it has in the past." The title of the article refers to a *Life* cartoon which appeared during the prohibition era bearing the caption, "Officer, arrest that man; he seems to be thinking of beer."

Sherburne, E. G., Jr. *The Need to Know of Science*. Columbia, Mo., Freedom of Information Center, School of Journalism, University of Missouri, 1963. 5 p. (Publication no. 92)   **S 326**
Speech by the director of Studies in the Public Understanding of Science, American Association for the Advancement of Science, before the Northwestern University Science Public Information Seminar, 21 March 1962.

Sherek, Henry, and John Mortimer. "End or Change Stage Censorship." *Plays and Players*, 9:22, September 1962.   **S 327**
Sherek favors licensing of stage plays by the Lord Chamberlain but believes "dirty plays" should be permitted, provided people are warned beforehand of the nature of the play as in the case of films. Mortimer objects to the "antique power" of stage censorship by the Lord Chamberlain which he terms "irresponsible, childish and an insult to artists working seriously in the theatre."

———, et al. "Why Censor the Theatre?" *Author*, 69:39–43, Winter 1958.   **S 328**
A variety of opinion on the present control of the English theater, expressed by Henry Sherek (licensing for adults), Sir Donald Wolfit (compromise), Wynard Browne (reform), Ivan Brown (abolition), Charles Landstone (anomaly), and Kenneth Tynan (who needs a censor?).

Sherman, Stuart C. "Defending the Freedom to Read." *Library Journal*, 87:479–83, 1 February 1962.   **S 329**
The librarian of Providence Public Library reviews the action taken to keep Henry Miller's *Tropic of Cancer* available to readers in spite of the threat of the Attorney General to arrest the librarian and borrower. Includes a statement of the library's position, supported by the Board of Trustees.

Sherman, Stuart P. "Unprintable." In his *Points of View*. New York, Scribner's, 1924, pp. 49–74. (Reprinted from *Atlantic Monthly*, July 1923)   **S 330**
A literary critic believes that the obscenity laws should not apply to "books issued by regular publishers, through the regular channels." Such action is "futile and mischievous." While expressing sympathy for the vice societies and their motives, he believes it is impossible to make the reading-world safe for children and adolescents. He also objects to the analogy of the Comstock Act and the Volstead Act, since the effect of alcohol can be measured scientifically; the effect of reading cannot. While he decries the salacious trends in modern fiction, he believes the solution is not in legislation and court action but in the development of "independent and dispassionate criticism," instead of the "violation partisan combats between champions of literature who express their contempt for public morals, and champions of public morals who express their contempt for literature."

Sherman, William F. "Motion Picture Censorship: Social Control and the Constitution." *Ohio State Law Journal*, 17:227–39, Spring 1956.   **S 331**
A review of recent court decisions on movie censorship with special reference to the State of Ohio. The author concludes that a constitutional pre-exhibition motion picture censorship law could be drawn by a state legislature under Supreme Court ruling, but care must be taken not to infringe on religious, antireligious, or political expression. Obscenity and incitement to crime are justification for censorship if they are properly circumscribed.

Sherrard, Owen A. *A Life of John Wilkes*. London, Allen & Unwin, 1930. 319 p.   **S 332**
This modern biography of Wilkes "attempts to see him as he was, neither straining his virtues nor defending his vices." The work is written mainly from original manuscript sources, supplemented by printed journals, letters, and histories of the times.

Shientag, Bernard L. "From Seditious Libel to Freedom of the Press." *Brooklyn Law Review*, 11:125–54, April 1942. (Reprinted in *Moulders of Legal Thought*, pp. 159–97)   **S 333**
On the 150th anniversary of the Fox Libel Act, the author traces the liberalization of the English and American libel laws from the strict views of Lord Mansfield and Lord Kenyon in eighteenth-century England to modern times. Lord Kenyon had protested that the Fox Libel Act would prove the confusion and destruction of the libel law of England. The author, a justice of the New York Supreme Court, gives special attention to the New York statutes relating to freedom of speech and of the press.

———. "The Struggle for a Free Press." *New York State Bar Association Bulletin*, 17:62–70, April 1945.   **S 334**
How the New York Libel Act of 1805 came to be enacted and the influence that it brought about.

Shillito, Edward, "Alfred Noyes Defies Church." *Christian Century*, 55:1102, 14 September 1938.   **S 335**
Discussion of the threat of Catholic Church condemnation of Alfred Noyes's *Voltaire* and Noyes's letter of defiance.

Shils, Edward A. *The Torment of Secrecy; the Background and Consequences of American Security Policies*. Glencoe, Ill., Free Press, 1956. 238 p.   **S 336**
A sociological study of peacetime restriction of information by the government in the interest of national security.

Shipler, Guy E. "Freedom of Press vs. Freedom of Pulpit." *Outlook*, 108:774–82, 2 December 1914.   **S 337**
The author tells how he left the newspaper

field to become an Episcopalian clergyman because of the control of newspapers by advertisers and businesses, particularly by department stores, in the city where he was located.

Shipley, Carl L. ["Libel"]. *Editor & Publisher*, 92(30):58–59, 25 July 1959; 92(31):49, 1 August 1959; 92(33):50, 15 August 1959; 92(34):48–49, 22 August 1959. **S 338**
Part 1 discusses the general concept of laws that protect man's good name in society; part 2 discusses the principles of libel as applied by judges; part 3 considers some injurious statements that are not deemed libelous; and part 4 explores the fine line between freedom of the press and liability for libel. A talk given by a Washington attorney at the Pennsylvania Press Conference, May 1959.

Shipley, Maynard. *The War on Modern Science; a Short History of the Fundamentalist Attacks on Evolution and Modernism.* New York, Knopf, 1927. 415 p. **S 339**

Shipley, Parker. "Obscene Publication Prohibition." *Nebraska Law Review*, 40: 481–91, April 1960. **S 340**
A discussion of problems in the regulation of publication and sale of obscene material in Nebraska; the present state laws; two local ordinances; and recent Nebraska Supreme Court decisions.

[Shipley, William D.]. *The Proceedings in the Cause of the King against the Dean of St. Asaph, on the Prosecution of William Jones, for a Libel, at the Great Session Held at Wrexham, for the county of Denbigh, on Monday, September the First, 1783. Taken in Short-Hand by W. Blanchard . . .* Printed and distributed gratis by the Society for Constitutional Information. London, 1783. 36 p. (Society's Tracts, vol. 2, pp. 41–77) **S 341**

[———]. *The Whole of the Proceedings at the Assizes at Shrewsbury, on Friday August the Sixth, 1784, in the Cause of the King on the Prosecution of William Jones, Attorney at Law, against the Rev. William Davies Shipley, Dean of St. Asaph. For a Libel. Before the Hon. Francis Buller, esq. . . . Taken in Short-Hand by William Blanchard . . .* London, Printed by H. Goldney, and sold by J. Johnson. 1784. 112 p. With the *Proceedings in the Cause of the King against the Dean of St. Asaph . . . 1783.* (Also reported in Howell, *State Trials*, vol. 21, pp. 847 ff.; in Borrow, *Celebrated Trials*,

vol. 5, pp. 106–15; and in the Reeves and Turner edition of Erskine's *Speeches*, vol. 1, pp. 137–393. The last named contains the complete speeches of Erskine and Justice Buller's charge to the jury) **S 342**
The Dean of St. Asaph was brought to trial in 1784 on charges of seditious libel for publishing and distributing *Principles of Government, in a Dialogue between a Gentleman and a Farmer,* by his brother-in-law, Sir William Jones. The work was a serious tract urging constitutional reform in parliamentary representation. Thomas Erskine represented the Dean in what was to become one of the most noteworthy libel trials in British history. Justice Buller ruled that the jury was limited to deciding whether or not the work had been published and not to consider its subject matter. The jury found the defendant "guilty of publishing only" which confused the judge and led to the request for a new trial. Erskine's eloquent arguments for the expanded rights of the jury in libel cases were answered point by point by Lord Mansfield. The case led to the adoption of Erskine's views in a revision of the libel law in 1792 (Fox Libel Act). The case against the Dean of St. Asaph was ultimately dismissed.

Shoemaker, Floyd C. "Anthony Haswell, Patriot Printer." *Quill*, 31(3):7, 14, 17, March 1941. **S 343**
Sigma Delta Chi honored the Vermont printer for his championship of Matthew Lyon, first victim of the Sedition Act, and his own consequent imprisonment.

Shoniker, F. R. "Censorship and the Library." In David Martin, *ed.*, *Catholic Library Practice.* Portland, Ore., University of Portland Press, 1947, pp. 185–91. **S 344**

Shore, Viola B. "You Can't Say That." *New Theatre & Film*, 4(11):37, 48, April 1937. **S 345**
Censorship of the movies, including a list of expressions taboo in English films.

Shortt, John. *Law Relating to Works of Literature and Art; Embracing the Law of Copyright, the Law Relating to Newspapers, the Law Relating to Contracts between Authors, Publishers, Printers, etc., and the Law of Libel; with the Statutes Relating Thereto, Forms of Agreements between Authors, Publishers, etc., and Forms of Pleadings.* London, H. Cox, 1871. 780 p. **S 346**

"Should Moving Pictures Be Censored?" *Current Opinion*, 70:652–55, May 1921. **S 347**
Summary of debate in the periodical press between the proponents of movie censorship (principally Wilbur F. Crafts of the Inter-

national Reform Bureau) and opponents (including Theodore A. Schroeder and the *Ladies Home Journal*). The New York *Evening Mail* is quoted as calling for a "purgation in taste rather than morals." Includes a picture of Mr. Crafts.

"Should Newspapers Tell the Truth?" *Christian Century*, 42:273–75, 26 February 1925. **S 348**
An editorial criticizing the American press for playing up the sordid side of the news disproportionately to other news events, thus creating a "lie of perspective."

"Should School Books Be Censored?" *School and Society*, 48:405–7, 24 September 1938. (Reprinted from the Educational Supplement of the London *Times*). **S 349**
A review of a report on provision of school textbooks in various nations, issued by the International Bureau of Education. The reply from the English Board of Education indicates that there is no law or regulation governing the selection or use of textbooks in Great Britain; the choice rests with local authorities, school managers, and teachers. This is in contrast with controls in Germany and Italy and even in the United States where half the states prescribe school textbooks.

"Should the Press be Censored?" *Goodwin's Weekly*, 19:1, 19 August 1911. **S 350**
The question is answered with a hesitating "yes" and the argument is based on materials in the Mormon controversy.

Showerman, Grant. "Art and Decency." *Yale Review*, 11(n.s.):304–14, January 1922. **S 351**
The author rejects the claim of the modern "sex novelist" that "whatever is, is matter for art." The essence of the sex novelist's offense "lies not in the illegality or in the immorality of the matter he represents, but in its ugliness." There are certain things in the world which are necessities in nature but which are inherently offensive and indecent "when they are obtruded upon the perception of other men."

Shriver, Harry C., and Cedric Larson. "Books, Bullets, and Blue-Pencils." *Publishers' Weekly*, 142:828–33, 5 September 1942. **S 352**
A survey of government wartime censorship as it applies to the importation of foreign books. Many consignments of books to American universities have been destroyed at the port of entry in accordance with rulings that should not apply to research institutions. Includes a review of book banning in World War I and censorship in Canada in World War II.

———. "Halt! What Book Goes There?" *Bill of Rights Review*, 2:43–53, Fall 1941. **S 353**

A discussion of the Army's "Index Expurgatorius," the list of books banned from army camps during World War I as violating the Sedition and Espionage Acts. A list of such books, compiled from official records is given on pages 46–50. The objectionable books were also banned from export. The article quotes several contemporary reports of the book banning.

———. "Mars with a Blue Pencil: The U.S. Censorship Board of 1917–18." *Bill of Rights Review*, 1:293–302, Summer 1941. **S 354**

Brief description of the operation of censorship in World War I. It "operated silently and effectively" in censoring foreign mail.

———. "Office of Censorship." *Bill of Rights Review*, 2:189–200, Spring 1942. **S 355**

An account of the establishment and operation of the World War II agency for directing censorship of information harmful to the prosecution of the war. Discussion of some of the problems faced in protecting the war effort and at the same time preserving essential freedom of the press.

Shryock, Richard H. "Freedom and Interference in Medicine." *Annals of the American Academy of Political and Social Science*, 200:32–59, November 1938. **S 356**

Discusses suppression of information by the state, by the church, by the organized public, and by the profession itself. Includes references to bans on information on birth control and venereal diseases.

Shufeldt, Robert W. "Critique of the Trial of Ida C. Craddock." *Boston Investigator*, 82:4–5, 5 April 1902; *Truth Seeker*, 29:170, 15 March 1902. **S 357**

A review of the obscenity trial in New York City. "History has one more record to make of a backslide in science, and a distinct restriction of personal liberty to the American citizen. Vice, indeed, won a victory, and tyranny scored a brilliant success." Miss Craddock had written a pamphlet on sex education, entitled, *The Wedding Night*.

———. "Enemies of Art and Literature in America." *Boston Investigator*, 69:2, 3 March 1900. **S 358**

A discussion of attacks by the Post Office Department and the courts on scientific works and art pictures involving nudity of the human form.

———. "Enemies of Art, Sculpture and Anatomy in the Law Courts of Washing-

ton, D.C." *Medical Review of Reviews*, 25:599–604, October 1919. **S 359**

A criticism of the trial of Professor H. M. B. Moens, an anthropologist who was fined and sentenced to prison for having in his possession a series of anthropological photographs of nude native women, intended to illustrate a book he was writing.

———. "On the Study of the Question of Sex." *Alienist and Neurologist*, 39:109–17, April 1918. **S 360**

Dr. Shufeldt stresses the importance of sex studies and his objection to placing those studies under taboo.

———. "Release of Miss Craddock." *Boston Investigator*, 72:8–9, 5 July 1902. **S 361**

Account of a dinner given by the Free Speech League to Ida C. Craddock on her release from prison, including an address made by Dr. Shufeldt, criticizing the action of the court. Miss Craddock was rearrested for sending her book, *The Wedding Night*, through the mails. She committed suicide rather than serve another jail sentence.

———. "Suppression of the Literature of Human Topographical Anatomy in This Country." *Pacific Medical Journal*, 52:146–53, March 1909. **S 362**

The author opposes censorship of medical books which contain anatomical illustrations.

———. "Where the Impurists Would Lead Us." *Pacific Medical Journal*, 55:402–9, July 1912. **S 363**

A defense of sex education for the general public.

Shumaker, W. A. "Clean Books." *Law Notes*, 29:104–6, September 1925. **S 364**

The writer, while disclaiming sympathy for the purveyors of filth, is in favor of abolishing all restrictions on literature based on "moral" grounds. Obscenity is in the mind of the reader, not in the words of the writer. "Free will to choose with inescapable responsibility for choice is the divine law, and it is at least doubtful if man can improve on it."

Shuman, Edwin L. "The Librarian and Public Taste." *Public Libraries*, 18:179–82, May 1913; 18:223–27, June 1913; 18:271–74, July 1913. **S 365**

The literary editor of the Chicago *Record-Herald* advises public librarians on book selection, drawing the analogy of a square, which represents a barrier that keeps out books on four sides—trashy books, too technical books, ill-written books, and immoral books. He discusses changing points of view on what is immoral in literature, cautioning against narrowness. Moralists who lack a sense of proportion do not make good librarians. While acknowledging that evil reading is doing "incalculable harm to the

young," it is the price we pay for a free press. The juvenile book that inculcates false standards of life is more objectionable than one that treats frankly with sex. It is the great privilege of the librarian to counteract the evil of bad books with good books.

Shurlock, Goeffrey. "The Motion Picture Production Code." *Annals of the American Academy of Political and Social Science*, 254:140–46, November 1947. **S 366**

———. *Movie Self-Regulation*. Columbia, Mo., Freedom of Information Center, School of Journalism, University of Missouri, 1964. 4p. (Publication no. 125) **S 367**

The director of the Production Code Administration of the Motion Picture Association of America highlights the historical developments leading to current movie control by the industry.

———. *Movies and Morality*. New York, Motion Picture Association of America, 1962. 10p. mimeo. **S 368**

In a talk before the New York Chapter, Order of Military Chaplains, Mr. Shurlock defends the Production Code as exemplifying "the best way of protecting public morality in a free society."

Shuster, George N. "Letters and Censorship." *Commonweal*, 10:176–78, 19 June 1929. **S 369**

"How morals and art are related is not an easy matter to determine. The following paper makes no effort to arrive at a complete solution of the problem, but analyzes Catholic negative and positive teaching. The contention is that censorship, however exercised, is only a prelude to a realization of what is good and beautiful, and that the value of art lies in the rightness of its aspiration and in its sanity."

Sibley, Frank. "When Is a Book Pure?" *Independent*, 118:467–68, 30 April 1927. **S 370**

Deals with the censorship wave that swept Boston in 1927. If officials and the courts were to be consistent in the application of the Massachusetts obscenity laws even the English version of the Bible would be actionable.

Sidmouth, Henry Addington, *Viscount*. *Circular Letter from Lord Viscount Sidmouth to His Majesty's Lieutenants of Counties in England and Wales . . .* [re circulation of blasphemous and seditious pamphlets and writings]. London, Ordered printed by the House of Commons, 1817. 2p. (Report 287, vol. 15) **S 371**

In the opinion of the law officers of the Crown "a Warrant may be issued to apprehend a Party, charged on oath for publishing a Libel, either by the Secretary of State, a Judge, or a Justice of the Peace."

Sidney, Algernon. *Discourses concerning Government . . . with His Letters, Trial, Apology, and Some Memoirs of His Life.* London, A. Miller, 1763. 46 p., 496 p., 198 p. (*Memoirs*, pp. 1–46); also in Howell, *State Trials*, vol. 9, pp. 817 ff.) **S 372**
"This was the first indictment of high treason upon which any man lost his life writing anything without publishing it." An unpublished manuscript, believed to have been written by Sidney, stated that the king is subject to the laws of God, as he is a man, and to the people who made him, as he is a king. The manuscript may have been a part of his *Discourses concerning Government.* Sidney was beheaded in 1683.

Siebert, Fredrick S. "Communications and Government." In Schramm, *Mass Communications.* Urbana, Ill., University of Illinois Press, 1949, pp. 138–44. **S 373**
The author discusses four areas in which government might participate in communications—as a restricting agency, a regulating agency, a facilitating agency, and a participating agency. He recommends "hands off" content; efficient but cautions regulating of the "market-place"; greater facilitating of existing media; and the development of government-owned facilities to supplement commercial channels.

———. "The Confiscated Revolutionary Press." *Journalism Quarterly,* 13:179–81, June 1936. **S 374**
In browsing through records in the Public Record Office, London, the author discovered what happened to the confiscated press of the *Norfolk Gazette,* seized by the British at the outbreak of the Revolutionary War.

———. "Contemporary Regulations of the British Press." *Journalism Quarterly,* 8:235–56, June 1931. **S 375**
A compilation of current press regulations. "The statutes have been annotated by the author to the decisions of the English courts."

———. "Contempt of Court and the Press." *Journalism Quarterly,* 5(2):22–33, June 1928. **S 376**

———. "Freedom of Propaganda." *Journalism Quarterly,* 12:27–36, March 1935. **S 377**
"To what extent does the doctrine of freedom of the press protect the dissemination of propaganda? or, conversely, would any restriction on the free dissemination of propaganda constitute an interference with the guarantees of intellectual liberty such as liberty of speech and of the press?"

———. *Freedom of the Press in England, 1476–1776; the Rise and Decline of Government Controls.* Urbana, Ill., University of Illinois Press, 1952. 411 p. (Reprinted in Illini Books, paperback edition) **S 378**
A study of the development of freedom of the press in England from the introduction of printing to the drafting of the American Bill of Rights. In tracing the growth and gradual decline of government control of the press in England, Siebert considers three main lines of development: first, the number and variety of government controls; secondly, the efforts at enforcement; and third, the degree of compliance. In his introduction, he identifies three theories of press control in England during the three-hundred-year period: the Tudor-Stuart theory, the Blackstone-Mansfield theory, and the Camden-Erskine-Jefferson theory. In addition, he cites three theories that have developed in modern times: the Holmes-Brandeis "clear and present danger" standard; the point of view of press responsibility expressed in the Hutchins commission report; and the totalitarian theory of the U.S.S.R. Siebert's work is based on firsthand examination of basic documents in various English libraries and depositories. A calendar of important dates in the history of English press freedom is given on pages 14–17.

———. "The Future of a Free Press." *Journalism Quarterly,* 32:6–9, Winter 1955. **S 379**
"International tensions and possible shifts of power within the United States will bring threats to press freedom which can be offset only by improved press performance."

———. "Historical Pattern of Press Freedom." *Nieman Reports,* 7(3):43–47, July 1953. **S 380**
In an address at the University of Iowa on receiving the research award of Kappa Tau Alpha, Professor Siebert discusses the four theories of press freedom: the authoritarian, the libertarian, the Communist, and the social-responsibility theories.

———. "The Law and Journalism." *Virginia Law Review,* 32, 771–80, June 1946. **S 381**
The author discusses "areas in which law and journalism might mutually profit from joint study and cooperation and some possible contributions which the law might make toward assisting the profession of journalism to fulfill more adequately its important social functions." Includes a discussion of the law of libel, "trial by newspaper," and the right of privacy.

———. "Legal Developments Affecting the Press." *The Annals of the American Academy of Political and Social Science,* 219:93–99, January 1942. **S 382**
"Today the press of the United States finds itself in possession of greater freedom to gather, publish, and comment on the news than ever before in its history. It has also found that the courts are reluctant to extend the meaning of the constitutional guarantees of freedom of the press to cover social and economic regulations, or to grant any special immunities to publish because of the nature of their service to the public."

———. "News Sources Must Be Protected." *Quill,* 21(12):3–4, 12, December 1933. **S 383**
Newspapermen should have the legal right to withhold identity of informants.

———. "Persons' Right to Privacy and Public Right to Know Is Still Unsettled Problem." *Quill,* 45(4):17, 20, April 1957. **S 384**
"Radio and television have created new areas of dispute in invasion of privacy question, as has increased use of pictures in the press."

———. "Professional Secrecy and the Journalist." *Journalism Quarterly,* 36:3–11, Winter 1959. **S 385**
"The problem of obtaining legislation to protect the journalist from compulsion to reveal his news sources is reviewed in detail. In the United States refusal to testify before administrators and legislators is recognized, but in only 12 states are newspapermen protected from demands of courts."

———. "The Regulation of Newsbooks, 1620–1640." *Journalism Quarterly,* 16:151–62, June 1939. **S 386**
An account of the Royal licensing of early newspapers ("newsbooks" or "corontos") in England.

———. "Regulation of the Press in the Seventeenth Century; Excerpts from the Records of the Court of the Stationers' Company." *Journalism Qaurterly,* 13:381–93, December 1936. **S 387**
Notes from unpublished records of the Court of the Stationers' Company, 1602–1717, relating to press regulations.

———. "Research in Press Law and Freedom of the Press." *Journalism Quarterly,* 19:69–70, March 1942. **S 388**
A professor of journalism considers the need for research in nine areas—historical, law of libel, contempt, trial by newspaper, confidence laws, state statutes, economic factors, labor, and wartime controls. He calls for "more case studies and fewer studies of cases."

———. "The Right to Know." *ILA Record,* 2:13–17, December 1948. **S 389**
An account of the world struggle for freedom of the press which is taking place in the United Nations. The author reviews developments within the Commission on Human Rights and the Subcommission of Freedom

of Information and of the Press. The vast differences in the Soviet and American understanding of the meaning of *freedom* has created an ideological impasse.

————. "The Right to Report by Television." *Journalism Quarterly*, 34:333–37, Summer 1957.   **S 390**
The author discusses the right of access of TV cameramen and newsmen, and the right to report by television in the areas of straight news, features, and entertainment. He also applies the law of privacy to those areas of TV program content, and to advertising.

————. *The Rights and Privileges of the Press*. New York, Appleton, Century, 1934. 429 p.   **S 391**
"An attempt to define the limits of the rights and privileges of the press as they have been laid down by legislatures and courts." Intended as a guide for practicing journalists. An introductory chapter relates to Freedom of the Press. Part 1 deals with The Right to Gather News; Part 2, The Right to Print News; and Part 3, The Right to Comment on the News. The appendix includes the text of the *Near v. Minnesota* case and a Table of Cases.

————. "Taxes on Publications in England in the Eighteenth Century." *Journalism Quarterly*, 21:12–24, March 1944.   **S 392**
The stamp tax replaced the earlier licensing as a government means of press control. A chapter from the author's book *Freedom of the Press in England*.

————, Theodore Peterson, and Wilbur Schramm. *Four Theories of the Press*. Urbana, Ill., University of Illinois Press, 1956. 153 p. (Reprinted in Illini Books, paperback edition)   **S 393**
The authors have identified four systems of social control in which the media of mass communications have operated from the beginning of printing to the present day: *Authoritarian theory*, represented by the Tudors and Stuarts, in which the state is in control; *libertarian theory*, guaranteed by the Bill of Rights and in which the press is conceived as a partner in the search for truth; the *social responsibility theory*, an outgrowth of the libertarian theory, which assures that neither powerful government nor private monopoly prevent the press from carrying out its responsibility to the people. This is the theory advocated by the Hutchins commission. The fourth, the *Soviet Communist theory* of the press, is a modification of the earlier authoritarian system, with the state in control.

Siebert, Sara, and Linda Lapides. "Shuddered to Think . . ." *Top of the News*, 22: 259–64, April 1966.   **S 394**

A letter to the editor of a local newspaper complained of the presence of the book, *The Prisoners of Combine D* by Len Giovannitti, in the young adult section of Enoch Pratt Free Library, Baltimore. This article describes how the incident was handled in light of the book evaluation and selection policy of that library.

Siegel, Seymour N. "Censorship in Radio." *Air Law Review*, 7:1–24, January 1936. (Excerpted in Summers, *Radio Censorship*, pp. 58–62)   **S 395**
The assistant director of radio broadcasting for the city of New York discusses the formation of the law governing radio, including the Radio Act of 1927 and the Communications Act of 1934, and the operation of subsequent punishment by means of refusal to grant renewal of a license.

Siepmann, Charles A. "Moral Aspects of Television." *Public Opinion Quarterly*, 24: 12–18, Spring 1960.   **S 396**
Testimony presented at hearings held by the FCC, 11 December 1959. Siepmann recommends reform in the FCC and its controls of the broadcasting industry to ensure that the public interest in television is guaranteed.

————. "Propaganda and Information in International Affairs." *Yale Law Journal*, 55:1258–80, August 1946.   **S 397**
A survey of international communications. The author cites the need for international agreements that will ensure the freedom of all media of mass communications.

————. *The Radio Listener's Bill of Rights: Democracy, Radio and You*. New York, Anti-Defamation League of B'nai B'rith, 1948. 52 p.   **S 398**
Public ignorance, indifference, and inertia are the three dangers to democracy as they apply to radio broadcasting. Siepmann urges public participation in listeners' councils and in other action groups to make radio more responsive to its social obligations.

————. *Radio, Television and Society*. New York, Oxford University Press, 1950. 410 p.   **S 399**
One of the purposes of the book is "to deal with broadcasting as a reflection of our time and to throw light upon the problems of free speech, propaganda, public education, our relations with the rest of the world, and upon the concept of democracy itself." Chapter 9 deals with Freedom of Speech—In Theory; Chapter 10 with Freedom of Speech—In Practice. The latter discusses the various regulations and court decisions that have led to present practices.

————. *Radio's Second Chance*. Boston, Little, Brown, 1946. 282 p.   **S 400**
The author develops the theme that the

airways belong to the people and that networks, under government license, have not fulfilled their public responsibility. He warns that the greatest danger to freedom in communication is public apathy; he stresses the role of the FCC in assuring balanced programs. FM and television offer the broadcasting industry a second chance to develop an agency sensitive to public needs.

————, and Sidney Reisberg. "'To Secure These Rights': Coverage of a Radio Documentary." *Public Opinion Quarterly*, 12:649–58, Winter 1948–49.   **S 401**
"Origination of a valuable radio program does not alone insure good coverage. Participation by affiliated stations in a network and adequate promotion are equally necessary." Less than half the stations, it was determined, carried this civil rights documentary.

Sifton, Victor. *Rights and Citizenship. The Threat to Our Freedom*. Winnipeg, Can., Winnipeg Free Press, [1954]. 8 p. (Winnipeg Free Press Pamphlet no. 49)   **S 402**
An address by the chancellor of the University of Manitoba. "We think we have free speech, freedom of person, free assembly, a free press, and freedom of religion. What we forget is that in one way or another they have been challenged several times within recent years." He discusses the Padlock Law, the Alberta Press Act, and the Jehovah's Witnesses case in Quebec.

Sigler, Jay A. "Customs Censorship." *Cleveland—Marshall Law Review*, 15:58–74, January 1966.   **S 403**
A review of the history and administration of Customs censorship in the United States as applied against obscenity and Communist propaganda, with brief comments on Customs censorship in Great Britain and Commonwealth countries.

————. "Freedom of the Mails: A Developing Right." *Georgetown Law Journal*, 54:30–54, Fall 1965.   **S 404**
"Concluding that a freedom of the mails is implicit in the first amendment's freedom of speech guarantee, the author explores various activities of the Post Office Department which tend to abridge this freedom. Professor Sigler notes that the postal censorship power is growing more popular with Congress, but he voices cautious optimism about an eventual recognition of a freedom of the mails. The recent Supreme Court decision in *Lamont v. Postmaster General* is largely responsible for this optimism."

Sigma Delta Chi. Committee on Advancement of Freedom of Information. *Annual Reports*. Chicago, The Society, 1948–date.   **S 405**
The first (1948) report stated: "The whole structure of human rights in a world of free

men with governments of their own choosing rests upon one basic right—the right to know. We believe that this basic right includes freedom to speak freely upon all matters without fear; freedom to gather and disseminate information and opinion without censorship or suppression, and freedom of choice of sources of information without dictation, either by government or by private monopoly." Annual reports have included such topics as the federal government, government in the states, reporter confidence law, freedom of information in Latin America, freedom of information in radio and television, and the press and the bar.

Sikes, Herschel M. "William Hone: Regency Patriot, Parodist, and Pamphleteer." *Newberry Library Bulletin*, 5:281–94, July 1961. **S 406**
An account of the political pamphleteering of William Hone, "a noisy advocate of political change whose bold style and concrete, vivid language were used in numerous and well-illustrated (George Cruikshank) pamphlets ranging from exposés of the horrifying conditions in insane asylums and jails to ringing defenses of freedom of the press and religious tolerance." The article is based on the large collection of Hone's writings in the Newberry Library.

Silber, Jules C. *The Invisible Weapons, With a Foreword by Major-General Edward Gleichen*. London, Hutchinson, 1932. 288 p. **S 407**
Propaganda and censorship in World War I.

Silverstein, Hyman C. "Freedom of the Press." *Boston University Law Review*, 16: 919–22, November 1936. **S 408**
An account of the case (*Grosjean v. American Press Co.*, 56 Sup. Ct. 444) which declared unconstitutional the Louisiana law licensing newspapers and magazines.

Simkins, T. M., Jr. "Remarks on Censorship by Sheriffs." *North Carolina Libraries*, 16:44–47, February 1958. **S 409**

Simmons, E. B. "Obscene Publication." *Solicitors' Journal*, 107:165–67, 1 March 1963. **S 410**
Suggested changes to plug the loopholes in the Obscene Publications Act, 1959, based on case experience and the French Penal Code.

Simon, Paul. "Elijah Lovejoy: Minister, Editor, Martyr." *Presbyterian Life*, 18(21): 13–15, 36–37, 1 November 1965. **S 411**
"The first United States martyr for freedom of the press was a Presbyterian minister and editor, Elijah Lovejoy, who was buried on his thirty-fifth birthday, November 9, 1837."

———. *Lovejoy: Martyr to Freedom*. St. Louis, Concordia, 1964. 150 p. **S 412**

A dramatic account of the martyrdom of the antislavery editor of Alton, Ill., who in 1837 gave his life in defending his press from a proslavery mob. The story unfolds the chain of events that led to Lovejoy's antislavery sentiments and, more significantly, to his championship of freedom of the press. Lovejoy became the first martyr to freedom of the press in America.

Simpkins, John D. *A Comparative Study of Four State Laws Affecting Access to News*. Athens, Ohio, Ohio University, 1965. 154 p. (Unpublished Master's thesis) **S 413**
A study of the four laws of the state of Ohio which are concerned with access to public information: open records law, open meetings law, reporter confidence law, and right to advertise law. Includes a brief statement on access laws of other states and the text of the Sigma Delta Chi model laws.

Simpson, Jerome D. "Censorship: The Profession's Response." *ALA Newsletter on Intellectual Freedom*, 13:41–42, July 1964. **S 414**
A statistical examination of the literature on censorship in the library profession to determine how much literature is being published and whether there has been an increase or decrease. The author finds a rather steady growth in "censorship" citations culminating in 568 entries in the past 3 years.

Sinclair, Robert. *The British Press; the Journalist and His Conscience*. London, Home & Van Thal, 1949. 271 p. **S 415**
A veteran journalist discusses freedom of the press and the ethics of British journalism, giving examples in the handling of specific news stories. He recommends a "court of honor," more informal than that proposed by the Royal Commission, to enforce press standards.

Sinclair, Upton. *Brass Check; a Study of American Journalism*. Pasadena, Calif., The Author, 1920. 445 p. **S 416**
A novelist and Socialist writer attacks the American press. His bitter and violent criticism is based largely on his own unhappy experience and represents his attitudes toward efforts made by the owners, advertisers, and press associations to control public opinion.

———. "Censorship and Secret Treaties." *Appeal to Reason*, 1219:2, 12 April 1919. **S 417**
How military intelligence arranged to have the British censor exclude Upton Sinclair's works from England during World War I.

———. "How Censorship Actually Works." *Everybody's Magazine*, 26:135–36, January 1912. **S 418**
An account of J. Wesley Glasgow's publication

of a work on sexual purity, his arrest and trial on obscenity charges, and the confiscation of all copies of the book. Any person who wishes to investigate the matter, writes Sinclair, "is not only powerless to get any information but is liable himself to arrest for trying to find out about it." Sinclair had interviewed Glasgow in the Newcastle County Workhouse.

———. "The Library Censorship." *Athenaeum*, 4428:247, 7 September 1912. **S 419**
Sinclair protests the suppression of his novel, *Love's Pilgrimage*, in England by the Circulating Libraries Association.

———. *Oil! A Novel*. New York, Albert & Charles Boni, 1926. 527 p. ("Fig Leaf" edition) **S 420**
In May of 1927 a bookstore clerk in Boston was arrested for selling a copy of *Oil!* The book was offensive to authorities on several counts: it attacked organized religion, it openly attacked the graft in the Harding Administration, and it referred to birth control and free love. A municipal court judge found the book "manifestly tending to corrupt the morals of youth." Sinclair persuaded the judge to drop action against the clerk and, instead, to take action against the book and author. To insure his own arrest, Sinclair sold a copy of *Oil!* on the streets of Boston to a member of the police vice squad. It was this special "fig leaf" edition, and Sinclair appropriately wore a fig leaf sandwich board. Certain objectionable pages in the edition were either greyed or blacked out by large fig leaves printed over the original text. The following note (in red) appears on the title page of the edition: "This novel has won the praise of some of the world's greatest writers and critics, but a censorship of the city of Boston has banned it, and we have therefore prepared this special edition for sale throughout Massachusetts. We point out to the reader that there are still a great many pages not blacked out; and these are the really important pages, full of the political and social information which is the real cause of the attack upon the book. It is interesting to note that the greater part of the material on pages 328–329 consists of passages from the Song of Solomon, which you may read in any copy of the Old Testament." Sinclair's scheme failed, however, when a different judge appeared in court, refused to accept the case against Sinclair, but found the bookstore clerk guilty and fined him $100.

———. "Poor Me and Pure Boston." *Nation*, 124:713–14, 29 June 1927. **S 421**
Sinclair, who called himself the "prize prude of the radical movement," considers the irony of his book, *Oil!* being banned in Boston as obscene. He speculates on the reasons and describes his fun in selling a copy of the Bible to a Boston policeman, under the jacket of a copy of *Oil!*

Singer, George A., *pseud. Judicial Scandals and Errors.* London, The University Press, 1899. 58 p. (Also bound with Democritus' *Darwin on Trial at the Old Bailey*, pp. 45–86) **S 422**

An account of the Bedborough trial in London for the sale of Havelock Ellis' *Studies in the Psychology of Sex.* Ellis, in a foreword to the 1936 edition of his *Studies*, declares Singer to be the fictitious creation of Dr. Roland de Villiers, actually the pseudonym of George F. S. von Weissenfeld. Villiers, as von Weissenfeld was best known, published Ellis' *Studies.* He later was found to be a notorious forger and confidence man and committed suicide when apprehended.

Singh, Ram N. P. *The All India Radio.* Columbia, Mo., Freedom of Information Center, School of Journalism, University of Missouri, 1961. 6 p. (Publication no. 52) **S 423**

A discussion of the state-owned and state-operated All India Radio (A.I.R.).

————. *The Story of India's Free Press.* Columbia, Mo., Freedom of Information Center, School of Journalism, University of Missouri, 1961. 6 p. (Publication no. 55) **S 424**

Singleton, M. K. "The Hatrack Controversy." In his *H. L. Mencken and the American Mercury Adventure.* Durham, N.C., Duke University Press, 1962, pp. 167–81. **S 425**

Sington, Derrick. *Freedom of Communication.* London, Ampersand, 1963. 126 p. **S 426**

A German journalist presents a concise survey of the current status of freedom in the various media—the press, films, and radio-television—giving a brief historical background in the area of sedition, obscenity, and libel. He examines in some detail the charges against the profit motive as a threat to a free press. While his remarks deal largely with the British scene, he also comments on mass communications in America, the British Commonwealth, and the totalitarian countries, by way of comparison or contrast.

"The Sinister Assault on the Freedom of the Press." *Arena*, 41:358–65, March 1909. **S 427**

A collection of excerpts from American newspapers referring to the growing efforts of government and business interests to shackle the American press. Reference to President Theodore Roosevelt's fight with Pulitzer and the *New York World* and to Lincoln's refusal to suppress the *Chicago Times* during the Civil War.

Sirluck, Ernest. "*Areopagitica* and a Forgotten Licensing Controversy." *Review of English Studies*, 11(n. s.):260–74, August 1960. **S 428**

The author maintains that the controversy that was waged in 1697, whether or not to reinact the licensing act that had been allowed to lapse 2 years earlier, was a direct reflection of the influence of Milton's *Areopagitica*, written in 1644 against the licensing of printing. The 32-page document which inspired the parliamentary opposition to licensing in 1698 was entitled *A Letter to a Member of Parliament, Shewing, that a Restraint On the Press Is inconsistent with the Protestant Religion, and dangerous to the Liberties of the Nation.* The pamphlet is believed to be the work of Matthew Tindal, but is taken almost entirely from *Areopagitica*, without giving credit to Milton. The author shows by parallel readings the similarities of the two texts. Tindal is believed to have read *Areopagitica* for the first time from one of the collected editions of 1697 and 1698. He may also have made use of Charles Blount's adaptation of Milton's work, *A Just Vindication of Learning*, 1679.

Sisk, John P. "The Human Management of News." *Ramparts*, 4:59–63, October 1965. **S 429**

"We are by nature, then, news managers, news manipulators, which is only to say that we are embattled by time. The need to manage or manipulate the news is in proportion not only to the amount of it but to the strain it imposes on the structures we have already made out of the messages that have come to us. If time is to move at a manageable pace the messages must be managed. . . . But however we manage or manipulate the news there are too many messages for most of us, and time like water through a leaking dike breaks through on us everywhere."

Sitney, P. Adams. "[Film Censorship]: United States." *Censorship*, 2(2):48–50, Spring 1965. **S 430**

Censorship troubles of the avant-garde cinema in the United States, including the case of Jack Smith's *Flaming Creatures*, Jean Genet's *Un Chant d'Amour*, and Kenneth Anger's *Scorpio Rising.*

Sitwell, *Sir* Osbert. "On the Burning of Books as Private Pastime and Public Recreation." In his *Penny Foolish.* London, Macmillan, 1935, pp. 328–33. (Reprinted in Downs, *The First Freedom*, pp. 270–71) **S 431**

"To those who know and hate literature, there is no satisfaction comparable to that of poking some special volume's glowing ashes." In this humorous bit of satire, the British author describes the sport of book burning as practiced in Germany and England.

Six Hours to Deadline: A Free and Responsible Press. 20 min., b/w movie. New York, Prepared by a Committee of the National Council of Teachers of English to Cooperate with Teaching Film Custodians, 1964. (Accompanied by study guide) **S 432**

A fictionalized dramatization of a small-town editor faced with the decision whether or not to publish a news story that would bring grief to a respected member of the community. Presents an analysis of social and ethical problems of journalism.

Skeffington, Owen S. "McGahern Affair." *Censorship*, 1(2):27–30, Spring 1966. **S 433**

"The most striking thing about the victimisation of John McGahern for the crime of writing a book [*The Dark*] that was banned by the Irish Censorship Board, is the closed-circuit clerical machine which wielded its absolute power to cut off his right to earn his living in Ireland as a primary school teacher."

Skiba, Francis. "Access to Legislative Department Records." *Marquette Law Review*, 44:230–34, Fall 1960. **S 434**

Notes on *Trimble v. Johnston*, 173 F. Supp. 651 (D.D.C. 1959), relating to inspection of a government payroll record by a reporter. "The *Trimble* case, in conjunction with the concept of executive privilege, leads to the conclusion that the release of government records must be determined by the branch of government which controls them."

Skousen, W. Cleon. "Obscene Literature: What Can the Police Do About It?" *Law and Order*, 9(8):10–14, August 1961. **S 435**

An outline of the program of the national Citizens for Decent Literature. The author recommends that police departments take the initiative in setting up local citizens' committees to police magazines and books on newsstands. He answers a group of questions that are commonly asked: Isn't obscenity censorship unconstitutional? (He cites the Roth case in answering in the negative.) Isn't reading of pornography an adult pastime? (He shows that 75 per cent of the readers are minors.)

Skow, John. "Is Love, Sweet Love, A Crime?" *Saturday Evening Post*, 239:82, 87, 12 February 1966. **S 436**

The story of Ralph Ginzburg and the legal action against his publication, *Eros.*

Slack, Henry J. *State of Prosecutions of the Press at the Instigation of a Foreign Government; a Defense of the Free Press in England, a Lecture Delivered at St. Martin's Hall, 28 April, 1858.* London, Published for the Press Defence Committee by J. Pattie, 1858. 32 p. **S 437**

Slafter, Edmund F. *John Checkley; or, The Evolution of Religious Tolerance in*

Massachusetts Bay. Including Mr. Checkley's Controversial Writings; His Letters and Other Papers ... With Historical Illustrations and a Memoir by the Rev. Edmund F. Slafter ... Boston, The Prince Society, 1897. 2 vol. (Publications of the Prince Society, vols. 22–23) **S 438**

Volume 2 contains the libel proceedings against Mr. Checkley for publishing Leslie's *Short and Easy Method with the Deists* (1724), including Mr. Checkley's speech at the trial. There is a bibliography of the controversy in America relating to episcopacy, in which the above book also played a part.

Sledd, Andrew. "Dismissal of Professor Banks." *Independent*, 70:1113–14, 25 May 1911. **S 439**

Professor Enoch M. Banks was dismissed from the University of Florida in 1911 because of an article he wrote for the *Independent*, which stated that if the intellectuals of the South had taken the slavery question in hand the Civil War would have been unnecessary. An article by Professor James W. Garner of the University of Illinois criticizing the action appeared in the 27 April issue.

Slivka, William J. "Obscenity Through the Mails." *Western Reserve Law Review*, 11:480–92, June 1960. **S 440**

"This note will concern itself with the authority of the United States Post Office Department, emanating from the Constitution, legislation, and postal regulations, to investigate and terminate the sending of obscene material through the mails."

Sloan, Frank K. "The Case for the Right of Privacy." *University of South Carolina Selden Society Yearbook*, 9:45–62, Fall 1948. **S 441**

Following a definition of the "right of privacy" the author discusses the legal problems involved, recommending wider recognition of the right in common law. Among the objections to acceptance are: injury to feelings are too nebulous; the right opens up a vast field of litigation; equity is not a proper method of dealing with rights that do not involve tangible property and any recognition of this right of privacy infringes upon freedom of speech and of the press.

Sloan, George W. "Censorship in Historical Perspective." *Top of the News*, 22:269–72, April 1966. **S 442**

History has demonstrated that the only "acceptable censor" is one's conscience. "The conscience which is in every one of us is the only thing to which any child, adult, or librarian should submit."

Sloss, Robert. *An American's View of the British Mail Censorship.* London, W. Speaight, 1916. 31 p. **S 443**

The author was a correspondent of the *Chicago Daily News.*

Slough, M. C., and P. D. McAnany. "Obscenity and Constitutional Freedom." *St. Louis University Law Journal*, 8:279–357, Spring 1964; 8:449–532, Summer 1964. **S 444**

Part one deals with the historic developments of efforts to establish definitions and standards in the area of obscenity in Great Britain and the United States and with the constitutional issues of obscenity versus freedom of the press. Part two deals with the structure and dimensions of obscenity as perceived by the courts, the public issue of obscenity in theory, and the controversy over effect and where to draw the line. It also discusses the position of the Catholic Church in matters of obscenity. The authors summarize private and public action against obscenity and suggest a middle ground of self regulation. They conclude with an outline of procedural requirements—pretrial and trial procedures, and independent judicial review.

Small, Collie. "Too Many Self-Appointed Censorship Groups." *Reader's Digest*, 59:109–12, September 1951. (Condensed from *Redbook*, July 1951) **S 445**

An increase in censorship is attributed to the large number of minority groups organized and active in recent years and to the growing fear on the part of publishers, and radio and motion pictures officials of offending them. The author mentions specifically a Texas threat against the Negro-problem film, *Pinky*; Catholic pressures against the movie, *The Miracle*; Jewish opposition to the movie, *Oliver Twist*; and the Bartlesville, Okla., "vigilante committee" action against *The Nation* and *New Republic*.

Smead, Elmer E. *Freedom of Speech by Radio and Television.* Washington, D.C., Public Affairs, 1959. 182 p. **S 446**

A general summary of legislation, court rulings, and FCC regulations relating to broadcasting. Such issues as public interest, equal time, and censorship are included.

Smelser, Marshall. "George Washington and the Alien and Sedition Acts." *American Historical Review*, 59:322–34, January 1954 **S 447**

A review of events leading to passage of the Alien and Sedition Acts, from the point of view of George Washington as president. The author points out Washington's exasperation at the many and bitter attacks on him and his administration by newspaper editors and his mistrust of the politics of immigrants, particularly of a French conspiracy. After the laws were passed Washington approved and defended them.

———. "The Jacobin Phrenzy: Federalism and the Menace of Liberty, Equality, and Fraternity." *Review of Politics*, 13:457–82, October 1951. **S 448**

A study of the first years of the American Federal republic when American relations

with France became strained and many thought our country endangered by mismanagement of foreign relations. In the resulting bitter debate the aristocratic Federalists, because of "distaste for having their acts and motives minutely reviewed by the vulgar mass," began to show symptoms of "social paranoia." Repressive legislation seemed the defense against this. Out of this climate came the Sedition Act.

Smith, Alice K. "Secrecy and the Army." *Midway*, 23:2–26, Summer 1965. **S 449**

A discussion of the controversy between scientists and the military over the control of information on atomic energy following World War II.

Smith, Bernard B. "The People's Stake in Radio." *New Republic*, 111:11–13, 3 July 1944. **S 450**

An appeal to the radio broadcasting industry and the FCC to consider the public interest with which they are charged by law.

Smith, Beverly. "Keeping of Our Morals." *American Magazine*, 123:24–25+, January 1937. **S 451**

Includes comments on the work of John S. Sumner of the New York vice society.

Smith, Bruce L. "Scientific and Semi-Scientific Literature on War Information and Censorship." *Journalism Quarterly*, 20:1–20, March 1943. **S 452**

Includes a bibliography on censorship and propaganda.

———, Harold D. Lasswell, and Ralph D. Casey. *Propaganda, Communication, and Public Opinion; a Comprehensive Reference Guide.* Princeton, N.J., Princeton University Press, 1946. 435 p. **S 453**

Prefaced by four essays on mass communications, this is a comprehensive, annotated bibliography on propaganda, part 7 of which deals with control and censorship of communications. This is a continuation of the work begun in *Propaganda and Promotional Activities: An Annotated Bibliography*, compiled by Lasswell, Casey, and Smith.

Smith, C. R. F. "Freedom of the Press on the Campus." *Quill*, 24(4):10–11, April 1936. **S 454**

A journalism professor suggests that the university act as publisher, with student staff as paid hirelings, which will give students a taste of the censorship of ownership that every newspaperman recognizes.

Smith, Calvin S. "How Much Freedom?" *Utah Libraries*, 6:19–20, Spring 1963. **S 455**

Smith, Charles E. *The Freedom of the Press. Governor Samuel W. Pennypacker's Message Approving the Bill in Restraint of Its Liberty, and Charles Emery Smith's Editorial in Protest.* [Philadelphia, 1903]. 28 p. **S 456**

Smith was editor of the Philadelphia *Press*; he had been Postmaster General in the McKinley Administration. The bill criticized was aimed at political cartoons and grew out of Governor Pennypacker's outrage at attacks on him by cartoonists during his gubernatorial campaign. The brochure includes a cartoon by F. T. Richards from the Philadelphia *Press* of 13 May 1903 entitled The Gag and the Gauntlet.

————. "Press: Its Liberty and License." *Independent*, 55:1371–75, 11 June 1903. **S 457**

When Judge Samuel W. Pennypacker became governor of Pennsylvania in 1902 he signed into law a severe libel bill, passed without hearings. It was aimed to prevent criticism of state officials. "The viciousness of the new Pennsylvania law is that it is a backward step flying in the face of the whole course of libel legislation in other states; that it is a deliberate attempt to terrorize the press and to stifle public criticism; and that it is the joint product of public pique and private piracy."

[Smith, Delavan, et al.]. *The Indianapolis News Panama Libel Case. Circumstances Preceding the Return of the Indictments and Proceedings for the Removal to the District of Columbia for Trial of Delavan Smith and Charles R. Williams, Publishers of the Indianapolis News. Order for Removal Denied October 13, 1909, by the United States District Court for the District of Indiana, Hon. Albert B. Anderson, Judge.* Indianapolis, 1909. 352 p. **S 458**

In the only attempt of the federal government to sue a newspaper for libel since the Alien and Sedition Acts, President Theodore Roosevelt instructed Attorney General William N. Cromwell to enter a libel suit against Delavan Smith of the *Indianapolis News* and Joseph Pulitzer of the *New York World*. The papers had carried hints that an American syndicate, including Cromwell, had made illegal profits from the purchase of Panama Canal rights. The federal courts dismissed the suits, ruling that such action violated the First Amendment of the Constitution. The offending article from the *World* is reprinted in Don C. Seitz' biography of Joseph Pulitzer.

Smith, Desmond. "American Radio To-day—The Listener Be Damned." *Harper's Magazine*, 229:57–63, September 1964. **S 459**

The author suggests internal reform of broadcasting standards and practices to remind the advertisers and their Washington allies of the public interest.

Smith, Dorothea. *Press Commission in Other Countries.* Columbia, Mo., Freedom of Information Center, School of Journalism, University of Missouri, 1960. 8 p. (Publication no. 35) **S 460**

A survey of press councils and commissions in Sweden, Denmark, Switzerland, Netherlands, Germany, Pakistan, India, South Africa, Australia, Italy, France, Chile, Indonesia, and Great Britain. The patterns of the British Royal Commission of the Press, 1947–49, were followed by South Africa, India, and Pakistan.

Smith, Edward. *William Cobbett: a Biography.* London, Low, Marston, Searle & Rivington, 1872. 2 v. **S 461**

G. D. H. Cole describes this biography of the mercurial champion of press freedom as "good, but somewhat uncritically laudatory."

Smith, Everett E. "Constitutional Aspects of Censorship." *Dicta*, 32:305–11, July–August 1955. **S 462**

Brief report on constitutional problems relating to censorship of books on the grounds of obscenity.

[Smith, Francis]. *An Impartial Account of the Tryal of Francis Smith upon an Information Brought against Him for Printing and Publishing a Late Book Commonly Known by the Name of Tom Ticklefoot, Etc. As Also of the Trial of Jane Curtis upon an Information Brought against Her for Publishing and Putting to Sale a Scandalous Libel, Called A Satyr upon Injustice; or Scroggs upon Scroggs.* [London], 1680. 6 p. (Also in Howell, *State Trials*, vol. 7, pp. 931 ff., and in Hart, *Index Expurgatorius Anglicanus*, p. 184) **S 463**

One of the chief victims of Censor Roger L'Estrange, "old Frank Smith" spent many months in jail for printing matter offensive to the government. George Kitchen, in his biography of L'Estrange, calls this work "one of the most interesting documents on the tyrannous side of the press." Smith was entrapped by L'Estrange's messenger agent, Robert Stephens, and brought to trial before the severe Judge Scroggs. *Tom Ticklefoot* was a satire on the trial of Sir George Wakeman.

Smith, G. K. "Censorship of Instructional Material." In National Conference on Higher Education. *Current Issues in Higher Education, 1952.* Washington, D.C., Department of Higher Education, National Education Association, 1953, pp. 138–39. **S 464**

Smith, George M. "Lawful Pleasures." *Critic*, 38:256–64, March 1901. **S 465**

Autobiographical account of personal libel cases in which the author was involved as proprietor of the *Pall Mall Gazette* and *The Cornhill Magazine*.

[Smith, Harrison]. "Censorship Can Be Stopped." *Saturday Review of Literature*, 32(16):28–29, 16 April 1949. **S 466**

A summary of Judge Curtis Bok's decision in the Philadelphia trial over works of Farrell, Faulkner, and Caldwell. Obscenity, he states, has no inherent meaning and "is not indictable unless actual or imminent criminal behavior can be traced to it."

Smith, Helena H. "Boston's Bogy-Man." *Outlook*, 149:214–16+, 6 June 1928. **S 467**

This journalist spent two weeks in Boston in the heat of the police campaign against modern novels. The censor, she found, was the bookseller himself and all that it took to bar a book was a suggestion. While works of literature were being banned, she observed obscene magazines being sold to high school students with no attempt being made to stop this traffic.

Smith, Hugh. *Theory and Regulation of Public Sentiment; an Address Delivered before the Alumni of Columbia College . . .* New York, Lane, 1842. 48 p. **S 468**

Smith, James M. "Alexander Hamilton, the Alien Law, and Seditious Libels." *Review of Politics*, 16:305–33, July 1954. **S 469**

————. "The Aurora and the Sedition Laws." *Pennsylvania Magazine of History and Biography*, 77:3–23, January 1953; 77:123–55, April 1953. **S 470**

Part I deals with the editorship of Benjamin Franklin Bache; part II with the editorship of William Duane, both victims of the Sedition law during the administration of President Adams. An expanded account appears in the author's book, *Freedom's Fetters*.

————. *Freedom's Fetters; the Alien and Sedition Laws and American Civil Liberties.* Ithaca, N.Y., Cornell University Press, 1956. 464 p. Published in Co-operation with the Institute of Early American History and Culture. (Cornell Studies in Civil Liberty) **S 471**

The dramatic story of the struggle between the elements of freedom and order that took place in the United States with the passage of the Alien and Sedition Laws of 1798, legislation which Woodrow Wilson wrote "cut perilously near the root of freedom of speech and the press." This first volume of a projected two-volume study on the Alien and Sedition Laws deals with "the enactment and enforcement of the Federalist measures of 1798 and attempts to assess their influence in shaping the development of the political process of republicanism, with its dual goals of majority rule and individual rights." The second volume will deal with the Kentucky and Virginia Resolutions. Together, the volumes "will form an integrated investigation of the relationship between liberty and authority in a popular form of government." This volume includes cases on Benjamin Franklin Bache (Philadelphia *Aurora*), John Daly (New York *Time-Piece*), Matthew Lyon (*Vermont Gazette*), Thomas Adams (Boston *Independent Chronicle*), William Duane (Philadelphia *Aurora*), Thomas Cooper and President Adams, James T. Callender (Richmond *Examiner*), Anthony Haswell (*Vermont Gazette*), Charles Holt (New London, Conn., *Bee*), William Durrell (Mt. Pleasant, N.Y., *Register*), and Jedidiah Peck, a New York legislator. The text of the Alien and Sedition Laws is given in the appendix.

———. "President John Adams, Thomas Cooper, and Sedition: A Case Study in Suppression." *Mississippi Valley Historical Review*, 42:438–65, December 1955.
S 472
Thomas Cooper's prosecution under the Sedition Act, 1799–1800. A shorter version of a chapter in the author's book, *Freedom's Fetters*.

———. "Sedition in the Old Dominion: James T. Callender and *The Prospect Before Us*." *Journal of Southern History*, 20:157–82, May 1954.
S 473
Notes on the trial and conviction of Callender under the Sedition Law of 1798, presided over by Justice Samuel Chase, 1800; with some account of Callender's works as a newspaperman in Virginia. The article is expanded in the author's book, *Freedom's Fetters*.

———. "The Sedition Law, Free Speech and the American Political Process." *William and Mary Quarterly*, 9:497–511, October 1952.
S 474
"If people cannot communicate their thoughts to one another without running the risk of prosecution, no other liberty can be secure because freedom of speech and of the press are essential to any meaning of liberty. The years between 1798 and 1801 afford the first instance under the Constitution in which American political leaders faced the problem of defining the role of public criticism in a representative government. This paper deals with the solution which the Federalists proposed and acted upon and the response of the American people to it."

———. "Sedition, Suppression, and Speech: a Comic Footnote on the Enforcement of the Sedition Law of 1798." *Quarterly Journal of Speech*, 40: 284–87, October 1954.
S 475

An account of the prosecution of Luther Baldwin for expressing the wish, when a cannon was accidentally discharged close to the person of President John Adams, that the shot "had lodged in the President's posterior," and the "basic language" in which the issue was discussed in the Republican newspapers.

Smith, Jeremiah. "Are Charges against the Moral Character of a Candidate for an Elective Office Conditionally Privileged?" *Michigan Law Review*, 18:1–15, November 1919; 18:104–26, December 1919.
S 476

———. "Disparagement of Property." *Columbia Law Review*, 13:13–36, January 1913; 13:121–42, February 1913.
S 477
A discussion of this legal issue, sometimes considered as slander of property, to include patent rights, copyright, and the right to use a trade name. The legal area is divided into two parts: disparagement of title or interest and disparagement of quality. The second article deals with actual damages resulting therefrom.

Smith, John. *Trial of John Smith, Bookseller . . . December 6, 1796, for Selling a Work Entitled, "A Summary of the Duties of Citizenship."* London, Mrs. Smith, [1797]. 35p.
S 478

Smith, John E. "A Statewide Experience with Pressure Groups." In *Freedom of Communication; Proceedings of the First Conference on Intellectual Freedom . . .* Chicago, American Library Association, 1954, pp. 89–96.
S 479
Deals with pressures exerted against schools and libraries in California.

———, and Evelyn B. Detchon. "It Happened in Burbank." *ALA Bulletin*, 46:3, 85–87, March 1952.
S 480
A proposal by the Burbank Public Library Board that the League of California Cities approve labeling of subversive and immoral books in California public libraries stirred state-wide controversy. The California Library Association passed a resolution against labeling and sent it to the League, which did not adopt the controversial proposal.

Smith, Judith A. "The Reporter's Right to Shield His 'Reliable Source.'" *PEAL*, 1:31–48, June 1961.
S 481
Favors the legal protection of a reporter's news source, within reasonable limits.

Smith, Margaret Chase. "Fair Trial and Free Press: Pressures Exerted on Courts and Jurors." *American Bar Association Journal*, 42:341–43+, April 1956.
S 482

Pressures that "trial by newspaper" exert on courts and jurors; the need for maintaining a proper balance between free press and fair trial. Address by the U.S. senator before the American Bar Association, section on Judicial Administration.

Smith, Michael. *Glenview and the Birch Society*. Columbia, Mo., Freedom of Information Center, School of Journalism University of Missouri, 1966. 5p. (Publication no. 159)
S 483
A case study indicating the climate of opinion in one community (Glenview, Illinois) when faced with establishment of a John Birch Society bookstore and headquarters.

Smith, Mortimer J. *Important and Interesting Trial of Mortimer J. Smith, on an Indictment for Libel on Miss Emma Williams in Having Connected Her Name with the Separation of David Groesbeck (the New York Wall Street broker), from his Wife, in the Albany Court of Sessions, December 16, 1847. . . .* Albany, Castigator Press, 1847. 16p.
S 484
A later edition (1870) contained an added item: "the Bill of Complaint by Mary W. Groesbeck against David Groesbeck, for Repeated Acts of Adultery, and the Decree of the Court Adjudging a Separation and Divorce."

Smith, Paul. "Secrecy in Local Government." *Censorship*, 2(2):18–21, Spring 1966.
S 485
"One of the main causes of discontent with British local government today is its over-indulgence in secrecy." The author offers seven recommendations to remedy the situation.

Smith, Payson, *et al. Book Censorship in Massachusetts; a Responsible Statement.* Boston, The Author, 1928. 8p.
S 486
A pamphlet in support of an obscenity bill before the Massachusetts legislature, sponsored by Ellery Sedgwick, editor of the *Atlantic Monthly*. The bill, which failed to pass, was intended to liberalize Massachusetts obscenity laws by requiring that a book be judged as a whole. Smith was Massachusetts Commissioner of Education.

Smith, Robert M. *Modern Dramatic Censorship: George Bernard Shaw.* Bloomington, Ind., Indiana University, 1953. 208p. (Ph.D. dissertation, University Microfilms, no. 6452)
S 487
Censorship of Shaw's plays in England and the United States as reflected in the playwright's own writings attacking stage censorship.

Smith, Roger H. "Cops, Counselors and *Tropic of Cancer*." *Publishers' Weekly*, 180:35, 23 October 1961. **S 488**
"The rash of local censorship drives which have been launched against *Tropic of Cancer* without court authorization or adjudication of any kind are irresponsible and, quite likely, unconstitutional."

————. "If Ever a Library Needed a Friend." *Publishers' Weekly*, 183:55, 4 February 1963. **S 489**
Editorial concerning the efforts of a member of the board of library trustees of New City, Rockland County, N.Y., to censor public library books.

————. "A Summer of Censorship." *Publishers' Weekly*, 184:38, 29 July 1963. **S 490**

Smith, S. W. "Propaganda and the Library." *Library Journal*, 64:13–15, 1 January 1939. **S 491**
"If librarians as a group are believers in the democratic dogma and wish to be consistent in their actions and carry out their convictions, they can hardly avoid permitting entry to their libraries of all forms of propaganda. Democracy presupposes toleration and can only hope to function in a *milieu* in which opinions circulate freely and in which the individual is exposed to all sides of public questions and given an opportunity to make up his own mind."

[Smith, Samray]. "The Best/Worst Television Can Do." *ALA Bulletin*, 57:377–78, May 1963; "Censorship or Fair Play?" *ALA Bulletin*, 57:477, June 1963. **S 492**
Two editorials concerning the controversy over the unfavorable portrayal of a smalltown librarian in a censorship case, *A Book for Burning*, on the C.B.S. television program, "The Defenders."

Smith, Sydney. "Proceedings of the Society for the Suppression of Vice." In his *Works*. Philadelphia, Carey and Hart, 1844, vol. 2, pp. 282–93. (Reprinted from *Edinburgh Review*, 1809; also in *Selected Writings of Sydney Smith*, New York, Farrar, Straus, Cudahy, 1956, pp. 287–97) **S 493**
"It is hardly possible," writes the Rev. Mr. Smith, "that a society for the suppression of vice can ever be kept within the bounds of good sense and moderation . . . Beginning with the best intentions in the world, such societies must, in all probability, degenerate into a receptacle for every species of tittle-tattle, impertinence and malice. Men whose trade is rat-catching, love to catch rats."

Smith, Vernon W. "Studies in the Control of Student Publications." *College Press Review*, 4(1):19–33, Winter 1964. **S 494**

Smith, William G. "Puritans Will Rise." *Books and Bookmen*, 7(1):11, October 1961. **S 495**
The editor, in a review of Dianne Doubtfire's *Reasons for Violence*, pleads for more restraint in exercising freedom in treatment of sex in novels. Without it, he forecasts a Puritan revolt. In the November issue the author responds: "To put sex into a novel, purely as a selling point, is unforgivable. But surely it is equally reprehensible to leave it out for fear of shocking the Puritans? A writer of integrity cannot allow himself to be hampered by restrictions of any kind."

————, et al. "Living in Sin." *Assistant Librarian*, 49:185–206, December 1956. **S 496**
Entire issue devoted to censorship: Living in Sin, editorial comments by W. G. Smith on his delight in reading certain banned books and seeing certain banned plays; The Sins of Puritans by John L. Broom; What Is Censorship by R. L. Collison; The Dam Busters, comments pro and con on Eric Moon's reference in a recent review to "a damned good book;" Who Killed Cock Robin? by Alan R. Eager; the Catholic Point of View by V. P. Richards; Censorship in Ireland (various quotes); Danger to Libraries by Edward Dudley; and New Light on Lear by Brian R. Ingram.

Smith, William H. *Charles Hammond and His Relations to Henry Clay and John Quincy Adams; or Constitutional Limitations and the Contest for Freedom of Speech and the Press. An Address delivered before the Chicago Historical Society, May 20, 1884.* Chicago, Chicago Historical Society, 1885. 72 p. **S 497**
The efforts of Hammond, a Cincinnati editor, in behalf of the freedom to criticize slavery and the slave trade.

"Smith, the Censor." *University Magazine and Free Review*, 5:337–51, 1 January 1896. **S 498**
Criticism of the censorship activities of Smith and Sons, one of the largest English circulating libraries that participated in the voluntary Victorian censorship of impure books.

"Smoking and News; Coverage of a Decade of Controversy." *Columbia Journalism Review*, 2(2):6–11, Summer 1963. **S 499**
"Has American journalism given a full, fair, and intelligent account of the complex debate over the effects of smoking on health?"

Snaith, Stanley. "Censorship." *Library Assistant*, 21:128–42, June 1928. **S 500**

Censorship can be approached from three standpoints: the believer, i.e. the man who demands protection for his daughters or his neighbor's daughters; the nonbeliever or atheist "who looks on censorship somewhat as a Chicago bar-tender looks upon prohibition"; and the agnostic or equivocater who sits on the fence. The evil of censorship is fourfold: it is an uncalled-for limitation of the field of the artist, it makes for pruriency in the reader, it sets up invidious class distinction, and it exalts into undue prominence the amatory material of books.

Snyder, Earl A. "Liability of Station Owners for Defamatory Statements Made by Political Candidates." *Virginia Law Review*, 39:303–17, April 1953. **S 501**
Notes on cases tried from 1927–52.

Snyder, Orville C. "Freedom of the Press—Personal Liberty or Property Liberty?" *Boston University Law Review*, 20:1–22, January 1940. **S 502**
The usual argument for freedom of the press "assumes that the liberty of an individual to have thoughts and to express them and the rights of an individual or corporate owners in his or its newspaper are one and the same thing. . . . All that is contended for [in this study] is that in deciding issues involving the business of publishing the news for profit, property rights only are being dealt with, and that, in determining the issues, confusing property rights and personal liberty, in laudatory acclaim of the latter, is not a satisfactory instrument of inquiry."

Snyder, William, *ed. Great Speeches by Great Lawyers; a Collection of Arguments and Speeches before Courts and Juries; by Eminent Lawyers; with Introductory Notes, Analyses, etc.* New York, Baker, Voorhis, 1881. 748 p. **S 503**
William Pinkney, law of constructive treason in the defense of John Hodges; Thomas Erskine, for the prosecution of Thomas Williams for publishing Paine's *Age of Reason;* James Mackintosh, in behalf of Jean Peltier, indicted for a libel against Napoleon Bonaparte.

Soames, Jane. *The English Press; Newspapers and News.* 2d ed. London, Drummond, 1938. 181 p. **S 504**
The author believes that the British press is in danger from increasing commercialization which lowers its standards and encourages uniformity. The French press represents more diversity in opinion, despite its frank subvention to special interests, and it offers better-informed foreign news.

Sobeloff, Simon E. "Free Press and Fair Trial." *Nieman Reports*, 10(1):3–5, January 1956. **S 505**
"The editor and the judge are set apart from other citizens only that they may act as guardians of other men's liberties."

Sobiloff, Stephen J. "The Jury and the Press." *Washburn Law Journal*, 2:142–57, Winter 1962. **S 506**
"The need has arisen as evidenced in these pages to gives the courts further control over the activities of the press. To deny the courts this weapon, is to make a mockery of justice and an empty ritual of the jury trial."

"Social Problems Books in the Small Library." *Wilson Bulletin*, 7:495–99, April 1933; 7:565–68, May 1933. **S 507**
"The librarian cannot hope to keep the facts of life from a sophisticated younger generation bred on the sensational cinema and the scandalous newspapers . . . The day is past when a book is considered bad because of the author's lack of reticence in the treatment of universal experiences and problems."

Society for the Suppression of Vice (London). *Reports*. London, The Society, 1803–85. Annual. **S 508**
During the reign of George IV and with his blessing a movement of evangelical revival developed to encourage piety and to suppress profaneness and immorality. A royal proclamation (1 June 1787) suggested the need "to suppress all loose and licentious prints, books, and publications, disbursing poison to the minds of the young and unwary; and to punish the publishers and vendors thereof." A Proclamation Society, under the leadership of William Wilberforce, took action, among other things, against the issuing of Sunday newspapers and financed the prosecution of Paine's *Age of Reason*. In 1802 there was established a Society for the Suppression of Vice and the Encouragement of Religion and Virtue throughout the United Kingdom, to consist of members of the Established Church. The Proclamation Society was subsequently merged with the Vice Society. The first annual report (1803) noted that the purpose of the Society was prevention rather than punishment, and a major activity was to check "the circulation of obscene books and prints, especially in seminaries of education, into which they have been most artfully introduced." The Earl of Dartmouth was president, Augustus Pitcher was secretary, and John Bowdler was a charter member. The work of the Society was well-received so long as it limited its activities to suppressing obscene works, but when it began a campaign against blasphemy in 1819, prosecuting Richard Carlile and his associates, it came in for severe public criticism. Between 1817 and 1825 the Society prosecuted 14 blasphemy cases as well as 20 obscenity cases. In 1857, after more than a half-century of activity, the Society reported 159 prosecutions, with convictions in all but 5 cases. The work of the Society was subsequently taken over by the National Vigilance Association for the Repression of Criminal Vice and Public Immorality (1885) and the Public Morality Council (1899). Other publications of the Society include: *Proposal for Establishing a Society for the Suppression of Vice* (1802); *Address to the Public from the Society* (1803); and *Second Address to the Public from the Society* (1803).

———. *Seventy-Sixth Annual Report for*

1879. (Abstract) London, The Society, 1879. 24p. **S 509**
The report complains of the difficulty in suppressing obscene literature, since its distribution is largely via the mails. Catalogues of such literature are often circulated in schools. "Your Committee do not pretend to arrogate to themselves the position of censors of the press; but they feel that literature and art have in all ages required strong moral supervision and restraint." Two societies have served this purpose in London: The Society for the Suppression of Vice suppresses bad literature; the Society for Promoting Useful Knowledge, established in 1830 but no longer existing in 1879, sought to offer good literature. The report lists titles of cheap periodicals suppressed (*Paul Pry, Polly Pree, Women of London*, etc.) and gives a statistical report of seizure since 1834 (380,569 prints, 63,487 books, etc.). The recent reduction in paper duty has served to encourage cheap pornography.

Socolow, Abraham. *The Law of Radio Broadcasting*. New York, Baker, Voorhis, 1939. 2 vols. **S 510**
A comprehensive study covering regulation of radio by federal and state laws and the operation of the FCC. Volume II includes chapters on privacy, defamation, copyright, and censorship.

Sokolsky, George. "Open Letter to the Post Office." *Saturday Review of Literature*, 38(17):9–10, 23 April 1955. **S 511**
Opposition to the Post Office policy of "increasing ignorance by refusing to permit Russian publications to pass through the mails." "I cannot know what I am talking about [in opposing communism], unless I have freedom to read what the other side publishes. . . . The best method is the American method, which is to use no means [in fighting communism] that violate the freedom and dignity of the individual American citizen."

"The Soldiers Vote Act and its Effect on the Distribution of Books." *Publishers' Weekly*, 145:2244–49, 17 June 1944. **S 512**
Concern by the Council on Books in Wartime, which issues book editions to the Armed Services, that its publishing program might be impaired as a result of the Act. Contains an analysis of the section of the Act pertaining to distribution of political propaganda, made by the Adjutant General's Office.

Solinger, David M. "Television and the Law." *Fortune*, 38:161–62, December 1948. **S 513**
Discusses the rights and obligations of the new television industry with respect to others—libel, defamation, and the right of privacy.

Some Account of a Very Seditious Book, Lately found upon Wimbledon Common,

by One of His Majesty's Secretaries of State, with a Commentary, By the Right Hon. Gentleman, and Notes By the Editor. London, J. Owen, 1794. 38p. **S 514**
An amusing satire on the government's attack on seditious literature, closing with this advertisement: "The Editor requests the favour of any Gentlemen who may be fortunate enough to find any Political Treatises in their hunting or shooting parties, and of any Traveller, who may meet with them upon any highway or common, to transmit them to him via Mr. Owen, for castration, translation, and publication."

"Some Legislative Aspects of the Birth-Control Problem." *Harvard Law Review*, 45:723–29, February 1932. **S 515**
A review of the varying and often contradictory policies of the 26 states that have statutes relating to birth control information and devices.

"Some Views on State Censorship of Literature." *South African Libraries*, 21:71–72, January 1954. **S 516**
Excerpts from commentaries on state censorship appearing in African, British, and American papers.

Somers, Gerald A. "The Librarian's Syndrome." *Library Journal*, 89:4672–74, 1 December 1964. **S 517**
Librarians ought to know more about themselves, their prejudices, motivations, weaknesses, as well as about their books, if they are to perform a sound job in book selection.

Somers, John. *The Security of Englishmen's Lives: or the Trust, Power, and Duty of Grand Juries of England Explained . . .* London, J. Almon, 1771. (First edition, 1681) **S 518**
Lord Somers' tract on the right of trial by jury was reprinted during a period when criminal libel charges were being filed against authors, publishers, and booksellers "without so much as suffering a Grand Jury to inquire whether the case be criminal or not."

Somerville, Don S. *A Study of Local Regulations and Group Actions in the Circulation of Newsstand Publications*. Urbana, Ill., University of Illinois, 1956. 246p. (Ph.D. dissertation, University microfilms, no. 18,199) **S 519**

"Something Burning." *Newsweek*, 41:23, 29 June 1953. **S 520**
Report of book burning by U.S. government officials in overseas information libraries, an outgrowth of the McCarthy attacks on communism.

Sommer, Frank H. "The Fading Bill of Rights." *New York University Law Quarterly Review*, 4:10–34, February 1927. **S 521**
State rather than federal legislation constitutes the major legal threat to freedom of speech and the press.

Sonderegger, Leo. "Right to Read." *Minnesota Libraries*, 17:205–7, September 1953. **S 522**

Sonntag, Nathaniel. "Canon 1399, Related Canons, and the College and University Library." In Catholic Library Association, *Proceedings, 1957*. Louisville, Ky., CLA, 1957, pp. 85–90. **S 523**

"Sound and Fury over Free Speech." *Literary Digest*, 123:3–4, 1 May 1937. **S 524**

"Liberty of expression in the United States won a needed victory a few days ago. Public outcry forced the Kansas State Board of Review to cancel an order eliminating a blast of Sen. Burton K. Wheeler of Montana against the Supreme Court plan from the current issue of 'The March of Time.'"

South Africa. Commission of Enquiry in Regard to Undesirable Publications. *Report*. Pretoria, South Africa, Govt. Printer, 1957. 285 p. **S 525**
Chapters 1 and 2 consider the nature of the problem; chapter 3 analyzes specific objectionable aspects in books, magazines, and newspapers; chapters 4 through 11 consider combating and regulating measures; chapter 12 through 22 discuss preventive measures including the responsibility of family, schools, universities, libraries, churches, the book trade, and the South African Institute for Literature.

———. Parliament. House of Assembly. Select Committee on the Newspaper Libel Bill. *Report . . . [with Special Report, Proceedings and Minutes of Evidence]*. Cape Town, South Africa, Cape Town Times, 1931. 10 p. (Published by order of the House of Assembly) **S 526**

"South African Censorship Bill." *Bookseller*, 2990:1582–83, 13 April 1963. **S 527**
Account of the passage of a bill setting up a Publications Control Board.

[South African Library Association]. "Report of the Commission on Undesir- able Publications; Memorandum Sent by the Council of the South African Library Association to the Hon. the Minister of the Interior." *South African Libraries*, 25:113–15, April 1958. **S 528**

Southern Baptist Convention. Christian Life Commission. *Speeches from Daily Conferences on the Traffic in Obscene Literature*. Glorieta Baptist Assembly [Nashville, Tenn.?]. 1957. 44 p. mimeo. **S 529**
The Assembly was held at Glorieta, New Mexico.

Southey, Robert. *A Letter to William Smith, Esq. M.P. from Robert Southey, Esq.* 3d ed. London, John Murray, 1817. 45 p. **S 530**

The poet laureate of England is aggrieved that his poem, *Wat Tyler*, written in his youth and published without his approval, has been brought up in Parliament to his discredit. The piece was mischievous, he said, and "written under the influence of opinions which I have long since outgrown, and repeatedly disclaimed." Both Richard Carlile and W. T. Sherwin published the poem and gave it wide circulation. Southey attempted to stop publication on the basis of his literary property rights. The court, however, ruled the work libelous and not subject to protection. *Wat Tyler* was critical of taxes, the church, the king, and the courts.

Southwell, Charles. "Plain Answer to the Query, ought there to Be a Law against Blasphemy?" Birmingham, Eng., J. Taylor, 1842. 23 p. **S 531**

———. *The Trial of Charles Southwell, (Editor of "The Oracle of Reason") for Blasphemy. Before Sir Charles Wetherall . . . January the 14th, 1842. Specially Reported by William Carpenter*. London, Hetherington, 1842. 104 p. **S 532**
In 1841 Southwell started publishing in Bristol, Eng., the *Oracle of Reason*, a journal of free thought with the avowed purpose of challenging existing legal and social restrictions on dissemination of atheist thought. The fourth number was critical of the Bible, which he derisively called the "Jew Book." Southwell was brought to trial for blasphemous libel, was convicted and sentenced to a year in prison. A committee, including such free press advocates as Hetherington and Holyoake, was formed to protest this "interference with speculative opinion." Holyoake took over as editor of *The Oracle* during Southwell's imprisonment, until he also was sent to jail.

Sowle, Claude R. "Press-Created Prejudice in Criminal Trials—A Mirage?" *Nieman Reports*, 18(3):16–17, September 1964. **S 533**
Pretrial prejudice is rarely a factor in a fair trial, unless the case is highly unusual or the persons involved enjoy a special status in the community.

Spangler, Raymond. "Open Court & Fair Press." *Nation*, 202:421–24, 11 April 1966. **S 534**

"Spanking the Movies." *Literary Digest*, 122(2):20–21, 11 July 1936. **S 535**
Reaction of the Legion of Decency and the Federal Council of Churches to the work of the Hays office. It has done some good but not enough.

Spargo, John. *Anthony Haswell, Printer-Patriot-Ballader; A biographical Study with a Selection of his Ballads and an Annotated Bibliographical List of His Imprints*. Rutland, Vt., Tuttle, 1925. 293 p. (Limited to 300 copies, signed by author) **S 536**
In 1800 Haswell, editor of the *Vermont Gazette* and popular ballader, was brought to trial under the Sedition Act for passages appearing in his paper. Judge Patterson practically demanded conviction in his charge to the jury. Haswell was found guilty and imprisoned for two months. He made the most of his confinement, issuing frequent letters from prison, which were widely used against the Federalists in the campaign of 1800. On his release from prison Haswell was received as a hero by his Bennington friends. He celebrated his martyrdom by composing a ballad entitled, A Review of Past Scenes.

[Sparke, Michael]. *Scintilla, or A Light Broken Into darke Warehouses. With Observations upon the Monopolists of Seaven severall Patents, and Two charters. Practiced and performed, By a Mistery of some Printers, Sleeping Stationers, and Combining Booksellers . . .* London, [Michael Sparke]. 1641. **S 537**
An attack by the Puritain publisher against the monopoly practices of the printing trade, particularly against Robert Barker, the king's printer, the principal Bible patentee who spared no efforts in fighting infringements of his monopoly. Sparke, the printer of Prynne's banned *Histrio-Mastix*, was involved in almost every case of "seditious" printing of his time. He was committed to prison at least 11 times for objectionable printing, yet continued to challenge the authority of both Church and Crown to control the press.

[———]. *A Second Beacon fired by Scintilla . . . Wherein is remembered the former Actings of the Papists in their secret Plots: And now discovering their wicked Designes to set up, advance, and cunningly to usher in Popery; By introducing Pictures to the Holy Bible: . . . Also Shewing and setting forth the Misery Of the whole Company of Station-*

ers . . . *in these sad times, when Blasphemy, Negromancy, Popery, and all Heresies be Printed and Publiquely Sold, in a most horrid manner without controll or Punishment.* London, [Sparke]. 1652. 11 p. **S 538**

Sparrow, John. "The Censor as Aedile." In his *Independent Essays.* London, Faber and Faber, 1963, pp. 193–209. **S 539**

An essay, based on a review of *Regina v. Penguin Books Ltd.,* the *Transcript of the Trial,* edited by C. H. Rolph, and *Censorship,* the 1961 Rede Lecture by Lord Radcliffe. Sparrow criticizes the trial of *Lady Chatterley's Lover* and the biased, though vivid, reporting of the trial by Mr. Rolph. If the book had been tried under common law on grounds of public mischief rather than under the Jenkins Act, the "sheer indecency of the book" would have been brought into focus. He agrees with Lord Radcliffe's broader perspective. Is not the real reason for prosecuting an indecent book, he asks, the fact that it is indecent, not that the public is being corrupted or depraved? Prosecutions for obscenity should not be used to protect public morals but should be considered in the same department of law that forbids "solicitation" and indecent exposure, or, to use Lord Radcliffe's expression, to adopt "the old aedile business of keeping the roads clean and the air sweet."

Sparrow-Simpson, W. J. "Roman *Index* of Prohibited Books." *Quarterly Review,* 247:1–15, July 1926. **S 540**

A general review of the Catholic *Index* with special reference to English authors and readers. "We English people, conscious of the reduction of authority among ourselves to a shadow and a name, may well look with wonder on an authority which excommunicates a man if he dares to read a book. . . . We may still have misgivings whether this imperious despotic rule is after all the better state."

Spaulding, William E. "Can Textbooks Be Subversive?" *Educational Record,* 34:297–304, October 1953. **S 541**

A textbook publisher explains the procedures that go into the making of textbooks and the adoption of textbooks by schools. He feels that we should give people an understanding of the procedures in order to refute the claim of subversiveness in textbooks, which he feels is most improbable under the present system of publishing.

Speight, Harold E. B. "The Case of John Peter Zenger, a Momentous Trial." *American German Review,* 2:11–12+, September 1935. **S 542**

A brief summary of the Zenger libel trial, New York, 1735.

Speirs, Charles H. *The Effects of Political Censorship in the United States on Public Libraries and Librarians from 1945 to 1955.* Cleveland, Western Reserve University,

1957. 55 p. (Unpublished Master's thesis) **S 543**

[Spence, Thomas]. *The Important Trial of Thomas Spence for a Political Pamphlet, Entitled "The Restorer of Society to Its Natural State," on May 27th 1801, at Westminster Hall before Lord Kenyon and a Special Jury . . .* London, Printed by A. Seale for T. Spence. 1803. 47 p. **S 544**

Spence was indicted in 1801 for writing and publishing a seditious libel concerning land ownership. Spence's proposal for the distribution of land to the parishes, Lord Kenyon ruled, was a threat to hereditary landlordship and Spence was given a year's imprisonment. He defended himself with great ability and published this account of the trial after his release.

[———]. *Trial of Thomas Spence in 1801, together with his Description of Spensonia, Constitution of Spensonia, End of Oppression. Recantation of the End of Oppression, Newcastle on Tyne Lecture Delivered in 1775, also a Brief Life of Spence and a Description of his Political Token Dies. By Arthur W. Waters. . . .* Leamington Spa, Eng., Privately printed at the Courier Press, 1917. 131 p. (Seventy-five copies of this book were printed and signed by Arthur W. Waters) **S 545**

Spence, who conducted a private school, was expelled from the Newcastle Philosophical Society in 1775 for delivering an offensive paper on the English landlord system. In 1792 he opened a bookstore in London and in the following year was arrested for selling Paine's *Rights of Man,* but was acquitted on a technicality. Between 1792 and 1795 he was arrested four times for publication and sale of objectionable works.

Spencer, Harry C. "The Christian and the Censorship of Television, Radio and Films." *Religion in Life,* 30:17–31, Winter 1960–61. **S 546**

The author is general secretary of the Television, Radio and Film Commission of the Methodist Church. Obscenity, he stated, is a terrible disease, but censorship is only treating the symptoms. The deeper evil lies in man's loneliness in a vast universe, in the long history of prudery and shocked modesty which the Church has had toward sex, and the unsatisfactory personal relations which result in persistent frustrations for vast numbers. It is the job of the Church to help people mature, to build integrity in relationships, and to enhance individual self-respect.

Spencer, Herbert. "The Rights of Free Speech and Publication." In his *Principles of Ethics.* New York, Appleton, 1893.

vol. 2, pp. 141–47. (First published in 1879) **S 547**

"So long as he does not suggest the commission of crimes, each citizen is free to say what he pleases about any or all of our institutions— even to the advocacy of a form of government utterly different from that which exists, or the condemnation of all governments."

Spender, John A. "Liberty of the Press." *Spectator,* 155:857–58, 22 November 1935. **S 548**

"The really important freedom is not that of dancing on the edge of Campbell's Act, but freedom to write fearlessly on matters of public importance, freedom, above all, to express unpopular opinions—opinions which the established authorities may think dangerous." A free and courageous press is needed to prevent conservatism from slipping into fascism, and radicalism into revolution. This entire issue of the *Spectator* is devoted to various aspects of freedom.

———. "On the Freedom of the Press." In his *Last Essays.* London, Cassell, 1944, pp. 7–9. **S 549**

A general statement on the importance of a free press in the life of the nation, from a broadcast talk, 25 March 1938.

———. "The Press in Wartime." In his *Last Essays.* London, Cassell, 1944, pp. 72–85. (Reprinted from the *Yorkshire Observer,* 22 September 1940) **S 550**

"We submit without demur to all discipline that is necessary in war for the safety of the public and the fighting forces. But we remain the eyes and ears of the Government, and we ask it to bear in mind that it would run the risk of becoming deaf and blind if it encroached unnecessarily on our activities."

Spingarn, Jerome H. "Huntington Cairns, Federal Censor." *American Mercury,* 68:683–91, June 1949. **S 551**

A description of the man who had served (at time of writing) for 15 years as advisor to the U.S. Customs in matters of censorship, under the authority of the Tariff Act.

———. *Radio Is Yours.* New York, Public Affairs Committee, 1946. 31 p. (Public Affairs Pamphlet no. 121) **S 552**

The public who ultimately pays the bill is entitled to a free and responsible radio. The pamphlet suggests ways in which the public can influence radio programs and policies, citing the Winston-Salem (N.C.) Community Radio Council as an example of listener participation.

Spingarn, Lawrence P. "Censorship by Sensation; the Case Against Publishers."

Trace, 35:1–6, January–February 1960.

S 553

The author, concerned with the decline of the American short story, claims publishers are guilty of censorship in their selection of material for publication. They "regard magazine stories as ephemera, and rather woo the public in terms of the novel, which they manipulate for greater profit toward Hollywood production."

Spitz, David. "Milton's Testament." *Antioch Review*, 13:290–302, September 1953. (Reprinted in Downs, *The First Freedom*, pp. 8–14)

S 554

A professor of political science discusses Milton's *Areopagitica*.

Sprading, Charles T. *Freedom and Its Fundamentals*. Los Angeles, Libertarian Publishing Co., 1923. 255 p.

S 555

A presentation based on the Law of Equal Freedom, as adopted by the Libertarian League. This embraces principles of freedom of thought, speech, press, assembly, education, science, literature, amusements, religion, and initiative. A chapter on freedom of the press consists of a series of epigrams followed by brief statements of eminent "libertarian thinkers": John Milton, John Locke, David Hume, Jeremy Bentham, Robert Hall, James Mill, John Stuart Mill, Herbert Spencer, and Thomas Cooper. The author's libertarian theories on freedom of the press are developed further in his book, *Real Freedom*, Los Angeles, 1954.

Sprague, Charles A. "Our Free Press. How Free?" *Nieman Reports*, 7(1):3–4, January 1953.

S 556

The editor of the *Oregon Statesman* and alternate delegate to the UN Assembly answers Soviet charges against the United States press, made before the UN Committee on Freedom of Information.

————. "UN Considers Freedom of Information." *U.S. State Department Bulletin*, 27:789–94, 17 November 1952.

S 557

The author describes the events that have taken place in recent years, following the Geneva Conference on Freedom of Information, as "among the most significant in the long history of man's struggle for free expression and of his efforts to safeguard the freedom already attained. But what has happened is quite different from what we hoped would happen."

Sprague, Homer B. "Societies for the Suppression of Vice." *Education*, 3:70–81, September 1882.

S 558

The first president of the New England Society for the Suppression of Vice defends the work of vice societies in general and Anthony Comstock in particular, in an impassioned, and melodramatic attack on obscenity. He charges the "dirt eaters" with "finding nutriment in *Leaves of Grass*, but not in fig leaves." Sprague, a classical scholar and principal of the Boston Girls' High and Normal School, had just taken part in the suppression of the Boston publication of Whitman's work.

Sprague, Stuart. "Freedom of the Air." *Air Law Review*, 8:30–45, January 1937. (Excerpted in Summers, *Radio Censorship*, pp. 121–23)

S 559

————. "More Freedom of the Air." *Air Law Review*, 11:17–28, January 1940. (Reprinted in New York University School of Law Pamphlets, series 1, no. 26)

S 560

The radio networks have imposed a rigid self-censorship because of state laws under which they may be sued for libel even where there is no negligence, such as when a speaker deviates from a script. The author recommends the rule of due care and liability through fault only. Five states have already, by court decision or legislation, adopted more moderate liability standards.

Spring, Samuel. "Invasion of Privacy and the Use of Photos in Books." *Publishers' Weekly*, 162:19–21, 5 July 1952.

S 561

————. *Risks & Rights in Publishing, Television, Radio, Motion Pictures, Advertising, and the Theater*. 2d ed., rev. New York, Norton, 1956. 365 p.

S 562

A comprehensive work on the legal aspects of privacy, slander, libel, copyright, and unfair competition, written for persons engaged in mass communications. Chapter 23 deals with obscenity and censorship, citing a number of significant court decisions.

Sproul, Robert G. "First Amendment; Allow New Freedom to Be Flanked." *Vital Speeches*, 10:89–90, 15 November 1943.

S 563

The president, University of California, speaks in behalf of the freedom of the American newspaper.

Spry, Graham. "Case for Nationalized Broadcasting." *Queens Quarterly*, 38:151–69, Winter 1931. (Reprinted in Buehler, *America vs. British System of Radio Control*, pp. 190–92)

S 564

"This paper is a statement of the case for the establishment of a Canadian Radio Broadcasting Company to own and operate all broadcasting stations, under a Royal Charter or an Act of Parliament."

[Squire, Francis]. *A Faithful Report of a Genuine Debate Concerning the Liberty of the Press, Addressed to a Candidate at the Ensuing Election, Wherein a Sure and Safe Method Is Proposed of Restraining the Abuse of That Liberty Without the Least Encroachment upon the Rights and Privileges of the Subject*. London, Printed for J. Roberts, 1740. 58 p. (Reprinted in 1764 by T. Becket and P. A. DeHondt)

S 565

The author believes in strict press control, fairly imposed. He would provide such safeguards as: (1) the right for a defendant to make public his defense, (2) the right to accuse, if the accuser can prove the charge, and (3) the right to public reporting of parliamentary proceedings, if accurate.

Squire, *Sir* John C. "On Destroying Books." In his *Life at the Mermaid*. London, Collins' Clear-Type Press, [1927], pp. 92–96.

S 566

A whimsical essay on the difficulty but necessity of destroying one's old books which may make fools of themselves for posterity. At midnight the author takes a sack of old books, slinks down to the Thames and drops them in. When he gets home he regrets his harsh deed but remarks that at least "I should not have sent you to the soldiers."

Squires, Grant. "Experiences of a War Censor." *Atlantic Monthly*, 83:425–32, March 1899.

S 567

Account of the 110-day military censorship exercised by the United States during the Spanish-American War through control of all telegraph and cable lines.

Srygley, Sara M. K. "Schools under Fire." *Library Journal*, 76:2049–50, 15 December 1951.

S 568

Suggestions to help school librarians combat censorship pressures and to encourage free access to controversial materials and their intelligent use by young people.

[Stable, *Sir* Wintringham N.]. *The Summing Up by Mr. Justice Stable. Regina v. Martin Secker & Warburg, Ltd., Frederic J. Warburg, The Camelot Press, Ltd. "The Philanderer" Case*. [New York], Printed by Clarke & Way for Blanche and Alfred Knopf, 1954. 16 p. (Edition limited to 600 copies)

S 569

The text of Justice Stable's decision in Central Criminal Court, London, in 1954, freeing the book, *The Philanderer*, of charges of obscene libel.

"Stage Censorship Is Certain Unless . . ." *Theatre Guild Magazine*, 8(5):11–17, February 1931. (Reprinted in *Journal of Social Hygiene*, March 1931)

S 570

"An inquiry among all shades of representative opinion concerning control of the stage to discover whether there is not some common ground on which all reasonable persons can unite." Includes opinions of Arthur Brisbane, H. L. Mencken, John S. Sumner, Heywood Broun, Amos Pinchot, Chief of Police Edward P. Mulrooney, Canon William S. Chase, John Dewey, Roger Baldwin, Norman Thomas, Rev. John Haynes Holmes, Elmer Davis, Herbert Bayard Swope, and others. Questions asked: Would voluntary stage censorship obviate licensing boards? If obscenity for profit were banned should the stage then be free to present serious plays? Is precensorship of manuscripts practicable in view of alterations made in rehearsals? Does a play jury system as advocated by Actors' Equity offer a reasonable guarantee against indecent exhibitions? A wide difference in opinion was reflected in the answers, and was summarized as follows: "The theatrical profession should and probably can exercise an effectual voluntary control to obviate obscenity on the stage. If the theatrical profession does not voluntarily take steps to this end, legal censorship of the New York stage is inevitable."

Stage the High Road to Hell: Being an Essay on the Pernicious Nature of Theatrical Entertainments; Shewing them to be at Once Inconsistent with Religion, and Subversive of Morality . . . London, Nicoll, [1767?]. 43 p.
S 571

Stallings, Laurence. "F.D.R.: Censor-in-Chief." *Esquire*, 35(3):35, 111–12, March 1951. **S 572**
Reminiscence of a 1934 preview of a film history of World War I by President Roosevelt, with the President's comments on the Chief Executive's powers as censor.

"The Stamped Press: The Mighty Organ of Good and Evil." *Tait's Edinburgh Magazine*, 2(n.s.):167–75, March 1835.
S 573

Standing, Paul. "Nipples on the Newsstand." *Canadian Forum*, 41:155–56, October 1961. **S 574**
Humorous commentary on the so-called "skin books," such as *Playboy, Swank, Gent, Rogue,* which the author considers an encouraging phenomenon. The publishers of the skin books "like the breasts, which it is their pleasure and pride to present, ought to be supported."

Stanley, Earl R. "Revocation, Renewal of License, and Fines and Forfeiture Cases before the Federal Communications Commission." *Journal of Broadcasting*, 3: 371–82, Fall 1964. **S 575**
A tabulation of radio and television stations, which in the past 4 years, were in jeopardy because of alleged violations of FCC rules or the Communications Act, shows that 26 stations had their licenses revoked or renewal denied.

Stansbury, Arthur J. *Report of the Trial of James H. Peck, Judge of the United States District Court for the District of Missouri, before the Senate of the United States, in an Impeachment Preferred by the House of Representatives against him for High Misdemeanors in Office.* Boston, Hilliard, Gray, 1833. 592 p. **S 576**
In 1831 impeachment proceedings were brought against Federal District Judge Peck who had suspended an attorney from practice and had him imprisoned for criticizing one of the judge's opinions. Judge Peck was acquitted, but James Buchanan, who had been prosecutor, introduced a bill in the House of Representatives to limit the power to punish contempts.

Stanton, Frank. "Free Press v. Fair Trial: The Broadcaster's View." *North Dakota Law Review*, 47:7–13, November 1964.
S 577
"Electronic communications, in this time of social unrest, offer the higher courts of the states and the nation an opportunity fully to bring the people, whom they serve and to whom they are ultimately answerable, within reach of their presence, their intellectual influence, and their moral force. To realize this opportunity is clearly in the intent of the court. It is overwhelmingly in the intent of the people." Television would not necessarily interfere with the orderly conduct of a trial, but would serve a useful educational purpose. This article is followed by the judge's point of view, presented by Bernard S. Meyer.

———. *Suspend 315.* New York, Columbia Broadcasting System, 1961. 7 p. **S 578**
The president of C.B.S., in an address before the Broadcast Advertising Club of Chicago, recommends suspension of the equal time rule for political candidates.

———. "Would Bricker Choke TV's Bloodstream?" *Broadcasting-Telecasting*, 50: 66–68, 21 May 1956. **S 579**
A condensation of the C.B.S. executive's talk before the American Marketing Association in Philadelphia. Stanton defends television and marketing and opposes Senator Bricker's proposal for government regulation of the networks as a public utility.

Stanton, Herbert E. "Prohibition Is Back—For Books" and "Censor's Choice: A Checklist of Banned Books." *Antiquarian Bookman*, 12:1487–91, 21 November 1953. (Reprinted from booklets published by the author) **S 580**
Includes an editorial on banned books decrying the plight of the bookseller who is the chief victim of the censorship system.

Stapleton, Larrick B. "Testimony Privilege of Journalist." *West Virginia Law Review*, 61:220–24, April 1959. **S 581**

Notes on the case, *Garland v. Torre,* 259 F. 2d 545.

Starck, Kenneth. "Trial by Jury; from 1735 . . . to 1966." *Grassroots Editor*, 7(2):5–7, April 1966. **S 582**
The trial of Eugene H. Wirges, editor of the Morrilton, Ark., *Democrat,* on charges of perjury growing out of a libel suit and involving Wirges' investigations of county government. The article compares Wirges' trial with that of John Peter Zenger. Zenger was found not guilty; Wirges was found guilty.

Stark, Alexander. "Newspapers and the Law of Libel." *Canadian Bar Review,* 24: 861–78, December 1946. **S 583**
A general review of the law of libel as applied to the press in England, the United States, and Canada. The paper, delivered to the Lawyers Club of Toronto, contains an amusing incident of an elderly Toronto lawyer who managed, by means of a clever poem, to get the Toronto *Daily Star* to acknowledge a libel.

Starkie, Thomas. *A Treatise on the Law of Slander, Libel, Scandalum Magnatum, and False Rumours; including Rules which Regulate Intellectual Communications, Affecting the Characters of Individuals and the Interests of the Public* . . . *1st American edition with notes and references to American and the late English cases. By Edward D. Ingraham.* New York, G. Lamson, 1826. 616 p. **S 584**
The first generally recognized treatise on English libel law, the basis for many subsequent works. First published in London by J. S. W. T. Clarke, 1812. Unlike Blackstone, Starkie believes that the absence of prior restraints does not constitute a free press. The "pains and penalties inflicted for that which has been published" may be "so unwarrantably severe" as to prevent future publication. "Something more than the mere absence of previous restraint is essential to the liberty of the press."

Starr, Isidore. "Recent Supreme Court Decisions: Censorship of Film." *Social Education,* 26:19–22, January 1962.
S 585
A review of the U.S. Supreme Court decision in the *Times Film Corp. v. the City of Chicago,* 365 U.S. 43 (1961) and an analysis of the majority and minority reports. The author concludes: "The movie censor has been given a lease on life by five of the justices."

"State Court Upholds Constitutionality of Refusal to License *Lady Chatterley's Lover* under Recently Amended Motion Picture Licensing Statute." *Columbia Law Review,* 59:337–51, February 1959.
S 586

The case of *Kingsley International Pictures Corp. v. Regents of the University of New York,* 1958.

State Law: Or, the Doctrine of Libels, Discussed and Examined. London, Printed by E. & R. Nutt and R. Gosling for T. Wotton and J. Shuckburgh, [1730?]. 136 p. **S 587**
Reports on a variety of libel cases: Henry Care, *Weekly Packet of Advice from Rome;* William Hurt, *Flying Post;* and Edmund Curll, *Ker of Kersland's Memoirs.* Includes opinions on seditious libel by Justices Hale, Holt, and Parker.

"State Sedition Laws: Their Scope and Misapplication." *Indiana Law Journal,* 31:270–85, Winter 1956 **S 588**

State Trials for High Treason, Embellished with Portraits . . . Reported by a Student in the Temple to which is prefixed Lord Chief Justice Eyre's Charge to the Grand Jury. London, B. Crosby, 1794. 3 pts. bound together, separately paged. **S 589**
Pt. 1, Trial of Thomas Hardy, 275 p. Pt. 2, Trial of John Horne Tooke, 152 p. Pt. 3, Trial of John Thelwall, 126 p.

"Statutory Prohibition of Group Defamation." *Columbia Law Review,* 47:595–613, May 1947. **S 590**

Staudacher, Lucas G. "Public's Right to Know is Denied at the Grass Roots, This Survey Shows." *Quill,* 44(10):9–14, October 1956. **S 591**
"A study of 409 Wisconsin newspapers, radio and television stations reveals that censorship exists for 24 media with some secrecy problems continuing over long periods."

Steadman, J. M., Jr. "Language Taboos of American College Students." *English Studies* (Amsterdam), 17:81–91, April 1935. **S 592**

———. "A Study of Verbal Taboos." *American Speech,* 10:93–103, April 1935. **S 593**

Steadwell, B. S. "J. Frank Chase." *Light,* 173:11, January–February 1927. **S 594**
An obituary of the long-time secretary of the New England Watch and Ward Society, by the editor of *The Light.*

Steamer, Robert J. "Freedom of Information: a Constitutional Right." *Nieman Reports,* 14(3):24–26, July 1960. **S 595**

Talk at the Southwestern Journalism Congress at Baton Rouge, 11 March 1960. "Establishing the theoretical constitutional right of the people to be informed means nothing unless that right can be vindicated, and the chief means of vindication is, of course, the press. . . . The people are no longer being informed; they are merely being told what some official thinks they ought to know. This is little better than the secret government of absolute monarchs, and tends to become dangerously like the press of the Soviet Union."

———. "Mr. Justice Jackson and the First Amendment." *University of Pittsburgh Law Review,* 15:193–221, Winter 1954. **S 596**
Opinions of Supreme Court Justice Robert H. Jackson.

———. *A Self-Evident Assumption.* Columbia, Mo., Freedom of Information Center, School of Journalism, University of Missouri, 1960. 3 p. (Publication no. 32) **S 597**
A government professor considers freedom of the press as "a self-evident assumption" for a democratic government.

Stearns, Charles. "Memoir of William Pynchon." *New England Historical and Genealogical Register,* 13:289–97, October 1959. **S 598**
Pynchon's book, *The Meritorious Price of Our Redemption,* was the first book banned in the American colonies, 1650–51. Portrait of Pynchon, opposite page 289. An account of the action against the book also appears in Samuel Eliot Morison's article on Pynchon in Proceedings of the Massachusetts Historical Society, February 1931. A photo-reproduction of one of the four extant copies of *The Meritorious Price* (in the Congregational Library, Boston) was produced by Harry A. Wright of Springfield, Mass., in 1931.

Stechhan, H. O. "Censoring Shakespeare." *Authors' League Bulletin,* 15(1):19, April 1927. **S 599**
The Merchant of Venice is no longer permitted to be taught in the Los Angeles high schools because of pressures brought by Jewish groups.

Steed, Henry W. *The Press.* London, William Clowes; Penguin Books, 1938. 250 p. **S 600**
A critical survey of the significance, influence, and workings of the British press. Mr. Steed does not believe that "commercial journalism" has provided the independence and freedom that is necessary for serving the British public. He lauds the B.B.C., which, unhampered by money-making, is doing a better job of public communication.

Steed, Wickham. "Watchdogs and Morals; an English View of Censorship." *Outlook,* 155:3–5, 7 May 1930. **S 601**

One way out of the censorship dilemma may "lie in the education of a healthy public taste by self-discipline on the part of the artists themselves."

Steele, Wilbur Daniel. "As to Censorship." *Authors' League Bulletin,* 15(1): 14–15, April 1927. **S 602**
A lampooning of all forms of prohibition, including censorship.

Steff, Alfred L., Jr. "Constitutional Law—Defamation." *University of Pittsburgh Law Review,* 25:752–55, June 1964. **S 603**
New York Times Co. v. Sullivan, 376 U.S. 254 (1964), in which the U.S. Supreme Court reverses the Alabama libel decision against the *New York Times.*

Steffens, Joseph L. *Suppression of Free Speech in New York and in New Jersey . . . together with the Full Text of the Suppressed Lecture by Emma Goldman and the Addresses by Leonard Abbott and Alden Freeman . . .* [East Orange, N.J., East Orange Record, 1909]. 28 p. **S 604**

Steffens, Lincoln. ["Free Speech v. Censorship"]. *Everybody's Magazine,* 25: 717–20, November 1911; 25:796–99, December 1911. **S 605**
In the October 1911 issue of *Everybody's Magazine,* the publisher, Erman J. Ridgway, had urged a ban on two current broadway plays and recommended censorship of plays and magazines injurious to the morals of youth. Steffens answers Ridgway in two letters endorsing complete freedom of speech and press. People cannot be made good by force of law; only self-censorship is effective. He cites the teachings of Jesus as argument against the use of force. In the January 1912 issue Hugh Black, professor of theology, Union Theological Seminary, agrees with Steffens' opposition to censorship, believing that criticism and the force of public opinion is more effective.

Steichen, Edward. ["Defense of *Evergreen Review* and Cadoo"]. *Evergreen Review,* 33:32, August–September 1964. **S 606**
The director-emeritus of photography at the Museum of Modern Art defends the portfolios of nudes by Emil J. Cadoo, appearing in the April-May issue of *Evergreen Review,* which had resulted in the seizure of 21,000 copies of that issue by a Nassau County vice squad.

Steigleman, Walter A. "Newspaper Confidence Laws—Their Extent and Provisions." *Journalism Quarterly,* 20:230–36, September 1943. **S 607**

————. *The Newspaperman and the Law.* Dubuque, Iowa, W. C. Brown, 1950. 427 p. **S 608**

Stein, Fritz. *The Censoring of Books in the United States.* Cleveland, Western Reserve University, 1955. 98 p. (Unpublished Master's thesis) **S 609**

Steinberg, Morton. "Only a Free Press Can Enable Democracy to Function." *Journalism Quarterly,* 23:11–19, March 1946. **S 610**

Steiner, Bernard C. "Andrew Hamilton and John Peter Zenger." *Pennsylvania Magazine,* 20:405–8, 1896. **S 611**
Newly uncovered biographical data on John Peter Zenger and his lawyer, Andrew Hamilton, in the famous New York libel trial.

Steiner, Franklin. "Exclusion of the *Truth Seeker.*" *Truth Seeker,* 45:634–35, 5 October 1918. **S 612**
Several issues of the *Truth Seeker* were excluded from the mails for criticising the YMCA on the grounds that this organization is part of the military establishment of the United States and to criticize it during wartime is an act of sedition.

————. "Genesis of Joseph." *Truth Seeker,* 44:695, 3 November 1917. **S 613**
Deals with the prosecution of the editor of the *Twin City Reporter,* Minneapolis, for publishing a "blasphemous" poem entitled "The Ballad of Joseph."

————. "Old Bailey Prisoners; an Account of Some Who Went There a Generation Ago as 'Blasphemers.'" *Truth Seeker,* 44:769–70, 8 December 1917. **S 614**
Deals mainly with the case of G. W. Foote and reproduces his portrait.

————. "Purity Law vs. Free Press." *Truth Seeker,* 43:150, 4 March 1916; 43:166, 11 March 1916; 43:182, 18 March 1916; 43:198, 25 March 1916; 43:214, 1 April 1916. **S 615**
The issue of 4 March deals with a general discussion of obscenity, "an undefined crime, but generally involving unorthodox opinion"; the 11 March issue discusses the work of Anthony Comstock, including the Bennett and Heywood cases; the issues for 18 and 25 March consider the censorship practices of the Catholic Church, including the attacks on J. J. Crowley and *The Menace;* the 1 April issue considers the Catholic boycott (pressure on advertisers) against Thomas E. Watson's *Jeffersonian* and *Watson's Jeffersonian Magazine.* The article about Watson was reprinted in *Watson's Jeffersonian Magazine,* July 1916.

Steiner, George. "Night Words." *Encounter,* 25:14–19, October 1965. **S 616**
The present danger to freedom of literature "is not censorship or verbal reticence. The danger lies in the facile contempt which the erotic novelist exhibits for his readers, for his personages, and for the language . . . It is not a new freedom that they bring, but a new servitude."

Stella, Stefanie R. *Subversive Literature and Unofficial Censorship: A Study of Organized Patriotic Groups' Tactics and Philosophy, 1960–62.* Chapel Hill, N.C., University of North Carolina, 1965. 67 p. (Unpublished Master's thesis) **S 617**

Stephen, *Sir* James F. "Blasphemy and Blasphemous Libel." *Fortnightly Review,* 35(n.s.):289–318, March 1884. **S 618**
Justice Stephen discusses the origin and interpretations of the present (1884) law of blasphemy and blasphemous libel and calls for its repeal.

————. *History of Criminal Law in England.* London, 1883. 3 vols **S 619**
Commentary on English criminal law by one of Britain's leading jurists. In chapters 24 and 25 (vol. 3) he summarizes the development of law on seditious libel and blasphemy. He cites noteworthy statutes and court decisions from the sixteenth century to date of publication. Included are brief comparisons of English libel law with French and German law.

————. *Liberty, Equality, Fraternity.* London, Smith, Elder, 1873. 350 p. **S 620**
In chapter 2 the author answers John Stuart Mill's *Essay on Liberty.* He declares that Mill is naïve to urge toleration of a variety of opinion and free discussion, for such toleration will give rise to fanatics who, when they get to power, will not tolerate the tolerant.

Stephen, *Sir* Leslie. "The Suppression of Poisonous Opinions." *Nineteenth Century,* 13:493–508, March 1883; 13:653–66, April 1883. **S 621**
It may be right, say some utilitarians, to suppress a poisonous opinion when the evil of opinion is measured by the corruption of a whole social order. Sir Leslie suggests that "criminal laws should not be brought into play to punish people for outrages upon good taste, but only for directly inciting to violence. The fact that an opinion is offensive to a majority is so far a reason for leaving it to public opinion, which in most cases is perfectly capable of taking care of itself; and we are certainly not impartial or really tolerant till we are equally anxious to punish one of the majority for insulting the minority."

Stephens, Alexander. *Memoirs of John*

Horne Tooke. London, J. Johnson, 1813. 2 vols. **S 622**
Biography of the English theologian, political agitator, and philologist. Tooke was involved in several incidents relating to freedom of the press, including the defense of John Wilkes and opposition to the stamp tax. In 1794 he was tried for treason for publishing tracts advocating parliamentary reform; he was acquitted with the forensic aid of Thomas Erskine.

Stephens, Harmon B. "The Relation of the Motion Picture to Changing Moral Standards." *Annals of the American Academy of Political and Social Science,* 128:151–57, November 1928. **S 623**
The recreation of the young can never be safely left to commercial exploitation. Regulation cannot be left to the industry for its self-cleansing has not been entirely effective.

Stephenson, William. *F.O.I. As People See It.* Columbia, Mo., Freedom of Information Center, School of Journalism, University of Missouri, 1965. 4 p. (Publication no. 144) **S 624**
A summary of the author's study of what the public thinks of press freedom, freedom of information, and the "people's right to know." The information was gathered by a combination of "free-talk" and questionnaire (Q-sort).

Stern, J. David. "The Free Press: An Obit." *Fact,* 1(3):53–59, May–June 1964. **S 625**
A publisher looks back at how newspaper monopolists—himself among them—turned the voice of the press into a chorus of castrati. "Whatever the causes, this change from a competitive to a monopoly press is unhealthy, sinister. It is making a travesty of our vaunted freedom of the press."

Stern, Philip V. "More on Censorities." *Saturday Review of Literature,* 27(31):13–14, 29 July 1944. **S 626**
The general manager of Editions for the Armed Services, Inc., charges that certain newspapers and magazines containing political material can be distributed to the troops while political material in book form is forbidden.

Stern, Robert H. *The Federal Communications Commission and Television: the Regulatory Process in an Environment of Rapid Technical Innovation.* Cambridge, Mass., Harvard University, 1951. 368 p. (Unpublished Ph.D. dissertation) **S 627**

Sterry, Ernest V. "Blasphemous Libel." *Canadian Bar Review,* 5:362–65, May 1927. **S 628**

Charge to the jury by Judge Coatsworth in the case of *King v. Ernest V. Sterry*, 1927. Sterry was convicted and given a prison sentence for publishing and distributing a paper libeling God and the Bible.

[Stevens, Abel.]. "The Devil in Literature." *National Magazine*, 2:124–28, 1853. **S 629**

The author is a Methodist clergyman.

[———]. "Licentiousness in the Fine Arts." *National Magazine*, 6:422–24, 1855. **S 630**

[———]. "Satanic Literature." *National Magazine*, 2:25–28, 1853. **S 631**

Stevens, Leonard A. "The Top-Secret Mania." *Nation*, 197:218–21, 12 October 1963. **S 632**

The misuse of Executive Order 10501 in the unnecessary restriction of scientific data and the cover-up of errors, waste, and inefficiency.

Stevenson, Adlai E. "Suppression of News." In his *New America*, edited by Seymour E. Harris, *et al.* New York, Harper, 1957, pp. 203–6. **S 633**

In a presidential campaign speech in Philadelphia, 18 April 1956, Stevenson spoke of the suppression of public information by the Eisenhower Administration. "I think it is pretty plain that there is today greater suppression of public information by the national government than there has ever been in the history of this country, except in time of war." He offers two solutions: more and better leg work by the working press instead of dependence upon government news handouts, and support of his candidacy for President.

———, and Barry Bingham. "Two Tributes to Elijah Lovejoy." *Quill*, 41(1): 10–11, 16, January 1953. (Reprinted in Stevenson, *What I Think*. New York, Harper, 1956, pp. 153–56) **S 634**

The governor of Illinois and the editor of the Louisville *Courier-Journal* spoke at Alton, Ill., at the dedication of a Sigma Delta Chi memorial tablet to the memory of the abolitionist editor.

[Stevenson, Duncan]. *Report of Trial of the Issues, in the Action of Damages for Libel in the Beacon, James Gibson of Ingliston, Esq. Clerk to the Signet-Pursuer against Duncan Stevenson, Printer in Edinburgh—Defender*. Edinburgh, Archibald Constable, 1822. 139 p. **S 635**

The proprietor of the *Beacon* was found guilty of publishing a libelous letter suggesting improprieties in handling of a forgery case.

Stevenson, E. R. "What Is Freedom of the Press?" *Special Libraries*, 32:205–8 July–August 1941. **S 636**

A newspaper editor discusses freedom in wartime. Freedom of the press belongs to the people as a basic right in a democracy. "Fight for it against the government if need be; fight for it against any newspaper, if need be."

Stewart, Alva W. "North Carolina's Gag Law." *Christian Century*, 81:1336–38, 28 October 1964. **S 637**

Stewart, George. "The Catholic Question in Canada. II. The *Index Expurgatorius* in Quebec." *Arena*, 17:747–51, April 1897. **S 638**

"The *Index* is a powerful weapon with which to scourge the recalcitrant." It is more frequently used and more potent in Quebec than in Europe. It may mean social and economic ruin to those who defy it.

Stewart, Gilbert W., Jr. "World Threat to A Free Press." *Quill*, 39(7):5–7, 20–21, July 1951. **S 639**

A discussion of the efforts within the United Nations for American standards of a free press and the rebuffs these efforts have met.

Stewart, Herbert L. "Freedom of Speech in Wartime." *Dalhousie Review*, 20:114–20, April 1940. **S 640**

A defense of wartime restrictions on freedom of speech and the press in Canada. While freedom of discussion is essential during an election, once a decision is reached democratically the course of truth is not served by unlimited debate.

Stewart, Irvin. "The Public Control of Radio." *Air Law Review*, 8:131–52, April 1937. **S 641**

Stewart, James. "Censorship in Canada." *Food for Thought*, 10:4–8, March 1950. **S 642**

Official censorship in Canada now operates in two well-defined fields. The first is the federal organization under the Department of National Revenue which censors publications entering Canada. The second is that exercised under the Criminal Code, which is administered by the Attorneys-General of the individual provinces.

Stewart, Kenneth. "Freedom to Read: Newspapers." *Survey Graphic*, 35:452–55, 513–14, December 1946. **S 643**

A newspaper editor warns that this is no time in world history to take freedom of the American press for granted. He considers that the threat to a free press is from monopoly of newspaper ownership, concentration in national and international news gathering,

and profit making. "If Americans want to speak to the rest of the world, we must make sure that our newswpapers—and the agencies which represent us to the world—speak for all of our *own* people."

Stewart, Lucy. "What Do the Censors Want?" *Adult*, 2:232–34, September 1898. **S 644**

Criticizes suppression of *The Adult*, a journal devoted to combating sex ignorance, while cheap and lascivious works are allowed to be freely distributed.

Stewart, Nathaniel. "Georgia Challenge." *Wilson Library Bulletin*, 16:166–67, October 1941. **S 645**

A letter protesting against the statement by Governor Talmadge of Georgia who had urged the burning of books dealing with the betterment of race relations.

Stewart, William. *John Lennox and the "Greenock Newsclout." A Fight against the Taxes on Knowledge*. Glasgow, James Maclehose, 1918. 44 p. **S 646**

"Against these taxes [on knowledge], John Lennox, first at Dumbarton and then at Greenock, for a period covering roughly a score of years, waged deliberate and uncompromising war. It was not only the Government that he had to convince of the vexatious character and anti-social effect of these taxes, but many even of the newspaper owners." Some of the proprietors actually drafted a memorial to Parliament opposing the remission of the tax as lowering the character of the press.

"Stifling War Correspondents." *Literary Digest*, 49:585–87, 589, 16 September 1914. **S 647**

Stigler, George J. "United States v. Lowe's Inc., A Note on Block-Booking." In *The Supreme Court Review*. Chicago, University of Chicago Press, 1963, pp. 152–57. **S 648**

The author examines the economic practices of block-booking of movies in light of the recent case, *United States v. Lowe's Inc.*, 371 U.S. 38, 52 (1962), in which the Court again struck down the practice as the compounding of a statutorily conferred monopoly.

"Still More Censorship—Case of H. L. Mencken." *Virginia Law Review*, 12:35–39, May 1926. **S 649**

A discussion of the "Hatrack" case involving censorship of Mencken's *American Mercury* in Boston.

Stillman, James W. *Rhode Island Justice*. Boston, The Author, 1912. 27 p. **S 650**

The article relates to the case of *Joseph C. Moore v. James W. Stillman*, asking for damages for an alleged libel published in the *Westerly Times*, 26 August 1905.

Stilwell, Clara, *pseud.* "America's School-book Scandal." *Christian Herald,* 73: 17–18+, September 1950. (Reprinted in Daniel, *Censorship of Books,* pp. 135–38) **S 651**

A textbook editor reveals the many pressures brought by interest groups on publishers to omit, include, or slant school textbooks, and the politics that sometimes enters into "state adoption."

Stockbridge, Frank P. "Censorship War Raging in Washington." *American Press,* 50(1):1, 40, October 1931. **S 652**

Newspaper correspondents are asking for investigation of charges that officials in Washington are trying to muzzle the press. The writer believes the conservative views of the Hoover administration and the liberal views of some of the young correspondents, both sides honest, have come into conflict. But from their clashes "is bound to come the truth of the matter as the truth eventually comes out."

[Stockdale, John]. *Four Letters on the Subject of Mr. Stockdale's Trial for a Supposed Libel on the House of Commons. By "A Briton."* London, 1790. 52 p. **S 653**

[———]. *Nightingale versus Stockdale. Report of the Trial in an Action for a Libel, Contained in a Review of the "Portraiture of Methodism:" Tried at Guildhall, before the Right Hon. Lord Ellenborough, and a Special Jury, Saturday, March 11, 1809 . . .* London, Johnson, 1809. 99 p. **S 654**

A review in the *Annual Register* for 1807 stated: "The Methodists may be fools but their present historian is obviously a knave." Mr. Stockdale, publisher of the *Annual Register,* was fined $200.

[———]. *Vindication of the Privilege of the People, Respect to the Constitutional Right of Free Discussion.* London, Stockdale, 1796. 80 p. **S 655**

———. *The Whole Proceedings on the Trial of an Information Exhibited Ex Officio, by the King's Attorney General, against John Stockdale; for a Libel on the House of Commons, Tried in the Court of King's-Bench, Westminster, on Wednesday, the Ninth of December, 1789, before the Right Hon. Lloyd Lord Kenyon, Chief Justice of England. Taken in Short-Hand by Joseph Gurney. To Which Is Subjoined, an Argument in Support of the Rights of Juries.* London, Printed for John Stockdale, 1790. 228 p. (Various editions of the trial were published in England and Ireland. The trial is also reported in Thomas Erskine, *Speeches,* vol. 2, pp. 205–88) **S 656**

Stockdale, a London bookseller, was brought to trial on the complaint of Mr. Fox for publishing the Rev. Mr. Logan's pamphlet, *A Review of the Principal Charges against Warren Hastings, Esquire, Late Governor General of Bengal.* The pamphlet was in defense of Mr. Hastings and implied criticism of Parliament in handling the impeachment. Thomas Erskine's plea for the defense embodied many of the liberal principles of free speech and rights of juries in libel trials, for which he became famous. His ideas on the latter were embodied in the Fox Libel Act, passed two years later. Judge Kenyon instructed the jury to "look at the whole book" in passing judgment. Stockdale was acquitted. Attached to this edition is Erskine's argument, in the trial of the Dean of St. Asaph, regarding libels.

Stockdale, Percival. *A Letter to a Gentleman of the Philanthropick Society; on the Liberty of the Press.* London, Jordan, 1794. 28 p. **S 657**

The letter from this English author and poet was occasioned by refusal of the Society to publish his work containing sentiments "obnoxious to an English printing-office." The work, a satire on the Bishop of Durham, exposed spiritual wickedness in high places. Stockdale attacks the existing censorship as an offense against the "indisputable liberties of Englishmen." It is not clear whether the Society was actually a threat to the freedom of the press or merely exercised its prerogative of rejecting an unsuitable manuscript.

Stocker, Bram. "Censorship of Fiction." *Nineteenth Century,* 64:479–87, September 1908. **S 658**

The author of *Dracula,* while deploring censorship, believes that the lack of restraint in modern fiction may require it. If no other method can be found to eradicate the "plague-spot" in fiction, even police censorship, as obnoxious as it is, may be inevitable.

———. "Censorship of Stage Plays." *Nineteenth Century,* 66:974–89, December 1909. **S 659**

Stocker, Joseph. "Freedom's Frightened People." *Library Journal,* 81:318–25, 1 February 1956. **S 660**

Freedom's frightened people are those who look with suspicion at everything that is evidence of the human intellect. The writer comments on the Bartlesville, Okla., Public Library censorship case (his home town) and reviews the ground lost in the battle for free expression. Librarians must stand fast against censorship, loyalty oaths, and other encroachments on freedom.

Stockton, Adrian. "Books That Shocked—21: *The Black Book.*" *Books and Bookmen,* 6(9):23–24, June 1961. **S 661**

Account of attacks on Lawrence Durrell's *The Black Book.* (Earlier articles in the series were written by Desmond Elliott and Godfrey Harrison.)

Stokes, Anson P. *Church and State in the United States . . . Introduction by Ralph Henry Gabriel.* New York, Harper, 1950. 3 vols. rev. ed. by Stokes and Leo Pfeffer. New York, Harper, 1964. 3 vols. in one (660 p.) **S 662**

In this comprehensive and critical study of religious freedom, the author makes frequent reference to freedom of religious expression in the press, beginning with the foundation laid by John Milton and the Levellers in Cromwellian England. The author refers to the Lovejoy martyrdom, the work of the Federal Council of Churches, the censorship position of the Catholic Church, the action of vice societies, and the case of Jehovah's Witnesses. There are also references to blasphemy cases (including the Kneeland trial), and suppression of birth control information.

Stone, Abraham, and Harriet F. Pilpel. "Social and Legal Status of Contraception." *North Carolina Law Review,* 22: 212–25, April 1944. **S 663**

In the second part of the article Mrs. Pilpel reviews the prohibitions against information on birth control, from the Comstock laws of the 1870's to the present, with special attention to the restrictive laws of Connecticut and Massachusetts.

Stone, Donald L. "Press and Mail Censorship in Wartime." *Editor and Publisher,* 59:5–6+, 14 August 1926; 59:7–8, 21 August 1926. **S 664**

Description of American censorship in World War I, with explanation of the rules that governed the press. A firsthand account by the chief American press censor in Paris.

Stone, E. T. "Is a Free Press Out of Date?" *Bulletin,* American Society of Newspaper Editors, 413:1, 8, October 1958. **S 665**

A Seattle editor points out that the battle for freedom of the press is not for the rights of the press but the rights of the people.

Stone, Eugenia. *Free Men Shall Stand.* New York, Nelson, 1944. 264 p. **S 666**

Fictionized biography of John Peter Zenger.

Stone, Judy. "The Legion of Decency: What's Nude?" *Ramparts,* 4:43–55, September 1965. **S 667**

A detailed and candid report on the history and operation of the Legion of Decency, film censorship agency of the Catholic Church.

The author is drama critic of the *San Francisco Chronicle*.

Stone, Leo. "On the Principal Obscene Word of the English Language (An Inquiry, with Hypothesis, Regarding Its Origin and Persistence)." *International Journal of Psycho-Analysis*, 35:30–56, 1954.
S 668

Stone, Thomas T. *The Martyr of Freedom. A Discourse Delivered at East Machias, November 30, and at Machias, December 7, 1837. . . .* Boston, I. Knapp, 1838. 31 p.
S 669
A eulogy on Elijah P. Lovejoy, delivered the year following his murder in Alton, Ill., in defense of his printing press.

Stone, Wilbur M. "Emasculated Juveniles." *American Book Collector*, 5:77–80, March 1934.
S 670
Examples of nineteenth-century guardians of children's reading such as Maria and Richard Lovell Edgeworth's *Practical Education*, and Sarah Trimmer's magazine, *The Guardian of Education*, that, through their critical reviews, held a tight rein on the moral tone of children's literature.

Stone, William T. *Atomic Information.* Washington, D.C., Editorial Research Reports, 1953. (*Editorial Research Reports*, 2[15]:709–25, 1953)
S 671
Discusses the rising pressure against the wall of secrecy surrounding atomic data, military secrecy v. public understanding, the secrecy provisions of the Atomic Energy Act and the publicity limitations of the 1951 amendment, control of technical information, and international exchange of atomic information.

——. *Secrecy in Government.* Washington, D.C., Editorial Research Reports, 1955. (*Editorial Research Reports*, 2:895–912, 1955)
S 672
Discusses complaints and investigations on suppression of news by executive agencies, information practices of federal agencies, proposals to counteract secrecy trend (i.e. press conferences and revisions of laws on access to news).

Stopes, Marie C. *A Banned Play and a Preface on the Censorship.* London, John Bale, 1926. 144 p.
S 673
Relates to the banning of Mrs. Stopes's play, *Vectia*, in England by the Lord Chamberlain. The play deals with an undersexed male, a theme which, according to the author offended the male censor. Mrs. Stopes discusses British stage censorship in general and proposes that censorship could be made more effective against pornography and at the same time protect the serious writer if "a married woman of the world" were added to the official advisors to the Lord Chamberlain.

——. *Contraception (Birth Control) Its Theory, History and Practice; a Manual for the Medical and Legal Professions. . . .* London, J. Bale & Danielsson, 1923. 418 p.
S 674
Includes an account of the trial of Charles Bradlaugh and Annie Besant, together with earlier and later birth control propaganda and its reception.

——. *The Evidence of Dr. Marie C. Stopes to the Royal Commission on the Press.* London, The Author, 1953. 33 p. **S 675**
In her testimony before the Commission, not published in the official report, Dr. Stopes, the author of *Married Love* and a leader in the birth control movement, accuses the *Times* and a number of other British papers of refusal to accept advertisements of her books on sex education. She proposes an act of Parliament to make consistent refusal of a legitimate advertisement of any reputable individual, society, company, or cause, as an act of libel. The report includes documents relating to the refusal to accept advertising.

Storey, Moorfield. *Libel Suits of Frank P. Bennett vs. John Donohoe and Hastings & Sons Publishing Co.; Closing Argument.* [Boston, 1902?]. 37 p.
S 676

Story, Joseph. *Commentaries on the Constitution of the United States.* 5th ed. Edited by Melville M. Bigelow. Boston, Little, Brown, 1905. 2 vols.
S 677
Paragraphs 1880–91 (vol. 2) deal with liberty of the press. Judge Story criticizes the loose thinking about freedom of the press "as if its inviolability were constitutionally such, that, like the King of England, it could do no wrong and was free from every inquiry and afforded a perfect sanctuary for every abuse; that, in short, it implied a despotic sovereignty to do every sort of wrong, without the slightest accountability to private or public justice." He asks whether liberty of the press is so much more valuable than other rights of society that public safety and the very existence of government should yield to it?

The Story That Couldn't Be Printed. 10 min., b/w movie. New York, Teaching Film Custodians. (Passing Parade Series)
S 678
The story of the trial of John Peter Zenger. Recommended for junior high school age level; restricted to classroom use.

Stowell, Ellery C. "Courtesy to our Neighbors vs. Freedom of the Press." *American Journal of International Law*, 36:99–103, January 1942.
S 679
Discussion of President Franklin D. Roosevelt's denunciation of *Time* for its criticism of the Chilean president, and the implications for freedom of the press.

[Strachey, John St. Loe]. "Mr. Strachey's Speech on Demoralizing Literature." *Spectator*, 108:147–48, 27 January 1912.
S 680
John St. Loe Strachey, editor of *Spectator*, introduced a deputation on decency in literature to the Home Secretary, which is printed here along with an introduction. In the introduction Strachey notes that he does not personally take so extreme a view as the deputation, but agrees on the need to do something to stop the flood of obscene books. The deputation asks that books that are rightfully obscene be suppressed by police action; books that are demoralizing but not legally obscene be left to public action, including boycott. Newspapers, not covered by the deputation, should be warned that they will be treated as a public nuisance if they offend the public standard of decency. The publisher and author as well as the less culpable distributor should be indicted for obscenity violations. The deputation calls for the creation of a Joint Select Committee of the Parliament to study obscenity and for legislation to require the Home Office and the police to be more vigilant.

Straham, J. Andrew. "Is the Press Free?" *Law Magazine and Review*, 23(4th ser.): 83–92, February 1898. **S 681**
English law does not afford the same freedom of discussion of private affairs as it does of public affairs. The vagueness, rather than the severity of the law, leaves the way open to considerable damage and annoyance by frivolous actions.

Straus, Ralph. *The Unspeakable Curll, Being Some Account of Edmund Curll, Bookseller; to Which Is Added a Full List of His Books.* London, Chapman and Hall, 1927. 322 p. (Edition limited to 535 copies)
S 682
Edmund Curll (1675–1747) was a London bookseller who published, in addition to many works of literary importance, a number of obscene items. In 1727 he was convicted and condemned to the pillory for publishing a pornographic work, *Venus in the Cloister or the Nun in her Smock*. Twenty years earlier in the Read case (1708) the judge had ruled obscenity to be a matter for the ecclesiastical courts and not subject to civil law. The conviction of Curll established the misdemeanor of "obscene libel" as an offense at common law. Curll also incurred the displeasure of the Parliament when he published works involving its members.

Strauss, Leo. "Prosecution and the Art of Writing." In Chapter 2 of his book by the same title. Glencoe, Ill., Free Press, 1952, pp. 22–37. **S 683**

The author's thesis is that the threat of persecution of the writer has resulted historically in "a peculiar technique of writing, and therewith to a peculiar type of literature, in which the truth about all crucial things is presented exclusively between the lines. That literature is addressed, not to all readers, but to trustworthy and intelligent readers only."

Strauss, Walter A. "Sense and Nonsense in Censorship." *Emory University Quarterly*, 20:183–86, Fall 1964.   **S 684**
Law and literature speak a different language in considering obscenity. Law wants a quantitative yardstick; literature wants qualitative evaluation. Law is by nature protective and conservative; the arts are aggressive and rebellious. The author defines "obscene" as being that which goes counter to accepted standards of propriety at a given time and place; an erotic work is one which gives serious consideration to physical love; a pornographic work is the degradation and distortion of the erotic. In a healthy society, obscenity should be met with laughter, pornography with a yawn.

Street, A. L. H. "Right to Regulate Objectionable Performances in Theaters." *American City*, 30:677, 679, June 1924.
S 685
Brief review of pertinent laws and court decisions.

Street, G. S. "The Censorship of Plays." *Fortnightly Review*, 124:348–57, September 1925.   **S 686**
The British "reader of plays" since 1914 writes an inside account of his experience as censor. "The right course for censorship is to hold a really enlightened balance, extending freedom where, to the best of its intelligence, it judges freedom to be right, but guarding this freedom, by its own careful discrimination, from being drowned in a deluge of protest. My ideal of its function is to extend freedom, up to the limit where protest would be reasonable, to all genuinely artistic or even didactic efforts, and to curb sharply the efforts to attract by pruriency or mere salacity or intolerable vulgarity."

Stringer, William H. "Censorship Censured: News Blackouts Cast Shadow on West." *Christian Science Monitor*, 40:9, 26 August 1948. (Reprinted in Summers, *Federal Information Controls in Peacetime*, pp. 167–70)   **S 687**
"There is genuine danger today that the world's international sparring match is leading to increased censorship, less news, and more blocking of the usual avenues of journalistic information along the western diplomatic front . . . It can perilously restrict a nation's knowledge of what its own diplomats are up to."

Stritch, Samuel, *Cardinal*. "Freedom of Speech, Censorship and the Responsibility of a Free Press." *Books on Trial*, 12:323–24, 358–60, June 1954.   **S 688**
Freedom of the press carries the obligation to "keep within the limitations which the moral law imposes on its freedom." The Cardinal discusses the "imperatives" of a Catholic press, consistent with "right freedom." He approves of the holy crusade of the Catholic press against obscene books and films.

Stroud, George M. *Sketch of the Laws Relating to Slavery in the Several States of the United States of America*. Philadelphia, Kimber & Sharpless, 1827. 180p.   **S 689**
The final chapter deals with the encroachments of slavery on freedom of speech and press.

Strout, Donald E. "Are Librarians Censors?" *Nation*, 189:379–81, 21 November 1959.   **S 690**

———. "Censorship." In the *American Library and Book Trade Annual, 1960*. New York, Bowker, 1959, pp. 129–32.   **S 691**
A summary of the year's events involving libraries and the work of the American Library Association's Committee on Intellectual Freedom.

———. "Intellectual Freedom Landmarks: 1955–60." *Library Journal*, 86:2035–42, 1 June 1961; 86:2575–79, August 1961.   **S 692**
Summary of major court decisions, incidents, and policy statements pertaining to intellectual freedom as related to libraries during the five-year period, 1955–60. Part 1 deals with Causes for Comfort; part 2 with Causes for Concern.

Stryker, Lloyd P. *For the Defense: Thomas Erskine, the Most Enlightened Liberal of His Times, 1750–1823*. Garden City, N.Y., Doubleday, 1947. 624p.   **S 693**
A biography of the British jurist and champion of freedom of the press. Erskine defended Thomas Paine, John Stockdale, Thomas Hardy, John Horne Tooke and others on charges of sedition or criminal libel. His courageous and eloquent defense of the Dean of St. Asaph before a hostile judge not only convinced a jury but led in 1792 to the liberalization of the British law of libel. Includes full accounts of many of the censorship trials.

Stuart, *Sir* Campbell. *Secrets of Crewe House, the Story of a Famous Campaign*. London, Hadder & Stoughton, 1920. 240p.   **S 694**
References to British censorship and propaganda efforts in World War I.

Stuart, Lyle. "Crab Grass of Book Censorship Grows in Many Places." *Independent*, 122:3, May 1962.   **S 695**

A review of widespread censorship by pressure groups in the United States, particularly in the area of obscenity. Criticism of the lack of effort by the publishing industry to fight censorship.

"Student Freedom: Censorship of Articles in *Scholastic*." *Commonweal*, 78:269–70, 31 May 1963. (Reply by O. P. Kretzman, 78:379, 28 June 1963)   **S 696**
An editorial criticizing the suppression of a student magazine at Notre Dame. University administrators must realize that "one of the penalties for having good students and exposing them to a good education is that they are going to be critical of their elders." In reply, the Lutheran president of Valparaiso University defends the university administrators. "Here is the outcropping on a Catholic campus of the heresy of freedom without responsibility."

Sturgion, John. *A Plea for Tolleration Of Opinions and Perswasions In Matters of Religion, Differing from the Church of England . . . Shewing the unreasonablenesse of Prescribing to other mens Faith, and the evil of persecuting differing Opinions. . . .* London, Printed by S. Dover for Francis Smith, 1661. 20p. (Reprinted in Edward B. Underhill, *Tracts of Liberty of Conscience and Persecution*, pp. 311–41)   **S 697**

Styles, John. *An Essay on the Characters and Influence of the Stage*. 3d ed. London, R. Williams, 1815. 234p.   **S 698**
An attack on the immorality of the stage and its dangerous tendencies.

"Subversive Literature." *New Zealand Libraries*, 4:1, August 1940.   **S 699**
The Customs Department in New Zealand has asked librarians to restrict books and periodicals that might be of a subversive character.

[Sullivan, Alexander M., and Richard Pigott]. *Report of the Trials of Alexander M. Sullivan and Richard Pigott, for Seditious Libels on the Government, at the County of Dublin Commission . . . Edited by T. Pakenham Law*. Dublin, Printed by Alexander Thom, 1868. 286p.   **S 700**
Sullivan, the publisher of the *Weekly News* was brought to trial in 1868 for seditious libel contained in pictures and articles criticizing the administration of justice in a murder trial. He was convicted and sentenced to six months in prison. The case against Richard Pigott followed immediately. Pigott, publisher of the *Irishman*, was brought to trial for reporting in some detail the activities of the Fenian Conspiracy for an independent

Ireland. He was convicted and given a year's sentence.

Sullivan, Harold W. *Contempt by Publication: The Law of Trial by Newspaper.* 3d ed. New Haven, Conn., Privately printed, 1941. 230 p.   **S 701**
Cases in the United States and Great Britain in which editors, publishers, and writers have been cited for contempt by publishing. The author holds that "trial by newspaper is a shabby form of jury tampering" and that the United States courts should follow the British rule in citing newspapers for contempt. He denies that such action would be an infringement on the freedom of the press.

————. *Trial by Newspaper.* Hyannis, Mass., Patriot Press, 1961. 250 p.   **S 702**
"There is scarcely one inmate of our fifty state penitentiaries who has had a fair and impartial trial, doubly guaranteed by our federal and state constitutions, and this because of Trial by Newspaper." The author cites such notable examples as the Morro Castle case, the Hopson case, the Lindbergh kidnapping case, the Mooney case, and the Manton case. He believes the courts should use the contempt power against the press and against police, district attorneys, and anyone who furnishes information to the press that results in trial by newspapers.

[Sullivan, James]. *A Dissertation upon the Constitutional Freedom of the Press in the United States of America. By an Impartial Citizen . . .* Boston, Printed by David Carlisle for Joseph Nancrede, 1801. 54 p.   **S 703**
Sullivan was a leader of the Democratic-Republican party in Massachusetts, serving as attorney general and later as governor. In 1791 he conducted the first prosecution for criminal libel under the new state constitution. His ideas on seditious libel, expressed in this pamphlet, are more akin to those of the Federalists than such Jeffersonian writers as George Hay and Tunis Wortman. He defends the constitutionality of the Sedition Act insofar as it is applied to malicious libel of the government, but not against the officer of the government. The latter, he believes, is a private matter. His pamphlet is a legalistic attempt to achieve a balance between the traditional Blackstonian views and those of the Jeffersonian libertarians. "A reasonable, constitutional restraint, judiciously exercised, is the only way in which the freedom of the press can be preserved, as an invaluable privilege to the nation."

Sullivan, John J. "Obscenity: Police Enforcement Problems." *Catholic Lawyer,* 10:301–8, Autumn 1964.   **S 704**
A New York City police officer discusses problems that law officials face in attempting to enforce state laws relating to obscene literature. Police find themselves, on the one hand, accused of being censors; on the other hand, of being lax in suppressing harmful material. Police action alone is insufficient to stem the flow of salacious literature; the entire community must accept responsibility.

Sullivan, John P. "Editorials and Controversy: The Broadcaster's Dilemma." *George Washington Law Review,* 32:719–68, April 1964.   **S 705**
The author believes the FCC's fairness doctrine is unconstitutional and "neither ensures fairness nor respects the freedom necessary for a democratic society."

Sullivan, Kay. "Cincinnati vs. Pornography." *Catholic Digest,* 23(8):12–19, June 1959.   **S 706**
Story of the operation of the Citizens for Decent Literature in Cincinnati, under the leadership of Charles H. Keating, Jr.

Sullivan, Mark. "Creel-Censor." *Collier's,* 60:13+, 10 November 1917.   **S 707**
"Creel ought never to have taken the (World War I) censorship job. And before that President Wilson ought to have known better than to have appointed him." Article showing how unsuited Creel was to the job because of his violent personality and his inability to see other than plain black or plain white.

Sullivan, Sheila. "The Anti-Secrecy Law in Wisconsin." *Nieman Reports,* 17?(1): 25–28, March 1963.   **S 708**
The Wisconsin law (1959) guarantees open public meetings and unopposed admittance of newsmen except in certain cases specifically excepted in the law.

Sullivan, Walter. "U.S. Purges Libraries It Runs in Germany." *Nieman Reports,* 7(3):34, July 1953. (Reprinted from *New York Times,* 11 June 1953)   **S 709**
Censorship of U.S. information libraries overseas.

Sulloway, Alvah W. *Birth Control and Catholic Doctrine. Preface by Aldous Huxley.* Boston, Beacon, 1959. 257 p.   **S 710**
Legislation against birth control, according to the author, grew out of a Victorian preoccupation with obscenity; it was later supported by the Catholic Church. There are frequent references to efforts at suppression of birth control information in England and America and a section on the legal aspects.

Sulzberger, Arthur H. *Man's Right to Knowledge and the Free Use Thereof.* [Honolulu], University of Hawaii, 1954. 11 p. (University of Hawaii Occasional Paper 61)   **S 711**
Charter Day address by the publisher of the *New York Times* at the University of Hawaii, 16 February 1954, as part of Columbia University Bicentennial celebration.

————. "Newspaper—Its Making and Meaning." *Vital Speeches,* 11:539–43, 15 June 1945.   **S 712**
The editor of the *New York Times,* in an address to New York teachers, denies charges that the American press is dominated by economic pressure groups. He appeals to his audience to teach that a free press is the right of the people and not the publishers.

————. "Where We Stand on Freedom." *Nieman Reports,* 7(2):3–6, April 1953.   **S 713**
"Discussion is being restricted. . . . A smoke screen of intimidation dims essential thought. . . . It isn't the super-zealots who bother me so much as the lack of plain old-fashioned guts in those who capitulate to them." From a talk upon receiving the Columbia College award for distinguished service in 1952.

Summerfield, Arthur C. *The Great Menace to America's Children: What You Can Do About It.* Washington, D.C., U.S. Post Office Department, 1959. 10 p. (Mimeographed release no. 114)   **S 714**
An address by the Postmaster General before a conference of women leaders of civic, educational, parent, and religious organizations, and women members of the Congress and government agencies. He calls for parents to report any pornography received by their children to local postmasters for action.

————. *Mail-Order Obscenity vs. Decency, Our Responsibility to Our Children. Address by Postmaster General Arthur E. Summerfield, before Detroit Federation of Womens' Clubs, . . . Jan. 14, 1960.* Washington, D.C., Govt. Print. Off., 1960. 15 p.   **S 715**

————. *Our Challenge, Decency and Dignity for Our Children. Address by . . . Postmaster General . . . 2d National Conference, Citizens for Decent Literature, Cincinnati, Ohio, Feb. 27, 1960.* Washington, D.C., Govt. Print. Off., 1960. 21 p.   **S 716**

Summers, Harrison B., comp. *Radio Censorship.* New York, Wilson, 1939. 297 p. (Reference Shelf, vol. 12, no. 10)   **S 717**
A compilation of articles and extracts, pro and con, dealing with the proposed amendments to the Communications Act of 1934, prepared as a guide for debaters. Includes extracts from newspaper editorials, not readily available elsewhere. Bibliography, pp. 285–97.

Summers, Joseph P. "Freedom of the Press—Court Orders Forbidding Photography, Television, and Radio Facilities on Streets and Sidewalks Surrounding Courthouse Is Constitutional." *Notre Dame Lawyer*, 36:78–81, December 1960. **S718**

Comments on the Georgia case, *Atlanta Newspapers, Inc. v. Grimes*, 114 S.E. 2d 421 (1960).

Summers, Robert C. "Constitutional Protection of Obscene Material against Censorship as Correlated with Copyright Protection of Obscene Material against Infringement." *Southern California Law Review*, 31:301–12, April 1958. **S719**

Summers, Robert E., *comp. Federal Information Controls in Peacetime.* New York, Wilson, 1949. 301 p. (Reference Shelf, vol. 20, no. 6) **S720**

A collection of articles and official documents relating to government control of information in the interest of national security—the military force, atomic energy, and the federal loyalty investigations—and the implication of such restrictions to freedom of the press.

———. *Wartime Censorship of Press and Radio.* New York, Wilson, 1942. 297 p. (Reference Shelf, vol. 15, no. 8) **S721**

A collection of articles and extracts relating to the development of censorship in World War II. Limited to news control as it affects radio and the press. Most of the material is taken from the trade journals of the news industry: *Variety* and *Broadcasting* for radio; *Editor & Publisher* for the press. Articles are presented under such headings as: history of censorship, development of controls, censorship in operation, self-censorship, censorship controversies, problems of censorship, editorial comment, and philosophy of censorship. The appendix includes text of executive orders and wartime codes of radio broadcasting.

Sumner, John S. "Activities against Obscene Literature." *Light*, 189:10–13, July–August 1929. **S722**

The secretary of the New York Society for the Suppression of Vice discusses recent censorship cases including that of Mrs. Mary Ware Dennett.

———. "Are American Morals Disintegrating?" *Current Opinion*, 70:608–12, May 1921. **S723**

An appraisal of sexual immorality in America and the efforts of the New York vice society to suppress immoral literature.

———. "The Clean Books League: Mr. Justice Ford and Obscene Literature." *Light*, 152:21–24, May–June 1923. **S724**

Justice Ford introduced a "clean books" bill in the New York legislature. Sumner's picture appears on the front cover of this issue.

———. "Comstock and Sumner." *Journal of Education* (Boston), 82:458–59, 11 November 1915. (Reprinted from the Philadelphia *Public Ledger*) **S725**

Written on the death of Comstock, by his successor. "I shall go after the sellers and distributors of indecent pictures and cards and 'literature' just as fiercely as he ever did." Since the trade in pornography has been forced underground, greater secrecy is now required to ferret out the offenders.

———. "Criticising the Critic." *Bookman*, 53:385–88, July 1921. **S726**

The secretary of the New York vice society defends the society against its critics, principally Heywood Broun (*Bookman*, May 1921). "The Society is an agency to enforce the law where it is violated—not a censor."

———. "The Decency Crisis; a Summing Up." *Good Housekeeping*, 107:26–27, 140–42, August 1938. **S727**

"I see the need of protection for the young from the temptations of pandering enterprises which assault their eyes and ears." Sumner calls for the public to take action against the spread of filthy literature.

———. "Effective action against Salacious Plays and Magazines." *American City*, 33:553–55, November 1925. **S728**

The author calls for an end to the delays of legal action against offending literature. The judiciary should be "aroused to the fact that the safeguarding of public morals is much more important than upholding alleged 'freedom of expression' or 'freedom of the press.'"

———. "The New York Society for the Suppression of Vice." *Publishers' Weekly*, 117:2516–18, 17 May 1930. **S729**

The secretary of the Society describes its work. Photograph of the author on page 2517.

———. "Obscene Literature—Its Suppression." *Case and Comment*, 23:16–19, June 1916. (Reprinted in *Publishers' Weekly*, 8 July 1916) **S730**

"The suppression of obscene literature and pictures is an ever present necessity." Sumner defends a rigid enforcement of present laws on obscene literature.

———. "The Suppression of Vice." *Fra*, 17:198–99, September 1916. **S731**

In defense of the law prohibiting circulation of birth control propaganda.

———. "The Truth about 'Literary Lynching.'" *Dial*, 71:63–68, July 1921. **S732**

In answer to an article by Ernest Boyd (April 1921) Secretary Sumner defends the activities of the New York vice society in its

attack on obscene works of literature and art. References to the suppression of the *Little Review*.

The Suppressed Book about Slavery! Prepared for Publication in 1857,—Never Published Until the Present Time. New York, Carleton, 1864. 432 p. **S733**

The reason for including this title, an exposé and denunciation of slavery, is that the work was suppressed, according to a statement on p. 6. The book was written in 1857, sterotype plates made, but for seven years it "slumbered, unknown, unnoticed, and undisturbed, beneath the surface of the earth." We no longer have to fear the slave power, the editor proclaims. "We can print, publish, read, speak, and listen to exactly what we please."

"Suppression." *Nation*, 68:388–89, 25 May 1899. **S734**

An editorial criticizing the McKinley Administration for attempting to suppress publication of letters from soldiers in the Philippines, which are critical of the United States government.

"Suppression of Malicious, Scandalous, and Defamatory Newspapers and Periodicals by Injunction or Suit of the State Held to Violate the Constitutional Guarantee of Freedom of the Press." *Law and Labor*, 13:153–58, July 1931. **S735**

"Supreme Court Decision Limits Censorship." *Publishers' Weekly*, 186:48–49, 6 July 1964. **S736**

The decision of the U.S. Supreme Court in the Jacobellis case, which declared the movie, *The Lovers*, not obscene, limits movie censorship.

"Supreme Court Upholds Estes Appeal; Photo Ban Qualified." *FOI Digest*, 7(2): 4-page supplement, July–August 1965. **S737**

A report and analysis of the decision of the U.S. Supreme Court in June 1965 that Billie Sol Estes, in a Texas trial for theft and embezzlement in September 1962, had been deprived of his right to due process by the telecasting of the trial. Includes press commentary on the decision.

"Supreme Court Upholds Validity of Municipal Ordinance Requiring Submission of All Motion Pictures for Censorship Prior to Exhibition." *Columbia Law Review*, 61:921–26, May 1961. **S738**

The case of *Times Film Corp. v. City of Chicago*, 365 U.S. 43 (1961).

Suren, Victor T. "Obscene Literature:

a Theological Opinion." *Guild of Catholic Psychiatrists Bulletin*, 8:73–77, April 1961.

S 739

Obscene literature makes a frontal attack on the protective virtues of modesty and shame. "It tends inevitably to progressively disarm the unsuspecting and curious adolescent until it leaves him the unguarded victim of his lower passions." Dissemination of obscene literature can be curtailed only by concerted effort of the Church, parents, schools, the courts, and the legislature.

Sutherland, James. *Defoe*. Philadelphia, Lippincott, 1938. 300 p.   **S 740**

Daniel Defoe's lifetime efforts at political satire and his frequent indiscretions in print brought him often into conflict with the authorities, both Tories and Whigs. For his *The Shortest Way with Dissenters* (1703), a pamphlet favoring the Protestant succession, Defoe served a term in prison and was pilloried. For many years he was engaged in a feud with Ridpath, the editor of the Whig *Flying Post*, who tried repeatedly to "queer" Defoe with the authorities. As secret agent of the Whigs, Defoe served on the Tory paper, *Mist's Journal*, in an attempt to tone down its anti-Whig sentiments.

Sutton, Horace. "The Art of Censorship." *Saturday Review of Literature*, 38(11):24, 12 March 1955.   **S 741**

While current literature enjoys relative freedom from censorship there are hidden censors, ghost writers, editors, and a "censorship of silence" in government affairs that is extremely dangerous.

Svirsky, Leon, *ed. Your Newspaper: Blueprint for a Better Press; by Nine Nieman Fellows, 1945–1946*. New York, Macmillan, 1947. 202 p.   **S 742**

The nine Fellows reach the conclusion that the press must assume responsibility for public service or face government control; that it is the readers, in the final analysis, who must decide what kind of press the nation is to have.

Swacara, Frank. "Fundamentalism and the Law." *United States Law Review*, 65: 592–604, November 1931.   **S 743**

Archaic blasphemy laws are used to suppress radical literature that may only incidentally refer to atheism.

————. *Obstruction of Justice by Religion; a Treatise on Religious Barbarities of the Common Law, and a Review of Judicial Oppressions of the Non-Religious in the United States*. Denver, W. H. Courtright, 1936. 298 p.   **S 744**

Chapter 17, Blasphemy Laws in the United States; Chapter 18, Some Alleged "Reasons" for Blasphemy Laws; Chapter 19, Some Victims of the Religious Gag Laws (the cases of Daniel Isaac Eaton, Thomas Tunbridge, Mary Ann Carlile, Thomas Williams, George Holyoake in England, and Abner Kneeland and Anthony Bimba in the United States).

Sweeney, John. *At Scotland Yard. Experience during Twenty-seven Year's Service*. London, Grand Richards, 1904. 368 p. Edited by Francis Richards.   **S 745**

Includes the detective's account of the prosecution of Havelock Ellis' *Studies in the Psychology of Sex*.

Sweet, Justin. "The Right of Privacy." *Wisconsin Law Review*, 1952:507–20, May 1952.   **S 746**

Sweet and Maxwell, Ltd., London. *Complete Law Book Catalogue*. London, Sweet & Maxwell, 1925–49. 7 vols.   **S 747**

Vol. 1, A Bibliography of English Law to 1651; vol. 2, A Bibliography of English Law, 1651 to 1800; vol. 3, A Bibliography of English Law, 1801 to 1932. Sections in each deal with freedom of the press and the law of libel.

————. *Legal Bibliography of the British Commonwealth of Nations*. 2d ed. London, Sweet & Maxwell, 1955. 7 vols.   **S 748**

Vol. 1, English Law to 1800; vol. 2, English law from 1801–1954; vol. 3, Canadian and British-American colonial law from earliest times to 1956; vol. 4, Irish law to 1956; vol. 5, Scottish law to 1956; vol. 6, Australia, New Zealand to 1958; vol. 7, Law of the colonies, protectorates, and mandated territories to 1958. References throughout to works dealing with freedom of the press and the law of libel.

Swezey, Robert D. "Give the Television Code a Chance." *Quarterly of Film, Radio and Television*, 7:13–24, Fall 1952.   **S 749**

Written from the point of view of the Television Board of the National Association of Radio and Television Broadcasters.

————. *The Sight and Sound of Justice*. Washington, D.C., National Association of Broadcasters, 1958. 12 p.   **S 750**

The chairman of the Association's Freedom of Information Committee appeals to the House of Delegates of the American Bar Association to grant the broadcasting industry equal access to coverage of court trials.

————. *Television Broadcasting in the Public's Interest; the Role of Self-Regulation*. Washington, D.C., National Association of Broadcasters, 1962. 12 p. mimeo.   **S 751**

Remarks by the director of code authority, National Association of Broadcasters, at the Television Conference on Broadcasting in the Public's Interest, Illinois Commission on Children.

[Swift, Jonathan]. *The Importance of the Guardian Considered, in a Second Letter to the Bailiff of Stockbridge. By a Friend of Mr. St——le*. London, Printed for John Morphew, 1713. 25 p.   **S 752**

In a mild and sometimes amusing attack on his "brother-scribbler," Richard Steele, Swift lists the various devices authors use to avoid incurring charges for libel, such as the use of the dash for part of a man's name, the use of cases and insinuations, the use of nicknames, and "celebrating the Actions of others, who acted directly contrary to the Persons we would reflect on."

Swift, Lucius B. *How We Got Our Liberties*. Indianapolis, Bobbs-Merrill, 1928. 304 p.

S 753

A popular presentation of the foundations of political and religious liberty, including a section on freedom of speech and press.

Swindler, William F. "The AP Anti-Trust Case in Historical Perspective." *Journalism Quarterly*, 23:40–57, March 1946.   **S 754**

"Almost a century of communications law, literally and figuratively, was rounded out in June 1945, with the Supreme Court's historic opinion in the Federal government's anti-trust suit against the Associated Press." The author gives background information and analysis of the decision which brought to an end the long debate on exclusive membership in newsgathering associations.

————. *A Bibliography of Law on Journalism*. New York, Columbia University Press, 1947. 191 p.   **S 755**

An annotated bibliography, with a bibliographic essay tracing the development of published works on the law of the press. Of special interest are the sections on freedom of the press and radio, censorship and control of speech and press, access to public records, libel, and privacy—all relating to the United States—and the section on press freedom and press control dealing with other countries. Includes both books and periodical literature.

————. "Commentary on Press Photographers and the Courtroom." *Nebraska Law Review*, 35:13–16, November 1955.

S 756

The author suggests modification of Canon 35 of the American Bar Association "to permit non-flash camera coverage under certain well-defined conditions and within definite physical limits inside the courtroom."

————. "Newspaper Libel in Canada—a Note in Comparative Press Law." *Journalism Quarterly*, 21:25–36, March 1944.

S 757

Compares Canadian libel laws with those of

England and the United States, noting modifications from those of the mother country.

————. *Phases of International Law Affecting the Flow of International Communications.* Columbia, Mo., University of Missouri, 1942. 223 p. (Ph. D. dissertation, University Microfilms, no. 435) **S 758**
Includes the right to gather and transmit international news, protection of news as property, and laws relating to censorship and propaganda.

————. *Problems of Law in Journalism.* New York, Macmillian, 1955. 551 p. **S 759**
A casebook for use of journalism students. Each section gives a background note, principles involved, and a selected list of readings in addition to the text of appropriate cases. Includes such topics as: press freedom, freedom to gather news, libel, law of privacy, law of contempt, and law relating to radio. The introduction discusses the basic nature of newspaper law and the concept of press freedom.

————. "Wartime News Control in Canada." *Public Opinion Quarterly*, 6: 244–49, Fall 1942. **S 760**
"In three years of war Canada has maintained an ever-tightening surveillance over the freedom of its minority press and over civil liberties generally."

Swing, Raymond G. "Birth Control and Obscenity." *Nation*, 140:621–22, 29 May 1935. **S 761**
The author objects to a proposed modification of the Comstock law of 1873 to permit the Post Office authorities to prosecute at destination of mail as well as place of mailing. This would prevent the spread of scientific birth control knowledge from a city where it was considered legal to a city where it was considered obscene.

————. "Only One Truth." *Vital Speeches*, 4:78–80, 15 November 1937. (Also in Lew R. Sarett and W. T. Foster, comps., *Modern Speeches on Basic Issues*, Boston, Houghton Mifflin, 1939, pp. 34–36) **S 762**
A discussion of the controlled press of Europe in contrast to that of democratic nations. The title is based on the comment of a young Communist who remarked that it was strange that in old Russia there were thousands of newspapers and periodicals expressing many different points of view when there was really "only one truth." If this were true, Swing comments, a controlled press in which falsehood was suppressed would be the logical answer. "The democracies live by the theory that there is no one truth, that truth is something that comes out of experience, and that since experience is often painful, the individuals that make up the nation must have a voice in choosing the experience."

Swisher, Carl B. "Civil Liberties in Wartime." *Political Science Quarterly*, 55: 321–47, September 1940. **S 763**
Action in the United States against newspapers and pamphlets under the Espionage Act during World War I.

Swope, E. B. "Censorship in the Prison Library." American Prison Association, *Proceedings of the Annual Congress*, 1940, pp. 457–61. **S 764**

While it is necessary to exclude from prison libraries works that are likely to encourage antisocial attitudes and behavior and upset the mental health of the prisoners, we ought not go beyond this by excluding works of religion, politics, and social problems merely because they are controversial. Careful positive selection of useful books and individual guidance in their use is the sensible approach.

Sylvester, Arthur. "Public Information and National Security: A Government View." *Yale Political*, 3(1):18, 33–35, Autumn 1963. **S 765**
The assistant secretary for defense presents the twofold purpose of the Defense Department in this matter: to insure national security and to provide public information. A journalist's point of view is presented in an accompanying article by Arthur Krock.

Symon, J. D. *The Press and Its Story. An Account of the Birth and Development of Journalism up to the Present Day, with the History of all the Leading Newspapers . . .* London, Seeley Service, 1914. 327 p. **S 766**
Chapter 20, in this general history of the British press, deals with freedom of the press.

Symonds, R. V. *The Rise of English Journalism.* Exeter, A. Wheaton, 1952. 191 p. **S 767**
A history of the British press through Daniel Defoe. Includes references to licensing and the work of press censor, Roger L'Estrange.

T

T., J. H., Jr. "Postal Power and Its Limitation on Freedom of the Press." *Virginia Law Review*, 28:634–48, March 1942. **T1**
A review of the history of postal powers, particularly in time of crisis. While the Supreme Court generally is moving toward greater freedom of expression, there is no single unifying decision in the matter of encroachment of postal power on freedom of the press. The author hopes that the Supreme Court in 1942 will take a more tolerant view than in 1919.

"Tact, Taste, and Libel." *Outlook*, 103:245–46, 1 February 1913. **T2**
Comments on the *New York Evening Post*'s defense of a man convicted of slander against the King of England. The *Post* "does not regard as morally reprehensible slanderous attacks upon those with whom it politically disagrees."

Taft, Henry W. "Freedom of Speech and the Espionage Act." *American Law Review*, 55:695–721, September–October 1921. **T3**
"Now that the war is over . . . and such propaganda cannot weaken our military resources, I believe that Communism can best be fought by argument, and not by repression." Address before the New Jersey State Bar Association.

———. "Press and the Courts." *American Law Review*, 58:595–617, July–August 1924. **T4**
Criticism of newspaper coverage of the courts and a recommendation for the establishment of standards of professional ethics rather than the use of contempt to enforce fair treatment.

"Taft and Army Disagree over Books in Soldiers' Vote Act." *Publishers' Weekly*, 146:177–78, 15 July 1944. **T5**
Senator Taft objects to the Army's exclusion of books from overseas libraries, as a misinterpretation of the legislative intent in the Soldiers' Vote Act.

"Taft-Hartley and Press Freedom." *Nieman Reports*, 1(4):27–28, October 1947. **T6**
Relates to the restriction of communications activities of labor unions under the Taft-Hartley labor act.

"Take the Shackles Off Television News." *Broadcasting*, 67(24):54–55, 14 December 1964. **T7**
Robert W. Sarnoff, board chairman of N.B.C., and Frank Stanton, C.B.S. president, call for the revision of Section 315 of the Communications Act to eliminate the equal time rule in broadcasting. Stanton calls for an end to discrimination against television in the coverage of public proceedings.

Talbert, Samuel S. "A Basic Threat to Freedom." *Quill*, 51(8):14–15, August 1963. **T8**
"Apathy, timidity, fear, and a desire for popularity on the part of the individual citizen are probably greater threats to freedom of expression than orders and policies issued by bureau officials."

Talbot, Francis. "More on Smut." *America*, 48:500–501, 25 February 1933; "More Smut," *America*, 48:460–61, 11 February 1933. **T9**
A priest appeals to Catholics to take action against the sale of immoral literature.

Talfourd, *Sir* Thomas N. *Laws against Blasphemy; Speech for the Defendant, in the Prosecution of the Queen v. Moxon for the Publication of Shelley's Works.* . . . London, Edward Moxon, 1841. 58 p. (Also published with an introduction by Telfourd in *Roberts' Semi-Monthly Magazine*, 1 January 1842) **T10**
The offending work was Shelley's first poem, *Queen Mab*. The prosecution, according to Talfourd in an introduction to the publication, was prompted by Henry Hetherington, who had himself been sentenced to four months in prison for the publication of *Queen Mab* and wanted the law to apply equally to the aristocratic bookseller, Edward Moxon. Despite the eloquent plea of Sir Thomas ("I commend into your hand the cause of the defendant, the cause of Genius, the cause of Learning, the cause of History, the cause of Thought"), Moxon was convicted and fined.

Tallmer, Jerry. "The Silent Treatment." *Nation*, 169:59–60, 16 July 1949. **T11**
An account of the "silent treatment" given to Paul Blanshard's *American Freedom and Catholic Power* by many book reviewers.

Tamblyn, Eldon W. "They Play It Safe: A Report of a Survey on Book Selection and Censorship in North Carolina Public Libraries." *Library Journal*, 90:2495–98, 1 June 1965. **T12**
"Is there censorship in North Carolina public libraries? How do they handle controversial books? And how do their book selection practices compare with those of California public libraries as indicated in the Fisk study? A 1963 questionnaire to selected libraries was designed to supply answers to these questions." This article is a summary of a Master's thesis in library science at the University of North Carolina.

Tanenhaus, Joseph. "Group Libel." *Cornell Law Quarterly*, 35:261–302, Winter, 1950. **T13**
Commentary on laws pertaining to group defamation, 1815–1949.

[Tanner, Henry]. *The Martyrdom of Lovejoy. An Account of the Life, Trials and Perils of Rev. Elijah P. Lovejoy. Who Was Killed by a Pro-Slavery Mob, at Alton, Ill., on the Night of November 7, 1837. By an Eye-Witness* . . . Chicago, Fergus Printing Co., 1881. 233 p. **T14**
Cited by Gill in *Tide Without Turning*, as one of the five major sources of material on Elijah Lovejoy. In addition to contemporary newspaper accounts and discussions in Congress, Tanner's book includes notes by Dr. Samuel Willard, who had been witness to the events of 1837.

Tanner, Sheldon C. "Developments in Newspaper Libel Laws." *Journalism Quarterly*, 12:245–54, September 1935. **T15**

The article discusses three contemporary milestones in freedom of the press: the libel suit against the *Chicago Tribune*, the Minnesota "gag" law, and the Florida court decision on libelous stories received from a news agency.

Tanselle, G. Thomas. "The Thomas Seltzer Imprint." *Papers of the Bibliographical Society of America*, 58:380–416, Fourth Quarter 1964. **T16**
A large portion of the article deals with censorship cases in which Seltzer was involved. In the summer of 1922 John S. Sumner of the New York vice society seized 772 copies of 3 books from Seltzer's offices in New York. They were Arthur Schnitzler's *Casanova's Homecoming*, D. H. Lawrence's *Women in Love*, and an anonymous work, *A Young Girl's Diary*. A New York municipal judge subsequently dismissed the obscenity charge against Seltzer after hearing testimony from such critics as Carl Van Doren and Gilbert Seldes. Two years later Seltzer was again indicted for sale of Schnitzler's book and *A Young Girl's Diary* and charges were dropped only when the publisher agreed to withdraw the books from sale and destroy the plates. The article also deals with the formation by George Creel, World War I censor, of an anticensorship organization known as the Joint Committee for the Protection of Art and Literature, and with Justice John Ford's efforts in behalf of censorship in the formation of the Clean Books League and sponsorship of the Clean Books Bill in the New York legislature.

Tapper, Colin. "Freedom and Privilege." *Modern Law Review*, 26:571–74, September 1963. **T17**
Relates to the case of the three British journalists, who were sentenced to prison for refusal to disclose the source of information relating to the William Vassall trial.

Tarkington, Booth. "When Is It Dirt?" *Collier's*, 79:8–9+, 14 May 1927. **T18**
Based on two plays he has seen, Tarkington considers what is art and what is dirt and where the two meet. His conclusion: "I perceived that a thing is not art if a pinch of dirt is deliberately added to it to make it sell."

Tarr, H. A. "Builders of American Democracy: John Peter Zenger and Freedom of the Press." *Scholastic*, 37:15–16, 30 September 1940. **T19**

Tauber, Maurice F. *A Study of Motion Picture Censorship in Pennsylvania*. Philadelphia, Temple University, 1939. 151 p. (Unpublished Master's thesis) **T20**

Tavel, Emilie. *Fair Trial and Free Press*. Columbia, Mo., Freedom of Information Center, School of Journalism, University of Missouri, 1962. 4 p. (Publication no. 71) **T21**

Reprint of three articles appearing in the *Christian Science Monitor* on the eve of the lurid murder trial of Willem Van Rie in Boston. The *Monitor* and Miss Tavel each received a Gavel Award from the American Bar Association for making an "outstanding contribution to public understanding of the American legal and judicial systems."

Tawse, George. "James Watson—the Edinburgh Printer." *Bibliographer*, 2:124–30, October 1882. **T22**
The story of the Edinburgh newspaper and book printer (James Watson, the younger) who led a somewhat precarious life under threats of civil suits and royal displeasure. He served a short jail sentence in 1700 for publication of his book, *Scotland's Grievance Respecting Darien*.

The Tax upon Paper: The Case Stated for Its Immediate Repeal. Published under the direction of the Committee of the Newspaper and Periodical Press Association for Obtaining the Repeal of the Paper Duty. London, The Committee, 1858. **T23**

"Taxes on Knowledge and the Newspaper Press." *Tait's Edinburgh Magazine*, 15:351–56, June 1848; 15:499–503, August 1848. **T24**
"We have no censors for the press, except those astute gentlemen, the commissioners of stamps and taxes. Our fetters are made of copper, with silver chains." The press is the only educational institution in Britain that is taxed. "Tax on knowledge is treasonable to good government. The penny stamp is seditious, and the eighteen penny duty is a misdemeanor against the best interest of the State. That red penny stamp on the corners of the newspaper is a badge of slavery, a barricade of knowledge as the window-tax is a barricade to health and light—and the country cannot be free where both exist."

Taylor, Charles E. "The New Standard of Obscenity: *Roth v. United States*, 354 U.S. 476 (1957)." *Ohio State Law Journal*, 19:137–42, Winter 1958. **T25**

Taylor, Charles H., and Eliot Lord. "Libel and Signed Articles." *Writer* (Boston), 1:177–89, December 1887. **T26**
In an address at the Boston Press Club dinner, Taylor, the managing editor of the *Boston Globe*, urges that newspaper articles be signed as a means of assessing both credit and blame. Greater personal responsibility, accuracy, and fewer libel suits would be the result. Eliot Lord, managing editor of the Boston *Evening Record*, defends anonymity. The writer can feel freer to be frank. Furthermore, because of editing and cutting, and the composite story, a writer would not care to sign his name to the finished product. In any event, the paper should stand behind its writers.

Taylor, E. G. "Intellectual Liberty and the Blasphemy Laws." *Westminster Review*, 143:117–39, February 1895. **T27**
In an age and nation that boasts of its freedom, there is an exception to the rule of toleration. Freethinkers and secularists are still victims of oppression. The author reviews the laws and court decisions that have deprived this class of their civil and political rights, including freedom to speak and publish. References are made to such leading blasphemy cases as Foote, Ramsey, and Besant and Bradlaugh.

Taylor, Frank L. "Broadcasting in the Courtroom." *West Virginia Law Review*, 60:312–19, April 1958. **T28**
Discussion of Canon 35 of the Canons of Judicial Ethics of the American Bar Association.

Taylor, G. Rattray. *Sex in History*. rev. ed. London, Thames and Hudson, 1959. 338 p. **T29**
A history of changes in attitudes toward sex, which includes numerous references to heresy, obscene libel, and pornography.

Taylor, Glen E. "Obscenity not Entitled to Constitutional Protection as Free Speech under First or Fourteenth Amendment." *Texas Law Review*, 36:226–29, December 1957. **T30**
Notes on the U.S. Supreme Court decision in *Roth v. United States*, 354 U.S. 476 (1957).

Taylor, Hannis. "Blow at Freedom of the Press." *North American Review*, 155:694–705, December 1892. **T31**
Criticism of the recent Supreme Court decision (*Dupré*, 143 U.S. 110–35) which gives Congress "despotic power" over the intellectual content of all communication passing through the mail, in contradiction to the freedom guaranteed by the First Amendment. Taylor writes of the "fiction" created by the Court that, since citizens have a right to transmit mail through other than the United States mails, the First Amendment is satisfied. Instead, the ruling "takes away the only substantial right which the First Amendment was ever intended to guarantee to him."

Taylor, Henry A. *The British Press: A Critical Survey*. London, Arthur Barker, 1961. 176 p. **T32**
A British journalist appraises the nation's press in light of the report of the Royal Commission on the Press (1947–49). A large portion of the commentary deals with the freedom of the press—external and internal disciplines. Taylor discusses the work of the Press Council, particularly in "counselling a chartered libertine." "The reputation of the Press as a libertine arises from the circumstance that whereas the ordinary citizen is

seldom in a position that requires him to exercise his rights to the extreme limit, the newspaper Press in its day-to-day activities is always ranging near the frontier that separates liberty from license." In Britain, he observes, there is no specific law guaranteeing the freedom or independence of the Press. "What passes as its charter is the recognition, long accorded by the dicta of judges, to the concept of the Press as a free institution endowed with the rights of the ordinary citizen."

————. *Freedom Number One: Liberty of Expression and the British Press.* London, Signpost Press, 1944. 30p. (Signpost Booklet no. 16)   **T 33**

A defense of the British press, written by a Conservative editor who believes that the financial basis of the newspaper industry, i.e. income from advertising, does not interfere with the freedom of expression. "The newspaper community is inspired by a sense of service which is entirely unrelated to the commercial structure on which its organization rests." The real control of the press rests with the readers. The author discusses the effect of the press and the B.B.C. on public opinion, stresses the importance of press freedom, and warns of the dangers of State-imposed ideas.

Taylor, Howard B. *The Theory of Privacy as It Affects Advertising and News in the Press of the United States.* Columbia, Mo., University of Missouri, 1937. 125p. (Unpublished Master's thesis)   **T 34**

[Taylor, John E.]. *A Full and Accurate Report of the Trial of Mr. John Edward Taylor, of Manchester, for an Alleged Libel on Mr. John Greenwood . . . at Lancaster, on Monday, March 29, 1819, before Mr. Baron Wood.* Manchester, Eng., W. Cowdroy, 1819. 34p.   **T 35**

Although the case involved an alleged libel in letters written by Taylor to Greenwood rather than anything appearing in the public press, the case is of interest because, according to the defendant in his lengthy introduction on libel, it is "the first instance, in cases of criminal prosecution for libel in which the defendant has been allowed to call evidence in justification, and to prove the truth of the alleged libellous matter." Despite strict instructions from the judge for conviction, the jury found the defendant not guilty.

Taylor, Michael A. 'The Censorship Bugaboo: Radio-TV Programming and the FCC." *New Republic*, 146:17–21, 2 April 1962.   **T 36**

The physical limitations of the broadcasting medium together with the "public interest" mandate from Congress necessitate some licensing power in the FCC. The courts

have conclusively declined to limit the Commission's power to technical matters but have included program content as well. There is no prior censorship, only action after an extended series of acts that indicate the station is not operating in the public interest.

Taylor, Peter A. *Burning a Theology Book. Libraries of Mechanical Institutes: should they be free, or subject to theological censorship? A speech delivered . . . at the Halstead Literary . . . Institute, June 30, 1858.* London, E. Wilson, 1858. 16p.   **T 37**

[Taylor, Robert]. *Trial of the Reverend Robert Taylor . . . upon a charge of Blasphemy, with his defence, as Delivered by Himself, before the Lord Chief Justice and a Special Jury, on Wednesday, October 24, 1827. To which is now added, the Judgment of the Court of King's Bench, and the Reverend Defendant's Address to the Court . . .* London, R. Carlile, 1828. 48p.   **T 38**

This unorthodox minister was brought to trial for a blasphemous sermon, advertised in the press and by handbill, on the character of Christ, an exposure of "the atrocious villanies that characterize the Jewish vampire." Taylor was convicted and sentenced to a year in prison.

Taylor, Thurston. "Keep Calm and Support the Library Bill of Rights." *Library Journal*, 76:2063–64, 15 December 1951. (Reprinted in Daniels, *The Censorship of Books*, pp. 174–75)   **T 39**

The librarian of the Free Public Library, Worcester, Mass., questions the policy of Ralph Ulveling of the Detroit Public Library in handling pro-Communist materials. Ulveling's statement had appeared in the August 1951 *Library Journal*.

Taylor, W. S. "Why Not Censureship?" *Sewanee Review*, 43:311–26, July 1935.   **T 40**

Instead of censorship or unlimited intellectual freedom the author proposes a third alternative—"censureship." "Censureship would demand *complete freedom of publication*; but recognizing the rights of governments as much as authors, critics, publishers, and customers, for the sake of consumers, censureship would provide *opportunity for the government's opinion* of any intellectual or artistic production to reach the consumer *along with the production itself.*" The scheme would not require prior censorship, but prior submission of the manuscript to a government agency in time for the agency to prepare its opinion. The producer of the work would be required to give the opinion of the government verbatim along with his own publicity.

Taylor, Winchell. "Secret Movie Censors." *Nation*, 147:38–40, 9 July 1938.   **T 41**

An account of the drive in the United States against *Blockade*, a Spanish Civil War story with an anti-Fascist theme. Opposition was from Catholic groups, from the International Alliance of Theatrical Stage Employees, and the Fox West Coast theater chain.

The Tears of the Press, with Reflections on the Present State of England. London, Printed and Sold by Richard Janeway, 1681. 9p. (Also in *The Harleian Miscellany*, vol. 8, pp. 527–29)   **T 42**

"The tears of the press were but the livery of its guilt . . . the ink has poison in it." The enormities of the press are caused partly by writers and partly by readers. The cure lies not so much in "breaking" the press but in "prophylactical" measures, employment of the press as "a battering-ram to destroy and overthrow the mighty walls of heresy and error" and to communicate "all wholesome knowledge and science."

Tebbel, John. "Freedom of the Air: Myth or Reality?" *Saturday Review*, 45(15):56–57, 15 April 1962.   **T 43**

Problems raised by editorializing on the air.

"Television and the Accused." *New York County Lawyers Association Bar Bulletin*, 21:166–74, 1964.   **T 44**

A report of the Association's Committee on Civil Rights dealing with the balancing of television's freedom of the press with the right of the accused to a fair trial. The report was approved by the Association's Board of Directors.

Television Information Office. The Library. *Television: Freedom, Responsibility, Regulation. A Bibliography.* New York, TIO, 1962. 8p. (TIO Bibliography Series, no. 2)   **T 45**

A selected and annotated bibliography.

————. *Television in Government and Politics. A Bibliography.* New York, TIO, 1964. 63p. (TIO Bibliography Series, no. 3)   **T 46**

A selected and annotated bibliography.

Teller, Edward. "Perilous Illusion: Secrecy Means Security." *New York Times Magazine*, 13 November 1960, pp. 29+.   **T 47**

A scientist criticizes government classification of scientific secrets as inimical to our interests and those of our allies.

[Tennessee v. John Thomas Scopes]. *The World's Most Famous Court Trial, Tennessee Evolution Case.* 3d ed. Cincinnati, National Book Co., 1925, 339p.   **T 48**

A verbatim report of the Scopes trial, including speeches and arguments of attorneys, testimony of scientists, and William Jennings Bryan's last speech. In Irving Stone's *Clarence Darrow for the Defense*, chapter 12, entitled *Your Old Man's a Monkey!* deals with Darrow's part in the trial. The case involved the use of a high school textbook discussing evolution.

Tennyson, Charles. "The Libraries' Censorship." *Contemporary Review*, 97:476–80, April 1910.　　　　**T 49**
Deals with censorship imposed by such circulating libraries as Mudie's, W. H. Smith, Booklovers' Library, the *Times* Book Club, etc., who classify all books submitted to them by the publisher as (a) satisfactory, (b) doubtful, and (c) objectionable.

Terrou, Fernand, and Lucien Solal. *Legislation for Press, Film and Radio*. Paris, UNESCO, 1951. 420p. (Press, Film, and Radio in the World Today)　　**T 50**
A comparative study of the main types of regulations governing the information media, including professional codes.

Terry, Hugh B. "Electronic Journalism in the Colorado Courts." *Journalism Quarterly*, 34:341–48+, Summer 1957.　　　　**T 51**
"When John Gilbert Graham planted a time-bomb aboard an airliner, he indirectly aided in a substantial victory by Colorado news broadcasters over restrictions of Canon 35. State radio and television newsmen banded together to convince their judges that electronic reporters can cover a trial with fairness."

Terwilliger, W. Bird. "William Goddard's Victory for the Freedom of the Press." *Maryland Historical Magazine*, 36:139–49, June 1941.　　　　**T 52**
A Baltimore editor in 1777 withstood the vigilante pressures of a local Whig Club and refused to reveal the name of the writer of an article in his paper, *Maryland Journal*. He received the support of the Committee of Grievances of the Maryland House of Delegates to whom he referred the case.

"Test for Obscenity—Requirement of Patent Offensiveness and Necessity of Judicial Determination Prior to Postal Censorship." *Rutgers Law Review*, 17: 213–17, Fall 1962.　　　　**T 53**
Notes on the decision, *Manual Enterprises, Inc. v. Day*, 370 U.S. 478 (1962).

"The Test of Obscenity." *Author*, 65: 1–5, Autumn 1954.　　　　**T 54**
A report of the decision of the Central Criminal Court of England in freeing the publishers of Stanley Kauffmann's *The Philanderer* of charges of obscene libel. Excerpts from the text of Mr. Justice Stable's decision, which "may prove a classic statement in English law." The case of *Regina v. Martin Secker & Warburg, Ltd.*, et al.

"Textbooks Brought to Book." *Time*, 37(9):39–40, 3 March 1941.　　**T 55**
An account of the controversial report of the National Association of Manufacturers' study of social science textbooks used in American high schools, conducted by Ralph W. Robey.

Thackrey, Russell I. "Legal Controls of Communications as America Enters World War II. *Journalism Quarterly*, 19: 24–27, March 1942.　　　　**T 56**
While legal controls of the press in wartime are a heritage of World War I, the Attorney General in World War II "has charted a liberal course with respect to opinion, and a widely respected newspaperman has been made censor."

Thaxton, Carlton J. *An Analysis of the Twenty-four Novels Published between 1947 and 1957 Which Were Reported in Either the Censorship Bulletin or the Newsletter on Intellectual Freedom as Having Been Banned or Blacklisted in the United States in the Years 1956 or 1957*. Tallahassee, Florida State University, 1958. 188p. (Unpublished Master's thesis)　　　　**T 57**

Thayer, Frank. "Cited for Contempt." *Quill*, 27(12):10–13 December 1939.
　　　　T 58
Suggestions to journalists for avoiding citation for contempt, offered by a professor of journalism and law.

————. "Defamation and Freedom of Expression." *Quill*, 52(1):18–22, January 1964.　　　　**T 59**
First in a series of articles on defamation, libel, and slander.

————. "Fair Comment as a Defense." *Wisconsin Law Review*, 1950:288–307, March 1950.　　　　**T 60**
Part of a larger study on libel being proposed by the author. "Fair criticism, though embarrassing and often severe, helps to crystallize public opinion and focus attention on merits and defects in human activity. To comment fairly on what is in the public interest tends to make better art, government, or business. The limits of fair comment are broad, yet every individual is not destined to suffer injury to reputation because these limits are extended. It is still fundamental law that every man is entitled to a good reputation."

————. *Legal Control of the Press; Concerning Libel, Privacy, Contempt, Copyright, Regulation of Advertising, and Postal Laws*. With Cooperation on Research by Eugene O. Gehl and Harold L. Nelson. 4th ed. Brookyln, The Foundation Press, 1962. 795p.　　　　**T 61**

A legal casebook "based upon the experience gained in conducting classes and seminars in law of the press in the School of Journalism at the University of Wisconsin . . . Examples are based on actual cases, public records of judicial decisions." The appendix includes a selected bibliography, second-class mail regulations, and a table of cases cited.

————. "Libel Per Se and Libel Under Special Circumstances." *Quill*, 52(2): 20–23, February 1964.　　　　**T 62**
Second article in a series.

————. "Principal Defense in Civil Libel." *Quill*, 52(3):22–26, March 1964.　　**T 63**
Third article in a series.

————. "Shifting Concepts in Laws Affecting the Press." *Journalism Quarterly*, 28:24–30, Winter 1951.　　　　**T 64**
An examination of recent decisions by courts and regulating agencies suggests that newspapers are clearly facing more controls.

[Thayer, Scofield]. "Comments [on Censorship]." *Dial*, 72:446–48, April 1922.
　　　　T 65
Comments by the editor on censorship of the stage. The basis for all prohibitions "is not so much hatred of the thing to be prohibited as the love of the power to destroy." A work of art is let alone if it has a moral purpose, "it may be damned and burned if it intends nothing but amusement." The artist should be independent just as the scientist is independent.

Theisen, Roman. *A Moral Evaluation of the American Law Regarding Literary Obscenity*. Rome, Catholic Book Agency, 1957. 109p.　　　　**T 66**
The author of this thesis generally agrees with the Congressional Investigation Committee which found that "the legislation, both Federal and State, is sufficient," except in the protection of children, and that citizens should insist on the enforcement of existing laws.

Thelwall, John. *Natural and Constitutional Right of Britons to Annual Parliaments and Universal Suffrage, and the Freedom of Popular Association; Being a Vindication of the Motives and Political Conduct of John Thelwall and the London Corresponding Society in General . . .* London, The Author, 1795. 96p.　　　　**T 67**
Thelwall did not use this speech at his treason trial but left the defense to his lawyer, Thomas Erskine.

————. *Political Lectures, containing the Lecture on Spies and Informers and the First*

Lecture on Prosecutions for Political Opinions, to which is prefixed a narrative of facts relative to the recent attempts to wrest from the people the palladium of their natural and constitutional rights, Liberty of Speech. London, 1795. **T 68**

Thelwall, publisher of the weekly *Champion* and active in the London Corresponding Society, was a stout advocate of parliamentary reform and defender of the freedom of expression. He was tried for sedition along with other Jacobin pamphleteers. This work was intended to be followed by another volume, but volume 2 did not appear because the Attorney General seized Thelwall's notes and did not return them after the trial.

[————]. [*Trial of John Thelwall for Seditious Libel, 1821*]. In *Annual Register*, 1822, p. 351. *Commons Journals*, 1821, vol. 76, pp. 943 ff.; *Champion*, 6 May 1821. **T 69**

For attacking the Constitutional Association in the columns of the *Champion*, Thelwall was brought to trial on charges of seditious libel. He was freed by the court and the Chief Justice declared that officers of the Association who took part in the arrest and imprisonment had been unnecessarily harsh. Following his arrest, Thelwall wrote in the *Champion*: "This is, in fact, the commencement only of a great warfare about to be waged between the Liberty of the Press and the usurping tyranny of a detestable self-constituted inquisition."

[————]. *Trial of Mr. John Thelwall, Reported by a Student in the Temple. . . . In State Trials for High Treason. . . . Part Third.* London, Printed for B. Crosby, [1794?]. 126 p. **T 70**

Thelwall was arrested in May 1794 along with Hardy, Tooke, and nine others for their activity in behalf of parliamentary reform and their sympathies for the French Revolution. Thelwall's papers, manuscripts, personal library, and etchings were all seized in a raid by the king's "messengers," never to be returned. After more than six months in prison, the last month in the charnel house of Newgate among corpses of dead prisoners, Thelwall was brought to trial. Thomas Erskine defended him and, as in the case of Hardy and Tooke who had been tried before him, Thelwall was found not guilty.

"They Snoop to Conquer." *Saturday Review* (London), 147:309–10, 9 March 1929. **T 71**

Opposition to a proposal made by the London Council of Public Morality for legislation that anyone knowingly selling books to persons under 18 years of age should be punished under summary jurisdiction if such books are calculated to corrupt morals. "The wretched bookseller," the writer remarks, "will have to calculate not only the age of the recipient but the corruptive power of the book!" The Home Secretary cannot be depended upon as a judge, for he once said that "the coarser remarks in Shakespeare, if published in penny form" would undoubtedly be indecent.

"This Hush-Hush War." *Christian Century*, 59:1281–82, 21 October 1942. **T 72**

The Navy's announcement that it would celebrate the first anniversary of the attack on Pearl Harbor by revealing the full story of the event, leads the editor to criticize the withholding of important information for a year. Censors should keep in mind the danger of loss of public confidence which it produces as well as the effect on the enemy.

Thomas, A. V. "Newspaper Control." *Dial*, 66:121–24, 8 February 1919. **T 73**

The author charges that coercive ownership controls over editorial policy caused Canadian papers to desert Laurier in the last election.

Thomas, Alan W. "Complaints and Answers." *Library Journal*, 88:510–12, 1 February 1963. **T 74**

One of three papers relating to selection of controversial materials, given at a staff meeting of librarians working with young adults at the Free Library of Philadelphia.

————. "Damned If You Do and Damned If You Don't." *Pennsylvania Library Association Bulletin*, 18:13–16, May 1963. **T 75**

The official responsible for adult book selection in the Free Library of Philadelphia discusses that library's handling of certain controversial titles—the basis for selection or rejection and the response of the public—pro and con.

Thomas, Augustus. "A Playwright's Views." *Review of Reviews*, 75:402, April 1927. **T 76**

A playwright gives his reasons for opposing censorship. "The natural progress of things is for liberty to yield and government to gain ground."

Thomas, Donald. "Hicklin: Deprave and Corrupt." *Censorship*, 3:38–42, Summer 1965. **T 77**

A discussion of the hypothesis, established as a tenet of English obscenity law by Lord Cockburn in 1868, that pornography corrupts its readers. The concept "still remains the fundamental justification of censorship by means of the Obscene Publications Act."

————. "Leigh Hunt's *Examiner*." *Censorship*, 2(2):38–42, Spring 1966. **T 78**

The clash of Leigh Hunt and his brother John with the political censorship of the early nineteenth century.

————. "Licensing in England, 1538–1695." *Censorship*, 4:37–41, Autumn 1965. **T 79**

"This system of licensing grew from a decree of Henry VIII, issued in 1538, and continued with modifications until the House of Commons refused to prolong the final Licensing Act in 1695." A brief history of a century-and-a-half of licensing of printing.

Thomas, Ella C. *Libel and Slander and Related Action.* 2d ed., Dobbs Ferry, N.Y., Oceana, 1963. 73 p. (Legal Almanac series 15) **T 80**

Thomas, Isaiah. *The History of Printing in America, with a Biography of Printers and an Account of Newspapers.* Worcester, Mass., 1810; rev. ed., Albany, N. Y., Munsell, 1874. 2 vols. **T 81**

An important source of information on suppression of early American newspapers, written by a printer with firsthand knowledge of eighteenth-century journalism.

Thomas, Ivor. *The Newspaper.* London, Oxford University Press, 1943. 32 p. (Oxford Pamphlets on Home Affairs) **T 82**

In a general survey of the British press Thomas, former editorial writer for the *Times*, believes the high standards of newspaper ownership are likely to prevent the British press from becoming a sinister instrument of a few press lords. He believes that lack of objectivity in presenting the news is more the result of the speed of work than any deliberate malice.

Thomas, John L. *Law of Constructive Contempt; the Shepherd Case Reviewed.* St. Louis, F. H. Thomas, 1904. 270 p. **T 83**

A criticism of the decision in the case *Missouri v. Shepherd*, 177 Mo. 205, 76 S.W. 79 (1903) in which the editor of the Warrensburg, Mo., *Standard-Herald* was convicted of contempt of court. J. M. Shepherd, in an editorial published during the case of *H. R. Oglesby v. Missouri Pacific Railway Co.*, had charged the Missouri Supreme Court with bribery and corruption. The trial report in Shepherd's case includes a lengthy review of the history of the power of the court in matters of contempt by publication.

————. *Lotteries, Frauds and Obscenity in the Mails.* Columbia, Mo., E. W. Stephens, 1900. 358 p. **T 84**

Includes abstracts of court decisions and statutes.

Thomas, John P. *A Legal and Constitutional Argument against the Alleged Judicial Right of Restraining the Publication of Reports of Judicial Proceedings, as assumed in King vs. Thistlewood and others, enforced against the Proprietor of The Observer by a Fine of*

£500, and afterwards Confirmed by the Court of King's Bench . . . London, Printed by I. L. Turner for S. Sweet, 1822. 148 p. **T 85**

In the trial of Arthur Thistlewood and others for treason, April 1820, Lord Chief Justice Abbott prohibited publication of the proceedings of the court until subsequent trials should be concluded. William Clement, proprietor of *The Observer* published a report of the proceedings on the day following the conclusion of the Thistlewood trial. Clement was fined £500 for violating the order of the Court. Following an account of the case, Thomas presents arguments against such court restraints and concludes with publication of a "Proposal for An Act for the declaring and confirming the right and lawfulness of publishing without restraint, all fair and complete reports of the proceedings in the several courts of record."

Thomas, Joseph M. "Swift and the Stamp Act of 1712." *Publications of Modern Language Association*, 31(n. s.):247–63, 1916. **T 86**

Rejects charge that Swift was author of the suggestion for a tax on publications.

Thomas, Peter D. G. "The Beginning of Parliamentary Reporting in Newspapers, 1768–1774." *English Historical Review*, 74:623–36, October 1959. **T 87**

Study based on newspapers of the period, particularly those of London.

———. "John Wilkes and the Freedom of the Press, 1771." *Bulletin, Institute for Historical Research*, 33:86–98, 1960. **T 88**

Thomas, Ralph C. "Libel and Slander: Defamation of Class." *Oklahoma Law Review*, 2:377–87, August 1949. **T 89**

Thompson, Charles A. H. "Television, Politics and Public Policy." In *Public Policy: A Yearbook of the Graduate School of Public Administration*. Cambridge, Mass., Harvard University Press, 1958, pp. 368–406. (Reprint no. 25, Brookings Institution) **T 90**

In discussing Section 315 of the Communications Act of 1934, which deals with equal time for political candidates, the author points out that the industry has demonstrated its capability and intention of providing adequate time for the major parties and could take care of minor parties, "so long as it does not have to give substantially equal access to all legally qualified candidates who come forward."

Thompson, Craig F. "The Christian Science Censorship." *New Republic*, 61:59–62, 11 December 1929. **T 91**

Concerns the efforts of the Christian Science Church to suppress Edwin F. Dakin's book, *Mrs. Eddy: The Biography of a Virginal Mind*, published by Charles Scribner's. Subsequent issues of the *New Republic* carry editorials and letters to the editor on the subject: 15 January 1930, 22 January 1930, 29 January 1930, and 19 February 1930.

———. "Christian Science Censorship Again." *New Republic*, 62:44–46, 26 February 1930. **T 92**

The author describes efforts being made by the local publications committees of the Christian Science Church to keep Dakin's biography of Mrs. Eddy off the library shelf.

Thompson, Denys. "Beaverbrook for Beginners." *School Library Review*, 2(4):126–27, Summer 1939. **T 93**

The answer to the challenge to protect young people from the sinister propaganda rife in the world today is not censorship but education of children to discriminate in their reading. Before they leave school they should have an "emotional balance" that will serve as a protection against propaganda.

Thompson, Dorothy. "The Climate of a Free Press." *Ladies' Home Journal*, 65:11–12+, September 1948. **T 94**

Discusses the widespread doubts that exist today about press freedom because of centralization of ownership and advertising control, and considers the extent to which such criticisms are justified. "A free press is indeed a press which appeals to reason in the light of facts, and one in which ownership and direction respect truth and reason. In our country it seeks to pay its bill by pleasing readers. And if readers also respect truth, they will keep it free and make it more so."

Thompson, Elbert N. S. *The Controversy between the Puritans and the Stage*. New York, Holt, 1903. 275 p. Reprinted in 1966 by Russell & Russell, New York. (Yale Studies in English, vol. 20) **T 95**

A study in the conflict between morality and art reflected in the Puritan literature and sermons which resulted in the theater closure act of 1642. Includes a critical account of William Prynne's attack on the stage in his *Histrio-Mastix* and a section on the dramatists' replies to their critics.

Thompson, Helen. "Censorship Defeated in Riverside Drive." *Library Journal*, 84:388–89, 1 February 1959. **T 96**

Account of an attempt by a member of the Library Board of the Riverside, Calif., Public Library, to ban from the shelves all books by persons who had been unfavorably mentioned by the Un-American Activities Committee of the California legislature. The local newspaper reported the efforts and there was widespread opposition. A firm stand against censorship by the Library Board and the staff defeated the attempt.

Thompson, J. W. M. "The Press." *Spectator*, 212:244–45, 21 February 1964. **T 97**

The author examines numerous press comments in Great Britain concerning the condemnation of *Fanny Hill* as obscene by the chief metropolitan magistrate. "What has emerged most strongly from the press comments has been a healthy uneasiness over the way the case was handled by the prosecution."

[Thompson, Nathaniel, *et al.*]. *Tryal of Nathaniel Thompson, William Pain and John Farwell; for Writing, Printing and Publishing Libels, Reflecting upon the Justice of the Nation, in the Proceedings against the Murderers of Sir Edmond-Bury Godfrey; Added by Way of Appendix Several Affidavits* . . . London, T. Simmons, 1682. 53 p. (Also in Howell, *State Trials*, vol. 8, pp. 1359 ff.) **T 98**

Thompson, a Catholic printer, had published two letters in his *Domestick Intelligence* defending Catholics against murder charges in an episode of the Popish Plot. The letters were written by Pain and Farwell. Publisher and authors were brought to trial and found guilty. Thompson and Farwell were sentenced to stand upon the pillory. A contemptuous mob hurled refuse and abuse on the men. Each defendant was fined £100.

Thompson, Ralph. "Deathless Lady." *Colophon*, 1(n. s., 2):207–20, Autumn 1935. **T 99**

History of the often-banned *Fanny Hill*, with a biography of the author, John Cleland.

Thompson, W. H., *et al.* "Press Freedom in Wartime; a Symposium." *Labour Monthly*, 23:115–25, March 1941. **T 100**

"In view of the grave issues raised by the suppression of the 'Daily Worker' and 'The Week,' we have approached a number of representatives of democratic opinion for expressions of their viewpoint. While these contributors in several cases make clear their criticisms of the viewpoint of the 'Daily Worker,' they are united in protesting against the Government's action in suppressing this organ of working-class and democratic opinion." The contributors are: W. H. Thompson, George Bernard Shaw, H. G. Wells, Sir Richard Acland, Sir Hugh Roberton, Lord Ponsonby, H. W. Nevinson, L. C. White, S. O. Davies, Ronald Kidd, and the Dean of Canterbury.

Thomson, James. *Mr. Thomson's Preface to a Speech of Mr. John Milton, for the Liberty of Unlicensed Printing.* (Printed with George Walker's *Substance of a Speech at the General Meeting of the County of Nottingham* . . . 28 February 1780.) [London]. Society for

Constitutional Information, 1780, pp. 9–12. **T101**

Thomson's preface to the 1738 edition is also printed in T. Holt White's edition of Milton's *Areopagitica*, 1819, pp. lxv–lxxi, along with White's comments about the Thomson edition.

Thomson, John. *An Enquiry, Concerning the Liberty, and Licentiousness of the Press, and the Uncontroulable Nature of the Human Mind: containing an investigation of the right which government have to controul the free expression of public opinion, Addressed to the People of the U. States* . . . New York, Printed by Johnson & Stryker, for the Author, 1801. 84p. (Text reprinted with commentary in Levy, *Freedom of the Press from Zenger to Jefferson*, pp. 284–317) **T102**

"Let the whig and tory, the royalist and aristocrate, the republican and democrat, or by whatever other name the partizans of political parties are designated . . . be allowed to express their opinions, whether by speech or press, with the same unconstrained freedom with which men of science discuss their subjects of investigation. No more danger will result from one discussion, than arises from the other . . . Give unto all opinions the same freedom and the same effects will follow. . . . It is of no consequence to enquire who writes a paper or a pamphlet, where principles and not individuals are the subject of investigation. The only reasonable enquiry is, are the principles contended for just? If they are, let them have their due weight; if otherwise, they will meet with their merited contempt. In all cases, however, where specific or general charges are exhibited against an individual, or individuals; the person's name ought to be affixed to the publication. In this case, wilful culumny and abuse would never dare to make their appearance. He who had been once convicted of publishing a malicious falsehood, would forever after be deprived of the means of giving currency to his culumnies. Let not Government interfere. The laws of society, as before observed, are fully sufficient to the purpose." This pamphlet was written after the expiration of the Alien and Sedition Acts, with the hope of the author that we will "guard ourselves from being again fettered by a measure of that kind."

Thomson, John M. "Obscenity Statutes—Freedom of Speech." *Miami Law Quarterly*, 11:523–26, Summer 1957. **T103**

Comments on *Butler v. Michigan*, 352 U.S. 963 (1956). The U.S. Supreme Court held the obscenity statute under which a Michigan bookseller was convicted in violation of the due process clause of the Fourteenth Amendment.

Thornton, John L. "The Censorship of Books." *Library Journal*, 59:313–14, 1 April 1934. **T104**

"It will be a long time before all librarians are agreed upon the subject of sex literature in the public library. Meanwhile they will have to study the individual requirements of their neighborhoods, the status of the people using the library, and attempt the impossible, of satisfying every member of the community concerned." A letter from a London college librarian.

Thornton, Richard H. "English Authors Placed on the Roman *Index* (1600–1750)." *Notes and Queries*, 12(11th ser.):333, 30 October 1915. **T105**

Thorp, Willard. "Defenders of Ideality." In Spiller, *et al. Literary History of the United States*. 3d ed. rev. New York, Macmillan, 1963, pp. 809–26. **T106**

Thorp discusses the conservative literary critics, including the neohumanists, who reacted strongly against the uninhibited expression of the twenties. The group included Bliss Perry, Irving Babbitt, Paul Elmer More, Stuart Pratt Sherman, and Brander Matthews. Perry and the author, Hamlin Garland, supported the Watch and Ward in its efforts at collective action against "debasing forms of art." Sherman and Matthews, while disgusted with the trend in modern literature, believed the solution lay in improvement of taste rather than in suppression.

Thrasher, Frederic M. "The Comics and Delinquency: Cause or Scapegoat?" *Journal of Educational Sociology*, 23:195:205, December 1949. **T107**

Criticism of the writings of Fredric Wertham on the effects of comic books on juvenile delinquency. The author maintains that there is no acceptable evidence that the reading of comic books has, or has not a significant relation to delinquent behavior.

———. "Education versus Censorship." *Journal of Educational Sociology*, 13:285–306, January 1940. **T108**

A consideration of the motion picture—its effect on the viewer, the problems of encouraging better movies, and the fallacies of some of the current ideas on the social control of the movies.

"Threat to a Free Press." *Nation*, 139:467–68, 24 October 1934. **T109**

Editorial charges that the attitude of the American Newspaper Publishers' Association in criticizing news handouts in the Roosevelt administration is hypocritical. "Nobody censors news and suppresses more freely than do many of the newspaper publishers of this country."

"Threat to Liberty." *Library Association Record*, 40:101–2, March 1938. **T110**

An editorial critical of the action of a library committee that excluded propaganda periodicals and required committee review of the book collection to eliminate all books "propagandist in character."

"Threats of Federal Censorship Send a Shudder Through the Movie World." *Current Opinion*, 62:185–86, March 1917. **T111**

"Throwing the Rule Book." *Time*, 57:70–72, 22 January 1951. **T112**

American military censorship in Korea.

Thurtle, Ernest. "The Printing Press and Truth." *Rationalist Annual*, 1939:49–55, 1939. **T113**

Discusses difficulty that unorthodox ideas have in getting into print. While there is freedom from state censorship or control, lack of funds (in the case of books) and monopoly control (in the case of newspapers) weigh heavily on the side of the status quo.

Tidball, Eugene C. "The Censorship of Moving Pictures: An Open Question." *Montana Law Review*, 17:193–203, Spring 1956. **T114**

A survey of the U.S. Supreme Court's decisions with respect to movie censorship. The author believes that censorship is still upheld by the Court but only after three requirements are filled: (1) The statutes must be limited so that no picture is censored that is not violative of an interest that the state has a right to protect. (2) The picture must present a "clear and present danger." (3) A movie charged as "obscene" must violate the "primary requirements of decency."

Tiercel, *pseud.* "Press Control in War Time." *Nation* (London), 17:568–69, 31 July 1915; 17:607–8, 7 August 1915; 17:637–39, 14 August 1915. **T115**

The first article is an historical review of press control or the lack of it in the Balkan War; the second describes the inadequate control of the press in the present war (World War I); the final article describes the many sources used by the enemy to secure and piece together information.

Tilsley, Hugh. *Treatise on the Stamp Laws in Great Britain and Ireland.* . . . 2d ed. London, Stevens & Norton, 1849. 896p. **T116**

A digest of statutes and cases.

Timberg, Eleanor E. "The Mythology of Broadcasting." *Antioch Review*, 6:354–67, Fall 1946. **T117**

A critique of the FCC report, *Public Service Responsibility of Broadcast Licensees.*

Timbs, John. "Books Burnt." *Notes and Queries* 8(ser.2):37–38, 21 January 1860. **T118**
Relates to the destruction of copies of Lord Bolingbroke's *Essay on a Patriotic King*.

"Time to Clean Up Movie Morals." *Literary Digest*, 71:28–29, 15 October 1921. **T119**

Timmis, Michael T. "The Right of the Press to Refuse to Disclose Confidential Sources of Information." *Wayne Law Review*, 10:599–61, Spring 1964. **T120**
The case of the refusal of the Philadelphia *Evening Bulletin* to turn over to an investigating grand jury documentary sources of information used in writing articles on corruption in city government, 412 Pa. 32, 193 A. 2d 181 (1963).

Timperley, Charles H. *Encyclopaedia of Literary and Typographical Anecdote; Being a Chronological Digest of the Most Interesting Facts Illustrative of the History of Literature and Printing from the Earliest Period to the Present Time* . . . 2d ed. London, H. G. Bohn, 1842. 996p., 116p., 12p. **T121**
This chronological reporting of the events in the history of printing and bookselling from earliest times until about the middle of the nineteenth century is a source of detailed information on events relating to freedom of the press and on such figures as Lilburne, Prynne, L'Estrange, Wilkes, Erskine, Carlile, Almon, Cobbett, Bingley, Wooler, Woodfall, and others. It is one of the few sources of information on the activities of minor figures for which there is no full-length account, and for identifying the printers whose names appear in early accounts of trials.

Tindal, Matthew. *An Essay Concerning the Power of the Magistrate, and the Rights of Mankind, in Matters of Religion.* London, Printed by J. D. for Andrew Bell, 1697. 204p. **T122**
The essay is a plea for religious tolerance, with casual reference to freedom of the press. In a *Postscript* in answer to Atterbury's *Letter to a Convocation-Man*, appended to the main work, Tindal argues against giving the clergy the power of licensing the press.

———. *Four Discourses on the Following Subjects: Viz. 1. Of Obedience to the Supreme Powers, and the Duty of Subjects in all Revolutions; 2. Of the Laws of Nations, and the Rights of Sovereigns; 3. Of the Power of the Magistrate, and the Rights of Mankind in Matters of Religion; 4. Of the Liberty of the Press.* London, 1709. 329p. **T123**

———. *A letter to a Friend: Occasioned by the Presentment of the Grand Jury for the County of Middlesex, of the Author, Printer and Publisher of a Book Entitled the Rights of the Christian Church Asserted.* London, 1708. 24p. **T124**
Tindal (or Tindall), a prominent lawyer and theologian, and Richard Sare, the bookseller, were brought to trial for this work (first published in 1706) that dared to criticize the High-Church party. In 1710 the House of Commons ordered the book burned.

[———]. *A Letter to a Member of Parliament, Shewing, that a Restraint On the Press Is Inconsistent with the Protestant Religion, and dangerous to the Liberties of the Nation.* London, Printed for J. Darby, 1698. 32p. (Reprinted in *A Collection of State Tracts . . .,* 1705–7, vol. 2, pp. 614–26, and in Cobbett, *Parliamentary History of England, 1806–12,* vol. 5, col. 1164) **T125**
This work, attributed to Tindal, was written in opposition to parliamentary proposals to re-enact the licensing law that was allowed to lapse in 1694. It is taken almost entirely from Milton's *Areopagitica*, without giving credit. The only way to discover truth, Tindal wrote, is to exercise the God-given quality of reason in the examination of many and diverse ideas. Restraint of the press requires men to "blindly submit to the Religion they chance to be educated in," it deprives men of the best means to discover truth, it hinders truth from having an influence on men's minds, it "tends to make us hold the truth guiltily," it prevents men from sharing their ideas in "mutual love and kindness," and it increases the chance of error. The Reformation would not have been possible with press restraint; censorship is a popish device. Licensing will not prevent seditious and blasphemous works; there were more such works printed when the law for regulating the press was in force than before.

[———]. *Reasons against Restraining the Press.* London, 1704. 15p. (Also in Baron, *The Pillars of Priestcraft and Orthodoxy Shaken,* 1768, vol. 4, pp. 279–99 and in Somers, *Tracts* vol. 12, pp. 462–66) (This is an abridgment of Tindal's *A Letter to Members of Parliament . . .,* 1698) **T126**
Tindal, a prominent legal scholar and deist at the turn of the seventeenth century, was an early exponent of the freedom of the press as a natural right. He believed in the application of this right in civil as well as religious controversy and expressed his opinion that if members of the parliament have the right to publish their proceedings "why should they deny those they Represent the same Liberty?" Restraint of the press is "consistent enough with Popery" but strikes at the very foundation of Protestantism. Where the freedom of the press is securely maintained, all other freedoms, civil and ecclesiastical, are safe. Tindal defends anonymity of publications as necessary for writers to speak freely of government abuses without fear of recrimination. (Somers attributes this work to Toland or Tindal)

———. *Second Defence of the Rights of the Christian Church, Occasioned by Two Late Indictments against a Bookseller and His Servant for Selling One of Said Books; in a Letter from a Gentleman in London to a Clergyman in the Country* . . . London, 1708. 150p. **T127**
Relates to the prosecution of Tindal and the bookseller, Sare, for publication of Tindal's *The Rights of the Christian Church asserted, Against the Romish and other Priests who claim an Independent Power over it with A Preface concerning the Government of the Church of England, as by Law Established.*

Tinker, Edward L. "Whitewashing." *Bookman,* 60:719–22, February 1925. **T128**
The author writes of a visit to a famous privately-owned library where the lady in charge told of destroying letters of George Washington because they were "smutty" and might destroy the ideal of our first President. The article deals with the ethics of destroying letters and manuscripts of dead men of note. We must sternly oppose "that colorless class of persons who believes that, once a man of genius dies, he should at once be canonized and clothed with all the conventional virtues."

"To Censor Popular Songs." *Literary Digest,* 46:1181, 24 May 1913. **T129**
Maud Powell, violinist, would have our song-makers disciplined by a board of censorship, because of the disrepute of American music through the "unspeakably depraved modern popular song." The Washington *Times* calls for song censorship by the Post Office Department the same as for books, but other newspapers quoted do not approve.

"To Define Obscenity." *Truth Seeker,* 33:676–77, 27 October 1906. **T130**
An editorial on the meeting of the National Purity Federation.

"To Fight Censorship." *Literary Digest,* 74:32–33, 2 September 1922. **T131**
A collection of critical comments on John Sumner's proposals for voluntary censorship.

Tobin, A. I., and Elmer Gertz. *Frank Harris; a Study in Black and White.* Chicago, Madelaine Mendelsohn, 1931. 393p. **T132**
One of a number of biographies of an often-suppressed writer. Numerous references to action against Harris' *My Life and Loves.*

Tobin, Charles J., Jr. "State and Federal Censorship." *Catholic Lawyer,* 3:312–21, Autumn 1957. **T133**

The author discusses the "violent period of change" that is taking place in federal and state censorship; he believes that the Roth and Kingsley Books decisions of the U.S. Supreme Court "have given new encouragement to those forces in the community which are concerned with the elimination of indecency and obscenity from our various communications media." In the last analysis, the people, acting through their designated officials, can obtain the kind of law enforcement against obscenity that they desire.

Tobin, Maurice J. [*Liberty of the Press*]. *Address of Maurice J. Tobin, Secretary of Labor, May 1, 1949, New York City before New York Catholic Writers' Association.* Washington, D.C., U.S. Department of Labor, 1949. 6 p. **T134**

Tobin, Richard L. "It Did Happen Here." *Saturday Review*, 46:65–66, 14 September 1963. Discussion, 46:49, 12 October 1963; 46:82, 9 November 1963. **T135**
Concerns the threat to subpoena the reporting and editorial staff of the Register Publishing Co., Danville, Va., as witnesses in civil rights cases and the implications of such action to freedom of the press.

———. "Just How Free Is the Press?" *Saturday Review*, 45(36):59–60, 8 September 1962. **T136**
The author sees a potential threat to a free press in labor union action against newspapers. He cites as an example the Teamsters' refusal to deliver an edition of the *Cleveland Press* until certain advertising copy was deleted. He also believes that the Newspaper Guild's convention vote committing its members to the endorsement of certain controversial measures in Congress threatens "the traditional dispassionate objectivity of those who write and edit the news."

———. "*New York Times*' Vital Victory." *Saturday Review*, 47:69–70, 11 April 1964. **T137**
"In overturning the notorious Alabama libel award against the *Times*, our highest court has handed a stunning victory not only to all communicators in this country but to the American public in re-etching the fundamental principles of the U.S. Constitution's free press guarantee."

———. "News as a Weapon." *Saturday Review*, 45:61–62, 8 December 1962. **T138**
Criticism of government news policy in the Cuban crisis of mid-October 1962, as expressed by Arthur Sylvester, assistant secretary of defense for public affairs.

———. "On Revealing the Source of News." *Saturday Review*, 66(15):55–56, 9 December 1961. **T139**
Commentary following the case of the Hawaiian Supreme Court ruling that the reporter does not have a right to conceal his news source when the information is sought in legal matters.

———. "Two Hits and a Strikeout." *Saturday Review*, 47(19):59–60, 9 May 1964. **T140**
The hits: an advertisement in the *San Francisco Chronicle* that saved the *Portland Reporter* from having to cease publication and the courage of Xerox Corp. in sponsoring a UN program without product advertising. The strikeout was the recent announcement of the Justice Department that it is going to investigate the newspaper syndicate business.

[Tocker, Mary A.]. *The Trial of Miss Mary Ann Tocker, for an Alleged Libel on R. Gurney. . . .* New York, Printed for William Cobbett, 1818. 48 p. **T141**
Miss Tocker was tried for an alleged libel in the *West Briton and Cornwall Advertiser*. The trial took place 5 August 1818 in the town of Bodmin, County of Cornwall. She served as her own lawyer. The judge declared the statement libelous, but the jury insisted in reading it and declared her not guilty. Cobbett wrote (from America) an introduction to the trial: To English Jurymen, On their Duties on Trials for Civil Libel. He praised both Miss Tocker and the jury. A London edition of the trial was published by John Fairburn under the title *A Female Orator and Politician at the Bar!* Fairburn also published a satirical poem based on the trial, entitled *Miss Mary Ann Ticklewig; Or, Truth No Libel.*

Tocqueville, Alexis de. *Democracy in America.* New York, Vintage, 1954. 2 vols. (The Henry Reeve text as revised by Francis Bowen and Phillips Bradley) **T142**
A classic study of American democracy by a French liberal who visited the United States in the 1830's and recorded with great insight and vision his observations of the working of the new democracy. In chapter 11, Liberty of the Press in the United States, Tocqueville examines the strengths and weaknesses of the press; he observes the violent language of the periodicals; he records the attitude of the people toward judicial repression; and he compares the press of America with that of France. Chapter 11 is reprinted in McCormick, *Versions of Censorship.* pp. 141–45.

To-Day's Cinema News and Property Gazette. London, Cinematograph Exhibitors' Association. 1912–date. Weekly. Title varies. **T143**
Contains numerous news articles on film censorship in Great Britain and elsewhere, and dossiers of cuttings of such films as *Mother* (31 January 1930), *All Quiet on the Western Front* (9 April 1930), and *For the Prosecution* (24 November 1930).

Toland, John. "Proposal for Regulating ye News-papers." In Hanson, *Government and the Press, 1695–1763.* Oxford, Eng., Oxford University Press, 1936, pp. 135–38. **T144**
About 1717 Toland proposed a measure that would plug the loopholes in the law that now permitted many scandalous and seditious newspapers to evade the tax. This, he said, could be done "without encroaching in the least on the Liberty of the press (which ought to be sacred)." Taken from a manuscript in the British Museum.

———. *Vindicious Liberius: Or, M. Toland's Defence of himself, Against the late Lower House of Convocation, and Others; Wherein (Besides his Letters to the Prolocutor) Certain Passages of the Book, Intitul'd Christianity not Mysterious, are Explain'd, and others Corrected: With a Full and clear Account of the Authors Principles realting to Church and State; and a Justification of the Whigs and Commonwealthsmen, against the Misrepresentations of all their Opposers. . . .* London, Bernard Lintott, 1702. 166 p. **T145**
Toland had been accused by the lower house of writing a pernicious and theistical book and a representative was sent to the bishops to advise suppression. The bishops, however, found they were without license to censor and refused to do so.

Tomlinson, H. M. "The Black Shade." *Atlantic Monthly*, 165:506–12, April 1940. **T146**
Wartime censorship as seen by a reporter in World War I.

Tomlinson, John D. *The International Control of Radio Communications.* Ann Arbor, Mich., J. W. Edwards, 1945. 314 p. **T147**

Tompkins, Jerry R., *ed. D-Days at Dayton: Reflections on the Scopes Trial.* Baton Rouge, La., Louisiana State University, 1965. 189 p. **T148**
Recollections from persons involved in the Dayton, Tenn., "evolution" trial, including Roger Baldwin, H. L. Mencken, Watson Davis, W. C. Curtis, Kirtley Mather, and John T. Scopes himself.

Tompkins, Raymond S. "Dangers Facing the Press." *Public Utilities Fortnightly*, 34:201–6, 17 August 1944. **T149**
The author believes there is danger in government control of criticism of foreign governments in the interest of the United States foreign policy.

Tonnsen, John J., Jr. "Scienter Required in Post Office Censorship Proceedings

under 18 U.S.C., Par. 1461." *Montana Law Review*, 24:65–71, Fall 1962. **T150**
Analysis of a ruling of the U.S. Supreme Court that magazines under suit (containing male nudes and seminudes) do not affront the current community standards of decency and hence are not obscene in themselves, *Manual Enterprises, Inc. v. Day*, 82 Sup. Ct. 1432 (1962). The diverse opinions expressed by the justices makes it difficult to interpret the impact of the decision.

"Too Dangerous for Us to Read." *Literary Digest*, 54:1413, 12 May 1917. **T151**
Comments on the ban of the British weekly, *Nation*.

[Tooke, John Horne]. *The Trial (at large) of John Horne . . . for a Libel . . .* London, Published by the defendant from Mr. Gurney's shorthand notes, 1777. 69p. (Also in Howell, *State Trials*, vol. 20, pp. 651 ff.) **T152**
John Horne (later John Horne Tooke) was brought to trial on charge of seditious libel for publishing a criticism of Britain's prosecution of the war with America. As a member of the Constitutional Society, Horne had been responsible for the publication of the Society's resolution for raising funds for the Americans who had been "inhumanly butchered by the king's troops" at Lexington and Concord. Horne was convicted and served three years in prison.

[————]. *The Trial of John Horne Tooke for High Treason at . . . the Old Bailey . . . 1794, Taken in Short-Hand by Joseph Gurney.* London, 1795. 2 vols. (Another edition, "reported by a student in the Temple," was published by B. Crosby (152p.) as part 2 of *State Trials for High Treason*. A two-volume report, "taken in shorthand by J. H. Blanchard," was published by J. S. Jordan) **T153**
In 1794 Tooke was arrested, along with Thomas Hardy, John Thelwall, and others associated with the constitutional reform societies. The excesses in the French Revolution caused the English government to fear the speech and writings of members of even the most moderate reform groups. Hardy was the first to be tried and was acquitted; the Tooke trial followed. Tooke was defended by Thomas Erskine and Major John Cartwright testified in his behalf. Tooke was acquitted as was John Thelwall whose trial followed. This marked the end of the sedition trials which were widely condemned by the public press.

Toomey, John A. "Some Pages in Our Magazines Should Be Labeled 'Poison.'" *America*, 66:516–17, 14 February 1942. **T154**

Torpey, William G. *Judicial Doctrines of Religious Rights in America.* Chapel Hill, N.C., University of North Carolina Press, 1948. 376p. **T155**
A useful reference work in locating cases and decisions relating to blasphemy, religious content of public school textbooks, and regulations on distribution of religious literature. The index is not an adequate guide to the book's content.

Torre, Marie. *Don't Quote Me.* Garden City, N.Y., Doubleday, 1965. 254p. **T156**
The reporter who went to jail to protect a news source in the Judy Garland-C.B.S. dispute, gives an account of the events of this case that ended with a decision by the U.S. Supreme Court.

Toulmin, Joshua. *A Review of the Life, Character and Writings of Rev. John Biddle, M.A., who was Banished to the Isle of Scilly, in the Protectorate of Oliver Cromwell.* London, 1789. 186p. **T157**
Biddle, the "father of Unitarianism" was often persecuted for his doctrinal works.

Tourtellot, Arthur B. "In Defense of the Press." *Atlantic Monthly*, 174:83–87, August 1944. **T158**
In a democracy "a free press vindicates the special right guaranteed it in direct proportion to the truth of its news and the honesty of its opinions. . . . The concern of our democracy should be less with the organizational or commercial nature of the press than with its sense of moral responsibility to fulfill its functions." More adequately educated readers are the greatest need of a free press.

"Toward Sense in Censorship." *Art News*, 50:17, April 1951. **T159**
Editorial critical of censorship of the films *The Miracle* and *Oliver Twist*, but suggesting a federal board or state boards composed of creative artists, writers, educators, and clergymen to advise licensing authorities as to artistic and other values of films. Letters to the editor in the 15 May issue are mostly opposed to such a board.

Tower, Charles H. *The Fairness Doctrine.* New York, Corinthian Broadcasting Corp., 1963. 13p. **T160**
The executive vice-president of Corinthian Broadcasting, in an address before the Indiana Broadcasters Association, calls the fairness doctrine in broadcasting "highly controversial, time consuming, awkward and aggravating for both the regulator and regulatee."

[Towers, Joseph]. *An Enquiry into the Question, Whether Juries are, or are not, Judges of Law, as well as of Fact; With a particular Reference to the case of Libels. . . .* London, Printed for J. Wilkie, 1764. 31p. **T161**

————. *Observations on the Rights and Duty of Juries in Trials for Libels; Together with Remarks on the Origin and Nature of the Law of Libels.* London, J. Debrett, 1784. 147p. (Reprinted in Towers, *Tracts on Political and Other Subjects.* London, Cadell and Davies, 1796, vol. 2, pp. 1–174) **T162**
Towers' work reflects the liberal views of Thomas Erskine—that juries should take into consideration the law as well as the facts in libel suits.

————. *Remarks on the Conduct, Principles, and Publications, of the Association at the Crown and Anchor, in the Strand, for preserving Liberty and Property against Republicans and Levellers. . . .* London, 1793. 52p. (Reprinted in Towers, *Tracts on Political and Other Subjects.* London, Cadell and Davies, 1796, vol. 3, pp. 247–98) **T163**
An account of the Association for Preserving Liberty and Property, against Republicans and Levellers, established in London in 1792 during the hysteria over the French Revolution. The object of the Society and its branches was "to check the circulation of seditious publications of all kinds, whether newspapers or pamphlets, or the invitations to club-meetings, by discovering and bringing them to justice, not only the authors of them, but those who kept them in shops, or hawked them in the streets for sale; or, what was much worse, were employed in circulating them from house to house in any manner whatever." Towers denounces the Society as a dangerous threat to the freedom of the English people. "Under the pretence of maintaining and preserving the constitution, their conduct and publications are in direct opposition to its genuine principles. . . . The period is not far distant, when even the lowest of the vulgar will discern, that depriving men of the freedom of the press, and of the freedom of speech, is not maintaining liberty and the constitution."

Townsend, Charles C. "English Law Governing the Right of Criticism and Fair Comment." *American Law Register*, 30(n.s.):517–55, 1891. **T164**

Townsend, William C. *Modern State Trials.* London, Longman, Brown, Green, and Longmans, 1850. 2 vols. **T165**
Vol. 1 includes the trial of John Frost; vol. 2 includes the trial of John Ambrose Williams for a libel on the Durham clergy, 1822, and the trial of Edward Moxon for blasphemy in publishing Shelley's *Queen Mab*, 1841.

[Townshend, Charles]. *A Defence of the Minority in the House of Commons, on the Question Relating to General Warrants.*

London, Printed for J. Almon, 1764. 38 p. (Reprinted in *A Collection of Scarce and Interesting Tracts . . .*, vol. 1, pp. 50–73) **T166**

As an outgrowth of the seizure of the papers of John Wilkes under a general warrant issued by Lord Halifax, the Whigs in the House of Commons introduced a measure to prohibit the use of the general warrant for seizing authors, printers, publishers, and their papers. The measure was defeated. Townshend, although no supporter of Wilkes, defends the efforts of the Whigs (the minority) to outlaw the general warrant. Among the cases cited is that of the House of Commons in 1680, censuring Lord Chief Justice Scroggs for such use of warrants.

[Townshend, George F., *plaintiff*]. *Crimination and Recrimination. . . .* London, A. Macpherson, 1809. 41 p. **T167**

Townshend, Earl of Leicester, sued the *Morning Herald* for an alleged libel in that paper, authorship unacknowledged. The jury found for the plaintiff.

Townshend, John. *A Treatise on the Wrongs Called Slander and Libel, and on the Remedy by Civil Action for those Wrongs, together with a Chapter on Malicious Prosecution.* 4th ed. New York, Baker, Voorhis & Co., 1890. 848 p. **T168**

Swindler describes this work as the "first American treatise on libel law and leading authority on the subject in the United States in the nineteenth century." First published in 1868.

Tozer, Basil. "The Coming Censorship of Fiction." *National Review*, 51:236–42, April 1908. (Reprinted in *Living Age*, 2 May 1908) **T169**

The alarming increase in fleshpot novels brings with it the danger of a censorship of fiction comparable to the English censorship of plays. Tozer criticizes authors, publishers, and booksellers for prostituting the English novel and thereby imperiling their own future. An editorial in *Current Literature*, June 1908, quotes the *New York Evening Post* in disagreement with Tozer. Indecent novels says the editorial, are merely the result of poor authors unsuccessfully copying good authors. Their work will be eliminated by time and not by censorship.

[Trachtenberg, Alexander]. *Books on Trial; The Case of Alexander Trachtenberg, Director, International Publishers.* [New York, International Publishers], 1952. 23 p. **T170**

Together with 15 others, Trachtenberg was indicted under the Smith Act for conspiring "to advocate and teach" the principles of Marxism-Leninism and for publishing and circulating books "advocating the principles of Marxism-Leninism." Some 40 titles issued by International Publishers are mentioned. The pamphlet deals with the story of the man, the publishing company, and the issue of a free press. A biography of Trachtenberg on the occasion of the trial appeared in the October 1952 issue of *Masses & Mainstream*.

————, ed. "Labor in the War." In *The American Labor Year Book*, 1919–1920. New York, Rand School of Social Science, 1920, pp. 7–140. **T171**

This general summary of American labor in World War I, edited by Alexander Trachtenberg, includes a section on wartime restrictions on freedom of speech, press, and assemblage. Roger Baldwin has written the account of postal censorship, including a listing of cases; Floyd Dell has an article on the trial of *The Masses*; Harry Weinberger has an article on the trial of Emma Goldman and Alexander Berkman for articles in *Mother Earth* and *The Blast*; and Walter Nelles and William E. Williams have articles on the trial of Scott Nearing for his pamphlet, *The Great Madness*.

Tracy, Robert. "Literature and Obscenity." *Christian Century*, 82:769–72, 16 June 1965. **T172**

"For a literary critic the question is not 'Is it shocking or disgusting?' but 'Is it relevant?'"

Trapnell, H. C. "The Indian Press Prosecutions." *Law Quarterly Review*, 14:72–91, January 1898. **T173**

Summary of Indian press laws from the British point of view. While court action was sometimes harsh, the legislation was intended to promote press freedom as well as to curb incitement to disaffection.

Traubel, Horace L. "Freedom to Write and to Print." *Poet-Lore*, 2:529–31, October 1890. **T174**

An impassioned appeal for freedom of literary expression prompted by the Post Office ban on Tolstoi's *Kreutzer Sonata*. "Take from literature its freedom, and it is a disgraceful rag. . . . Take from literary journalism its capacity to resent the dictation of official hypocrisy or public bigotry, and it is a bloodless skeleton, valueless as a force, and useful only in museums of the last resort. . . . With Tolstoi in danger, who is exempt?"

Treason Arraigned in Answer to Plain English; Being a Trayterous and Phanatique Pamphlet which Was Condemned by the Counsel of State, Suppressed by Authority; and the Printer Declared against by Proclamation. It is Directed to the Lord General Monck, and Officers of His Army. London, 1660. 31 p. **T175**

"Treason Scented by Suffragettes." *Literary Digest*, 52:166–68, 22 January 1916. **T176**

Deals with the suppression of an issue of *Britannia*, organ of the Women's Social and Political Union that dropped their suffragette campaign during World War I in favor of service to their country. The issue had accused Sir Edward Grey and Mr. Asquith in the English government of being pro-German.

Trebbel, John. "Journalism: Public Enlightenment or Private Interest." *Annals of the American Academy of Political and Social Science*, 363:79–86, January 1966. **T177**

"Journalism in America occupies a unique position because it is protected by the First Amendment to the Constitution, which by implication gives it a public responsibility. The dilemma of the publisher, however, is that he is also a private businessman who must make a profit to survive, and in the conflict between public enlightenment and private interest, he is found too often on the side of the conservative business interests which sustain his newspaper and whose viewpoints he usually shares. Advertising and public relations have come to dominate the output of the press in many respects. In government, newspapers have become particularly the willing partners of the image-makers. Advertising dominates the magazine business even more completely, while broadcasting has government regulation to contend with as well. In sum, the public interest and the responsibility of the media have been the victims of economic pressures which have made the private interest paramount. In spite of some advances, the outlook is not hopeful."

Treble, J. F. "Federal Radio Commission—Censorship—Broadcast of Information Concerning Lotteries—Application of Sec. 237 of the Federal Criminal Code to Such Broadcasts." *Air Law Review*, 2:256–60, April 1931. **T178**

Tree, Viola. "Censorship of Stage Plays; Another Point of View." *Nineteenth Century*, 67:164–72, January 1910. **T179**

Commentary on the present discussion of stage censorship, including the opinions of leading writers, producers, and statesmen. The author praises the report of the Joint Committee and approves amending the present law on stage censorship to permit alternate procedures. The producer could elect to have his play precensored ("The present nursing policy") or produce the play without license, but at the risk of subsequent prosecution. This proposal is the first step toward the realization of the ideal state where no censorship is needed. The author suggests, along with Israel Zangwill, that someone write a play with the censor as the chief character.

Treloar, William P. "*The North Briton*, No. 45." In *Wilkes and the City*. London, John Murray, 1917, pp. 13–41. **T180**

An account of the suppression of the objectionable issue of Wilkes's paper and action taken against the publisher.

[Trenchard, John, and Thomas Gordon]. *Cato's Letters: or, Essays on Liberty, Civil and Religious.* London, Printed for W. Wilkins, T. Woodward, J. Walthoe, and J. Peele, 1723–24. 4 vols. **T181**

Beginning in November 1720 two English journalists, John Trenchard and Thomas Gordon, writing under the pseudonym "Cato," produced a series of essays which were first published in the *London Journal*. The letters represent popular expression of the libertarian theory of a free press in the eighteenth century. Cato's letters were widely quoted on both sides of the Atlantic, and were printed by Benjamin Franklin at the time of his brother's imprisonment. Cato's thoughts were well ahead of the times. He believes that suppression of the press is a greater threat to the state than the evils it attempts to suppress. Without freedom of the press there can be "neither Liberty, Property, true Religion, Arts, Sciences, Learning, or Knowledge." He criticizes the existing laws of seditious libel, believing that truth should be offered as a defense, an idea introduced in the Zenger case in 1735. Publication of so-called libels, if true, has a salutory effect on government affairs because they check the behavior of public officials. Most so-called libels, he believes, are not worthy of serious attention; they should be ignored or laughed at. The Cato letters, some 158 in all, continued through the year 1723; they were from time to time gathered into collections and at least 7 such groups of the letters were published. In 1723–24 most of the letters were brought together in a 4-volume work with a dedication by Mr. Trenchard and an unsigned preface.

Trent, W. P. "Some Remarks on Modern Book-Burning." In his *Greatness in Literature*, New York, Crowell, 1905, pp. 185–218. **T182**

In a talk before the English Club at Amherst College, 27 April 1905, the author discusses modern intolerance of heterodox ideas, developing his theme around the burning of James A. Froude's *The Nemesis of Faith* by a lecturer at Exeter College in 1849.

"Trial by Newspaper." *Fordham Law Review*, 33:61–76, October 1964. **T183**

"The enactment of a statute which would deter all those responsible from continuing to deprive the accused of his right to a fair trial is the only effective answer to the question of what can be done to free the defendant from the prejudiced effects of 'trial by newspaper.'"

"Trial by Newspaper: The Supreme Court Rebukes the Press." *Nieman Reports*, 15(3):3–4, July 1961. **T184**

Text of statements of Justices Clark and Frankfurter (in *Irvin v. Dowd*) relating to inflammatory pretrial newspaper publicity in a murder trial.

Tribune Association, New York. *The Law of Libel. What Every Tribune Employee Is Expected to Know About It. How to Guard against Libel Suits and How to Be Prepared to Defend Them When Brought.* [New York]. The Tribune Association, 1885. 10p. **T185**

"Tributes to the Ideal of Freedom of Expression." *Annals of the American Academy of Political and Social Science*, 200:292–306, November 1938. **T186**

Includes statements from Plato, Peter Wentworth, John Milton, John Locke, John Stuart Mill, Walter Bagehot, William E. Channing, Calvin Coolidge, E. R. A. Seligman, Charles E. Hughes, Charles H. Cooley, Everett D. Martin, J. B. Bury, Henry Ward Beecher, Wendell Phillips, J. G. Schurman, A. Lawrence Lowell, Thomas S. Gates, James Conant, Robert M. Hutchins, Robert G. Sproul, Frank Aydelotte, Abraham Flexner, Campbell West-Watson, Edwin G. Conklin, and Justices Brewer, Harlan, Holmes, Brandeis, and Hughes.

[Triggs, Oscar L.]. "Libel: Unjustifiable Criticism." In *American Newspaper Publishers Association Bulletin*, 1215:397–406, 4 October 1904. **T187**

A colorful libel case involving literary criticism. Professor Oscar L. Triggs of the University of Chicago sued the Sun Printing and Publishing Co. for ridiculing his literary criticism and attacking him as a "presumptuous literary freak." Triggs had been critical of Longfellow and Whittier. The Court of Appeals reversed a lower court decision for the paper, finding that the paper had exceeded the privilege of reasonable literary criticism. The *Bulletin* gives the text of the decision and reprints the offending articles and editorial comment on the decision.

Troper, R. E. "The U.N. Is Strangling the Free Press!" *American Mercury*, 89:3–18, November 1959. (Reprinted by the National Defense Committee of the DAR) **T188**

The author maintains that the Soviet Union has "quietly, slowly but surely taken over the strategic areas of press, radio and television at the United Nations." He charges censorship and interference in the preparation of UN documents and news reports and cites difficulties created for outside reporters who may be critical of the UN.

Tropic of Cancer Banned as Obscene in N.Y. State." *Publishers' Weekly*, 184:25–26, 22 July 1963. **T189**

A report of the 4 to 3 decision of the New York State Court of Appeals (New York's highest court) reversing a lower court ruling and finding Henry Miller's book obscene under the state's antiobscenity law.

"*Tropic of Cancer* before the U.S. Supreme Court." *ALA Bulletin*, 58:291–98, April 1964. **T190**

The abridged text of the American Library Association's *amicus curiae* brief in the *Tropic of Cancer* case (*Smith v. California*) before the U.S. Supreme Court. The brief is introduced by a background statement by Archie L. McNeal, chairman of the ALA Committee on Intellectual Freedom.

"Tropics of Book Selection: Two Censorship Attempts in Pennsylvania." *Pennsylvania Library Association Bulletin*, 18:17–18, May 1963. **T191**

Relates to two titles: Robert Heinlein's *Starman Jones* and Nikos Kazantzakis' *The Last Temptation of Christ*.

True Briton. London, Nos. 1–74, 3 June 1723—17 February 1724. Semiweekly. **T192**

The organ of the outspoken Duke of Wharton, who wrote most of its articles. Almost every issue evoked a warrant for its criticism of the government and there were frequent references to freedom of the press. The Duke hoped to be arrested so that he might plead his case in court, but the government instead took action against the printers, Sharpe and Payne. The paper folded in February 1724 after Payne was fined £3,000. This paper is not to be confused with a later *True Briton*, established in 1794 with subsidies from the Pitt government, and which supported the state sedition trials.

[Truelove, Edward]. *In the High Court of Justice, Queen's Bench Division, February 1, 1878. The Queen v. Edward Truelove for Publishing the Hon. Robert Dale Owen's "Moral Physiology," and a Pamphlet, Entitled "Individual, Family, and National Poverty."* London, Edward Truelove, 1878. 125p. **T193**

Two years after Annie Besant and Charles Bradlaugh had been acquitted of obscenity charges for republishing an 1833 pamphlet on birth control, Edward Truelove was brought to trial for republishing Robert Dale Owen's 1830 treatise on family limitation. The jury failed to agree on a verdict. The argument of prosecutor and defense counsel and the summing up by Lord Chief Justice Cockburn present a good picture of the prevailing thoughts on birth control literature in nineteenth-century England.

Trumbo, Dalton. *The Devil in the Book.* Los Angeles, Emergency Defense Committee, 1956. 42p. **T194**

The author, in support of the 14 persons convicted as Communists under the Smith Act (Alien Registration Act of 1940), argues that the defendants were prosecuted because of the books they read.

Trumbull, Charles G. *Anthony Comstock, Fighter; Some Impressions of a Lifetime of Adventure in Conflict with the Powers of Evil.* New York, Revell, 1913. 240 p. **T195**
A eulogistic biography of the founder of the New York Society for the Suppression of Vice and the national leader of the crusade against obscene and immodest literature. The author describes the organizing of the vice society and relates many of the cases in which Comstock appeared over a period of 40 years.

"Truth is Forbidden—Censorship in Chicago." *New Theatre*, 3(6):16, 17, 22, May 1934. **T196**

Truth Seeker; a Magazine for Freethinkers. New York, 1873–1919. Monthly, semimonthly, weekly. **T197**
Founded by D. M. Bennett in Paris, Ill., as a monthly journal "devoted to science, morals, free thought, free inquiry and the diffusion of liberal sentiments." With vol. 1, no. 4, December 1873, the publication was moved to New York, where it remained. Over the years *The Truth Seeker* changed from monthly, to semimonthly, to weekly frequency. With Bennett's death in 1882, E. M. Macdonald became editor and served until 1909. He was succeeded by George E. Hussey. To the original purpose was added: "sexual equality, labor reform, and free education." In 1909 Theodore A. Schroeder said of the *Truth Seeker*, "A quarter of a century ago this paper pioneered the opposition against the abridgment of sex-discussion." An editorial in the issue of 16 March 1918 relates to the suppression of the *Truth Seeker* by the U.S. Army.

Truth Seeker Annual and Freethinkers Almanac. New York, Truth Seeker Office, 1884–88. Annually. **T198**
The 1884 annual has a section on the National Liberal League, an organization dedicated to opposition to the Comstock laws. The 1885 annual reports on the activities of the League and contains a memorial to D. M. Bennett, founder of the *Truth Seeker* (photograph of Bennett on p. 29). The 1887 annual has an article on Sunday Oaths and Blasphemy Laws and includes the text of state blasphemy laws. The 1888 annual carries an account of the Reynolds blasphemy case in which Robert G. Ingersoll served as defense attorney.

Tucker, St. George. "Of the Right of Conscience; and of the Freedom of Speech and of the Press." In *Blackstone's Commentaries . . . Edited by St. George Tucker.* Philadelphia, Birch and Small, 1803. Appendix to vol. 1, pt. 2, Note G, pp. 1–30. (Reprinted in Schroeder, *Constitutional Free Speech*, pp. 122–49, and with commentary in Levy, *Freedom of the Press from Zenger to Jefferson*, pp. 317–26) **T199**
This distinguished American law professor edited Blackstone in light of American concepts of intellectual liberty and freedom of the press, reflecting the opinions of Jefferson and those adopted by the Commonwealth of Virginia. In his extensive Note G, Tucker discusses the development of freedom of the press in England and the new American nation, with its Bill of Rights and its recent experience with the Sedition Act. He discusses the latter in detail—the debates over the Act, its operation, the persecutions, and the Kentucky and Virginia resolutions. "Liberty of speech and of discussion in all speculative matters," writes Tucker, "consists in the absolute and uncontrollable right of speaking, writing, and publishing our opinions concerning any subject, whether religious, philosophical, or political; and of inquiring into and examining the nature of truth, whether moral or metaphysical; the expediency or inexpediency of all public measures, with their tendency and probable effect; the conduct of public men, and generally every other subject, without restraint, except as to the injury of any other individual, in his person, property, or good name."

Tugman, W. M. "The People's Right to Know." *State Government*, 27:225–26, November 1954. **T200**
Reviews briefly the main causes for concern with secrecy in government and suggests ways for developing better understanding and mutual confidence between the press and public officials, with both recognizing their responsibilities to the public.

Tumpane, Frank. "I'm in Favor of Censorship." *Maclean's Magazine*, 69:4, 83–84, 24 November 1956. **T201**
An attack on the anticensorship zealots who either (1) believe anybody should have the right to read anything he wishes, or (2) who dislike pornography but believe that it is better to suffer smut than to risk banning what might turn out to be tomorrow's literary masterpiece. To protect a *Ulysses* you don't have to protect pornography. The author defends action of pressure groups including boycotts as proper democratic expressions.

[Tunbridge, William]. *A Report of the Proceedings, in the Mock Trial . . . against William Tunbridge, for the Publication of a Book Called "Palmer's Principles of Nature," as an alleged blasphemous libel upon the Christian Religion, and the Holy Scriptures . . . before a Packed Jury and Lord Chief Justice Abbott . . . to which is added the whole of the suppressed part, of the Defendant's Defence . . .* London, R. Carlile, 1823. 160 p. (Also in Macdonell, *Report of State Trials*, vol. 6, p. 515) **T202**
Tunbridge was one of Carlile's volunteer shopmen, brought to trial through efforts of the Society for the Suppression of Vice. He was given two years' imprisonment.

Turano, Anthony M. "Birth Control and the Law." *American Mercury*, 34:466–72, April 1935. **T203**
Discussion of birth control and the legal restrictions on it. The author concludes that "the only legislative concern should be the purity and fair representation of the various products and the suppression of the quack advertising now fostered by the contraband nature of the subject."

———. "Is Sex Lawful?" *American Mercury*, 45:323–29, November 1938; Discussion, 46:253–54, February 1939. **T204**
Deals with the difficulties encountered by general periodicals in disseminating sex education, for example, *Life*'s Birth of a Baby pictures. Propriety in print depends upon "the subjective taste of each individual. Private conscience can never be regulated by theological fulmination or judicial writ."

Turnbull, George. *An Oregon Editor's Battle for Freedom of the Press.* Portland, Ore., Binfords & Mort, 1952. 91 p. **T205**
A biographical tribute to George Putnam, the editor of the Medford, Ore., *Tribune*. Putnam was brought to trial on charges of criminal libel growing out of a newspaper crusade against the actions of local government officials. His case was taken before the Oregon Supreme Court, where he was vindicated.

Turner, Arthur C. *Free Speech and Broadcasting.* Oxford Eng., Blackwell, 1943. 32 p. **T206**
The author believes that broadcasting does not enjoy the same freedom as the press, partly because of technical limitations. Both British and American broadcasting are remarkably free. Under the British system, however, there is a tendency to avoid controversial expression; under the American system, radio suffers from a cultural paucity. Turner recommends for American radio a relaxation of the broadcasting libel laws. This essay was awarded the Blackwell Prize for 1943 by the University of Aberdeen, the announced subject being, *Does Broadcasting Restrict the Free Expression of Opinion?*

Turner, G. W. "Some Implications of the 'Comics Question Fiasco.'" *New Zealand Libraries*, 17:236–37, November–December 1955. **T207**
References to the "bad" legislation to control comics, enacted by the New Zealand Parliament. Librarians are criticized for tolerating poor quality, "half-alive recreational" books in their rental collections.

Turner, Max W. *State Regulation of the Motion Picture Industry.* Iowa City, State University of Iowa, 1947. 399 p. (Unpublished Ph. D. dissertation) **T208**

Chapters 3 and 4 deal with motion picture censorship, state and municipal, covering legislation and court decisions. Chapter 8 discusses alternative methods of control (self or state), dealing with the Production Code of the Motion Picture Producers Association and the advertising code of a subsidiary organization. A table of cases cited is included in the appendix.

Tutchin, John. *An Account of the Proceedings on the Tryall of Mr. John Tutchin, at the Guild-Hall of the City of London, on the 4th Day of November, 1704. For Several Pamphlets Entitled the Observator.* London, 1704. 2 p. (Also in Howell, *State Trials*, vol. 14, p. 1095 ff.) **T 209**
Tutchin, publisher of the newspaper, *Observator*, was brought to trial for seditious libel. He had charged corruption in high circles, including the Navy. The jury found him guilty of publishing, but not writing, the offensive articles, and the case was dropped. It was in this case that Chief Justice Holt rendered his famous decision on the rules for judgment in cases of seditious libel. The jury was to determine only whether the accused was the publisher and whether the words expressed the meaning alleged by the prosecution. The judge was left to determine whether the work was libelous. In Judge Holt's opinion anything was seditious if it tended to make a citizen think ill of his government. Parliament, not the press, was the place for free discussion. Tutchin died in Queen's Bench prison in 1707, a prisoner for debt. J. G. Muddiman, in his *The Bloody Assizes*, treats Tutchin as a malicious liar rather than as a martyr for a free press.

"TV Censor and Subsidies." *Author*, 4–5, Spring 1963. **T 210**
Objection to a proposed television bill because of the clause on censorship and the additional payment of the companies to the Exchequer that might reduce cultural grants to theaters, drama schools, etc.

"TV Station Yields to Catholic Pressure." *Christian Century*, 74:4, 2 January 1957. **T 211**
An editorial on the cancellation by WGN-TV of the world television premiere of the award-winning film, *Martin Luther*, because of "emotional reaction" to its plan to show the film. A telephone blitzkrieg was organized by the Chicago diocese of the Roman Catholic Church, protesting the showing of the film.

"Twin Bed Trouble." *Life*, 22:142–44, 19 May 1947. **T 212**
An American movie in which husband and wife occupy twin beds is refilmed for British showing, with the beds a foot apart. Illustrations before and after.

"Two Hundred Publishers and Authors Sign Freedom to Read Statement."

Library Journal, 87:2339–41, 15 June 1962. **T 213**

Two Letters; the First Containing Some Remarks on the Meeting . . . to Celebrate the Acquittal of Messrs. Hardy, J. H. Tooke, Thelwall and Others . . . the Second Containing a Short Comparative Sketch of Our Practical Constitution in Ancient Times and the Present; with Some Observations on Certain Assertions Made by the Modern Reformers; by a Freeholder of Cornwall. London, J. Hatchford, 1810. 57 p. **T 214**

"Two Massachusetts Anti-Censorship Bills." *Library Journal*, 53:356, 15 April 1928. **T 215**
Compares the Sedgewick bill and the Book Trade bill, both of which were before the Massachusetts legislature, as attempts to remedy the censorship situation in Massachusetts.

Twomey, John E. "The Citizens' Committee and Comic-Book Control: a Study of Extragovernmental Restraint." *Law and Contemporary Problems*, 20:621–29, Autumn 1955. **T 216**
This study is concerned with the organization and dynamics of the Citizens' Committee for Better Juvenile Literature of Chicago.

————. "New Forms of Social Control over Mass Media Content." *Studies in Public Communications*, 1:38–44, Summer 1957. **T 217**
The author notes a growing public attitude which favors censorship and other forms of social control. Chief among the causes is the increase in publications dealing with sex, crime, violence, and sadism that are freely available to children. He discusses the crusade against the comic book—the Congressional investigations, and the work of the NODL and other citizen groups.

Twyman, Margaret G. *Freedom and Responsibility.* Columbia, Mo., Freedom of Information Center, School of Journalism, University of Missouri, 1963. 4 p. (Publication no. 112) **T 218**
The director of community relations for the Motion Picture Association of America, in a speech at Ohio Wesleyan University, discusses censorship threats to the movie industry. Self-appointed censors are often persons who are not regular movie attenders, do not support good movies when they are available, want the government to make decisions for them, are personally impervious to damage, but fear for their fellowmen.

————. *You . . . and Movies.* New York, Motion Picture Association of America, 1961. 11 p. **T 219**

An address to the Buffalo Federation of Women's Clubs on 26 January 1961, describing the work of the motion picture industry's production code in regulating the moral standards of the movies.

Twyn, John. *An Exact Narrative of the Tryal and Condemnation of John Twyn, for Printing and Dispersing of a Treasonable Book, With the Tryals of Thomas Brewster, Bookseller, Simon Dover, Printer, Nathan Brooks, Bookbinder, for Printing, Publishing, and Uttering of Seditious, Scandalous, and Malitious Pamphlets . . .* London, Printed by Thomas Mabb for Henry Brome, 1664. 78 p. (Also in Howell, *State Trials*, vol. 6, pp. 513 ff., and in Borrow, *Celebrated Trials*, vol. 2, pp. 228–60) **T 220**
Twyn was brought to trial under the prosecution of Roger L'Estrange, government surveyor of the press, on charge of high treason. Twyn had published a book, *A Treatise of the Execution of Justice*, in which he had asserted the right of the people to revolt under an oppressive government. He was convicted, hanged, drawn, and quartered. Brewster, the bookseller, Dover, the printer, and Brooks, the binder were found guilty of sedition, and were fined and pilloried. Siebert states that Twyn and Anderton "were the only printers to be executed for high treason in England during the later Stuart period." An introduction to the publication of the proceedings states that it was published to prevent secret and incorrect reporting of the trial; "to manifest the insufferable liberties of the press, and bring it into better order"; and to warn others of the hazard of printing treasonous works.

Tyler, Keith. "Freedom of Access to Broadcasting." In National Society for the Study of Education, *Mass Media and Education*, 53d Yearbook. Chicago, University of Chicago Press, 1954. Part 2, pp. 80–109. **T 221**
"The concept of libertarian theory as meaning protection of a medium from the tyranny of government has developed into a concern for protecting listeners and viewers in their right of access to all important points of view, with a government agency made responsible by Congress for ensuring that stations thus operate in the public interest."

Tyler, Poyntz, ed. *Television and Radio.* New York, Wilson, 1961. 192 p. (Reference Shelf, vol. 33, no. 6) **T 222**
The editor's introduction, One Hundred and Eighty Million Censors, discusses questions of obscenity, satire and antisocial expression, ethnic and racial groups, violence, and other areas where there are public pressures for control.

Tynan, Kenneth. "The Royal Smut-Hound." *Playboy*, 13:121, 166, 180–83, January 1966.   **T 223**
   "Since the time of the tudors, the lord chamberlain—britain's censor supreme—has done his prudishly prurient and ludicrous best to muzzle the english theater."

[Työmies Publishing Co., *et al.*]. *Arguments of Nicholas Klein, Attorney for Plaintiffs in Error, and Delivered before the United States Circuit Court of Appeals, sitting at Cincinnati, Ohio, January 6, 1914.* Hancock, Mich., Työmies Publishing Co., 1914. 16p.   **T 224**
   The publishers of the Finnish-American humor magazine, *Lapatossu*, were convicted by the U.S. District Court of Michigan (*Työmies Publishing Co. v. U.S.*) for publishing obscene caricatures in the 12 April and 13 December 1912 issues.

U

"U+A+X=Y." by B. D. L., Member no. 12981. *Drama*, 71:35–37, Winter 1963.

U 1

Deals with the controversy aroused by the resolution at the Drama Conference of the Edinburgh Festival urging the public to bring pressure upon the government by all possible means to establish a theater equivalent of the Cinema X Certificate. The British Board of Film Censors and its three certificates (A-Adult, U-Universal, X-no person under 16) are discussed, including the dangers to the theater of an X certificate. The tolerance of Lord Chamberlains in recent years in licensing plays, even though stage censorship is not satisfactory or desirable, is to be preferred to the difficulties facing playwrights, producers, and managers concerned with whether their work is to be certified U, A or X. The only test should be the public reaction to good cinema or good theater.

Udall, John. "Trial for Publishing a Seditious Book." In Howell, *State Trials*, vol. 1, pp. 127 ff.

U 2

Udall, a Puritan minister, was convicted in 1589 for writing an anti-episcopal tract, *Diotrephes*, seized by authority of the Star Chamber from the print shop of Robert Waldegrave. Udall was found guilty and sentenced to death. Popular sentiment led to the granting of a pardon, but Udall died shortly thereafter from the effect of harsh prison treatment.

Ulman, Ruth, *ed. University Debaters' Annual, 1949–1950*. New York, Wilson, 1950. 355 p.

U 3

Chapter 10 consists of a "public discussion" on film censorship, conducted in the form of a congressional hearing by a class at Albion College.

Ulveling, Ralph A. "Book Selection Policies." *Library Journal*, 76:1170–71, August 1951. (Reprinted in Daniels, *The Censorship of Books*, pp. 173–74)

U 4

The director of the Detroit Public Library referred to his library's policy on limited circulation of controversial material that aroused librarians and resulted in numerous comments in the library press. "Communist expressions of opinion or misleading propaganda," Ulveling stated, "would be found in only the Reference service ˌnot in the Home Reading serviceˌ where duplication of titles is limited." Thurston Taylor and Paul Bixler answer Ulveling in the 15 July issue of *Library Journal*.

"Uncle Sam as Censor." *Fortune*, 19(6): 109–10, June 1939. (Fortune Survey XXII)

U 5

The survey asked: Do you think our government should or should not establish a bureau to supervise what should be produced in moving pictures? Radio? Newspapers and Magazines? The answer is an emphatic "no." A generalization from the answer: the lower the income, the higher the sentiment for federal control.

Underhill, Edward B., *ed. Tracts on Liberty of Conscience and Persecution, 1614–1661*. London, Printed for the Hanserd Knollys Society by T. Haddon, 1846. 401 p.

U 6

According to the prospectus of the Hanserd Knollys Society, "to the Baptists belongs the honour of first asserting in this land, and of establishing on the immutable basis of just argument and scripture rule, the right of every man to worship God as conscience dictates, in submission only to divine command." The editor has brought together the text of the earliest Baptist writings in the English language dealing with freedom of religious expression, supplying an introduction to each tract. The book contains Leonard Busher's *Religious Peace: or A Plea for Liberty of Conscience, 1614*; ˌThomas Helwys'ˌ *Persecution for Religion Judg'd and Condemn'd, 1615*; Samuel Richardson's *The Necessity of Toleration in Matters of Religion, 1647*; and John Sturgion's *A Plea for Toleration of Opinions and Persuasion in Matters of Religion, 1661*.

Underhill, Frank A. "*Peyton Place*: Evidence of Frank A. Underhill before the Tariff Board, 29 January 1958." *Canadian Library Association Bulletin*, 15:13–16, July 1958.

U 7

A defense of *Peyton Place* as a serious modern novel dealing with a theme of sex, violence, and a decaying society. The book is not immoral by standards laid down by Judge Woolsey.

United Nations. Conference on Freedom of Information, Geneva, 1948. *Draft Rules of Procedure*. Lake Success, N.Y., The UN, 1948. 8 p. mimeo. **U 8**

In May 1946, at the request of the American Delegation to the UN, the Commission on Human Rights created a Sub-Commission on Freedom of Information. The General Assembly subsequently called for an international Conference on Freedom of Information to be held in 1947–48. It adopted 3 conventions and 43 resolutions. The work of the Conference and the related documents are described in The Library of Congress, *Freedom of Information; A Selective Report on Recent Writings*, 1949, pp. 23–40.

———. *Memorandum Concerning Codes of Honor for Journalists and Encouraging Standards of Professional Conduct*. Lake Success, N.Y., 1949. 33 p. (UN Document E/Conf. 6/10) **U 9**

Texts of the codes of International Federation of Journalists, International Union of Press Associations, First National and Pan-American Press Congress, Mexico, 1942, American Society of Newspaper Editors, National Union of Journalists (Great Britain), National Association of Broadcasters, Association of Radio News Analysts, and Inter-American Association of Broadcasters.

———. *Report of the United States Delegation with Related Documents*. Washington, D.C., Govt. Print Off., 1948. 45 p. (U.S. State Department Publication 3150; International Organization and Conference Series, III 5) **U 10**

The appendix includes the Draft Convention on the Gathering and International Transmission of News (the U.S. Convention), Draft Convention Concerning the Institution of an International Right of Correction (the French Convention), Draft Convention on Freedom of Information (the British Convention), Resolutions (nos. 12 and 13 on "censorship," no. 26 on "libel," and no. 28 on "freedom to listen"). William Benton was chairman of the delegation which included Sevellon Brown, Erwin D. Canham, Zechariah Chafee, Jr., and Harry Martin.

————. *Request for Information.* Lake Success, N.Y., The UN, 1947. 8 p. mimeo. (UN Document E/Conf. 6/2) **U 11**
Invitation to member nations to supply answers to a series of questions relating to freedom of information in their respective countries. The replies were published in two volumes by the UN Secretariat.

————. *Summary Record of the 1st–13th Meeting, Mar. 23–Apr. 21, 1948.* [Geneva?], The UN, 1948. 15 nos. in 1 vol. (UN Document E/Conf. 6/SR/1–E/Conf. 6/SR/13) **U 12**

United Nations. Economic and Social Council. *Freedom of Information: Agenda Item 15.* Lake Success, N.Y., The UN, 1955. 107 p. **U 13**
Survey prepared by the Secretary General on the legal aspects of the rights and responsibilities of the communications media.

————. *Report on Developments in the Field of Freedom of Information since 1954.* [Lake Success, N.Y.], The UN, 1961. 155 p., 11 p., 4 p. mimeo. (UN Document E/3443) **U 14**
Chapter 1, Freedom of Information and the United Nations. Chapter 2, The Concept of Freedom of Information—the Legal Approach. Chapter 3, The Pragmatic Approach. Chapter 4, Facilities for the Free Flow of Information. Chapter 5, Obstacles to the Free Flow of Information (newsprint production, tariff, copyright, legislation, telecommunication press rates, access to news sources, censorship of dispatches). Chapter 6, Content and Quality of Information. Chapter 7, The Extent to Which the People Receive News of the United Nations and Its Specialized Agencies and their Work for Peace. Chapter 8, Brief Note on the Inter-Relationship of Problems. Annex, Chronology of UN Activities in the Field of Information since 1954. The report was prepared by Dr. Hilding Eek, professor of international law, University of Stockholm.

————. *Suggestions to Member States on Measures to Promote the Free Flow of Information and Ideas.* Lake Success, N.Y., The UN, 1965. 14 p. (UN Document CL/1772, Annex) **U 15**

————. *Tentative International Bibliography of Works Dealing with Press Problems, 1902–1952.* Paris, The UN, 1954. 46 p.

(Reports and Papers on Mass Communications) **U 16**

————. *Traffic in Obscene Publications. Summary of Annual Reports for 1946–47.* Lake Success, N.Y., The UN, [1948?] 7 p. **U 17**
A similar summary was published for 1947–48.

United Nations. Economic and Social Council. Sub-Commission on Freedom of Information and of the Press. *Discussion of the Concept of Freedom of Information in Organs of the United Nations.* [Lake Success, N.Y.], 1948. 49 p. (UN Document E/CN. 4/sub. 1/38) **U 18**

————. *Final Act.* Lake Success, N.Y., The UN [1948]. 41 p. (UN Document E/Conf. 6/79) **U 19**
Includes texts of resolutions, draft conventions, articles for draft declaration, and draft covenant on human rights. The drafted clauses concerned (1) gathering and transmission of news, (2) institution of an international right of correction, and (3) freedom of information. The Draft Convention in the gathering and transmission of international news was incorporated in the Declaration of Human Rights. It was revised by an *ad hoc* committee of the General Assembly.

————. *Report* [1st]–*5th sess; May 19–June 4, 1947—Mar. 3–21, 1952.* [Lake Success, N.Y.]. Issued 1950–52 as Supplements to the Official Records of the Economic and Social Council. 5 vols. Various paging. (UN Document E/441) **U 20**
Includes agenda, memoranda, drafts, texts of statements of delegates, resolutions, draft rules, discussions, and suggested programs covering the five sessions.

————. *Report of the Subcommission . . . Transmitted by UNESCO.* [Lake Success, N.Y.], The UN, 1947, 18 p. (UN Document E/507) **U 21**

United Nations. General Assembly. Committee on the Draft Convention. *Reports. . . . Legal Problems Raised by Certain Amendments to the Draft Convention. Memorandum by the Secretary-General.* [Lake Success, N.Y.], The UN, 1951. 21 p. plus 41 p. (UN Document E/2046 and E/2046/Add 1) **U 22**
The Draft Convention on Freedom of Information originated in a proposal made by the delegation of the United Kingdom to the UN Conference on Freedom of Information. The text of the Draft Convention as approved by the Conference is contained in the *Final Act* of the Conference, 1948. In 1950 the

Third Committee of the UN General Assembly appointed an *ad hoc* Committee for revision of the text of the Draft Convention. The Committee held its first meeting at Lake Success in January 1951. Numerous mimeographed reports were issued by the Committee during the course of deliberation; a new draft was submitted in February 1959. The Third Committee of the General Assembly subsequently adopted the four articles of the Draft Convention. A complete account of the Draft Convention is given in Michael Wei, *UN FOI Draft Convention.* Columbia, Mo., Freedom of Information Center, School of Journalism, University of Missouri, 1962. 32 p. (Publication no. 85)

United Nations. Secretariat. *Agreement for the Suppression of Obscene Publications. Signed at Paris on 4 May 1910, amended by the Protocol signed at Lake Success, New York, 4 May 1949.* Lake Success, N.Y., The UN, 1950. 5 p. **U 23**

————. *The Freedom of the Press. Some Historical Notes.* Lake Success, N.Y., The UN, 1948. 29 p. mimeo. (UN Document E/Conf. 6/4) **U 24**
A summary of previous conferences on freedom of the press: Chapter 1, Early Non-Government Conferences. Chapter 2, Proposals at the Paris Peace Conference, 1919–1920. Chapter 3, The League of Nations and the Press. Chapter 4, Other Conferences and Organizations. Chapter 5, Freedom of the Press in The Americas—A Regional Study (including statement on Free Access to Information in the Chapultepec Declaration).

————. *International Convention for the Suppression of the Circulation of and Traffic in Obscene Publications, Opened for Signature at Geneva from 12 September 1923 to 31 March 1924, Amended by the Protocol Signed at Lake Success, New York, 12 November 1947.* Lake Success, N.Y., The UN, 1948. 13 p. **U 25**

————. *Protocol Amending the Convention of 12th September 1923, for the Suppression of the Circulation and Traffic in Obscene Publications.* Lake Success, *12th November, 1947.* London, H.M. Stat. Off., 1952. 25 p. (Cmd. paper 8438) **U 26**

United Nations. Secretariat. Department of Social Affairs. *Freedom of Information. A Compilation.* Lake Success, N.Y., The UN, 1950. 2 vols. **U 27**
Vol. 1 consists of replies from 33 governments in response to a request from the Secretary-General to supply information on the status of freedom of information in their respective countries. Chapter 9 includes reports submitted on "measures to combat the diffusion of false or distorted reports likely to injure

friendly relations between States." Vol. 2 includes relevant articles of constitutions, legislative enactments and regulations, judicial decisions, codes of honor, and other related materials submitted with the replies published in volume one.

United Nations. Seminar on Freedom of Information, New Delhi, 1962. *Seminar on Freedom of Information, New Delhi, India, 20 Feb.–5 Mar., 1962. Organized by the United Nations in Co-operation with the Government of India.* New York, The UN, 1963. 149 p. (UN Document ST/TAO/HR/13) **U 28**

United Nations. Seminar on Freedom of Information, Rome, 1964. *Seminar on Freedom of Information Organized by the United Nations in Co-operation with the Government of Italy.* New York, The UN, 1964. 44 p. (UN Document ST/TAO/HR/20) **U 29**

United Nations. Educational, Scientific and Cultural Organization. *Freedom of Information; Development of Information Media in Under-Developed Countries. Report by the Director-General.* [Paris?], UNESCO, 1961. 196 p. plus tables. (UNESCO Document E/CN.4/814) **U 30**
Contents: Review of past efforts and problems; conclusions and recommendations in various media. I Southeast Asia, II Latin America, III Development of press, film, radio, and television throughout the world.

———. *Freedom of Information; Development of Information Media in Under-Developed Countries. Report by the Director-General of UNESCO. Meeting on Development of Information Media in Latin America.* Paris, UNESCO, 1961. 50 p. mimeo. (UN Document E/3437/Add.1;E/CN.4/814/Add.1) **U 31**

United Nations. Educational, Scientific and Cultural Organization. Department of Mass Communications. Division of Free Flow of Information. *Trade Barriers to Knowledge; a Manual of Regulations Affecting Educational, Scientific and Cultural Materials.* Paris, UNESCO, 1951. 167 p. New and revised edition. New York, Columbia University Press, 1955. 364 p. (UNESCO Publication 847) **U 32**
This manual, intended to enlist public support for the UNESCO convention designed to remove duties, quotas, licenses, and other obstacles to the exchange of cultural materials, lists by country import restrictions for

newspapers and periodicals, works of art, films, scientific apparatus, and materials for the blind.

———. *World Communications, Press, Radio, Film; Report.* New and rev. ed. [Paris], UNESCO, 1951. 223 p. (UNESCO Publication 942) **U 33**

United States. Attorney General. *Annual Report, 1918.* Washington, D.C., Govt. Print. Off., 1918. 782 p. (House Document 1437, 65th Cong., 3d sess.) **U 34**
A summary is given (pp. 20–24, 47–54) of 37 selected cases prosecuted under the wartime Espionage Act, including those involving free speech and freedom of the press or political or religious liberty. Includes the case against the Masses Publishing Co., The Jeffersonian Publishing Co., and the Milwaukee Social Democrat Publishing Co.

———. *The Freedom of the Press from Unlawful Restraints and Monopoly. In the Matter of the Complaint of the Sun Printing and Publishing Company against the Associated Press.* New York, 1914. 84 p. **U 35**

United States. Censorship Office. *Code of Wartime Practices for American Broadcasters.* Washington, D.C., Govt. Print. Off., 1942. 8 p. **U 36**
Handbook outlining rules for voluntary radio censorship in America during World War II. The first edition appeared 15 June 1942. Revised editions were issued 1 February 1943 and 1 December 1943. (Reprinted in Summers, *Wartime Censorship*, pp. 266–75)

———. *Code of Wartime Practices for the American Press.* Washington, D.C., Govt. Print. Off., 1942. 6 p. **U 37**
Handbook outlining the rules for voluntary censorship of the American press during World War II. The first edition appeared 15 June 1942. Revised editions were issued 1 February 1943, 1 December 1943, and 15 May 1945. (Reprinted in Summers, *Wartime Censorship*, pp. 259–66, and as Publication no. 72 of the Freedom of Information Center, School of Journalism, University of Missouri)

———. *Code of Wartime Practices for the American Press and Radio.* Washington, D.C., Govt. Print. Off., 1945. 4 p. **U 38**
"This Code covers everything published—newspapers, press services, periodicals, magazines, books, newsletters, reports, directories, almanacs, trade and financial papers and all else—and everything broadcast by standard, point-to-point nonmilitary, frequency modulation, facsimile and television stations and all else in the United States. This is the guide by which you are expected to censor your own operations." This edition reflects changes resulting from victory in Europe and combines

the previous separate editions for press and radio.

———. *A Report on the Office of Censorship.* Washington, D.C., Govt. Print. Off., 1945. 54 p. (Historical Reports on War Administration, Office of Censorship, series 1) **U 39**
Official history of U.S. government censorship in World War II. Introduction by Byron Price, director of the Office of Censorship.

———. *Rules for Operating Companies.* Washington, D.C., Govt. Print. Off., 1942. 11 p. **U 40**
Instructions for operating overseas cable and radio circuits and affiliated landwire companies concerned with international traffic under wartime censorship.

———. *U.S. Cable and Radio Censorship Regulations.* Washington, D.C., Govt. Print. Off., 1942. 7 p. **U 41**
Includes a list of subjects forbidden for transmission during wartime.

———. *U.S. Postal Censorship Regulations.* Washington, D.C., Govt. Print. Off., 1942. 5 p. **U 42**
Wartime restrictions on mail and films to foreign countries.

———. *U.S. Radiotelephone Censorship Regulations.* Washington, D.C., Govt. Print. Off., 1942. 3 p. **U 43**
Wartime code of restrictions on international radiotelephone calls.

United States. Commerce Department. *Self-Regulation in Advertising. A Report on the Operations of Private Enterprise in an Important Area of Public Responsibility. Submitted by the Advertising Advisory Committee to the Secretary of Commerce.* Washington, D.C., U.S. Department of Commerce [1964?]. 105 p. **U 44**
"The immediate purpose of this document is to provide, for the first time, a clear, accurate report of the many types of activities, instituted and carried out by private businessmen, which operate in our society to regulate American advertising. . . . What you find here is a factual record of the efforts of literally thousands of responsible men—advertisers, agencies, farm publications, magazines, newspapers, TV and radio stations and networks, trade associations, and industry groups—to set up standards, maintain controls, and operate advertising in the public interest."

United States. Congress. House of Representatives. *Proceedings of the House of Repre-*

sentatives of the United States, with Respect to the Petitions Praying for a Repeal of the Alien and Sedition Laws; including the Report of a Select Committee, and the Speeches of Messrs. Gallatin and Nicholas, Thereon. Philadelphia, Printed by J. Gales, 1799. 34 p. (Also in *Annals of Congress*, 5th Cong., 3d sess. and, with commentary, in Leonard W. Levy, *Freedom of the Press from Zenger to Jefferson*, pp. 171–86) **U 45**

A debate over the Sedition Act of 1798, with the Federalists represented in the majority report by Chauncey Goodrich of Connecticut and the Republicans in the minority report by John Nicholas of Virginia. Levy writes of the debate (p. 171): "In their opposition the Republicans were driven to originate so broad a theory of freedom of expression that the concept of seditious libel was at last repudiated, common-law concepts were abandoned, and the overt-acts test was advocated in order to protect all political opinion."

———. *Report on Freedom of the Mails by Representative William Kellogg.* Washington, D.C., Govt. Print. Off., 1863. 15 p. (House Report 51, 37th Cong., 3d sess.) **U 46**

Relates to the Postmaster General's authority over mailable matter.

———. *Resolution on Freedom of the Mails by Representative J. A. Bingham.* Washington, D.C., Govt. Print. Off., 1863. 15 p. (House Document 16, 37th Cong., 3d sess.) **U 47**

Relates to the Postmaster General's authority over mailable matter.

———. ["Resolutions Declaring the Sedition Law of 1798 a Violation of the Constitution"]. In *Gales & Seaton's Register of Debates in Congress, 1827–28*, vol. 4, pt. 1, col. 859, 24 December 1827. (20th Cong., 2d sess.) **U 48**

The resolution, introduced by James Hamilton, Jr. of Charleston, S.C., also provided for a restoration of the fines paid by those convicted under the Act. A review in the May 1829 issue of *Southern Review* stated: "We have always considered that adequate atonement was not made for the violation of the Constitution of the United States, perpetuated by the passing of the . . . Sedition Law, in the mere fact of its being permitted to expire by its own limitation; and that effective securities ought to be obtained against any effort, in future, to make what are generally called political libels, punishable by the authority of the United States, and consequently, cognizable in the Federal Courts."

———. "The Sedition Law." In *Annals of the Congress of the United States.* (2 December 1799 to 3 March 1801). Washington, D.C., Gales & Seaton, 1851. pp. 404–26; 916–40; 946–76. (6th Cong.) **U 49**

Congressional debate on the controversial Sedition Act which was aimed at silencing criticism of the federal government.

United States. Congress. House of Representatives. Education Committee. *Federal Motion Picture Commission; Briefs and Statements Filed with the Committee on Education, on H. R. 456 to Create a New Division of the Bureau of Education, to be Known as the Federal Motion Picture Commission and Defining Its Powers and Duties.* Washington, D.C., Govt. Print. Off., 1916. 65 p. (64th Cong., 1st sess.) **U 50**

A second Congressional proposal to create federal controls over motion pictures.

———. [*Federal Motion Picture Commission*] *Hearings on H.R. 456.* Washington, D.C., Govt. Print. Off., 1916. 303 p. (64th Cong., 1st sess.) **U 51**

———. *Minority Views to Accompany H. R. 15462, Submitted by Mr. F. W. Dallinger.* [*Re: Motion Picture Commission*]. Washington, D.C., Govt. Print. Off., 1916. 5 p. (House Report 697, 64th Cong., 1st sess.) **U 52**

"In our opinion every reasonable protection to the public morals can be secured by the proper exercise of the local police power supplemented by the amendment to the Federal Penal Code. . . . The extraordinary power vested in the commission proposed to be created by this bill will not only prove ineffective to protect public morals . . . but it is utterly un-American in its character."

———. *Motion Picture Commission. Hearings on H. Res. 14805 and H. Res. 14895 to Establish a Federal Motion Picture Commission.* Washington, D.C., Govt. Print. Off., 1914. 234 p. (63d Cong., 3d sess.) **U 53**

The first congressional consideration of a federal Commission to control motion pictures.

———. *Proposed Federal Motion Picture Commission. Hearings . . . on H.R. 4094 and H. R. 6233, . . .* Washington, D.C., Govt. Print. Off., 1926. 467 p. (69th Cong., 1st sess.) **U 54**

———. *Report* [*on Resolutions to Establish a Federal Motion Picture Commission*]. Washington, D.C., Govt. Print. Off., 1914. 3 p.

(House Report 1411, 63d Cong., 3d sess.) **U 55**

The Committee recommended unanimously the creation of a federal board for movie censorship.

———. *Report to Accompany H.R. 15462, Submitted by Mr. D. M. Hughes* [*Re: Motion Picture Commission*]. Washington, D.C., Govt. Print. Off., 1916. 5 p. (64th Cong., 1st sess.) **U 56**

The majority of the Committee recommended the passage of the bill regulating motion pictures "for the protection of the public, and particularly the children, against vicious and immoral pictures." The measure, according to the report, "has the endorsement of leading producers of motion picture films and others engaged in the industry."

United States. Congress. House of Representatives. Education and Labor Committee. Subcommittee on Special Education. *Commission on Noxious Printed and Pictured Material. Hearings . . . on H.R. 11454, A Bill to Establish a Commission on Noxious Printed and Pictured Material.* Washington, D.C., Govt. Print. Off., 1960. 160 p. (86th Cong., 2d sess.) **U 57**

Statements by Francis R. Cawley, president of Magazine Publishers' Association; Monsignor Thomas J. Fitzgerald, NODL; Congressmen E. C. Gathings, James C. Oliver, Edward H. Rees; psychologists Eberhard and Phyllis Kronhausen; Senator Karl E. Mundt; James R. Norris, Jr., assistant attorney general of Maryland; Lawrence Speiser of the American Civil Liberties Union, and others.

United States. Congress. House of Representatives. Foreign Affairs Committee. *Expressing the Sense of the Congress Desiring Freedom of Speech and Freedom of Press in Countries Receiving Mutual Security Aid.* Washington, D.C., Govt. Print. Off., 1959. 4 p. (House Report 542, 86th Cong., 1st sess.) **U 58**

———. *World Freedom of News.* Washington, D.C., Govt. Print. Off., 1945. 37 p. (Committee Print, 79th Cong.) **U 59**

A collection of articles, resolutions and other data gathered by the Committee.

United States. Congress. House of Representatives. Government Operations Committee. *Availability of Information from Federal Departments and Agencies.* Washington, D.C., Govt. Print. Off., 1956–59. 17 pts. (84th Cong., 1st sess. through 86th Cong., 1st sess.) **U 60**

Hearings were held to investigate charges that executive agencies have denied or withheld public information from newspapers, radio, television, and other communication media, from qualified research workers, and from the Congress. Part 1 consists of a panel discussion with editors, including statements from Joseph Alsop, Jr., William L. Beale, Jr., Hugh Boyd, Harold L. Cross (counsel for the American Society of Newspaper Editors), Guy Easterly, Theodore F. Koop, Clark Mollenhoff, V. M. Newton, Jr., Wade H. Nichols, James S. Pope, James Reston, Richard W. Slocum, and J. R. Wiggins. Part 3 is a panel discussion with legal experts; parts 4 and 15 deal with scientific and technical information; part 12 is a panel discussion with government lawyers. Other parts deal with specific executive departments.

———. *Availability of Information from Federal Departments and Agencies (Air Force Refusal to the General Accounting Office).* Washington, D.C., Govt. Print. Off., 1959. 121 p. (House Report 234, 86th Cong., 1st sess.)   **U 61**

———. *Availability of Information from Federal Departments and Agencies (Department of Defense).* Washington, D.C., Govt. Print. Off., 1958. 295 p. (House Report 1884, 85th Cong., 2d sess.)   **U 62**

A report submitted by the special subcommittee on Government Information following 15 days of hearings and testimony from 72 witnesses, developing from charges in an earlier report (House Report 2947) that "information policies and practices of the Department are the most restrictive—and at the same time the most confused—of any major branch of the Federal Government." The report covers attitudes of officials, censorship practices of the several services, administrative secrecy, news leaks, security classification and declassification, and the providing of information to Congress. "Under the prevailing attitude in the Pentagon, [the report concludes] an employee must justify the release of even the most innocuous nonsecurity information. Unless this attitude is reversed . . . Congress will face the difficult task of framing suitable legislation to guarantee the public's right to know—a right so obviously fundamental to our form of government that it should require no legislative protection."

———. *Availability of Information from Federal Departments and Agencies. (The First Five Years and Progress of Study, August 1959–July 1960).* Washington, D.C., Govt. Print. Off., 1960. 222 p. (House Report 2084, 86th Cong., 2d sess.)   **U 63**

"The 5-year summary of the subcommittee's work indicates that a significant trend has, indeed, developed—that a sweeping claim of 'executive privilege' is advanced as justification, in spite of laws to the contrary, to deny Congress and the public any information which executive branch officials prefer to hide."

———. *Availability of Information from Federal Departments and Agencies (Navy Refusal to the General Accounting Office).*

Washington, D.C., Govt. Print. Off., 1960. 57 p. (House Report 1224, 86th Cong., 2d sess.)   **U 64**

———. *Availability of Information from Federal Departments and Agencies (Progress of Study, February 1957—July 1958).* Washington, D.C., Govt. Print. Off., 1958. 243 p. (House Report 2578, 85th Cong., 2d sess.)   **U 65**

This report covers three areas of special interest—a study of continued complaints that military officials are assuming police power at military accident sites in civilian areas outside their jurisdiction; a partial study of specific restrictions on information to Congress; and a study of the availability of information about federal loan programs.

———. *Availability of Information from Federal Departments and Agencies. (Progress of Study, July–December 1960).* Washington, D.C., Govt. Print. Off., 1961. 197 p. (House Report 818, 87th Cong., 1st sess.)   **U 66**

Included in the report is an analysis of the Executive Order establishing the system of restriction on military information and a case study of a dramatic resolution of an attempt to use the claim of executive privilege to withhold information from Congress. Of the 28 cases discussed in the report, definite improvement is reported in 11 instances.

———. *Availability of Information from Federal Departments and Agencies. (Progress of Study, January–August 1961).* Washington, D.C., Govt. Print. Off., 1961. 191 p. (House Report 1257, 87th Cong., 1st sess.)   **U 67**

This report covers the attempt to clear up past information problems as well as efforts to remove new information restrictions which arose during the first 8 months of the Kennedy Administration. Summaries of 34 information cases are presented.

———. *Availability of Information from Federal Departments and Agencies. (Progress of Study, Sept. 1961—Dec. 1962).* Washington, D.C., Govt. Print. Off., 1963. 223 p. (House Report 918, 88th Cong., 1st sess.)   **U 68**

"The effect of the Cuban crisis on government information policies was probably the most important, and certainly the most controversial, development in this area for the past several years. . . . The specific items described in this report generally are of two types. Most of them involve subcommittee investigation into complaints about specific incidents of information withholding. With some exceptions, the other developments resulted from positive congressional action, either in the form of an expression of congressional will through legislation or by active subcommittee

participation in the formulation of new information policies. Of the 40 cases included in this report, restrictions were removed or information policies were otherwise improved in . . . 34 instances."

———. *Availability of Information from Federal Departments and Agencies (Scientific Information and National Defense).* Washington, D.C., Govt. Print. Off., 1958. 94 p. (House Report 1619, 85th Cong., 2d sess.)   **U 69**

The report supports "the conclusion that excessive secrecy regulations—issued in the name of national security—have stifled the Nation's scientific progress."

———. *Availability of Information from Federal Departments and Agencies (Telephone Monitoring).* Washington, D.C., Govt. Print. Off., 1961. 39 p. (House Report 1215, 87th Cong., 1st sess.)   **U 70**

———. *Clarifying and Protecting the Right of the Public to Information. Report to Accompany S. 1160.* Washington, D.C., Govt. Print. Off., 1966. 14 p. (House Report 1497, 89th Cong., 1st sess.)   **U 71**

———. *Executive Branch Practices in Withholding Information from Congressional Committees. Hearing . . .* Washington, D.C., Govt. Print. Off., 1960. 48 p. (86th Cong., 2d sess.)   **U 72**

An investigation into the delay by the State Department in supplying information requested by Congress, which "can be for all practical purposes tantamount to denial of information requested."

———. *Executive Branch Practices in Withholding Information from Congressional Committees. Report.* Washington, D.C., Govt. Print. Off., 1960. 16 p. (House Report 2207, 86th Cong., 2d sess.)   **U 73**

———. *Federal Public Records Law. Hearings . . .* Washington, D.C., Govt. Print. Off., 1965. 528 p. (2 pts.) (89th Cong., 1st sess.)   **U 74**

Includes testimony, statements, and letters from members of the press, bar and press associations, American Civil Liberties Union, representative government agencies. Concerns bills to amend the law with respect to authority of federal officers and agencies to withhold information and limit availability of records.

———. *Federal Statutes on the Availability of Information.* Washington, D.C., Govt.

Print. Off., 1960. 303 p. (Committee Print, 86th Cong., 2d sess.) **U 75**
A compilation of federal statutes that control the gathering, keeping, and disseminating information by the government. The list is arranged in three major groupings: statutes on information to Congress, statutes on information for other public officials, and statutes affecting the availability of information to the public.

————. *Freedom of Information Legislation during the 85th Congress.* Washington, D.C., Govt. Print. Off., 1958. 24 p. (Committee Print, 85th Cong., 2d sess.) **U 76**
A summary of activities of the Moss Committee, appointed to investigate specific complaints of the withholding of timely and pertinent information by federal executive and independent agencies. This is a summary of the five reports adopted by the full committee.

————. *Government Information Plans and Policies. Hearings . . .* Washington, D.C., Govt. Print. Off., 1963. 5 pts. (88th Cong., 1st sess.) **U 77**
Part 1, News media panel discussion (19 March 1963), Department of State and Department of Defense (25 March 1963). Part 2, Office of Emergency Planning (5 June 1963). Part 3, Information Procedures in the Department of Defense (27–28 May 1963). Part 4, Vietnam News Coverage (24 May 1963). Part 5, National Aeronautics and Space Administration (23 May and 6 June 1963).

————. *Government News from Anonymous Sources.* Washington, D.C., Govt. Print. Off., 1964. 12 p. (Committee Print, 88th Cong., 2d sess.) **U 78**
"The study developed two basic conclusions: (1) that the anonymous news source can be useful in making more information available to the public, or (2) it can be a self-serving device to convey distorted information which the public seldom can evaluate."

————. *Investigation of Charges that Proposed Security Regulations under Executive Order 9835 Will Limit Free Speech and a Free Press. Hearing before a Subcommittee of the Committee on Expenditures in the Executive Departments.* Washington, D.C., Govt. Print. Off., 1948. 68 p. (80th Cong., 2d sess.) **U 79**

————. *Overseas Military Information Programs.* Washington, D.C., Govt. Print. Off., 1962. 144 p. (House Report 1549, 87th Cong., 2d sess.) **U 80**
The study found duplication of communi-

cations services in several areas and a lack of centralized administrative authority and responsibility which makes more difficult the task of eliminating possible information conflicts between the armed forces and official policies of the United States.

————. *The Right of Congress to Obtain Information from the Executive and from Other Agencies of the Federal Government. Study by the Staff of the Committee on Government Operations.* Washington, D.C., Govt. Print. Off., 1956. 26 p. (Committee Print, 84th Cong., 2d sess.) **U 81**
Consideration of the right of Congress to obtain information from federal agencies, department heads, and their subordinates, and the judicial determination of this right. The report concludes that "if Congress can grant control over public records and documents by statute it follows that it can also regulate the release of such information and, in fact, require the release of such information by the heads of the agencies upon terms and conditions prescribed by the Congress."

————. *Safeguarding Official Information in the Interests of the Defense of the United States (The Status of Executive Order 10501).* Washington, D.C., Govt. Print. Off., 1962. 48 p. (House Report 2456, 87th Cong., 2d sess.) **U 82**
"This current study is concerned with the procedures under which the Federal Government imposes necessary restrictions on the availability of sensitive defense information in the face of the democratic ideal that the public has a right and a need to know the facts of government. These considerations are embodied in Executive Order 10501 (18 F. R. 7049) and its amendments. . . . After a careful study of the use of the new order, the House Government Operations Committee concluded that it embodied a 'negative' approach by giving blanket authority to hundreds of agencies . . . to classify information as important to the Nation's security and to withhold it from the public."

————. *United States Information Problems in Vietnam.* Washington, D.C., Govt. Print. Off., 1963. 14 p. (House Report 797, 88th Cong., 1st sess.) **U 83**
"The restrictive U.S. press policy in Vietnam—drafted in the State Department's public relations office by an official with an admitted distrust of the people's right to know—unquestionably contributed to the lack of information about conditions in Vietnam which created an international crisis. Instead of hiding the facts from the American public, the State Department should have done everything possible to expose the true situation to full view."

United States. Congress. House of Representatives. Interstate and Foreign Commerce Committee. *Amending Section 315 of the Communications Act of 1934.*

Report of the Committee . . . Washington, D.C., Govt. Print. Off., 1959. 34 p. (House Report 802, 86th Cong.) **U 84**
Section 315 provides for equal broadcast time for political candidates.

————. *Broadcast Advertisements; Hearings . . . on H.R. 8316, 8381, 8729, 8896 8980, and 9042. November 6, 7, and 8, 1963.* Washington, D.C., Govt. Print. Off., 1963. 381 p. (88th Cong., 1st sess.) **U 85**
Bills to amend the Communications Act of 1934 to prohibit the FCC from making certain rules relating to the length or frequency of broadcast advertising.

————. *Broadcast Editorializing; Hearings . . . on Broadcast Editorializing Practices, July 15–Sept. 20, 1963.* Washington, D.C., Govt. Print. Off., 1964. 458 p. (88th Cong., 1st sess.) **U 86**
"The purpose of the hearing is to ascertain for the record the practices being pursued by radio and television broadcast stations with regard to editorializing, whether or not legislation is needed on the subject, and if so, the approach that should be followed. . . . The matter was brought into focus in the recent past in the actions of a Chairman of the Federal Communications Commission advocating editorializing by radio and television stations. Some station owners felt that this was a good policy and one that should be followed. Others, I am advised, felt that it was an infringement upon their freedom of action, that they and they alone should make the determination as to the editorial policies, and that their failure to editorialize should not be considered in the renewal of their license."—Chairman Walter Rogers. Testimony includes that of representatives of the radio and television networks and stations, the FCC, the Congress, and the American Civil Liberties Union. Includes text of FCC report on editorializing and the fairness doctrine adopted in 1949.

————. *Communications Act Amendments. Hearings . . . January 31–April 19, 1956.* Washington, D.C., Govt. Print. Off., 1956. 360 p. (84th Cong.) **U 87**
Testimony and documents relating to Section 315 of the Communications Act of 1934, the National Association of Broadcasters' station survey dealing with libel and slander, and the text of libel and slander laws of the various states.

————. *Equal-Time Amendments to Communications Act of 1934. Report.* Washington, D.C., Govt. Print. Off., 1959. 20 p. (House Report 1069, 86th Cong.) **U 88**

————. *Investigation of Radio and Television Programs. Hearings on H. Res. 278.*

Washington, D.C., Govt. Print. Off., 1952. 493 p. (82nd Cong., 2d sess.)

U 89

———. *Investigation of Radio and Television Programs. Report pursuant to H. Res. 278.* Washington, D.C., Govt. Print. Off., 1952. 15 p. (House Report 2509, 82nd Cong., 2d sess.)

U 90

The report on the extent to which radio and television programs contain immoral or otherwise offensive matter, or place improper emphasis upon crime, violence, and corruption. The committee believes that self-regulation by the industry is preferable to government-imposed regulation and that there is no good reason why controls should be imposed at this time. The report recommends that industry be given more time to solve its own problems but that Congress make continued studies of the issues.

———. *Motion-Picture Films (Compulsory Block Booking and Blind Selling). Hearing . . . on S. 280 . . .* Washington, D.C., Govt. Print. Off., 1940. 1139 p. (2 pts.) (76th Cong., 3d sess.)

U 91

———. *Motion-Picture Films. Hearing . . . on Bills to Prohibit and Prevent Trade Practices Known as Compulsory Block-booking and Blind Selling in Leasing of Motion Picture Films in Interstate and Foreign Commerce, March 9–26, 1936.* Washington, D.C., Govt. Print. Off., 1936. 526 p. (74th Cong., 2d sess.)

U 92

———. *Political Broadcasts—Equal Time. Hearings . . . June 29–July 1, 1959.* Washington, D.C., Govt. Print. Off., 1959. 277 p. (86th Cong., 1st sess.)

U 93

Hearings on an amendment to the Communications Act of 1934 to modify "equal time" provisions in political broadcasts.

———. *Political Broadcasts—Equal Time. Hearings . . . March 4–22, 1963.* Washington, D.C., Govt. Print. Off., 1963. 188 p. (88th Cong.)

U 94

———. *Prohibiting Certain Coercive Practices Affecting Radio Broadcasting.* Washington, D.C., Govt. Print. Off., 1946. 10 p., 2 p. (House Report 1508, 79th Cong., 2d sess.)

U 95

Relates to alleged coercive methods taken in the name of the American Federation of Musicians. The report recommends amending Title V of the Communications Act of 1934 to prohibit such practices. Congressman Vito Marcantonio, in a minority report, objects to the proposal as "anti-labor."

———. *Proposed Changes in the Communications Act of 1934. Hearings.* Washington, D.C., Govt. Print. Off., 1942. 3 vols. (77th Cong., 2d sess.)

U 96

Includes testimony of broadcasting officials and a memorandum of C.B.S. wartime standards for sponsored news programs.

———. *Regulation of Community Antenna Television. Hearings before the Subcommittee on Communications and Power . . . on H.R. 7715.* Washington, D.C., Govt. Print. Off., 1965. 534 p. (89th Cong., 1st sess.)

U 97

———. *Suspension of Equal Time Provisions of Communications Act for 1964 Presidential Campaign. Report . . . to Accompany H.J. Res. 247.* Washington, D.C., Govt. Print. Off., 1963. 7 p. (House Report 359, 88th Cong.)

U 98

United States. Congress. House of Representatives. Interstate and Foreign Commerce Committee. Subcommittee on Legislative Oversight. *Regulation of Broadcasting; Half a Century of Government Regulation of Broadcasting and the Need for Further Legislative Action.* Washington, D.C., Govt. Print. Off., 1958. 171 p. (Subcommittee print, 85th Cong., 2d sess., prepared by Robert S. McMahon; excerpted in *Journal of Broadcasting*, Winter, 1958–59)

U 99

United States. Congress. House of Representatives. Judiciary Committee. *Birth Control; Hearings . . . on H.R. 5978, Jan. 18, 19, 1934.* Washington, D.C., Govt. Print. Off., 1934. 245 p. (73d Cong., 2d sess.)

U 100

———. *Censorship between Territories and the United States. Report (to Accompany H.R. 7151).* Washington, D.C., Govt. Print. Off., 1952. 3 p. (House Report 2397)

U 101

———. *Dr. Thomas Cooper.* Washington, D.C., 1850. 2 p. (House Report 11, 31st Cong., 1st sess.)

U 102

A recommendation for refunding the fine imposed upon Dr. Cooper in 1800 under the Sedition Act. Similar recommendations had been made in almost every Congress since 1825.

———. *Proposed Federal Group Libel Legislation.* Washington, D.C., Govt. Print.

Off., 1963. 23 p. (Staff report prepared by Benjamin L. Zelenko and Theodore Sky, 88th Cong., 1st sess.)

U 103

Deals with the constitutionality and desirability of curbing the dissemination through the mails of materials that disparage various groups on grounds of racial, religious, or ethnic characteristics.

———. *Sedition. Hearings on S. 3317, H.R. 10650 and 12041, February 4 and 6, 1920.* Washington, D.C., Govt. Print. Off., 1920. 288 p. (66th Cong., 2d sess.)

U 104

———. *Sedition, Syndicalism, Sabotage, and Anarchy. Hearings on H.R. 10210, 10235, 10379, 10614, 10616, 10650, and 11089* Washington, D.C., Govt. Print. Off., 1919. 64 p. (66th Cong., 2d sess.)

U 105

———. [*Sedition, Syndicalism, Sabotage and Anarchy*]. *Report to Accompany S. 3317.* Washington, D.C., Govt. Print. Off., 1920. 9 p. (House Report 542, 66th Cong., 2d sess.)

U 106

While seeking to give the Government adequate power to "crush out this spirit of force, violence, and destruction [against anarchy and sedition] . . . the bill is confined to the restraint and punishment of the use of force and violence and leaves 'free speech' and a 'free press' untrammeled and the right to advocate or teach any reform or change by peaceful and lawful methods without limitation." The two bills, as amended, are recommended for passage.

———. *To Punish Offenses Against the Existence of the Government of the United States. Report to Accompany H.R. 11430.* Washington, D.C., Govt. Print. Off., 1920. 7 p. (House Report 536, 66th Cong., 2d sess.)

U 107

———. *Western Newspaper Union.* [*Hearings*] *June 11, 1912.* Washington, D.C., Govt. Print. Off., 1912. 293 p. (62d Cong., 2d sess.)

U 108

Relates to the controversy between the Western Newspaper Union and the American Press Association.

United States. Congress. House of Representatives. Merchant Marine and Fisheries Committee. *Government Control of Radio Communication. Hearings before the Committee on H.R. 13159 . . . December 12, 13, 17, and 19.* Washington, D.C., Govt.

Print. Off., 1919. 476p. (65th Cong., 3d sess.) **U 109**

United States. Congress. House of Representatives. Post Office and Civil Service Committee. *Circulation of Obscene and Pornographic Material. Hearing before the Subcommittee on Postal Operations.* Washington, D.C., Govt. Print. Off., 1960. 60p. (86th Cong., 2d sess.) **U 110**
Appendix includes the report from the Select Committee on Obscene Publications to the British House of Commons, 1958.

———. *Detention of Mail for Temporary Periods. Hearing . . . on H.R. 4383 . . .* Washington, D.C., Govt. Print. Off., 1958. 19p. (85th Cong., 2d sess.) **U 111**
Testimony of Congressman John Dowdy and Herbert B. Warburton, general counsel of the Post Office Department, relating to a bill to close a loophole in the laws preventing the mailing of obscene matter.

———. *Detention of Mail for Temporary Periods. Hearings . . . on H.R. 7379 and similar bills . . .* Washington, D.C., Govt. Print. Off., 1959. 101p. (86th Cong., 1st sess.) **U 112**
Hearings on legislation recommended by the Post Office Department to assist in carrying out the existing law which provides for the exclusion of obscene matter from the mails. Includes testimony from representatives of the American Civil Liberties Union, the American Book Publishers Council, the Post Office Department, various church groups, and members of the Congress.

———. *Exclusion of Communist Political Propaganda from the U.S. Mails. Hearings . . .* Washington, D.C., Govt. Print. Off., 1963. 64p. (88th Cong., 1st sess.) **U 113**
Statements by Tyler Abell of the Post Office Department and Irving Fishman of the U.S. Customs.

———. *Improving Enforcement of Laws Prohibiting Use of Mails to Defraud and Send Obscene Literature. Hearings on H.R. 560.* Washington, D.C., Govt. Print. Off., 1954. 35p. (83d Cong., 2d sess.) **U 114**

———. *Obscene Matter Sent Through the Mails. Hearings before the Subcommittee on Postal Operations . . .* Washington, D.C., Govt. Print. Off., 1959. 3 pts. (86th Cong., 1st sess.) **U 115**

Testimony before the Granahan Committee from more than 100 persons, including representatives from churches, welfare, civic, patriotic, and women's organizations, customs and postal officials, psychiatrists, judges, law enforcement officers, and others concerned with the problem of obscenity and pornography.

———. *Obscene Matter Sent Through the Mails, Hearings, Nov. 13–Dec. 6, 1961.* Washington, D.C., Govt. Print. Off., 1962. 355p. (87th Cong., 2d sess.) **U 116**
Includes testimony from representatives of the Boston Police Department, Sunshine Publishing Co., Knights of Columbus, Philadelphia Citizens Committee against Obscenity, Citizens for Decent Literature, postal and customs inspectors, juvenile court judges, and district attorneys.

———. *Obscene Matter Sent Through the Mails. Report to the Committee . . .* Washington, D.C., Govt. Print. Off., 1959. 61p. (Committee Print, 86th Cong., 1st sess.) **U 117**

A report of the findings of the Subcommittee on Postal Operations (Granahan Committee), together with a suggested program for community action in the crusade against obscenity. Recommendations of the Committee include suggestions that "State governments consider adopting legislation to provide more effective and more uniform antiobscenity statutes" and that "local governments consider adopting more effective ordinances."

———. *Protecting Postal Patrons from Obscene and Obnoxious Mail and Communist Propaganda. Hearings . . . on H.R. 142, H.R. 319 and Similar Bills, June 25–July 24, 1963.* Washington, D.C., Govt. Print. Off., 1964. 207p. (88th Cong., 2d sess.) **U 118**

———. *Protecting Postal Patrons from Obscene Mail. Hearings on H.R. 980 and Related Bills.* Washington, D.C., Govt. Print. Off., 1965. 34p. (89th Cong., 1st sess.) **U 119**
Bills provide for the return of obscene mail matter. Included are statements from the Citizens for Decent Literature, the American Civil Liberties Union, the American Library Association, the Direct Mail Advertising Association (text of their standards of business practices), the American Book Publishers Council, the Magazine Publishers' Association, and the Los Angeles County Commission Against Indecent Literature.

———. *Protection of Postal Patrons from Morally Offensive Mail Matter.* Washington, D.C., Govt. Print. Off., 1964. 15p. (House Report 1506, 88th Cong., 2d sess.) **U 120**

Recommends the passage of H.R. 319.

———. *Return of Obscene Mail. Report to the Committee.* Washington, D.C., Govt. Print. Off., 1965. 13p. (House Report 219, 89th Cong., 1st sess.) **U 121**
Concerns H.R. 980. "The purpose of this legislation is to give every person, particularly a parent, served by the U.S. mail an effective and urgently needed means to prevent the forced entry into his home, or into the hands of his children, of mail matter which in his opinion is obscene, lewd, lascivious, indecent, filthy, or vile." The Committee recommends passage.

———. *Self-Policing of the Movie and Publishing Industry. Hearing before the Subcommittee on Postal Operations . . .* Washington, D.C., Govt. Print. Off., 1960. 178p. (86th Cong., 2d sess.) **U 122**
Statements by Richard Brandt, Independent Film Importers & Distributors of America; John G. Broumas, Theater Owners of America; Congressman Ken Hechler; Eric Johnston, Mrs. Margaret G. Twyman, Gordon S. White, and Geoffrey Shurlock, Motion Picture Association of America; Robert E. Kenyon, Jr., Magazine Publishers' Association; Dan Lacy, American Book Publishers Council; and Abram F. Myers, Allied States Association of Motion Picture Exhibitors.

United States. Congress. House of Representatives. Post Office and Public Roads Committee. *Exclusion of Certain Publications from the Mails. Hearings on H.R. 20644 and 21183.* Washington, D.C., Govt. Print. Off., 1915. 59p. (63d Cong., 3d sess.) **U 123**
Proposal to make postal censorship include matter considered libelous.

———. *Offense Against Postal Service. Hearings . . . H.R. 5370, providing penalty for anyone who shall knowingly cause obscene matter to be delivered by mail or to be delivered at place to which it is directed to be delivered . . .* Washington, D.C., Govt. Print. Off., 1935. 113p. (74th Cong., 1st sess.) **U 124**

———. *Restricting the Size of Newspapers. Hearings . . . on H.R. 10960. December 15, 1919.* Washington, D.C., Govt. Print. Off., 137p. (66th Cong., 2d sess.) **U 125**

United States. Congress. House of Representatives. Rules Committee. *Rule Making in Order Consideration of S. 3317, Hearings on H. Res. 438* [*for consideration of S. 3317, to prohibit and punish certain seditious acts against the Government of the United States, and to Prohibit use of mails for purpose of promoting such acts*]. Washington, D.C., Govt. Print. Off., 1920. 203p. (66th Cong., 2d sess.) **U 126**

Includes article by Alfred Bettman and Swinburne Hale, Do We Need More Sedition Laws?

United States. Congress. House of Representatives. Select Committee on Current Pornographic Materials. *Investigation of Literature Allegedly Containing Objectionable Material. Hearings on S. Res. 596 and 597.* Washington, D.C., Govt. Print. Off., 1953. 388 p. (82d Cong., 2d sess.)

U 127

The investigation centered largely on paperbacks, "cheesecake" magazines, and "comics." The Committee heard from publishers, distributors, churchmen, police officers, and postal officials. Statements were made by the following associations: National Council of Catholic Men, American Book Publishers Council, American Civil Liberties Union, Mystery Writers of America, Women's Christian Temperance Union, National Association of Photographic Manufacturers, and The Society of Magazine Writers. Annual reports of the censor detail of the Detroit Police Department (1950, 1951, and 1952) are included.

———. *Report of the Select Committee on Current Pornographic Materials.* Washington, D.C., Govt. Print. Off., 1952. 137 p. (House Report 2510, 82d Cong., 2d sess.)

U 128

The "Gathings Committee" was directed to conduct an investigation "(1) to determine the extent to which current literature—books, magazines, and comic books—containing immoral, obscene, or otherwise offensive matter, or placing improper emphasis on crime, violence, and corruption, are being made available to the people of the United States through the United States mails and otherwise; and (2) to determine the adequacy of existing law to prevent the publication and distribution of books containing immoral, offensive, and other undesirable matter." After hearing numerous witnesses the Committee made two recommendations: enactment of legislation to prohibit interstate shipment of obscene matter by private carriers (already prohibited by public carriers); and enactment of legislation authorizing the Postmaster General to impound mail addressed to distributors of obscene matter and to exempt the Post Office Department from the provisions of the Administrative Procedures Act. A minority report, while agreeing with the serious extent of pornographic literature, objects to the investigation that has "embarked upon an ambitious expedition to determine the intrinsic and extrinsic nature of contemporary literature." The minority report questions the advisability of permitting the Postmaster General to impound mail and exempting the Department from the Administrative Procedures Act. Adequate federal and state legislation already exists for dealing with obscenity. The Appendix contains two articles: This Literature We Distribute by Samuel Black, vice-president, Atlantic Coast Independent Distributors Association, and Filth on the Newsstands by Margaret Culkin Banning, novelist.

United States. Congress. House of Representatives. Select Committee to Investigate the Federal Communications Commission. *Investigation of Port Huron Decision and Scott Decision.* Washington, D.C., Govt. Print. Off., 1948. 5 p. (House Report 2461, 80th Cong., 2d sess.) **U 129**

The *Port Huron* decision of FCC held in effect that radio stations have no right to censor libelous or slanderous statements in political broadcasting; the Scott decision was concerned with the rights of atheists to equal time on the air to reply to religious broadcasts. The Select Committee objects to the decisions. The *Port Huron* decision left broadcasters in the unenviable position between the FCC decision and state libel laws. With respect to the Scott decision the Committee asserted that "the broadcast of a regular religious worship . . . does not present a public controversy which in the public interest requires that time be granted to those who would destroy the church in America."

United States. Congress. House of Representatives. Special Committee . . . Concerning Right of Victor L. Berger to Be Sworn in as Member of the 66th Congress. *Hearings.* Washington, D.C., Govt. Print. Off., 1919. 2 vols. (66th Cong., 1st sess.) **U 130**

Berger, a founder of the Socialist Party in the United States, editor of the *Milwaukee Leader*, and a member of Congress (1911–13), actively opposed American participation in World War I. In September 1917 the *Leader* was deprived of its second-class mailing privilege by the Postmaster General and the U.S. Supreme Court ultimately upheld the decision (*U.S. ex. rel. Milwaukee Social Democrat Publishing Co. v. Burleson*, 258 Fed. 282, 1919). In February 1918, Berger was indicted for conspiracy under the wartime Espionage Act for 5 editorials in the *Leader*. He was convicted and sentenced to 20 years' imprisonment. In January 1921 the Supreme Court reversed the conviction because of the prejudicial conduct of Judge Landis. Volume 2 of the hearings, conducted when Berger was seeking a seat in the House of Representatives, contains the full record of the trial.

United States. Congress. House of Representatives. Un-American Activities Committee. *Cumulative Index to Publications of the Committee on Un-American Activities, 1938–1954.* Washington, D.C., Govt. Print. Off., 1962. 1344 p. (87th Cong.) **U 131**

The index lists individuals, organizations, and publications (including motion pictures, plays, radio and television programs, and songs) that have been mentioned in testimony or have submitted a report to the Committee. The Un-American Activities Committee was organized in 1938, under the chairmanship of Martin Dies, for the purpose of conducting an investigation of "the extent, character, and objects of un-American propaganda

activities in the United States; the diffusion within the United States of subversive and un-American propaganda that is instigated from foreign countries or of domestic origin and attacks the principle of the form of government as guaranteed by our Constitution; and, all other questions in relation thereto that would aid Congress in any necessary remedial legislation." (House Resolution 282, 75th Cong., 3d sess.) The index covers more than 38,00 pages of testimony.

United States. Congress. House of Representatives. Ways and Means Committee. *Birth Control. Hearings . . . on H.R. 11082, May 19 and 20, 1932.* Washington, D.C., Govt. Print. Off., 1932. 149 p. (72d Cong., 1st sess.) **U 132**

United States. Congress. Senate. *Alien and Sedition Laws; Debates in the House of Delegates of Virginia in December, 1798, on Resolutions before the House on the Acts of Congress Called the Alien and Sedition Acts.* Washington, D.C., Govt. Print. Off., 1912. 187 p. (Senate Document 873, 62d Cong., 2d sess.) **U 133**

"To keep alive the memory of the doctrines which actuated the Republicans of those days, as well as to extend the reputation of the able speakers who appeared on that occasion, the present edition of the debate has been committed to press." This constitutes a reissue of the verbatim record of debates on the Virginia Resolutions, drafted by James Madison, opposing the passage of the Alien and Sedition Acts by Congress.

———. "Breach of Privilege." In *Annals of the Congress of the United States.* (2 December 1799 to 3 March 1801). Washington, D.C., Gales & Seaton, 1851, pp. 67–97, 114–25, 183–84. (6th Cong.) **U 134**

Proceedings in Congress relating to the case of William Duane, Republican editor of the *Aurora*, charged with a "breach of privilege" for publishing the text of a bill before Congress. The right of Congress to protect its deliberations versus the liberty of the press was the issue at stake.

United States. Congress. Senate. Armed Services Committee. *Defense Security. McNamara on S. Res. 191. Hearings . . .* Washington, D.C., Govt. Print. Off., 1961. 246 p. (87th Cong., 1st sess.) **U 135**

Resolution to authorize the Committee on Armed Services to study the use of military personnel and facilities to arouse the public to the meaning of the cold war, 6–7 September 1961.

United States. Congress. Senate. Armed Services Committee. Special Preparedness

Subcommittee. *Military Cold War Education and Speech Review Policies. Hearings . . .* Washington, D.C., Govt. Print. Off., 1962. 8 pts. (87th Cong., 2d sess.) **U 136**
Hearings held pursuant to a Committee resolution "to study and appraise the use of military personnel and facilities to arouse the public to the menace of the cold war and to inform and educate armed services personnel on the nature and menace of the cold war." Much of the testimony revolved around policies for clearing speeches to be delivered by military personnel. A Department of Defense memorandum on clearance appears in part 1, pp. 294–97. Part 8 is an index to the hearings.

———. *Military Cold War Education and Speech Review Policy. Report . . .* Washington, D.C., Govt. Print. Off., 1962. 203 p. (87th Cong., 2d sess.) **U 137**

United States. Congress. Senate. Commerce Committee. *Equal Time Amendment to Communications Act of 1934. Report . . .* Washington, D.C., Govt. Print. Off., 1959. 20 p. (Senate Report 562, 86th Cong.) **U 138**

———. *Equal Time. Hearings . . . June 26–28, 1963.* Washington, D.C., Govt. Print. Off., 1963. 266 p. (88th Cong., 1st sess.) **U 139**

———. *Freedom of Communications. Final Report of the Committee on Commerce . . . prepared by its Subcommittee of the Subcommittee on Communications Pursuant to S. Res. 305, 86th Congress.* Washington, D.C., Govt. Print. Off., 1961–62. (Senate Report 994, part 6, 87th Cong., 1st sess.) **U 140**
In 1959 a subcommittee on Freedom of Communications was appointed under the chairmanship of Senator Yarborough, to receive information and complaints concerning the treatment of news by media operating under government license, in order to insure freedom, fairness, and impartiality in news presentations. In 1960 the subcommittee was authorized to examine the dissemination of political opinions, news, and advertising and to accept complaints during the presidential campaign of that year. The subcommittee recommendations included: (1) The adoption by the FCC of the report on editorializing. Licensees should editorialize; strong convictions should be encouraged, but with fair treatment to news of the other side. (2) The adoption of ground rules for editorializing in behalf of or against a candidate. (3) Candidates should not be required to file scripts of speeches in advance. (4) A study in depth in the use of broadcasting for discussion of controversial issues is sug-

gested. (5) "Censorship by the licensee by refusal to sell time for the presentation of a news commentary program by a commentator who may espouse a viewpoint contrary to that held by the licensee, or refusal to sell time for a speech or discussion program to be made by a public figure who, in the licensee's opinion may be 'controversial,' may be a denial to the public of its right to hear those contrary viewpoints which are so necessary for the formation of intelligent opinion and sound judgment." (6) The FCC should reform its procedures for handling "equal time" and "editorial fairness" complaints. Part 1 constitutes campaign speeches of John F. Kennedy; part 2, speeches of Richard M. Nixon; part 3, Kennedy-Nixon debates; part 4, network newscasts; and part 5, hearings before the subcommittee.

———. *Political Broadcasting. Hearings . . . July 10–12, 1962.* Washington, D.C., Govt. Print. Off., 1962. 236 p. (87th Cong., 2d sess.) **U 141**
Hearings on an amendment to the equal time provision (Section 315) of the Communications Act of 1934.

———. *Suspension of Equal Time Provisions of the Communications Act for 1964 Presidential Campaign. Report. . . .* Washington, D.C., Govt. Print. Off., 1963. 13 p. (Senate Report 501, 88th Cong.) **U 142**

United States. Congress. Senate. Foreign Relations Committee. *The United States Information Service in Europe. Report . . .* Washington, D.C., Govt. Print. Off., 1948. 2 pts. (Senate Report 855, 80th Cong., 2d sess.) **U 143**
The first part of the report states the role of the U.S. Information Service and recommends a vigorous program to "tell the truth about communism just as directly as we seek to tell the truth about ourselves . . . that we shall gain confidence and respect and thereby help to spread the area of freedom and extend hope to the world for the solution of its problems through truly democratic and peaceful means." The second part discusses in detail the propaganda climate of various European countries.

United States. Congress. Senate. Government Operations Committee. Permanent Subcommittee on Investigations. *State Department Information Program—Information Centers. Hearing . . . Pursuant to S. Res. 40.* Washington, D.C., Govt. Print. Off., 1953. 9 pts. (83d Cong., 1st sess.) **U 144**
An investigation of charges that U.S. Information Libraries abroad contain Communist books or books written by Communists. Testimony by authors, publishers, editors, and government officials.

United States. Congress. Senate. Inter-

state and Foreign Commerce Committee. *Condemning Communist, Fascist, or Nazi Film Exhibition in the United States . . . Report to accompany S. Res. 321.* Washington, D.C., Govt. Print. Off., 1950. 3 p. (Senate Report 2365, 81st Cong., 2d sess.) **U 145**
Expression of disapproval of exhibition in the United States of motion pictures produced or directed by Fascists, Nazis, or Communists. No recommendation for censorship.

———. *The Network Monopoly. Report Prepared for Use of the Committee . . . by Senator John W. Bricker.* Washington, D.C., Govt. Print. Off., 1956. 27 p. (Committee Print, 84th Cong., 2d sess.) **U 146**
"The information contained herein outlining the economic grip on the TV industry held by two major networks and a selected group of large affiliate TV stations is as foreboding as it is graphic."

———. *Political Broadcasting. Hearings . . . June 18–25, 1959.* Washington, D.C., Govt. Print. Off., 1959. 324 p. (86th Cong., 1st sess.) **U 147**
Hearings on an amendment to the equal time provision (Section 315) of the Communications Act of 1934.

———. *Review of Section 315 of the Communications Act (1960 Temporary Suspension of Equal Time Provision). Hearings . . . January 31–February 1, 1961.* Washington, D.C., Govt. Print. Off., 1961. 117 p. (87th Cong.) **U 148**

———. *Television Inquiry. Hearings before the Committee . . . pursuant to Senate Resolutions 13 and 163 . . .* Washington, D.C., Govt. Print. Off., 1956. 8 pts. (84th Cong., 2d sess.) **U 149**
Parts 1 and 2, UHF-VHF allocation problem; part 3, subscription TV; part 4, network practices; part 6, FCC regulation of networks; part 7, TV rating services, and part 8, TV allocation problems. In part 3, proponents of toll-TV argue it will increase the diversity of programs; opponents see it as a means of transferring cost of television from advertisers to the public. AFL-CIO believes it will "curtail greatly free use of a medium, which has become part of the American home." The American Civil Liberties Union believes that, despite imperfections, the pay-TV system should have a trial, if certain safeguards are provided.

———. *The Television Inquiry. Television Network Practices. Staff Report.* Washington, D.C., Govt. Print. Off., 1957. 102 p. (Committee Print, no. 2, 85th Cong., 1st sess.) **U 150**
This staff report deals primarily with network practices that have been challenged or

criticized in hearings before the Committee. Includes examination of charges of restrictive practices, failure to comply with public service programming responsibilities, and the proposal that networks be subjected to direct regulation.

————. *To Amend Communications Act of 1934. Hearings . . . June 17–24, 1947.* Washington, D.C., Govt. Print. Off., 1947. 671 p. (80th Cong., 1st sess.) **U 151**
Discusses radio freedom and editorializing.

United States. Congress. Senate. Interstate Commerce Committee. *Anti-Block-Booking and Blind Selling in Leasing of Motion-Picture Films. Hearings before Subcommittee . . . on S. 280 . . . April 3–17, 1939.* Washington, D.C., Govt. Print. Off., 1939. 651 p. **U 152**

————. *Compulsory Block-booking and Blind Selling in Motion-Picture Industry. Hearings . . . on S. 3012 to Prohibit and to Prevent Trade Practices Known as Compulsory Block-Booking and Blind Selling on Leasing of Motion-Picture Films in Interstate and Foreign Commerce, Feb. 27 and 28, 1936.* Washington, D.C., Govt. Print. Off., 1938. 219 p. (74th Cong., 2d sess.) **U 153**

————. *Hearings on S. 6, for Regulation of Transmission of Intelligence by Wire or Wireless.* Washington, D.C., Govt. Print. Off., 1930. 2 vols. (71st Cong., 2d sess.) **U 154**
Includes testimony of Oswald F. Schuette, Joseph Pierson, and Kenneth R. Cox.

————. *Propaganda in Motion Pictures, Hearings . . . on S. Res. 152, Authorizing Investigation of War Propaganda. Disseminated by Motion-Picture Industry and of any Monopoly in Production, Distribution, or Exhibition of Motion Pictures, Sept. 9–26, 1941.* Washington, D.C., Govt. Print. Off., 1942. 449 p. (77th Cong., 1st sess.) **U 155**

————. *Report to Accompany S. 3012.* Washington, D.C., Govt. Print. Off., 1936. 11 p. (Senate Report 2378, 74th Cong., 2d sess.) **U 156**
S. 3012 relates to the prohibition of block-booking of films and other restrictive practices.

————. *To Prohibit and to Prevent Trade Practices Known as Compulsory Block-Booking and Blind Selling in Leasing of Motion-Picture Films in Interstate and Foreign*

Commerce. *Report to Accompany S. 153.* Washington, D.C., Govt. Print. Off., 1938. 11 p. (Senate Report 1377, 75th Cong., 3d sess.) **U 157**
The primary purpose of the bill is to "establish community freedom in the selection of motion-picture films. A secondary purpose is to relieve the independent motion-picture theater operator of a burdensome and monopolistic trade practice."

————. *To Prohibit and to Prevent Trade Practices Known as Compulsory Block-Booking and Blind Selling of Motion-Picture Films in Interstate and Foreign Commerce; Report [and Minority Views] to Accompany S. 280.* Washington, D.C., Govt. Print. Off., 1939. 2 pts. (Senate Report 532, 76th Cong., 3d sess.) **U 158**
"The primary purpose of the bill is to establish community freedom in the selection of motion picture films." Similar bills were introduced in the 70th, 72d, 74th, and 75th Congresses and hearings held in the 70th, 74th and 76th. The majority favored the bill outlawing block-booking and were backed in this stand by the National Motion Picture Research Council. The minority opposed the bill and cited widespread industry opposition.

United States. Congress. Senate. Judiciary Committee. *Birth Control, Hearings . . . on S. 4582 . . .* Washington, D.C., Govt. Print. Off., 1931. 84 p. (71st Cong., 3d sess.) **U 159**
To amend the tariff act and the criminal code to permit dissemination of birth control information and objects.

————. *Birth Control Hearings . . . on S. 4436 . . . [to allow, under certain conditions, use of mails to disseminate information on contraception . . .] May 12–20, 1932.* Washington, D.C., Govt. Print. Off., 1932. 151 p. (72d Cong., 1st sess.) **U 160**

————. *Birth Control, Hearings . . . on S. 1842 to Amend sec. 211, 245, and 312 of Criminal Code . . .* Washington, D.C., Govt. Print. Off., 1934. 175 p. (73d Cong., 2d sess.) **U 161**

————. *Censorship. Hearing before the Committee on H.R. 7151, An Act to Amend the First War Powers Act, 1941, by Extending the Authority to Censor Communications between the Continental United States and any Territory or Possession of the United States, or between any Territory or Possession and any Other Territory or Possession. December 14, 1942.* Washington, D.C., Govt. Print.

Off., 1943. 32 p. (77th Cong., 2d sess.) **U 162**

————. *Clarifying and Protecting Right of Public to Information and for Other Purposes.* Washington, D.C., Govt. Print. Off., 1964. 17 p. (Senate Report 1219, 88th Cong., 2d sess.) **U 163**
Recommends that Senate Bill 1666 with amendments pass.

————. *Comic Books and Juvenile Delinquency. Interim Report . . . Pursuant to S. Res. 89 and S. Res. 190 . . .* Washington, D.C., Govt. Print. Off., 1955. 50 p. (Senate Report 62, 84th Cong., 1st sess.) **U 164**
An investigation to determine whether certain publications dealing with "crime and horror" contribute to juvenile delinquency. Includes a brief history of the so-called "comic book," a case history of crime and horror comic books, and testimony on the relation of the reading of the crime comics to juvenile delinquency. The study explored self-regulation within the industry and the responsibility of distributors and publishers. Appendix includes Code of the National Cartoonists Society, Code of the Association of Comic Magazine Publishers (1948), Code of the Comic Magazine Association of America (1954), and a list of comic book publishers and comic book titles, spring 1954.

————. *Cummins-Vaile Bill, Joint Hearings before Subcommittees of Committees on Judiciary on H.R. 6542 and S. 2290, April 8 and May 9, 1924.* Washington, D.C., Govt. Print. Off., 1924. 79 p. (68th Cong., 1st sess.) **U 165**
Relates to a birth control bill sponsored by the Voluntary Parenthood League.

————. *Free Press and Fair Trial. Hearings before the Subcommittee on Constitutional Rights and the Subcommittee on Improvements in Judicial Machinery.* Washington, D.C., Govt. Print. Off., 1966. 762 p. (2 pts.) (89th Cong., 1st sess.) **U 166**
The relation between the constitutional right of free press and the constitutional guarantees of an impartial trial.

————. *Freedom of Information. Hearings before the Subcommittee on Administrative Practice and Procedure . . . on S. 1666 and S. 1663 (in part), Oct. 28–31, 1963.* Washington, D.C., Govt. Print. Off., 1963. 322 p. (88th Cong., 1st sess.) **U 167**

————. *Repealing Certain Provisions of Espionage Act. Report to Accompany S. 1058.*

Washington, D.C., Govt. Print. Off., 1932. 11 p. (72d Cong., 1st sess.) **U 168**

The report calls for the repeal of wartime acts that "invest the post office authorities with the power to determine whether an article or articles in a newspaper does or does not offend against the statute, a question often so delicate that learned judges of the Supreme Court have differed in conclusion." The act to be repealed "has been so administered as to make it to all intents and purposes a censorship law." A similar bill for repeal (Senate Report 83) was introduced in the 71st Cong., 2d sess.

———. *Transportation of Obscene Matters (Phonograph Records) . . . Report to Accompany S. 2811.* Washington, D.C., Govt. Print. Off., 1950. 6 p. (Senate Report 1305, 81st Cong., 2d sess.) **U 169**

Recommendation for extending the federal obscenity law specifically to include phonograph records. Includes text of U.S. Supreme Court decision in the Alpers case.

United States. Congress. Senate. Judiciary Committee. Subcommittee on Constitutional Rights. *Freedom of Information and Secrecy in Government. Hearing . . . on S. 186 and the extent to which constitutional rights are being infringed by undue secrecy in government.* Washington, D.C., Govt. Print. Off., 1959. 64 p. (86th Cong., 1st sess.) **U 170**

Includes testimony of Arthur V. Burrowes, John W. Colt, William H. Fitzpatrick, James S. Pope, Eugene S. Pulliam (editors), Earl English, dean of the University of Missouri School of Journalism, and Edwin M. Williams, director, Freedom of Information Center, University of Missouri.

———. *The Power of the President to Withhold Information from the Congress. Memorandum of the Attorney General.* Washington, D.C., Govt. Print. Off., 1958. 2 pts. (Committee Print, 85th Cong., 2d sess.) **U 171**

The views of the Attorney General on the power of the President to withhold information from the Congress.

———. *Withholding of Information from the Congress. A Survey* . . . Washington, D.C., Govt. Print. Off., 1961. 99 p. (86th Cong., 2d sess.) **U 172**

A collection of letters from senators expressing views on the power of the President to withhold information from Congress. These letters bring up-to-date a similar survey made by the subcommittee in 1956.

United States. Congress. Senate. Judiciary Committee. Subcommittee to Investigate Juvenile Delinquency. *Juvenile Delinquency (Comic Books) . . . Hearings . . . pursuant to S. 190 . . .* Washington, D.C., Govt. Print. Off., 1954. 310 p. (83d Cong., 2d sess.) **U 173**

Testimony and statements from psychiatrists, publishers, newsdealers, cartoonists, and persons studying juvenile delinquency, given before the Kefauver subcommittee. A survey of literature dealing with the issue of crime movies, crime comic books, and crime radio programs as a cause of crime, prepared by the Library of Congress, is given on pp. 12–23. Also included in the "exhibits" are reports of the New York legislative committee to study the publication of comics, an evaluation of comic books made by a Cincinnati committee, the Code of the Comics Magazine Association of America, the Code of the National Cartoonists Society, and reprints of a number of articles dealing with the comics and juvenile delinquency.

———. *Juvenile Delinquency. Hearings . . . pursuant to S. Res. 274 . . . Part 16. Effects on Young People of Violence and Crime Portrayed on Television.* Washington, D.C., Govt. Print. Off., 1965, pp. 3729–3860. (89th Cong., 2d sess.) **U 174**

———. *Juvenile Delinquency (Motion Pictures). Hearings . . . pursuant to S. Res. 62 . . .* Washington, D.C., Govt. Print. Off., 1955. 242 p. (84th Cong., 1st sess.) **U 175**

Includes statements from representatives of the film industry, editors, ministers, dealing pro and con with effect of the movies on delinquency. The Advertising Code for Motion Pictures is given on pages 169–72.

———. *Juvenile Delinquency (Obscene and Pornographic Materials). Hearings . . . pursuant to S. Res. 62 . . .* Washington, D.C., Govt. Print. Off., 1955. 531 p. (84th Cong., 1st sess.) **U 176**

Includes testimony from police officials, post-office and customs officials, and persons charged with selling pornography. Exhibits include a summary of state obscenity laws, advertisements, and reports of police investigation. Part 2 relates to hearings conducted in Providence, R.I.

———. *Juvenile Delinquency (Television Programs). Hearings . . . pursuant to S. Res. 62 . . .* Washington, D.C., Govt. Print. Off., 1955. 141 p. (84th Cong., 2d sess.) **U 177**

Includes statements by psychiatrists, educators, sociologists, and representatives from the television industry and the FCC commenting on the causal relationship between viewing crime and violence on TV and juvenile delinquency.

———. *Motion Pictures and Juvenile Delinquency. Report of the Committee . . . pursuant to S. Res. 173 . . .* Washington, D.C., Govt. Print. Off., 1956. 122 p. (Senate Report 2055, 84th Cong., 2d sess.) **U 178**

Factors underlying the present trend toward criminal violence in American films; relationship between brutality and violence in motion picture advertising; working of the Motion Picture Production Code Administration; conclusions and recommendations. The appendix includes the text of the television code and the standards of practice of the National Association of Radio and Television Broadcasters and the code of the Comics Magazine Association of America; a tabulation by class of films reviewed by the Code Administration; lists of public previewing groups and motion picture councils (by state and city); and a list of state and city censor boards.

———. *Obscene and Pornographic Literature and Juvenile Delinquency. Interim Report . . . Pursuant to S. Res. 62 and S. Res. 173 . . .* Washington, D.C., Govt. Print. Off., 1956. 71 p. (Senate Report 2381, 84th Cong., 2d sess.) **U 179**

Includes testimony of psychiatrists, ministers, post office and customs officials, and persons accused of trafficking in pornography. The Committee expressed its serious concern for the effect on the adolescent from the estimated $500 million a year racket in pornography. The Committee recommended enactment of stricter federal laws to curtail the production, distribution, sale, and possession of pornography. It recommended reevaluation of state laws and city ordinances on obscene matter, the setting up of a National Advisory Crime Commission to provide data on violation of laws relating to pornography and narcotics. It also urged aggressive leadership in religious and civic groups in the fight against pornography and encouraged the giving of adequate sex education through the home, the church, and the school. Bibliography on pp. 68–70.

———. *Television and Juvenile Delinquency. Interim Report . . . Pursuant to S. Res. 274.* Washington, D.C., Govt. Print. Off., 1965. 74 p. mimeo. (88th Cong., 2d sess.) **U 180**

Recommendations include suggestions for development of a plan to devote specific prime time each week to good programs for children, a revision of the license renewal requirement to consider programs for children, more effective sanctions against violators under the NAB code, a system of encouraging community comment on children's programs, and a research attack on more precise information as to the impact of television on juvenile delinquency. The concern of the subcommittee for freedom of speech and the press is given on pages 3–4.

———. *Television and Juvenile Delinquency. Report of the Committee . . . pursuant to S. Res. 62 . . .* Washington, D.C., Govt.

Print. Off., 1956. 128 p. (Senate Report no. 1466, 84 th Cong., 2d sess.) **U 181**

The Kefauver Committee explored the causal relationship between viewing of crime and violence on TV and delinquency behavior. While unable to establish proof of a direct causal relationship, it considered it wise to minimize the risk. Its recommendations included the setting up of citizens' listening councils, the assumption by the FCC of additional responsibility for program content, additional industry efforts to improve program content, the modification of the TV code, and the need for further research. The appendix includes the text of the NARTB Code, the Standards of Practice for Radio Broadcasters of the USA, a statement on Children and Television made by the National Association for Better Radio and Television, the Motion Picture Production Code, letters from various psychiatrists, and a bibliography (pp. 125–28).

United States. Congress. Senate. Post-Offices and Post-Roads Committee. *Report to Accompany S. 2834.* Washington, D.C., Govt. Print. Off., 1892. 4 p. (52d Cong., 1 st sess.) **U 182**
The bill proposed certain restrictions on the transmission of obscene publications. The Committee "finds the fact that there is now on the statute books ample prohibitive legislation on this subject" and reports back the bill with recommendation for indefinite postponement.

United States. Congress. Senate. Special Committee to Study Problems of American Small Business. *Survival of Free Competitive Press. Small Newspaper, Democracy's Grass Roots. Report of Chairman to Members of Committee, January 2, 1947.* Washington, D.C., Govt. Print. Off., 1947. 72 p. (Committee Print 17, 80th Cong., 1st sess.) **U 183**

United States. Defense Department. *Armed Forces Censorship.* Washington, D.C., Govt Print. Off., 1964. 58 p. (Army FM 30–28; Navy OPNAVINST 5530.10; Air Force AFM 205–9) **U 184**

————. *D. O. D. Information Policies.* Columbia, Mo., Freedom of Information Center, School of Journalism, University of Missouri, 1965. 4 p. (Publication no. 142) **U 185**

"This paper is designed to provide a general explanation of United States Department of Defense policies concerning release of information. The department's control ranges from the Secretary of Defense to a small-unit adviser in South Vietnam; therefore, policies on specific questions can become complex. This paper, therefore, can do little more than serve as a basic 'primer.' Confusions as to

policy and terminology occur even among those who work daily in these turbulent and often muddy waters."

————. *Military Security; Armed Forces Censorship, Sept. 24, 1954.* Washington, D.C., Govt. Print. Off., 1954. 49 p. (Army SR 380–80–1, Navy OPNAVINST 5530.6; Air Force Regulations 205–30) **U 186**

————. *Military Security; Civil Censorship Oct. 22, 1954.* Washington, D.C., Govt. Print. Off., 1954. 8 p. (Army Regulations 380–83) **U 187**

————. *Public Information: Establishment and Conduct of Field Press Censorship in Combat Areas: Aug. 15, 1952.* U.S. Govt. Print. Off., 1952. 20 p. (Army Regulation 360–65; Navy OPNAVINST 5530.3; Air Force Regulations 190–11) **U 188**

————. *Report.* [Press Release]. Washington, D.C., Office of the Secretary of Defense, 1948. (Reprinted in Summers, *Federal Information Controls in Peacetime,* pp. 104–8) **U 189**
Report of the Media Subcommittee, representing various media of the press, radio, and moving pictures, appointed in response to an invitation of Secretary of Defense Forrestal to advise on "how far we may go in keeping the American public informed about technical progress while protecting our secret and scientific projects."

United States. Federal Communications Commission. *Broadcast Licensees Advised Concerning Stations' Responsibilities under the Fairness Doctrine as to Controversial Issue Programming.* (FCC 62–1019, Public Notice-B.) Washington, D.C., The Commission, 1963. 2 p. **U 190**
Clarification of the fairness doctrine of 1949.

————. *In the Matter of Editorializing by Broadcast Licensees.* Washington, D.C., The Commission, 1949. 25 p. (Report no. 8516) **U 191**
This report holds that broadcasters have the right to editorialize, subject to affording opportunity for opposing views. A reversal of the Mayflower decision of 1941. Includes text of the original fairness doctrine.

————. [*Letter to NAB on FCC's July 26 Fairness Notice*]. Washington, D.C., The Commission, 1963. 3 p. (Report no. 4802) **U 192**

————. *Public Service Responsibility of Broadcast Licensees.* Washington, D.C., Govt. Print. Off., 1946. 59 p. **U 193**
This "Blue Book" outlines the responsibilities of stations and networks to operate "in the public interest, convenience, or necessity." The report recommends the creation of professional radio criticism such as that published in *Variety,* the establishment of radio listeners' councils such as those in Madison, Wis., and Cleveland, and continued experimentation and reasearch in educational broadcasting.

————. *Report on Chain Broadcasting.* Washington, D.C., Govt. Print. Off., 1941. 153 p. (Commission Order no. 37, Docket no. 5060) **U 194**
While the United States has rejected government ownership of broadcasting facilities in the interest of free enterprise, concentration of control in the hands of a few powerful networks can become a dangerous pitfall in the freedom of communications. The report resulting from monopoly investigations in the radio broadcasting industry, led to limitations in the powers of the three networks (N.B.C., C.B.S., and Mutual) and to the separation of N.B.C.'s Blue and Red networks.

United States. Federal Radio Commission. *Commercial Radio Advertising. Letter from the Chairman of the Federal Radio Commission Transmitting in Response to Senate Resolution No. 129, a Report Relative to the Use of Radio Facilities for Commercial Advertising Purposes, together with a List Showing the Educational Institutions Which Have Been Licensed.* Washington, D.C., Govt. Print. Off., 1932. 201 p. (Senate Document 137) **U 195**

The Senate resolution asked 15 questions of the Commission including the feasibility of government ownership and operation of broadcasting facilities and what plans might be adopted to limit, control, and perhaps eliminate the use of radio facilities for commercial advertising purposes. To the last question the FCC responded: "Any plan the purpose of which is to eliminate the use of radio facilities for commercial advertising purposes will, if adopted, destroy the present system of broadcasting."

United States. Library of Congress. *List of References on Censorship of the Press during the Civil War.* Washington, D.C., The Library, 1917. 12 p. **U 196**

————. *Select List of References on the Regulation and Control of Radio Broadcasting in the United States and Foreign Countries.* Washington, D.C., The Library, 1933. 34 p. mimeo. **U 197**

United States. Library of Congress. Division of Bibliography. *List of References on Freedom of the Press and Speech and Censorship in War (with Special Reference to the European War)*. Washington, D.C., The Library, 1917. 9p. typewritten. (Select List 184)   **U 198**

———. *A Selected List of References on Freedom of Speech and the Press (Supplementary to Typewritten List of April 14, 1930)*. Compiled by Grace Hadley Fuller. Washington, D.C., The Library, 1938. 27p.   **U 199**

United States. Library of Congress. Legislative Reference Service. *Obscene Literature. Digest of Laws Enacted in the Various States Relating to the Possession, Circulation and Sale of Obscene Literature*. Compiled by Alice Brown. Washington, D.C., Govt. Print. Off., 1929. 22p. (Senate Document 54, 71st Cong., 2d sess.)   **U 200**

A compilation of the laws in the 48 states "relating to obscene literature in books, pamphlets, magazines, and newspapers and of laws on publications made up of criminal news, police reports, and accounts of criminal deeds. It does not include laws on prohibited advertising or on prohibited publications relating to sexual diseases, or provisions relating specifically to birth control, indecent posters, or prints."

United States. Library of Congress. Reference Department. European Affairs Division. *Freedom of Information; a Selective Report on Recent Writing*. Compiled by Helen F. Conover. Washington, D.C., The Library, 1949. 153p.   **U 201**

"The illustrations and examples are chosen with a view to avoidance, insofar as possible, of repetitive expression; with very few exceptions the literature examined is work produced in the last ten years . . . First place is given to the examination of the issue on the international level, in form of considerations, implementations and comment. Next, the question of freedom of information is examined on national levels, the United States, Great Britain, France and other states of Western Europe. . . . A short section on Latin America is intended to show that the considerable smaller body of writing does not indicate a less acute realization of the issue or a lack of yearning for freedom of expression." A particularly valuable contribution is the survey of various international press conferences, beginning with 1893, and their attention to press freedom. The bibliography interprets freedom of the press to cover all the mass media of communications.

———. *Freedom of Information; a Revised Supplementary Survey of Recent Writings*. Compiled by Helen F. Conover. Washington, D.C., The Library, 1952. 40p.   **U 202**

A supplement to the previous bibliography, covering the past three years.

United States. Mayors' Conference. *Municipal Control of Objectionable Comic Books*. Washington, D.C., The Conference, 1948. 12p. (Report no. 298)   **U 203**

United States. National Archives. *Records of the Office of Censorship*. Compiled by Henry T. Ulasek. Washington, D.C., The National Archives, 1953. 16p. (Preliminary Inventories, no. 54)   **U 204**

Inventory of official records of the government agency charged with censorship in the United States during World War II. A seven-page introduction surveys the organization and operation of the office.

United States. National Commission for UNESCO. *Our Interest in Freedom of Information and Communications*. Washington, D.C., The Commission, 1953. 4p.   **U 205**

Prepared by Kenneth N. Stewart in cooperation with the Association for Education in Journalism for the 4th national conference, U.S. Commission for UNESCO.

United States. Navy Department. Office of Naval Intelligence. *Cable Censorship Digest*. Compiled by F. D. Pryor. Washington, D.C., Govt. Print. Off., 1933. 269p.   **U 206**

United States. Post Office Department. *Report on Exclusion of Newspapers from the Mails*. Washington D.C., Govt. Print. Off., 1863. 2p. (Senate Document 19, 37th Cong., 3d sess.)   **U 207**

Instructions to deputy postmasters with regard to excluding certain newspapers from the mails, and for restoring mailing privilege.

United States. President. *Repression of the Circulation of Obscene Publications. Message from the President of the United States Transmitting an Arrangement Relative to the Repression of the Circulation of Obscene Publications, Signed at Paris on May 4, 1910*. [Washington, D.C., Govt. Print. Off., 1910]. 4p. (61st Cong., 3d sess.; confidential)   **U 208**

United States. President's Commission on the Assassination of President Kennedy.

Report. Washington, D.C., Govt. Print. Off., 1964. 888p.   **U 209**

The report includes a recommendation that "representatives of the bar, law enforcement associations, and the news media work together to establish ethical standards concerning the collection and presentation of information to the public so that there will be no interference with pending criminal investigations, court proceedings, or the right of individuals to a fair trial."

United States. Public Information Committee. *Complete Report of the Chairman of the Committee on Public Information, 1917: 1918: 1919*. Washington, D.C., Govt. Print. Off., 1920. 290p.   **U 210**

This World War I committee was created by Executive Order, 13 April 1917, and terminated 21 August 1919. Its chairman was George Creel. Among its duties was the control of information about American participation in the war.

———. *Official Bulletin*. Washington, D.C., Govt. Print. Off., Vol. 1–Vol. 3, no. 575, 10 May 1917—31 March 1919. 8p. or 16p. each.   **U 211**

The 31 December issue contains the Request for Censorship by Press of Certain War News, as Revised and Urged upon All American Publishers.

———. *Preliminary Statement to the Press of the United States*. Washington, D.C., Govt. Print. Off., 1917, 20p.   **U 212**

An outline of the program for supervising voluntary censorship of the press in World War I.

United States. State Department. "Arrangement between United States and Other Powers relative to Repression of Circulation of Obscene Publications; Signed Paris, May 4, 1910, proclaimed April 18, 1911." In *State Department Foreign Relations, 1911* (1918), pp. 94–97; in *U.S. Statutes at Large*, vol. 37, pt. 2, pp. 1511–15; in *U.S. Treaty Series*, no. 559; and issued as a separate 9-page pamphlet by the State Department in 1911. The British publication of the agreement appears in the *Treaty Series*, 1911, no. 11, issued by H.M. Stat. Off.   **U 213**

A treaty whereby contracting countries centralize through the French government information facilitating the tracing and seizing of obscene drawings, writings, pictures, and objects.

———. *Concerning Freedom of Information*. Washington, D.C., Govt. Print. Off., 1947. 13p. (Publication 2977)   **U 214**

Contains: Address of Warren R. Austin, U.S. Representative to the United Nations,

"U.S. Rejects Resolutions Limiting Free Flow of Information"; statement of Mrs. Franklin D. Roosevelt, U.S. Representative to the General Assembly, opposing Yugoslav resolution to restrict offensive propaganda.

United States. State Department. Office of Public Affairs. Division of Historical Policy Research. *Freedom of Information in American Policy and Practice*. By William Gerber and Letitia A. Lewis. Washington, D.C., The Department, 1948. 65 p. **U 215**
A review of the history of American policy and practice as regards freedom of information, including public rights, rights of reporters and other writers, and rights of media of mass communications from 1776 to the present. These rights are subject to government limitations only in the interest of such goals as national security, public morals, and prevention of personal libel. The report was prepared in anticipation of the Geneva Conference on Freedom of Information.

United States. Temporary National Economic Committee. *The Motion Picture Industry: A Pattern of Control*. By Daniel Bertrand, W. Duane Evans, and E. L. Blanchard. Washington, D.C., Govt. Print. Off., 1941. 92 p. (TNEC Monograph 43, Senate Committee Print, 76th Cong., 3d sess.) **U 216**
A study of the concentration of economic power in the movie industry as it existed at the time of the investigation. Five major companies and 3 satellites produce and distribute 70 per cent of American movies. The industry utilizes such restrictive practices as block booking, blind selling, and forcing of shorts, which, unlike some monopolies, does not result in a savings for the consumer. The appendix includes a description of the self-censorship activities of the Hays Office.

United States. Treasury Department. *Report on the Cost of Libel Prosecutions*. Washington, D.C., The Department, 1807. 15 p. (Executive Document, 9th Cong., 2d sess.) **U 217**
Albert Gallatin, Secretary of the Treasury, reports on expense incurred in libel prosecutions against the following publishers in Connecticut in 1806: Thaddeus Osgood, Tapping Reeve, Barzillai Hudson, George Goodwin, and Azel Backus.

United States. War Department. Adjutant General. *Censorship: Some Important Facts You Must Know ₁When you Write Home₁*. Washington, D.C., Adjutant General's Department, 1942. 4 p. **U 218**

United States. War Department. General Staff Corps. War College Division. *The Proper Relationship between the Army and the Press in Time of War*. Washington, D.C.,

Army War College, 1916. 13 p. (Supplement to *Statement of a Proper Military Policy for the United States*; also published as War Department Document no. 528) **U 219**
A statement of military law as it relates to war correspondents, release of military information, and censorship.

United States. War Information Office. *OWI Regulation No. 4*. Washington, D.C., OWI, 1942. 4 p. (Reprinted in Summers, *Federal Information Controls in Peacetime*, pp. 141–46) **U 220**
The wartime directive establishing security classification over government information "which might prove of aid or comfort to the enemy."

"U.S. Supreme Court Reexamines Precedents in Hearings on Three Book Censorship Cases." *Publishers' Weekly*, 188:61–66, 27 December 1965. **U 221**
"On December 7 and 8, the U.S. Supreme Court heard testimony on three cases involving allegedly obscene books. At issue: Is 'expert' testimony admissible? Is the court itself the supreme censor?"

"U.S. Supreme Court Rules Pro-Censorship in Two of Three Cases Involving Books." *Publishers' Weekly*, 189(13):43–44, 28 March 1966. **U 222**
"Affirming two publishers' convictions, the court expanded the scope of its anti-obscenity purview to include book advertising and promotion. Only *Fanny Hill* escaped the deluge, as the court held for G. P. Putnam's and overturned a Massachusetts ban."

University of Chicago Round Table. *Book Burning and Censorship*. Chicago, University of Chicago Press, 1953. 18 p. (Radio Forum no. 795) **U 223**
A radio discussion by Robert Faulhaber and others; includes The Menace of Free Journalism in America by Mary McCarthy.

———. *Censorship*. Chicago, University of Chicago Press, 1942. 29 p. (Radio Forum no. 201) **U 224**
Participants: Byron Price, William Benton, and Harold D. Lasswell. American philosophy of censorship in wartime should incorporate the negative aspect of guarding military secrets from the enemy and the positive aspect of keeping the American public well-informed. There is also a need to guard against unnecessary local censorship.

———. *A Free and Responsible Press*. Chicago, University of Chicago Press, 1947. 29 p. (Radio Forum no. 472) **U 225**
Wilbur Forrest, Robert Hutchins, and George N. Shuster, the latter two members of the

Commission on Freedom of the Press, discuss the Commission's recommendations. Mr. Forrest believes that the report, prepared by academicians rather than practicing journalists, is too critical of the American press. Mr. Hutchins and Mr. Shuster defend the report, believing that vigorous criticism of the press is healthy to a democratic institution.

———. *Free Flow of News and World Peace*. Chicago, University of Chicago Press, 1946. 21 p. (Radio Forum no. 453) **U 226**
Participants: Seymour Berkson, Palmer Hoyt, and Quincy Wright. There was agreement among the three journalists that more communications facilities, lower costs, less censorship, and higher standards were needed to provide free international flow of information.

———. *Freedom of Information*. Chicago, University of Chicago Press, 1949. 33 p. (Radio Forum no. 612) **U 227**
Participants: Benjamin Cohen, Gerrit Jan Van Heuven Goedhart, Carlos Romulo, and David Sarnoff. A discussion of the free flow of information among the peoples of the world as one of the fundamental human rights. Includes an address by David Sarnoff, Freedom to Listen and Freedom to Look, presented at a Chicago meeting in honor of the U.S. National Commission for UNESCO, 12 September 1947, and an address, The Word Is Freedom, by William Benton, before the UN Conference on Freedom of Information and of the Press, Geneva, 24 March 1948.

———. *The Press*. Chicago, University of Chicago Press, 1942. 29 p. (Radio Forum no. 240) **U 228**
A radio discussion by M. C. Krueger and R. P. McKeon of the University of Chicago and Samuel E. Thomason, publisher of the *Chicago Times*. Professor Krueger submitted that the basic issue in the problem of a free press is that of reconciling its duties as a public service with its rights as a private business. Mr. Thomason stated that a good newspaper should neither lead nor follow the public, but should present the facts from which the public can form its own conclusions.

———. *Radio in Wartime*. Chicago, University of Chicago Press, 1942. 29 p. (Radio Forum no. 218) **U 229**
Participants: William Benton, James L. Fly, Harold D. Lasswell. There should be as little control of radio as possible during wartime, yet enough to protect military secrecy. Free flow of information is essential for democracies waging war.

———. *Social Responsibilities of Radio*. Chicago, University of Chicago Press, 1947. 28 p. (Radio Forum no. 476) **U 230**
Participants: Barbara Ward, member of the

Board of Governors of the B.B.C.; Clarence Moore, station KOA, Denver; Ray C. Wakefield of the FCC; and Louis Wirth, University of Chicago. There was general agreement with the findings of the Commission on Freedom of the Press that radio has a responsibility to entertain, disseminate information, and foster discussion of public issues, but the participants differed on the extent to which these responsibilities had been met. Mr. Moore believed radio is giving the public what it wants; Miss Ward believed the American public was getting what the advertisers want; Mr. Wakefield believed the major responsibility for content control is with the individual stations and the networks, with the FCC enforcing only minimum standards.

————. *What Freedom of Information Means to You.* Chicago, University of Chicago Press, 1950. 33 p. (Radio Forum no. 620) **U 231**

Participants: William Benton, Erwin D. Canham, and Harold D. Lasswell. Includes an address, Freedom of Information, by Senator Benton, given before the Connecticut Editorial Association, 4 February 1950.

————. *World-Wide Freedom of News?* Chicago, University of Chicago Press, 1944. 21 p. (Radio Forum no. 347) **U 232**

Claude Jagger, Robert D. Leigh, and Hans J. Morgenthau discuss concepts of international freedom of the press, a necessity for world organization.

"The 'Unstamped Press' in London." *Tait's Edinburgh Magazine*, 1(n.s.):614–25, October 1834. **U 233**

A survey and defense of the lawless penny publications, issued to the working class in defiance of the "odius taxes upon knowledge." The author notes the significant contribution of these unstamped publications, too often considered by the educated people "in the same degraded light as the Unwashed." Beginning with the papers of Cobbett and Wooler, the publications have served a useful purpose in English reform.

Unwin, *Sir* Stanley. *The Truth About a Publisher; an Autobiographical Record.* New York, Macmillan, 1960. 455 p. **U 234**

An autobiography of one of Britain's leading publishers refers to a number of incidents of censorship, from the time of World War I, when censorship was mismanaged, to World War II where a more enlightened policy prevailed. He also discusses his difficulties with the director of public prosecution over the publication of *A Young Girl's Diary* and his experience as head of the Council of the Publishers' Association in dealing with book seizures under British obscenity laws.

[Upham, Timothy, *plaintiff*]. *Libel Trial. Report of the Trial. Timothy Upham vs. Hill & Barton, for an Alleged Libel, at the Court of Common Pleas, Rockingham County, October term. 1830. Compiled from Notes Taken at the Trial, and the Original Papers in the Case. To which is Added an Appendix, Containing the Evidence Ruled out by the Court . . .* Concord, N.H., Hill and Barton, 1831. 96 p., 24 p. **U 235**

[————]. *Report of the Case of Timothy Upham against Hill & Barton, Publishers of the New-Hampshire Patriot, for Alleged Libels, at the Court of Common Pleas, Rockingham County . . . 1830.* Dover, N.H., G. W. Ela, 1830. 159 p. **U 236**

Upham brought action against the publishers of the *New Hampshire Patriot and State Gazette*, who had charged him with misconduct as collector of the United States Customs.

"Upward Trend in Congressional Secrecy." *Congressional Quarterly Weekly Report*, 16:638–41, 16 April 1963. **U 237**

Closed sessions by Congressional committees are on the increase.

Utah Council of Teachers of English. "The Censorship Roundup in Utah." *Utah Council of Teachers of English Bulletin*, 5(5):3–5, September 1966. **U 238**

Results from a questionnaire on censorship in Utah schools, circulated by a committee of the Association. Thirty per cent of the schools reported censorship incidents; most of the pressures were from individual parents, not groups.

Utley, Freda. "The Book Burners Burned." *American Mercury*, 77:35–39, December 1953. **U 239**

Attack on the United States Information Service overseas as being administered by "woolly liberals" and that its libraries contain books about communism, but none presenting the Republican or conservative point of view. Article is critical of the American Library Association and its "Freedom to Read" manifesto, claiming it discriminates against the books it considers "bad."

V

V., P. "Une Menace pour la Litterature en Angleterre." *Journal des Débats*, 35(2): 705–6, 2 November 1928. **V1**
A report on the attacks by England's censor, Sir William Joynson-Hicks, on "immoral" literature. "Quant on pense qu'il est des Anglais qui osent critiques le siècle de Victoria! Mais sous le règne de cette illustre souveraine on était libre en Angleterre."

Vagts, Detlev. "Free Speech in the Armed Forces." *Columbia Law Review*, 57:187–218, 1957. **V2**

Vainstein, Rose. "Book Selection or Censorship?" *California Librarian*, 16: 235–37, July 1955. **V3**

Vamis, John. "Newspaper Interference in Judicial Proceedings." *Cleveland-Marshall Law Review*, 10:59–69, January 1961. **V4**
The author appeals for higher standards of journalistic ethics which will protect the right of the individual from sensationalism and the overaggressive behavior of reporters. "There should be a right to damages from the press when individual rights are unlawfully invaded by overaggressive journalism."

Vance, E. L. "Freedom of the Press for Whom?" *Virginia Quarterly Review*, 21: 340–54, July 1945. **V5**
Most questions involving freedom of the press are really questions of freedom of business enterprise and bear no relationship to protection under the First Amendment. The author recommends that some newspapers be endowed as educational institutions so that they might publish without having to please their corporate ownership. Schools and colleges should help to create informed readers by providing for the study of the newspaper as a social institution.

Vance, W. R. "Freedom of Speech and of the Press." *Minnesota Law Review*, 2:239–60, March 1918. **V6**
Discussion of the sedition laws of World War I and their interpretations by the courts. The author shows where and how the line can be drawn between legitimate criticism of the government and its measures and opposition to the government and resistance to the laws. He concludes that "a sedition law, supported by public sentiment, will be enforceable; while one violating the public sense of justice and freedom will register unfitness in verdicts of acquittal."

Vandenberg, Arthur H. "Freedom of the Press." In *Problems of Journalism; Proceedings of the American Society of Newspaper Editors, 1930.* Washington, D.C., ASNE, 1930, pp. 80–85. **V7**
An address by the United States Senator from Michigan, a former newspaper publisher.

Van den Haag, Ernest. "Quia Ineptum." *Ethics*, 72:266–76, July 1962. **V8**
The author offers "some hypotheses to explain censorship in principle, and particularly its origin, function, and effects, as well as its peculiar ambivalence." Censorship is a compromise "between the original wish to indulge infantile, anal, oral, and ultimately all sexual desires, and the later wish to control them. . . . Censorship serves both to curb and to stimulate, to intensify desire while restraining it. Above all it reduces anxiety." He likens censorship to fashion—it makes the hidden more alluring, and, like fashion, it is capricious. He sees little harm in most censorship of sex in television or the movies. He would require children to have permission of a guardian to see adult movies and he would prohibit printing anything about the sexual life of an identifiable living person without his permission. One of the many arguments against censorship that is "defective, not to say silly" is that "no girl has ever been corrupted by a book" (to quote New York's Mayor Walker), implying that literature is uninfluential and, therefore, harmless. This is wrong. "The thoughts and feelings which literature articulates and produces are quite influential. . . . Ultimately they influence conduct more perhaps than anything else," although the effect is difficult to measure. The liberal assumption is that individuals are capable of withstanding influences that may lead to unlawful acts. The acts are held illegal, but not the reading of a book that may prompt the act. The author likewise challenges the axioms of Jefferson and Mill that truth will prevail over error.

Van der Weyde, William M. "Brave Richard Carlile; the Year 1917 Marks the Centenary of His Battle for Freedom of the Press." *Truth Seeker*, 44:561–63, 8 September 1917. **V9**

Van Doren, Carl E., and Carl Carmer. "Freedom of the Press." In *American Scriptures*. New York, Boni & Gaer, 1946, pp. 234–38. **V10**
Excerpts from a radio broadcast of dramatic episodes in the American history of press freedom, leading to the First Amendment.

Van Doren, Mark. "Anthony Comstock." In *Dictionary of American Biography*. New York, Scribner, 1930. vol. 4, pp. 330–31. **V11**
A biography of the sponsor of the first federal laws against obscenity in the United States and founder of the New York vice society.

———. "If Anybody Wants to Know." *American Scholar*, 20:396–405, Autumn 1951. (Reprinted in Downs, *The First Freedom*, pp. 370–74 and Daniels, *The Censorship of Books*, pp. 103–6) **V12**
An American poet replies to his critics in an address before the Hudson County Chapter of Americans for Democratic Action, Jersey City, N.J., 20 February 1951. Van Doren's books were banned from the Jersey City Junior College presumably because of "objectionable" organizations Van Doren had belonged to at one time. Van Doren defends the American people and their government and warns against those who would destroy our freedom because of fear of communism.

———. *Man's Right to Knowledge and the Free Use Thereof. With an Introduction by Richard R. Powell.* New York, Columbia University, 1954. 60 p. **V13**
Commentary on a graphic exhibit of 60 panels prepared to explain and illustrate the theme of the Columbia University Bicentennial celebration, "Man's Right to Knowledge and the Free Use Thereof," with reproductions of the panels.

Van Loon, Hendrik W. "Sense or Censorship?" *Woman Citizen*, 9:9–10, 4 April 1925. **V14**
While opposed to all forms of literary censorship of books, the author favors stemming the tide of "mushy filth" on the newsstand— the so-called "confessionals," which threaten to destroy the less intelligent members of our younger generation. These magazines are dangerous because, unlike books, they are cheap and therefore likely to be read by the average citizen who may be corrupted. Van Loon objects to his name having been used in behalf of the Clean Books bill in New York, preferring parental watchfulness to police protection. To his own children he says: while you may read any book or see any play, "if I ever find you with one of those vile little confessionals I shall take you behind the barn and I shall beat Hades out of you."

———. "Uplift Journals Please Copy." *Commonweal*, 1:202–3, 31 December 1924. (Reprinted in Beman, *Selected Articles on Censorship*, pp. 417–22) **V15**
The author tells of his attempt to interest newspapers in crusading against "filth" on newstands. He attacks the magazines of "revelations," "dreams," "romances," and "confessions" "which in their true nature are nothing but thinly veiled pornography."

Van Os, George J. "Defamation by Broadcast: A Lively Dispute." *Houston Law Review*, 2:238–50, Fall 1964. **V16**

Van Patten, Nathan. "Exclusion from the Mails." *ALA Bulletin*, 35:401–2, June 1941. **V17**
The Post Office Department informs the librarian of Stanford University, in answer to his inquiry regarding the failure of the University to receive shipments of Russian and Japanese books, that scientific and academic works are not being delayed or interfered with.

———. "Librarian and Censorship." *California Library Association Bulletin*, 3: 33–35, September 1941. **V18**
The librarian should be familiar with federal and state laws dealing with importation, sale, distribution, and possession of controversial printed matter. He should submit to suppression of such material by authorized agents of the government, reserving the right to court appeal. He should not submit to pressures from individuals or groups. He should restrict certain types of material in the best interests of the country, making known his reason for doing so. He should advise readers in the use of library materials, without making critical comment upon the reader's interests. The librarian should determine his course in the matter of censorship "by reason and not by hysteria."

Van Schaick, F. L. *Press and State.* Washington, D.C., Editorial Research Reports, 1948. (*Editorial Research Reports*, 2(11): 651–66, 21 September 1948) **V19**
Divergent points of view between the Soviet doctrine of a captive press and the American doctrine of a free press with right to criticize the government and to present diverse points of view.

Van Sooy, Neal. "James King of William." *Quill*, 31(8):10–12, 16, November–December 1943. **V20**
An account of the martyred San Francisco, Calif., editor whose memory Sigma Delta Chi honored with the designation of his print shop as an historic site in journalism.

[Vane, *Sir* Henry, the Younger]. *The Tryal of Sir Henry Vane. At the King's Bench, Westminster, June the 2nd and 6th, 1662. Together with What He Intended to Have Spoken the Day of His Sentence (June 11) for Arrest of Judgment . . . and His Bill of Exceptions. With Other Occasioned Speeches, &c. Also His Speech and Prayer, &c., on the Scaffold.* [London], 1662. 134p. (Reprinted as Old South Leaflets no. 62 [24p.] and in Howell, *State Trials*, vol. 5, pp. 791ff.) **V21**
In 1656 Sir Henry Vane, the younger, a Puritan author and government official, had submitted his pamphlet, *Healing Question*, to a member of Cromwell's Council prior to publication. On hearing no objection after a month he had the book printed. On its appearance Sir Henry was charged with sedition and sent as prisoner to the Isle of Wight. He was later released. In 1662 Sir Henry was accused of treason under the Restoration government and executed.

Vanek, E. V. "Survey of Controversial Books." *ILA Record*, 10:27–29, October 1956. **V22**
An examination of "the areas in which controversial books are most likely to occur," and what makes a book controversial.

Variety. New York, Variety, Inc., 1905–date. Weekly. **V23**
This major newspaper of the entertainment business in the United States frequently carries news items relating to freedom of the press (or lack of it) as it relates to the movies, radio, television, and the stage.

Varma, Babu Ishwari Prasad, *comp.* *Hyderabad Sensational Case; Complete and Detailed Proceedings of the Well-Known Pamphlet Scandal Case, with Full Speeches of the Counsels.* Lucknow, India, G. P. Varma, 1893. 579p. **V24**

"The Vatican on Obscene Literature."

Literary Digest, 93:31–32, 4 June 1927. **V25**
Comments on the directive of Pius XI to Catholic bishops to protect their flocks from immorality on the printed page and to call the attention of Catholics to the fact that the reading of immoral books constitutes a sin whether or not such books have been expressly condemned by the ecclesiastical authorities or listed in the *Index of Forbidden Books*.

Vaughan, Bernard, *plaintiff.* "[The Jesuit Libel Case] . . . *Vaughan v. The Rock Newspaper Printing and Publishing Co.*" In *Concerning Jesuits.* London, Catholic Truth Society, 1902. 64p. **V26**
Father Vaughan recovered damages for an alleged libel published in *The Rock*, 23 August 1902, under the title, Jesuit Outlaws.

Veeder, Van Vechten. "Absolute Immunity in Defamation: Judicial Proceedings." *Columbia Law Review*, 9:463–91, June 1909. **V27**

———. "Absolute Immunity in Defamation: Legislative and Executive Proceedings." *Columbia Law Review*, 10:131–46, February 1910. **V28**

———. "Freedom of Public Discussion." *Harvard Law Review*, 23:413–40, April 1910. **V29**
"The process of continual readjustment between the needs of society and the protection of individual rights is nowhere more conspicuous than in the history of the law of defamation. . . . Yet the law defining the affirmative offense, with its rigorous presumptions of falsity, malice, and damage, remains practically unchanged." The author considers the nature and extent of freedom which the law permits in the discussion of matters of public interest.

———. "The History of the Law of Defamation." In *Select Essays in Anglo-American Legal History . . . edited by a Committee of the Association of American Law Schools . . .* Boston, Little, Brown, 1907. vol. 3, pp. 447–73. **V30**

———. "The Judicial History of Individual Liberty." *Green Bag*, 16:23–32, January 1924; 16:101–12, February 1924; 16:177–87, March 1924; 16:247–53, April 1924; 16:317–21, May 1924; 16:395–404, June 1924; 16:471–77, July 1924; 16: 529–38, August 1924; 16:591–94, September 1924; 16:673–79, October 1924; 16:725–31, November 1924. **V31**
A popularly written account of the development of civil liberties in England from the seventeenth century to the beginning of the

twentieth century, based on official records of trials for sedition and blasphemy. Includes portraits of men who figured in the trials—Lord Chief Justices Holt, Jeffreys, Kenyon, Eyre, Ellenborough, and Mansfield; John Lilburne, John Tutchin, John Wilkes, Thomas Erskine, William Cobbett, Thomas Hardy, Thomas Muir, Thomas Paine, John Frost, and Richard Carlile.

Velie, Lester. "You Can't See That Movie: Censorship in Action." *Colliers*, 125:11–13+, 6 May 1930. **V 32**
Censorship of the movies as it is practiced in various parts of the country, with special reference to Memphis and its chief censor, 83-year-old Lloyd T. Binford, who describes himself as "America's most notorious censor."

Verani, John R. "Motion Picture Censorship and the Doctrine of Prior Restraint." *Houston Law Review*, 3:11–57, Spring–Summer 1965. **V 33**
The study attempts to show that the U.S. Supreme Court's decisions with respect to prior censorship of motion pictures have been incompatible with its traditional doctrine of prior restraint. The author suggests a solution to the constitutional problems raised by motion picture censorship and relates his conclusions to the techniques currently employed by Boston to deter the showing of obscene films in that city. A full account of the Boston experience is given in the appendix.

Verinder, Frederick. "L[ondon] C[ounty] C[ouncil] Censorship." *Freethinker*, 39: 541–42, 2 November 1919. **V 34**
A report on the controversy over prohibition of the sale of free-thought, Socialist, and Communist literature in public parks.

Viator, *pseud.* "Literature and Pornography." *Colosseum*, 3:287–90, December 1936. **V 35**

"Vice Report and the Mails." *Outlook*, 99:353–54, 14 October 1911. **V 36**
While approving in principal the withholding of obscene literature from the mails, the author objects to action of the Post Office in suppressing the official report of the Chicago Vice Commission.

Vickers, Robert H. *Martyrdoms of Literature*. Chicago, Charles H. Sergel, 1891. 456 p. **V 37**
The story of the development of great libraries, private and public, and their willful destruction by religious zealots, vandals, war, revolution, and government action. The narrative begins with the ancient Egyptian civilization and extends to modern times. The author is a member of the Chicago Bar.

Victor, Jon, *pseud.* "Restraints on American

Catholic Freedom." *Harper's Magazine*, 227:33–39, December 1963. **V 38**
A close observer of affairs of the Catholic Church, writing pseudonymously, discusses "how some of the Church's leading scholars —and spokesmen for Pope John's reform movement—have had their voices muffled . . . and how the news of their banning was kept from much of the Catholic press."

"A Victory for a Free Press." *Saturday Evening Post*, 237:78, 4 April 1964. **V 39**
Editorial approval of the decision of the U.S. Supreme Court unanimously reversing the $500,000 libel judgment of an Alabama court against the *New York Times* and 4 Negro ministers. "The decision made it clear that excessive libel awards of any kind are a grave threat to the boldness and initiative of a free press."

"Vigilante Censorship Is Spreading." *Christian Century*, 70:404, 8 April 1953. **V 40**
Editorial comments on the spread of extralegal attacks on sellers of "objectionable" literature, with special attention to the Minneapolis scene.

"Vigilantes Object to Books in the Newark Public Library." *Library Journal*, 43:117–18, February 1918. **V 41**
An editorial on the efforts of a vigilante committee to remove eight books from the Newark Public Library because they allegedly contained enemy propaganda. Librarian John Cotton Dana and the trustees refused to comply with the censorship demands.

The Village Voice. New York, 1955–date. Weekly. **V 42**
This Greenwich Village weekly newspaper regularly carries news and feature stories of threats against freedom of the arts and letters, particularly the difficulties faced by producers and distributors of avant-garde films, magazines, and books. For example, in his Movie Journal for 12 March 1964 and 23 April 1964, Jonas Mekas reports on the action of city police against the film, *Flaming Creatures*, and his own arrest. Feature writer Stephanie G. Harrington covers the Mekas trial in the issue of 18 June 1964, and in the issue of 6 July 1964 the obscenity trial of Lenny Bruce (How Many 4-Letter Words Can a Prosecutor Use?). The issue for 30 April 1964 carried a lengthy report on demonstrations in front of Lincoln Center "to protest government limitations on freedom of the arts."

Villard, Oswald Garrison. "Freedom of the Press." In *Public Opinion in a Democracy Proceedings of the Institute of Human Relations . . .* (A special supplement to the January 1938 issue of *Public Opinion Quarterly*, pp. 56–59) **V 43**
"The average owner—thank Heaven there are many notable exceptions—does not really consider his newsgathering and publication

as public functions at all. Far from it. It is solely his affair what news he shall print, or how it shall be displayed."

———. "The New Fight for Old Liberties." *Harper's Magazine*, 151:440–47, September 1925. **V 44**
The article cites the Yenowsky case of Waterbury, Conn., and the magistrate involved, as an "example of what may happen if one begins to save the country by imprisoning doctrines and punishing thoughts." Our sedition law is "skillfully drawn to give authority control of public opinion," and its most dangerous feature is "that it makes any magistrate the judge of what is propaganda, or doctrine, and whether it is or is not inimical to the State of Connecticut or to the United States."

———. "The Newspaper and Government." *Journalism Bulletin*, 2(3):11–16, November 1925. **V 45**
Most newspapers have long since freed themselves of party domination, but have a new bondage to government and its propaganda. "We of the profession were merely agents of government propaganda, much of it lying and false, during the World War." This propaganda is still being carried on by news conferences, handouts, and news leaks.

———. "The Press and the War." *Christian Century*, 59(1):214–16, 18 February 1942. **V 46**
A veteran newspaper correspondent and editor recounts the difficulties newspapers encounter during wartime. He makes a case for less government censorship so that the American people can know the truth about the war situation, including casualty lists.

———. "The Press and the War News." *Christian Century*, 61:267–68, 1 March 1944. **V 47**
The author condemns Roosevelt's policy of secrecy in release of war information, and the newspapers for agreeing to voluntary censorship. There has been too much suppression of vital facts in the interest of a false optimism, "and the journalism that continues to give entirely misleading impressions renders a great disservice to itself, to the profession, and to the nation."

———. "The Press as Affected by the War." *American Review of Reviews*, 51: 79–83, January 1915. **V 48**
A review of the financial burdens war imposes on the press through the increased costs in gathering war news, and the loss of advertising. Villard criticizes the "stupidity" of the English control of war news, which is "turning from a military into a political" censorship.

———. "A Responsible Press?" *Forum*, 105:706–9, April 1946. **V 49**

"The record of the American press during World War II and in the half year which has followed the end of hostilities is replete with sordid distortions of the truth. It is a record of shameful suppression, of too easy acquiescence in censorship, of apologizing and covering up for the mistakes of the military, of fanning hatreds against whole peoples even when the war was over, and of miserable incompetence and inadequacy in reporting the occupation of conquered countries and the struggle for freedom in colonial areas."

————. "Sex, Art, Truth and Magazines." *Atlantic Monthly*, 137:388–98, March 1926. **V 50**

The editor of *The Nation* examines the "true story," the "confession," the "snappy story," the "artists and models," and the out-and-out vulgar group of magazines on the newsstands. He believes that "anything like wholesale suppression would be a mistake. They will run their course in due time." If they should be firmly established and make money (as Bernarr Macfadden's *True Story* does) they will become increasingly conservative.

————. "What the Blue Menace Means." *Harper's Magazine*, 157:529–40, October 1928. **V 51**

Villard criticizes the DAR, the American Legion, and the ROTC for engaging in "heresy-hunting and padlocking the lips of speakers." He quotes from *Scabbard and Blade* which denounces Jane Addams as "the most dangerous woman in America."

Vint, John, *et al.* "Trial of John Vint with George Ross and John Parry for a Libel upon Paul the First, Emperor of Russia, Published in the Courier Newspaper, 1799." (In Howell, *State Trials*, vol. 27, pp. 627 ff.) **V 52**

Proprietor, printer, and publisher were all found guilty and given prison sentences.

Virginia. Division of Motion Picture Censorship. *Annual Reports.* Richmond, The Division, 1924–date. **V 53**

The General Assembly created the Virginia State Board of Censors in 1922. It was redesignated the Division of Motion Picture Censorship under the Attorney General's Office in 1930. Its first report was for 1922 through 1924 and it has made annual reports since that date.

Virginia. General Assembly, 1799–1800. House of Delegates. *Communications from Several States, on the Resolutions of the Legislature of Virginia Respecting the Alien & Sedition Laws; Also Instructions from the General Assembly of Virginia, to Their Senators in Congress and, the Report of the Committee to Whom Was Committed the Proceedings of Sundry of the Other States in Answer to the Resolutions of the General Assembly, of the 21st day of Dec. 1798 . . .* Richmond, Printed by M. Jones, [1800]. 104 p. **V 54**

[————]. *Virginia and Kentucky Resolutions of 1798 and 1799; with Jefferson's Original Draught thereof; Also, Madison's Report, Calhoun's Address, Resolutions of the Several States, With Other Documents in Support of the Jeffersonian Doctrines of '98 . . .* Washington, J. Elliot, 1832. 82 p. (Another edition of the Virginia and Kentucky Resolutions, edited by Robert I. Smith, was published in Richmond by Samuel Shepherd in 1835) **V 55**

————. *The Virginia Report of 1799–1800, Touching the Alien and Sedition Laws; together with the Virginia Resolutions of December 21, 1798, The Debates and Proceedings thereon, in the House of Delegates of Virginia, and Several Other Documents Illustrative of the Report and Resolutions.* Richmond, J. W. Randolph, 1850. 264 p. (In 1912 the debates were reprinted by order of the U.S. Senate as Senate Documents, vol. 39, no. 873; an extract of the Madison report with commentary appears in Levy, *Freedom of the Press from Zenger to Jefferson*, pp. 197–229) **V 56**

In opposition to the odious Alien and Sedition Acts the Virginia House of Delegates adopted a series of resolutions (1798) and James Madison prepared a notable paper in behalf of freedom of the press, the Virginia Report of 1799–1800. These documents have appeared in numerous editions, in Richmond, Washington, Philadelphia, and Albany, since the first publication in 1800. This edition includes similar resolutions from Kentucky (drawn by Thomas Jefferson), comments from other states, and correspondence between Madison and Everett concerning the first Virginia resolutions.

Vitullo, Vincent F. "Censorship of Motion Pictures on Grounds of Obscenity." *Illinois Bar Journal*, 43:504–7, March 1955. **V 57**

Vizetelly, Ernest A. *Emile Zola, Novelist and Reformer; an Account of His Life & Work.* London, Lane, 1904. 560 p. **V 58**

In chapter 9, The British Pharisees, the author deals with the celebrated trial of his father, Henry Vizetelly, for publishing English translations of Zola's works. Although the works were severely expurgated in translation, the National Vigilance Society objected to Zola's portrayal of French vice and the matter was eventually brought to discussion in the House of Commons where Vizetelly was declared "the chief culprit in the spread of pernicious literature" and his prosecution demanded. At the trial Judge Cockburn's obscenity test was invoked. Vizetelly was found guilty and served three months in prison. The trial cost him both his business and his health. One of the great disappointments in the affair was the lack of support in the newspaper press.

[Vizetelly, Henry]. *Debate in the House of Commons: Trial and Conviction of Henry Vizetelly for Sale of Zola's Novels.* London, National Vigilance Association, 1889. **V 59**

[————]. *Extracts Principally from English Classics: Showing that the Legal Suppression of M. Zola's Novels Would Logically Involve the Bowdlerizing of Some of the Greatest Works in English Literature.* London, [Compiled by and privately printed for Henry Vizetelly], 1888. 87 p. **V 60**

This pamphlet was prepared as a mock memorial to the Solicitor to the Treasury at the time charges were made against Vizetelly for publishing novels by Zola. Vizetelly's purpose was to show the inconsistency of suppressing Zola's work while permitting circulation of famous English classics which contain so-called obscene passages. The extracts, believed to have been selected by George Moore, include quotations from the works of Wycherley, Congreve, Shakespeare, Beaumont, Fletcher, Ben Jonson, Ford, Dryden, Defoe, Swift, Fielding, Smollett, Sterne, and Byron. Also included is Lord Macaulay's suggested suppression of the works of Wycherley and Congreve. Vizetelly, then a sick old man, was condemned to prison, and died shortly after his release. A four-page text of Vizetelly's letter to the Solicitor to the Treasury was also published as a separate leaflet. A list of the works extracted is reprinted in Ernst, *To the Pure . . . ,* pp. 305–8.

————. *Glances Back Through Seventy Years: Autobiographical and Other Reminiscences.* London, Paul, Trench, Trübner, 1893. 2 vols. **V 61**

The memoirs of this British publisher include references to the persecution of Richard Carlile and his shopmen for their "swing" pamphlets, Cobbett's trial for libel (1831–32), the struggle against "taxes on knowledge," Hetherington's imprisonment, and the prosecution of Moxon for selling *Queen Mab* (1832–36), all in volume one. Volume two ends with 1870, short of the celebrated case of prosecution of the author for publishing the works of Zola.

Vizzard, John A. "The Production Code of the Motion Picture Association." In *Lectures in Communications Media, Legal and Policy Problems Delivered at University of*

The author is assistant to the director,
Production Code Administration, Motion
Picture Association of America.

Vleeschauwer, Herman J. *Censorship and
Libraries.* Pretoria, Union of South Africa,
1959. 165 p. **V 63**

A professor of library science at the University
of South Africa considers the rising tide of
censorship and the pressures on libraries
throughout the world, in the setting of a
broad historical background. The library
should stand as a neutral institution in a
world of ideological conflict. Its duty is to
make its collection truly reflect the ideological
conflict taking place outside its walls. The
library is "a haven of tolerance in respect of
people, ideas and books. In principle it should
be capable of bearing witness to everything
that thinkers have in the past committed
to paper and thus presented for communication
to their fellow-men and to posterity. . . . The
social body should adopt the same attitude
towards the library as the library has adopted
towards the book, namely to allow it to be an
institution which to a certain extent lives in
and by the majesty of death." Professor
Vleeschauwer rejects the idea expressed by
Louis N. Ridenour (American Library Association, *Freedom of Book Selection*) with respect
to rejection by libraries of the "pseudo-
scientific book." Instead of an "arsenal for
democracy" the library should be an "arsenal
from which all ideological parties draw their
weapons."

Vogelbach, Arthur L. "The Publication
and Reception of *Huckleberry Finn* in
America." *American Literature*, 11:260–72,
October 1939. **V 64**

Includes references to the exclusion of the
work from public libraries.

Vold, Lawrence. "Defamation by Radio."
Journal of Radio Law, 2:673–707, October
1932. **V 65**

The article is a condensation of a brief submitted in the case of *Sorenson v. Wood*, decided
by the Supreme Court of Nebraska, 10 June
1932. The court contended, and the author
agrees, that the broadcasting station actively
participates with the speaker in carrying out
publication by radio and shares the responsibility for utterances. Exercise of due care is
not a defense if the utterance is defamatory.
Publication by radio, because of its wide
diffusion, must be governed by the laws of
libel rather than slander.

———. "Defamatory Interpolations in
Radio Broadcasts." *University of Pennsylvania Law Review*, 88:249–96, January
1940. **V 66**

"The purpose of this article is to support the
view that radio stations under the common
law of defamation should properly be held to
the same liability for defamatory interpolations
as they are for defamatory utterances contained
in written or printed manuscripts transmitted
to radio listeners by their broadcasting
operations."

Volkart, Edmund H. *Censorship of the Press
in the United States; a Study of Social
Control.* New Haven, Yale University,
1947. 555 p. (Unpublished Ph. D. dissertation) **V 67**

The study considers censorship as a factor in
social control. The author finds that most
postpublication censorship in America today
is in the area of sex expression. It consists of
either quasi-legal or nonlegal action, with the
vice societies and NODL as the chief practitioners. Such agencies have tended to avoid
legal sanctions in favor of extralegal methods
such as boycott and pressure tactics. He finds
that censorship is a barrier to cultural change
because it limits the variation of ideas and
reduces the amount of deviant behavior.
Part 1 deals with legal censorship by federal,
state, and local government; part 2 discusses
the quasi-legal censorship of the vice societies,
the New York and New England societies in
particular; part 3 discusses the nonlegal
censorship of the Roman Catholic Church,
relating to heresy, birth control, and obscenity.

"Voluntary Censorship of the Cleveland
Movies." *Survey*, 30:639–40, 23 August
1913. **V 68**

The chief of police authorizes patrolmen to
serve as censors and make arrests. Movie
managers ask for the appointment of a
competent movie censor.

"Volunteer Censorship." *Independent*, 67:
1460–61, 23 December 1909. **V 69**

A defense of the Circulating Libraries Association of England which the author believes
"is guilty of no censorship." It is simply
conducting "a limited boycott." The author
supports censorship of plays in Great Britain.

Von Hilsheimer, George. "Christians
and Censors." *Nugget*, 9:4, 54, February
1965. **V 70**

The general superintendent of Humanitas,
a brotherhood of service, sees in the censor at
work a man dominated by sex, his world
"populated with copulating monstrosities."
To censor works of art and literature that

deal with the joyfulness of nature and that
"elevates and redeems marriage from its too
common state of a legalized prostitution is
demon worship at its most corrupting."

Voorhees, Melvin B. *Korean Tales.* New
York, Simon & Schuster, 1952. 209 p.
V 71

One of the "tales" in this outspoken book on
the Eighth Army in Korea deals with actions
and attitudes of war correspondents; another
deals with military censorship, imposed by the
premature reporting of the death of General
Walker, two days before Christmas when the
Army was striving to halt the onrushing
Chinese. There had been press revelations
that endangered plans or lives ever since the
war began, and 90 per cent of the press
correspondents in Korea said they wanted
press censorship and a good many campaigned
to get it. For the publication of this controversial book without approval by military
authorities the author, a lieutenant colonel,
was court-martialed, found guilty, and dismissed from the service.

Vorpe, W. G. "What Is Freedom of the
Press?" *Quill*, 29(2):3–4+, February 1941.
V 72

A veteran newspaper editor defines freedom
of the press as "the right of any editor, writer
or publisher of any newspaper, magazine or
pamphlet to express an opinion whether it be
endorsement, denunciation, praise, criticism
or suggestion, so long as these expressions are
not treasonable." If individuals are unjustly
accused they have recourse to the libel laws.
He rejects the charges that the National
Recovery Administration of the depression
years was a menace to a free press and that
"the desire for profit" threatens a free press.
He also disagrees with the charges against the
press made by Harold Ickes.

*Vox Senatus. The Speeches at Large Which
Were Made in a Great Assembly . . . When
J. C. Phipps Made a Motion, "For Leave to
Bring in a Bill to Amend the Act of William
the Third, Which Empowers the Attorney
General to File Informations Ex Officio,"
and . . . When Serjeant Glynn Made a
Motion, "That a Committee Should be
Appointed to Enquire into . . . the Proceedings
of the Judges in Westminster Hall, Particularly
in Cases relating to the Liberty of the Press,
and the Constitutional Power and Duty of
Juries."* London, W. Woodfall, 1771. **V 73**

W

[W., G.]. *Remarks Upon the Rights and Duties of Jurymen, in Trials for Libel, in a Letter Addressed to Jeremy Bentham.* . . . London, Heward, 1831. 24p. (Signed G. W.) **W1**

The author maintains that in "matters of law, as well as matters of fact, by express written law, the jury are the sole judges in trials for libel, in whatever shape brought before them, by means of criminal process, as information, indictment, or by means of civil process, as an action at law for damages." From the beginning, the law of libel was intended to put down discussion, written and spoken, and to prevent the spread of intelligence. The power to suppress opinion, whether "possessed and exercised by one, few, or many, is equally indefensible; for it is tyranny and being tyranny, cannot be the rule of right."

W., W. R. "Extralegal Censorship Held Valid." *Utah Law Review*, 8:70–74, Summer 1962. **W2**

Regarding *Bantam Books, Inc. v. Sullivan* and the constitutionality of the Rhode Island Commission to Encourage Morality in Youth.

[Waddington, Samuel]. "Trial of Samuel Waddington for Publishing a Blasphemous Libel. Judgment of Abbott, C.J., Bayley, Holroyd, and William D. Best, J.J., on November 14, 1822, on Motion for a New Trial." In Macdonell, *Report of State Trials*, vol. 1, pp. 1339–43. **W3**

The defendant published a pamphlet in which Jesus Christ was referred to as an "imposter" and "a murderer in principle." Chief Justice Abbott directed the jury that the publication was a blasphemous libel; and the jury found Waddington guilty.

Wade, E. C. S. "Obscene Publications Act, 1959." *Cambridge Law Journal*, 1959: 179–82, November 1959. **W4**

A discussion of the change in the British obscenity laws and the implication to protection of morals and freedom of literature.

Wadsworth, William S. "Newspaper and Crime." *Bulletin*, American Academy of Medicine, 12:316–25, October 1911. **W5**

The effect of the publication of crime news on behavior.

Wagman, Frederick H. "Freedom to Read—Active Voice." *ALA Bulletin*, 58:473–81, June 1964. **W6**

The president of the American Library Association in various meetings across the nation decided to talk about the freedom to read because it seemed "to lie at the very heart of our philosophy of librarianship, because the defense and the extension of this freedom are the most profound obligations we have and, for some of us, the most trying." One of the strongest weapons against censorship pressures, he writes, "would be a library accreditation system that had the respect of library and school boards and that could make it difficult to mistreat a librarian for doing his professional duty." He suggests an advisory service that could blacklist a library as an undesirable place to work, much as the American Association of University Professors is able to make a university squirm by issuing an unfavorable report if that university violates academic freedom. Freedom to read is also abridged by the scarcity of libraries —both public and school—in many parts of the nation, and by the denial of service to citizens because of race. "Of all our inadequacies," he writes, "the weakness of our college libraries seems to me the most distressing." Students who face an impoverished college library "are not truly free to read."

Wagner, Geoffrey A. *Parade of Pleasure: A Study of Popular Iconography in the USA.* New York, Library Publishers, 1955. 192p. **W7**

A British critic defends American freedom of expression despite the fact that this tolerance has permitted certain vulgar expressions in popular iconography—in the movies, television, the comic books, and the pin-up magazines. The book is a critical review of sex and sadism in American mass media.

Wagner, Robert W. "Motion Pictures in Relation to Social Control." In National Society for the Study of Education. *Mass Media and Education*, 53d Yearbook. Chicago, University of Chicago Press, 1954, pp. 54–79. **W8**

"Censorship of the motion pictures takes many forms. It is found in federal laws such as those regulating the import and export of films, in state and local censorship rulings, and in the self-imposed censorship of scripts and films by the Production Code Administration. Special-interest groups . . . may also voice disapproval of certain films . . . And finally, there is a kind of censorship which grows from the fact that truth is hard to portray."

Wagner, Ruth H. "What About Those Attacks on UNESCO?" *Midland Schools*, 67:12–13+, October 1952. (Reprinted in Daniels, *The Censorship of Books*, pp. 128–32) **W9**

Waisbrooker, Lois. "The Great Conspiracy." *To-morrow* (Chicago), 2:68–72, September 1906. **W10**

Criticizes postal censorship of radical sex and labor reformers.

———, and Mattie D. Penhallow. "Our New Contest." *Discontent*, 4:1, 26 March 1902. **W11**

The account of an arrest because of an article, The Awful Fate of a Fallen Woman, published in *Clothed in the Sun*, December 1901. Miss Penhallow was postmistress at Home, Wash., and was arrested for forwarding the paper.

Waite, John B. "Administrative Censorship—the *Esquire* Decisions." *Michigan Law Review*, 43:1172–80, June 1945. **W12**

Relates to the denial by the Post Office Department of the second-class mailing privileges to *Esquire* and the disposal of the order by Judge Arnold of the Court of Appeals (*Esquire, Inc. v. Walker, Postmaster General*, App. D.C., 1945). Partial text of the hearing and the decision.

Wakefield, Dan. "An Unhurried View of Ralph Ginzburg." *Playboy*, 12:95–96, 172–77, October 1965. **W13**

"... in which the trials, tribulations and temperment of the sorely pressed publisher of eros, fact and assorted erotica are dispassionately probed."

[Wakefield, Gilbert]. "Proceedings on the Trial of an Information . . . against Gilbert Wakefield, Clerk, for a Seditious Libel . . ., 1799." In Howell, *State Trials*, vol. 27, pp. 679 ff. **W14**
Reverend Wakefield, a church scholar, was convicted and given two years in prison for writing and publishing a pamphlet that was critical of the king, the Pitt administration, and the clergy. At the trial he spoke in his own behalf, adding fuel to the fire. He maintained his Christian right and duty to speak and write thusly. He was found guilty, imprisoned, and died shortly after his release.

Wakeman, Thaddeus B. *Administrative Process of the Postal Department, A Letter to the President.* [New York, Free Speech League, 1906]. 16 p. **W15**
A letter to President Theodore Roosevelt from one of the nation's leading opponents of the Comstock postal laws. Wakeman considers these laws and their administration by the Post Office Department as a threat to the freedom of the press in America, a violation of the Bill of Rights, a uniting of Church and State, and an offense against humanity. He cites particularly the recent cases against Dr. Alice B. Stockman and Moses Harman, editor of *Lucifer.* The latter, aged 76, was given a year's sentence at hard labor for his publication on sex education for married women. Wakeman calls on President Roosevelt to instruct the Post Office Department to attend to postal affairs, leaving censorship to the courts.

———. *The Comstock Laws Considered as to Their Constitutionality; Being T. B. Wakeman's Faneuil Hall Speech, Replies to the Index, Judge E. P. Hurlbut's "Liberty of Printing," Mr. Wakeman's Reply, the Laws in Question, Various Letters from Eminent Men . . .* New York, D. M. Bennett, 1880. 61 p.; 67 p. (Truth Seeker Tracts nos. 144 and 150 bound together with a common title page and an introduction by T. B. Wakeman) **W16**
Contents: (1) A letter from T. B. Wakeman to the officers of the third Convention of the National Liberal League (New York), 8 August 1878, in which he reiterates his opposition to the Comstock act. (2) Reprint of Wakeman's address delivered at the "Indignation Meeting," Faneuil Hall, Boston, 1878, on the arrest of Ezra H. Heywood, editor of *The Word.* (3) Justice Field's opinion in the case of A. Orlando Jackson (1877), Supreme Court of the United States, affirming the constitutionality of the Comstock act. (4) Wakeman's answers to criticism of his Faneuil Hall speech in *The Index.* (5) E. P. Hurlbut's address to the second convention of the National Liberal League, 1878. The address, entitled

The Liberty of Printing, endorsing the Blackstone view that freedom of the press consists of freedom from prior restraint, not freedom from penalties after publication. Hurlbut defends the Post Office action against obscenity. (6) Wakeman's reply to the Hurlbut speech in a letter entitled, The Campaign against Unconstitutional Postal Laws and Espionage over the Mails. (7) Letters recommending repeal of the Comstock laws from James Parton, O. B. Frothingham, Elizur Wright, and others.

———. *Liberty and Purity. How to Secure Both Safely, Effectively, and Impartially. An Address before the Committee on Charitable and Religious Societies of the Assembly of the State of New York in Opposition to a Bill to Largely Increase the Criminal Jurisdiction and Powers of the Society for the Suppression of Vice. March 23, 1881.* New York, Liberal Publishing Co., 1881. 92 p. **W17**
A bill before the legislature called for sweeping police powers to be given to the New York Comstock society. Mr. Wakeman, a New York lawyer and leader in the National Liberal League, presented to the Committee a substitute bill to return the enforcement of the obscenity laws to local district attorneys and to limit the vice society to "persuasive, advisory, charitable, educational, missionary, and religious means" of suppressing vice. The testimony is a strong attack on vice societies in general and the tactics of Anthony Comstock in particular. Wakeman brings testimony against the Comstock bill from members of the National Liberal League and cites the attacks of the vice society against such liberals as Ezra Heywood, Elizur Wright, Robert Ingersoll, Dr. E. B. Foote, O. B. Frothingham, and others.

[Wakley, Thomas]. *Report of the Trial, Cooper versus Wakley, for Libel. From the Notes of W. B. Gurney, Esq. . . . with Remarks on the Evidence, by Bransby B. Cooper, Surgeon, and Lecturer on Anatomy at Guy's Hospital.* London, Printed for S. Highley, 1829. 182 p. **W18**
Bransby Blake Cooper, surgeon at Guy's Hospital, London, charged the defendant, Mr. Wakley, editor of *Lancet,* with publishing two articles in that journal allegedly ridiculing his professional conduct in an operation for lithotomy. The articles, written for the *Lancet* by a surgeon who witnessed the operation, further suggested that Cooper was incompetent and held his position because he was the nephew of Sir Ashley Cooper, noted surgeon. Wakley conducted his own defense, and in an unusual procedure was permitted by the judge, Lord Tenterden, to present his case before that of the plaintiff. The jury found Wakley guilty, but damages were so small (£100) as to establish Wakley's main contention of malpractice. Wakley's expenses were defrayed by public subscription. In a long career of crusading for medical and hospital reform Wakley was often involved in litigation. In 1826 he was awarded £100 damages for a libel on him in the *Medico-Chirurgical Journal.*

Wakley founded the *Lancet* in 1823 to publish accounts of medical lectures, hitherto regarded as the exclusive property of members of hospital staffs who received lucrative fees. Attempts were made to secure an injunction against publication, but Lord Elden ruled that lectures given in public places were public property. The Cooper articles were part of a series in the *Lancet* intended to reveal evidence of malpractice, incompetence, and nepotism in London hospitals. This edition of the trial is liberally footnoted by Cooper, who considered the outcome of the trial a complete vindication of his professional competence.

Wald, Jerry. "Movie Censorship: The First Wedge." *Saturday Review,* 44(14): 53–54, 8 April 1961. **W19**
The recent decision of the U.S. Supreme Court in upholding (4 to 5) the right of the Chicago Police Commissioner to require censorship of films is "a shock to anyone who cherishes the provisions of our Constitution's First Amendment. . . . It is, in effect, a backhanded tribute to the unique power of film as a medium of communication that the film has been singled out to be censored in this fashion." The author disapproves of film censorship by local, state, or national boards, preferring the self-censorship of the industry. "The Code seems to remain the most valid way of dealing with the ever-hovering threat of censorship." Wald also disapproves the adoption of the British system of film classification. The best solution to the problem of preventing children from seeing undesirable films is for parents to exercise their authority and judgment as to what films their children are permitted to see.

Walford, Edward. "Life of Lord Erskine." In *Speeches of Thomas Lord Erskine . . . With Memoir of His Life by Edward Walford.* London, Reeves & Turner, 1870. vol. 1, pp. vii–xxiv. **W20**
"It is almost superfluous to remind the legal reader what great services Lord Erskine rendered to posterity by his advocacy and assertion of the Liberty of the Press, and by his definition of the Law of Libel, or that, in his day [1750–1823] he was the principal agent in the work of improving the state of the law on these all-important subjects."

[Walker, Clement]. *The Triall of Lieut.-Collonell John Lilburne at the Guild-Hall of London, 24, 25, 26 Oct. [1649].* London, Published by Thoedorus Verax, [1649]. 166 p. (Verax is the pseudonym for Clement Walker) **W21**
One of the numerous contemporary accounts of the sedition trial of Lilburne.

Walker, Edwin A. *Censorship and Survival.* New York, Bookmailer, 1961. 67 p. **W22**

The text of Major General Walker's statement to the U.S. Senate Armed Services Committee charging censorship, following his removal from command of the 24th Infantry Division in the controversy over his "Pro-Blue" indoctrination program. Included is the text of the controversial training circular and commentary by Ike McAnally.

Walker, Edwin C. "The Country's Postal Censor." *Lucifer, The Light Bearer*, 12(35): 2, 14 December 1896.   **W 23**
Anthony Comstock and the vice societies.

———. *The Ethics of Freedom. You and the Other Man is The Covenant of Liberty . . .* New York, Walker, 1913. 24 p.   **W 24**
Dinner address at the Sunrise Club, 24 February 1913. Appendix includes Walker's letter to *The Globe*, What Does "Free Speech" Include?

———. *The Revival of Puritanism.* New York, Free Speech League, 1903. 13 p.
                                          W 25
In a paper read before the Sunrise Club, Walker predicts a revival of puritan repression in the twentieth century. Among the prohibitive measures he cites are censorship of the mails under the Comstock law, and local pressures against newsstands and theaters. He quotes Frances Willard, in her address before the WCTU, as advocating the creation of a cabinet position, Secretary of Amusements, whose duty would be to determine what plays would be presented.

———. *Who Is the Enemy; Anthony Comstock or You?* New York, The Author, 1903. 63 p.   **W 26**
This caustic criticism of Comstock and the work of the vice societies was written by a crusading freethinker who was active in the National Liberal League and associated with the papers, *Lucifer* and *The Truth Seeker*.

Walker, George. *Substance of the Speech of the Rev. Mr. Walker at the General Meeting of the County of Nottingham, held at Mansfield, on Monday, the 28th of February, 1780. To Which Is Added Mr. Thomson's Preface to a Speech of Mr. John Milton, for the Liberty of Unlicensed Printing, to the Parliament of England. First Published in the Year 1644.* London, The Society for Constitutional Information, 1780. 12 p.   **W 27**

Walker, J. "The Censorship of the Press during the Reign of Charles II." *History*, 35(n.s.):219–38, October 1950.   **W 28**
Discussion of the creation and operation of the Licensing Act of 1662 and the monopolistic activities of the Stationers' Company. In 1668

the Stationers' Company was made responsible for suppressing the trade in libels.

Walker, Jerry. "Civil Liberties Union Considers Free Radio." *Editor and Publisher*, 78:34, 1 December 1945.   **W 29**
A report on needed changes in the regulation of federal laws on freedom of the air as discussed at the 25th annual conference of the American Civil Liberties Union.

Walker, Roy. "Sense and Censorability." *Twentieth Century*, 163:554–57, June 1958.
                                          W 30
"The case against British stage censorship is not that Bowdler is now in control and our stage is fast becoming one dark repertory of repressions in consequence. It is that compulsory licensing is an effective standing deterrent to the composition of new plays dealing directly with what are, for obvious reasons, the dynamic sources for contemporary drama—controversial beliefs, politics and sex."

Walker, Stanley. "'Book Branding'; a Case History." *New York Times Magazine*, 12 July 1953, pp. 11, 20–21.   **W 31**
An account of the crusade against Communist books in the San Antonio, Texas, public library led by Mrs. Myrtle Glasscock Hance and opposed by M. M. Harris, head of the library's board of trustees. Mrs. Hance proposed that library books written by Communist sympathizers bear a warning stamp.

———. "The Newspaper and Crime." In *Attorney General's Conference on Crime. Proceedings, 1934.* Washington, D.C., Govt. Print. Off., 1936, pp. 98–103.   **W 32**
"In general . . . I am in favor of the merciless, complete printing of all the news of crime, even of crime photographs. In no other way can the public be shaken out of its natural lethargy . . . I believe it is better for the public to be fully informed, whether the facts are pleasant or shocking, than to remain ignorant." He also defends the gangster picture. Walker was then city editor of the New York *Herald Tribune*.

Wall, Bernard T. "Ordinance Requiring Submission of Motion Pictures for Examination and Licensing Prior to Exhibition Not Void Per Se." *University of Illinois Law Forum*, 1961:332–36, Summer 1961.
                                          W 33
Times Film Corp. v. City of Chicago, 365 U.S. 43 (1961).

Wall, James M. "Toward Christian Film Criteria." *Christian Century*, 82:775–78, 16 June 1965.   **W 34**
"How are we to obtain freedom of artistic expression in view of the temptation to exploit salaciousness for its own sake?"

Wall, Patrick M. "Obscenity and Youth: The Problem and a Possible Solution." *Criminal Law Bulletin*, 1(8):28–39, October 1965.   **W 35**
Includes text and analysis of New York State's new obscenity statute, intended to protect youth but liberalize freedom for adult literature.

Wall, Thomas H. "Program Evaluation by the Federal Communications Commission: an Unconstitutional Abridgement of Free Speech?" *Georgetown Law Journal*, 40:1–40, November 1951.   **W 36**

Wallace, *Mrs.* George R. "It *Has* Happened in Massachusetts." *Massachusetts Library Association Bulletin*, 43:4–5, January 1953.   **W 37**
An account of the attack on the Boston Public Library for allegedly possessing and circulating Communist propaganda. The author is president of the Trustee Association of the MLA.

Wallace, Irving. "A Problem Author Looks at Problem Librarians." *Library Journal*, 87:2293–97, 15 June 1962.   **W 38**
Too many librarians judge modern works of fiction "not for what they say, or have to say, but because their central theme troubles the reviewer or librarian, or rubs his or her neurosis the wrong way, or makes his life uneasy when he or she simply wants it easy—smooth, slick, and easy." Wallace believes that librarians and authors have much in common and a mutual need for each other. While recognizing the leadership of many librarians in upholding the freedom to read, he addresses his criticism to those who stand guard between an author and his public. He concludes: "If you will accept into your vocabulary one seven letter word—*courage*— you will need worry less about all our four letter words."

Wallas, Graham. *The Life of Francis Place, 1771–1854.* London, Longmans, Green, 1898. 415 p. (Reprinted in New York by Burt Franklin, 1951)   **W 39**
Place was a radical reformer, remembered for his efforts in behalf of Chartism, the trade union movement, and birth control. He also joined with Henry Hetherington, James Mill, and Richard Carlile in opposing the newspaper stamp tax. He was associated with Roebuck in publishing the unstamped weekly pamphlet series, which are said to have reached a sale of 10,000. The stamp tax was not repealed until 1855, a year after Place's death. This biography has numerous references to Place's efforts in behalf of freedom of the press.

———. "The Price of Tolerance." *Atlantic Monthly*, 125:116–18, January 1920. **W 40**
The author reports on the suppression of Thorstein Veblen's *Imperial Germany*, and pleads for greater tolerance for radicals.

Waller, Theodore. "Paper-Bound Books and Censorship." *ALA Bulletin*, 47: 474–76, November 1953. **W 41**
"The censors argue that the low price and wide availability of paper-bound books make them more a threat to the immature and impressionable reader than the more expensive original editions of the same books." The author objects to the double standard. The only tenable position is to take a book as a book whatever the format and to deal with censorship as an invidious process wherever it is found. The American Book Publishers Council of which the author is managing director, "is militantly opposing censorship, whether it strikes first at the newsstand, library or bookstore."

Wallis, C. Lamar. "Too Much Ado About Too Little." *ALA Bulletin*, 59: 100, February 1965. **W 42**
The director of the Memphis Public Library takes issue with Ervin Gaines's charges of censorship in Memphis, made in the Intellectual Freedom column of the *ALA Bulletin*. No library or bookstore has been visited by police and, except for a flurry of activity over a handful of "girlie" magazines, Memphis is relatively free of censorship by organized citizen groups or the police. "Contrary to the expressed belief of some librarians, I do not feel it my duty to defend to death every scrap of paper which happens to be run through a printing press. If private individuals want to sell for profit the girlie magazines let them do so at their own risk before the courts."

Walpole, *Sir* Hugh. *The Freedom of Books.* [London, National Book Council, 1940?]. 4 p. Reprinted in *Classics in Sociology*, pp. 145–50. **W 43**
"For many centuries now the Englishman has enjoyed perfect freedom in the reading of any kind of literature. . . . So the freedom of books is indestructible, and the men and women of our country, with all their faults and lacks, are made of this freedom. No government is tolerable to them for a moment that tries to prevent their right to think for themselves, often studying all the evidence, past and present. That trust in their independence is their right, won through years of conflict, and never again, to any power on this earth will they surrender it."

Walsh, J. Herbert. "Is the New Judicial and Legislative Interpretation of Freedom of Speech, and of the Freedom of the Press, Sound Constitutional Development?" *Georgetown Law Journal*, 21:35–50, November 1932; 21:161–91, January 1933. **W 44**
Beginning with the Sedition Act of 1798, the author traces the judicial and legislative development of the modern concept of freedom of the press. The First Amendment prevents Congress from abridging freedom of speech or of the press, but under the Sedition Act and as late as 1907 freedom meant only freedom from prior restraint. This Blackstonian inter-

pretation was overruled by cases decided under the Espionage Act of 1917. Our protection today rests in the hands of the U.S. Supreme Court which contains judges who look first to the protection of the people. One group acts as a counterbalance to the other.

Walsh, William T. "Cut Out By the 'Movie' Censor." *Illustrated World*, 27: 14–19+, March 1917. **W 45**
The author observes a film being cut by eight censors and by the motion picture producer. He proposes that movies be divided into two classes—those which are uncensored to be forbidden to minors, and those passed by the censor to be open to all classes and ages. The photoplay is fighting for recognition, for freedom as a legitimate medium of expression.

Walters, Basil. *An Editor Asks a Big "Why?"* Columbia, Mo., Freedom of Information Center, School of Journalism, University of Missouri, 1958. 3 p. (Publication no. 7) **W 46**
Referring to a Purdue University poll which showed that 41 per cent of high school students polled would cancel freedom of the press, the executive editor of the *Chicago Daily News* asks the question: How did these children get that way? Excerpts from his remarks in a panel discussion at a PTA meeting.

Walters, Fred. "The Supreme Court Ruling on *The Miracle* and *Pinky* . . ." *Theatre Arts*, 36:74–77, August 1952. **W 47**
Comments on the U.S. Supreme Court decision lifting bans imposed by local censorship boards against the movies, *The Miracle* and *Pinky*.

Walther, Louis R. *Freedom of the Press in the Americas.* Stanford, Calif., Stanford University, 1939. 45 p. (Unpublished Master's thesis) **W 48**

Walton, Clyde C. "Intellectual Freedom for Librarians." *Iowa Library Quarterly*, 16:195–96, April 1952. **W 49**

[Walwyn, William]. *The Compassionate Samaritane . . .* 2d ed. London, 1644. 79 p. (Reproduced in Haller, *Tracts on Liberty in the Puritan Revolution*, vol. 3, pp. 61–104) **W 50**
Walwyn, a member of the Levellers, was one of the first Englishmen to write forcefully in behalf of freedom of conscience. This tract, published anonymously without license earlier in the same year that Milton's more famous *Areopagitica* appeared, was a criticism of printing regulations. While recognizing the need for some form of regulation of the press, Walwyn believed that the Puritan divines went too far in suppressing religious opposition. He was one of the first to point out the

impracticality of a licensing system and to question the judgment of the licensers.

———. *The Fountain Of Slaunder Discovered. By William Walwyn, Merchant With Some passages concerning his present Imprisonment in the Tower of London. Published for satisfaction of Friends and Enemies.* London, Printed by H. Hils, 1649. 26 p. **W 51**
The author's account of his arrest and conviction, along with Lilburne, Overton, and Prince, for circulation of Leveller pamphlets.

[———]. *To the right Honourable and supreme Authority of this Nation, the Commons in Parliament Assembled.* London, 1647. 7 p. **W 52**
This pamphlet, believed to have been written by Walwyn, was one of several petitions submitted by the Levellers to the House of Commons to secure basic freedoms, including the right to publish religious opinions. It presented a 13-point program of civil liberties. The pamphlet was ordered burned by the common hangman. (Reproduced in Haller, *Tracts on Liberty in the Puritan Revolution*, vol. 3, pp. 399–405)

"War Against the Smut Peddlers." *Changing Times*, 14:19–22, August 1960. **W 53**
A detailed plan for community action against the pornographer who preys on youngsters. Recommends legal action rather than economic boycotts.

"War and a Free Press." *Outlook*, 116: 56–57, 9 May 1917. **W 54**
"Congress ought to protect the right of the Administration to prevent the publication of news which it deems injurious to the public interest; and it ought to protect the right of the public through the press to criticize freely the public acts and public policies of the Administration."

"The War on the Minnesota Law." *Literary Digest*, 104:13, 1 February 1930. (Reprinted in Beman, *Censorship of Speech and the Press*, pp. 212–15) **W 55**
An attack on the Minnesota "gag law" which has reduced press freedom in Minnesota "to about the freedom of a strait-jacket." The text of the statute is reprinted in Beman, pp. 216–18.

Warburg, Frederic J. "Onward and Upward with the Arts: A Slight Case of Obscenity." *New Yorker*, 33:106–33, 20 April 1957. **W 56**
An account of the author's trial in 1954 in London's Old Bailey for publishing "an

obscene book," Stanley Kauffmann's *The Philanderer*. The defendant, a member of the publishing firm of Martin Secker & Warburg, London, was acquitted.

Ward, Harry F. "Repression of Civil Liberties in the United States." *Publications of the American Sociological Society*, 18:127–46, 1924. **W 57**
"This discussion summarizes recent developments in relation to free speech, in the field of law—federal, state and municipal. . . . It assembles the evidence concerning administrative interference with civil liberties—from the Department of Justice down through state officials to municipal authorities. It then reviews the attitudes of the public mind as shown by mob violence, anti-radical propaganda, attacks upon the American Civil Liberties Union, and the relations of the legal profession to our constitutional guarantees of freedom."

[Ward, William V.]. "*Provincetown Review on Trial . . .*" *Provincetown Review*, 5, Winter 1961. 62 p. plus. **W 58**
The entire issue is devoted to the trial of the editor of the *Provincetown Review* (*Commonwealth of Massachusetts v. William V. Ward*), 17 August 1961, for publication of an offending short story, *Tralala*, by Herbert Selby, Jr. This issue reprints the story together with a transcript of the trial.

Warfield, Ethelbert D. *Kentucky Resolutions of 1798, an Historical Study*. New York, Putnam's, 1887. 203 p. **W 59**
A study of the Kentucky Resolutions composed by Thomas Jefferson in opposition to the Alien and Sedition Acts of 1798.

Warne, Colston E. *Caveat Venditor*. Columbia, Mo., Freedom of Information Center, School of Journalism, University of Missouri, 1961. 6 p. (Publication no. 51) **W 60**

A professor of economics discusses the ethical and social responsibilities in advertising and sales practices. To protect the consumer he argues for a legally enforced responsibility for accurate information about a firm's product (caveat venditor) to supplement the prohibitions against false advertising. "The truth is not a residue left after falsehood has been eliminated; information does not necessarily fill the gap left when misinformation has been erased."

Warner, Bob. "Canon 35: The Case for the Defendant." *U.S. Camera*, 26(7): 64–65, 92, 97, July 1963. **W 61**
In the conflict between the right of the photographer to take pictures and the right of the defendant to have a fair trial, the defendant's right should take precedence.

Warner, H. C. *Threatened Standards: Erotic Elements in Current Publications*. London, S. C. M. Press, [1954?]. 11 p. (Sex Education Booklets). **W 62**
The author is a canon of the church.

Warner, Harry P. *Radio and Television Law*. Albany, Matthew Bender, 1948. 1 vol. loose-leaf. **W 63**
A standard reference book on the legal and regulatory structure of the radio industry, kept up-to-date by cumulative supplements.

Warner, Rex. "Freedom in Literary and Artistic Creation." In UNESCO's *Freedom and Culture*. New York, Columbia University Press, 1951, pp. 305–28. **W 64**
The sphere in which the creative writer works is "beyond politics and different from religion" and "any dictation or control exercised over writers and artists by political or religious bodies is bound to be both dangerous and constricting." Education, leisure, and freedom from outside censorship, control, or dictation are the chief demands that the creative artist makes on society.

Warren, C. Henry. "Freedom at the B.B.C." *Bookman* (London), 86:38, April 1934. **W 65**
An account of William Ferrie, who, instead of giving a talk over the B.B.C. as arranged, made an impromptu protest of the censorship of his text by B.B.C. until he was cut off.

Warren, Charles. *Jacobin and Junto; or, Early American Politics as Viewed in the Diary of Dr. Nathaniel Ames, 1758–1822*. Cambridge, Mass., Harvard University Press, 1931. 324 p. **W 66**
The frank diary of this fiery partisan of the Antifederalist party, devotes considerable attention to the conflict over the Alien and Sedition Acts and the libel trials that resulted.

Warren, Fred D. *Suppressed Information and Federal Court Speech*. Chicago, Charles H. Kerr, [1910?]. 63 p. **W 67**
Warren was convicted of sending a publication by mail with a wrapper containing scurrilous matter.

Warren, Samuel D., and Louis D. Brandeis. "The Right to Privacy." *Harvard Law Review*, 4:193–220, 15 December 1890. **W 68**
A classic statement on the Anglo-American law relating to the individual's right to withhold or to communicate his thoughts and feelings.

Warren, Sidney. *American Freethought, 1860–1914*. New York, Columbia University Press, 1943. 257 p. (Studies in History, Economics and Public Law no. 504) **W 69**
Since the American free-thought movement was often concerned with issues of free speech and press, this history of the movement contains numerous references to censorship, both in matters of religion (blasphemy) and obscenity. Included is an account of the Charles Reynolds blasphemy case and the schism in the National Liberal League in 1878 over an attack on the Comstock acts (modification or repeal). The publication, *Truth Seeker*, representing the extreme left wing of the free-thought movement, and a long-time champion of a free press (D. W. Bennett was once its editor) is mentioned throughout.

Warren, William C., *et al*. "Community Security vs. Man's Right to Knowledge." *Columbia Law Review*, 54:667–837, May 1954. **W 70**
The dean of the School of Law, Columbia University, wrote the introduction to this issue which contains symposium papers delivered as part of Columbia's bicentennial. Dean Warren reviews the historic struggle of "man's right to the free use of knowledge," the theme of the bicentennial. This is followed by articles on the experience of religious groups in freedom of expression: Judaism (Robert Gordis); Roman Catholicism (Francis J. Connell); Islam (Saba Habacky); and Protestantism (Robert T. Handy). The experience of national states is reported for Great Britain (Sir Hartley Shawcross), The Soviet Union, France, China, Canada (Ivan C. Rand), Italy, Spain, Switzerland, and The Netherlands.

Warshow, Robert. "Paul, and Horror Comics, and Dr. Wertham." In Rosenberg and White. *Mass Culture*. Glencoe, Ill., Free Press, 1957, pp. 199–211. **W 71**
While disagreeing with Dr. Wertham on the serious affect of comic books on juvenile delinquency, the author favors some form of regulation of the worst of the comic books and believes that no real problem of freedom of expression is involved, except that it may be difficult to frame a law that would not open the way to a wider censorship. The problem of regulation is more difficult than Dr. Wertham imagines.

Wasby, Stephen L. "Public Law, Politics, and the Local Courts: Obscene Literature in Portland." *Journal of Public Law* (Emory University Law School), 14:105–30, 1965. **W 72**
A case study of a campaign against obscene literature which took place in Portland, Ore., in 1959. "In addition to portraying the impact of local courts on politics, the case study also illustrated the utilization of an advisory committee by executive officials in an attempt to secure their goals."

Washington Library Association. "Statement on Freedom to Read." *Library*

Wasilewski, Vincent T. *Payola and Government Controls.* Columbia, Mo., Freedom of Information Center, School of Journalism, University of Missouri, 1960. 4 p. (Publication no. 30) **W 74**
An official of the National Association of Broadcasters lists objections and counter-proposals by that organization to the various recommendations for regulating the broadcast industry in light of "payola" and other abuses.

"The Watch and Ward Society of Censorship." *Massachusetts Library Club Bulletin,* 17:70–71, October 1927. **W 75**
A review of the recent history of the vice society, the appointment of Charles S. Bodwell to succeed the late J. Frank Chase as secretary, and the text of Bodwell's statement to the press on the future of the organization.

Watchet, H. Mitchell. "The Arrest and Trial of the Editor." *Physical Culture,* 15:582–84, June 1906. **W 76**
Bernarr Macfadden, editor of *Physical Culture,* was arrested in his editorial office by Anthony Comstock for "giving away obscene prints." Macfadden appeared before the Court of Special Sessions where he was found guilty, but because of a divided Court no punishment was fixed. The Court refused to admit expert witnesses to testify on whether or not the work was obscene.

Watkins, A. T. L. "Film Censorship in Britain." In *Penguin Film Review,* 9:61–66, 1949. **W 77**
The secretary of the British Board of Film Censors discusses the work of that agency. In judging films the Board considers three main questions: Is it likely to impair the moral standards of the audience? Is the story, incident, or dialogue likely to give offense to any reasonably minded section of the public? What will be the effect of the movie on children? "Censorship is only news when it makes a mistake."

Watrous, A. E. "The Newspaper and the Individual: a Plea for Press Censorship." *Lippincott's Monthly Magazine,* 45:267–70, February 1890. **W 78**
As an editor "the fact that has struck me with the greatest force in the relation of the newspaper to the individual is the utter inadequacy of the present libel law to protect either party." The author calls for the creation of an extrajudicial body which shall, with the approval of the legislative body, erect its own code, defining the functions of a newspaper, protecting its use of these functions, and punishing its abuse. The author was editor of the Philadelphia *Press.*

Watrous, George D. "The Newspaper before the Law." *Yale Law Journal,* 9:1–16,

October 1899. **W 79**
A brief history of press freedom during the nineteenth century.

Watson, E. H. L. "A Censorship of Fiction, and Some Other Matters." *Dial,* 50:296–98, 16 April 1911. **W 80**
A letter from the London correspondent describes present literary and stage censorship in England. He discusses George Bernard Shaw's relationship to the Select Committee of Parliament and the pressures for censorship by certain groups. The only remedy for censorship is to wait for public taste to improve.

Watson, Francis. "Thou Shalt Not Read. . . ." *Bookman* (London), 84:290–91, September 1933. **W 81**
The writer examines two parallel lists: the *Index* of the Catholic Church and a French publication listing approved and disapproved books on surrealism. He argues that to neglect to study the opposing case "implies either unjustifiable self-sufficiency or else an admission of the weakness of one's own case, which must thus deliberately be protected from criticism. Such consideration, of course, applies directly to any form of literary censorship."

Watson, G. B. "Periodicals of Change—Propaganda." *Pacific Northwest Library Association Proceedings,* 27:85–87, 1936. **W 82**
To refuse to handle periodicals advocating a fundamental change in our social system "is for the library to disclaim the necessity of inquiry, to be glaringly undemocratic." The library "would become an agent of repression and would ally itself with the very forces causing the discontent . . . The function of a periodical collection is, among other things, to present a cross section of contemporary opinion."

[Watson, James]. *A Report of the Trial of James Watson for Having Sold a Copy of Palmer's Principles of Nature, at the Shop of Mr. Carlile . . . on the 24th Day of April, 1823, before Mr. Const, as chairman, and a Common Jury.* London, R. Carlile, 1825. 28 p. **W 83**
Watson was found guilty and sentenced to a year in prison.

Watson, John S. *Biographies of John Wilkes and William Cobbett.* Edinburgh, Blackwood, 1870. 407 p. **W 84**
An English clergyman interprets two figures in the fight for freedom of the press. He considers Wilkes a selfish, indulgent, fraudulent charmer, without a redeeming quality. Cobbett, he finds, was a man of good character and temperate habits, but erratic and mischievious in his attacks on the popular opinions of his day. G. D. H. Cole characterizes Watson's work on Cobbett as "poor stuff."

Watson, Richard. *Sermon Preached before the Society for the Suppression of Vice in the*

Parish Church of St. George, Hanover Square, on Thursday, the 3d of May, 1804 . . . to which are added the Plan of the Society, a Summary of the Proceedings and a List of Its Members. London, Printed for the Society by T. Woodfall, [1804]. 72 p. **W 85**

[Watson, Thomas E.]. "Attorney General Does Not Realize the Lawlessness of His Threatened Proceedings Against Watson." *Watson's Jeffersonian Magazine,* 22:302–7, April 1916. **W 86**
Watson, a self-styled Jeffersonian democrat and twice candidate for the presidency on the Populist ticket, used his two journals, *Watson's Jeffersonian Magazine* (monthly) and *The Jeffersonian* (weekly), to express violent opposition to socialism and Catholicism and to promote his own economic and social views. He was three times indicted but never convicted on obscenity charges for his book, *The Roman Catholic Hierarchy* (1910), and articles in his papers "exposing" the confessional. This article deals with efforts of the attorney general to prosecute Watson outside the jurisdiction (Atlanta, Ga.) where his magazine was published.

[———]. "The End of the Watson Case; or, How the Roman Catholic Priests Strive to Crush Those Who Expose Their Vices, their Crimes, and their Systematic Underhanded Work, Against Civil and Religious Liberty." *Watson's Jeffersonian Magazine,* 24:129–230, January 1917. **W 87**

[———]. "How the Liberty of the Press is Attacked in the Watson Case." *Jeffersonian,* 12:1–4, 9 December 1915. **W 88**
Editor Watson discusses behind-the-scenes and extralegal motives for prosecuting him on the "obscene" exposure of the Catholic confessional. His own speech at the trial is reported in the 2 December 1915 issue.

[———]. "Official Record of Case of United States v. Thomas E. Watson." *Watson's Jeffersonian Magazine,* 22:111–68, February 1916. **W 89**
A report of Watson's trial on charges of obscenity for sending through the mail a book entitled, *The Roman Catholic Hierarchy,* which was critical of the Catholic confessional. The jury disagreed and Watson was acquitted.

Watt, D. C. "Foreign Affairs, the Public Interest and the Right to Know." *Political Quarterly,* 34:121–36, April 1963. **W 90**

While retired service officers and former ministers are free to consult and publish recent documents, historians are generally restricted to documents not less than 50 years old.

Watts, Alan. "Sculpture by Ron Boise: The Kama Sutra Theme." *Evergreen Review*, 9(36):64–65, June 1965. **W 91**
A transcript of Alan Watts's impromptu talk at a showing of Ron Boise's sculpture at Big Sur Hot Springs. Eleven of his sculptures from the Kama Sutra theme, exhibited at the San Francisco Vorpal Gallery in April 1964, brought about the arrest of the gallery owners and a salesman on obscenity charges, and confiscation of the statuary. After a nine-day trial the jury acquitted the defendants and released the statuary. Watts speaks of the statuary as "pushing the line back" in the same way that Miller, Lawrence, and Joyce did in literature. Where do we draw the line in the expression of intimacy—what is "on-scene" and what is "off-scene" or "obscene"? The article is illustrated with photographs of eight of the statues.

Watts, G. T. "Some Great Advocates: Thomas Erskine." *Law Times*, 223:175–77, 5 April 1957. **W 92**

Way, H. Frank, Jr. "Freedom of the Press: Censorship and Obscenity." In his *Liberty in the Balance: Current Issues in Civil Liberties*. New York, McGraw-Hill, 1964, pp. 29–51. **W 93**
Part of a series, Foundations of American Government and Political Science, to serve the need of an introductory course in American government.

"The 'Ways of Love' Controversy." *Life*, 30:59–60+, 15 January 1951. **W 94**
Controversy over the showing of the film, *The Miracle*, with a brief account of the story and scenes from it.

"We Refuse to Review This Book." *Time & Tide*, 44(14):21, 10 April 1963. **W 95**
An attack on Henry Miller's *Tropic of Cancer* as "the dirtiest book ever to reach British bookstalls." The author considers the prospects for its prosecution in Great Britain under the Obscene Publications Act of 1959.

Weatherford, John. "Drapery for Diego." *Library Journal*, 91:646, 1 February 1966. **W 96**
In his On the Grindstone column the author deals whimsically with the theme of censorship. The title comes from the suggestion by a citizen that a curtain be hung over the Diego Rivera murals in the art museum until the Communist menace passed.

Weaver, George. "Revolving Obscenity: Nudists and Prudes." *Open Road*, 42(2): 4–6+, February 1942. **W 97**

Weaver, Robert. "*Lady Chatterley* and All That." *Tamarack Review*, 21:49–57, Autumn 1961. **W 98**
The editor reviews current censorship practices in Canada, the efforts of pressure groups, the semiofficial action of advisory committees on obscene literature, and the official action of Canadian Customs. He considers recent court decisions and contrasts the strict Canadian interpretation of obscenity statutes with the liberalized interpretation in England under the Obscene Publications Act of 1959.

Weaver, Sylvester L., Jr. "Why Suppress Pay TV? The Fight in California." *Atlantic*, 214(4):55–59, October 1964. **W 99**
The president of Subscription TV, Inc., describes pay TV and the fight for it that is taking place in California, where opposition comes from motion picture exhibitors. The TV broadcasters, an unofficial spokesman for the Federation of Women's Clubs, and a large portion of the public has been led to believe (falsely) that they would be required to pay for commercial programs now on the air.

Webb, Julian. "Conscripting the News: What the Brass Hats Are Trying to Keep 100,000,000 Newspaper Readers from Learning; The Censorship Technique and the Men Behind It; Shades of the Creel Committee." *New Masses*, 39(9):9–11, 20 May 1941. **W 100**
Charges that government censors are going beyond that necessary for the war.

Webb, Philip C., *comp. Copies taken from the Records of the Court of King's Bench . . . the original Office Books of the Secretaries of State, or from the Originals under Seal, of Warrants issued by Secretaries of State, for seizing persons suspected of being guilty of various crimes, particularly of being the authors, printers and publishers of Libels, from the Restoration to the present time, Etc.* London, 1763. 80 p. **W 101**

[———]. *Some Observations on the Late Determination for Discharging Mr. Wilkes from his Commitment to the Tower of London; for being the Author and Publisher of a Seditious Libel, called the North Briton, Number XLV. By a Member of the House of Commons.* London, Sold by A. Millar, 1763. 114 p. **W 102**

Weber, Francis J. "John J. Cantwell and the Legion of Decency." *American Ecclesiastical Review*, 151:237–47, October 1964. **W 103**
An account of the part played by Bishop Cantwell in the formative years of the Legion of Decency, the first nationwide attempt by the Catholic Church "to discipline, according to Catholic moral standards," the nation's film industry.

Webster, Daniel. ["A Free Press"]. In his *Works*. Boston, Little, Brown, 1890. vol. 1, pp. 263–66. **W 104**
In a speech delivered before the National Republican Convention at Worchester, Mass., 12 October 1832, Webster decries the "open attempt to secure the aid and friendship of the public press, by bestowing emoluments of office on its active conductors" as a threat against the freedom of the press, turning "the palladium of liberty into an engine of party." In a speech on the Constitution and the Union, delivered in the U.S. Senate, 7 March 1850, Webster discusses (pp. 358–59) complaints from Southerners against the Northern press: "The press violent! Why, sir, the press is violent everywhere. . . . They think that he who talks loudest reasons the best. And this we must expect when the press is free, as it is here—and I trust always will be—for, with all its licentiousness and all its evil, the entire and absolute freedom of the press is essential to the preservation of government on the basis of a free Constitution. Wherever it exists there will be foolish paragraphs and violent paragraphs in the press, as there are, I am sorry to say, foolish speeches and violent speeches in both Houses of Congress."

———. "Freedom of the Mails." In M. M. Miller, *ed., Great American Debates*. New York, Current Literature Publishing Co., 1913. vol. 4, pp. 129–30. **W 105**
Senator Webster opposed the bill, introduced into the U.S. Senate by Calhoun, to prohibit the Post Office from accepting publications critical of slavery. Webster charges that the wording of the bill is vague and obscure and that, should it pass, even the Constitution of the United States might be prohibited. The bill is in conflict with the First Amendment of the Constitution prohibiting the abridgment of the freedom of speech and press. The circulation of papers through the mails, he maintains, constitutes an ordinary mode of publication. Furthermore, no paper should be pronounced unlawful without a legal trial.

Wedderburn, Robert. *The Address of the Rev. R. Wedderburn, to the Court of King's Bench at Westminster, on appearing to receive Judgment for Blasphemy, when he was sentenced to Two Years Imprisonment in Dorchester Jail. . . . Edited by Erasmus Perkins*. London, T. Davison, [1820]. 15 p. **W 106**

[———]. *The Trial of the Rev. Robt. Wedderburn, (A Dissenting Minister of the*

Unitarian Persuasion) *for Blasphemy. . . . Edited by Erasmus Perkins.* London, Printed for the editor and sold by Mrs. Carlile, 1820. 23 p. **W107**

The defendant, who claimed to be the off-spring of a female slave by a Scotsman, was sentenced to two years in prison for a "blasphemous" talk he made in Hopkins Street Chapel in Soho, commenting on the trial of Richard Carlile. His subject was: "Whether the refusal of the Chief Justice to allow Mr. Carlile to read the Bible in his defense, was to be attributed to the sincere respect he had for the sacred writings, or to a fear lest the absurdities it contained should be exposed?"

[Weed, Thurlow]. *The Great Libel Case. Geo. Opdyke Agt. Thurlow Weed. A Full Report of the Speeches of Counsel, Testimony, etc.* New York, American News, 1865. 156 p. **W108**

Thurlow Weed was sued for libel for articles appearing in his *Albany Evening Journal*, accusing George Opdyke, prominent civic leader and politician, of fraudulent dealings in Army contracts. The jury could not agree and Mr. Weed was freed of the charge.

[————]. *The Opdyke Libel Suit. A Full Metrical, Juridical, and Analytical Report of the Extraordinary Suit for Libel of George Opdyke "Versus" Thurlow Weed . . . in the New York Supreme Court Circuit, before Judge Charles Mason . . . By a Full Corps de Bully, Short and Long Metre Reporters.* New York, 1865. 62 p. **W109**

A satirical poem on the Opdyke-Weed libel suit together with excerpts from newspaper opinion on the trial.

Weeks, Edward. "The American Public Trusts the Bookseller." *Publishers' Weekly,* 163:2384–86, 6 June 1953. (Reprinted in Daniels, *The Censorship of Books,* pp. 74–76) **W110**

The editor of the *Atlantic Monthly,* in an address to the convention of the American Booksellers' Association, deals with the position of the bookseller in the fight against the current wave of book censorship.

————. "The Practice of Censorship." *Atlantic Monthly,* 145:17–25, January 1930. **W111**

A review of recent censorship in Boston and Massachusetts written by the editor of the *Atlantic Monthly* who was serving on a committee to reform Massachusetts laws relating to obscene literature. Weeks shows how English and American book censorship laws were derived from statutes originally framed as a protection against deliberate pornography.

————. "Sex and Censorship." In his

This Trade of Writing. Boston, Little, Brown, 1935, pp. 126–47. (Reprinted in Downs, *The First Freedom,* pp. 162–67; also in W. Bower, *ed., New Directions,* pp. 346–57) **W112**

Standards of morality change over the years so that literature that is deemed indecent in one generation may become a classic in another. Writers 50 years ago adhered to the "closed-door policy" in sex expression; today many writers have pushed the door wide open. Weeks describes censorship in Boston in recent years and the efforts to change the Massachusetts obscenity law to embrace the principles laid down by Judge Woolsey in the *Ulysses* case, a test of obscenity which Weeks endorses.

Weems, John E., *et al.* "Talking Back to the Censors." *Southwestern Review,* 47:201–19, Summer 1962. **W113**

John Weems of the University of Texas Press introduces a group of statements in opposition to textbook censorship from five members of the Texas Institute of Letters, who appeared in January 1962 as witnesses before an investigating committee of the Texas House of Representatives: J. Frank Dobie (dean of Texas writers), Lon Tinkle (book critic), Ernest Mossner (English professor), Frank Wardlow (director of the University of Texas Press), and Joseph Dawson (retired Baptist minister). Also included are statements by Frank E. Vandiver (president of the Institute), which were read at the hearing; a statement from Professor Paul F. Boller, Jr., whose history textbook was under attack; and resolutions condemning textbook censorship passed by the American Studies Association of Texas and the Texas Library Association. The editor of *Southwestern Review* notes that "the 1961–62 hearings of the Texas Legislature's five-man Textbook Investigating Committee ended in confusion and futility on June 25, 1962, when the committee terminated its own existence by a 4–1 vote."

————. "Textbooks under Fire." *Publishers' Weekly,* 180:22–24, 2 October 1961; 180:21, 23 October 1961; 181:43–45, 19 February 1962. **W114**

An account of political censorship of textbooks in Texas.

Wei, Michael. *UN FOI Draft Convention.* Columbia, Mo., Freedom of Information Center, School of Journalism, University of Missouri, 1962. 33 p. (Publication no. 85) **W115**

This monograph traces the development of the draft convention on freedom of information in the United Nations from the argued proposals at the conference held in Geneva in 1948 to the present, showing the difficulties rising out of the different concepts and interpretations of "freedom of information" held by member nations. The 4 articles (out of 19) already adopted varied considerably from that originally prepared in Geneva, and were regarded by western journalists as curtailing

freedom of information. Text and chronology of events are given along with a bibliography.

Weil, Gilbert H. *Legal Rules of the Road to Honest Advertising.* New York, Association of National Advertisers, 1960. 19 p. **W116**

The general counsel for the Association of National Advertisers presents the basic concepts for self-appraisal of honesty in advertising, regardless of rules of an enforcing agency. "An advertisement is honest when objective facts which bear upon the product or service advertised fulfill in all material respects the understanding regarding them that is generated in people by the advertisement when observed in the way or ways that they normally perceive it."

Weinberger, Harry. *Clarion Call. A Free Press Play in One Act.* New York, Dramatic Play Service, 1941. 23 p. **W117**

The John Peter Zenger story. The play received honorable mention in the 1939 one-act play contest conducted by the American Civil Liberties Union.

————. *The First Casualties in War.* Washington, D.C., American Union against Militarism, [1917]. 7 p. (Reprinted from the New York *Evening Post,* 10 April 1917) **W118**

Freedom of the press is among the first casualties of war.

————. "Free Speech and Free Press." *Fra,* 18:130–31, January 1917. (Also published separately by the author) **W119**

"Governmental authorities, majorities, the newspapers do not understand that all criticism should be expressed, for expression itself is a form of relief to those who have complaints to make." The author quotes such writers as Milton, Jefferson, and Phillips on a free press.

————. *The Liberty of the Press; Two Addresses.* Berkeley Heights, N.J., Oriole Press, 1934. 40 p. (Includes reproductions of three records from Zenger's trial) **W120**

The addresses commemorate the public service of Andrew Hamilton, the attorney who defended John Peter Zenger in the celebrated libel trial and whose defense has become a classic. The addresses were delivered to the Philadelphia and New York bar associations on the 200th anniversary of Zenger's arrest. Weinberger is a New York lawyer, prominent in civil liberties cases. The volume was printed by Joseph Ishill in an edition of 565 copies.

————. "Reitman and Rochester." *Mother Earth*, 12:44–46, April 1917. **W121**
The trial and acquittal of Benjamin Reitman at Rochester, N.Y., on charge of giving birth control information.

Weisberger, Bernard A. "Keeping the Free Press Free: Who Watches the Watchmen?" *Antioch Review*, 13:329–40, September 1953. **W122**
A study of the problems involved in maintaining a free press, including the need for vigorous self-criticism.

Weiss, Lawrence G. "Goldwater and Colorado U." *Nation*, 195:402–4, 8 December 1963. **W123**
Discussion of the episode of the dismissal of the editor of the *Colorado Daily* for that paper's articles on Senator Goldwater.

Weker, Meyer. "The Power to Exclude from the Mails." *Boston University Law Review*, 10:346–50, June 1930. **W124**
A review of court decisions which established the power of the postmaster general to censor the mail. This power "to determine what matter is non-mailable under the several acts of Congress is not an unconstitutional power."

Welbourn, Donald J. "Censorship and the Law in Canada." *Saskatchewan Bar Review*, 24:29–37, June 1959. **W125**

Welch, Colin. "Black Magic, White Lies." *Encounter*, 16(2):75–79, February 1961. **W126**
An attack on *Lady Chatterley's Lover* and criticism of the defense of the work at the recent Penguin Books trial. Welch considers the work "not about love and marriage but the worship of the phallus." "It is unlikely to corrupt anyone who reads it with as little attention and understanding as that displayed by most of those who spoke up on its behalf at the trial . . . The people it is most likely to corrupt are those few who are going to read it 'for the right reasons,' the earnest ones who will read it carefully with sympathy and respect." Comments on Welch's article by Rebecca West, William Emrys Williams, Richard Hoggart, and Martin Jarrett-Kerr appear in the March 1961 issue of *Encounter*.

Welch, Francis X. "Who Will Regulate Radio Broadcasting and How?" *Public Utilities Fortnightly*, 3:90–99, 24 January 1929. (Reprinted in Buehler, *American vs. British System of Radio Control*, pp. 135–50) **W127**

Welch, Robert. "Censorship and Political Ideology." *Yale Political*, 3(1):14, 30, Autumn 1963. **W128**
The founder of the John Birch Society explains that the subtle techniques of censorship used by the "Liberal Establishment" are those perfected by Stalin in his purge of Leon Trotsky. These methods are far more dangerous than overt information control.

Welch, Robert G. "The *Martin Luther* Film." *America*, 96:698–700, 23 March 1957. **W129**
A criticism of the film as unfair and designed to perpetuate known falsehoods about the Catholic Church.

Welliver, Judson C. "Divorce Publicity Here and Abroad." *Review of Reviews*, 75:257–61, March 1927. **W130**
Discussion of a bill in the New York legislature to curb reporting of divorce proceedings, similar to the restrictions in Great Britain. Such a bill contains an entering wedge of censorship, even though it is "sanitation rather than restriction."

Wellman, Hiller C. "Book Censorship." *Library Journal*, 69:507–8, 1 June 1944. (Reprinted from the Springfield *Republican*, 2 April 1944) **W131**
The librarian of the Springfield (Mass.) city library disapproves of the present censorship in Massachusetts. He concludes that "probably the least censorship of serious literature that we can get along with, is best. The real remedies, and in the long run the only effective remedies, are education and public opinion."

————. "Massachusetts Censorship Law Changed." *Library Journal*, 70:526, 1 June 1945. **W132**
A leader in the fight against censorship summarizes the features of the new Massachusetts book bill which provides for action against the book itself rather than the bookseller.

————, comp. "Free Speech, Obscenity, and Censorship." *Massachusetts Library Association Bulletin*, 39:49–50, June 1949. **W133**
An annotated reading list. Interest in the subject, the compiler notes, grows out of "disgust with the lack of restraint in much current fiction, increasing concern regarding the effect of 'comics' on the young, and the consequent rising tide of censorship."

Wellman, Paul I. "The First Freedom." *Library Journal*, 80:509–13, 1 March 1955. **W134**
In an address before the Missouri Library Association, the novelist and historian calls for vigilance in support of our first freedom against demagogues and pressure groups. Americans must "recognize what that freedom really is based upon—the right to individual, and original, and even divergent thought, and expression, and written words."

Wenning, Dorothy W. *Books Removed from the United States Information Service Libraries: An Analysis and Appraisal.* Tallahassee, Florida State University, 1956. 213 p. (Unpublished Master's thesis) **W135**

Werkmeister, Lucyle. *The London Daily Press, 1772–1792.* Lincoln, Nebr., University of Nebraska Press, 1963. 470 p. **W136**
A history of the British press during two decades of political controversy in England embracing the American and French Revolutions. The period witnessed the John Wilkes affair, the suppression of Parliamentary reporting, and the frequent prosecution of newspapermen and pamphleteers that flourished in the unrest of revolutionary sentiment.

Werne, Benjamin. "Freedom of Speech and Press—Some Recent Restraints." *Editor & Publisher*, 72:28, 26 August 1939. **W137**
A labor economist considers recent rulings of the National Labor Relations Board affecting newspaper business activities as a potential threat to the freedom of the press.

————. "Radio Censorship and Federal Regulation." *Editor and Publisher*, 72:16, 8 July 1939. **W138**
A new regulation of the Federal Communications Commission directed at the licensee of an international broadcasting station is considered by the author to extend government interference in program making and broadcasting.

Wertham, Fredric. "The Curse of the Comic Books; the Value Patterns and Effects of Comic Books." *Religious Education*, 49:394–406, November–December 1954. **W139**
"The comic book publishers, racketeers of the spirit, have corrupted children in the past, they are corrupting them now, and they will go on corrupting them unless we actively prevent it." The author, a New York psychiatrist, recommends a public health law forbidding the display and sale of comic-book smut and trash to children under 15.

————. "It's Still Murder; What Parents Still Don't Know About Comic Books." *Saturday Review of Literature*, 38(15):11–12, 46–48, 9 April 1955. **W140**
A New York psychiatrist, whose writings on the terror comics helped to bring about the adoption of an industry code, comments on changes under the code: "At present it is far safer for a mother to let her child have a comic book without a seal of approval than one with a seal. If comic books, as the industry claims, are the folklore of today, then the codes are the fables." He calls for legal action.

———. "Psychiatry and Censorship." *American Journal of Psychotherapy*, 11: 249–53, April 1957. **W141**
The author charges as antiquated and unscientific both the earlier official attitude of psychiatry embodying a prudish censorship of sexual matters and the present attitude of condemning all legal controls of printed matters.

———. "Reading for the Innocent." *Wilson Library Bulletin*, 29:610–13, April 1955. **W142**
A condemnation of horror comics, along the line of the argument in his book, *Seduction of the Innocent*.

———. *Seduction of the Innocent*. New York, Rinehart, 1954. 400 p. **W143**
A New York psychiatrist finds that many of the so-called "comic books" have a pernicious influence on children. They contribute to illiteracy; they create an atmosphere of cruelty and deceit; they stimulate unwholesome fantasies; they suggest criminal and sexually abnormal ideas; they contribute to moral disarmament. Dr. Wertham urges legislative control based on public health considerations. His shocking exposé contributed to the attempts within the industry to establish a code of ethics and to community campaigns to clean up the newsstands. (Reviewed by Anita L. Mishler in *Public Opinion Quarterly*, Spring 1955)

Wesberry, James P. "The Case Against Obscenity." *Congressional Record*, 99(12): A 4650–52, 24 July 1953. **W144**
The author is chairman of the Georgia State Literature Commission. He sets forth "a comprehensive report of the dangers of obscene literature to the moral standards of our society and the practical and effective means by which this evil may be remedied."

———. "Georgia Scrubs Its Newsstands." *Christian Century*, 70:1498–1500, 23 December 1953. **W145**
The work of the Georgia Literature Commission, "the first state to attempt to deal officially with the problem created by the presence on its newsstands of a plague of pornographic publications."

Wescott, Glenway, *et al*. "Statements on Censorship Read at Council Meeting, February 3, 1959." In American Academy of Arts and Letters, *Proceedings*, *Second Series*, no. 11, pt. 3. New York, The Academy, 1961, pp. 76–80. **W146**
Statements by Glenway Wescott, Malcolm Cowley, Mark Van Doren, and Robert Penn Warren disapproving literary censorship.

Wessel, Milton R. "Controlling Prejudicial Publicity in Criminal Cases." *Journal American Judicature Society*, 48:106–9, October 1964. **W147**

"The Ruby murder trial furnishes a textbook example of the causes and effects of unwarranted prejudicial publicity in criminal cases."

West, Albert. "Shadow on American Justice." *ASNE Bulletin*, 446:11–14, 1 October 1961. **W148**
Discussion of "trial by newspaper" in America as compared with British and French coverage of trials. Includes text of the preamble to a code of ethics being developed jointly by the Massachusetts press and bar.

West, Charles R. *Fair Comment and Criticism, a Defense in Libel Cases*. Austin, Tex., University of Texas, 1935. 166 p. (Unpublished Master's thesis) **W149**

West, Henry L. "Democracy and a Free Press." *Bookman*, 52:116–21, October 1920. **W150**
"We want, and always will have a free press, but it must be a press that deserves its freedom through respecting and upholding the principles that make us a free nation."

———. "The Suppression of Books." *Bookman*, 51:460–65, June 1920. **W151**
The author objects to policemen, some librarians, and the paid employees of vice societies passing judgment on what is fit for a community to read. He suggests, instead, a committee selected from among the citizens of the community.

West, James T. "The Present Status of the 'Clear and Present Danger' Test as Applied to Freedom of Speech." *Arkansas Law Review*, 4:52–60, Winter 1950. **W152**

West, Mabel G. "Is Censorship a Librarian's Function?" In California Library Association, *Handbook and Proceedings*, 1923, pp. 51–54. (Publication of the California Library Association, no. 23) **W153**
It is the librarian's duty "to guard against the introduction of cheap, trashy, sensational books, the reading of which is neither elevating, educational, nor instructional . . . and to establish and maintain a source of information for the public which is reliable and trustworthy."

West, Rebecca, Richard Hoggart, *et al*. "*Chatterley*, the Witnesses, and the Law." *Encounter*, 16(3):52–56, March 1961. **W154**
"Among the contributors to this discussion, Dame Rebecca West, Richard Hoggart, and Sir William Emrys Williams (a director of Penguin Books) were all witnesses for the defence [the British trial of *Lady Chatterley's Lover*]. The Rev. Martin Jarrett-Kerr, C.R.,

is a colleague of the Bishop of Woolwich who also testified (and was later reprimanded by the Archbishop of Canterbury)." Largely a response to Colin Welch's attack on *Lady Chatterley's Lover*, in the February issue.

West, Theresa H. "Improper Books; Methods Employed to Discover and Exclude Them." *Library Journal*, 20:32, Denver Conference of Librarians, 1895. **W155**
"Books which speak truth concerning normal, wholesome conditions may be safely bought, however plain-spoken." Others are not bought, and any tabooed books which happen to be purchased are given only to those who definitely ask for them and not to children. Comments of the librarian of the Milwaukee Public Library in one of a series of papers on undesirable books in public libraries.

Westen, Ronald E. "Constitutional Law —Freedom of Speech in Motion Pictures—Doctrine of Prior Restraint." *Wayne Law Review*, 7:589–96, Summer 1961. **W156**
Notes on *Times Film Corp. v. City of Chicago*, 365 U.S. 43 (1961) and related cases.

Westerway, Peter B., and J. de Lissa. "O, Victoria!" *Censorship*, 4:42–44, Autumn 1965. **W157**
Interview with J. de Lissa, editor of *Squire* magazine, broadcast on Australian television, 19 July 1965. The interview dealt with action of the Victoria (Australia) government censors against illustrations in *Squire*.

Westin, Alan F. *The Miracle Case: The Supreme Court and the Movies*. University, Ala., University of Alabama Press, 1961. 38 p. (Inter-University Case Program, Case Series no. 64) **W158**
An account of the U.S. Supreme Court case dealing with state censorship of a motion picture entitled *The Miracle* (*Burstyn v. Wilson*). "This study raises questions about censorship of motion pictures by government agencies and about the way in which private groups associate themselves with constitutional cases as they progress upward through the courts. It depicts the way in which judges balance values in deciding cases—precedent versus social change, freedom of expression versus community morals, religious freedom versus state enforcement of religious doctrines, and 'subjective' judicial rules versus 'objective' standards."

Westmacott, Charles M. *The Stamp Duties. Serious Considerations on the Proposed Alteration of the Stamp Duty on Newspapers: Addressed to the Right Honourable Thomas Spring Rice, Chancellor of the Exchequer*.

London, The Age Office, 1836. 15 p.
W 159

The author opposes abolishing the tax on newspapers on the grounds that it would encourage "a restless band of desperate adventurers" who are motivated by political and mercenary reasons. Instead, he recommends reduction of the duty on paper, which will materially benefit and encourage literature.

Weston, Emily. "Boston's Battle of the Books." *Nation*, 175 : inside cover, 1 November 1952.
W 160

Account of the two-week battle between the Boston *Post* and the Public Library over the *New World Review*, which the editors of the *Post* discovered in the periodical room. The *Post* attempted to have it removed and all subversive publications either removed or labeled. The Board of Trustees, although divided, upheld the Library's position.

Wettach, Robert H. "Restrictions on a Free Press." *North Carolina Law Review*, 4 : 24–38, February 1926.
W 161

Special references to legal restrictions and court cases involving the North Carolina press.

Weybright, Victor. "Attack on Books; a Publisher's Analysis." *Publishers' Weekly*, 163 : 1511–13, 4 April 1953. (Reprinted in Daniels, *The Censorship of Books*, pp. 69–72)
W 162

Excerpts from an address before the Conference on College Composition and Communication, an affiliate of the National Council of Teachers of English. The author, chairman of the New American Library of World Literature, defends publishers, particularly paperback and reprint publishers, from attacks by censors.

————. *The Complete and Unabridged Statement to the Gathings Committee by the New American Library of World Information, Inc.* [New York, The New American Library, 1952]. 44 p.
W 163

The statement of the chairman of the board of New American Library which he was not permitted to make before the House of Representatives Select Committee on Current Pornographic Materials. Weybright recommends punishment of obscenity under present statutes rather than special regulation directed against the paperbacks. He likewise objects to the imposition of any sort of industry code, favoring the self-restraint of individual publishers. An appendix includes a complete list of the Signet and Mentor books and "our commentary on each of the titles which your counsel selected to enter into the record as evidence of alleged pornographic material."

Wharton, Don. "The Battle against Mail-Order Pornography." *Reader's Digest*, 84(502) : 147–54, February 1964.
W 164

An account of the Post Office Department's all-out effort to prosecute under the criminal laws dealers in hard-core pornography who use the mails to distribute their wares.

Wharton, Francis. "'Obscene' Indictments." In his "Disputed Questions of Criminal Law." *Southern Law Review*, 4(n.s.) : 252–61, June 1878.
W 165

Involves the practice of setting out an allegedly "obscene" document in the indictment. The author concludes that the law does not require a document which is the basis of a prosecution to be set out in the indictment, when there is sufficient reason given in the indictment to excuse the omission.

————. *State Trials of the United States during the Administrations of Washington and Adams. With References, Historical and Professional, and Preliminary Notes on the Politics of the Times* . . . Philadelphia, Carey and Hart, 1849. 727 p.
W 166

Summaries of libel trials against William Cobbett, Matthew Lyon, David Frothingham, Thomas Cooper, Anthony Haswell, and James W. Callender.

"What Constitutes Obscene Literature?" *Human Fertility*, 10 : 122–25, December 1945.
W 167

A publication of the Research Bureau, New York Birth Control Clinic.

"What Is a Free Press and What Are Its Perils? Ten Views." *Newsweek*, 37 : 50–51, 30 April 1951.
W 168

Newsweek asked ten journalists to answer two questions: (1) In these days of ideological warfare, both at home and abroad, what do you consider the chief responsibility of a free press? (2) Do you see any specific threats to a free press in this country? The journalists are: Hugh Baillie, Frank Starzel, Seymour Berkson, Arthur Hays Sulzberger, Walter Winchell, George Sokolsky, Ray Tucker, Robert R. McCormick, Helen Rogers Reid, and Dorothy Thompson.

"What Is Free Speech under the Constitution?: A Debate between Sveinbjorn Johnson and the American Civil Liberties Union." *Illinois Law Review*, 19 : 124–47, November 1924.
W 169

A series of letters between the Attorney General of North Dakota and Roger N. Baldwin of the American Civil Liberties Union. The Attorney General urged consideration of measures by the state legislature to suppress sabotage activities of the I.W.W. and other revolutionary organizations. Mr. Baldwin asserted that such legislation interfered with the right of free speech.

"What of the Destiny of Books?" *Medical Library Association Bulletin*, 30 : 93–94, January 1942.
W 170

"Today, suppression of books in general and of medical books in particular is still a lawful procedure in many countries, democratic and totalitarian."

"What Others Think of Censorship." *Wilson* [*Library*] *Bulletin*, 2 : 311–13, November 1924.
W 171

Comments on censorship by Arthur E. Bostwick, Corinne Bacon, Mary V. Rothrock, and Willard Huntington Wright.

"What Sense Censorship?" *Time*, 39 : 58–60, 22 June 1942. (Reprinted in Summers, *Wartime Censorship*, pp. 188–90)
W 172

Criticism of the application of the government's wartime censorship policy, citing four incidents of debatable restrictions on the press.

"What Shall Librarians Do About Bad Books—Contributed by Various American Librarians." *Library Journal*, 33 : 349–54, September 1908; 33 : 390–93, October 1908.
W 173

Thirteen statements from public librarians concerning the handling of "literature of immoral or unwholesome character." Reports how such books are treated in libraries and offers suggestions for treatment in bookstores or the press.

[Whately, Richard]. *Considerations on the Law of Libel, as Related to Publications on the Subject of Religion. By John Search* [*pseud.*]. London, 1833. 86 p.
W 174

The author, Archbishop of Dublin, is critical of the law of libel in which "any writing whatever, which shall tend to impeach the evidence of the Christian faith, or in any manner to impugne Christianity as a whole, is indictable as a blasphemous libel, and punishable as such by fine and imprisonment, or other infamous corporal punishment." Christianity should be maintained, he argues, by its supporters on the grounds of its truth and not by force of law. The pamphlet is favorably reviewed in the January 1834 issue of *Edinburgh Review*.

Wheatley, C. S., Jr. "Some Legal Aspects of Birth Control." *Law Notes*, 36 : 45–47, October 1932.
W 175

"The legal status of birth control is by no means clear. The confusion in this regard is probably as much of an obstacle to the movement as the restrictive and prohibitory legislation itself."

Whelan, Charles M. "Censorship and the Constitutional Concept of Morality." *Georgetown Law Review*, 43 : 547–81, June 1955.
W 176

The author considers cultural and religious pluralism in America, which accounts for a multitude of moral codes governing the citizenry. "In the exercise of their undoubted power to preserve the public morals, the states must be mindful that the content of this concept is determined by those standards which are generally and currently accepted throughout their communities. As long as publication of all types stop short of inciting violations of the existing laws which express the considered moral judgment of society, the public should be free to see, consider and decide on the wisdom and propriety of innovations for itself. If this liberty involves the risk of temptation, it is also the price of maturity in morals and progress in civic virtue."

Whelan, Russell. "The Legion of Decency." *American Mercury*, 60:655–63, June 1945; Discussion, 61:246, 380, 507, 636, August–November, 1945.   **W177**
A history and discussion of the work of the Catholic organization, Legion of Decency, which exerts pressures on the moral content of movies. "With such acknowledged power the Legion can almost dictate what we shall not see in our movie theaters. This is clearly minority rule over mass entertainment in America." The discussion consists largely of letters in support of the Legion.

"When Annie Oakley 'Shot the Papers.'" *Frontier Times*, 27:52–55, November 1949.   **W178**
Deals with the libel suit filed by the famous marksman of Buffalo Bill's Wild West Show, against newspapers that confused her with a drug addict of the same name.

"When Is a Nude?" *Art Digest*, 13:56, 15 March 1939.   **W179**
Brief editorial commenting on the banning of the February issue of *The Studio* from the mails. Protests brought about a reversal of the ban.

"Whig Prosecutions of the Press." *Blackwood's Edinburgh Magazine*, 35:295–310, March 1834.   **W180**
While the Whigs have long "laid exclusive claim to the privilege of vindicating" the liberty of the press, the writer, a Tory, cites numerous examples of press prosecution at the hands of the Whigs. While respecting the liberty of the press, he observes: "We have never felt that it was so essential to our existence as the air we breathed—or that without it we should have died."

[Whipple, Leon R.]. "Censorship." In *Encyclopaedia Britannica.* 14th ed., 1929. vol. 5, pp. 114–17.   **W181**
General account of censorship in the United States and Great Britain.

———. "Gags and Shackles." *Survey*, 64:154–56, 1 May 1930.   **W182**
Review of the following books: Mary Ware Dennett's *Who's Obscene*, Ernst and Lorentz' *Censored*, H. M. Kallen's *Indecency and the Seven Arts*, James Mackaye's *Thoreau*, H. W. Nevinson's *The Voice of Freedom*, and H. I. Brock's *Meddlers*.

———. *Our Ancient Liberties; the Story of the Origin and Meaning of Civil and Religious Liberty in the United States.* New York, Wilson, 1927. 153 p.   **W183**
A popularized account of the history of civil liberties, including the English origins and the American contributions down to 1917. Chapter 7 deals with Freedom of Speech and of the Press.

———. "Plans and Censors." *Survey*, 66:446–47, 1 August 1931.   **W184**
Praise for the National Council on Freedom from Censorship and some general comments on movie censorship.

———. *The Story of Civil Liberty in the United States.* New York, Vanguard Press and American Civil Liberties Union, 1927. 366 p.   **W185**
This popular summary of civil liberties contains numerous references to freedom of the press—the Alien and Sedition Acts, early prosecutions for blasphemy and obscenity, the suppression of abolitionist literature, and the threats against the newspaper press during the Civil War. The concluding chapter deals with the suppression of social nonconformity during the 1920's—birth control, anarchism, and evolution.

White, Albert L. "Liberty and the Local Press." *Contemporary Review*, 200:465–68, September 1961.   **W186**
To the local editor freedom of the press means something more than keeping an eye on the legislative and executive; it means seeing that the town council and other local statutory bodies in the United Kingdom keep open the channels of information. The Guild of British Newspaper Editors played a leading part in getting the Public Bodies Act passed, establishing more firmly the right of the public to hear and the press to report council meetings.

White, Andrew D. *A History of the Warfare of Science with Theology in Christendom.* New York, Appleton, 1896. 2 vols. (Reprinted in 1960 by Dover Publications)   **W187**
An American scholar (onetime professor of history and president of Cornell University, minister to Germany and to Russia) traces the struggle between scientific knowledge of man and the universe and dogmatic theology. His account begins with the Middle Ages and closes with the end of the nineteenth century. He refers to the Church's attacks on scientific theories of the universe, the geology of the earth, and theories of evolution, which were considered blasphemous. Such opposition frequently resulted in suppression of speech and press and in persecution of the holder of unorthodox beliefs.

White, George A. *Shall Speech be Free?* Toronto, 1910. 23 p. (Reprinted from *Secular Thought*)   **W188**

A brief history of man's struggle with the censors and an impassioned plea for complete "freedom to write and publish anything on any conceivable subject—not one bar, not one tiniest taboo, not one darksome cranny or corner hidden from the frankest scrutiny."

White, Henry. "Trial with John Harriott Hart for Libels upon Sir Simon Le Blanc and the Administration of Justice . . . Published in the *Independent Whig*, 1808." In Howell, *State Trials*, vol. 30, pp. 1131 ff., 1194 ff.   **W189**
Following the first trials the defendants, publisher and proprietor of the *Independent Whig*, stood trial again for criticism of the presiding judge, Lord Ellenborough. They were found guilty in both trials and given 18-month prison sentences.

White, Isaac D. *Freedom of the Press and Its Limitations.* New York, Bureau of Accuracy and Fair Play, World Editorial News Rooms, 1914. 24 p.   **W190**
An address read at the National Newspaper Conference, University of Kansas.

White, Joseph B. *The Law of Anti-Religious Libel Reconsidered in a Letter to the Editor of the Christian Examiner, in Answer to an Article . . . Against a Pamphlet Entitled, Considerations on the Law of Libel . . . by John Search [pseud. for Richard Whately].* London, Richard Milliken, 1834. 106 p.   **W191**
White defends Archbishop Whately against his critics, protesting against intolerance of religious thought.

White, Llewellyn. *The American Radio, a Report on the Broadcasting Industry in the United States.* Chicago, University of Chicago Press, 1947. 260 p. (Report from the Commission on Freedom of the Press)   **W192**
The history, development, and self-regulatory aspects of the American broadcasting industry. A detailed account of FCC rulings and court decisions affecting the role of government in regulating radio communications.

———, and Robert D. Leigh. *Peoples Speaking to Peoples; A Report on International Mass Communications from the Commission on Freedom of the Press.* Chicago, University of Chicago Press, 1947. 120 p. (Report from the Commission on Freedom of the Press)   **W193**
A survey of the problems of transmitting information across national boundaries so that an accurate and fair picture of life in each country can be achieved. References to private

monopoly and government restrictions, to Hollywood control of the motion picture industry and the British challenge. Kenneth Stewart reviews the work in the 27 April 1946 issue of *Saturday Review of Literature*, commending its impartial scholarship.

White, Melvin R. *History of Radio Regulations Affecting Program Policy.* Madison, Wisc., University of Wisconsin, 1948. 3 vols. (Unpublished Ph. D. dissertation) **W 194**

White, Newman I. "Literature and the Law of Libel: Shelley and the Radicals of 1840–1842." *Studies in Philology*, 22: 34–47, January 1925. **W 195**
An account of the blasphemy trial of Edward Moxon in 1841 for publishing *Queen Mab*. The trial, the author notes, "is simply an incident in a campaign waged with considerable resourcefulness by Henry Hetherington and his radical friends, partly for the protection of radicals from discriminatory treatment under the law of libel and partly to widen the limits of free speech under English law."

White, Pliny H. *The Life & Services of Matthew Lyon* . . . Burlington, Vt., General Assembly of Vermont, 1858. 26 p. (Printed with *The Marbles of Vermont* by Albert D. Hager) **W 196**
An address before the Vermont Historical Society in the presence of the General Assembly of Vermont, 29 October 1858. Lyon was the first to be imprisoned under the Sedition Act of 1798.

White, Thomas R. "Constitutional Provisions Guaranteeing Freedom of the Press in Pennsylvania." *American Law Register*, 52:1–21, January 1904. **W 197**
The author discusses the provisions for freedom of the press contained in Pennsylvania's constitutions of 1790 and 1873 and the cases tried under each.

White, William. "Detroit Police Censorship." *American Book Collector*, 12(4):23–24, December 1961. **W 198**
An account of Detroit police censorship written by a member of the faculty of Wayne State University who attempted to break the censorship.

[White, William Allen]. "A Document on 'Liberty.'" *Literary Digest*, 74:32, 19 August 1922. **W 199**
Editor White's open letter to Governor Allen in defense of a free press.

———. "How Free Is Our Press?"

Nation, 146:693–95, 18 June 1938. **W 200**
Editor White reviews the changing threats to the liberty of the press over the past 50 years. The present menace comes from organized control of newspaper opinion by the political advisers of national advertisers.

"A 'White List' for Plays." *Literary Digest*, 48:434, 28 February 1914. **W 201**
The newly organized Catholic Theater Movement is trying "the method of preparing a 'white list' of plays deemed suitable for its members and exacting a pledge that they will abstain from any that do not appear on this list."

Whitebait, William. "This Censorship." *New Statesman*, 60:153–54, 30 July 1960. **W 202**
A criticism of recent film censorship in England and the use of the "X" certificate "ostensibly for the protection of children."

———. "This Nanny!" *New Statesman*, 60:48, 9 July 1960. **W 203**
The author recommends that the British Board of Film Censors be either drastically overhauled, or abolished. "Novels and the Press get along, not too calamitously, without this Nanny; why shouldn't films?"

Whitehead, William B. *Prosecutions of Infidel Blasphemers Briefly Vindicated in a Letter to David Ricardo.* 2d ed. London, 1823. 25 p. (Also in *Pamphleteer*, vol. 22, pp. 495–520) **W 204**
Criticism of Whitehead's thesis in *Westminster Review*, July 1824, is thought to be by John Stuart Mill.

Whitehorn, Katharine. "Swinging the Censor." *Spectator*, 205:320–21, 26 August 1960. **W 205**
Objection to the British classification of *Ben Hur* as an "A" film (suitable for families) because of its horror and violence. The film board seems more concerned in protecting children from sex than from sadism.

Whiting, George W. "Pareus, The Stuarts, Laud, and Milton." *Studies in Philology*, 50:215–29, April 1953. **W 206**
Because David Pareus had advocated calling rulers to account for their actions, in 1622, authorities at Oxford were ordered to search private and public libraries and bookshops, and burn every copy of his work. Similar orders were carried out at Cambridge and London. Six years later (1628) when Roger Manwaring, the king's chaplain, in his *Religion and Allegiance*, maintained that imposing taxes by the king without consent of Parliament was justified, Parliament turned the tables as if in retaliation. They ordered Manwaring sent to prison, fined £1,000, stripped of his clerical rights, and his book burned. The king's ministers did not carry out the sentence; Manwaring was pardoned and given a pastorate.

[Whiting, James, *et al.*]. *Trial of James Whiting, John Parsons, and William Congreve, for a Libel against the Hon. G. C. Berkeley, Rear Admiral of the Red* . . ., *June 27th, 1804* . . . *together with the Letters and Papers Which Are Referred to in the Course of the Trial.* Buckingham, Eng., J. Seeley, 1804. 132 p. **W 207**

Whitley, William T. *Baptist Bibliography; Being a Register of the Chief Materials for Baptist History, Whether in Manuscript or in Print, Preserved in Great Britain and Ireland* (*comp. for the Baptist Union of Great Britain and Ireland*). London, Kingsgate Press, 1916. 236 p. **W 208**
The index refers to some 300 entries relating to freedom to print, speak, teach, and worship.

Whitman, Bernard. *Two Letters to the Rev. Moses Stuart; on the Subject of Religious Liberty.* Boston, Gray and Bowen, 1830. 165 p. **W 209**
The author supports charges made by Dr. Channing that orthodox Christians were attempting to suppress free religious inquiry, a statement which Stuart had refuted in his *Letter on Religious Liberty.* Whitman attempts to prove that the leaders of the orthodox denominations have attempted measures subversive of free inquiry and religious liberty.

Whitman, Walt. "A Memorandum at a Venture." *North American Review*, 132: 546–50, June 1882. **W 210**
There are two prevailing attitudes toward the discussion of sexual matters, Whitman wrote. One is the conventional puritan attitude of "repressing any direct statement of them." The other, and by far the most prevalent among common people everywhere, is "to talk, to excite, express and dwell on that merely sexual voluptuousness." Whitman saw the need for a third point of view in which sex would be treated with "the same freedom and faith and earnestness which, after centuries of denial, struggle, repression, and martyrdom, the present-day brings to the treatment of politics and religion." It was this attitude that the poet had attempted to present in his *Leaves of Grass*.

[Whitmarsh, Joseph A.]. *Letter to* . . . *Jurors Empanelled to Try the Indictment against Joseph A. Whitmarsh, for an Alleged Crime of Libel.* Boston, Beals and Greene, 1838. 12 p. **W 211**
The author, who signs himself "A Friend to the Constitutional Rights of the Citizen," denounces the decision of the jury against Whitmarsh "as a blow against the liberty of the press, not founded, nor justified by, the law of the land." He recites at length the history of libel law in England and the United States, concluding that "no criminal libel law, neither common nor statute libel

law, exists in this commonwealth ... and none can be made until our constitution is altered."

Whitmer, Dana P. "When Someone Complains." *Scholastic Teacher*, 83:27+, 17 January 1964. **W 212**
The superintendent of schools in Pontiac, Mich., reviews the situation and action taken in that city when a group of parents objected to two books used in senior high school English, *Drums Along the Mohawk* and *The Good Earth.*

Whitmore, Harry. "Australian Censorship 1964." *Sydney Law Review*, 4:396–403, August 1964. **W 213**

———. "Obscenity in Literature: Crime or Free Speech." *Sydney Law Review*, 4:179–204, March 1963. **W 214**
A survey of the development of the obscenity law in Australia, the United States, and Great Britain and an account of modern federal and state censorship in Australia.

Whitton, John B. "Efforts to Curb Dangerous Propaganda." *American Journal of International Law*, 41:899–903, October 1947. **W 215**
"Rather than to embark upon an apparently fruitless attempt to reach an agreement on the broader question of freedom of the press, our government, we submit, should rather take the Russians at their word, and call a conference for the more restricted but no less important matter of curbing the use of propaganda for aggression and war."

———. "United Nations Conference on Freedom of Information and the Movement against International Propaganda." *American Journal of International Law*, 43:73–87, January 1949. **W 216**

———, and Arthur Larson. *Propaganda.* New York, Oceana, 1964. 305 p. (Published for the World Rule of Law Center, Duke University) **W 217**
The authors are concerned largely with bad propaganda, that which is subversive and defamatory of other nations. Such propaganda that imperils the peace of the world should be suppressed as an international crime. They recommend "propaganda disarmament," with adequate monitoring machinery and an international right of reply.

Whitworth, Frank. "Law As to Obscenity." *Law Journal*, 80:397–98, 14 December 1935. **W 218**
Criticism of the present obscenity law that, as currently interpreted, might land an innocent solicitor in trouble for the wording of a brief in a bigamy case, wording that "might corrupt some low-minded fellow."

"Who is 'Tainted.'" *Commonwealth*, 58:480–81, 21 August 1953. **W 219**
Criticism of the Los Angeles City Board of Education for banning a UNESCO pamphlet from the city's schools.

"Who Is to Control the BBC?" *New Statesman and Nation*, 26:97, 14 August 1943. **W 220**
A call for a parliamentary investigation of the B.B.C., which, the article charges, stifles all extremes of opinion in order to avoid offending anyone and hence becomes a mouthpiece for the party in power.

"Whose Responsibility Is It?" *Library Journal*, 64:744–45, 1 October 1939. **W 221**
Comments on the banning of Steinbeck's *Grapes of Wrath* from the Kansas City Public Library.

"Why Stop with Shylock?" *Outlook*, 98:607, 22 July 1911. **W 222**
Criticizes the movement of Jewish citizens to eliminate Shakespeare's *Merchant of Venice* from the public schools on the ground that the portrait of Shylock tends toward ridicule of the Jewish race. The "success of such a movement, so far from doing away with prejudice against the Jews, would be apt to increase it."

Whyte, Alexander. *An Account of the Trial of A. Whyte, for a False, Malicious, and Seditious Libel; of Which Charge He Was Honourably Acquitted* . . . Newcastle, 1793. 19 p. (Also in Howell, *State Trials*, vol. 22, pp. 1238 ff.) **W 223**
Whyte was accused of lending a seditious paper to a man in a "pub." The trial was held after the passage of the Fox Libel Act and the jury found him not guilty.

[Wickes, Edward Z. F.]. *Alpha and Omega . . . Plea for Liberty, the Divine Right of Man, Freedom of Person, Pen, Press and Mail . . . Arrest, Trial, and Complete Vindication of Dr. E. Z. Franklin* [*pseud.*]. New York, Mutual Benefit Publishing Co., 1884. 112 p. **W 224**
Edward Zeus Franklin Wickes was brought to trial in Boston Municipal Court in 1883 at the instigation of Henry Chase, agent of the New England Society for the Suppression of Vice. He was charged with the sale of an alleged obscene work entitled, *Illustrated Domestic Medical Counsellor*, a marriage guide. An impressive array of witnesses testified that the book was a serious attempt at sex education. The case was referred to a grand jury for decision and that body denied the charges. In addition to a reprint of the trial, this volume contains favorable "letters to the editor" from Elizur Wright and others and several long poems, including "Alpha and Omega," and others by Wickes commemorat-

ing his triumph and "exposing" the tactics of the vice society. Two phrenology charts are included. One of Wright's letters to the *Boston Herald* complains of the "New England Goodocracy."

[———]. *Free Speech, Press, and Mails; the Divine Right of Man; Plea for Light, Liberty, Purity, and Justice; Satan in Society, His Modern Inquisition Exposed; Persecution, Cruelty, and Crime . . . by Dr. E. Z. Franklin* [*pseud.*]. New York, Mutual Benefit Publishing Co., 1884. 188 p. **W 225**
Another account of the "obscenity" trial o "Dr. Franklin" for his *Medical Counsellor*, and general observations on the right of free speech and press in the realm of sex education.

[Wickham, Littleton M.]. "Alleged Obscenity as a Cause for Suppression." *Virginia Law Review*, 9:216–20, January 1923. **W 226**
Activities of the New York Society for the Suppression of Vice.

Wickhem, John C. "The 'Clear and Present Danger' Test in Constitutionality of Proceedings to Punish for Contempt by Publication during Pending Cases." *Wisconsin Law Review*, 1948:125–32, January 1948. **W 227**
Notes on the case *Craig v. Harney* (1947), and other recent cases.

Wicklein, John F. "Citations for Contempt: The Courts versus the Press." *Journalism Quarterly*, 26:51–56, March 1940. **W 228**

Wickliffe, John. *Remarks Upon two late Presentments of the Grand Jury of the County of Middlesex: Wherein are shewn, The Folly and Injustice of Men's persecuting one another for Difference of Opinion in Matters of Religion. And the ill Consequences wherewithin that Practice must affect any State in which it is encouraged.* London, Printed for A. Moore, 1729. 28 p. **W 229**
The author publishes the text of the two grand jury condemnations (1723, 1728) of Bernhard Mandeville for his "blasphemous" *Fable of the Bees.* The second presentment also cited Thomas Woolston for five "blasphemous" pamphlets. Wickliffe criticizes the grand jury action in a series of six letters and a preface. He thinks it strange that a grand jury that should be the guardian of man's liberties should take away their liberties in matters of conscience. Theirs is an "illguarded Zeal for the Honour of God." Wick-

liffe is shocked to think that "there should be any men so deaf to Religion and common Sense, so regardless of the natural Rights of Mankind, as to attempt to break in upon that Liberty which every Man ought freely to enjoy, of thinking for himself, and of publishing such Thoughts to the World, in all Instances where such Publication is not prejudicial to Society." "I do not write in behalf of Infidelity; but, I am, I contend for a Liberty for other men to unite in behalf of it, if they think fit."

Wickwar, William H. *The Struggle for the Freedom of the Press, 1819–1832.* London, G. Allen & Unwin, 1928. 325 p. **W 230**
This work covers one of the most important periods in English history with respect to freedom of the press, the 12 years (1819–32) that followed the Napoleonic wars. This was an era that witnessed the transition from press persecution to press freedom. Wickwar reviews the conditions that prevailed at the beginning of the nineteenth century, when the English press still suffered from the hysteria that gripped the nation during the French Revolution. He discusses the sedition trials arising from the Peterloo massacre of 1819 and the libel charges against such pamphleteers and newspapermen as William Hone, John Hunt, Richard Carlile, Thomas Wooler, and James Watson. He treats the work of James Mill, Francis Place, Jeremy Bentham, and Major Cartwright and others who wrote and campaigned in behalf of more liberal libel laws and against the "taxes on knowledge." The work contains numerous references to the short-lived but influential radical papers such as *Black Dwarf, Cap of Liberty, Champion, Patriot, Republican,* and others which supported and practiced freedom of expression.

Widmer, Kingsley, and Eleanor Widmer, eds. *Literary Censorship: Principles, Cases, Problems.* San Francisco, Wadsworth, 1961. 182 p. **W 231**
A collection of readings representing various points of view on literary censorship, intended to serve as a basis for discussion in courses in literature and contemporary affairs. Part I, Principles of Literary Censorship, quotes from Plato, Saint Paul, John Milton, John Stuart Mill, Supreme Court Justices Brennan and Douglas, Walter Berns, Walter Lippmann, and Henry Miller. Part II, "Censorship" of Literature by a Private Organization, deals with the activity of the National Office of Decent Literature, an agency of the Catholic Church, with excerpts from works by John Fischer, John Courtney Murray, Harold C. Gardiner, Robert W. Haney, and the American Civil Liberties Union. Part III deals with Censorship of Comic Books and contains statements from Frederic Wertham, Judge Jerome Frank, Terrence J. Murphy, Leslie Fiedler, and the American Civil Liberties Union. Part IV deals with the American Censorship of *Lady Chatterley's Lover,* and quotes from D. H. Lawrence, Malcolm Cowley, Alfred Kazin, Harry T. Moore, Judges Frederick Van Pelt Bryan,

Charles E. Clark, and Leonard P. Moore, and others. Part V, The Cultural Context of American Censorship, quotes from Margaret Mead, Eric Larrabee, and Ernest van den Haag.

Wieland, Christopher. "On the Liberty and Licentiousness of the Press." In *Varieties of Literature, from Foreign Journals and Original MSS.* London, J. Debrett, 1795, pp. 252–56. **W 232**

Wiener, Frederick B. "'Freedom for the Thought that We Hate': Is It a Principle of the Constitution?" *American Bar Association Journal,* 37: 177–80, 241–45, March 1951. **W 233**
The author examines this constitutional argument, a phrase from Justice Holmes's dissenting opinion in *United States v. Schwimmer,* tracing the concept from the records of the Constitutional Convention, through the philosophy of Jefferson, the opinions of Holmes and Brandeis, to Judge Learned Hand's opinion in *United States v. Dennis.*

Wiener, Stanley. "Final Curtain Call for the Motion Picture Censor?" *Western Reserve Law Review,* 4: 148–58, Winter 1953. **W 234**
A survey of recent court decisions. "In all probability, . . . motion picture censorship is not at an end as a result of the Burstyn case, but rather the problems in this new area of civil liberties are just beginning."

[Wiffen, Jeremiah H.]. *Verses Written in the Portico of the Temple of Liberty at Woburn Abbey, on Placing Before It the Statues of Locke and Erskine in the Summer of 1835.* [London, James Moyes], 1836. 39 p. **W 235**
Only 50 copies printed. Introduction signed J.H.W.

Wiggins, James R. "Do Public Officials Withhold the News Because They Do Not Trust the Public?" *Quill,* 42(11): 10–11, 24, 26 November 1954. **W 236**
The managing editor of the *Washington Post* and *Times Herald* fears that even honest office-holders may lack faith in the people's judgment to a degree that threatens our basic freedom.

———. "Free Press *and* Fair Trial." *Nieman Reports,* 17(1): 2+, March 1964. **W 237**
An answer to an earlier article in the *Reports* that suggested the public has no "right to know."

———. *Freedom or Secrecy.* New York, Oxford University Press, 1956. 242 p. rev. ed., Oxford, 1964. 289 p. **W 238**

The chairman of the Freedom of Information Committee of the American Society of Newspaper Editors discusses the growing secrecy in American government and the threat of such secrecy to the maintenance of democratic society. The revised edition includes references to results of the Administrative Procedures Act.

———. *An Historical Summary of Some of the Conflicts between the Press and the Legislative Branches of Government.* n.p. [American Society of Newspaper Editors, 1953]. 14 p. (Reprinted in *Nieman Reports,* October 1953) **W 239**
The account begins with the William Duane case of 1800 and comes down to the Rumely case (*U.S. v. Edward A. Rumely*) of 1952. Rumely was cited for contempt by the Lobbying Committee of the House of Representatives for refusal to disclose names of persons who had purchased books from his organization, the Committee on Constitutional Government. The U.S. Supreme Court upheld a reversal of conviction made by the U.S. Court of Appeals for the District of Columbia.

———. "On Making Martyrs: The Elements of Press Freedom." *Vital Speeches,* 21: 883–88, 1 December 1954. **W 240**
As the annual Elijah P. Lovejoy lecturer at Colby College, the speaker reviews the contribution of the Alton martyr to the cause of freedom of the press and examines some of the threats made against a free press, historically and currently. He reviews the three basic facets of freedom: the right of access to information, the right to print without prior restraint, and the right to print without menace of arbitrary reprisal either from government or lawless citizenry.

———. "The Power and Responsibility of the Press." *Journalism Quarterly,* 37: 29–34+, Winter 1960. **W 241**
Criticism of the failure of the press to provide the public with adequate information, particularly in government affairs.

———. "The Press and Conflicts of Interest." *Federal Bar Journal,* 24: 358–68, Summer 1964. **W 242**
"It is doubtful that anyone can devise a set of rules or a code of ethics that would free the press from this burden of life. The best for which we can hope is a press with a sense of values that will inspire them to resolve conflicts of interest in favor of their larger public responsibility as opposed to their narrow individual interests."

———. "The Printed Word." *Library Journal,* 78: 1359–65, 1 September 1953. **W 243**
"Men must have the right to discover the truth. They must have the right to print it without the prior restraint or pre-censorship of government . . . They must have the right

to put printed material into the hands of readers without obstruction by government, under cover of law, or obstruction by citizens acting in defiance of the law."

————. *A Right to Hold, Not Give Away.* Columbia, Mo., Freedom of Information Center, School of Journalism, University of Missouri, 1958. 4p. (Publication no. 6) **W 244**

At a recognition dinner in honor of Professor Ralph D. Casey, Editor Wiggins asks the question: Whose freedom is it? Freedom of the press does not belong to newspapermen as private property to give or withhold. The right to know belongs to the people. He criticizes the "cozy arrangements" between the press and government to regulate news.

————. "The Right to Know." *Nieman Reports*, 6(3):27–33, July 1952. **W 245**

"There is evidence enough that there is abroad in government at every level a spirit of secrecy that is inciting public men to attitudes toward the disclosure of public business not unlike those exhibited in government generations ago." An address to the National Conference of Farm Bureau Editors.

————. "The Right to News; Only Constant Struggle Protects and Extends It." *Nieman Reports*, 4(3):7–10, October 1950 **W 246**

Discussion of the practical aspects of the exercise of press freedom from an address by the managing editor of the *Washington Post* at the University of Minnesota.

————. "The Role of the Press in Safeguarding the People's Right to Know Government Business." *Marquette Law Review*, 40:74–82, Summer 1956. **W 247**

————. *Secrecy, Security and Freedom.* Tucson, Ariz., University of Arizona Press, 1958. 16p. (The John Peter Zenger Award for Freedom of the Press, 1957; excerpted in *Nieman Reports*, July 1958) **W 248**

The 1957 recipient of the award was the executive editor of the *Washington* (D.C.) *Post* and *Times Herald*, a national leader in the battle against secrecy in government and onetime chairman of the Committee on Freedom of Information of the American Society of Newspaper Editors.

————. "Wise Censorship Must Be a Compromise." *Quill*, 38(10):26–27, October 1950. **W 249**

Since hostilities began in Korea, the country has been working toward a practical compromise between the achievement of military security and the citizens' right to know. If there is to be any considerable domestic censorship, it should follow the rules laid down by Byron Price when he terminated World War II censorship.

Wilcock, John. "The Publisher of *Eros* Answers Some Questions." *Village Voice*, 9(15):2, 20, 30 January 1940. **W 250**

In his column, The Village Square, the author interviews Ralph Ginzburg, recently sentenced to a five-year jail term by a Philadelphia judge on obscenity charges for his magazine *Eros.* To the question regarding what subjects are most in need of exposure Ginzburg answers: big business, the cigarette industry, our military complex, the antidemocratic measures of the Catholic Church, and "our spook establishment" (CIA, FBI, etc.). Ginzburg blames the hierarchy of the Catholic Church for action against *Eros.* He reveals his intention of publishing a new magazine of controversy—*Fact.*

————. "The Small Knife: Studies in Censorship." *Sight and Sound*, 25:206–11, 220, Spring 1956. **W 251**

Censorship of motion pictures in Great Britain and France. "What one jibs at is the number of cuts now being made by the British Board (one film cut in three is a disturbingly high proportion); the inability of the film-goer to know, except by internal evidence, whether the film he is watching has been cut and, if so, to what extent; the power of the Board virtually to ban a film without the public knowing anything about it."

Wild, Nelson H. "Presumption of Constitutionality—Application to Regulation of Obscene Motion Pictures." *Wisconsin Law Review*, 1961(4):659–64, 1961. **W 252**

"This note will analyze the presumption of constitutionality in the area of regulation of obscene motion pictures, as illustrated by *Times Film Corp. v. City of Chicago*, 365 U.S. 43 (1961)."

Wiley, William F. *Riding a Wave of Fanaticism in a Sea of Paternalism, the Creatures of Our Own Making Seek Our Destruction. The Vaunted Power of the Press Is No More, an Address, January 30, 1917, Columbus, Ohio.* Cleveland, United Press Association, 1917. 8p. **W 253**

The managing editor of the Cincinnati *Inquirer* attacks the various elements in government that are "sweeping down on the press of America" in a "relentless, cold, merciless un-American avalanche of government censorship."

Wilkerson, Marcus M. "The Press and the Spanish-American War.' *Journalism Quarterly*, 9:129–48, June 1932. **W 254**

Wilkes, George. *The Mysteries of the Tombs; a Journal of Thirty Days Imprisonment in the New York City Prison, for Libel.* New York, The Author, 1844. 64p. **W 255**

Wilkes, imprisoned on a conviction of obscene libel under circumstances that may have been unjust, writes his observations on the case and on life in prison in a series of letters. In a general observation on obscene libel he anticipates a point of view expressed by Gershon Legman a century later: "Is it criminal to *incite* to an act (fornication), the *actual commission* of which is innocent by law?" At most, he thinks, obscenity should be considered an offense against good taste. He concludes with an amusing list of the books in the prison library.

[Wilkes, John]. *An Authentick Account of the Proceedings against John Wilkes, Esq. . . . Containing All the Papers Relative to this Interesting Affair . . . with an Abstract of That Precious Jewel of an Englishman, the Habeas Corpus Act. Addressed to All Lovers of Liberty.* London, Printed for J. Williams, [1763]. 39p. **W 256**

[————]. *The Battle of the Quills; or Wilkes Attacked and Defended. An Impartial Selection of all the most Interesting Pieces Argumentative, Declamatory, and Humorous, in Prose and Verse relative to John Wilkes, Esq; Written by his Adversaries, his Partisans, and Himself . . . to which is prefixed an Account of the Nature of Outlawry.* London, J. Williams, 1768. 74p. **W 257**

[————]. *Comparative View of the Conduct of John Wilkes, Esq.; as contrasted with the Opposite Measures during the Last Six Years.* By ————. London, J. Williams, 1768. 27p. **W 258**

A sympathetic account of Wilkes trials and tribulations.

[————]. *Conduct of the Administration in the Prosecution of Mr. Wilkes.* London, J. Wilkie, 1764. 31p. **W 259**

————. *The Correspondence of the Late John Wilkes, Printed from the Original Manuscripts, in which are introduced Memoirs of His Life, by John Almon.* London, Printed for Richard Phillips, 1805. 5 vols. **W 260**

The biography of Wilkes by John Almon, his publisher, contains a history of *North Briton*, and an account of the various legal actions taken against him for his criticism of the government.

[————]. *English Liberty; or The British Lion Roused; Containing the Sufferings of John Wilkes, Esq., from the First of His*

Persecutions down to the Present Time. London, T. Marsh, [1770?]. 367 p.
W 261

A collection of letters, speeches, newspaper accounts, and other documents relating to the Wilkes trial. A poem on Wilkes and Liberty, ascribed to Wilkes, appears on pages 59–69 of vol. 2.

[———]. *An Epistle from Col. John Lilburn, In the Shades, to John Wilkes, Esq.; Late a Colonel in the Buckinghamshire Militia.* London, F. Freeman, [179—?]. 45 p.
W 262

A letter supporting John Wilkes, purporting to come from the Leveller, John Lilburne, deceased. In a light vein the writer compares Wilkes' struggle for freedom of the press with that of his own, more than a century earlier. He closes with this statement: "I am desired to inform you, that all the friends of liberty in the shades are willing to encourage the work, and that you may make the price to subscribers in the nether world, as high as you think proper."

———. *An Essay on Woman, and Other Pieces, printed at the private press in Great George-street, Westminster, in 1763, and now reproduced in fac-simile from a copy believed to be unique. To which are added, Epigrams and Miscellaneous Poems now first collected, by the Right Hon. John Wilkes . . . Preceded by an introductory narrative of the extraordinary circumstances connected with the prosecution of the author in the House of Lords, digested and compiled from contemporary writers.* London, Privately printed [by J. C. Hotten], 1871. 263 p.
W 263

When the king's ministers were unable to convict Wilkes of seditious libel for his publication, *North Briton*, because of his Parliamentary immunity, they accused him before the House of Commons of publishing an obscene libel. Wilkes had printed on his private press a few copies of *Essay on Woman*, a risqué parody on Pope's *Essay on Man*, intended for his friends. By bribing the printer, a government agent secured a proof copy of the poem as evidence. This contributed to Wilkes's expulsion from Parliament. In addition to reprinting the famous *Essay on Woman*, together with the author's original introduction (advertisement), the volume includes the affidavits and statements of Michael Curry and Thomas Farmer, printers, an account of the proceedings against Wilkes for publication of the essay, comments on the case by Lord Macaulay and Horace Walpole, the narrative of the Rev. Mr. Kidgell and details of his part in the affair, and other related documents.

[———]. "A Letter on the Public Conduct of Mr. Wilkes." In *A Collection of Scarce and Interesting Tracts*, vol. 3, pp. 76 ff., and in *The Correspondence of the Late John Wilkes*, vol. 1, pp. 244–71.
W 264

Wilkes's own account of his various prosecutions for libel and a justification for his conduct at the trials. The account, told in the third person, was written by Wilkes from prison and first published anonymously in the *Political Register*, November 1768.

[———]. *A Letter to William Lord Mansfield . . . Upon some late Star Chamber Proceedings in the Court of King's Bench. Against the Publishers of the Extraordinary North Briton, No. IV. By the Author of those Papers.* London, 1768.
W 265

Upon his return to England from a four-year exile in Paris, Wilkes was determined to test his outlawry and arranged to have himself arrested on the four-year-old charge of seditious and obscene libel (Wilkes had criticised the king's ministers in his *North Briton*). There was high feeling among friends of Wilkes and a bloody clash between Wilkesites and troops delayed the trial before Lord Mansfield until June 1768, when he was found guilty. For publication of the *Essay on Woman* he was fined £500 and sentenced to a year in prison; for no. 45, *North Briton* he was fined £500 and sentenced to 10 months in prison. He was incarcerated for a total of 22 months. This open letter to the judge who sentenced him was written from prison and relates to the conduct of the trial.

[———]. *A Narrative of the Proceedings against John Wilkes, Esq. from his Commitment in April 1763, to his Outlawry. With a full View of the Arguments used in Parliament and out of Doors, in canvassing the various important Questions that arose from his Case.* London, Printed for Richardson & Urquhart, 1768. (Also in Howell, *State Trials*, vol. 19, pp. 981 ff.)
W 266

Wilkes, along with more than 40 of his associates, was arrested in the spring of 1763 on a "general warrant" for publication of seditious libels in issue no. 45 of *North Briton*. He was confined to prison for 6 days, then released on the basis of his Parliamentary immunity. All who had been arrested ultimately sued and recovered damages for illegal arrest. Wilkes was later found guilty of seditious libel by the House of Commons and expelled. When he failed to attend his trial (he was in Paris recovering from a duel wound) the court declared him an outlaw. Popular opinion favored Wilkes and, overnight, he became a champion of the freedom to criticize an unpopular government.

[———]. *Observations upon the Authority, Manner and Circumstances of the Apprehension and Confinement of Mr. Wilkes Addressed to Free-Born Englishmen.* London, J. Williams, 1763. 36 p.
W 267

Wilkinson, Clennell. "The Cinema and the Puritan." *Outlook* (London), 51:13, 6 January 1923.
W 268

"Penny dreadfuls" used to be blamed for juvenile delinquency; now it is the films that are responsible. Why prohibit showing sex films to those under 16—they would only go to sleep; it is those just over 16 for whom the film will "put ideas into their heads." The notion that the movies are "any more capable than the penny dreadful and the melodrama of making saints or sinners is a theory that still remains to be proved." The modern puritan treats adults and children as having the same kind of mind.

Wilkinson, Donald M., Jr. "Constitutional Law—Censorship of Obscene Literature." *Michigan Law Review*, 52:575–82, February 1954.
W 269

Prior restraint may be constitutional, "but it would seem that before the court would sanction prior censorship of obscene literature, it would demand extremely definite standards for determining what would constitute obscenity—a requirement which appears quite difficult to meet."

Wilkinson, Louis U. *Blasphemy and Religion; a Dialogue about John Cowper Powys' "Wood and Stone," and Theodore Powys' "The Soliloquy of a Hermit"* . . . New York, G. A. Shaw, [1916]. 12 p.
W 270

Will, Hubert L. "Free Press vs. Fair Trial." *Nieman Reports*, 17(3):16–21, September 1963. (Reprinted from *De Paul Law Review*, Spring–Summer 1963)
W 271

A U.S. District Court judge demonstrates that "existing remedies are less than adequate to cope with the growing problem of prejudicial publicity" and recommends that unless voluntary means of restraint are put into effect, "the constitutional right to a fair trial will have to be secured by means which the press may find repugnant but which will have been brought on by its own disregard of this fundamental right."

"Will the Catholic Church Screen TV/Radio Programming? Pope [Pius XII] Calls for Setting up of National Offices to Evaluate Broadcast Entertainment." *Sponsor*, 11:38–41, 26 October 1957.
W 272

Willert, *Sir* Arthur. "British News Controls." *Foreign Affairs*, 17:712–22, July 1939.
W 273

The author reviews the "heavy handed" treatment of the British press under the Chamberlain government. There has been no deliberate design to throttle the press, just the reaction of a weak government under stress of criticism.

Williams, Arnold. "*Areopagitica* Revisited." *University of Toronto Quarterly*, 14:67–74, October 1944.   **W 274**
A consideration of the importance of Milton's classic defense of freedom of the press on the tercentenary of its first publication.

[Williams, Benjamin W., *et al.*]. *Trial of B. W. Williams and Others, Editor and Printers of the Dew Drop, a Temperance Paper Published at Taunton, Mass., for an Alleged Libel upon William Wilbar, a Rumseller of Taunton, before the Supreme Judicial Court at New Bedford . . .*, 1845. . . . Taunton, Mass., Hack & King, 1846. 60 p.   **W 275**
The offending article, for which Wilbar sued for $3,00 damages, was entitled A Dream and is reprinted here as court evidence. Williams calls Wilbar's tavern a "house of human slaughter" in the January 1845 issue of his temperance paper. The judge posed these questions for the jury: (1) Is it a libel? (2) Was it published concerning the plaintiff? (3) Was it published by the defendant? (4) Is it true? Williams was found not guilty.

Williams, Bernard. "Censorship and Reading." In *Proceedings, Papers and Summaries of Discussions at the Hastings Conference, The Library Association*. London, The Association, 1961, pp. 64–74.   **W 276**
"A first class discussion, in depth, of censorship of various types—moral, political, etc. The meaning of censorship, going beyond the philosophical into the present state of English law on the question of obscenity, is dissected and examined with thoroughness. . . . Mr. Williams believes that, in the esthetic sense, no really great work of art can be obscene. The law, of course, considers obscenity in a social, psychological concept." From a review in *ALA Newsletter on Intellectual Freedom*, April 1962.

Williams, C. Dickerman. "What's Wrong in Libel." *National Review*, 10:185–86, 25 March 1961.   **W 277**
The plaintiff in a libel trial is relieved of the burden of proof as to its falsity; the defendant must justify his defamatory assertions. The publisher as defendant has many possible defenses—truth, privilege of reporting on official proceedings, fair comment on facts, good faith, credibility, and reputation of the plaintiff. Newspapers, the author charges, rarely report libel cases against their own or other papers, thus avoiding the suggestion of evil.

Williams, Chester S. *Liberty of the Press*. Evanston, Ill., Row, Peterson, 1940. 72 p. (Our Freedoms Series)   **W 278**
Popular dramatization of episodes in the struggle for a free press including the Junius letters, the histories of William Prynne, Thomas Cooper, Elijah P. Lovejoy, and espionage cases in World War I. Written for use in schools.

Williams, Edward B. *One Man's Freedom*. New York, Atheneum, 1962. 344 p. Introduction by Eugene V. Rostow.   **W 279**
Chapter 16, Neither Snow Nor Rain Nor Heat . . ., deals with postal censorship; chapter 17, The Well-Meaning Man of Zeal, deals largely with the work of NODL. The author's point of view is that the organization has a right to object to publications but not to take action that would limit the right of others to have access to the publications.

[Williams, Elisha]. *A seasonable Plea for the Liberty of Conscience, and The Right of Private Judgment, in Matters of Religion, without any Controul from human authority. Being a Letter, From a Gentleman in the Massachusetts-Bay to his Friend in Connecticut . . . By a Lover of Truth and Liberty . . .* Boston, S. Kneeland and T. Green, 1744. 66 p. (Signed "Philalethes")   **W 280**
A judge and former president of Yale argues for "the Right that every one has to speak his Sentiments openly concerning such Matters as Affect the good of the whole." He would exclude "Papists." He defends the right of each individual to read and make his own interpretation of the Scriptures, without interference from civil or religious authorities.

Williams, Francis. "Curbing Press Freedom." *New Statesman*, 65:366, 68, 15 March 1963.   **W 281**
The author (Baron Francis Williams) discusses a case in which the Tribunals of Inquiry Act was invoked by the government against journalists who refused to disclose the source of their information.

———. "Danger from Within." *Nieman Reports*, 17?(1):22–25, March 1963.   **W 282**
Excerpts from a paper on Responsibilities of the Mass Media presented at the tenth-anniversary convocation of the Fund for the Republic. The author, historian and critic of the British press, believes that the greatest threat to confine or diminish the independence of the press in democratic countries now comes from the inside and such threats are more difficult to repel.

———. *Dangerous Estate; The Anatomy of Newspapers*. New York, Macmillan, 1958. 304 p.   **W 283**
The author traces British newspaper history "from the days of the illegal Press, and the battles with Church, Crown and Parliament, to the extraordinary influence on the social life exerted by Steele and Addison in the early eighteenth century; through the bribery and corruption of the rest of the century to the position of respectability and political power which leading newspapers had achieved by the end of the nineteenth century; then into the twentieth century with the rapid development of commercialization and advertising, culminating in the fantastic mass-circulation battles of the twenties and thirties."

———. *Press, Parliament and People*. London, Heinemann, 1946. 254 p.   **W 284**
The controller of news and censorship in England during World War II examines the relationship of the government and the press in providing freedom of information. He considers the government's role in the release of public information, and the role of the commercial press, influenced by its owners, its advertisers, and its sensitivity to public appeal. The high standards and code of the professional journalist provides the main safeguard against pressures from both government and the newspaper industry.

———. "The Right to Know." *Twentieth Century*, 170:6–17, Spring 1962.   **W 285**
"Is intrusion by the press 'an intolerable invasion of private rights' or is it a necessary part of the newspaper's job in holding up a mirror to society, irrespective of private feelings?" These complicated and controversial ethics are discussed by a leading historian and commentator on the British press.

Williams, G. "Censorship and Sex." *Sexology*, 9:631–35, March 1942; 684–87, April 1942.   **W 286**

Williams, George G. "The Future, Censorship and Librarians." *Texas Library Journal*, 31:10–14, 50, March 1955.   **W 287**
Discussion of the liberal and conservative methods of bringing about changes in society, changes which the author says are inevitable. He notes the liberal artitude in writing on sex matters which has not yet extended to matters of social and economic ideas.

Willimas, Harold, Jr. "Case for the Boston Booksellers." *Publishers' Weekly*, 113:444–47, 4 February 1928.   **W 288**
The attorney for the Boston booksellers praises the new obscenity bill that would give "liberty of access to all that is legal, and the fullest protection against all that is illegal." The bill, sponsored by the Boston booksellers, would relieve the bookseller who has been prosecuted under the criminal laws for crimes of which he was not guilty. It would place responsibility where it belongs, with the authors and publishers. The booksellers' bill and a more liberal one sponsored by Ellery Sedgwick of the *Atlantic Monthly* both failed of passage.

———. "The Decision in the *Strange Fruit* Case." *Publishers' Weekly*, 148:1831–32, 20 October 1945.   **W 289**
Comments on the Massachusetts Supreme Judicial Court decision against *Strange Fruit*, by the attorney for the Old Corner Book Store of Boston.

Williams, J. E. Hall. "The Obscene

Publications Act, 1959." *Modern Law Review*, 23:285–90, May 1960.　　**W 290**

An analysis of the law which superseded the Lord Campbell Act of 1857—"a compromise measure, the result of a long struggle between the Home Office and the would-be reformers." It was intended "to provide for the protection of literature; and to strengthen the law concerning pornography."

———. "Obscenity in Modern English Law." *Law and Contemporary Problems*, 20:630–47, Autumn 1955.　　**W 291**

The author, an English barrister and lecturer in law at the London School of Economics and Political Science, discusses the history of the English law relating to obscene publications, including the famous *Hicklin* case, the procedure under the Obscene Publications Act of 1857, and finally, the recent developments, including proposals for reform culminating in the Obscene Publications Bill of 15 March 1955.

[Williams, James]. "Law Relating to Theatres." In *Encyclopaedia Britannica*. 11th ed., 1911. vol. 26, pp. 736–39.　**W 292**

Williams, Jerre S. "Parliamentary Privilege Limitation on Freedom to Criticize the British House of Commons." *Texas Law Review*, 42:1–38, November 1963.　**W 293**

"The newspaper and periodical publisher in Great Britain is subject to a restriction upon his comments concerning the actions of Parliament which constitutes a significant limitation upon his freedom of speech. A comparable restriction is unknown in this country. While the precise lines of the British restriction are not ascertainable, the over-all effect is to keep the British press in a state of frequent concern lest the proper bounds of comment on Parliamentary activity be transgressed." The author, studying the problem in England under a Ford Foundation grant, describes the current state of restrictions on reporting of Parliamentary activities and some of the cases that have arisen. While criticizing some of the judgments that he considers too stringent, the author concludes that, while the system "would clearly be unacceptable under the American constitutional system," there is "no insistance, that the principle itself is faulty for Britain," where "the tradition of liberty is in the hands of the people and is protected by the people's representatives in the House of Commons."

Williams, Jesse L. "If Censorship Comes." *Authors' League Bulletin*, 15(1):6–8, April 1927.　**W 294**

The author urges that plays be appraised by their social effect—the object rather than the subject of the play, and in light of the changing times.

Williams, John. "Films and the Blue Pencil." *World Review* (London), 1948: 48–51, September 1948.　**W 295**

No Orchids for Miss Blandish was "passed by the Board of film Censors, cut by the L.C.C. and banned altogether by at least one local authority. *No Orchids* caused questions in Parliament and—inevitably—drew packed houses. It was an interesting example of the untidy working of our censorship." If censorship must be used it should be "used promptly, consistently and sparingly."

[Williams, John A.]. *Letter to Henry Brougham upon his Durham Speech [in the trial of J. A. Williams for a Libel on the Durham Clergy] and the Three Articles in the Last Edinburgh Review upon the Subject of the Clergy*. London, 1823. 28 p.　**W 296**

[———]. *Trial of John Ambrose Williams, for a Libel on the Clergy, contained in the Durham Chronicle of August 18, 1821. Tried at the Summer Assizes, at Durham, on Tuesday, August 6th, 1822, before Mr. Baron Wood and a Special Jury. Including a Report of the Preliminary and Subsequent Proceedings in the Court of King's Bench, London*. 2d ed. Durham, Eng., Printed by J. A. Williams and published by Ridgway, 1823. 63 p. (Appeared in various separate editions and in Macdonell, *Report of State Trials*, vol. 1, pp. 1294–1338. Lord Brougham's speech is reprinted in Veeder, *Legal Masterpieces*. St. Paul, Keefe-Davidson, 1903)　**W 297**

Williams, publisher of the *Durham Chronicle*, was charged with attempting to bring the Church of England into contempt and vilifying its clergy. Lord Brougham, in his defense of Williams, argued that the clergy and the church were no more freed from criticism than any other public functionary or institution. Furthermore, the Protestant religion itself was the product of free discussion. The judge urged conviction, stating that freedom of the press, if carried to the extreme, endangered the establishments of the nation. The jury found no cause for criminal libel, only "defamatory libel," and no sentence was passed.

Williams, Joseph C., and Arthur Brown. "Is Censorship Justifiable in a Democracy?" *Forum*, 110:228–34, October 1948.　**W 298**

Williams supports the affirmative: "Freedom of expression is the right of every citizen; it is a right because such expression is of benefit to the community. Obviously, then, the community through the government, may at any time limit this right for its own protection. This protection is called censorship and such censorship is vital to democracy." Brown supports the negative: "The democratic philosophy is based on man's ability to reason, to decide for himself his own best interest, on man's educability, and his conscience. Censorship denies all these premises. . . . Regardless of the issues of truth and falsehood, danger or obscenity, free expression is invaluable for progress. Censorship cannot be justified in a democracy."

Williams, Michael. "Views and Reviews: Alfred Noyes." *Commonweal*, 28:555–56, 23 September 1938.　**W 299**

Editor Williams criticizes Alfred Noyes's refusal to submit to the rulings of the Holy Office with respect to his study of Voltaire. "Everything written by any Catholic should be at least implicitly subjected to the ruling authority of the Church; and if that authority should be exercised in a way that seems harsh, or even mistaken, nevertheless the writer should submit, with complete good will."

———. "Views and Reviews: [Irish Censorship]." *Commonweal*, 34:423–24, 22 August 1941; 34:565, 3 October 1941.　**W 300**

"Under the Irish censorship, it is abundantly clear that what the Irish people are permitted to know about the great issues at stake in the world conflict is heavily weighted in favor of Hitlerism." A Dublin government spokesman replies in the 3 October issue that "no sort of propaganda for or against either belligerent is permitted in Ireland."

Williams, Pat. "Enemies of the Imagination." *Twentieth Century*, 171:79–88, Spring 1963.　**W 301**

"Are censors really necessary? Pat Williams, a South African journalist who is radio critic of the *Sunday Telegraph*, describes some aspects of British Censorship and makes a plea for more freedom to play 'imagination games.'" Censors "are highly sensitive regulators of the rate of change. And in the case of official censors, they are part of a social feedback system prohibiting more emotion, and consequently more change, than the social machine can manage without breaking down. Censors are the enemies of unlicensed imagination . . . unlicensed, that is, by society." The author describes present aspects of British censorship and concludes that so many things are censored unconsciously, such as facts of birth, death, old age, etc., that it is difficult to be sure what they are. We should have more "imagination games" to uncover "hidden areas of ugliness and pain" which writers can help us explore.

[Williams, Paul]. "Danger in a 'Constitutional Gap.'" *Bar Bulletin*, New York County Lawyers' Association, 13:196, 200–201, March 1956.　**W 302**

A U.S. attorney opposes efforts to amend Canon 20 of the American Bar Association because it would extend the "constitutional gap"—the area between the ethical limits placed on lawyers' statements by their own professional canons and the constitutional limits which the government can impose on newspaper coverage of trials.

Williams, Roger. *The Bloudy Tenent, of Persecution, for cause of Conscience, discussed, in a Conference betweene Truth and Peace . . .* [London?]. 1644. 247 p. (An edition, with introduction by Edward B. Underhill, was published by the Hansard Knollys Society, London, 1848 [439 p.]; it is also reprinted in Joseph L. Blau, *Cornerstones of Religious Freedom in America.* Boston, Beacon, 1949, pp. 36–51) **W 303**
The *Bloudy Tenent*, while not strictly directed to freedom of the press, was a strong statement of the theory of the natural rights of man and the principle of religious toleration. It marks the beginning of religious freedom in America. Williams wrote the work when his controversy with John Cotton and the Massachusetts clergy forced him to flee to Rhode Island. He shocked the orthodox churchmen in England and America by extending tolerance even to Jews, pagans, and Turks. Cotton responded to Williams' work in *The Bloudy Tenent washed and made white in the bloude of the Lambe* (1647) and Williams followed with *The Bloudy Tenent yet More Bloudy* (1652). In England *The Bloudy Tenent* was ordered by the House of Commons to be publicly burned by the hangman.

Williams, S. M. ["Freedom of the Press"]. In *Problems of Journalism; Proceedings of the American Society of Newspaper Editors, 1932.* Washington, D.C., ASNE, 1932, pp. 59–62. **W 304**

An account of an Aberdeen, S.D., contempt case.

Williams, T. Harry. "Civil War Papers Spilled Secrets." *Quill*, 32(1):5, 12, January–February 1944. **W 305**
Newspapers operated during the Civil War under little or no restraint and sometimes revealed military secrets.

Williams, Walter. "International Free Press." *Public*, 20:1011–12, 19 October 1917. **W 306**
The achievement of a permanent peace will depend largely upon an internationally free press.

Williams, Wythe. "The Sins of the Censor; an Open Letter to Americans." *Collier's*, 60(18):6–7, 12 January 1918. **W 307**

The Paris correspondent of the *New York Times* asserts that "the American censorship which should be the fairest and best, is acutally the worst—and with less reason, for America has had time to find the perfect form of censorship if there is one." He urges that civilian control of censorship replace that imposed by the "West Point mind."

Williamson, Arleigh B. "Safeguarding Channels of Communications." *Annals of the American Academy of Political and Social Science*, 250:1–11, March 1947. **W 308**
The arguments for safeguarding communication channels are: development of codes of social responsibility, improvement of standards of accuracy, enlargement of the group that can discriminate between opinion and fact, and "expansion of consciousness in the general public that welfare of the individual or the group is inseparable from the welfare of the whole."

Williamson, Geoffrey. *Morality Fair; Vagaries of Social Conduct as Reflected in the Press.* London, Watts, 1955. 260 p. **W 309**
A popular survey of "the ever-changing attitude of the public and the growing tendency of the Press to deal frankly with all the facts of life, pleasant and unpleasant." There are frequent references to obscenity, censors and censorship, the issue of birth control, and criminal libel. Chapter 10 deals with Exploitation [of sex] in Print, and chapter 11 with Some Ardent Reformers.

Williamson, George C. *Lodowick Muggleton, A Paper Read before ye Sette of Odd Volumes, at ye 337th Meeting, January 27, 1915.* London, Chiswick Press, 1919. 84 p. (Sette of Odd Volumes no. 71) **W 310**
Muggleton, in 1652, was imprisoned on a blasphemy charge for denying the Trinity.

Williamson, Hugh R. *"Who Is for Liberty?"* London, Michael Joseph, 1939. 291 p. **W 311**
The author denounces the conservative press of Great Britain, "owned as it is by a few irresponsible millionaires." Censorship of the press in the interests of the plutocracy, the writer claims, is unnecessary. "Those Left papers outside the millionaire-control and who do, on occasion, manage to defy even advertiser-control, are kept in their place by a Government which uninterruptedly exerts 'the power of the hint' and which keeps in reserve, and on occasion does not scruple to use a series of repressive measures." The measures referred to are contempt of court, libel, application of the Official Secrets Act, and employment of police raids.

Williamson, T. Raworth. "Validity of Court Order Banning Newspaper Photographers from Court House Area." *Georgia Bar Journal*, 23:406–8, February 1961. **W 312**

The author defends the decision, *Atlanta Newspapers Inc. v. Grimes*, 216 Ga. 74, in the interest of the proper administration of justice.

Williford, Imogene. *The Development of Radio Regulation; Its Historical, Economic and Legal Phases.* Washington, D.C., American University, 1933. 114 p. (Unpublished Master's thesis) **W 313**

Willis, Delbert. "A Brass Curtain Fell in Texas." *Quill*, 39(7):18, 22–23, July 1951. (Also in *Nieman Reports*, July 1951) **W 314**
The *Fort Worth Press* won after a six-day news blackout imposed by an Air Force general who didn't like the way the newspaper was edited.

Willis, Hugh E. "Freedom of Speech and the Press." *Indiana Law Journal*, 4:445–87, April 1929. **W 315**
Relates to the application of restrictions on freedom of the press "in the public interest."

Wills, Elbert V. "Case of Doctor Cooper." *South Atlantic Quarterly*, 18:6–14, January 1919. **W 316**
Wartime interest in the Espionage Act recalls the case of Dr. Thomas Cooper, the second trial under the Sedition Law of 1798. Cooper was brought to trial for libel of President Adams. He was found guilty and given 6 months in prison and a fine of $400. In 1840 the fine was repaid by Congress to Cooper's heirs.

[Wilson, Effingham]. *On the Taxes on Knowledge.* London, Robert Heward, 1831. 32 p. (Reprinted from the *Westminster Review*, July 1, 1831) **W 317**
A speech by Wilson declaring the newspaper stamp tax a "moral and political evil."

Wilson, Kenneth E. "The Great Secrecy Case." *Nieman Reports*, 8(2):3–6, April 1954. **W 318**
The San Francisco press kept the story of the Leonard Moskovitz kidnapping a secret for 61 hours. Was it suppression or service?

Wilson, Lyle C. "A Government Press Agent Need Not Be a Barrier to News." *Quill*, 39(7):10–11, 22 July 1951. **W 319**
It isn't the system but the man who makes information service good or bad.

Wilson, Quintus C. *A Study and Evaluation of the Military Censorship in the Civil War.* Minneapolis, University of Minnesota, 1945. 292 p. (Unpublished Master's thesis) **W 320**
The study begins with a background of the social and military conditions that made censorship necessary in the Civil War. The major body of the thesis consists of a detailed examination of records of the war to determine what censorship action was taken by military commands. Finally, the author appraises the effectiveness of censorship in relation to the war effort. Development of Civil War censorship, he notes, may be divided into three periods. First, the frantic, fumbling efforts to

prevent information from reaching the enemy; second, a basic plan developed by army commanders but faulty in execution, and which was sometimes used to prevent release of information which would reflect discredit to a commander; and, third, a limited but effective censorship effort directed soley for purpose of military security.

————. "Voluntary Press Censorship during the Civil War." *Journalism Quarterly*, 19:251–61, September 1942. **W 321**
A forerunner of the censorship codes of later wars.

Wilson, Richard B. *Freedom of Speech and Public Opinion*. Berkeley, Calif., University of California, 1952. 193 p. (Unpublished Ph.D. dissertation) **W 322**
The study attempts to determine to what extent public intolerance of unpopular persons and groups operated as a limitation on freedom of speech. It also considers the seemingly contradictory objectives of controlling such intolerance and at the same time preserving the essential guarantees of the First Amendment. The author finds that: (1) Widespread public intolerance of specific doctrines and groups leads ultimately to the destruction of democratic government; (2) our judicial system is not now dealing adequately with those contributors to the growth of public intolerance who come under its surveillance; and (3) it is possible to strengthen rather than impair the freedoms guaranteed by the First Amendment by developing judicial principles which will at least partially control these contributors. Chapter III deals with the problem of group defamation in the American law of libel. The author concludes that the "clear and present danger" interpretation of the First Amendment, which accepts unrestrained clashes between interest groups, is a mechanistic notion that is no more than a myth and is a dangerous concept in a pluralistic society. Instead, he poses an ethnocentric interpretation, which recognizes that "whenever intergroup hostility reaches a certain level of intensity . . . democratic institutions can no longer operate."

Wilson, Robert A. "The *National Enquirer*: 'All the News That's *Un*fit to Print.'" *Fact*, 1(4):19–23, July–August 1964. **W 323**
"By catering to America's growing thirst for sadism, the *National Enquirer* has become the nation's best-selling weekly newspaper." The author observes that, while various organizations oppose the pornography of sex, "no group of Americans has banded together to combat sadism in literature."

Wilson, Robert R. "International Law and Proposed Freedom of Information." *American Journal of International Law*, 39: 790–93, 1945. **W 324**

A general discussion of proposals for world news freedom as they relate to the principles of international law. Includes the resolution adopted by representatives of 20 American republics at the Inter-American Conference on Problems of War and Peace, held in Mexico City in 1945.

Winant, John G., *ed.* "Right of All People to Know; A Symposium." *Survey Graphic*, 35:429–504+, December 1946. **W 325**
Fifteen advocates of world freedom of information contribute to this symposium. They include: Morris L. Ernst, Senator James E. Murray, Frederic G. Melcher, James T. Shotwell, and Ferdinand Kuhn, Jr.

Winchell, Walter. "Blueprint for Disaster." *Collier's*, 123:13–15+, 18 June 1949. **W 326**
The author opposes the Tydings-Vinson bills before Congress, that would give increased powers to the Department of Defense, because of the present policy of military censorship that requires clearance with the department before a member of the armed forces can give information to Congress.

Winfield, P. H. "Law of Libel and the Press." *Fortnightly*, 164:374–77, December 1948. **W 327**
The author considers the present position of the British press in light of two modern decisions unfavorable to it under the libel law, and recommends legal reforms.

Winger, Howard W. "Public Library Holdings of Biased Books about Russia." In *Occasional Papers*, no. 1, University of Library School, July 1949. 12 p. mimeo. **W 328**
The results of this study show that in the case of selecting books on Russia, librarians have adhered to the principle of balance expressed in the *Library Bill of Rights*.

Winick, Charles. "Censor and Sensibility: A Content Analysis of the Television Censor's Comments." *Journal of Broadcasting*, 5:117–35, Spring 1961. **W 329**
The article "is intended to convey the flavor of the censor's work, and provide an adequate introduction to this important phase of broadcasting self-regulation and management. It is possibly the only study of the broadcasting executive as a decision-maker." Tables classify the number of deletions and comments of censors by categories. The author concludes: "The matter-of-fact work of the network censors does not seem to represent the sort of interference with free expression around which the 'great debate' on censorship has raged."

————. *Taste and the Censor of Television*. New York, Fund for the Republic, 1959. 34 p. **W 330**

The author discusses the self-regulatory code of the television industry which covers such areas of controversy as violence, sex, religion, and politics.

Winslow, Edward. *Hypocrasie Unmasked: By A true Relation of the Proceedings of the Governor and Company of the Massachusetts against Samuel Gorton (and his Accomplices) a notorious disturber of the Peace and quiet of the severall Governments wherein he lived: With the grounds and reasons thereof, examined and allowed by their Generall Court holden at Boston in New England in November last, 1646* . . . London, Printed by Rich. Cotes for John Bellamy, 1646. 103 p. (A reprint of the original edition, with an introduction by Howard Millar Chapin, was published in Providence, R.I., by the Club for Colonial Reprints, 1916) **W 331**
Samuel Gorton had been convicted of blasphemy in the Massachusetts colony and, upon his return to England, wrote an exposé of religious intolerance in Massachusetts. Winslow was sent to England to defend the colony against Gorton's charges. *Hypocrasie Unmasked* is Winslow's refutation of the accusations.

Winslow, John. *The Battle of Lexington as Looked at in London before Chief-Justice Mansfield and a jury in the trial of John Horne, Esq., for libel on the British Government*. New York, New York Society of the Order of the Founders and Patriots of America, 1897. 39 p. (Publications no. 2) **W 332**
Address read before the Society, 13 May 1897. Horne (later Horne Tooke) had denounced the battle as murder and proposed a subscription for the widows and orphans of the colonists killed at Lexington and Concord. Winslow gives a full account of the trial in 1775 in which Horne defended himself. He was found guilty of seditious libel and was sentenced to a year in prison and fined £200.

Winter, Calvin. "*Index* of Prohibited Books." *Bookman*, 34:185–90, October 1912. **W 333**
A popular account of the origin and development of the Catholic *Index*. "There is nothing in the published index to give any hint as to the nature of the offense given by any particular book or the amount of correction necessary before the prohibition may be removed." The secretary of the *Index* is empowered to inform the author of the reason for the objection if he so requests.

[Winterbotham, William]. *Trials of William Winterbotham for Seditious Words*. London, 1794. 132 p. **W 334**

Wirt, Frederick M. "To See or Not to

See: The Case Against Censorship."
Film Quarterly, 13(1):26–31, Fall 1959.
W 335

"Films have been censored in the United States, as in other countries, for many years. Recently, however, censorship statutes have proved increasingly unenforceable in court, as well as increasingly unpopular. In this article we present the principle case for abolishing censorship entirely."

Wisconsin. Legislative Reference Library. *Legislation to Control the Distribution of Obscene Materials with Special Reference to Wisconsin*. Madison, Wis., The Library, 1960. 11 p. (Bulletin 192) **W 336**

Wisconsin. University. Extension Division. *University of Wisconsin through the University Extension Division Lends Its Auspices to Newspaper and Magazine Men for the First National Newspaper Conference, to Consider the Question: Are Newspaper and Magazine Writers Free to Tell the Truth? If Not, Why Not, and What Can Be Done About It?* [Madison, Wis.]. 1912. 8 p.
W 337

The conference (29 July–1 August 1912) dealt mostly with censorship by advertisers. The *Proceedings* were published in the *Bulletin* of the University of Wisconsin, General Series, 1913.

Wisconsin Free Library Commission. "Free Library Commission Issues Statement on Freedom of Inquiry and Expression." *Wisconsin Library Bulletin*, 46: 3–4, September 1950. **W 338**

Wisconsin Library Association. Intellectual Freedom Committee. *Intellectual Freedom*. Madison, Wis., The Association, 1964. 55 p. (A reprint from the *Wisconsin Library Bulletin*, May–June 1964) **W 339**

Contents: ALA Library Bill of Rights, School Library Bill of Rights, Intellectual Freedom in Libraries (A Statement of Policy for the Wisconsin Library Association), The Sleeping Dog vs. The Stolen Horse by Margaret E. Monroe, To Hold in Trust (trustees responsibility) by Elizabeth J. Fabry, Municipal Administration and the Freedom to Read by John Colson, The Novel in the High School Library (Censorship or Selection), Arsenal of the Librarian (bibliography) by Leonard B. Archer, Jr.

"Wisconsin Policy as to the Literature of Disloyalty." *Wisconsin Library Bulletin*, 14:39–40, February 1918. **W 340**

Text of a letter from the Wisconsin Library Commission to guide public libraries in handling literature relating to the war.

Withers, Philip. *Alfred; or, A Narrative of the Daring and Illegal Measures to Suppress a Pamphlet, Intituled, Strictures in the Declaration of Horne Tooke, Esq., respecting "Her Royal Highness the Princess of Wales," Commonly Called Mrs. Fitzherbert, etc.* London, Philip Withers, 1789. 48 p.
W 341

Chaplain Withers had written a pamphlet, signed "Alfred," exposing the secret marriage of the Prince of Wales to Mrs. Maria Ann Fitzherbert, whom he termed a "Catholic Whore." He delivered copies to James Ridgway, bookseller, who, instead of selling them, used them for political extortion. Richard B. Sheridan, a friend of Mrs. Fitzherbert, arranged for the suppression of the pamphlet. In the above signed pamphlet, in which he repeats his charges, Withers explains that he was "reduced to the alternative of publishing his own name, or of exposing honest men to the resentments of the Whig Party." Withers followed this with an anonymous pamphlet, *Nemesis, or a Letter to Alfred*, in which he continued to attack Mrs. Fitzherbert, charging her with intimacies with the Marquis de Bellois in Paris. For this work Mrs. Fitzherbert brought charges against Withers for libel, and the pamphleteer was imprisoned. While in prison he issued another tract, *Alfred to the Bishop of London*, defending his earlier charges, which he stated were made out of a sense of duty to Church and State. The London *World* supported Withers and it is likely that he was subsidized by certain government officials. At the trial Mrs. Fitzherbert was represented by Thomas Erskine, Withers by himself. When he was convicted of libel, but before sentencing, Withers published yet another pamphlet, *Alfred's Apology, Second Part . . . with a Summary of the Trial of the Editor of Nemesis, on the Prosecution of Mrs. Fitzherbert, for a Libel*. In the pamphlet Withers repeated his charges of immorality and defended his own motives in exposing the Prince's "wife." Withers was convicted and sentenced to serve twelve months in Newgate Prison and to pay a fine of £50.

———. *Alfred's Appeal, Containing His Address to the Court of King's Bench, on the Subject of the Marriage of Mary Anne Fitzherbert, and Her Intrigue with Count Bellois*. [London], 1789. 88 p. **W 342**

Withers protested his conviction for libel of Mrs. Fitzherbert (see previous entry), complaining that the law was hostile to the discovery of truth and the freedom of the press, and that he had only done his duty as a "good Citizen and a Protestant Minister." A full account of the Withers affair is given in Werkmeister, *The London Daily Press, 1772–1792*.

Withers, Samuel. "The Library, the Child and the Censors." *New York Times Magazine*, 8 April 1962, pp. 53–58.
W 343

An account of recent trends toward censorship in school libraries. Reports on the dropping of *Huckleberry Finn* from the approved textbook list of the New York schools, which turned out to be objection to the expurgated edition.

Witherspoon, John. *Serious Inquiry into the Nature and Effects of the Stage: and a Letter Respecting Play Actors . . . Also a Sermon on the Burning of the Theatre at Richmond; by Samuel Miller . . . together with an Introductory Address, by Several Ministers in New York, etc.* New York, Whiting & Watson, 1812. 199 p. (First published in Glasgow, 1757) **W 344**

Dr. Witherspoon was principal of Princeton University.

Witman, Arthur L. "Canon 35 Abridges Freedom of Press and Denies Public Its Right to Know." *Quill*, 46(6):8–9, 19–20, June 1958. **W 345**

"Gains are being made in some states in relaxing restrictions against courtroom cameras but photographers believe now is the time to launch frontal attack on this outmoded barrule."

Witt, Marion. "'Great Art Beaten Down': Yeats on Censorship." *College English*, 13:248–58, February 1952. (Reprinted in Downs, *The First Freedom*, pp. 382–88) **W 346**

"From the beginning to the end of his life, as poet, playwright, theatre manager, and public man, Yeats never surrendered to the forces of repression . . . he repeatedly stated that unless the Abbey [Theatre] could be free of government or mob interference, he preferred to close its doors." An account of Yeat's battle against Irish censorship, a battle which he lost.

Wittenberg, Philip. *Dangerous Words; a Guide to the Law of Libel*. New York, Columbia University Press, 1947. 335 p.
W 347

Consideration of the law of libel from the point of view of prevention. "What libel is, what words or groupings of words are libelous, how such words are construed, against what background they are scrutinized in point of time and place of utterance." Truth as a defense, libel of the dead, group libel, libel of minority groups, and defamation by radio are among the topics covered. The author is a New York patent and copyright lawyer.

———. *The Law of Literary Property*. Cleveland, World Publishing Co., 1956. 284 p. **W 348**

Chapters on Literature and Censorship, Right of Privacy, and Libel.

Wittmer, Felix, and Thomas F. Hunt. "Slow Poison for the Young Idea; Two Educators Report on Pro-Soviet Texts." *Freeman*, 2:142–45, 3 December 1951.
W 349

Wittmer criticizes as pro-Soviet the Oxford Social Studies pamphlet, *Our Stake in the Far East*, and recommends it be prohibited from the schools. Hunt criticizes as pro-Soviet the National Education Association publication, *Building America*.

Wolfe, Don M., *ed. Leveller Manifestoes of the Puritan Revolution* . . . Foreword by Charles A. Beard. New York, Nelson, 1944. 440 p. **W 350**
Contains text and commentary of the major documents of the Levellers, including several attacks and remonstrances against the licensing of the press. One of the principle documents relating to the free press is: *To the . . . Commons of England*, dated 1648 (pp. 322–30). "To put the least restraint upon the Press, seems altogether inconsistent with the good of the Commonwealth, and expresly opposite and dangerous to the liberties of the people, and to be carefully awarded." The petition asks that the people be permitted to express themselves freely in "speaking, writing, printing, and publishing . . . without seting of Masters, Tutors, and Controulers over them."

———. "Milton and Mirabeau." *PMLA*, 49:1116–28, December 1934. **W 351**
A comparison of Milton's *Areopagitica* (1644) and Mirabeau's *Sur la liberté de la Presse imité de l'Anglais de Milton* (1788).

———. *Milton in the Puritan Revolution.* New York, Nelson, 1941. 496 p. **W 352**
The author devotes a chapter to the *Areopagitica* which he calls "the most drastically radical tract of its day." In opening free discussion of revolutionary ideas, "Milton was arguing for a principle so far-reaching that even he himself was unwilling in practice to accept it: the right to agitate for the overthrow of the dominant political and economic interests." In other chapters the author deals with Lilburne, Goodwin, Prynne, Overton, and Walwyn, including their views on press freedom.

Wolfram, Harold W. "John Lilburne: Democracy's Pillar of Fire." *Syracuse Law Review*, 3:213–58, Spring 1952. **W 353**

"A Woman and a Book." *Bookman*, 60: 385–86, December 1924. **W 354**
An editorial in The Point of View section, comparing the exploitation and advertising for public sale of an indecent book to the prostitution of a woman, and calling for censorship of the author or publisher who abets such prostitution.

The Woman Rebel. New York. March 1914—August 1914. Monthly. Edited by Margaret Sanger. **W 355**
The paper served as the news organ for Mrs. Sanger's fight for freedom of birth control information. In the first issue she attacked Anthony Comstock and the vice societies and announced the intention of publishing contraception information. She was informed by the New York Postmaster that the issue was unmailable on grounds of obscenity. The story of her indictment and exile to Canada is told in her biography, *My Fight for Birth Control*, as well as in issues of *The Woman Rebel*.

Wood, A. L. S. "Keeping the Puritans Pure." *American Mercury*, 6:74–78, September 1925. **W 356**
A Springfield (Mass.) newspaperman describes the censorship practices of the New England Watch and Ward Society and particularly the tactics of its secretary, the Rev. J. Frank Chase. Following H. L. Mencken's brush with the Society in Boston, April 1926, this article was reprinted for distribution.

Wood, Charles E. S. *Free Speech and the Constitution in the War . . . being Substantially a Reprint of the Argument against the Constitutionality of the Espionage Act, from the Brief Filed in the Marie Equi Case, no. 3328 U.S. Circuit Court of Appeals Ninth Circuit,* James E. Fenton, Attorney. [Portland, Ore., The Author, 1919]. 29 p. **W 357**

Wood, Dallas E. "To Print, or Not to Print." *Quill*, 27(12):3–4+, December 1939. **W 358**
A California editor advises how to handle the request: "Please keep it out of the paper!"

Wood, Eric F. "The British Censorship." *Saturday Evening Post*, 189:5–7, 101–2, 28 April 1917; 189:18–19, 105–6, 5 May 1917. **W 359**
Censorship in Great Britain during World War I.

Wood, H. H. "Books Burnt." *Notes and Queries*, 11(1st ser.):288–89. **W 360**
A list compiled principally from the Acts and Orders of the Commonwealth and supplementing the list of B. H. Cooper, appearing in earlier issues of *Notes and Queries*.

Wood, John. *A Correct Statement of the Various Sources from Which the History of the Administration of John Adams was Compiled, and the Motives for Its Suppression by Col. Burr: With Some Observations on a Narrative, by a Citizen of New-York By John Wood, Author of the Said History.* New York, Printed and sold for the author by G. F. Hopkins, 1802. 49 p. **W 361**
A reply to James Cheetham's *A Narrative of the Suppression by Col. Burr, of the History of the Administration of John Adams.* In June 1801, Wood writes, he entered into agreement with Barlas and Ward, booksellers, to publish this history of the Adams administration to be finished that fall. Wood found the truth difficult to establish because of so much partisanship in the press and required more time for research. The publishers insisted that it be ready on time or forfeit a penalty. Wood said he gathered information mainly from the *Aurora*, Mr. Duane, and Mr. Callender. Their information proved to be "false and libellous," particularly with respect to the relation of Adams to Franklin. By November, because of inaccuracies, Wood began to doubt whether the book should be published. He and the publishers decided to submit it to an independent judge, Brockholst Livingston, who let Burr see it. They agreed it should not be published and Burr suggested that the edition be purchased, but that his name be withheld from the transaction. The publishers agreed.

———. *The History of the Administration of John Adams* . . . New York, 1802. 506 p. **W 362**
"This book was printed and ready for publication in December, 1801, but was suppressed at the instigation of Aaron Burr as being incorrect and also libelous. Overtures were made to the publishers, Messrs. Barlas and Ward, by Burr and his friends, for the purchase of the edition and it was finally given up to them. The book was subsequently issued . . . When . . . placed on sale a new title page was added bearing the imprint, 'New York printed 1802.'" Quoted from Tomkins' *Bibliography Jeffersoniana*, 1887. Aside from the facts of suppression, the original work is of some interest because of its observations on the sedition trials, including the cases against Callender, Cooper, Duane, Fries, Frothingham, Lyon, Reynolds, Robbins, and Williams.

———. *The Suppressed History of the Administration of John Adams, (from 1797 to 1801) as Printed and Suppressed in 1802. By John Wood . . . Now Republished with Notes, and an Appendix, by John Henry Sherburne. . . .* Philadelphia, Published for the Editor, 1846. 392 p. **W 363**
The original work, highly critical of the second President, was published in 1802 but, according to Sherburne's introduction to this edition, all but a few copies were burned. The copy used in this reprinting was presumably presented to the editor's father (Judge Sherburne of New Hampshire) by Thomas Jefferson. The story of the suppression of the first printing is related by Sherburne as follows: While the work was in the hands of a New York printer, a copy of the printed sheets was mysteriously conveyed by a "renowned political star of that day" to "a certain lady conspicuous at that period for her deep political intrigue," who, in turn, showed the sheets to "another political luminary" who appeared unfavorably in the work. The latter commissioned two of his friends to purchase the entire edition, which was done and the copies were burned. A few copies escaped the flames, however, and came

into the possession of various political figures. The incident, according to Sherburne, was the commencement of hostilities between Aaron Burr and Alexander Hamilton, which terminated in the fatal duel. In 1802 James Cheetham and the author, John Wood, both wrote their somewhat different versions of the episode, but both involve Aaron Burr.

Wood, William R. "Newspaper Censorship." *Congressional Record*, 55(App.):269, 2 June 1917. **W 364**
"In my opinion the real purpose of this measure [wartime censorship of the press] is not so much for prevention of the publication of information that would be of comfort to our enemies or detrimental to our own Army as it is to shield the inefficiency of those who will be in high places in the conduct of the affairs of the nation during the present crisis." The author is a representative from Indiana.

Woodcock, George. "The Critic's Freedom." *Now*, 9:3, July–August 1947.
W 365
The great cinema combines are beginning to attempt control not only over film production, but over film criticism, witness the action of MGM in trying to persuade the B.B.C. to drop a film critic.

[Woodfall, Henry S.]. "Trial in London for Publishing Junius's Letter to the King, 1770." In Howell, *State Trials*, vol. 20, pp. 895 ff. Pleadings of the crown lawyers and defense counsel are given in *A Collection of Scarce and Interesting Tracts*, vol. 4, pp. 114–25. **W 366**
In this historic trial Judge Mansfield directed the jury to disregard the intention of the writer or the truth or falsehood of the assumed libel. Instead, the jury disregarded the judge's directions and found the editor of the *Public Advertiser* guilty of publication only, which was a virtual acquittal. A subsequent letter by Junius criticized Judge Mansfield's opinion.

Woodin, Glenn W. "Contributions of Mr. Justice Gaynor to the Law of Libel and Slander." *Bench and Bar*, 12(n.s.): 102–15, July 1917. **W 367**

Woodlock, Thomas F. "Make Responsibility Real." *Commonweal*, 1:201–2, 31 December 1924. **W 368**
The author advocates jury trial for obscenity cases, with the jurors reading and deciding on the publications themselves.

Woodruff, Clinton R. "Indictment against the Bill-Board. *Outlook*, 87:582–86, 16 November 1907. **W 369**
In support of a court decision enjoining an offensive billboard. The author argues that the government should protect the public against an aesthetic offense as well as against a moral offense or an infectious disease.

Woods, Amy. "Boston and the 'Movie' Censorship." *Survey*, 44:108–9, 17 April 1920. **W 370**
A member of the executive committee of the Massachusetts State Committee on Motion Pictures favors a Massachusetts bill creating a state censorship board to preview all movies and claims backing by 347 organizations. She objects to the so-called "Boston Plan" (*Survey*, 1 May), sponsored by the National Board of Review of Motion Pictures.

———. "Shall We Have State Censorship of Motion Pictures?" Boston, State Committee on Motion Pictures [in Massachusetts], 1920. 4 p. **W 371**

Woods, Harriett. "It's *Candy*-Time in St. Louis." *Focus/Midwest*, 3(10–11): 18–21, 1965. **W 372**
When the St. Louis County Council set up a Decent Literature Commission in 1963, Dr. William Landau, neurologist and local civil liberties leader, accepted appointment on the Committee to prevent censorship. This is an account of the problems and conflicts that developed.

Woodson, Fred W. "Newspaper Publication of Names of Juvenile Offenders." *Focus*, 33:146–55, Fall 1954. **W 373**
"One of the fundamental principles of juvenile court philosophy and practices is that files on juveniles within the court's jurisdiction should not be opened to persons having no legitimate interest therein. To reveal the names of juvenile offenders through the press violates this principle; in some jurisdictions to do so would violate an explicitly worded statute." The article reviews this issue in light of the recent attacks on the principle by the press.

Woodsworth, J. S. "Bible a Seditious and Libelous Book in Canada." *Crucible*, 3:1–2, 14 March 1920. **W 374**
Woodsworth is indicted for quoting from the Bible, Isaiah 10:1–2 and 65:21–22. The passages relate to the right of the poor and needy and the right of the workman to reap the benefit of his labor: "They shall not build, and another inhabit."

Woody, Thomas. "Affirmation versus Negation in American Education." *School and Society*, 79:33–39, 6 February 1954.
W 375
The "spirit of eternal negation" dominates American thought today—censorship, loyalty oaths, blacklists, investigations, suspicion of strange ideas, etc. The author cites numerous examples of the denial of the free flow of ideas, taken from scanning the pages of the *New York Times*. He calls for affirmation of faith in the American doctrine of freedom. "Affirmation is the rule of life; negation that of death."

Wooler, Thomas J. *Appeal to the Citizens*

of London against the Alleged Lawful Mode of Packing Special Juries . . . London, Wooler, 1817. 32 p. **W 376**
Following the trial of John Horne Tooke attention was drawn by Mr. Wooler and by the city solicitor, Charles Pearson, to the illegal preparation of jury lists by the king's attorney and coroner which led to the packing of juries in a number of libel cases. With the support of the Court, the corrupt system was brought to an end. Wooler's *Black Dwarf*, 26 November 1817, published this verse describing the court corruption in libel cases:

This is the jury that cast (convicted),
Which was picked by the Master,
Who held his place of the Judge,
Who was appointed by the Minister,
That accused the man of libel.

The Master was the official who compiled the jury list.

[———]. *A Verbatim Report of the Two Trials of Mr. T. J. Wooler, Editor of the Black Dwarf, for Alledged Libels, before Mr. Justice Abbott, and a Special Jury, on Thursday, June 5, 1817. Taken in Short-Hand by an eminent writer, and Revised by T. J. Wooler.* London, T. J. Wooler, 1817. 143 p. **W 377**
Wooler's *Black Dwarf*, a radical reform paper, was the subject of extensive government persecution during its brief life. Booksellers and other vendors who offered it for sale were arrested and held at high bail; stocks were seized; and the publisher was finally brought to trial on charges of seditious libel against the character of Lord Castlereagh and Mr. Canning. Wooler spoke in his own behalf, attacking the doctrine of "constructive libel" and the practices of employing "ex-officio informations." He was found guilty, but because of a technicality the verdict was set aside.

[———, and James Watson, Sr.]. *A Narrative of the Trial of Thomas Jonathan Wooler, for a Libel on His Majesty's Ministers; and of Dr. James Watson, Senior, for High Treason. With an account of the acquittal of Thistlewood, Preston and Hooper and Remarks by the Publisher.* Glasgow, Printed by R. Chapman for W. M. Borthwick, 1817. 155 p. **W 378**
An unsympathetic reporting of the trials of Wooler and Watson before Lord Ellenborough, *et al.* Wooler was found guilty, but the verdict was set aside because of a technicality; Watson was found not guilty.

Woolf, S. J. "Interview with Our Unofficial 'Censor.'" *New York Times Magazine*, 20 October 1946, pp. 24, 65. **W 379**
"Mr. [John] Sumner of the Anti-Vice Society talks of his career in suppressing the 'impure.'"

"'Broadmindedness,' he is quoted as saying, 'is all right so long as it does not strike home.'" The article includes a drawing of Sumner by the author. Another article about Sumner by the same author appears in the *New York Times*, 9 October 1932, section 8, p. 2.

Woolfolk, William. *A Book for Burning.* 1 hour television movie produced by Plautus Productions, New York, for "The Defenders" (created by Reginald Rose) and presented over the C.B.S. television network, 1963. (Production no. 60; Not available for distribution) **W 380**

Many of the basic issues in censorship are brought out in this courtroom drama in which the fictional father-and-son team, Lawrence and Ken Preston, defend an author against charges of obscenity. The case involves the arrest of the author by a local police officer at the instigation of the mayor. Despite threats from the mayor, who is his father-in-law, the judge (the hero of the episode), following an extensive airing of the issues, dismisses the case. The small-town librarian favors censorchip; the bookstore owner is afraid to defend the book; the newspaper editor defends the author in his editorial, but is afraid to testify because of possible retaliation.

Woolley, William. *Trials . . . W. Woolley for Publishing a Libel on Sir Richard Hill and Rev. Rowland Hill. . . . Intitled A Cure for Centing, etc.* London, 1794. 82 p. **W 381**

Woolsey, John M. "The Monumental Decision of the United States District Court Rendered December 6, 1933, By Hon. John M. Woolsey Lifting the Ban on *Ulysses.*" In James Joyce, *Ulysses.* New York, Modern Library, 1934, pp. ix–xiv. **W 382**

The Woolsey decision and the affirming decision of Judge Augustus N. Hand of the U.S. Circuit Court of Appeals, appear in many other sources, including the appendix of the John Lane edition of *Ulysses* (1936), Downs, *The First Freedom*, pp. 83–89, a recent German periodical, *Akzente* (July 1965), and in 5 *Federal Supplement* 182–85 and 72 *Federal Reporter*, 2d ser., 706–9.

Woolston, Thomas. *A Defence of the Miracle of the Thundering Legion.* London, 1726. 112 p. **W 383**

The *Dictionary of National Biography* describes the *Defence* as "a remarkable *tour de force* that ends with a fine appeal for liberty of publication, on the ground that 'it is the opposition of others that sharpens wit and brightens truth.'" Woolston wrote the work when he was under attack for blasphemy for his

A Moderator between an Infidel and an Apostate. His light and sometimes witty treatment of sacred themes seems to have been the real basis for his persecution.

[——]. "Trial for Writing and Publishing Four Books on the Miracles, 1729." In Borrow, *Celebrated Trials*, vol. 3, pp. 432–39. **W 384**

In 1725 Woolston, an enthusiastic freethinker, published *A Moderator between an Infidel and an Apostate*, relating to a theological quarrel between Anthony Collins and Edward Chandler. This was followed by two supplements. In these works Woolston interpreted as an allegory the story of the Resurrection and the Virgin Birth. For this and *A Defence of the Miracle of the Thundering Legion* he was brought to trial and, in 1729, was fined and sentenced to a year in prison. At the end of the year, being unable to pay his fine he remained in prison where he died in 1733.

Wooster, Harold A. "A Few Thoughts on Libraries and the Spirit of Censorship." *Library Journal*, 69:917–18, 1 November 1944. **W 385**

"Libraries are primarily concerned in making wholesome constructive reading available on a community-wide basis. They disapprove of the commercial exploitation of 'goodness' or 'badness' by authors and publishers, respect honesty and sincerity in literary expression, and feel that the adult individual reader has full power of necessary censorship, within himself, through selective reading." Matthew A. McKavitt criticizes the article in *Library World*, May 1945.

Worcester, Leonard. *A Discourse on the Alton Outrage, Delivered at Peacham, Vermont, December 17, 1837.* Concord, N.H., A. McFarland, 1838. 16 p. **W 386**

Relates to the murder of Elijah P. Lovejoy in defense of his printing press.

"Worcester Library Directors Support Their Librarian." *Library Journal*, 74: 649, 15 April 1949. **W 387**

Directors of the Free Public Library in Worcester, Mass., accept and endorse the Library Bill of Rights. Action followed removal of *Serenade* and *God's Little Acre* from the library by action of the Attorney General of Massachusetts. Directors instructed the librarian to surrender no books in the future without a court order.

The Word; a Monthly Journal of Reform. Princeton, Mass., 1872–93. **W 388**

This little paper, sometimes only a few pages, was edited by Ezra Heywood and his wife Angela, who campaigned for freedom in sexual expression and the sexual emancipation of women. It figured in various prosecutions of Heywood on obscenity charges, including the August 1882 issue in which appeared two poems of Whitman's from *Leaves of Grass*.

A Word to the Wise: Or, Some Seasonable Cautions about Regulating the Press. London, n.p., 1712. 22 p. **W 389**

The anonymous author calls for a stop to the scandalous licentiousness of the press which has libeled both king and church. He urges that the author's name be required on every publication as a method of insuring the truth. Licensing is not the answer; persons should not be punished before any crime is committed. "The Church which has Truth on her side, cannot be shaken by any Attacks from the Press that Error can make, while she has Liberty to defend herself the same way." The church and monarchy have gained more than they have lost by freedom of the press. To prohibit a work is to make it more attractive. It has been said "that none can be against truth, but when Truth is against 'em." Only a guilty government would consider restraint of the press.

Work, Telford. "Something is Lacking in 'Public Disclosure.'" *California Publisher*, 45(2):24, November 1965. **W 390**

The case for publishing lists of tax assessments in newspapers, inspired by bribery indictments of two California assessors.

"Work of the War Censor on the Field and at Home." *Literary Digest*, 57:46–53, 20 April 1918. **W 391**

The *World*, (New York). *The Roosevelt Panama Libel Case against the New York World [The United States v. The Press Publishing Co.]. A Brief History of the Attempt of President Roosevelt by Executive Usurpation to Destroy the Freedom of the Press in the United States, together with the Text of the Unanimous Decision of the United States Supreme Court Handed down by Mr. Chief Justice White, Affirming the Action of Judge Hough of the United States Court in Quashing the Indictment.* [New York], Published for the New York *World*, 1911. 88 p. **W 392**

[——]. *The Roosevelt Panama Libel Case against the New York World and Indianapolis News; Decision of Hon. Charles M. Hough, Judge of the United States Court for the Southern District of New York, and Hon. Albert B. Anderson, Judge of the United States Court for the District of Indiana. Together with an Account of the Circumstances That Led to the Unprecedented Prosecutions on the Part of the United States Government, and a Stenographic Report of the Trial of the New York World.* [New York], Printed for the New York *World*, 1910. 109 p. **W 393**

World League for Sexual Reform, 3rd Congress, London, 1929. *Sexual Reform Congress. Proceedings of the Third Congress. Edited by Norman Haire.* London, Paul, Trench, Trübner, 1930. 670p. **W394**
Includes discussions of the British law of obscene libel by H. F. Rubenstein and Laurence Housman, censorship of literature by Desmond MacCarthy, suppression of birth control information in United States, Ireland, and France by Marie C. Stopes, British stage censorship by John Van Druten, British film censorship by Ivor Montagu, taboos leading to the suppression of literature by Bertrand Russell and George Ives, and discussions of sex and censorship by F. P. Streeton and Hertha Riese.

World's Press News and Advertisers' Review. London, 1929–date. Weekly. **W395**
This organ of the British press industry (advertising, press, publicity, printing, and paper) regularly carries news dealing with freedom of the press.

Worthington, George. *An Inquiry into the Power of Juries to Decide Incidentally on Questions of Law.* London, S. Sweet, 1825. 197p. **W396**
It is the object of this inquiry to demonstrate that, on every point of law, libel juries are bound to obey the direction of the judge presiding at the trial. A lengthy critical review of the work in the *Westminster Review* (October 1827) charges the author with attempting to reverse the doctrine settled by the Fox Libel Act of 1792, establishing the rights of juries in libel cases. The reviewer suggests the work be retitled, after Defoe, *The Shortest Way with Juries; or Proposal for the Establishment of Absolute Judges.*

Worthington, George E. "Statutory Restrictions on Birth Control." *Journal of Social Hygiene,* 9:458–65, November 1923. (Excerpts in Johnsen, *Selected Articles on Birth Control,* pp. 36–44) **W397**

Wortman, Tunis. *A Treatise Concerning Political Enquiry, and the Liberty of the Press.* New York, Printed by George Forman for the Author, 1800. 296p. (Excerpts in Theodore A. Schroeder, *Free Press Anthology,* pp. 36–38) **W398**
"The freedom of speech and opinion, is not only necessary to the happiness of Man, considered as a Moral and Intellectual Being, but indispensibly requisite to the perpetuation of Civil Liberty. To enforce and advocate that inestimable right, is the principal object of the present Treatise." In a careful appraisal of Wortman's contribution to an American libertarian theory, Leonard W. Levy writes in his *Legacy of Suppression:* "It is, in a sense, the book that Jefferson did not write but should have." Wortman, a New York lawyer, expresses the libertarian views held, though not always practiced, by the Jeffersonian

administration. He defends the unlimited natural right of people to express opinion in government. Freedom of thought and open debate is the only basis for intelligent management of human affairs, particularly of a democratic government. Like John Locke, Wortman espouses the theory of involuntary belief, that one's ideas are the natural and inevitable product of association and environment. The individual should have unlimited freedom to pursue knowledge, to form his own opinions, and to transmit his ideas to others. Even willful and seditious libels should not be prosecuted unless an overt act is involved. Honest government and wide publication of the truth are more effective than prosecution in combating libel. Like Milton, Wortman believed that truth would ultimately triumph over falsehood. This classic work on freedom of the press was published the same year as Madison's *Virginia Report* on the Alien and Sedition Acts and reflects somewhat similar ideas.

Wright, Andrew. *A Report of the Trial of Andrew Wright, Printer of the "Republican Spy," on an Indictment for Libels against Governor Strong, before the Hon. Theophilus Parsons, Chief Justice of the Supreme Judicial Court of the Commonwealth of Massachusetts, at Northampton, Sept. Term 1806.* Northampton, Published by Andrew Wright, 1806. 32p. **W399**

Wright, H. G. *The Life and Works of Arthur Hall of Grantham, Member of Parliament, Courtier, and First Translator of Homer into English.* Manchester, Eng., University of Manchester Press, 1919. 233p. (Publications of the University of Manchester, English Series no. 9) **W400**
In 1580 Hall was sentenced to imprisonment for five months and deprived of his membership in the House for publishing a pamphlet reflecting upon the late Speaker of the House and criticizing the proceedings. Any unofficial reporting of Parliamentary proceedings was prohibited. The account of Hall's trial appears as a document in the appendix, pp. 187–89.

Wright, Herbert. "Henry Brooke's *Gustavus Vasa.*" *Modern Language Review,* 14:173–82, April 1919. **W401**
Henry Brooke's play about a fictional Swedish king was the first stage production to be banned by the Lord Chamberlain under the Licensing Act of 1737 (Walpole Administration). Following the ban (in 1737) the book appeared and sold in much greater quantities as a result of the publicity from the ban. Samuel Johnson supported Brooke and opposed the ban in an article appearing in the *Gentleman's Magazine.*

Wright, J. Skelly. "A Judge's Views: The News Media and Criminal Justice." *American Bar Association Journal,* 50: 1125–29, December 1964. **W402**

"To lessen dangers of trial by mass media, newspapers, radio and television should broaden their perspective of criminal coverage with the cooperation of judges. The first televised cases should be carefully chosen, with proceedings of appellate courts a likely place to begin."—*FOI Digest.*

Wright, John. *Sermon Delivered at the Long Room, Marble Street, Liverpool, on . . . April 8th, 1817 . . . for Which a Prosecution Is Commenced on a Charge of Blasphemy.* Liverpool, F. B. Wright, 1817. 26p. **W403**
After this publication of the offending sermon the prosecution was discontinued.

Wright, Kenneth D. "Henry Fielding and the Theatres Act of 1737." *Quarterly Journal of Speech,* 50:252–58, October 1964. **W404**
"In 1737 . . . Henry Fielding devoted his genius to the task of exposing and destroying parliamentary corruption, then at its height. Walpole, unable to govern without corruption, promptly gagged the stage by a censorship which is in full force at the present moment."

Wright, Richard. "Freedom to Read: An Author's View of a Library." *Library Journal,* 85:4421–22, 15 December 1960. **W405**
Reprint of a passage from the author's *Black Boy* about his experience as a Negro boy trying to get books by H. L. Mencken from a public library, which did not admit Negroes.

[Wright, Susannah]. *Report of the Trial of Mrs. Susannah Wright, for Publishing, in his shop, the Writings and Correspondences of R. Carlile; before Chief Justice Abbott, and a Special Jury; in the Court of King's Bench, Guildhall, London, on Monday, July 8, 1822. Indictment at the Instance of the Society for the Suppression of Vice.* London, Printed and published by R. Carlile, 1822. 59p. (Also in Macdonald, *Report of State Trials,* vol. 6, pp. 213 ff.) **W406**
Mrs. Wright, a Nottingham laceworker, was a volunteer in Richard Carlile's shop and was prosecuted for selling a twopenny pamphlet, *Addresses to the Reformers.* She was convicted and imprisoned along with her 6-month-old baby. For her insistence that Christianity could not be a part of the law she was given an additional 18 months' sentence.

———. *Speech of Mrs. Susannah Wright before the Court of King's Bench, on the 14th of November, 1822; in the course of reading which she was continually interrupted by the Court, and before she had finished it Committed to Newgate for persisting to read, to be brought up again for judgment, on the fourth day of Hilary Term, 1823.* London, R. Carlile, 1822. 24 p. **W 407**

Wright, Willard H. "Is Library Censorship Desirable?" *ALA Bulletin,* 5:59–60, July 1911. **W 408**
The literary editor of the *Los Angeles Times* believes that librarians should permit on their shelves "any book whatsoever that the law countenances; provided, of course, there is a sufficient demand to warrant its purchase."

Wronski, Stanley P. "Use of 'Slanted' Materials in the Classroom." *Educational Leadership,* 10:26–30, October 1952. **W 409**
"Should a wide variety of materials which advocate or protect vested interest be used in classrooms? This article discusses the right of students to free inquiry—and to the exercise of the critical thinking capacity which accompanies such inquiry."

Wyatt, Robert H. *Coping with the Vigilantes, Censors, and Critics in 1963.* Washington, D.C., National Education Association, 1963. 3 p. mimeo. **W 410**
The president-elect of the NEA, addressing the Association's convention in Detroit, 4 July 1963, discusses the forces that are today seeking to restrict the free flow of ideas in the public schools.

Wyatt, Sibyl W. *Nineteenth Century English Novels and Austrian Censorship.* Houston, Tex., Rice University, 1964. 224 p. (Ph. D. dissertation, University Microfilm, no. 63–7177) **W 411**
Titles of 32 English novels appeared on Metternich's Austrian index between 1820 and 1847, largely works with reference to rebellion against established authority, advocacy of democracy, and any kind of mass movement considered dangerous to the Empire.

Wylie, D. M. "Indecent Publications Act, 1954." *New Zealand Libraries,* 17: 229–35, November–December 1954. **W 412**
Criticism of the Act, which, the author states, was passed in haste, one week after receipt of the report of the Special Committee on Moral Delinquency in Children and Adolescents. A library, under the Act, runs the risk of prosecution, if any objectionable work, even intended for adults, is seen by an adolescent who might be depraved by it.

Wylie, Philip. "Sex and the Censor." *Nation,* 159:39–40, 8 July 1944. **W 413**
"Censorship is epidemic at the moment." Wylie discusses cases involving the "application of the prude's scissors and the prig's blue pencil" as well as the authoritarianism of the Army in rejecting such titles as *Yankee from Olympus* and Charles Beard's *The Republic* from the list prepared by the Council for Books in Wartime.

———. "What Freedom of What Press?" *Quill,* 39(2):10–12+, February 1951. **W 414**
The writer denies that the American press practices freedom and that the press is uninfluenced by its advertisers. Those who write for the press operate under a system of taboos. To tamper with such taboos, to violate self-censorship, "is not within the power of most journalists since none can subsist *sans* bread and butter."

Wynne, J. C. "Fighting Lady: Congresswoman Granahan's Efforts to Combat Pornography." *Catholic Preview of Entertainment,* 6:25–28, April 1962. **W 415**
Kathryn Granahan, as chairman of the House of Representatives subcommittee on Postal Operations, conducted an investigation of pornography being sent through the mails.

Y

Y., J. T. "Bibliography of the *North Briton.*" *Notes & Queries*, 9(7th ser.):104–6, 8 February 1890. **Y 1**
A bibliographic study of the suppressed newspaper of John Wilkes.

Yankwich, Leon R. *The Doctrine of Privilege in the Law of Libel*. Los Angeles, n.p., 1926. 36p. **Y 2**

———. *Essays in the Law of Libel*. Los Angeles, Parker, Stone & Baird, 1929. 310p. **Y 3**
A reference book on problems in the law of civil and criminal libel for the use of lawyers and newspaper workers, written by a California judge who has specialized in newspaper law. He discusses the nature of libel and the legal privilege of newspapers; what is and what is not libelous; some of the defenses in the law of libel; the doctrine of privilege; newspapers and the law of contempt; the character of the plaintiff as an issue in libel; and the law of criminal libel.

———. "Freedom of the Press in Prospect and Retrospect." *Southern California Law Review*, 15:322–39, March 1944. **Y 4**
The author reviews the development of freedom of the press in America, particularly with respect to libel and contempt, and cites examples of present-day efforts to curtail press freedom. Special attention is given to the Minnesota gag law of 1925, the attempts to limit distribution of pamphlets (sometimes fostered by selfish newspapers), and the contempt cases of Harry R. Bridges and the *Los Angeles Times*. Throughout, the emphasis is on California cases.

———. *It's Libel or Contempt If You Print It. A Practical Book on Libel, Contempt, and Kindred Topics for Lawyers, and for Students and Workers in the Newspaper Field*, Los Angeles, Parker, 1950. 612p. **Y 5**
Part I, The Newspaper and the Law of Libel. Part II, Freedom of the Press and Its Limitations and Responsibilities. The author is a federal judge.

———. "Protection of Newspaper Comment on Public Men and Public Affairs." *Louisiana Law Review*, 11:327–46, March 1951. **Y 6**
"To obtain the optimum of the wider scope of coverage and criticism of public men and matters, which the courts now concede to the newspaper editor and writer, two cardinal rules should be observed: (1) Comment should be limited to what is essential to the special situation . . . (2) Facts should be made to speak and non-essential comments should be avoided —especially those fulminating epithets."

———. "Recent Developments in the Law of Creation, Expression, and Communication of Ideas." *Northwestern University Law Review*, 101:721–39, April 1953. **Y 7**
Notes on developments in law of defamation, privacy, and copyright since about 1940, especially as they pertain to radio and television.

———. "The Right of Privacy: Its Development, Scope and Limitations." *Notre Dame Lawyer*, 27:499–527, Summer 1952. **Y 8**

———. "The Trial of John Peter Zenger: The Beginnings of Free Speech in America and Its Meaning Today." *Los Angeles Bar Bulletin*, 24:360–61, 371–72, 374–76, 378, August 1949. **Y 9**

Yarborough, Minnie C. *John Horne Tooke*. New York, Columbia University Press, 1926. 252p. (Columbia University Studies in English and Comparative Literature) **Y 10**
Biography of the versatile eighteenth-century cleric, reformer, and linguist (*Diversions of Purley*). Tooke was a friend of John Wilkes. He championed the cause of the colonies (for which he served three years in prison), and figured prominently in the treason trials of 1794, in which he was acquitted. While Tooke was cantankerous and quarrelsome, the biographer considered him "an honest patriot, impelled in all of his self-imposed tasks by a keen sense of justice." Chapter 6 deals with Tooke's trial for treasonable writings.

Yarros, Victor S. "The Chicago Socialist Trial." *Nation*, 108:116–18, 25 January 1919. **Y 11**
An account of the trial in The Federal Court in Chicago of Victor Berger and four other Socialists for conspiracy under the wartime Espionage Act. The overt acts which Berger was said to have committed consisted of publishing in the Milwaukee *Leader* five editorials opposing the draft.

Yauch, John H. "The Bar's Side of Canon 35." *Saturday Review*, 46(10):61–62, 9 March 1963. **Y 12**
The chairman of the Special Committee on Proposed Revision of Judicial Canon 35 of the American Bar Association, answers Herbert Brucker's criticism of the Canon (8 December issue). Text of the controversial Canon is given on page 61.

Yeaman, Elizabeth. "Catholic Movie Censorship." *New Republic*, 96:233–35, 5 October 1938. **Y 13**
An account of Joseph I. Breen, "one-man censor of the movies," who enforces the morals code, carrying "the portfolio of the Legion of Decency." The head of the Eastern Branch, Production Code, objects to the statements in a letter to the editor in the 9 November issue.

Yeats, William Butler. "Censorship of Films." In Donald R. Pearce, ed. *The Senate Speeches of W. B. Yeats*. Bloomington, Ind., Indiana University Press, 1960, pp. 51–52. **Y 14**
Senator Yeats speaks against a proposed amendment to the Censorship of Films Bill requiring that minors should not be permitted to go to the cinema unattended by adults. "I think you can leave the arts, superior or inferior, to the general conscience of mankind." The amendment failed of passage.

———. "The Irish Censorship." *Spectator*, 141:391–92, 29 September 1928. Discussion: 141:435–36, 6 October 1928; 141:488, 13 October 1928; 141:528, 20 October 1928. (Reprinted in Downs, *The First Freedom*, pp. 388–91) **Y 15**
The noted Irish poet and playwright, then serving as senator in the Dáil Éireann, expressed eloquent and vigorous opposition to the Irish Censorship of Publications Bill of

1928, which he states will create "an instrument of tyranny" and place "control over the substance of our thought" in the hands of one man, the Minister of Justice.

"You Can't Censor Nonsense." *Collier's*, 70:15–16, 4 November 1922.   **Y 16**
Second in a series of articles written anonymously by a producer of motion pictures. The first, Little Men Behind the Big Screen (*Collier's*, 70:11–12+, 30 September 1922), gives the view that the movies have outgrown the men who control them, that stupidity of those in control is the main trouble of the movies. This article says you cannot censor stupidity and cites pettiness and difficulties encountered by movie-censorship groups. A third article, You'll Get What You Ask for (*Collier's*, 70:9–10+, 18 November 1922), points out ways the public can help obtain more intelligent movies.

Young, Donald R. *Motion Pictures; A Study in Social Legislation.* Philadelphia, Westbrook Publishing Co., 1922. 109 p. (Ph. D. dissertation, University of Pennsylvania) **Y 17**
The author examines the conformity and the deviations of motion pictures from the standards established by the various censorship boards. He considers the work of the National Board of Review of Motion Pictures and the various state and municipal regulatory bodies. He concludes that legal censorship is justified by conditions in the motion picture industry which have been unavoidable, and that for many years to come the most desirable form of censorship will be that which is under direct state control. Appendices include: English censorship rules, standards of the Pennsylvania Board of Censors, samples of eliminations by the National Board of Review, and the text of the U.S. Supreme Court decision, *Mutual Film Corp. v. Industrial Commission of Ohio.*

————. "Social Standards and the Motion Picture." *Annals of the American Academy of Political and Social Science*, 128:146–50, November 1926.   **Y 18**
An enlightened public opinion, not government or industry censorship, is the most effective method of counteracting the false standards portrayed in the movies. A change in public attitude toward films is basic to reform of the industry.

Young, Eugene J. *Looking Behind the Censorship.* New York, Lippincott, 1938. 368 p. **Y 19**
An examination of the forces responsible for political censorship and propaganda met by American news correspondents in Europe during the period leading up to World War II.

Young, Julius R. "Should Democracy Curb Propaganda?" *Common Sense*, 9:8–10, March 1940.   **Y 20**
Can propaganda be curbed in a democracy without abrogating the principles of freedom? The author believes it can and proposes a federal law with a threefold purpose: (1) To eradicate obnoxious and vicious practices in propaganda and establish a code of fair practices; (2) to reduce the disparity of influence among propagandizing forces by the creation of a tribunal where equal consideration can be given to two or more sides of a question; and (3) to provide the public with a reliable opportunity to get at the undoctored truth.

Young, Kimball. "Censorship in Wartime." *ALA Bulletin*, 38:439–42+, 15 October 1944.   **Y 21**
A sociologist discusses censorship as a system of social control. He offers advice to librarians in dealing with threats of censorship.

————, and Raymond D. Lawrence. *Bibliography on Censorship and Propaganda.* Eugene, Ore., University of Oregon Press, 1928. 133 p. (University of Oregon Publication. Journalism Series, vol. 1, no. 1)   **Y 22**
Part I of this selected bibliography covers censorship: political, wartime (largely World War I), and literary. Young has written an introductory essay, Censorship and Propaganda as Factors in Social Control, pp. 7–14. Except for foreign material and newspaper articles, most of the items have been included in the present bibliography.

Young, Stark. "Censorshipping." *New Republic*, 91:101–2, 2 June 1937.   **Y 23**
An essay on censorship of the stage, prompted by the passage of the Dunnigan Bill in the New York legislature setting up a state system for licensing of plays. The bill was vetoed by Governor Lehman.

Young, Wayland. "The Adventures of *Eros Denied.*" *Censorship*, 2(2): 2–13, Spring 1966.   **Y 24**
The author of *Eros Denied* reports on the difficulties he had in getting his book published.

————. *Eros Denied; Sex in Modern Society.* New York, Grove, 1964. 415 p. (A chapter, Excluded Words, is reprinted in *Evergreen Review*, April–May 1964) **Y 25**
The author considers the "unfreedom to discuss, describe, depict—in a word, to possess—sex and love with the full resources of the individual imagination in Anglo-Saxon countries." The book "places itself in the tradition which holds that the unfreedom to love hurts more than is justified by the countervailing gains." Part II deals with "excluded words" in English, French, German and Italian; Part III deals with "excluded images," forthright descriptions and depictions of the act of physical love in writings and pictorial matter. Pornographic works and taboo words are quoted throughout. Felix Pollak, in a lengthy letter to the editor in the August–September issue of *Evergreen Review*, considers this work and similar clinical studies as having the net effect of "a de-sexing of sex, far more effective than all the sincantings of the censors."

————. "Obscenity." *Twentieth Century*, 157:237–43, March 1955.   **Y 26**
Comments on the British obscenity bill, drafted by the Herbert Committee.

A Young Gentleman of the Temple, pseud. *Arguments Relating to a Restraint upon the Press, Fully and Fairly handled in a Letter to a Bencher, from a Young Gentleman of the Temple, With Proposals Humbly offer'd to the Consideration of Both Houses of Parliament.* London, Printed for R. and F. Bonwicke, 1712. 51 p.   **Y 27**
An anonymous lawyer refutes the usual arguments for freedom of the press. The Bible, he believes, contains all the religious truth needed by men; the Lords and Commons are capable of deciding all political truth; controversial ideas only lead to trouble and should be suppressed. The solution offered is the restoration of a strict licensing system, and he submits a proposed act for "accommodating the Regulation of the Press, to the Sentiments of Moderate Men."

Yorke, *Sir* Philip C. *The Life and Correspondence of Philip Yorke, Earl of Hardwicke, Lord High Chancellor of Great Britain.* Cambridge, Eng., Cambridge University Press, 1913. 3 vols.   **Y 28**
As Attorney General, Sir Philip prosecuted Thomas Woolston for publishing a blasphemous tract (1725), the publishers of *The Craftsman* for seditious libel (1728), and the bookseller, Edmund Curll, for obscene libel. In the case of the latter (*Rex v. Curll*) Sir Philip established obscenity as a temporal offense, reversing the earlier decision in the *Queen v. Read.* He also upheld the opinion that in libel cases the jury was limited to determining the fact of publishing only. In addition to comments on the above cases, this work includes Sir Philip's opinions on the John Wilkes affair.

————. "Remarks on the Legal Meaning of the Liberty of the Press." In Howell, *State Trials*, vol. 17, pp. 670 ff.   **Y 29**

Yurasko, Frank N. "The Right to be Let Alone." *Progressive*, 28:29–33, September 1964.   **Y 30**
Because of modern electronic devices for eavesdropping, the old common law method of protecting privacy is no longer adequate.

Yust, William F. "Censorship—a Library Problem." *Library Journal*, 57:176–79, 15 February 1932.   **Y 31**
Brief discussion of legislation pertaining to censorship in New York State, particularly the "clean books bill" which was defeated. The author concludes that "absolute rules on the subject of book censorship are unwise and unwarranted. What we need . . . is an attitude . . . of open mindedness that will adjust itself to conditions and cases as they arise."

Z

Zacherle, Hedo M. "Pretrial Fact Press Reports as Contempt." *Iowa Law Review*, 39:738–49, Summer 1953. **Z1**
Notes on cases, 1858–1953.

Zall, Paul M. "Lord Eldon's Censorship." *PMLA*, 68:436–43, June 1953. **Z2**
Action taken against Byron's *Don Juan* and *Cain* as well as Southey's *Wat Tyler*, and Shelley's *Queen Mab*, "lay in the moral and legal principles of the Chancellor, Lord Eldon." The author reviews Lord Eldon's career as "licenser of the press." The Chancellor, using the argument that a work of "injurious nature" was not entitled to protection under the copyright law, refused to grant injunction for piratical publishing of Southey's *Wat Tyler* (*Southey v. Sherwood*). The failure of the Chancellor to grant an injunction from publication of a work which he thought censurable, actually resulted in the broader dissemination of such literature.

Zeitlin, Jake. "Who Shall Silence All the Airs and Madrigals?" *Library Journal*, 90:2479–83, 1 June 1965. **Z3**
An American bookseller discusses censorship in a paper delivered at the California Library Association Conference. While admitting his own embarrassment at the careless use of four-letter words and his revulsion to violence, brutality, and sexual depravity depicted in some books, he concludes that no one is so wise and universally competent to tell others: "You shall not express yourself thus, you shall not describe your own experiences; or depict the fantasies which your mind has created; or laugh at what others have set up as respectable; or question old beliefs; or contradict the dogmas of the church, of our society, our economic system, and our political orthodoxy."

Zelermyer, William. *Invasion of Privacy*. Syracuse, N.Y., Syracuse University Press, 1959. 161 p. **Z4**
The purpose of this work is to present for the enlightenment of the general public "the development of the right of privacy as a concept in the realm of civil wrongs called torts." Included are chapters on invasion by advertising; invasion by magazines, newspapers, and books; and invasion by moving pictures, radio, and television.

[Zenger, John Peter]. *A brief Narrative of the Case and Tryal of John Peter Zenger, Printer of the New-York Weekly Journal*. New York, Printed and sold by John Peter Zenger, 1736. 40 p. **Z5**
John Peter Zenger was the printer of the *New-York Weekly Journal*, which opposed the administration of Governor Cosby, thereby incurring his wrath. The publisher of the *Journal* and author of most of the offending articles was the brilliant young politician and lawyer, James Alexander. Because of the libel laws, however, it was Zenger the printer who stood trial. After other methods of silencing the paper had failed, Governer Cosby had the printer arrested for seditious libel. The bail was set so high that Zenger had to remain in jail. His wife continued to print the paper in his absence. Alexander planned Zenger's defense, but was summarily removed by Chief Justice James Delancy. At this point the distinguished Andrew Hamilton took over for the defense, conducting what is considered a classic performance. Zenger was acquitted by the jury, despite an unfriendly judge, and the results were widely acclaimed throughout the colonies and in England. The trial is important in the development of freedom of the press in America because of several precedents it set: it challenged the official censorship of the representative of the Crown; it introduced for the first time in an American court the proposition that the people have a right to know the facts about their government; it established "truth" as a mitigating factor in libel cases; and it established the right of the jury in libel cases to consider the law as well as the fact of publication, a practice not established in England until after the Fox Libel Act of 1792. Three heroes emerged from this celebrated trial: Zenger for his courage in standing trial, Alexander for the brilliant planning of the trial and the careful recording of the proceedings, and Hamilton for his notable forensic performance in court. Leonard W. Levy describes Alexander as "the first colonial figure to develop a philosophy of a free press," and the report of the trial as "the most widely known source of libertarian thought in England and America during the eighteenth century." This is the first edition of the Zenger trial, believed to have been written by James Alexander. Numerous editions followed both in America and England. These are recorded, along with a reprinting of the text of the first edition, in Rutherfurd's *John Peter Zenger* (1904). The text of the first edition is also reprinted in the Crippled Turtle edition, edited by Frank Luther Mott (1954), and in the Belknap Press edition, edited by Stanley N. Katz (1963).

[————]. *A Brief Narrative of the Case and Trial of John Peter Zenger, Printer of the New York Weekly Journal. By James Alexander*. Edited by Stanley Nider Katz. Cambridge, Mass., Belknap Press of Harvard University Press, 1963. 238 p. (The John Harvard Library) **Z6**
"The present edition supplements the *Brief Narrative* with other major documents of the Zenger case. It is also the first to attempt a full identification of the documents, people, and ideas that appear in the pamphlet. It seeks in this way to explain the case more completely than before by restoring it to its original context." A lengthy introduction brings the consideration of modern scholarship to the implications of the Zenger trial. Katz points out that Attorney Hamilton, refuting current English law, contended that truth was a defense against an accusation of libel and that the jury had the right to return a general verdict. While Alexander's law was weak, his logic was strong and his plea for the right to criticize the government appealed to the jury. Zenger was freed amidst great public acclaim, but the case did not immediately change the law of libel. "It was seventy years before the doctrine prophetically annunciated in 1735 by Andrew Hamilton became law in New York, and then the formulation was not his but Alexander Hamilton's." Editor Katz believes the account of the trial was probably Alexander's reworking of Hamilton's rough draft. The following documents are printed in this edition: Appendix A, Selections from Zenger's Press. Appendix B, The briefs of James Alexander and John Chambers, and the drafts of Zenger's speeches, prepared by Alexander. Appendix C, Two essays published in 1737—Anglo-Americanus' attack on the handling of the Zenger case, appearing originally in the *Barbados Gazette*, and James Alexander's response to the attack, appearing in four issues of Benjamin Franklin's *Pennsylvania Gazette*.

[————]. "Trial of John Peter Zenger, for Libel, New York City, 1735." In *American State Trials*, vol. 16, pp. 1–39; in Chandler's *American Criminal Trials*, vol. 1, pp. 151–209; and in Howell, *State Trials*, vol. 17, pp. 675 ff.) **Z7**

[————]. *The Trial of John Peter Zenger, of New York, Printer: Who was charged with having printed and published a libel against the Government; and acquitted. With a narrative of his case. To which in now added, being never printed before, the Trial of Mr. William Owen, Bookseller, near Temple-Bar, Who was also charged with the Publication of a Libel against the Government; of which he was honourably acquitted by a Jury of Free-born Englishmen, Citizens of London.* London, Printed by J. Almon, 1765. 59 p. (This edition was reissued by the Works Projects Administration in 1940 as an *Occasional Paper* of the Sutro Branch, California State Library, San Francisco) **Z8**

This "new" edition of the Zenger trial, issued by J. Almon in 1765, includes the 1752 trial of William Owen, bookseller, acquitted of having published a seditious libel entitled, The Case of Alexander Murray. In the case of Mr. Owen, the jury ignored the judge's instructions to consider only the fact of publication and not the nature of the content, and found Owen "not guilty" on the whole of the case—facts, law, and justice.

[————]. *The Tryal of John Peter Zenger, of New-York, Printer, Who was lately Try'd and Acquitted for Printing and Publishing a Libel against the Government. With the Pleadings and Arguments on both Sides . . .* 2d ed. London, Printed for J. Wilford, 1738. 32 p. **Z9**

The first edition of the Zenger trial was published in New York by the printer himself in 1736 and given wide circulation throughout the colonies and in England. In 1738 four separate editions of the trial were published in London by J. Wilford. In the same year two other London publishers, Thomas Fleet and J. Roberts, brought out editions.

[————]. *Zenger's Own Story: A Brief Narrative of the Case and Tryal of John Peter Zenger . . . A Literal Reprint of the Original Pamphlet Printed by Zenger in New York in 1736.* Columbia, Mo., Press of the Crippled Turtle, 1954. 45 p. **Z10**

A preface and introduction by Frank Luther Mott describes the publishing history of the original pamphlet, and gives a brief biographical sketch of Zenger, including an imaginary conversation with James Alexander, leading to the publishing of the *New-York Weekly Journal.*

Zenger and Freedom of the Press. 35 mm filmstrip, 41 frames, b/w. Rego Park, N.Y., Heritage Filmstrips, 1954. **Z11**

The trial of John Peter Zenger, its implications and effects on the American Revolution and the Bill of Rights.

The Zenger Trial. 30 min., 7-inch phonotape. Boulder, Colo., National Tape Repository, University of Colorado. (American Adventure Series) **Z12**

For junior and senior high school use.

Zimmerman, Isabella M. "What About Paul Blanshard?" *Bay State Librarian*, 52:7–8, 14–18, 20, October 1962. **Z13**

A reference librarian at Boston University visited ten public libraries to discover how they handled nine titles considered objectionable to Roman Catholics—books by Paul Blanshard, Emmett McLoughlin, and Nikos Kazantzakis. She found that the anticipation of a complaint or protest by one religious group, or fear of an accusation of censorship from another such group has a tendency to influence a librarian's decision on selection of books. This influence depends, in almost direct proportion, on the vociferousness, strength, influence, and size of the complaining group, but it is sometimes counteracted by the strength, prestige, and professional stature of the library in the eyes of the community.

Zins, Thomas A. "Constitutional Law—Freedom of Speech—Not all Prior Restraints are Invalid." *University of Cincinnati Law Review*, 30:386–90, Summer 1961. **Z14**

Notes on *Times Film Corp. v. City of Chicago*, 81 Sup. Ct. 391 (1961).

Zinsser, William K. "The Bold and Risky World of 'Adult Movies.'" *Life*, 48:79–89, 29 February 1960. **Z15**

Franker films attract a more mature audience but put censorship responsibility on the home. "Classification" is suggested as one solution.

[Zola, Emile]. *The Trial of Emile Zola Containing M. Zola's Letter to President Faure Relating to the Dreyfus Case, and a Full Report of the Fifteen Days' Proceedings in the Assize Court of the Seine, including the Testimony of the Witnesses and Speeches of Counsel.* New York, Benjamin R. Tucker, 1898. 355 p. **Z16**

The publication of Zola's open letter, *J'Accuse*, initiated the inquiry into the notorious Dreyfus Affair which rocked the French government. For his accusations against high officials of the army, the novelist Zola was convicted of libel. He fled to England, where a decade before his English publisher, Vizetelly, had been imprisoned for publishing Zola's novels. Benjamin Tucker, the American publisher of the report of the Zola trial, had been identified with freedom of the press since 1882 when, as a young man, he had offered to go to jail in Boston for publishing Whitman's *Leaves of Grass.*

Zuckman, Harvey L. "Censorship of Defamatory Political Broadcasts: The Port Huron Doctrine." *New York University Law Review*, 34:127–40, January 1959. **Z17**

Relates to the doctrine established by the FCC in the *Port Huron Broadcasting Co.* decision, 12 F.C.C. 1069 (1948), to the effect that broadcast licensees are not responsible for defamatory statements made during political broadcasts.

————. "The Law of Obscenity and Military Practice." *Military Law Review*, 1963:43–64, April 1963. **Z18**

Two recent Army obscenity cases raise questions about legal practices with respect to obscenity under the Uniform Code of Military Justice. The author discusses problems of special concern to the military in the light of civilian court decisions. Despite the difficulties in creating a precise legal doctrine, he urges the military lawyer, in the interest of society, to make the effort with intelligence and discrimination to enforce the obscenity laws.

————. "Obscenity in the Mails." *Southern California Law Review*, 33:171–88, Winter 1960. **Z19**

"This article is devoted to an analysis of the present status of postal obscenity law and makes recommendations for legislative change where such action seems necessary or desirable."

ADDENDUM

A. B. C. Television. *Libel: A Note for Television Producers and Others.* London, A. B. C. Television, 1963. 14 p. **A1**
A practical guide for writers and producers, on the British law of libel as applied to television.

Ablard, Charles D. "Obscenity, Advertising, and Publishing: The Impact of *Ginzburg* and *Mishkin*." *George Washington Law Review*, 35:85–92, October 1966. **A2**
Relates to *Ginzburg v. United States, Mishkin v. United States.*

Adair, Donald R. "Free Speech and Defamation of Public Persons: The Expanding Doctrine of *New York Times Co. v. Sullivan*." *Cornell Law Quarterly*, 52: 419–32, Winter II, 1967. **A3**

Adamo, S. J. "Painless News Control." *America*, 115:190–92, 20 August 1966. **A4**
Comparison of the blunt amateurism in control of news in the Catholic press and the smooth news management of the federal government.

Affleck, W. B. "Free Press—Fair Trial." *Criminal Law Quarterly* (Canada), 8:163–71, October 1965. **A5**
The author recommends for Canada contempt of court proceedings in flagrant cases of prejudicial publicity, encouragement of the press in drafting a code of ethics in the area, a press-ban study committee, and the establishment of a National Press Council similar to Great Britain's.

Agree, Rose H. "The Freedom to Read on Long Island." *Top of the News*, 22: 285–87, April 1966. **A6**
An account of the establishment, by school librarians, of the Long Island Intellectual Freedom Committee and the adoption of a resolution on freedom to read.

Ahrens, Nyla H. *Censorship and the Teachers of English: A Questionnaire Survey of a Selected Sample of Secondary School Teachers of English.* New York, Teachers College, Columbia University, 1965. 137 p. (Ed. D. dissertation) **A7**
The study indicated that teachers who encountered censorship were generally those "doing a good job of teaching English" who were trying to introduce realistic fiction into the classroom. The study also revealed that a fairly low percentage of schools had an established policy for dealing with complaints about textbooks.

Aldridge, Alfred O. *Man of Reason: The*

Life of Thomas Paine. Philadelphia, Lippincott, 1959. 348 p. **A8**
A definitive and scholarly work based on original research in France and England as well as in America. Chapters 9, 12, and 13 deal with the controversy and trial over Paine's *The Rights of Man.* Chapter 19 deals with the controversy and trial over *The Age of Reason.*

[Alexander, James?]. ["Essays on Freedom of the Press"]. In Levy, *Freedom of the Press from Zenger to Jefferson*, pp. 24–43, 61–74. **A9**
"The [*New York Weekly*] *Journal* essays reprinted here are original compositions, almost certainly by James Alexander, reflecting the influence of both *Cato's Letters* and the *Craftsman*. . . . Taken as a group, and including the four by Alexander in 1737 (Document 10), these essays constitute the finest and broadest libertarian statements published in America until after the Sedition Act of 1798." The four essays of 1737 were first published in Franklin's *Pennsylvania Gazette.*

Alisky, Marvin. "Cuban Press: Censorship Replaces Bribery." *Nieman Reports*, 11(2): 17–18, April 1957. **A10**
"The Batista regime of Cuba during January and February [1957] switched from the big carrot to the big stick, from widespread bribery to overt censorship of the press."

[Allestree, Richard?]. *The Government of the Tongue By the Author of the Whole Duty of Man, &c.* Oxford, At the Theater, 1674. 224 p. **A11**

Alpert, Hollis. "Talk with a Movie Censor." *Saturday Review*, 35:21, 50–54, 22 November 1952. **A12**
An interview with New York State's film censor, Dr. Hugh M. Flick, reveals the point of view, the problems, and the technique of prior censorship of films by New York Motion Picture Division.

Aly, Bower, and Gerald D. Shively, *eds. Debate Handbook on Radio Control and Operation.* Columbia, Miss., Staple, 1933. 224 p. **A13**
Material for debaters on private versus government control of radio.

American Bar Association. "Report of the Special Committee on Cooperation Between Press, Radio and Bar, as to Publicity Interfering with Fair Trial of Judicial and Quasi-Judicial Proceedings." In American Bar Association, *Annual Report*, Chicago, 1937, vol. 62, pp. 851–66. **A14**
The committee represented the American Bar Association, the American Newspaper Publishers Association, and the American Society of Newspaper Editors and was headed by

Newton D. Baker. The Committee considered, among other factors, the unpublished report of an earlier committee, headed by Judge Oscar Hallam to examine the pretrial publicity attending the trial of Bruno Richard Hauptmann, which made 16 specific recommendations. Seven of the recommendations are quoted and the point of view of the present committee is given. Among the general recommendations of the Baker committee is that "local bar associations appoint continuing committees on press relations to function with corresponding committees representing the Press and other means of publicity." The Committee recommended that the Court use its power to punish for contempt to protect the fairness of trial, but at the same time use it sympathetically to protect that portion of the press which spurns the sensational, scandalous, and inflamatory treatment of trial proceedings.

American Bar Association. Project on Minumum Standards for Criminal Justice. *Standards Relating to Fair Trial and Free Press. Recommended by the Advisory Committee on Fair Trial and Free Press. . . .* [Chicago, American Bar Association, 1966]. 265 p. (Tentative draft, December 1966) **A15**
"This Committee was charged to consider the impact of news reporting on the administration of criminal justice and to seek methods of preserving and strengthening the right to a fair trial without abridging freedom of speech and of the press." Standards recommended cover conduct of attorneys, conduct of law enforcement officers, conduct of judicial proceedings, and exercise of the contempt power. There is also a statement on Matters of Joint Concern to the Bench, the Bar, Law Enforcement Officers, and the News Media. The Committee was headed by Judge Paul C. Reardon of the Massachusetts Supreme Court. The report received considerable criticism from the press because of its restrictions on press freedom. In July 1967 the Committee published a 36-page *Revisions of Tentative Draft*, liberalizing certain sections of the recommendations and including in the appendix: Bench-Bar-Media Cooperation in the State of Washington and Guidelines Issued by the Prosecuting Attorney, St. Louis County, Missouri.

American Civil Liberties Union. *Statement, Board of Directors on Fair Trial and Free Press.* New York, ACLU, 1966. 9 p. mimeo. **A16**

American Historical Association and Organization of American Historians. "The Joint Committee for the Defense of the Rights of Historians under the First Amendment." *PMLA*, 81:A6–A8, December 1966. **A17**

The Committee was formed as an outgrowth of legal action taken by the daughter of Henry Clay Frick to suppress a scholarly book by Sylvester K. Stevens, *Pennsylvania: Birthplace of a Nation.* "It is the first case we know of in which a serious work has been challenged in the Courts, in which the Court has been asked to ban a book, and in which the Court has proceded to hear the suit on the merits. . . . A victory for Miss Frick would be a crippling blow to scholarly study and would eventually shake the very foundation of our great democracy which depends so much on the free and unfettered flow and exchange of ideas. . . . An attack on one book is an attack on all learning. A challenge such as this case presents is a challenge to all historians." On 25 May, Judge Clinton R. Weidner of the Court of Common Pleas, Cumberland, Pa., dismissed the request for an injunction against the book, delivering a 51-page opinion in which he analyzed the issues. "The courts cannot restrain writings on the historical development of . . . public issues. They are part of the heritage of every citizen and each is entitled to know them." (*Publishers' Weekly,* 5 June 1967.)

American Law Institute and American Bar Association. Joint Committee on Continuing Legal Education. *The Problem of Drafting an Obscenity Statute.* [Philadelphia, The Committee, 1961]. 104 p. (Problems in Criminal Law and Administration, no. 9) **A 18**

American Library Association. Intellectual Freedom Committee, *et. al.* "Intellectual Freedom and the Teenager." *ALA Bulletin,* 61:833, July–August 1967. **A 19**
A brief résumé of a conference, sponsored by the Intellectual Freedom Committee, the Young Adult Services Division, and the American Association of School Libraries. Speakers were Edgar Z. Friedenberg, Rev. Larry Beggs, Kenneth Rexroth, Robert Kirach, Mrs. Helen Cyr, Stanley Fleishman, Mrs. Harriet R. Covey, David Cohen, Mrs. Doris Watts, Alex Allain, and Esther Helfand. A summary of the conference by Ervin J. Gaines appears in the September 1967 *ALA Newsletter on Intellectual Freedom.* Also reported in *Library Journal* and *Wilson Library Bulletin.*

American Newspaper Publishers Association. *Free Press and Fair Trial.* New York, The Association, 1967. 143 p. **A 20**
Report of a study made by a Special Committee on Free Press and Fair Trial. The report concludes there is no real conflict between the First and Sixth Amendments, a free press requires not only freedom to print without prior restraint but free access to public information that should be public; there are grave dangers to the public in censorship at the source; the press is a positive influence in assuring fair trial; isolated cases should not serve as a cause for censorship; court rules restricting release of information by law enforcement officers are an unwarranted judicial invasion of the executive branch of government; there can be no codes which compromise the principles of the Constitution; and neither the press nor the Bar has a right to sit down and bargain away the right of the people to know. Appendices include a history of the First and Sixth Amendments, the law as enunciated by Supreme Court decisions, a review of representative codes relating to reporting of trials, and a review of the *Estes* and *Sheppard* cases.

American Society of Newspaper Editors. Freedom of Information Committee. "Freedom of Information Report, 1964." In *Problems of Journalism; Proceedings of the American Society of Newspaper Editors, 1964.* Washington, D.C., 1964, pp. 253–56. **A 21**

Creed C. Black was chairman.

———. "Freedom of Information Report, 1965." In *Problems of Journalism; Proceedings of the American Society of Newspaper Editors, 1965.* Washington, D.C., 1965, pp. 219–21. **A 22**
Creed C. Black was chairman.

———. "Freedom of Information Report, 1966." In *Problems of Journalism; Proceedings of the American Society of Newspaper Editors, 1966.* Washington, D.C., 1966, pp. 213–16. **A 23**

Eugene Patterson was chairman.

American Society of Newspaper Editors. Press-Bar Committee. *Report of Press-Bar Committee, American Society of Newspaper Editors, 1964–1965.* New York, ASNE, 1965. 14 p. mimeo. **A 24**
The Committee found almost totally lacking evidence that press coverage of criminal proceedings injures the chances of fair trial for defendants. The Committee takes issue with the *Warren Report* criticism of the press, which it finds unfair and in a large part unfounded. "The press has no wish to conduct 'trial by newspaper'; by the same token, it has no desire for lawyers and police to attempt 'trial by publicity.'" The problem would not be solved by voluntary press codes, which are more harmful than the evil complained of. "To perform its functions the press must not be bound by the same regulations that govern the operation of the law enforcement agencies and the courts." It has an obligation to society to report and criticize. The solution to the problem will be found not in codes or law but in "energetic, frequent and continuing conversations among those concerned." The Committee consisted of Creed C. Black, Herbert Brucker, Alfred Friendly (Chairman), and Felix R. McKnight.

Anderson, Maxwell. "The Blue Pencil." *New Republic,* 17:192–94, 14 December 1918. **A 25**
The story of an imaginary (?) California newspaper publisher (H. N. De Smith) and the four rigid censorships he maintained over the contents of that paper—commercial, political, philosophical, and personal.

"Anything goes: Taboos in Twilight." *Newsweek,* 70(20):74–78, 13 November 1967. **A 26**
"A new, more permissive society is taking shape. Its outlines are etched most prominently in the arts—in the increasing nudity and frankness in today's films, in the blunt, often obscene language seeming endemic in American novels and plays, in the candid lyrics of pop songs and the undress of the avant-garde ballet, in erotic art and television talk shows, in freer fashions and franker advertising."

Arkadin, *pseud.* "Film Clips." *Sight and Sound,* 34:98–100, Spring 1965. **A 27**
Notes on cutting done, particularly on American films, by the British Board of Film Censors.

Armbrister, Trevor. "The Embattled Crusader of Conway County." *Saturday Evening Post,* 239(24):25–29, 90–94, 19 November 1966. **A 28**
Eugene H. Wirges, the crusading editor of the Morrilton, Ark., *Democrat,* faces a three-year prison term for perjury, the latest in a long series of legal and financial defeats that have stripped him of his job, his funds, and his freedom. He has been found guilty at one conspiracy trial and two libel trials and twice cited for contempt of court. An attempt has been made to burn his newspaper; his office and home have been damaged. He has been shot at and beaten up by a county official—all because he used his weekly paper to level charges of corruption against county political bosses. On 5 June 1967 Wirges was completely cleared when the Arkansas Supreme Court dismissed the three-year sentence on perjury conviction.

Armstrong, O. K. "Damning Case against Pornography." *Reader's Digest,* 87:131–34, December 1965. **A 29**
"Police chiefs, judges, doctors, psychiatrists and leaders of religious, educational and civic groups all over the nation testify to the causal relationship between crime and the tide of obscenity in publications and motion pictures."

———. "Filth for Profit: The Big Business of Pornography." *Reader's Digest,* 88:73–76, March 1966. **A 30**

———. "A Victory Over the Smut Peddlers." *Reader's Digest,* 90:147–52, February 1967. **A 31**

Arnstein, Walter L. *The Bradlaugh Case A Study in Late Victorian Opinion and*

Politics. Oxford, Clarendon, 1965. 348 p.
A 32

A scholarly study of the life and work of the nineteenth-century English reformer who, as editor of the *National Reformer*, carried on a fight against "taxes on knowledge," and suppression of unorthodoxy in religion, politics, and sex. The Bradlaugh-Besant trial involving the publication of the Knowlton tract on birth control "did much to make legal the general distribution of contraceptive knowledge within England."

Asencio, José Benito Díaz. "Freedom of Speech and Obscenity Standards in the United States: Their Applicability to Puerto Rico." *Revista Jurídica de la Universidad de Puerto Rico*, 35:423–50, 1966.
A 33

Ashmore, Harry, "Has Our Free Press Failed Us?" *Saturday Evening Post*, 233(18): 36–37, 50–52, 29 October 1960.
A 34

"I am not . . . so much concerned with what the press is doing as with what it is not doing. There is too little diversity, and there are too many total gaps of information and of advocacy." There is no simple cure—by law, subsidy, organized pressure, and those within the press cannot be solely relied upon to affect a cure. "The inadequacy of mass communications in our threatened society is not a matter of internal concern for the press alone, but an issue of great urgency for the public at large."

Association for Preserving Liberty and Property against Republicans and Levellers. *Proceedings* . . . London, Printed and Sold by J. Sewell, 1792. 16 p. (Number 1; "to be continued.")
A 35

A group of gentlemen met at the Crown and Anchor Tavern in the Strand on 20 November 1792 to form "a Society for discouraging and suppressing Seditious Publications." John Reeves was chairman. The group called for the organizing of neighborhood societies throughout London and other cities. They agreed to "check the circulation of seditious publications of all kinds whether newspapers or pamphlets, or the invitation to club meetings." Authors, printers, booksellers, and house-to-house salesmen of the radical publications should be apprehended and the Society should counter with their own chap books and papers that would "undeceive those poor people who have been mislead" by the radicals who threaten the country and Constitution. The resolution called for working in aid of magistrates and not on their own. In subsequent meetings—29 and 30 November, 1, 4, and 9 December, the Society passed resolutions against disloyal newspapers and called for a boycott of them. They quoted Justice Blackstone on the penalties for sedition and treason. Among the members was John Bowles, an active pamphleteer against radical publications. Four years after the formation of the Society, Chairman Reeves was himself the victim of prosecution for a publication when Whigs came to power. On 22 December

a countersociety, Friends to the Liberty of the Press, was formed at Free Masons Tavern and subsequently met at Crown and Anchor under the chairmanship of Gerald Noel Edwards (later with R. B. Sheridan as chairman) with support of Thomas Erskine.

Association of the Bar of the City of New York. Special Committee on Radio, Television, and the Administration of Justice. *Freedom of the Press and Fair Trial: Final Report with Recommendations*. New York, Columbia University Press, 1967. 99 p.
A 36

The report of the Committee, headed by Judge Harold R. Medina, suggests "action that we hope may result in appropriate controls of the lawyers and the law enforcement officials, under the auspices of the lawyers and the police themselves, more positive and effective action by the courts and the judges, and a larger measure of self-restraint by the news media." The Committee recognizes that "the First Amendment guarantees of free speech and free press and the critical importance of the concept of freedom of communication that underlies this guarantee preclude, on both constitutional and policy grounds, direct controls of the mass media by a governmental scheme of legislative or judicial establishment, understood as including the courts and the judges." The report deals largely with Canon 20 of the American Bar Association and recommends revisions dealing with the conduct of lawyers; it does not deal with Canon 35 relating to the use of radio and television in the court. The text of *Sheppard v. Maxwell*, 384 U.S. 333 (1966), is given in the appendix.

———. *Radio, Television, and the Administration of Justice; a Documented Survey of Materials*. New York, Columbia University Press, 1965. 321 p.
A 37

Part I constitutes a documented survey of the effect of radio and television coverage of civil and criminal trials. Part II includes the text of such documents as canons of ethics, court rules, statutes, court opinions, voluntary codes, and various proposals for resolving the conflict between fair trial and a free press. Introduction by Judge Harold R. Medina, chairman.

Audience Unlimited News. Rochester, N.Y., Audience Unlimited, Inc., 1964–date. Monthly.
A 38

This news sheet reports on censorship incidents in the Rochester area.

Austin, Alvin E. *Codes, Documents, Declarations Affecting the Press*. Grand Forks, N.D., University of North Dakota, 1964. 61 p.
A 39

———. *The Situation in Latin America. The Throttling of the Free Press and the Free Flow of Information in Cuba and Elsewhere in Latin America*. Grand Forks,

N.D., University of North Dakota, 1962. 45 p.
A 40

Austin, Douglas V. "Governmental Censorship in Radio and Television Broadcasting." *Public Utilities Fortnightly*, 76: 27–42, 19 August 1965.
A 41

"The prohibition against restraint censorship is recognized by the FCC, the industry, and Congress. But does the commission have the right to review program performances as a criterion for judging performance in the public interest? A historical review of the role of governmental intervention into broadcasting programing reveals that there are problems and questions that need to be explicitly answered by court review on legislation."

Authors League of America. "A Licensing System: A Proposal by the Authors League of America, Inc." *Library Journal*, 91:892–93, 15 February 1966.
A 42

"Under the system described below, authors and publishers would license the making of copies of material from books and periodicals on a royalty basis." Payment procedure involves the use of copyright stamps.

Ayling, Ronald. "W. B. Yeats on Plays and Players." *Modern Drama*, 9:1–10, May 1966.
A 43

Account of Yeats' concern for the preservation of a free theater in Ireland, including his and Lady Gregory's resistance to attempts (1909) to prevent the playing at the Abbey of Shaw's *The Shewing-Up of Blanco Posnet*.

Badger, Ronald K. "Unsworn and Unfettered Witness in Our Courtrooms: Prejudicial Publicity." *American Criminal Law Quarterly*, 4:5–19, Fall 1965.
B 1

The article deals with specific problems likely to confront the practicing attorney whose client's case has been affected by adverse publicity in the news media.

Bagdikian, Ben H. "Houston's Shackled Press." *Atlantic*, 218(2):87–93, August 1966.
B 2

"Over the years, among the most insistent alarmists of the internal threat to freedom has been the Houston *Chronicle* . . . But so far in this decade the greatest contribution the Houston *Chronicle* has made to the maintenance of native American institutions is to conduct a continuing and depressing demonstration on how not to operate a free paper in a free society, and to remind its brethren in the trade that the most immediate threat to a free press in this country is their own conflict of interest."

[Bain, Kenneth B. F.]. *Banned! A Review of Theatrical Censorship in Britain. By Richard*

Findlater, pseud. London, Macgibbon & Kee, 1967. 238 p. **B 3**

A critic and historian of the British theater surveys two centuries of the Office of Lord Chamberlain as British theatrical censor. Bain cites action taken against specific plays and the reaction of authors and critics, quoting from the statements of theatrical figures involved. He refers to the Parliamentary investigations of stage censorship (1866, 1909) and sums up the case for and against the Lord Chamberlain and the present system, suggesting possible solutions. Reviewed by Norman Marshall in the Summer 1967 issue of *Drama.*

Baker, Leonard. "Fair Trial and a Free Press: Balancing the First and the Sixth Amendments." *New Leader*, 49:15–17, 17 January 1966. **B 4**

Baker, Merrill T. *A Rhetorical Analysis of Thomas Erskine's Courtroom Defenses in Cases Involving Seditious Libel.* Iowa City, State University of Iowa, 1952. 303 p. (Ph. D. dissertation, University Microfilms, no. 4042) **B 5**

Balk, Alfred. "The Racial News Gap." *Saturday Review*, 49(33):53–54, 13 August 1966. **B 6**

Lack of comprehensive news coverage in the nation's press of life in the American ghetto and lack of coverage of the day-to-day affairs of Negro citizens are described as the racial news-gap.

Barnes, James J. *Free Trade in Books; a Study of the London Book Trade Since 1800.* Oxford, Clarendon, 1964. 198 p. **B 7**

A study of the "bookselling question" in England, efforts of the booktrade to control prices, beginning with the London Booksellers' Committee and regulations of 1829 and closing with the 1962 Decision of Restrictive Practices Court vindicating the Net Book (price control) Agreement of 1899.

Barnstein, Fred J. "Right of Privacy—Protection Against Publication of Newsworthy Information." *Washington and Lee Law Review*, 2:133–41, Fall 1940. **B 8**

Sidis v. F-R Publishing Co. (1940).

Baron, George. "A British View of Brimstone." *Teachers College Record*, 65:667–70, May 1964. **B 9**

A British educator views the Paradise, Calif., case of a teacher who was persecuted for encouraging her students to read varying points of view on current issues.

Barron, Jerome A. "Free Press v. Fair Trial: A Continuing Dialogue." *North Dakota Law Review*, 41:177–84, January 1963. **B 10**

A law professor presents the "brood of constitutional quandries" in the controversy between the press and the bar, pointing out the need for development of an accommodation between the competing constitutional issues.

————. "In Defense of 'Fairness': A First Amendment Rationale for Broadcasting's 'Fairness Doctrine.'" *University of Colorado Law Review*, 37:31–48, Fall 1964. **B 11**

Bartelme, Elizabeth. "Let It Be Printed." *Commonweal*, 81:701–3, 26 February 1965. **B 12**

A discussion of the imprimatur of the Catholic Church and the difficulties it imposes. Although designed to protect the reader, its chief effect is on the writer. The imprimatur has lost its usefulness.

Barth, J. Robert "Four Viewpoints on Literary Censorship." *Homiletic and Pastoral Review*, 67:293–300, January 1967. **B 13**

Barzun, Jacques. "Venus at Large; Sexuality and the Limits of Literature." *Encounter*, 26:24–30, March 1966. **B 14**

The author distinguishes between *sexuality*, "the very atmosphere in which all literature breathes and lives," and *sex*, the actual or imaginable act of copulation, which is "terribly limited." He believes that "the glut of sex in our prose and verse fiction will remain as the special mark of our work, the band of the times on our genius."

Bass, Abraham Z. *Ginzburg: Intent of the Purveyor.* Columbia, Mo., Freedom of Information Center, School of Journalism, University of Missouri, 1967. 4 p. (Report no. 182) **B 15**

The author finds a new and important legal test for obscenity in the U.S. Supreme Court's decision in the case of Ralph Ginzburg—the intent of the purveyor. In the case of borderline obscenity, the *Ginzburg* test will be applied first. If pandering is shown at this point, there is no need to put the material to further test. The *Ginzburg* test makes it possible to regulate the dissemination alone, and not cut off access to the material, which in and of itself may not be obscene.

Batroukha, M. Ezzedin. "A Comparative Study of Responsibility in Libel." *Journalism Quarterly*, 39:333–38, Summer 1962. **B 16**

"Who is held responsible for libelous publication? The author examines American, French and Italian laws and then compares them with Egyptian law. He finds the Egyptian and Italian laws to be most severe in fixing responsibility, and American law the most free in its treatment of individuals."

Beagle, Peter S. "Wayward Reader." *Holiday*, 37:35–38, June 1965. **B 17**

"My own opinion about pornography is that it ought to be permitted." But the author is depressed to realize that "the only development in literary content in our time has been in our freedom to describe the sexual relationship."

Beale, Howard K. *A History of Freedom of Teaching in American Schools.* New York, Scribner's, 1941. 343 p. (Report of the Commission on the Social Studies in the Schools, American Historical Association, Part 16. Reprinted by Octagon Books, New York, 1966) **B 18**

Throughout this volume are references to suppression and control of school textbooks, particularly in the South in the years preceding the Civil War when the "incendiary textbooks" of the Yankee publishers were banned and Southern authors and publishers were subsidized. There are also references to attacks on Darwinism and the discouragement of the treatment of controversial issues.

Beausang, Michael F., Jr. "A New Look at Prejudicial Publicity in Criminal Cases." *Criminal Law Bulletin*, 1(7):14–23, September 1965. **B 19**

Beer, Max. "Freedom of Information: ECOSOC [Economic and Social Council of the United Nations] Discussions and Resolutions Reflect Conflicts Which Divide World Today." *IPI Report* (International Press Institute), 3(2):6–8, June 1954. **B 20**

The article reviews the discussions on freedom of information that took place in the meeting.

Begeman, Jean. "Bigotry in Bartlesville." *New Republic*, 123(22):13–14, 27 November 1950. **B 21**

The case of fifty-nine year old Ruth Brown, town librarian of Bartlesville, Okla., for thirty-one years, fired for having liberal magazines in the library. The list included the *Nation*, *New Republic*, *Negro Digest*, *Consumers' Research*, and *Soviet Russia Today*.

Bellew, Henry. "Censorship, Law, and Conscience." *Bell*, 3:140–48, November 1941. **B 22**

Criticism of the interpretation and administration of Irish censorship under the Censorship of Publications Act.

Bellman, *pseud.* "Meet Dr. Hayes." *Bell*, 3:106–14, November 1941. **B 23**

An interview with Dr. Richard Hayes, the Irish censor.

Benjamin, Curtis G. "Copyright and Government." *Library Journal*, 91:881–86, 15 February 1966. **B 24**
Section 8 of the U.S. Copyright Act states that "no copyright shall subsist . . . in any publication of the United States Government," but the interpretation of this law has brought "a sea of troublesome questions." The chairman of the board of McGraw-Hill Book Company explores this sea, concluding that unless Congress can present "some precise but flexible guidelines" in the new copyright law, the vagueness will preclude the chance for effective and mutually profitable cooperation between the Government and the publishing industry on literally hundreds of publishing projects of crucial importance to science, technology, and education.

Beotra, B. R. *Law of Cinematograph (Central and States)*. Allahabad, India, Bar Book Co., 1965. 379 p. **B 25**

Berk, Philip E. *Canon 35: An Experimental Study of the Conflicts of Principles between Fair Trial and Free Press*. Iowa City, State University of Iowa, 1963. 300 p. (Ph.D. dissertation, University Microfilms, no. 63-7988) **B 26**
"This study traces the background and history of Canon 35 and the controversy surrounding it, quotes extensively from the many arguments on both sides of the Canon, and establishes four distinct types of viewpoints toward Canon 35 as applied to the greater conflict between fair trial and free press."

Bernas, Joaquin G. "Legal Censorship: Problems and Principles." *Philippine Studies*, 11:267–82, April 1963. **B 27**
In light of the Revitalized Movie Censorship Law of 1962 and the recent customs hassle over *Lady Chatterley* in the Philippines, the author considers the problems of prior restraint and obscenity. He concludes that there is need for a way of protecting children without doing harm to adults.

Berney, Arthur L. "Libel and the First Amendment—A New Constitutional Privilege." *Virginia Law Review*, 51:1–58, January 1965. **B 28**
The author examines the various state libel laws that governed criticism of public officials prior to *New York Times Co. v. Sullivan* and the various interests that have to be weighed, finally supporting the First Amendment on the side of the "absolutists" rather than the "balancers."

Bertelsman, William O. "Libel and Public Men." *American Bar Association Journal*, 52:657–62, July 1966. **B 29**
A critique of *New York Times Co. v. Sullivan*. The author suggests a test for applicability of the *New York Times* rule in libel cases, to determine whether there is a legitimate

public interest in free discussion of the events from which defamation arises.

Beste, R. Vernon. "Faces for the TV Censors." *Censorship*, 4(2):22–24, Autumn 1966. **B 30**
An account of the activities of the Censorship Appeals Committee, set up by the British Screenwriters Guild in 1962 to inquire into censorship of films and television, to represent members in censorship disputes, and to evolve some bridge mechanism between censors and censored in TV.

Beth, Loren P. "Group Libel and Free Speech." *Minnesota Law Review*, 39:167–84, January 1955. **B 31**
A reassessment of the validity and utility of group libel laws in light of the U.S. Supreme Court approval of the Illinois group libel statute in the case of *Beauharnais v. Illinois*, 343 U.S. 250 (1952).

Biberman, Herbert. *Salt of the Earth*. Boston, Beacon, 1965. 373 p **B 32**
The author is one of the "Hollywood Ten" who spent six months in jail for contempt of Congress because he refused to answer questions about his political beliefs. This is the story of Biberman's struggle to produce the film *Salt of the Earth* and to distribute it against blacklisting and boycott within the film industry. It deals at length with the conspiracy trial brought by the producers of the film against various groups within the film industry that had interfered with production and distribution.

Bickel, Alexander M. "Obscenity Cases." *New Republic*, 46:15–17, 27 May 1967. **B 33**
Comment on *Ginzburg, Mishkin* and *Fanny Hill* decisions by the U.S. Supreme Court.

Bird, George L., and Frederic E. Merwin. *The Newspaper and Society: A Book of Readings*. New York, Prentice-Hall, 1946. 627 p. **B 34**
Chapter 3, Freedom of Press in the United States; Chapter 6, How and Why News Is Suppressed; and Chapter 24, Pressure Groups Attempts on the Press.

Birley, Robert. *Printing and Democracy*. London, Privately Printed for the Monotype Corp., 1964. 31 p. **B 35**
The author traces the gradual growth of the liberty of the press in England over a period of a hundred years, beginning in 1641 with the abolishing of the Star Chamber. During the next two years, until 14 June 1643, he points out, Parliament was too busy with "distractions" to devote itself to the control of the press and it was during this two-year period that the "surge of political literature began." Plates accompanying the article include the title page of several contemporary pamphlets.

Birnbaum, Harold L. "Libel by Lens." *American Bar Association Journal*, 52:837–39, September 1966. **B 36**
Truth is not necessarily a defense for libel in photographic reporting.

Black, Shirley Temple. "Sex at the Box Office." *McCall's*, 94:45, 110, January 1967. **B 37**

Blakey, G. Robert. "Obscenity and the Supreme Court." *America*, 115:152–56, 13 August 1966. **B 38**
A review of the decisions of the U.S. Supreme Court in the area of obscenity, beginning with the acceptance of the so-called *Hicklin* dictum through the most recent *Ginzburg* decision. The author, a Notre Dame law professor, concludes: "An honest accommodation between the requirements of free speech, the hopes of legitimate artistic expression and the simple demands of common decency has been, and is being, worked out—though it is not yet perfectly realized. The thoughtful observer must surely conclude that the work of the Supreme Court in the obscenity area will rank as one of its finest achievements in recent years."

Blanchard, Robert O. "A Watchdog in Decline." *Columbia Journalism Review*, 5(2):17–21, Summer 1966. **B 39**
Suggests two broad courses of action for those who would "re-establish an effective Congressional check on federal withholding of information and news management."

Blashfield, Albert E. "Case of the Controversial Canon." *American Bar Association Journal*, 48:429–34, May 1962. **B 40**
There is need for a careful re-examination of the validity of Judicial Canon 35 in the light of the present-day American mind and the technological advances in the fields of electronics and photography.

Blumer, Herbert, and Philip M. Hauser. *Movies, Delinquency, and Crime*. New York, Macmillan, 1933. 233 p. **B 41**
The conclusion of the study is that it is probable that movies influence about 10 per cent of delinquent boys and 25 per cent of delinquent girls.

Bobrakov, Yuri. "War Propaganda: A Serious Crime against Humanity." *Law and Contemporary Problems*, 31:473–78, Summer 1966. **B 42**
The Soviet press-attaché in Washington urges nations to adopt legislation outlawing war propaganda as an important contribution to world peace. Since such propaganda represents a threat against society he sees no justification for protection under principle of freedom of speech.

Bogle, Allan G. *"The Times" Testimonial. Report of the Trial of the Action Bogle versus Lawson, for a Libel Published in "The Times" . . . Tried at . . . Croydon . . . August 16, 1841 . . . Together with the Proceedings of a Public Meeting . . . Edited, and with a Preface, by W. Hughes Hughes.* London, J. Hatchard, 1841. 180p. **B 43**

Boll, John J. *The American Library Association and Intellectual Freedom.* Urbana, Ill., University of Illinois Library School, 1953. 17p. (Occasional Papers no. 35) **B 44**

Bottini, Ronald L. *Regulation of TV Sex and Violence.* Columbia, Mo., Freedom of Information Center, School of Journalism, University of Missouri, 1966. 6p. (Publication no. 165) **B 45**
This report examines the effectiveness of special departments in all three networks and the Code Authority of the National Association of Broadcasters to regulate sex and violence in television programming.

Bradbury, Ray. *Fahrenheit 451.* New York, Ballantine Books, 1953. 147p. **B 46**
In this work of science fiction the central character is a "fireman" who, in this civilization of the future, is employed by the government to burn books and the houses that contain them. His frightening difficulties come about when curiosity about ideas prompts him secretly to save from the flame some books for his own use. Fahrenheit 451 is the temperature at which book-paper catches fire and burns. A motion picture has been made from the book.

Braden, Thomas. "Why My Newspaper Lied." *Saturday Review,* 41(14):11–13, 42–43, 5 April 1958. **B 47**
The difficulty in getting accurate news through the bureaucratic security policy. "It would be well for Americans to bear in mind that the battle of the press to get the whole truth from Government is their battle, and that the people own this right to know."

Bradlaugh, Charles. *Heresy: Its Utility and Morality.* London, Freethought Publishing Co., 1882. 64p. **B 48**
"My plea is, that modern heresy, from Spinoza to Mill, has given brain-strength and dignity to every one it has permeated—that the popular propagandists of this heresy, from Bruno to Carlile, have been the true redeemers and saviors, the true educators of the people. And if to-day we write with higher hope, it is because the right to speak and the right to print has been partly freed from the fetters forged through long generations of intellectual prostration, and almost entirely freed from the statutory limitations, which under pretence of checking blasphemy and sedition, have really gagged honest speech against Pope and Emperor, against Church and Throne."

Bradley, Duane. *The Newspaper, Its Place in a Democracy.* Princeton, N.J., Van Nostrand [1965] 113p. **B 49**
Written for young readers, the book gives a concise history of freedom of the press in the United States; it considers the importance of a free press in a democracy; and it examines such issues as press monopoly, libel, and government management of the news.

Branard, Robert S. "Of Opportunity & Timidity (Censorship)." *Choice; Books for College Libraries,* 2:145–48, May 1965. **B 50**
The college librarian has a standard duty to make certain his collection contains the important controversies of all time, and recent court decisions clear almost everything of literary or cultural value. Yet timidity and fear of controversy has prevented many college librarians from accepting this responsibility. "The worst censors in the field of college librarianship are the librarians themselves . . . To truly provide for his community of scholars the college librarian must not give way at any point, for any reason, to timidity, that secret, insidious censor. To do this is to betray his high responsibility."

Brand, Thomas B. "Defamation of a Group—Civil and Criminal." *Oregon Law Review,* 33:68–77, December 1953. **B 51**

Brant, Irving. *The Bill of Rights; Its Origin and Meaning.* Indianapolis, Bobbs-Merrill, 1965. 567p. **B 52**
In the first part of this work, Brant, a journalist-historian and authority on James Madison, traces the concept of freedom of the press in British common law, from the struggle against the decrees of the Star Chamber in the suppression of heresy and sedition, through the contributions of the Levellers, the abolition of the press licensing system, the eighteenth-century trials that challenged Justice Blackstone's limited concept of press freedom, and the influence on press freedom of the ideas of Cato, Junius, and Wilkes. Part two deals with the immediate background of the creation of the Bill of Rights, especially the First Amendment, the threat to press freedom under the Sedition Act of 1798, and the interpretation of the First Amendment by successive decisions of the U.S. Supreme Court, beginning in 1907 with *Patterson v. Colorado.* Unlike Leonard W. Levy (*Legacy of Suppression*), who believes that the framers of the First Amendment accepted Blackstone's interpretation of press freedom, Brant defends the libertarian intention of the framers.

———. "Seditious Libel: Myth and Reality." *New York University Law Review,* 39:1–19, January 1964. **B 53**
In exploring the American attitudes back of the adoption of the First Amendment, Brant traces the concept of the English common law of seditious libel from the days of the Star Chamber and the licensing system. Legal minds in England and America could be divided into two groups—those who supported the Coke-Blackstone-Mansfield notion of limited freedom and those who were opposed. Brant argues that the framers of the First Amendment intended to reject the eighteenth-century English common law of libel. The "balancing test" was developed in America with the Sedition Act of 1798 and has been brought up from time to time by those who have been skeptical of complete freedom of expression.

Braumueller, Gerd. *Das Ringen um die Pressefreiheit in den U.S.A.; eine historische Darstellung und Untersuchung der wichtigsten Phasen.* Munich, 1952. 148p. (Inaugural dissertation; typescript in Library of Congress) **B 54**

Brechner, Joseph L. *News Media and the Courts.* Columbia, Mo., Freedom of Information Center, School of Journalism, University of Missouri, 1967. 6p. (Report no. 004) **B 55**
"American justice must be protected not from the indiscretions of our free news media who are likewise guardians of truth and justice—but from malicious, unconscionable self-serving and gullible members of the legal profession and the subverted judgment of those in our courts who sustain and approve the efforts of lawyers to restrict the free flow of information to our citizens."

Brennan, William J., Jr. "The Supreme Court and the Meiklejohn Interpretation of the First Amendment." *Harvard Law Review,* 79:1–20, November 1965. **B 56**
The author is associate justice of the U.S. Supreme Court.

Briant, Keith. *Marie Stopes; a Biography.* London, Hogarth, 1962. 286p. **B 57**
A biography of the British birth control crusader and author of *Married Love.* Includes an account of the difficulty in publication of the work, its ban in the United States, and the various battles for freedom of birth control information.

Brickman, David. "Sanctity and Sources." *American Editor,* 3(1):27–34, April 1959. **B 58**
Commentary on the implications of the Marie Torre case, relating to the protection of news sources.

Brooke, Jocelyn. "A Pyrrhic Victory?" *London Magazine,* 4:54–60, October 1964. **B 59**
"I am opposed . . . to any form of censorship, but I would suggest that novelists, now that

the battle for freedom is won, might with advantage impose on themselves a certain degree of self-censorship, merely in the interests of art."

Brown, Charles H. "Press Censorship in the Spanish-American War." *Journalism Quarterly*, 42:581–90, Autumn 1965.　**B 60**

"Censorship during the 1898 war against Spain was more extensive and effective than historians have been inclined to grant. But the press was incautions in reporting troop and ship movements." References to censorship also appear in the author's book, *The Correspondents' War: Journalists in the Spanish-American War* (Scribner's, 1967).

Brown, Gene D. "Florida's Obscenity Statutes—Some Recommendations." *University of Florida Law Review*, 18:135–44, Summer 1965.　**B 61**

Relates to movie censorship and obscene literature.

Browne, Malcom W. "The New Face of Censorship: Viet Nam Report." *True*, 48:30–39, 91–95, April 1967.　**B 62**

"By and large, Americans are getting the truth about Viet Nam, despite official efforts to warp it out of shape." The article reports the "disturbing facts about Washington's news manipulation."

Brueggeman, Arlene A. *Analysis of Alexander Meiklejohn's Interpretation of the First Amendment of the Constitution As It Applies to A New Theory of the Press.* Urbana, Ill., University of Illinois, 1963. 76 p. (Unpublished Master's thesis)　**B 63**

Bryant, Barbara E. "Continuing Education Confronts the Controversial; a Course in Censorship." *Adult Leadership*, 13:319+, April 1965.　**B 64**

A report on a lively noncredit course called "Problems of Literary Censorship" offered as a community service by Oakland University.

Bryer, J. R. "Joyce, *Ulysses*, and the Little Review." *South Atlantic Quarterly*, 66:148–64, Spring 1967.　**B 65**

An account of the first trial of James Joyce's *Ulysses* brought about in New York in 1921 by publication in the *Little Review*. The prosecution was prompted by the New York Society for the Suppression of Vice.

Burgess, Wells D. "Obscenity Prosecution: Artistic Value and the Concept of Immunity." *New York University Law Review*, 39:1063–86, December 1964.　**B 66**

"It would appear, therefore, that even if the uncertainty and unfairness involved in distinguishing between work of artistic merit and artistically worthless work is overcome, the Court's refusal to extend first amendment protection to nonartistic work is open to question. This remains true whether the Court presently adheres to the balance of interest approach or to the absolute approach in ascertaining the scope of the first amendment."

Burke, Albert E., *et al.* "Free Press v. Fair Trial: A Panel." *Connecticut Bar Journal*, 39:140–95, March 1965.　**B 67**

Third Annual Connecticut Bar Association Seminar for the Connecticut Press. Speakers: Albert E. Burke, Judge MacDonald, Alfred Friendly, and F. Lee Bailey.

Cade, Dozier C. *A Critical Analysis of the Role of American Daily Newspapers in the Current Encroachment by Government and Society on Freedom of Expression in the United States.* Iowa City, State University of Iowa, 1954. 525 p. (Ph. D. dissertation, University Microfilms, no. 10,197)　**C 1**

Cahn, Edmond. "Freedom of the Press: The Libertarian Standard" and "Freedom of the Press: Responsibility for Defamation." In *Confronting Injustice: The Edmond Cahn Reader*, edited by Lenore L. Cahn. Boston, Little, Brown, 1966, pp. 134–60.　**C 2**

Two lectures delivered in Israel, December 1962, under the joint auspices of the Hebrew University of Jerusalem and the Association of Journalists. Those who proclaim the libertarian standard of press freedom "submit that the proper function of government is to regulate men's conduct, not the expression of their opinions and beliefs; that a press is not free unless we respect its right to publish thoughts that we disapprove, reject, and detest; and that a free people will never permit government officials—their hired servants and employees—to tell them what they can or cannot read." Cahn considers in some detail, by way of example, the case of J. M. Near and the Minnesota gag law. In his discussion of defamation Cahn considers libel against public officials and social groups. Laws against group libel "are equally unacceptable whether the court admits evidence to support a defense of truth or excludes it." He discusses the Beauharnais case, noting that despite the fact that the court upheld the group-libel laws not a single state subsequently enacted such a statute and so far as he knows not a single prosecution has been instituted since Beauharnais's.

Campbell, Lawrence M., *et al.* "Bar-Press Guidelines Discussion Widening." *Quill*, 53(3):12–17, March 1965.　**C 3**

A roundup of news events and attitudes toward pretrial publicity including a discussion of the controversial Philadelphia Bar Association "guidelines."

Canada. Committee on Broadcasting. *Report, 1965.* Ottawa, Queen's Printer, 1965. 416 p.　**C 4**

The so-called Fowler Committee makes this report on the system of broadcasting in Canada. "The State should not restrict its participation in broadcasting to the essential grant of frequencies and channels, but should control, supervise, and encourage an excellent performance in the use the broadcasters make of the public assets they have been granted." In furtherance of this principle, the Committee makes recommendations on licensing, control, and programming of both public and private sectors of radio and television.

Canada. Special Committee on Hate Propaganda in Canada. *Report . . .* [Ottawa, Queen's Printer, 1966]. 327 p.　**C 5**

Social-psychological effects of hate propaganda and the role of law and education as controls; the condition of the law in Canada and elsewhere; conclusions and recommendations. Appendix includes a survey of libel and related offenses in England, the United States, and Canada; United Nations action against hate propaganda; and samples of hate propaganda circulated in Canada.

Cardwell, Richard W. "Finding a Definition for Obscenity." *National Publisher*, 46(6):2, 4–25, June 1966.　**C 6**

A review of the Supreme Court decisions on the *Ginzburg*, *Fanny Hill*, and *Mishkin* cases.

Carey, Kevin W. "Tom Swift and His Electric Electorate: Legislation to Restrict Election Coverage." *Notre Dame Lawyer*, 40:191–202, February 1965.　**C 7**

Several bills before Congress would withhold the broadcast of early election returns and predictions in areas where polls remain open, because of effect of the information on the vote. The author believes such legislation will not violate the First Amendment. "That which corrupts the electoral process ought not to be blindly tolerated in the name of freedom."

Carmen, Ira H. *Movies, Censorship, and the Law.* Ann Arbor, Mich., University of Michigan Press, 1966. 339 p.　**C 8**

This study presents an analysis of "the several Supreme Court holdings that are relevant to an understanding of what film censorship may constitutionally accomplish or which will give insight into the rights of the motion picture industry as opposed to those of the other media of speech and press under the First Amendment." This is followed by a detailed examination of motion picture censorship programs in four large cities (Detroit, Chicago, Atlanta, and Memphis) and of the four state-wide agencies which, as of March 1965, were involved in prior restraint (New York, Virginia, Kansas, and Maryland). A concluding chapter evaluates "how successful the American political system has been in transmitting the Court's views on free expression in this area into legislative and administrative policy-making at the local level," and what kind of censorship, if any, is desirable.

————. *State and Local Motion Picture Censorship and Constitutional Liberties with Special Emphasis on the Communal Acceptance of Supreme Court Decision-Making.* Ann Arbor, Mich., University of Michigan, 1964. 458 p. (Ph.D. dissertation, University Microfilms, no. 65–5280)   **C 9**

Carroll, William A. "Natural Law and Freedom of Communication under the Fourteenth Amendment." *Notre Dame Lawyer*, 42:219–23, December 1966. **C 10**
"Although the Supreme Court has developed some subsidiary principles in elaborating the general principle that freedom of speech and press is included within the liberty of the due process clause, it is proposed that the questions suggested in this paper as derived from the natural law offer additional guidance to the Court."

Carter-Ruck, P. F. "Libel and Slander." *Director*, 18:450–53, March 1966.   **C 11**
The British laws of defamation as they relate to the businessman.

Carver, Charles. *Brann and the Iconoclast.* Austin, Tex., University of Texas Press, 1957. 196 p.   **C 12**
The story of William Cowper Brann, newspaperman of Waco, Texas, whose vitriolic pen built the *Iconoclast* into a nationwide circulation, but sowed bitter seeds of hatred in Waco. Brann took out after hypocrisy and organized virtue as exemplified in Baylor University and the Baptist Church. He defended the Catholics when they were attacked by an anti-Catholic organization, known as the American Protective Association. He was horsewhipped, kidnapped by a lynch mob of Baylor students, and eventually silenced by a shot in the back by a prominent citizen on a street in Waco. See also his *Collected Works*.

Cary Memorial Library, Lexington, Massachusetts. Board of Trustees. ["Controversial Books"] *Library Journal*, 91:4572, 1 October 1966.   **C 13**
A reprinting of the Board's statement on selection of controversial books, particularly those in the area of sex frankness.

"Censorship and the Arts." *Arts in Society* (University of Wisconsin), 4:195–358, Summer 1967.   **C 14**
Contents: Editorial comment by Edward L. Kamarck; How to Write "The Marriage of Figaro" by Irving W. Kreutz; The Music of Frustration: McClure's *The Beard*; Literature and the Supreme Court by Elmer Gertz; The Supreme Court and the Social Redemption of Pornography by Tom Robischon; Censorship: But Deliver Us from Evil by Eugene F. Kaelin; Censorship and Creativity by Campbell Crockett; The Ambiguity of Censorship by Peter Yates; and Market and Moralist Censors of a Rising Art Form: Jazz by Richard A. Peterson. Censorship 1967 (a series of symposia designed to suggest the prevailing attitudes and viewpoints held by a number of key occupational groups): Psychiatrists and Psychologists (Bryant H. Roisum, Leon A. Jakobovits, Daniel Starch, and Donald M. Kaplan); Social Scientists (Gerald Marwell and Mulford Q. Sibley); Creative Writers (Wallace Stegner, Richard Eberhart, Karl Shapiro, Erskine Caldwell, Irving Wallace, John Barth, Rex Stout, R. V. Cassill, James Drought, and Archibald MacLeish); Television Writers (Jerry McNeely, Lou Hazam, Loring Mandel, and Robert Richter); Art Gallery Directors and Concert Managers (Bret Waller, Donald Goodall, James R. Carlson, Norman A. Geske, Harold W. Lavender, and Betty Crowder); and Librarians (Edwin Castagna, Margaret Monroe, Helen Dirtadian, Ferris J. Martin, Ervin J. Gaines, William F. Hayes, Doris L. Shreve, Everett T. Moore, Gordon H. Bebeau, and Emerson Greenaway).

Center for the Study of Democratic Institutions. *Blacklist: A Failure of Political Imagination.* Santa Barbara, Calif., The Center, 1967. (Tape recording no. 260)   **C 15**
Although blacklisting is no longer practiced as it was in the 1950's, an insidious and subtle form, far more dangerous, remains today, according to once-blacklisted television artists Millard Lampell and John Henry Faulk. The discussion is approximately 30 minutes long.

————. *Freedom of the Press.* Santa Barbara, Calif., The Center, 1966. (Tape recordings nos. 123 and 124)   **C 16**
In the first discussion, the Center staff, led by Robert M. Hutchins, consider *The New York Times Co. v. Sullivan* decision which gives citizens immunity to criticize public officials unless malice can be proven. Although the decision met with approval in general from those discussing it, there were misgivings about its usefulness in future cases. In the second discussion, Harry Kalven, Jr. hails the decision as the gretest First Amendment decision in the history of the Court. He suggests that the Negro protest-movement was in large measure repsonsible for forcing the Court to reach such high ground in defense of First Amendment rights. Each discussion is about 60 minutes long.

Charles, W. H. "Obscene Literature and the Legal Process in Canada." *Canadian Bar Review*, 44:243–92, May 1966.   **C 17**
Why has Canada's highest court so frequently had to adjudicate problems of obscenity? In answering this, the author explores the relationship between the courts and the legislature in their historical development to determine how the legal process operates within the field of obscene literature. He discusses the nature of obscenity itself and some of the underlying assumptions which have prompted Canada and other countries to prohibit free circulation of obscene matter. He concludes that the present state of the law is unsettled and will probably remain so unless further legislative action is taken.

Chernoff, George, and Hershel Sarbin. *The Photographer and the Law.* Philadelphia, Chilton, 1965. 128 p.   **C 18**
Includes discussion of legal restraints on taking pictures (including courtroom prohibitions), invasion of privacy, nudes in photography, copyright, and libel by photography. Discusses case of *Manual Enterprises v. Day*.

Chleboun, William S. "California Booksellers Join Forces to Combat Censorship." *Publishers' Weekly*, 188:30–31, 16 August 1965.   **C 19**
Action of California booksellers in opposition to 23 obscenity censorship bills in the 1965 state legislature.

Christenson, Reo M., and Robert O. McWilliams. *Voice of the People: Readings in Public Opinion and Propaganda.* New York, McGraw-Hill, 1962. 585 p.   **C 20**
Chapter 7, Censorship and Freedom, includes selections from J. S. Mill, *On Liberty*; the *Ulysses* case; the *Miracle* case; John Fischer, The Harm Good People Do; Walter Lippmann, Violent Entertainment: Stimulus to Violence? *Winters v. New York*, The ALA-ABPC Freedom to Read statement; The Right Not to Be Lied To (*New York Times* editorial, 10 May 1961 relating to the Cuban crisis); William J. Jorden, A Western View of Soviet Censorship; Francis E. Rourke, How Much Should the Government Tell? and Arthur Schlesinger, Jr., Censorship: the Russian Rationale.

Ciardi, John. "Expert Witness." *Saturday Review*, 49(1):22, 1 January 1966.   **C 21**
Report, via John Pekkanen of the Middletown, Conn., *Press*, of an obscenity case against *The National Insider*, featuring testimony of a self-styled expert, questioned by defense attorney Elmer Gertz.

————. "The Marquis de Sade, II." *Saturday Review*, 48(40):36, 2 October 1965.   **C 22**
"The works of the Marquis de Sade, whether in the present Grove Press edition or in any subsequent selection, should be permitted full legal freedom to circulate for the simple reason that every book should have that freedom." Because the work represents the detailed sexual orgies of a sick mind, Ciardi would withhold the work from children.

————. "Taboo Languages." *Saturday Review*, 49:14–15, 20 August 1966. **C 23**

"Why are we so uneasy about the root words that describe bodily functions? . . . By ethnic agreement it is not only shocking to use taboo language but it is sometimes held to be sinful and sometimes even to be criminal. It is, therefore, exactly such taboo language that will best express our feelings when we are enraged or socially mutinous."

Cihlar, Frank P. *et al.* "[Survey Note] on Obscenity." *Notre Dame Lawyer*, 41:753–85, June 1966. **C 24**
Part of an anlysis of the church-state relationship in America. Particular emphasis has been given to the field of obscenity, as major evolutions have occurred culminating with the recent Supreme Court pronouncements in the *Ginzburg*, *Fanny Hill*, and *Mishkin* cases.

Cipes, Robert M. "Controlling Crime News; Sense or Censorship?" *Atlantic*, 220(2):47–53, August 1967. **C 25**
"Without noticeable movement toward a meeting of minds, the American press and bar have been debating the conflict between a free press and the right to a fair trial. . . . Mr. Cipes here examines the controversial Reardon Committee report of the American Bar Association and the press's general outraged and sometimes fatuous response to it."

Clayton, Charles C. "Default of a Public Trust." *Grassroots Editor*, 8(3):3–5, 27, May–June 1967. **C 26**
The author examines the public's right in newspaper strikes, concluding that "either management and labor accept their responsibility to serve the public, or the people will demand legal measures to ban newspaper strikes." A subsequent article, Blackout in Carbondale, is a case study of the 128-day strike of the *Southern Illinoisan*.

Clemons, L. S. "The Right of Privacy in Relation to the Publication of Photographs." *Marquette Law Review*, 14:193–98, June 1930. **C 27**

Clissitt, William. "The British Press Council; Its Work with the Public." *Grassroots Editor*, 7(3):24–26, July 1966. **C 28**
Excerpts from an address by the secretary of the Council before the Manchester Literary and Philosophical Society.

Cochran, W. Thad. "Pre-Trial Publicity As Denial of Due Process." *Mississippi Law Journal*, 36:369–91, May 1965. **C 29**
The author concludes that the only real protection is the elimination of prejudicial publicity, which might be achieved by passing laws that would extend the contempt power. This should not be necessary if the legal profession and news media would formulate and follow mutually satisfactory standards governing publicity in criminal cases.

Cockcroft, George P., and James D. "The High Cost of Dissent." *Frontier, The Voice of the New West*, 17(9):7–9, July 1966. **C 30**
How dissenting views by scholars may result in the withholding of government or private grants and subsidies.

"Codes and Censorship." In *International Motion Picture Almanac, 1965*. Charles S. Aaronson, *ed.* New York, Quigley Publications, 1965, pp. 775–91. **C 31**
Includes: Motion Picture Production Code, Motion Picture Advertising Code, Censorship Boards in the U.S., Public Reviewing Groups, and Motion Picture Councils.

Cole, Georgia. "Controversial Areas in Library Materials." *Bulletin of the National Association of Secondary School Principals*, 50:31–36, January 1966. **C 32**

Colquhoun, Iain. "Trial by the Press; Crime Reporting Stirs Widespread Controversy." *IPI Report* (International Press Institute), 6(2):7–8, June 1957. **C 33**
Discussion in Britain following the trial of Dr. John Bodkin Adams.

Columbia Broadcasting System. *Network Practices; Memorandum Supplementing Statement of Frank Stanton, President, Columbia Broadcasting System, Inc. Prepared for the Senate Committee on Interstate and Foreign Commerce.* New York, C.B.S., 1956. 143 p., 66 p. **C 34**
Includes a section which examines the several charges against the networks and proposals for change including the licensing and regulation of networks. Of the latter the report states: "Nothing in the nature of television broadcasting or of current practices warrants, or even permits, so radical a departure from existing concepts and so dangerous a philosophy of Government intervention."

A Commentary on the Licentious Liberty of the Press, In which the recent Publication, entitled "Memoirs of Harriet Wilson," is severely censured. By a student of the Inner Temple. London, Sold by J. Robins. 1825. 24 p. **C 35**
An attack on the abuse of freedom of the press. The author charges that, with the publication of the *Memoirs*, "the press is now the asylum for those retiring from the public lewdness of their despicable scenes. It is open to all vice and uninfluenced by every virtue." He calls for moral controls of the press.

"Constitutional Limitations to Long Arm Jurisdiction in Newspaper Libel Cases." *University of Chicago Law Review*, 34:436–52, Winter 1967. **C 36**

New York Times Co. v. Connor, 365 F. 2d 567 (5th Cir. 1966).

"Constitutional Problems in Obscenity Legislation Protecting Children." *Georgetown Law Journal*, 54:1379–1414, Summer 1966. **C 37**
"Together, the two New York statutes represent the most carefully reasoned and precisely drafted attempt to date to prohibit the dissemination of material deemed objectionable to minors."

"Constitutionality of the Law of Criminal Libel." *Columbia Law Review*, 52:521–34, April 1952. **C 38**
"Fundamentally, the concept of criminal prosecution for the publication of defamatory statements is inimical to the principle of freedom of the press embodied in the Federal Constitution." A solution lies not in a frontal attack on this body of law but "in reading into the Federal Constitution some of the major limitations imposed by state courts and legislatures upon the stricture of criminal libel as originally developed by Star Chamber."

"Contempt by Publication." *Northwestern Law Review*, 60:531–49, September–October 1965. **C 39**
Recommends that the Supreme Court abandon the "clear and present danger" test and return to the "reasonable tendency" test for punishing contempt by publication.

Cope, J. P. "Shadow of Censorship over South Africa." *IPI Report* (International Press Institute), 1(10):1–2, February 1953. **C 40**
Clash between the Malan government and the English press brings threats of control on papers and correspondents.

Corbett, Edward P. J. "Raise High the Barriers, Censors." *America*, 54:441–44, 7 January 1961. (Reprinted in Laser and Fruman, *Studies in J. D. Salinger*. New York, Odyssey, 1963, pp. 134–41) **C 41**
An examination of various charges made against the novel, *The Catcher in the Rye*, together with arguments in its defense.

Coren, Alan. "Yes, Filth, M'Lud, but Beautiful Filth." *Punch*, 252:223–24, 1 February 1967. **C 42**
A whimsical piece, complaining that the author had not been invited to testify in court on behalf of certain banned books because he was unable to get hold of advance copies to read.

Corry, John. "The Manchester Papers."

Esquire, 67(6):82–91, 124–27, 164–71, June 1967. (Also published in book form by Putnam's.)　**C43**

From documents, memoranda, and calculated news leaks "a disinterested observer seeks the truth" in the complex and tortuous story of William Manchester's book, *The Death of a President*. In the same issue (pp. 92–94) Gay Talese describes in The Corry Papers—"what happened to the disinterested observer who sought the truth."

Cossart, Theophilus, *pseud. A Full and True Account of the Prodigious Experiment Brought to perfection in Boston at Father Burke's Academy to the Glory of God, The Propagation of Truth and the Suppression of Venery.* New York, Printed by Marchbank Press for the Author, 1928. 19 p.　**C44**

A humorous tale in verse of "Father" Burke who conducted an academy in Boston where the young were forced to read risqué books and denied the usual Dickens, Eliot, and Scott. Such fare inoculated them against evil books in later life and encouraged them to read the good books formerly banned. "They're through with vicious ways and sinful,/Who've known the worst, and had a skinful." The verse is preceded by an Introduction to Father Burke's Academy, Being a Short Life of Father Burke by Montague Glass.

Coupe, Bradford. "The Roth Test and Its Corollaries." *William and Mary Law Review*, 8:121–32, Fall 1966.　**C45**

Commentary on the obscenity rulings of the U.S. Supreme Court in *Roth v. United States* (1957) and later decisions in the *Ginzburg, Mishkin,* and *Fanny Hill* cases. "Under the present status of the law, it is unclear whether the evils of obscenity are that it criminally arouses the minds of men, or that it is without any redeeming value to society such as to warrant its distribution."

"Court Stirs a Hornet's Nest." *Christian Century*, 83:451–52, 13 April 1966.　**C46**

Comments on the three split decisions on obscenity rendered by the U.S. Supreme Court on 21 March 1966.

Cowen, Zelman. "Prejudicial Publicity and the Fair Trial: A Comparative Examination of American, English and Commonwealth Law." *Indiana Law Journal*, 41: 69–85, Fall 1965.　**C47**

—————, *et al. Fair Trial vs. A Free Press.* Santa Barbara, Calif., Center for the Study of Democratic Institutions, 1965. 36 p. (Occasional Paper on the Free Society)　**C48**

The nationwide debate on the issues of a fair trial versus a free press that grew out of the events of the Kennedy assassination, led to a series of discussions at the Center, which are reported here. Zelman Cowen, dean of the University of Melbourne Law School, discusses the comparative English, British Commonwealth, and American approaches; there are statements of two practicing journalists, Alfred Friendly, managing editor of the Washington *Post* and chairman of the Press-Bar Committee of the American Society of Newspaper Editors, and Gene Blake of the Los Angeles *Times*. W. H. Parker, chief of police of Los Angeles contributes a paper on the problems from the standpoint of the law enforcement officer; and Donald H. McGannon, president of Westinghouse Broadcasting Co. contributes a paper on the role of television. The appendix contains the text of Canon 20 of the American Bar Association Canons of Ethics, the Oregon Bar-Press-Broadcasters Joint Statement of Principles, and the Massachusetts Guide for the Bar and News Media.

Coyne, John R., Jr. "The Pornographic Convention." *Library Journal*, 91:2768–73, 1 June 1966.　**C49**

The author argues that the librarian's world and literature itself is threatened by the "pornographic convention" and that it is up to the librarian to speak out. He criticizes the American Library Association for helping to destroy one set of standards in selection of better books without substituting another, for viewing controversial literature as something sociological which acts upon man in society, rather than for the effect such work has upon literature itself.

Crow, Peter. *Fair Trial—Free Press Case Study.* Columbia, Mo., Freedom of Information Center, School of Journalism, University of Missouri, 1966. 4 p. (Publication no. 158)　**C50**

A study of the Hackworth murder case, showing the influence of the Katzenbach guidelines in the relation between bar and press.

—————. *New York "Times" Strike, 1965.* Columbia, Mo., Freedom of Information Center, School of Journalism, University of Missouri, 1965. 8 p. (Publication no. 151)　**C51**

Consideration of the forces at work in the 25-day strike of New York papers in the fall of 1965.

—————. *Toward a New Copyright Law.* Columbia, Mo., Freedom of Information Center, School of Journalism, University of Missouri, 1966. 4 p. (Publication no. 156)　**C52**

A discussion of the points of conflict in the proposed revision of the copyright law.

[Cullen, Paul *Cardinal*]. *Report of the Action of Libel brought by the Rev. Robert O'Keefe, P. P. against His Eminence Cardinal Cullen. With an Introduction by Henry Clare Kirkpatrick.* London, Longmans, Green, 1874. 600 p.　**C53**

A charge of published libel was brought by a parish priest against Cardinal Cullen, Primate of Ireland. The case is significant because it calls into account in a court of civil law an ecclesiastical superior of the Roman Catholic Church. Under advice of the Lord Chief Justice, the jury found for the plaintiff and assessed damages of one farthing.

[Cunliffe, David A.]. ["Golden Convolvulus Trial"]. *Poetmeat*, No. 11, Summer 1966.　**C54**

Most of the issue of this avant-garde magazine, published in Blackburn, England, deals with the trial of the editor (*Regina v. David Alexander Cunliffe*) for an article entitled The Golden Convolvulus in the summer 1965 issue. The present issue quotes from defense testimony, contains a censorship cartoon by Arthur Moyce, and a statement protesting police censorship (the offices of the magazine had been raided) signed by various American and English authors and editors. Cunliffe was found not guilty of publishing an obscene article, but guilty of sending an indecent book through the mail and was fined £50.

Cyr, Helen. "Case of the Book That Wasn't There." *Top of the News*, 22:265–68, April 1966.　**C55**

Account of an organized effort to remove certain books on the background and history of the Negro from Oakland (Calif.) school libraries. Members of the Citizens Committee for Common Sense in the Schools attacked the books as "atheistic" and "communistic."

Danna, Sammy R. *Death of Broadcasting Option Time.* Columbia, Mo., Freedom of Information Center, School of Journalism, University of Missouri, 1965. 5 p. (Publication no. 150)　**D1**

A history of the practice of broadcast networks requiring their affiliated stations to set aside certain hours for network programs, from the advent of television until the elimination of the practice in 1962.

Dash, Samuel, Richard F. Schwartz, and Robert E. Knowlton. The *Eavesdropper.* New Brunswick, N.J., Rutgers University Press, 1959. 484 p.　**D2**

A report on a nationwide fact-finding study of wiretapping, involving eavesdropping by county and state law enforcement, by private parties, and by the racketeers. The report is arranged in three parts: The Practice, by Samuel Dash; The Fools, by Richard F. Schwartz; and The Law, by Robert E. Knowlton.

Davidson, Donald. "Notes: Zona Gale, Censorship." In his *The Spyglass; Views and Reviews, 1924–1930*, edited by John T. Fain. Nashville, Tenn., Vanderbilt University Press, 1963, pp. 153–58.　**D3**

Observations on the absurdity of censorship in the author's column, The Spyglass, in the *Nashville Tennessean*, 6 February 1927. "Censorship . . . gets nowhere, because nobody can decide with any sort of accuracy what really ought to be censored . . . I know of no person I would trust as a literary censor."

Davis, A. G. "Law of Defamation in New Zealand." *University of Toronto Law Journal*, 16:37–54, 1965. **D4**

Davis, Norris G. "Invasion of Privacy: A Study in Contradictions." *Journalism Quarterly*, 30:179–88, Spring 1953. **D5**
"Court decisions in right of privacy cases are completely contradictory and have seldom brought justice, contends the author after extensive study."

Day, J. Edward. "Mailing Lists and Pornography." *American Bar Association Journal*, 52:1103–9, December 1966. **D6**
The author was Postmaster General in the Kennedy Administration.

"Defamation a Deux: Incidental Defamation and the *Sullivan* Doctrine." *University of Pennsylvania Law Review*, 114:241–48, December 1965. **D7**
"Does the qualified privilege to make defamatory remarks about a public official in his official capacity also immunize defamation of a private party incidental to that of a public official?"

"Defamation of the Public Official." *Northwestern University Law Review*, 61: 614–39, September–October 1966. **D8**
Analysis of the implications of the U.S. Supreme Court decision in *New York Times Co. v. Sullivan*, 376 U.S. 254 (1964).

de Graffenried, William R. "Torts—Invasion of Right of Privacy." *Alabama Law Review*, 1:124–27, Fall 1948. **D9**
The author explores the implications of *Smith v. Doss*, 37 So 2d 118 (1948), which relates to an Alabama Supreme Court ruling involving the radio broadcast of a 1905 story about the disappearance of the father of the plaintiff. The Court ruled that the subject matter was of legitimate public interest and that the passage of time did not give privacy to his acts which were "imbedded in the public record."

Del Porto, Joseph A. *Thomas Erskine and Alexander Hamilton.* Iowa City, Iowa, Association for Education in Journalism, 1966. 15 p. mimeo. (Presented at convention of the Association, University of Iowa) **D10**
An account of the two eighteenth-century lawyers, Erskine in England and Hamilton in America, who challenged the existing laws of seditious libel.

De Mott, Robert. "The Right of Privacy in Relation to Radio Broadcasts." *Rocky Mountain Law Review*, 12:127–33, February 1940. **D11**
Regarding *Mau v. Rio Grande Oil, Inc.* 28 F. Supp. 845 (S.D.Cal. 1939), which recognizes that there can be an invasion of personal privacy by oral publication through the medium of radio.

Dempsey, David. "S.E.X. and the P.E.N." *Saturday Review*, 49(11):31, 12 March 1966. **D12**
Report of a frank discussion of pornography by a panel composed of authors Elizabeth Janeway and Marya Mannes, Professor Leslie Fiedler, and publisher Barney Rosset, given before the P.E.N. Club.

"Deprive and Corrupt, I and II." *Times Literary Supplement*, no. 3,393, 9 March 1967, p. 193; no. 3,394, 16 March 1967, p. 219. **D13**
In the first issue the reviewer discusses hidden public library censorship in England as referred to in an article by B.-H. Yemini in *Censorship* and reviews Pamela H. Johnson's book, *On Iniquity*, "an energetic and despondent meditation on the power of literature to deprave and corrupt." Part II deals with recent activities of the Lord Chamberlain in the censorship of plays and the possible outcome if this official were divested of his censorship duties.

Derby, E. Stephen. "Section 315: Analysis and Proposal." *Harvard Journal on Legislation*, 3:257–321, February 1966. **D14**
The author considers four policy questions raised by Section 315 of the Federal Communications Act of 1934 which relate to grants of broadcast time to candidates for public office: What is the proper definition of legally qualified candidate? To what uses of broadcast facilities should the section apply? What is the proper role for the concept of equal opportunities? How may rights created under this section be effectively enforced?

Deutsch, Eberhard P. "From Zenger to Garrison: A Tale of Two Centuries." *New York State Bar Journal*, 38:409–19, October 1966. **D15**
A comparison of the Zenger libel case of 1734 with the defamation case against New Orleans District Attorney Jim Garrison in 1964.

Devereux, E. J. "Elizabeth Barton and Tudor Censorship." *Bulletin of the John Rylands Library, Manchester*, 49:91–106, Autumn 1966. **D16**
In the affair of *The Nun's Book* in 1533 the author relates "what may be the first case of really successful suppression of books and ideas in England." In July of that year King Henry VIII ordered Cromwell to take action against a book, probably written by Edward Thwaites, recounting the revelations and

miraculous cures of a nun of St. Sepulcre's, Elizabeth Barton. The book also contained criticism of Henry's divorce and marriage to Anne Boleyn. Some 700 copies of the book printed by John Skot were seized and probably destroyed since no copies are extant, and the nun and five clerics were executed.

Devol, Kenneth S. "Libel and the Student Press." *The Collegiate Journalist*, 3(2):10, 12, Winter 1966. **D17**
Who would be involved in a libel suit against a student publication?

———. *Major Areas of Conflict in the Control of College and University Daily Student Newspapers in the United States.* Los Angeles, University of Southern California, 1965. 294 p. (Unpublished Ph.D. dissertation) **D18**

Dibble, J. Rex. "Obscenity: A State Quarantine to Protect Children." *Southern California Law Review*, 39:345–77, 1966. **D19**
"It is the premise of this article that society today has the constitutional power to protect children from obscene materials within reasonable limitations of certainty and fairness, and that this power exists even though there may not be definite scientific proof of actual injury to children . . . The area of state power over obscenity and children is the subject of the present discussion . . . The principal purpose of this article is to suggest a possible statutory scheme, recognizing that some points in discussion, and several important parts of the draft statute, are subject to argument."

Dilliard, Irving. "The Greatest Freedom of All." *Grassroots Editor*, 7(4):8–12, October 1966. **D20**
In this 1966 Elijah Parish Lovejoy Lecture at Southern Illinois University Dilliard pays tribute to four editors of "unusual courage and integrity and long devotion to journalism." Josiah William Gitt, editor and publisher of the *York* (Penn.) *Gazette*, John Theodore Evjue, editor and publisher of the *Madison* (Wis.) *Capital Times*, John Netherland Heiskell, editor and publisher of the *Arkansas Gazette* (Little Rock), and Thomas More Starke, editor and publisher emeritus of the *Santa Barbara News Press*.

Disraeli, Isaac. "War against Books." In his *Amenities of Literature . . .* New York, Widdleton, 1874, pp. 425–46. (Also issued by Stratford Press, Cincinnati, 1942 as vol. 3 of *A Trilogy on Printing*) **D21**
An essay on the war waged against early English printers by Church and State, the Star Chamber, the Stationers' Office, and the Licensers of the Press. The essay was first published in 1841.

Doan, Edward N. "The Newspaper and the Right of Privacy." *Journal of the Bar Association of Kansas*, 5:203–14, February 1937. **D 22**
A professor of law summarizes the existing legal situation in attempting to answer questions on the right of privacy raised by Lee A. White of the Detroit *News* in *Editor and Publisher*, 25 April 1936.

Dobbs, Kildare. "Eros on Yonge Street: Impressions of the Dorothy Cameron Trial." *Saturday Night*, 81:18–21, February 1966. **D 23**
A Toronto art gallery owner is tried for exhibiting "obscene" pictures.

Dobyns, Frank L. *Cigarette Advertising Code*. Columbia, Mo., Freedom of Information Center, School of Journalism, University of Missouri, 1967. 6 p. (Report no. 179) **D 24**
The story of the cigarette advertising code, imposed by the industry to forestall government regulation.

Donigan, Robert L., and Edward C. Fisher. "Fair Trial vs. Freedom of the Press." *Traffic Digest and Review*, 14(10):18–24, October 1966. **D 25**
A discussion of the recent court rulings in the *Sheppard* and *Estes* cases.

Doubles, M. Ray. "A Camera in the Courtroom." *Washington and Lee Law Review*, 22:1–16, Spring 1965. **D 26**
"Giving the widest latitude to arguments on behalf of the television industry that what transpires in a courtroom is news, and that it should be televised under the right of freedom of the press . . . the overwhelming conclusion is that a Canon prohibiting such television is proper." But the Canon should not be based on television techniques detracting from the dignity of the court, but rather that knowledge of the telecasting may distract the witnesses.

Dowd, Donald W., *et al*. "Free Press and a Fair Trial—A Symposium." *Villanova Law Review*, 11:677–741, Summer 1966. **D 27**
Introduction by Donald W. Dowd, A Newspaperman's View by Fred Graham, A Radio and Television Newsman's View by William B. Monroe, A Prosecutor's View by Arlen Specter, A Defense Attorney's View by Percy Foreman, A Bar Association View by Robert L. Trescher, A Judicial View by Judge William F. Smith, and An Academic View by Robert B. McKay. Comments on *Sheppard v. Maxwell*, 384 U.S. 333, are given by McKay and Graham.

Doyle, Henry G. "Censorship and Student Publications." *School and Society*, 28:78–80, 21 July 1928. **D 28**
"The ideal system, my inquiries seem to indicate, is one of complete editorial control by students, with strict accountability for the exercise of that control both as members of the college community and as citizens."

[Drennan, William]. *A Full Report of the Trial at Bar, in the Court of King's Bench, of William Drennan, M. D. upon an Indictment, Charging Him with Having Written and Published a Seditious Libel . . .* Dublin, J. Rea, G. Johnson, 1794. 96 p. **D 29**
Dr. Drennan was brought to trial along with Archibald H. Rowan for having written the *Address to the Volunteers* by the Dublin United Irishmen, published in the *Northern Star*.

Driver, Tom F. "Obscenity and the Court." *Christianity and Crisis*, 26:81–83, 2 May 1966. **D 30**
Criticism of the Supreme Court decisions in the *Ginzburg*, *Mishkin*, and *Fanny Hill* cases. *Fanny Hill* was freed, but for the wrong reasons. The jailing of Ginzburg and Mishkin "does not seem to be part of any process that protects the freedom and order of the rest of society." While holding no brief for their motives, they should not be considered criminals. "We believe that this hypocrisy [allowing *Fanny Hill* on the basis of its redeeming social value] has a worse moral effect than does the free distribution of erotic literature."

Dumbauld, Edward. "State Precedents for the Bill of Rights." *Journal of Public Law*, 7:323–44, Fall 1958. **D 31**
A table (p. 343) indicates topics including freedom of press and freedom of debate, appearing in state constitutions.

Dunn, Robert H. "The Right to Read." *New Jersey Libraries*, 4:13–16, March 1966. (Reply by P. J. Hayes appears in the June 1966 issue) **D 32**
An account of the work of the New Jersey Committee for the Right to Read in combating extralegal censorship in that state. The same issue contains Governor Richard J. Hughes's veto message of an antiobscenity bill (pp. 9–12) and the opposition to the bill by the New Jersey School Library Association (pp. 30–31).

Durgnat, Raymond. "Horror, Violence and Catharsis." *Censorship*, 2:51–54, Spring 1965. **D 33**
Discusses the paradox in the motion picture viewing theory that must accommodate the concepts of both "catharsis" and "reinforcement."

Du Shane, Graham. "Their (Un) Appointed Rounds." *Saturday Review*, 44(13):47, 1 April 1961. (Reprinted from *Science*, 24 February 1961) **D 34**
The story of a censorship that harrassed science for 20 years—impounding of mail deemed to be foreign political propaganda—a practice ordered ended by President Kennedy.

Dutch Treat Club. *Censored: The Dutch Treat Blue Book*, 1940. New York, The Club, 1940. 82 p. **D 35**
The theme of the 1940 yearbook of the famous New York club of writers, artists, publishers, producers, etc. (established in 1905) was censorship. In mock seriousness the ribald cartoons, articles, and poetry that usually appear in the club's yearbook are subjected to a form of censorship.

Dworkin, Gerald. "Privacy and the Press." *Modern Law Review*, 24:185–89, January 1961. **D 36**
Regarding *Williams v. Settle*, a British case involving the unauthorized publication of a wedding group photograph.

Dyson, Richard B. "Looking-glass Law: An Analysis of the Ginzburg Case." *University of Pittsburgh Law Review*, 28:1–18, October 1966. **D 37**
"The recent case of *Ginzburg v. United States* has reawakened the continuing legal dispute around obscene publications and the first amendment. In the course of a critical and exposing analysis of the decision, Professor Dyson arrives at the novel interpretation that the familiar doctrine of estoppel lies behind the *Ginzburg* rationale."

Easterly, Elenora. *CMAA: Experiment in Self-Regulation*. Columbia, Mo., Freedom of Information Center, School of Journalism, University of Missouri, 1967. 4 p. (Report no. 178) **E 1**
A discussion of self-regulation in the comic magazine industry imposed under the Code Authority of the Comics Magazine Association of America (CMAA).

Edenhofer, Lawrence E. "The Impartial Jury—Twentieth Century Dilemma: Some Solutions to the Conflict Between Free Press and Fair Trial." *Cornell Law Quarterly*, 51:306–27, Winter 1966 **E 2**
Proposals of alternate solutions to muzzling the press include changes in the methods of selecting impartial juries.

Edwards, Frank. *Flying-Saucers—Serious Business*. New York, Stuart, 1966. 319 p. **E 3**
Throughout this journalistic account of evidence in support of "flying saucers," gathered largely from eyewitness accounts, the author criticizes the Air Force for its efforts to deny or censor all reports of UFO investigations.

Elman, Richard M. "Consensus TV."

Censorship, 4(2):42–45, Autumn 1966.
E 4

"Unless some means is found to ensure absolute press freedom (without further empowering the television monopolies) one cannot rule out the possibility that the medium will increasingly become the monolithic voice of the bureaucratic state."

Ely, John H. "Trial by Newspaper & Its Cure." *Encounter*, 28(3):80–92, March 1967.
E 5

"My purpose in this article is to suggest that the problem [trial by newspaper] is in fact *not* capable of easy solution, that the English answer—contempt of court—although it goes a long way towards safeguarding the right to be tried by an impartial jury and may on balance be the best answer to the problem, in fact falls short of its goal of ensuring trials uninfluenced by publicity and, into the bargain, pays dearly by diminishing the contribution the press can make to the efficient and fair administration of justice."

Emerson, Howard. *Access to Medical News.* Columbia, Mo., Freedom of Information Center, School of Journalism, University of Missouri, 1966. 6 p. (Publication no. 163)
E 6

A consideration of the conflict between access to medical news on the one hand and the patient's right to privacy and the doctor's fear of publicity on the other.

Emerson, John, S. *A Full & Faithful Report of the Proceedings in His Majesty's Court of Exchequer in Ireland in the Case of the Hon. Mr. Justice Johnson.* Dublin, Thomas Burnside, 1805. 196 p., 34 p., 8 p.
E 7

Johnson was charged with publishing at Westminster certain "scandalous and malicious libels" concerning His Majesty's government of Ireland.

Emery, Walter B. "Broadcasting Rights and Responsibilities in a Democratic Society." *Centennial Review*, 8:306–22, Summer 1965.
E 8

Epstein, Jason. "The Obscenity Business." *Atlantic*, 218(2):56–60, August 1966. (Reprinted in *Library Journal*, 1 October 1966)
E 9

"The tortuous, not altogether articulate attempt of the Supreme Court to deal with the growing traffic in obscenity and pornography must be examined in detail if its latest decision scrutinizing the motives of authors, editors, publishers, and booksellers, is to be understood. Mr. Epstein, a vice president of Random House, takes on that exacting task in this article and demonstrates that the issue at stake is not only individual freedom but the responsibility with which we use that freedom."

An Essay on the Liberty of the Press: Chiefly as it respects Personal Slander. Dublin, M. Williamson, 1755. 44 p.
E 10

Essex, Harold. "Responsibility and Respectability in the Public Interest." *Journal of Broadcasting*, 9:285–90, Fall 1965.
E 11

Estrin, Herman A., and Arthur M. Sanderson, *eds. Freedom and Censorship of the College Press.* Dubuque, Iowa, W. C. Brown, 1965. 310 p.
E 12

"This book is a collection of seminal essays on functions and concepts for the student press, exploring its complex areas of freedom, censorship, and responsibilities." Includes Code of Ethics of the National Council of College Publications Advisors and the U.S. Student Press Association, a statement on Faculty Responsibility for the Academic Freedom of Students by the American Association of University Professors, a statement on Freedom of the College Press, by the AAUP, and Basic Policy Declaration on Freedom and Responsibility of the Student Press passed by the U.S. Student Press Association. Extensive bibliography includes many articles from college press sources not listed in this bibliography.

Fain, Gerald G., John Guman, and Frederick M. Tobin. "The Law of Defamation in Connecticut." *Connecticut Bar Journal*, 38:420–93, September 1964.
F 1

Faircloth, Earl. "Free Press—Independent Judiciary: Neither Has Primacy Over the Other." *Florida Bar Journal*, 39:928–32, September 1965.
F 2

Falk, Richard A. "On Regulating International Propaganda: A Plea for Moderate Aims." *Law and Contemporary Problems*, 31:622–34, Summer 1966.
F 3

"It is the position of this article to oppose the use of international law to regulate international propaganda at the present time, except in very selective instances."

False Steps of the Ministry after the Revolution; Shewing that the Lenity and Moderation of that Government was the Occasion of All the Factions Which Have Since Endanger'd the Constitution. With Some Reflections on the License of the Pulpit and the Press. In a Letter to My Lord. London, Printed for J. Roberts, 1714. 34 p.
F 4

Fanning, Odom. "Lifting the Lid on Science News." *Quill*, 47(9):11, 19–20, September 1959.
F 5

Farley, John J. *Book Censorship in the Senior High School Libraries of Nassau County, New York.* New York, New York University, 1964. 386 p. (Ph.D. dissertation, University Microfilms, no. 65–969)
F 6

"Pressure to censor existed in the Nassau County senior high school libraries in the sense that the majority of the librarians had had experience with censorship attempts made in the past by members of the community. Present pressures to censor, however, consisted mainly in vague expectations of complaints if certain books were to be circulated. . . . Voluntary censorship, the censorship performed because of the librarians' own convictions, was more prevalent than was involuntary censorship."

Featherer, Esther J. *CATV: Problems and Promise.* Columbia, Mo., Freedom of Information Center, School of Journalism, University of Missouri, 1964. 4 p. (Publication no. 122)
F 7

A study of the pros and cons of community antenna television. A second report from the Center appeared in 1965 (Publication no. 135), and a third report of developments was reported in 1966 (Publication no. 152).

Feibelman, Herbert U. "How Can 'Trial by Newspaper' Be Avoided? A League Committee Explores the Question." *Commercial Law Journal*, 70:100–101+, April 1965.
F 8

Report of a committee of the Commercial Law League.

Felsher, Howard, and Michael Rosen. *The Press in the Jury Box: The Case Against Trial by Newspaper.* New York, Collier-Macmillan, 1966. 239 p.
F 9

Using numerous examples from press coverage and court decisions the authors show how excessive pretrial publicity in newspapers, radio, and television has interfered with a fair trial for the defendants. In a final chapter the authors offer possible remedies. A critical review of the book appears in the May 1966 issue of the *ALA Newsletter on Intellectual Freedom*.

Ferry, W. H., Harry S. Ashmore, *et al. Mass Communications* with a View of our press by 14 foreign journalists and a discussion by Center staff members. Drawings by Robert Osborn. Santa Barbara, Calif., Center for the Study of Democratic Institutions, 1966. 39 p. (Occasional Paper).
F 10

"One of the basic issues defined by the Center as central to the well-being of the free society arises from political, social, and cultural responsibilities of mass communications. This publication brings together a wide variety of disparate views of the media, and discusses possible cures for what most thoughtful Americans agree is one of the most serious of our contemporary afflictions."

Fey, Harold E. "Truth and Censorship." *Library Occurrent*, 21:283–88, December 1965. **F11**
The speed of change, the advances in technology and communication enlarge the arena in which decisions must be made. "They also heighten the danger of mistake and make necessary the most careful examination of ideas." The author, a professor of theology, believes that our peril is created not by the wholly ignorant but by the half-educated who hold a conspiratorial view of history. "Our salvation lies in keeping our nerve, in holding open against all challengers the doors of knowledge through maintaining the freedom and integrity of our libraries, our schools, our news media, our ministries of service to people at home and abroad."

Finman, Ted, and Stewart Macaulay. "Freedom to Dissent: The Vietnam Protests and Words of Public Officials." *Wisconsin Law Review*, 1966:632–723, Summer 1966. **F12**
The article deals with public statements directed at the propriety of protests against American government policies in Vietnam.

Fischer, Ruth. "TV: No Place for Satire." *Nation*, 202:470, 18 April 1966. **F13**
A burlesque of Peyton Place (Parma Place) over a Cleveland TV station brought protests from residents of Parma, Ohio, and the program was banned.

Fisher, Paul. "The Press, the Government and Society." *Grassroots Editor*, 8(1):3–6, January–February 1967. **F14**
The major reason for the press not doing a better job of informing its readers is not government control or news management, but the response or lack of response in readers. A good newspaper is rendered impossible by "their general conservatism, their resistance to change and mental effort in the reading process, their willingness to accept the bland and oleaginous, their unwillingness to view the unpleasant except where personalities are involved, their distaste for dissent, and their willingness to punish the dissenter."

Fishman, Andrew M. "Libel—Newspapers—A New First Amendment Safeguard." *Western Reserve Law Review*, 15:803–7, September 1964. **F15**
New York Times Co., v. Sullivan, 376 U.S. 254 (1964).

Fleishman, Stanley. "Obscenity: The Exquisitely Vague Crime." *Law in Transition*, 2:97–110, Spring 1965. **F16**

The author reviews recent Supreme Court cases on obscenity, finding that there is "no judicial consensus as to the verbal formula to be utilized in separating obscene from constitutionally protected speech, and even less agreement as to the meaning of the words used." He concludes that the final solution to the obscenity dilemma will come only when the court affords works dealing with sex the same rights accorded all other expression.

Fleming, Thomas J. "'A Scandalous, Malicious and Seditious Libel.'" *American Heritage*, 19(1):22–27, 100–106, December 1967. **F17**
An account of the case of Harry Croswell, editor of the New York *Wasp*, and his trial for alleged libel of Thomas Jefferson.

Forkosch, Morris D. "Freedom of the Press: Croswell's Case." *Fordham Law Review*, 33:415–48, March 1965. **F18**
An analysis of the case of Harry Croswell, editor of *The Wasp*, a Federalist newspaper of Hudson, N.Y., indicted in 1803 for criminal libel.

Foxe, John. *Acts and Monuments of John Foxe . . . With a Preliminary Dissertation, by the Rev. George Townsend . . . Edited by the Rev. Stephen Reed Cottley . . .* London, Seeley and Burnside, 1837–41. Vol. 4, pp. 557–704. (First published in 1563) **F19**
In Book VIII of his *Acts*, Foxe reports on the action taken against the clergy and laity by Henry VIII and his bishops for publishing, selling, and reading heretical books. "Seven godly martyrs" burned at Coventry for teaching their children the Lord's Prayer and the Ten Commandments in English (1519), and Thomas Harding burned for reading an English book of prayers and for possessing English books of scripture under the boards of his floor (1532). Foxe also reports on the controversy over the book, *The Supplication of Beggers* by Simon Fish (1531), and the prohibition against the Tyndale translation of the New Testament by Cuthbert Tonstall, Bishop of London, and gives the text of Henry VIII's first proclamation containing a list of prohibited books, drawn up in 1529 with the help of the clergy. He tells the documented story of the martyrdom of Thomas Bilney, Richard Bayfield, John Teukesbury, and James Bainham, all burned in 1531 or 1532 under the authority of the proclamation. "Occasional executions for circulation of Reformation literature took place," writes Fredrick Siebert, "until Henry's final breach with Rome in 1534; then begins the list of executions of the adherents of Rome headed by Sir Thomas More and Bishop Fisher."

Frank, John P. "Obscenity: Some Problems of Values and the Use of Experts." *Washington Law Review*, 41:631–75, August 1966. **F20**

The author favors the "pandering test"; he concludes that under the current court decisions the standards of obscenity are so low as to make experts superfluous; he discusses unanswered questions on the relationship of obscenity to social values of crime control and family life.

———, and Robert F. Hogan. *Obscenity, the Law, and the English Teacher.* Champaign, Ill., National Council of Teachers of English, 1966. 62 p. **F21**
Two position papers dealing with the obscenity problem. Lawyer Frank considers the legal basis for determining obscenity in reading materials; NCTE Associate Executive Secretary Hogan responds in terms of the unique problems faced by teachers of English. Both conclude that the answer lies in educating the reader rather than suppressing the literature.

Frankhauser, Mahlon M., and P. Dennis Belman. "The Right to Information in the Administrative Process: A Look at the Securities and Exchange Commission." *Administrative Law Review*, 18:101–35, Winter–Spring 1966. **F22**
"The Securities and Exchange Commission administers a complex of statutes with a predominant regulatory objective of protection of investors. In the performance of its functions the Commission has considerable discretion in requesting and obtaining sensitive corporate information. The authors examine the Commission's dispensing information."

"'Free Press-Fair Trial' Revisited: Defendant-Centered Remedies as a Publicity Policy." *University of Chicago Law Review*, 33:512–30, Spring 1966. **F23**
"This comment will review several measures designed to immunize criminal proceedings from the prejudicial effects of publicity and suggest a system based on automatic relief to defendants as the appropriate next step in limiting the prejudicial effects of extensive coverage of crimes."

"Free Press vs. Fair Trial." *Civil Liberties*, 241:4–6, November 1966. **F24**
A review of this issue since the assassination of President Kennedy, including the Ruby trial, the Sheppard case, the report of the American Bar Association, and the activity of the American Civil Liberties Union.

Freedman, Janet. "The Birch Tree Grows." *Library Journal*, 91:624–28, 1 February 1966. **F25**
"The conviction that libraries and other communications agencies are controlled by Communists and their sympathizers has led the John Birch Society to establish a massive literature distribution program designed to appraise Americans of the 'truth' about the extent and threat of the internal Communist conspiracy."

Freedom of Information Conference. University of Missouri. School of Journalism. *Freedom of Information in the Market Place. A Collection of Opinions Expressed during the Ninth Annual Freedom of Information Conference Held December 4–6, 1966 . . .* Columbia, Mo., Freedom of Information Center, School of Journalism, University of Missouri, 1967. 182 p.　　　**F 26**

Fridman, G. H. L. "Press: Conflicts of Interest." *Law Journal*, 115:509–11, 30 July 1965.　　　**F 27**
Discussion of the report, *The Law and the Press*, issued by *Justice* and the British Committee of the International Press Institute and the book by David Williams, *Not in the Public Interest.*

Friedman, Leon. "The *Ginzburg* Decision and the Law." *American Scholar*, 36:71–91, Winter 1966–67.　　　**F 28**
The author believes that the U.S. Supreme Court was offended by Ginzburg's "taunting and truculant claim to going as far as they had allowed him to" and that the decision "will unquestionably be treated as an aberration in the future." On the other hand, the *Fanny Hill* decision "established a rule that can stay with us for many years to come."

Friendly, Alfred, and Ronald Goldfarb. *Crime and Publicity. The Impact of News on the Administration of Justice.* Washington, D.C., Twentieth Century Fund, 1967. 325 p.　　　**F 29**
"How far, on the one hand, may society go to limit public observation, and, on the other hand, how much impact on the processes of justice resulting from publicity about criminal cases can society tolerate? How can the conflict be resolved or diminished? What accommodations can be made?" A newspaper editor and a trial lawyer in this analysis of actual cases, find that "with all its faults, the press serves the cause of justice far more than it subverts it. For it is the agency of public scrutiny." They call for self-regulation rather than imposed restrictions on the press. Their recommendations include procedures for the Bar and law enforcement agencies, legal filtering procedures, experimentation in the use of television in the courtroom, advice on use of contempt power (they oppose use in the British manner), and remedies within the press for handling news of crime in a more responsible manner. Appendix: Responses from Prosecutors, Press Regulation by Law, and Prejudice at Dallas.

Fritchey, Clayton. "The Leakiest Winter on Record." *Harper's*, 232:42–48, March 1966.　　　**F 30**
A discussion of news leaks.

Frost, John *The Trial of John Frost, for Seditious Words, at Hilary Term, 1793.*

Taken in Short Hand by Ramsey. London, Printed for J. Ridgway and H. D. Symonds, 1794. 54 p.　　　**F 31**
Frost, a lawyer, was brought to trial, accused of shouting in a coffee house: "I am for equality; I see no reason why any man should not be upon a footing with another; it is every man's birth right." He further declared that the English constitution was bad and that he favored having no kings. He was found guilty of seditious libel, despite the eloquent defense of Thomas Erskine, and was sentenced to six months in prison.

Fryer, Peter. *The Birth Controllers.* New York, Stein and Day, 1966. 384 p.　　　**F 32**
"This book gives an account of the chief pioneers of birth control, as family planning used to be called, showing the sort of opposition they encountered and describing their other public activities." The pioneers include: Jeremy Bentham, James Mill, John Stuart Mill, Richard Carlile, Francis Place, Charles Bradlaugh, Annie Besant, and Marie Stopes in England; Robert Dale Owens, Charles Knowlton, Ezra Heywood, Dr. William J. Robinson, and Margaret Sanger in America. Bibliography.

———. "Censorship at the British Museum: The 'Private Case' & Other Mysteries." *Encounter*, 27(4):68–77, October 1966.　　　**F 33**
A complaint that some 5,000 sexological and erotic works kept in the "private case" are not made readily available to the scholar. "Research in erotica at Bloomsbury is a jigsaw puzzle in which the missing pieces are kept from the solver until he knows what is on them."

———. *Private Case-Public Scandal.* London, Secker & Warburg, 1966. 160 p.　　　**F 34**
Good-humored criticism of the practices of the British Museum in shielding the "cupboard books," works of erotica, both from the would-be mutilators and the serious scholars. He lists and describes some 250 erotic books from the collection of some 5,000 pornographic items in the "private case." By means of selected quotations the author analyzes the contents of the clandestine library, exposing some of the uneasy attitudes of the Museum toward its embarrassing secrets. In Chapter 10 the author discusses the contents of the SS collection, books suppressed because they have been withdrawn by their publishers or authors, because they have been the subject of successful libel action, or because they have been deposited on condition that they not be issued for a certain period. Included are *The Fall of Tsingtau* by Jefferson Jones (Boston, Houghton Mifflin, 1915), suppressed by Scotland Yard because it offended the Japanese government; Charles R. Mackay's *Life of Charles Bradlaugh* (1888), considered libelous by the Bradlaugh family; *The Beecher-Tilton Scandal*, and a number of other works considered libelous of Victoria Claflin Woodhull whose husband, John Biddulph Martin, sued the Museum (1894) to prevent its circulation of the *Beecher-Tilton* book which he charged

libeled his wife; *Coronation Commentary* (1937) by Geoffrey Dennis because it libeled the Duke of Windsor; the 1882 Christmas number of *The Freethinker* for which its editor, G. W. Foote, went to prison for blasphemy; and a copy of *Rib Ticklers*, subject of the 1911 blasphemy trial of William Gott.

———. "'To Deprave & Corrupt'" *Encounter*, 28(3):41–44, March 1967. **F 35**
Shortcomings and anomalies in the British Obscene Publications Act of 1959, with special reference to the trial of *Last Exit to Brooklyn*, by Hubert Selby, Jr., before a London magistrate.

Fuller, John G. *Incident at Exeter: The Story of Unidentified Flying Objects over America Today.* New York, Putnam, 1966. 251 p.　　　**F 36**
A report of the author's investigation of a rash of flying-saucer sightings in Exeter, N.H., which he considers a serious business worthy of national attention by science and government. He charges the Air Force with suppressing information. "The censorship of the political powers of the Air Force seems to be exercising authority far beyond the powers assigned to it by the civilian control under which it is supposed to be operating." One of a number of books and articles calling for further investigations and an end to government secrecy.

Gabel, Émile. "Freedom of Information." *America*, 109:133–35, 10 August 1963.　　　**G 1**
Freedom of information has a place in the church today as well as in the world of secular affairs.

Gagnon, Joseph H., and William Simon. "Pornography: Raging Menace or Paper Tiger?" *Trans-action*, 4(8):41–48, July–August 1967.　　　**G 2**
"Pornography is only a minor symptom of sexuality and of very little prominence in people's minds most of the time. Even among those who might think about it most, it results either in masturbation or in the 'collector' instinct." In confronting pornography "agencies of criminal justice, and especially the courts, behave in a very curious manner that is quite dangerous for the freedom of ideas as they might be expressed in other zones of activity such as politics, religion, or the family." The problem is not that pornography represents a "clear and present danger" but that "the kind of thinking prevalent in dealing with pornography will come to be prevalent in controlling advocacy of other ideas as well." The authors are on the staff of the Indiana University Institute for Sex Research.

Gaines, Ervin J. "In the Trenches." *ALA Bulletin*, 60:229–30, March 1966.　　　**G 3**

"Within the scope of our professional competence as librarians, the emphasis must be that we take no sides, that we insist on keeping the lines of communication from being blocked. Pornography is not the real issue at all, for the growth of pornographic literature is only a superficial symptom of the more profound movements . . . In defending the freedom of the press, the only end we envision is the safety of open discussion." Librarians will probably have to "endure with a certain fortitude the charge that we who stand for freedom are antisocial, abnormal, demented, or perverse." In almost every recent case where librarians have stood fast, they have prevailed over the censors.

————. "A Proposed Revision of the Library Bill of Rights." *ALA Bulletin*, 61:409–10, April 1967. **G 4**
Text of present and revised form approved by the ALA Executive Board in January 1967 and by the ALA Council in July 1967.

————. "Spring Harvest Festival." *ALA Bulletin*, 60:551–52, June 1966. **G 5**
Commentary on the U.S. Supreme Court's "three-act musical comedy on obscenity, 'Mishkin, Ginzburg, and Fanny Hill.'"

Gazette: International Journal for Mass Communications Studies. Leiden, Holland. 1955–date. Quarterly. **G 6**
In addition to carrying occasional articles relating to press freedom, each issue includes a general bibliography, listing international literature.

Geis, Gilbert. "Identifying Delinquents in the Press." *Federal Probation*, 29:44–49, December 1965. **G 7**
This sociologist concludes that "a program involving the publication of identifying information about youths appearing before the juvenile court is likely to cause more social and individual harm than it is likely to eliminate."

Gerber, Albert B. *Sex, Pornography and Justice.* New York, Lyle Stuart, 1965. 349 p. **G 8**
A history of literary censorship, with emphasis on the contemporary scene in the United States and Great Britain. Includes recent Supreme Court decisions and the difficulties the courts have found over the years in trying to establish a definition of the obscene. The book includes the text of two early banned works, *The Fifteen Plagues of a Maidenhead* and John Wilkes's *Essay on Woman*, and extracts from *Fanny Hill*, *Candy*, the homosexual magazine, *One*, and a number of pornographic novels. The author is an American lawyer, with experience in cases involving pornography. The publishers plan annual supplements to keep the book up-to-date. Reviewed in the

May 1966 issue of the *ALA Newsletter on Intellectual Freedom.*

Getz, Leon. "Problem of Obscenity." *University of British Columbia Law Review*, 2:216–32, March 1965. **G 9**
"It is the purpose of this article to explore some of the implications of the new ⌐obscenity⌐ test. Specifically, attention will be directed to the problem of ascertaining community standards of acceptance, and to some of the factors relevant to a determination of the extent to which they are or should be relevant for legal purposes. Some general comments will then be offered about the problem of controlling obscene literature." Particular reference to the Canada Supreme Court decision, *Brodie, Dansky and Rubin v. R.,* Can. Sup. Ct. 681 (1962).

Giglio, Ernest D. *The Decade of "The Miracle," 1952–1962: A Study in the Censorship of the American Motion Picture.* Syracuse, N.Y., Syracuse University, 1964. 361 p. (D.S.S. dissertation, University Microfilms, no. 65–3418) **G 10**

Gillard, William A. "Freedom to Read: Censorship with Responsibilities." *Hospital Progress*, 45:92–96, December 1964. **G 11**
"Censorship represents a prudent solicitude on the part of responsible adults to protect the innocent against anything that may be psychically harmful. The author ⌐Director of Libraries, St. John University⌐ makes some observations on the moral evaluation of modern realistic literature, particularly as it involves the so-called controversial books. He says censorship is not to be construed as harshly condemnatory but as a benevolent guide. He offers eight basic guidelines for Catholic novelists and readers."

Gillette, Paul J. *An Uncensored History of Pornography.* Los Angeles, Holloway House, 1965. 224 p. **G 12**
A witty but scholarly survey of pornographic literature from the Golden Age of Greece where it flourished, through its subsequent decline in the Middle Ages, its secret revival in the eighteenth and nineteenth centuries, and its meteoric rise in the post-Freudian world of the twentieth century. The author defines and analyzes the role of pornography and comments throughout on efforts to control and suppress it. The appendix lists authors and works of erotica.

Gillis, Kenneth L. "Obscenity: The Man, Not the Book." *Illinois Bar Journal*, 55:462–72, February 1967. **G 13**
The *Ginzburg* case emphasizes the freedom not to read, or be annoyed by unsolicited obscene material. The *Roth* test can be short-circuited "if the disseminator's only sales pitch—for an item of minimal social value—is a brazen boast that his wares are obscene."

Gillmor, Donald M. "The Puzzle of Pornography." *Journalism Quarterly*, 42:363–72, Summer 1965. **G 14**
"The author discusses the philosophic conflict, the legal aspects and the definitional dilemma involved in the areas of obscenity and hard-core pornography, and challenges some current beliefs."

————. "Reardon Report: A Journalist's Assessment." *Wisconsin Law Review*, 1967:215–30, Winter 1967. **G 15**
A criticism of the report of the Advisory Committee on Fair Trial and Free Press of the American Bar Association. "In spite of considerable resources, prestige, and what might have been rare access to real and prospective jurors, the committee's effort shows no evidence of any systematic analysis of the crucial, cause-effect relationship between news reports and jury verdicts."

⌐Ginzburg, Ralph⌐. "Playboy Interview: Ralph Ginzburg." *Playboy*, 13(7):47–54, 120–24, July 1966. **G 16**
"A candid conversation with the convicted publisher of *Eros* and other erotica, condemned by a new Supreme Court criterion for obscenity." The Playboy Forum in the same issue (pp. 41—44, 140–44) is devoted to the *Ginzburg* decision.

Gipe, George A. *Nearer to the Dust; Copyright and the Machine. With A Foreword by Felix Morley.* Baltimore, Williams and Wilkins, 1967. 290 p. **G 17**
A discussion of American copyright law and the recent developments in photocopying and computer storage and retrieval which the author believes threatens independent publishing. In his foreword Felix Morley writes: "Books have often been burned by tyrants who did not agree with the views expressed. A more efficient censorship is to eliminate profit from publishing and then bring that business under political control." The appendix includes the Authors League of America proposal for a licensing system and the Williams and Wilkins Company proposal for a Royalty Clearinghouse Facility. The book represents the point of view of authors and publishers in the controversy over protection of literary property versus wider dissemination of published material, the latter being espoused by librarians and educators.

Girodias, Maurice. "The Erotic Society." *Evergreen Review*, 10(39):64–69, February 1966. **G 18**
An essay in defense of the erotic society and in response to an article by George Steiner attacking the erotic novelist, appearing in *Encounter*, October 1965.

————. "Introduction." In his *The Olympia Reader.* New York, Ballantine Books, 1965, pp. 15–33. **G 19**
The founder of the Olympia Press, Paris, relates his experience in publishing books in

English that were often banned. The editor's introductions to the various selections from the Traveller's Companion Series also frequently refer to the experience with the censor.

Goggin, Terrence P. "Publicity and Partial Criminal Trials: Resolving the Constitutional Conflict." *Southern California Law Review*, 39:275–95, 1966. **G 20**

——, and George M. Hanover. "Fair Trial v. Free Press: The Psychological Effect of Pre-Trial Publicity on the Juror's Ability to Be Impartial; a Plea for Reform." *Southern California Law Review*, 38: 672–88, 1965. **G 21**

Goldberg, Arthur J. "Freedom and Responsibility of the Press." In *Problems of Journalism; Proceedings of the American Society of Newspaper Editors, 1964.* Washington, D.C., 1964, pp. 50–57. **G 22**
"The first and primary responsibility of the press, in my opinion, is therefore as protector and promoter of all the rights and liberties of Americans. The entire Bill of Rights is in the press's charge—not only the free speech clause of the First Amendment . . . Our Constitution has made the press free. You have it in your charge to make it responsible. It is for you to demonstrate that press freedom and responsibility are viable and indivisible concepts." Address to the 1964 ASNE convention when the speaker was associate justice of the U.S. Supreme Court.

Goldberg, Isaac. "A Move to Censor Music." *Haldeman-Julius Monthly*, 1:30–31, December 1924. **G 23**
Ridicule of a proposal in the Kansas City *Star* that music should be censored. "There is a censorship for the film and for the stage [according to the *Star*] yet none for music, for which it is even more needed."

Goldman, Peter. "Supreme Court Decisions." *Censorship*, 2(3):2–9, Summer 1966. **G 24**
Commentary on the *Ginzburg, Fanny Hill,* and *Mishkin* decisions on obscenity made by the U.S. Supreme Court.

Goldsmith, Adolph O. "The Roaring Lyon of Vermont." *Journalism Quarterly*, 39:179–86, Spring 1962. **G 25**
"Matthew Lyon was convicted under the Sedition Act of 1798, was re-elected to Congress while in jail, and cast the vote which made Thomas Jefferson president instead of Aaron Burr in the disputed election of 1800."

Goldstein, Richard. "The Good-Guy Censors." *Village Voice*, 11(43):10, 16, 22, 11 August 1966. **G 26**
An account of censorship of pop music played over radio stations by disc jockeys.

Goodrick, Richard P. "Blackouts vs. Public's Right to Know." *Grassroots Editor*, 7(3):12–13, 36, July 1966. **G 27**
The publisher-enforced newspaper blackout as a weapon against strikes.

Gordon, Giles. "Smith's Choice." *Censorship*, 2(3):37–39, Summer 1966. **G 28**
How the book selection and rejection policies of W. H. Smith & Sons, Ltd., Britain's largest wholesale booksellers, dominate the trade.

Gothberg, Helen. "YA Censorship; Adult or Adolescent Problem?" *Top of the News*, 22:275–78, April 1966. **G 29**
The author recommends that high school librarians give greater attention to the "reaction of the student himself when he first encounters ideas in opposition to his own beliefs." She suggests ways of dealing with situations where the adolescent approaches adult literature for the first time.

Gottesman, Irving. "Ralph Ginzburg Goes to Jail." *Catholic Digest*, 30(12): 70–73, October 1966. **G 30**
"When he admitted that pornography was his business the Supreme Court rejected his appeal."

Grassroots Editor. Carbondale, Ill., International Conference of Weekly Newspaper Editors, 1959–date. Quarterly. **G 31**
The pages of this "journal for editorial writers" frequently carry accounts of weekly newspaper editors subjected to pressures and persecution for expression of their views or for attacking graft, corruption, or vested interests.

Gray, Richard G. *Freedom of Access to Government Information.* Minneapolis, University of Minnesota, 1965. 674p. (Ph.D. dissertation, University Microfilms, no. 65–7882) **G 32**
A study of the federal executive indicates the general level of knowledge about public affairs in the United States has not kept pace with the needs of society. "In a large measure this is because the people's right to know about the Executive Branch has been encroached upon until there is serious danger that the democratic way of life will be rendered unworkable if present trends continue." The author concludes that laws and regulations will not be effective unless there is a government-wide program to educate government officials in releasing information wherever possible.

Gray, Tony. "'Indecent and Obscene': Censorship." In *The Irish Answer.* Boston, Little, Brown, 1966, pp. 241–57. **G 33**
A review of Irish censorship as it exists today.

Great Britain. Court of King's Bench. *Copies Taken from the Records of the Court of King's Bench, at Westminster; the Original*

Office—Books of the Secretaries of State, Remaining in the Paper, and Secretaries of State's Offices, or from the Originals under Seal. Of Warrants Issued by Secretaries of State for Seizing Persons Suspected of Being Guilty of Various Crimes, Particularly, of Being the Authors, Printers, and Publishers of Libels, from the Restoration to the Present Time. . . . London, 1763. 80p. (Compiled by Philip Carteret Webb) **G 34**

Great Britain. Parliament. *The Humble Answer of the Lords and Commons Assembled in Parliament, to the Message of the 25 of August, Received from His Majesty . . . with a Perfect Copy of His Majesties Message . . . With an Order of Both Houses Concerning Irregular Printing and for the Suppression of All False and Scandalous Pamphlets . . .* London, Printed for John Wright, 1642. 4p. **G 35**

Greatorex, Wilfred. "Power Games." *Censorship*, 4(2):25–28, Autumn 1966. **G 36**
The writer discusses his experience with television censorship (Independent Television Authority) in the suppression of a drama series, "The Power Game."

Green, Ervine. "The Right of Privacy—Nature and Extent of Liability for Unauthorized Publication of Pictures." *Nebraska Law Bulletin*, 19:177–89, June 1940. **G 37**
A study of the nature and extent of liability for the unauthorized publication of the picture of another, or the legal right of the person whose picture is published, or another claiming injury from such publication, to prevent or recover damage for such publication.

Greenberg, Henry C. *The Bench, the Bar and the Press: The Main Currents of Our Democracy.* Kingsport, Tenn., Kingsport Press, 1951. 39p. **G 38**
While recognizing the need in a democracy for the total dissemination of knowledge, Justice Greenberg recommends that "reporting be categorized, and exposed to those who have a legitimate need to know the event." He discusses the danger to the judicial process by improper newspaper publicity, praising the British practice of withholding editorial comment pending the outcome of a trial. "The court and the press by working out an agreement to safeguard the freedom that both are dedicated to protect can do so without denying to the people its right to see the processes of justice at work, or infringing upon the liberties of the press."

Greenfield, Jeff. "College Newspapers in Search of Their Own Voice." *Harper's*, 232:87–93, May 1966. **G 39**

The author believes a school should "let its students run the risk of making up their own minds, however mistakenly, however immaturely, and let them offer those opinions at large."

Gropper, Mitchell. "Hate Literature— The Problem of Control." *Saskatchewan Bar Review*, 30:181–94, September 1965. **G 40**

Grossman, James W. "Curbing Obscenity." *Book Week (Washington Post)*, 3(36): 1, 10, 15 May 1966. **G 41**

Commentary on the *Mishkin, Ginzburg* and *Fanny Hill* decisions of the U.S. Supreme Court.

Guback, Thomas H. *Control and Censorship of the Northern Press during the Civil War.* New Brunswick, N.J., Rutgers University, 1958. 226p. (Unpublished B.A. thesis) **G 42**

Gustafson, Gustaf J. "Censorship." *Priest*, 20:295–99, April 1964; 20:401–5, May 1964. (Replies, 20:550–53, June 1964; 20:623, July 1964) **G 43**

Hager, Philip. "A Cat Called Jesus." *Progressive*, 30(4):31–33, April 1966. **H 1**

The public furor in San Diego, Calif., caused by a play, *A Cat Called Jesus*, written by a high school drama teacher. When the school board refused to take action against her the California State Department of Education crudentials committee sat in judgment, questioned the teacher's qualifications to continue in the teaching profession, but found no legal ground for punishment.

Haigh, F. H. "The Indecent Publications Act 1963 and Censorship." *Landfall*, 68:379–83, December 1963. **H 2**

Comparison of the British Act with that of New Zealand.

Haiman, Franklyn S. "Legal and Social Limitations on Freedom of Communication." *Grassroots Editor*, 8(1):9–12, January–February 1967. **H 3**

Despite a remarkable degree of freedom existing in America today there are still limitations. He cites the Supreme Court ruling against Ralph Ginzburg, the self-censorship in radio and television broadcasting, and the public's lack of sympathies with dissenters over Vietnam. He calls for efforts to "narrow the cultural gap between those who understand what freedom of communications is all about and those who do not."

Haldeman-Julius, Emanuel. "The Blight of Censorship and Intolerance in the 'Movies.'" *Haldeman-Julius Monthly*, 1: 3–10, December 1924. **H 4**

An attack on censorship which "robs the movies of virtually every vestige of freedom save that of the indiscriminate throwing of pies." He describes the curious and idiotic inconsistencies of state and city censors, performing in the area of sex and patriotism.

Haley, James O. "Fair Trial and Free Press." *Alabama Lawyer*, 27:374–87, October 1966. **H 5**

"The Irwin, Rideau, Estes and Sheppard decisions, all handed down since 1960, reflect a growing awareness by the Supreme Court that the news media can represent a serious threat to the orderly administration of criminal justice. The latter two cases have greatly strengthened the right of the accused to be free from prejudicial outside interference during his trial."

Halloran, J. D. "TV Violence." *Censorship*, 4(2):15–21, Autumn 1966. **H 6**

The article considers what is known, through research, of the effects on the child of violence and aggression in television programs. The author stresses the need for media education and for support of those creative people in the television industry who, given a change in the existing system of control, would present less stereotyped material.

Hamlin, William R. "Trial by Newspaper: Should It Continue?" *Kentucky Law Journal*, 54:141–54, Fall 1965. **H 7**

"The answer must come, if at all, from the legislatures through the enactment of a law preventing the printing of certain types of prejudicial information, along with the use of the contempt power by a wise and intelligent judiciary."

Hanson, Arthur B. "Developments in the Law of Libel: Impact of the *New York Times* Rule." *William and Mary Law Review*, 7:215–23, May 1966. **H 8**

New York Times Co. v. Sullivan, 376 U.S. 254 (1964).

Harlan, Robert D. "David Hall and the Stamp Act." *Papers of the Bibliographical Society of America*, 61:13–37, First quarter 1967. **H 9**

The effect of the Stamp Act crisis of 1765–66 on the career of a Philadelphia printer.

Harrigan, Anthony. "The Surrender of Privacy." *Nieman Reports*, 12:6–8, July 1958. **H 10**

The growing invasion by agencies of the federal government, poll takers, television cameras, and newspaper photographers prying into human emotions, is a threat to the privacy of the American citizen.

Harrison, John M. "The Press vs. The Courts." *Saturday Review*, 38(42):9–10, 35, 15 October 1955. **H 11**

How sensational coverage of a case by the press injures a defendant's right of trial by jury.

Hartz, F. R. "Combatting Library and Textbook Censorship in Schools." *Clearing House*, 41:264–67, January 1967. **H 12**

Harum, Albert E. "Free Press, Fair Trial Controversy." *Florida Bar Journal*, 40: 231–39, April 1966. **H 13**

Since the use of discretion by the trial judge is a major factor in resolving this conflict, "bar and media alike should bring their powerful forces to bear on seating judicious, learned, and unassailable judges."

Harvey, Arthur. "The Right of Privacy in Fields of Communication and Entertainment." *Intramural Law Review of New York University*, 8:129–53, January 1953. **H 14**

"The plan of the paper is to outline briefly the history of the right of privacy beginning with the incidents leading to the passage of the New York Right of Privacy Statute, and continuing to a comparison of a number of decisions under the statute with holdings in iurisdictions which recognize a common law right of privacy, in an attempt to determine whether any consistent pattern can be found and definite rules established."

Harvey, C. P. "Fair Trial v. Free Press— A British Lawyer's View." *Los Angeles Bar Bulletin*, 42:109–13, January 1967. **H 15**

Harvey, Joseph M. "Trial by Newspaper." *Nieman Reports*, 11(2):18–19, April 1957; 11(3):3–4, July 1957. **H 16**

Taken from a talk made to the Boston Bar Association.

Hastings, Patrick. "Libel and Slander." In his *Cases in Court*. London, Heinemann, 1949, pp. 22–106. **H 17**

This chapter recounts six celebrated British libel cases in which the lawyer-author participated, together with brief commentary on the law of libel: Princess Irena Alexandrovna Youssupoff (the *Rasputin* film), Robert Sievier (race track libel), Harold Laski (*Newark Advertiser*), Mr. Chapman (*Racing Calendar*), Mr. Lambert (B.B.C.), and Mr. Blennerhassett ("Yo-Yo" case against the *Evening Standard*).

Havighurst, Clark C., *ed.* "International Control of Propaganda." *Law and Contemporary Problems*, 31:437–637, Summer 1966. **H 18**

Symposium on the present state of international propaganda and what can be done to "curb the worst abuses to achieve controls in peripheral tension spots, and to reduce even slightly the risks of war inflamed by propaganda."

————. "Privacy." *Law and Contemporary Problems*, 31:251–435, Spring 1966. **H 19**
A symposium on privacy as "a single right entitled to protection against a variety of conflicting interests." Includes articles on The Right to Privacy and American Law by William M. Beaney; Privacy and the Law: A Philosophical Prelude by Milton R. Konvitz; Privacy: Its Constitution and Vicissitudes by Edward Shils; Some Psychological Aspects of Privacy by Sidney M. Jourard; Philosophical Views on the Value of Privacy by Glenn Negley; Privacy in Tort Law—Were Warren and Brandeis Wrong? by Harry Kalven, Jr.; "The Files": Legal Controls Over the Accuracy and Accessibility of Stored Personal Data by Kenneth L. Karst; Privacy in Welfare: Public Assistance and Juvenile Justice by Joel F. Handler and Margaret K. Rosenheim; and The Privacy of Government Employees by William A. Creech.

Hawkins, Gordon J. "Problem of Pornography." *Sydney Law Review*, 5:221–38, September 1966. **H 20**
The author poses the question: "Shall any limits be imposed on the writer's freedom to present and dwell on sexual detail?" He states the case for and against censorship. In the final section he considers the question, Can Pornography Be Literature?

Hayes, John C. "A Position on the Control of Obscenity." *Kentucky Law Journal*, 51:641–55, Summer 1963. (Erroneously published under the name of John C. Levy) **H 21**
The position of the author is that obscene publications "exert a substantial adverse effect on *public* morality and must, therefore, be controlled." Since legal controls can be only minimal, "extra-legal control by private agencies of society which are non-officially concerned with the public welfare and which themselves act only withhin the law is necessary for the common good." The author is dean of the School of Law, Loyola University and, since 1958, legal consultant to the National Office for Decent Literature.

————. "The Recent Obscenity Cases before the Supreme Court." *NODL Newsletter*, 11(1):1–6, Summer 1966. **H 22**
Regarding the *Ginzburg*, *Mishkin*, and *Fanny Hill* cases.

Headingley, Adolph S. *The Biography of Charles Bradlaugh*. 2d ed. London, G. P. Varma, 1889. 332p. **H 23**

Healey, John R. *The California Press and the Brown Act*. Los Angeles, University of California, 1964. 77p. (Unpublished Master's thesis) **H 24**
The Brown Act provides for open access to public records.

[Hefner, Hugh M.]. *The Playboy Philosophy, III*. [Chicago, Playboy Magazine, 1964], pp. 100–158. **H 25**
Installments thirteen through eighteen of editorials by Editor Hefner, appearing in *Playboy* magazine. The editorials deal with aspects of sexual morality and individual freedom, with considerable attention to anti-sexuality in America. Very little deals explicitly with censorship.

[————]. *The Playboy Philosophy, IV*. [Chicago, Playboy Magazine, 1967], pp. 159–94. (Index for series, pp. 95–98) **H 26**
Installments nineteen through twenty-two of Editor Hugh M. Hefner's editorials present a panel discussion on the American Sexual Revolution. Panelists are: Father Norman J. O'Connor, Roman Catholic priest; Reverend Richard E. Gary, Episcopal minister; Rabbi Marc H. Tannenbaum; and Editor Hefner. Topics discussed include sex and the mass media, freedom of and from religion, the nature of obscenity, protecting the young, a censor-free society, self-censorship, and pornography and delinquency. Plans call for publication of the completed series in book form.

Helwig, Gilbert J. "Fair Trial versus Free Press: Must We Choose?" *Judicature* 50:149–52, January 1967. **H 27**
"There is no sensible reason why an increased sensitivity to the rights of defendants in criminal cases demands any reduction in our sensitivity for a free press . . . Our goal should be no less than to be both fair *and* free."

————. "Should Special Facilities Be Provided for Courtroom Photography and Broadcasting?" *Judicature*, 50:163–67, January 1967. **H 28**
In the planning of courtrooms we should not omit provision for the intelligent and effective use therein of photography and broadcasting facilities.

Hennion, Reeve L. *A Survey of the Ralph M. Brown Act*. Palo Alto, Calif., Stanford University, 1965. 94p. (Unpublished Master's thesis) **H 29**
The Brown Act provides for open access to public records.

Herndon, James. "*Sheppard v. Maxwell*: The Sufficiency of Probability." *North Dakota Law Review*, 43:1–16, Fall 1966. **H 30**
Relating to *Sheppard v. Maxwell*, 384 U.S. 333, and the issue of pretrial publicity.

Herr, Dan. "Catholics, Censorship, and Common Sense." *U.S. Catholic*, 31:39–41, September 1965. **H 31**
"Catholics have not always taken a sensible stand on the problem of censorship." Dan Herr offers his ideas on how to avoid excesses for and against freedom of expression.

Herron, Russell L. *Freedom of the College Press: A Moral and Educational Justification*. Urbana, Ill., University of Illinois, 1963. 59p. (Unpublished Master's thesis) **H 32**

H[ess] T. B. "Art, Government and Dirty Books." *Art News*, 65(3):25, May 1966. **H 33**
An editorial satire, suggesting government subsidy for free dirty books, prompted by the Supreme Court decision. It isn't so much what is sold as how it is sold. "The 'panderers' . . . are urged, under the penalty of a stiff jail sentence, to wipe the 'prurient leer' . . . off their faces before they undertake to peddle their wares."

[Hewitt, Cecil R.]. "The Literary Censorship in England." *Kenyon Review*, 29:401–22, June 1967. Written under the pseudonym, C. H. Rolph. **H 34**
A statement on the British Obscene Publications Act of 1959 as it has been administered, the present climate of public feeling about obscenity, and the current trends among publishers and booksellers. The author discusses the proposal of a "publishers' censorship board," the so-called "Cleanup TV" campaign, and observes that the English theater "is on the point of getting rid of the Lord Chamberlain as its censor." While grudging complete freedom to the "septic scribblers" he believes that prosecution of books and pictures under the criminal law is "both pathetic and ridiculous."

[Heywood, George B.]. *Abel Heywood, Abel Heywood & Son, Abel Heywood & Son, Ltd., 1832–1932*. [Manchester, Eng., The Company, 1932?]. 7p. **H 35**
In this brochure issued on the occasion of the centennial of this wholesale news agency, the present head recounts the experience of his grandfather, Abel Heywood, imprisoned in 1832 for distributing the *Poor Man's Guardian* in defiance of the Newspaper Stamp Act.

Hibschman, Harry. "Sex in American Law." *Modern Thinker*, 1:175–85, May 1932. **H 36**
Includes examples of curious legal interpretations of the obscenity laws including an 1877 statement of the Indiana Supreme Court tracing common law of obscenity back to Adam and Eve.

Hildebrand, Berthold. *Der Gedanke der Pressefreiheit im öffentlichen Recht Englands. Eine Studie über ein Grundprinzip des volkssouveränen Staates und Mittel gesellschaftlichen Fortschritts.* Singen s. H., Oberlander Zeitung, 1932. 132 p. (Heidelberg, Jur. Diss., 1932) **H 37**

Hill, Gladwin. "Free Press and Fair Trial—The Witch Hunt." *Frontier, The Voice of the New West,* 18(3):19–21, January 1967. **H 38**
The writer concludes that trials are for the benefit of society, not for the defendant, and that the "peoples' right to know" is paramount.

Hills, Lee. "Free Press AND Fair Trial." *Nieman Reports,* 20(2):15–17, June 1966. **H 39**
The author, executive editor of Knight Newspapers, believes that free press versus fair trial is not a major problem, that the issue arises in a comparatively few sensational cases.

———. "Justice by Daylight—Law and Press Are Allies, Not Antagonists." *Oklahoma Bar Association Journal,* 37:1023–27, 28 May 1966. **H 40**
"It seems self-evident that justice is more likely to be done in the light of day than in the dark."

Hiner, James. "Remembering *Eros.*" *Trace,* 1966–67:481–83, Fall–Winter 1966–67. **H 41**
A reader of Eros criticizes the Supreme Court decision in the *Ginzburg* case.

Hofland, J. A. "The Fight Against the Horror Comics." *Gazette: International Journal of the Science of the Press,* 1:123–24, 1955. **H 42**
Review of action taken in the United States, Great Britain, West Germany, France, and the Netherlands.

Hofstadter, Samuel H. *The Development of the Right of Privacy in New York.* Edited by George Horowitz. New York, Grosly Press, 1954. 92 p. **H 43**
Includes a reprinting of the classic Warren-Brandeis article on the right of privacy.

———, and Shirley R. Levittan. "No Glory, No Beauty, No Stars—Just Mud." *New York State Bar Journal,* 37:38–47, February 1965; 37:116–25, April 1965. **H 44**
"The line to be drawn between pornography and art, obscenity and literature, is often

surrounded by fog. Our readers will find this article . . . sheds new light on a subject now receiving a great deal of judicial attention."

———. "Obscenity; *Roth v. United States;* Summary." *Catholic Lawyer,* 11:225–27, Summer 1965. **H 45**

Hogan, R. F. "Book Selection and Censorship." *Bulletin of the National Association of Secondary School Principals,* 51:67–77, April 1967. **H 46**

Holbrook, David. "Enlightenment or Demoralisation? Literature and the New Morality." *Twentieth Century,* 175:24–26, Summer 1966. **H 47**
"I recognize censorship as a danger . . . . I also believe that a degree of censorship is inevitable. The reason why I believe this is that some human beings have an impulse to harm others, and that we have a problem of hate. . . . The utterance of mind sex, in pornography and near pornography for instance, is both lucrative, and a means of satisfying the unconscious impulse to build one's own identity at the expense of others." The liberal mind is a victim of good-natured belief in human nature, ignoring the destructive evil of hate in sex-expression.

Holley, Ira H. "Obscenity Law—The Bane of the Courts." *Criminal Law Bulletin,* 1(6):3–26, July–August 1965. **H 48**

Hollis, Christopher. "The Roman *Index.*" *History Today,* 16:712–19, October 1966. **H 49**
On 14 June 1966 the Vatican announced the abolition of the *Index of Prohibited Books* the forerunner of which began in the year 405. The article constitutes a brief history of the *Index.*

Holmes, John C. "The Last Cause." *Evergreen,* 44:28–32, 93–99, December 1966. **H 50**
Personal recollection of the author's association in New York with Gershon Legman, book collector and student of erotica and sex literature.

Holmes, Joseph L. "Crime and the Press." *Journal of Criminal Law and Criminology,* 20:6–107, May and August 1929. **H 51**
Newspaper abuses in reporting crime and divorce cases can be met in part by a journalist code of ethics and in part by legislation limiting the press to a mere statement of facts of a crime or divorce case without discussion or pictures.

Hood, Stuart. "Two Approaches." *Censor-*

ship, 2(4):2–5, Autumn 1966. **H 52**
Contrast in the extent of formal censorship of television in Great Britain between B.B.C. and I.T.V. There is whithin the B.B.C no written code or formal machinery of censorship; B.B.C. operates under a very liberal charter which leaves it free to manage its own affairs. The position of I.T.V. differs radically, governed by terms of an Act which requires I.T.V. to serve as watchdog over the companies. In order to discharge its duties, I.T.V. has set up a machinery for censorship.

Hoover, J. Edgar. "Combating Merchants of Filth: The Role of the FBI." *University of Pittsburg Law Review,* 25:469–78, March 1964. **H 53**
"It is essential that high standards of decency be zealously maintained in every phase of community life; for to lower the barriers of good taste and moral acceptability in *any* way—and in the highly vulnerable fields of entertainment, literature and art in particular—is to invite an eventual floodtide of moral corruption and spiritual decay."

———. "The Fight against Filth." *American Legion Magazine,* 70(5):16–18, 48–49, May 1961. **H 54**
The director of the FBI describes the obscenity business in America, its harmful effect on youth, and advises on how the citizen can protect his family and community against obscenity.

Huggins, Roy B. "The Bloodshot Eye: A Comment on the Crisis in American Television." *Television Quarterly,* 1(3):6–22, August 1962. **H 55**
"Huggins suggests that government control of television is a frightening reality. Not only will such interference in programming wash out the fertile acreage commercial television has nurtured, it will leave behind only a thin residual of the silt of conformity, to be tilled inexpertly by nervous licensees and apprehensive program entrepreneurs as they await the next cultural decree from 'The State.'"

Hunnings, Neville M. "Censorship of Lantern Slides." *Cinema Studies,* 2:38, June 1966. **H 56**
A brief note on Canadian legislation of 1912 to bring slides within the film censorship law.

———. *Film Censors and the Law.* Foreword by *Frede Castberg.* London, Allen & Unwin, 1967. 474 p. **H 57**
A comprehensive study of comparative law in the censorship of films in England, the United States, India, Canada, Australia, Denmark, France, and Russia. Appendix contains a list of presidents and secretaries of the British Board of Censors, a list of "x" films distributed, T. P. O'Connor's 43 rules, tables of statutes, and tables of films. Bibliography.

———. "The Silence of *Fanny Hill.*"

Sight and Sound, 35:134–38, Summer 1966.

H 58

The author observes that film censorship and criminal obscenity "have all but fallen in the United States and Scandinavia, and strong liberalizing tendencies can be seen in Britain too." He describes the recent liberalizing tendencies in film and theater censorship in Britain and summarizes events in the United States, Sweden, Denmark, Canada, and New Zealand.

Hunter, Edward. *Attack by Mail*. Linden, N.J., Bookmailer, 1966. 252 p.

H 59

An attack on American policy which permits free flow of Communist propaganda into the United States.

Huntley, R. E. R., and C. F. Phillips, Jr. "Community Antenna Television: A Regulatory Dilemma." *Alabama Law Review*, 18:64–81, Fall 1965.

H 60

"The need for regulation seems insistent, and yet the only convenient criteria for regulatory policy are those drawn from the existing pattern of the industry—criteria which will necessarily yield a policy tending to solidify the existing pattern in perpetuity."

Hyatt, William D. "Fair Trial v. Free Press: The Need for Compromise." *University of Cincinnati Law Review*, 34:503–24, Fall 1965.

H 61

"The inescapable conclusion seems to be that the British system of suppressing publicity during the pendency of a criminal trial affords an accused in Britain a substantially fairer trial than his American counterpart, and the American system of dealing with prejudicial publicity, in its present form, is inadequate to afford an accused a fair trial in the face of heavy news coverage."

Hyman, Lawrence W. "Obscene Words and the Function of Literature." *College English*, 28:432–34, March 1967.

H 62

The author attempts to explain why college students feel impelled to use shocking scenes and obscene language in their college literary efforts, which prompt censorship action.

Inter-American Press Association. *Report of the Committee on Freedom of the Press*. Montego Bay, Jamaica, The Association, 1965 (Doc. 6, English). 28 p. mimeo.

I 1

A country by country discussion of press freedom in North and South America, with lengthy reports on Bolivia and the United States.

International Press Institute. British Committee. *The Law and the Press*. London, Stevens, 1965. 52 p.

I 2

Report of a joint working party of representatives of *Justice* (British Section of the International Commission of Jurists) and of the British Committee of the IPI, headed by Lord Shawcross, recommends changes in British libel laws, official secrets acts, and laws of contempt of court by publication.

Irvine, Keith. "The Film You Won't See; Unofficial Censors at Work." *Nation*, 181:109–10, 6 August 1955.

I 3

Censorship of the French film, *Wages of Fear*, by American film distributors because it showed friction between an American company on foreign soil and the local population. Twenty-two minutes of essential action were deleted.

Jackson, Andrew. ["Seventh Annual Message to Congress, 7 December 1835"]. In James D. Richardson, *ed. Messages and Papers of the Presidents*, vol. 2, New York, Bureau of National Literature, 1907, pp. 1394–95.

J 1

Recommendation for the passage of legislation to "prohibit circulation in the Southern States, through the mail, of incendiary publications intended to instigate the slaves to insurrection." A contemporary illustration (opp. p. 1394) shows the robbing of the United States mails in Charleston, S.C., in order to burn abolitionist literature. Correspondence between Postmaster General Amos Kendall and President Jackson concerning the suppression of abolitionist papers appears in *Correspondence of Andrew Jackson* ed., John S. Bassett, vol. 5, 1931, pp. 359–61. Letters concerning the issue from Postmaster General Kendall to Petersburg, Va., and New York postmasters are published in *Niles' Register*, 49(1, 250):8–9, 5 September 1835.

Jacobson, Dan. "An End to Pornography?" *Commentary*, 42(5):76–82, November 1966.

J 2

An essay on pornography revolving around a favorable review of Steven Marcus' *The Other Victorians*.

Jacobson, David L., *ed. The English Libertarian Heritage from the Writings of John Trenchard and Thomas Gordon in* The Independent Whig *and* Cato's Letters. Indianapolis, Bobbs-Merrill, 1965. 284 p. (American Heritage Series)

J 3

The first American edition of *Cato's Letters*, the work of two eighteenth-century Englishmen, John Trenchard and Thomas Gordon, whose thoughts on freedom of the press were widely read and quoted in both England and America but have only recently been "rediscovered." Also reprinted are selections from Trenchard and Gordon's *The Independent Whig* and an extensive introduction dealing with the careers of the two authors, their philosophy, and their impact on American thought. The editor also provides a publishing history of *Cato's Letters* and *The Independent Whig*.

"Jacqueline B. Kennedy, Plaintiff." *Newsweek*, 68(26):39–43, 26 December 1966.

J 4

An account of the controversy over the publication of William Manchester's *The Death of a President* and the efforts of Mrs. Kennedy to block publication of the book which she had asked the author to write.

Jaffe, Louis L. "Trial by Newspapers." *New York University Law Review*, 40:504–24, May 1965.

J 5

The author concludes that the canons of ethics should be amended to forbid attorneys and police from communicating information except in performance of their duties bearing upon guilt or innocence of accused, and that it be made a crime to publish such information during the course of the trial unless it has been admitted into evidence.

Jameson, John. "Colorado Courts Extend the First Amendment to the Camera." *Quill*, 44(4):7–8, 14 April 1956.

J 6

Following a hearing the Colorado Supreme Court ruled out Canon 35 in Colorado courts.

Janeway, Elizabeth. "'The Toad Beneath the Harrow Knows . . .'" *Library Journal*, 91:887–91, 15 February 1966.

J 7

An author discusses some aspects of copyright revision, and the potential impact upon writers of the technological revolution that is taking place in publishing and library service.

[Jefferson, Thomas]. "The Special Case of Thomas Jefferson." In Leonard W. Levy, *Freedom of the Press from Zenger to Jefferson*. Indianapolis, Bobbs-Merrill, 1966, pp. 327–76.

J 8

Levy considers Jefferson more of a democrat than a libertarian and his comments on the subject more felicitous than profound. Jefferson's thoughts and actions on freedom of the press "revealed ambiguity and tension, contradictions and conflict, as the following documents will show." Included are: the Virginia Bill for Establishing Religious Freedom, draft of the Virginia Constitution (1783), letters to Edward Carrington, James Madison, Noah Webster, Samuel Smith, Elbridge Gerry, Benjamin Rush, Levi Lincoln, Monsieur Pictet, John Tyler, Thomas McKean, Abigail Adams, Thomas Seymour, John Norvell, Walter Jones, N. G. Dufief, and Adamantios Coray, the Kentucky Resolutions of 1798 and excerpts from Jefferson's inaugural addresses.

Jenkins, Dan. "A Trial That Has the South Seething." *Sports Illustrated*, 19(6):18–21, 5 August 1963.

J 9

"Published charges [*Saturday Evening Post*] of a college football fix will be challenged in court next week when ex-Georgia Coach Wally Butts confronts accuser George Burnett in a case nearly as decisive as the 1925 monkey trial." *Wally Butts v. Curtis Publishing Co.* A sketch of the courtroom scene appears in the 19 August issue; the verdict ($3,060,000 to Butts) is reported in the 2 September issue.

Jennings, W. Ivor. *The Sedition Bill Explained by W. Ivor Jennings . . . With a Preface by J. B. Priestly.* London, New Statesman and Nation, 1934, 31 p. **J 10**

"If there is any case for freedom of thought, freedom of expression, and the sanctity of the home, there is a strong and indeed overwhelming case for inducing the Government to withdraw this Bill." Under the bill, the author notes, printers would be held responsible for the opinions they put into print and might expect to have their shops raided by the police.

Jennison, Peter S. "National Service Organization Proposes a Nationwide Survey." *ALA Bulletin,* 59:89–90, February 1965. (Discussion, 59:239, April 1965) **J 11**

The director of National Library Week rejects a proposal from a national service organization that National Library Week be used as a focal point for a nationwide survey of newsstands and libraries to uncover questionable books.

Jensen, Jay W. "Freedom of the Press: A Concept in Search of a Philosophy." In Marquette University, College of Journalism. *Social Responsibility of the Newspress.* [Milwaukee, The College, 1962], pp. 71–88. **J 12**

"What is most urgently required for the rehabilitation of the concept of freedom of the press is a new metaphysics—a metaphysics that will restore what Positivism, Romanticism, Collectivism, and other derivative isms have lately destroyed: an image of the self as ontologically independent of Culture and existentially related to an objective order of values."

———. *William Cobbett: John Bull as Journalist and Defender of Press Freedom.* Iowa City, Iowa, Association for Education in Journalism, 1966. 18 p. mimeo. (Presented at convention of the Association, University of Iowa) **J 13**

Cobbett was not one to theorize on press freedom but asserted his principles when his own freedom or that of others was being threatened.

Jensen, Oliver. "Filial Piety and the First Amendment." *American Heritage,* 18(6):2–4, October 1967. **J 14**

The editor of *American Heritage* discusses the case of *Frick v. Stevens.* The magazine is a member of an *ad hoc* committee "to fight this and any other infringement of the constitutional rights of historians to publish freely."

Johnson, Lawrence R. "The Limits of Political Speech: *New York Times v. Sulivan*

Revisited." *UCLA Law Review,* 14:631–52, January 1967. **J 15**

Comments on *New York Times Co. v. Sullivan,* 376 U.S. 254 (1964). The author suggests areas for expansion of the *New York Times* rule to promote communication of values vital to a free society.

Johnson, Miles B. *The Government Secrecy Controversy; a Dispute Involving the Government and the Press in the Eisenhower, Kennedy, and Johnson Administrations.* New York, Vantage, 1967. 136 p. **J 16**

Johnson, Pamela Hansford. *On Iniquity, Some Personal Reflections Arising Out of the Moors Murder Trial.* London, Macmillan, 1967. 142 p. **J 17**

A discussion of the power of literature to deprave and corrupt. While concerned with the "near-license" in sex expression that exists, she is reluctant to recommend any extension or relaxation of present censorship until effects of "total license" have had a serious public examination. Kenneth Allsop criticizes Miss Johnson's views in the July 1967 issue of *Encounter.*

———. "We Need More Censorship." *Saturday Evening Post,* 240:8, 10, 14 January 1967. **J 18**

"Total license in the arts at best engenders boredom and produces a kind of ghastly sameness; at worst it produces a combination of sex and sadism. . . . A sensibility blunted by cruelty in art will become blunted to it in life." The author objects particularly to the presentation of cruelty for the purpose of kicks. While opposed to police censorship, she suggests for the theater "a small censoring body which could, with wisdom, apply an initial check" and "a powerful Court of Appeals, consisting of open-minded persons, preferably attached to learned institutions." There is no evidence that complete freedom from censorship will produce great art but considerable evidence that great works of art and literature were produced during periods when some censorship prevailed.

Johnson, Pyke, Jr. "Censorship, Critical Thinking, and the Paperback." *Library Journal,* 90:296–301, 15 January 1965. **J 19**

A paperback publisher discusses censorship of children's books, emphasizing the need to expand the scope of the child's reading. He cites a stement in defense of *The Catcher in the Rye* by the Hamden, Conn., Public Library. He notes the vulnerability of paperbacks to the censor because their low price makes them more likely to fall into the hands of children.

Jones, Bill R. "Defamation of a Public Official in Texas." *Baylor Law Review,* 18:583–605, Fall 1966. **J 20**

The current status of the law in Texas concerning the recovery of damages by a public

official for libelous newspaper articles relating to his official conduct, in light of *New York Times Co. v. Sullivan* decision.

Jones, D. A. N., Peter Fryer, and C. H. Rolph [pseud. for C. R. Hewitt]. "The Trouble with Censorship." *New Statesman,* 72:912–13, 16 December 1966. **J 21**

Three writers comment separately on the present state of affairs on obscenity censorship in Britain, including the case against *The Last Exit to Brooklyn.*

Jones, Nancy. *Press Codes, American and Foreign.* Columbia, Mo., Freedom of Information Center, School of Journalism, University of Missouri, 1966. 6 p. (Publication no. 160) **J 22**

A review of codes of ethics of American news organizations in relation to press codes and press councils abroad.

Jones, Penry. "Important Moral Issues: The Censorship of Books, Radio and Television." *Expository Times,* 75:333–37, August 1964. **J 23**

Joseph, Helen. "Letter from Captivity." *Atlas,* 7:138–41, March 1964. **J 24**

"Helen Joseph is a victim of South Africa's earlier censorship laws. In this article · she predicts that the new law will completely suppress all opinion—in politics as well as in the arts—displeasing to the government. In 1962 Miss Joseph was sentenced to five years' house arrest. From her confinement she managed to forward the manuscript [of this article] to the Australian weekly [*Nation*] in which it appeared."

Journal of Broadcasting. Los Angeles, Association for Professional Broadcasting Education, 1956–date. Quarterly. **J 25**

Issues frequently carry articles dealing with aspects of freedom and controls in broadcasting. Also a source of information on new books and articles.

Kahn, Gordon. *Hollywood on Trial; the Story of the 10 Who Were Indicted.* Foreword by Thomas Mann. New York, Boni & Gaer, 1948. 229 p. **K 1**

The House Un-American Activities Committee publicly accused ten leading Hollywood writers and directors with being agents of un-American propaganda in the motion picture industry. When the accused refused to testify they were indicted for contempt and were blacklisted by the film industry.

Kansas Bar Association, *et al. Fair Trial & Free Press. A Dialogue Sponsored by the Kansas Bar Association in Cooperation with the University of Kansas Law School and the*

William Allen White School of Journalism, University of Kansas . . . Columbia, Mo., Freedom of Information Center, University of Missouri, 1967. 52 p. **K 2**
"Moderator John Colburn introduces the program. Ernest C. Friesen, Jr., argues for withholding certain types of evidence; thinks remedies provided to ensure fair trial are no longer adequate. F. Lee Bailey places the onus upon those in a position to disclose information; believes greater respect for the presumption of innocence should be preserved by all. Professor Fred E. Inbau describes misconceptions about the state of criminal justice; suggests that ultra civil libertarians now bring on a greater evil. Glen E. King replies to suggestions that the bar set up penalties against police officers who reveal information. J. Edward Murray speaks for press scrutiny of the law at the arrest stage; thinks over-reactions to Sheppard [decision] and Reardon [report] may encourage secret law enforcement. Morris A. Shenker says some information serves no purpose in keeping society informed and should not be released. Bruce Dennis points out radio and television news directors' objections to proposals of the Reardon Committee . . . Professor David L. Shapiro discusses the work and recommendations of the ABA advisory Committee on Fair Trial and Free Press. Arthur B. Hanson criticizes the work and recommendations of the Reardon Committee. W. Theodore Pierson states reforms desirable in parts II and IV of the Reardon report . . . Justice Tom C. Clark discusses opinions of the Supreme Court that pertain to inherent prejudice and pre-trial publicity."

Kaplan, Benjamin. *An Unhurried View of Copyright.* New York, Columbia University Press, 1967. 142 p. **K 3**
Analysis of the law of copyright in light of technical and social developments. *Copyright and Intellectual Property* by Julius J. Marke (Fund for the Advancement of Education, 1967), received too late for a separate entry, discusses the conflict between publishers and educators over the right to copy.

Katzenbach, Nicholas deB. "Fair Trial and Free Press." In *Problems of Journalism; Proceedings of the American Society of Newspaper Editors, 1965,* pp. 94–101. **K 4**
The talk by Attorney General Katzenbach was followed by a panel discussion by Clifton Daniel, *New York Times*; Edward W. Brooke, Massachusetts Attorney General; Judge J. Skelly Wright, and Felix R. McKnight of the Dallas *Times Herald.*

Keating, Charles H., Jr., and James J. Clancy. *Commentaries on the Law of Obscenity.* Cincinnati, Citizens for Decent Literature, 1965. 95 p. (Vol. 1, no. 1) **K 5**
Contents: Propriety of Judicial Criticism; A General Criticism of United States Supreme Court Obscenity Decisions; A Criticism of *Arizona v. Locks*; A Model Obscenity Statute; and Scienter.

Keyhoe, Donald E. *Flying Saucers: Top Secret.* New York, Putnam, 1960. 283 p. **K 6**
In this and other books by Major Keyhoe charges are made that the Air Force is deliberately suppressing news about unidentified flying objects (UFO's).

Kimble, Theodore H. *Freedom of the Press in the American Constitution.* Urbana, Ill., University of Illinois, 1947. 142 p. (Unpublished Master's thesis) **K 7**

Kingsley, Robert G. *Canon 35 : IV.* Columbia, Mo., Freedom of Information Center, School of Journalism, University of Missouri, 1966. 5 p. (Publication no. 162) **K 8**
Events of the past three years relating to the American Bar Association's prohibition of photography in the courtroom.

——— . *Injunctions against Media.* Columbia, Mo., Freedom of Information Center, School of Journalism, University of Missouri, 1966. 7 p. (Publication no. 172) **K 9**
"Not content with seeking damages for libel or invasion of privacy, an increasing number of 'injured parties' have tried to muffle the media with injunctions halting dissemination of the material in question." An examination of recent cases involving this type of legal action.

Kingston, Jeremy. "Criticism: Theatre." *Punch*, 250:550–51, 13 April 1966. **K 10**
Proposal for a Select Committee of Censors, made up of "genial, permissive men and women of the world, indulgent when in doubt," to which management might turn for advice on whether or not a play was objectionable.

Kintner, Earl W. "Federal Trade Commission Regulation of Advertising." *Michigan Law Review*, 64:1269–84, May 1966. **K 11**
Deals with the origin of federal regulation of advertising, the expansion of FTC jurisdiction and enforcement powers, and typical patterns of deception.

Klein, Robert J. "Film Censorship: The American and British Experience." *Villanova Law Review*, 12:419–56, Spring 1967. **K 12**
The author examines the historical development of film censorship in the United States, with its city and state regulations and industry controls through the Production Code, and the British experience in film censorship through the Board of Film Censors and using a film classification scheme.

Knight, Arthur, and Hollis Alpert. "The History of Sex in Cinema." *Playboy*,

12(4):127–37, April 1965; 12(5):134–38, May 1965; 12(6):155–60, 174–81, June 1965; 12(8):114–20, 126–32, August 1965; 12(9):170–77, 244–55, September 1965; 12(11):150–57, 208–21, November 1965; 13(2):134–40, 167–72, February 1966; 13(4):142–50, 201–17, April 1966; 13(8): 120–28, 149–54, August 1966; 13(9): 172–78, 206–16, September 1966; 13(10): 150–60, 164–87, October 1966; 13(11): 162–85, November 1966; 13(12):232–58, December 1966; 14(1):95–108, 130, 222–34, January 1967; 14(4):136–43, 196–212, April 1967; 14(6):124–36, 177–88, June 1967; and three subsequent issues. (To be published in book form.) **K 13**
Contents: 1. The Original Sin. 2. Compounding the Sin. 3. The Twenties—Hollywood's Flaming Youth. 4. The Twenties—Europe's Decade of Decadence and Delirium. 5. Sex Stars of the Twenties. 6. The Thirties—Censorship and Depression. 7. The Thirties—Europe's Decade of Unbuttoned Erotica. 8. Sex Stars of the Thirties. 9. The Forties—War and Peace in Hollywood. 10. War and Peace in Europe. 11. Sex Stars of the Forties. 12. The Fifties—Hollywood Grows Up. 13. The Fifties—Sex Goes International. 14. Sex Stars of the Fifties. 15. Experimental Films. 16. The Nudies. 17. Stag Movies. 18. The Sixties—Hollywood Unbuttons. 19. The Sixties—Eros Unbound in Foreign Films. 20. Sex Stars of the Sixties.

Knudson, Rozanne. "And the Years Pass Away." *Journal of Secondary Education*, 41:43–44, January 1966. **K 14**
Despite three years passing after the issuance of "The Students' Right to Read" by the National Council of Teachers of English, censorship continues in the English classroom and the school library.

——— . *Censorship in English Programs of California's Junior Colleges.* Palo Alto Calif., Stanford University, 1967. 236 p. (Ph. D. dissertation) **K 15**

——— . "My Mother, the Censor." *Teachers College Record*, 67:363–66, February 1966. (Reprinted in *ALA Bulletin* 60:6113–16, June 1966) **K 16**
An almost fictionized account, written in terms of affection, of the author's mother, a book-lover who in the name of maternal love and a determination to protect all children from "unworthable" books, has extended her censorship activities to the community. Her methods are unorthodox—"to snatch the book or urge, implore, wheedle, cajole, bully, pay, drive, nag, lead, and expect

teachers, librarians, and administrators to snatch them *in loco* mother."

——. "'Phonography' or the Humorous Side of Censorship." *California School Libraries*, 37(2):7–8, January 1966. **K 17**
A collection of humorous anecdotes involving censors and censorship.

Konvitz, Milton R. "Censorship of Literature." In his *Expanding Liberties; Freedom's Gains in Postwar America.* New York, Viking, 1966, pp. 168–242. **K 18**
An extensive review of the problem of obscenity as considered by the American courts. The author concludes that we need to know more about the effects of obscene publications and suggests an Anglo-American study of the problem. He considers the Supreme Court's use of "contemporary standards," its difficulties in defining the term "obscene," and its use of the criterion of "social importance." Despite the Court's denial that obscenity is constitutionally protected, the acts of the Court say it is protected. Konvitz asks for basic sympathy for the Court as it continues to strive for a solution to this difficult problem.

Kopkind, Andrew. "May It Please the Court." *New Republic*, 153:9–10, 18 December 1965. **K 19**
Account of the testimony given before the U.S. Supreme Court in the *Ginzburg, Mishkin,* and *Fanny Hill* cases.

Kopple, Robert. "Balancing of Free Press and Fair Trial—Inherent Prejudice from Mass Publicity." *DePaul Law Review*, 16:203–9, Autumn–Winter 1966. **K 20**
Sheppard v. Maxwell, 384 U.S. 333 (1966).

Krahling, William D. "Labor's Charge of 'Unfair': A Libel Risk for Newsmen." *Journalism Quarterly*, 38:347–50, Summer 1961. **K 21**
"The author examines six court cases involving publication of charges by a labor union that a business was 'unfair' to labor. He concludes that the outcome of the most recent suit, against a Kentucky newspaper, indicates a need for caution in the handling of references to 'unfair to labor' lists."

Krueger, Robert. "What's All This . . . About Pornography?" *Los Angeles Law Bulletin*, 40:505–20, August 1965. **K 22**
An exploration of some of the nonlegal source material about pornography brought out through extensive footnotes. The author concludes that we should accept pornography and put it in its inferior place and not attempt to collectively draw a line around it. "Let the reader do it—let him decide whether it is erotic realism, hard-core pornography, or whether it is worth reading at all."

Kruger, Frederick. *Privacy and the Press.* Columbia, Mo., Freedom of Information Center, School of Journalism, University of Missouri, 1967. 8p. (Report no. 176) **K 23**
"The increasing trend toward privacy (as opposed to libel) actions has posed new problems for media in the area of false or 'fictionalized,' but non-defamatory reports. The background of this situation and implications of the most recent court decisions—including *Time, Inc. v. Hill*—are presented here."

Kruger, Helen N. *The Access to Federal Records Law.* Columbia, Mo., Freedom of Information Center, School of Journalism, University of Missouri, 1967. 7p. (Center Report, no. 186) **K 24**
"Critics say the language of the new Freedom of Information Act is vague and wonder if the law goes far enough. Nine categories of records are exempted."

Kuh, Richard H. *Foolish Figleaves: Pornography In and Out of Court.* New York, Macmillan, 1967. 352p. **K 25**
The author, a lawyer, discusses court decisions on pornography and the problems in attempting to censor it. He suggests "reasonably precise statutes" that will combat pornography and yet meet constitutional objections: control of public displays of nudity or sexual activity for advertising purposes, control of public shows, and control over presentations of nudity or sexual activity to minors for profit. The author would focus attention on the audience for whom contraband is intended.

Kurtz, Robert S. "The Right to Privacy: A Legal Guidepost to Television Programming." *Journal of Broadcasting*, 6: 243–54, Summer 1962. **K 26**
The article is designed "to provide the non-lawyer broadcaster with some guides for minimizing the influence of the 'right to privacy' on the 'right to know.'"

LaFarge, Oliver. "A Ban on *Laughing Boy*." In his *The Man with the Calabash Pipe.* Edited by W. T. Scott. Boston, Houghton Mifflin, 1966, pp. 101–3. **L 1**
The author expresses his surprise and sadness that his first novel has been removed from the libraries of the public schools of Amarillo, Tex., on grounds of obscenity. He considers the action a "false smirching."

Lambert, J. W. "The Folly of Censorship." *Encounter*, 29(1):60–62, July 1967. **L 2**
The literary editor of the *Sunday Times* defends his views on censorship—that in the field of the arts and entertainment any form of censorship is undesirable and unnecessary.

Lambert, Richard S. *Propaganda.* London,
Nelson, 1938. 165p. (Discussion Books, no. 13) **L 3**
Chapter 8 deals with censorship, "the negative form of propaganda," with special reference to Britain in World War I.

Lapid, Joseph. "The *Exodus* Trial." *Fact*, 3(3):59–61, May–June 1966. **L 4**
The British libel trial against Leon Uris, author of the best-seller *Exodus*, brought by Dr. W. A. Dering, accused of performing experiments in human sterilization in Auschwitz prison. The jury awarded Dering damages of "one ha'penny" and the judge made Dering responsible for the $75,000 incurred by the defense. The author criticizes the American press for printing virtually nothing about the trial.

Larsen, Otto N. "Controversies about the Mass Communication of Violence." *Annals of the American Academy of Political and Social Science*, 364:37–49, March 1966. **L 5**
"Few would dispute that American mass communication dispenses large doses of violence to audiences ever growing in size. Two related controversies stem from this fact. One concerns the question of effects and the other the problem of control. An inventory of relevant research is inconclusive about effects, partly because of varying conceptions of what constitutes evidence. A dynamic opinion process leads to control efforts. Critics play a vital part in defining discontent. A reciprocal relationship emerges between the public, the critic, and the media. American media respond to controversy and threat of censorship with systems of self-regulation. These grow out of public opinion and are sustained by it in a delicate balance dependent somewhat on developing knowledge of the effects of violence."

Larson, Arthur. "The Present Status of Propaganda in International Law." *Law and Contemporary Problems*, 31:439–51, Summer 1966. **L 6**
"As to warmongering, subversive, and defamatory propaganda by states, the illegality of propaganda is established. As to the liability of states for acts of individuals, the special circumstances under which responsibility exists can be identified, with non-liability in other circumstances remaining the current role. Finally, as to individuals themselves, they are substantively responsible for illegal acts committed on behalf of states, when the states themselves would be responsible, but for acts of private propaganda their responsibility is less clear, except where domestic statutes have dealt with the topic."

Larson, Orvin. *American Infidel: Robert G. Ingersoll.* New York, Citadel, 1962. 316p. **L 7**
This biography of a flamboyant American agnostic includes chapters dealing with Ingersoll's defense of freedom of speech and of the press. A chapter on obscenity treats of Ingersoll's participation in the conventions

of the National Liberal League, his quarrel with other liberals over repeal of the Comstock laws (Ingersoll favored amendment, not repeal), and his defense of Ezra Heywood, convicted of obscenity. It also deals with Ingersoll's defense of De Robigne M. Bennett on obscenity charges and his eventual break with Bennett and withdrawal from the National Liberal League over objections to free love. Elsewhere are accounts of Ingersoll's lifelong confrontation with the blasphemy laws—both for his own statements and in behalf of others, particularly Charles B. Reynolds of Morristown, N.J. In the latter case, Reynolds was convicted despite an eloquent defense by Ingersoll.

Laser, Marvin, and Norman Fruman. "Not Suitable for Temple City." In their *Studies in J. D. Salinger*. New York, Odyssey, 1963, pp. 124–29.   **L8**
The editors relate the controversy over *The Catcher in the Rye* in the high school at Temple City, Calif.

Lassiter, William C. *Law and the Press; The Legal Aspects of News Reporting, Editing and Publishing in North Carolina*. Rev. ed. Raleigh, N.C., Edwards and Broughton, 1956. 262 p.   **L9**
Chapters on civil and criminal libel, contempt, right of privacy, access to public records, and a free press and the right to a fair trial.

Lawlor, Pat. "Censorship Problem." *New Zealand Law Journal*, 1964:440–44, 20 October 1964; 1964:464–68, 3 November 1964.   **L10**
A New Zealand author and critic reviews literary censorship in New Zealand, deploring the surge of obscene works which menace our freedom. There must be some sensible control of books, but thus far efforts have failed. "Let us all face this problem bravely and broad-mindedly: forget that word censorship and replace it with a sense of responsibility, one to another."

Lawton, Sherman P. "Who's Next?: The Retreat of Canon 35." *Journal of Broadcasting*, 2:289–94, Fall 1958.   **L11**
"Three hundred attorneys and judges in Oklahoma's seventy-seven counties were queried as to their attitudes on still photography, motion pictures and live television in the courtroom. It became clear that the more experience lawyers and judges had with such coverage, the more favorable they were toward it."

Lazarus, Jonathan G. *American Military Control of News during World War II*. New Brunswick, N.J., Rutgers University, 1964. 136 p. (Unpublished Bachelor's thesis)   **L12**

League of Nations. International Bureau. *International Convention concerning the Use of Broadcasting in the Cause of Peace*. (Geneva, *September 23rd, 1936*). Geneva, The League, 1936. 11 p. (League of Nations Publications, 1936. XII. B. 10)   **L13**
The Convention covers the prohibition of broadcasting that would incite violence or illegal acts in another nation or encourage another nation to wage war.

Leavy, Zad. "Protection from Group and Class Defamation by Extremists." *Los Angeles Bar Bulletin*, 40:23–29, November 1964.   **L14**
"What reason is there to deny to members of large groups and classes the right to protection from inflammatory defamation designed to weaken through hatred their prestige and position in the community?" The author believes there is need for a balance to be struck between the interests of freedom of speech and class defamation.

Leder, Lawrence H. "The Role of Newspapers in Early America 'In Defense of Their Own Liberty.'" *Huntington Library Quarterly*, 30:1–16, November 1966.   **L15**
The author examines the American colonial press prior to 1762 to determine the editors' own attitudes toward press freedom. Speculation did not appear during the first three decades, but only as new papers attempted to break a news monopoly. The author finds references in James Franklin's *New-England Courant* (Boston), Benjamin Franklin's *Pennsylvania Gazette*, Andrew Bradford's *American Weekly Mercury* (Philadelphia), John Peter Zenger's *Weekly Journal* (New York), Lewis Timothy's *Gazette* (Charleston, S.C.), William Bradford's *New-York Gazette*, the Boston *Independent Advertiser*, and the *New-York Mercury*. References are made to the newspaper debate between Jonathan Blenman and James Alexander over the Zenger trial, the essay by Jeremiah Gridley in *American Magazine and Historical Chronical*, and the articles by James Parker in the *New-York Gazette* and the *Connecticut Gazette*.

Lederer, William J. *A Nation of Sheep*. New York, Norton, 1961. 192 p.   **L16**
Caustic criticism of the government and the press by one of the authors of *The Ugly American* for misinforming, censoring, and failing to inform the American people about foreign affairs. Lederer also criticizes the American people for their "dumb sheeplike acceptance" of what is offered them in the press. "Decisions are being made on the basis of second-hand rumors, guesses, and propaganda supplied by ill-informed amateurs." Journalism has become an industry rather than a profession.

Leflar, Robert A. "The Social Utility of the Criminal Law of Defamation." *Texas Law Review*, 34:984–1035, October 1956.   **L17**
The author, from an analysis of reported American criminal defamation cases from 1920 to 1955, attempts to determine what function the law serves when so many violations of the law produces so few prosecutions,

and still fewer convictions that stand up on appeal.

"Legal Responsibility for Extra-Legal Censure." *Columbia Law Review*, 62: 475–500, March 1962.   **L18**
Extralegal censure includes group attempts to prevent dissemination of literature deemed offensive, picketing of business organizations, and blacklisting of suspected subversives by prospective employers.

Legman, Gershon. *The Fake Revolt*. New York, Breaking Point, 1967. 32 p.   **L19**
This powerful statement condemns "the perversion of the sexual freedom we have all —or many of us—fought to achieve," by the sadistic sexual orgies in the mass media that serve to detract from the real social problems of America.

Leigh, L. H. "Aspects of the Control of Obscene Literature in Canada." *Modern Law Review*, 27:669–81, November 1964.   **L20**

Lerner, Max. "Literature vs. Trash: Where Can We Draw the Line?" *Redbook*, 129(4):60–61, 124–26, August 1967.   **L21**
Lerner describes the breakthrough in publishing erotic literature, including *Lady Chatterley's Lover*, *Tropic of Cancer*, and *Fanny Hill*, and believes that for reader and writer alike the gain will "far outweigh any possible damage to unready minds." He favors a limited censorship as established by the Supreme Court, for "freedom operates best when we can set up safeguards against the destructiveness of those who don't care about freedom but advocate freedom so they can exploit it." He draws a line between "the obviously cheap exploitive junk" and "serious literature by serious writers."

Lever, Harold. "Libel & Contempt." *Censorship*, 2(2):14–17, Spring 1966.   **L22**
A member of Parliament discusses proposed reforms in the British libel law.

Levy, H. Phillip. *The Press Council: History, Procedure and Cases. With a Preface by Rt. Hon. the Lord Devlin*. London, Macmillan, 1967. 505 p.   **L23**

Le Wine, Jerome M. "What Constitutes Prejudicial Publicity in Pending Cases?" *American Bar Association Journal*, 51: 942–48, October 1965.   **L24**
The author examines the methods employed by both English and American courts in dealing with prejudicial publicity in pending cases. He concludes that restraints on the media of communications are possible under the "clear and present danger" test used by the U.S. Supreme Court.

Lewis, Anthony. "British Verdict on Trial-by-Press." *New York Times Magazine*, 114:14–15, 46–47, 20 June 1965. **L 25**
"The United States needs to attack problems other than the surface one of press comment. It should worry about police corruption, political prosecutors, incompetent judges, regional bias, and many other deficiencies in American criminal justice."

"Liability for Defamation of a Group." *Columbia Law Review*, 34:1322–35, November 1934. **L 26**
Notes on the applicability of civil and criminal law in prosecution for libel of a group of persons or a corporation.

Line, Bryant W. *A Study of Incidents and Trends in the Censorship of Books Affecting Public and School Libraries in the United States, 1954–1964.* Washington, D.C., Catholic University of America, 1965. 249 p. (Unpublished Master's thesis) **L 27**

Lippmann, Walter. "The Credibility Gap." Washington *Post*, 113:A17, 28 March 1967; 115:A21, 30 March 1967. **L 28**
In his column, Today and Tomorrow, Lippmann criticizes President Johnson for a "deliberate policy of artificial manipulation of official news. The purpose of this manipulation is to create a consensus for the President, to stifle debate about his aims and his policies, to thwart deep probing into what has already happened, what is actually happening, what is going to happen . . . There has been damaged also the credibility of the State Department on the conduct of the [Vietnam] war."

——. "On the Importance of Being Free." *Encounter*, 25:88–90, August 1965. **L 29**
"A free press exists only where newspaper readers have access to other newspapers which are competitors and rivals, so that editorial comment and news reports can regularly and promptly be compared, verified, and validated. A press monopoly is incompatible with a free press . . . if there is a monopoly of the means of communication—of radio, television, magazines, books, public meetings—it follows that this society is by definition and in fact deprived of freedom." Lippmann discusses such problems as the public's right to know and the government's need for secrecy; the conflict between the professional journalist's duty to seek the truth and his human desire to get on in the world; the conflict between seeking the truth and being on good terms with the powerful; between seeking the truth and the human desire to say "my country right or wrong."

Lipton, Laurence. "50 Million Censors Can't Be Wrong." *Frontier; The Voice of the New West*, 8(10):9–11, 14, August 1957. **L 30**
"No matter how you may try to hedge it about with safeguards, legal censorship is the imposition of force, police force, on thought art, judgment and conscience On such matters 50 million censors, or more, acting for themselves alone, are better than any one censor with legal police power . . . At the newsstand or in the book store, as in the polling booth, the people have a right to make their own mistakes."

Livingston, William. "Of the Use, Abuse, and Liberty of the Press." In Levy, *Freedom of the Press from Zenger to Jefferson*, pp. 75–82. **L 31**
This essay, first appearing in *The Independent Reflector*, 30 August 1753, "reflects mid-century American libertarian theory at its best."

Lloyd, Brian, and George Gilbert. *Censorship and Public Morality; an Australian Conspectus.* Sydney, N.S.W., Angus, 1930. 60 p. **L 32**

Loades, D. M. "The Press Under the Early Tudors; a Study in Censorship and Sedition." *Transactions of the Cambridge Bibliographical Society*, 4(1):29–50, 1964. **L 33**
The efforts of Henry VIII and Mary Tudor to control the press, including the establishment of the Stationers' Company.

Loftis, John. *The Politics of Drama in Augustan England.* Oxford, Clarendon, 1963. 173 p. **L 34**
Chapter 6, Fielding and the Stage Licensing Act of 1737.

Lofton, John. *Justice and The Press.* Boston, Beacon, 1966. 462 p. **L 35**
"One aim of this book is to examine how newspapers flout the right of due process. Another aim is to note how the courts themselves abuse the rights of due process and obstruct the rights of a free press. The final objective is to suggest under what circumstances and in what ways the individual right to due process should take precedence over the collective public right to know and, conversely, when the right to know should take precedence." In developing an understanding of the problem the author reviews the historic conflict between press and bar going back to the 1807 treason trial of Aaron Burr. The appendix includes: The Oregon Bar-Press-Broadcasters joint statement on fair trial and freedom of the press, the Massachusetts guidelines, the Kentucky Press Association statement on pretrial reporting, the New York County Lawyers Association Code on Fair Trial and Free Press, the Philadelphia Bar Association statement, the joint statement of the Cleveland Bar Association and the Cleveland *Plain Dealer*, the U.S. Department of Justice statement on release of information relating to criminal proceedings, and the U.S. Supreme Court decision in *Sheppard v. Maxwell*.

London. Stationers' Company. *Records of the Court of Stationers' Company, 1576 to 1602—from Register B. Edited by W. W. Greg & E. Boswell.* London, The Bibliographical Society, 1930. 144 p. **L 36**
The first of two volumes of transcription of the Records, followed by transcription for the years 1602–40, edited by W. A. Jackson.

——. *Records of the Court of Stationers' Company, 1602 to 1640. Edited by William A. Jackson.* London, The Bibliographical Society, 1957. 555 p. (Bibliographical Society Publication for the Years 1955 and 1956) **L 37**
This installment "includes part of the first separate volume of the records of the Court, *Court-Book C*, as well as the same part of the letter book entitled 'Orders of Parliam^t. & Ld Mayor Liber A' and the whole of the 'Book of Entraunce of Fines.' The letter book contains much material of an earlier date which it is to be hoped will some day be published, while *Court-Book C* continues on to 1654/5, and together with the succeeding books and supplementary documents, ought likewise to be published."

Long, Howard R. "Straight Thinking on Freedom of the Press." *Grassroots Editor*, 7(1):3, 38, January 1966. **L 38**
Justice Hugo L. Black and Lord Shawcross on the extension of freedom of the press.

"Long-Arm Jurisdiction over Publishers: to Chill a Mocking Word." *Columbia Law Review*, 67:342–65, February 1967. **L 39**
Deals with the problem of courts exercising jurisdiction over nonresident publishers. Includes a critique of the cases of *Curtis Publishing Co. v. Birdsong* (1966), *New York Times Co. v. Connor* (1962), and *Time, Inc. v. Manning* (1966).

Low, Rachel. *The History of the British Film.* London, Allen & Unwin, 1948–50. 3 vols. to date. (Published under the joint auspices of the British Film Institute and the British Film Academy) **L 40**
Vol. I (with Roger Manvell) covers the years 1896–1906. Vol. II, 1906–14, includes a section on official regulation which began with concern for public safety, an account of the organization of the British Board of Film Censors, and a list of causes of film censorship by the Board for 1913. Vol. III, 1914–18, contains a section on the activities of the British Board of Film Censors and the work of the Cinema Commission of Inquiry. Vol. IV, 1919–29 is in preparation.

Lowenstein, Ralph L. *PICA: Measuring*

World Press Freedom. Columbia, Mo., Freedom of Information Center, School of Journalism, University of Missouri, 1966. 6 p. (Publication no. 166) **L 41**

An explanation of a Freedom of Information Center project for the annual measurement of the extent of press freedom in independent nations of the world—Press Independence and Critical Ability (PICA) Index.

———. *World Press Freedom, 1966.* Columbia, Mo., Freedom of Information Center, School of Journalism, University of Missouri, 1967. 8 p. (Report no. 181) **L 42**

The findings of the Press Independence and Critical Ability (PICA) Survey for 1966. Four hundred and thirty newsmen, broadcasters, and journalism editors throughout the world participated in the survey. Twenty-three criteria were used for measuring press freedom. The survey concluded that "a plurality of the world's nations and the world's population lives under conditions of press freedom."

Luce, Clare Boothe. "Problem of Pornography." *McCall's,* 94:15, October 1966. **L 43**

"Censorship, like charity, should begin at home, but, unlike charity, it should end there."

McClellan, Grant S., *ed. Censorship in the United States.* New York, Wilson, 1967. 222 p. (The Reference Shelf, vol. 39, no. 3) **M 1**

A compilation of current articles on such topics as the nature and effect of pornography, the United States Supreme Court and obscenity, fair trial and a free press, news management, and motion picture and television censorship.

MacCracken, Henry N. *Prologue to Independence: The Trials of James Alexander, 1715–1756.* New York, James H. Heineman, 1964. 187 p. **M 2**

Chapters 7 and 8 deal with Lawyer Alexander's part in the defense of John Peter Zenger, charged with seditious libel.

McCullough, Dan H. "Trial by Newspaper—Free Press and Fair Trial." *South Dakota Law Review,* 12:1–61, Winter 1967. **M 3**

"Newspapers, radio stations and the operators of television stations are part of the power complex of a community, and as such they would like to take control of the economy, the political machinery, and the courts. It is this attempt of the press, radio and television to intervene in the judicial process with which we are concerned." The appendix contains the text of Guidelines on Publicity in Criminal Proceedings adopted by the *Toledo Blade* and *Toledo Times.*

McCullough, Robert G. "Torts—Right of Privacy as Subject to Qualified Privilege of Television News Broadcaster." *Washington and Lee Law Review,* 13:255–64, 1956. **M 4**

Discussion of *Jacova v. Southern Radio and Television Co.,* 83 S. (2d) 34 (Fla. 1955), the first decision on the precise point of invasion of privacy by means of a television news program.

Macdonagh, Michael. *The Reporters' Gallery.* London, Hodder and Stoughton, [1913]. 452 p. **M 5**

An account of "the long and dramatic struggle between Parliament and those who, as printers, publishers, editors and reporters, sought to satisfy the curiosity of the people as to the conduct of their representatives in Parliament, and, at the same time, of course, make a commercial profit for themselves, by reporting the Debates in the magazines and newspapers."

McDonald, Ben F. "TV and News Coverage of the Courtroom." *Texas Bar Journal,* 30:169–70, 220–27, March 1967. **M 6**

The author advocates balance between the right of fair trial and a free press in the dilemma over press coverage guidelines.

[McDougall, Alexander]. "The McDougall Case as a Libertarian Cause." In Levy, *Freedom of the Press from Zenger to Jefferson,* pp. 105–27. **M 7**

Text and commentary of documents relating to the case of Captain McDougall, charged with seditious libel in 1770. The documents, appearing originally in James Parker's *New-York Gazette,* consist of a defense of Zengerian principles by Judge William Smith (published anonymously), an attack on "Star Chamber doctrines" by an unknown author, and McDougall's own statement written in jail.

McDougall, Gordon. "To Deprave and Corrupt? An Examination of the Method and Aim of Film Censorship in Britain." *Motion,* 2:5–8, Winter 1961–62. **M 8**

McFadden, Monte. "Changing Standards for Obscenity." *Santa Clara Lawyer,* 6:206–15, Spring 1966. **M 9**

MacGall, Rex. "How Your Films Are Censored." *Bell,* 10:493–501, September 1945. **M 10**

A detailed account of the procedures of the Irish censorship of films, which have already been passed by the British Board of Censorship and, in the case of American imports, by the Hays Office. (Will Hays as distinguished from Dr. Richard Hayes, the Irish censor.) The author advocates a film classification system for Ireland, which would make it unnecessary to reject any film except on grounds of its being utter pornography.

MacGillivray, Royce. "Note on a Case of Seventeenth-Century Censorship." *Notes and Queries,* 211:262–63, July 1966. **M 11**

Concerns part 2 of John Rushworth's *Historical Collections,* London, 1680.

McGinn, Donald J. *John Penry and the Marprelate Controversy.* New Brunswick, N.J., Rutgers University Press, 1966. 274 p. **M 12**

"In this first complete account of the controversy and Penry's relationship to it, Mr. McGinn has examined both literary style and content of all writers attacking and defending the Church in this period. Also appraised are the depositions to the Crown made by other suspects in the Martinist conspiracy." Text of seven Marprelate Tracts, 1588–89, are reproduced in facsimile in a volume published by Scolar Press, Leeds, Eng., 1967.

McKaig, Dianne L. "Public Interest as a Limitation of the Right to Privacy." *Kentucky Law Journal,* 41:126–33, November 1952. **M 13**

Relates to the case of *Leverton v. Curtis Publishing Co.,* 192 F 2d 974. Factors to be considered in determining whether the subject matter is of legitimate public interest and therefore privileged: the nature of the publication, the informative value of the article, the degree of public prominence of the plaintiff, and the effect of publication on plaintiff's relation to third person.

[McKean, Thomas]. "Chief Justice McKean Interprets the Constitutional Guarantee of a Free Press." In Levy, *Freedom of the Press from Zenger to Jefferson,* pp. 131–42. **M 14**

In the libel case against Eleazer Oswald, editor of the *Independent Gazetteer,* Chief Justice McKean ruled that the constitutional guarantee of freedom of the press meant only what it had meant in England for a century. Other opinions upholding these views are included: a speech by James Wilson, a letter from Richard Henry Lee, an extract from Alexander Hamilton's essay in *The Federalist,* No. 84, an exchange of letters between William Cushing and John Adams, Franklin's article on abuses of the press (*The Pennsylvania Gazette,* 12 September 1789), and "Camillus Junius" articles relating to the New York libel case of William Keteltas (*The Argus,* 15 March and 6 April 1796).

MacLeod, Daniel G. "Fair Trial and Free Press—the *Sheppard* Case." *Massachusetts Law Quarterly,* 51:130–33, June 1966. **M 15**

Sheppard v. Maxwell, 384 U.S. 333.

Macmillan, Dougald. "The Censorship

in the Case of Macklin's *The Man of the World.*" *Huntington Library Bulletin*, 10: 79–101, October 1936. **M 16**

An account of the refusal of the Lord Chamberlain to license Charles Macklin's comedy, in 1770 and again in 1779. In 1781 the play in revised form was approved and performed at Covent Garden. While the suppression is widely cited as an example of obstruction in the path of English drama, Macmillan notes that the enforced revisions resulted in a play "greater in conception, more economical in presentation, and more effective in every scene than that which had originally been refused a license."

McNeill, Don. "Coast Police Crackdown on City Lights Bookshop." *Village Voice*, 12(8):16, 31–32, 8 December 1966. **M 17**

Arrest by San Francisco police of a clerk in Lawrence Ferlinghetti's City Lights Bookstore for sale of Lenore Kendel's five-page poem bound as *The Love Book.*

Magrath, C. Peter. "Obscenity Cases: Grapes of Roth." In *Supreme Court Review*, 1966. Chicago, University of Chicago Press, 1966, pp. 7–77. **M 18**

In this essay on the confused legal status of obscenity, the author reviews the 1957 case of *United States v. Roth*, which marked the Supreme Court's first confrontation with the constitutionality of obscenity laws and its first effort to define obscenity. He follows with a critical review of the 1966 cases, *Ginzburg v. United States*, *Mishkin v. New York*, and *Memoirs v. Massachusetts*, in which the Court released 14 separate opinions. The root problem he finds is the Court's inability to provide an intelligible definition of obscenity, yet discussing what it has failed to define, and making decisions based upon the discussion. As a possible solution to the impasse the author recommends that the Court reject the "basic appeal formula" of the 1867 *Regina v. Hicklin* case in favor of the adoption of a clear and reasonably objective definition of "hardcore pornography," which he believes is possible. Such a definition should incorporate the elements of "patent offensiveness" in relation to a "national standard of decency" and would recognize the hallucinatory object of pornography.

———. "*Tropic of Cancer*: the Biography of a Book." In Rocco J. Tresolini, and Richard T. Frost, *Cases in American National Government and Politics*. Englewood Cliffs, N.J., Prentice-Hall, 1966, pp. 174–82. **M 19**

The *Tropic of Cancer* case is presented as an example of how the Supreme Court in settling a legal dispute helps to fashion public policy. What is obscenity and can our government regulate it without infringing on freedom of speech and press?

Maheu, René. "The Right to Information and the Right to the Expression of Opinion." In UNESCO, *Human Rights, Comments and Interpretation; A Symposium edited by UNESCO with an Introduction by Jacques Maritain*. New York, Columbia University Press, 1949, pp. 218–22. **M 20**

Mallik, Jyotsna N. *Law of Obscenity in India*. Calcutta, Eastern Law House, [1966]. 119p. **M 21**

Manchester, William. "William Manchester's Own Story." *Look*, 31(7):62–77 4 April 1967. **M 22**

The author's account of the writing of *The Death of a President* at the request of the Kennedy family and the bitter conflict that developed when the family attempted, ultimately through the New York state court, to block publication of the work.

Marcus, Steven. *The Other Victorians: A Study of Sexuality and Pornography in Mid-Nineteenth Century England*. New York, Basic Books, 1966. 292p. **M 23**

The book consists of "a series of related studies in the sexual culture—more precisely, perhaps, the sexual subculture—of Victorian England." The author deals first with the official attitude toward sex as expressed by Dr. William Acton, then with an analysis of the work of Henry Spencer Ashbee (Pisanus Fraxi), scholar-bibliographer of sexual and pornographic literature. A major portion of the book deals with the 11-volume autobiography, *My Secret Life*, a work important because of its authenticity, its social and cultural significance, and because "it helps to demonstrate the connection between an authentic account of sexual experience in the Victorian period and the fantasies and language of pornography." The author also analyses four pornographic novels of the period and some of the immense literature describing flagellation appearing in Victorian England. In a final chapter, Pornotopia, he reaches certain theoretical conclusions concerning the nature and function of pornography.

———. "Pornotopia." *Encounter*, 27(2): 9–18, August 1966. **M 24**

"The literary genre that pornographic fantasies—particularly when they appear in the shape of pornographic fiction—tend most to resemble is the utopian fantasy. For our present purposes I call this fantasy pornotopia." Pornography is not literature because of its endless repetition; it exists less in its language than any other kind of creative writing; unlike literature it is not interested in persons but in organs, in sex without human emotions. The author discusses three breakthroughs in the nineteenth-century subculture of pornography: the discovery of modern psychology, the novelists' assault on the hypocritical sexual life of the bourgeois, and the liberalization of sexual life and social attitude toward sexuality now taking place.

The open publication of pornography today is both inevitable, necessary, and benign. It marks "the end of an era in which pornography had a historical meaning and even a historical function."

Margolin, Malcolm. "Censorship of Advertising by the Mass Media." *Fact* 4(4):49–55, July–August 1967. **M 25**

"The communications industry wields a heavy blue pencil not only to screen harmful products, but, perhaps more significantly, to suppress ideas, control thought and muzzle dissent."

Markel, Lester. "The Management of News." *Saturday Review*, 46(6):50–51, 61, 9 February 1963. **M 26**

"Newspapers should recognize that it is not enough, in these critical days, to ask: Is it news? They must also ask: Is it in the national interest? It is not enough that the press be free; it must be responsible also. Government should recognize that there are grave dangers in overclassification and in censorship under any guise and that such procedures are to be used with the utmost caution and under constant scrutiny."

Markmann, Charles L. *The Noblest Cry; A History of the American Civil Liberties Union*. New York, St. Martin's Press, 1965. 464p. **M 27**

A history of America's foremost agency in defense of the freedom of the press, with reports on numerous cases where the ACLU came to the defense of the right to speak and publish. The author discusses the role of Roger N. Baldwin in founding and directing the Union, actions in espionage cases in World War I, the Palmer raids of the 1920's, the Scopes evolution trial, the several Jehovah's Witnesses cases, opposition to the House Un-American Activities Committee and the various suppressions that took place during the hysteria of the McCarthy era. Markmann also discusses the role of the Union in combating post office and customs censorship, blacklisting practices in the communications industry, and the controversy within the Union over the issue of fair trial versus a free press. In the latter, the author supports the right of the accused as taking precedence over the right of the general public to know details. He is also concerned with the increasing invasions of privacy. A chapter entitled "Unclean! Unclean!" deals with the relatively late efforts by the Union to combat censorship of obscenity by vigilante groups and administrative agencies. He recounts the work of Morris Ernst on behalf of the Union in the cases of Dreiser's *American Tragedy*, Joyce's *Ulysses*, *Esquire* magazine, and many others, and criticizes the application of the "clear and present danger" dictum as being "as pernicious in the field of obscenity as in that of political censorship." The author reviews the Roth obscenity case, various cases before the Supreme Court relating to city and state motion picture censorship boards, including *Jacobellis v. Ohio*, and the then pending Ginzburg case before the Supreme Court. There is an account of

ACLU's work in behalf of academic freedom in schools and colleges, censorship of textbooks and library books, and particularly the attacks on publications of UNESCO. The book constitutes a review of most of the issues on freedom of the press that arose in the United States during almost a half century.

Marks, Stan. "The Comstock Ghost." *Sundial*, 5(2):5+, September 1966. **M 28**
The story of the court fight waged by Dr. Ilsley Boone to permit publication of nudist pictures. This "Free Press" issue also carries an article on Pornography and Freedom by R. W. Wescott, and the Nudist Picture by Robert L. Schwarz, all freely interspersed with pictures of nudes.

Marowitz, Charles. "An End to Censorship, But Not to Its Spirit." *Village Voice*, 12(38):18, 6 July 1967. **M 29**
News of a joint Parliamentary Committee recommendation for the abolition of the two-hundred-and-thirty-year-old play censorship by the Lord Chamberlain prompts these observations on the work of the office. The Lord Chamberlain in recent years has been mainly concerned with niceties of language. "As for the really radical, destructively subversive plays, the plays that might topple the empire or excoriate the sensibility of the Mothers' Union . . . those plays aren't being written."

Martin, John B. "Murder of a Journalist." *Harper's*, 193:271–82, September 1946. **M 30**
An account of the murder of Don Mellett, young crusading editor of the Canton, Ohio, *Daily News* on the night of 15 July 1926, the victim of his crusade against crime and corruption in Canton, and the investigation and trials that followed.

Martin, L. John. *International Propaganda: Its Legal and Diplomatic Control.* Minneapolis, University of Minnesota Press, 1958. 284 p. **M 31**
An account of legal and diplomatic maneuvers in the attempt to control international propaganda. The author concludes that "international propaganda has little chance of being controlled or adjudicated at the international level." At present international propaganda is controlled by domestic courts, under the laws of individual states of the world.

Mathews, Joseph J. *Reporting the Wars.* Minneapolis, University of Minnesota Press, 1957. 322 p. **M 32**
Chapter 12 deals with Censorship and Control. References to censorship also appear in chapters 10 and 11, on World War I and II.

Mayer, Michael F. *Foreign Films on American Screens.* New York, Arco, 1965. 119 p. **M 33**
Three chapters relate to freedom of the films:

Chapter 8, The Censorship Problem, Chapter 9, The Decline of Prior Restraint, and Chapter 10, Classification or Clarification. There are a number of illustrations of films that met with censorship troubles. Examples of rating and classification services including the NODL list are given in the appendix.

Mead, Margaret. "Right to Privacy; The Public Need To Be Informed." *Redbook*, 128:30–34, April 1967. **M 34**
Implications of the prepublication controversy over William Manchester's *The Death of a President* on the reporting about public figures—living and dead.

Meier, Ernst. "The Licensed Press in the U.S. Occupation Zone of Germany." *Journalism Quarterly*, 31:223–31, Spring 1954. **M 35**
The development of an entirely new press in Germany between 1945 and 1949 was a great victory for the licensing system, but in reorienting the people toward democracy it was less successful.

Meiklejohn, Donald. *Freedom and the Public: Public and Private Morality in America.* Syracuse, N.Y., Syracuse University Press, 1965. 163 p. **M 36**
Chapter 4 deals with Responsible Government—The Freedom of Public Discussion.

Meister, Stanley. "Hidden Censors." *Nation*, 189:207–10, 10 October 1959. **M 37**
A review of the long history of post-office censorship, culminating with the recent action of Postmaster General Summerfield against *Lady Chatterley's Lover*. "At present the Post Office's administrative procedures have no solid authorization from Congress. This is true of its campaigns against both obscenity and foreign political propaganda." Until the courts or the Congress act, "poor judgment, like that of Postmaster General Summerfield, is all that keeps the problems and procedures of postal censorship in public view."

"Men from CLEAN: California Smut Trade." *Newsweek*, 68:23–24, 5 September 1966. **M 38**
California League Enlisting Action Now (CLEAN).

Merrill, John C. *Is There a Right to Know?* Columbia, Mo., Freedom of Information Center, School of Journalism, University of Missouri, 1967. 3 p. (Publication no. 002) **M 39**
An essay which examines the basis and implications of the people's right to know. If this right exists, is there not a concurrent duty on the part of the government and press to inform the people?

Merryman, John H. "Defamation of a Group." *Notre Dame Lawyer*, 21:21–25, September 1945. **M 40**

Meyer, Richard J. "'The Blue Book'" and "Reaction to the 'Blue Book.'" *Journal of Broadcasting*, 6:197–207, Summer 1962; 6:295–312, Fall 1962. **M 41**
An overview of the content and effect of the controversial FCC report, *Public Service Responsibility of Broadcast Licensees*.

[Mill, James]. ["Review of] *Memoires de Candide, sur la Liberté de la Presse . . . Par le Docteur Emmanuel Ralph . . .*" *Edinburgh Review*, 18:98–123, May 1811. **M 42**
Mill briefly reviews this satire on press freedom (or lack of it) in France under the Directory, devoting much of the article to a comparison between restrictions of the press under French law and the restricted law of libel in England, which he considers odious and without statutory authority.

Miller, Helen H. "Freedom of the Press." In her *The Case for Liberty*. Chapel Hill, N.C., University of North Carolina Press, 1965, pp. 29–66. **M 43**
The story of the William Bradford case (Philadelphia, 1692) and the John Peter Zenger case (New York, 1735). A portrait of Zenger's lawyer, Andrew Hamilton, is on p. 59.

Minneapolis Public Library. "Adult Book Selection Policy: A Model." *Illinois Libraries*, 48:402–4, May 1966. **M 44**
A positive expression of one library's interpretation of the Library Bill of Rights, developed by the staff of the Minneapolis Public Library and approved by their Board of Trustees on 20 May 1965.

Mollenhoff, Clark R. "The Federal FOI Law: Meaningful If . . ." *Quill*, 54(8): 22–23, August 1966. **M 45**
A leader in the crusade for newspaper access to public information believes S1160, signed by the President, "will be meaningful if it is understood by the press and the public and is used as a device to force government agencies to produce documents." The text of the law follows.

———, and Lester Markel. "Managing the News." *IPI Report* (International Press Institute), 12(1):4–6, May 1963. **M 46**
Two newspaper men debate the alleged management of news by the Kennedy Administration.

Molz, Kathleen. "Implications of the

Ginzburg Affair." *Wilson Library Bulletin*, 40:941–47, June 1966.　　**M 47**

The editor of the *Bulletin* analyzes the decisions of the U.S. Supreme Court in three obscenity cases: *Ginzburg v. U. S.*; *Mishkin v. New York*; and *Memoirs of a Woman of Pleasure v. The Attorney General of the Commonwealth of Massachusetts*, considering the implications to libraries of these and other federal censorship cases. The problem of the controversial novel still remains and "I would hope that librarians could strive for a review of fiction which would ask questions pertaining not so much to the book, but to the reader."

———. "The Public Custody of the High Pornography." *American Scholar*, 36: 93–103, Winter 1966–67.　　**M 48**

The role of the public librarian in the selection of "high pornography." The author traces the attitude of the librarian from that of discouraging the novel as a questionable genre, to the present libertarian status, evidenced by the American Library Association entering an *amicus curiae* brief in defense of the *Tropic of Cancer*. In handling controversial books the librarian is caught in a dilemma between public demands and professional standards, made more confusing because of the "topsy-turvy scheme of things, in which the jurist adjudicates our national aesthetic and the [literary] critic serves as watchdog of our national ethic."

Monaghan, Henry P. "Obscenity, 1966: The Marriage of Obscenity Per Se and Obscenity Per Quod." *Yale Law Journal*, 76:127–57, November 1966.　　**M 49**

"Like *Roth*, the 1966 cases do not succeed in fitting obscenity prosecution within any comprehensive theory of the First Amendment. But, in principle, they do permit the states wide leeway to move against the commercial exploiters of erotica . . . It is . . . safe to assume that the censors will take the 1966 decisions as further encouragement to go about their good works. But, as yet, obscenity prosecutions are still of marginal concern; it still remains unlikely that any 'significant' book will be suppressed. That may not be enough, but it is a good deal."

Monsen, Per. "Attacks on Press Freedom Take New Pattern." *IPI Report* (International Press Institute), 13(9):1–3, January 1965.　　**M 50**

The new pattern is the statutory press council and repressive laws to "discipline" newspapers, adopted by governments as far apart politically and geographically as Ceylon, South Africa, Nigeria, and Korea.

Montgomery, Reid H. *Libel Laws and South Carolina Newspapers*. New York, New York University, 1955. 256p.

(Ph.D. dissertation, University Microfilms, no. 13, 628)　　**M 51**

"The purpose of this study is to trace the historical development of libel laws as applied to newspapers of South Carolina, and to examine critically the areas from which proposals for changes in the statutes have been or may be made."

Moore, Everett T. "Clean Down the Drain." *Library Journal*, 92:83–84, 1 January 1967.　　**M 52**

Account of the astonishing defeat by California voters of an antiobscenity proposal sponsored by an *ad hoc* organization called CLEAN, Inc. (California League Enlisting Action Now).

———. "Libraries." *Censorship*, 2(3): 10–14, Summer 1966.　　**M 53**

A summary of censorship pressures against public and school libraries and the role librarians are taking in resisting censorship.

Moore, John R. "Defoe in the Pillory: A New Interpretation." In his *Defoe in the Pillory*. Indiana University Publications, Humanities Series no. 1, 1939, pp. 3–32.　　**M 54**

"The final cause of Defoe's humiliation was the personal resentment of his judges at the Old Bailey on July 7, 1703. These judges were men whom he had satirized in print, in the most scathing terms, for public and private vices."

"More Ado About Dirty Books." *Yale Law Journal*, 75:1364–1409+, July 1966.　　**M 55**

"A new legal test for obscenity was born during the Supreme Court's 1965 term. Joining the already crowded household of indicia and criteria, the 'pandering' test added a distinctive trait: for the first time, the offensive character of the defendant became relevant along with the noxious quality of his speech. In the process, First Amendment values—supposedly sheltered by the 1957 decision in *Roth v. United States*—were again left without protection." A critique of the *Fanny Hill*, *Ginzburg*, and *Mishkin* cases. The author concludes: "First Amendment theory will thus require a clear understanding of the evil feared from erotic literature. Once the evil is identified, the judges can ask whether the state's censorship is suited to achieve the legitimate goal and no more." Appendixes: A Review of U.S. Obscenity Statutes (Criminal) and Representative Depiction of U.S. Obscenity Statutes. These tables are arranged by state.

Morgan, Richard. "The Court and Obscenity." *New Leader*, 49:15–17, 11 April 1966.　　**M 56**

A discussion of the *Ginzburg*, *Mishkin*, and *Fanny Hill* cases before the U.S. Supreme Court.

Morgenthau, Hans J. "Freedom, Free-

dom House and Vietnam." *New Leader*, 50:17–19, 2 January 1967.　　**M 57**

A political scientist attacks the statement o Freedom House (*New York Times* advertisement of 30 November 1966) which "urges the responsible critics of the Vietnam war to disassociate themselves from wild charges being made against the nation and its leaders." He examines the five charges and concludes that the Freedom House document is trying to establish a political orthodoxy with regard to Vietnam policy and is attempting to limit freedom of legitimate speech and criticism. Leo Cherne of Freedom House defends the statement in the 16 January issue and criticizes Morgenthau's position. Morgenthau responds in the 30 January issue, characterizing Cherne's reply as "a thoroughly disreputable document," which justifies his own forebodings about the Freedom House statement.

Morning Chronicle (London). *Report of the Trial of the Printer of the Morning Chronicle, and Others, for a Supposed Libel*. [Derby, England, 1793]. 48p.　　**M 58**

The defendant was judged "not guilty" for supposed libel contained in an advertisement from the Association at Derby.

Morris, Earl F. "Justice and the News Media." *Illinois Bar Journal*, 55:554–57, March 1967.　　**M 59**

A rebuttal by the president-elect of the American Bar Association to the report of the American Newspaper Publishers Association on the "fair trial-free press" dialogue.

Morrison, Joseph L. "Editor for Sale: A World War II Case History." *Journalism Quarterly*, 43:34–42, Spring 1966.　　**M 60**

"The story of how the *Living Age*, with a proud history dating back to 1844, fell into the hands of an editor financed by the Japanese from July 1938 to August 1941. The magazine died; the editor went to jail."

Morse, Howard N. "A Critical Analysis and Appraisal of *Burstyn v. Wilson*." *North Dakota Law Review*, 29:38–41, January 1953.　　**M 61**

The case involved the motion picture, *The Miracle*.

Moser, J. G., and Richard A. Lavine. *Radio and the Law*. Los Angeles, Parker, 1947. 386p.　　**M 62**

Includes chapters on program control, advertising, obscene and indecent language, defamation, right of privacy, presentation of public issues, unfair competition, copyright, and a brief section on censorship.

Mosk, Stanley. "Free Press and Fair Trial—Placing Responsibility." *Santa Clara Lawyer*, 5:107–20, Spring 1965.　　**M 63**

A general review of the issue with special reference to the New Jersey case, *State v.*

Van Duyne, 204 A 2d 841 (N.J. 1964), which "helpfully warned police officers and the bar. It is hoped that other jurisdictions will be similarly resolute. Perhaps then the current trend of irresponsibility can be reversed."

Mowrer, Richard Scott. "Where Americas Lead Way in Censorship." *IPI Report* (International Press Institute), 13(9):5, January 1965. **M 64**
"An aspect of the U.S. military presence in Spain is the suppression of news. It has existed in varying degrees since the defense agreements were signed with General Franco's government 11 years ago. Lately it has become more noticeable."

Muddiman, Joseph G. *The King's Journalist, 1659–1689; Studies in the Reign of Charles II.* London, Lane, 1923. 294 p. **M 65**
An account of the regulation of the newspaper press during the Restoration, achieved through Royal monopoly held by Henry Muddiman, Roger L'Estrange, and Oliver Williams, who competed among themselves for monopoly power. L'Estrange became the first Surveyor of the Press, when that office was established in 1663, serving as both publisher and censor. The work includes a brief account of Benjamin Harris, first American newspaper publisher, whose efforts in both England and America were suppressed.

Murphy, Terrence J. *et al.* "Fighting the Obscenity Racket: Special Issue." *Mary Today*, 55:4–10+, September–October 1964. **M 66**
Contents: Who Shall Censor? by Terrence J. Murphy, Give Them a Chance by Ralph Guyatte, Repercussions by Charles Lees, The Playboy Philosophy by Francis Lawlor, No Matter How Good the Seed by Margaret Rowland, Our Brother's Keeper by C. Doherty, and The Law We Live by Julius G. Neumann.

Naeser, Vincent. "Some Aspects of the Social Function and Ethical Responsibilities of the Newspaper Press." *Gazette; International Journal for Mass Communications Studies*, 9:171–75, 1963. **N 1**
The author discusses seven decisive factors in world-wide freedom of the press: freedom from dictatorship, freedom guaranteed under the Constitution, freedom from government control, freedom from labor conflicts, freedom from curbs on editorial departments, freedom from obstacles to the flow of news, and freedom from outside economic control.

Naftzger, Roger V. "Gulliver: The Right to Read." *Top of the News*, 22:389–95, June 1966. **N 2**
A discussion of the philosophy of censorship, particularly as applied to high school readers, drawing an analogy to the position of Gulliver, held captive by the threadlike ropes of the Lilliputian.

Namurois, Albert. "Some Aspects of Freedom of Information." *E.B.U. Review* (European Broadcasting Union), 59:25–31, January 1960. **N 3**
Following a review of the fundamental source of the right of freedom of expression, the author considers whether the media of information, particularly broadcasting and the cinema, are in a position to fulfill the mission assigned to them by virtue of the existing law. The inquiry is confined to the question of access to the event and includes Britain and the Commonwealth countries.

Natarajan, Swaminath. *Democracy and the Press.* Bombay, India, Manaktalas, 1965. 38 p. **N 4**

Nathan, George Jean. "Coprophilia." In his *Art of the Night*. New York, Knopf, 1928, pp. 80–92. (Reprinted in *The Magic Mirror, Selected Writings on the Theatre by George Jean Nathan.* Edited by Thomas Q. Curtiss. New York, Knopf 1960, pp. 92–96) **N 5**
Irreverent comments on Anthony Comstock's crusade against morality in literature and drama. In the eighties the vice societies objected to depicting countless human frailties; now "drama may safely violate all the Commandments but the Seventh." Nathan accuses the professional vice crusader of enjoying the pursuit of vice. "You will never find a sewer repairer who can't stand the smell of sewage."

[Nathan, John]. "San Francisco Censorship—Michael McClure's *The Beard*." *Evergreen Review*, 11:16–20, February 1967. **N 6**
Arrest of the playwright and the cast by police following the first performance in Berkeley.

Neider, Charles. "On Mark Twain Censorship." In his *Mark Twain*. New York, Horizon, 1967, pp. 133–55. **N 7**

Nelson, Harold L., ed. *Freedom of the Press from Hamilton to the Warren Court.* Indianapolis, Bobbs-Merrill, 1967. 420 p. (American Heritage Series) **N 8**
A collection of essays, court decisions, newspaper editorials, and laws relating to general principles of freedom of the press, limits of freedom, criminal libel, contempt of court, abolitionist press, wartime press controls, sex and obscenity, sedition, newspaper monopoly, and secrecy in government. Includes text of the following court cases: *Schenck v. United States, Gitlow v. People of New York, Near v. Minnesota, New York Times Co. v. Sullivan, Commonwealth v. Clap, Beauharnais v. Illinois, Arkansas v. Morrill, Bridges v. California, U.S. v. One Book Called "Ulysses," Roth v. United States,* and *Grosjean v. American Press Co.* There are excerpts from general works on freedom of the press by Thomas Cooper,

Francis L. Holt, Zechariah Chafee, Jr., and Henry Schofield; comments on criminal libel by Theodore Roosevelt and Judge A. B. Anderson; statements on control of abolitionist literature by Amos Kendall, William Leggett, Andrew Jackson, and Postmaster General Holt; references to wartime censorship by General George B. McClelland and Abraham Lincoln (Civil War), William Hard (World War I), and the American Civil Liberties Union (World War II); comments on sex and obscenity censorship by Anthony Comstock and Theodore A. Schroeder; comments on radicalism by the National Civil Liberties Bureau and Zechariah Chafee, Jr.; and comments on secrecy in government by Francis Lieber and Dwight D. Eisenhower. A final chapter on freedom and responsibility quotes from the Commission on Freedom of the Press, the Warren Commission, and from various codes and credos.

New Jersey Committee for the Right to Read. *A Survey of New Jersey Psychiatrists and Psychologists Pertaining to the Proscription by Legislation of Sexually Oriented Publications for Persons under 18 Years. Final Report, January 1967.* Caldwell, N.J., The Committee, 1967. 32 p. **N 9**
"The tenor of the response to this survey is that the reasons for passage of a law such as New Jersey Bill A-768 [distribution of obscene matter to children under 18 years of age] are invalid in the eyes of most psychiatrists and psychologists who responded to this request for information." Eighty-three percent did not believe exclusion of sex literature from libraries and stores would encourage healthier attitudes toward sex in young people, and 62 percent said concealment of sexual and anatomical information might promote pathological curiosity. The appendix includes the text of the Bill and statements from respondents.

New York (City). Mayor's Citizens Anti-Pornography Commission. *Report.* [New York, The Commission], 1965. 11 p. **N 10**
The Commission consisted of 21 members representing diverse occupations and professions, appointed by Mayor Robert F. Wagner, who served as chairman. Members were presented with a number of books and magazines to see whether in their judgment they were obscene. The members unanimously judged as obscene *Tropic of Cancer, Fanny Hill, Touch Magazine,* and *Candy.* The Commission recommended an 11-point program to combat the evil of obscenity, which called for vigorous enforcement of existing laws, passage of additional laws to protect the morals of children, and establishment of federal, state, and city obscenity commissions to read and pass judgment on books alleged to be salacious.

"The New York Law Controlling the Dissimination of Obscene Materials to Minors." *Fordham Law Review*, 34:692–710, May 1966. **N 11**

Efforts to draft a New York law that would be constitutionally acceptable.

[New York *Sun*]. *The Freedom of the Press from Unlawful Restraints and Monopoly.* [*In the Matter of the Complaint of the Sun Printing and Publishing Company against the Associated Press*]. [New York], 1914. 84 p. **N12**

Appeal of the New York *Sun* to the Attorney General of the United States to invoke the provisions of the Sherman Anti-Trust Law against the Associated Press.

Newhouse, Wade J., Jr. "The Constitution and International Agreements or Unilateral Action Curbing 'Peace-Imperiling' Propaganda." *Law and Contemporary Problems*, 31:506–26, Summer 1966. **N13**

On the basis of ordinary First Amendment doctrine, the author concludes that "there are serious questions as to the constitutional validity of language which might be included in proposed treaties and statutes proscribing warmongering, subversive, and defamatory propaganda." He also concludes that such proscription of warmongering propaganda by treaty "would face the same scrutiny as comparable domestic legislation when first amendment interests are invoked." Comments on Professor Newhouse's paper, by Nathaniel L. Nathanson are given on pp. 526–29.

Nixon, Raymond B. "Freedom in the World's Press: A Fresh Appraisal with New Data." *Journalism Quarterly*, 42:3–14, Winter 1965. **N14**

"Analysis of experts' ranking of 117 countries on a 9-point scale from freedom to control indicates economic level is most significant factor. Comparison with earlier studies shows more gains than losses in last five years."

Norman, Albert E. "Press Freedom Falters 'Down Under.'" *IPI Report* (International Press Institute), 2(12):3–4, April 1954. **N15**

The Australian Bureau chief of the *Christian Science Monitor* finds that all is not well with press freedom in Australia.

Norris, Hoke, James R. Squire, and Robert F. Hogan. "Should We Censor What Adolescents Read? A Symposium-in-Print." *PTA Magazine*, 59:10–12, March 1965. (Reprinted in *Education Digest*, May 1965) **N16**

Suggestions for study and discussion and for a PTA program on censorship are given on page 36.

"Not on the List." *ALA Bulletin*, 60:691, 700, July-August 1966. **N17**

An instructive and amusing brouhaha over school library censorship in Hanover County, Va.

"Notable Prosecutions of the English Press of the Past." In *Progress of British Newspapers in the Nineteenth Century*. London, Simpkin, Marshall, Hamilton, Kent, [ca. 1900], pp. 177–83. **N18**

A popular account containing portraits of John Wilkes, John Horne Tooke, William Cobbett, and John Hunt.

Oaks, Dallin H. "Suppression of the *Nauvoo Expositor*." *Utah Law Review*, 9:862–903, Winter 1965. **O1**

An account and interpretation of the suppression of the *Nauvoo Expositor* by the Mormons in Nauvoo, Illinois, in 1844, which was the first in a series of events that lead directly to the murder of the Mormon prophet, Joseph Smith.

O'Brien, Francis W. "Movie Censorship: A Swiss Comparison." *Duke Law Journal*, 1966:633–68, Summer 1966. **O2**

An examination of the approach to movie censorship under Swiss laws as compared with American. The Swiss Tribunal Federal exercises minimum restraint in judging acts by the cantons to censor movies, believing that local conditions and community standards ought to determine what restrictions are to be imposed.

O'Brien, William V. "International Propaganda and Minimum World Public Order." *Law and Contemporary Problems*, 31:589–600, Summer 1966. **O3**

The author's contention is that "meaningful legal regulation of international propaganda is so difficult at best and so inconceivable in the present divided world, that international law is not well served by encouraging the belief among its supporters that substantial progress in this problem area is imminent."

"Obscenity and Minors: Another Attempt." *Albany Law Review* 30:133–44, January 1966. **O4**

The problems of drafting a New York law controlling dissemination of obscene materials to minors, in light of the 1964 court decision in *People v. Bookcase, Inc.*, 14 N.Y. 2d 409.

O'Casaide, Séamus. "Watty Cox and his Publications." In Bibliographical Society of Ireland. *Publications*, 7(2):17–38, 1935. **O5**

For seditious libel in his *Irish Magazine* (1807–15) Walter (Watty) Cox was harassed in various ways, pilloried, and repeatedly fined and imprisoned. After spending more than three years in prison, where he continued to publish his paper, Cox accepted a government pension on condition that he leave the country. He spent some years in New York, but eventually returned to Ireland. The issue of *Irish Magazine* for April 1811 contains an engraving of Watty Cox on the pillory "for a wicked and seditious libel."

[O'Connell, Daniel, *et al.*]. *A Special Report of the Proceedings in the case of the Queen against Daniel O'Connell* [*et al.*] *in the Court of Queen's Bench, Ireland, Michaelmas term, 1843, and Hilary term, 1844; on an Indictment for Conspiracy and Misdemeanour*. Edited by John Flanedy. Dublin, James Duffy, 1844. 484 p. **O6**

O'Connell, a Catholic member of Parliament, was brought to trial along with eight others on charge of creating disaffection among the people for published speeches made in behalf of repeal of the union of Great Britain and Ireland. He was imprisoned for a time, but released by the House of Lords.

Oettinger, Elmer R., *et al.* "Press Court Reporting Seminar." *Popular Government*, 30(5–6):1–28+, February–March 1964. **O7**

Contents: Free Press Can Guarantee Better Government by Judge Hamilton H. Habgood, Free Press and Fair Trial Are Not Incompatible by Sam Ragan, Press Freedom Is Not Absolute by John W. Scott, Libel-Qualified Privilege of Reporting Judicial Proceedings by William Lassiter, The Press and the Defendant by James R. Nance, John B. Adams, and Charles Hauser, Photographing and Broadcasting Proceedings in Court by Judge Leo Carr, The Press and the Prosecution by Judge E. Maurice Braswell, Thomas W. Christopher, and Weimar Jones.

[O'Faolain, Sean]. "The Senate and Censorship." *Bell*, 5:247–52, January 1943. **O8**

Comment on the censorship debates in the Irish Senate. O'Faolain criticizes the legalistic arguments of the chairman of the Censorship Board (Professor Megennis) in defense of the Board's ban of Dr. Halliday Sutherlands' *The Laws of Life*, despite the fact that the book bore an imprimatur. O'Faolain predicts that authors will ultimately extract the fundamental rights of the individual from the mass of superficial verbiage of the defenders of censorship.

Olson, Kenneth E. "The Press of the British Isles: Oldest Battlers for Freedom." In his *The History Makers: The Press of Europe From Its Beginnings Through 1965*. Baton Rouge, La., Louisiana State University Press, 1966, pp. 5–32. **O9**

O'Neil, Robert M. *Free Speech: Responsible Communication under Law*. Indianapolis, Bobbs-Merrill, 1966. 123 p. **O10**

Deals with legal rights and limitations on speech, including radio and television.

O'Neill, James M. "Catholics and Censorship." In his *Catholics in Controversy.* New York, McMullen, 1954, pp. 107–54. **O11**
The author refutes the charges of censorship made against the Catholic hierarchy, the Legion of Decency, the National Organization of Decent Literature, and other Catholic groups. Particularly, he takes to task Paul Blanshard and Elmer Rice. He discusses the film cases of *The Miracle, Pinky, M,* and *La Ronde.*

O'Neill, William L., ed. *Echoes of Revolt: The Masses, 1911–1917. Introduction by Irving Howe, Afterword by Max Eastman.* Chicago, Quadrangle Books, 1966. 303 p. **O12**
A collection of excerpts from *The Masses,* the magazine that became the rallying center for almost everything that was irreverent in American culture in the decade before World War I. In its attacks on the capitalist system, militarism, and sexual traditions, the journal was almost continuously involved in controversy and was sometimes confronted with censorship. One section of the anthology discusses the legal battle with the Associated Press on charges of criminal libel (Floyd Dell) and the Arthur Young cartoons that prompted the controversy; another section deals with *The Masses* and the censor (Anthony Comstock), the New York subway system that dropped the paper from its stands, and an article on post office censorship. Comstock caricatures by Robert Minor and George Bellows are included. There is a section on birth control, including support of Margaret Sanger and Emma Goldman, whose speech in her own defense is included; John Reed's account of the Berkman-Goldman trial, and finally, an account of the end of the *The Masses,* the result of an indictment under the World War I Espionage Act.

Osborne, John. *William Cobbett: His Thought and His Time.* New Brunswick, N.J., Rutgers University Press, 1966. 272 p. **O13**
An analysis of Cobbett's ideas and their relation to the England of his time, concentrating on his career as a political journalist during the first thirty-five years of the nineteenth century. A chapter on the press and scattered references throughout record Cobbett's ardent championing of a free press.

O'Sullivan, Richard. *The Law of Defamation.* London, Sweet & Maxwell, 1958. 188 p. **O14**

Otto, Herbert A. "Sex and Violence on the American Newsstand." *Journalism Quarterly,* 40:19–26, Winter 1963. **O15**
"Three studies tracing the scope and incidence of themes of 'sex' and 'violence' in mass media of communications are reported. The studies include content analyses of 55 magazines and of the covers of 296 paperback books available on newsstands, as well as an analysis of 10 leading U.S. newspapers."

Parker, F. T. "Word Portrayal of Events in the Life of a Living Person in a Work of Fiction as a Violation of the Right of Privacy." *Rocky Mountain Law Review,* 21:114–18, December 1948. **P1**
Regarding *Toscani v. Hersey,* 271 App. Div. 445, 65 N.Y.S. (2d) 814 (1946), involving John Hersey's *A Bell for Adano.*

Percy, H. R. "Literature and the Law." *Chitty's Law Journal,* 12(10):18–22, October 1964. **P2**
Suggests that an obscenity law should allow a publisher or author to prosecute those who level unproved charges.

Perrin, Noel. "Real Bowdler." *Notes & Queries,* 13(n.s.):141–42, April 1966. **P3**
The author offers evidence that Thomas Bowdler's sister, Henrietta, did the "Bowdlerizing" of the first edition of *Family Shakespeare.*

Perry, Stuart H. "The Courts, the Press, and the Public." *Michigan Law Review,* 30:228–37, December 1931. **P4**
"Trial by newspaper could be stopped tomorrow if judges would use the contempt powers that are in their hands." They do not do so for fear of the political power of the newspapers, and judges depend for re-election upon political support of the press. "The popular election of judges for fixed terms is the greatest single evil of our judicial system."

Peterson, H. C., and Gilbert C. Fite. *Opponents of War, 1917–1918.* Madison, Wis., University of Wisconsin Press, 1957. 399 p. **P5**
Chapter 9 deals with Purging the Movies and the Press. "The censorship exercised by the Postmaster General, Albert Sidney Burleson, was perhaps more effective than all of the other individuals and organizations combined." The author deals with Burleson's authority to withhold mailing privileges from publications under the Espionage Act.

Pew, Marlen E. *Local Government and the Press; Address Delivered at the Twentieth Annual Journalism Week at the University of Missouri, May 5–11, 1929.* Columbia, Mo., School of Journalism, University of Missouri, 1929. 14 p. (University of Missouri Bulletin, v. 29, no. 40; Journalism Series no. 55) **P6**
The first Don Mellett memorial lecture.

Pfeffer, Leo. "The Supreme Court and the Bill of Rights, I: Freedom of Expression." *Nation,* 203:315–18, 3 October 1966. **P7**

Phelps, Robert H., and E. Douglas Hamilton. *Libel: Rights, Risks, Responsibilities.* New York, Macmillan, 1966. 405 p. **P8**
"What libel is—and what it is not—and how to communicate the maximum information with the minimum risk. With case histories illustrating potential danger areas." Cases include: *Reynolds v. Pegler, The Saturday Evening Post's* Story of a College Football Fix, *The New York Times Co. v. Sullivan,* and action against various magazines and newspapers not generally reported in the public press. "The picture that emerges from this study of libel," the authors conclude, "is one that heartens and at the same time appalls the observer. He is heartened by the trend in the law toward more freedom to speak out on public affairs. He is appalled by the possible use of that freedom to wreck an innocent man's reputation." An alphabetical index of libel cases is appended.

Pierce, Samuel R., Jr. "Anatomy of an Historic Decision: *New York Times Co. v. Sullivan.*" *North Carolina Law Review,* 43: 315–63, February 1965. **P9**
"*New York Times Co. v. Sullivan* is a landmark decision in the law of libel and in the field of civil liberties, because the United States Supreme Court, for the first time, determined 'the extent to which the constitutional protections for speech and press limit a State's power to award damages in a libel action brought by a public official against critics of his official conduct.'"

Pigot, Robert of Chetwynd. *Liberty of the Press; A Letter Addressed to the National Assembly of France by Robert Pigot . . . and Published by their Order, with Notes and Supplement Afterwards Added; and Offered to the Consideration of Every English-man.* London, Printed for the Booksellers, 1790. 32 p. **P10**

Pische, Vail W. "How Far Will the Law of Privacy Extend In Radio?" *Notre Dame Lawyer,* 19:148–54, December 1944. **P11**

Porter, Katherine Anne. "A Wreath for the Gamekeeper." In *Encounters; an Anthology from the First Ten Years of Encounter Magazine.* New York, Basic Books, 1963, pp. 277–90. **P12**
In this devastating criticism of D. H. Lawrence's *Lady Chatterley's Lover* are numerous observations on censorship. While defending the loud protests of literary critics against censorship of the work, she objects to the defense of *Lady Chatterley* as a work of art, which it is not.

Post, Albert. *Popular Freethought in America, 1825–1850.* New York, Columbia University Press, 1943. 258 p. (Studies in History, Economics and Public Law, no. 497) **P13**

The development of religious radicalism in America from 1825 to 1850 and the freedom generally extended to its press by civil authorities. Opposition was largely in the form of counterattacks in press and pulpit, but Abner Kneeland and Charles Knowlton were brought to trial for their blasphemies and Dr. Thomas Cooper was forced to resign his presidency of South Carolina College because of his heterodoxy.

"Postal Privacy." *Playboy*, 13(8):39–44, August 1966; 13(12):89–93, December 1966. **P14**

A series of letters in the Playboy Forum citing experiences with postal censorship.

Potamkin, Harry A. *The Eyes of the Movie.* [New York, International Pamphlets, 1934]. 32 p. (International Pamphlets, no. 38) **P15**

The author, one of the founders of the John Reed Club and member of the National Board of Review, charges the film industry with a bourgeois conspiracy to promote capitalist thought and suppress films that encourage social advancement.

[Pountney, E. R., et al.]. *Citrine & others v. Pountney: The Daily Worker Libel Case.* [London, Modern Books, 1940?]. 48 p. **P16**

Summary of the six-day trial for libel action brought by Sir Walter Citrine and six other members of the Trades Union Congress against E. R. Pountney, proprietor of the *Daily Worker.* The court awarded for the plaintiff and granted an injunction to restrain the publishing of further libels. Mr. Justice Stable awarded damages of a sum that would not have the effect of putting the paper out of business, declaring that so long as the *Daily Worker* expounded its views and refrained from libeling other people it was desirable that it should be in a position to do so.

Powell, Lawrence C. *You, John Milton.* Norman, Okla., The Library, University of Oklahoma, 1966. 12 p. **P17**

An address by the Dean of the School of Library Service, University of California, Los Angeles, on the occasion of the presentation of a copy of Milton's *Areopagitica* as the millionth volume at the University of Oklahoma.

Powell, Richard P. "Nobody Loves a Censor." *Infantry Journal*, 58:17–20, March 1946. **P18**

The chief news censor for the Southwest Pacific theater in World War II writes of the trials of a military censor.

Powsner, Robert H. "Libel in Limbo: Another Conquest for the Right of Privacy?" *Los Angeles Bar Bulletin*, 30:365–75, September 1955. **P19**

Reference to California's right of privacy law and the cases of *Gill v. Curtis Publishing Co.*, 38 Cal. 2nd 273, and *Gill v. Hearst*, 40 Cal. 2nd 224.

Prasher, A. LaVonne. "The Censorship of Landor's *Imaginary Conversations.*" *Bulletin of the John Rylands Library*, 49:427–63, Spring 1967. **P20**

The long and involved controversy over deletions in William S. Landor's manuscript that took place between the author and his publisher, John Taylor. Julius Hare, as negotiator, demonstrated the firmness of his dedication to freedom of expression; the poet, Robert Southey, assisted in the censoring.

Priestly, J. B. "Censor and Stage." *New Statesman*, 70:967, 17 December 1965. **P21**

Pringle, Henry F. ". . . *Guard It, Cherish It and Work for It . . .*" *An Address Broadcast over the Columbia Network During National Journalism Week, October 6, 1941.* [New York, Columbia Broadcasting Co., 1941?]. 16 p. **P22**

"Publicity Controls Imposed on Newsmen in Murder Case." *Editor & Publisher*, 99(30):9–10, 44, 23 July 1966. **P23**

Relates to the Peoria, Ill., trial of *People v. Richard Franklin Speck.*

Pulitzer, Joseph, Jr. "The Press Lives by Disclosures." *Nieman Reports*, 15(3):7–9, July 1961. **P24**

A discussion of President Kennedy's proposal of voluntary censorship, occasioned by the ill-fated Cuban invasion. The editor of the St. Louis *Post-Dispatch* believes that "it would be better to conclude that maneuvers of this sort should not be undertaken by an open society than that our society should become less open."

[Pynchon, William]. *The Meritorious Price of Our Redemption by William Pynchon, London, 1650 . . .* 158 p. (Facsimile reproduction of one of four known copies, made in June 1931 under the direction of Harry A. Wright, Springfield, Mass.) **P25**

Bound with the facsimile reproduction is a nine-page account of the action taken by the colonial authorities against the book, the first to be burned in the American colonies.

"Race Defamation and the First Amendment." *Fordham Law Review*, 34:653–75, May 1966. **R1**

Minority groups will not be protected if the race-baiter is driven underground. The airing of obnoxious attacks aids rather than harms the group by rallying the majority on the side of those attacked. Legislators should recognize this and refrain from class libel legislation.

Radin, Max. "Freedom of Speech and Contempt of Court." *Illinois Law Review*, 36:599–620, 1942. **R2**

"It is respectfully suggested to Superior Courts everywhere, that contumely, no matter how offensive, which falls short of an organized conspiracy to impede justice, may be treated not as contempt of court but with contempt by the court."

Rajan, K. R. S. "India's Free Press in Peril." *New Statesman*, 72:818–20, 2 December 1966. **R3**

Raney, William. "San Francisco." *Censorship*, 2(3):15–18, Summer 1966. **R4**

Despite recent censorship activities against books, films, and nightclubs, San Francisco remains the most liberal major city in America.

Raywid, Mary Anne. "Operation Textbook." In *The Ax-Grinders: Critics of Our Public Schools.* New York, Macmillan, 1962, pp. 123–54. **R5**

An account of pressures brought to bear by patriotic or idealogical groups to suppress or influence selection of public school textbooks.

Reed, David. *Canon 35: Flemington Revisited.* Columbia, Mo., Freedom of Information Center, School of Journalism, University of Missouri, 1967. 5 p. (Report no. 177) **R6**

"Much of the impetus for the 1937 passage of the American Bar Association's Canon 35, which bars photographers and electronic media from the courtroom, was provided by accusations against the press in its coverage of the 1935 kidnapping trial of Bruno Richard Hauptmann." The author revisits the scene in an attempt to determine whether conduct of photographers at the trial deserved such a rebuke.

———. *Pre-Trial Publicity in England.* Columbia, Mo., Freedom of Information Center, School of Journalism, University of Missouri, 1966. 4 p. (Publication no. 167) **R7**

This report considers the limits placed upon the English press in reporting pretrial information and compares the English system with the American system.

———. *Toils of the College Press.* Columbia, Mo., Freedom of Information Center,

School of Journalism, University of Missouri, 1967. 6p. (Report no. 180) **R 8**
A survey of the difficulties with censorship faced by the college press across the nation. The author concludes that, although "student newspapers and magazines make little progress toward any sort of permanent guarantees of absolute freedom from control, [their status fluctuates with administrations, the changing political scene, and periodic restaffing] the college press seems to be holding its ground."

Reeves, R. Ambrose. "Dangers of Censorship." *Forum*, 4(18):18–21, November 1955. **R 9**
The Bishop of Johannesburg, South Africa, believes that censorship of literature, the press, and broadcasting by the state "cuts at the roots of the moral life because it destroys one of the essential foundations of all morality, namely, the respect for truth." Under censorship truth becomes something laid down by the authority. When freedom of expression goes, a loss of the meaning of truth follows, and book burning is not far away. References are to South Africa.

Regan, John J. "Supreme Court and Obscenity; Censorship a Defensive Weapon." *Vital Speeches*, 31:592–95, 19 July 1965. **R 10**

Reichardt, Jasia. "Censorship, Obscenity and Context." *Studio*, 172:222–23, November 1966. **R 11**
The author considers censorship of works of art in England under the Vagrancy Acts of 1824 and 1838 (public exhibition of indecent prints) and the Obscene Publications Act of 1959, as amended in 1964. The occasion is police action against works of Jim Dine in a London exhibition. References are also made to contemporary exhibitions of Aubry Beardsley, Stass Paraskos, Hermann Nitsch, and, historically, to Ruskin's burning of the Turner nudes and the 1929 confiscation of D. H. Lawrence paintings.

Reiss, Bernard F. "The Supreme Court and Obscenity: *Mishkin* and *Ginzburg*—Expansion of Freedom of Expression and Improved Regulation Through Flexible Standards of Obscenity." *Rutgers Law Review*, 21:43–55, Fall 1966. **R 12**

Rhode Island. Legislative Council. *Obscenity and Censorship*. Providence, R.I., The Council, 1966. 41p. (Research Report no. 15) **R 13**

Rice, Elmer. "How We Muzzle the Movies." *This Week*, 6 March 1949, pp. 5, 35. **R 14**
Rice charges the Production Code Administration with being "probably the most effective private censorship agency ever devised" and

with being "a sounding board for all organized pressure groups in the country."

Richman, Richard. "Coexistence: The Press and Courts." *Grassroots Editor*, 7(3): 21–23, July 1966. **R 15**

"Right of Privacy—Relative's Interest in a Deceased's Name or Likeness." *Ohio State Law Journal*, 22:438–41, Spring 1961. **R 16**
Bradley v. Cowles Magazines, Inc., 168 N.E. 2d 64 (1960).

"Right of Privacy vs. Free Press: Suggested Resolution of Conflicting Values." *Indiana Law Journal*, 28:179–94, Winter 1953. **R 17**
The over-zealous protection of the individual's privacy and the exaggerated concern for this new tort grew out of "a journalistic era characterized by extreme callousness for the feeling of the individual."

"The Right to Know." *Economist*, 206: 1085–86, 23 March 1963. **R 18**
"Freedom of the press means access for its readers to views as well as news. The important thing is that views ought not, any more than trivia, to drive out information." Freedom to report news and views should be given equally to the press and the broadcasting agencies.

Roberts, Charles. "LBJ's Credibility Gap." *Newsweek*, 68(25):24–26, 19 December 1966. **R 19**
"The list of outright pervarications, half-truths, concealments and misleading denials by the [Johnson] Administration is almost as long as its impressive list of achievements."

Roberts, Edwin A., Jr. *The Smut Rakers: A Report in Depth on Obscenity and the Censors*. Silver Springs, Md., The National Observer, 1966. 143p. (Newsbook no. 9) **R 20**
Contents: Free expression v. obscenity—the dilemma of a reasonable society. The long bookshelf of sex and the various aims of erotica. Movies keep their sex quotient high but public is partial to corn, not porn. Postal inspectors vigorously pursue major violators of Mr. Comstock's Law. Customs Bureau's criteria change to reflect contemporary ideas. When smut moves between states J. Edgar Hoover's men move in. The magistrate's reluctance frustrates the prosecutor, baffles the patrolman. The "Citizens for Decent Literature." Geri Turner Davis and her *Cat Called Jesus*. Father Hill and Operation Yorkville. The *Ginzburg* Opinions of the U.S. Supreme Court (text). The work includes an account of the publishing trials of Grove Press, attacks on the *Dictionary of American Slang*, exposés of the nudist press and nudist movie industry, and a view of the operations against obscenity by the cities of New York, Boston, and Washington, D.C.

Robischon, Thomas. "A Day in Court with the Literary Critic." *Massachusetts Review*, 6:101–10, Autumn 1964. **R 21**
The author finds disappointing the testimony of literary critics in behalf of books accused of being obscene, citing as an example the Massachusetts trial of *Tropic of Cancer*. "Purely literary or esthetic defenses of books do a disservice to literature. They divorce the moral potential of literature from our sexual lives, and thereby foster a moral irrelevant approach to literature."

Rogers, Charles H. "Police Control of Obscene Literature." *Journal of Criminal Law*, 57:430–82, December 1966. **R 22**
"In this article Mr. Rogers traces the development of the American law of obscenity from its common law antecedents to the most recent decisions of the Supreme Court of the United States. Particular emphasis is placed upon the role of the police in the suppression of obscenity, and the special problems created for law enforcement personnel by court decisions. An examination of the work of the Chicago police department in this area is included, as is a detailed analysis of the obscenity market, a subject usually, but inexplicably, ignored by past law review commentaries." There is considerable information about the work of the NODL, CDL, and other citizens groups opposing obscenity, and a review of the major obscenity cases before the courts. The author concludes: "It is time that the courts, the legislatures and the public, including the booksellers and publishers, accept the responsibility for pornography as their own. The first step is to recognize that the sole responsibility is not that of the police and the solution is not the placing of additional restrictions and responsibility on the police."

Rothenberg, Ignaz. "Invasion of Privacy, in the Codes of Journalists." *Nieman Reports*, 13:5–7, October 1959. **R 23**
A comparison of canons of journalism and active newspaper practices in the United States with those of other countries in the matter of invasion of privacy. Great Britain, Sweden, France, and South Africa are included. The author suggests how intrusions of privacy are avoided in the foreign press.

———. "Newspaper Sins Against Privacy." *Nieman Reports*, 11:41–44, January 1957. **R 24**
Among the sins against privacy practiced by American newspapers are: recalling expiated violations of the law, refusing anonymity to juvenile and to first offenders in minor cases, prejudicial pretrial publicity, and unnecessary involvement of families of accused or convicted.

Rowat, D. C. "How Much Administrative Secrecy?" *Canadian Journal of Economics and Political Science*, 31:479–98, Novem-

ber 1965. (Reply by K. W. Knight and rejoinder, February 1966)   **R 25**
A recommendation for relaxation of present restrictions on access to public documents. The logic of democracy "demands that the long-term trend be in the direction of the principle of publicity."

Royster, Vermont. "Free Press and a Fair Trial." *North Carolina Law Review*, 43:364–71, February 1965.   **R 26**

Rucker, Bryce W. *The First Freedom.* Carbondale, Ill., Southern Illinois University Press, 1968. 322 p. Introduction by Morris Ernst.   **R 27**
The author traces monopoly, chain, and cross-media ownership trends in mass communications and surveys developments related to a reduction in the diversity of voices in the marketplace of ideas. Although a grim picture of the use of legal and illegal means to achieve monopoly control emerges, the author offers hope in the form of the weekly newspaper press, which, he argues, has the greatest potential to remain the public's watchdog over government and its agencies.

———. "What Solutions Do People Endorse in Free Press—Fair Trial Dilemma?" *Journalism Quarterly*, 44:240–44, Summer 1967.   **R 28**
"This experimental study using the Q technique shows five distinct groups of people holding divergent opinions on the free press-fair trial issue, rather than two opposing camps."

Russell, *Sir* Charles. *The Parnell Commission. The Opening Speech for the Defense.* London, Macmillan, 1889. 615 p.   **R 29**
Russell was defense attorney for the Irish nationalist, Charles Parnell, in his libel case against *The Times.* The full account of the affair appears in 35 volumes published by the Special Commission appointed to inquire into Parnellism and Crime.

Rust, William. *Lift the Ban on the Daily Worker.* [London, Daily Worker League, 1942?]. 24 p.   **R 30**
The editor of London's *Daily Worker*, suspended 21 January 1941 by the British Home Secretary under wartime Regulation 2D for "systematically impeding the successful prosecution of the war," criticizes the act as an offense against a free press. A Declaration of Authors and an Actors' Declaration favoring removal of the ban are included, as well as the result of a Gallup Poll showing that less than one-third of the British public supports the ban.

Ruszkowski, Andrew, Oto Denes, and Barbara Scott. "Screen Censorship: Three Views." *Television Quarterly*, 5:31–41, Winter 1967.   **R 31**
Ruszkowski is president of the International Catholic Cinema Office with headquarters in Brussels; Denes is general secretary of the Yugoslavian Film Workers Union; Barbara Scott is associate counsel of the Motion Picture Association of America.

Ryan, Leo A. "Canada." *Censorship*, 2(3): 30–33, Summer 1966.   **R 32**
The author notes that censorship in Canada divides itself nationally along geographic lines—in the East (Ontario and Quebec) there has been a sweeping liberalized trend, whereas in the West and the Maritimes, puritanical values still reign supreme.

Sachs, Emanie. "*The Terrible Siren.*" *Victoria Woodhull (1838–1927).* New York, Harper, 1928. 423 p.   **S 1**
This biography of the colorful Victoria Claflin Woodhull, stockbroker, spiritualist, free love advocate, candidate for the Presidency, and, in later life, the wife of a respectable English banker, has references throughout to issues of free speech, censorship, and libel. Mrs. Woodhull, with her sister Tennessee Claflin, published *Woodhull & Claflin* weekly in New York during the 1870's. The paper attacked many revered institutions and personages and in 1872 was suppressed by Anthony Comstock for its charges of infidelity against the Rev. Henry Ward Beecher. The sisters were sent to a New York jail. Many years later Victoria's English husband, John Biddulph Martin, brought suit for libel against the British Museum for possessing a copy of *The Beecher-Tilton Scandal.* The libel trial is reported in Chapter 17. Two recent biographies of Victoria Woodhull are: (1) Johanna Johnston, *Mrs. Satan; The Incredible Saga of Victoria C. Woodhull.* New York, Putnam's, 1967. 319 p. (2) M. M. Marberry, *Vicky; A Biography of Victoria C. Woodhull.* New York, Funk & Wagnalls, 1967. 344 p.

St. John-Stevas, Norman. "Censorship in the Church." *Books and Bookmen*, 12(7) 15–16, April 1967.   **S 2**
While the Roman index of forbidden books was abolished by the Vatican Council, "the Catholic Church has not dismantled its general system of prior censorship which remains fully in force . . . It seems to me that the disadvantages now far outweigh the advantages and the ecclesiastical system of compulsory censorship should be abolished."

Salisbury, Harold E. *A Survey and Analysis of Current Attitudes toward Censorship of the Legitimate Theatre in the United States.* Los Angeles, University of Southern California, 1961. 176 p. (Ph.D. dissertation, University Microfilms, no. 61–3825)   **S 3**
According to this study, current American attitudes are based upon Christian rather than Puritan objections to the theater, with major concern over protecting the young from obscenity.

Sargent, John A. *Self Regulation: The Motion-Picture Production Code, 1930–1961.* Ann Arbor, Mich., University of Michigan, 1963. 277 p. (Ph.D. dissertation, University Microfilms, no. 63–5013)   **S 4**
"The main object of this dissertation is to document the history of the Motion Picture Production Code through an examination of the Code in theory and the Code in practice. A further purpose is to determine how critics affected the administration and application of Code regulations."

Schauerte, Bud. *Yes, There Is the Right to Know.* Columbia, Mo., Freedom of Information Center, School of Journalism, University of Missouri, 1967. 3 p. (Report no. 003)   **S 5**
The writer takes issue with J. C. Merrill (Report no. 002) in defining "the people's right to know."

Schechner, Richard. "Pornography and the New Expression." *Atlantic*, 219:74–78 January 1967.   **S 6**
The author reports on a new "atavistic, cohesive and participatory revolution"—a revolution of the flesh which is engulfing the culture of the Western world. "The new expression seems pornographic and obscene only when it threatens our sexual taboos . . . The least interesting part of the new expression is its literature . . . At best, publication of new, sexy titles and the reissuing of classics are efforts to keep up with change . . . When authentic, the new expression rejects the sequential logic of print for the simultaneous tumult of experience."

Scheiber, Harry N. *The Wilson Administration and Civil Liberties, 1917–1921.* Ithaca, N.Y., Cornell University Press, 1960. 69 p. (Cornell Studies in American History, Literature, and Folklore, no. 6)   **S 7**
Chapter 3 deals with the censorship practices of Postmaster General Burleson under the Espionage Act.

Schmidtchen, P. W. "Progress, Where Is Thy Sting? History of Book Censoring." *Hobbies*, 71:108–9+, March 1966.   **S 8**

"Schools Ban Art Magazine." *Artscan*, 109/10:1, 11, June–July 1967.   **S 9**
Edmonton, Canada, public schools ban *Artscan* magazine because of its alleged emphasis on "eroticism and sexual allusions."

Schramm, Wilbur, Jack Lyle, and Edwin B. Parker. *Television in the Lives of Our Children. With a Psychiatrist's Comment on the Effects of Television by Lawrence Z. Freedman.* Stanford, Calif., Stanford University Press, 1961. 324 p.   **S 10**
Responses from 6,000 children, 2,000 parents,

and several hundred teachers. Questions asked include: Does television often frighten children? Does it teach violence to children? Does it cause juvenile delinquency? To the last the answer is: Television can contribute but can hardly be the basic cause.

Schultheiss, Thomas. "Conrad on Stage Censorship." *American Notes & Queries*, 5:117–18, April 1967.   **S11**
Reference to Conrad's attitude toward the stage censor expressed in 1907 in a *Daily Mail* article and in a letter to Galsworthy.

Schultz, James. *Editorials and Electioneering Laws*. Columbia, Mo., Freedom of Information Center, School of Journalism, University of Missouri, 1967. 4p. (Publication no. 174)   **S12**
The case of the Birmingham editor arrested for violating the Alabama Corrupt Practices Act by publishing an election-day editorial favoring a referendum on the city's form of government. The U.S. Supreme Court declared the law unconstitutional.

"Scope of Supreme Court Review in Obscenity Cases." *Duke Law Journal*, 1965:596–608, Summer 1965.   **S13**

Scopes, John T., and James Presley. *Center of the Storm: Memoirs of John T. Scopes*. New York, Holt, Rinehart, and Winston, 1967. 277p.   **S14**
Scopes was the defendant in the famous "monkey trial" of 1925 in which the constitutionality of Tennessee's antievolution act was tested.

Scott, Barbara. "Motion Picture Censorship and the Exhibitor." *Film Comment*, 2(4):56–60, Fall 1965.   **S15**
A review of the legal progress made in recognizing freedom for motion pictures, with special attention to the case of *Freedman v. Maryland* involving the constitutionality of the Maryland censorship statutes and prior licensing of a nonobscene film. "I predict that with total industry cooperation, motion picture censorship in the next ten years will be only a subject for the history books."

Seaton, Richard H. "Obscenity: The Search for a Standard." *University of Kansas Law Review*, 13:117–24, October 1964.   **S16**
Roth v. United States, 354 U.S. 476 (1957).

Sebastian, Raymond F. "Obscenity and the Supreme Court: Nine Years of Confusion." *Stanford Law Review*, 19:167–89, November 1966.   **S17**
"Whether the Supreme Court has promulgated intelligible standards for identifying obscenity and for determining in what circumstances obscenity, when once identified, may be

constitutionally suppressed is the question which this Note attempts to answer." Regarding *Mishkin v. New York*, *Ginzburg v. United States* and *Fanny Hill v. Attorney General*.

Segal, Robert M. "Fair Trial and Free Press—An Analysis of The Problem." *Massachusetts Law Quarterly*, 51:101–16, June 1966.   **S18**
One of the escapes from the dilemma posed by the desire to keep the press free of restraint and to assure fair trial for the accused is the Bar-Press Code. The Massachusetts version is appended.

Seldes, George. *One Thousand Americans*. New York, Boni & Gaer, 1947. 312p. **S19**
One thousand Americans, interested in property rights rather than the general welfare, stand in the way of progress. Control is effected through the National Association of Manufacturers to the press and hence to Congress. In a section on "big magazines" Seldes shows that "a few men, whose interests are identical with that of the National Association of Manufacturers," are in control. The appendix lists newspaper press controls of radio stations, press in chains, DuPont influence on the press, ownership statements on *Time* and the Curtis Publishing Co., and "the suppressed U.S. War Department exposé of fascism."

———. *You Can't Do That: A Survey of the forces attempting, in the name of patriotism, to make a desert of the Bill of Rights*. New York, Modern Age Books, 1938. 307p.
                S20
The forces include the American Legion, the DAR, Chambers of Commerce, the American Navy League, the National Security League, and certain large business organizations, particularly newspaper publishers. Almost all newspapers of the country, Seldes charges, are business concerns, placing profits above public welfare. "The history of the American Newspaper Guild offers the best proof that the press is the enemy of the people and that the bulwark of our liberties is therefore collapsing." Appendix includes a list of organizations defending civil liberties in the United States and a bibliography on civil liberties.

Semonche, John E. "Definitional and Contextual Obscenity: the Supreme Court's New and Disturbing Accomodation." *UCLA Law Review*, 13:1173–1213, August 1966.   **S21**
"The new contextual test for obscenity [Ginzburg case] by-passes the patent offensiveness and social value elements of *Roth* and considers prurient interest only in an imprecise way. If the promotion and marketing methods of the disseminator of material that would be protected under the definitional approach is such that he is found to be making an appeal, successful or not, to the prurient interest of his potential customer, then his own evaluation of the material, as determined by the court, will convict him."

Sha, Shiva C. *A Concept of a Planned Free Press*. Calcutta, India, Bookland Private Press, 1958. 92p.   **S22**

Shaffer, Helen B. *Protection of Privacy*. Washington, D.C., Editorial Research Reports, 1966. (*Editorial Research Reports*, 1:283–99, 1966)   **S23**
Includes new controls to protect the privacy of the U.S. mails.

Shaw, Bernard. "The Censor Censured." *Shavian*, 13:20–23, September 1958. **S24**
In a letter to Bache Matthews of the Birmingham Repertory Theatre, Shaw comments on the Lord Chamberlain's censorship requirement for licensing of *Back to Methuselah*. The parody of the Athanasian Creed must be withdrawn, two characters must not be made up to resemble Lloyd George and H. H. Asquith (these gentlemen will be disappointed, Shaw observes), and "usual conventionalities of dress" should be observed in representing Adam and Eve.

Shaw, Robert M. "The Danger of Getting Used to Lies." *Vital Speeches*, 32:332–34, 15 March 1966.   **S25**
The manager of the Minnesota Newspaper Association accuses many government leaders of not only managing the news but bragging about it. He urges newspapermen to speak up and defend their profession.

Shaw, Roy. "TV Control and Responsibility." *Censorship*, 2(4):6–14, Autumn 1966.   **S26**
"The accusation of censorship *within* the [British] broadcasting organisation is not proven, and may simply reflect a creative artist's impatience with complex editorial controls. The claim, at the other extreme that there is urgent need for *external* control from a Broadcasting Council and a consumer movement seems equally ill-founded. Despite the Press Council, there are far more abuses of freedom in the popular press than there are in television."

Shawcross, Hartley W., *baron*. "The Shadow of the Law." *Encounter*, 26:78–89, March 1966. (Comment by Sir Linton Andrews, July 1966)   **S27**
Lord Shawcross, who chaired the 1962 Royal Commission on the Press, examines various issues involving press freedom in Great Britain—the right of privacy, the law of libel, qualified privilege, contempt by publication, and the protection of state secrets. He notes differences between British and American law relating to the press and calls for certain legal reforms. "Newspapers in seeking to obtain and publish information which it is in the public interest to know are beset on all sides with doubts and arguments as to what

they may properly disclose. Often these have to be resolved at once, perhaps late at night, or the news becomes stale. Newspapers generally take care to prevent the publication of anything untrue. When they act in good faith and with a true sense of public responsibility they should be protected if occasionally they go wrong."

Shenker, Morris A., and Cordell Siegel. "Cause Célèbre: The Problem and The Solutions." *St. Louis University Law Journal*, 11:152–79, Winter 1967.　**S 28**
In solving the problem of free press versus fair trial there must be an all-out effort. "The professions must police themselves internally; legislatures must enact statutes giving the courts the power to punish summarily in limited cases; the courts must use their contempt powers as well as the procedural remedies."

Sheridan, Thomas. *An Humble Appeal to the Public, together with some considerations on the present critical and dangerous state of the Stage in Ireland . . .* Dublin, 1758. 46p.　**S 29**

Sherwin, Robert V. *Legal Aspects of Photography.* Philadelphia, Chilton, 1957. 126p. (Modern Camera Guide Series)　**S 30**
Includes sections on obscenity, libel, invasion of privacy, and copyright.

Shipley, Carl L. "Privacy Invasion by Telecast." *Federal Bar Journal*, 15:186–93, April–June 1955.　**S 31**
In the absence of television case law the station manager must rely on the analogous experience of the motion picture, newsreel, and news photograph industries.

"Showdown Coming on the Billion-Dollar 'Smut Industry.'" *U.S. News*, 59:68+, 6 December 1965.　**S 32**
"There is growing concern over the torrent of obscene material sent to youngsters. Supreme Court may set a border between free speech and smut."

"Showdown in the Southwest." *Time*, 87(6):44, 11 February 1966.　**S 33**
Concerns a New Mexico weekly editor's successful libel suit against a reader who claimed his written views followed the Communist line.

Siepmann, Charles. *Radio in Wartime.* New York, Oxford, 1942. 32p. (America in a World at War no. 26)　**S 34**
Deals with radio propaganda, the monitoring of both domestic and foreign broadcasts, and

the work of the Defense Communications Board to meet the national defense requirements.

Sigourney, Andre R. "Fair Trial and Free Press—A Proposed Solution." *Massachusetts Law Quarterly*, 51:117–29, June 1966.　**S 35**
Includes text of a proposed bill in the Massachusetts House that would restrict only the most prejudicial publicity items and impose only mild sanctions for their divulgence and publication.

Silber, Alan. "The Supreme Court and Obscenity: The *Ginzburg* Test—Restriction of First Amendment Freedoms Through Loss of Predictability." *Rutgers Law Review*, 21:56–72, Fall 1966.　**S 36**
"The achievement of the *Ginzburg* formulation most likely will be to increase confusion in an already intolerably confused area. The role of the individual judge's value judgment of the material—and now his evaluation of the defendant's business—is not bridled by meaningful judicial standards."

Silver, Isadore. "Privacy and the First Amendment." *Fordham Law Review*, 34:553–68, May 1966.　**S 37**
"While libel 'interests' are known, privacy is a bit more mysterious . . . Invasion of privacy, at least by communications media, is a relatively new area of law, with its own amorphous principles, and some clearing of the mystery concerning the interest it is designed to protect is necessary. It is only then that constitutional problems can be fruitfully analysed."

Silverman, Betsy M. "Sale of Smut Can Be Stopped." *Parents Magazine*, 40:48, 98, January 1965.　**S 38**
"Here's what local groups should do to protect children from mail-order and newsstand pornography."

Smith, Charles W., Jr. *Public Opinion in a Democracy; A Study in American Politics.* New York, Prentice-Hall, 1939. 598p.　**S 39**
Includes chapters on propaganda and censorship, pressure groups, artificial restraints on opinion, patriotism and radicalism, public opinion in wartime, and public opinion and the Supreme Court.

Smith, Francis. *An Account of the Injurious Proceedings of Sir G. Jeffreys . . . late Recorder of London, against F. Smith, Bookseller, with his arbitrary carriage towards the Grand-Jury at Guildhall, Sept. 16, 1680, upon an Indictment then exhibited against . . . F. Smith for publishing a Pretended Libel: entituled, An Act of Common-Council for Retrenching the Expenses of the Lord Mayor and Sheriffs of the City of London, etc.* London, [1681?].　**S 40**

Smith, J. W. B. "Subversive Propaganda, the Past and the Present." *Georgetown Law Journal*, 29:809–28, April 1941.　**S 41**
"The immediate adoption of a program to counteract subversive propaganda, placing primary emphasis on publicity and information . . . coupled with vigorous enforcement of existing legislation . . . should, if properly administered and coordinated, go far toward defeating this elusive attack." The propaganda of acts in redressing economic and social problems is more effective than the propaganda of words.

Smith, William R., Jr. "Free Press-Fair Trial: First Duty of the Bar Is To Correct Its Own Failings." *Florida Bar Journal*, 39:921–27, September 1965.　**S 42**
"Prosecutors and defense counsel alike must exercise enlightened self-restraint and in the absence of the courts and disciplinary committees must act to enforce Canon 20." The press, he believes can promulgate and honor a voluntary code.

Smythe, Dallas W. "Freedom of Information: Some Analysis and a Proposal for Satellite Broadcasting." *Quarterly Journal of Economics and Business*, 6:7–24, August 1966.　**S 43**
Proposals relate to a world-wide broadcasting system.

Some Thought Upon the Prosecutions of Libels by Way of Information. Addressed to All Persons Who May Be Summoned to Serve upon Juries. London, J. Walker, 1719. 1p.　**S 44**

Sontag, Susan. "Feast for Open Eyes." *Nation*, 198:374–76, 13 April 1964.　**S 45**
An analysis and defense of the avant-garde film, *Flaming Creatures*, which met with police hostility.

Sowle, Claude R. "Free Press and Fair Trial: Some Predictions and Suggestions." *Nieman Reports*, 20(4):18–20, December 1966.　**S 46**
The author recommends that newspaper publishers employ an able member of the Bar as a paid consultant in the area of free press-fair trial problems, to work with the newspaper's decision makers in drawing up a sound policy on news coverage of criminal matters, and once such guidelines are established to monitor the paper's adherence to them.

Spock, Benjamin. "How Can We Protect Our Children from Obscenity." *Redbook*, 124:18+, April 1965.　**S 47**
Until obscenity laws are enforced or changed to give greater protection for children and until popular taste becomes revolted by excess license and swings back toward propriety, it is up to parents to protect their children

from the shock of obscenity. Parents should keep track of what their children are reading and viewing. They should make their feelings known to neighborhood newsdealers and movie houses that are patronized by children and teenagers.

———, and Paul Goodman. "Civil Liberties and the Juvenile: In the Library & Bookstore." *Civil Liberties*, 244:4–6, March 1967. **S 48**

Dr. Spock argues that "men must have moral values—however relative—and that society cannot afford to let them be destroyed or even changed too abruptly." He advocates two levels of tolerance. "What is allowed to be displayed openly on newsstands and in bookstores, shown on television during children's viewing hours, shown in theaters open to all ages should only be what average citizens would consider not disturbing to children, not debasing to children's ideals. This would not mean that immorality could not be honestly dealt with. For adults over 18, plays, movies, late TV programs, books, magazines should be allowed to deal seriously or lightly with sexual or other categories of immorality, for the purpose of edifying, producing catharsis of emotions, amusing or providing escape." Such works should be labeled and reserved for adults only, and a presentation should not be allowed if in a court's opinion it would degrade or tantalize the feeling of the average citizen or offend his moral values. Goodman disagrees with Dr. Spock's protection of the adolescent. "The young will conspiratorially get what they want anyway, whether pornography or drugs, but the atmosphere of conspiracy prevents moral maturation, as well as the possibility of advising them." There is a use for high-grade pornography, but sadistic images are unhygienic to masturbate to since guilt prevents relaxation and release, and censorship increases the prevalance of the sadistic association. Instead of suppressing the obscene we must help young people to "cope with brute realities by common reason, justice, compassion, and affection."

Steigleman, Walter A., and Paul Jess. "Publication of Names of Juvenile Offenders." *Journalism Quarterly*, 37:393–97, Summer 1960. **S 49**

"A national survey of newspaper policies indicates that an increasing number of youthful criminals may expect to see their names in print in the future, particularly where editors view publication as a deterrent to crime. Even in states with restrictive statutes many editors find ways to lessen the limitations."

Stein, M. L. *Freedom of the Press; A Continuing Struggle.* New York, Messner, 1966. 190 p. **S 50**

Commentary on current issues dealing with press freedom in the United States—censorship and national security, libel, post-office censorship, influence of advertisers and pressure groups on the news, responsibility of the press in presenting a variety of views on controversial issues, and free press and fair trial. There are chapters on freedom of the press in other countries; television broadcasting, and the movies.

Steinberg, Harris B., *et al.* "Symposium: Fair Trial—Free Press." *Criminal Law Bulletin*, 2:3–37, April 1966. **S 51**

Panelists: Justice Bernard S. Meyer, Herbert Brucker, Frank G. Raichle, and Harris B. Steinberg, moderator.

[Stephen, *Sir* James F.]. "The Law of Libel." *Cornhill Magazine*, 15:36–46, January 1867. **S 52**

A brief sketch of the historical development of British libel law together with appraisal of the present (1867) statutes. "We do not believe that the law has ever before been stated in a manner so favourable to journalists."

[Stephen, *Sir* Leslie]. "Art and Morality." *Cornhill Magazine*, 32:91–101, July 1875. **S 53**

The author examines the "pretentious fallacy" used by authors accused of writing an immoral book that "art and morality are two different things, and that a critic has no business to judge a poem by the rules which he would apply to a sermon."

Stephens, Kenneth D. "Privileged Communications—News Media—A 'Shield Statute' for Oregon?" *Oregon Law Review*, 46:99–112, December 1966. **S 54**

An analysis of a proposed "shield statute" model supported by the Oregon Newspaper Publishers Association.

Stern, Gerald. "The Two Forums of a Criminal Trial: The Courtroom and the Press." *Syracuse Law Review*, 14:450–71, Spring 1963. **S 55**

Stevens, John D., Robert L. Bailey, Judith F. Krueger, and John Mallwitz. "Criminal Libel vs. Seditions Libel, 1916–65." *Journalism Quarterly*, 43:110–13, Spring 1966. **S 56**

"This study undertakes to examine some aspects of criminal libel cases that resemble seditious libel prosecutions, as reported in West's *American Digest* system, during the last half-century. Of the 148 criminal libel cases reported during this period, the study examines the 31 which were brought for criticism of public officials and which found their ways to the highest courts in their states or to the federal courts."

Straton, H. H. "The Church Faces the Problem of Pornography." *Church Today*, 9:3–5, 24 September 1965. **S 57**

Struve, John G. "Contempt by Publication—Fair Trial v. Freedom of the Press."

Willamette Law Journal, 4:31–53, Spring 1966. **S 58**

Sullenberger, Lloyd. "*Sheppard v. Maxwell*: Free Speech and Press v. Fair Trial." *William and Mary Law Review*, 8:143–51, Fall 1966. **S 59**

Sheppard v. Maxwell, 86 S. Ct. 1507 (1966).

Sullivan, Ann. "Annette Buchanan's Fight to Protect a Reporter's Sources." *Quill*, 54(8):12–14, August 1966. **S 60**

The case of the managing editor of University of Oregon's *Daily Emerald*, found guilty of contempt of court for shielding news sources in an article on student use of marijuana.

Sulzberger, E. J., Jr. "Privacy Invaded by Wrongful Presentation of Privileged News." *Washington and Lee Law Review*, 17:279–86, Fall 1960. **S 61**

Concerns *Aquino v. Bulletin Co.*, 154 A. 2d 422 (Pa. 1959), whether an otherwise privileged newspaper article can be made so sensational as to constitute an unwarranted invasion of privacy by going beyond the recognized limits of decency.

Summers, Robert E., and Harrison B. Summers. *Broadcasting and the Public.* Belmont, Calif., Wadsworth, 1966. 402 p. **S 62**

Chapter 7 deals with Broadcasting and Government; Chapter 13 with The Public Interest.

"Survival of Right of Privacy Action." *Illinois Law Review*, 41:114–18, May–June 1946. **S 63**

Notes on an Arizona Supreme Court decision, *Reed v. Real Detective Publishing Co., Inc.*, 162 P. (2d) 133 (1945).

Süssman, Irving, and Cornelia Süssman. *How to Read a Dirty Book, or The Way of the Pilgrim Reader. Preface by Anne Fremantle.* Chicago, Franciscan Herald, 1966. 139 p. **S 64**

"Examining arguments for and against reading dirty books, the authors offer a way out of the morass of misunderstanding particularly the misunderstandings of the Judaeo-Christian cultural perspectives. Literature, whether dirty or clean, is presented as something to be read not only as history, but as life itself. The dictum that there are no dirty books, only dirty minds, is qualified by a clear discussion of the distinction between a dirty book and those pornographic (non-literature) commodities printed by smut-peddlers."

Sutherland, Arthur E. "Crime, Courts,

and Newspapers." *Nieman Reports*, 10(2): 39–45, April 1956.　　　**S 65**

Memorandum prepared by Professor Sutherland of the Harvard Law School to brief the Nieman Fellows for a seminar. He raises questions relating to the conflict of interest between the right of a fair trial and the right of the people to know.

Taylor, Henry A. "British Concept of the Freedom of the Press." *Gazette: International Journal for Mass Communications Studies*, 11(2/3):123–38, 1965.　　**T 1**

"Evolution of press freedom in Britain and recent activities of the General Council of the Press in assuring that abuses of freedom by the press do not lead to restrictive government legislation." The author traces the evolution of the concept of freedom of the press in England from the beginning of printing to 1861, when the present-day concept was established. "The state of continual alertness is natural and necessary because, in Britain, the freedom of the Press is not guaranteed, as it is in some countries, by inclusion in a written constitution. Nor is it established by any specific Act of Parliament." It is the result of four centuries' struggle in common law.

Taylor, Telford. "Crime Reporting and Publicity of Criminal Proceedings." *Columbia Law Review*, 66:34–61, January 1966.　　**T 2**

The primary purpose of the author has been to select and specify those problems which are of concern both in American and British law. The appendix includes the text of the Massachusetts Guide for the Bar and News Media and a statement of the Justice Department policy on release of information relating to criminal proceedings.

Teeter, Dwight L. *Press Freedom and the Public Printing: Pennsylvania, 1775–1783*. Boulder, Col., Presented at the History Division, National Convention of the Association for Education in Journalism, 1967. 14 p. mimeo.　　**T 3**

"The Television Code." In *International Television Almanac, 1967*. Charles S. Aaronson, *ed.* New York, Quigley Publications, 1967, pp. 752–61.　　**T 4**

Text of the Code of the National Association of Broadcasters.

Thai, Nguyen. "'News' in Vietnam: A Case of Underdeveloped Freedom to Know." *Nieman Reports*, 16(1):19–21, March 1963.　　**T 5**

Thomas, Donald. "L'Escole des Filles." *Censorship*, 2(3): 42–46, Summer 1966.　**T 6**

A account of how a little book, "a remarkable piece of Renaissance pornography, maintained its international reputation throughout the sixteenth and much of the seventeenth centuries."

———. "Vice Society." *Censorship*, 3(1): 34–40, Winter 1967.　　**T 7**

An account of the formation of the vice society in England, from the Society for the Reformation of Manners (1692), the Proclamation Society (1788), the Society for the Suppression of Vice (1802), the National Vigilance Association (1886), and followed by the London Council for the Promotion of Morality (later known as the Public Morality Council). References are made to some of the attacks of the vice societies on works of literature. An editor's note states that Thomas is at work on a large-scale historical study of censorship in Britain.

Thompson, E. P. *The Struggle for a free press*. London, People's Press, 1952. 24 p.　　**T 8**

Largely a criticism of the monopolistic practices of the capitalist press, and the fight for freedom by the socialist press. There is a brief history of earlier fighters for a free press in England—the Levellers, John Wilkes, Richard Carlile, and the antistamp tax crusade.

Thomson, George P. *Blue Pencil Admiral; the Inside Story of the Press Censorship*. London, Low, Marston, 1947. 216 p.　**T 9**

Rear Admiral Thomson tells how censorship problems were handled in Britain during World War II. The major censorship problems appear to have arisen with domestic rather than field censorship.

Treloar, William P. *Wilkes and the City*. London, Murray, 1917. 299 p.　　**T 10**

Chapters 3, 4 and 5 deal with the prosecution of John Wilkes for publication of *The North Briton* and his expulsion from Parliament.

Trimmer, C. Stephen, Jr. "Criminal Law—Obscenity—A New Dimension in Which to Judge Previous Criteria." *Alabama Law Review*, 19:187–93, Fall 1966.　　**T 11**

Relates to the *Ginzburg* obscenity case, 383 U.S. 463 (1966).

Tynan, Kenneth. "Forbidden Horror." *Atlas*, 11:310–11, May 1966. (Reprinted from *The Observer*, London)　　**T 12**

The author deplores the timidity of the British Broadcasting Corp. for refusing to televise *The War Game*, a film depicting the outbreak of nuclear conflagration, which B.B.C. had itself commissioned.

Underwood, Robert C. "Observations Regarding Canon 35." *Illinois Bar Journal*, 55:194–203, November 1966.　　**U 1**

Justice Underwood cites reasons why Canon 35 should not be eliminated or modified despite technological advances in broadcasting and television.

United Nations Educational, Scientific and Cultural Organization. *The Effects of Television on Children and Adolescents*. Paris, The UN, 1964. 54 p. (Reports and Papers on Mass Communications, no. 43)　**U 2**

An annotated bibliography with an introductory overview of research results, prepared by the International Association for Mass Communications Research, Amsterdam; edited by Wilbur Schramm. Includes sections on television and delinquency, the effect of violence, and television and maladjustment.

———. *The Influence of the Cinema on Children and Adolescents; an Annotated International Bibliography*. Paris, The UN, 1961. 106 p. (Reports and Papers on Mass Communications, no. 31)　　**U 3**

Annotations of 491 titles, including both research and commentary.

United States. Attorney General. *Attorney General's Memorandum on the Public Information Section of the Administrative Procedure Act*. Washington, D.C., Govt. Print. Off., 1967. 47 p.　　**U 4**

A memorandum for the executive departments of the government on methods of implementing Public Law 89–487, which imposes on the executive branch an affirmative obligation to adopt new standards and practices for publication and availability of information. Disclosure is to be the general rule, not the exception; all individuals are to be given equal rights of access; the burden of justifying withholding a document is that of the government; and persons improperly denied access have the right to seek injunctive relief in the courts.

United States. Congress. House of Representatives. Education and Labor Committee. *To Create a Commission on Noxious and Obscene Matters and Materials; Hearings before the Select Subcommittee on Education . . . on H. R. 7465 . . .* Washington, D.C., Govt. Print. Off., 1965. 143 p. (89th Cong., 1st sess.)　　**U 5**

Includes statements from representatives of Citizens for Decent Literature, Knights of Columbus, American Civil Liberties Union, Department of Justice, Post Office Department, and the American Library Association.

———. Judiciary Committee. *Copyright Law Revision. Hearings before Subcommittee 3 . . . on H. R. 4347, H. R. 5680, H. R. 6831, H. R. 6835, Bills for the General Revision of the Copyright Law . . .* Washington, D.C., Govt. Print. Off., 1966. 3 pts. (2056 p.) (89th Cong., 1st sess.)　　**U 6**

A series of hearings on the proposed revision

of the 1909 copyright law (H. R. 4347). Testimony was given by scores of persons representing, on the one hand, the interest of authors, composers, publishers, printers, and producers of copyrightable works (e.g. Authors League of America, American Book Publishers' Council, and the American Society of Composers, Authors, and Publishers) and, on the other hand, the consumers including educators, scholars, and librarians (e.g. Ad Hoc Committee [of Educational Organizations] on Copyright Law, American Library Association Committee on Copyright Issues, Association for Higher Education, and the Joint Libraries Committee on Fair Use in Photocopying).

————. *Copyright Law Revision. Part 1. Report of the Register of Copyrights on the General Revision of the U.S. Copyright Law.* Washington, D.C., Govt. Print. Off., 1961. 160p. (House Committee Print, 87th Cong., 1st sess.) **U 7**

————. *Copyright Law Revision. Part 2. Discussion and Comments on Report of the Register of Copyrights on the General Revision of the U.S. Copyright Law.* Washington, D.C., Govt. Print. Off., 1963. 419p. (House Committee Print, 88th Cong., 1st sess.) **U 8**
Transcripts of four meetings of the panel of consultants (1961–62) and comments received by the Committee on the Report of the Register of Copyrights on the proposed revision of the 1909 law. Comments were from persons representing producers and users of copyrighted materials as well as from such legal experts as Harriet F. Pilpel.

————. *Copyright Law Revision. Part 3. Preliminary Draft for Revised U.S. Copyright Law and Discussions and Comments on the Draft.* Washington, D.C., Govt. Print. Off., 1964. 457p. (House Committee Print, 88th Cong., 2d sess.) **U 9**

————. *Copyright Law Revision. Part 4. Further Discussions and Comments on Preliminary Draft for Revised U.S. Copyright Law.* Washington, D.C., Govt. Print. Off., 1964. 477p. (House Committee Print, 88th Cong., 2d sess.) **U 10**
Transcripts of four meetings of the panel of consultants (1963–64) and comments received.

————. *Copyright Law Revision. Part 5. 1964 Revision Bill with Discussion and Comments.* Washington, D.C., Govt. Print. Off., 1965. 350p. (House Committee Print, 89th Cong., 1st sess.) **U 11**
Text of the revised copyright bill, transcripts of a meeting of the panel of consultants, and comments from individuals and organizations.

————. *Copyright Law Revision. Part 6.*

Supplementary Report of the Register of Copyrights on the General Revision of the U.S. Copyright Law: 1965 Revision Bill. Washington, D.C., Govt. Print. Off., 1965. 338p. (House Committee Print, 89th Cong., 1st sess.) **U 12**
Includes a comparative table: the 1965 revision bill, the present law, the 1964 revision bill, and the preliminary draft.

————. *Copyright Law Revision . . . Report to Accompany H. R. 2512.* Washington, D.C., Govt. Print. Off., 1967. 254p. (House Report no. 83, 90th Cong., 1st sess.) **U 13**
Background history, summary of principal provisions, sectional analysis and discussion, and a comparative table giving the text of the bill as reported, the existing law, and the 1965 bill. H. R. 2512 corresponds to H. R. 4347 in the earlier Congress. After extensive hearings and study the Committee attempted to reach a compromise between the often conflicting interests of the producers and consumers of copyrighted works.

United States. Congress. House of Representatives. Post Office and Civil Service Committee. *Obscene and Pandering Advertisement Mail Matter. . . Hearing before Subcommittee on Postal Operations . . . on H. R. 426.* Washington, D.C., Govt. Print. Off., 1967. 34p. (90th Cong., 1st sess.) **U 14**

United States. Congress. Senate. Foreign Relations Committee. *News Policies in Vietnam. Hearings . . ., August 17 and 31, 1966.* Washington, D.C., Govt. Print. Off., 1966. 161p. (89th Cong., 2d sess.) **U 15**
An investigation of the extent of freedom and censorship of news coverage in Vietnam, the role of the U.S. Information Agency and the public affairs agencies in the Department of Defense. The appendix includes text of a series of Voice of America programs on freedom of the press.

————. Judiciary Committee. Subcommittee on Administrative Practice and Procedure. *The Newsman's Privilege.* Washington, D.C., Govt. Print. Off., 1966. 62p. (Committee Print, 89th Cong., 2d sess.) **U 16**
A study of the proposals for a federal law on "newsmen's privilege," with historical background and legal effect. Twelve states recognize this privilege which allows a newsman in certain instances to protect his sources. Although the common law recognizes privileges in certain areas, such as between an attorney and his client, there is no special privilege for newsmen at the common law. The study

was prepared by Freeman W. Sharp, American Law Division, Library of Congress.

————. Subcommittee on Antitrust and Monopoly. *The Failing Newspaper Act. Hearings . . .* Washington, D.C., Govt. Print. Off., 1968. 2 vols. (90th Cong., 1st sess.) **U 17**
The bill would exempt from federal antitrust laws certain newspaper combinations, if necessary to secure the survival of a "failing newspaper." The press was badly divided over whether or not the bill would have the effect of preserving a diversity in press voice or the opposite.

————. Subcommittee on Constitutional Rights. *Freedom of Information and Secrecy in Government. Hearings . . . on S921 and Power of President to Withhold Information from Congress.* Washington, D.C., Govt. Print. Off., 1958. 2pts., 513p., 1022p. (85th Cong. 2d sess.) **U 18**

————. Subcommittee on Patents, Trademarks, and Copyrights. *Copyright Law Revision—CATV. Hearings . . . on S.1006.* Washington, D.C., Govt. Print. Off., 1966. 252p. (89th Cong., 2d sess.) **U 19**
Testimony from the Register of Copyrights, Chairman of the FCC, and representatives of writers, and broadcasting and motion picture organizations.

————. *Copyright Law Revision. Hearings . . . on S.1006.* Washington, D.C., Govt. Print. Off., 1967. 242p. (89th Cong., 2d sess.) **U 20**
Includes testimony from the Organization of American Historians, the American Newspaper Publishers' Association, the Register of Copyrights, American Bar Association, Ad Hoc Committee of [Educational Organizations] on Copyright Law Revision, Committee on Copyright Issues of the American Library Association, and the American Council on Education.

United States. State Department. *Suppression of the Circulation of Obscene Publications. Protocol, with Annex, between the United States of America and Other Governments Amending Agreement of May 4, 1910, Opened for Signature at Lake Success May 4, 1949 . . . Proclaimed by the President of the United States of America November 25, 1950, Entered into Force with Respect to the United States of America, August 14, 1950.* Washington, D.C., Govt. Print. Off., 1951. 38p. (U.S. Department of State Publication 4085, Treaties and Other International Acts Series 2164) **U 21**

Valenti, Jack. "The Motion Picture Code and the New American Culture." *PTA Magazine*, 61:16–19, December 1966. **V1**

The author is president of the Motion Picture Association of America.

Vamplew, J. L. K. "Obscene Literature and Section 150A." *Criminal Law Quarterly*, 7:187–92, August 1964. **V2**

Court authorization of the seizure of obscene publications under the Canadian Criminal Code.

Van Alstyne, William W. "The First Amendment and the Suppression of War-mongering Propaganda in the United States: Comments and Footnotes." *Law and Contemporary Problems*, 31:530–52, Summer 1966. **V3**

"I cannot agree . . . that there are no substantial constitutional issues which hedge the power of government significantly to curtail war-mongering propaganda within the United States, to control the domestic consumption of subversive or defamatory propaganda sent from abroad, or even to silence its own official-dom. Beyond that, I despair of attempts to legislate virtuous speech in debates of public policy, and I doubt whether the policies of government will permit the merely neutral application of anti-propaganda laws."

van den Haag, Ernest. "The Case for Pornography Is the Case for Censorship and Vice Versa." *Esquire*, 67(5):134–35, May 1967. **V4**

While recognizing the need that some people have for pornography, the author also sees the need for censorship, provided it is limited to protecting "vulnerable people from injury or, at least, from distressing shock to their sensibilities." He concludes: "If we indulge pornography, and do not allow censorship to restrict it, our society at best will become ever more coarse, brutal, anxious, indifferent, deindividualized, hedonistic; at worst its ethics will disintegrate altogether."

Vanet, M. Randall. "Right of Privacy—Unauthorized Use of Photograph." *Missouri Law Review*, 24:567–70, November 1959. **V5**

Annerino v. Dell Publishing Co., 149 N.E. 2d. 761 (1958).

Vigne, Randolph. "Censorship: South Africa." *Censorship*, 3(1):8–14, Winter 1967. **V6**

An account of the widespread censorship of literature taking place in South Africa as evidenced in the Pretoria commercial publication, *Index of Objectionable Literature*, a list of some 11,000 titles covering ten years of government censorship. "It is important to realize that in South Africa publications are also suppressed by suppressing the writer, by banning, 'naming' him, or, if abroad, listing him as a person whom it is unlawful to quote."

Virginia Commission on Constitutional Government. *The Right Not to Listen.* [Richmond, The Commission, 1964]. 23 p. **V7**

A commentary on the conflict between property rights and freedom of speech that have collided head-on. The report concurs with the belief of Justice Hugo Black that the Constitutional guarantee of freedom of expression does not carry with it "a right to force a private property owner to furnish his property as a platform to criticize the property owner's use of that property."

von Glahn, Gerhard. "The Case for Legal Control of 'Liberation' Propaganda." *Law and Contemporary Problems*, 31:553–88, Summer 1966. **V8**

The author concludes that "since the Charter of the United Nations does not spell out human rights and freedoms related to the control of propaganda, since the one convention adopted does not relate directly to subversive propaganda, and since the Universal Declaration of Human Rights ought to be regarded either as a consensus or, better, as a species of moral preachment not bound up at all with legal obligations or norms of law, any attempt to regulate subversive propaganda would not conflict with legally established human rights and freedoms of speech or information. The latter simply do not exist as rights under either customary or convenient international law."

Wagner, Geoffrey. "The End of the 'Porno'—Or, No More Traveling Companions." *Sewanee Review*, 75:364–76, Spring 1967. **W1**

"In a society as committed to liberty as the American, *mere* license may fail to provoke; for it comes within the anti-authoritarian mode, and so can all too often emerge as cliché." The author analyzes and compares American and French attitudes toward "the literature of sexual trespass," noting the reversal of the French/Anglo-Saxon attitude toward pornography. New pornography in America has to be "far more brutal to reverberate and the truth is that although the traffic is heavier than it has ever been, the *porno* is vanishing because it no longer represents a transgression."

Wainwright, Loudon. "Dissent to the High Court's Harsh Verdict." *Life*, 60:26, 22 April 1966. **W2**

Comment on the *Ginzburg* obscenity case.

Waite, Edward F. "The Debt of Constitutional Law to Jehovah's Witnesses." *Minnesota Law Review*, 28:209–46, March 1944. **W3**

Includes a discussion of the following Supreme Court decisions relating to distribution of literature: *Douglas v. City of Jeannette*, 319 U.S. 157, (1943), *Lovell v. City of Griffin*, 303 U.S. 444, (1938), *Schneider v. New Jersey*, 308 U.S. 147, (1939), *Jones v. City of Opelika*, 316 U.S. 584, (1942), *Largent v. Texas*, 318 U.S. 418, (1943), and *Marten v. City of Struthers*, 319 U.S. 141 (1943).

[Wakem, Hugh], *pseud. Hugh Wakem; the Diary of a Smut-Hound. A Crusade for Morality in Literature Supplies the World with a Valuable Insight Into His Life and Habits.* Philadelphia, William Hodgson, 1930. 63 p. **W4**

A mock diary describing the imaginary antics of vice society agent Hugh Wakem and his assistant, Otto Klotz, against six booksellers for selling such works as *Lysistrata, Fanny Hill, Lady Chatterley's Lover,* and *The Confessions of Monsieur Montcairn.* "The truth is that disgusting as are these books and the lascivious drawings which illustrate them it is not at all difficult to go through them. I have not missed a single word or a single drawing."

Wald, Emil W. "Obscene Literature Standards Re-Examined." *South Carolina Law Review*, 18:497–503, Spring 1966. **W5**

Comment on the *Ginzburg, Mishkin,* and *Fanny Hill* decisions of the U.S. Supreme Court. "In *Mishkin* and *Ginzburg* the Court did not abandon the concept embodied in the *Roth* standard; rather, it recognized its shortcomings and emphasized that it will not ignore the setting and circumstances which may be the determinative factor for questionable materials in the application of *Roth*."

Walker, Alexander. *The Celluloid Sacrifice: Aspects of Sex in the Movies.* New York, Hawthorn, 1967. 241 p. **W6**

Chapter 8, One Man's Meat, deals with British film censorship which the author describes as singular (the work of the secretary of the British Board of Film Censors). Chapter 9 deals with American film censorship, basically plural, because the Hollywood Production Code Administration is only one among many censorship groups—state, local, official and unofficial. He compares the operation of the British film board and the American code administration, finding British censorship more flexible, more enlightened, and more liberal in the treatment of serious sex themes. The Hollywood censor is governed by rigid rules and is torn between the demands of the industry and the demands of pressure groups, principally the Legion of Decency, since 1965 known as the National Catholic Office for Motion Pictures.

Walker, Dean. "Canadian TV—The Wasteland and the Pasture." *Television Quarterly*, 1(3):23–38, August 1962. **W7**

"Canadian television, operating under a complex system of both government and private controls, has produced a veritable 'pasture' of ideas and excitement. Creative initiative has not wilted."

Warburton, Herbert B. "Pornography and Youth." In Eli Ginzburg, ed. *Values and Ideals of American Youth*. New York, Columbia University Press, 1961, pp. 157–67. **W 8**
Covers a definition of pornography and obscenity, legal background, and effect of obscenity on youth. The author is former General Counsel, U.S. Post Office Department.

[Warren, Fred D.]. *Warren's Defiance to the Federal Courts . . . Full Text of Fred D. Warren's Speeches Before the Federal Courts at Fort Scott and St. Paul*. Chicago, Charles H. Kerr, n.d. 29p. **W 9**
The editor of the Socialist paper, *Appeal to Reason*, Girard, Kan., was brought to trial charged with mailing envelopes bearing a libelous statement about a former Kentucky governor. When Warren's lawyers attempted to acquit him by means of legal technicalities, Warren took over his own defense, based on the issue of freedom of the press. This is a printing of his two speeches, together with a brief description of the Fort Scott trial by George H. Shoaf.

Wasby, Stephen L. *The Pure and the Prurient: The Politics of Obscene Literature in Oregon*. Eugene, Ore., University of Oregon, 1962. 402p. (Ph.D. dissertation, University Microfilms, no. 63–1085) **W 10**
"The purposes of this study were to determine the impact of United States Supreme Court opinions on policy-making and to examine intensively the development of obscene literature policy in Oregon from 1958 through 1961."

Wellman, Tom. "Student Expression Censored at Missouri University." *Focus/Midwest*, 5(5):24–29, 1967. **W 11**
The coeditor of the *Columbia* (Mo.) *Free Press* describes the efforts of campus and city police to ban sale of his newspaper.

Westin, Alan F. *Privacy and Freedom*. New York, Atheneum, 1967. 487p. Foreword by Oscar M. Ruebhausen. **W 12**
The work explores the basic concept of privacy in American democracy, examines the uses of the various devices (the exposé press, hidden cameras, questionnaires, eavesdropping mechanisms, etc.) by government, industry, and private individuals, and shows how the legislatures, the courts, and the press have responded. The author, director of the Center for Research and Education in American Literature of Columbia University, considers what can be done to safeguard against the assault on privacy and still maintain adequate security for the state and the individual.

Whalen, Ray. *Crime and Violence on Television . . .* Ottawa, Canadian Broadcasting Corp., 1959. 27p. **W 13**
Content analysis reveals that two U.S. networks devoted nine and one-half hours weekly to programs containing crime and violence; the third network carried six and one-half hours. Canadian Broadcasting Corp. carried five and one-half hours, but with fewer hours on the air, its percentage was higher. Despite this, juvenile crimes in Canada decreased since 1942.

White, David M. "The 'Gatekeeper': A Case Study in the Selection of News." *Journalism Quarterly*, 27:383–90, Fall 1950. (Reprinted in L. A. Dexter, and D. M. White, *People, Society, and Mass Communications*, Glencoe, Ill., Free Press, 1964, pp. 160–72) **W 14**
A case study of the activities of the wire editor of a large daily newspaper whose job it is to select and reject news from an avalanche of wire copy. The study was made to determine why this particular editor selected or rejected news stories and thereby to gain some diagnostic notions about the general role of "gatekeeper."

White, William. "On Collecting 'Dirty' Books: Some Notes on Censorship." *American Book Collector*, 17(7):20–26, March 1967. **W 15**
The author discusses the bibliography of erotica and pornography, and describes the "adults only" paperbacks, nudist magazines, sex-dominated tabloids, and the vast field of literature and nonliterature of sex that was once subterranean but is now sold openly in city "bookstores."

Whitehouse, Mary. *Cleaning-up T. V.; from Protest to Participation*. London, Blandford, 1967. 240p. **W 16**

Whitton, John B. "The Problem of Curbing International Propaganda." *Law and Contemporary Problems*, 31:601–21, Summer 1966. **W 17**
"The ideal way to deal with a specific case of inflammatory communication across frontiers would be to seek out and alleviate the cause of the underlying tension." Since this is seldom possible, "our goal must be the more limited one of preventing specific international disputes from worsening and thus increasing the risks of war. . . . International efforts must continue toward finding methods of inhibiting propaganda's function as a means of creating and exacerbating conflicts among nations."

"Why I Am [For] [Against] Pornography." *Fact*, 4(3):15–19, May–June 1967. **W 18**
Twenty-eight famous Americans answer these questions: Is pornography bad or good? If bad, should it be censored?

Whyte, George K., Jr. "Use of Expert Testimony in Obscenity Litigation." *Wisconsin Law Review*, 1965:113–32, Winter 1965. **W 19**

Widmer, Kingsley. *Censorship and the Teacher: The Experience of Freedom*. Chicago, American Federation of Teachers, n.d. 16p. (A Grassroots Research Project) **W 20**
In addition to the censorship of teaching materials that comes from community pressure groups, the author attacks censorship within the teaching profession—the academic and administrative special interest groups—the censorship by school administrators out of fear of conflict or change, and the effort of textbook publishers to avoid controversy. He recommends that teachers use supplementary paperbacks, recognize ideological propaganda and counterbalance it. Freedom in the use of teaching materials should become part of a broader educational freedom. "To be truly against censorship—our own as well as others—means to drastically pursue the critical variousness and lively responsiveness which encourage the experience of freedom."

Wiggins, James R. "The Press and the Courts." In Archibald Cox, *et al.*, *Civil Rights, the Constitution, and the Courts*. Cambridge, Mass., Harvard University Press, 1967, pp. 57–76. **W 21**
The importance of the press in continuing public scrutiny in the proper administration of justice. Paper presented before the Massachusetts Historical Society

———. "Top Secret! Secret! Confidential!" *Bulletin of the American Society of Newspaper Editors*, 417:9, 12, 1 February 1959. **W 22**
"There is more than one way to endanger the country's security. And I think presently we are pursuing a way that is more insidious than espionage and we may be weakening our country far more than any of us can perceive." Deals with the misuse of security classification.

Williams, D. G. T. "Control of Obscenity." *Criminal Law Review*, 1965:471–79, August 1965; 1965:522–31, September 1965. **W 23**
A review of recent court decisions in Britain under the Obscene Publications Acts of 1959 and 1964.

Williams, David. *Not in the Public Interest; the Problem of Security in Democracy*. London, Hutchinson, 1965. 224p. **W 24**
The purpose of the book is to point to some of the areas of conflict in the controversy about

executive secrecy in Great Britain, with special emphasis on the workings of the Official Secrets Acts.

Williams, George L. "School Censorship in Fascist Italy and the U.S." *School and Society*, 95:185–88, 18 March 1967. **W 25**
The author finds book censorship in local communities throughout the United States today reminiscent in some respects of censorship in Fascist Italy in 1922–43.

Williams, Wythe. *Passed by the Censor; the Experience of an American Newspaper Man in France.* New York, Dutton, 1916. 270 p. **W 26**

Williamson, E. G., and John L. Cowan. *The American Student's Freedom of Expression: A Research Appraisal.* Minneapolis, University of Minnesota Press, 1966. 193 p. **W 27**

Editorial Freedom section, pp. 125–34.

Wilmer, Lambert A. *Our Press Gang; or, a Complete Exposition of the Corruptions and Crimes of the American Newspapers.* Philadelphia, J. T. Lloyd, 1860. 394 p. **W 28**
Among the many charges the writer makes against the press are tyranny of editors, deception, obscene reporting of crime, trial by newspaper, encouragement of treason, and slander and defamation of character. Specific examples are given throughout. One section deals with editorial duels, another with flogging of editors. Freedom of the press, the author maintains, is a farcical illusion. "Our journalism is both tyrannical and slavish; it succumbs to every powerful influence, and it is bold and independent only when it attacks the weak and defenseless."

Wirt, Frederick M. *State Film Censorship, with Particular Reference to Ohio.* Columbus, Ohio State University, 1956. 492 p. (Ph.D. dissertation, University Microfilms, no. 20,738) **W 29**

Wolff, Geoffrey. "Government Book Control." *Book Week (World Journal Tribune)*, 4(22):2, 15, 5 February 1967. **W 30**

"There is much evidence that books [written by public officials] are used increasingly as engines of propaganda, that highly-placed persons are pre-censoring books they find repellant or embarrassing, and that they are commissioning and controlling the writing of books without disclosing the facts of such control." Much of the article deals with the Book Development Program of the U.S.I.A. as revealed in a congressional hearing, in which the U.S.I.A. subsidizes the secret production of manuscripts, published by private companies and sold in this country without any government imprimatur or acknowledgment of the circumstances of their origin. "It is not Government money or Government interest itself that sullies books. All one wants is that Government acknowledge its involvement and keep its hands off the writer's work."

Wolfram, Harold W. "Free Press, Fair Trial, and the Responsibility of the Bar." *Criminal Law Review*, 1(1):3–17, Spring 1954. **W 31**

Woodward, W. E. *Tom Paine: America's Godfather, 1737–1809.* New York, Dutton 1945. 359 p. **W 32**
Chapter 8, Paine as a Propagandist; Chapter 10, The Rights of Man; Chapter 11, More Books—More Trouble; Chapter 12, Outlawed in England; and Chapter 13, The Age of Reason, dealing with the challenge in England to Paine's unorthodox political and religious ideas.

Wyatt-Brown, Bertram. "The Abolitionists' Postal Campaign of 1835." *Journal of Negro History*, 50(4):227–38, October 1965. **W 33**

Yale Reports. *Obscenity and the First Amendment.* New Haven, Conn., Yale Reports, Yale University, 1966. 10 p. (Report no. 404) **Y 1**
A discussion over station WTIC, Hartford, by John Hollander, Professor of English at Yale, Professor Ronald Dworkin and Dean Louis H. Pollak of the Yale Law School.

Yang, T. L. "Privacy: A Comparative Study of English and American Law." *International and Comparative Law Quarterly*, 15:175–98, January 1966. **Y 2**
Includes a proposed statute on invasion of privacy.

Yemini, B.-H. "Censorship: Public Libraries." *Censorship*, 3(1):20–27, Winter 1967. **Y 3**
A study of self-censorship practiced by British public libraries and recommendations for changes in book selection policies which will give the public a clear picture of why certain books are not selected.

Yevish, I. A. "Attack on *Jude the Obscure*: A Reappraisal Some Seventy Years After." *Journal of General Education*, 18:239–48, January 1967. **Y 4**
An attempt to understand what it was in Thomas Hardy's novel that caused it to be attacked and banned as immoral when it appeared in 1895. Hardy was so deeply offended that he never wrote another novel.

Yoakam, Richard D., and Ronald T. Farrar. "The *Times* Libel Case and Constitutional Law." *Journalism Quarterly*, 42:661–64, Autumn 1965. **Y 5**
New York Times Co. v. Sullivan.

Young, Gordon. "Freedom of the Press in 1963—and Some Lessons for 1964." *IPI Report* (International Press Institute), 12(9):1–3, January 1964. **Y 6**
An appraisal of gains and losses in press freedom among countries of the world.

Zagri, Sidney. *Free Press, Fair Trial.* Chicago, Charles Hallberg, 1966. 115 p. **Z 1**
The author charges that the government used the mass media as an instrument in its campaign to "get" James R. Hoffa. Statements not admitted as evidence in the courts were planted in the nation's press. The author proposes changes in the law to prevent trial by newspaper.

INDEX

B657; religions (world) compatible with, G106; reveals designs of evil men, H165; right of dissent, C477, C479–C480, R27; Robinson (Henry) on, R174; satire, H168; Stephen (Sir James F.) on, S620; Sulzberger (Arthur) on, S711–S713; theory and philosophy of, J73, S378, S380, S393; totalitarian view, P181; truth defeats falsehood, M378–M379; truth only, L374; usefulness of matter not criterion, F11. *See also* International freedom in communications

—Great Britain: S378, S426; Bentham (Jeremy) on, B201–B203; bibliography, S130, S747, U201–U202, Y22; Blackstone (William) on, B303, F384, H149–H150, P18; Buckle (Henry T.) on, B614; *Cato's Letters*, L213, T181, °J3; Civil War and Commonwealth, P205–P206; Commonwealth countries, H302; control with safeguards, S565; Cooper (Thomas) on, C556; *Craftsman, The*, A243, C614–C616, F274, G68, G201, H22, H217–H221, P352, R14, S10–S12; decline of (1916), H155; defense against revolution, S548; Defoe (Daniel) on, D77–D81; Dicey (Albert V.) on, D147–D148; documents relating to, M428; *English Review* under attack, K139; Erskine (Thomas) on, E140–145, S126; foreign government interferes with, S437; French and British compared, °M42, °P10; French interpretation (1817), M443; French urged to adopt English policy (1815), C513; Furneaux (Philip) on, F384; Gentz (Friedrich von) on, G69; German interpretation, P31, °H37; Goodwin (John) on, G176; government criticism needed, L187; Hall (Robert) on, H36; Hayter (Thomas) on, H165; history, A194 A269, B339, B425, C399, F207, H2, H28, H83, H414, J8, K95, L345, M256, M561, P51, R283, S135, S378, S426, S766, T121, W230, W283, °B35, °O9, °T1; Hone (William) parodies on, H332–H335; Hume (David) on, H409; law, comparative study of, C136; legislative history, D147–D148, P51; Leveller theories on, B474, F265, G47, G91, G279, H41, H43–H44, H317, M572, P81, W52, W350, W352; liberal, totalitarian, socialist concepts, B479; libertarian views, B202–B203, D57–D58, E140, E144–E145, H36, M224, S547, T181, W389, °J3; "liberty" v. "license," sham distinction, B201; Lilburne (John) on, L275–L277, L279; Macaulay (Thomas B.) on, L371; Meek (Thomas) on, M272; Meredith (Sir William) on, M299; Mill (James) on, M336; °M42; Milton (John) on, M378–M379; National Conference (1941) on, N42; natural law, A255, C452, H165, L319, T126; Nazi views, M277; news events, A204, B395, N44, S258, W395; other countries compared, A28, K55, M36, °M42, °P10; Overton (Richard) on, O127–O129; Palmer (Elihu) on, P20; pamphleteering, eighteenth-century, B339, R36; PEP survey on, P103; Priestley (Joseph) on, P18, P319; restraint needed, L248, L262, °F4; right to complain, L319; Roman times, history from, F317; Shaw (G. B.) on, S292; Shawcross (Lord) on, G221, W70, °S27; socialist press, B167, °T8; Spencer (Herbert) on, S547; Spender (John A.) on, S548–S550; Squire (Francis) on, S565; Stockdale (John) on, S655; Stockdale (Percival) on, S657; theory of, S378, S380, S393; Tindal (Matthew) on, T122–T127; UN Draft Convention (British), U10; usefulness of matter not criterion, F11; Whigs v. Tories, W180; Williams (Francis) on, W282–W285; Yorke (Sir Philip C.) on, Y28–Y29

—United States: B173, B592, C695, C697, D242, F341, H16, J86, L216, M61, N147, P138, S104, °N8, °S50; abuses cause censorship, B471, P145; affirmation v. negation, W375; Alexander (James) on, A63, B623–B624, R309, °A9, °L15, °M2; American heritage, B450, C245, C297, C307, G76, H396, J9, L213, L216, S753, W183–W185, °B52–°B53, °N8; American Society of Newspaper Editors, A162–A167, °A21–°A24; antidemocratic views protected by, M512, W233; balancing of interest doctrine, A64, C71, F276, G78, G85, M296–M297, S197, S677, W44; Benton

(William) on, B207–B208, U231; bibliography, B533, C58, S130, U199, U201–U202, Y22, °S20; Brucker (Herbert) on, B590–B597; Cahn (Edmond) on, °C2; Canham (Edwin D.) on, C49–C56, U231; change, speed of, requires, °F11; changing concepts, F254, H98, S104; Colonial editors on, °L15; common law basis, C138; Congress and M594, W105, W239; constitutional limitations on, M244, O54, P182, R102, S677, W190, W315; constitutional problems, C699, F256, G75, G146, K30, K180–K182, M274–M276, P51, P57, P182, R206, S104, S138, S317, W233, °K7; Cooper (Thomas) on, C556–C558; court decisions (text, summaries), F255–F256, H16, K180–K182, N138, T61; courts v. state legislatures, R126; democracy requires, B95, B592, B595, C51, C53, C393, E163, F377, L4, L286, L298, O76, S597, S610, W287, W298, °F11; documents relating to, M428, P138, °N8; Douglas (Justice William O.) on, D225–D226, D228, M470; Drinker (Henry S.) on, D254; Ernst (Morris) on, E116–E118, E122, S189; false issue, I1; fear of subversion threatens, E155, E159; Fisk (Theophilus) on, F132–F133; Frank (Glenn) on, F260–F261; Frank (Jerome) on, F260–F263; freedom of association and, E88; Garfield (James A.) on, G42; Garrison (William L) on, G49; German dissertation on, °B54; German editors, seminar for, K133; Gertz (Elmer) on, G84–G89; Goldberg (Arthur J.) on, °G22; Great Britain and United States compared, A28; Hamilton (Alexander) on, H52, L216; Hay (George) on, H149–H150, L213, L216; Hays (Arthur Garfield) on, H158–H161, S189; high school teachers attitudes on, R204; history, B132, B399, B425, B480, C236, C242–C244, C260, C697, E55, E58, E87, G75, H45, H396, J69, K63, L213–L214, L216, L345, M326, M517, P51, P57, P70, P74, S104, U215, W44, W48, W183, W185, °B49, °B52–°B53, °N8; Hocking (William E.) on, H289–H290; Holmes (Oliver W.) on, H314; Hoover (Herbert) on, H342; Illinois, C312; Industrial Relations Commission testimony, S168; Inter American Press Association, reports on, I38–I40, °I1; Jefferson (Thomas) on, B451, J27–J30, L212–L213, L216, M548, °J8; Johnson (Gerald W.) on, J69–J73; journalists comment on, W168; judicial independence and, S87; judicial tests authorizing abridgment, A215; Krueger (M. C.) on, U228; labor unions and, F301, P98, S320; law, comparative study of, C136; Lasswell (Harold D.), I2, U231; Leigh (Robert D.) on, L161; libel not protected, O4; liberal, totalitarian, socialist concepts, B479; libertarian views, A63, D161, G84–G85, H149–H150, L213–L214, L216, S604, T102, T181, T199, W188, W398, °A9, °J3, °L31; librarians and booksellers, common stake, K144; library's stake in, A148, K144, M48; limited obligation of press, F300, K100; Lippmann (Walter) on, L304–L308, °L29; lobby in Congress needed, S145; local government and, °P6; Luce (Clare Booth) on, °L43; McCormick (Robert R.) on, M30–M35; McGill (Ralph) on, M77; McKean (Justice Thomas) on, °M14; McKeon (R. P.) on, M96, U228; MacLeish (Archibald) on, M105, M107–M109; Madison (James) on, B52, L216, M143–M144; means to an end, H289; Meiklejohn (Alexander) on, C231, M274–M276, °B56, °B63; Melcher (Frederic G.) on, M279, W325; metaphysical concept, °J12; Miller (Edward G., Jr.) on, M345; natural law, R232, °C10; news events, A102, A110, A115, A150, A162, A218, E31, F177, L261, N178, P351, Q8, V23, V42; newspaper role in defense of, C55, C71, C322, N162, °C1; newspapers abuse of, F8, F328, I1–I2, K63, P289; officials kept honest, K104; opinion polls, C64, P294, S624; other countries compared, B425, K55, M36; Pennsylvania, W197; philosophical aspects, B368, C558, H216, H289, J73, L213, M96, W233, W398, °B52; Phocion supports (1821), P153; political expression, threats to, E87; Pope (James S.) on, P239–P244; prior restraint doctrine, E86, H353, R98; public apathy as

threat, J71, T8, °F13; public intolerance, W322, °F13; public safety takes precedence over, S677; public v. private issues, M276; publishers' responsibility, M279; quotations, F341, S26, S555, T186; reader's (not newspaper's) right, B104, B399, E117, H177, S502, S665, S712, W244; Reed (Sen. James A.) on, R58; responsibility for wise use, B142, B370, B585, C279, J69, T158, °G22, °M36; restrictions on, D207, E86–E87, H353, J71, L167, M185, S138, S176, S231, S233–S234, S521; right of dissent, C477, C479–C480; Rogge (R. John) on, R215–R216; Roosevelt (Franklin D.) on, R224–R225; Rosenberg (James N.) on, R251–R253; Sarnoff (David) on, F300; Schroeder (Theodore A.) on, S121, S138, S148, S159, S165, S168, S177; Seldes (George) on, S230–S231, S233–S234, S236–S238; Siebert (Fredrick S.) on, S373, S377, S379–S380, S382, S388, S393; Sigma Delta Chi reports, S405; socially unimportant protected, F153; South Carolina, B43, H153; Soviet v. U.S., I23, K32, P253, S762; state constitutional provisions, R185; state court negation of federal right, A214; state laws abridging, S176, S521; Story (Judge Joseph) on, S677; Stritch (Samuel Cardinal) on, S688; Sullivan (James) on, S703; Supreme Court interpretations, B527, C251, F256, H396–H397, K180–K182, P133, P304, R215–R216, S104, S277, S317; Swing (Raymond Gram) on, S762; Thomason (Samuel E.) on, U228; Thompson (Dorothy) on, T94; Thomson (John) on, T102; Tobin (Maurice J.) on, T134; Tocqueville (Alexis de) on, T142; Tucker (St. George) on, S123, T199; UN Draft Convention (U.S.), U10; Vandenberg (Arthur H.) on, V7; Walker (Edwin C.) on, W24–W26; wartime protection, L146, S129; Webster (Daniel) on, W104–W105; Weinberger (Harry) on, W118–W120; West Virginia, M322; White (William Allen) on, I2, W199–W200; Wiggins (James R.) on, W236–W249; Williams (Elisha) on, W280; Wortman (Tunis) on, L216, W398; youths' attitudes on, H178, W46; Zenger (John Peter) lectures, H390, J53. *See also* Commission on Freedom of the Press, Report of

Freedom of the Press, The; a Farce (play), B23

Freedom of thought: B419, C502, M170, R121, W134; Douglas (Justice William O.) on, D225–D226; history of, B655. *See also* Freedom of speech; Freedom of the press; Religious expression, freedom of

Freedom to Read (film), F338

Freedom to read: G191, L227, M96, M128; American Bar Association statement, A98; American Book Publishers Council statement, A154, T213; Australian library association, B619; bibliography, G285, O10, W133; California Library Association, M310; children's and adolescents', E153, M137, M444; Constitutional guarantee, B104, B399, E117, H177, S665, S712, W244; Eisenhower (Dwight D.) on, E52–E53; Ernst (Morris) on, E117; Intellectual Freedom Conference, A149; Kennedy (John F.) on, K67; Miller (Henry) on, M347; municipal administration, C464; New York, Association of the Bar of the City of, A275; not to read, L390; people's right to choose, J83; public libraries as guardians, B310, B493; responsibility to teach and, G199; restrictions on (mock), B628; students, F311, M120, N54; Walpole (Sir Hugh) on, W43; Washington (State) Library Association, W73; Wisconsin Free Library Commission, W338

Freedom to write: Authors League of America statement, A296; Bruce (Archibald) on, B589; Collins (Anthony) on, C451–C452; culture and political pressures, M165; International writers' Conference, I49; literary responsibility and, H71; literature, same freedom as history, L234; P.E.N. conferences, O120–O121; prosecution threat to, S683; Rice (Elmer L.) on, R121

C644, E130, H376, I64, K88, L240, N176, R166, R231, S427, S458, W392–W393

New Zealand, censorship in: G289, H339, N139; *Another Country*, I18, N141; broadcasting, Q2; comic books, T207; Customs, B391, H339, S699; favors responsible, °L10; history, P115; Indecent Publications Act, B390, B392, B515, C30, H351, P41, S208, W412, °H2; Indecent Publications Tribunal, I18, N141, P115; labeling, L2; libel, A67, °D4; Library Association report, N140; *Lolita*, L337, S208; motion pictures, H96, °H58; obscenity laws, P115, P191; public libraries, H339, S699; World War I, A187

Newark (Eng.) *Advertiser*, L64, °H17

Newark Public Library, V41

Newett, George A., trial, A2, M392–M393, N160, R227, R229–R230

News, management of (Great Britain): Chamberlain government, W273; "crisis week," C227; Official Secrets Act, A24, K107, M208–M210, N80, R183, °F27, °W24

News, management of (United States): B11, B13, B154, B266, C321, F81, F308, H373, K196–K198, L400, M410, M417, M421, M423–M425, N165, N167, N169, O2, P49, R30, R284, S595, S672, S720, S741, °B47, °M1, °M26, °M39, °N8, °S25; anonymous sources, U78; Armed Forces, U61–U62, U185, W314; Catholic press, °A4; Congressional investigation, F53, M418, U60–U83, U163, U167, U170–U172, °B39; Cuban invasion, E31, H375, L399, N153, T138; Cuban missile crisis, B13, E31, M92, M422, T138; education of officials needed, °G32; Eisenhower (Pres. Dwight D.) Administration, C200, E31, M423, S633, °J16; favors, C125; federal statutes, U75; Freedom of Information Act, 1967, °M45, °U4; Hoover (Pres. Herbert) Administration, S652; human need to, S429; investigation by ACLU, R31; Johnson (Pres. Lyndon) Administration, B12, °J16, °L28, °R19; Kennedy (Pres. John F.) Administration, B33, E31, H373, H375, L399, M92, M422, N153, T138, °J16, °M46; lack trust in people, W236; news leaks, F52, G190, °F30; newspaper problems in confronting, °B47; Pope (James) on, P239–P243; press can counteract, K190, M417; public indifferent, M410; Roosevelt (Pres. Franklin D.) Administration, M321; satire, J124; secrecy v. publicity, R280–R282; Stevenson (Adlai E.) on, S633; Truman (Pres. Harry S.) Administration, E31; Villard (Oswald G.) on, V45; Washington correspondents comment on, G23; Wiggins (James R.) on, W236, W238, W243–W248. *See also* News handouts; Public Records, right of access to; Security restrictions on news

News, overcoverage of, F54

News copy, immune from control, F119

News handouts, F310, M321, W319

News service, monopoly in: Associated Press, A272–A273, C550, F100, F119, K120, L59, L77, M226, S754, U35; restrictive practices of, K59; Reuters, C545; threat to free press, S643

Newsam, Frank (Sir), G241

Newscasts, B24, C567, H383

Newspaper censorship: Canada, A65, B555, E47, F318, F335, G282, I27, R162, S402, T73
—Great Britain: advertising as threat, I28, S504, W311; contempt of court, B273–B274, F247, F293, G1, G166, K107, M79, P103, T85; diversity lacking, S504; divorce news, G81, R128; extent of freedom, F186, G74, H119, T32–T33, T82, W284; false news, J114; foreign correspondents, B100; government controls, B101, B178, G74, I44, K107, P250, T32, W284; labor as threat, I28; monopoly controls, B167, H119, L169, P103, W284, W311; Sayers (Dorothy L.) on, S77; scandal, I17; self-imposed, A45, B168, D18, P290, S77, W282. *See also* Licensing of printing (Great Britain); Newspaper law; Newspaper libel cases (Great Britain)

—Ireland: C664, C684, I29, M142, M146–M147, R137
—United States: H350, H428, I2, K85, N162, °B34; advertiser influence and control, A172, B196, B644, E36, G170, G186, G206, I2, L60, M167, R68, R263, R288, S337, W200, W337, W414; advertising, refusal of, B315, R152; blackout of news, G13; business pressures, B641, G206, R68, R288, S233, S259, S416, S427, S643, V72, °S19–°S20; case studies needed, S388; Central Information Bureau opposed, K197, U5; circulation restrictions, B133, J21, S408, S519; Congress, conflicts with, W239; contempt of court, B45, B91, B626, C416, E32, E49, F75, F103, F309, F372, G75, H76, H81, H118, H341, I4, L85, L217, L299, L357, M23, M79, M400, M530, M615, N99, O69, P29, P59–P60, P120, R46, R91, R139, R168, R192, S316, S376, S505, S576, S701, T4, T58, W227–W228, Y4; crime news, B164, C431, D260, F74, R94, °F26, °H51; disbarment of lawyer-editor, M23; editorial control, I19, L58, L336, S233, T109; election day editorial, °S12; favored, S350; "gatekeeper" as censor, C116, °W14; government controls opposed, A303, B596, F130, H79–H80, I5, R73; government imposed, B552, B574, K196–K198, M244, S108, S521, U5; "honor-bound" censorship, F76; *Iconoclast* (W. C. Brann), °C12; investigation by ASNE, B572; licensing under NIRA, H195; Marxian views on, M184–M185; Mellett (Don) martyrdom, D202, °M30; Minnesota "gag" law, A128, B79, B173, C114, F179, F232, F333, G75, H400, K120, K182, M33, M550, P281, P306, T15, W55, Y4, °C2, °N8; monopoly controls, A173, B472, B592, B596, C151, C249, C255, E116–E117, F100, F170, G75, G170, L20, L45, L47, N186, P142, S189, S625, S643, U183; NRA code, A188, H173, H195, M31–M32, M35, N161, N206, V72; National Labor Relations Board, W137; North Carolina, S637, W161; personal liberty v. property liberty, B399, E117, S502, S665, S712, T177, W244; political news banned, B509; political pressures, B196, F285, M136, P289, R68, S427, W104; pressures influencing, B196, B198, I2, M136, S233; prior restraint, R98; reader pressures, C667, R288, W358; rightist pressures, S236; Seldes (George) on, S231, S233, S236; self-imposed, B10, B159, B196, B334, B509, B598, C116, K146, M132, M136, W318, W414, °A25, °B2; self-restraints urged, B557, B596, D62, D221, M132, °H51; Sinclair (Upton) on, S416; size of newspaper, restriction on, U125; state laws threat to, S521; steel strike (1919–20) coverage, I41; Tennessee, M377; Union pressures, N206, T136; Webster (Daniel) on, W104; Wylie (Philip) on, W414. *See also* Espionage Act of 1917; Fair trial v. free press; News, management of (United States); Newspaper tax (United States); Post Office censorship (United States); Sedition Act of 1798; Wartime control of press; World War I censorship (United States); World War II censorship (United States)

Newspaper editors: crusaders for freedom, H386, L344; liability of, L235, P196

Newspaper history (Great Britain): A194, B423, C399, G201, R283, S378, S766–S767, W283; bibliography, B378, C58, P315; eighteenth-century, A269, H13, H83, J8, R36, R283, S378, W136; nineteenth-century, A269, S573, W230; seventeenth-century, C399, F264, M561, S378

Newspaper history (United States): B198, B331, E91, J99, M547, P70, W79; bibliography, P315. *See also* Civil War censorship; Colonial press censorship (United States); World War I censorship (United States); World War II censorship (United States)

Newspaper law: Australia, S75; comparative, R272
—Great Britain: D66, F128, M443, P51, P301, R272, S346, S375; bibliography, P315, S747, S755; contempt of court, B273–B274, F247, F293, G166, K107, M79, P103, T85, °S27; equity jurisdiction in libels, E111, F340; fair trial v. free press, G103, G107, G166,

H355; handbook, M121, P167, P275; injunctions, F180, L232; jury prejudice against press, H345; Law of Defamation, Committee on the, G211; liability of editor, L235, P196; libel, B39–B40, D158, G210–G211, G239, K107, L236–L237, P103, R33, S346, °S27; Newspaper Libel and Registration Act of 1881, P254; Official Secrets Act, A24, K107, M208–M210, R183, °S27; public v. private affairs, S681; Shawcross (Lord) on, °S27. *See also* Libel laws, Great Britain
—international: °M50; leading countries, S306; sixty countries, S279
—United States: A252, B508, B574, E31, H27, H357, J100, M61, P51, R272, S279, S382, T61, T64; bibliography, P315, S755; Bowles (Samuel) on libel, F98; Colorado, P347; Field (David D.) on libel, F98–F99; Florida, B44, L126, T15; handbook, L291, P178, S391, S608, S759, °L9; Iowa, J48; libel law, B661, C660, F98–F99, F340, J48, K54, M61, M304, M370, N156, S759, T15, T59, T61, W78; Louisiana, B133, J21, K182, S408; Minnesota "gag" law, A128, B79, B173, C114, F179, F232, F333, G75, H400, K120, K182, M33, M550, P281, P306, T15, W55, Y4, °C2, °N8; North Carolina, S637, W161; Ohio, P229; South Carolina, M442, °M51; Tennessee, M377; Texas, D47–D48, D219, P150; West Virginia, M322, P184. *See also* Contempt of court by publication; Fair trial v. free press; Privacy, right of; Public records, right of access to; Qualified privilege (newspapers)

Newspaper libel cases (Great Britain): *Armstrong et al. v. Armit, et al.*, P292; Cambridge *Intelligencer*, F161; *County Chronicle* (Bury St. Edmunds), B180; *Daily Mirror*, H447; *Daily Worker*, °P16; *Evening Standard*, °H17; *Gee v. Pritchard*, E111; Liverpool *Post and Mercury*, R304; *Milisich v. Lloyds*, L236; *Morning Chronicle*, °M58; *Morning Herald*, T167; *Newark Advertiser*, L64, °H17; *Pall Mall Gazette*, H421, S465; *People, The* (London), C330; *Pinero v. Goodlake*, P180; *Queen v. Holbrook*, L236; *Racing Calendar*, °H17; *Salisbury Journal*, S221; *Times, The*, E161, G256, °R29; *West Briton and Cornwall Advertiser*, T141; *Western Times* (Exeter), L27. *See also* Libel cases; Seditious libel

Newspaper libel cases (Ireland): M142, M156; *Dublin Evening Post*, M146–M147; *Mayo Constitution*, B272

Newspaper libel cases (Scotland): *Blackwood's Edinburgh Magazine*, B305; *Edinburgh Beacon*, S635; *Tait's Edinburgh Magazine*, R130

Newspaper libel cases (United States): A157, M547, N213, P170; Albany *Evening Journal*, D92, W108–W109; *Argus* (New York), F367; *Bennett (Frank P.) v. John Donohoe*, S676; Brooklyn *Daily Times*, B194; Charleston (S.C.) *News and Courier*, D59; *Chicago, City of v. Chicago Tribune*, C314, F126, M33, T15; *Connecticut Journal*, C526; editor sues reader, °S33; *Lapatossu*, T224; Lowell (Mass.) *Courier*, L238; Morrilton (Ark.) *Democrat*, R64, S582, °A28; *National Advocate* (New York), N193; *New England Galaxy*, B613, K104, O112; *New Hampshire Patriot and State Gazette*, U235–U236; New York *Evening Mirror*, D74; New York *Evening Post*, C434; New York *Evening Signal*, E130; New York *Sun*, A157, T187; *New York Times v. Sullivan*, B9, D153, D218, E162, F122, F315, K15, L397, M21, M123, N114, P83, P222, S603, T137, V39, °A3, °B29, °C16, °C36, °D7–°D8, °F15, °H8, °J15, °J20, °N8, °P8–°P9, °Y5; New York *Tribune*, C543, E130, G261, O124, S260; New York *World*, C644, E130, H376, I64, K88, L240, N176, R166, R231, S427, S458, W392–W393; Oakley (Annie), W178; Paterson (N.J.) *Weekly Issue*, N121; Pennsylvania cases, M174; *Polynesian* (Honolulu), J22; *Porcupine Gazette* (Philadelphia), C406, N96, W166; *Republican Chronicle* (New York), B32;

R198, S22, S128, S153, S204, T29, °G8, °G12, °H36; Hoover (J. Edgar) on, °H53–°H54; humor, lacking in, L392; hysteria over, not justified, L9; Indiana Supreme Court, °H36; informal government action against, C210; intensity of objection to, L4; inter-, national control of, F258, G223, L118, L121–L123, U17, U23, U25–U26, U208, U213, °U21; Johnson (Pamela H.) on, °J17–°J18; judge and prosecutor as critics, B540, C334, S139, S146, S201; jury trial recommended, W368; Konvitz (Milton R.) on, °K18; Larrabee (Eric) on, L50–L52; Lawrence (D. H.) on, F224, L97–L101, P247; Lerner (Max) on, °L21; libel laws applied to, B491, C363, D258; "liberal opponents and conservative friends," S143; libraries and court decisions, °M47; limited censorship favored, A183, B470, B665, E56, E64, G185, K102–K103, °H47, °K25, °L21; literary aspects, A12, B365, B459, C334, D51, F151, I76, K102, L52, M101, M140, M407, M593, S201, S204, T172, V35, °H44, °R21; literary style factor in, F153, I36, S137, °B66, °R21; Luce (Clare Booth) on, °L43; Mead (Margaret) on, M269; Miller (Henry) on, M347–M350; mind of viewer, in, H240, I13, R51, S124, S139, S143, S167, S364; minority imposed, B137; mock trial, S146; Molz (Kathleen) on, °M47–°M48; morality and, L50–L52, W176; Murray (Gilbert) on, M593; newsstand survey, °O15; opposes censorship, A84, A88, B87, B366, B538, C470, E137, F153, G85, G172, H448, K86, S153, S158, S180–S181, S204, S364, °F16; origin, E134, H445, S22, S204; pandering test, U222, °A2, °B15, °B33, °B38, °F18, °F25, °G13, °M55, °S21; paperbacks, A183, C62, J43, R241, W41, U127–U128, °O15; *per se* v. *per quod*, °M49; Philippine Islands, °B27; phonograph records, J67, U169; *Playboy* philosophy on, H185–H186, °H25–°H26, °M66; police censorship, A205, C210, C310, G72, H124, L6, L48, M327, N69, P218–P220, P264, S5, S435, S704, U127, W198, °R22; Post Office censorship, A135, A247, B500, C234, C300, C496, C691, D84, D101–D103, E150–E151, G96, G198, H102, H395, L10, L155, L395, M64, M67–M68, M85, M117, O17, O23, P65–P67, P172, S98, S155, S194, S440, S714–S716, U111–U112, U114–U121, U124, U128, U176, U182, W12, W15–W16, W91, W164, Z19, °P14; producers of, C347, C349, G116–G119, K36, M3, R24, °R20; Protestant Churches and, C62–C63, C609–C610, F241, M445–M446, O46, P179, S529, S546, V70, W34, W62, °H26; prudery encourages, G20; psychodynamic aspects, A8, H293, H338, K199–K200, M593, W141; psychologists and psychiatrists (poll) on, °N9; public library case study, B235; public opinion, role of, B62, B366; publishers self-censorship, B137, °H34; radicalism and, K164, S218–S219, S615; radio and television, D61, U90, °B45; religious basis of ban, H200; repression a cause of, M593; research needed, J12, K42, R104, °K18; Rhode Island legislature report, °R13; sadism and, C470, L50, L52, L156, M445, P317, W323, °H47, °L19, °W1; satire, °H33; Schroeder (Theodore A.) on, R179, S120, S124, S133, S139, S142–S143, S146, S153, S167, S172–S175, S180–S181; scientific work judged obscene, B510; Seagle (William) on, S218–S219; social basis of, C62–C63, K227, L52, M593, S139, S546; social control of, B491, L4; Spock (Dr. Benjamin) on, °S47–°S48; stage code on, C361; Strachey (J. St. Loe) on, F102, K139, L341, S680; Sumner (John S.) on, S722–S723, S727–S728, S730, S732; Supreme Court decisions on, B62, B79, C68, C346, D82, F149, F153, F351, G85, G114, H17, K14, K92, K130, K182, L3, L270, L328–L330, M531, N69, O26, S331, T25, T30, U221–U222, °B38, °C45, °F16, °F25, °G8, °K18, °K25, °M19, °M47, °M49, °R10, °S13, °S17, °W10; tests and standards, A189, B528, C310, F233, F235, L93, L320, L328–L330, M85, O18, P89, P251, P264, R161, S124, S133, S139, S153–S154, S172–S173, S175, T53–T54, °A2, °B15, °C45, °F20, °F25, °G9, °G14, °K25, °M9, °M18, °M55, °R12,

°S16–°S17, °S21, °W5; witchcraft and, F153, S120, S181; women support, E84; Woolf (Virginia) on, E73; Yapp (Darsie) on, M593. *See also* Birth control information, dissemination of; Citizens for Decent Literature; Legion of Decency, National; Morality and literature; National Office for Decent Literature; New England Watch and Ward Society; New York Society for the Suppression of Vice; Pornography; Sex education, censorship of; Society for the Suppression of Vice (London)

—and blasphemy: criticism of compound offense, K147

—and subversion: criticism of association, K164

Obscenity and the Law (Norman St. John-Stevas), K16, S22

Obscenity cases (Australia): C433; Chidley (William J.), C317; *We Were the Rats*, F205

Obscenity cases (Canada): M89; Britnell (Albert) trial, P220; *Brodie, Dansky and Rubin v. R.*, °G9; *R. v. American News Co., Ltd.*, M88

Obscenity cases (Great Britain): C618, C620–C621, E137, S22; *Adult, The*, A39, B148, M145, S644; Bedborough (George) trial, A39, B147–B148, C583–C584, C620, D60, E68, E71–E72, F286, J127, P123, P197, P199, S22, S265–S267, S291, S422, S745; Benbow (William) trial, B175; Conway (Moncure D.) criticizes prosecution, C529; Curll (Edmund) trial, C620, C681, F213, F251, S22, S587, S682, Y28; *Fanny Hill*, B427, G131, H445, L82, N183, T97; Gott (J. W.) trials, G188–G189, P2; Hicklin trial, C620, F213, M88, S22; *Last Exit to Brooklyn*, °F35, °J21; Moxon (Edward) trial, F222, L108, M59, M557, T10, T165; National Vigilance Association, C442, C561–C562, N81, S508, °T7; Obscene Publications Act of 1959, 1964, °W23; *Philanderer, The*, E62, K28, M89, S569, T54, W56; *Poet-meat*, N196, °C54; Potocki (Count G. W. V.) trial, C620, P269; *R. v. Bradlaugh (Charles) and Annie Besant*, B245, B467–B468, C620, F198, L91, M9, N108, S22; *R. v. Penguin Books, Ltd.* (*Lady Chatterley's Lover*), B153, C363, C620, H227, H230, H233, H239, L18, L198, M106, M181, R2, S539, W126; Read (James) trial, C620, F251, S22; satire, °C42; scientific work banned, B510; *Sexual Impulse, The*, H443; *Sleeveless Errand*, C620, E62, M13, P43; Society for the Suppression of Vice (London), B175, C86, C90, C561–C562, S508–S509, W85, °T7; Truelove (Edward) trial, R178, T193; Vizetelly (Henry) trial, B611, C561, E137, M492, V59–V61; *Well of Loneliness*, B469, B495, C129, C216, C620, E62, E102, F225, M13, *See also* Wilkes, John

Obscenity cases (United States): C68, C137, C346, E129, E134, E137, H66, K180–K182, R198, S182, °N8; *Alberts v. California*, B62, B79, F153, H17, K14, K182; *American Mercury* ("Hatrack" case), A253, B454, E110, G203, H161, K57, M38, M162, M288, M291, N117, S425, S649; *Arizona v. Locks*, °K5; *Attorney General (Mass.) v. The Book Named "Tropic of Cancer,"* A6, F111, G109, K182, L221, M234, M475, °R21; *Bantam Books, Inc. v. Sullivan*, C201, C205, C566, D279, F268, K182, L220, M498, W2; *Barnes v. The Book Named "Forever Amber,"* C137, D129, D133, E131, G109, L292, M38, M522; Bennett (D. M.) trial, B187–B192, M52, S182, S615; *Bookcase, Inc. v. Broderick*, P175; Bruno (Guido) trial, K192; *Bunis v. Conway* (*Tropic of Cancer*), G300, M257, T189; *Burstyn v. Wilson* (*The Miracle*), B79, C357–C358, C514, C672, H108, K23, K182, L29, L230, M4, M386–M387, M456, M543, N62, N147, O57, P132, R82, R118, S187, S241, T159, W47, W94, W158, W234, °C20, °M61; *Butler v. Michigan*, K14, K182, T103; *California v. Ferlinghetti* (*Howl*), E50, F83, P109; *Chant d'Amour, Un* (film), S430; *Cincinnati v. Marshall*, C645; Clark (William L.) trial, C369–C370, S82; *Commercial Pictures Corp. v. Regents*, L151, M542, S312; *Commonwealth (Mass.) v. Buckley* (*Three Weeks*), D55, F213, G203, M38, N117; *Commonwealth (Mass.) v. Delacey* (*Lady Chatterley's Lover*) B454, B658, D137, G109, G203–G204, J3,

L136, M38, N116–N117; *Commonwealth (Mass.) v. Friede* (*American Tragedy*), B454, B620, G109, G204, M38, M502, N117, S111; *Commonwealth (Mass.) v. Holmes* (*Fanny Hill*), E134, G109, G203, M38, Q4; *Commonwealth (Mass.) v. Isenstadt* (*Strange Fruit*), C46, C137, D126–D127, D134–D135, E131, G109, H282, J37, L171, M38, P350, S201, W289; *Commonwealth (Mass.) v. McCance*, G109; *Commonwealth (Mass.) v. Ward*, J117, R198, W58; *Commonwealth (Mass.) v. Wright*, M90; *Commonwealth (Pa.) v. Blumenstein* (film), B221, M154; *Commonwealth (Pa.) v. Gordon*, B367, B369, F22, H424, K182, S466; *Commonwealth (Pa.) v. Landis*, L34; *Commonwealth (Pa.) v. Sharpless*, E134; Craddock (Ida) case, C499, F192, M52, S182, S357, S361; Doty (Elias) trial, D220; *Doubleday v. New York* (*Memoirs of Hecate County*), A229, M531, P274; *Dreiser v. John Lane Co.* (*The Genius*), A229, A285, C504, D250–D252, D285, M287, R67, R258; *Evergreen Review*, B204, S606; *Excelsior Pictures Corp. v. Regents*, K140, S187; *Flaming Creatures* (film), S430, V42, °S45; *Ginzburg v. U.S.*, G114, O26, S436, U221–U222, °A2, °B15, °B33, °B38, °C6, °C45–°C46, °D30, °D37, °F28, °G5, °G13, °G16, °G24, °G30, °G41, °H22, °H41, °K19, °M18, °M47, °M55–°M56, °R12, °R20, °S17, °S21, °S36, °T11, °W2, °W5; *Glasgow v. Moyer*, G122, S418; *Grove Press v. Christenberry* (*Lady Chatterley's Lover*), B602, G303, K27, K182, L100, M29, M106, M181, M514, P177, °M37; *Grove Press v. Gorstein* (*Tropic of Cancer*), G87, M487; *Haiman, et al v. Morris* (*Tropic of Cancer*), E108–E109, G84, G86–G89, N151, N205; *Halsey v. Sumner* (*Mademoiselle de Maupin*), A229, C700, E128; *Hannegan v. Esquire*, A135, A247, B500, C234, E150–E151, J37, K182, L395, M117, N147, P172, W12; *Harman* (Moses) trial, B553, C264, C629, D64, F213, F289, H100–H101, H103, H148, J13, L378, N170, S166, S182, S254, W15; Heywood (Ezra H.) trials, B187, C241, C265, H148, H241–H243, M38, P168, R178, S615, W388. °L7; Hurt (Walter H.) trial, H432; *Jacobellis v. Ohio* (film), A189, F153, O77, S736, °M27; *Kingsley Books, Inc. v. Brown*, B79, B569, K182; *Kingsley International Pictures v. Regents*, B239, F352, G197, H17, K14, K182, L128, M4, M429, N69, S187, S586; Knowles (Freeman T.) trial, K164, S168; *Leaves of Grass*, B86, H104, H253, K73–K74, M38, M500, N117, O35–O37; *Lobert Picture Corp. v. City of Atlanta*, A91; *McCauley v. Tropic of Cancer*, C191, N199; *Manual Enterprises v. Day*, F59, F150, K182, O25, S190, T53, T150, °C18; *Marcus v. Search Warrant*, N201; *Memoirs v. Massachusetts*, O26, U221–U222, °A2, °B33, °C6, °C45–°C46, °D30, °F28, °G5, °G24, °G41, °H22, °K19, °M18, °M47, °M55–°M56, °R12, °S17, °W5; *Menace, The*, B29, C370, F163, F167, H431, M283, R221, S82, S615; *Mishkin v. New York*, O26, U221–U222, °A2, °B33, °C6, °C45–°C46, °D30, °G5, °G24, °G41, °H22, °K19, °M18, °M47, °M55–°M56, °R12, °S17, °W5; Moens (Professor H. M. B.) trial, M411–M412, S359; Nation (Carrie) trial, N12; National Defense Association, N67–N68; *New Library of World Literature v. Allen*, L320; New York *Daily Call*, S168; *Nudism in Modern Life*, P36; *One, Inc. v. Olesen*, G284, O83, S261; Penhallow (Mattie D.) trial, W11; *People (N.Y.) v. Eastman*, E11, R167; *People (N.Y.) v. Finkelstein*, O18; *People (N.Y.) v. Holt, McBride, et al.* (*Jurgen*), A44, A229, B66, B257–B258, B446 B545, C1, H320, K11, M289, P365; *People (N.Y.) v. Kennerley* (*Hagar Revelly*), C127, L312; *People (N.Y.) v. Muller*, F213; *People (N.Y.) v. Viking Press, et al.* (*God's Little Acre*), C6–C7; *Physical Culture*, A9, I14, M67–M68, S124, S136, W76; Polish People's Publishing Co., S160; *Quantity of Copies of Books v. Kansas*, A189, A217; *Roth v. Goldman*, D82, F262; *Roth v. United States*, B79, C68, F153, F351, H17, K14, K92, K182, L3, L270, M155, N69, T25, T30,

White, Lincoln, F310
White, T. Holt, M379
White, William Allen, E51, I2, L76, M550, P111, W199–W200
Whited Sepulchres (Count Potocki), C620, P269
Whitman, Walt, I25, K73–K74, O36, W210
Whitney, A. F., I2
Wierzbianski, Boleslaw, F307
Wiggins, J. Russell, F306, M194, U60, W236–W249, °W21–°W22
Wightman, Edward, L150
Wilberforce, William, S508
Wilde, Oscar, E62
Wilde, William (Sir), G56
Wilkes, John: B328, B444, E149, H414, P266, R283, R293, S332, W84, W260, W264, °T10; Bingley (William) and, B273–B274, S1; Churchill (Charles) and, B136; *Essay on Woman, An,* A258, K96, W263, W265, °G8; expulsion from Parliament, G287, S73, °T10; honoring of, J54; Kidgell (John) charges, K96, W263; letters, speeches, W260–W261, W265; *North Briton,* K79, L90, M428, N194, N207, R113–R114, T180, W260, W266, Y1; portrait of, V31; trials, A85, B423, C438–C439, C620–C621, D11, G201, L191, M25, M256, R36, R171, S224, T88, T166, T180, W102, W136, W256–W267, °T10
Wilkinson v. Chicago Tribune (1868), E158
Willard, Frances, W25
William Goldman Theatres, Inc. v. Dana (1962), B96
Williams, Charles R., trial, S458
Williams, John, F35
Williams, John A., trial, B541, M59, T165, W296–W297
Williams, Oliver, °M65
Williams, Paul, O118, W302
Williams, Roger, S116, S123, W303
Williams, Thomas, E141, E144, S503
Williams, William E., T171
Williams, William Emrys, W126, W154
Williams v. Settle (1960), °D36
Willis, R., N80
Wilmans, Helen, B632
Wilson, George E., F269
Wilson, James, L216
Wilson, Richard L., I2
Wilson, Woodrow (Pres.) Administration: censorship policies criticized, B556, °P5, °S7; Creel (George) on, C641; Peace Conference news coverage, A231, C185, C415
Winchell, Walter, C291, W168, W326
Winslow, Amy, G191
Winters v. New York (1948), N147, °C20
Wire service: monopoly of, C545, F100, F119, K59, K120, L59, L77
Wirges, Eugene H., trial, R64, S582, °A28
Wirth, Louis, U230
Wisconsin: Library Commission statement on freedom of inquiry, W338; obscenity act, C422, H171, W336; public meetings law, R111, S591, S708; school library censorship survey, B649; *Tropic of Cancer,* C191, G93, N199
Witchcraft and blasphemy, S171
Witchcraft and obscenity, F153, S120, S181
Without Magnolias (Bucklin Moon), F10
Wittome, M. G., G241
Wizard of Oz (Frank Baum), D216, E148
Wolf, Hazel C., B249
Wolfe, John, H347
Wolfit, Donald (Sir), S328
Wolseley, Roland E., M607
Woman Rebel (Margaret Sanger), S46, S50, S53, S168, W355
Woman Thou Gavest Me, The (Hall Caine), B396, L312, M391
Woman's Farm Journal, M523
Women: excluded as movie censors, C168
Women in Love (D. H. Lawrence), C189, F213, T16
Women's Christian Temperance Union, U127

Women's Clubs, General Federation of: campaign against pronography by, M360, M579; censorship pressures by, H194; motion picture censorship by, B312
Wood, John, C294, W361–W363
Wood and Stone (John Cowper Powys), W270
Woodfall, Henry S., trial, C438, D11, E149, R36, W366
Woodhull, Victoria C., B187, B550, I13, °F34, °S1
Woodhull and Claflin's Weekly, B187, B550, °S1
Woolcott, Alexander, K142
Wooler, Thomas J.: H337, K79, R283, W230; *Black Dwarf, The,* B298, W230; Carlile (Richard) on, C88; jury packing, W376; trial, B298, W230, W377–W378
Woolf, Virginia, E73, F225
Woolsey, John M. (Justice), E120, J112, J116, O92, W382
Woolston, Thomas: W383; trial, S123, W229, W384
Worcester, Mass., Public Library, W387
Word, The, H241, K74, W388
Worde, Wynkyn de, R56
Words, libelous, B504, B661, S323, S752, W334, W347
Words, obscene: H249, K65, S668, Y25; humorous essay, D1; Lawrence (D. H.) on, L97, L99–L101; Lewis (C. S.) on, C609, L223–L224; Miller (Henry) on, M350; taboo against use of, D128, F371, H269, S8, Y25, °H61; washing them clean, H240. *See also Dictionary of American Slang*
Words, scurrilous: right to use, I36, S137
Words, seditious, T165, °F31
Words, taboo: Y25, °C23; college students use of, S592, °H62; television ban of, M382; verbal usage, C361, S593
Words of Pearl for Married People Only (Edward B. Foote), F187
Words tantamount to action, L366
Work, Martin H., C358
Worker: freedom of inquiry and discussion, B428, D141
Worker's Voice, G143
World freedom of information. *See* International freedom in communications
World I Never Made, A (James T. Farrell), A229, E129, L92
World League for Sexual Reform, R179, W394
World Purity Federation, L272
World War I censorship: Allied military forces in Paris, B210, C148; Canada, B49, B505; Catholic Index influence, K101; India, C271; New Zealand, A187
—Great Britain: A199, C24, F223, H86, J51, K172–K173, K194, L135, M251, M434, N3, R13, R131, R218, S694, W359; American correspondent arrested, B195; bibliography, Y22; *Britain's Deadly Peril,* C156; *Britannia,* T176; censor's comments, C533–C534; controls inadequate, T115; criticism, B158, B536, C29, D166, E103, H123, H126, L170, L251, M57, M330, M332, P19, R49, R54, R306, S36; *Daily News* attacks on Lord Kitchener criticized, B535; decline of freedom, H154; docility of press, D56; false news to delude enemy, C177, P320; field orders, G222; futility of, P296, R306; German newspapers to U.S. seized, K40; German science books seized, B523; history, C204, C678, F211, G249, H169; Indian precedent, L183; journalists' proposal, G316; lampooning, B347, B667, E97; liberal press suppressed, A200; limited censorship favored, B654; living with it, B186; mail seized from neutral ships, A79, C149, G217–G220, H215, H254; Miles (Nelson A.) on, M332; Ministry of Information, L54; Montague (Charles E.) on, M434; *Nation, The,* H122; naval censor's memoirs, B587; Parliamentary debate, reporting of, D290, *Polish Review,* H95; Press Bureau policy, G257–G258, L254; postal censorship, G249, N109, S443; professional and trade journals reveal, N3; propaganda

and, S407, S694, °L3; publications of enemy censored, K40, K172–K173; *R. v. Russell,* R301; Sinclair (Upton) on, S417; trade advantage charges refuted, C186
—United States: A73, B156, J99, K184, L55, L135, M372–M373, M401–M404, N3, P367, P312, S30, S129, S207, T56, T146, W391, °W26; balancing rights, W54; bibliography, N2, U198, Y22; *Blast, The,* B213, T171; book banning, S352; British and German censorship effect on U.S., S229; Bromberg (F. G.) on, B529; *Bull, The,* O65–O66; "censorate" recommended, G61; censor's autobiography, P22; Censorship Board, S354; Committee on Public Information, A73, C206, C637, C640, D138, L56, M401–M403, U210–U212; court decisions, C242, C244, G175; Creel (George), C635, C637–C642, S707; criticism, A265, B581, C206, D140, F327, G266, K25, P217, P344, P346, R193, W100, W307, W364; Dewey (John) on, D140, D142; Espionage Act cases, A73, A131, B109–B110, C110, C242, C244, M600, M613, N128, O13, O65–O66, P305, S763, T171, V6, W278 (play), W357, Y11; favors, O40, O54, S322; foreign correspondents in war zones, F19; foreign journals barred, A73, A106, C181, C217, K40; General Staff proposal, A207; German-American press, G304, H175; history, F211, H270, M401–M403; libraries, H247, M329; Lippmann (Walter) on, L305, L308; mental effect of, D142; Mexico relations, M402; Milam (Carl) on, M329; military authorities in France, B544, C148, F281, G113, J81, K25, M225, P21–P22, S664, W307; Morel (E. D.) case, M504–M505; naval censorship, J88; Peace Conference, Paris, A73, A231, C185, C415, F76, U25; periodical press regulations, C181, C211; political prisoners, M63; Post Office policies on seditious publications, B640, J63, P303, R207, S7, S763, °P5, °S7; postwar policy, E98, M401; proposals evaluated, B445, S62; public officials, right to criticize, F202; Roosevelt (Theodore) on, R228; Schroeder (Theodore A.) on, S148; Seldes (George) on, S238; soldiers' reading "index," A242, M501, S7; state sedition laws, C246; territories (U.S.), U162; voluntary censorship, U211–U212; Weinberger (Harry) on, W118; Wilson administration criticized in handling war news, B556, C185, °S7; World War II censorship contrasted, A110, L288; YMCA, criticism of, S612. *See also* Anarchist publications, censorship of; Espionage Act of 1917; Post Office censorship (United States)
World War II censorship: Australia, P99; France, P105; Germany, P105; Ireland, K78
—Canada: F145, P354, S352; British less severe, C44, C354; criticism of, S760; defense of, S640; French-Canadian press, L143; German periodicals, L43; U.S. World War I compared, S207
—Great Britain: B462, H8, K159, K194, K207, M109, N43, P105, °T9; book censorship, H8; Canadian censorship compared, C354; criticism of, H258, N45–N47, P280, T100, V48; *Daily Worker,* D3, L63, N46, T100, °R30; Freedom Press raids, R40; gossip, E101; *Mirror, The,* C197; newsprint rationing, L114; Official Secrets Act, M208–M210, O50, R183; Regulation 2D, L62, N46; U.S. business affected, J68; U.S. mail seized, E4, G215; vigilance needed, S550; Villard (Oswald G.) on, V48
—United States: A14–A17, A78, A139, A174–A175, C553, C588, D189, H15, J72, J99, K184, L146, L294, M404, M547, M549, N209, S76, S636, S721, U224, U229; academic libraries, V18; advertising copy, A219, C157; bibliography, S81, S452; British censorship and U.S. business, J68; British correspondent criticizes, F38; business and industrial data, C223, J68; cables, overseas, U40–U41; codes, U36–U38, U40–U43; criticism of, A14, L197,